MW01528177

A TELUGU–ENGLISH DICTIONARY

Oxford TELUGU-ENGLISH Dictionary

By

J.P.L. GWYNN

Assisted by

J. VENKATESWARA SASTRY

OXFORD
UNIVERSITY PRESS

Oxford University Press is a department of the University of Oxford.
It furthers the University's objective of excellence in research, scholarship,
and education by publishing worldwide. Oxford is a registered trademark of
Oxford University Press in the UK and in certain other countries

Published in India by
Oxford University Press
YMCA Library Building, 1 Jai Singh Road, New Delhi 110001, India

© Oxford University Press 1991

The moral rights of the author have been asserted

First Edition published in 1991
Fourth impression August 2012

All rights reserved. No part of this publication may be reproduced, stored in a retrieval system, or transmitted, in any form or by any means, without the prior permission in writing of Oxford University Press, or as expressly permitted by law, by licence, or under terms agreed with the appropriate reprographics rights organization. Enquiries concerning reproduction outside the scope of the above should be sent to the Rights Department, Oxford University Press, at the address above

You must not circulate this book in any other form
and you must impose this same condition on any acquirer

ISBN-13: 978-0-19-562863-0
ISBN-10: 0-19-562863-2

Typeset by All India Press, Kennedy Nagar, Pondicherry
Printed in India by Yash Printographics, Noida

To Peggy

CONTENTS

INTRODUCTION

సుప్రసిద్ధ భాషావేత్త గిడుగు వెంకట సీతాపతిగారు చెప్పినట్లు మారుతున్న భాషకు తగినట్లు నిఘంటువులు కనీసం ప్రతి యిరవై సంవత్సరాల కొకసారి సంస్కరణ జరగాలి. అలా జరిగినప్పుడే నిఘంటువులు సజీవ భాషకు యోగ్యమైన ప్రాతినిధ్యం వహిస్తాయి.

suprasiddha bhaaSaaweetta giDugu wenkaTa siitaapatigaaru ceppinaTLu maarutunna bhaaSaku taginaTLu nighaNTuwulu kaniisam prati yiraway samwatsaraala kokasaari samskaraNa jaragaali. alaa jariginappuDee nighaNTuwulu sajiiwa bhaaSaku yoogyamayna praatinidhyam wahistaayi.[1]

As the renowned linguist Gidugu Venkata Sitapatigaru has said, dictionaries should be revised at least once in every twenty years so as to conform with the changes in a language. Only if this is done will they present a true image of the living language.

Compilation of the Dictionary.

1. I consider the words quoted above to be my justification for undertaking the task of compiling a new Telugu–English dictionary. At Hyderabad in the middle 1960s while collaborating with Professor Bh. Krishnamurti on *A Grammar of Modern Telugu*[2] I began to read Telugu literature and found I was unable to understand many passages without the help of a Telugu speaker because the existing Telugu–English dictionaries were thoroughly out of date. C. P. Brown's *Telugu–English Dictionary* (Madras 1852) was re-edited by M. Venkata Ratnam, W. H. Campbell and K. Veeresalingam (Madras 1903), but has not been revised since then. P. Sankaranarayana's *Telugu–English Dictionary* (first edition Madras 1900) has not been effectively modernised although later editions have appeared. Galletti's *Telugu Dictionary* (Oxford 1935) is more up to date, but owing to its restricted purpose it contains only a small selection of words from the enormous vocabulary range of Telugu. Those were the dictionaries that I found most useful at the time, but as they gave no help regarding many modern words and idiomatic expressions I began to prepare a list for my own use. By the time I left India in 1968 it had filled four manuscript volumes.

2. In the London suburb of Bromley when I took up preparation of the dictionary in earnest I spent four and a half years compiling an inventory of rough entries with draft meanings. This involved making a thorough study of certain literary works by various authors and also a selection of other writings dealing with administrative, journalistic, scientific and technical subjects. At the same time I perused all the Telugu–English dictionaries, vocabularies, glossaries and word lists that I could obtain and also certain English–Telugu dictionaries and glossaries, including the *Glossary of Administrative and Legal Terms* (Telugu Akademi, Hyderabad 1980). I found the compendious *Glossary of Journalistic Terms* by Dr Budaraju Radhakrishna to be very valuable (a copy was kindly supplied by the author in advance of its publication by Eenaadu). I also made use of certain monolingual glossaries and dictionaries including (after the arrival of Dr J. V. Sastry) the first five volumes of *telugu*

[1] *V. Venkatappayya, telugu nighaNTu wikaasam*, Andhra Pradesh Sahitya Akademi, Hyderabad 1975, page 4.
[2] Bh. Krishnamurti and J. P. L. Gwynn, *A Grammar of Modern Telugu*, Oxford University Press, Delhi 1985.

wyutpatti koośam (*Telugu Etymological Dictionary*) published by the Andhra University, Waltair. The authors of that dictionary deserve praise for their industry in having collected a large number of words and phrases which occur in everyday speech but which had not been cited in any dictionary previously. My only regret is that by the time my work was finished the final part of the *Etymological Dictionary* had not yet appeared. A list of the books that I made most use of for the purposes of the dictionary will be found on page xxiii below. I have given the list with much hesitation, lest it create the impression that those were the only publications consulted, apart from dictionaries and glossaries. In fact many useful words, phrases and examples of usage were drawn here and there from other sources too many to mention. Of the books in the list I studied selected passages from items 10, 13 to 16 and 20, and the others from cover to cover.

3. Here I would like to acknowledge my special debt of gratitude to Dr Gutala Krishnamurti, a resident of London whose scholarly interests extend to both Telugu and English literature. Contact with him from the early 1970s helped to keep alive my interest in Telugu, and later on he helped me with the dictionary in various ways. He supplied me with several books which I studied intensively, such as Rachakonda Viswanadha Sastry's '*rattaalu raambaabu*' and Narla Venkateswara Rao's '*muuDu daśaabdaalu*'. During a visit to Visakhapatnam he obtained for me a pre-publication copy of Volume 5 of the Telugu Etymological Dictionary from Andhra University. I put many questions to him at his flat in London concerning passages in books whose meanings I found obscure. He introduced me to visiting literary figures whom I was also able to consult about difficult words and passages, and I had many meetings and discussions with Sri Sri (Srirangam Srinivasa Rao) and Dr Puripanda Appalaswami at Dr Gutala Krishnamurti's flat when they were staying there in 1980.

4. Work on the dictionary was furthered by my visits to India in 1982, 1984, 1985, 1988 and 1990 and to Madison, U.S.A., the home of the University of Wisconsin, in May 1983.

5. In September 1984 Dr (then Shri) Jonnalagedda Venkateswara Sastry, Reader in Linguistics, Osmania University, Hyderabad, whose mother tongue is Telugu, came to London at my behest with a grant from the Charles Wallace India Trust and spent the academic years 1984–5 to 1986–7 assisting me in the compilation of the dictionary, and in the same period acquiring a Ph.D. degree in Phonetics at the School of Oriental and African Studies, London University. During those years all the material that I had collected was gone through by Dr Sastry and myself, additions were made and the work of compiling the dictionary was completed.

6. The method adopted was as follows. From the material that I had prepared previously Dr Sastry wrote out the headwords and draft meanings in a series of exercise books. We then met and discussed each entry and agreed on matters like grammatical classification and on the meanings and the examples of usage requiring to be cited, if any. Dr Sastry suggested additional entries such as words or expressions found in monolingual Telugu dictionaries, scientific terms taken from relevant glossaries and a variety of classical, literary and other words found in existing Telugu–English dictionaries. He supplemented my stock of illustrative examples with other useful examples of usage where necessary, and marked the status of entries as classical, obsolescent, dialect or colloquial where appropriate. When all this had been settled, I composed the entries in manuscript in the exercise books, which became a back up copy of the dictionary after Dr Sastry had copied them on to manuscript slips. Those slips were despatched in batches to Hyderabad for typing. By keeping a close watch on progress and adhering to a strict timetable it was possible to get through the whole

operation in just three years. All this involved hard thinking, attention to detail and a great deal of scriptory work. I am deeply grateful to Dr Sastry both for his valuable intellectual contribution and for the willing way in which he shouldered an ample share of the writing work. Taking part in the compilation of the dictionary was clearly as much a labour of love for him as it has been for me.

Purpose and Scope of the Dictionary; Selection of Entries.

7. The dictionary is intended to serve the practical needs of English speakers who want to learn to read, write and converse in Telugu on subjects of general interest and to read and appreciate modern Telugu prose literature; it is also intended to be useful to Telugu speakers who refer to it for English equivalents of the Telugu words and expressions that are cited. Entries have been selected with the object of including words which occur with at least a fair degree of frequency in Modern Telugu and are likely to be encountered in conversation or general reading. I have taken care not to overload the dictionary with rare literary words belonging to the classical language or with scientific or technical terms that are only used by specialists. As a result the total number of entries is estimated to be over 28,000 and I hope that the selection will meet the needs of most users. To make the dictionary fully comprehensive would mean multiplying its size many times.

8. In the dictionary the word 'Telugu', where it refers to language, should be taken to mean the modern and not the classical style of the language. An account of the evolution of Modern Telugu and its relationship with Classical Telugu will be found in the Introduction to *A Grammar of Modern Telugu*, together with some observations on Classical Telugu which include the following:"The classical style, known as *graanthika*, has kept a strong hold on Telugu and is occasionally used in literary works, public notices and some school text books even today, although it is purely a written medium and diverged from speech centuries ago."

9. The question of how far to go in including in a dictionary of this type classical words which do not belong properly to the modern language is a difficult one to answer. It may arise in any language which possesses an ancient literature. In Arabic, where the situation is quite similar to that of Telugu, the question has been posed thus:

> Classicisms are a further special problem. Arab authors, steeped in classical tradition, can and do frequently draw upon words which were archaic in the Middle Ages. The use of classical patterns is by no means limited to belles-lettres. Archaisms may crop up in the middle of a spirited newspaper article. Wherever an aesthetic or rhetorical effect is intended, wherever the language aims more at expressiveness than at imparting information, authors tend to weave in ancient Arabic and classical idioms. They are artistic and stylistic devices of the first order. They awaken in the reader images from memorised passages of ancient literature and contribute to his enjoyment....It is clear from the foregoing that it is not possible to make a sharp distinction between living and obsolete usage.[3]

In Telugu, obsolete terms are perpetuated in contexts such as proverbs and quotations, and authors draw on the classical language freely to suit their individual tastes and styles. That makes it obligatory for this dictionary to contain a range of classical terms which occur not too infrequently in present-day literature and journalism. Based partly on my experience and

[3] Hans Wehr, *A Dictionary of Modern Written Arabic* edited by J. Milton Cowan, Wiesbaden, Otto Harrassowitz; London, George Allen and Unwin 1966.

helped by Dr Sastry's guidance I have included a selection of classical terms in the dictionary, which are marked *class.* to indicate their status.

10. In the Introduction to *A Grammar of Modern Telugu* an outline of the four main dialects is given. They are (i) the Central Dialect, current in the central coastal districts of Andhra Pradesh (East and West Godavari, Krishna, Guntur and Prakasam), which has become the standard language employed in the media and the main body of modern literature and which can be referred to as Modern Standard Telugu or *śiSTawyaawahaarika*; (ii) the Northern Dialect, current in Visakhapatnam, Vizianagaram and Srikakulam Districts; (iii) the Southern Dialect, current in Nellore District and Rayalasima; and (iv) the Telangana Dialect current in the Telugu-speaking districts of the former Hyderabad State. The present work is primarily a dictionary of Modern Standard Telugu but certain dialect words have been included based on the frequency of their use and they are marked *dial.*

11. The main thrust of the dictionary has been towards making it "present a true image of the living language" by citing a wide range of Telugu words and phrases that occur commonly in modern communication, and presenting their English equivalents in translation. Special attention has been paid to certain features of the Telugu vocabulary which are important but which had either not manifested themselves when previous lexicographers were at work or were overlooked by them. These are:

(i) citing of a very large number of words which have come into existence in recent times or have acquired new meanings in order to express modern concepts;

(ii) citing of modern colloquialisms, including for example verbs like *eeDcu, aghoorincu, maNDu, tagulu* and *tagalabeTTu* which can be substituted idiomatically for other verbs in colloquial speech;

(iii) detailed treatment of basic words in common use whose translation presents problems and of many particles, clitics and connecting words with illustrations of their usage; for examples see under the headwords *maaTa, lekka, cellu, anaka, anagaa, alaa ani, aTTu, aTTee, intakuu, kanuka, pootee, poonii, poonu* and *pooyi*;

(iv) citing and treatment of interrogative and indefinite pronouns and adverbs with prefixation of *ad-* or *all-* or *ill-* together with instances of their usage; see entries under *adeemiTi, adeedoo, adeppuDoo, adoo, adoka, adoolaa, adaynaa, allakkaDa, allappuDu, alleppuDoo, illikkaDa* and *illidigoo*;

(v) citing of a selection of idiomatic phrases, proverbs, quotations and other homely expressions which are part of everyday intercourse between Telugu speakers but whose meaning is obscure to outsiders; it is essential for a Telugu–English dictionary to cite such phrases with their meanings and I have included many of these collected from various sources.

Presentation.

12. *Arrangement and labelling of entries.* Each entry begins with a headword (single word or phrase) in Telugu and Roman script followed by a grammatical category label in abbreviated form in italics (*n., adj., vb., adv.,* etc.). When a headword can function in more than one grammatical category, e.g., as a noun and also as a transitive or intransitive verb, each category is marked with a large Roman figure (I, II, III, etc.); for examples see *aakharu, uDuku, heccu.*

This is followed when appropriate by a status label in italics, denoting level of usage (e.g., *class., colloq., dial.*) or field of knowledge or activity (*phys., chem., maths., econ., polit.*) together with any other special information about the headword that may be relevant.

Thereafter the meanings are given with examples of usage, if any. Meanings which are synonyms or near synonyms are separated by commas; see *arikaTTu, santr̥pti, parihaasam.* When major differences of meaning occur, they are distinguished by Arabic numerals in bold type (**1, 2, 3,** etc.); see *mandu, uuhincu, sangrahincu.*

Words which are identical in spelling but differ in basic meaning and origin (homonyms) are indicated by separate headword entries with superscript numbers; see *aDugu, aadi, uuru.*

13. *Headwords with alternative forms.* Attention is particularly invited to the fact that in order to save space *alternative forms of headwords are cross-referenced only if they are separated from each other by more than six intervening entries*—see further in paragraph 23 below. In cases where an alternative form cannot be used for all the meanings of a headword but only for some, this is indicated in the entry concerned; see for example *santa,* where the alternative form *santagoola* can only be used for the group of meanings bearing the number 2. So also with *sandhya* and its alternative form *sandhyaawandanam.*

14. The status labels mentioned in paragraph 12 above may apply to all the meanings in an entry or only to some; this is indicated by the place allotted to them in the entry. For example, in the entry *seewanam* the label *class.* applies to all the meanings; in the entry *suucii* the label *class.* applies only to meanings bearing number 2; in the entry *suDi* the label *colloq.* applies only to meanings bearing number 3; in the entry *darśini* the label *class.* applies to the meaning bearing number 1 and the label *journ.* to the meaning bearing number 3.

15. *Examples of usage.* These are cited to fulfil one or more of the following purposes:

(i) to bring out a meaning clearly with the help of an illustration;
(ii) to explain an idiomatic expression;
(iii) to illustrate a grammatical construction;
(iv) to suggest a translation into natural-sounding English;
(v) to substantiate the range of meanings that a word or phrase can convey;
(vi) some sentences are quoted because they convey the flavour of the language.

As far as possible these have been taken from literary and other writings, but where ready-to-hand examples were not available, they have been composed. Examples quoted from printed sources have been reproduced unaltered or with the minimum alteration required to make them self-contained.

16. In some cases the context in which a term can be used is indicated by a word or words in brackets; see *eerparacu.* The purpose of this is to provide an illustration. It does not imply that the use of the term is restricted to that particular context; see for instance

aNTottu.... 2 to press or crush together (thorn branches).

17. Correspondence between postpositions in Telugu and prepositions in English is indicated within brackets in certain cases where such guidance is likely to be helpful; see *tapincu, pratigaa, bhayapaDu.*

18. *Child language.* The marking '*child language*' against certain headwords generally means that the words are used by grown-ups when speaking to children; examples are *aampeTTu, cicci, bajjuNDu.* In a few cases it indicates a game or custom or some other activity special to children, e.g., *kaakaNTu ceeyu, paNTalu weeyu.*

19. *Square brackets* are used in many places (though not uniformly throughout the dictionary) for the purpose of avoiding repetition. They indicate that the entry can be read with or without the portion enclosed in square brackets. Thus 'to be[come] cold' is equivalent to 'to be cold *or* to become cold'; '*santooSam*[*ayna*]' is equivalent to '*santooSam or santooSamayna*'; *sama*[*taa*]*sthiti* is equivalent to '*samasthiti or samataasthiti*'; '[praise]worthy' is equivalent to 'praiseworthy *or* worthy'. A headword in which square brackets occur is placed in alphabetical order in the position it would occupy if the portion in square brackets was omitted.

omitted.

20. *Tilde or swung dash* (~). When a headword has to be repeated in the text of an entry, the symbol ~ is used in its place unless the headword is a monosyllable, in which case it is repeated in full.

21. *Roman script.* Roman symbols used to transcribe the Telugu alphabet are the same as in *A Grammar of Modern Telugu*. The Telugu symbols with their Roman counterparts arranged in the traditional order of the Telugu alphabet are shown below:

Vowels

అ	ఆ	ఇ	ఈ	ఉ	ఊ	ఋ	ఎ	ఏ	ఐ	ఒ	ఓ	ఔ
a	aa	i	ii	u	uu	ṛ	e	ee	ay	o	oo	aw

Consonants

క	ఖ	గ	ఘ	ఙ	చ	ఛ	జ	ఝ	ఞ	ట	ఠ
k	kh	g	gh	ŋ	c	ch	j	jh	ñ	T	Th
డ	ఢ	ణ	త	థ	ద	ధ	న	ప	ఫ	బ	భ
D	Dh	N	t	th	d	dh	n	p	ph	b	bh
మ	య	ర	ల	వ	శ	ష	స	హ	ళ	క్ష	
m	y	r	l	w	ś	S	s	h	L	kS	

The following points from the 'Note on Transcription' prefaced to *A Grammar of Modern Telugu* should be borne in mind:

(a) Telugu diphthongs are represented as *ay* and *aw*[4];
(b) Phonemic EE is represented, where Telugu uses only *aa* or *ee* for want of a symbol;
(c) The anuswaara (o) is represented by the appropriate nasal phoneme, i.e.
'n' before velars (k,g), palatals (c,j) and dentals (t,d)
'N' before retroflexes (T,D)
'm' before labials (p,b), before y, r, l, w, s, ś, h and also in the word-final position;
(d) 'ś' is represented as s before front vowels (i, ii, e, ee, EE) in native Telugu words.

22. *Orthography.* In Telugu dialectal differences of pronunciation account for many spelling variations. An example is the occurrence of *-LL-* (as in *peLLi, baLLu*) in the central and northern coastal districts, whereas *-NDL-* (as in *peNDLi, baNDLu*) prevails elsewhere in Andhra Pradesh. Stylistic and literary variations also occur, as in the alternation between

[4] When the combination *aww* occurs, it almost always stands for *a* followed by consonantal *w* reduplicated, as in *awwa*. In a very few headwords it stands for the diphthong *aw* followed by consonantal *w*, as in *yawwaraajyam*, *sawwarNakaraNi*. In order to tell which those rare cases are, the version of the headword in Telugu script should be referred to.

initial *o-* and initial *wa-* in certain words. In this dictionary some common variations in spelling are noted but many have had to be omitted in the interest of saving space. When a headword is cited with alternative spellings, e.g., *peLLi* or *peNDLi*, it should be assumed that similar alternative spellings apply to closely-connected words, e.g., *peLLikuuturu* and *peLLikoDuku* have alternatives *peNDLikuuturu* and *peNDLikoDuku*.

23. *Cross-referencing.* It is important to note that in order to save space *cross-referencing has been dispensed with for entries which come close to each other in alphabetical order.* Thus, if a headword is cited in two alternative forms, e.g., *śani, sani,* which are far apart in alphabetical order, the entry for *śani* will show the meaning and other details, and *sani* will be cited again at the appropriate place with a cross-reference reading '*same as śani*'. *But if the two alternative forms come close to each other in alphabetical order and are separated by not more than six intervening entries, then no cross-reference is made.* For this reason it is advisable to scan the immediately preceding and following seven entries if a headword is not found in its expected place, in view of the possibility of its being cited as an alternative to one of those entries.

24. *Grammar.* The grammatical terminology used in the dictionary is the same as in *A Grammar of Modern Telugu.* Certain points regarding the classification of headwords as parts of speech should be borne in mind when consulting the dictionary. They are: (i) most Telugu nouns, which are cited as such in the dictionary, can be used as adjectives if they occupy the adjectival position (*grammar*, 12.11); (ii) adverbs of time and place can function as nouns and may also be described as adverbial nouns (*grammar*, 10 and 23.2); (iii) echo words, which are a special feature of Telugu, are cited in the dictionary as 'onomatopoeic nouns *or* adverbs' (*grammar*, 23.8).

25. *Translation from Telugu into English.* The principle I have followed is to translate examples as literally as possible, but if a literal translation sounds unnatural in English I have had no hesitation in preferring a free translation which still preserves the essence of the original. Many instances of this will be found in the dictionary. It means that for some Telugu headwords English meanings are cited which at first sight appear far removed from the basic or literal meaning of the word. In such cases the free rendering is generally justified by furnishing one or more examples; see for instance *tayaaru awu*, which in some contexts has to be translated 'to appear', and *maaTa*, which is used in a wide range of senses.

Some thoughts on learning Telugu.

26. The mellifluous sound of spoken Telugu has justly earned it the title of 'the Italian of the East', but, sad to say, this phrase can generally be taken to represent the limit of what foreigners know about the language. They have little idea even of the region of India where it is spoken and none at all of its literature or the names of its great writers. This ignorance concerning the language which stands next to Hindi in the number of its mother-tongue speakers in India, besides being widely spoken in a number of countries overseas, is a product of the lack of interest in learning Telugu that is displayed in the world at large. It is a great pity, because the cultural wealth of Andhra Pradesh, which contains so much to be admired, can only become fully accessible to outsiders through a knowledge of the Telugu language. To remedy this situation would be to the benefit of all and in order to bring that about a far greater effort needs to be made to encourage and promote the learning of Telugu as a second or third language by increasing the facilities for its study both within the State and outside.

27. Looking at the matter of learning Telugu from an English-speaking student's point of

view, there are two basic practical difficulties which may discourage him initially. The first is the problem of mastering the grammatical structure, which may appear strange and baffling at first sight to someone whose mother tongue is not a Dravidian language. For one thing, Telugu has no relative pronouns, their part being played by verbal adjectives. For another, English and Telugu differ widely in their systems of sentence construction: whereas the main clause of an English sentence containing the main verb tends to come first, followed by subordinate clauses, in Telugu it is the other way round, with the subordinate clauses preceding the main clause and the main verb occurring at the very end of the sentence. But for a student with motivation challenges like these can be overcome.

The second practical difficulty is the need to acquire a large vocabulary, and on this I must comment in some detail. A noteworthy feature of Telugu, which it shares with English, is the great size of its vocabulary. This can partly be ascribed to the ease with which Telugu accepts and assimilates words derived from Sanskrit. Just as English, a Germanic language, has a high proportion of words that are of Latin or Greek origin, so Telugu, a Dravidian language, abounds in words derived from Sanskrit roots. Most of the concepts which occur in everyday speech can be expressed equally well by a word derived from a Telugu root or by one or more Sanskrit-based synonyms. Telugu contains many compound words and draws freely on Sanskrit for their formation. Furthermore, the Sanskrit-based corpus is constantly being added to by new coinages whenever they are required to express scientific, technical, journalistic or other newly-arising concepts which proliferate in the modern world and to which names have to be attached. This is one cause for the richness of the Telugu vocabulary. The well-known facility of Telugu to borrow from modern languages like Hindi, Urdu and English is another.

29. The copiousness of the vocabulary may act as a disincentive to persons embarking on the study of Telugu. To illustrate what I mean, let us consider the Telugu rendering of the word 'dog'. Five synonyms come readily to mind — *kukka, śunakam, śwaanam, graama-simham* and *beepi*. None of them is in any sense a rare word. No less than four of them are cited in the short but otherwise excellent *Emesco Pocket Telugu–English Dictionary*,[1] which testifies to their being in common use. When an English-speaking student comes across such a wide variety of names for a common animal, he may well exclaim in despair, "What kind of a language is this?" But he should nevertheless persist with his studies, and may reflect that his own mother tongue has several synonyms for 'dog'—remember Oliver Goldsmith's

> mongrel, puppy, whelp and hound
> and curs of low degree

— not to mention a score of names for different breeds of dogs, such as spaniel, terrier, alsatian, etc., which are household words among English speakers.

30. A third difficulty that students encounter, and one that is not so much a real obstacle as a psychological block, must also be mentioned. It has its roots far in the past. Right from the early years of the British raj would-be learners of Telugu have been cautioned by their teachers and also in textbooks and the like to concern themselves with the colloquial language and steer clear of 'literary Telugu', which was held to be over-Sanskritised and too highflown to be worth studying for practical purposes. This advice to learners was and still is sound upto a point, as indicating the proper approach when starting on the study of Telugu, but it has been misconstrued into meaning that they should not seriously try to get beyond the stage of

[1] Bommakanti Srinivasacharyulu, *Emesco Pocket Telugu – English Dictionary*, M. Sesachalam and Company, Machilipatnam, 1977.

being able to engage in straightforward conversation on simple topics. Nowadays this attitude needs to be reversed, because even to be able to read newspapers and books of general interest and to follow public speeches and programmes on television and radio requires a much wider knowledge than was formerly aimed at. Unfortunately the view that foreigners are not expected to know more than a smattering of Telugu has remained very much alive to the present day, and is often apparent when educated Telugu speakers express surprise at a learner's trying to extend his vocabulary, instead of realising that they ought to be on their guard against discouraging him, however unintentionally, from making progress.

31. Telugu is in fact an extremely versatile and flexible language; in that respect it has qualities and features akin to those of Ancient Greek, as for instance in its reflexive verbs in -*konu* meaning 'to do something *for oneself*', reminiscent of the Greek middle voice. Both languages have the facility of expressing shades of meaning very neatly by the use of particles, and both can impart subtle degrees of emphasis by varying the order of words in a sentence. In its oral range Telugu abounds in vivid, lively and elliptical turns of phrase, while in its literature, both poetry (which I mention only in passing because it is outside the scope of this dictionary) and prose, it achieves a truly high standard. In all the qualities that make for good creative writing — descriptive and narrative composition, character drawing and portrayal of the range of human emotions — Telugu writers have produced works of quality which not only have a high intrinsic value as literature but also mirror the daily life of the people in a way that is arresting, attractive, and often very entertaining. The Telugu public have a deep affection for their own literature and it deserves to have a wider readership.

32. Having paid to the Telugu language the tribute to which I feel it is entitled I cannot forbear from adding that having spent a great deal of time reading printed Telugu on and off for over fifty years I still do not feel at home with the Telugu script. Fully realising its intimate association with both the classical and modern styles of the language and also appreciating the beauty of Telugu type at its best, I still am unable to read it comfortably because many of the symbols resemble each other so closely and the syllabic nature of the script causes problems in the separation of words. Besides this, some new kinds of type distort both the form and arrangement of the symbols, and much of the present-day outpouring of popular literature and journalism is a real strain to read because the print is so small and the ink and paper are so poor in quality. I have therefore come to regard the Telugu script as to some extent standing in the way of acquiring a knowledge of the language. Whether or not there is any value in advocating a change at this time, I would still like to remind the Telugu public that two possible ways of tackling the problem are either to undertake script reform, perhaps on the lines discussed in chapter 5 of *A Grammar of Modern Telugu*, or to move towards making more use of the Roman script. It was at my publishers' request that the Telugu script has been used in the dictionary only for the headword of each entry, and accordingly all the rest of the text appears in Roman. I believe that users of the dictionary, if the method of transcription is new to them, will nevertheless have little difficulty in accustoming themselves to it after a small amount of practice.

ACKNOWLEDGEMENTS

My particular thanks foi assistance rendered in connection with the dictionary go to Dr Jonnalagedda Venkateswara Sastry and Dr Gutala Krishnamurti for their help which has been mentioned with gratitude already; to Professor Bhadriraju Krishnamurti, Professor G. N. Reddi and Professor Velcheru Narayana Rao for their comments on and criticisms of certain entries in the dictionary and also for the encouragement they gave at an early stage when I was feeling particularly diffident at having taken on such a daunting task; Professor Narayana Rao spared a good many days going through parts of the dictionary with me at Madison in 1983 and later on at Bromley in 1986.

I am grateful to Shri M. Gopalakrishnan, I.A.S., one of my successors in the post of Education Secretary to the Government of Andhra Pradesh, for his invaluable help in organising the arrangements for getting the typescript prepared from the manuscript slips which I sent to him at Hyderabad and for despatching the typescript back to me for correction; likewise to his personal assistant, Shri D. Nateshwar Rao, for his part in attending to the work under Shri Gopalakrishnan's supervision.

I owe my thanks to three persons who shared almost all the typing work between them, Shrimati S. Bhaskar, who typed a section in London which it was not convenient to send to Hyderabad, the late Shri M. L. Raghaviah, who used to be my personal assistant when I was Education Secretary at Hyderabad and whose unexpected death in 1987 came as very sad news; and Shri S. Chalapati Rao, who carried out the major part of the typing work.

Thanks are also due to the Telugu Akademi, the Andhra Pradesh Sahitya Akademi and the Andhra University for making some of their publications available to me free of cost for use in preparing the dictionary; to the Charles Wallace India Trust for a grant which enabled Dr J. V. Sastry to come and spend three years in London assisting me with the dictionary and carrying out his own research in phonetics leading to a Ph. D. degree, and for grants to cover Professor V. Narayana Rao's stay in London in 1986 and my dictionary-related expenses from 1983 to 1987; to the INTACH UK Trust for a grant to cover my air fare from London to India and back in 1990.

I am grateful to Messrs. John King and Son Ltd through Mr D. J. O'Reilly of Bromley for the supply of stationery used for manuscript slips containing the dictionary entries; to Mr P. S. Falla of Bromley for his guidance in the method of correcting dictionary proofs.

I am also deeply indebted to all the authors whose writings I have drawn on in order to cite interesting illustrative examples of modern usage in the dictionary.

Many other persons have helped towards the completion of the dictionary in various ways — by the loan or gift of books or periodicals, by answering my questions and by providing useful information and advice. I am very grateful to them all and if I have not named them individually they must on no account think that their kindness has been forgotten.

Now finally I have an opportunity to say thank you to my wife Peggy for the part she has played in seeing the dictionary into print. During all these years she has never complained of the time I have given up to the dictionary or the extent to which it has diverted me from playing a full part in our home life. Having seen the need for the task to be fulfilled she provided the atmosphere and background in our home which made it not only possible but also easy for me to carry the work through to the end. When a husband on reaching retirement devotes himself to studies which are even more distracting than the job he had been doing before, and yet is about the house all day, it is far more taxing for his wife than when his working hours followed a fixed schedule and he was free to share in family life for the rest of the time. It is late now to try to make up for it, but I can at least acknowledge the debt that I owe my wife by expressing how fully I appreciate that she supported me with so much unselfishness and at so great a personal sacrifice while the dictionary was being composed. Now that it is over I want to leave on record these thoughts which have been with me for a long time. It is fitting that the book should be dedicated to her.

ABBREVIATIONS

A.	answer
abl.	ablative
adj.	adjective
admin.	administrative term
adv.	adverb
advbl.	adverbial
alt.	alternative
fig.	figurative[ly]
fut.	future
gen.	generally
geom.	geometrical term
gram.	grammatical term
hab.	habitual
hon.	honorific
i.e.	*id est* (Latin: that is)
indef.	indefinite
interrog.	interrogative
intr.	intransitive
journ.	journalistic term
ling.	linguistic term
lit.	literally
literary	literary usage
masc.	masculine

maths.	mathematical term
med.	medical term
met.	meteorological term
mil.	military term
mod.	in modern usage
n.	noun
neg.	negative
obs.	obsolescent (*note*: when 'obsolete' is intended, the word is written in full)
o.-i	okari of someone (genitive case)
o.-ki	okariki to someone (dative case)
o.-ni	okarini someone (accusative case)
orom.	onomatopoeic
per.	person
phys.	physics term
poet.	poetical
polit.	political term
p.p.	postposition
pron.	pronoun
pronom.	pronominal
Q.	question
ref.	reference
sci.	scientific term
sing.	singular
sp.	species
sug.	suggesting
theat.	theatrical term
tr.	transitive
v., vb.	verb
vbl.	verbal
vet.	veterinary term
viz.	*videlicet* (Latin: namely)
zool.	zoological term

SYMBOLS

〉 *or* >	becomes
〈 *or* <	derived from
*	asterisk: this denotes an obsolete form, an ungrammatical form or an intermediate form in the application of grammatical rules
[ ]	square brackets: see Introduction, paragraph 19
~	tilde or swung dash: see Introduction, paragraph 20
/	oblique stroke or slash: this is used to link together two alternative words or phrases

Principal Books Studied

(See Introduction, paragraph 2)

Fiction

1 Kodavatiganti Kutumba Rao, *caduwu* (novel).
2 K. Kutumba Rao, *ayświaryam* (novel).
3 Rachakonda Viswanadha Sastri (Ravi Sastri) *alpajiiwi*, (novel).
4 Ravi Sastri, *rattaalu raambaabu* (novel).
5 Ravi Sastri, *raaju mahiSi* (novel).
6 Potukuchi Sambasiva Rao, *eeDu roojula majilii* (novel).
7 K. Kausalya Devi, *cakrabhramaNam* (novel).
8 Sripada Subramania Sastri, *waDLaginjalu* (novel).
9 Srirangam Srinivasa Rao (Sri Sri), *carama raatri* (stories and sketches).

Non- Fiction

10 *śri śri saahityam*, collected works of Sri Sri, volumes 2 and 3, edited by K. V. Ramana Reddi.
11 C. Narayana Reddi, *maa uuru maaTLaaDindi* (essays).
12 V. R. Narla, *muuDu daśaabdaalu* (editorials).
13 A. B. K. Prasad, *A. B. K. sampaadakiiyaalu* (editorials).
14 *brawn leekhalu–aadhunikaandhra saahitya śakhalaalu*, C. P. Brown's letters selected by Bangoorey.
15 *brawn jaabulloo sthaanika caritra śakhalaalu*, C. P. Brown's Cuddapah letters selected by Bangoorey.
16 Prakasachandra Sathapati, *telugu palukubaDula tiirutennulu* (essays).
17 *śriikakulam prajala bhaaSa*, survey compiled by V. C. Balakrishna Sarma for the district level committee, First World Telugu Conference.
18 *paatikeeLLa aandhra pradeeS 1956–1980*, survey edited by T. Nageswara Rao for the Telugu Akademi, Hyderabad.
19 *maaNDalika wṛttipadakoośam — Telugu Dialect Dictionary*, volume I, *Agriculture*, by Bhadriraju Krishnamurti.
20 G. V. Ramamurti Pantulu, *śrii suuryaraayaandhra nighaNTuwu wimarśanamu* (pamphlet).
21 Budaraju Radhakrishna, *ii naaDu bhaaSaaswaruupam*, treatise on Telugu usage for journalists.
22 *Graded Readings in Modern Literary Telugu*, selected by G. N. Reddi and B. Matson.
23 *Graded Readings in Newspaper Telugu*, selected by G. N. Reddi and B. Matson.
24 Bhadriraju Krishnamurti, *Telugu Verbal Bases*.
25 Leigh Lisker, *Introduction to Spoken Telugu*.

అ - a

అంకం **ankam** *n.* 1 numerical figure, digit. 2 act (in a play). 3 lap.

అంకగణితం **ankagaNitam** *n.* arithmetic.

అంకడాలు **ankaDaalu** *n.pl.* figures, numbers.

అంకణం **ankaNam** *n.* space between two beams or pillars in a house.

అంకనం **ankanam** *n.* 1 *ling.* notation. 2 trade mark.

అంకపొంకాలు **ankaponkaalu** *n.pl.* fierceness, fury; **ankaponkaalatoo jwaram waccindi** the fever was fierce.

అంకమ్మ **ankamma** *n.* name of a village goddess; **ardharaatri wEELa ~ siwaalu laagaa undi** it sounds like s.o. possessed by the goddess Ankamma dancing at midnight (said by persons who are disturbed by others with noise at an unwelcome time).

అంకవన్నె, అంకెవన్నె **ankawanne, ankewanne** *n.* stirrup.

అంక [గణిత] శ్రేఢి **anka[gaNita] śreeDhi** *n. maths.* arithmetic progression.

అంకసిరి **ankasiri** *n.* illness developed in old age.

అంకించు **ankincu** *v.t.* 1 to raise, lift up. 2 to praise, extol. 3 to brandish, flourish.

అంకిత **ankita** *adj.* 1 dedicated, devoted; **ankita padyaalu** dedicatory verses. 2 discerned, discernible, apparent, visible; **aayana cuupulloo maatram saaraLyam ankitam kaaleedu** but in his looks gentleness was not discernible. 3 **birudaankituDu** person conferred with a title.

అంకితం **ankitam** *n.* dedication, devotion.

అంకితం ఇచ్చు, అంకితం చేయు **ankitam iccu, ankitam ceeyu** *v.t.* to dedicate, devote; *see* **cuupu**[1].

అంకిలి **ankili** *n.* 1 cheekbone. 2 *pl.* **ankiLLu** joints of the jaws.

అంకురం **ankuram** *n.* sprout, bud.

అంకురణం **ankuraNam** *n. bot.* germination.

అంకురార్పణ **ankuraarpaNa** *n.* 1 ceremony preceding any main worship. 2 beginning of any event.

అంకురించు **ankurincu** *v.i.* 1 to sprout, germinate. 2 (of emotion, disease) to manifest itself, break forth.

అంకురోత్పత్తి **ankurootpatti** *n. bot.* germination.

అంకుశం **ankuśam** *n.* 1 goad. 2 check, bar, s.g which restrains.

అంకె **anke** *n.* 1 numerical figure, digit. 2 control; **aa eddu naa ~ ku raawaDam leedu** that bullock is not under my control.

అంకెం **ankem** *n.* 1 measure of volume amounting to 40 manikas. 2 bag, sack.

అంకెవన్నె **ankewanne** *same as* **ankawanne.**

అంగ **anga** *n.* stride, step; **angaapangaa weestuu weLLEEDu** he strode away.

అంగం **angam** *n.* 1 body. 2 limb. 3 part, component. 4 branch (of literature). 5 *slang* genital organ.

అంగచ్ఛేదం **angaccheedam** *n.* amputation.

అంగచ్ఛేదం చేయు **angaccheedam ceeyu** *v.t.* to amputate.

అంగడి **angaDi** *n.* shop.

అంగణం **angaNam** *n.* 1 (= **naDawa**) entrance leading to the main door (**simhadwaaram**) of a house, flanked by the pial or raised platform (**arugu**) on either side. 2 *fig.* arena; **jiiwita samaraangaNam** the arena of life's conflict.

అంగదం **angadam** *n.* bracelet worn on the upper arm.

అంగన **angana** *n.* woman.

అంగన్యాసం **anganyaasam** *n.* ceremony of touching the various parts of the body with the hands or fingers, accompanied by prayers.

అంగప్రదక్షిణం **angapradakSiNam** *n.* making a circuit of a temple clockwise (= **pradakSiNam**) by rolling the body over and over.

అంగబలం **angabalam** *n.* 1 physical strength. 2 material support; **~ arthabalam** material and financial support.

అంగబిళ్ళ **angabiLLa** *n. class.* leaf-shaped ornament worn by a girl round the waist.

అంగరంగ వైభవం **angaranga waybhawam** *n.* pomp, grandeur.

అంగరకా, అంగర్ఖా **angarakaa, angarkhaa** *n.* long coat.

అంగరక్ష **angarakSa** *n.* 1 bodyguard. 2 charm to ward off evil.

అంగరక్షకుడు **angarakSakuDu** *n.* bodyguard.

అంగరాగం **angaraagam** *n.* scented cosmetic ointment for the body.

అంగలార్చు **angalaarcu** *v.i.* to grieve, cry, lament (**-koosam,** for).

అంగవస్త్రం, అంగోస్త్రం **angawastram, angoostram** *n.* man's upper cloth, towel.

అంగవికల **angawikala** *adj.* 1 physically handicapped. 2 disabled, incapacitated.

అంగవైకల్యం **angawaykalyam** *n.* 1 physical handicap, deformity. 2 disablement, mutilation.

అంగహీన **angahiina** *adj.* mutilated, maimed, disabled, incapacitated.

అంగహీనత **angahiinata** *n.* disablement, incapacity.

అంగారం **angaaram** *n.* 1 live coal or charcoal. 2 fire.

అంగారక గ్రహం, అంగారకుడు **angaaraka graham, angaarakuDu** *n.* the planet Mars.

అంగారకవారం **angaarakawaaram** *n. class.* Tuesday.

అంగారుబొట్టు **angaaruboTTu** *n.* mark on the forehead made with saffron as a sign of the wearer's community.

అంగి **angi** I. *suffix meaning* having a body or limbs, e.g., **sundaraangi** having a beautiful body or limbs. II. *n.dial.* shirt. III. *adj. class.* important.

అంగిలి **angili** *n.* palate (of the mouth).
అంగీ **angii** *n.* 1 long coat, gown. 2 *dial.* shirt.
అంగీకరించు **angiikarincu** *v.t.* 1 to agree to, consent to 2 to accede to, accept (proposal). 3 to admit, acknowledge (mistake).
అంగీకారం **angiikaaram** *n.* 1 agreement, consent. 2 acceptance, adoption. 3 approval. 4 admission, acknowedgement.
అంగుళం **anguLam** *n.* inch.
అంగుళి **anguLi** *n.* finger, toe.
అంగుళీయకం **anguLiiyakam** *n.* finger ring.
అంగుష్ఠం **anguSTam** *n.* thumb, big toe.
అంగుష్ఠమాత్రుడు **anguSTamaatruDu** *n. colloq.* 1 person of small stature. 2 weak person who is habitually guided by others. 3 illiterate person.
అంగూరు **anguuru** *n.* grape.
అంచ **anca** *n. class.* swan.
అంచనా **ancanaa** *n.* guess, estimate, valuation.
అంచనా కట్టు, అంచనా వేయు **ancanaa kaTTu, ancanaa weeyu** *v.t.* to make an estimate of, guess; **ekkuwa/takkuwa ancanaa weeyu** to over-/under-estimate.
అంచలం **ancalam** *n. class.* 1 edge, border. 2 loose end of a sari (**kongu**).
అంచు **ancu**[1] *n.* 1 edge, border; **arugu ~ na nilabadi kaaLLu kaDukkoo** stand at the edge of the platform and wash your feet. 2 brim, rim (of pot). 3 hem (of garment). 4 *pl.* **~ lu** borders, limits; **aakaaśapuT ~ lu** the borders of the sky, the far distance; **~ lu kammulu leeni baTTa** plain cloth with no border either lengthwise or breadthwise.
అంచు **ancu**[2] *v.t.* to send.
అంచె [టపా] **ance[Tapaa]** *n. class.* post carried in stages by relays of runners; **idi ~ parugulamiida weLLaali** this must be delivered by postal runners.
అంచెలంచెలుగా **ancelancelugaa** *adv.* in stages, in instalments, stage by stage, gradually.
అంచెలవారీగా **ancelawaariigaa** *adv.* in stages, one after another, one by one.
అంచెలుకట్టు **ancelukaTTu** *v.i.* to keep in line, move in file (one behind the other).
అంచేత **anceeta** *same as* **anduceeta.**
అంజ **anja** *n.* 1 footstep, footprint. 2 stride.
అంజనం **anjanam** *n.* 1 eye-salve, collyrium. 2 magic ointment for discovering hidden objects or creating illusions.
అంజలి **anjali** *n.* 1 folded hands, i.e., hands with palms together and fingers pointing upwards as in prayer. 2 hands held together to form a cup. 3 (*in compounds*) tribute to the dead; *see* **ghaTincu.**
అంజలించు **anjalincu** *v.i.* to fold o.'s hands in prayer or reverence.
అంజలి బంధం **anjali bandham** *n.* joining of hands together in prayer or respect.
అంజాయించు **anjaayincu** *v.i.* to hesitate, doubt.
అంజి **anji** *n.* game played by a group of five girls.
అంజూరు **anjuuru** *n.* fig (fruit).
అంట **anTa**[1] *p.p.* 1 to; **ciwaraNTaa** to the very end; **modal ~** down to the root. 2 on, at, along; **daar ~ pooniwwaru** they will not allow you to go on the road. 3 from; **kaLL ~ niiLLu kaarutunnaayi** tears are flowing from (her) eyes.
అంట **aNTa**[2] *same as* **aTa.**
అంటకట్టు **aNTakaTTu** *v.t.* 1 to join, fasten together, tie together. 2 to attribute, ascribe; **aayana awakatawakalu aayana taabeedaarulakee aNTakaTTeewaaru** they would ascribe his misdeeds to his underlings. 3 to foist, force (s.g on s.o.); **naaku leenipooni baadhyata miiree aNTakaTTEEru** it was you who forced on me (*or* saddled me with) an unwanted responsibility.
అంటకట్టుకొను **aNTakaTTukonu** *v.i.* to be[come] clotted or matted.
అంటకాక **aNTakaaka** *n.* heat which pervades a kiln when pots are fired.
అంటగు **aNTagu** *v.i.* 1 to be defiled. 2 to be in menses.
అంటపెట్టు **aNTapeTTu** *v.t.* 1 to stick [together]; **kaayitaalu jigurutoo ~** to stick papers together with gum. 2 to set fire to, set on fire, light, ignite; **ii pullalu aNTapeTTaNDi** please light these sticks *or* please set these sticks on fire.
అంటరాని **aNTaraani** *adj.* untouchable, fit to be shunned.
అంటరానితనం **aNTaraanitanam** *n.* untouchability.
అంటి **aNTi** *n. dial.* plantain, banana.
అంటించు **aNTincu** *v.t.* 1 to stick, paste, fasten (a cover). 2 to unite, join, attach. 3 to light, set on fire. 4 *colloq.* **reNDu aNTincEEnu** I gave (him) two blows.
అంటిపెట్టుకొను **aNTipeTTukonu** *v.t.* to cling to, stick to, adhere to; **idi yaawajjiiwamuu ataNNi aNTipeTTukonee undi** this (habit) has clung to him all his life.
అంటు **aNTu** I. *n.* 1 touch. 2 dirt, unclean[li]ness, impurity; **~ guDDalu** dirty clothes; **aNTLu** unwashed dishes. 3 defilement, pollution; **annam tiNTuu tiNTuu ceeyi annam ginneloo peTTEEDu. "adi ~ kaaduu? waaDi engili ewaru tiNTaaru?" ani andaruu leecipooyEEru** while eating he put his hand in the vessel. "is that not defilement? who will eat the defiled food?" they asked, and got up and went away. 4 infection, contagion; **~ roogam** infectious disease. 5 grafting, grafted plant or branch; **~ maamiDi** grafted mango. II. *v.i. and t.* 1 to touch. 2 to stick to, adhere to, be attached to; **rangu baTTalaki ~ tundi. duurangaa kuureoo** the (wet) paint will stick to your clothes. sit far away from it; **koosTaa tiiraanni aNTuNDee bhuumulu** the land contiguous to the coastline; **kaSTaalaloo, sukhaalaloo naa wennaNTi unnaaDu** he stood by me through thick and thin (*lit.* he stood right at my back in my joys and sorrows); **waaDiki aa caduwu aNTadu** that kind of learning will not stick in his mind.
అంటుకట్టు, అంటుతొక్కు **aNTukaTTu, aNTutokku** *v.t.* to graft.
అంటుకొను **aNTukonu** I. *v.i.* 1 to stick or adhere (to). 2 to catch fire. 3 to catch on, take hold; **satyagraha udyamam ikkaDa kuuDaa baagaa aNTukondi** here too the satyagraha movement took a firm hold. 4 (of interest, attention) to be fixed; **waaDi buddhi aa neercukonee akSaraalaku aNTukupooyindi** his mind became fixed on the letters he was learning; **pustakaalaku aNTukupooyee waaNNi** I was devoted to books. 5 **ataniki kannu** (*or* **reppa**) **aNTukoodu** his eye will not close, i.e., he will not get sleep; **kaLLu aNTukuNTunnaayi** his eyelids are sticking (due to conjunctivitis). II. *v.t.* 1 to rub on, smear on; **nettina nuune aNTukoni snaanam ceeyu** to rub oil on the head and take a bath; *see* **talaNTukonu.** 2 (of disease) to infect; **waaDu ekkaDoo tirigi ii jwaram paTTukonnaDu. ippuDu adi**

illantaa aNTukondi he wandered somewhere and caught this disease. now it has infected the whole house.

అంటుడు **aNTuDu** *adj.* contagious.

అంటుపోగులు **aNTupoogulu** *n.pl.* small close-fitting earrings.

అంటురాయి **aNTuraayi** *n.* magnet.

అంటురోగం, అంటువ్యాధి **aNTuroogam, aNTuwyaadhi** *n.* infectious disease.

అంటూ **aNTuu** I. *present participle of* **anu** to say. II. *particle used to emphasise or draw attention to the preceding word or phrase*; **aandhrapradeeśloo 1935 warakuu pancadaara phyaakTarii ~ eemii leedu** till 1935 there was not a single sugar factory in Andhra Pradesh.

అంటూశొంటూ, అంటూసొంటూ **aNTuuśoNTuu, aNTuusoNTuu** *n.* impurity.

అంటే **aNTee** I. *conditional form of* **anu** to say. II. *idiomatic usages:* (i) *in a verbless sentence* ~ = means, signifies; **oka kiloomiiTar~ weyyi miiTarlu** a kilometre means a thousand metres; (ii) *two clauses, one containing ~ and one containing another part of* **anu**, *may signify competition* or *rivalry*; **hrdayamloo eeDupuu, koopam neenu mundu~ neenu mundu aNTunnaayi** grief and anger are competing with each other in his heart; (iii) *a simple sentence + ~ may replace a conditional clause*: **maLLii waccEEw ~ cuusukoo!** if you come back again, mind out!; (iv) *the conditional of* **[w]aali** *is formed by adding ~* ; **maa tammuNNi cuuDaal~ pilustaanu** if you want to see my brother, I will call him; (v) ~ *following a noun in the nominative may be used to express the object of emotional feelings*; **nuwwu ~ waaDiki praaNam** he is devoted to you; **waaDu ~ pillalaku bhayangaa uNDeedi** children used to be afraid of him.

అంటొత్తు **aNTottu** *v.t.* 1 to propagate (a plant) by layering. 2 to press or crush together (thorn branches).

అండ **aNDa**[1] *n.* assistance, protection, support, patronage.

అండ **aNDa**[2] *dial. variant form of* **aNDi.**

అండం **aNDam** *n.* 1 egg, ovum. 2 *class.* testicle. 3 *class.* world, globe, universe.

అండకోశం **aNDakoośam** *n.* 1 scrotum, testicle. 2 *bot.* pistil.

అండచేసుకొను **aNDa ceesukonu** *v.t.* to take help from, rely on.

అండదండలు **aNDadaNDalu** *n.pl.* material and moral assistance, backing, support.

అండా **aNDaa** *n. dial.* large metal vessel.

అండాకార **aNDaakaara** *adj.* 1 oval. 2 spheroid.

అండాశయం **aNDaaśayam** *n. sci.* ovary.

అండి **aNDi** I. *suffix used to form imperative plural or polite imperative singular* **iTu raNDi**! come here! (*pl.*) *or* please come here (*sing.*) II. *clitic (always in suffix position) signifying a polite form of address* **eem~**! sir! *or* madam! **uNTaanaNDi** I will stay here, sir/madam.

అంత **anta** I. *det. n.* 1 so much, so many; **~ mandi** so many people; **~ seepu** so much time, so long; **nuwwu enta aDigitee ~ istaanu** I will give as much as you ask. 2 *with certain postpositions* upto that point, that far (in distance or time): **~ waraku, ~ maTTuku** upto that, so far; **~ ku puurwam** before that, previously. II. *particle suffixed to a noun, adv. or vbl.adj.* as. . . . .as **naa ~ waaDu** a man as big/tall/old as I am; **lank ~ illu** a huge house (*lit.* a house as big as an island); **idiwarak ~ gaTTigaa** as strongly as before; **naaku telisin ~ waraku** as far as I know; **aame pani ceestunn~ seepuu** as long as she keeps on working; **waaLLu tinn~ tini takkinadi paareeśEEru** they ate as much as they wanted and threw away the rest; **tan~ taanee** of his accord; **neenu purugunu kaanu, maniS~ maniSini** I am a grown man, not an insect.

అంతం **antam** *n.* 1 end, limit; **ikaaraanta padaalu** words ending in the letter *i*; **maasaantam** end of a month. 2 death.

అంతం అవు **antam awu** *v.i.* to end, terminate, cease, be finished, be over.

అంతం చేయు, అంతం ఒందించు **antam ceeyu, antam ondincu** *v.t.* 1 to put an end to, finish, abolish. 2 to kill.

అంతంత **antanta** *adj.* 1 so much, so great; **roojuu ~ seepu eem ceppukoNTaaru?** what do they talk about for so long every day? 2 so little; **naaTakaracanalu ~ gaa unna mana telugu naaTa nuutana prakriyala koosam wetakapoowaDam śramatoo kuuDina pani** when even dramas are so scarce in our Telugu land, to go searching for new art forms is a difficult task.

అంతంత మాత్రం **antanta maatram** *adj.* just enough to manage with; **iNTipaTTuna kuurconi unna polam cuusukoomanu. asalee ~ gaa uNTee inkaa kaaleejii caduwu ekkaDa ceppistaawu?** tell him to stay at home and look after the land that you have. really when you have only just enough to manage with, how will you be able to educate him further at college?; **pariikSaloo antantamaatrapu maarkulu waccEEyi** he only just passed the examination.

అంతః **antah** *see* **antar.**

అంతఃకరణ[ం] **antaḥkaraNa[m]** *n.* 1 mind, heart, inner consciousness; **antaḥkaraNa jñaanam** innate knowledge. 2 conscience. 3 kindheartedness.

అంతఃపురం **antaḥpuram** *n.* women's apartments in a palace, harem.

అంతఃప్రజననం **antaḥ prajananam** *n. sci.* inbreeding.

అంతకం **antakam** *adjvl. suffix meaning* causing the end of, e.g., **paytyaantakam** causing the end of bile; **praaNaantakam** causing the end of life, lethal.

అంతకంత, అంతకు అంత **antakạnta, antaku anta** *adv.* as much again; **wiiDu manaki uurikee iccEEDeemiTi? ~ puccukooDuu?** has he given it to us free? will he not take as much again from us?

అంతకంతకు **antakantaku** *adv.* 1 gradually, step by step, little by little. 2 increasingly, more and more.

అంతగా **antagaa** *adv.* so much, to that extent; **~ kaawaalaNTee istaanu** if he wants it so much, I will give it; **~ upakarincani** not so very useful.

అంతట **antaTa** *adv.* afterwards, then, next.

అంతటా **antaTaa** *p.p. and adv.* everywhere, throughout, all over; **diini ~ daTTamayna nuugu uNTundi** there is thick down all over it; **deeśam~** all over the country.

అంతటి **antaTi** *oblique form of* **anta/antaa**: **~ too uurukooru** they will not be content with that much; **bhaaraddeeśam ~ loonuu** in the whole of India. 2 *dialectal and literary variant of* **anta.**

అంతటిలో, అంతట్లో **antaTiloo, antaTLoo** *adv.* in the mean time.

అంతదాకా, అంతదనుక **antadaakaa, antadanuka** *adv.* 1 up to that, so far. 2 till then.

అంతనే **antanee** *particle·suffixed to past relative participle* 1 as soon as; **aa waarta telisin~** as soon as he heard that news. 2 for the sole reason that, just because, simply because; **DiTekTiw pustakaalu cadiwin~ widyaarthulu ceDipootaaraa?** will students be corrupted simply as a result of reading detective novels?

అంతమంది **antamandi** *det.n.pl.* so many persons, that number of persons.

అంతమందీ **antamandii** *det.n.pl.* all those persons.

అంతమాత్రంచేత **antamaatramceeta** *adv.* only for that reason.

అంతమాత్రాన **antamaatraana** *adv.* just for that reason, just because of, just as a result of; **bhikSulanu aresTu ceesin~samasya pariSkaaram kaadu** just as a result of of arresting the beggars, the problem will not be solved.

అంతమాత్రానికి **antamaatraaniki** *adv.* only for that, just for that reason, only because of that; **~muncuku-pooyeedi eemii leedu** as a result of that small thing nothing will be lost.

అంతర్, అంతః : **antar, antaḥ** *adjvl. prefix* 1 internal, inner; **antaḥ preeraNa** inner urge. 2 inter- **antarjaatiiya** international.

అంతరం **antaram**[1] I. *n.* 1 difference, disparity, space, gap, interval, hiatus. 2 rank; **cinn~ pedd ~uNDakkara leedaa?** should there be no difference in rank between young and old? II. *suffix* 1 other, another; **kaaryaantaram-miida ii uuru wacci paDDaanu** I came here on some other business; **grahaantara yaanam** voyage to another planet; **ruupaantaraalu arthaantaraalu** variations of form and meaning; **kaaraNaantaraalawalla** due to various causes; **kaalaantaramloo** in the course of time. 2 outside, beyond; **kulaantara wiwaham** marriage outside o.'s own community; **deeśaantaram weLLEEDu** he left the country; **mana deeśamloo puTTi, samudraantaraalaku wyaapincina bawddha matam** the Buddhist religion which was born in our country and spread to lands beyond the seas.

అంతరం **antaram**[2] *suffix meaning* inner part or deep recess, e.g., **guhaantaram** deep cave.

అంతరం **antaram**[3] *n. dial.* storey, floor (of a building).

అంతరంగం **antarangam** *n.* mind, heart.

అంతరంగిక, ఆంతరంగిక **antarangika, aantarangika** *adj.* 1 inner[most], interior, internal. 2 confidential; **~mitruDu** confidant, confidential adviser on personal matters.

అంతరణం **antaraNam** *n.* 1 transfer. 2 *ling.* translation.

అంతరాంతరాలు **antaraantaraalu** *n.pl.* 1 heart. 2 core.

అంతరాత్మ **antaraatma** *n.* 1 conscience. 2 inner self, spirit, soul.

అంతరాయం **antaraayam** *n.* 1 impediment, obstacle, obstruction, hindrance. 2 interruption.

అంతరాళం **antaraaLam** *n.* interval, distance, depths; **wiśwaantaraaLam** distant parts of the universe; **hṛdanta-raaLam** depths of o.'s heart.

అంతరించు **antarincu** *v.i.* 1 to perish, die. 2 to come to an end, pass away, pass off.

అంతరిక్షం **antarikSam** *n.* space.

అంతరువు **antaruwu** *n.* difference, distinction.

అంతర్గత **antargata** I. *adj.* 1 inner. 2 hidden. 3 intermediate. II. *adjvl. suffix meaning* contained in, forming part of, e.g., **padmapuraaN~** forming part of the Padmapuranam.

అంతర్గమనం **antargamanam** *n.* infiltration.

అంతర్గర్భిత **antargarbhita** *adj.* hidden inside, concealed.

అంతర్జంఘిక **antarjanghika** *n. med.* tibia.

అంతర్జాతీయ **antarjaatiiya** *adj.* international.

అంతర్జాతీయత **antarjaatiiyata** *n.* internationalism.

అంతర్జీవ ద్రవ్యం **antarjiiwa drawyam** *n. biol.* endoplasm.

అంతర్దర్శనం **antardarśanam** *n.* introspection.

అంతర్దశ **antardaśa** *n.* interphase.

అంతర్ధానం **antardhaanam** *n.* disappearance.

అంతర్ధానం అవు **antardhaanam awu** *v.i.* to disappear.

అంతర్నిర్మాణం **antarnirmaaNam** *n.* internal structure.

అంతర్బుద్ధి **antarbuddhi** *n.* 1 cunning. 2 intuition.

అంతర్భాగం **antarbhaagam** *n.* constituent part, integral part.

అంతర్భూత **antarbhuuta** *adj.* 1 included, contained. 2 embodied, incorporated. 3 embedded.

అంతర్భూతం చేయు **antarbhuutam ceeyu** *v.t.* to embody, incorporate.

అంతర్భేదం **antarbheedam** *n.* internal variation.

అంతర్మథనం **antarmadhanam** *n.* agitation of mind.

అంతర్ముఖుడు **antarmukhuDu** *n.* inward looking person, introspective person.

అంతర్యామి **antaryaami** *n.* indwelling spirit, soul; *cf.* **sarwaantaryaami.**

అంతర్యుద్ధం **antaryuddham** *n.* civil war.

అంతర్రాష్ట్ర **antarraaSTra** *adj.* interstate.

అంతర్లీన[ం] **antarliina [m]** *adj.* 1 innate. 2 lying hidden.

అంతర్వర్ణ **antarwarNa** *same as* **warNaantara.**

అంతర్వాణి **antarwaaNi** *n.* inner voice, conscience.

అంతర్వాహిని **antarwaahini** *n.* 1 *class.* river that flows underground. 2 undercurrent.

అంతర్వేదన **antarweedana** *n.* inwardly felt grief.

అంతర్వేశనం **antarweeśanam** *n.* interpolation.

అంతల పొంతల **antala pontala** *adj.* far, distant; **~cuTTam** distant relative.

అంతలు **antalu** *noun suffix meaning* times *attached to numerals*; **reND~** twice, double; *cf.* **intalu.**

అంతలేసి **antaleesi** *adj.* so big, so great; **~panulu** such great works *or* such wicked works.

అంతలో **antaloo** *adv.* 1 just then, suddenly. 2 meanwhile, in the mean time, within that time. 3 within that limit (referring to quantity, size, price, etc.)

అంతవట్టు **antawaTTu** *dial. form of* **antawaraku.**

అంతవరకు **antawaraku** *adv.* 1 upto that, as far as that, to that extent, till then. 2 *following an affirmative vbl. adj.* as far as, as long as; **saadhyamayn~** as far as possible. 3 *following a negative vbl. adj.* so long as; **adhikaara sthaanaalanu sanyasincan~** so long as they do not give up their official positions.

అంతశయ్య **antaśayya** *n. class.* deathbed.

అంతశ్చర్మం **antaścarmam** *n. zool.* endodermis.

అంతశ్శత్రువు **antaśśatruwu** *n.* 1 hidden foe, secret enemy. 2 evil passions which are enemies of the self.

అంతస్తు **antastu** *n.* 1 position, status, standing, dignity. 2 rank (in society). 3 storey (of a building).

అంతస్థం **antastham** *n. gram.* one of the semivowels *y, r, l, w*.

అంతస్సు **antassu** *n.* 1 heart. 2 inner content.

అంతా **antaa** I. *det.n.* 1 all, everything, everyone. 2 **~ aytee** if it comes to that. II *adv.* afterwards, later; **pillalu koTTukonnaaru. kaaseepaTik ~ maLLi kalisi aaDukonnaaru** the children quarrelled; after a little time they joined together again and played.

అంతిపురం **antipuram** *colloq. alt. form of* **antaḥpuram**.

అంతిమ **antima** *adj.* last, final, latest.

అంతిమంగా **antimangaa** *adv.* finally.

అంతు **antu** *n.* end; **nii ~ cuustaanu** *or* **nii ~ kanukkoNTaanu** I will see the end of you; **nii ~ muuDindi** your end is near; (*these threats are equivalent to* I will punish you); **bhaaSaaśaastram ~ cuusEEDu** he studied linguistics thoroughly.

అంతుచిక్కు **antucikku** *v.i.* to be grasped or understood; **aayana enduku alaa maaTLaaDEEDoo enta aaloocincinaa naaku antucikka leedu** no matter how hard I thought I could not make out why he talked like that.

అంతుపట్టు **antupaTTu** *v.i.* to be understood or discerned.

అంతుపొంతు, అంతుపంతు **antupontu, antupantu** *n.* 1 end, limit; **~ leeni caduwu** endless study. 2 place, position, situation, whereabouts; (**pontu/pantu**, *an echo word, may be connected with* **ponta** nearness).

అంతే **antee** I. *det. n. + emphatic suffix* **-ee** just that much, just so much. II. *adjvl. use* **~ parimaaNam / poDugu / ettu** the same amount/length/height; **maa abbaayi kuuDaa ~ ettu uNTaaDu: pEENTu saripootundi** my son is the same height: the pants will fit him. III. *minor sentence* that is all.

అంతేకాకుండా **antee kaakuNDaa** *adv.* not only that, in addition, besides.

అంతేకాని, అంతేగాని, అంతేతప్ప **anteekaani, anteegaani, anteetappa** *conj. connecting two sentences, one affirmative and one negative* and, but, apart from that, however; **miiru caduwukoowaali, anteekaani allari ceeyakuuDadu** you must study and not create a noise; **waaDitoo tirupati wellaali anteekaani inkekkDiki kaadu** you must go with him to Tirupati but not to anywhere else; **neenu wini uurukunnaanu anteetappa eemii maaTLaaDaleedu** I listened in silence and did not say anything; **nuwwu aayanatoo weLLaali anteetappa naatoo raakuuDadu** you must go with him and not come with me; **intee telusu, anteetappa inkeemii teliyadu** I know this much, apart from that I know nothing more.

అంతేవాసి **anteewaasi** *n. class.* disciple of a guru.

అంతో ఇంతో **antoo intoo** I. *adj.* some little [amount of]. II. *adv.* just a little, only a little; **~ sarigaa** fairly correctly; **~ caduwukonnawaaDu** a semi-educated person.

అంత్య **antya** *adj.* last, final, ultimate, concluding; **~ niSThuuram kanna aadi niSThuuram meelu** it is better to be harsh at the beginning than at the end (proverb).

అంత్యక్రియలు **antya kriyalu** *n.pl.* last rites, funeral obsequies.

అంత్రం **antram** *n.* bowel, intestine.

అంత్రమూలం **antramuulam** *n. med.* duodenum.

అందం **andam** *n.* beauty, handsomeness.

అందగత్తె **andagatte** *n.* beautiful woman.

అందగాడు **andagaaDu** *n.* handsome man.

అందచందాలు **andacandaalu** *n. pl.* beauty, good looks, handsome appearance.

అందచేయు **andaceeyu** *v.t.* 1 to hand over, supply, deliver. 2 to convey (news, congratulations). 3 to provide (education). 4 to hand out, distribute (books). 5 to serve (notice).

అందనుక **andanuka** *adv.* (= **antadaakaa**) upto that, that far, so far.

అందరు **andaru** *det. n. pl.* so many persons, that number of persons.

అందరూ **andaruu** *det.n.pl.* all (persons), everyone.

అందలం **andalam** *n.* palanquin; **andaruu ~ ekkitee mooseewaaLLu ewaru?** if everyone climbs into the palanquin, who will there be to carry it? (proverb).

అందలి **andali** *adj.* of that, in that; **~ paatralu** characters in it (a story).

అందవికారం **andawikaaram** *n.* ugliness.

అందాకా **andaakaa** *adv.* 1 so far, so long, till then. 2 for the time being.

అందాజు **andaaju** I. *n.* estimate, valuation. II. *adv.* approximately.

అందాల **andaala** *adj.* beautiful, charming, graceful.

అందించు **andincu** *v.t.* 1 to give, hand over, provide, deliver. 2 to make available, supply. 3 to convey, render (information). 4 to offer, hand (cup).

అందిక **andika** *n.* nearness, proximity.

అందిచ్చు **andiccu** *variant form of* **andincu**.

అందిపొందనివాడు **andipondaniwaaDu** *n.* stranger, outsider.

అందిపొందినవాడు **andipondinawaaDu** *n.* distant relative.

అందివచ్చు **andiwaccu** *v.i.* to be a help, be of assistance; **pillawaaDu ceetiki andiwaccEEDu** the boy has come in order to be of assistance.

అందు **andu**[1] *defective pronoun occurring bound to certain cases and postpositions,* e.g., **anduceeta, anduwalla**; *cf.* **indu**[2].

అందు **andu**[2] *p.p., mostly class., mod. only in literature and formal speech* **maayandu daya wuncaNDi** please be sympathetic to us.

అందు **andu**[3] I. *v.i.* to be reached, achieved or received, be within reach; **mii uttaram andindi** your letter has been received; *used with shades of meaning varying according to* *the context*, e.g., **naaku TikaT andaleedu** I did not get a ticket; **naaku bassu andaleedu** I did not catch the bus; **caritraku andani kaalamloo** in prehistoric times; **uuhaku andani wiSayam** something inconceivable; **dhanaruupamloo ancanaaku andani** incapable of being estimated in money terms; **sthala kaalaalaku andani mahaakawulu** poets whose dates and places of abode have not been ascertained. II. *v.t.* to reach, achieve, attain.

అందుకని **andukani** *adv.* therefore.

అందుకనే, అందుకే **andukanee, andukee** *adv.* for that very reason.

అందుకొను **andukonu** *v.i. and t.* 1 to reach, attain: **anukonna lakSyaalanu andukooleeka pooyEEm** we could not reach the targets that we expected. 2 to catch up with, overtake (vehicle). 3 to take into o.'s hands, receive, accept. 4 to take up, pick up (phone, sitar). 5 to perceive, imbibe, appreciate; **artham andukunnaaDu** he perceived the meaning. 6 to begin, take up, go on with (song, story). 7 to answer, reply, retort.

అందుచేత, అంచేత **anduceeta, anceeta** *adv.* therefore, for that reason.

అందునిమిత్తం **andunimittam** *adv.* on account of that.

అందుబాటు **andubaaTu** *n.* reach, availability; **~loo** available, ready to hand, within reach; **~loo unna wanarulu** available resources.

అందుబాటుగా **andubaaTugaa** *adv.* within reach, conveniently near, accessible.

అందుమీదట **andumiidaTa** *adv.* thereupon.

అందులో **anduloo** *adv.* 1 in it, therein. 2 moreover, furthermore; **~ aame ippuDu ayśwaryawanturaalu** moreover now she is a rich woman.

అందులోనూ **anduloonuu** *adv.* 1 besides, moreover, furthermore. 2 particularly, in particular; **tanu cuusina wiSayam ewarikaynaa ~ J. baabuki ceppaalanipincindi** he wanted to tell what he had seen to someone, and in particular to J. Babu.

అందువల్ల **anduwalla** *adv.* because of that, due to that, for that reason.

అందె **ande** *n.* anklet, armlet; **~ weesina ceyyi** a competent person, expert; *in former days a person of great skill or competence was honoured by the king with the award of an armlet.*

అంధ[ం] **andha[m]** *adj.* blind; **andhayugam** dark age.

అంధకారం **andhakaaram** *n.* darkness.

అంధకారబంధుర **andhakaarabandhura** *adj.* gloomy, dismal.

అంధత్వం **andhatwam** *n.* blindness.

అంధప్రాయంగా **andhapraayangaa** *adv.* blindly, as if (one) was blind.

అంధవిశ్వాసం **andhawiśwaasam** *n.* blind belief, superstition.

అంధానుకరణ **andhaanukaraNa** *n.* slavish imitation.

అంధానుకర్త **andhaanukarta** *n.* slavish imitator.

అంధుడు **andhuDu** *n.* blind person.

అంధురాలు **andhuraalu** *n.* blind woman.

అంప **ampa** *n. class.* arrow.

అంపశయ్య **ampaśayya** *n.* bed of arrows (on which Bhishma lay, as described in the Mahabharata).

అంపకాలు **ampakaalu** *n.* the final ceremony in a marriage when parents of the bride bid farewell to her.

అంపు, అంపించు **ampu, ampincu** *v.t.* to send, despatch; **kabur~** to send a message, send word.

అంబ **amba** *n.* 1 *dial.* mother. 2 *affix attached to certain women's names*, e.g., **pullamaamba**. 3 a name of the Goddess Durga.

అంబడి **ambaDi** *p.p., another form of* **wembaDi** *used only with inanimate nouns*; **rooDD ~ tiragaku, eNDagaa undi** do not walk along the road, the sun is very hot.

అంబరం **ambaram** *n.* 1 sky. 2 cotton cloth.

అంబరు **ambaru** *adj.* wheat coloured, golden yellow.

అంబలి **ambali** *n.* porridge, gruel; **ambaTipoddu, ambaTipuuTa, ambaTiweeLa, ambaTeeLa** time for taking **ambali**, i.e., about noon.

అంబా **ambaa** *n.* sound of a cow mooing or lowing; **aawu ~ ani aricindi** the cow lowed; **~ rawaalu winipincEEyi** the sound of cows lowing was heard.

అంబాడు **ambaaDu** *v.i.* (of an infant) to crawl.

అంబారం **ambaaram** *n.* 1 heap of grain on the threshing floor. 2 grain brought home after harvest. 3 landlord's share of a crop. 4 yield of grain from a field.

అంబారి **ambaari** *n.* howdah, seat on an elephant's back.

అంబు **ambu** *n. class.* arrow, dart.

అంబుధి **ambudhi** *n.* sea.

అంభోజం **ambhoojam** *n. class.* lotus.

అంశ **amśa** *n.* 1 part. 2 feature, trait; **waaDiki taata ~ konta waccindi** he has inherited his grandfather's traits to some extent.

అంశం **amśam** *n.* 1 share, part, portion. 2 constituent, component, element; **samaajaśaastramloo muulaamśaalu** basic elements of sociology. 3 subject, topic. 4 point, item; **iraway amśaala aarthika kaaryakramam** twenty point economic programme. 5 *pl.* **amśaalu** minutes (of a meeting). 6 subject (in a syllabus). 7 degree of latitude or longitude.

అంశకాలిక **amśakaalika** *adj.* part time.

అంశదానం **amśadaanam** *n.* small contribution, mite.

అంశిక **amśika** *adj.* fractional.

అంశువు **amśuwu** *n.* ray or beam of light.

అకటావికటం **akaTaawikaTam** I. *n.* obstinacy, perverseness, wilfulness, contrariness. II. *adj.* contrary; **waaDu ~ maniSi** he is a contrary person.

అకర్బన **akarbana** *adj. chem.* inorganic.

అకర్మక **akarmaka** *adj. gram.* intransitive.

అకలంక, అకళంక **akalanka, akaLanka** *adj.* undefiled, pure, spotless.

అకలుషం **akaluSam** *adj.* stainless, unspotted, sinless.

అకశేరుకం **akaśeerukam** *n.sci.* invertebrate.

అకస్మాత్తు **akasmaattu** *adj.* abrupt, sudden.

అకస్మాత్తుగా **akasmaattugaa** *adv.* 1 suddenly, unexpectedly. 2 accidentally, by chance.

అకస్మిక, ఆకస్మిక **akasmika, aakasmika** *adj.* sudden, abrupt, unexpected, unforeseen, fortuitous.

అకారం **akaaram** *n.* the letter *a*.

అకారణ **akaaraNa** *adj.* without cause, without reason.

అకారణంగా **akaaraNangaa** *adv.* without cause, without reason, unjustifiably.
అకారాదిక్రమం **akaaraadikramam** *n.* alphabetical order.
అకారాదిగా **akaaraadigaa** *adv.* in alphabetical order.
అకార్యం **akaaryam** *n.* misdeed, evil deed, criminal act.
అకాల **akaala** *adj.* untimely, unseasonable; ~ **kaalamloo kaalam ceesEEru** he met an untimely death.
అకాలం **akaalam** *n.* wrong time or season.
అకించనుడు **akincanuDu** *n.* penniless person, pauper.
అకుంఠిత **akuNThita** *adj.* 1 unchecked, unhindered. 2 continuous, steady.
అకృత్యం **akṛtyam** *n.* 1 wrong, evil. 2 misdeed.
అక్క **akka** *n.* 1 elder sister. 2 *polite term of address used to a woman.*
అక్కజం **akkajam** *n. class.* wonder, surprise, astonishment.
అక్కటా! **akkaTaa!** *interj. class.* alas!
అక్కడ **akkaDa** *advbl. n.* that place, there; **akkaDiwaaLLu** people of that place.
అక్కడక్కడ **akkaDakkaDa** *adv.* here and there.
అక్కడికక్కడే **akkaDikakkaDee** *adv.* on the spot, right there, then and there.
అక్కర **akkara**[1] *n.* need, want, necessity; **naaku Dabbu ~ leedu** I do not want / need money; **miiru pilawan~ leedu** you need not call; **idi ~ ku wastundi** this will come in useful; **waaLLa ~ tiirutundi** the need they felt will be over; **neeneemaypooyinaa niik~ leedu kaduu?** whatever happens to me, you do not care, do you?
అక్కర **akkara**[2] *n.* 1 occasion, function, celebration; ~ **paTLa iNTiki cuTTaalu wastaaru** relatives will come to the house for the function. 2 consummation of marriage.
అక్కర **akkara**[3] *n.* a kind of poetic metre, used in modern Telugu by Viswanatha Satyanarayana in his '**madhya akkaralu**'.
అక్కరం **akkaram** *n.* letter of the alphabet.
అక్కలకర్ర **akkalakarra** *n.* a medicinal root, *anthemis pyrethrum.*
అక్కళించు **akkaLincu** *v.i.* (of stomach muscles) to be drawn in or contracted.
అక్కసు **akkasu** *n.* 1 spite, malice, anger, jealousy. 2 strong desire.
అక్కిడి **akkiDi** *n.* 1 sowing one crop between lines of another. 2 crop sown between lines of another crop.
అక్కిడికట్టె **akkiDikaTTe** *n.* implement for sowing between lines of crops.
అక్కు *n. class.* chest, breast; ~ **na ceeru** to be embraced; ~ **na ceercu** to embrace, hold close to the chest.
అక్కుపక్షి **akkupakSi** *n.* 1 lean or emaciated person (*corruption of* **wakku pakSi**). 2 *colloq., used as a mild term of abuse.*
అక్కుళ్ళు **akkuLLu** *n.pl.* superior variety of paddy grown mainly in delta areas.
అక్రమ **akrama** *adj.* 1 irregular, wrongful. 2 *maths.* ~ **bhinnam** improper fraction. 3 illegitimate; ~ **santaanam** illegitimate offspring.
అక్రమం **akramam** *n.* irregularity.
అక్రమంగా **akramangaa** *adv.* irregularly, by irregular means, by unlawful means.
అక్రోటు **akrooTu** *n.* walnut tree, *juglans regia.*
అక్షం **akSam** *n.* 1 axis. 2 axle. 3 dice.
అక్షతలు, అక్షింతలు **akSatalu, akSintalu** *n.pl.* 1 grains of rice mixed with turmeric or saffron used for blessings or salutations in certain ceremonies. 2 *slang* abuse, scolding.
అక్షయ **akSaya** *n.* name of the final year in the Hindu cycle of sixty years.
అక్షయం **akSayam awu** *v.i.* to continue to flourish without perishing.
అక్షయపాత్ర **akSayapaatra** *n.* inexhaustible vessel, giving an unfailing supply of food that is wished for.
అక్షర **akSara** *adj.* eternal.
అక్షరం **akSaram** *n.* 1 *in Telugu script* graphic syllable; **naalugu ~ mukkalu waccinanta maatraana prayoojanam leedu** there is no use in acquiring just a smattering of education. 2 *in Roman Script* letter of the alphabet.
అక్షరక్రమం **akSarakramam** *n.* alphabetical order.
అక్షరజ్ఞానం **akSarajñaanam** *n.* literacy.
అక్షరమాల **akSaramaala** *n.* alphabet chart.
అక్షరశః **akSaraśaḥ** *adj.* literally, as laid down by written precept.
అక్షరాభ్యాసం **akSaraabhyaasam** *n.* ceremony of giving the first lesson in writing to a child.
అక్షరాస్యత **akSaraasyata** *n.* literacy.
అక్షరాస్యుడు **akSaraasyuDu** *n.* literate person.
అక్షాంశ[ం] **akSaamśa[m]** *n.* [degree of] latitude.
అక్షి **akSi** *n.* eye; ~ **paTalam** retina.
అక్షింతలపురుగు **akSintalapurugu** *n.* small red coloured insect occurring as a pest on chillies, brinjals, etc., *epilachna.*
అక్షింతలు **akSintalu** *same as* **akSatalu.**
అక్షీణ **akSiiNa** *adj.* lasting, permanent.
అక్షీయ **akSiiya** *adj.* axial.
అక్షౌహిణి **akSawhiNi** *n.* large army.
అఖండ **akhaNDa** *adj.* 1 whole, entire, intact, indivisible. 2 abounding, immense, mighty. 3 *journ.* landslide (victory).
అఖండం **akhaNDam** *n.* long stone slab.
అఖండజ్యోతి **akhaNDajyooti** *n.* lamp which burns continuously, esp. in a temple.
అఖండత్వం **akhaNDatwam** *n.* wholeness, entirety, oneness.
అఖండుడు **akhaNDuDu** *n.* 1 genius, expert. 2 champion (in sports and games).
అఖాతం **akhaatam** *n.* bay, gulf.
అఖిల **akhila** *adj.* all, whole, entire, complete; ~ **bhaarata** (pertaining to) All India.
అఖిలం **akhilam** *n.* whole.

అగచాట్లు **agacaaTLu** *n.pl.* evils, afflictions, troubles, distress.

అగడు **agaDu** *n.* 1 blame, fault. 2 craving (for liquor, gambling, etc.)

అగడ్త **agaDta** *n.* ditch, trench, moat.

అగణిత **agaNita** *adj.* countless, innumerable.

అగణ్య **agaNya** *adj.* uncountable.

అగత్యం **agatyam** I. *n.* need, necessity. II. *adv.* urgently.

అగపడు, అగపరచు **agapaDu, agaparacu** *same as* **agupaDu, aguparacu.**

అగమ్య **agamya** *adj.* 1 inaccessible, impenetrable. 2 aimless.

అగమ్యగోచర[ం] **agamyagoocara[m]** *adj.* inexplicable, confused, in confusion.

అగరు **agaru** *n.* kind of sweet-scented wood.

అగరునూనె **agarunuune** *n.* kind of perfume.

అగరువత్తి **agaruwatti** *n.* incense stick.

అగసాలి **agasaali** *n.* goldsmith.

అగస్త్యభ్రాత **agastyabhraata** *n.* 1 obscure or unknown person who tries to pretend that he is a great personage (*lit.* brother of the sage Agastya). 2 person who is overshadowed by his brother. 3 *colloq.* idiot, fool.

అగస్త్యుడు **agastyuDu** *n.* Agastya, the sage who brought Aryan culture to South India.

అగాధ **agaadha** *adj.* unfathomable, very deep, bottomless.

అగాధం **agaadham** *n.* 1 chasm. 2 *fig.* gulf, gap.

అగాధమండలం **agaadhamaNDalam** *n.* abyss.

అగారం **agaaram** *n.* 1 *class.* house, apartment, building. 2 *mod. only as second part of a compound,* e.g., **karmaagaaram** factory, **kaaraagaaram** prison.

అగావు **agaawu** *n.* advance (in cash or kind).

అగుడుచేయు **aguDuceeyu** *v.t.* to belittle, show (s.o.) in a bad light.

అగుపడు, అగపడు, ఔపడు **agupaDu, agapaDu, awpaDu** *v.i.* to appear, seem, be found, be perceived.

అగుపరచు, ఔపరచు **aguparacu, awparacu** *v.t.* to show, display.

అగుపించు, ఔపించు **agupincu, awpincu** *v.i.* to appear, seem.

అగులుబొగులుగా **agulubogulugaa** *adv.* hurriedly; **aaTala randhiloo paDi pillalu annam ~ tiNTunnaaru** the children are gulping down their food, being very keen to go out and play.

అగోచర **agoocara** *adj.* invisible, intangible, imperceptible.

అగౌరవం **agawrawam** *n.* disregard, contempt, disgrace, dishonour, humiliation, ignominy.

అగౌరవపరచు **agawrawaparacu** *v.t.* 1 to shock, scandalise. 2 to show disrespect to, insult, disgrace, humiliate. 3 to bring into disrepute. 4 to disparage, denigrate.

అగౌరవించు **agawrawincu** *v.t.* to dishonour, disgrace, humiliate.

అగ్గగలాడు **aggaggalaaDu** *v.i.* to tremble.

అగ్గి, అగ్ని **aggi, agni** *n.* fire; **aggimiida guggilam pooyu** *or* **agniloo aajyam pooyu** *expression meaning* to stir up further trouble, *cf. the English expression* to pour fat on the fire.

అగ్గికుండ, అగ్గిదాక **aggikuNDa, aggidaaka** *n.* pot containg burning coals carried before a corpse on the way to the cremation ground.

అగ్గి తెగులు **aggi tegulu** *n.* name of a group of pests which attack crops and cause withering.

అగ్గిపిడుగు **aggipiDugu** *n.* physically strong person.

అగ్గిపుల్ల **aggipulla** *n.* match [stick].

అగ్గిపెట్టె **aggipeTTe** *n.* match box.

అగ్గిబరాటా **aggibaraaTaa** *n.* kind of fire work.

అగ్గిరాముడు **aggiraamuDu** *n.* 1 folk hero of the type of Robin Hood. 2 angry person.

అగ్గువ **agguwa** I.*n. dial.* cheapness. II. *adj. dial.* cheap.

అగ్గైపోవు **aggaypoowu** *v.i.* 1 to turn to fire. 2 to be very angry.

అగ్ని **agni** *same as* **aggi.**

అగ్నికణం **agnikaNam** *n.* spark.

అగ్నికుండం **agnikuNDam** *n.* fire pit made for religious ceremonies.

అగ్నిక్రియ **agnikriya** *n.* cremation.

అగ్నిజ్వాల **agnijwaala** *n.* flame.

అగ్నిపరీక్ష **agnipariikSa** *n.* crucial test (*lit.* ordeal by fire).

అగ్నిపర్వతం **agniparwatam** *n.* volcano.

అగ్నిప్రమాద సూచన **agnipramaada suucana** *n.* fire alarm.

అగ్నిప్రవేశం **agnipraweeśam** *n.* self-immolation.

అగ్నిమాంద్యం **agnimaandyam** *n.* indigestion, dyspepsia, want of appetite; *cf.* **mandaagni.**

అగ్నిమాపకం **agnimaapakam** *n.* fire extinguisher.

అగ్నిమాపకదళం **agnimaapakadaLam** *n.* fire brigade.

అగ్నిసంస్కారం **agnisamskaaram** *n.* cremation in fire which has been purified by a religious rite.

అగ్ని సాక్షి[కం]గా **agnisaakSi[kan]gaa** *adv.* in the presence of fire as witness.

అగ్నిహోత్రం **agnihootram** *n.* 1 fire. 2 sacred fire maintained in certain brahman households.

అగ్నిహోత్రుడు **agnihootruDu** *n.* a name of the God of fire.

అగ్ర **agra** *adj.* first, highest, topmost, chief, principal, leading.

అగ్రం **agram** *n.* 1 top, peak, summit, apex. 2 *geog.* cape.

అగ్రగణ్యుడు **agragaNyuDu** *n.* foremost person.

అగ్రగామి **agragaami** *n.* 1 one who is in the forefront, leader. 2 one who precedes, precursor, forerunner.

అగ్రజుడు **agrajuDu** *n.* eldest brother in a family.

అగ్రణి **agraNi** I. *n.* leader. II. *adj.* principal, chief.

అగ్రతాంబూలం **agrataambuulam** *n.* greatest honour, highest honour.

అగ్రనాయకుడు **agranaayakuDu** *n.* top leader.

అగ్రపూజ **agrapuuja** *n.* reverence paid to the most respected person present on an occasion.

అగ్రభాగం **agrabhaagam** *n.* top position.

అగ్రవర్ణం **agrawarNam** *n.* higher or upper caste or community.

అగ్రసరుడు **agrasaruDu** *same as* **agreesaruDu.**

అగ్రసైన్యాలు **agrasaynyaalu** *n. pl. mil.* advance guard.

అగ్రస్థావరం **agrasthaawaram** *n. mil.* advance base.

అగ్రస్థిత **agrasthita** *adj.* foremost.

అగ్రహాయనం **agrahaayanam** *n. class.* another name for the month Margasira.

అగ్రహారం **agrahaaram** *n.* **1** street or quarter in which brahmans live. **2** landed property (gen. a whole village) gifted by a ruler or landholder in former times to a brahman for his maintenance.

అగ్రహారీకుడు **agrahaariikuDu** *n.* holder of an agraharam.

అగ్రేసరంగా **agreesarangaa** *adv.* at the head, in the lead.

అగ్రేసరత్వం **agreesaratwam** *n.* pre-eminence, leadership.

అగ్రేసరుడు, అగ్రసరుడు **agreesaruDu, agrasaruDu** *n.* leader, prominent person.

అఘాయిత్యం **aghaayityam** *n.* **1** atrocity, outrage. **2** disaster, calamity.

అఘోరించు **aghoorincu** *v.i. and t.* **1** to lament loudly or violently. **2** *colloq., substituting for another verb,* e.g., **mundu nuwwu tondaragaa akkaDiki aghooristee** (*for* **weLtee**) if first you go there very quickly; **pilla annam aghooristunnadi** (*for* **tiNTunnadi**) the girl is eating food. **3** *as an expletive or to indicate a poor opinion* **aghoorincinaTTundi** it is lamentable; **caallee, aghoorincEEwu**! that's enough, damn it!; *cf.* **eeDcu.**

అఘోరింపు **aghoorimpu** *n.* bad conduct or behaviour.

అచంచల **acancala** *adj.* firm, steady.

అచంచలంగా **acancalangaa** *adv.* steadily, unremittingly.

అచర **acara** *adj.* immoveable.

అచల **acala** *adj.* immoveable, immobile, motionless, fixed.

అచలం **acalam** *n.* mountain.

అచింత్య **acintya** *adj.* incomprehensible, unimaginable, inconceivable.

అచిర[ం] **acira[m]** *adj.* short (duration); **acira kaalamloo** in a short time.

అచేతన **aceetana** *adj.* **1** inanimate. **2** insensible, lifeless. **3** immobile, inactive.

అచైతన్యం **acaytanyam** *n.* inanimateness, lifelessness.

అచ్చ **acca** *adj.* pure; ~ **telugu maaTalu** words of pure Telugu origin.

అచ్చకాలు బుచ్చకాలు, అచ్చికలు బుచ్చికలు **accakaalu buccakaalu, accikalu buccikalu** *n. pl.* friendly talk, pleasant conversation.

అచ్చగా, అచ్చం, అచ్చంగా **accagaa, accam, accangaa** *adv.* only, merely, purely, totally, completely, exactly; **accangaa niikee** only for you; **abbaayi accam miilaagee unnaaDu** the boy is exactly like you.

అచ్చట ముచ్చట **accaTamuccaTa** *n.* pleasure, enjoyment, fun, humour; **pillawaaDiki mupphayyeeLLu waccEEka waDugu ceestee ~ eem uNTundi?** if you celebrate the boy's coming of age when he is 30 years old what fun will there be?; **wiyyapuraali meDaloo aaDapeLLiwaaLLu waDiyaala daNDa weestee ~ leeni aa maniSi wisiri koTTindaTa** when some of the bride's party hung a garland of crisps round the mother-in-law's neck, that humourless woman tore it off, they say.

అచ్చట్లు ముచ్చట్లు **accaTLumuccaTLu** *n.pl.* pleasant conversation, passing the time pleasantly; **raatri caalaa poddu pooyee daakaa ~ ceppukoNTuu kuurcunnaaru** they sat chatting happily till very late at night.

అచ్చనగండ్లు, అచ్చనగాయలు **accanagaNDLu, accanagaayalu** *n.pl.* game played by girls (= **ammanaalu**).

అచ్చాళి **accaaLi** *n.* **1** person who has no cares or worries. **2** person free from family encumbrances, bachelor. **3** fool.

అచ్చి ఉండు **acci uNDu** *v.i., always in neg.sense, either expressed or implied* to owe, be indebted; **neenu niiku acci unnaanaa?** do I owe anything to you? (implying that nothing is owed).

అచ్చిక, అచ్చిక **accika, acchika** *n.* want, deficiency.

అచ్చివచ్చు **acciwaccu** *v.i.* to prove good or successful, be advantageous, be auspicious or lucky; **acciwaccina illu** an auspicious house.

అచ్చు **accu**[1] *n. gram.* vowel.

అచ్చు **accu**[2] I.*n.* **1** stamp, form, mark, mould; **kaaLLa ~ lu paDDaayi** there were footmarks. **2** print, printing. II. *adv.* exactly (like).

అచ్చు అవు **accu awu** *v.i.* to be printed.

అచ్చుకట్టు **accukaTTu** I.*n.* plot of wet (irrigated) land surrounded by banks. II. *v.i.* **1** to prepare land for wet cultivation by dividing it into plots surrounded by banks. **2** to prepare a mould.

అచ్చుకూర్పు **accukuurpu** *n.* typesetting.

అచ్చుకొను **accukonu** *same as* **aacukonu.**

అచ్చుగుంటక **accuguNTaka** *n.* kind of harrow for levelling ground after ploughing.

అచ్చుగుద్దు **accuguddu** *v.t.* to print; **accuguddinaTTu waaLLa naanna poolika** exactly like his father *or* the exact image of his father.

అచ్చుతప్పు **accutappu** *n.* misprint, printing mistake.

అచ్చుదించు **accudincu** *v.i.* to make a copy; **pariikSaloo naa peeparu cuusi waaDu accudincEEDu** in the examination he looked at my paper and copied it.

అచ్చుపడు **accupaDu** *v.t.* to be imprinted.

అచ్చుపోయు **accupooyu** *v.t.* **1** to stamp, mark; **accoosina aambootu** bull that is marked and let loose in the name of God Siva. **2** to cast (statue).

అచ్చుబాటు **accubaaTu** *n.* family custom or practice.

అచ్చువేయు **accuweeyu** *v.t.* to print.

అచ్చెరపాటు, అచ్చెరువు **accerapaaTu, acceruwu** *n.* astonishment.

అచ్చెరువొందు **acceruwondu** *v.i.* to wonder, be astonished.

అచ్చొత్తు **accottu** *v.t.* to print.

అచ్చోటు **accooTu** *n. class.* that place.

అచ్ఛిక **acchika** *same as* **accika.**

అచ్యుత **acyuta** *adj. class.* 1 firm, unyielding, permanent, imperishable. 2 epithet of Vishnu.

అజ, అజాపతా **aja, ajaapataa** *n.* whereabouts; **waaDu ~ leekuNDaa pooyinaaDu** his whereabouts are not known.

అజం **ajam** *n.* 1 pride. 2 shock, fright.

అజంత **ajanta** *adj. gram.* ending in a vowel.

అజగరం **ajagaram** *n.* python.

అజర **ajara** *adj.* not subject to old age, ageless.

అజరామర **ajaraamara** *adj.* ageless and deathless.

అజాఅంబారా **ajaa ambaaraa** *n.* care, protection; **tallidaNDrulu uuruku weLLEEru. pillalu ~ leekuNDaa gaaliki tirugutunnaaru** the parents have gone away and the children are wandering about with no one to take care of them.

అజాగరూక **ajaagaruuka** *adj.* careless, heedless, negligent, reckless.

అజాగ్రత, అజాగ్రత్త **ajaagrata, ajaagratta** *n.* carelessness, heedlessness, negligence, recklessness.

అజాగ్రతగా, అజాగ్రత్తగా **ajaagratagaa, ajaagrattagaa** *adv.* 1 carelessly. 2 off o.'s guard, unawares.

అజాతశత్రువు **ajaata śatruwu** *n.* person without enemies, inoffensive person.

అజాది **ajaadi** *adj. gram.* beginning with a vowel.

అజాపతా **ajaapataa** *same as* **aja.**

అజిత **ajita** *adj.* 1 unconquered. 2 unrestrained.

అజితేంద్రియుడు **ajiteendriyuDu** *n.* person who does not restrain his passions.

అజీర్ణం, అజీర్తి **ajiirNam, ajiirti** *n.* indigestion, dyspepsia.

అజేయ **ajeeya** *adj.* unconquered, invincible.

అజ్జాయించు **ajjaayincu** *v.i.* to draw back, hesitate.

అజ్ఞత **ajñata** *n.* ignorance.

అజ్ఞాత **ajñaata** *adj.* unknown; **~ waasam** living incognito, esp. the incognito life of the Pandavas during the last year of their exile.

అజ్ఞాతంగా **ajñaatangaa** *adv.* without o.'s knowledge, unbeknown.

అజ్ఞానం **ajñaanam** *n.* ignorance.

అజ్ఞాని **ajñaani** *n.* ignorant person.

అజ్మధ్య **ajmadhya** *adj. ling.* intervocalic.

అజ్మాయిషీ **ajmaayiSii** *n.* 1 supervision, superintendence. 2 control, authority. 3 inspection of crops by revenue officials.

అట **aTa**[1] *adv.* there.

అట, అంట, ట **aTa**[2]**, aNTa, Ta** *clitic* it is said, he/she/it says, they say.

అటక **aTaka** *n.* loft, storage space under the roof of a house; **~ ekkincu** to put in the loft, discard.

అటకాయించు **aTakaayincu** *v.t.* to stop, hinder, obstruct, prevent.

అటమట **aTamaTa** *n.* 1 trickery, fraud. 2 grief.

అటమటకాడు **aTamaTakaaDu** *n.* cheat, deceiver.

అటమటలాడిపోవు **aTamaTalaaDipoowu** *v.i.* to be distressed or worried.

అటమటించు **aTamaTincu** *v.i.* 1 to suffer, be distressed. 2 to be deceived.

అటవి **aTawi** *same as* **aDawi.**

అటావలి ఎల్లుండి **aTaawali elluNDi** *adv.* four days hence.

అటిక **aTika** *n.* small earthen pot with a large mouth (= **caTTi**).

అటు **aTu** *adv.* thus, in that way (manner or direction).

అటు ఇటూ **aTu iTuu** *adv.* this way and that; **aaTalu aaDaniwaaLLu ~ weLLa kuuDadu** those who are not playing games must not wander here and there.

అటు ఉంచు, అటుంచు **aTu uncu, aTuncu** *v.t.* to set aside, put aside, leave aside; **debbala baadha aTunci caalaa awamaanangaa uNTundi** leaving aside (*or* apart from) the pain of the blows, it will be very humiliating.

అటుకులు **aTukulu** *n.pl.* 1 flattened rice. 2 grain not quite ripe but fit for eating.

అటుపక్క **aTupakka** *adv.* on that side, on the other side, over there.

అటుపెట్టు **aTupeTTu** *v.t.* to set aside, put aside, leave aside; **ii bhaawaalannii aTupeTTi asalu wiSayamlooki waddaam** setting aside all these thoughts, let us come to the real matter.

అటుపైన **aTupayna** *adv.* 1 over and above that. 2 after that.

అటుమొన్న **aTumonna** *adv.* the day before the day before yesterday, three days ago.

అటువంటప్పుడు **aTuwaNTappuDu** *adv.* that being so, in that case.

అటువంటి **aTuwaNTi** *adj.* that kind of.

అటువంటిది **aTuwaNTidi** *adv.* that being the case.

అట్ట **aTTa** *n.* 1 cardboard. 2 pad for writing on. 3 book cover.

అట్టకట్టు **aTTakaTTu** *v.i.* to be[come] caked or matted; **aTTakaTTina śiroojaalu** matted hair.

అట్టడుగు **aTTaDugu** I.n. the very bottom. II.*adj.* lowest, humblest, extreme; **~ biidarikam** extreme poverty; **samaajamloo ~ wargaalawaaru** people of the lowest class in society.

అట్టహాసం **aTTahaasam** *n.* 1 pomp, show, ostentation. 2 conceit, self-satisfaction. 3 loud or noisy laughter.

అట్టి **aTTi** *adj.* that kind of.

అట్టిట్టుగా ఉండు **aTTiTTugaa uNDu** *v.i.* to be in a precarious state, hover between life and death.

అట్టిట్టు చేయు **aTTiTTu ceeyu** *v.i.* to cause uncertainty, worry or anxiety; **raatrallaa roogi aTTiTTu ceesEEDu, ippuDu baagaanee unnaaDu** all night long the patient caused anxiety, now he is quite all right.

అట్టిట్టుపడు **aTTiTTupaDu** *v.i.* to be in a state of uncertainty, worry or anxiety.

అట్టిపెట్టు **aTTipeTTu** *v.t.* to keep, retain.

అట్టియెడ **aTTiyeDa** *adv.* in that case, that being so.

అట్టు **aTTu**[1] *n.* 1 pancake; **kooDiguDD ~** omelette; **pesar ~** greengram pancake; **minap ~** blackgram pancake. 2 mark left on the skin after receiving a blow; **~ teelindi** a mark on the skin was left (of the size and shape of a pancake).

అట్టు, అట్లు **aTTu**[2]**, aTLu** *particle suffixed to vbl. adj.* 1 like, as if; **eenuguni cuusi kukkalu morigin ~** like dogs barking at an elephant; **aayana raan ~ ndi** it seems as if he has not come. 2 that (reporting or recording a statement or event); **miiku neenu waccin ~ ewaru ceppEEru**? who told you that I had come? **waaDu waaLLu kSeemangaa ceerin ~ uttaram raasEEDu** he wrote a letter that they had arrived safely. 3 as; **neenu ceppin ~ ceyyi** do as I say; **jaabulanu unnawi unn ~ gaa eTTi pariSkaraNaluu leekuNDaa iwwaDam jarigindi** the letters are presented just as they are without any revision. 4 *with fut.vbl.adj.* so that, with the result that; **widyaarthulu grahinceeT ~ upaadhyaadhyaayulu śraddha tiisukoowaali** teachers must take care that the students understand. 5 *in a special type of rhetorical question* **asalu intakuu manam ikkaDiki enduku waccin ~** ? now why did we really come here?; *see* **aTTee, annaTTu.**

అట్టుడుకు, అట్టుడికిపోవు, అట్టుడికినట్లుడికిపోవు **aTTuDuku, aTTuDikipoowu, aTTuDikinaTLuDikipoowu** *v.i.* 1 *lit.* to be fried like a pancake. 2 (of persons) to seethe or boil with rage inwardly. 3 (of atmosphere, situations) to threaten to explode, be potentially explosive.

అట్టు పుట్టాన వాళ్ళు **aTTupuTTaanawaaLLu** *n.pl.* full description, history and antecedents.

అట్టుబడి ఇట్టుబడి **aTTubaDi iTTubaDi** *adv. dial.* hesitating, wavering.

అట్టే **aTTee** *adv.* 1 just so much, just as it was, as before; **noppi ~ unnadi** the pain is no better; **~ uNDanii** leave it as it was; **~ peTTu** to leave aside, keep aside, keep in reserve. 2 *in neg. constr.* very little, only a little; **~ baagaaleedu** not very well.

అట్ల, అట్లు, అట్లా, అట్లాగు **aTLa, aTLu, aTlaa, aTLaagu** *adv.* thus, like that, in that way.

అట్లకాడ **aTLakaaDa** *n.* kitchen utensil with a broad flat blade, spatula.

అట్లతద్దె, అట్లతద్ది, అట్లతదియ **aTLatadde, aTLataddi, aTLatadiya** *n.* women's festival celebrated in the lunar month of Asviyuja.

అట్లనోము **aTLanoomu** *n.* vow undertaken on the day of **aTLatadde.**

అట్లపెనం **aTLapenam** *n.* pan for frying pancakes.

అట్లా[ం]టప్పుడు **aTLaa[N]TappuDu** *same as* **alaa[N]TappuDu.**

అట్లా[ం]టిది **aTLaa[N]Tidi** *same as* **alaa[N]Tidi.**

అట్లు **aTLu**[1] *pl. of* **aTTu**[1].

అట్లు **aTLu**[2] *same as* **aTTu**[2].

అడ **aDa** *n.* redgram pancake.

అడంగల్ **aDangal** *n.* name of the village register in the Andhra region in which the crops cultivated in each field are noted annually after inspection.

అడంగు **aDangu** *n.* 1 destination. 2 terminus. 3 halting place, camp. 4 place of residence. 5 birth place.

అడకత్తెర **aDakattera** *n.* arecanut cracker.

అడకువ **aDakuwa** *same as* **aNakuwa.**

అడగారు, అడగార్చు **aDagaaru, aDagaarcu** *same as* **aNagaaru, aNagaarcu.**

అడచు **aDacu** *same as* **aNacu.**

అడపట్టె **aDapaTTe** *n.* board used for smoothing a ploughed field after grain is sown.

అడతిదారు, అడితీదారు **aDatidaaru, aDitiidaaru** *n.* agent, broker.

అడపాదడపా **aDapaadaDapaa** *adv.* now and then, from time to time, occasionally, off and on, intermittently.

అడబాల **aDabaala** *n.* cook (man or woman).

అడమానం **aDamaanam** *n.* mortgage.

అడలకొట్టు **aDalakoTTu** *same as* **haDalakoTTu.**

అడలిపోవు **aDalipoowu**[1] *same as* **haDalipoowu.**

అడలిపోవు **aDalipoowu**[2] *v.i.* (of milk) to be about to turn sour.

అడలు **aDalu** *same as* **haDalu.**

అడవి, అటవి **aDawi, aTawi** I.*n.* forest, jungle. II.*adj.* wild (not domesticated); **~ jantuwu** wild animal; **~ goola** loud confused noise; **~ kaacina wennela** moonlight which shines in the forest, i.e., something that is wasted.

అడవికాకర, ఆరగాకర **aDawikaakara, aaragaakara** *n.* wild bitter gourd, *momordica cochinchinensis.*

అడవితుమ్మ **aDawitumma** *n. acacia arabica,* silver thorned babul tree.

అడవిమనిషి **aDawi maniSi** *n.* 1 ape. 2 boorish or uncivilised person.

అడవీకరణ **aDawiikaraNa** *n.* afforestation.

అడసాల **aDasaala** *n.* improvised kitchen set up when space is needed to cook for extra guests.

అడాయించు **aDaayincu** *v.t.* to hinder, obstruct, get in the way of (s.o.).

అడితీ **aDitii** *n.* 1 timber depot. 2 broker's commission.

అడిదం **aDidam** *n. class.* sword.

అడిదం బడిదం **aDidam baDidam** *adv., colloq.* in great haste, in a great hurry.

అడియాస **aDiyaasa** *n.* vain desire, vain hope.

అడుక్కొను **aDukkonu** *v.i. and t.* 1 to beg (as a beggar), live by begging. 2 *dial.* to ask for, request.

అడుగంట **aDugaNTa** *adv.* down to the bottom.

అడుగంటిపోవు **aDugaNTipoowu** *v.i.* to reach the lowest limit; **R-ki aaśalannii aDugaNTi pooyEEyi** R.'s hopes were all dashed.

అడుగంటు **aDugaNTu** *v.i.* 1 to sink to the bottom, be exhausted; **baawiloo niiLLu aDugaNTEEyi** the water in the well has been exhausted. 2 **annam aDugaNTindi** the rice was scorched (at the bottom of the pot during cooking).

అడుగడుగునా, అడుగడుక్కీ **aDugaDugunaa, aDugaDukkii** *adv.* at every step, constantly.

అడుగిడు **aDugiDu** *v.i.* to set foot.

అడుగు **aDugu**[1] I.*n.* 1 foot, step, pace; **~ jaaDa** footprint; **~ peTTu** to place o.'s foot, set foot; **~ loo ~ weeyu** to walk very slowly. 2 foot, bottom, base; **koNDa ~ na** at the foot of the hill. 3 foot (twelve inches). 4 beginning, start; **~ loonee hamsapaadu** a correction at the very start. II. *adj.* bottom, inferior, low, under; **~ pakka** the underside.

అడుగు **aDugu**[2] *v.t.* to ask, enquire, request, beg.

అడుగుబద్ద **aDugubadda** *n.* measuring rod one foot in length.

అడుగుబొడుగు **aDuguboDugu** *n.* whatever remains, anything that may be left over; **~ [migilinawi] tinaali waaDu** he must eat whatever is left over.

అడుగుమాడిపోవు, అడుగుమాలిపోవు **aDugu-**

maaDipoowu aDugumaalipoowu, v.i. to be completely destroyed.

అడుసు aDusu *n.* mud, clay.

అడ్డ aDDa¹ *n.* 1 *bauhinia racemosa,* a forest tree whose leaves are used to make leaf plates for serving food. 2 cross beam of a harrow to which other parts are fixed. 3 a measure of grain equal to two manikas in volume.

అడ్డ aDDa² *n.* stand, halting, halting place.

అడ్డం **aDDam** *n.* 1 obstacle, hindrance, obstruction. 2 screen, shield; **peeparu mukhaaniki ~ peTTukoni** screening his face with a newspaper (*lit.* putting a newspaper as a screen for his face); **eNDaki ceyyi ~ peTTukoni** putting his hand [up] as a shield against the sun. 3 pawn, pledge.

అడ్డం ఆడు **aDDam aaDu** *v.t.* to obstruct, oppose.

అడ్డంకి **aDDanki** *n.* hindrance, obstruction.

అడ్డంకొట్టు **aDDam koTTu** *v.t.* to frustrate, thwart.

అడ్డంగా **aDDangaa** *adv.* 1 across, crosswise. 2 in the way. 3 as a shield or screen.

అడ్డంచెప్పు, అడ్డంమాట్లాడు **aDDam ceppu, aDDam maaTLaaDu** *v.i. dial.* to contradict.

అడ్డంతగులు **aDDam tagulu** *v.i.* to come in the way of, oppose, obstruct.

అడ్డంతొక్కు **aDDam tokku** *v.i.* to take a short cut.

అడ్డంపడు **aDDam paDu** *v.i.* 1 to intervene, interfere; **waaLLu koTTukunTuu uNTee neenu aDDam paDDaanu** when they were quarrelling I intervened. 2 to obstruct; **gontuku eedoo aDDam paDindi** something has obstructed the throat.

అడ్డంపెట్టుకొను **aDDam peTTukonu** *same as* **aDDuweesukonu.**

అడ్డంవచ్చు **aDDam waccu** *v.i.* 1 to get in the way, be an obstacle, obstruct. 2 to interrupt; **naa maaTalaki aDDam raaku** do not interrupt me.

అడ్డకట్టు **aDDakaTTu** *n.* 1 method of tying a lungi in the form of a skirt (=**guNDaaru**). 2 iron ring round the hub of a cartwheel.

అడ్డకత్తి **aDDakatti** *n.* broadsword.

అడ్డకమ్మి **aDDakammi** *n.* lintel.

అడ్డకర్ర **aDDakarra** *n.* 1 cross piece of timber. 2 obstacle.

అడ్డకాలువ **aDDakaaluwa** *n.* branch channel leading from a main irrigation channel.

అడ్డకొలత, అడ్డుకొలత **aDDakolata, aDDukolata** *n.* diameter.

అడ్డగాడిద **aDDagaaDida** *n.* ass, worthless person (*mild term of abuse*).

అడ్డగించు **aDDagincu** *v.t.* to stop, hinder, obstruct, block.

అడ్డగుణకారం **aDDaguNakaaram** *n. maths.* cross multiplication.

అడ్డగొడ్డం **aDDagoDDam** *n.* contradiction.

అడ్డ గొడ్డంగా మాట్లాడు **aDDagoDDangaa maaTLaaDu** *v.i.* to talk in a self-contradictory or illogical manner.

అడ్డగోలుగా **aDDagoolugaa** *adv.* (of speaking) unbefittingly, inopportunely.

అడ్డచాలు **aDDacaalu** *n.* cross furrow; **niluwu dunnina tarawaata aDDangaa dunnina caalu ~ aNTaaru** after ploughing lengthwise the furrow that is ploughed crosswise is called a cross furrow.

అడ్డదారి, అడ్డుదారి **aDDadaari, aDDudaari** *n.* short cut.

అడ్డదిడ్డం **aDDadiDDam** *adj.* 1 strange, curious, odd, awkward, unnatural. 2 unaccountable, unpredictable.

అడ్డదిడ్డంగా **aDDadiDDangaa** *adv.* this way and that, haphazard, crisscross, crosswise, crookedly; **marikonni paTaalloo ii reekhalu okadaanikokaTi kramarahitangaa ~ daaTipootunnaTLu kanipistaayi** in some other maps these lines can be seen to crisscross each other irregularly; **~ maaTLaaDu** to talk in a self-contradictory manner.

అడ్డదిడ్డి **aDDadiDDi** *adj.* meaningless, purposeless; **~ maaTalu / ceeSTalu** meaningless words / deeds.

అడ్డనామం **aDDanaamam** *n.* horizontal lines marked on the forehead, a sign of the Saivite sect.

అడ్డపంచె **aDDapance** *n.* man's skirt, lungi.

అడ్డపచ్చన **aDDapaccana** *n.* tinge of green on furrows ten days after sowing the seed.

అడ్డపట్టె **aDDapaTTe** *n.* crossbar or crossbeam in a cot, cart, etc.

అడ్డమాను **aDDamaanu** *n.* 1 lintel. 2 crossbar.

అడ్డమైన **aDDamayna** *adj.* in the way, encountered, met with, come across; **S.gaaru ~ waaLLandarnii salahaa aDigindi** S. sought advice from everyone whom she met; **~ gaDDi tiNTee wireecanaaluu waantuluu paTTukoNTaayi** if you eat whatever poor food you come across, you will get purging and vomiting.

అడ్డమొద్దు **aDDamoddu** *n.* main crossbeam of a cart.

అడ్డాకులు **aDDaakulu** *n.pl.* adda leaves, used for making leaf plates for serving food.

అడ్డాట **aDDaaTa** *n.* name of a game of cards.

అడ్డాలు **aDDaalu** *n.pl.* arms held crosswise for carrying an infant; **cinnappuDu waaDu naa aDDaalaloo perigEEDu** he grew up in my arms; **aDDaala biDDa** babe in arms.

అడ్డిగలు, అద్దిగలు **aDDigalu, addigalu** *n.pl.* kind of jewellery worn round the neck.

అడ్డు **aDDu** I. *n.* 1 obstacle, obstruction, impediment, hindrance. 2 screen, protection. 3 security, pledge; **tamaki bhayam waddu, tama praaNaalaku naa praaNaalu** ~ do not afraid, my life will be a security for yours. II. *in first part of a n. compound, dial. variation of* **aDDa[m]** cross, e.g., **~ kolata, ~ daari.** III. *v.t.* to prevent, obstruct, hinder, impede.

అడ్డు ఆపు, అడ్డూ ఆపూ **aDDu aapu, aDDuu-apuu** *n., in neg. or interrog. constr.* stoppage, limit, control; **waaDi nooTiki aDDaa aapaa?** is there any limit to his talk? **dharala perugudalaki ~ leeka pooyindi** there was no control on rising prices.

అడ్డుకట్ట **aDDukaTTa** *n.* 1 dam. 2 crossbund, temporary construction interrupting and diverting flow of water.

అడ్డుకమ్మి **aDDukammi** *n.* 1 crossbar or beam in a frame. 2 cross stripe in a cloth. 3 kind of jewellery.

అడ్డుకొను **aDDukonu** *v.t.* 1 *same as* **aDDu** *sense III.* 2 to protect.

అడ్డుకొలత **aDDukolata** *same as* **aDDakolata.**

అడ్డుకోత **aDDukoota** *n.* cross section.

అడ్డుగ **aDDuga** *n. dial.* half rupee, fifty paise.

అడ్డుగా **aDDugaa** *adv.* 1 across, crosswise. 2 in the way. 3 as a screen or shield: **mukhaaniki guDDa ~ peTTukoni** putting a cloth as a screen for his face *or* hiding his face behind a cloth.

అడ్డుగోడ **aDDugooDa** *n.* parapet wall, boundary wall, barrier.

అడ్డు చెప్పు **aDDuceppu** *v.i.* to speak against, oppose.

అడ్డుతగులు **aDDutagulu** *v.i.* 1 to obstruct, hinder. 2 to impede. 3 to object. 4 to intervene, interrupt.

అడ్డుతొలగించు **aDDutolagincu** *v.t.* to remove, get rid of (obstacle, hindrance).

అడ్డుతొలగు **aDDutolagu** *v.i.* to get out of the way, remove o.s., depart.

అడ్డుదారి **aDDudaari** *same as* **aDDadaari.**

అడ్డుపడు **aDDupaDu** *v.i.* 1 to intervene, help, come to the rescue. 2 to obstruct, hinder, impede. 3 **eeTiki~** to swim against the current, encounter difficulties.

అడ్డుపాటు **aDDupaaTu** *n.* obstruction, hindrance.

అడ్డుపుల్ల **aDDupulla** *n.* 1 petty obstruction; **~ lu weeyu** to create minor difficulties, cause petty obstructions, put a spoke in (s.o.'s) wheel. 2 crossbar in the middle of the beam of a picota (baling machine).

అడ్డుపెట్టు **aDDupeTTu** *v.t.* to stop, hold up, halt.

అడ్డుపోవు **aDDupoowu** *v.i.* to go between, intervene, obstruct.

అడ్డువచ్చు **aDDuwaccu** *v.i.* to come in the way, intervene, interrupt.

అడ్డువేసుకొను, అడ్డం పెట్టుకొను **aDDuweesukonu, aDDampeTTukonu** *v.t.* 1 to pawn, pledge; **Dabbu kaawaali, gaDiyaaram aDDuweesukonnaanu** I wanted money, so I pawned my watch. 2 to keep (s.g or s.o.) as a screen; **nannu aDDuweesukoni tappincukonnaaDu** he escaped by keeping me as screen *or* he escaped by sheltering behind me.

అడ్డుసమాధానం **aDDusamaadhaanam** *n.* retort, rejoinder.

అడ్డుసవాళ్ళు **aDDusawaaLLu** *n. pl.* cross-questions, cross-examination.

అడ్డెడు **aDDeDu** *adj.* one **aDDa** in quantity; **~ kaDawa** pot in which one **aDDa** of rice can be cooked.

అణకువ, అణుకువ, అడకువ **aNakuwa, aNukuwa, aDakuwa** I. *n.* humbleness, humility, obedience, submissiveness. II. *adj.* humble, submissive.

అణగదొక్కు **aNagadokku** *v.t.* to crush, suppress.

అణగారు, అడగారు **aNagaaru, aDagaaru** *v.i.* 1 to be pressed down, be crushed, be suppressed, be repressed. 2 to be subdued, subside.

అణగార్చు, అడగార్చు **aNagaarcu, aDagaarcu** *v.t.* to suppress.

అణగి పెణగి **aNagi peNagi** *adv.* mixing freely.

అణగిపోవు **aNagipoowu** *v.i.* 1 to die down, subside. 2 to be compressed, be confined, be restricted.

అణగిమణగి ఉండు **aNagimaNagi uNDu** *v.i.* to be subdued, be submissive.

అణగు **aNagu** *v.i.* to be suppressed, subdued, repressed, curbed or humbled.

అణచివేత **aNaciweeta** *n.* suppression.

అణచు, అడచు **aNacu, aDacu** *v.t.* to suppress, subdue, humble, bring or keep under control.

అణా **aNaa** *n.* one anna (an obsolete coin, one sixteenth of a rupee).

అణిమ **aNima** *n.* supernatural power of becoming invisible; **~ laghima widyalu** supernatural powers of assuming invisibility and weightlessness.

అణు **aNu** *adj. sci.* 1 molecular. 2 (*in non-technical language*) atomic.

అణుకువ **aNukuwa** *same as* **aNakuwa.**

అణుమాత్రమైనా **aNumaatramaynaa** *adv., in neg. constr.* not at all, not in the least (*lit.* as little as a particle); **naaku ~ sandeeham leedu** I have not the least doubt *or* I have no doubt at all.

అణుయుగం **aNuyugam** *n.* atomic age.

అణులేశం **aNuleeśam** *n.* a little, a small amount.

అణువు **aNuwu** *n.* 1 molecule. 2 (*in non-technical language*) atom.

అణుశక్తి **aNuśakti** *n.* atomic energy.

అణ్వస్త్రం **aNwastram** *n.* atom[ic] bomb.

అతఃపూర్వ **ataḥ puurwa** *adj.* previous.

అతఃపూర్వం **ataḥ puurwam** *adv.* before that, previously.

అతగాడు **atagaaDu** *n.* 1 *dial. variant of* **atanu** he, that man. 2 *colloq., referring to s.o. contemptuously* he, that man.

అతడు, అతను **ataDu, atanu** *pron.* he, that man.

అతర్కికంగా, అతార్కికంగా **atarkikangaa, ataarkikangaa** *adv.* without rational consideration.

అతర్కితంగా, అతార్కితంగా **atarkitangaa, ataarkitangaa** *adv.* impulsively, unpremeditatedly.

అతలం **atalam** *n.* the first of the seven legendary subterranean regions, lying just below the earth.

అతలాకుతలం **atalaakutalam** *n.* 1 seething, boiling. 2 disorder, confusion, bustle.

అతార్కిక **ataarkika** *adj.* irrational, illogical.

అతి **ati** *adj.* very, very much, too much, overabundant, superfluous, excessive.

అతికించు **atikincu** *v.t.* 1 to join, unite. 2 to weld or solder together.

అతిక్రమం **atikramam** *n.* transgression, wickedness.

అతిక్రమణ **atikramaNa** *n.* 1 transgression, wickedness. 2 *sci.* deviation.

అతిక్రమించు **atikramincu** *v.t.* to transgress, go beyond, exceed (limit), surpass (record).

అతిగా **atigaa** *adv.* 1 very much, a great deal. 2 too much; **prati pani ~ ceeyaku** do not overdo things.

అతిథి **atithi** *n.* guest; **aayana A.ku ~ gaa unnappuDu** when he was A.'s guest.

అతిథిమర్యాదలు **atithimaryaadalu** *n.pl.* hospitality.

అతిథి సత్కారం **atithisatkaaram** *n.* hospitality.

అతిధ్వానిక **atidhwaanika** *adj.* supersonic.

అతినవీన **atinawiina** *adj.* ultramodern.

అతినిద్రావ్యాధి **atinidraawyaadhi** *n.* sleeping sickness.

అతినీలలోహిత **atiniilaloohita** *adj.* ultraviolet.

అతిపరావలయం **atiparaawalayam** *n. maths.* hyperbola.

అతిబాహుళ్యం **atibaahuLyam** *n.* plethora, overabundance.

అతిమిక్కిలి **atimikkili** *adj. and adv.* **1** very much. **2** too much.

అతిమూత్రవ్యాధి **atimuutrawyaadhi** *n.* diabetes.

అతిరథుడు **atirathuDu** *n.* **1** *class.* great and unrivalled warrior (charioteer) of the days of the Mahabharata. **2** *mod.* great expert or authority.

అతిరిక్త **atirikta** *adj. class.* **1** excessive. **2** other, different.

అతిరేకం **atireekam** *n.* abundance, excess; *gen. as last part of a compound*, e.g., **santooSaatireekam** abundance of joy.

అతివ **atiwa** *n.* woman.

అతివస **atiwasa** *n. aconitum ferox*, a medicinal plant.

అతివాదం **atiwaadam** *n.* extremism.

అతివాది **atiwaadi** *n.* extremist.

అతివాసం **atiwaasam** *n.* fast observed on the night previous to an annual death cermony (**śraaddham**).

అతివృష్టి **atiwṛSTi** *n.* excessive rain; **eedi modalupeDitee, adee pani. ~ anaawṛSTi** whatever work he takes up, it is always the same; he does it without moderation.

అతివ్యయం **atiwyayam** *n.* extravagance, overexpenditure.

అతివ్యాపనమవు **atiwyaapanamawu** *v.i.* to overlap.

అతిశయం **atiśayam** I. *n.* pride, self-esteem (either in a good or bad sense). II. *as last part of a n. compound* **1** excess. **2** greatness, superiority; **prajñaatiśayam** greatness of intellect.

అతిశయంగా **atiśayangaa** *adv.* **1** excessively. **2** wonderfully, marvellously.

అతిశయత్వం **atiśayatwam** *n. ling.* domination.

అతిశయించు **atiśayincu** I. *v.i.* **1** to increase, multiply. **2** to increase excessively. **3** to speak proudly. **4** to exaggerate. II. *v.t.* to exceed, surpass, transcend, excel.

అతిశయోక్తి **atiśayookti** *n.* exaggeration, hyperbole, overstatement.

అతిశీతలీకరణం **atiśiitaliikaraNam** *n. sci.* supercooling.

అతిసారం **atisaaram** *n.* diarrohoea, dysentery.

అతీంద్రియ **atiindriya** *adj.* imperceptible to the senses, extrasensory.

అతీత **atiita** I. *adj.* **1** beyond the reach, scope or comprehension of: **~ śakti** a power beyond o.'s control; **manaku ~ngaa unna eewoo kaaraNaala muulangaa pratidii jarugutundi** everything takes place due to causes that are beyond our comprehension; **kulawarga bheedaalaku ~ mayna wyawastha** an organisation free from caste and class differences. **2** above, superior to, unaffected by, surpassing: **'naadi' anee mamakaaraaniki ~ngaa nilawaali** we must stand superior to the selfishness of the word 'mine'; **mottam miida poo kaawyaracanalanniNTiloo oka ~ mahassunnadi** overall there is a surpassing splendour in all Poe's poetry; **~ maanawuDu** superman. II. *as last element of an adjvl. compound* past, beyond, above, surpassing; **warNanaatiita** beyond description, indescribable; **kulaatiita** free from caste, casteless.

అతుకు **atuku** I. *n.* **1** joining, junction, union. **2** joint (in a sugarcane). **3** seam (in a cloth). **4** patch (in a cloth). **5** *pl.* **~ lu** defects. II. *v.i.* **1** to stick, adhere, be stuck, be fixed, be fastened; **andari cuupulu aayana iNTimiida atukkupooyEEyi** the eyes of all were fixed on his house. **2** to suit, fit, match. III. *v.t.* **1** to join, unite. **2** to stick, fasten, attach; **sTaampulu kawaruku sarigaa atikEEraa?** have you stuck the stamps on the cover correctly? **3** to weld, solder.

అతుకుబడి **atukubaDi** *n.* system of cultivation by yearly lease.

అతుకుబొతుకు **atuku botuku** *adj.* (of a cloth) torn, ragged.

అతుకులబతుకు **atukulabatuku** *n.* sponging, living on s.o. else or at s.o. else's expense.

అతుకులబొంత **atukula bonta** *n.* rug made of patchwork.

అతుకులమారి పని **atukulamaari pani** *n.* patchwork.

అతుకులువేయు **atukuluweeyu** *v.t.* to mend (cloth); **cokkaa cirigipooyindi, atukuluweesEEnu** the shirt was torn, I stiched it up.

అతుల, అతులిత **atula, atulita** *adj.* matchless.

అతోడ, హతోడ **atooDa, hatooDa**, *n.* medium sized hammer used by stonecutters.

అత్త **atta** *n.* **1** mother-in-law; **~ maamalu** mother-in-law and father-in-law. **2** father's sister. **3** maternal uncle's wife.

అత్తం **attam** *n.* cluster (part of a bunch) of plantains (= **ciipu**).

అత్తపత్తి **attapatti** *n.* touch-me-not, *mimosa pudica*, a medicinal plant sensitive to touch.

అత్తరం **attaram** *n.* haste.

అత్తరు **attaru** *n.* attar, scented oil, perfume.

అత్తరుబిళ్ళ **attarubiLLa** *n.* gulkand, a kind of paste made with rose petals which is taken along with betel and nut.

అత్తా కోడలంచు **attaakooDalancu** *n.* **~ ciire/pance** sari/dhoti having two borders in different colours, generally one red and the other green.

అత్తారిలు **attaarillu** *n.* mother-in-law's house.

అత్తారు బొత్తంగా **attaarubottangaa** *adv.* very carefully.

అత్తి **atti** *n.* fig tree, *ficus glomerata.*

అత్తిపిత్తిమాటలు **attipittimaaTalu** *n.pl.* imperfect speech of a child or of a nervous or mentally backward person; **ippuDippuDee ~ wastunnaayi pillaaDiki** the child is just learning to speak; **inta wayasu waccinaa ~ pooleedu waaDiki** though he has reached this age, he has not stopped speaking child language; **~ maaTLaaDaku, sarigaa ceppu eemayindoo** stop stammering and tell me clearly what happened.

అత్తెసరు **attesaru** *n.* **1** quantity of water used for boiling rice, just sufficient to evaporate by the time the rice is cooked, leaving no cunjee to be drained off—*a quick method of cooking, hence* ~ **paDeestaanu, weLLipooku** don't go away! I will cook a quick meal (said by a housewife to a casual visitor). 2 *colloq.* just enough of anything; ~ **maarkulatoo pariikSa paasayyEEDu** he passed the examination with just enough marks *or* with grace marks.

అత్యంత **atyanta** *adj.* 1 very, very much, very great, extreme. 2 most, utmost, greatest. 3 excessive.

అత్యధిక **atyadhika** *adj.* 1 biggest, most, greatest, largest. 2 excessive, superfluous.

అత్యధికంగా **atyadhikangaa** *adv.* 1 mostly. 2 excessively.

అత్యయిక **atyayika** *adj.* critical, crucial.

అత్యల్ప **atyalpa** *adj.* smallest, least.

అత్యవసర **atyawasara** *adj.* 1 most urgent; ~ **paristhiti** emergency: ~ **caryalu** emergency measures. 2 essential; ~ **seewalu** essential services.

అత్యాచారం **atyaacaaram** *n.* 1 crime. 2 rape.

అత్యావశ్యక **atyaawaśyaka** *adj.* indispensible, essential.

అత్యాశ **atyaaśa** *n.* greed, covetousness.

అత్యుక్తి **atyukti** *n.* exaggeration, overstatement.

అత్యుత్తమ **atyuttama** *adj.* highest, best.

అత్యుత్పాదన **atyutpaadana** *n.* overproduction.

అత్యుష్ణ **atyuSNa** *adj. geog.* torrid.

అథర్వణం **atharwaNam** *n.* name of the fourth Veda.

అథవా **athawaa** *adv.* or, otherwise.

అదటు **adaTu** *n.* pride, arrogance, presumption.

అదనంగా **adanangaa** *adv.* 1 very much, exceedingly. 2 in addition.

అదనపు **adanapu** *adj.* additional, extra.

అదను **adanu** *n.* 1 time, season, opportunity, occasion. 2 suitable, right, opportune or appropriate time; **adanu cuusi appu aDigEEDu** he watched for the right moment and asked for a loan; **manci~ku waccEEwu** you have come at an opportune time. 3 ~ **miida unna polam waanaki naaśanam ayyindi** the field that was just ripe (ready for harvest) was spoilt by the rain.

అదమాయించు **adamaayincu** *v.t.* to admonish.

అదమాయింపు **adamaayimpu** *n.* 1 admonition. 2 control.

అదరగొట్టు **adaragoTTu** *v.t.* to startle, frighten, alarm.

అదరిపడు **adaripaDu** *v.i.* 1 to be startled or alarmed. 2 to be boastful, give o.s. airs; ~ **tunnaaDu Dabbu cuusukoni** (*or* **udyoogam cuusukoni**) he is giving himself airs on account of his money (*or* his position).

అదరిపాటు **adaripaaTu** *n.* boasting, presumption.

అదరు, అదురు, ఉదరు **adaru, aduru, udaru**) I. *n.* shaking, trembling, tremor, concussion. II. *v.i.* 1 to tremble, shake; **bhuumi adirindi** the earth shook. 2 to tremble, shiver, quake, quiver (out of fear or other emotion). 3 to receive a shock, be shaken or concussed; **debbaki tala koncem adirindi** his head was slightly concussed by the blow.

అదరుగుండె **adaru guNDe** *n.* timid-hearted person.

అదరుబెదరు **adaru bedaru** *n.* fear, hesitation.

అదలించు, అదరించు **adalincu, adarincu** *v.t.* to frighten, menace. 2 to reprove, rebuke, chastise.

అదలింపు **adalimpu** *n.* warning shout, rebuke.

అదలుబదలు **adalu badalu** *n.* exchange; **pustakaalu** ~ **ceesukonnaaru** they exchanged their books.

అదవ **adawa** *n.* rent; ~ **seedyam** cultivation of land on lease.

అదవబతుకు **adawabatuku** *n.* life of poverty, life of wretchedness.

అదాటు[న] **adaaTu[na]** *adv.* suddenly.

అదాలతు **adaalatu** *n.* law court, court of justice.

అదాహ్య **adaahya** *adj. chem.* non-inflammable, incombustible.

అది **adi** *pron.* 1 she, that woman. 2 it, that thing; *see* **adee.**

అదికాక, అదికాకుండా **adikaaka, adikaakuNDaa** *adv.* in addition, besides [that], moreover.

అదిగదీ! **adigadii!** *interj.* that's it!

అదిగో! **adigoo!** *interj.* there is .... (pointing to s.g); ~ **maa illu!** there is our house!

అదిమిపట్టుకొను, అదుముకొను **adimi paTTukonu, adumukonu** *v.t.* to grip, clasp, clutch; **pillalanu tana guNDelaku adimipaTTukonnaaDu** he clasped the children to his chest.

అదిమొదలు **adimodalu** *adv.* since then.

అదిరించు **adirincu** *v.t.* 1 to shake. 2 *dial.* to move, shift; **aa iTikaraayini koncem** ~ , **baaguNTundi** shift that brick a little, then it will be all right.

అదివరకు, అదివరలో **adiwaraku, adiwaraloo** *adv.* previously, in the past.

అదుపు **adupu** *n.* control, restraint.

అదుపుచేయు **adupuceeyu** *v.t.* to control, regulate.

అదుపుతప్పు **aduputappu** *v.i.* to go out of control, get out of hand, run riot.

అదుపులో ఉంచు **adupuloo uncu** *v.t.* to keep under control, keep in check.

అదుపులోకి తీసుకొను **adupulooki tiisukonu** *v.t.* to take into custody.

అదుపూ ఆజ్ఞలు లేకుండా **adupuu aajñalu leekuNDaa** *advbl. phrase* freely, uncontrolled.

అదుము **adumu** *v.t.* to press, squeeze; **baadhanu paNTi biguwuna adimipaTTEEDu** he bore the pain, gritting his his teeth.

అదుముకొను **adumukonu** *same as* **adimipaTTukonu.**

అదుముడు **adumuDu** *n.* pressing, squeezing.

అదురు **aduru** *same as* **adaru.**

అదూష్య **aduuSya** *adj.* irreproachable, unblameable.

అదృఢ **adṛDha** *adj.* flexible.

అదృఢత **adṛDhata** *n.* flexibility.

అదృశ్య **adṛśya** *adj.* 1 invisible. 2 untraceable.

అదృశ్యం అవు **adṛśyam awu** *v.i.* to disappear, vanish.

అదృష్టం **adṛSTam** *n.* luck, good fortune; ~ **kalisi wastee naDiciwaccee koDuku puDataaDu** if fortune is favourable a healthy son will be born.

అదృష్టవంతుడు **adṛSTawantuDu** *n.* lucky person.

అదృష్టవశాత్తూ **adṛSTawaśaattuu** adv. luckily, fortunately.

అదృష్టశాలి **adṛSTaśaali** *n.* lucky person.

అదృష్టహీనుడు **adṛSTahiinuDu** *n.* unlucky person.

అదెప్పుడో **adeppuDoo** *adv.* long ago, some time in the past.

అదే **adee** I. = **adi** *pron.* + ee *emphatic suffix* that itself, just that; ~ **neenu anukonnaanu** that is just what I thought; ~ **padiweelu** *lit.* that itself is (worth) ten thousand; *here* **padiweelu** *stands for a large number in general and the phrase means* that is something very good or very satisfactory; **biccam peTTaka pooyinaa, kukkanu kaTTeestee** ~ **padiweelu** you may not give alms to the poor but if you tie up your dog that at least is worth something (by way of merit); ~ **parugu parigettEEDu** *or* ~ **parugu tiisi pooyEEDu** he ran without stopping. II. *adjvl. use* the same; ~ **samwatsaramloo** in the same year *or* in that very year; **naalugu roojuluu aydu roojuluu** ~ **baTTalu weesukoNTaaru** they wear the same clothes for four or five days at a time. III. *advbl. use* by itself, of its own accord; **kaasta pullagaa eedannaa naalukki raasukoo,** ~ **taggutundi** rub anything sour on your tongue and it (feeling of sickness) will subside of its own accord.

అదేదో **adeedoo** *det. adj., often used deprecatingly* some or other; ~ **udyoogam ceestunnaaDu** he is doing some job or other; **adi caalaa nallagaa** ~ **naalukkaaLLa jantuwulaa undi** it was very black and like some four legged animal or other.

అదేపనిగా **adeepanigaa** *adv.* 1 non-stop, ceaselessly, continuously. 2 persistently. 3 repeatedly.

అదేప్రకారంగా, అదేవిధంగా **adeeprakaarangaa, adeewidhangaa** *adv.* in the same manner, accordingly.

అదేమిటి **adeemiTi** *interrog. pron., advbl.use* how, why; ~ **aa moham aTLaa peTTEEwu?** why are you looking like that? ~ **alaa uupiri tiistunnaawu?** why are you gasping like that?

అదయినా **adaynaa** I. *adv.* and that too, moreover; **poyyi,** ~ **boggula poyyi wisaraDam** to fan a hearth, and that too a charcoal hearth. II. *tag word introducing a rhetorical question* and, but, well then; **laNDan waccEEDu** — ~ **eppuDu?** — **neenu waccina tarawaata** he came to London — and when was that? — after I came.

అదో, అదోక **adoo, adoka** *det.adj., variant forms of* **oka** one *used to convey shades of meaning such as strangeness, indefiniteness, uncertainty, dislike, distaste, sadness*; **aayana** ~ **rakam maniSi** he is an odd kind of person; **aame wenakku tirigi** ~ **widhangaa nannu cuusindi** she turned round and looked at me in a peculiar way; **miiru** ~ **rakangaa unnaaru** you look strange; **puwwula puwwula lungii maatram kaTTukonna M. naDawaloonci waraNDaa looki** ~ **rakam elugubaNTi laagaa waccEEDu** dressed only in a flower patterned skirt, M. came through the passage to the veranda looking like some sort of bear; **aaśalu tiiraka pootee manaki** ~ **baadha** if our hopes are not fulfilled, we shall have much sadness.

అదోలా **adoolaa** *adv.* 1 strangely; ~ **mukham peTTEEDu** he put on a strange expression. 2 disagreeably, unpleasantly; **aameki** ~ **anipincindi** it was disagreeable to her *or* she was upset; **maa iNTiki wacci** ~ **maaTLaaDEEDu** he came to my house and spoke unpleasantly.

అద్ద **adda** *n.* 1 half. 2 rick of straw not yet threshed. 3 measure of grain by volume.

అద్దం **addam** *n.* 1 mirror, looking glass. 2 pane of glass; **kaLLaddaalu** [pair of] spectacles.

అద్దకం **addakam** *n.* 1 printing on cloth. 2 printed cloth.

అద్దగోడ **addagooDa** *n.* parapet wall, screen wall.

అద్దద్ద **addadda** *adv.* at once.

అద్దమరేయి, అద్దమరాతిరి **addama reeyi, addama raatiri** *n. class.* middle of the night, dead of night.

అద్దరి **addari** *n.* the other or opposite shore; **aa nadiki** ~ **ni eemunnadi?** what is on the opposite shore of that river?

అద్దలించు **addalincu** *v.t.* to pat, slap (mortar with a trowel to make it smooth).

అద్ది **addi** *pron., variant form of* **adi.**

అద్దించు **addincu** *v.t.* to get s.g stamped, impressed or printed.

అద్దిగలు **addigalu** *same as* **aDDigalu.**

అద్దిరపాటున **addirapaaTuna** *adv.* suddenly, unexpectedly.

అద్దిరమ్మ! **addiramma!** *interj. gen. used in speaking to children* wonderful!

అద్దిరయ్య! **addirayya!** *interj. expressing apprehension.*

అద్దిరా! **addiraa!** *interj.* wonderful!

అద్దు **addu**[1] *v.t.* 1 to press gently, dab, blot. 2 to stamp, print (on cloth).

అద్దు **addu**[2] *same as* **haddu.**

అద్దు **addumuddu** *n.* **pillala** ~ children's playing, children's games.

అద్దె **adde** *n.* rent, hire; ~ **illu** rented house; ~ **kaTTu** to pay rent; ~ **ki iccu** to give on rent; **meemu addekunna waaLLam** we are tenants.

అద్భుత **adbhuta** *adj.* wonderful, marvellous, fabulous, amazing, remarkable.

అద్భుతం **adbhutam** *n.* wonder, marvel.

అద్భుతంగా **adbhutangaa** *adv.* wonderfully, marvellously.

అద్రి **adri** *n.* mountain; **sahyaadri** the Sahya mountain range.

అద్వితీయ **adwitiiya** *adj.* unparallelled, unequalled, unique.

అద్వైతం **adwaytam** *n.* monism.

అద్వైతి **adwayti** *n.* monist.

అధః **adhaḥ** *Sanskrit prefix meaning* lowest, bottom; ~ **paataaLam** the bottom of hell.

అధఃకరణం **adhahkaraNam** *n.* degradation, downgrading.

అధఃపతనం **adhahpatanam** *n.* decline, degeneration.

అధమ **adhama** *adj.* inferior, low, mean, base, least, lowest.

అధమం **adhamam** *adv.* at least, at the minimum.

అధమపక్షం **adhamapakSam** *adv.* at the very least.

అధమాధముడు **adhamaadhamuDu** *n.* very base person, meanest of the mean.
అధముడు **adhamuDu** *n.* mean or base person.
అధరం **adharam** *n.* lip, lower lip.
అధరస్పందనం **adharaspandanam** *n.* trembling of the lips.
అధర్మ[ం] **adharma[m]** I.*n.* anything contrary to **dharmam**, injustice, wrong, evil. II. *adj.* unjust, unrighteous, wrongful, evil.
అథవా **adhawaa** *adv.* or, otherwise.
అధస్తరం **adhastaram** *n. sci.* substratum.
అధార్తుగా **adhaartugaa** *adv.* suddenly.
అధార్మిక **adhaarmika** *adj.* irreligious. impious.
అధిక **adhika** *adj.* 1 much, many, great, abundant; ~**janulu śaakhaahaarulu awutunnaaru** many people are becoming vegetarians. 2 greater, more, additional. 3 too much, excessive, superfluous, surplus, redundant.
అధికం **adhikam** *n.* 1 much, greatness. 2 superiority; **okari ~ okari takkuwa emii leedu; andaruu samaanamee** there is no superiority or inferiority among them, they all are equal.
అధికంగా **adhikangaa** *adv.* much, abundantly, more, excessively (*with shades of meaning varying according to the context*); **widyaarthigaa unnappuDu maa iNTiki ~wastuNDeewaaDu** when he was a student he used to come to our house often; **naakaNTee waaDiki naalugu markulu ~waccEEyi** he got four marks more than I did.
అధికత **adhikata** *n.* superiority.
అధికతరకోణం **adhikatara kooNam** *n. maths.* reflex angle.
అధికప్రసంగం **adhikaprasangam** *n.* meddling, officious interference.
అధికమాసం **adhikamaasam** *n.* additional or intercalary lunar month occurring once in three calendar years.
అధికరణం **adhikaraNam** *n. admin.* article or schedule (of Constitution).
అధికరణకారకం **adhikaraNa kaarakam** *n. gram.* locative case.
అధికసంఖ్య **adhika sankhya** *n.* majority, greater number.
అధికసంఖ్యాకపక్షం **adhika sankhyaaka pakSam** *n.* majority party.
అధికసంఖ్యాకులు **adhika sankhyaakulu** *n.pl.* majority, greater number (of persons).
అధికాధికంగా **adhikaadhikangaa** *adv.* increasingly, more and more.
అధికార **adhikaara** *adj.* official.
అధికారం **adhikaaram** *n.* 1 authority, power, charge; ~**loo** in charge; **ii pani ceeyaDaaniki neenu ataniki ~iccEEnu** I authorised (*or* empowered) him to do this work; **eemiTi mii ~?** what authority have you? 2 *as second part of a n. compound* title, claim, right; **jhaansii lakSmibaayiki tana datta putruni raajyaadhikaaranni gurticananduku aagraham kaligindi** Jhansi Lakshmibai was incensed because her adopted son's right to rule was not recognised.
అధికారంపొందిన **adhikaaram pondina** *adj.* authorised, empowered.
అధికారపక్షం **adhikaarapakSam** *n. polit.* party in power.
అధికారపత్రం **adhikaarapatram** *n.* 1 letter of authority, authorisation. 2 charter.
అధికారపరిధి **adhikaaraparidhi** *n.* jurisdiction.
అధికారపూర్వకంగా **adhikaarapuurwakangaa** *adv.* authoritatively.
అధికారప్రాంతం **adhikaarapraantam** *n.* jurisdiction.
అధికారభాష **adhikaarabhaaSa** *n.* official language.
అధికారవర్గం **adhikaarawargam** *n.*1 officials, officialdom. 2 *pl.* **adhikaarawargaalu** official circles.
అధికారహోదా **adhikaarahoodaa** *n.* official capacity.
అధికారి **adhikaari** *n.*1 person in authority; **graamaadhikaarulu** village officers; **tanikhii adhikaarulu** inspecting officials. 2 master. 3 owner (of property); **lakS~** lakhaire, person owning property worth a lakh of rupees.
అధికుడు **adhikuDu** *n.* superior person; **waarikaNTee taanu adhikuNNi anukoonaarambhincEEDu** he began to think he was superior to them.
అధికృత **adhikṛta** *adj. econ.* authorised (capital).
అధికేంద్రం **adhikeendram** *n.* epicentre.
అధికోత్పత్తి **adhikootpatti** *n.* overproduction.
అధిక్షిప్త **adhikSipta** *adj.* condemned, censured.
అధిక్షేపణ, అధిక్షేపం **adhikSeepaNa, adhikSeepam** *n.* 1 blaming, condemnation, censure, reproach. 2 ridiculing, mocking, taunting.
అధిక్షేపించు **adhikSeepincu** *v.t.* 1 to condemn, censure, reproach. 2 to ridicule, mock, taunt.
అధిగణనం **adhigaNanam** *n.* preferment, advancement.
అధిగమించు **adhigamincu** *v.t.* 1 to exceed, excel. 2 to overcome, surmount.
అధిదేవత **adhideewata** *n.* presiding deity.
అధినాథుడు **adhinaathuDu** *n.* ruler, governor, lord, chief, head.
అధినాయకుడు **adhinaayakuDu** *n.* leader, presiding person.
అధినివేశం **adhiniweeśam** *n.* dominion.
అధినేత **adhineeta** *n.* chief, head, manager, person in charge (of a company or institution).
అధిపతి **adhipati** *n.* 1 chief; **śaakhaadhipati** head of a department. 2 master, owner.
అధిరోహణ **adhiroohaNa** *n.* climbing to the top, surmounting.
అధిరోహించు **adhiroohincu** *v.t.* 1 to climb to the top of, scale (mountain). 2 to surmount (difficulties).
అధివసించు **adhiwasincu** *v.t.* 1 to occupy (a place). 2 to make (a place) o.'s abode.
అధివాస్తవిక **adhiwaastawika** *adj.* surrealist.
అధివాస్తవికత **adhiwaastawikata** *n.* surrealism.
అధివేదనం **adhiweedanam** *n. class.* marrying a second wife during a first wife's lifetime.
అధిష్ఠానం **adhiSThaanam** *n.* abode, dwelling place.

అధిష్ఠానదేవత **adhiSThaana deewata** *n.* presiding deity.

అధిష్ఠాన వర్గం **adhiSThaana wargam** *n.* 1 governing body. 2 *polit.* high command.

అధిష్ఠించు **adhiSThincu** *v.t.* to step up and occupy (a higher position).

అధిసంఖ్య **adhisankhya** *adj.* supernumerary.

అధీన **adhiina** *adj.* subordinate.

అధీనం, ఆధీనం **adhiinam, aadhiinam** *n.* 1 possession, power. 2 control, authority. 3 charge, custody; **pooliisula~loo** in police custody.

అధీనత **adhiinata** *n.* dependence, subjection.

అధీశుడు **adhiiśuDu** *n.* ruler, master, lord.

అధీశ్వరుడు **adhiiśwaruDu** *n.* God.

అధునాతన **adhunaatana** *same as* **aadhunaatana.**

అధైర్యం **adhayryam** *n.* cowardice, timidity.

అధైర్యపడు **adhayryapaDu** *v.i.* to be disheartened or discouraged.

అధైర్యపరచు **adhayrya paracu** *v.t.* to dishearten, discourage.

అధో **adhoo** *Sanskrit prefix meaning* downward[s]: **samudra prawaahaala swabhaawam, uurdhwa ~jalagamanaalanu gurincina pariśoodhanalu jarigEEyi** researches were conducted into the nature of ocean currents and the upward and downward motion of water.

అధోగతి **adhoogati** *n.* 1 downward path, degeneration, degradation. 2 low state, disastrous condition, state of perdition.

అధోజ్ఞాపిక **adhoojñaapika** *n.* footnote.

అధోముఖ **adhoomukha** *adj. sci.* inverted.

అధోముఖి, అధోవదన **adhoomukhi, adhoowadana** *adv.* looking downwards, with downcast eyes (due to shyness, grief or shame).

అధో హనువు **adhoo hanuwu** *n.* lower jaw.

అధ్యక్షత **adhyakSata** *n.* presidency, chairmanship; ~ **wahincu** to take the chair, preside.

అధ్యక్షుడు **adhyakSuDu** *n.* President, Chairman, Chancellor, Speaker.

అధ్యయనం **adhyayanam** *n.* 1 study, learning. 2 traditional learning, esp. study of the Vedas.

అధ్యయనంచేయు **adhyayanam ceeyu** *v.t.* to study, ponder [over].

అధ్యయనపరుడు **adhyayana paruDu** *n.* student, researcher, scholar.

అధ్యయనించు **adhyayanincu** *v.t.* to study.

అధ్యాత్మ **adhyaatma** I.*n.* 1 the Supreme Spirit or universal soul that pervades the entire created order. 2 the Supreme Spirit as manifested in the personal soul or individual self. II. *adj.* spiritual, relating to the soul or spirit.

అధ్యాత్మరామాయణం **adhyaatma raamaayaNam** *n.* the Ramayana explained as an allegory relating to the Supreme Spirit.

అధ్యాత్మిక, ఆధ్యాత్మిక **adhyaatmika, aadhyaatmika** *adj.* spiritual, relating to the soul or spirit.

అధ్యాపకుడు **adhyaapakuDu** *n.* teacher.

అధ్యాపన[ం] **adhyaapana[m]** *n.* teaching, instruction.

అధ్యాపనశాస్త్రం **adhyaapanaśaastram** *n.* (science of) education.

అధ్యాయం **adhyaayam** *n.* chapter, section (of a book).

అధ్వర్యం **adhwaryam** *same as* **aadhwaryam.**

అధ్వానం, అధ్వాన్నం, అర్ధాన్నం **adhwaanam, adhwaannam, ardhaannam** *adj.* 1 bad, worse, terrible, dreadful, wretched, miserable; **waaDi ayyakaNTee ~** even worse than his father; **reepee iNTarwyuuku weLLaali. ~ jwaram ippuDee raawaalEE?** tomorrow I have to go for an interview. must this wretched fever come just now? **kuuliila batukulu adhwaannapu batukulu** labourers' lives are miserable lives; **waaLLa illu ekkaDoo maarumuula ardhaanapu aDawiloo undi. akkaDiki weLLaDam kaSTam** their house in some out of the way deserted place. it is difficult to go there. 2 spoilt, ruined; **bassu doowaloo ceDipooyindi. neenu weLLina pani ~ayindi** the bus broke down on the way and the work I went for was ruined.

అన **ana** *n. poet.* 1 sprout. 2 twig, young shoot; **~lu toDigi konalu saagi** flourishing (*lit.* sprouting young shoots and extending the tips of branches).

అనంగక్రీడ **ananga kriiDa** *n.* amorous sport.

అనంగరంగా భాష **anangarangaa bhaaSa** *n.* obscene language.

అనంగీకారం **anangiikaaram** *n.* 1 disapproval, disapprobation. 2 disagreement.

అనంగుడు **ananguDu** *n.* a name of Manmatha or Cupid.

అనంత **ananta** *adj.* endless, unending, infinite.

అనంతం **anantam** *n.* infinity.

అనంతంగా **anantangaa** *adv.* endlessly, ceaselessly.

అనంతత్వం, అనంత్యం **anantatwam, anantyam** *n.* infinity.

అనంతర **anantara** *adj.* next, following, succeeding, subsequent.

అనంతరం **anantaram** *adv.* afterwards, thereafter.

అనక **anaka** *negative participle of* **anu** without thinking, without considering; **raatr~ pagal~ muuDu samwatsaraalu ataniki naanaa caakirii ceesEEnu** day and night I did all kinds of menial work for him for three years (*lit.* without considering whether it was day or night I did, etc.); **waan~ eND~ pagalallaa pani ceestaaDu** whether the weather is wet or fine, he works all day long; **waaD ~ wiiD ~ andari kaaLLu paTTukunnaaDu Dabbukoosam** he begged for money from everyone, whoever they might be.

అనగా **anagaa** *particle* 1 that is to say, namely. 2 when it is/was said, just when; **dasaraa paNDaga daggara paDutundi** ~ just when Dasara was approaching (*lit.* when it was said that Dasara was approaching); **paNDaga reepu~** on the day before the festival. 3 *emphasising a preceding adv. of time* **eemiraa bhiimayyaa! madhyaannam~ weLLi intadaakaa eem eem ceesEEwu raa?** hey Bhimayya! you went out (as long ago as) this afternoon. what have you been doing upto now? **ninnu cuuDaalani ninnan~ mii amma wacci paśuwula doDLoo kaacukkuucunnadi** your mother has come to see you and has been sitting in the cattle yard ever since yesterday. 4 ~ ~ once upon a time (a traditional opening for a story).

అనగిపెనగి **anagi penagi** *adv.* mixing freely.

అనఘుడు **anaghuDu** *n.* sinless person.

అనతి **anati** *adj.* not much, a little (*only of time or distance*) ~ **duuram** not far: ~ **kaalamloo** in a short time.

అనధికార **anadhikaara** *adj.* unofficial, nonofficial.

అనధికారంగా **anadhikaarangaa** *adv.* **1** unofficially. **2** unauthorisedly.

అననుకూల **ananukuula** *adj.* **1** unfavourable. **2** inconvenient, disadvantageous.

అననుకూలత **ananukuulata** *n.* inconvenience, disadvantage.

అననుపాత **ananupaata** *adj.* disproportionate.

అననురక్తి **ananurakti** *n.* lack of love or affection.

అననేల **ananeela** *see* **eela.**

అనన్య **ananya** *adj.* matchless, incomparable.

అనన్యసామాన్య **ananyasaamaanya** *adj.* not shared by others, unique.

అనన్యాదృశ్య **ananyaadṛśya** *adj.* not seen elsewhere, marvellous, unique.

అనన్వయ **ananwaya** *adj.* **1** unconnected, disjointed, inconsistent. **2** not applicable to others, not matching with others.

అనభిలషణీయ **anabhilaSaNiiya** *adj.* undesirable.

అనపత్యుడు **anapatyuDu** *n.* person without issue, childless person.

అనయం **anayam** *adv. class.* always.

అనర్గళ **anargaLa** *adj.* unimpeded, unrestrained.

అనర్గళంగా **anargaLangaa** *adv.* (*gen. of speech*) without stopping, without a pause, non-stop.

అనర్ఘ **anargha** *adj.* costly, invaluable, priceless.

అనర్థ[ం] **anartha[m]** *n.* **1** evil, harm. **2** disaster, calamity.

అనర్థక **anarthaka** *adj.* meaningless, nonsensical,

అనర్థదాయక **anarthadaayaka** *adj.* wrong, harmful, damaging.

అనర్హ **anarha** *adj.* **1** unfit, unworthy, undeserved, undeserving. **2** unqualified, ineligible. **3** disqualified.

అనర్హత **anarhata** *n.* **1** ineligibility. **2** disqualification.

అనర్హుడు **anarhuDu** *n.* **1** undeserving or unfit person. **2** ineligible or unqualified person. **3** disqualified person.

అనలం **analam** *n.* fire.

అనల్ప **analpa** *adj.* much, great.

అనవధానత **anawadhaanata** *n.* inadvertence, inattention, lack of concentration.

అనవధి[క] **anawadhi[ka]** *adj.* unbounded.

అనవరత **anawarata** *adj.* perpetual, endless, incessant, ceaseless.

అనవరతం **anawaratam** *adv.* always.

అనవసర **anawasara** *adj.* unnecessary, needless, superflous.

అనవసరంగా **anawasarangaa** *adv.* **1** unnecessarily, needlessly. **2** without cause, for no reason, wantonly.

అనశ్వర **anaśwara** *adj.* imperishable, eternal.

అనాకార **anaakaara** *adj.* ugly.

అనాకారి **anaakaari** *n.* ugly person.

అనాక్షేపణీయ **anaakSeepaNiiya** *adj.* indisputable.

అనాగతం **anaagatam** *n.* future.

అనాగతవేది **anaagataweedi** *n.* prophet.

అనాగరిక **anaagarika** *adj.* uncivilised, uncultured, barbarous.

అనాగరికుడు **anaagarikuDu** *n.* uncivilised person, barbarian.

అనాచారం **anaacaaram** *n.* **1** defiance of tradition. **2** unorthodox practice.

అనాచ్ఛాదిత **anaacchaadita** *adj.* bare, uncovered, denuded, undisguised.

అనాడి, ఆనాడి **anaaDi, aanaaDi** *n.* **1.** village yokel, uncultured person. **2** *dial.* ~ **ceeyu,** ~ **gaa cuucu** to look down on, despise.

అనాథ **anaatha** I.*n.* orphan. II. *adj.* **1** without a protector, orphaned, destitute; ~ **preeta** unclaimed or unidentified corpse. **2** forlorn, wretched.

అనాథశరణాలయం, అనాథాశ్రమం **anaathaśaraNaalayam, anaathaaśramam** *n.* orphanage.

అనాథుడు **anaathuDu** *n.* s.o. without a protector.

అనాదరం **anaadaram** *n.* **1** disrespect, disregard. **2** coldheartedness, lack of affection.

అనాదరణ **anaadaraNa** *n.* disrespect, disregard; ~ **ku paalpaDu,** ~ **ku guri awu** to suffer from disrespect or disregard.

అనాదరణచేయు **anaadaraNa ceeyu** *v.t.* to disregard.

అనాది **anaadi** *n. and adj.* without a beginning, existing from eternity; ~ **nunci** from time immemorial.

అనాదిగా **anaadigaa** *adv.* from time immemorial.

అనామక **anaamaka** *adj.* nameless, anonymous.

అనామకుడు **anaamakuDu** *n.* obscure person, s.o. unknown to the public or without a reputation.

అనామతు **anaamatu** *n.* suspense account.

అనామధేయుడు **anaamadheeyuDu** *n.* anonymous writer or author.

అనామిక **anaamika** *n.* ring finger.

అనాయాస **anaayaasa** *adj* **1** painless **2** trouble free.

అనాయాసం **anaayaasam** *adv.* **1** painlessly. **2** effortlessly.

అనారోగ్య **anaaroogya** *adj.* unhealthy.

అనారోగ్యం **anaaroogyam** *n.* sickness, ill health, unhealthiness.

అనార్జిత **anaarjita** *adj.* unearned.

అనార్ద్ర **anaardra** *adj. sci.* dry.

అనాలోచనంగా **anaaloocanangaa** *adv.* without thinking, absent-mindedly.

అనాలోచిత **anaaloocita** *adj.* thoughtless, careless, uncaring, inconsiderate.

అనావశ్యక **anaawaśyaka** *adj.* unnecessary, superfluous.

అనావృష్టి **anaawṛSTi** *n.* failure or lack of rain, drought; *see* **atiwṛSTi.**

అనాస **anaasa** *n.* pineapple.

అనాసక్త **anaasakta** *adj.* detached, dispassionate; ~ **pariśiilana** dispassionate consideration.

అనాహూత **anaahuuta** *adj.* uninvited.

అని **ani**[1] *n., class.* war, battle.

అని **ani**[2] *past participle of* **anu** 1 *lit.* having said, having thought, saying, thinking. 2 *used as a connecting particle* (i) *as a marker of indirect report or command* **Dabbu istaanu ~ ceppEEDu** he said he would give money; **weNTanee bayaldeeram ~ aajña waccindi** an order came to start immediately; (ii) *to subordinate a clause to a verb expressing* knowledge, thinking, fearing, etc. **adi elaa ceeyaalaa ~ digulu paDutunnaanu** I am worried about how I should do it; **kanna talli manassu baadha peTTaDam enduku ~ neenu aa wiSayaaleemii maaTLaaDaleedu** thinking, why should I worry my own mother (*or* not wanting to worry my own mother), I talked of none of those things; **puujak ~ teccina bellam gaDDalanu engili ceesEEDu** he defiled the jaggery balls that had been brought for (use in) worship; (iii) *to subordinate a causal clause to a main clause in which the subject is human* **oNTiki mancidi kaad ~ sigareTLu taagaDam maaneesEEnu** I gave up smoking cigarettes because it was not good for my health. 3 *other usages* (i) 'to want' *is expressed by an infinitive* + **[w]aali** + **ani**, e.g., **naaku sinimaa cuuDaal ~ undi** I want to see a movie; (ii) *suffixed to onomatopoeic words ~ gives adverbial force*, e.g., (of snakes) **bussum ~** hissingly; (iii) **~ kaadu** *negates a preceding clause or sentence*, e.g., **andukani paraayi padaalanu anniTinii neTTaDam ~ kaadu** that is not to say (*or* that does not mean) that for that reason we should reject all foreign words.

అనింద్య **anindya** *adj.* irreproachable, faultless.

అనిచిపుచ్చు **anicipuccu** *v.t. class.* to bid farewell to.

అనిత్య **anitya** *adj.* 1 not permanent, temporary. 2 not continuous, intermittent.

అనితరసాధ్య **anitarasaadhya** *adj.* unequalled, unparallelled.

అనిపించు **anipincu** *v.i. and t.* 1 to cause s.o. to say, think or feel; **naa sneehituDitoo muuDu saarlu istaanu ~ koni weLLipooyEEDu** he went away after making my friend say three times that he would give; **C. ati canuwu eemiToo cikaaku anipincindi** C.'s familiarity somehow caused (him) to feel irritated. 2 to seem, appear; **aayana maaTLaaDutuNTee miiree maaTLaaDutunnaTTanipincindi** when he was talking it seemed as if (*or* it was just as if) you yourself were talking. 3 (of emotions) to be felt; **naaku caalaa kaSTam anipincindi** I felt very much grieved. 4 ~ *with infinitive* + **[w]aali** *means* to want to, feel inclined to; **atanni cuusi yoogakSeemaalu kanukkoowaalani aameki anipincindi** when she saw him, she felt inclined to ask about his welfare.

అనిపించుకొను **anipincukonu** *v.i.* 1 to be considered to be, be seen as, be taken as. 2 to be called (some good or bad epithet).

అనిమితి **animiti** *n.* inference.

అనిమిష[ం] **animiSa[m]** *n.* staring without blinking the eyes.

అనిమిషత్వం **animiSatwam** *n.* divinity.

అనిమిషుడు **animiSuDu** *n.* God.

అనియత **aniyata** *adj.* disorderly, erratic, irregular, desultory, random, haphazard, arbitrary.

అనియతంగా **aniyatangaa** *adv.* at random.

అనియమిత **aniyamita** *adj.* 1 irregular, not according to rule. 2 unappointed.

అనిర్ణీత **anirNiita** *adj.* undetermined.

అనిర్ధారిత **anirdhaarita** *adj.* indeterminate.

అనిర్వచనీయ **anirwacaniiya** *adj.* 1 indefinable. 2 beyond description.

అనిలం **anilam** *n. class.* wind, breeze.

అనివర్తనీయ **aniwartaniiya** *adj.* irrevocable.

అనివార్య **aniwaarya** *adj.* 1 unavoidable, inevitable. 2 binding, obligatory.

అనిశ్చయ **aniścaya** *adj.* uncertain, unsettled.

అనిశ్చిత **aniścita** *adj.* 1 undecided, uncertain, undetermined, unsettled. 2 *gram.* indefinite.

అనిషిక్తజననం **aniSiktajananam** *n. biol.* parthenogenesis.

అనిష్ట **aniSTa** *adj.* disliked, undesired.

అనిష్టంగా **aniSTangaa** *adv.* 1 unwillingly, grudgingly. 2 ~ **tala tippEEDu** he shook his head in dissent.

అనిష్టత **aniSTata** *n.* dislike, aversion, antipathy; ~ **wyaktam ceeyu**, ~ **welipuccu** to express dislike.

అను **anu** *v.t.* 1 to say, speak. 2 to call; **naa anee waaLLu ewaruu leeru** I have no one whom I can call my own. 3 *used to form verbs from certain onamotopoeic nouns/adverbs*, e.g., **jhallum ~** to receive a shock; **gaNagaNam ~** (of bells) to jingle.

అనుంగు **anungu** *same as* **anugu.**

అనుకరణ **anukaraNa** *n.* imitation, copying, mimicry; ~**ku longani** inimitable; **dhwany ~** mimicry of a person's speech.

అనుకరించు **anukarincu** *v.t.* to imitate, copy, mimic.

అనుకూల **anukuula** *adj.* 1 favourable, beneficial, advantageous. 2 congenial, amenable, suitable, well suited; ~ **mayna jaNTa** a well matched pair. 3 agreeable, acceptable. 4 benign, friendly.

అనుకూలం **anukuulam** *n.* good, benefit, convenience; **mii[ku] ~ cuucukoni okasaari akkaDiki weLLaNDi** please go there at your convenience.

అనుకూలం అవు, అనుకూలపడు, అనుకూలించు **anukuulam awu, anukuulapaDu, anukuulincu** *v.i.* 1 to be favourable; **annii anukuulistee** if everything turns out favourably. 2 to be suitable. 3 to be of use, have effect, prove successful. 4 to adapt, conform.

అనుకూలంగా **anukuulangaa** *adv.* 1 suitably. 2 favourably; **mii pratipaadanaku ~ maaTLaaDEEnu** I spoke in favour of your proposal; **naaku ~ uttaruwu iccEEDu** he gave an order in my favour.

అనుకూలత **anukuulata** *n.* 1 suitability. 2 favourability.

అనుకూలనం **anukuulanam** *n.* adaptation, accommodation.

అనుకూలనశీలత **anukuulanaśiilata** *n.* adaptibility.

అనుకూలింపచేయు **anukuulimpaceeyu** *v.t.* to adapt.

అనుకృతి **anukṛti** *n.* 1 imitation. 2 reproduction; **nṛtyabhangimaloo unna winaayaka śilpaaniki citraanukṛti** pictorial reproduction of a statue of Vinayaka in a dancing pose.

అనుకొను **anukonu** *v.i. and t.* 1 to say to o.s., think, consider. 2 to suppose, expect. 3 to intend; **anukonna kaaryakramam anukonnaTLugaa naDawadu** the intended programme does not proceed in the way that was intended. 4 (of more than one person) to say to each other. 5 *in neg. constr.* to mind, take amiss; **niiku eemaynaa panundEE? panuNTee ceppu. raanakkaraleedu. neeneemii anukoonu.** have you some work to do? if you have, say so, then you need not come. I will not mind.

అనుకో, అనుకొండి, అనుకోండి **anukoo, anukoNDi, anukooNDi** *imperative of* **anukonu** 1 suppose; **warSam wastundi ~ miiru eem ceestaaru?** suppose it rains, what will you do? 2 to be sure, for sure; **miiru naatoo aa maaTa idiwarakee ceppEEru ~ kaanii neenu ceeyaleedu** you told me that already, to be sure, but I did not do it.

అనుకోకుండా **anukookuNDaa** *adv.* 1 unexpectedly. 2 without premeditation, on the spur of the moment.

అనుకోని **anukooni** *adj.* unexpected.

అనుక్త **anukta** *adj.* unspoken, unuttered, tacit.

అనుక్రమం **anukramam** *n.* series, sequence, succession.

అనుక్రమణిక **anukramaNika** *n.* list (of contents); **wiSayaanukramaNika** index.

అనుక్రమిక **anukramika** *adj.* successive.

అనుక్రోశం **anukroośam** *n.* compassion, sympathy.

అనుక్షణ **anukSaNa** *adj.* constant, ceaseless; **aa naaTinunci aayana jiiwitam oka ~ samaram** from that day his life was a constant struggle.

అనుక్షణం **anukSaNam** *adv.* at every moment, every minute, from moment to moment, constantly, ceaselessly.

అనుగతంగా **anugatangaa** *advbl. suffix meaning* through or by means of a number of stages, e.g., **kramaanugatangaa** by degrees, gradually; **kaalaanugatangaa** in course of time; **wamśaanugatangaa** hereditarily.

అనుగు, అనుంగు **anugu, anungu** *adj.* dear, beloved.

అనుగుణ **anuguNa** *adj.* fit, proper, suitable, appropriate.

అనుగుణంగా **anuguNangaa** *adv.* 1 in accordance with, in conformity with, consistent with; **widyaarangamlooni nuutana dhooraNulaku ~** in accordance with recent trends in the field of education. 2 in tune with. 3 corresponding to.

అనుగ్రహం **anugraham** *n.* mercy, favour, grace, bounty, kindness, benignity.

అనుగ్రహించు **anugrahincu** *v.t.* 1 to favour, show kindness to. 2 to grant, bestow.

అనుఘటకం **anughaTakam** *n. chem.* component.

అనుచరుడు **anucaruDu** *n.* follower, supporter.

అనుచిత **anucita** *adj.* 1 unseemly, improper, unsuitable, undue, inappropriate. 2 unfair, inequitable; **~ pampakam** maldistribution.

అనుచితి **anuciti** *n.* impropriety.

అనుచ్ఛేదం **anuccheedam** *n. admin.* article (of Constitution).

అనుజనితం **anujanitam** *n. chem.* by product.

అనుజ్ఞ, అనుజ్ఞానం **anujña, anujñaanam** *n.* 1 order, command. 2 permission, sanction, leave.

అనుజ్ఞాత **anujñaata** *adj.* permitted.

అనుతాపం **anutaapam** *n.* regret, penitence, remorse.

అనుత్క్రమణీయ **anutkramaNiiya** *adj.* irreversible.

అనుత్తేజనం **anutteejanam** *n. sci.* deactivation.

అనుత్పాదక **anutpaadaka** *adj.* unproductive, non-productive.

అనుదాత్తస్వరం **anudaattaswaram** *n.* 1 *ling.* falling tone. 2 falling pitch in Vedic recitation.

అనుదినం **anudinam** *adv.* daily, every day.

అనుదైర్ఘ్య **anudayrghya** *adj. maths.* longitudinal.

అనుద్దిష్ట **anuddiSTa** *adj.* unintended, accidental.

అనునయ **anunaya** *adj.* soothing, conciliatory; **~ waakyaalu** soothing phrases.

అనునయం **anunayam** *n.* conciliation, propitation, endearment.

అనునయంగా **anunayangaa** *adv.* soothingly, endearingly.

అనునయించు **anunayincu** *v.t.* to placate, pacify, soothe, conciliate.

అనునాసికం **anunaasikam** *n. ling.* nasal.

అనునిత్యం **anunityam** *adv.* 1 continuously. 2 regularly. 3 daily.

అనుపమ **anupama** *adj.* incomparable.

అనుపమానంగా **anupamaanangaa** *adv.* incomparably.

అనుపయుక్త, అనుపయోగ **anupayukta, anupayooga** *adj.* not in use, disused.

అనుపస్థితి **anupasthiti** *n.* absence.

అనుపల్లవి **anupallawi** *n.* verse of a song which follows the **pallawi** or refrain.

అనుపాకం **anupaakam** *n.* preparation of dishes accompanying the main dish of a meal.

అనుపాత **anupaata** *adj.* proportional, proportionate.

అనుపాతం **anupaatam** *n.* proportion.

అనుపానం **anupaanam** *n. med.* 1 vehicle, i.e., liquid or other substance added to the active ingredient to give bulk to medicine or make it palatable. 2 secondary ingredient (for example milk or honey) added to the main ingredient in Ayurvedic medicine.

అనుపార్జిత **anupaarjita** *adj.* unearned.

అనుప్రయుక్త **anuprayukta** *adj.* applied (science).

అనుప్రయోగం **anuprayoogam** *n.* application.

అనుప్రాస **anupraasa** *n.* rule of poetical composition governing rhyming of syllables at the end of a line and alliteration within the lines of a stanza.

అనుబంధ **anubandha** *adj.* 1 connected, attached, affiliated. 2 supplementary, subsidiary. 3 auxiliary, accessory; *see* **anubandhita.**

అనుబంధం **anubandham** *n.* 1 connection, relationship. 2 addendum, appendix, annexe, supplement (to a book or document). 3 tie, bond, attachment (of love or affection). 4 *gram.* auxiliary(verb). 5 *pl.* **anubandhaalu** accessories, attachments, extra parts (of a machine).

అనుబంధించు **anubandhincu** *v.t.* 1 to join, attach, annex. 2 to affiliate.

అనుబంధిత **anubandhita** *adj.* 1 affiliated; ~ (*or* **anubandha**) **kaLaaśaala** affiliated college. 2 supplementary; ~ (*or* **anubandha**) **praśnalu** supplementary questions.

అనుభవం **anubhawam** *n.* 1 experience (**-loo**, of). 2 knowledge gained from or based on experience. 3 enjoyment. 4 suffering.

అనుభవజ్ఞుడు **anubhawajñuDu** *n.* experienced person, expert.

అనుభవపూర్వక, అనుభవసిద్ధ **anubhawapuurwaka, anubhawasiddha** *adj.* empirical.

అనుభవపూర్వకంగా **anubhawa puurwakangaa** *adv.* by or from experience.

అనుభవయోగ్య **anubhawayoogya** *adj.* able to be used, of practical value.

అనుభవవాదం **anubhawawaadam** *n.* empiricism.

అనుభవశాలి **anubhawaśaali** experienced person, expert.

అనుభవించు **anubhawincu** *v.t.* 1 to experience. 2 to enjoy; **aastini anubhawistunnaaDu** he is enjoying the property. 3 to suffer, undergo; **ceesina paapaaniki śikSa anubhawistunnaaDu** he is undergoing punishment for the sin he has committed.

అనుభవైక్య **anubhawaykya** *adj.* (knowledge) gained by experience.

అనుభావం **anubhaawam** *n.* indication of emotion or passion by look or gesture.

అనుభూత **anubhuuta** *adj.* enjoyed.

అనుభూతి **anubhuuti** *n.* 1 experience. 2 impression, feeling, sentiment; **aayana uttaram waccindi. adi cuustee aayannee cuusin~ kaligindi** his letter arrived and when I saw it I had the impression of having seen him himself: **anubhuutulu leeni maniSi eem maniSi?** what kind of a man is he if he has no sentiments (*or* feelings)? 3 **madhuraanubhuutulu** sweet memories.

అనుభోగం **anubhoogam** *n.* enjoyment.

అనుభోగ హక్కు **anubhooga hakku** *n. legal* easement.

అనుమతి **anumati** *n.* 1 agreement, consent, leave, permission. 2 *legal* admission.

అనుమతించు **anumatincu** *v.i.* 1 to consent, allow, give permission, permit. 2 *legal* to admit; **anumatinca tagina** admissible.

అనుమస్తిష్కం **anumastiSkam** *n.* cerebellum.

అనుమానం **anumaanam** *n.* 1 doubt, suspicion. 2 conjecture, surmise.

అనుమానపడు **anumaanapaDu** *v.i.* to suspect, doubt.

అనుమానాస్పద **anumaanaaspada** *adj.* doubtful, questionable, suspicious.

అనుమానించు **anumaanincu** *v.i.* 1 to suspect, doubt. 2 to infer.

అనుమిత **anumita** *adj.* inferred.

అనుమితి **anumiti** *n.* inference, deduction.

అనుములు **anumulu** *n.pl.* a minor variety of pulses.

అనుమోదం, అనుమోదించు **anumoodincu** *same as* **aamoodam, aamoodincu.**

అనుయాయి **anuyaayi** *n.* follower, adherent, supporter.

అనుయోగ **anuyooga** *adj.* appropriate.

అనురంజన **anuranjana** *adj.* pleasing.

అనురక్త **anurakta** *adj.* devoted, attached.

అనురక్తి **anurakti** *n* love, affection, attachment, devotion.

అనురణనం **anuraNanam** *n. sci.* resonance.

అనురాగం **anuraagam** *n.* love, affection.

అనురూప **anuruupa** *adj.* conforming, corresponding, similar.

అనురూపంగా **anuruupangaa** *adv.* in conformity with.

అనురూపత **anuruupata** *n.* similitude.

అనురోధం **anuroodham** *n. class.* conformity, compliance.

అనులేఖనం **anuleekhanam** *n. ling.* 1 citation. 2 transcription.

అనులోమ **anulooma** *adj.* 1 regular. 2 *lit.* following the direction of the hair or grain. 3 *maths.* ~**niSpatti** direct ratio; ~**calatwam** direct variation.

అనుల్లంఘనీయ **anullanghaniiya** *adj.* not to be transgressed.

అనువంశిక **anuwamśika** *adj.* hereditary.

అనువదించు **anuwadincu** *v.t.* to translate, interpret.

అనువర్తనం **anuwartanam** *n.* application.

అనువర్తి **anuwarti** *n.* one who follows (a path): **satyamaargaanuwarti** follower of the path of truth.

అనువర్తించు **anuwartincu** I. *v.i.* to apply, be applicable. II. *v.t.* to apply, make applicable.

అనువర్తింపచేయు **anuwartimpaceeyu** *v.t.* 1 to cause to apply. 2 to extend (aid).

అనువర్తిత **anuwartita** *adj.* applied.

అనువాదం **anuwaadam** *n.* translation.

అనువాదకుడు **anuwaadakuDu** *n.* translator.

అనువు **anuwu** I. *n.* suitability, facility, convenience; **mii~ cuusukoni uuriki weLLiraNDi** go to your home town at your convenience. 2 *dial.* low position, humble status; **nii ~cuusi eemaynaa aNTaaDu aa wedhawa** that villain will say anything, taking account of your humble status. II. *adj.* suitable, convenient, appropriate, conducive.

అనువుగా **anuwugaa** *adv.* 1 conveniently, suitably. 2 as a means towards, for the purpose of: **pariśramaalanu sthaapincaDaaniki** ~ as means towards establishing industries.

అనుశాసనం **anuśaasanam** *n.* 1 command, order, rule or precept governing an individual's conduct. 2 *gram.* rules governing the grammar and vocabulary of a language; **iTuwaNTi maaTalu neeTi teluguloo aneekamulu unnaayi. awi lawkika bhaaSalooniwi. śabdaanuśaasanam ceeseewaaru aTTi śabdaalannii anuśaasincawalenu** there are many words like these in modern Telugu. they belong to the colloquial language. those who make rules for the language must frame them so as to govern all these words.

అనుశాసనికపర్వం **anuśaasanika parwam** *n.* the final parwam of the Mahabharata, in which rules of conduct are laid down.

అనుశాసించు **anuśaasincu** *v.t.* 1 to cite in an authoritative manner. 2 *gram.* to frame rules for a language governing its grammar and vocabulary.

అనుశిష్ట **anuśiSTa** *adj.* cited, quoted.

అనుశీలన[ం] **anuśiilana[m]** *n.* survey.

అనుశ్రుత **anuśruta** *adj.* pertaining to traditional learning acquired orally; **waaDu peddagaa caduwukoo leedu. ~ widya. pawroohityam ceestunnaaDu** he has not studied much. he has picked up some traditional learning and lives as a purohit.

అనుషంగం **anuSangam** *n. class.* attachment, love.

అనుషంగికం **anuSangikam** *adj.* 1 following as a result, consequential. 2 consistent, comforming, consonant; **oka cinna lakSyaanni pedda lakSyaaniki ~ ceeyaDam** making a lesser purpose conform to greater purpose.

అనుషక్త **anuSakta** *adj. maths.* concurrent.

అనుష్ఠానం **anuSThaanam** *n.* observance, practice, performance (of religious rites).

అనుష్ఠించు **anuSThincu** *v.t.* 1 to practise, observe (custom). 2 to celebrate, perform (festival).

అనుసంధానం **anusandhaanam** *n.* 1 joining, linking, connecting. 2 liaison.

అనుసంధించు **anusandhincu** *v.t.* to unite, join, link, connect.

అనుసరణ **anusaraNa** *n.* adaptation.

అనుసరణచేయు **anusaraNaceeyu** *v.t.* to adapt.

అనుసరణీయ **anusaraNiiya** *adj.* 1 fit or worthy to be followed. 2 adaptable.

అనుసరణీయత **anusaraNiiyata** *n.* adaptability.

అనుసరించి **anusarinci** *past participle of* **anusarincu** in accordance with, in pursuance of, in conformity with, as per: **sandhini** ~ in accordance with the treaty.

అనుసరించు **anusarincu** *v.t.* 1 to follow, attend on, accompany. 2 to conform to.

అనుసారం [గా] **anusaaram[gaa]** *adv.* 1 accordingly. 2 following, in accordance with, according to: **niyamaaniki anusaarangaa** *or* **niyamaanusaaram** according to rule; **naaku tana aasti iSTaanusaaram raasi iccEEDu** he left me his property to deal with at my discretion.

అనుసూచి **anusuuci** *n.* schedule.

అనుస్యూత **anusyuuta** *adj.* regular, continuous, uninterrupted.

అనుస్వరత **anuswarata** *n.* harmony, concordance.

అనుస్వారం **anuswaaram** *n.* anusvara, the nasal letter ం in the Telugu alphabet; *see* **sunna.**

అనూచానం **anuucaanam** *n.* traditional learning, esp. study of the Vedas and Vedangas, handed down hereditarily by word of mouth.

అనూచానంగా **anuucaanangaa** *adv.* traditionally.

అనూహ్య **anuuhya** *adj.* unimaginable, inconceivable.

అనృత **anṛta** *adj.* false, untrue.

అనృతం **anṛtam** *n.* lie, falsehood.

అనే **anee** *fut. vbl. adj. of* **anu 1 neenu ~ maaTa** the word which I [will] say; **sontangaa tanadi ~ aasti eemii leedu** he has no property that he can call his own; **raamaaraawu ~ aayana** a man called Rama Rao. 2 *in some situations ~ is translatable by the connecting particle* 'that' *in English, or its meaning may be completely neutralised,* e.g., **aayana tirigi raaD~ bhayam aameni piiDistoondi** the fear that he will not return afflicts her; **balapamtoo i ii ~ reNDu akSaraalu raasindi** she wrote the two letters *i* and *ii* with a slate pencil: *cf.* **anna**[2].

అనేక **aneeka** *adj.* many.

అనేకం **aneekam** *n. occurring in apposition* much, many; **daaniki prabalamayna kaaraNaalu ~ leeka pooleedu** many good reasons for that were not lacking; **awaka tawakalu ~ jarigEEyi** many inconsistencies occurred.

అనేకులు **aneekulu** *n.pl.* many persons.

అనేది **aneedi** *fut. vbl. adj. of* **anu + di 1 neenu ~ eemaNTee** what I [will] say is as follows. 2 that is to say, namely; **wiiTanniTiloo reNDeesi rakaalu unnaayi, pyuur aND applayD~** there are two varieties in all these (sciences), namely, pure and applied. 3 *in neg. constr.* such a thing; **waaDiki Dabbu kodawa~leedu** for him there is no such thing as shortage of money.

అనైక్యత, అనైక్యమత్యం **anaykyata, anaykyamatyam** *n.* disunity, discord.

అనైచ్ఛిక **anaycchika** *adj.* involuntary, spontaneous; ~ **kaNDaraalu** involuntary muscles.

అనౌచిత్యం **anawcityam** *n.* impropriety.

అన్న **anna**[1] I. *honorific suffix attached to a man's name,* e.g., **raamanna** Ramanna. II. *n.* elder brother.

అన్న **anna**[2] *past vbl. adj. of* **anu 1 sarigaa neenu ~ samayaaniki waccEEDu** he came exactly at the time that I said. 2 *in some situations ~ is translatable by the connecting particle* 'that' *in English or its meaning may be completely neutralised,* e.g., **niiku paaTa wacc~sangati andarikii ceppeesEEnu** I have told everyone (the fact) that you can sing; **wiiTiloo eedi mundaa eedi wenakaa ~tikamaka awasaram leedu** there is no need for confusion about which of these comes first and which comes afterwards; *cf.* **anee.**

అన్నం **annam** *n.* cooked rice, food; **biDDaku ~peTTu** give the child food; **~ginne** utensil for cooking rice.

అన్నం ముట్టించు **annam muTTincu** *v.t. dial.* to perform the ceremony of giving solid food to a baby for the first time.

అన్నకోశం **annakoośam** *n. zool.* stomach.

అన్నట్టు **annaTTu** 1 *sentence opener* by the way, oh! (*said by a person remembering something*). 2 as if; **deewuDu pampEEDu ~miiru waccEEru** you came (unexpectedly) as if sent by God. 3 *tag phrase* as the proverb says; **andaru andalam ekkitee mooseewaLLewaru~** as the proverb says, if all climb into the palanquin, who will there be to carry it?

అన్నట్టుగా **annaTTugaa** *adv.* 1 same as **annaTTu** *sense* 1. 2 as said; **aayana ~ nee jarigindi** it happened just as he said.

అన్నదాత **annadaata** *n.* person who gives food as charity.

అన్నదానం **annadaanam** *n.* free distribution of food.

అన్నద్వేషం **annadweeSam** *n.* aversion to food, nausea.

అన్నన్నా! **annannaa!** *interj. expressing surprise or grief.*

అన్నపూర్ణ **annapuurNa** *n.* a name of Durga in her manifestation as Goddess of plenty.

అన్నపూర్ణచెంబు **annapuurNa cembu** *n.* 1 bowl of a certain shape. 2 begging bowl.

అన్నప్పుడల్లా **annappuDallaa** *adv.* readily, whenever you want: **aa udyoogaalu~dorakutaayaa?** will those jobs be readily available?

అన్నపుపొడి, అన్నప్పొడి, కమ్మ[టి] పొడి **annap[u]poDi, kamma[Ti] poDi** *n.* powder made of gram and mixed spices ground together and eaten with rice.

అన్నప్రాశన **annapraaśana** *n.* ceremony of giving solid food to a baby for the first time.

అన్నభేది **annabheedi** *n. sci.* sulphate of iron.

అన్నమాట **annamaaTa** *tag particle indicating that the speaker is confident of what he or she is saying, roughly equivalent to* I am telling you, it is a fact that, so, then: **iTLaa telugu-ingliiSu nighaNTuwu waypu brawn manassu maLLind** ~ it is a fact that in this way Brown's mind turned towards a Telugu-English dictionary; **ayitee naaku paaTham ceputunnaaw** ~ ! so you are teaching me a lesson!

అన్నవస్త్రాలు **annawastraalu** *n.pl.* food and clothing.

అన్నవాహిక **annawaahika** *n.* gullet, oesophagus.

అన్నా **annaa**[1] I. *concessive form of* **anu 1 neenu wadd~ TikaT konnaaDu** he bought a ticket, although I told him not to. 2 *a simple sentence* + ~ *may replace a concessive clause;* e.g., **waaDu bediristunnaaDu ~ naaku bhayam leedu** I will not be afraid, even though he threatens me. II. *particle similar to* **aynaa** *and indefinite clitic* **oo**; *usages:* (i) *to express indefiniteness, when added to an* **e-** *question word,* e.g., **inkewarin ~ pilawaNDi** please call anyone else; (ii) *to express alternatives,* e.g., **miir ~ neen ~ ii pani ceyyaali** either you or I must do this work.

అన్నా **annaa**[2] *interj.* no! (*often said to children and accompanied by the gesture of wagging the finger*) ~ ! **aTLaa parigettakuuDadu** no! you must not run like that!; ~ ! **aTLaa kaadu** no! it is not like that.

అన్నార్తులు **annaartulu** *n.pl.* hungry persons.

అన్ని **anni** *det. n. pl. and adj.* (*of non-human things*) 1 that number, so many. 2 *idiomatic usage:* ~ **kaaLLatoo iNTLoo tiragaku** do not walk about the house with unwashed feet (*meaning* with feet in different kinds of condition); ~ **gari-Telu ii annamloo peTTaku** do not put unwashed spoons in this rice (*meaning* spoons that have been used in different dishes).

అన్నిందాలా **annindaalaa** *adv., corruption of* **anniwidhaalaa** from all aspects, in all respects or ways.

అన్నిటా **anniTaa** *adv.* 1 in all respects, ways, places or matters: **jillaa kaaryaalayaal~** in all district offices; **panul~ sahaayam ceesEEDu** he helped in all the works.

అన్నివైపులా **anniwaypulaa** *adv.* all around, on all sides.

అన్నీ **annii** *det.n.pl.* (*of non-human things*) everything, all; ~ **kalisi waccEEyi** everything turned out well; **maanawuDu paDutunna paaTLu ~ innii kaawu** *lit.* the ills that man suffers are not just that many or this many, i.e., man's ills are innumerable.

అన్నెంపున్నెం **annem punnem** *n.* wrong and right; ~ **eragani biDDa** child who cannot distinguish wrong from right, innocent or simple-minded child.

అన్య **anya** *adj.* another, other, different, strange.

అన్యం **anyam** *n. in neg. constr.* anything else; **aadhyaatma cinta tappa ~ eragani rsi pungawuni wale toocEEDu** he appeared to be like a saint who understood nothing else but spiritual thought.

అన్యత్ర **anyatra** *adv.* elsewhere, somewhere else.

అన్యథా **anyathaa** *adv.* in a different manner, differently, otherwise; ~ **bhaawincakaNDi** please do not think otherwise.

అన్యదేశం **anyadeeśam** *n.* another country, foreign country.

అన్యదేశ్య **anyadeeśya** *adj.* pertaining or belonging to a foreign country, foreign.

అన్యదేశ్యం **anyadeeśyam** *n. ling.* foreign or borrowed word.

అన్యధ్యాస **anyadhyaasa** *n.* diverted attention.

అన్యపరతంత్ర **anyaparatantra** *adj.* dependent on others.

అన్యమనస్కంగా **anyamanaskangaa** *adv.* thinking of or concentrating on s.g else.

అన్యమనస్కత **anyamanaskata** *n.* distraction, lack of concentration.

అన్యవిధాల **anyawidhaala** *adv.* in other ways or respects.

అన్యాక్రాంతం **anyaakraantam** *n.* 1 alienation (of property). 2 occupation (of property) by others.

అన్యాక్రాంతంచేయు **anyaakraantamceeyu** *v.t.* to alienate (property).

అన్యాపదేశం **anyaapadeeśam** *n.* indirect reference, implication.

అన్యాపదేశంగా **anyaapadeeśangaa** *adv.* indirectly, by indirect means.

అన్యాయం **anyaayam** *n.* 1 injustice, wrong. 2 wickedness, lawlessness. 3 unfair means, foul play.

అన్యాయంగా **anyaayangaa** *adv.* 1 unjustly, unfairly, wrongfully. 2 unjustifiably, for no [good] reason; **baabuu, wiiDi aakataayatanaanni miiru sarididdaali. leekapootee ~ ceDipootaaDu** sir, you must correct this boy's mischievousness. otherwise he will get spoilt for no reason.

అన్యోన్య **anyoonya** *adj.* 1 mutual, reciprocal. 2 affectionate, intimate, mutually attached.

అన్యోన్యంగా **anyoonyangaa** *adv.* 1 mutually, reciprocally. 2 affectionately, intimately, on very friendly terms, getting on well together.

అన్యోన్యచర్య **anyoonyacarya** *n.* interaction.

అన్యోన్యత **anyoonyata** *n.* mutual affection, concord.

అన్వయం **anwayam** *n.* 1 comparison, correspondence. 2 constructing, understanding. 3 *gram.* agreement, accord. 4 *gram.* syntax.

అన్వయపరచు **anwayaparacu** *v.t.* to adapt, fit in.

అన్వయాంతరం **anwayaantaram** *n.* paraphrase.

అన్వయించు **anwayincu** I. *v.i.* 1 to apply, be applicable, correspond in meaning, be in accordance, be in agreement; **wiiru wraasinadi akSaraalaa wiiri wraataalakee anwayistundi** what he has written (about others) applies literally to his own writings. II. *v.t.* 1 to apply, make applicable. 2 to interpret with reference to, consider in relation to; **waaTini unna paristhitulatoo anwayinci cuustee, ennoo kliSTa samasyalu sunaayaasangaa awagaahana kaagalawu** if we consider them in relation to existing circumstances, ever so many difficult problems can be comprehended. 3 *gram.* to relate (verbs to nouns).

అన్వయించుకొను **anwayincukonu** I. *v.i.* to apply, be applicable, correspond in meaning. II.*v.t.* 1 to apply, make applicable, relate, adapt. 2 to interpret, construe with reference to; **1866 eDiSanloo ii krindi waakyaalanu ii sanghaTanatoo anwayincukoowaalsi uNTundi** we must construe the following sentences in the 1866 edition with reference to this incident.

అన్వయింపచేయు **anwayimpa ceeyu** *v.t.* to adapt, apply.

అన్వర్థ **anwartha** *first part of a noun compound* true to the sense or meaning; ~**naamam** a fitting or appropriate name.

అన్వీత **anwita** *last part of an adjvl. compound* possessed of, imbued with; **mahimaanwita** imbued with glory.

అన్వేషణ **anweeSaNa** *n.* 1 search, quest. 2 enquiry. 3 exploration, prospecting.

అన్వేషించు **anweeSincu** *v.t.* to look for, search for, explore, prospect; **upaayam**~ to search out a means or method.

అపకర్ష **apakarSa** *adj.* pejorative.

అపకర్షం **apakarSam** *n.* 1 detraction. 2 diminution. 3 deterioration. 4 decadence.

అపకారం **apakaaram** *n.* 1 harm, injury. 2 disservice. 3 detraction.

అపకారి **apakaari** I.*n.* ill doer. II.*adj.* harmful.

అపకిరణం **apakiraNam** *n. phys.* dispersion.

అపకీర్తి **apakiirti** *n.* bad reputation, ill fame, infamy, disgrace.

అపకేంద్ర **apakeendra** *adj.* centrifugal.

అపకేంద్రీకరణ **apakeendriikaraNa** *n.sci.* centrifugation.

అపక్రమభిన్నం **apakramabhinnam** *n. maths.* improper fraction.

అపక్వ **apakwa** *adj.* 1 raw, uncooked. 2 unripe.

అపఖ్యాతి **apakhyaati** *n.* bad report, ill fame, discredit; ~**paalawu** to be discredited.

అపగతం **apagatam** *adj.* gone, departed.

అపగుణం **apaguNam** *same as* **awaguNam.**

అపఘాతం **apaghaatam** *n.* sudden, violent or untimely death.

అపచక్రవాతం **apacakrawaatam** *n. met.* anticyclone.

అపచయక్రియ **apacayakriya** *n. sci.* catabolism.

అపచారం **apacaaram** *n.* 1 crime, offence. 2 insult, affront, slight, incivility. 3 wrong; **mukhyawiSayam intawarakuu itanninci daaci itani eDala**~ **ceesEEnu** in hiding an important matter from this man for so long I have done him a wrong.

అపజయం **apajayam** *n.* failure, defeat.

అపథ్యం **apathyam** *adj.* unwholesome, contrary to the prescribed diet.

అపదాది **apadaadi** *adj. ling.* non-initial.

అపనమ్మకం, అపనమ్మిక **apanammakam, apanammika** *n.* mistrust, disbelief.

అపనమ్మకంగా **apanammakangaa** *adv.* 1 disbelievingly; **neenu ceeppinadantaa wini** ~**naawaypu cuusEEDu** after hearing all I said, he looked at me disbelievingly. 2 uncertain; **okaToo teedii Dabbu wastundoo leedoo** ~ **undi** it is uncertain whether the money will come on the first of the month or not.

అపనింద, అపదూరు **apaninda, apaduuru** *n.* slander, false accusation, undeserved blame, calumny.

అపప్రథ **apapratha** *n.* bad name or reputation.

అపప్రయోగం **apaprayoogam** *n. gram.* wrong usage.

అపభ్రంశ **apabhramśa** *adj. colloq.* low, mean, objectionable, unseemly; ~**pu wedhawa** mean fellow (term of abuse); ~**pu maaTalu** vulgar words.

అపభ్రంశం **apabhramśam** *n.* 1 the lowest or most colloquial form of Prakrit. 2 (of language) corruption, degeneration.

అపభ్రంశంచేయు **apabhramśam ceeyu** *v.t.* to misuse, spoil.

అపభ్రష్ట **apabhraSTa** *adj.* corrupt, degenerate, deteriorated, inferior.

అపమానం **apamaanam** *same as* **awamaanam.**

అపమార్గం **apamaargam** *n.* wrong road.

అపమృత్యువు **apamṛtyuwu** *n.* sudden, violent or untimely death.

అపయశస్సు **apayaśassu** *n.* ill fame, bad reputation.

అపర **apara** *adj.* other, another; **neeneemii** ~**karNuDini kaadu nuwwu aDiginawannii iwwaDaaniki** I am not another Karna to give all you ask for (Karna, a hero of the Mahabharata, was renowned for his selfsacrifice and charity).

అపరంజి **aparanji** *n.* fine gold.

అపరకర్మలు, అపరక్రియలు **aparakarmalu, aparakriyalu** *n.pl.* funeral rites, obsequies.

అపరపక్షం **aparapakSam** *n.* second half of the lunar month.

అపరబుద్ధి **aparabuddhi** *n.* evil notion, bad idea; **waaDu roojuu naa gadiki wacceewaaDu. iwwEELa naa reeDiyoo ettukupooyEEDu. waaDiki enduku ii**~**puTTindoo teliyaDam leedu** he would come to my room daily; today he has stolen my radio. I do not know how this evil notion occurred to him.

అపరాజితుడు **aparaajituDu** *n.* one who is not defeated, an epithet of Iswara.

అపరాత్రి **aparaatri** *n.* later part of the night; **artharaatri**~ **rooDLa wembaDi tiragakuuDadu** you should not wander about on the roads at midnight or later; (the night is divided into three phases—**tolijaamu, artharaatri** and **malijaamu** or **aparaatri**); *cf.* **aparaahnam.**

అపరాధ[ం] **aparaadha[m]** *n.* 1 crime, offence. 2 fault, sin. 3. fine, punishment, penalty.

అపరాధ పరిశోధన **aparaadhapariśoodhana** *n.* detection (of crime); ~**nawala** detective novel.

అపరాధి **aparaadhi** *n.* offender, culprit, criminal, delinquent, miscreant.

అపరాలు **aparaalu** *n. pl.* pulses (peas, beans and other leguminous foodgrains); **pawitra samayaalaloo** ~**braahmaNulaku daanam ceestaaru** they make gifts of pulses to brahmans on auspicious occasions.

అపరాహ్ణం **aparaahnam** *n.* afternoon and evening; (the day is divided into three phases — **udayam, madhyaannam** and **aparaahnam**); *cf.* **aparaatri.**

అపరిచిత **aparicita** *adj.* unfamiliar.

అపరిచితుడు **aparicituDu** *n.* unknown person, unfamiliar person, stranger.

అపరిపక్వం **aparipakwam** *adj.* 1 unripe. 2 immature. 3 incomplete, unsettled, unfinished; **wyawahaaram inkaa ~ gaa undi** the affair is still unsettled.

అపరిమిత **aparimita** *adj.* 1 boundless, limitless, unlimited, infinite. 2 immense.

అపరివర్తనీయ **apariwartaniiya** *adj. sci.* irreversible.

అపరిశుద్ధ **apariśuddha** *adj.* dirty, unclean, insanitary.

అపరిశుద్ధం చేయు **apariśuddham ceeyu** *v.t.* to defile.

అపరిష్కృత **apariSkṛta** *adj.* un[re]solved (problem).

అపరిహార్య **aparihaarya** *adj.* unavoidable, indispensible.

అపరూప **aparuupa** *adj.* ugly.

అపలపించు **apalapincu** *v.t. class.* to deny.

అపలాపం, అపలాపన **apalaapam, apalaapana** *n.* vain or idle talk.

అపవర్తనం **apawartanam** *n. sci.* deflection

అపవాదం **apawaadam** *n.* 1 imputation, aspersion, calumny, slanderous report, scandal. 2 *gram.* exception to a rule.

అపవాదు **apawaadu** *n.* slander, slanderous report.

అపవారించు **apawaarincu** *v.t.* to cover up, hide, conceal.

అపవిత్ర **apawitra** *adj.* impure.

అపవిత్రంచేయు **apawitram ceeyu** *v.t.* to defile, desecrate.

అపవేళ **apaweeLa** *adj.* untimely.

అపశకున **apaśakuna** *adj.* ill omened; **~ pu sankhya** unlucky number.

అపశకునం **apaśakunam** *n.* bad omen.

అపశబ్దం **apaśabdam** *n.* 1 vulgar word. 2 ungrammatical word.

అపశృతి **apaśṛti** *n.* discordant note; **mahootsawa sandarbhamloo okee oka ~ wina waccindi** on the occasion of the celebration only one discordant note was heard.

అపసత్యం **apasatyam** *n.* lie, untruth, falsehood.

అపసరణం **apasaraNam** *n.* divergence.

అపసవ్యం **apasawyam** I.*n.* wearing the sacred thread in the wrong way, i.e., over the right shoulder and not the left, as is done when performing a funeral or death anniversary ceremony. II.*adj.* contrary, perverse.

అపసవ్యంగా **apasawyangaa** *adv.* 1 anticlockwise, counterclockwise. 2 wrong, awry, in the wrong way; **neenu ceppina maaTalu winakapootee waaDiki antaa ~ gaa jarigindi** when he did not listen to me, everything went wrong for him.

అపస్మార[క] **apasmaara[ka]** *adj.* unconscious, subconscious; **~ manassu** the subconscious mind.

అపస్మారం **apasmaaram** *n.* 1 unconsciousness, fainting, swooning. 2 epilepsy.

అపస్వరం **apaswaram** *n.* 1 false, wrong or discordant tone. 2 inappropriate or untimely remark liable to be regarded as a bad omen.

అపహరణ **apaharaNa** *n.* 1 theft, stealing, robbery. 2 *legal* abduction.

అపహరించు **apaharincu** *v.t.* 1 to steal, rob, make away with, seize, take by violence. 2 *legal* to abduct.

అపహర్త **apharta** *n.* thief, robber, person who carries away by force or violence.

అపహసించు **apahasincu** *v.t.* to deride, laugh at, ridicule, sneer at.

అపహాస్యం **apahaasyam** *n.* 1 derision, ridicule, sneering. 2 buffoonery.

అపాత్ర **apaatra** *adj.* undeserving, unworthy.

అపాత్రదానం **apaatradaanam** *n.* charity to an undeserving person.

అపాదానం **apaadaanam** *n.* 1 taking away, removing. 2 *gram.* meaning conveyed by the ablative case.

అపాదానకారకం **apaadaanakaarakam** *n. gram.* ablative case.

అపానం **apaanam** *n.* anus.

అపామార్గం **apaamaargam** *same as* **uttareeNi.**

అపాయం **apaayam** *n.* 1 danger, peril. 2 risk, hazard. 3 harm, injury. 4 accident; **~ loo maraNincEEDu** he died in an accident.

అపాయకర, అపాయకారి **apaayakara, apaayakaari** *adj.* dangerous, hazardous, perilous.

అపార **apaara** *adj.* 1 limitless, boundless. 2 immense, enormous, tremendous, abundant.

అపారంగా **apaarangaa** *adv.* endlessly, abundantly, profusely, tremendously.

అపారపారావారం **apaarapaaraawaaram** *n.* 1 *class.* ocean. 2 *colloq.* **waaDiki ~ gaa Dabbu undi** he has enormous wealth (*lit.* he has oceans of money).

అపార్థం **apaartham** *n.* 1 misinterpretation. 2 misunderstanding.

అపార్థంచేసుకొను **apaartham ceesukonu** *v.t.* 1 to misunderstand, misconstrue. 2 to misinterpret.

అపుణ్య **apuNya** *adj. class.* wicked, bad.

అపుత్రుడు **aputruDu** *n.* person who has no son.

అపురూప **apuruupa** *adj.* 1 unusual, extraordinary, exceptional. 2 rare; **~ mayna taaLapatra granthaalu** rare palmleaf manuscripts.

అపురూపం **apuruupam** *n.* 1 s.g unusual, rare or precious; **miiru maa iNTiki raawaDamee ~** it is s.g rare for you to come to our house; **~ ayipooyEEwu** you are seldom to be seen. 2 extreme fondness; **waaDiki pillalu aNTee ~** he has a great fondness for (*or* he is extremely fond of) children.

అపూపం **apuupam** *n.* kind of sweet cake.

అపూర్వ **apuurwa** *adj.* novel, unprecedented, unique.

అపేక్ష **apeekSa** *n.* 1 desire, wish, hope. 2 felt need.

అపేక్షించు **apeekSincu** *v.t.* 1 to desire, wish for. 2 to require, demand.

అపోహ **apooha** *n.* 1 misconception. 2 misapprehension.

అపౌరుషేయ **apawruSeeya** *adj.* (of the Vedas) divinely revealed.

అపౌరుషేయత్వం **apawruSeeyatwam** *n.* divine revelation.

అప్ప **appa** I. *suffix added to names as a mark of respect*, e.g., **raamappa** Ramappa. II. *n.* 1 *dial.* gentleman; **pustakam aa ~ki icciraa** go and give the book to that gentleman. 2 *dial.* elder sister (= **akka**).

అప్పం **appam** *n.* 1 kind of savoury snack. 2 (*also* **aapam**) sweet cake of rice flour.

అప్పగించు, వప్పచెప్పు, ఒప్పచెప్పు, అప్పచెప్పు, ఒప్పగించు, వప్పగించు

appagincu, wappaceppu, oppaceppu, appaceppu, oppagincu, wappagincu *v.t.* 1 to entrust, commit, consign, deliver, hand over; **kaLLappaginci cuucu** to fix o.'s eyes on, stare fixedly at. 2 to repeat back (s.g learnt by heart).

అప్పగింత **appaginta** *n.* 1 handing over, delivery. 2 *pl.* **~lu** ceremony of handing over the bride to the bridegroom at a wedding.

అప్పగింతపెట్టు **appaginta peTTu** *v.t.* 1 to hand over, make over, deliver, consign; **aayana naaku appagintalu peTTEEDu** he handed over all his assets and affairs to me (said of s.o. expecting to die). 2 to repeat back (s.g learnt); **ii padyam cadiwi naaku~** learn this poem by heart and recite it back to me.

అప్పచ్చి **appacci** *n.* 1 any dish made with flour. 2 *in child language* any kind of eatable. 3 *slang* slap; **reNDu appacculu waDDistee allari taggutundi** if you give him two slaps his naughtiness will subside.

అప్పటంగా **appaTangaa** *adv.* unaltered, in its original or existing state, as it is.

అప్పటికప్పుడు **appaTikappuDu** *adv.* immediately, then and there, straight away; **appaTikappuDee** just then, at that very moment.

అప్పటికి **appaTiki** I. *adv.* 1 by that time. 2 *dial.* by evening time. II. *advbl. n. suffixed to vbl. adj.* 1 by the time that; **miiru wacceeT~ neenu akkaDee unnaanu** by the time that you came, I was at that very place. 2 since (= because); **miiru uttaram raaseeT~ aayana ceeyaka tappaleedu** since you wrote him a letter, he had to do it without fail.

అప్పటికీ **appaTikii** I. *adv.* 1 even then, even at that time. 2 even so, nevertheless. 3 **~ ippaTikii miiru maaraleedu** you have not changed between then and now. II. *advbl.n.suffixed to vbl. adj.* although; **atanu aalasyangaa waccin~, raylu dorikindi** although he came late, he caught the train.

అప్పట్లో **appaTLoo** *adv.* at that time, in those days, then (covering a period of time).

అప్పడం, అప్పళం, వప్పడం, పాపడ్

appaDam, appaLam, pappaDam, paapaD *n.* thin wafer of black gram flour, papad.

అప్పడాలకర్ర **appaDaala karra** *n.* rolling pin used in cookery.

అప్పనం **appanam** *n.class.* gift, offering.

అప్పనంగా **appanangaa** *adv.* free, for nothing; **~wastee entayna caaladu** if it is given free, any amount will not be enough.

అప్పలమ్మచీర **appalamma ciira** *n.* white sari made of coarse yarn, with coloured borders.

అప్పసం **appasam** *n.* cut or breach in bank of a channel to let water into a field.

అప్పు **appu** *n.* debt, loan; **~ iccu** to give a loan, lend; **~ ceeyu, ~ tiisukonu** to take a loan, borrow; **~ tiircu** to repay a debt; **o.-ki ~ uNDu** to be indebted to s.o.; **o.-ki ~ peTTu** to advance a loan to s.o.; **~la waaDu** creditor.

అప్పుడప్పుడు **appuDappuDu** *adv.* now and then, sometimes.

అప్పుడప్పుడే **appuDappuDee** *adv.* only just then; **~ maamiDipaLLu bajaarlooki wastunnaayi** mangoes were only just then coming into the market.

అప్పుడు **appuDu** *advbl.n.* 1 then, that time. 2 *suffixed to vbl. adj.* when; **aayana wacceeT~ iTu pilawaNDi** when he comes, please call him here.

అప్పుడెప్పుడో **appuDeppuDoo** *adv.* a long time ago.

అప్పుడే **appuDee** *adv.* 1 just then. 2 straight away, promptly.

అప్పోసప్పో **appoosappoo** *n.* debts and the like; **~ ceesi biDDalaku pedda caduwulu ceppincinaaDu** he gave his children a good education by incurring debts and so on.

అప్యర్థం **apyartham** *n. gram.* concessive form (of a verb).

అప్రచలనం **apracalanam** *n.* obsolescence.

అప్రచలిత **apracalita** *adj.* obsolete.

అప్రతిమ **apratima** *adj.* unrivalled; **~ paraakramaśaali** an unrivalled warrior.

అప్రతిమాన **apratimaana** *adj.* unrivalled.

అప్రతిష్ఠ **apratiSTa** *n.* 1 bad reputation, ill fame. 2 disgrace, dishonour.

అప్రతిహత **apratihata** *adj.* 1 irresistible. 2 unobstructed, unconstrained.

అప్రత్యక్ష **apratyakSa** *adj.* indirect.

అప్రదక్షిణంగా **apradakSiNangaa** *adv.* anticlockwise.

అప్రధాన **apradhaana** *adj.* 1 of minor importance, secondary; **~ paatra** minor part(in a play). 2 *gram.* subordinate.

అప్రభావిత **aprabhaawita** *adj.* unaffected.

అప్రమత్త **apramatta** *adj.* alert, vigilant.

అప్రమత్తత **apramattata** *n.* alertness, vigilance.

అప్రమాణ **apramaaNa** *adj.* non-standard, substandard.

అప్రమేయ **aprameeya** *adj.* immeasurable, inconceivable.

అప్రయత్న **aprayatna** *adj.* involuntary, spontaneous, unintentional.

అప్రయత్నంగా **aprayatnangaa** *adv.* involuntarily, spontaneously, unintentionally.

అప్రయోజక **aprayoojaka** *adj.* useless, unserviceable, ineffective, ineffectual, inefficient.

అప్రయోజకత్వం **aprayoojakatwam** *n.* uselessness, unserviceableness, incapacity.

అప్రయోజకుడు **aprayoojakuDu** *n.* useless or good-for-nothing person.

అప్రవేశ్య **apraweeśya** *adj.* impermeable, impervious.

అప్రశస్త **apraśasta** *adj.* bad, worthless.

అప్రసన్న **aprasanna** *adj.* dejected.

అప్రసన్నత **aprasannata** *n.* dejection, displeasure.

అప్రసిద్ధ **aprasiddha** *adj.* not known to the world, obscure, insignificant.

అప్రస్తుత **aprastuta** *adj.* irrelevant, out of place, inopportune.

అప్రాచ్యపు **apraacyapu** *adj.* low, mean, worthless.

అప్రియ **apriya** *adj.* 1 unpleasant, disagreeable, disliked, distasteful. 2 unpalatable, unwelcome, unpopular.

అప్సరస **apsarasa** *n.* 1 damsel. 2 mythological heavenly nymph.

అబందర **abandara** *adj.* disorderly, confused, haphazard.

అబక **abaka** *n.* ladle made of a half coconut shell.

అబద్ధ **abaddha** *adj.* false, untrue.

అబద్ధం **abaddham** *n.* lie, falsehood.

అబద్ధం ఆడు **abaddham aaDu** *v.i.* to tell a lie.

అబద్ధీకుడు **abaddhiikuDu** *n.* liar, unprincipled person.

అబల **abala** *n.* 1 weak person. 2 woman.

అబాసు **abaasu** *same as* **abhaasu.**

అబోధవేళ **aboodhaweeLa** I.*n.class.* dead of night, midnight. II. *adv.* at the wrong time, esp. with reference to asking for alms at an inappropriate time of day.

అబోరు **abooru** *adj.* 1 empty. 2 (of a house) uninhabited, untenanted.

అబ్దం, అబ్ధి **abdam, abdi** *n. class.* year; *mod. only in compounds*, e.g., **śataabdi** centenary.

అబ్ధి **abdhi** *n. class.* sea.

అబ్బ **abba**[1] *n.* 1 father. 2 *dial.* gentleman.

అబ్బ, అబ్బా **abba**[2], **abbaa** *mode of address by one woman or girl to another.*

అబ్బబ్బా **abbabbaa!** *interj. expressing distress or displeasure.*

అబ్బరం, అబ్బురం **abbaram**[1], **abburam** *n.* surprise, astonishment.

అబ్బరం **abbaram**[2] *n.* 1 affection, fondness. 2 excessive fondness, overindulgence, pampering, spoiling; **cinnappuDu ~ gaa periginaa peddayyEEka aa buddhulu raaleedu** although he was pampered as a child he did not show that mentality when he grew up; **abbaraalu pootunnaadu** he is getting spoilt.

అబ్బా! **abbaa!** *interj. expressing surprise, pain or displeasure.*

అబ్బాయి **abbaayi** *n.* 1 boy; **maa/mii ~** our/your son. 2 *dial.* man (of any age).

అబ్బి! **abbi!** *informal mode of address to a man* hey!

అబ్బించు **abbincu** *v.t.* to cause (a quality) to be acquired; **manaki sahanam abbistundi** it accustoms us to patience.

అబ్బు **abbu** *v.i.* to be gained, obtained, acquired or imbibed, to accrue; **ataniki caduwu abba leedu** he did not acquire education; **daanni cuuDagala mahadbhaagyam manaku abbindi** the good fortune of being able to behold it has accrued to us.

అబ్బురపడు **abburapaDu** *v.i.* to be surprised, startled or astonished.

అబ్బురపాటు **abburapaaTu** *n.* astonishment.

అబ్బే! **abbee!** *interj. expressing negation* ~ ! **neenu weLLa leedu** no! I did not go.

అబ్బో **abboo!** *interj. used as widely as* oh! *in English.*

అభంగుర **abhangura** *adj.* eternal, imperishable.

అభయం **abhayam** *n.* feeling of security, freedom from fear.

అభం **abham** *n.* 1 s.g inauspicious. 2 wrong, evil; ~ **śubham teliyani pasiwaaDu** a child who cannot tell good from evil, an innocent child.

అభయహస్తం **abhayahastam** *n.* holding up the hand with the palm open, to indicate 'have no fear!' (a posture in dancing).

అభాండం **abhaaNDam** *n.* unjust accusation, slander.

అభాగిని **abhaagini** *n.* unfortunate woman.

అభాగ్యం **abhaagyam** *n.* misfortune.

అభాగ్యుడు **abhaagyuDu** *n.* unfortunate person.

అభాజ్య **abhaajya** *adj.* indivisible; ~ **sankhya** *maths.* prime number.

అభావ **abhaawa** *adj.* 1 non-existent. 2 blank, void; ~ **dṛSTulu** blank or inexpressive looks.

అభావం **abhaawam** *n.* 1 non-existence, absence, lack, want; **sthal ~ walla iwEELa wyaasam puurtigaa weeyaDam leedu** for want of space the article is not being printed in full today. 2 privation.

అభాసు, అబాసు **abhaasu, abaasu** *n.* disaster, fiasco, calamity.

అభి **abhi** *Sanskrit prefix, etymologically related to Greek epi-,* (i) *meaning* on, above, onto, e.g., ~ **keendra** centripetal (ii) *used as an intensifier*, e.g., ~ **warNincu** to describe with appreciation.

అభికరించు, అభిఘరించు **abhikarincu, abhigharincu** *v.t.* to sprinkle ghee on food before beginning a meal.

అభికారం, అభిఘారం **abhikaaram, abhighaaram** *n.* ceremonial sprinking of ghee on food before beginning a meal.

అభికేంద్ర **abhikeendra** *adj.* centripetal.

అభిక్రియ **abhikriya** *n. chem.* reaction.

అభిగృహీత **abhigṛhiita** *adj.* putative.

అభిఘాతం **abhighaatam** *n.* 1 collision. 2 impact.

అభిచర్య **abhicarya** *n. sci.* treatment.

అభిజాత్యం **abhijaatyam** *n.* pride, selfesteem.

అభిజ్ఞ **abhijña** *adj.* 1 intelligent, learned, scholarly. 2 *journ.* well informed; ~ **wargaalu** reliable sources (of information).

అభిజ్ఞత, అభిజ్ఞానం **abhijñata, abhijñaanam** n. 1 intelligence, skill. 2 mark, sign.

అభిజ్ఞుడు **abhijñuDu** *n.* 1 learned person, scholar, genius. 2 experienced or well informed person.

అభినందన **abhinandana** *n.* 1 felicitation. 2 *pl.* ~ **lu** felicitations, congratulations.

అభినందించు **abhinandincu** I.*v.i.* to rejoice, be delighted. II.*v.t.* 1 to congratulate, felicitate. 2 to applaud, appreciate, show appreciation for. 3 to greet, pay respects to.

అభినతి **abhinati** *n. maths.* bias.

అభినయం **abhinayam** *n.* gestures or poses practised in dancing or acting to express emotions.

అభినయించు **abhinayincu** *v.i. and t.* 1 to express emotions by gestures, gesticulate. 2 to act a part in a play. 3 to pretend, feign.

అభినవ **abhinawa** *adj.* modern, present day; ~ **aandhra bhoojuDu** a modern Andhra Bhoja (to call s.o. this is to equate him with the emperor Krishnadevaraya of Vijayanagar who like king Bhoja in ancient times was a patron of literature).

అభిని **abhini** *n.* opium.

అభినివేశం **abhiniweeśam** *n.* 1 zeal, enthusiasm. 2 commitment, dedication; **mataabhiniweeśam** religious fervour. 3 determination, insistence.

అభిన్నం **abhinnam** *adj.* 1 unbroken, undivided. 2 unchanged, identical.

అభిన్నత **abhinnata** *n.* 1 unbrokenness. 2 sameness, identicalness, identity.

అభిన్నాంకం **abhinnaankam** *n. maths.* integer.

అభిప్రాయం **abhipraayam** *n.* 1 opinion, estimation. 2 intention.

అభిప్రాయబేధం **abhipraayabheedam** *n.* 1 difference of opinion. 2 dissent, dissension.

అభిప్రాయసామ్యం **abhipraayasaamyam** *n.* consensus.

అభిమంత్రణ **abhimantraNa** *n.* consecration by reciting the prescribed mantras.

అభిమంత్రించు **abhimantrincu** *v.t.* to consecrate by reciting mantras.

అభిమతం **abhimatam** *n.* 1 wishes, desires, will; **prajaabhimatam** will of the people. 2 trend of (o.'s) opinion, impressions; **eeweewoo saahitya wiSayaalagurinci naa ~ koorinaaru** they requested my impressions about some literary matters.

అభిమాన[పాత్రమైన] **abhimaana[paatramayna]** *adj.* beloved, cared for, favourite; ~ **naTuDu** favourite actor.

అభిమానం **abhimaanam** *n.* 1 love, devotion, affection. 2 regard, liking, care. 3 favour, patronage; **kulaabhimaanam** showing favouritism towards o.'s community. 4 pride (in a good sense), self-respect, self-esteem. 5 pride (in a bad sense), arrogance.

అభిమాని **abhimaani** *n.* 1 one who loves or cares, one who has affection or regard. 2 admirer.

అభిమానించు **abhimaanincu** *v.t.* 1 to love, have affection for. 2 to honour, favour. 3 to protect, patronise.

అభిముఖం **abhimukham** *adj.* facing, fronting; **daTTincina tupaakii puccukoni wacci ataniki ~ gaa oka yoodhuDu nuncunnaaDu** a warrior was standing facing him holding a loaded gun.

అభియోగం **abhiyoogam** *n. legal* criminal case, complaint, charge, accusation.

అభిరంజనం **abhiranjanam** *n. biol.* staining.

అభిరామ **abhiraama** *adj.* pleasing, sweet.

అభిరుచి **abhiruci** *n.* 1 taste, relish. 2 inclination, desire. 3 preference.

అభిలక్షణం **abhilakSaNam** *n. sci.* characteristic.

అభిలషణీయ **abhilaSaNiiya** *adj.* 1 desirable. 2 prudent; **ii wyuuhaaniki niiru, bhuumi, paśusampadala ~ upayoogam aayuwupaTTu** for this strategy the prudent use of water, land and cattle wealth is vital.

అభిలషణీయంగా **abhilaSaNiiyangaa** *adv.* prudently.

అభిలషించు **abhilaSincu** *v.t.* 1 to desire, wish for. 2 to aspire after.

అభిలాష **abhilaaSa** *n.* 1 desire, wish, aspiration, inclination. 2 love, attachment, appreciation; **sangiitamloo ~** love of music.

అభిలాషగల **abhilaaSagala** *adj.* desirous.

అభిలాషి **abhilaaSi** *n.* person who wishes, desires or loves.

అభివందనం **abhiwandanam** *n.* greeting, salutation; **abhiwandana pratyabhiwandanaalu** exchange of greetings.

అభివర్ణించు **abhiwarNincu** *v.t.* to describe with warmth or praise or appreciation.

అభివాదం **abhiwaadam** *n.* reverential salutation.

అభివాదన **abhiwaadana** *n.* greeting, salutation; ~ **pratyabhiwaadanalu** exchange of greetings.

అభివృద్ధి **abhiwṛddhi** *n.* 1 increase, growth, expansion. 2 progress, improvement, development.

అభివృద్ధికర **abhiwṛddhikara** *adj.* developmental.

అభివృద్ధిచెందు **abhiwṛddhicendu** *v.i.* 1 to be developed or improved. 2 to flourish.

అభివృద్ధిచేయు, అభివృద్ధిపరచు **abhiwṛddhiceeyu, abhiwṛddhiparacu** *v.t.* to develop, improve.

అభివృద్ధినిరోధక **abhiwṛddhiniroodhaka** *adj.* reactionary.

అభివ్యంజక **abhiwyanjaka** *last part of an adjvl. compound* expressive of.

అభివ్యక్త **abhiwyakta** *adj.* revealed, expressed, declared.

అభివ్యక్తం చేయు **abhiwyaktam ceeyu** *v.t.* to reveal, express.

అభివ్యక్తి **abhiwyakti** *n.* revealing, making clear, expression, expressiveness; **ii maaTalaloo intaTi ~ undi** there is such great expressiveness in these words.

అభిశంసన **abhiśamsana** *n.* censure.

అభిశంసించు **abhiśamsincu** *v.t.* to censure, condemn.

అభిశాపం **abhiśaapam** *n.* curse.

అభిషిక్తుడు **abhiSiktuDu** *n.* person who is anointed or installed by being anointed.

అభిషేకం **abhiSeekam** *n.* 1 worship of God Siva. 2 anointing as part of a religious ceremony. 3 installation by anointing, coronation (of a king).
అభిషేకించు **abhiSeekincu** *v.t.* to bathe, anoint.
అభిసరణం **abhisaraNam** *n.* 1 *chem.* osmosis. 2 *phys.* convergence.
అభిసారి **abhisaari** *adj.* convergent.
అభిసారిక **abhisaarika** *n.* woman who goes to meet her lover at an appointed place.
అభీప్స, అభీప్సితం **abhiipsa, abhiipsitam** *n.* desire, wish.
అభీష్టం **abhiiSTam** *n.* desire, inclination.
అభూత **abhuuta** *adj.* 1 non-existent. 2 hitherto not known or experienced. 3 ~ **kalpanalu** (i) unprecedented happenings; (ii) trumped up charge.
అభేదం **abheedam** *n.* 1 similarity. 2 identity.
అభేద్య **abheedya** *adj.* 1 not to be divided, broken or pierced. 2 impenetrable, (of a fort) impregnable.
అభోజనం **abhoojanam** *n.* abstaining from food.
అభ్యంగనం, అభ్యంజనం **abhyanganam, abhyanjanam** *n.* oil bath.
అభ్యంతరం **abhyantaram** *n.* 1 objection. 2 obstacle, hindrance, impediment. 3 gap, interval.
అభ్యంతరమందిరం **abhyantara mandiram** *n.* private apartments in a palace.
అభ్యర్థన[ం] **abhyarthana[m]** *n.* request.
అభ్యర్థనపత్రం **abhyarthana patram** *n.* 1 application form. 2 memorandum of requests.
అభ్యర్థి **abhyarthi** *n.* 1 candidate. 2 applicant.
అభ్యర్థించు **abhyarthincu** *v.t.* to request, ask, solicit, desire, beg, pray.
అభ్యర్థిత్వం **abhyarthitwam** *n.* candidacy, candidature.
అభ్యసన **abhyasana** *n.* 1 practice. 2 study.
అభ్యసించు *v.i. and t.* 1 to practise, exercise. 2 to learn, study.
అభ్యాగతి **abhyaagati** *n.* uninvited casual visitor.
అభ్యాసం **abhyaasam** *n.* 1 practice, exercise; **mawkhika** ~ oral practice (of lessons). 2 study.
అభ్యుత్థానం **abhyutthaanam** *n.* rising from o.'s seat as a mark of respect, rising to greet a person.
అభ్యుదయ **abhyudaya** *adj.* progressive.
అభ్యుదయ[ం] **abhyudaya[m]** *n.* 1 welfare, prosperity. 2 development, progress, uplift.
అభ్యున్నతి **abhyunnati** *n.* 1 development, progress, uplift, advancement. 2 prosperity.
అభ్రకం **abhrakam** *n.* mica.
అమంగళ **amangaLa** *adj.* inauspicious, unlucky.
అమందానందం **amandaanandam** *n.* extreme happiness.
అమర **amara** *adj.* 1 eternal, immortal, heavenly; ~ **jiiwi awu** *is a poetic phrase meaning* to die (*lit.* to become an immortal). 2 ~ **bhaaSa** the Sanskrit language.
అమరం **amaram** *n.* 1 name of the most famous Sanskrit dictionary, also called **amarakoośam**, written by Amarasimha. 2 *obs.* grant of land on feudal tenure.
అమరకం **amarakam** *n.* 1 lease of land. 2 *class.* grant of land on feudal tenure.
అమరత్వం **amaratwam** *n.* immortality.
అమరవాణి *n.* the Sanskrit language.
అమరించు **amarincu** *same as* **amarcu.**
అమరిక **amarika** *n.* 1 fitness, suitability, appropriateness, correspondence, compatibility. 2 arrangement.
అమరికగా **amarikagaa** *adv.* suitably, fittingly.
అమరు **amaru** *v.i.* 1 to fit into, onto or round; **aa peTTeloo aa pustakaalu amaraleedu** the books do not fit into the box; **gadiloonci cuustee aa gummam ataniki paTam kaTTinaTTugaa amarindi** seen from inside the room, the doorway fitted round him as if it was a picture frame. 2 to suit, be suitable, fitting or appropriate; **aa weTakaarapu nawwu aayanaki caalaa sahajangaa baagaa amaripooyindi** the scornful smile suited him very naturally. 3 to be arranged, provided or made available; **waccee eedaadi aakharikaynaa daanangaa amarina bhuumi pampiNii puurti kaagaladu** the distribution of land made available by gift can be completed at least by the end of next year; **Dabbutoo amarani panulu caalaa unnaayi** there are many things that cannot be arranged (*or* provided) by money; **waaDiki annii amari unnaayi** he has all that he requires *or* he wants for nothing.
అమరుడు **amaruDu** *n.* 1 immortal. 2 speaker of a divine language, i.e., Sanskrit.
అమర్చు, అమరించు **amarcu, amarincu** *v.t.* 1 to provide, supply, furnish, instal. 2 to arrange, set out; **tellaTi baTTanu parici bommalanniTinii andangaa amarustaaru** they spread a white cloth and set out all the dolls beautifully; **amśaalanu wibhajanagaa amarci peTTincEEru** they arranged the items in sections.
అమర్త్యుడు **amartyuDu** *n. class.* immortal.
అమర్యాద **amaryaada** *n.* dishonour, disrespect, impoliteness, impertinence.
అమర్యాదగా **amaryaadagaa** *adv.* disrespectfully, impolitely, impertinently.
అమలు **amalu** *n.* implementation, enforcement, execution, putting into force or practice; ~ **looki waccu** to come into force; ~ **loo unna wyawastha** the established order; ~ **loo leeni** not in force, not current, defunct, expired.
అమలుచేయు, అమలుజరుపు, అమలుపరచు **amaluceeyu, amalujarupu, amaluparacu** *v.t.* to implement, bring into effect, bring into force, enforce, carry out, execute.
అమలుదారు **amaludaaru** *n.* revenue official of the rank of a tahsildar.
అమహత్తు **amahattu** *n. gram.* non-masculine gender.
అమాంఖానా **amaamkhaanaa** *n. dial.* bathroom.
అమాంతంగా **amaantangaa** *adv.* 1 all at once, suddenly, all of a sudden. 2 wholly, totally.
అమాందస్తా **amaandastaa** *n.* small mortar used for pounding and grinding ayurvedic medicines, spices, areca nut, etc.

అమాంబాపతు **amaambaapatu** *adv.* including sundry amounts, all told.

అమాత్యుడు **amaatyuDu** *n.* minister.

అమానుష **amaanuSa** *adj.* inhuman, dreadful.

అమానుషత్వం **amaanuSatwam** *n.* inhumanity.

అమాయక, అమాయిక **amaayaka, amaayika** *adj.* innocent.

అమాయకంగా **amaayakangaa** *adv.* innocently.

అమాయకత్వం **amaayakatwam** *n.* innocence.

అమాయకుడు **amaayakuDu** *n.* innocent person, simpleton.

అమావాస్య **amaawaasya** *n.* last day of **kr̥SNa pakSa** when there is no moon in the sky.

అమిత **amita** *adj.* 1 boundless, limitless, unlimited. 2 immense, enormous.

అమిరె **amire** *n.* kind of eye disease.

అమీతుమీ **amiitumii** *adv.* this way or that; **nuwwu ~ teelcukoowaali** you must decide one way or the other.

అమీనా **amiinaa** *n.* executive officer of a civil court.

అమీర్ **amiir** *n.* 1 Muslim nobleman. 2 wealthy person.

అముద్రిత **amudrita** *adj.* 1 unprinted. 2 unpublished.

అమూర్త **amuurta** *adj.* abstract.

అమూల్య **amuulya** *adj.* priceless, invaluable, precious.

అమృతం **amr̥tam** *n.* 1 nectar, ambrosia. 2 immortality.

అమృతత్వం **amr̥tatwam** *n.* immortality.

అమృతవల్లి **amr̥tawalli** *n.* a medicinal plant also called **tippatiige.**

అమృతపాణి **amr̥tapaaNi** *n.* kind of plantain or banana.

అమృతహృదయుడు **amr̥tahr̥dayuDu** *n.* kindhearted person.

అమృతాంశువు **amr̥taamśuwu** *n. class.* moon.

అమృతుడు **amr̥tuDu** *n.* loveable person, likeable person.

అమేయ **ameeya** *adj.* immeasurable, immense.

అమోఘ **amoogha** *adj.* 1 efficacious, successful, fruitful. 2 wonderful, splendid.

అమ్మ **amma** I. *n. suffix* 1 *denoting the female sex*, e.g., **pantulamma** school mistress. 2 *added to proper names as a mark of respect*, e.g., **raamamma** Ramamma. II. *n.* 1 mother. 2 woman, lady.

అమ్మకం **ammakam** *n.* sale.

అమ్మకందారు **ammakamdaaru** *n.* seller, vendor.

అమ్మకంపన్ను **ammakam pannu** *n.* sales tax.

అమ్మతల్లి **ammatalli** *n.* 1 goddess who is the patroness of a village. 2 goddess of smallpox.

అమ్మనాలు, అచ్చనగాయలు **ammanaalu, accanagaayalu** *n.pl.* game played by girls with **gaccakaayalu.**

అమ్మన్న, అమ్మణ్ణి **ammanna, ammaNNi** *n.* little girl.

అమ్మమ్మ **ammamma** *n.* grandmother, mother's mother; **~ kaburlu** oldfashioned ideas.

అమ్మయ్య **ammayya**[1] *n.* 1 mother's elder sister. 2 *dial* lady.

అమ్మయ్య ! **ammayya!**[2] *interj. expressive of relief.*

అమ్మరో! **ammaroo!** *interj. expressive of surprise.*

అమ్మలక్కలు **ammalakkalu** *n.pl.* womenfolk.

అమ్మలు **ammalu** *n: pet name for a little girl.*

అమ్మవారు **ammawaaru** *n.* 1 goddess, esp. the goddess of smallpox. 2 consort of either Vishnu or Siva.

అమ్మా **ammaa** 1 *vocative case of* **amma.** 2 *interj. expressive of pain.*

అమ్మాయి **ammaayi** *n.* 1 girl. 2 daughter.

అమ్మి **ammi** I. *n.* 1 little girl. 2 *dial.* daughter. II. *polite form of address to a woman of lower status than the speaker.*

అమ్ము **ammu**[1] *n.* arrow, dart; **~ podi** quiver.

అమ్ము **ammu**[2] *v.t.* to sell.

అమ్ముడు **ammuDu** *n.* selling, sale.

అమ్ముడు అవు, అమ్ముడు పోవు **ammuDu awu, ammuDu poowu** *v.i.* to be sold.

అయత్నకృత **ayatnakr̥ta** *adj.* spontaneous.

అయనం **ayanam** *n.* the sun's passage or duration of such passage from one tropic to another during half a year.

అయనరేఖా మండలం **ayanareekhaa maNDalam** *n. geog.* the tropics, i.e., the tropical zone bounded by the tropics of Cancer and Capricorn.

అయనరేఖలు **ayanareekhalu** *n.pl.* the tropics of Cancer and Capricorn.

అయస్కాంతం **ayaskaantam** *n.* magnet.

అయస్కాంతత్వం *n.* **ayaskaantatwam** magnetism.

అయాచిత **ayaacita** *adj.* unasked, unsolicited.

అయారే!, అయ్యారే! **ayaaree!, ayyaaree!** *interj. expressing surprise or admiration.*

అయిష్ట **ayiSTa** *adj.* not wanted, disliked, disfavoured, disapproved.

అయిష్టంగా **ayiSTangaa** *adv.* unwillingly, reluctantly.

అయిష్టత **ayiSTata** *n.* unwillingness, dislike, distaste.

అయిష్టపడు **ayiSTa paDu** *v.i.* to be unwilling.

అయుక్త **ayukta** *adj.* wrong, unfit, improper.

అయోగ్య **ayoogya** *adj.* 1 unfit, unbecoming. 2 undeserving, unworthy.

అయోగ్యుడు **ayoogyuDu** *n.* undeserving person.

అయోమయ **ayoomaya** *adj.* 1 in a state of complete confusion, mystified, unable to understand, stupefied, looking blank. 2 abstruse, difficult to understand, mystifying, incomprehensible.

అయోమయం **ayoomayam** *n.* state of complete confusion, blankness.

అయోధ్య **ayoodhya** *n.* 1 name of the capital of the Ikshawaku kings. 2 *journ.* strained relations (*opposite of* **sayoodhya**).

అయ్య **ayya** I. *suffix* 1 *attached to man's name as a mark of respect*, e.g., **raamayya** Ramaiah. 2 *indicating the male sex*, e.g., **musalayya** old man. II. *n.* father.

అయ్యంగారు **ayyangaaru** *n.* name of a sect of Vaishnavite brahmans.

అయ్యయ్యో! అయ్యో! **ayyayyoo!, ayyoo!** *interj. expressive of sorrow* alas!

అయ్యవారు **ayyawaaru** *n., with different meanings in different dialects* **1** brahman beggar. **2** temple priest, pujaari. **3** teacher. **4** cook.

అయ్యా! **ayyaa!** *mode of address* sir!

అయ్యారే **ayyaaree** *same as* **ayaaree.**

అర **ara**[1] *n. and adj.* half.

అర **ara**[2] *n.* **1** drawer. **2** compartment. **3** shelf. **4** trough or manger for feeding cattle. **5** *dial.* room.

అరక **araka** *n.* plough complete with bullocks; ~ **kaTTu** to yoke a plough; ~ **wippu** to unyoke a plough.

అరకన్ను **arakannu** *n.* half shut eye.

అరకపూజ **arakapuuja** *n.* worship of a plough and bullocks, performed annually at the start of the ploughing season.

అరకబియ్యం **arakabiyyam** *n.* grain not quite ripe but fit for eating.

అరకు **araku**[1] *n.* hearts (in playing cards).

అరకు, అరుకు, అరుఖు **araku**[2], **aruku, arukhu** *n.* **1** liquid medicine. **2** alcoholic liquor.

అరకొర **arakora** *n.* defect, deficiency.

అరకొర[గా] **arakora[gaa]** *adv.* incompletely, imperfectly.

అరక్షిత **arakSita** *adj.* unprotected.

అరగతీయు **aragatiiyu** *v.t.* to grind, rub, wear away.

అరగాడి, అరగాణి **aragaaDi, aragaaNi** *n.* bed of an irrigation reservoir or tank.

అరగూడు **araguuDu** *n.* niche in a wall.

అరచేయి, అరిచేయి **araceeyi, ariceeyi** *n.* palm of the hand; **araceeta peTTukonu** *lit.* to hold in o.'s palm, *hence* to caress, fondle; **praaNaalu araceetiloo peTTukonu** to fear for o.'s life, be mortally afraid.

అరటి, అరిటి **araTi, ariTi** *n.* plantain, banana.

అరణం **araNam** *n.* gifts to a bride by her parents at her wedding.

అరణ్యం **araNyam** *n.* forest; **araNyaroodanam** cry in the wilderness (which no one will hear).

అరణ్యకుడు **araNyakuDu** *n.* forest dweller.

అరతి **arati** *n. literary* distaste for everything, one of the ten mental states which a lover is liable to experience.

అరత్ని **aratni** *n. med.* ulna.

అరదం **aradam** *n. class.* chariot.

అరదండ **aradaNDa** *n.* **1** wooden doorlatch. **2** handcuffs, fetters.

అరప **arapa** *n.* raised platform in a field for watching crops.

అరపావు **arapaawu** *n.* one eighth.

అరబ్బీ **arabbii** I.*n.* the Arabic language. II. *adj.* Arab, Arabian.

అరబ్బుడు **arabbuDu** *n.* Arab.

అరమర, అరమరిక **aramara, aramarika** *n.* reservation, reticence; ~ **leekuNDaa anni wiSayaaluu ceppindi** she told everything without reservation.

అరమోడ్పు **aramooDpu** *adj.* half-closed.

అరయిక **arayika** *n. class.* examination, search.

అరయు, ఆరయు **arayu, aarayu** *v.t. class.* **1** to search, examine. **2** to see, observe. **3** to know, understand.

అరవ **arawa** *adj.* Tamil.

అరవం **arawam** *n.* the Tamil language.

అరవందం **arawandam** *n.* state of confusion, state of mystification, blankness, inability to understand.

అరవచాకిరీ **arawacaakirii** *n.* drudgery.

అరవరలు **arawaralu** *n.pl.* bits, fragments.

అరవింద[ం] **arawinda[m]** *n.* lotus.

అరవిచ్చిన **arawiccina** *adj.* (of a flower) half-opened, half in bloom.

అరవై **araway** *n.* sixty.

అరస **arasa** *adj.* tasteless.

అరసికత **arasikata** *n.* lack of culture or good taste.

అరసు, అరుసు **arasu, arusu** *n.* king.

అరసుకొను, అరుసుకొను **arasukonu, arusukonu** *v.t.* to learn about; **wiSayam** ~ to investigate or find out about a matter.

అరసున్న **arasunna** *n.* 'half sunna', also called **ardhaanuswaaram,** denoted by the symbol (in Telugu script and standing for nasalisation of the preceding vowel in classical Telugu; it has been lost everywhere in modern standard Telugu but persists even today in certain literary writings.

అరాజకం, అరాచకం **araajakam, araacakam** *n.* **1** anarchy. **2** disorderliness.

అరాజకత్వం **araajakatwam** *n.* anarchy.

అరాజకవాది **araajakawaadi** *n.* anarchist.

అరాతి **araati** *n. class.* enemy, foe.

అరాయించుకొను, హరాయించుకొను **araayincukonu, haraayincukonu** *v.i. and t.* to digest, be digested.

అరారగా **araaragaa** *adv.* **1** at intervals. **2** little by little.

అరి **ari** *n.* enemy, foe.

అరిందముడు **arindamuDu** *n. class.* one who has conquered his foes.

అరిక **arika** *same as* **aarika.**

అరికట్టు **arikaTTu** *v.t.* to check, stop, prevent, obstruct.

అరికాలు **arikaalu** *n.* sole of the foot.

అరిగించుకొను **arigincukonu** *v.t.* to digest.

అరిచేయి **ariceeyi** *same as* **araceeyi.**

అరిటాకు **ariTaaku** *n.* plantain leaf.

అరిటి **ariTi** *same as* **araTi.**

అరిపాదం **aripaadam** *n.* sole of the foot.

అరివాణం, హరివాణం **ariwaaNam, hariwaaNam** *n.* bowl or tray used for collecting water which has been used during religious worship.

అరిషడ్వర్గాలు **ariSaDwargaalu** *n.pl.* the six deadly sins which are a person's enemies: lust, anger, avarice, covetousness, pride and envy.

అరిష్టం **ariSTam** *n.* misfortune, disaster, calamity.

అరిసమాసం **arisamaasam** *n.* hybrid word, compound made up of two words whose roots originate from different languages, e.g., **aalayatalupu** temple door.

అరిసె **arise** *n.* rice cake made for auspicious ceremonies: **aDugulaku ~ lu pancipeDataaru** they distribute rice cakes when a child takes its first steps.

అరుంధతి, ఆరంజోతి **arundhati, aaranjooti** *n.* a star in the constellation of the Pleiades, named after the wife of the sage Vasishta; (at marriage ceremonies **arundhati** is invoked by the bridegroom as a pattern of conjugal excellence and the star in the Pleiades is pointed out to the bride and bridegroom).

అరుకు, అరుఖు **aruku, arukhu** *same as* **araku.**

అరుగు **arugu**[1] *n.* pial, raised platform or terrace serving as a seat in front of a house.

అరుగు **arugu**[2] *v.i.* 1 to be worn away, be worn down, be abraded, be worn out; **arigipooyina ceppulu** worn out shoes. 2 to be digested. 3 to waste away. 4 *class.* to go, proceed.

అరుగుదల **arugudala** *n.* 1 abrasion. 2 digesting, digestion.

అరుచి **aruci** *n.* 1 tastelessness. 2 unpalatableness. 3 aversion, distaste.

అరుచు **arucu** *v.i.* to shout, cry out, bawl.

అరుణ **aruNa** *adj.* red.

అరుణరాగం **aruNa raagam** *n.* blushing, flushing (i) of the human face (ii) of the sky at dawn or sunset.

అరుణిమ **aruNima** *n.* red or pink colour.

అరుణుడు **aruNuDu** *n.* sun.

అరుణోదయం **aruNoodayam** *n.* sunrise.

అరుదు **arudu** *adj.* rare, scarce, uncommon.

అరుదెంచు **arudencu** *v.i. class.* to come, go, proceed.

అరుపు **arupu** *n.* 1 noise, clamour, shouting. 2 animal's cry.

అరులుమరులు **arulumarulu** *n.pl.* 1 dotage, childishness in old age. 2 doting, excessive fondness.

అరువు **aruwu** *n.* loan, credit.

అరువు ఇచ్చు **aruwu iccu** *v.t.* to give on credit, lend.

అరుసు **arusu** *same as* **arasu.**

అరుసుకొను **arusukonu** *same as* **arasukonu.**

అరె!, అరే! **are!, aree!** 1 *form of address to equals, inferiors or young people* hallo! 2 *exclamation of surprise.*

అరెరే! **are ree!** *interj.* is that so?

అర్కం, అర్కుడు **arkam, arkuDu** *n.* sun.

అర్ఘ్యం **arghyam** *n.* taking water in o.'s cupped hands and offering it reverentially to a god accompanied by prayers.

అర్ఘ్యపానాలు **arghyapaanaalu** *n.pl.* water for washing followed by a drink offered to a venerable person on arrival or to a god during worship.

అర్చకుడు **arcakuDu** *n.* temple priest.

అర్చన **arcana** *n.* worship, temple ceremonies.

అర్చించు **arcincu** *v.t.* to worship, adore.

అర్జీ **arjii** *n.* petition, representation, application; ~ **peTTukonu** to present or send a petition.

అర్జీదారు **arjiidaaru** *n.* petitioner, applicant.

అర్జున **arjuna** *adj. class.* white.

అర్జునుడు **arjunuDu** *n.* name of one of the five Pandavas.

అర్ణవం **arNawam** *n.* sea, ocean.

అర్థం **artham** I. *n.* 1 meaning, sense, significance. 2 wealth, money. 3 thing, object. II. *postpositional use* for [the sake of], on account of, intended for, involving; **aayana smrty ~** in memory of him; **aayana gawrawaartham** in his honour; **kaaryaarthamayi wijayawaaDa wacci nannu kalisEEDu** he met me when he came to Vijayawada on business.

అర్థం అవు **artham awu** *v.i.* to be understood; **naaku artham ayindi** I understood.

అర్థంచేసుకొను **artham ceesukonu** *v.t.* to understand.

అర్థక **arthaka** *adjvl. suffix meaning* containing, involving, indicating, e.g. **praśnaarthaka** interrogative; **aaścaryaarthaka** exclamatory.

అర్థగౌరవం **arthagawrawam** *n.* credibility.

అర్థచ్ఛాయ **arthacchaaya** *n.* shade of meaning, nuance.

అర్థమైన **arthamayna** *adj.* understood, significant.

అర్థయుక్త, అర్థవంత **arthayukta, arthawanta** *adj.* with meaning, meaningful.

అర్థయుక్తంగా, అర్థవంతంగా **arthayuktangaa, arthawantangaa** *adv.* meaningfully, in a meaningful way.

అర్థరహిత **artharahita** *adj.* meaningless.

అర్థవ్యక్తీకరణం **arthawyaktiikaraNam** *n.* expression of meaning.

అర్థశాస్త్రం **arthaśaastram** *n.* (science of) economics.

అర్థశాస్త్రజ్ఞుడు, అర్థశాస్త్రవేత్త **arthaśaastrajñuDu, arthaśaastraweetta** *n.* economist.

అర్థసంబంధి **arthasambandhi** *adj. ling.* semantic.

అర్థహీన **arthahiina** *adj.* weak.

అర్థహీనుడు **arthahiinuDu** *n.* poor person, pauper.

అర్థాంతరం **arthaantaram** *n.* another meaning.

అర్థించు **arthincu** *v.i. and t.* 1 to ask for, request. 2 to beg (for alms).

అర్ధ **ardha** *adj.* half, semi-, hemi-.

అర్ధం **ardham** *n.* half.

అర్ధగోళం **ardhagooLam** *n.* hemisphere.

అర్ధచంద్రప్రయోగం **ardhacandra prayoogam** *n.* 1 turning s.o. out by scruff of his neck. 2 curling o.'s lip as a sign of displeasure.

అర్ధచంద్రుడు **ardhacandruDu** *n.* half-moon.

అర్ధనారీశ్వరుడు **ardhanaariiśwaruDu** *n.* God Siva in his manifestation as half male and half female.

అర్ధప్రవేశ్య **ardhapraweeśya** *adj. sci.* semipermeable.

అర్ధరాత్రి **ardharaatri** *n.* midnight.

అర్ధవృత్తం **ardhawṛttam** *n.* semicircle.

అర్ధశేరు **ardhaśeeru** *n.* half a seer.

అర్ధాంగి **ardhaangi** *n.* wife.

అర్ధాంతరంగా **ardhaantarangaa** *adv.* (of s.g done unexpectedly in the middle of a proceeding) abruptly; **sabha jarugutuuNTee ~leeci weLLipooyEEDu** he got up and left abruptly while the meeting was going on.

అర్ధాకలి **ardhaakali** *n.* half satisfied hunger; **~too leecipooyEEDu** he got up with his appetite half satisfied.

అర్ధాధికార **ardhaadhikaara** *adj. admin.* demiofficial.

అర్ధానుస్వారం **ardhaanuswaaram** *same as* **arasunna.**

అర్ధాన్నం **ardhaannam**[1] *same as* **adhwaanam.**

అర్ధాన్నం **ardhaannam**[2] *n.* half a meal; **ewarinii ~peTTi leepakuuDadu** do not disturb anyone in the middle of his meal.

అర్ధాసనం **ardhaasanam** *n.* half of the throne (offered by a king in olden times to a person as token of highest respect or appreciation).

అర్ధోక్తి **ardhookti** *n.* half finished utterance.

అర్పణం **arpaNam** *n.* offering.

అర్పించు **arpincu** *v.t.* 1 to make a gift of, bestow, contribute. 2 to offer [up] sacrifice.

అర్భకం **arbhakam** adj. weak, thin, lean.

అర్భకుడు **arbhakuDu** *n.* weak person, weakling.

అర్ర **arra** *n. dial.* room.

అర్రాజు, హర్రాజు **arraaju, harraaju** *n.* auction.

అర్రు **arru** *n.* 1 neck of an animal; *used for the human neck only in the phrase* **~lu caacu** to stretch out (their) necks (for), strive (for), crave (for), e.g., **asaadhyaaniki ~lu caacaDam maanawa prawṛttiloo oka bhaagam** to strive for the impossible is a part of man's disposition. 2 sore on a bullock's neck caused by a yoke.

అర్రెం **arrem** *n.* sixth day of the festival of **batukamma**, on which no celebrations take place.

అర్వాచీన **arwaaciina** *adj.* recent, modern.

అర్హ **arha** *adj.* 1 worthy, deserving, deserved, fit[ting]. 2 eligible, qualified, entitled.

అర్హత **arhata** *n.* 1 worthiness, fitness. 2 eligibility, qualification, entitlement.

అర్హతగల **arhatagala** *adj.* eligible, qualified.

అర్హుడు **arhuDu** *n.* 1 worthy or deserving person. 2 eligible or qualified person.

అల **ala** *n.* 1 wave. 2 tide.

అలం **alam** *n.* weeds which spread by creeping; *cf.* **aaku~.**

అలంకరణ[ం] **alankaraNa[m]** *n.* 1 act or way of adorning. 2 ornamentation, adornment.

అలంకరణసామగ్రి **alankaraNasaamagri** *n.* cosmetics.

అలంకరించు **alankarincu** *v.t.* to adorn, decorate, embellish.

అలంకారం **alankaaram** *n.* 1 ornament, adornment, decoration. 2 figure of speech; **alankaaragrantham** book dealing with figures of speech.

అలంకారికంగా **alankaarikangaa** *adv.* figuratively.

అలంగం **alangam** *n.* rampart, bulwark of a fort.

అలంగం తిరుగు **alangam tirugu** *v.i.* to move aimlessly; **nidra paTTaleedu, mancam miida ~tunnaaDu** he is tossing about on his bed unable to sleep; **Dabbu koosam ~tunnaaDu** he is wandering about in search of money

అలంఘ్య, అలంఘనీయ **alangh[anii]ya** *adj.* insurmountable, impassable.

అలక, అలుక **alaka**[1], **aluka** *n.* 1 anger, displeasure; **~wahincu** to show displeasure. 2 son-in-law's complaint or demand; **~paanpu ekkEEDu** he sat on his bed and made demands (it being traditional for a son-in-law to make demands when staying in his father-in-law's house).

అలక; అల్క **alaka**[2], **alka** *adj. dial.* 1 light. 2 easy.

అలకలు **alakalu** *n.pl.* ringlets, curls.

అలక్ష్యం **alakSyam** *n.* disregard.

అలక్ష్యం చేయు **alakSyam ceeyu** *v.t.* to disregard, ignore, slight.

అలగా **alagaa** *adj.* mean, low; **~buddhi** low mental calibre.

అలగాజనం **alagaajanam** *n.* people of low social or economic standing, the poor.

అలజడి **alajaDi** *n.* agitation.

అలదు **aladu** *v.t.* to apply, rub on (oil, scent).

అలనాడు **alanaaDu** *adv.* once upon a time, some time ago.

అలనాడేనాడో **alanaaDeenaaDoo** *adv.* long ago, some time ago.

అలపు, అలుపు **alapu, alupu** *n.* tiredness, fatigue, weariness.

అలభ్య **alabhya** *adj.* unobtained, unobtainable.

అలమటించు **alamaTincu** *v.i.* to suffer, be in distress; **aakalitoo~** to suffer from starvation.

అలమర, అల్మారా **alamara, almaaraa** *n.* almirah, wardrobe.

అలము, అలుము **alamu, alumu** I *v.i.* (of clouds, darkness) to spread, gather. II. *v.t.* to pervade, surround, envelop, cover.

అలయు, అలసిపోవు, అలిసిపోవు **alayu, alasipoowu, alisipoowu** *v.i.* to be tired or weary.

అలరారు **alaraaru** *v.i.* (of the arts) to flourish.

అలరించు **alarincu** *v.t.* to please, gratify.

అలరు **alaru** *v.i.* to be pleased or gratified.

అలవడు **alawaDu** *v.i.* (of habits, skills, accomplishments) to be learnt or acquired; **waaritoo sahawaasam ceesewaariki aa śiSTa bhaaSa alawaDutundi** those who associate with them will acquire that educated way of speaking.

అలవరచు **alawaracu** *v.t.* to habituate, accustom.

అలవరచుకొను **alawaracukonu** *v.t.* to habituate or accustom o.s. to, cultivate; **deeśa prajalu ii śaastriiya drSTinee alawarcukoowaali** the people of our country must accustom themselves to (*or* cultivate) this same scientific outlook.

అలవాటు **alawaaTu** *n.* habit, custom, practice; **ceTLu ekkaDam naaku ~ leedu** I am not in the habit of climbing trees; **aameki ii kotta waataawaraNam ~ kaaleedu** she has not become accustomed to this new atmosphere; **aawiDa maanipincina alawaaTLu maLLii enduku ceesukoNTaaru?** why are you again adopting the practices that she made you give up?

అలవాటుపడు **alawaaTupaDu** *v.i.* to become accustomed; **anniTikii alawaaTu paDipootaaru** you will grow accustomed to everything.

అలవి, అలివి **alawi, aliwi** *n.* possibility, practicability, power, capability.

అలవికాని **alawikaani** *adj.* impossible.

అలవిమాలిన **alawimaalina** *adj.* excessive; **~ koopam** excessive anger; **~ neppi** unbearable pain.

అలవోకగా **alawookagaa** *adv.* 1 easily; **yaabhay kiloola baruwunu ~ ettEEDu** he lifted fifty kilos weight with ease. 2 casually; **~ nawwindi** she smiled casually.

అలసంద[లు] **alasanda[lu]** *n., gen. pl.* a minor variety of pulse, *dolichos catjang* (= **bobbarlu**).

అలసట **alasaTa** *n.* tiredness, weariness, exhaustion.

అలసత్వం **alasatwam** *n.* slackness, sluggishness, laziness, sloth.

అలసభావం **alasabhaawam** *n.* disdain; **itarulapaTLa ~** disdain for others.

అలసిపోవు **alasipoowu** *same as* **alayu.**

అలసుడు **alasuDu** *n.* tired, inactive or idle person.

అలా[గా/గు], అట్టా[గా/గు], అట్లా[గా/గు] **alaa[gaa/gu], aTTaa[gaa/gu], aTlaa[gaa/gu]** *adv.* like that, thus, in that way; **alaa cuusEEDu** he looked in that direction; **alaa ceppEEDu** he said like that; **alaa kuurcooNDi** please sit there (polite request).

అలా అని, అలాగని, అలాని **alaa ani, alaagani, alaani** *adv.* having said that, nevertheless; **ii uurantaTikii baakii ~ aayanaki duralawaaTLu eewii leewu sumaNDii** he is in debt to everyone in this village, nevertheless he has no bad habits *or* he is in debt to everyone in the village, but that is not to say that he has any bad habits.

అలా అలా **alaa alaa** *adv.* 1 continually, on and on; **~ aaDukoni aaDukoni akkaDee alasipooyi nidrapooyeedi** she would go on and on playing, grow tired and fall asleep in that same place.

అలాగే **alaagee** *minor sentence, in reply to a request* all right, as you wish.

అలా[ం]టప్పుడు, అట్లా[ం]టప్పుడు **alaa[N]TappuDu, aTLaa[N]TappuDu** *adv.* when that is so, in that case.

అలా[ం]టిది, అట్లా[ం]టిది **alaa[N]Tidi, aTLaa[N]Tidi** I. *adv.* 1 that being so, in that case. 2 in the same way, similarly. II. *pron.* the same as that; **~ naaku kaawaali** I want one like that.

అలాటి **alaaTi** *adj.* that kind of.

అలాములు పలాములు చేయు **alaamulu palaamulu ceeyu** *v.t.* to squander

అలాయిదాగా **alaayidaagaa** *adv.* separately, apart.

అలికి **aliki** *n. dial.* gasping.

అలికిడి **alikiDi** *n.* noise, sound (used of a sound which attracts attention) **aDugula ~ wini iNTLoonunci bayaTaku waccEEnu** on hearing the sound of footsteps I came out of the house; **~ ki meelukonna rawiindra appuDee kaLLu tericEEDu** Ravindra who was awakened by the sound opened his eyes just then.

అలిఖిత **alikhita** *adj.* unwritten.

అలిపిరి **alipiri** I.n. thin or lean person. II.*adj. dial.* poor, mean, scanty.

అలివి **aliwi** *same as* **alawi.**

అలివేణి **aliweeNi** *n. class.* woman.

అలిసిపోవు **alisi poowu** *same as* **alayu.**

అలీన **aliina** *adj.* 1 *polit.* non-aligned. 2 unconcerned. 3 disinterested.

అలీనం **aliinam** *n. polit.* non-alignment.

అలుక **aluka** *same as* **alaka**[1].

అలుకు **aluku** *v.t.* 1 to smear a floor with cowdung. 2 to scatter, sprinkle. 3 to sow seeds broadcast. 4 to transplant seedlings.

అలుగు **alugu**[1] *v.i.* 1 to be angry or annoyed. 2 (esp. of a son-in-law) to grumble, complain (**-payna, against**).

అలుగు **alugu**[2] *n.* 1 surplus weir of an irrigation tank. 2 blunt edge (non-cutting edge) of a sickle blade. 3 flattened tip of a crowbar.

అలుగ్గుడ్డ **alugguDDa** *n.* torn or dirty cloth used for cleaning a house floor.

అలుపు **alupu** *same as* **alapu.**

అలుపుసొలుపు **alupusolupu** *n.* tiredness and so on.

అలుము **alumu** *same as* **alamu.**

అలుసు **alusu** *n.* 1 demeaned or humble status; **~ ceeyu** to degrade or humble (a person). 2 leniency; **~ iccu** to be lenient.

అలైంగిక **alayngika** *n., zool.* asexual.

అలోహం **alooham** *n.* non-metal.

అలౌకిక **alawika** *adj.* 1 spiritual. 2 heavenly. 3 other wordly. 4 supernatural.

అల్క **alka** *same as* **alaka**[2].

అల్ప **alpa** *adj.* little, small, trifling, mean, meagre.

అల్పజ్ఞత **alpajñata** *n.* smallness of intellect.

అల్పజ్ఞుడు **alpajñuDu** *n.* person with little wisdom or understanding.

అల్పత్వం **alpatwam** *n.* pettiness, meanness.

అల్పప్రాణం **alpapraaNam** *n. ling.* unaspirated sound.

అల్పప్రాణి **alpapraaNi** *n.* petty creature.

అల్పబుద్ధి **alpabuddhi** *n.* smallness of intellect.

అల్పసంఖ్యాక **alpasankhyaaka** *adj.* few in number.

అల్పసంఖ్యాకులు **alpasankhyaakulu** *n.pl.* persons in a minority.

అల్పసంతోషి **alpasantooSi** *n.* one who is content with little.

అల్పాచమానం **alpaacamaanam** *n.* urine.

అల్పాయుష్కుడు **alpaayuSkuDu** *n.* short-lived person.

అల్పాహారం **alpaahaaram** *n.* snack, light meal.

అల్పుడు **alpuDu** *n.* worthless person.

అల్మారా **almaaraa** *same as* **alamara.**

అల్లం **allam** *n.* ginger, *zingiber officinale.*

అల్లంత **allanta** *adj.* some (amount): ~**duuram** some distance, a certain distance.

అల్లకం **allakam** *n.* plaiting, weaving.

అల్లకల్లోలం **allakalloolam** *n.* confusion, disorder, disturbance.

అల్లక్కడ **allakkaDa** *adv.* over there.

అల్లటపెట్టు **allaTapeTTu** *v.t.* to annoy, harass.

అల్లదిగో! **alladigoo!** *interj.* look there!

అల్లన **allana** *adv.* gently, softly, slowly: **gaali allan~wiistunnadi** the breeze is blowing softly.

అల్లనేరేడు **allaneereeDu** *n.* kind of black plum, *myrtus communis.*

అల్లప్పుడు **allappuDu** *adv.* some time back, some time ago.

అల్లరి **allari** I. *n.* 1 commotion, noise, confusion. 2 affray, riot. 3 naughtiness. 4 trouble, annoyance. II. *adj.* naughty, mischievous, noisy, troublesome.

అల్లరిచిల్లరి **allaricillari** *adj.* worthless, mischievous; ~**maniSi** mischievous vagabond.

అల్లరిపడు **allaripaDu** *v.i.* to incur trouble, get into trouble.

అల్లరిపెట్టు, అల్లరిచేయు **allaripeTTu, allariceeyu** *v.t.* to trouble, disturb, worry, annoy, tease.

అల్లరిమూక **allarimuuka** *n.* rabble.

అల్లలాడు, అల్లాడు **allalaaDu, allaaDu** *v.i.* 1 to wander about in want or distress. 2 to wave, flap, flutter (in the wind). 3 (of parts of the body) to tremble, quiver, shake.

అల్లా **allaa**[1] *n.* the principal Muslim name for God.

అల్లా **allaa**[2] *suffix meaning* all, every, only; **manaku kanabaDDad~** all that we see; **waaDiki kanabaDDa waaLLatoo ~** with everyone whom he saw; **pagal~** all day long; **aame moguDiki unna loopam ~taaguDu** the only defect in her husband is drunkenness; **waaDiki~Dabbu kaawaali** money is the only thing he wants; *cf.* **kallaa.**

అల్లాటప్పయ్య **allaaTappayya** *n.* name of a stock comic character in a puppet show.

అల్లాటప్పా **allaaTappaa** *adj.* mean, worthless.

అల్లాటప్పాలు **allaaTappaalu** *n.pl.* boasting, bragging.

అల్లాబిల్లి **allaabilli** *n.* game played by children.

అల్లారుముద్దుగా **allaarumuddugaa** *adv.* 1 sweetly, pleasantly. 2 fondly, dearly.

అల్లార్చు **allaarcu** *v.t.* to wave, shake, flap.

అల్లి **alli** *n.* 1 kind of lotus, *nymphaea alba.* 2 wild shrub like broom, *memecylon edule.*

అల్లిక **allika** *n.* 1 embroidery. 2 intertwining, interweaving. 3 knitting.

అల్లికాయలు **allikaayalu** *n.pl.* marbles.

అల్లితెమ్మెర **allitemmera** *n.* cool breeze.

అల్లిబిల్లి **allibilli** *adj.* interwined; ~**kaburlu** gossip.

అల్లు **allu** *v.t.* 1 to weave together. 2 to weave (mat). 3 to embroider. 4 to knit (sweater). 5 **padyaalu ~** to compose verses. 6 **kathalu ~** to invent, make up, compose, concoct or fabricate stories.

అల్లుకొను **allukonu** *v.i.* 1 to intertwine. 2 (of creeping plants and other things) to grow, spread, expand; **poTLa paadu jaaliimiidiki allukoNTunnadi** the gourd is climbing up the trellis. 3 to permeate, penetrate.

అల్లుడు **alluDu** I. *n.* son-in-law. II. *adj.* twining.

అల్లుపెట్టు **allupeTTu** *v.t.* to train (a plant) to climb; **iNTimiidiki allupeTTee tiige mokka** a creeper that is trained to climb over a house.

అల్లె[తాడు] **alle[taaDu]** *n.* bowstring.

అల్లెప్పుడో **alleppuDoo** *adv.* a long time ago.

అల్లే **allee** *adv.* like, as if; **aa wacceewaaDu maa tammuD~unnaaDu** that person who is coming is like my younger brother; **ibbandi tappad ~undi** it appears as if trouble will come without fail.

అళాకు **aLaaku** *n.* measure of volume, one eighth of a **paDi.**

అవ **awa** *Sanskrit prefix signifying* bad, evil, not normal, e.g., **awaguNam** bad quality, **awalakSaNam** bad characteristic.

అవకతవక **awakatawaka** *adj.* absurd, nonsensical, untoward, odd, queer.

అవకతవకగా **awakatawakagaa** *adv.* in a disorderly manner, not properly.

అవకతవకలు **awakatawakalu** *n.pl.* 1 absurdities, incongruities, inconsistencies. 2 irregularities, errors, defects.

అవకరం **awakaram** *n.* 1 *class.* dust, sweepings. 2 *pl.* **awakaraalu** defects, bad traits.

అవకలనం **awakalanam** *n. sci.* differentiation.

అవకాశం **awakaaśam** *n.* 1 opportunity, occasion, chance. 2 interval, space, gap, lacuna.

అవకాశవాదం **awakaaśawaadam** *n.* opportunism.

అవకుంఠనం **awakuNThanam** *n. class.* veil, covering.

అవకృష్టం **awakr̥STam** *adj.* hopeless, degraded.

అవక్రమ **awakrama** *adj. class.* straightforward, honest, upright.

అవక్షేపం **awakSeepam** *n.* 1 residue. 2 *sci.* precipitate.

అవక్షేపకం **awakSeepakam** *n. sci.* precipitant.

అవక్షేపణం **awakSeepaNam** *n. sci.* precipitation.

అవగణనం **awagaNanam** *n.* disregard, disdain.

అవగత **awagata** *adj.* known, understood, perceived.

అవగతంచేసుకొను **awagatam ceesukonu** *v.t.* to understand, perceive.

అవగతి **awagati** *n. class.* knowledge, perception, comprehension.

అవగాహన[ం] **awagaahana[m]** *n.* **1** mastering, learning, comprehension, understanding. **2** view, outlook. **3** *class.* bathing, immersion.

అవగాహన[ం]చేసుకొను **awagaahana[m] ceesukonu** *v.t.* to come to know, get to know, comprehend, understand.

అవగుంఠనం **awaguNThanam** *n.* covering, veiling, hiding.

అవగుణం, అపగుణం **awaguNam, apaguNam** *n.* bad quality (mental or physical), demerit, defect.

అవఘాతం **awaghaatam** *n.* violent blow, mortal blow.

అవచూషక[ం] **awacuuSaka[m]** *adj. chem.* absorbant.

అవచూషణం **awacuuSaNam** *n. chem.* absorption.

అవచ్ఛేదం **awaccheedam** *n. sci.* cross section.

అవజ్ఞ[త] **awajña[ta]** *n.* disrespect, contempt.

అవజ్ఞుడు **awajñuDu** *n.* person who deserves no respect.

అవటు **awaTu** *same as* **awTu.**

అవతంసం, వతంసం **awatamsam, watamsam** *n. class.* flower or ornament worn on the ear.

అవతంసుడు, వతంసుడు **awatamsuDu, watamsuDu** *n.* chief, leader, person of excellence; **naTanaawatamsuDu** prince of actors.

అవతరణ **awataraNa** *n.* coming into existence.

అవతరించు **awatarincu** *v.i.* **1** to be born, appear, put on a form, become incarnate, come into being. **2** to emerge, be formed or constituted; **sudiirgha wideeśii paripaalana tarwaata mana deeśam swatantra deeśangaa awatarincindi** after prolonged foreign rule our country emerged as an independent state.

అవతల **awatala** I. *adj., same as* **awatali.** II.*adv.* **1** further, beyond, on the other side. **2** afterwards, next, besides, in addition; **twaragaa ceppu, ~ naaku caalaa panulu unnaayi** tell me quickly, I have many other things to attend to; **"naaku weeree pani undi. inkewarinannaa pilawaNDi" "miikanna nipuNulu leeru. ~ oka maanawa praaNam DaakTar!"** "I have some other work, call anyone else." "there are no greater experts than you, and besides it is (for the sake of) a human life, doctor!" **3** **~ oka waypu waana kurustuu uNTee miiru eTLaa weDataaru?** if it is raining how will you go? *here* **~ oka waypu** *is used idiomatically to express one alternative, while the other alternative is left unexpressed.* III. *p.p.* beyond, after; **weesawi śalawala ~ waaNNi hayskuulloo praweeśapeTTaDaaniki oppukunnaaDu** he agreed to admit him to the high school after the summer vacation.

అవతలి, అవతల **awatali, awatala** *adj.* **1** next, following. **2** other; **~ waari jiitam telistee kSeemangaa uNTaamu** if we know the salaries of other people we will feel at ease (when talking to them).

అవతలికి, ఆవలకి **awataliki, aawalaki** *adv.* further off, away; **miiraantaa ~ poNDi!** get out all of you! **ataNNi ~ pilici aDigEEDu** he called him aside and asked.

అవతారం **awataaram** *n.* **1** incarnation, metamorphosis. **2** guise, appearance, dress.

అవతారం ఎత్తు **awataaram ettu** *v.i.* **1** to become incarnate, be born. **2** *colloq.* to appear, come on the scene.

అవతారం చాలించు **awataaram caalincu** *v.i.* to die, end o.'s days.

అవతారపురుషుడు **awataara puruSuDu** *n.* godlike person, god in human form.

అవతారిక **awataarika** *n.* **1** preface (to a book) **2** *pl.* **~ lu** customary attributes (dress, make up, etc.) associated with stock characters in a drama.

అవధరించు **awadharincu** *v.t.* to spare attention to, listen to

అవధానం **awadhaanam** *n.* **1** attention, care, regard, intentness, devotion. **2** the skill of remembering many different matters or replying to many different questions at the same time.

అవధాని **awadhaani** *n.* **1** person who has acquired the skill of performing **awadhaanam. 2** title attached to certain brahman names. **3** Hindu astrologer.

అవధారు! **awadhaaru!** *interj. called out before worship starts in a temple* attention!

అవధి **awadhi** *n.* **1** boundary, limit. **2** period of time.

అవధూత **awadhuuta** *n.* ascetic who has renounced all connection with the world.

అవధ్య **awadhya** *adj. class.* not to be killed, not meriting death.

అవనతం **awanatam** *adj.* bowed, bent, lowered; **pataakam ~ ceeyu** to lower a flag to halfmast.

అవనతి **awanati** *n.* **1** decline, degradation. **2** downfall.

అవనిచ్చు **awaniccu** *same as* **kaaniccu.**

అవనీనాథుడు, అవనీపతి, అవనీపాలుడు, అవనీశుడు **awaniinaathuDu, awaniipati, awaniipaaluDu, awaniiśuDu** *n. class.* king, ruler.

అవనీమండలం **awanii maNDalam** *n.* the globe, the earth.

అవనీరుహం **awaniiruham** *n. class.* tree.

అవనీసురుడు **awaniisuruDu** *n. class.* brahman.

అవపథ్యం, ఔపథ్యం **awapathyam, awpathyam** *n.* violation of prescribed diet.

అవపాతం **awapaatam** *n.* **1** *sci.* dip. **2** *met.* precipitation.

అవభృథస్నానం **awabhṛdha snaanam** *n.* ceremonial bathing in river or sea on completing a sacrifice or other religious duty.

అవమర్యాద **awamaryaada** *n.* impoliteness, disrespect, dishonour.

అవమానం, అపమానం **awamaanam, apamaanam** *n.* **1** shame, disgrace, ignominy, humiliation. **2** dishonour, disrespect, insult, affront.

అవమానం చేయు **awamaanam ceeyu** *v.t.* to insult, affront, humiliate.

అవమానకర **awamaanakara** *adj.* insulting, humiliating, ignominious.

అవమానపరచు, అవమానించు **awamaanaparacu, awamaanincu** *v.t.* **1** to shame, disgrace, humiliate. **2** to insult, affront, dishonour.

అవమూల్యం **awamuulyam** *n. econ.* devaluation.

అవయవం **awayawam** *n.* **1** limb, member. **2** component part. **3** organ (of the body).

అవయోగం **awayoogam** *n. astrol.* inauspicious conjunction of influences.

అవరం **awaram** *n.* 1 hind part, rear. 2 aft part of a boat or ship.

అవరోధం **awaroodham** *n.* 1 obstruction, obstacle, hindrance, impediment, restraint. 2 barrier, barricade.

అవరోధకం **awaroodhakam** *n.* barrier.

అవరోధించు **awaroodhincu** *v.t.* to obstruct, hamper, hinder, restrain.

అవరోహణం **awaroohaNam** *n.* descent; **swaraalu awroohaNa kramamloo aalaapincu** to play musical notes in descending order.

అవరోహి **awaroohi** *adj.* descending, falling.

అవల **awala** *same as* **aawala.**

అవలంబం **awalambam** *n.* support, protection.

అవలంబకుడు **awalambakuDu** *n.* adherent.

అవలంబనం **awalambanam** *n.* embracing, adoption, profession (of opinions, beliefs). 2 *phys.* suspension.

అవలంబించు **awalambincu** *v.t.* 1 to embrace, adopt, profess, adhere to (opinions, beliefs). 2 to practise, follow (methods, skills).

అవలక్షణం **awalakSaNam** *n.* bad feature, trait or characteristic (mental or physical), deformity.

అవలి **awali** *same as* **aawali.**

అవలీలం **awaliilam** *n.* s.g that is done effortlessly.

అవలీలగా **awaliilagaa** *adv.* easily, effortlessly, deftly, dexterously.

అవలేపం **awaleepam** *n. class.* 1 smearing, anointing. 2 pride.

అవలేపనం **awaleepanam** *n.* smearing, anointing.

అవలోకనం **awalookanam** *n.* 1 looking. 2 survey, study.

అవలోకనం చేయు **awalookanam ceeyu** *v.t.* to look into, have a careful view of, study.

అవలోకించు **awalookincu** *v.t.* to look at, behold, review.

అవశిష్ట **awaśiSTa** *adj.* remaining, left over, residual; **salyaawaśiSTamayna roogi** a patient reduced to skin and bone.

అవశేషం **awaśeeSam** *n.* 1 remainder, residue. 2 *pl.* **awaśeeSaalu** remains, vestiges, traces, aftermath (of floods, war).

అవశేషక **awaśeeSaka** *adj. sci.* vestigial.

అవశ్య **awaśya** *adj.* necessary, indispensible.

అవశ్యం **awaśyam** *adv.* certainly, necessarily, of necessity; **taariikuluu dastaaweejuluu leeni ii samiikSa ~ asamagram** this review without dates or documents is necessarily not comprehensive.

అవశ్యంగా **awaśyangaa** *adv.* necessarily, positively.

అవశ్యక **awaśyaka** *adj.* necessary, essential; ~ **wastuwulu** essential goods.

అవశ్యకం **awaśyakam** *n.* need, necessity; **jiiwitaawaśyakaalu** necessities for life.

అవశ్యకత **awaśyakata** *n.* need, necessity; ~ **eem waccindi?** what is the need?

అవశ్యాయాంకం **awaśyaayaankam** *n. phys.* dew point.

అవసర **awasara** *adj.* 1 necessary. 2 urgent.

అవసరం **awasaram** *n.* 1 need, requirement, necessity; **aameki naatoo ~ undi** she has need of me. 2 haste, hurry, urgency. 3 occasion, opportunity.

అవసరనైవేద్యం **awasara nayweedyam** *n.* **nayweedyam** presented to a deity for the time being, before the main **nayweedyam** offering.

అవసరపడు **awasarapaDu** *v.i.* to hasten, hurry.

అవసరపెట్టు **awasarapeTTu** *v.t.* to hasten, hurry, expedite.

అవసానం **awasaanam** *n.* end, conclusion, termination; **awasaana kaalam** hour of death.

అవస్థ **awastha** *n.* 1 troublesome situation, difficulty, struggle. 3 *as last part of a n. compound* state, condition, situation, e.g., **baalyaawastha** childhood.

అవస్థపడు **awasthapaDu** *v.i.* to struggle, suffer difficulties.

అవస్థపెట్టు **awasthapeTTu** *v.* to cause trouble or difficulties (to s.o.).

అవస్థాపనసౌకర్యాలు **awasthaapana sawkaryaalu** *n. econ.* infrastructure.

అవస్థితి **awasthiti** *n. sci.* duration.

అవహేళన **awaheeLana** *n.* 1 mockery, ridicule. 2 disregard, contempt.

అవహేళన చేయు **awaheeLana ceeyu** *v.t.* to mock, ridicule.

అవాంఛనీయ **awaanchaniiya** *adj.* undesirable.

అవాంఛిత **awaanchita** *adj.* unwanted, undesired.

అవాంతరం **awaantaram** *n.* misfortune, mishap, unforeseen difficulty, setback.

అవాకులూ చెవాకులూ **awaakuluucewaakuluu** *n.pl.* ~ **waagu** to talk inconsequentially, talk irrelevantly, talk incoherently.

అవాచ్య **awaacya** *adj.* unspeakable, unutterable, taboo.

అవాచ్యం **awaacyam** *n.* s.g unspeakable.

అవాస్తవ **awaastawa** *adj.* unreal, unnatural, abnormal.

అవాస్తవిక **awaastawika** *adj.* unreal, not true to reality.

అవిఘ్న **awighna** *adj.* unobstructed, unhindered; **awighnam astu**! let it not be impeded! (*form of words used to invoke the blessing of providence on an auspicious occasion*).

అవిచ్ఛిన్న **awicchinna** *adj.* 1 continuous, unbroken, uninterrupted, undisturbed. 2 unbreakable.

అవిచ్ఛిన్నంగా **awicchinnangaa** *adv.* uninterruptedly, without a break, continously, in a stream.

అవిచ్ఛిన్నత **awicchinnata** *n.* continuance, continuity.

అవిజ్ఞత **awijñata** *n.* ignorance.

అవిటి **awiTi** *n.* disabled or physically handicapped person.

అవిటి బతుకు **awiTi batuku** *n.* mean or wretched life.

అవిద్య **awidya** *n.* lack or want of education.

అవిధేయ **awidheeya** *adj.* unmanageable, disobedient, insubordinate.

అవిధేయత **awidheeyata** *n.* disobedience, insubordination.

అవినయం **awinayam** *n.* want of humility, presumptuousness.

అవినాభావ **awinaabhaawa** *adj.* inseparable, indissoluble; ~ **sambandham** integral connection.

అవినీతి **awiniiti** *n.* 1 dishonesty, corruption. 2 immorality, depravity.

అవిభక్త **awibhakta** *adj.* 1 undivided, composite. 2 unpartitioned, joint (family).

అవిభాజ్య **awibhaajya** *adj.* indivisible; ~ **sankhya** prime number.

అవిభాజ్యత **awibhaajyata** *n.* indivisibility.

అవియు, అవిసిపోవు **awiyu, awisipoowu** *v.i.* to break, burst, be destroyed; **naa guNDelu** (*or* **naa praaNaalu**) **awisipooyEEyi** my heart burst *or* I was overwhelmed (with emotion or shock).

అవిరళ **awiraLa** *adj.* 1 ceaseless, untiring; ~ **kṛSi** untiring effort. 2 *class.* thick, dense.

అవిరళంగా **awiraLangaa** *adv.* continuously.

అవిరళత **awiraLata** *n. sci.* continuity.

అవిరి **awiri** *n.* 1 a disease of the eye. 2 **kannu** ~ **peTTu** to remove a particle lodged in the eye by touching the eye with a gold object which has been dipped in water.

అవిరుద్ధ **awiruddha** *adj.* compatible.

అవిరేణి **awireeNi** *n.* ~ **kuNDalu** coloured pots used in a marriage ceremony.

అవిలంబ[న]ం **awilamba[na]m** *n.* promptness.

అవిలంబిత **awilambita** *adj. class.* quick, prompt.

అవివాహిత **awiwaahita** *adj.* unmarried.

అవివేక **awiweeka** *adj.* foolish, stupid.

అవివేకం **awiweekam** *n.* foolishness, stupidity.

అవివేకి **awiweeki** *n.* fool.

అవిశ్వసనీయ **awiświsaniiya** *adj.* untrustworthy.

అవిశ్వాసం **awiśwaasam** *n.* distrust, doubt; **awiśwaasa tiirmaanam** no confidence motion.

అవిశె **awise** *n.* flax, *linum usitatissimum.*

అవిశె [చెట్టు] **awise[ceTTu]**[2] *n.* tree known as *sesbania grandiflora.*

అవు **awu** *v.i.* 1 to be, become: *irregular verb with an alternative root* **kaa** *occurring in the negative and in certain non-finite forms; several forms of this verb are used as particles, conjunctions, etc., and as such are cited seperately,* e.g., **aytee** if so, but; **aynaa** nevertheless, even; **kaani** but; **kaakuNDaa** without. 2 to come to pass: *see* **giita**[2].

అవేద్యం **aweedyam** *adj.* (that) which cannot be known or experienced.

అవ్యక్త **awyakta** *adj.* 1 not clear, indistinct. 2 imperceptible, invisible. 3 not perceived, unknown. 4 implicit.

అవ్యక్తగణితం **awyaktagaNitam** *n.* algebra.

అవ్యయం **awyayam** *n. gram.* indeclinable word, conjunction, adverb, particle, clitic.

అవ్యవధానంగా **awyawadhaanangaa** *adv.* without a moment's pause, without any delay.

అవ్యయాత్మ **awyayaatma** *n. class.* imperishable soul.

అవ్యవస్థ **awyawastha** *n.* disorder, state of disorganisation.

అవ్యవస్థిత **awyawasthita** *adj.* disorganised.

అవ్యవహిత **awyawahita** *adj.* 1 direct, immediate (cognition). 2 continuous. 3 contiguous.

అవ్యాప్తి **awyaapti** *n.* narrowness.

అవ్యాహతంగా **awyaahatangaa** *adv.* steadily, continuously, uninterruptedly.

అవ్యాజ్య **awyaajya** *adj.* honest, guileless, true, genuine.

అవ్యుత్పన్నుడు **awyutpannuDu** *n.* person who is not well versed in language or literature.

అవ్వ **awwa** *n.* 1 grandmother, old woman. 2 *dial.* woman (of any age).

అవ్వాయిచువ్వ **awwaayicuwwa** *n.* kind of firework.

అశక్తత, అశక్తి **aśaktata, aśakti** *n.* weakness, disability, incapacity.

అశక్య **aśakya** *adj.* impossible, impracticable.

అశనం **aśanam** *n. dial.* 1 food. 2 eating, feeding.

అశనిపాతం **aśanipaatam** *n. class.* thunderbolt.

అశరీర **aśariira** *adj.* bodiless, disembodied; ~ **waaNi** disembodied voice.

అశాంతి **aśaanti** *n.* restlessness, unrest, disorder.

అశాశ్వత **aśaaśwata** *adj.* impermanent, temporary, transient.

అశాశ్వతం **aśaaśwatam** *n.* impermanence.

అశాస్త్రీయ **aśaastriiya** *adj.* 1 unscientific. 2 not in accordance with the traditional authority of the Sastras.

అశిరెమ్మ, అసిరెమ్మ **aśiremma, asiremma** *n.* name of a village goddess.

అశుద్ధం **aśuddham** I. *n. colloq.* excrement. II. *adj.* impure, unclean.

అశుద్ధత **aśuddhata** *n.* uncleanliness.

అశుచి **aśuci** I.*n.* dirt, uncleanliness, impurity. II.*adj.* dirty.

అశుభ **aśubha** *adj.* inauspicious, unlucky, unfortunate.

అశుభ్రం **aśubhram** *adj.* unclean, dirty, insanitary.

అశేష *adj.* whole, all, entire: ~ **janam** all the people, a great crowd of people.

అశోక **aśooka** *adj. class.* without sorrow.

అశోకచెట్టు **áśooka ceTTu** *n.* the Asoka tree, *jonesia asoka.*

అశోకవనం **aśookawanam** *n.* pleasure park; ~ **loo siita laagaa undi** she is like Sita in Asokavanam *i.e.*, she is in deep sorrow (Sita, the heroine of the Ramayana, spent her time of sorrow in Asokavanam).

అశౌచం **aśawcam** *n.* period of twelve days after a death when members of the family do not mingle with others on account of pollution.

అశ్రద్ధ **aśraddha** I.*n.* neglect, inattention, carelessness, negligence. II.*adj.* careless, negligent, remiss.

అశ్రావ్య **aśraawya** *adj.* discordant, cacophonous.

అశ్రావ్యత **aśraawyata** *n.* discordant sound, cacophony.

అశ్రువు **aśruwu** *n.* tear; **aśrutarpaNam arpincu** to offer a tribute of tears (a phrase used to signify mourning); *see* **tarpaNam.**

అశ్లీల **aśliila** *adj.* vulgar coarse, obscene, ribald; ~ **saahityam** pornography.

అశ్లీలం, అశ్లీలత **aśliilam, aśliilata** *n.* vulgarity, coarseness, obscenity, ribaldry.

అశ్వం **aśwam** *n. class.* horse.

అశ్వత్థం **aśwattham** *n.* pipal tree, *ficus religiosa.*

అశ్వబలం **aśwabalam** *n.* cavalry.

అశ్వశక్తి **aśwaśakti** *n.* horse power.

అశ్వమేధం **aśwameedham** *n.. class.* 1 traditional horse sacrifice. 2 great achievement.

అశ్విని **aświni** *n. astrol.* first of the 27 lunar mansions, consisting of 3 stars.

అష **aSa** *dial. variant form of* **aTa.**

అష్ట **aSTa** *n.* eight.

అష్టకం **aSTakam** *n.* 1 any group of eight things. 2 a poem composed in eight lines. 3 a form of dancing with eight poses. 4 one of the eight divisions of the Rigveda.

అష్టకష్టాలు **aSTakaSTaalu** *n.pl.* all kinds of troubles, overwhelming difficulties.

అష్టదిక్పాలకులు **aSTadikpaalakulu** *n.pl., astrol.* regents of the eight points of the compass.

అష్టదిగ్గజాలు **aSTadiggajaalu** *n.pl.* 1 the eight mythological elephants supporting the earth. 2 group of eight great poets in the court of the emperor Krishna Deva Raya.

అష్టదిగ్బంధనం **aSTadigbandhanam** *n.* total blockade (*lit.* blockade in all the eight directions).

అష్టపది **aSTapadi** *n.* kind of poetic metre consisting of eight lines, used by Jayadeva in his 'Gita Govinda.'

అష్టభుజి **aSTabhuji** *n.* octagon.

అష్టమ **aSTama** *adj.* eighth.

అష్టమి **aSTami** *n.* eighth day after the new or full moon.

అష్టవంకరలు **aSTawankaralu** *n.pl.* contortions; **siggutoo ~ tirigipooyEEDu** he twisted himself into knots on account of shyness.

అష్టాచెమ్మ **aSTaacemma** *n.* 'eights and fours', a game played with shells.

అష్టాదశ **aSTaadaśa** *adj.* eighteenth.

అష్టాదశం **aSTaadaśam** *n.* eighteen.

అష్టావక్రం **aSTaawakram** I. *adj.* crooked, awkward, clumsy. II. *adv.* awkwardly, clumsily.

అష్టావక్రుడు **aSTaawakruDu** *n.* name of a hermit in the Ramayana whose limbs were deformed and contorted.

అష్టావధానం **aSTaawadhaanam** *n.* the art of attending to eight different matters simultaneously.

అష్టావధాని **aSTaawadhaani** *n.* person who can practise the art of **aSTaawadhaanam.**

అసంకల్పిత **asankalpita** *adj.* involuntary, reflex; ~ **carya** reflex action.

అసంక్రమకరణం **asankramakaraNam** *n. med.* immunisation.

అసంక్రామ్యత **asankraamyata** *n. med.* immunity.

అసంఖ్యాక **asankhyaaka** *adj.* numberless, countless, innumerable.

అసంగత **asangata** *adj.* 1 incoherent. 2 irrelevant. 3 anomalous, incompatible, inconsistent.

అసంగతి **asangati** *n.* inconsistency, anomaly.

అసంజనం **asanjanam** *n. sci.* adhesion.

అసంతత **asantata** *adj. sci.* discontinuous.

అసంతుష్టి **asantuSTi** *n.* dissatisfaction, displeasure.

అసంతృప్త **asantrpta** *adj.* 1 dissatisfied, discontented, disgruntled. 2 *chem.* unsaturated; ~ **draawaNam** unsaturated solution.

అసంతృప్తి **asantrpti** *n.* dissatisfaction, discontent[ment].

అసంతృప్తికర **asantrptikara** *adj.* unsatisfactory.

అసంతోషం **asantooSam** *n.* displeasure.

అసందర్భ **asandarbha** *adj.* inappropriate, irrelevant.

అసందర్భత **asandarbhata** *n.* inappropriateness.

అసందిగ్ధ **asandigdha** *adj.* unambiguous, unequivocal.

అసంపాదిత **asampaadita** *adj.* unearned.

అసంపీడ్య **asampiiDya** *adj.* incompressible.

అసంపూర్ణ **asampuurNa** *adj.* 1 incomplete, partial; ~ **sweedanam** *chem.* fractional distillation. 2 *gram.* defective, elliptical.

అసంపూర్తిగా **asampuurtigaa** *adv.* incompletely.

అసంబంధ **asambandha** *adj.* unconnected, incongruous.

అసంబద్ధ **asambaddha** *adj.* 1 unconnected, irrelevant. 2 absurd, nonsensical. 3 incoherent, inconsistent.

అసంభవ **asambhawa** *adj.* 1 impossible, impracticable. 2 improbable, unlikely.

అసంభవత **asambhawata** *n.* impossibility.

అసంభావ్య **asambhaawya** *adj.* 1 impossible. 2 improbable.

అసంభావ్యత **asambhaawyata** *n.* 1 impossibility. 2 improbability.

అసంయమనం **asamyamanam** *n.* lack of control.

అసంలగ్న **asamlagna** *adj.* discrete.

అసంశయంగా **asamśayangaa** *adv.* without doubt.

అసంస్కారం **asamskaaram** *n.* lack of culture or refinement.

అసంస్కారి, అసంస్కారుడు **asamskaari, asamskaaruDu** *n.* uncultured or unrefined person.

అసక్తుడు **asaktuDu** *n.* person who has no attachment to or involvement in worldly affairs.

అసత్య **asatya** *adj.* false.

అసత్యం **asatyam** *n.* falsehood.

అసదృశ asadṛśa *adj.* incomparable.

అసనాటు **asanaaTu** *adj.* weak, feeble; ~ **batuku** insecure life.

అసఫలత **asaphalata** *n.* defeat, failure.

అసభ్య **asabhya** *adj.* 1 low, base, vulgar. 2 uncivilised.

అసభ్యంగా **asabhyangaa** *adv.* 1 impolitely, vulgarly. 2 in an uncivilised manner.

అసమ **asama** *adj.* unequal.

అసమంజస **asamanjasa** *adj.* 1 absurd. 2 unreasonable.

అసమగ్ర **asamagra** *adj.* incomplete, not comprehensive.

అసమతౌల్యం **asamatawlyam** *n.* imbalance, disequilibrium.

అసమనేయుడు, అసమనేత్రుడు **asamaneeyuDu, asamaneetruDu** *n.* epithet of God Siva, who possesses a third eye.

అసమయం **asamayam** I.*n.* unfavourable or unsuitable time. II.*adj.* untimely, inopportune.

అసమర్థ **asamartha** *adj.* incapable, incompetent, useless, ineffective, inefficient.

అసమర్థత **asamarthata** *n.* incapacity, incompetence, inefficiency.

అసమశరుడు **asamaśaruDu** *n.* epithet of Manmatha or Cupid.

అసమస్త **asamasta** *adj.* imperfect, not complete or comprehensive.

అసమాన **asamaana** *adj.* 1 unequal, disparate. 2 unequalled, unrivalled.

అసమానత **asamaanata** *n.* inequality, disparity.

అసమాపక **asamaapaka** *adj. gram.* non-finite.

అసమాప్త **asamaapta** *adj.* incomplete, unfinished.

అసమ్మతి, అసమ్మతం **asammati, asammatam** *n.* disapproval, disagreement.

అసలు **asalu** I. *n.* capital sum, principal. II.*adj.* 1 real, actual, true, genuine; ~ **dhara** the real price; **ii pani taracu jariginappuDu, ~ śaasanaalapaTLanee gawrawam sannagillutundi** when this thing happens often, the very respect for law (*or* the respect for law itself) is undermined. 2 main, principal, original; ~ **artham** the original meaning. III. *adv.* 1 really, absolutely, actually; **niiku ~ buddhi undEE?** have you really got any sense? 2 *in neg. constr.* at all; ~ **neenu saaraa taaganu** I do not drink liquor at all.

అసలు సిసలు **asalu sisalu** *adj.* 1 real, true, genuine. 2 original.

అసహజ **asahaja** *adj.* unnatural, artificial.

అసహనం **asahanam** *n.* impatience, intolerance, lack of forbearance.

అసహనంగా **asahanangaa** *adv.* in a quandary, nonplussed.

అసహాయ **asahaaya** *adj.* helpless, unaided.

అసహాయత **asahaayata** *n.* helplessness.

అసహాయశూరుడు **asahaayaśuuruDu** *n.* warrior who fights alone and unaided.

అసహిష్ణుత **asahiSNuta** *n. class.* impatience, intolerance.

అసహ్యం **asahyam** I. *n.* 1 hatred, loathing, disgust. 2 dislike; **ii goDawa haaku ~ weestunnadi** I cannot stand this shouting; **wankaaya kuura miida waaDiki ~ puTTindi** he is tired of brinjal curry. II. *adj.* 1 intolerable, unbearable, hateful, loathsome, odious, disgusting, repugnant, repulsive. 2 unpleasant, disliked, disagreeable, ugly, unsightly; **ninaadaalatoo gooDalu annii ~ ceesEEru** they disfigured all the walls with slogans.

అసహ్యంగా **asahyangaa** *adv.* 1 with disgust. 2 with dislike, disapprovingly.

అసహ్యకర **asahyakara** *adj.* 1 hateful, abominable. 2 irksome, unpleasant, distasteful.

అసహ్యపడు **asahyapaDu** *v.i.* to feel detestation or dislike (-**miida**, for).

అసహ్యించు **asahyincu** *v.t.* 1 to hate, loathe, detest. 2 to feel distaste for.

అసాంప్రదాయ **asaampradaaya** *adj.* deviating from custom, unconventional.

అసాధారణ **asaadhaaraNa** *adj.* 1 uncommon, rare. 2 unusual, extraordinary, exceptional, abnormal.

అసాధు[వు] రూపం **asaadhu[wu] ruupam** *n. gram.* incorrect or ungrammatical form.

అసాధ్య **asaadhya** *adj.* 1 impossible, impracticable; ~ **paristhiti** desperate situation. 2 unbeatable, unconquerable; ~ **pu aaTagaaDu** topranking or unbeatable player.

అసాధ్యత **asaadhyata** *n.* impossibility.

అసాధ్యుడు **asaadhyuDu** *n.* 1 unbeatable or insuperable person. 2 person with extraordinary gifts or talents.

అసామర్థ్యం **asaamarthyam** *n.* inefficiency.

అసామాన్య **asaamaanya** *adj.* unusual, abnormal, rare.

అసి **asi** *n.* sword.

అసింట **asiNTa** *adv.* on that side, to that side.

అసిధార **asidhaara** *n.* edge of a sword blade.

అసిధారావ్రతం **asidhaaraawratam** *n.* 1 *lit.* vow to stand on the edge of a sword. 2 being engaged in a hopelessly difficult task; **neenu traaTimiida naDustunnaTTugaa ~ gaa sancarincaali** I must move as if I was walking on a tight rope or on the edge of a sword.

అసిరెమ్మ **asiremma** *same as* **aśiremma.**

అసివారులు **asiwaarulu** *n. class.* gentle walk, stroll.

అసుర, అసురుడు, ఆసురుడు **asura, asuruDu, aasuruDu** *n.* demon, giant.

అసురసంధ్య, అసురసంజె **asurasandhya, asurasanje** *n.* dusk, evening.

అసుర్రి, ఆసురి **asuri, aasuri** *n.* female demon.

అసువు **asuwu** *n., gen.pl.* ~ **lu** life; ~ **lu koolpoowu** to lose o.'s life, die.

అసూయ **asuuya** *n.* 1 envy, jealousy. 2 malice, malignity.

అసూర్యంపశ్య **asuuryampaśya** *n.* woman who lives in purdah (*lit.* woman who is never seen by the sun).

అసౌకర్యం **asawkaryam** *n.* inconvenience.

అసౌష్టవ **asawSTawa** *adj.* 1 without charm or grace. 2 *sci.* asymmetrical.

అసౌష్టవం **asawSTawam** *n.* 1 lack of charm or grace. 2 *sci.* asymmetry.

అస్ఖలిత **askhalita** *adj.* chaste; ~ **brahmacaari** strict bachelor.

అస్తమయం **astamayam** *n.* 1 setting of the sun and other heavenly bodies. 2 death, decease.

అస్తమానం **astamaanam** I. *n.* sunset, evening. II.*adv.* all day long.

అస్తమించు **astamincu** *v.i.* 1 (of the sun and other heavenly bodies) to set. 2 to die.

అస్తరు **astaru** *n.* lining [cloth].

అస్తవెస్త **astawesta** *adj.* 1 *same as* **astawyasta**. 2 foolish.

అస్తవ్యస్త **astawyasta** *adj.* disorderly, confused, topsy turvy, chaotic, haphazard.

అస్తవ్యస్తంగా **astawyastangaa** *adv.* in confusion, higgledy piggledy.

అస్తవ్యస్తత **astawyastata** *n.* chaos, disorderliness, confusion.

అస్తాద్రి, అస్తాచలం **astaadri, astaacalam** *n. class.* the legendary mountain behind which the sun sets.

అస్తిత్వం **astitwam** *n.* existence, entity.

అస్తిత్వవాదం **astitwawaadam** *n.* existentialism.

అస్తిమార్దవరోగం **astimaardawa roogam** *n.* rickets.

అస్తేయం **asteeyam** *n.* honesty.

అస్త్రం **astram** *n.* 1 weapon; **naa miida sammoohanaastram prayoogicEEDu** he practised the weapon of cajolery on me. 2 missile. 3 arrow charged with magical power.

అస్త్రకరి **astrakari** *n.* plastering.

అస్త్రసన్యాసం **astrasanyaasam** *n.* laying down of arms in token of surrender.

అస్థి **asthi** *n.* bone.

అస్థిక **asthika** *n.* bone, *gen.pl.* ~ **lu** bones.

అస్థినిమజ్జనం **asthinimajjanam** *n.* immersion of mortal remains in a river or stream on the twelfth day after a cremation.

అస్థిపంజరం **asthipanjaram** *n.* skeleton.

అస్థిమజ్జ **asthimajja** *n. sci.* marrow.

అస్థిమిత **asthimita** *adj.* unsteady, unstable, unsettled.

అస్థిమితత్వం **asthimitatwam** *n.* instability.

అస్థిర **asthira** *adj.* unstable, fickle, volatile.

అస్పష్ట **aspaSTa** *adj.* 1 indistinct, unclear, blurred, hazy. 2 vague, ambiguous.

అస్పష్టత **aspaSTata** *n.* 1 indistinctness, haziness. 2 vagueness, ambiguity.

అస్పృశ్యత **asprśyata** *n.* untouchability.

అస్పృశ్యుడు **asprśyuDu** *n.* untouchable person.

అస్ఫుట **asphuTa** *adj.* indistinct.

అస్మత్, అస్మదీయ **asmat, asmadiiya** *pron. and adj. class.* mine, my.

అస్మదర్థక **asmadardhaka** *adj. gram.* exclusive.

అస్మదాదులు **asmadaadulu** *n.pl.* myself and others, we.

అస్మాదృశులు **asmaadrśulu** *n.pl. class.* persons like me.

అస్యకుహరం **asyakuharam** *n. zool.* buccal cavity.

అస్వతంత్ర **aswatantra** *adj.* dependent.

అస్వరిత **aswarita** *adj. ling.* unaccented.

అస్వస్థత **aswasthata** *n.* ill health, indisposition.

అస్వాధీన **aswaadhiina** *adj. class.* not in o.'s control, not in o.'s possession or power.

అస్వాభావిక **aswaabhaawika** *adj.* unnatural.

అహం **aham** *n.* ego, pride, self-conceit; **waaDi ~ debba tiNTundi** his ego will be wounded; **waaDiki enta ~ !** how egoistic he is! *see* **haamu.**

అహంకరించు, హంకరించు **ahankarincu, hankarincu** *v.i.* to be proud, be overbearing.

అహంకారం, హంకారం **ahankaaram, hankaaram** *n.* 1 egoism, pride, self-conceit, vanity, arrogance. 2 selfishness.

అహంకారి **ahankaari** *n.* proud, vain or arrogant person, egoist.

అహంకృతి **ahankrti** *n.* egoism, arrogance.

అహంభావం **ahambhaawam** *n.* pride, egoism, self-conceit.

అహమిక, అహమహమిక **ahamika, ahamahamika** *n.* 1 arrogance, pride. 2 emulation, competition; **nalabhay mandi widyaarthuluu ~ too caduwutunnaaru** all the forty students are studying competitively.

అహరహం **aharaham** *adv.* daily, regularly, steadily, continuously.

అహర్నిశం, అహర్నిశలు **aharniśam, aharniśalu** *adv.* day and night.

అహింస **ahimsa** *n.* non-violence.

అహిత **ahita** *adj.* hurtful, injurious, disadvantageous.

అహితం **ahitam** *n.* 1 damage, injury, harm, detriment. 2 enmity.

అహితుడు **ahituDu** *n.* 1 enemy. 2 s.o. who is disliked.

అహేతుక **aheetuka** *adj.* groundless.

అహోరాత్రులు, అహోరాత్రం **ahooraatrulu, ahooraatram** *adv.* day and night.

ఆ - aa

ఆ **aa**[1] *interrog. suffix used in questions expecting yes/no type answers*, e.g., **aayana waccEEDaa**? has he come?

ఆ **aa**[2] *pronom. adj.* that, those; **aa aa** or **aayaa** those various (things or persons — *see* **aayaa**).

ఆ **aa**[3] *Sanskrit prefix meaning* till, until, up to, as far as, e.g., **aamaraNa niraahaara diikSa** fast unto death.

ఆంక్ష **aankSa** *n.* **1** restraint, restriction; ~**lu widhincu** to impose restrictions or sanctions. **2** excommunication.

ఆంగికం **aangikam** *n.* gesture, action.

ఆంగీరస **aangiirasa** *n.* sixth year of the Hindu cycle of sixty years.

ఆంగ్ల, ఆంగ్లేయ **aangla, aangleeya** *adj.* English.

ఆంగ్లం **aanglam** *n.* the English language.

ఆంగ్లేయుడు **aangleeyuDu** *n.* English person.

ఆంజనేయుడు **aanjaneeyuDu** *n.* a name of Hanuman, devoted servant of Rama.

ఆండ్రెబ్బ **aaNDrebba** *n.* spoilt behaviour, behaviour of a spoilt or pampered child; **taatayya wastee nii ~ wadilistaaDu** if your grandfather comes he will put a stop to your spoilt behaviour.

ఆంతరంగిక **aantarangika** *same as* **antarangika.**

ఆంతరాయిక **aantaraayika** *adj.* intermittent.

ఆంతరిక **aantarika** *adj.* inner.

ఆంతర్యం **aantaryam** *n.* **1** heart. **2** mind. **3** opinion. **4** true meaning, real intention.

ఆంత్రం **aantram** *n.* intestine, bowel.

ఆంత్రప్రకోపం **aantraprakoopam** *n.* enteritis, typhoid fever.

ఆంత్రమూలం **aantramuulam** *n. med.* duodenum.

ఆంత్రవృద్ధి **aantrawṛddhi** *n. med.* hernia.

ఆందోళన **aandooLana** *n.* **1** agitation, alarm. **2** worry, anxiety. **3** grief, sorrow.

ఆందోళనకారుడు **aandooLanakaaruDu** *n.* agitator.

ఆంధ్యం **aandhyam** *n.* blindness.

ఆంధ్ర **aandhra** *adj.* Telugu; ~**prajalu** the Telugu people; ~ **samskrti** Telugu culture.

ఆంధ్రం **aandhram** *n.* **1** the Telugu country. **2** the Telugu language.

ఆంధ్రీకరించు **aandhriikarincu** *v.t.* to translate into Telugu.

ఆంధ్రుడు **aandhruDu** *n.* Andhra, person belonging to the Telugu country.

ఆంపెట్టు **aampeTTu** *v.i. used in speaking to a child.* (< **annam peTTu**) to give food; **aampeDataanu daa**! come! I will give you food.

ఆంబోతు **aambootu** *n.* bull.

ఆంశిక **aamśika** *adj.* partial.

ఆంశికంగా **aamśikangaa** *adv.* partially, fractionally.

ఆక **aaka** *advbl. suffix attached to past vbl. adj. meaning* when, e.g., **adi winnaaka bhayapaDDaaDu** when he heard it, he was afraid; *when the verb root is not a monosyllable ending in* **-n**, *as in* **win** *above, the termination* **inaaka** >**EEka** *in coastal Andhra dialect, e.g.*, **waccinaaka** (*other dialects*), **waccEEka** (*coastal dialect*).

ఆకట్టుకొను **aakaTTukonu** *v.t.* **1** to attract. **2** to stop, hold up, withhold: **naa jiitam raawaali. aaDiT braanciiwaaLLu aakaTTukoni kuurcunnaaru** my salary is due, but the audit branch is holding it up.

ఆకతాయ **aakataaya** *adj.* (of children) naughty, mischievous.

ఆకతాయతనం **aakataayatanam** *n.* (of children) naughtiness, mischievousness.

ఆకరం **aakaram** *n.* source, basis, authority.

ఆకరిత **aakarita** *adj. class.* called, summoned.

ఆకర్ణనం **aakarNanam** *n.* hearing, listening.

ఆకర్ణించు **aakarNincu** *v.t.* to listen to, attend to.

ఆకర్షణ **aakarSaNa** *n.* attraction, attractiveness, temptation, enticement.

ఆకర్షణపత్రం **aakarSaNa patram** *n. bot.* petal (of a flower).

ఆకర్షణపత్రావళి **aakarSaNa patraawaLi** *n. bot.* corolla.

ఆకర్షణశక్తి **aakarSaNa śakti** *n.* power of attraction, attractiveness; **bhuumy~** force of gravity.

ఆకర్షణీయ **aakarSaNiiya** *adj.* attractive, tempting, enticing.

ఆకర్షించు **aakarSincu** *v.t.* to attract, appeal to, tempt, entice.

ఆకలనం **aakalanam** *n.* understanding, comprehension, estimation.

ఆకలి **aakali** *n.* hunger, appetite; ~**maNTalu** pangs of hunger; ~**dappulu** hunger and thirst.

ఆకలికొను **aakalikonu** *v.i.* to be hungry.

ఆకళించు **aakaLincu** *v.t.* to comprehend or understand thoroughly.

ఆకళించుకొను **aakaLincukonu** *v.t.* to master (a subject of study).

ఆకళింపు **aakaLimpu** *n.* understanding, comprehension.

ఆకళింపుచేసుకొను **aakaLimpu ceesukonu** *v.t.* to get to know, come to understand.

ఆకసం **aakasam** *n.* sky.

ఆకస్మిక **aakasmika** *same as* **akasmika.**

ఆకాంక్ష **aakaankSa** *n.* wish, desire, aspiration.

ఆకాంక్షించు **aakaankSincu** *v.t.* to desire, aspire (after).

ఆకార **aakaara** *adjvl. suffix meaning* shaped, e.g., **tribhuj** ~ triangle shaped, triangular.

ఆకారం **aakaaram** *n.* 1 shape, form, figure. 2 look, appearance.

ఆకారరేఖ **aakaara reekha** *n.* contour.

ఆకాశం **aakaaśam** *n.* sky; ~ **madum aytee, ii polam paNDutundi** if we have good rains (*lit.* if the sky becomes a floodgate) this field will yield a crop.

ఆకాశగంగ **aakaaśaganga** *n.* the river of heaven, the celestial Ganges.

ఆకాశరామన్న **aakaaśaraamanna** *n. an imaginary person, i.e. nobody; used as a fictitious name.*

ఆకాశవాణి **aakaśawaaNi** *n.* 1 *lit.* voice from the sky. 2 All India Radio.

ఆకీర్ణం **aakiirNam** *suffix meaning* crowded with, abounding in.

ఆకు **aaku** I. *n.* 1 leaf. 2 betel leaf; ~ **lu weesukooDamwalla aame pedawulu erupekkEEyi** her lips were red from chewing betel: ~ **ku andani pookaku pondani jawaabulu** irrelevant answers, answers that are neither here nor there. 3 leaf plate; ~ **loo annam waDDinci aame bhartanu pilicindi** she served food on a leaf plate and called her husband; *cf.* **wistaraaku.** 4 pendant, ear ornament; *cf.* **loolaaku.** 5 palmyra leaf formerly used for writing; *cf.* **taaTEEku.** 6 letter (epistle). 7 spoke in a wheel. 8 slat in a shutter or venetian blind. 9 seedlings for transplantation. 10 cutting edge of a sharp instrument. II. *adjvl. prefix meaning* green, e.g., ~ **pacca rangu** leaf green colour.

ఆకు అలం **aaku alam** *n.* greens and herbs.

ఆకుకూరలు **aakukuuralu** *n. pl.* green leafy vegetables.

ఆకుచెప్పులు **aakuceppulu** *n.pl.* sandals with thin soles.

ఆకుతోట **aakutooTa** *n.* garden of betel vines.

ఆకుపచ్చ **aakupacca** *adj.* leaf green.

ఆకుపసరు **aakupasaru** *n.* sap drawn from leaves.

ఆకుపూజ **aakupuuja** *n.* worship of Hanuman performed with betel leaves.

ఆకుమడి **aakumaDi** *n.* bed of seedlings.

ఆకుముడత **aakumuData** *n.* leaf curl, a disease of cholam caused by aphids.

ఆకురాయి **aakuraayi** *n.* file, rasp.

ఆకురాలే, ఆకురాల్చే **aakuraalee, aakuraalcee** *adj. bot.* deciduous.

ఆకుసన్నం **aakusannam** *n.* a superior variety of rice.

ఆకృతి **aakṛti** *n.* form, shape.

ఆకొను **aakonu** *v.i.* to be hungry.

ఆక్రందన[ం] **aakrandana[m]** *n.* weeping, crying, lamenting.

ఆక్రమణం **aakramaNam** *n.* 1 encroachment, usurpation. 2 occupation. 3 attack.

ఆక్రమించు **aakramincu** *v.t.* 1 to encroach on, usurp. 2 to occupy.

ఆక్రాంతం **aakraantam** *suffix meaning* seized, appropriated, occupied, taken possession of.

ఆక్రోశం **aakroośam** *n.* 1 anger. 2 cursing, imprecation.

ఆక్రోశించు **aakroośincu** *v.i.* 1 to show anger. 2 to curse, revile.

ఆక్షేపక **aakSeepaka** *adj.* objectionable.

ఆక్షేపకుడు **aakSeepakuDu** *n.* 1 objector. 2 member of the Boya community.

ఆక్షేపణ **aakSeepaNa** *n.* 1 objection, criticism. 2 censure, blame, reproach.

ఆక్షేపణీయ **aakSeepaNiiya** *adj.* objectionable.

ఆక్షేపించు **aakSeepincu** *v.i. and t.* 1 to object, remonstrate, take exception. 2 to find fault with, criticise, take to task.

ఆక్షోటం **aakSooTam** *n.* walnut tree, *juglans regia.*

ఆఖరు **aakharu** I. *n.* end, termination, finish. II. *adj.* last, final.

ఆఖ్యాత **aakhyaata** *n.* person who tells or narrates.

ఆఖ్యానం **aakhyaanam** *n.* 1 story, legend. 2 saying, declaring. 3 *ling.* predicate.

ఆఖ్యాయిక **aakhyaayika** *n.* a story based on fact.

ఆగం **aagam** *n.* offence, misbehaviour; ~ ~ **ceeyu** to behave badly, create trouble, make a scene.

ఆగంతుక **aagantuka** *adj.* 1 unexpected, unforseen, adventitious. 2 ad hoc, incidental.

ఆగంతుకుడు **aagantukuDu** *n.* 1 unexpected guest. 2 newcomer, stranger.

ఆగడం **aagaDam** *n.* 1 mischief, naughtiness, misbehaviour. 2 misdeeds, wrong doing.

ఆగడపలు **aagaDapalu** *n.pl.* thick layers of clouds.

ఆగడీడు **aagaDiiDu** *n.* mischievous person.

ఆగతం **aagatam** *n.* 1 that which has come or been obtained. 2 that which is to come, fortune.

ఆగమం **aagamam** *n.* 1 coming, arrival. 2 treatise on religious rites. 3 *gram.* grammatical increment or inserted syllable. 4 increase of property.

ఆగమనం **aagamanam** *n.* 1 coming, approach, arrival. 2 induction.

ఆగాయిత్యం, ఆఘాయిత్యం **aagaayityam, aaghaayityam** *n.* outrageous behaviour.

ఆగు **aagu** *v.i.* 1 to stop, stay. 2 to abstain, refrain. 3 to wait. 4 to bear, tolerate, endure, withstand; **gaali paaTuku aagee rakam** a variety which tolerates the force of the wind; **ii kooTu caliki** ~ **tundaa?** will this coat keep out the cold? **uttaram raaleedu, manassu aagaka phoonu ceesEEnu** your answer did not come; as I was anxious in my mind, I telephoned.

ఆగ్నేయ **aagneeya** *adj.* southeast.

ఆగ్నేయాస్త్రం **aagneeyaastram** *n.* a mythical fiery weapon.

ఆగ్రహం **aagraham** *n.* 1 anger, displeasure, resentment. 2 wrath, rage.

ఆగ్రహించు **aagrahincu** *v.i.* 1 to be angry, resent. 2 to be in a rage.

ఆఘమేఘాలమీద **aaghameeghaalamiida** *adv.* very quickly; **phoonu ceeyagaanee** ~ **waccEEDu** when I phoned he came in an instant.

ఆఘాతం **aaghaatam** *n.* blow, stroke, shock.

ఆఘాయిత్యం **aaghaayityam** *same as* **aagaayityam.**

ఆఘోషణం **aaghooSaNam** *n.* proclamation.

ఆఘోషించు **aaghooSincu** *v.t.* to shout.

ఆఘ్రాణం **aaghraaNam** *n.* sense of smell.

ఆఘ్రాణించు **aaghraaNincu** *v.t.* to smell (flowers, etc.).

ఆచంద్రతారార్కంగా **aacandrataaraarkangaa** *adv.* for ever (*lit.* as long as the sun, moon and stars endure).

ఆచమనం **aacamanam** *n.* sipping water three times and reciting the names of Vishnu on prescribed occasions.

ఆచమించు **aacamincu** *v.i.* to perform **aacamanam.**

ఆచరణ **aacaraNa** *n.* 1 practice, performance, implementation; ~ **loo peTTu** to put into practice. 2 observation (of a custom).

ఆచరణయోగ్య, ఆచరణసాధ్య, ఆచరణీయ **aacaraNayoogya, aacaraNasaadhya, aacaraNiiya** *adj.* practicable.

ఆచరణయోగ్యత **aacaraNayoogyata** *n.* practicability.

ఆచరణాత్మక **aacaraNaatmaka** *adj.* 1 practical. 2 operative.

ఆచరించు **aacarincu** *v.t.* 1 to practise, perform, implement. 2 to observe (a custom).

ఆచారం **aacaaram** *n.* 1 practice, custom. 2 traditional practice, religious observance, ritual; ~ **maniSi** a strictly orthodox person.

ఆచారపరాయనుడు **aacaaraparaayaNuDu** *n.* traditionalist.

ఆచారపరుడు **aacaaraparuDu** *n.* orthodox person.

ఆచారి **aacaari** *n.* 1 craftsman belonging to the community of goldsmiths, blacksmiths and carpenters. 2 *same as* **aacaarya.**

ఆచార్య, ఆచార్యుడు **aacaarya, aacaaryuDu** *n.* 1 professor. 2 spiritual guide, priest, preceptor (generally a Vaishnavite). 3 ayurvedic doctor.

ఆచార్యత్వం **aacaaryatwam** *n.* status of an **aacaarya.**

ఆచిపెట్టికొట్టు **aacipeTTikoTTu** *v.t.* to strike s.o. a hard blow.

ఆచు **aacu** *v.t.* stop, check; **nooru aacitee jwaram taggutundi** if you check your appetite the fever will subside.

ఆచుకొను, అచ్చుకొను **aacukonu, accukonu** *v.i.* to hold o.s. responsible (for a loss or debt); **doowaloo pustakaalu pootee ewaru aacukoNTaaru?** who will hold himself responsible if the books are lost on the way?

ఆచూకీ, ఆచోకీ **aacuukii, aacookii** *n.* 1 trace, sign, clue; **ataNNi ewaru campEEroo eemiToo ewarikii ~ teliyadu** no one has a clue as to who killed him. 2 inkling, information, intimation; **neenu raastunnadaaniloo kaastaynaa abaddham unnaTLu miiku ~ dorikindaNTee** if you get an inkling that there is the slightest falsehood in what I am writing. 3 whereabouts; **V. saayamtoo aame ~ tiisi aamenu kalusukonnaaDu** with the help of V. he traced her whereabouts and met her.

ఆచ్ఛాదనం **aacchaadanam** *n.* 1 lid, cover[ing]. 2 cloak. 3 sheath.

ఆచ్ఛాదిత **aacchaadita** *adj.* covered, hidden, concealed.

ఆచ్ఛికం **aacchikam** *n.class.* pure Telugu word; **aacchika samaasam** pure Telugu compound.

ఆజన్మ **aajanma** *adj.* existing since birth, lifelong.

ఆజానుబాహుడు **aajaanubaahuDu** *n.* 1 *lit.* person of tall stature whose arms reach down to his knees (traditionally regarded as a sign of greatness). 2 *colloq.* tall well built person.

ఆజి **aaji** *n. class.* war, battle.

ఆజుబాజు **aajubaaju** *adj.* close, nearby, neighbouring; ~ **iLLaloo manuSyulu naa sneehitulee** the people living in the neighbouring houses are my friends.

ఆజ్ఞ **aajña** *n.* 1 order, command. 2 leave, sanction, permission.

ఆజ్ఞానుసారం **aajñaanusaaram** *adv.* as ordered, according to orders.

ఆజ్ఞాపన **aajñaapana** *n.* order, command.

ఆజ్ఞాపించు **aajñaapincu** *v.t.* to order, command.

ఆజ్ఞాబద్ధుడు **aajñaabaddhuDu** *n.* person who is bound by an order.

ఆజ్యం **aajyam** *n.* ghee; **agniloo ~ poosinaTLu** like adding fuel to the fire (proverb: *lit.* like pouring ghee on the fire).

ఆట **aaTa** *n.* 1 game, sport, play[ing]; ~ **kaTTindi** the game was finished *or* the game ended; **naa ~ kaTTeesEEru** (i) (in chess) you have checkmated me, (ii) (in general) you have defeated me; **neenu waaDi ~ kaTTincaali** (i) (in chess) I must checkmate him, (ii) (in general) I must defeat him *or* I must put a stop to his tricks. 2 dance, dancing.

ఆటంకం **aaTankam** *n.* obstacle, hindrance, interruption, obstruction.

ఆటంకపరచు **aaTankaparacu** *v.t.* to hinder, stop, obstruct, impede, inhibit.

ఆటకట్టు **aaTakaTTu** *n.* (in chess) checkmate.

ఆటకత్తె **aaTakatte** *n.* 1 player in a game (woman). 2 dancer (woman).

ఆటకాడు **aaTakaaDu** *n.* player in a game (man).

ఆటగొర్రు **aaTagorru** *n.* harrow or rake used to break up clods after ploughing.

ఆటపట్టించు **aaTapaTTincu** *v.t.* to tease, make fun of.

ఆటపట్టు **aaTapaTTu** *n.* 1 playground. 2 abode, place.

ఆటపాట **aaTapaaTa** *n.* 1 *gen.pl.* ~ **lu** amusements; **aaTapaaTalaloo paDi pillalu annam tinaDam maricipooyEEru** the children were engrossed in playing and forgot to eat their meal. 2 (*singular*) singing and dancing; **aameki ~ waccu** she can sing and dance.

ఆటలమ్మ **aaTalamma** *n.* chicken-pox.

ఆటలాడు **aaTalaaDu** *v.i.* 1 to play. 2 to toy (**-too**, with).

ఆటవస్తువు **aaTa wastuwu** *n.* plaything, toy.

ఆటవిక **aaTawika** *adj.* 1 belonging to or living in a forest. 2 savage, barbarous.

ఆటవికుడు **aaTawikuDu** *n.* 1 forest dweller. 2 uncivilised person, savage, barbarian.

ఆటవిడుపు **aaTawiDupu** *n.* holiday (from school or work).

ఆటవీశాస్త్రం **aaTawiiśaastram** *n.* (science of) forestry.

ఆటవెలది **aaTaweladi** *n.* 1 name of a poetic metre (in which Vemana wrote his poems). 2 dancing girl, prostitute.

ఆటస్థలం **aaTasthalam** *n.* playing field, playground.

ఆటి **aaTi** *suffix used to form adjs.*, e.g., **laaw**~ fat.

ఆటివచ్చు **aaTiwaccu** *v.i.* 1 to be sufficient, last longer, go a long way (of food, etc.); **kotta biyyam koNTee aaTiraawu paata biyyam aytee aaTiwastaayi** if you buy new rice it will not go a long way (when cooked), if you buy old rice it will go further. 2 to be saved; **ii miThaayilu ekkuwa pancadaara paTTawu. pancadaara aaTiwastundi** in these sweets not much sugar is used; sugar will be saved.

ఆటు **aaTu** *n.* falling or ebbing tide.

ఆటుపోటులు **aaTupooTulu** *n.pl.* rising and falling (like tides); **ii udyoogamloo aaTupooTulaku taTTukooleeka paaripooyEEDu** he ran away because he could not stand the ups and downs in this job.

ఆటుబడి **aaTubaDi** *n.* 1 sufficiency, lasting power. 2 saving, economising; **karuwukaalamloo ~ maaTalaa?** economising is not a trivial matter in times of scarcity.

ఆటే **aaTee** *adv., in neg. constr.* not so much, not very much.

ఆఠీన్ **aaThiin** *n.* hearts (in card games); ~ **raaNi** (i) queen of hearts (ii) *colloq.* prostitute.

ఆడ **aaDa**[1] *adv. dial.* there.

ఆడ **aaDa**[2] *adj.* female, woman's.

ఆడంగి **aaDangi** I.*n., gen.pl.* **aaDangulu** women. II.*adj.* effeminate, womanish.

ఆడంబరం **aaDambaram** *n.* pomp and ceremony, show, ostentation.

ఆడంబరపూరిత **aaDambarapuurita** *adj.* ceremonious.

ఆడంబరపూర్ణ **aaDambarapuurNa** *adj.* grandiose.

ఆడంబరపూర్వక **aaDambarapuurwaka** *adj.* pretentious.

ఆడకట్టు చీరె/పంచె **aaDakaTTu ciire/pance** *n.* white sari worn by a widow.

ఆడతనం **aaDatanam** *n.* 1 femininity. 2 weakness.

ఆడతోడు **aaDatooDu** *n.* help provided by a woman.

ఆడది **aaDadi** *n.* woman.

ఆడపడుచు **aaDapaDucu** *n.* 1 female member of a **gootram** by birth; **aame maa iNTi**~ she is a member of our **gootram** (spoken by a man or woman). 2 husband's sister; **aame maa**~ she is my sister-in-law (spoken by a woman); *cf.* **haarati paLLem.**

ఆడపాప **aaDapaapa** *n.* servant maid.

ఆడపెత్తనం **aaDapettanam** *n.* woman's rule.

ఆడబిడ్డ **aaDabiDDa** *n.* sister-in-law (husband's sister).

ఆడబొట్టె **aaDaboTTe** *n.* girl.

ఆడా **aaDaa** *n.* 1 control, authority. 2 protection, patronage.

ఆడారివాడు **aaDaariwaaDu** *n.* impotent man, eunuch.

ఆడి **aaDi** *feminine suffix added to certain nouns indicating a trait or characteristic*, e.g., **maayal**~ deceitful woman; **wannel**~ lovely woman.

ఆడించు **aaDincu** *v.t.* 1 to cause to move or dance or play; **kukka tooka aaDistundi** the dog wags its tail; **tala**~ to nod or shake o.'s head; **Dabbu/taaLaalu galagala**~ to jingle money/keys. 2 **o.-ni tegan**~ to criticise s.o severely. 3 to grind, crush or otherwise process material in a mill; **aaDincina sunnam** lime that has been ground in a mortar; **aaDincina biyyam** milled rice.

ఆడితప్పు **aaDitappu** *v.i.* to break a promise.

ఆడిపోయు **aaDipooyu** *v.t.* to reproach or vilify s.o. behind his back.

ఆడు **aaDu** *v.i. and t.* 1 to play. 2 to dance. 3 to move, shake, do, act, practise, perform: *used to form verbs from a wide variety of nouns with meaning varying according to the context*, e.g., **abaddhaalu/bonkulu**~ to tell lies; **sarasaalu**~ to make jokes; **maaTL**~ (< **maaTalu**~) to talk; **muddul**~ to kiss; **peLL**~ to marry; **maa waDLu ~ tunnaayi maraloo** our paddy is being ground in the mill; **podduna leecinappaTinunci waaDi nooru~ tuuneee undi** ever since he got up in the morning he has been munching s.g; **aa gurrammiida aaDaDam mancidi kaadu** it is not a good thing to bet on that horse; **aarindaalaa ippuDu kaaTan markeTTu~ tunnadi** she is betting on the cotton market nowadays as if she was an expert.

ఆఢ్యుడు **aaDhyuDu** *suffix meaning* owner or possessor of; **guN**~ man of all virtues; **bal**~ man possessing great strength.

ఆణి **aaNi** I.*n.* nail, pin. II *adj.* round, spherical; ~ **puusa/mutyam** round or faultless pearl.

ఆణె, ఆనె **aaNe, aane** *n. med.* hardening of the skin due to pressure or friction, corn.

ఆతతాయి **aatataayi** *n.* 1 villain, rogue. 2 sadist.

ఆతపం **aatapam** *n.* heat, sunshine.

ఆతపస్నానం **aatapa snaanam** *n.* sunbath.

ఆతిథేయి **aatitheeyi** *n. class.* host.

ఆతిథ్యం **aatithyam** *n.* hospitality.

ఆతిథ్య ధర్మం **aatithyadharmam** *n.* a host's duty to his guests.

ఆతురం, ఆతురత, ఆత్రుత, ఆత్రం **aaturam, aaturata, aatruta, aatram** *n.* 1 haste, eagerness, ardour. 2 anxiety.

ఆతురతగా **aaturatagaa** *adv.* eagerly.

ఆత్మ **aatma** I. *n.* 1 soul, spirit. 2 self. 3 mind, reason, intellect. 4 body. II. *adj.* 1 own, personal. 2 self-, e.g., ~ **stuti** self-praise.

ఆత్మక **aatmaka** *suffix meaning* consisting of, of the nature of, of the character of, e.g., **caritr**~ historical, **sangiit**~ musical, **wiwaraN**~ detailed, descriptive, **sandeeś**~ having a message to convey.

ఆత్మకథ **aatmakatha** *n.* autobiography.

ఆత్మగతం **aatmagatam** *adj. theat.* aside, spoken to o.s.

ఆత్మగౌరవం **aatmagawrawam** *n.* self-respect.

ఆత్మజ **aatmaja** *n.* daughter.

ఆత్మజుడు **aatmajuDu** *n.* son.

ఆత్మజ్ఞానం **aatmajñaanam** *n.* spiritual knowledge.

ఆత్మత్యాగం **aatmatyaagam** *n.* self-sacrifice, altruism.

ఆత్మనాశక **aatmanaaśaka** *adj.* self-destructive, suicidal.
ఆత్మనింద **aatmaninda** *n.* self-reproach.
ఆత్మనిగ్రహం **aatmanigraham** *n.* self-control.
ఆత్మనేపదం **aatmaneepadam** *n.gram.* 1 the middle voice of a verb in Sanskrit. 2 a verb formed with **-konu** in Telugu.
ఆత్మపరిశోధన **aatmapariśoodhana** *n.* self-examination, introspection.
ఆత్మప్రశంస **aatmapraśamsa** *n.* self-praise.
ఆత్మబంధువు **aatmabandhuwu** *n.* close or bosom friend
ఆత్మవంచన **aatmawancana** *n.* self-delusion.
ఆత్మవిశ్వాసం **aatmawiśwaasam** *n.* self-confidence.
ఆత్మశక్తి **aatmaśakti** *n.* will power.
ఆత్మశుద్ధిగా **aatmaśuddhigaa** *adv.* honestly, truthfully.
ఆత్మసంయమనం **aatmasamyamanam** *n.* self-control.
ఆత్మస్తుతి **aatmastuti** *n.* self-praise, boasting.
ఆత్మహత్య **aatmahatya** *n.* suicide.
ఆత్మారాముడు **aatmaaraamuDu** *n.* the inner man, appetite; **bhoojanaantaram ~ callabaDDaaDu** after dinner the inner man felt contented.
ఆత్మార్థం **aatmaartham** *adv.* for [the sake of] o.s.
ఆత్మార్థక **aatmaarthaka** *adj. gram.* reflexive.
ఆత్మార్పణ **aatmaarpaNa** *n.* self-sacrifice, altruism.
ఆత్మాభిమానం **aatmaabhimaanam** *n.* self-respect, self-esteem.
ఆత్మాశ్రయ **aatmaaśraya** *adj.* subjective.
ఆత్మాశ్రయత **aatmaaśrayata** *n.* subjectivity.
ఆత్మాహుతి **aatmaahuti** *n.* self-immolation.
ఆత్మీయ **aatmiiya** *adj.* 1 o.'s own, personal. 2 affectionate, loving, near and dear.
ఆత్మీయత **aatmiiyata** *n.* 1 friendliness, cordiality, affection. 2 close friendship, intimacy.
ఆత్మీయుడు **aatmiiyuDu** *n.* 1 close or bosom friend. 2 *pl.* **aatmiiyulu** o.'s nearest and dearest.
ఆత్మోన్నతి **aatmoonnati** *n.* spiritual exaltation.
ఆత్యయిక **aatyayika** *adj.* **~ paristhiti** *polit.* emergency.
ఆత్రం **aatram** *same as* **aaturam.**
ఆత్రగాడు **aatragaaDu** *n.* hasty person.
ఆత్రుత **aatruta** *same as* **aaturata.**
ఆదమరచి **aadamaraci** I. *past participle of* **aadamaracu.** II. *adv.* 1 soundly; **~ nidra pootunnaaDu** he is sleeping soundly *or* he is sound asleep. 2 taken unawares, off o.'s guard: **~ asalu wiSayam ceppeesEEDu** he let out the true facts when off his guard.
ఆదమరచు **aadamaracu** *v.i.* 1 to become unconscious, lose consciousness, become oblivious. 2 to be overwhelmed by emotion.
ఆదమరపు **aadamarapu** *n.* unconsciousness, oblivion.
ఆదరం **aadaram** *n.* 1 respect, regard. 2 kindness, love, attachment, devotion.
ఆదరణ **aadaraNa** *n.* 1 respect, careful attention. 2 approval, favourable reception, appreciation.
ఆదరణీయ **aadaraNiiya** *adj.* worthy of being treated with respect or consideration.
ఆదరాబాదరా **aadaraabaadaraa** *adv.* confusedly, in a great hurry.
ఆదరాభిమానాలు **aadaraabhimaanaalu** *n.pl.* friendliness, goodwill.
ఆదరించు **aadarincu** *v.t.* 1 to treat kindly, cherish, befriend; *see* **aadaruwu.** 2 to show respect for, give support or encouragement to: **telugu prajaaniikam maatram wyawahaarikoodyamaanni hṛdayapuurwakangaa aadarincindi** but the Telugu people gave wholehearted support to the colloquial language movement.
ఆదరింపు **aadarimpu** *adj.* approving, appreciative.
ఆదరువు **aadaruwu** *n.* 1 shelter, support, help. 2 protection, refuge. 3 livelihood, subsistence; **aadarincina aa musalaayanee oka ~ cuupeTTaalani G.ki oka kaNTraakTar daggira gumaastaa pani ippincEEDu** the same old man who befriended G. got him a clerk's job under a contractor in order to provide him with a livelihood.
ఆదర్శ **aadarśa** *adj.* ideal.
ఆదర్శం **aadarśam** *n.* 1 ideal. 2 model, pattern.
ఆదర్శకం **aadarśakam** *n.* mirror.
ఆదర్శప్రాయం **aadarśapraayam** *adj.* ideal.
ఆదర్శవంత **aadarśawanta** *adj.* 1 ideal. 2 idealistic.
ఆదర్శవాదం **aadarśawaadam** *n.* idealism.
ఆదర్శవాది **aadarśawaadi** *n.* idealist.
ఆదా **aadaa** *n.* saving, economy.
ఆదాచేయు **aadaa ceeyu** *v.t.* to save, economise; **Dabbu aadaa ceeyaDaaniki tana uuriki naDici weLLEEDu** in order to save money he went walking to his home town.
ఆదాన[ం] **aadaana[m]** *n.* 1 receiving. 2 *ling.* borrowing.
ఆదానప్రదానాలు **aadaana pradaanaalu** *n. pl.* receiving and giving.
ఆదాయం **aadaayam** *n.* income, revenue.
ఆదాయపు పన్ను **aadaayapu pannu** *n.* income tax.
ఆది **aadi**[1] I. *Sanskrit prefix meaning* first, initial, original, chief, principal, e.g., **~ puruSuDu** founder; **~ waasi** aboriginal inhabitant. II. *suffix* 1 *meaning* beginning with, e.g., **cakaar ~ śabdaalu** words beginning with the letter 'c'. 2 *meaning* and other (things or persons), e.g., **paaNinyaadulu** Panini and others; **nannay ~ mahaakawulu** Nannaya and other great poets. 3 *added to* **uttaram** *and* **daksiNam** *to form adjs.*: **uttar ~** northern; **daksiN ~** southern. 4 *added to certain round numerals to form quantitative adjs.*, e.g., **weel ~ prajalu** thousands of people. III. *n.* beginning **~ madhyaantam** the beginning, the middle and the end.
ఆది **aadi**[2] *n.* 1 measurements given for making anything that can be worn, viz., clothes, shoes, jewellery, etc.; **darjii daggiraki weLLi ~ icciraaraa!** go and give measurements to the tailor; **mii abbaayiki meemu tiisukeLLina cokkaa ~ saripooyindEE?** does the shirt that we brought

for your son fit him? 2 a sample of anything that can be worn, given for copying: **mii ungaram ~istee nagala wyaapaarastuDiki icci wastaanu** if you will lend me your ring as a sample I will take it to the jeweller.

ఆదికం **aadikam** *suffix meaning* and so on, and the like, etcetera, e.g., **kuśala praśn~** welfare enquiries and the like.

ఆదికవి **aadikawi** *n.* the first poet (in Sanskrit, Valmiki; in Telugu, Nannaya).

ఆదికావ్యం **aadikaawyam** *n.* the first literary work (the Ramayana in Sanskrit).

ఆదిగా **aadigaa** *suffix meaning* 1 beginning with, starting from: **samskrta bhaaSalooni śabdaalannii akaar ~paTTiilu wraasi** writing lists of all the words in Sanskrit, starting from the letter 'a'. 2 since the time of: **srST~ bhuugooLamloo tananu bandiigaa ceesiweestunna gurutwaakarSaNanu jayinci** overcoming the force of gravity which had been holding him captive on earth since the time of creation.

ఆదితాళం **aaditaaLam** *n.* one of the modes of measuring time in music.

ఆదినారాయణం **aadinaaraayaNam** *n.* a game similar to chess.

ఆదిపురుషుడు **aadipuruSuDu** *n.* 1 founder. 2 originator.

ఆదిభౌతిక **aadibhawtika** *adj.* metaphysical.

ఆదిమ **aadima** *adj.* 1 first, earliest. 2 primitive, aboriginal.

ఆదివారం **aadiwaaram** *n.* Sunday.

ఆదివాసి **aadiwaasi** *n.* aboriginal inhabitant.

ఆదిశక్తి **aadiśakti** *n.* Durga, the goddess of primordial energy.

ఆదుకొను **aadukonu** *v.t.* 1 to come to the rescue, relieve, aid, assist. 2 to treat kindly, care for, look after. 3 to back up, support.

ఆదుర్దా **aadurdaa** *n.* 1 worry, fear, alarm, anxiety, concern. 2 agitation, excitement.

ఆదేశం **aadeeśam** *n.* 1 order, command, direction, instruction, ruling, mandate, teaching. 2 *gram.* conversion of one sound into another; *see* **guN~** *and* **gasaDadaw~**. 3 *gram.* insertion of a consonant between vowels for for euphony, e.g., **ceppu + ooy 〉 ceppawooy.**

ఆదేశక **aadeeśaka** *adj.* mandatory, directive; **~suutraalu** directive principles.

ఆదేశించు **aadeeśincu** *v.t.* to order, command, direct, instruct, teach.

ఆద్యంతాలు **aadyantaalu** *n.pl.* beginning and end.

ఆద్యుడు **aadyuDu** *n.* 1 founder. 2 originator.

ఆధరువు **aadharuwu** *n.* an item to go with rice in food; **iwwEELa annamlooki eem~lu ceesEEru?** what dishes have you cooked to go with the rice today?

ఆధార **aadhaara** *adj.* basic.

ఆధారం **aadhaaram** *n.* 1 support, prop, basis, base, foundation. 2 source, authority.

ఆధారంగా **aadhaarangaa** *adv.* with the help of, relying on: **oNTarigaa naa gadiloo kuurcuNDi jñaapakaalu maatramee~** sitting alone in my room, relying only on my memories.

ఆధారపడు **aadhaarapaDu** *v.i.* to depend (**-pay** *or* **-miida**, on).

ఆధారబిందువు **aadhaarabinduwu** *n. sci.* fulcrum.

ఆధారిత **aadhaarita** *adj.* dependent.

ఆధికారిక **aadhikaarika** *adj.* 1 official. 2 authorised, authoritative.

ఆధిక్యం **aadhikyam** *n.* 1 greatness, superiority. 2 abundance. 3 excess, superabundance, surfeit.

ఆధిక్యత **aadhikyata** *n.* superiority, supremacy.

ఆధిపత్యం **aadhipatyam** *n.* 1 dominion, command, sovereignty, control. 2 aegis, auspices.

ఆధిరాజ్యం **aadhiraajyam** *n.* autocracy.

ఆధీనం **aadhiinam** *same as* **adhiinam.**

ఆధునాతన, అధునాతన **aadhunaatana, adhunaatana** *adj.* modern, contemporary.

ఆధునిక **aadhunika** *adj.* modern, upto date, recent.

ఆధునికం చేయు **aadhunikam ceeyu** *v.t.* to modernise.

ఆధునికత్వం **aadhunikatwam** *n.* modernity.

ఆధునికీకరణ **aadhunikiikaraNa** *n.* modernisation.

ఆధునికీకరించు **aadhunikiikarincu** *v.t.* to modernise.

ఆధ్యాత్మిక **aadhyaatmika** *same as* **adhyaatmika.**

ఆధ్యాత్మికత **aadhyaatmikata** *n.* spirituality.

ఆధ్వర్యం, అధ్వర్యం **aadhwaryam, adhwaryam** *n.* 1 leadership, direction, control; **aayana ~loo** under his control or direction; **~wahincu** to assume leadership or direction, be in control or command. 2 aegis, auspices.

ఆన **aana**[1] *n.* 1 order. 2 oath.

ఆన **aana**[2] *n.* mark, trace.

ఆనంద **aananda**[1] *n.* forty-eighth year of the Hindu cycle of sixty years.

ఆనంద **aananda**[2] *adj.* pleasant, delightful.

ఆనందం **aanandam** *n.* joy, happiness, delight, pleasure.

ఆనందదాయక **aanandadaayaka** *adj.* giving or bringing joy.

ఆనందమయ **aanandamaya** *adj.* full of joy, festive.

ఆనంద రంగు **aananda rangu** *n.* a shade of green.

ఆనందించు **aanandincu** I. *v.i.* to rejoice, be glad or happy. II. *v.t.* to enjoy.

ఆనందిత **aanadita** *adj.* cheerful.

ఆనక **aanaka** *adv.* afterwards, later on.

ఆనకట్ట **aanakaTTa** *n.* anicut, dam, barrage.

ఆనతి **aanati** *n.* command, instruction, order.

ఆనపకాయ **aanapakaaya** *n.* bottle gourd, *cucurbita sp.*

ఆనపకాయ బుర్ర, ఆనపకాయ బూరా **aanapakaaya burra, aanapakaaya buuraa** *n.* kind of wind instrument made from a dried bottle gourd, played by snake charmers.

ఆనపెట్టు **aana peTTu** *v.t.* to order.

ఆనవాయితీ **aanawaayitii** *n.* convention, tradition, custom.

ఆనవాలు, ఆనమాలు **aanawaalu, aanamaalu** *n.* 1 sign, mark, token, indication. 2 identification, recognition.

ఆనవాలుపట్టు **aanawaalu paTTu** *v.t.* to identify, recognise.

ఆనవైచు **aanawaycu** *v.i.* to swear an oath, promise.

ఆనాటి **aanaaTi** *adj.* former.

ఆనాడి **aanaaDi** *same as* **anaaDi.**

ఆనాడు **aanaaDu** *adv.* on that day, at that time.

ఆనాడేనాడో **aanaaDeenaaDoo** *adv.* long ago.

ఆనించు, ఆన్చు **aanincu, aancu** *v.t.* to cause to rest on or against; **gooDaki wiipu ~koni kuurcunnaaDu** he sat leaning his back against a wall.

ఆనిక **aanika** *n.* support, rest; **bangaaram paatra aynaa~ kaawaali** even if it is a golden vessel, it still needs a support to rest on (proverb).

ఆను **aanu** *v.i. and t.* 1 to rest on, press against, touch; **waaDi kaaLLu bhuumiki aanaleedu** his feet did not touch the ground. 2 (of vision) to reach, extend; **cuupu aanee duuramloo illu leedu** there is no house as far as the eye can see; **DaakTarugaaruu, cuupu sarigaa aanaDam leedu, kaLLajooDu kaawaali** Doctor, my eyes are not able to see properly, I need spectacles. 3 **kaNTiki~** to appeal to, be approved of, be fancied, be liked; **miiru cuusina suuTu kaNTiki aanindEE miiku?** do you like the suit that you have seen? 4 to appear; **aa reNDu koNDala madhya agaadhamayna looya unnaTLu duuraanaku~tundi** there appears in the distance to be a deep valley between those two hills.

ఆనుకర్ర **aanukarra** *n.* walking stick.

ఆనుకూల్యం **aanukuulyam** *n.* 1 coordination, convenience, suitability. 2 compatibility, consonance.

ఆనుకొను **aanukonu** *v.i. and t.* 1 to be close to, lean against or on; **tallini aanukoni kuurcunnaaDu** he sat close to his mother. 2 to adjoin, abut, be next to, be adjacent to, border on; **naa gadiki aanukoni unna haalu** the hall which adjoins my room.

ఆనుగుణ్యం **aanugunNyam** *n.* 1 fitness, suitability. 2 consonance, conformity.

ఆనురూప్యం **aanuruupyam** *n. sci.* correspondence.

ఆనువంశిక **aanuwamśika** *adj.* hereditary.

ఆనుషంగిక **aanuSangika** *adj.* 1 accompanying, concomitant; **~saakSyam** collateral evidence. 2 incidental.

ఆనుషంగికంగా **aanuSangikangaa** *adv.* incidentally, casually.

ఆనూపానూ, ఆనుపానులు **aanuupaanuu, aanupaanulu** *n.* origin and antecedents; **~kanipeTTu** to find out the ins and outs of (s.g).

ఆనె **aane** *same as* **aaNe.**

ఆనోటా ఆనోటా **aanooTaa aanooTaa** *adv.* orally, from mouth to mouth, by word of mouth; **idi weedam~wallincukonna deeśam** this is the country in which the Vedas have been passed down by word of mouth.

ఆన్చు **aancu** *same as* **aanincu.**

ఆపం **aapam** *n.* (*also* **appam**) cake of riceflour.

ఆపంచా ఆపంచా **aapancaa aapancaa** *adv.* **~paTTukonu** to wander about aimlessly; **aameki ewaruu leeru,~ paTTukoni kaalakSeepam ceestunnadi** she has no-one to look after her, so she spends her life wandering here and there.

ఆపట్టున, ఆపట్టాన **aapaTTuna, aapaTTaana** *adv.* thereupon.

ఆపడంగా, ఆపళంగా **aapaDangaa, aapaLangaa** *adv.* immediately afterwards, just then.

ఆపత్కర **aapatkara** *adj.* dangerous, perilous, hazardous.

ఆపత్కాలం **aapatkaalam** *n.* time of distress.

ఆపద, ఆపత్తి, ఆపత్తు **aapada, aapatti, aapattu** *n.* 1 disaster, calamity. 2 misfortune, adversity. 3 danger, peril, hazard.

ఆపదమొక్కులవాడు **aapadamokkulawaaDu** *n.* the God who is invoked in times of misfortune, Sri Venkateswara.

ఆపద్ధర్మ **aapaddharma** *adj.* stopgap, caretaker.

ఆపద్ధర్మం **aapaddharmam** *n.* procedure not usually allowable but which is adopted in an emergency.

ఆపద్బాంధవుడు **aapadbaandhawuDu** *n.* one who comes to the rescue in a disaster, friend in need.

ఆపన్న **aapanna** *adj.* unfortunate, distressed.

ఆపసోపాలుపడు **aapasoopaalu paDu** *v.i.* to display self-pity, moan and groan over o.'s ailments or misfortunes.

ఆపాట, ఆపాటున, ఆపాట్న, ఆపాడాన, ఆపాళాన **aapaaTa, aapaaTuna, aapaaTNa, aapaaDaana, aapaaLaana** *adv.* immediately afterwards, just then.

ఆపాటి **aapaaTi** *adj.* that much, so much, so great.

ఆపాతమధురం **aapaata madhuram** *adj.* pleasing to the senses.

ఆపాదమస్తకం **aapaada mastakam** *adv.* from tip to toe.

ఆపాదించు **aapaadincu** *v.t.* 1 to assign, refer, attribute, ascribe. 2 to confer, accord, bestow.

ఆపాదిల్లు **aapaadillu** *v.i.* to happen, take place.

ఆపాళాన **aapaaLaana** *same as* **aapaaTa.**

ఆపు **aapu** I.*n.* stopping, restraining, preventing; *see* **aDDu.** II.*v.t.* 1 to stop, curtail, restrain, check, hold back, hold up, detain, prevent; **koopam~konnaaDu** he controlled his anger. 2 **layT aapiweeyu** to put out a light.

ఆపుచేయు **aapuceeyu** *v.t.* 1 to stop, check, prevent; **o.-ni paDakuNDaa ~** to prevent s.o. from falling.

ఆపుదల **aapudala** *n.* stopping, stoppage, stay.

ఆపేక్ష **aapeekSa** *n.* liking, love, affection.

ఆపోక **aapooka** *n.* satisfaction, fulfilment of desire.

ఆపోరు **aapooru** *dial. form of* **aapoowu.**

ఆపోవు **aapoowu** *v.i.* to satisfy, be sufficient; **inta koncem perugu waaDiki eem aapoorutundi?** how will he be satisfied with this small amount of curds?

ఆపోశన **aapoośana** *same as* **awpoosana.**

ఆప్కోర, ఆపుకోరా **aapkoora, aapukooraa** *n.* round-bottomed drinking bowl.

ఆప్త **aapta** *adj.* intimate, dear; **~mitruDu** close friend.

ఆప్తత **aaptata** *n.* kindness, lovingness, good nature.

ఆప్తుడు **aaptuDu** *n.* near and dear person.

ఆప్యాయం[గా] **aapyaayam[gaa]** *adv.* 1 affectionately, good naturedly. 2 **paayasam ~ tinnaaDu** he ate the pudding with relish.

ఆప్యాయత **aapyaayata** *n.* friendliness, good nature, goodwill, kindness, fondness, affection.

ఆఫారం **aaphaaram** *n.* half arm shirt.

ఆబ **aaba** *n.* 1 greed[iness]. 2 pupil of the eye.

ఆబగా **aabagaa** *adv.* 1 greedily, avidly. 2 hungrily, thirstily, ravenously.

ఆబాది **aabaadi** *n.* village lands held in common.

ఆబారున **aabaaruna** *adv.* continuously, non-stop.

ఆబాలగోపాలం **aabaalagoopaalam** *n.pl.* all and sundry, anybody and everybody.

ఆబి **aabi** *n.* kharif crop, sown in the southwest monsoon season.

ఆబోతు **aabootu** *n.* bull.

ఆబోరు **aabooru** *n.* honour, character, prestige, reputation; **baabbaabuu! naa ~ kaasta dakkincu! ii pani tondaragaa ceesipeTTu!** boy! please do the work quickly and save my reputation.

ఆబ్కారి **aabkaari** *n.* excise tax on liquor.

ఆబ్దికం **aabdikam** *n.* anniversary death ceremony.

ఆభరణం **aabharaNam** *n.* ornament, decoration.

ఆభాసం **aabhaasam** *n.* 1 fallacy, illusion. 2 unreal or fallacious appearance, semblance. 3 likeness, resemblance.

ఆభిజాత్యం **aabhijaatyam** *n.* 1 nobility of birth. 2 self-respect, pride, self-esteem.

ఆమంత్రణ **aamantraNa** *n.* invocation, invitation.

ఆమంత్రించు **aamantrincu** *v.t.* to invoke, invite.

ఆమ, ఆము **aama, aamu** *n.* kiln for firing pottery.

ఆమట్టునే **aamaTTunee** *adv.* immediately afterwards.

ఆమడ **aamaDa** *n.* measure of distance equal to about 8 miles or 13 kilometres.

ఆమధ్య **aamadhya** *adv.* 1 recently. 2 some time ago.

ఆమని **aamani** *n.* spring season.

ఆమరణ **aamaraNa** *adj.* leading to death; **~ niraahaara diikSa** fast unto death.

ఆమాత్రం **aamaatram** *adj.* that much.

ఆమాశయం **aamaaśayam** *n.* stomach.

ఆముఖం **aamukham** *n.* prelude to a drama.

ఆముదం **aamudam** *n.* 1 castor oil plant. 2 *pl.* **aamudaalu** castor oil seeds.

ఆముష్మిక **aamuSmika** *adj.* spiritual.

ఆమూలంగా **aamuulangaa** *adv.* completely; **neenu ceppinadi ~ winnaaDu** he listened right through to what I had to say.

ఆమూలాగ్రం **aamuulaagram** *adv.* from beginning to end, thoroughly.

ఆమె **aame** *pron.* she, that woman.

ఆమెత, ఆమిత **aameta, aamita** *n. class.* feast, festive occasion.

ఆమోదం, అనుమోదం **aamoodam, anumoodam** *n.* 1 consent, assent, approval, sanction. 2 acceptance. 3 ratification. 4 *class.* joy, pleasure.

ఆమోదకర, ఆమోదయోగ్య **aamoodakara, aamoodayoogya** *adj.* acceptable, agreeable.

ఆమోదించు, అనుమోదించు **aamoodincu, anumoodincu** *v.t.* 1 to approve, adopt, sanction, pass (law, resolution). 2 to recognise, acknowledge (talent). 3 to accept (argument). 4 to confirm, ratify.

ఆమ్నాయం **aamnaayam** *n.* 1 the Vedas. 2 scripture.

ఆమ్రేడితం **aamreeDitam** *adj.* 1 repeated, reiterated. 2 *ling.* iterative.

ఆమ్లం **aamlam** *n.* 1 acid. 2 sourness.

ఆమ్లజని **aamlajani** *n. chem.* oxygen.

ఆమ్లజనీకరణం **aamlajaniikaraNam** *n. chem.* oxidation.

ఆమ్లిత **aamlita** *n.* acidity.

ఆయం **aayam** *n.* 1 share of the harvest given by custom to the village officials and artificers. 2 measurement of distance between beams in the roof of a house.

ఆయకం **aayakam** *n.* mortgage.

ఆయకట్టు **aayakaTTu** *n.* 1 irrigated area watered by an irrigation source. 2 land for which patta (occupancy right) is held jointly by several cultivators.

ఆయకాడు **aayakaaDu** *n.* 1 village officer. 2 *pl.* **aayagaaLLu** village officials, including both officers and artificers.

ఆయతం, ఆయతనం **aayatam, aayatanam**[1] *n. and adj.* oblong.

ఆయతన **aayatana** *adj.* volumetric.

ఆయతనం **aayatanam**[2] *n.* 1 abode, house. 2 sacred place. 3 *sci.* volume, cubic content.

ఆయత్త **aayatta** I. *n.* readiness, preparation. II. *adj.* ready, inclined, prepared.

ఆయత్తపడు **aayattapaDu** *v.i.* to be ready or prepared.

ఆయత్తపరచు **aayattaparacu** *v.t.* to prepare, make ready.

ఆయన **aayana** *pron.* he, that man; **mii/maa ~** your/my husband.

ఆయమ **aayama** *pron.* she, that woman.

ఆయమం **aayamam** *n.* length, expansion, extension, amplitude.

ఆయవారం **aayawaaram** *same as* **yaayawaaram**

ఆయవ్యయపట్టిక **aayawyayapaTTika** *n.* budget.

ఆయా, ఆ ఆ **aayaa**[1], **aa aa** *adj.* those various: **pariśoodhakulu ~ uuLLanunci raasina uttaraalu konniTini cuustee ii wiSayam wyaktam awutundi** this matter will be plain if you see the letters which researchers have written from those various villages.

ఆయా **aayaa**[2] *n.* woman servant who looks after children, ayah.

ఆయాసం **aayaasam** *n.* fatigue, exhaustion.

ఆయిందా **aayindaa** *adv.* 1 next time. 2 in future.

ఆయుధం **aayudham** *n.* 1 weapon. 2 tool, instrument.

ఆయుధశాల, ఆయుధాగారం **aayudhaśaala, aayudhaagaaram** *n.* arsenal, armoury.

ఆయుర్దాయం **aayurdaayam** *n.* a person's remaining life span; **padinimiSaalu kaadu, padi roojulu, padi nelalu, ~ uNTee padi samwastaraalu ceppagalanu** I could talk (about Telugu culture) not just for ten minutes but for ten days, ten months or even ten years if my life lasted long enough; **aayana ~ gaTTidi** *lit.* his life span is strong (an expression used when a person has a lucky escape from an accident).

ఆయుర్వేదం **aayurweedam** *n.* Ayurveda, the science of Indian Medicine.

ఆయువు **aayuwu** *n.* age, length of life, life span; **aayana ~ tiirindi** his life came to an end; **nii ~ muuDutundi** the end of your life is near *or* this will be the end of you! (a threat made to a naughty child); **naa ~ kuuDaa poosukunibatuku!** may my life span be added to yours! *or* may you live long! (a blessing spoken by an elder to a younger person).

ఆయువుపట్టు **aayuwupaTTu** *n.* centre of life, vital point, key point, vital matter; **prajaaswaamyaaniki caTTabaddhamayna paalana ~** the rule of law is a vital matter for democracy.

ఆయుష్కర **aayuSkara** *adj.* life lengthening, promoting long life.

ఆయుష్కర్మం **aayuSkarmam** *n. class.* shaving, hair-cutting.

ఆయుష్మంతుడు **aayuSmantuDu** *n.* man of great age.

ఆయుష్షు, ఆయుస్సు **aayuSSu, aayussu** *n.* life.

ఆయొక్క **aayokka** *demonstrative pron. class., but occurring sometimes mod.* a certain *or* a particular (person or thing).

ఆర **aara** *n.* 1 shoemaker's awl. 2 whip.

ఆరంజోతి **aaranjooti** *same as* **arundhati**.

ఆరంభం **aarambham** *n.* beginning.

ఆరంభశూరుడు **aarambhaśuuruDu** *n.* person whose initial enthusiasm for an undertaking is not sustained to the end.

ఆరంభించు **aarambhincu** *v.t.* to begin, start, commence.

ఆరకాగు **aarakaagu** *v.i. dial.* to be fully boiled.

ఆరగాకర **aaragaakara** *same as* **aDawikaakara.**

ఆరగించు **aaragincu** *v.t.* to eat, drink, consume.

ఆరగింపు **aaragimpu** *n.* 1 eating. 2 ceremonial offering of food to a deity in a temple at regular times each day.

ఆరడి **aaraDi** *n.* 1 scolding, reviling. 2 *pl.* **aaraLLu** torment.

ఆరడిపడు **aaraDipaDu** *v.i.* to be scolded, be tormented by scolding.

ఆరడిపెట్టు **aaraDipeTTu** *v.t.* to scold, revile, torment by scolding.

ఆరపెట్టు, ఆరవేయు **aarapeTTu, aaraweeyu** *v.t.* to put or spread (clothes) out to dry.

ఆరపోయు **aarapooyu** *v.t.* to put or spread (grain) out to dry.

ఆరముగ్గిన **aaramuggina** *adj.* 1 fully ripe. 2 overripe.

ఆరయు **aarayu** *same as* **arayu.**

ఆరా **aaraa**[1] (< **aaran**, *obsolete infinitive of* **aaru** to be full) *suffix added idiomatically to certain nouns to form adverbs conveying the sense* 'fully, completely', e.g., **kaLL ~ cuusEEDu / cewul ~ winnaaDu** he looked to his heart's content / he listened to his heart's content (*lit.* eye-fillingly / ear-fillingly *or* so as to fill his eyes / ears); **ii paaDu pani ceetul ~ ceesEEDu** he did this bad work with his own hands *or* he himself did this bad work.

ఆరా **aaraa**[2] *vocative pl. suffix* **mitrulaaraa**! friends!

ఆరా **aaraa**[3] *n.* 1 trace, whereabouts (of a person). 2 clue. 3 *pl.* **~ lu** details, particulars; **~ lu tiiyu** to make enquiries, ascertain details, question, investigate.

ఆరాటం **aaraaTam** *n.* 1 worry, anxiety, distress; **nii aaraaTaanni upasamimpa ceestundi** it will soothe your anxiety. 2 uncomfortable feeling, restlessness; **kaDupuloo ~ gaa undi** there is an uncomfortable feeling in my stomach.

ఆరాటపడు **aaraaTapaDu** *v.i.* 1 to be worried, troubled or disturbed; **antaraatma aaraaTapaDa saagindi** his conscience began to be troubled. 2 to long, yearn; **ii winuutna anubhuutikoosam mana hṛdayam ~ tunnadi** our heart is yearning for this new experience.

ఆరాధన **aaraadhana** *n.* 1 worship, adoration. 2 death anniversary of a person who in his lifetime renounced the world and entered **sanyaasam.**

ఆరాధించు **aaraadhincu** *v.t.* 1 to worship, adore, pray to. 2 to appreciate (beauty).

ఆరాధ్య **aaraadhya** *adj.* worthy to be worshipped.

ఆరాధ్యదైవం **aaraadhya daywam** *n.* deity to whom one is personally devoted.

ఆరాధ్యులు **aaraadhyulu** *n.pl.* 1 name of a group of Saivites. 2 name of a sub-community of brahmans.

ఆరామం **aaraamam** *n.* 1 grove, garden. 2 Buddhist monastery.

ఆరి ! **aari!** *interj. of surprise or alarm.*

ఆరిందా **aarindaa** *n.* expert.

ఆరిక, అరిక **aarika, arika** *n., gen. pl.* **~lu** a small-grained millet.

ఆరితేరు **aariteeru** *v.i.* to be accomplished, experienced, adept, expert, well versed (in).

ఆరు **aaru**[1] *n.* six.

ఆరు **aaru**[2] *n.* lower part of the stock of a wooden plough to which the iron share is fixed.

ఆరు **aaru**[3] *n.* line of hair on the abdomen extending upwards from the navel.

ఆరు **aaru**[4] *v.i. archaic* to be[come] full, increase; *mod. occurring as an intensifier in compounds,* e.g., **eep~** to grow sturdily.

ఆరు **aaru**[5] *v.i.* 1 to become dry, (of a wound) be healed; **aaraaragaa mandu raasukoowaali** you must rub on the medicine (repeatedly) as and when it dries up. 2 to go out, be put out, be extinguished (lamp, fire). 3 to become cool. 4 to be calmed, soothed, appeased, allayed, alleviated or assuaged.

ఆరుగురు **aaruguru** *n. pl.* six persons.

ఆరుద్రపురుగు **aarudra purugu** *n.* cochineal insect.

ఆరున్నొకటి **aarunnokaTi** *n.* seven (*circumlocution to avoid use of the word* **eeDu**).

ఆరుబయట **aarubayaTa** *adv.* in the open air.

ఆరుబైలు **aarubaylu** *adj.* outdoor, open; ~ **sthalam** an open place.

ఆరువేల[వారు] **aaruweela[waaru]** *n.* subsect of Niyogi brahmans.

ఆరూఢం **aaruuDham** *adj.* mounted, seated.

ఆరూమూడు అవు **aaruumuuDu awu** *v.i.* to fail, come to grief; **neenu weLLina pani aaruumuuDu ayindi** the work that I went for is in a hopeless state.

ఆరె **aare** [1] *n.* potter's wheel.

ఆరె[చెట్టు] **aare[ceTTu]**[2] *n.* species of bauhinia tree.

ఆరెకుడు **aarekuDu** *n.* watchman.

ఆరోగ్యం **aaroogyam** *n.* health, hygiene.

ఆరోగ్యకర **aaroogyakara** *adj.* 1 health giving, healthy, salubrious. 2 sanitary, hygienic.

ఆరోగ్యరక్షణ **aaroogyarakSaNa** *n.* sanitation.

ఆరోగ్యవంత **aaroogyawanta** *adj.* healthy.

ఆరోగ్యశాస్త్రం **aaroogyaśaastram** *n.* (science of) hygiene.

ఆరోపం **aaroopam** *n. ling.* entry, citation.

ఆరోపణ **aaroopaNa** *n.* 1 accusation, charge, allegation. 2 imputation, attribution (of any quality).

ఆరోపించు **aaroopincu** *v.t.* 1 to impute, allege. 2 to attribute, ascribe. 3 to accuse, charge.

ఆరోహణం **aaroohaNam** *n.* 1 climbing, mounting, ascent, ascension. 2 *music* ascending scale of notes.

ఆరోహి **aaroohi** *adj. ling.* ascending, rising.

ఆరోహించు **aaroohincu** *v.t.* 1 to ascend, climb. 2 to mount.

ఆర్చు **aarcu**[1] *v.t. transitive of* **aaru**[5] 1 to dry. 2 to put out, extinguish (lamp, fire). 3 to cool; **kaaphii [call]~ku taagEEDu** he drank the coffee after cooling it.

ఆర్చు **aarcu**[2] *v.t. causative of* **aaDu** to move, shake; **kanureppalu** ~ to blink o.'s eyes; **pakSi rekkalaarcindi** the bird flapped its wings.

ఆర్చు **aarcu**[3] *v.t. class., another form of* **aarayu** to investigate, *occurring mod. in the expression* **nuwwu aarcee waaDiwaa tiirceewaaDiwaa**? are you the right person to investigate or fulfil my needs? (spoken in anger or irritation).

ఆర్చుకుపోవు **aarcukupoowu** *v.i.* to dry up, wither, waste away; **nooru aarcukupootunnadi ceppiceppi** I am tired of repeating the same thing, *lit.* my mouth is getting dried up on account of saying and saying; **waaDiki taaguDu ekkuwayindi andukee aarcuku pootunnaaDu** he drinks too much, that is why his figure is wasting away.

ఆర్జన[ం] **aarjana[m]** *n.* 1 earnings. 2 acquisition.

ఆర్జించు **aarjincu** *v.t.* 1 acquire, gain, accumulate. 2 to earn; **aarjincani aadaayam** unearned income.

ఆర్త **aarta** *adj.* distressed, afflicted.

ఆర్తనాదం **aartanaadam** *n.* sound of wailing or lamenting.

ఆర్తవం **aartawam** I. *n. class.* menstrual discharge. II. *adj. class.* seasonal, vernal.

ఆర్తి **aarti** *n.* grief, sorrow, distress, misery; ~ **gaa aDugu** to ask plaintively.

ఆర్తుడు **aartuDu** *n.* distressed or afflicted person.

ఆర్థిక **aarthika** *adj.* 1 economic; ~ **maandyam** economic depression. 2 financial.

ఆర్థికవ్యవస్థ **aarthika wyawastha** *n.* economy, economic state or condition.

ఆర్థికశాఖ **aarthika śaakha** n. Finance Department.

ఆర్థికశాస్త్రం **aarthika śaastram** *n.* (science of) economics.

ఆర్థిక[శాస్త్ర]వేత్త **aarthika[śaastra]weetta** *n.* economist.

ఆర్థికసంవత్సరం **aarthika samwatsaram** *n.* financial year.

ఆర్థిక సహాయం **aarthika sahaayam** *n.* economic assistance, subsidy.

ఆర్ద్ర **aardra** *adj.* 1 wet, damp, moist, humid. 2 gentle, soft, kindly.

ఆర్ద్రత **aardrata** *n.* 1 dampness, moisture, humidity. 2 softness, kindness, gentleness.

ఆర్పు **aarpu**[1] *v.t.* to put out, extinguish (lamp, fire).

ఆర్పు **aarpu**[2] *v.t.* to move, shake; **reppalu aarpaka cuucu**; to stare without blinking.

ఆర్భాటం **aarbhaaTam** *n.* 1 loud noise, roar, hubbub, furore. 2 fuss, bustle, to do, much ado; **maagurinci eemii ~ waddu, iha roojuu wacceewaaLLameegaa!** don't make fuss over us, in future we will be coming daily, won't we? 3 empty talk, outward show, display; **aacaraNa suunyam, ~ ekkuwa** performance nil, but lots of outward show.

ఆర్య **aarya** *adj.* 1 Aryan. 2 noble.

ఆర్యా! **aaryaa!** *mode of address, formal, gen. used in writing* Sir!

ఆర్యావర్తం **aaryaawartam** *n.* home of the Aryans, an ancient name of North India.

ఆర్యులారా! **aaryulaaraa!** *mode of address, formal* Ladies and Gentlemen!

ఆర్యోక్తి **aaryookti** *n.* saying, proverb.

ఆర్ష **aarSa** *adj.* 1 relating to rishis (ascetics). 2 traditional.

ఆలంకారికుడు **aalankaarikuDu** *n.* person who practises the art of **alankaaram** or ornamental prose writing.

ఆలంబ[న]ం **aalamba[na]m** *n.* support, prop, basis.

ఆలకాపరి **aalakaapari** *n. class.* cowherd.

ఆలకించు **aalakincu** *v.t.* to listen to, pay attention to, heed.

ఆలగోడుబాలగోడు **aalagooDubaalagooDu** *n.* lamentation, clamour due to distress; *lit.* lowing of cattle and wailing of children.

ఆలనపాలన **aalanapaalana** *n.* care and attention.

ఆలపించు **aalapincu** *v.i. and t.* 1 *same as* **aalaapincu.** 2 to sing, recite, declaim.

ఆలమంద **aalamanda** *n.* herd of cattle.

ఆలయం **aalayam** *n.* 1 abode, dwelling. 2 temple.

ఆలవట్టం **aalawaTTam** *n.* umbrella or sunshade held over a deity or an important person in a procession.

ఆలవాలం **aalawaalam** *n.* 1 garden bed, basin for water formed round the foot of a tree. 2 source, breeding ground, nursery. 3 **awiniitiki~** den of corruption.

ఆలసించు **aalasincu** *v.i.* to delay.

ఆలస్యం **aalasyam** *n.* delay; **ceppaDamee ~** (*or* **ceppaDamee taDawugaa) parigettEEDu** he ran as soon as he was told; *see* **taDawu**¹ *sense 3.*

ఆలస్యంచేయు **aalasyam ceeyu** *v.i.* to delay, take a long time.

ఆలాగా **aalaagaa** I. *adv.* like that. II. *minor sentence* ~ ? is that so?

ఆలాపం **aalaapam** *n.* 1 prelude in music. 2 talk, conversation; **nii kaThina ~wini waaDu illu wadili weLLi pooyEEDu** hearing your harsh talk, he left the house and went away.

ఆలాపన **aalaapana** *n.* 1 *same as* **aalaapam.** 2 apprehension, imagination, fancy. 3 delirious talk.

ఆలాపనగా **aalaapanagaa** *adv.* 1 faintly, indistinctly; **pakka gadiloo ewaroo maaTLaaDutunnaaru. ~naaku maaTalu winipistunnaayi** some people are talking in the next room. I can their words indistinctly. 2 **~nidra paTTindi, ewaroo talupu taTTEEru** I was just falling asleep when s.o. knocked on the door.

ఆలాపించు, ఆలపించు **aalaapincu, aalapincu** *v.i.* to sound notes appropriate to a raga as a prelude to performing a vocal or instrumental musical piece.

ఆలి **aali** *irregular impersonal present indicative of* **walayu,** *used as an auxiliary vb. added to an infinitive* must, is necessary; **miiru cepp~** you must say: *cf.* **waali. walenu.**

ఆలింగనం **aalinganam** *n.* embrace.

ఆలించు **aalincu** *v.t.* to listen to, give ear to.

ఆలిచిప్ప, ఆల్చిప్ప **aalicippa, aalcippa** *n.* shellfish, mollusc.

ఆలు **aalu**¹ *n.* 1 woman. 2 wife; *class. except in compounds,* e.g., **illaalu** mistress of a house.

ఆలు **aalu**² *class pl. of* **aawu.**

ఆలుగడ్డ **aalugaDDa** *n.* potato.

ఆలె **aale** *variant form of* **aali.**

ఆలెపొయ్యి **aalepoyyi** *n.* long hearth for cooking several dishes at a time.

ఆలేఖనం **aaleekhanam** *n.* writing; **śil~** inscription on stone.

ఆలేప[న]ం **aaleepa[na]m** *n.* anointing, smearing.

ఆలోక[న]ం **aalooka[na]m** *n.* seeing, looking.

ఆలోకించు **aalookincu** *v.t.* to see, view, behold.

ఆలోచన **aaloocana** *n.* 1 thought, consideration, reflection. 2 advice.

ఆలోచించు **aaloocincu** *v.i. and t.* to think, consider, reflect, ponder, ruminate.

ఆలోన, ఆలోపల **aaloona, aaloopala** *adv.* within that time, in the mean time.

ఆల్చిప్ప **aalcippa** *same as* **aalicippa.**

ఆళి **aaLi** *n.* 1 *class.* row, range. 2 *mod. only as last part of a compound,* e.g., **windhy~** the Vindhya mountain range.

ఆళ్ళు **aaLLu** *n.pl.* a kind of millet.

ఆళ్వారు **aaLwaaru** *n. title given to each of the twelve chief Vaishnavite saints, e.g.,* **garuDaaLwaaru.**

ఆవ **aawa**¹ *n.* low marshy ground forming a large natural lake.

ఆవ **aawa**² *n.* mustard;**~ peTTi waNDina kuura** a vegetable cooked with mustard seasoning.

ఆవం **aawam** *n.* potter's kiln.

ఆవంత **aawanta** *adj.* very little, very small (*lit.* as small as a mustard seed);**~ wicaaram kuuDaa leedu Dabbu pooyindani** he was not in the least sorry at having lost his money.

ఆవకాయ **aawakaaya** *n.* kind of mango pickle made with with mustard powder in oil.

ఆవగింజ **aawaginja** *n.* 1 mustard seed. 2 tiny particle or quantity.

ఆవటిల్లు **aawaTillu** *v.i. class.* to happen, occur.

ఆవడ **aawaDa** *n.* kind of blackgram cake soaked in curds.

ఆవపచ్చడి **aawapaccaDi** *n.* chutney made of curds seasoned with mustard, gen. prepared on a death anniversary.

ఆవపిండి **aawapiNDi** *n.* mustard powder.

ఆవరణ **aawaraNa** *n.* enclosure, compound, precinct, premises.

ఆవరణశాస్త్రం **aawaraNaśaastram** *n.*(science of) ecology.

ఆవరించు **aawarincu** *v.t.* 1 to cover, surround, envelop, pervade. 2 (of sleep, emotion) to overcome, overwhelm.

ఆవర్జా **aawarjaa** *n.* ledger.

ఆవర్తం **aawartam** *n.* whirlpool, vortex, eddy.

ఆవర్తక, ఆవర్తి **aawartaka, aawarti** *adj.* 1 periodical. 2 recurring.

ఆవర్తత, ఆవర్తిత్వం **aawartata, aawartiwam** *n. phys.* periodicity.

ఆవర్తనం **aawartanam** *n.* 1 revolving, rotation. 2 repeating. 3 *phys.* oscillation.

ఆవర్ధనం **aawardhanam** *n.* magnification.

ఆవల, అవల **aawala, awala** *adv.* 1 beyond. 2 outside.

ఆవలకి **aawalaki** *same as* **awataliki.**

ఆవలి, అవలి **aawali,**¹ **awali** *adj.* further;**~ oDDu, ~ tiiram** the other/further bank or shore.

ఆవలి, ఆవళి **aawali**², **aawaLi** *n.* 1 row, line. 2 group, collection (of poems, stories, etc.)

ఆవలించు, ఆవులించు **aawalincu, aawulincu** *v.i.* to yawn, gape.

ఆవలింత, ఆవులింత **aawalinta, aawulinta** *n.* yawn[ing].

ఆవలిమొన్న **aawalimonna** *n.* the day before the day before yesterday.

ఆవలెల్లుండి, ఆవులెల్లుండి **aawalelluNDi, aawulelluNDi** *adv.* the day after the day after tomorrow.

ఆవశ్యక **aawaśyaka** *adj.* necessary, needful, requisite.

ఆవశ్యకం, ఆవశ్యకత **aawaśyakam, aawaśyakata** *n.* necessity, need.

ఆవహం **aawaham** *suffix denoting* bringing, producing or creating, e.g., **mudaawaham** (that) which brings happiness, **śubhaawaham** auspicious.

ఆవహించు **aawahincu** *v.t.* 1 (of emotional feelings) to overcome, overwhelm. 2 (of a spirit or demon) to possess.

ఆవహుడు **aawahuDu** *last part of a n. compound meaning* one who is possessed, e.g., **bhiit~** one who is possessed by fear.

ఆవాపం **aawaapam** *n.* 1 trough of water round the foot of a tree. 2 sowing, scattering (seed).

ఆవాపనం **aawaapanam** *n.* sowing, scattering (seed).

ఆవాలు **aawaalu** *n.pl.* mustard seed.

ఆవాసం **aawaasam** *n.* 1 habitation, house, abode. 2 *sci.* habitat.

ఆవాహన **aawaahana** *n.* 1 calling, inviting. 2 invocation to a deity by means of Vedic mantras to enter into an idol and receive worship.

ఆవి **aawi** *n.* 1 steam, vapour. 2 heat.

ఆవిడ, ఆవిడే **aawiDa, aawiDe** *pron.* she, that woman.

ఆవిరి **aawiri** *n.* steam, vapour; **inta pasupu weesukoni~ paTTu. jalubu taggutundi** mix a little turmeric powder in boiling water and inhale the vapour; your cold will get better.

ఆవిర్భవించు **aawirbhawincu** *v.i.* to be produced, come into being or existence, arise, originate.

ఆవిర్భవిల్లు **aawirbhawillu** *v.i.* to be produced or generated.

ఆవిర్భావం **aawirbhaawam** *n.* birth, appearance, manifestation.

ఆవిర్భూత **aawirbhuuta** *adj.* born, arisen, manifest.

ఆవిష్కరణ **aawiSkaraNa** *n.* 1 unconvering. 2 unfurling (flag). 3 unveiling (statue). 4 releasing (publication). 5 discovery.

ఆవిష్కరించు **aawiSkarincu** *v.t.* 1 to reveal. 2 to unfurl (flag). 3 to unveil (statue). 4 to release (publication). 5 to discover.

ఆవు **aawu** *n.* cow.

ఆవురావురుమని **aawuraawurumani** *adv.* very hungrily or thirstily, ravenously.

ఆవురుమను **aawurumanu** *v.i.* to weep, lament.

ఆవృత **aawṛta** *adj.* enclosed, surrounded, covered, overcast, beset; *often as second part of a compound*, e.g., **meegh~** overcast by clouds.

ఆవృత్తంగా **aawṛttangaa** *adv.* periodically.

ఆవృత్తి **aawṛtti** *n.* 1 return, recurrence, repetition. 2 learning by repeating many times. 3 time, occasion; **weedam padi aawṛttulu ceppukonnaaDu** he repeated the Veda ten times (in the process of learning it). 4 *phys.* frequency.

ఆవేగం **aaweegam** *n.* haste, hurry.

ఆవేదన **aaweedana** *n.* grief, sorrow, distress, anguish.

ఆవేళ **aaweeLa** *adv.* then, at that time.

ఆవేశం **aaweeśam** *n.* 1 emotion, passion. 2 excitement, agitation. 3 inspiration.

ఆవేశాత్మక **aaweeśaatmaka** *adj.* emotional.

ఆవేశించు **aaweeśincu** *v.i.* (of fear, evil spirits) to enter into, possess.

ఆవేశుడు **aaweeśuDu** *second part of a n. compound meaning* s.o. who is fully possessed by, e.g., **aagrah~** s.o. full of anger.

ఆశ, ఆస **aaśa, aasa** *n.* 1 desire, wish. 2 hope; **~lu peTTukonu** to nourish hopes. 3 greed, avarice.

ఆశంక **aaśanka** *n.* doubt, apprehension.

ఆశంస **aaśamsa** *n.* expectation.

ఆశగా **aaśagaa** *adv.* longingly, hopefully.

ఆశపడు **aaśapaDu** *v.i.* to covet, desire; **inkokari Dabbuki aaśapaDakuuDadu** you must not desire another person's wealth.

ఆశపాశాలు **aaśapaaśaalu** *n.pl.* expectations and attachments.

ఆశపెట్టు **aaśapeTTu** *v.t.* to tempt, raise (s.o.'s) hopes.

ఆశపోతు **aaśapootu** *n.* greedy person.

ఆశయం **aaśayam** *n.* 1 aim, object[ive], goal, purpose, intention. 2 desire. 3 ideal. 4. *as second part of a n. compound* container, receptacle, e.g., **jal~** reservoir, **muutr~** bladder.

ఆశయసాధన **aaśayasaadhana** *n.* practice of (o.'s) ideals, putting (o.'s) ideals into practice.

ఆశయసిద్ధి **aaśayasiddhi** *n.* attainment of (o.'s) objects.

ఆశాజనక **aaśaajanaka** *adj.* giving rise to hopes, encouraging.

ఆశాభంగం **aaśaabhangam** *n.* disappointment.

ఆశాభావం **aaśaabhaawam** *n.* hope.

ఆశావాదం **aaśaawaadam** *n.* optimism.

ఆశావాది **aaśaawaadi** *n.* optimist.

ఆశాహీన **aaśaahiina** *adj.* giving rise to despair, hopeless.

ఆశించు **aaśincu** *v.i. and t.* 1 to wish, desire, covet, long for. 2 to hope, expect.

ఆశీర్వచనం, ఆశీర్వాదం, ఆశీస్సు **aaśiirwacanam, aaśiirwaadam, aaśiissu** *n.* blessing, benediction.

ఆశీర్వదించు **aaśiirwadincu** *v.t.* to bless.

ఆశుకవిత్వం **aaśukawitwam** *n.* extempore or impromptu verse.

ఆశుధార **aaśudhaara** *n.* flow of spontaneous expression.

ఆశుధారగా **aaśudhaaragaa** *adv.* spontaneously, extempore.

ఆశువు **aaśuwu** *n.* extempore or impromptu verse; **annitikii ~gaa padyaalu ceppEEDu** tō all (the questions) he gave answers in extempore verse.

ఆశ్చర్యం **aaścaryam** I. *n.* surprise, wonder, astonishment, amazement. II. *interj.* how wonderful!

ఆశ్చర్యంగా **aaścaryangaa** *adv.* **~winnaaDu** he listened with astonishment or surprise.

ఆశ్చర్యజనక **aaścaryajanaka** *adj.* surprising, astonishing.

ఆశ్చర్యపడు, ఆశ్చర్యపోవు **aaścaryapaDu, aaścaryapoowu** *v.i.* to be surprised, astonished, amazed or astounded.

ఆశ్చర్యపరచు **aaścaryaparacu** *v.t.* to surprise, astonish, amaze, astound.

ఆశ్చర్యార్థకం **aaścaryaarthakam** *n. gram.* interjection, exclamation.

ఆశ్రమం **aaśramam** *n.* 1 ashram, place where monastic life is led, retreat or abode of ascetics. 2 one of the four periods into which a man's life is traditionally divided, namely, **brahmacaryam, gaarhastyam, waanaprastham** and **sanyaasam.**

ఆశ్రమపాఠశాల **aaśrama paaThaśaala** *n.* school where traditional learning is imparted.

ఆశ్రయం **aaśrayam** *n.* 1 refuge, asylum, retreat. 2 place, abode. 3 support, protection, patronage; **naaku~ iccEEDu** he gave me protection. 4 dependence.

ఆశ్రయించు **aaśrayincu** *v.t.* 1 to depend on, rely on, be dependent on: **nannu ~ koni batikeewaaLLu naluguru unnaaru** four persons are dependent on me. 2 to take advantage of, make use of, have recourse to, fall back on. 3 to approach, pay court to; **unnataadhikaarula darśanam ceesukoowaalaNTee endarnoo aaśrayinci ennennoo tippalu paDaali** to gain access to the highest authorities you have to approach ever so many persons and encounter ever so many difficulties.

ఆశ్రిత **aaśrita** *adj.* dependent.

ఆశ్రితపక్షపాతం **aaśritapakSapaatam** *n.* favouritism.

ఆశ్రితుడు **aaśrituDu** *n.* dependant, protégé.

ఆశ్లేష **aaśleeSa** *n. astrol.* ninth lunar mansion.

ఆశ్లేషం **aaśleeSam** *n.* embrace; **gaaDha ~** tight embrace, hug.

ఆశ్లేషించు **aaśleeSincu** *v.t.* to embrace.

ఆశ్వయుజం, ఆశ్వీయుజం **aaśwayujam, aaświiyujam** *n.* seventh lunar month.

ఆశ్వాసం **aaśwaasam** *n.* 1 chapter or canto in a book. 2 consolation.

ఆశ్వాసించు **aaśwaasincu** *v.t.* to console, comfort.

ఆశ్విక **aaświka** *adj.* equestrian.

ఆశ్వికదళం **aaświkadaLam** *n.* cavalry.

ఆశ్వికుడు **aaświkuDu** *n.* horseman, rider, cavalry man.

ఆషాఢం **aaSaaDham** *n.* fourth lunar month.

ఆషాఢపట్టి **aaSaaDhapaTTi** *n.* gifts sent by parents-in-law to their son-in-law in the month of Ashadam following his marriage.

ఆషాఢభూతి **aaSaaDhabhuuti** *n.* cheat, deceiver, swindler, crook.

ఆషామాషీ **aaSaamaaSii** *adj.* 1 informal, casual. 2 inconsequential, trivial; **~ kaburlu** empty or idle talk.

ఆస **aasa** *same as* **aaśa.**

ఆసకొను **aasakonu** *v.i.* to hope, have expectations.

ఆసకొలుపు **aasakolupu** *v.i.* to create hopes or expectations.

ఆసక్త **aasakta** *adj. second half of a compound* inclined for, devoted to, e.g., **nidr ~** inclined for sleep.

ఆసక్తి **aasakti** *n.* 1 interest. 2 keenness, eagerness; **caduwumiida ~** keenness on study. 3 desire, inclination.

ఆసక్తికర, ఆసక్తిదాయక **aasaktikara, aasaktidaayaka** *adj.* interesting.

ఆసక్తిగల **aasaktigala** *adj.* interested, having an interest.

ఆసత్తి **aasatti** *n. ling.* juxtaposition.

ఆసనం **aasanam** *n.* 1 seat, sitting. 2 mode of sitting, posture. 3 rump.

ఆసనాస్థి **aasanaasthi** *n. med.* ischium.

ఆసన్న **aasanna** *adj.* 1 near at hand, approaching, imminent; **~ mrtyuwu** the hour of approaching death. 2 *maths.* approximate.

ఆసరా **aasaraa** *n.* 1 help, support; **waaLLaki payki raawaDaaniki maroo ~ uNDaali** they need some other support in order to rise. 2 assurance: **R. kukkawaypu bedurutoo cuusindi. adeemii ceyyadani aameki ~ iccEEDu R.** looked fearfully towards the dog but he assured her that it would do nothing.

ఆసరాచేసుకొను **aasaraa ceesukonu** *v.t.* to take advantage of, make use of, rely on.

ఆసాంతంగా **aasaantangaa** *adv.* from beginning to end, totally, entirely.

ఆసాది **aasaadi** *n.* 1 cobbler, shoemaker. 2 priest who serves a village deity.

ఆసామి **aasaami** *n.* 1 individual. 2 landowner, wealthy person.

ఆసియా **aasiyaa** *n.* Asia.

ఆసీనుడవు **aasiinuDawu** *v.i.* to be seated.

ఆసీనుడు **aasiinuDu** *n.* person who is seated.

ఆసు **aasu** *n.* 1 ace (in cards). 2 framework of sticks used by weavers for preparing the warp for a loom.

ఆసుపోయు **aasupooyu** *v.i.* 1 (of a weaver) to wind thread on a framework (which involves running back and forth). 2 to go back and forth: **pooyina wastuwula koosam pooliisu sTeeSanki iNTiki aasupoostunnaaDu** he has been going back and forth between his house and the police station to recover his stolen property.

ఆసురం **aasuram** I. *n.* one of the eight traditional forms of marriage, in which the bridegroom purchases the bride. II. *adj.* belonging or pertaining to Asuras or Rakshasas or demons.

ఆసురి **aasuri** *same as* **asuri.**

ఆసురుడు **aasuruDu** *same as* **asura.**

ఆసేకం **aaseekam** *n.* sprinkling, wetting.

ఆసేతుహిమాచలం **aaseetuhimaacalam** *n.* the whole of India (*lit.* the country stretching from Adam's Bridge to the Himalayas).

ఆస్కారం **aaskaaram** *n.* 1 scope, basis. 2 *in neg. constr.* possibility, opportunity, chance; **maa iNTLoo digaDaaniki eemaatram ~ leedu** there is absolutely no possibility (for them) to stay in our house.

ఆస్తి **aasti** *n.* 1 property, wealth. 2 *pl.* **aastulu** assets.

ఆస్తికుడు **aastikuDu** *n.* one who believes in the existence of God.

ఆస్తిపరుడు **aastiparuDu** *n.* man of property.

ఆస్తిపాస్తులు **aastipaastulu** *n.pl.* property and possessions; **baagaa aastipaastulunnawaaDu** wealthy man.

ఆస్థ **aastha** *n.* desire, inclination.

ఆస్థానం **aasthaanam** *n.* court of a king.

ఆస్థానకవి **aasthaanakawi** *n.* poet laureate.

ఆస్థానికుడు **aasthaanikuDu** *n.* courtier.

ఆస్పత్రి **aaspatri** *n.* hospital.

ఆస్పద **aaspada** *last part of an adjvl. compound meaning* giving room, support, ground or basis, e.g., **anumaan** ~ giving ground for suspicion, suspicious; **haasy** ~ ridiculous.

ఆస్పదం **aaspadam** *n.* 1 place, room, situation. 2 ground for a supposition, basis.

ఆస్యం **aasyam** *n.* 1 face. 2 mouth.

ఆస్యకుహరం **aasyakuharam** *n. ling.* oral cavity.

ఆస్వాదించు **aaswaadincu** *v.t.* to taste, experience, enjoy.

ఆస్వాద్య **aaswaadya** *adj.* delightful.

ఆహరించు **aaharincu** *v.t.* steal, rob, snatch away.

ఆహవం **aahawam** *n.* 1 war, fighting. 2 Vedic sacrifice.

ఆహారం **aahaaram** *n.* food, nourishment.

ఆహారధాన్యాలు **aahaaradhaanyaalu** *n.pl.* food grains.

ఆహారనాళం **aahaaranaaLam** *n. med.* alimentary canal.

ఆహారపదార్థం **aahaarapadaartham** *n.* foodstuff.

ఆహార్యం **aahaaryam** *n. theat.* dress and make up worn by an actor or actress suiting the character that he or she represents.

ఆహితాగ్ని **aahitaagni** *n.* orthodox person who maintains a sacred fire in his home and performs daily Vedic rites.

ఆహుతి **aahuti** *n.* 1 offering, oblation, sacrifice. 2 victim; **aakali caawuku aahutulu ayyEEru** they became victims of (*or* they fell a prey to) death from hunger.

ఆహూతుడు **aahuutuDu** *n.* 1 invited visitor, guest. 2 *pl.* **aahuutulu** guests, persons who assemble, spectators.

ఆహ్లాద **aahlaada** *adj.* beautiful, appealing, pleasant.

ఆహ్లాదం **aahlaadam** *n.* delight, joy, pleasure.

ఆహ్లాదకర **aahlaadakara** *adj.* delightful, enjoyable.

ఆహ్వానం **aahwaanam** *n.* invitation.

ఆహ్వానించు **aahwaanincu** *v.t.* 1 to invite. 2 to greet, welcome.

ఆహ్వానితుడు **aahwaanituDu** *n.* invitee.

ఇ - i

ఇంక, ఇక, ఇహ **inka, ika, iha** *particle* 1 now, next; ~ **miiru weLLaNDi** now you must go; ~ **telugu maaTalanu gurinci wraastaanu** next I will write about Telugu words; ~ **caalu** that's enough! *or* no more!; **aayana ceppina katha winnaam gadaa,** ~ **neenu cebataanu** we have heard his story, now I will speak. 2 in future, hereafter, henceforth; ~ **nuwwu abaddham ceppawaddu** hereafter you must not tell a lie.

ఇంకా **inkaa** *particle* more, some more, even more, yet, still; ~ **kondaru** some more persons; ~ **pedda kuTumbam** an even bigger family; ~ **wastunnaaru** they are still coming; ~ **raaleedu** they have not come yet; ~ **caduwu, telustundi** read some more (*or* read further) and you will understand; **talanoppi** ~ **perigindi** the headache increased still more; *note: before an* **e-** *question word the final* **-aa** *of* ~ *is dropped*, e.g., ~ + **ewaru** 〉 **inkewaru** who else? ~ + **ekkaDa** 〉 **inkekkaDa** where else? *so also* ~ + **oka** 〉 **inkoka** one more, another; *see* **ika.**

ఇంకు **inku** *v.i.* (of water, etc.) to sink, dry up, evaporate, be absorbed.

ఇంకొక, ఇంకో **inkoka, inkoo** *adj.* another (additional) *or* another (different); **inkoka maaTa, inkoo maaTa** another (one more) word *or* a different word; **inkoka maniSi, inkoo maniSi** another (one more) person *or* a different person.

ఇంగ **inga** *dial. variant form of* **inka.**

ఇంగం **ingam** *n. class.* hint or indication of sentiment by gesture.

ఇంగలం **ingalam** *n. dial.* fire.

ఇంగితం **ingitam** *n.* 1 mood, inclination, disposition, hint or gesture indicating feelings; **sabha antaa kalayacuusi andari** ~ **gurtincEEDu** he looked around the whole meeting and observed the mood of all the people. 2 intention, purpose; **miiru ii wiSayam naaku ceppaDamloo mii** ~ **arthamayindi** I have understood your intention in telling me this. 3 good sense, intelligence; **aaruguru biDDala talliki aamaatram** ~ **leekuNDaa eTTaa pooyindoo?** how could a mother of six children have such little sense?

ఇంగితజ్ఞానం **ingitajñaanam** *n.* 1 keenness of intellect, shrewdness, common sense. 2 intuition, perspicacity.

ఇంగితజ్ఞుడు **ingitajñuDu** *n.* person skilled in reading the moods or intentions of others.

ఇంగిలికం, ఇంగిలీకం **ingilikam, ingiliikam** *n.* vermilion, cinnabar.

ఇంగుది **ingudi** *n. class.* name of a certain fruit mentioned in ancient literature.

ఇంగువ **inguwa** *n.* asafoetida.

ఇంచు **incu** *suffix for forming* (i) *causative verbs*, e.g., **ceeyincu** to cause s.o. to do s.g, cause s.g to be done, (ii) *verbs from nouns of Sanskrit origin*, e.g., **santooSincu** < **santooSam** to rejoice, **puSpincu** < **puSpam** to flower, (iii) *verbs from certain Telugu nouns*, e.g., **lekkincu** < **lekka** to count, **maLLincu** < **maLLu** to turn, (iv) *verbs from roots of Hindi-Urdu origin*, e.g., **badalaayincu** < **badlaanaa** to transfer.

ఇంచుక **incuka** *adj. and adv., obs.* a little; ~ **oopika paTTu** have a little patience.

ఇంచుమించు[గా] **incumincu[gaa]** *adv.* approximately, about, more or less.

ఇంట **iNTa**[1] *suffix meaning* out of *added to numerals in order to form fractions*, e.g., **muuD~ reNDu wantulu** *or* **muuD~ reNDu bhaagaalu** two out of three, two thirds.

ఇంట **iNTa**[2] *obs. locative case of* **illu.**

ఇంటరం **iNTaram** *same as* **iNTram.**

ఇంటాయన, ఇంటి ఆయన **iNTaayana, iNTi aayana** *n.* 1 house owner, landlord. 2 **maa/mii~** my/your husband *or* my/your landlord.

ఇంటావంటా **iNTaawaNTaa** *adv., in neg. constr., lit.* in (o.'s) house and in (o.'s) tradition; **ii alawaaTu maa~ leedu** this practice has never been customary in my family.

ఇంటావిడ, ఇంటి ఆవిడ **iNTaawiDa, iNTi aawiDa** *n.* 1 mistress of a house. 2 **maa/mii~** my/your wife.

ఇంటి **iNTi**[1] (*also* **iTi**) *suffix forming oblique stems of numerals; if added to a human noun, only* **iNTi** *is used*, e.g., **aydiNTiwaraku** *or* **aydiTiwaraku nidra pootaaDu** he sleeps till 5 o'clock; **maniSi okiNTiki padi ruupaayalu iccEEnu** I gave ten rupees to each of them.

ఇంటి **iNTi**[2] *genitive of* **illu.**

ఇంటికప్పు **iNTikappu** *n.* roof.

ఇంటికాపు **iNTikaapu** *n. obs.* householder, head of a family.

ఇంటిపాప **iNTipaapa** *n. dial.* servant maid in a house.

ఇంటిపేరు **iNTipeeru** *n.* family name, surname; *in Telugu names the* **iNTipeeru** *comes first, then the given name, then, if there is one, a name suffix, as in* Gurajada Appa Rao *or* Kandukuuri Viresalingam Pantulu.

ఇంటిల్లిపాది **iNTillipaadi** *n.* all the family, the entire household.

ఇంట్రం, ఇంటరం **iNTram, iNTaram** *n. class.* difficulty.

ఇంట్రపడు **iNTrapaDu** *v.i. class.* to be in difficulty or trouble.

ఇండె **iNDe** *n. class.* crack, split.

ఇంత **inta** *det.n.and adj.* this much; **~pedda** so great (as this); **~poDugu** so long /tall (as this); **~raatriweeLa** so late at night; **~annam tini weLLu** eat this much (i.e., just a little) rice before you go; **~caalaa?** is this enough?

ఇంతంత, ఇంతా అంతా **intanta, intaa antaa** *det.n. and adj.* 1 *lit.* this much. 2 just so much. 3 *in neg. constr.* not just a moderate amount, very great; **ataDu intantaTiwaaDu kaaDu** he is not just an ordinary person; **waaDi koopam intaa antaa kaadu** his anger is terrible.

ఇంతకీ, ఇంతకూ **intakii, intakuu** *advbl. particle.* 1 (*turning to a new subject or returning to a former train of thought*) well then, well now, after all. 2 but, yet, still, nevertheless. 3 besides, moreover, in addition. 4 in substance, in essence.

ఇంతకుముందు, ఇంతకుపూర్వం **intakumundu, intakupuurwam** *adv.* before this, previously (in the recent or distant past).

ఇంతక్రితం **intakritam** *adv.* before this, previously (in the recent past).

ఇంతగా **intagaa** *adv.* so much, to this extent.

ఇంతట **intaTa** *adv.* at this stage, at this point, thus far; **~mugincu** stop at this stage.

ఇంతటి **intaTi** 1 *oblique form of* **inta.** 2 *dial. and literary variant of* **inta; ii maaTalaloo~ abhiwyakti undi** there is such great expressiveness in these words.

ఇంతటిలో, ఇంతట్లో, ఇంతలో **intaTiloo, intaTLoo, intaloo** *adv.* 1 just now, right now; **kaani intaTLoo siitayya gurinci cebutaanani miiranukoNTee, caalaa porapaaTu paDDawaaLLawtaaru** but if you think I am going to tell you about Sitayya just now, you are much mistaken. 2 meanwhile, in the mean time; **nuwwu leekapootee naa gati eemaypootundoo anukoneedaanni. intaTLoo haThaattugaa weLLipooyEEwu** I was pondering what my fate would be without you; in the mean time you suddenly departed.

ఇంతదాకా **intadaakaa** *adv.* 1 till now, up to this (time). 2 thus far, upto this (place).

ఇంతమాత్రం **intamaatram** *det.n. and adj.* only this much.

ఇంతలు **intalu** *n.suffix meaning* times *attached to numerals*; **waaDu naa kaNTe muuD~ baruwu** he is 3 times as heavy as I am; *cf.* **antalu.**

ఇంతలేసి **intaleesi** *adj.* so big, so great; *used with reference to parts of the human body or acts of human beings in a limited number of phrases*, e.g., **~kaLLu** such beautiful large eyes; **~juTTu** such beautiful long hair; **~panulu** such great deeds *or* such wicked deeds.

ఇంతవట్టు **intawaTTu** I. *det.n. and adj., dial.* all this, so much. II *adv.* upto this, upto now, thus far, to this extent.

ఇంతవరకు, ఇంతవరదాకా **intawaraku, intawaradaakaa** *adv.* upto this point, till now.

ఇంతి **inti** *n.* woman.

ఇంతింత **intinta** *adj., used only with pl. nouns* of this size.

ఇంతే **intee** I. *det. n.* only this much, just so much; **~kaaka** not only this; **~kaakuNDaa** moreover, in addition. II. *minor sentence* quite so, just so, exactly, precisely; **~sangatulu** that's all the news.

ఇంతోటి **intooTi** *adj., colloq.* so great (*gen. with a sarcastic implication*): **daani paryawasaanam eemaNTee, aa~ baawagaaru aame peTTina SaratulanniTikii talawancEEDu** the upshot was that her brother-in-law, great as he was, submitted to all her conditions.

ఇంద! **inda!** *minor sentence* take this!, here it is!

ఇందందు **indandu** *adv. class.* here and there.

ఇందరు **indaru** *det.n.pl.* so many persons, this number of persons.

ఇందలి **indali** *adj.* of this, in this; **~paatralu** characters in it (a play).

ఇందాక **indaaka** *adv.* just recently, a little time ago, a short while ago.

ఇందాకటి **indaakaTi** *adj.* previous, preceding.

ఇందాకటినుంచి **indaakaTinunci** *adv.* for some time past, all this time.

ఇందాకటిలా[గే], ఇందాట్లా[గే] **indaakaTilaa[gee], indaaTLaa[gee]** *adv.* as before; **raambaabu atani waypu indaaTLaagee inkaa cuustuu uNDipooyEEDu** Rambabu continued looking in his direction exactly as before.

ఇందాకా **indaakaa** *adv.* upto this time, till now, hitherto.

ఇందిర **indira** *n.* a name of the Goddess Lakshmi.

ఇందిరం, ఇందీవరం **indiram, indiiwaram** *n.* blue lotus.

ఇందు **indu**[1] *n. class.* moon.

ఇందు **indu**[2] *defective pron. occurring bound to certain case endings and postpositions,* e.g., ~ **ku** for this; ~ **ku gaanu** for this reason or purpose; ~ **miidaTa** hereupon; ~ **loo** in this; ~ **induwalla** by means of this.

ఇందుగోపం **indugoopam** *n.* cochineal insect, a kind of bright red mite.

ఇంద్రజాలం **indrajaalam** *n.* conjuring, magic.

ఇంద్రజిత్తు **indrajittu** *n.* name of the son of Ravana in the Ramayana, noted for his magical powers.

ఇంద్రధనస్సు **indradhanassu** *n.* rainbow.

ఇంద్రనీల **indraniila** *n.* sapphire.

ఇంద్రలోకం **indralookam** *n.* abode of the God Indra.

ఇంద్రియం **indriyam** *n.* **1** organ of sense or action. **2** semen.

ఇంద్రియజ్ఞానం **indriyajñaanam** *n.* perceiving, perception.

ఇంద్రియలోలత్వం **indriyaloolatwam** *n.* devotion to sexual pleasure, womanising (colloq.)

ఇంద్రుడు **indruDu** *n.* **1** Indra, lord of Gods. **2** *second part of a n. compound meaning* finest, greatest, e.g., **raajendruDu** king of kings, **nareendruDu** king of men, **mṛgendra** king of the beasts, lion.

ఇంధనం **indhanam** *n.* fuel.

ఇంధనవాయువు **indhana waayuwu** *n.* fuel gas.

ఇంపారు **impaaru** *v.i.* to be pleasant or agreeable.

ఇంపు **impu** I. *n.* **1** pleasingness, pleasantness, agreeableness, beauty. **2** pleasure, satisfaction. **3**. fondness, liking. II. *adj.* sweet, attractive, pleasant.

ఇంపొలయు **impolayu** *v.i. class.* to be pleasing or agreeable.

ఇక, ఇహ **ika, iha** *particle* **1** ~ *can alternate freely with* **inka** *in all situations.* **2** ~ *can alternate with* **inkaa** *only in situations where the final* **-aa** *of* **inkaa** *is dropped before an* **e-** *question word,* e.g., **inkewaru** or **ikewaru** who else? **inkekkaDa** or **ikekkaDa** where else?

ఇకమీదట, ఇహమీదట, ఇకముందు, ఇహముందు **ikamiidaTa, ihamiidaTa, ikamundu, ihamundu** *adv.* in future, henceforth, hereafter.

ఇక్కం **ikkam** *n.* narrow place.

ఇక్కట్టు **ikkaTTu** *n., gen.pl.* **ikkaTLu** difficulty, trouble, hardship.

ఇక్కడ **ikkaDa** I. *n.* this place. II. *adv.* here.

ఇక్కడక్కడపడు **ikkaDakkaDapaDu** *v.i.* to be[come] perplexed.

ఇక్కడిక్కడ **ikkaDikkaDa** *adv.* around here, hereabouts.

ఇక్కుపాటు **ikkupaaTu** *n. class.* difficulty.

ఇక్కువ **ikkuwa** *n. class.* **1** place. **2** existence, being alive.

ఇక్షుధన్వుడు **ikSudhanwuDu** *n.* Cupid, God of Love (whose bow is made of sugarcane).

ఇక్షువు **ikSuwu** *n. class.* sugarcane.

ఇక్ష్వాకులు **ikSwaakulu** *n.pl.* name of a mythological dynasty, ancestors of Sri Rama, founded by king Ikshavaku; **ikSwaakula baarasaalanaaDu** *lit.* the naming ceremony of the Ikshavakus, *hence colloq.* long, long ago.

ఇగ **iga** *dial. variant of* **inka.**

ఇగం **igam** *n.* biting cold, frost; **niiLLu igaallaa unnaayi** the water is freezing cold.

ఇగిరించు, ఇగురుకొను, ఇగురొత్తు **igirincu**[1], **igurukonu, igurottu** *v.i.* to sprout, produce buds.

ఇగిరించు **igirincu**[2] *same as* **igurcu.**

ఇగిలించు **igilincu** *v.i.* to grin, show o.'s teeth.

ఇగిలింత, ఇగిలింపు **igilinta, igilimpu** *n.* grin.

ఇగురు **iguru**[1] *n.* gum (surrounding teeth).

ఇగురు **iguru**[2] *n.* sprout, shoot, young red-coloured leaf.

ఇగురు **iguru**[3] *v.i.* **1** (of water) to dry up, evaporate, boil away. **2** (of food being cooked) to boil until the moisture has evaporated. **3** to fade away, disappear, perish.

ఇగురు **iguru**[4] (*also* ~ **kuura**) *n.* vegetable curry prepared without tamarind juice.

ఇగురుకూర **igurukuura** *n.* curry cooked by slow boiling until the moisture has evaporated.

ఇగురుకొను, ఇగురొత్తు **igurukonu, igurottu** *same as* **igirincu**[1].

ఇగురుబోడి **iguruhooDi** *n.* woman.

ఇగుర్చు, ఇగిరించు **igurcu, igirincu** *v.t.* to cause (s.g) to dry up.

ఇగో **igoo** *alt. dial.* form of **idigoo.**

ఇగ్గులాట **iggulaaTa** *n.* jerking, struggling, dragging, pulling backwards.

ఇగ్గులాడు **iggulaaDu** *v.i. and t.* to pull, drag, jerk, struggle, resist by pulling backwards.

ఇచ్చకం **iccakam** *n., gen.pl.* **iccakaalu** **1** cajolery, flattery, wheedling. **2** pampering.

ఇచ్చకాలమారి **iccakaalamaari** *n.* one who flatters in order to persuade.

ఇచ్చగించు **iccagincu** *v.t.* to wish for, desire, like, fancy.

ఇచ్చగొండి **iccagoNDi** *n.* flatterer.

ఇచ్చరూపాయి, ఇచ్చురూపాయి, విచ్చరూపాయి, విచ్చురూపాయి **iccaruupaayi, iccuruupaayi, wiccaruupaayi, wiccuruupaayi** *n.* rupee coin.

ఇచ్చిపుచ్చుకోలు **iccipuccukoolu** *n.* **1** *lit.* giving and taking. **2** (*also* **iipooti**) (i) giving and taking brides and grooms in marriage; (ii) intermarrying between communities or groups; **śaakha bheedamwalla iccipuccukooLLu uNDeewi kaawu aa roojulloo in those days they would** not intermarry, due to belonging to different sects. **3** negotiations for a marriage. **4** custom of marrying a boy and a girl from one family to a girl and a boy from another. **5** negotiations for a bribe.

ఇచ్చు **iccu** *v.t.* **1** to give, grant, confer, bestow. **2** *with vb. in infinitive* to allow, let, permit; **nannu raaniwwaNDi** let me come, please. **3** to lend; **ii pustakam naaku nelaroojulapaaTu istaaraa**? will you lend me this book for a month? **4 pariikSa** ~ to appear (*or* sit) for an examination.

ఇచ్ఛ **iccha** *n.* inclination, propensity, love, liking, desire, wish, will.

ఇచ్ఛాపూర్వకంగా **icchaapuurwakangaa** *adv.* wholeheartedly, willingly.

ఇచ్ఛార్థకం **icchaarthakam** *n. gram.* optative.

ఇజం **ijam** *n. Eng.* -ism.

ఇజారా **ijaaraa** *n. obs.* farming or renting the right to collect taxes or the proceeds of a monopoly.

ఇజారాదారు **ijaaraadaaru** *n. obs.* farmer (of taxes), renter, contractor.

ఇజారు **ijaaru** *n.* trousers.

ఇజ్జతు **ijjatu** *n. dial.* prestige, status.

ఇటి **iTi** *see* **iNTi**[1].

ఇటిక, ఇటికె **iTika, iTike** *n.* brick.

ఇటీవల **iTiiwala** *adv.* recently, in the recent past.

ఇటీవలి **iTiiwali** *adj.* recent.

ఇటు **iTu** *adv.* thus, this way (manner or direction).

ఇటు అటూ **iTu aTuu** *adv.* this way and that; **gadiloo~ tirigEEDu** he paced back and forth (*or* to and fro) in the room; **paristhiti ~ gaa undi** the situation is in an uncertain state (*or* in a fluid state).

ఇటునుంచి **iTununci** *adv.* from this side.

ఇటుపక్క **iTupakka** *adv.* on this side.

ఇటుపైన **iTupayna** *adv.* 1 above this. 2 beyond this. 3 hereafter henceforth, henceforward.

ఇటువంటి **iTuwaNTi** *adj.* this kind of, such.

ఇటువలె **iTuwale** *adv.* similarly.

ఇట్టట్టు **iTTaTTu** *adv.* this way and that; **praaNam~ ayndi** his life hung in the balance *or* he was hovering between life and death.

ఇట్టలం **iTTalam** *adj. class.* great, abundant.

ఇట్టా [గా/గు], ఇట్లా [గా/గు], ఇలా [గా/గు], ఇల్లా [గా/గు] **iTTaa[gaa/gu], iTLaa[gaa/gu], ilaa[gaa/gu], illaa[gaa/gu]** *adv.* 1 like this, thus; **ilaa ceeyaNDi** do it like this. 2 in this direction; **ilaa raNDi** come this way, come over here.

ఇట్టి **iTTi** *adj.* this kind of, such.

ఇట్టియెడ [ల] **iTTiyeDa[la]** *adv.* in this case.

ఇట్టే **iTTee** *adv.* 1 just so, just like this. 2 at once. 3 quite, very; **~ suluwugaa** quite easily, very easily.

ఇట్లాంటి, ఇట్లాటి, ఇలాంటి, ఇలాటి **iTLaaNTi, iTLaaTi, ilaaNTi, ilaaTi** *adj.* this kind of, such.

ఇట్లు **iTLu** *advbl. particle, used as a formal way of ending a letter, equivalent to* yours *or* I remain.

ఇడు **iDu** *v.t.* to put, make, give; *this verb occurs only after certain nouns,* e.g., **aDug ~** to set foot; **modal~** to begin; **peer~** to give a name, **taakaTT ~** to mortgage, pawn.

ఇడుగడ **iDugaDa** *n. class.* envy.

ఇడుగు **iDugu** *v.i.* (of new earthenware pots) to burst as soon as used due to faulty firing; *cf.* **wiccu** *sense II. 5.*

ఇడుము **iDumu** *n., gen. pl.* **~ lu** misfortune, calamity.

ఇడుముడిపాటు **iDumuDipaaTu** *n.* suffering.

ఇడ్లీ, ఇడ్డెన **iDLii, iDDena** *n.* rice cake cooked by steaming.

ఇతఃపరం **itaḥparam** *n.* other than this.

ఇతఃపూర్వ **itaḥpuurwa** *adj.* previous.

ఇతఃపూర్వం **itaḥpuurwam** *adv.* previously.

ఇతడు, ఇతను **itaDu, itanu** *pron.* he, this man.

ఇతర **itara** I. *adjvl. suffix signifying negative or opposite,* e.g., **prabhutwa + ~ 〉 prabhutweetara** non-governmental, **wyawasaaya + ~ 〉 wyawasaayeetara** non-agricultural; *on this analogy* **eetara**, *not~, is suffixed to certain stems not ending in* **-a**, *to form compounds like* **kaangreseetara** non-Congress. II. *adj.* 1 other, different. 2 additional.

ఇతరం **itaram** *n.* 1 another thing, s.g else; **nyaayangaa waccee jiitapu raaLLu tappa itaraaniki aaśapaDa leedu** he desired nothing other than the salary which he earned honestly; **ataniki ii pani tappa~ teliyadu** apart from this work, he does not know anything. 2 *pl.* **itaraalu** other items *or* miscellaneous items (often cited at the end of a list of specified items).

ఇతరత్రా **itaratraa** I. *adv.* in other places, elsewhere; **dwitiiya wibhakti pratyayam 'ni/nu', ikaaraanta padaala tarawaata 'ni',~ 'nu'** the accusative case suffix is **'ni/nu'**, after words ending in **'i'** it is **'ni'**, elsewhere **'nu'**. 2 in other respects or ways. II. *adj.* other kinds of, various, miscellaneous.

ఇతరేతర **itareetara** *adj.* 1 reciprocal, mutual. 2 irrelevant, extraneous; **~ śaktulu leestee, paDipooyenu peekameeDalay** when extraneous powers rose up, they collapsed like card houses.

ఇతవరి, హితవరి **itawari, hitawari** *n.* person who gives wholesome advice, adviser, counsellor, wellwisher.

ఇతవు **itawu** *n.* 1 advantage, benefit. 2 good counsel.

ఇతివృత్తం **itiwrttam** *n.* subject matter, plot (of a story).

ఇతిహాసం **itihaasam** *n.* 1 history. 2 heroic tradition as recounted in the Hindu epics.

ఇతోధిక **itoodhika** *adj.* more than at present, greater than at present.

ఇతోధికంగా **itoodhikangaa** *adv.* 1 more abundantly. 2 to a great extent.

ఇత్తడి **ittaDi** *n.* brass.

ఇత్యాది **ityaadi** *particle* et cetera, and other things, beginning with this.

ఇదమిత్థం **idamittham** *adj.* exact, precise, definite.

ఇదమిత్థంగా, ఇదమిత్థమని **idamitthangaa, idamitthamani** *adv.* clearly, exactly, precisely.

ఇది **idi** *pron.* 1 she, this woman (*note: this usage is impolite*). 2 it, this thing; *see* **idee.** 3 **~** *is used colloquially whenever the speaker is at loss for a suitable n. or adj.*; **aayana aNTee naaku caalaa~** I have much respect for him (here~ = **gawrawam**). 4 *colloquially* **~** *may refer to an uncertain, inexplicable or perturbed situation, feeling, etc.*; **naakadoo ~ gaa undi** I feel unaccountably uneasy; **nuwwemii idawaku raa!** don't be at all disturbed!; **weLLaniwwaleedani C. gaaDiki entoo ~ gaa uNDaali** poor C. must feel very put out at not being allowed to go; **elaagayinaa wiiDi**

pani paTTincaalani R.-ki caalaa ~ gaa undi R. is very particular about somehow getting his own back on this man: **miiru mari inta ~ gaa iNTiloo paDi uNDaDam M. aajñaanusaaramee anukoNTaanu** I believe that your being so very particular about remaining indoors is due to M.'s instructions.

ఇదిగో **idigoo** *minor sentence* look (at this)!, here it is!; ~ **naNDii adde**! here is the rent, sir!

ఇదివరకు, ఇదివరలో **idiwaraku, idiwaraloo** *adv.* **1** upto now, till now. **2** hitherto, previously.

ఇదివరకే **idiwarakee** *adv.* already.

ఇదివరదాకా **idiwaradaakaa** *adv.* until recently.

ఇదే **idee** I.*pron.* (= **idi** + *emphatic suffix* **ee**) this very thing, the very same thing. II. *adj.* this very, the same: ~ **samayaaniki** just at this time, at this very time. **aytee naaku maatram DaakTarugaaraNTee ~ abhipraayam uNDeedi kaadu** but I did not hold the same opinion about the doctor.

ఇద్దరి **iddari**[1] *n.* (= **ii dari**) this bank or shore.

ఇద్దరి **iddari**[2] *genitive of* **iddaru.**

ఇద్దరు **iddaru** *n.pl.* two persons.

ఇద్దుం **iddum** *n.* two tooms, an obsolete measure equal to about 30 bushels.

ఇద్దులాట **iddulaaTa** *n. dial.* mischievousness, tomfoolery.

ఇద్ధం **iddham** I.*n.* brightness, radiance, splendour. II.*adj.* glowing, shining.

ఇనప **inapa** *genitive of* **inum.**

ఇనపకచ్చ[డం] **inapakacca[Dam]** *n.* chastity belt.

ఇనపగజ్జెల తల్లి **inapagajjela talli** *n. colloq.* goddess of poverty.

ఇనపగుగ్గిళ్ళు **inapa guggiLLu** *n.pl.* uneatable dhall (*lit.* dhall that is as hard as iron).

ఇనపదారి **inapadaari** *n.* railway line.

ఇనపరజను **inaparajanu** *n.* iron filings.

ఇనాం, ఈనాం **inaam, iinaam** **1** *n.* gift, present. **2** *obs.* inam land granted by the government or a landholder on favourable terms for services rendered.

ఇనాందారు **inaamdaaru** *n.* holder of an inam.

ఇను **inu** *adjvl. prefix meaning* two[fold] *or, by extension,* much, many; *cf.* **iru.**

ఇనుం **inum** *n.* iron; **inapa golusu** iron chain.

ఇనుమడి, ఇబ్బడి, ఇమ్మడి **inumaDi, ibbaDi, immaDi** *n.and adj.* double, twice as much, twice as great.

ఇనుమడించు, ఇబ్బడించు **inumaDincu, ibbaDincu** *v.t.* to double.

ఇనుమారు **inumaaru** *adv.* twice.

ఇనుమిక్కిలి **inumikkili** *adv.* **1** twice as much. **2** very much.

ఇన్నాళ్ళకి, ఇన్నినాళ్ళకి **innaaLLaki, inni naaLLaki** *adv.* after such a long time.

ఇన్ని **inni** *det. n.pl.and adj.* this many, this number (of non-human things or animals).

ఇన్నిందాల **innindaala** *adv. dial.* in so many ways.

ఇన్నీ **innii** *det.n.pl.* all these things.

ఇన్నూరు **innuuru** *n.* two hundred.

ఇన్నో **innoo** *adj. lit.* this many-eth; ~ **taariikhu wastaanani kaccitangaa ceppu: neenu sTeeSanuku wastaanu** tell me definitely that you will come on such and such a date, and I will come to the station; *cf.* **ennoo.**

ఇప్ప **ippa** *n.* the mahwa tree, *bassia longifolia,* from whose flowers intoxicating liquor is produced.

ఇప్పటి **ippaTi** *genitive of* **ippuDu** of the present time, current.

ఇప్పటికి **ippaTiki** *adv.* by now, only now, till now, upto now.

ఇప్పటికే **ippaTikee** *adv.* already: ~ **Tayam daaTi pooyindi** it is already late.

ఇప్పించు **ippincu** *v.t.* **1** to cause (s.g) to be given. **2** to procure. **3** to give, *used deferentially, as in* **koddigaa Tayam ippicaNDi** please allow me a little time.

ఇప్పుడప్పుడే **ippuDappuDee** *adv.* **1** soon, straight away, in the near future. **2** *in neg. constr.* so soon; **sundaram modalu peLLikee peecii peTTEEDu. ~ tanaku peLLi waddannaaDu** at first Sundaram objected to the whole idea of marriage. he said he did not want to get married so soon.

ఇప్పుడిప్పుడు **ippuDippuDu** *adv.* **1** about this time, nowadays. **2** just now, very recently.

ఇప్పుడు **ippuDu** I.*n.* this time; *cf.* **ippaTi.** II. *adv.* **now.**

ఇబ్బంది **ibbandi** *n.* **1** trouble, difficulty. **2** inconvenience, discomfort; **niiLLaku baagaa ~ gaa undi** there is much inconvenience for want of water. **3** awkwardness, embarrassment. **4** nuisance, bother; ~ **pani** a troublesome affair.

ఇబ్బందిపడు **ibbandi paDu** *v.i* to suffer trouble, inconvenience or discomfort; **baagaa caligaa undi kadaa, ibbandi paDipootaawee!** it's very cold, isn't it? you will be uncomfortable.

ఇబ్బందిపెట్టు **ibbandipeTTu** *v.t.* **1** to make (s.o.) uncomfortable. **2** to trouble, worry, put pressure on (s.o.)

ఇబ్బట్టు **ibbaTTu** *n.* **1** scarcity. **2** dearness, costliness.

ఇబ్బడి, ఇబ్బడించు **ibbaDi, ibbaDincu** *same as* **inumaDi, inumaDincu.**

ఇముడు **imuDu** *v.i.* **1** to fit (into), adjust (o.s. to); **okka waraloo reNDu kattulu imaDawu** two swords will not fit into one scabbard (proverbial saying).

ఇముడ్చు, ఇమిడ్చు, ఇమిడించు **imuDcu, imiDcu, imiDincu** *v.t.* **1** to fit into, insert, implant, compress; **saametalu padyaalaloo imuDcaDamu koosamu kawulu konni maarpulu ceeyaka tappadu** for the sake of fitting proverbs into verse, poets are bound to make some changes in them: **ii arthaalannii okee okka padyapaadamloo imiDinci racistee** if you compress all these meanings into one verse. **2** to confine, restrict.

ఇముడ్చుకొను **imuDcukonu** *v.t.* to comprise, contain, hold, include, accommodate, embrace, have room for; **enni kathalu imuDcukoo galadu?** how many stories can it accommodate?

ఇమ్మడి **immaDi** *same as* **inumaDi.**

ఇమ్ము **immu**[1] I. *n.* **1** *gen.pl.* ~ **lu** comfort, convenience. **2** place, home. **3** ease, happiness. **4** contrivance, expedient. II. *adj.* (of a house) comfortable, convenient, suitable.

ఇమ్ము immu[2] *class. alt. form of* **iyyi** *imperative sing. of* **iccu.**

ఇయ్య[కోరు] iyya[kooru] *n. class.* 1 giving. 2 consent.

ఇయ్యకొను **iyyakonu** *v.i. class.* to agree, consent.

ఇరకటం **irakaTam** I. *vbl.n. of* **iruku.** II. *n.* (*also* **irakaaTam**) 1 narrowness. 2 narrow place, straits. 3 difficulty.

ఇరవారు, ఇరవుకొను **irawaaru, irawukonu** *v.i.* to become fixed, become firmly established, become settled.

ఇరవు **irawu** I. *n.* place. II. *adj.* firm, fixed, settled.

ఇరవై **iraway** *n.* twenty.

ఇరస **irasa** *n.* a grain measure equal to five quintals.

ఇరికించు **irikincu** *v.t.* 1 to insert, thrust (in), poke (in), stick (in), wedge (in); **kuDiceeti weeLLa sanduloo cuTTa irikinci** wedging a cigar between the fingers of his right hand. 2 to involve, entangle; **o.-ni taguwuloo~** to involve s.o. in a quarrel. 3 to push, press or squeeze (s.g) into a confined space.

ఇరిణం **iriNam** *n.* saline soil, barren land.

ఇరు **iru** *adjvl. prefix meaning* two, both, e.g., **~waypulaa** on both sides; *cf.* **inu.**

ఇరుకు **iruku**[1] I.*n.* 1 narrowness. 2 difficulty, distress; **~napaDu** to get into difficulty. 3 narrow V-shaped entrance/outlet of a cattle pen, allowing humans but not cattle to pass through. II. *adj.* narrow, tight, cramped, confined, congested. III. *v.i.* (*also* **irukkonu**) 1 to be sqeezed, pressed, compressed, confined. 2 to be caught, get stuck. 3 to be entangled or involved (in). 4 to force o.'s way (into), intrude; **miiru ilaa madhyaloo irakaTam baagaa leedu** it is not right for you to force your way in like this.

ఇరుకు **iruku**[2] *same as* **iluku.**

ఇరుకుమాను **irukumaanu** *n.* rough wooden bridge across a stream.

ఇరుకులాటపడు **irukulaaTapaDu** *v.i.* to get into trouble.

ఇరుక్కంత, ఇరుక్కొయ్య **irukkanta, irukkoyya** narrow V-shaped passage-way through a fence; *cf.* **iruku**[1].

ఇరుగడలు **irugaDalu** *n.pl.* two sides.

ఇరుగు **irugu** I. *n.* 1 nearness. 2 the neighbourhood. II.*adj.* neighbouring, adjoining.

ఇరుగుపొరుగు **iruguporugu** I. *n.* 1 the neighbourhood. 2 *pl.* **~ lu** (*also* **~ waaLLu**) neighbours. II. *adj.* neighbouring.

ఇరుపంచల **irupancala** *adv.* on both sides, round about, all round; **aa~ki raaniwwaru** they will not let you go anywhere near there.

ఇరుము, ఇరువు **irumu, iruwu** *n.* room, space, place; **naaku kaalu peTTaDaaniki~ eedii?** where is there any room for me (in such a crowded place)?

ఇరులు **irulu** *n.pl.* shades, shadows, darkness.

ఇరులుకొను **irulukonu** *v.i., poet.* (of shadows, darkness) to close in, gather in:

ఇరువైపులా **iruwaypulaa** *adv.* on both sides.

ఇరువురు **iruwuru** *n.pl.* two persons.

ఇరుసాలు **irusaalu** *n.* remittance of government money; **aa sommu khajaanaaku ~ ayndi** the money was remitted to the treasury.

ఇరుసు **irusu** *n.* 1 axle. 2 axis. 3 pivot or crossbar in the beam of a picota (baling apparatus).

ఇర్రి **irri** *n.* buck, deer, antelope.

ఇర్రిగోరజం **irrigoorajam** *n.* musk.

ఇల **ila** *n.* the earth, the world; **kalaloo jarigindi ~ loo jaragadu** what happens in a dream will never happen in the real world (proverbial saying).

ఇలకరచు **ilakaracu** *v.i.* 1 to grit o.'s teeth (in order to bear pain). 2 to gnash o.'s teeth (in anger).

ఇలకోడి **ilakooDi** *n.* cricket, cicada.

ఇలపీట **ilapiiTa** *same as* **kattipiiTa.**

ఇలా[గా/గు] **ilaa[gaa/gu]** *same as* **iTTaa[gaa/gu]**

ఇలాంటి, ఇలాటి **ilaaNTi, ilaaTi** *same as* **iTLaaNTi, iTLaaTi.**

ఇలాకా **ilaakaa** *n.* 1 territory. 2 jurisdiction. 3 belonging; **neenu aayanagaari ~leNDi** I am one of his men; **aame waaDi~ loo undi** she is being kept by him.

ఇలారం **ilaaram** *n.dial.* (*also* **iluwaram**) 1 raised platform in a field for watching crops. 2 round-shaped cattle shelter.

ఇలార్చుకొను **ilaarcukonu** *v.i.* (of the mouth or throat) to become parched.

ఇలి **ili** *n.* grain of food left over; **illii balii leedu waaDiki** he does not give to anyone (i.e., he is a miser, who does not give a morsel to the humblest or a sacrifice to God).

ఇలు **ilu** *alt. form of* **illu.**

ఇలుకు, ఇరుకు **iluku, iruku** *n. med.* sprain; **~ paTTu** to be sprained.

ఇలువడి **iluwaDi** *n.* 1 high birth. 2 good conduct, decency, respectability.

ఇలువేలుపు, ఇలవేలుపు **iluweelpu, ilaweelupu** *n.* household god.

ఇల్లటం, ఇల్లరికం **illaTam, illarikam** *n.* (of a married man) living in his father-in-law's house.

ఇల్లడ **illaDa** *n.* 1 dwelling, residing. 2 entrusting.

ఇల్లడపెట్టు **illaDapeTTu** *v.t. dial.* to mortgage.

ఇల్లరి **illari** *n.* house tax.

ఇల్లా[గా/గు] **illaa[gaa/gu]** *same as* **iTTaa[gaa/gu].**

ఇల్లామల్లి **illaamalli** *n.* tale bearer, scandal monger; **~ suddulu** backbiting, scandal.

ఇల్లాలు **illaalu** *n.* housewife, mistress of a house.

ఇల్లిక్కడ **illikkaDa** *adv.* just here, right here.

ఇల్లిదిగో! **illidigoo!** *minor sentence* here it is!

ఇల్లు **illu** *n.* house, home; **iNTidaggara** at home, in o.'s house; **illuuwaakili** house and home; **gollumani goDawa ceesi ~ tiisi** (*or* **~ piiki**) **pandira weestunnaaru** they are turning the house into a shambles with all this noise; *see* **cewi.**

ఇవక **iwaka** *n.* 1 wet[ness], damp[ness]. 2 cold.

ఇవతల **iwatala** *adv.* 1 (of place) on this side; **gooDaku~** on this side of the wall. 2 (of time) hereafter, next.

ఇవతలి **iwatali** *adj.* 1 (of place) on or relating to this side: ~ **waaru** the people on this side. 2 (of time) of or relating to recent times.

ఇవతళించు **iwataLincu** *v.i.* to be[come] cool.

ఇవ్వాళ, ఇవేళ **iwwEELa, iweeLa** *adv.* today.

ఇష్ట **iSTa** *adj.* dear, beloved, desired, favourite; ~ **deewata** tutelary deity.

ఇష్టం **iSTam** *n.* wish, desire, inclination, volition, liking, affection, fondness; **naaku ii pani ceeyaDaaniki ~ undi** I would like to do this work; **naaku ii pani aNTee ~** I like [doing] this work; **nii miida daaniki ~ undi** she has a liking for you; **waLLu ~ waccina pani ceeyawaccu** they may do as they please *or* let them do what they like; **nii ~** *minor sentence* [do] as you please; **meekalaku baagaa ~ ayna alam** greenery much loved by goats.

ఇష్టంగా **iSTangaa** *adv.* agreeably, to o.'s liking.

ఇష్టపడు **iSTapaDu** I. *v.i.* to like, want, desire, be willing, consent (to do s.g); **aa samayamloo tagawu teccukonduku R. iSTapaDaleedu** R. did not want to pick up a quarrel at that time. II. *v.t.* to wish for, desire, want (a person, object).

ఇష్టసఖి **iSTasakhi** *n.* confidante.

ఇష్టాగోష్ఠి **iSTaagooSTi** *n.* informal discussion.

ఇష్టాగోష్ఠిగా **iSTaagooSTigaa** *adv.* informally, agreeably.

ఇష్టానిష్టాలు, ఇష్టాయిష్టాలు **iSTaaniSTaalu, iST-aayiSTaalu** *n.pl.* likes and dislikes.

ఇష్టానుసారం **iSTaanusaaram** *adv.*; *see* **anusaaram.**

ఇష్టుడు **iSTuDu** *n.* friend, favoured man.

ఇష్టురాలు **iSTuraalu** *n.* 1 favoured woman. 2 mistress, kept woman.

ఇసక, ఇసుక **isaka, isuka** *n.* sand: ~ **weestee raalanaTTu** *is a proverb, said of things so tightly packed that if you pour sand it will not sink through*: ~ **weestee raalakuNDaa** (*or* **raalananta**) **janam miiTingku waccEEru** a tightly packed throng attended the meeting.

ఇసకదిన్నె, ఇసకదిబ్బ **isakadinne, isakadibba** *n.* sand hill, sand bank.

ఇసకపఱ్ఱ **isakaparra** *n.* sandy waste.

ఇసడిలు **isaDilu** *v.i.* to be tired or disgusted.

ఇసిరో! **isiroo!** (*also* **isii!**) *interj. expressive of disgust.*

ఇసుమంత **isumanta** *particle, in neg. constr.* even a little, at all, in the least; **anduceeta guruwugaaru ceesina apa-haasyaaniki isumantaynaa cintinca leedu** for that reason he was not in the least put out by his guru's ridicule.

ఇసుము **isumu** *n.* grain or particle of sand.

ఇసుళ్ళు **isuLLu** *n.pl.* flying ants, a kind of termite.

ఇస్త్రి, ఇస్త్రీ **istiri, istrii** *n.* ironing (of clothes); ~ **ceeyu** to iron (clothes); ~ **peTTe** an iron (for pressing clothes); ~ **baTTalu** clothes that have been ironed.

ఇస్తిహారు **istihaaru** *n.* proclamation.

ఇస్పేట్లు **ispeeTLu** *n.pl.* spades (in playing cards).

ఇహ, ఇహమీదట, ఇహముందు **iha, ihamiidaTa, ihamundu** *same as* **ika, ikamiidaTa, ikamundu.**

ఇహం, ఇహలోకం **iham, ihalookam** *n.* 1 the material world, this world (*contrasted with* **param** the next world). 2 *by extension* **iham param** *means* benefits in this world and the next, i.e., material and spiritual benefits: **ee panaynaa ceeseeTappuDu iham param cuucukoowaali** every act that you perform must be conducive to both material and spiritual benefits (*lit.* when you perform any act you must be mindful of the material and spiritual benefits [arising from it]). 3 *colloq.* **ii sinimaa cuustee ihamaa para-maa? eem wastundi? pooyi caduwukoo!** if you watch this movie what will it benefit you in this world or the next? what will come of it? go and study! *or* what earthly or heavenly good will it do you to watch this movie? go and study!

ఇహిహీ **ihihii**! *interj* ha! ha! (*laughter*).

ఈ - ii

ఈ **ii**[1] *demon. adj.* this, these; **iiyii kuuralu** these various vegetables; *see* **saari.**

ఈ **ii**[2] *imperative sing. of* **iccu** to give, allow, *contracted from* **iyyi**, *as in* **poonii, kaanii.**

ఈండ్ర, ఈడిగ **iiNDra, iiDiga** *n.* name of the toddy tappers' community in Andhra Pradesh.

ఈండ్రం **iiNDram** *n.* trouble, worry.

ఈండ్రపడు **iiNDrapaDu** *v.i.* to hang on, cling on.

ఈక **iika** *n.* feather; *pl.* ~ **lu** feathers, plumage; ~ **kalam** quill pen.

ఈగ **iiga** *n.* fly; ~ **la moota** buzzing of flies.

ఈగపులి **iigapuli** *n.* spider.

ఈచ **iica** I. *n.* (of limbs) crookedness caused by withering. II. *adj.* withered, misshapen.

ఈచపడు, ఈచపోవు, ఈచుకుపోవు **iicapaDu, iicapoowu, iicukupoowu** *v.i.* 1 to wither; **weeru purugulu paDitee, mokka iicabaDi cacci pootundi** if root worms come, the plant will wither and die. 2 (of a cow's udder) to dry up.

ఈచు **iicu** *v.i.* to wither, shrivel.

ఈటార్చు **iiTaarcu** *v.t.* to boil (s.g) dry, boil (s.g) till it is free from moisture.

ఈటు **iiTu** *adj.* useless, empty.

ఈటె **iiTe** *n.* spear, lance.

ఈడ **iiDa** *dial. alt. form of* **ikkaDa.**

ఈడిగ **iiDiga** *same as* **iiNDra.**

ఈడిగిలు, ఈడిగిలపడు **iiDigilu, iiDigilapaDu** *v.i.* 1 to halt owing to weakness. 2 to hang back, draw back. 3 to refuse to stir owing to fear, resist being dragged. 4 to sink down, subside, drop. 5 **iiDigalapaDi kuurcuNDu** to sit leaning backwards, lounge.

ఈడు **iiDu**[1] *personal suffix, class.*, e.g., **kummar~** potter.

ఈడు **iiDu**[2] I.*n.* 1 age; **tana~ waaLLani kuuDagaTTi** assembling some persons of his own age; **ii ~na waaDiki ee buddhuluu puTTanakkara leedu** at this age there is no need for him to conceive any ideas. 2 marriageable age; **aameki~ waccindi** she attained puberty. 3 **iiDuu jooDuu** correct matching of persons of the same age; **waaLLiddariki iiDuu jooDuu baagundi** those two will suit each other. II. *adj.* (of partners) suitable, well matched; **miiku iiDayna pilla** she is a suitable match for you.

ఈడుచు **iiDucu** *same as* **iiDcu.**

ఈడుపు **iiDupu** *same as* **iiDpu.**

ఈడేరు **iiDeeru** *v.i.* 1 to come to maturity. 2 to be effected, attained, accomplished, completed or fulfilled. 3 (of a girl) to attain puberty.

ఈడేర్చు **iiDeercu** *v.t.* 1 to effect, complete, accomplish. 2 to fulfil (wants, needs). 3 **kaSTam~** to cause distress to be relieved.

ఈడ్చు, ఈడుచు **iiDcu, iiDucu** *v.t.* 1 to pull, draw, drag. 2 to attract. 3 *colloq.* to get through, cope with (studies).

ఈడ్చుకువచ్చు **iiDcukuwaccu** *v.i.* to keep going, carry on, manage, drag out o.'s life: **neenu aahaarapaaniiyaalaynaa leekuNDaa iiDcukaraagalanu gaani gaali leekapootee kSaNamaynaa gaDawadu** I can carry on even without food or drink but without air I cannot survive for even a moment.

ఈడ్చుకొను, ఈడ్చుకుపోవు **iiDcukonu, iiDcukupoowu** *v.i.* 1 (of legs) to feel weak. 2 (of eyes) to be hollow or sunken.

ఈడ్పు, ఈడుపు **iiDpu, iiDupu** *n.* 1 pulling, dragging; ~ **mokham** haggard face; ~ **kaaLLu** weary legs. 2 convulsion, spasm.

ఈత **iita**[1] *n. also* ~ **ceTTu** date tree; ~ **kallu** date toddy.

ఈత **iita**[2] *n.* swimming; ~ **kaaDu** swimmer; ~ **koTTu** to swim.

ఈత **iita**[3] *n.* (of animals, plants) bearing, yielding; **iipaaTiki muuDu ~ lu iinawalasina goDDu** a cow that ought to have borne three calves by now; **wari ~ ku waccee samayamloo aakumiida erraTimaccalu ceerpaDataayi** when it is time for the paddy to yield, red spots (disease) appear on the leaf.

ఈతి **iiti** *n.* plague, evil; ~ **baadhalu** troubles, afflictions, conventionally the six traditional plagues: floods, drought, epidemics, rats, locusts, threat of war.

ఈద్ **iid** *n.* the festival of Id.

ఈద **iida** *n.* strong cold rainy wind.

ఈదర, ఈదరు, ఈదురు **iidara, iidaru, iiduru** *adj.* ~ **gaali** strong cold rainy wind; **cali gaali~ keraTaalugaa wiistoondi** a cold wind is blowing in violent gusts.

ఈదాడు **iidaaDu** *n.* kind of date tree; **wiiDu~ aNTee, waaDu koodaaDu aNTaaDu** if A says one thing B will be sure to say the opposite.

ఈదు **iidu** I. *v.i.* 1 to swim. 2 to push o.'s way, struggle (through storm or difficulty). 3 to manage successfully in spite of difficulties; **aaphiisu paniloo ~ tunnaaDu** he is managing to cope with his work in office. II. *v.t.* (*also* ~ **koniwaccu**) to maintain or support (a family) with difficulty: **ippaTidaakaa kuuDaa ii samsaaram elaa ~ kostunnaanoo miiku telusu** you know how I have been maintaining this family against odds to this very day; **ika mundu ii samsaaram eTLaa ~ taanu?** how can I possibly support this family hereafter? (family life (**samsaaram**) is traditionally regarded as an ocean (**saagaram**) to be swum through).

ఈదురో **iiduroo** *same as* **iisuroo.**

ఈనాం **iinaam** *same as* **inaam.**

ఈనాడు **iinaaDu** *adv.* today.

ఈనిక **iinika** *n.* (of animals) bearing offspring, yeaning, calving.

ఈను **iinu** *v.t.* 1 (of animals) to bear, yean, calve, produce offspring. 2 (of crops) to produce, yield; **korra maadiri ennu iinee gaDDi mokka** a grass which produces ears like korra; **neela iininaTTu** as if the land had given birth (an expression to indicate huge numbers); **iinagaaci nakkalapaalu ceesinaTTu** all o.'s care is thrown away *or* all o.'s trouble is wasted (proverb — *lit.* like letting a flock that has yielded well fall a prey to jackals).

ఈనె **iine** *n.* rib or vein of a leaf, esp. the midrib.

ఈపట్టు[న] **iipaTTu[na]** *adv.* this time, now: ~ **pariikSa paasawaali** this time you must pass the examination.

ఈపాటి **iipaaTi** *adj.* this much, to this extent.

ఈపాటికి **iipaaTiki** *adv.* 1 now, for the present. 2 by now; ~ **wacci uNTaaDu** by now he will have arrived.

ఈపి, ఈరు **iipi, iiru** *n.* 1 louse, nit. 2 egg of a louse or fly.

ఈపె **iipe** *pron. class.* she, this woman.

ఈపోతి **iipooti** *same as* **iccipuccukoolu.**

ఈప్స, ఈప్సితం **iipsa, iipsitam** *n.* wish, desire.

ఈబరి[గొట్టు] **iibari[goTTu]** *n.* useless person, stupid fellow.

ఈమధ్య **ii madhya** *adv.* 1 recently. 2 nowadays.

ఈమరి **iimari** *n.* wet[ness], moisture.

ఈమాత్రం **iimaatram** *adj.* this much.

ఈమాత్రంగా **iimaatrangaa** *adv.* 1 like this (in a deprecatory sense). 2 at least.

ఈమె **iime** *pron.* she, this woman.

ఈయన **iiyana** *pron.* he, this man.

ఈరకాడు/ఈరకత్తె **iirakaaDu/iirakatte** *n.* father mother of o.'s son-in-law or daughter-in-law: *cf.* **wiyyankuDu/wiyyapuraalu.**

ఈరస **iirasa** *n.* spite, malice, anger.

ఈరిక **iirika** *n.* sprout, shoot.

ఈరు **iiru** *same as* **iipi.**

ఈరెండ **iireNDa** *n.* soft sunlight.

ఈరెలుగు **iirelugu** *n.* soft, low or gentle voice.

ఈరేడు లోకాలు **iireeDu lookaalu** *n.pl.* the fourteen worlds of Hindu mythology (= **caturdaśa bhuwanaalu**).

ఈర్చు, ఈరుచు **iircu, iirucu** *v.t.* to comb nits or lice from the hair.

ఈర్పెన, ఈరుపెన **iirpena, iirupena** *n.* comb for removing nits or lice.

ఈర్ష్య **iirSya** *n.* jealousy, envy, spite, illwill, malice; **o.-i miida** ~ jealousy against s.o.

ఈర్ష్యాళువు **iirSyaaLuwu** *n.* jealous or envious person.

ఈల **iila** *n.* whistle, whistling.

ఈలకొట్టు, ఈలవేయు **iila koTTu, iila weeyu** *v.i.* to whistle.

ఈలపీట **iilapiiTa** *same as* **kattipiiTa.**

ఈలువు **iiluwu** *n.* respectability, honour, chastity.

ఈలో[పు]గా **iiloo[pu]gaa** *adv.* during this time, meanwhile, in the mean time.

ఈలోపల, ఈలోపున **iiloopala, iiloopuna** *adv.* meanwhile, in the mean time.

ఈవరకి **iiwaraki** *adv. colloq.* 1 by now, already (= **idiwarakee**). 2 only now (= **ippaTiki**); *see* **kuduTapaDu.**

ఈవల **iiwala** I. *n.* this side. II. *adv.* 1 on this side. 2 recently.

ఈవలావల **iiwalaawala** *adv.* on this side and on that.

ఈవాళ, ఈవేళ **iiwEELa, iiweeLa** *adv.* today.

ఈవిడ **iiwiDa** *pron.* she, this woman.

ఈశాన్యం **iiśaanyam** *n.* northeast.

ఈశుడు **iiśuDu** *n.* 1 name of the God Siva. 2 master, lord.

ఈశ్వర **iiśwara** *n.* eleventh year of the Hindu cycle of sixty years.

ఈశ్వరవేరు **iiśwaraweeru** *n. aristolochia indica,* an aromatic herb.

ఈశ్వరి **iiśwari** *n.* name of the Goddess Parvati, wife of Siva.

ఈశ్వరుడు **iiśwaruDu** *n.* 1 God, the Supreme Ruler of creation. 2 name of the God Siva. 3 *in compounds* lord, master, king, e.g., **bhuum**~ lord of the earth.

ఈషణం **iiSaNam** *n. class.* desire.

ఈషణత్రయం **iiSaNatrayam** *n. class.* the three strongest desires of a man: a wife, wealth, a child.

ఈషత్ **iiSat** *prefix used in Sanskrit compounds meaning* small, slight, e.g., **iiSadbheedam** slight difference.

ఈసడం **iisaDam** *n.* 1 blame. 2 reproach.

ఈసడించు **iisaDincu** I. *v.i.* (*also* ~ **konu**) 1 to speak mockingly. 2 to show anger, dislike or distaste. 3 to grumble. II. *v.t.* 1 to deride, disparage, regard with contempt. 2 to hate, dislike, have distaste for. 3 to reproach.

ఈసడింపు **iisaDimpu** *n.* 1 disapproval, dislike. 2 disdain, contempt.

ఈసడింపుగా **iisaDimpugaa** *adv.* with dislike, critically, unfavourably.

ఈసపోవు **iisapoowu** *v.i.* to shrivel, wither.

ఈసరికి **iisariki** *adv.* at this moment, just now.

ఈసరికే **iisarikee** *adv.* by now, already.

ఈసు **iisu** *n.* 1 envy, jealousy. 2 dislike. 3 anger.

ఈసురో, ఈదురో **iisuroo, iiduroo** *adv.* weakly, feebly.

ఈహీ!, ఈహూ! **iihii!, iihuu!** *interj.* for shame!

ఉ - u

ఉంకించు unkincu *v.i.* to try, attempt.

ఉంకు unku I. *n.* consent. II. *v.i.* to jump, leap.

ఉంకుటుంగరం unkuTungaram *n.* ring presented to a bride at the time of her marriage; *cf.* **baTuwu.**

ఉంకువ unkuwa *n.* bride price (=**ooli**).

ఉంగ unga *n.* coaxing sound made by a mother to her baby when giving **uggu** (castor oil and milk).

ఉంగటం, ఉంగుటం ungaTam, unguTam *n.* toe strap of a sandal into which the big toe is inserted.

ఉంగరం ungaram *n.* ring; **ungarapu weelu** ring finger, fourth finger; **ungaraala ceyyi** *colloq.* hand that wields power, hand of a person in authority; **ungaraala juTTu** curly hair.

ఉంగిడి ungiDi *n. vet.* bloat, abnormal distention of stomach in cattle, sheep, etc., caused by eating certain kinds of green fodder.

ఉంచు uncu *v.t.* 1 to place, put, set, lay; **daya uncaNDi** please show favour. 2 to let be, leave; **aa sangati aTLaa uncaNDi** leave that matter aside.

ఉంచుకొను uncukonu *v.t.* to keep, retain, deposit, reserve, preserve; **ceTLu waaDipooyina aakulu uncukoowu** trees do not keep their withered leaves. 2 to keep as a mistress.

ఉంఛం uncham *n.* 1 extreme poverty. 2 living by gleaning.

ఉంఛవృత్తి unchawrtti *n.* living by gleaning or begging.

ఉంట uNTa *n.* ball.

ఉంటగాలం uNTagaalam *n.* fisherman's hook with ball attached as a sinker.

ఉండ uNDa I. *n.* 1 lump, ball; **daarapu~** ball or roll of thread; **miThaayi~** ball-shaped sweet; **~ki waccu** (of sweets being cooked) to come to the right consistency for forming into balls. 2 *dial.* pill. II. *adj.* round.

ఉండకట్టు uNDakaTTu *v.i.* to form a lump, conglomerate.

ఉండకట్టుకొను, ఉండచుట్టుకొను unDakaTTukonu, uNDacuTTukonu *v.i.* to curl up, roll up like a ball.

ఉండబట్టలేక uNDabaTTaleeka *advbl. phrase* not being able to restrain o.s., not being able to endure; **nannu endukuraa alaa tiTTinaawani ~ aDigindi** "why did you abuse me like that?" she could not help asking.

ఉండి uNDi *same as* **huNDi.**

ఉండిఉండి uNDi uNDi *adv.* 1 from time to time, at intervals, on and off. 2 after [waiting for] a long time. 3 all of a sudden.

ఉండిపోవు uNDipoowu *v.i.* to continue, remain; **peLLikaakuNDaa uNDipooyEEru** they remained unmarried.

ఉండు uNDu *v.i.* 1 to be, exist, be alive. 2 to remain, stop, stay; **padi roojulu akkaDa unnaanu** I stayed there for ten days. 3 to reside, dwell, live. 4 to last, endure. 5 to wait. 6 (*with dat.*) to have; **waaDiki paTTaNamloo illu unnadi** he has a house in town; **unnawaaDu** rich person.

ఉండేలు uNDeelu *n.* sling or bow for discharging stones at birds.

ఉండ్ర uNDra *n.* white mimosa tree.

ఉండ్రం uNDram *adj.* round, spherical; **ceyyi uNDrapu mukkallee undi, debba tagala leedu** the hand is perfectly all right, it is quite uninjured.

ఉండ్రాళ్లతద్దె uNDraaLLatadde *n.* third day after the full moon in the lunar month of Bhadrapadam, a festival celebrated by women.

ఉండ్రాలు, ఉండ్రాళ్లు uNDraalu, uNDraaLLu *n.pl.* a kind of sweet cake.

ఉంపడం umpaDam *n.* being kept as a mistress; **aayana daggiriki ~ weLLindi** she went to him as his mistress.

ఉంపించు umpincu *v.t.* to cause to be placed.

ఉంపుడు umpuDu *adj.* kept (as a mistress).

ఉంపుడుకత్తె umpuDukatte *n.* mistress, concubine.

ఉంభనం umbhanam *n.* filling.

ఉక్క ukka I. *n.* heat, sultriness. II. *adj.* hot, stuffy, sultry, oppressive.

ఉక్కడచు, ఉక్కడిగించు ukkaDacu, ukkaDigincu *v.t.* to humble, crush the pride of (s.o.).

ఉక్కపోయు ukkapooyu *v.i.* (of atmosphere) to become hot and stifling.

ఉక్కిపోవు ukkipoowu *v.i.* 1 to feel oppressed or suffocated (by sultry weather). 2 to die. 3 to be crushed.

ఉక్కిరిబిక్కిరి అవు ukkiribikkiri awu *v.i.* 1 to be suffocated or stifled. 2 to be exhausted. 3 to be choked with emotion. 4 to be speechless (unable to answer).

ఉక్కిస ukkisa *n.* dry cough.

ఉక్కు ukku *n.* 1 steel; **~ karmaagaaram** steel plant; **~ tunaka** piece of steel; **~ maniSi** active and valiant man, man of courage and determination. 2 *class.* courage, spirit, mettle.

ఉక్కెర ukkera *n.* kind of sweet cake made for children consisting of rice flour, sugar and ghee.

ఉక్తం uktam *adj. class.* spoken, said, uttered; *mod. only in* **punaruktam** said again, repeated.

ఉక్తి ukti *n.* 1 speech, speaking. 2 word. 3 expression, saying, utterance; *often used in Sanskrit compounds*, e.g., **atiśayookti** exaggeration, **chalookti** joke, funny story.

ఉక్రోషం ukrooSam *n.* resentfulness, resentment, rancour, anger.

ఉగాది ugaadi *n.* Telugu New Year's Day, celebrated on the first day of Chaitra at the beginning of **wasanta rtuwu.**

ఉగాదిపచ్చడి ugaadi paccaDi *n.* a dish prepared on

Ugadi day from neem flowers, new jaggery and pieces of raw mango, signifying that life is a mixture of those flavours.

ఉగాదిసారె **ugaadi saare** *n.* presents given to a bride by her parents or her parents-in-law on the first Ugadi day after her wedding.

ఉగ్గం **uggam** *n.* cord tied round the mouth of a pot to enable it to be carried.

ఉగ్గడించు **uggaDincu** *v.t.* **1** to utter, declare, proclaim. **2** to speak of, mention. **3** to praise, speak in praise of.

ఉగ్గబట్టు **uggabaTTu** *v.t.* to control (emotions).

ఉగ్గు **uggu** *n.* **1** breast milk and castor oil mixed and given to young children as a dose; **~ paalatoo neerpina widya** knowledge taught from (o.'s) earliest childhood. **2** wrinkle or fold in a cloth.

ఉగ్గుగిన్నె **ugguginne** *n.* small vessel made of silver or other metal for giving **uggu.**

ఉగ్గుపడు **uggupaDu** *v.i.* to be folded.

ఉగ్రం **ugram** I. *n.* **1** fierceness, fiery temper. II. *adj.* **1** fierce, angry, wrathful. **2** frightful, terrible, violent, ferocious.

ఉగ్రత **ugrata** *n.* ferocity.

ఉగ్రవాది **ugrawaadi** *n.* terrorist.

ఉగ్రాక్షుడు **ugraakSuDu** *n.* the fierce eyed, epithet of Siva.

ఉగ్రాణం **ugraaNam** *n.* storehouse, treasury.

ఉగ్రుడు **ugruDu** *n.* fierce or fiery tempered person.

ఉచిత **ucita** *adj.* **1** proper, suitable, fit[ting], apposite, appropriate, felicitous, advisable. **2** *colloq.* free of cost, for nothing. **3** liberal, plentiful. **4** equitable, fair. **5** deserving.

ఉచితంగా **ucitangaa** *adv.* **1** appropriately, suitably. **2** free of cost.

ఉచ్చ **ucca**[1] *n.* urine; **~ poosukonu** to pass urine.

ఉచ్చ **ucca**[2] *prefix meaning* high, tall, lofty, elevated; **~ sthiti** high position.

ఉచ్చం **uccam** *n.* zenith, the highest point in the heavens.

ఉచ్చగుంట **uccaguNTa** *n.* pit of urine, cess pit; **~ loo ceepalu paDataaDu** he will even try to catch fish in a cess pit (i.e., he is very miserly).

ఉచ్చత **uccata** *n.* elevation.

ఉచ్చబుడ్డ **uccabuDDa** *n.* bladder.

ఉచ్చయం **uccayam** *n. class.* crowd.

ఉచ్చరించు **uccarincu** *v.t.* **1** to pronounce. **2** to utter, enunciate.

ఉచ్చాటనం **uccaaTanam** *n.* **1** routing, driving away. **2** exorcising (of evil spirits).

ఉచ్చారం, ఉచ్చారణ **uccaaram, uccaaraNa** *n.* **1** pronunciation, articulation. **2** utterance.

ఉచ్చావచం **uccaawacam** *n.* fluctuation, wavering.

ఉచ్చావచంగా **uccaawacangaa** *adv.* in all sorts of ways: **~ tiTTu** to curse s.o. up and down.

ఉచ్చి **ucci** *n.* crown of the head.

ఉచ్చిష్ట **ucciSTa** *adj.* highest.

ఉచ్చు **uccu**[1] *n.* slip knot, noose, halter. **2** trap.

ఉచ్చు **uccu**[2] *v.i. and t.* **1** to enter, penetrate, pierce, rush in. **2** to send.

ఉచ్చుచ్చిరే **uccucciree!** *sound made in coaxing a dog.*

ఉచ్చైశ్రవం **uccayśrawam** *n.* name of Indra's horse.

ఉచ్చైస్స్వరం **uccayswaram** *n.* high pitched voice, loud voice.

ఉచ్ఛాదనం **ucchaadanam** *n. chem.* exposure to light.

ఉచ్ఛిత్తి **ucchitti** *n.* extermination, extirpation.

ఉచ్ఛిష్టం **ucchiSTam** *n.* scraps of food left over after a meal and therefore defiled.

ఉచ్ఛుష్క **ucchuSka** *adj.* dried up, evaporated.

ఉచ్ఛూణ **ucchuuNa** *adj. class.* **1** swollen. **2** turgid, close, thick.

ఉచ్ఛృంఖల **ucchṛnkhala** *adj.* self-willed, unrestrained.

ఉచ్ఛేదనం **uccheedanam** *n.* cutting off, destruction.

ఉచ్ఛేషం **uccheeSam** *n.* remainder, residue.

ఉచ్ఛోషం **ucchooSam** *n.* drying up, parching.

ఉచ్ఛ్వాసం **ucchwaasam** *n.* breath, breathing in, inhalation.

ఉజ్జ, ఉజ్జా **ujja, ujjaa** *n.* guess, rough estimate.

ఉజ్జకొను **ujjakonu** *v.t.* to guess, think, consider.

ఉజ్జగించు **ujjagincu** *v.i. and t.* to cease from, lay aside.

ఉజ్జగిల్లు **ujjagillu** *v.i.* to be removed.

ఉజ్జనం, ఉజ్ఝనం **ujjanam, ujjhanam** *n.* abandonment, giving up, leaving.

ఉజ్జాపనం **ujjaapanam** *n. same as* **udyaapanam.**

ఉజ్జాయించు **ujjaayincu** *v.t.* to guess, conjecture.

ఉజ్జాయింపు **ujjaayimpu** *n.* guess, conjecture, rough estimate.

ఉజ్జాయింపుగా **ujjaayimpugaa** *adv.* approximately.

ఉజ్జీ **ujjI** *same as* **uddI**[1].

ఉజ్జీవనం **ujjiiwanam** *n.* animating, inspiring with life.

ఉజ్జీవించు **ujjiiwincu** *v.i.* to live, subsist.

ఉజ్జువకల్లు **ujjuwakallu** *n.* pumice stone.

ఉజ్జృంభిత **ujjṛmbhita** *adj.* **1** bursting forth. **2** (of emotions) displayed, manifested.

ఉజ్జృంభితం **ujjṛmbhitam** *n.* effort, exertion.

ఉజ్జ్వల **ujjwala** *adj.* **1** bright, shining. **2** splendid, glorious.

ఉజ్ఝనం **ujjhanam** *same as* **ujjanam.**

ఉటంకం **uTankam** *n.* summing up, summary, abstract.

ఉటంకి, ఉటంకు **uTanki, uTanku** *n.* clever, active, lively or bold person.

ఉటంకించు, ఉట్టంకించు **uTankincu, uTTankincu** *v.t.* **1** to assert, declare. **2** to propound (doctrine, thesis).

3 to summarise, make an abstract of. 4 to quote, repeat, reproduce (s.g said or written). 5 to praise, compliment.

ఉటజం **uTajam** *n.* hermitage, hut made of leaves.

ఉట్టప్పుడు **uTTappuDu** *same as* **uttappuDu.**

ఉట్టి **uTTi** *n.* 1 sling made of network in which pots are hung up in a house; ~ **miida wenna peTTukoni uurantaa neetiki deewulaaDinaTLu** (proverb) like searching the whole village for ghee, when you have butter in your own sling. 2 pl. **uTlu** (i) slings, (ii) fibres inside a ripe tamarind.

ఉట్టిపడు **uTTipaDu** *v.i.* 1 to issue forth, exude; **praśaanta waataawaraNam** ~ **tunnadi** a peaceful atmosphere exudes. 2 to be expressed or displayed; **teliwiteeTalu uTTipaDee mukham** a face in which intelligence is displayed.

ఉట్రవడియం **uTrawaDiyam** *n.* kind of thin blackgram cake.

ఉట్రవడియంగా **uTrawaDiyangaa** *adv. colloq.* very easily.

ఉట్లపండగ **uTLapaNDaga** *n.* festival of Krishnastami, in which slings (**uTLu**) play a part.

ఉఠాణి **uThaaNi** *adj.* great, high.

ఉఠాయించు **uThaayincu** *v.t.* to cause s.o. to quit a place.

ఉడకపెట్టు **uDakapeTTu** *v.t.* to boil, cook by boiling.

ఉడత **uData** *same as* **uDuta.**

ఉడాం **uDaam** *n.* leap; ~ **weeyu** to leap.

ఉడాయించు **uDaayincu** *v.i.* to run away.

ఉడికించు **uDikincu** *v.t.* 1 to tease, cause s.o. to feel hurt or irritated. 2 to cook by boiling.

ఉడిగించు **uDigincu** *v.t.* 1 to remove, do away with. 2 to check, stop.

ఉడుం **uDum** *n.* iguana; **aayana paTTu ~ paTTu** *lit.* his grip is like an iguana's (i.e., he is very obdurate).

ఉడుక **uDuka** *n.* small drum shaped like an hourglass.

ఉడుకు **uDuku** I. *n.* boiling, heat; **annam~ paTTindi** the rice has begun to boil. II. *adj.* boiling, hot. III. *v.i.* 1 to boil, seethe, be cooked by boiling. 2 to get enraged, boil with rage. 3 to smart with anger or envy; *see* **pappu.**

ఉడుకెక్కు, ఉడుకెత్తు **uDukekku, uDukettu** *v.i.* 1 to boil, become hot. 2 to grow hot with anger.

ఉడుకుబోతు, ఉడుకుమోతు **uDukubootu, uDukumootu** *n.* 1 envious or jealous person. 2 quick-tempered or irritable person.

ఉడుకుబోతుతనం, ఉడుకుమోతుతనం **uDukubootutanam, uDukumootutanam** *n.* taking offence, feeling offended. 2 sulking.

ఉడుకులెక్కించు, ఉడుకులెత్తించు **uDukulekkincu, uDukulettincu** *v.t.* to boil.

ఉడుగర **uDugara** *n.* present, esp. a wedding gift.

ఉడుగు **uDugu** *v.i.* 1 to pass away, abate, cease, depart; **udreekaalu uDigee waardhakyamloo** in old age when emotions will have passed away. 2 to fail, wane, be lacking or wanting; **śakti uDigipoo coccindi** his strength began to fail. 3 (of hunger, thirst) to pass off, be relieved or satiated. 4 (of hope) to fade.

ఉడుత, ఉడత **uDuta, uData** *n.* squirrel; ~ **bhakti** a squirrel's devotion, what little help one can give (this refers an episode in the Ramayana); ~ **bhaktigaa** as a small contribution.

ఉడుపు **uDupu** *n., gen. pl.* ~ **lu** clothes, dress, clothing.

ఉడ్డ, ఉడ్డా **uDDa, uDDaa** *n.* 1 four. 2 heap, pile, collection.

ఉడ్డీనం **uDDiinam** *n.* flying, soaring.

ఉడ్డుకుడుచు **uDDukuDucu** *v.i.* 1 to feel suffocated, have o.'s breath taken away. 2 to be at o.'s wits' end.

ఉడ్డోలం **uDDoolam** *adj.* very much, very great.

ఉతక **utaka** *n.* bottom pivot on which a door turns.

ఉతుకు **utuku** *v.t.* 1 to wash (clothes). 2 to beat, thrash.

ఉత్కంఠ **utkaNTha** *n.* eagerness, longing, interest, curiosity; **paaThakulu śiirSikalu maatramee cadiwi mottam wiSayam grahistee waariki patrika cadawaalanee~ uNDadu** if readers can understand the whole matter simply from the headlines, they will have no desire to read the newspaper.

ఉత్కంపం **utkampam** *n.* shaking, trembling.

ఉత్కటం **utkaTam** *adj.* very great, abundant, extreme, excessive.

ఉత్కరం **utkaram** *n.* 1 heap, mass. 2 crowd.

ఉత్కర్ష **utkarSa** *n.* 1 excellence. 2 progress, prosperity. 3 *ling.* crescendo.

ఉత్కలం, ఉత్కళం **utkalam, utkaLam** *n.* the State of Orissa.

ఉత్కలిక **utkalika** *n.* desire, longing.

ఉత్కృష్ట **utkṛSTa** *adj.* excellent, best, outstanding, eminent, noble.

ఉత్కేంద్రక, ఉత్కేంద్రీయ **utkeendraka, utkeendriiya** *adj. maths. sci.* eccentric.

ఉత్కేంద్రత *n. maths. sci.* eccentricity.

ఉత్క్రతనం **utkratanam** *n. chem.* ebullition.

ఉత్క్రమణం **utkramaNam** *n.* 1 ascent. 2 departure. 3 *sci.* reversion.

ఉత్క్రమణీయ **utkramaNiiya** *adj. sci.* reversible.

ఉత్క్షిప్త **utkSipta** *adj. class.* thrown up, tossed up.

ఉత్క్షేపం **utkSeepam** *n. class.* throwing up, tossing up.

ఉత్ఖాటనం **utkhaaTanam** *n.* digging up, excavation.

ఉత్త, ఉత్తి, వట్టి, ఒట్టి **utta, utti, waTTi, oTTi** *adj.* 1 empty, void, vacant, mere, plain, simple, bare; ~ **kaaLLatoo waccEEDu** he came barefooted; ~ **ceetulatoo weLLakuuDadu** do not go empty-handed; **utta kaaphii taagi weLLi pooyEEDu** he left after taking some coffee and nothing else; ~ **puNyaaniki** (i) for no reason at all, (ii) free of charge, for nothing; **ippuDu aame ~ maniSi kaadu** now she is pregnant. 2 utter, downright, absolute; ~ **wedhawa** an utter wretch; ~ **abaddham** a downright lie. 3 *in a contrasting situation* ~ = others, the rest; **bhoon ceestunna waaruu ~ waaruu** those taking food and the rest; **maDikaTTukonnawaaruu ~ waaruu** those wearing **maDi** and the rest. 4 useless, vain, idle, not serious; ~ **kaburlu** idle talk. 5 false, groundless; **adi ~ maaTa** (i) that is an untrue saying, (ii) that is s.g that will not happen.

ఉత్తండాలు **uttaNDaalu** *n.pl.* kind of gold necklace worn by women.

ఉత్తంభించు **uttambhincu** *v.t.* to uphold, support.

ఉత్తంశం **uttamśam** *n.* 1 earring. 2 tiara.

ఉత్తనే, ఉత్తినే, వట్టినే, ఒట్టినే **uttanee, uttinee, waTTinee, oTTinee** *adv.* 1 simply, merely, for no special reason. 2 to no purpose, in vain.

ఉత్తప్పుడు, ఉట్టప్పుడు **uttappuDu, uTTappuDu** *adv.* normally, on ordinary occasions, when (one) is at leisure, when (one) is at ease; ~ **baagaanee maaTLaaDataaDu, sabhaloo bigusukupootaaDu** on ordinary occasions he speaks well, but in a meeting he becomes tense.

ఉత్తమ **uttama** *adj.* 1 excellent, first, best. 2 ~ **puruSa** *gram.* first person.

ఉత్తమాంగం **uttamaangam** *n.* head.

ఉత్తముడు **uttamuDu** *n.* excellent person, most worthy person.

ఉత్తర **uttara** I. *first part of a n. compound meaning* second, latter, following, e.g., **uttaraartham** second half, ~ **raamaayaNam** latter part of the Ramayana. II. *n. same as* ~ **phalguNi.**

ఉత్తరం **uttaram** *n.* 1 answer, reply. 2 letter (epistle). 3 north.

ఉత్తరకుమార ప్రజ్ఞలు **uttarakumaara prajñalu** *n.pl.* conceitedness, vain boasting (like that of Uttara, son of Virata, in the Mahabharata).

ఉత్తరక్రియలు **uttarakriyalu** *n.pl.* funeral rites, obsequies.

ఉత్తరజందెం **uttarajandem** *n.* cord made of gold or silver worn along with the sacred thread by a brahman bridegroom at his wedding and for sixteen days thereafter.

ఉత్తరణం **uttaraNam** *n.* passing, crossing.

ఉత్తరధ్రువం **uttaradhruwam** *n.* North Pole.

ఉత్తరపక్షం **uttarapakSam** *n.* second part of an argument, defendant's reply.

ఉత్తరప్రత్యుత్తరాలు **uttarapratyuttaraalu** *n.pl.* correspondence.

ఉత్తరఫల్గుణి **uttaraphalguNi** *n. astrol.* (*also* **uttara**) twelfth lunar mansion.

ఉత్తరమీమాంస **uttaramiimaamsa** *n.* name given to Vedanta philosophy.

ఉత్తరవాదం **uttarawaadam** *n.* 1 responsibility, answerability. 2 *legal* answer.

ఉత్తరవాది **uttarawaadi** *n.* 1 person who is responsible or answerable. 2 *legal* defendant, respondent.

ఉత్తరవాసం **uttarawaasam** *n.* upper garment.

ఉత్తరసర్కార్లు **uttarasarkaarlu** *n.pl.* Northern Circars, the northern and central coastal districts of Andhra Pradesh.

ఉత్తరహనువు **uttara hanuwu** *n.* upper jaw.

ఉత్తరాధికారి **uttaraadhikaari** *n.* successor in power, heir.

ఉత్తరాపథం **uttaraapatham** *n.* North India.

ఉత్తరాభద్ర **uttaraabhadra** *n. astrol.* twenty-sixth lunar mansion.

ఉత్తరాయణం **uttaraayaNam** *n.* period of six months from mid-January during which the point where the sun rises each day moves from the south towards the north.

ఉత్తరాషాఢ **uttaraaSaaDha** *n. astrol.* twenty-first lunar mansion.

ఉత్తరాసంగం **uttaraasangam** *n. class.* upper garment.

ఉత్తరాసి, ఉత్రాసి **uttaraasi, utraasi** *n.* lintel, the horizontal beam forming the top of a door frame.

ఉత్తరించు **uttarincu** *v.t.* 1 to cut, esp. to cut cloth into lengths or pieces. 2 to pass over, cross. 3 to kill by cutting the throat.

ఉత్తరీయం **uttariiyam** *n.* man's upper cloth, cloak, mantle.

ఉత్తరువు **uttaruwu** *n.* 1 order, command. 2 permission, leave.

ఉత్తరేణి **uttareeNi** *n. achyranthes aspera,* a medicinal plant used for skin diseases, also called **apaamaargam.**

ఉత్తరోత్రా **uttarootraa** *adv.* 1 at some future time, hereafter, in course of time. 2 gradually.

ఉత్తలం, ఉత్తలపాటు **uttalam, uttalapaaTu** *n.* distress, agitation, sorrow.

ఉత్తానం **uttaanam** *adj.* lying on o.'s back, supine.

ఉత్తారకుడు **uttaarakuDu** *n.* 1 person who enables another to cross or pass over. 2 deliverer, saviour.

ఉత్తాలం **uttaalam** *adj.* 1 long. 2 high. 3 formidable.

ఉత్తి[నే] **utti[nee]** *same as* **utta[nee].**

ఉత్తీర్ణ **uttiirNa** *adj.* passed, crossed over.

ఉత్తీర్ణుడు **uttiirNuDu** *n.* 1 person who has passed; **pariikSaloo** ~ **awu** to pass an examination. 2 competent person.

ఉత్తుంగ **uttunga** *adj.* high, tall, great.

ఉత్తుడు **uttuDu** *n.* fit person.

ఉత్తుత్త, ఉత్తుత్తి **uttutta, uttutti** *adj.* 1 mock, sham, make believe, pretended; ~ **yuddham** sham fight; ~ **peLLi** mock marriage. 2 *intensive form of* **utta, utti.**

ఉత్తేజ[న]ం **utteeja[na]m.** *n.* 1 excitement, stimulation, inspiration, motivation. 2 *sci.* stimulus, activation.

ఉత్తేజక[ర] **utteejaka[ra]** *adj. sci.* stimulating, activating.

ఉత్తేజక[ర]ం **utteejaka[ra]m** *n.* stimulant.

ఉత్తేజపరచు **utteejaparacu** *v.t.* to excite, arouse, stir up, enthuse, encourage, inspire, stimulate, activate, motivate.

ఉత్తేజిత **utteejita** *adj. sci.* stimulated, activated.

ఉత్థానం **utthaanam** *n.* 1 standing up, rising. 2 effort, exertion. 3 war, battle. 4 army.

ఉత్థాపనం **utthaapanam** *n.* raising, elevating, elevation, lifting.

ఉత్పతనం **utpatanam** *n.* 1 flying, leaping. 2 birth, production. 3 fall from a high position; **aayanaku** ~ **tappadu** he is heading for a fall. 4 *chem.* sublimation.

ఉత్పత్తి **utpatti** *n.* 1 production, output; **wyawasaayaka** ~ agricultural production. 2 *pl.* **utpattulu** products; **aTawii utpattulu** forest products. 3 birth, creation. 4 source, origin.

ఉత్పత్తిచేయు **utpatticeeyu** *v.t.* to produce.

ఉత్పత్తిదారు **utpattidaaru** *n.* producer.

ఉత్పన్న **utpanna** *adj.* produced, created, derived.

ఉత్పన్నం అవు **utpannamawu** *v.i.* to arise, occur, result, be caused, be created, be produced; **haykoorTu tiirpuwalla utpannamayna paristhiti** the situation created by (*or* resulting from) the High Court's judgement.

ఉత్పరివర్తకం **utpariwartakam** *n. biol.* mutagen.

ఉత్పరివర్తన **utpariwartana** *n. biol.* mutation.

ఉత్పలం **utpalam** *n.* 1. lotus. 2 *maths., sci.* gradient.

ఉత్పలమాల **utpalamaala** *n.* kind of verse composed in four lines each of twenty syllables.

ఉత్పాటనం **utpaaTanam** *n.* eradication, uprooting.

ఉత్పాతం **utpaatam** *n.* 1 widespread disaster or calamity. 2 prodigy, portent.

ఉత్పాదక **utpaadaka** *adj.* of production, productive, generative; ~ **pathakaalu** schemes of production; ~ **śakti** productive capacity; ~ **wastuwulu** capital goods; ~ **kanaalu** *biol.* germinating cells.

ఉత్పాదకం **utpaadakam** *n.* productive element, input; **wyawasaayadaaruDu rasaayanika eruwulu modalayna utpaadakaalu koNTaaDu** the cultivator buys chemical fertilisers and other inputs.

ఉత్పాదకత **utpaadakata** *n.* productivity.

ఉత్పాదకుడు **utpaadakuDu** *n.* producer.

ఉత్పాదన **utpaadana** *adj.* productive; ~ **śakti** productivity, productive capacity.

ఉత్పాదనం **utpaadanam** *n.* production, manufacture, creation.

ఉత్పాదించు **utpaadincu** *v.t.* to produce, create, bring about, generate, derive.

ఉత్పాదిల్లు **utpaadillu** *v.i.* 1 to be produced or created. 2 to occur, arise.

ఉత్ప్రాసం **utpraasam** *n.* laughter or joking directed against a person.

ఉత్ప్రేక్ష **utpreekSa** *n.* 1 a certain figure of speech, a kind of fanciful comparison. 2 exaggeration, hyperbole, high-flown language.

ఉత్ప్రేక్షించు **utpreekSincu** *v.t.* 1 to make a fanciful comparison. 2 to exaggerate.

ఉత్ప్రేరకం **utpreerakam** *n. chem.* catalytic agent.

ఉత్ప్రేరణ[ం] **utpreeraNa[m]** *n. chem.* catalysis.

ఉత్ప్లవనం **utplawanam** *n. phys.* buoyancy.

ఉత్ఫుల్ల **utphulla** *adj.* (of a flower) expanded, open.

ఉత్రాసి **utraasi** *same as* **uttaraasi.**

ఉత్సంగం **utsangam** *n.* 1 thigh, lap. 2 association, union. 3 embrace.

ఉత్సన్న **utsanna** *adj.* 1 uprooted, destroyed, ruined. 2 neglected, out of use.

ఉత్సరణం **utsaraNam** *n. bot.* osmosis.

ఉత్సర్గం, ఉత్సర్జనం **utsargam, utsarjanam** *n.* 1 abandoning, relinquishing, resigning. 2 freeing, letting loose, discharging.

ఉత్సవం **utsawam** *n.* festival, festivity, feast, celebration, jubilee; **śatajayanti utsawaalu** centenary celebrations; **wajrootsawam** diamond jubilee.

ఉత్స[వ]విగ్రహం **utsa[wa]wigraham** *n.* 1 small temple idol used for taking in procession as a representative of the main presiding deity. 2 small personality representing s.o. greater.

ఉత్సహించు **utsahincu** *v.i.* 1 to endeavour, attempt. 2 to rejoice, feel happy. 3 to be enthused.

ఉత్సాదనం **utsaadanam** *n.* 1 rooting out, abolition. 2 elevating.

ఉత్సారగ్రాసం **utsaara graasam** *n.* concentrated fodder.

ఉత్సారణం **utsaaraNam** *n.* moving (people) aside in order to clear a path.

ఉత్సాహం **utsaaham** *n.* 1 zeal, enthusiasm, excitement, eagerness, keenness, zest, ardour, relish. 2 joy, merriment. 3 spirit, mettle, alacrity. 4 effort, energy.

ఉత్సాహంగల **utsaahangala** *adj.* eager, enthusiastic.

ఉత్సాహపరచు **utsaahaparacu** *v.t.* to encourage, enthuse.

ఉత్సాహపూరిత **utsaahapuurita** *adj.* 1 thrilled, excited, filled with excitement. 2 eager, enthusiastic.

ఉత్సాహవంత **utsaahawanta** *adj.* excited, enthusiastic.

ఉత్సుక **utsuka** *adj.* eager, keen, desirous.

ఉత్సుకం, ఉత్సుకత **utsukam, utsukata** *n.* 1 eagerness, keenness, zeal, enthusiasm. 2 love, longing.

ఉత్సృజం **utsṛjam** *n. bot.* secretion.

ఉత్సృష్ట **utsṛSTa** *adj.* abandoned, left.

ఉత్సేకం **utseekam** *n.* 1 increase, excess. 2 pride, haughtiness. 3 sprinkling of water.

ఉత్సేధం **utseedham** *n.* 1 height, loftiness. 2 *sci.* protuberance, swelling.

ఉత్స్ఫోటక **utsphooTaka** *adj. bot.* explosive.

ఉత్స్వేదనం **utsweedanam** *n. bot.* transpiration.

ఉదంతం **udantam** *n.* 1 story, narrative, fable. 2 news, message, account. 3 subject matter. 4 *gram.* word ending in the vowel *u*.

ఉదకం **udakam** *n.* water.

ఉదగ్ర **udagra** *adj.* 1 high. 2 fearful, terrible. 3 *bot.* acuminate. 4 *maths.* **udagraakSam** vertical axis.

ఉదజని **udajani** *n. chem.* hydrogen.

ఉదత్యాగం **udatyaagam** *n. chem.* efflorescence.

ఉదయం **udayam** *n.* 1 morning. 2 rising of sun and other heavenly bodies. 3 birth. 4 advancement, prosperity.

ఉదయాద్రి **udayaadri** *n.* name of the mythological eastern mountain from behind which the sun rises.

ఉదయించు **udayincu** *v.i.* 1 (of the sun) to rise. 2 to originate, begin, be born.

ఉదరం **udaram** *n.* stomach, abdomen.
ఉదరపోషణం **udarapooSaNam** *n.* sustaining o.s., earning o.'s living.
ఉదరు **udaru** *same as* **adaru.**
ఉదర్కం **udarkam** *n.* 1 future. 2 remote consequence. 3 conclusion, outcome.
ఉదహరించు **udaharincu** *same as* **udaaharincu.**
ఉదాత్త **udaatta** *adj.* 1 generous, liberal. 2. noble, glorious. 3 (of passions) lofty, elevated, sublime. 4 great, vast.
ఉదాత్తత **udaattata** *n.* 1 generosity. 2 nobility.
ఉదాత్తస్వరం **udaattaswaram** *n.* 1 *ling.* rising tone. 2 rising pitch in Vedic recitation.
ఉదాత్తుడు **udaattuDu** *n.* great, noble or generous person.
ఉదార **udaara** *adj.* generous, munificent, charitable, liberal, nobleminded.
ఉదారత **udaarata** *n.* generosity, munificence, liberality.
ఉదార[తా]వాదం **udaara[taa]waadam** *n.* *polit.* liberalism.
ఉదారపూరిత **udaarapuurita** *adj.* benevolent.
ఉదాసి **udaasi** *n.* stoic, s.o. devoid of passion.
ఉదాసించు **udaasincu** *v.t.* 1 to despise. 2 to browbeat, bully.
ఉదాసీనం, ఉదాసీనత **udaasiinam, udaasiinata** *n.* indifference, disregard, coldness, apathy, unconcern.
ఉదాహరణ[ం] **udaaharaNa[m]** *n.* example, instance, illustration; **udaaharaNaatmakamayna naDawaDika** exemplary good conduct.
ఉదాహరించు, ఉదహరించు **udaaharincu, udaharincu** *v.t.* 1 to cite or quote (as an example or authority). 2 to instance, mention. 3 to illustrate, exemplify.
ఉదాహృత **udaahrta** *adj.* instanced, mentioned, cited, quoted.
ఉదిరి **udiri** I. *n.* fine gold. II. *adj.* fine, pure.
ఉదిల **udila** *n.* grief.
ఉదీచి **udiici** *n.* *class.* north.
ఉదీర్ణం **udiirNam** *adj.* generous, noble, great.
ఉదుకుష్టం **udukuSTam** *adj.* *colloq.* wretched, miserable, hopeless.
ఉదుటు **uduTu** *n.* vigour, strength, force; **okka ~na** leeci **waakiTLooki weLLEEDu** he sprang up and went outside.
ఉదురు **uduru** *same as* **adaru.**
ఉద్గతి, ఉద్గమనం **udgati, udgamanam** *n.* 1 rising. 2 birth, production.
ఉద్గమించు **udgamincu** *v.i.* 1 to rise, fly. 2 to emerge, burst out.
ఉద్గారం **udgaaram** *n.* 1 vomiting, belching, spewing. 2 *chem.* emission.
ఉద్గారించు **udgaarincu** *v.t.* to vomit, belch, spew out.
ఉద్గ్రంథం **udgrantham** *n.* 1 big book. 2 great book, masterpiece of literature.
ఉద్గ్రహణ **udgrahaNa** *n.* extraction (of minerals).
ఉద్గ్రీవుడు **udgriiwuDu** *n.* proud, haughty person.
ఉద్ఘట్టనం **udghaTTanam** *n.* striking against.
ఉద్ఘాటన **udghaaTana** *n.* emphasis.
ఉద్ఘాటనం **udghaaTanam** *n.* 1 breaking open. 2 water lift, picota. 3 key.
ఉద్ఘాటించు **udghaaTincu** *v.t.* 1 to break open. 2 to assert, say emphatically, emphasise.
ఉద్ఘాతం **udghaatam** *n.* 1 beginning. 2 blow, stroke, wound. 3 iron rod or club. 4 stumbling.
ఉద్ఘోషం **udghooSam** *n.* 1 crying out, shouting. 2 proclaiming. 3 generally believed rumour, popular report.
ఉద్ఘోషించు **udghooSincu** *v.t.* 1 to cry out, shout. 2 to proclaim, enunciate.
ఉద్ద **udda** *adj.* and *adv.* *class.* much, very.
ఉద్దండ **uddaNDa** I. *n.* (*also* ~ **ta**) violence, fierceness. II. *adj.* great, *as in* ~ **paNDituDu** great scholar.
ఉద్దర **uddara** *n.* *dial.* credit; **Dabbu iwwaali, ~ leedu** pay in cash, no credit is given.
ఉద్దరి **uddari** *n.* steep bank.
ఉద్దరువు **uddaruwu** *n.* mortgage of a crop.
ఉద్దవడి **uddawaDi** I.*n.class.* speed, haste. II *adv.* *class.* 1 very fast. 2 soon after[wards].
ఉద్దాముడు **uddaamuDu** *n.* 1 irresistible person or being. 2 name of Yama or Varuna.
ఉద్దాలకుడు **uddaalakuDu** *n.* Uddalaka, a Hindu sage, husband of Chandika, a proverbial shrew.
ఉద్దాలు **uddaalu** *n.pl.* sandals.
ఉద్ది, ఉజ్జీ **uddi[1], ujjii** I. *n.* 1 equal, match. 2 rival, competitor. 3 equality. II. *adj.* equal, paired, coupled.
ఉద్ది **uddi[2]** *n.* 1 bank with a channel on it to convey water raised by baling. 2 resting platform for baling bullocks.
ఉద్దిష్ట **uddiSTa** *adj.* 1 intended, designed, proposed, contemplated. 2 mentioned, designated.
ఉద్దీపక **uddiipaka** *adj.* 1 burning, inflaming, lighting. 2 enlightening, exciting, intensifying, arousing.
ఉద్దీపన[ం] **uddiipana[m]** *n.* 1 burning, inflaming, making more tense. 2 enlightening, exciting, arousing.
ఉద్దీపించు **uddiipincu** *v.t.* 1 to cause to shine or burn. 2 to illuminate. 3 to excite, arouse.
ఉద్దు, ఉద్దిపప్పు **uddu, uddipappu** *n.* *dial.* blackgram.
ఉద్దేశం **uddeeśam** *n.* 1 intention, meaning, design. 2 object, purpose, motive. 3 opinion, idea, belief.
ఉద్దేశపూర్వకంగా **uddeeeśapuurwakangaa** *adv.* intentionally, deliberately.
ఉద్దేశించు **uddeeśincu** *v.t.* to intend, design, aim at, have in mind, address; **talettakuNDaance ramaNayya raambaabuni uddeeśinci aDigEEDu** addressing Rambabu, Ramanayya asked, without even raising his head. . . .
ఉద్దేశ్యం **uddeeśyam** *n.* s.g that is intended.
ఉద్ధతి **uddhati** *n.* haughtiness, arrogance, pride, insolence.

ఉద్ధరణ[ం]**uddharaNa[m]** *n.* 1 raising, uplift[ing]; **harijanooddharaNa** harijan uplift. 2 establishment, support. 3 revival, restoration, rehabilitation, rescue; **taamu patita janooddharaNa ceestunnaamanna manastatwam powaali** they must stop thinking of themselves as rescuers of fallen humanity.

ఉద్ధరణి **uddharaNi** *n.* small spoon (specially designed) used in making oblations.

ఉద్ధరించు **uddharincu** *v.t.* 1 to raise, uplift; **aarthikangaa wenakabaDina wargaalawaarini uddharincaDaaniki pathakaalu ceepaTTEEru** they have undertaken schemes for the uplift of members of economically backward classes. 2 to support, uphold. 3 to rescue, restore, revive, rehabilitate. 4 to save, preserve, deliver. 5 *ironical use* **uddharincEEwulee!** how helpful you have been! (meaning the opposite).

ఉద్ధారకుడు **uddhaarakuDu** *n.* 1 person who uplifts or sustains. 2 saviour, deliverer.

ఉద్ధుర **uddhura** *adj.* 1 heavy. 2 firm, intrepid. 3 unrestrained.

ఉద్ధూత **uddhuuta** *adj.* driven off, shaken off, scattered.

ఉద్ధృత **uddhrta** *adj.* 1 raised. 2 drawn out, extracted.

ఉద్బుద్ధ **udbuddha** *adj.* 1 awakened. 2 enlightened. 3 stirred, excited.

ఉద్బోధ[నం] **udboodha[nam]** *n.* 1 awakening. 2 reminding. 3 exhortation.

ఉద్బోధించు **udboodhincu** *v.t.* 1 to exhort. 2 to awaken. 3 to remind.

ఉద్భవం **udbhawam** *n.* birth, origin.

ఉద్భవించు **udbhawincu** *v.i.* 1 to be born, produced or created. 2. to originate.

ఉద్భాసిత **udbhaasita** *adj.* splendid, glorious.

ఉద్భిజ్జం, ఉద్భిదం **udbhijjam, udbhidam** *n.* 1 sprouting, germinating. 2 anything which sprouts or germinates, any plant, tree, etc., belonging to the vegetable kingdom.

ఉద్భిదవ్యాధిశాస్త్రం **udbhidawyaadhi śaastram** *n.* plant pathology.

ఉద్భిన్న **udbhinna** *adj.* 1 sprouting. 2 (of a flower) open, blossoming.

ఉద్భూత[ం] **udbhuuta[m]** *adj.* 1 produced. 2 manifested.

ఉద్భేద[ం] **udbheeda[m]** *adj.* breaking or bursting through.

ఉద్భ్రమణం **udbhramaNam** *n.* whirling, brandishing.

ఉద్యమ[ం] **udyama[m]** *n.* 1 *polit.* movement, campaign. 2 effort, exertion. 3 attempt, endeavour. 4 (*also* **udyami**) enterprise, initiative, dynamism.

ఉద్యమకారుడు **udyamakaaruDu** *n.* agitator, campaigner.

ఉద్యమించు **udyamincu** *v.i.* 1 to strive (-**ku**, for), make an attempt (-**ku**, at). 2 to set about, begin.

ఉద్యమిదారు, ఉద్యమదారు **udyamidaaru, udyamadaaru** *n.* 1 *econ.* enterpreneur. 2 agitator.

ఉద్యానం **udyaanam** *n.* garden, park.

ఉద్యానకృషి **udyaanakrSi** *n.* horticulture.

ఉద్యానవనం **udyaanawanam** *n.* garden or park consisting of land with trees and shrubs.

ఉద్యాపనం, ఉజ్జాపనం **udyaapanam, ujjaapanam** *n.* closing rite of a penance or devotion.

ఉద్యుక్త **udyukta** *adj.* keen, determined, ready.

ఉద్యుక్తుడు **udyuktuDu** *n.* one who is ready or prepared.

ఉద్యోగం **udyoogam** *n.* 1 job, work, occupation, profession, employment; ~**ceeyu** to be employed; **udyoogaawakaaśaalu** job opportunites; **udyooga saadhaka kaaryaalayam** employment exchange. 2 effort, exertion. 3 attempt, endeavour.

ఉద్యోగరీత్యా **udyoogariityaa** *adv. ex officio.*

ఉద్యోగస్థుడు **udyoogasthudu** *n.* 1 employee. 2 government official.

ఉద్యోగి **udyoogi** *n.* employee.

ఉద్యోగించు **udyoogincu** *v.i.* to strive, undertake, apply o.s.; **manam udyooginci pani ceeyaali** we must work with all our might.

ఉద్యోగిస్వామ్యం **udyoogiswaamyam** *n.* bureaucracy.

ఉద్యోతనం **udyootanam** *n. phys.* irradiation.

ఉద్రథం **udratham** *n.* linchpin of a chariot wheel.

ఉద్రిక్త **udrikta** *adj.* 1 excited, tense, stirred up, aroused; **koopoodriktuDu** s.o. roused to anger. 2 increased, abundant.

ఉద్రిక్తత **udriktata** *n.* [state of] tension; ~**saDali sawmanasya waataawaraNam nelakonaali** tension must be relaxed and a climate of good will must be established.

ఉద్రిక్తపడు **udriktapaDu** *v.i.* to be stirred up, aroused, incensed.

ఉద్రేకం **udreekam** *n.* 1 emotional tension, passion, excitement. 2 excess, increase.

ఉద్రేకపడు **udreekapaDu** *v.i.* to get excited.

ఉద్రేకపరచు **udreekaparacu** *v.t.* to excite.

ఉద్రేకించు **udreekincu** *v.i.* 1 to get excited, flare up, be enraged. 2 to increase, intensify.

ఉద్వర్తనం **udwartanam** *n.* 1 ointment applied to the body before bathing or to relieve pain. 2 rubbing the body with ointment. 3 rising up.

ఉద్వహనం **udwahanam** *n. class.* 1 supporting, bearing. 2 marrying.

ఉద్వాసం **udwaasam** *n.* expulsion, banishment.

ఉద్వాసన[ం] **udwaasana[m]** *n.* 1 same as **wisarjana** *sense 2.* 2 expulsion, banishment, displacement, removal; ~**ceppu** to banish, expel, remove, get rid of, bid farewell to; **ii mEEsTaru muuDu nelalaynaa uNDaka puurwamee aayanaku~ceppEEru kamiTiiwaaru** before this master had been there even for three months the committee members got rid of him.

ఉద్వాహం **udwaaham** *n. class.* marriage.

ఉద్విగ్న **udwigna** *adj.* 1 animated, thrilled, excited: **atani manasu aa nṛtyakheelaku ~mayindi** his mind was thrilled by the dancing performance. 2 enthusiastic, passionate, zealous. 3 anxious, agitated, tense.

ఉద్విగ్నత **udwignata** *n.* zeal, enthusiasm; **lakSyamleeni** ~ zeal without an objective.

ఉద్వీక్షణం **udwiikSaNam** *n.* looking up at.

ఉద్వృత్తి **udwṛtti** *n.* 1 haughtiness, pride. 2 rudeness, bad manners.

ఉద్వేగం **udweegam** *n.* 1 agitation, excitement. 2 fear, anxiety.

ఉద్వేజనం **udweejanam** *n.* fear, anxiety.

ఉద్వేల **udweela** *adj.* vast, surpassing the limit.

ఉధృత **udhṛta** *adj.* (relating to any unwelcome occurrence or situation, misfortune, natural calamity, etc.) great, strong, violent, turbulent, mighty, powerful, serious, severe; **aneeka kaaraNaala walla maleeriyaa ~ngaa tala ettindi** due to many reasons malaria appeared on an intense scale; **gaaliwaana ~ngaa undi** the cyclone was severe.

ఉధృతం **udhṛtam** *n.* greatness, muchness.

ఉనికి **uniki** *n.* 1 being, living, existence; **suukSmajiiwula ~ni kanipeTTina śaastraweetta** the scientist who discovered the existence of microorganisms; **ii praśnalu keewalam arthamleeni aaloocanalu kaawu, maanawuni~ni praśninci, uuginci, śaasincee sawaaLLu** these questions are not just meaningless thoughts, they are challenges which question, sway and direct men's existence. 2 remaining, stay, presence, occurrence; **bengaal, biihaar, malabaarlaloo Dacwaari paripaalanaakaalaaniki sambandhincina granthaalu aneekam uNDagaa, aandhra praantamloo wiiri~ ki sambandhincina grantham okaTaynaa raaleedu** whereas there are many books relating to the time of Dutch rule in Bengal, Bihar and Malabar, not one has appeared which deals with their presence in the Andhra region. 3 *geog.* position, situation, location. 4 state, condition.

ఉనికిపట్టు **unikipaTTu** *n.* place of habitation, home, habitat.

ఉన్నట్లుండి, ఉన్నట్టుండి **unnaTLuNDi, unnaTTuNDi** *adv.* suddenly, all of a sudden, all at once.

ఉన్నత **unnata** *adj.* high, lofty; ~ **śikSaNa** advanced training; ~ **paaThaśaala** high school, *but* ~ **widya** higher (i.e., university) education; ~ **sthaayi** high level.

ఉన్నతి **unnati** *n.* 1 height, altitude, elevation. 2 exaltation, eminence. 3 increase, prosperity, headway, development.

ఉన్నతోపరి **unnatoopari** *adj. and adv.* aloft.

ఉన్నదున్నట్లుగా **unnadunnaTLugaa** *same as* **yathaa tathangaa.**

ఉన్నపళంగా, ఉన్నమట్టున **unnapaLangaa, unnamaTTuna** *adv.* in the state or condition just then existing; **aayana phoon ceesEEDu. neenu~ TEEksiiloo ekki akkaDiki weLLEEnu** he telephoned and I got into a taxi and went there just as I was.

ఉన్నపాటున **unnapaaTuna** *adv.* 1 *same as* **unnapaLangaa.** 2 just for the moment, all of a sudden, on the spur of the moment; **widyaarthulu udaaharaNalu teluguloo ceppamannaaru. ~ naaku okaTii taTTaleedu** the students asked for examples in Telugu, but on the spur of the moment I could not think of even one.

ఉన్నమిత[ం] **unnamita[m]** *adj.* raised, exalted.

ఉన్నరూపు **unnaruupu** *n.* original form, original shape.

ఉన్నవాడు **unnawaaDu** *see* **uNDu** *sense 6.*

ఉన్ని **unni** I. *n.* wool. II. *adj.* made of wool, woollen.

ఉన్నిఅల్లిక **unni allika** *n.* wool knitting.

ఉన్నిద్ర **unnidra** *adj.* awakened.

ఉన్మత్త[ం] **unmatta[m]** *adj.* 1 crazy, mad, insane. 2 *fig.* drunk, intoxicated; **dhanoonmatta** drunk with riches.

ఉన్మాదం **unmaadam** *n.* madness, insanity, mania, psychosis.

ఉన్మాది **unmaadi** *n.* madman, lunatic, maniac.

ఉన్మీలనం **unmiilanam** *n.* 1 opening, expanding, blooming. 2 revealing, unfolding.

ఉన్మీలిత **unmiilita** *adj.* 1 fully opened, blooming. 2 revealed, unfolded, made clear.

ఉన్ముఖ[ం] **unmukha[m]** *adj., occurring in compounds, often in noun form* **unmukhuDu** *pl.* **unmukhulu** 1 ready for, prepared for, inclined to; **ii mahaanubhaawulu manalni kaaryoonmukhulugaa ceestaaru** these great men make us feel inclined to take action. 2 directed, oriented, tending towards, headed towards; **waaru weLLi kaaruloo kuurconi gṛhoonmukhulu ayyEEru** they went and sat in the car and headed for home; **udyoogoonmukha koorsulu** job-oriented courses.

ఉన్ముఖత **unmukhata** *n.* tendency, propensity.

ఉన్మూల **unmuula** *adj.* from the root, radical.

ఉన్మూలంగా **unmuulangaa** *adv.* radically.

ఉన్మూలించు **unmuulincu** *v.t.* to uproot, eradicate, destroy.

ఉన్మేషణ[ం] **unmeeSaNa[m]** *n.* 1 (of a flower) opening, blooming. 2 (of knowledge, progress) expanding, spreading.

ఉప **upa** *Sanskrit prefix meaning* lower, subordinate (in place or degree); *cf. English 'sub', to which it is etymologically related.*

ఉప ఉత్పత్తి **upa utpatti** *n.* by-product.

ఉప ఎన్నిక **upa ennika** *n.* by-election.

ఉపకరణం **upakaraNam** *n.* 1 tool, implement, instrument. 2 *sci.* apparatus, appliance. 3 agent, means.

ఉపకరించు **upakarincu** *v.i.* to benefit, serve, be of help or use, facilitate.

ఉపకల్పన **upakalpana** *n.* hypothesis.

ఉపకారం, ఉపకృతి **upakaaram, upakṛti** *n.* aid, help, kindness, favour, benefit, benefaction, service.

ఉపకారవేత[న]ం **upakaara weeta[na]m** *n.* 1 student's scholarship or stipend. 2 retirement gratuity. 3 pension

ఉపకారి **upakaari** I. *n.* benefactor. II. *adj.* 1 helpful, beneficial. 2 charitable.

ఉపకార్యదర్శి **upakaaryadarśi** *n.* deputy secretary.

ఉపకులాలు **upakulaalu** *n.pl.* subcastes, subcommunities.
ఉపకృతం **upakrtam** *n.* **1** favour. **2** help, usefulness.
ఉపక్రమం **upakramam** *n.* **1** beginning, start, inception. **2** *class.* practice of medicine.
ఉపక్రమణిక **upakramaNika** *n.* introduction, preface (to a book), preamble.
ఉపక్రమించు **upakramincu** *v.i.* to begin, undertake, embark on; **wiiDi paripuurNa citram miimundu uncaalanee ii raataki upakramincEEnu** I have undertaken this writing in order to place a complete picture of him before you.
ఉపక్రోశం **upakroośam** *n.* censure, blame.
ఉపఖండం **upkhaNDam** *n.* subcontinent.
ఉపగూహనం **upaguuhanam** *n.* lovers' embrace, kiss.
ఉపగోత్రాలు **upagootraalu** *n.pl.* subclans.
ఉపగ్రహం **upagraham** *n.* **1** satellite. **2** *colloq.* follower, dependant.
ఉపచయం **upacayam** *n.* **1** increase, rise. **2** heap, accumulation.
ఉపచరించు **upacarincu** *v.i. and t.* **1** to serve, be of help, be useful. **2** to attend, wait upon. **3** to honour.
ఉపచారం **upacaaram** *n.* **1** service, attendance, good offices. **2** respect, honouring. **3** medical treatment.
ఉపచేతనం **upaceetanam** *n.* subconscious mind.
ఉపచ్ఛాయ **upacchaaya** *n.* penumbra.
ఉపజాతి **upajaati** *n.* **1** subclass. **2** subspecies. **3** kind of poetic metre.
ఉపజిహ్వక **upajihwaka** *n.* uvula.
ఉపజీవకుడు **upajiiwakuDu** *n.* dependant.
ఉపజీవి **upajiiwi** *n.* person who lives parasitically on others.
ఉపజ్ఞ **upajña** *n.* **1** innate knowledge, natural intelligence, instinct. **2** genius, originality.
ఉపతాపం **upataapam** *n.* **1** grief. **2** trouble. **3** disease.
ఉపత్యక **upatyaka** *n.* land at the foot of a hill.
ఉపద, ఉపదానం **upada, upadaanam** *n.* present, bribe.
ఉపదేశం **upadeesam** *n.* **1** teaching, instruction, guidance. **2** precept, maxim. **3** lecture, discourse, preaching. **4** **~awu, ~pondu** (i) to receive guidance or instruction, (ii) to receive religious instruction leading to attainment of salvation.
ఉపదేశించు **upadeesincu** *v.t.* **1** to teach, instruct, guide. **2** to advise, prompt. **3** to suggest, hint. **4** to preach, lecture. **5** to give religious instruction leading to attainment of salvation.
ఉపదేష్ట **upadeeSTa** *n.* teacher, instructor, preceptor, esp. a religious preceptor.
ఉపద్రవ **upadrawa** *adj.* troublesome, dreadful, violent, severe, serious, distressing.
ఉపద్రవం **upadrawam** *n.* **1** trouble, difficulty, affliction. **2** misfortune, disaster, calamity. **3** injury, harm, damage. **4** violence, disorder. **5** terrorising. **6** revolt.
ఉపధ **upadha** *n. gram.* second last letter in a word.
ఉపధా **upadhaa** *same as* **upaantya.**
ఉపధాతువు **upadhaatuwu** *n. chem.* metalloid.
ఉపధానం **upadhaanam** *n.* pillow, cushion.
ఉపధి **upadhi** *n.* fraud, cheating.
ఉపధ్మానీయం **upadhmaaniiyam** *n. gram.* name given to visarga or voiceless sound occurring before a bilabial stop, as in **praata-h-pawanam.**
ఉపనగరం **upanagaram** *n.* suburb.
ఉపనది **upanadi** *n.* tributary (of a river).
ఉపనయనం **upanayanam** *n.* ceremony of investiture with the sacred thread.
ఉపనిధి **upanidhi** *n.* **1** pledge. **2** sealed deposit.
ఉపనియమావళి **upaniyamaawaLi** *n.* byelaws.
ఉపనిషత్తు **upaniSattu** *n.* sacred philosophical treatise attached to the Vedas, forming part of the Hindu scriptures.
ఉపనీతుడు **upaniituDu** *n.* person who has been invested with the sacred thread.
ఉపన్యసించు **upanyasincu** *v.i. and t.* **1** to deliver a speech, lecture or address. **2** to explain, expound, inculcate, preach (doctrine).
ఉపన్యాసం **upanyaasam** *n.* speech, lecture, discourse, address.
ఉపపతి **upapati** *n.* married woman's paramour.
ఉపపత్తి **upapatti** *n.* **1** possessing, gaining. **2** birth. **3** cause, reason. **4** *maths.* demonstration, proof (of a proposition).
ఉపపత్ని **upapatni** *n.* mistress, concubine.
ఉపపత్రం **upapatram** *n. bot.* leaflet, pinna.
ఉపపదం **upapadam** *n. ling.* **1** prefix. **2** article.
ఉపపన్న **upapanna** *adj.* possessed of, furnished with.
ఉపపాదనం **upapaadanam** *n.* **1** demonstrating. **2** proposal, proposition.
ఉపపాదించు **upapaadincu** *v.t.* to put forward a proposition.
ఉపపాద్యం **upapaadyam** *n.* proposal, proposition.
ఉపప్రమాణం **upapramaaNam** *n. sci.* reference.
ఉపప్రమేయం **upaprameeyam** *n.* corollary.
ఉపప్లవం **upaplawam** *n.* **1** misfortune, disaster, calamity. **2** evil omen, portent signifying disaster.
ఉపఫలం **upaphalam** *n.* by-product.
ఉపబలం **upabalam** *n. class.* aid, assistance.
ఉపబలక **upabalaka** *adj. class.* supporting (evidence).
ఉపభోగం **upabhoogam** *n.* enjoyment, use.
ఉపమ **upama**[1] *n.* **1** contrivance. **2** skill.
ఉపమ **upama**[2] *n.* **1** likeness, resemblance. **2** comparison. **3** simile.
ఉపమంత్రి **upamantri** *n.* deputy minister.
ఉపమరి **upamari** *n.* person who is quick with expedients, ingenious or resourceful person.
ఉపమానం **upamaanam** *n.* **1** example, illustration. **2** comparison. **3** likeness, resemblance, similarity. **4** simile.
ఉపమార్గం **upamaargam** *n.* byway.
ఉపమించు **upamincu** *v.t.* to compare.

ఉపమితి **upamiti** *n.* resemblance, similarity.

ఉపమృత్తిక **upamṛttika** *n.* subsoil.

ఉపమేయం **upameeyam** I. *n.* subject of a comparison, s.g which is compared with a standard or another object. II. *adj.* fit to be compared.

ఉపయుక్త **upayukta** *adj.* 1 useful, serviceable, practical; **wiiriki konta saamaanya widya, aneeka ~ wṛttulaloo śikSana istaaru** they give these persons some general education along with training in many useful occupations. 2 fit, suitable. 3 employed, used, made use of. 4 (of books) consulted; **~grantha suucika** index of books consulted, bibliography. 5 applied; **~gaNitaśaastram** applied mathematics.

ఉపయోక్త **upayookta** *n.* user; **sangraahakuDu entawarakuu kṛtakṛtyuDu kaagalindii nirNayincawalasindi nighaNTuwu~lu** it is the users of the dictionary who must decide how far the compiler has been successful.

ఉపయోగం **upayoogam** *n.* 1 use[fulness], advantage, benefit, utility. 2 applicability, application.

ఉపయోగకర **upayoogakara** *adj.* 1 useful, practical. 2 applicable.

ఉపయోగపడు **upayoogapaDu** *v.i.* 1 to be useful, be of use. 2 to apply, be applicable.

ఉపయోగపరచు **upayoogaparacu** *v.t.* 1 to make use of. 2 to put to use, apply.

ఉపయోగించు **upayoogincu** I. *v.t.* to use, make use of, employ, utilise. II. *v.i.* 1 to be used, be useful, serve. 2 to apply, be applicable.

ఉపయోగితావాదం **upayoogitaawaadam** *n. econ.* utilitarianism.

ఉపయోజనం **upayoojanam** *n. biol.* adaptation.

ఉపయోజనీయ **upayoojaniiya** *adj.* utilisable, available: **~śakti** available energy.

ఉపరాగం **uparaagam** *n.* eclipse.

ఉపరాష్ట్రపతి **uparaaSTrapati** *n.* Vice President of India.

ఉపరి **upari** *adv.* over and above.

ఉపరితలం **uparitalam** *n.* surface.

ఉపరిభాగం **uparibhaagam** *n.* 1 upper part. 2 surface.

ఉపలం **upalam** *n.* 1 stone, rock. 2 precious stone, jewel.

ఉపలంబం **upalambam** *adj. maths. sci.* sub-normal.

ఉపలక్షకంగా **upalakSakangaa** *adv.* as a sign, token or indication.

ఉపలక్షణం **upalakSaNam** *n.* sign, token, indication, characteristic.

ఉపలక్షించు **upalakSincu** *v.t.* 1 to survey, observe. 2 to watch over. 3 *admin.* to designate.

ఉపలక్షీకరించు **upalakSiikarincu** *v.t.* to characterise.

ఉపలబ్ధ **upalabdha** *adj.* 1 obtained, gained. 2 understood.

ఉపలభ్య **upalabhya** *adj.* available, procurable.

ఉపలాలనం **upalaalanam** *n.* 1 lulling to sleep. 2 coaxing.

ఉపలేపనం **upaleepanam** *n.* smearing, rubbing on (ointment).

ఉపవనం **upawanam** *n.* garden, backyard.

ఉపవసించు **upawasincu** *v.i.* to fast.

ఉపవాక్యం **upawaakyam** *n. gram.* [subordinate] clause.

ఉపవాసం **upawaasam** *n.* fast[ing], abstinence from food; **~ uNDu, ~ ceeyu** to fast.

ఉపవిభక్తి **upawibhakti** *n. gram.* inflectional increment; *see* **awpawibhaktikam.**

ఉపవిష్ట **upawiSTa** *adj.* seated, sitting.

ఉపవీతం **upawiitam** *n.* sacred thread.

ఉపవృక్కం **upawṛkkam** *n. med.* adrenal gland.

ఉపవృక్కి **upawṛkki** *n. med.* adrenalin.

ఉపశమనం **upaśamanam** *n.* 1 relief, alleviation, abatement. 2 calmness, quiet (of passions).

ఉపశమించు **upaśamincu** I. *v.i.* 1 to be calmed, relieved, alleviated, assuaged or soothed. 2 (of emotions) to subside. II. *v.t.* to calm, relieve.

ఉపశమిల్లు **upaśamillu** *v.i.* to become calm or quiet.

ఉపశాంతి **upaśaanti** *n.* 1 calmness, tranquillity. 2 relief.

ఉపశ్రుతి **upaśṛti** *n.* dissenting voice.

ఉపసంఘం **upasangham** *n.* subcommittee.

ఉపసంహరించు **upasamharincu** *v.t.* 1 to withdraw, retract, (proposal), countermand (order), recall, take away. 2 to sum up in conclusion.

ఉపసంహారం, ఉపసంహరణ[ం] **upasaṁhaaram, upasaṁharaNa[m]** *n.* 1 withdrawal (of a proposal). 2 recalling, averting. 3 final summing up, end, conclusion; **grantha~** epilogue.

ఉపసభాపతి **upasabhaapati** *n.* Deputy Speaker.

ఉపసరణ **upasaraNa** *n. sci.* transfusion.

ఉపసర్గ[ం] **upasarga[m]**[1] *n. ling.* prefix.

ఉపసర్గం **upasargam**[2] n. portent.

ఉపసర్పంచ్ **upasarpanc** *n.* vice president of a village panchayat.

ఉపసర్పణం **upasarpaNam** *n. class.* 1 approaching. 2 courting, wooing.

ఉపసిద్ధాంతం **upasiddhaantam** *n.* corollary.

ఉపసూర్యకం **upasuuryakam** *n.* halo round the sun.

ఉపస్తరణం **upastaraNam** *n.* 1 spreading out. 2 bed cover.

ఉపస్థ **upastha** *n.* external organs of generation in either sex.

ఉపస్థానం **upasthaanam** *n.* 1 nearness, closeness, proximity. 2 attendance, service. 3 worship[ing]. 4 obeisance made on departure.

ఉపస్థితి **upasthiti** *n.* 1 nearness. 2 recollection. 3 presence, appearance, occurrence.

ఉపస్పర్శం **upasparśam** *n.*1 touching, contact. 2 ceremonial bathing.

ఉపహతం **upahatam** *adj.* 1 struck, smitten, injured. 2 overpowered, destroyed.

ఉపహారం **upahaaram** *n.* 1 complimentary gift to a superior. 2 offering to a deity, sacrifice.

ఉపహాసం **upahaasam** *n.* ridicule, joking.

ఉపాంగం **upaangam** *n.* 1 subsidiary part, appendage. 2 drone forming the accompaniment to a musical performance. 3 class of writings supplementary to the Vedangas. **4** mark made with sandal paste on the forehead to indicate the Vaishnavite sect.

ఉపాంత **upaanta** *adj.* near, close, marginal.

ఉపాంతం **upaantam** *n.***1** close proximity. **2** edge, border, margin.

ఉపాంత్య, ఉపధా **upaantya, upadhaa** *adj.* last but one, second last, penultimate.

ఉపాంశువు **upaamśuwu** *n.* **1** reciting of prayer in a low voice. **2** prayer so recited.

ఉపాకర్మ[ం] **upaakarma[m]** *n.* ceremony performed on full moon day of Sravanam before beginning ceremonial reading of the Vedas.

ఉపాఖ్యానం **upaakhyaanam** *n.* episode or illustrative story introduced as part of a longer tale.

ఉపాదానం **upaadaanam** *n.* **1** receiving alms. **2** alms, charity. **3** cause, motive. **4** withdrawing the organs of sense and perception from the external world.

ఉపాదేయం **upaadeeyam** *adj.* fitting, useful, worth while, acceptable; **pariśoodhakulaku, jijñaasuwulaku idi ~gaa uNTundani aaśistunnaamu** we trust that this (book) will be useful to researchers and scholars; **jaatiiya bhaaSa weeraynaa, maatṛbhaaSaloo widyaaboodhana awaśyamani, ~ani caalaamandi angiikaristaaru** though the national language may be different, many people agree that education in the mother tongue is necessary and fitting.

ఉపాధానం **upaadhaanam** *n.* **1** keeping. **2** covering. **3** wearing.

ఉపాధి **upaadhi** *n.* subsistence, means of livelihood, means of living, employment.

ఉపాధ్యక్షుడు **upaadhyakSuDu** *n.* Vice President, Vice Chairman, Vice Chancellor, Deputy Speaker.

ఉపాధ్యాయ **upaadhyaaya** *adj.* relating to teachers; **~śikSaNa** teachers' training; **~sangham** teachers' association.

ఉపాధ్యాయిని **upaadhyaayini** *n.* school mistress, lady teacher.

ఉపాధ్యాయుడు **'upaadhyaayuDu** *n.* school master, teacher.

ఉపాయం **upaayam** *n.* **1** means, method, way. **2** contrivance, device, artifice. **3** clever idea, easy solution.

ఉపాయనం **upaayanam** *n.* complimentary gift.

ఉపాయశాలి **upaayaśaali** *n.* clever, ingenious or resourceful person.

ఉపార్జన[ం] **upaarjana[m]** *n.* gaining, acquiring, earning, achievement.

ఉపార్జిత **upaarjita** *adj.* acquired.

ఉపాలంభం **upaalambham** *n.* abuse, taunting, censure.

ఉపాశ్రయం **upaaśrayam** *n.* **1** support, asylum, refuge. **2** reliance, dependence.

ఉపాశ్రిత **upaaśrita** *adj.* relied upon.

ఉపాసకుడు **upaasakuDu** *n.* worshipper, devotee; **deewi~** worshipper of the Goddess Devi; **saahityoopaasakuDu** devotee of literature.

ఉపాసనం **upaasanam** *n.* **1** worship, cult. **2** service. **3** meditation. **4** wooden seat. **5** practice of archery.

ఉపాసి **upaasi** *n.* worshipper, devotee.

ఉపాసించు **upaasincu** *v.t.* to worship, be a devotee or follower of.

ఉపాహారం **upaahaaram** *n.* light refreshment, breakfast.

ఉపేంద్రుడు **upeendruDu** *n.* a name of the God Vishnu in his Vamana incarnation.

ఉపేక్ష **upeekSa** *n.* indifference, disregard, apathy, neglect, negligence, lack of interest; **eedoo ceestunnaaDu poonii ani ~cuupinawaaru caalaamandi** there are many who display lack of interest, thinking he is getting on with the job.

ఉపేక్షచేయు, ఉపేక్షించు **upeekSa ceeyu, upeekSincu** *v.t.* to disregard, ignore, neglect, overlook, be indifferent to.

ఉపేక్షణం **upeekSaNam** *n.* overlooking, ignoring, disregarding.

ఉపేక్షణీయ **upeekSaNiiya** *adj.* negligible, fit to be ignored.

ఉపేత **upeeta** *adjvl. suffix meaning* endowed with, possessing, comprising; **waybhawoopeetangaa** splendidly, handsomely; **saahasoopeetangaa** with valour, daringly.

ఉపోద్ఘాతం **upoodghaatam** *n.* preface, introduction, beginning.

ఉపోషం, ఉపోష్యం **upooSam, upooSyam** *n.* fasting, abstinence; **upooSam uNDu** to fast, abstain from food.

ఉప్పదనం, ఉప్పన **uppadanam, uppana** *n.* saltiness, salinity.

ఉప్పని **uppani** *adj.* salty, saline.

ఉప్పర **uppara** *n.* name of a community of persons who make tanks, dig wells, do other kinds of earthwork and make baskets; **ceruwuku gaNDi paDDappuDu puuDcee upparalaku inaam icceewaaru** they used to give an inam to Upparas who repaired the tank bund when it was breached.

ఉప్పరం **upparam** *n.* **1** sky. **2** top, upper part.

ఉప్పలవాయి **uppalawaayi** *n.* space between the forefinger and thumb.

ఉప్పళం **uppaLam** *n.* **1** salt marsh. **2** place where salt is manufactured.

ఉప్పిడి **uppiDi** *adj.* unsalted, saltless; **~cappiDi maaTalu** nonsense.

ఉప్పు **uppu**[1] *n.* **1** salt; **~waNDu** to manufacture salt from brine; **mii ~tinnaanu** *lit.* I have eaten your salt, i.e., I am under an obligation to you for giving me protection. **2** *colloq.* intimation, tip off (colloq.), hint or warning based on inside information; **kotta aaphiisaru reyDu gappuna areenjii ceesEEDu, kindi waaLLaki mundugaa ~anda leedu** the new officer arranged the raid suddenly and the subordinates did not get a tip off in advance. **3** *idiomatic expression*: **~too tommidi papputoo padi pooguceesi waNTa ceesukonnaaDu** he collected everything right from the very start and cooked his meal.

ఉప్పు **uppu**[2] *dial., corrupt form of* **wippu.**

ఉప్పుకండ **uppukaNDa** *n.* salted meat.

ఉప్పుకయ్య **uppukayya** *n.* expanse of brackish water, backwater.

ఉప్పుకల్లు **uppukallu** *n. dial.* grain of salt.

ఉప్పుకాగితం **uppukaagitam** *n.* sandpaper.

ఉప్పుకాయ **uppukaaya** *n.* pickle.

ఉప్పుకొఠారు **uppukoThaaru** *n. obs.* salt warehouse.

ఉప్పుచేప **uppuceepa** *n.* salt fish.

ఉప్పుచౌడు **uppucawDu** *n.* salty soil.

ఉప్పుటేరు **uppuTeeru** *n.* 1 salt stream, salt creek. 2 name of the waterway connecting the Collair Lake with the sea.

ఉప్పుడు **uppuDu** *dial., corrupt form of* **ippuDu.**

ఉప్పుడుబియ్యం **uppuDu biyyam** *n.* parboiled rice.

ఉప్పుపఱ్ఱ **upuparra** *n.* salt marsh.

ఉప్పుపాతరవేయు **uppupaataraweeyu** *v.t.* 1 *lit.* to bury a corpse in salt. 2 *when used in anger or jest the nearest English equivalent is* to bury s.o. alive; **waaDi nooTLoonin-ci maaTa raadu, uppupaatara weesinaa waaDu palakaDu** not a word comes from his mouth, even if you bury him alive, he will not utter a sound.

ఉప్పు[డు]పిండి **uppu[Du]piNDi** *n.* rice flour cooked with a pinch of a salt (simple food traditionally taken by some widows).

ఉప్పుమడి **uppumaDi** *n.* salt pan.

ఉప్పుమావు, ఉప్మా **uppumaawu, upmaa** *n.* dish made like **uppupiNDi** but flavoured with spices.

ఉప్పురాయి **uppuraayi** *n.* grain of salt.

ఉప్పురియు **uppuriyu** *v.i.* to moulder, crumble (of walls affected by efflorescence of salt.)

ఉప్పురేవు **uppureewu** *n.* place where salt is manufactured by evaporation.

ఉప్పూకారం **uppuukaaram** *n.* salt and chilly powder.

ఉప్పెన **uppena** *n.* tidal wave.

ఉప్పొంగు **uppongu** *v.i.* 1 to surge, swell, burst forth, overflow, flood; **ii loopugaa goodaawari nadi uppongi apaara-mayna aastinaSTam kaligincindi** meanwhile the River Godavari burst its banks and caused terrible damage to property. 2 to be thrilled, overjoyed, proud, elated.

ఉప్మా **upmaa** *same as* **uppumaawu.**

ఉబలాటం **ubalaaTam** *n.* 1 strong or keen desire, zeal. 2 craze, childish fancy.

ఉబలాటపడు **ubalaaTapaDu** *v.t.* to be very keen or desirous; **kotta peLLaamtoo wiDigaa kaapuram peTTaalani ~ tunnaaDu** he is longing to set up a home separately with his newly wedded wife.

ఉబీకిన **ubiikina** *adj.* 1 convex. 2 embossed.

ఉబుకు **ubuku** I. *n.* 1 swelling, bulging, bulge, protuberance. 2 heaving. II. *v.i.* 1 to swell, bulge. 2 to heave. 3 to jut out, project. 4 to well up, burst forth, overflow.

ఉబుసు **ubusu** *n.* 1 spare time, leisure time. 2 chit chat, talk, gossip; *cf.* **uusu.**

ఉబుసుపుచ్చు, ఉబుసుపోక, ఉబుసుపోని, ఉబుసుపోవు **ubusupuccu, ubusupooka, ubusupooni, ubusupoowu** *same as* **uusupuccu, uusupooka, uusupooni, uusupoowu.**

ఉబ్బ **ubba** *n.* closeness, sultriness (of weather).

ఉబ్బకం **ubbakam** *n.* increase, swelling.

ఉబ్బనీరు **ubbaniiru** *same as* **ummaniiru.**

ఉబ్బనేల **ubbaneela** *n.* marshy soil.

ఉబ్బరం **ubbaram** *n.* 1 swelling, esp. of the stomach. 2 increase. 3 heat, sultriness (of weather).

ఉబ్బరపోవు **ubbarapoowu** *v.i.* to be shocked or stunned with emotion.

ఉబ్బరించు **ubbarincu** *v.i.* 1 to swell. 2 to increase. 3 *dial.* (of weather) to be hot, be sultry.

ఉబ్బవేయు, ఉబ్బేయు **ubbaweeyu, ubbeeyu** I. *v.i.* (of weather) to be sultry. II. *v.t.* to flatter, cajole; **waaNNi ubbeesi pani ceeyincEEru** they cajoled him into doing the work.

ఉబ్బసం **ubbasam** *n.* asthma.

ఉబ్బించు **ubbincu** *v.t.* 1 to inflate. 2 to flatter.

ఉబ్బితబ్బిబ్బవు **ubbitabbibbawu** *v.t.* to feel flattered, be pleased by flattery.

ఉబ్బు **ubbu** I. *n.* 1 swelling, distension, bulge, bump, protrusion. 2 joy, exuberance. 3 haughtiness, arrogance, being puffed up with pride. II. *v.i.* 1 to swell, be distended, bulge, protrude. 2 to rise, overflow. 3 (of tears, laughter) to well up, burst forth. 4 to be delighted or overjoyed. 5 to be puffed up with pride. 6 (*also* **ubbitabbibbayi poowu**) to be pleased by flattery. 7 **kaDup~** (i) **wiiLLu janaanni kaDupubba nawwincEEru** these (performers) made the people burst with laughter, (ii) **udyoogam naaku dori-kindani waaDiki kaDup~tunnadi** (*or* **waaDiki kaDup~ [gaa undi]**) he is envious at my getting a job.

ఉబ్బురోగం **ubburoogam** *n.* dropsy.

ఉబ్బెత్తు **ubbettu** *n.* 1 swelling, bulge, protrusion. 2 (in sculpture or architecture) embossing; **~gaa uNDee muur-tulu** embossed figures, figures modelled or carved in relief. 3 **~gaa unna** convex.

ఉభయ **ubhaya** *adj.* both; **~bhaaSaaprawiiNuDu** scholar in both languages, i.e., Telugu and Sanskrit.

ఉభయం **ubhayam** *n.* paying for a ceremony or festival to be conducted at a shrine or temple.

ఉభయచర, ఉభయజీవ **ubhayacara, ubhayajiiwa** *adj. sci.* amphibious.

ఉభయచరాలు, ఉభయజీవాలు **ubhayacaraalu, ubhayajiiwaalu** *n.pl. sci.* amphibia.

ఉభయతారక **ubhayataaraka** *adj.* mutually beneficial.

ఉభయత్రా **ubhayatraa** *adv.* on both sides.

ఉభయధర్మి **ubhayadharmi** *n. chem.* substance having both acid and alkaline qualities.

ఉభయపక్ష **ubhayapakSa** *adj.* bilateral.

ఉభయలింగి **ubhayalingi** *adj. bot.* androgynous.

ఉభయలైంగిక **ubhayalayngika** *adj. sci.* bisexual.

ఉభయవాదులు **ubhayawaadulu** *n. pl. legal* both parties to a suit or proceedings.

ఉభయసంకటం **ubhayasankaTam** *n.* dilemma.

ఉభయులు **ubhayulu** *n.pl.* both persons, both parties.

ఉభేతుగా **ubheetugaa** *adv. class.* suddenly, unexpectedly.

ఉమ **uma** *n.* a name of the Goddess Parvati.

ఉమియు **umiyu** *v.t.* to spit.

ఉమ్మ **umma** *n.* heat, warmth, closeness, sultriness.

ఉమ్మగిల్లు **ummagillu** *v.i.* **1** to be hot or sultry. **2** (of rice) to be boiled in such a way that when cooking is finished the grains separate freely and no water remains unabsorbed.

ఉమ్మడం **ummaDam** *n.* heat, sultriness (of atmosphere).

ఉమ్మడి **ummaDi** I.*n.* **1** partnership, fellowship. **2** anything held or done jointly or in common. II. *adj.* **1** joint; **~kuTumbam** joint family; **~wyawasaayam** joint cultivation; **~śatruwu** common enemy. **2** *polit.* composite; **~madraasu raaSTram** the Composite Madras State. **3** *maths.* simultaneous; **~samiikaraNam** simultaneous equation.

ఉమ్మతిత్తి **ummatitti** *n.* kind of musical instrument fitted with bellows.

ఉమ్మనీరు, ఉబ్బనీరు **ummaniiru, ubbaniiru** *n.* the water that precedes childbirth.

ఉమ్మరం, ఉమ్మలం **ummaram, ummalam** *n.* grief, sorrow.

ఉమ్మరించు, ఉమ్మలించు **ummarincu, ummalincu** *v.i.* to grieve.

ఉమ్మి **ummi** *n.* spittle, saliva.

ఉమ్మివేయు, ఉమ్మేయు **ummi weeyu, ummeeyu** *v.i.* to spit.

ఉమ్మెత్త **ummetta** *n.* plant known as *datura stramonium.*

ఉమ్మెత్తలు **ummettalu** *n.pl.* **1** drops of saliva sprayed from the mouth while talking. **2** dribbling of saliva from the mouth.

ఉయాల, ఊయల, ఉయ్యాల, ఊయాల **uyaala, uuyala, uyyaala, uuyaala** *n.* **1** cradle. **2** swing. **3** hammock.

ఉయాలతొట్టి **uyaalatoTTi** *n.* cradle.

ఉరం, ఉరస్సు **uram, urassu** *n.* **1** breast, chest, bosom. **2** *med.* (*also* **urahpanjaram**) thorax.

ఉరక **uraka** *n.* run[ning], leaping, eagerness; **~weeyu, ~lu tiiyu** to leap, jump, bound; **~lu parugulugaa waccu** to come in great haste.

ఉరడించు **uraDincu** *v.i.* to hasten.

ఉరణం **uraNam** *n.* ram.

ఉరఫ్ **uraph** *n.* alias.

ఉరలు, ఉర్లు **uralu, urlu** *v.i.* **1** to roll down, flow down, exude. **2** (of water from a canal) to escape. **3 payna TEEnk undi, kinda gooDa uralipootundi** there is a tank above, the wall below is soaking wet. **4 piNDi uralipooyindi** the dough rose and overflowed (i.e., swelled and overflowed due to fermentation.)

ఉరవడి **urawaDi** *n.* **1** speed, rushing, careering. **2** force, violence, e.g., of rushing water.

ఉరవు **urawu** *n.* **1** beauty. **2** fitness. **3** abundance.

ఉరస్సు **urassu** *same as* **uram.**

ఉరామరిక **uraamarika** *adv.* approximately.

ఉరి **uri** *n.* **1** noose, slipknot, halter. **2** trap, snare. **3** death by hanging.

ఉరికంబం, ఉరికొయ్య, ఉరిమాను **urikambam, urikoyya, urimaanu** *n.* gallows.

ఉరికించు **urikincu** *v.t.* to make (s.o.) run.

ఉరికొల్పు **urikolpu** *v.t.* to incite, egg on.

ఉరితాడు **uritaaDu** *n.* hangman's rope.

ఉరితీయు **uritiiyu** *v.t.* to hang, execute by hanging.

ఉరిపోసుకొను **uripoosukonu** *v.i.* to hang o.s.

ఉరియాడు **uriyaaDu** *v.i.* **1** to waver, hesitate. **2** to swing to and fro.

ఉరియు **uriyu** *v.i.* **1** to leak, sweat, seep, ooze; **Daabaa cuuruki niiru urisi aaripooyina marakalu** stains made by water that had seeped through the eaves and dried up. **2** (of rain) to pour.

ఉరిశిక్ష **uriśikSa** *n.* death penalty, execution by hanging.

ఉరుకు **uruku** *v.i.* **1** to jump, leap, bound, spring. **2** to run.

ఉరుకుడుబొడ్డు **urukuDuboDDu** *n.* protruding navel.

ఉరుతాడు **urutaaDu** *n.* rope with which a cow's legs are tied while being milked.

ఉరుపు **urupu** *n.* leaking, seeping, soaking through.

ఉరుము **urumu** I. *n.* (*also* **urum**) thunder, roar. II. *v.i.* to thunder, roar; **urimi cuucu** to look like thunder (as result of anger), glare at, glower at.

ఉరుముడు **urumuDu** *n.* *cassia marginata*, a forest tree.

ఉరువడు **uruwaDu** *v.i. class.* to be accomplished, be fulfilled

ఉరువు **uruwu** *n.* **1** piece, item. **2** *pl.* **~lu** *dial.* pieces of baggage. **3** trace; **ataDu ~leedu** *or* **ataDu pattaa leedu** he is not to be found.

ఉరుసు **urusu** *n.* festival conducted at the burial place of a Muslim saint.

ఉరోజం **uroojam** *n.* woman's breast.

ఉర్రూతలూగించు **urruutaluugincu** *v.t.* to sway or stir the emotions, rouse, excite, thrill, inspire; **baLLaari raaghawaacaari tana naTanatoo yaawadaandhra deeśaanni urruutaluugincEEru** Bellary Raghavachari thrilled the entire Andhra country by his acting.

ఉర్లగడ్డ **urlagaDDa** *n. dial.* potato.

ఉర్లు **urlu** *same as* **uralu.**

ఉర్వి **urwi** *n.* the earth.

ఉర్వీపతి **urwiipati** *n.* king.

ఉలక **ulaka** *adj.* **1** light, easy. **2** slight, trifling.

ఉలకన **ulakana** *n.* **1** lightness, easiness. **2** disregard.

ఉలవలు **ulawalu** *n.pl.* horsegram, *dolichos uniflorus.*

ఉలస, ఉలూపి, ఉలూచి **ulasa, uluupi, uluuci** *n.* hilsa, a kind of fish.

ఉలి **uli** *n.* chisel.

ఉలికిపాటు **ulikipaaTu** *n.* shock, start, being startled.

ఉలిక్కిపడు **ulikkipaDu** *v.i.* to jump (due to shock), start, be startled; **ulikkipaDi leecu** to wake up with a start.

ఉలిపి **ulipi**[1] *n.* person suffering from oedema.

ఉలిపి, ఉలిపికట్టె, ఉలిపిగొట్టు **ulipi**[2], **ulipikaTTe, ulipigoTTu** *n.* **1** pig-headed, perverse or contrary person. **2 ulipi cilipi** (of children) noisy, rowdy, naughty.

ఉలిపిరి **ulipiri** *adj.* very thin; **~kaayitam** manifolding paper; **~battalu** thin muslin cloth; *cf.* **ullipora.**

ఉలుకు **uluku** I. *n.* fear, fright, timidity. II. *v.i.* **1** to start, be startled. **2** to quiver, quake, fear; **kondaru guNDelloo**

gunapaalu dincutunnaa ulakaru palakaru some (very brave) persons, even when their hearts are speared with crowbars, do not quake or utter a sound; **enni uttaraalu raasinaa ulukuu leedu palukuu leedu** however many letters you write, there is not a word in reply.

ఉలుచు **ulucu** *v.t. class.* to brandish, wave, shake.

ఉలుఫా, ఉల్ఫా **uluphaa, ulphaa** *adj.* free, without payment.

ఉలూకం **uluukam** *n.* owl.

ఉలూఖలం **uluukhalam** *n.* mortar for pounding grain.

ఉలూఖలసంధి **uluukhalasandhi** *n.* ball and socket joint.

ఉలూచి, ఉలూపి **uluuci, uluupi** *same as* **ulasa.**

ఉలేమా **uleemaa** *n.* body of Muslim scholars or religious leaders.

ఉల్క **ulka** *n.* **1** meteor, shooting star. **2** torch.

ఉల్టా **ulTaa** *adj. and adv.* opposite, contrary, the other way round, the wrong way round, inside out; **cokkaa ~ gaa weesukonnaaDu** he wore his shirt inside out; **adee praśna ~ gaa aDigEEDu** he asked the same question the other way round (i.e., in a different form).

ఉల్ఫా **ulphaa** *same as* **uluphaa.**

ఉల్బణం **ulbaNam** *n.* **1** excess. **2** increase. **3** *econ.* **drawyoolbaNam** inflation.

ఉల్లం **ullam** *n.* heart, mind.

ఉల్లంఘనం **ullanghanam** *n.* transgression, defiance, disregard, violation, breach, contravention (of laws, codes of conduct).

ఉల్లంఘించు **ullanghincu** *v.t.* to defy, destroy, break, contravene, disregard (laws, etc.).

ఉల్లకుట్టు **ullakuTTu** *n.* offensive remark.

ఉల్లడ **ullaDa** *n.* canopy.

ఉల్లలం **ullalam** *n.* movement, shaking.

ఉల్లసం **ullasam**[1] **1** *n.* taunting, censure. **2** ridicule, derision. **3** teasing.

ఉల్లసం **ullasam**[2] *n.* **1** joy, pleasure, fun. **2** light, splendour.

ఉల్లసం ఆడు **ullasam aaDu** *v.t.* **1** to censure, scold. **2** to taunt, ridicule, deride. **3** to tease.

ఉల్లసించు **ullasincu** *v.i.* **1** to rejoice, be glad, be pleased. **2** to shine, gleam.

ఉల్లాకు **ullaaku** *n.* note or invoice accompanying a parcel or consignment of goods.

ఉల్లాపం **ullaapam** *n.* change in tone of voice indicating the speaker's emotional feelings.

ఉల్లాభం **ullaabham** *n.* canopy carried over the bride and bridegroom or over wedding presents in a wedding procession.

ఉల్లారు **ullaaru** *n.* **1** saddle cloth. **2** multi-coloured cushion.

ఉల్లాసం **ullaasam** *n.* **1** joy, happiness, rejoicing, jubilation; **iwi sundaraaniki caalaa ullaasapu roojulu** these were very happy days for Sundaram. **2** pleasure, amusement. **3 ullaasa puruSuDu** playboy, man of pleasure.

ఉల్లి[గడ్డ], ఉల్లిపాయ **ulli[gaDDa], ullipaaya** *n.* onion.

ఉల్లిపొర **ullipora** I. *n.* outer skin of an onion. II. *adj.* very thin; **~ kaagitam** manifolding paper; **~ baTTalu** thin muslin cloth; *cf.* **ulipiri.**

ఉల్లిపాషాణం **ullipaaSaaNam** *n.* arsenic.

ఉల్లె **ulle** *n.* crust at the bottom of a cake called **appam.**

ఉల్లేఖనం **ulleekhanam** *n.* **1** utterance, description, mention, allusion, reference. **2** writing. **3** rubbing out, scraping off. **4** name of a rhetorical figure of speech.

ఉల్లేఖించు **ulleekhincu** *v.t.* **1** to describe, mention, discourse on. **2** to state emphatically, assert.

ఉల్లోలం **ulloolam** *n.* large wave.

ఉళక్కి **uLakki** *same as* **huLakki.**

ఉవాచ **uwaaca** *n.* remark, statement, pronouncement.

ఉవిద **uwida** *n.* woman.

ఉవ్వన **uwwana** *adv.* unexpectedly, all at once.

ఉవ్వాయి **uwwaayi** *n.* joy, delight.

ఉవ్విళ్ళూరు **uwwiLLuuru** *v.i.* **1** to long, yearn; **aa prayaaNaanni maLLii warNincaDaaniki itaDu ~ tunnaaDu** he is longing to describe that journey over again. **2** to be impatient or eager; **raatrantaa candroodayaaniki ~ tuu niriikSistunnaTTugaa undi** it was as if the whole night was waiting impatiently for moonrise. **3** to be thrilled, be filled with excitement; **patrikalaloo ii upanyaasam cuucinappuDu deeśaaniki tagina naayakuDu dorikEEDani yuwakalookam uwwiLLuurindi** on seeing this speech in the newspapers, young people felt thrilled that a real leader for the country had been found. **4.** to water at the mouth, salivate.

ఉవ్విళ్ళూరుచు **uwwiLLuurcu** *v.t.* to tempt, incite, rouse (s.o.'s) appetite.

ఉవ్వు **uwwu** *n.* attempt, exertion, effort.

ఉవ్వెత్తు, ఉవ్వెత్తుగా, ఉవ్వెత్తున **uwwettu, uwwettugaa, uwwettuna** *adv.* **1** suddenly, all at once; **uwwettugaa leeci** getting up suddenly. **2** entirely, completely.

ఉష[స్సు] **uSa[ssu]** *n.* dawn, daybreak.

ఉష్ట్రం **uSTram** *n.* camel.

ఉష్ట్రపక్షి **uSTrapakSi** *n.* ostrich.

ఉష్ణం **uSNam** I. *n.* **1** heat, warmth. **2** sunshine. **3** hot weather, hot season, summer. **4** *dial.* fever [ishness]. II. *adj.* **1** hot, warm. **2** tropical. **3** hot tempered.

ఉష్ణగతికశాస్త్రం **uSNagatikaśaastram** *n. sci.* thermodynamics.

ఉష్ణగ్రాహక **uSNagraahaka** *adj. chem.* endothermic.

ఉష్ణజిత **uSNajita** *adj.* heat proof.

ఉష్ణత **uSNata** *n.* heat, warmth.

ఉష్ణతాధారణ శక్తి **uSNataadhaaraNa śakti** *n. phys.* thermal capacity.

ఉష్ణతాప్రసారం **uSNataaprasaaram** *n. phys.* transmission of heat.

ఉష్ణతామాపకం **uSNataamaapakam** *n. phys.* calorimeter.

ఉష్ణతాసంవహనం **uSNataasamwahanam** *n. phys.* convection.

ఉష్ణదక్షత **uSNadakSata** *n. phys.* thermal efficiency.

ఉష్ణనిరోధకం, ఉష్ణబంధకం **uSNaniroodhakam, uSNabandhakam** *n. phys.* heat insulator.

ఉష్ణమండలం uSNamaNDalam *n. geog.* tropical zone, the tropics.

ఉష్ణమాపకం uSNamaapakam *n.* thermometer.

ఉష్ణమోచక uSNamoocaka *adj. chem.* exothermic.

ఉష్ణరక్త uSNarakta *adj. zool.* warm blooded.

ఉష్ణవాహకం uSNawaahakam *n.* conductor of heat.

ఉష్ణసంవహనం uSNasamwahanam *n. phys.* convection.

ఉష్ణీషం uSNiiSam *n.* **1** turban, diadem. **2** distinguishing mark in the form of an auspicious curl of hair above the forehead.

ఉష్ణోగ్రత uSNoograta *n.* temperature.

ఉష్ణోగ్రతా మాపకం uSNoogrataamaapakam *n.* thermometer.

ఉష్మాకం uSmaakam *n.* **1** heat, warmth. **2** hot season. **3** hot temper, anger. **4** ardour, zeal.

ఉసి usi[1] *n.* hissing sound made when exciting a dog.

ఉసు usi[2] *n.* (*also* **nusi**) dust, powder, trash.

ఉసికొల్పు usikolpu *v.t.* to incite, urge on, spur on (*lit.* to excite a dog to attack s.o.).

ఉసిడి usiDi *n., gen. pl.* **usiLLu** flying ant(s).

ఉసిరిక usirika *n.* emblic myrobalan, a tree with acid fruits used for pickles.

ఉసుము usumu *v.t.* to cleanse, wash (clothes).

ఉసురు usuru *n.* **1** breath, life. **2** retribution, recompense, curse, esp. an evil effect or curse suffered for having harmed s.o.: **waaDu taagubootani waaNNi udyoogamnunci tiiseestee, waaDi peLLaam pillala ~ naaku tagulutundi** if I sack him for being a drunkard, the curse of his wife and children will fall upon me.

ఉసురుపోసుకొను usurupoosukonu *v.i.* to invite a curse upon o.s.; **ewarikaynaa okaDi walana haani jarigitee, enduku waaDi usuru poosukuNTaawaNTaaru** when harm is caused to s.o. by s.o. else, people say, "why do you invite his curse upon you?"

ఉసులు usulu *n.* **1** ease, convenience. **2** recovery of health.

ఉసూరు usuuru *n.* sighing, distress.

ఉసూరుమను usuurumanu *v.i.* to distressed or disgusted, feel fed up (colloq); **pillalu [annam] tini tinnanta paarees-EEru, naa praaNam usuurumanipincindi** the children wasted as much[food] as they ate. I felt distressed.

ఉస్సూరు ussuru *n.* sigh of tiredness and exasperation; **entani ceppanu? praaNam ussuranipincindi** how often must I tell you? I am completely fed up (with repeating the same thing).

ఉస్తె uste *n. bot.* gigantic swallow wort, *solanum trilobatum.*

ఊ - uu

ఊ! uu! *interj. pronounced with nasalisation* (i) *indicating acceptance of an order or agreement with a statement,* (ii) *expressing anger or similar emotion,* (iii) *denoting that the listener is paying attention; see* **uukoTTu.**

ఊక uuka *n.* husk (of grain).

ఊకతీయు uuka tiiyu *v.t.* to dehusk.

ఊకదంపు[డు] uukadampu[Du] *adj.* (of words or talk) useless, pointless, worthless, senseless.

ఊకదంపుడుగా uukadampuDugaa *adv.* uselessly (*lit.* like pounding husk).

ఊకపొయ్యి uukapoyyi *n.* kiln in which husk is burnt as fuel.

ఊకబంతి uukabanti *n.* flower called bachelor's button.

ఊకర uukara *n.* shouts of excitement or joy.

ఊకించు uukincu *v.i. and t.* **1** to shake, move. **2** *class.* to endeavour, make an effort.

ఊకు uuku[1] I. *n.* effort, endeavour. II. *v.i.* to make an effort.

ఊకు uuku[2] *v.t. dial.* to sweep.

ఊకొట్టు uukoTTu *v.i.* to punctuate s.o.'s remarks with the sound *uu* nasalised (*cf.* 'm-hm' in English) to indicate that one is paying attention but not necessarily agreeing with what is said.

ఊగించు uugincu *v.t.* **1** to swing, wave, sway. **2** to shake, agitate.

ఊగిసలాడు uugisalaaDu *v.i.* (of a rickety chair) to shake, sway, rock, totter.

ఊగు uugu *v.i.* **1** to swing, rock, sway, waver. **2** to reel, totter. **3** to be shaken or agitated. **4** to dangle.

ఊగులాడు, ఊగాడు uugulaaDu, uugaaDu *v.i.* **1** to rock, sway; **paDaga ettina naagulu uugaaDutunnaayi** cobras with their hoods raised are swaying to and fro. **2** to waver, hesitate, vacillate; **reNDu aloocanala madhya ~** to vacillate between one thought and another. **3 paTTukoni ~** to hang onto, cling desperately to; **inkaa aa paata wyawasthanee paTTukoni ~ taareem?** why cling desperately to that outmoded system?

ఊచ uuca[1] *n.* **1** stalk or stem of a tall millet such as cholam. **2** soft core or pith of a plantain tree. **3** thorn bush. **4** metal bar or rod. **5 ~ koota kooyu** to cut down, mow down, kill (*lit.* to cut down s.g like a cholam stalk that can be cut easily).

ఊచ uuca[2] *adj.* lean, withered, emaciated; **~ kaaLLu** withered legs.

ఊచగొళ్ళెం uucagoLLem *n.* door latch made of iron.

ఊచపడు, ఊచపోవు uucapaDu, uucapoowu *v.i.* to become lean or withered.

ఊచబియ్యం uucabiyyam *n.* grain, esp. cholam, that is not quite ripe.

ఊచముట్టు uucamuTTu *adv.* wholly, entirely, to the core.

ఊచముట్టుకొను uucamuTTukonu *v.i.* to be entirely ruined.

ఊచు uucu[1] *v.i.* (of hair) to fall out due to illness.

ఊచు uucu[2] *v.t.* to wave, swing, rock, shake.

ఊజ **uuja** *n.* basket for holding fish.

ఊట **uuTa** *n.* 1 spring of water. 2 pickling juice. 3 strength. 4 ~ **kalam** fountain pen.

ఊట ఊరు **uuTa uuru** *v.i.* 1 to be damp. 2 to exude (like pickling juice).

ఊట ఎత్తు **uuTa ettu** *v.i.* 1 to be damp. 2 to spring up (like water in a well).

ఊటలూరు **uuTaluuru** *v.i.* to spring up (like water in a well); **waaDiki noorantaa uuTaluurindi** he watered at the mouth.

ఊటించు **uuTincu** *v.t.* to deceive.

ఊటు **uuTu** I. *n.* moisture caused by rain. II. *v.t.* 1 to water cattle, give cattle water to drink. 2 to pierce.

ఊటుగా **uuTugaa** *adv. colloq.* completely; ~ **taaginawaaDu** person who is completely drunk.

ఊడ **uuDa** *n.* aerial root of a banyan tree.

ఊడకొట్టు **uuDakoTTu** *v.t.* 1 to take out, root out. 2 to tear up. 3 to dismiss, depose.

ఊడతీయు **uuDatiiyu** *v.t.* 1 to pull out, extract. 2 to loosen, untie. 3 to remove, take off, cast off, strip off; *see* **kiilu.**

ఊడపీకు **uuDapiiku** *v.t.* to pull out, root out.

ఊడపెరుకు **uuDaperuku** *v.t.* to pull out, extract.

ఊడలాగు **uuDalaagu** *v.t.* to pull out.

ఊడి **uuDi** *n.* basket-like trap for fish.

ఊడిగం **uuDigam** *n.* 1 drudgery, menial work. 2 task, job, service.

ఊడిపడు **uuDipaDu** *v.i.* 1 to arrive unexpectedly from a place unknown, appear from nowhere. 2 to emerge forcibly. 3 to lose o.'s grip and fall.

ఊడు **uuDu** *v.i.* 1 to slip down, slip, fall, drop off (of clothes, etc.); **okantaTa uuDakuNDaa nilustundi** it stays without suddenly slipping down. 2 to slip away, be lost; **paNDluuDipooyinawaaru** persons who have lost their teeth; **waaDi baDipantulu udyoogam uuDindi** he was dismissed from his job as a schoolmaster. 3 (*also* **uuDiwaccu, uuDoccu**) to be detached, unfastened, relaxed, loosened or separated, come off, come out; **meeku uuDiwaccindi** the nail came out *or* the nail came loose; **talupu goLLem daanantaTadee uuDoccindi** the door latch came unfastened of its own accord. 4 to give way, fail; **phyuuj uuDipooyindi** the fuse failed. 5 to run away, flee. 6 to leak.

ఊడుకొను **uuDukonu** *v.i.* (of earth) to become moist.

ఊడ్చు **uuDcu** *v.t.* 1 to sweep. 2 to transplant (paddy seedlings). 3 to loosen, untie. 4 to pull off (feathers). 5 **ginneloo annam undi. ~ ku peTTukoo** there is rice in the vessel, take all of it! (*lit.* sweep it up! *cf. the English expression* polish it off!).

ఊడ్పు **uuDpu** *n.* 1 sweeping. 2 transplanting, transplantation (of paddy seedlings).

ఊడ్పుచేను, ఊడ్పుపొలం **uuDpuceenu, uuDpupolam** *n.* field that has been transplanted with paddy seedlings.

ఊడ్పుదమ్ము **uuDpudammu** *n.* ploughing a wet (irrigated) field in preparation for sowing seed.

ఊఢ **uuDha** *n. class* married woman, wife.

ఊత **uuta** *n.* 1 support, prop; **karra ~ puccukoni** with the help of a [walking] stick. 2 *ling.* stress.

ఊతం **uutam** *n.* 1 strength, force, pressure. 2 stress, emphasis. 3 prop, support; **waaru ~ iyyaka pootee ii pustakam weluwaDeedi kaadu** but for his support this book would not have been published.

ఊతకర్ర, ఊతకోల, ఊతగడ **uutakarra, uutakoola, uutagaDa** *n.* walking stick, crutch.

ఊతకొను **uutakonu** *v.t.* to keep as a support.

ఊతపదం **uutapadam** *n.* 1 pet phrase, catch phrase or cliché used by s.o. habitually. 2 meaningless echo word, jingle.

ఊతప్పం **uutappam** *n.* kind of thick pancake made with spices.

ఊతి **uuti** *n. class.* 1 weaving. 2 sewing. 3 protection.

ఊద **uuda** *n.* 1 swelling of part of the body, esp. the stomach. 2 envy, malice.

ఊదర **uudara**[1] *n.* smoke for fumigation or for ripening fruit.

ఊదర[గడ్డి] **uudara[gaDDi]**[2] *n.* grass-like weed growing in wet (irrigated) land.

ఊదరకొట్టు **uudarakoTTu** *v.t.* 1 to fumigate. 2 to ripen fruit by means of smoke. 3 to talk on and on in an attempt to persuade. 4 to praise s.o. unduly.

ఊదారంగు **uudaarangu** *n.* purple or violet colour.

ఊది **uudi** *n.* trap for fish.

ఊదు **uudu** I. *n.* 1 swelling of part of the body. 2 trap for fish made of basketwork. 3 incense. II. *v.t.* 1 to blow (with breath or bellows). 2 to whisper, breathe; **naaku telusu, waaDi cewiloo rahasyangaa ~ taaru** I know they whisper secretly in his ear. 3 to play, blow or sound a wind instrument; **oka kEEpTen heccarika buuraa uudamani aajñaapincEEru** a captain ordered a warning trumpet to be sounded. 4 *gram.* to stress, emphasise. 5 to blow out, extinguish (lamp). 6 to refine gold with the help of a blow pipe. III. *v.i.* to be[come] inflated or swollen.

ఊదుగొట్టం **uudugoTTam** *n.* blow pipe.

ఊదుడు **uuduDu** *n.* 1 whispering. 2 swelling. 3 blowing.

ఊదువత్తి, ఊదుబత్తి, ఊదొత్తి, ఊదుకడ్డీ **uuduwatti, uudubatti, uudotti, uudukaDDi** *n.* incense stick.

ఊదువాద్యం **uuduwaadyam** *n.* wind instrument.

ఊధం, ఊధస్సు **uudham, uudhassu** *n. class.* udder.

ఊధస్యం **uudhasyam** *n. class.* milk.

ఊనం **uunam** *n.* 1 loss. 2 deficiency; **kincittu ~ gaa lakSa ruupaayalu poogu paDDaayi** a little short of a lakh of rupees has been collected.

ఊనిక **uunika** *n.* 1 support. 2 *ling.* stress.

ఊను **uunu** *v.i. and t.* 1 *class.* to have, take, bear, lean on, rest on. 2 *mod. only in a few set phrases such as* **kaal ~** to set foot; **weer ~** to take root; **candralookampay kaaluunaDam maanawuni uurdhwayaatraloo prathama ghaTTam maatramee** setting foot on the moon is only the first episode in man's journey to the heavens.

ఊప **uupa** *n. class.* undergrowth in a forest.

ఊపి ఊపి **uupi uupi** *adv.* shaking continuously; ~ **nawwincu** to make s.o. laugh hilariously.

ఊపిరి uupiri *n.* 1 breath, respiration; ~ **aaDu**, ~ **piilcu** to draw breath, breathe; ~ **[biga] paTTu** to hold o.'s breath. 2 ~ **tirugu / aadu** (*with dat.*) to [be able to] breathe: **waaDiki ~ tirugutundi / aaDutundi** he breathes *or* he is able to breathe. 3 ~ **tiiyu** (i) to draw breath, breathe; **aayana nidrapootuu peddagaa ~ tiistunnaaDu** he is breathing heavily while sleeping, (ii) to take away s.o.'s breath, *hence* to worry, pester; **pillalu sinimaaki weLdaamani naa ~ tiistunnaaru** the children have been pestering me to take them to the cinema. 4 ~ **poowu** to cease to breathe, die, be near to death; **ii pani ceesi ceesi naa ~ pooyindi** I was quite exhausted after doing this work continuously. 5 ~ **salupu** (i) to breathe freely or easily; **duhkhamwalla ~ salipeedi kaadu** he could hardly breathe on account of sorrow, (ii) to provide rest or relief; **lakSalaadi cinna raytulaku idi ~ salipee carya kaagalugutundi** this can be an action bringing relief to lakhs of small cultivators. 6 ~ **poosukonu** to recover (from a difficulty); **ceesina appulu tiirci ippuDee ~ poosukoNTunnaDu** he is just recovering after clearing off his debts.

ఊపిరికుట్టు **uupirikuTTu** *n.* stitch in o.'s side (causing painful breathing).

ఊపిరితిత్తి **uupiritittI** *n.* lung.

ఊపు **uupu** I. *n.* 1 swing, swinging blow. 2 shaking. 3 setting in motion, push[ing]. 4 *idiomatic usages*: **oka ~ loo ii pani ceesEEDu** he did this work at one stretch; **koDuku puTTEEDu anna waarta winagaanee aayanaki manci ~ waccindi** on hearing the news of his son's birth he was in a jubilant mood. II. *v.t.* 1 to wave, swing, sway, rock (cradle). 2 to shake. 3 to put in motion, push. 4 **tala ~** to nod o.'s head (in assent) *or* to shake o.'s head (in dissent).

ఊబ **uuba** *adj.* stout.

ఊబి **uubi** I. *n.* bog, marsh, morass, quagmire. II. *adj.* marshy, boggy.

ఊయల, ఊయాల **uuyala, uuyaala** *same as* **uyaala.**

ఊయాలవంతెన **uuyaala wantena** *n.* suspension bridge.

ఊయు **uuyu** *v.i.* 1 to whistle. 2 to spit.

ఊరంత **uuranta** *adj. lit.* as big as a (whole) village, *hence* great, large, big; **aayana ii maaTalu wini ~ nawwu nawwEEDu** when he heard this, he burst out laughing. ~ **gontutoo maaTLaaDaDam aameki alawaaTu** she is in the habit of talking at the top of her voice.

ఊరక[నే] **uuraka[nee]** *same as* **uurikee.**

ఊరకుక్క **uurakukka** *n.* stray dog.

ఊరగాయ **uuragaaya** *n.* pickled fruit or vegetable.

ఊరట **uuraTa** *n.* 1 rest, ease, leisure. 2 relief, consolation.

ఊరటపడు **uuraTapaDu** *v.i.* to be consoled.

ఊరడించు **uuraDincu** *v.t.* to comfort, console, soothe.

ఊరడింపు **uuraDimpu** *n.* consolation.

ఊరడింపుగా **uuraDimpugaa** *adv.* consolingly.

ఊరడిల్లు **uuraDillu** *v.i.* to be comforted, consoled or soothed.

ఊరపంది **uurapandi** *n.* pig which roams freely round a village.

ఊరపిచ్చుక **uurapiccuka** *n.* bird (of any kind) which frequents a village; ~ **laa tirugutaaDu** he roams about idly in the village.

ఊరపెట్టు, ఊరవేయు **uurapeTTu, uuraweeyu** *v.t.* to pickle, preserve.

ఊరబావి **uurabaawi** *n.* 1 well used by villagers in common. 2 *slang* prostitute.

ఊరించు **uurincu** *v.t.* 1 to make (s.o.'s) mouth water, make (s.o.) long for (s.g). 2 to cause to swell; **buggalu ~** to puff out o.'s cheeks.

ఊరికే, ఊరక[నే] **uurikee, uuraka[nee]** *adv.* 1 for no reason, simply, merely. 2 in vain, for no purpose. 3 free (of payment), for nothing. 4 spontaneously, voluntarily. 5 alone, unaccompanied. 6 (of a house) empty, unoccupied. 7 free, at leisure, unemployed.

ఊరిదేవర **uurideewara** *n.* village deity.

ఊరు **uuru**[1] *n.* village, town; **aa roojulloo ingliiSuku ~ peeru uNDeedikaadu** English used to be quite unknown in those days.

ఊరు **uuru**[2] *v.i.* 1 to become fat or stout. 2 (of a root) to swell. 3 to be crammed or crowded to the extent of overflowing; **iNTiniNDaa janam ekkii tokkiigaa ~ tunnaaru** the house is filled to overflowing with people. 4 to leak, seep, ooze, exude, trickle; **nuutiloo niiLLuurinaTTu atani kaLLaloo niiLL ~ tunnaay** as water seeps into a well so does water trickle from his eyes; **nooru ~ tundi** the mouth waters. 5 to soak in, sink in. 6 (of emotions) to be aroused, increase, overflow; **kamala keesi koorikaluurakuNDaa cuuDaleeka pooyEEDu** he could not look at Kamala without his desires being aroused.

ఊరుకొను **uurukonu** *v.i.* 1 to be silent, keep silence. 2 to be calm; **aDakkuNDaa uurukoNTaaDaa?** he is sure to ask (*lit.* will he keep quiet without asking?)

ఊరుకోపెట్టు **uurukoopeTTu** *v.t.* to silence; **pillalu eeDustuNTee miThaayilu icci uurukoopeTTEEnu** when the children were crying, I silenced them by offering sweets.

ఊరుపిండి **uurupiNDi** *n.* preparation made from flour mixed into dough and left overnight.

ఊరువు **uuruwu** *n.* thigh.

ఊరుసంధి **uurusandhi** *n.* hip joint.

ఊరేగించు **uureegincu** *v.t.* to take in procession.

ఊరేగింపు **uureegimpu** *n.* procession.

ఊరేగు **uureegu** *v.i.* to go in procession.

ఊర్చు **uurcu** *v.t.* to gather up s.g scattered.

ఊర్ధ్వ **uurdhwa** *adj.* 1 upper, upward; ~ **śwaasa** gasp, intake of breath. 2 *maths. sci.* vertical.

ఊర్ధ్వకోణం **uurdhwakooNam** *n. maths. sci.* angle of elevation.

ఊర్ధ్వతాన, ఊర్ధ్వగతి **uurdhwataana, uurdhwagati** *adj.* vertical.

ఊర్ధ్వపుండ్రం **uurdhwapuNDram** *n.* vertical mark on the forehead worn by Vaishnavites.

ఊర్ధ్వరేఖ **uurdhwareekha** *n.* vertical line.

ఊర్ధ్వలోకం **uurdhwalookam** *n.* heaven.

ఊర్పు **uurpu** *n.* breath, sigh.

ఊర్మిళ **uurmiLa** *n.* Lakshmana's wife in the Ramayana, who was granted the boon of sleep to enable her to forget her sorrow at her husband's prolonged absence for fourteen years.

ఊర్వశి **uurwaśi** *n.* name of a mythical dancer in Indra's court.

ఊర్వస్థి **uurwasthi** *n. med.* femur, thigh bone.

ఊలు **uulu** *n.* wool. II. *adj.* woollen.

ఊళ **uuLa** *n.* howl; **nakkalu ~ peDtunnaay** jackals are howling.

ఊషర, ఊసర **uuSara, uusara** *adj.* (of soil) salty; **~ kSeetram** saline land.

ఊష్ణం **uuSNam** *n. dial.* fever.

ఊష్మం **uuSmam** *n. ling.* fricative, spirant, sibilant.

ఊసరవెల్లి **uusarawelli** *n.* chameleon.

ఊసు **uusu** *n.* **1** (*also* **ubusu**) spare time, leisure time. **2** (*also* **ubusu**) chit-chat, talk, gossip. **3** news, information, particulars; **jarigina uusantaa ceppindi** she narrated all that had occurred; **nuuti capTaamiida kuurconi talaarabeT-TukoNTuuNTee appuDuu N. eeweewoo ~ lu aDigindi** when she was sitting on the well platform drying her hair, N. asked her for some particulars even at that time. **4** concern, affairs; **naa ~ niiku enduku**? what have you got to do with my affairs? *or* mind your own business! **ceer-mangaariNTLoo kuuDaa raajamma geedeluusenduku ma-naki**? what concern have we in the chairman's house with Rajamma's buffaloes? **5** consideration, thought, mention.

ఊసుపుచ్చు, ఉబుసుపుచ్చు **uusupuccu, ubusupuccu** *v.i.* to while away the time, pass the time agreably in chatting, etc.

ఊసుపోక, ఉబుసుపోక **uusupooka, ubusupooka** I. *n.* **1** gossip. **2** passing the time; **waaLLa naannatoo ~ ku peekaaDaDaaniki weLLeewaNNi** in order to pass the time I used to go and play cards with his father. II. *adv.* casually, for no special reason; **weemana ~ analeedu** it was not without purpose that Vemana said. . . .

ఊసుపోని, ఉబుసుపోని **uusupooni, ubusupooni** *adj.* idle, trifling, trivial; **~ kaburlu** gossip.

ఊసుపోవు, ఉబుసుపోవు **uusupoowu, ubusupoowu** *v.i.* (of time) to pass by pleasantly; **waaLLandari gurincee aaloocistuu kathalu kalpincukoNTuu wiidhi waraNDaaloo kuurcuNTee subbayyaki uusupootundi** when he was sitting in the street veranda thinking about all of them and making up stories, the time passed pleasantly for Subbayya; **naannaki manyapu deeśaalloo uusupooyeedi kaa-danukoNTaanu** I think our father was bored (when living) in the hill areas.

ఊసులాడు **uusulaaDu** *v.i.* to chat, gossip.

ఊసెత్తు **uusettu** *v.t.* to mention, make mention of; **ekkaDa 'dharmam' uusettinaa, pradhaanangaa aayana warNaaśra-ma dharmaalanee manasuloo peTTukoNTunnaaDu** wherever he mentions 'duty' he principally has in mind religious duties. **2** to think of, have consideration for; **tanaku rangu buDDii teppincukonnaaDu gaani, mana uusettaleedu** he sent for a drink for himself, but never thought of us.

ఊహ **uuha** *n.* **1** thought, idea, concept. **2** reasoning, inference. **3** guess, conjecture, supposition. **4** imagination, fancy. **5** contrivance. **6** awareness; *see* **graahi.**

ఊహనం **uuhanam** *n. sci.* assumption.

ఊహాకల్పన **uuhaakalpana** *n.* speculation, fancy.

ఊహాగానం **uuhaagaanam** *n.* [flight of] fancy; **wiiTini kee-walam uuhaagaanaalugaa toosiweeyaDaaniki wiilu leedu** it is impossible to dismiss these (ideas) as mere flights of fancy.

ఊహాజనిత **uuhaajanita** *adj.* imaginary, conjectural, hypothetical.

ఊహాతీత **uuhaatiita** *adj.* unimaginable.

ఊహాత్మక **uuhaatmaka** *adj.* imaginary.

ఊహాదృశ్యం **uuhaadṛśyam** *n.* mental picture.

ఊహాదృష్టి **uuhaadṛSTi** *n.* imagination, forethought.

ఊహామయ **uuhaamaya** *adj.* fantastic.

ఊహాశక్తి **uuhaaśakti** *n.* imagination, power to imagine.

ఊహించు **uuhincu** *v.i. and t.* **1** to think, reason, reflect, consider, presume. **2** to guess, conjecture. **3** to conceive, infer. **4** to think of, visualise, imagine. **5** to assess. **6** to contrive.

ఊహించుకొను **uuhincukonu** *v.i. and t.* **1** to imagine. **2** to to guess.

ఊహ్యం **uuhyam** *n.* s.g conceivable, s.g imaginable.

ఋ - ṛ

ఋ vocalic r, seventh letter of the Telugu alphabet, a sound borrowed from Sanskrit, transcribed as ṛ. all forms starting with ṛ can be said to be classical; in modern spelling ṛ may be replaced by consonantal r + u, i.e., ru.

ఋక్కు ṛkku *n.* 1 the Rigveda, the first of the four Vedas. 2 *pl.* ~ lu verses from the Rigveda.

ఋక్షం ṛkSam *n.* 1 bear. 2 star. 3 constellation.

ఋగ్వేదం ṛgweedam *n.* the Rigveda.

ఋజు ṛju *adj.* 1 straight. 2 straightforward, upright, honest. 3 *sci.* rectilinear.

ఋజుకణవిభాగం ṛjukaNawibhaagam *n. biol.* amitosis.

ఋజుత్వం ṛjutwam *n.* 1 straightness. 2 honesty, straightforwardness, sincerity.

ఋజురేఖ ṛjureekha *n.* straight line.

ఋజురేఖీయ ṛjureekhiiya *adj.* rectilinear.

ఋజువర్తనం ṛjuwartanam *n.* straightforwardness.

ఋజువు ṛjuwu *n.* proof, demonstration.

ఋజువుఅవు ṛjuwu awu *v.i.* to be proved, be established, be demonstrated.

ఋజువుచేయు ṛjuwuceeyu *v.t.* to prove, establish, demonstrate.

ఋణం ṛNam *n.* 1 debt, obligation: **miiru ceesina saayaaniki mii ~ neenu eppuDuu tiircukooleenu** I can never repay my obligation to you for the help you have given me. 2 loan. 3 *maths.* minus. 4 *phys.* negative.

ఋణంచేయు ṛNamceeyu *v.t.* to incur a debt.

ఋణకర్త, ఋణగ్రస్తుడు ṛNakarta, ṛNagrastuDu *n.* debtor, borrower.

ఋణత్వరణం ṛNatwaraNam *n. sci.* deceleration.

ఋణదాత ṛNadaata *n.* creditor, lender.

ఋణధ్రువం ṛNadhruwam *n. sci.* cathode.

ఋణపడు ṛNapaDu *v.i.* to be[come] indebted.

ఋణసంజ్ఞ ṛNasanjna *n. maths. phys.* minus sign, negative sign,

ఋణాక్రాంత ṛNaakraanta *adj.* laden with debt, encumbered.

ఋణాత్మక ṛNaatmaka *adj. maths. phys.* negative.

ఋతం ṛtam I. *n.* truth, reality. II. *adj.* true, real.

ఋతుకాలం ṛtukaalam *n.* 1 duration of a season. 2 menstruous period.

ఋతుపవనం ṛtupawanam *n.* monsoon.

ఋతువు ṛtuwu *n.* 1 season lasting about two months, there being six seasons in the Telugu year. 2 menstruation, menstruous discharge.

ఋతుశాంతి ṛtuśaanti *n.* ceremony performed at the first menstruation of a girl after her marriage.

ఋతుస్నాత ṛtusnaata *n.* woman who has bathed ceremonially after menstruation.

ఋతుస్నానం ṛtusnaanam *n.* ceremonial bathing performed as purification after menstruation.

ఋతుస్రావం ṛtusraawam *n.* menstruation.

ఋత్వం ṛtwam *n. gram.* secondary form of the vocalic letter *ṛ*.

ఋత్విక్కు, ఋత్విజుడు ṛtwikku, ṛtwijuDu *n.* priest appointed to perform particular rites at a sacrifice.

ఋషభం ṛSabham *n.* 1 bull. 2 name of a raga.

ఋషి ṛSi *n.* holy man, ascetic, sage, rishi.

ఋషిపంచమి ṛSipancami *n.* ceremony performed by women on the fifth day of the first fortnight of Bhadrapada.

ఎ - e

ఎంకిపాట **enki paaTa** *n.* lyric composed by Nanduri Subba Rao in the style of a folk song.

ఎంగిలి **engili** I. *n.* 1 defilement by contact with mouth or saliva. 2 scraps of food remaining after a meal. 3 **koncem ~ paDi weLLaNDi** take a little food before you go. II. *adj.* unclean, dirty, esp. of plates, etc., after a meal; **~ maaTalu** vulgar language.

ఎంగిలి అవు **engili awu** *v.i.* 1 to be[come] defiled. 2 *colloq.* to commit adultery.

ఎంచు **encu** *v.t.* 1 to count, reckon, enumerate. 2 to think, reflect, consider; **kiiDenci meelencaali** consider the disadvantages first and then the advantages (proverb). 3 to choose, select. 4 to regard, esteem. 5 to prefer.

ఎం[దు]చేత **en[du]ceeta** *interrog. and det. particle* why, for what reason.

ఎంటి, వెంటి **eNTi, weNTi** *n.* straw rope used to secure a rick by tying it down.

ఎండ **eNDa** *n.* sunshine, sunlight, sun's heat; **~ kaastunnappuDu** when the sun is hot; **eNDaawaanaa anakuNDaa tirigEEDu** he wandered about not caring if it was wet or fine; **~ kanneragani sukumaari** person who leads a pampered and sheltered life.

ఎండకట్టు **eNDakaTTu** *v.t.* 1 to dry up or dry out by stopping supply of water. 2 to put an end to, put a stop to.

ఎండకాలం **eNDakaalam** *n.* hot weather, summer.

ఎండకొట్టు **eNDakoTTu** *v.t.* to dry up, wither.

ఎండదెబ్బ **eNDadebba** *n.* sunstroke.

ఎండపెట్టు, ఎండవేయు **eNDapeTTu, eNDaweeyu** *v.t.* to expose to the sun, dry in the sun.

ఎండపోయు **eNDapooyu** *v.t.* to spread out (grain) to dry in the sun.

ఎండమావి **eNDamaawi** *n.* mirage.

ఎండు **eNDu** I. *adj.* 1 dry, dried up; **~ gaDDi** dried grass, hay. 2 lean, emaciated, withered; **~ nakka** lean, hungry fox; **~ roogam** wasting disease. II. *v.i.* 1 to dry up, become dry or parched. 2 to become lean, emaciated or withered.

ఎండుకయ్యి **eNDukayyi** *n.* pool that has dried up.

ఎండుగులు **eNDugulu** *n.pl.* grain spread out to dry in the sun.

ఎండ్రకాయ, ఎండ్రి **eNDrakaaya, eNDri** *n.* crab.

ఎంత **enta** *interrog. and det. n. and adj.* how[ever] much, how[ever] great; **~ duuram?** how far? **~ anyaayam!** what an injustice! **~ maaTa!** what a thing to say! **ippuDu ~ ayindi Tayam?** what time is it now? **miiku ceppaDaaniki neenu ~ waaNNi?** am I a great enough person to advise you? **~ twaragaa aytee anta mancidi** the sooner, the better; **~ ku ammEEDu?** how much did he sell it for? **~ laa cikkipooyEEwuraa!** how thin you have become! **muuDu roojulanunci cebutunnaanu ii pani ceyyamani, entani ceppaali?** I have been telling you to do this for three days, how long must I go on telling you? **neenu ~ daaca prayatnincinaa, bayTapaDDadi** no matter how much (*or* however much) I tried to hide it, it came out; **~ leedannaa** however much anyone denies it; **nuwwu ceptee ~ ceppakapootee ~ , naaku teliyadanukonnaawaa?** it makes no difference (*or* it is all the same) whether you tell me or not: do you think I do not know? **aame baDinunci iNTiki ~ ku wastundi?** at what time will she come home from school? **~ loo peddawaaDiwi ayyEEwu!** how quickly you have grown up!

ఎంతకీ, ఎంతకూ **entakii, entakuu** *adv., always in neg. constr.* for (*or* until after) a long time; **neenu enni saarlu aDiginaa, aayana ~ jawaabu ceppa leedu** although I asked ever so many times, he did not reply for a long time.

ఎంతటి **entaTi** *dialectal and literary alt. form of* **enta.**

ఎంతమంది, ఎందరు **entamandi, endaru** *interrog. and det. n.pl.* how[ever] many persons.

ఎంతమాత్రం, ఏమాత్రం **entamaatram, eemaatram** I. *interrog. and det. n. and adj.* 1 how great, how much; **aa iNTi dhara ~ uNTundi?** *or* **aa illu ~ ceestundi?** how much will be the cost of that house? **aa naaTi paristhitiki ii naaTi paristhitiki ~ wyatyaasam unnadii ii uttaraalu cuustee telustundi** if you look at these letters you will understand how great is the difference between the situation then and now. 2 the least amount of, any amount at all; **~ awakaaśam unnaa neenu wastaanu** if there is any opportunity at all, I will come; **~ atiśayookti leekuNDaa** without the least exaggeration. II. *adv., in neg. constr.* by any means, on any account, in the least; **naaku daanni gurinci ~ teliyadu** I do not know anything about it at all; **~ neenu oppukoonu** I will not agree on any account.

ఎంతెంత, ఎంతలేని **ententa, entaleesi** *intensive forms of* **enta** how[ever] much, how[ever] great.

ఎంతైనా **entaynaa** I. *det. n.* ever so much, any amount; **miiru ~ ceppaNDi, neenu oppukoonu** say whatever you like (*or* however much you say) I will not agree; **Dabbu ~ saree, istaanu** whatever the cost may be, I will pay it. II. *det. adj.* ever so (much, great, etc.); **~ baagundi** it is ever so good; **~ peddawaaLLu** they are ever such great people. III. *adv.* however that may be, anyhow, any way, after all; **~ waaDu mii tammuDu** after all, he is your younger brother.

ఎంతో **entoo** *det. n. and adj.* ever so (much, great, etc.)

ఎందరు **endaru** *same as* **entamandi.**

ఎందాక, ఎంతదాక **endaaka, entadaaka** *adv.* how far, how long.

ఎందు **endu** *bound pron. occurring with certain case suffixes and postpositions,* **e.g., enduku, endunimittam.**

ఎందుకు **enduku** *interrog. and det. particle* why, for what reason; **endukaNTee** *lit.* if you ask 'why?', *hence* because; **aayana koorika kaadanaDam endukani sareenannaanu** I agreed, in order to avoid refusing his request (*lit.* thinking 'why should I refuse his request?' I said, 'all right!'): **endukaynaa mancidani** for safety's sake *or* to be on the safe side; **manak ~ ?** what is that to us? *or* what do we care?

ఎందుచేత **enduceeta** *same as* **enceeta.**

ఎందునిమిత్తం **endunimittam** *interrog. and det. particle* for what reason.

ఎంపిక **empika** *n.* 1 choice, selection. 2 preference.

ఎంపికచేయు **empikaceeyu** *v.t.* to choose, select.

ఎంబె[న్న] **embe[nna]** *n. colloq.* fool, worthless person.

ఎంబెరికం **emberikam** *n. colloq.* foolishness.

ఎంబెరుమాళ్ళు **emberumaaLLu** *n.* exponent of the Visishtadvaita system of philosophy.

ఎకరం, ఎకరా **ekaram, ekaraa** *n.* acre.

ఎకసక్కెం, ఎకసక్కేలాడు **ekasakkem, ekasakkEElaaDu** *same as* **wekkasakkem, wekkasakkEElaaDu.**

ఎకాయెకి[ని] **ekaayeki[ni]** *adv.* directly, straight away, without stopping.

ఎక్కం **ekkam** *n.* multiplication table.

ఎక్కడ **ekkaDa** I. *interrog. and det. n.* what place; *genitive* **ekkaDi** of *or* from what place: **ekkaDiwaaLLu akkaDee uNDipooyEEru** the people stopped just where they were; **nuwwu ekkaDi waaDiwi?** where are you from? **aa paaTa miikekkaDidi?** where did you get that song from? **aayanekkaDi guruwu? aayanaki paaTham ceppaDam raadu** what kind of a teacher is he? he cannot explain a lesson. II. *adv.* where; **idi ~ adi ~** ? what is the comparison between this and that? (*lit.* where is this and where is that?); **niiw ~ sangiitam ~** ? what do you know about music? (*meaning* music is s.g much beyond your comprehension); **~ leeni** *adj.* unique, unequalled, extreme, rare: *see* **naakam.**

ఎక్కడా **ekkaDaa** *adv., in neg. constr* anywhere ~ **dorakadu** it is not found anywhere.

ఎక్కడికక్కడ **ekkaDikakkaDa** *adv.* 1 in the appropriate place, wherever required. 2 at every place, at every point.

ఎక్కడికి **ekkaDiki** *adv.* whither.

ఎక్కడైనా **ekkaDaynaa** *adv.* anywhere.

ఎక్కడో **ekkaDoo** *adv.* somewhere.

ఎక్కతీయు **ekkatiiyu** *v.t.* 1 *dial.* to raise, increase the height of (e.g., a wall). 2 to pull off, pull out, peel off; **nii cemaDaalu ekkadiistaanu jaagratta!** be careful, or I will skin you!

ఎక్కా **ekkaa** *n.* kind of horsedrawn carriage.

ఎక్కాడు **ekkaaDu** *v.t.* 1 to spur on, incite. 2 to increase.

ఎక్కించు **ekkincu** *v.t.* 1 to cause to rise, help up, raise. 2 **o.-ni koorTuk ~** to take s.o. to court, involve s.o. in litigation. 3 to stack, load (goods onto a vehicle). 4 **suudiloo daaram ~** to thread a needle. 5 to enter, insert, include (in a book, file, ledger, etc.). 6 to inculcate (ideas); **miiru waaDi burralooki leenipooni uuhalu ekkinci ceDagoDataaru** you will spoil him by putting wrong ideas into his head. 7 to get (s.o.) over (s.g); **nuwwu nannu elaagaynaa gaTTekkincaaliraa!** you must somehow get me over the difficulty. 8 to thrust into or through. 9 to incite, stir up, rouse.

ఎక్కిడితొక్కిడిగా **ekkiDitokkiDigaa** *adv.* amply; **ataniki ~ aasti unnadi** he has ample property *or* he has enough property and to spare.

ఎక్కిరించు, ఎక్కిరింత **ekkirincu, ekkirinta** *alt. forms of* **wekkirincu, wekkirinta.**

ఎక్కిళ్ళు, వెక్కిళ్ళు **ekkiLLu, wekkiLLu** *n.pl.* 1 hiccoughs. 2 gasping sobs.

ఎక్కీతొక్కీ **ekkiitokkii** *adv.* 1 crammed, crowded; **iNTiniNDaa janam ~ [gaa] uurutunnaaru** the house is filled to overflowing with people. 2 plentifully, in plenty; **roojuu iNTillipaadii ~ naTTu kuuralu tiNTunnaaru** every day the whole household eats its fill of vegetables.

ఎక్కు **ekku** I. *n.* bowstring, esp. in a strung bow. II. *v.i.* 1 to rise, go up, come up; **poddu ekki nidra leecEEDu** he awoke after sunrise; **ii panilooki ewaruu ekkaleedu** no one has turned up for this work. 2 to get into; **koorTuku ~** to go to court, start litigation; **waartalaku ~** to get into the news; **aa uuha atani talaku ekkaleedu** that idea did not enter his head; **paamu karici wiSam payki ekkindi** a snake bit him and the poison entered his body; **nighaNTuwuloo ~** to be entered in a dictionary. 3 **kiirtik ~** to become famous, renowned or celebrated. 4 to increase, grow, swell. 5 (of interest) to accumulate, accrue. 6 to become; **waaDiki picci ekkindi** he became mad; **waaDi medaDu padunekkindi** his brain became keen; **Deegisaaloo niiLLu weeDekkaleedu** the water in the pan has not become hot; **waaDu iDLiilu tini laawekkEEDu** he grew fat through eating idlies. 7 to prevail, avail, be acceptable; **atani maaTa ekkadu** his word will not avail. 8 to be successful; **waaDu teliwigalawaaDu, jiiwitamloo ekkiwastaaDu** he has got brains, he is sure to do well in life. III. *v.t.* to ascend, climb, mount, get onto; **mancam ~** *lit.* to take to o.'s bed, *hence* to fall sick.

ఎక్కుడు **ekkuDu** I. *n.* 1 ascent. 2 greatness. 3 bowstring. II. *adj.* 1 great, mighty. 2 excessive. 3 *bot.* **~ tiige** creeping or climbing plant.

ఎక్కుదించు **ekkudincu** *v.t.* to unstring (a bow).

ఎక్కుపెట్టు **ekkupeTTu** *v.t.* to string (a bow).

ఎక్కువ **ekkuwa** I. *n.* 1 greatness, eminence, superiority. 2 excess, superfluity. II. *adj.* 1 great, much, large, high; **~ loo ~** highest of all, maximum. 2 greater, more, larger, superior; **pillalu sundaraanni kaasta ~ gaa cuuseewaaLLu** the children used to look up to Sundaram with some respect. 3 too much, too great, excessive, surplus; **ceruwuloo ekkuwayna niiLLu** the surplus water in the irrigation tank.

ఎక్కువతక్కువ **ekkuwatakkuwa** *n.* unevenness, irregularity; **~ lu ceeyakuNDaa** without making distinctions, without showing discrimation; **~ maaTLaaDaku** restrain your language.

ఎక్కువ తక్కువగా **ekkuwatakkuwagaa** *adv.* roughly, more or less.

ఎగ **ega** *adv.* up[wards].

ఎగఊపిరి **ega uupiri** *n.* gasp[ing], panting.

ఎగకట్టు **egakaTTu** *v.t.* to tie up, hitch up (clothes as far as the knee).

ఎగకొట్టు **egakoTTu** *v.t.* to evade, dodge, intentionally avoid.

ఎగచల్లు **egacallu** *v.t.* to sprinkle, spray.

ఎగచిమ్ము **egacimmu** *v.i. and t.* to spout, spurt, gush; **raktam egacimmindi** blood spouted (or spurted) out.

ఎగచేపు **egaceepu** *v.t.* (of a cow) to withhold milk.

ఎగతన్ను **egatannu** I. *v.i.* to force a way up; **mandu imaDaleedu, egatannindi** the medicine did not go down, it was vomited back; **paraayi neelaloo kuuDaa molaketti weeL-Luuni payki egadannukoni wastunna wittanaalu** seeds which sprout, strike root and keep on forcing their way up even in a foreign soil. II. *v.t.* to kick upwards.

ఎగతాళి **egataaLi** *n.* derision, mockery, ridicule, raillery.

ఎగతాళిచేయు, ఎగతాళిపట్టించు **egataaLi ceeyu, egataaLi paTTincu** *v.t.* to tease, mock, ridicule, make fun of, jeer at, gibe at.

ఎగతోయు **egatooyu** *v.t.* 1 to push up; **watti~** to turn up the wick (of a lamp). 2 to urge on, instigate.

ఎగదువ్వు **egaduwwu** *v.t.* 1 to comb upwards. 2 to stroke hair or fur in the wrong direction, *hence* to incite, irritate stir up; **naamiidiki waaNNi egaduwwEEDu** he stirred him up against me.

ఎగదొబ్బు **egadobbu** *v.t. slang* 1 to make away with, run off with (money, etc.). 2 to evade, dodge (an obligation).

ఎగపడు **egapaDu** *v.i.* to go after (s.g) eagerly, run after, seek to obtain, want, demand; **gumaastaa udyoogaalaku~taaru** they seek after clerks' jobs; **okaToo taariiku appula-waaru Dabbukoosam~taaru** on the first day of the month creditors come and demand their money.

ఎగపాకు **egapaaku** *v.i.* to creep up, crawl up, climb [up], ascend, rise [up].

ఎగపీల్చు[కొను] **egapiilcu[konu]** *v.i.* to sniff, inhale through the nose.

ఎగపెట్టు, ఎగవేయు **egapeTTu, egaweeyu** *v.t.* to dodge, avoid, evade (payment, etc.)

ఎగపోత **egapoota** *n.* 1 (*also* **egarapoota**) winnowing. 2 incitement, instigation. 3 a disease of the lungs.

ఎగపోయు **egapooyu** *v.i. and t.* 1 (*also* **egarapooyu**) to winnow grain by pouring it from a height. 2 to carry tales or spread rumours; **naamiida egapoosEEDu** he carried tales against me.

ఎగయు **egayu** *v.i.* 1 to rise, spring [up], fly [up]. 2 to jump, leap, bound. 3 to drift or float in the air; **gaali waaluloo aa śabdam egasiwacci naa cewiloo paDDadi** the sound came floating downwind and struck my ear.

ఎగరకొట్టు **egarakoTTu** *v.t.* 1 to finish off, polish off (colloq.), cause to vanish; **sommantaa wenkaTraawukee iddaam aNTee, muuDu nimiSaalloo antaa egarakoTTees-taaDatanu** if all the money was given to Venkatrao, he would polish it off in three minutes. 2 to pooh-pooh, disdain; **naa maaTa egarakoTTeesEEDu** he dismissed what I said with scorn.

ఎగరవేయు, ఎగరేయు **egaraweeyu, egareeyu** *v.t.* to toss up, toy with (s.g held in the hand), fly (kite), hoist (flag), shrug (shoulders), wave (hands), raise (eyebrows).

ఎగరేసుకుపోవు **egareesukupoowu** *v.t.* to run away with, carry off.

ఎగరొప్పు **egaroppu** *n.* panting (due to tiredness after exercise).

ఎగరోజు **egarooju** *v.i.* to gasp (due to eating hot spices).

ఎగవేత **egaweeta** *n.* evasion.

ఎగవేయు **egaweeyu** *same as* **egapeTTu.**

ఎగశ్వాసం **egaśwaasam** *n.* heavy breathing.

ఎగసన **egasana** *adv.* up[wards].

ఎగసన తోయు **egasana tooyu** *v.t.* 1 to push up, lift up. 2 to turn up (wick of a lamp); raise (flame in a fire). 3 to encourage, instigate.

ఎగసిపడు **egasipaDu** *v.i.* 1 to jump, leap; **guNDelu~tunnaayi** his heart is beating hard (due to shock). 2 to flare up, be enraged; **naamiida egasipaDDaaDu** he flared up against me. 3 to be proud or arrogant, give o.s. airs.

ఎగసిపాటు **egasipaaTu** *n.* 1 jumping, leaping. 2 passion, rage. 3 pride, arrogance.

ఎగాదిగా **egaadigaa** *adv.* from head to foot, from top to toe.

ఎగిరిపడు **egiripaDu** *v.i.* to flare up, show o.'s temper (**-miida**, against).

ఎగిరిపోవు **egiripoowu** *v.i.* 1 to fly away. 2 to disappear, be lost. 3 to be stolen.

ఎగుడు **eguDu** *adj.* ascending.

ఎగుడుదిగుడు **eguDudiguDu** *adj.* uneven, at different levels; **ii ~samaajam** this unequal society; **~maaTalu** incoherent words.

ఎగుదల **egudala** *n.* 1 upper region, upper part. 2 rise, ascent. 3 increase.

ఎగుబోటు **egubooTu** *n. and adv.* uphill.

ఎగుమతి **egumati** *n.* export.

ఎగుమతి చేయు **egumati ceeyu** *v.t.* to export.

ఎగురు **eguru** I. *n.* 1 flight. 2 leap. II. *v.i.* 1 to fly; **gaaliki~** (of clothes) to float or flap in the wind. 2 to jump [up], dance (with excitement or enthusiasm). 3 to flare up in anger (**–miida**, against); **intettuna egirEEDu** he flared up this much.

ఎగువ **eguwa** I. *n.* 1 top, upper part. 2 upstream; **aanakaT-Tuku 24 miiTarla~na** 24 metres upstream of the anicut. II. *adj.* upper, higher; **~sabha** Upper House (of Parliament).

ఎగ్గు **eggu** *n.* 1 shame, disgrace; **sigguu egguu leekuNDaa tirugutunnaaDu** he goes about without any feeling of disgrace or shame. 2 harm, injury.

ఎచ్చిపచ్చి **eccipacci** *adj.* half dry; **baTTalu~gaa eND-EEyi, kaasseepaagi testaanu** the clothes are half dry, I will bring them in a little time.

ఎచ్చిరిల్లు **eccirillu** *v.i. class.* to thrive, prosper, increase.

ఎచ్చులు **ecculu** *dial. variant of* **hecculu.**

ఎజమాని, ఎజమానురాలు **ejamaani, ejamaanuraalu** *same as* **yajamaani, yajamaanuraalu.**

ఎట **eTa?** *adv. class.* where? *mod. only in* **waaD~ ? wiiD ~ ?** *lit.* where is that man and where is this man? *meaning* there is no comparison between these men.

ఎటమటం **eTamaTam** *n.* disorder, turning upside down; **neenu ceppindeemiTi? nuwwu ceesindeemiTi? ~ ceesEEwantaa** what did I tell you? what have you done? you have spoilt everything *or* you have done everything in the wrong way.

ఎటు **eTu** *adv.* how, in what way, manner or direction; **tuurpu ~** ? in what direction is the east? **~ nunci cuusinaa** from whatever standpoint you look; **~ tirigi** however.

ఎటుపక్క **eTupakka** *adv.* on which side.

ఎటువంటి **eTuwaNTi** *interrog. and det. adj.* what kind of, any kind of.

ఎటూ **eTuu** *adv.* 1 anyhow, in any case; **neenu phoonu ceeyaleedu ~ miiru wastaaru gadaa ani** I did not phone because in any case I thought you would come. 2 **~ toocaka** not knowing what to think.

ఎటొచ్చీ **eToccii** *adv.* 1 in any case. 2 however, nevertheless; **miirumiiruu okaTee, ~ neenee bayTadaanni** you are all one (family), whereas I am a stranger.

ఎటో **eToo** *adv.* in some direction.

ఎట్టఎదురు **eTTa eduru** *adv.* right in front.

ఎట్టకేలకు **eTTakeelaku** *adv.* at last, in the end, finally.

ఎట్టా[గా/గు], ఎట్లా[గా/గు], ఎలా[గా/గు], ఎల్లా [గా/గు] **eTTaa[gaa/gu], eTLaa[gaa/gu], elaa [gaa/gu], ellaa[gaa/gu]** *adv.* in what way, how.

ఎట్టి **eTTi** *interrog. and det. adj.* what kind of, any kind of.

ఎట్టియెడ **eTTiyeDa** *adv.* in what cases, in what situations.

ఎట్టెట్టా ! **eTTeTTaa!** *interj. of surprise.*

ఎట్లా[ం]టి, ఎలా[ం]టి **eTLaa[N]Ti, elaa[N]Ti,** *interrog. and det. adj.* what kind of, any kind of.

ఎట్లాగయినా, ఎలాగయినా **eTLaagaynaa, elaagaynaa** *adv.* somehow or other.

ఎట్లాగో, ఎలాగో **eTLaagoo, elaagoo** *adv.* somehow.

ఎట్లు **eTLu** *adv.* how.

ఎడ **eDa** I. *n.* space, room, interval, distance; **~ duuDa** weaned calf; **~ pilla** last but one child. II. *p.p.* towards; **anaadhula ~ aadaram cuuputaaru** they show kindness towards orphans.

ఎడం **eDam** *n.* space, room, gap, interval.

ఎడంగా **eDangaa** *adv.* apart, some way off, separately, at a distance, leaving an interval; **ginnelu ~ peTTaNDi** please put the vessels in a separate place; **~ kuurcuNDu** to sit separately (not crowded together); **o.-ni ~ tiisukuweLLu** to take s.o. aside.

ఎడకట్టు **eDakaTTu** *v.i.* (of old sores, etc.) to appear again, come to a head again; **kurupu ~ ku waccindi** the old boil has come to a head again; **paata pagalu maLLii ~ ku waccEEyi** old enmities have raised their heads again.

ఎడతీయు **eDatiiyu** I. *v.t.* 1 to remove, take away. 2 to abstract. II. *v.i.* to cease, break off.

ఎడతెగని **eDategani** *adj.* ceaseless, incessant, continuous, chronic.

ఎడతెగకుండా **eDategakuNDaa** *adv.* ceaselessly, incessantly, continuously.

ఎడతెగు, ఎడపడు **eDategu, eDapaDu** *v.i.* to cease, break off.

ఎడతెరపి **eDaterapi** *n.* interval, break, pause.

ఎడల **eDala** I. *p.p.* regarding, towards, for, relating to, in the matter of; **aa kampenii ~ tanakuNDee gawrawam** the respect which he felt towards that company; **jaanapada sangiitam ~ abhiruci** taste for folk music. II. *advbl. particle suffixed to past vbl. adj.* if; **aayana ceppina ~ miiru aTLa ceeyaali** if he says so, you must do accordingly.

ఎడాపెడా **eDaapeDaa** *adv.* 1 this way and that; **~ cuucu** to look one way and then the other. 2 on both sides (as in playing a drum); **~ cempalu waayincu** to beat s.o. on both cheeks; **~ koTTEEnu** *or* **~ waayincEEnu** I beat him soundly; **waana ~ kurustunnadi** it is raining cats and dogs.

ఎడ్డి, ఎడ్డె **eDDi, eDDe** *n.* fool, ignorant person.

ఎడ్లబండి **eDLa baNDi** *n.* bullock cart; *see* **eddu.**

ఎతడు, ఎతను **etaDu, etanu** *interrog. and det. pron.* who, which person.

ఎత్తించు **ettincu** *v.t.* 1 to lift, raise. 2 to erect, build. 3 to cause, bring on, arouse (feelings, emotions).

ఎత్తికట్టు **ettikaTTu** *v.t.* to cut short, give up, abandon (studies).

ఎత్తిచూపు **etticuupu** *v.t.* 1 to bring to light, reveal, point out, demonstrate, expose. 2 to publicise, draw attention to (faults, defects).

ఎత్తిపెట్టు **ettipeTTu** *v.t.* 1 to put in order, make tidy; **neenu ii gadi ettipeTTaali** I must tidy this room. 2 to put or set aside; **neenu aalasyangaa wastaanu, miiru bhoonceesi naaku waNTa ettipeTTaNDi** I shall be late, finish your meal and put mine aside for me; **aa wiSayam ettipeTTaNDi, naa praśnaku jawaabu ceppaNDi** put that matter aside and answer my question.

ఎత్తిపొడుచు **ettipoDucu** *v.t.* 1 to ridicule, deride, jeer at. 2 to taunt, reproach.

ఎత్తిపొడుపు **ettipoDupu** *n.* 1 ridicule, jeering. 2 taunting, reproach.

ఎత్తిపోత **ettipoota** *n.* ceremony of immersion of ashes after a funeral.

ఎత్తివచ్చు **ettiwaccu** *v.i.* to attack; **mana deeśampay ettiwaccina wijaatiiya śaktuku** foreign powers which attacked our country.

ఎత్తివేయు **ettiweeyu** *v.t.* to abolish, stop, terminate, wind up, remove.

ఎత్తు **ettu** I. *n. suffix meaning* of a certain quantity or size; **wiisam ~** (*or* **cinnam ~**) **saayam ceeyaleedu** he did not give even a tiny amount of help; **pall ~ maaTa anakuNDaanee** without even uttering a word; **weeleD ~ maniSi** a very short person (*lit.* a person only as tall as o.'s finger): **taaD ~ maniSi** a very tall person (*lit.* s.o. as tall as a palmyra tree). II. *n.* 1 height, tallness; **ekkaDa paDitee akkaDa gaDDi molici sundaram ~ naa perigindi** grass sprang up everywhere and grew as tall as Sundaram; **nii oNTimiida maTTi aydaDugula ~ [na] undi** you are covered with mud (*lit.* the mud on your body is five feet thick); **pani naa ~ [na] undi, eppaTiki awutundoo teliyadu** I am up to my eyes in work, I do not know when it will be finished. 2 elevation, altitude. 3 weight; **naa ~ bangaaram iccinaa ii pani ceyyanu**

I will not do this, even if you offer me my weight in gold; **aaphiisuloo dammiDii ~ pani ceyyaleewu** the work you do in office is not worth a farthing (*lit.* in office you cannot do work equal to the weight of one paysa). 4 scale; **bhaarii ~ na** on a mass scale. 5 (*in two clauses stressing a contrast*) (i) matter, thing; **paaśćaatya deeśaalloo pillalanu kanaDam oka ~, waarini pencaDam maroka ~** giving birth to children in western countries is one thing, bringing them up is quite another thing, (ii) level, stage; **anni samwatsaraalaloonu maanawuDu saadhincina wayjñaanika pragati oka ~, kaDacina 100, 150 samwatsaraalaloo ataDu saadhincagaligindi maroka ~** the scientific progress that man achieved in all those years was one stage, what he has been able to achieve in the last 100–150 years is another stage. 6 move in chess. 7 trick, device, manoeuvre; **~ ku pay ~ weeyu** to outwit, play one trick in return for another. 8 weight of about $1^1/_2$ kilograms. 9 prop, support; **baNDicakram uuDadiisinappuDu irusukinda ~ peTTina karra** a stick placed under the axle for support when a cartwheel is removed; **talakinda ~ kaawaali, inkoo diNDu iwwaNDi** I need a support for my head, give me another pillow please. III. *adj.* 1 high, elevated; **~ maDamala jooLLu** high heeled shoes. 2 prominent: **~ paLLu** prominent or protruding teeth. 3 heavy. IV. *v.i.* to happen, occur, come on, arise; **naaku picci etteeTaTLugaa undi** it was as if madness was coming upon me. V. *v.t.* 1 to lift, raise, take up, pick up; **kaalu ~** to raise o.'s foot in order to kick; **gont ~** to raise o.'s voice; **daNDu ~** to invade; **hiTLar phraansumiida daNDettEEDu** Hitler invaded France. 2 to take away, remove; **kancaalu etti niiLLu callu** to remove plates and sprinkle water (cleaning up after a meal). 3 **maaTa ~** to mention, make mention of, bring up, refer to, allude to (a person, matter, subject); **pariikSalu daggira paDutunnaayi, tega cadiweestunnaanu, sinimaala maaTaa, naaTakaala maaTaa ettawaddu** exams are approaching, I am working very hard, don't breathe a word about cinemas or dramas; *see* **uusu.** 4 to take on o.s., assume; **awataaram ~** to undergo incarnation, be incarnated; **janmam ~** to be born; **ruupam ~** to assume a shape or form. 5 **nooru ~** to open o.'s mouth to speak. 6 **bhikSam ~** to live by begging.

ఎత్తుకొను **ettukonu** *v.t.* 1 to pick up, lift up. 2 to carry away, steal. 3 to hold (a child) in o.'s arms. 4 to make a start with, launch into, undertake, attempt; **ii pani talakettukoNTee, miiwalla awutundaa?** if you undertake this work, will you be able to finish it? **paaTa ~** to start to sing a song, launch into a song.

ఎత్తుగడ **ettugaDa** *n.* 1 contrivance, device, trick, manoeuvre. 2 tactics.

ఎత్తుగొలుసులు **ettugolusulu** *n.pl.* kind of ear ornament.

ఎత్తుబడి **ettubaDi** *n.* beginning, opening, exordium (of a poem, story, etc.).

ఎత్తుబిడ్డ **ettubiDDa** *n.* foster child.

ఎత్తుభారం **ettubhaaram** *n.* harassment, ruin.

ఎత్తుమానం **ettumaanam** *n.* maintenance allowance.

ఎత్తువేయు **ettuweeyu** *v.t.* 1 to weigh (precious metals). 2 to make a move (in chess).

ఎత్తుసరి **ettusari** *n.* equivalent weight; **paawalaa ~** weight equivalent to a quarter of a rupee.

ఎద **eda**[1] *n.* 1 heart, mind. 2 chest, breast; **naa Dabbu waaDu edaana weesukonnaaDu** he got away with my money; **neenu kaSTapaDi sampaadincina Dabbu waaDi edaana** (*or* **waaDi mohaana**) **weeśEEnu** (*or* **peTTEEnu** *or* **koTTEEnu**) I surrendered my hard earned money to him. 3 fear.

ఎద **eda**[2] *n.* period when a cow is fit to be crossed by a bull.

ఎదపడు **edapaDu** *v.i.* to be alarmed, be afraid.

ఎదర **edara** *same as* **eduTa.**

ఎదర్పు **edarpu** *n.* second loan given by a creditor to a debtor to enable repayment of the first loan.

ఎదవ **edawa** *n.* (*a mispronunciation of* **wedhawa** *indicating extreme contempt*) fool, useless person.

ఎదావు **edaawu** *n.* cow ready to be crossed by a bull.

ఎదిగిన మనిషి **edigina maniSi** *n.* grown up, adult.

ఎదిరి **ediri** *n.* opponent.

ఎదిరించు **edirincu** *v.t.* to oppose, resist, confront, encounter.

ఎదుగు **edugu** *v.i.* (of living things) to grow [up], grow to maturity.

ఎదుగుదల **edugudala** *n.* (of living things) growth, growing up, developing.

ఎదుగుబొదుగు **edugubodugu** *n.*, *always in neg. constr.* growth, increase, improvement; **adi puurtigaa giDasabaari pooyindi, daanikinka ~ lu leewu** it has been completely stunted, there is no more growth in it.

ఎదుట, ఎదర **eduTa, edara** *adv.* in front.

ఎదుటి **eduTi** *adj.* opposite.

ఎదురవు **edurawu** *v.i.* to be met, confronted, encountered or experienced; **aayana naaku bajaaruloo edurayEEDu** I came across him in the bazaar.

ఎదురాడు **eduraaDu** *v.i.* to oppose, resist.

ఎదురీదు **eduriidu** *v.i.* to swim against the current.

ఎదురు **eduru** I. *n.* front. II. *adj.* opposite, opposing, facing, confronting; **edurillu** the opposite house; **~ sawaalu** counter question; **kiTikii talupulu weyyaNDi, ~ jallu paDutunnadi** shut the doors and windows, the rain is beating in; **edureNDaloo** against the sunlight, with the sun in o.'s eyes. III. *adv.* 1 in return, in turn. 2 nevertheless, on the other hand, on the contrary; **taanu tappu ceesi ~ nannee duuSincEEDu** he committed the fault himself, nevertheless he blamed me.

ఎదురుకెదురు **edurukeduru** *adv.* on the other hand, on the contrary; **waaDu nannu appaDugudaamani waccEEDu, ~ neenee waaNNi aDigEEnu** he came to ask me for a loan but on the contrary I asked him for one.

ఎదురుగుండా **eduruguNDaa** *adv.* before, in front, facing, opposite.

ఎదురుచూచు **edurucuucu** *v.t.* to wait for, await, look out for, look forwards to, expect, anticipate, envisage, foresee.

ఎదురుతిరుగు **edurutirugu** *v.i.* 1 to resist, oppose, turn against, go against (s.o.'s wishes). 2 to revolt, rebel (-**ki**, against).

ఎదురుదాడి **edurudaaDi** *n.* counterattack, counteroffensive.

ఎదురుపడు **edurupaDu** *v.i.* to be met, be encountered; **aayana naaku doowaloo edurupaDDaaDu** I came across him on the road.

ఎదురుబదురు **edurubaduru** *n.* custom whereby a boy and a girl from one family are married to a girl and a boy from another; *cf.* **iccipuccukoolu.**

ఎదురుబదురుగా **edurubadurugaa** *adv.* facing each other, facing one another.

ఎదురుమేనరికం **edurumeenarikam** *n.* 1 (of a man) marriage with his paternal aunt's daughter. 2 (of a woman) marriage with her maternal uncle's son.

ఎదురురొమ్ము **edururommu** *n.* chest, breast.

ఎదురువచ్చు, ఎదురొచ్చు **eduruwaccu, eduroccu** *v.i.* to come towards, approach from the opposite direction.

ఎదురుసన్నాహం **edurusannaaham** *n.* 1 preparations for **edurkoolu** (reception of a bridegroom). 2 preparations for reception of s.o. important.

ఎదురెదురుగా **eduredurugaa** *adv.* face to face.

ఎదురేగు **edureegu** *v.i.* 1 to approach, go to meet. 2 to step forward in order to receive s.o.

ఎదురొడ్డు **eduroDDu** *v.t.* to put at stake; **praaNaalu**~ to stake or wager o.'s life.

ఎదుర్కొను **edurkonu** *v.i. and t.* 1 to go to meet, encounter. 2 to face, confront. 3 to oppose.

ఎదుర్కోలు **edurkoolu** *n.* 1 reception offered to a bridegroom when he arrives at the bride's house for the wedding ceremony. 2 reception offered to a guest.

ఎద్దడి **eddaDi** *n.* want, scarcity, shortage.

ఎద్దు **eddu** *n.* bullock, ox; *pl.* **eDLu** *or* **eddulu.**

ఎద్దుమొద్దు **eddumoddu** *n.* ruffian.

ఎద్దేవా **eddeewaa** *n.* 1 mockery. 2 heckling.

ఎద్దేవాచేయు **eddeewaa ceeyu** *v.t.* 1 to mock, tease, insult. 2 to heckle.

ఎనభై **enabhay** *n.* eighty.

ఎనమండుగురు **enamaNDuguru** *n.pl.* eight persons.

ఎనలేని **enaleeni** *adj.* matchless, incomparable.

ఎనిమిది **enimidi** *n.* eight.

ఎనియు **eniyu** *v.i. colloq. (esp. of boiled pulses)* to be well mixed.

ఎనుం, ఎనుము **enum[u]** *n.* she buffalo.

ఎనుచు, ఎనుపు **enucu, enupu** *v.t. colloq.* 1 to mash boiled pulses into dhall. 2 to mix thoroughly.

ఎనుబోతు **enubootu** *n.* male buffalo.

ఎన్నడు **ennaDu** *adv.* when.

ఎన్నడూ **ennaDuu** *adv., in neg. constr.* never.

ఎన్నడైనా **ennaDaynaa** *adv.* at any time.

ఎన్నడో **ennaDoo** *adv.* 1 at some time or other. 2 long ago.

ఎన్నదగిన, ఎన్నదగు **ennadagina, ennadagu** *adj.* notable, noteworthy.

ఎన్నాళ్ళు **ennaaLLu** *n.pl. and adv.* 1 *lit.* how many days. 2 how long.

ఎన్ని **enni** *interrog. and det. adj.* how many (things, not persons); **glEEsuloo**~**niiLLu/paalu unaayi**? how much water/milk is there in the glass?

ఎన్నిక **ennika** *n.* 1 election, *often pl.* ~**lu**; ~**la sangham** Election Commission; ~**pracaaram** election campaign. 2 selection, choice. 3 esteem, estimation.

ఎన్నిక చేయు **ennika ceeyu** *v.t.* 1 to elect. 2 to select, choose. 3 to [hold in] esteem.

ఎన్నికైన **ennikayna** *adj.* 1 elected. 2 selected, chosen. 3 esteemed.

ఎన్ను, వెన్ను **ennu**[1], **wennu** *n.* ear of corn.

ఎన్ను **ennu**[2] *v.t.* 1 to count, reckon. 2 to think. 3 to esteem, care for. 4 to criticise, find fault with.

ఎన్నుకొను **ennukonu** *v.t.* 1 to count, enumerate, reckon. 2 to choose, select. 3 to elect.

ఎన్నూరు **ennuuru** *n. dial.* eight hundred.

ఎన్నెమ్మ **ennemma** *n.* name of an evil spirit harmful to newborn children.

ఎన్నో **ennoo** I. *interrog. adj. lit.* the how many-eth? **iiwEELa** ~**taariiku**? what is the date today? II. *det. adj.* ever so many.

ఎప్పటట్లా, ఎప్పట్లా, ఎప్పటట్లు, ఎప్పటిలాగే **eppaTaTLaa, eppaTLaa, eppaTaTLu, eppaTilaagee** *adv.* as before, as usual.

ఎప్పటి **eppaTi** *interrog. and det. adj.* 1 of which period, of what time; **idi** ~**racana**? what period does this writing belong to? 2 former, old, usual; ~**maaTa** old or out of date saying.

ఎప్పటికప్పుడు **eppaTikappuDu** *adv.* 1 then and there. 2 now and then, from time to time.

ఎప్పటికప్పుడే **eppaTikappuDee** *adv.* 1 then and there (*emphatic*). 2 on every occasion, all the time.

ఎప్పటికి **eppaTiki** *adv.* by what time; ~**pani awtundi?** by what time will the work be over?

ఎప్పటికీ, ఎప్పుడూ **eppaTikii, eppuDuu** *adv.* 1 always. 2 *in neg. constr.* never.

ఎప్పుడు **eppuDu** *adv.* when.

ఎప్పుడైనా **eppuDaynaa** *adv.* at any time.

ఎప్పుడో **eppuDoo** *adv.* at some time or other (past or future.)

ఎప్పుడో తప్ప **eppuDoo tappa** *adv. only in neg. constr.* hardly ever.

ఎబ్బె! **ebbe!** *interj. expressing disapproval or disgust.*

ఎబ్బెట్టు **ebbeTTu** *adj.* 1 ugly, awkward, strange, odd. 2 objectionable, shocking, repulsive. 3 disreputable, not respectable.

ఎముక **emuka** *n.* bone ~**leeni ceyyi** a person of generous nature.

ఎమ్ములు **emmulu** *n.pl. slang* excessive talkativeness.

ఎర **era** *n.* 1 bait, enticement, lure. 2 victim.

ఎరక్క, ఎరగక **erakka, eragaka** *neg. participle of* **erugu** unwittingly, unknowingly.

ఎరికె **erike** *n.* range of knowledge, purview.

ఎరుక **eruka** *n.* 1 knowledge, acquaintance, understanding, cognisance; **aayana naaku erikee** I know him (**erikee** *here*

= **eruka** + *emphatic suffix* **ee**). 2 consciousness. 3 fortune telling; ~ **ceppu** to tell fortunes.

ఎరుకత, ఎరుకలసాని **erukata, erukalasaani** *n.* woman fortune teller of the Erukala tribe.

ఎరుకపరచు **erukaparacu** *v.t.* to make known, familiarise.

ఎరుకల **erukala** *n.* name of a tribe in Andhra Pradesh.

ఎరుగు **erugu** *v.t.* 1 to know, be acquainted with. 2 *in neg. constr. following a past participle* to be in the habit of; **waaDu baDi pustakaalu cadiwi eragaDu** he is not in the habit of reading school books.

ఎరుపు **erupu**[1] *n.* redness.

ఎరుపు[కొను] **erupu [konu]**[2] *v.t. colloq.* to tease, worry, trouble.

ఎరుపుచేయు **erupu ceeyu** *v.i.* **kaaliki debba tagilitee, erupuceesi kaTTEEnu** when his leg was injured, I applied lime and turmeric paste and bandaged it (a spoonful of turmeric mixed with lime and water and heated to form a paste is a home remedy for cuts and boils).

ఎరుపెక్కు **erupekku** *v.i. with dat.* 1 to blush (with shyness). 2 to flush (with anger).

ఎరువు **eruwu**[1] *n.* manure.

ఎరువు **eruwu**[2] *n.* loan.

ఎరువుయిచ్చు, ఎరువిచ్చు **eruwu iccu, eruwiccu** *v.t.* to lend.

ఎరువు తెచ్చుకొను **eruwu teccukonu** *v.t.* to take on loan, borrow.

ఎర్ర **erra**[1] I. *n.* (*also* ~ **na**) red[ness]. II. *adj.* (*also* ~ **Ti**, ~ **ni**) 1 red, reddish brown; ~ **gaa kaalcina** red hot; ~ **kaLLu** red eyes (due to anger or passion); ~ **Ti eNDaloo paDi** suffering from the extreme heat; *see* **eegaani.**

ఎర్ర **erra**[2] *n.* earthworm.

ఎర్ర[రక్త]కణాలు **erra[rakta]kaNaalu** *n.pl.* red blood cells, red blood corpuscles, erythrocytes.

ఎర్రగడ్డ **erragaDDa** *n.* onion.

ఎర్రగావురు **erragaawuru** *n.* mixture of red and black colours seen in clouds.

ఎర్రచవుడు **erracawuDu** *n.* red salty soil.

ఎర్రడాలు **erraDaalu** *n.* redness, esp. of clouds.

ఎర్రపుండు **errapuNDu** *n.* scab on a cut which is healing; **gaayam** ~ **paDindi** the wound has formed a scab.

ఎర్రబడు, ఎర్రబారు **errabaDu, errabaaru** *v.i.* to turn red.

ఎర్రముల్లంగి **erramullangi** *n.* carrot.

ఎల **ela** *adj.* young, tender; ~ **niiru** tender coconut water.

ఎలక **elaka** *same as* **eluka.**

ఎలనవ్వు **elanawwu** *n.* smile.

ఎలపల ఉండు **elapala uNDu** *v.i. dial.* to be in menses.

ఎలా[గా/గు] **elaa[gaa/gu]** *same as* **eTTaa[gaa/gu].**

ఎలాగో ఓలాగా **elaagoo oolaagaa** *adv.* somehow or other.

ఎలా[ం]టి **elaa[N]Ti** *same as* **eTLaa[N]Ti.**

ఎలానూ **elaanuu** *adv.* 1 anyhow. 2 in any case. 3 somehow or other.

ఎలి[గట్టు]దుక్కి **eli[gaTTu]dukki** *n.* ploughed dry (unirrigated) land.

ఎలుక, ఎలక **eluka, elaka** *n.* rat.

ఎలుగు **elugu**[1] *n.* voice; **elugetti arucu, elugetti pilucu** to call out aloud.

ఎలుగు **elugu**[2] *n.* (*also* ~ **goDDu,** ~ **baNTi**) bear.

ఎలుగు, వెలుగు **elugu**[3], **welugu** *n.* fence.

ఎలువు **eluwu** *n.* deep ploughing.

ఎలువుపీట **eluwupiiTa** *n.* wooden wedge in a plough stock to adjust the depth of ploughing.

ఎల్ల **ella**[1] *n.* 1 limit, boundary; ~ **raayi** boundary stone. 2 measuring rod used in the game **biLLankooDu.** 3 ~ **lu eerparacu** to demarcate.

ఎల్ల **ella**[2] *n.* white[ness].

ఎల్ల **ella**[3] (*also* **ellaa**) *adj.* all; **kr̥SNaagoodaawari nadulu ~ kaalam prawahistaayi** the rivers Krishna and Godavari flow perennially.

ఎల్లప్పుడు **ellappuDu** *adv.* always.

ఎల్లరు, ఎల్లవారు **ellaru, ellawaaru** *det.n.pl.* everybody.

ఎల్లా[గా/గు] **ellaa[gaa/gu]** *same as* **eTTaa[gaa/gu].**

ఎల్లుండి **elluNDi** *n. and adv.* the day after tomorrow.

ఎళువు సుళువులు **eLuwusuLuwulu** *n.pl.* inconveniences and conveniences.

ఎవరు **ewaru** *interrog. and det. pron. sing. or pl.* who (*note: the sing. forms* **ewaDu** *masc. and* **ewate** *fem. are informal and impolite*); ~ **cuusEEru**? who knows? *or* who can tell? **ewariki kaawaali**? (i) who needs? (ii) *rhetorical question* who cares?

ఎవరూ **ewaruu** *det. pron., in neg. constr.* no one.

ఎవరైనా **ewaraynaa** *det. pron.* anyone, anybody.

ఎవరో **ewaroo** *det. pron.* someone, somebody, anyone, anybody; **aa waccinawyakti ~ kaadu** that person who came was not just anybody (i.e., he was s.o. of importance or some particular person.)

ఎసరు **esaru** *n.* water boiled to cook food, esp. rice; **kotta biyyam waNDitee mundu ~ peTTaali, kaagitee biyyam pooyaali** if you are cooking new rice, first put the water on the fire to boil, when it is boiling, pour in the rice; **naaku ~ peDutunnaaDu** he is planning to do me harm; *see* **attesaru.**

ఏ- ee

ఏ ee[1] *emphatic suffix* **1** *emphasising the n./pron./vb./adv. to which it is attached;* **aa samwatsaramee** that very year (and no other); **aa tarwaatee** only after that (not at any other time); **okee uttaram andindi** only one letter has been received (not any more); **miiree jawaabu raayaali** only you (*or* you yourself) must write the answer (none else). **2** *less commonly, to indicate surprise or excitement, emphasing a whole sentence* **DaakTaru waccinaTTundee!** it seems that the doctor has come! **3 eekaaka** (*or* **eekaadu**) *suffixed to a noun signifies* not only; **ii wiSayamloo aayanee kaaka** (*or* **aayanee kaadu**) **migataa waaLLu kuuDaa adee abhipraayamtoo unnaaru** in this matter not only he but also others are of the same opinion; *see* **adee.**

ఏ ee[2] *interrog. and det. adj.* **1** which: **ee peejii miida** on which page; **ee widhangaa** by which means, how. **2 ee** + *noun* **aynaa** *signifies* any; **ee ceTTaynaa koTTawaccu** you may cut down any tree. **3 ee** + *noun* + **oo** *signifies indefiniteness in certain contexts*: **ee koddimandoo** just a few persons: **ee briTanloonoo amerikaaloonoo** in some place like Britain or America: **ee** + *noun* + **ku** + **aa** + *noun repeated signifies* each; **ee payrukaa payru wiDiwiDigaa roogalakSaNaalu raayaali** write down the symptoms of the diseases of each crop separately: **ii widhangaa aame kSeema samaacaaraalu naaku ee roojukaa rooju telustunnaayi** by these means I get news of her state of health every day.

ఏం, ఏమి[టి] eem, eemi[Ti] I. *interrog. and det. pron.* **1** what; **eemayindi?** what has happened? **eemiTi wiśeeSaalu?** what is the [latest] news? **miireem anukookuuDadu** you must not think anything of it. **2** *in rhetorical questions* **daaniki eemundi?** what is the difficulty about that? (*implying* nothing is wrong with it); **ee deeśamnuNDi wasteeneemi?** what does it matter what country it comes from? **nuwwu melligaa naDistee baNDi weLLipook[a]eem ceestundi?** if you walk slowly you are sure to miss the train (*lit.* if you walk slowly, what else will the train do except depart?); **pillalu allari ceestee amma koTTak[a] eem ceestundi?** if the children are naughty their mother is sure to beat them (*lit.* if the children are naughty, what else will their mother do except beat them?); *see also* **mooyina. 3** *advbl. use* how, why: **eem ilaa waccEEru?** how come you are here? (a greeting); "**aayana wastaaDaa?**" "**raakeem?**" "will he come?" "of course he will" (*lit.* why won't he come?); "**maaku cooTu undEE?**" "**leekeem?**" "will there be room for us?" "of course there will" (*lit.* why won't there be?): **neenerakkeem?** *or* **naaku teliyakeem?** of course I know; **beeDaa muuDaNaalu rooju kuuliitoo waaLLeem bataggalaru?**) how can they live on a daily wage of 2 or 3 annas? II. *interj., with suffix of address* **eemaNDii** *or* **eemayya**! hallo! *or* sir! III. *clictic joining two or more nouns* . . . **eemi** . . . **eemi** both . . . and . . . . . . either . . . or . . ., neither . . . nor . . .; **widyawallaneemi paaNDiti kaaraNangaaneemi naayakatwam labhincadu** leadership is not acquired either through education or through scholarship.

ఏక eeka *adjvl. prefix meaning* one, single, only: ~ **kaalamloo** at one and the same time, simultaneously.

ఏకం eekam *n.* one.

ఏకం అవు eekam awu *v.i.* to be united, unified, combined; **aayana illu kaalipooyindi. uuruuwaaDaa antaa eekamayi niiLLu poosinaa eemii migalaleedu** his house was burnt down. although the whole village joined together and poured water on it, nothing was saved.

ఏకంగా eekangaa *adv.* **1** united[ly], jointly, combining together. **2** just, simply, only, once for all; **eeDoo nelanu ~ puriTikee tiisukeLLaNDi** take her in the seventh month once for all for her confinement. **3** straight[away]; **~ naa iNTiki waccEEDu** he came to my house straightaway. **4** continuously, incessantly; **raatri antaa ~ waana kurisindi** it rained steadily all night long.

ఏకంచేయు eekam ceeyu *v.t.* **1** to unite, combine. **2** to gather, collect.

ఏకకణ eekakaNa *adj. biol.* unicellular.

ఏకకాలిక eekakaalika *adj.* synchronous.

ఏకకేంద్రక eekakeendraka *adj.* concentric.

ఏకగ్రీవ eekagriiwa *adj.* unanimous.

ఏకగ్రీవంగా eekagriiwangaa *adv.* unanimously, with one accord.

ఏకగ్రీవత eekagriiwata *n.* unanimity.

ఏకఘాత eekaghaata *adj. maths. sci.* linear.

ఏకచ్ఛత్రాధిపత్యం eekacchatraadhipatyam *n.* **1** absolute authority (of a ruler). **2** monopoly of power.

ఏకజాతీయత eekajaatiiyata *n.* homogeneity.

ఏకటాకీగా, ఏకటాకీన eekaTaakiigaa, eekaTaakiina *adv.* continuously, nonstop.

ఏకత eekata *same as* **aykyam.**

ఏకతలీయ eekataliiya *adj. maths.* coplanar.

ఏకతానం eekataanam *adj.* concentrated.

ఏకతాళం eekataaLam *n.* one of the modes of beating time in music.

ఏకతాసూత్రం eekataasuutram *n.* unitary principle.

ఏకత్రపరచు eekatraparacu *v.t.* to unite, consolidate.

ఏకత్వం eekatwam *n.* unity, singleness, oneness; **bhinnatwamloo ~** unity in diversity.

ఏకదంతుడు eekadantuDu *n.* epithet of the God Vinayaka.

ఏకదీక్షగా eekadiikSagaa *adv.* with concentrated attention, singlemindedly.

ఏకదేవతారాధన eekadeewataaraadhana *n.* monotheism.

ఏకదేశం eekadeeśam *n.* part, portion.

ఏకధాటిగా, ఏకధాటిన eekadhaaTigaa, eekadhaaTina *adv.* ceaselessly, continuously; **eekadhaaTigaa kuNDapootagaa** (of rain) pouring continuously.

ఏకధారగా eekadhaaragaa *adv.* flowing or pouring continuously.

ఏకపక్ష, ఏకపార్శ్విక **eekapakSa, eekapaarświka** *adj.* unilateral.

ఏకపత్నీవ్రతుడు **eekapatniiwratuDu** *n.* monogamist.

ఏకబిగిన, ఏకబిగువున **eekabigina, eekabiguwuna** *adv.* nonstop, continuously, at one stretch.

ఏకమాత్ర **eekamaatra** *adj.* single.

ఏకముఖ **eekamukha** *adj.* 1 homogeneous. 2 ~ **prawaaham** direct (electric) current.

ఏకమొత్తం **eekamottam** *n.* lump sum.

ఏకరక్త **eekarakta** *adj.* consanguineous.

ఏకరీతి **eekariiti** *adj.* constant, steady, uniform; ~ **mandam** uniform thickness.

ఏకరువుపెట్టు **eekaruwu peTTu** *v.t.* 1 to repeat, reproduce, utter, enunciate; **waaLLatoo ceppawalasina naalugu maaTaluu taDumukookuNDaa eekaruwu peTTeesEEnu** I repeated without faltering the few words that I had to say to them. 2 to narrate in great detail and at a stretch; **aa peLLi sambandhamtoo praarambhinci graamamloo unna anni kuTumbaala aTTupuTLu aanawaaLLuu aayana eekaruwu peDuTunnaaDu** beginning with that marriage relationship he is narrating in detail all the relationships between all the families in the village.

ఏకరూప **eekaruupa** *adj.* uniform; ~ **saandrata** uniform density.

ఏకరూపత **eekaruupata** *n.* 1 uniformity. 2 *sci.* isomorphism.

ఏకలింగ **eekalinga** *adj. sci.* unisexual.

ఏకవచనం **eekawacanam** *n. gram.* singular number; **eekawacana prayoogam** using the singular to address a person, *i.e.*, addressing a person impolitely or informally.

ఏకవాక్యత **eekawaakyata** *n.* unanimity, agreement.

ఏకవార్షికం **eekawaarSikam** *n. bot.* annual, plant which completes its life cycle in one year.

ఏకవింశతి **eekawimśati** *see* **wimśati.**

ఏకవీరుడు **eekawiiruDu** *n.* unchallenged hero.

ఏకశిలానగరం **eekaśilaanagaram** *n.* a name of the city of Warangal.

ఏకసంతగ్రాహి, ఏకసంధాగ్రాహి **eekasantagraahi, eekasandhaagraahi** *n.* person who has the power to memorise and repeat back any (literary or other) material after only one hearing.

ఏకస్వం **eekaswam** *n.* patent.

ఏకస్వామ్యం **eekaswaamyam** *n.* monopoly.

ఏకాంకిక **eekaankika** *n.* one act play.

ఏకాండం **eekaaNDam** *adj.* made in one piece.

ఏకాంత **eekaanta** *adj.* 1 lonely, solitary, secluded, isolated; ~ **waasa śikSa** solitary confinement. 2 secret.

ఏకాంతం **eekaantam** *n.* 1 loneliness, solitude, seclusion, isolation. 2 secrecy, privacy.

ఏకాంతంగా **eekaantangaa** *adv.* 1 alone, apart. 2 *theat.* aside. 3 secretly, in secret, privately.

ఏకాంతర **eekaantara** *adj.* alternate; ~ **prawaaham** alternating current.

ఏకాంతరీకరణ **eekaantariikaraNa** *n.* alternation.

ఏకాంతవాసి **eekaantawaasi** *n.* recluse.

ఏకాకి **eekaaki** *n.* solitary person, recluse.

ఏకాక్షరం **eekaakSaram** *n.* monosyllable.

ఏకాగ్ర **eekaagra** *adj.* intent, concentrated; ~ **dṛSTi** concentrated attention.

ఏకాగ్రత **eekaagrata** *n.* intentness, concentration, single-mindedness; ~ **too winu** to listen with rapt attention.

ఏకాత్మక **eekaatmaka** *adj.* unitary.

ఏకాదశ **eekaadaśa** *adj.* eleventh.

ఏకాదశి **eekaadaśi** *n.* eleventh day of the lunar fortnight, observed by some persons as a day of fasting.

ఏకాభిప్రాయం **eekaabhipraayam** 1 *n.* agreement, accord. 2 consensus.

ఏకీకరణ[ం] **eekiikaraNa[m]** *n.* uniting, unification, consolidation, integration.

ఏకీకరించు **eekiikarincu** *v.i.* to unite, become one.

ఏకీకృత **eekiikṛta** *adj.* unified, united, consolidated, integrated.

ఏకీకృతపరచు **eekiikṛta paracu** *v.t.* to consolidate, unite, integrate, unify.

ఏకీభవించు **eekiibhawincu** *v.i.* 1 to agree, concur, be of one mind. 2 (of opinions) to coincide.

ఏకీభావం **eekiibhaawam** *n.* agreement, concurrence, concord.

ఏకీయ **eekiiya** *adj. maths. sci.* unitary.

ఏకు **eeku** I. n. flock of cotton or wool cleaned and prepared for spinning. II. *v.t.* 1 to gin or clean cotton. 2 *colloq.* to criticise, condemn.

ఏకేశ్వరవాదం **eekeeśwarawaadam** *n.* monotheism.

ఏకైక **eekayka** *adj.* 1 pure, simple; ~ **pakSapaatam** sheer partiality. 2 unique, one and only.

ఏకైకత **eekaykata** *n. maths. sci.* uniqueness.

ఏకోదర **eekoodara** *adj.* of the same womb.

ఏకోదరులు **eekoodarulu** *n. pl.* uterine brothers and sisters.

ఏకోశానా, ఏకోశంలో ఐనా **eekoośaanaa, eekoośamloo aynaa** *adv., in neg. constr., lit.* in no place or corner, *hence* nowhere, to no extent, not in the least, not at all; ~ **waaDiki dhayryam leedu** he has no courage in him at all.

ఏక్కు **EEkku** *n.* utter disgust.

ఏగాని **eegaani** *n.* small copper coin worth two pies, no longer current; **errani ~ naa wadda leedu** I haven't a penny on me.

ఏగు **eegu** *v.i.* to go, *literary and classical but also occurring mod. in* **uur ~** to go in procession *and* **edur ~** to go to receive.

ఏగుడ్డూ **eeguDDuu** *n. slang, in neg. constr.* nothing at all, none at all; ~ **pramaadam leedannamaaTa** there is no danger at all, I am telling you.

ఏగుదెంచు **eegudencu** *v.i.* to come, go, proceed.

ఏట **eeTa**[1] *n.* 1 ram. 2 he goat. 3 *dial.* meat, esp. mutton. 4 any animal offered as a sacrifice.

ఏట **eeTa**[2] *abl. case of* **eeDu** year; **reNDoo**~ in the second year.

ఏటవాలు **eeTawaalu** I. *n.* slant, slope. II. *adj.* 1 steep, sloping. 2 *maths.* oblique (angle).

ఏటవాలుగా **eeTawaalugaa** *adv.* slanting, sloping, at an angle.

ఏటా **eeTaa** *adv.* every year, annually.

ఏటి **eeTi**[1] *genitive case of* **eeDu** year.

ఏటి **eeTi**[2] *genitive case of* **eeru** river.

ఏటి **eeTi**[3] *colloq. form of* **eemiTi.**

ఏటికాలువ **eeTikaaluwa** *n.* irrigation channel bringing water from a stream.

ఏటికీ కోటికీ **eeTikii kooTikii** *adv.* on rare occasions.

ఏటు, వేటు **eeTu, weeTu** *n.* blow, stroke.

ఏటో **eeToo** *colloq. form of* **eemiToo.**

ఏడడుగులు **eeDaDugulu** *n.pl.* seven steps taken round the sacrificial fire during a marriage ceremony; (=**saptapadi**).

ఏడాది **eeDaadi** *n.* year's time; ~ **poDawunaa** all the year round, for a whole year.

ఏడికర్ర, ఏడికోల **eeDikarra, eeDikoola** *n.* pole or shaft of a plough.

ఏడిపించు **eeDipincu** *v.t.* to tease, annoy, make (s.o.) cry.

ఏడిపించుకుతిను **eeDipincukutinu** *v.t.* to annoy, worry, irritate, bother; *see* **tinu** *sense 5.*

ఏడీ? **eeDii?** *composite question word* where is (some male person)?

ఏడు **eeDu**[1] *n.* seven.

ఏడు **eeDu**[2] *n.* year; **aa eeTiki aa**~ from year to year; **eeLLuupuuLLuu** years and years, many years; **eeTiki eeDaadi** all the year round, all through the year.

ఏడు **eeDu**[3] *imperative sing. of.* **eeDcu.**

ఏడుకొండలవాడు **eeDukoNDalawaaDu** *n.* Lord of Seven Hills, Sri Venkateswara, deity of the temple at Tirupati-Tirumala.

ఏడుగడ **eeDugaDa** *n.* safety, protection.

ఏడుపు **eeDupu** *n.* weeping, crying; **naaku~waccinanta pani ayindi** I almost cried *or* I felt like crying; **waaDi ~ eemiTi?** what is his opinion/attitude/version (regarding some happening)? **nii~mukham naaku cuupincaku!** don't look so miserable! *see* **eeDcu** *sense 4.*

ఏడువారాల నగలు **eeDu waaraala nagalu** *n.pl.* collection of jewellery consisting of seven separate sets, each one to be worn on one day of the week.

ఏడూరి **eeDuuri** *n.* ceremonies performed on the first anniversary of a death, consisting of the final monthly ceremony (**maasikam**) followed by the first annual ceremony (**taddinam**).

ఏడో **eeDoo** *adj.* seventh.

ఏడ్చు **eeDcu** *v.i.* 1 to cry, weep, shed tears, lament; **eeDceedaani moguDu wastee, naa moguDu wastaaDu** if the husband of that weeping woman comes (back to life), so will mine (*proverbial saying meaning* if so and so succeeds in something he or she is doing, I will also benefit); **eeDci mukham kaDukkunnaTTundi** you look as if you had washed your face after crying (*proverbial saying meaning* you seem to be trying to hide something). 2 to be resentful: **wiiLLantaa naa miida paDi eeDustaaru** they will all be resentful against me. 3 *with a past participle to give intensive force* **ceppi eeDu!** speak out! **aytee matoo ceppi eeDawakuudaduu!** then why on earth could not he tell us? **waaDiki lookam gurinci okaTi teliseeDcuneemiTi niiku ceppaDaaniki?** is there anything at all that he can tell you about the world? *see* **kanuka** *sense II. 2.* 4 *colloquially, substituting for another verb* **aa maaTa wastuunee enduku eeDawakuuDadu?** (*for* **ceppakuuDadu?**) why could he not have said that as soon as he came? **neenu ii gadiloo eeDawaali** (*for* **uNDaali**) I must stay in this room; **jeebuloo Dabbulu eeDistee** (*for* **uNTee**) **ee pani aynaa ceyyawaccu** you can do anything if there is money in your pocket; **nii eeDupu nuwwu eeDu, waaDi sangati wadileeyi** do your own part (of the work), do not think about him; *cf.* **aghoorincu, caccu.** 5 *as an expletive or to indicate a poor opinion* **eeDicEEwulee!** nonsense!; **ii pustakam eeDcinaTTundi** this book is useless.

ఏడ్చుకొను **eeDcukonu** *v.i.* to be envious and resentful.

ఏణా **eeNaa** *suffix used to form adverbs from certain Sanskrit nouns,* e.g., **ruupeeNaa, krameeNaa.**

ఏణ్ణర్థం **eeNNardham** *n.* a year and half, one and a half years.

ఏతం, ఏతాం **eetam, eetaam** *n.* picota, a device for baling water for irrigation.

ఏతర **eetara** *see* **itara.**

ఏతావాతా **eetaawaataa** *adv.* summing up, finally, in conclusion.

ఏతెంచు **eetencu** *v.i. class.* to come, go, proceed.

ఏత్వం **eetwam** *n.* secondary form of the vowel *ee* in Telugu script.

ఏదన్నా, ఏదైనా **eedannaa, eedaynaa** I. *pron.* something, anything. II. *pronom. adj., sing. or pl.* some, any.

ఏది **eedi** I. *interrog. pron.* which thing? II. *adv.* where? **pustakam~? naadaggira leedu** where is the book? I have not got it.

ఏదీ? **eedii?** *composite question word* where is ..... (s.g)?

ఏదుం **eedum** *n.* obsolete measure of grain, five tooms.

ఏదుపంది **eedupandi** *n.* porcupine.

ఏదువాసన **eedu waasana** *n.* foul smell.

ఏదైనా **eedaynaa** *same as* **eedannaa.**

ఏదో **eedoo** I. *pron.* 1 anything, something; **ii pustakaalaloo ~okaTi tiiyaNDi** take any one of these books; **sabhaloo~ okaTi maaTLaaDaNDi** say something or other at the meeting. 2 *adverbial use* (i) somewhat, a little, rather; **peekaaTa ~ koddigaa waccu** I can play cards just a little; **~ paradhyaanangaa** somewhat absentmindedly; **~ pharawaa leedu** *minor sentence* not bad! (ii) somehow; **indrayyagaari praapuna ~ bratukutunnaanu baabuu**! I am somehow managing to live with Indrayya's help sir! (iii) just, just about; **~ ninnoo, monnoo jariginaTTundi** it is as though it happened only (*or* just) yesterday or the day before. 3 *as a sentence opener when giving a reason or explanation* you see! **~ miiru peddamaniSi gadaa ani ceppEEnu, ewaritooTii ceppakaNDi** you see, I have told you this considering you to be a gentleman, do not tell anyone else: **~ śarmagaaru naa guruwu, aayana ceppEEDani ceesEEnu** you see, Sarma is my guru, I did it because he told me to. II. *adj., sometimes used deprecatingly* some: **ceetulaku ~ gaajulu unnaayi** she has bangles of a sort on her arms; **ikkaDee ~ uuLLoo uNTaaDu, naaku teliyadu** he lives in some village near here but I do not know where.

ఏదోగా, ఏమిటోగా **eedoogaa, eemiToogaa** *adv.* a little strange, not quite normal; **~ anipistundi** it will seem rather odd.

ఏనాడో **eenaaDoo** *adv.* 1 *in past constr.* long ago; **~ jarigindi** it happened long ago. 2 *in future constr.* one day, some day; **~ waaDu nii pratyarthi kaawaccu** one day he may be your rival.

ఏనాది **eenaadi** *n.* name of a tribe in Andhra Pradesh.

ఏనుగు **eenugu** *n.* elephant; **~ balam** great strength; **~ daaham** greed (= **peeraaśa**); **~ kaalu** elephantiasis (= **boodakaalu**).

ఏపాటి **eepaaTi** *interrog. and det. adj.* how much, how great, to what extent, what amount of.

ఏపారు **eepaaru** *v.i.* to increase, bloom, flourish.

ఏపి,ఏపె[చెట్టు] **eepi, eepe [ceTTu]** *n.* sal tree, *hardwickia binata.*

ఏపు **eepu** I. *n.* 1 blooming or flourishing condition. 2 strength. II. *adj.* fine, sturdy, vigorous.

ఏబలం, ఏబులం **eebalam, eebulam** *n.* obsolete weight equal to five palams or a quarter of a viss.

ఏబ్రాసి **eebraasi** *n.* filthy, nasty looking or slovenly person.

ఏమంత **eemanta** *adv., in neg. constr.* not so much, not so very; **wasanta ~ manci pilla kaadu** Vasanta is not such a very good girl.

ఏమన్నా **eemannaa** *same as* **eemaynaa.**

ఏమరించు, ఏమార్చు **eemarincu, eemaarcu** *v.t.* to distract s.o.'s attention, make s.o. forget himself.

ఏమరుపాటు **eemarupaaTu** *n.* inattention.

ఏమరుపాటున **eemarupaaTuna** *adv.* casually, unawares, inattentively, carelessly; **~ poyyiloo ceyyi peTTEEnu** I put my hand in the fire without paying attention; **~ uNDu** to be careless, be off o.'s guard, be taken unawares.

ఏమర్చు **eemarcu** *v.i. and t.* to forget s.g temporarily.

ఏమాత్రం **eemaatram** *same as* **entamaatram.**

ఏమారు **eemaaru** *v.i.* to be off o.'s guard, be neglectful or careless, be caught unawares.

ఏమి[టి] **eemi[Ti]** *same as* **eem.**

ఏమిటో **eemiToo** *det. pron.* 1 something; **kaaru naDawaDam leedu, ~** (*or* **eemoo**) **ayindi** the car will not move, something has happened to it; **~ anukunnaanu, idi baagaanee undi** I expected something different, but this is quite all right. 2 *adverbial use* (i) somehow: **~ ikkaDa uNTee haayigaa anipincindi** somehow it seemed that it would be pleasant to remain here; (ii) perhaps; **waana wastundoo ~** (*or* **eemoo**), **tondaragaa weLLaNDi** perhaps it will rain (*or* it may rain), go quickly.

ఏమిటోగా **eemiToogaa** *same as* **eedoogaa.**

ఏమిట్లు **eemiTLu** *interrog. pron.* of what community? **~ miiru**? what is your community?

ఏమూలో **eemuuloo** *adv.* in some corner, somewhere or other; **~ waaDiki manasuloo śanka uNDanee undi** somewhere in his mind there certainly lurked a doubt.

ఏమైనా, ఏమన్నా **eemaynaa, eemannaa** I. *interrog. and det. pron.* something, anything. II. *pronom. adj.* some, any; **~ saayam ceyyaNDi** please give some help. III. *adv.* 1 all the same, nevertheless, however. 2 (*also* **~ saree**) whatever happens, in any case, come what may. 3 in any way **~ nyaayangaa undEE?** is that in any way right?

ఏమో **eemoo** *det. pron.* 1 something; *see* **eemiToo.** 2 *advbl. use, indicating uncertainty or doubt in the speaker's mind* perhaps; **atanu raaleed~** perhaps he has not come; Q. **aayana iNTidaggara unnaaDaa**? A. ~ ! Q. is he at home? A. I am not sure (*or* he may or may not be); *see* **eemiToo.**

ఏరకట్ట **eerakaTTa** *n.* ploughing equipment, ploughing bullocks, harness, etc.

ఏరాలు **eeraalu** *n.* co-daughter-in-law, husband's brother's wife.

ఏరీ? **eerii?** *composite question word* where are . . . . (some persons)?

ఏరు **eeru[1]** *n.* plough complete with bullocks; **~ kaTTu** to yoke a plough.

ఏరు **eeru[2]** *n.* river, rivulet; **eeTikaDDapaDu, eeTikeduriidu** to swim against the current, encounter difficulties; **eeTikokaru kaaTikokaruu laagutaaru** if one pulls one way, the other will pull another way (proverbial saying).

ఏరు **eeru[3]** *v.t.* 1 to pick up (things) one by one, pull up (weeds), gather up (papers). 2 to clean (rice). 3 to glean.

ఏరుకొను **eerukonu** *v.t.* to choose, select.

ఏరుకోల **eerukooLa** *n.* shaft of a bullock cart.

ఏరుగు **eerugu** *v.i.* to ease o.s., excrete, defecate.

ఏరుగుడు **eeruguDu** *n. dial.* excretion.

ఏరువాక **eeruwaaka** *n.* ceremony performed annually before the beginning of the cultivation season.

ఏరువాక పున్నమ **eeruwaaka punnama** *n.* full moon day in the month of Jeshta, when the cultivation season begins.

ఏర్చు **eercu** *v.t.* to choose, select, pick out, sort out; **eercikuurci** selecting and assembling.

ఏర్పడు **eerpaDu** *v.i.* 1 to be formed, take shape; **asalu gooLaalu eewidhangaa ~ tunnaayi**? how are spheres really formed? **ennuleerpaDee modaTi daśa** the first stage of formation of the ears of corn. 2 to be caused, brought about or produced; **pustaka prapancamtoo sambandham eerpaDindi** a link was forged with the world of books; **aneeka wayyaakaraNula pariśramawalla trimuni wyaa-**

karaNam eerpaDDadi the Trimuni Vyakaranam was produced by the efforts of many grammarians. **3** to happen, occur, come about; **kSaamam eerpaDindi** famine broke out. **4** to be felt or experienced; **aameloo ceppaleenanta jaali eerpaDindi** she felt an unutterable sense of pity. **5** to be established, set up or created; **aandhrapradeeS eerpaDina naaTinunci** since the establishment of Andhra Pradesh. **6** to be drawn up, arranged, laid down, fixed or determined; **waaTini lawkika bhaaSaloo kalapa kuuDadanee niyamam eerpaDDadi** a rule was laid down that they (classical words) should not be included in the everyday language; **kaaryakramam eerpaDutunnadi** a programme is being arranged.

ఏర్పరచు **eerparacu** *v.t.* **1** to form (ideas). **2** to make, build (roads). **3** to create, establish (factories). **4** to arrange, fix, settle (targets).

ఏర్పాటు **eerpaaTu** *n.* **1** arrangement. **2** formation, establishment, setting up.

ఏల **eela** *adv. mainly used in rhetorical questions* why? **iwi awi anan ~ ?** *or* **int ~ ?** *or* **weey ~ ?** why do I say all these things? **idantaa jaragan ~** ? why should all this happen?

ఏలం **eelam** *same as* **weelam.**

ఏలకి **eelaki** *n.* cardamom plant.

ఏలకులు **eelakulu** *n. pl.* cardamom seeds.

ఏలపదం, ఏలపాట **eelapadam, eelapaaTa** *n.* kind of folk song.

ఏలిక **eelika** *n.* ruler, prince, king.

ఏలికపాము **eelikapaaamu** *n.* tape worm.

ఏలినవారు **eelinawaaru** *n.pl. lit.* rulers, *a complimentary term sometimes used when referring to a person in authority.*

ఏలు [కొను] **eelu[konu]** *v.t.* **1** to rule, govern. **2** to control, manage. **3.** to accept, admit, take care of, entertain. **4** to look after (a wife or mistress).

ఏలుగుపాము **eelugupaamu** *n.* kind of thorny cactus.

ఏలుబడి **eelubaDi** *n.* rule, government.

ఏల్నాటిశని **eelnaTi śani** *n. phrase* seven years of misfortune caused by the planet Saturn.

ఏవ **eewa** *n.* dislike.

ఏవగించు **eewagincu** *v.t.* **1** to hate, dislike, be disgusted by *or* at. **2** to despise, scorn, speak contemptuously of.

ఏవగింపు **eewagimpu** *n.* **1** dislike, distaste, disgust. **2** scorn, contempt.

ఏవి *interrog. and det. pron.* which things.

ఏవిధంగానైనా **eewidhangaanaynaa** *adv.* by some means other, somehow or other.

ఏవీ? **eewii?** *composite question word* where are . . . (certain things)?

ఏవురు **eewuru** *class. alt. form of* **ayduguru.**

ఏస, యాస **eesa, yEEsa** I.*n.* accent, way of speaking; **ee praantamwaaLLu aa praantapu ~ nu sahajangaanuu itarula ~ nu wintagaanuu cuustaaru** the people of every region regard their own accent as normal and the accents of other people as strange. II. *adj.* irregular in shape; **~ mancam** irregularly shaped cot.

ఏసి **eesi** *distributive suffix, attached to a numeral, meaning* each, at a time, at the rate of; **okkokka puuTiiki reND ~ aakulu unnaayi** there are two spokes for each felloe (of a cartwheel); **okkokka balla daggara pad ~ mandi, irawayy ~ mandi naluguLLupaDDaaru** at each (chess) board ten or twenty people at a time struggled with the problem; **samwatsaraaniki muuD ~ jillaalu coppuna** at the rate of three districts per year; **iddar ~ muggur ~ gaa tirugutunnaaru** they are going about in twos and threes; **wandal ~ pillalu** children by the hundred, hundreds of children.

ఏహ్య **eehya** *adj.* hateful.

ఏహ్యం, ఏహ్యభావం **eehyam, eehyabhaawam** *n.* hatred.

ఐ - ay

ఐ, అయి ay[i] *past participle of* **awu** to be[come] **1 tappanisari~** having become inevitable. **2** *adverbial use* concerning, about: **oka wiSayam~naaku ceppaDaaniki waccEEDu** he came to tell me about something; **oka wiSayam~ eekiibhawistunnaaru** they agree about one matter. **3** *equivalent to* **gaa** *advbl. suffix* **naakoosam~ ceyyaNDi** please do it for me; **tamaku taam~** for themselves.

ఐంద్రజాలికుడు **ayndrajaalikuDu** *n.* magician.

ఐకమత్యం **aykamatyam** *n.* unity, agreement, harmony, concord.

ఐక్య **aykya** *adj.* united.

ఐక్యం, ఏకత, ఐక్యత **aykyam, eekata, aykyata** *n.* unity, union, oneness, unitedness.

ఐక్యం అవు **aykyam awu** *v.t.* to become one, become united.

ఐక్యరాజ్యం **aykyaraajyam** *n.* unitary state.

ఐక్యరాజ్యసమితి **aykyaraajya samiti** *n.* United Nations Organisation (UNO).

ఐక్య సంఘటన **aykya sanghatana** *n. polit.* **1** coalition. **2** United Front.

ఐచ్ఛిక **aycchika** *adj.* optional, voluntary.

ఐతిహాసిక **aytihaasika** *adj.* **1** historical. **2** (of poetry) epic.

ఐతిహ్యం **aytihyam** *n.* traditional or legendary account.

ఐతే **aytee** I. *conditional participle of* **awu** to be[come]; **neenu ~aDakkuNDaa Dabbu icceewaaNNi** if it had been myself, I would have given the money without being asked. II. *adv.* **1** if so, then, in that case. **2** but, however. **3** provided that. III. *clitic, emphasising the n., pron. or n. phrase to which it is attached* as for, indeed; **konni graamaalaloo~ waariki smaśaana waaTikalu kuuDaa leewu** indeed in some villages they do not even possess burial grounds; **naak~ teliyadu** as for me (*or* for my part) I do not know; **swaraajyam ~waccindi gaani, waari swaraaSTra waancha gaganakusumangaanee migilindi** independence did indeed come, but their desire for a separate state remained a dream.

ఐతేనేమి **ayteeneemi** *minor sentence* **1** what does it matter?, what of it?, never mind! **2** *conjunctive use* whether . . . . or . . . . ; **pustakaala dwaraa~ śeeSagiri waNTi waaLLu ceesee pracaaram wallan~** whether it was through books or because of publicity conducted by people like Seshagiri.

ఐత్వం **aytwam** *n.* secondary form of the diphthong *ay* in Telugu script.

ఐదు **aydu** *n.* five.

ఐదుగురు **ayduguru** *n.pl.* five persons.

ఐదుపదికావించు **aydu padi kaawincu** I. *v.i.* to join the two hands together in prayer or salutation. II. *v.t. colloq.* to break in pieces, destroy.

ఐదువ **ayduwa** *n.* married woman.

ఐదోతనం **aydootanam** *n.* status of a married woman.

ఐన **ayna** I. *suffix for forming adjectives from nouns, e.g.,* **andam~** beautiful, **teliw~** intelligent. II. *relative participle of* **awu** to be[come] **1 naa sneethituDu~phalitangaa waaDiki udyoogam dorikindi** as a result of his being my friend, he got a job; **pariikSa pEEs~widyaarthi** a student who has passed his examination; **raamuDi bhaarya ~siita** Rama's wife Sita. **2~ dii kaanidii** this or that, insignificant matters; **saree, taruwaata eemii~dii kaanidii waagakaNDi, telisindEE?** all right, after this do not talk irrelevantly, do you understand? **3 ~weeLaa kaaniweeLaa** (i) at all times, (ii) at favourable and unfavourable times.

ఐనప్పటికీ **aynappaTikii** *adv.* nevertheless, all the same.

ఐనప్పుడు **aynappuDu** *adv.* when that is so, then, therefore, in that case.

ఐనవారు **aynawaaru** *n.pl.* **1** o.'s relations and friends. **2** o.'s supporters and backers.

ఐనా **aynaa** I. *concessive form of* **awu** to be[come] **1 goppawaaD~** although he is a great man. **2** *conjunctive use* (i) but, however, nevertheless; (ii) that being so, moreover, besides; **naaku pani undi, ~neenenduku?** I am busy and besides, why involve me? **3** *adverbial use* even, at least; **koddi mottaanik~ saree** even for a small amount. **4** *in idiomatic construction, giving strong negative meaning* **neenu eppuDuu sigareTLu muTTukoon~muTTukooleedu** I have never so much as touched cigarettes. II. *particle similar to* **annaa** *and indefinite clitic* **oo**; *usages*: (i) *to express indefiniteness, when added to an* **e-** *question word,* e.g., **ewaru?** who? **ewar~** anyone; (ii) *to express alternatives,* e.g., **miir~neen~ii pani ceeyaali** either you or I must do do this work.

ఐనిల్లు **aynillu** *n.* family with a good standing and reputation, respectable family.

ఐపు **aypu** *n.* sign, trace; *cf.* **aanawaalu.**

ఐపోవు **aypoowu** *v.i.* **1** to be finished, be over. **2** to be exhausted, run out (colloq.).

ఐమూల **aymuula** *adj.* oblique, diagonal, diagonally opposite.

ఐరావతం **ayraawatam** *n.* the elephant on which the God Indra rides.

ఐరేనికుండలు **ayreeni kuNDalu** *n.pl.* painted earthenware pots used for worship in a marriage ceremony.

ఐవేజు **ayweeju** *n.* **1** rent for land paid in cash or kind. **2** yield from a field. **3** income.

ఐశ్వర్యం **ayśwaryam** *n.* wealth, prosperity.

ఐశ్వర్యవంతుడు **ayśwaryawantuDu** *n.* rich person.

ఐసరబజ్జ! **aysarabajja!** *interj., often in children's language, expressing satisfaction when s.g is finished.*

ఐసాపైసా **aysaapaysaa** *adv.* this way or that; **~teelci ceppaNDi** make up your mind one way or the other.

ఐహిక **ayhika** *adj.* **1** temporal, pertaining to the present world. **2** secular, material, wordly.

ఒ - O

ఒంకె **onke** *n.* hook, peg.

ఒంగు **ongu** *same as* **wangu.**

ఒంటపట్టు, వంటపట్టు **oNTapaTTu, waNTapaTTu** *v.i.* 1 to be digested, assimilated or absorbed; **waaDiki tiNDi oNTapaTTindi** he digested his food; **kaasta naagarikata oNTapaTTina waaLLuu caduwukonna waaLLuu maaTLaaDee bhaaSani wyawahaarika bhaaSa aNTaaru** the speech of those who have absorbed some culture and those who are educated is called '**wyawahaarika bhaaSa**'. 2 to become used, accustomed or familiarised.

ఒంటరి **oNTari** I. *n.* single or lonely person. II. *adj.* alone. single, lonely.

ఒంటరికాడు **oNTarikaaDu** *n.* single or lonely person.

ఒంటరిపాటు **oNTaripaaTu** *n.* loneliness, seclusion.

ఒంటి **oNTi**[1] *adj.* one, single; ~**ankelu** single figures; ~**gaNTa** one o'clock; ~**peeTa** single string or strand (in a necklace); ~**pora** single fold or layer; **naa maaTalu wini~ kaalimiida naa miidiki waccEEDu** hearing what I said, he came towards me in a rage; ~**uupiriwaaDu** physically weak person; ~**kaNTi raamalingam** jealous or envious person.

ఒంటి, వంటి **oNTi**[2], **waNTi** *genitive of* **oLLu.**

ఒంటిగా **oNTigaa** *adv.* alone, on o.'s own, by o.s.

ఒంటిగాడు, ఒంటివాడు **oNTigaaDu, oNTiwaaDu** *n.* 1 bachelor. 2 single person, s.o. who is alone.

ఒంటిపూట **oNTipuuTa** *n.* 1 *same as* **okkapoddu.** 2 half a day; **saniwaaram~baDi** on Saturday there is school for half a day.

ఒంటు **oNTu** *v.i.* to be fit, suitable to o.'s constitution, congenial, agreeable.

ఒంటె **oNTe** *n.* camel.

ఒంటెత్తు **oNTettu** *adj.* ~**maniSi** self-centred or egoistic person.

ఒంట్లు **oNTLu** *n. pl.* figures, numbers; **waaDiki ~kuuDaa raawu** he is not even able to count.

ఒండు **oNDu**[1] *same as* **waNDu**[1].

ఒండు, ఒండ్రు, వండు, వండ్రు **oNDu**[2], **oNDru, waNDu**[2], **waNDru** *n.* alluvium, silt; ~**neela** alluvial soil.

ఒండు **oNDu**[3] *n. and adj.* 1 *class.* one. 2 *in neg. or interrog. constr.* any[thing]; **weer~ kaaraNaalu ceppakaNDi** do not give any more reasons; **oNDananeela?** why should I say anything more? (*rhetorical question—see* **eela**).

ఒండొంటి **oNDoNTi** *det. n. colloq.* (of animals, things) of each other.

ఒండొంటికి **oNDoNTiki** *adv.* mutually, reciprocally.

ఒండొక **oNDoka** *adj.* another, one more, additional.

ఒండొరులు **oNDorulu** *det. n. pl., colloq.* (of persons) each other

ఒందించు **ondincu** *v.t., literary and formal* to cause, bring about; **antam~** to bring to an end, contrive the destruction of, put an end to.

ఒందు **ondu** *v.t.* 1 *class.* to obtain, possess, have. 2 *mod. only in compounds* **gelup~** to be victorious, **peerondina** famous.

ఒక **oka** *adj.* 1 one; *sometimes equivalent to the indefinite article in English,* e.g., **~uuLLoo~raaju unnaaDu** there was a king in a town. 2 **okee** one (emphatic), only one.

ఒకంతకు **okantaku** *adv., in neg. or interrog. constr.* after a little time, in a short time; **bassu~raaleedu** the bus did not come within a short time.

ఒకంతట **okantaTa** *adv.* as quickly as that, so quickly.

ఒకందుకు **okanduku** *adv.* for one reason.

ఒకటి **okaTi** *det. n.* 1 one, one thing, something; ~**ki reNDu** not one but two (emphatic); ~**ki padi saarlu** time and again, over and over again; **okaTeemiTi?** why (do I mention) only one thing? (*rhetorical question*); **adrSTawa-śaattu~jarigindi** by good fortune something occurred. 2 one and the same, all the same; ~**awu** to become one, be united; ~**ceeyu** to mix together, join together, unite. 3 **okaTee** only one; **wedhawa wiidhibaDi! okaTee koTTaDam!** that wretched street school! nothing but beatings! 4 **okaTii araa** one or two, a few (*lit.* one and a half).

ఒకటొకటిగా **okaTokaTigaa** *adv.* one by one.

ఒకడు **okaDu** *pron.* one man, someone.

ఒకతె **okate** *pron.* one woman.

ఒకదగ్గర **okadaggara** *adv.* in one place; **iwannii ~peTTaN-Di** put all these together in one place.

ఒకనాడు **okanaaDu** *adv.* 1 at one time, once, formerly. 2 one day, at some time in the future.

ఒకపక్క, ఒకమూల **okapakka, okamuula** *adv.* on the one hand; *often used without specifically expressing* on the other hand, e.g., ~**waanakurustuu uNTee weLLipooyEE-Du** even though it was raining, he went away; ~**paDi neenu eeDustuu uNTee, eTLaa paDDaarani aDugutunnaaru migataa waaLLu** when I have fallen down and am weeping, the others are simply asking, "how did you fall?"

ఒకపట్టాన, ఒకపట్టున **okapaTTaana, okapaTTuna** *adv.* all at once, straight away.

ఒకప్పుడు **okappuDu** *adv.* on one occasion, formerly, once upon a time; ~**kaakapootee~** once in a while, occasionally.

ఒకమాత్రపు **okamaatrapu** *adj.* 1 ordinary; **idi ~jabbu kaadu** this is not an ordinary illness. 2 mediocre; ~**paaTakaaDu** a mediocre singer.

ఒకరు **okaru** *pron. pl.* 1 some persons. 2 *polite pl. used for sing,* someone, some person. 3 **okarinokaru** each other, one another.

ఒకలా[గా], ఒకలాగు **okalaa[gaa], okalaagu** *adv.* in a certain way.

ఒకలా[ం]టి **okalaa[N]Ti** *adj.* a certain kind of

ఒకళ్లు **okaLLu** *pron. pl. always with singular meaning* someone.

ఒకవేళ **okaweeLa** *adv.* **1** perhaps. **2** by chance. **3** supposing.

ఒకసారి **okasaari** *adv.* **1** once. **2** *used to introduce a polite request*, e.g., ~ **naaku istaaraa?** would you lend it to me, please?

ఒకానొక **okaanoka** *adj.* a certain; ~ **deeśam** a certain country, some country or other.

ఒకానొకప్పుడు **okaanokappuDu** *adv.* at a certain time, once upon a time.

ఒకింత **okinta** *adj.* some, a little.

ఒకేసారి **okeesaari** *adv.* simultaneously.

ఒకేదగ్గర **okee daggara** *adv.* at the same place.

ఒక్క **okka** *adj. emphatic form of* **oka** only one, just one; ~ **abbaayi** only one boy; ~ **phalitamee pariśiilistee** if you examine only the result; ~ **kaawyaalee kaakuNDaa ennoo itara pustakaalu** not just poems but ever so many other books also.

ఒక్కపెట్టున **okkapeTTuna** *adv.* suddenly, all at once, at one stroke.

ఒక్క పొద్దు **okkapoddu** *n.* day of partial fasting; ~ **uNDu** to eat only one meal per day.

ఒక్కమారే **okkamaaree** *adv.* at all once.

ఒక్కలాగే **okkalaagee** *adv.* exactly alike.

ఒక్కసారిగా **okkasaarigaa** *adv.* all at once.

ఒక్కుమ్మడిగా **okkummaDigaa** *adv.* all together, in a rush, all at the same time.

ఒక్కొక్క **okkokka** *adj.* each.

ఒక్కొక్కటి **okkokkaTi** *pron.* **1** each one. **2** *adverbial use* singly, one by one; **iNTLoo unna saamaanlu okkokkaTee paTTukupooyi ammeesEEDu** taking the household things one by one, he sold them off.

ఒక్కొక్కప్పుడు **okkokkappuDu** *adv.* occasionally.

ఒక్కొక్కరోజు, ఒక్కోరోజు **okkokkarooju, okkoorooju** *adv.* on certain days.

ఒక్కొక్కళ్లే **okkokkaLLee** *adv.* one after the other; **pillalu ~ weLLi paDukonnaaru** the children went one by one and lay down.

ఒక్కొక్కసారి, ఒక్కోసారి **okkokkasaari, okkoosaari** *adv.* at certain times.

ఒగరు **ogaru** *n.* acrid or astringent taste.

ఒగుడు **oguDu** *n.* dried leaves of cholam, cumbu, etc.

ఒగ్గు **oggu**[1] *v.i. and t.* **1** to yield, submit, offer, present; **wiipu ~** to turn o.'s back (in order to run away or show indifference). **2** to be prepared, undertake (to do s.g). **3** to apply (o.'s mind), lend (o.'s ear, hand). **4** to bend, bow: **balaprayoogaaniki tala ~** to bow o.'s head (*or* yield) to force.

ఒగ్గు **oggu**[2] *v.i. and t., slang* (=**wadalu**) to leave, let go; **oggi!** *imperative, slang* let go!

ఒగ్గుకథ **oggukatha** *n.* a legend narrated by weavers about the founders of their community.

ఒచ్చు **occu** *alternative form of* **waccu.**

ఒజ్జ **ojja** *n.* **1** teacher, tutor. **2** priest, purohit.

ఒజ్జబంతి **ojjabanti** *n.* **1** example. **2** top line written by a teacher as an example to be copied by a pupil.

ఒట్టి[నే] **oTTi[nee]** *same as* **utta[nee].**

ఒట్టు **oTTu** *n.* **1** oath. **2** imprecation or spell liable to be incurred if an oath is falsely sworn: **naa pillalamiida ~** I swear by my children (*lit.* may a spell fall on my children if I swear falsely); **deewuDimiida ~** I swear by God (who will punish me if I swear falsely); **erraTi eegaaNaynaa wasuulaytee ~** I swear I have not (*or* may a spell fall on me if I have) collected a single pie.

ఒట్టుపెట్టు **oTTu peTTu** *v.t.* to make (s.o.) swear an oath.

ఒట్టువేయు **oTTuweeyu** *v.i.* to swear an oath, take an oath: **idee jarigindani oTTuweesi ceppEEDu** he swore that this had happened.

ఒట్టు తీయు **oTTu tiiyu** (*or* **oTTu tiisi gaTTuna peTTu**) *v.t.* to revoke a spell.

ఒడంబడిక **oDambaDika** *n.* **1** agreement, accord. **2** contract; **saamaajika ~** social contract.

ఒడంబడు **oDambaDu** *v.i.* to agree, come to an agreement.

ఒడకొట్టు **oDakoTTu** *v.t.* to empty, drain, exhaust (water from a well, any liquid from a drinking vessel).

ఒడలు **oDalu** *class. alt. form of* **oLLu.**

ఒడి **oDi** *n.* **1** lap. **2** pouch formed in o.'s clothing on the lap or at the waist; **oDiloo eedoo daacukuni bayTiki weLLipooyindi** she went out hiding s.g at her waist.

ఒడికట్టు **oDikaTTu** *v.i.* to prepare o.s., get ready, undertake (gen. to do some evil): **enta paapaaniki oDikaTTa dalacukunnaawu?** what mischief are you preparing to commit?

ఒడినింపు **oDinimpu** *v.i.* to honour (s.o.) with gifts.

ఒడిపట్టు **oDipaTTu** *v.i.* to reap the result of an action; **neenu ceesina paapaalaki aame oDipaTTindi** she has reaped the result of my misdeeds.

ఒడిదుడుకులు **oDiduDukulu** *n.pl.* **1** ups and downs, variations, fluctuations, unevenness, unsteadiness, instability. **2** troubles, difficulties. **3** complications, hurly burly.

ఒడిబియ్యం, వడిబియ్యం **oDibiyyam, waDibiyyam** *n.* rice given by a mother to her daughter when she first goes to live with her husband.

ఒడియం, వడియం **oDiyam, waDiyam** *n.* cake of black gram, dried in sunlight and fried.

ఒడియు **oDiyu** I. *v.i.* **1** to be used up or exhausted. **2** (of water) to flow away, sink down. II. *v.t.* to catch, seize, snatch.

ఒడిసిపట్టు, వడిసిపట్టు **oDisipaTTu, waDisipaTTu** *v.t.* to hold firmly.

ఒడిస్సీ **oDissii** *n.* style of dancing special to Orissa.

ఒడుచు **oDucu** *v.t.* to seize, catch, snatch, grab; **peekaaTaloo naa Dabbu antaa ~ konnaaru** they took all my money at cards.

ఒడుపు **oDupu** *n.* **1** skill, ability, ingenuity, cleverness, dexterity. **2** reaping, harvesting.

ఒడుపుగా **oDupugaa** *adv.* skilfully, dexterously.

ఒడ్డి[మంగలి] **oDDi[mangali]** *n.* barber and masseur from Orissa, recognised as an expert.

ఒడ్డిగ **oDDiga** *n.* pile of pots one above the other.

ఒడ్డు **oDDu** I. *n.* **1** bank, shore. **2** stake in gambling. II. *adj.* large, big, great, wide, broad. III. *v.t.* **1** to place, put, lay. **2** to bet, wager; **praaNaalu~** to wager o.'s life, put o.'s life at stake.

ఒడ్డూపొడుగూ **oDDuupoDuguu** *n.* physical proportions of a person.

ఒడ్డె[ర], వడ్డెర **oDDe[ra], waDDera** *n.* member of a community of irrigation tank diggers and building workers.

ఒడ్డెక్కించు **oDDekkincu** *v.t.* to help (s.o.) out of a difficulty.

ఒడ్డెక్కు **oDDekku** *v.i.* to be settled, be brought to a successful conclusion; **naalugu nelalu wyawadhi leekuNDaa wyawahaaraalu oDDekkaDam leedu** transactions are only concluded after an interval of four months.

ఒడ్డోలగం **oDDoolagam** *n.* king's court.

ఒత్తరి, వత్తరి **ottari, wattari** *n.* fat person.

ఒత్తాసు **ottaasu** *same as* **wattaasu.**

ఒత్తిగించు **ottigincu** I. *v.i.* **1** to lie on o.'s side. **2** to step aside, stand back, get out of the way. II. *v.t.* to pull aside, push aside.

ఒత్తిగిల్లు **ottigillu** *v.i.* **1** to lie on o.'s side. **2** to lean to one side.

ఒత్తిచెప్పు **otticeppu** *v.i.* to press, urge; **waaLLa iNTiki rammani otti ceppEEDu** he pressed me to come to his house.

ఒత్తిడి **ottiDi** *n.* pressure.

ఒత్తు, వత్తు **ottu, wattu** I. *n.* **1** thickness, denseness of texture. **2** support, pad, cushion. **3** *gram.* aspiration of a consonant, vertical stroke below a consonant as a sign of aspiration. **4** *gram.* secondary form of a consonant, e.g., ్య = **yawattu.** II. *adj.* **1** thick, dense (hair). **2** closely woven(rug). III. *v.i.* **1** to make way, yield. **2** to leave a mark, be imprinted (**-ki**, on). IV. *v.t.* **1** to press, squeeze. **2** to dab, blot, wipe clean or dry. **3** *gram.* to aspirate a consonant.

ఒత్తుపొయ్యి **ottupoyyi** *n.* hearth made of baked mud or bricks for cooking inside a house.

ఒత్తులొత్తు **ottulottu** *v.t.* to flatter as a means of persuasion.

ఒదుగు **odugu**[1] I. *n. dial.* increase; **biyyam~ ayndi** the rice swelled (when being cooked). II. *v.i.* to increase.

ఒదుగు **odugu**[2] *v.i.* to move aside, make room. **2** to move, stir. **3** *ling.* (of a sound) to shift or change. **4** to shrink from.

ఒద్దిక **oddika** *n.* **1** concord, harmony, union. **2** friendship, familiarity, intimacy. **3** movement, gesture. **4** counterpoise weight.

ఒద్దికగా **oddikagaa** *adv.* amenably; **aame attagaariNTa entoo~ uNTundi** she is very amenable in her mother-in-law's house.

ఒనగూడు **onaguuDu** *v.i.* **1** to come about, take place, happen. **2** to accrue, be secured, be acquired; **aastihakku striiki kuuDaa onaguuDinappuDu** when women also acquired a right to property. **3** to be suited. **4** to prosper, go well; **annii onaguuDitee** if all goes well.

ఒనగూర్చు **onaguurcu** *v.t.* **1** to effect, accomplish. **2** to obtain, procure.

ఒనర్చు,ఒనరించు **onarcu, onarincu** *v.t. class.* to do, perform.

ఒప్పందం **oppandam** *n.* agreement, contract; **~ kudurcukonu** to make or enter into an agreement.

ఒప్పగించు **oppagincu** *same as* **appagincu.**

ఒప్పచెప్పు **oppaceppu** *same as* **appaceppu.**

ఒప్పించు **oppincu** *v.t.* **1** to persuade, prevail on, convince. **2** to make (s.o.) agree.

ఒప్పిదం **oppidam** *n.* grace, beauty, agreeableness.

ఒప్పు **oppu** I. *n.* **1** fitness, right, propriety, correctness. **2** elegance, beauty, charm, grace; *see* **kuppa. 3** correct form (in a list of errata). II. *v.i. and t.* **1** to agree, admit, accept. **2** to own, acknowledge. **3** to be suitable, fitting or becoming. **4** *class.* to be, exist.

ఒప్పుకొను **oppukonu** *v.i. and t.* **1** to confess, admit, avow. **2** to consent, agree.

ఒప్పుకోలు **oppukoolu** *n.* **1** consent, agreement. **2** confession, admission, acknowledgement.

ఒప్పుదల **oppudala** *n.* agreement, consent, acceptance.

ఒబ్బిడి **obbiDi** I. *n.* threshing of grain. II. *adj.* complete, finished.

ఒయ్యారం, వయ్యారం **oyyaaram, wayyaaram** *n.* **1** grace, beauty, shapeliness. **2** affectation, coquettishness.

ఒయ్యారంగా, వయ్యారంగా **oyyaarangaa, wayyaarangaa** *adv.* alluringly, seductively.

ఒర **ora** *n.* **1** sheath, scabbard. **2** ring of cement or baked clay for lining a well; **~la baawi** ring well.

ఒరగపెట్టు **oragapeTTu** *v.t.* (*often in a negative sense, indicated by scorn, sarcasm or a rhetorical question*) to do some good, provide some benefit; **miiru wiiraadhiwiirulayi naaku enta oragabeTTEEroo cuustuu** seeing how much good you great heroes have done to me.

ఒరగవేయు, వరగవేయు **oragaweeyu, waragaweeyu** *v.t.* to bend, slant.

ఒరగల్లు **oragallu** *n.* touchstone.

ఒరగు **oragu**[1] *same as* **orugu**[1].

ఒరగు[దిండు] **oragu**[2] **[diNDu]** *n.* cushion to lean against.

ఒరపు, ఒరుపు **orapu, orupu** *n.* **1** touch, contact. **2** feel, texture. **3** rubbing, testing on a touchstone.

ఒరపుడురాయి **orapuDuraayi** *n.* touchstone.

ఒరయు **orayu** I. *v.i.* **1** to rub together, touch. **2** to be bruised. II. *v.t.* **1** to rub (against), graze. **2** to test (with a touchstone or yardstick).

ఒరిగిపడు,ఒరిగిపోవు **origipaDu, origipoowu** *v.i.* to fall over, tumble down.

ఒరిపిడి **oripiDi** *n.* **1** rubbing, abrasion. **2** irritation; **ii~ ki neenu taTTukooleenu** I cannot endure this irritation.

ఒరిబీజం, వరిబీజం **oribiijam, waribiijam** *n.* hydrocele.

ఒరియు **oriyu** *v.i.* (of water) to spring up, well up; **baawini enta lootu tawwinaa niiLLu oriyaDam leedu** no matter how deep we dig the well, there are no springs of water.

ఒరిసికొను, ఒరిసికొనిపోవు **orisikonu, orisikonipoowu** I. *v.i.* 1 to rub or graze (against). 2 to be bruised. II. *v.t.* to rub against, touch.

ఒరుగు, ఒరగు, వరుగు, వరగు **orugu[1], oragu, warugu[1], waragu** *v.i.* 1 to lean [over], bend, slant, incline. 2 to lie down, recline. 3 *dial.* to sleep. 4 (*often in a negative sense, indicated by scorn, sarcasm or a rhetorical question*) to do good, be of benefit; **oDiduDukulu jarigitee saawadhaanangaa maaTLaaDukoni diddukoowaccu kadaa! okarinokaru duyyabaTTukoNTee origindeemiTi?** if troubles arise, surely people can put them right by talking over them calmly. what good does it do if they abuse each other? *see* **oluku.**

ఒరుగు, వరుగు **orugu[2], warugu[2]** *n.* dried vegetables, fruit, or fish.

ఒరుగుచేప **oruguceepa** *n.* salt fish.

ఒరుగుచేయు **oruguceeyu** *v.t.* to dry (vegetables, etc.).

ఒరుడు **oruDu** *n. class.* another person, *pl.* **orulu** others.

ఒరులు, ఒర్లు **orulu, orlu** *v.i., dial.* to cry, shout.

ఒరే, ఒరేయ్ **oree, oreey** *term of address to a boy, a close friend or an inferior(male)* hey!

ఒర్ర, వర్ర **orra, warra** I. *n.* pungency. II. *adj.* 1 hot, spicy; ~ **guNDa** chilli powder. 2 reddish.

ఒలకపోయు, వలకపోయు **olakapoyu, walakapooyu** *v.t.* to spill, pour [out]; **naa miida koopam antaa olakapoosEEDu** he poured out all his anger on me; **kotta suuTu konukkoni kulukulu olakapoostunnaaDu** he is showing himself off after buying a new suit.

ఒలికించు, వలికించు **olikincu, walikincu** *v.t.* to sprinkle, shower.

ఒలియు **oliyu** *v.i.* (of rind, bark, skin) to be peeled off, stripped off, flayed.

ఒలుకు **oluku** *v.i.* (of liquid) to run away, pour out, be spilt, overflow; **ruculu olikee padarthaalu waDDincEEru** they served dishes overflowing with tastiness. 2 (of tears) to be shed. 3 *same as* **orugu[1]** *sense 4* **"niikewarannaa unnaaraa?" "uNDakeem baaboo! uNTee eem olikindi?"** "have you any relatives?" "of course I have, sir, but what good are they to me?"

ఒలుకులు **olukulu** *n.pl.* burial ground; **uuriki uttaraana olukulamiTTa undi** there is a burial ground on the north side of the village.

ఒలుచు **olucu** *v.t.* to peel, skin, flay; **naannagaaru wastee carmam oliceestaaru, buddhigaa uNDaNDi!** if your father comes, he will beat the skin off your backs, behave properly! **aadhunika wijñaanaanni araTipaNDu olici araceetiloo peTTinaTTugaa andincEEru** he explained modern science very easily and simply (*lit.* as if a banana has been peeled and put in the hand—which makes eating it a simple task).

ఒల్లు **ollu** *v.t., gen. used in neg. sense* to love, like, fancy, be in harmony with; **aalini ollani waaDiki kuuraloo uppu ekkuwa** the man who does not love his wife complains that there is too much salt in the curry (proverb, meaning he complains of even the smallest thing.)

ఒల్లుకొను **ollukonu** *v.i.* to keep quiet, be silent.

ఒళ్ళు **oLLu** *n.* 1 body. 2 o.'s self, o.'s person; **naaku oNTLoo bagaa leedu** I do not feel well; ~ **ceeyu** to grow fat, put on weight. 3 *idiomatic usages*: **oLLantaa kaLLu ceesukonu** to stare intently or with concentration; ~ **telisi maaTLaaDu** to talk carefully or responsibly; ~ **maraci maaTLaaDu** to talk intemperately or excitedly; ~ **maraci** (*or* ~ **teliyakuNDaa) nidra poowu** to sleep soundly; **naaku~ teliyani koopam waccindi** I became furiously angry; ~ **wanci paniceeyu** to work strenuously; ~ **wirucukonu** (i) to stretch o.'s limbs, (ii) to strive hard, exert o.s.; **gaNaacaari aNTee ammawaaru oNTimiidiki waccinawaaDu** 'Ganachari' means a person who is possessed by the goddess; ~ **daacukookuNDaa paniceesEEDu** he worked unflinchingly; ~ **guNDa ceesukonu** *or* ~ **piNDi ceesukonu** to work strenuously.

ఒసంగు **osangu** *v.t. class.* to give.

ఒసే, ఒసేయ్ **osee, oseey** *term of address to a girl, a close friend or an inferior (female)* hey!

ఓ - OO

ఓ oo[1] *interj. used with vocative case*, e.g., **oo ammaa**! mother!

ఓ oo[2] *adjvl. suffix added to cardinal numerals to form ordinals*, e.g., **reNDu** two, **reNDoo** second.

ఓ oo[3] *indefinite clitic, usages:* **1** *in conveying indefiniteness when added to an* **e-** *question word*, e.g., **ekkada** where, **ekkaDoo** somewhere. **2** *in conveying doubt, when added at the end of a sentence*, e.g., **reepu wastaaDoo** perhaps he will come tomorrow *or* he may come tomorrow. **3** to express alternatives, e.g., **reepoo elluNDoo madraasu weLtaaDu** he will go to Madras either tomorrow or the next day. **4** *idiomatic usage*: **aDawiloo kaalu peTTEEnoo leedoo, peddapuli kanabaDindi** I had scarcely set foot in the forest, when a tiger appeared. **5** *to form indirect questions*, e.g., **enduku waccEEDoo naaku teliyadu** I do not know why he has come.

ఓ oo[4] *suffix used in calling out wares*, e.g., **perugoo perugu**! curds for sale!

ఓ oo[5] *colloq. contraction of* **oka** *one*.

ఓంకారం **oomkaaram** *n.* the sacred syllable **oom.**

ఓండ్ర **ooNDra** *n.* braying of a donkey.

ఓండ్రపెట్టు **ooNDrapeTTu** *v.i.* to bray.

ఓంపొడి **oompoDi** *n.* medicinal powder prepared from **waamu** and given to a woman after childbirth.

ఓంప్రథమంగా **oomprathamangaa** *adv.* at the very beginning.

ఓంబాయిపట్టు **oombaayipaTTu** *v.i.* **1** to praise highly. **2** to praise unduly, overpraise. **3** to serve; (**oombaayi** repeated rhythmically was the sound uttered by journeying palanquin bearers in former times).

ఓకరించు **ookarincu** *v.t.* to retch while vomiting.

ఓకులు **ookulu** *n.pl.* points in a card game.

ఓకులాడు **ookulaaDu** *v.i. dial.* to play cards.

ఓగు **oogu** *n.* **1** evil, harm, misfortune; *cf.* **baagoogulu. 2** fool, weak person.

ఓజస్సు **oojassu** *n.* strength, vigour, energy.

ఓజోమయ **oojoomaya** *adj.* vigorous.

ఓటమి **ooTami** *n.* defeat, failure.

ఓటమితత్వం **ooTamitatwam** *n.* defeatism.

ఓటి **ooTi**[1] *adj.* **1** cracked, leaky (pot). **2** dried up, empty (irrigation tank). **3 gaTTi maaTa kaadu, ~ maaTa** not a reliable statement but an unsure, unsound one.

ఓటి **ooTi**[2] *colloq. contraction of* **okaTi** one.

ఓటు **ooTu** *n.* defeat, failure.

ఓటుపడు **ooTupaDu** *v.i. dial.* to be defeated.

ఓటుపోవు **ooTupoowu** *v.i.* to be defeated.

ఓంట్రించు **ooTrincu** *v.t.* to deny falsely; **tappu ceesinaa ceyyaleedani ooTristunnaaDu** although he has committed the fault he is vehemently denying it.

ఓడ **ooDa** *n.* **1** ship, vessel. **2** *dial.* large earthenware jar for storing grain.

ఓడదొంగ **ooDadonga** *n.* pirate.

ఓడరేవు **ooDareewu** *n.* port, harbour.

ఓడించు **ooDincu** *v.t.* to defeat, conquer, overcome, vanquish.

ఓడినక్క **ooDinakka** *n.* cunning little fox.

ఓడిపోవు **ooDipoowu** *v.i.* to lose, be defeated, be beaten, be vanquished, be conquered; **krikaTaaTaloo maa jaTTu ooDipooyindi** our team was beaten in the cricket match.

ఓడు **ooDu** I. *n.* **1** defeat, loss, failure. **2** crack, chink, hole. II. *v.i. and t.* **1** to lose, fail, be beaten, be defeated. **2** to flow, trickle, run, drip, ooze, exude; **pakooDiilu camuru ~ tunnaayi** the cakes are dripping with oil. **3** to be diffident, shrink, hesitate, be frightened.

ఓడ్చు **ooDcu** *v.t.* **1** to pour out. **2** to shed (tears).

ఓఢ్ర **ooDhra** *adj.* Oriya, belonging to Orissa.

ఓఢ్రం **ooDhram** *n.* **1** the State of Orissa. **2** the Oriya language.

ఓణీ, వాణీ **ooNii, waaNii** *n.* **1** half sari, a dress worn by girls on attaining puberty before they begin to wear a full sari. **2** *dial.* man's upper cloth.

ఓదార్చు **oodaarcu** *v.t.* to console, comfort.

ఓదార్చుకొను **oodaarcukonu** *v.i.* to endure, put up with.

ఓదార్పు **oodaarpu** I. *n.* comfort, solace, consolation. II. *adj.* comforting, consoling.

ఓదె **oode** *n.* **1** rick made of bundles of straw. **2** single sheaf of straw.

ఓనమాలు **oonamaalu** *n.* alphabet.

ఓనికట్టు **oonikaTTu** *n.* **1** dark ravine or gully. **2** narrow pass between mountains.

ఓపిక **oopika** *n.* **1** strength, endurance, stamina; **leeni~ teccukoni gabagaba naDici weLLEEnu** summoning up my strength I walked quickly away. **2** patience, toleration.

ఓపికచేయు **oopikaceeyu** *v.i.* to have patience; **koncem oopika ceesukoni ii pani ceeyaNDi naakoosam** please take the trouble to do this work for me.

ఓపికపట్టు **oopikapaTTu** *v.i.* to be patient, keep o.'s patience; **inta kaalam oopikapaTTEEnu, aayana raaleedu** I waited patiently for so long, but he did not come.

ఓపికపెట్టు **oopikapeTTu** *v.i.* to be patient; **koncem oopika peTTi naa maaTalu ciwaridaaka winaNDi** listen patiently until I finish speaking.

ఓపు **oopu** I. *n.* same as **oopika**. II. *v.t., always in neg. or interrog. constr.* to bear, endure, tolerate; **oopaleenanta** unbearable; **oopaleeni** unable to tolerate. III. *v.i.* **1** to be able or competent. **2** to be fit, suitable or worthy.

ఓమం **oomam** *same as* **waamu**[2].

ఓర **oora** *n.* edge, side, border; **mukham ~ ceesukonu** to turn o.'s face aside; **~ cuupu** sidelong glance; **~ moomutoo kuurcunnaaDu** he sat with his face averted *or* he sat looking away.

ఓరకంట **oorakaNTa** *adv.* sidelong **o.-ni ~ cuucu** to look at s.o. sidelong or out of corner of o.'s eye.

ఓరగా **ooragaa** *adv.* aside, sideways, obliquely, towards one side; **~ cuucu** to look sidelong; **talupu terici ~ unci** opening the door and leaving it ajar.

ఓరవాకిలి **oorawaakili** *n.* partly closed door; **talupu ~ gaa weesi loopaliki weLLEEnu** I set the door ajar and went inside.

ఓరి **oori** *interj. addressed to a male person* hey!

ఓరిమి **oorimi** *n.* patience.

ఓరుగల్లు **oorugallu** *n.* a name of the city of Warangal.

ఓరుగాలి **oorugaali** *same as* **hoorugaali.**

ఓర్చు **oorcu** *v.i.* 1 to be patient, bear, endure, suffer, tolerate; **neenu maanahaaniki oorcukooleenu** I cannot endure a disgrace to my honour. 2 to forgive.

ఓర్పరి **oorpari** *n.* patient person.

ఓర్పు **oorpu** *n.* patience, endurance.

ఓర్వమి, ఓర్వలేనితనం **oorwami, oorwaleenitanam** *n.* 1 intolerance. 2 impatience. 3 envy, jealousy.

ఓలగం **oolagam** *n. class.* king's court.

ఓలలాడు **oolalaaDu** *v.i.* to live luxuriously, revel: **aanandamloo ~** to revel in happiness; **ayśwaryamloo ~** to be rolling in money.

ఓలి **ooli** *n.* bride price.

ఓషధి **ooSadhi** *n.* medicinal herb.

ఓష్ఠం **ooSTham** *n.* lip.

ఓష్ఠ్య, ఓష్ట్య **ooSThya, ooSTya** *adj. gram.* labial.

ఓసరించు, ఓసరిల్లు **oosarincu, oosarillu** *v.i.* to move aside, get out of the way.

ఓసి! **oosi!** *interj. addressed to a female person* hey!

ఓహో! **oohoo!** *interj. expressing surprise or wonder.*

ఔ - aw

ఔచితి, ఔచిత్యం **awciti, awcityam** *n.* 1 fitness, suitability. 2 propriety, correctness, decorum. 3 appropriateness, aptness.

ఔటు, అవటు **awTu, awaTu** *n.* kind of fire work.

ఔడు **awDu** *n.* lip.

ఔడుకరుచు **awDukarucu** *v.i.* to bite o.'s lip due to fear, shock, anger or tiredness.

ఔత్కృష్ట్యం **awtkrSTyam** *n.* excellence, eminence.

ఔత్తరాహిక **awttaraahika** *adj.* northern.

ఔత్తరాహుడు **awttaraahuDu** *n.* Northerner.

ఔత్వం **awtwam** *n.* the letter *aw* in Telugu script.

ఔత్సాహిక **awtsaahika** *adj.* 1 enthusiastic. 2 amateur, nonprofessional.

ఔత్సాహికుడు **awtsaahikuDu** *n.* 1 enthusiast. 2 amateur.

ఔత్సుక్యం **awtsukyam** *n.* 1 eagerness, ardent desire, earnest interest or attention. 2 anxiety.

ఔదల **awdala** *n.* crown of the head.

ఔదలదాల్చు **awdala daalcu** *v.t.* to respect, bow o.'s head in acceptance (of a pronouncement).

ఔదార్యం **awdaaryam** *n.* generosity, liberality, bounty.

ఔదాసీన్యం **awdaasiinyam** *n.* indifference, inactivity, carelessness.

ఔను **awnu** *minor sentence* yes.

ఔన్నత్యం **awnnatyam** *n.* 1 greatness, grandeur. 2 height, eminence.

ఔపడు **awpaDu** *same as* **agupaDu.**

ఔపథ్యం **awpathyam** *same as* **awapathyam.**

ఔపరచు **awparacu** *same as* **aguparacu.**

ఔపవిభక్తికం **awpawibhaktikam** *n. gram.* noun that is declined with the aid of an inflectional increment, e.g., **anniN-Ti-ki, nuuriN-Ti-ki.**

ఔపించు **awpincu** *same as* **agupincu.**

ఔపోసన, ఆపోశన **awpoosana, aapoośana** *n.* 1 ceremonial sipping of water from the palm of the hand and invoking the gods before and after meals. 2 nuptial ceremony.

ఔపోసనపట్టు **awpoosanapaTTu** *v.t.* 1 to begin to eat (a meal). 2 to sample the essence of (art, literature, etc.)

ఔరసపుత్రుడు **awrasaputruDu** *n.* legitimate offspring or descendant.

ఔరా! ఔరౌరా! **awraa!, awrawraa!** *interj. expressing wonder or surprise.*

ఔషధం **awSadham** *n.* medicine.

ఔషధశాల **awSadhaśaala** *n.* chemist's shop, pharmacy.

ఔషధశాస్త్రం **awSadhaśaastram** *n.* pharmacology.

ఔషధసేవ[నం] **awSadhaseewa[nam]** *n.* 1 consumption of medicine. 2 *colloq.* consumption of alcohol, drinking.

ఔషధీయ **awSadhiiya** *adj.* pharmaceutical.

క - ka

కంకం **kankam** *n. class.* comb.

కంకటిల్లు, కక్కటిల్లు **kankaTillu, kakkaTillu** *v.i.* to weep uncontrolledly.

కంకణం **kankaNam** *n.* 1 bangle. 2 bracelet. 3 sacred thread tied round the wrist by a person taking a vow after invoking the God of Fire; **~ kaTTukonu, kankaNa dhaaraNa ceeyu** to take a vow, dedicate or devote o.s.; **waaNNi rakSincaalani ~ kaTTukonnanu** I vowed to save him; **strii janooddhaaraNaku ~ kaTTukonnaaDu** he devoted himself to the upliftment of women; **kankaNa wisarjana** formal relinquishment of a vow after its fulfilment; *cf.* **baddha kankaNuDu.**

కంకర **kankara** *n.* 1 gravel. 2 rubble, road metal.

కంకాలం, కంకాళం **kankaalam, kankaaLam** *n.* skeleton.

కంకి **kanki** *n.* 1 ear or head of any kind of grain. 2 *pisonia aculeata*, a thorny bush.

కంకిపురుగు **kanki purugu** *n.* climbing cutworm.

కంగారు, ఖంగారు **kangaaru, khangaaru** *n.* agitation, confusion, worry, alarm, anxiety.

కంగారు చేయు, కంగారు పెట్టు **kangaaru ceeyu, kangaaru peTTu** *v.i. and t.* to worry, confuse, perplex, cause anxiety; **ninnallaa kangaaru ceesEEDu, iwwaaLa baagaanee unnaaDu** all yesterday he caused anxiety, today he is all right.

కంగారుపడు **kangaaru paDu** *v.i.* to be agitated, confused or worried.

కంగాళీ **kangaaLii** I. *n.* 1 quarrel, disturbance. 2 confusion, noise. II. *adj.* nasty, untidy, dirty.

కంగించు **kangincu** *v.i* to coax (s.o.) to reveal a fact or opinion, to wheedle; **enta kangincinaa tana peLLi wiSayam maaTLaaDaleedu** no matter how much I coaxed him, he would not speak about his marriage.

కంగుతిను **kangutinu** *v.i. colloq.* to be stunned or flabbergasted.

కంచం **kancam** *n.* metal dish or tray or plate.

కంచరగాడిద **kancaragaaDida** *n.* mule.

కంచరపురుగు **kancarapurugu** *n.* deathwatch beetle.

కంచరి **kancari** *n.* coppersmith.

కంచి **kanci** *n.* the town of Kanchipuram (Conjeevaram) in Tamil Nadu; **katha ~ ki weLLindi** that is the end of the story (a traditional way of ending the narration of a folk tale).

కంచు **kancu** *n.* bronze, bell metal; **~ gontu** shrill voice.

కంచుకం **kancukam** *n.* blouse, tunic.

కంచుకాగడా **kancukaagaDaa** *n.* brightly shining torch; **~ weesi wetikinaa kanabaDaleedu** although I searched very thoroughly, I could not find it.

కంచుకి **kancuki** *n. class.* attendant or guard over women's apartments.

కంచుకోట **kancukooTa.** *n.* strong fort, stronghold.

కంచుయుగం **kancuyugam** *n.* bronze age.

కంచె **kance** *n.* 1 fence, hedge; **~ ceenu meesindi** the fence devoured the crop (instead of protecting it — proverb). 2 grazing land, pasture. 3 wire fence; **muLLa ~** thorn fence *or* barbed wire fence.

కంజాతం **kanjaatam** *n. class.* lotus.

కంజీరా **kanjiiraa** *n.* kind of stringed musical instrument.

కంట **kaNTa** *locative of* **kanu** in the eye; **waaDu naa ~ paDitee tsaalu** it is enough if he comes into my view; **oka ~ kanipeTTaali miiru** you must keep a watchful eye.

కంటకం **kaNTakam** *n.* 1 thorn, barb. 2 fish bone. 3 pest, plague, evil.

కంటక రోమం **kaNTaka roomam** *n.* bristle.

కంటకుడు **kaNTakuDu** *n.* tormentor.

కంటగించు **kaNTagincu** *v.t.* to hate.

కంటగింపుగా **kaNTagimpugaa** *adv.* hatefully, distastefully.

కంట తడిపెట్టు **kaNTa taDipeTTu** *v.i.* to shed tears.

కంటికీ మంటికీ **kaNTikii maNTikii** *adv.* (of weeping) continuously, steadily; **~ eekadhaaragaa eeDcu** to weep continuously.

కంటిపాప **kaNTipaapa** *n.* pupil of the eye.

కంటిపువ్వు **kaNTipuwwu** *n.* xerophthalmia, a disease of the eye.

కంటు **kaNTu** *n.* aversion, hatred, enmity.

కంటె **kaNTe**[1] *n.* 1 woman's gold collar. 2 wooden beam placed across the top of a well.

కంటె, కన్న **kaNTe**[2], **kanna** *p.p.* than, rather than, other than; **waaDu naa ~ cinna** he is younger than I; **pagaTi weluguloo illu ceerukooDam ~ saayankaalapu ciikaTiloonee iNTiki weLLaDam mancidanipincindi** rather than arriving home in daylight, it seemed better to go home in the evening darkness; **koDuku yuddham ceestunnappuDu talli iNTidaggira deemuDiki daNDam peTTukooDam ~ inkeem ceeyagaladu?** when her son is fighting what can a mother do, other than pray to God at home?

కంఠం **kaNTham** *n.* 1 throat. 2 voice.

కంఠగతం **kaNThagatam** *adj.* (of life) having reached the throat, i.e., ready to depart; **eNDaloo waccEEnu, koncem manci niiLLu ippincaNDi, praaNaalu ~ ay unnaayi** I have come in the hot sunshine, please get me some water, I feel exhausted.

కంఠతాపట్టు **kaNThataa paTTu** *v.t.* to learn by heart.

కంఠపాఠం **kaNThapaaTham** *n.* learning by heart.

కంఠబిలం **kaNThabilam** *n. ling.* glottis.

కంఠమణి **kaNThamaNi** *n.* Adam's apple.

కంఠమూలీయ **kaNThamuuliiya** *adj. ling.* glottal.

కంఠశోష **kaNThaśooSa** *n.* useless, vain or profitless talk.

కంఠస్థం **kaNThastham** *adj.* learnt by heart, committed to memory.

కంఠస్థం చేయు **kaNThastham ceeyu** *v.t.* to learn by heart.

కంఠస్వరం **kaNThaswaram** *n.* 1 tone of voice. 2 sound of a voice.

కంఠాణి **kaNThaaNi** *n.* implement for boring and stitching.

కంఠీరవం **kaNThiirawam** *n. class.* lion.

కంఠోక్తిగా **kaNThooktigaa** *adv.* definitely, with authority.

కంఠోపాఠం **kaNThoopaaTham** *n.* s.g learnt by heart; ~**gaa ceppu** to repeat over and over again.

కంఠ్య **kaNThya** *adj. ling.* back, glottal.

కంఠ్యాచ్చు **kaNThyaaccu** *n. ling.* back vowel.

కండ **kaNDa** *n.* 1 flesh, muscle; **maniSi~ paTTEEDu** he has put on flesh; ~**lu tirigina śariiram** muscular body. 2 flesh of a fruit or vegetable.

కండకావరం **kaNDakaawaram** *n.* hotheadedness, arrogance, haughtiness.

కండచక్కెర **kaNDacakkera** *n.* sugar candy.

కండచీమ, గండుచీమ **kaNDaciima, gaNDuciima** *n.* large black ant.

కండరం **kaNDaram** *n.* muscle.

కండువా **kaNDuwaa** *n.* man's upper cloth worn draped over one shoulder.

కండూతి **kaNDuuti** *n.* itch[ing]; **waaDiki kiirti~ paTTukondi** the itch for fame gripped him.

కండె **kaNDe** *n.* 1 ripe head of cholam. 2 ball or roll of thread wound on a spindle.

కండ్రిగ, ఖండ్రిక **kaNDriga, khaNDrika** *n.* small village, hamlet.

కండ్ల కలక **kaNDLa kalaka** *n.* 1 rheum. 2 disease of the eyes.

కంత, క్రంత **kanta, kranta** *n.* 1 hole, chink. 2 gap, aperture, fissure. 3 passage, alley way.

కంతి, కనితి, కణితి **kanti, kaniti, kaNiti** *n.* 1 bump, swelling, lump made by a bruise. 2 tumor.

కంతుడు **kantuDu** *n.* a name of Manmatha or Cupid.

కంద, కందగడ్డ, కందదుంప, కందమూలం **kanda, kandagaDDa, kandadumpa, kandamuulam** *n.* red edible root like a beetroot; **koopamtoo mukham kandagaDDa ayyindi** his face was as red as a beetroot with anger.

కందం **kandam** *n.* kind of poetic metre.

కందకం **kandakam** *n.* ditch, trench.

కందళిత **kandaLita** *class., second part of an adjvl. compound meaning* sprouting, budding, giving rise to; **aananda~** giving rise to joy.

కందాయం **kandaayam** *n. astrol.* period of four months.

కంది **kandi** *n., gen. pl.* **kandulu** red gram, *cajanus indicus*; ~**pappu** red gram dhall; ~**kaTTe** red gram stalks; ~**pullalu** red gram twigs.

కంది మొరుం **kandi morum** *n.* fine gravel, grit.

కందిరీగ **kandiriiga** *n.* hornet.

కంది సున్ని **kandi sunni** *n.* kind of dry chutney powder made of red gram, black gram, bengal gram and spices.

కందు **kandu** I. *n.* 1 *class.* infant. 2 *mod only in the compounds* **pasi~** *and* **kasi~**. II. *v.i.* to turn red, be inflamed (e.g., as a result of a blow); **muTTukoNTee kandipooyeeTaTTu unnaaDu** if you only touch him, it will leave a red mark (a way of saying that a child's flesh is very tender).

కందుకం **kandukam** *n.* ball.

కందెన **kandena** *n.* 1 grease, lubricant. 2 lubrication; ~**taylam** lubricating oil.

కంప **kampa** *n.* thornbush; ~**na paDDa kaakilaa tirugutunnaaDu** *lit.* he is moving about like a crow caught in a thornbush, i.e., he is in extreme difficulties.

కంపం **kampam** *n.* trembling, shaking, tremor, irritation.

కంపన[ం] **kampana[m]** *n.* 1 *same as* **kampam.** 2 *sci.* vibration.

కంపరం **kamparam** *n.* dislike, aversion; **cuuDagaanee waaDiki ~ ettindi** as soon as he saw it, he had a feeling of aversion.

కంపించు **kampincu** *v.i.* to tremble, shake, shudder, be agitated.

కంపిత ధ్వని **kampita dhwani** *n. ling.* trill.

కంపు **kampu** *n.* bad or foul smell, stink, stench.

కంపు కొట్టు **kampu koTTu** *v.i.* to stink.

కంబం **kambam** *n.* pillar, post; **uri~** gallows; **ooDa~** mast of a ship.

కంబళం **kambaLam** *n.* woollen rug or blanket.

కంబళి **kambaLi** *n.* rug or blanket of wool or finer material.

కంబళి పురుగు **kambaLi purugu** *n.* hairy caterpillar.

కంబు **kambu** *n.* spiked millet, *panicum spicatum* (= **sajja**)

కంసాలి **kamsaali** *n.* goldsmith.

కకవికలు, కకావికలు **kakawikalu, kakaawikalu** *adj.* confused, scattered, tumultuous.

కకుదం **kakudam** *n. class.* bull's hump.

కక్క **kakka**[1] *n.* morsel or piece of meat or fish.

కక్క **kakka**[2] *n.* father's younger brother, uncle.

కక్కటిల్లు **kakkaTillu** *same as* **kankaTillu.**

కక్కసం **kakkasam** *n.* harshness, roughness, gruffness.

కక్కసపడు **kakkasapaDu** *v.i.* to be angry with o.s.

కక్కసు **kakkasu** *same as* **kakkoosu.**

కక్కించు **kakkincu** *v.i.* 1 to cause (s.o.) to vomit. 2 to force (s.o.) to cough up illegal gains.

కక్కిరిబిక్కిరి **kakkiribikkiri** *n.* confusion, disorder.

కక్కు **kakku**[1] *n.* 1 notch, dent. 2 tooth of a saw.

కక్కు **kakku**[2] *v.t.* 1 to vomit, spew [out]. 2 **nippulu~** to spit fire, i.e., to be very angry. 3 **Dabbu~** *slang* to pay up money that is due. 4 **kaaphii pogalu** (*or* **aawirlu**) ~**tunnadi** the coffee is emitting a smell (*lit.* the coffee is emitting steam or vapour).

కక్కుడు **kakkuDu** *n.* vomit.

కక్కుర్తి, కక్కూర్తి **kakkurti, kakkuurti** *n.* 1 stooping down, demeaning o.s.; ~**maniSi** servile person, one who demeans himself. 2 greed, avarice; **Dabbu~** greed for for money; **kaDupu~** demeaning o.s. for the sake of getting a living. 3 rush, hurry, urgency.

కక్కుర్తిపడు, కక్కూర్తిపడు **kakkurtipaDu, kakkuurtipaDu** *v.i.* 1 to stoop down, demean or lower o.s. 2 *colloq.* to take bribes: **eedoo ~ tunnaaDu, naalugu Dabbulu wenakeesEEDu** he accepts some bribes and has accumulated some money.

కక్కువాయు దగ్గు **kakkuwaayu daggu** *n. dial.* whooping cough.

కక్కోసు, కక్కసు **kakkoosu, kakkasu** *n.* lavatory, latrine.

కక్ష **kakSa** *n.* spite, malice, enmity, rivalry; **naa miida** (*or* **naa payna**) **~ kaTTEEDu** he had enmity towards me; **~ raajakiiyaalu** party or factional politics; **~ saadhimpu caryalu** *journ.* reprisals.

కక్షి **kakSi** *n.* party, faction; **~ daaruDu** member of a party or faction.

కక్ష్య **kakSya** *n.* 1 orbit. 2 *class.* girdle. 3 *class.* apartment in a palace. 4 *sci.* chamber.

కగ్గు **kaggu** *v.i.* 1 to lose colour or brightness. 2 to turn black.

కచడా **kacaDaa** *adj. and n.* bad, evil, wrong, wicked[ness].

కచేరీ, కచ్చేరీ **kaceerii, kacceerii** *n.* 1 office 2 musical recital or entertainment.

కచ్చ **kacca**[1] *n.* truss; **~ poosi ciire kaTTukonnadi** she wore her sari tied in a truss.

కచ్చ, కచ్చి **kacca**[2], **kacci** *n.* quarrels, anger, bad temper; **anta kacci endukaNDii miiku?** why are you in such a bad temper?

కచ్చడం **kaccaDam** *n.* 1 cart with a hood. 2 loin cloth.

కచ్చా **kaccaa** *adj.* 1 raw, unripe. 2 rough, inferior; **~ daari** rough road; **~ rangu** colour that fades, non-fast colour.

కచ్చిక **kaccika** *n.* tooth powder made from ashes of dried cowdung cakes.

కచ్చితం, ఖచ్చితం **kaccitam, khaccitam** *adj.* 1 strict, exact, definite. 2 accurate, precise; **~ ayna saankhya wiwaraalu** accurate statistical details.

కచ్చితంగా, ఖచ్చితంగా **kaccitangaa, khaccitangaa** *adv.* 1 definitely, strictly, exactly; **~ aydu gaNTalaku** exactly at five o'clock. 2 directly; **~ aDigEEDu** he asked point blank. 3 certainly, undoubtedly. 4 accurately, precisely.

కచ్చితత్వం, ఖచ్చితత్వం **kaccitatwam, khaccitatwam** *n.* precision.

కచ్చె **kacce** *n.* quarrel, fight.

కచ్చెపోతు **kaccepootu** *n.* quarrelsome person.

కచ్చేరీ **kacceerii** *same as* **kaceerii.**

కచ్ఛపం **kacchapam** *n. class.* tortoise.

కజ్జం **kajjam** *n.* kind of cake with sweet stuffing, also called **kajjikaayalu.**

కజ్జలం **kajjalam** *n.* lamp black used as black paint for the eyes, collyrium.

కజ్జా **kajjaa** *n.* quarrel.

కజ్జాకోరు **kajjaakooru** *n.* troublemaker, quarrelsome person.

కజ్జికాయలు **kajjikaayalu** *see* **kajjam.**

కజ్జూరం **kajjuuram** *same as* **kharjuuram.**

కటక **kaTaka** *n. dial.* door or window latch.

కటకం **kaTakam** *n.* 1 lens. 2 ridge. 3 *class.* bracelet, girdle. 4 the town of Cuttack.

కటకట **kaTakaTa** I. *n.* 1 distress. 2 want, scarcity. II. *interj.* alas!

కటకటపడు, కటకటలాడు **kaTakaTapaDu, kaTakaTalaaDu** *v.i.* 1 to suffer, be in distress. 2 to be in want. 3 to feel tired or weak. 4 to be angry.

కటకటమను **kaTakaTamanu** *v.i.* to rattle.

కటకటాలు **kaTakaTaalu** *n.pl.* 1 bars; **kaTakaTaallooki toosEEru** them put him behind [prison] bars. 2 railings. 3 trellis work.

కటాకటీగా **kaTaakaTiigaa** *adv.* 1 definitely, certainly; **~ enimidi gaNTalaku wastaaDu** he will definitely come at 8 o'clock. 2 with difficulty, barely, only just; **aaDabbutoo ~ batukutunnaaDu** he is barely able to live on that income.

కటాక్షం **kaTaakSam** *n.* 1 glance. 2 kindness, favour.

కటాక్షించు **kaTaakSincu** *v.t.* to look with favour on (s.o.).

కటారి, కటారు, కఠారి **kaTaari, kaTaaru, kaThaari** *n.* dagger.

కటి **kaTi** *n. class.* waist; **~ siimaloo unna bangaara waDDaaNam** a gold belt round the region of the waist.

కటిక **kaTika** adj. total, complete, downright; **~ karuwu** severe famine; **~ ciikaTi** pitch darkness; **~ neela** bare ground, hard ground; **~ daridruDu** downright pauper; **~ peeda raytulu** desperately poor farmers; **~ upawaasam** complete fast.

కటువు **kaTuwu** *adj.* 1 hard, unpleasant. 2 (of language, tone of voice) harsh. 3 (of taste) pungent.

కటూక్తి **kaTuukti** *n.* harsh utterance.

కటోని **kaTooni** *n. dial.* pincer used for extracting nails.

కటోర **kaToora** *n. dial.* small pottery plate with handles.

కట్ట **kaTTa**[1] *n.* 1 bank, shore, dam, embankment; **ceruwu~** tank bund, dam for retaining water in an irrigation reservoir. 2 bundle, pack, office file; **pustakaalu ~ kaTTu** to tie books in a bundle; **miirantaa ~ kaTTuku caawaNDi** you can all go to hell, for all I care (*lit.* all of you bundle up yourselves and die!); **twaragaa mugguru oka ~ ayipooy naTTiNToo lookaabhiraamaayaNam maaTLaaDaDam praarambhincEEru** three of them quickly formed into a bunch and began talking about this and that in the interior of the house.

కట్ట, కట్ల, గట్ల **kaTTa**[2], **kaTLa, gaTLa** I. *p.p.* at; *mod. only in* **tellawaari ~** at dawn. II. *adjvl. prefix meaning* barred, i.e., with cross stripes; **kaTLa paamu** Russell's viper.

కట్టకడకు **kaTTakaDaku** *adv.* at the very end, finally.

కట్టడం **kaTTaDam** *n.* building, edifice, construction; **raati~** stone masonry.

కట్టడి **kaTTaDi** *n.* rule, restriction, constraint; **graamamloo ~** the rule that is followed in the village.

కట్టడిచేయు **kaTTaDiceeyu** *v.t.* to restrict, constrain, regulate, control.

కట్టబెట్టు **kaTTabeTTu** *v.t.* 1 to put together, unite (esp. of a marriage which the speaker disapproves of): **nikSeepamlaaNTi ammaayini oka kunikiSTiwaaDiki kaTTabeTTEEru** they married a jewel of a girl to a chronically sick man. 2 to deliver, hand over, consign, confer, bestow.

కట్టించు **kaTTincu** *v.t.* 1 *causative of* **kaTTu** to have s.g built, tied, etc. 2 **aaTa[lu]** ~ to put an end to s.o.'s game, checkmate s.o., cause s.o.'s tricks to be stopped. 3 **paTam** ~ to frame (a picture or similar object).

కట్టించుకొను **kaTTincukonu** *v.t.* 1 *causative of* **kaTTukonu** to have s.g built, tied, etc. for o.s. 2 **rikSaa**~ to hire or arrange a rickshaw: **eDLabaNDi**~ to harness a bullock cart; **baTTalu**~ to get o.s. dressed.

కట్టిపెట్టు **kaTTipeTTu** *v.t.* to end, stop, finish, put a stop to, have done with, dispense with.

కట్టివేయు, కట్టేయు **kaTTiweeyu, kaTTeeyu** *v.t.* 1 to stop; **eeDupu kaTTeeyu** to stop weeping. 2 to shut; **nooru kaTTeesukonu** to close o.'s mouth.

కట్టు **kaTTu** I. *adjvl. prefix meaning* complete, whole, downright; ~**amaawaasya** dark night (with no moon at all): **kaTTedurugaa** exactly opposite; ~**pogarumootu** a downright boaster. II. *n.* 1 knot, fastening, band, bond, bondage. 2 **naDi**~ waistband worn by a woman after childbirth. 3 ~**kaaluwa** supply channel to an irrigation tank. 4 restriction, regulation, rule; ~**gaa uncu** to keep within bounds, keep under control; **kula**~ community custom. 5 ring, hoop (of a bucket). 6 tyre (of a cartwheel). 7 setting (of a jewel). 8 style (of dress); **kaTTuuboTTuu** dress and general appearance; ~**kooka** sari worn for everyday use; ~**baTTalatoo bayaldeerEEDu** he set out with only the clothes he was wearing. 9 composition, fabrication; ~**katha** concocted story, fiction. 10 **mundari**~ front elevation of a building. 11 banding together, uniting; **naamiida** ~**kaTTi ewaruu maaTLaaDaleedu** they banded together against me and no one spoke to me. 12 stopping, stoppage; **aaTa**~ checkmate (in chess); **niiru**~ stoppage of urine. 13 dam, bund, embankment. 14 water in which any kind of pulse has been boiled. III. *v.i.* 1 to stop, cease, pass off; **waaDi tala pagilindi, sunnam weestee raktam kaTTipooyindi** his head was broken, when I applied lime the bleeding stopped. 2 to gather, come together, form into a lump or bump; **mabbulu kaTTEEyi** clouds gathered; **kooDiguDDanta boppi kaDutundi** a bump as big as an egg is forming; **juTTu aTTalu kaTTindi** the hair was matted. 3 to appear, be formed, take shape; **tuuTu kaTTindi** a hole was formed; **kaarina niiru cinna maDugu kaTTindi** the dripping water formed into a small pool; **kaLLaku** ~ to appear. 4 to flow; **raktam dhaara kaTTindi** blood flowed in a stream. 5. (of animals) to be pregnant. IV. *v.t.* 1 to tie, fasten, bind. 2 to build, construct. 3 to stop, shut. 4 to wear. 5 *idiomatic usages are many and various and include the following:* **keesu**~ *legal* to file or institute a case; **Dabbu**~ to pay money; **tappu**~ to impute a fault; **doowa**~ to obstruct a road; **dhara**~ to estimate a price; **naDum**~ to gird o.'s loins and get ready; **padyam**~ to compose a poem; **pannu**~ (i) to pay a tax (ii) to levy a tax; **prayaaNam** ~to start on a journey; **beeram**~ to strike a bargain; **lekka**~ to reckon, calculate; **wiluwa**~ to attach, assess or attribute value or importance; **werriwaaDi kinda**~ to class (s.o.) as a madman; **samme**~ to go on strike.

కట్టుకొంగు **kaTTukongu** *n.* loose end of a sari tied round the waist when doing manual work.

కట్టుకొను **kaTTukonu** *v.t.* 1 to build. 2 to bind. 3 to fold (arms). 4 to credit: **Dabbu appukinda kaTTukonnaaDu** he credited the money towards the loan. 5 **kaDupu kaTTukoni pillalni pencutunnaaru tallidaNDrulu** the parents are bringing up their children by stinting themselves.

కట్టుకొయ్య **kaTTukoyya** *n.* stake for tethering cattle.

కట్టుగుంజ **kaTTugunja** *n.* post to which an animal is tethered.

కట్టుడు **kaTTuDu** *adj.* 1 ~**paLLu** artificial teeth, dentures. 2 ~**ciire** sari worn for everyday use (as opposed to **daapuDu ciire**).

కట్టుదిట్టం **kaTTudiTTam** I. *n., gen.pl.* **kaTTudiTTaalu** strict measures, strict arrangements, strict limits, restraints, restrictions; **pillalanu caalaa kaTTudiTTaalaloo pencEEru** they brought the children up very strictly. II. *adj.* strict, strictly arranged.

కట్టుదిట్టంగా **kaTTudiTTangaa** *adv.* strictly.

కట్టుబడి **kaTTubaDi** *n.* 1 construction. 2 social rule or convention. 3 kind of lease of agricultural land.

కట్టుబడిదారు **kaTTubaDidaaru** *n.* tenant.

కట్టుబడు **kaTTubaDu** *v.i.* to be tied or bound (**-ki**, by *or* to) *with shades of meaning varying according to context*; **konni suutraalaku kaTTubaDi** subject to certain principles; **prajaaswaamyaaniki kaTTubaDi** devoted or pledged to democracy; **andaaniki kaTTubaDi** entranced by beauty; **oka maaTa aNTee aa maaTaku kaTTubaDi uNDaali** if you say s.g you must adhere to it; **mantraaniki kaTTubaDi** spellbound.

కట్టుబాటు **kaTTubaaTu** *n.* 1 control, regulation, discipline; ~**loo** under control; **saanghika kaTTubaaTLu** social restrictions or conventions. 2 ~**raayi** stone used for construction work.

కట్టె **kaTTe**[1] *n.* 1 stick, piece of wood. 2 bamboo stick. 3 dry stalks and leaves of pulses used as cattle fodder. 4 *pl.* ~**lu** (*or* ~**peeLLu**) firewood.

కట్టె **kaTTe**[2] *n.* lifeless body, corpse.

కట్టె చిట్టె **kaTTe ciTTe** *n.* bolt for fastening a window.

కట్టెదుట, కట్టెదురుగా **kaTTeduTa, kaTTedurugaa** *adv.* right in front, directly opposite.

కట్టెపొంగలి **kaTTepongali** *n.* dish made of rice and green gram eaten as breakfast in rural areas and also offered as **prasaadam** in Vaishnavite temples.

కట్టెబొగ్గు **kaTTeboggu** *n.* charcoal.

కట్టెవిరుపు, పుల్లవిరుపు **kaTTewirupu, pullawirupu** *adj.* harsh (*lit.* like the snapping of a stick); ~**maaTa** or ~**ceesTa** harsh word or action.

కట్నం **kaTNam** *n.* 1 present, gift. 2 dowry.

కట్ల **kaTLa** *same as* **kaTTa**[2].

కఠారి **kaThaari** *same as* **kaTaari.**

కఠిన **kaThina** *adj.* 1 hard, severe, difficult; ~**wyaayaamam** strenuous exercise. 2 cruel, harsh, stern, grim. 3 rigorous, stringent, strict, inflexible; ~**sikSa** rigorous imprisonment.

కఠోర **kaThoora** *adj.* 1 dreadful, terrible. 2 cruel, harsh, stern, grim.

కడ **kaDa**[1] I. *n.* end; **~ daakaa** till the end. II. *adj.* last, final; **~ saari** the last time; **~ jaati** the lowest community.

కడ **kaDa**[2] *p.p.* by, near, at; **naa ~ Dabbu leedu** I have no money on me; **waaDi ~ku weLLi neenu ceppEEnani ceppu** go to him and say that I said so.

కడకంట **kaDakaNTa** *adj. and adv.* from the corner of the eye.

కడకు **kaDaku** *adv.* at last, finally.

కడగండ్లు **kaDagaNDLu** *n. pl.* afflictions, troubles, calamities, evils, dangers, miseries, sufferings.

కడగా **kaDagaa** *adv.* away, aside; **ii Dabbu ~ peTTu** put this money aside; **kaalu tiisi ~ peTTu** keep your leg aside (a phrase used in a children's game similar to 'odd man out').

కడగొట్టు **kaDagoTTu** *adj.* youngest (in a family); **~ biDDa** the last child to be born in a family.

కడచీల **kaDaciila** *n.* linchpin.

కడచు, గడచు, గడుచు **kaDacu, gaDacu, gaDucu** I. *v.i.* 1 (of time, distance) to pass, go by, elapse; **reNDu mayLLu gaDawagaanee** as soon as two miles had passed; **oka reNDu nelalu gaDistee gaanii ceppaleemu** we cannot say until about two months are over. 2 (of difficulties) to be overcome or surmounted. 3 (of needs, etc.) to be met or supplied; **maa kharculu sarigaa gaDawaDam leedu** our expenses are not being properly met; **ajñaatawaasamloo uNTee S.ki awasaraalu gaDawawu** when S. is in hiding his needs are not supplied; **eedoo oka pani ceeyaka uurikee kuurcuNTee elaa gaDustundi raa bhukti?** if you just sit and do no work, how do you manage for food? **samsaaram cinnadee kaabaTTi ippuDeTLagoo gaDustunnadi** (our) family is small, so now we get along somehow; **gaali leekapootee naaku kSaNamaynaa gaDawadu** I cannot survive for even a moment without air; *see* **kaDupu** *sense 4*. II. *v.t.* to pass (time), cross (sea), get over (difficulties, obstacles).

కడతేరు **kaDateeru** *v.i.* 1 to be accomplished, concluded or finished, come to an end. 2 to die.

కడతేర్చు **kaDateercu** *v.i.* 1 to finish, put an end to, see the end of. 2 to fulfil (duty).

కడదాటు **kaDadaaTu** *v.t.* to overcome, surmount.

కడప, గడప **kaDapa, gaDapa** *n.* 1 threshold, gateway, doorstep. 2 *fig.* house; **weyyi~ unna uuru** a village with a thousand houses; **podduTinunci ekkee~digee~** from early morning onwards (he) goes from one house to another.

కడపట, కడపటికి **kaDapaTa, kaDapaTiki** *adv.* in the end, finally.

కడపటి **kaDapaTi** *adj.* last, final.

కడబట్టు **kaDabaTTu** *v.i.* to come to an end; *mod. only in the expression* **praaNam/praaNaalu~**, e.g., **praaNaalu kaDabaTTinaTTayindi** I felt as if I was at the point of death; **waaDu iNTiki naDicipooyee sariki praaNam kaDabaTTi pooyindi** by the time he reached the house walking, he was exhausted; **kaDabaTTi eeDustunnaaDu** he is weeping copiously (*here* **praaNam** *is understood but not expressed*).

కడమ, కడాం, కొడమ, కొడం **kaDama, kaDaam, koDama, koDam** I. *n.* rest, remainder. II. *adj.* last, final, remaining.

కడలి **kaDali** *n.* sea, ocean.

కడవ **kaDawa** *n.* pot for drawing or storing water.

కడవెళ్లు **kaDaweLLu** *v.i.* to be finished or ended.

కడసారం **kaDasaaram** *adj.* last; **~ pilla peLLi ceestunnaanu** I am performing the marriage of my youngest daughter; **naa ~ koorika** *or* **naa kaDasaarapu koorika** my last wish.

కడాం **kaDaam** *same as* **kaDama.**

కడాకి **kaDaaki** *adv.* finally, in the end.

కడి **kaDi** *n.* 1 morsel. 2 white lime paste used for drawing **muggu.** 3 **peeDa ~** lump of cowdung.

కడిగించు **kaDigincu** *v.t.* to get s.g washed or cleaned.

కడిగేయు **kaDigeeyu** *v.t.* 1 to wash, clean. 2 *colloq.* to give a scolding to.

కడియం **kaDiyam** *n.* 1 anklet. 2 bracelet.

కడీ **kaDii** *n.* long stone slab.

కడు **kaDu** *adv.* much, very much, greatly.

కడుగు **kaDugu** I. *n.* water in which rice or pulses have been washed. II. *v.t.* to wash (body and other articles but not clothes).

కడుపాత్రం **kaDupaatram** I. *n.* greed, voraciousness. II. *adj.* greedy.

కడుపారా **kaDupaaraa** *adv., lit.* so as to fill the stomach; **~ tinu** to eat o.'s fill.

కడుపు **kaDupu** *n.* 1 stomach; **pilawanakkaraleedu, ~ loo kaalitee waaDee wastaaDu** no need to call him; when he is hungry (*lit.* if there is burning in his stomach) he will come of his own accord. 2 womb; **~ too uNDu** to be pregnant. 3 heart, mind; **~ loo eem undoo ewariki telusu?** who knows what is in his mind? **kasi prastutaaniki ~ loo peTTukonnaaDu** he kept his anger hidden in his heart for the time being. 4 *other idiomatic usages:* **~** (*or* **poTTa**) **cekkalayyeeTaTTu nawwu** to burst o.'s sides with laughing; **~** (*or* **poTTa**) **ceetapaTTukoni leecipoowu**; to go elsewhere for a living; **~ jaragaka** (*or* **~ gaDawaka**) being unable to manage/carry on/support o.s.; **~ loo niiLLu** (*or* **~ loo c[illegible]a**) **kadalakuNDaa** without exerting o.s.; **nannu ~ loo peTTukonnaaDu** he kept me under his wing; **nii ~ bangaaram kaanu!** may you (*lit.* your womb) be blessed! **nii~ kaala/maaDa/uDaka!** may you (*lit.* your womb) be cursed!

కడుపుకోత **kaDupukoota** *n.* loss of o.'s child[ren]; **aayana pedda koDuku miliTariloo ceeri cacci pooyEEDu, ii wayassuloo aayanaki ii~** his eldest son joined the army and was killed, he has lost his son at this age.

కడుపు చేయు **kaDupu ceeyu** *v.i.* to make pregnant; **waaDu peLLi wiSayam maaTLaaDakuNDaa kaDupu ceesi paaripooyEEDu** without speaking of marriage he has deserted her after making her pregnant.

కడుపు పోవు **kaDupu poowu** *v.i. with dative* to have a miscarriage or abortion; **aameki pillalu leeru, naalugu saarlu kaDupu pooyindi** she has no children, she has had four miscarriages.

కడుపుబ్బ నవ్వు **kaDupubba nawwu** *v.i.* to laugh heartily.

కడుపుబ్బు **kaDupubbu** *n.* 1 jealousy; **~ too maaTLaaDaleeDu** he is speechless on account of jealousy. 2 swelling of the stomach due to illness.

కడుపుమంట **kaDupumaNTa** *n.* 1 grief for the loss of o.'s child. 2 jealousy. 3 starvation, pangs of hunger.

కడ్డీ **kaDDii** *n.* metal bar, ingot.

కణం **kaNam** *n.* 1 particle; **nippu~** spark; **niiTi~** drop of water; **uppu~** grain of salt. 2 *sci.* cell of an organism, corpuscle; **jiiwa~** living cell.

కణకణలాడు, గణగణలాడు **kaNakaNalaaDu, gaNagaNalaaDu** *v.i.* (of fire) to glow; **kaNakaNalaaDee nippuloo naDicipoyEEDu** he walked through glowing coals of fire.

కణకవచం **kaNakawacam** *n. sci.* cell wall.

కణజం **kaNajam** *n. dial.* grain cellar, underground granary.

కణజన్యుశాస్త్రం **kaNajanyuśaastram** *n. zool.* cytogenetics.

కణజాలం **kaNajaalam** *n. biol.* tissue.

కణత **kaNata** *n.* temples (of the head).

కణద్రవ్యం **kaNadrawyam** *n. zool.* cytoplasm.

కణరహిత **kaNarahita** *adj. zool.* acellular.

కణశాస్త్రం **kaNaśaastram** *n. zool.* cytology.

కణిక **kaNika** *n.* 1 bit, piece; **nippu~** piece of burning charcoal. 2 *sci.* granule.

కణితి, కణుజు **kaNiti**[1], **kaNuju** *n.* sambar deer, *cervus hippelaphus.*

కణితి **kaNiti**[2] *same as* **kanti.**

కణీకరించు **kaNiikarincu** *v.i.* to atomise.

కణుం, కనుం **kaNum, kanum** *n.* 1 festival held on the day after Sankranti. 2 blouse piece of handloom cloth.

కణుపు **kaNupu** *same as* **kanupu.**

కణుసుఎక్కు, కణుసుతేలు **kaNusu ekku, kanNusu teelu** *v.i. dial.* to become coarse or rough.

కణేల్మని, కణేల్మను **kaNeelmani, kaNeelmanu** *same as* **khaNeelmani, khaNeelmanu.**

కత **kata** *n.* tale, story; **aame ~lu wetalu winnaanu** I listened to her tales of woe.

కతం **katam** *n. class.* reason, cause.

కతిపయ **katipaya** *adj.* some, a few.

కతుకు **katuku** *v.t.* to eat; gen. used of animals; if of human beings it implies eating with haste or reluctance or carries a derogatory meaning; **eedoo reNDu metukulu katiki bayaTa paDDaanu** I ate a little food and went out; **katikitee atakadu** 'eating means failing' (a proverb incorporating the belief that prospective in--laws should not be offered any food while marriage negotiations are proceeding, otherwise they may fail).

కత్తాళి **kattaaLi** *n.* aloe plant.

కత్తి **katti** *n.* 1 knife, sword. 2 measure of land, about 17 acres.

కత్తికట్టు **kattikaTTu** *v.i.* 1 to draw a sword (in order to attack). 2 *fig.* to declare enmity against, to attack; **tamatoo kiibhawincani waaripayna kattikaDataaru** they attack persons who do not agree with them.

[కత్తిదూ]యు **katti duuyu** *v.i.* to draw a sword.

కత్తిపీట **kattipiiTa** *n.* knife blade fixed to a wooden plank, used for cutting vegetables (= **ilapiiTa, iilapiiTa**).

కత్తిరించు **kattirincu** *v.t.* to cut, shear or prune with scissors or similar implement.

కత్తిరింపు **kattirimpu** *n.* cutting.

కత్తిరిగూడు **kattiriguuDu** *n.* triangular niche in a wall.

కత్తివాటు **katti waaTu** *n.* blow of a sword or knife; **R. mukhamloo ~ku netturu cukka leedu** R.'s face is very pale (*lit.* even at the blow of a sword, not a drop of blood will come from R.'s face).

కత్తుకలుపు, ఖత్తులు కలుపు **kattukalupu, khattukalupu** *v.i.* to make friends, become acquainted.

కత్తిసాము **kattisaamu** *n.* sword play, fencing.

కత్తె **katte** *suffix denoting the female sex*; **anda~** beautiful woman; **oNTari~** lonely woman.

కత్తెర **kattera**[1] *n.* 1 scissors, shears; **tirupati koNDamiida aydu ~lu juTTu istaanani mokkukonnaaDu** he vowed to give five clippings of his hair to the God (Sri Venkateswara) on Tirupati hill. 2 **juTTu~ weeyu** to cut s.o.'s hair; **juTTu~ weeyincukonu** to have o.'s hair cut. 3 **peeka mukkalu~ weeyu** to shuffle playing cards.

కత్తెర **kattera**[2] *n. corruption of* **kartari.**

కథ **katha** *n.* story, tale, narrative, fable; **ii wiSayam miida caalaa~** (*or* **caalaa grantham**) **naDicindi** there has been much confabulating about this affair; *cf.* **kaakamma ~lu.**

కథకుడు **kathakuDu** *n.* story teller, narrator.

కథనం **kathanam** *n.* narration, story, account.

కథనాత్మక **kathanaatmaka** *adj.* narrative.

కథాకమామీషు **kathaakamaamiiSu** *n.* story and such other things, story and so on; **aa wiSayamgurinci ceppukoowalasina~ caalaa undi** there is a long story and so on to be told about that matter.

కథాక్రమం **kathaakramam** *n.* sequence of events in a story.

కథానాయకుడు **kathaanaayakuDu** *n.* hero of a story.

కథానాయిక **kathaanaayika** *n.* heroine of a story.

కథానిక **kathaanika** *n.* short story.

కథావస్తువు **kathaawastuwu** *n.* plot of a story, story material.

కథితం **kathitam** *n.* narration.

కదం **kadam** *n.* 1 step, stride. 2 outlet at the bottom of a baling bucket.

కదం తొక్కు, కదను తొక్కు **kadam tokku, kadanu tokku** *v.i.* 1 to trot. 2 *fig.* to move ahead, advance.

కదంబం **kadambam** *n.* 1 garland or bunch of mixed flowers. 2 miscellany; **kadamba kaaryakramam** variety programme.

కదంబవృక్షం **kadambawrkSam** *n.* plant called *nauclea cadamba.*

కదనం **kadanam** *n.* battle, combat.

కదనకుతూహలం **kadanakutuuhalam** *n.* combativeness.

కదనరంగం **kadanarangam** *n.* battlefield.

కదను **kadanu** *n.* step, stride.

కదను తొక్కు **kadanu tokku** *same as* **kadam tokku.**

కదపా **kadapaa** *n.* **1** bond, written agreement. **2** rent agreement.

కదపాయించు **kadapaayincu** *v.t* to bet, stake, wager; **aaTa gelawaka pootee naa cewi ~ koNTaanu** if I do not win, I will eat my hat (*lit.* if I do not win, I will offer my ear as a stake).

కదపు, కదుపు **kadapu, kadupu** *v.t.* **1** to move, stir, set in motion. **2** to raise (matter for discussion); **waaDitoo peLLi wiSayam kadipEEnu** I raised the matter of marriage with him.

కదలబారు **kadalabaaru** *v.i.* to stir, begin to move.

కదలాడు **kadalaaDu** *v.i.* to be in motion, move continuously; **atani ceetiloo eppuDuu poDugaaTi ceepaaTi karra ~ tuu uNTundi** a long walking stick is always swaying in his hand; **aame cuusina dṛśyam aame kaLLamundu kadalaaDagaa aameloo ceppaleenanta jaali eerpaDindi** when the scene that she had witnessed passed before her eyes again, she had an indescribable feeling of pity.

కదలిక **kadalika** *n.* motion, movement, stirring, mobility.

కదలు **kadalu** *v.i.* **1** to stir, move. **2** to shake, totter. **3** to set out on a journey, move off. **4** to be displaced; **kadilina iTikalu** loose bricks. **5** (of emotion) to be stirred or roused.

కదల్చు, కదిలించు **kadalcu, kadilincu** *v.t.* to move, shift, stir, shake.

కదళం, కదళి **kadaLam, kadaLi** *n. class.* banana, plantain.

కదళీపాకం **kadaliipaakam** *n.* style of writing that is simple, straightforward and easy to understand.

కదా, గదా, కా, గా **kadaa, gadaa, kaa, gaa** *particle* for sure, to be sure, is not it? *and related forms* are not they? etc.; **iwwEELa aadiwaaram ~** today is Sunday, isn't it? **neenu weLtunnaanu ~ aayanni tiisukuwastaanu** I am going (am I not?) so I will bring him; *see* **eTuu.**

కదుం **kadum** *n.* **1** lump, bump, swelling. **2 raktapu ~** blood clot.

కదుం కట్టు **kadum kaTTu** *v.i.* **1** (of limbs) to swell, become stiff. **2** (of blood) to clot.

కదుపు **kadupu** *same as* **kadapu.**

కదురు **kaduru** *n.* spindle.

కదుష్ణం **kaduSNam** *n.* slight warmth, tepidness.

కద్దు **kaddu** *irregular 3rd per. sing. neuter of* **kalugu** *used with a vbl. n. to denote habitual action,* e.g., **aayana maa iNTiki raawaDam ~** he comes to our house regularly.

కనక **kanaka** *same as* **kanuka.**

కనకం **kanakam** *n.* gold.

కనకన **kanakana** *n.* glow of fire or live coals.

కనకవర్షం కురిపించు **kanakawarSam kuripincu** *v.i.* to shower gold.

కనకాంబరం **kanakaambaram** *n.* name of a saffron coloured flower.

కనకాభిషేకం **kanakaabhiSeekam** *n.* lavishing wealth on s.o. (*lit.* pouring a shower of gold pieces on the head of of s.o.).

కనపడు **kanapaDu** *v.i.* to be seen, appear, seem, come to light, turn up (colloq.), be found.

కనపరచు **kanaparacu** *v.t.* to show, exhibit, display.

కనమ, కనుమ **kanama, kanuma** *n.* **1** pass, defile. **2** *pl.* **~ lu** ghats

కనరు **kanaru** *n.* itching sensation in the mouth felt when eating a vegetable like **durada kanda.**

కనాకత్తు **kanaakattu** *adv. and adj. dial.* approximately.

కనికట్టు **kanikaTTu** *same as* **kanukaTTu.**

కనికరం, కనికారం **kanikaram, kanikaaram** *n.* pity, mercy, clemency, compassion.

కనికరించు **kanikarincu** *v.t.* to have mercy on, take pity on.

కనితి **kaniti** *same as* **kanti.**

కనిపించు **kanipincu** *v.i.* **1** to seem, appear, be seen, be visible. **2** to appear before, come to see; **naalugu roojulu pooyEEka naaku kanipincaNDi** come to see me after a few days.

కనిపెట్టు **kanipeTTu** *v.t.* **1** to find out, discover, invent. **2** to observe, perceive, notice, discern. **3** to watch over, tend, guard, look after, take care of. **4** to watch for, wait for; **samayam kanipeTTi aa wiSayam ettEEnu** I waited for the right moment and raised the matter.

కనిపెట్టుకొని ఉండు **kanipeTTukoni uNDu** *v.t.* to be dependent on; **musalitanam waccinaa inkaa batikunnaawu, maa iNTinee kanipeTTukoni unnaawu** old as you are you are still living and still a dependant of our house.

కనిపెట్టుకొను **kanipeTTukonu** I. *v.i.* to wait. II. *v.t.* to look after, watch over, take care of.

కని విని ఊహించని, కని విని ఎరగని **kani wini uuhincani, kani wini eragani** *adj.* unheard of and undreamt of, never before experienced.

కనిష్ఠ **kaniSTha** *adj.* **1** minimal, minimum, least. **2** youngest. **3** lowest.

కనిష్ఠ సామాన్య గుణిజం **kaniSTha saamaanya guNijam** *n. maths.* least common multiple (LCM).

కనిష్ఠిక **kaniSThika** *n.* little finger.

కనిష్ఠుడు **kaniSThuDu** *n.* youngest male member of a family.

కనీనిక **kaniinika** *n. class.* pupil of the eye.

కనీనికాపటలం **kaniinikaa paTalam** *n. med.* iris diaphragm.

కనీస **kaniisa** *adj.* minimum, least.

కనీసం **kaniisam** *adv.* **1** at least. **2** *in neg. constr.* even; **neenu niiku kaLankam aapaadinca leenu, ~ uuhincanaynaa uuhinca leenu** I cannot impute any defect to you, nor even imagine one.

కనీసపక్షంగా **kaniisa pakSangaa** *adv.* to the least extent.

కను **kanu** I. *n. same as* **kannu.** II. *v.t.* **1** to bear, give birth to, beget. **2** *class.* to see, observe, attain, obtain; *mod. in this sense only in certain set phrases,* e.g., **kalalu ~** to dream, **prakhyaatiganna** *and* **peeruganna** famous.

కనుం **kanum** *same as* **kaNum.**

కనుక, కనక, గనుక, గనక **kanuka, kanaka, ganuka, ganaka** I. *conj.* therefore, for that reason. II. *particle*

1 *inserted in a conditional clause to emphasise the preceding word* **miiru Dabbistee~** (*or* **miiru Dabbistee kaanii**) **neenu ceestaanu** if you give me money, I will do it; **waaDu~** (*or* **waaDu kaanii**) **waccinaTTayitee neenu weLLEEnani ceppu** if he comes, tell him I have gone. 2 *added to a question sentence to imply the speaker's scepticism or pessimism concerning the matter* **miiru okkaruu eTLaa uNTaaru~?** how will you (be able to) stay here alone? **neenu cebitee miiru eppuDu ceesEEru~?** as a result of my telling you to do it, when did you ever do it? **niikokappuDu lekkalu wacci eeDicEEyi~?** could you ever do arithmetic?

కనుకట్టు, కనికట్టు **kanukaTTu, kanikaTTu** *n.* 1 sleight of hand, conjuring, jugglery. 2 hypnotism, mesmerism.

కనుకలుపు **kanukalupu** *v.i.* (of two persons) to make a sign with the eyes; **preemikulu iddaru kanukalipEEru** the two lovers made a sign to each other with their eyes.

కనుకుట్టుతనం **kanukuTTutanam** *n.* envy, jealousy.

కనుకొట్టు, కనుగిలుపు, కనుగీటు **kanukoTTu, kanugilupu, kanugiiTu** *v.i.* to wink.

కనుకొలుకులు **kanukolukulu** *n.pl.* inner corners of the eyes.

కనుకొసలు **kanukosalu** *n.pl.* outer corners of the eyes.

కనుక్కొను, కనుకొను **kanukkonu, kanukonu** *v.t.* 1 to enquire, find out. 2 to discover, detect.

కనుగుడ్డు **kanuguDDu** *n.* eyeball.

కనుచాటు **kanucaaTu** *n.* being out of sight, concealment, privacy.

కనుచీకటి **kanuciikaTi** *n.* twilight, half darkness.

కనుచూపు **kanucuupu** *n.* sight, vision; **~meeraloo** within sight, as far as the eye can see.

కనుతుడుపు **kanutuDupu** *n.* eyewash.

కనుదమ్ములు **kanudammulu** *n. pl.* lotus-like eyes.

కనుపాప **kanupaapa** *n.* pupil of the eye.

కనుపు, కణుపు, గనుపు **kanupu, kaNupu, ganupu** *n.* 1 finger joint, knuckle. 2 node (of bamboo).

కనుబొమ, కనుబొమ్మ **kanuboma, kanubomma** *n.* eyebrow; **~la madhya muDi** frown.

కనుమ **kanuma** *same as* **kanama.**

కనుమరుగవు **kanumarugawu** *v.i.* to disappear, vanish.

కనుమరుగు **kanumarugu** *n.* disappearance from sight.

కనుమలుపు **kanumalupu** *v.i.* to shut o.'s eyes in sleep.

కనుమూత **kanumuuta** *n.* death.

కనుమూయు **kanumuuyu** *v.i.* 1 to shut o.'s eyes. 2 to sleep. 3 to die.

కనురెప్ప **kanureppa** *n.* eyelid.

కనురెప్పపాటు **kanureppa paaTu** *n.* instant, moment, twinkling of an eye.

కనువిప్పు **kanuwippu** *n.* opening of the eyes, sudden realisation.

కనుసన్న, కనుసైగ **kanusanna, kanusayga** *n.* wink.

కన్న **kanna**[1] *same as* **kaNTe**[2].

kanna[2] *vbl. adj. of* **kanu** *v.t.* to give birth to; **naa~ talli** own mother (who gave birth to me); **naa~pillalu** my children (whom I gave birth to).

కన్నం **kannam** *n.* hole; **doDDigooDaki~weesi donga loopaliki waccEEDu** a thief made a hole in the back wall and entered the house; **gampaki~peTTi elukalu waDLannii tinnaayi** rats made a hole in the basket and ate all the paddy.

కన్నడ **kannaDa** *n. class.* disregard, neglect.

కన్నడం **kannaDam** *n.* the Kannada or Canarese language.

కన్నయ్య **kannayya** *n.* 1 corrupted form of the name Krishna. 2 pet name of a child.

కన్నాకు **kannaaku** I.n. the outside leaf in a bundle of betel leaves. II. *adj.* chief, leading, best, excellent.

కన్నీరు **kanniiru** *n.* tear, *gen. pl.* **kanniiLLu** tears.

కన్ను, కను **kannu, kanu** *genitive* **kaNTi,** *locative* **kaNTa,** *pl.* **kaLLu, kaNDLu** *or* **kannulu** 1 eye; **waaDiki kaLLu lootuku** (*or* **kuuruku**) **pooyEEyi** his eyes are sunken. 2 *idiomatic expressions*: **mii koosam cuusi cuusi kaLLu kaayalu kaasEEyaNDii** I have been waiting for a long time for you, sir! (*lit.* my eyes have become swollen and sore with waiting for you, sir!); **kaLLu peddagaa ceeyu** to open o.'s eyes wide (in surprise, anger or wakefulness); **naaku kaLLu tirigEEyi** I felt giddy; **kaLLu erra ceeyu** to be very angry (*lit.* to make o.'s eyes red); **kaLLu teelaweeyu** (i) to stare blankly, (ii) to die; **kaLLu appaginci cuucu** to gaze or stare fixedly at; **nuwwu waari kaLLabaDaali** you must appear before him *or* you must be seen by him; **nii raktam kaLLa cuustaanu** I will see the end of you *or* I will punish you; **nelaki 2000 ruupaayilu culaaggaa kaLLa cuustaawu** you will easily get (*or* earn) Rs. 2000 per month; **nannu cuusi waariki kaLLukuTTEEyi** they were envious of me; **kaLLaloo nippulu poosukonnaaru** they felt mortified or envious; **kaLLaki addukonu** (i) *lit.* to touch s.g to o.'s eyes as a sign of reverence, (ii) to show great respect for, (iii) to show appreciation or gratitude for; **kaLLaku addukoni tiisukonee waaLLu unnaaru** there are people who will gladly accept it (*lit.* there are people who will take it and touch it to their eyes in reverence); **kaLLaku wattulu peTTi wetuku** to search diligently, earnestly or very carefully; **aa dr̥syam atani kaLLaku kaTTinaTTundi** that sight remains vividly before his eyes (*lit.* it is as if that sight was bound to his eyes); **kaLLaku kaTTinaTTugaa wiwarincu** to describe vividly; **kaLLaku koTTawaccee ciire** (*or simply* **koTTawaccee ciire**) a striking or attractive sari; **kaLLaaraa** *lit.* so as to fill the eyes, *hence* **kaLLaaraa cuusEEDu** he gazed to his heart's content. 3 eye in a peacock's feather. 4 small hole or aperture, e.g., the origin of a spring of water. 5 knot or node in a bamboo, sugarcane, etc.

కన్నుగిలుపు, కన్నుగీటు **kannu gilupu, kannu giiTu** *v.i.* to wink, make a sign by winking.

కన్నె **kanne**[1] *n.* maiden, virgin.

కన్నె **kanne**[2] *n.* rope for tethering cattle.

కన్నెరికం **kannerikam** *n.* virginity, maidenhood.

కన్నెరికం పెట్టు **kannerikam peTTu** *v.i.* to deflower.

కన్నెర్ర **kannerra** *n.* anger (*lit.* redness of the eyes).

కన్నెర్ర అవు **kannerra awu** *v.i.* to be jealous.

కన్నెర్ర చేయు **kannerra ceeyu** *v.i.* to be angry.

కన్య **kanya** *n.* 1 maiden, virgin. 2 *astrol.* constellation of Virgo.

కన్యక **kanyaka** *n. class. same as* **kanya.**

కన్యాదానం **kanyaadaanam** *n.* handing over a maiden in marriage.

కన్యాశుల్కం **kanyaaśulkam** *n.* bride price, the name of a famous Telugu play by Gurujada Appa Rao.

కపట **kapaTa** *adj.* cunning, deceitful, bogus, fraudulent.

కపటం **kapaTam** *n.* deceit, guile, cunning, fraud, trickery, dissimulation, hypocrisy; **kallaa ~ eraganiwaaDu** person who does not know falsehood or deceit, i.e., innocent or naïve person.

కపటనాటకం **kapaTanaaTakam** *n.* trickery, imposture.

కపటి **kapaTi** *n.* deceitful person, hypocrite.

కపర్దం **kapardam** *n. class.* braided or matted hair.

కపాలం **kapaalam** *n.* skull, cranium.

కపాలమోక్షం **kapaala mookSam** *n.* 1 breaking s.o.'s head, cracking s.o.'s skull. 2 *class.* breaking the skull of a corpse to allow the spirit to depart.

కపి **kapi** *n.* monkey, ape.

కపిత్థం **kapittham** *n. class.* woodapple tree.

కపిధ్వజుడు **kapidhwajuDu** *n. class.* one who bears a flag with the emblem of a monkey, i.e., Arjuna.

కపిల **kapila** *n.* kind of baling apparatus known as a mhote.

కపిల[ం] **kapila[m]** *adj.* dun, dark brown, copper coloured.

కపోతం **kapootam** *n.* dove, pigeon.

కపోలం **kapoolam** *n. class.* cheek.

కప్ప **kappa** *n.* frog.

కప్పం **kappam** *n.* tax, tribute.

కప్పగంతులు **kappagantulu** *n. pl.* jumping fire crackers.

కప్పతాళం, తాళంకప్ప **kappa taaLam, taaLam kappa** *n.* padlock.

కప్పదాట్లు **kappadaaTLu** *n. pl.* evasiveness, dodging.

కప్పలతక్కెడ **kappala takkeda** *n. phrase expressive of the humorous situation likely to arise if a person has the task of weighing live frogs on a scale,* hilarious confusion.

కప్పి **kappi** I. *n.* pulley. II. *past participle of* **kappu.**

కప్పి పుచ్చు **kappi puccu** *v.t.* 1 to cover up, hide, conceal. 2 to set aside; **ii wiSayam kappi pucci migataa wiSayaalu maaTLaaDEEDu** setting this matter aside, he talked about other things.

కప్పి పెట్టు **kappi peTTu** *v.t.* to cover up, hide.

కప్పు **kappu** I. *n.* 1 cover[ing], lid. 2 shutter. 3 roof. 4 cup. 5 *dial.* black colour. II. *v.i.* (of clouds, smoke) to spread, extend, come on, collect. III. *v.t.* 1 to cover; **atani oNTi-miida guDDa kappindi** she covered his body with a cloth. 2 to block up, fill up (hole, crack).

కప్పెర **kappera** *n.* earthen pot or coconut shell used as a begging bowl.

కఫం **kapham** *n.* phlegm.

కఫరి, కఫారి **kaphari, kaphaari** *n. class.* dried ginger (= **śoNThi**).

కబంధుడు **kabandhuDu** *n.* Kabandha, a blind giant in the Ramayana who put volleys of questions to his victims and devoured them if they could not answer, and who could stretch his arms to any length.

కబడి, కబడ్డి **kabaDi, kabaDDi** *n.* a game played by two teams (= **ceDuguDu**).

కబరి **kabari** *n. class.* bun of hair (=**koppu**).

కబళం **kabaLam** *n.* mouthful, morsel.

కబళించు **kabaLincu** *v.t.* to swallow, gulp down, devour.

కబురు **kaburu** *n.* 1 message, news, information. 2 *pl.* **kaburlu** idle talk, chatting, gossip; **kaburlu ceppukonu** to chat, talk, gossip.

కబురు చేయు, కబురు పంపు, కబురంపు, కబురుపెట్టు, కబురెట్టు **kaburu ceeyu, kaburu pampu, kaburampu, kaburu peTTu, kabureTTu** *v.i.* to send a message, send word.

కబేళా **kabeeLaa** *n.* slaughter house.

కబోది **kaboodi** *n.* blind person.

కబ్జా, ఖబ్జా **kabjaa, khabjaa** *n.* 1 possession. 2 land possessed by a cultivator.

కబ్బం **kabbam** *n., corruption of* **kaawyam** literary work (of poetry or prose).

కమండలం, కమండలువు **kamaNDalam, kamaNDaluwu** *n.* vessel used by ascetics for carrying drinking water.

కమటం, కమ్మటం **kamaTam, kammaTam** *n.* goldsmith's portable furnace for melting precious metal.

కమతం **kamatam** *n.* a holding of agricultural land; **sonta ~** land cultivated by an owner directly and not through tenants; **kamataala cekiikaraNam** consolidation of agricultural holdings.

కమతగాడు **kamatagaaDu** *n.* 1 agricultural labourer. 2 crop sharing tenant.

కమనీయ **kamaniiya** *adj.* charming, graceful, pleasing, delightful, lovely.

కమరు **kamaru** I. *n.* singeing; **~ waasana** smell of singeing (of hair, skin, etc.) II. *v.i.* to be singed or charred.

కమల[ం] **kamala[m]** *n.* lotus.

కమలాకరం **kamalaakaram** *n.* tank full of lotuses, lotus pond.

కమలాపండు **kamalaapaNDu** *n.* sweet loose-jacket orange.

కమలు, కములు **kamalu, kamulu** *v.i.* 1 to be scorched, burnt or singed. 2 to turn black, be blackened.

కమాటీ **kamaaTii** *n.* labourer.

కమాను **kamaanu** *n.* 1 arch. 2 bow of a violin. 3 bowlike instrument used for teasing cotton.

కమానుపోవు **kamaanu poowu** *v.i.* to go on tour or circuit, go to camp.

కమామీషు **kamaamiiSu** *see* **kathaa ~**

కముకు దెబ్బ **kamuku debba** *n. dial.* bruise.

కమ్చీ **kamcii** *n.* whip.

కమ్మ **kamma** I. *n.* 1 palmyra leaf. 2 earring. 3 name of a community in Andhra Pradesh. 4 *dial.* letter. II. *adj.* pleasing, pleasant, sweet.

కమ్మచ్చు **kammaccu** *n.* steel plate or die made with holes for drawing wire; ~ **na tiisinaTLunnaaru** (*lit.* they look as if they had been drawn through a die) *is an expression used of persons subjected to a regime of extreme discipline.*

కమ్మటం **kammaTam** *same as* **kamaTam**.

కమ్మ[టి] పొడి **kamma[Ti]poDi** *same as* **annap[u]poDi**.

కమ్మర, కమ్మరి **kammara, kammari** *n.* blacksmith.

కమ్మి **kammi** *n.* 1 wire. 2 bar. 3 iron tyre of a cartwheel. 4 wooden crossbar of a cart frame. 5 border at the end of a length of cloth; *see* **aDDu~**, **mukku~**, **ancu**[1] *sense 4.*

కమ్ము **kammu** *v.t.* 1 to cover [up]. 2 to hide, veil, conceal, 3 to beat out into wire.

కమ్ముకొను **kammukonu** *v.i. and t.* 1 to cover, overspread. 2 to pervade. 3 to hide, veil, conceal.

కయ్య **kayya** *n.* 1 bed for plants in a garden or field. 2 stream.

కయ్యం **kayyam** *n.* fight, quarrel.

కర **kara**[1] *n.* 1 shore, bank, embankment. 2 mark, stain; **cokkaa antaa ~ kaTTindi** the shirt was all stained. 3 scab; **raktam ~ kaTTindi** the blood formed a scab.

కర **kara**[2] *suffix for forming adjs. from certain nouns*; **laabha~** profitable.

కరం **karam** *n. class.* hand, arm; **karacaraNaalu** arms and legs.

కరండం **karaNDam** *n. class.* 1 casket. 2 beehive.

కరక **karaka** *n. class.* hailstone.

కరకజ్జం **karakajjam** *n.* kind of sweet.

కరకట్ట **karakaTTa** *n.* bank, bund; **waradala~** floodbank.

కరకమలాలు **karakamalaalu** *n. pl. class.* lotus-like hands.

కరకర, గరగర **karakara, garagara** *adv.* 1 with a munching or crunching sound. 2 ~ **namalu** to crunch or munch loudly. 3 **biskaTLu Dabbaaloonee uncitee ~ laaDataayi** if you keep biscuits in a tin, they will be crisp. 4 **naaku aakali ~ laaDutannadi** I am beginning to feel hungry. 5 brightly gleaming; ~ **poddu poDicindi** the sun rose gleaming.

కరకు **karaku** I. *n.* 1 sharpness, harshness, roughness. 2 stage of a crop's growth when the ear is developing. II. *adj.* sharp, rough, harsh; ~ **maaTalu** harsh words.

కరకుతనం **karakutanam** *n.* harshness.

కరక్కాయ **karakkaaya** *n.* gallnut or chebulic myrobalan used as a medicine for coughs and colds and also for making black dye; ~ **siraa** *obs.* a kind of black ink.

కరక్కాయవైద్యం **karakkaaya waydyam** *n.* use of home remedies, practice of home medicine; **cinna cinna jwaraalaku DaakTaru daggariki poowaDam enduku? iNTLoo~ too awee taggutaayi** why go to the doctor for petty illnesses? if you practise home medicine, they will go away by themselves.

కరక్కున **karakkuna** *adv.* with a popping or rasping sound.

కరగించు, కరిగించు **karagincu, karigincu** *v.t.* to melt [down], dissolve.

రగు, కరుగు **karagu, karugu** *v.i.* 1 to melt, be dissolved. 2 (of a boil, abscess) to be dispersed.

కరగగొట్టు, కరగబెట్టు **karagagoTTu, karagabeTTu** *v t.* to melt, dissolve.

కరగ్రహణం చేయు **karagrahaNam ceeyu** *v.t.* to marry.

కరచాలనం **karacaalanam** *n.* shaking hands.

కరిచాలనం చేయు **karacaalanam ceeyu** *v.i.* to shake hands.

కరచు, కరుచు **karacu, karucu** *v.t.* 1 to bite. 2 (of ill-fitting shoes) to pinch.

కరచుకొను, కరుచుకొను **karacukonu, karucukonu** I. *v.i.* to stick, adhere, cling (like paste); **neenu ciiwaaTLu peTTEEnu, gooDaku ballilaa karucukoni kuurcunnaaDu bikkacacii** I scolded him, he sat cowed down like a lizard sticking to the wall. II. *v.t.* 1 to bite, take or hold s.g in o.'s teeth; **pilli pillalanu nooTa karacukoni pootundi** the cat takes its kittens in its mouth and carries them. 2 **karacukoni taagu** to drink touching the vessel with o.'s mouth.

కరడు, కరుడు **karaDu, karuDu** *n.* lump, mass, ball, clot; **annam~** lump or ball of rice grains adhering together.

కరడు కట్టిన, కరుడు కట్టిన **karaDu kaTTina, karuDu kaTTina** *adj.* 1 congealed, solidified. 2 *fig.* inflexible, hidebound, stick-in-the-mud, fossilised; ~ **saampradaayaalu** inflexible traditions.

కరణం **karaNam** I. *suffix equivalent to* -isation; **keendrii~** centralisation. II. *n.* 1 karnam, village accountant. 2 *gram.* instrumental case.

కరణకారకం **karaNakaarakam** *n. gram.* instrumental case.

కరణి **karaNi** *n.* manner, mode, way.

కరణీకం **karaNiikam** *n.* office of karnam.

కరతలం **karatalam** *n.* palm of the hand.

కరతలామలకం **karatalaamalakam** *n.* s.g very plain or easy (*lit.* a berry placed in the hand, ready for eating).

కరతాళ ధ్వనులు **karataaLa dhwanulu** *n. pl.* sound of hand clapping, applause.

కరదీపిక **karadiipika** *n.* torch carried by hand.

కరపత్రం **karapatram** *n.* pamphlet, leaflet, handout.

కరపించు, కరిపించు **karapincu, karipincu** *v.t.* to cause to eat; **o.-ni gaDDi~** to humiliate s.o. (*lit.* to make s.o. eat grass).

కరపు, కరుపు, గరుపు **karapu, karupu, garupu** *v.t.* to teach, impart, provide (education, training, knowledge); **prajalandarikii widya garapaDam** providing education for all the people.

కరవాక **karawaaka** *n.* marsh near the sea, salt marsh.

కరవాలం **karawaalam** *n. class.* sword.

కరసంకేతం **karasankeetam** *n.* gesture made by hand.

కరసంచాలనం **karasancaalanam** *n.* shaking hands.

కరాఖండీగా **karaakhaNDiigaa** *adv.* 1 firmly. 2 precisely, definitely. 3 adamantly.

కరారు[నామా], ఖరారు[నామా] **karaaru[naamaa], kharaaru[naamaa]** n. written agreement, contract, bond.

కరాళ **karaaLa** *adj. class.* horrible, dreadful.

కరి **kari** *n.* elephant.

కరిగట్టు **karigaTTu** *n. dial.* irrigated land.

కరిగించు **karigincu** *same as* **karagincu.**

కరిపించు **karipincu** *same as* **karapincu.**

కరివేప **kariweepa** *n.* tree called *murraya koenigii.*

కరివేపాకు **kariweepaaku** *n.* 1 leaves of **kariweepa** used for flavouring and as an aid to digestion. 2 *slang* money.

కరుకు **karuku** *n.* sharpness, harshness, roughness.

కరుకుదేరు **karukudeeru** *v.i.* to be[come] rough.

కరుగు **karugu** *same as* **karagu.**

కరుచు[కొను] **karucu[konu]** *same as* **l aracu[konu].**

కరుడు **karuDu** *same as* **karaDu.**

కరుణ **karuNa** *n.* mercy, grace, pity, compassion.

కరుణరసం **karuNarasam** *n.* pathos.

కరుణామయ **karuNaamaya** *adj.* compassionate.

కరుణించు **karuNincu** *v.t.* to have pity on, have mercy on, favour.

కరుపు **karupu** I. *n.* bite. II *v.t. same as* **karapu.**

కరువు **karuwu** I. *n.* famine, scarcity, shortage. II. *adj.* rare, scarce, lacking, wanting; **naaku pitrpreema karuwayindi** I lacked a father's love.

కరువుకాలం **karuwukaalam** *n.* period of famine or scarcity.

కరువుబత్తెం **karuwubattem** *n.* dearness allowance.

కర్కశ **karkaśa** *adj.* 1 harsh, rough. 2 cruel. 3 (of sound) strident.

కర్కశత్వం **karkaśatwam** *n.* harshness, roughness, cruelty.

కర్కాటకం **karkaaTakam** *n.* 1 crab. 2 *astrol.* the sign of Cancer.

కర్కాటకరేఖ **karkaaTaka reekha** *n.* tropic of Cancer.

కర్కోటక **karkooTaka** *adj.* cruel, hard, harsh.

కర్కోటకుడు **karkooTakuDu** *n.* cruel person.

కర్ణం **karNam** *n.* 1 ear. 2 *maths.* hypotenuse.

కర్ణకఠోరం **karNakaThooram** *adj.* harsh sounding, dreadful sounding, hideous (to listen to).

కర్ణధారి **karNadhaari** *n. class.* helmsman, pilot.

కర్ణపిశాచం, కర్ణపిశాచి **karNapiśaacam, karNapiśaaci** *n.* an ear devil, *used jokingly to suggest an unnaturally keen sense of hearing,* e.g., **meem enta rahasyangaa maaTLaaDukonnaa, waaDu winnaaDu. ~ undoo eempaaDoo?** although we talked ever so secretly, he heard us: has he a devil in his ear, I wonder?

కర్ణపేయం, కర్ణరసాయనం **karNapeeyam, karNarasaayanam** *n.* s.g pleasing to the ear.

కర్ణభేరి **karNabheeri** *n.* eardrum, tympanum.

కర్ణాకర్ణిగా **karNaakarNigaa** *adj.* 1 *lit.* from ear to ear. 2 orally, by word of mouth.

కర్ణాటక **karNaaTaka** I. *n.* 1 the modern State of Karnataka. 2 *class.* the Carnatic, i.e., the Telugu and Kannada speaking areas of South India. II. *adj.* belonging to the culture and tradition of the Carnatic; **~ sangiitam** Carnatic music, classical South Indian music.

కర్ణిక **karNika** *n. sci.* auricle.

కర్ణుడు **karNuDu** *n.* name of a character in the Mahabharata noted for his generosity; **daana~** generous donor to charities.

కర్త **karta** *n.* 1 doer, maker, performer, originator, creator; **manam deenikii kartalam kaamu** we are not creators of anything; *often in compounds,* e.g., **sankalana~** compiler. 2 *gram.* subject. 3 *gram.* nominative case.

కర్తనం **kartanam** *n. class.* cutting, severing.

కర్తరి **kartari**[1] *adj. gram.* active.

కర్తరి, కత్తెర **kartari**[2], **kattera**[2] *n.* season of early summer.

కర్తర్యర్థకం **kartaryarthakam** *n. gram.* active voice.

కర్తవ్యం **kartawyam** *n.* 1 that which has to be done, duty, obligation. 2 function. 3 course of action.

కర్తృకారకం **kartrkaarakam** *n. gram.* nominative case.

కర్పరం **karparam** *n.* 1 skull. 2 begging bowl. 3 *sci.* orbit.

కర్పూరం **karpuuram** *n.* camphor; **pacca~** menthol.

కర్పూరతైలం **karpuura taylam** *n.* turpentine.

కర్పూరహారతి **karpuura haarati** *n.* an offering of lighted camphor made to a deity.

కర్బన **karbana** *adj. sci.* organic; **~rasaayanaśaastram** organic chemistry.

కర్బనం **karbanam** *n. sci.* carbon.

కర్బనేతర **karbaneetara** *adj.* inorganic.

కర్బూజ **karbuuuja** *n.* watermelon.

కర్మ **karma** *n. gram.* object.

కర్మ[ం], ఖర్మ[ం] **karma[m], kharma[m]** *n.* 1 action. 2 the fruit of good and evil actions in previous lives, fate, destiny; **waaDi ~ aTLaa undi** *or* **waaDi ~ loo aTLaa undi** such is his fate; **waaDi~ kaalipooyindi** his luck was against him; **~ caalaka** unfortunately. 3 misfortune, hard lot, affliction. 4 religious rites. 5 obsequies, funeral rites. 6 **~ !** *or* **ayyoo ~ !** alas! 7 **oka saareem ~ ? reNDu muuDu saarlay cuusEEnu** why [do you say] only once? I have seen them two or three times *or* I have seen them not only once but two or three times; **anaDam eemi ~ ? raasEEru kuuDaanu** they not only said it but wrote it also.

కర్మకాండ[ం] **karmakaaNDa[m]** *n.* 1 funeral rites, obsequies. 2 ceremony; **karmakaaNDantaa mugisee sariki raatri padi gaNTalayindi** by the time the whole ceremony was over it was 10 p.m. 3 *colloq.* untidiness, disarray; **ii karmakaaNDantaa eemiTi iNTLoo? tondaragaa tiyyaNDi!** what is all this untidiness in the house? clear it away quickly! 4 portion of the Vedas relating to the performance of ceremonies and sacrifices.

కర్మకారకం **karmakaarakam** *n. gram.* accusative case.

కర్మకారుడు **karmakaaruDu** *n.* craftsman, artisan.

కర్మక్షేత్రం, కర్మభూమి **karmakSeetram, karmabhuumi** *n.* 1 India, the land where religious rites hold the most important place in life. 2 field of activity.

కర్మణా **karmaNaa** *adv.* by deed, actively; **manasaa waacaa ~** by thought, word and deed.

కర్మణి **karmaNi** *adj. gram.* passive; ~ **prayoogam** use of the passive voice (in sentence construction).

కర్మధారయం **karmadhaarayam** *n. gram. name of a compound consisting of an adj. and a noun*, e.g., **peddapuli.**

కర్మపరిపాకం **karma paripaakam** *n.* maturing of o.'s fate; **nii ~ aytee kaSTaalanunci bayaTapaDataawu** if the time is ripe for it, you will get over your difficulties.

కర్మయోగం **karmayoogam** *n.* performance of worldly tasks purely out of a sense of duty without any feeling of personal interest.

కర్మర్థకం **karmarthakam** *n. gram.* passive voice.

కర్మవశాత్తూ **karmawaśaattuu** *adv., gen. in neg. constr.* by fate, due to ill luck, unluckily.

కర్మసాక్షి **karmasaakSi** *n.* the sun (*lit.* the witness of human actions).

కర్మసిద్ధాంతం, ఖర్మసిద్ధాంతం **karmasiddhaantam, kharmasiddhaantam** *n.* the doctrine of predestination.

కర్మాంతరాలు **karmaantaraalu** *n. pl.* obsequies, funeral rites.

కర్మాగారం **karmaagaaram** *n.* factory.

కర్మిష్ఠి **karmiSThi** *n.* diligent performer of religious rites, pious person.

కర్మేంద్రియాలు **karmeendriyaalu** *n. pl.* organs of the body which perform actions.

కర్ర **karra** I. *n.* 1 wood, timber. 2 piece of wood, stick. 3 stalk of a grain such as cholam. II. *adj.* wooden; ~ **saamagri** wooden articles.

కర్రపెండలం **karrapeNDalam** *n.* tapioca.

కర్రపెత్తనం చేయు **karrapettanam ceeyu** *v.i.* to be overbearing towards others.

కర్రాబిళ్లా **karraabiLLaa** *n.* game played by boys, *same as* **biLLangooDu** *or* **gilliidaNDu.**

కర్రి **karri** *adj.* 1 black; ~ **aawu** black cow. 2 dark (complexion).

కర్రు **karru** *n.* 1 ploughshare. 2 share of a drill plough (**gorru**).

కర్విణ్ణత **karwiNNata** *n.* feeling of shock.

కర్షం **karSam** *n.* a weight of about ten grammes.

కర్షకుడు **karSakuDu** *n.* agriculturist, cultivator, farmer.

కర్షణం **karSaNam** *n. phys.* traction.

కర్షితం **karSitam** *n.* that which is pulled or attracted.

కల **kala**[1] *n.* dream; ~ **[lu] kanu** to dream.

ల, గల **kala**[2], **gala** *irregular vbl. adj. of* **kalugu** 1 *follow-* *a noun* having, possessing, containing, e.g., **Dabbu ~** althy; **Dabbu ~ waaru** *or simply* **~ waaru** wealthy pers; **santooSam ~** joyful. 2 *following a noun + p.p. (formal and literary)* being, existing, e.g., **sabhaloo ~ waaru harsincEEru** the people in the meeting approved; **okaToo padyamnunci arawayeeDoo padyam waraku ~ bhaagam** the portion (of a poem) from verse 1 to verse 67. 3. *following an infinitive* able to, about to; **miiru cadawa ~ pustakaalu** books which you can read; *see* **raagala, kaagala.**

కలం **kalam** *n.* pen; ~ **giiTu** stroke of a pen; ~ **peeru** pen name.

కలంకం, కళంకం **kalankam, kaLankam** *n.* 1 defect, blemish, stigma, slur. 2 spot, mark, stain.

కలంకారి **kalankaari** *n.* a kind of printed or patterned cotton cloth.

కలక **kalaka** *n.* 1 turbidness, turbidity; **kaNTi ~** ophthalmia, a disease of the eye. 2 perturbation, trouble, confusion.

కలకంఠి **kalakaNThi** *n.* woman.

కలకండ **kalakaNDa** *n.* sugar candy.

కలకతేరు **kalakateeru** *v.i.* (of water) to settle, become calm and clear.

కలకపాటు **kalakapaaTu** *n.* 1 turbidness. 2 disturbance, agitation, confusion, trouble.

కలకపారు **kalakapaaru** *v.i.* 1 to be turbid. 2 to be disturbed or agitated. 3 to be confused or troubled.

కలకల[ం] **kalakala[m]** *n.* 1 subdued noise or murmuring indicating a disburbance. 2 chirping, calling (of birds).

కలకలలాడు, కళకళలాడు **kalakalalaaDu, kaLakaLalaaDu** *v.i.* 1 to gleam, shine. 2 to be lively, bright or cheerful.

కలకాలం **kalakaalam** *adv.* for a long time, for ever; **aayana peeru ~ nilicipootundi** his name will endure for long.

కలగచేయు **kalagaceeyu** *v.t.* 1 to create, bring about. 2 to provide, furnish.

కలగచేసుకొను **kalagaceesukonu** *v.i.* to intervene, interfere.

కలగలసి **kalagalasi** *adv.* mixed, mingled.

కలగలుపు **kalagalupu**[1] *n.* 1 mixing, blending, intermingling. 2 intimacy, familiarity, sociability. 3 *pl.* ~ **lu** curry made of mixed vegetables.

కలగలుపు, కలయగలుపు, కలియగలుపు, కలేగలుపు **kalagalupu**[2], **kalayagalupu, kaliyagalupu, kaleegalupu** *v.t.* to mix together, combine, make a mixture of.

కలగలుపుచేయు **kalagalupu ceeyu** *v.t.* to mix together, make a mixture of.

కలగాచు **kalagaacu** *v.i.* to dream (<**kala + kaancu**).

కలగాపులగం **kalagaapulagam** *n.* mixture, assortment.

కలగాపులగంగా **kalagaapulagangaa** *adv.* mixed up, higgedly piggedly, jumbled together, intermingled.

కలగాపులగం చేయు **kalagaapulagam ceeyu** *v.t.* to mix up, jumble together.

కలగుండుపడు **kalaguNDupaDu** *v.i.* to be stunned, shocked or thrown into confusion.

కలగుమ్ము **kalagummu** *v.t.* to mix by crushing and pounding.

కలగూర **kalaguura** *n.* 1 a kind of green vegetable. 2 wild herbs in general.

కలగూరగంప **kalaguura gampa** *n.* 1 basket of green vegetables. 2 medley, miscellany.

కలచు **kalacu** *v.t.* to agitate, disturb, trouble, stir.

కలత **kalata** *n.* 1 agitation, confusion, disturbance. 2 dispute, misunderstanding.

కలతచెందు, కలతబడు, కలతబారు **kalatacendu, kalatabaDu, kalatabaaru** *v.i.* to be distressed, disturbed, troubled, ruffled or agitated.

కలతనిద్ర **kalatanidra** *n.* 1 disturbed sleep. 2 state of being half asleep; **pillawaaDu ardharaatri puuTa ~ loo leeci eeDustunnaaDu** the child has got up at midnight half asleep and is crying.

కలతొక్కు **kalatokku** *same as* **kalayatokku.**

కలధౌతం **kaladhawtam** *n. class.* 1 gold and silver. 2 pleasing tone.

కలధ్వని **kaladhwani** *n.* low sweet tone.

కలనగణితం **kalana gaNitam** *n. maths.* calculus.

కలనేత **kalaneeta** *n.* cloth woven with threads of one colour in the warp and another in the woof.

కలప **kalapa** *n.* wood, timber.

కలబంద **kalabanda** *n.* aloe plant.

కలబడు **kalabaDu** *v.i.* 1 to combine, join in with others; **iNTiki waccina cuTTam kalabaDi pani ceestunnaaDu** the relative who has come to the house is joining in and working. 2 *same as* **kaliyabaDu.**

కలబెట్టు, కలియబెట్టు **kalabeTTu, kaliyabeTTu** *v.t.* 1 to mix, stir together (ingredients). 2 to pay visits to, call on (friends, relations); **uuLLoo cuTTaalu nalugurinii kaliyabeTTi waccEEDu** he returned after having visited several of his relations in the village.

కలబోయు **kalabooyu** *v.t.* to pour together, mix.

కలయంపి, కళ్లాపు, కల్లాపు **kalayampi, kaLLaapu, kallaapu** *n.* cowdung and water mixed together and sprinkled in front of a house to settle the dust; **~ callu** to sprinkle that mixture in the front yard of a house early in the morning.

కలయగలుపు **kalayagalupu** *same as* **kalagalupu.**

కలయచూచు, కలియచూచు **kalayacuucu, kaliya cuucu** *v.t.* 1 to look all round (for s.g). 2 to look at (s.g) carefully.

కలయతిరుగు **kalayatirugu** *v.i. and t.* to roam around, go about.

కలయతొక్కు, కలతొక్కు **kalayatokku, kalatokku** *v.t.* to mix by crushing and pounding or trampling.

కలయబడు **kalayabaDu** *same as* **kaliyabaDu.**

కలయిక **kalayika** *n.* 1 meeting, uniting, joining, junction. 2 mixing, mixture, blending, combining, combination. 3 *bot.* **reNDu wangaDaala ~** crossing of two strains.

కలయు **kalayu** *same as* **kaliyu.**

కలరా **kalaraa** *n.* cholera.

కలవరం **kalawaram** *n.* confusion, puzzlement, anxiety.

కలవరపడు **kalawarapaDu** *v.i.* to be confused, puzzled, perplexed or anxious.

కలవరచు, కలవరపరచు, కలవరపెట్టు **kalawaracu, kalawaraparacu, kalawarapeTTu** *v.t.* 1 to confuse. 2 to worry, disturb, distress.

కలవరపాటు, కళవళపాటు **kalawarapaaTu, kaLawaLapaaTu** *n.* confusion, turmoil.

కలవరించు **kalawarincu** *v.i.* 1 to talk in o.'s sleep. 2 to dream of, long for.

కలవిలపడు **kalawilapaDu** *v.i.* to be agitated, worried or confused.

కలశం **kalaśam** *n.* 1 jar, water pot, urn. 2 ornament in the form of an inverted pot which surmounts a temple tower. 3 jar containing an offering worshipped as a preliminary to a main ceremony.

కలస్వనం **kalaswanam** *n. class.* melodious tone.

కలహం **kalaham** *n.* quarrel, dispute.

కలహంస **kalahamsa** *n. class.* swan; **~ naDaka** elegant or swanlike gait.

కలహకంఠి **kalahakaNThi** *n.* quarrlesome woman.

కలహకారక **kalahakaaraka** *adj.* causing quarrels.

కలహప్రియుడు, కలహభోజనుడు **kalahapriyuDu, kalahabhoojanuDu** *n. class.* one who incites quarrels, like Narada in the Puranas.

కలహించు **kalahincu** *v.i.* to quarrel, fight, dispute, contend.

కలాపం **kalaapam** *n.* affair, activity; **prema~** love affair, **rahasya kalaapaalu** secret activities.

కలాయి **kalaayi** *same as* **kaLaayi.**

కలి **kali**[1] *n.* 1 the age of Kali, also called **~ yugam** or **ghoora ~** the iron age, the last of the four ages of the world, the age in which we live. 2 name of the deity who presides over everything that is unworthy, sinful and dreadful; **niiloo ~ puruSuDu praweeśincEEDu** Kali has entered into you, i.e., you have become very wicked.

కలి **kali**[2] *n.* water used for washing rice and left to ferment: **kaloo ganjoo taagi batukutunnaaDu** he lives only on rice water and gruel, i.e., he lives in extreme poverty.

కలికం **kalikam** *n.* 1 eye salve. 2 magic ointment for discovering hidden objects or creating illusions; **kaNTLoo ~ weesinaa kaanaraadu** even if you put magic ointment in your eye, you cannot see it. 3 **kaNTLoo kalikaaniki leedu** *lit.* even for eyesalve in the eye there is not (enough); *eyesalve is a medicine of which only a tiny amount is needed, hence this expression means* not even the least amount is available; *see* **mandu** *sense 7 for a similar usage.*

కలికాలం **kalikaalam** *n.* 1 difficult times, hard times. 2 *same as* **kaliyugam**; *see* **kali**[1].

కలికి **kaliki** *n.* woman.

కలిగించు, కల్గించు **kaligincu, kalgincu** I. *v.i.* to happen, occur, arise. II. *v.t.* to cause, bring about, provide.

కలితీ **kalitii** *same as* **kaltii.**

కలిపి **kalipi** *past participle of* **kalupu**[2].

కలిపించు **kalipincu** 1 *variant form of* **kalpincu.** 2 *causative of* **kalupu**[2].

కలిమి **kalimi** *n.* wealth, riches; ~ **leemulu kaawaDi kuNDalu** wealth and poverty are like the two pots on a carrying pole, i.e., equally balanced (proverb); *see* **kaawaDi.**

కలియగలుపు **kaliyagalupu** *same as* **kalagalupu[2].**

కలియచూచు **kaliyacuucu** *same as* **kalayacuucu.**

కలియబడు, కలయబడు, కలబడు, కలేబడు **kaliyabaDu, kalayabaDu, kalabaDu, kaleebaDu** *v.i.* to rush at or against, fall upon.

కలియు, కలయు **kaliyu, kalayu** *v.i. and t.* 1 to mix, mingle, merge, join, be mixed, merged or joined; **reegaDi isaka kalisina neela** soil composed of mixed sand and clay. 2 to join together, be[come] united; **koTTukonna waarandaruu kalisipoyEEru** all those who had quarrelled have become united. 3 to agree; **mana aaloocanalu kalisEEyi** our ideas agreed. 4 to collect, assemble. 5 to be included; **B. too kalisi aaruguru sabhyulu unnaaru** there are six members including B. 6 to meet; **aayananu kalawaDaaniki entoo mandi wacci unnaaru** ever so many people have come to meet him. 7 *imper., with dative* to match, suit; **manakii daanikii kalawadu** we and she do not get on well together *or* are not suited to each other; **iddarikii kalisipooyinaTTundi** they both seem to have got on well together. 8 **kalisi** *past participle used adverbially* together; **iddaruu kalisi madraasu weLLEEru** they both went to Madras together.

కలియుగం **kaliyugam** *see* **kali[1].**

కలివిడిగా **kaliwiDigaa** *adv.* 1 mixing or joining together. 2 jointly, unitedly.

కలిసి **kalisi** *past participle of* **kaliyu**; *see* **kaliyu** *sense 8.*

కలిసికట్టుగా **kalisikaTTugaa** *adv.* 1 together, jointly, unitedly. 2 in a friendly way, intimately.

కలిసిమెలిసి **kalisimelisi** *adv.* amicably, affably, mixing and mingling on friendly terms.

కలిసివచ్చు **kalisiwaccu** *v.i.* 1 to come together, join, unite. 2 to come in addition, be added or included. 3 to come as a blessing or favour of fortune; **waaDiki caduwu, udyoogam, manci bhaarya annii kalisi waccEEyi** he is blessed with education, a job and a good wife; **anni immuluu kalisoccina jaagaa** a site favoured with all conveniences; **kaalam naaku kalisiraawaDam leedu** the time is not propitious for me. 4 to be spared or saved; **enta kluptangaa waartalu andincagaligitee anta sthalam kalisiwastundi** the more briefly the news can be conveyed, the more space is saved.

కలు **kalu** *imperative sing. of* **kaliyu.**

కలుక్కుమను **kalukkumanu** *v.i.* to feel a twinge of pain (mental or physical); **aa maaTalu jñaapakam wastee ippaTikii guNDe kalukkumaNTundi** when I remember those words my heart feels a twinge of pain even now.

కలుగ చేసుకొను **kaluga ceesukonu** *v.i.* to interfere, intervene.

కలుగు **kalugu[1]** *n.* hole, pit; **eluka ~ looki duurindi** the rat ran into the hole.

కలుగు **kalugu[2]** *v.i. with irregular present tense* **kalanu,** **lanu** 1 *obs., literary* to be, exist; **amaraawati anee uuru** **du** there is a town called Amaravati. 2 to happen, r, arise, accrue; **awasaram kaliginappuDu** when need 3 to be born; **naaku iddaru pillalu kaligEEru** two were born to me. 4 *with dative* to have, get, obtain; **aayam kaligindi** I got justice. 5 *following an infini-* able; **taanu peddawaaDay pooyinaTTu tana-** **awaaLLanu nammincagalaDu gaani tanakanna caalaa pedda waLLanu nammincaleeDu** he can convince those younger than himself that he has grown up but he cannot convince those much older than himself. 6 *following an infinitive* to be prepared, be willing, be liable; **aTuwaNTi paristhitulloo neenu raajakiiyarangamnunci tappukoogalanu, miiru mii udyoogaaniki raajiinaama peTTagalaraa?** in those circumstances, I am prepared to quit the political arena, are you prepared to resign your job? *for other irregular forms of this verb see* **kala[2], kaddu.**

కలుజు **kaluju** *n.* surplus weir of an irrigation tank.

కలుపు **kalupu[1]** *n.* weeds; ~ **mokka** weed, wild plant.

కలుపు **kalupu[2]** *v.t.* 1 to join, connect, link; **jaatiiya giitam paaDutunnappuDu naluguritoo gontukalipEEDu** he joined in the chorus with others in singing the national anthem. 2 to combine, unite, bring together. 3 to add. 4 to mix, blend; **annam ~ konu** to mix food on o.'s plate; **peeka mukkalu ~** to shuffle playing cards. 5 to include, incorporate, assimilate; **naatoo kalipi aaruguru** six persons including myself; **maa ammaayini waaru ~ konnaaru** they have taken my daughter into their family. 6 *idiomatic usages*: **cuTTarikam ~ konu** to establish relationship (between persons or families); **naatoo maaTa kalipEEDu** he entered into conversation with me; **waaDitoo ceetulu kalipi ii pani ceesEEnu** I joined hands with him and did this work; **iddarimadhya gharsaNa wacci ceetulu kalapaDamdaakaa pooyindi** friction arose between them and they came to blows.

కలుపుకోలు **kalupukoolu** *adj.* sociable, affable, friendly, intimate.

కలుపుకోలుతనం **kalupukoolutanam** *n.* friendliness, sociability, affability, intimacy.

కలుపుతీత **kaluputiita** *n.* weeding, removing weeds.

కలుపు సేద్యం **kalupu seedyam** *n.* stage of cultivation consisting of removing weeds and loosening the soil with a harrow or hoe.

కలురొట్టె **kaluroTTe** *n. dial.* a cheap kind of bread.

కలువ **kaluwa** *n.* water lily, lotus.

కలుషం **kaluSam** I *n.* foulness, impurity. II. *adj.* foul, turbid, muddy.

కలుషితం **kaluSitam** *adj.* 1 spoilt, defiled, corrupted, polluted. 2 *fig.* ruined, poisoned.

కలుషితం చేయు **kaluSitamceeyu** *v.t.* to spoil, adulterate, pollute.

కలుసుకొను **kalusukonu** *v.i. and t.* to meet, join; **miiru aayananu kalusukoni maaTLaaDaali** you must meet him and talk; **daarulu kalusukonnaayi** the roads joined together.

కలేగలుపు **kaleegalupu** *same as* **kalagalupu[2].**

కలేజా **kaleejaa** *n.* courage, heart; ~ **uNDaalooyi!** take heart! *or* take courage!

కలేబడు **kaleebaDu** *same as* **kaliyabaDu.**

కల్కం **kalkam** *n. class.* oily sediment, paste.

కల్తీ, కలితీ **kaltii, kalitii** *n.* adulteration; ~ **leeni** unadulterated.

కల్తీ చేయు **kaltii ceeyu** *v.t.* to adulterate.

కల్దారు **kaldaaru** *n.* name by which coinage issued by the Government of India was formerly known in the Nizam's Dominions.

కల్పం **kalpam** *n.* mythological age, a cycle of 432 million years, equivalent to one day of Brahma.

కల్పన **kalpana** *n.* 1 creation. 2 imagination.

కల్పనకర్త, కల్పకుడు **kalpanakarta, kalpakuDu** *n.* inventor.

కల్పనచేయు **kalpana ceeyu** *v.t.* 1 to imagine. 2 to concoct.

కల్పనాత్మక **kalpanaatmaka** *adj.* creative (writing).

కల్పనాశక్తి **kalpanaa śakti** *n.* 1 ingenuity. 2 power of imagination.

కల్పవృక్షం **kalpa wṛkSam** *n.* 1 heavenly tree that grants any wish. 2 very generous donor.

కల్పించు, కలిపించు **kalpincu, kalipincu** *v.t.* 1 to devise, create, form, bring about, cause. 2 to invent, make up, fabricate.

కల్పించుకొను **kalpincukonu** *v.i.* 1 to come and join, take part. 2 to intervene, interfere.

కల్పిత **kalpita** *adj.* invented, made up, fictional, fictitious.

కల్మషం **kalmaSam** *n.* 1 dirt, defilement, contamination, impurity. 2 sin.

కల్యాణం **kalyaaNam** *same as* **kaLyaaNam.**

కల్ల **kalla**[1] *n.* 1 lie, falsehood. 2 *in constr. with a vbl. n.* improbability, absurdity, s.g out of the question: **neenu akkaDiki raawaDam ~** my coming there is out of the que

కల్ల **kalla**[2] *n.* hedge, fence.

కల్లబొల్లి **kallabolli** *adj.* false, fictitious.

కల్లా **kallaa** *suffix denoting* (i) within (of time), e.g., **eeDu gaNTala ~** by seven o'clock, (ii) *a superlative*, e.g., **anni nagaraalloo ~ pedda nagaram** the biggest city of all.

కల్లాపు **kallaapu** *same as* **kalayampi.**

కల్లు **kallu** *n.* 1 toddy, fermented juice drawn by tapping from a palmyra, date or coconut tree. 2 *class.* stone; *mod. only in compounds*, e.g., **uppu ~** grain of salt.

కల్లోలం **kalloolam** *n.* 1 turmoil, disturbance, turbulence, confusion. 2 **samudram ~gaa undi** the sea is rough.

కల్లోలపరచు, కల్లోలపెట్టు **kalloolaparacu, kalloolapeTTu** *v.t.* to plunge into turmoil.

కల్వం **kalwam** *n.* 1 grinding stone. 2 apothecary's mortar.

కల్హారం **kalhaaram** *n.* pink lotus.

కళ **kaLa** *n.* 1 art; **kaLaabhyaasam ceeyu** to study art. 2 *class.* ray of light. 3 brightness, radiance, lustre; **waaDi mukhamloo ~leedu** there is no brightness in his face. 4 grace, charm. 5 look, sign, appearance; **iNTLoo peLLi ~ leedu** there is no sign of a wedding in the house. 6 phase of the moon, the degree of difference between the moon's brightness on one night and the next. 7 *gram.* word not ending with the letter *n.*

కళంకం **kaLankam** *same as* **kalankam.**

కళకళ **kaLakaLa** *adj.* shining, radiant.

కళకళలాడు **kaLakaLalaaDu** *same as* **kalakalalaaDu.**

కళత్రం **kaLatram** *n. class.* wife.

కళపెళలాడు **kaLapeLalaaDu** *v.i.* to boil violently.

కళవళపాటు **kaLawaLapaaTu** *same as* **kalawarapaaTu.**

కళవళించు **kaLawaLincu** *v.i.* to be confused, talk nonsense, babble.

కళాకాంతి **kaLaakaanti** *n. pl., only in neg. constr.* look of happiness, joy or well-being; **waaDi mohamloo ~ leewu** there is no joy or well-being in his face.

కళాకారుడు **kaLaakaaruDu** *n.* artist.

కళాఖండం **kaLaakhaNDam** *n.* 1 work of art. 2 masterpiece.

కళాత్మక **kaLaatmaka** *adj.* artistic.

కళాత్మకంగా **kaLaatmakangaa** *adv.* artistically.

కళానైపుణ్యం **kaLaanaypuNyam** *n.* artistry, artistic skill.

కళాయి, కలాయి **kaLaayi, kalaayi** *n.* 1 round bottomed metal cooking vessel. 2 tin plating (of vessels), silver plating (of mirrors).

కళారచన **kaLaaracana** *n.* artistic creation.

కళారూపం **kaLaaruupam** *n.* art form.

కళావతి **kaLaawati** *n.* 1 woman well versed in the arts. 2 prostitute.

కళావరు **kaLaawaru** *n.* club (in playing cards).

కళావస్తువు **kaLaawastuwu** *n.* work of art.

కళావిహీన **kaLaawihiina** *adj.* lustreless, lifeless.

కళాశాల **kaLaaśaala** *n.* college.

కళాశాలి **kaLaaśaali** *n.* artist.

కళాసి **kaLaasi** *n.* 1 boatman, sailor. 2 worker in a factory.

కళింగ **kaLinga** I. *n.* surplus weir of an irrigation tank. II. *adj.* belonging to the Kalinga region.

కళింగం **kaLingam** *n.* the ancient region of Kalinga centred around Visakhapatnam, Vijayanagaram and Srikakulam districts.

కళిక **kaLika** *n.* 1 bud. 2 **diipa ~** flame.

కళేబరం **kaLeebaram** *n.* 1 body. 2 corpse.

కళ్యాణం, కల్యాణం **kaLyaaNam, kalyaaNam** *n.* 1 prosperity, well-being; **wiśwa ~, looka ~** the well-being of society, the general good. 2 any auspicious ceremony or festival. 3 marriage.

కళ్యాణి **kaLyaaNi** *n.* 1 woman whose husband is living. 2 name of a raga.

కళ్ళ, కళ్లె **kaLLa, kaLLe** *n.* phlegm.

కళ్ళం **kaLLam** *n.* threshing floor.

కళ్ళాపు **kaLLaapu** *same as* **kalayampi.**

కళ్ళి **kaLLi** *n. euphorbia tirucalli*, a cactus-like plant grown as a hedge.

కళ్ళెం **kaLLem** *n.* reins, bridle.

కవకవ **kawa kawa** *adv.* (of laughter or speech) loudly; **~nawwu** to laugh aloud.

కవచం **kawacam** *n.* armour.

కవచకుండలాలు **kawacakuNDalaalu** *n. pl.* the protective armour and earrings possessed by Karna, a hero in the Mahabharata.

కవటం **kawaTam** *n.* main branch of a tree.

కవటాకు **kawaTaaku** *n.* tender leaf.

కవన[ం] **kawana[m]** *n.* poetic composition, poetry.

కవయిత్రి **kawayitri** *n.* poetess.

కవర **kawara** *n., always suffixed to a word denoting a colo*[r] tinge, tint; **ciire niiLLaloo peTTagaanee, aakupac**[ca] **niiLLu waccEEyi** as soon as the sari was put in wat[er] water became tinged with green.

కవరు **kawaru** *n.* cover, envelope.

కవలపిల్లలు, కవలలు **kawalapillalu, kawalalu** *n.pl.* twins.

కవళిక **kawaLika** *n.* 1 facial features. 2 *pl.* **mukha ~ lu** facial expressions.

కవాచీ బల్ల **kawaacii balla** *n.* bench.

కవాటం **kawaaTam** *n.* 1 door. 2 valve.

కవాతు **kawaatu** *n.* 1 military drill. 2 physical exercise.

కవి **kawi** *n.* poet, bard.

కవిజనం **kawijanam** *n.pl.* poets.

కవిత, కవిత్వం **kawita, kawitwam** *n.* 1 poem. 2 poetry.

కవితాగానం **kawitaagaanam** *n.* recital of poetry.

కవితాత్మక **kawitaatmaka** *adj.* poetic.

కవిత్రయం **kawitrayam** *n.* the three great Telugu classical poets, Nannaya, Tikkana and Errana.

కవియు **kawiyu** *v.i.* 1 to rush upon, attack; **naa miidiki kawisi waccEEDu** he rushed at me. 2 *class.* to approach. 3 *class.* to spread.

కవిరి **kawiri** *n.* catechu (**kaacu**[5]) mixed with sediment of boiled arecanut made into pills for chewing with betel leaves.

కవిలె **kawile** *n. class.* 1 ledger. 2 **~ kaTTa** bundle or pile of books.

కవోష్ణం **kawooSNam** *n.* warmth.

కవ్వం **kawwam** *n.* churning stick.

కవ్వడి **kawwaDi** *n.* 1 ambidextrous person. 2 epithet of Arjuna.

కవ్వించు **kawwincu** *v.t.* 1 to provoke. 2 to tease. 3 to stir, arouse.

కశ **kaśa** *n.* whip, cord.

కశ్మలం **kaśmalam** *n.* foulness, nastiness, dirt, impurities.

కషాయం **kaSaayam** *n.* 1 decoction, potion, mixture (of liquids), brew. 2 Ayurvedic liquid medicine. 3 astringent taste.

కషాయి **kaSaayi** *adj.* red; **rooSa ~ neetraalu** eyes red with fury.

కష్టం **kaSTam** I. *n.* 1 trouble, difficulty; **kaSTaalanu anubhawincu** to experience difficulties. 2 labour, fatigue, effort; **naa rekkala ~ too illu kaTTEEnu** I built the house by my own efforts. 3 distress, sorrow, feeling hurt or offended; **naaku ~ weesindi** *or* **naaku ~ anipincindi** I felt distressed *or* I felt offended. II. *adj.* 1 hard, difficult. 2 distressful, unpleasant, painful; **naaku ~ gaa undi** it is difficult for me *or* it is painful to me; **daanitoo naaku manasu ~ aypooyindi** I took it to heart.

కష్టజీవి **kaSTajiiwi** *n.* one who lives a hard life.

కష్టతర **kaSTatara** *adj.* painstaking.

కష్టపడు **kaSTapaDu** *v.i.* to toil, work hard, exert o.s., take pains, take trouble, struggle.

...పెట్టు **kaSTapeTTu** *v.t.* to trouble, bother.

...పెట్టుకొను **kaSTapeTTukonu** *v.i.* to feel offended.

...ితం **kaSTaphalitam** *n.* result of suffering.

...ారాలు **kaSTaniSThuuraalu** *n.pl.* hardships and ...s.

...**kaSTasaadhya** *adj.* difficult to achieve.

కష్టార్జిత **kaSTaarjita** *adj.* hard-earned.

కష్టాలమారి **kaSTaalamaari** *n.* person who is beset by difficulties.

కష్టించు **kaSTincu** *v.i.* to work hard, labour, toil.

కసకస **kasakasa** *onom. adv. sug.* munching *or* chewing.

కసకసనమలు **kasakasa namalu** *v.t.* to munch, chew.

కసకసలాడు **kasakasalaaDu** *v.i.* to grind o.'s teeth in anger.

కసగు **kasagu** *same as* **kasugu.**

కసపిసలాడు **kasapisalaaDu** *v.i.* to be anxious.

కసరత్తు **kasarattu** *n.* 1 exercise. 2 gymnastics.

కసరత్తు చేయు **kasarattu ceeyu** *v.i.* to take exercise.

కసరు **kasaru** I. *n.* illhumour, sharp words, scolding. II. *v.t.* to scold, abuse, rebuke.

కసాయి **kasaayi** *n.* butcher.

కసాయితనం **kasaayitanam** *n.* mercilessness.

కసి **kasi** *n.* 1 spite, malice, grudge; **~ tiircukonu** to give vent to o.'s spite; **~ paTTu** to be spiteful. 2 itching, desire. 3 vengeance. 4 passion, anger.

కసింత, కాసింత, కుసింత **kasinta, kaasinta, kusinta** *adj. dial.* a little (= **koncem**).

కసికందు **kasikandu** I. *n.* infant, baby. II. *v.i.* 1 to change colour. 2 *colloq.* to become weak or tired: **ii maatram panikee kasikandipooyEEDu, eTLaa batukutaaDoo eemoo!** he has been tired by only this much work, how will he live, I wonder?

కసికాయ **kasikaaya** *n.* unripe fruit.

కసిగా **kasigaa** *adv.* 1 spitefully. 2 angrily. 3 vengefully, in revenge.

కసిడికోత **kasiDikoota** *n.* 1 cutting into small pieces. 2 constant torture.

కసిన్ని, కాసిన్ని, కుసిన్ని **kasinni, kaasinni, kusinni** *adj. dial.* some, a few (= **konni**).

కసీదాపని **kasiidaa pani** *n. dial.* embroidery.

కసుకాయ **kasukaaya** *n.* 1 *same as* **kasikaaya.** 2 little child; **amma caccipooyindi, pillalantaa ~ lu** the mother has died, the children are all young.

కసుక్కున **kasukkuna** *onom. adv. sug. sound made by* piercing *or* stabbing with a knife *or* biting with the teeth.

కసుగు, కసగు **kasugu, kasagu** I. *v.i. dial.* to be got or found. II. *v.t. dial.* 1 to give, yield. 2 to trouble. 3 to crush.

కసురు **kasuru** *n.* unripe fruit.

కసువు **kasuwu** *n.* 1 dust, dirt, sweepings. 2 straw and other sweepings left over after threshing. 3 hay, cattlefodder.

కసువుచిమ్ము, కసువూడ్చు **kasuwu cimmu, kasuwuuDcu** *v.i.* to sweep up dust.

కస్తూరి **kastuuri** *n.* musk.

కస్తూరిమృగం **kastuuri mrgam** *n.* musk deer.

కస్బా **kasbaa** *n.* headquarters town of a district.

కస్బీలు **kasbiilu** *n. pl. dial.* tips, bribes.

కస్సుమను **kassumanu** *v.i.* 1 to hiss. 2 to be angry.

కా - kaa

కా **kaa**[1] *adjvl. prefix meaning* bad, mean, insignificant, *as in* **kaapuruSuDu** bad man.

కా **kaa**[2] *n.* caw, the sound made by a crow.

కా **kaa**[3] *imperative sing. and infinitive of* **awu.**

కా **kaa**[4] *particle, same as* **kadaa.**

కాంక్ష **kaankSa** *n.* wish, desire, inclination.

కాంక్షించు **kaankSincu** *v.t.* to wish, desire, long for.

కాంక్షితం **kaankSitam** *n.* requirement.

కాంచన[ం] **kaancana[m]** *adj.* gold[en].

కాంచనం **kaancanam** *n.* gold.

కాంచి **kaanci** *n.* girdle made of gold worn by a woman or child.

కాంచు, గాంచు **kaancu, gaancu** *v.t.* 1 *class.* to have, obtain, acquire, achieve; *mod.* **peeru kaancina** famous. 2 *class* to see, behold; *cf.* **kalagaacu.**

కాంజి **kaanji** *n. dial., same as* **kali**[2].

కాంటు **kaaNTa** *n. dial.* safety pin.

కాంటా **kaaNTaa** *n. dial.* simple balance.

కాంటాయించు **kaaNTaayincu** *v.t.* to get (s.g) weighed.

కాండ **kaaNDa** *n.* 1 rite, ritual, custom. 2 *journ., suffixed to certain words denoting violence, it expresses widespread or continuous activities* **dahana~** incendiarism; **hatyaa~** succession of killings; **himsaa~** reign of terror.

కాండ[ం] **kaaNDa[m]**[1] *n. class.* 1 division, chapter, section. 2 one of the six sections of the Ramayana.

కాండం **kaaNDam**[2] *n.* 1 stem, stalk, trunk. 2 core.

కాండ్రించు **kaaNDrincu**[1] *v.i.* to hawk, clear o.'s throat.

కాండ్రించు **kaaNDrincu**[2], **gaaNDrincu** *v.i.* to roar (like a tiger).

కాండ్రింపు, గాండ్రింపు **kaaNDrimpu, gaaNDrimpu** *n.* swelling or flushing of the face due to anger or fever;~**moham peTTEEDu** he wore an angry or grim look:**jwaram tagginaa mohamloo~taggaleedu** although the fever went down, his face was still flushed.

కాండ్రు, గాండ్రు **kaaNDru, gaaNDru** *n.* tiger's roar.

కాంత **kaanta** *n.* woman.

కాంతారం **kaantaaram** *n. class.* forest.

కాంతి **kaanti** *n.* 1 brilliancy, lustre, gleam. 2 light; ~**kiraNam** ray or beam of jight.

కాంతినిరోధక **kaantiniroodhaka** *adj.* opaque.

కాంతివంత **kaantiwanta** *adj.* brilliant.

కాంతిశాస్త్రం **kaantiśaastram** *n.* (science of) optics.

కాంతి హీన **kaantihiina** *adj.* dull, tarnished, lustreless.

కాంతుడు **kaantuDu** *n.* 1 lover. 2 husband.

కాందిశీకం **kaandiśiikam** *n.* fleeing.

కాందిశీకుడు **kaandiśiikuDu** *n.* refugee, displaced person, evacuee.

కాంస్య **kaamsya** *adj.* bell metal, bronze:~**wigraham** bronze statue; ~**patakam** bronze medal.

కాక **kaaka**[1] *neg. participle of* **awu** not[being]; **marunaaDu~muuDoo naaDu** not the next day but the one after that; **payna wiwarincina bhuumulu~migataa praantam caalaawaraku erra bhuumi** apart from (*or* other than) the soils described above, the remaining area is mainly red soil; **guNamulee~dooSamulu kuuDaa prakaTincaka tappadu** I must proclaim not only the good points but also the defects.

కాక **kaaka**[2] *n.* 1 fever[ishness]: **caNTipillawaaDoki~tagilindi** the baby caught fever. 2 heat, warmth. 3 anger, harshness: ~**miida unnaaDu** he is hot with anger.

కాక **kaaka**[3] *particle with optative force, class., mod. only in formal utterances* **miiku śubham agu~!** may you be fortunate! **miiru weLLee pani jarugu~!** may the work that you are going for be accomplished!

కాకం **kaakam** *n.* crow.

కాకంటు చేయు, కాకెంగిలి చేయు **kaakaNTu ceeyu, kaakengili ceeyu** *v.i., child language* to cover s.g eatable with a cloth, bite a piece off and give it to another person to eat, thus avoiding saliva pollution.

కాకతాళీయం **kaakataaLiiyam** *n.* mere chance, coincidence.

కాకతాళీయంగా **kaakataaLiiyangaa** *adv.* by mere chance.

కాకమ్మ కథలు **kaakamma kathalu** *n.pl.* invented imaginary stories, fables.

కాకమ్మ కబుర్లు **kaakamma kaburlu** *n.pl.* vain or idle talk, gossip.

కాకర **kaakara** *n.* bitter gourd, *momordica charantia.*

కాకర పువ్వొత్తు, కాకర పువ్వొత్తి **kaakara puwwottu, kaakara puwwotti** *n.* kind of firework.

కాకలి **kaakali** *n. class.* sweet tone or sound.

కాకలు తీరిన **kaakalu tiirina** *adj. journ.* sobered, matured.

కాకాక్షన్యాయం **kaakaakSanyaayam** *n.* argument that cuts both ways.

కాకాపట్టు **kaakaa paTTu** *v.t.* to curry favour (with s.o.).

కాకి **kaaki** *n.* crow; ~**ceeta kaburu pampistee neenu rekkalu kaTTukuni wacci waalataanu** if you send a message by any means at all, I will come at once.

కాకి గోల **kaaki goola** *n.* clamour.

కాకి చావు **kaaki caawu** *n.* sudden death from apoplexy.

కాకితం **kaakitam** *same as* **kaagitam.**

కాకి బంగారం **kaaki bangaaram** *n.* imitation gold, tinsel.

కాకిరాయి **kaakiraayi** *n. geol.* quartzite.

కాకిసొమ్మ **kaakisomma** *n.* epilepsy.

కాకీ **kaakii** *same as* **khaakii.**

కాకుండా **kaakuNDaa** *neg. participle of* **awu** 1 without being, not being, not; **aayana ingliiSu maaTLaaDitee itara mEESTarlu maaTLaaDinaTLu ~ inkoo rakangaa uNDeedi** when he spoke English, it was not as the other schoolmasters spoke it, but differently. 2 besides, in addition.

కాకువు **kaakuwu** *n.* change in tone of voice or intonation pattern to indicate the speaker's mood or convey his intention.

కాకెంగిలిచేయు **kaakengili ceeyu** *same as* **kaakNTu ceeyu.**

కాకేం? **kaakeem?** *minor sentence* why not?, of course!

కాకోదరం **kaakoodaram** *n. class.* snake, serpent.

కాగడ, కాగడా **kaagaDa, kaagaDaa** *n.* torch.

కాగల **kaagala** *adj.* about to be, about to happen, future; ~ **kaaryam** event that is about to happen.

కాగా **kaagaa** *infinitive of* **awu** + *particle* **gaa** *used with conjunctive force* 1 this being so, while this is/was so, however, nevertheless, on the other hand, but now, and now, moreover; ~ **ii sankalanamloo ceercina sampaadakiiyaalanu gurinci kuuDaa konta ceppaali** but now I must also say something about the editorials gathered in this collection. 2 whereas, although; **sangiita muurtitrayamloo modaTi waaru tyaagayya ~ takkina iddaruu muttuswaami diikSitulu, śyaama śaastri** whereas the first member of the trio of great musicians is Tyagaraja, the other two are Muthuswamy Dikshit and Syama Sastri. 3 compared with, as against; **mottam widyaku peTTina kharcu nuuTa arawai aaru kooTla ruupaayalu ~, okka praathamika widyaku maatramee debbhay reNDu kooTLu keeTaayincinaaru** as against the total expenditure on education of Rs. 166 crores, they allotted Rs. 72 crores for primary education alone.

కాగితం, కాయితం, కాకితం **kaagitam, kaayitam, kaakitam** *n.* paper.

కాగు **kaagu** I. *n.* 1 vessel for boiling water, etc. 2 large vessel for storing grain. II. *v.i.* 1 to grow hot, be heated. 2 to boil. 3 to be angry.

కాగుడు **kaaguDu** *n.* heating, boiling; **niiLLu ippDee ~ paTTEEyi** the water is just now beginning to boil.

కాచం **kaacam** *n. class.* glass.

కాచాభ **kaacaabha** *adj. sci.* glassy, transparent.

కాచివడబోయు **kaaciwaDabooyu** *v.t.* to experience or know thoroughly; **kaSTaalanu kaaciwaDaboosina waaLLu** persons who have had their fill of troubles; **miiru ceppakkaraleedu, aayanni kaaciwaDaboosEEnu** you need say nothing, I know him through and through.

కాచు, కాయు **kaacu,[1] kaayu[1]** *v.i.* (of a tree) to bear fruit, (of fruit) to ripen on a tree; **ceTTu wiraga kaacindi** the tree is in full bearing *or* the tree has produced a heavy crop; *see* **iinu.**

కాచు, కాయు **kaacu[2], kaayu[2]** *v.i.* (of sun, moon) to shine, (of sun, fever) to be hot; **eNDa baagaa kaastunnadi** the sun is shining brightly *or* the sun is very hot; **ataniki jwaram kaastunnadi** he has a raging fever; **aDawi kaacina wennela** moonlight shining in the forest (a proverbial phrase for wasted effort).

కాచు, కాయు **kaacu[3], kaayu[3]** *v.t.* to heat, warm, boil; **saaraa ~** to distil arrack.

కాచు, కాయు **kaacu[4], kaayu[4]** *v.t.* 1 to watch, guard. 2 to save, preserve, keep, retain; **neela cemma kaastundi** the soil retains moisture. 3 to ward off, keep off, stave off; **nidra kaacaleewu** you cannot stave off sleep *or* you cannot remain awake. 4 to protect, tend, look after. 5 to spare, forgive, excuse; **tappu ~** to excuse a mistake. 6 to bear, endure; **tannulu/debbalu ~** to suffer blows. 7 **pandem ~** to place or make a bet or wager. 8 **kommu ~** to support, assist, give or lend support to.

కాచు **kaacu[5]** *n.* catechu, juice of an acacia tree called **khadiram** used for mixing with betel and nut.

కాచుకొను **kaacukonu** I. *v.i.* 1 to watch out, be on o.'s guard, guard o.s., take care. 2 to warm o.s.; *see* **cali.** II. *v.t.* 1 to watch, tend, mind (cattle). 2 to ward off (blows).

కాజా **kaajaa** *n.* 1 kind of sweet. 2 *colloq.* ~ **lu tinu** to suffer blows. 3 button hole.

కాజీ **kaajii** *n.* kazi, Muslim priest or judge.

కాజు **kaaju** *n. dial.* cashewnut.

కాజేయు **kaajeeyu** *v.t.* 1 to make away with, misappropriate, steal. 2 to get s.g done or finished; **mundu ii pani kaajeesi, taruwaata maaTLaaDu** first get this work finished, then talk.

కాటకం **kaaTakam** *n.* famine, dearth, scarcity.

కాటమరాజు **kaaTamaraaju** *n.* a village god worshipped by cowherds; ~ **kathalu** folk tales told about **kaaTamaraaju.**

కాటా **kaaTaa** *n.* large weighing scales; ~ **bastaa** standard bag of rice weighing one quintal.

కాటా కట్టు, కాటా వేయు **kaaTaa kaTTu, kaaTaa weeyu** *v.t.* to weigh.

కాటిపాపడు **kaaTipaapaDu** *n.* cowherd.

కాటు **kaaTu** *n.* 1 bite; **paamu ~** snake bite. 2 sting (of a scorpion). 3 notch, indentation.

కాటుక **kaaTuka** *n.* lamp black, eye salve, collyrium.

కాటుక తెగులు **kaaTuka tegulu** *n.* crop disease called smut.

కాటుక పిట్ట **kaaTukapiTTa** *n.* wagtail.

కాటుపోవు **kaaTu poowu** *v.i.* (of food) to be overboiled or scorched while cooking.

కాటువాసన **kaaTu waasana** *n.* smell of food which has been overboiled or scorched.

కాటువేయు **kaaTu weeyu** *v.t.* 1 to bite. 2 (of a scorpion) to sting.

కాట్రగడ **kaaTragaDa** *n. class.* stockade.

కాట్రేటి చీర **kaaTreeTiciira** *n.* black and red sari worn by pregnant women to ward off evil omens.

కాట్రేడు **kaaTreeDu** *n.* lord of the burial ground, an epithet of Siva.

కాట్లకుక్క **kaaTLakukka** *n.* vicious dog (likely to bite); **aayana ~ laagaa wiidhina paDDaaDu** he goes about the street like a vicious dog, i.e., he is a quarrelsome person.

కాట్లమారి **kaaTLamaari** *n.* quarrelsome person.

కాట్లాట **kaaTLaaTa** *n.* quarrel, wrangling.

కాఠిన్యం **kaaThinyam** *n.* harshness, roughness, severity, sternness, grimness, cruelty.

కాడ **kaaDa**[1] *n.* 1 stem, stalk, shoot. 2 handle, haft; **gariTe~** handle of a spoon or ladle. 3 **mulak~** drumstick pod.

కాడ **kaaDa**[2] *p.p. dial.* at, with, near, by; **aayana~** with him; **iNTi~** at home.

కాడి **kaaDi** *n.* 1 yoke. 2 *colloq.* **neenu weLLamani ceppinaa kadalakuNDaa ~laa nilabaDDaaDu** although I told him to go, he stood there stolidly without moving (*lit.* he stood there like a yoke).

కాడికి **kaaDiki** *p.p. and adv.* 1 to (=**daggira**); **iNTi~pooyi tiisukuraa** go home and bring it. 2 to the extent that (= **meeraku**) **naaku kaligina~istaanu** I will give as much as is possible for me. 3 for a (certain) price, at a (certain) rate (=**coppuna**); **waaLLu ee~aDigitee nuwwu aa~istaawu** you will give it for the price (*or* at the rate) that they demand. 4 **aa~** if it comes to that, in that event; **miiru waariki ceppaleekapootee, aa~ neenee cebtaanu** if you cannot tell them, then if it comes to that I will tell them myself. 5 **ee kaDikii waaDu manciwaaDee, neenee ceDDawaaNNi ani miiru cebutunnaaru** you are saying that in every way he is a good person and only I am bad.

కాడిగట్టు **kaaDigaTTu** *n.* boundary ridge between fields.

కాడిపీట **kaaDipiiTa** *n.* short piece of wood under a yoke.

కాడిరాయి **kaaDiraayi** *n.* boundary stone between fields.

కాడు, గాడు **kaaDu**[1], **gaaDu**[1] *n. suffix denoting the male sex* **jiita~** male servant, salaried man; **moosa~** cheat, impostor; *cf.* **atagaaDu.**

కాడు **kaaDu**[2] *n.* 1 burial ground, cemetery, graveyard. 2 forest.

కాణాచి **kaaNaaci** *n.* 1 abode. 2 repository, storehouse, treasury. 3 inherited right. 4 source, origin.

కాణీ, కాని **kaaNi, kaani** *n.* obsolete small coin equal to 1/64 of a rupee; **naadaggara cilli~kuuDaa leedu** I have not even a pie with me.

కాతర **kaatara** *adj.* timid, confused; **~drSTi** timid look.

కాతా, ఖాతా **kaataa, khaataa** *n.* running account.

కాతాదారు,ఖాతాదారు **kaataadaaru, khaataadaaru** *n.* customer with a running account, regular customer.

కాదంబరి **kaadambari** *n.* name of a famous collection of stories in Sanskrit.

కాదంబిని **kaadambini** *n. class.* line or bank of clouds.

కాదను **kaadanu** *v.i. and t.* 1 to deny, contradict, gainsay. 2 to say no to, refuse; **anumaanangaanee unnaa awatali wyakti maaTanu kaadanaleeDu** although he was doubtful, he could not refuse the other person's request.

కాదాచిత్కంగా **kaadaacitkangaa** *adv.* occasionally.

కాదుకూడదను **kaadukuuDadanu** *v.i.* to deny or refuse flatly.

కాన[నం] **kaana[nam]** *n. class.* forest.

కానమి **kaanami** *n.* 1 not seeing. 2 omission, oversight.

కానవచ్చు **kaanawaccu** *v.i.* to appear, be visible, be found.

కానా **kaanaa** *n.* 1 channel. 2 groove. 3 small hole.

కాని **kaani**[1] *same as* **kaaNi.**

కాని, గాని **kaani**[2], **gaani** I. *neg. vbl. adj. of* **awu** not being, not, other than, non-; **granthastham~ śiSTabhaaSa** educated speech that is not book language; **wiwaadagrastam~** non-controversial; **uuru~uuru** a town that is not o.'s own. II. *adj.* bad, wicked, hard, difficult; **~panulu** wicked acts; **~kaalam** hard times; **~waaDu** (i) person who is not related or not a close friend, (ii) person who is difficult to deal with, tough character. III. *particle* 1 (*with adversative meaning*) but, yet, however. 2 (*with alternative meaning*) either. . . or; **miiru~neenu~weLLaali** either you or I must go. 3 *following a conditional form* + **nee** unless; **cuusteenee ~ nammanu** unless I see I will not believe. 4 *following a time expression in neg. constr.* until; **V kaapuraaniki weLLEEka~ asalu wiSayaalu ewarikii artham kaaleedu** until V. went to live with her husband, no one understood the real facts; **padi roojulaku~raaDu** he will not come for ten days *or* he will not come until ten days have passed. 5 *in neg. constr.* except, but for; **antee~ naaku mareemii teliyadu** except for that much I know nothing more; **eppuDoo~ ciirelu kaTTaru** they do not wear saris except on some occasions. 6 *at the end of a clause or sentence or attached to a n., pron. or vb.* ~ *contributes to the indefiniteness of the utterance, e.g.,* **ewaroo** someone; **ewaroo~** someone or other; **peTTeloo~ peTTEEnaa?** did I put in a box, perhaps? **eem cuTTa kampu! ewaDu kaalacEEDoo~** what a smell of cigars! someone must have been smoking; **miiku~ii wiSayam ceppEEnaa?** did I ever tell you this? *see* **kanuka.**

కానిచ్చు, అవనిచ్చు **kaaniccu, awaniccu** *v.i.* to let s.g happen or be done, get s.g done or finished, allow s.g to proceed.

కానీ, కానివ్వండి **kaanii**[1], **kaaniwwaNDi** *infinitive of* **awu** + *imperative of* **iccu**, *with the force of a minor sentence or particle* 1 so be it, so let it be, let it be done, all right, very well. 2 whether it be; **adi kawitwam ~, gaNitaśaastram~, citraleekhanam~, waydyaśaastram~, wiiTanniTiloo reNDeesi rakaalu unnayi, pyuur aND aplayD aneedi** whether it be poetry, mathematics, painting or medical science, there are two varieties in each, namely, pure and applied.

కానీ **kaanii**[2] *variant form of* **kaani**[2].

కానీనుడు **kaaniinuDu** *n. class.* son of a virgin.

కాను **kaanu**[1] *v.t. class.* to see, behold; *mod. in certain phrases, e.g.,* **kannu minnu kaanaka** without having any consideration for others, arrogantly.

కాను, గాను **kaanu**[2], **gaanu** *particle added to dative case* for the purpose of (= **koosam**) **ii ceesindantaa endukugaanu?** for what purpose was all this done?

కానుండు **kaanuNDu** *v.i.* to be going to be, be going to happen; **mundeem kaanundaa ani talacukoNTee bhayangaa undi** it is frightening to think what is going to happen.

కానుక **kaanuka** *n.* gift, offering, present[ation].

కానుకొను **kaanukonu** *v.t.* 1 to foresee. 2 to consider carefully. 3 to think twice (colloq)..

కానుగ **kaanuga** *n.* pungam tree, *pongamia glabra.*

కానుపు **kaanupu** *n.* delivery, childbearing.

కానుపు పోయు **kaanupu pooyu** *v.i.* to perform a delivery.

కానైతే **kaanaytee** *conj.* but then, however.

కాపట్యం **kaapaTyam** *n.* deceitfulness, hypocrisy.

కాపరి **kaapari** *n.* keeper, watcher, guard; **kaaTi~** caretaker of a burial ground; **gorrela~** shepherd; **paśula~** herdsman.

కావలా **kaapalaa** *n.* keeping watch, guarding.

కావలా ఉంచు, కావలా పెట్టు **kaapalaa uncu, kaapalaa peTTu** *v.t.* to place s.o. as a guard.

కావలా కాచు **kaapalaa kaacu** I. *v.i.* to keep watch. II. *v.t.* to watch over, guard.

కావలాదారు[డు] **kaapalaadaaru[Du]** *n.* watchman.

కాపాడు **kaapaaDu** *v.t.* 1 to guard, watch. 2 to keep, preserve, safeguard. 3 to save, rescue.

కాపాలి[కుడు] **kaapaali[kuDu]** *n.* one who wears a garland of skulls.

కాపీనం **kaapiinam** *n.* miserliness.

కాపు **kaapu** *n.* 1 name of a community in Andhra Pradesh. 2 cultivator, farmer. 3 protection, watch[ing], guard[ing]. 4 productiveness, bearing; **ii eeDaadi ceTTu ~ku waccindi** this year the tree has come into bearing. 5 crop, fruit. 6 heat, warmth.

కాపుకాచు **kaapukaacu** *v.i. and t.* 1 to guard, watch over. 2 to bear fruit.

కాపుగడ, కాపుదల **kaapugaDa, kaapudala** *n.* guarding, watching, protection.

కాపుబాన, కాపుకుండ **kaapubaana, kaapukuNDa** *n* large earthen pot with a thick base.

కాపురం **kaapuram** *n.* 1 residing, esp. of a wife residing with her husband. 2 family life; **waaLLa kaapuraalu nilawawu ilaa aytee** if it goes on like this, their family life will not last. 3 home, dwelling, residence. 4 household; **ii wiidhiloo iraway kaapuraalu unnaayi** there are twenty households in this street. 5 *dial.* agriculture.

కాపురస్థుడు **kaapurasthuDu** *n. admin.* inhabitant, resident; **marripuuDi graama~ yeggayyagaaru** Yeggayya, a resident of Marripudi village.

కాపురుషుడు **kaapuruSuDu** *n.* bad or wicked person.

కాఫీ **kaaphii** *n.* coffee; **~ kalupu** to prepare coffee; **~ ginjalu** coffee seeds; **~ biLLalu** coffee powder cubes.

కాబట్టి **kaabaTTi** *conj.* therefore, for that reason.

కాబడు **kaabaDu** *v.i.* to become, be made.

కాబోయే **kaabooyee** *fut. vbl. adj. of* **kaapoowu** going to be, future, prospective; **~ moguDu** future husband.

కాబోలు, కామోసు, గావును, గామాలు **kaaboolu, kaamoosu, gaawunu, gaamaalu** *adv.* perhaps, probably, surely.

కామ **kaama** *n.* handle or haft of an axe, hoe or similar implement.

కామం **kaamam** *n.* lust, passion.

కామంచిగడ్డి **kaamanci gaDDi** *n.* lemon grass, *andropogon nardus.*

కామంచి చెట్టు **kaamanci ceTTu** *n. solanum nigrum,* a plant used in Indian medicine.

కామందు, ఖామందు **kaamandu, khaamandu** *n.* owner, master, boss; **bhuu~** land owner, landlord.

కామక **kaamaka** *adv.* certainly, definitely, positively.

కామకూటం **kaamakuuTam** ~~*n.*~~ prostitution.

కామకేళి, కామక్రీడ **kaamakeeLi, kaamakriiDa** *n.* amorous sport, copulation.

కామధేనువు **kaamadheenuwu** *n.* mythical cow which gives all that is desired.

కామపిశాచి **kaamapiśaaci** *n.* demon of lust.

కామరూపవిద్య **kaamaruupa widya** *n. class.* the power to assume any shape or form that is desired.

కామల **kaamala** *n.* jaundice.

కామవాంఛ **kaamawaancha** *n.* passion, lust.

కామా **kaamaa** *n.* comma.

కామాంధుడు **kaamaandhuDu** *n.* person blinded by passion and lust.

కామాటం **kaamaaTam** *n.* 1 obsession. 2 worry, bother; **enduku waccina ~?** why bother about it? 3 involvement in family ties; **illu peLLaam pillalu anee ~loo paDDaaDu, kanipincaDam leedu** he is entirely occupied with family matters, so he is not to be seen.

కామాటి **kaamaaTi** *n.* field labourer, sundry labourer.

కామాతురుడు **kaamaaturuDu** *n.* person who is sick with passion.

కామాత్ముడు **kaamaatmuDu** *n.* lustful person.

కామాపు చేయు, కైమాపు చేయు **kaamaapu ceeyu, kaymaapu ceeyu** *v.t.* to hush up (crimes).

కామాల **kaamaala** *n. dial.* jaundice.

కామి **kaami** *n.* loving or passionate person.

కామిని **kaamini** *n.* 1 woman. 2 passionate woman. 3 **~ dayyam** ghost.

కాముక **kaamuka** *adj.* lustful.

కాముకత్వం **kaamukatwam** *n.* lustfulness.

కాముకి **kaamuki** *n.* 1 lustful woman. 2 prostitute.

కాముకుడు **kaamukuDu** *n.* 1 lustful person. 2 *in compounds* person desirous of or attracted by s.g; **śaanti~** peace lover; **abhyudaya~** progressive-minded person.

కాముడు **kaamuDu** *n.* 1 a name of Cupid. 2 demon of lust.

కామెర్లు **kaamerlu** *n.pl.* jaundice.

కామోష్! **kaamooS!** *interj.* hush!, be quiet!, silence!

కామోసు **kaamoosu** *same as* **kaaboolu.**

కామ్యం **kaamyam** I. *n.* s.g desirable. II. *adj.* desirable.

కాయ **kaaya** *n.* 1 green unripe fruit; **maamiDi~** green mango. 2 nut, pod, bulb; **Ten~** coconut; **śenak~** groundnut; **doosa~** cucumber; **mirapa~** chilli. 3 any round object (e.g. ball, knob); **gooli~** marble; **tala~** head; **poDum~** snuff box; **taabeTi~** tortoise shell. 4 wart, callus, lump or swelling on the body; **waaDi ceetulu ~lu kaasEEyi** his hands are covered with swellings. 5 bottle; **sooDaa~** soda water bottle. 6 playing piece or 'man' in a game like chess or carroms. 7 *affixed to certain nouns, it contributes nothing to the meaning,* e.g., **pilla~** child; **gontu~** (*or* **meDa~**) neck; **enDra~** crab.

కాయం **kaayam**[1] *n. class.* body.

కాయం **kaayam**[2] *n.* medicine containing asafoetida given to a woman at time of childbirth.

కాయకం **kaayakam** *n.* deceitfulness; **Dabbu ekkaDoo~ ceesEEDu** he has caused the money to disappear somewhere.

కాయకన్ను **kaayakannu** *n.* blind eye.

కాయకల్పన చికిత్స **kaayakalpana cikitsa** *n.* Ayurvedic treatment designed to bring about rejuvenation.

కాయకష్టం **kaayakaSTam** *n.* physical labour, hard work.

కాయగూరలు **kaayaguuralu** *n. pl.* vegetables.

కాయధాన్యాలు **kaayadhaanyaalu** *n. pl.* pulses (produce of legumes).

కాయపురుగు **kaayapurugu** *n.* pod borer.

కాయ వేయు **kaaya weeyu** *v.i.* 1 to bear fruit. 2 to make a move in chess or strike a playing piece in carroms.

కాయ[బారు] శరీరం **kaaya[baaru] śariiram** *n.* strong body.

కాయస్థుడు **kaayasthuDu** *n.* 1 member of a community of accountants. 2 the Supreme Soul as indweller in a body.

కాయితం **kaayitam** *same as* **kaagitam.**

కాయిలా **kaayilaa** *n.* illness, sickness.

కాయు **kaayu**1,2,3,4 *same as* **kaacu.**

కారం **kaaram**1 *n.* 1 pungency, hot taste. 2 spices, hot stuff.

కారం **kaaram**2 *particle added to a letter in naming it, e.g.,* **ikaaram** the letter *i*.

కారక **kaaraka** *adj.* 1 *gram.* relating to a case; ~ **pratyayam** case suffix. 2 *last part of an adjvl. compound* causing, making, creating, contributing to; **kalaha**~ creating quarrels.

కారకం **kaarakam** *n.* 1 *gram.* case. 2 factor; **manoowayjnaanika kaarakaalu** psychological factors.

కారకుడు **kaarakuDu** *n.* responsible person.

కారణం **kaaraNam** *n.* 1 cause, reason, ground. 2 source. 3 motive.

కారణంగా **kaaraNangaa** *p.p.* by reason of, because of, as a result of, due to.

కారణజన్ముడు **kaaraNajanmuDu** *n.* s.o. who was destined at birth to fulfil a certain purpose.

కారణభూతం **kaaraNabhuutam** *n.* cause.

కారణభూతుడు **kaaraNabhuutuDu** *n.* originator.

కారణాంతరాలు **kaaraNaantaraalu** *n. pl.* different reasons, other reasons.

కారాకిల్లీ **kaaraakillii** *same as* **khaaraakillii.**

కారాకు **kaaraaku** *n.* withering yellow leaf.

కారాగారం, కారాగృహం **kaaragaaram, kaaraagrham** *n.* prison, jail.

కారాగారవాసం, కారాగృహవాసం **kaaraagaarawaasam, kaaraagrhawaasam** *n.* imprisonment.

కారి **kaari**1 I. *n: suffix denoting* actor *or* agent, e.g., **upa**~ benefactor: **moosa**~ cheat. II. *adjvl. suffix meaning* making, causing: **doohada**~ making a contribution, contributing: **rooga**~ causing disease.

కారి **kaari**2 *n.* saline soil containing an admixture of clay.

కారిక **kaarika** *n. class.* explanatory verse.

కారిజం **kaarijam** *n. class* liver.

కారు **kaaru**1 I. *n.* 1 season, time of year, rainy season; **waana**~**roojulu** the rainy season; ~**paNTa** crop grown during the rains; **naalugu**~**la gitta** heifer four years (*lit.* four seasons) old; **ii gaDDa munigitee**~ **paNDutundi** if this land is submerged, the season will be a good one. 2 forest. 3 black colour. 4 saltiness, brackishness. 5 blade of a hoe. 6 type, kind, class, group; **gaDee**~**maniSi** tall thin person (*lit.* bamboo type person): **skuulu wyawahaaraalu nirwahincaDaaniki kotta**~ **waccindi** a new group (of people) came to run the affairs of the school; **kurra**~ young people, youth; **sanna**~**raytulu** small farmers. II. *adj.* 1 black; ~**mabbulu** black clouds; ~**nalla** pitch black, jet black. 2 of the forest, wild; ~**ciccu** wild fire, forest fire; **kaaraDawi** jungle. 3 brackish, salty. 4 ~ **waasana** smell of singeing, stale smell, rancid smell. 5 **kaaraaku** withered leaf. 6 ~**cawka** very cheap. 7 ~ **kuutalu** foul language, abuse.

కారు **kaaru**2 *v.i.* to flow, trickle, leak, exude.

కారుకొను **kaarukonu** *v.i.* (of clouds) to turn black.

కారుణ్యం **kaaruNyam** *n.* mercy, pity.

కారుపోతు **kaarupootu** *n.* wild buffalo (male).

కారుసీసం **kaaru siisam** *n.* black lead.

కారెం **kaarem** *n.* curved palmyra trough used for baling.

కారెనుము **kaarenumu** *n.* wild buffalo (female).

కార్కశ్యం **kaarkaśyam** *n. class.* hardness, harshness, roughness, cruelty.

కార్ఖానా **kaarkhaanaa** *n.* workshop, factory.

కార్చు **kaarcu** *v.t.* 1 to cause to flow or drip. 2 to shed (tears), exude (sap). 3 **conga**~ to dribble.

కార్తికం, కార్తీకం **kaartikam, kaartiikam** *n.* the eighth Telugu lunar month.

కార్తె **kaarte** *n. astrol.* period of about $13^1/_2$ days spent by the sun in each one of the 27 constellations through which it passes during the course of a year; **roohiNi** ~**loo eNDaku rooLLu baddalawutaayi** in Rohini karte even mortars will crack in the sun's extreme heat (proverbial saying).

కార్పణ్యం **kaarpaNyam** *n.* malice, ill-will, spite, ill-feeling.

కార్మిక **kaarmika** *adj.* relating or belonging to labourers or workers; ~**sangham** trade union.

కార్మికుడు **kaarmikuDu** *n.* worker, labourer.

కార్ముకం **kaarmukam** *n. class.* 1 bow. 2 bamboo.

కార్యం **kaaryam** *n.* 1 act, action, deed, work. 2 business, affair, deal. 3 object, purpose. 4 effect; **kaarya kaaraNa sambandham** the connection between cause and effect. 5 celebration, function, festive occasion; ~**paTLa naluguruu wastaaru** many people will come for the function. 6 **pitr**~ father's death ceremonies. 7 celebration marking the consummation of a marriage, nuptial ceremony; *see* **sandhi**~

కార్యంచీర **kaaryam ciira** *n.* sari given to the bride by the bridegroom's family on the occasion of the nuptial ceremony.

కార్యం పెళ్లికొడుకు **kaaryam peLLikoDuku** *n.* the groom at the nuptial ceremony.

కార్యకర్త **kaaryakarta** *n.* 1 active worker, organiser. 2 office bearer.

కార్యకలాపాలు **kaaryakalaapaalu** *n. pl.* affairs, activities, proceedings.

కార్యకారి **kaaryakaari** *adj. admin.* acting (for a temporary period).

కార్యక్రమం **kaaryakramam** *n.* programme.

కార్యక్షేత్రం **kaaryakSeetram** *n.* field of activity, walk of life.

కార్యదక్షత **kaaryadakSata** *n.* practical wisdom, practicality.

కార్యదక్షుడు **kaaryadakSuDu** *n.* practical person.

కార్యదర్శి **kaaryadarśi** *n.* secretary.

కార్యదీక్ష **kaaryadiikSa** *n.* dedication, devotion, commitment (to an object or goal).

కార్యనిర్వహణ **kaaryanirwahaNa** *n.* execution (of work).

కార్యనిర్వాహక **kaaryanirwaahaka** *adj.* executive; ~ **wargam** executive committee.

కార్యనిర్వాహకుడు **kaaryanirwaahakuDu** *n.* executive.

కార్యభారం **kaaryabhaaram** *n.* 1 workload. 2 duty, responsibility.

కార్యరంగం **kaaryarangam** *n.* field of action, field of activity.

కార్యరూపం **kaaryaruupam** *n.* material form.

కార్యరూపం ధరించు, కార్యరూపం దాల్చు **kaaryaruupam dharincu, kaaryaruupam daalcu** *v.i.* to materialise, fructify.

కార్యవర్గం **kaaryawargam** *n.* committee.

కార్యవర్తన **kaaryawartana** I. *n. legal* operation. II. *adj. legal* operative.

కార్యవాదం **kaaryawaadam** *n.* pragmatism.

కార్యవాది **kaaryawaadi** *n.* 1 practical person. 2 pragmatist. 3 man of action.

కార్యవిధి **kaaryawidhi** *n.* function.

కార్యశూరత్వం **kaaryaśuuratwam** *n.* determination, persistence.

కార్యసమీక్ష **kaaryasamiikSa** *n.* review (of action taken).

కార్యసాధక **kaaryasaadhaka** *adj.* effective.

కార్యసాధకుడు **kaaryasaadhakuDu** *n.* competent person.

కార్యసాధన[ం] **kaaryasaadhana[m]** *n.* achievement (of an object), implementation.

కార్యసిద్ధి **kaaryasiddhi** *n.* accomplishment, completion, fulfilment (of a task).

కార్యాచరణ **kaaryaacaraNa** n. implementation.

కార్యార్థి **kaaryaarthi** *n.* person who has a purpose to fulfil.

కార్యాలయం **kaaryaalayam** *n.* office.

కార్యాలయ సామగ్రి **kaaryaalaya saamagri** *n.* stationery.

కాల **kaala** *same as* **kaaLa.**

కాలం **kaalam** *n.* 1 time, occasion, period; **waaDikeem pooyee kaalamoo!** *lit.* is it going time for him? *or* is it time for him to die? *this phrase is used as a form of expostulation*; **aa munasabukeem pooyee kaalamoo kaanii monna utta puNyaaniki subbamma geedelni bandelaDoDDiki toolincEEDu!** the day before yesterday the munsiff—confound him!—had Subbamma's buffaloes driven to the cattle pound for no reason at all. 2 season; **maamiDi paLLu ~ kaani ~ loo wastunnaayi** mangoes are arriving out of season. 3 *gram.* tense.

కాలంచేయు **kaalam ceeyu** *v.i.* to die, pass away.

కాలకంఠుడు **kaalakaNThuDu** *n.* epithet of Siva.

కాలకూటం **kaalakuuTam** *n.* kind of deadly poison.

కాలకృత్యాలు **kaalakṛtyaalu** *n. pl.* daily routine: ~ **tiirucukonu** to perform o.'s morning routine.

కాలక్రమ **kaalakrama** *adj.* gradual.

కాలక్రమం **kaalakramam** *n.* chronology.

కాలక్రమంలో, కాలక్రమేణా **kaalakramamloo, kaalakrameeNaa** *adv.* in course of time.

కాలక్షేపం **kaalakSeepam** *n.* 1 passing or spending time. 2 entertainment. 3 means of livelihood.

కాలక్షేపం చేయు **kaalakSeepam ceeyu** *v.i.* 1 to spend time, pass the time. 2 to live, make a living, maintain o.s.: **unna koddipaaTi bhuumimiidaa eedoo wastee atanu daantoo kaalakSeepam ceestunnaaDu** he lives on whatever he gets from the little land he owns.

కాలగతి **kaalagati** *n.* passing of time.

కాలగర్భం **kaalagarbham** *n.* 1 womb of time. 2 the past; ~ **loo kalisipoowu** to perish, pass away.

కాలచక్రం **kaalacakram** *n.* wheel of time.

కాలజ్ఞానం **kaalajñaanam** *n.* 1 *lit.* knowledge of time. 2 power to forecast or prophesy.

కాలజ్ఞుడు **kaalajñuDu** *n.* astrologer.

కాలత్రయం **kaalatrayam** *n.* past, present and future times.

కాలదండం **kaaladaNDam** *n.* rod of the God of Death.

కాలదన్ను **kaaladannu** *v.t.* 1 *lit.* to kick away. 2 to reject, discard, refuse.

కాలదోషంపట్టు **kaaladooSampaTTu** *v.i.* 1 to be[come] out of date, outdated or antiquated. 2 *legal* to be[come] time barred.

కాలధర్మం **kaaladharmam** *n.* 1 characteristic feature of a time or season. 2 death.

కాలధర్మం చేయు, కాలధర్మం చెందు **kaaladharmam ceeyu, kaaladharmam cendu** *v.i.* to die.

కాలపరిమితి **kaalaparimiti** *n.* time limit.

కాలపాశం **kaalapaaśam** *n.* noose of the God of Death.

కాలబోధక ప్రత్యయం **kaalaboodhaka pratyayam** *n. gram.* tense suffix.

కాలమహిమ **kaala mahima** *n.* portent, portentous event

కాలమానం **kaalamaanam** *n.* 1 state of the climate or season; **kaalamaana paristhitulu** climatic conditions, seasonal conditions. 2 time standard; **sthaanika** ~ local time; **griinwic** ~ Greenwich mean time.

కాలమాపకం **kaalamaapakam** *n.* chronometer.

కాలయాపన[ం] **kaalayaapana[m]** *n.* delay, waste of time, prolonging or spinning out time, procrastination.

కాలయుక్తి **kaalayukti** *n.* fifty-second year of the Hindu cycle of sixty years.

కాలరాచు **kaalaraacu** *v.t.* to crush or grind under foot.

కాలవ **kaalawa** *same as* **kaaluwa.**

కాలవ్యవధి **kaalawyawadhi** *n.* interval (of time).

కాలహరణ[ం] **kaalaharaNa[m]** *n.* waste of time.

కాలాంతక **kaalaantaka** *adj.* mischievous, prankish; ~ **pu panulu ceesi kompa miidiki teecEEDu** he played some pranks and stirred up a host of complaints.

కాలాంతకుడు **kaalaantakuDu** *n.* 1 *class.* epithet of Siva. 2 very acute or capable person, s.o. capable of anything; **cuuDaDaaniki waaDu pillawaaDee kaanii ~, teliwi caalaa undi** he appears only a boy but he is extremely acute, he has great intelligence.

కాలాతీత **kaalaatiita** *adj.* 1 beyond the bounds of time; ~ **wyaktulu** immortals. 2 out of time, delayed, overdue.

కాలావధి **kaalaawadhi** *n.* duration.

కాలింది **kaalindi** *same as* **kaaLindi.**

కాలిక **kaalika** I. *adjvl. suffix signifying* for a period of time; **alpa** ~ short term; **diirgha** ~ long term. II *adj.* seasonal.

కాలిగోరు **kaaligooru** *n.* toenail; **waaDu naa kaaligooriki kuuDaa saaTi kaadu** he is far inferior to me (*lit.* he is not even a match for my toenail).

కాలిజోడు **kaalijooDu** *n.* boot.

కాలిదారి **kaalidaari** *n.* footpath.

కాలినడక **kaalinaDaka** *n.* going on foot, walking.

కాలిపట్టా **kaalipaTTaa** *n.* anklet.

కాలిబాట **kaalibaaTa** *n.* trodden path, track.

కాలివేలు **kaaliweelu** *n.* toe.

కాలు **kaalu** I. *n.* 1 leg, foot. 2 *idiomatic expressions:* **aame ~ jaarindi** she became pregnant out of wedlock (*lit.* her foot slipped); ~ **nilawadokkukonu** to establish o.s., make a name for o.s.; **kaaliki buddhi ceppu** to run away; **kaalimiida ~ weesukoni kuurcuNDu** to enjoy an easygoing and comfortable life (*lit.* to sit at ease with one leg crossed over the other); **kayyaaniki ~ duwwu** to be spoiling for a fight; **N.ki kaaluu ceyyii aaaDindi kaadu** N. could not stir a muscle; **kaaLLa beeraaniki waccu** to come to the stage of begging and entreating; **yoogiiśwaruNNi tana gṛham paawanam ceyyamani kaaLLaa weeLLaa paDDaaDu** he begged and entreated the great yogi to graciously enter his abode; **waaDiki kaaLLuu ceetuluu callabaDDaayi** he suffered a great shock *or* he died ((*lit.* his hands and feet grew cold); **kaaLLu balapaalu kaTTeelaagaa uurantaa tirigEEDu** he went around the whole town until he was exhausted (*lit.* until his legs developed swellings like slate pencils); *see* **iiDcu.** 3 one of the two parallel bars forming the sides of a ladder. 4 quarter, one fourth part; ~ **ruupaayi** quarter of a rupee, 25 paise. 5 stubble (of a crop), stump (of a tree). 6 burning; **mii maaTalu wiNTee ~ ku wastundi** when I hear what you say, I feel very angry (*lit.* when I hear what you say, it comes to burning). II. *v.i.* 1 to burn, be burnt, be on fire; **kaalina bobba** blister caused by a burn. 2 to burn with fever.

కాలుమడి **kaalumaDi** *n.colloq.* urine.

కాలువ, కాలవ **kaaluwa, kaalawa** *n.* channel, canal.

కాలుష్యం **kaaluSyam** *n.* 1 foulness, turbidity, murkiness. 2 contamination, pollution.

కాలూను **kaaluunu** *v.i.* to set foot; *see* **uunu.**

కాలేయం **kaaleeyam** *n.* liver.

కాల్చివేత **kalciweeta** *n.* 1 burning. 2 firing, shooting.

కాల్చు **kaalcu** *v.t.* 1 to burn, set on fire, ignite. 2 to roast. 3 to fire, discharge (gun). 4 to light, let off (firework). 5 to smoke (cigarette).

కాల్చుకుతిను **kaalcukutinu** *v.t.* 1 to roast and eat (food). 2 to illtreat, maltreat, oppress.

కాల్పనిక **kaalpanika** *adj.* 1 invented, artificial, made up, contrived. 2 inventive, creative (writing).

కాల్పు **kaalpu** *n.* 1 (*often pl.* ~ **lu**) firing, shooting; ~ **lu jarupu** to open fire. 2 baking, roasting; *see* **leeta** *sense 3.*

కాల్బలం **kaalbalam** *n.* infantry.

కాళ, కాల **kaaLa, kaala** *adj.* black; ~ **raatri** pitch dark night.

కాళి[క] **kaaLi[ka]** *n.* the goddess Kali.

కాళింది, కాలింది **kaaLindi, kaalindi** *n. class.* seven hooded serpent.

కాళీ, ఖాళీ **kaaLii, khaaLii** I. *n.* emptiness, vacancy, blank space, hiatus. II. *adj.* 1 empty, blank, vacant, free; ~ **samayam** spare time. 2 unemployed, jobless. 3 *slang* finished, done with; **okka aakaaśaraamanna piTiiSanu guddeesEEnaNTee wiiDu ~** if I send off one anonymous petition, this man will be finished.

కాళీచేయు, ఖాళీచేయు **kaaLiiceeyu, khaaLiiceeyu** *v.t.* to empty, deplete, vacate.

కావడి, కావిడి, కావిడీ **kaawaDi, kaawiDi, kaawiDii** *n.* carrying pole, i.e., pole borne on a man's shoulder from which two burdens of equal weight are suspended, one at either end; ~ **weesukoni manci niiLLu tiisukuraawaDam aa uuLLoo andarikii alawaaTee** it is the custom for everyone in that village to fetch water on a carrying pole; *see* **kalimi.**

కావరం **kaawaram** *n.* pride, arrogance.

కావలసిన **kaawalasina** *infinitive of* **awu** + *past vbl. adj.* of **walayu** (that) which is wanted; ~ **panimuTLu** tools that are required.

కావలసినవాడు **kaawalasina waaDu** *n.* person who is dearly loved, friend.

కావలి **kaawali** *n.* watching, guarding, custody.

కావలి ఉంచు **kaawali uncu** *v.t.* to put (s.o.) as a guard.

కావలించు, కావిలించు **kaawalincu, kaawilincu** *v.t.* to embrace, put o.'s arms around, hug.

కావలికాచు **kaawali kaacu** *v.i.* to keep watch.

కావలికాడు, కావలివాడు **kaawalikaaDu, kaawaliwaaDu** *n.* watchman.

కావలిస్తే **kaawalistee** *infinitive of* **awu** + *irregular conditional form of* **walayu** if necessary, if wanted, if needed; **miiku ~ Dabbu istaanu** if you want, I will give you money.

కావాలని **kaawaalani** *adv.* deliberately, intentionally, on purpose; **neenu waddannaa waaDu ~ ceesEEDu** although I told him not to, he did it deliberately.

కావాలి **kaawaali** *infinitive of* **awu** + *irregular impersonal present indicative form of* **walayu** 1 must be; **aragaNTa loopala sabha puurti ~** the meeting must be finished in half an hour. 2 *with dative* to be wanted or needed; **naaku Dabbu ~** I want money *or* I need money. 3 *with dative* to matter, concern; **"pillalaku kuuDaa iTuwaNTi wiSayaalu kaawaalEE?" anukondi aa praśna wiNTunna R. talli** "Do things like that matter to children too?" thought

R.'s mother when she heard that question; **ewariki ~?** who is concerned? *or* who cares? **4 aayana miiku eem ~?** how is he related to you?

కావి **kaawi** I. *n.* red colour. II. *adj.* red, russet, tawny; **niiru ~ rangu guDDalu** pale red coloured clothes.

కావించు **kaawincu** *v.t.* 1 to do, perform. 2 to make, produce, create, cause to become.

కావింపు **kaawimpu** *n. colloq.* action, activity, thing; **waaDini eeDipincaDaaniki wiiDu eedoo ~ kaawistunnaaDu** he is doing something in order to tease him; **pillalu baDinunci wacceesariki amma eedaynaa ~ kaawincaali** by the time the children return from school, the mother should make something ready (meaning something for them to eat).

కావిడి, కావిడీ **kaawiDi, kaawiDii** *same as* **kaawaDi.**

కావు **kaawu** *n.* caw, the sound made by a crow.

కావున **kaawuna** *same as* **gaawuna.**

కావును **kaawunu** *adv. colloq.* may be, perhaps (= **kaaboolu**)

కావేషం **kaaweeSam** *n.* spite, malice, animosity, illwill.

కావ్యం **kaawyam** *n.* 1 poetry. 2 poetical composition. 3 literary composition in verse or ornamental prose.

కావ్యత్వం **kaawyatwam** *n.* poetic quality.

కాశీ **kaaśii** *n.* Kasi, Varanasi, Benares, ancient city of India important for religious and cultural life; **~ loo gaaDida kuuyaDam** *lit.* a donkey braying in Benares (a stock phrase for an extraordinary happening); **eeDupu modalu peDitee ~ loo gaDida kuusinaa wadaladu** once she starts crying, no matter what happens, she will not stop; **~ aawu / geede** cow / buffalo of a superior breed called after the city of Kasi.

కాశీ చెంబు **kaaśiicembu** *n.* round bottomed brass pot with a narrow mouth.

కాశీతాడు, కాశీదారం **kaaśiitaaDu, kaaśiidaaram** *n.* black thread worn round the wrist to ward off evil spirits (originally only brought from Kasi, now from any holy place).

కాశీ మజిలీ కథలు **kaaśii majilii kathalu** *n. pl.* stories told on a pilgrimage to Kasi (these are proverbially reputed to continue indefinitely).

కాశీయాత్ర **kaaśiiyaatra** *n.* 1 pilgrimage to Kasi. 2 part of the wedding ritual, when the bridegroom professes a desire to go on a pilgrimage to Kasi, but is persuaded to stay.

కాషాయం **kaaSaayam** *n.* 1 reddish colour. 2 cloth dyed reddish brown, worn by ascetics; **~ dharincu** to put on an ascetic's dress, adopt an ascetic's life.

కాషాయధారి **kaaSaayadhaari** *n.* one who wears the reddish robes of an ascetic.

కాష్ఠం **kaaSTam** *n.* 1 wood used for cremation. 2 funeral pyre; **nadii jalaala samasya inkaa ~ laa kaalutuunee unnadi** the river waters dispute is still raging (*lit.* still burning like a funeral pyre). 3 stick, log of wood.

కాస **kaasa**[1] *n.* **~ roogam** asthma.

కాస, ఖాస **kaasa**[2], **khaasa** *adj.* own; **naa ~ tammuDu** my own younger brother.

కాసంత **kaasanta** *adj.* only a little.

కాసా **kaasaa** *n.* servant, attendant.

కాసారం **kaasaaram** *n. class.* pond, lake.

కాసింత **kaasinta** *same as* **kasinta.**

కాసిన్ని **kaasinni** *same as* **kasinni.**

కాసినో కూసినో **kaasinoo kuusinoo** *adj.* just a few.

కాసీసం **kaasiisam** *n.* sulphate of iron, green vitriol.

కాసు **kaasu** *n.* 1 coin; **paawalaa ~** quarter rupee coin. 2 pie (smallest copper coin); **~ ku koragaaDu** s.o. not worth even a pie, worthless person. 3 gold coin, sovereign; **muuDu ~ la bangaaram** three sovereigns weight of gold. 4 money; **~ ku loobaDi waaDu hatya ceesEEDu** yielding to (the power of) money, he committed murder.

కాసె **kaase** *n.* truss; **aaDawaaLLu ciirelu ~ poosi kaTTukoni panilooki digEEru** the women tied their saris in a truss and went to work.

కాసేపటికి, కాస్సేపటికి **kaaseepaTiki, kaasseepaTiki** *adv.* for a short time.

కాసేపు, కాస్సేపు **kaaseepu, kaasseepu** *n. and adv.* some time, a little time, a short while.

కాస్త **kaasta**[1] I. *det. n.* a little, a small amount; **~ loo** in a short time *or* by a small amount. II. *adj.* a little, some; **~ annam tiniweLLu** eat a little food and then go. III. *adv.* a little, somewhat, rather; **adi naaku ~ wintagaa uNDeedi** that was rather strange to me. IV. *particle used as a courtesy marker in a polite request*; **~ uttaram poosTu ceestaaraa?** would you post the letter, please?

కాస్త **kaasta**[2] *n. dial.* cultivation.

కాస్తంత **kaastanta** *det. n. and adj.* just a little.

కాస్తకూస్త, కాస్తాకూస్తా **kaastakuusta, kaastaakuustaa** *adj.* only a little; **~ duuram kaadu, aydu mayLLu undi** it is five miles, not just a short distance.

కాస్తదారు **kaastadaaru** *n. dial.* cultivator.

కాస్తా **kaastaa** I *det. n.* a little, a small amount; **unnadi ~ pooyindi** what little there was has been lost. II. *adv.* to a small extent, by a small amount or margin, just; **neenu enta parigettinaa baNDi ~ tappi pooyindi** although I ran so fast, I just missed the train. 3 ~ *can be used to imply that s.g has happened or been done which in the speaker's opinion ought not to have happened or been done, cf. the use of 'go and' in English*, e.g., **neenu daacipeTTamannaa, waaDu naluguriloo aa wiSayam ~ bayTapeTTEEDu** although I told him to keep it secret, he went and revealed that matter to everyone (*implying that he ought not to have revealed it*); *similarly* **baNDi ~ tappipooyindi** *above could also mean* I unfortunately missed the train.

కాస్తో కూస్తో **kaastoo kuustoo** *adj. and adv.* just a little, only a little, somewhat.

కాస్సేపటికి, కాస్సేపు **kaasseepaTiki, kaasseepu** *same as* **kaaseepaTiki, kaaseepu.**

కాహళ[ం] **kaahaLa**[m] *n. class.* trumpet, clarion.

కి - ki

కి/కు **ki/ku** *dative suffix* **1** to, for; **manaki, manaku** to us, for us; **iNTLooki** into the house; **oka ruupaayiki istaawaa**? will you sell it for a rupee? **2** *other usages*: (i) *with impersonal verbs* **naaku illu undi** I have a house (*lit.* there is to me a house); **naaku illu kaawaali** I want/need a house (*lit.* a house is needed for me); **aayana naaku telusu** I know him (*lit.* he is known to me); (ii) *relating to possession, association, content or number* **raamuDu siitaku bharta** Rama is Sita's husband; **rooDDuki reNDu pakkalaa** on both sides of the road; **goodaawariki wantena** a bridge over the Godavari; **ruupaayiki nuuru paysalu** there are 100 paise in a rupee; **mii waddanunna bommalu rakaaniki okaTi coppuna pampaNDi** of the toys that you have, send me one of each kind; **roojuku padi saarlu** ten times per day; (iii) *relating to time* **padi gaNTalaku kalusukondaam** let us meet at 10 o'clock; **padi gaNTala baNDiki waccEEDu** he came by the 10 o'clock train; **raatri meyiluku bayaldeeri guNTuuru waccEEnu** leaving by the night mail I came to Guntur; **aydaaru roojulaku jawaabu waccindi** an answer came after five or six days; (iv) *indicating a natural cause* **ceTTu gaaliki paDipooyindi** the tree fell down on account of the wind; *see also* **maayu** *sense 1*; (v) *a n.* + **ki/ku** *followed by the same n. repeated results in strong emphasis* **mana deeśamnunci kooTLaku kooTLa ruupaayalu waaru doocukupootunnaaru** they are plundering crores and crores of rupees from our country; **pustakaalu cadawaDamloo aanandam sagaaniki sagam taggipooyindi** his joy in reading books was reduced by at least a half; **aa raatriki raatri S. raylwee sTeeSanuku weLLEEDu** that same night S. went to the railway station; (vi) *adverbial use* **nijaaniki/waastawaaniki** in truth, really, actually.

కింక **kinka** *n.* convulsions; ~**paTTu** to suffer from convulsions.

కింకరుడు **kinkaruDu** *n.* servant, slave; **yama**~ servant of the God of Death.

కింకర్తవ్యం **kinkartawyam** *n. phrase* what is to be done; **kinkartawya wimuuDhuDay** being uncertain what to do.

కింకిణి **kinkiNi** *n. class.* small tinkling bell.

కించ **kinca** *n.* sorrow, sadness, grief, dejection.

కించపడు **kincapaDu** *v.i.* **1** to feel sad. **2** to feel offended or put out. **3** to feel remorse or regret.

కించపరచు **kincaparacu** *v.t.* to belittle, criticise, denigrate.

కించిత్తు **kincittu** *det. n. and adv.* very little, the least amount, to the least extent.

కింద, క్రింద **kinda, krinda** I. *p.p.* **1** under[neath], below, beneath, down; **atani ceeti**~ **maniSi** a person under his thumb, under his control, in his power. **2** under the heading of, as; **appu**~**jama kaTTEEDu** he credited it towards (i.e., under the heading of) the loan; **nannu sanghadroohi**~ **jamakaTTi weliweesEEru** they classed me as a traitor to society and expelled me; **ii naaTi baDi okappuDu paśuwula śaala**~ **upayooginceedi** today's school was once used as a cattle shed; **śikSa**~ as a punishment; **mandu**~ as medicine. **3** *with a vb. denoting change* into; **bangaaram antaa Dabbu**~ **maarcEEDu** he converted all the gold into money; **paccaDi**~ **koTTi wadileesEEru** they gave him a sound beating (*lit.* they beat him into chutney) and let him go. II. *adv.* **1** underneath, below. **2** ago; **eeDaadi**~ one year ago.

కిందట **kindaTa** *adv.* formerly, ago; **eeDaadi**~ one year ago.

కిందటి **kindaTi** *adj.* last, former, previous; ~**samwatsaram** last year.

కిందామీదా **kindaamiidaa** *adv.* uncertain, confused, now up and now down, in doubt, at a loss, in two minds; **iNTiki weLLaalaa waddaa ani**~**paDDaaDu** he was in two minds whether to go home or not; **aayana paristhiti**~**gaa undi** his condition is uncertain; **wyaapaaramloo**~ **awutunnaaDu** he is having ups and downs in his business.

కిందామీదా పడు **kindaamiidaa paDu** *v.i.* to strive by all possible means; **eedoo kindaamiidaa paDi aaDapillala peLLiLLu ceesEEDu** he strove by all possible means and managed to marry off his daughters.

కింది **kindi** *adj.* down, downwards.

కిందిచూపు **kindicuupu** *n.* downcast look.

కిందుగా **kindugaa** *p.p.* below, beneath, under[neath].

కిందు మీదు **kindumiidu** *adv.* bowled over (colloq.), gasping (with exhaustion, astonishment or being disconcerted).

కింవదంతి **kinwadanti** *n.* generally believed rumour, common talk.

కిక్కిరిబిక్కిరి మాటలు **kikkiribikkiri maaTalu** *n pl.* foolish babble.

కిక్కిరియు **kikkiriyu** *v.i.* to be crowded; **kikkirisi** crowded, crammed, jammed or packed together.

కిక్కురుమను **kikkurumanu** *v.i., always in neg. constr.* to say s.g in reply; **kikkurumanakuNDaa** without a word in reply, silently.

కిచకిచ **kicakica** *n.* **1** chirping (of birds). **2** chattering, screeching (of monkeys).

కిచకిచలాడు **kicakicalaaDu** *v.i.* **1** (of birds) to chirp, chirrup. **2** (of monkeys) to chatter, screech.

కిచిడీ, కిచ్చిడీ **kic[c]iDii** *n.* **1** one of the best known varieties of superior rice grown in South India. **2** mixed vegetables and fried rice (used for breakfast or a snack).

కిటకిటలాడు **kiTakiTalaaDu** *v.i.* to teem, be crowded.

కిటికీ **kiTikii** *n.* window.

కిటుకు **kiTuku** *n.* **1** trick, device, secret, knack. **2** clue for solving a problem.

కిట్టం **kiTTam** *n. class.* excretion.

కిట్టు, కిట్టుబాటు, కిట్టుబడి **kiTTu, kiTTubaaTu, kiTTubaDi** *same as* **giTTu**[2], **giTTubaaTu, giTTubaDi.**

కిణం **kiNam** *n. class.* wart, corn.

కిణ్వం **kiNwam** *n.* yeast.

కిణ్వనం, కిణ్వ[ప్ర]క్రియ **kiNwanam, kiNwa[pra]kriya** *n. sci.* fermentation.

కితకితలు **kitakitalu** *n.pl.* tickling, titivation.

కితకితలుపెట్టు **kitakitalupeTTu** *v.i.* to tickle, titivate.

కితాబు **kitaabu** *n.* title, honour, token of approval or appreciation.

కిత్తనార **kittanaara** *n.* fibre made from the **kittali** plant; ~ **baTTa** canvas cloth.

కిత్తలి **kittali** *n. agave americana*, a kind of aloe.

కినియు **kiniyu** *v.i.* to be irritated, displeased or angry (-**ku**, at).

కినుక **kinuka** *n.* anger, displeasure, disapproval.

కినుకగా **kinukagaa** *adv.* disapprovingly.

కిన్నెర **kinnera** *n.* 1 lute. 2 lute player in Indra's court.

కిన్నెరసాని **kinnerasaani** *n.* 1 female lute player in Indra's court. 2 a tributary of the River Krishna. 3 a poetical work by Viswanatha Satyanarayana.

కిమ్మతు **kimmatu** *n.* price, value.

కిమ్మను **kimmanu** *v.i., always in neg. constr.* to say (s.g) in response; **kimmanakuNDaa** without saying a word.

కిమ్మన్నాస్తి **kimmannaasti** *minor sentence and n. phrase* **neenu enta aricinaa wəaDu jawaabu cebitee kadaa?~** however much I shouted, did he answer me? no, not a word.

కియిక్కుమనిపించు **kiyikkumanipincu** *v.t.* to make s.o. accept defeat.

కియ్కుయ్మను **kiykuymanu** *v.i. always in neg. constr.* to grumble, complain, demur; **kiykuymanakuNDaa** without demur.

కిరకిర **kirakira** *n.* creaking.

కిరణం **kiraNam** *n.* ray or beam of light.

కిరణజన్య సంయోగక్రియ **kiraNajanya samyoogakriya** *n. bot.* photosynthesis.

కిరసనాయిలు **kirasanaayilu** *n.* kerosene oil.

కిరస్తానం **kirastaanam** *n.* Christianity.

కిరస్తానీ **kirastaanii** *adj.* Christian.

కిరాత[క] **kiraata[ka]** *adj.* savage, barbarous, barbarian.

కిరాతకంగా **kiraatakangaa** *adv.* savagely, barbarously.

కిరాతకుడు **kiraatakuDu** *n.* 1 barbarian, savage. 2 cruel person.

కిరాయి **kiraayi** *n.* rent, hire, fare.

కిరీట[ం] **kiriiTa[m]** *n.* 1 crown. 2 *sci.* corona.

కిర్రు **kirru** I. *n. colloq.* pride, conceitedness. II. *adj.* 1 creaking, creaky; ~ **ceppulu** creaking shoes. 2 *dial.* fresh, blooming.

కిలకిల **kilakila** *onom. n. and adv. sug.* (i) sound of laughter; **pillalu ~ nawwutunnaaru** the children are laughing gaily; (ii) sound of birds twittering; ~ **laaDu** (of birds) to chirp, twitter.

కిలుం **kilum** *n.* verdigris, tarnishing of copper or brass.

కిలుంపట్టు **kilumpaTTu** *v.i.* to be[come] tarnished.

కిలుక్కున **kilukkuna** *same as* **kilakila** *sense(i).*

కిల్లీ, కిళ్ళీ **killii, kiLLii** *n.* betel and nut, pan.

కిల్లీకొట్టు, కిళ్ళీకొట్టు, కిల్లీబడ్డీ, కిళ్లీబడ్డీ **killiikoTTu, kiLLiikoTTu, killiibaDDi, kiLLiibaDDi** *n.* panshop, where betel and nut and other sundry articles are sold.

కిల్లేదారు **killeedaaru** *n.* commander of a fort.

కిశోరం **kiśooram** *n.* young of any animal; **simha~** young lion.

కిశోరప్రాయం **kiśoora praayam** *n.* adolescence.

కిశోరి **kiśoori** *n.* girl.

కిశోరుడు **kiśooruDu** *n.* young man, youth, lad.

కిసలయం **kisalayam** *n. class.* tender leaf.

కిస్మిసి **kismisi** *n.* raisins.

కిస్తీ **kistii** *n.* 1 instalment of any payment. 2 instalment of land revenue.

కీ - kii

కీ **kii** *n.* key.

కీ ఇచ్చు **kii iccu** *v.i.* 1 to wind (clock, etc.). 2 to instigate.

కీకారణ్యం **kiikaaraNyam** *n.* wild forest, wilderness.

కీగంట **kiigaNTa** *adv.* (looking) sidelong; *cf.* **kreegannu.**

కీచకుడు **kiicakuDu** *n.* name of a villain in the Mahabharata.

కీచరబాచర **kiicarabaacara** *same as* **kiisarabaasara.**

కీచు **kiicu** *n.* shrill cry, screech; ~ **gontuka** shrill voice.

కీచుమను **kiicumanu** *v.i.* to screech.

కీచురాయి **kiicuraayi** *n.* cricket, grasshopper, cicada.

కీచులాట **kiiculaaTa** *n.* quarrel, dispute, altercation.

కీచులాడు **kiiculaaDu** *v.i.* to quarrel, dispute.

కీటకం **kiiTakam** *n.* insect.

కీటకనాశకం **kiiTakanaaśakam** *n.* pesticide.

కీటకశాస్త్రం **kiiTakaśaastram** *n.* (science of) entomology.

కీటు **kiiTu** *n.* horizontal course or stratum in a wall, between one and one and a half feet in height.

కీడు **kiiDu** *n.* 1 evil, misfortune. 2 harm, danger; **kiiDenci meelencaali** consider the disadvantages before the advantages (proverb).

కీడుపడు **kiiDupaDu** *v.i.* to be vanquished.

కీత **kiita** *adj.* inferior.

కీతు **kiitu** *n.* coconut bough with the leaves plaited to form a mat.

కీనీడ **kiiniiDa** *n.* 1 shadow or darkness immediately under a lamp. 2 silhouette; **kiTikiimundu ewaroo niilabaDinaTTu ~gaa kanipincindi** someone appeared as a silhouette standing in front of the window.

కీర **kiira** *n.* kind of cucumber.

కీరం **kiiram** *n.* 1 bird. 2 parrot.

కీర్ణం **kiirNam** *adj., in composition* strewn, scattered, pervaded: **meeghaa~** pervaded by clouds.

కీర్తన **kiirtana** *n.* hymn, psalm, devotional song.

కీర్తనం **kiirtanam** *n.* song of praise, encomium.

కీర్తనీయ **kiirtaniiya** *adj.* praiseworthy.

కీర్తి **kiirti** *n.* fame, renown, reputation, glory.

కీర్తించు **kiirtincu** *v.t.* to praise, extol, glorify.

కీర్తికాయుడు **kiirtikaayuDu** *n., gen. honorific pl.* **kiirtikaayulu,** *lit.* person who has departed this life leaving his fame behind him; **ii nela padoo teediina aayana kiirtikaayulu ayyEEru** he died on the tenth of this month.

కీర్తిశేషుడు **kiirtiśeeSuDu** *n., gen. honorific pl.* **kiirtiśeeSulu** 1 *same as* **kiirtikaayuDu.** 2 deceased, late; **kiirtiśeeSulu jawaharlaal nehruu** the late Jawaharlal Nehru.

కీల **kiila** *n.* flame.

కీలం **kiilam** *n.* 1 pin, peg, wedge, pivotal point. 2 *bot.* style.

కీలక **kiilaka**[1] *adj.* crucial, of key importance.

కీలక **kiilaka**[2] *n.* forty-second year of the Hindu cycle of sixty years.

కీలకం **kiilakam** *n.* 1 s.g of vital importance. 2 key to a puzzle, clue, device. 3 secret. 4 pin, peg, wedge, pivotal point.

కీలాభేదం **kiilaabheedam** *n. colloq.* petty difference; **iddaru manci sneehitula madhya ~ peTTEEDu, ippuDu waaLLu śatruwulu ayyEEru** he created a petty difference between two good friends and now they have become enemies.

కీలించు **kiilincu** *v.t. class.* to bring into contact, join together.

కీలు **kiilu** *n.* joint, hinge; **reeDiyoo ee ~kaa~ uuDatiisEEDu** he took the radio to pieces.

కీలుబొమ్మ **kiilubomma** *n.* puppet.

కీలుముట్టుగా **kiilumuTTugaa** *adv.* shakily, creaking at the joints.

కీస **kiisa**[1] I. *n.* 1 a little. 2 one anna (obsolete coin). II. *adj.* little.

కీస[ర] **kiisa**[2], **kiisara** *n.* pouch or pocket in a purse or bag.

కీసరబాసర, కీచరబాచర **kiisarabaasara, kiicarabaacara** *n.* 1 confusion, disorder. 2 strange or unintelligible language.

కు - ku

కు **ku**[1] *Sanskrit prefix denoting* bad, inferior, small, e.g., **kugraamam** small wretched village; **kuwimarśa** hostile criticism.

కు **ku**[2] *suffix, same as* **ki**.

కుంక **kunka** *n.* 1 *term of abuse* **kurra ~** stupid boy. 2 widow. 3 prostitute.

కుంకం, కుంకుమ **kunkam, kunkuma** *n.* red powder made of turmeric, alum and lime juice used as a cosmetic; *see* **pasupu ~**.

కుంకటి **kunkaTi** I. *n.* tuft of hair. II. *adj.* (*also* **kuukaTi**) chief, main, principal; **~ weeru** main root, taproot.

కుంకు **kunku** *same as* **kuuku**.

కుంకుడు **kunkuDu** *n.* soapnut, *sapindus marginatus*; **~ pikka** soapnut kernel.

కుంకుడు పురుగు **kunkuDu purugu** *n.* kind of red insect.

కుంకుమ **kunkuma** *same as* **kunkam**.

కుంకుమ పువ్వు **kunkuma puwwu** *n.* saffron.

కుంగతీయు, క్రుంగతీయు **kungatiiyu, krungatiiyu** *v.t.* 1 to force down, reduce, diminish (hopes). 2 to reduce (s.o.) to wretchedness; **aTLaa ammani kungatiiyakaNDi** do not torment your mother like that.

కుంగు, క్రుంగు **kungu, krungu** *v.i.* 1 to feel depressed, feel wretched (**-ki**, at *or* on account of). 2 to sink, bend, stoop. 3 to shrink, contract; **baTTa kungipooyindi** the cloth has shrunk.

కుంచం **kuncam** *n.* 1 measure of volume equal to four manikas. 2 plug or stopper of an irrigation tank sluice. 3 hole in the head of an axe through which the handle passes. 4 hub of a cart wheel.

కుంచనం **kuncanam** *n. sci.* constriction.

కుంచించు **kuncincu** *v.t.* to abridge, restrict.

కుంచించుకొను **kuncincukonu** *v.i.* to contract, bend down (with shame, cold, etc.).

కుంచిత **kuncita** *adj. class.* bent, crooked, curved.

కుంచుకొను **kuncukonu** *v.i.* to contract.

కుంచె **kunce** *n.* painter's brush.

కుంజం **kunjam** *n.* place overgrown with shrubs or creepers, thicket, bower, arbour.

కుంజరం **kunjaram** *n. class.* elephant.

కుంట **kuNTa** *same as* **guNTa**[2].

కుంటతూము **kuNTatuumu** *n.* outlet for drainage water from a house.

కుంటి **kuNTi** *adj.* lame, crippled.

కుంటించు **kuNTincu** *v.t.* to cripple.

కుంటితనం **kuNTitanam** *n.* lameness.

కుంటు **kuNTu** I *n.* lameness. II. *v.i.* to limp, be[come] lame.

కుంటుపడు **kuNTupaDu** *v.i.* 1 to be[come] lame, maimed or crippled. 2 *fig.* to be impaired, dislocated or hindered; **waaDu raakapoowaDamwalla pani kuNTupaDindi** the work was dislocated by his not coming.

కుంటెన **kuNTena** *n.* leather thong for tying a bullock's yoke to the pole of a cart, plough, etc.

కుండ **kuNDa** *n.* 1 round pot or jar; **warSam ~ pootagaa kurustunnadi** it is raining cats and dogs (*lit.* it is raining as if pots were being poured). 2 pot in which fire is carried to a cremation and broken to signify the breaking of connection with the departed spirit; **kuNDaa karraa siddham ceeyu** to get ready the pot and firewood (for s.o.'s funeral), i.e., to expect s.o. to die; **~ pagaleesi ceppu** *or* **~ baddalu koTTinaTTu ceppu** to say s.g outright, once and for all, finally or unequivocally. 3 ball or globe surmounting a temple tower. 4 hub of a cartwheel.

కుండం **kuNDam** *n.* 1 pit for receiving sacred fire, generally in a temple. 2 pot for the same purpose.

కుండబొజ్జ **kuNDabojja** *n.* pot belly.

కుండమార్పు **kuNDamaarpu** *n.* giving and taking in exchange, barter; **~ peLLi** wedding performed by exchange between families.

కుండలం **kuNDalam** *n.* earring.

కుండలి **kuNDali** *n.* 1 *sci.* coil. 2 *astrol.* planetary circle.

కుండలీకరణం **kuNDaliikaraNam** *n.* bracket, parenthesis.

కుండా **kuNDaa** *neg. participial suffix meaning* (i) not being, not doing, etc., *or* without being, without doing, etc.; **oka maaTa ana ~ alaa kuurcoo** sit there without saying a word; (ii) (*an elliptical construction in Telugu*) in order to prevent, so as to prevent; **kaaLLaku muLLu guccukoo ~ ceppulu dharistaam** we wear shoes to prevent thorns from piercing our feet; **o.-ni paDa ~ aapuceeyu** to prevent s.o. from falling.

కుండీ **kuNDii** *n.* pot, jar, vase, bowl, bin; **puula ~** flower vase; **cetta ~** rubbish bin.

కుంతం **kuntam** *n. class.* lance.

కుంతలం **kuntalam** *n. class.* 1 hair of the head. 2 *pl.* **kuntalaalu** tresses, curls.

కుంద **kunda** *n.* post, pillar; **o.-ni ~ pooTLu poDucu** to buffet s.o.

కుందనం **kundanam** *n.* gold.

కుంది **kundi** *n.* brass lamp stand.

కుందు **kundu** *v.i.* to pine, be sad or dejected.

కుందుకుట్లాడు **kundukuTLaaDu** *v.i.* to move restlessly, fidget.

కుందేలు **kundeelu** *n.* hare; **kundeeTi kommu** *lit.* a hare's horn, *hence* an absurdity, s.g that does not exist.

కుంపటి **kumpaTi** *n.* small iron stove for burning charcoal; **~ biLLa** grate.

కుంఫిణీ **kumphiNii** *n.* company, esp. the East India Company.

కుంభం **kumbham** *n.* 1 water pot. 2 *astrol.* constellation of Aquarius. 3 heap of cooked rice.

కుంభకం **kumbhakam** *n.* yogic exercise involving suspending the breath by closing the mouth and nostrils with the fingers of the right hand.

కుంభకర్ణుడు **kumbhakarNuDu** *n.* a brother of the demon Ravana in the Ramayana to whom sleep was granted as a boon, *hence* **kumbhakarNuDi nidra** deep or profound sleep.

కుంభకారుడు **kumbhakaaruDu** *n.* potter.

కుంభవర్షం, కుంభవృష్టి **kumbhawarSam, kumbhawrSTi** *n.* very heavy rain.

కుంభవృష్టిగా **kumbhawrSTigaa** *adv.* copiously.

కుంభాకార **kumbhaakaara** *adj.* convex.

కుంభాభిషేకం **kumbhaabhiSeekam** *n.* consecration of an idol by pouring water from pots and reciting appropriate mantras.

కుంభించు **kumbhincu** *v.i.* to draw in and retain o.'s breath.

కుంయోమను **kumyoomanu** *v.i.* to groan with pain.

కుకవి **kukawi** *n.* poetaster.

కుక్క **kukka** *n.* dog; **waaDi buddhi ~ tooka** his mind is crooked or twisted (like a dog's tail); **~ caawu caccEEDu** he died uncared for and unattended (*lit.* he died a dog's death).

కుక్కగొడుగు **kukkagoDugu** *n.* kind of fungus.

కుక్కజట్టీలు **kukkajaTTiilu** *n. pl.* dog fights (partly serious, partly in play).

కుక్కపిల్ల **kukkapilla** *n.* puppy.

కుక్కముట్టిన **kukkamuTTina** *adj.* fouled, polluted.

కుక్కమూతి పిందె **kukkamuuti pinde** *n.* blasted fruit.

కుక్కి **kukki** 1 *past participle of* **kukku.** 2 **~ mancam** loose or sagging string cot.

కుక్కు **kukku** *v.t.* 1 to crush with the thumb nail; **kukkina peenu laagaa unnaaDu** he is like a crushed louse, i.e., he is thoroughly subdued. 2 to pack tightly, stuff, cram, push, thrust, stow; **annam mukkunaa nooTanaa ~ koni leeci weLLipooyEEDu** he stuffed some food anyhow into his mouth and got up and went away; **eeDupu ~ koni maaTLaaDu** to talk suppressing a sob.

కుక్షి **kukSi** *n.* stomach; **nirakSara ~** uneducated person (*lit.* person who has no alphabet in his stomach).

కుక్షింభరత్వం **kukSimbharatwam** *n.* gluttony.

కుంక్షింభరులు **kukSimbharulu** *n. pl.* gluttons.

కుచం **kucam** *n.* woman's breast.

కుచేలుడు **kuceeluDu** *n.* Kuchela (*or* Sudama), a friend of Krishna famous proverbially for his poverty and the large number of his offspring.

కుచ్చిత, కుత్సిత **kuccita, kutsita** *adj.* 1 rotten. 2 low, mean, vile.

కుచ్చితం, కుత్సితం **kuccitam, kutsitam** *n.* 1 rottenness. 2 meanness.

కుచ్చిళ్లు, కుచ్చెళ్లు **kucciLLu, kucceLLu** *n. pl.* folds made in the front of a sari or dhoti when tying it round the waist.

కుచ్చు **kuccu** *n.* tassel; **~ la talapaagaa** turban worn with a sash hanging down at the back; *see* **jaDa ~ lu.**

కుచ్చెల **kuccela** *n.* heap of unthreshed millet straw stacked with the ears of corn pointing upwards.

కుజుడు **kujuDu** *n.* the planet Mars.

కుటి **kuTi** *n. class.* hut, cottage.

కుటిల **kuTila** *adj.* 1 crooked. 2 illnatured. 3 insincere, dishonest.

కుటీరం **kuTiiram** *n.* hut, cottage; **kuTiira pariśrama** cottage industry.

కుటుంబం **kuTumbam** *n.* family, household; **kuTumba niyantraNa** family planning.

కుటుంబీకుడు **kuTumbiikuDu** *n.* family person, *gen. as second part of a compound* **bahu ~** person with a large family.

కుట్టు **kuTTu** I. *n.* 1 sharp pain in the side, stitch; **muTTu ~ noppi** pain felt at the time of menstruation. 2 stitch (in sewing). 3 prick, puncture. 4 sting. 5 *fig.* grudge; *cf.* **kanukuTTutanam, kannu** *sense 2.* II. *v.i.* to ache, be sore. III. *v.t.* 1 to sew, stitch; **baTTalu ~** to stitch clothes; **nooru kuTTeesukonnaaDu** he kept silent (*lit.* he stitched up his mouth). 2 to prick, bore, pierce, puncture. 3 to sting; **ciima nannu kuTTindi** an ant stung me. 4 **paNDLu ~ konu** to pick o.'s teeth.

కుట్టుపని **kuTTupani** *n.* tailoring, needlework.

కుట్టుపనివాడు **kuTTupaniwaaDu** *n.* tailor.

కుట్టుపోయు **kuTTupooyu** *v.t.* to stitch together loosely.

కుట్టుయంత్రం **kuTTuyantram** *n.* sewing machine.

కుట్టుసురు **kuTTusuru** *n.* last remaining breath, last gasp.

కుట్ర **kuTra** *n.* 1 plot, conspiracy, intrigue. 2 evildoing, mischief.

కుట్రదారు **kuTradaaru** *n.* conspirator, plotter.

కుట్రపన్ను **kuTrapannu** *v.i.* to conspire, plot.

కుడి **kuDi** *n.* right; **~ ceeyi** right hand; **~ bhujam** right shoulder, righthand man, supporter; **~ eDangaa** round about, approximately.

కుడితి **kuDiti** *n.* a drink for cattle containing nourishing elements.

కుడుం **kuDum** *n.* kind of cake cooked in steam.

కుడుచు **kuDucu** *v.t.* 1 to suck (as a baby does); **abbaayi muddulu kuDustunnaaDu enni eeLLu waccinaa** the boy behaves like a baby although he is so many years old. 2 to eat.

కుడుపు **kuDupu** *v.t.* to suckle, feed.

కుడ్తా **kuDtaa** *same as* **kurtaa.**

కుడ్యం **kuDyam** *n. class.* wall.

కుడ్యచిత్రం **kuDyacitram** *n.* wall painting, fresco.

కుతంత్రం **kutantram** *n.* trickery, intrigue.

కుతకుత **kuta kuta** *onom. adv. sug.* sound made by boiling.

కుతకుత ఉడుకు, కుతకుతలాడు **kutakuta uDuku, kutakutalaaDu** *v.i. and t.* 1 to boil. 2 fig. to boil with anger or emotion.

కుతర్కం **kutarkam** *n.* false logic, fallacy.

కుతలం **kutalam** *n. class.* one of the seven legendary subterranean regions.

కుతి **kuti** *n.* 1 desire, urge, eagerness, inclination; **bombaayi weLLaDaaniki naaku ~ leedu** I have no urge to go to Bombay; **laDDulu caalaa ceesEEnu, ~ tiiraa** (*or* **~ miiraa**) **tinu** I have made a big quantity of laddus, eat your fill. 2 inquisitiveness, curiosity; **~ campukooleeka aDigEEnu** unable to suppress my curiosity, I asked.

కుతిక, కుత్తుక **kutika, kuttuka** *n.* throat, gullet; **~ pisiki campu** to strangle, throttle.

కుతికంటు **kutikaNTu** *n.* necklace worn close round the throat.

కుతుకం **kutukam** *n.* desire, inclination, eagerness, curiosity.

కుతూహలం **kutuuhalam** *n.* eagerness, impetuosity, curiosity, enthusiasm, interest.

కుత్త **kutta** *n.* vagina.

కుత్తుక **kuttuka** *same as* **kutika.**

కుత్సిత[ం] **kutsita[m]** *same as* **kuccita[m].**

కుదప **kudapa** *same as* **kudupa.**

కుదించు **kudincu** *v.t.* 1 to shorten, abridge, condense, compress, restrict, confine. 2 to shake, toss, shake up (a sack in order to settle its contents); *see* **maTTam** *sense I. 1.*

కుదింపు **kudimpu** *n.* abridgement, shortening, condensing.

కుదిమట్టసంగా **kudimaTTasangaa** *adv.* steady at the base, stable; **sanci ~ undi, paDadu** the sack is steady at the base, it will not fall over.

కుదిరిక **kudirika** *n.* steadiness, stability, constancy.

కుదిలించు, కుదుల్చు **kudilincu, kudulcu** *v.t.* to shake, jolt.

కుదుట పడు **kuduTapaDu** *v.i.* to settle down, become calm, be settled or pacified, feel at ease; **ippaTiki praaNam** (*or* **manassu**) **koncem kuduTa paDDadi** by now I am feeling somewhat at ease; **podduTinunci tirugutunnaanu, kaaLLu reNDuu kuduTa paDDaayi iiwaraki** I have been going about since the morning, only now my legs are having some rest.

కుదుటపరచు **kuduTaparacu** *v.t.* to calm, pacify.

కుదుప, కుదప **kudupa, kudapa** *n.* clot (of blood).

కుదుపు **kudupu** I. *n.* jolting, shaking. II. *v.t.* to jolt, shake, nudge.

కుదురు **kuduru** I *n.* 1 shapeliness, gracefulness. 2 steadiness, stability. 3 prop, support. 4 cure, recovery from sickness. 5 coming to o.'s senses, recovery of mental balance; **inta jarigEEka kuuDaa aayanaki ~ raaleedu** even after all this has happened, he has not come to his senses; **~ eeDisteegaa, aaTalee aaTalu!** won't you come to your senses? you think of nothing but games! 6 ring of rope or cloth placed under a round-bottomed pot to keep it steady. 7 ring placed round a mortar to keep grain from spilling. 8 garden bed or plot (=**paadu**). 9 branch of a family, stock; **maa kuduTLoo waaDee** a member of our stock, a member of our branch of the family. 10 root, foundation, origin. II *adj.* well formed, shapely. III *v.i.* 1 to be settled, arranged, adjusted, fixed, established, well grounded, confirmed; **beeram kudirindi** a bargain was struck; **waNTaku kudirEEDu** he was engaged as a cook (*lit.* he was engaged for cooking); **pempuku kudirEEDu** he was adopted. 2 to fit, suit, be suitable; **waaLLiddarikii kudirindi** they suit each other. 3 to be possible; **neenu reepu raawaDam kudaradu** it is impossible for me to come tomorrow. 4 (of illness) to be cured. 5 to be improved, rectified or set right. 6 to become calm or quiet, be pacified. 7 to turn out successfully. 8 (of handwriting) to be well formed.

కుదురుకొను **kudurukonu** *v.i.* 1 to settle, be settled. 2 to be engaged (as employee or servant).

కుదురుగా **kudurugaa** *adv.* 1 properly, comfortably, gracefully, symmetrically; **~ kuurcoo!** sit properly! **kokkiraayi laagaa raayaku, akSaraalu ~ raayi!** don't scribble, form the letters properly! 2 suitably, conveniently.

కుదుర్చు, కుదురుచు **kudurcu, kudurucu** *v.t.* 1 to settle, arrange, adjust, fix, place. 2 to rectify, improve. 3 to cure, heal. 4 to engage (s.o.) for work.

కుదుర్చుకొను **kudurcukonu** *v.t.* 1 to arrange, engage (rickshaw). 2 **samaadhaanam ~** to contract (*or* enter into) an agreement.

కుదులు **kudulu** *v.i.* to shake, tremble.

కుదుల్చు **kudulcu** *same as* **kudilincu.**

కుదువ **kuduwa** *n.* mortgage, pledge; **~ paTTu** to take as security for a loan.

కుదువ పెట్టు **kuduwa peTTu** *v.t.* to mortgage, hypothecate, pawn.

కుదువ విడిపించు **kuduwa wiDipincu** *v.t.* to redeem a mortgage.

కుదేళ్ళు బేస్తులు **kudeeLLu beestulu** *same as* **beestu.**

కునారిల్లిపోవు **kunaarillipoowu** *v.i.* to sink, decline.

కుని **kuni** *n.* corner of a field or sloping bit of land, awkward for ploughing.

కునికిపాటు **kunikipaaTu** *n.* nodding with sleep, dropping asleep, drowsiness, dozing.

కునికిపాట్లుపడు **kunikipaaTLupaDu** *v.i.* to drop off to sleep, doze.

కునికివేయు, కునికేయు **kunikiweeyu, kunikeeyu** *v.i. colloq.* to die.

కునికిష్టి **kunikiSTi** *n.* chronically sick person, invalid.

కునుకు **kunuku** I. *n.* nodding, dropping asleep, dozing. II. *adj.* ill, sick diseased. III. *v.i.* 1 to nod, doze, drop asleep. 2 *colloq.* to die.

కునుకుపట్టు **kunukupaTTu** *v.i.* to get a little sleep; **aayanaki ippuDee sannagaa oo kunuku paTTindi** just now he has fallen lightly asleep.

కుపిత **kupita** *adj.* angry.

కుపితభావం **kupita bhaawam** *n.* anger.

కుపితుడు **kupituDu** *n.* angry person.

కుప్ప **kuppa** *n.* **1** heap, pile, esp. of threshed corn. **2** assemblage, collection; **oppula~** collection of charms and graces. **3 peNTa~** rubbish heap.

కుప్పం **kuppam** *n.* small village, hamlet.

కుప్ప[గా]కూలు **kuppa[gaa] kuulu** *v.i.* to collapse, fall in a heap.

కుప్పకొట్టు **kuppakoTTu** *v.i.* to thresh corn; **waana raakamundee maa ceeloo kuppa koTTEEru** they threshed the corn in our field before it rained.

కుప్పతెప్పలుగా **kuppateppalugaa** *adv.* abundantly.

కుప్పించు **kuppincu** *same as* **guppincu.**

కుప్పిగంతులు **kuppigantulu** *n. pl.* **1** leaps, jumps. **2** pranks, antics.

కుప్పు **kuppu**[1,2] *same as* **guppu**[1,2].

కుప్పె **kuppe** *n.* **1** brass knob fixed on the end of a bullock's horn as an ornament. **2 gaaju~** glass jar or bottle or flask; *see* **jaDa~**.

కుబుద్ధి **kubuddhi** *n.* wicked or bad natured person.

కుబుసం **kubusam** *n.* snake's cast skin; **paamu~ wadilindi** the snake sloughed [off] its skin.

కుబేరుడు **kubeeruDu** *n.* the God of wealth.

కుబ్జం **kubjam** *n.* hunchback, dwarf.

కుమార **kumaara** *adj.* young, youthful; **~ praayam** youthful age, teenage.

కుమారి **kumaari** *n.* **1** daughter, girl. **2** (*in addressing a letter, etc.*) Miss.

కుమారుడు **kumaaruDu** *n.* **1** son. **2** *second part of a n. compound* young person; **kawi~** young poet.

కుమార్తె **kumaarte** *n.* daughter.

కుముదం **kumudam** *n.* white lotus.

కుములు **kumulu** *v.i.* **1** to smoulder. **2** to pine, be consumed with passion, grief or sorrow.

కుముల్చు **kumulcu** *v.t.* to cause to smoulder.

కుమ్మక్కవు **kummakkawu** *v.i.* to conspire or collude together.

కుమ్మక్కు **kummakku** *n.* conspiring, colluding.

కుమ్మరపురుగు **kummarapurugu** *n.* mole cricket, a kind of beetle.

కుమ్మరవాడు **kummarawaaDu** *n.* potter.

కుమ్మరసారె **kummarasaare** *n.* potter's wheel.

కుమ్మరాము **kummaraamu** *n.* potter's kiln.

కుమ్మరి **kummari** *n.* potter, member of the potters' community.

కుమ్మరించు, క్రుమ్మరించు **kummarincu, krummarincu** I. *v.i.* to pour or gush out. II. *v.t.* **1** to pour [out]. **2** to shower (s.g on s.o.).

కుమ్మరిబట్టి **kummaribaTTi** *n.* potter's kiln.

కుమ్ము **kummu**[1] *n.* **1** smouldering ashes; **~loo wankaayalaagaa** like a brinjal in smouldering ashes, *i.e.*, blackened. **2** bother, trouble. **3** plague, pest.

కుమ్ము **kummu**[2] I. *n.* thrust, poke. II. *v.t.* to butt, gore, pierce, poke.

కుమ్ములాట **kummulaaTa** *n.* fight, quarrel, wrangle.

కుమ్ములాడుకొను **kummulaaDukonu** *v.i.* **1** to fight each other. **2** to elbow or buffet one another.

కుయుక్తి **kuyukti** *n.* trick, dodge.

కుయ్యోమొర్రో! **kuyyoomorroo!** *interj. indicating* weeping or wailing due to pain or grief.

కురంగం **kurangam** *n. class.* deer, antelope.

కురంజివాము, కురాసానివాము **kuranjiwaamu, kuraasaaniwaamu** *n.* seeds of henbane (*hyoscyamus nigrum*) used in Ayurvedic medicine.

కురదలా **kuradalaa** *adj.* left over, remaining, surplus.

కురమ **kurama** *n.* **1** a cattle disease. **2** *same as* **kuruma.**

కురిడీ **kuriDii** *n.* dried coconut kernel, copra.

కురిపించు **kuripincu** *v.t.* to shower, cause to rain; **preema~** to shower affection; **atani kaLLu nippulu kuripincEEyi** *or* **atani kaLLu nippulu kurisEEyi** his eyes flashed fire (due to anger—*lit.* his eyes showered fire).

కురియు **kuriyu** I. *v.i.* **1** to rain, shower, fall like rain. **2** to leak; **waana wastee kappu kurustundi** if rain comes the roof will leak. II. *v.t. same as* **kuripincu.**

కురుక్షేత్రం **kurukSeetram** *n.* **1** the famous battlefield where the Pandavas fought the Kauravas in the Mahabharata. **2** great and decisive battle.

కురుచ, కురచ **kuruca, kuraca** *adj.* short.

కురుచవు **kurucawu** *v.i.* to be shortened.

కురుపు **kurupu** *n.* boil, sore, abscess.

కురుమ, కురమ **kuruma, kurama** *n.* name of a community of weavers of woollen blankets.

కురులు **kurulu** *n. pl.* hair of the head, curls.

కురువింద **kuruwinda** *n.* corundum.

కురువృద్ధుడు **kuruwṛddhuDu** *n.* **1** *class.* Bhishma, the eldest among the Kauravas in the Mahabharata. **2** aged and experienced person, very old person.

కురూపత **kuruupata** *n.* malformation.

కురూపి **kuruupi** *n.* ugly person.

కుర్చీ **kurcii** *n.* chair.

కుర్తా, కుడ్తా **kurtaa, kuDtaa** *n.* shirt without a collar.

కుర్ర **kurra** I. *n.* **1** boy, child. **2** young male buffalo. II. *adj.* young, junior; **~laayaru** junior lawyer.

కుర్రకారు **kurrakaaru** *n. pl.* young people, youths, teenagers.

కుర్రతనం **kurratanam** *n.* youth, childhood, boyhood.

కుర్రతనపు **kurratanapu** *adj.* **1** youthful. **2 ~ceeSTalu** childish acts.

కుర్రది **kurradi** *n.* girl.

కుర్రవాడు, కుర్రాడు **kurrawaaDu, kurraaDu** *n.* boy.

కులం **kulam** *n.* **1** community, caste. **2** family.

కులం తక్కువ **kulamtakkuwa** *adj.* belonging to a lower community.

కులకట్టు **kulakaTTu** *n.* rule or custom followed by a community.

కులచిహ్నం **kulachihnam** *n.* caste-mark, community mark.

కులతత్వం **kulatatwam** *n.* community mindedness, caste-ism.

కులధర్మం **kuladharmam** *n.* duty or practice observed by a community.

కులపతి **kulapati** *n.* **1** patriarch, head of a family. **2** Vice Chancellor of a university.

కులపెద్ద **kulapedda** *n.* leader or head of a community.

కులవంతుడు **kulawantuDu** *n.* man of respectable family.

కులవతి **kulawati** *n.* woman of respectable family.

కులవ్యవస్థ **kulawyawastha** *n.* community or caste system.

కులస్త్రీ, కులకాంత, కులవధువు, కులసతి **kulastrii, kulakaanta, kulawadhuwu, kulasati** *n.* **1** woman who is well regarded. **2** woman of a good family.

కులస్థుడు **kulasthuDu** *n.* casteman, member of a community; **iiDiga~** member or the toddy tappers' community.

కులహీనుడు **kulahiinuDu** *n.* outcaste.

కులాసా, ఖులాసా **kulaasaa, khulaasaa** I. *n.* happiness, wellbeing, comfort, good health. II. *adj.* happy, comfortable; **~kaburlu** pleasant talk. III. *minor sentence* ~? are you keeping well?

కులాసాగా, ఖులాసాగా **kulaasaagaa, khulaasaagaa** *adv.* well, comfortable, at ease.

కులీనత, కులీనత్వం **kuliinata, kuliinatwam** *n.* high or noble birth, respectability.

కులీనుడు **kuliinuDu** *n.* s.o. of a noble family, well born person.

కులుకు **kuluku** I. *n.* **1** graceful and affected movement of the body. **2** attitudinising, giving o.s. airs, self-pride. II. *v.i.* **1** to move gracefully and affectedly. **2** to put on airs, attitudinise. **3** to have illicit enjoyment. **4** to flourish, luxuriate. III. *v.t. class.* to pour, scatter, spread; *see* **olakapooyu.**

కుల్య **kulya** *n. class.* canal, channel.

కుల్లా, ఖుల్లా **kullaa, khullaa** *adj.* **1** vacant. **2** open; **~jaagaa** vacant land, empty space.

కుళాయి, కొళాయి **kuLaayi,**[1] **koLaayi** *n.* water tap.

కుళాయి **kuLaayi**[2] *n.* cap (gen. handwoven) for the head.

కుళ్ళగించు **kuLLagincu** *v.t.* to loosen, disturb (soil, etc.).

కుళ్లబొడుచు **kuLLaboDucu** *v.t.* to thrash, beat up, belabour.

కుళ్లు **kuLLu** I. *n.* **1** rottenness, decay; **~kaaluwa** drainage channel. **2** envy, jealousy. **3** slovenliness. II. *adj.* **1** rotten, decayed, putrid. **2** slovenly. III. *v.i.* **1** to rot, decay, turn putrid, fester. **2** to envy, be envious or jealous. **3** to pine with grief or sorrow; **kuLLi kuLLi eeDcu** to weep silently keeping o.'s grief to o.s.; *see* **kṛśincu.**

కుళ్లుబోతు, కుళ్లుమోతు **kuLLubootu, kuLLumootu** *n.* jealous person, envious person.

కువకువలాడు **kuwakuwalaaDu** *v.i.* (of doves, pigeons) to coo.

కువలయం **kuwalayam** *n. class.* **1** lotus. **2** the earth, the world.

కువాక్కు **kuwaakku** *n.* vulgar abuse.

కుశం **kuśam** *n. class.* a kind of grass, *poa cynosuroides.* used in religious rituals.

కుశంక **kuśanka** *n.* unnecessary or frivolous objection, cavilling.

కుశల **kuśala** *adj.* **1** happy, prosperous. **2** skilful, clever, expert, ingenious.

కుశలం **kuśalam** *n.* welfare, wellbeing.

కుశలత **kuśalata** *n.* **1** cleverness, ability, ingenuity. **2** expertness, dexterity; **kaarya~** executive ability.

కుశలప్రశ్నలువేయు **kuśalapraśnalu weeyu** *v.i.* to ask after s.o., make enquiries about s.o.'s health, welfare, etc.

కుశలుడు **kuśaluDu** *n.* skilful person, expert.

కుశాగ్రబుద్ధి **kuśaagrabuddhi** *n.* **1** wit as sharp as the point of a blade of **kuśam** grass. **2** sharp witted person.

కుషామత్తుచేయు, ఖుషామత్తుచేయు **kuSaamattu ceeyu, khuSaamattu ceeyu** *v.t.* to flatter.

కుష్టురోగం, కుష్టువ్యాధి **kuSTuroogam, kuSTuwyaadhi** *n.* leprosy, Hansen's disease.

కుష్టురోగి **kuSTuroogi** *n.* sufferer from leprosy or Hansen's disease.

కుసంస్కారి **kusamskaari** *n.* uncultured person.

కుసి **kusi** *n.* tenon.

కుసింత **kusinta** *same as* **kasinta.**

కుసిన్ని **kusinni** *same as* **kasinni.**

కుసిబెజ్జం **kusi bejjam** *n.* mortise.

కుసీదుడు, కుసీదకుడు **kusiid[ak]uDu** *n. class.* usurer.

కుసుమ[ం] **kusuma[m]** *n.* **1** safflower; **kusuma nuune** safflower oil. **2** any flower. **3** name of a fine variety of rice.

కుసుమించు **kusumincu** *v.i.* to flower, blossom, bloom.

కుసులు **kusulu** *v.i.* to grumble, be discontented.

కుసృతి **kusṛti** *n.* fraud, cheating.

కుస్తీ **kustii** *n.* wrestling.

కుస్తీచేయు, కుస్తీపట్టు **kustiiceeyu, kustiipaTTu** *v.i.* to wrestle.

కుహకం, కూహకం **kuhakam, kuuhakam** *n.* deception, jugglery, trickery.

కుహనా **kuhanaa** I. *n.* deception. II *adj.* false, imitation, bogus.

కుహరం **kuharam** *n.* cave, hole, cavity.

కుహు, కూహూ **kuhu, kuuhuu** *n.* cry of the cuckoo.

కూ - kuu

కూక **kuuka** *n.* 1 cry, shout. 2 *pl.* ~ **lu** scolding.

కూకటి, కుంకటి **kuukaTi, kunkaTi** *adj.* main, chief, principal; ~ **weeru** main root, taproot.

కూకలువేయు, కూకలేయు **kuukaluweeyu, kuukaleeyu** *v.t.* to chide, blame, scold.

కూకు, గూకు, కుంకు **kuuku, guuku, kunku** *v.i.* (of sun, moon) to set.

కూచం **kuucam** *same as* **kuuśam.**

కూచుండు, కూచొను **kuucuNDu, kuuconu** *same as* **kuurcuNDu, kuurconu.**

కూజా **kuujaa** *n.* earthen pot (bottle shaped), goglet.

కూజాబిందె **kuujaabinde** *n.* brass pot in the shape of a goglet.

కూజితం **kuujitam** *n.* birds' song, warbling.

కూట **kuuTa** *adj.* false, fictitious; ~ **saakSyam** false evidence.

కూటం **kuuTam** *n.* 1 meeting, assembly, gathering. 2 group, gang, bloc.

కూటకరణం **kuuTakaraNam** *n.* fraud.

కూటమి **kuuTami** *n.* 1 union, meeting. 2 society, association, league.

కూటు **kuuTu** *n.* dish of mixed vegetables and dhal.

కూడకట్టుకొను **kuuDakaTTukonu** *v.t.* 1 to gather, collect, assemble. 2 to take the support of, enlist the help of.

కూడతీయు **kuuDatiiyu** *v.t.* to assemble, collect, gather together (forces); **praaNaalu kuuDatiisukoni maaTLaaDindi** summoning all her strength, she spoke.

కూడదు **kuuDadu** *3rd per. sing. neg. tense of* **kuuDu** 1 *impersonal use following an infinitive* must not, should not; **miiru ii pani ceeya** ~ you must not do this work. 2 (subject) is/are not fitting, is/are not proper; **ilaaNTiwi kuuDadani racayitanu mettagaa mandalincEEru** they gently rebuked the author, saying that such things were not proper.

కూడని **kuuDani** *neg. vbl. adj. of* **kuuDu** improper, unsuitable; ~ **pani** an improper act.

కూడపలుక్కొను **kuuDapalukkonu** *v.i. and t.* 1 to come to an agreement or understanding (with other persons). 2 to learn to read by a method involving repetition.

కూడబెట్టు **kuuDabeTTu** *v.t.* to collect, amass, accumulate (wealth).

కూడలి **kuuDali** *n.* joining, coming together, meeting, junction, fusion.

కూడా **kuuDaa** *adv.* 1 too, also. 2 *in neg. constr.* even. 3 along with, together with; **naatoo** ~ **raa** come along with me; ~ **tiisukeLLu** to take along with one.

కూడిక **kuuDika** *n.* 1 *maths.* addition. 2 *maths.* sum total. 3 junction. 4 partnership.

కూడు **kuuDu** I. *n.* cooked rice, food (gen. in a deprecatory sense); ~ **guDDa** food and clothing. II *v.i.* 1 to be associated with, be accompanied by, be combined with, involve; **pustakaalu wiDiwiDigaa pampaDam caalaa wyayaprayaasalatoo kuuDi uNTundi** to send the books separately will involve much expense and trouble. 2 to consist of, be comprised, composed or made up of; **naalugu deeśaala pratinidhulatoo kuuDina samaaweeśam** a meeting composed of (*or* made up of) representatives of four countries. 3 to be mixed with, be accompanied by; **awamaanamtoo** ~ **konna koopam** anger mixed with shame. 4 to be filled with, be full of; **aawiDa manassu antaa aandooLanatoo** ~ **konee undi** her whole mind is filled with grief. 5 to contain, have; **okee oka elekTraantoo kuuDina hayDroojan aNuwu** a hydrogen atom which has only one electron; **muLLa ceTLatoo kuuDina poda aDawulu** scrub jungles containing thorny trees. 6 to meet, join. 7 to gather, collect, join together. 8 to accumulate. 9 to be possible. 10 to be fit, proper; *see* **kuuDadu, kuuDani.** III. *v.t.* 1 to add [together], join; **ekkaalannii kuuDikalee. warasagaa naalugu muuLLu weesi kuuDitee, panneNDu wastundi** all multiplication is (the same as) addition; if you put four threes in a row and add them together, you get twelve. 2 to collect, amass, accumulate.

కూత **kuuta** *n.* 1 shout. 2 animal's cry. 3 whistle, hoot, siren (of a train).

కూతవేటు దూరం **kuutaweeTu duuram** *n.* 1 *lit.* the distance within which a shout can be heard. 2 a short distance; **pooliisulu** ~ **loo unnaaru** the police are in the proximity (*or* at a short distance).

కూతురు **kuuturu** *n.* daughter.

కూతురుబుడమ **kuuturu buDama** *n. bryonia scabrella*, a kind of wild cucumber.

కూన **kuuna** *n.* 1 little one. 2 young of an animal or insect; **pilli** ~ kitten. 3 **pasi** ~ human child.

కూనపులివాళ్లు, కూనపులోళ్లు **kuunapuliwaaLLu, kuunapulooLLu** *n.* community of wandering beggars who live by telling the story of Bhavana rishi, founder of the weavers' community.

కూనలమ్మ **kuunalamma** *n.* name of a village goddess worshipped by women who desire children.

కూనిరాగం **kuuniraagam** *n.* humming, singing in a low voice.

కూనిరాగం ఆలాపించు, కూనిరాగం తీయు **kuuniraagam aalaapincu, kuuniraagam tiiyu** *v.i.* to hum a tune, sing softly to o.s.

కూనీ, ఖూనీ **kuunii, khuunii** *n.* murder.

కూనీ అవు, ఖూనీ అవు **kuunii awu, khuunii awu** *v.i.* to be murdered.

కూనీకోరు, ఖూనీకోరు **kuuniikooru, khuuniikooru** *n.* murderer.

కూనీచేయు, ఖూనీచేయు **kuuniiceeyu, khuuniiceeyu** *v.t.* to murder.

కూపం **kuupam** *n.* 1 pit, hole, hollow. 2 well.

కూపస్థమండూకం **kuupastha maNDuukam** *n.* 1 *lit.* a frog in a well. 2 s.o. who is hemmed in on all sides and believes the whole world to be no bigger than his own surroundings.

కూపీ **kuupii** *n.* 1 secret, true fact. 2 investigation.

కూపీ తీయు, కూపీలాగు **kuupiitiiyu, kuupiilaagu** *v.i.* to investigate, detect (crime).

కూబి **kuubi** *n.* secretive or uncommunicative person; **waaDoo ~ maniSi. loopala unnadi payki ceppaDu** he is a secretive person who does not disclose his thoughts.

కూయు **kuuyu** *v.i.* to cry, call; **nakkalu kuuseeweeLa** the time when jackals howl.

కూర **kuura** *n.* 1 a herb. 2 herbs or vegetables in general. 3 vegetable or meat curry.

కూరగాయలు **kuuragaayalu** *n.* 1 vegetables which produce pods or fruit, e.g., beans or brinjals, as opposed to **aakukuuralu** green leafy vegetables.

కూరగాయవైద్యం **kuuragaaya waydyam** *n.* naturopathy, medical treatment by herbal remedies.

కూరగుత్తి **kuuragutti** *n.* set of four small vessels in which curries, etc., are kept, cruet.

కూరానారా **kuuraanaaraa** *n.* vegetables and such other things.

కూరిమి, కూర్మి **kuurimi, kuurmi** *n.* love, affection, friendship.

కూరు **kuuru** *v.t.* to pack, stuff, cram (s.g into a confined space); **tana paypuloo pogaaku ~ taaDu** he stuffs tobacco into his pipe *or* he fills his pipe with tobacco; **nooTiniNDaa laDDuulu kuurukoNTaaDu** he crams his mouth full of laddus.

కూరుకు **kuuruku** *n.* sleep, dozing, falling or dropping asleep; **naaku nidra ~ waccindi** I dropped off to sleep; **waaDi kaLLu ~ pootunnaayi** his eyes are heavy with sleep *or* he is falling asleep.

కూరుకుపోవు, కూరుకొనిపోవు **kuurukupoowu, kuurukonipoowu** *v.i.* 1 to sink down, get stuck (in mud,sand). 2 (of a channel, drain) to be choked.

కూర్చి **kuurci** *same as* **gurinci.**

కూర్చు **kuurcu** *v.t.* 1 to collect, gather, assemble; *see* **eercu.** 2 to join, combine. 3 to add. 4 to put together, compile, arrange. 5 to compose (literature), set (type). 6 to provide, confer, furnish.

కూర్చుండబెట్టు, కూర్చోబెట్టు **kuurcuNDabeTTu, kuurcoobeTTu** *v.t.* to make s.o. sit down, offer s.o. a seat.

కూర్చుండు, కూర్చొను, కూచును, కూచొను **kuurcuNDu, kuurconu, kuucunu, kuuconu** *v.i.* 1 to sit [down], be seated. 2 *following the past participle of another verb ~ is used idiomatically as follows: (i) it may serve to make the utterance definite and emphatic* **miiru sahaayam ceestaamani haamii iccEEru. prajalu daanni nammi kuurcunnaaru. nelalu gaDicinaa eemii jaragaleedu** you promised to help. the people believed it implicitly, but although months have passed nothing has happened; (ii) *it may indicate the continuing nature of a state or action described* **kaaLahasti ceerEEnu. digaDamtoonee ekkaDa basa ceeyaalaneedi samasyayi kuurcunnadi** I reached Kalahasti. from time of my arrival the problem of where to stay has remained unsolved; (iii) *it may imply that an event described was regrettable from the speaker's point of view* **maa abbaayi pariikSa tappi kuurcunnaaDu** our son has gone and failed his examination.

కూర్చుకొను **kuurcukonu** *v.t.* to amass, accumulate.

కూర్పరి **kuurpari** *n.* composer, compiler.

కూర్పు **kuurpu** *n.* 1 joining, putting together. 2 adding, addition. 3 fitting, arranging, arrangement, setting; **cekka** ~ fitting (*or* arrangement) of wooden planks; **accu~** type setting. 4 editing, edition (of a book). 5 sewing, stitching, seam (of a garment).

కూర్మం **kuurmam** *n. class.* turtle, tortoise.

కూర్మా **kuurmaa** *n.* a spicy mixed vegetable dish.

కూర్మావతారం **kuurmaawataaram** *n.* incarnation of Vishnu in the form of a tortoise.

కూర్మి **kuurmi** *same as* **kuurimi.**

కూలం **kuulam** *n. class.* edge, bank, shore.

కూలంకషంగా **kuulankaSangaa** *adv.* in full, from first to last, thoroughly.

కూలతోయు, కూలత్రోయు **kuulatooyu, kuulatrooyu** *v.t.* to overthrow, topple.

కూలపడు **kuulapaDu** *v.i.* to collapse, fall down, slump; **kurciiloo kuulapaDDaaDu** he sank back into a chair.

కూలి, కూలీ **kuuli, kuulii** *n.* 1 daily wages. 2 labourer.

కూలినాలి **kuulinaali** *n.* casual labour, doing odd jobs.

కూలు **kuulu** *v.i.* to fall down, to sink down, collapse.

కూల్చు **kuulcu** *v.t.* 1 to knock down, shoot down, kill. 2 to overthrow, bring down.

కూళ **kuuLa** *adj.* wicked, vile, cruel.

కూష్మాండం **kuuSmaaNDam** *n.* gourd, pumpkin.

కూసం, కూచం **kuusam, kuucam** *n.* wooden post, pole or pillar.

కూసు **kuusu** *adj.* 1 infant, childlike. 2 inferior. 3 trifling. 4 **abhyaasam ~ widya** practice makes skill come easily, i.e., practice makes perfect.

కూహకం **kuuhakam** *same as* **kuhakam.**

కూహూ **kuuhuu** *n.* cry of the cuckoo.

కృ - kṛ

కృతం **kṛtam** I. *suffix used to form adjs. from agentive nouns in* **karaNa** *or* **kaaram**, e.g., **angiikaaram** agreement, **angiikṛtam** agreed. II. *n.* act, deed, s.g done.

కృతక[ం] **kṛtaka[m]** *adj.* **1** artificial, unnatural. **2** spurious.

కృతకత, కృతకత్వం **kṛtakata, kṛtakatwam** *n.* artificiality.

కృతకృత్యుడు, కృతార్థుడు **kṛtakṛtyuDu, kṛtaarthuDu** *n.* successful person.

కృతఘ్నత **kṛtaghnata** *n.* ingratitude, ungratefulness.

కృతఘ్నుడు **kṛtaghnuDu** *n.* ungrateful person.

కృతజ్ఞత **kṛtajñata** *n.* gratitude, gratefulness, thanks; ~ **ceppu** *or* ~ **teliyaceeyu** to convey gratitude or thanks.

కృతజ్ఞుడు **kṛtajñuDu** *n.* grateful person.

కృతనిశ్చయం **kṛtaniścayam** *n.* firm decision, determination, resolve.

కృతనిశ్చయుడు **kṛtaniścayuDu** *n.* determined person.

కృతయుగం **kṛtayugam** *n.* the golden age, first of the four mythological ages of the world.

కృతాంజలి **kṛtaañjali** *n.* hands held with palms together and fingers pointed upwards in a gesture of reverence or soliciting a favour.

కృతార్థత **kṛtaarthata** *n.* success.

కృతార్థుడు **kṛtaarthuDu** *same as* **kṛtakṛtyuDu.**

కృతి **kṛti** *n.* **1** act[ion], doing. **2** literary or artistic work or composition of any kind; ~ **karta** creator of an artistic or literary work; ~ **bharta** person to whom a work is dedicated, dedicatee. **3** devotional song; **tyaagaraaja kṛtulu** devotional songs composed by Tyagaraja.

కృత్తి **kṛtti** *n. class.* hide, skin; ~ **waasuDu** epithet of Siva.

కృత్తిక **kṛttika** *n. astrol.* third lunar mansion.

కృత్యం **kṛtyam** *n.* act, deed, action; **nitya**~ daily activity or routine.

కృత్యాద్యవస్థ **kṛtyaadyawastha** *n.* preparatory stage, introductory phase.

కృత్రిమ **kṛtrima** *adj.* unnatural, artificial, synthetic, spurious.

కృత్రిమంగా **kṛtrimangaa** *adv.* **1** artificially. **2** deceitfully.

కృత్రిమత్వం **kṛtrimatwam** *n.* artificiality.

కృదంతం **kṛdantam** *n. gram.* verbal noun.

కృప **kṛpa** *n.* **1** favour, grace. **2** mercy, pity, compassion.

కృపణ **kṛpaNa** *adj. class.* **1** low, mean. **2** miserly.

కృపణుడు **kṛpaNuDu** *n. class.* miser.

కృపాణం **kṛpaaNam** *n. class.* sword.

కృపాళువు **kṛpaaLuwu** *n. class.* one who is kindhearted, gracious and merciful.

కృశత్వం **kṛśatwam** *n.* leanness, thinness.

కృశించు **kṛśincu** *v.i.* to become lean or thin, languish, waste away; **kuLLi**~ to pine away.

కృషి **kṛSi** *n.* **1** labour, exertion, hard work, effort. **2** cultivation, agriculture.

కృషిచేయు **kṛSiceeyu** *v.i.* to work hard, strive.

కృషి సంబంధ **kṛSisambandha** *adj.* agrarian.

కృషీవలుడు **kṛSiiwaluDu** *n.* cultivator, farmer.

కృష్ణ **kṛSNa** I. *n.* **1** God Krishna. **2** a name of Draupadi, wife of the Pandavas in the Mahabharata. **3** River Krishna. II. *adj.* black, dark.

కృష్ణకాటుకలు **kṛSNakaaTukalu** *n.pl* name of a fine variety of rice.

కృష్ణజన్మస్థానం **kṛSNajanmasthaanam** *n.* **1** *lit.* Krishna's birthplace. **2** prison.

కృష్ణతులసి **kṛSNa tulasi** *n. ocymum sanctum*, the sacred basil plant, used in Ayurvedic medicine.

కృష్ణపక్షం **kṛSNapakSam** *n.* dark fortnight, the fortnight of the waning moon.

కృష్ణయజుర్వేదం **kṛSNa yajurweedam** *n.* the Taittiriya part of the Yajurveda.

కృష్ణవేణి **kṛSNaweeNi** *n.* **1** she who has black hair. **2** a name of the River Krishna.

కృష్ణసర్పం **kṛSNasarpam** *n.* black snake, cobra.

కృష్ణాజినం **kṛSNaajinam** *n.* hide of the black buck **jinka** which used to be worn during performance of religious ceremonies.

కె - ke

కెంజాయ **kenjaaya** *n.* red colour.

కెంజిగురు **kenjiguru** *n.* young red-coloured leaf.

కెందామర, కెందమ్మి **kendaamara, kendammi** *n.* red lotus.

కెంపు **kempu** *n.* 1 ruby. 2 red colour; **aame cempalloo ~ lu puucEEyi** she blushed.

కెరటం **keraTam** *n.* 1 wave. 2 gust; *see* **iidara.**

కెరలు **keralu**[1] *v.i. class.* to increase, rise, swell.

కెరలు **keralu**[2] *v.i. class.* 1 to cry out in alarm. 2 to be angry.

కెలుకు, కెలకు **keluku, kelaku** *v.t.* 1 to stir [up], disturb, scratch (as a chicken does), meddle with. 2 to finger, touch, stir with the fingers; **wistarimundu kuurconi annam keliki leeci weLLEEDu** after sitting in front of his plate and just fingering his food, he got up and left, i.e., he ate hardly anything; **bindeloo niiLLannii keliki paaDucees-EEDu** he spoilt all the water in the binde by stirring it with his fingers. 3 to stir, rouse, provoke.

కెళ్లగించు **keLLagincu** *v.t.* 1 to stir up (soil), disturb (plants). 2 to enrage, exasperate.

కెవ్వు[న] **kewwu[na]** *adv.* loudly, shrilly.

కెవ్వుమను **kewwumanu** *v.i.* to cry out, scream, shriek.

కే - kee

కేంద్ర **keendra** *adj.* central; **~ prabhutwam** the Central Government.

కేంద్రం **keendram** *n.* centre; **pariśoodhana ~** research centre; **reeDiyoo ~** radio station.

కేంద్రక **keendraka** *adj.* nuclear; **~ bhawtika śaastram** nuclear physics.

కేంద్రకం **keendrakam** *n.* nucleus.

కేంద్రస్థానం **keendrasthaanam** *n.* headquarters.

కేంద్రాపసారక **keendraapasaaraka** *adj.* centrifugal.

కేంద్రాభిముఖ **keendraabhimukha** *adj.* convergent.

కేంద్రాభిసారక **keendraabhisaaraka** *adj.* centripetal.

కేంద్రిక **keendrika** *n. biol.* centriole.

కేంద్రీకరణ **keendriikaraNa** *n.* 1 concentration. 2 centralisation. 3 focussing.

కేంద్రీకరించు **keendriikarincu** *v.i.* 1 to concentrate. 2 to centralise. 3 to focus.

కేంద్రీకృత **keendriikṛta** *adj.* 1 concentrated. 2 centralised. 3 focussed.

కేంద్రీయ **keendriiya** *adj.* central; **~ widyaalayam** central school.

కేక **keeka** *n.* 1 cry, shout. 2 *class.* peacock's call.

కేకపెట్టు **keekapeTTu** *v.i.* to shout, call out.

కేకరించు **keekarincu** *v.i.* 1 to cry out, shout. 2 to hawk, clear o.'s throat.

కేకలువేయు **keekaluweeyu** *v.i. and t.* 1 to shout, call out (due to fear). 2 to scold, admonish.

కేకవేయు **keekaweeyu** *v.i. and t.* 1 to shout, call out. 2 to call, summon.

కేకి **keeki** *n. class.* peacock.

కేకిసలుకొట్టు **keekisalukoTTu** *v.i.* to be in a happy or triumphant mood (due to a success).

కేటా **keeTaa** *n.* separation; **nannu ~ ceesEEDu** he separated me (from others).

కేటాగా **keeTaagaa** *adv.* separately; **paTamloo aa paTTa-Nam ~ cuupawalasi uNTundi** it will be necessary to show that town separately on the map.

కేటాయించు **keeTaayincu** *v.t.* 1 to allot, allocate, assign; **nidhulu keeTaayincEEru** they have allotted (*or* allocated) funds. 2 to keep separate, set apart; **waaLLantaa okaTi ayi nannu keeTaayincEEru** they all joined together and kept me apart.

కేటాయింపు **keeTaayimpu** *n.* 1 allocation, allotment. 2 separating, keeping apart.

కేటు **keeTu** *n,* rogue, villain.

కేడీ **keeDii** *n.* hardened criminal (=K.D. or known depredator in police records).

కేతకం, కేతకి **keetakam, keetaki** *n. class.* screwpine, *pandanus odoratissimus* (= **mogali puwwu, geedangi, gojjangi**)

కేతనం **keetanam** *n. class.* flag.

కేతిగాడు **keetigaaDu** *n.* **~, bangaarakka** and **juttupoo-ligaaDu** are three stock characters who provide light relief in traditional puppet shows.

కేతువు **keetuwu** *n. astrol.* name of the ninth planet; **waaLLu iddaruu raahu ~ llaagaa aDDu wastunnaaru** those two are coming like Rahu and Ketu (unlucky planets) to cause obstruction.

కేదారం **keedaaram** *n.* rice field.

కేదారగౌళ **keedaaragawLa** *n.* name of a raga.

కేయూరం **keeyuuram** *n.* epaulet, ornament worn on the shoulder.

కేరడం **keeraDam** *n.* scorn, derision, disregard, indifference.

కేరళం **keeraLam** *n.* the State of Kerala.

కేరింతలు **keerintalu** *n.pl.* 1 gusts or outbursts of laughter. 2 joyfulness, merriment, laughing and joking.

కేరింతలు కొట్టు **keerintalu koTTu** *v.i.* to behave hilariously, have fun, laugh and joke.

కేరుమను **keerumanu** *v.i.* (of a baby) to burble, gurgle, crow, sob.

కేలు **keelu** *n. class.* hand.

కేళి **keeLi** *n. class.* 1 play, sport. 2 amorous sport.

కేళ్ళురుకు **keeLLuruku** *v.i.* to rush, dash; **śriinaathuDee raasEEDanukoNTunna kriiDaabhiraamam kaLLamundu ~ tunnadi** 'Kridabhiramam', which we believe was written by Srinatha himself, comes rushing before our eyes.

కేవలం **keewalam** I. *adj.* pure, simple, unmixed, mere, sheer. II. *adv.* 1 altogether, absolutely. 2 entirely, completely. 3 merely, only, simply.

కేవలుడు **keewaluDu** *n.* 1 the Supreme Spirit. 2 the common man.

కేవు **keewu** *n.* freight, cost of transport.

కేశం **keeśam** n. hair of the head.

కేశనాళిక **keeśanaaLika** *n. biol.* capillary.

కేశపాశం **keeśapaaśam** *n.* mass or quantity of hair, beautiful hair.

కేశబంధం **keeśabandham** *n.* bun of hair (= **koppu**).

కేసరం **keesaram** *n.* 1 *bot.* stamen. 2 lion's or horse's mane.

కేసరి **keesari** *n.* 1 lion. 2 horse. 3 saffron.

కేసి **keesi** *p.p.* towards, in the direction of; **naa ~ cuusEEDu** he looked towards me.

కేసు **keesu** *n. legal* case (civil or criminal).

కై - kay

కై **kay**[1] *p.p.* for [the sake of]; **abhiwṛddhi ~** for the sake of improvement; **cuuDaDaani ~** for the sake of seeing.

కై **kay**[2] *n.* hand.

కైంకర్యం **kaynkaryam** *n.* 1 service, divine service. 2 *class.* misappropriation.

కైకొను, గైకొను **kaykonu, gaykonu** *v.t.* 1 to take on, undertake. 2 to take, receive, accept.

కైజారు **kayjaaru** *n.* small dagger.

కైత[ం] **kayta[m]** *n. class.* poetry.

కైదండ **kaydaNDa** *n.* help, assistance, providing a helping hand.

కైదీ, ఖైదీ **kaydii, khaydii** *n.* prisoner.

కైదు, ఖైదు **kaydu, khaydu** *n.* prison.

కైదుచేయు, ఖైదుచేయు **kayduceeyu, khayduceeyu** *v.t.* to imprison.

కైపు **kaypu** *n.* intoxication.

కైపు ఎక్కు **kaypu ekku** *v.i. with dative* to get intoxicated; **koncem taagagaanee waaDiki kaypekkindi** as soon as he had drunk a little, he became intoxicated.

కైఫియ్యత్ **kayphiyyat** *n.* statement in writing.

కైమాపు చేయు **kaymaapu ceeyu** *same as* **kaamaapu ceeyu.**

కైమోడ్పు **kaymooDpu** *n.* greeting with folded hands.

కైలాసం **kaylaasam** *n.* Siva's abode, Siva's heaven.

కైలు **kaylu** *n.* measurement of harvested grain before sharing it.

కైలుగడ్డి **kaylugaDDi** *n.* straw that is not completely threshed.

కైలుచేయు **kaylu ceeyu** *v.i.* to hand over landlord's share of harvest.

కైవడి **kaywaDi** *n. class.* manner, likeness.

కైవల్యం **kaywalyam** *n.* final liberation of the soul from the body, union with the Supreme Spirit, eternal bliss (= **mookSam**).

కైవసం **kaywasam** *n.* possession.

కైవసం చేయు **kaywasam ceeyu** *v.t.* to hand over.

కైవసం చేసుకొను **kaywasam ceesukonu** *v.t.* to take over, take possession of, sequester.

కైవారం **kaywaaram** *n.* 1 circumference, perimeter. 2 encomium, praise, flattery.

కైసన్న **kaysanna** *n.* gesture with the hand; **~ ceesi nannu pilicEEDu** he beckoned and called me.

కొ - ko

కొంకనక్క **konka nakka** *n.* small fox.

కొంకర **konkara** *n.* crookedness, bending.

కొంకరబారు, కొంకర్లుపోవు **konkarabaaru, konkarlupoowu** *v.i.* 1 (of limbs) to be twisted, bent, stiffened or contracted by cold. 2 to crouch or cower due to cold, weakness or fear.

కొంకి, కొంకె **konki, konke** *n.* 1 hook, peg (for hanging clothes, etc.) 2 *pl.* **konkulu** jointed bones; **meDakonkulu** collarbones; **mookaali konkulu** kneebones.

కొంకికర్ర **konkikarra** *n.* hooked stick.

కొంగ **konga** *n.* bird of the stork, heron or crane type.

కొంగజపం **konga japam** *n.* insincere hypocritical prayers intended to deceive others; *cf.* **baka dhyaanam.**

కొంగు **kongu** *n.* hem, border, end of a sari or dhoti; **waaDu daani** ~ (*or* **cengu**) **paTTuku tirugutunnaaDu** he is tied to her apron strings *or* he is under her thumb (*lit.* he is going about holding the end of her sari).

కొంగుబంగారం **kongu bangaaram** *n.* ready money.

కొంగుమాయు **kongumaayu** *v.i.* to be in menses.

కొంగొత్త, క్రొంగొత్త **kongotta, krongotta** *adj.* brand new.

కొంచపోవు **koncapoowu** *v.t.* to take away.

కొంచెం **koncem** *det. n. and adj.* some [thing], a little; **nannu** ~ **ceesi maaTLaaDEEDu** he belittled me.

కొంచెంకొంచెంగా **koncem koncemgaa** *adv.* gradually, little by little.

కొంచెంలో **koncemloo** *adv., lit.* within a small amount; ~ **mugincaNDi** (i) finish it in a short time, (ii) finish it at little expense; **pramaadam** ~ **tappindi** the accident was narrowly averted.

కొంచెతనం **koncetanam** *n.* littleness, pettiness.

కొంచెపడు **koncepaDu** *v.i.* 1 to fall short, be wanting. 2 to be belittled, feel belittled.

కొంచెపువాడు **koncepuwaaDu** *n.* low or mean person.

కొంజా **konjaa** *n.* wooden framework supporting a roof over a wall.

కొంజెర **konjera** *n.* feeder channel bringing water to fields from a main channel.

కొంటె **koNTe** *adj.* naughty, mischievous, lewd.

కొంటెకోణంగి **koNTekooNangi** *n.* mischievous or buffoonlike person.

కొంటెతనం **koNTetanam** *n.* naughtiness, mischievousness, lewdness.

కొండ **koNDa** *n.* hill, mountain; **diipam** ~ **ekkindi** the light has been extinguished *or* the light has gone out (paraphrase to avoid a taboo expression; *cf.* **golusu, biiyam**).

కొండంత **koNDanta** *adj.* as big as a mountain, very great, enormous; ~ **koorika** great desire; ~ **saayam** enormous help; *see* **gooranta.**

కొండకసింద **koNDakasinda** *n. toddalia aculeata*, a medicinal plant.

కొండకాలువ **koNDakaaluwa** *n.* hill stream.

కొండకొమ్మ **koNDakomma** *n.* peak or summit of a mountain.

కొండకోన **koNDakoona** *n.* wild hilly area.

కొండగాలి **koNDagaali** *n.* cool breeze from the mountains.

కొండగుర్తు **koNDagurtu** *n.* means or mark of identification, landmark; **maa iNTi edurugaa muuDu guDiselunnaayi, adee** ~ opposite our house there are three huts, that is an identification mark.

కొండగోగు **koNDagoogu** *n.* yellow tree cotton, *cochlospermium gossypium.*

కొండచిలువ **koNDaciluwa** *n.* python.

కొండజాతి **koNDajaati** *n.* hill tribe.

కొండదారి **koNDadaari** *n.* canyon.

కొండనాలుక **koNDanaaluka** *n.* uvula.

కొండపోడు **koNDapooDu** *n.* slash and burn method of cultivation.

కొండముచ్చు **koNDamuccu** *n.* lion-tailed monkey.

కొండరాయి **koNDaraayi** *n.* granite.

కొండలాదిగా **koNDalaadigaa** *adv.* enormously.

కొండవాగు **koNDawaagu** *n.* hillstream.

కొండవాడు **koNDawaaDu** *n.* hillman, member of a hill tribe.

కొండవీటి చేంతాడు **koNDawiiTi ceentaaDu** *n.* s.g very long (like the proverbially long ropes of the wells in the town of Kondavidu in Guntur district).

కొండవెల్లుగాలి **koNDawellugaali** *n.* strong cold rainy wind.

కొండి **koNDi** *n.* 1 hook, staple. 2 scorpion's tail containing the sting.

కొండిక **koNDika** I. *n. class.* little boy, child II. *adj. class.* young.

కొండెం **koNDem** *n.* slander, backbiting; **koNDEElu ceppu** to carry tales (against a person).

కొండెకత్తె, కొండెకాడు **koNDekatte, koNDekaaDu** *n.* (woman/man) tale bearer.

కొండొక **koNDoka** *det. adj.* (= **okaanoka**) a certain; **S. anee** ~ **rSi akkaDa uNDeewaaDu** a certain saint named S. used to live there.

కొండ్ర **koNDra** *n.* land fit for cultivation, cultivable land.

కొంత **konta** I. *det.n. and adj.* some[thing], a little; ~ **loo** the very least. II. *adv.* to some extent, partly.

కొంతగా **kontagaa** *adv.* to some extent.

కొంతమట్టుకు **kontamaTTuku** *adv.* to some extent.

కొంతవరకు **kontawaraku** *adv.* to some extent, for some distance, for some time.

కొందరు **kondaru** *det. n. pl.* some persons.

కొండలపడు **kondalapaDu** *v.i. class.* to be confused, anxious or sorry.

కొంప **kompa** *n.* 1 house (in a deprecatory sense), hut, hovel. 2 **naa ~ tiisEEDu / tagalabeTTEEDu / muncEEDu** he has ruined me. 3 **~ tiisi** *is used as an expletive roughly equivalent to* heaven forbid!, e.g., **mabbu muusukostunnadi, ~ tiisi warSam paDutundeemoo!** clouds are gathering, perhaps it will rain — heaven forbid! 4 *other idiomatic expressions:* **naa ~ munigipootundi** I shall be ruined; **ippuDu eem ~ munigindani nuwwu waccEEwu?** now what disaster has happened so as to cause you to come? **kompaagooDuu paTTakuNDaa tirugutunnaaDu** he is wandering about without considering his house and family; **~ miidiki teccEEDu** he stirred up a host of complaints (*lit.* he brought (everyone) to his house complaining).

కొంపోవు **kompoowu** *variant form of* **konipoowu.**

కొక్కిరాయి **kokkiraayi** *n.* heron, crane; *see* **kudurugaa.**

కొక్కిరాయి మాటలు **kokkiraayimaaTalu** *n.* ludicrous words, nonsense.

కొక్కిరిగీతలు **kokkirigiitalu** *n.* clumsy writing.

కొక్కిరిబిక్కిరి **kokkiribikkiri** *adj.* clumsy, awkward.

కొక్కీ, కొక్కెం **kokkii, kokkem** *n.* 1 buckle, hook. 2 staple, clamp.

కొక్కెర **kokkera** *n.* heron, crane.

కొక్కొరోకో **kokkorookoo** *n.* sound of a cock crowing.

కొక్కోకం **kokkookam** *n.* study of erotics.

కొజ్జా **kojjaa** *n.* eunuch.

కొటారు, కొఠారు **koTaaru, koThaaru** *n.* 1 storage place; **uppu ~** salt storage depot. 2 granary. 3 *dial.* threshing floor.

కొట్టం, కొట్టాం **koTTam, koTTaam** *n.* 1 cattle shed. 2 shed, hut.

కొట్టకొన, కొట్టకొన **koTTakosa, koTTakona** *n. and adj.* extreme end or tip, furthest point.

కొట్టడి, కొట్టీడు **koTTaDi, koTTiiDu** *n.* 1 store room. 2 *dial.* room (of any kind).

కొట్టవచ్చు **koTTawaccu** *v.i.* to strike the eye, be noticeable or conspicuous; **koTTawaccee ciire** a striking or attractive sari; **koTTawaccinaTLu kanipincu** to appear obviously, plainly or glaringly.

కొట్టించు **koTTincu** *v.t.* to cause to beat; *see* **buriDii ~**

కొట్టిపారవేయు, కొట్టిపారేయు **koTTipaaraweeyu, koTTipaareeyu** *v.t.* 1 to throw away. 2 to get rid of, do away with. 3 to dismiss, reject (an idea as being of no value). 4 *legal* to dismiss (case, complaint), quash (conviction, sentence).

కొట్టివేత **koTTiweeta** *n.* 1 correction, crossing out. 2 *legal* quashing.

కొట్టివేయు **koTTiweeyu** *v.i.* 1 to throw away, reject. 2 to discard. 3 to cross out, correct. 4 *legal* to quash (conviction, sentence), repeal (law). 5 to steal, misappropriate. 6. *colloq.* to make off with, run away with.

కొట్టీడు **koTTiiDu** *same as* **koTTaDi.**

కొట్టు **koTTu**[1] *n.* 1 shop; **~ ciikuDu guDDa** shop-soiled cloth. 2 storehouse, storeroom, granary. 3 room. 4 prison cell.

కొట్టు **koTTu**[2] I. *v.i.* to strike (*with shades of meaning varying according to the context*); **iidurugaali koDutunnadi** a strong cold wind is blowing; **eNDa baagaa koDutunnadi** the sun's heat is severe; **waaDiki waDa debba koTTindi** he suffered [from] heat stroke; **kampu koDutunnadi** there is a bad smell; **naalugu gaNTalu koTTindi** it is four o'clock; **naa pariikSa goowindaa koTTindi** I have failed my examination; **daridra ~ waaDu** *or* **daridra ~ mukham** s.o. who is the embodiment of poverty. II. *v.t.* 1 to strike, beat, hit, thump, knock (*with shades of meaning varying according to the context*); **talupu ~** to knock on a door; **cappaTLu ~** to clap o.'s hands, applaud; **piNDi ~** to pound into flour or powder, pulverise, smash to pieces; **ii rooDDu waaDiki koTTina piNDi** this is a road that he knows very well (*lit.* this road is like pounded flour to him); **Dabbu naa mukhaana koTTEEDu** he flung the money in my face; **gooDaki sunnam ~** to apply whitewash to a wall *or* to whitewash a wall; **aDawulu ~** to cut down a forest; **kaTTelu ~** to cut up firewood (into convenient lengths); **keesu ~** *legal* to dismiss a case; **jeebulu ~** to pick pockets; **daarlu ~** to commit highway robbery; **aTu iTu pacaarlu ~** to pace back and forth; **Sikaaru ~** to go for a walk; **Dabbu undani pooju koDutunnaaDu** he is giving himself airs because he has got money. 2 **~** *is used to form verbs from certain nouns*, e.g., **accu ~** to print; **iita ~** to swim; **busa ~** to hiss. 3 **~** *is used as an auxiliary to form tr. from intr. vbs.*, e.g., **ceDu** to be spoilt, **ceDagoTTu** to spoil; **weLLu** to go, **weLLagoTTu** to chase, drive out; **ekkuwa maaTLaaDitee nii paLLu raalagoDataanu** if you talk any more, I will knock your teeth out.

కొట్టుకొను **koTTukonu** I. *v.i.* 1 to beat, pulsate, thump, knock; **aame guNDelu koTTukuNTunnaayi** her heart is beating hard (due to emotion); **waaDi muNukulu koTTukuNTunnaayi** his knees are knocking together. 2 to struggle; **pani puurticeeyaalani mahaa koTTukupootunnaaDu** he is struggling hard to finish the work. 3 to be at a loss, be perplexed, writhe or flounder in difficulties; **eemii teliyaka koTTukoNTunnaanu** I am completely perplexed; **walaloo koTTukoNTunna ceepalaa** like a fish floundering in a net. 4 (of wind, water) to come with a rush; **koNDa looyallooncí niiru koTTukoccinaTTu** like water rushing down from mountain valleys. 5 to be blown or tossed about, carried forward, carried away, washed away, swept away; **gaaliki koTTukupoowu** to be blown away by the wind; **tiiraaniki koTTukuwaccu** to be washed up on shore *or* to be washed ashore; **nadiloo koTTuku waccina puuDika** silt washed down by the river. 6 (of the heart, mind) to be agitated by desire; **aamekoosam praaNam koTTuku pooyeedi** he used to long for her; **eemannaaDoo telusukoowaalani naa manasu koTTukupootunnadi** my mind is agog to know what he said. 7 **kowwekki** (*or* **madamekki**) **koTTukoNTunaaDu** he is behaving arrogantly. II. *v.t.* 1 to strike, beat, hit, thump; **mukkunaa nooTanaa annam koTTukoni skuuluku ceerukoneesariki pariikSakinkaa araganTa Taymunnadi** when he reached school after cramming food anyhow into his mouth, it was still half an hour before the exam; **daani kaaLLuu ceetuluu gawnuu antaa burada koTTukoni uNDeewi** her legs, hands and dress were all splashed with mud. 2 *colloq.* **uuLLoo andarinii bhoojanaaniki koTTuku waccEEDu** he brought the whole village in for a meal.

కొట్టుమిట్టాడు **koTTumiTTaaDu** *v.i.* to waver, hesitate, tremble in the balance.

కొట్లాట **koTLaaTa** *n.* fight, quarrel.

కొట్లాడు **koTLaaDu** *v.i.* to fight, quarrel.

కొఠారు **koThaaru** *same as* **koTaaru.**

కొడమ, కొడం **koDama, koDam** *same as* **kaDama.**

కొడవలి **koDawali** *n.* sickle.

కొడి **koDi** *n.* 1 tip, end. 2 burnt tip of a wick; **diipam~ kaTTindi** the lamp wick is covered with soot.

కొడుకు **koDuku** *n.* son.

కొణామణి **koNaamaNi** *n.* name of a fine variety of rice having a long grain.

కొణుజు **koNuju** *n.* tick (insect).

కొతిమేర, కొత్తిమీర **kotimeera, kottimiira** *n.* coriander plant, *coriandrum sativum.*

కొతుకు **kotuku** *v.i.* to mumble, mutter, hesitate in speaking.

కొత్త, క్రొత్త **kotta, krotta** I. *n.* newness; **~ tiirindi** newness wore off; **peLLi ayna~loo** in the period just after the marriage. II. *adj.* new, fresh, strange, unfamiliar; **~ mukhaalu kanipincaayi** unfamiliar faces appeared; **~ niiru** freshes (in a river); **~ waaDu** a stranger.

కొత్తమాస, కొత్తామాస **kottamaasa, kottaamaasa** *n.* worship on the new moon day after Ugadi at the start of the new ploughing season.

కొత్తరికం **kottarikam** *n.* newness.

కొత్తిమీర **kottimiira** *same as* **kotimeera.**

కొత్తెం **kottem** *n.* 1 pulp of palmyra fruit. 2 tuft of hair on the head (= **pilaka**).

కొత్వాలు **kotwaalu** *n.* chief of police in a town.

కొదమ **kodama** I. *n.* young male buffalo. II. *adj.* (of animals) young; **~simham** young lion.

కొదవ **kodawa** *n.* deficiency, want, scarcity, dearth; **manci niiTiki~** scarcity of drinking water.

కొదవపెట్టు **kodawapeTTu** *v.t.* to leave as remainder, omit, leave out; **annii ceesEEDu, adi okaTii kodawapeTTEEDu** he has done it all, he has left out only that.

కొద్ది **koddi** I. *n.* a little, something; **bahu~** a very little. II. *adj.* little, small, a few; **~ mandi** a few people.

కొద్దిగా **koddigaa** *adv.* a little, slightly, to a small extent; **~ Dabbu undi** there is a little money.

కొద్దిపాటి **koddipaaTi** *det. adj.* little, small, slight, partial, meagre; **~ warSam** slight rainfall; **~ akSaraasyata** partial literacy.

కొద్దీ, కొలది **koddii, koladi** *suffix* 1 [in proportion] as; **manuSulu perigina~ duuram awtaaru**; as people grow up, they become further apart; **talacukonna~ naaku aaścaryam ayndi** the more I thought over it, the more surprised I was (*lit.* in proportion as I thought over it, I became surprised); **sattuwa~ koTTEEDu** he struck with all his strength. 2 as a result of, due to, out of; **maaremma kalaloo kanipistundeemoonanna bhayam~ S.ki caalaa roojulu nidra kuuDaa paTTeedi kaadu** as a result of fear that Maremma would appear to him in a dream S. got no sleep for many days; **niimiida wiroodham~ cebutunnaamanukonnaawaa?** do you think we are speaking out of enmity towards you? 3 as much as, as many as; **kooTLa~ janam winnaaru** crores of people heard it; **siisaala~ kaSaayam kaluputaaru** they make bottlefuls of the mixture; **ewaritoonuu maaTLaaDakuNDaa gaNTala~ kuurcuNTaaDu** he sits for hours on end without talking to anybody.

కొద్దోగొప్పో **koddoogoppoo** *adj. and adv.* just a little, some amount, to some extent; **~caduwukunnaaDu** he has studied just a little.

కొన **kona** I *n.* end, point, tip. II. *adj.* last, final; **~ uupiri** last breath; **konaakulu meeyaku** do not [try to] graze the topmost leaves (which are beyond your reach), i.e., do not talk about things which you are not able to understand.

కొనగోరు **konagooru** *n.* tip of the finger nail; **naa konagooTiki sari kaaDu** he is not worth so much as the tip of my fingernail.

కొనతేరు, కొనతేలు **konateeru, konateelu** *v.i.* to form a point, become pointed; **kurupu konateerindi** the boil has come to a head; **konateerina cubukam** pointed chin.

కొనసాగించు **konasaagincu** *v.t.* 1 to continue, carry on, pursue. 2 to transact (business).

కొనసాగింపు **konasaagimpu** *n.* continuing, continuation.

కొనసాగు **konasaagu** *v.i.* 1 to proceed, continue, be carried on, be pursued. 2 (*also* **konalusaagu**) to extend the tips, grow.

కొనితెచ్చుకొను **koniteccukonu** *v.t.* to cause, bring about, create, give rise to; **kaSTaalu koniteccukonnaaDu** he brought troubles on himself; **praaNaalamiidaki** (*or* **tanamiidaki**) **koniteccukonnaaDu** he got himself into serious difficulty; **cirunawwu pedawulamiidaki koniteccukonnaaDu** he forced himself to smile.

కొనిపించు **konipincu** *v.t.* to cause s.g to be brought.

కొనిపోవు, కొంపోవు **konipoowu, kompoowu** *v.t.* to take away, carry off.

కొనియాడు **koniyaaDu** *v.t.* to praise, extol.

కొను **konu**[1] *v.t.* 1 *mod. only in compounds* (i) to take, e.g., **ceekonu** to take (ii) to feel, experience, e.g., **aakalikonu** to feel hungry. 2 to buy, purchase.

కొను **konu**[2] *auxiliary vb. signifying* (i) *reflexive force*, e.g., **koTTukonnaaru** they beat each other, **maaTLaaDukonnaaru** they talked to each other; (ii) to do s.g for o.'s own benefit, e.g., **paNDLu ammukoNTundi** she sells fruit (for her benefit).

కొనుగోలు **konugoolu** *n.* buying, purchasing, purchase; **~śakti** purchasing power; **~dhara** purchase price.

కొనుగోలు చేయు **konugoolu ceeyu** *v.t.* to purchase.

కొనుగోలుదారు **konugooludaaru** *n.* purchaser, customer.

కొనుబడి **konubaDi** *n.* purchase.

కొన్నాళ్ళు **konnaaLLu** I. *n.pl.* some days. II. *adv.* for some days, for some time.

కొన్ని **konni** *det.n.pl. and adj.* some number (of non-human things).

కొన్నిట **konniTa** *adv.* in some respects, ways, places or matters; **waaDiki~ anubhawam undi** he has experience of some matters.

కొప్పు **koppu** *n.* 1 bun (of hair). 2 crest (of a roof).

కొబ్బరి **kobbari** *n.* copra, kernel of coconut.

కొబ్బరి కాయ **kobbari kaaya** *n.* coconut fruit.

కొబ్బరి చెట్టు **kobbari ceTTu** *n.* coconut tree.

కొబ్బరి తాడు **kobbari taaDu** *n.* coconut rope.

కొబ్బరి నార **kobbari naara** *n.* coir, coconut fibre.

కొబ్బరి నూనె **kobbari nuune** *n.* coconut oil.

కొబ్బరి పీచు **kobbari piicu** *n.* coconut husk.

కొమరితె **komarite** *dial. same as* **kumaarte.**

కొమరుడు **komaruDu** *dial. same as* **kumaaruDu.**

కొమిరె **komire** *n.* upright post supporting the axle or pivot of a baling apparatus.

కొమ్మ **komma** *n.* 1 branch. 2 *class.* maiden, woman. 3 **kooTa ~lu** battlements of a fort.

కొమ్ము **kommu**[1] 1 horn or tusk of an animal. 2 horn (musical instrument). 3 root or tuber of ginger or turmeric. 4 handle of a palanquin or bier. 5 *gram.* secondary form of the vowel *u* in Telugu script. 6 **ceruwu~** surplus weir of an irrigation tank. 7 spout of a kettle; *see* **kaacu**[4].

కొమ్ము **kommu**[2] *a form of the imperative sing. of* **konu**[2].

కొయ్య **koyya** I n. 1 log of wood. 2 staff, stick. 3 **waaDoo moNDi~** he is an obstinate individual. II. *adj.* wooden.

కొయ్యకండ **koyyakaNDa** *n. med.* trachoma.

కొయ్యకాలు **koyyakaalu** *n.* stubble.

కొయ్య[తోట] కూర **koyya[tooTa]kuura** *n.* kind of spinach, *amaranthus tristis.*

కొయ్యబారిపోవు **koyyabaari poowu** *v.i.* to be transfixed or stunned.

కొయ్యబారు **koyyabaaru** *v.i.* to stiffen, become rigid.

కొర **kora** *n.* 1 *class.* profit, use, advantage. 2 *mod. only in neg. constr.* **endukuu~kaakuNDaa pootunnaaDu** he is not going in for anything useful.

కొరకంచు **korakancu** *n.* 1 firebrand, burning piece of wood. 2 headstrong, obstinate or fiery tempered person.

కొరకరానికొయ్య **korakaraanikoyya** *n.* 1 s.g unintelligible. 2 stupid and obstinate person.

కొరకు **koraku** *p.p.* for [the sake of].

కొరకొర **korakora** *n.* 1 anger. 2 hatred.

కొరకొర చూచు **korakora cuucu** *v.t.* to glare at, look angrily at.

కొరకొరలాడు **korakoralaaDu** *v.i.* to be angry or irritable.

కొరగాని **koragaani** *adj.* good for nothing, useless.

కొరగామి **koragaami** *n.* uselessness, worthlessness.

కొరడా **koraDaa** *n.* whip, scourge.

కొరడు **koraDu** *n.* rainbow.

కొరడుబారు **koraDubaaru** *v.i.* 1 to become numb. 2 to become hardened.

కొరత **korata**[1] *n.* want, deficiency, insufficiency, paucity, scarcity, shortage.

కొరత **korata**[2] *locative of* **korru** on an impaling stake.

కొరతవేయు **korataweeyu** *v.t.* 1 to impale. 2 to torture.

కొరదల **koradala** *n.* imperfection, defect.

కొరపోవు **korapoowu** *v.i.* (of food, drink) to be swallowed the wrong way so as to cause a fit of coughing (=**polamaaru, porapoowu**).

కొరమాలిన **koramaalina** *adj.* useless, good for nothing.

కొరవడు **korawaDu** *v.i.* to be absent, missing or lacking.

కొరవలు **korawalu** *n. pl.* Koravas, members of a tribe who live by basketmaking.

కొరవి, కొరివి **korawi, koriwi** *n.* 1 firebrand, burning stick, burnt stick. 2 *fig.* firebrand (human).

కొరవిదయ్యం **korawidayyam** *n.* will o' the wisp.

కొరుకు **koruku** I. *n.* 1 bite. 2 syphilis. II. *v.t.* to bite, gnaw, munch; **paLLu~** to grind or gnash o.'s teeth; **neenu aayana ceppina pani ceeyakapootee korukku tineeseelaa cuusEEDu** when I did not do the work he said, he looked at me very angrily (*lit.* he looked at me as if he would devour me); **waaLLu cewulu korukkoNTunnaaru** they are talking to each other in whispers.

కొరుకుడు **korukuDu** *n. and adj.* gnawing, grinding: **~purugu** cut worm; **paLLu~** grinding the teeth.

కొరుకుడుపడు **korukuDupaDu** *v.i.* to be understood, comprehended, fathomed, mastered; **ii grantham naaku korukuDupaDaDam leedu** I cannot make head or tail of this book; **maniSi naaku korukuDupaDaDam leedu** I cannot fathom him.

కొరుకుడుపుండు **korukuDupuNDu** *n.* ulcer.

కొర్నా **kornaa** *n.* hyena.

కొర్ను **kornu** *n.* unploughed land (=**kooNDra**).

కొర్ర **korra** *n. panicum italicum*, a kind of millet.

కొర్రు **korru** *n.* 1 impaling stake. 2 hook, thorn. 3 small tear or hole in a cloth; **cokkaa~ paTTindi** there is tear in the shirt.

కొర్రెక్కు **korrekku** *v.i.* (of persons) to become obstinate; **eduru ceppinakoddii ~taaDu** the more you contradict him the more obstinate he will become.

కొలకర్ర **kolakarra** *n.* measuring rod.

కొలత **kolata** *n.* 1 measuring, measure[ment]; **tuunika ~lu** weights and measures. 2 dimension.

కొలతవేయు **kolataweeyu** *v.t.* to measure, survey.

కొలది **koladi** *class., same as* **koddii.**

కొలను **kolanu** *n.* lake, pond.

కొలపాత్ర **kolapaatra** *n.* measuring vessel.

కొల[త]బద్ద **kola[ta]badda** *n.* ruler, measuring rod, standard (for measuring).

కొలమానం **kolamaanam** *n.* system of measurement; **meTrik~** metric system of weights and measures.

కొలికి **koliki** *n.* 1 loop, hook. 2 inner corner of the eye. 3 end; **ippaTiki ii pani oka kolikki waccindi** by now this work has reached a certain stage *or* by now this work has come to fruition. 4 **~puusa** *or* **mutyaala~** leading or best bead in a chain.

కొలిపించు **kolipincu** *v.t.* to get s.g measured.

కొలిమి **kolimi** *n.* furnace, forge.

కొలుచు **kolucu**[1] *v.t.* to measure.

కొలుచు **kolucu**[2] *v.t.* to serve, worship.

కొలుపు **kolupu** I. *n.* festival of a village goddess. II. 1 *transitive/causative form of the auxiliary verb* **konu**[2], e.g., **meelukonu** to wake (*intr.*), **meelu~** to awaken (*tr.*) 2

literary usage to create, cause, bring on; **haayikolipee gaali** soothing and refreshing breeze; **ewaroo kadulutunnaTLu sphurinci koncem bhayam ~tunnadi** by making it appear that s.o. is moving about, it causes some alarm.

కొలువు **koluwu** *n.* 1 service, employment. 2 hall of audience, royal court; **~ tiircu** *class.* to summon a court. 3 **bommala ~** religious exhibition of dolls.

కొలువుకూటం **koluwukuuTam** *n.* royal court.

కొల్ల **kolla** *n.* 1 loot, plunder, pillage, booty. 2 plenty; **adee naaku~** that is quite enough to satisfy me; **miiru raawaDamee~, inkeemii ceyyakkaraleedu** your coming itself is sufficient, you need do nothing more. 3 *pl.* **~lu** plenty, plentiful; **udaaharaNalu~lu, kaawaalaNTee dorukutaayi** examples are plentiful and are available if wanted: **~lugaa** plentifully, in abundance, in large numbers.

కొల్లకొట్టు, కొల్లకొను **kollakoTTu, kollakonu** *v.t.* to loot, plunder.

కొల్లపోవు **kollapoowu** *v.i.* to be plundered or robbed; **neenu kollapooyina manaśśaanti** the peace of mind which I lost; **kollapooyina mukham** a face which has lost its lustre.

కొల్లలాడు **kollalaaDu** *v.t.* 1 to plunder. 2 to revel in, enjoy to the full.

కొల్లాయి **kollaayi** *n.* small handloom cloth used for covering the body.

కొల్లేరు **kolleeru** *n.* the Collair lake, between the Krishna and Godavari deltas.

కొళాయి **koLaayi** *same as* **kuLaayi**[1].

కొవ్వు **kowwu** I. *n.* 1 fat, grease; **~padaartham** fatty substance. 2 pride, insolence, presumption, arrogance. II. *v.i.* to be fat; **kowwina gorre** fattened sheep.

కొవ్వుబలుసు **kowwu balusu** *v.i.* to be[come] proud, arrogant or insolent.

కొవ్వువత్తి, కొవ్వొత్తి **kowwu watti, kowwotti** *n.* candle.

కొవ్వెక్కు **kowwekku** *v.i.* to be[come] proud, haughty, arrogant, overbearing or overweening.

కొశ, కొశ్శ **kośa, kośśa** *adj. dial.* sharp, pointed.

కొస **kosa** *n.* 1 end, tip; **~merupu** final flash. 2 **puri~** rope made of hemp.

కొసరు **kosaru** I. *n.* small extra quantity asked for by a purchaser and given by a trader in addition to what has been purchased; **~leekapootee rucileedu** unless you add a little extra, it will have no taste (so says the purchaser). II. *adj.* extra, additional, marginal. III. *v.i.* to ask for a little extra quantity after purchasing any article.

కో - koo

కో **koo** *syllable used in echo phrases to indicate a wish easily fulfilled, support readily given, etc.* **'koo' aNTee kooTimandi unnaaru, ewaroo okarini ennukoNTaanu** if I only say 'koo' there will be crores of people, I will choose any one of them; **'koo' anagaanee 'kookoo' aNTuu kooTaanukooTLa janam maarupalukutaaru** as soon as I say 'koo' crores of people will say 'koo koo' in reply.

కోండ్ర **kooNDra** *n.* 1 ploughing in a circuit and leaving an interval. 2 the interval so left.

కోక **kooka** *n.* sari.

కోకిల **kookila** *n.* Indian cuckoo.

కోకొల్లలు **kookollalu** *n.pl.* very many (persons or things); **cinna wyaapaarasthulu ~gaa unnaaru** small business people are very many.

కోట **kooTa** *n.* fort; **~loo paagaa weeyu** to become established or stabilised.

కోటానుకోట్లు **kooTaanukooTLu** *n.pl.* crores upon crores.

కోటి **kooTi** *n.* 1 crore, ten millions. 2 host, multitude, class; **jiiwa~** the animal kingdom; **maanawa~** the human race; **piiDita prajaa~** the class of oppressed people; **bhakta~** a host of devotees; **raama~** writing the name 'Rama' ten million times (a form of devotion); **~ki paDaga[lu] ettu** to be[come] very wealthy (*lit.* to raise a serpent's hood over a crore of rupees).

కోటీశ్వరుడు **kooTiiśwaruDu** *n.* 1 owner of property worth a crore of rupees. 2 very rich man.

కోటేరు **kooTeeru** *n.* 1 plough placed and tied upside down on top of the bullocks' yoke, when being brought to and from the fields. 2 **~laaNTimukku** pointed nose.

కోఠా **kooThaa** *n.* warehouse.

కోడండ్రికం, కోడరికం **kooDaNDrikam, kooDarikam** *n.* state of being a daughter-in-law; **~peTTu** to harass a daughter-in-law.

కోడలు **kooDalu** *n.* daughter-in-law.

కోడి **kooDi** *n.* 1 fowl. 2 *pl.* **kooLLu** poultry. 3 surplus weir of an irrigation tank, which allows excess water to escape by overflowing.

కోడికునుకు **kooDikunuku** *n.* dozing, nodding, dropping off to sleep.

కోడిపిల్ల **kooDipilla** *n.* chick[en].

కోడిపీటలు **kooDipiiTalu** *n.pl.* wooden supports (one at either end) for the upper cross beam of a bullock cart.

కోడిపుంజు **kooDipunju** *n.* cock.

కోడిపెట్ట **kooDipeTTa** *n.* hen.

కోడిపోయు **kooDi pooyu** *v.i.* (of an irrigation tank) to overflow, surplus.

కోడు **kooDu** I *n.* leg of a bed, chair, bench or table. II. *v.t.* to toss or winnow rice so as to separate whole grains from broken rice, paddy grains, stones, etc.

కోడె **kooDe** I. *n.* young bull aged about 2 years. II *adj.* young.

కోడెకాడు **kooDekaaDu** *n.* paramour, lover.

కోడెకారు **kooDekaaru** *adj.* young, teenage.

కోడెతాచు **kooDetaacu** *n.* young cobra.

కోడైకూయు **kooDaykuuyu** *v.t.* to shout, proclaim, trumpet; **prapancam antaa kooDaykuustunnadi ii wiSayaanni** the whole world is trumpeting this matter.

కోణం **kooNam** *n.* 1 angle. 2 corner; **ciikaTi ~** dark corner.

కోణంగి **kooNangi** *n., used only in the phrase* **koNTe~** mischievous or buffoonlike person.

కోణంగితనం **kooNangitanam** *n.* buffoonery.

కోణమాని **kooNamaani** *n. maths.* protactor.

కోణాంకం **kooNaankam** *n. phys. and maths.* amplitude.

కోణీయ **kooNiiya** *adj.* angular.

కోత **koota** *n.* **1** cutting; **ii rampapu ~ neenu paDaleenu** I cannot bear this agony (*lit.* I cannot bear this saw cutting). **2** harvest, reaping. **3** erosion (of river bank). **4** cut (in expenditure, electricity, etc.) **5** pl. **~ lu** boasting; *see* **kaDupu ~, raata ~ lu.**

కోతదోనె **koota doone** *n.* shoe dony, kind of flat bottomed boat used in the Godavari delta.

కోతలు కోయు **kootalu kooyu** *v.i.* to boast.

కోతి **kooti** *n.* monkey, ape.

కోదండం **koodaNDam** *n.* **1** bow, esp. Rama's bow. **2** sling from which a person is hung as a punishment.

కోదాడు **koodaaDu** *n.* kind of palm tree; *see* **iidaaDu.**

కోన **koona** *n.* **1** valley, gorge. **2** glade, dell. **3** forest. **4** corner of a field.

కోనసీమ **koonasiima** *n.* central part of the Godavari delta.

కోనేరు **kooneeru** *n.* temple tank, square in shape and surrounded by stone steps.

కోన్‌కిస్కా **koonkiskaa** *n.* **1** nonentity. **2** stranger, unknown person.

కోపం **koopam** *n.* anger.

కోపంతెచ్చుకొను **koopam teccukonu** *v.i.* to get angry.

కోపగించు **koopagincu** *v.i.* to get angry, be angry.

కోపగిల్లు **koopagillu** *v.i.* to be angry or displeased.

కోపదారి **koopadaari** *adj.* bad tempered.

కోపపడు, కోప్పడు **koopapaDu, kooppaDu** *v.t.* to scold, admonish, be angry with (s.o.).

కోపాలుతాపాలు, కోపతాపాలు **koopaalutaapaalu, koopataapaalu** *n. pl.* anger (*lit.* anger and heat generated by anger).

కోపి **koopi** *n.* angry person.

కోపించు **koopincu** *v.i.* to be angry.

కోపిష్ఠి **koopiSTi** *n.* angry or bad tempered person.

కోపు **koopu** *n.* **1** point, sharp end of a stick, stone, etc., which has been shaped into a point. **2** tip, tuft, crest. **3** any sticklike object, e.g., **balapapu~** slate pencil. **4 ii waana walla neelaku ~ waccindi** the earth has become soft as a result of this rain.

కోపుదారు **koopudaaru** *n.* travelling salesman, hawker.

కోపుపారు **koopu paaru** *v.i.* to be[come] beautiful or good looking.

కోమటి **koomaTi** *n.* merchant, shopkeeper, member of the Vysya community.

కోమల **koomala** *adj.* delicate, tender, blooming.

కోమలత్వం **koomalatwam** *n.* delicacy, tenderness.

కోమలాంగి, కోమలి **koomalaangi, koomali** *n.* beautiful woman.

కోయ **kooya** *n.* name of a tribe of forest dwellers in Andhra Pradesh.

కోయించు **kooyincu** *v.t.* **1** to cause s.g to be cut. **2** *colloq.* **TikaT~** to purchase a ticket.

కోయిల **kooyila**[1] *n.* Indian cuckoo.

కోయిల **kooyila**[2] *same as* **koowila.**

కోయు **kooyu** *v.t.* **1** to cut. **2** to pick, pluck (flowers). **3** to harvest, reap (crop). **4** to slaughter, kill (animals for food). **5** *colloq.* **TikaT~** to issue a ticket; *see* **kootalu~.**

కోర **koora**[1] I. *n.* fang, tusk. II. *adj.* sharp, pointed; **~ paLLu** fangs, sharp protruding teeth; **~ cuupulu** fierce or angry looks; **~ miisaalu** curled and pointed moustaches.

కోర **koora**[2] *n.* drinking bowl, goblet.

కోరం **kooram** *n.* toothed instrument for scraping or grating; **kobbari~** coconut scraper or grater.

కోరంగి **koorangi** *n.* small variety of cardamum.

కోరకం **koorakam** *n.* bud.

కోరడి **kooraDi** *n.* earthen ridge planted with thorns or cactus to form a fence.

కోరా **kooraa** *adj.* unbleached.

కోరి **koori** *past participle of* **kooru** **1** asking, desiring, having asked, having desired. **2** *following a noun in the accusative* **~** *or* **kooree** (i.e., **koori** + *emphatic suffix* **ee**) *is used with postpositional force to mean* for, for the benefit of, for the sake of, in favour of; **nuwwu tammuDu laaNTiwaaDawu ganaka nii manci~ niiku salahaa istunnaanu antee** you are like my younger brother, so I am just advising you; **Dabbunu~ kaaka preemanu~** not for money but for love. **3** *advbl. use* deliberately, intentionally, to please o.s., of o.'s own accord, wantonly; **udyaanawanam weeseesEEDu, andulooki aame tana geedeni kooree pampincindi** he laid out a garden and she deliberately sent her buffalo into it; **ahankaari aatmawidhwamśaanni ~ teccukoNTaaDu** an egoist brings destruction on himself of his own accord.

కోరింతదగ్గు **koorinta daggu** *n.* whooping cough.

కోరిక **koorika** *n.* wish, desire, request.

కోరు **kooru**[1] *v.i. and t.* **1** to ask, request, demand. **2** to wish, desire.

కోరు **kooru**[2] I. *n.* **1** any grated substance, e.g., coconut kernel. **2** cropsharing agreement between landowner and tenant. **3** system of cultivation by cropsharing. II. *v.t.* to grate, scrape (coconuts, etc) with a grater.

కోరు **kooru**[3] *suffix signifying agent, actor or doer,* e.g., **abaddhaala~** liar, **dagaa~** cheat.

కోల **koola** I. *n* **1** rod, staff, stick, arrow. **2** ploughshaft. **3** jujube tree (= **reegi**). II. *adj.* elongated, oblong, oval-shaped; **~ mukham** oval-shaped face.

కోలాటం **koolaaTam** *n.* dance performed with sticks by people forming a ring.

కోలాహలం **koolaahalam** *n.* **1** uproar, hubbub, confused noise. **2** excitement.

కోలు **koolu** *suffix for forming nouns from certain verbs,* e.g., **iccu~** giving; **konugoolu** purchase.

కోలుకర్ర **koolukarra** *n.* measuring rod.

కోలుకొను **koolukonu** *v.i.* to recover (from illness), be cured.

కోలుపోవు, కోల్పోవు **koolupoowu, koolpoowu** *v.t.* to lose.

కోళ్ళగంప **kooLLagampa** *n.* chicken basket.

కోళ్ళగూడు **kooLLa guuDu** *n.* hen house.

కోవ **koowa** *n.* 1 class, category. 2 lineal descent, succession (in a family).

కోవా[బిళ్ళ] **koowaa [biLLa]** *n.* kind of sweet made with milk.

కోవిదత్వం **koowidatwam** *n.* scholarship, learnedness, erudition.

కోవిదుడు **koowiduDu** *n.* learned person, scholar.

కోవిల, కోవెల, కోయిల **koowila, koowela, kooyila** *n.* temple.

కోశం **koośam** *n.* 1 receptacle, repository. 2 treasury. 3 dictionary, lexicon, glossary; *see* **eekoośaanaa.**

కోశసంబంధ **koośasambandha** *adj.* fiscal.

కోశస్థ **koośastha** *adj.* included in a glossary.

కోశాగారం **koośaagaaram** *n.* treasury.

కోశాధికారి **koośaadhikaari** *n.* treasurer.

కోష్ఠిక **kooSThika** *n. chem.* chamber.

కోసం, కోసరం **koosam, koosaram** *p.p.* for the sake of, on account of, for.

కోసు, క్రోసు **koosu**[1], **kroosu** *n.* coss, obsolete measure of distance, about 2 miles.

కోసు **koosu**[2] *adj.* 1 sharp, pointed. 2 narrowing to a point.

కోసుకొనితిను **koosukonitinu** *v.t.* 1 to cut and eat (fruit, etc.) 2 *fig.* to torture.

కోసుకొనిపోవు **koosukoni poowu** *v.i.* to be worn away or eroded (e.g., by floods).

కోసుగడ్డ **koosugaDDa** *n.* cabbage.

కోసుపువ్వు **koosupuwwu** *n.* cauliflower.

కోస్తా **koostaa** I *n.* coast. II. *adj.* coastal.

కౌ - kaw

కౌకులు **kawkulu** *n.pl. dial.* troubles, difficulties.

కౌగిలి, కౌగిలింత **kawgili[nta]** *n.* embrace, hug.

కౌగిలించు **kawgilincu** *v.t.* to embrace, hug.

కౌజు **kawju** *n.* partridge.

కౌటిల్యం **kawTilyam** *n.* 1 crookedness, curvedness. 2 deceitfulness.

కౌటిల్యుడు **kawTilyuDu** *n.* Kautilya or Chanukya, adviser to king Chandragupta and author of the 'Artha Sastra', a treatise on political economy.

కౌతూహలం, కౌతుకం **kawtuuhalam, kawtukam** *n.* eagerness, impetuosity, curiosity.

కౌపీనం **kawpiinam** *n.* loin cloth.

కౌమార **kawmaara** *adj.* adolescent.

కౌమారం **kawmaaram** *n.* youth, bloom.

కౌముది **kaumudi** *n.* moonlight.

కౌమోదకి **kaumoodaki** *n.* Vishnu's club or mace.

కౌరవ **kawrawa** *adj.* pertaining to the Kauravas.

కౌరవులు **kawrawulu** *n.pl.* the Kauravas, descendants of Kuru, esp. the sons of Dhrutarashtra in the Mahabharata.

కౌలు **kawlu** *n.* lease of land, agreement in writing between tenant and landowner.

కౌలుదారి **kawludaari** *n.* tenancy.

కౌలుదారు **kawludaaru** *n.* lease holder, tenant, lessee:

కౌశలం, కౌశల్యం **kawśalam, kawśalyam** *n.* skill, dexterity, proficiency.

క్త్వా, క్యా - ktwaa, kyaa

క్త్వార్థకం **ktwaarthakam** *n. gram.* past participle ending in *i* e.g., **wacc-i, cees-i.**

క్యావడి **kyaawaDi** *n.* secondary form of the letter *y* in Telugu script.

క్ర, క్రా - kra, kraa

క్రంత **kranta**[1] *n.* presents taken to a future bride from her future bridegroom's house before the betrothal ceremony.

క్రంత **kranta**[2] *same as* **kanta.**

క్రందనం **krandanam** *n.* weeping, lamentation.

క్రతువు **kratuwu** *n.* 1 religious sacrifice, religious occasion. 2 *colloq.* any religious or social function performed on a large scale.

క్రమం **kramam** *n.* 1 order, series, sequence, line, course: **akSara~** alphabetical order: **kaalakramaana** in course of time. 2 rule, regularity, arrangement.

క్రమంగా **kramangaa** *adv.* gradually.

క్రమక్షయం **kramakSayam** *n.* erosion.

క్రమచయనం **kramacayanam** *n. maths.* permutation.

క్రమణిక **kramaNika** *n.* list, *always as second part of a compound*, e.g., **kaala~** list of dates; **wiSaya~** list of topics.

క్రమపద్ధతి **kramapaddhati** *n.* 1 orderly way, manner, fashion or system. 2 regular method.

క్రమపరిణామం **kramapariNaamam** *n.* gradual development.

క్రమబద్ధ **kramabaddha** *adj.* orderly, regular, well-regulated, systematic, phased.

క్రమబద్ధం చేయు **kramabaddham ceeyu** *v.t.* to reduce to order, regulate, systematise.

క్రమబద్ధీకరణ **kramabaddhiikaraNa** *n.* regulating, regulation.

క్రమభంగం **kramabhangam** *n.* deviation, irregularity.

క్రమభిన్నం **kramabhinnam** *n. maths.* proper fraction.

క్రమభుజి **kramabhuji** *n. maths.* regular polygon.

క్రమ[వి]రహిత **krama[wi]rahita** *adj.* disorderly, irregular.

క్రమ[వి]రహితంగా **krama[wi]rahitangaa** *adv.* irregularly, in disorderly fashion.

క్రమ[వి]రాహిత్యం **krama[wi]raahityam** *n.* disorder.

క్రమశః **kramaśaḥ** *adv.* regularly, gradually.

క్రమశిక్షణ **kramaśikSaNa** *n.* discipline.

క్రమశిక్షణారాహిత్యం **kramaśikSaNaaraahityam** *n.* indiscipline, lack of discipline.

క్రమస్యా **kramasyaa** *adv.* gradually.

క్రమాంకనం **kramaankanam** *n. phys.* **1** calibration. **2** graduation.

క్రమాంకిత **kramaankita** *adj. phys.* **1** calibrated. **2** graduated.

క్రమానుగత **kramaanugata** *adj.* phased; **~sankhyalu** consecutive numbers, serial numbers.

క్రమానుగతంగా **kramaanugatangaa** *adv.* gradually, by degrees, step by step.

క్రమాలంకారం **kramaalankaaram** *n.* figure of speech involving arrangement of words in a prescribed manner.

క్రమేణ, క్రమేపి **krameeNa, krameepi** *adv.* gradually, by degrees.

క్రమ్మర **krammara** *adv. class.* again.

క్రయం **krayam** *n.* purchase, buying.

క్రయధనం **krayadhanam** *n.* cost.

క్రయవిక్రయాలు **krayawikrayaalu** *n.pl.* buying and selling, trade.

క్రయపత్రం **krayapatram** *n.* deed of purchase.

క్రయించు **krayincu** *v.t.* to buy, purchase.

క్రయికుడు **krayikuDu** *n.* buyer, purchaser.

క్రయ్య **krayya** *n.* canal.

క్రాంతి **kraanti** *n.* **1** turning. **2** transgression. **3** revolution. **4** *astron.* declination.

క్రాప **kraapa** *n.* (= **diSTibomma**) object displayed to ward off the evil eye from a house, field, etc.

క్రాపు **kraapu** *n.* haircutting, hairstyle.

క్రాపుచేయు **kraapuceeyu** *v.i.* to cut s.o.'s hair.

క్రావడి **kraawaDi** *n.* secondary form of the letter *r* in Telugu script.

క్రి, క్రీ - kri, krii

క్రింద **krinda** *same as* **kinda.**

క్రితం **kritam** I. *adj.* last, previous; **naa~janmaloo** in my last birth; **~śataabdapu tudiloo** at the end of the last century. II. *adv.* ago; **reNDeeLLa~** two years ago (= **kindaTa**).

క్రిమి **krimi** *n.* **1** insect, worm. **2** germ or other micro-organism.

క్రిమిసంహారక **krimisamhaaraka** *adj.* insecticidal, germicidal, pesticidal, disinfectant.

క్రియ **kriya** *n.* **1** act, action, activity; **rasaayanika~** chemical action. **2** *gram.* verb. **3** funeral ceremony, obsequies.

క్రియాజన్యవిశేషణం **kriyaajanya wiśeeSaNam** *n. gram.* verbal adjective.

క్రియాత్మక **kriyaatmaka** *adj.* active, constructive, creative, functional.

క్రియాపదం **kriyaapadam** *n. gram.* verb.

క్రియారంగం **kriyaarangam** *n.* executive field.

క్రియారూపం **kriyaaruupam** *n.* active form; **ii bhaawam mari reNDeeLLaku~dharincindi** this idea took shape (*or* materialised) after two more years.

క్రియావంతుడు **kriyaawantuDu** *n.* assiduous or practical person.

క్రియావిశేషణం **kriyaawiśeeSaNam** *n. gram.* adverb.

క్రియాశీల **kriyaaśiila** *adj.* **1** active. **2** practical, constructive.

క్రియాశీలత **kriyaaśiilata** *n.* activity, activeness.

క్రీడ **kriiDa** *n.* sport, games.

క్రీడాకారుడు **kriiDaakaaruDu** *n.* sportsman.

క్రీడారంగం **kriiDaarangam** *n.* playing ground, sports field, arena.

క్రీడించు **kriiDincu** *v.i. class.* to play.

క్రీస్తు **kriistu** *n.* Christ.

క్రీస్తుపూర్వం **kriistupuurwam** *n.* before Christ; **krii. puu.** B.C.

క్రీస్తు శకం **kriistuśakam** *n.* Christian era; **krii. śa.** A.D.

క్రు, క్రూ - kru, kruu

క్రుంగు **krungu** *same as* **kungu.**

క్రుద్ధుడు **kruddhuDu** *n.* angry person.

క్రుమ్మరించు **krummarincu** *same as* **kummarincu.**

క్రూరం **kruuram** *adj.* 1 harsh, hard, stern. 2 cruel, brutal, wicked, malignant.

క్రూరత్వం **kruuratwam** *n.* cruelty.

క్రే, క్రై - kree, kray

క్రేంకారం **kreenkaaram** *n.* piercing cry of an animal or bird; **mayuura~** peacock's call.

క్రేగన్ను **kreegannu** *n. class.* outer corner of the eye; **kreegaNTa cuusi** *class.* looking sidelong; cf. **kiigaNTa.**

క్రైస్తవ **kraystawa** *adj.* Christian.

క్రైస్తవ మతం **kraystawa matam** *n.* Christianity.

క్రొ, క్రో, క్రౌ,- kro, kroo, kraw

క్రొంగొత్త **krongotta** *same as* **kongotta.**

క్రొత్త **krotta** *same as* **kotta.**

క్రోడీకరణ[ం] **krooDiikaraNa[m]** *n.* 1 codification. 2 compilation.

క్రోడీకరించు **krooDiikarincu** *v.t.* 1 to codify (laws). 2 to collect, compile. 3 to consolidate, make an abstract of. 4 to list, classify.

క్రోధం **kroodham** *n.* anger, wrath.

క్రోధన **kroodhana** *n.* fifty-ninth year of the Hindu cycle of sixty years.

క్రోధావేశం **kroodhaaweeśam** *n.* fury.

క్రోధి **kroodhi** *n.* thirty-eighth year of the Hindu cycle of sixty years.

క్రోలు **kroolu** *same as* **groolu.**

క్రోవి **kroowi** *n. class.* 1 tube. 2 flute.

క్రోసు **kroosu** *same as* **koosu**[1].

క్రౌంచపక్షి **krawnca pakSi** *n.* heron.

క్రౌర్యం **krawryam** *n.* cruelty.

క్లా, క్లి, క్లీ - klaa, kli, klii

క్లాంతి **klaanti** *n.* weariness, fatigue.

క్లిష్ట **kliSTa** *adj.* 1 complex, complicated. 2 intricate, elaborate, puzzling. 3 difficult.

క్లిష్టత **kliSTata** *n.* complexity, difficulty.

క్లీబం **kliibam** *adj. class.* 1 impotent. 2 unmanly.

క్లు, క్లే, క్లో - klu, klee, kloo

క్లుప్తం **kluptam** *adj.* brief, concise, short.

క్లుప్తంగా **kluptangaa** *adv.* briefly, concisely, in brief.

క్లుప్తత **kluptata** *n.* 1 brevity. 2 abridgement.

క్లుప్తపరచు **kluptaparacu** *v.t.* to abridge, make a précis of.

క్లుప్తసరిగా **kluptasarigaa** *adv.* briefly, curtly, abruptly.

క్లుప్తీకరణ **kluptiikaraNa** *n.* shortening, abridging.

క్లేశం **kleeśam** *n.* 1 affliction, distress, suffering. 2 difficulty, trouble; **kleeśaniwaaraNa** redressal of grievances.

క్లేశపడు **kleeśapaDu** *v.i.* to be afflicted or distressed.

క్లోమం **kloomam** *n. med.* pancreas.

క్వ, క్ష, క్షా - kwa, kSa, kSaa

క్వచిత్కంగా **kwacitkangaa** *adv.* occasionally, rarely.

క్వణం **kwaNam** *n. ling.* click.

క్వథనాంకం **kwathanaankam** *n.* boiling point.

క్షంత **kSanta** *n.* patient person.

క్షంతవ్య **kSantawya** *adj.* forgiveable, excusable, pardonable.

క్షంతవ్యుడు **kSantawyuDu** *n.* person fit to be forgiven, pardoned or excused.

క్షణం **kSaNam** *n.* 1 second (of time). 2 moment, instant.

క్షణక్షణానికి **kSaNa kSaNaaniki** *adv.* from one moment to the next.

క్షణభంగుర **kSaNabhangura** *adj.* transient, passing, fleeting.

క్షణిక **kSaNika** *adj.* momentary.

క్షతం **kSatam** *n.* wound, sore, hurt.

క్షతగాత్రుడు **kSatagaatruDu** *n.* injured person.

క్షత్రియ **kSatriya** *adj.* pertaining to the Kshatriya or warrior community.

క్షత్రియుడు **kSatriyuDu** *n.* member of the Kshatriya community.

క్షమ **kSama** *n.* 1 patience. 2 forgiveness.

క్షమాపణ, క్షమార్పణ **kSamaa[r]paNa** *n.* 1 apology; ~ **ceppukonu** to apologise. 2 pardon, forgiveness; ~ **kooru** to ask for pardon, ask to be forgiven.

క్షమాభిక్ష **kSamaabhikSa** *n.* forgiveness (*lit.* pardon given like alms).

క్షమార్హం **kSamaarham** *adj.* excusable.

క్షమించు **kSamincu** *v.t.* to pardon, excuse, forgive, condone; **kSamincaNDi** excuse me! *or* I beg your pardon.

క్షయం **kSayam** *n.* 1 decrease, wasting, decline, decay. 2 *biol.* atrophy. 3 waning (of moon).

క్షయకరణం **kSayakaraNam** *n. chem.* reduction.

క్షయచర్య **kSayacarya** *n. geol.* erosion.

క్షయరోగం **kSayaroogam** *n.* tuberculosis.

క్షరం **kSaram** *adj. class.* perishable.

క్షాత్రధర్మం **kSaatra dharmam** *n.* the duty of a Kshatriya or warrior.

క్షామం **kSaamam** *n.* famine.

క్షామదేవత **kSaamadeewata** *n.* goddess of famine.

క్షారం **kSaaram** *n.* 1 alkali; **kSaara dharmaalu** alkaline properties (of chemicals). 2 any caustic substance.

క్షారస్వభావం, క్షారత **kSaaraswabhaawam, kSaarata** *n.* alkalinity.

క్షాళన[ం] **kSaaLana[m]** *n.* washing away, cleansing.

క్షాళనచేయు **kSaaLanaceeyu** *v.t.* to cleanse, purify.

క్షి, క్షీ - kSi, kSii

క్షితి **kSiti** *n. class.* the earth.

క్షితిజం **kSitijam** *n.* horizon.

క్షితిజలంబ **kSitijalamba** *adj.* vertical.

క్షితిజసమాంతర **kSitijasamaantara** *adj.* horizontal.

క్షితిపతి **kSitipati** *n. class.* king.

క్షిపణి **kSipaNi** *n.* missile.

క్షీణ **kSiiNa** *adj.* 1 declining, decaying, wasting, fading away; ~ **candruDu** waning moon; ~ **sthiti** declining phase. 2 wasted, emaciated, decayed, exhausted; ~ **yugam** age of decadence.

క్షీణించు **kSiiNincu** *v.i.* to decline, decay, waste away, grow weak, deteriorate.

క్షీరం **kSiiram** *n. class.* milk.

క్షీరదం **kSiiradam** *n.* mammal.

క్షీరమాపకం **kSiiramaapakam** *n.* lactometer.

క్షీరసాగరం, క్షీరసముద్రం, క్షీరాబ్ధి **kSiirasaagaram, kSiirasamudram, kSiiraabdi** *n.* the sea of milk in Hindu mythology.

క్షీరాన్నం **kSiiraannam** *n.* pudding made of milk and rice.

క్షీరాబ్ధి ద్వాదశి **kSiiraabdi dwaadaśi** *n.* festival celebrated by women on the 12th day of the lunar month of Kartika before the full moon day.

క్షీరోదకన్యాయం **kSiiroodakanyaayam** *n.* intimate union or association (like the mixing of milk and water).

క్షీరోపలం **kSiiroopalam** *n.* opal.

క్షు - kSu

క్షుణ్ణం **kSuNNam** *adj.* thorough, complete; ~**ayna carca** exhaustive discussion.

క్షుణ్ణంగా **kSuNNangaa** *adv.* thoroughly, carefully, completely.

క్షుత్తు **kSuttu** *n. class.* hunger.

క్షుత్పీడితుడు **kSutpiiDituDu** *n.* s.o. afflicted by hunger.

క్షుద్బాధ **kSudbaadha** *n.* pangs of hunger.

క్షుద్ర **kSudra** *adj.* **1** little, small, insignificant; ~**deewata** minor deity. **2** mean, base, nasty; ~**saahityam** worthless literature.

క్షుద్రుడు **kSudruDu** *n.* s.o. who has been demeaned or disgraced.

క్షుధ **kSudha** *n.* hunger, appetite.

క్షుధాతురుడు, క్షుధార్తుడు **kSudhaaturuDu, kSudhaartuDu** *n. class.* hungry or starving person.

క్షుధార్తి **kSudhaarti** *n.* misery caused by hunger.

క్షుబ్ధ, క్షుభిత **kSubdha, kSubhita** *adj.* agitated, disturbed, restive.

క్షురకుడు, క్షురి **kSurakuDu, kSuri** *n.* barber.

క్షురిక **kSurika** *n. class.* **1** barber's razor. **2** knife.

క్షే, క్షో, క్షౌ - kSee, kSoo, kSaw

క్షేత్రం **kSeetram** *n.* **1** holy place, sacred spot, place of pilgrimage. **2** place where some activity is carried out, e.g., **kaLaa**~ institution where artists are trained and performances given; **paariśraamika**~ industrial estate. **3** *class.* field.

క్షేత్రగణితం **kSeetragaNitam** *n.* geometry.

క్షేత్రజ్ఞుడు **kSeetrajñuDu** *n.* **1** person who travels to centres of pilgrimage. **2** the human soul. **3** *colloq.* wanderer.

క్షేత్రమితి **kSeetramiti** *n.* mensuration.

క్షేత్రయాత్ర **kSeetrayaatra** *n.* pilgrimage.

క్షేత్రశాస్త్రం **kSeetraśaastram** *n.* agronomy.

క్షేపణి **kSeepaNi** *n. class.* paddle (=**teDDu**).

క్షేమం **kSeemam** I. *n.* wellbeing, welfare, happiness, good health, safety. II. *adj.* **1** happy, well, prosperous. **2** prudent, safe.

క్షేమకర **kSeemakara** *adj.* beneficial.

క్షోభ **kSoobha** *n.* **1** grief, sorrow, distress, misery. **2** agitation, disturbance.

క్షోభ్యత **kSoobhyata** *n.* agitation, disturbance.

క్షౌరం **kSawram** *n.* **1** hair-cutting. **2** shaving of the head.

క్షౌరం అవు **kSawram awu** *v.i.* **1** (of hair) to be cut or shaved. **2** *fig.* to fail, be lost; *used idiomatically in sentences like* **naa pariikSa kSawram ayindi** I failed my exam **maa paarwatiiśam ii peLLitoo puurtigaa kSawram ayipootee pooyinaaDu gaani manci aLLuNNee sampaadincEEDulee!** our friend Parvatisam may have exhausted his whole fortune on this marriage, but he has got a good son-in-law, to be sure!

క్షౌరం చేయించుకొను **kSawram ceeyincukonu** *v.i.* **1** to have o.'s hair cut. **2** to have o.'s head shaved; *but* to have o.'s face or chin shaved *is* **gaDDam giiyincukonu** *or* **gaDDam ceeyincukonu.**

ఖ - kha

ఖంగారు **khangaaru** *same as* **kangaaru.**

ఖంగు ఖంగు **khangu khangu** *n.* **1** sound made by weapons or other metal objects clanging or clashing together. **2** ~**daggutunnaaDu** he is coughing hoarsely.

ఖంగున **khanguna** *adv.* with a clanging sound.

ఖంగుమను **khangumanu** *v.i.* to clang, resound like a bell.

ఖంజరీటం **khanjariiTam** *n.* wagtail (= **kaaTuka piTTa**).

ఖండం **khaNDam** *n.* **1** anything cut off or separated, piece, part, fragment, excerpt, sector, section, portion, division; **śilaa**~ lump of rock; **kaLaa**~ work of art, art object; **śilpa**~ piece of sculpture; **khaNDa khaNDalugaa naruku** to cut into pieces; **waaDiki padi ekaraala maagaaNi eeka~gaa undi** he has ten acres of irrigated land all in one block. **2** land, country; **bharata**~ the land of India. **3** continent; **ayroopaa**~ the continent of Europe.

ఖండకావ్యం **khaNDakaawyam** *n.* literary composition consisting of a collection of short poems.

ఖండన[ం] **khaNDana[m]** *n.* **1** refutation. **2** denial. **3** censure, stricture, condemnation. **4** criticism.

ఖండనతీర్మానం **khaNDanatiirmaanam** *n.* censure motion.

ఖండనబిందువు **khaNDanabinduwu** *n. maths.* point of intersection.

ఖండనమండన **khaNDanamaNDana** *n.* hostile or destructive criticism.

ఖండబిందువు **khaNDabinduwu** *n.* arthanusvara, half sunna.

ఖండసర్కర, ఖండశర్కర **khaNDasarkara, khaNDaśarkara** *n.* sugar candy.

ఖండసారి **khaNDasaari** *n.* khandasari, a kind of sugar.

ఖండాంతర **khaNDaantara** *adj.* foreign, pertaining to foreign lands.

ఖండాంతరాలు **khaNDaantaraalu** *n. pl.* 1 other continents. 2 foreign lands.

ఖండించు **khaNDincu** *v.t.* 1 to confute, refute, contradict. 2 to reject, deny. 3 to criticise, censure, impugn, condemn. 4 to cut off, cut to pieces, mutilate. 5 to divide, cleave.

ఖండిక **khaNDika** *n.* 1 essay, short piece of literary work. 2 cutting, extract (from a longer piece of writing).

ఖండితంగా **khaNDitangaa** *adv.* 1 decidedly, definitely. 2 clearly, forcibly. 3 strictly.

ఖండ్రిక **khaNDrika** *same as* **kaNDriga.**

ఖగం **khagam** *n. class.* bird.

ఖగోళం **khagooLam** *n.* the heavens.

ఖగోళశాస్త్రం **khagooLaśaastram** *n.* astronomy.

ఖగోళశాస్త్రవేత్త **khagooLaśaastraweetta** *n.* astronomer.

ఖచిత[ం] **khacita[m]** *adj.* inlaid, inset, studded; **wajra~** diamond studded.

ఖచ్చితం, ఖచ్చితంగా, ఖచ్చితత్వం **khaccitam, khaccitangaa, khaccitatwam** *same as* **kaccitam, kaccitangaa, kaccitatwam.**

ఖజానా **khajaanaa** *n.* treasury.

ఖడ్గం **khaDgam** *n.* 1 sword, scimitar. 2 rhinoceros' horn.

ఖడ్గమృగం **khaDgamrgam** *n.* rhinoceros.

ఖణేల్మని, కణేల్మని **khaNeelmani, kaNeelmani** *onom. adv. sug.* any sharp, sudden sound, clang, bang, crack, thud, etc.; **ewaroo raayi wisiritee,~naa talaki tagilindi** when someone threw a stone, it hit my head with a thud.

ఖణేల్మను, కణేల్మను **khaNeelmanu, kaNeelmanu** *v.i.* to make a clang, bang, crack, thud or other sharp, sudden sound; **kaalu jaari paDDaanu, maDama daggira eedoo khaNeelmandi, emuka wirigindeemoo?** my foot slipped and I fell down, it made a cracking sound near my heel, I wonder if the bone is broken.

ఖత్తు **khattu** *n.* letter, epistle.

ఖత్తుకలుపు **khattu kalupu** *same as* **kattu kalupu.**

ఖత్రి **khatri** *n.* name of a community of silk weavers.

ఖదిరం **khadiram** *n.* kind of acacia tree from which catechu (= **kaacu**[5]) is obtained.

ఖద్దరు **khaddaru** *n.* khaddar, homespun cloth.

ఖనకం **khanakam** *n. class.* 1 mine (= tunnel). 2 rat.

ఖనకుడు **khanakuDu** *n.* 1 digger, esp. a member of the community of tank diggers. 2 *colloq.* burglar.

ఖననం **khananam** *n.* 1 digging. 2 burying.

ఖని **khani** *n.* mine, quarry.

ఖనిజ **khanija** *adj.* mineral.

ఖనిజం **khanijam** *n.* mineral [ore]; **khanijaanweeSaNam** prospecting for minerals.

ఖనిజవిజ్ఞానం **khanijawijñaanam** *n.* mineralogy.

ఖబ్జా **khabjaa** *same as* **kabjaa.**

ఖబ్జాదార్ **khabjaadaar** *n. dial.* landowner.

ఖర **khara** *n.* twenty-fifth year of the Hindu cycle of sixty years.

ఖరం **kharam** *n. class.* ass, donkey.

ఖరా **kharaa** I. *n.* accuracy, preciseness. II. *adj.* accurate. precise, exact.

ఖరాఖండిగా, ఖరాగా **kharaa khaNDigaa, kharaagaa** *adv.* 1 firmly, definitely. 2 precisely, accurately. 3 adamantly.

ఖరాబు **kharaabu** *adj.* bad.

ఖరాబు చేయు **kharaabu ceeyu** *v.t.* to spoil.

ఖరారు[నామా] **kharaaru[naamaa]** *n.* written agreement, contract, bond.

ఖరారుగా **kharaarugaa** *adv.* definitely, clearly.

ఖరారుచేయు **kharaaru ceeyu** *v.t.* to decide definitely.

ఖరీదు **khariidu** *n.* price, value, cost.

ఖరీదుచేయు **khariidu ceeyu** *v.t.* 1 to buy; **ii pustakaalu neenu khariidu ceesEEnu** I have bought these books. 2 to cost, be worth; **ii ceppulu wanda ruupaayalu khariidu ceestaayi** these shoes will cost a hundred rupees.

ఖరీదైన **khariidayna** *adj.* expensive, costly.

ఖరీఫ్ **khariiph** *n.* khariff, south-west monsoon agricultural season starting in May-June.

ఖర్చవు **kharcawu** *v.i.* to be spent, be expended, be used up.

ఖర్చు **kharcu** *n.* expense, expenditure, cost.

ఖర్చుచేయు,ఖర్చుపెట్టు **kharcu ceeyu, kharcu peTTu** *v.t.* to spend, incur expenditure; **aa rakam wastuwulakinda kharcu ceeyaDam alawaaTee leedu** it is not at all the custom to spend money on things like that.

ఖర్జూరం, కజ్జూరం **kharjuuram, kajjuuram** *n.* date palm.

ఖర్మ[ం] **kharma[m]** *same as* **karma[m].**

ఖర్మసిద్ధాంతం **kharmasiddhaantam** *same as* **karmasiddhaantam.**

ఖలుడు **khaluDu** *n. class.* wicked person, sinner.

ఖా - khaa

ఖాకీ, కాకీ **khaakii, kaakii** *n.* khaki colour.

ఖాతరు **khaataru** *n.* attention, care, regard; **neenu aNTee waaDiki~leedu** he has no regard for me.

ఖాతరుచేయు **khaataru ceeyu** *v.t.* to care for, pay attention to, have regard for.

ఖాతా, ఖాతాదారు **khaataa, khaataadaaru** *same as* **kaataa, kaataadaaru.**

ఖాదీ **khaadii** *n.* khadi, homespun cloth.

ఖాద్య[ం] **khaadya[m]** *adj.* edible, eatable.

ఖామందు **khaamandu** *same as* **kaamandu.**

ఖాయం **khaayam** *adj.* confirmed, fixed, settled, sure.

ఖాయం చేయు **khaayam ceeyu** *v.t.* to fix, settle, confirm, ensure, make sure; **debba tagalleedani khaayam ceesukonnaaDu** he made sure that there was no injury.

ఖాయిదా **khaayidaa** *n.* care, protection, security; **pillalanu ~ ceeyu** to keep children under careful control.

ఖారాకిల్లీ, కారాకిల్లీ **khaaraakillii, kaaraakillii** *n.* pungent way of preparing betel and nut.

ఖాళీ[చేయు] **khaaLii[ceeyu]** *same as* **kaaLii[ceeyu]**.

ఖాస **khaasa** *same as* **kaasa**[2].

ఖి, ఖు, ఖూ - khi, khu, khuu

ఖిన్న **khinna** *adj.* distressed, dejected.

ఖిన్నత **khinnata** *n.* distress, dejection.

ఖిన్నుడు **khinnuDu** *n.* distressed person.

ఖిల **khila** *adj.* 1 waste, uncared for. 2 ruined, dilapidated.

ఖిలీభూత **khiliibhuuta** *adj. class.* ruined, dilapidated.

ఖుద్దున **khudduna** *adv.* 1 personally, in person. 2 directly, without an intermediary.

ఖురం **khuram** *n. class.* hoof.

ఖులాసా[గా] **khulaasaa[gaa]** *same as* **kulaasaa[gaa]**.

ఖుల్లా **khullaa** *same as* **kullaa.**

ఖుషామత్తు చేయు **khuSaamattu ceeyu** *same as* **kuSaamattu ceeyu.**

ఖుషీ **khuSii** *n.* happiness, pleasure, delight.

ఖుషీగా **khuSiigaa** *adv.* happily.

ఖుష్కి **khuSki** *n.* dry or unirrigated land.

ఖూనీ **khuunii** *same as* **kuunii.**

ఖే, ఖై, ఖ్యా - khee, khay, khyaa

ఖేచర[ం] **kheecara[m]** *n.* bird.

ఖేచరత్వం **kheecaratwam** *n.* ability to fly like a bird or a demigod.

ఖేచరుడు **kheecaruDu** *n.* demigod.

ఖేదం **kheedam** *n.* grief, sorrow.

ఖేదకర **kheedakara** *adj.* saddening.

ఖేదపడు, ఖేదించు **kheedapaDu, kheedincu** *v.i.* to grieve, feel sad or sorrowful.

ఖేల **kheela** *n. class.* sport, game; **nṛtya~** dancing performance.

ఖైదీ, ఖైదు **khaydii, khaydu** *same as* **kaydii, kaydu.**

ఖ్యాతి **khyaati** *n.* fame, reputation.

గ - ga

గంగ **ganga** *n.* 1 River Ganges. 2 water in general; **pacci~** cold drinking water; **naa paruwu pratiSTa ~loo kalisi pootaayi** my standing and reputation will be completely ruined. 3 **~ bhaagiirathi samaanuraalu** *is a formal term for* widow.

గంగడోలు **gangaDoolu** *n.* dewlap.

గంగబాయిలికూర **gangabaayilikuura** *n. portulaca oleracea*, a green vegetable used extensively in Telangana.

గంగవెర్రి **gangawerri** *n.* 1 state of stupefaction due to mental derangement. 2 nervous disease of cattle.

గంగవెర్రులెత్తు **gangawerrulettu** *v.i.* to become mentally deranged.

గంగాళం **gangaaLam** *n.* large brass or copper vessel for storing water.

గంగిగోవు **gangigoowu** *n.* 1 mild tempered cow. 2 pure, innocent person.

గంగిరెద్దు **gangireddu** *n.* bull consecrated to a temple, dressed with ornaments and exhibited by beggars after being trained to perform tricks; *see* **DuuDuu basawanna.**

గంగిరేగి **gangireegi** *n.* umbrella tree, *thespesia populnea.*

గంజ్, గంజి **ganj, ganji**[1] *n.* wholesale market for grains and foodstuffs other than vegetables.

గంజాయి **ganjaayi** *n.* ganja, Indian hemp, cannabis; **~ dammu koTTu** to smoke ganja.

గంజి **ganji**[2] *n.* 1 cunjee, gruel, water in which rice has been boiled. 2 *fig.* very poor meal, very poor diet. 3 starch; **baTTalu ~ peTTi utikEEru** they washed and starched the clothes.

గంజిగుంట **ganjiguNTa** *n.* kitchen sink (used for pouring away waste liquids from the kitchen); **~loo ceepalu dorukutaayaa**? can you catch fish in the kitchen sink? *meaning* are you not looking for something that cannot be found?

గంజు **ganju** *n.* urine of cattle.

గంట, ఘంట **gaNTa**[1], **ghaNTa** *n.* 1 bell, gong. 2 hour, time, o'clock; **oka~** one hour; **~ enta ayindi?** *or* **enni~lu ayindi?** what time is it? **oNTi~ ayindi** it is one o'clock; **padi ~lu ayindi** it is ten o'clock; **~ stambham** clock tower.

గంట **gaNTa**[2] *n.* stubble, shoots growing round the main stem of a plant of paddy or cholam or other grain.

గంటం **gaNTam** *n.* iron pen or stylus. esp. one for writing on palm leaves.

గంటి **gaNTi** *n.* small hole; **gaNTLu gaNTLugaa** pitted.

గంటు **gaNTu** *n.* 1 cut, wound, hurt. 2 dent, notch, indentation: **nooTitoo ~ peTTu** to bite and leave a toothmark. 3 bump, excrescence (= **buDipe**). 4 knot. 5 *class., also mod. slang* bag containing money or valuables; **idi nii abba gaNTaa**? is this your patrimony? 6 **mukham ~ peTTukonu** to put on an angry look; **nannu Dabbu aDigEEDu, naadaggira leedannaanu, mukham ~peTTukoni weLLEEDu** he asked me for money, I said I had none, he went away frowning.

గంటె, గరిట, గరిటె **gaNTe**[1], **gariTa, gariTe** *n.* spoon, ladle, scoop.

గంటె **gaNTe**[2] *n.* kind of millet, *holcus spicatus*, also known as **kambu** or **sajja**.

గండం **gaNDam**[1] *n.* 1 evil hour, *lit.* baleful influence of a star: **~ gaDicindi** the evil hour has passed. 2 serious danger; **koddipaaTiloo ~ tappindi** a serious danger has just been averted.

గండం **gaNDam**[2] *n.* side of the head, upper part of the cheek.

గండకం, గండకమృగం **gaNDakam, gaNDaka mṛgam** *n.* rhinoceros.

గండకిశిల **gaNDakiśila** *n.* saligrama stone used in worship.

గండగత్తెర **gaNDagattera** *n.* dire straits.

గండదీపం **gaNDadiipam** *n.* lighted lamp placed in the tower of a temple in fulfilment of a vow.

గండపెండేరం **gaNDapeNDeeram** *n.* anklet awarded to a warrior or learned scholar as a mark of honour.

గండభేరుండం **gaNDabheeruNDam** *n.* large fabulous bird or beast.

గండమాల **gaNDamaala** *n.* goitre.

గండరగండడు **gaNDaragaNDaDu** *n.* hero of heroes.

గండరించు **gaNDarincu** I. *v.i.* to issue, spring, be produced. II. *v.t.* to produce.

గండశైలం **gaNDaśaylam** *n.* boulder, rock.

గండాగొండి **gaNDaagoNDi** *adj.* quarrelsome.

గండి **gaNDi** *n.* breach, hole, opening, gap.

గండికొట్టు, గండిపెట్టు **gaNDikoTTu, gaNDipeTTu** *v.i.* to cause a breach.

గండిపడు **gaNDipaDu** *v.i.* (of a dam) to breach, be breached, burst.

గండు **gaNDu** *adj.* 1 male. 2 big, large, stout. 3 brave, courageous.

గండుకోయిల **gaNDukooyila** *n.* cuckoo.

గండుచీమ **gaNDuciima** *same as* **kaNDaciima**.

గండుతుమ్మెద **gaNDutummeda** *n.* large black bee.

గండుపిల్లి **gaNDupilli** *n.* tomcat.

గండురోమం **gaNDuroomam** *n.* bristle.

గండ్రగొడ్డలి **gaNDragoDDali** *n.* battle-axe.

గండ్రిసక **gaNDrisaka** *n.* coarse sand.

గంత **ganta** *n.* 1 pack saddle, burden; **ii ~lu mooyaleeka castunnaam** we cannot bear these burdens. 2 quilt: **~ku tagga bonta sambandham cuusi peLLi ceeseeyi** perform the wedding after finding a suitable match. 3 bandage over the eyes; **waaDikaLLaku ~lu kaTTi tiisuku weLLEEru** they blindfolded him and took him away. 4 blinkers (to restrict an animal's lateral vision); **gurram kaLLaki ~lu kaTTi baNDi naDipistaaru** they put blinkers on the horse and drive the cart.

గంతు, గెంతు **gantu, gentu** I. *n.* jump, leap. II. *v.i.* to jump, leap.

గంథోలిగాడు **ganthooLigaaDu** *n.* clown.

గందరగోళం **gandaragooLam** *n.* utter confusion, complete disorder; **~ loo** at sixes and sevens.

గంధం **gandham** *n.* 1 sandalwood. 2 smell, scent, odour; **waaDiki widyaa ~ leedu** he has no semblance of education. 3 sandal paste.

గంధకం **gandhakam** *n.* sulphur.

గంధకాశ్మం **gandhakaaśmam** *n.* brimstone.

గంధకితం **gandhakitam** *n. chem.* sulphate.

గంధకితామ్లం **gandhakitaamlam** *n. chem.* sulphuric acid.

గంధకిదం **gandhakidam** *n. chem.* sulphide.

గంధప్రవరాలు **gandhaprawaraalu** *n. pl. biol.* olfactory capsules.

గంధయుత **gandhayuta** *adj. sci.* odoriferous.

గంధర్వకన్య **gandharwakanya** *n.* celestial nymph.

గంధర్వగానం, గంధర్వసంగీతం **gandharwa gaanam, gandharwa sangiitam** *n.* celestial music.

గంధర్వుడు **gandharwuDu** *n.* Gandharva, celestial singer.

గంప **gampa** I. *n.* 1 basket. 2 large basket for storing grain. II. *adj.* large; **waaDidi ~ samsaaram, ii jiitam ee muulaki?** his is a large family, what use will this salary be?

గంపంత **gampanta** *adj.* 1 as big as a basket. 2 very large, very much; **kaastanta uNTee ~ ceestunnadi** she is exaggerating (*lit.* when there is only so much, she is making it very much).

గంపగయ్యాళి **gampagayyaaLi** *n.* quarrelsome woman.

గంపెడు **gampeDu** *adj.* 1 a basketful of. 2 much, plenty of; **eedaynaa udyoogam cuusukondaamani ~ aaśatoo haydaraabaadu waccEEDu** he came to Hyderabad with high hopes, seeking for some job.

గంభీర **gambhiira** *adj.* 1 serious, solemn, grave. 2 deep, profound. 3 inscrutable. 4 impressive, dignified, imposing. 5 calm, placid, staid.

గంభీరత **gambhiirata** *n.* calmness, seriousness, solemnity.

గగనం **gaganam** *n.* 1 sky, heavens. 2 s.g impossible; **adi dorakaDam aameki ~ayipooyindi** to find it was impossible for her.

గగనకుసుమం **gagana kusumam** *n., lit.* sky blossom, i.e., a mere nothing, an empty dream, unreality.

గగనమండలం **gaganamaNDalam** *n. astron.* space.

గగుర్పాటు **gagurpaaTu** *n.* tingling, glowing sensation, thrill.

గగుర్పొడుచు **gagurpoDucu** *v.i.* to tingle, quiver, shiver with excitement.

గగ్గి **gaggi** *n.* threshed heads of corn used for cattle fodder.

గగ్గోలు **gaggoolu** *n.* 1 uproar, clamour, hubbub. 2 wailing, weeping.

గచ్చకాయ **gacca kaaya** *n.* fruit of the physic nut, *caesalpina bonducella*; its grey seeds are used medicinally and in a game played by girls; **gaccaaku puccaaku waydyam** treatment by herbal remedies.

గచ్చు **gaccu** *n.* cement or lime mortar or plaster; ~ **neela** floor plastered with lime or cement.

గజ **gaja** *adj.* great; ~ **donga** great thief; ~ **iitakaaDu** strong swimmer.

గజం **gajam** *n.* 1 yard, three feet; ~ **badda** yard stick. 2 *dial.* bar, rod. 3 elephant.

గజకర్ణం **gajakarNam** *n.* 1 kind of fan. 2 power of moving or waving the ears, as an elephant does. 3 **gajakarna gookarNa widyalu** (*or* **gookarNa gajakarNa widyalu**) trickery, deception, cheating.

గజగజ **gajagaja** *onom. adv. sug.* trembling, shivering *or* shuddering.

గజగజలాడు **gajagajalaaDu** *v.i.* to tremble (from fear or cold).

గజగామిని, గజయాన **gajagaamini, gajayaana** *n.* woman.

గజనిమ్మ **gajanimma** *n.* lemon, large lime with thick skin.

గజారోహణం **gajaaroohaNam** *n.* 1 *lit.* climbing on to the back of an elephant. 2 the honour of being seated on an elephant.

గజిబిజి **gajibiji** *n.* haste, confusion, muddle.

గజిబిజిగా **gajibijigaa** *adv.* 1 in haste; **sTeeSanuloo andaruu ~ unnaaru** in the station all are hurrying hither and thither. 2 confusedly, haphazardly; **taanu ~ wraasipeTTukonna DikSanarii nooTsulloonunci oka kramapaddhatiloo pheer kaapii ceesEEDu** from the dictionary notes that he had written down haphazardly he made a fair copy in a systematic way.

గజ్జ **gajja** *n.* groin, inner part of the thigh.

గజ్జి **gajji** *n.* eczema, mange, scabies; ~ **kukka** mangy dog.

గజ్జె **gajje** *n. gen. pl.* ~ **lu** tinkling ornaments, bells worn by dancers.

గజ్జెకట్టు **gajje kaTTu** *v.i.* to wear tinkling ornamental bells, i.e., to dance.

గజ్జెపూజ **gajje puuja** *n.* worship performed at the initiation of s.o. into dancing.

గట్టి **gaTTi** *adj.* 1 hard, firm, rigid, strong; ~ **prayatnam** hard effort; **paaTham ~ ceeyu** to learn a lesson thoroughly. 2 tight; *cf.* **mandi** *sense II.* 3 strict. 4 (of cloth) not torn, in good repair. 5 loud. 6 able, clever, expert. 7 difficult. 8 ~ **ancu ciire** sari with an ornate border. 9 *idiomatic expressions:* (i) **idee ~ maaTa** this is the final word (i.e., this saying is not to be modified or contradicted); (ii) **waaDidi ~ praaNam** he has a strong hold on life (said of s.o. who is none the worse after escaping from an accident or surviving a serious illness).

గట్టిగా **gaTTigaa** *adv.* 1 well, properly, firmly, strongly. 2 loudly. 3 definitely; **miiru ~ maa iNTiki raawaali reepu** you must definitely come to my house tomorrow. 4 emphatically. 5 *in neg constr.* hardly, scarcely, barely, not even (= **paTTumani**); **waaDiki ~ padi eeLLu leewu, sigareTLu taagutunnaaDu** he is scarcely ten years old, but he is smoking cigarettes.

గట్టితనం **gaTTitanam** *n.* 1 hardness, firmness, rigidity, strength. 2 ability, cleverness.

గట్టిపడు **gaTTipaDu** *v.i.* to become hard, solidify.

గట్టు **gaTTu** *n.* 1 bank, shore. 2 bund (=ridge) between plots of land. 3 bund (=dam) of an irrigation tank. 4 parapet wall (of a well).

గట్టెక్కించు **gaTTekkincu** *v.t.* to help (s.o.) out of difficulties.

గట్టెక్కు **gaTTekku** *v.t.* to get over, get free from, surmount; **kaSTaalu gaTTekkee naaTiki** by the time he surmounted his difficulties.

గట్టెక్కేయు **gaTTekkeeyu** *v.i. colloq.* to die.

గట్ర **gaTra** *n. suffix meaning* and such (similar) things, etcetera, e.g., **Dabbu~** money and such things.

గట్ల **gaTLa** *same as* **kaTTa**[2].

గట్లా **gaTLaa** *dial. variant form of* **aTLaa.**

గడ, గెడ **gaDa, geDa** *n.* 1 stick, staff, pole. 2 long bamboo stick or pole.

గడంగు **gaDangu** *v.i. class.* to resort to, have recourse to.

గడకర్ర **gaDakarra** *n.* bamboo stick or pole.

గడకొయ్య **gaDakoyya** *n.* wooden pole; ~ **laa kuurconnaaDu** he sat motionless *or* he sat without stirring.

గడగడ **gaDagaDa** *adv.* 1 violently (trembling). 2 rapidly (speaking); ~ **wallincu** to repeat rapidly.

గడగడలాడు **gaDagaDalaaDu** *v.i.* to tremble, shiver, shake.

గడచు **gaDacu** *same as* **kaDacu.**

గడప **gaDapa** *same as* **kaDapa.**

గడబిడ, గడిబిడి **gaDabiDa, gaDibiDi** *n.* commotion, fuss.

గడమంచె **gaDamance** *n.* wooden frame like a bench to keep sacks on.

గడవు, గడువు **gaDawu, gaDuwu** *n.* 1 period, term, time limit, time span (for payment, etc.). 2 duration.

గడసరి **gaDasari** *n.* 1 clever, intelligent person. 2 sharp, smart, shrewd person. 3 firm, tough, stubborn person.

గడసరితనం **gaDasaritanam** *n.* 1 shrewdness, smartness, sharpness. 2 firmness, toughness.

గడి **gaDi**[1] *n.* 1 square. 2 *pl.* **gaLLu** checks; **gaLLacokkaa** checked shirt; **gaLLanuDikaTTu** crossword puzzle.

గడీ **gaDi**[2] *n. dial.* fort.

గడించు **gaDincu** *v.t.* to earn, acquire, gain.

గడిగడికీ **gaDigaDikii** *adv.* 1 every now and then. 2 very often, time and again.

గడియ **gaDiya**[1] *same as* **ghaDiya.**

గడియ **gaDiya**[2] *n.* bolt or bar to secure a door.

గడియ పెట్టు, గడియ వేయు **gaDiya peTTu, gaDiya weeyu** *v.t.* to bolt (a door).

గడియారం **gaDiyaaram** *n.* watch, clock.

గడియారస్తంభం **gaDiyaarastambham** *n.* clock tower.

గడుగ్గాయి **gaDuggaayi** *n. colloq.* mischievous fellow.

గడుచు **gaDucu** *same as* **kaDacu.**

గడుపు **gaDupu** I. *v.i.* to spend time, pass time, carry on. II. *v.t.* **1** to pass, spend (time, etc.). **2** to get over, get through.

గడుపుకొను **gaDupukonu** *v.i.* to manage, carry on.

గడువు **gaDuwu** *same as* **gaDawu.**

గడుసు **gaDusu** *adj.* **1** clever, intelligent. **2** sharp, smart, shrewd. **3** firm, tough, stubborn.

గడుసుతనం **gaDusutanam** *n.* **1** cleverness, shrewdness. **2** firmness, toughness.

గడేకారి **gaDeekaari** *n.* **1** building worker, stone mason. **2** labourer.

గడ్డ, గెడ్డ **gaDDa, geDDa** *n.* **1** lump, clod. **2** boil, abscess. **3** land, country. **4** bulbous root. **5** stream, hill stream.

గడ్డకట్టు **gaDDakaTTu** *v.i.* **1** to solidify. **2** (of blood) to clot. **3** to freeze, be frozen stiff.

గడ్డం, గెడ్డం **gaDDam, geDDam** *n.* beard, chin; ~ **paT-Tukoni batimaalu** to beseech.

గడ్డం చేయించుకొను, గడ్డం గీయించుకొను **gaD-Dam ceeyincukonu, gaDDam giiyincukonu** *v.i.* to get o.s. shaved; *see* **kSawram ceeyincukonu.**

గడ్డం చేయు, గడ్డం గీయు **gaDDam ceeyu, gaD-Dam giiyu** *v.i.* to shave; **mangaliwaaDu aayanaki gaDDam ceesEEDu** *or* **gaDDam giisEEDu** the barber shaved him.

గడ్డం చేసుకొను, గడ్డం గీసుకొను **gaDDam cee-sukonu, gaDDam giisukonu** *v.i.* to shave o.s.

గడ్డపలుగు, గడ్డపార **gaDDapalugu, gaDDapaara** *n.* crowbar.

గడ్డాల **gaDDaala** *adj.* bearded.

గడ్డి **gaDDi** *n.* **1** grass, straw, hay. **2** rubbish.

గడ్డిగట్రా **gaDDigaTraa** *n.* hay and similar things.

గడ్డిగాదర, గడ్డిగాదం **gaDDigaadara, gaDDigaadam** *n.* weeds, trash, rubbish.

గడ్డితిను **gaDDi tinu** *v.i.* **1** *lit.* to eat grass. **2** to eat s.g indigestible; **aDDamayna gaDDi tiNTee niiku jabbu cees-tundi** if you eat anything that you come across, you will get ill. **3** *fig.* to swallow s.g illegally; **aa udyoogamloo naanaa gaDDi tini baagaa sampaayincEEDu** he made a fortune by swallowing many bribes in that job.

గడ్డిపరక, గడ్డిపోచ **gaDDiparaka, gaDDipooca** *n.* **1** blade of grass. **2** a trifle, very little.

గడ్డిపువ్వు **gaDDipuwwu** *n.* **1** wild flower. **2** *fig.* attractive flower with no fragrance.

గడ్డిమేటు **gaDDimeeTu** *n.* rick of hay or straw.

గడ్డు **gaDDu** I. *n.* hardness, toughness. II. *adj.* hard, diffi-cult, tough, serious, testing; **ii ~ roojulloo** in these difficult days *or* in these hard times; ~ **samasya** tough or difficult problem; ~ **roogam** serious disease.

గణం **gaNam** *n.* assemblage, collection, group, circle, number, flock, troop. **2** body, class, kind; **widyaarthi ~** student body; **paśu ~** cattle (in general). **3** foot, metre in prosody; **gaNaalu tappina padyam** verse which does not comply with the rules of metre and versification, verse which does not scan correctly.

గణకశాస్త్రం **gaNakaśaastram** *n.* accountancy.

గణకాధికారి **gaNakaadhikaari** *n.* accountant, accounts officer.

గణగణ **gaNagaNa** *onom. n. and adv. sug. sound of* ringing; **gaNTa ~ mannadi** *or* **gaNTa ~ moogindi** the bell rang.

గణగణలాడు **gaNagaNalaaDu** *v.i.* **1** (of a bell) to ring. **2** *same as* **kaNakaNalaaDu.**

గణతంత్రరాజ్యం **gaNatantra raajyam** *n.* republic.

గణన[ం] **gaNana[m]** *n.* **1** counting, reckoning, calculation. **2** earning[s].

గణనీయ **gaNaniiya** *adj.* noteworthy, notable, significant, appreciable.

గణనీయుడు **gaNaniiyuDu** *n.* notable person.

గణరాజ్యం **gaNaraajyam** *n.* name given to a form of government prevailing in ancient India, comprising a system of loosely knit mainly autonomous village units.

గణాంక **gaNaanka** *adj.* statistical.

గణాంకశాస్త్రం **gaNaankaśaastram** *n.* (science of) statis-tics.

గణాంక శాస్త్రజ్ఞుడు **gaNaankaśaastrajñuDu** *n.* statis-tician.

గణాంకాలు **gaNaankaalu** *n.pl.* figures, statistics.

గణాచారి **gaNaacaari** *n.* priest who enters into a trance and becomes possessed by a goddess; **waanaloo taDisi ~ laa iNTiki waccEEDu** he came home soaked with rain like a **gaNaacaari** (who is soaked with water by onlookers during a trance).

గణించు **gaNincu** *v.t.* **1** to reckon, calculate, compute. **2** to acquire, gain, earn.

గణిక **gaNika** *n. class.* prostitute.

గణికుడు, గణితజ్ఞుడు **gaNikuDu, gaNitajñuDu** *n.* mathematician.

గణితం **gaNitam** *n.* mathematics.

గణితయంత్రం **gaNitayantram** *n.* computer.

గణితశాస్త్రం **gaNitaśaastram** *n.* (science of) mathematics.

గణియం **gaNiyam** *n.* ornaments, artificial jewellery.

గణ్య **gaNya** *adj.* estimable, [praise]worthy.

గణ్యత **gaNyata** *n.* estimability, [praise]worthiness.

గత **gata** I. *suffix used to form adjs. conveying the meaning* resulting from, embedded in, involving, in accordance with, e.g., **sandhi ~ ruupaalu** forms involving sandhi; **abhiwṛddhi ~ mayna praNaalika** developmental plan; **antar ~** internal; **bahir ~** external. II. *adj.* last, previous; ~ **padeeLLugaa** for the last ten years; *cf.* **paramayna.**

గతం **gatam** *n.* past.

గతంగా **gatangaa** *suffix used to form adverbs conveying the meaning* in the course of, as a result of, relating to, e.g., **sandhi ~** as a result of sandhi; **wyakti ~** individually; *cf.* **parangaa.**

గతజలసేతుబంధనం **gatajalaseetubandhanam** *see* **see-tubandhanam.**

గతానుగతికంగా **gataanugatikangaa** *adv.* in a stereo-typed manner.

గతానుగతికత్వం **gataanugatikatwam** *n.* habit of following the past blindly, uninventiveness.

గతి **gati** *n.* 1 going, movement, motion. 2 manner of moving, gait. 3 path (of sun, moon), course (of time, river). 4 contrivance, expedient, resource, means of obtaining: **nuuTiki parwaaleedu, kaasuki ~ leedu** (outwardly) they have no difficulty for a hundred rupees (but in fact) they have no way of getting a pie (i.e., they appear to be very well off but in fact they are penniless — proverb). 5 refuge, help, aid, remedy, hope; **diipam buDDiiyee ~ , kareNTu ghaDighaDikki pootundi** lanterns are all we have (as a remedy), the current goes on and off; **~ leeni, ~ maalina** helpless, wretched, destitute; **maaku bhoojanaaniki ~ leedu** there is no hope of a meal for us. 6 fate, lot, destiny, fortune; **mana ~ eemayuNDeedoo**? what might have been our fate?

గతితార్కిక **gatitaarkika** *adj.* dialectic.

గతించు **gatincu** *v.i.* 1 to pass, elapse. 2 to pass away. 3 to die.

గతిశక్తి **gatiśakti** *n. phys.* kinetic energy.

గతిశాస్త్రం **gatiśaastram** *n. sci.* dynamics.

గతిశీల **gatiśiila** *adj.* mobile.

గతిశీలత **gatiśiilata** *n.* mobility.

గతుకు **gatuku**[1] *v.t.* to lap up, gobble up (like a dog); *cf.* **katuku.**

గతుకు **gatuku**[2] *n.* pit; **rooDDantaa ~ lu** the road is all pits.

గతుక్కుమను **gatukkumanu** *v.i.* to be startled, have a great shock.

గత్తర **gattara** *n.* outbreak of a serious disease such as cholera.

గత్యంతరం **gatyantaram** *n.* other means, alternative.

గత్వాగత్వా **gatwaagatwaa** *adv.* as (s.g) progresses or proceeds; *cf.* **piitwaapiitwaa.**

గద **gada** *n.* mace, club.

గదం **gadam** *n. class.* disease.

గదమాయించు **gadamaayincu** *v.t.* to scold, rebuke.

గదాధరుడు **gadaadharuDu** *n.* club or mace bearer.

గది **gadi** *n.* 1 room, apartment. 2 compartment. 3 square on a chess board.

గదుము **gadumu** *v.t.* to scold, rebuke, check, admonish.

గద్గదం **gadgadam** *n.* choking sound, choked voice.

గద్గదంగా **gadgadangaa** *adv.* with a choking voice.

గద్గదస్వరం **gadgadaswaram** *n.* choked or strangled voice.

గద్ద, గెద్ద **gadda, gedda** *n.* kite, eagle.

గద్దగోరు **gaddagooru** *n.* 1 *lit.* kite's claw or talon. 2 hook for fastening a door. 3 implement used by thieves for housebreaking. 4 clawlike tool used for plucking betel leaves.

గద్దరి **gaddari** *adj.* 1 quarrelsome, cantankerous. 2 impudent, impertinent.

గద్దించు **gaddincu** *v.t.* to scold, rebuke, chide.

గద్దె **gadde** *n.* throne, high seat.

గద్దె దించు **gadde dincu** *v.t.* to depose, dethrone.

గద్య[ం] **gadya[m]** *n.* 1 ornamental literary prose. 2 prose.

గని **gani** *n.* mine, quarry.

గనిగడ్డ **ganigaDDa** *n.* 1 mine. 2 source of wealth, s.g very valuable; **aa roojulloo oka ruupaayiki konnadi ippuDu dhara perigi ~ ayindi** what one bought for a rupee in those days has become very valuable now because of the rise in price.

గనిమ **ganima** *n.* ridge or bund between fields.

గనుక, గనక **ganuka, ganaka** *same as* **kanuka.**

గనుపు **ganupu** *same as* **kanupu.**

గన్నేరు **ganneeru** *n.* oleander.

గప్‌చిప్, గుప్‌చిప్ **gap cip!, gup cip!** *interj.* hush!, be quiet!, be silent! **~ gaa kuurcuNDu** to sit silently.

గప్పాలు **gappaalu** *n.pl.* boasting, bragging.

గప్పాలుకొట్టు **gappaalukoTTu** *v.i.* to boast, brag.

గప్పున **gappuna** *adv.* suddenly, quickly.

గప్పుమను **gappumanu** *v.t.* to flare up, blaze.

గఫ్‌కీలు **gaphkiilu** *n.pl.* barefaced lies and boasting.

గబగబ, గబగబా **gabagaba, gabagabaa** *adv.* quickly, rapidly, hurriedly, in a hurry.

గబాలున **gabaaluna** *same as* **gabhaaluna.**

గబుక్కున, గభుక్కున **gabukkuna, gabhukkuna** *adv.* suddenly, hastily.

గబ్బిలం **gabbilam** *n.* bat (small animal that flies by night).

గబ్బు **gabbu** *n.* bad smell, stench.

గబ్బుచీకటి **gabbu ciikaTi** *n.* pitch darkness.

గబ్బులేపు **gabbuleepu** *v.i.* 1 to stir up a bad smell. 2 *dial.* to create a furore.

గభాలున, గబాలున, గుభేలున **gabhaaluna, gabaaluna, gubheeluna** *adv.* suddenly, hurriedly, quickly, hastily; *cf.* **dabhaaluna.**

గభీమని **gabhiimani** *adv.* violently, explosively, suddenly; **niiLLalooki ~ gentu** to dive into water with a splash; *cf.* **dabhiimani.**

గభీరం **gabhiiram** *adj. class.* deep, profound.

గమకం **gamakam** *n. music* sequence of notes.

గమగమ, ఘమఘమ **gamagama, ghamaghama** *adv.* sweetly smelling.

గమనం **gamanam** *n.* 1 motion, movement, progress. 2 course (of river). 3 passing, passage (of time).

గమన నియమాలు **gamana niyamaalu** *n.pl. sci.* laws of motion.

గమనశీల **gamanaśiila** *adj.* mobile.

గమనార్హం **gamanaarham** *adj.* noteworthy, worthy of attention.

గమనించు **gamanincu** *v.t.* to pay attention to, attend to, notice, observe, take notice of, note.

గమనిక **gamanika** *n.* notice, attention.

గమళ్ల, గౌండ్ల **gamaLLa, gawNDLa** *n.* a name of the toddy tappers community.

గమికొను **gamikonu** *v.i.* to form together into a crowd.

గమిడి **gamiDi**[1] *n.* village boundary.

గమిడి **gamiDi**[2] **~geede** *n.* buffalo of large size such as a murra buffalo.

గమేళా **gameeLaa** *n.* iron bowl-shaped implement for carrying earth, sand, cement, etc.

గమ్మత్తు **gammattu** *n.* 1 fun, amusement, jest. 2 s.g strange, odd or peculiar.

గమ్మత్తుగా **gammattugaa** *adv.* in jest, for fun, jokingly; **uurikee~ pilicEEnu** I just called you for fun *or* I just called you as a joke.

గమ్ము **gammu** *n.* fragrance.

గమ్మున **gammuna** *adv.* 1 quickly, suddenly; "**~raa**" **annaaDu** "come quickly", he said. 2 quietly; **~kuurcoo** sit quietly.

గమ్యం **gamyam** *n.* goal, objective.

గమ్యస్థానం **gamyasthaanam** *n.* destination.

గయాళు **gayaaLu** *n.* waste land.

గయ్యాళి **gayyaaLi** I. *n.* nagging woman, shrew. II. *adj.* shrewish.

గరపనేల **garapaneela** *n.* light gravelly soil.

గరజు, గర్జు **garaju, garju** *n.* necessity, need; **naakeem ~paTTindi maaTLaaDaDaaniki?** what need is there for me to talk?

గరళం **garaLam** *n.* poison.

గరాటు **garaaTu** *n.* funnel.

గరానా, ఘరానా **garaanaa, gharaanaa** *adj.* respectable, honourable, *often used ironically*, e.g., **caTTaalanu tamaku anukuulangaa maarcukoni samaajamloo~gaa calaamaNii awutaaru** they alter the laws in their own favour and pass for respectable people in society.

గరిక **garika** *n.* kind of grass used as fodder for cattle and horses.

గరికె వడ్లు **garike waDLu** *n.pl.* name of a variety of paddy usually grown as second crop.

గరిట, గరిటె **gariTa, gariTe** *same as* **gaNTe**[1].

గరిడీ **gariDii** *n.* 1 fencing, sword play. 2 fencing school, gymnasium.

గరిత **garita** *n.* woman, housewife.

గరిపొడుచు **garipoDucu** *v.i.* to tingle; **naa oLLantaa garipoDustoondi** my whole body is tingling.

గరిమ **garima** *n.* weight, greatness, abundance, *often as second part of a compound*, e.g., **wiśwaasa~** abundance of faith; **bhaawanaa~gala maaTalu** words containing an abundance of imagination.

గరిమనాభి **garimanaabhi** *n. phys.* centre of gravity.

గరిష్ట **gariSTa** *adj.* 1 heavy, weighty. 2 venerable. 3 greatest, maximum.

గరిష్టం **gariSTam** *n.* maximum.

గరిష్టసామాన్య కారణరాశి **gariSTa saamaanya kaaraNa raaśi** *n. maths.* highest common factor, HCF.

గరిష్టీకరణ **gariSTiikaraNa** *n.* maximisation.

గరిష్టుడు **gariSTuDu** *n.* most esteemed or venerable person.

గరిసె **garise** *n.* 1 basket for storing grain. 2 building for storing grain, granary. 3 grain measure equal to 600 kunchams.

గరుకు **garuku** *adj.* 1 rough, rugged. 2 coarse.

గరుడ **garuDa** *n.* eagle, lord of all the birds in mythology.

గరుడకంబం, గరుడస్తంభం **garuDakambam, garuDastambham** *n.* post erected before a Vaishnavite temple, surmounted by bells; *cf.* **dhwajastambham.**

గరుడధ్వజుడు **garuDadhwajuDu** *n.* epithet of Vishnu, whose emblem is an eagle.

గరుడపచ్చ **garuDa pacca** *n.* inferior kind of emerald, a medicinal stone used as an antidote for snake bite.

గరువం **garuwam** *same as* **garwam.**

గరువు **garuwu** *n.* light gravelly soil.

గర్జన[ం] **garjana[m]** *n.* roar; **meegha~** thunder.

గర్జించు **garjincu** *v.i.* to roar.

గర్జు **garju** *same as* **garaju.**

గర్తం **gartam** *n.* 1 *class.* hole, hollow, pit, cave. 2 *class.* crack, fissure. 3 *sci.* trough.

గర్దభం, గార్దభం **gardabham, gaardabham** *n.* ass, donkey.

గర్భం **garbham** *n.* 1 womb, uterus; **aameki~waccindi** she became pregnant; **aameki ~** (*or* **aameki kaDupu**) **ceesEEDu** he made her pregnant. 2 embryo, foetus. 3 stomach. 4 interior, innermost part of anything; **samudra~** depths of the ocean; **nadii~** deepest part of a riverbed.

గర్భం ధరించు, గర్భంతో ఉండు **garbham dharincu, garbhamtoo uNDu** *v.i. and t.* to conceive, be[come] pregnant.

గర్భకోశం **garbhakoośam** *n.* uterus.

గర్భగుడి **garbhaguDi** *n.* innermost shrine of a temple, sanctum sanctorum.

గర్భగృహం **garbhagṛham** *n.* inner part of a house.

గర్భగ్రహణం **garbhagrahaNam** *n.* impregnation, conception.

గర్భదరిద్రుడు **garbha daridruDu** *n.* poverty stricken person, s.o. in dire poverty.

గర్భధారణ[ం] **garbhadhaaraNa[m]** *n.* 1 insemination, fertilisation. 2 conception.

గర్భపాతం, గర్భస్రావం **garbhapaatam, garbhaśraawam** *n. med.* miscarriage, abortion.

గర్భవతి, గర్భిణి **garbhawati, garbhiNi** *n.* pregnant woman.

గర్భశత్రువు **garbhaśatruwu** *n.* lifelong enemy.

గర్భస్థ **garbhastha** *adj.* 1 in the womb. 2 in the interior or depths of anything.

గర్భాదానం **garbhaadaanam** *n.* nuptial ceremony. 2 *slang* intercourse.

గర్భావధి **garbhaawadhi** *n.* gestation; **~kaalam** gestation period.

గర్భాశయం **garbhaaśayam** *n.* uterus.

గర్భిత **garbhita** *adj.* 1 hidden, concealed, latent, implicit, inherent; **ii heccarika prapanca caritraloonee ~ mayunnadi** this warning is implicit in world history itself. 2 full of, pregnant with; **bhaawa~** pregnant with meaning.

గర్భోత్పత్తి **garbhootpatti** *n.* insemination.

గర్రు **garru** *n.* noise made in belching; **~ mani teencu** to belch loudly.

గర్వం, గరువం **garwam, garuwam** *n.* pride, vanity, arrogance, haughtiness.

గర్వపడు **garwapaDu** *v.i.* to feel proud, feel vain.

గర్వి **garwi** *n.* proud person.

గర్వించు **garwincu** *v.i.* to be proud.

గర్వితుడు **garwituDu** *n.* proud person, *gen. as second part of a compound,* e.g., **widyaa~** s.o. who is proud of his education.

గర్విష్ఠి **garwiSTi** *adj.* proud, arrogant.

గర్హణీయ, గర్హ్య **garhaniiya, garhya** *adj.* fit to be condemned, base, scandalous.

గర్హించు **garhincu** *v.t.* 1 to condemn, denounce, revile. 2 to blame, censure.

గల **gala** *same as* **kala**[2].

గలగల **galagala** *onom. n. and adv. sug. the sounds of* tinkling (bells, bangles), jingling (keys), clinking (coins), rattling (seeds in a pod), flapping (papers in a breeze); **gaajulu ~ laaDutunnaayi** *or* **gaajulu ~ maNTunnaayi** the bangles are tinkling.

గలనపత్రం **galanapatram** *n.* filter paper.

గలని **galani** *n.* filter funnel.

గలపరించు **galaparincu** *v.t.* to rinse out (a bottle); **siisaa galaparinci kaDigEEnu** I washed the bottle by rinsing it out.

గలబరించు **galabarincu** *v.i.* to grumble.

గలభ, గలాభా **galabha, galaabhaa** *n.* commotion, disturbance, hubbub.

గలాటా **galaaTaa** *n.* noise, fuss, hubbub, row, disturbance.

గలిబిలి **galibili** *n.* confusion, fuss.

గలీబు **galiibu** *n.* pillow case.

గల్పిక **galpika** *n.* sketch (short literary composition).

గల్ల **galla**[1] *n.* grain.

గల్ల, గల్లా, గల్లగురుగు, గల్లపెట్టి, గల్లబుడ్డి **galla**[2]**, gallaa, gallagurugu, gallapeTTi, gallabuDDi** *n.* money box, cash box.

గల్లంతు **gallantu** *n.* 1 confusion, disturbance, noise. 2 naughtiness, mischievous behaviour (of children).

గల్లంతు అవు **gallantu awu** *v.i.* to disappear, be missing; *see* **śaalti.**

గల్లీ **gallii** *n.* alley, lane.

గల్లు, ఘల్లు **gallu, ghallu** *onom. n. and adv. sug.* tinkling sound of bells, jewels, broken glass, broken chains, etc.; **gajjelu ~ maNTunnaayi** the ankle bells are tinkling; **siisaa penkulu ~ na cediripaDDaəyi** the broken pieces of the bottle scattered with a tinkling sound.

గళం **gaLam** *n.* throat, neck.

గళగండం **gaLagaNDam** *n.* diphtheria.

గళధమని **gaLadhamani** *n.* carotid artery.

గళ్ల, గళ్లు **gaLLa, gaLLu** *see* **gaDi.**

గవదబిళ్లలు **gawada biLLalu** *n.pl.* mumps.

గవదలు **gawadalu** *n.pl.* 1 glands of the throat. 2 mumps.

గవను **gawanu** *n. class.* entrance gate of a fort.

గవయం **gawayam** *n. class.* wild ox.

గవాక్షం **gawaakSam** *n.* window.

గవిసెన **gawisena** *n.* cloth cover placed over a bullock's back during a festival.

గవేషణ[ం] **gaweeSaNa[m]** *n.* search, enquiry.

గవేషించు **gaweeSincu** *v.t.* to search.

గవ్వ **gawwa** *n.* 1 sea shell, cowrie. 2 pl. **~ lu** money (since cowries were used as money in olden times).

గవ్వకన్ను **gawwakannu** *same as* **tappakannu.**

గవ్వలాట **gawwalaaTa** *n.* a game played with shells.

గవ్వసున్నం **gawwa sunnam** *n.* lime mortar made from shells.

గస **gasa** *n.* asthma.

గసగసాలు **gasagasaalu** *n.pl.* poppy seeds.

గసడదవాదేశం **gasaDadawaadeeśam** *n. gram.* sandhi rule by which the sounds *k,c,T,t,p* become *g,s,D,d,w* under certain conditions in Telugu.

గసి **gasi** *n.* residue (in a cup of tea, coffee, ghee, etc.).

గసిక **gasika** *n.* 1 *same as* **gasi.** 2 wooden spike or wedge. 3 peg for tying cattle. 4 wooden or iron digging implement.

గస్తీ **gastii** *n.* patrol; **~ waaDu** *or* **~ saynikuDu** sentry.

గస్తీ తిరుగు **gastiitirugu** *v.i.* to go on patrol.

గహన[ం] **gahana[m]** I. *n. class.* forest. II. *adj.* dense, thick, deep, impenetrable.

గహ్వరం **gahwaram** *n.* cave.

గా - gaa

గా **gaa** *originally* **kaa** *infinitive of* **awu** to be[come] *used as an adverbial suffix* **1** *equivalent to the adverbial termination* -ly *in English*, e.g., **tondaragaa** hastily. **2** like, as; **neela erragaa undi** the soil is red (*lit.* the soil is red-like); **1-11-56 haydaraabaad raajadhaani nagarangaa aandhra pradeeś awatarincindi** on 1-11-1956 Andhra Pradesh came into existence with Hyderabad as the capital. **3** *idiomatic translation may require the use of a preposition in English*, e.g., **adiwarakugala jaali gawrawangaa maarindi** his former pity changed into respect; **186 puTalaloo maatramu imiDina granthamu meemu 1000 puTalugaa pencinaamu** we have expanded into 1000 pages a book that was previously contained in only 186 pages; **goodaawari nadi reNDu paayalugaa ciilutundi** the River Godavari splits into two branches; **nadi tuurpugaa paarutundi** the river flows eastwards; **dawaLeeśwaram graamaaniki dakSiNangaa paarutundi**; it flows south of the village of Dowleshwaram; **aa praajekTuku 1.54 kooTLa ruupaayalu wyayangaa ancanaa weesinaaru** they made an estimate of Rs. 1.54 crores for expenditure on that project; **gata 25 samwatsaraalugaa** for (*or* during) the last 25 years; **aneeka kaaraNaalugaa** for many reasons; **muuDu daśalugaa** in three stages. **4** *following an infinitive* (i) when, since, as a result of; **paristhitulu iTLaa uNDagaa** when circumstances are like this; **lakSalaadi kuuliilu reeyimbawaLLu kaSTam ceeyagaa aanakaTTa aydeeLLaloo puurtayindi** as a result of lakhs of labourers working strenuously by day and night, the anicut was finished in five years; (ii) as against, whereas; **1975-76 loo 36,633 Tannula senaga paNDincagaa, 1976-77 loo 20,995 Tannulu maatramee paNDicaDam jarigindi** whereas 36,633 tonnes of groundnuts were harvested in 1975–76, only 20,995 tonnes were harvested in 1976–77; *see* **kaagaa. 5 gaanee** *following an infinitive* as soon as; **DaakTarugaaru raagaanee ceppaNDi** tell me as soon as the doctor comes.

గాంచు **gaancu** *same as* **kaancu.**

గాండీవం **gaaNDiiwam** *n.* Arjuna's bow.

గాండ్రించు, గాండ్రింపు, గాండ్రు **gaaNDrincu, gaaNDrimpu, gaaNDru** *same as* **kaaNDrincu, kaaNDrimpu, kaaNDru.**

గాంధర్వ[ం] **gaandharwa[m]** *n.* **1** form of marriage by mutual consent. **2** the art of music.

గాంధారి **gaandhaari** *n.* **1** name of the wife of King Dhrutarastra. **2** cannabis, bhang, ganja.

గాంభీర్యం **gaambhiiryam** *n.* **1** depth. **2** grandeur. **3** seriousness.

గాజర, గాదెర **gaajara, gaadera** *n.* carrot.

గాజు **gaaju** *n.* **1** glass; ~**palaka** pane of glass. **2** bangle, bracelet.

గాజురొయ్య **gaajuroyya** *n.* crayfish, prawn.

గాజులమలారం **gaajulamalaaram** *n.* bundle of different kinds of bangles carried by bangle sellers from place to place when selling their wares.

గాజుసామాను **gaaju saamaanu** *n.* glassware.

గాటిగుంజ, గాటికంబం **gaaTigunja, gaaTikambam** *n.* post or stake for tying cattle near a feeding trough.

గాటు **gaaTu** *n.* mark or dent caused by biting.

గాటుపడి **gaaTupaDi** *see* **raaTupaDi.**

గాడి **gaaDi** *n.* **1** ditch, trench, groove; ~**tiiyu** to dig a trench; ~**tappu** to go off the track, miss the groove. **2** feeding trough for cattle, manger. **3** thread of a screw.

గాడిద, గాడిదె **gaaDida, gaaDide** *n.* ass, donkey.

గాడిదగుడ్డు **gaaDidaguDDu** *n. slang* nonsense.

గాడిపొయ్యి **gaaDipoyyi** *n.* hearth made in the form of a trench for cooking a line of pots.

గాడు **gaaDu**[1] *n. suffix* **1** same as **kaaDu**[1]. **2** *colloq. when added to the names of male persons and certain occupations it may indicate contempt* **bicca**~ beggar. **3** *colloq. when added to the names of male persons it may indicate informality or friendliness* **weLLaniwwaleedani C.gaaDiki entoo idigaa uNDaali** poor C. must feel very put out at not being allowed to go.

గాడు **gaaDu**[2] *n.* **1** lust, longing. **2** *colloq.* itch, hankering; **oLLu** ~**paTTi gurrappandEElaku weLLEEDu** he went to to the horse races because he had a hankering for it.

గాడ్పు **gaaDpu** *n.* wind; **waDa**~ hot wind.

గాఢ **gaaDha** *adj.* strong, firm, tight, deep, extreme, intense; ~**mooham** intense or vehement passion; ~**andhakaaram** pitch darkness; ~**mayna erupu** deep red, dark red; ~**nidra** deep sleep, sound sleep; ~**aamlam** concentrated acid; **o.-ni** ~**ngaa kawgalincukonu** to embrace (s.o.) tightly, give (s.o.) a tight hug.

గాఢత **gaaDhata** *n.* intensity, concentration.

గాఢవాంఛ **gaaDhawaancha** *n.* ambition.

గాఢ్య **gaaDhya** *adj.* firm, strong.

గాత **gaata** *n.* **1** groove, channel or opening which allows water to flow out of a building from within. **2** ditch or channel dug in a field to distribute water to crops.

గాతం **gaatam** *n.* pit, hole.

గాత్రం **gaatram** *n.* **1** singer's voice. **2** *colloq.* **peekaaTaloo**~ **paniki raadu, Dabbu kaawaali** you cannot play cards on credit (*lit.* in a card game voice is not enough, you must have ready money).

గాత్రకచేరి **gaatrakaceeri** *n.* recital of songs, music party.

గాత్రసంగీతం **gaatra sangiitam** *n.* vocal music.

గాథ **gaatha** *n.* long tale or story, narrative.

గాదం **gaadam** *n.* kind of grass that infests fields, known as knot grass; *cf.* **gaDDi**~.

గాదె **gaade** *n.* basket for storing grain.

గాదెర **gaadera** *same as* **gaajara.**

గాద్గదిక **gaadgadika** *adj.* (of voice) choked, emotional.

గాద్గదికంగా **gaadgadikangaa** *adv.* in a choked or emotional voice.

గానం **gaanam** *n.* **1** music, singing. **2** **kawitaa**~ poetry recital.

గానకచేరి **gaanakaceeri** *n.* music recital, concert; ~ **ceeyu** to give a concert.

గానమందిరం **gaanamandiram** *n.* concert hall.

గానసభ **gaanasabha** *n.* music recital, concert.

గానాభజానా **gaanaabhajaanaa** *n.* singing and drumming; ~ **gaaLLu** *colloq.* vagabonds, wasters.

గాని **gaani** *same as* **kaani**².

గాను **gaanu**¹ *n.* cartwheel.

గాను **gaanu**² *same as* **kaanu**².

గానుగ, గానిగ **gaanuga, gaaniga** *n.* oilmill, sugarcane crusher.

గానుగ ఆడించు, గానుగ పట్టు **gaanuga aaDincu, gaanuga paTTu** *v.t.* to mill (oilseeds), crush (sugarcane).

గానుగపిండి **gaanugapiNDi** *n.* oilcake.

గానే **gaanee** *see* **gaa** *sense 5.*

గాబు **gaabu** *n.* **1** *dial.* weeds. **2** large jar or trough for storing grain or watering cattle.

గాభరా, గాబరా **gaabharaa, gaabaraa** *n.* fright, confusion, perplexity.

గాభరాపడు **gaabharaapaDu** *v.i.* to be very upset, feel frightened, feel confused, feel perplexed.

గాభరాపెట్టు **gaabharaapeTTu** *v.i.* to cause alarm or perplexity.

గామాలు **gaamaalu** *same as* **kaaboolu.**

గామి **gaami** *suffix denoting* follower, traveller, e.g., **wyooma**~ space traveller; **gaandhii maarga**~ follower in the path of Mahatma Gandhi.

గాయం **gaayam** *n.* wound, cut, injury; **naaku~ayindi** *or* **naaku~tagilindi** I was injured.

గాయకం **gaayakam** I. *n.* secret. II. *adj.* costly, scarce.

గాయకుడు **gaayakuDu** *n.* singer (man).

గాయత్రి **gaayatri** *n.* **1** name of a goddess. **2** name of a mantra in which the sun is invoked.

గాయని **gaayani** *n.* singer (woman).

గాయపడు **gaayapaDu** *v.i.* to be hurt, injured or wounded.

గాయపరచు **gaayaparacu** *v.t.* to hurt, injure, wound.

గార **gaara** *n.* mortar, plaster. **2** tartar on teeth.

గారం, గారాబం, గారాము **gaaram, gaaraabam, gaaraamu** *n.* **1** affection, fondness. **2** indulgence, excessive fondness, spoiling, pampering.

గారచెక్క **gaaracekka** *n.* implement for smoothing plaster, trowel.

గారడి **gaaraDi** *n.* conjuring, jugglery; ~**waaDu** conjurer, juggler.

గారాల, గారాబు **gaaraala, gaaraabu** *adj.* (of a child) darling.

గారు **gaaru** *honorific suffix added to names of persons* (*equivalent to* Mr., Mrs., *in English*) *and to names of professions.*

గారుడం **gaaruDam** *adj. class.* pertaining to Garuda.

గారె **gaare** *n.* kind of cake made of black gram, a delicacy (= **waDa**²).

గార్దభం **gaardabham** *same as* **gardabham.**

గార్హస్త్యం **gaarhastyam** *n.* state of being a householder, married state; **gaarhastya jiiwanam** domestic life.

గాల **gaala** *n.* trench, ditch, groove.

గాలం, గేలం **gaalam, geelam** *n.* **1** fishing hook; ~ **weeyu** *or* ~ **wisuru** to cast a baited fishing hook. **2** implement with hooks for recovering things fallen into a well.

గాలనం **gaalanam** *n.* filtration.

గాలని **gaalani** *n.* filter.

గాలి **gaali** *n.* air, wind, breeze; ~**kaburlu** *or* ~**maaTalu** vain or senseless words, idle or meaningless talk; ~**peeni** (*or* ~**pooguceesi**) **kathalu allu** to compose stories from hardly any material; ~**ki tirugu** to roam about idly and aimlessly; **nannu tiTTEEDu, neenu** ~**ki wadileesEEnu** he abused me, but I ignored it; **pillalu**~**ki puTTi dhuuliki perugutunnaaru** the children are growing up neglected and uncared for; **aayana**~**waariki sookindi** they have come under his influence. **2** ghost, evil spirit. **3** scent of an animal (= **pasi**).

గాలించు **gaalincu** *v.t.* **1** to search thoroughly, ransack; **illantaa gaalincEEru** they ransacked the whole house. **2** to sift stones, etc., from grain (by soaking in water to allow stones to sink).

గాలింపు **gaalimpu** *n.* **1** thorough search. **2** sifting.

గాలికుంటు **gaalikuNTu** *n.* infectious disease affecting the hooves of horses and cattle.

గాలిగుడి **gaaliguDi** *n.* halo round the sun or moon.

గాలిగుమ్మటం **gaaligummaTam** *n.* parachute.

గాలిగోపురం **gaaligoopuram** *n.* temple tower.

గాలిదుమారం **gaalidumaaram** *n.* dust storm.

గాలిపటం **gaalipaTam** *n.* paper kite.

గాలిపోత **gaalipoota** *n.* winnowing by pouring grain from a height so that wind carries away the chaff.

గాలిబిళ్లలు **gaalibiLLalu** *n.pl.* mumps.

గాలిమర, గాలియంత్రం **gaalimara, gaaliyantram** *n.* windmill.

గాలిమేడ **gaalimeeDa** *n.* castle in the air, hope unlikely to be fulfilled; **aayana kanna kalalannii** ~**layi pooyEEyi** all his dreams vanished into thin air.

గాలివాటు బతుకు **gaaliwaaTu batuku** *n.* life with no security or stability.

గాలివాన **gaaliwaana** *n.* cyclone, typhoon.

గాళ్లరోగం **gaaLLaroogam** *n. vet.* foot and mouth disease.

గావంచా **gaawancaa** *n.* small piece of cloth worn round the waist while bathing.

గావు **gaawu** *n.* **1** sacrifice of an animal in a village ceremony. **2** blood of a sacrificed animal.

గావుకేక **gaawukeeka** *n.* loud shout, cry of alarm.

గావున, కావున **gaawuna, kaawuna** *conj. class.* therefore.

గావును **gaawunu** *same as* **kaaboolu.**

గాసం **gaasam** *same as* **graasam.**

గాసటబీసట **gaasaTabiisaTa** *n.* meaningless gabbling.

గాసిల్లు **gaasillu** *v.i.* to labour, struggle.

గి - gi

గి, గీ **gi, gii** *prefix used when, in speaking slightingly, a word is repeated with its initial syllable changed to* **gi** *if it is short or* **gii** *if it is long*, e.g., **Dabbu gibbu naa daggira leedu** I haven't a pie on me; **nii koopam giipam naa daggira paniki raadu** your tantrums make no impression on me.

గింగురు **ginguru** *adv.* resoundingly.

గింగురుమను **gingurumanu** *v.i.* **1** to resound, ring in o.'s ears. **2** to reel with dizziness.

గింజ **ginja** *n.* **1** grain, seed. **2** *pl.* ~ **lu** grain, corn, seeds.

గింజుకొను **ginjukonu** *v.i.* **1** to twitch, writhe, be restless, toss about. **2** to struggle, strive. **3** to say (s.g) grudgingly. **4** to beg, wheeedle; **enta ginjukonnaa, niiku nagalu iwwanu** however much you wheedle me, I will not give you the jewels.

గింజులాట **ginjulaaTa** *n.* restlessness.

గిండి **giNDi** *n.* kind of narrownecked vessel.

గిచ్చు **giccu** *v.t.* to pinch, nip.

గిచ్చులాట **gicculaaTa** *n.* pinching in play, teasing.

గిజగిజ **gijagija** *adv.* agitatedly, convulsively.

గిజగిజకొట్టుకొను **gijagijakoTTukonu** *v.i.* to wriggle, writhe.

గిజగిజలాడు **gijagijalaaDu** *v.i.* **1** to be agitated, struggle, writhe, squirm, wriggle, flutter. **2** to shiver (from fear or cold).

గిజాటుగా **gijaaTugaa** *adv. colloq.* confused, perplexed, at o.'s wits' end; **Dabbuku naaku ~ undi** I am at my wits' end for want of money.

గిజాటుపడు **gijaaTupaDu** *v.i. colloq.* to be confused, be perplexed, be at o.'s wits' end.

గిజిగాడు, గిజ్జిగాడు **gij[j]igaaDu** *n.* the weaver bird, whose nest is suspended from the end of a branch over water.

గిజురు, గుజురు, గుంజు, గుజ్జు **gijuru, gujuru, gunju, gujju** *n.* flesh or pulp of fruit.

గిటక, గిటకబారు **giTaka, giTakabaaru** *same as* **giDasa**[1], **giDasabaaru.**

గిటగిట **giTagiTa** *onom. n. and adv. signifying* teeth chattering (from anger or cold).

గిట్ట **giTTa** *n.* hoof.

గిట్టు **giTTu**[1] *v.i.* to die, expire, perish.

గిట్టు, కిట్టు **giTTu**[2], **kiTTu** *v.i.* **1** to suit, be agreeable or pleasing; **ii waasana [aNTee] naaku giTTadu** I do not like this smell; **waaDikii naakuu giTTadu** he and I do not get on well together. **2** to be earned or acquired; **ii baDimiida R.ku nelaku ee padi panneNDu ruupaayaloo giTTeewi** from this school R. used to earn some Rs. 10 or Rs. 12 per month. **3** (of money) to be enough to cover expenses; **kaniisam kharculu giTTinaa caalu** it will be enough if at least the expenses are covered; **aa kaaDikistee naaku elaa giDutundi?** if I give at that rate how will my expenses be met? "**muppaawalaa istaanu, wastaawaa?**" "**muppaawalaa giTTadaNDii!**" "I will pay 75 paise, will you come?" "75 paise will not be enough, Sir!"

గిట్టుబాటు, కిట్టుబాటు, గిట్టుబడి, కిట్టుబడి **giTTubaaTu, kiTTubaaTu, giTTubaDi, kiTTubaDi** *n.* **1** availability; ~ **loo** within reach, within a person's means, available; ~ **gaa** in demand, saleable. **2** constituting a fair transaction, providing a fair return; ~ **dhara** fair price; ~ **kuulii** fair wages; **oka wanda ruupaayilu TikaTLu amminaa manaku ~ awutundi** even if Rs. 100 worth of tickets are sold, it will give us a fair return.

గిట్లా **giTLaa** *dial. variant of* **iTlaa.**

గిడస, గిటక **giDasa**[1], **giTaka** *adj.* short, dwarfed, stunted.

గిడస **giDasa**[2] *n.* kind of fish.

గిడసబారు, గిటకబారు **giDasabaaru, giTakabaaru** *v.i.* to be stunted.

గిడుగు **giDugu** *n.* small palmyra leaf umbrella without a handle.

గిడ్డ, గిడ్డు **giDDa, giDDu** *adj.* short, dwarfish.

గిడ్డంగి **giDDangi** *n.* warehouse, depot, godown, storehouse.

గిత్త **gitta** *n.* young bull.

గిద్ద **gidda** *n.* measure of volume, one sixteenth of a manika.

గిన్నీముంతా **ginniimuntaa** *n.pl.* pots and pans.

గిన్నె **ginne** *n.* cup, bowl.

గిరక **giraka** *n.* pulley wheel.

గిరగిర **giragira** *adv.* round and round.

గిరజాలు **girajaalu** *n.pl.* long hair style worn by some children and men.

గిరవు, గిరివి **girawu, giriwi** *n.* mortgage.

గిరాకీ **giraaki** *n.* commercial demand.

గిరాటువేయు, గిరాటుకొట్టు **giraaTuweeyu, giraaTukoTTu** *v.t.* **1** to hurl, fling. **2** to throw down with contempt. **3** to throw away, discard.

గిరి **giri**[1] *n.* hill, mountain.

గిరి **giri**[2] *n.* line drawn round a thing, line drawn to mark a division.

గిరి **giri**[3] *last part of a n. compound* status, position, office, -ship; **munasabu~** office of munsiff; **gumaastaa~** clerkship.

గిరిగీయు **girigiiyu** *v.i.* to fix a limit, circumscribe; **girigiisukoni kuurcuNDu** to cut o.s. off, isolate o.s.

గిరిజనుడు **girijanuDu** *n.* member of a hill tribe, girijan.

గిరివాసి **giriwaasi** *n.* mountain dweller.

గిరివి **giriwi** *dial., same as* **girawu.**

గిరుక్కున **girukkuna** *adv.* turning round; ~ **tirugu** to turn round suddenly, wheel round quickly.

గిర్ని **girni** *n.* **1** mill. **2** factory.

గిర్రున **girruna** *adv.* **1** whirling round. **2 atani kaLLaloo niiLLu ~ tirigEEyi**; tears welled up in his eyes.
గిర్రునతిప్పు **girruna tippu** *v.t.* to whirl round.
గిర్రుమను **girrumanu** *v.i.* to whirl round.
గిలక **gilaka** *n.* **1** pulley wheel. **2** toy rattle.
గిలకకొట్టు **gilakakoTTu** *v.t.* to churn.
గిలకరించు **gilakarincu** *v.t.* **1** to churn, beat (buttermilk). **2** to rinse by shaking (bottle). **3** *dial.* to sprinkle.
గిలక్కాయ **gilakkaaya** *n.* toy rattle.
గిలగిలకొట్టుకొను, గిలగిలతన్నుకొను **gilagila koTTukonu, gilagila tannukonu** *v.i.* **1** to struggle, writhe. **2** to squirm, wriggle. **3** to wheedle (= **ginjukonu**).
గిలి **gili** *n.* doubt, fear, hesitation; **aayana raaDeemoonanna ~ undi naaku** I had a doubt about his coming.
గిలిగింత, గిలిగిలి **giliginta, giligili** *n.* tickling.
గిలిగింతలు పెట్టు **giligintalu peTTu** *v.t.* to tickle.
గిలుకు **giluku** *v.t.* to scribble.
గిలుపు **gilupu** *see* **kannu~**.
గిల్లీదండు **gilliidaNDu** *n.* a boys' game (= **karraabiLLaa**).
గిల్లు **gillu** I. *n.* pinch, nip. II. *v.t.* to pinch, nip[off]; **gooLLu ~ koNTuu kuurcuNDu** to sit idly, waste time.
గిల్లుడు **gilluDu** *n.* pinch[ing], nip[ping].
గిళనం **giLanam** *n.* *class.* swallowing.

గీ - gii

గీ **gii** *see* **gi.**
గీకు **giiku** *v.t.* **1** to scrape, scratch. **2** to instigate.
గీచు **giicu** *v.t.* **1** to scrape, scratch. **2** to draw (picture). **3** to tap (palm tree for toddy).
గీటడగు **giiTaDagu** *v.i.* *class.* to die, perish.
గీటు **giiTu** I. *n.* line, stroke; **kalam ~** stroke of a pen; **kannu ~** wink. II. *v.i.* **kannu ~** to wink.
గీటుపెట్టు **giiTupeTTu** *v.t.* to test by a touchstone or yardstick.
గీటుబద్ద **giiTubadda** *n.* yardstick.
గీత **giita**[1] *n.* the Bhagawadgita.
గీత **giita**[2] *n.* **1** (drawn) line. **2** line by which to tell s.o.'s fate; **nii ~ loo uNTee awutundi** if it is in your fate, it will happen. **3** scratch, scrape. **4** scratch made for tapping toddy from a palm tree; **~ kaarulu** or **~ paniwaaLLu** toddy tappers.
గీతం **giitam** *n.* **1** song, hymn, poem; **jaatiiya ~** national anthem. **2** name of a very simple musical composition for beginners.
గీతి **giiti** *n.* song, poem; **teeTa ~** name of a kind of poetical metre.
గీతిక **giitika** *n.* short song.
గీపెట్టు **giipeTTu** *v.i.* **1** to scream; **arici giipeTTinaa laabham leedu** there is no use in shouting and screaming. **2** (of an elephant) to trumpet.
గీయించుకొను **giiyincukonu** *v.i.* to get o.s. shaved.
గీయు **giiyu** *v.t.* **1** to draw, trace (line). **2** to sketch (picture). **3** to tap (toddy from a palm tree). **4** to shave. **5 aggipulla ~** to strike a match.
గీర **giira** *n.* **1** line, stripe (on cloth). **2** *dial.* cartwheel. **3** pride, arrogance; **~ cuupistunnaaDu** he is exhibiting arrogance.
గీరు **giiru** *v.t.* to scratch, scrape.
గీర్వాణం **giirwaaNam** *n.* **1** the Sanskrit language. **2** haughtiness, pride, arrogance.

గు - gu

గుంజ **gunja** *n.* **1** post, pillar, prop, pole. **2** peg, stake.
గుంజాటన **gunjaaTana** *n.* worry, anguish.
గుంజాటనపడు **gunjaaTanapaDu** *v.i.* **1** to be beset with difficulties. **2** to be worried or anguished. **3** to hesitate, dither (= **mallaagullaalupaDu, majjugujjulupaDu**).
గుంజాయించు **gunjaayincu** *v.t.* **1** to pull, drag, haul. **2** to pull this way and that, pull first to one side and then to another.
గుంజాయిషీ **gunjaayiSii** *n.* flaw, defect.
గుంజీలు, గుంజిళ్లు **gunjiilu, gunjiLLu** *n.pl.* a kind of punishment for children involving kneeling on the ground and standing up again for a number of times while holding both ears; also performed by worshippers in a temple as a mark of respect to the deity.
గుంజీలుతీయు **gunjiilutiiyu** *v.i.* to perform **gunjiilu.**
గుంజు **gunju**[1] *v.t.* **1** to pull, drag, haul. **2** to grab, extort, extract (money).
గుంజు **gunju**[2] *n. same as* **gijuru.**
గుంట **guNTa**[1] *n.* (*used to convey contempt or disrespect*) girl.
గుంట, కుంట **guNTa**[2], **kuNTa** *n.* **1** pond, pool. **2** hole, pit, hollow. **3** measure of land, gen. one fortieth of an acre.
గుంటక **guNTaka** *n.* harrow.
గుంటగలగర **guNTagalagara** *n.* a shrub, *eclipta prostrata.*
గుంటడు **guNTaDu** *n. slang* fellow (*used contemptuously of a boy or man*).
గుంటనక్క **guNTanakka** *n.* **1** fox. **2** cunning person.
గుంటపూలు పూయు **guNTapuulu puuyu** *v.i.* **1** *lit.* to yield a crop of weeds or wild flowers. **2** to produce a poor result; **waaDi caduwu guNTapuulu puustunnadi** his education is not progressing well.
గుంటి, గుంటు **guNTi, guNTu** *n.* portion of a field intended for ploughing.
గుండ **guNDa** *n.* powder; **mirapa~** chilli powder; **kandi~** red gram flour; **biskaT~** biscuit crumbs.
గుండం **guNDam** *n.* **1** fire pit. **2** pit of any kind.
గుండగొయ్య **guNDagoyya** *n.* wicked or daring person.
గుండడు **guNDaDu** *n.* servant.
గుండా **guNDaa**[1] *p.p.* through, by, by means of.
గుండా, గూండా **guNDaa**[2], **guuNDaa** *n.* rowdy, villain.
గుండారు **guNDaaru** *n. dial.* method of tying a lungi or sari, *also called* **aDDakaTTu.**
గుండిగ **guNDiga** *n.* large metal pot for cooking, storing water, etc.
గుండీ **guNDii** *n.* button.
గుండు **guNDu** I. *n.* **1** cylindrical or spherical object; **raati~** *or* **kanki~** stone roller used for threshing corn. **2** bullet, cannonball, shot. **3** weight for scales or for a plumbline; **~koTTu** to suspend a plumbline. **4** [shaven] head. **5** iron hoop round the rim of a baling bucket. **6** whole cashewnut (not split in half). II. *adj.* round, spherical.
గుండుకొట్టించుకొను, గుండుచేయించుకొను **guNDukoTTincukonu, guNDuceeyincukonu** *v.i.* to have o.'s head completely shav
గుండుపెంకు **guNDupenku** *n.* curved tile (half-cylinder in shape).
గుండుసూది **guNDusuudi** *n.* pin.
గుండె **guNDe** *n., often pl.* **~lu** **1** heart, chest, breast; **~lu baadukonu** to beat o.'s breast, lament; **atani~lloo raayi paDindi** he was greatly disturbed *or* he was greatly shocked; **~lamiida kumpaTi** heavy burden of responsibility, source of great anxiety; **ammaku~ceruwaypooyindi** the mother's heart was overwhelmed with sorrow; **~lu tiisina baNTu** utterly heartless person, one capable of any wickedness. **2** boldness (in good or bad sense), courage; **enni~lu raa niiku?** how bold you are! **aa maaTa anaDaaniki niiku guNDEE, ceruwaa?** how dare you say that? **waaDi~jaari pooyindi** his courage failed.
గుండెధైర్యం **guNDedhayryam** *n.* courage.
గుండెనిబ్బరం **guNDenibbaram** *n.* staunchness.
గుండెపోటు **guNDepooTu** *n.* heart attack.
గుండ్ర[ం], గుండ్రని **guNDra[m], guNDrani** *adj.* round, circular, spherical; **guNDra balla samaaweeśam** round table conference.
గుండ్రం **guNDram** *n.* roundness.
గుండ్రాయి **guNDraayi** *n.* **1** pestle. **2** round stone.
గుంత **gunta** *n.* **1** pond, pool. **2** hole, pit, hollow.
గుంపు **gumpu** I. *n.* **1** crowd, group; **leeLLa~** herd of deer. **2** *dial.* thick end of a stick, by which the stick is held. II. *adj. dial.* stout, bulky.
గుంపుచేయు **gumpuceeyu** *v.t.* to collect, assemble.
గుంపుచేరు **gumpuceeru** *v.i.* to come together, gather, assemble.
గుంపెన **gumpena** *n. class.* leap.
గుంఫనం **gumphanam** *n.* **1** *class.* tying or stringing together. **2** **pada~** arrangement of words, composition.
గుంభనం **gumbhanam** *n.* obscurity, secrecy.
గుంభనగా **gumbhanagaa** *adv.* secretly.
గుక్క **gukka** *n.* **1** gulp, sip, mouthful (of anything liquid). **2** drawing breath, a lungful of breath; **~tippukonu** to breathe; **~tippakuNDaa** *or* **~tiragakuNDaa** ceaselessly, without pausing for breath; **~paTTu** to hold o.'s breath; **~paTTi eeDcu** to weep convulsively.
గుక్కెడు **gukkeDu** *adj.* gulp of, mouthful of (any liquid).
గుగ్గిలం **guggilam** *n.* gum or resin of *shorea robusta*; *see* **aggi.**
గుగ్గిళ్లు **guggiLLu** *n. pl.* boiled horsegram for feeding to cattle and horses.
గుచ్చిగుచ్చి **guccigucci** *adv.* persistently (asking), intently (gazing).

గుచ్చు **guccu** *v.t.* 1 to pierce, prick, attach by pricking; **cokkaaku baaDjii ~ toondi** she pins a badge onto his coat. 2 to string together, thread (beads, garland of flowers). 3 to insert, push in, stick in; **kancu looTaaloo biyyam poosi oka kaTTa uuduwattulu gucci uncEEDu** he poured rice into a bronze lota and stuck a packet of incense sticks into it; **suudiloo daaram ~** to thread a needle.

గుచ్చుకొను **guccukonu** *v.i.* to penetrate, pierce, prick; **ceetulaku muLLu guccukonnayi** the thorns pricked his hands.

గుచ్ఛం **guccham** *n.* bunch; **puSpa~** bunch of flowers, bouquet; **kathaa~** collection of stories.

గుజగుజపోవు **gujagujapoowu** *v.i.* to talk in a whisper.

గుజగుజలాడు **gujagujalaaDu** *v.i.* to be at a loss, be confused.

గుజురు, గుజ్జు **gujuru, gujju**[1] *same as* **gijuru.**

గుజ్జనగూళ్లు **gujjanaguuLLu** *n.pl.* name of a children's game.

గుజ్జు **gujju**[2] *n.* dwarf.

గుజ్జు **gujju**[3] *n.* 1 tooth of a harrow. 2 *pl.* **~ lu** upright posts fixed along the sides of a cart.

గుటక **guTaka** *n.* gulp.

గుటకలుమింగు **guTakalumingu** *v.i.* 1 to falter, hesitate (to reply); **neenu praśnalu aDigitee jawaabu ceppaleeka guTakalu mingEEDu** when I questioned him he faltered, being unable to reply. 2 to wait hopefully, be full of expectation; **~ tuu kuurcunnaaDu** he sat waiting hopefully.

గుటగుట **guTaguTa** *onom. n. and adv. sug.* (i) drinking rapidly, gulping, (ii) bubbling, simmering.

గుటగుటలాడు **guTaguTalaaDu** *v.i.* to flicker (in a figurative sense); **praaNam ~ tunnadi** his life is flickering, he is on the point of death.

గుటి[క] **guTi[ka]** *n.* pill, tablet.

గుటుక్కున **guTukkuna** *adv.* with a gulp; **mandu ~ mingEEDu** he swallowed the medicine with a gulp.

గుటుక్కుమను **guTukkumanu** *v.i. slang* to die.

గుట్ట **guTTa** *n.* 1 hill, hillock. 2 heap.

గుట్టకూలు **guTTakuulu** *v.i.* to be ruined.

గుట్టు **guTTu** *n.* secrecy, privacy; **roogam raTTu, kaapuram ~** tell people about your illness but keep your home life private (proverb); **~ cappuDu kaakuNDaa** without informing other persons, without any noise or fuss.

గుట్టుగా **guTTugaa** *adv.* secretly, privately.

గుడం **guDam** *n.* jaggery, gur (= **bellam**).

గుడక **guDaka** *n.* shell of a coconut or similar fruit.

గుడగుడ **guDaguDa** *onom. n. and adv. sug.* boiling or bubbling.

గుడగుడలాడు **guDaguDalaaDu** *v.i.* to talk in a whisper.

గుడారం, గుడారు **guDaaram, guDaaru** *n.* tent.

గుడి **guDi** *n.* 1 temple. 2 circle. 3 halo round the sun or moon. 4 swollen portion round a boil or abscess. 5 secondary form of the vowel *i* in Telugu script.

గుడింతం, గుణింతం **guDintam, guNintam** *n.* combination of primary symbol of a consonant with secondary symbol of a vowel to form a graphic syllable (**akSaram**); *cf.* **baLLu.**

గుడిగి **guDigi** *n.* loin cloth reaching down to the knees.

గుడిగుడిగుంజం, గుడుగుడుగుంజం **guDiguDigunjam, guDuguDugunjam** *n.* name of a children's game.

గుడిచుట్టు **guDicuTTu** *n.* halo round the sun or moon.

గుడిజెల్ల **guDijella** *n.* kind of small fish.

గుడిపూడి జంగాలు **guDipuuDi jangaalu** *see* **jangam.**

గుడిసె **guDise** *n.* hut.

గుడిసేటి **guDiseeTi** *adj.* immoral; **~ di** prostitute; **~ maniSi** immoral scoundrel.

గుడుగుడు **guDuguDu** *n.* huqqa, hubble bubble; **~ taagu** to smoke a huqqa.

గుడ్డ **guDDa** *n.* cloth, clothing; *pl.* **~ lu** clothes; **~ lu wippukuraa, annam tinduwugaani** change your clothes and come and take a meal.

గుడ్డం, గుడ్డాం **guDDam, guDDaam** *n.* field, plot of land.

గుడ్డంతపిల్లి **guDDantapilla** *n.* little brat.

గుడ్డగుడుసు **guDDaguDusu** *n.* cloth and such things.

గుడ్డి **guDDi** *adj.* 1 blind; **~ waaDu** blind person; **~ nammakam** blind trust; **guDDeddu ceeloo paDDaTTu** like a blind bull entering a field (proverb, said of s.o. who is hoodwinked or who cannot take care of himself); **wiiDu ~ gawwapaaTi kuuDaa ceeyaDu** he is not worth a pie (*lit.* he is not worth as much as a damaged cowrie). 2 pale, dim; **~ wennela** pale moonlight; **~ diipam** dim light.

గుడ్డితనం **guDDitanam** *n.* blindness.

గుడ్డీబొడ్డీ **guDDii boDDii** *n.* rubbish.

గుడ్డు **guDDu** *n.* 1 egg; **guDLu peTTu** to lay eggs; **guDLu podugu** to hatch eggs; *see* **gaaDida ~ , ee ~ .** 2 any young thing, human or animal; **aaru nelala ~** a six months old baby; *cf.* **pasi ~ .** 3 eyeball; **guDLurumu** to glare or glower angrily; **guDLerraceeyu** to be very angry (*lit.* to make o.'s eyes red with anger); **nannu cuusi guDLaloo peTTukoNTunnaaDu** he is envious of me. 4 *colloq.* zero, nil.

గుడ్లగూబ **guDLa guuba** *n.* owl.

గుణం **guNam** I. *suffix attached to certain numerals meaning* -fold, e.g., **dwi~** twofold, **daśa~** tenfold. II. *n.* 1 quality, property, character, disposition. 2 trait of character, characteristic, attribute. 3 virtue, merit; **guNadooSaalu** good and bad points of character. 4 effect, influence. 5 one of the three basic qualities of beings in nature; these are *sattwa* (goodness or purity), *rajas* (activity or passion) and *tamas* (darkness or ignorance). 6 improvement in health; **aa mandu waaDitee ~ kanipincindi** when I too that medicine there was an improvement. 7 delirium; **waaDiki ~ puTTindi** he became delirious.

గుణకం **guNakam** *n. sci.* 1 coefficient. 2 multiple. 3 modulus.

గుణకారం **guNakaaram** *n. maths.* multiplication; **guNakaara labdham** product.

గుణగణాలు **guNagaNaalu** *n. pl.* 1 characteristics, qualities. 2 good qualities, virtues.

గుణగానం **guNagaanam** *n.* praise of s.o.'s character.

గుణపాఠం **guNapaaTham** *n.* lesson learnt by experience.

గుణవంత **guNawanta** *adj.* possessing good qualities.

గుణవంతుడు **guNawantuDu** *n.* man of good qualities and character.

గుణవతి **guNawati** *n.* woman of good qualities and character.

గుణశ్రేఢి, గుణోత్తరశ్రేఢి **guNa śreeDhi, guNoottara sreeDhi** *n. maths.* geometric progression.

గుణాత్మక **guNaatmaka** *adj.* qualitative.

గుణాదేశం **guNaadeeśam** *n. sandhi rule governing changes occurring in vowels when they merge*, e.g., a + i > ee *as in* **deewa indruDu > deeweendruDu.**

గుణించు **guNincu** *v.t.* to multiply.

గుణింతం **guNintam** *same as* **guDintam.**

గుణిజం **guNijam** *n. sci.* multiple.

గుణుచు, గునుచు **guNucu, gunucu** *v.i.* to murmur, grumble.

గుత్త **gutta** *n.* 1 lease, contract; ~ **ku iccu** to lease out, give on rent or contract; ~ **paTTu,** ~ **tiisukonu** to take on contract. 2 monopoly. 3 *dial.* land revenue.

గుత్తం **guttam** *n.* tightness; **guttapu rawika** tight or close-fitting blouse.

గుత్తంగా **guttangaa** *adv.* thickly, densely, in a bunch; **molakalu ~ unnaayi** the seedlings are bunched close together; **gaajulu ~ weeyincukoo** cover your arm with bangles (*lit.* put on your bangles thickly).

గుత్తకూలి **guttakuuli** *n.* contract labourer.

గుత్తగా **guttagaa** *adv.* firmly, tightly.

గుత్తగైకొను **guttagaykonu** *v.t.* 1 to take on contract. 2 to monopolise.

గుత్తదారుడు **guttadaaruDu** *n.* 1 contractor. 2 monopolist. 3 lessee, tenant.

గుత్తవ్యాపారం **guttawyaapaaram** *n.* monopoly business.

గుత్తసొత్తు, గుత్తసొమ్ము **guttasottu, guttasommu** *n.* monopoly, exclusive possession.

గుత్తాధిపతి, గుత్తాధికారి **guttaadhipati, guttaadhikaari** *n.* monopolist.

గుత్తాధిపత్యం **guttaadhipatyam** *n.* monopoly.

గుత్తి **gutti** *n.* 1 bunch, cluster. 2 ankle joint.

గుత్తికాయ **guttikaaya** *n.* pickle made of mangoes stuffed with spices.

గుత్తివంకాయ **guttiwankaaya** *n.* brinjal stuffed with spices and cooked.

గుదం **gudam** *n.* anus.

గుది, గుదికర్ర, గుదికొయ్య, గుదిబండ **gudi**[1], **gudikarra, gudikoyya, gudibaNDa** *n.* hobble to prevent cattle from straying.

గుది **gudi**[2] *n.* bunch, cluster.

గుదిగుచ్చు **gudiguccu** *v.t.* 1 to string together. 2 to narrate in detail.

గుద్ద **gudda** *n.* anus.

గుద్దలి **guddali** *n.* 1 single or double headed pickaxe. 2 kind of hoe.

గుద్దలిపూజ **guddali puuja** *n.* worship performed at the laying of a foundation stone.

గుద్దు **guddu** I. *n.* blow with the fist, box, cuff, punch. II. *v.t.* 1 to strike, hit, knock against, collide with, bump into; **kaaru ceTTuku guddeesindi** the car collided with a tree; **appuDee iNTLooki wastunna J.ni guddeesEEDu** he bumped into J. who was just entering the house. 2 to strike with the fist, cuff. 3 *slang* to send (report, petition); *see* **accu ~**.

గుద్దులాట **guddulaaTa** *n.* 1 fighting with fists. 2 fighting; **musuguloo ~** infighting, internal bickering, internal wrangling.

గునగున **gunaguna** *adv.* 1 (of human beings) moving slowly and with effort; ~ **naDucu** to plod, waddle, totter. 2 (of plants) growing lushly or delicately; **mokkalu ~ molakettEEyi** the plants grew lushly.

గునపం, గునపాం **gunapam, gunapaam** *n.* crowbar.

గునియు **guniyu** *v.i.* 1 to grumble, murmur, be discontented. 2 to speak coaxingly.

గునుచు **gunucu** *same as* **guNucu.**

గునుపు **gunupu** *n.* grumbling, dissatisfaction, discontent.

గున్న **gunna** I. *n. in apposition to another n.* young one; **eenugu ~** young elephant; **maamiDi ~** young mango tree. II. *adj.* short and broad, dumpy, squat; ~ **eenugu** small stout elephant; ~ **maamiDi** variety of mango tree which is low and bushy.

గుప్చిప్ **gupcip** *same as* **gapcip.**

గుప్త **gupta** *adj.* 1 hidden, secret. 2 *sci.* latent; **guptooSNam** latent heat.

గుప్పించు, కుప్పించు, గుప్పు, కుప్పు **guppincu, kuppincu, guppu**[1], **kuppu**[1] *v.t.* to shower, scatter freely or plentifully, compose (verses, etc.) freely; **haridaasu haasyam tega kuppincEEDu raa!** Haridas made ever so many jokes; **anyadeeśyaalu guppinci waakyaalu raayawaccu** you may write sentences making free use of foreign words.

గుప్పిలి, గుప్పిడి **guppili, guppiDi** *n.* fist, grasp; **guppiTLoo** in the grasp of, in the clutches of.

గుప్పు, కుప్పు **guppu**[2], **kuppu**[2] *v.t.* to butt with the head.

గుప్పుగుప్పున **guppuguppuna** *adv.* (of cigar smoking) in puffs or whiffs.

గుప్పున **guppuna** *adv.* suddenly, all at once.

గుప్పుమను **guppumanu** *v.i.* 1 (of a sweet smell) to be emitted; **puula waasana guppumannadi aame talaloonunci** a sweet smell of flowers came from her hair. 2 to envelop, engulf, pervade, spread through; **ii wiSayam uurantaa guppumannadi** this news spread through the entire village.

గుప్పెడు **guppeDu** *adj.* a fistful of.

గుబగుబలాడు **gubagubalaaDu** *v.i.* (of the heart) to quake.

గుబాళించు, గుబాళింపు **gubaaLincu, gubaaLimpu** *same as* **gubhaaLincu, gubhaaLincu.**

గుబాలున **gubaaluna** *same as* **gabhaaluna.**

గుబిలి, గులిమి **gubili, gulimi** *n.* wax in the ear.

గుబుక **gubuka** *n.* boss, knob.

గుబుక్కున **gubukkuna** *adv.* suddenly.

గుబుక్కుమను **gubukkumanu** *v.i.* (of the heart) to beat fast, quake.

గుబురు **guburu** I. *n.* (of foliage) thickness, denseness, dense growth; **ceTLa ~** cluster of trees. II. *adj.* (of foliage) thick, dense.

గుబులు **gubulu** *n.* 1 melancholy, mental depression: **naa** guNDelloo ~ ~gaa unnadi I am sick at heart. 2 whim, fancy.

గుబ్బ gubba I. *n.* 1 knob, stud, protuberance. 2 canu~ woman's breast. II. *adj.* rounded.

గుబ్బటిల్లు gubbaTillu *v.i.* to turn round suddenly, wheel round.

గుబ్బెత, గుబ్బలాడి gubbeta, gubbalaaDi *n.* young woman.

గుభాళించు, గుబాళించు gubhaaLincu, gubaaLincu *v.i. and t.* to emit a scent of, be fragrant with.

గుభాళింపు, గుబాళింపు gubhaaLimpu, gubaaLimpu *n.* fragrance.

గుభిల్లుమను gubhillumanu *v.i.* to be shocked or horrified.

గుభులుగుభులు gubhulu gubhulu *adv.* with a crashing noise.

గుభేలున gubheeluna *same as* gabhaaluna.

గుభేలుమను gubheelumanu *v.i.* 1 (of the heart) to sustain a shock. 2 (of a crash or similar sound) to echo, resound, be heard; niiTikuNDa nuutiloo paDDaTTu gubheelmandi a crash resounded as of a water pot falling down a well.

గుమగుమ, ఘుమఘుమ gumaguma, ghumaghuma *n.* sweet scent.

గుమగుమలాడు, ఘుమఘుమలాడు gumagumalaaDu, ghumaghumalaaDu *v.i.* to smell sweetly or pleasantly.

గుమాను gumaanu *n.* suspicion.

గుమాయించు, ఘుమాయించు gumaayincu, ghumaayincu *v.i.* (of scent) to spread, pervade.

గుమాస్తా gumaastaa *n.* clerk.

గుమి gumi *n.* crowd, multitude.

గుమికీ gumikii *n.* blow with a fist.

గుమిగూడు gumiguuDu *v.i.* to gather together, assemble, crowd around.

గుమ్మ gumma *n.* 1 spurt of milk from the teat of a cow; ~paalu milk still warm from a cow's udder. 2 muddu~ darling girl.

గుమ్మం gummam *n.* doorway (= door frame and threshold); ~loo nuncunnaaDu he is standing in the doorway; ~talaki koTTukondi he hit his head against the door frame; ~tagili kinda paDDaaDu he tripped and fell on the threshold; praaNam miidikostee tappa irugiNTi~ tokkadaawiDa unless it is something vitally important she will not cross her neighbour's threshold.

గుమ్మటం gummaTam *n.* 1 dome, cupola. 2 anything shaped like a balloon or dome; aayana ~laa unnaaDu he is as round as a balloon. 3 paper lantern, Chinese lantern; *see* gaali~.

గుమ్మడి gummaDi *n.* pumpkin, gourd; tiyya~ *cucurbita maxima*; buuDida~ *cucurbita pepo*.

గుమ్మడు gummaDu *n.* foppish person, dandy.

గుమ్మను, ఘుమ్మను gummanu, ghummanu *v.i.* to smell strongly of s.g fragrant.

గుమ్మి gummi[1] *n.* swamp, morass.

గుమ్మి, గుమ్ము gummi[2], gummu[1] *n.* tall basket for storing grain.

గుమ్ము gummu[2] *adj.* pleasant, enjoyable; ~aypooyEEDu he was struck with amazement and delight.

గుమ్మెట, గుమ్మెత gummeTa, gummeta *n.* kind of small drum.

గుయ్యారం guyyaaram *n.* ciikaTi~ dark hole, dungeon.

గురక guraka *n.* snore, snoring.

గురకపెట్టు, గుర్రుపెట్టు gurakapeTTu, gurrupeTTu *v.i.* to snore.

గురగుర guragura *n.* grunt[ing] (of a pig).

గురి guri *n.* 1 aim, mark. 2 goal, object[ive], target. 3 esteem, respect, trust, faith; roogiki kaawalasindi DaakTarupayna (*or* DaakTarumiida *or* DaakTaraNTee)~ what a patient needs is faith in his doctor.

గురి అవు guri awu *v.i.* to be a target for, be a victim of, be subjected to, be an object of, suffer from; paaThya pustakaalu konukkoowaalaNTee aarthikangaa caalaa ibbandulaku ~taaru if they want to buy textbooks for themselves, they will be put to much trouble financially.

గురించి, కూర్చి, గూర్చి gurinci, kuurci, guurci *p.p., suffixed to genitive or accusative case of a noun* about, concerning.

గురిగి gurigi *n.* small pot used for oil, oilcan.

గురిగింజ, గురివెంద, గురివింద guriginja, guriwenda, guriwinda *n.* small red and black seed of *abrus precatorius*.

గురి చూచు, గురిపెట్టు guri cuucu, guri peTTu *v.i. and t.* to [take] aim; ceetiloo pisTal naaku guri peTTEEDu he aimed the pistol in his hand at me.

గురి చేయు guri ceeyu *v.t.* 1 to subject to; konni cooTLa tupaanlu raaSTraanni sankSoobhaaniki guri ceesinaayi in some places cyclones subjected the state to a crisis. 2 to point or aim (a weapon) at.

గురి తప్పు guri tappu *v.i.* to miss the mark, miss o.'s aim.

గురు guru[1] *adjvl. prefix signifying* great, heavy, important, venerable.

గురు guru[2] *suffix added to certain cardinal numbers to form human numerals*, e.g., aydu~ five persons.

గురుకులం gurukulam *n.* residential school imparting education according to traditional Indian principles.

గురుకోణం gurukooNam *n. maths.* obtuse angle.

గురుచాపరేఖ gurucaapareekha *n. maths.* major arc.

గురుజనం gurujanam *n.pl.* venerable persons.

గురుజు guruju *n.* handle of a grinding mortar.

గురుడు guruDu *n.* the planet Jupiter.

గురుతర gurutara *adj.* 1 *class.* heavier. 2 *mod. restricted to certain phrases*, e.g., ~mayna wiSayam weighty or important matter; ~baadhyata heavy responsibility.

గురుతుల్యుడు gurutulyuDu *n.* one who is equivalent to a teacher or entitled to the same respect as a teacher.

గురుత్వం gurutwam *n. class.* 1 weight. 2 importance. 3 venerableness.

గురుత్వకేంద్రం gurutwakeendram *n.sci.* centre of gravity.

గురుత్వనియమం gurutwaniyamam *n.* law of gravity.

గురుత్వాకర్షణ gurutwaakarSaNa *n. sci.* gravity.

గురుత్వాకర్షణశక్తి **gurutwaakarSaNa śakti** *n. sci.* gravitation, force of gravity.

గురుదక్షిణ **gurudakSiNa** *n.* offering or reward to a teacher on completion of a pupil's education.

గురుధాతు **gurudhaatu** *n.* heavy metal.

గురుముఖతః, గురుముఖతా **gurumukhataḥ, gurumukhataa** *adv.* with the aid of a teacher; **samskṛtam ~ caduwukoNTee kaani raadu** Sanskrit cannot be learnt except with the help of a teacher.

గురువర్యుడు **guruwaryuDu** *n.* esteemed or venerable teacher.

గురువారం **guruwaaram** *n.* Thursday.

గురువు **guruwu** *n.* **1** teacher, mentor, spiritual guide, guru. **2** *gram.* long syllable. **3** weightiness; **bhoojanam ~ ayindi** the meal was a heavy one. **4** the planet Jupiter.

గుర్తించు **gurtincu** *v.t.* **1** to notice. **2** to recognise, perceive, understand (fact, situation). **3** to recognise, identify (person, object). **4** to recognise officially. **5** to take note of, make a note of, note. **6** to mark (place on a map, passage in a book).

గుర్తింపు **gurtimpu** *n.* **1** notice, noticing, noting. **2** recognition, identification.

గుర్తింపుపొందు **gurtimpu pondu** *v.i.* to be (officially) recognised.

గుర్తు **gurtu** *n.* **1** mark, sign, token, symbol. **2** trace. **3** identification mark. **4** memory, s.g remembered; **aayana maaTalu naaku baagaa ~** I remember his words well.

గుర్తుంచుకొను, గుర్తుపెట్టుకొను **gurtuncukonu, gurtu peTTukonu** *v.t.* to keep in mind, bear in mind.

గుర్తుండు, గుర్తుకువచ్చు **gurtuNDu, gurtuku waccu** *v.i.* to come to mind, be recalled.

గుర్తుచేయు, గుర్తుకుతెచ్చు **gurtu ceeyu, gurtuku teccu** *v.t.* to remind; **aa wiSayam naaku gurtu ceesEEDu** he reminded me of that matter.

గుర్తుపట్టు **gurtupaTTu** *v.t.* to recognise, identify.

గుర్తెరుగు **gurterugu** *v.t.* to perceive and understand, recognise.

గుర్రం **gurram** *n.* **1** horse; **gurrapu pandem** horse race; **gurrapu pedaalu** thick or coarse lips. **2** trigger of a gun. **3** knight in chess.

గుర్రం ఎక్కు **gurram ekku** *v.i.* **1** to mount a horse. **2** *slang* to get drunk.

గుర్రప్పిల్ల **gurrappilla** *n.* foal, colt.

గుర్రు **gurru** *n.* **1** snore, snoring. **2** grunt. **3** growl, snarl (of anger). **4** anger.

గుర్రుపెట్టు **gurru peTTu** *v.i.* to snore.

గుల **gula** *n.* **1** itching. **2** *colloq.* strong desire, hankering.

గులకరాయి **gulakaraayi** *n.* **1** pebble. **2** gravel, rubble.

గులగులలాడు, గులగుల్లాడు **gulagulalaaDu, gulagullaaDu** *v.i.* to desire strongly, hanker for.

గులాం, గులాలు **gulaam[1], gulaalu** *n.* rose coloured powder sprinkled at a marriage and in Dasara and Holi festivals.

గులాం **gulaam[2]** *n.* servant, slave.

గులాబి **gulaabi** *n.* rose.

గులాబ్‌జాం **gulaabjaam** *n.* kind of sweet.

గులామి **gulaami** *n.* slavery, servitude, bondage.

గులిమి **gulimi** *same as* **gubili.**

గుల్ఫం, గుల్భం **gulpham, gulbham** *n.* ankle.

గుల్మం **gulmam** *n.* **1** bush, shrub. **2** spleen. **3** enlargement of the spleen.

గుల్మనాశకం **gulmanaaśakam** *n. bot.* herbicide.

గుల్ల **gulla** I. *n.* **1** shell; **naa illu ~ ceesEEDu** he made me a pauper *or* he ruined me (*lit.* he made my house into an empty shell). **2** anything hollow, e.g., empty cotton pod after the cotton is removed. **3** basket. **4** bump, swelling. II. *adj.* **1** hollow, empty. **2** soft. **3** (of soil) loose.

గుల్లపారు **gullapaaru** *v.i.* to become soft.

గుల్లసున్నం **gullasunnam** *n.* lime mortar or plaster made from shells.

గుల్లాగుట్రా **gullaaguTraa** *n. dial.* petty things, knick knacks.

గుళిక **guLika** *n.* pill, capsule, pellet.

గువ్వ **guwwa** *n.* dove.

గుసగుస **gusagusa** *n.* whisper[ing].

గుసగుసలాడు **gusagusalaaDu** *v.i.* to whisper.

గుహ **guha** *n.* cave, cavern.

గుహాంతరం **guhaantaram** *n.* interior of a cave.

గూ - guu

గూండా guuNDaa *same as* **guNDaa**[2].
గూండ్ర guuNDra *n.* hoot, cry of an owl.
గూకు guuku *same as* **kuuku**.
గూటం guuTam *n.* 1 pestle. 2 peg, wedge. 3 post, stake. 4 wooden mallet.
గూటం దింపు **guuTam dimpu** *v.i. colloq.* to worry, pester; **ninnaTinunci ~ tunnaaDu** he has been pestering me since yesterday.
గూటాయించు **guuTaayincu** *slang, same as* **guuTincu.**
గూటించు **guuTincu** *v.t.* to put pressure on, worry, pester.
గూడ **guuDa**[1] *n.* 1 swing basket for baling water for irrigation. 2 basket for carrying grain, etc. 3 canvas hood to keep off dust or rain. 4 socket of shoulder or hip joint.
గూడ **guuDa**[2] *n.* small village; *cf.* **guuDem.**
గూడకట్టు **guuDakaTTu** *n.* fashion of wearing a dhoti like a skirt.
గూడకొంగ, గూడబాతు **guuDakonga, guuDabaatu** *n.* pelican.
గూడు **guuDu** *n.* 1 nest; **guuTipiTTa** young bird, nestling, fledgling; **saale~** spider's web; **~kaTTukonu** *or* **~kaTTukoni kuurcuNDu** to remain fixed and immovable; **atani mukhamloo durmaargam~kaTTukonnadi** wickedness has made its abode in his face. 2 niche or recess in a wall, pigeonhole. 3 hood (of cart, rickshaw). 4 case, cage; **jwaram taggEEka maniSi emukala ~laa migilEEDu** when the fever subsided he was only skin and bone (*lit.* he was left looking like a cage of bones). 5 storage basket. 6 store room. 7 **iTikala~** brick kiln. 8 socket of shoulder joint or hip joint. 9 **kurupu ~ poosukoccindi** the sore developed an abscess. 10 **kooLLa~** hen house.
గూడుపుఠాణీ **guuDupuThaaNii** *n.* plot, conspiracy.
గూడెం **guuDem** *n.* village, hamlet.
గూఢ **guuDha** *adj.* hidden, secret, abstruse, crypto-.
గూఢం **guuDham** *n.* secret.
గూఢచారి **guuDhacaari** *n.* spy, secret agent.
గూఢార్థం **guuDhaartham** *n.* hidden meaning.
గూన **guuna** *n.* 1 storage jar, gen. for pickles. 2 large pot or tub for watering cattle.
గూని **guuni** *adj.* hunchbacked.
గూనివాడు **guuniwaaDu** *n.* hunchbacked person.
గూను **guunu** *n.* hump, crooked back, hunchback.
గూబ **guuba** *n.* 1 (*also* **guDLa~**) owl. 2 eardrum; **~giymanipincu** to make s.o.'s eardrum reverberate (with a blow). 3 **induloo naaku laabham eemundi? laabham~looki waccindi** what is my profit in this? I have made no profit at all.
గూర్చి **guurci** *p.p. same as* **gurinci.**

గృ -gṛ

గృధ్రం **gṛdhram** *n. class.* vulture, bird of prey.
గృహం **gṛham** *n.* house, dwelling.
గృహకృత్యాలు **gṛhakṛtyaalu** *n. pl.* housework.
గృహచ్ఛిద్రం **gṛhacchidram** *n.* domestic disputes, domestic strife.
గృహనిర్వహణ **gṛhanirwahaNa** *n.* housekeeping.
గృహప్రవేశం **gṛhapraweeśam** *n.* 1 ceremony performed on coming to live in a new house. 2 ceremony performed when a bride comes to stay in the bride-groom's house for the first time.
గృహమేధి **gṛhameedhi** *same as* **gṛhasthuDu.**
గృహవిజ్ఞానశాస్త్రం **gṛhawijñaanaśaastram** *n.* domestic science, home science.
గృహస్థ **gṛhastha** *adj.* domestic.
గృహస్థాశ్రమం **gṛhasthaaśramam** *n.* period of a man's life spent as a householder.
గృహస్థు[డు] **gṛhasthu[Du]** *n.* householder.
గృహిణి **gṛhiNi** *n.* mistress of a house, housewife.
గృహోపకరణం **gṛhoopakaraNam** *n.* article used for domestic purposes.

గె, గే, గై - ge, gee, gay

గెంటు **geNTu** *v.t.* 1 to push, thrust, shove. 2 **awataliki geNTiweeyu** to expel, drive away, turn out, eject.

గెంతు **gentu** *same as* **gantu.**

గెడ **geDa** *same as* **gaDa.**

గెడ్డ **geDDa** *same as* **gaDDa.**

గెడ్డం **geDDam** *same as* **gaDDam.**

గెద్ద **gedda** *same as* **gadda.**

గెనుసు **genusu** *n.* sweet potato.

గెల **gela** *n.* bunch (of plantains, coconuts and certain other fruit).

గెలుచు **gelucu** *v.i. and t.* to win (contest, prize), be successful.

గెలుపు **gelupu** *n.* victory, success.

గేడికాళ్లు **geeDikaaLLu** *n.pl.* thin legs, spindle shanks.

గేదంగి **geedangi** *n.* screw pine, *pandanus odoratissimus.*

గేదె **geede** *n.* she buffalo.

గేయం **geeyam** *n.* lyric, song.

గేలం **geelam** *same as* **gaalam.**

గేలి **geeli** *n.* mockery, ridicule, derision.

గేలిచేయు **geeliceeyu** *v.t.* to ridicule, mock, deride, make fun of.

గేస్తు **geestu** *alternative form of* **grhasthu.**

గేహం **geeham** *n.* house.

గైకొను **gaykonu** *same as* **kaykonu.**

గైగడ్డ **gaygaDDa** *n. dial.* kind of root vegetable (= **peNDalam**).

గైమను **gaymanu** *v.i.* to shout angrily, flare up in anger.

గైరాన్ **gayraan** *n.dial.* government land reserved for communal use in a village.

గైరికం **gayrikam** *n.* gold in the form of ore.

గైర్‌హాజరు **gayrhaajaru** *adj.* absent.

గొ - go

గొంకు **gonku** I. *n.* 1 fear, timidity. 2 hesitation. 3 crouching or cowering due to cold, weakness or fear; *cf.* **konkarlupoowu.** II. *v.i.* 1 to be timid, fear. 2 to hesitate; **gonkakuNDaa** (*or* ~ **leekuNDaa**) **nirbhayangaa ceppu** speak without hesitation or fear.

గొంగళి **gongaLi** *n.* rug or blanket made of coarse material; **ekkaDaweesina ~ akkaDee uNTundi** the rug will remain wherever you put it (proverbial saying meaning that nothing new will transpire *or* there will be no progress).

గొంగళిపురుగు **gongaLipurugu** *n.* hairy caterpillar.

గొంజ **gonja** *n.* barren woman.

గొండి **goNDi**[1] *n. suffix giving a meaning of* evil *or* banefulness; **durada** ~ stinging nettle; **dummula** ~ hyena (*lit.* bone eater); **lanca** ~ bribe taker.

గొండి **goNDi**[2] *n.* waste pipe to allow drainage water to escape from a house.

గొంతు[క] **gontu[ka]** *n.* 1 throat. 2 voice.

గొంతుకలుపు **gontu kalupu** *see* **kalupu**[2].

గొంతుకూర్చుండు **gontukkuurcuNDu** *v.i.* to squat on o.'s heels.

గొంతుచించుకొను **gontu cincukonu** *v.i.* to shout loudly, scream, yell; **gontucincukoni keekalu weeyu** to shout at the top of o.'s voice (*lit.* to shout so as to tear o.'s voice).

గొంతునులుము, గొంతుపిసుకు **gontu nulumu, gontu pisuku** *v.t.* to strangle.

గొంతుసర్దుకొను **gontu sardukonu** *v.i.* to clear o.'s throat.

గొంతెమ్మ **gontemma** *n.* name of a village goddess.

గొంతెమ్మకోరికలు **gontemma koorikalu** *n.pl.* impossible desires, impossible demands.

గొంది **gondi** *n.* bylane, alley[way]; **sandulu gondulu** lanes and bylanes.

గొగ్గిపళ్లు **goggipaLLu** *n.pl.* overlapping teeth.

గొగ్గులుగొగ్గులుగా **goggulu goggulugaa** *adv.* uneven, irregular.

గొజ్జంగి **gojjangi** *n.* a scented flower, *pandanus odoratissimus*, screw pine.

గొట్టం **goTTam** *n.* 1 tube, pipe, duct; **goTTapu baawi** tube well. 2 barrel of a gun. 3 factory siren. 4 *pl.* **goTTaalu** *colloq.* pills, capsules (medicine).

గొట్టికాయ **goTTikaaya** *n.* marble (glass ball); ~ **laaDukuNTunnaawaa?** are you playing marbles?

గొట్టు **goTTu** I. *n. suffix meaning* wretch, e.g., **pisini** ~ miser; **daridra** ~ pauper. II. *adj.* hard, difficult; ~ **praśnalu** difficult questions.

గొడగరి, గొడారి **goDagari, goDaari** *n.* cobbler.

గొడవ **goDawa** *n.* 1 trouble, problem, difficulty; **naa ~ wineewaaDu leeDu** there is no-one to listen to my problem. 2 noise, nuisance; **wiiDitoo wedhawa ~ waccipaDindi** a wretched nuisance was caused by this fellow. 3 confusion, commotion. 4 agitation. 5 business, affairs, concern; **naa ~ neenu paDataanu** I will see to my own affairs. 6 mention, information; **ataDi ~ eemii teliyadu naaku** I have no information concerning him; **maLLii ataDi ~ raaleedu** he was not mentioned again.

గొడవపడు **goDawapaDu** *v.i.* to quarrel; **naatoo goDawa paDDaaDu** he picked up a quarrel with me.

గొడుగు **goDugu** *n.* umbrella; **~ karra, ~ kaama** umbrella handle; **okariki ~ paTTu** to respect s.o. *or* to protect s.o.

గొడుగుగడ్డి **goDugugaDDi** *n.* kind of fragrant grass growing in marshy places.

గొడుగుతుమ్మ **goDugutumma** *n.* umbrella tree (species of acacia or babul tree).

గొడ్డంబలి **goDDambali** *n.* gruel or cunjee containing no broken rice; **~ taagi batikEEDu** he lived on a starvation diet.

గొడ్డలి **goDDali** *n.* axe, hatchet.

గొడ్డు **goDDu** I. *n.* **1** beast, animal. **2** head of cattle, buffalo. **3** *dial.* lump. II. *adj.* barren, sterile.

గొడ్డు అమావాస్య **goDDu amaawaasya** *n.* completely dark night when there is no moon.

గొడ్డుకారం **goDDukaaram** *n.* very hot chilli powder, very hot spicy food.

గొడ్డుగోదా, గొడ్డూగాదం **goDDugoodaa, goDDuugaadam** *n.pl.* cattle.

గొడ్డుచాకిరీ **goDDucaakirii** *n.* drudgery.

గొడ్డుపోతు, గొడ్డుబోతు, గొడ్డుమోతు **goDDupootu, goDDubootu, goDDumootu** *n.* **1** useless person. **2** barren woman.

గొడ్డుపోవు **goDDupoowu** *v.i.* to become sterile or barren.

గొడ్రాలు **goDraalu** *n.* barren woman.

గొణుకు, గొణుగు **goNuku, goNugu** *v.t.* to mutter, murmur.

గొణుక్కొను **goNukkonu** *v.i.* to mutter to o.s., murmur, grumble.

గొణుగుడు **goNuguDu** *n.* muttering, murmuring. mumbling.

గొద్దె[లు] **godde[lu]** *n.pl. dial.* sheep and goats' droppings.

గొప్ప **goppa** I. *n.* (*also* **~ tanam**) **1** greatness, respectability. **2** pride, self-conceit. II. *adj.* **1** great. **2** noble; **~ manassutoo ii pani ceesEEDu** he did this with a noble heart.

గొప్ప[లు] చెప్పుకొను **goppa[lu] ceppukonu** *v.i.* to boast, brag.

గొప్పవాడు **goppawaaDu** *n.* **1** respectable person. **2** wealthy person.

గొప్పు **goppu** *n.* small raised plot of land in a vegetable garden or rice field.

గొప్పుతవ్వు **goppu tawwu** *v.i.* to remove weeds from a vegetable garden.

గొబ్బరం **gobbaram** *n.* manure.

గొబ్బి **gobbi** *n.* dance performed at the time of Sankranti by girls clapping hands and singing in chorus.

గొబ్బిపాటలు, గొబ్బిళ్లు **gobbi paaTalu, gobbiLLu** *n.pl.* songs sung by girls while performing **gobbi.**

గొబ్బున **gobbuna** *adv.* quickly, instantly.

గొయ్యి, గోయి **goyyi, gooyi** *n.* **1** pit, hole in the ground. **2** grave.

గొరగొర **goragora** *onom. adv. and n. sug.* speed *or* haste.

గొరిగించుకొను **gorigincukonu** *v.i.* to have o.'s head completely shaved.

గొరిగేయు, గొరిగివేయు **gorigeeyu, gorigi weeyu** I. *v.i. colloq.* to be a failure, fail; **neenu weLLina pani gorigeesindi** the work that I went for was a failure; **naa pariikSa gorigeesindi** I failed my examination. II. *v.t. colloq.* to deprive s.o. of money, goods, etc.; **unna Dabbantaa gorigeesi bayaTaku toosEEru** they cleaned out all his money and drove him away.

గొరిజ. **gorija** *n.* hoof.

గొరుగు **gorugu** *v.t.* to shave.

గొర్రు **gorru** *n.* **1** harrow. **2** drill plough. **3** measure of land equal to about three acres.

గొర్రుకొట్టు **gorrukoTTu** *v.t.* to harrow.

గొర్రె **gorre** *n.* sheep.

గొర్రెపిల్ల **gorrepilla** *n.* lamb.

గొర్రెపోతు, గొర్రెపొట్టేలు **gorrepootu, gorrepoTTeelu** *n.* ram.

గొలుసు **golusu** *n.* **1** chain; **~ perigipooyindi** the chain broke (*lit.* the chain became larger — paraphrase to avoid a taboo expression); *cf.* **koNDa, biyyam. 2** measure of length in land survey equal to 22 yards.

గొలుసుకట్టు రాత, గొలుసుమోడి రాత **golusukaTTuraata, golusumooDiraata** *n.* cursive writing.

గొల్ల **golla** I. *n.* **1** name of the sheperds' and herdsmen's community. **2** rustic; **werri ~** simple rustic.

గొల్లం **gollam** *n.* deep pit.

గొల్లతనం **gollatanam** *n.* boorishness.

గొల్లదరువులు, గొల్లసుద్దులు **golladaruwulu, gollasuddulu** *n.pl.* kind of song sung by shepherds.

గొల్లభామ **gollabhaama** *n.* **1** shepherdess. **2** grasshopper, cricket, mantis.

గొల్లవాడు **gollawaaDu** *n.* shepherd, herdsman.

గొల్లుమను **gollumanu** *v.i.* to burst out (weeping or laughing): **gollumani eeDcu** to weep copiously, burst out crying; **gollumani nawwu** to laugh heartily, burst out laughing.

గొళ్లెం **goLLem** *n.* doorlatch, hasp, bolt; **talupu ~ weeyu/peTTu** to bolt a door.

గో - goo

గో goo[1] *adjvl. prefix meaning* of cattle; ~ **jaati** race of cattle.

గో goo[2] *advbl. suffix meaning* look there!, there is. . . , *see* **adigoo.**

గోంకారం **goonkaaram** *n.* howling (of dog, jackal).

గోంగూర **goonguura** *n. dial.* Indian hemp plant, a green vegetable, *hibiscus cannabinus* (= **puNTikuura, googaaku, googu**).

గోండు **gooNDu** *n.* Gond, name of a hill tribe.

గోండ్రించు, గోండ్రిల్లు **gooNDrincu, gooNDrillu** *v.i.* to roar, bellow.

గోండ్రుకప్ప **gooNDrukappa** *n.* bullfrog, toad.

గోందు **goondu** *n. dial.* gum, adhesive.

గోకర **gookara** *same as* **goorucikkuDu.**

గోకర్ణం **gookarNam** *n.* **1** kind of bowl for serving liquids during a feast. **2** power of twitching the ears as cattle do; *see* **gajakarNam.**

గోకు, గోదారి **gooku[1], goodaari** *n.* residue formed in the process of making ghee from butter.

గోకు **gooku[2]** *v.t.* to scratch, scrape.

గోకుడు పార **gookuDu paara** *n.* small hoe used for digging up or cutting grass.

గోకులం **gookulam** *n.* **1** shepherds' and herdsmen's community; *cf.* **golla. 2** legendary village where Krishna spent his childhood.

గోగు, గోగాకు **googu, googaaku** *n.* Indian hemp plant, a green vegetable, *hibiscus cannabinus* (= **goonguura, puN-Tikuura**).

గోగునార **googunaara** *n.* hemp fibre.

గోచర **goocara** *adj.* perceptible, visible, cognisable, evident.

గోచరించు **goocarincu** I. *v.i.* to be visible, be evident, appear. II. *v.t.* to show.

గోచారం **goocaaram** *n. astrol.* the motion of planets in the different signs of the zodiac.

గోచీ **goocii** *n.* **1** loincloth. **2** ~ **poosi kaTTu** to wear a loincloth tucked up and tied in a truss.

గోచీపాత **gooc iipaata** *n.* old and shabby loincloth.

గోచీపాతరాయుడు **gooc iipaata raayuDu** *n.* poor man (*lit.* one who wears only an old and shabby loincloth).

గోజాట **goojaaTa** *n.* harassing, pestering.

గోటిబిళ్ల **gooTibiLLa** *n.* a boys' game, *also called* **gilliidaNDu** *or* **karraabiLLaa.**

గోటు **gooTu** *n.* **1** ornamental fringe or hem of a cloth. **2** kind of bangle or bracelet. **3** affectedness, haughtiness, self-conceit.

గోడ **gooDa** *n.* wall.

గోడాడు **gooDaaDu** *v.i.* to lament.

గోడిగ **gooDiga** *n.* mare.

గోడు **gooDu** *n.* **1** grief, wailing. **2** affliction. **3** sorrowful tale.

గోణి **gooNi[1]** *n. class.* bull.

గోణి **gooNi[2]** *n.* sacking, sack-cloth, hessian.

గోతం, గోతాం **gootam, gootaam** *n.* sack, bag.

గోత్రం **gootram** *n.* family, lineage.

గోద **gooda** *n. dial.* bull, bullock, head of cattle.

గోదా **goodaa** *n.* boxing ring.

గోదాం **goodaam** *n.* godown, storage shed, warehouse.

గోదారి **goodaari[1]** *same as* **gooku[1].**

గోదావరి, గోదారి **goodaawari, goodaari[2]** *n.* River Godavari.

గోదురుకప్ప **gooduru kappa** *n.* bullfrog, toad.

గోధుమ **goodhuma** *n.* wheat; ~ **rangu** light brown, golden colour, colour of wheat.

గోధూళివేళ **goodhuuLi weeLa** *n.* evening time, time when cattle return and cause dust to rise.

గోనెగుడ్డ, గోనిగుడ్డ **gooneguDDa, gooniguDDa** *n.* **1** sacking, sackcloth. **2** coarse cloth of any kind.

గోనెపట్ట, గోనిపట్ట **goonepaTTa, goonipaTTa** *n.* sacking, sackcloth, hessian.

గోనెసంచీ, గోనిసంచీ **goonesancii, goonisancii** *n.* sack, bag.

గోపనం **goopanam** *n.* **1** hiding, concealing. **2** preserving secretly. **3** secrecy.

గోపాలం ఎత్తు **goopaalam ettu** *v.i.* to beg for food.

గోపాలకుడు, గోపాలుడు **goopaal[ak]uDu** *n. class.* cowherd, herdsman.

గోపిక **goopika** *n.* shepherdess, esp. a Gopika or shepherdess of Gokulam, the legendary village where Krishna spent his childhood.

గోపిచందనం **goopicandanam** *n.* yellow ochre.

గోపురం **goopuram** *n.* temple tower.

గోప్యం **goopyam** *n.* secrecy.

గోప్యంగా **goopyangaa** *adv.* secretly.

గోప్యత **goopyata** *n.* confidentiality, secrecy.

గోబి [గడ్డ] **goobi[gaDDa]** *n.* cabbage.

గోమయం **goomayam** *n.* cowdung.

గోమాంసం **goomaamsam** *n.* beef.

గోమాయువు **goomaayuwu** *n. class.* jackal.

గోమారి **goomaari** *n.* kind of tick which infests cattle.

గోము **goomu** *n.* **1** brightness, freshness. **2** fondness, affection. **3** felicity.

గోముఖం **goomukham** *n.* spout for water in the form of a cow's head placed in a temple wall.

గోముఖ వ్యాఘ్రం **goomukha wyaaghram** *n.* **1** tiger disguised as a cow. **2** hypocrite.

గోముగా **goomugaa** *adv.* endearingly, appealingly, invitingly.

గోమేధికం **goomeedhikam** *n.* topaz.

గోయి **gooyi** *same as* **goyyi.**

గోరంక **gooranka** *same as* **goorinka.**

గోరంచు **goorancu** *n.* narrow border (of a sari, dhoti, etc.).

గోరంట **gooraNTa** *n.* henna plant.

గోరంత **gooranta** *n. and adj.* very little, a tiny amount(of) (*lit.* as little as a finger nail); **naaku ~saayam ceyyaleedu** he did not give me even the least amount of help; **~lu koNDantalu ceeyu** to make mountains out of molehills.

గోరచెక్క **gooracekka** *n.* implement for levelling irrigated fields after ploughing.

గోరింక, గోరంక, గోరువంక **goorinka, gooranka, gooruwanka** *n.* myna, a bird of the starling family.

గోరీ **goorii** *n.* tomb; **aa samasyalaku ~kaTTeesEEDu** he laid those problems to rest.

గోరు **gooru** *n.* nail, claw, talon.

గోరుచిక్కుడు **goorucikkuDu** *n.* kind of bean, *cyamopsis tetragonoloba.*

గోరుచుట్టు **goorucuTTu** *n.* whitlow.

గోరువంక **gooruwanka** *same as* **goorinka.**

గోరువెచ్చని **gooruweccani** *adj.* lukewarm.

గోరెత్తు **goorettu** *adj.* very little, a tiny amount of.

గోరోజనం **gooroojanam** *n.* 1 ox gall. 2 *colloq.* pride, arrogance.

గోర్జె **goorje** *n.* path, cattle track.

గోల **goola** *n.* 1 moan[ing], weeping, wailing, lamenting. 2 howl, yell, clamour, confused noise; **phoonuloo eedoo ~gaa winipincindi, maaTalu sarigaa winapaDaleedu** I heard some confused noise on the phone, I could not hear the words distinctly.

గోలచేయు **goolaceeyu** I. *v.i.* to make a noise, clamour or outcry. II. *v.t.* to tease.

గోలపెట్టు, గోలెత్తు **goola peTTu, goolettu** *v.i.* to wail, lament.

గోలాంగూలం **goolaanguulam** *n.* lion-tailed monkey.

గోలీ **goolii** *n.* 1 tablet, pill. 2 (*also* **~kaaya**) marble (glass ball).

గోలీలాట **gooliilaaTa** *n.* game of marbles.

గోలుగోలున **goolugooluna** *adv.* lamenting loudly.

గోలెం **goolem** *n.* 1 large jar for storing grain. 2 tub for watering cattle.

గోళం **gooLam** *n.* globe, ball, sphere.

గోళకుడు **gooLakuDu** *n.* (*term of abuse*) widow's bastard.

గోళకేంద్రం **gooLakeendram** *n. phys.* centre of curvature.

గోళాకార **gooLaakaara** *adj.* spherical.

గోళిక **gooLika** *n.* globule.

గోళికూర **gooLikuura** *n.* spinach.

గోవ **goowa** *n.* 1 *dial.* scaffolding. 2 *dial.* heap of winnowed grain on a threshing floor.

గోవకట్టు **goowa kaTTu** *v.i. dial.* to erect scaffolding.

గోవతాడు **goowataaDu** *n.* flexible belt made of gold or silver.

గోవిందాకొట్టు **goowindaa koTTu** *v.i.* 1 *lit.* to bid final farewell to a departed spirit at a funeral. 2 *colloq.* to be defeated, fail; **waaDi parikSa goowindaa koTTindi** he failed his examination (*lit.* his examination bade him farewell).

గోవు **goowu** *n.* cow.

గోష **gooSa** *n.* purdah.

గోష్ఠం **gooSTham** *n.* cattle pen, cowhouse.

గోష్ఠి **gooSThi** *n.* discussion meeting, seminar, symposium; *see* **isTaa~**.

గోష్పాదం **gooSpaadam** *n.* s.g of the size of a cow s footprint; **~antapilaka** tuft of hair the size of a cow's footprint (worn with the rest of the head shaved by some orthodox brahmans).

గోసాయి **goosaayi** *n.* wandering religious mendicant; **~ciTkaa** treatment of illness by home remedies.

గౌ - gaw

గౌండ్ల **gawNDLa** *same as* **gamaLLa.**

గౌడిగేదె **gawDigeede** *n.* large kind of buffalo.

గౌణ **gawNa** *adj.* 1 *class.* unimportant, secondary, subsidiary. 2 *gram.* subordinate.

గౌద్దలీకం **gawddaliikam** *n. class.* large axe.

గౌరం, గౌరవర్ణం **gawram, gawrawarNam** *n.* 1 pale straw colour. 2 rosy red.

గౌరవ **gawrawa** *adj.* honorary.

గౌరవం **gawrawam** *n.* 1 respect, honour, esteem; **aayanapaTLa ~cuupincEEru** they showed respect for (*or* towards) him. 2 dignity. 3 nobility, nobleness, respectability.

గౌరవనీయ **gawrawaniiya** *adj.* (of persons) honourable.

గౌరవప్రద **gawrawaprada** *adj.* honourable, conferring honour; **~mayna pariSkaara saadhana** achievement of an honourable settlement.

గౌరవార్థం **gawrawaartham** *p.p.* in honour of, out of respect for.

గౌరవాస్పద **gawrawaaspada** *adj.* honourable, being a source of honour.

గౌరవించు **gawrawincu** *v.t.* to respect, honour, esteem.

గౌలు **gawlu** *n.* bad smell, stink, stench.

గ్ర - gra

గ్రంథం **grantham** *n.* book; *see* **katha.**

గ్రంథకర్త **granthakarta** *n.* 1 author. 2 *slang* person of notorious character.

గ్రంథచౌర్యం **granthacawryam** *n.* plagiarism.

గ్రంథనం, గ్రథనం **granthanam, grathanam** *n.* 1 stringing or tying together. 2 arranging, compiling, composing.

గ్రంథపాతం **granthapaatam** *n.* lacuna, omission of a passage from a book or manuscript.

గ్రంథప్రచురణ హక్కు, గ్రంథస్వామ్యం **granthapracuraNa hakku, granthaswaamyam** *n.* copyright.

గ్రంథమాల **granthamaala** *n.* series of books.

గ్రంథరాజం **grantharaajam** *n.* great book.

గ్రంథసాంగుడు **granthasaanguDu** *n. slang* 1 person of notorious character. 2 womaniser.

గ్రంథస్థ **granthastha** *adj.* pertaining to, recorded in or derived from books; **~bhaaSa** book language.

గ్రంథస్థంచేయు **granthastham ceeyu** *v.t.* to record in a book.

గ్రంథాలయం **granthaalayam** *n.* library.

గ్రంథి **granthi** *n. med.* gland.

గ్రంథులసిరలు **granthula siralu** *n.pl.* varicose veins.

గ్రక్కు **grakku** *v.t.* to shoot out, emit; **aame cuupulloo nippulu grakkindi** she flashed fire by means of her looks; *cf.* **weligrakku.**

గ్రక్కున **grakkuna** *adv.* quickly, immediately.

గ్రథనం **grathanam** *same as* **granthanam.**

గ్రసిక **grasika** *n. sci.* gullet.

గ్రస్త[ం] **grasta[m]** *adjvl. suffix meaning* swallowed by, consumed by, seized by, involved in; **roogagrastuDu** s.o. taken ill; **bhayagrastuDu** person overcome by fear; **rNagrastuDu** indebted person.

గ్రహం **graham** *n.* 1 planet. 2 evil spirit; *see* **grahaNam.**

గ్రహకూటమి **grahakuuTami** *n. astrol.* conjunction of planets.

గ్రహచారం **grahacaaram** *n.* 1 fate. 2 misfortune. 3 planetary motion, position of the planets as a affecting a person's fortune.

గ్రహణం **grahaNam** *n.* 1 understanding, comprehension; **~awu** to be understood. 2 taking, seizing, seizure; **eedoo~** (*or* **eedoo graham**) **paTTindi, wipariitangaa prawartistunnaaDu** something has taken possession of him (*or* some evil spirit has come over him) and he is behaving unnaturally. 3 eclipse; **candruDiki ~paTTindi** the moon is eclipsed. 4 recording; **śabda~** sound recording; **chaayaacitra~** photography.

గ్రహణశూల **grahaNa śuula** *n.* pain in the abdomen believed to be caused by having eaten food during an eclipse.

గ్రహణి **grahaNi** *n.* diarrohoea, dysentry.

గ్రహపతి, గ్రహరాజు **grahapati, grahàraaju** *n.* sun.

గ్రహపీడ[నం] **grahapiiDa[nam]** *n. astrol.* evil influence exerted by a planet.

గ్రహశాంతి **grahaśaanti** *n. astrol.* propitiation of the planets by performing ceremonies.

గ్రహించు **grahincu** *v.t.* 1 to understand, comprehend, grasp. 2 to take, seize. 3 to receive, accept, adopt.

గ్రహించుకొను **grahincukonu** *v.i.* to perceive, understand, realise.

గ్రహింపు **grahimpu** *n.* 1 understanding, perception. 2 perspicacity, sagacity.

గ్రహీత **grahiita** *n.* acceptor, receiver, grantee; **bahumati~** recipient of an award.

గ్రా - graa

గ్రాంథిక **graanthika** *adj.* 1 relating or pertaining to books. 2 (of language, esp. the Telugu language) classical.

గ్రాంథికం **graanthikam** *n.* classical style of Telugu.

గ్రామం **graamam** *n.* village; **graamaantaram weLLEEDu** he went away from (*or* he left) his village.

గ్రామకంఠం **graamakaNTham** *n.* 1 village site. 2 waste land in which villagers have rights in common.

గ్రామకరణం **graama karaNam** *n.* village accountant, karnam.

గ్రామదేవత **graama deewata** *n.* village goddess.

గ్రామనత్తం **graama nattam** *n.* village site.

గ్రామ పెద్దలు **graama peddalu** *n.pl.* village elders.

గ్రామమునసబు **graama munasabu** *n.* village headman.

గ్రామ సింహం **graamasimham** *n.* dog.

గామ సీమ **graamasiima** *n.* rural parts, rural area, countryside.

గ్రామీణ **graamiiNa** *adj.* pertaining to villages, rural.

గ్రామీణుడు **graamiiNuDu** *n.* villager.

గ్రామ్య[ం] **graamya[m]** *adj.* 1 pertaining to a village, rustic, crude. 2 (of speech) common, vulgar, uneducated.

గ్రాసం, గాసం **graasam, gaasam** *n.* 1 grass. 2 food; **paśu~** cattle fodder.

గ్రాసవాసాలు **graasawaasaalu** *n.pl.* 1 food and shelter. 2 food and clothing.

గ్రాహకం **graahakam** *n. phys.* receiver.

గ్రాహి **graahi** *n.* awareness, discretion; **naaku~** (*or* **naaku uuha) telisinappaTinunci aayanni cuustunnaanu** for as long as I have been aware (*or* for as long as I can remember) I have been encountering him; **~telisina pillalani tiTTakuuDadu** do not scold children who have reached the age of discretion.

గ్రాహ్య **graahya** *adj.* comprehensible, understandable.

గ్రాహ్యతశక్తి **graahayata śakti** *n.* absorptive capacity.

గ్రీ, గ్రో, గ్లా - grii, groo, glaa

గ్రీవ **griiwa** *adj. med.* cervical.

గ్రీవం **griiwam**[1] *n.* 1 neck, throat. 2 *bot.* axil.

గ్రీవం **griiwam**[2] *n.* ray of light.

గ్రీష్మం **griiSmam** *n.* 1 heat, warmth. 2 hot season, hot weather, summer.

గ్రీష్మకాలం , గ్రీష్మఋతువు **griiSma kaalam, griiSma ṛtuwu** *n.* hot season, hot weather, summer.

గ్రీష్మసుప్తి **griiSmasupti** *n. biol.* aestivation.

గ్రోలు,క్రోలు **groolu, kroolu** *v.t. class.* 1 to eat, drink, consume. 2 *fig.* to drink in, absorb.

గ్లాని **glaani** *n.* 1 fatigue. 2 grief.

గ్లాసు **glEEsu** *n.* tumbler; **gaaju~** glass tumbler; **weNDi~** silver tumbler.

ఘ - gha

ఘంట **ghaNTa** *same as* **gaNTa**[1].

ఘంటాకంకణం **ghaNTaa kankaNam** *n.* award or honour in the form of a wrist band ornamented with small bells.

ఘంటాపథం **ghaNTaapatham** *n. class.* highway.

ఘంటాపథంగా **ghaNTaapathangaa** *adv.* definitely, emphatically, without doubt; ~ **cebutaanu** I affirm without hesitation.

ఘంటారవం **ghaNTaarawam** *n.* ringing or clanging sound made by a bell.

ఘటం **ghaTam** *n.* 1 earthen jar. 2 musical instrument shaped like an earthen jar and played as a drum. 3 body, person; **moNDi** ~ obstinate person; **naa~ unnantawarakuu ii aacaaraalu ilaa saagipoowalasindee** as long as I am alive these customs must continue in this manner.

ఘటకం **ghaTakam** *n. sci.* 1 constituent. 2 component.

ఘటజట **ghaTajaTa** *n.* the first two portions of the Vedas, required to be memorised by a student embarking on Vedic studies; ~ **walle weestunnaaDu** he is starting to learn the Vedas *or, colloq.*, he is blindly repeating what he has heard.

ఘటన **ghaTana** *n.* 1 happening, occurrence, episode, incident. 2 disposition, dispensation; **daywa~** dispensation of Providence; **iśwara~** God's will. 3 *class.* bringing together, joining; **ghaTanaa~ samarthuDu** highly skilled or competent person (*lit.* one who is able to bring together or break apart).

ఘటశ్రాద్ధం **ghaTaśraaddham** *n.* funeral rites.

ఘటశ్రాద్ధంచేయు, ఘటశ్రాద్ధంపెట్టు **ghaTaśraaddham ceeyu, ghaTaśraaddham peTTu** *v.i.* 1 to perform funeral rites. 2 to perform a mock funeral of s.o. who has been excommunicated.

ఘటించు **ghaTincu** *v.t.* 1 *class.* to join together. 2 *mod. only in the phrase* **anjali~** to join the hands together in a gesture of reverence or devotion, to offer tribute of reverence or devotion.

ఘటిక **ghaTika** *n.* Indian measure of time equal to 24 minutes.

ఘటికుడు **ghaTikuDu** *n.* clever, able, astute or competent person.

ఘటిల్లు **ghaTillu** *v.i.* to happen, occur.

ఘటీకారం **ghaTiikaaram** *n. class.* clock.

ఘటీయంత్రం **ghaTiiyantram** *n.* 1 clockwork. 2 *class.* apparatus for baling water.

ఘట్టం **ghaTTam** *n.* 1 incident, happening, event, occasion. 2 period, stage, phase. 3 scene in a play. 4 landing place; **snaana~** bathing place, bathing ghat.

ఘట్టన[ం] **ghaTTana[m]** *n.* ramming down; **paada~** trampling.

ఘడియ, గడియ **ghaDiya, gaDiya** *n.* Indian measure of time equal to 24 minutes; **kaLyaaNa ~lu** auspicious time for a marriage; **wiSapu ~lu** time of misfortune, bad time caused by an unfavourable omen.

ఘన **ghana** *adj.* 1 great, grand, excellent, noble; ~ **swaagatam** rousing reception. 2 solid, hard, firm: ~ **sthiti** solid state. 3 cubic[al].

ఘనం **ghanam** *n.* 1 greatness, honour. 2 cube.

ఘనంగా **ghanangaa** *adv.* grandly, nobly.

ఘనకార్యం **ghanakaaryam** *n.* great or important deed, mighty action, heroic deed.

ఘనత **ghanata** *n.* 1 greatness, eminence. 2 fame, renown, distinction; ~ **ku ekku** to achieve fame.

ఘనతవహించు **ghanata wahincu** *v.i.* to become famous or eminent, achieve fame or distinction.

ఘనత్వం **ghanatwam** *n.* greatness.

ఘనపదార్థం **ghanapadaartham** *n.* solid [matter].

ఘనపరిమాణ **ghanaparimaaNa** *adj.* cubical.

ఘనపరిమాణం **ghanaparimaaNam** *n. maths. sci.* volume.

ఘనపు **ghanapu** *adj.* cubic; ~ **TaDugu** cubic foot.

ఘనమూలం **ghanamuulam** *n. maths.* cube root.

ఘనాఘన **ghanaaghana** *n. class.* floating cloud, rainy cloud.

ఘనాపాఠీ **ghanaapaaThii** *n.* expert, proficient person, esp. a scholar proficient in the Vedas.

ఘనీభవనస్థానం **ghaniibhawana sthaanam** *n. sci.* freezing point.

ఘనీభవించు **ghaniibhawincu** *v.i.* 1 to become solid or hard, solidify, congeal, harden. 2 to become firm. 3 to freeze.

ఘనుడు **ghanuDu** *n.* great, important, respectable person.

ఘమఘమ **ghamaghama** *same as* **gamagama.**

ఘరానా **gharaanaa** *same as* **garaanaa.**

ఘర్మం, ఘర్మజలం **gharmam, gharmajalam** *n.* sweat, perspiration.

ఘర్షణ[ం] **gharSaNa[m]** *n.* 1 friction. 2 dispute, contention, argument, quarrel; **naatoo ~ paDDaaDu** he quarrelled with me.

ఘర్షణశక్తి **gharSaNa śakti** *n.* frictional force.

ఘర్షించు **gharSincu** *v.i.* to dispute, quarrel.

ఘల్లు **ghallu** *same as* **gallu.**

ఘా to ఘ్రా - ghaa to ghraa

ఘాటు **ghaaTu** I. *n.* strength (of tastes, smells, words, etc., not physical strength). II. *adj.* 1 pungent, spicy, acrid. 2 strong, powerful; ~**maaTalu** strong words; ~**preema** passionate love.

ఘాటుగా **ghaaTugaa** *adv.* 1 strongly, powerfully. 2 vehemently, severely, fiercely.

ఘాతం **ghaatam** *n.* 1 blow, stroke. 2 *maths.* power.

ఘాతకుడు **ghaatakuDu** *n.* villain, murderer, slayer.

ఘాతక్షమత **ghaatakSamata** *n. chem.* malleability.

ఘాతుక **ghaatuka** *adj.* cruel, savage, villainous, devilish.

ఘీంకరించు **ghiinkarincu** *v.i.* (of an elephant) to trumpet.

ఘీంకారం **ghiinkaaram** *n.* trumpeting of an elephant.

ఘుటిక **ghuTika** *n.* ball, pill.

ఘుమఘుమ[లాడు] **ghumaghuma[laaDu]** *same as* **gumaguma[laaDu].**

ఘుమాయించు **ghumaayincu** *same as* **gumaayincu.**

ఘుమ్మను **ghummanu** *same as* **gummanu.**

ఘుసృణం **ghusṛNam** *n. class.* saffron.

ఘూకం **ghuukam** *n. class.* owl.

ఘూర్జర **ghuurjara** *adj.* of Gujarat.

ఘూర్ణిల్లు **ghuurNillu** *v.i.* 1 to roll. 2 to turn round.

ఘృణ **ghṛNa** *n. class.* 1 pity, compassion. 2 dislike, aversion.

ఘృతం **ghṛtam** *n.* ghee.

ఘొల్లున, ఘొల్లుమని **ghelluna, ghollumani** *adv.* (of shouting or wailing) loudly, clamorously.

ఘోటకం **ghooTakam** *n. class.* horse.

ఘోటకబ్రహ్మచర్యం **ghooTaka brahmacaryam** *n. class.* enforced bachelordom.

ఘోరం **ghooram** I. *n.* evil deed, atrocity, terrible event. II. *adj.* frightful, horrible, terrible, tremendous.

ఘోరంగా **ghoorangaa** *adv.* terribly, tremendously; **naaku aakali ~ awutunnadi** I am terribly hungry.

ఘోరదేశద్రోహం **ghoora deeśadrooham** *n. legal* high treason.

ఘోష **ghooSa** *n.* 1 loud cry, noise, shouting, tumult, uproar. 2 wailing, lamenting. 3 **weeda~** sound of chanting the Vedas in chorus. 4 affairs, concern; **naa~ niiku enduku?** what have you to do with my affairs? ~**leeni** unconcerned, disinterested. 5 retribution or curse due to the envy or malice of others or to having harmed others; **waaLLa ~ maaku tagilindi** (*or* **koTTindi**) their curse fell upon me; **enta~ paDipooyEEwuraa!** what an amount of envy you have incurred!

ఘోషణ **ghooSaNa** *n.* proclamation; ~**patram** proclamation notice.

ఘోషా **ghooSaa** *n.* purdah.

ఘోషించు **ghooSincu** I. *v.i.* to roar, resound. II. *v.t.* to proclaim.

ఘ్రాణం **ghraaNam** *n.* smell, odour.

ఘ్రాణేంద్రియం **ghraaNeendriyam** *n.* sense of smell.

చ - ca

చంక **canka** *n.* 1 armpit; **aaTalloo paDi waaDi caduwu~ naaki pooyindi** *slang* because he was involved in sport his education went to the dogs; **waaDi pariikSa ~naaki pooyindi** *slang* he failed his exam. 2 *dial.* udder.

చంకన పెట్టుకొను **cankana peTTukonu** *v.t.* 1 to carry on or under o.'s arm. 2 *colloq.* to steal, make off with.

చంకన వేసుకొను, చంకన ఎత్తుకొను **cankana weesukonu, cankana ettukonu** *v.t.* to carry on or under o.'s arm; **pillanu cankana weesukoni bajaaruku weLLindi** she went to the bazaar carrying her child on her arm.

చంక్రమణం **cankramaNam** *n. class.* going about, moving from place to place; *cf.* **śaakhaa~.**

చంచల **cancala** *adj.* unsteady, unstable, fickle, volatile, inconstant.

చంచా, చెంచా **cancaa, cencaa** *n.* spoon.

చంటి **caNTi** *genitive of* **cannu** breast; ~**biDDa** (*or* ~**pilla**) baby, infant.

చంటి[బిడ్డ]గుణం **caNTi[biDDa]guNam** *n.* convulsions.

చండ **caNDa** *adj.* violent, terrible; ~**maarutam** violent wind, gale; **caNDooSNam** extreme heat.

చండశాసనం **caNDaśaasanam** *n.* strict discipline, strict orders.

చండశాసనుడు **caNDaśaasanuDu** *n.* strict disciplinarian, martinet.

చండప్రచండంగా **caNDapracaNDangaa** *adv.* 1 brightly (shining). 2 profusely (spreading).

చండాలం **caNDaalam** *n.* 1 nonsense, rubbish. 2 s.g unpleasant, disagreeable, nasty or horrible; **beeram aaDaDam~** it is unpleasant to bargain; **sinimaa parama ~gaa undi** the movie was dreadfully bad; **poddunnee caNDaalapu waana paTTukondi** wretched rain started in the early morning; **caNDaalapu wedhawalu** riffraff.

చండాలుడు **caNDaaluDu** *n.* outcast.

చండి, చెండి **caNDi, ceNDi** *n.* epithet of the Goddess Parvati.

చండితనం, చెండితనం **caNDitanam, ceNDitanam** *n.* stubbornness, obstinacy.

చండ్ర **caNDra** *n.* kind of acacia tree.

చందం **candam** *n.* 1 manner, likeness. 2 state, form, condition. 3 **andam~** beauty and charm; *cf.* **andacandaalu.**

చందంగా **candangaa** *same as* **candaana.**

చందనం **candanam** *n.* sandalwood, sandal paste.

చందన చర్చ **candana carca** *n. class.* traditional way of offering hospitality to guests by rubbing sandal paste on the hands or neck.

చందమామ **candamaama** *n.* 1 *child language* moon. 2 yolk of an egg.

చందా **candaa** *n.* money subscription.

చందాదారుడు **candaadaaruDu** *n.* subscriber.

చందాన, చందంగా **candaana, candangaa** *adv.* in the manner of, like; **tana weelitoo tana kaNTinee poDucukonna candaana wyawaharincaDam tagunaa**? is it fitting to behave as if one was poking o.'s finger into o.'s own eye?

చందావేయు **candaa weeyu** *v.t.* to subscribe.

చందుగుపెట్టె **candugu peTTe** *n.* small chest or safe.

చంద్రకాంత, చెంద్రకాంత **candrakaanta, cendra kaanta** *n. mirabilis jalapa*, a flower of varying colour with black seeds and medicinal leaves.

చంద్రకాంతశిల **candrakaanta śila** *n.* marble.

చంద్రకాంతాలు **candrakaantaalu** *n. pl.* kind of sweet made of sugar, coconut and greengram.

చంద్రమండలం **candramaNDalam** *n.* moon (the term used for the moon in astronomy).

చంద్రవంక **candrawanka** *n.* 1 crescent moon. 2 crescent, cresent-shaped object.

చంద్రహారం **candrahaaram** *n.* necklace.

చంద్రహాసం **candrahaasam** *n.* 1 radiance. 2 *class.* sword, esp. Ravana's sword in the Ramayana.

చంద్రిక **candrika** *n.* 1 moonlight, moon's rays. 2 *as second part of a compound in certain literary words* light, e.g., **śabdaartha~** lexicon, dictionary (*lit.* light of word meaning); **wijñaana ~** light of knowledge.

చంద్రుడు **candruDu** *n.* moon (the traditional name for the moon); **candruniki oo nuulu poogu** (an offering of) a piece of thread to the moon (proverbial expression meaning whatever little one has to offer); *cf.* **uDatabhakti.**

చంద్రోదయం **candroodayam** *n.* moonrise.

చంపక **campaka** *n.* the sampangi or champak tree, *michelia champaka.*

చంపకమాల **campakamaala** *n.* kind of poetic metre.

చంపు **campu**[1] *v.t.* 1 to kill, slay; *see* **kuti.** 2 to harass, tease; *~ is often used in a very much weaker sense than is suggested by the original meaning of* to kill; **campakaNDooy**! don't tease me (e.g., by keeping me in suspense, refusing to answer my question); **campeesEEwu**! you are asking too much! *or simply* oh, no! 3 (in chess) to take (a pawn, knight or any other piece on the board).

చంపు **campu**[2] *n.* kind of literary work containing both poetry and prose.

చంపుకొనితిను, చంపుకుతిను **campukoni tinu, campuku tinu** *v.t.* to keep on worrying or pestering.

చంపుడు **campuDu** *n.* killing, slaying.

చకచక, చెకచెక **cakacaka, cekaceka** *adv.* 1 quickly, fast, briskly. 2 brilliantly.

చకిత **cakita** *adj.* surprised, astonished, taken aback, struck by wonder.

చకోరం **cakooram** *n.* kind of partridge often mentioned in poetic literature; **candruDikoosam cakoorapakSi laagaa aame bhartakoosam kaacukoni undi** she is waiting for the coming of her husband as a patridge yearns for the moon.

చక్క **cakka** *adj.* 1 nice, beautiful, pretty, good-looking. 2 direct, straight. 3 right, correct, due, proper.

చక్కగా **cakkagaa** *adv.* 1 straight, directly. 2 beautifully, prettily.

చక్కతనం **cakkatanam** *n.* 1 straightness. 2 beauty.

చక్కదిద్దు[కొను] **cakkadiddu[konu]** *v.t.* 1 to put right, rectify, settle, put in order. 2 to trim.

చక్కపడు **cakkapaDu** *v.i.* to be settled or set right.

చక్కపరచు **cakkaparacu** *v.t.* to set right, rectify, remedy.

చక్కపెట్టు **cakkapeTTu** *v.t.* to arrange, settle, set right, put in order; **diipam uNDagaa illu ~koowaali** put your house in order while the light lasts (proverb). 2 *colloq.* to make off with, steal.

చక్కర్ **cakkar** *n. dial.* giddiness.

చక్కా **cakkaa** *adv.* 1 straight, on o.'s own initiative, without reference to others; **neenu sTeeSanuku weLLeeloopala aayana iNTiki ~waccEEDu** before I reached the station, he came home on his own. 2 *after a past participle ~ implies performing a certain action and nothing else*, e.g., **paaDadalacukonna paaTalu paaDi ~pooyEEru** they left straightaway after singing the songs they had intended.

చక్కిలం **cakkilam** *n.* kind of savoury, ring shaped.

చక్కిలి **cakkili** *n.* armpit.

చక్కిలిగింత, చక్కిలిగిలి **cakkiliginta, cakkiligili** *n.* tickling.

చక్కిలిగింతలుపెట్టు, చక్కిలిగిలిపెట్టు **cakkiligintalupeTTu, cakkiligilipeTTu** *v.t.* to tickle.

చక్కీ **cakkii** *n. dial.* 1 frame. 2 set of things fixed together in a frame.

చక్కెర **cakkera** *n.* sugar.

చక్కెరకేళీ, చక్రకేళీ **cakkerakeeLii, cakrakeeLii** *n.* kind of plantain or banana.

చక్ర **cakra** *adj.* rotatory, rotary.

చక్రం **cakram** *n.* 1 wheel, any flat round object, disc, esp. Vishnu's disc; **~aDDu weeyu** to come to the rescue (*lit.* to put a wheel as a protection — referring to an episode in the Mahabharata). 2 circle, cycle; **wiSama ~** vicious circle; **jiiwita ~** life cycle. 3 potter's wheel. 4 diagram in astrology; **~weeyincu** to have a horoscope cast. 5 in traditional Indian medicine, one of the six glands of the body, influencing psychic activity.

చక్రబంధం **cakrabandham** *n.* closed circle from which there is no way of escape.

చక్రవడ్డీ **cakra waDDii** *n.* compound interest.

చక్రవర్తి **cakrawarti** *n.* emperor.

చక్రవాకం **cakrawaakam** *n.* brahminy duck.

చక్రవాతం **cakrawaatam** *n.* whirlwind, cyclone.

చక్రవాళం **cakrawaaLam** *n.* horizon.

చక్రి **cakri** *n.* epithet of Vishnu.

చక్రిక **cakrika** *n.* disc.

చక్షువు **cakSuwu** *n. class.* eye.

చచ్చు **caccu** I. *n.* paralysis, numbness, weakness (of limbs). II. *adj.* 1 rotten; ~ **ullipaayalu** rotten onions. 2 poor, weak, insipid, wretched, useless; ~ **maaTa** weak word; ~ **praśna** pointless question; ~ **beeram** unacceptably low offer made in a bargain. 3 dull, uninteresting, lifeless. 4 ~ **baakii** irrecoverable debt. 5 ~ **gaDDi** straw that has been threshed. III *v.i.* 1 to die, expire, perish; **guNDu debbalaki** ~ to die of bullet wounds. 2 to suffer difficulties, be in misery, be in urgent need; **prastutam ii gantalu moyyaleeka castunnaamu** at present we are suffering greatly because we cannot bear these burdens; **rangu pensilu leeka castunnaanu** I desperately need a coloured pencil. 3 *with the past participle of another verb* ~ *lends intensive force*, e.g., **enta seepu cuusinaa kanapaDi caawaleedu** no matter how long I searched, the wretched thing was not to be found; **mEESTaru raaleedu, pillalu tannukoni castunnaaru** the master has not come and the children are squabbling like anything; *cf.* **eeDcu** *sense 3.* 4 *colloq., substituting for another verb* **wiiDitoo elaa cacceedi?** how are we to get along with this man? *cf.* **eeDcu** *sense 4.* 5 *some nonfinite forms of* ~ *are used idiomatically*: (i) **caccee[Tanta]**, **caccinanta** terrible (*lit.* great enough to kill), e.g., **caccee eNDalu** terrible heat; **cacceeTanta talanoppi** a terrible headache; (ii) **castee** *or* **caccinaa** *before a neg. vb. adds emphasis*, e.g., **castee anukooru** they are certain not to think; **caccinaa raadu** it will certainly not come; **castee iwwanu** I will certainly not give; (iii) **caccinaTTu** certainly, to be sure, undoubtedly, unfailingly; **waaDu ippuDu khariidu nuuru annaa caccinaTTu manam teccukoowalasindee** now even if he says the price is a hundred rupees, we will undoubtedly have to bring it; *see* **caawu.**

చచ్చుపడు **caccupaDu** *v.i.* to be[come] numb or paralysed: **naa kaaLLu caccupaDDaayi** my legs are paralysed *or* I cannot move my legs.

చటాకు **caTaaku** *n.* a grain measure, one sixteenth of a seer.

చటాలున **caTaaluna** *adv.* suddenly.

చటుక్కున **caTukkuna** *adv.* 1 quickly, suddenly. 2 quietly; ~ **kuurcunnaaDu** he sat quietly.

చటులం **caTulam** *adj class.* trembling, glancing, tremulous.

చట్ట **caTTa** *n. slang* hip, thigh.

చట్టం **caTTam** *n.* law, act, statute.

చట్టన, చట్టున **caTTana, caTTuna** *adv.* quickly, promptly, on the spur of the moment.

చట్టనిర్మాణం **caTTanirmaaNam** *same as* **śaasana nirmaaNam.**

చట్టబద్ధ **caTTabaddha** *adj.* legal, lawful, statutory.

చట్టబద్ధంగా, చట్టరీత్యా **caTTabaddhangaa, caTTariityaa** *adv.* legally, lawfully, in accordance with law.

చట్టవిరుద్ధ **caTTawiruddha** *adj.* illegal, unlawful.

చట్టశాసనం **caTTaśaasanam** *n.* legislation, enactment of laws.

చట్టి **caTTi** *n.* small earthen pot with a wide mouth.

చట్టిముక్కు **caTTimukku** *same as* **cappiDimukku.**

చట్టు **caTTu** *n.* 1 rock. 2 stone slab. 3 base; **ii kuNDaki** ~ **leedu** this pot has no base (to stand on).

చట్టుతనం **caTTutanam** *n.* rocklike stubbornness.

చట్టున **caTTuna** *same as* **caTTana.**

చట్టుబండలు **caTTubaNDalu** *echo word* and all that, and the like; **saamaanluu**~ luggage and all that; **pillaki iraway eeLLu weLLEEyi, caduwuu~ aNTuu amma eedoo kaalakSeepam ceeseestoondi** the girl is twenty years old, her mother keeps her occupied with a little education and the like.

చట్టురాయి, చట్రాయి **caTTuraayi, caTraayi** *n.* living rock.

చట్నీ **caTNii** *n.* chutney.

చట్రం **caTram** *n.* 1 frame [work]; **phooTooki** ~ **kaTTistaanu** I will have the photo framed. 2 perforated ladle used in frying.

చడి **caDi** *n.* sound, noise; **caDii cappuDu leekuNDaa** silently, without a sound.

చతికిలపడు, చదికిలబడు **catikilapaDu, cadikilabaDu** *v.i.* 1 to slump, subside, sink back (-**miida,** onto). 2 to feel depressed, collapse with shock. 3 to fall or lie flat on the ground. 4 to sit on the ground with legs outstretched.

చతుర **catura** *adj.* 1 clever, intelligent. 2 ingenious, skilful.

చతురంగం, చదరంగం **caturangam, cadarangam** *n.* chess.

చతురంగబలం **caturanga balam** *n.* an army in ancient times equipped with all the four arms—infantry, cavalry, elephants and war chariots.

చతురత **caturata** *n.* cleverness.

చతురస్రం **caturasram** *n.* 1 quadrilateral. 2 square.

చతురుడు **caturuDu** *n.* clever, intelligent or skilful person.

చతురోక్తి, చతుర్వచనం **caturookti, caturwacanam** *n.* 1 anecdote. 2 amusing or quickwitted reply, repartee.

చతుర్థ **caturtha** *adj.* fourth.

చతుర్థి **caturthi** *n.* 1 *gram.* dative case. 2 *class.* fourth day of a lunar fortnight (= **cawiti**).

చతుర్దశభువనాలు **caturdaśa bhuwanaalu** *n. pl. class.* the fourteen worlds depicted in Hindu mythology.

చతుర్దశి **caturdaśi** *n.* fourteenth day of a lunar fortnight.

చతుర్భుజం **caturbhujam** *n.* quadrilateral.

చతుర్ముఖపురాణం,చతుర్ముఖపారాయణం **caturmukha puraaNam, caturmukha paaraayaNam** *n. colloq.* game of cards.

చతుర్ముఖుడు **caturmukhuDu** *n. class.* epithet of God Brahma, the creator of the world.

చతుర్వచనం **caturwacanam** *same as* **caturookti.**

చతుష్పాద **catuSpaada** *adj.* four legged; ~ **jantuwu** quadruped.

చతుష్షష్టి **catuSSaSTi** *n. class.* sixty-four.

చతుష్షష్టికళలు **catuSSaSTi kaLalu** *n. pl.* the sixty-four forms of art constituting all human knowledge.

చత్వారం **catwaaram** *n.* 1 long sight. 2 astigmatism.

చద **cada** *same as* **ceda.**

చదర **cadara** *n.* small mat.

చదరం **cadaram** I. *n.* square. II. *adj.* 1 square. 2 level, even; **neela** ~ **ceestaaru** they level the ground.

చదరంగం **cadarangam** *same as* **caturangam.**

చదరంగంబల్ల **cadarangam balla** *n.* chess board.

చదరంగ[పు]బలం **cadaranga[pu]balam** *n.* set of chess men.

చదరంగా **cadarangaa** *adv.* 1 squarely. 2 at one level, evenly.

చదరపు **cadarapu** *adj.* square; ~**gajam** square yard; **cadarapillu** a well-appointed house.

చదివించు **cadiwincu** *v.t.* 1 to cause (s.g) to be read or learnt. 2 to teach (a lesson). 3 to educate (a person). 4 to make a gift at a wedding or similar occasion and have it announced by the priest.

చదివింపులు **cadiwimpulu** *n.pl.* presents given and formally announced at weddings and similar occasions.

చదును **cadunu** *adj.* even, level, flat.

చదునుచేయు **cadunu ceeyu** *v.t.* to level, make even.

చదురాడు, చతురాడు **caduraaDu, caturaaDu** *v.i. dial.* to make jokes.

చదురు **caduru** I. *n. class.* 1 assembly, prince's court. 2 entertainment consisting of music and dancing. II. *v.i. dial.* to crack a joke.

చదువరి **caduwari** *n.* reader.

చదువు **caduwu** I. *n.* 1 learning, study. 2 education, studies. 3 reading. II. *v.t.* 1 to read. 2 to read out loud, recite.

చదువుకొను **caduwukonu** *v.i. and t.* 1 to read to o.s. 2 to study, educate o.s.; **caduwukonnawaaru** educated persons.

చదువుసంధ్యలు **caduwu sandhyalu** *n.pl.* 1 learning of hymns and other studies begun by a brahman boy as soon as his upanayanam has been performed. 2 education; **caduwuu sandhyaa leeni** without any education. uneducated.

చద్ది, చల్ది **caddi, caldi** *n.* 1 stale food. 2 (*also* **caddannam**) food cooked overnight and eaten cold next morning for breakfast.

చద్దినైవేద్యం **caddinayweedyam** *n.* offering made to a village goddess of cold freshly cooked food mixed with yoghurt.

చనిపోవు **canipoowu** *v.i.* to die, pass away, expire.

చను **canu** *v.i. class.* 1 to go. 2 to be fit or proper.

చనుకట్టు **canukaTTu** *n.* 1 breast. 2 bodice.

చనుదెంచు **canudencu** *v.i class.* to go, come, proceed.

చనుబాలు **canubaalu** *n.pl.* mother's milk.

చనువు **canuwu** *n.* familiarity, informality; **okariki** ~ **iccu** to behave in a kindly and informal way towards s.o.; **okaritoo** ~ **tiisukonu** to presume on or take undue advantage of s.o.'s friendship or good nature.

చన్నీళ్లు **canniiLLu** *n.pl.* cold water (= **calla niiLLu**).

చన్ను **cannu** *n.* breast, nipple, teat; *see* **caNTi.**

చపల **capala** *adj.* unsteady, fickle, wavering, unstable, volatile, inconstant.

చపలత్వం **capalatwam** *n.* fickleness, inconstancy.

చపాటి, చపాతి **capaaTi, capaati** *n.* flat cake of unleavened flour baked on a pan.

చప్టా **capTaa** I. *n.* flat platform; **nuuti**~ platform round a well. II. *adj.* flat.

చప్ప **cappa** *adj.* 1 tasteless, insipid. 2 weak, feeble. 3 dull, boring.

చప్పగా **cappagaa** *adv.* 1 spiritlessly, feebly. 2 quietly.

చప్ప చల్లారు **cappa callaaru** *v.i.* 1 (of food) to become tasteless and cold. 2 (of emotions) to calm down, cool, subside.

చప్పట **cappaTa** *n.* clap of the hand, *gen. pl.* **cappaTLu** clapping, applause.

చప్పట్లుకొట్టు **cappaTLukoTTu** *v.i.* to clap o.'s hands, applaud.

చప్పబడు **cappabaDu** *v.i.* to become passive or quiescent. subside.

చప్పరం **capparam** *n.* canopied seat in which an idol is carried in procession.

చప్పరించు **capparincu** *v.i. and t.* 1 to relish, smack o.'s lips. 2 to suck s.g, e.g., a sweet, by letting it dissolve in the mouth. 3 **pedimalu** ~ to purse o.'s lips in disapproval.

చప్పిడి **cappiDi** *adj.* 1 tasteless, insipid, dull. 2 ~**mukku, caTTimukku** snub nose.

చప్పుడు **cappuDu** *n.* noise, sound.

చప్పుడు చేయు **cappuDu ceeyu** *v.i.* to make a noise or sound, be noisy.

చప్పున **cappuna** *adv.* quickly, immediately, promptly.

చప్పుమని **cappumani** *adv.* abruptly.

చబుకు **cabuku** *n.* whip.

చమక్‌చమక్ **camakcamak** *onom. adv. and n. sug.* glittering; ~**manu** to flash, glitter.

చమత్కరించు **camatkarincu** I. *v.i.* to speak jokingly, say (s.g) jokingly, say (s.g) with a laugh. II. *v.t.* to make fun of, mock.

చమత్కారం **camatkaaram** *n.* 1 wit, humour. 2 ingenuity.

చమత్కారంగా **camatkaarangaa** *adv.* wittily, funnily, humorously, comically, jokingly, with a laugh.

చమత్కృతి **camatkṛti** *n.* 1 wit. 2 ingenuity.

చమరీమృగం **camariimṛgam** *n. class.* yak.

చమురు **camuru** I. *n.* 1 oil. 2 *colloq.* money, wealth; **ceeti~ wadilindi** my money was exhausted *or* my money ran out. 3 **~kaaLLa peddamma** stupid fellow (*term of reproach or abuse, lit.* person with slippery feet). II. *v.t.* to smear, rub with oil.

చమ్కీ **camkii** *n.* embroidery; **~Toopii** embroidered cap.

చర **cara** *adj.* 1 movable. 2 *maths. sci.* variable.

చరకం **carakam** *n.* science of Indian medicine; **caraka samhita** name of a treatise on Indian medicine.

చరచర **cara cara** adv. quickly, in a hurry, with a rush.

చరచు **caracu** *v.t.* 1 to pat, slap. 2 **cappaTLu~** to clap, applaud. 3 **piDakalu~** to make cowdung cakes by patting them into shape.

చరణ[ం] **caraNa[m]** *n.* 1 *class.* foot; **caraNa kamalaalu** lotus-like feet. 2 verse of a song; *see* **karam**.

చరపు **carapu** *n.* 1 slap, clap. 2 buffeting, pounding.

చరమ **carama** *adj.* last, final, ultimate.

చరమూలధనం **caramuula dhanam** *n. econ.* liquid capital.

చరరాశి **cararaaśi** *n. maths. sci.* variable.

చరలాడు **caralaaDu** *v.i.* 1 to play. 2 to roll about, toss from side to side.

చరాంశం **caraamśam** *n. maths. sci.* variable.

చరాస్తి **caraasti** *n.* movable property.

చరించు **carincu** *v.i. class.* 1 to wander, roam. 2 to behave.

చరిత[ం] **carita[m]** *n.* 1 nature, character; **waaDi~ mancidi kaadu** his character is not good. 2 history, tale, narrative; *see* **wiira~**.

చరితుడు **carituDu** *second part of a n. compound* person who has a certain nature or character; **puNya~** person of meritorious character; **paawana~** person of pious character.

చరితార్థ **caritaartha** *adj.* 1 meaningful, purposeful, significant. 3 historically important.

చరితార్థత **caritaarthata** *n.* 1 meaning, purpose, significance. 2 historical importante.

చరిత్ర **caritra** *n.* 1 history. 2 tale, story, account, narrative.

చరిత్రకారుడు **caritrakaaruDu** *n.* historian.

చరిత్రపూర్వ **caritrapuurwa** *adj.* prehistoric.

చరిత్రాత్మక **caritraatmaka** *adj.* historic.

చరియ **cariya** *n.* 1 gorge or valley in a mountain range. 2 cliff, precipice.

చరుపుడు **carupuDu** *n.* pounding.

చర్చ **carca** *n.* 1 discussion, debate, argument, deliberation. 2 smearing with sandal paste; *see* **candana carca.**

చర్చనీయ **carcaniiya** *adj.* debatable.

చర్చించు **carcincu** *v.t.* to discuss, debate.

చర్మం **carmam** *n.* skin, hide, leather.

చర్మకారుడు **carmakaaruDu** *n.* leather worker, tanner.

చర్మీయ **carmiiya** *adj.* dermal.

చర్య **carya** *n.* 1 action, act, activity. 2 *chem.* reaction.

చర్రన, చర్రున **carrana, carruna** *adv.* quickly, hurriedly, with a rush.

చర్రుమని **carrumani** *adv.* quickly, suddenly.

చర్వణం **carwaNam** *n.* chewing; **taambuula~** chewing betel leaf; **carwita~** going over the same ground again (*lit.* chewing what has been chewed already), tautology.

చలం **calam**[1] *n.* shaking, trembling.

చలం **calam**[2] *n.* 1 determination, insistence, persistence, obstinacy. 2 *class.* envy, malice.

చలంవేయు **calam weeyu** *v.i.* to behave obstinately; **eNDaloo tirigi waddannaa calam weesi niiLLu taagutunnaaDu** although it is forbidden he is obstinately insisting on drinking cold water after going out in the hot sun.

చలత్వం **calatwam** *n. maths.* variation.

చలనం **calanam** *n.* 1 movement, [loco]motion, activity. 2 stirring, shaking, trembling, instability. 3 wandering, roaming.

చలనచిత్రం **calanacitram** *n* film, motion picture, movie.

చలనశీలత **calanaśiilata** *n.* mobility.

చలపట్టు **calapaTTu** *v.i.* 1 to be determined, be insistent, be obstinate. 2 *class.* to be envious, be malicious.

చలపాది **calapaadi** *adj.* 1 determined, insistent, obstinate. 2 *class.* envious, malicious.

చలరాశులు **calaraaśulu** *n. pl. maths.* variables.

చలవ **calawa** *same as* **caluwa.**

చలవరాయి **calawaraayi** *n.* white marble.

చలాకీ **calaaki** *adj.* 1 lively, vivacious. 2 pert, saucy.

చలాత్ముడు **calaatmuDu** *n.* fickleminded person.

చలాన **calaana** *n.* 1 memorandum of money paid into the treasury serving as a receipt for the amount paid. 2 police charge memo.

చలామణీ, చెలామణీ **calaamaNi, celaamaNi** *n.* currency, circulation; **telugu naaDantaTaa ii maaTa~loo undi** this word is in currency (*or* in current use) all over the Telugu country; **~loo unna drawyam** money that is in circulation.

చలామణీ అవు **calaamaNi awu** *v.i.* 1 to be current, be in circulation. 2 to be regarded as, be considered as, pass for; **caTTaalanu tamaku anukuulangaa maarcukoni samaajamloo gharaanaagaa ~taaru** they alter the laws in their own favour and pass for respectable people in society.

చలాయించు, చెలాయించు **calaayincu, celaayincu** *v.t.* to wield, exercise (authority).

చలాయింపు **calaayimpu** *adj.* authoritarian.

చలి **cali** I. *n.* cold; **boccutoo neesinadi aytee ~ ki aagutundi** if it is woven of wool it will withstand the cold; **bhoogimaNTadaggira kuurcuni ~ kaacukoneewaaDu** he used to warm himself by sitting next to a bonfire. II. *adj.* cold; **~ kaalam** cold weather; **~ eNDa** winter sunlight; **~ dustulu** winter clothes, woollen clothes.

చలించు **calincu** *v.i.* 1 to stir, move. 2 to shake, be shaken, receive a shock; **waaDiki mati calincindi** he became insane.

చలిగాడ్పు **caligaaDpu** *n.* cold wind.

చలిచీమ **caliciima** *n.* kind of black ant.

చలిజ్వరం **calijwaram** *n.* malaria, ague.

చలిమంట **calimaNTa** *n.* bonfire.

చలిమిడి **calimiDi** *n.* sweet made of rice flour and jaggery.

చలిమిడి సుద్ద **calimiDisudda** *n.* 1 ball of **calimiDi**. 2 lethargic person.

చలివేంద్రం **caliweendram** *n.* place where in hot weather a drink of water or buttermilk is offered to travellers.

చలువ, చలవ **caluwa, calawa** I. *n.* 1 coolness, cooling effect; **eNDaakaalamloo munjelu ~ ku tiNTaaru** in summer people eat palmyra fruits for their cooling effect. 2 cold [ness]; **~ lu kammutunnayi** coldness is spreading (over a person's body, as a sign of approaching death). 3 beneficence, benignity, liberality. 4 (*in complimentary expressions*) goodness, kindness, blessing; **miiru weLLina pani ayindEE?" "mii [ceeti/nooTi] ~ walla"** "did you finish the work that you went for?" "yes, thanks to your blessing". 5 clean clothes newly washed and ironed. II. *adj.* cold, cool[ing]; **~ gadi** a cool room; **~ kaLLaddalu** sun glasses, dark glasses.

చల్ది **caldi** *same as* **caddi.**

చల్ల **calla** I. *n.* buttermilk. II. *adj.* 1 cool, cold. 2 soothing, pleasant. 3 benign, kindly. 4 happy, blessed.

చల్లకం **callakam** *n.* 1 sprinkling, scattering. 2 watering, irrigation.

చల్లగా **callagaa** *adv.* 1 coolly. 2 gently, quietly, calmly. 3 favourably, benignly. 4 unconcernedly.

చల్లగుంజ **callagunja** *n.* churning rod for making buttermilk.

చల్లతనం **callatanam** *n.* 1 coolness. 2 benignity, goodness.

చల్లనయ్య **callanayya** *n.* a god or other benign being.

చల్లపడు **callapaDu** *v.i.* 1 to become cool. 2 to be pacified. 3 to be happy, be blessed.

చల్లారపెట్టు **callaarapeTTu** *v.t.* to make cool.

చల్లారు **callaaru** *v.i.* 1 to become cool, grow cool. 2 to calm down, become calm. 3 (of fire, lamp) to be extinguished, be quenched, be put out.

చల్లార్చు **callaarcu** *v.t.* 1 to cool. 2 to calm, pacify. 3 to extinguish, quench, put out (fire, lamp).

చల్లు **callu** *v.t.* 1. to sprinkle, scatter, spray. 2 to sow (seeds). 3 to spatter, splash (ink).

చవ **cawa** *n.* pink colour of a new born baby (= **nelamuriki**).

చవట **cawaTa** *n.* fool, idiot, stupid person.

చవి **cawi** *n.* taste; **nooru ~ caccipooyindi** the mouth has lost its sense of taste.

చవిచూచు **cawicuucu** *v.t.* to taste.

చవిటి **cawiTi** *adj.* saline, salty; **~ neela** salty soil.

చవితి **cawiti** *n.* fourth day of a lunar fortnight.

చవిమరుగు **cawimarugu** *v.i.* to be infatuated.

చవులూరించు **cawuluurincu** *v.i.* to make s.o. water at the mouth.

చషకం **caSakam** *n. class.* goblet, wine cup.

చా - caa

చాంగురే! **caanguree!** *interj.* well done!, excellent!

చాంచల్యం **caancalyam** *n.* instability, fickleness, unsteadiness, inconstancy.

చాందినీ **caandinii** *n.* awning, canopy.

చాంద్రమానం **caandramaanam** *n. astrol.* calendar of lunar months.

చాంద్రమాసం **caandramaasam** *n. astrol.* lunar month.

చాంద్రాయనం **caandraayaNam** *n.* 1 kind of religious penance. 2 wandering, roaming about; **~ tirigi waccEEDu** he went roaming from place to place.

చాకంటి **caakaNTi** *adj.* pertaining to a washerman; **~ baTTalu** clean clothes (which have been washed by a washerman).

చాకచక్యం **caakacakyam** *n.* 1 wit, sharpness, alertness. 2 skill, proficiency, dexterity.

చాకరు **caakaru** *n., gen. pl.* **caakarlu** servants.

చాకలి **caakali** *n.* washerman.

చాకలిగూన, చాకిబాన **caakaliguuna, caakibaana** *n.* large pot used by washermen for boiling clothes.

చాకలి పిట్ట **caakalipiTTa** *n.* wagtail.

చాకిత, చాకలిది **caakita, caakalidi** *n.* washerwoman.

చాకిరి **caakiri** *n.* drudgery.

చాకిరేవు **caakireewu** *n.* washermen's ghat or washing place on the bank of a stream or river.

చాకు **caaku** *n.* penknife: **~ laaNTiwaaDu** quick-witted person, sharp person.

చాక్షుష **caakSuSa** *adj. class.* pertaining to the eye, observable by the eye.

చాగనార **caaganaara** *see* **saaganaara.**

చాగోరు **caagooru** *v.i. dial.* to lie down, take rest.

చాచు caacu *v.t.* to extend, stretch [out]; **caacipeTTi ooTi** (= **okaTi**) **iccukonnaaDu** he drew back his hand and dealt him a blow; **kaaLLu ~ koni kuurcunnaaDu** he sat with his legs stretched out *or* he abandoned his efforts.

చాటించు, చాటు **caaTincu, caaTu** *v.t.* to proclaim, declare, announce, make known.

చాటింపు **caaTimpu** *n.* declaration, announcement.

చాటిచెప్పు **caaTiceppu** *v.t.* to announce by beat of drum.

చాటు **caaTu**[1] I. *n.* 1 covering, shelter, screen. 2 hidden place, hiding place. 3 hiding, secrecy, privacy, stealth. II. *adj.* 1 covered. 2 hidden. 3 secret. III. *postpositional use* screened by, hidden by, protected by; **aaku ~ pinde** young fruit hidden by leaves (proverb); **talli ~ biDDa** child protected by its mother; **tera ~** behind a screen; **ciikaTi ~** under cover of darkness.

చాటు **caaTu**[2] *v.t. same as* **caaTincu.**

చాటు **caaTu**[3] *adj.* (of verse) stray, extempore; **~ padyaalu** stray or detached verses composed extempore.

చాటుకు **caaTuku** *adv.* aside, to one side.

చాటుగా **caaTugaa** *adv.* 1 secretly, furtively, on the sly. 2 aside, out of the way; **~ uNDaNDi** please stand aside.

చాటుగోడ **caaTugooDa** *n.* partition wall.

చాటున **caaTuna** *p.p.* beyond, behind, hidden by; **koN-Dala ~** on the other side of the hills.

చాటుమాటుగా **caaTumaaTugaa** *adv.* stealthily, clandestinely, surreptitiously, in hiding, in secrecy.

చాటువులు **caaTuwulu** *n. pl.* stray verses, extempore verses, epigrams.

చాడీ **caaDii** *n., gen. pl.* **~ lu** telling tales, backbiting, slandering.

చాడీకోరు **caaDiikooru** *n.* backbiter, slanderer.

చాణక్యం **caaNakyam** *n.* 1 skill, dexterity, ability. 2 shrewdness, cunning.

చాణుక్యుడు **caaNukyuDu** *n.* 1 *same as* **kawTilyuDu.** 2 shrewd, intelligent and determined person.

చాతకం **caatakam** *n.* black cuckoo.

చాతుర్మాస్యం **caaturmaasyam** *n.* name of the four months period from October to January when certain religious sacrifices and ceremonies are performed annually.

చాతుర్యం, చాతురి **caaturyam, caaturi** *n.* skill, cleverness.

చాతుర్వర్ణ్యం **caaturwarNyam** *n.* division of Hindu society into four castes.

చాదస్తం **caadastam** *n.* 1 orthodoxy, traditionalism, old-fashionedness. 2 ceremonialism, bigotry. 3 impracticability, unworldliness, silliness. 4 eccentricity, whimsi--cality. 5 zeal, keenness.

చాదస్తపు **caadastapu** *adj.* orthodox, traditional-minded.

చాదు **caadu** *n.* preparation made of black paste for cosmetic use.

చాదుబొట్టు, చాదుచుక్క **caaduboTTu, caaducukka** *n.* beauty spot, mark made of black paste placed on the forehead. 2 black mark placed on a child's cheek to ward off the evil eye.

చాన **caana** *n.* woman.

చాప **caapa** *n.* mat; **~ kinda niiru** water under the mat (proverbial expression for discreditable actions that are kept hidden).

చాపం **caapam** *n.* 1 *maths.* arc of a circle. 2 bow.

చాపకర్ణం **caapakarNam** *n. maths.* chord.

చాపరాయి **caaparaayi** *n.* stone slab.

చాపల్యం, చాపలం **caapalyam, caapalam** *n.* fickleness, inconstancy.

చాపు **caapu**[1] *n.* (*also* **pancala ~**) full piece of cloth equivalent in length to two dhotis.

చాపు, జాపు **caapu**[2], **jaapu** *v.t.* to stretch out, extend; **nooru ~** *colloq.* to look blank, be unable to answer; **kaaLLu ~** *colloq.* to admit defeat.

చామ **caama** *n.* sama, a kind of millet.

చామనచాయ **caamanacaaya** *n.* fair complexion.

చామరం **caamaram** *n. class.* fly whisk.

చాయ **caaya** *n.* 1 colour, tint, hue. 2 complexion. 3 shadow, shade. 4 likeness, resemblance. 5 (of wood) grain. 6 nearness, vicinity; **maa iNTi ~ laloo** near about my house; **1880 ~ laloo** round about the year 1880. 7 direction, side, quarter.

చాయపప్పు **caayapappu** *n.* polished pulses with husk removed.

చార **caara** *n.* stripe, line, streak; **~ la payjaamaa** striped pyjamas.

చారచర్యలు **caaracaryalu** *n. pl.* secret service work, undercover activities.

చారిక **caarika**[1] *n.* streak.

చారిక **caarika**[2] *n.* woman attendant, woman messenger.

చారిత్రక **caaritraka** *adj.* historic[al].

చారిత్రకత **caaritrakata** *n.* historicity.

చారిత్రకుడు **caaritrakuDu** *n.* historian.

చారిత్రాత్మక **caaritraatmaka** *adj.* historic[al].

చారు **caaru**[1] *n.* pepper water, kind of thin soup made of coriander, tamarind, pepper and spices (= **rasam**).

చారు **caaru**[2] *adj.* beautiful, lovely, charming.

చారుడు **caaruDu** *n.* secret agent, spy.

చారులవ **caarulawa** *n.* kind of horsegram.

చార్వాకం **caarwaakam** *n.* atheism, scepticism.

చార్వాకుడు **caarwaakuDu** *n.* name of a philosopher who preached atheism and scepticism.

చాలనం **caalanam** *n.* shaking.

చాలనీ **caalanii** *n. sci.* sieve.

చాలమి **caalami** *n.* insufficiency, inadequacy.

చాలా **caalaa** I. *adj.* much, many, very. II. *advbl. n.* much, many, great[ly].

చాలామటుకు, చాలావరకు **caalaamaTuku, caalaawaraku** *adv.* to a large extent, to a great extent.

చాలించు **caalincu** I. *v.i.* to stop, cease, come to an end. II. *v.t.* 1 to leave off, stop, give up (job). 2 to close, bring to an end (meeting); *see* **awataaram ~.**

చాలినంత **caalinanta** *adj.* adequate.

చాలీచాలని **caaliicaalani** *adj.* scarcely sufficient, meagre, scant.

చాలు **caalu**[1] *n.* 1 line, row, stripe. 2 furrow. 3 ploughing; **pattiki padi caaLLu, aamudaku aaru** cotton needs ten ploughings, castor needs six; *see* **talli~.**

చాలు **caalu**[2] *v.i.* 1 to suffice, be enough, be sufficient, be adequate. 2 ~ *is used as an impersonal vb. meaning* it is enough; **ruupaayi istee** ~ it is enough if you give a rupee. 3 **caal~!, caallee!** enough!, stop! 4 *in neg. constr.* to be equal **B.ku ewaruu caalaru** no-one can equal B *or* no-one is as good as B. 5 *in neg. constr.* to be able; **aayana paaTham ceppajaalaDu** he cannot teach the lesson.

చాలూఖాతా **caaluu khaataa** *n.* running account.

చావగొట్టు **caawagoTTu** *v.t.* to beat severely.

చావదన్ను **caawadannu** *v.t.* to beat or kick severely.

చావబాదు **caawabaadu** *v.t.* to beat severely (with a stick).

చావమోదు **caawamoodu** *v.t.* to beat severely (with a heavy instrument).

చావిడి, చావడి, సావిడి **caawiDi, caawaDi, saawiDi** *n.* 1 rest house, headman's office in a village. 2 porch, portico. 3 **goDLa~** cattle shed.

చావు **caawu** I. *n.* 1 death; **~kaburu** news of death, any bad news; **~kaburu callagaa ceppEEDu** he broke the bad news gently. 2 s.g almost amounting to death, exhaustion; **ii pani ceeseesariki ~waccipaDindi** I was exhausted by the time I finished this work; **caccina~ ayndi, ii pani ceeseesariki** by the time I finished doing this work, I was utterly exhausted. 3 funeral; **~ku pooyi tirigi waccEEDu** *or* **~ceesi waccEEDu** he attended the funeral. II. *irregular imperative sing. of* **caccu**; *following the past participle of another vb., it conveys impatience, annoyance impoliteness or informality,* e.g., **tondaragaa ceppi~ naaku bassu Tayam ayindi** tell me quickly, it is time for me to catch the bus.

చావుదెబ్బ **caawudebba** *n.* mortal blow, mortal wound.

చి - ci

చింకి **cinki** *adj.* torn, ragged, tattered.

చింకిరి **cinkiri** *adj.* 1 ragged, tattered. 2 **~kaLLu** bleary eyes, half-open eyes.

చించు, చింపు **cincu, cimpu** *v.t.* to tear; **reNDu mukkalugaa~** to tear in half; **kaDupu~koNTee [nii] kaaLLamiida paDutundi** if you divulge s.g, it will recoil against you (proverbial saying); *see* **gontu~konu.**

చింటా **cimTaa** *same as* **cimaTaa**[1].

చింత **cinta**[1] *n.* 1 sorrow, grief. 2 thought, reflection. 3 care, worry; **naa~niiku waddu** do not worry about me.

చింత, చింతమాను, చింతచెట్టు **cinta**[2], **cintamaanu, cintaceTTu** *n.* tamarind tree.

చింతకాయ **cintakaaya** *n.* unripe tamarind fruit.

చింతకుడు, చింతనుడు **cintakuDu, cintanuDu** *n.* pensive person, thoughtful person, thinker.

చింతచిగురు **cintaciguru** *n.* tender tamarind leaves, which are cooked as a vegetable.

చింతచిగురురంగు **cintaciguru rangu** *n.* pea green colour.

చింతన[ం] **cintana[m]** *n.* thinking, thought, reflection; *see* **dharma~, śubha~.**

చింతనిప్పులు **cintanippulu** *n.pl.* fierce heat (*lit.* extreme heat from charcoal made from tamarind wood); **~ciimalni cuusinaTTu** in the way that a fierce fire looks at ants, i.e., contemptuously and ferociously; **cintanippulaaNTi koopam** fierce anger, fury.

చింతనీయ **cintaniiya** *adj.* fit to be meditated on or pondered over.

చింతపండు **cintapaNDu** *n.* ripe tamarind fruit.

చింతపిక్క **cintapikka** *n.* tamarind seed.

చింతపిక్కలాట **cintapikkalaaTa** *n.* game with tamarind seeds played by girls.

చింతాక్రాంతుడు **cintaakraantuDu** *n.* griefstricken person.

చింతామణి **cintaamaNi** *n.* 1 wishing stone. 2 (in titles of books) key, guide; **waydya~** guide to medicine.

చింతించు, చింతిల్లు **cintincu, cintillu** *v.i.* 1 to grieve, be worried. 2 to think, muse, reflect.

చింత్యం **cintyam** *n.* s.g regrettable.

చిందరవందరగా **cindarawandaragaa** *adv.* pellmell, in confusion, confusedly, topsy turvy, helter skelter, at random.

చిందరవందరచేయు **cindarawandara ceeyu** *v.t.* to plunge into confusion or disorder.

చిందించు **cindincu** *v.t.* 1 to spread, scatter, sprinkle. 2 **[ciru]nawwulu~** to radiate smiles. 3 **raktam~** to shed or spill blood.

చిందు **cindu** I. *n.* dance. II. *v.i.* to be scattered, be spilt, be spread.

చిందులుతొక్కు **cindulutokku** *v.i.* 1 to dance. 2 to dance with excitement or emotion. 3 to dance with rage.

చిందులాడు **cindulaaDu** *v.i.* 1 to dance about, jump about. 2 **ciikaTLoo~** to move about uncertainly in the dark.

చింపి **cimpi** *adj.* 1 torn, tattered, ragged. 2 **~tala** dishevelled or tousled hair.

చింపిరి **cimpiri** *adj.* 1 dishevelled, tousled (hair). 2 tattered, ragged (clothes).

చింపు **cimpu** *same as* **cincu.**

చికాకు, చీకాకు **cikaaku, ciikaaku** *n.* annoyance, irritation, vexation, displeasure.

చికాకుపడు, చీకాకుపడు **cikaakupaDu, ciikaakupaDu** *v.i.* to be annoyed, be irritated, be bothered.

చికాకుపెట్టు, చీకాకుపెట్టు **cikaakupeTTu, ciikaakupeTTu** *v.t.* to irritate, annoy, bother.

చికిత్స **cikitsa** *n.* 1 medical treatment, therapy. 2 remedy.

చికిత్సాశాస్త్రం **cikitsaśaastram** *n.* therapeutics.

చికిలి **cikili** I. *n.* polishing, burnishing. II. *adj.* 1 polished, bright, shining, gleaming. 2 (of eyes) leering.

చికిలించు **cikilincu** *v.i.* (*also* **kaLLu~**) 1 to wink. 2 to leer.

చికిలింతగడ్డి **cikilintagaDDi** *same as* **cigirintagaDDi.**

చికిలీ చేయు **cikiliiceeyu** *v.t.* to polish, cause to shine or gleam.

చికిలీపట్టు **cikiliipaTTu** *v.i.* to be polished, shine, gleam.

చిక్క, చిక్కటి, చిక్కని **cikka, cikkaTi, cikkani** *adj.* 1 (of texture) thick, dense, close. 2 (of liquid) thick, heavy, viscous; **cikkaTi paalu** undiluted milk. 3 strong, intense; **cikkaTi eNDa** strong sunlight; **cikka[Ti] ciikaTi** thick or intense darkness; **cikkaTi kaaphii** strong coffee; **cikkaTi niili rangu** dark blue colour.

చిక్కం **cikkam** *n.* 1 purse. 2 bag of network. 3 muzzle of wickerwork. 4 mould for cement blocks.

చిక్కతనం **cikkatanam** *n.* thickness, denseness, compactness.

చిక్కపట్టుకొను **cikkapaTTukonu** *v.t.* 1 to take hold of, recover; **uDigina śaktulni cikkapaTTukonnaaDu** he recovered his faded strength; **dhayryam cikkapaTTukonnaaDu** he plucked up courage. 2 to use sparingly; **Dabbu cikkapaTTukonnaaDu** he eked out his money.

చిక్కపడు **cikkapaDu** *v.i.* to become thick (e.g., liquids during cooking).

చిక్కించుకొను **cikkincukonu** *v.t.* to catch, secure.

చిక్కిరిబిక్కిరి **cikkiribikkiri** *adj.* disordered, jumbled; **~juTTu** dishevelled or unkempt hair; **~raata** scribbling, scrawling.

చిక్కు **cikku**[1] I. *n.* 1 tangle, entanglement; **tala~ tiisukonu** to comb out the knots from tangled hair. 2 difficulty, trouble; **~laloo paDu** to run into difficulties; **~laloo peTTu** to involve (s.o.) in difficulties. 3 confusion, perplexity, puzzle, problem; **ii ~wippaali** you must solve this problem. II. *adj.* puzzling, perplexing, difficult, intricate; **~praśna** difficult question; **~muDi** knot that is hard to untie. III. *v.i.* 1 to be caught, be [en]tangled. 2 to remain, be left [over]. 3 to be found, be obtained; **niiku nammakam cikkadu** you will not believe. 4 to be found out, be detected. 5 *dial.* to be met or encountered; **aayana naaku cikkEEDu** I met him. IV. *v.t. dial.* 1 to pinch. 2 **peelu ~** to crush lice with the fingernail.

చిక్కు **cikku**[2] *v.i.* to become thin, lean or emaciated.

చిక్కుకొను **cikkukonu** *v.i.* to be involved, be caught up.

చిక్కుడు **cikkuDu** *n.* kind of bean, *dolichos lablab.*

చిక్కుపడు **cikkupaDu** *v.i.* 1 to be caught, be ensnared. 2 to be [en]tangled; **daaram cikkupaDindi** the thread became tangled.

చిగిరింతగడ్డి, చికిలింతగడ్డి **cigirintagaDDi, cikilintagaDDi** *n.* burgrass, spear grass.

చిగురాకు **ciguraaku** *n.* young tender leaf.

చిగురించు, చిగుర్చు **cigurincu, cigurcu** *v.t.* to sprout, bud.

చిగురు **ciguru** *n.* 1 sprout, shoot. 2 young tender leaf. 3 gum (of teeth). 4 quick (of nail).

చిగురుపెట్టు, చిగురువేయు **cigurupeTTu, ciguruweeyu** *v.i.* to sprout.

చిగురుబోడి **cigurubooDi** *n. class.* maiden.

చిగురొత్తు **cigurottu** *v.i.* to sprout, bud.

చిచ్చి **cicci** *n. child language* patting.

చిచ్చికొట్టు **ciccikoTTu** *v.t.* to pat (a child) to sleep.

చిచ్చు **ciccu** *n.* fire, flame, fierce heat; **enabhay eeLLa talli kaDupuloo ~peTTi canipooyEEDu** when he died he caused deep sorrow to his eighty year old mother.

చిచ్చుబుడ్డి **ciccubuDDi** *n.* 1 flowerpot (a kind of fire work). 2 high spirited person.

చిటచిటలాడు **ciTaciTalaaDu** *v.i.* 1 to crackle, sputter (like salt in a frying pan). 2 to itch, smart, tingle; **waaDi wiipu~ tunnadi** his back is itching. 3 to be in an angry mood.

చిటపటలాడు **ciTapaTalaaDu** *v.i.* 1 to crackle, sputter (like salt in a frying pan). 2 to tingle. 3 to be quick tempered or fiery tempered.

చిటారు **ciTaaru** *adj.* highest, topmost; **~komma** topmost branch.

చిటిక, చిటికె **ciTika, ciTike** *n.* 1 snap of fingers. 2 instant, moment of time; **~loo waccEEDu** he came in an instant.

చిటికెడు **ciTikeDu** *adj.* pinch of, small quantity of, **~uppu** a pinch of salt.

చిటికెన[వేలు] **ciTikena[weelu]** *n.* 1 little finger. 2 little toe.

చిటికెలు వేయు **ciTikelu weeyu** *v.i.* to snap o.'s fingers; **ciTikelu weestuu weLLEEDu** he went away in a very cheerful mood.

చిటుక్కున **ciTukkuna** *adv.* suddenly.

చిటుక్కుమను **ciTukkumanu** *v.i.* to make a slight sound; *mod. only in the phrase* **ciima ciTukkumaNTee** *or* **ciima ciTukkumannaa** (*lit.* if an ant makes a slight sound) **ciima ciTukkumaNTee melukuwa wastundi** he will wake at the slightest sound.

చిట్కా **ciTkaa** *n.* 1 device, contrivance, clue (for solving a problem); **grhinulaku~lu** helpful suggestions for housewives. 2 remedy, nostrum; *see* **goosaayi.**

చిట్టచివర **ciTTaciwara** *n.* the very end.

చిట్టచీకటి **ciTTaciikaTi** *n.* pitch darkness.

చిట్టడవి **ciTTaDawi** *n.* 1 sparse forest, scrub jungle. 2 dense forest.

చిట్టా **ciTTaa** *n.* day book, daily account of money transactions.

చిట్టాముదం **ciTTaamudam** *n.* castor oil plant.

చిట్టి **ciTTi** I. *n.* measure of volume, one sixteenth of a seer. II. *adj.* 1 little, small, tiny, young; ~**talli** darling little girl: ~**poTTi maaTalu/ceeSTalu** dear little words/acts (of young children). 2 ~**praśna** (i) short question; (ii) petty or trivial question.

చిట్టిగూబ **ciTTiguuba** *n.* scops owl.

చిట్టిముత్యాలు **ciTTimutyaalu** *n.pl.* name of a fine variety of rice having a short grain.

చిట్టీ **ciTTii** *same as* **ciiTLu.**

చిట్టు **ciTTu** *n.* mixed husk and bran fed to cattle.

చిట్టుడుకు **ciTTuDuku** *adj.* parboiled; ~**niiLLu** water in which rice has been parboiled.

చిట్టె **ciTTe** *n.* door stopper.

చిట్టెం **ciTTem** *n.* scum or dross of melted metal, slag.

చిట్టెంకట్టు **ciTTemkaTTu** *v.i.* to become caked or fused together.

చిట్టెలుక **ciTTeluka** *n.* mouse.

చిట్రంకట్టు **ciTramkaTTu** *v.i.* to solidify, become hard.

చిట్లించు **ciTLincu** *v.i. fig.* to be lined or furrowed; **mukham**~ to frown; **kaLLu**~ to put on a wry face.

చిట్లింపు **ciTLimpu** *n.* frown.

చిట్లు **ciTLu** *v.i.* (of glass, etc.) to crack, split or fracture without breaking into pieces; **nii wiipu** ~**tundi** *lit.* your back is going to crack, i.e., you going to get a beating.

చిట్లుకట్టె **ciTLukaTTe** *n.* very angry person.

చిడత, చిరత **ciData, cirata** *n.* 1 castanet. 2 pincers; ~**weeyu** to torture with pincers. 3 block of wood, wedge.

చిడి **ciDi** *n. dial.* 1 ladder. 2 staircase, steps.

చిడిముడిపాటు **ciDimuDipaaTu** *n.* irritation, vexation, anger.

చిడుం **ciDum** *n.* itch[ing] due to skin disease.

చిత, చితి **cita, citi** *n.* funeral pyre.

చితక **citaka** *same as* **cituku**[3].

చితకతొక్కు **citakatokku** *v.t.* to beat down, trample.

చితకబాదు **citakabaadu** *v.t.* 1 to give (s.o.) a sound beating. 2 to pound (vegetables).

చితకలు **citakalu** *n.pl. dial.* flesh.

చితక్కొట్టు, చిదగ్గొట్టు **citakkoTTu, cidaggoTTu** *v.t.* 1 to crush, smash to pieces. 2 to beat soundly; **wiipu cidaggoDataanu** I will give you a beating.

చితచితలాడు **citacitalaaDu** *v.i.* to be damp or moist.

చితి **citi** *same as* **cita.**

చితుకు, చిదుకు **cituku**[1], **ciduku**[1] *n., gen. pl.* ~**lu** dry sticks or twigs, firewood.

చితుకు, చిదుకు **cituku**[2], **ciduku**[2] *v.i.* 1 to burst; **kurupu citikindi** the boil burst. 2 to be crushed, smashed or broken to pieces. 3 to lose o.'s wealth, be ruined; **wyaapaaramloo cidikipooyEEDu** he was ruined in his business.

చితుకు, చితక **cituku**[3], **citaka** *adj.* very small, tiny, very young; **aayanadi pedda samsaaram, pillalantaa ciimaacitukuu** (*or* **cinnaacitakaa**) his is a large family, his children are all very young; **cinnawaaDiwEE citakawaaDiwEE? nalabhay eeLLu nettimiidiki waccinay!** are you a just little child? no, you are fully forty years old!

చిత్త **citta** *n. astrol.* name of the 14th asterism; ~**kaarte** season occurring at the onset of the rains about July.

చిత్తం **cittam** I. *n.* 1 mind, heart. 2 inclination, pleasure. II. *minor sentence* as you wish! *or* yes, sir!

చిత్తగించు **cittagincu** *v.t.* 1 to pay attention, keep in mind, consider. 2 to observe, note; *see* **palaayanam**~, **paraaru**~.

చిత్తడి **cittaDi** I. *n.* wetness, dampness, moisture. II. *adj.* wet, soaked, swampy; ~**neela** morass; ~**kaalam** rainy season.

చిత్తమోహం **cittamooham** *n.* 1 infatuation. 2 illusion.

చిత్తరువు **cittaruwu** *n.* picture, painting, portrait; ~**laa nilabaDipooyEEDu** he stood stock still (with amazement).

చిత్తవికారం **cittawikaaram** *n.* new mood, change of mood (usually for the worse); **eppuDaynaa cittawikaaraaniki loonaytee taagutaaDu** he drinks whenever the mood comes over him.

చిత్తవిభ్రమం **cittawibhramam** *n.* insanity.

చిత్తవృత్తి **cittawṛtti** *n.* frame of mind, mentality, mental outlook, mental attitude, mood; ~**gaNTagaNTakii maaritee eTLaa?** how can I cope if your mood changes from hour to hour?

చిత్తశాంతి **cittaśaanti** *n.* peace of mind.

చిత్తశుద్ధి **cittaśuddhi** *n.* 1 devotion. 2 sincerity. 3 integrity.

చిత్తస్థిరత **cittasthirata** *n.* sanity, soundness of mind.

చిత్తు **cittu** I. *n.* draft of a document. II. *adj.* rough; ~**kaayitaalu** rough sheets of paper.

చిత్తుగా **cittugaa** *adv.* excessively, severely; ~**ooDipoowu** to be severely defeated; ~**taagu** to drink to excess.

చిత్తుచేయు **cittuceeyu** *v.t.* to beat, defeat, overcome.

చిత్తుపత్తు **cittupattu** *n. dial.* heads and tails; ~**weesi paNDu ewarikoo teelcukondam** let us decide by tossing a coin who will get the fruit; *cf.* **bomma, borusu.**

చిత్తైపోవు **cittaypoowu** *v.i.* to be beaten, defeated or overcome.

చిత్ర **citra** *n. astrol.* name of the 14th asterism.

చిత్రం **citram** I. *n.* 1 picture, painting, photograph. 2 curiosity, wonder, marvel, s.g strange. 3 motion picture, movie. II. *adj.* odd, strange.

చిత్రంగా **citrangaa** *adv.* strangely.

చిత్రం వేయు **citram weeyu** *v.i.* 1 to draw or paint a picture. 2 *with dative* to feel strange; **aayana ceppindantaa winnatarwaata naaku citram weesindi** when I heard all that he said, I felt strange.

చిత్రకంబళి **citrakambaLi** *n.* patterned rug or carpet.

చిత్రకథ **citrakatha** *n.* 1 interesting story or episode. 2 plot or story of a motion picture.

చిత్రకళ **citrakaLa** *n.* the art of painting.

చిత్రకవిత్వం **citrakawitwam** *n.* ingenious poetry.

చిత్రకారుడు **citrakaaruDu** *n.* artist, painter.

చిత్రణ **citraNa** *n.* sketching, portraying, delineation, portraiture.

చిత్రపటం **citrapaTam** *n.* 1 picture. 2 figure, diagram. 3 map.

చిత్రభాను **citrabhaanu** *n.* sixteenth year of the Hindu cycle of sixty years.

చిత్రలిపి **citralipi** *n.* pictography.

చిత్రలేఖనం **citraleekhanam** *n.* painting, drawing, sketch[ing].

చిత్రవధ **citrawadha** *n.* death by torture.

చిత్రవధ చేయు **citrawadha ceeyu** *v.t.* to torture to death.

చిత్రవస్తు[ప్రదర్శన]శాల **citrawastu[pradarśana] śaala** *n.* museum.

చిత్రవస్త్రం **citrawastram** *n.* patterned cloth.

చిత్రవిచిత్రం **citrawicitram** *adj.* 1 wonderful, strange. 2 varied, variegated.

చిత్రశాల, చిత్రాలయం **citraśaala, citraalayam** *n.* art gallery.

చిత్రహింస **citrahimsa** *n.* torture.

చిత్రాన్నం **citraannam** *n.* rice cooked and mixed with turmeric, tamarind and other spices (= **pulihoora**).

చిత్రాసనం **citraasanam** *n. class.* small carpet used as a seat during prayer.

చిత్రించు **citrincu** *v.t.* 1 to draw, paint. 2 to portray, depict, describe.

చిత్రిక **citrika** *n.* carpenter's plane.

చిత్రికపట్టు **citrikapaTTu** *v.t.* to plane, smooth; **citrika paDataanu jaagrata**! if you do not take care, I will punish you!

చిత్రీకరణ **citriikaraNa** *n.* 1 portraying, delineation. 2 shooting of a motion picture.

చిత్రీకరించు **citriikarincu** *v.t.* to portray, depict.

చిదంబరం **cidambaram** *n.* Chidambaram, name of a town and pilgrimage centre in Tamilnadu.

చిదంబర రహస్యం **cidambara rahasyam** *n.* unfathomable secret.

చిదగ్గొట్టు **cidaggoTTu** *same as* **citakkoTTu.**

చిదుకు **ciduku**[1,2] *same as* **cituku**[1,2].

చిదుపు **cidupu** *v.t.* 1 to break up (a lump); **annampeLLa ~, neyyi weestaanu** break up your lump of rice, I will pour ghee on it. 2. to break off a piece from a lump.

చిదుము **cidumu** *v.t.* to squeeze, crush, pinch, nip off; **mukku cidimi diipam peTTaali** first trim the end of the wick and then light the lamp (proverbial saying).

చిద్విలాసం **cidwilaasam** *n.* bliss[fulness], contentment.

చిద్విలాసంగా **cidwilaasangaa** *adv.* blithely, blissfully.

చిన, చిని **cina, cini** *alt. forms of* **cinna, cinni.**

చినబాబు **cinabaabu** *n.* younger son, youngest son.

చినుకు **cinuku** *n.* 1 rain drop. 2 sprinkling of rain. 3 *gen. pl.* **~lu** drizzling.

చినుకులుపడు **cinukulu paDu** *v.i.* to drizzle.

చినుగు **cinugu** I. *n.* tear, rent; **ii cokkaa antaa ~lee** this shirt is all torn. II. *v.i.* to be torn.

చిన్న **cinna** *adj.* 1 little, small; **~ tarahaa pariśrama** small scale industry. 2 short. 3 young. 4 slight, trifling, insignificant. 5 mean; **mukham ~di ceesukonu** to feel slighted or belittled.

చిన్నం **cinnam** *n.* 1 one thirtieth of a tola; *see* **ettu** *sense I.* 2 *dial.* one hundred rupees.

చిన్నకారు **cinnakaaru** I. *n.pl.* youth, young people. II. *adj.* young, youthful.

చిన్నగా **cinnagaa** *adv.* slightly, gently, lightly, softly.

చిన్నచూపు **cinnacuupu** *n.* belittlement.

చిన్నచూపు చూచు **cinnacuupu cuucu** *v.t.* to look down on, despise, belittle, regard with contempt.

చిన్నతనం **cinnatanam** *n.* 1 smallness. 2 youth, childhood. 3 disgrace, dishonour. 4 shame, embarassment.

చిన్ననాటి **cinnanaaTi** *adj.* relating to o.'s younger days.

చిన్నన్న **cinnanna** *n.* younger of two elder brothers.

చిన్నపుచ్చు **cinnapuccu** *v.t.* to make s.o. feel or appear small, offend, humiliate.

చిన్నపుచ్చుకొను **cinnapuccukonu** *v.i.* 1 to feel slighted or humiliated or offended. 2 to feel crestfallen.

చిన్నపోవు **cinnapoowu** *v.i.* to be downcast or dispirited.

చిన్నబుద్ధి **cinnabuddhi** *n.* mean mentality, narrow-mindedness.

చిన్నాయన **cinnaayana** *n.* father's younger brother.

చిన్నారి **cinnaari** I. *n.* little girl, daughter. II. *adj.* young, infant; *cf.* **ponnaari.**

చిన్ని **cinni** *adj.* little, tiny.

చిన్నె **cinne** *n.* sign, token, mark; *see* **wanne.**

చిన్నెలాడి **cinnelaaDi** *n.* coquette.

చిన్మయ **cinmaya** *adj.* spiritual, mental, intellectual.

చిన్మయత్వం **cinmayatwam** *n.* pure thought, spiritual contemplation.

చిప్ప **cippa** *n.* 1 shell made of any non-metal material, saucer, cup, bowl. 2 begging bowl. 3 **raa~** stone bowl. 4 **kobbari~** (i) coconut shell; (ii) half coconut with kernel. 5 **mutyapu~** (i) mother of pearl; (ii) pearl oyster. 6 **mookaali~** knee cap.

చిప్పకత్తి **cippakatti** *n.* woodcutter's knife.

చిప్పర[గడ్డి] **cippara[gaDDi]** *n.* kind of grass useful for grazing.

చిప్పిలు **cippilu** *v.i.* to gush forth, surge, overflow.

చిబుకం **cibukam** *same as* **cubukam.**

చిబుకు **cibuku** *v.t.* 1 to smack the lips. 2 to suck.

చిమచిమ, తిమతిమ **cimacima, timatima** *n.* smarting, burning or itching sensation.

చిమచిమలాడు **cimacimalaaDu** *v.i.* to smart with pain, itch; **oLLu ~ tunnadaa?** *lit.* is your body itching (for blows)? i.e., do you want a beating?

చిమట, చిమ్మట, చిమ్మెట **cimaTa, cimmaTa, cimmeTa** *n.* clothes moth.

చిమటా, చింటా **cimaTaa**[1], **cimTaa** *n. dial.* girl of low status, wench.

చిమటా **cimaTaa**[2] *n.* tongs, pincers, tweezers.

చిముడు **cimuDu** *v.i.* (of rice, etc.) to be overboiled or overcooked.

చిముడ్చు **cimuDcu** *v.t.* to overboil, overcook.

చిమ్నీ **cimnii** *n.* 1 chimney. 2 **~ diipam** lantern, lamp; **~ guuDu** niche for a lamp in a wall.

చిమ్మచీకటి **cimmaciikaTi** *n.* pitch darkness.

చిమ్మట, చిమ్మెట **cimmaTa, cimmeTa** *same as* **cimaTa.**

చిమ్మనగ్రోవి **cimmanagroowi** *n.* syringe, sprayer.

చిమ్మిలి, చిమ్మిరి **cimmili, cimmiri** *n.* sweet dish made with dry coconut and jaggery, distributed at the time of a girl's attaining puberty.

చిమ్ము, జిమ్ము **cimmu, jimmu** I. *n.* 1 thrusting, butting. 2 squirting, gushing forth. II. *v.i.* 1 to overflow. 2 to spurt, squirt, ooze, gush forth. III. *v.t.* 1 to butt (with horns). 2 to fling, toss. 3 to scatter, spread (dust). 4 to spout, give off (flames, sparks). 5 to blow, waft (smoke). 6 to spray, squirt. 7 to sweep (floor).

చిమ్ములాట **cimmulaaTa** *n.* squirting coloured water as part of a game at the time of Holi.

చియ్య **ciyya** *n.* 1 flesh, muscle. 2 *dial.* excrement.

చిర[ం] **cira[m]** *adj.* long (of time).

చిరంజీవి **ciranjiiwi** *n. and adj.* long-lived, a term of affection implying a blessing of long life on the person addressed or spoken of; **mii ciranjiiwulu kulaasaagaa unnaaraa?** are your children well? **~ subbaaraawuku** dear Subba Rao (a way of starting a letter).

చిరంతన **cirantana** *adj. class.* old, ancient, antiquated.

చిరకాలిక, చిరకాలీన **cirakaalika, cirakaaliina** *adj.* old, longstanding (friendship).

చిరచిర **ciracira** *n.* peevishness.

చిరచిరలాడు **ciraciralaaDu** *v.i.* to be peevish, surly, sullen, cross or ill-humoured.

చిరత **cirata** *same as* **ciData.**

చిరతలు **ciratalu** *n. pl.* dazzling; **aaayana kaLLu ~ kammEEyi** his eyes were dazzled.

చిరదీర్ఘ **ciradiirgha** *adj.* lengthy (of time).

చిరమర **ciramara** *n.* difference of opinion, misunderstanding.

చిరమిత్రుడు **ciramitruDu** *n.* old friend.

చిరస్థాయిగా **cirasthaayigaa** *adv.* 1 for a long time. 2 for ever.

చిరస్మరణీయ **cirasmaraNiiya** *adj.* memorable, unforgettable.

చిరాకు **ciraaku** *n.* 1 annoyance, crossness, irritation. 2 dislike, aversion.

చిరాకుపడు **ciraakupaDu** *v.i.* to be irritated, annoyed or cross; **naa miida** (*or* **neenaNTee**) **ciraakupaDDaaDu** he was annoyed with me.

చిరాయువు **ciraayuwu** *adj.* long-lived.

చిరిచాప **ciricaapa** *n.* small mat of fine texture.

చిరు, చిరి **ciru, ciri** *adj., occurring only with certain nouns* small, trifling, little, slight.

చిరుకప్ప **cirukappa** *n.* tadpole.

చిరుకోపం **cirukoopam** *n.* slight irritation or annoyance.

చిరుగు **cirugu** I. *n.* tear, rent. II. *v.i.* to tear, be torn.

చిరుగుపట్టు **cirugupaTTu** *v.i.* to be torn.

చిరుత, చిరుతపులి **ciruta**[1], **cirutapuli** *n.* panther, leopard.

చిరుత **ciruta**[2] *adj. class.* young; *mod. only in the phrase* **~ praayam** tender age, youth.

చిరుతిండి **cirutiNDi** *n.* (*also pl.* **cirutiLLu**) light refreshment, snacks.

చిరునవ్వు **cirunawwu** *n.* smile.

చిరునామా **cirunaamaa** *n.* address (on a letter).

చిరునాలిక, చిరునాలుక **cirunaalika, cirunaaluka** *n.* uvula.

చిరుమంటలు **cirumaNTalu** *n.pl.* burning sensation in the eyes due to feverishness.

చిర్ర **cirra** *n.* anger; **waaDiki cirrettindi** *or* **waaDiki cirrettuku waccindi)** he felt irritated, annoyed or impatient.

చిర్రి **cirri** *n.* kind of leafy vegetable, *amaranthus sp.*

చిర్రు **cirru** *n.* anger.

చిర్రుబుర్రుమను, చిర్రుబుర్రులాడు **cirruburrumanu, cirruburrulaaDu** *v.i.* 1 to have clogged up nostrils. 2 to speak angrily, behave angrily, be irritable, peevish or petulant.

చిర్రుమను **cirrumanu** *v.i.* to be angry.

చిలక, చిలుక **cilaka, ciluka** *n.* 1 parrot. 2 *slang* beautiful girl. 3 *slang* prostitute. 4 pan, betel leaf and nut. 5 **pancadaara ~** sugar doll in the shape of a parrot, distributed at the Holi festival and when a child begins to talk; **aDugulaku ariselu, palukulaku ~ lu** rice cakes for a child's first steps, sugar dolls for a child's first words.

చిలకలకొలికి **cilakalakoliki** *n.* graceful woman, woman with beautiful eyes.

చిలకపలుకులు **cilakapalukulu** *n.pl.* words repeated in parrotlike fashion.

చిలకపచ్చ, చిలకాకుపచ్చ **cilakapacca, cilakaakupacca** *n.* olive green colour, parrot green colour.

చిలకరించు **cilakarincu** *v.t.* to sprinkle (water), radiate (smiles).

చిలకేటుగా **cilakeeTugaa** *adv.* now and then, once in a way, sporadically.

చిలక్కొయ్య **cilakkoyya** *n.* wooden or iron peg fixed in a wall.

చిలగడదుంప **cilagaDa dumpa** *n.* sweet potato (= **ratnapuri gaDDa**).

చిలచిల **cilacila** *onom. n. sug.* hissing sound made when water is poured on a hot surface and becomes steam.

చిలవలుపలవలు **cilawalu palawalu** *n.pl.* 1 luxuriant growth, rapid increase or expansion; **wyaapaaram ~gaa wistaristunnadi** the business is expanding by leaps and bounds. 2 exaggeration; **asalu katha cinnadee kaanii waaDu~ceesi ceppEEDu** the original story was a small matter but he exaggerated it.

చిలికించు **cilikincu** *v.t.* 1 to sprinkle. 2 to churn.

చిలిపి **cilipi** *adj.* 1 naughty, cheeky, saucy, mischievous. 2 joyful, witty, fun-loving; **~kayyam** fake quarrel.

చిలిపికొయ్య **cilipikoyya** *n. dial.* mischievous or cheeky person.

చిలిపితనం **cilipitanam** *n.* naughtiness, cheekiness.

చిలుం **cilum**[1] *n.* 1 verdigris, metal tarnish. 2 metallic taste. 3 *colloq.* money.

చిలుం **cilum**[2] *n.* huqqa; **~piilcu, ~taagu** to smoke a huqqa.

చిలుం ఎక్కు **cilum ekku** *v.i.* 1 to become tarnished, become coated with verdigris. 2 to acquire a metallic taste.

చిలుకు **ciluku**[1] *v.t.* 1 to sprinkle. 2 to churn.

చిలుకు **ciluku**[2] *n. class.* remainder, balance, residue; *mod. only in* **pay~** and a little more, and odd, e.g., **muuDu kiloola pay~** three kilos and odd; **ii samwatsaram pay~loonuu** in this year and a little longer.

చిలుకుడు **cilukuDu** *n.* 1 sprinkling. 2 churning.

చిలువ **ciluwa** *n.* snake; **koNDa~** python.

చిల్ల **cilla** *n.* 1 bit, fragment. 2 spar of wood, wooden bar. 3 wooden tooth of a rake or harrow.

చిల్లంగి **cillangi** I. *n.* casting of spells, sorcery. II. *adj.* capable of bewitching or casting a spell; **~kaLLu** eyes that can cast a spell; **~widya, ~waydyam** sorcery, necromancy.

చిల్లకంప **cillakampa** *n.* clearing nut tree, *strychnos potatorum.*

చిల్లకుండ **cillakuNDa** *n.* pot that is ceremonially broken at a funeral; *see* **kuNDa.**

చిల్లగింజ **cillaginja** *n.* clearing nut.

చిల్లపెంకు **cillapenku** *n.* potsherd, piece of broken pottery.

చిల్లర **cillara** I. *n.* loose money, [petty] change; **nuuru ruupaayala [pay]~** a hundred rupees and odd; **~mahaalakSmi aNTaaru** they (shopkeepers, creditors) say that petty change is wealth, i.e., wealth is earned by collecting sundry amounts; *cf. the English proverb* little drops makes an ocean. II. *adj.* 1 sundry, stray, random, miscellaneous; **~kharculu** miscellaneous expenses; **~raayi** odd stone or brick used to fill up a gap in a wall. 2 petty, trifling, trivial, insignificant; **~manuSulu** insignificant persons, riffraff, nonentities. 3 retail; **~koTTu** retail shop; **~wartakuDu** retail shopkeeper, petty merchant.

చిల్లరమల్లర **cillaramallara** *adj.* miscellaneous, sundry; **~udyoogaalu** odd jobs.

చిల్లి **cilli** *n.* small hole, perforation, puncture, crack, fissure, cleft.

చిల్లిగవ్వ **cilligawwa** *n.* the smallest coin, a pie (now obsolete): **waaDu~ku maaraDu** he is not worth a pie.

చిల్లిపడు, చిల్లులుపడు **cillipaDu, cillulupaDu** *v.i.* to develop holes, be cracked, punctured or perforated; **cewulu cillulu paDutunnaayi** *lit.* my ears are being punctured (*expression meaning* "I am tired of hearing the same thing over and over again").

చివర **ciwara** I. *n.* end, tip, extremity, point. II. *adj.* last, final. III. *postpositional use* at the end of: **spaSTatakoosam konni bhaagaala~ reekhaacitraalu ponduparacabaDDaayi** for the sake of clarity diagrams have been provided at the end of some parts (of a book).

చివరంటా **ciwaraNTaa** *adv.* to the very end.

చివరకు **ciwaraku** *adv.* 1 in the end, at last, finally. 2 *in neg. constr.* even; **aa roogi ewaroo maaku teliyadu, maa bandhuwuu, sneehituDuu kaadu, sarikadaa~paricituDu kuuDaa kaadu** we do not know who that sick man is, he is not a relation or a friend of ours, he is not even an acquaintance; *cf.* **kaniisam.**

చివరి **ciwari** *adj.* last, final.

చివాలున **ciwaaluna** *adv.* suddenly, abruptly, all of a sudden.

చివుకు **ciwuku** *v.i.* to rot, decay, be spoilt; **ciwiki pooyina baTTa** cloth spoilt by getting wet.

చివుక్కుమను **ciwukkumanu** *v.i.* to feel pain, feel sad, regret; **aame antaraatma ciwukkumannadi** her conscience pricked her.

చివ్వున, జివ్వున **ciwwuna, jiwwuna** *adv.* all of a sudden.

చిహ్నం **cihnam** *n.* mark, sign, token; **waaDi asamarthataku ~ koopam** anger is a sign of his incompetence.

చీ - cii

చీ!, ఛీ! **cii!, chii!** *interj. of disgust or disapproval.*

చీకటి **ciikaTi** I. *n.* darkness, gloom; **~ too nidra leecEEDu** he woke up before daylight. II. *adj.* dark, obscure, hidden; **~ tappu** adultery; **~ bajaaru** black market.

చీకాకు, చీకాకుపడు, చీకాకుపెట్టు **ciikaaku, ciikaakupaDu, ciikaakupeTTu** *same as* **cikaaku, cikaakupaDu, cikaakupeTTu.**

చీకిరి **ciikiri** *adj.* blinking.

చీకిరించు **ciikirincu** *v.i.* to blink.

చీకు **ciiku**[1] *v.t.* to suck (e.g., a mango) with the lips.

చీకు **ciiku**[2] *v.i.* to rot, decay, be spoilt, esp. by damp.

చీకుడు **ciikuDu** *n.* spoiling; **koTTu ~ baTTa** shopsoiled cloth; **peTTe ~ baTTa** cloth spoilt by long storage.

చీకూచింతా **ciikuucintaa** *n.* cares and worries.

చీకొట్టు, ఛీకొట్టు **c[h]iikoTTu** I. *v.i.* to express disgust. II. *v.t.* to condemn, rebuke, scold.

చీటికిమాటికి **ciiTikimaaTiki** *adv.* every now and then, from time to time.

చీటీ, చీటి **ciiTii, ciiTi** *n.* 1 (*also* **~ mukka**) short letter, note, chit. 2 whistling; **~ weeyu, ~ koTTu** to whistle. 3 **~ guDDa** rough unbleached printed cloth piece.

చీట్లపేక **ciiTLapeeka** *n.* pack of cards.

చీట్లు, చిట్టీ **ciiTLu, ciTTii** *n. colloq.* 1 playing cards. 2 chit fund.

చీడ **ciiDa** *n.* pest, blight.

చీడపురుగు **ciiDa purugu** *n.* insect pest.

చీడీ **ciiDii** *n.* 1 cement platform used as a seat. 2 *dial. same as* **ciDi.**

చీత్కరించు, చీత్కారంచేయు, ఛీత్కరించు, ఛీత్కారంచేయు, సీత్కారంచేయు **c[h]iitkarincu, c[h]iitkaaram ceeyu, siitkaaram ceeyu** *v.t.* to express scorn or disgust (at s.g).

చీదర **ciidara** *n.* 1 dislike, abhorrence, loathing, nausea; **aayana manassu eppuDuu ~ gaa uNDeedi** he was always irritable *or* he was always out of sorts. 2 confusion, disturbance.

చీదరగా **ciidaragaa** *adv.* confusedly, in confusion, in disorder, in disarray.

చీదరించు **ciidarincu** *v.t.* to rebuke.

చీదరించుకొను **ciidarincukonu** *v.i.* to show dislike, show displeasure, speak angrily.

చీదరింపు **ciidarimpu** *n.* reproach, rebuke.

చీదు **ciidu** *v.i.* 1 to blow o.'s nose. 2 *slang* to feel resentment. 3 *slang* **waaDi pariikSa ciideesindi** he failed his examination.

చీనం **ciinam** *n. class.* 1 gold. 2 gold thread.

చీని **ciini** *n.* 1 sugar. 2 batavian orange, *limonia trifoliata* (= **battaayi**).

చీనిచీనాంబరం **ciini ciinaambaram** *n. class.* silk interwoven with gold thread (imported from China in olden times).

చీపు **ciipu** *n.* cluster (part of a bunch) of plantains or bananas (= **attam**).

చీపురు **ciipuru** *n.* 1 broom, brush. 2 *cyperus sp., aristida sp.* (plants from which brooms are made).

చీపురుకట్ట **ciipurukaTTa** *n.* broom.

చీపురుపుల్లలు **ciipurupullalu** *n. pl.* twigs used for making a broom.

చీమ **ciima** *n.* ant; **naalugu daraawulu weesukonnaa waaDiki ~ kuTTinaTTu leedu** although he drank several drams, it had no effect on him (*lit.* it was not even like an ant stinging him); *see* **ciTukumanu.**

చీమిడి, చీముడు **ciimiDi, ciimuDu** *n.* mucus of the nose.

చీము **ciimu** *n.* pus; **kurupu ~ paTTindi** the boil formed pus.

చీముపొక్కు **ciimupokku** *n.* 1 pimple. 2 boil with pus.

చీరానారా **ciiraa naaraa** *n.pl.* saris and other such things.

చీరు **ciiru** *v.t.* to tear, rend, scratch, scrape, split.

చీరుకుపోవు **ciirukupoowu** *v.i.* to be torn, rent, scratched or split.

చీరె, చీర **ciire, ciira** *n.* 1 sari. 2 *class.* any cloth.

చీరేసారే **ciireesaaree** *n.* a sari and other such gifts presented to a daughter by her parents every time she returns from their house to her husband's house; *cf.* **saare.**

చీర్చు **ciircu** *v.t.* to split.

చీల **ciila** *n.* 1 nail, pin. 2 linch pin.

చీలమండ **ciilamaNDa** *n.* ankle.

చీలిక, చీరిక **ciilika, ciirika** *n.* 1 split, rupture. 2 slit, slice. 3 *sci.* cleft.

చీలు **ciilu** *v.i.* 1 to split, rupture. 2 to crack, divide. 3 to branch off, split off, separate.

చీల్చు **ciilcu** *v.t.* 1 to split, crack, tear. 2 to divide.

చీవాట్లు **ciiwaaTLu** *n.pl.* scolding, rebuke, reproach, reproof.

చీవాట్లు తిను, చీవాట్లు పడు **ciiwaaTLu tinu, ciiwaaTLu paDu** *v.i.* to be scolded, be rebuked, be reproached, be reproved.

చీవాట్లు పెట్టు, చీవాట్లు వేయు **ciiwaaTLu peTTu, ciiwaaTLu weeyu** *v.t.* to scold, rebuke, reprove, grumble at; **mukka ~** to scold with foul language.

చు - cu

చుంగులు **cungulu** *n. pl.* folds made in the front of a sari or dhoti when tying it round the waist (= **kucceLLu**).

చుంచు, చుంచెలుక **cuncu**[1], **cunceluka** *n.* muskrat.

చుంచు **cuncu**[2] *n.* projecting eaves of a house.

చుంచు మొహం పెట్టుకొను **cuncumoham peTTukonu** *v.i.* to pout (*lit.* to make a face like a muskrat).

చుంచురాయి **cuncuraayi** *n.* kind of slate used for roofs.

చుండు, చుండ్రు **cuNDu, cuNDru** *n.* dandruff.

చుండెలుక **cuNDeluka** *n.* mouse.

చుంబనం **cumbanam** *n. class.* kiss[ing].

చుంబించు **cumbincu** *v.t.* to kiss.

చుంయ్ **cumyi** *onom. n. sug.* hissing sound made by water turning to steam when poured on a hot surface.

చుక్క **cukka** *n.* **1** point, dot, spot. **2** drop. **3** star: **eemiTi ~ uuDipaDDaTTu waccEEwu?** why have you come like a star falling? i.e., why have you come unexpectedly out of the blue? **4** the planet Venus, whose appearance in front of a traveller starting on a journey is considered unlucky: **~ tirigindi** *lit.* the star has turned, i.e., Venus is no longer in front and the auspicious time has begun: *cf.* **cukkeduru. 5** beautiful woman. **6** alcohol, liquor.

చుక్కకూర, చుక్కాకు **cukkakuura, cukkaaku** *n.* kind of green leafy vegetable, *rumex vesicarius.*

చుక్కబొట్టు **cukkaboTTu** *n.* beauty spot, mark on the forehead made with **caadu.**

చుక్కలరేడు **cukkalareeDu** *n.* the moon (*lit.* king of the stars).

చుక్క వేసుకొను **cukka weesukonu** *v.i.* **1** to drink liquor. **2** to get drunk.

చుక్కాని, చుక్కాను **cukkaani, cukkaanu** *n.* rudder, steering oar, helm.

చుక్కెదురు **cukkeduru** *adv.* dead against, diametrically opposed: **aayanakii naakuu ii wiSayamloo ~** he and I are diametrically opposed to each other in this matter; *cf.* **cukka.**

చుచుకం, చూచుకం **cucukam, cuucukam** *n.* nipple.

చుచ్చుకొట్టు **cuccukoTTu** *v.i.* to make an alveolar click with the tongue in token of pity or sympathy.

చుట్ట **cuTTa** *n.* **1** roll, coil, ring, anything rolled up; **pakka ~** bedding roll. **2** cigar.

చుట్టం **cuTTam** *n.* relation, relative.

చుట్టం చూపు, చుట్టపు చూపు **cuTTam cuupu, cuTTapu cuupu** *n.* visit paid casually and once in a way (as is done by relatives).

చుట్టకుదురు **cuTTakuduru** *same as* **maTTu**[2].

చుట్టగా **cuTTagaa** *adv.* in a roll, in a circle.

చుట్టచుట్టు **cuTTacuTTu** *v.t.* to roll up, make into a roll.

చుట్టపక్కాలు **cuTTapakkaalu** *n. pl.* relatives, kith and kin.

చుట్టపెట్టు **cuTTapeTTu** *v.t.* **1** to surround; **oNTiki guDDa ~konu** to wrap a cloth round o.'s body. **2** to engulf, envelop. **3** to go round visiting (friends, relations).

చుట్టముక్క **cuTTamukka** *n.* anything that is smoked, esp. a cigar or beedi.

చుట్టరికం **cuTTarikam** *n.* relationship, kinship; **~ kalupu** to establish relationship, establish how one is related to a person.

చుట్టిల్లు **cuTTillu** *n.* circular shaped hut.

చుట్టివచ్చు **cuTTiwaccu** *v.t.* to walk round (e.g., a temple).

చుట్టు **cuTTu** I. *n.* **1** time; **aydu cuTLu** five times; **oka ~ weLLiraa** go once and come back. **2** turn, circuit. II. *v.t.* **1** to surround, encircle. **2** to roll, wrap, wind. III. *adv.* round about.

చుట్టుకొను **cuTTukonu** *v.t.* **1** to surround, wrap round, coil round, encircle. **2 paagaa ~** to tie o.'s turban.

చుట్టుకొలత **cuTTukolata** *n.* circumference, perimeter.

చుట్టుపక్కలు **cuTTupakkalu** *n. pl.* surroundings, vicinity.

చుట్టుపట్ల, చుట్టుపక్క[ల], చుట్టుపట్టు **cuTTupaTLa, cuTTupakka[la], cuTTupaTTu** *adv.* in the neighbourhood, in the vicinity, all around, round about.

చుట్టు[డు]బట్ట **cuTTu[Du] baTTa** *n.* wrapping cloth.

చుట్టుముట్టు **cuTTumuTTu** I. *v.i. and t.* **1** to surround, hem in, encircle. **2** to besiege. II. *adv.* in the vicinity, nearby; **~ unna waaru dongani paTTukonnaaru** nearby people caught the thief.

చుట్టూ, చుట్టూరా, చుట్టూతా **cuTTuu, cuTTuur cuTTuutaa** *adv.* all around.

చుడిదారి, ఛుడిదారి **cuDidaari, chuDidaari** *n.* churidars, breeches.

చుప్పనాతి **cuppanaati** *n.* hardhearted or jealous or selfish person (often used in referring to **śuurpaNakha** a female demon in the Ramayana).

చుబుకం, చిబుకం **cubukam, cibukam** *n. class.* chin.

చుమీ, చుమ్మి **cumii!, cummi!** *interj. class.* look!, see!, for sure!, indeed!

చురక, సురక **curaka, suraka** *n.* branding, scorching, burning; **maaTalatoo ~ weesEEDu** he scorched (them) by his words.

చురకత్తి, సురకత్తి, సూరకత్తి **curakatti, s[u]urakatti** *n.* small knife.

చురచుర, సురసుర **curacura, surasura** *adv.* fiercely: **~ kaalu** to burn fiercely or quickly; **~ cuucu** to look angrily, glower.

చురిక **curika** *n. class.* dagger.

చురుకు **curuku** I. *n.* 1 smartness, sharpness, intelligence, briskness. 2 heat, burning sensation: **muTTukoNTee~ tagilindi** when I touched it I got burnt. II. *adj.* 1 sharp, keen, hot, fierce. 2 brisk, smart, active, efficient; **pilla-waaDu caalaa~** the boy is very smart. III. *v.i.* to feel hot, burn (with fever).

చురుకుగా **curukugaa** *adv.* 1 actively, smartly, briskly. 2 keenly, sharply, intently. 3 fiercely.

చురుకుతనం **curukutanam** *n.* smartness, efficiency, activeness.

చురుక్కున **curukkuna** *adv.* fiercely, keenly, sharply.

చురుక్కుమనిపించు **curukkumanipincu** *v.i.* to cause pain or a burning sensation; **maaTa ataniki curukku-manipincindi** the word stung him.

చురుక్కుమను **curukkumanu** *v.i.* (of sharp pain) to sting, smart, tingle.

చుర్రున **curruna** *adv.* fiercely, sharply, keenly (of heat or wind striking).

చుర్రుమను **currumanu** *v.i.* 1 (of fire, boiling water) to sputter, hiss. 2 to be hot to taste. 3 to tingle; **naaku naalika currumandi** my tongue tingled. 4 to be scalded, scorched or stung; **weeNNiiLLu poosukoNTee oLLu currumandi** when I poured the hot water I was scalded; **aa maaTatoo waaDiki currumandi** he felt stung by that word.

చులకన, చులుకన **culakana, culukana** I. *n.* lightness, ease. II. *adj.* 1 easy, light. 2 not serious.

చులకన అవు **culakana awu** *v.i.* to be belittled, be treated lightly, be treated with contempt.

చులకనగా చూచు **culakanagaa cuucu** *v.t.* to treat with contempt, look down on.

చులకనచేయు **culakana ceeyu** *v.t.* to belittle, disparage, denigrate, regard with contempt, make light of.

చులాగ్గా **culaaggaa** *adv.* easily.

చుల్ల, చుల్లి **culla, culli** *n.* penis.

చుల్లా **cullaa** *n.* fireplace, stove.

చువ్వ, జువ్వ **cuwwa, juwwa** *n.* 1 iron rod, iron bar. 2 canc.

చూ - cuu

చూచాయగా **cuucaayagaa** *adv.* 1 slightly, indistinctly, vaguely. 2 suggestively, roughly, in outline.

చూచావాచాయగా **cuucaawaacaayagaa** *adv.* vaguely, indistinctly, indirectly, by means of hinting.

చూచిరాత **cuuciraata** *n.* copying exercise.

చూచు **cuucu** *v.t.* 1 to see, look [at], watch, observe; **cuusEEraa**! *interj.* did you observe this? do you know this? **cuustuuNTee, cuustuNDagaanee** *lit.* even while you are watching, i.e., very quickly and promptly; **cuus-tuucuustuu** being fully aware of the situation (*lit.* seeing and seeing); **cuucirammaNTee kaalciwacceewaaDu** *expression used of a person who takes matters into his own hands or acts on his own initiative* (alluding to an incident in the Ramayana about Hanuman who returned having laid waste Ravana's kingdom after being sent only to observe and report). 2 to perceive or experience through any sense; **ruci~** to taste; **naaDi~** to feel (a patient's) pulse. 3 *gen. with vbl. n. in dative* to try; **taguwu penca-Daaniki cuusEEDu** he tried to foment a quarrel. 4 to regard, consider; **lookuwagaa~** to regard as inferior, look down on. 5 **cuustee** *as a clitic means* if you consider the matter *or* come to think of it; **nuwwu cuustee yoogyu-Diwanee toostundi** (when I) come to think of it, you seem to be a worthy person. 6 *gen. in present continuous tense* to treat, care for, look after; **atanni kaasta jaagrattagaa cuustuNDaNDi** please look after him carefully.

చూచుకం **cuucukam** *same as* **cucukam.**

చూచుకొను **cuucukonu** *v.i. and t.* 1 to observe, look carefully at, examine. 2 to see to, attend to, look after. 3 to be careful, take care, consider carefully. 4 to look for, avail o.s. of; **wiilu/awakaaśam~** to take an opportunity; **wiilu cuucukoni maa iNTiki raNDi** come to my house at your convenience.

చూడామణి **cuuDaamaNi** *n. class.* jewel worn in a diadem.

చూడి **cuuDi** *n.* pregnancy in cattle.

చూడ్కు **cuuDku** *n. class.* look, stare.

చూతం **cuutam** *n. class.* mango tree.

చూపరులు **cuuparulu** *n. pl.* spectators, onlookers.

చూపించు **cuupincu** *v.t.* 1 to show, demonstrate, display, evince, exhibit. 2 **weelu peTTi ~** to point out.

చూపు **cuupu**[1] *n.* look, glance, sight, gaze, vision, power of seeing: **~maralcaleeka pooyEEDu** he could not turn his gaze away: **~lu appaginci nilabaDDaaDu** (*or* **~lu ankitam ceesi nilabaDDaaDu**) he stood gazing; *see* **peLLi, meera, cinna~.**

చూపు **cuupu**[2] *v.t. class.* to show; *also mod. with ref. to a quality*, e.g., **dhayryam~** to show courage; **paTTudala~** to exhibit determination; **neerpu~** to show o.'s skill.

చూపుడుగుర్రం **cuupuDugurram** *n.* worthless person, one who is all outward show.

చూపుడువేలు **cuupuDuweelu** *n.* index finger.

చూపు[ల]తూపులు **cuupu[la]tuupulu** *n. pl.* looks, glances.

చూపెట్టు **cuupeTTu** *v.t.* to show, exhibit.

చూపోపమి **cuupoopami** *n.* envy, jealousy.

చూపోపు **cuupoopu** *v.t.* to bear or endure the sight of.

చూర **cuura** *n.* 1 powder. 2 crumbs.

చూరకొను **cuurakonu** *v.t.* 1 to plunder. 2 to win, gain (s.o.'s appreciation or affection). 3 to attain.

చూరు **cuuru** I. *n.* 1 eaves. 2 underside of a roof, ceiling. II. *v.i.* (*also* **poga~**) to be begrimed, be black with soot or smoke, be charred.

చూర్ణం **cuurNam** *n.* 1 powder. 2 ayurvedic medicine made from powder without burning; *cf.* **bhasmam.**

చూర్ణంచేయు **cuurNam ceeyu** *v.t.* to pulverise.

చూలు **cuulu** *n.* pregnancy.

చూషణం **cuuSaNam**[1] *n. sci.* suction.

చె - ce

చెంగట **cengaTa** *adv. class.* near, close by.

చెంగనాలు **cenganaalu** *n.pl. dial.* skipping, dancing, jumping about.

చెంగల్వ **cengalwa** *n. class.* red lotus.

చెంగావి **cengaawi** *n.* light reddish brown colour.

చెంగు, చెరగు, చెరుగు **cengu, ceragu, cerugu** *n.* end of sari worn over the breast and shoulder; **~ paTTi aDugu** (of a woman) to beg (by holding out the end of her sari for the receipt of alms); **~ muDiweeyu** to get married (because at a wedding the bride's sari and the bridegroom's upper cloth (**uttariiyam**) are tied together in a knot): *see* **kongu.**

చెంగుచెంగున **cengu cenguna** *adv.* jumping, skipping, leaping about.

చెంగున **cenguna** *adv.* suddenly.

చెంచా **cencaa** *same as* **cancaa.**

చెంచు **cencu** *n.* Chenchu, name of a hill tribe in Andhra Pradesh.

చెంచెత **cenceta** *n.* woman member of the Chenchu tribe.

చెండాడు **ceNDaaDu** I. *v.i.* to play with a ball. II. *v.t.* to cut to pieces.

చెండి, చెండితనం **ceNDi, ceNDitanam** *same as* **caNDi, caNDitanam.**

చెండు **ceNDu** I. *n.* **1** bunch or ball of flowers. **2** ball for play. **3** bull's hump. II. *v.t. class.* to cut to pieces, destroy.

చెండుకుతిను **ceNDuku tinu** *v.t.* **1** to maltreat, illtreat. **2** to torture.

చెండుకొను **ceNDukonu** *v.i.* **1** to show irritation. **2** to speak grudgingly.

చెండుమల్లె **ceNDumalle** *n.* marigold.

చెంత **centa** I. *n.* nearness. II. *adv.* by, at, beside, along, near; **waari ~ ku** to[wards] them.

చెందు **cendu** I. *v.i.* **1** to pertain, belong; **aa pustakaalu naaku cendinawi** those books belong to me. **2** *class.* to be felt or experienced: **cendina bhayam** the fear that is felt. II. *v.t.* **1** to experience, undergo; **maarpulu ~** to undergo change; **abhiwṛddhi ~** to experience development, be developed. **2** to feel, enjoy, suffer; **asantṛpti ~** to feel dissatisfaction; **aagraham ~** to become angry. **3** to achieve, attain; **prasiddhi ~** to attain fame.

చెంద్రకాంత **cendrakaanta** *same as* **candrakaanta.**

చెంప **cempa** *n.* **1** cheek. **2** side, direction, region, area; **mii gadiki aa ~ ii ~ ewaru unnaaru?** who stays on either side of your room? **maa ~ aTLaa maaTLaaDaru** people do not speak like that in our area. **3 oka ~** (*sentence opener meaning* on the one hand, *the other alternative being unexpressed*) *signals an adversative relationship in the clauses that are to follow*, e.g, **oka ~ waana kurustunnadi, iNTiki eTLaa weLtaawu?** it is raining, then how will you go home? **oka ~ Taym aypootunnadi, bassu raaleedu** time is passing, but the bus has not come.

చెంపకాయ **cempakaaya** *n.* slap on the cheek.

చెంప చెళ్లుమనిపించు **cempa ceLLumanipincu** *v.i.* to give a hard slap on the cheek.

చెంపలేసుకొను **cempaleesukonu** *v.i.* to make a gesture of apology and repentance by touching o.'s cheeks.

చెంబు **cembu** *n.* small round metal water pot.

చెకచెక **cekaceka** *same as* **caka caka.**

చెకడా **cekaDaa** *n.* **1** bullock cart. **2** cart with solid wheels.

చెకపికలాడు **cekapikalaaDu** *v.t.* to hurry, hasten.

చెకుముకి[రాయి] **cekumuki[raayi]** *n.* flint.

చెక్క **cekka** *n.* **1** wood. **2** wooden plank or board. **3** wooden chip. **4** broken piece, small piece or bit; **kaDupu ~ layyeeTaTTu nawwu** to burst o.'s sides with laughter. **5 pooka ~** *dial.* piece or slice of arecanut. **6 gaanuga ~** oilcake made from ground oil seeds.

చెక్కడం **cekkaDam** *n.* setting (of a jewel), engraving (of a picture).

చెక్కసున్నం **cekkasunnam** *n.* rough plaster.

చెక్కిపారేయు **cekkipaareeyu** *v.t.* **1** to scrape thoroughly. **2** *colloq.* to criticise severely.

చెక్కిలి **cekkili** *n.* cheek.

చెక్కు **cekku** I. *n.* **1** skin, peel, rind (of fruit, vegetable). **2** flake; **~ lu uuDina bommalu** toys whose paint has flaked off. **3** scab; **gaayam ~ kaTTindi** the wound has formed a scab. **4** cheque (on a bank). **5** *dial.* currency note. II. *v.i. slang* to run away, abscond. III. *v.t.* **1** to carve, engrave. **2** to scrape, trim. **3** to sharpen (chisel, pencil). **4** to thrust, insert, tuck in. **5** to set (jewels). **6** *slang* to run away with, steal.

చెక్కుచెదరకుండా **cekkucedarakuNDaa** *adv.* unharmed, unscathed, untouched, intact.

చెక్కుచెదరు **cekkucedaru** *v.i., always in neg. constr.* to be harmed, disturbed or unsettled; **rayilununci paDipooyinaa cekkucedaraleedu** even though he fell from a train, he was unscathed; **meem kadili pooyEEm gaanii waaDu maatram cekkucedara leedu** we were in a panic but he was undaunted.

చెక్కుడు **cekkuDu** *n.* **1** carving, shaping (stone). **2** scraping.

చెక్కేయు **cekkeeyu** I. *v.i. slang* to run away, abscond. II. *v.t. slang* to run away with, steal.

చెట్టపట్టాలేసుకొను, చెట్టపట్టాలుపట్టుకొను **ceTTapaTTaaleesukonu, ceTTapaTTaalu paTTukonu** *v.i.* (of two persons) to join hands, hold each other by the hand.

చెట్టపట్టు **ceTTapaTTu** *v.t. class.* to marry.

చెట్టు **ceTTu** *n.* tree, shrub, plant; **~ kindi pliiDaru** pettifogging lawyer.

చెట్టుచేమలు **ceTTuceemalu** *n.pl.* trees and the like.

చెడగొట్టు ceDagoTTu *v.t.* 1 to ruin, destroy. 2 to spoil, disrupt, damage. 3 to upset, cause inconvenience (to s.o.). 4 to break up; **golusu ceDagoTTi gaajulu ceeyincukonnadi** she broke up the chain and had bangles made (from it).

చెడతిట్టు ceDatiTTu *v.t.* 1 to scold (a person) severely. 2 to criticise severely, condemn (book, opinion).

చెడతిరుగు ceDatirugu *v.i.* to wander idly for a long period.

చెడనాడు ceDanaaDu *v.t.* 1 to scold. 2 to curse.

చెడు ceDu I. *n.* evil. II. *adj.* bad, vile, worthless. III. *v.i.* 1 to be spoilt, damaged or ruined, become worthless. 2 to become bad or wicked. 3 (of fruit) to go bad, become rotten. 4 (of a machine) to break down, get out of order. 5 **maa iddarikii ceDindi** we fell out *or* we quarrelled with each other. 6 **ceDibatikinawaaDu** s.o. who has become rich after having been poor; *see* **talaceDu**.

చెడుగు ceDugu I. *n.* evil. II. *adj.* bad, vile, worthless.

చెడుగుడు ceDuguDu *n.* a boys' game (= **kabaDDi**).

చెడ్డ ceDDa I. *adj.* 1 bad, evil. wicked. 2 tremendous, terribly great; **~ciraaku** great irritation; **mahaa~iSTam** great yearning, craze. II. *past vbl. adj. of* **ceDu** (*also* **ceDina**) **kulam~waaDu** person who has lost his caste; **batiki ~waaDu** person who has been rich and has become poor; **tala ~ maniSi** widow.

చెడ్డతనం ceDDatanam *n.* badness, wickedness.

చెడ్డీ ceDDii *n.* short trousers, pants.

చెణుకు, చెణకు ceNuku, ceNaku I. *n.* 1 small particle. 2 spark of fire. 3 *pl. colloq.* **~lu** jokes, lively comments. II. *v.t.* to stir up, excite, provoke; **~lu ~** to crack jokes.

చెత్త cetta I. *n.* dirt, trash, sweepings, rubbish, refuse. II. *adj.* rubbishy, worthless.

చెత్తకుండీ cettakuNDii *n.* dustbin.

చెత్తాచెదారం cettaacedaaram *n.* dirt and rubbish.

చెద, చద ceda, cada *n.* white ant, termite; **pustakaalaku ~lu paTTEEyi** white ants attacked the books.

చెదరు, చెదురు cedaru, ceduru I. *adj.* scattered, sporadic. II. *v.i.* 1 to be scattered, dispersed or dissipated. 2 (of clothes, hair) to be dishevelled. 3 (of eyes) to be dazzled.

చెదరకొట్టు cedarakoTTu *v.t.* 1 to scatter, disperse. 2 to splash (water). 3 to shatter, dispel (solitude).

చెదురుగా cedurugaa *adv.* sporadically, at random.

చెదురుమదురుగా cedurumadurugaa *adv.* here and there.

చెదురువాటుగా ceduruwaaTugaa *adv.* sporadically.

చెనటి cenaTi I. *n. class.* foolish or wicked person. II. *adj. class.* 1 empty, vain, useless. 2 wicked, wretched, foolish.

చెన్నపట్నం, చెన్నపురి cennapaTNam, cennapuri *n.* city of Madras.

చెన్ను cennu *n. class.* grace, beauty.

చెప్పబడు ceppabaDu *v.i.* (*passive of* **ceppu**) to be said.

చెప్పించు ceppincu *v.t.* 1 to cause to say. 2 **caduwu~** to educate; **pillalaku caduwu ~konu** to get o.'s children educated.

చెప్పు ceppu[1] *n.* sandal, slipper, shoe.

చెప్పు ceppu[2] *v.t.* 1 to say, speak, tell, inform; **maa kurraaDitoo ceppaNDi** please speak to our son; **miitoo ceppi poodaamani waccEEru** they have come to take leave of you *or* they have come to say goodbye to you. 2 to narrate (story). 3 to teach (lesson). 4 (of an astrologer) **praśna~** to answer a question about the future.

చెప్పుకొను ceppukonu *v.t.* 1 to speak of, tell of, express, convey (thoughts). 2 to complain (to s.o. for sympathy or redress); **ewaritoo naa baadhalu ceppukoonu?** to whom shall I tell my miseries? **pooyi nii taatatoo ceppukoo!** go and complain to your grandfather! (*meaning* complain to anyone you like, I don't care!) 3 to mention, refer to; **iTuwaNTi naaTakaalanu gurinci manam sagarwangaa ceppukoowaccu** we can mention plays like these with pride. 4 to guess. 5 **paaThaalu~** (i) to give lessons; (ii) to take lessons. 6 to admit, confess, acknowledge. 7 **kSamaapaNa~** to apologise, make an apology. 8 **artham~** to assign a meaning.

చెప్పుకోతగిన ceppukootagina *adj.* noteworthy, worthy of mention.

చెప్పుచేతలు ceppuceetalu *n. pl.* command, control; **o.-i ceppuceetalaloo uNDu** to be under s.o.'s orders, be at s.o.'s beck and call.

చెప్పుడుమాట ceppuDumaaTa *n.* 1 words heard second-hand. 2 malicious report.

చెప్మా cepmaa! *interj.* I wonder?

చెమట cemaTa *n.* sweat, perspiration.

చెమటకాయ cemaTakaaya *n.* 1 pustule. 2 prickly heat.

చెమటపట్టు, చెమటపోయు cemaTapaTTu, cemaTapooyu *v.i.* to sweat.

చెమటోడ్చు cemaTooDcu *v.i.* to pour with sweat (due to hard labour).

చెమడాలు cemaDaalu *n. pl. colloq.* skin.

చెమరకాయ cemarakaaya *n.* pimple.

చెమర్చు cemarcu *v.i.* 1 to be wet or damp; **aame kaLLu cemarcEEyi** her eyes watered. 2 to be porous.

చెమర్పు cemarpu *n.* porosity.

చెముడు cemuDu *same as* **cewuDu.**

చెమ్మ cemma *n.* damp, moisture.

చెమ్మగిల్లు cemmagillu *v.i.* 1 to be damp, wet or moist. 2 to ooze.

చెమ్మచెక్క cemma cekka *n.* a girls' game.

చెయిదం ceyidam *n. class.* deed, action.

చెయివాటు ceyiwaaTu *adj.* light fingered, prone to stealing.

చెయ్యి, చేయి ceyyi, ceeyi *n.* 1 hand, arm; **~etti namaskarincu** to salute, pay homage to; **~cuucu** (i) to feel (s.o.'s) pulse; (ii) to read (s.o.'s) palm; **awakaaśam ~ jaaripooyindi** the opportunity was lost *or* the opportunity slipped from (his) grasp; **~tirigina racayita** a skilled writer; **~ceesukonu** (i) to assault, beat; **aayanamiida ~ ceesukonnaaru** they assaulted him; (ii) to take part (in), have a hand (in); **ii paniki** (*or* **ii paniloo**) **akaDamiilu~ ceesukoowaali** the Akadamis must take part in this work; **~daaTu, ~miiripoowu** to get out of hand, pass out of control; **o.-ki ~taDiceeyu** to offer s.o. a bribe; **aayana**

ceetiki emuka leedu he is very charitable and generous (*lit.* his hand has no bone it it); **pillalu ceetiki andiwaccEEru** his children came to his aid *or* his children gave him support; **taginanta bhuumi seedyaaniki ceetiki wastundi** enough land will become available for cultivation; **ceetulu ettu** to accept defeat, throw in o.'s hand; **ceetulu kaTTukoni cuucu** to look on with folded arms; **ceetulu kalupu** (i) to join hands in friendship; (ii) to quarrel, come to blows; **ceetulu tippu** to gesture with o.'s hands, gesticulate; **ceetulu nalupukonu** to rub o.'s hands together making a nervous or apologetic gesture; **cirigina guDDaynaa paaraweeyaDaaniki naaku ceetulu raawu** I have not got the capacity (*or* I cannot bring myself) to discard even a torn cloth; **uuLLoo padimandi padi ceetulu weestee pani tondaragaa jarugutundi** if everyone in the village helps, the work will be done quickly; *see* **kinda.** 2 sleeve (of a garment). 3 **taaLam~** *or* **taaLamcewi** key. 4 *in selling fruit ~ is used for a number (of fruits to be sold), usually five or less, depending on circumstances, e.g.,* **ruupaayaki reNDu ceetulu** two 'hands' (*meaning ten fruits*) for a rupee.

చెర **cera** *n.* prison, imprisonment.

చెరకు **ceraku** *same as* **ceruku.**

చెరగని **ceragani** *adj.* indelible.

చెరగు **ceragu** *n.* 1 direction, quarter, corner; **neela naalugu ~laa** in all directions, far and wide. 2 *same as* **cengu.**

చెరగుమాయు, చెంగుమాయు **ceragumaayu, cengumaayu** *v.i.* to be menstruous.

చెరచెర **ceracera** *adv.* quickly, speedily.

చెరపట్టు, చెరపెట్టు **cerapaTTu, cerapeTTu** *v.t.* to imprison, take (s.o.) prisoner.

చెరలాటం **ceralaaTam** *n.* game; **nipputoo ~aaDutunnaawu** you are playing with fire.

చెరలాడు **ceralaaDu** *v.i.* to play.

చెరసాల **cerasaala** *n.* prison.

చెరి **ceri** *adj.* each; **waaLLu ~ sagam tiisukonnaaru** they took a half share each.

చెరుకు, చెరకు **ceruku, ceraku** *n.* sugarcane; **~gaDa** sugarcane stick.

చెరుగు **cerugu**[1] I. *v.i.* to be rubbed out, be obliterated. II. *v.t.* 1 to winnow, fan. 2 to sift.

చెరుగు **cerugu**[2] *same as* **cengu.**

చెరుచు **cerucu** *v.t.* 1 to spoil. 2 to rape, ravish.

చెరుపు **cerupu** I. *n.* 1 damage, harm, spoiling, ruin. 2 something harmful or ill-omened. II. *v.t.* 1 to spoil, damage, ruin; **~konna tala** dishevelled hair. 2 to erase, rub out, wipe clean. 3 to ravish, rape.

చెరువు **ceruwu** *n.* tank, irrigation reservoir; **o.-ni muuDu ceruwula niiLLu taagincu** *lit.* to make s.o. drink three tankfuls of water, i.e., to cause him extreme difficulty and suffering.

చెర్నాకోల, చెలకోల **cernaakoola, celakoola** *n.* cart driver's whip.

చెర్ర **cerra** *n.* ball bearings in a wheel.

చెర్రుమను **cerrumanu** *v.i.* (of anger) to be aroused; **aa maaTa wiNTee naaku cerrumandi** when I heard that I was extremely angry.

చెలక, చెలిక **celaka, celika** *n.* dry (unirrigated) land.

చెలకదుక్కి **celakadukki** *n.* ploughing of dry land; **aayana ~ wyawasaayam ceestunnaaDu** he cultivates dry (unirrigated) land.

చెలగాటం **celagaaTam** *n.* game, sport; **pilliki ~ elikki praaNa sankaTam** sport for the cat means danger to its life for the mouse (proverb).

చెలగాటం ఆడు, చెలగాటాలాడు **celagaaTam aaDu, celagaaTaalaaDu** *v.i.* to play, toy (**-too,** with).

చెలగు **celagu** *v.t.* to cut down; **araNyaalu celaginawaaDu** he who cut down the forests.

చెలమ **celama** *n.* 1 small pit dug in a dry riverbed for water. 2 spring of water.

చెలరేగు **celareegu** *v.i.* 1 to burst forth, break out. 2 (of a crowd) to become excited and inflamed.

చెలామణి, చెలాయించు **celaamaNi, celaayincu** *same as* **calaamaNi, calaayincu.**

చెలి **celi** *n.* 1 woman. 2 girl friend.

చెలిక **celika** *same as* **celaka.**

చెలికత్తె **celikatte** *n.* confidante, girl's playmate or companion.

చెలికాడు **celikaaDu** *n.* 1 friend; **nammakamayna~** faithful friend or associate. 2 young friend, boy friend.

చెలిమి **celimi** *n.* friendship.

చెలియ **celiya** *n.* girl friend.

చెలియలికట్ట **celiyalikaTTa** *n.* coast, sea shore.

చెలువ **celuwa** *n.* beautiful woman.

చెలువం **celuwam** *n.* beauty, loveliness.

చెల్లాచెదరు **cellaacedaru** *adj.* scattered, dispersed.

చెల్లాచెదరుగా **cellaacedarugaa** *adv.* scattered in all directions, pell-mell.

చెల్లించు **cellincu** *v.t.* 1 to pay off (debt), disburse (salary). 2 to fulfil (desire). 3 (*causative of* **cellu**) to cause to circulate or be current. 4 *colloq.* to eat up, finish off (food); **ginne cellincEEDu** he has finished off the bowl (of food).

చెల్లింపులు **cellimpulu** *n.pl.* 1 expenditure. 2 disbursements, payments.

చెల్లు **cellu** I. *n.* 1 payment; **~ciiTii** acknowledgement or receipt for payment. 2 equivalent, quits; **niiku naaku baakii~** you and I are quits *or* you and I owe each other nothing (*lit.* to you and to me the debt is equal); **~ki~ aypootundi** it will be tit for tat. 3 s.g appropriate; **tana aajanma parisaraala prabhaawaalni dhikkarinci, samucita kartawyaanni nirNayincagalagaDam ee gaandhiikoo ~** to be able to reject the influence of o.'s native surroundings and decide o.'s proper duty is s.g appropriate for a person like Gandhi. 4 end[ing], finish; **aayana maa iNTiki raawaDam aa roojee modalu aa roojee~kuuDaanu** that was the first and last day that he came to my house; **appaTi maaTa appaTiki~** *lit.* the promise given on that day expired on that same day, i.e., you must forget about what was promised previously; *cf.* **sari** *sense I. 1.* II. *v.i.* 1 to be acceptable, prevail, have power and influence; **aayana maaTa ikkaDa~tundi** he has power and influence here; **anyaayaalu dawrjanyaalu inkaanaa ikapay cellawu** injustice and violence will not prevail any more. 2 to be fit, proper, appropriate, permissible or possible. 3 to pass (as), be reckoned (as); **atiita maanawulugaa cellagaligEEru** they were able to pass as supermen. 4 (of a document) to be valid. 5 (of a coin) to pass, be current; **cellani dammiDi** a bad penny. 6 to be finished, used up, spent, consumed, exhausted; **mottamloo atyadhika bhaagam jiitanaataala kindanee cellipootundi** the greater part of the whole (budget) will be spent on salaries and allowances; **kancam cellindi kaani kancam mundununci leewa leedu** he has cleared his plate but he has not got up from his place (after eating). 7 (of time) to pass; **wayassu cellinawaaru** elderly people; **aayana kaalam cellindi** he died. 8 (of desire) to be fulfilled. 9 (of debt) to be paid, be discharged. 10 **aayanni kalawaDaaniki naaku moham celleedu** I have not the face to meet him.

చెల్లుపెట్టు[కొను] **cellupeTTu[konu]** *v.t.* 1 to settle (a debt). 2 to credit money to an account or towards repayment of a loan.

చెల్లుబడి **cellubaDi** *n.* 1 authority, influence. 2 currency, current use, validity.

చెల్లుబడి అవు **cellubaDi awu** *v.i.* 1 to prevail, have authority, have influence. 2 to be current, be in use, be in circulation.

చెల్లుబాటు **cellubaaTu** *n.* 1 currency, validity, current use. 2 acceptability, fitness, appropriateness. 3 capability, capacity; **idi waaDikee ~ awtundi inkewaruu ceeyaleeru** he alone has the capability to do this, no-one else can. 4 completion, end.

చెల్లెలు, చెల్లి, చెల్లాయి, చెల్లె **cellelu, celli, cellaayi, celle** *n.* younger sister (*these are formal, informal, affectionate and substandard terms respectively*).

చెళ్లున **ceLLuna** *adv.* 1 resoundingly. 2 quickly, in a flash; **~ jawaabu ceppEEDu** he replied in a flash.

చెళ్లుమను **ceLLumanu** *v.i. fig.* to deal a sharp blow; **aayana jawaabu ceLLumannaTTu ayindi** his reply was as if he had given me a sharp blow.

చెవలవేధవ, చెవలాయ్ **cewalawedhawa, cewalaay** *interj., term of abuse* **eeraa ~** ! you stupid fellow!

చెవి **cewi** *n.* 1 ear. 2 *idiomatic expressions:* **sangiitam cewulaaraa winnadi** *lit.* she listened to music so as to fill the ears, *hence* she listened to music to her heart's content; **kawitwamaNTee ~ koosukoNTaaDu** he is very fond of poetry; **aayana sangiitamtoo waaLLa cewula tuppu antaa wadilindi** their ears were charmed by his music; **dharmoopanyaasaalu winaleeka maa cewulu cillulu paDutunnayi** we are sick of hearing moral lectures; **naa ~ korikEEDu** he whispered s.g in my ear *or* he told me s.g secretly; **~ ni illu kaTTukonu** *lit.* to build a house in s.o.'s ear, *hence* to repeat s.g to s.o. over and over again, to din s.g into s.o.; **~ kooyincukoNTaanu** *or* **~ kadapaayincukoNTaanu** (*lit.* I will have my ear cut off) *corresponds to the English expression* "I will eat my hat", e.g., **saayantram aaroogaNTakallaa sommu nii ceetiloo uNDakapootee ~ kadapaayincuku pootaanu** if the money is not in your hands by six p.m. I'll eat my hat. 3 **taaLam ~** *or* **taalam ceyyi** key. 4 ringshaped handle of a vessel.

చెవిటి **cewiTi** *adj.* deaf.

చెవుడు, చెముడు **cewuDu, cemuDu** *n.* deafness.

చెవులపిల్లి **cewulapilli** *n.* hare.

చే - cee

చే **cee** I. *nominal prefix derived from* **ceyyi, ceeyi** hand, e.g., **ceejaaru, ceeneeta.** II. *p.p. alt. form of* **ceeta.**

చేంతాడు **ceentaaDu** *n.* 1 rope for drawing a water bucket from a well. 2 **kaalee ~** piece of smouldering string kept for lighting beedies, etc., in a shop.

చేకాపు **ceekaapu** *n.* safeguard, precaution; **ciikaTLoo weLLutunnaaru, diipam karra ~ku tiisukuweLLaNDi** you are going in the dark, take a light and stick as a precaution.

చేకూరు **ceekuuru** *v.i.* 1 to be gained, accrue. 2 to be attained, be reached.

చేకూర్చు **ceekuurcu** *v.t.* 1 to procure, bring about. 2 to arrange, give, provide.

చేగోడీ **ceegooDii** *n.* fried preparation of black gram flour and rice flour made in ring shape.

చేచిక్కించుకొను, చేజిక్కించుకొను **ceecikkincukonu, ceejikkincukonu** *v.t.* 1 to take over, take charge of, take into o.'s hands, win, capture, get control of. 2 *colloq.* to grab, get hold of.

చేచిక్కు, చేజిక్కు **ceecikku, ceejikku** *v.i.* to be caught, obtained, captured or won.

చేజారు **ceejaaru** *v.i.* to slip from o.'s grasp.

చేజేతులా **ceejeetulaa** *adv.* 1 with o.'s own hands, by o.'s own actions. 2 wilfully, deliberately.

చేట **ceeTa** *n.* winnowing tray; **ceeTanta mokham ceesukonu** to look very pleased or happy.

చేటు **ceeTu** I. *n.* 1 evil, harm, misfortune. 2 danger. 3 spoiling, ruin, disaster. II. *adj.* bad, evil, harmful; **~ kaalam** bad time, time of misfortune. III. *particle* **inta ~** *and* **anta ~** *sometimes alternate for* **intagaa** this much *and* **antagaa** that much, e.g., **miiru inta ~ ceppanakkara leedu, tappakuNDaa wastaanu** you need not say so much, I will certainly come; **taaguDu maaneeddaam anukoNTee mari inta ~ alawaaTaypooyEEka maanaDam elaa**? if he wants to stop drinking how will he be able to when he has grown accustomed to it to this extent?

చేత **ceeta** I. *n.* 1 act, action. 2 deed. II. *p.p.* by [means of], through, with.

చేత అవు **ceeta awu** *v.i.* to be possible; **nii[ku] ~ naa?** can you do it? **naaku ~ nu** I can do it; **naa[ku] ceeta kaadu** I cannot (ever) do it; **naa[ku] ceeta kaawaDam leedu** I cannot do it (at the present time); **ceetanaynantagaa** as much as possible, to the extent possible; **waaDiki ceetanayna widhangaa** in the way that was possible for him, as best he could; **ceetakaani** incapable, incompetent, useless.

చేత ఇనుము **ceeta inumu** *n.* wrought iron.

చేతకూలి **ceetakuuli** *n.* making charges, cost of labour involved.

చేతన **ceetana** *n.* **1** consciousness. **2** life, vitality.

చేతనం **ceetanam** *n.* living or animate creature.

చేతపట్టు **ceetapaTTu** *v.t.* to obtain, get possession of.

చేతపడు **ceetapaDu** *v.i.* to be obtained, come to hand.

చేతబడి **ceetabaDi** *n.* **1** spell, charm. **2** invoking of evil spirits.

చేతావాతాకాని **ceetaawaataa kaani** *adj.* incompetent, useless (*lit.* wanting in both deeds and words).

చేతికర్ర **ceetikarra** *n.* walking stick.

చేతిగడియారం **ceetigaDiyaaram** *n.* wrist watch.

చేతిగుడ్డ **ceetiguDDa** *n.* handkerchief.

చేతిబిడ్డ **ceetibiDDa** *n.* infant, child in arms.

చేతివేలు **ceetiweelu** *n.* finger.

చేతివృత్తులు, చేతిపనులు **ceetiwṛttulu, ceetipanulu** *n.pl.* handicrafts.

చేతులారా **ceetulaaraa** *adv.* with (o.'s) own hands, by (o.'s) own effort.

చేతోవికారం **ceetoowikaaram** *n. class.* strong emotion.

చేద **ceeda** *n.* bucket and rope for drawing water from a well.

చేదండ **ceedaNDa** *n.* help, support.

చేదంతె **ceedante** *n.* implement like a hoe for forming ridges round small irrigated plots.

చేదర్థ[క]ం **ceedartha[ka]m** *n. gram.* conditional form (of a vb.).

చేదు **ceedu**[1] I. *n.* bitterness, s.g bitter; **adi ceedaa, wiSamaa**? is it so unpleasant? (*rhetorical question, lit.* is it bitter or poisonous?) II. *adj.* bitter; **~mandu** bitter medicine.

చేదు **ceedu**[2] *v.t.* to draw (water from a well).

చేదుకొను **ceedukonu** *v.t.* to draw to o.s.; **aadukoo, ceedukoo**! come to my rescue and draw me to thee! (a prayer recited by pilgrims).

చేదుబావి **ceedubaawi** *n.* draw well, well from which water is drawn with a bucket and rope.

చేదోడు **ceedooDu** *n.* help, support, assistance.

చేదోడువాదోడుగా **ceedooDu waadooDugaa** *adv.* as a help and support by both words and deeds.

చేను **ceenu** *n.* field containing a crop.

చేనేత **ceeneeta** *n.* hand weaving; **~pariśrama** handloom industry.

చేప **ceepa** *n.* fish.

చేపట్టు **ceepaTTu** I. *n.* help, support. II. *v.t.* **1** to undertake, take charge of, take over. **2** to assume (office). **3** to adopt, embrace (profession, way of living). **4** to marry.

చేపడు **ceepaDu** *v.i.* to fall into the hands (**-ki**, of).

చేపపిల్ల **ceepapilla** *n.* fish fingerling.

చేపరెక్క **ceeparekka** *n.* fin.

చేపాటికర్ర **ceepaaTikarra** *n.* walking stick or staff.

చేపు **ceepu** I. *n.* gush or flow of milk. II. *v.i.* to lactate, give milk.

చేపెక్కు **ceepekku** *v.i.* (of a mother) to have a supply of milk.

చేబదులు **ceebadulu** *n.* hand loan, loan for a small sum given without written security.

చేబియ్యం **ceebiyyam** *n.* **1** hand pounded rice. **2** rice not highly polished.

చేమ **ceema** *n.* (*also* **~kuura**) kind of green vegetable, *arum esculentum*.

చేమంతి **ceemanti** *n.* chrysanthemum.

చేమంతిబిళ్ల **ceemanti biLLa** *n.* flower-like gold ornament studded with jewels worn in plaited hair.

చేమగడ్డ, చెమదుంప **ceemagaDDa, ceemadumpa** *n.* kind of root vegetable, *calladium esculentum*.

చేమగ్గం **ceemaggam** *n.* handloom.

చేమిరి **ceemiri** *n.* sour buttermilk used for curdling milk.

చేయి **ceeyi** *same as* **ceyyi.**

చేయించు **ceeyincu** *v.i.* to cause to be made or done; **peLLi~** to have a marriage performed.

చేయించుకొను **ceeyincukonu** *v.t.* **1** to get s.g made or done for o.s. **2** to engage, hire (conveyance).

చేయు **ceeyu** I. *v.i.* **1** to act, work, behave; **jaDjii[gaa] ceesi riTayr ayyEEDu** he retired after working as a judge. **2** to happen, be caused, become; **naaku jabbu ceesindi** I became ill *or* I am ill; **naaku ajiirNam ceesindi** I have indigestion; **taDistee niiku jalubu ceestundi** if you get wet, you will catch cold; **oLLu ceesEEDu** be became/grew fat. **3** to be worth; **nii lekkaloo ii gaDiyaaram enta ceestundi?** what is the cost of this watch in your estimation? II. *v.t.* to do, perform, make, form, create; **racanalu~** to compose writings; **mahaabhaaratam telugu ceesEEru** they rendered the Mahabharata into Telugu; **Ph.D ceeyu** to work for a Ph.D.; **appu~** to incur a debt, become indebted; **biyyam~** to clean rice; **Tiphin~** to prepare/eat a light meal; **goolu~** to score a goal; **neenu raakuNDaa ceesEEru** they stopped/prevented me from coming; **ika ceeseedileeka, naDiciweLLEEDu** being unable to do anything else (*or* having no other course) he went walking.

చేయూత **ceeyuuta** *n.* help, assistance.

చేర **ceera** *n.* hollow of the hand.

చేరగిలపడు **ceeragilapaDu** *v.i.* **1** to lean back, recline. **2** to fall back (**-ki**, against).

చేరదీయు **ceeradiiyu** *v.t.* **1** to become friendly with, admit to o.'s friendship or company. **2** to befriend, take into o.'s household, take under o.'s wing. **3** *slang* to keep as a paramour. **4** to collect, gather, assemble (a number of persons).

చేరపడు **ceerapaDu** *v.i.* to sink back, fall back (**-ki**, against).

చేరపిలుచు **ceerapilucu** *v.t.* to invite s.o. into o.'s group or party.

చేరపోవు **ceera poowu** *v.t.* to go near, approach.

చేరవేత **ceeraweeta** *n.* supplying, bringing in.

చేరవేయు **ceeraweeyu** *v.t.* to [cause to] rest or lean; **rikSaa wenakki atanu tala ceereesEEDu** he rested his head against the back of the rickshaw; **talupu~** to set a door ajar, leave it slightly open. **2** to convey, carry (information): **ewaroo aayanaki ii waarta ceeraweesEEru** s.o. has carried this news to him. 3 to transport, supply (goods). 4 to carry away, purloin, steal.

చేరిక **ceerika** *n.* 1 joining, junction. 2 *gram.* addition, attachment (of an affix). 3 nearness, closeness, contiguity. 4 access. 5 arrival. 6 familiarity.

చేరు **ceeru**[1] I. *v.i.* 1 to assemble, gather, come together, collect. 2 to approach, come near. 3 to arrive, be received. 4 to be included. 5 to be added, be attached. 6 to join, become a member (of); **kampeniiloo sTenoogaa ceerEEnu** I joined the company as a stenographer. 7 to belong, pertain, be part (of). II. *v.t.* to reach, arrive at.

చేరు **ceeru**[2] *n.* 1 string, cord. 2 string of pearls or flowers. 3 cord by which a net bag (**uTTi**) is suspended; **naalugu ceerlu tegi neelaki paDDaaDu wyaapaaramloo naSTam raawaDamtoo** he was ruined by the loss in his business (*lit.* when the four cords of his net bag broke he fell to the ground due to loss in his business).

చేరుకొను **ceerukonu** I. *v.i.* to join, associate with, combine with. II. *v.t.* to arrive at, reach, attain.

చేరుగడ **ceerugaDa** *n.* 1 nearness. 2 refuge, shelter.

చేరుగొండి **ceerugoNDi** *n.* kept woman, concubine.

చేరువ **ceeruwa** *n.* nearness, proximity.

చేరువగా **ceeruwagaa** *adv.* nearby, close; **mancaaniki~** close to the bed.

చేరెడు **ceereDu** *adj.* handful of, i.e., as much as can be held in the hollow of the hand; **~kaLLu, ceereDeesi kaLLu** large eyes (*lit.* eyes as big as the hollow of the of the hand).

చేర్చు **ceercu** *v.t.* 1 to join, unite, combine, mix together, put together, assemble, accumulate. 2 to add, include. 3 to enrol (as a member), admit (to school, hospital). 4 to cause to reach; **rawini ati kaSTamtoo oDDuki ceercEEDu** with great difficulty he brought Ravi to the shore. 5 to place, put, fit, rest; **diNDu tecci mellagaa maadhawi talakinda ceercEEDu** he brought a pillow and gently placed it under Madhavi's head; **kinda pustakaalu ceerci balla ettuceesEEDu** he fitted books underneath and raised the bench; **gooDaku wiipu ceerci nuncunnaaDu** he stood resting his back against a wall.

చేర్పించు **ceerpincu** *v.t.* to cause to be joined, assembled, included or admitted.

చేర్పు **ceerpu** *n.* 1 addition, inclusion. 2 support.

చేర్లబడు **ceerlabaDu** *v.i.* 1 to lean, rest (**-ki**, on *or* against). 2 to sink back (**-ki** *or* **-loo**, onto *or* into).

చేర్లవేయు **ceerlaweeyu** *v.t.* to leave (a door) ajar, leave (a door) slightly open.

చేవ **ceewa** *n.* 1 strength. 2 courage. 3 heart or core of a tree.

చేవగల **ceewagala** *adj.* strong, having a hard core.

చేవచచ్చు **ceewacaccu** *v.i.* to lose vigour, strength or courage.

చేవచెట్టు, చేవమాను **ceewaceTTu, ceewamaanu** *n.* timber tree known as redwood.

చేవదేరు **ceewadeeru** *v.i.* to increase in strength, grow stronger.

చేవాటి **ceewaaTi** *adj.* light-fingered, prone to stealing.

చేవాటితనం **ceewaaTitanam** *n.* light-fingeredness.

చేవ్రాలు **ceewraalu** *n.* 1 signature. 2 handwriting.

చేష్ట **ceeSTa** *n.* 1 deed, act. 2 behaviour, action. 3 gesture; **śrngaara ~lu** romantic gestures. 4 prank; **koNTe ~lu** tricks, pranks.

చేష్టితం **ceeSTitam** *n.* activity, action, behaviour.

చేసుకొను **ceesukonu** *v.t.* 1 to do (s.g) for o.s.; **bajaaru~** to go shopping; **peLLi~** to marry; **rikSaa~** to engage a rickshaw.

చై - cay

చైతన్యం **caytanyam** *n.* 1 consciousness, awareness. 2 vitality, liveliness, activity, dynamism.

చైతన్యవంత **caytanyawanta** *adj.* 1 conscious, aware. 2 active.

చైత్యం **caytyam** *n.* Buddhist shrine or place of worship.

చైత్రం **caytram** *n.* 1 Chaitra, the first Telugu lunar month (corresponding to March-April). 2 *fig.* spring.

చొ - co

చొంగ **conga** *n.* dribbling.

చొంగకార్చు **congakaarcu** *v.i.* to dribble.

చొక్కం **cokkam** *adj.* excellent, pure.

చొక్కా **cokkaa** *n.* shirt, jacket.

చొక్కు **cokku** *v.i.* 1 to be drunk, be intoxicated. 2 to be beside o.s. (with emotion), be infatuated.

చొక్కునీరు **cokkuniiru** *n.* intoxicating drink, liquor.

చొక్కుపెట్టు **cokkupeTTu** *v.t.* to entrance a person into falling in love, captivate, infatuate.

చొక్కుపొడి, చొక్కుమందు **cokkupoDi, cokkumandu** *n.* love powder, love potion.

చొచ్చు **coccu** *v.i. and t.* 1 to enter, find a way into, penetrate, infiltrate. 2 to go in, recede, turn in[wards]; **paLLu uuDipooyi aayana pedimalu loopaliki ~ku pootaayi** because his teeth are lost, his lips turn inwards. 3 to jut out, protrude. 4 **śaraNu~** to seek protection or asylum, surrender; **raamuni śaraNu coccinaaDu** he sought Rama's protection. 5 *with infinitive* to begin; **śakti uDigipoo-coccindi** his strength began to fail.

చొటచొట **coTacoTa** *same as* **boTa boTa.**

చొట్ట, సొట్ట **coTTa, soTTa**[1] *adj.* lame, crippled.

చొనుపు, జొనుపు **conupu, jonupu** *v.t.* to thrust in, insert.

చొప్ప, చొప్పకట్టె, చొప్పదంటు **coppa, coppakaTTe, coppadaNTu** *n.* millet straw after being threshed.

చొప్పదంటుప్రశ్నలు **coppadaNTu praśnalu** *n. pl.* trashy or meaningless questions.

చొప్పించు, జొప్పించు **coppincu, joppincu** *v.t.* to insert, implant, introduce, incorporate.

చొప్పున **coppuna** *adv. and p.p.* 1 at the rate of; **ruupaayiki reNDu ~ konnaanu** I bought them at the rate of two for a rupee; **okkokkaTi yaabhay paysala ~ istaaru** they sell them at the rate of fifty paise each. 2 agreeably to, according to, in accordance with; **miiru ceppina ~** in accordance with what you said. 3 by reason of, through; **bhayam ~** through fear.

చొరగొట్టు **coragoTTu** *v.t. dial.* to insert.

చొరబడు, జొరబడు **corabaDu, jorabaDu** *v.i.* to enter, rush into, break into, make (*or* find) a way into, intrude on.

చొరబాటు, జొరబాటు **corabaaTu, jorabaaTu** *n.* penetration, intrusion.

చొరబారు, జొరబారు **corabaaru, jorabaru** *v.i.* to enter, encroach, find a way into.

చొరవ **corawa** *n.* 1 daring, boldness, forwardness. 2 aptitude. 3 enterprising nature, initiative. 4 empty place. 5 opportunity; **naaku ~ dorikinappuDalla antoo intoo prajaasamasyalni siniipaaTalloo testuunee unnaanu** whenever I have an opportunity I am introducing a little of the people's problems into my cinema songs.

చొరు **coru** *v.i.* to enter, force a way in.

చొరుగు **corugu** *same as* **sorugu.**

చో - coo

చో **coo** *conditional particle, class.* **aayana ceppinacoo neenu ceesedanu** if he says so, I will do it.

చోటు **cooTu** *n.* 1 place. 2 room, space, unoccupied area.

చోటుచేసుకొను **cooTuceesukonu** *v.i.* to find place, find room.

చోడంబలి **cooDambali** *n.* ragi porridge.

చోడి **cooDi** *n., often pl.* **cooLLu** *eleusine corocama*, a millet known as ragi.

చోదకుడు **coodakuDu** *n.* driver.

చోద్యం **coodyam** I. *n.* 1 wonder, marvel. 2 interesting sight, spectacle. II. *adj.* wonderful, marvellous; *see* **sooddem.**

చోపుదారు **coopudaaru** *n.* mace bearer.

చోరీ **coorii** *n.* theft, robbery; **~ aasti** stolen property.

చోరుడు **cooruDu** *n.* thief, robber.

చోళీ **cooLii** *n.* blouse.

చోషణం **cooSaNam** *n.* sucking, suction.

చౌ - caw

చౌక **cawka** I. *n.* cheapness. II. *adj.* 1 cheap; **~ dharala dukaaNam** fair price shop. 2 tenuous, slight.

చౌకం **cawkam** *n.* square.

చౌకట్టు **cawkaTTu** *n.* door frame or window frame fixed into a wall.

చౌకనేల **cawkaneela** *n.* red sandy soil.

చౌకబారు **cawkabaaru** *adj.* cheap, shoddy.

చౌకీ **cawkii** *n.* chowki, tollgate, customs post.

చౌకీదారు **cawkiidaaru** *n.* 1 chowkidar, watchman. 2 person in charge of a chowki.

చౌకు **cawku** *n.* chowk, crossroads.

చౌకుచెట్టు **cawkuceTTu** *n.* casuarina tree (= **saruguDu**).

చౌట **cawTa** *adj.* (of colour) pale, light.

చౌటి, చవిటి **cawTi, cawiTi** *genitive case of* **cawDu.**

చౌటీరాయి **cawTiiraayi** *n.* keystone of an arch.

చౌడు **cawDu** *n.* 1 saline or saltish land. 2 saltiness, salinity.

చౌరాస్తా **cawraastaa** *n.* crossroads.

చౌర్యం **cawryam** *n.* theft; **grantha ~** unauthorised copying, infringement of copyright, plagiarism.

చ్యు - cyu

చ్యుత **cyuta** *adj.* fallen.

చ్యుతి **cyuti** *n.* fall, decline; **pada ~** fall from a high position or rank.

ఛ, ఛా - cha, chaa

ఛ!, ఛా! **cha!, chaa!** *interj. of disapproval, disquiet or exasperation.*

ఛందం, ఛందస్సు **chandam, chandassu** *n.* prosody, poetic metre, metrical arrangement; **deeśiiya chandassulu** indigenous metres.

ఛంధశ్శాస్త్రం **chandaśśaastram** *n.* science of prosody.

ఛందోబద్ధ **chandoobaddha** *adj.* (of poetry) metrical.

ఛందోభంగం **chandoobhangam** *n.* violation of laws of poetic metre.

ఛట్‌ఫట్‌మను **chaTphaTmanu** *v.i.* to make a snapping or crackling sound.

ఛత్రం **chatram** *n. class.* umbrella, esp. an umbrella as a token of sovereignty.

ఛద్దర్ **chaddar** *n.* bedspread.

ఛద్మ **chadma** *n.* trick[ery], fraud, deceit, guile; **~ weeSamloo weLLEEDu** he went in disguise.

ఛప్పన్న **chappanna** *n.* fifty-six.

ఛలం **chalam** *n. class.* deception, deceit, trick, stratagem.

ఛలోక్తి **chalookti** *n.* 1 joke; **~ weeyu, ~ wisuru** to make a joke. 2 innuendo. 3 funny story.

ఛా! **chaa!** *same as* **cha!**

ఛాందస **chaandasa** *adj.* orthodox, traditional-minded.

ఛాందసం **chaandasam** I. *n.* 1 orthodoxy, bigotry. 2 simplicity, awkwardness, stupidity of a mere bookworm.

ఛాందసుడు **chaandasuDu** *n.* 1 orthodox person. 2 ritualistic pedant, obscurantist, reactionary.

ఛాతీ **chaatii** *n.* 1 chest. 2 breasts; *see* **wirucukonu.**

ఛాత్కారి **chaatkaari** *adj. used as a term of abuse* wretched, miserable.

ఛాత్రుడు **chaatruDu** *n.* disciple, student.

ఛాదనం **chaadanam** *n.* cover[ing].

ఛాది **chaadi** *n. zool.* pellicle.

ఛాయ **chaaya** *n.* 1 shadow, shade. 2 colour, hue, shade of colour; **erupu oka ~ ekkuwa uNDaali** it must be a shade more red. 3 complexion, esp. fair complexion. 4 reflection. 5 trace, vestige. 6 *pl.* **~ lu** nearness, vicinity; **maa iNTi ~ lalooki raaku** do not come anywhere near our house.

ఛాయగ్రహాలు **chaayagrahaalu** *n.pl. astrol.* the shadowy planets Rahu and Ketu.

ఛాయాచిత్రం **chaayaacitram** *n.* photograph.

ఛి - chi

ఛిద్రం **chidram** *n.* 1 hole, slit, cleft. 2 splitting, schism. 3 fault, defect.

ఛిద్రంచేయు **chidramceeyu** *v.i.* to cleave.

ఛిన్నం **chinnam** *adj.* cut, divided.

ఛిన్నాభిన్నం **chinnaabhinnam** *adj.* 1 cut to pieces. 2 scattered. 3 mangled, mutilated.

ఛీ, ఛు - chii, chu

ఛీ[కొట్టు] **chii[koTTu]** *same as* **cii[koTTu].**

ఛీత్కారంచేయు, ఛీత్కరించు **chiitkaaram ceeyu, chiitkarincu** *same as* **ciitkaaram ceeyu, ciitkarincu.**

ఛుడిదారి **chuDidaari** *same as* **cuDidaari.**

ఛె, ఛే - che, chee

ఛెడ **cheDa** *adjvl. prefix occurring before certain vbs. and advs. to denote the meaning* great, excessive, e.g., **~ tiTTu** to scold severely; **~ huSaarugaa** very happily.

ఛెడీ... ఫెడీ **cheDii. . . .pheDii** *expression to denote* tit for tat, retorting or answering back; **waaDu cheDiimannappuDu nuwwu pheDii aNTee wedhawa caccinaTTu uurukoNNu** if you had answered him back when he spoke, the wretch would undoubtedly have kept quiet.

ఛెత్తు **chettu** *n. dial.* roof of a house.

ఛెన్ని **chennii** *n.* pointed instrument for engraving on stone.

ఛేదం **cheedam** *n.* 1 cutting, dividing: **padac~** division of words: **śirac~** beheading. 2 part, piece.

ఛేదించు **cheedincu** *v.t.* 1 to cut, sever, divide. 2 to cut up (into pieces), cut down (forest), cut away, cut out (unwanted material). 3 to break (chains), dispel (silence).

జ - ja

జంకించు **jankincu** *v.t.* to frighten, intimidate.

జంకు **janku** I. 1 *n.* fear. 2 hesitation. 3 shrinking. II. *v.i.* 1 to fear, be afraid. 2 to hesitate, shrink; **wenakki~** to shrink back. 3 to shake, tremble. 4 (of a wall) to be shaky, totter.

జంగం **jangam** *n.* 1 name of a Saivite sect of wandering people. 2 **guDipuuDi jangaalu** a stock phrase used of persons who habitually make plans but fail to carry them out. it derives from the story of the Jangams of Gudipudi, who would assemble together in the evenings and plan to build a house for their mother, but never did so because next day each would go away on his own business.

జంగమ, జంగమాత్మక **jangama, jangamaatmaka** *adj.* movable, mobile.

జంగమం **jangamam** *n.* 1. movable object. 2. living and moving creature.

జంగమదేవర, జంగమయ్య **jangamadeewara, jangamayya** *n.* member of the Jangam sect.

జంగిలి **jangili** *n.* herd of cattle.

జంగుపిల్లి **jangupilli** *n.* kind of wild cat.

జంఘ **jangha** *n.* calf of the leg.

జంజాటం, జంఝాటం **janjaaTam, janjhaaTam** *n.* worry, trouble, annoyance, esp. due to preoccupation with o.'s family affairs.

జంజెరం **janjeram** *n.* sacred thread worn by members of the weavers' community.

జంఝనక జంఝనక **janjhanaka janjhanaka** *onom. n. sug.* sound of beating drums.

జంఝానిలం, ఝంఝానిలం **janjhaanilam, jhanjhaanilam** *n.* strong wind.

జంట **jaNTa** I. *n.* pair, couple. II. *adj.* twin, joint; **~nagaraalu** twin cities (of Hyderabad and Secunderabad); **~padam** compound word.

జంటగా **jaNTagaa** *adv.* along with.

జండా **jaNDaa** *same as* **jeNDaa.**

జంతికలు **jantikalu** *n.pl.* kind of crisp savoury made of rice flour fried in oil.

జంతుకృషి **jantukṛSi** *n.* animal husbandry.

జంతుజాలం **jantujaalam** *n.* fauna.

జంతుప్రదర్శనశాల **jantupradarśanaśaala** *n.* zoological gardens, zoo.

జంతుమాంసకృత్తులు **jantumaamsakṛttulu** *n.pl.* animal proteins.

జంతువు **jantuwu** *n.* 1 animal, beast. 2 chessman.

జంతుశాస్త్రం **jantuśaastram** *n.* zoology.

జంతుసముదాయం **jantusamudaayam** *n.* fauna.

జంత్రం **jantram** *n.* machine, instrument.

జంత్రగాత్ర సంగీతం **jantragaatra sangiitam** *n.* instrumental and vocal music

జంత్రవాద్యం **jantrawaadyam** *n.* musical instrument.

జంత్రి **jantri** *n.* 1 almanac. 2 *colloq.* **bhoojanaaniki pilistee mottam jantri weesukoni waccEEDu** when I invited him to dinner he came with his whole household.

జందెం, జంధ్యం **jandem, jandhyam** *n.* sacred thread worn by brahmans.

జంపకానా, జంబుఖానా **jampakaanaa, jambukhaanaa** *n.* carpet.

జంపాల **jampaala** *n.* lullaby, cradle song.

జంపాలలు **jampaalalu** *echo word*; **uyyaala~uugincu** to swing or rock a cradle.

జంపు **jampu** *n.* long gold ornament linking earring to plaited hair.

జంబీరం **jambiiram** *n. class.* lime tree.

జంబుకం **jambukam** *n.* jackal.

జంబూద్వీపం **jambuudwiipam** *n. class.* poetical name for the central division of the world which contains India.

జంభాలు **jambhaalu** *n.pl.* boasting, bragging.

జక్కవ **jakkawa** *n.* brahminy duck.

జక్కించు **jakkincu** *v.i.* to be penitent.

జక్కిణి **jakkiNi** *n.* kind of wild dance.

జక్కులవాళ్లు **jakkulawaaLLu** *n.* members of a hill tribe who worship Kameswari and claim descent from Yakshas.

జగం, జగత్తు, జగతి **jagam, jagattu, jagati** *n.* 1 the world, the earth. 2 *colloq.* people in general; **jagam ẹem anukoNTundi?** what will people think?

జగజెట్టి **jagajeTTi** *n.* great or famous wrestler.

జగడం **jagaDam** *n.* dispute, quarrel, fight, affray.

జగడగొండి, జగడాలమారి **jagaDagoNDi, jagaDaalamaari** *n.* quarrelsome person.

జగడమాడు **jagaDamaaDu** *v.i.* to fight, quarrel.

జగదేక **jagadeeka** *adj.* greatest in the world; **~sundari** most beautiful woman in the world.

జగ్గుమను **jaggumanu** *v.i.* (of eyes) to dazzle, be dazzlingly bright.

జఘనం **jaghanam** *n.* hips, loins.

జజ్జు **jajju** *adj.* 1 mild, timid. 2 (of soil) soft, loose. 3 (of cloth) ragged, torn.

జట **jaTa** *n. class.* caked or matted hair.

జటాజూట **jaTaajuuTa** *n. class.* mass of caked or matted hair.

జటామాంసి **jaTaamaamsi** *n.* Indian spikenard.

జటాధారి **jaTaadhaari** *n.* hermit (*lit.* person with matted hair).

జటిల **jaTila** *adj.* 1 complicated, complex, hard to understand. 2 twisted.

జట్కా **jaTkaa** *n.* jutka, small horse-drawn conveyance.

జట్టిమిడత **jaTTimiData** *n.* locust.

జట్టీ **jaTTii** *n.* 1 fight, quarrel. 2 contract whereby money is paid in advance for the supply of goods or produce.

జట్టు **jaTTu** *n.* 1 team. 2 group, gang. 3 friendship; **naa~ uNTaawaa?** will you be my friend?

జట్టుకట్టు,జట్టుకూడు **jaTTukaTTu, jaTTukuuDu** *v.i.* to become friendly, make friends (**-too**, with).

జఠరం **jaTharam** *n. class.* 1 stomach, belly, abdomen. 2 womb.

జఠర రసం **jaThara rasam** *n.* gastric juice.

జఠరాగ్ని **jaTharaagni** *n.* pangs of hunger.

జఠరిక **jaTharika** *n. zool.* ventricle.

జడ **jaDa**[1] *n.* 1 plaited or braided hair. 2 matted hair.

జడ **jaDa**[2] *adj.* 1 inanimate, immobile, motionless. 2 insensible, inert. 3 dull, stupid.

జడకుచ్చులు **jaDakucculu** *n.* tassel attached to the end of a girl's plait.

జడకుప్పె **jaDa kuppe** *n.* bell-shaped ornament attached to plaited hair.

జడత **jaData** *n.* 1 immobility. 2 insensibility, inertness.

జడత్వం **jaDatwam** *n.* 1 immobility. 2 inertness, insensibility. 3 *phys.* inertia.

జడదారి **jaDadaari** *n.* hermit, ascetic (*lit.* person with matted hair).

జడపదార్థం **jaDapadaartham** *n.* inanimate object.

జడప్రాయం **jaDapraayam** *adj.* inert, paralysed.

జడబిళ్ల **jaDabiLLa** *n.* ornament worn in plaited hair.

జడభరతుడు **jaDabharatuDu** *n.* 1 idiot. 2 name of a sage who appeared to act like an idiot.

జడముడి **jaDamuDi** *n.* knot of braided hair.

జడవేసుకొను **jaDaweesukonu** *v.i.* to plait o.'s hair.

జడి **jaDi** *n.* 1 flood, stream, torrent (of rain, tears, words) 2 (*also* **~waana**) downpour, steady continuous rain.

జడిపించు **jaDipincu** *v.t.* to frighten, alarm, startle, intimidate.

జడియు **jaDiyu** *v.i.* to fear, be frightened, be afraid; **waanaku jaDisi bayaTaku weLLaleedu** he did not go out because he was afraid of the rain.

జడుడు **jaDuDu** *n.* stupid person, idiot.

జడుపు **jaDupu** *n.* fear, fright.

జడ్డక్షరం **jaDDakSaram** *n.* double or geminate consonant.

జడ్డి **jaDDI** *adj.* 1 stupid, obstinate. 2 dumb.

జడ్డిగం **jaDDigam** *n.* funnel of a drill plough (**wedagorru**) through which the seed is poured and distributed to the furrows.

జడ్డు **jaDDu** *adj.* dull, sluggish, lazy, inactive.

జత **jata** *n.* 1 pair. 2 fellow, mate, match.

జతకట్టు **jatakaTTu** *v.i. and t.* 1 to make a pair. 2 to make friends; **naatoo jata kaTTEEDu** he made friends with me.

జతకూర్చు **jatakuurcu** *v.i. and t.* 1 to arrange a match. 2 to attach, join.

జతచేయు **jataceeyu** *v.t.* 1 to combine. 2 to attach. 3 to enclose (in a letter).

జతపడు **jatapaDu** *v.i.* 1 to suit, be suitable. 2 to be got, be obtained, be found; **aayana miiku ekkaDaynaa jatapaDitee, neenu aDigEEnani ceppaNDi** if you come across him anywhere, tell him I asked. 3 to come together, materialise, eventuate; **neenu weLLina pani jatapaDaleedu** the purpose for which I went did not materialise.

జతపరచు **jataparacu** *v.t.* 1 to attach, enclose (in a letter). 2 to put together, join, connect. 3 to arrange to produce; **waccee soomawaaram loopala Dabbu jataparacaali** you must arrange to produce the money by next Monday.

జతి **jati** *n.* accompaniment in harmony with a singer's voice.

జత్రువు **jatruwu** *n. class.* collarbone.

జనం **janam** *n.pl.* people, folk.

జనక **janaka** *adj. second part of a compound meaning* creating, producing, e.g., **santooSa~** producing happiness.

జనకత **janakata** *n.* producing, engendering.

జనకుడు **janakuDu** *n.* 1 father. 2 name of the father of Sita.

జనగణమన **janagaNamana** opening words of the Indian national anthem, composed by Rabindranath Tagore.

జనత **janata** I. *n.* people, folk. II. *adj.* people's, popular.

జననం **jananam** *n.* 1 birth. 2 origin.

జననవిద్య **jananawidya** *n.* (science of) genetics.

జననావయవ,జననేంద్రియ **jananaawayawa, jananeendriya** *adj.* genital.

జనని,జనయిత్రి **janani, janayitri** *n.* mother.

జననేంద్రియాలు, జననావయవాలు **jananeendriyaalu, jananaawayawaalu** *n.pl.* sex organs, reproductive organs, genitals.

జనప **janapa** I. *genitive case of* **janum.** II. *adj.* made of jute.

జనపతి **janapati** *n.* king.

జనపదం **janapadam** *n.* rural area, countryside.

జనపనార **janapanaara** *n.* hemp, jute fibre.

జనప్రవాదం, జనశ్రుతి **janaprawaadam, janasrti** *n.* common saying, rumour.

జనప్రియ, జనరంజక **janapriya, janaranjaka** *adj.* popular, liked by the people.

జనబాహుళ్యం **janabaahuLyam** *n.* 1 crowd or throng of people. 2 the masses, the general public.

జనసంఖ్య **janasankhya** *n.* population.

జనసంచారం **janasancaaram** *n.* movement of people; **eNDalaki wiidhulloo~leedu** these is no movement of people in the streets because of the hot sun.

జనసందోహం **janasandooham** *n.* 1 the masses, the general public. 2 crowd, multitude.

జనసమర్దం **janasamardam** *n.* crowd or throng of people.

జనసాంఖ్యకశాస్త్రం **janasaankhyakaśaastram** *n.* demography.

జనసాంద్రత **janasaandrata** *n.* density of population.
జనసాంద్రతగల **janasaandratagala** *adj.* populous, thickly populated.
జనసామాన్యం **janasaamaanyam** *n.* ordinary people, the public, the populace.
జనాంతికంగా **janaantikangaa** *adv.* aside (*stage direction, indicating words spoken by an actor to the audience not intended to be heard by other actors*).
జనానీకం **janaaniikam** *n.* the people, the populace.
జనాభా **janaabhaa** *n.* population.
జనాభా లెక్కలు **janaabhaa lekkalu** *n.pl.* census.
జనావాసం **janaawaasam** *n.* inhabited place, populated place.
జని **jani** *n.* birth, production.
జనించు **janincu** *v.i.* **1** to be born. **2** to be produced. **3**(of a river) to rise. **4** (of a thought) to occur.
జనిత **janita** *adj., second part of a compound meaning* born of, produced by, e.g., **ajñaana~** born of ignorance.
జనుం **janum** *n.* **1** jute. **2** sunhemp used for green manure.
జనుడు **januDu** *n.* man.
జనులు **janulu** *n.pl.* people, persons.
జన్నం **jannam** *n.* Vedic sacrificial ritual (= **yajñam**).
జన్మ[ం] **janma[m]** *n.* **1** birth, rebirth. **2** origin. **3** life, o.'s life span; **naa janmaloo neenu inta waana cuuDaleedu** I have not seen so much rain in all my life.
జన్మం ఎత్తు **janmam ettu** *v.i.* to undergo incarnation, be born.
జన్మజ **janmaja** *adj.* congenital.
జన్మతః **janmatah** *adv.* by virtue of birth.
జన్మదినం **janmadinam** *n.* birthday.
జన్మపత్రిక **janmapatrika** *n.* horoscope.
జన్మభూమి **janmabhuumi** *n.* native country, country of birth.
జన్మసార్థక్యం **janmasaarthakyam** *n.* self-fulfilment.
జన్మసార్థక్యం అవు **janma saarthakyam awu** *v.i.* to fulfil (o.'s) life purpose, justify (o.'s) existence.
జన్మాంతర **janmaantara** *adj.* postnatal.
జన్మాష్టమి **janmaaSTami** *n.* festival of the birth of Krishna celebrated in the month of Sravana.
జన్మించు **janmincu** *v.i.* to be born.
జన్యం **janyam** *second part of an adjvl. compound meaning* derived from, originating from, e.g., **samskṛta ~ayna bhaaSa** a language derived from Sanskrit.
జన్యుశాస్త్రం **janyuśaastram** *n.* (science of) genetics.
జన్యువు **janyuwu** *n.biol.* gene.
జపం **japam** *n.* **1** prayer. **2** repetition of charms. **3** repetition (in general).
జపతపాలు **japatapaalu** *n.pl.* prayers and penance.
జపించు **japincu** *v.i.* **1** to mutter prayer or incantations. **2 waaDi cewiloo japistunnaaDu** he is repeatedly urging him.
జప్తీ, జప్తు **japtii, japtu** *n.* attachment (of property).
జప్తీ చేయు **japtii ceeyu** *v.t.* to attach, confiscate.
జబర్దస్తీ **jabardastii** I. *n.* **1** force, violence, compulsion. **2** right, authority; **eemiTi nii~? naa isTam waccinaTTu ceestaanu** what authority have you over me? I will do as I like. II. *adj.* physically strong, well built.
జబ్బ, జెబ్బ **jabba, jebba** *n.* upper arm.
జబ్బ బలం, జబ్బ పుష్టి, జబ్బ సత్తువ **jabba balam, jabba puSTi, jabba sattuwa** *n.* **1** physical strength. **2** brute force.
జబ్బు **jabbu** I. *n.* disease, illness, sickness, ailment. II. *adj.* ill, sick, ailing.
జబ్బు చేయు **jabbu ceeyu** *v.i. with dative* to be[come] ill; **adi tiNTee niiku jabbu ceestundi** if you eat that, you will become ill.
జబ్బుపడు **jabbupaDu** *v.i.* to become ill, fall sick.
జమ, జమా **jama, jamaa** *n.* collection, receipt, crediting (of money); **waaDimundu nii lekkeemiTi, jameemiTi?** what is your value when compared to him?
జమకట్టు **jamakaTTu** *v.t.* **1** to credit (to an account). **2** to reckon, count. **3** to take account of, take into account.
జమఖర్చులు **jamakharculu** *n.pl.* receipts and disbursements, income and expenditure.
జమపడు **jamapaDu** *v.i.* (of money) to be accounted or credited.
జమవేసుకొను **jamaweesukonu** *v.t.* to reckon, count.
జమాచేయు **jamaaceeyu** *v.t.* to collect, amass, make a collection of; **sTaampulu jamaa ceestunnaaDu** he collects stamps.
జమాజెట్టీ **jamaajeTTii** *n.* strong and well built person.
జమానతు **jamaanatu** *n.* security, bail.
జమాను **jamaanu** *same as* **jawaanu.**
జమాబంది **jamaabandi** *n. admin.* annual settlement of revenue accounts of a village.
జమాయించు **jamaayincu** *v.t.* **1** to put together, join. **2** to shake things into place (e.g., a pack of cards).
జమిలి **jamili** I. *n.* (*also* **jamulu**) pair, couple. II. *adj.* **1** joined, coupled together, intertwined. **2** jumbled, mixed up, confused: **~ pani** jumbled work: **~ maaTalu** stammering words.
జమిలించు **jamilincu** *v.t.* to combine together.
జమిలిదారం **jamilidaaram** *n.* coarse thread made of two strands intertwined.
జమీ **jamii** *n.* landholder's estate.
జమీందారి **jamiindaari** *n.* Zamindari, landed estate held by a Zamindar under a system now abolished.
జమీందారు **jamiindaaru** *n.* Zamindar, proprietor of a landed estate.
జముకులు **jamukulu** *n. pl.* kind of drums.
జముకులోళ్లు **jamukulooLLu** *n.pl.* ballad singers, story tellers.
జముడు **jamuDu** *same as* **yamuDu.**
జములు **jamulu** *same as* **jamili** *sense I.*

జమేదారు **jameedaaru** *n.* Jamadar, title of a rank in the army below that of Subadar.

జమ్మి **jammi** *n. acacia suma* or *prosopis spicigera*, a plant whose leaves are used in a religious ceremony on Vijyadasami day.

జమ్మున **jammuna** *adv. dial.* quickly.

జయ **jaya** *n.* name of the twenty-eighth year of the Hindu cycle of sixty years.

జయం **jayam** *n.* victory, triumph, success.

జయంతి **jayanti** *n.* birth anniversary, birthday.

జయప్రద **jayaprada** *adj.* successful.

జయభేరి **jayabheeri** *n.* victory drum, drum sounded to announce victory.

జయించు **jayincu** I. *v.i.* to succeed, win, be victorious. II. *v.t.* to conquer, defeat, overcome.

జర **jara** *n.* old age, senility, decrepitude.

జరజరా **jarajaraa** I. *adv. dial.* quickly. II. *onom. adv. expressive of* sound of dragging or of a snake crawling.

జరఠ **jaraTha** *adj.* old, decayed, infirm.

జరాభారం **jaraabhaaram** *n.* burden of old age.

జరాయువు **jaraayuwu** *n. sci.* 1 placenta. 2 afterbirth.

జరి, జరీ **jari, jarii** *n.* gold or silver thread used to weave an ornamental border for a sari or dhoti; **~ ancu** a border so woven.

జరిపించు **jaripincu** *v.t.* 1 to carry out, perform, conduct. 2 to celebrate (wedding). 3 to bring about, cause to happen.

జరిమానా, జుల్మానా **jarimaanaa, julmaanaa** *n.* fine, penalty.

జరుగు **jarugu** *v.i.* 1 to slip, slide. 2 to move aside, make room. 3 to move, shift; **kaLingapu sarihaddu raajakiiya kaaraNaala walla ilaa ~ tuu waccindi** the boundary of Kalinga was continuously shifting in this way for political reasons. 4 (of time) to pass, elapse, expire. 5 to happen, occur. 6 to take place, be performed, be carried out, (of a festival) be celebrated. 7 to go on, continue, proceed: **keesu ~ tunnadi** the case is going on. 8 *impersonal use, gen. in neg. constr.* to subsist, be maintained, be afforded; **naaku illu jaragaDam leedu** I cannot maintain my household; **kaDupu jaragaka ii panilooki digEEnu** being unable to subsist I entered upon this work; **pustakaalu modalayna saradaaleewii daaniki leewu, iSTam leekanoo, jarakkanoo sundaraaniki teliidu** she had no books or such other amusments, whether because she did not want them or because she could not afford them, Sundaram did not know.

జరుగుబడి, జరుగుబాటు **jarugubaDi, jarugubaaTu** *n.* living, subsistence, livelihood; **waaDiki udyoogam tappitee weeree ~ leedu** apart from his job he has no other means of livelihood.

జరుగురు **jaruguru** *adj. colloq.* 1 urgently needed. 2 important.

జరుపు **jarupu** *v.t.* 1 to push, move; **balla munduku jaripi kuurcoo** push the table forwards and sit down. 2 to conduct (meeting), perform, celebrate (festival). 3 to spend, pass (time); **appuDu ippuDu ani cebutuu kaalam ~ tuu waccEEDu** he went on prolonging the time by making vague promises; *see* **amalu ~**.

జరూరు **jaruuru** *adj.* urgent.

జర్రున **jarruna** *adv.* quickly, suddenly; **~ jaari paDDaaDu** he slipped and fell suddenly.

జల, జెల **jala, jela** *n.* spring of water (in a well or stream); **baawiloo manci niiLLa ~ paDindi** a spring of good drinking water was struck in the well.

జలం **jalam** *n. class.* water.

జలకం **jalakam** 1 bath, bathing. 2 water for bathing.

జలకడుగు **jalakaDugu** *v.t. colloq.* to squander; **waaDu unna aastantaa ~ tunnaaDu** he is squandering all his property.

జలకమాడు, జలకాలాడు **jalakamaaDu, jalakaalaaDu** *v.i.* to bathe.

జలకాలాట **jalakaalaaTa** *n.* bathing (in river, canal, lake or sea).

జలగ **jalaga** *n.* leech.

జలగవ్యాధి **jalaga wyaadhi** *n.* wasting disease of cattle.

జలచర **jalacara** *adj. sci.* aquatic.

జలచరం **jalacaram** *n.* aquatic creature.

జలజ **jalaja** *n. class.* lotus.

జలజంత్రం **jalajantram** *n.* 1 fountain. 2 *colloq.* **illantaa ~ ayindi** the entire house was dripping with water.

జలజల **jalajala** *onom. adv. suggesting* sound of water dripping.

జలదరించు **jaladarincu** *v.i.* 1 to shudder, tremble, shiver. 2 to tingle with fear.

జలదారి **jaladaari** *n.* drain, gutter, gully, water course.

జలధరం **jaladharam** *n. class.* cloud.

జలధి **jaladhi** *n. class.* ocean.

జలనిధి **jalanidhi** *n. class.* sea, ocean.

జలపాతం **jalapaatam** *n.* waterfall.

జలప్రళయం **jalapraLayam** *n.* deluge.

జలప్రవేశం **jalapraweeśam** *n.* launching (of a ship).

జలమ **jalama** *corrupt form of* **janma.**

జలమయం **jalamayam** *n.* flood, inundation.

జలమార్గం **jalamaargam** *n.* waterway.

జలరాశి **jalaraaśi** *n.* sea.

జలవిద్యుత్తు **jalawidyuttu** *adj.* hydroelectric.

జలవిశ్లేషణ **jalawiśleeSaNa** *n. sci.* hydrolysis.

జలశాస్త్రం **jalaśaastram** *n. sci.* hydrology.

జలస్తంభనం **jalastambhanam** *n.* the art (acquired by magic) of surviving during prolonged submersion under water.

జలాంతర్గామి **jalaantargaami** *n.* submarine.

జలాధారం **jalaadhaaram** *n.* water source, source of irrigation.

జలాశయం **jalaaśayam** *n.* reservoir.

జలుబు **jalubu** *n.* cold, catarrh; **naaku ~ paTTindi** or **naaku ~ ceeSindi** I have a cold; *cf.* **maniSi** *sense 1.*

జలూక **jaluuka** *n.* leech.

జలోదరం **jaloodaram** *n. class.* dropsy.

జల్తారు **jaltaaru** *n.* gold or silver lace woven as the border or hem of a garment, gen. of foreign manufacture.

జల్దుకొను **jaldukonu** *v.i.* to bestir o.s., rouse o.s.

జల్ల **jalla** *n.* **1** long basket placed on a cart for holding materials transported. **2** large basket for storing or transporting grain, etc. **3** kind of fish. **4** *dial.* blow on the cheek.

జల్లి, జల్లీ **jalli, jallii** *n.* mesh, gauze, tracery.

జల్లించు **jallincu** *v.t.* to sift, sieve.

జల్లిగంటె, జల్లిగరిటె **jalligaNTe, jalligariTe** *n.* perforated ladle.

జల్లిబుట్ట **jallibuTTa** *n.* loosely woven basket, sometimes used for muzzling cattle.

జల్లిమూకుడు **jalli muukuDu** *n.* perforated bowl, strainer.

జల్లు **jallu** I. *n.* **1** shower, drizzle. **2** sprinkling, spraying, scattering. II. *v.i. dial.* (of disease) to spread; **waanalu kurisEEka uurantaa kalaraa jallindi** after the rains cholera spread through the entire village. III. *v.t.* to sprinkle, spray, scatter.

జల్లుమను, ఝల్లుమను **jallumanu, jhallumanu** *v.i.* to shudder, feel a shock; **aayana guNDelu jallumannaayi** he (*lit.* his heart) felt a shock.

జల్లెడ **jalleDa** *n.* sieve.

జల్లెడపట్టు **jalleDa paTTu** *v.t.* **1** to sift, sieve. **2** *colloq.* to abuse, rebuke, scold.

జల్లెడ పోయు **jalleDa pooyu** *v.t.* to sift, sieve.

జల్సా **jalsaa** *n.* enjoyment, merriment, pleasure, lightheartedness.

జల్సాగా **jalsaagaa** *adv.* **1** lightheartedly. **2** frivolously.

జళిపించు **jaLipincu** *same as* **jhaLipincu.**

జళిపింపు **jaLipimpu** *n.* brandishing.

జవ **jawa** *n.* **1** strength. **2** youth. **3** speed.

జవజవ **jawajawa** *adv.* quivering, trembling.

జవజవలాడు **jawajawalaaDu** *v.i.* to quiver.

జవదాటు **jawadaaTu** *v.t.* to transgress, disobey, defy.

జవనిక **jawanika** *n.* screen, curtain.

జవరాలు **jawaraalu** *n.* young woman.

జవళి, జౌళి **jawaLi, jawLi** *n.* **1** cloth or drapery kept for sale, textiles. **2** ~**neeta ciire** sari made of coarse cloth.

జవళిదుకాణం **jawaLi dukaaNam** *n.* cloth shop.

జవళిపరిశ్రమ **jawaLi pariśrama** *n.* textile industry.

జవసత్త్వాలు **jawasatwaalu** *n. pl.* youthful vigour.

జవాది **jawaadi** *n.* civet.

జవాను, జమాను **jawaanu, jamaanu** *n.* **1** soldier. **2** constable. **3** peon, messenger. **4** **poosTu**~ postman.

జవాబు **jawaabu** *n.* answer, reply.

జవాబుగా **jawaabugaa** *adv.* **1** in answer to, in reply to. **2** corresponding to; **meeDamiidi waraNDaaki~ kindani anta weDalpugaanu waraNDaa undi** corresponding to the upstair veranda there is a veranda downstairs of the same width.

జవాబుదారీ **jawaabudaarii** *n.* responsibility, accountability.

జవాబుదారుడు **jawaabudaaruDu** *n.* responsible person.

జవాహిరీ **jawaahirii** *n.* valuables.

జవుకు **jawuku** *v.i.* to be shaky, be loose, totter.

జవురు **jawuru** *v.i. and t.* to sweep into a heap, collect (things) together by sweeping.

జవురుకొను **jawurukonu** *v.i. and t. colloq., used contemptuously* to collect for o.s., lay hands on; **ceetiki andinantawaraku jawurukoni wenakki waccEEDu** he returned after laying hands on everything within his reach.

జవ్వనం **jawwanam** *n.* youth[fulness].

జవ్వని **jawwani** *n.* girl, maiden.

జా - jaa

జాకెటు, జాకెట్టు **jaakeTu, jaakeTTu** *n.* blouse.

జాకెటుగుడ్డ, జాకెటుముక్క **jaakeTu guDDa, jaakeTu mukka** *n.* blouse piece, piece of cloth for making a blouse.

జాగరం, జాగరణం, జాగారం **jaagaram, jaagaraNam, jaagaaram** *n.* **1** waking, watching, staying awake all night. **2** vigil, staying awake as part of a religious duty. **3** **śawa**~ vigil beside a dead body.

జాగరితం **jaagaritam** *n.* awakening.

జాగరితంచేయు **jaagaritam ceeyu** *v.t.* to awaken.

జాగరూకత **jaagaruukata** *n.* **1** wakefulness, watchfulness, wariness, vigilance. **2** care, caution.

జాగరూకుడు **jaagaruukuDu** *n.* cautious, wary or vigilant person.

జాగా **jaagaa** *n.* **1** place, locality, spot; **ii ~loo** on this spot. **2** space, (vacant) room; **peTTeloo kuurcooDaaniki~ leedu** there is no room to sit down in the compartment.

జాగారం **jaagaaram** *same as* **jaagaram.**

జాగారంచేయు **jaagaaramceeyu** *v.i.* to stay awake all night.

జాగిలం **jaagilam** *n.* hound.

జాగిలపడు **jaagilapaDu** *same as* **saagilapaDu.**

జాగీర్ **jaagiir** *n.* Jagir, landed estate held on feudal tenure under a system now abolished.

జాగీర్దార్ **jaagiirdaar** *n.* Jagirdar, proprietor of a Jagir (originally a feudal chief owing allegiance to a Muslim overlord.)

జాగు **jaagu** *n.* delay.

జాగుచేయు **jaagu ceeyu** *v.i.* to delay.

జాగుమేళం **jaagumeeLam** *n. colloq.* person who is regularly slow in doing things, procrastinator.

జాగృతం **jaagṛtam** *adj.* aroused, awakened.

జాగృతి **jaagṛti** *n.* awakening.

జాగ్రత, జాగ్రత్త **jaagrat[t]a** *n.* 1 care[fulness], caution, wariness, vigilance. 2 *pl.* ~**lu** precautions.

జాగ్రత్తగా **jaagrattagaa** *adv.* carefully, cautiously, attentively.

జాగ్రత్తచేయు **jaagrattaceeyu** *v.t.* to preserve, keep carefully.

జాగ్రత్తపడు **jaagrattapaDu** *v.i.* to be careful, take care, take precautions, be on o.'s guard, be wary.

జాగ్రత్తపరుడు **jaagrattaparuDu** *n.* cautious person.

జాగ్రత్తపెట్టు **jaagrattapeTTu** *v.t.* to preserve carefully, protect.

జాగ్రత్తవహించు **jaagrattawahincu** *v.i.* to take care, be on o.'s guard, be cautious.

జాగ్రదావస్థ **jaagradaawastha** *n.* state of awareness.

జాజి **jaaji** *n.* dealwood; ~**cekkalapeTTe** dealwood box.

జాజికాయ **jaajikaaya** *n.* nutmeg.

జాజిపువ్వు **jaajipuwwu** *n.* jasmine flower, *jasminum grandiflorum.*

జాజు **jaaju** *n.* iron oxide, (colour of) red ochre.

జాజువారు **jaajuwaaru** *v.i.* to grow red.

జాజ్వల్యమాన **jaajwalyamaana** *adj.* radiant, brilliant, shining brightly.

జాటీ **jaaTi** *n.* whip.

జాడ **jaaDa** *n.* 1 mark, trace. 2 track, clue. 3 **aDugu**~ footprint.

జాడించు, ఝాడించు **j[h]aaDincu** *v.t.* 1 to swing, toss, wave, flap about, shake; **[oTTi] ceetulu**~**koNTuu waccEEDu** he returned with his task unaccomplished (*lit.* he came swinging his arms empty-handed). 2 **niiLLaloo** ~ to rinse (clothes) in water. 3 *colloq.* to rebuke, scold.

జాడీ **jaaDii** *n.* jar.

జాడు **jaaDu** *n.* stalks of cholam and other grains which have not produced heads of corn.

జాడుకట్ట **jaaDukaTTa** *n. dial.* broom.

జాడ్యం **jaaDyam** *n.* 1 disease, illness, sickness. 2 foolishness. 3 sluggishness.

జాణ **jaaNa** I. *n.* clever woman. II. *adj.* 1 clever, shrewd. 2 artful, cunning.

జాణతనం **jaaNatanam** *n.* artfulness, cunning[ness].

జాతకం **jaatakam** *n.* 1 horoscope. 2 *colloq.* history, record; **dongala jaatakaalu pooliisuwaaLLaku telusu** the police know the thieves' record.

జాతకకథలు **jaataka kathalu** *n.pl.* jatakas, legends concerning Buddha in his earlier incarnations.

జాతకర్మం **jaatakarmam** *n. class.* ceremonies performed at the time of a child's birth.

జాతకుడు **jaatakuDu** I. *second part of a n. compound meaning* one who is born, e.g., **kaSTa**~ one who is born to suffer trouble. II. *n.* 1 lucky person. 2 person to whom a horoscope relates; *see* **śubhuDu.**

జాతర **jaatara** *same as* **jaatra.**

జాతి **jaati** I. *n.* 1 kind, sort. 2 class, community, race, breed. 3 tribe. 4 nation. 5 *sci.* species. II. *adj.* high class, superior, highly bred; ~**mutyam** pearl of highest quality; ~**kukka** pedigree dog.

జాతిధర్మాలు **jaati dharmaalu** *n.pl.* duties of a caste or community.

జాతివిధ్వంసం **jaati widhwamśam** *n.* genocide.

జాతివివక్షత **jaati wiwakSata** *n.* communalism.

జాతిహీనుడు **jaatihiinuDu** *n.* person of low caste.

జాతీయ **jaatiiya** *adj.* 1 national; ~**giitam** national anthem. 2 nationalised. 3 belonging to a class or community.

జాతీయం **jaatiiyam** *n.* 1 nationalisation. 2 *ling.* idiom[atic expression].

జాతీయకరణం, జాతీయీకరణం **jaatiiyakaraNam, jaatiiyiikaraNam** *n.* nationalisation.

జాతీయం చేయు **jaatiiyam ceeyu** *v.t.* to nationalise.

జాతీయత, జాతీయవాదం **jaatiiyata, jaatiiyawaadam** *n.* national feeling, nationalism.

జాతీయవాది **jaatiiyawaadi** *n.* nationalist.

జాత్యం **jaatyam** *adj.* 1 well-born, highly born. 2 fine, excellent.

జాత్యంధుడు **jaatyandhuDu** *n.* one who has been blind from birth.

జాత్ర, జాతర **jaatra, jaatara** *n.* folk festival, village festival.

జాన, జేన **jaana, jEEna** *n.* span, a measure of length, about eight inches.

జానకి తాడు **jaanakitaaDu** *n.* piece of smouldering string used for lighting fireworks, etc.

జానపద **jaanapada** *adj.* rural, pertaining to a village; ~**geeyam** folk song; ~**sangiitam** folk music; ~**citram** folklore movie.

జానపదం **jaanapadam** *n.* countryside, rural area.

జానపదులు **jaanapadulu** *n.pl.* villagers, rural folk.

జాని **jaani** *n. class.* 1 old age. 2 woman, wife.

జాను **jaanu** *adj. class.* 1 graceful, beautiful. 2 pure: ~**telugu**; pure (i.e., non-sanskritised) Telugu.

జానుక **jaanuka** *n. med.* fibula.

జానుఫలకం **jaanu phalakam** *n.* knee cap.

జానువు **jaanuwu** *n. class.* knee.

జాపత్రి **jaapatri** *n.* mace (spice).

జాపు **jaapu** *same as* **caapu**[2].

జాప్యం **jaapyam** *n.* delay, loitering.

జాబితా, జాపితా **jaabitaa, jaapitaa** *n.* 1 list, inventory. 2 category.

జాబిల్లి **jaabilli** *n.* moon.

జాబు **jaabu** *n.* letter, epistle.

జామ, జామి **jaama, jaami** *n.* guava fruit.

జామాత **jaamaata** *n.* son-in-law.

జామారు **jaamaaru** *n.* 1 *dial.* pair of dhotis. 2 plain cloth without a coloured border.

జామీను **jaamiinu** *n.* 1 security, surety, 2 bail. 3 *dial.* cultivator's holding of land.

జాము, ఝాము **jaamu, jhaamu** *n.* watch, period of time equal to about three hours; **tellawaaru**~ early hours of the morning; ~**poddekkEEka** at 9 a.m. (i.e., about three hours after sunrise).

జాయ **jaaya** *n.* wife.

జాయమాన **jaayamaana** *adj. class.* (that) which is produced; **nirhetuka~ kaTaakSam** unmerited kindness.

జారజ **jaaraja** *adj.* (of offspring) illegitimate.

జారత్వం **jaaratwam** *n.* adultery.

జారించు **jaarincu** *v.t.* to allow to slip down.

జారిణి **jaariNi** *n.* adulteress, prostitute.

జారీ **jaarii** *n.* pot with a spout; **neeti~** pot for serving ghee.

జారీచేయు **jaariiceeyu** *v.t.* **1** to publish, proclaim, promulgate. **2** to issue (order, licence).

జారు, జారిపోవు **jaaru, jaaripoowu** *v.i.* **1** to slip, slide, glide; **nooru jaari ceppEEnu** *or* **maaTa jaari ceppEEnu** I let slip a word *or* I divulged (s.g) unintentionally; **waaDi guNDe jaaripooyindi** *lit.* his heart slipped down, i.e., his courage failed; *cf.* **kaalu** *sense I. 2.* **2** to subside, come down, decline, be reduced; **jwaram jaarindi** the fever came down *or* the fever subsided; **N. miida waaDikigala abhipraayam marikonta jaarindi** his estimation of N. declined a little further. **3** to run away, slip away, sneak off. **4** to go back (on), resile (from); **tana maaTa miida nilabaDakuNDaa jaaripooyEEDu** without keeping to his word he went back on it. **5** (of time) to elapse, pass slowly. **6** to ooze, be liquid.

జారుడు **jaaruDu** I. *n.* slipperiness. II. *adj.* **1** slippery. **2** liquid, oozing.

జారుడుబండ **jaaruDubaNDa** *n.* children's slide (for play).

జారుముడి **jaarumuDi** *n.* slip knot.

జార్చు **jaarcu** *v.t.* **1** to let slip, let fall; **takkina mukhya pathakaalanu puurtigaa jaarciweeya kuuDadu** you must not drop the other important schemes completely. **2** **jaarci paTTukonu** to hold (s.g) lightly or loosely.

జార్లగిలపడు **jaarlagilapaDu** *v.i.* to sink or fall back (**-ku**, against).

జార్లపడు **jaarlapaDu** *v.i.* to lean back, sink (into a chair).

జాల **jaala** *n.* line or stripe on an animal's body (= **caara**).

జాలం **jaalam**[1] *n.* assemblage, collection; **pada**~vocabulary; **wrkSa~** flora.

జాలం **jaalam**[2] *n. class.* delay, procrastination.

జాలం **jaalam**[3] *second part of a n. compound meaning* magic, conjuring, e.g., **indra~**

జాలకం **jaalakam** *n.* **1** lattice, trellis. **2** netting, gauze.

జాలకకణజాలం **jaalaka kaNajaalam** *n. biol.* reticular tissue.

జాలరి **jaalari** *n.* fisherman.

జాలరు **jaalaru** *n.* netting, mesh.

జాలవిద్య **jaalawidya** *n.* art of conjuring.

జాలారి **jaalaari** *n.* **1** bathroom. **2** trellis.

జాలి **jaali** *n.* **1** pity, compassion (**-pay** *or* **-miida**, on *or* for). **2** sorrow, regret. **3** mercy.

జాలిగా **jaaligaa** *adv.* **1** pitifully, piteously, pathetically. **2** pityingly, sympathetically, with pity or compassion.

జాలి తల్చు **jaali talcu** *v.i. and t.* to feel pity for, feel sorry for, take pity on; **waaNNi jaali talci padi ruupaayalu iccEEnu** I felt sorry for him and gave him ten rupees.

జాలి పడు **jaali paDu** *v.i.* to feel pity (**-pay** *or* **-miida**, for).

జాలీ **jaalii** *n.* **1** trellis[work], lattice[work]. **2** netting, mesh, gauze.

జాలు **jaalu**[1] *n.* stream; ~**kaaluwa** watercourse, hillstream; **wennela~** stream of moonlight.

జాలు **jaalu**[2] *n.* trellis.

జాలు **jaalu**[3] *n.* sciatic pain.

జాలువారు **jaaluwaaru** *v.i.* **1** to flow, stream, pour. **2** to hang, be suspended, dangle.

జావ **jaawa** *n.* porridge or gruel made of boiled broken rice or sago.

జావకారు **jaawakaaru** *v.i.* to become soft, become flabby, lose heart, lose initiative (*lit.* to become as soft as porridge).

జావజావ అవు **jaawajaawa awu** *v.i.* to become very soft, melt, be weakened; **antaloonee koopamantaa kuuDaa jaawajaawagaa bhayamkinda maaripooyindi** suddenly all his anger melted and turned into fear.

జావళీ **jaawaLii** *n.* song with erotic lyrics.

జాస్తి **jaasti** *adj. and adv.* many, much, more.

జి - ji

జింక **jinka** *n.* black buck, *antilope cervicapra.*

జిగజిగ **jigajiga** *onom. adv. sug.* gleaming, e.g., **~ merayu** to gleam, glitter.

జిగట **jigaTa** I. *n.* stickiness. II. *adj.* 1 sticky; **~ mannu** clay; **~ wiroocanaalu** dysentry. 2 gelatinous.

జిగమిష **jigamISa** *n. class.* desire to go.

జిగి **jigi** *n.* 1 brightness. 2 vigour. 3 fertility (of soil).

జిగినీనాను **jiginiinaanu** *n.* kind of jewellery worn round the neck.

జిగీబిగీ **jigiibigii** *adj.* bright and strong.

జిగీష **jigiiSa** *n.* will to win, ambition.

జిగురు **jiguru** I. *n.* 1 gum, paste. 2 stickiness. II. *adj.* sticky; **~ maTTi** clay.

జిగురుతెగులు **jiguru tegulu** *n. bot.* gummosis.

జిగురుపొడి **jigurupoDi** *n.* gum arabic.

జిగేలుమను **jigeelumanu** *v.i.* 1 to flash, gleam, glitter, dazzle. 2 to be dazzled.

జిజ్ఞాస **jijñaasa** *n.* 1 desire for knowledge, curiosity. 2 investigation, research.

జిజ్ఞాసువు **jijñaasuwu** *n.* seeker after knowledge, research worker, scholar.

జిట్రేగు **jiTreegu** *n.* rosewood, *dalberghia latifolia.*

జిడ్డి **jiDDi** *adj.* coarse.

జిడ్డు **jiDDu** *n.* 1 grease, oil, greasiness; **~ paTTina** oily, greasy. 2 trouble, worry; **aayanatoo maaTLaaDaDam aamudamtoo ceyyi kaDukkunanta ~ pani** talking to him is as troublesome as washing your hand in castor oil (an effort doomed to failure).

జిడ్డుకారు, జిడ్డోడు **jiDDukaaru, jiDDooDu** *v.i.* to ooze oil or grease; **~ tunna moham** face dripping with (sweat and) greasiness (due to heat or hard labour).

జితాత్ముడు **jitaatmuDu** *n.* one who has conquered his own self.

జితించు **jitincu** *v.i.* 1 to win, succeed, conquer. 2 to be digested, be instilled, become part of (= **jiirNincu**).

జితుడు **jituDu** *n.* one who is conquered.

జితేంద్రియుడు **jiteendriyuDu** *n.* one who has subdued his passions.

జిత్తు **jittu** *n.* trick, prank.

జిత్తులమారి **jittulamaari** *n.* sly or cunning rogue.

జినుగు **jinugu** *same as* **jilugu.**

జినుడు **jinuDu** *n.* generic name given to the chief saints of the Jain religion.

జిమ్మడ **jimmaDa** *term of abuse* **nannu enni tiTTEEDu! waaDi ~!** how badly he abused me! may he be struck dumb for it! **(waaDi ~! = waaDi jihwa paDa!).**

జిమ్ము **jimmu** *same as* **cimmu.**

జియ్య **jiyya** *n. class.* god, king, lord, master.

జియ్యరు **jiyyaru** *n.* Vaishnavite saint.

జిరాయితి **jiraayiti** *n.* cultivation; **~ hakku** occupancy right; **~ bhuumi** land held by a cultivator.

జిర్రున **jirruna** *adv.* 1 all at once, suddenly. 2 **~ ciideesEEDu** he blew his nose loudly.

జిల **jila** *n.* itch[ing].

జిలజిల **jilajila** *onom. adv. sug.* tingling, tickling.

జిలార్చుకుపోవు **jilaarcukupoowu** *v.i.* to feel a sharp tingling sensation (*used with ref. to the funnybone in the elbow*); **mooceetimiida debba tagilitee praaNam jilaarcukupooyindi** when I was struck on the elbow I felt a sharp tingling sensation.

జిలిబిలి **jilibili** *adj.* 1 sweet, agreable, nice. 2 romantic.

జిలుగు, జినుగు **jilugu, jinugu** *n.* fine embroidered cloth.

జిలుగురాత **jiluguraata** *n.* crabbed handwriting (which is difficult to decipher).

జిలుగువాన **jilugu waana** *n.* continuous drizzling.

జిలేబి **jileebi** *n.* kind of sweet.

జిల్లపురుగు **jillapurugu** *n. dial.* cockroach.

జిల్లా **jillaa** *n.* district, the administrative jurisdiction of a Collector.

జిల్లాపరిషత్ **jillaa pariSat** *n.* Zilla Parishad, the highest tier in local government, having jurisdiction over the non-municipal area of a district.

జిల్లాయి **jillaayi** *n.* kind of excommunication generally practised by children and incurred by a person whose foot or other bodily part is defiled by contact with dirt; **~ annaaru pillalu** the children declared (him) untouchable.

జిల్లుమను **jillumanu** *v.i* to be or feel very cold; **ceyyi niiLLaloo peTTagaanee jillumandi** as soon as I put my hand into the water, it felt very cold.

జిల్లేడు **jilleeDu** *n. calatropis gigantea*, a plant with milky sap.

జిల్లేడుకాయ **jilleeDukaaya** *n.* 1 unripe fruit of *calatropis gigantea.* 2 kind of sweet cake offered to Ganesha on Vinayakachaturthi day.

జివ్వున **jiwwuna** *same as* **ciwwuna.**

జివ్వుమను **jiwwumanu** *v.i.* to be or feel very cold; **caligaaliki bayaTaki raagaanee praaNam jiwwumandi** when I came out into the cold wind I was nearly frozen.

జిహ్వ **jihwa** *n.* tongue; **~ koo ruci, purrekoo buddhi** each tongue has its own taste, each brain has its own opinion (i.e., tastes differ – proverb); *see* **jimmaDa.**

జిహ్వాచాపల్యం **jihwacaapalyam** *n.* inordinate liking for a taste, greediness; **~ (*or* jihwa) campukooleeka antaa tinnaanu** not being able to overcome my greediness, I ate it all.

జీ - jii

జీండ్రం **jiiNDram** *n. class.* miserable state.

జీడి **jiiDi** *n.* **1** kernel of a mango stone. **2** sap of a mango tree (which is sticky and causes a stain).

జీడికాయ, జీడిపండు **jiiDi kaaya, jiiDi paNDu** *n* fruit of the marking nut tree, *semicarpus anacardium.*

జీడిపప్పు **jiiDipappu** *n.* cashewnut.

జీడిమామిడి **jiiDimaamiDi** *n.* a variety of mango.

జీతం **jiitam** *n.* **1** salary, wages, pay. **2** school fees.

జీతగాడు **jiitagaaDu** *n.* **1** servant. **2** field labourer. **3** *colloq.* wage earner; **nelaku weyyi ruupaayala~** person who earns Rs. 1000 per month.

జీతపురాళ్లు **jiitapuraaLLu** *n.pl. colloq.* salary.

జీను **jiinu** *n.* saddle.

జీనువ, జీనువాయి **jiinuwa, jiinuwaayi** *n.* white throated munia or tailor bird.

జీబు **jiibu** *n.* **1** thicket. **2** woman's sari. **3** fibrous sheath surrounding the base of a coconut or palmyra leaf.

జీబుకొను **jiibukonu** *v.i.* to thicken, grow thick.

జీబుగా **jiibugaa** *adv.* thickly, densely.

జీబూతం **jiibuutam** *n. colloq. form of* **jiimuutam**; **~laa unnaaDu** his appearance is untidy and dishevelled.

జీమూతం **jiimuutam** *n.* **1** mountain. **2** cloud.

జీర **jiira**[1] *n.* streak, line, stripe.

జీర **jiira**[2] *n.* hoarseness, harshness, roughness (of voice).

జీరంగి **jiirangi** *n.* green beetle, whose emerald wing cases are fastened on embroidery for adornment.

జీరపోవు **jiirapoowu** *v.i.* (of voice) to be choked with emotion.

జీరాడు **jiiraaDu** *v.i.* to trail on the ground, sweep the ground; **kongu neelaku (*or* neelamiida) ~tunnadi** the end of the sari is sweeping the ground.

జీరు **jiiru** *v.i. class.* to hang down, dangle, trail on the ground.

జీర్ణ **jiirNa** *adj.* **1** digested. **2** tattered, worn. **3** ruined, dilapidated. **4** old, worn out, decrepit.

జీర్ణం **jiirNam** *n.* **1** digestion. **2** becoming old, worn out, ruined or dilapidated.

జీర్ణం అవు **jiirNam awu** *v.i.* **1** to be digested. **2** to be absorbed, be assimilated.

జీర్ణకోశం **jiirNakoośam** *n.* stomach.

జీర్ణక్రియ **jiirNakriya** *n.* (process of) digestion.

జీర్ణమండలం **jiirNamaNDalam** *n.* digestive system.

జీర్ణశూల **jiirNaśuula** *n.* stomach pain, colic.

జీర్ణించు **jiirNincu** *v.i.* **1** to be digested. **2** to be assimilated, be absorbed; **paata paddhatulu paata sampradaayaalu waariloo jiirNincipoowaDamee induku kaaraNam kaawaccu** the reason for this may be that old habits and old traditions had been assimilated by them. **3** to grow old, wear away, be obliterated; **telugu patrikala kaapiilu tiiyincakapootee, aadhunikaandhra caritra racanaku kaawalasina 'orijinal soorses' jiirNincipoogalawu** unless copies of Telugu newspapers are taken, the original sources required for writing modern Andhra history may be obliterated.

జీర్ణించుకొను **jiirNincukonu** *v.t.* **1** to digest. **2** to absorb, assimilate.

జీర్ణోద్ధారణం **jiirNooddhaaraNam** *n.* rebuilding a ruined house or temple.

జీలకర్ర **jiilakarra** *n.* cummin seed.

జీలుగు **jiilugu** *n. sesbania sp.*, its stem is used to make stoppers for bottles, etc.: **~beNDu** pith of the **jiilugu** shrub.

జీవ **jiiwa** *adj., occurring as first part of a compound* living, bio-; **~kaNam** living cell: **~śaastram** biology.

జీవం **jiiwam** *n.* **1** life: **ii bhumimiida ~ ee widhangaa aawirbhawincindoo manam aakaLimpu ceesukoowaccu** we may come to understand how life originated on this earth. **2** vitality; **waaDi mukhamloo ~ leedu** there is no vitality in his face. **3** living being, living creature.

జీవకణం **jiiwakaNam** *n.* living cell.

జీవకణశాస్త్రం **jiiwakaNaśaastram** *n.* cytology.

జీవకళ **jiiwakaLa** *n.* **1** liveliness, vitality. **2** lifelike appearance; **bommalu~uTTipaDutunnaayi** the dolls exhibit a lifelike appearance.

జీవకోటి **jiiwakooTi** *n.* living things (in general).

జీవగర్ర **jiiwagarra** *n.* essential means of support; **wywasaayam bhaarata deeśapu aarthika wyawasthaku~** agriculture is the mainstay of the Indian economy.

జీవచ్ఛవం, జీవన్మృతుడు **jiiwacchawam, jiiwanmr̥tuDu** *n.* living corpse, useless or worthless person.

జీవజాలం **jiiwajaalam** *n.* multitude of living creatures, living things (in general).

జీవద్భాష **jiiwadbhaaSa** *n.* living language.

జీవద్రవ్యం **jiiwadrawyam** *n. sci.* plasma.

జీవనం **jiiwanam** *n.* **1** life, existence. **2** mode of living, livelihood, means of subsistence; **ceppulu kuTTi~ceestunnaaDu** he earns his living (*or* he lives) by making shoes.

జీవనక్రియ **jiiwanakriya** *n. sci.* metabolism.

జీవనది **jiiwanadi** *n.* regularly flowing river, perennial river.

జీవనప్రమాణం, జీవనస్థాయి **jiiwanapramaaNam, jiiwanasthaayi** *n.* standard of living.

జీవనవ్యయం **jiiwanawyayam** *n.* cost of living.

జీవనాడి **jiiwanaaDi** *n.* pulse which gives life or animates.

జీవనోపాధి, జీవనోపాయం **jiiwanoopaadhi, jiiwanoopaayam** *n.* livelihood, means of living.

జీవనౌషధం **jiiwanawSadham** *n.* medicine that revives life.

జీవన్ముక్తి **jiiwanmukti** *n.* final liberation from the present state of life.

జీవన్మృతుడు **jiiwanmrtuDu** *same as* **jiiwacchawam.**

జీవపదార్థం **jiiwapadaartham** *n. sci.* protoplasm.

జీవపరిమాణం **jiiwaparimaaNam** *n.* organic evolution.

జీవభౌతికశాస్త్రం **jiiwabhawtika śaastram** *n.* biophysics.

జీవయాత్ర **jiiwayaatra** *n.* journey through life.

జీవరసాయనశాస్త్రం **jiiwarasaayanaśaastram** *n.* biochemistry.

జీవరాసి **jiiwaraasi** *n.* living things (in general).

జీవశాస్త్రం **jiiwaśaastram** *n.* biology.

జీవాణువు **jiiwaaNuwu** *n. biol.* nucleus of a cell.

జీవాత్మ **jiiwaatma** *n.* human soul.

జీవాధారం **jiiwaadhaaram** *n.* **1** life support. **2** vital organ.

జీవావరణశాస్త్రం **jiiwaawaraNaśaastram** *n.* (science of) ecology.

జీవి **jiiwi** *n.* **1** living thing, living creature, organism. **2** *second part of a compound* one who lives by: **sangha~** social being.

జీవించు **jiiwincu** *v.i.* to live, exist, subsist.

జీవిక **jiiwika** *n.* **1** livelihood. **2** *class.* maintenance.

జీవితం **jiiwitam** *n.* life[time], duration of life, length of life, period of life, life span.

జీవితఖైదు **jiiwita khaydu** *n.* life imprisonment.

జీవితచక్రం **jiiwitacakram** *n. biol.* life cycle.

జీవితచరిత్ర **jiiwitacaritra** *n.* biography.

జీవితబీమా **jiiwitabiimaa** *n.* life insurance.

జీవితయాత్ర **jiiwitayaatra** *n.* life's journey, course of (o.'s) life.

జీవితరంగం **jiiwitarangam** *n.* **1** day to day life. **2** *poet.* arena of life.

జీవితాంతం **jiiwitaantam** *adv.* till the end of (o.'s) life.

జీవితాశంస **jiiwitaaśamsa** *n. sci.* expectation of life.

జీవితేశుడు **jiiwiteeśuDu** *n. class.* husband.

జీవుడు **jiiwuDu** *n.* **1** living being or creature. **2** life (= **praaNam**). **3** human soul.

జు - ju

జుంకీలు, జుంకాలు, జూకాలు **junkiilu, junkaalu, juukaalu** *n.pl.* earrings.

జుంటితేనె **juNTi teene** *n.* kind of honey.

జుగుప్స **jugupsa** *n.* **1** abhorrence, aversion. **2** dislike, reviling.

జుట్టు **juTTu** *n.* hair of the head.

జుట్టుజుట్టుపట్టుకొను **juTTujuTTupaTTukonu** *v.i.* (of two persons) to quarrel with each other.

జుట్టుజుట్టుముడివేయు **juTTujuTTumuDiweeyu** *v.i.* to create a quarrel (between two persons; *lit.* to tie two persons' hair together).

జుట్టుతీయు **juTTutiiyu** *v.i.* to cut the hair, esp. of a widow as a token of widowhood.

జుత్తు **juttu** *dial. form of* **juTTu.**

జుత్తుపోలిగాడు **juttupooligaaDu** *see* **keetigaaDu.**

జునపాలు **junapaalu** *same as* **julapaalu.**

జున్ను **junnu** *n.* kind of cheese.

జున్నుపాలు **junnupaalu** *n.* biestings, milk of a cow or buffalo that has recently calved.

జుబ్బా **jubbaa** *n.* shirt with no collar.

జుమలా **jumalaa** I. *n. dial.* total. II. *adv. dial.* jointly, together.

జుమాయించు, ఝుమాయించు **jumaayincu, jhumaayincu** *v.t.* to hold tightly.

జుమ్మను **jummanu** *v.i.* to hum.

జుమ్ము **jummu** *n.* humming sound.

జుర్రు, జూరు **jurru, juuru** *v.t.* **1** to drink with a slurping sound. **2** *fig.* to drink in, absorb, enjoy.

జులపాలు, జునపాలు **julapaalu, junapaalu** *n. pl.* curly hair.

జులపాలు తిరుగు **julapaalu tirugu** *v.i.* (of hair) to be curly.

జులాయి **julaayi** *n.* loafer.

జులుం **julum** *n.* **1** force, violence. **2** oppression.

జుల్మానా **julmaanaa** *n.* fine, penalty.

జువ్వ **juwwa** *same as* **cuwwa.**

జువ్వి **juwwi** *n.* kind of fig tree, *ficus tisela.*

జువ్వున **juwwuna** *adv.* quickly.

జూ, జృ - juu, jṛ

జూకాలు **juukaalu** *same as* **junkaalu.**
జూటం **juuTam** *n. class.* matted hair of Siva or of an ascetic.
జూదం **juudam** *n.* gambling, a gamble.
జూదం ఆడు **juudam aaDu** *v.i.* to gamble.
జూదకాడు, జూదరి **juudakaaDu, juudari** *n.* gambler.
జూరు **juuru** *same as* **jurru.**
జూలు **juulu**[1] *n.* mane (of horse or lion).
జూలు **juulu**[2] *n.* cloth to cover a horse's back.
జృంభణం **jṛmbhaNam** *n. class.* 1 yawning, stretching the limbs. 2 opening, expansion, spreading.
జృంభించు **jṛmbhincu** *v.i. class.* 1 to yawn. 2 to spread, expand.
జృంభితం **jṛmbhitam** *n. class.* yawn.

జె - je

జెండా, జండా **jeNDaa, jaNDaa** *n.* flag, banner.
జెండాకొయ్య **jeNDaakoyya** *n.* flagstaff.
జెట్టి **jeTTi** *n.* 1 wrestler. 2 hero, champion.
జెబ్బ **jebba** *same as* **jabba.**
జెమాజెట్టి **jemaajeTTi** *same as* **jamaajeTTii.**
జెముడు **jemuDu** *n.* bush or plant of the cactus family.
జెముడుకాకి **jemuDukaaki** *n.* crow pheasant, *centropus sinensis.*
జెర్రి **jerri** *n.* centipede.
జెర్రిపోతు **jerripootu** *n.* 1 centipede. 2 kind of snake.
జెల **jela** *same as* **jala.**
జెల్ల **jella**[1] *n.* kind of fish.
జెల్ల **jella**[2] *n. dial.* blow with the knuckles struck on the back of the head.
జెల్లా **jellaa** *echo word; see* **pillaa ~**.
జెష్ట **jeSTa** *n.* 1 plague, pest, evil. 2 goddess of misfortune. 3 whitlow.

జే, జై - jee, jay

జేగంట **jeegaNTa** *n.* bell, gong.
జేగీయమానం **jeegiiyamaanam** *adj.* splendid, magnificent, spectacular.
జేగురించు **jeegurincu** *same as* **jeewurincu.**
జేగురు **jeeguru** *n.* 1 red ochre, iron oxide. 2 reddish brown colour.
జేజె **jeeje** *n.* 1 *child language* god, goddess. 2 *dial.* grandfather.
జేజెమ్మ **jeejemma** *n.* 1 goddess. 2 oldest woman member of a family. 3 grandmother; **nii ~ waccinaa neenu Dabbu iwwanu** I will not give you money on any account (*lit.* even if your grandmother comes, I will not give you money).
జేజేలు **jeejeelu** *n. pl.* hurrahs, salutations.
జేత **jeeta** *n. class.* conqueror, victor.
జేన **jEEna** *same as* **jaana.**
జేబు **jeebu** *n.* pocket; **~ koTTu** to pick s.o.'s pocket.
జేబుగుడ్డ **jeebuguDDa** *n.* pocket handkerchief.
జేబుదొంగ **jeebudonga** *n.* pickpocket.
జేవురించు, జేగురించు **jeewurincu, jeegurincu** *v.i.* to grow red, redden, flush.
జేష్టం, జ్యేష్ఠం **jeeSTam, jyeeSTham** *n.* third Telugu lunar month corresponding to June-July.
జైత్ర **jaytra** *adj.* victorious, triumphant; **~ yaatra** triumphant march.
జైనం **jaynam** *n.* Jainism, the Jain religion.
జైనుడు **jaynuDu** *n.* Jain, follower of the Jain religion.
జైవిక **jaywika** *adj. sci.* biological.

జొ - jo

జొంపం **jompam** *n.* cluster of leaves with flowers and branches.

జొనుపు **jonupu** *same as* **conupu.**

జొన్న **jonna** *n., gen. pl.* **~lu** millet known as jowar or cholam.

జొన్నగడ్డ **jonnagaDDa** *n.* cholam stalk.

జొన్ననాగు **jonnanaagu** *n.* kind of snake.

జొప్పించు **joppincu** *same as* **coppincu.**

జొరబడు, జొరబాటు **jorabaDu, jorabaaTu** *same as* **corabaDu, corabaaTu.**

జొరబారు **jorabaaru** *same as* **corabaaru.**

జొర్రీగ **jorriiga** *same as* **jooriiga.**

జొల్లు **jollu** *n.* spittle, slaver.

జో, జౌ - joo, jaw

జో! **joo!** *interj. used for lulling a child to sleep* hush!

జోకు **jooku** *v.t. dial.* to weigh.

జోకొట్టు **jookoTTu** *v.t.* **1** to lull to sleep. **2** to soothe, pacify.

జోక్యం **jookyam** *n.* connection, concern.

జోక్యం కల్పించుకొను, జోక్యం కల్గించుకొను **jookyam kalpincukonu, jookyam kalgincukonu** *v.i.* to interfere, meddle.

జోక్యం చేసుకొను **jookyam ceesukonu** *v.i.* to interfere, meddle.

జోగి **joogi** *n.* Saivite religious mendicant.

జోగిని, జోగిరాలు **joogini, joogiraalu** *n.* religious beggar and fortune teller (woman).

జోగు **joogu**[1] I. *n.* drowsiness. II. *v.i.* **1** to stagger. **2** to doze, be drowsy.

జోగు **joogu**[2] *n.* alms.

జోగు ఎత్తు, జోగు తిరుగు **joogu ettu, joogu tirugu** *v.i.* to go round collecting alms in order to fulfil a religious vow.

జోడా **jooDaa** *n.* **1** pair, couple. **2** equal, match.

జోడాయించు **jooDaayincu** *v.t.* to join, fit together, couple together.

జోడించు **jooDincu** *v.t.* **1** to join, couple, put together, combine, unite. **2** to add.

జోడింపు **jooDimpu** *n.* joining, jointing, coupling.

జోడీ **jooDii** *n.* pair, couple.

జోడీగా **jooDiigaa** *adv.* in pairs, two at a time.

జోడు **jooDu** *n.* **1** pair, couple; **~ gurraalu** pair of horses; **kaLLa~** pair of spectacles. **2** (*also pl.* **jooLLu**) pair of boots or shoes. **3** (*a single*) boot or shoe. **4** match, equal.

జోడు కూర్చు **jooDu kuurcu** *v.t.* to unite, join.

జోతి **jooti** *substandard form of* **jyooti.**

జోదు **joodu** *n.* hero, warrior.

జోరవు **joorawu** *v.i.* to be intensified.

జోరిగాడు **joorigaaDu** *n.* kind of lark (bird).

జోరీగ, జొర్రీగ **jooriiga, jorriiga** *n.* gadfly, horsefly.

జోరు **jooru** I. *n.* **1** force. **2** speed. II. *adj.* **1** strong, fierce, intense (wind, sun's heat). **2** forceful. **3** fast, brisk.

జోల[పాట] **joola[paaTa]** *n.* lullaby, cradle song.

జోలపాడు **joolapaaDu** *v.i.* **1** to sing a lullaby. **2** to speak soothingly.

జోలి **jooli** *n., gen. in neg. constr.* affair, concern, matter, business, connection, proximity; **naa~ki nuwwu raawaddu** do not meddle in my affairs; **DitekTiv nawala cadiwi hantakuDewaDoo telisipooyina tarwaata maLLi manam aa nawala ~ ki poomu** after we have read a detective novel and found out who the murderer was, we do not want to have anything more to do with that novel; **aa kukka karustundi, daani~ki pooku** that dog bites, do not go near it.

జోలిశొంఠి **jooliśoNThi** *n.* (*more emphatic than* **jooli**) concern, affair, connection; **ataDi~naaku akkaraleedu** I will have nothing to do with him *or* I am not concerned with him at all; **adi nii jooli kaadu śoNThi kaadu** that is no concern of yours whatever.

జోలె **joole** *n.* bag for receiving alms hung round the neck or shoulder.

జోస్యం **joosyam** *n.* **1** astrology. **2** prophecy, forecast

జోస్యం చూచు **joosyam cuucu** *v.i.* to look into a horoscope.

జోస్యం చెప్పు **joosyam ceppu** *v.i.* to make a forecast or prophecy.

జోస్యుడు **joosyuDu** *n.* astrologer.

జోహారు **joohaaru** *n.* **1** salutation. **2** *pl.* **joohaarlu** tribute, homage.

జౌళి **jawLi** *same as* **jawaLi.**

జ్ఞ, జ్ఞా - jña, jñaa

జ్ఞప్తి **jñapti** *n.* recollection, memory, remembrance.

జ్ఞాత **jñaata** *n.* one who knows or understands.

జ్ఞాతం **jñaatam** *adj.* known, understood.

జ్ఞాతి **jñaati** *n.* male blood relation on the father's side (= **daayaadi**).

జ్ఞానం **jñaanam** *n.* **1** knowing, cognition, perception, understanding. **2** wisdom, knowledge, religious or spiritual knowledge. **3** *as second part of a n. compound* sense, e.g., **sparśa** ~ sense of touch.

జ్ఞానకాండం **jñaanakaaNDam** *n.* esoteric portion of the Vedas relating to spiritual knowledge.

జ్ఞానచక్షువు **jñaanacakSuwu** *n.* **1** the inner eye, giving the power of clairvoyance. **2** the eye of knowledge.

జ్ఞానదృష్టి **jñaanadṛSTi** *n.* second sight, clairvoyance.

జ్ఞానపిత **jnaanapita** *n.* godfather.

జ్ఞానమాత **jñaanamaata** *n.* godmother.

జ్ఞానమీమాంస **jñaanamiimaamsa** *n. class.* epistemology.

జ్ఞానవంతుడు **jñaanawantuDu** *n.* wise person.

జ్ఞానస్నానం **jñaanasnaanam** *n.* baptism.

జ్ఞాని **jñaani** *n.* man of wisdom, sage, philospher.

జ్ఞానేంద్రియాలు **jñaaneendriyaalu** *n.pl.* organs or senses of perception.

జ్ఞానోదయం **jñaanoodayam** *n.* revelation, enlightenment.

జ్ఞాపకం **jñaapakam** *n.* memory, recollection, remembrance; **naa maaTalu aameki ~ waccEEyi** she remembered my words; **jnaapakaaniki teccukonu, ~ ceesukonu** to recall; **~ peTTukonu** to keep in o.'s memory, keep in mind; **waaDiki daanni ~ ceesEEnu** I reminded him of it; **jñaapakaalu** (i) memories; (ii) memoirs.

జ్ఞాపకార్థం **jñaapakaartham** *adv.* in memory of, as a reminder of; **puurwapu mahaatmula ~** in memory of holy men of former days.

జ్ఞు, జ్ఞే - jñu, jñee

జ్ఞుడు **jñuDu** *n. suffix meaning* learned in, e.g., **śaastra ~** scientist.

జ్ఞేయం **jñeeyam** *adj. class.* knowable, known.

జ్యా, జ్యే - jyaa, jyee

జ్యా **jyaa** *n.* chord of a circle.

జ్యామితి **jyaamiti** *n.* geometry.

జ్యేష్ఠ **jyeeSTha**[1] *n. astrol.* the 18th lunar mansion, name of a kaarte in the month of Margasira.

జ్యేష్ఠ **jyeeSTha**[2] *adj.* elder, eldest; **~ putruDu** eldest son.

జ్యేష్ఠ, జెష్ట **jyeeSTha**[3], **jeSTa** *n.* goddess of ill luck.

జ్యేష్ఠం **jyeeSTham** *same as* **jeeSTam.**

జ్యేష్ఠభ్రాత **jyeeSThabhraata** *n.* fool, idiot, useless person; *cf.* **agastyabhraata** *sense 3.*

జ్యేష్ఠుడు **jyeeSThuDu** *n.* elder, eldest or seniormost man; **maa ~** my eldest brother *or* my eldest son; **maa iNTi ~** the eldest male member of our family.

జ్యో - jyoo

జ్యోతి **jyooti** *n.* **1** light, lustre, radiance. **2** lamp.

జ్యోతిర్మయ **jyootirmaya** *adj.* full of radiance.

జ్యోతిశ్చక్రం **jyootiścakram** *n.* zodiac.

జ్యోతిశ్శాస్త్రం **jyootiśśaastram** *n.* astrology.

జ్యోతిశ్శాస్త్రజ్ఞుడు **jyootiśśaastrajñuDu** *n.* astrologer.

జ్యోతిషం **jyootiSam** *n.* astrology.

జ్యోతిషుడు, జ్యోతిష్కుడు **jyootiSuDu, jyootiSkuDu** *n.* astrologer.

జ్యోత్స్న **jyootsna** *n.* **1** moonlight. **2** moonlit night.

జ్యోత్స్ని **jyootsni** *n.* moonlit night.

జ్వ, జ్వా - jwa, jwaa

జ్వరం **jwaram** *n.* fever; *see* **peTTukonu** *sense II. 3.*

జ్వలనం **jwalanam** *n.* 1 burning, blazing, flaming. 2 ignition.

జ్వలనశీల **jwalanaśiila** *adj.* inflammable.

జ్వలించు **jwalincu** *v.i.* 1 to burn. 2 to shine.

జ్వలిత **jwalita** *adj.* 1 burnt. 2 shining.

జ్వాజ్వల్యమానంగా **jwaajwalyamaanangaa** *adv.* brilliantly, spectacularly.

జ్వాల **jwaala** *n.* flame, blaze.

జ్వాలకం **jwaalakam** *n. sci.* burner.

జ్వాలముఖి **jwaalamukhi** *n.* volcano.

ఝ, ఝా, ఝు - jha, jhaa, jhu

ఝంకారం, ఝంకృతి **jhankaaram, jhankrti** *n.* humming sound (of bees, spinning wheel).

ఝంఝ **jhamjha** *adj.* (of wind) stormy, tempestuous; **jhamjhaanilam, jhamjhaamaarutam** stormy or tempestuous wind.

ఝణఝణలాడించు **jhaNajhaNalaaDincu** *v.i.* 1 to give a shaking (to s.o.) 2 to speak threateningly or warningly; **ewaraynaa dorikitee iNTiki pampistaanu annaaDu jhaNajhaNalaaDistuu pariikSa haaluloo mEESTarugaaru** "if anyone is detected I will send him home" said the teacher in the examination hall, as a warning.

ఝణాయించు **jhaNaayincu** *v.t.* to urge forcefully, browbeat.

ఝమాయించు **jhamaayincu** *v.t.* to say forcefully, assert.

ఝరం, ఝరి **jharam, jhari** *n.* 1 mountain stream. 2 waterfall.

ఝర్ఝరం, ఝర్ఝరి **jharjharam, jharjhari** *n. class.* kind of drum.

ఝల్లుమను **jhallumanu** *same as* **jallumanu.**

ఝళిపించు, జళిపించు **jhaLipincu, jaLipincu** *v.t.* to brandish, wave, flourish.

ఝాడించు **jhaaDincu** *same as* **jaaDincu.**

ఝామను, ఝామ్మను, ఝుమ్మను **jhaamanu, jhaammanu, jhummanu** *v.i.* 1 to boil, burn (*lit. and fig.*); **niiLLu kaagaDam modalu peTTaka mundu jhaamani śabdam ceestaayi** before water begins to boil it makes a hissing sound; **wiidhiloo reNDu kaagadaalu jhaammaNTunnaayi** two torches are blazing in the street; **ii maaTa wiNTee mii naanna jhaamani egurutaaDu** if your father hears this, he will be furiously angry. 2 *the figurative meaning is extended to cover other kinds of strongly expressed emotion*, e.g., **aame tinnagaa jhaammani raaju iNTiki weLLindi** she went proudly (*or* grandly) straight to Raju's house; **waaDu jhummani weLLEEDu** he went away full of cheerfulness; **praaNaalanu jhummanipincee teliwi** intelligence that exhilarates the heart.

ఝాము **jhaamu** *same as* **jaamu.**

ఝుమాయించు **jhumaayincu** *same as* **jumaayincu.**

ఝుమ్మున **jhummuna** *adv.* forcefully, vigorously.

ట - Ta

ట Ta *alt. form of* **aTa.**

టంకం **Tankam** *n.* 1 an obsolete coin. 2 borax. 3 solder. 4 stone mason's chisel.

టంకసాల **Tankasaala** *n.* mint.

టంకారం **Tankaaram** *n.* twang of a bowstring.

టంకు **Tanku** *n.* pretentious person.

టంకుతనం **Tankutanam** *n.* pretention.

టంగు[వారు] **Tangu[waaru]** *n.* saddle girth.

టంగున, టంగుమని **Tanguna, Tangumani** *onom.adv.* with a bang, with a loud report (*sug. the sound of a blow or a clock striking*); **Tangumani okka moTTikaaya moTTeesEEDu** he struck one blow with his fist.

టంచనుగా, ఠంచనుగా **T[h]ancanugaa** *adv.* 1 directly, straight out, outright. 2 (of time) exactly, punctually; ~ **padi gaNTalaku maa iNTiki waccEEDu** punctually at ten o'clock he came to my house.

టకటక **TakaTaka** *onom. adv. expressive of* rattling, chattering, clattering *or* knocking; ~ **talupu koTTEEDu** he knocked briskly on the door; **waaDi paLLu caliki ~laaDutunnaayi** his teeth are chattering with cold.

టకాయించు **Takaayincu** *v.t.* 1 to confront, put a straight question to. 2 to stop, hinder. 3 to cut off.

టకార **Takaara** *n.* shallow iron basket.

టకీమని, ఠకీమని **T[h]akiimani** *adv.* at once, straight away, promptly.

టకోరా **Takooraa** *n.* 1 kind of drum. 2 ornamental rim round the top of a **tulasi kooTa.** 3 *dial.* kind of haircut in which the front part of the head is shaved.

టక్కరి, తక్కరి **Takkari, takkari** I. *n.* cheat, rogue, cunning person, thief, hypocrite. II. *adj.* mischievous, cunning, wily, tricky.

టక్కు **Takku** I. *n.* pretence, trick[ery]. II. *adj.* feigned, pretended.

టక్కుటక్కు **TakkuTakku** *onom. adv. sug.* tapping *or* knocking; **kinda eedoo ~maNTunnadi** there is some knocking sound below.

టక్కుటమారాలు **TakkuTamaaraalu** *n. pl.* 1 cheating, deceiving. 2 trickery, cunning.

టక్కున **Takkuna** *adv.* 1 suddenly, quickly, promptly. 2 abruptly, briefly, curtly.

టక్కుపెట్టు **TakkupeTTu** *v.i.* to pretend; **nela tappEEnani Takku peTTeesindi** she pretended that she was pregnant.

టక్కుబాజీ **Takkubaajii** *n.* deceiver, cheat.

టక్కుమని, ఠక్కుమని **T[h]akkumani** *adv.* suddenly.

టక్కులాడి **TakkulaaDi** *n.* deceitful woman.

టపటప **TapaTapa** *onom. adv. sug.* (i) tears being shed; **kanniiLLu ~ raalEEyi** tears poured down; (ii) rattling; **gaaliki talupu ~ koTTukondi** the door rattled in the wind.

టపా[లు], టప్పా, తపాలా **Tapaa[lu], Tappaa, tapaalaa** *n. and adj.* post, mail; **tanti tapaalaa śaakha** Post and Telegraph Department.

టపాకట్టు **TapaakaTTu** *v.i. colloq.* to die (*lit.* to clear the post, despatch the mail).

టపాకాయ, టపాసు **Tapaakaaya, Tapaasu** *n.* firework, cracker.

టపేటా **TapeeTaa** *n.* taffeta.

టప్పుని **Tappuni** adv. suddenly.

టమటమకొట్టు **TamaTamakoTTu** *v.t.* to proclaim by beat of drum.

టమాటా, తమాటా **TamaaTaa, tamaaTaa** *n.* tomato.

టముకు, తముకు **Tamuku, tamuku** *n.* large drum (= **daNDooraa**).

టర్టరాయణం **TarTaraayaNam** *n.* croaking of frogs.

టస్సా, ఠస్సా **T[h]assaa** *n.* 1 plot, stratagem. 2 trace. 3 *dial.* likeness. 4 stamp, mould.

టా - Taa

టాంటాంచేయు **TaamTaam ceeyu** *v.t.* to proclaim or publish (s.g) widely.

టాకా **Taakaa** *n.* stitch; **cokkaa ciriginappuDallaa reNDu ~lu weeyinci kuTTistuu waccEEnu** whenever my shirt was torn I used to get it repaired with a couple of stitches.

టాకీ **Taakii** *n.* motion picture; *cf.* **muukii.**

టాపు **Taapu** *n.* 1 top. 2 *dial.* deck of a boat.

టాపులేపు **Taapuleepu** *v.i. and t.* to yell, clamour, create an uproar, scold severely; **pillawaaDu paalakoosam TaapuleepeestunnaaDu** the child is clamouring for milk; **paaTham cadawaleedu kaabaTTi mEESTarugaaru waaDi TaapuleepeesEEru** the master scolded him because he had not learnt the lesson.

టాళాటోళీ, ఠాళాఠోళీ **T[h]aaLaaT[h]ooLii** *adj.* lightweight, insignificant, inconsiderable.

టాళాటోళీగా, ఠాళాఠోళీగా **T[h]aaLaaT[h]ooLiigaa** *adv.* lightheartedly, lightly, not seriously.

టి, టీ - Ti, Tii

టింగణా **TingaNaa** *n.* dwarf.

టింగురంగా అంటూ **Tingurangaa aNTuu** *advbl. phrase* carefree, having no worries or responsibilities.

టికాణా, ఠికాణా **T[h]ikaaNaa** *n.* 1 place, room; **waana kuristee tala daacukooDaaniki ~leedu** if it rains there is no place to shelter. 2 possibility, hope, scope; **maaku puuTaki ~leedu** there is no hope of a meal for us. 3 trace; **ekkaDiki pooyEEDoo ~leedu** there is no trace of where he has gone.

టిట్టిభం **TiTTibham** *n.* kingfisher (bird).

టిప్పణం, టిప్పణి **TippaNam, TippaNi** *n.* note or gloss explaining a difficult passage in a text.

టిఫిను **Tiphinu** *n.* 1 light meal, snack. 2 tiffin carrier, lunch box for carrying a meal from home to work place.

టిర్రి **Tirri** *n.* 1 cry to cattle causing them to turn to the left. 2 beast of burden. 3 fish basket.

టీక **Tiika** *n.* commentary or glossary explaining the meaning of each word in a text.

టీకా **Tiikaa** *n.* vaccination, inoculation; **~mandu** vaccine; **~lu weeyu** to vaccinate, inoculate.

టీకు **Tiiku** *n.* haughtiness.

టు, టూ - Tu, Tuu

టుగాగమం **Tugaagamam** *n. gram.* insertion of the letter *T* for euphony, e.g., **aakaaśapu-T-anculu** the borders of the sky, **teene-T-iiga** bee.

టుప్పు **Tuppu** *n. dial.* huqqa, hubble bubble.

టుమ్రి **Tumri** *n.* kind of Hindustani musical composition.

టూకి **Tuuki** *n.* tree whose broad leaves are used in manufacture of beedies, *diospyrum sp.*

టూకీ **Tuukii** *adj.* brief, concise.

టూకీగా **Tuukiigaa** *adv.* briefly, concisely, in brief, in a nutshell.

టె, టే - Te, Tee

టెంక **Tenka** *n.* 1 stone of a mango. 2 shell of a palmyra fruit.

టెంకణం **TenkaNam** *n. class.* salutation.

టెంకాయ **Tenkaaya** *n.* coconut; **~ceTTu** coconut tree.

టెంకి **Tenki**[1] *n.* place, house, home.

టెంకి **Tenki**[2] *n. dial.* back of the head.

టెంకి, టెంకె **Tenki**[3], **Tenke** *n.* 1 cobbler's awl for boring leather. 2 large needle for stitching palmyra leaves.

టెక్క, టెక్కు **Tekka, Tekku** *n.* 1 pride, haughtiness, arrogance. 2 showing off (colloq.).

టెక్కులాడి **TekkulaaDi** *n.* coquette, woman who puts on airs.

టెక్కులుపోవు **Tekkulupoowu** *v.i.* 1 to be proud, be arrogant, be boastful. 2 to show off (colloq.)

టెక్కెం **Tekkem** *n. class.* flag, banner.

టేకు **Teeku** *same as* **teeku.**

టొ, టో -To, Too

టొంప **Tompa 1** *same as* **kompa** *sense 1.* **2** *dial.* unwelcome burden. **3** hobble to prevent cattle from straying.

టొకాయించు **Tokaayincu** *v.i. and t.* **1** to knock, tap. **2** (in speaking) to drive home a point, make a point clear by special emphasis.

టొక్కాయమ్మ **Tokkaayamma** *n. dial.* fool.

టొపారం **Topaaram** *n. colloq.* roof.

టోకరా **Tookaraa** *n.* **1** cheating, misleading, deception; **naaku balee ~iccEEDu** he deceived me thoroughly; *see* **thakaraa. 2** upsetting, overturning, capsizing.

టోకరా కొట్టు, టోకరా వేయు **Tookaraa koTTu, Tookaraa weeyu** *v.t.* to cheat, deceive.

టోకు **Tooku** *adj.* wholesale.

టోకున **Tookuna** *adv.* **1** on the whole, altogether. **2 ~ konu** to buy in wholesale quantities.

టోకురు **Tookuru** *n. dial.* snoring.

టోపీ **Toopii** *n.* **1** hat, cap. **2** *colloq.* cheating, deceiving, duping.

టోపీ పెట్టు, టోపీ వేయు **Toopii peTTu, Toopii weeyu** *v.i. colloq.* to deceive, cheat; **naaku Toopiiweesi naa Dabbulu tiisukuweLLEEDu** he deceived me and made off with my money.

టోలా, ఠోలా **T[h]oolaa** *n. class.* crowd.

టోలి, ఠోలి **T[h]ooli** *n.* **1** half a pie, very small coin now obsolete. **2** s.g of trifling value or no value.

థ, థా - Tha, Thaa

థంచనుగా **Thancanugaa** *same as* **Tancanugaa.**

థకీమని **Thakiimani** *same as* **Takiimani.**

థక్కుమని **Thakkumani** *same as* **Takkumani.**

థపీమని **Thapiimani** *adv.* suddenly, at once, straight away, promptly.

థలాయించు **Thalaayincu** *v.i. and t.* **1** to pay no attention to, take no account of. **2** to dodge, evade. **3** to go to and fro.

థవథవలాడు **ThawaThawalaaDu** *v.i.* to feel very tired.

థస్సా **Thassaa** *same as* **Tassaa.**

థా అయిపోవు **Thaa ayipoowu** *v.i.* to die.

థాకూరు **Thaakuuru** *n.* **1** lord, nobleman. **2** religious preceptor, religious teacher.

థాథా అయిపోవు **ThaaThaa ayipoowu** *v.i., dial.* to be exhausted; **aa pani ceesi waceeTappaTiki naa pani ThaaThaa ayipooyindi** by the time that I finished that work I felt quite exhausted.

థానా **Thaanaa** *n.* police station.

థానేదారు **Thaaneedaaru** *n.* officer in charge of a police station.

థాప్మని **Thaapmani** *onom. adv.* with a cracking, knocking, banging, snapping or similar sound; **~talupu weesukonnaaDu** he shut the door with a bang.

థారు **Thaaru** *n.* alarm, fright; **naannanu cuustee pillalaku~** the children are frightened when they see their father.

థారుమను, థారెత్తు **Thaarumanu, Thaarettu** *v.i.* **1** to be greatly frightened, scared, terrified; **aa keeka wini Thaarumannaadu/ThaarettipooyEEDu** when he heard that shout he was terrified. **2** to be amazed, be greatly astonished, be struck with wonder.

థాళాథోళీ[గా] **ThaaLaaThooLii[gaa]** *same as* **TaaLaaTooLii[gaa].**

థావు **Thaawu**[1] *n.* full sheet of white paper of double foolscap size.

థావు **Thaawu**[2] *n. class.* place.

థి to థో - Thi to Thoo

థికాణా **ThikaaNaa** *same as* **TikaaNaa.**

థీ **Thii** *see* **ThiikoTTu.**

థీకు **Thiiku** *adj. dial.* proper, just, fitting, correct; **nuwwu ceppeedi~** what you say is quite right.

థీకొట్టు **ThiikoTTu** *v.i.* **1** to end o.'s friendship or break off o.'s relations (with s.o.) **2** *child language* **niikuu naakuu Thii** *or* **nii saawaasam Thii** I will not be friends with you any more.

థీవి **Thiiwi** I. *n.* **1** splendour, grandeur. **2** pose. **3** prestige. II. *adj.* splendid, grand.

థీవిణీ **ThiiwiNii** *n.* sitting comfortably; **~weesukoni kuurconnaaDu** he is sitting at ease, he is making himself comfortable.

థువ్వుమను **Thuwwumanu** *v.i. class.* (of the heart) to beat fast, tremble.

థేవ **Theewa** *n. class.* **1** beauty. **2** manner.

థోలా, థోలి **Thoolaa, Thooli** *same as* **Toolaa, Tooli.**

డ, డా - Da, Daa

డంకా **Dankaa** *same as* **Dhakkaa.**

డంగు, దంగు **Dangu, dangu** I. *n.* mill in which lime mortar is ground for use in building; the mill is in the form of a circular groove like the rim of a large wheel, mortar is poured into it and ground by a stone roller which is dragged round and round by a bullock. II. *v.i.* (of grain) to be crushed or pounded.

డంగుబిళ్ల **DangubiLLa** *n.* wheel-shaped roller used to crush lime for making mortar.

డంగైపోవు, డంగు వాయించు **Dangaypoowu, Dangu waayincu** *v.i.* to be amazed, be shocked, be surprised.

డంబం **Dambam** *n.* ostentation, show.

డంబాచారి **Dambaacaari** *n.* boastful person.

డక్క **Dakka** *n.* 1 small drum. 2 rush or force of wind.

డక్కా **Dakkaa** *n.* damage, harm, injury, loss.

డక్కి **Dakki** *n.* small drum shaped like an hour glass.

డగ్గుత్తిక, దగ్గుత్తిక **Dagguttika, dagguttika** *n.* choked voice.

డచ్చీలు, డప్పాలు **Dacciilu, Dappaalu** *n.pl.* boasting; ~ **koTTu** to boast.

డజను **Dajanu** *n.* dozen.

డప్పు **Dappu** *n.* large drum; ~ **moogutunnadi** the big drum is being sounded (gen. indicating either a funeral or the festival of a village goddess).

డప్పు[లు]కొట్టు **Dappu[lu]koTTu** *v.i.* 1 to announce by beat of drum, publish widely. 2 to boast.

డబుడక్కు, డుబుడుక్కు **DabuDakku, DubuDukku** *n.* small drum carried in the hand by beggars making a sound like a rattle.

డబ్బా **Dabbaa** *n.* 1 tin, bin, barrel. 2 box; **poosTu**~ post box. 3 *colloq.* boaster. 4 *dial.* compartment in a train.

డబ్బాకొట్టుకొను **DabbaakoTTukonu** *v.i.* to boast.

డబ్బావాయించు **Dabbaawaayincu** *v.t. colloq.* to praise inordinately.

డబ్బీ **Dabbii** *n.* tin box of small size; **poDum**~ snuff box.

డబ్బు **Dabbu** *n.* 1 money; ~**kalawaaDu** rich man. 2 *fig.* rupee; **naalugu**~**lu sampaayincu** to earn a few rupees. 3 a pie.

డబ్బుదస్కం **Dabbudaskam** *n.* money (*lit.* small and large coins).

డమరకం **Damarakam** *n.* small drum shaped like an hourglass and making a sound like a rattle; it is held in the hand by Siva while dancing.

డలాయతు **Dalaayatu** *n.* messenger, attendant.

డల్లయిపోవు **Dallayipoowu** *v.i.* to feel downhearted, feel discouraged.

డవాలా, డవాళీ **Dawaalaa, DawaaLii** *n.* peon's belt or badge; ~ **baNTrootu** peon (attendant) wearing a badge.

డస్సిపోవు **Dassipoowu** *v.i.* to be[come] tired.

డాంబరు **Daambaru** *n.* coal tar; ~ **rooDDu** tarred road.

డాంబికం **Daambikam** *n.* pride, pretentiousness.

డాకు **Daaku** *n. dial.* thief.

డాగు **Daagu** *n.* mark, stain, blemish.

డాగుతెగులు **Daagutegulu** *n.* plant disease causing fruit to rot.

డాగుపడు **DaagupaDu** *v.i.* to be[come] stained.

డాగులువేయు **Daaguluweeyu** *v.i.* to brand.

డాబా **Daabaa** *n.* 1 terrace or flat roof of a house. 2 house with a flat roof.

డాబు **Daabu** I. *n.* false pride, ostentation, boasting; ~ **lukoTTu** to boast; ~ **laraayuDu** boaster. II. *adj.* pompous, grand, showy, ostentatious.

డాబుసరి **Daabusari** *n.* ostentation.

డాలు **Daalu**[1] *n.* shield.

డాలు **Daalu**[2] *suffix added to nouns denoting* colour, tinge, shade; **tella**~ tinge of white; **erra**~ shade of red, reddish tinge.

డి, డీ - Di, Dii

డింకీ **Dinkii** *n.* 1 a fall in wrestling. 2 somersault; ~[lu] **koTTu** (i) to turn somersaults; (ii) *slang* to fail (e.g., in an examination); (iii) *slang* ~ **koTTeesEEDu** he died.

డింగరి **Dingari** *n.* 1 servant, slave. 2 *colloq.* faithful follower.

డిండిమ **DiNDima** *n.* drum (for playing).

డింభం **Dimbham** *n. class.* 1 egg. 2 young animal.

డింభకం **Dimbhakam** *n. entom.* larva.

డింభకుడు **DimbhakuDu** *n. colloq.* fool, idiot.

డింభోషణం **DimbhooSaNam** *n. zool.* incubation.

డిగ్గున, దిగ్గున **Digguna, digguna** *adv.* suddenly.

డిప్ప **Dippa** *n.* 1 half of a fruit; **battaayi**~ half an orange; **kobbari**~ half a coconut. 2 *colloq.* head; ~**koTTincukonu,** to have o.'s hair cut. 3 *colloq.* ~ **kaTTipoowu** to become stubborn.

డిప్పకాయ, దిప్పకాయ, తిప్పకాయ **Dippakaaya, dippakaaya, tippakaaya** *n. colloq.* mischievous child.

డిబ్బి **Dibbi** *n.* small tin container with a lid.

డిల్ల, దిల్ల **Dilla, dilla** *n.* timidness.

డిల్లపడు, దిల్లపడు **DillapaDu, dillapaDu** *v.i.* to lose heart, be unmanned or unnerved.

డిసా **Disaa** *n. dial.* delay.

డీ, డీకొట్టు, డీకొను **Dii, DiikoTTu, Diikonu** *same as* **Dhii, DhiikoTTu, Dhiikonu.**

డీడిక్కి **DiiDikki** *n.* butting with the head.

డీలా **Diilaa** I. *n.* weakness, tiredness, timidness, dejection. II. *adj.* weak, tired, timid, dejected.

డీలా అవు, డీలా పడు **Diilaa awu, Diilaa paDu** *v.i.* to break down, collapse (due to weakness, exhaustion, fear or dejection).

డీలు **Diilu** *adj. dial.* 1 loose. 2 lean, thin.

డు, డూ - Du, Duu

డుబికీ **Dubikii** *n.* 1 overturning. 2 tricking, deceiving.

డుబుక్ **Dubuk** *onom. adv. and n. sug.* bubbling or gurgling.

డుబుక్కున **Dubukkuna** *adv.* with a bubbling or gurgling sound; ~**munigi pooyEEDu** he sank with a gurgling sound.

డుబుడుక్కు **DubuDukku** *same as* **DabuDakku.**

డుమ్మాకొట్టు **DummaakoTTu** *v.i.* 1 to run away. 2 to absent o.s. (from school or duty), play truant.

డూడూబసవన్న **DuuDuubasawanna** I. word of command to a performing bull (= **gangireddu**) to cause it to nod its head. II. *n. colloq.* person who nods his head and assents to whatever is said to him.

డె, డే, డై - De, Dee, Day

డెందం **Dendam** *n. class.* heart, mind.

డెక్క **Dekka** *n.* hoof.

డెక్కు **Dekku** *v.t.* 1 to strike, smite. 2 *dial.* to shave.

డెక్కుపట్టు **DekkupaTTu** *v.i.* to gasp for breath.

డెబ్బై **Debbhay** *n.* seventy.

డేగ **Deega** *n.* hawk, falcon.

డేగిస **Deegisa** *n.* degchi, saucepan, cooking pot.

డేరా **Deeraa** *n.* tent; **ikkaDa**~ **ettiweesi akkaDiki weLLEEDu** he has migrated from this place to that place; **waaLLa alluDu wacci iNTLoo**~ **weesi kuurcunnaaDu** their son-in-law has come and ensconced himself in their house.

డైమను **Daymanu** *n.* diamonds (in playing cards).

డొ, డో, డౌ - Do, Doo, Daw

డొంక **Donka** *n.* 1 thicket, clump of bushes; **tiiga kadilistee ~ antaa kadilindi** when I stirred one creeper the whole thicket was shaken (expression used when a small step taken in the beginning leads to widespread consequences which had not been anticipated). 2 patch of waste land with bushes. 3 pathway, cattle track.

డొంకతిరుగుడు **DonkatiruguDu** *n.* behaving or talking in a roundabout way, beating about the bush, circumlocution; **enduku ii ~ ?** why beat about the bush?

డొంకదారి **Donkadaari** *n.* short cut.

డొక్క **Dokka** *n.* 1 flank. 2 stomach; **ekkaDikoo pooyEEDu, ~ maaDitee waaDee wastaaDu** he has gone somewhere, when he is hungry he will come of his own accord; **rekka aaDiteegaani ~ aaDadu** *lit.* unless your arm is active your stomach will not be active, i.e., unless you work hard your stomach will not be filled (proverb). 3 shell or stone of a nut or fruit; **aawakaaya ~** piece of pickled mango with a piece of the stone attached. 4 **waaDiki ~ śuddhi leedu** he has not much education; *see* **Doolu, medalu** *sense 4.*

డొక్కి **Dokki** *n.* wooden ladle.

డొక్కు **Dokku** I. *n.* tin, box or other container. II. *adj.* 1 (of things) old, dilapidated, useless. 2 (of persons) weak, emaciated, thin, skinny, decrepit.

డొలుపు **Dolupu** *n.* main cross beam of a bullock cart which rests on the axle and supports the frame.

డొల్ల **Dolla** I. *n.* 1 cavity, hollow. 2 long basket placed on a cart (= **jalla**). II. *adj.* hollow, empty.

డొల్లు **Dollu**[1] *n.* pod of beans, peas, pulses, etc., containing no seeds.

డొల్లు **Dollu**[2] *v.i.* to roll.

డోకు **Dooku** I. *n.* vomiting, nausea; **naaku ~ waccindi** (i) I felt like vomiting; (ii) I felt disgusted. II. *v.i.* to vomit, be sick.

డోకుకుపోవు, డోక్కుపోవు, డోక్కొనిపోవు **Dook[u]kupoowu, Dookkonipoowu** *v.i.* to be scraped or scratched.

డోరియా **Dooriyaa** *n.* cloth woven for saris with metal threads for ornament at regular intervals.

డోలకం **Doolakam** *n. sci.* oscillator.

డోలక్కు **Doolakku** *n.* kind of drum (for playing).

డోలనం **Doolanam** *n. sci.* oscillation.

డోలాందోళన **DoolaandooLana** *n.* repeated worries, succession of troubles.

డోలాయమాన **Doolaayamaana** *adj. sci.* oscillating.

డోలాయమానుడు **DoolaayamaanuDu** *n.* wavering or irresolute person.

డోలి[క] **Dooli[ka]** *n.* swing cot, cradle.

డోలీ **Doolii** *n.* litter, palanquin.

డోలు **Doolu** *n.* kind of drum (for playing); **nii toolu oliceesi** (*or* **nii Dokka cinceesi**) **~ kaTTeestaanu!** *is a threat equivalent to* "I will flay you alive!"

డౌలు **Dawlu** *n.* tinge of colour.

ఢ to ఢో - Dha to Dhoo

ఢం ! **Dham!** *interj.* bang!

ఢక్కా, ఢంకా, డంకా **Dhakkaa, Dhankaa, Dankaa** *n.* kind of drum (for playing); **~ bajaayinci ceptaanu** I will assert (*or* I will proclaim) definitely.

ఢక్కాముక్కీలు **Dhakkaamukkiilu** *n. pl.* 1 hard knocks, hard blows. 2 difficulties, calamities.

ఢాకా **Dhaakaa** *n.* 1 violence. 2 attack.

ఢాకిని **Dhaakini** *n.* female evil spirit (= **śaakini**).

ఢిల్లీభోగాలు **Dhillii bhoogaalu** *n. pl.* name of a fine variety of rice.

ఢీ, డీ **Dhii, Dii** *particle used with certain verbs in the sense of* challenge, competition, opposition *or* collision; **ewaru ~ annaa waaDu ~ aNTaaDu** if anyone challenges him he will accept the challenge.

ఢీకొట్టు, డీకొట్టు **DhiikoTTu, DiikoTTu** *v.t.* to collide violently with.

ఢీకొను, డీకొను **Dhiikonu, Diikonu** *v.t.* 1 to charge, rush towards, collide with, knock against. 2 to impinge on.

ఢోకా **Dhookaa** *n.* 1 danger. 2 difficulty, trouble. 3 impediment.

ఢోకా యిచ్చు **Dhookaa iccu** *v.i.* to play mischief, cheat, deceive.

త - ta

త **ta** *suffix used in forming feminine nouns*, e.g., **caakita** washerwoman; **erukata** woman fortune teller.

తంగేడు **tangeeDu** *n.* senna, *cassia auriculata*, a shrub whose bark is used for tanning; **puucina ~laa uNDu** *lit.* to be like a flowering **tangeeDu**, i.e., to be happy and prosperous.

తంజావూరు సత్రం **tanjaawuuru satram** *n.* Tanjore choultry; **aayana illu oo~** his house is (like) a Tanjore choultry (meaning a place where food is given indiscriminately to all who come, regardless of their merit).

తంటా **taNTaa** *n.* **1** trouble, difficulty. **2** contention, dispute; **ii maaTa ee ~leeni nijam** this statement is true beyond dispute.

తంటాలమారి **taNTaalamaari** *n.* **1** troublemaker, creator of problems. **2** slanderer.

తంటాలుపడు **taNTaalupaDu** *v.i.* **1** to undergo difficulty, suffer. **2** to take trouble. **3** to cope, manage with difficulty; **aa pani S.-ki kotta kaanii eedoo ~tuu wastunnaaDu** the work is new to S. but somehow he is managing it with difficulty.

తండం **taNDam** *n. class.* crowd, collection, mass, group.

తండా **taNDaa**[1] *n.* **1** crowd or village composed of Lambadis, a tribal community in Andhra Pradesh. **2** group, party.

తండా **taNDaa**[2] *n. dial.* satisfaction, satiety, fullness.

తండు, దండు **taNDu, daNDu** *v.i.* **1** to demand repayment of debt, demand money as due. **2** to collect contributions. **3** to beg.

తండులాలు **taNDulaalu** *n. pl.* **1** *class.* rice. **2** *colloq.* money, cash.

తండోపతండాలు **taNDoopataNDaalu** *n.pl.* crowds upon crowds.

తండోపతండాలుగా **taNDoopataNDaalugaa** *adv.* **1** in crowds, in multitudes. **2** in large quantities, prodigiously.

తండ్రి **taNDri** *n.* **1** father. **2** ~is used (i) as a term of affection for any male person either older or younger than the speaker; **naa taNDree, manci pani ceesEEwu** my dear man! (*or* my dear boy!) you have done a marvellous job; (ii) as a term of respect when addressed to a male person older than the speaker. **3** as a term of address ~may convey sarcasm.

తంతి **tanti** *n.* **1** wire. **2** string of a musical instrument. **3** telegram.

తంతికురుపు, నారికురుపు **tantikurupu, naarikurupu** *n.* abscess caused by a guinea worm.

తంతితపాలాశాఖ **tanti tapaalaa śaakha** *n.* Post and Telegraph Department.

తంతు **tantu** *n.* **1** proceedings, procedure, ritual, ceremony; **mottam peLLi~** the entire marriage proceedings. **2** trick, ruse, device. **3** life style. way of living, way of behaving, way of carrying on (colloq). **4** state of affairs; **prati cooTaa aalasyam, podduTinunci idee~**! delay everywhere! since this morning this is the state of affairs!

తంతుకరణం **tantukaraNam** *n.* spinning.

తంతుయుత **tantuyuta** *adj.* fibrous.

తంతువు **tantuwu** *n.* filament, thread, fibre.

తంత్రం **tantram** *n.* **1** device, contrivance, means. **2** trick, stratagem. **3** scheme, plan. **4** ceremonial, ritual. **5** *class.* magical or mystical formula for obtaining supernatural powers.

తంత్రగొట్టు **tantragoTTu** *n.* wicked person.

తంత్రగ్రంథాలు **tantragranthaalu** *n. pl.* books which teach secret rites and methods for obtaining supernatural powers.

తంత్రజ్ఞుడు **tantrajñuDu** *n.* one who possesses supernatural powers.

తంత్రి **tantri** *n.* **1** stringed musical instrument resembling a vina. **2** wire. **3** string of a musical instrument; **hrdaya tantrulu** heartstrings.

తందనం **tandanam** *n.* dancing or prancing awkwardly, lurching or reeling about; **taagi tandanaalaaDutunnaaDu** he is reeling about in a drunken state.

తందనాలుతొక్కు **tandanaalu tokku** *v.i.* to dance awkwardly, prance (due to rage, drunkness, etc.).

తందానతాన **tandaanataana** *n.* a meaningless refrain; **paywaaLLu ceppinadaanikallaa wiiDu~ aNTaaDu** he supports blindly whatever his superiors say.

తందానపదాలు **tandaanapadaalu** *n.pl.* kind of folk song in which every verse sung by the lead singer is followed by a meaningless refrain **tandaanataana** sung by the support singer.

తంపట, తంపటి **tampaTa, tampaTi** *n.* fire used for roasting peanuts, etc.

తంపి **tampi** *n.* **1** hearth for burning cowdung cakes as fuel. **2** quarrel.

తంపులమారి **tampulamaari** *n.* person who stirs up quarrels.

తంపులుపెట్టు **tampulu peTTu** *v.i.* to create quarrels.

తంబళ్లు **tambaLLu** *n. pl.* name of a community of Saivite priests.

తంబురా **tamburaa** *n.* stringed instrument providing a drone to accompany music.

తకతకలాడు **takatakalaaDu** *v.i.* **1** to hurry, hasten. **2** to be distressed, be agitated, be restless.

తకతైతకతైమను **takataytakataymanu** *v.i. colloq.* to gesticulate excitedly.

తకపికలాడించు **takapikalaaDincu** *v.t.* **1** to deceive. **2** to cause worry or anxiety.

తకపికలాడు **takapikalaaDu** *v.i.* **1** to move this way and that, **2** to deceive.

తకరారు **takaraaru** *n.* dispute, quarrel, altercation

తకావి, తక్కావి **tak[k]aawi** *n.* loan given by the government for purpose of cultivation.

తకిట, తక్కిట **tak[k]iTa** *onom. adv. sug.* beating of a drum.

తకిలీ **takilii** *n. dial.* spindle.

తక్క **takka** *adv. class.* except[ing] (= **tappa**).

తక్కటి **takkaTi** *adj.* remaining, left over.

తక్కరి **takkari** *same as* **Takkari.**

తక్కలపడు **takkalapaDu** *v.i.* to be in trouble.

తక్కాలు **takkaalu** *n. dial.* tomato.

తక్కావి **takkaawi** *same as* **takaawi.**

తక్కించు **takkincu** *v.t.* 1 to remove. 2 to divert. 3 to set aside.

తక్కించుకొను **takkincukonu** *v.t.* to keep or preserve for o.s.

తక్కిట **takkiTa** *same as* **takiTa.**

తక్కిడికాడు **takkiDikaaDu** *n.* cheat, deceiver.

తక్కిన **takkina** *adj.* remaining, other; ~**waaru** other persons, others; ~**di** (*sing.*), ~**wi** (*pl.*) remainder, the rest.

తక్కు **takku**[1] *v.i. and t., class. except for vbl. adj.* **takkina** (*see above*) 1 to remain, be left over. 2 to refrain, give up, omit.

తక్కు **takku**[2] *v.i. and t. class.* to pretend, deceive.

తక్కువ **takkuwa** I. *n.* 1 shortage deficiency, lack; **bhuulookamloo durmaargulaki eem~**? what shortage of wicked people is there in the world? **annii ceesEEnu, niiku eem~ ayindi**? I have done everything, what else do you want? 2 inferiority. 3 meanness, baseness. 4 defect. II. *adj.* 1 deficient; ~**ancanaa ceeyu** to underestimate. 2 little, small, few[er], less; **teliwi~** stupid (*lit.* having little intelligence); **nuuTiki~** *or* **nuuTikaNTee~** less than a hundred; **paawu~eeDayindi** it is a quarter to seven (*lit.* it is a quarter (of an hour) less than seven). 3 inferior, lower (in rank, estimation); **waaDiki kulam takkuwaa, guNam takkuwaa**? is he inferior either in his community or in good qualities? 4 mean, base.

తక్కువగా చూచు **takkuwagaa cuucu** *v.t.* to look down on, despise.

తక్కువ చేయు **takkuwa ceeyu** *v.t.* 1 to make (s.g) smaller, make (s.g) less, reduce. 2 to look down on, despise.

తక్కువ తిను **takkuwa tinu** *v.i.* 1 *in interrog. constr., often in rhetorical questions* to be worse, be inferior; **waLLiddariloo ewaru takkuwa tinnaaru**? which of those two is the worse? 2 *in neg. constr.* to be a match (for others); be similar (to others); be the same (as others); be no worse (than others); *see* **tagaadaa.**

తక్కువపడు **takkuwapaDu** *v.i.* 1 to be insufficient, be deficient; **sommu takkuwapaDindi** the money was not enough. 2 to feel-belittled.

తక్కువపరచు **takkuwaparacu** *v.t.* to belittle, look down on, regard with contempt.

తక్కువపాటు **takkuwapaaTu** *n.* 1 deficiency. 2 belittlement.

తక్కువలో తక్కువ **takkuwaloo takkuwa** *adv.* at the very least.

తక్కెడ, తక్కిడి, తక్కిట **takkeDa, takkiDi, takkiTa** *n.* balance, pair of scales.

తక్కెడు **takkeDu** *n.* a weight of one viss, about one and a half kilograms.

తక్షకుడు **takSakuDu** *n.* name of a king of the serpents in mythology, a proverbially wicked character.

తక్షణ **takSaNa** *adj.* immediate, instant[aneous]; ~**samasyalu** current problems.

తక్షణం **takSaNam** I. *adv.* immediately. II. *particle suffixed to a past vbl. adj.* as soon as; **paaTham winna~ appaceppEEDu** as soon as he had heard the lesson, he repeated it back.

తఖ్తు **takhtu** *n.* seat, throne.

తగని **tagani** *neg. vbl. adj. of* **tagu** 1 unbefitting, unbecoming, inappropriate, improper. 2 great, huge, enormous, tremendous, vast.

తగరం **tagaram** *n.* tin.

తగల[బ]డు **tagala[ba]Du** *v.i.* 1 to be [set] on fire, burn. 2 *fig. usage* **oLLu~tunnadi** *or* **oLLu tagala[ba] Deesukoni wastunnadi** I am extremely angry. 3 *in colloq. speech~ can substitute for* **uNDu** *to be or other verbs when used disparagingly* **nuwwu ikkaDininci~**! go away from here! **mana caduwulu andukee iTLaa~tunnaay!** so this is the state of our education! **poonii daani koDukoo! paankooDDokkulaa moham waaDuunuu! waaDaynaa tagalaDi caawaleedaa akkaDa**? well then her son; the boy with a face like an old wooden sandal, is not he there either? *cf.* **eeDcu, caccu.**

తగలబెట్టు, తగలెట్టు **tagal[ab]eTTu** *v.t.* 1 to burn, set on fire. 2 *in colloq. speech~ can substitute for other verbs when used disparagingly* **ii Dabbu tiisukeLLi waaDi mohaana ~** go and give him this money (spoken unwillingly).

తగలేయ!, తగలేసిరి! **tagaleeya!, tagaleesiri !** *optative of* **tagaleeyu** (*lit. meaning* may (s.g) burn!, may (s.g) be burnt!) *used as interj. expressive of disapproval or disgust* **waaDu antee! ceppina maaTa winaDu, waaNNi tagaleesiri!** he is like that, he won't listen to what you say, confound him! **nii teliwi~, ii pani tondaragaa ceyyi!** do this quickly, confound you!

తగలేయు, తగలవేయు **tagaleeyu, tagalaweeyu** *v.i. and t.* 1 to burn, set on fire, set fire to. 2 *colloq.* to spend wastefully, squander; **naakinda Dabbu tagaleeseewaaDu** he used to squander money on me. 3 *in colloq. speech~ can substitute for other vbs. when used disparagingly* **aa sanci iTLaa tagileey!** give me that bag! 4. *colloq.* to spoil; **ceppina pani tagaleesEEDu** he spoilt the work that was given to him.

తగవరి **tagawari** *n.* judge, arbitrator.

తగవు, తగువు **tagawu, taguwu** *n.* 1 dispute, fight, quarrel; ~**lu paDu** to be involved in quarrels. 2 trouble, disturbance.

తగాదా, తగాయిదా **tagaadaa, tagaayidaa** *n.* dispute, quarrel; **aayana ~weesukonnaaDu, neenu takkuwa tina**

leedu, maaTaki maaTa jawaabu ceppEEnu he started a quarrel, I was a match for him, I answered him word for word.

తగిన, తగ్గ **tagina, tagga** *past vbl. adj. of* **tagu 1** proper, fit[ting], suitable, appropriate, reasonable; **~ sambandham** a suitable match; **cadawa ~ pustakam** a book worth reading; **~ waaTaa** a fair share; **~ Dabbu icci pampinceesEEnu** I sent him away with a reasonable (*or* appropriate) sum of money. **2** likely, probable, possible; **jiiwitamloo raa ~ maarpulu** changes which may occur during o.'s lifetime; **reNDu widhaala waaDa ~ kriyalu** verbs that may be used in two ways. **3** proportional, corresponding; **anduku ~ prayoojanam** the advantage corresponding to it; **aa kharjiiduku ~ paalu** a quantity of milk proportional to that price.

తగినంత **taginanta** *adj.* as much as is needed, adequate, sufficient.

తగినట్టు[గా], తగ్గట్టు[గా] **taginaTTu[gaa], taggaTTu[gaa]** *adv.* **1** fittingly, appropriately, suitably; **praśnaku ~ jawaabu iccEEDu** he answered the question fittingly. **2** corresponding to, in proportion to, consistent with; **andukanee sampaadincina sampaadanaku ~ Dabbu migalaleedu** for that reason money was not saved in proportion to the income that was earned.

తగినన్ని **taginanni** *adj.* as many as are needed; **~ kaaraNaalu** a sufficient number of reasons.

తగిలించు **tagilincu** *v.t.* **1** to apply, attach, fix, fasten; **tana kooTu gooDaku tagilincEEDu** he hung his coat on the wall. **2** to join, connect, link. **3** *slang* to start a quarrel between two persons; **waaLLiddarikii tagilinci tanu tappukunnaaDu** having provoked a quarrel between them, he slipped away.

తగిలించుకొను **tagilincukonu** *v.t.* **1** to wear, put on (attachable items like glasses, wrist watch, jewellery). **2** to catch, contract (disease).

తగిలేయు **tagileeyu**[1] *same as* **tagalaweeyu.**

తగిలేయు **tagileeyu**[2] *v.t.* to drive away, drive out.

తగు **tagu** I. *adj.* fit[ting], suitable, appropriate, right, sufficient, adequate; **~ jaagratta tiisukoowaali** you must take sufficient care; **~ mootaadu** the correct dose; **miiru ceeya ~ pani** the right work for you to do. II. *v.i.* to be fit[ting], suitable, appropriate, sufficient, right, proper, worthy; **ii prawartana miiku tagadu** this conduct is unworthy of you; **iTLaa ceeya tagunaa?** is it right to do this? **idi iraway ruupaayala welaki tagi unnadaa?** is this worth twenty rupees? *see* **tagani, tagina, tagga.**

తగుదునమ్మా అను **tagudunammaa anu** *v.i.* to claim to be fit, capable, competent or eligible; **ewaDeenaa wacci tagudunammaa ani manaki niiti boodhincabootee manaki tala noppigaa uNTundi** if anyone comes claiming to be a fit person and proceeds to preach morals to us, it will give us a headache; *this verb is derived from* **tagudunu** *1st per. sing. indefinite tense of* **tagu** *meaning* 'I am fit' + **ammaa** *(particle)* + **anu** to say.

తగుమనిషి **tagumaniSi** *n. dial.* **1** an equal (in social status). **2** gentleman.

తగుమాత్రం **tagumaatram** *adj.* moderate, adequate.

తగుమాత్రంగా **tagumaatrangaa** *adv.* moderately, adequately, just enough.

తగు[వు]లాట **tagu[wu]laaTa** *n.* quarrel.

తగులాటం **tagulaaTam** *n.* **1** bondage. **2** hindrance, obstruction. **3** trouble, bother.

తగు[వు]లాడు **tagu[wu]laaDu** *v.i.* to quarrel.

తగులు **tagulu** I. *v.i.* **1** to come in contact with, touch, hit, strike; **waaDiki debba tagilindi** he received a blow; **naaku kaaliki raayi tagilindi** my foot hit against a stone; **waaDi manasuki tagileelaa ceppaali** you must speak so as as to impress this on his mind; **ikkaDa gaali ~ tunnadi** the wind strikes here *or* there is a wind here; **waaDi tiTLu naaku tagala leedu** his abuse had no effect on me; *see* **usuru.** **2** (of disease) to be caught; **rawiki jwaram tagilindi** Ravi caught fever. **3** to happen, occur, appear, turn up, take place (more or less by chance); **ii uuLLoo naaku pani tagilindi, andukoosam waccEEnu** I happened to get a job in this place and have come for it; **aayanaku prayaaNam tagilindi** he went on a journey; **ii waaram maaku bayaTa bhoojanaalu naalugu roojulu tagilinaayi** this week we have had four invitations to dinner. **4** to be met or encountered (more or less by chance); **atanu doowaloo naaku tagilEEDu** I happened to meet him on the road. **5 naaku ceeticamuru tagilindi** I had to spend my money. II. *v.t.* **1** to send. **2 aDDam ~** to come in the way of, oppose, obstruct. **3 weNTa ~** to run after, pursue.

తగులుకొను **tagulukonu** I. *v.i.* to be[come] involved, entangled or ensnared. II. *v.t.* **1** to involve, entangle, ensnare. **2** to run after or run away with (a loved one), fall in love with.

తగులుబడి **tagulubaDi** *n.* expenditure, outgoings.

తగుల్చు **tagulcu** *v.t.* to attach.

తగుల్చుకొను **tagulcukonu** *v.t.* to sustain (injury); **aame kaaliki debba tagulcukonnadi** she sustained an injury to her leg.

తగువు **taguwu** *same as* **tagawu.**

తగ్గ **tagga** *same as* **tagina.**

తగ్గట్టు[గా] **taggaTTu[gaa]** *same as* **taginaTTu[gaa].**

తగ్గించు **taggincu** *v.t.* **1** to lessen, reduce, deplete, decrease, curtail, diminish. **2** to lower; **diipam ~** to turn down a lamp. **3** to shorten, abridge. **4** to belittle, degrade.

తగ్గింపు **taggimpu** *n.* **1** fall, sinking. **2** lessening, curtailment, reduction; **~ dhara** reduced price.

తగ్గు **taggu** I. *n.* **1** reduction, decrease, abatement, lessening, lowering, diminishing; **heccu ~ lu** increases and decreases, ups and downs; **~ sthaayiloo** at a reduced level, on a modest scale; **ninna nadi udhṛtangaa undi, ii wEELa koncem ~ loo undi** yesterday the river was flowing turbulently, today it is a little reduced; **~ mukham paTTu** to decline, diminish, decrease, be on a downward trend. **2** shortage in measuring; **ginneloo neyyi ~ undi, niNDaa pooyaNDi** there is a shortage of ghee in the ginne, fill it to the brim. II. *v.i.* to decrease, diminish, be reduced, dwindle, be lessened, decline, abate, (of floods) recede, (of prices) fall, (of fire, disease) die down, subside. **2 wenakaku ~** to draw back, withdraw, retire, retreat.

తగ్గుదల **taggudala** *n.* decrease.

తచ్చాడు, తచ్చాట్లాడు **taccaaDu, taccaaTLaaDu** *v.i.* to walk about, move about. **2** to loiter, linger, hang about (colloq.)

తజ్ఞుడు **tajñuDu** *n. class.* knowledgeable person.

తటం **taTam** *n.* **1** shore, bank. **2** valley. **3** place.

తటతట **taTataTa** *onom. adv. sug.* flapping of wings.

తటపటా **taTapaTaa** *onom. adv. sug.* rattling, shaking (e.g., of doors in wind).

తటపటాయించు **taTapaTaayincu** *v.i.* to hesitate, waver, dither.

తటపటాయింపు **taTapaTaayimpu** *n.* hesitation, wavering, vacillation.

తటమట **taTamaTa** *n.* deceit.

తటమటించు **taTamaTincu** *v.t.* to deceive.

తటస్థ **taTastha** *adj.* neutral, impartial.

తటస్థపడు **taTasthapaDu** *v.i.* 1 to appear. 2 to happen, occur. 3 *with dat.* to come across, meet; **aayana miiku doowaloo taTasthapaDitee maa iNTiki tiisukuraNDi** if you meet him on the way please bring him to my house; **Dabbu taTasthapaDitee peLLi ceestaanu** if I can raise some money, I will celebrate the marriage.

తటస్థభావం **taTasthabhaawam** *n.* neutral stance.

తటస్థవిధానం **taTasthawidhaanam** *n. polit.* non-alignment.

తటస్థించు **taTasthincu** *v.i.* to happen, occur, take place.

తటస్థీకరణం **taTasthiikaraNam** *n.* neutralisation.

తటస్థీకరించు **taTasthiikarincu** *v.t.* to neutralise.

తటస్థుడు **taTasthuDu** *n.* neutral person, impartial person.

తటాకం **taTaakam** *n.* tank, pond, reservoir.

తటాయించు **taTaayincu** *v.i.* (of an irrigation tank) to be full to the brim.

తటాలున, తటాల్న, తటుక్కున **taTaaluna, taTaalna, taTukkuna** *adv.* suddenly, abruptly.

తటి **taTi** *n. class.* bank, edge, shore.

తటిత్తు **taTittu** *n. class.* lightning.

తటిద్దండం **taTiddaNDam** *n.* lightning rod.

తటిల్లత **taTillata** *n. class.* streak of lightning.

తట్ట **taTTa** *n.* 1 flat basket. 2 metal plate or tray. 3 *dial.* eating plate.

తట్టగోలెం **taTTagoolem** *n.* basket-shaped earthen vessel for holding cattle fodder.

తట్టతగలేయు **taTTatagaleeyu** *v.i.* to sever relationships; **aa uuLLoo taTTatagaleesukoni ii uuru waccEEru** they severed their relationships in that village and came to this one.

తట్టాబుట్టా **taTTaabuTTaa** *n.* all o.'s belongings; **~ paTTuku bayaldeeru** to take all o.'s belongings and start.

తట్టి **taTTi** *n.* 1 dish, plate. 2 small cup or bowl. 3 screen of khaskhas grass (moistened and hung in a doorway or in front of a fan to cool the air in a room by evaporation).

తట్టు **taTTu** I. *n.* 1 side, direction, quarter. 2 bank, shore. 3 *dial.* riddle; **mii praśna oka ~ laagunnadi** your question is like a riddle. 4 *dial.* area; **maa ~ iTLanee maaTLaaDataaru** in our area people speak like this. 5 mark left on the skin as a result of a blow; **oNTimiida ~ teelindi** a welt appeared on the body. 6 (*also* **taTTammawaaru**) chicken pox; **waaDiki ~ poosindi** he developed (*or* he caught) chicken pox. II. *v.i.* (of an idea) to occur, strike; **aawiDaki oka aaloocana taTTindi** an idea occurred to her. III. *v.t.* 1 to strike, knock; **talupu ~** to knock on a door. 2 to pat, tap, slap.

తట్టుకొను **taTTukonu** I. *v.i.* 1 to strike against; **kaaliki raayi taTTukoni kinda paDDaaDu** he struck his foot against a stone and fell down. 2 to get over, recover from; **ii debbaki taTTukonnaaDu** he recovered from this blow. II. *v.t.* 1 to bear, withstand, tolerate, put up with. 2 to overcome, surmount, cope with.

తట్టుబడి **taTTubaDi** *n. dial. same as* **taakiDi.**

తడక, తడిక, తడికె **taDaka, taDika, tadike** *n.* 1 screen of interlaced palm leaves, bamboo slats, etc. 2 open framework of criss-crossing wooden slats serving as a screen, partition or fence. 3 *idiomatic usages*: **~ aarcil** two upright posts surmounted by a flat lintel; **~ wippukonu** to lay everything bare, keep nothing secret; **pillalu aayanaki ~lu kaTTEEru** the children ridiculed him; *see* **tappu** *sense I.1.*

తడపర **taDapara** *n.* chicken pox; **waaDiki ~ poosindi** he caught chicken pox.

తడబడు **taDabaDu** *v.i.* to falter (in moving, making progress, speaking).

తడబాటు **taDabaaTu** *n.* faltering, irresolution.

తడవ **taDawa** *n.* time, occasion; **reNDu ~lu** twice.

తడవు, తడువు **taDawu**[1], **taDuwu**[1] *n.* 1 (period of) time; **konta ~** a little time, a short while. 2 delay; **~ oorcu** to wait patiently. 3 (*idiomatic usage*) as soon as; **ceppaDamee ~ gaa** (*or* **ceppaDamee aalasyam**) **parigettEEDu** he ran as soon as he was told; *the underlying thought in this elliptic expression is*: his being told was the (only) delay; *further examples are*: (i) **aame atani anni wyawahaaraalaloonu ataniki salahaalu icceedi, phalaanaa widhangaa ceyyaNDi ani aame ceppaDam ~ gaa aa prakaaram atanu ceeseewaaDu** she used to advise him in all his affairs, as soon as she said "do this in a certain way" he would do it accordingly; (ii) **"eem Sawkaarugaaruu! eTLa undi wyaapaaram?" ani aDagaDamee ~ "eem beerasaaraalu leewu baabuu! eedoo roojulu dorlincukostunnaam" aNTaaDu** as soon as you ask "what mr. shopkeeper? how is your business?" he will reply "no business at all sir! we are just letting the days go by".

తడవు, తడువు, తడుము **taDawu**[2], **taDuwu**[2], **taDumu** *v.i. and t.* 1 to touch, pat, handle, finger. 2 to feel about with the hands, grope. 3 to pause for thought, hesitate for want of confidence, falter, stumble; **taDumukookuNDaa maaTLaaDEEDu** he talked fluently without hesitating. 4 *dial.* to grab; **naa jeebuloo Dabbulu taDumukonnaaDu** he grabbed the money in my pocket. 5 **bhujaalu ~konu** (*lit.* to pat o.'s shoulders) *is used of a person who fancies that a chance remark was aimed at himself.*

తడవులాడుకొను **taDawulaaDukonu** *v.i.* to grope; **ciikaTLoo tadawulaaDukoNTuu weLLEEDu** he went groping his way in the dark.

తడాఖా **taDaakhaa** *n.* strength, force, power.

తడి **taDi** I. *n.* 1 wetness, damp[ness], moistness, moisture. 2 watering, irrigation (of a field); **naaru weesina tarwaata reNDoo ~** the second watering after the seedlings are sown. II. *adj.* wet, damp, moist.

తడిక, తడికె **taDika**, **tadike** *same as* **taDaka**.

తడిక దాసరి **taDika daasari** *n.* bogus religious mendicant, cheat.

తడిగుడ్డ **taDiguDDa** *n.* 1 wet or damp cloth; **~too gontu[ka] kooyu** *lit.* to cut s.o.'s throat with a damp cloth, i.e., to deceive s.o. by means of soft words. 2 ceremonial damp cloth worn by a person before dressing himself in **maDi**.

తడిచేయు **taDiceeyu** *v.t.* 1 to make wet, moisten. 2 to water, irrigate. 3 *slang* **o.-ki ceyyi~** to give s.o. a bribe.

తడిపెట్టు **taDipeTTu** *v.i.* to moisten; **aame kaNTa taDi peTTindi** she dissolved in tears.

తడిపొడి **taDipoDi** *adj.* slightly wet, damp; **~cinukulu** light rain, drizzle.

తడిబారు **taDibaaru** *v.i.* to become damp.

తడిమడి **taDimaDi** *n.* ceremonially pure wet cloth ordained to be worn on certain occasions.

తడియారు **taDiyaaru** *v.i.* to be[come] dry.

తడియార్చు **taDiyaarcu** *v.t.* to dry; **juTTu ~koNTuu kuurcunnadi** she sat drying her hair.

తడియు **taDiyu** *v.i.* to be wet, get wet; **taDisi gaani guDise kaTTaDu** he will not build a hut till he gets wet (said of a person who lacks foresight); **naa baTTalu annii taDisimudda aypooyEEyi** all my clothes are wet through; **tiisukonna appu koncamee gaani ippuDu waDDiitoo taDisimoopeDu ayyindi** the loan which he took was small but now with interest it has become a heavy burden (in the way that a dry load becomes heavier when it gets wet).

తడివెండి **taDiweNDi** *n.* mercury.

తడుపు **taDupu** *v.t.* 1 to wet, moisten, make wet. 2 *slang* **o.-ki ceyyi~** to bribe s.o.

తడుప్పాత **taDuppaata** *n.* small cloth worn when taking a bath.

తడుము **taDumu** *same as* **taDawu**[2].

తత్ **tat** *Sanskrit prefix meaning* it, that, the same, the aforesaid; **tatsambandhamayna** connected with that, connected therewith; **tadbhinnam** different from that, different therefrom; **aa naaTi kawulu prakr̥tini tatsawndaryaanni warNincEEru** the poets of those days described nature and its beauty.

తతం **tatam** *n. phys.* stretched string or wire.

తతంగం **tatangam** *n.* 1 affairs, business, rigmarole; **ingliiSuwaaLLu wartakamtoo iNDiyaanu doostunnaaru, ii doopiDi koosamee paripaalana~antaanuu** the English are plundering India with trade, all the rigmarole of government is for the sake of this plundering. 2 paraphernalia; **reNDu swaarii baNDLu, aaru gurraalu wagayraa ~antaa uNDeedi** there was all the paraphernalia of two carriages, six horses and so on. 3 procession of events, proceedings, procedure; **brndam naayakuDu laanchanapraayamayna tatangaalu mugincEEka mugguru wyoomagaamulu roodasii nawkalooki praweeśincEEru** when the leader of the team had completed the regular procedures, the three astronauts entered the spaceship.

తతిమ, తతిమ్మా **tatima**, **tatimmaa** *adj.* other, remaining.

తత్తరపడు **tattarapaDu** *v.i.* to be perplexed or disconcerted.

తత్తరపాటు **tattarapaaTu** *n.* perplexity, disconcertedness.

తత్తరబిత్తర **tattarabittara** *adj.* bewildered, baffled.

తత్తరబిత్తరవు **tattarabittarawu** *v.i.* to be at a loss.

తత్తురుబుత్తురుగా **tatturubutturugaa** *adv.* (of walking, writing) irregularly, unsteadily, not following a straight line.

తత్తుల్యం **tattulyam** *adj.* similar, equivalent.

తత్పరత **tatparata** *n.* single-minded devotion.

తత్పరుడు **tatparuDu** *n.* devoted or single-minded person.

తత్పూర్వం **tatpuurwam** *adj.* previous, preceding.

తత్ఫలితంగా **tatphalitangaa** *adv.* as a result of that, consequently.

తత్వం **tatwam** *n.* 1 true or real state, reality. 2 entity. 3 nature, essence. 4 *pl.* **tatwaalu** kind of song.

తత్వజ్ఞానం, తత్వశాస్త్రం **tatwajñaanam**, **tatwaśaastram** *n.* philosophy.

తత్వజ్ఞానజ్ఞుడు, తత్వశాస్త్రజ్ఞుడు, తత్వవేత్త **tatwajñaanajñuDu**, **tatwaśaastrajñuDu**, **tatwaweetta** *n.* philosopher.

తత్వోపదేశం **tatwoopadeeśam** *n.* 1 philosophical instruction. 2 mantra or prayer taught by a guru to a disciple by reciting which the disciple can attain salvation.

తత్సంబంధ **tatsambandha** *adj.* 1 relating to, connected with. 2 *legal* relevant; *see* **tat**.

తత్సమం **tatsamam** *n. gram.* unassimilated borrowing into Telugu from Sanskrit; *cf.* **tadbhawam.**

తథాగతుడు **tathaagatuDu** *n.* epithet of Buddha.

తథాస్తు! **tathaastu!** *interj.* so let it be!

తథ్యం, తధ్యం **tathyam**, **tadhyam** I. *n.* truth, fact reality. II. *adj.* 1 true, real, actual. 2 certain, definite.

తదనంతర **tadanantara** *adj.* next, following; **~kaaryakramam** the next programme.

తదనంతరం **tadanantaram** I. *p.p.* after. II. *adv.* later on, afterwards.

తదర్థ **tadartha** *adj.* intended for a particular purpose, ad hoc.

తదితర **taditara** *adj.* and other.

తదియ **tadiya** *n.* third day of a lunar fortnight, third day after a new or full moon.

తదీయ **tadiiya** *pronom. adj.* his, her, its, their.

తదుపరి **tadupari** *adv.* 1 after that, thereafter, afterwards. 2 over and above that.

తదేక **tadeeka** *adj.* fixed, intent, concentrated; **~drSTi** fixed or intent gaze; **~dhyaanam** concentrated attention.

తదేకంగా **tadeekangaa** *adv.* fixedly, intently.

తద్జ్ఞులు **tadjñulu** *n. pl.* persons with wide experience.

తద్ద, తద్దయు **tadda**,[1] **taddayu** *adv. class.* much, very.

తద్ద **tadda**[2] *n.* kind of tree, *grewia tiliaefolia*, whose wood is used for cart making.

తద్దినం **taddinam** *n.* annual ceremony commemorating a person's death; ~ **koniteccukonu** to invite difficulties upon o.s.

తద్దె **tadde** *n. corrupt form of* **tadiya** *occurring in names of festivals held on* **tadiya** *day,* e.g., **aTLa ~, koomaTLa ~**.

తద్ధర్మార్థకం **taddharmaarthakam** *n. gram.* indefinite aorist tense.

తద్ధర్మార్థక ప్రత్యయం **taddharmaarthaka pratyayam** *n. gram.* fut. habitual vbl. adj. suffix ending in ee, e.g., **pooy-ee, wacc-ee.**

తద్ధిత **taddhita** *adj. gram.* derivative; ~ **pratyayam** derivative suffix.

తద్భవం **tadbhawam** *n. gram.* word borrowed from Sanskrit or Prakrit assimilated into Telugu; *cf.* **tatsamam.**

తద్భిన్నం **tadbhinnam** *n. and adj.* different, otherwise: **eedi śaaswatam? eedi kSaNikam? eedi sundaram? eedi ~ ?** what is eternal? what is transitory? what is beautiful? what is otherwise?

తద్భిన్నంగా **tadbhinnangaa** *adv.* differently; **neenu anukonnadi okaTi gaani ~ jarigindi** I thought of something but it turned out differently.

తద్రూపం[గా] **tadruupan[gaa]** *adv.* in an identical manner, in exactly the same way; **maaTalloo ceppinadi ceetalloo tadruupam ceesi cuupincEEDu** what he had said verbally he demonstrated in an identical manner in his actions; **waaLLa naannaki wiiDu tadruupam** he is exactly like his father *or* he is the living image of his father; **neenu ceppindi ceppinaTTu tadruupangaa winipincEEDu** he recited word for word just as I had told him.

తద్వారా **tadwaaraa** *adv.* thereby, by means of that, through that.

తధిగిణతై తధిగిణతై **tadhigiNatay tadhigiNatay** rhythmical sounds uttered by a dancing master for keeping time.

తధ్యం **tadhyam** *same as* **tathyam.**

తన **tana** *genitive of* **tanu, taanu**[1].

తనం **tanam** *suffix used for forming abstract nouns from adjectives,* e.g., **goppa ~** greatness.

తనఖా **tanakhaa** *n.* mortgage.

తనబ్బి, తనాబి **tanabbi, tanaabi** *n.* niche in a wall.

తనయ **tanaya** *n. class.* daughter.

తనయుడు **tanayuDu** *n. class.* son.

తనరు **tanaru** *v.i. class.* 1 to appear. 2 to shine.

తనలో **tanaloo** *adv. theat.* (in stage directions) spoken to o.s., aside.

తనికీ, తనిఖీ **tanikii, tanikhii** *n.* inspection, examination.

తనివారు **taniwaaru** *v.i.* to be satisfied; **niiku ippaTiki taniwaarindaa?** now are you satisfied?

తనివి **taniwi** *n.* satisfaction, contentment.

తనివితీరా **taniwitiiraa** *adv.* to (o.'s) heart's content.

తనివితీరు **taniwitiiru** *v.i., gen. in neg. or interrog. constr.* to be satisfied; **waaDiki taniwi tiiraleedu** he was not satisfied *or* it was not enough for him.

తను, తాను **tanu, taanu**[1] *reflexive pron.* 1 himself, herself, *pl.* **taamu** themselves; **taanu** (*or* **taanee**) **waccEEDu** he himself came; **aayana nannu tana tooTaku tiisukupooyEEDu** he took me to his (own) garden; **tamalootaamu waadincukoNTunnaaru** they are arguing among themselves; **tanantataanee** of his own accord. 2 *the use of* **tanu** *as substitute for a demonstrative pron. is becoming increasingly common in colloq. speech,* e.g., **tanu ekkaDiki weLLEEDoo naaku teliyadu** I do not know where he has gone.

తనుకులాట **tanukulaaTa n.** death throes.

తనుపు **tanupu** *n. class.* coolness, cold.

తనువు **tanuwu** *n.* body.

తనువుచాలించు **tanuwu caalincu** *v.i. class.* to die.

తన్ను **tannu** I. *n.* kick, blow, beating; ~ **lu tinu** to be beaten or thrashed. II. *v.i.* 1 **ega ~, payki ~** to rise up, rear up, force a way up. 2 *slang* to fail; **naa pariikSa tanneesindi** I failed my examination. III. *v.t.* 1 to kick, beat, thrash. 2 to strike against. 3 *slang* **baalcii tanneesEEDu** he died.

తన్నుకొను **tannukonu** *v.i. t.* 1 to beat one another. 2 to strike against. 3 to struggle or flutter in anguish. 4 *idiomatic usages convey various shades of meaning,* e.g., (i) **wiidhulloo tannuku castunnaaru** they are quarrelling in the streets; (ii) **wenakku jaragabooyi Saraayiloo kaaLLu tannukoni kinda paDipooyEEDu** when he started to move backwards he caught his feet in his trousers and fell over; (iii) **ceetiloodaanni ceetiloonuncee tannuku pootaarayye!** they will snatch away what we have from out of our very hands!

తన్నుబిళ్ల **tannubiLLa** *n.* a girls' game.

తన్నులాడుకొను **tannulaaDukonu** *v.i.* to exchange blows.

తన్మయత, తన్మయత్వం **tanmayata, tanmayatwam** *n.* bliss, ecstasy; **aananda ~** transports of joy.

తన్మయుడు **tanmayuDu** *n.* person wholly absorbed in ecstasy or meditation.

తన్యజ **tanyaja** *adj.* tensile.

తన్యత **tanyata** *n. sci.* tension.

తన్వి **tanwi**[1] *corrupt from of* **taniwi.**

తన్వి **tanwi**[2] *n. class.* graceful woman.

తపం **tapam** *same as* **tapassu.**

తపతప **tapatapa** *onom. adv. sug.* fluttering of birds' wings *or* pattering of raindrops.

తపన **tapana** *n.* 1 distress, anguish. 2 yearning. 3 heat.

తపనపడు, తపనచెందు **tapanapaDu, tapanacendu** *v.i.* 1 to feel anxious or anguished. 2 to strive, do o.'s utmost.

తపల, తబల **tapala, tabala** *n.* spherical mud pot played as a musical instrument.

తపశ్చరణం, తపశ్చర్య **tapaścaraNam, tapaścarya** *n.* 1 practice of austerity. 2 performing penance.

తపశ్శాలి **tapaśśaali** *n.* person who performs penance.

తపస్వి **tapaswi** *n.* ascetic, devotee (male).

తపస్విని **tapaswini** *n.* ascetic, devotee (female).

తపస్సు, తపం **tapassu, tapam** *n.* 1 penance, self-mortification. 2 meditation. 3 self-appointed task accompanied by austerity.

తపస్సు చేయు **tapassu ceeyu** *v.i.* 1 to do penance. 2 to practise meditation with self-denial.

తపారం, తపారు **tapaaram, tapaaru** *n.* kind of cap.

తపాలా **tapaalaa** *same as* **Tapaa[lu].**

తపించు, తపిల్లు **tapincu, tapillu** *v.i.* 1 to be distressed, be in anguish, be distraught. 2 to yearn, long (**-koosam,** for). 3 to perform penance.

తపిక్కున **tapikkuna** *onom. adv. sug.* sound of s.g falling on the ground with a bump, thump, clang or clatter.

తపేలచెక్క, తపేలరొట్టె **tapeela cekka, tapeela roTTi** *n.* kind of cake made of rice flour.

తపేలా, తప్పేలా **tapeelaa, tappeelaa** *n.* metal vessel gen. made of brass.

తపోధనుడు **tapoodhanuDu** *n.* person who has acquired merit by good deeds.

తపోవనం **tapoowanam** *n.* place of penance.

తప్త **tapta** *adj.* heated, burnt.

తప్ప **tappa** I. *n.* empty ear of grain; **ii waDLaloo taaluu tappaa poogaa eemundi?** what is there in this paddy apart from husk and empty ears? II. *advbl. particle* 1 except; **nuwwu ~ naaku ewaruu dikku leeru** I have no-one as protector except you.' 2 unless; **neenu cuusteenee ~ nammanu** unless I see I will not believe. III. *disjunctive particle* and not, but not; **boppaayi ceTTuki aakulu kaaDalu ~ kommalu uNDawu** the papaya tree has leaves and stalks but no branches.

తప్పక, తప్పకుండా **tappaka, tappakuNDaa** *adv.* 1 without fail, unfailingly. 2 undoubtedly.

తప్పకన్ను, గవ్వకన్ను **tappakannu, gawwakannu** *n.* sightless eyeball.

తప్పటడుగులు **tappaTaDugulu** *n. pl.* faltering steps.

తప్పతాగు **tappataagu** *v.i.* to be dead drunk.

తప్పనిసరి **tappanisari** *adj.* 1 unavoidable, inevitable. 2 indispensable, essential.

తప్పనిసరిగా **tappanisarigaa** *adv.* 1 without fail, unfailingly. 2 surely, inevitably, perforce. 3 invariably.

తప్పించు **tappincu** *v.t.* 1 to cause (s.o.) to miss or lose (s.g); **naa baNDi tappincEEDu** he made me miss my train; **nannu doowa tappincEEDu** he misled me. 2 to save, keep safe, **naaku caawu tappincEEDu** he saved me from death. 3 to extricate, set free. 4 to take away, remove; **neenu Dabbu istaanu ani ceppi mokham tappincEEDu** after saying "I will pay the money", he made himself scarce. 5 to omit, miss out, leave out; **reNDu wiidhulu tappinci nannu muuDoo wiidhilooki tiisukuwaccEEDu** after missing out (*or* after passing by) two streets, he brought me to the third; **reNDu tappinci muuDu roojulloo wastaanu** I will come in three days if not in two. 6 to change, alter; **neenu praśnalu adugutuNTee maaTa tappincEEDu** when I was putting questions, he changed the subject. 7 **tappinci** (*past participle*) *is used adverbially to mean* excepting, excluding, apart from, other than; **ciiTlu paTTuku tiragaDam tappinci waaLLaki weeree pani eemii leedu** they have no other work than to go about carrying messages.

తప్పించుకొను **tappincukonu** I. *v.i.* to get free, escape. II. *v.t.* to avoid, elude, dodge, shirk.

తప్పిచ్చుకొను **tappiccukonu** *v.i.* 1 to get free, escape. 2 to admit o.'s mistake and pay a forfeit.

తప్పిజారి **tappijaari** *adv.* by chance.

తప్పితం, తప్పిదం **tappitam, tappidam** *n.* error, fault, wrong, mistake.

తప్పు **tappu** I. *n.* 1 mistake, error, fault, misdeed; **~ la taDaka** mass of errors; **~ lu encu, ~ lu etti cuupu** to point out mistakes. 2 offence, crime. II. *adj.* wrong, mistaken, faulty. III. *v.i.* 1 to err, go wrong, fail, be missed; **waaDi lekka tappindi** his calculation was wrong; **peLLi koncemloo tappi pooyindi** the marriage just failed to take place; **aame nela tappindi** *lit.* she missed a month, i.e., she is pregnant. 2 to be averted, be avoided; **gaNDam koncemloo tappindi** the danger was narrowly averted; **adi waaDiki tappadu** that is sure tobefall him; **tapputundaa?** can it be avoided? (*rhetorical question*). 3 **tappadu** *following a neg. participle gives the meaning* must . . . . without fail; **miiru raaka tappadu** you must come without fail. IV. *v.t.* 1 to miss; **guri ~** to miss the mark; **daari ~** to miss or lose o.'s way. 2 *colloq.* to fail; **waaDu pariikSa tappEEDu** he failed his examination. 3 to avoid, escape from. 4 **maaTa ~** to break o.'s promise.

తప్పుకొను **tappukonu** *v.i.* 1 to make way, get out of the way. 2 to retreat, withdraw. 3 to slip away, evade.

తప్పుడు **tappuDu** *adj.* wrong, mistaken, incorrect.

తప్పుతోయు **tapputooyu** *v.i.* to impute blame (**-miidiki,** on).

తప్పు[లు]పట్టు **tappu[lu]paTTu** *v.t.* to find fault with, blame.

తప్పెట **tappeTa** *n.* kind of drum.

తప్పేలా **tappeelaa** *same as* **tapeelaa.**

తప్పొప్పుల పట్టిక **tappoppula paTTika** *n.* corrigenda, errata.

తప్సీలు, తబ్సీళ్లు **tapsiilu, tabsiiLLu** *n. dial.* details.

తబల **tabala** *same as* **tapala.**

తబుకు **tabuku** *n.* plate, tray, dish.

తబ్బిబ్బు **tabbibbu** *n.* confusion, flurry.

తబ్బిబ్బు అవు, తబ్బిబ్బు పడు **tabbibbu awu, tabbibbu paDu** *v.i.* to be confused, be in a flurry.

తభావతు **tabhaawatu** *n.* 1 discrepancy, contradiction. 2 deficiency.

తమ **tama**[1] *Sanskrit adjvl. termination signifying the superlative degree,* e.g., **uccha ~** highest.

తమ **tama**[2] *genitive of* **taamu.**

తమకం **tamakam** *n.* 1 eagerness, enthusiasm. 2 desire, lust.

తమరు, తాము **tamaru, taamu** *obs. honorific form of* **miiru.**

తమలం **tamalam** *n.* 1 betel leaf. 2 betel vine.

తమలపాకు tamalapaaku *n.* betel leaf; ~ **tiige** betel vine; ~ **tooTa** betel garden; ~ **aarcii** pointed arch recalling the shape of a betel leaf.

తమస్సు tamassu *n.* 1 darkness. 2 *tamas*, darkness or ignorance, one of the three gunas; *see* **guNam.**

తమాం tamaam *adj.* all, whole.

తమాట tamaaTa *same as* **TamaaTa.**

తమాయించు tamaayincu *v.i.* to control o.s., control o.'s emotions, be patient.

తమాషా tamaaSaa *n.* 1 joke. 2 fun, joking. 3 spectacle, stunt. 4 oddity, peculiarity, s.g odd or intriguing.

తమాషాగా tamaaSaagaa *adv.* 1 in jest, for fun. 2 oddly, strangely; **ninna swayangaa wastaanannawaaDu ~ iwwEELa raanani phoonu ceesEEDu** after saying yesterday that he would come in person, strangely he phoned today to say that he would not come.

తమి tami *n.* eagerness, desire, lust; ~ **puTTindi** desire/lust was kindled.

తమికొను tamikonu *v.i.* 1 to be eager, be desirous. 2 to be lustful.

తమికొల్పు tamikolpu *v.i.* to arouse desire (in s.o.).

తమిద, తమిదె tamida, tamide *n., gen. pl.* ~ **lu** ragi, a kind of millet, *eleusine coracana.*

తమిరె tamire *n.* pin in the middle of a bullock's yoke.

తమిళం tamiLam *n.* the Tamil language.

తముకు tamuku *same as* **Tamuku.**

తమ్మ tamma[1] *n.* chewed betel leaves.

తమ్మ tamma[2] *n.* kind of bean, *canavalia ensiformis.*

తమ్మకర tammakara *n.* stain caused by betel leaf juice.

తమ్మట్లు, తమ్మెట్లు tammaTLu, tammeTLu *n.pl.* kind of gold earrings with precious stones.

తమ్మరసం tammarasam *n.* betel leaf juice.

తమ్మి tammi *n. class.* lotus.

తమ్మికంటి tammikaNTi *n. class.* fair-eyed woman.

తమ్ముడు tammuDu *n.* 1 younger brother. 2 *form of address to a male person* brother!, friend!, my lad!

తమ్మె tamme *n.* 1 lobe of the ear. 2 part of a halter which goes round an animal's neck.

తయారవు tayaarawu *v.i.* 1 to be ready, get ready, be prepared. 2 to be produced, be manufactured. 3 to come on the scene, appear, turn up; *informant* **wembaDi tayaarayyee waaLLatoo konta ibbandi** there was some trouble with those who turned up along with the informant. 4 to turn into, develop into, take shape, become, turn out to be; **appuDu waydyuni maatra roogiki nijangaanee waykuNTha yaatragaa tayaarawutundi** then the doctor's pill will really turn out to be a journey to heaven for the patient; **ii wibhaagam puroogaminci iinaaDu entoo peerupondina śaakhagaa tayaarayindi** this section progressed and has today become a most renowned department; **śriikaakuLam jillaa 16wa śataabdam daakaa kaLinga raajyamloo uNDipooyindi, anceeta bhaaSa wilakSaNangaa tayaarayindi** Srikakulam district was part of the Kalinga kingdom till the 16th century, for that reason the language developed separately; **aa eeDu sekaND phaaramloo widyaarthulu wipariitangaa waccipaDDaaru, okkokka sekSanulonuu yaabhayyeesi mandi daakaa tayaaraynaaru** in that year students joined the second form in large numbers, they came to as many as fifty in each section.

తయారీ tayaarii *n.* 1 preparation, making ready; ~ **loo** under preparation. 2 manufacturing, production, processing; **ceeneeta ~ lu** handloom manufactures, handloom products.

తయారు tayaaru I. *n.* readiness. II. *adj.* ready, prepared.

తయారు చేయు tayaaru ceeyu *v.t.* 1 to make ready, prepare. 2 to create, produce, manufacture, process.

తర tara *Sanskrit adjvl. termination signifying the comparative degree*; **tiiwratara** more severe.

తరం taram *n.* 1 generation; *see* **taaTikaaya.** 2 *in neg. or interrog. construction* possibility, s.g possible; **ii looyala sawndaryam warNincaDam naa ~ aa?** is it possible for me to describe the beauty of these valleys? 3 *class.* kind, sort.

తరంగం tarangam *n.* 1 wave. 2 *pl.* **tarangaalu** kind of devotional song.

తరంగణం tarangaNam *n. phys.* undulation.

తరంగదైర్ఘ్యం tarangadayrghyam *n. sci.* wavelength.

తరంగలేఖిని tarangaleekhini *n. med. ling.* kymograph.

తరంగిణి tarangiNi *n.* 1 river, stream. 2 *in a book title ~ denotes* material compiled and arranged for purpose of reference or study.

తరంగిత tarangita *adjvl. suffix meaning* wavy, surging; **aananda~** surging with joy.

తరక taraka *n.* skin which forms on a hot liquid, e.g. milk, when it cools; **miigaDa ~ lu** blobs of cream.

తరగ taraga *n.* wave.

తరగతి taragati *n.* grade, set, rank, class, form.

తరగతిగుళ్లు taragatiguLLu *n.pl.* kind of necklace.

తరగరి, తరుగరి taragari, tarugari *n.* broker, commission agent.

తరగు taragu *same as* **tarugu.**

తరచు taracu[1,2] *same as* **tarucu**[1,2].

తరణం taraNam *n. class.* 1 crossing. 2 deliverance, extrication.

తరణోపాయం, తరుణోపాయం taraNoopaayam, taruNoopaayam *n.* means, expedient.

తరతమ taratama *adj.* varying, differing, different; **ii aaru deesaalu ~ bheedaalatoo tiiwramayna drawyoolbaNa paristhitini edurkoNTunnayi** these six countries are encountering a severe inflationary situation in different degrees.

తరతర taratara *n.* alarm, panic.

తరఫు taraphu *n.* side.

తరఫున taraphuna *p.p.* on behalf of, on the side of; **atanu rayitula~ kommu kaasEEDu** he gave support on the side of (*or* on behalf of) the cultivators.

తరబడి tarabaDi *advbl. suffix* at the rate of; **weela~** at the rate of thousands, by the thousand; **gaNTala~ kaacukonnaaru** they waited for hours on end; **eeLLa~** for years at a time, year after year; **śataabdaala~ waaDukaloo undi** it has been in use for centuries.

తరబీతు, తర్ఫీతు, తర్ఫీదు **tarabiitu, tarphiitu, tarphiidu** *n.* training.

తరలించు, తర్లించు **taralincu, tarlincu** *v.t.* 1 to move, shift. 2 to take forcibly.

తరలించుకొను, తర్లించుకొను **taralincukonu, tarlincukonu** *v.t.* to transport, convey.

తరలింపు, తర్లింపు **taralimpu, tarlimpu** *n.* transfer (of resources).

తరలిపోవు **taralipoowu** *v.i.* 1 to start out in a group, migrate. 2 (of a marriage party) to go in procession.

తరలివచ్చు **taraliwaccu** *v.i.* 1 to immigrate. 2 (of a marriage party) to come in procession.

తరలు, తర్లు **taralu, tarlu** *v.i.* 1 to start out in a group. 2 to stir, move, proceed.

తరలుచీరె **taraluciire** *n.* sari presented to the bride by the bridegroom's party, worn by her when she first goes to the bridegroom's house.

తరళపదార్థం **taraLapadaartham** *n. chem.* emulsion.

తరళాక్షి **taraLaakSi** *n.* woman with tremulous eyes.

తరళిత **taraLita** *second part of an adjvl. compound* tremulous, trembling, shaking; **aananda~** trembling with joy.

తరవ కొరవ **tarawa korawa** *n.* shortage occurring at the end of a sequence; **~ eemaynaa uNTee neenu istaanu** if any shortage is found at the end, I will make it good.

తరవాణి **tarawaaNi** *n.* sour or fermented gruel.

తరవాత, తరువాత, తర్వాత **tarawaata, taruwaata, tarwaata** I. *p.p.* after. II. *adv.* afterwards, later, next. III *adj.* (*also* **tarawaati**) next, following, ensuing, later, subsequent. IV. *advbl. particle suffixed to past vbl. adj.* after: **neenu waccina ~ waana paDindi** it rained after I came.

తరవాత్తరవాత **tarawaattaarawaata** *adv.* later on, after some time.

తరవాయి **tarawaayi** *n.* 1 continuation, sequel; **gata sancika ~** continuation from the previous issue. 2 remainder, what remains, what is left over; **ikkaDa pani antaa aypooyinaTTee, inkeem ~ undi?** all the work here is over, what is there still remaining? 3 repetition, recitation. 4 **śaastram ceppina ~ gaa undi** (*or* **śaastram ceppinaTTundi**) that is like reciting the Sastras without regard to their meaning, i.e., that is a meaningless sentence; "**widwattu uNTee tiNDi akkaraleedu, nidra akkaraleedu, peLLaamoo?**" "**śaastram ceppina ~ gaa undi, nidraahaaraalee akkaraleekapooyEEka ika peLLaam endukuu?**" "a man immersed in the search for knowledge needs neither food nor sleep, what about a wife?" "that is meaningless: why should a man who needs neither food nor sleep want a wife?" 5 *advbl. use* apart from, except for, short of; **baahaaTangaa oppukoowaDam ~ gaa maharaaju ooDipooyee unnaaru** short of admitting it in public, the king has been defeated.

తరహా **tarahaa** *n.* 1 kind, sort, type, scale, category; **cinna ~ pariśrama** small scale industry. 2 manner; **mii ~ naaku artham kaawaDam leedu** I am not able to understand your manner.

తరహాగా **tarahaagaa** *adv.* in the manner of, after the fashion of; **peddamaniSi ~** like a gentleman; **oka ~** in a manner, in a way, more or less, to some extent; **oka ~ iSTam leenaTTu moham peTTEEDu** he put on an expression showing that to some extent he was unwilling; **naaku iimadhya oNTLoo oka ~ uNTunnadi** nowadays I am feeling only moderately well.

తరాజు **taraaju** *n.* scales, balance (= **traasu**).

తరి **tari** *n.* 1 irrigated land, wet land. 2 *class.* time, occasion; **aTTi ~** at that time.

తరించు **tarincu** *v.i.* 1 to be surmounted or got over. 2 to earn salvation; **kolanuloo bhaktulu snaanam ceesi taristaaru** the worshippers bathe in the lake and earn salvation. 3 *colloq.* **kotta sinimaa TikaTTu dorikitee waaDi janma taristundi** he will be in the seventh heaven if he gets a ticket for the new movie.

తరికంబం **tarikambam** *n.* churning staff.

తరిచల్ల, తరిమజ్జిగ **taricalla, tarimajjiga** *n.* freshly churned buttermilk.

తరిచి అడుగు **tarici aDugu** *v.t.* to enquire closely into, probe into, investigate throughly.

తరిచి అవు **tarici awu** *v.i.* 1 to become dense. 2 to become frequent.

తరిచి చూచు **tarici cuucu** *v.t.* to took closely into, investigate thoroughly.

తరితీపు **taritiipu** *n.* 1 fondness, liking. 2 lust. 3 pride. 4 neglect, indifference.

తరినాగలి **tarinaagali** *n.* plough used on irrigated land.

తరిపాలు **taripaalu** *n.* fresh milk, still lukewarm after milking.

తరిపి **taripi** *n.* calf that has been weaned.

తరిమెన **tarimena** *n.* lathe.

తరీఖు **tariikha** *n.* method, manner, way.

తరుకృషి **tarukṛSi** *n.* arboriculture.

తరుగరి **tarugari** *same as* **taragari.**

తరుగు, తరగు **tarugu, taragu** I. *n.* shortage, deficit, deficiency. II. *adj.* deficit, deficient, short (in weight, quantity). III. *v.i.* 1 to be worn away, be eroded. 2 to grow less, be reduced, diminish, decline; **pani perigindi kaani taragaleedu** the work grew more rather than less; **taragani gani** an inexhaustible mine. 4 **naaku kaDupu tarukkupootunnadi** I feel sad at heart. IV. *v.t.* to cut up into pieces, slice, carve, mince; **aame kuuralu ~ koNTunnadi** she is cutting up vegetables.

తరుగుదల **tarugudala** *n.* 1 decrease. 2 depreciation. 3 deficit.

తరుచు, తరచు **tarucu**[1], **taracu**[1] *v.t. class.* 1 to stir, agitate. 2 to churn.

తరుచు, తరచు **tarucu**[2], **taracu**[2] I. *n.* denseness, density, compactness. II. *adv.* (*also* **~ gaa**) often, frequently.

తరుణ **taruNa** *adj.* 1 young, tender, youthful. 2 new, fresh

తరుణం **taruNam** *n.* time, occasion, opportunity.

తరుణి **taruNi** *n.* young woman.

తరుణుడు **taruNuDu** *n.* young man, youth.

తరుణోపాయం **taruNoopaayam** *same as* **taraNoopaayam.**

తరుము **tarumu** *v.t.* 1 to chase, pursue, follow. 2 to drive away, drive out. 3 (*also* **tarimi pampu**) to send or despatch (s.o.) in haste.

తరువాత **taruwaata** *same as* **tarawaata.**

తరువు **taruwu** *n. class.* tree.

తరువోజ **taruwooja** *n.* kind of poetical metre.

తర్కం **tarkam** *n.* 1 logic. 2 discussion, argument.

తర్కబద్ధ **tarkabaddha** *adj.* logical.

తర్కవితర్కాలు **tarkawitarkaalu** *n.pl.* arguments and counter-arguments, polemics.

తర్కవిరుద్ధ **tarkawiruddha** *adj.* illogical.

తర్కశాస్త్రం **tarkaśaastram** *n.* (science of) logic.

తర్కించు **tarkincu** *v.i.* 1 to argue, discuss. 2 (*also* ~ **konu**) to ponder, consider, debate in o.'s mind.

తర్జనం **tarjanam** *n. class.* pointing at, blaming, threatening.

తర్జనభర్జన **tarjanabharjana** *n.* discussion, debate, controversy, arguing this way and that.

తర్జని **tarjani** *n.* index finger, forefinger.

తర్జుమా **tarjumaa** *n.* translation, interpretation.

తర్పణ[ం] **tarpaNa[m]** *n.* 1 *class.* offering of water to the spirits of deceased ancestors. 2 offering made as a tribute; **deeśamkoosam rakta ~ ceesEEDu** he offered up his life for his country; *see* **aśruwu.**

తర్ఫీతు, తర్ఫీదు **tarphiitu, tarphiidu** *same as* **tarabiitu.**

తర్బూజా **tarbuujaa** *n.* watermelon.

తర్రాయి బుర్రాయి **tarraayi burraayi** *n.* meaningless syllables; ~ **taaTikaaya ceeyu** *v.t. colloq. dial.* to deceive, cheat.

తర్లు, తర్లించు[కొను], తర్లింపు **tarlu, tarlincu[konu], tarlimpu** *same as* **taralu, taralincu[konu], taralimpu.**

తర్వాత **tarwaata** *same as* **tarawaata.**

తల **tala** I. *n.* 1 head. 2 *idiomatic usages*: (i) **aayanni ~ miida peTTukonnaaru** they paid him great respect; (ii) ~ **ku mincina bhaaram** a burden too heavy to bear; (iii) ~ **taDiwi cuucukonu** to feel a sense of relief; (iv) ~ **loo naaluka** person who gives sound advice; (v) ~ **waaceeTaTTu ciiwaaTLupeTTu** to scold (s.o.) severely; (vi) **naaku ~ praaNam tookaku waccindi** I felt completely exhausted; (vii) **naaku ~ boppi kaTTindi** I faced many difficulties; (viii) **naa ~ miida ceyyipeTTEEwu** you have deceived me. 3 hair of the head; **waaDi ~ ciidaragaa undi** his hair is unwashed and dishevelled. 4 top, highest point; **rooDDu ~ na nilabaDDaaDu** he stood at the top of the road. 5 shoot, sprout (of tree, plant); **mokka ~ ettina daggaranunci** from the time when the plant puts forth a shoot; ~ **lu tuncu** to nip off the ends of shoots; **werri ~** shoot (of a plant) that is not true to type; **wyaktigata wibheedaalu miti miiri werri ~ lu weesi paraspara nindaaroopaNalawaraku weLLipooyEEyi** individual differences exceeded the limits, put forth untypical shoots and led to mutual recriminations. II. *adj.* chief, main, front; ~ **maanikam** chief jewel; ~ **waakili** front entrance; ~ **komma** leading branch (of a tree).

తల అడ్డంగా ఊపు **tala aDDangaa uupu** *v.i.* to shake o.'s head.

తల ఊపు **tala uupu** *v.i.* to nod o.'s head.

తల ఎత్తు **tala ettu** *v.i.* to raise (its) head, appear; **aayanaloo anumaanam tala ettindi** suspicion was aroused in him *or* his suspicion was aroused.

తలం **talam** *n.* surface.

తలంచు **talancu** *same as* **talacu.**

తలంటి, తలంటు స్నానం **talaNTi, talaNTusnaanam** *n.* oiling and washing o.'s hair.

తలంటుకొను, తలంటి పోసుకొను, తలకుపోసుకొను **talaNTukonu, talaNTipoosukonu, talakupoosukonu** *v.i.* to oil and wash o.'s hair.

తలంపు **talampu** *same as* **talapu.**

తలంబ్రాలు **talambraalu** *same as* **talabraalu.**

తలకట్టు **talakaTTu** *n.* 1 hair of the head; **aamedi pedda ~** hers is a fine head of hair. 2 crest. 3 *gram.* the mark ✓ signifying the vowel *a* in its secondary form. 4 turban.

తలకాయ **talakaaya** *n. slang* head; **nii ~** ! you ass! (*a mild expletive*).

తలకిందులు **talakindulu** *adv.* upside down, topsy turvy, inverted.

తలకిందులు అవు **talakindulu awu** *v.i.* 1 to overturn, capsize, be inverted, be turned upside down. 2 (of a plan, policy) to be upset, be reversed. 3 to be in a quandary.

తలకిందులు చేయు **talakindulu ceeyu** *v.t.* 1 to overturn, invert, turn upside down. 2 to upset, reverse (plan, policy).

తలకు **talaku** *adv. same as* **talaa.**

తలకు ఎక్కు **talaku ekku** *v.i.* to be understood; **neenu ceppindi niiku talaku ekkindEE?** do you understand what I have said?

తలకు ఎత్తుకొను **talaku ettukonu** *v.t.* 1 to elevate, exalt. 2 to take upon o.s.; **ii pani talaku ettukonnaDu** he has taken this work upon himself *or* he has undertaken the responsibility for this work.

తలకుదువపెట్టు, తలతాకట్టుపెట్టు **talakuduwa peTTu, talataakaTTupeTTu** *v.i., lit.* to mortgage o.s., i.e., to perform the humblest tasks for the sake of a living.

తలకు మాయు **talaku maayu** *v.i.* to have dirty and unkempt hair; **talaku maasina waaDaa!** *lit.* you dirty headed fellow! (*a mild term of abuse*).

తలకూడు **talakuuDu** *v.i.* to be fulfilled, be attained, be accomplished.

తలకూర్చు **talakuurcu** *v.t.* to accomplish.

తల[లు] కొట్టు **tala[lu]koTTu** *v.t.* 1 *lit.* to behead; **talalukoTTi batuku** to live by robbing and murdering. 2 **naa[ku] talakoTTeesinaTTundi** I feel disgraced *or* I have been put to shame.

తలకొను **talakonu** *v.i.* to endeavour, attempt.

తలకొరివి పెట్టు **talakoriwi peTTu** *v.i.* to light a funeral pyre.

తలకొవ్విన **talakowwina** *adj.* arrogant, proud, overweening.

తలగంప **talagampa** *n.* first basket of grain from a newly harvested crop, which is offered to the gods.

తలగడ **talagaDa** *n.* pillow.

తలగుడ్డ, తలపాగా **talaguDDa, talapaagaa** *n.* turban.

తలగొడుగు **talagoDugu** *n.* umbrella held over a deity or an important personage in a procession.

తల[ం]చు **tala[n]cu** *v.i. and t.* 1 to think, consider, reflect. 2 to intend, propose, contemplate. 3 to want, wish, desire (to do s.g); **aame eemii maaTLaaDa ~ kooleedu** she had no wish to say anything. 4 to think of, remember; **mimmalni ~ konnaam** we thought of you. 5 **daya ~** to be gracious; *see* **jaali talcu.**

తలచూపు **talacuupu** *v.i.* to show o.s., appear, be seen.

తలచెడు **talaceDu** *v.i.* 1 *with dative* to become insane, go mad; **waaDiki talaceDipooyindi** he has become mad. 2 **talaceDina maniSi** widow (person whose head is shaven).

తలతాడు **talataaDu** *n.* leading rope for cattle.

తలతిక్క **talatikka** *n.* 1 eccentricity, craziness. 2 arrogance, stubbornness. 3 tipsiness.

తలతిరుగు **talatirugu** *v.i. with dative* 1 to feel giddy, have a reeling sensation. 2 to be angry; **allari ceeyyakaNDi! naaku talatirigitee leeci tantaanu** be quiet! if I get angry I will come and beat you. 3 to lose o.'s senses; **niiku ~ tundEE?** have you lost your senses?

తలతిరుగుడు **talatiruguDu** *n.* eccentricities, idiosyncracies.

తలదన్ను **taladannu** *v.t.* to excel, surpass.

తలదాచుకొను **taladaacukonu** *v.i.* 1 to hide o.s. 2 to take shelter, take refuge.

తలదూర్చు **taladuurcu** *v.i.* to get o.s. involved in, meddle in, interfere in; **naa wyawahaaraalaloo taladuurcaku** do not meddle in my affairs.

తలధరించు **taladharincu** *v.t. class.* to submit to, obey.

తలనాదు **talanaadu** *n.* feeling of heaviness in the head caused by a cold.

తలనిక్కు **talanikku** *n.* pride, haughtiness.

తలనీలాలు **talaniilaalu** *n.pl.* hair of the head.

తలనెరిసిన, తలపండిన **talanerisina, talapaNDina** *adj.* 1 grey haired. 2 aged. 3 experienced.

తలపండు **talapaNDu** *n. slang* head.

తలపట్లు **talapaTLu** *n.pl.* quarrelling, quarrels; **talapaTLaku digu** to be involved in quarrels.

తలపడు **talapaDu** *v.i.* 1 to begin, engage in. 2 to attack, oppose (s.o.) head on.

తలపన్ను **talapannu** *n.* poll tax.

తలపించు **talapincu** *v.t.* to call to mind.

తల[ం]పు **tala[m]pu** *n.* 1 thinking, reflection. 2 thought, idea. 3 recollection, remembrance; **~ ku waccu** to come to mind, be recalled.

తలపెట్టు **talapeTTu** *v.t.* 1 to think of. 2 to intend. 3 to begin, start. 4 to devise, conceive (plan). 5 to undertake.

తలపొగరు **talapogaru** *n.* arrogance.

తలపోటకం **talapooTakam** *n. cassia auriculata,* a shrub (= **tangeeDu**).

తలపోటు **talapooTu** *n.* throbbing pain in the head.

తలపోయు **talapooyu** *v.i. and t.* 1 to think [over], reflect [on], ponder, consider. 2 to devise, contrive.

తలబరువు **talabaruwu** *n.* 1 headload carried by a porter. 2 obstinacy, pigheadedness.

తలబిరుసు **talabirusu** I. *n.* 1 pride, arrogance, haughtiness. 2 obstinacy. II. *adj.* headstrong, wilful.

తలబీకనకాయ **talabiikanakaaya** *same as* **talawiipanakaaya.**

తల[ం]బ్రాలు **tala[m]braalu** *n.* rice soaked in turmeric poured over the heads of the bride and bridegroom by each other during a wedding.

తలమానికం **talamaanikam** I. *n.* finest jewel. II. *adj.* most excellent.

తలమీరు **talamiiru** *v.i.* to go beyond, trangress, exceed the limit.

తలమునక **talamunaka** *n.* 1 bathing by submerging o.s. completely 2 *pl.* **~ lu** troubles, difficulties.

తలమునకలవు **talamunakalawu** *v.i.* to be submerged, be immersed, be overwhelmed.

తలరాత **talaraata** *n.* fate, destiny.

తలవంచు **talawancu** *v.i.* 1 to bow the head in submission, surrender. 2 to bow the head in shame.

తలవంపు **talawampu** *n.* shame, humiliation.

తలవనితలంపుగా **talawanitalampugaa** *adv.* unexpectedly, out of the blue.

తలవిసురు **talawisuru** *n.* arrogance.

తలవీపనకాయ, తలబీకనకాయ **talawiipanakaaya, talabiikanakaaya** *adj.* confused, perplexed.

తలసరి **talasari** *adj.* per head, per capita; **~ aadaayam** per capita income.

తలా, తలకు **talaa, talaku** *adv.* per head, each; **~ padi ruupaayalu iccEEnu** I gave ten rupees to each.

తలాటం **talaaTam** *n. class.* crest.

తలాపు **talaapu** *n.* head of a bed.

తలారా **talaaraa** *adv.* including the head; **~ snaanam ceesEEDu** he bathed himself head and all: *see* **aaraa[1].**

తలారి **talaari** *n.* village servant, attendant on the village headman.

తలికి **taliki** *dial., particle affixed to vbl. adj. in* **ee** by the time that; **naa kaaDakoccee ~ eemii migili caawwu!** by the time it comes to me, nothing at all will be left! (= **sariki**).

తలిదండ్రులు **talidaNDrulu** *same as* **tallidaNDrulu.**

తలిపెకాల్వ, తలిపెర **talipekaalwa, talipera** *n.* spring channel.

తలిరు **taliru** I. *n. class.* sprout, shoot. II. *adj. class.* fresh, tender, sprouting; **~ jompam** tender cluster of leaves; **taliraaku** tender leaf.

తలిరొత్తు **talirottu** *v.i. class.* (of leaves) to sprout.

తలుగు **talugu[1]** *n.* halter for tying cattle.

తలుగు **talugu[2]** *dial. variant form of* **tagulu.**

తలుపు **talupu[1]** *n.* 1 door. 2 shutter.

తలుపు **talupu[2]** *alternative form of* **tala[m]pu.**

తలేటిమడక **taleeTimaDaka** *n.* heavy plough drawn by two or more pairs of bullocks.

తలేరు **taleeru** *n.* leading pair of bullocks used when two or more pairs are required to draw a heavy cart or plough.

తల్పం **talpam** *n. class.* bed.

తల్మాయించు **talmaayincu** *v.i.* to suffer o.'s woes in silence.

తల్లంటుతీగె **tallaNTutiige** *n.* yellow-flowered wild convolvulus, *ipomoea chrysis.*

తల్లడం, తల్లడపాటు **tallaDam, tallaDapaaTu** *n.* 1 anxiety, trouble, agitation. 2 turmoil, commotion, consternation.

తల్లడపెట్టు **tallaDapeTTu** *v.t.* to trouble, throw into confusion or turmoil, cause anxiety.

తల్లడిల్లు **tallaDillu** *v.i.* 1 to be troubled, be harassed, be agitated. 2 to tremble, quiver.

తల్లి **talli** I. *n.* 1 mother. 2 form of address to a woman of any age. 3 term of endearment to a girl child. 4 *dial.* chickenpox. II *adj.* 1 maternal, mother's; ~ **preema** mother's love. 2 main, principal; ~ **weeru** main root, taproot.

తల్లిదండ్రులు, తలిదండ్రులు **tallidaNDrulu, talidaNDrulu** *n.pl.* parents.

తల్లిచాలు **tallicaalu** *n.* 1 daughter's resemblance to her mother: ~ **waccindi iddaruu tommidoo nelaloo pasupukumkum ceesEEru** like mother like daughter! they both performed the **pasupukumkum** ceremony in the ninth month of pregnancy. 2 first furrow made when ploughing in a circuit (**kooNDra**).

తళతళ **taLataLa** *onom. adv. sug.* glittering.

తళతళమెరయు, తళతళలాడు **taLataLamerayu, taLataLalaaDu** *v.i.* to gleam, sparkle, glint.

తళుకు **taLuku** *n.* 1 flash, gleam. 2 glitter, lustre. 3 scintillation.

తళుకుబెళుకు **taLukubeLuku** *n.* glitter[ing], scintillation.

తళుక్కున **taLukkuna** *adv.* with a flash.

తళుక్కుమను **taLukkumanu** *v.i.* to flash, gleam, scintillate.

తవగంప **tawagampa** *n.* basket of paddy offered to the sister or daughter (**iNTi aaDapaDucu**) of the owner of a house before a new crop is stored in the granary.

తవిట, తొగట **tawiTa, togaTa** *n.* name of a community of weavers.

తవుడు, తౌడు **tawuDu, tawDu** *n.* bran.

తవ్వ **tawwa** *n.* seer; *see* **śeeru.**

తవ్వకం **tawwakam** *n.* 1 digging, excavation. 2 dredging.

తవ్వితలకెత్తు **tawwi talakettu** *v.i. colloq.* to do a benefit: **aayana niiku eeemaynaa tawwi talakettEEDaa?** has he benefited you in any way? **eem tawwi talakettukondaamani ii pani ceesEEwu**? how did you expect to benefit yourself by doing this?

తవ్వు **tawwu** *v.t.* to dig [up], excavate; **tama waadaanni balaparacukonaDam koosam manawaaru paata caritranu tawwipooseewaaru** in order to support their argument our people used to resurrect past history.

తవ్వుకోల **tawwukoola** *n.* spade.

తవ్వెడు **tawweDu** *adj.* one seer of; ~ **ginne** pot which can hold a seer of a cooked rice.

తవ్వోడ **tawwooDa** *n.* dredger.

తసద్దీకు **tasaddiiku** *n.* tasdik, annual grant or allowance.

తసుకు **tasuku** *n.* trickery, deception, falsehood.

తసులు **tasulu** *n.* gentle and quiet cough.

తస్కరణ **taskaraNa** *n.* theft.

తస్కరించు **taskarincu** *v.t.* to steal.

తస్కరుడు **taskaruDu** *n.* thief.

తస్మదీయ **tasmadiiya** *pron. and adj. class.* yours, your.

తస్మాత్ **tasmaat** *adv.* for that reason; ~ **jaagratta** therefore be careful.

తస్స **tassa** *n.* proud flesh, granulation tissue; **wiiDi tassaa diyyaa!** *or* **wiiDi tassaa goyyaa!** *are expletives equivalent to* blast him!

తహకత్తు **tahakattu** *alternative form of* **taahatu.**

తహజీమ్, తాజీమ్ **tahajiim, taajiim** *n.* 1 ceremonial gift. 2 felicitation.

తహతహ **tahataha** *n.* 1 eagerness, keenness. 2 anxiety, curiosity. 3 haste.

తహతహపెట్టు **tahatahapeTTu** *v.t.* to hurry, hasten.

తహతహలాడు, తహతహపడు **tahatahalaaDu, tahatahapaDu** *v.i.* 1 to be eager or keen. 2 to be anxious, excited or curious. 3 to hasten.

తహశీల్ **tahaśiil** *n.* 1 one of the territorial units into which a revenue district is subdivided (taluk). 2 tax levied on landed or house property.

తహశీల్దార్ **tahaśiildaar** *n.* tahsildar, official of the Revenue Department in charge of a taluk or tahsil.

తా - taa

తాండవం **taaNDawam** *n.* violent form of dance; **śiwa~** the dance of Siva.

తాండవించు **taaNDawincu** *v.i.* 1 to dance violently. 2 (of natural disasters, misfortunes) to prevail; **kSaamam taaNDawincina roojulaloo** in the days when famine prevailed.

తాండ్ర **taaNDra** *n.* jam, jelly; **maamiDi~** mango jelly.

తాండ్రచెట్టు **taaNDra ceTTu** *n. terminalia bellerica*, a tree.

తాంతవం **taantawam** *n. zool.* fibrin.

తాంబాళం **taambaaLam** *n.* large plate gen. for serving betel and nut.

తాంబూలం **taambuulam** *n.* betel leaf and arecanut; **maa iNTiki wacci~tiisukeLLaNDi** please come to our house and take some betel and nut (a way of inviting s.o. to attend a ceremony in the house); **taambuulaalu puccukonnaaru** they exchanged betel and nut (this signifies that a marriage has been arranged and the betrothal performed).

తాంబేలు **taambeelu** *same as* **taabeelu.**

తాంబ్రేలు **taambreelu** *n. dial.* tin.

తా.క. **taa. ka.** *see* **taajaa kalam.**

తాకట్టు **taakaTTu** *n.* mortgage; **~waakaTTu ayndi** is an alliterative phrase signifying that a debt with interest added has become more than the value of the property originally pledged for the debt.

తాకట్టుపెట్టు **taakaTTupeTTu** *v.t.* to mortgage, pawn, hypothecate.

తాకత్తు **taakattu** *n.* strength, power, capacity, ability.

తాకిడి **taakiDi** *n.* 1 force. 2 onslaught, onrush; **tupaanu~ki taTTukooleeka** unable to withstand the onslaught of the cyclone. 3 crowding, throng, rush; **anduwalla satraaniki~eemii leedu, eppuDannaa peLLiwiDidigaa upayooga paDadam tappistee** therefore there was no rush at the village inn, except when it was used as a lodging for wedding guests. 4 strong demand, pressure; **Dabbu~aTTee leeni panaytee ceestaanu** if it is a work involving no great demand for money, I will do it.

తాకీదు, తాఖీదు **taakiidu, taakhiidu** *n.* order, command.

తాకు **taaku** I. *n.* 1 touch, contact. 2 attack. II. *v.i. and t.* 1 to touch. 2 to hit, strike; **waaDiki eNDadebba taakindi** he suffered heat-stroke. 3 to encounter, oppose in battle.

తాకుడు **taakuDu** *n.* touching; **~kaaLLa waaDu** knock-kneed person.

తాకొను **taakonu** *v.i.* to catch fire.

తాకొలుపు **taakolupu** *v.t.* 1 to cause to touch. 2 to infect, cause infection; **uuLLoo jwaram tecci maa iNTini taakolipFEDu** he brought the illness from the village and infected our house.

తాగు **taagu** *v.t.* 1 to drink. 2 **cuTTa~** to smoke a cigar.

తాగుడు **taaguDu** *n.* 1 drink[ing]. 2 drunkenness.

తాగుబోతు **taagubootu** *n.* drunkard.

తాచు [పాము] **taacu[paamu]** *n.* cobra.

తాచ్చారం **taacchaaram** *same as* **taatsaaram.**

తాజా **taajaa** *adj.* 1 fresh, new. 2 latest, uptodate (news).

తాజా కలం, తా.క. **taajaa kalam, taa.ka.** *n.* postscript, P.S.

తాజాగా **taajaagaa** *adv.* newly, freshly, recently.

తాజీమ్ **taajiim** *same as* **tahajiim.**

తాజుగా **taajugaa** *adv.* 1 steadily, firmly, self-confidently. 2 slowly, calmly, seriously, grandly.

తాట **taaTa**[1] *n.* ear ornament.

తాట **taaTa**[2] *n.* skin.

తాటకి **taaTaki** *n.* 1 hag; **juTTu wiraboosukoni ~laagaa tirugutunnadi** she goes about like a hag with her hair dishevelled. 2 name of a female demon in the Ramayana.

తాటస్థ్యం **taaTasthyam** *n.* neutrality.

తాటాకు **taaTEEku** *n.* 1 palmyra leaf; **aayanaki ~lu kaDutunnaaru** they are ridiculing him. 2 tongue scraper (orignally made from a palmyra leaf).

తాటి[చెట్టు], తాడి[చెట్టు], తాడు **taaTi[ceTTu], taaDi[ceTTu], taaDu**[1] *n.* palmyra tree.

తాటించు **taaTincu** *v.i. and t.* 1 to pat, tap. 2 (of wings) to flutter 3 (of breeze) to strike. 4 **tala~konu** to shake or nod o.'s head.

తాటికట్టెడ **taaTikaTTeDa** *n.* poisonous snake that lives in palmyra trees.

తాటికల్లు **taaTikallu** *n.* palmyra toddy.

తాటికాయ **taaTikaaya** *n.* palmyra fruit; **aayana taraalanaaTi~** (*or* **aayana kaalamnaaTi~**) he is one of the old guard.

తాటిచన్నులు **taaTicannulu** *n.pl.* flowers of the palmyra tree.

తాటిదోనె **taaTidoone** *n.* hollowed out palmyra stump used for directing the flow of water baled from a well or as a canoe for transport.

తాటిబెల్లం **taaTibellam** *n.* jaggery made from palmyra juice.

తాటిమట్ట **taaTimaTTa** *n.* palmyra leaf.

తాడనం **taaDanam** *n. class.* beating, striking.

తాడి[చెట్టు] **taaDi[ceTTu]** *same as* **taaTi[ceTTu].**

తాడితం **taaDitam** *n. ling.* flap sound.

తాడు **taaDu**[1] *same as* **taaTi[ceTTu].**

తాడు **taaDu**[2] *n.* rope, cord, string; **annadammulu naluguru okka taaTipay nilicEEru** the four brothers agreed on a common course of action; **pasupu~** tali (woman's token of marriage).

తాడోపేడో **taaDoopeeDoo** *adv.* in this manner or in that, this way or that; **~teelcukonu** to decide one way or the other.

తాత **taata** *n.* grandfather; **nii~too ceppukoo!** I don't care! *see* **ceppukonu** *sense 2*; **~ku daggulu neerpaDam** giving instructions that are not needed (*lit.* teaching o.'s grandfather to cough).

తాతా! **taataa!** *vocative of* **taata** *used as a form of address to an elderly person* Sir!

తాత్కాలిక **taatkaalika** *adj.* temporary, ephemeral, of the moment, ad hoc, provisional.

తాత్పర్యం **taatparyam** *n.* intention, purport, meaning.

తాత్త్విక **taatwika** *adj.* 1 true, real. 2 concerned with truth, concerned with reality, metaphysical.

తాత్సారం, తాచ్చారం **taatsaaram, taacchaaram** *n.* neglect, disregard.

తాదాత్మ్యం **taadaatmyam** *n.* absorption in o.'s own thoughts, reverie.

తానం **taanam**[1] *n.* 1 musical note. 2 a style of musical composition.

తానం **taanam**[2] *variant form of* **snaanam** *and of* **sthaanam.**

తానం **taanam**[3] *n.* bed for retaining water round a plant.

తానకల్పన **taanakalpana** *n. ling.* intonation, tonality.

తాను **taanu**[1] *same as* **tanu.**

తాను **taanu**[2] *n.* roll of cloth of standard length, gen. 40 yards.

తాపం **taapam** *n.* 1 heat, feverishness. 2 emotional suffering.

తాపకం **taapakam** *n. chem.* bath.

తాపక్రమం **taapakramam** *n. sci.* temperature.

తాపక్రమమాపి **taapakrama maapi** *n. sci.* thermometer.

తాపత్రయం **taapatrayam** *n.* 1 bother, trouble. 2 anxiety, worry. 3 strong desire, urge, craze, passion.

తాపదీప్తి **taapadiipti** *n. phys.* incandescence.

తాపసుడు **taapasuDu** *n.* hermit, ascetic.

తాపస్థాపకం **taapasthaapakam** *n.* thermostat.

తాపించు **taapincu** *v.t.* to fix, establish.

తాపిత **taapita** *n.* a variety of silk; **paTTu~** silk cloth.

తాపీ **taapii**[1] *n.* mason's trowel.

తాపీ **taapii**[2] *n.* quietness, calmness, steadiness; **naa manassu ~ni paDindi** my mind is at rest.

తాపీగా **taapiigaa** *adv.* 1 quietly calmly, coolly. 2 in a leisurely manner, without hurrying. 3 steadily, firmly.

తాపీపని **taapiipani** *n.* mason's work, bricklaying, plastering.

తాపీపనివాడు **taapiipaniwaaDu** *n.* mason, bricklayer.

తాపీయ **taapiiya** *adj. sci.* thermal.

తాపు **taapu** I. *n.* kick, blow. II. *v.t.* 1 to inlay, set (jewels); **raaLLu taapina gaajulu** bangles set with precious stones; **rawikalaku mutyaalu taapi toDigeewaaLLu** they used to wear dresses inlaid with pearls. 2 to make watertight by plastering; **kaaluwaku tagu widhangaa simeNTutoo, raatitoo taapaDam ceesukoowaalsi uNTundi** it will be necessary to line the canal with stone and cement in the proper manner.

తాబందు **taabandu** *n.* petticoat.

తాబి **taabi** *n.* the rabi crop, sown in the northeast monsoon season.

తాబె **taabe** *n.* 1 possession. 2 control.

తాబేటికాయ,తాబేటిచిప్ప **taabeeTikaaya, taabeeTicippa** *n.* 1 tortoiseshell. 2 vessel shaped like a tortoiseshell used for drinking water.

తాబేదారుడు **taabeedaaruDu** *n.* subordinate, dependant, minion, underling.

తాబేలు, తాంబేలు **taabeelu, taambeelu** *n.* tortoise, turtle.

తామర **taamara** 1 lotus. 2 ringworm, a skin disease.

తామరతంపర **taamaratampara** *n.* cluster of lotuses; **~gaa perugu** to grow by leaps and bounds, increase profusely (*lit.* to increase or multiply like a cluster of lotuses).

తామసం **taamasam** *n.* 1 delay. 2 *colloq.* anger.

తామసించు **taamasincu** *v.i. colloq.* to be angry.

తామసుడు **taamasuDu** *n.* 1 angry person. 2 wicked person.

తాము **taamu** 1 *pl. of reflexive pron.* **taanu.** 2 *same as* **tamaru.**

తామ్ర **taamra** *adj.* (made of) copper; **~śaasanam** copper plate inscription.

తామ్రం **taamram** *n.* copper.

తాయం, తాయిలం **taay[il]am** *n. child language* something special (a way of referring to a gift promised to a child as an enticement); **nuuwwu wastee~peDataanu** if you come, I will give you something special.

తాయారు **taayaaru** *n.* 1 mother. 2 a name of the Goddess Lakshmi.

తాయి **taayi** *n.* mother.

తాయెత్తు, తాయత్తు, తాయిత్తు **taayettu, taayattu, taayittu** *n.* amulet, talisman, charm.

తార **taara** *n.* 1 star. 2 cinema star. 3 beautiful woman. 4 pupil of the eye. 5 round earthen pot used in making a kind of firework called **ciccubuDDi.**

తారం **taaram** *n.* tare in merchandise, weight allowance to cover packing, etc.

తారక[ం] **taaraka[m]** *n. class.* rescue, saving, salvation.

తారకుడు **taarakuDu** *n. class.* saviour, redeemer, rescuer.

తారట్లాడు **taaraTLaaDu** *v.i.* 1 to move about, walk about. 2 to move hesitantly, move furtively.

తారణ **taaraNa** *n.* eighteenth year of the Hindu cycle of sixty years.

తారతమ్య **taaratamya** *adj. sci.* 1 relative. 2 specific.

తారతమ్యం **taaratamyam** *n.* difference, distinction.

తారళ్యం **taaraLyam** *n.* gleam[ing], brightness.

తారస, తారసు **taarasa, taarasu** *n.* flat rectangular roof tile.

తారసపడు **taarasapaDu** *v.i.* **1** *with dative* to be met or encountered; **naDucukostuuNTee kurraaDokaDu aayanaki taarasapaDDaaDu** as he was coming along walking, he met a boy. **2** to approach, face.

తారసిల్లు, తారసించు **taarasillu, taarasincu** I. *v.i.* **1** *with dative* to be met or encountered by chance; **aa uuLLoo aayana aameki taarasillEEDu** she met him by chance in that village. **2** to turn up, appear or occur unexpectedly.

తారస్వరం **taaraswaram** *n. phys. music* high pitched note.

తారాజువ్వ **taaraajuwwa** *n.* rocket (firework).

తారాడు **taaraaDu** *v.i.* **1** to move about. **2** to lurk. **3** to be evasive. **4** to be hesitant, boggle.

తారాపథం **taaraapatham** *n.* the Milky Way.

తారామండలం **taaraamaNDalam** *n.* the heavens.

తారావళి **taaraawaLi** *n.* cluster of stars.

తారాస్థాయి **taaraasthaayi** *n. lit.* level of the stars, *hence* highest level, climax; **pillaaDi eeDupu taaraasthayi[ni] andukondi** the child's crying reached a climax.

తారికాడు **taarikaaDu** *v.i.* **1** to abscond (from work). **2** to play truant (from school).

తారీఖు, తారీకు **taariikhu, taariiku** *n.* date, day of the month.

తారీఫు **taariiphu** *n. dial.* praise.

తారు **taaru** *n.* (coal) tar.

తారుకొను **taarukonu** *v.t.* **1** to approach. **2** to oppose, face.

తారుణ్యం **taaruNyam** *n. class.* youthfulness, bloom, freshness.

తారుమారవు **taarumaarawu** *v.i.* to be in confusion or disorder, be upset, be overturned, be reversed.

తారుమారు **taarumaaru** *n.* disorder, confusion, upsetting, turning upside down.

తారుమారుగా **taarumaarugaa** *adv.* confusedly, in disorder, in disarray, in the wrong order.

తారుమారుచేయు **taarumaaruceeyu** *v.t.* to upset, overturn, reverse.

తార్కాణం **taarkaaNam** *n.* **1** instance, example, illustration. **2** proof, demonstration.

తార్కాణించు **taarkaaNincu** *v.t.* to prove, demonstrate.

తార్కికంగా **taarkikangaa** *adv.* logically, rationally.

తార్కికుడు **taarkikuDu** *n.* logician.

తార్కులాడు, తారుకులాడు **taar[u]kulaaDu** *v.i.* to behave evasively, keep out of the way.

తార్కొల్పు, తారుకొల్పు **taar[u]kolpu** *v.t.* to fit in; accommodate.

తార్చు **taarcu** *v.t.* to procure for prostitution.

తార్పుడు **taarpuDu** *n.* procuring for prostitution.

తాలం **taalam** *same as* **taaLam.**

తాలవ్య **taalawya** *adj. ling.* palatal.

తాలవ్యం **taalawyam** *n. ling.* palatal sound.

తాలవ్యీకరణ **taalawyiikaraNa** *n. ling.* palatalisation.

తాలి **taali** *same as* **taaLi.**

తాలింఖానా **taalimkhaanaa** *n.* gymnasium.

తాలించు **taalincu** *same as* **taaLincu.**

తాలింపు **taalimpu** *n.* **1** seasoning a dish with spices. **2** curry that has been seasoned.

తాలింపుదినుసులు **taalimpu dinusulu** *n. pl.* condiments.

తాలు **taalu** *n.* **1** empty ears of corn. **2** straw or green stalks and leaves fed to cattle.

తాలువు **taaluwu** *n.* palate.

తాలూకా **taaluukaa** *n.* taluk or tahsil, a subdivision of a district.

తాలూకు **taaluuku** *p.p.* concerning, pertaining to, belonging to, relating to, having to do with; **DaakTarugaari~ maniSi** one of the doctor's men.

తాల్చు, దాల్చు **taalcu**[1], **daalcu** *v.t.* to bear, wear, put on, take, assume; **ruupu~** to take shape, evolve.

తాల్చు **taalcu**[2] *v.t.* to sieve.

తాల్మి **taalmi** *same as* **taaLimi.**

తాళం, తాలం **taaLam**[1], **taalam** *n.* **1** lock. **2** cymbal. **3** beat or time in music.

తాళం **taaLam**[2] *n. class.* palmyra tree.

తాళంకప్ప **taaLamkappa** *n.* padlock.

తాళంచెవి **taaLamcewi** *n.* key; (*pl.* **taaLamcewulu** *or* **taaLamceetulu**).

తాళం తీయు **taaLam tiiyu** *v.i.* to unlock.

తాళం పెట్టు **taaLam peTTu** *v.i.* to lock.

తాళం వేయు **taaLam weeyu** *v.i.* **1** to lock. **2** to beat time (in music). **3** *fig.* **aame ceppina maaTalanniTikii aayana taaLam weesEEDu** he backed up every word that she said.

తాళపత్రం **taaLapatram** *n.* palm leaf; **taaLapatra granthaalu** palm leaf manuscripts.

తాళి, తాలి, మంగళసూత్రం **taaLi, taali, mangaLasuutram** *n.* tali, sacred thread with a small gold locket (**taaliboTTu** *or* **puste**) attached, which is tied round the bride's neck by the bridegroom at the wedding ceremony and worn by her as her marriage token; **aameki ~kaTTEEDu** he married her.

తాళించు, తాలించు **taaLincu, taalincu** *v.t.* **1** to shake dice before casting them. **2** to stir food in a frying pan while adding condiments.

తాళిబొట్టు, పుస్తె **taaLiboTTu, puste** *n.* small gold locket forming part of a woman's tali or marriage token.

తాళిమి, తాల్మి **taaLimi, taalmi** *n.* patience, endurance, courage.

తాళు **taaLu** *v.i.* **1** to bear, endure, withstand, suffer; **aakaliki taaLaleeka** being unable to endure hunger. **2** to be patient, have patience.

తావలం, తావరం **taawalam, taawaram** *n.* 1 place. 2 abode, home.

తావళం, తావడం **taawaLam, taawaDam** *n.* necklace of beads worn by religious devotees.

తావి **taawi** *n. class.* fragrance, scent.

తావికొను **taawikonu** *v.t. class.* to smell.

తావీజు, తావీదు, తావేజు **taawiiju, taawiidu, taaweeju** *n.* amulet, charm, talisman.

తావు **taawu** *n.* place, room, space.

తావు ఇచ్చు **taawu iccu** *v.i.* to give room, give scope (**-ki**, for).

తాశామార్పు, తాషామార్పు **taaśaamaarpu, taaSaamaarpu** *n.* earthen pot with a leather-covered mouth played as a drum.

తాష్ట్రం **taaSTram** *n.* dissolute person, rake.

తాహతు **taahatu** *n.* 1 status. 2 capacity, means; **mii ~ ku taggaTTu candaa iwwaNDi** please make a contribution according to your means.

తి - ti

తిండి **tiNDi** *n.* 1 food. 2 meal; **~ tippalu** meals and so on; **unnadi okka gadi. waNTaapeNTaa, tiNDiitippalu, pillala caduwuusandhyaa, mii kaceerii raatakootalu annii induloonee** we have just this one room, cooking and so on, meals and so forth, the children's studies and your office work — they all take place here.

తిండిపోతు **tiNDipootu** *n.* glutton.

తింపు **timpu** *n.* pride, arrogance.

తికమక **tikamaka** *n.* 1 confusion, perplexity. 2 intricacy. 3 tottering, wavering.

తికమకచేయు, తికమకపెట్టు **tikamakaceeyu, tikamakapeTTu** *v.i. and t.* to confuse, perplex, upset, cause worry or anxiety.

తికమకపడు **tikamakapaDu** *v.i.* to be upset, be confused, be at a loss, be perplexed.

తికమకపరచు **tikamakaparacu** *v.t.* to upset, confuse, perplex.

తిక్క **tikka** *n.* 1 madness, craziness. 2 strangeness of manner, eccentricity. 3 **waaDiki eedi waccinaa tikkee** whatever mood he is in, he goes to extremes.

తిక్కపట్టు **tikkapaTTu** I. *n.* obstinate determination. II. *v.i. with dative* to go mad, go crazy; **waaDiki tikkapaTTindi** he became mad.

తిక్కబుచ్చిగాడు **tikkabuccigaaDu** *n.* innocent harmless fellow.

తిక్కమేళం **tikkameeLam** *n.* 1 group of crazy persons. 2 simpleton.

తిక్కశంకరయ్య **tikkaśankarayya** *n.* 1 person who goes to extremes. 2 eccentric person.

తిట్టిపోయు **tiTTipooyu** *v.t.* to abuse.

తిట్టు **tiTTu** I. *n.* abuse, scolding, cursing, violent or obscene language; **tiTLu tinu** to suffer abuse. II. *v.t.* to abuse, scold, curse, use obscene language.

తిట్టుపోతు **tiTTupootu** *n.* person who uses foul language.

తిట్లమారి **tiTLamaari** *n.* person who habitually abuses others.

తిత్తి **titti** *n.* 1 leather bag. 2 bellows. 3 any baglike thing. 4 skin of an animal.

తిత్తి ఒలుచు, తిత్తి తీయు **titti olucu, titti tiiyu** *v.i.* to skin, flay.

తిత్తికాడు **tittikaaDu** *n.* person who works the bellows.

తిత్తిపెట్టు **tittipeTTu** *same as* **tiripeTTu.**

తిత్తిపోయు **tittipooyu** *v.i.* to work the bellows.

తిత్తివ **tittiwa** *n.* story.

తిథి **tithi** *n.* 1 lunar date, i.e., date reckoned by the moon's phases. 2 annual death ceremony.

తినిపించు **tinipincu** *v.i.* 1 to give s.g to s.o. to eat. 2 to bribe.

తిను **tinu** *v.t.* 1 to eat, consume; **nuwwu tineedi annamaa, gaDDEE?** are you a man or beast? (*lit.* is what you eat rice or grass?); **aDukku ~** to live (*lit.* to eat) by begging; **lancaalu ~** to take (*lit.* to eat) bribes; **tinnanta tini leecEEDu** he ate his fill and stood up. 2 to swallow, devour (s.o. else's property). 3 to eat away, destroy little by little. 4 to suffer (blows, abuse); *see* **debba[lu] ~, tiTTu. 5 piikku ~, weedhincuku ~, campuku ~** to worry or pester continually. 6 *other idiomatic usages*: (i) **tinikuurcuNDu** to live in comfort; (ii) **tini uNDa[baTTa] leeka, tini kuurcooleeka** being unable to restrain o.s., for no reason, unnecessarily; **tini uNDabaTTaleeka waaDu weLLi nuuru ruupaayalu tagalabeTTEEDu** he went and spent Rs. 100 unnecessarily; (iii) **tini tiragaDam tappa waaDiki pani leedu** he has nothing to do except to wander about; *see* **takkuwa ~**

తినుకు **tinuku** *v.i.* to strain at stool.

తినుబండారాలు **tinubaNDaaraalu** *n.pl.* eatables.

తిన్న **tinna**[1] *adj.* 1 straight, direct. 2 straightforward, upright. 3 right, proper.

తిన్న, తిన్నె, దిన్నె **tinna**[2], **tinne, dinne** *n.* 1 heap, mound; **isuka ~** sandbank, sand hill. 2 pial, raised platform or terrace serving as a seat in front of a house.

తిన్నగా **tinnagaa** *adv.* 1 straight, direct[ly]; **~ weLLaNDi** keep straight on. 2 honestly, uprightly, fairly, properly; **~ sampaadincu** to earn by fair means; **~ uNDu** to behave properly. 3 gently, slowly, steadily. 4 (of health) well, all right, normal; **mii aaroogyam ~ undaa?** is your health all right? *or* are you keeping well?

తిపారం, తీపరం **tipaaram, tiiparam** *a form of expostulation*; **eem ~ aa?** *or* **eem ~ waccindi?** *or* **eem pooyeekaalam waccindi?** what[ever] has come over you? *see* **kaalam** *sense 1.*

తిప్ప **tippa** *n.* 1 hillock, mound. 2 small river island; **isuka**~ sand hill, sandbank. 3 difficulty, stumbling block. 4 *pl.* (i) difficulties; (ii) *echo word occurring in* **tiNDi**~**lu** meals and such things.

తిప్పకాయ **tippakaaya** *same as* **Dippakaaya.**

తిప్పట **tippaTa** *n.* 1 roving, wandering. 2 care, worry. 3 difficulty, trouble.

తిప్పతిమ్మరి **tippatimmari** *n.* monkey.

తిప్పతీగ **tippatiiga** *n.* kind of creeper, *tinospara cordifolia.*

తిప్పలుపడు **tippalu paDu** *v.i.* 1 to be in difficulties. 2 to make efforts, try hard, strive.

తిప్పి **tippi** (*past participle of* **tippu**) *followed by a tr. vb. gives the meaning of* again; ~ **aDugu** to ask again *or* to ask in a different form; ~ **pampu** to send back, return; ~ **raayu** to rewrite; ~ **paaDu** to sing (a song) over and over again.

తిప్పికొట్టు **tippikoTTu** *v.t.* to send back, drive back, repulse.

తిప్పివేయు **tippiweeyu** *v.t.* 1 to return, reject. 2 to turn away.

తిప్పు **tippu** I. *n.* 1 turn, circuit, round; **oka**~ **tippi kuurcoopeDataanu** I will take you on one round and then make you sit down; **daaram pulla cuTTuu reNDu** ~ **lu tippEEru** they wound a thread twice round the stick. 2 fainting, swooning. 3 pride, arrogance. II. *v.i.* 1 to turn. 2 to reel, feel giddy. 3 (of illness) to be checked; **mandu weesEEka jwaram tippindi** when he gave medicine the fever went down; *see* **gukka.** III. *v.t.* 1 to turn [round], turn back. 2 to brandish, whirl, twirl. 3 to lead about, lead round; **aameni uurantaa tippEEDu** he led her round the whole village. 4 to wind (watch), coil (rope). 5 to reverse, revoke (order).

తిప్పుకొను **tippukonu** I. *v.i.* to recover o.s., collect o.'s wits. II. *v.t.* 1 to turn; **kaLLu tippukooleeka pooyEEDu** he could not turn his eyes away. 2 to wave, brandish; **ceetulu**~ to gesture with the hands, gesticulate. 3 to make others associate with o.s.; **mammalni tana cuTTuu tippukoneewaaDu** he used to make us associate with him *or* he used to make us revolve around him.

తిప్పులాడి **tippulaaDi** *n.* woman who attracts men.

తిమతిమ **timatima** *same as* **cimacima.**

తిమింగలం **timingalam** *n.* 1 whale. 2 sea monster.

తిమిరం **timiram** *n.* 1 darkness. 2 name of an eye disease.

తిమురు **timuru** I. *n.* 1 pride. 2 numbness. II. *v.i.* 1 to be proud or arrogant. 2 to hasten, hurry.

తిమురువాతరోగం **timuruwaataroogam** *n.* rheumatism.

తిమ్మడు, తిమ్మన్న **timmaDu, timmanna** *n.* name given to a monkey; **rammannaaru timmanna bantiki!** *lit.* they have invited you to a monkey's feast! *a saying meaning* "quite impossible!" *gen. used by a mother refusing a child's request.*

తిమ్మనం **timmanam** *n. dial.* 1 thin porridge made of milk, rice flour and sugar. 2 preparation made with buttermilk. 3 **manam manam**~ let's all stick together.

తిమ్మరి **timmari** *same as* **dimmari.**

తిమ్మరితనం **timmaritanam** *n.* tendency to wander restlessly without settling down.

తిమ్మిరి, తిమిరి **timmiri, timiri** *n.* 1 numbness, palsy. 2 itching. 3 desire. 4 excessive desire, lust. 5 pride, arrogance.

తియ్య, తీయ **tiyya, tiiya** *adj.* sweet, pleasant.

తియ్యకంద **tiyyakanda** *n.* an edible root.

తియ్యకూర **tiyyakuura** *n.* curry prepared without tamarind.

తియ్యదనం **tiyyadanam** *n.* sweetness.

తియ్యనిమ్మ **tiyyanimma** *n.* sweet lime.

తిరం **tiram** *alt. form of* **sthiram.**

తిరకాసు **tirakaasu** *n.* 1 dispute, argument. 2 difference.

తిరగకలుపు **tiragakalupu** *v.t.* to mix thoroughly and completely.

తిరగగొట్టు **tiragagoTTu** *v.t.* 1 to send back, return. 2 to reject, repel.

తిరగతిప్పు **tiragatippu** *v.t.* to turn round, reverse.

తిరగదోడు **tiragadooDu** *v.t.* 1 to drag up once again, revive (old grievances). 2 to start again from the beginning, recast, reconstruct.

తిరగదోయు **tiragadooyu** *v.t.* to knock over.

తిరగనాటు **tiraganaaTu** *v.t.* to transplant.

తిరగబడు **tiragabaDu** *v.i.* 1 to fall down, fall over, overturn. 2 to turn against, revolt, rebel.

తిరగబెట్టు **tiragabeTTu** *v.i.* (of illness) to return, recur.

తిరగమరగ **tiragamaraga** *adv.* inside out, upside down.

తిరగమోత, తిరగబోత **tiragamoota, tiragaboota** *n. dial.* seasoning with spices (= **taalimpu**).

తిరగరాయు **tiragaraayu** *v.t.* 1 to rewrite, revise. 2 **nooTu**~ to revalidate a promissory note.

తిరగలి **tiragali** *n.* handmill.

తిరగేయు, తిరగవేయు **tirageeyu, tiragaweeyu** *v.t.* 1 to turn round, turn over; **pustakam peejiilu**~ to scan (*or* turn) the pages of a book; **cokkaa tirageesi toDugukonu** to wear a shirt the wrong way round (back to front *or* inside out). 2 to recount, recite, rehearse; **maa akkayya paata bhaagootam antaa tirageesindi** my sister recounted all the past history.

తిరపడు **tirapaDu** *alt. form of* **sthirapaDu.**

తిరస్కరించు **tiraskarincu** *v.t.* 1 to despise, scorn, treat with contempt. 2 to refuse, reject.

తిరస్కారం **tiraskaaram** *n.* 1 scorn, disregard, contempt. 2 rejection, refusal.

తిరస్కృతి **tiraskṛti** *n.* rejection.

తిరస్కృతుడు **tiraskṛtuDu** *n.* s.o. rejected or despised.

తిరిగి **tirigi** I. *past participle of* **tirugu** having turned. II. *adv.* again, back; ~ **pampu** to send again, send back, return.

తిరిపెం **tiripem** *n.* 1 alms, charity. 2 begging.

తిరిపెకాడు **tiripekaaDu** *n.* beggar.

తిరిపెట్టు, తిత్తిపెట్టు **tiripeTTu, tittipeTTu** *v.i.* to twist a piece of cloth and insert it in the ear.

తిరు **tiru** *adjvl. prefix* holy, sacred.

తిరుకళ్యాణమంటపం **tirukaLyaaNamaNTapam** *n.* pandal or canopy erected for performing the ceremony of a god's marriage.

తిరుక్షవరం **tirukSawaram** *n.* complete shaving of the head.

తిరుక్షవరం అవు **tirukSawaram awu** *v.i.* 1 to have the head completely shaved. 2 to fail completely in an undertaking.

తిరుగాడు, తిరుగులాడుకొను **tirugaaDu, tirugulaaDukonu** *v.i.* to move about, wander.

తిరుగు **tirugu** I. *n.* 1 turn[ing], return[ing], turning back, going back; ~ **prayaanam** return journey; ~ **Teligraam** reply telegram; **naa nirNayaaniki ~ leedu** there is no going back on my decision. 2 turning round, going round. 3 opposition, disputing, gainsaying; **mii maaTaku ~ leedu** there is no disputing what you say. II. *v.i.* 1 to turn [round]. go round; **kaawali ~** to go round on patrol, be on guard as a sentry. 2 to revolve, spin, reel; **waaDi oLLu tirigindi** *or* **waaDiki kaLLu tirigEEyi** he felt giddy (*lit.* his body reeled *or* his eyes reeled). 3 to go back, come back, return, come again; **tirugu! get back!** (command addressed to an animal such as a dog); **nela tiragaka mundu** before a month comes round again *or* before a month has passed; **maaTamiida nilabaDaka tirigi pooyEEDu** he did not keep his word but went back on it. 4 to wander, roam. 5 (of illness) to pass off. 6 to be well developed (with ref. to strength, skill, experience); **aa peddamaniSi sayjuloo kuuDaa peddamaniSee, atani ceetulu kaNDalu tirigi unnaayi** that gentleman (*lit.* that big man) was big in size too, his arms had well developed muscles; **ceyyitirigina racayita** a well versed writer; **kommulu tirigina** well established, experienced, expert. 7 *idiomatic usages*: (i) **waaDi adṛSTam tirigipooyindi** his luck has changed; (ii) **waaDi tala ~ tunnadi** he has become conceited; (iii) **mii pani miidee ~ tunnaaDu** he is engaged on your work only; (iv) **nooru tiragaka** not being able to pronounce words correctly; (v) **aame kaLLalloo niiLLu tirigEEyi** tears welled up in her eyes *or* her eyes brimmed with tears; *see* **gukka, cukka.**

తిరుగుడు **tiruguDu** *n.* 1 going round, going about, wandering. 2 revolving, turning round, spinning round.

తిరుగుబాటు **tirugubaaTu** *n.* 1 rebellion, revolt, insurrection, uprising. 2 turning against, disobedience.

తిరుగుబాటుదారు **tirugubaaTudaaru** *n.* rebel.

తిరుగుమొహంపట్టు **tirugumoham paTTu** *v.i.* 1 to turn back, go back, return. 2 (of illness) to pass off. 3 (of floods) to recede, subside.

తిరుగులాడుకొను **tirugulaaDukonu** *dial., same as* **tirugaaDu.**

తిరుగులేని **tiruguleeni** *adj.* 1 unanswerable, incontrovertible, undeniable. 2 unwavering, unfaltering, unswerving, unfailing.

తిరుచూర్ణం **tirucuurNam** *n.* paste made of turmeric and rice flour smeared on the forehead to denote the Vaishnavite sect.

తిరునగరం **tirunagaram** *n.* prosperous town.

తిరునామం **tirunaamam** *n.* mark on the forehead indicating the Vaishnavite sect.

తిరునాళ్ల **tirunaaLLa** *n.* 1 temple festival. 2 auspicious day on which a temple festival is performed.

తిరుపతిక్షవరం **tirupati kSawaram** *n.* work left unfinished (a proverbial saying derived from a practice resorted to by barbers at Tirupati).

తిరుమాళిగ **tirumaaLiga** *n.* house of a Vaishnavite religious teacher.

తిరువాయిమొళి **tiruwaayimoLi** *n.* name of a sacred work in Tamil.

తిరువారాధన **tiruwaaraadhana** *n.* worship of the gods.

తిరుసన్నిధి **tirusannidhi** *n.* God's presence.

తిరోగమనం **tiroogamanam** *n.* 1 retreat, withdrawal, regression. 2. *sci* retrogression.

తిరోగమనశీల **tiroogamanaśiila** *adj.* 1 regressive, retrogressive. 2 retrograde.

తిరోగమించు **tiroogamincu** *v.i.* to retreat, withdraw, retire.

తిరోధానం **tiroodhaanam** *n. class.* 1 cover, veil. 2 concealment, vanishing, disappearing.

తిర్యక్కు **tiryakku** I. *n. class.* 1 animal, brute. 2 *pl.* ~ **lu** the animal kingdom. II. *adj. class.* horizontal, oblique, transverse.

తిర్రి **tirri** *n.* kind of palmyra leaf basket for catching fish.

తిలకం **tilakam** *n.* 1 red mark worn on the forehead by a woman as adornment, also by a man to mark an auspicious occasion. 2 *as second part of a n. compound* best, greatest; **naTa ~** greatest of actors.

తిలకించు **tilakincu** *v.t.* to view, survey, behold.

తిలయంత్రం **tilayantram** *n.* oil press, oil mill.

తిలలు **tilalu** *n.pl.* seeds of gingelly, *sesamum indicum.*

తిలాదానం **tilaadaanam** *n.* charity to brahmans in the form of gingelly seeds and money given at the time of an eclipse.

తిలోదకాలు **tiloodakaalu** *n.pl.* offering of gingelly seeds and water to the spirits of deceased ancestors; ~ **iccu** to bid goodbye to s.o. (*lit.* to offer gingelly seeds and water to s.o., indicating that connections have been broken).

తిల్రమల్ర **tilramalra** *dial., same as* **talakindulu.**

తివాసి, తివాచి **tiwaasi, tiwaaci** *n.* carpet.

తిష్టవేయు **tiSTaweeyu** *v.i.* to establish o.s., instal o.s., ensconce o.s.

తీ - tii

తీండ్ర **tiiNDra** *n.* 1 heat, fierceness. 2 *class.* brightness.

తీండ్రించు **tiiNDrincu** *v.i.* 1 to blaze with anger or rage. 2 *class.* to shine.

తీంతారి, తీన్తారు **tiintEEri, tiintaaru** *adv.* 1 in confusion. 2 in a state of ruin.

తీక్ష్ణ **tiikSNa** *adj.* 1 sharp, keen, severe. 2 hot.

తీక్ష్ణం, తీక్షణం **tiikSNam, tiikSaNam** *n.* 1 sharpness, keenness. 2 heat.

తీక్ష్ణంగా **tiikSNangaa** *adv.* severely, keenly, intensely, fiercely.

తీక్ష్ణత **tiikSNata** *n.* intensity, fierceness, severity.

తీక్ష్ణలోహం **tiikSNalooham** *n. class.* steel.

తీక్ష్ణామ్లం **tiikSNaamlam** *n.* strong acid.

తీగ, తీగె **tiiga, tiige** *n.* 1 creeping plant, creeper. 2 spray, tendril. 3 string of a musical instrument. 4 wire. 5 item of jewellery. 6 strip or ribbon of a syrupy or gummy substance which links cup and spoon when a spoonful is taken from the cup; **paakam ~ saageeTappudu anduloo piNDi pooyaNDi** when the syrup becomes sticky add the flour to it. 7 **~ tiistuu maaTLaaDutunnaaDu** he talks in a drawling fashion *or* he talks with a drawl.

తీగచుట్ట **tiigacuTTa** *n.* coil.

తీగబచ్చలి **tiigabaccali** *n.* climbing spinach, *basella cordifolia.*

తీగబోడి **tiigabooDi** *n. class.* woman.

తీట **tiiTa** *n.* 1 itch[ing]. 2 urgent wish or desire.

తీత **tiita** *n.* 1 plucking, pulling, extracting. 2 pain. 3 wound, blow.

తీతువ, తీతువు, తీతుకపిట్ట **tiituwa, tiituwu, tiitukapiTTa** *n.* lapwing (bird).

తీన్తారు **tiintaaru** *see* **tiintEEri.**

తీపరం **tiiparam** *same as* **tipaaram.**

తీపి **tiipi**[1] I. *n.* 1 sweetness. 2 liking, fondness. II. *adj.* sweet.

తీపి, తీపు **tiipi**[2], **tiipu** *n.* pain, aching; **kaaLLu tiipulu** aching of legs.

తీయ **tiiya** *same as* **tiyya.**

తీయు **tiiyu** I. *v.i.* 1 to pass off, leave off, cease, be dispelled, disappear; **tiiyakuNDaa** ceaselessly, without intermission, without stopping; **tiiyani** ceaseless. 2 to diminish, grow less, be reduced, subside; **jwaramtoo maniSi tiisEEDu** he became thin as a result of illness. II. *v.t.* 1 to take, pull, draw; **paalu~** to draw milk from a cow; **phoToo~** to take a photograph. 2 to take out, extract; **iinelu~** to take out midribs from a palm leaf. 3 to take away, deduct, subtract. 4 to remove, do away with, abolish. 5 to open; **talupu~** to open a door; **taaLam~** to unlock. 6 *with different nouns ~ acquires different meanings;* **kaaluwa~** to dig or excavate a channel; **kuuniraagaalu~** to hum tunes; **gandham~** to rub sandalwood into a paste; **gooLLu tiisukonu** to cut o.'s nails; **citram~** to make a movie; **daari~** to go forward, lead the way; **diipam~** to put out or extinguish a light; **debba~** to deal or strike a blow; **nuulu ~** to spin thread; **parugulu~** to run; **gunjiilu~** to perform **gunjiilu**; **raagaalu~, śookaalu~** to wail, weep; **wedurubaddalu~** to make bamboo slats; **dukaaNamloo saruku tiisukonu** to buy goods from a shop; *see* **ceera~, bayaldeera~, wenaka~, weelaaDa~.**

తీరం **tiiram** *n.* shore, bank, coast.

తీరస్థదీవి **tiirasthadiiwi** *n.* offshore island.

తీరా **tiiraa** I. *advbl. suffix indicating* completeness, contentment *or* satisfaction; **karuwu~nidrapoo** sleep as long as you like (so as to make up for loss of sleep). II. *adv.* 1 in the end, after all. 2 at length, finally.

తీరిక **tiirika** *n.* leisure; **~cuusukoni maa iNTiki raa** come to our house when you are free.

తీరికగా, తీరిగ్గా **tiirikagaa, tiiriggaa** *adv.* at ease, at leisure, free from work.

తీరికూర్చొను **tiirikuurconu** *v.i.* to sit at ease (*lit.* to sit down after finishing o.'s work); **pani tiirindaa? tiirikuurconnaawu** you are taking it easy, have you finished your work?

తీరు **tiiru** I. *n.* 1 manner, way, style, fashion, method; **ii~na ceyyaali** you must do it in this way; **Dabbuleeni~na maaTLaaDEEDu** he talked as if there was no money. 2 arrangement, shape, outline, appearance. 3 **wyayam~** pattern of expenditure. 4 nature, state, condition; **niiLLa~cuustee, iTLaa undi** if you look at the state of water supply, it is like this. 5 **waaDu oka ~ maniSi** he is an odd man. 6 **waaDu oka ~ gaa unnaaDu** (i) he is in a strange mood; (ii) he in moderately good health. II. *adj.* pretty, beautiful, shapely, well proportioned. III. *v.i.* 1 to finish, stop, end, cease, be over, be completed, be exhausted; **naa baakii tiirindi** my debt has been discharged; **aayanaki nuukalu tiirinaayi** his allotted life-span is over. 2 (of needs) to be fulfilled, be met. 3 (of desire, animosity, vengeance) to be satisfied, be satiated; **naa muccaTa tiirindi** I am content. 4 to be ordered, be arranged; **panktulu tiiri bhoojanaalu ceesEEru** they took meals seated in rows. 5 *following a past participle ~ gives the meaning* to do s.g without fail; **neenu wacci~taanu** I will come with out fail *or* I will certainly come. IV. *impersonal vb.* 1 to have leisure, be free; **kSaNam tiiraka** not being free for a moment *or* without resting for a moment; **aameki pillalatoo tiiraka weLLaleedu** she did not go because she had no leisure on account of the children. 2 *following a neg. participle* **tiiradu** *gives the meaning* is certain to, must .... without fail; **aame aDagaka tiiradu** she is sure to ask; *cf.* **tappu** *sense III. 3.*

తీరుగడ **tiirugaDa** *n.* end, finish.

తీరుగా **tiirugaa** *adv.* 1 in the manner of. 2 properly, duly.

తీరుతీయాలు **tiirutiiyaalu** *n. pl.* niceties.

తీరుతెన్నులు **tiirutennulu** *n.pl.* 1 features, characteristics. 2 tendencies. 3 style, manner.

తీరుదల **tiirudala** *n.* ending.

తీరుబడి, తీరుబాటు **tiirubaDi, tiirubaaTu** *n.* leisure.

తీరువ, తీర్వ **tiiruwa, tiirwa** *n.* 1 tax, duty, assessment, cess. 2 orderliness, system, method; **~leeni pani** unsystematic work; **~dibba** (*or* **~paaDu**) **leekuNDaa annii kalipi ceestunnaaDu** he jumbles everything together without any method; *here* **dibba** *and* **paaDu** *are equivalent to echo words.*

తీర్చిదిద్దు **tiircididdu** *v.t.* 1 to train, regulate. 2 to mould, fashion. 3 to steer, guide. 4 to adorn, decorate.

తీర్చు **tiircu** *v.t.* 1 to order, arrange, regulate, rectify. 2 to end, finish. 3 to repay, liquidate (debt). 4 to satisfy, meet, fulfil (desire, need). 5 to relieve (thirst). 6 to remove, resolve, (doubt, fear). 7 to hold (meeting, court). 8 to decorate, adorn. 9 to assuage, satisfy (spite). 10 to settle.

తీర్థం **tiirtham** *n.* 1 holy water offered to devotees at a temple. 2 holy place, place of pilgrimage. 3 *slang* liquor.

తీర్థం ఆడు **tiirtham aaDu** *v.i. class.* to bathe.

తీర్థంకరుడు **tiirthankaruDu** *n.* saint of the Jain religion.

తీర్థయాత్ర **tiirthayaatra** *n.* pilgrimage.

తీర్థరాజం **tiirtharaajam** *n.* holiest of all holy places.

తీర్థవాసి **tiirthawaasi** *n.* resident of a pilgrimage centre.

తీర్థవిధి **tiirthawidhi** *n.* rites to be observed at a pilgrimage centre.

తీర్పరి **tiirpari** *n.* judge, umpire.

తీర్పు **tiirpu** *n.* decision, judgement, verdict.

తీర్పుచెప్పు **tiirpu ceppu** *v.i.* to pronounce judgement.

తీర్పు చేయు **tiirpu ceeyu** *v.t.* to settle, decide.

తీర్మానం **tiirmaanam** *n.* settlement, decision, conclusion, resolution; **rNaala~** settlement of debts.

తీర్మానం చేయు **tiirmaanam ceeyu** *v.t.* 1 to resolve. 2 to settle, repay (debt).

తీర్మానించు **tiirmaanincu** *v.t.* to resolve.

తీవ **tiiwa** *alt. form of* **tiiga.**

తీవ్ర **tiiwra** *adj.* 1 fast, rapid. 2 sharp, acute, virulent, intense, severe; **~gaayam** grievous injury; **~ruupam daalcu** to become acute, serious or critical. 3 hot, scorching.

తీవ్రం, తీవ్రత **tiiwram, tiiwrata** *n.* 1 speed. 2 sharpness, acuteness, intensity, severity, seriousness, virulence. 3 heat.

తీవ్రతరం అవు **tiiwrataram awu** *v.i.* to become more severe or acute.

తీవ్రతరం చేయు **tiiwrataram ceeyu** *v.t.* to accelerate, aggravate, intensify.

తీసికట్టు **tiisikaTTu** *adj.* inferior, worse.

తీసికట్టుగా **tiisikaTTugaa** *adv.* slightingly, belittlingly.

తీసిపారవేయు **tiisipaaraweeyu** *v.t.* to ignore, disregard, reject, dismiss (argument, request).

తీసిపోవు **tiisipoowu** *v.i., in neg. or interrog. constr.* to be inferior; **mana raaSTram ee raaSTraanikii tiisipooleedu** our state is not inferior to any other state *or* our state is second to no other state.

తీసివేత **tiisiweeta** *n.* subtraction, deduction.

తీసివేయు, తీసేయు **tiisiweeyu, tiiseeyu** I. *v.i.* to diminish, decrease, subside, be reduced. II. *v.t.* 1 to take away, remove, eliminate. 2 to subtract, deduct. 3 to ignore, disregard, reject, dismiss. 4 to sever, cut off.

తీసుకొను **tiisukonu** I. *v.i.* to suffer continuously, suffer over a long period; **jabbutoo tiisukoNTunnaaDu** he suffers from illness continuously; **ii prayoogaalu wijayawantamay, pawSTikaahaara loopamtoo tiisukoNTunna saamaanya prajalandarikii kuuDaa ceeruwa kaawaali** these experiments must succeed and be made available also to all ordinary people who have endured the lack of nutritious food for so long. II. *v.t.* to take; **tiisukoni waccu, tiisukawaccu** to bring; **tiisukonipoowu, tiisukapoowu** to take away, *see* **canuwu.**

తు - tu

తుంగ **tunga**[1] *n.* kind of reed used for thatching or weaving mats, *cyperus sp.*

తుంగ **tunga**[2] *n.* name of a river of South India; ~ **loo tokku** to discard, throw away; *here* **tunga** *is used for water in general*; *cf.* **gangaloo kalupu.**

తుంగముస్త **tungamusta** *n.* kind of grass (*cyperus sp.*) with medicinal value.

తుంగిడీ **tungiDii** *same as* **tuugiDii.**

తుంచు, త్రుంచు **tuncu, truncu** *v.t.* **1** to nip off, cut off, break off. **2** to pluck (flower). **3** to break into small pieces. **4** to interrupt, cut short.

తుంట[రి]తనం **tuNTa[ri]tanam** *n.* naughtiness, mischief.

తుంటరి **tuNTari** I. *n.* naughty or mischievous person (gen. used of a child). II. *adj.* naughty, mischievous; ~ **maaTalu** mischievous talk.

తుంటి **tuNTi** *same as* **toNTi**[1].

తుండు **tuNDu**[1] *n.* **1** piece, bit. **2** block of wood; ~**laa unnaaDu** he is a fat fellow (*lit.* he is like a block of wood in shape).

తుండు[గుడ్డ] **tuNDuguDDa, tuNDu**[2] *n.* towel.

తుంపర, తుపర, తుప్పర **tumpara, tup[p]ara** *n.* **1** drop of spray. **2** spray. **3** drizzle, drizzling. **4** *pl.* **tumparlu, tup[p]arlu** drizzle, drizzling. **5 nooTi tumparlu** saliva sprayed from the mouth while talking.

తుంపు **tumpu**[1] I *n.* **1** bit, piece. **2** cut piece of cloth. II. *v.t. same as* **tuncu.**

తుంపు **tumpu**[2] *n. dial.* quarrel.

తుంబ **tumba** *n. shoria tumbaggaria*, a timber tree.

తుంబురుడు **tumburuDu** *n. class.* celestial singer.

తుకడ **tukaDa** *n.* piece of wood.

తుకడరాతు **tukaDarawtu** *n.* broken stone used for filling foundations, ballast.

తుకతుక **tukatuka** *onom. n. sug. sound of* (i) boiling, bubbling, (ii) laughing.

తుక్కు **tukku** I. *n.* **1** rubbish, trash, sweepings, scrap; **pramaadamloo baNDi ~ tukkayi pooyindi** in the accident the vehicle was totally wrecked (*lit.* in the accident the the vehicle became mere rubbish); ~ **reegakoTTu** to beat severely. **2** nonsense. II. *adj.* useless, worthless, trashy; ~ **muuka** mob, rabble.

తుక్కుగా **tukkugaa** *adv.* thoroughly, severely; ~ **taDiyu** to be soaked or drenched; **waana ~ kurisindi** the rain fell in torrents.

తుక్కూదూగర **tukkuuduugara** *n.* **1** rubbish, trash. **2** nonsense.

తు.చ.తప్పకుండా, తూ.చా.తప్పకుండా **tu[u].ca[a]. tappakuNDaa** *advbl. phrase, lit.* without omitting 'tu' or 'ca' (Sanskrit conjunctions meaning 'if' and 'and'), *hence* fully, thoroughly, meticulously, complete in every detail; **miiru iccina heccarikalannii ~ aacaristunnaanu** I am carrying out all your instructions to the letter.

తుచ్ఛం **tuccham** *adj.* mean, base, contemptible.

తుచ్ఛుడు **tucchuDu** *n.* mean person, wretch.

తుటుకుతుటుక్కు **tuTukutuTukku** *onom. adv. sug.* palpitation of the heart; **aame guNDe ~ na koTTukundi** her heart beat fast.

తుట్ట, తుట్టె **tuTTa**[1], **tuTTe** *n.* lump or clot of rice, flour, tamarind, etc., that has been spoilt by moisture.

తుట్ట **tuTTa**[2] *adj.* (of lips) thick, bulbous.

తుట్ట[లు]కట్టు, తుట్టె[లు]కట్టు **tuTTa[lu]kaTTu, tuTTe[lu]kaTTu** *v.i.* (of rice, flour, tamarind, etc.) to form into lumps when spoilt by moisture.

తుట్టతుది , తుట్టతుద **tuTTatudi, tuTTatuda** *adj.* last, final.

తుట్టపురుగు, తుట్టెపురుగు **tuTTapurugu, tuTTepurugu** *n.* kind of worm which lives on decaying material.

తుట్టు **tuTTu** *adj.* false.

తుడుం **tuDum** *n. class.* drum, tomtom; ~ **modalukoni deewataaraacanawaraku** *lit.* from the beating of the drum to the worship of the god, i.e., from the earliest stage to the very end.

తుడిచిపెట్టు **tuDicipeTTu** *v.t.* **1** to wipe away, blot out, obliterate. **2** to wipe out, annihilate.

తుడిచిపెట్టుకొనిపోవు **tuDicipeTTukonipoowu** *v.i.* to be wiped out, be annihilated.

తుడుచు **tuDucu** *v.t.* **1** to wipe or rub clean. **2** to wipe or rub dry. **3** to sweep, dust. **4** to rub out, erase. **5** to wipe away, sweep away; **waradalawalla paNTa antaa ~ ku pooyindi** the entire crop was swept away by the floods.

తుడుపు **tuDupu** *n.* wiping, rubbing, erasing.

తుతారా **tutaaraa** *n.* kind of trumpet.

తుత్తం **tuttam** *n.* sulphuric acid, vitriol.

తుత్తర **tuttara** *n.* extreme desire, extreme lust.

తుత్తిరిబెండ **tuttiribeNDa** *n.* kind of okra.

తుత్తునాగం **tuttunaagam** *n.* zinc.

తుత్తునియలు **tuttuniyalu** *n.pl.* small pieces, fragments; ~ **ceeyu** to break or cut into small pieces.

తుథూ, తూథూ **tuthuu, tuuthuu** I. *onom. n. sug.* spitting. II. *interj. expressive of disgust.*

తుద **tuda** *n.* end, finish, conclusion.

తుదకు **tudaku** *adv.* at last, in the end, finally.

తుదముట్టించు **tudamuTTincu** *v.t.* **1** to finish, put an end to.

తుదముట్టు **tudamuTTu** *v.i.* to finish, come to an end.

తుది **tudi** I. *n. same as* **tuda.** II. *adj.* last, final; ~ **merugulu diddu** to put finishing touches; ~ **heccarika** ultimatum.

తునక **tunaka** *n.* 1 bit, piece, fragment. 2 piece of meat. 3 vegetarian savoury food item. 4 **mabbu ~ lu** patches of cloud.

తునకాలు **tunakaalu** *n.pl. dial.* scales, balance.

తునాతునకలవు, తునాతునియలవు **tunaatunakalawu, tunaatuniyalawu** *v.i.* to disintegrate, be blown to pieces.

తునాతునకలు **tunaatunakalu** *n.pl.* broken pieces.

తుని **tuni** *n.* name of a town in East Godavari District; **~ tagawu pariSkaaram** *lit.* settlement of a dispute in Tuni; this refers to the story of a judge who settled a dispute between parties in Tuni by a compromise which satisfied both sides.

తునికి, తూకి **tuniki, tuuki** *n.* Coromandel ebony, a tree whose leaves are used for making beedies.

తునుము, తున్ము **tunumu, tunmu** *v.t. class.* 1 to cut. 2 to kill.

తుపర **tupara** *same as* **tumpara.**

తుపాకి **tupaaki** *n.* gun; **~ kaalcu** to fire a gun.

తుపాను, తుఫాను **tupaanu, tuphaanu** *n.* storm, hurricane, cyclone, typhoon; **~ gaali** cyclonic wind.

తుపారం **tupaaram** *n.* heavy drizzle.

తుపాసి, దుబాసి **tupaasi, dubaasi** *n.* interpreter.

తుపుక్కు **tupukku** *onom. adv. sug.* sound of spitting; **~ na / ~ mani / tupukmani / tuppuna ummeesEEDu** he spat.

తుప్ప **tuppa** *n.* bush, shrub.

తుప్పర **tuppara** *same as* **tumpara.**

తుప్పు **tuppu** *n.* rust; **~ paTTu** to be[come] rusty; **ceewula ~ wadilincu** to charm the ears; **naalika ~ wadilincu** to charm the palate.

తుఫాను **tuphaanu** *same as* **tupaanu.**

తుమర్థం **tumartham** *n. gram.* infinitive.

తుములం **tumulam** *n.* uproar, tumult.

తుమ్మ **tumma** *n.* babul tree, *acacia arabica*; **~ karra** babul wood; **~ kance** hedge of thorny babul branches.

తుమ్మజిగురు, తుమ్మబంక, తుమ్మగోది **tummajiguru, tummabanka, tummagoodi** *n.* gum arabic.

తుమ్మి **tummi** *n. leucas aspera,* an annual plant whose flowers are used in Dasara celebrations.

తుమ్ము **tummu** I. *n.* sneeze. II. *v.i.* to sneeze.

తుమ్మెద **tummeda** *n.* bee.

తుమ్మెదపదాలు **tummedapadaalu** *n.pl.* verses or songs having a retrain ending in "**tummedaa!**"

తురక **turaka** *adj.* Muslim.

తురకంచు **turakancu** *n.* rim of a pot made in Muslim fashion without decoration.

తురకసాయిబు **turakasaayibu** *n.* Muslim gentleman.

తురతురా **turaturaa** *onom. adv. sug.* burning, blazing; **~ kaalu** to burn fast, burn fiercely.

తురాయి **turaayi** *n.* headdress, crest, plume.

తురుఫు **turuphu** *n.* trump (in cards); **turuphaasu** ace of trumps; **~ mukka** trump card.

తురుము **turumu**[1] *v.t.* to adorn the head with flowers; **talloo mallepuulu ~ konnadi** she wound jasmine flowers in her hair.

తురుము **turumu**[2] I. *n.* grated substance; **kobbari ~** grated coconut. II. *v.t.* to grate, scrape.

తురుముపీట **turumupiiTa** *n.* instrument for grating or scooping out coconut, etc.

తుర్రిగడ్డి **turrigaDDi** *n.* kind of grass useful for fodder, *amphilophis pertusa.*

తుర్రు **turru** *n.* haste, speed.

తుర్రుపిట్ట **turrupiTTa** *n.* 1 woodpecker (bird). 2 kind of child's toy.

తుర్రుమని **turrumani** *adv.* hastily, speedily.

తుల **tula** *n.* 1 balance, scales. 2 *astrol.* the sign of Libra. 3 similarity, equality.

తులం **tulam** *n.* tola, the weight of a rupee coin.

తులతూగు **tulatuugu** *v.i.* 1 to match, be equal to, be on a par with; **perugutunna janaabhaatoo tulatuugee widhangaa udyoogaawakaaśaalu peragaDam leedu** employment opportunities are not increasing on a par with the growing population. 2 to be weighed; **ayśwaryamtoo ~** to be rich, be wealthy, be prosperous.

తులనం **tulanam** *n.* 1 weighing, lifting. 2 comparing, estimating.

తులనాత్మక **tulanaatmaka** *adj.* comparative.

తులసి, తులసెమ్మ **tulasi, tulasemma** *n.* sacred basil, *ocymum sanctum.*

తులసికోట **tulasikooTa** *n.* raised construction on which a tulasi plant is grown.

తులసిబృందావనం **tulasibrndaawanam** *n.* bed of tulasi plants.

తులాంశం **tulaamśam** *n.* longitude.

తులాదండం **tulaadaNDam** *n.* lever.

తులాభారం **tulaabhaaram** *n.* weighing against precious metal or other costly material.

తులిత **tulita** *adj.* equal, similar, rivalling.

తులువ, తుళువ **tuluwa, tuLuwa** I. *n.* villain, wretch, scoundrel, scamp. II. *adj.* badly-behaved, naughty.

తులువతనం **tuluwatanam** *n.* wickedness, villainy.

తుల్యం **tulyam** *adj.* equal to, similar to, like, equivalent to; **swarga ~** like heaven; **tulyaarthaalu** equivalent meanings.

తుల్యత **tulyata** *n.* equivalence.

తుల్యభారం **tulyabhaaram** *n. sci.* equivalent weight.

తుల్యాంకనం **tulyaankanam** *n. sci.* equivalent.

తుళు **tuLu** *n.* the Tulu language.

తుళ్లింత **tuLLinta** *n.* frisking, skipping, capering.

తుళ్లిపడు **tuLLipaDu** *v.i.* 1 to be startled, receive a shock 2 to shiver, tremble.

తుళ్లు **tuLLu** I. *n.* 1 jump, leap. 2 arrogance. II. *v.i.* 1 to frisk, caper about, jump or dance with joy. 2 to be arrogant.

తువ్వ, దువ్వ, దుబ్బ **tuwwa, duwwa, dubba** *n.* ash coloured sandy soil.

తువ్వాలు, తువాలు, తువ్వాల, తువాల **tuwwaalu, tuwaalu, tuwwaala, tuwaala** *n.* towel.

తువ్వాయి **tuwwaayi** *n.* calf.

తుషారం **tuSaaram** *n.* 1 dew. 2 snow. 3 mist.

తుష్టి **tuSTi** *n.* satisfaction, contentment.

తుస **tusa** *n.* husk.

తుసుక్కుమని **tusukkumani** *adv.* suddenly.

తుస్కారించు, తూస్కారించు **tu[u]skaarincu** *v.t.* to disregard, scorn, despise.

తుస్సు **tussu** *adj. colloq.* (of work, etc.) bad, poor, inferior.

తుస్సుమని **tussumani** *adv.* with a hissing sound.

తుహినం **tuhinam** *n.* frost.

తూ- tuu

తూ **tuu** 1 *same as* **tuthuu.** 2 *onom. n. sug.* sound of blowing a trumpet.

తూకం **tuukam** *n.* 1 weighing. 2 weight, **~ unna maniSi** s.o. of importance, s.o. to be listened to with deference. 3 weight suspended at the end of a builder's plumbline. 4 scales, balance.

తూకంగా **tuukangaa** *adv.* aptly.

తూకం వేయు **tuukam weeyu** *v.t.* to weigh.

తూకి **tuuki** *same as* **tuniki.**

తూకు **tuuku** *n.* time, occasion.

తూకుడురాయి, తూకంరాయి **tuukuDuraayi, tuukam raayi** *n.* weight used for weighing.

తూగిడీ, తుంగిడీ **tuugiDii, tungiDii** *n.* crowd.

తూగు **tuugu** I. *n.* 1 swinging, swaying; **~ Tuyyaala** swinging cradle; **~ diipam** lamp suspended between two upright poles. 2 dozing, drowsiness. II. *v.i.* 1 to weigh. 2 to match up, come up (to a standard, requirement or expectation); **unnapaaLangaa nannu bayaldeeramaNTee inta takkuwa wyawadhiloo neenu tuugaleenu** if you ask me to start just as I am, I shall not be able to do so in such a short interval; **waaLLu jaamiindaarlu, waaLLatoo sambandham manam tuuga galamaa?** they are zamindars, can we come up to the standard of a marriage with them? 3 to sleep, doze. 4 to rock or sway backwards and forwards or from side to side.

తూచి **tuuci** I. *past participle of* **tuucu.** II. *adv.* carefully, cautiously.

తూచినట్లు **tuucinaTLu** *adv.* exactly, precisely (*lit.* as if it has been weighed); **~ reNDee waakyaalu maaTLaaD-EEDu** he spoke precisely two sentences; **~ samangaa waccindi andarikii** all of them received exactly the same amount.

తూ.చా.తప్పకుండా **tuu.caa. tappakuNDaa** *same as* **tu.ca. tappakuNDaa.**

తూచు **tuucu** *v.t.* 1 to weigh. 2 *fig.* to weigh up, estimate.

తూటా **tuuTaa** *same as* **tooTaa.**

తూటు **tuuTu** *n.* hole.

తూటుకట్టు, తూటుపోవు **tuuTukaTTu, tuuTupoowu** *v.i.* to develop a hole or crack, become leaky.

తూట్లుపడు **tuuTLupaDu** *v.i.* 1 to be pierced, be perforated, be punctured. 2 **naa cewulu tuuTLupaDDaayi** (i) my ears were bombarded (by hearing the same thing again and again); (ii) my ears were deafened (by hearing a loud noise).

తూడు **tuuDu** *n. class.* root of a lotus.

తూతూబాకా **tuutuubaakaa** *n.* trumpet.

తూథూ, తూ, థూ **tuuthuu, t[h]uu** 1 *onom. n. sug.* spitting. 2 *interj. expressive of disgust.*

తూనిక **tuunika** *n.* 1 weight, weighing. 2 scales.

తూనికకొలతలు **tuunikakolatalu** *n.pl.* weights and measures.

తూనికకోల **tuunikakoola** *n.* arm of a balance.

తూనికరాయి **tuunikaraayi** *n.* weight used for weighing.

తూనీగ **tuuniiga** *n.* dragon fly.

తూపు **tuupu** *n. class.* arrow; *mod. in* **cuupula ~ lu** glances.

తూము **tuumu** *n.* 1 toom, a measure of grain (= 4 kunchams or 32 manikas). 2 sluice, outlet, drain hole. 3 iron ring to which the baling rope is attached for lifting the bucket of a mhote. 4 iron ring forming part of the head of a pickaxe, spade, etc., into which the handle fits. 5 measure of area, varying according to the region.

తూముకాగు **tuumukaagu** *n.* pottery vessel which can hold one toom of grain.

తూరి **tuuri** *n.* time, occasion; **oka ~** once.

తూరీగ **tuuriiga** *n.* dragon fly.

తూరు **tuuru**[1] *v.i.* 1 (of the sun) to rise. 2 to penetrate, enter. 3 to strive, endeavour.

తూరు **tuuru**[2] *n.* husk, empty ear of corn.

తూర్పార **tuurpaara** *n.* winnowing.

తూర్పారపట్టు, తూర్పారపోయు **tuurpaarapaTTu, tuurpaarapooyu** *v.t.* 1 to winnow. 2 to abuse, scold severely, rebuke. 3 to disparage, find fault with.

తూర్పిల్లు **tuurpillu** *n.* eastern part of a house in which a room is set aside for worship.

తూర్పు **tuurpu** I. *n.* east; **cadarangam aNTee naaku ~ pa-Damaralu teliyadu** I know nothing at all about chess. II. *adj.* east[ern.].

తూర్యం **tuuryam** *n. class.* brass trumpet.

తూలగొట్టు **tuulagoTTu** *v.t.* to knock over, strike down.

తూలనాడు **tuulanaaDu** *v.t.* 1 to scold, revile, speak contemptuously of. 2 to insult.

తూలిక **tuulika** *n.* 1 artist's pen, pencil or brush. 2 down of duck, goose or swan; **hamsa ~ talpam** feather bed.

తూలిక చిత్రం **tuulika citram** *n.* caricature.

తూలు **tuulu** *v.i.* to reel, stagger.

తూలుమాటలు **tuulumaaTalu** *n.pl.* vulgar words.

తూష్ణీభావం **tuuSNiibhaawam** *n.* disdain, showing contempt by ignoring.

తూస్కారంగా **tuuskaarangaa** *adv.* scornfully.

తూస్కారించు **tuuskaarincu** *same as* **tuskaarincu.**

తృ - tṛ

తృణం **tṛNam** *n.* 1 straw, grass. 2 blade of grass, trifle; **~ oophaNamoo** a trifling sum.

తృణప్రాయం **tṛNapraayam** *adj.* worthless, trifling (*lit.* equal to a straw).

తృణాహార **tṛNaahaara** *adj. zool.* herbivorous.

తృణీకరించు **tṛNiikarincu** *v.t.* 1 to despise, slight, disregard. 2 to make light of.

తృణీకార **tṛNiikaara** *adj.* contemptuous, slighting.

తృణీకారం **tṛNiikaaram** *n.* contempt, disregard.

తృతీయ **tṛtiiya** *adj.* third, tertiary.

తృతీయప్రకృతి **tṛtiiya prakṛti** *n.* eunuch.

తృప్తి **tṛpti** *n.* satisfaction, contentment.

తృప్తికర **tṛptikara** *adj.* satisfactory.

తృప్తిచెందు, తృప్తిపడు **tṛpticendu, tṛptipaDu** *v.i.* to feel satisfied, be content.

తృప్తుడు **tṛptuDu** *n.* contented person.

తృష్ణ **tṛSNa** *n.* 1 thirst. 2 desire.

తె - te

తెంచు, తెంపు **tencu, tempu** *v.t.* 1 to break, snap, cut, sever; **nadi gaTLu ~ konnadi** the river burst its banks. 2 *fig.* to cut off, put an end to.

తెంపరి **tempari** *n.* bold or daring person.

తెంపరితనం **temparitanam** *n.* daring, audacity.

తెంపి **tempi** *n.* 1 widow. 2 beggar woman. 3 ugly and slovenly woman.

తెంపు **tempu** 1 *v.t., same as* **tencu.** 2 *n., same as* **tegimpu.**

తెగ **tega** I. *n.* 1 class, sect, subsect, community. 2 tribe. 3 race. 4 set, subdivision. 5 *sci.* species. II. *adv.* greatly, very much, exceedingly, overmuch, excessively; **aame ~ santooSincindi** she was exceedingly glad; **sinimaalu ~ cuustunnaaDu** he is constantly going to the cinema; **~ janam waccEEru** people came in great numbers; **cuTTalu ~ kaalacaDam ceeta atani pedawulu nallabaDDaayi** his lips became black from smoking too many cigars.

తెగకొట్టు **tegakoTTu** *v.t.* to cut off.

తెగటార్చు **tegaTaarcu** *v.t.* to kill.

తెగడ **tegaDa** *same as* **temaDa.**

తెగడిక **tegaDika** *n.* blame, censure.

తెగతెంచు **tegatencu** *v.t.* to snap off, cut off, sever.

తెగతెంపులు **tegatempulu** *n.pl.* cutting off, breaking off.

తెగనాడు **teganaaDu** *v.t.* 1 to criticise harshly, revile. 2 to assert bluntly.

తెగనీలుగు **teganiilugu** *v.i.* to be very haughty or arrogant.

తెగబడిపోవు **tegabaDipoowu** *v.i.* (of animals from a herd) to become separated or detached.

తెగబడు, తెగబారు **tegabaDu, tegabaaru** *v.i.* to dare, venture, be bold, be daring.

తెగబారెడు **tegabaareDu** *adj.* (of hair) very long.

తెగవేయు **tegaweeyu** *v.t.* 1 to cut off. 2 **tegaweesi ceppu** to say boldly; **tegaweesi aDugu** to ask point blank.

తెగించు **tegincu** *v.i.* to dare, venture, be bold; **praaNaalaku ~** to risk o.'s life, put o.'s life in danger; **teginci kharcu peTTu** to be bold enough to spend money.

తెగింపు, తెంపు **tegimpu, tempu** *n.* courage, bravery, daring.

తెగు **tegu** *v.i.* 1 to break, snap. 2 (of a dam) to burst, be breached. 3 (of skin) to be cut, (of a limb) to be cut off, be severed. 4 (of soil in ploughing) to be broken. 5 (of a dispute) to be cut short, ended. 6 **naa aaloocanalu tegEEyi** my thoughts were broken off/interrupted/disrupted. 7 to be sharp. 8 to venture, dare.

తెగుదారి, తెగోదారి **tegudaari, tegoodaari** *n.* donor.

తెగులు, తెవులు **tegulu, tewulu** *n.* 1 pest, blight, plant disease. 2 epidemic. 3 *colloq.* irritation, worry; **mareem tegulaa niiku?** what else is bothering you?

తెగువ[తనం] **teguwa[tanam]** *n.* 1 daring, boldness. 2 determination, resolution. 3 sharpness. 4 liberality.

తెగువరి **teguwari** *adj.* 1 bold, daring. 2 sharp. 3 liberal, generous.

తెచ్చిపెట్టు **teccipeTTu** *v.t.* 1 to foist, inflict (s.g unwanted). 2 to bring about, induce (fear).

తెచ్చిపెట్టుకొను **teccipeTTukonu** *v.t.* 1 to pretend, simulate; **tecci peTTukonna nawwu** forced, unnatural or artificial smile. 2 to force on o.s.; **leeni kaaThinyam teccipeTTukonnaaDu** he put on a forced air of severity (*lit.* he forced on himself a severity that was not in him).

తెచ్చు **teccu** *v.t.* 1 to get, bring. 2 to bring about, cause; **maarpu~** to bring about a change.

తెచ్చుకొను **teccukonu** *v.t.* to bring on o.s., acquire, earn; **dhayryam~** to summon up courage; **koopam~** to get angry; **pedda peeru~** to acquire a great reputation; **eedoo oka naalugu Dabbulu teccukoNTunnaaDu** he is earning some small amount; **buddhi~** to come to o.'s senses, learn a lesson (after making a mistake).

తెచ్చుకోలు **teccukoolu** I. *n.* pretending, simulating. II. *adj.* pretended, simulated, unnatural; **~nawwu** forced laugh.

తెట్టు **teTTu**[1] *n.* scum, froth.

తెట్టు **teTTu**[2] *n.* 1 heap. 2 crowd. 3 swelling.

తెట్టె **teTTe** *n.* 1 beehive. 2 honeycomb.

తెడ్డు **teDDu** *n.* 1 paddle, oar. 2 wooden ladle.

తెనిగించు **tenigincu** *same as* **teligincu.**

తెనుగు **tenugu** *n. and adj., another form of* **telugu.**

తెన్ను **tennu** *n. class.* way, path; *mod. in certain phrases*, e.g., **daarii~** way and method; **eduru~lu cuucu** to wait anxiously, look out anxiously (for s.g); *see also* **tiiru~lu.**

తెపతెప **tepatepa** *adv.* backwards and forwards, this way and that.

తెప్ప **teppa** *n.* 1 raft, catamaran; **waaDi~munigipooyindi** *dial.* he was ruined. 2 rain cloud.

తెప్పరిల్లు **tepparillu** *v.i.* to recover o.'s senses, recover from a shock.

తెప్పలుగా **teppalugaa** *adv.* exceedingly, abundantly.

తెప్పించు **teppincu** *v.t.* 1 to send for, have (s.g) brought. 2 to procure, get, obtain. 3 **o.-ki koopam~** to make s.o. angry.

తెమడ, తెగడ **temaDa, tegaDa** *n.* thick saliva, mucus.

తెమర్చు, తెముల్చు **temarcu** (*dial.*), **temulcu** *v.i.* to have a sensation of retching or vomiting, have a feeling of nausea.

తెమలు, తెములు **temalu, temulu** I. *v.i.* 1 to move, stir. 2 to shake. 3 to get ready to go. 4 to start, set out. 5 to hasten. 6 to be finished or settled promptly or quickly. II. *impersonal vb. with dative* 1 to have spare time, have leisure; **pillalatoo naaku temalaDam leedu** on account of the children I cannot find enough time. 2 to feel nausea.

తెముల్చుకొను **temulcukonu** *v.t.* to finish, complete or finalise (s.g) quickly or promptly.

తెమ్మ **temma** *same as* **teema.**

తెమ్మెర **temmera** *n.* cool breeze.

తెయ్యిమను **teyyimanu** *v.i.* to be proud, be haughty; **teyteymani gentu** to dance with anger or other emotion.

తెర **tera** *n.* 1 curtain, screen; **~loo** *theat.* off-stage; **eNDa~ tiisindi** the sun broke through the clouds. 2 wave. 3 gust; **gaali~** gust of wind. 4 series, succession; **daggu~** fit or bout of coughing; *cf.* **~lu~lugaa.**

తెరకట్టు **terakaTTu** *v.i.* 1 (of a liquid) to form a layer on the surface; **paalu terakaTTEEyi** the milk has formed a layer of cream. 2 to set up a screen.

తెరకొయ్య **terakoyya** *n.* 1. ship's mast. 2 spar in a ship's rigging.

తెరగు **teragu** *n. class.* 1 way, path. 2 manner, fashion.

తెరగుడ్డ **teraguDDa** *n.* curtain cloth.

తెరచాప **teracaapa** *n.* ship's sail.

తెరచిరాజు **teraci raaju** *interj.* check! (in chess).

తెరచు, తెరుచు **teracu, terucu** *v.t.* to open, unfasten, unlock.

తెరచుకొను, తెరుచుకొను **teracukonu, terucukonu** *v.i.* to open.

తెరతీయు **teratiiyu** I. *v.i.* to draw back a curtain. II. *v.t.* to uncover, reveal.

తెరనోరు **teranooru** *n.* open mouth, gape.

తెరపట్టా **terapaTTaa** *n.* curtain made of thick canvas cloth.

తెరపి, తెరిపి **terapi, teripi** *n.* 1 interval, intermission, cessation, pause, break, respite; **~leekuNDaa waana dancutunnadi** the rain pours down ceaselessly. 2 leisure time, spare time. 3 vacant space, clear space, open space; **edurillu paDipooyEEka maaku baagaa ~gaa undi** now that the house opposite us has fallen down we have plenty of open space; **waaLLiddaruu janam ~gaa unna cooTa kalusukonnaaru** the two of them met in an unfrequented spot; **mabbulu cediripooyEEyi, aakaaśam ~ayyindi** the clouds have scattered and the sky has cleared.

తెరబొమ్మ **terabomma** *same as* **toolubomma.**

తెరలుతెరలుగా **teralu teralugaa** *adv.* in succession, one after the other, wave upon wave, layer upon layer.

తెరసెల్లా **terasellaa** *n.* curtain made of thin cloth.

తెరువరి **teruwari** *n.* traveller.

తెరువాటు **teruwaaTu** *n. class.* highway robbery.

తెరువు **teruwu** *n.* 1 way, path. 2 manner.

తెరువు ఇచ్చు **teruwu iccu** *v.i.* to show the way, lead the way.

తెర్ర **terra**[1] I. *n.* (*also* **~mokham**) fool, blockhead. II *adj.* open, gaping; **~nooru** gaping mouth.

తెర్ర **terra**[2] *same as* **torra.**

తెలంగాణం **telangaaNam** *n.* the Telangana region of Andhra Pradesh.

తెలంగాణ్యులు, తెలగాణ్యులు **telangaaNyulu, telagaaNyulu** *n.pl.* name of a sect of brahmans.

తెలకపిండి **telakapiNDi** *n.* steamed flour made from ground oil seeds used as cattle feed, oil cake.

తెలగ **telaga** *n.* name of a community in Andhra Pradesh.

తెలగదుంప **telagadumpa** *n.* sweet potato.
తెలతెలవారు, తెలవారు **telatelawaaru, telawaaru** *v.i.* to dawn.
తెలవారుఝాము, తెల్లవారుఝాము **telawaaru-jhaamu, tellawaarujhaamu** *n.* early dawn.
తెలి **teli** *adj.* white.
తెలిక **telika** *n.* gingelly, *sesamum indicum.*
తెలిగించు, తెనిగించు **teligincu, tenigincu** *v.t.* to translate or render into Telugu.
తెలియచెప్పు **teliyaceppu** *v.t.* 1 to inform. 2 to make known.
తెలియచేయు **teliya ceeyu** *v.t.* to make known, express, explain, intimate, convey, communicate, declare.
తెలియపరచు **teliyaparacu** *v.t.* to inform, explain, declare.
తెలియబడు **teliyabaDu** *v.i.* to be[come] known, be understood.
తెలియవచ్చు **teliyawaccu** *v.i.* to be[come] known, be[come] apparent.
తెలియు **teliyu** *v.i.* 1 to be known, be understood. 2 to be perceived, be clear, be intelligible.
తెలివి **teliwi** *n.* intelligence, wit, wisdom, knowledge, consciousness, awareness; **~na paDu** (i) to learn sense, come to o.'s senses; (ii) to recover consciousness.
తెలివిడి **teliwiDi** *n.* 1 knowledge, understanding. 2 explanatory example. 3 *same as* **smaarakam.**
తెలివితక్కువ **teliwitakkuwa** *adj.* stupid, unintelligent.
తెలివితక్కువతనం **teliwitakkuwatanam** *n.* stupidity, lack of intelligence.
తెలివితేటలు **teliwiteeTalu** *n. pl.* brains, intelligence.
తెలివైన **teliwayna** *adj.* intelligent, clever.
తెలిసితెలిసి **telisitelisi** *adv.* knowingly, with full knowledge, with intent.
తెలిసోతెలియకో **telisooteliyakoo** *advbl. phrase* knowingly or unknowingly, wittingly or unwittingly.
తెలుగు **telugu** *n.* the Telugu language.
తెలుగునాడు **telugunaaDu** *n.* the Telugu land.
తెలుగుమీరు **telugumiiru** *v.i. colloq.* 1 to become cultured or civilised. 2 to become proud or arrogant.
తెలుపు **telupu**[1] *n. and adj.* white.
తెలుపు **telupu**[2] *v.t.* 1 to make known. 2 to tell, inform. 3 to show, demonstrate. 4 to signify, indicate, denote. 5 to notify.
తెలుపుడు **telupuDu** *n.* knowledge, understanding.
తెలుపుడు చేయు **telupuDu ceeyu** *v.t.* to make known, signify, indicate.
తెలుసుకొను **telusukonu** *v.t.* 1 to learn, get to know, find out, ascertain, understand. 2 to observe, perceive.
తెల్ల **tella** *adj.* 1 white. 2 pale. 3 (of liquid) colourless.
తెల్లం **tellam** *adj. class.* apparent, evident, clear; *cf.* **teeTa~.**
తెల్లగడ్డ, తెల్లుల్లి, వెల్లుల్లి **tellagaDDa, tellulli, wellulli** *n.* garlic.
తెల్లపోవు **tellapoowu** *v.i.* to turn pale.
తెల్లబట్ట **tellabaTTa** *n. med.* whites, leucorrhoea.
తెల్లబారు, తెల్లబడు **tellabaaru, tellabaDu** *v.i.* to become white.
తెల్లమొహం వేయు **tellamoham weeyu** *v.i.* to look blank.
తెల్లవాడు, తెల్లాడు **tellawaaDu, tellaaDu** *n.* 1 white person, westerner. 2 Britisher; **tellaaLi baawuTaa** the British flag, union jack.
తెల్లవారగట్ట, తెల్లవారగట్ల **tellawaaragaTTa, tella-waaragaTLa** *adv.* at dawn.
తెల్లవారి, తెల్లారి **tellawaari, tellaari** *adv.* 1 at dawn. 2 next morning.
తెల్లవారు **tellawaaru** I. *n.pl.* white people. II. *v.i.* 1 to become white. 2 (*also* **tellaaru**) to dawn. 3 (*also* **tellaaru**) to fail, be lost, be ruined, be finished; **waaDi batuku tell-aaripooyindi** he has died.
తెల్లవార్చు, తెల్లార్చు **tellawaarcu, tellaarcu** *v.i. and t.* 1 to put an end to, settle (dispute). 2 to watch all night in sorrow, live through a period of sorrow; **ii batuku ilaa tellaarcuku poodaamaa?** are we to live all our lives like this?
తెల్లవార్లూ **tellawaarluu** *adv.* all night long.
తెల్లుల్లి **tellulli** *same as* **tellagaDDa.**
తెవులు **tewulu** *same as* **tegulu.**
తెస్సు **tessu** *adj. colloq.* blank; **~moham peTTukoni weLLi-pooyEEDu** he went away with a blank look on his face.

తే - tee

తేకు, టేకు **teeku, Teeku** *n.* teak tree, teakwood.
తేగ **teega** *n.* 1 young palmyra tree. 2 young edible palmyra sprout.
తేగుడు **teeguDu** *adj.* watery; **annam ~ayindi** the rice is watery.
తేజం, తేజస్సు **teejam, teejassu** *n.* 1 brilliance, lustre, splendour, brightness. 2 glory. 3 valour. 4 halo.
తేజరిల్లు **teejarillu** *v.i.* to shine, be glorious.
తేజస్వి **teejaswi** *n.* brilliant person, glorious person.
తేజి, తేజీ **teeji[i]** *adj. class.* rapid.
తేజిత **teejita** *adj.* bright, gleaming, sharp.
తేజోమండలం **teejoomaNDalam** *n.* halo.
తేజోమూర్తి **teejoomuurti** *n.* 1 brilliant or outstanding person. 2 sun.
తేట **teeTa** I. *n.* 1 clearness, purity, brightness. 2 (*also* **majjiga~**) clear buttermilk. II. *adj.* 1 clear, transparent. 2 pure; **~tenugu** pure Telugu; **~mutyam** pearl of good quality. 3 lively, vivacious.
తేటగీతి **teeTagiiti** *n.* kind of poetic metre.
తేటతెల్లం **teeTatellam** *adj.* very clear, evident.
తేటపరచు **teeTaparacu** *v.t.* 1 to make clear, expound. 2 to clarify.
తేటలూరు **teeTaluuru** *v.i.* 1 (of water) to flow from a clear spring. 2 (of poetry) to be pleasant, sweet and tasteful.
తేటి **teeTi** *n. class.* large black bee.
తేటికంటి **teeTikaNTi** *n. class.* beautiful woman with dark eyes.
తేడా **teeDaa** I. *n.* 1 difference; **~paaDaa** *see* **paaDaa.** 2 margin. II. *adj.* different; **~maaTa** a different word, another word.
తేదీ **teedii** *n.* date, day of the month.
తేనీరు **teeniiru** *n.* tea (drink).
తేనె, తేని **teene, teeni** *n.* honey.
తేనెటీగ **teeneTiiga** *n.* bee.
తేనెతెట్టు, తేనెపట్టు, తేనెగూడు, తేనెతుట్టె **teeneteTTu, teenepaTTu, teeneguuDu, teenetuTTe** *n.* beehive, honeycomb.
తేనె తొన **teene tona** *n.* kind of sweet dish.
తేనెపానకం **teenepaanakam** *n.* sugarcane juice boiled to the consistency of honey.
తేనెమంచుపురుగు **teenemancupurugu** *n.* mango hopper, a pest of the mango crop.
తేన్చు **teencu** *v.i.* to belch.
తేన్పు, తేపు **teenpu, teepu** *n.* belch[ing].
తేప **tEEpa** *n.* time; **nannu ~~pilustaaDu** he calls me very frequently.
తేభ్యం **teebhyam** *n.* useless fellow.
తేమ, తెమ్మ **teema, temma** I. *n.* moisture, damp[ness], humidity. II. *adj.* damp, moist, watery.
తేమగిల్లు, తేమ ఎక్కు **teemagillu, teema ekku** *v.i.* to become moist or damp.
తేయాకు **teeyaaku** *n.* tea leaves, tea.
తేర **teera** I. *n.* unconnectedness, unrelatedness. II. *adj.* 1 unconnected, unrelated. 2 free of payment; **~sommu biirapiicu** money that you get without any effort is like the fibre of a cucumber (i.e., s.g that you throw away casually — proverb). III. *adv.* (*also* **~gaa**) 1 free of payment. 2 easily, without effort, without trouble. 3 to no purpose; **~gaa kuurcuNDu** to sit idly.
తేరకత్తె **teerakatte** *n.* 1 strange woman, unrelated woman. 2 woman of loose character.
తేరిపారచూచు **teeripaaracuucu** *v.t.* to gaze intently at, stare steadily or fixedly at.
తేరు **teeru[1]** *v.i. with variant forms* **deeru, teelu, deelu** 1 to occur, be formed, develop, appear; **modaLLa daggira buDipelu deeri anduloo purugulu uNTaayi** swellings occur at the base of the stems and there are insects in them; **kinda guNDrangaa uNDi payna koosugaa teereeTTu unna gaDDikuppa** a hayrick round at the bottom and tapering upwards to a point; **kona deerina cubukam** pointed chin; **kaayalu deerina ceetulu** calloused hands; **marakalu deerina gooDalu** walls covered with stains. 2 to be[come] clear. 3 (of sediment) to settle. 4 (of scum, cream) to rise to the surface. 5 to come to an end, be finished. 6 (of illness, swooning) to pass off.
తేరు **teeru[2]** *n.* 1 temple car. 2 chariot.
తేరువీధి **teeruwiidhi** *n.* street through which the temple car is taken in procession.
తేరుకొను **teerukonu** *v.i.* to recover (from shock or illness).
తేర్చు **teercu** *v.t.* to make clear, clarify.
తేలగింపు **teelagimpu** *n.* infatuation.
తేలగిలపడు **teelagilapaDu** *v.i.* to be infatuated, be full of lust.
తేలవేయు **teelaweeyu** *v.i.* 1 to cause to float. 2 **kaLLu~** (i) to open o.'s eyes wide; (ii) to stare blankly due to fear, helplessness or exhaustion; (iii) *colloq.* to die. 3 **mokham teelaweesukonu** to wear a look of helplessness on o.'s face. 4 **ceetulu teelaweesukonu** to spread out o.'s hands in a gesture of helplessness.
తేలాడు, తేలియాడు **teelaaDu, teeliyaaDu** *v.i. class.* to float.
తేలించు **teelincu** *v.t.* to cause to float.
తేలిక **teelika** I. *n.* 1 lightness. 2 ease. II. *adj.* 1 light. 2 slight, trivial. 3 easy, simple. 4 inferior, poor in quality; **~rakam waDLu** inferior kind of paddy.

తేలికగా **teelikagaa** *adv.* **1** lightly. **2** easily. **3** scornfully, contemptuously.

తేలికపడు **teelikapaDu** *v.i.* **1** to become light, be lightened. **2** to be at ease, feel relieved. **3** to be treated lightly, be treated without respect.

తేలికపరచు **teelikaparacu** *v.t.* **1** to lighten. **2** to treat lightly, regard with contempt.

తేలిపోవు **teelipoowu** *v.i.* to float; **aanandamtoo gaaliloo teelipootuu waccEEDu** he came walking on air on account of happiness. **2** to reel, falter, waver; **aame niirasangaa undi, aDugulu teelipootunnaayi** she is weak and her steps are wavering. **3** to turn out, prove, emerge; **adi asaadhyamani teelipooyindi** that turned out to be impossible. **4** to be settled, be decided. **5** to fade away, fail to materialise, come to nothing. **6** to finish, end up; **kaaraagaaramloo uncitee inkaa moraTu teelipootundi** if you put her in prison she will end up even more hardened.

తేలు **teelu**[1] *alt. form of* **teeru**[1].

తేలు **teelu**[2] *v.t.* **1** to float. **2** to result, turn out, emerge.

తేలు **teelu**[3] *n.* scorpion.

తేల్చు **teelcu** *v.i. and t.* **1** to make up o.'s mind, decide; **aToo iToo teelci ceppaNDi** make up your mind one way or the other and tell me. **2** to settle, fix. determine; **kamiTiwaaru raytaanga ṛNabhaaram 218 kooTLu ani teelcEEru** the committee determined the rural debt burden to be Rs. 218 crores. **3** to cause to float. **4** (*also* **teelciweeyu**) to put an end to, finish.

తేల్చుకొను **teelcukonu** *v.t.* **1** to get to know, understand, fathom. **2** to settle, decide.

తై - tay

తైడంబలి **tayDambali** *n.* ragi porridge.

తైతక్కలాడు **taytakkalaaDu** *v.i.* **1** to dance with anger. **2** to dance wildly. **3** *fig.* to behave irresponsibly.

తైనాతీ **taynaatii** I. *n.* servant constantly in attendance. II. *adv.* ceaselessly, constantly.

తైపారు **taypaaru** *n.* comparing.

తైరు **tayru** *n.* **1** curds. **2** flattery; **~nawwu** flattering or ingratiating laugh.

తైరుకొట్టు **tayrukoTTu** *v.t.* to flatter.

తైలం **taylam** *n.* **1** oil. **2** ointment. **3** *slang* money.

తైలవర్ణచిత్రం **taylawarNacitram** *n.* oil painting.

తొ - to

తొంగిచూచు **tongicuucu** I. *v.t.* to peep at, peer at. II. *v.i.* 1 to peep [out], appear, emerge. 2 **tongicuuci poowu** to pay a flying visit, pay a casual visit.

తొంగు **tongu** *v.i.* 1 to bend. 2 to lie down.

తొంగుండు **tonguNDu** *v.i.* to lie down and sleep.

తొంటి, తుంటి **toNTi**[1], **tuNTi** *n.* hip, thigh; ~ **kiilu** hip joint; ~ **emuka** thigh bone, femur.

తొంటి, తొంట **toNTi**[2], **toNTa** *adj.* withered, deformed; ~ **ceyyi** withered hand.

తొండ **toNDa** *n.* chameleon.

తొండం **toNDam** *n.* 1 trunk of an elephant. 2 hose of a leather bucket used for baling from wells. 3. tongue of the lock of a suitcase.

తొందర **tondara** *n.* 1 haste, hurry. 2 trouble, annoyance. 3 confusion, perplexity.

తొందరగా **tondaragaa** *adv.* quickly, urgently.

తొందరచేయు, తొందరపరచు, తొందరపెట్టు **tondaraceeyu, tondaraparacu, tondarapeTTu** *v.t.* 1 to hurry, hasten. 2. to trouble, annoy.

తొందరపడు **tondarapaDu** *v.i.* 1 to hurry, hasten. 2 to be troubled. 3 to be confused, be perplexed.

తొందరపాటు **tondarapaaTu** *n.* 1 haste, hurry. 2 troublesomeness.

తొందళం **tondaLam** *n.* 1 dish of two or three vegetables cooked with tamarind juice. 2 *colloq.* miscellaneous group or assortment of people.

తొంబ **tomba** *n.* (gen. in a derogatory sense) crowd, group.

తొంభై **tombhay** *n.* ninety.

తొకతొక **tokatoka** I. *adj.* indistinct, jumbled (gen. of words spoken by young children). II. *onom. adv. sug.* sound of boiling water.

తొకతొకలాడు **tokatokalaaDu** *v.i.* to impede or jostle one another (e.g., persons in a crowd).

తొక్క **tokka** *n.* 1 skin, hide; ~ **reegakoTTu** to beat (s.o.) soundly. 2 bark, rind, peel. 3 crust of a pie.

తొక్కించు **tokkincu** *v.t.* 1 to cause to tread or trample. 2 **kuppa ~ konu** to have a heap of grain threshed.

తొక్కిడి **tokkiDi** *n.* congestion, crowding.

తొక్కిపట్టు **tokkipaTTu** *v.t.* 1 to trample on. 2 to repress, suppress (ideas). 3 to hold up, delay (business).

తొక్కిపెట్టు **tokkipeTTu** *v.t. fig.* to lock up, immobilise (funds), delay (business).

తొక్కిసలాట **tokkisalaaTa** *n.* 1 jostling, trampling, overcrowding. 2 disorder, turmoil.

తొక్కిసలాడు **tokkisalaaDu** *v.t.* to jostle, trample.

తొక్కు **tokku** I. *n. dial.* 1 chutney. 2 skin of a fruit (= **tokka**). II. *v.i. and t.* 1 to step, tread, trample. 2 to pedal, ride (cycle). 3 to perform a dance. 4 **gummam ~** to cross (*lit.* to tread on) a threshold; *see* **kadam ~**.

తొక్కుడు **tokkuDu** *n.* 1 trampling, treading, pounding. 2 straw, etc., trampled by cattle.

తొక్కుడుపచ్చడి **tokkuDupaccaDi** *n.* pounded mango pickle.

తొక్కుడుబండి **tokkuDubaNDi** *n. colloq.* pedal cycle.

తొక్కుడుబిళ్ల **tokkuDubiLLa** *n.* a girls' game.

తొక్కుడులడ్డు **tokkuDulaDDu** *n.* a kind of sweet (**laDDu**) first fried then crushed and cooked again after adding sugar.

తొక్కులాడు **tokkulaaDu** *v.i.* to dance with joy, dance with excitement.

తొగకంటి **togakaNTi** *n. class.* woman.

తొగట **togaTa** *same as* **tawiTa.**

తొగరు, తొగరి **togaru, togari** I. *n.* 1 red colour. 2 *dial.* red gram. II. *adj.* red; ~ **mannu** potter's clay.

తొగు **togu** *v.t. dial., alt. form of* **tawwu.**

తొట్ట **toTTa** *adj.* (of lips) thick, bulbous.

తొట్టతొలి **toTTa toli** *adj.* the very first.

తొట్టి, తొట్టె **toTTi, toTTe** *n.* 1 bin, tub, pot, trough; **puula ~** flowerpot. 2 child's cradle. 3 cradle made of ropes in the front part of a bullock cart serving as a seat for the driver. 4 *sci.* cistern.

తొట్టి ఉయ్యాల **toTTi uyyaala** *n.* 1 swinging cradle. 2 hammock.

తొట్టి తొంపరలాడు **toTTi tomparalaaDu** *v.t.* to mix up, scatter.

తొట్టిబండి **toTTibaNDi** *n.* bullock cart.

తొట్టిమంచం **toTTimancam** *n.* swinging couch.

తొట్రు, తొట్టు **toTru, toTTu** I. *n.* 1 confusion, perplexity. 2 stumbling, faltering. II. *v.i.* 1 to be confused. 2 to falter, stumble.

తొట్రుపడు **toTrupaDu** *v.i.* 1 to totter, stumble, falter. 2 to be confused, be perplexed, be bewildered.

తొట్రుపాటు **toTrupaaTu** *n.* 1 tottering, stumbling, faltering. 2 confusion, perplexity, bewilderment.

తొడ **toDa** *n.* thigh.

తొడకొట్టు, తొడచరచు **toDakoTTu, toDacaracu** *v.i.* to slap o.'s thigh (as a challenge to a fight).

తొడగిల్లు **toDagillu** *v.t.* to urge on, instigate (*lit.* to pinch the thigh).

తొడగు **toDagu** *same as* **toDugu.**

తొడతొక్కిడి **toDatokkiDi** *n.* congestion, crowding, rush or crush of people; **sTeeSanloo ~ gaa undi, Dabbu jaagrataa!** mind your money! there is a great crush at the station.

తొడపాశం, తొడపాయసం **toDapaaśam, toDapaayasam** *n.* pinching the thigh with thumb and finger as a punishment.

తొడలాగు **toDalaagu** *n.* pants.
తొడసంబంధం **toDasambandham** *n.* sexual relationship.
తొడిగించు **toDigincu** *v.t.* to clothe, cause to wear; **aameki gaajulu toDigincEEnu** I made her wear bangles *or* I gave her bangles to wear.
తొడిమ, తొడిమె **toDima, toDime** *n.* stalk or pedicel of a leaf, flower or fruit.
తొడుక్కొను **toDukkonu** *v.t.* to put on, wear (anything that is fitted, such as a coat, shoes, bangles).
తొడుగు, తొడగు **toDugu, toDagu** I. *n.* **1** dress, apparel, garb. **2** load of brushwood. **3** *class.* armour. **4** *class.* ornament. **5** *class.* sheath, covering. II. *v.i.* to sprout; **mokka aaku toDigindi** the plant sprouted leaves. III. *v.t.* to clothe (s.o.), dress (s.o.), put (clothes, shoes, jewellery, etc.) on s.o.; **aame kooTu tecci aayanaku toDigindi** she brought a coat and put it on him.
తొడుపు **toDupu** *n. class.* **1** armour. **2** covering, sheath. **3** ornament.
తొణకు, తొణుకు **toNaku, toNuku** *v.i.* **1** (of liquid) to be spilt. **2** *fig.* to be stirred, be agitated; **toNakakuNDaa** without a tremor.
తొణుకుబెణుకు **toNukubeNuku** *n.* fear and confusion.
తొత్తరికం **tottarikam** *n.* slavery.
తొత్తు **tottu** *n.* **1** prostitute. **2** servant, slave, menial; ~ **kinda baDi~** lesser menial serving under a menial.
తొత్తుకొడుకు **tottukoDuku** *n.* **1** son of a prostitute (*term of abuse*). **2** servant, slave, menial.
తొత్తుపడుచు **tottupaDucu** *n.* **1** prostitute (*term of abuse*). **2** slave girl, servant girl.
తొత్తులమారి **tottulamaari** *n.* libertine.
తొన **tona** *n.* **1** piece or division or segment of an orange or lime or jackfruit. **2** *class.* one who guards or protects.
తొనికిసలాడు, తొణికిసలాడు **tonikisalaaDu, toNikisalaaDu** *v.i.* **1** to be full to the brim. **2** to gleam, glint, glimmer.
తొనుకుడుబాన **tonukuDubaana** *n.* earthen pot filled with water into which during the marriage ceremony the bride and groom put their hands simultaneously in order to retrieve a gold article.
తొన్నూరు **tonnuuru** *n.* nine hundred.
తొపారం **topaaram** *n.* hood for the head of a hawk used in falconry.
తొప్పలుతొరలుగా **toppalutoralugaa** *adv.* in millions, by the million.
తొప్పి **toppi** *n.* cap.
తొబక **tobaka** I. *n.* **1** shell of a nut. **2** shell of a crab or other crustacean. II. *adj.* empty, seedless.
తొమ్మండుగురు **tommaNDuguru** *n. pl.* nine persons.
తొమ్మిది **tommidi** *n.* nine.
తొమ్మిదో **tommidoo** *adj.* ninth; ~**aSTakam** the ninth ashtakam, *a euphemism for vulgar language.*
తొయ్యలి, తోయలి **toyyali, tooyali** *n. class.* lady.
తొరక **toraka** *n.* skin which forms on the surface of a liquid (e.g., milk) when it cools.
తొరపు, తొరలించు, తొర్లించు **torapu, toralincu, torlincu** *v.t.* to regulate the heat of water by mixing hot and and cold.
తొర్ర, తెర్ర **torra, terra** *n.* **1** hole (in a tree trunk). **2** breach, gap. **3** loss; **wyaapaaramloo ~ paDindi** a loss was incurred in the business.
తొర్రి **torri** *n.* **1** gap, breach; **~paLLawaaDu** gaptoothed person. **2** defect, deformity; **~ pedawi** hare lip.
తొలకరి **tolakari** *n.* first rains, beginning of the rainy season.
తొలగతోయు **tolagatooyu** *v.t.* to drive away.
తొలగించు **tolagincu** *v.t.* **1** to remove, get rid of. **2** to delete, abolish, do away with. **3** to draw aside or raise (curtain).
తొలగింపు **tolagimpu** *n.* **1** removal, deletion, abolition. **2** *legal* **piiDa~** abatement of a nuisance.
తొలగు **tolagu** *v.i.* **1** to depart, be removed. **2** to cease, end, finish. **3** to vanish, disappear. **4** (of danger) to recede. **5** to step aside, get out of the way. **6** to get out of place, be displaced, be dislocated; **~ kiilu toligindi** the joint was dislocated. **7** (of a curtain) to be raised or drawn aside.
తొలచు **tolacu** *same as* **tolucu.**
తొలి **toli** I. *n.* beginning. II. *adj.* **1** first. **2** old, ancient. **3** former, previous; **paNDuga ~ naaDu** first day of a festival *or* the day before a festival. **4** initial; **~weegam** initial velocity.
తొలికలుపు **tolikalupu** *n.* first weeding of a seedbed.
తొలికోడికూత **tolikooDi kuuta** *n.* earliest cockcrow; **~ poddu** dawn.
తొలిచూలు **tolicuulu** *n.* first pregnancy.
తొలిజాము **tolijaamu** *n.* first part of the night; *see* **aparaatri.**
తొలితొలుత **tolitoluta** *adv.* first of all.
తొలిదిక్కు **tolidikku** *n.* east.
తొలిపలుకు, తొలినుడి **tolipaluku, tolinuDi** *n.* preface, foreword.
తొలిపించు **tolipincu** *v.t.* **1** to hollow out, bore. **2** *causative of* **tolucu.**
తొలిమబ్బు **tolimabbu** *n.* clouds which bring the first rains.
తొలిముద్ద **tolimudda** *n.* first morsel at a meal which is set aside ceremonially as an offering to a deity or to deceased ancestors.
తొలిసంధ్య **tolisandhya** *n.* morning twilight.
తొలుచు, తొలచు **tolucu, tolacu** *v.t.* **1** to bore (hole, tunnel). **2** to hollow out, scoop out. **3** to perforate. **4** to carve (wood). **5** to rinse, cleanse.
తొలుత **toluta** I. *n.* beginning. II. *adj.* first, former; ~ **raajulu paalincee roojulloo** in the days when former kings ruled. III. *adv.* [at] first.
తొల్లి **tolli** *adv.* formerly, at first, at the outset.
తొల్లిక, తొళ్లిక **tollika, toLLika** *n.* small hoe.

తొల్లిటి, తొల్లింటి **tolli[N]Ti** *adj.* previous, earlier, former; ~**katha** previous story, previous history.

తొవ్వ **towwa** *same as* **doowa.**

తొసల **tosala** *n. dial.* vessel with a wide mouth.

తొస్స, తొస్సి **tossa, tossi** I *n.* lisping, speech defect due to lack of teeth. II. *adj.* (*also* **tosse**) toothless; ~**nooru** toothless mouth; ~**paLLu** teeth with gaps occurring.

తో - too

తో **too** *p.p.* 1 with (instrumental); **paamunu karratoo koTTEEnu** I struck the snake with a stick. 2 with, along with, together with (comitative); **naatoo raNDi** come with me. 3 *other usages*: (i) *with nouns relating to psychosomatic states* **aame kaDuputoo undi** she is pregnant; **waaru upawaasamtoo unnaaru** they are fasting; (ii) *with vbs. meaning to speak, say* **aayana naatoo eppuduu teluguloonee maaTLaaDutaaDu** he always talks to me in Telugu; (iii) **saamaanyuDu kuuDaa guruwutoo awasaram leekuNDaa caduwukoni tanaku taanugaanee artham ceesukoowaccu** even an ordinary person can read and understand it without the need of a teacher; (iv) *see* **nimittam**; (v) **waaru leeci ciikaTitoo bayaludeerEEru** they got up and left before dawn.

తోక **tooka** *n.* 1 tail. 2 *slang* child.

తోక ఆడించు **tooka aaDincu** *v.i.* 1 to behave mischievously. 2 (of a dog) to wag its tail.

తోక ఎత్తు **tooka ettu** *v.i.* 1 to run away due to fear. 2 to oppose.

తోకకప్ప **tookakappa** *n.* tadpole.

తోకకోయు **tookakooyu** *v.i.* 1 to put to shame. 2 to cause loss. 3 to punish.

తోకచుక్క **tookacukka** *n.* comet.

తోక ఝాడించు **tooka jhaaDincu** *v.i.* to slip away, make o.s. scarce.

తోక పీకు **tooka piiku** *v.i.* to run away due to cowardice.

తోకపీకుళ్లు **tookapiikuLLu** *n.pl.* pest, plague.

తోక మడచు, తోక ముడుచు **tooka maDacu, tooka muDucu** *v.i.* to run away due to fear.

తోక మిరియాలు **tooka miiriyaalu** *n.pl.* cubebs.

తోకసన్నం **tookasannam** *n.* a variety of paddy.

తోచు **toocu** *v.i.* to occur to the mind, seem, be understood, be sensed, be perceived; **naaku toocindi idi** this is what appears to me *or* this is what I think; **naaku wintagaa toocindi** it seemed strange to me; **naaku artham toocaleedu** the meaning did not occur to me; **aa palletuuLLoo S.-ki eemii tooca leedu** S. found nothing with which to pass the time in that small village; **uurikee iNTLoo kuurcuNTee eem toostundi**? if we just sit at home, how will we pass the time?

తోట **tooTa** *n.* 1 garden. 2 plantation.

తోటకూర **tooTakuura** *n.* spinach.

తోటమాలి **tooTamaali** *n.* gardener.

తోటా, తూటా **tooTaa, tuuTaa** *n.* cartridge.

తోటా మందు **tooTaa mandu** *n.* dynamite.

తోటి, తోడి **tooTi**[1], **tooDi** *adjvl. prefix meaning* fellow, joint.

తోటి, తోటీ **tooTi**[2], **tooTii** *n.* 1 sweeper. 2 village servant working under the village headman.

తోటి అల్లుడు, తోడల్లుడు **tooTi alluDu, tooDalluDu** *n.* fellow son-in-law.

తోటికోడలు, తోడికోడలు **tooTikooDalu, tooDikooDalu** *n.* fellow daughter-in-law.

తోటిపెళ్లికూతురు **tooTipeLLikuuturu** *n.* relative or friend of the bride whose function is to be in attendance on the bride at a wedding.

తోటిపెళ్లికొడుకు **tooTipeLLikoDuku** *n.* relative or friend of the bridegroom whose function is to be in attendance on the bridegroom at a wedding.

తోటివాడు **tooTiwaaDu** *n.* 1 companion, mate; **baLLoo tooTiwaaLLatoo pooTLaaDaku** do not quarrel with your schoolmates. 2 person of the same age, contemporary (*fem.* **tooTidi**).

తోడవు **tooDawu** *v.i.* 1 to help, be of assistance. 2 to combine.

తోడా **tooDaa** *n.* ornamental bracelet worn as an honour or medal.

తోడితెచ్చు **tooDi teccu** *v.t.* to fetch.

తోడిపోయు **tooDipooyu** *v.t.* to dredge up; **maa akkayyalu paata kathalannii tooDipoosukonnaaru** my elder sisters recounted all the past history.

తోడు **tooDu**[1] I. *adjvl. prefix meaning* fellow, companion; ~**dongalu** fellow thieves, accomplices. II. *n.* 1 joining, coupling, accompaniment; **modaTa kaligina adhayryaaniki aaśaabhangam tooDaynadi** dejection was coupled with previously felt lack of confidence. 2 company, companion; **waaDiki mii abbaayini ~ peTTi waccEEnu** I have kept your son as a companion for him; **naa tallii tooDuu** my mother and my brothers and sisters. 3 aid, help. 4 curdling substance; **paalaloo ~ weeyu** to add curds to milk. III. *adv.* (*also* ~**gaa**) 1 besides, along with. 2 in addition to, over and above; **ii maaTalaku ~ gaa** in addition to these words. IV. *particle used in swearing an oath* **deewuni ~** I swear by God.

తోడు, తోడేయు **tooDu**[2], **tooDeeyu** I. *v.i.* (of nerves) to be stretched, be tense, suffer spasms. II. *v.t.* 1 to draw, bale (water from a well). 2 to dredge (mud). 3 to pull, draw (thread).

తోడుకొను **tooDukonu** I. *v.i.* 1 (of milk) to curdle. 2 (of nerves) to suffer spasms. II. *v.t.* 1 to draw (water) for o.s. 2 to bring along with one.

తోడునీడ **tooDuniiDa** *n.* constant companion and helper.

తోడుపోవు **tooDupoowu** *v.i.* 1 to accompany s.o. as a helper. 2 to be on a par with; **raamu ceppulu paareesukonnaaDu, tooDupooyinaTLu krSNuDu kuDaa ceppulu paareesukoni waccEEDu** Ramu lost his shoes, on a par with him Krishna lost his too.

తోడేలు **tooDeelu** *n.* wolf.

తోడ్పడు **tooDpaDu** *v.i.* to be of help, be of assistance.

తోడ్పాటు **tooDpaaTu** *n.* help, assistance, cooperation.

తోప **toopa** *n. dial.* badly cooked rice consisting of paste and lumps.

తోపడ **toopaDa** *n.* carpenter's plane.

తోపాటు **toopaaTu** *p.p.* along with.

తోపించు **toopincu** *v.i.* to appear, seem.

తోపు **toopu**[1] *n.* grove of fruitbearing trees.

తోపు **toopu**[2] *n.* 1 push, shove. 2 stuffing in a sweet or savoury dish such as **kajjam.**

తోపు **toopu**[3] *n.* dark red colour.

తోపు **toopu**[4] *n.* cannon.

తోపుఖానా **toopukhaanaa** *n.* arsenal, armoury.

తోపుడు **toopuDu**[1] *n.* push[ing].

తోపుడు **toopuDu**[2] *n.* discount.

తోపుదారు **toopudaaru** *n.* gunner.

తోపులాట **toopulaaTa** *n.* pushing, shoving, jostling.

తోపులాడు **toopulaaDu** *v.t.* to push, shove.

తోబుట్టు[వు] **toobuTTu[wu]** *n.* uterine brother or sister (*lit.* one who is born from the same womb).

తోమాల **toomaala** *n.* garland of flowers and leaves; **~ seewa** form of Vaishnavite worship.

తోము **toomu** *v.t.* 1 to clean, cleanse, scour, scrub; **aNTLu~** to clean plates and dishes; **paLLu~konu** to clean o.'s teeth. 2 to rub. 3 *colloq.* to tease, trouble, pester; **upanyaasakuDu mammalni toomi wadilipeTTEEDu** the speaker bored us to tears. 4 *colloq.* to flatter.

తోముడు **toomuDu** *n.* 1 rubbing. 2 *colloq.* troubling, worrying, pestering.

తోయం **tooyam** *n. class.* water.

తోయదం **tooyadam** *n. class.* cloud.

తోయలి **tooyali** *same as* **toyyali.**

తోయు **tooyu** *v.t.* 1 to push, shove, thrust, propel; **inkokarimiida tappu~** to shift the blame onto s.o. else. 2 to knock over; **pilli paala ginne toosindi** the cat has knocked over the cup of milk.

తోరణం **tooraNam** *n.* 1 festoon of leaves, gen. mango leaves, strung across an entrance. 2 string of tobacco leaves hung up to dry.

తోలు **toolu** I. *n.* leather, skin, hide. II. *v.t.* to drive [away]; **goDLu~** to drive cattle out to graze; **kapila~** to work a baling apparatus (mhote) pulled by bullocks.

తోలుతిత్తి **toolutitti** *n.* 1 leather or rubber bag for blowing air into a kiln or for pouring water, e.g., on plants or on cement being cured. 2 *colloq.* human body.

తోలుపని **toolupani** *n.* tanning, leather work.

తోలుబొమ్మ, తెరబొమ్మ **toolubomma, terabomma** *n.* [toy] puppet; **~laaTa** puppetry, puppet show.

తోసిపుచ్చు **toosipuccu** *v.t.* 1 to brush aside, refuse, reject (ideas, advice). 2 to break away from (influence). 3 to relinquish (leadership).

తోసిరాజను **toosiraajanu** *v.i. and t.* 1 to call "check!" in chess. 2 to reject, repudiate.

తోసిరాజు **toosiraaju** I. *n. lit.* a king that has to be moved. II. *interj.* check! (call in chess, a warning that the king must be moved).

తోసివేత **toosiweeta** *n.* dismissal (of an argument or case).

తోసుకువచ్చు, తోసుకొచ్చు **toosukuwaccu, toosukoccu** *v.i.* to surge forward, come of its own accord (referring to a benefit which comes adventitiously); **aayanaku adrSTam toosukoccindi** luck came his way.

తోసేయు, తోసివేయు **tooseeyu, toosiweeyu** *v.t.* 1 to reject, dismiss (argument, case). 2 to refute (allegation).

తౌ, త్య, త్యా - taw, tya, tyaa

తౌడు **tawDu** *same as* **tawuDu.**

తౌల్యం **tawlyam** *n. class.* similarity, equality.

త్యక్తం **tyaktam** *adj.* given up, abandoned.

త్యజించు **tyajincu** *v.t.* 1 to renounce. 2 to give up, quit, leave, desert, abandon.

త్యాగం **tyaagam** *n.* 1 giving up, abandoning. 2 renunciation, self-sacrifice, altruism.

త్యాగధని **tyaagadhani** *n.* philanthropist, very generous donor.

త్యాగశీలత **tyaagaśiilata** *n.* spirit of self-sacrifice.

త్యాగి **tyaagi** *n.* one who sacrifices himself, one who renounces worldly benefits.

త్యాజ్యం **tyaajyam** *n. class.* s.g fit to be abandoned.

త్ర, త్రా, త్రి - tra, traa, tri

త్రప **trapa** *n. class.* coyness, shyness.

త్రయం **trayam** *n. class.* trio.

త్రయి **trayi** *n. class.* the first three Vedas, i.e., the Rig-veda, Yajurveda and Samaveda.

త్రయోదశి **trayoodaśi** I. *n.* thirteenth day of a lunar fortnight. II. *adj.* thirteenth.

త్రాణ **traaNa** *n.* strength, vigour.

త్రాష్టి **traaSTi** *n.* ruffian.

త్రాసు **traasu** *n.* scales for weighing, balance.

త్రాహి! **traahi!** *interj. class.* save me!, help me!

త్రిక **trika** *adj.* triple, threefold.

త్రికం **trikam** *n.* **1** group of three, trio. **2** lower end of the spinal column.

త్రికరణం **trikaraNam** *n.* the three elements of action, i.e., **manasaa, wacaa, karmaNaa** (thought, word and deed).

త్రికరణశుద్ధిగా **trikaraNaśuddhigaa** *adv.* honestly, sincerely, scrupulously (*lit.* with purity in thought, word and deed).

త్రికోణం **trikooNam** *n.* triangle.

త్రికోణమితి **trikooNamiti** *n.* trigonometry.

త్రిజ్య **trijya** *n. maths.* radius.

త్రిత్వం **tritwam** *n.* trinity.

త్రిధాకరణం **trithaakaraNam** *n. maths.* trisection.

త్రిదోషం **tridooSam** *n.* disorder of all the three humours of the body — wind, bile and phlegm.

త్రినేత్రుడు **trineetruDu** *n.* **1** one who possesses three eyes, i.e., Siva. **2** *colloq.* angry person.

త్రిపరిమాణిక, త్రిపరిమితి **triparimaaNika, triparimiti** *adj.* three-dimensional.

త్రిపాది **tripaadi** *n.* **1** *sci.* tripod. **2** *colloq.* loafer, wanderer.

త్రిపీఠకం **tripiiThakam** *n.* collective title of three Buddhist sacred books.

త్రిపుండ్రం **tripuNDram** *n.* religious mark across the forehead indicating the Vaishnavite sect.

త్రిపుటతాళం **tripuTa taaLam** *n.* kind of poetic metre.

త్రిభుజం **tribhujam** *n.* triangle.

త్రిభువనం **tribhuwanam** *n.* the three worlds, i.e., heaven, earth and hell.

త్రిమితీయ **trimitiiya** *adj.* **1** three-dimensional. **2** stereoscopic.

త్రిమూర్తులు **trimuurtulu** *n.pl.* the three principal Hindu Gods, Brahma, Vishnu and Siva.

త్రిలింగ **trilinga** *n.* name suggesting a fanciful derivation of 'Telugu' given to the Telugu land by some later pandits.

త్రిలోకాలు **trilookaalu** *n.pl. class.* the three worlds, i.e., heaven, earth and hell.

త్రివర్ణ **triwarNa** *adj.* tricolour; ~ **pataakam** the tricolour, the Indian national flag.

త్రివేణి **triweeNi** *n.* junction of three rivers, esp. the junction of the Ganges, the Jamna and the mythical underground river Saraswati at Prayag.

త్రిశంకుస్వర్గం **triśanku swargam** *n.* uncomfortable situation experienced by s.o. on giving up his old position in favour of a new one, which he then fails to attain (*lit.* the uncomfortable kingdom ruled by the mythological king Trisanku midway between earth and heaven).

త్రిశూలం **triśuulam** *n.* the trident or three pointed weapon of Siva.

త్రు to త్వా - tru to twaa

త్రుంచు **truncu** *same as* **tuncu.**

త్రుటి **truTi** *n. class.* instant, moment of time.

త్రెళ్లు **treLLu** *v.i. class.* 1 to die. 2 to fall.

త్రేతాగ్ని **treetaagni** *n. class.* the three sacred fires of Vedic ritual.

త్రేతాయుగం, త్రేత **tretaayugam, treeta** *n. class.* the mythological second or silver age of the universe.

త్రైగుణ్యం **trayguNyam** *n.* the three gunas or qualities, **satwam** (tranquillity), **rajassu** (passion) and **tamassu** (mental blindness, darkness or sin), which make up the human character.

త్రైపక్ష **traypakSa** *adj.* 1 tripartite. 2 once in three fortnights.

త్రైపాక్షిక **traypaakSika** *adj.* tripartite.

త్రైజ్య **trayjya** *adj.* maths. radial.

త్రైమాస, త్రైమాసిక **traymaasa, traymaasika** *adj.* once in three months, three monthly, quarterly.

త్రైవార్షిక **traywaarSika** *adj.* triennial.

త్రోవ **troowa** *same as* **doowa.**

త్వచం **twacam** *n.* 1 *sci.* membrane. 2 skin, rind, bark.

త్వదీయ **twadiiya** *adj. class.* your.

త్వర **twara** *n.* speed.

త్వరకం **twarakam** *n.* accelerator.

త్వరగా **twaragaa** *adv.* quickly, fast, speedily, rapidly, swiftly.

త్వరణం **twaraNam** *n.* acceleration.

త్వరపడు **twarapaDu** *v.i.* 1 to make haste, hurry. 2 to be overhasty.

త్వరిత **twarita** *adj.* swift, fast, rapid.

త్వరితం **twaritam** *n.* speed, rapidity, swiftness.

త్వరితంచేయు **twaritamceeyu** *v.t.* to expedite, hasten, speed up, accelerate.

త్వరితగతి **twaritagati** *n.* speed, swiftness.

త్వరితగతిని **twaritagatini** *adv.* swiftly, speedily, quickly.

త్వాష్ట్రం **twaaSTram** *n.* useless person, scoundrel.

థ, థు - tha, thu

థకరా **thakaraa** *n. dial., variant form of* **Tookaraa** deception; **ee bEEnk eejeNTugaanoo wacceestaaDu, leedaa ee gawarnameNTu kampaniiloonaynaa aaphiisaraypootaaDu,** ~ **leedu** he will either become a bank agent or else an officer in some government company or other, believe me!

థుమథుమ **thumathuma** *onom. adv. sug.* anger; ~ **gaa** angrily; ~ **laaDu** to be angry; *cf.* **dhumadhumalaaDu.**

ద - da

దంక **danka** *dial. same as* **danuka.**

దంగిపోవు **dangipoowu** *v.i.* 1 to be pounded or crushed; **panulatoo~** to be overwhelmed by o.'s duties. 2 to slip away; **janamloonunci dangipooyEEDu** he slipped away from the crowd.

దంగు **dangu** *same as* **Dangu.**

దంగుడు **danguDu** *adj.* pounded.

దంచు **dancu** I. *v.i.* 1 (of weather conditions) to be intense or acute; **waana~tunnadi** rain is pouring down; **eNDa ~tunnadi** the sun's heat is excessive; **cali~tunnadi** the cold is intense. II. *v.t.* to pound (grain in a mortar); **biyyam~** to pound paddy so as to remove the husk. 2 to beat, thrash, belabour. 3 *colloq.* to persist in doing s.g; **upanayaasam ~tunnaaDu** he goes on and on delivering his lecture; **kaburlu ~tunnaaDu** he talks nonstop; **reNDee cokkaalu unnaayi waaDiki, awee dancutuu uNTaaDeppuDuunu** he has only two shirts and he wears them all the time.

దంటు **daNTu** *n.* 1 green or dried stalk of cholam or similar crop. 2 pith.

దంటుకూర **daNTukuura** *n.* kind of green vegetable, *amaranthus sp.*

దండ **daNDa**[1] *n.* 1 prop, support; *cf.* **aNDa~lu.** 2 garland, necklace. 4 side; **naalugu ~laa** on all four sides.

దండ **daNDa**[2] *n.* upper arm; **~lu tirigina wastaadu** strong-armed wrestler.

దండం, దణ్ణం **daNDam**[1], **daNNam** *n.* 1 bow, salutation. 2 respects, obeisance; **~peTTu** (i) to do obeisance, pay respects, salute as a token of gratitude; **paDipaDi daNNaalupeTTu** to bow again and again, bow repeatedly; (ii) *colloq.* to give up hope.

దండం **daNDam**[2] *n.* 1 rod, stick, staff. 2 punishment.

దండకం **daNDakam**[1] *n.* 1 poetical eulogy. 2 *colloq.* **~wippu** to utter abuse (**-miida**, against).

దండకం, దండకారణ్యం **daNDakam**[2], **daNDakaaraNyam** *n.* name of a famous forest in the Ramayana.

దండకడియం **daNDakaDiyam** *n.* bracelet worn on the upper arm.

దండకవిలె **daNDakawile** *n.* records relating to the accounts and other details of a village.

దండగ **daNDaga** *same as* **daNDuga.**

దండధరుడు **daNDadharuDu** *n. class.* epithet of Yama, God of Death.

దండన **daNDana** I. *n.* punishment, penalty. II. *adj.* penal.

దండనమస్కారం, దండప్రణామం **daNDanamaskaaram, daNDapraNaamam** *n.* prostrating o.s. in reverence.

దండనాథుడు, దండనాయకుడు **daNDanaathuDu, daNDanaayakuDu** *n.* military commander.

దండనీతి **daNDaniiti** *n.* political science, principles of government.

దండయాత్ర **daNDayaatra** *n.* 1 invasion. 2 campaign, expedition. 3 *colloq.* tirade.

దండాకోరి, దండాగొండి **daNDaakoori, daNDaagoNDi** *adj.* adamant, obstinate.

దండాడింపు **daNDaaDimpu** *n.* flower garland game (played by the bride and bridegroom at a marriage.)

దండాదండీ **daNDaadaNDii** *adj. and adv.* (of fighting) hand to hand, at close quarters; **waaLLiddaruu~ koTTukoNTunnaaru** they are fighting one another in close combat.

దండాసి **daNDaasi** *n.* name of a community in north-east Andhra Pradesh whose members act as village guards.

దండి **daNDi** I. *n.* 1 strength, power. 2 courage, daring. 3 abundance. 4 multitude, swarm. II. *adj.* abundant; **aayanadi~ceyyi** his is a generous hand, i.e., his is a generous disposition.

దండించు **daNDincu** *v.t.* to punish.

దండిగా **daNDigaa** *adv.* plentifully, abundantly.

దండీలు, దండేలు **daNDiilu, daNDEElu** *n. pl.* kind of physical exercise.

దండు **daNDu**[1] *n.* 1 army. 2 gang. 3 multitude. 4 swarm of insects.

దండు **daNDu**[2] *same as* **taNDu.**

దండుకొను **daNDukonu** *v.t.* 1 *slang* to collect (money) by force. 2 to beg.

దండుగ, దండగ **daNDuga, daNDaga** *n.* 1 waste. 2 penalty, fine. 3 loss; **~iccu** to pay compensation, make good a loss.

దండుగ చేయు, దండుగ పెట్టు **daNDuga ceeyu, daNDuga peTTu** *v.t.* to waste.

దండుపోవు, దండువెడలు **daNDu poowu, daNDu weDalu** *v.i.* to go on a campaign or expedition, wage war.

దండుముండ **daNDumuNDa** *n.* (*term of abuse*) quarrelsome woman.

దండె **daNDe** *n.* pole, esp. of a palanquin.

దండెం, దణ్ణెం **daNDem, daNNem** *n.* rope or stick for hanging up clothes to dry or for hanging clothes in storage.

దండెత్తు **daNDettu** *v.i.* to invade, attack.

దండోపాయం **daNDoopaayam** *n.* use of force or compulsion.

దండోరా **daNDooraa** *n.* tomtomming, announcing by beat of drum; **~weeyu** to announce by beat of drum.

దంతం **dantam** *n.* 1 ivory; **dantapu pani** ivory work. 2 tooth.

దంతకాష్ఠం **dantakaaSTam** *n.* twig for cleaning o.'s teeth.

దంతధావనం **dantadhaawanam** *n.* cleaning o.'s teeth.

దంతమూలీయ **dantamuuliiya** *adj. ling.* alveolar.

దంతవైద్యశాస్త్రం **dantawaydyaśaastram** *n.* dentistry.

దంతవైద్యుడు **dantawaydyuDu** *n.* dentist.

దంతసిరి **dantasiri 1** being in possession of sound teeth. **2 ~too puTTu** to be fortunate all through o.'s life.

దంతాకార **dantaakaara** *adj. bot.* dentate.

దంతె **dante** n. kind of harrow.

దంత్య **dantya** *adj. ling.* dental.

దండడీమూక **dandaDimuuka** *n.* gang of mischief makers.

దండనకత్తె **dandanakatte** *n.* mischievous woman.

దందా **dandaa** *n.* **1** business, trade. **2** *colloq.* underhand dealings.

దంపకం **dampakam** *n.* pounding of paddy.

దంపతి తాంబూలం **dampati taambuulam** *n.* part of the wedding ceremony in which the newly married couple offer fruit and betel and nut to other couples who invoke the blessing of offspring on them.

దంపతులు **dampatulu** *n.pl.* husband and wife, married couple; **raamamuurti ~** Mr. and Mrs. Ramamurti.

దంపనాగలి **dampanaagali** *n.* plough used for preparing irrigated land for cultivation.

దంపసాగు **dampasaagu** *n.* wet cultivation, cultivation of irrigated land.

దంపు **dampu** I. *n.* pounding. II. *v.t.* to pound.

దంపుడు **dampuDu** I. *n.* pounding. II. *adj.* pounded; **~biyyam** hand-pounded rice.

దంభ **dambha** *adj.* false, bogus; **~sanyaasulu** bogus saints.

దంభం **dambham** *n.* fraud, deceit.

దంభోళి **dambhooLi** *n. class.* **1** thunderbolt. **2** Indra's weapon (= **wajraayudham**).

దంభోళిగాడు **dambhooLigaaDu** *n.* **1** *class.* epithet of Indra. **2** *colloq.* boaster.

దంష్ట్ర **damSTra** *n. class.* large tooth, tusk.

దక్కను **dakkanu** *n.* Deccan.

దక్కించు **dakkincu** *v.t.* **1** to secure, obtain. **2** to keep in o.'s possession, save, retain. **3** to preserve; **maaTa** (*or* **maryaada**) **~konu** to preserve o.'s honour. **4** to retrieve, rescue, recover.

దక్కిస **dakkisa** *n. euphorbia antiquorum*, a kind of cactus.

దక్కు **dakku** *v.i.* **1** to be available. **2** to be secured, be obtained, come into (o.'s) possession. **3** to accrue: **aa kiirti naaku dakkaniwwaNDi** allow that fame to accrue to me. **4** to remain, be left [over], be kept, be retained. **5** to be retrieved, be recovered; **ii ciikaTLoo eedannaa paDipooyindaNTee dakkadu** in this darkness if anything falls down you will not be able to recover it. **6** to be saved, be spared; **puTTina pillalu ceetiki dakkagalaranna aaśa** the hope that his children will survive (and not die in infancy — *lit.* the hope that the children born to him will be saved for him). **7 ceeSTalu dakki nilabaDDaaDu** he stood rooted to the spot in amazement *or* he stood dumbfounded.

దక్షకన్య, దక్షతనయ **dakSakanya, dakSatanaya** *n. class.* epithet of Parvati (*lit.* daughter of Daksha).

దక్షత **dakSata** *n.* **1** skill, ability, cleverness. **2** competence, efficiency, proficiency. **3** protection, support, management; **iNTiki maga ~ leedu** there is no man to manage the household.

దక్షిణ **dakSiNa**[1] *adj.* south, southern, southerly; **~dhruwam** south pole; **~dikku** southern or southerly direction.

దక్షిణ **dakSiNa**[2] *n.* present or fee to a priest for officiating at a ceremony; *cf.* **guru~**.

దక్షిణం **dakSiNam** *n.* **1** south. **2** right-hand side.

దక్షిణాత్యుడు **dakSiNaatyuDu** *n.* southerner.

దక్షిణాది **dakSiNaadi** *adj.* southern.

దక్షిణాపథం **dakSiNaapatham** *n.* Deccan.

దక్షిణాయనం **dakSiNaayanam** *n.* the period of six months from mid-July during which the point where sun rises each day travels from the north towards the south.

దక్షుడు **dakSuDu** *n.* **1** clever or capable person, expert; **paripaalanaa~** able administrator. **2** *class.* Daksha, a character in mythology who was killed by Siva.

దఖలు, దాఖలు **dakhalu, daakhalu** *n.* **1** application, presentation, filing of records (in court, office). **2** proof.

దఖలుచేయు, దఖలుపరచు **dakhaluceeyu, dakhaluparacu** *v.t.* **1** to make over, assign, transfer. **2** to file, present (documents in court, office).

దఖలుదారు **dakhaludaaru** *n.* official.

దఖలుపడు **dakhalupaDu** *v.i.* to come into (o.'s) possession; **sommu naaku dakhalupaDindi** the money was credited to me.

దగ **daga** *n. class.* **1** thirst. **2** heat.

దగదగ **dagadaga** *same as* **dhagadhaga.**

దగా **dagaa** *n.* cheating, fraud, deceit.

దగాకోరు **dagaakooru** *n.* cheat, deceiver.

దగాచేయు **dagaaceeyu** *v.t.* to cheat, deceive, trick.

దగాపడు **dagaapaDu** *v.i.* to be cheated, deceived or tricked.

దగుల్బాజీ **dagulbaajii** *n.* **1** cheat, deceiver. **2** scoundrel.

దగ్గిర, దగ్గర **daggira, daggara** *adv. and p.p.* **1** near, close[to], at, by; **guDi ceruwukaTTa ~ undi** the temple is near the tankbund; **iNTi ~ unnaaDu** he is at home; **okee ~ annam tiNTaaru** they all take their meals at a common place. **2** with (one), on (o.'s) person (signifying temporary possession); **ippuDu naa ~ Dabbu leedu** I have no money with me (*or* on me) now. **3** from: **M. ~ appu tiisukonnaanu** I took a loan from M.; **aa alawaaTu S. daggiree neercukonnaDu** he learnt that habit from S. himself; **iiwiDa waccina ~ nuncii** from the time of her arrival *or* ever since she came. **4** to; **ilaaTi niitulu naa ~ ceppakaNDi** do not preach this kind of moral precepts to me. **5** about, concerning, with regard to, in respect of (money or valuables); **peLLiloo bangaaram ~ koncem bheedaabhipraayaalu waccEEyi** some misunderstandings concerning gold arose at the wedding; **iddaruu Dabbu ~ dongalee anna satyam iddarikii telusu** they both knew that in respect of money both of them had been thieves. **6 aa pappulu naa ~ uDakawu** that trickery will not work with me.

దగ్గిరతీయు **daggira tiiyu** *v.t.* to bring (s.o. or s.g) near, attract; **aayanaki pillalaNTee iSTam, pillalanu daggara[ki] tiistaaDu** he is fond of children and he collects them round him; **aameki pillalu leeru, anduceeta waaNNi daggira tiisindi** she has no children of her own, so she has taken him to her (*meaning* she has brought him up).

దగ్గిరపడు **daggirapaDu** *v.i.* to approach, come near, draw near.

దగ్గిరవాడు **daggirawaaDu** *n.* **1** close friend. **2** close relative.

దగ్గిరసా **daggirasaa** *adv. and p.p.* very near, very close.

దగ్గు **daggu** I. *n.* cough. II. *v.i.* to cough.

దగ్గుత్తిక **dagguttika** *same as* **Dagguttika.**

దగ్ధ[ం] **dagdha[m]** *adj.* burnt, consumed by fire.

దగ్ధపటలం అవు **dagdhapaTalam awu** *v.i.* to be engulfed in flames.

దటాయించు **daTaayincu** *v.t.* **1** to scold, chide, admonish. **2** *fig.* to beat down, crush.

దట్టం **daTTam** *adj.* thick, dense.

దట్టించు **daTTincu** *v.t.* **1** to press, ram, cram. **2** to load (gun, any container). **3** to reprove, rebuke, scold, intimidate, threaten with shouts or gestures.

దట్టీ[కోక] **daTTii[kooka]** *n.* **1** cloth worn by a young child tied round the waist. **2** coloured cloth tied round the waist over a dhoti or sari by a grown up person either for tightness or as ornament.

దడ **daDa** *n.* trembling, palpitation or thumping of heart.

దడచుకొను **daDacukonu** *v.i.* to fear, tremble, be afraid.

దడదడ **daDadaDa** *onom. adv. sug.* thumping or palpitation of heart.

దడదడకొట్టుకొను, దడదడమను, దడదడలాడు **daDadaDakoTTukonu, daDadaDamanu, dadadaDalaaDu** *v.i.* (of heart) to beat fast, thump, palpitate.

దడబడ **daDabaDa** *n.* fuss, bustle.

దడాదడి **daDaadaDi** *n. dial.* fuss, commotion, hubub, bustle.

దడాలన **daDaalana** *adv.* suddenly.

దడి **daDi** *n.* **1** fence, screen; **~kaTTu** to erect a fence. **2** framework.

దడిగోడ **daDigooDa** *n.* fence made of sticks.

దడియు **daDiyu** *v.i.* to tremble or shiver with fear.

దడివాన **daDiwaana** *n.* steady continuous downpour of rain.

దడీలుమని, దడేలుమని **daDiilumani, daDeelumani** *onom. adv. sug.* sound of a fall.

దడ్డు **daDDu** I. *n. slang* penis. II. *adj.* naked; **~sanyaasi** naked sanyasi.

దణ్ణం **daNNam** *same as* **daNDam.**

దణ్ణెం **daNNem** *same as* **daNDem.**

దత్తం **dattam** *adj.* given, granted, presented, assigned.

దత్తత, దత్తు **dattata**[1], **dattu** *n.* adoption.

దత్తత **dattata**[2] *n.* delegation; **adhikaara~** delegation of power.

దత్తతచేసుకొను, దత్తుచేసుకొను **dattataceesukonu, dattuceesukonu** *v.t.* to adopt.

దత్తపుత్రుడు, దత్తుడు **dattaputruDu, dattuDu** *n.* adopted son.

దత్తమండలం **dattamaNDalam** *n.* Ceded Districts, a historical name for the districts of Cuddapah, Kurnool, Bellary and Anantapur.

దత్తాంశాలు **dattaamśaalu** *n. pl.* data.

దత్తుతండ్రి **dattutaNDri** *n.* adoptive father.

దత్తువచ్చు **dattuwaccu** *v.i.* to come (into a family) by adoption.

దద్దమ్మ **daddamma** *n.* fool, simpleton.

దద్దయ్య, దద్ద **daaddayya, dadda** *n. dial.* father's younger brother, uncle.

దద్దడం, దద్దళం **daddaDam, daddaLam** *n.* small temple with flat roof and no **goopuram.**

దద్దరిల్లు **daddarillu** *v.i.* **1** to be alarmed, tremble. **2** to reverberate, resound.

దద్దు[రు] **daddu[ru]** *n.* small swelling on the body caused by a blow, insect bite, etc.

దనుక **danuka** *adv. class.* as far as, upto; until.

దన్నాసరి **dannaasari** *n. dial.* kind of **goonguura.**

దన్ను **dannu** *n.* help, support.

దన్నుదారు **dannudaaru** *n.* supporter.

దప్ప **dappa** *adj.* thick, fat.

దప్పడం, దప్పళం **dappaDam, dappaLam** *n.* sambar made with two or three vegetables.

దప్పా **dappaa** *n.* rap with the knuckles.

దప్పి[క] **dappi[ka]** *n.* thirst; **~tiirucukonu** to quench o.'s thirst.

దఫదఫాలుగా **daphadaphaalugaa** *adv.* in stages, stage by stage.

దఫా **daphaa** *n.* time, occasion; **oka~** once.

దఫ్తరు **daphtaru** *n.* office.

దబదబా, దబాదిబా **dabadabaa, dabaadibaa** *onom. adv. sug.* sound of pattering or rapid blows or footsteps; **~koTTEEru** they beat (him) resoundingly.

దబరాసట్టి **dabaraasaTTi** *n.* cup and bowl.

దబాటు **dabaaTu** *same as* **dabbaaTu.**

దబాయించు **dabaayincu** *v.t.* **1** to browbeat, bully, domineer over. **2** to insist, persist in saying. **3** to bluster, bluff. **4** to deceive, hoodwink.

దబాయింపు **dabaayimpu** *n.* **1** browbeating. **2** blustering. **3** hoodwinking.

దబాలున, దబుక్కున **dabaaluna, dabukkuna** *adv.* suddenly, all of a sudden.

దబ్బ **dabba**[1] *n.* citron, tree, *citrus medica*; **~kaaya** unripe citron fruit; **~paNDu rangu** colour of a ripe citron; **nimma~** slice of lime pickle.

దబ్బ **dabba**[2] *n.* thin strip of wood; **weduru~** bamboo slat; **aDDa~** wooden crossbar of a cart frame.

దబ్బనం **dabbanam** *n.* bodkin, large needle used for stitching gunny bags, etc.

దబ్బాటు, దబాటు **dabbaaTu, dabaaTu** *adv.* suddenly, unexpectedly; **~waana** sudden downpour.

దబ్బున **dabbuna** *adv.* 1 at once, quickly, soon. 2 *same as* **dabbumani.**

దబ్బుమని, దభీమని, దభేలున **dabbumani, dabhiimani, dabheeluna** *onom. adv. sug.* sound of falling; ~ **paDu** to fall with a crash. fall with a splash.

దమం **damam** *n. class.* 1 subduing, subjugation. 2 strict control, sternness. 3 subduing the passions, self-control; *see* **śamam.**

దమనం **damanam** *n.* subduing, subjugation, suppression.

దమననీతి **damananiiti** *n.* repression.

దమయంతి **damayanti** *n.* 1 dark green colour. 2 name of King Nala's queen in mythology.

దమాయించు **damaayincu** *v.t.* to smooth by patting or tapping with a wooden implement.

దమ్మ **damma** *n.* a cattle disease.

దమ్మిడి **dammiDi** *n.* a small coin, one pie, now obsolete; ~ **anta moham ceesukonu** to look gloomy or depressed; ~ **korakaakuNDaa** not worth a pie; *see* **kora.**

దమ్ము **dammu**[1] *n.* 1 mud, mire. 2 moisture, wetness. 3 ploughing of irrigated land.

దమ్ము **dammu**[2] *n.* 1 intake of breath, draught of air; **paTTumani padi gajaalu parigettitee waaDiki ~ wastundi** if he runs only for ten yards, he begins to pant. 2 strength, courage.

దమ్ము **dammu**[3] *n.* a respiratory disease.

దమ్ముకొట్టు, దమ్ముపట్టు, దమ్ముపీల్చు, దమ్ములాగు **dammukoTTu, dammupaTTu, dammupiilcu, dammulaagu** *v.t.* to breathe in, inhale; **aNTina cuTTani oo saari dammulaagEEDu** he took one puff at the lighted cigar.

దమ్ముచేయు **dammuceeyu** *v.t.* to irrigate land before ploughing.

దమ్మునాగలి **dammunaagali** *n.* plough used on irrigated land.

దయ **daya** *n.* 1 favour, kindness, grace. 2 mercy, clemency, pity. 3 goodness, amiability.

దయ ఉంచు **daya uncu** *v.i.* to be merciful, be gracious, be favourable (**-miida,** to[wards]).

దయచేయు **dayaceeyu** *v.i. and t.* 1 to be gracious, oblige. 2 to deign, condescend, be pleased (to do s.g): *in this sense ~ has a wide range of meanings,* e.g., **dayaceeyaNDi** please sit down; **ilaa dayaceeyaNDi** please come this way; **bayaTaki dayaceeyaNDi** please go out; **naaku padi ruupaayalu dayaceeyaNDi** please give me ten rupees.

దయచేసి **dayaceesi** *advbl. particle* please.

దయతలచు **dayatalacu** *v.i. and t.* to take pity, show clemency, show pity.

దయదాక్షిణ్యం, దయాదాక్షిణ్యం **daya[a]daakSiNyam** *n.* kindness and generosity.

దయనీయ **dayaniiya** *adj.* pitiful, piteous, pitiable, pathetic.

దయాధర్మ భిక్షం **dayaadharma bhikSam** *n.* charity.

దయాభిక్ష **dayaabhikSa** *n.* mercy, pity, clemency.

దయామయుడు **dayaamayuDu** *n.* merciful being, merciful person.

దయారసం **dayaarasam** *n.* spirit of kindness.

దయార్ద్ర **dayaardra** *adj.* benignant, merciful.

దయాళుత్వం **dayaaLutwam** *n.* kindness, humaneness, tenderness, graciousness.

దయాళువు **dayaaLuwu** *n.* kind, humane, gracious or tender-hearted person.

దయిత **dayita** *n. class.* beloved woman.

దయ్యం **dayyam** *n.* demon, devil, evil spirit; ~ **too jaagaaram** work which involves constant dangers (*lit.* an all-night vigil in company with a demon); *see* **debba.**

దయ్యంపట్టు **dayyampaTTu** I. *n.* tenacious grip. II. *v.i. with dative* to be possessed by an evil spirit; **waaDiki dayyam paTTinaTTunnadi, piccigaa maaTLaaDutunnaaDu** he is talking nonsensically, as if he was possessed by a spirit.

దయ్యపుతట్టుకాయ **dayyaputaTTukaaya** *n.* coconut shell which contains no kernel.

దయ్యపుమబ్బు **dayyapu mabbu** *n.* large black cloud.

దయ్యాలదండం **dayyaaladaNDam** *n.* rod used for exorcising spirits.

దరఖాస్తు, దర్ఖాస్తు **darakhaastu, darkhaastu** *n.* petition, application.

దరఖాస్తుదారుడు **darkhaastudaaruDu** *n.* applicant, petitioner.

దరహాసం **darahaasam** *n.* slight smile.

దరావత్తు, ధరావత్తు **daraawattu, dharaawattu** *n.* 1 deposit (of money). 2 investment, capital.

దరావు **daraawu** *n. dial.* dram (of liquor).

దరి **dari**[1] I. *n.* 1 bank, shore. 2 end, limit. 3 nearness. 4 shelter, refuge. II. *p.p.* near.

దరి **dari**[2] *n.* screen; *cf.* **daDi.**

దరికొను **darikonu** *v.i.* 1 to burn. 2 to happen.

దరికొల్పు **darikolpu** *v.t.* 1 to burn, set fire to. 2 to cause to happen.

దరిగా **darigaa** *adv.* near, close.

దరి చేరు **dari ceeru** *v.i.* 1 *lit.* to reach the shore, *hence* to succeed. 2 to reach the end, finish. 3 to come near. 4 to take shelter or refuge; **naa dari ceerEEDu** he came close to me *or* he took refuge with me.

దరిదాపు **daridaapu** I. *n.* nearness, proximity. II. *adv.* approximately.

దరిదాపులేని **daridaapuleeni** *adj.* endless; *cf.* **antupontu.**

దరిద్రం **daridram** *n.* 1 poverty, penury. 2 misfortune.

దరిద్రగొట్టు **daridragoTTu** *n.* 1 unfortunate person. 2 wretch (*term of abuse*).

దరిద్రత **daridrata** *n.* poverty, penury.

దరిద్రనారాయణుడు **daridranaaraayaNuDu** *n.* extremely poor person, poorest of the poor.

దరిద్రుడు **daridruDu** *n.* poor person, pauper.

దరిమిలా **darimilaa** I. *p.p.* after. II. *adv.* afterwards, later, subsequently.

దరివెం **dariwem** *n.* 1 grass mat made for a girl to sit on for three days after attaining puberty. 2 *fig.* **aayana ~ miida unnaaDu, miiru maaTLaaDakaNDi** he is very angry, do not speak to him.

దరువు **daruwu** *n.* 1 single beat in music. 2 kind of song; *see* **golla ~ lu.**

దరువు వేయు **daruwu weeyu** *v.i.* 1 to beat time in music. 2 *slang* to beat, hit, strike.

దర్ఖాస్తు **darkhaastu** *same as* **darakhaastu.**

దర్గా **dargaa** *n.* tomb of a Muslim saint.

దర్జా **darjaa** I. *n.* 1 rank, grade. 2 grandeur, ostentation. II. *adj.* grand, fine, showy, ostentatious.

దర్జాగా **darjaagaa** *adv.* grandly, in a grand manner, ostentatiously.

దర్జీ **darjii** *n.* tailor.

దర్జీపని **darjiipani** *n.* tailoring.

దర్జు **darju** *n.* gap between bricks or stones in a wall.

దర్పం **darpam** *n.* pride, arrogance, haughtiness.

దర్పణం **darpaNam** I. *n. suffix used in the title of a book to indicate that the work is explanatory.* II. *n.* mirror.

దర్బారు **darbaaru** *n.* 1 hall of audience. 2 durbar, court held by a king. 3 name of a raga.

దర్భ **darbha** *n.* 1 sacred grass used in religious rituals, *poa cynosuroides.* 2 **~ muLLu** sharp words, bitter words (*lit.* sharp pointed tips of darbha grass).

దర్యాప్తు **daryaaptu** *n.* enquiry, investigation.

దర్యాప్తు చేయు **daryaaptu ceeyu** *v.i.* to investigate, enquire, probe.

దర్వాజా **darwaajaa** *n.* door.

దర్శకత్వం **darśakatwam** *n. theat.* direction.

దర్శకుడు **darśakuDu** *n.* 1 *theat.* director. 2 spectator.

దర్శనం **darśanam** *n.* 1 sight, view, appearance; **aayana darśanaalu leewu ekkaDaa** he is not to be seen anywhere. 2 visit. 3 vision. 4 system of philosophy.

దర్శనం ఇచ్చు **darśanam iccu** *v.i.* 1 to grant an interview (to s.o.). 2 to appear.

దర్శనం చేసుకొను **darśanam ceesukonu** *v.i.* to come to see, meet, visit; **mii darśanam ceesukondaamani waccEEnu** I have come to see you; **mii darśanam ceesukoni ennaaLLu ayyindi?** how long is it since I met you?

దర్శనీయ **darśaniiya** *adj.* worth seeing or watching.

దర్శించు **darśincu** *v.t.* to see, look at, view, visit, have a sight of.

దర్శిని **darśini** *n.* 1 *class.* mirror. 2 display. 3 *journ.* review (periodical publication containing surveys, commentaries, etc.).

దల్లాలు **dallaalu** *n.* cheat.

దళం **daLam**[1] *n.* petal, leaf, esp. **tulasi** or **maareeDu** leaf with three leaflets, which is used in worship; **~ weesi puTTEEDu, Dabbuku looTu leedu** he was born fortunate, he has no lack of money; *here* **~ weesi** *means* having worshipped dutifully with **tulasi** or **maareeDu** in a previous life.

దళం **daLam**[2] *n.* 1 army. 2 contingent or detachment of troops. 3 gang, group, team. 4 thickness.

దళబీజం, బీజదళం **daLabiijam, biijadaLam** *n. bot.* cotyledon.

దళవాయి **daLawaayi** *n.* commander of an army.

దళసరి **daLasari** *adj.* 1 thick. 2 coarse.

దళారి, దళాలి **daLaari, daLaali** *n.* commission agent, broker.

దళిత **daLita** *adj.* depressed, downtrodden.

దవడ, దౌడ **dawaDa, dawDa** *n.* 1 jaw. 2 cheek; **~ nokkukonu** to clutch o.'s cheek (a gesture of surprise); **~ śuddhi ceeyu** to slap (s.o.) on the cheek.

దవనం **dawanam** *n.* southern wood, *artemisia vulgaris,* a plant with a fragrant leaf.

దవర **dawara** *same as* **doora.**

దవ్వ **dawwa** *n.* 1 tender shoot at the top of a sugarcane or cholam stem. 2 tender interior or pith of a plantain stem. 3 *zool.* medulla.

దవ్వు **dawwu** *n. class.* distance.

దశ **daśa** I. *n.* 1 state, condition, situation. 2 period, stage, phase; **ciwari ~** final phase; **baalya ~** childhood. 3 luck, fortune; **waaDi ~ ettukonnadi** his good luck has started. 4 *astrol.* position of a planet. II. *adj.* ten; **~ diśalu** in all the ten directions, all around, far and wide; **~ guNangaa** ten times.

దశకం **daśakam** *n.* ten (taken collectively); **muuDoo ~** the thirties (i.e., from 1930 to 1939).

దశమ **daśama** *adj.* tenth.

దశమంతుడు **daśamantuDu** *n.* lucky person.

దశమి **daśami** *n.* tenth day of a lunar fortnight.

దశలవారీ **daśalawaarii** *adj.* phased; **~ kaaryakramam** phased programme.

దశాంశ **daśaamśa** *adj.* decimal; **~ paddhati** decimal system.

దశాబ్దం, దశాబ్ది **daśaabdam, daśaabdi** *n.* decade.

దశావతారాలు **daśaawataaraalu** *n.pl.* the ten incarnations of Vishnu.

దశావతారీ **daśaawataarii** *n. class.* a game played with shells.

దశాహం, దెవసం **daśaaham, dewasam** *n.* ceremony performed on the tenth day after a death.

దష్టం **daSTam** *adj.* bitten; **sarpa ~** bitten by a serpent.

దసరా **dasaraa** *n.* name of a festival held on the eighth, ninth and tenth days of the first fortnight of Asviyuja (end of September), these days being known as Durgashtami, Maharnavami and Vijayadasami.

దస్కం **daskam** 1 a collective word for ten; *cf.* 'dozen' for twelve in English. 2 *dial. colloq.* ten rupees; *cf.* **Dabbu ~.**

దస్కతు, దస్కత్తు **daskatu, daskattu** *n.* signature.

దస్తరం, దస్త్రం **dastaram, dastram** *n.* 1 bundle of books, records or other documents. 2 cloth in which bundles of records, etc., are tied. 3 *colloq.* **~ wippu** to start a narration, start a tirade.

దస్తా **dastaa** *n.* quire (of paper).

దస్తాగిన్నె **dastaaginne** *n.* 1 brass pot used for keeping cunji. 2 cruet.

దస్తావేజు **dastaaweeju** *n. legal* 1 document. 2 written agreement.

దస్తీ **dastii** *n.* handkerchief.

దస్తు **dastu** *n.* **1** cash, money. **2** money that has been collected towards government tax or revenue.

దస్తూరి **dastuuri** *n.* handwriting.

దస్త్రం **dastram** *same as* **dastaram.**

దస్యుడు **dasyuDu** *n. class.* name given to a member of the aboriginal inhabitants of South India.

దహనం **dahanam** *n.* **1** burning. **2** cremation. **3** *chem.* combustion.

దహనంచేయు, దహనపరచు **dahanam ceeyu, dahanaparacu** *v.t.* to cremate.

దహనకాండ **dahanakaaNDa** *n.* conflagration.

దహనచర్య **dahanacarya** *n. chem.* combustion.

దహించు **dahincu** *v.t.* to burn; **naaku aakali ~ kupootunnadi** I am terribly hungry.

దా - daa

దా! **daa!** *interj.* come!

దాంపత్యం **daampatyam** *n.* married life, matrimony.

దాంపత్యసుఖం **daampatyasukham** *n.* married bliss.

దాంభికుడు **daambhikuDu** *n.* **1** pompous or ostentatious person. **2** cheat, deceiver.

దాక **daaka**[1] *n.* wide mouthed pot; **~ nooru** wide mouth: **daakallee nooru terucukoni kuurcunnaaDu** he sat with his mouth gaping.

దాక, దాకా **daaka**[2]**, daakaa** *p.p.* **1** until, as long as. **2** upto, as far as. **3** as much as. **4** as many as; **wandamandi ~** as many as a hundred persons.

దాకలి **daakali** *same as* **daagali.**

దాకొను **daakonu** *v.i.* **1** to approach, come near. **2** to attempt, try.

దాకొలుపు **daakolupu** *v.t.* to bring (gen. s.g unwanted) to or upon s.o.; **uuLLoo jwaram tecci maa iNTLoo daakolipEEDu** he introduced fever from the village into my house; **waaDu ceyyaleeni pani naa nettina daakolipEEDu** he left me with the work that he could not do himself.

దాక్కొను, దాగుకొను **daakkonu, daagukonu** *v.i.* to hide o.s.

దాక్షిణాత్య **daakSiNaatya** *adj.* southern.

దాక్షిణ్యం **daakSiNyam** *n.* kindness, compassion, mercy.

దాఖలా **daakhalaa** *n.* **1** proof. **2** sign, indication. **3** instance, example.

దాఖలు, దాఖలుచేయి, దాఖలుపరచు **daakhalu, daakhaluceeyu, daakhaluparacu** *same as* **dakhalu, dakhaluceeyu, dakhaluparacu.**

దాగర **daagara** *n.* large flat basket made of bamboo strips; **waaDiki daagaranta mohamayindi** he looked very pleased; *cf.* **ceeTa.**

దాగలి, దాకలి **daagali, daakali** *n.* anvil.

దాగు **daagu** *v.i.* to hide, be hidden, be concealed.

దాగుడుమూతలు, దాగిలిమూతలు **daaguDumuutalu, daagilimuutalu** *n.pl.* game of hide and seek.

దాచు **daacu** *v.t.* **1** to hide, conceal. **2** to keep safely, preserve.

దాచుకొను **daacukonu** *v.t.* **1** to hide (s.g) for o.s. **2** to save (money). **3** to keep away, put away (articles for safety).

దాటవేయు, దాటేయు **daaTaweeyu, daaTeeyu** *v.t.* **1** to get through, get over, pass over, skip over: **wiSayaalanniTinii tondaragaa daaTeeyaDaaniki prayatnincEEDu** he tried to pass over everything hurriedly; **padi peejiilu ~** to skip over ten pages. **2** to evade, dodge; **neenu eppuDu aDiginaa aayana maaTa daaTeestunnaaDu** whenever I ask, he dodges the subject. **3** to steal. **4** (of cattle) to cross, copulate.

దాటవేసిపోవు **daaTaweesipoowu** *v.t.* to leave behind, abandon.

దాటి **daaTi** *same as* **dhaaTi.**

దాటించు **daaTincu** *v.t.* **1** to cause to pass over or through. **2** to cause to escape, save (from difficulties); **nannu daaTinceewaaDu aa bhagawantuDu okkaDee** God alone can extricate me from my troubles. **3** to pass, spend (time). **4** to steal. **5** to have a cow crossed by a bull.

దాటిపోవు **daaTipoowu** I. *v.i.* **1** (of time) to pass. **2** to pass away, die. II. *v.t.* to go out of, go away from, leave; **deeśam daaTipooyi baagu paDDaaDu** after he left the country he fared well; **ceyyi daaTipootee Dabbu dorakadu** if the money goes out of your control, it will be lost.

దాటు **daaTu** I. *n.* **1** leap, jump. **2** crossing. II. *v.i. and t.* **1** to pass. **2** to cross. **3** to go out of, go away from, leave. **4** to go beyond, trangress. **5** to jump, leap.

దాటుకొను **daaTukonu** *v.i.* to run away, evade. **2** to jump, leap. **3** *colloq.* to die.

దాట్లమారి **daaTLamaari** *n.* prostitute.

దాట్లుదాట్లుగా **daaTLudaaTLugaa** *adv.* here and there, sporadically.

దాట్లువేయు **daaTLuweeyu** *v.i.* to jump, bound.

దాడి **daaDi**[1] *n.* invasion, incursion, raid, inroad.

దాడి **daaDi**[2] *n.* beard.

దాడి **daaDi**[3] *n.* game played on a board marked with squares.

దాడిచేయు **daaDiceeyu** *v.i.* to invade, attack.

దాడిమ్మ **daaDimma** *same as* **daanimma.**

దాణా **daaNaa** *n.* **1** feed for domestic animals and poultry. **2** food, sustenance.

దాత **daata** *n.* donor, giver.

దాతృత్వం **daatrtwam** *n.* generosity.

దాదా **daadaa** *n. dial.* hooligan.

దాదాపు **daadaapu** *adv.* approximately, about, more or less.

దాది, దాయి **daadi, daayi**[1] *n.* children's nurse.

దానం **daanam** *n.* 1 gift, donation. 2 charity.

దానంచేయు **daanamceeyu** *v.t.* to donate, grant, make a gift of.

దానకర్ణుడు **daanakarNuDu** *n.* 1 name of a character in the Mahabharata noted for his charity and generosity. 2 generous or charitable person.

దానధర్మం **daanadharmam** *n.* philanthropic acts, deeds of charity.

దానబుద్ధి **daanabuddhi** *n.* charitable disposition.

దానవత్వం **daanawatwam** *n.* devilry.

దానవుడు **daanawuDu** *n.* demon.

దానశీల **daanaśiila** *adj.* munificent.

దానా **daanaa** *vocative suffix added to feminine nouns or adjs.* **andamaynadaanaa!** oh fair lady!

దానాదీనా **daanaadiinaa** *adv.* in conclusion, on the whole.

దానికేముంది ? **daanikeemundi?** *interj.* of course, by all means, definitely (*lit.* what (objection) is there for that?).

దానిమ్మ, దాడిమ్మ **daanimma, daaDimma** *n.* pomegranate.

దాపట, దాపల **daapaTa, daapala** *adv.* on the left hand side.

దాపటెద్దు **daapaTeddu** *n.* the bullock on the left (usually the stronger one) in a pair of ploughing bullocks.

దాపరించు, దాపురించు **daaparincu, daapurincu** *v.i.* (*always of some unfortunate happening*) to befall, occur, light upon, descend upon.

దాపరికం **daaparikam** *n.* 1 hiding, concealment. 2 secrecy. 3 saving.

దాపలి **daapali** *adj.* left.

దాపు **daapu**[1] *n.* nearness, vicinity.

దాపు, దాపుడు **daapu**[2], **daapuDu** *n.* 1 hiding. 2 keeping, saving, preserving.

దాపుడుచీరె **daapuDuciire** *n.* sari kept for special occasions.

దాపున **daapuna** *adv.* near, close.

దామాషా **daamaaSaa** *n.* 1 proportion. 2 share; **ii paapamloo naa ~ eemii leedu** I have no share in this sin. 3 sharing, apportionment; **~ weestee naa waaTaa naalugu bastaalu** when the apportionment was made my share was four bags.

దాయం **daayam** *n.* share.

దాయక **daayaka** *adjvl. suffix meaning* giving, conferring; **santooSa ~** pleasing.

దాయాది **daayaadi** *n.* male blood relation on the father's side; **~ wayram** blood feud.

దాయి **daayi**[1] *same as* **daadi.**

దాయి ! **daayi!**[2] *interj. child language* come! (*variant form of* **daa!**).

దాయు **daayu** *v.i. and t. class.* to approach, draw near.

దార **daara**[1] *n. class.* wife.

దార **daara**[2] *alt. form of* **dhaara.**

దారం **daaram** *n.* thread, yarn.

దారం బండి **daaram baNDi** *n.* bobbin, reel.

దారకం, ధారకం **daarakam, dhaarakam** *n.* 1 mixture of buttermilk and rice made into pulp and given to a sick person. 2 thick cunjee. 3 any liquid diet given to a sick person.

దారపుండ **daarapuNDa** *n.* ball of thread.

దారపు కండె **daarapu kaNDe** *n.* spindle wound with thread.

దారి **daari** *n.* 1 way, road, path. 2 manner, mode, method, means, course.

దారి కాయు **daari kaayu** *v.i.* 1 to wait in ambush. 2 to wait for s.o.

దారికి వచ్చు **daariki waccu** *v.i.* to come into line, learn to behave properly.

దారికొట్టు **daarikoTTu** *v.i.* to commit highway robbery.

దారి తప్పు **daari tappu** *v.i.* to lose o.'s way, stray, be lost; **daari tappi ii udyoogamlooki waccEEDu** he is a misfit in this job.

దారి తీయు **daari tiiyu** *v.i.* 1 to lead the way. 2 to make o.'s way.

దారిద్ర్యం **daaridryam** *n.* 1 poverty, penury. 2 shortage, lack.

దారి పట్టు **daari paTTu** *v.i.* to take the road (in some direction), set off; **iNTi daari paTTEEDu** he set off for home.

దారీతెన్ను **daariitennu** *n.* way and method.

దారు[వు] **daaru[wu]** *n.* wood; **daaruśilpam** wood carving.

దారుణం **daaruNam** I *n.* 1 horror, terror. 2 crime, cruel act. II. *adj.* horrible, terrible, cruel, atrocious.

దారుణంగా **daaruNangaa** *adv.* cruelly, harshly.

దారుతంతువులు **daarutantuwulu** *n.pl.bot.* wood fibres.

దారుబోతు **daarubootu** *n.* useless person.

దారోగా **daaroogaa** *n.* 1 supervisor, superintendent. 2 *class.* military commander.

దార్ఢ్యం, దారుఢ్యం **daar[u]Dhyam** *n.* 1 strength, vigour (of body or mind). 2 strength of will, resolution, determination. 3 toughness, robustness, sturdiness (of materials).

దార్ఢ్యత **daarDhyata** *n.* resistance, ability to withstand.

దార్శనిక **daarśanika** *adj.* philosophical.

దార్శనికుడు **daarśanikuDu** *n.* philosopher.

దాలి **daali** *n.* 1 fire made of dried cowdung cakes. 2 hearth made for an indoor fire.

దాలిగుంట **daaliguNTa** *n.* hearth without a fire, small pit made for a hearth; **~ loo kukka** *is an expression used of a person who promises to mend his ways but soon afterwards breaks his promise.*

దాల్చిన **daalcina** *n.* cinnamon; *cf.* **daasincekka.**

దాల్చు **daalcu** *same as* **taalcu.**

దాళవా **daaLawaa** *n.* the coarse variety of paddy grown in the second crop season; *cf.* **saaruwaa.**

దావళీ, ధావళీ **d[h]aawaLii** *n.* woollen cloth used at the time of prayer or worship.

దావా **daawaa** *n.* law suit; ~ **weeyu** to file a suit.

దావాగ్ని **daawaagni** *n.* wildfire, forest fire.

దావాదారు **daawaadaaru** *n. legal* plaintiff.

దావానలం **daawaanalam** *n.* 1 wildfire, forest fire. 2 holocaust.

దావాపత్రం **daawaapatram** *n. legal* plaint.

దాశుడు **daaśuDu** *n. class.* fisherman.

దాష్టీకం **daaSTiikam** *n.* insolence, pride, arrogance.

దాసరి **daasari** *n.* Vaishnavite religious beggar.

దాసరిజంగాలు **daasari jangaalu** *n. pl.* sect of Lingayat beggars.

దాసరిపురుగు **daasaripurugu** *n.* kind of insect.

దాసి[కత్తె] **daasi[katte]** *n.* woman servant or slave.

దాసించెక్క **daasincekka** *n., colloq. form of* **daalcina cekka** cinnamon bark.

దాసుడు **daasuDu** *n.* 1 male servant or slave. 2 devotee.

దాసోహం అను, దాసోహం చెప్పు **daasooham anu, daasooham ceppu** *v.i.* 1 to be enslaved. 2 to behave in a servile manner (*lit.* to say 'I am your slave').

దాసోహం చేయు **daasooham ceeyu** *v.i. and t.* 1 to enslave. 2 to enslave o.s.; **waaDu aameki daasooham ceestunnaaDu** he has enslaved himself to her.

దాస్య **daasya** *adj.* enslaved.

దాస్యం **daasyam** *n.* slavery, servitude.

దాహం **daaham** *n.* 1 thirst. 2 eager desire, longing.

దాహం ఇచ్చు **daaham iccu** *v.i.* to quench thirst, give s.o. s.g to drink.

దాహం తీర్చు **daaham tiircu** *v.i.* 1 to quench thirst. 2 to satisfy longing.

దాహం పుచ్చుకొను **daaham puccukonu** *v.i.* to take s.g to drink.

దాహక **daahaka** *adj. chem.* caustic.

దాహ్యత **daahyata** *n. chem.* combustibility.

ది - di

ది **di** *feminine suffix added to certain nouns to denote an occupation or community,* e.g., **caakalidi** washerwoman.

దించిదిగువపెట్టు **dinci diguwa peTTu** *v.t.* to lower a dying person from the bed to the ground.

దించు **dincu** *v.t.* 1 to set down, put down, unload. 2 to pull down, drag down, lower. 3 to degrade. 4 **ginne poyyimiidanunci**~ to take off (*or* remove) a pot from the hearth. 5 to press, plunge; **baaku guNDellooki dincinaTTu** like plunging a dagger into the heart. 6 to pull, draw; **aa pantulni kramangaa sambhaaSaNalooki dincEEDu** he gradually drew the schoolmaster into (*or* engaged him in) a conversation. 7 to involve; **aa baabuni taguwullooki dinacaalaNTee** if you want to involve that gentleman in quarrels. 8 **garbham**~, **kaDupu**~ to cause a miscarriage.

దిఙ్మాత్రంగా **diŋmaatrangaa** *adv.* as a sample, as an indication.

దిండు **diNDu** *n.* 1 pillow, bolster. 2 any cylindrical shaped package or bundle; **reNDu diLLu wistaraakulu tiisukuraa** bring two bundles of leaf plates.

దిండుగలీబు **diNDugaliibu** *n.* pillow cover, pillowcase.

దింపు **dimpu** I. *n.* downward slope; ~**loo weLLee baNDi** a cart going on a downward slope *or* a cart going downhill. II. *v.t.* 1 **kobbarikaayalu ceTTununci**~ to take down (*or* pluck) coconuts from a tree. 2 *same as* **dincu** *senses 1 to 7.*

దింపుడు **dimpuDu** *adj.* downward.

దింపుడుకళ్లం **dimpuDu kaLLam** *n.* place on the way to a burial ground where a corpse is rested on the ground for a brief time; ~**aaśa** faint hope; ~**aaśatoo aayanni aasupatriki tiisuku weLLEEru** with faint hope they took him to hospital.

దిక్కు **dikku** *n.* 1 side, direction. 2 point of the compass. 3 shelter, refuge, protection asylum, help; ~**unnawaaDitoo ceppukoo!** *lit.* go and complain to s.o. who will protect you, i.e., go and complain to anyone you like, I don't care!

దిక్కుకానకుండు **dikkukaanakuNDu** *v.i.* to be bewildered.

దిక్కుదిక్కులా **dikkudikkulaa** *adv.* far and wide, in all directions.

దిక్కుమాలిన **dikkumaalina** *adj.* helpless, wretched (*a mildly abusive epithet*).

దిక్కులుచూచు **dikkulu cuucu** *v.i.* to gaze vacantly, look round in a bewildered manner.

దిక్కులేని **dikkuleeni** *adj.* helpless, shelterless, without protection.

దిక్కూమొక్కూ **dikkuumokkuu** *n.* help and so on; ~**leekuNDaa** without help of any kind.

దిక్చక్రం **dikcakram** *n.* horizon.

దిక్పాతం **dikpaatam** *n. astron.* declination.

దిక్సూచి **diksuuci** *n.* 1 weather cock. 2 compass needle, pointer, indicator.

దిగంతాలు **digantaalu** *n.pl.* farthest limits (*lit.* ends of the four quarters of the earth).

దిగంబర కవులు **digambara kawulu** *n.pl.* name adopted by a school of Telugu poets originating in the 1960's.

దిగంబరత్వం **digambaratwam** *n.* nakedness.

దిగంబరుడు **digambaruDu** *n.* 1 naked person. 2 Jain ascetic.

దిగంశ **digamśa** *n. astron.* azimuth.

దిగగుంజు **digagunju** I. *v.i.* (of liquid) to drain away. II. *v.t.* to pull down.

దిగగొట్టు **digagoTTu** *v.t.* 1 to knock down. 2 **gooDalooki meekulu**~ to hammer nails into a wall.

దిగచెమటపట్టు **digacemaTapaTTu** *v.i.* to sweat all over o.'s body.

దిగజారిపోవు, దిగజారు **digajaaripoowu, digajaaru** *v.i.* 1 to slip down, come down, descend; **inta niicaaniki digajaaripooyEEDu** he has descended to such meanness. 2 to decline, degenerate, decrease (courage, fever, etc.); **pramaaNaalu digajaari pootunnaayi** standards are declining.

దిగతుడుచు **digatuDucu** *v.i.* to counteract the evil eye by means of a charm, such as circulating a lighted wick or a mixture of salt and other things round the object to be protected.

దిగదీయు **digadiiyu** *v.t.* 1 to drag down, belittle, disparage. 2 to make (s.o.) sad or depressed.

దిగదుడుపు, దిగతుడుపు **digaduDupu, digatuDupu** *n.* 1 protection from the evil eye afforded by circulating salt, chillies, etc., round the object to be protected. 2 s.g throughly useless, s.g inferior in all respects; **R. mundu tanu puurtigaa digaduDupeenani kuuDaa aame anukoo saagindi** she also began to think that she was inferior to R. in all respects.

దిగదొబ్బు **digadobbu** *v.t.* to push down, push away, push out: **waaNNi kurciiloonunci digadobbEEDu** he pushed him out of the chair.

దిగనార్చు **diganaarcu** *v.t.* to shake down, knock down, pull down.

దిగనేత **diganeeta** *same as* **diguneeta.**

దిగబడిపోవు **digabaDipoowu** *v.i.* to be left behind, fall behind.

దిగబడు **digabaDu** *v.i.* 1 to fall down, slip down. 2 to descend, sink down; **naa kaalu buradaloo digabaDindi** my leg sank in the mud. 3 to come in[to], enter [into]; **waakiTLooki DaakTaru digabaDDaaDu** the doctor came in at the door; **neenu ii udyoogamloo digabaDDaanu** I entered into this employment. 4 to arrive (gen. of an unwelcome arrival): **maa iNTLoo cuTTaalu digabaDDaaru** relatives have arrived at my house (too many of them). 5 to stay, stop, remain behind; **miiru ikkaDa digabaDaNDi, neenu weLLagalanu** please stop here, I can go on by myself.

దిగబెట్టు **digabeTTu** *v.t.* 1 to leave (s.o.) at a place, escort (s.o.) to a place; **oNTLoo baagu leekapootee iNTiki digabeTTeestaanu** if you are not feeling well, I will escort you home.

దిగమింగు **digamingu** *v.t.* to gulp down, swallow down (food, *also* grief, anger, etc.).

దిగవిడుచు **digawiDucu** *v.t.* to leave (s.o.) at a place.

దిగవేయు **digaweeyu** *v.t.* to throw down, knock down.

దిగవేసుకొను **digaweesukonu** *v.t.* to put on (clothes, ornaments) in ample quantity.

దిగసన **digasana** *adv.* down[wards].

దిగాలు **digaalu** *same as* **digulu.**

దిగాలుపడు **digaalupaDu** *v.i.* to be worried, be downcast, be depressed, be crestfallen.

దిగు **digu** I. *v.i.* 1 to go down, come down, descend. 2 to arrive; **udayam padi gaNTalaki digEEDu** he arrived at ten a.m. 3 to stay, stop, halt (at a place on a journey). 4 to be unloaded, be disembarked. 5 to sink in, penetrate, be absorbed. 6 to abate, decrease, diminish. 7 (of sediment) to settle. 8 to enter into, become involved in; **ii panullooki digaku** do not get involved in these affairs; **yuddhaaniki~** to enter into a fight. 9 to go in for; **atani drSTi udyoogam miidiki pooleedu, kaaNTrEEkTullooki digEEDu** he did not look out for a job, he went in for contracts. 10 **ii maamiDi ceTTuki wanda kaaya digindi** this mango tree has yielded a hundred mangoes. II. *v.t.* to alight from, get down from, get off, leave; **rooDDu digi Donkaloo naaDawaali** you must leave the road and walk along a foot path; **ippuDee raylu digEEnu** I have just got down from the train.

దిగుడు **diguDu** *adj.* descending.

దిగుడుబావి **diguDubaawi** *n.* step well, large well with steps leading down to the water.

దిగుదల **digudala** *n.* 1 lower part. 2 falling, descent.

దిగునేత, దిగనేత **diguneeta, diganeeta** *n.* weaving done at night by lamplight.

దిగుబడి **digubaDi** *n.* yield.

దిగుబోటు **digubooTu** *n. and adv.* downhill.

దిగుభాగం **digubhaagam** *n.* lower part, lower portion.

దిగుమతి **digumati** *n.* import.

దిగుమతి అవు **digumati awu** *v.i.* to be imported.

దిగుమతి చేయు **digumati ceeyu** *v.t.* to import.

దిగుమాల **digumaala** *n. colloq.* sunset time.

దిగులు, దిగాలు **digulu, digaalu** *n.* 1 worry, trouble, anxiety. 2 fear, timidness. 3 grief, sorrow.

దిగులుపడు, దిగులువేయు, దిగులుచెందు **digulupaDu, diguluweeyu, digulucendu** *v.i* 1 to be anxious or worried. 2 to be downcast, depresse! or crestfallen. 3 to be afraid.

దిగువ **diguwa** I. *n.* underneath part, lower part. II. *adj.* lower, inferior. III. *p.p. and adv.* below; **ii~prakaTanalu** the following announcements.

దిగువన **diguwana** *adv.* below, down[stream].

దిగువ సభ **diguwa sabha** *n.* lower house (of legislature).

దిగ్గజం, దిగ్దంతి **diggajam, digdanti** *n. class.* 1 one of the eight mythological elephants supporting the eight corners of the earth. 2 mighty hero or warrior; *see* **aSTadiggajaalu.**

దిగ్గు **diggu**[1] *n. class.* fear.

దిగ్గు **diggu**[2] *v.i., alt.* form of **digu.**

దిగ్గున **digguna** *same as* **Digguna.**

దిగ్గుమని **diggumani** *adv.* all at once, without hesitation.

దిగ్బంధం, దిగ్బంధనం **digbandham, digbandhanam** *n.* blockade; *see* **aSTadigbandhanam.**

దిగ్భ్రమ[ం] **digbhrama[m]** *n.* perplexity, bewilderment, confusion, consternation.

దిగ్భ్రాంతి **digbhraanti** *n.* shock, consternation, bewilderment, perplexity.

దిగ్భ్రాంతుడు **digbhraantuDu** *n.* shocked or bewildered person.

దిగ్విజయం **digwijayam** *n.* total victory, world conquest.

దిటవు **diTawu** I. *n.* 1 courage. 2 mental stability, strength of mind, firmness, determination. II. *adj.* 1 firm, definite. 2 permanent.

దిటవుపడు, దిటవుచేసుకొను **diTawupaDu, diTawuceesukonu** *v.i.* to feel heartened or encouraged, rally o.s., recover or preserve o.'s mental stability.

దిట్ట **diTTa** *n.* **1** expert. **2** strong or capable person.

దిట్టం **diTTam** I. *n.* **1** firmness, stoutness. **2** good order, sound condition. II. *adj.* firm, strong, sturdy.

దిట్టంగా **diTTangaa** *adv.* **1** firmly, strongly. **2** fully, abundantly.

దిట్టతనం **diTTatanam** *n.* **1** courage. **2** capability, capacity.

దిట్టరి **diTTari** *n.* strong and determined person.

దిడ్డి **diDDi** *n.* **1** small entrance, backdoor. **2** small window. **3** niche for a lamp.

దిడ్డికంత **diDDikanta** *n.***1** small door. **2** narrow passage.

దిద్ది తీర్చు **diddi tiircu** *v.t.* **1** to mould, fashion. **2** to adorn.

దిద్దు **diddu**[1] *n.* kind of ear ornament (= **duddu**).

దిద్దు **diddu**[2] I. *n.* correction. II. *v.t.* **1** to correct, rectify, set right. **2** to adorn, trim. **3** to draw, trace, delineate. **4** to trace letters previously written by a teacher (the tradional way of learning to write the Telugu alphabet). **5** to train. **6 illu**~ to manage or conduct or run a household.

దిద్దుకొను **diddukonu** *v.t.* **1** to correct, put right, set right; **waaNNi diddukoowaali** you must correct him *or* you must set him on the right path. **2 illu**~ to clean and tidy o.'s house. **3 samsaaram**~ to set right (*or* set in order) o.'s family affairs. **4 ruupam** (*or* **ruupu**)~ (i) to assume a shape or form; (ii) to come into being, materialise.

దిద్దుబాటు **diddubaaTu** *n.* correction.

దినం **dinam** *n.* **1** day; **tiTLu tinanidi waaDiki**~**weLLadu** (*or* **gaDawadu**) a day does not pass (for him) without his being abused; **ii widhangaa aameki** ~**weLLutunnadi** (*or* **gaDustunnadi**) in this way she is able to subsist. **2** one of the ten days of mourning following a person's death.

దినకరుడు **dinakaruDu** *n. class.* sun.

దినకార్యం **dinakaaryam** *n.* funeral ceremony.

దినచర్య **dinacarya** *n.* **1** diary, daily journal. **2** daily routine.

దినదినం **dinadinam** *adv.* daily, every day, day by day.

దినదినగండం **dinadinagaNDam** *n.* daily peril.

దినపత్రిక **dinapatrika** *n.* daily newspaper.

దినబత్తెం **dinabattem** *n.* daily allowance for expenditure.

దినవారాలు **dinawaaraalu** *n.pl.* funeral ceremonies.

దినవెచ్చం **dinaweccam** *n.* daily expenditure.

దినసరి **dinasari** *adj.* daily; **lekka** daily account; ~**sarukulu** articles in daily use.

దినారి, దీనారం **dinaari, diinaaram** *n.* a gold coin.

దినుసు **dinusu** *n.* **1** article, thing, item. **2** ingredient. **3** commodity; **pappu**~**lu** pulses; **nuune**~**lu** oilseeds.

దినుసుగడ్డ **dinusugaDDa** *n.* an edible root vegetable.

దిన్నె **dinne** *same as* **tinna**[2], **tinne.**

దిప్పకాయ **dippakaaya** *same as* **Dippakaaya.**

దిబ్బ **dibba** I. **1** hillock, mound, heap; **isaka**~ sandhill, sand dune. **2** ~ is often used disparingly in a fig. sense, e.g., **peeru goppa uuru**~ the name (of the village) is big but the village is just a mound; **waradalaki polam**~ **cuupindi** due to the floods the field became (*lit.* showed) nothing but a mound (of sand and pebbles). II. *adj.* fat; ~**wedhawa** *term of abuse*; ~**muNDa** *term of abuse to a woman*; *see* **tiiruwa.**

దిబ్బకొక్కు **dibbakokku** *n. dial.* large rat, bandicoot.

దిబ్బడ **dibbaDa** *n.* stuffiness in the nose or ears due to a cold.

దిబ్బాదిరుగుండం **dibbaadiruguNDam** *n.* **1** s.g not worth mentioning, s.g insignificant. **2** this and that, odds and ends, trifles.

దిమాకి తీయు **dimaakitiiyu** *v.i.* to put down (s.o.'s) arrogance.

దిమాకు **dimaaku** *n.* **1** pride, arrogance. **2** strength, power.

దిమికిట, దిమిదిమి **dimikiTa, dimidimi** *onom. adv. sug.* sound of beating drums.

దిమ్మ, దిమ్మె **dimma**[1], **dimme**[1] *n.* **1** heap, mound. **2** pedestal, stand, frame. **3** slab (of wood, cement, etc.). **4** stopper (for bottle or flask).

దిమ్మ, దిమ్మె, దిమ్ము **dimma**[2], **dimme**[2], **dimmu** *n.* giddiness, dizziness, reeling sensation; **naa tala dimmugaa undi** my head is reeling (due to giddiness, illness or mental confusion).

దిమ్మతిరుగు **dimmatirugu** *v.i.* **1** to wander about aimlessly. **2** to feel dazed. **3** *with dat.* to be irritated; **naaku dimma tirigitee** if I get irritated.

దిమ్మరి **dimmari** *n.* (*also* **deeśa**~) **1** vagabond, wanderer, ragamuffin. **2** nomad.

దిమ్మరించు **dimmarincu** *v.t.* to pour (water, grain).

దిమ్మిస, దిమ్మెస **dimmisa, dimmesa** *n.* ram for stamping and consolidating earth, etc.

దిమ్మిసచేయు **dimmisa ceeyu** *v.t.* to ram, consolidate by ramming (e.g., a threshing floor).

దిమ్మెత్తిపోవు **dimmettipoowu** *v.i.* (of o.'s senses) to be numbed or deadened.

దిమ్మెరపోవు **dimmerapoowu** *v.i.* to feel dazed.

దిరదిరతిరుగు **diradiratirugu** *v.i.* to whirl round very fast.

దిలాసా **dilaasaa** *n.* **1** feeling of confidence or security. **2** encouragement; **aayana**~**iccEEDu, anduceeta neenu ii paniki puunukonnaanu** he gave me encouragement, so I ventured on this work.

దిల్‌పసందు **dilpasandu** *n.* name of a sweet kind of mango.

దిల్ల, దిల్లపడు **dilla[paDu]** *same as* **Dilla[paDu]**.

దివం **diwam** *n. class.* **1** sky. **2** heaven.

దివంగతుడవు **diwangatuDawu** *v.i.* to go to heaven, die.

దివంగతుడు **diwangatuDu** *n.* deceased person.

దివసం **diwasam** *n. class.* day.

దివాంధం **diwaandham** *n. class.* owl.

దివాణం **diwaaNam** *n.* **1** royal audience chamber. **2** palace.

దివాన్ **diwaan** *n.* dewan, raja's chief minister; ~**giri** office or post of dewan.

దివారాత్రాలు **diwaaraatraalu** *n. pl.* day and night.

దివాలా **diwaalaa** *n.* bankruptcy, insolvency.

దివాలా ఎత్తు, దివాలా తీయు **diwaalaa ettu, diwaalaa tiiyu** *v.i.* to become bankrupt, declare insolvency.

దివాలాకోరుతనం **diwaalaakoorutanam** *n.* bankruptcy.

దివి **diwi** *n. class.* heaven, sky.

దివిటీ **diwiTii** *n.* torch.

దివ్య **diwya** *adj.* 1 divine, supernatural. 2 charming, superb, splendid, delicious, delightful.

దివ్యంగా **diwyangaa** *adv.* 1 divinely. 2 charmingly. 3 gladly, with pleasure.

దివ్యచక్షువులు **diwyacakSuwulu** *n.pl.* eyes possessing spiritual insight.

దివ్యజ్ఞానం **diwyajñaanam** *n.* theosophy.

దివ్యజ్ఞానసమాజం **diwyajñaana samaajam** *n.* theosophical society.

దివ్యదృష్టి **diwyadṛSTi** *n.* 1 supernatural knowledge, second sight. 2 intuition.

దివ్యసుందర **diwyasundara** *adj.* divinely beautiful.

దివ్వె **diwwe** *n.* lamp, light.

దిశ **diśa** *n.* 1 direction. 2 point of the compass.

దిశాత్మక **diśaatmaka** *adj.* directional.

దిక్చక్రం **diścakram** *n.* horizon.

దిష్టి **diSTi** *n.* evil eye; **waaDiki ~ koTTindi** *or* **waaDiki ~ sookindi** *or* **waaDiki ~ tagilindi** he was affected by the evil eye; *see* **dṛSTi**.

దిష్టిచుక్క, దిష్టిబొట్టు **diSTicukka, diSTiboTTu** *n.* mark placed on the cheek or chin to ward off the evil eye.

దిష్టితాడు **diSTitaaDu** *n.* cord worn round the waist or upper arm as protection against the evil eye.

దిష్టి తీయు **diSTi tiiyu** *v.i.* to perform a rite for curing the evil eye.

దిష్టి పెట్టు **diSTi peTTu** *v.i.* to cast the evil eye (-ku, on).

దిష్టిబొమ్మ **diSTibomma** *n.* figure like a scarecrow displayed to avert the evil eye from crops, etc.

దిస **disa** *adj.* naked, nude.

దిసమొల **disamola** I. *n.* nakedness, nudity. II. *adj.* naked, nude.

దీ - dii

దీక్ష **diikSa** *n.* 1 vow. 2 devotion, dedication. 3 devoted attention, concentration.

దీక్షగా **diikSagaa** *adv.* 1 devotedly. 2 intently, deeply, with concentration.

దీక్షాయుత **diikSaayuta** *adj.* dedicated, devoted.

దీక్షావస్త్రాలు **diikSaawastraalu** *n. pl.* 1 *class.* clothes put on at the time of starting a religious ceremony and worn until the ceremony is over. 2 *colloq.* clothes worn for a long time; *cf.* **madhuparkaalu.**

దీక్షితుడు **diikSituDu** I. *n. class.* one who has performed a preliminary sacrificial ceremony. II. *second part of a n. compound* person who is devoted; **swaatantrya samara ~** one who is devoted to the struggle for independence.

దీటు **diiTu** *adj.* equal, similar, like; **diiTayna waarasuDu** worthy or fitting successor.

దీన[ం] **diina[m]** *adj.* 1 humble, poor, lowly. 2 wretched, dejected, miserable.

దీనత, దీనత్వం **diinata, diinatwam** *n.* wretchedness, lowliness, humility.

దీనారం **diinaaram** *same as* **dinaari.**

దీనుడు **diinuDu** *n.* humble or wretched person.

దీపం **diipam** *n.* lamp, light; **~ pedda[di] ceeyu** (*lit.* to make a lamp larger) *means* to extinguish a lamp; **~ koNDa ekkindi** (*lit.* the light went up the hill) *means* the light was extinguished; *these are euphemisms to avoid taboo expressions*, *cf.* **golusu, biyyam.**

దీపం పెట్టు, దీపం వెలిగించు **diipam peTTu, diipam weligincu** *v.i.* 1 to light a lamp. 2 **maa iNTa diipam peTTEEDu** *or* **maa iNTi diipam nilipEEDu** *lit.* he saw to it that there was a light in my house, i.e., he came to the rescue of my family in trouble.

దీపంగూడు **diipam guuDu** *n.* niche for a lamp.

దీపస్తంభం **diipastambham** *n.* lamp post; **~laa nilabaDDadi** she is wearing no jewellery or ornaments (*lit.* she is standing like a lamp post).

దీపాంతరం **diipaantaram** *n.* earthenware saucer filled with oil for use as a lamp.

దీపారాధన **diipaaraadhana** *n.* worship in the form of offering a light to a deity.

దీపాలంకరణ **diipaalankaraNa** *n.* illumination, floodlighting.

దీపాలమాస **diipaalamaasa** *n. colloq. form of* **diipaala amaawaasya** *or* **diipaawaLi.**

దీపావళి **diipaawaLi** *n.* Dipavali, festival of lights celebrated on the last day of the month of Asviyuja.

దీపించు **diipincu** *v.i.* to shine.

దీపింప చేయు **diipimpa ceeyu** *v.i.* to cause to shine.

దీపిక **diipika** *n.* 1 *class.* small lamp, torch. 2 *in book titles ~ is equivalent to* manual, e.g., **wijñaana ~** science manual.

దీప్త **diipta** *adj.* blazing, burning, flaming.

దీప్తి **diipti** *n.* 1 brightness, lustre, brilliance. 2 luminescence.

దీప్తిదం **diiptidam** *adj. sci.* luminous.

దీప్తిమయ **diiptimaya** *adj. sci.* luminescent.

దీర్ఘ **diirgha** *adj.* long.

దీర్ఘం **diirgham** *n.* length[ening].

దీర్ఘం తీయు **diirgham tiiyu** *v.i.* to lengthen, prolong: **asalu wiSayam ceppakuNDaa diirghaalu tiistuu maaTLaaDEEDu** without mentioning the real matter he dragged out the conversation.

దీర్ఘకాలిక **diirghakaalika** *adj.* long term.

దీర్ఘచతురస్రం **diirghacaturasram** *n. maths.* rectangle.

దీర్ఘత **diirghata** *n.* length.

దీర్ఘవర్తులం, దీర్ఘవృత్తం **diirghawartulam, diirghawrttam** *n.* ellipse.

దీర్ఘవృత్తాకార **diirghawrttaakaara** *adj.* elliptical.

దీర్ఘవ్యవధిక **diirghawyawadhika** *adj.* long range (forecast).

దీర్ఘవ్యాధి **diirghawyaadhi** *n.* chronic disease.

దీర్ఘాచ్చు **diirghaaccu** *n. gram.* long vowel.

దీర్ఘాయువు, దీర్ఘాయుష్షు **diirghaayuwu, diirghaayuSSu** *n.* long life.

దీర్ఘీకరించు **diirghiikarincu** *v.t.* to elongate.

దీవన, దీవెన **diiwana, diiwena** *n.* blessing, benediction.

దీవి **diiwi**[1] *n.* island.

దీవి **diiwi**[2] *n. dial.* longing to see; **maa abbaayimiida naaku ~ gaa undi** *or* **maa abbaayimiida naaku diiweestunnadi** I am longing to see my son.

దీవించు **diiwincu** *v.t.* to bless.

దు - du

దుంగ **dunga** *n.* log, block of wood.

దుండగం **duNDagam** *n.* villainy, mischief, wickedness, evil deed, crime.

దుండగీడు, దుండగాయ, దుండగుడు **duNDagiiDu, duNDagaaya, duNDaguDu** *n.* villain, wretch, bad character, rowdy.

దుందిలం **dundilam** *n.* kind of tree.

దుందుడుకు **dunduDuku** *same as* **duDuku.**

దుందుభి **dundubhi** *n.* **1** large drum. **2 deewadundubhulu** thunder in a clear sky (believed to be an auspicious sign). **3** name of the fifty-sixth year of the Hindu cycle of sixty years.

దుంప **dumpa** *n.* **1** edible root vegetable, tuber. **2** upper part of a plough stock.

దుంపకట్టుకుపోవు **dumpakaTTukupoowu** *v.i.* to harden, become congealed.

దుంపతెగు **dumpategu** *v.i. occurring in colloqial expressions* **1 sTeeSanninci naDiceesariki naa dumpa tegindi** by the time I had walked from the station I was dead tired. **2 oreey nii dumpa tega!** (conveying admonition) *and* **oreey nii dumpa weyya!** (conveying approval) *are informal sentence openers.*

దుంపనక్కు **dumpanakku** *n.* sullenness, sulkiness.

దుంపనాశనం **dumpanaaśanam** *n.* total ruin (*lit.* ruin from the roots).

దుంపరాష్ట్ర[క]ం **dumparaaSTra[ka]m** *n.* a medicinal root.

దుఃఖం **duḥkham** *n.* sorrow, grief, misery.

దుఃఖపడు, దుఃఖించు **duḥkhapaDu, duḥkhincu** *v.i.* to grieve, lament, feel sad.

దుఃఖపెట్టు **duḥkhapeTTu** *v.t.* to cause grief or sorrow.

దుఃఖభాజన **duḥkhabhaajana** *adj.* griefstricken, desolate.

దుఃఖమయ **duḥkhamaya** *adj.* sad, sorrowful.

దుఃఖోద్వేగం **duḥkhoodweegam** *n.* mental depression, neurosis.

దుఃఖోపశమనం **duḥkhoopaśamanam** *n.* consolation.

దుకాణం **dukaaNam** *n.* shop; **iwwaaLaTiki ~ kaTTipeTTaNDi** stop working for today (referring to any kind of work).

దుకూలం **dukuulam** *n. class.* robe made of fine cloth.

దుక్క **dukka** *n.* **1** log of wood. **2** trunk of a tree. **3** bar or ingot of metal.

దుక్క ఇనుము **dukka inumu** *n.* pig iron.

దుక్కబలియు **dukkabaliyu** *v.i.* to be fat.

దుక్కముక్క **dukkamukka** *adj.* stout, strong.

దుక్కి **dukki** *n.* **1** ploughing. **2** cultivation of land. **3** ploughed land. **4** a measure of rainfall which is sufficient for ploughing.

దుక్కిటెద్దు **dukkiTeddu** *n.* ploughing bullock.

దుక్కిపోతు **dukkipootu** *n.* ploughing buffalo.

దుక్కిముచ్చు **dukkimuccu** *n.* filthy or slovenly person.

దుక్కివాన **dukkiwaana** *n.* a measure of rainfall, i.e., the quantity needed to make the land wet enough to start ploughing; **reNDu dukkula waana kurisindi** the rainfall was twice as much as was needed to start ploughing.

దుగలం **dugalam** *n.* obsolete coin equivalent to one sixteenth of a pagoda.

దుగుణం **duguNam** *adj. class.* twice as much.

దుగ్గాని **duggaani** *n.* obsolete copper coin worth two pies.

దుగ్గు **duggu** *n.* straw that has been trampled by cattle in a shed.

దుగ్ధ, దుర్ధ **dugdha, durdha** *n.* **1** envy, heartburning. **2** resentment, disgruntlement, annoyance.

దుగ్ధం **dugdham** *n. class.* milk.

దుగ్ధరసం **dugdharasam** *n.* latex.

దుడుకు **duDuku** I. *n.* (*also* ~ **tanam**) **1** pride, arrogance. **2** rashness, haste, folly, intemperateness. **3** mischief.

wickedness. II. *adj.* 1 rash, foolish. 2 intemperate, imprudent. 3 wicked; ~ **naDaka** bad behaviour.

దుడ్డు **duDDu** *n.* 1 *dial.* money. 2 (*also* ~ **karra**) stout stick, club, bludgeon.

దుడ్డె **duDDe** *n.* calf.

దుత్త **dutta** *n.* small earthen pot.

దుద్దు **duddu** *same as* **diddu**[1].

దునియా **duniyaa** *n.* the world.

దున్న[పోతు] **dunna[pootu]** *n.* he buffalo (*also used as a mild term of abuse*); **dunnapootumiida waanakurisinaTTu** like rain falling on a buffalo (*proverbial expression for s.g that has no effect, cf. the English expression* 'like water off a duck's back').

దున్ను **dunnu** *v.t.* to plough.

దున్నుపదును **dunnupadunu** *adj.* (of land) moist enough to be ploughed.

దుప్పటి, దుప్పటం **duppaTi, duppaTam** *n.* 1 bed sheet. 2 *class.* sari. 3 *class.* upper cloth worn by a woman.

దుప్పి **duppi** *n.* spotted deer.

దుబారా **dubaaraa**[1] *n.* waste, extravagance, squandering, wasting; ~ **kharcu** extravagant expenditure.

దుబారా, దుబారు **dubaaraa**[2], **dubaaru** *n.* coarse sand.

దుబారాతనం **dubaaraatanam** *n.* wastefulness.

దుబాసి **dubaasi** *n.* interpreter.

దుబ్బ **dubba** *same as* **tuwwa.**

దుబ్బు **dubbu** I. *n.* 1 thick-growing vegetation such as grass or weeds. 2 tuft of grass. 3 stubble. II. *adj.* 1 (of vegetation, hair) thick, bushy. 2 (of persons) fat, stout.

దుబ్బుగడ్డి **dubbugaDDi** *n.* kind of grass, *agrostis lineoris.*

దుబ్బుచేయు **dubbuceeyu** *v.i.* (of grass) to produce tillers.

దుబ్బుమని, దుబ్బున **dubbumani, dubbuna** *onom. adv.* with a crash (sound made by a fall).

దుమారం **dumaaram** *n.* 1 dust storm. 2 storm, commotion.

దుముకు **dumuku** *v.i.* to jump, leap, spring.

దుముకులాడు **dumukulaaDu** *v.i.* (of children) to jump and play.

దుమ్ము **dummu** *n.* 1 dust. 2 *dial.* bone.

దుమ్ముచేయు **dummuceeyu** *v.t.* to waste (*lit.* to turn into dust); **Dabbantaa dummu ceesEEDu** he wasted all the money.

దుమ్ముదులుపు **dummudulupu** *v.t.* 1 to dust. 2 to beat. 3 to criticise.

దుమ్మురేగకొట్టు **dummureegakoTTu** *v.t.* to beat severely.

దుమ్ములగొండి **dummulagoNDi** *n.* hyena.

దుమ్మూదుడసరం **dummuuduDasaram** *n.* chaff.

దుమ్మెత్తిపోయు **dummettipooyu** *v.i.* to hurl abuse (-**miida**, at).

దుయ్యబట్టు, దూయబట్టు **duyyabaTTu, duuyabaTTu** *v.t.* to criticise severely, castigate (<**duuyu** to strip off + **paTTu**); *see* **orugu**[1] *sense 4.*

దుర్, దుశ్, దుష్, దుస్ **dur, duś, duS, dus** *adjvl. prefix signifying* 1 wrong *or* evil; **durabhipraayam** wrong opinion; **duSprabhaawam** evil influence. 2 difficulty *or* impossibility; **duruuhyam** difficult to imagine *or* unimaginable; **durbharam** hard to bear *or* unbearable.

దురంతం **durantam** *n.* brutality, excess, outrage.

దురంధరుడు **durandharuDu** *n.* veteran.

దురటిల్లు, దురపిల్లు **duraTillu, durapillu** *v.i* 1 to grieve, suffer. 2 to mourn, weep, lament, be distressed.

దురద **durada** *n.* 1 itch[ing]. 2 tingling.

దురదకంద **duradakanda** *n. amorphallus campanulatus*, a kind of yam which causes itching of the tongue when eaten.

దురదగొండి [ఆకు] **duradagoNDi[aaku]** *n.* stinging nettle.

దురదృష్టం **duradṛSTam** *n.* bad luck, ill luck, misfortune.

దురదృష్టవశాత్తు, దురదృష్టవశాన **duradṛSTawaśaattu, duradṛSTawaśaana** *adv.* unfortunately, by misfortune, due to ill luck.

దురపిల్లు **durapillu** *same as* **duraTillu.**

దురభిప్రాయం **durabhipraayam** *n.* wrong opinion, misconception.

దురభిమానం **durabhimaanam** *n.* 1 false pride. 2 prejudice.

దురభిమాని **durabhimaani** *n.* 1 arrogant person. 2 prejudiced person.

దురలవాటు **duralawaaTu** *n.* bad habit, bad custom.

దురవగాహం **durawagaaham** *adj.* 1 hard to understand. 2 incomprehensible.

దురవస్థ, దుస్థితి **durawastha, dusthiti** *n.* evil plight, miserable condition.

దురహంకారం **durahankaaram** *n.* 1 inordinate pride or arrogance. 2 bigotry, chauvinism.

దురాక్రమణ **duraakramaNa** *n.* aggression.

దురాక్షేపం, దురాక్షేపణం **duraakSeepa[Na]m** *n.* carping, cavilling, undue criticism.

దురాగతం **duraagatam** *n.* brutality, excess, outrage.

దురాగ్రహం **duraagraham** *n.* excessive anger.

దురాచారం **duraacaaram** *n.* bad custom, bad practice.

దురాత్ముడు **duraatmuDu** *n.* bad-natured person, evil-hearted person.

దురాపం **duraapam** *adj. class.* hard to attain.

దురాయి **duraayi** *n.* 1 command, order. 2 protestation. 3 veto.

దురాలోచన **duraaloocana** *n.* 1 bad intention. 2 evil counsel, plotting.

దురాశ, దురాస **duraaśa, duraasa** *n.* greed, avarice, covetousness.

దురాశయం **duraaśayam** *n.* bad intention, evil purpose.

దురిత **durita** *adj.* hasty, impetuous.

దురుద్దేశం **duruddeeśam** *n.* 1 bad intention, bad motive. 2 *legal* bad faith.

దురుసు **durusu** *adj.* 1 impetuous, hasty. 2 rude, harsh, rough.

దురుసు[తనం] **durusu[tanam]** *n.* 1 impetuosity, hastiness. 2 rudeness, harshness, roughness.

దురూహ్యం **duruuhyam** *adj.* 1 difficult to imagine. 2 unimaginable, unthinkable, inconceivable.

దుర్గ, దుర్గి **durga, durgi** *n.* Durga, Durgi, names of Parvati.

దుర్గం **durgam** *n.* 1 fort. 2 hill fort, citadel.

దుర్గంధం **durgandham** *n.* bad or foul smell, stench.

దుర్గతి **durgati** *n.* ruin, perdition, bad fate.

దుర్గమం **durgamam** *adj.* 1 difficult to reach, penetrate or pass through, hard to attain. 2 inaccessible, impossible to reach, unattainable.

దుర్గుణం **durguNam** *n.* bad quality, defect.

దుర్గ్రాహ్యం **durgraahyam** *adj.* hard to comprehend.

దుర్ఘటం **durghaTam** *adj.* 1 hazardous, hard. 2 impracticable.

దుర్ఘటన **durghaTana** *n.* accident, mishap, misadventure.

దుర్జనుడు **durjanuDu** *n.* bad or wicked person.

దుర్జయం **durjayam** *adj. class.* unconquerable, invincible.

దుర్జ్ఞేయం **durjñeeyam** *adj. class.* difficult to know or understand.

దుర్దశ **durdaśa** *n.* unhappy state, misfortune, plight.

దుర్దాంతం **durdaantam** *adj. class.* 1 difficult to restrain. 2 intractable.

దుర్దినం **durdinam** *n.* 1 time of misfortune. 2 *class.* rainy day.

దుర్ధ **durdha** *same as* **dugdha.**

దుర్ధరం **durdharam** *adj.* unbearable, intolerable.

దుర్నయం **durnayam** *n. class.* injustice, inequity.

దుర్నిమిత్తం **durnimittam** *n. class.* bad omen.

దుర్నిరీక్ష్యం **durniriikSyam** *adj.* 1 difficult to see, scarcely visible. 2 dazzling.

దుర్నివారం **durniwaaram** *adj. class.* unrestrainable.

దుర్నీతి **durniiti** *n.* immorality, vice, wickedness.

దుర్బలం **durbalam** *adj.* weak, feeble, frail.

దుర్బలత, దుర్బలత్వం **durbalata, durbalatwam** *n.* weakness, debility.

దుర్బీను, దుర్బిణీ, దుర్బినీ **durbiinu, durbiNii, durbinii** *n.* 1 magnifying glass. 2 field glass, telescope. 3 mason's spirit level.

దుర్బుద్ధి, దుర్మతి **durbuddhi, durmati** *n.* 1 evil intent or notion. 2 bad trait of character.

దుర్బోధ **durboodha** *n.* bad advice, evil counsel.

దుర్బోధ[లు] చేయు **durboodha[lu]ceeyu** *v.i.* to offer bad advice or evil counsel.

దుర్బోధనం **durboodhanam** *n.* evil counsel.

దుర్భరం **durbharam** *adj.* 1 hard to bear. 2 unedurable, unbearable, insupportable.

దుర్భావం **durbhaawam** *n.* ill feeling.

దుర్భాష **durbhaaSa** *n.* abuse, foul language, scurrilous language.

దుర్భాషలాడు **durbhaaSalaaDu** *v.t.* to scold, abuse.

దుర్భిక్షం **durbhikSam** *n.* famine, scarcity.

దుర్భేద్యం **durbheedyam** *adj.* 1 hard to pierce or penetrate. 2 impregnable.

దుర్భ్రమ **durbhrama** *n.* misconception, mistaken belief.

దుర్మతి **durmati** *n.* 1 *same as* **durbuddhi.** 2 fifty-fifth year of the Hindu cycle of sixty years.

దుర్మదం **durmadam** *n.* overweening pride or arrogance.

దుర్మరణం **durmaraNam** *n.* violent or untimely death, death due to an accident.

దుర్మాంసం **durmaamsam** *n.* 1 granulation tissue, proud flesh. 2 cataract (eye disease).

దుర్మార్గం **durmaargam** *n.* 1 vice, wickedness, wrongdoing. 2 misconduct, misbehaviour.

దుర్మార్గుడు **durmaarguDu** *n.* wicked person, villain.

దుర్ముఖి **durmukhi** *n.* thirtieth year of the Hindu cycle of sixty years.

దుర్యశం **duryaśam** *n.* infamy, disgrace.

దుర్లభం **durlabham** *adj.* 1 scarce, rare, hard to come by. 2 unobtainable.

దుర్వచనం **durwacanam** *n.* foul language.

దుర్వార్త **durwaarta** *n.* bad news.

దుర్వాసన **durwaasana** *n.* bad or foul smell, stench.

దుర్విదగ్ధుడు **durwidagdhuDu** *n. class.* foolish person who believes himself to be intelligent.

దుర్వినియోగం **durwiniyoogam** *n.* misuse, abuse; **adhikaara~** abuse of power.

దుర్వృత్తి **durwṛtti** *n.* unseemly or disreputable conduct.

దుర్వ్యయం **durwyayam** *n.* wasteful expenditure.

దుర్వ్యసనం **durwyasanam** *n.* vice, bad habit, addiction.

దుర్వ్యాపారం **durwyaapaaram** *n.* illicit business, improper transaction.

దులపరించు **dulaparincu** *v.t.* 1 to shake, scatter, spatter (ink). 2 *colloq.* to criticise, abuse.

దులపసన్నం **dulapasannam** *n.* a variety of paddy.

దులుపు **dulupu** I. *n.* shaking. II. *v.t.* 1 to shake off (dust), shake out (a cloth), shake (a tree in order to knock down the fruit). 2 to browbeat, give a scolding to; **waaNNi paTTuku dulipEEnu** I caught him and gave him a scolding.

దులుపుకొను **dulupukonu** *v.i. and t.* 1 to shake; **kukka oLLu dulupukonnadi** the dog shook itself. 2 *fig.* to shake off, shrug off, ignore; **ceppina pani ceesi ceetulu dulupukonnaaDu** he did what he was asked to do and washed his hands of the matter; **neenu waaNNi tiDitee dulupuku**

weLLEEDu when I abused him, he shrugged it off and went away.

దుళ్లగొట్టు **duLLagoTTu** *v.t. dial.* **1** to shake a tree in order to knock down the fruit. **2** to criticise.

దువ్వ **duwwa**[1] *n.* dust.

దువ్వ **duwwa**[2] *same as* **tuwwa.**

దువ్వు **duwwu** *v.t.* **1** to stroke. **2** to pat. **3 miisaalu~** *or* **kayyaaniki kaalu~** to challenge (persons) to a fight. **4** to comb. **5** to cajole.

దువ్వుకొను **duwwukonu** *v.t.* to ensnare (s.o.) by means of kind words.

దువ్వెన **duwwena** *n.* comb.

దుశ్చరితం **duścaritam** *n.* bad repute, bad character.

దుశ్చర్య **duścarya** *n.* misdeed, evil deed.

దుశ్చింత **duścinta** *n.* villainy.

దుశ్చింతనుడు **duścintanuDu** *n.* person with evil thoughts, villain.

దుశ్చేష్ట **duśceeSTa** *n.* evil deed, misdeed, wrongdoing, mischief.

దుశ్శాలువా **duśśaaluwaa** *n.* ornamental shawl.

దుష్కర **duSkara** *adj.* difficult, hard.

దుష్కర్మ **duSkarma** *n.* evil deed.

దుష్కాలం **duSkaalam** *n.* evil time, time of misfortune.

దుష్కృతం **duSkṛtam** *n.* sin, evil deed.

దుష్కృత్యం **duSkṛtyam** *n.* sin, crime.

దుష్ట **duSTa** *adj.* bad, wicked, vicious, cruel.

దుష్టత్వం **duSTatwam** *n.* evil, wickedness, vice.

దుష్టమృగం **duSTamṛgam** *n.* wild animal, beast of prey.

దుష్టసమాసం **duSTasamaasam** *n. gram.* irregularly formed compound made up of two words whose roots originate from two languages, e.g., **wasantagaali** spring breeze.

దుష్టాంగం **duSTaangam** *n.* deformed limb.

దుష్టుడు **duSTuDu** *n.* bad or wicked person, scoundrel, rascal villain.

దుష్ప్రచారం **duSpracaaram** *n.* **1** scandalmongering. **2** adverse publicity.

దుష్ప్రభావం **duSprabhaawam** *n.* evil influence.

దుష్ప్రయోగం **duSprayoogam** *n.* malapropism.

దుష్ప్రేరణ **duSpreeraNa** *n. legal* abetment.

దుష్ఫలం **duSphalam** *n.* evil result, bad effect.

దుష్ఫలితం **duSphalitam** *n.* evil result.

దుస్తంత్రం **dustantram** *n.* evil plot, guile.

దుస్తు **dustu** *n.* garment, dress; *gen. pl.* **~ lu** clothes.

దుస్తరం **dustaram** *adj.* difficult to cross.

దుస్థితి **dusthiti** *same as* **durawastha.**

దుస్సంఘటన **dussanghaTana** *n.* mishap, accident.

దుస్సహ **dussaha** *adj.* unbearable, intolerable.

దుస్సహనం **dussahanam** *n.* intolerance.

దుస్సాధ్య **dussaadhya** *adj.* **1** hard to accomplish. **2** impossible.

దుస్సాహసం **dussaahasam** *n.* daring or audacious or reckless act.

దుస్స్వప్నం **dusswapnam** *n.* bad dream, nightmare.

దుహిత **duhita** *n. class.* daughter.

దూ - duu

దూకు **duuku** *v.i.* to jump, leap, spring.

దూకుడు **duukuDu** I. *n.* **1** jumping. **2** (of a horse) galloping. II *adj.* arrogant.

దూట **duuTa** *n.* pith of a plantain tree.

దూటు **duuTu** *v.i. class.* to run, rush.

దూడ **duuDa** *n.* calf.

దూత **duuta** *n.* **1** messenger. **2** ambassador, envoy. **3** angel.

దూతీకరణం **duutiikaraNam** *n. slang* procurement for prostitution.

దూదర, దూదెర **duudara**[1], **duudera** *n.* pest affecting paddy and other grain crops.

దూదర **duudara**[2] *n. colloq.* cyclone.

దూది **duudi** *n.* cleaned cotton before spinning.

దూదిపింజ **duudipinja** *n.* cotton wool.

దూదేకు **duudeeku** *v.i.* to clean or gin cotton.

దూదేకులవాడు, దూదేకుల సాయెబు **duudeekulawaaDu, duudeekula saayebu** *n.* cotton cleaner.

దూప **duupa** *n. dial.* thirst.

దూబ **duuba** *n.* **1** mean fellow, contemptible person. **2** deformity; **~ oLLu** misshapen body.

దూబర **duubara** *n.* gentle drizzle.

దూబరతిండి **duubaratiNDi** *n.* **1** wasteful expenditure on food. **2** parasite, one who lives at the expense of others.

దూముడి, దూయుముడి **duu[yu]muDi** *n.* kind of knot that can be easily untied.

దూయబట్టు **duuyabaTTu** *same as* **duyyabaTTu.**

దూయు **duuyu** *v.t.* **1** to pierce, penetrate, go through. **2** to strip off (leaves from a branch); **katti~** to unsheath a knife or sword; *cf.* **duusukonu.**

దూరం **duuram** I. *n.* distance; **waariki nuwwu enta ~ loo unnaawu?** how far are you from them? II. *adj.* distant, far [off].

దూరం అవు **duuram awu** *v.i.* to be apart, be separated, be distant, be out of touch; **manuSulu periginakoddi ~ taaru** as people grow older they become further apart.

దూరంగా **duurangaa** *adv.* at a distance, distantly, apart.

దూరదర్శన్ **duuradarśan** *n.* television.

దూరదర్శిని **duuradarśini** *n.* telescope.

దూరదృష్టి **duuradṛSTi** *n.* foresight, prudence, farsightedness.

దూరభారం, దూరాభారం **duurabhaaram, duuraabhaaram** *n.* a great distance (*lit.* weight of distance); **bassuloo ~ prayaaNam ceeyakuuDadu, naDumulu paDipootaayi** do not travel for a long distance in a bus, you will get backache.

దూరశ్రవణ **duuraśrawaNa** *adj.* relating to telecommunications; **~ saakha** telecommunications department.

దూరు **duuru**[1] *v.i.* to enter, penetrate, rush in, creep in, be introduced, be inserted.

దూరు **duuru**[2] *v.t. class.* to reproach, rebuke, abuse.

దూరుడు **duuruDu** *second part of a n. compound meaning* person who is far removed from; **mana paNDitulu lookawyawahaaraaniki enta duuruloo telustunnadi** it is plain how far removed our scholars are from the affairs of everyday life.

దూర్చు, దూరించు **duurcu, duurincu** *v.t.* to thrust in, push in, introduce, insert; **suudilooki daaram duurcu** to thread a needle (*lit.* to push a thread through a needle).

దూర్వాసుడు **duurwaasuDu** *n.* **1** name of a rishi in mythology who had a fierce disposition. **2** person with a violent temper.

దూల **duula** *n.* **1** itching. **2** *slang* hankering.

దూలం **duulam** *n.* beam.

దూలగొండి **duulagoNDi** *n.* **1** (*also* **duulagoNDEEku**) stinging nettle, *tragia involucrata*. **2** irritable person.

దూలపు ఇల్లు, దూలపిల్లు **duulapu illu, duulapillu** *n.* house with beams in the roof.

దూలపు రాయి **duulapu raayi** *n.* stone placed above the beams of a house.

దూలాలు **duulaalu** *n. slang* prostitute.

ధూలి **duuli** *same as* **dhuuLi.**

దూవర **duuwara** *n.* gentle drizzle.

దూవలువ **duuwaluwa** *n.* muslin cloth.

దూషణ **duuSaNa** *n.* abuse, reproach, reviling, invective.

దూషించు **duuSincu** *v.t.* to abuse, reproach, revile, vilify.

దూష్య **duuSya** *adj.* reprehensible, blameworthy.

దూసరం **duusaram** *n.* dust.

దూసరితీగ **duusaritiiga** *n. cocculus villosus*, a wild plant.

దూసుకొను, దూసుకుపోవు **duusukonu, duusukupoowu** *v.i. and t.* to enter (gen. with some force or effort), pierce, penetrate, pass through, pass by; **DaakTarugaari kaaru rooDDumiida duusuku pootunnadi** the doctor's car is passing through the road. **2** to overtake, outstrip; **saykilu tecci rikSaani duusuku munduku pooyEEDu** he fetched a cycle, overtook the rickshaw and went on ahead.

దూసుకువచ్చు **duusukuwaccu** *v.i.* to pass out, emerge (gen. with some force or effort); **guNDelloo bhaawam sarruna bayaTiki duusuku raawaali** the idea in the mind must force its way out.

దృ - dṛ

దృక్కు **dṛkku** *n.* **1** sight. **2** look, glance.

దృక్కోణం **dṛkkooNam** *n.* **1** angle of vision. **2** point of view.

దృక్పథం **dṛkpatham** *n.* **1** point of view, viewpoint. **2** aspect. **3** attitude, approach, outlook.

దృగ్గోచర **dṛggoocara** *adj.* **1** visible. **2** visual; **~ duuram** visual range.

దృఢ **dṛDha** *adj.* **1** hard, solid. **2** strong, firm steady, rigid, fixed. **3** emphatic; **~ swaram** emphatic tone of voice. **4** confirmed.

దృఢంగా **dṛDhangaa** *adv.* **1** strongly, firmly. **2** emphatically.

దృఢత్వం, దృఢత **dṛDhatwam, dṛDhata** *n.* strength, firmness, steadiness, rigidity.

దృఢనిశ్చయం **dṛDhaniścayam** *n.* determination, resolve.

దృఢపడు **dṛDhapaDu** *v.i.* to be strengthened, be confirmed, be substantiated.

దృఢమతి **dṛDhamati** *n.* **1** strong or firm will. **2** strong-willed person.

దృఢీకరణ **dṛDhiikaraNa** *n.* confirmation.

దృశా **dṛśaa** *adj. sci.* optical.

దృశాశాస్త్రం **dṛśaaśaastram** *n.* (science of) optics.

దృశ్య **dṛŚya** *adj.* **1** visible; **~ prapancam** the visible world. **2** visual.

దృశ్యం **dṛsyam** *n.* view, scene, sight, look, appearance.

దృశ్యత **dṛśyata** *n.* visibility.

దృశ్యమాన **dṛśyamaana** *adj.* apparent.

దృశ్యశ్రవణ విద్య **dṛśyaśrawaNa widya** *n.* audio-visual education.

దృష్టాంతం **drSTaantam** *n.* 1 illustration, instance, example. 2 evidence, proof. 3 precedent.

దృష్టాంతరం **drSTaantaram** *n.* example.

దృష్టాంతీకరించు **drSTaantiikarincu** *v.t.* to illustrate, exemplify.

దృష్టి **drSTi** *n.* 1 sight, seeing, vision. 2 look, glance. 3 view, attention: **~loo peTTukonu** to keep in view. 4 outlook, attitude. 5 evil eye; *see* **diSTi.**

దృష్టితీయు **drSTi tiiyu** *v.t.* to perform a rite for counteracting the evil eye.

దృష్టిదోషం **drSTidooSam** *n.* harmful effect of the evil eye.

దృష్టిపథం **drSTipatham** *n.* range of view.

దృష్టి పారించు, దృష్టి సారించు **drSTi paarincu, drSTi saarincu** *v.i.* to cast a glance (at), turn o.'s eyes (towards).

దృష్ట్యా **drSTyaa** *adv.* from the point of view of, in view of, in the light of, having regard to, taking account of.

దె - de

దెంకువచ్చు, దెంగుకువచ్చు **denkuwaccu, dengukuwaccu** *v.i. and t. slang* 1 to procure s.g by stealing or by force. 2 to run away.

దెంగు **dengu** I. *n.* (*also* **~laaTa**) sexual intercourse. II. *v.t.* to have sexual intercourse with.

దెంగులు **dengulu** *n.pl. colloq.* abuse.

దెంగులు దెంగులుగా ఉండు **denguludengulugaa uNDu** *v.i.* to be in an angry, cross or irritated mood.

దెంగులుపెట్టు **dengulupeTTu** *v.t.* 1 to abuse. 2 to threaten.

దెత్తి **detti** *n.* 1 habit of being extravagant and overgenerous, esp. with regard to food. 2 *class.* ghost, female demon.

దెప్పం **deppam** *n. class.* object, aim.

దెప్పిపొడుచు **deppipoDucu** *v.t.* to ridicule, make fun of.

దెప్పు **deppu** I. *n.* (*also* **~Du**) taunt, gibe. II. *v.t.* to taunt, reproach, gibe at.

దెప్పుగా **deppugaa** *adv.* ironically, sarcastically, scornfully.

దెబ్బ **debba** *n.* blow, stroke; **tupaaki~** gunshot; **~ku dayyam wadilindi** *or* **~ku dayyam digiwaccindi** the blow (that he received) brought him to his senses (*lit.* as a result of the blow, the evil spirit left him).

దెబ్బ[లు] తిను **debba[lu] tinu** *v.i.* 1 to suffer blows, be beaten, be struck. 2 to suffer misfortune, damage or injury; **waradalawalla paNTalu debba tiNTaayi** the crops will be damaged by the floods; **waaDu wyaapaaramloo debba tinnaTLu mukhamloo kanabaDindi** it appeared from his face he had suffered a misfortune in business. 3 to fail, be a failure; **daadaapu nuuru sinimaalaloo padi sinimaalee aarthikangaa wijayawantam awutunnayi, migataawi debba tiNTunnaayi** out of about 100 cinema films only 10 are financially successful, the rest are failures; **waaLLa ancanaalu debba tinnaayi** their estimates turned out to be wrong.

దెబ్బ తీయు **debba tiiyu** *v.i.* to deal a blow; **debbaku~** to deal blow for blow.

దెబ్బలాట **debbalaaTa** *n.* fight, quarrel, dispute.

దెబ్బలాడు **debbalaaDu** *v.i.* to quarrel, fight.

దెయ్యం[పట్టు] **deyyam[paTTu]** *dial. variant of* **dayyam [paTTu].**

దెవసం **dewasam** *alt. form of* **daśaaham.**

దెవసంరాత **dewasamraata** *n. slang* atrociously bad handwriting.

దెస **desa** *alt. form of* **diśa.**

దేకు **deeku** *v.i.* 1 to slide along on o.'s haunches, scramble. 2 (of numbers, estimates) to creep up, rise up, mount up; **weyyi ruupaayala appu aydu weela daakaa deekindi** a debt of Rs. 1000 mounted up to Rs. 5000.

దేదీప్యమానం **deediipyamaanam** *adj.* glorious, splendid, noble.

దేనికది **deenikadi** I. *interrog. sentence* what is that for? (- **adideeniki**?). II. *adv.* individually; **atani mukhamloo ee bhaagamuukuuDaa sphuTangaa awupincadu kaani ~ cuustee kannuu mukkuu nooruu tiirugaanee uNTaayi** no part of his face appears striking, but if you regard them individually his eyes, nose and mouth are shapely.

దేపిరిగొట్టు, దేబిరిగొట్టు **deepirigoTTu, deebirigoTTu** *n.* groveller.

దేబిరించు, దేవురించు **deebirincu, deewurincu** *v.i.* to grovel, demean o.s., beg, entreat.

దేబిరింపు **deebirimpu** *n.* grovelling, demeaning o.s.

దేబె **deebe** *n.* simpleton, fool.

దేభ్యం, తేభ్యం **deebhyam, teebhyam** *n.* useless fellow.

దేముడు **deemuDu** *same as* **deewuDu.**

దేరిన **deerina** *see* **teeru**[1].

దేవకాంత **deewakaanta** *n.* goddess.

దేవగుమ్మడి **deewagummaDi** *n.* kind of pumpkin, *cucurbita maxima.*

దేవత **deewata** *n.* 1 goddess. 2 *pl.* ~ **lu** gods and goddesses, deities.

దేవతావస్త్రాలు **deewataawastraalu** *n.pl.* 1 *lit.* the robes of gods. 2 *slang* nudity.

దేవత్వం **deewatwam** *n.* divinity, godlike quality, godliness.

దేవదారు, దేవదారువు **deewadaaru[wu]** *n.* deodar, Himalayan cedar.

దేవదాసి **deewadaasi** *n.* temple dancing girl.

దేవదుందుభులు **deewadundubhulu** *see* **dundubhi** *sense 2.*

దేవదూత **deewaduuta** *n.* divine messenger, angel.

దేవదేవుడు **deewadeewuDu** *n.* chief of the gods.

దేవనాగరి **deewanaagari** *n.* Devanagari, the script used originally for Sanskrit and now for many Indo-Aryan languages in North India.

దేవమాతృకం **deewamaatṛkam** *n.* land dependent on rainfall, unirrigated land.

దేవయ్య **deewayya** *n.* good-for-nothing person.

దేవర **deewara** *n.* 1 god. 2 king, lord, master.

దేవర్షి **deewarSi** *n.* one of the seven celestial rishis or sages.

దేవలోకం **deewalookam** *n.* Indra's heaven.

దేవళం **deewaLam** *n.* temple.

దేవస్థానం **deewasthaanam** *n.* 1 temple. 2 temple trust board set up to manage the affairs of a temple and administer its endowments.

దేవస్వం **deewaswam** *n.* temple property.

దేవాంగిపిల్లి **deewaangipilli** *n.* slender loris, a nocturnal animal.

దేవాంగులు **deewaangulu** *n. pl.* members of a sect of weavers who worship Siva.

దేవాంతకుడు **deewaantakuDu** *n.* ingenious person (*lit.* person who can even defeat the gods in intelligence).

దేవాదాయ **deewaadaaya** *adj.* relating to endowments; ~ **saakha** endowments department.

దేవాదాయం **deewaadaayam** *n.* 1 endowment made to a temple. 2 income of a temple.

దేవానాంప్రియుడు **deewaanaampriyuDu** *n. colloq.* obstinate or foolish person.

దేవాలయం **deewaalayam** *n.* temple.

దేవి **deewi** *n.* goddess.

దేవిడీ, దేవడీ **deewiDii, deewaDii** *n.* 1 fort gate, palace gate. 2 government office building.

దేవిడీమన్నా **deewiDiimannaa** *n.* banishment from court.

దేవీ **deewii** 1 *term of affection to a woman* darling! 2 *term of respect to a woman* madam!

దేవు **deewu** *v.i. and t.* 1 to fish out, dredge up, take s.g out of water or other liquid. 2 to grope about; **kaDupuloo ceyyi peTTi deewinaTLu ayyindi** he suffered extreme mental anguish or agony (*lit.* it was as if a hand was groping in his intestines).

దేవుకొను **deewukonu** *v.t.* to help o.s. greedily, grab.

దేవుడిగది, దేవుడికొట్టీడు **deewuDigadi, deewuDikoTTiiDu** *n.* puja room, room set aside for worship in a house.

దేవుడు, దేముడు **deewuDu, deemuDu** *n.* god.

దేవురించు **deewurincu** *same as* **deebirincu.**

దేవులాట **deewulaaTa** *n.* 1 entreating, grovelling. 2 searching.

దేవులాడు **deewulaaDu** *v.t.* to search eagerly for, wander about in search of.

దేవేంద్రుడు **deeweendruDu** *n.* name of Indra.

దేవేరి **deeweeri** *n.* 1 queen. 2 lady.

దేశం **deeśam** *n.* 1 country, motherland. 2 land, region.

దేశకాలాలు **deeśakaalaalu** *n. pl.* time and place; **deeśakaala paristhitula prabhaawam** the influence of time, place and circumstance.

దేశదిమ్మరి **deeśadimmari** *same as* **dimmari.**

దేశద్రోహం **deeśadrooham** *n.* treason, sedition.

దేశద్రోహకర **deeśadroohakara** *adj.* treasonable, seditious.

దేశద్రోహి **deeśadroohi** *n.* traitor.

దేశపటం **deeśapaTam** *n.* map.

దేశభక్తి **deeśabhakti** *n.* patriotism.

దేశభక్తుడు **deeśabhaktuDu** *n.* patriot.

దేశభాష **deeśabhaaSa** *n.* **1** regional language. **2** language of a country.

దేశముఖ్ **deeśamukh** *n.* deshmukh, landed estate owner.

దేశవాళీ **deeśawaaLii** *adj.* indigenous, local.

దేశవ్యాప్తంగా **deeśawyaaptangaa** *adv.* countrywide.

దేశస్థుడు **deeśasthuDu** *n.* **1** inhabitant of a country; **Dac~** Dutchman. **2** *dial.* member of a subsect of potters.

దేశాంతరం **deeśaantaram** ***see*** **antaram.**

దేశాటనం **deeśaaTanam** *n.* wandering about in a country.

దేశాయి **deeśaayi** Desai, title given in former times to a hereditary revenue official.

దేశికవిత **deeśikawita** *n.* Telugu poetry composed in pure Telugu words displaying no Sanskrit influence.

దేశికుడు **deeśikuDu** *n. class.* **1** spiritual teacher. **2** person belonging to a country or land. **3** well-travelled person.

దేశిత్వం **deeśitwam** *n.* local traits, local characteristics, local style.

దేశీయ[ం] **deeśiiya[m]** *adj.* of a country, local, indigenous; **deeśiiya wyawahaaraalu** home affairs.

దేశీయుడు **deeśiiyuDu** *n.* countryman; **maa deeśiiyulu** my [fellow] countrymen.

దేశ్య **deeśya** *adj.* of or belonging to a country.

దేశ్యం **deeśyam** *n.* **1** *ling.* native word. **2** pure Telugu word.

దేహ **deeha** *adj.* of the body; **~ baadha tiircukonu** to ease o.s.; **~ śuddhi** *colloq.* beating.

దేహం **deeham** *n.* body.

దేహబలం **deehabalam** *n.* physique.

దేహయాత్ర **deehayaatra** *n.* life; **~ caalincu** to come to the end of o.'s life, die.

దేహి! **deehi!** *interj. class., used in begging, lit.* please give; **~ anu** to beg.

దై - day

దైత **dayta** *n. class.* woman.

దైత్యుడు **daytyuDu** *n. class.* demon.

దైనందిన **daynandina** *adj.* daily, regular.

దైనిక **daynika** *adj.* daily.

దైన్య **daynya** *adj.* low, mean.

దైన్యం **daynyam** *n.* **1** lowness, humility. **2** distress, low-spiritedness.

దైన్యంగా **daynyangaa** *adv.* **1** humbly. **2** pitifully.

దైర్ఘ్యం **dayrghyam** *n.* length.

దైర్ఘ్యవృద్ధి **dayrghyawrddhi** *n. sci.* elongation.

దైవం **daywam** *n.* **1** god, deity. **2** providence, destiny.

దైవగతి **daywagati** *n.* destiny.

దైవజ్ఞుడు **daywajñuDu** *n.* astrologer.

దైవతం **daywatam** *n.* deity.

దైవతుల్య **daywatulya** *adj.* godlike.

దైవత్వం **daywatwam** *n.* divine quality, divinity.

దైవదూషణ **daywaduuSaNa** *n.* blasphemy.

దైవభక్తి **daywabhakti** *n.* devotion to God, piety.

దైవభక్తుడు **daywabhaktuDu** *n.* devotee.

దైవవశమున, దైవవశాత్తు **daywawaśamuna, daywawaśaattu** *adv.* by chance, by an act of providence.

దైవాధీనం **daywaadhiinam** *adj.* in the hands of providence: **aa roojulloo wyawasaayam keewaalam ~ ayuN-Deedi** in those days agriculture used to be simply in the hands of providence.

దైవికం **daywikam** I. *n.* **1** act of providence. **2** accident, chance, coincidence. II. *adj.* **1** divine. **2** accidental, fortuitous.

దైవోపహతుడు **daywoopahatuDu** *n.* ill-fated person.

దైహిక **dayhika** *adj.* bodily.

దొ -do

దొంగ **donga** I. *n.* 1 thief, robber, burglar; **nii iNTa ~ lu doola!** may thieves plunder your house! (*an imprecation*; **~ lu doola** *is a set phrase*); **aayana illu ~ doocina kompalaa unnadi** his house is all in disarray (*lit.* his house is like one that has been plundered by thieves); **~ poddu** midnight (i.e., time when thieves are abroad). 2 rogue, villain, cheat, hypocrite. II. *adj.* 1 stolen; **~ sommu, ~ sottu** stolen property. 2 wicked, sinful, criminal, illicit; **~ ettu weestunnaaDu** he is plotting s.g; **~ laabhaalu** unfair profits; **~ niluwalu** hoarded stocks of goods; **~ saaraayi** illicitly distilled liquor; **~ meepu** illicit grazing of cattle; **~ goDDu** stray cattle. 3 false, deceitful, bogus; **~ nooTLu** forged notes; **~ sanyaasi** bogus sanyasi; **~ lekkalu** false accounts. 4 untrue, unreal, pretended; **~ aaśalu** false hopes; **~ nidra** pretended sleep. 5 hidden, concealed, clandestine, furtive, stealthy; **~ cuupulu** furtive glances; **~ pooTu** hidden blow, stab in the back.

దొంగచాటు **dongacaaTu** *adj.* furtive, clandestine, underhand.

దొంగతనం **dongatanam** *n.* theft, thieving, robbery.

దొంగతనంగా **dongatanangaa** *adv.* secretly, by stealth.

దొంగతొత్తులు **dongatottulu** *n.pl.* thievish or evil-minded persons.

దొంగరవాణా **dongarawaaNaa** *n.* smuggling.

దొంగవేషం **dongaweeSam** *n.* pretence; **nijangaa baadhapaTTindEE? leeka ~ weesEEwaa?** did it really hurt, or were you pretending?

దొంగాట **dongaaTa** *n.* a game like hide and seek.

దొంగాటకం **dongaaTakam** *n.* persistent thieving.

దొంగిలించు, దొంగిలు **dongilincu, dongilu** *v.t.* to steal.

దొండ[పండు] **doNDa[paNDu]** *n.* bryonia fruit.

దొండబలియు **doNDabaliyu** *v.i. dial.* to grow inordinately fat.

దొంతర **dontara** *n.* pile, heap.

దొంతరపొత్తు **dontarapottu** *n. dial.* joint cultivation by ten or more persons.

దొంతి **donti** *n.* heap.

దొందు **dondu**[1] *n. dial.* pair; **~ ku ~** equally matched.

దొందు, దొంద **dondu**[2], **donda** *n. dial.* fat person.

దొగ్గలి, దొగ్గలాకు **doggali, doggalaaku** *n.* broad leaved thorny dock, *amaranthus polygamus.*

దొటదొట, దొడదొడ **doTadoTa, doDadoDa** *onom. adv. sug.* sound of water dripping.

దొడ్డ **doDDa** I. *n.* (*also* **doDDamma**) mother's elder sister. II. *adj.* 1 great, large; **~ kaSTam** great difficulty. 2 good, excellent: **aawiDa bahu ~ maniSi** she is very noble-minded person.

దొడ్డతనం **doDDatanam** *n.* greatness.

దొడ్డయ్య **doDDayya** *n.* 1 **doDDamma's** husband (*see* **doDDa** *sense I*). 2 father's elder brother.

దొడ్డి **doDDi** *n.* 1 back yard. 2 open-air stable for cattle. 3 latrine. 4 excreta.

దొడ్డికాళ్లు **doDDikaaLLu** *n.pl.* bow legs.

దొడ్డిగుమ్మం, దొడ్డివాకిలి **doDDigummam, doDDiwaakili** *n.* back door, entrance via the back yard of a house.

దొడ్డిగోడ **doDDigooDa** *n.* boundary wall at the sides and back of a house.

దొడ్డిదారి **doDDidaari** *n.* back door, back entrance: **doDDidaarlu paTTu** to use back door methods.

దొడ్డు **doDDu** *adj.* 1 fat, stout, big, large. 2 coarse; **~ jalleDa** coarse sieve.

దొన్నె, దొప్ప **donne, doppa** *n.* cup made of leaves.

దొబ్బించుకొను **dobbincukonu** *v.i.* to copulate.

దొబ్బు **dobbu**[1] *n.* 1 stoutness, fatness. 2 *pl.* **~ lu** scolding; **waaNNi ~ lu peTTEEnu** I scolded him.

దొబ్బు **dobbu**[2] I. *n.* push, shove, thrust. II. *v.i.* 1 *in neg. constr.* to be suitable, be possible; **adeem dobbadu** that won't do; *cf.* **kuduru** *sense III. 3.* 2 to go away; **dobbeeyi!** get out! *or* go away! III. *v.t.* 1 to push, shove, thrust, poke. 2 to knock down. 3 *slang* to steal, snatch away. 4 to have sexual intercourse with.

దొబ్బుడాయి **dobbuDaayi** *n.* arrogance, insolence.

దొబ్బుతెగులు **dobbutegulu** *n.* obstinacy.

దొబ్బులాట **dobbulaaTa** *n. slang* embracing.

దొమ్మ **domma** *n.* serious cattle disease affecting the lungs.

దొమ్మర, దొమ్మరి **dommara, dommari** *n.* 1 name of a community of wandering acrobats and rope dancers; **~ samsaaram** a family which keeps on the move. 2 section of the Dommara community who are prostitutes.

దొమ్మరం **dommaram** *n.* mix up, state of confusion.

దొమ్మి **dommi** *n.* 1 swarm, rabble, mob, crowd. 2 affray, scuffle, mêlée.

దొమ్మి కయ్యం, దొమ్మి జగడం **dommi kayyam, dommi jagaDam** *n.* affray.

దొమ్మికూడు **dommikuuDu** *v.i.* to form into a group.

దొమ్మిగా **dommigaa** *adv.* tumultuously, confusedly, noisily.

దొమ్మి చేయు **dommi ceeyu** *v.i.* to make an attack (**-miida,** on).

దొమ్ములాట **dommulaaTa** *n.* fighting, scuffling.

దొమ్ములాడు **dommulaaDu** *v.i.* to fight, scuffle.

దొయ్యి, దోయి **doyyi, dooyi** *n. class.* pair.

దొర **dora** *n.* 1 ruler, lord, master, owner. 2 gentleman. 3 Englishman, westerner. 4 name signifying a community in some hill areas.

దొరకచేసుకొను, దొరికించుకొను **dorakaceesukonu, dorikincukonu** *v.t.* to find (time), create (opportunity); **inta bijiigaa tirugutunnaa roojuu konta wiśraanti dorakajeesukoneewaaDu wraatakootalakoosam** although he was going about so busily, he used to find some leisure time every day for his writings.

దొరకబడు **dorakabaDu** *v.i.* 1 to be found, be available. 2 to be found out, be detected.

దొరచుట్ట **doracuTTa** *n.* cigar.

దొరతనం **doratanam** *n.* 1 government, rule, sovereignty. 2 lordship.

దొరపొగాకు **dorapogaaku** *n.* Virginia tobacco.

దొరసాని **dorasaani** *n.* 1 mistress of a house. 2 Englishwoman, westerner.

దొరుకు, దొరకు **doruku, doraku** *v.i.* 1 to be found, be forthcoming, be available; **mahaasamudramloo timingalaalu ~ taayi** whales are found in the ocean; **neenu dorikEEnani pani ceppEEDu** because he came across me, he gave me work to do. 2 to be got, be obtained, be procured; **karnuuluuloo ataniki udyoogam dorikindi** he got a job at Kurnool. 3 to be detected, be found out, be caught: **ewaDoo donga pooliisuwaaLLaki dorikEEDu** the police have caught some thief.

దొరువు **doruwu** *n.* spring of water near a tank or riverbed.

దొర్లాడు **dorlaaDu** *v.i.* to roll down.

దొర్లించు **dorlincu** *v.t.* 1 to cause to roll. 2 to cause (time) to pass. 3 to shower, scatter freely; **niiLLu ~ koni waccEEDu** he threw some water over himself and came out.

దొర్లు **dorlu**[1] *v.i.* 1 to roll. 2 to turn up, crop up (colloq.), appear; **ii raataloo aneeka ingliiSu maaTalu ~ taayi** many English words turn up in this writing. 3 to happen, occur, befall, take place. 4 (of errors) to creep in. 5 (of talk, conversation) to proceed in a relaxed manner, flit from topic to topic.

దొర్లు **dorlu**[2] *v.i. class.* to die.

దొర్లుడు పుచ్చకాయ **dorluDupuccakaaya** *n.* 1 kind of pumpkin. 2 person who changes sides.

దొలుపు **dolupu** *v.t.* to cause to roll.

దొలుపుడు పురుగు **dolupuDupurugu** *n.* stem-boring insect.

దొల్లు **dollu** *dial. variant of* **dorlu.**

దొసగు **dosagu** *n. class.* 1 mistake, error. 2 trouble, difficulty; **~ labeTTu** to cause trouble.

దో - doo

దోకా, దోఖా **dookaa, dookhaa** *n.* cheating.

దోకి **dooki** *n. dial.* coconut shell ladle for scooping up water.

దోకు **dooku** *v.t.* 1 to scrape or dig slightly so as to loosen the ground for weeding. 2 to scuffle, grub up.

దోకు[డు]పార **dooku[Du] paara** *n.* spade for scuffling or weeding.

దోగాడు **doogaaDu** *v.i.* to crawl (like a baby), go on all fours, go on o.'s hands and knees.

దోచిపెట్టు **doocipeTTu** *v.t.* to hand over, make over, pass on (o.'s possessions); **aame aasti antaa kuutuLLaku doocipeTTindi** she has made over all her property to her daughters.

దోచు[కొను] **doocu[konu]** *v.t.* 1 to rob, plunder. 2 to exploit.

దోని **dooni** *n.* pipe for discharging waste water or rain water.

దోనె **doone** *n.* 1 small boat. 2 trough for discharging water baled from a well into a channel.

దోపిడి, దోపుడు **doopiDi**[1]**, doopuDu** *n.* 1 robbery, plunder, pillage, looting. 2 exploitation.

దోపిడి **doopiDi**[2] *see* **niluwu ~.**

దోపిడిదొంగ, దోపిడికారు, దోపిడిదారు **doopiDidonga, doopiDikaaru, doopiDidaaru** *n.* robber.

దోపు **doopu**[1] *n.* a ceremony performed in a temple.

దోపు **doopu**[2] I. *n.* pushing in, inserting. II. *v.t.* 1 to stick in, insert. 2 to tuck in.

దోపుడు **doopuDu**[1] *same as* **doopiDi**[1].

దోపుడు **doopuDu**[2] *same as* **doopu**[2].

దోబూచి **doobuuci** *n.* word used by a mother in a game to amuse her baby.

దోబూచులాడు **doobuuculaaDu** I. *v.i.* to appear, show itself, be displayed; **aspaSTangaa ~ tunna wiSaadacchaaya** a trace of sorrow faintly showing itself. II. *v.t.* to show, display, reveal.

దోమ **dooma** *n.* 1 mosquito. 2 small black insect which attacks grain crops; **~ musuru** swarm of those insects.

దోమతెర **doomatera** *n.* mosquito net or curtain.

దోయి **dooyi** *same as* **doyyi.**

దోయిలి **dooyili** *same as* **doosili.**

దోర, దవర **doora, dawara** *adj.* 1 half-ripened. 2 reddish, light red. 3 adolescent.

దోరపండు **doorapaNDu** *n.* half-ripened fruit.

దోరవయసు **doorawayasu** n. age of approaching or attaining puberty, teenage.

దోవతి **doowati** *same as* **dhoowati.**

దోవ, త్రోవ, తొవ్వ **doowa, troowa, towwa** *n.* road, path, way.

దోశ **doośa** *same as* **doose.**

దోషం **dooSam** *n.* 1 harm, evil: **dṛSTi ~** harmful effect of the evil eye. 2 error, mistake, fault. 3 blame. 4 guilt. 5 sin, crime, offence. 6 bad point or quality, defect, shortcoming, slur, blemish, imperfection.

దోషి **dooSi** *n.* criminal, guilty person.

దోస[కాయ] **doosa[kaaya]** *n.* 1 cucumber. 2 *dial.* melon.

దోసం doosam *corrupt form of* **dooSam.**

దోసిలి, దోయిలి **doosili, dooyili** *n.* two hands held together to form a cup in a gesture of begging or humility.

దోసిలి ఒగ్గు, దోసిలి పట్టు **doosili oggu, doosilipaTTu** *v.i.* to hold o.'s hands together in **doosili** pose as a mark of humility or in making a request.

దోసె, దోశ **doose, doośa** *n.* dosai, a South Indian pancake.

దోసెడు, దోసిడు **dooseDu, doosiDu** *n.* a measure of quantity, as much as can be held in two hands cupped together.

దోసెల పెనం **doosela penam** *n.* pan for frying dosais.

దోసెలు పోయు **dooselu pooyu** *v.i.* to fry dosais.

దోస్తీ **doostii** *n.* friendship.

దోస్తీగా **doostiigaa** *adv.* in a friendly manner.

దోహదం **doohadam** *n.* 1 physical support. 2 moral support, encouragement. 3 contribution.

దోహదం చేయు, దోహదపడు **doohadam ceeyu, doohadapaDu** *v.i.* 1 to give support. 2 to make a contribution, contribute.

దోహదకారి **doohadakaari** *n.* 1 supporter. 2 contributor.

దౌ - daw

దౌడ **dawDa** *same as* **dawaDa.**

దౌడు **dawDu** *n.* gallop.

దౌడు తీయు **dawDu tiiyu** *v.i.* 1 to run away. 2 to gallop.

దౌత్యం **dawtyam** *n.* diplomacy.

దౌత్యనీతి **dawtyaniiti** *n.* art of diplomacy.

దౌత్యవర్గం **dawtyawargam** *n.* diplomatic corps.

దౌత్యాలయం **dawtyaalayam** *n.* embassy.

దౌరు **dawru** *n. class.* lustre, brilliance.

దౌర్జన్యం **dawrjanyam** *n.* 1 force, violence, hooliganism. 2 misconduct, wickedness, wrongdoing.

దౌర్బల్యం **dawrbalyam** *n.* weakness, feebleness.

దౌర్భాగ్యం **dawrbhaagyam** *n.* misfortune, ill luck, ill-fatedness.

దౌర్భాగ్యుడు **dawrbhaagyuDu** *n.* penniless wretch.

దౌష్ట్యం **dawSTyam** *n.* 1 evil, wickedness. 2 evil deed.

దౌలత్తు **dawlattu** *n.* wealth.

దౌహిత్రి **dawhitri** *n. class.* granddaughter, daughter's daughter.

దౌహిత్రుడు **dawhitruDu** *n. class.* grandson, daughter's son.

ద్యు to ద్ర - dyu to dra

ద్యుతి **dyuti** *n. class.* light, brightness.

ద్యూతం **dyuutam** *n. class.* gambling.

ద్యోతకం **dyootakam** *adj.* clearly expressed, visible, evident.

ద్రవం **drawam** *n.* liquid, fluid.

ద్రవగతిశాస్త్రం **drawagatiśaastram** *n.* (science of) hydrodynamics.

ద్రవయంత్రశాస్త్రం **drawayantraśaastram** *n.* (science of) hydraulics.

ద్రవాభిసరణ **drawaabhisaraNa** *n. bot.* osmosis.

ద్రవించు **drawincu** *v.i.* 1 to melt, liquefy. 2 to seep out, ooze, trickle.

ద్రవిడ, ద్రావిడ **drawiDa, draawiDa** *adj.* Dravidian.

ద్రవీకరణం **drawiikaraNam** *n. chem.* liquefaction.

ద్రవీభవనం **drawiibhawanam** *n. sci.* 1 condensation. 2 melting.

ద్రవీభవనస్థానం **drawiibhawana sthaanam** *n.* sci. melting point.

ద్రవీభూత **drawiibhuuta** *adj.* melted.

ద్రవ్య **drawya** *adj.* consisting of or in the form of money or currency, monetary, financial; ~ **sahaayam** financial help; ~ **widhaanam** monetary policy.

ద్రవ్యం **drawyam** *n.* 1 matter, material, stuff, substance; **nirmaaNa** ~ construction material. 2 thing, object. 3 wealth, money. 4 currency.

ద్రవ్యత్వం **drawyatwam** *n.* liquidity.

ద్రవ్యరాశి **drawyaraaśi** *n. phys.* mass.

ద్రవ్యవేగం **drawyaweegam** *n. phys.* momentum.

ద్రవ్యాత్మక **drawyaatmaka** *adj. sci.* material.

ద్రవ్యోల్బణం **drawyoolbaNam** *n. econ.* inflation

ద్రష్ట **draSTa** *n.* 1 spectator, onlooker. 2 visionary.

ద్రష్టవ్య **draSTawya** *adj.* 1 perceptible, visible. 2 fit to be seen.

ద్రా to ద్వా - draa to dwaa

ద్రాక్ష **draakSa** *n.* **1** vine. **2** grape; ~ **gutti** bunch of grapes.

ద్రాక్షతీగ, ద్రాక్షవల్లి **draakSatiiga, draakSawalli** *n.* vine.

ద్రాక్షపాకం **draakSapaakam** *n.* style of poetry which is mellifluous and lucid.

ద్రాక్షరసం **draakSarasam** *n.* wine.

ద్రాక్షారిష్ట **draakSaariSTa** *n.* Ayurvedic tonic to promote vigour and strength.

ద్రావం **draawam** *n. chem.* solute.

ద్రావకం **draawakam** *n. chem.* solvent.

ద్రావణం **draawaNam** *n.* **1** *chem.* solution. **2** liquid.

ద్రావణీయ **draawaNiiya** *adj. chem.* soluble.

ద్రావిడ **draawiDa** *same as* **drawiDa.**

ద్రుతం **drutam** I. *n. gram.* the consonant *n* in Telugu script. II. *adj. class.* quick.

ద్రుతి **druti** *n. class.* **1** speed. **2** (in music) tempo.

ద్రుమం **drumam** *n. class.* tree.

ద్రోణి **drooNi** *n.* **1** *class.* basin. **2** *sci.* trough.

ద్రోహం **drooham** *n.* treachery, perfidy, betrayal.

ద్రోహంచేయు **drooham ceeyu** *v.t.* to commit treachery, betray.

ద్రోహచింతన **droohacintana** *n.* premeditated malice.

ద్రోహి **droohi** *n.* traitor, betrayer.

ద్వంద్వం **dwandwam** *n.* pair, couple.

ద్వంద్వపరిపాలన **dwandwaparipaalana** *n.* dyarchy.

ద్వంద్వయుద్ధం **dwandwayuddham** *n.* duel, single combat.

ద్వంద్వసమాసం **dwandwa samaasam** *n. ling.* copulative compound.

ద్వయం **dwayam** *n.* pair, couple.

ద్వాదశం **dwaadaśam** *n.* twelve.

ద్వాదశి **dwaadaśi** *n.* twelfth day of a lunar fortnight.

ద్వాపరం, ద్వాపర యుగం **dwaaparam, dwaapara yugam** *n.* the mythological third or bronze age of the universe.

ద్వారం **dwaaram** *n.* **1** door, entrance, gate. **2** *sci.* opening, vent.

ద్వారకం **dwaarakam** *n. biol.* aperture.

ద్వారపాలకుడు **dwaarapaalakuDu** *n.* doorkeeper.

ద్వారబంధం **dwaarabandham** *n.* door frame, doorway.

ద్వారా **dwaaraa** *p.p.* **1** through. **2** by means of.

ద్వి - dwi

ద్విఅక్షీయ **dwiákSiiya** *adj. sci.* biaxial.

ద్వికం **dwikam** *n.* doublet.

ద్వికుంభాకార **dwikumbhaakaara** *adj. sci.* biconvex.

ద్విగతిచర్య **dwigaticarya** *n. chem.* reversible reaction.

ద్విగుణనం **dwiguNanam** *n.* duplication.

ద్విగుణాత్మక **dwiguNaatmaka** *adj.* binary.

ద్విగుణిత, ద్విగుణీకృత **dwiguNita, dwinguNiikṛta** *adj.* doubled.

ద్విగుసమాసం **dwigusamaasam** *n. ling.* numerative compound.

ద్విజ **dwija** *adj. class.* twice-born, brahman.

ద్విజుడు **dwijuDu** *n. class.* brahman.

ద్వితీయ **dwitiiya** *adj.* second.

ద్వితీయావిభక్తి **dwitiiyaa wibhakti** *n. gram.* accusative case.

ద్విత్వ **dwitwa** *adj. ling.* double, reduplicated, geminate.

ద్విదళబీజం **dwidaLabiijam** *n. bot.* dicotyledon.

ద్విధా **dwidhaa** *adj.* binary.

ద్విధాకరించు **dwidhaakarincu** *v.t.* to bifurcate.

ద్వినాభి **dwinaabhi** *adj. sci.* bifocal.

ద్విపద **dwipada** *n.* **1** couplet of verses. **2** kind of poetic metre.

ద్విపార్శ్వక **dwipaarśwaka** *adj.* bilateral.

ద్విపుటాకార **dwipuTaakaara** *adj. sci.* biconcave.

ద్విభాజనం **dwibhaajanam** *n.* dichotomy.

ద్విభాషాభాషి **dwibhaaSaabhaaSi** I. *n.* bilingual person. II. *adj.* bilingual.

ద్విమితీయ **dwimitiiya** *adj.* two-dimensional.

ద్విరుక్త **dwirukta** *adj. ling.* double, reduplicated, geminated.

ద్విలింగిక **dwilingika** *adj.* bisexual.

ద్వివచనం **dwiwacanam** *n. gram.* dual number.

ద్విపర్ణ సమీకరణం **dwiwarNa samiikaraNam** *n. maths.* simultaneous equation.

ద్వివార్షిక **dwiwaarSika** *adj.* biennial.

ద్వివిధ **dwiwidha** *adj.* **1** of two kinds. **2** divided into two.

ద్విశతవార్షికం **dwiśatawaarSikam** *n.* bicentenary.

ద్విసమభుజత్రికోణం **dwisambhuja trikooNam** *n. maths* isoceles triangle.

ద్వీ to ద్వ్య - dwii to dwya

ద్వీపం **dwiipam** *n.* island.

ద్వీపకల్పం **dwiipakalpam** *n.* peninsula.

ద్వీపాంతరవాస శిక్ష **dwiipaantarawaasa śikSa** *n.* sentence of transportation.

ద్వేషం, ద్వేషభావం **dweeSam, dweeSabhaawam** *n.* enmity, hate, hatred, malice.

ద్వేషించు **dweeSincu** *v.t.* to hate.

ద్వైతం **dwaytam** *n.* **1** dualism. **2** duality.

ద్వైతి **dwayti** *n.* one who believes in dualism.

ద్వైధీభావం **dwaydhiibhaawam** *n.* dual nature.

ద్వైమాతృక **dwaymaatruka** *adj.* (of land) depending both on rain and irrigation.

ద్వైవార **dwaywaara** *adj.* biweekly, fortnightly.

ద్వైవిధ్యం **dwaywidhyam** *n.* dichotomy.

ద్వ్యర్థం **dwyartham** *n.* double meaning.

ద్వ్యర్థి, ద్వ్యార్థి **dwyarthi, dwyaarthi** *adj.* having a double meaning.

ధ - dha

ధగధగ **dhagadhaga** *onom. adv. sug.* burning or gleaming.

ధగిడీ **dhagiDii** *n.* mean or wicked person, bad character.

ధణధణ **dhaNadhaNa** *onom. adv. sug.* sound of rattling, clattering, beating of drums and such other things.

ధణుతెగిరిపోవు **dhaNutegiripoowu** *v.i. with dative* **1** to be unable to withstand; **musalaayanaki koopam wacci samskrtamloo tiTLu lankincukonee sariki iNTillipaadikii dhaNutegiri pooyindi** the household was cowed when the old man lost his temper and began to swear in Sanskrit. **2** to be thrilled, be amazed; **waaDu burrakatha cebutuu pay sthaayiloo oka raagam wisireesariki dhaNutegiripooyindi anukoo** I tell you I was thrilled when he threw in a raga in the classical style during his burrakatha recitation.

ధణేల్మని **dhaNeelmani** *adv.* with a bang.

ధన **dhana** *adj. maths. sci.* positive.

ధనం **dhanam** *n.* money, wealth, riches.

ధనధాన్యాలు **dhanadhaanyaalu** *n.pl., lit.* money and crops, i.e., prosperity, wealth.

ధనధ్రువం, ధనాగ్రం **dhanadhruwam, dhanaagram** *n. sci.* anode.

ధనమదం **dhanamadam** *n.* pride of wealth.

ధనరాసులు **dhanaraasulu** *n.pl., lit.* heaps of money, i.e., wealth, riches.

ధనరు **dhanaru** *n.* influence, effect.

ధనవంతుడు, ధనికుడు **dhanawantuDu, dhanikuDu** *n.* wealthy person.

ధన సంజ్ఞ **dhana sanjña** *n. maths. sci.* plus sign, positive sign.

ధనసంబంధ **dhanasambandha** *adj.* pecuniary.

ధనసహాయం **dhanasahaayam** *n.* financial help.

ధనసుడి **dhanasuDi** *n.* auspicious curl of hair on a bull's hump.

ధనస్వామ్యం, ధనికస్వామ్యం **dhanaswaamyam, dhanikaswaamyam** *n.* plutocracy.

ధనాగారం **dhanaagaaram** *n.* treasury.

ధనాత్మక **dhanaatmaka** *adj. maths. sci.* positive.

ధనాధిపతి **dhanaadhipati** *n.* **1** wealthy person. **2** *astrol.* a name of Kubera, God of wealth.

ధనాభావ **dhanaabhaawa** *adj.* lacking in resources, impecunious.

ధనార్జన **dhanaarjana** *n.* acquisition of wealth through earning money.

ధనాసరి **dhanaasari** *n.* **1** name of a raga. **2** woman. **3** variety of **goonguura** plant.

ధనిక వర్గాధిపత్యం **dhanikawargaadhipatyam** *n. polit.* plutocracy.

ధనియాలు **dhaniyaalu** *n. pl.* coriander seeds.

ధనిష్ఠ **dhaniSTa** *n. astrol.* twenty-third lunar mansion.

ధనుర్మాసం **dhanurmaasam** *n.* name of the solar month (December-January) when the sun is in the sign of Sagittarius.

ధనుర్ముమ్వా ఉండ **dhanurmuwwaa uNDa** *n. dial.* cake in the shape of a ball, made of puffed rice, coconut and sugar.

ధనుర్వాతం, ధనుర్వాయి **dhanurwaatam, dhanurwaayi** *n.* tetanus.

ధనుర్వేదం **dhanurweedam** *n. class.* **1** science of archery. **2** name of the subsidiary Veda in which the science of archery is taught.

ధనుస్సు **dhanussu** *n.* **1** bow. **2** *astrol.* Sagittarius.

ధన్నుమని **dhannumani** *adv.* with a bang.

ధన్య **dhanya** *adj.* fortunate, lucky, blessed, auspicious.

ధన్యత **dhanyata** *n.* good fortune, blessedness.

ధన్యవాదాలు **dhanyawaadaalu** I. *n. pl.* (expression of) thanks. II. *minor sentence* thank you!

ధన్యుడు **dhanyuDu** *n.* blessed or fortunate person.

ధన్యోస్మి, ధన్యోహం **dhanyóosmi, dhanyooham** *interj.* I am blessed! (gen. said sarcastically).

ధన్వంతరి **dhanwantari** *n.* **1** the divine physcian in mythology. **2** Ayurvedic physician.

ధబధబ **dhabadhaba** *onom. adv. sug.* sound of pattering footsteps.

ధబేల్మని **dhabeelmani** *adv.* with a crash.

ధమని **dhamani** *n.* **1** *med.* artery. **2** bellows.

ధమనిక **dhamanika** *n. med.* arteriole.

ధర **dhara**[1] *n.* **1** price, cost. **2** rate, valuation.

ధర **dhara**[2] *n. class.* the earth, the world.

ధరణం **dharaNam**[1] *n.* holding, possessing.

ధరణం **dharaNam**[2] *n.* an ancient coin.

ధరణి **dharaNi** *n. class.* the earth, the world.

ధరణీధరం **dharaNiidharam** *n. class.* mountain.

ధరవరలు **dharawaralu** *n.pl.* prices, rates.

ధరాధిపతి **dharaadhipati** *n.*lord of the earth, emperor.

ధరావత్తు **dharaawattu** *same as* **daraawattu.**

ధరించు **dharincu** *v.t.* **1** to put on, wear (clothes, ornaments, weapons). **2** to assume (name); **3 garbham~** to become pregnant. **4** *theat.* **paatra~** to play a part, act a part.

ధరిత్రి **dharitri** *n. class.* the earth.

ధర్నాచేయు **dharnaaceeyu** *v.i.* **1** to sit fasting on s.o.'s doorstep in order to induce him to comply with a demand. **2** to conduct a sit-down strike.

ధర్మ **dharma** *adjvl. prefix signifying* just, righteous, virtuous; **~wiiruDu** righteous hero.

ధర్మం **dharmam** *n.* **1** duty. **2** virtue, morality, propriety, rectitude. **3** good deeds, charitableness. **4** justice, right; **naalugu paadaalamiida~naDustunnappuDu** *lit.* when justice was walking on four feet, *i.e.* when justice reigned supreme *or* during the golden age. **5** law, rule, precept, guiding principle. **6** code of conduct, custom, usage or practice sanctioned by religion, tradition or society. **7** nature, property, characteristic feature; **yuga~** character *or* spirit of the age: **manoodharmaalu** behavioural features. **8** function; **deeha dharmaśastram** science of the functions of the body, physiology: *see* **kaala~**

ధర్మకర్త **dharmakarta** *n.* trustee.

ధర్మకర్తృత్వం **dharmakartrtwam** *n.* trusteeship.

ధర్మక్షేత్రం **dharmakSeetram** *n.* India, the land where religious duties are performed.

ధర్మచింతన **dharmacintana** *n.* right-mindedness.

ధర్మదర్శనం **dharmadarśanam** *n.* visit to a temple free of payment of a fee.

ధర్మదానం **dharmadaanam** *n.* charity.

ధర్మనిధి **dharmanidhi** *n.* charitable trust.

ధర్మనిష్ఠ **dharmaniSTha** *n.* piety.

ధర్మపత్ని **dharmapatni** *n.* legally married wife.

ధర్మపన్నాలు చెప్పు **dharmapannaalu ceppu** *v.i.* to preach morality.

ధర్మపిండం **dharmapiNDam** *n.* food earned by begging.

ధర్మపిత **dharmapita** *n.* god-father.

ధర్మబాధ్యత **dharmabaadhyata** *n.* legal responsibility or obligation.

ధర్మబోధ **dharmaboodha** *n.* preaching, moralising.

ధర్మభ్రష్ట **dharmabhraSTa** *n. and adj.* renegade.

ధర్మమా అని **dharmamaa ani** *see* **dharmaana.**

ధర్మమాత **dharmamaata** *n.* god-mother.

ధర్మరాజు **dharmaraaju** *n.* **1** just king. **2** noble, pious and dutiful person. **3** name of the eldest of the Pandavas in the Mahabharata.

ధర్మవిధి **dharmawidhi** *n.* legal duty or obligation.

ధర్మశాస్త్రం **dharmaśaastram** *n.* **1** the science of law, jurisprudence. **2** code of law. **3 manu~** ancient Hindu law, the law of Manu.

ధర్మసందేహం **dharmasandeeham** *n. colloq.* **1** small doubt or suspicion. **2** doubt concerning rectitude or propriety.

ధర్మసత్రం, ధర్మశాల **dharmasatram, dharmaśaala** *n.* charitable home for the poor, choultry.

ధర్మసమ్మతం **dharmasammatam** *adj.* just, fair (*lit.* in accordance with natural justice and propriety).

ధర్మసూక్ష్మం **dharmasuukSmam** *n.* fine point of law.

ధర్మసూత్రం **dharmasuutram** *n.* **1** moral precept. **2** legal principle.

ధర్మాత్ముడు **dharmaatmuDu** *n.* charitable, liberal and virtuous person.

ధర్మాదాయం **dharmaadaayam** *n.* endowment of land made for a charitable purpose.

ధర్మాదాయ సంస్థ **dharmaadaaya samstha** *n.* charitable institution.

ధర్మాన, ధర్మమా అని **dharmaana, dharmamaa ani** *advbl. particle, colloq.* by the grace of, by the kindness of, thanks to; **atani~ meem kSeemangaa iNTiki waccEEm** thanks to him we got home safely.

ధర్మాభినివేశం **dharmaabhiniweeśam** *n.* zeal or fervour for rectitude.

ధర్మాసనం **dharmaasanam** *n.* judge's seat, judgement seat.

ధర్మి **dharmi** *adj.* pious, virtuous; **mata~** obeying the precepts of religion.

ధర్మిష్ఠి **dharmiSThi** *n.* pious, virtuous and charitable person.

ధర్మోపదేశం **dharmoopadeeśam** *n.* sermon.

ధవళ **dhawaLa** *adj.* **1** white. **2** pure, clear.

ధవుడు **dhawuDu** *n. class.* master, lord, husband.

ధా - dhaa

ధాంధూంచేయు **dhaamdhuumceeyu** *v.i.* to act violently or outrageously.

ధాటి, దాటి **dhaaTi, daaTi** *n.* **1** force, energy, vigour. **2** onslaught.

ధాటిగా **dhaaTigaa** *adv.* forcefully, *cf.* **eeka~**.

ధాత **dhaata** *n.* **1** creator. **2** name of the tenth year of the Hindu cycle of sixty years; **~karuwu** severe famine which occurred in that year during the 19th century.

ధాతుమలం **dhaatumalam** *n. chem.* slag.

ధాతుమిశ్రం **dhaatumiśram** *n. chem.* alloy.

ధాతురసాయనశాస్త్రం **dhaaturasaayanaśaastram** *n.* metallurgical chemistry.

ధాతువు **dhaatuwu** *n.* **1** essence. **2** mineral. **3** *gram.* root. **4** *chem.* element. **5** a constituent element of the body.

ధాతుసాధనశాస్త్రం **dhaatusaadhanaśaastram** *n.* metallurgy.

ధాత్రి **dhaatri** *n. class.* the earth.

ధాన్యం **dhaanyam** *n.* grain, esp. paddy or rice in the husk; **nawadhaanyaalu** the nine kinds of grain used in certain auspicious ceremonies.

ధాన్యంకొట్టు **dhaanyamkoTTu** *n.* storage room for grain.

ధాన్యంవర **dhaanyamwara** *n.* large basket for storing grain.

ధాన్యాగారం, ధాన్యకోశం **dhaanyaagaaram, dhaanyakoośam** *n.* granary.

ధామం **dhaamam** *n. class.* house, abode, place.

ధార **dhaara** *n.* **1** stream, current, flow, jet. **2** cutting edge of a knife or other sharp instrument.

ధారకం **dhaarakam** *same as* **daarakam.**

ధారణ[ం] **dhaaraNa[m]** *n.* **1** maintaining, keeping, retention. **2** putting on, wearing. **3** (*also* **dhaaraNaśakti**) concentration. **4** (*also* **dhaaraNaśakti**) power of retaining in o.'s memory, retentivity.

ధారణశీల **dhaaraNaśiila** *adj.* retentive.

ధారణావధి **dhaaraNaawadhi** *n.* [period of] tenure.

ధారపోయు **dhaarapooyu** *v.t.* **1** to bestow as a solemn gift. **2 praaNaalu~** to sacrifice or give up o.'s life.

ధారాచాలనం **dhaaraacaalanam** *n.* jet propulsion.

ధారాదత్తం **dhaaraadattam** *n.* something given ceremonially, solemn gift.

ధారాధరం **dhaaraadharam** *n. class.* cloud.

ధారానాళిక **dhaaraanaaLika** *n. sci.* jet.

ధారాళం **dhaaraaLam** *adj.* free, fluent, unrestrained, plentiful.

ధారాళంగా **dhaaraaLangaa** *adv.* plentifully.

ధారావాహికంగా **dhaaraawaahikangaa** *adv.* (of publication, etc.) in serial form.

ధారాశుద్ధి **dhaaraaśuddhi** *n.* clarity of thought and expression.

ధారి, ధారుడు **dhaari, dhaaruDu** *n. suffix* person who bears, wears or carries.

ధార్మిక **dhaarmika** I. *adj.* moral, righteous, virtuous. II. *adjvl. suffix indicating possession of a certain nature or* character **reeDiyoo~** radio-active.

ధార్మిక చింతన **dhaarmika cintana** *n.* piety.

ధార్మికుడు **dhaarmikuDu** *n.* righteous person.

ధావనం **dhaawanam** *n. class.* washing, scrubbing.

ధావళీ **dhaawaLii** *same as* **daawaLii.**

ధాష్టీకం **dhaaSTiikam** *n.* browbeating, domineering.

ధి, ధీ - dhi, dhii

ధిక్కరించు **dhikkarincu** *v.t.* **1** to flout, treat with contempt, scorn. **2** to disregard, disobey, defy.

ధిక్కారం **dhikkaaram** *n.* **1** contempt, scorn. **2** defiance.

ధిమిధిమి **dhimidhimi** *onom. adv. sug.* sound of a dancer's movements on the stage: **tera tolagagaanee ~naaTyam ceestuu rangam miidiki waccindi** as soon as the curtain was raised she came on to the stage dancing with a sound of tinkling bells.

ధిషణ **dhiSaNa** *n. class.* **1** wisdom, understanding. **2** intellect.

ధీ **dhii** *n.* **1** understanding. **2** intellect.

ధీమంతుడు **dhiimantuDu** *n.* intelligent person, intellectual.

ధీమా **dhiimaa** *n.* **1** courage, boldness. **2** confidence, assurance, feeling of certainty.

ధీమాగా **dhiimaagaa** *adv.* **1** boldly. **2** confidently, with assurance.

ధీర **dhiira** *adj.* brave, steadfast.

ధీరత్వం, ధీరత **dhiiratwam, dhiirata** *n.* courage, bravery, steadfastness.

ధీరుడు **dhiiruDu** *n.* hero, brave person.

ధీరోదాత్తత **dhiiroodaattata** *n.* heroism.

ధీశక్తి **dhiiśakti** *n.* intellectual power, intelligence.

ధీశాలి **dhiiśaali** *n.* intellectual.

ధు to ధౌ - dhu to dhaw

ధుత్తరికే!, ధుత్తెరికే! **dhuttarikee!, dhutterikee!** *interj.* for shame!

ధుని **dhuni** *n. class.* river, stream.

ధుమధుమలాడు **dhumadhumalaaDu** *v.i.* to be extremely angry.

ధురంధరుడు **dhurandharuDu** *second part of a n. compound, lit.* one who bears a burden, *hence* an able and talented person; **raajaniiti~** shrewd and experienced politician.

ధురీణుడు **dhuriiNuDu** *second part of a n. compound. lit.* one who bears a burden, *hence* an able and talented person; **widyaa~** educated person.

ధూపం **dhuupam** *n.* incense.

ధూమం **dhuumam** *n.* **1** smoke. **2** fume.

ధూమకేతువు **dhuumakeetuwu** *n.* comet.

ధూమపానం **dhuumapaanam** *n.* smoking (cigarettes, etc.)

ధూర్త **dhuurta** *adj.* outrageous, mischievous, tricky, wily; **~goopaaluDu** Krishna the trickster.

ధూర్తత్వం **dhuurtatwam** *n.* trickery, knavishness.

ధూర్తుడు **dhuurtuDu** *n.* violent or mischievous person, deceiver.

ధూళి, దూళి **dhuuLi, duuLi** *n.* dust, dirt.

ధూళిదూసరం **dhuuLiduusaram** *n.* dust and grime.

ధూసరం **dhuusaram** *n.* ash colour, grey.

ధూసరద్రవ్యం **dhuusaradrawyam** *n. med., zool.* greyish tissue of the brain and spinal cord.

ధృతరాష్ట్రుడు **dhṛtaraaSTruDu** *n.* name of a blind king in the Mahabharata, father of the Kauravas.

ధేనువు **dheenuwu** *n. class.* milch cow.

ధైర్యం **dhayryam** *n.* **1** courage, valour, fortitude, bravery. **2** confidence.

ధైర్యంగా **dhayryangaa** *adv.* **1** bravely, valiantly. **2** confidently.

ధైర్యంచెప్పు **dhayryam ceppu** *v.i.* **1** to reassure, encourage. **2** to bid s.o. to be brave.

ధైర్యశాలి, ధైర్యవంతుడు **dhayryaśaali, dhayryawantuDu** *n.* brave or valiant person.

ధైర్యసాహసాలు **dhayryasaahasaalu** *n.pl.* **1** bold and daring deeds. **2** [spirit of] enterprise.

ధోరణి **dhooraNi** *n.* **1** manner, style. **2** mood, disposition. **3** trend, tendency. **4** trace, streak, strain. **5** series, succession, continuity; **ewari awasaraalu elaa unnaa kaalam tana ~loo taanu naDustuu uNTundi** whatever the needs of any persons may be, time continues on its own set course.

ధోవతి, దోవతి **dhoowati, doowati** *n.* dhoti, cloth worn by a man round the waist.

ధౌత **dhawta** *adj. class.* washed and clean.

ధౌతవస్త్రధారి **dhawtawastradhaari** *n. class.* person who wears washed and clean clothes.

ధౌర్త్యం **dhawrtyam** *n.* violent behaviour.

ధ్యా to ధ్వా - dhyaa to dhwaa

ధ్యానం **dhyaanam** *n.* 1 meditation, contemplation. 2 gaze, attention, concentration.

ధ్యానించు **dhyaanincu** *v.t.* to meditate on, think of, reflect on.

ధ్యాస **dhyaasa** *n.* 1 attention, concentration. 2 inclination, desire, yearning.

ధ్యేయం **dhyeeyam** *n.* goal, object, aim.

ధ్రువ **dhruwa** *adj.* 1 steady, firm. 2 (*also* **dhruwiiya**) *sci.* polar.

ధ్రువం **dhruwam** *n.* magnetic pole; **uttara~** north pole.

ధ్రువజ్యోతి **dhruwajyooti** *n.* aurora.

ధ్రువనం చేయు **dhruwanam ceeyu** *v.t. sci.* to polarise.

ధ్రువనక్షత్రం **dhruwanakSatram** *n.* pole star.

ధ్రువపత్రం **dhruwapatram** *n.* certificate, letter of confirmation.

ధ్రువపరచు **dhruwaparacu** *v.t.* 1 to establish, settle. 2 to confirm, affirm.

ధ్రువపరచుకొను **dhruwaparacukonu** *v.t.* to verify.

ధ్రువిత **dhruwita** *adj. sci.* polarised.

ధ్రువీకరణ **dhruwiikaraNa** *n.* establishing, confirmation, certification, affirmation, ratification.

ధ్రువీకరణం **dhruwiikaraNam** *n. phys.* polarisation.

ధ్రువీకరించు **dhruwiikarincu** *v.t.* to certify (after testing), confirm (minutes of meeting), affirm.

ధ్రువుడు **dhruwuDu** *n.* name of a child sage in mythology who became the pole star.

ధ్వంసం **dhwamsam** *n.* ruin, destruction, demolition, havoc.

ధ్వంసం అవు **dhwamsam awu** *v.i.* to be ruined, be destroyed, be demolished.

ధ్వంసం చేయు **dhawamsam ceeyu** *v.t.* to ruin, destroy, demolish.

ధ్వంసించు **dhwamsincu** *v.t. class.* to destroy.

ధ్వజం **dhwajam** *adj.* flag, banner.

ధ్వజం ఎత్తు **dhwajam ettu** *v.i., lit.* to raise a flag, *hence* (i) *class.* to invade, attack with an army; (ii) *colloq.* to make a personal attack; **naamiida dhwajam ettEEDu** he attacked me.

ధ్వజస్తంభం **dhwajastambham** *n.* 1 flagstaff. 2 brass pillar representing a flagstaff erected in front of a temple.

ధ్వని **dhwani** *n.* 1 sound. 2 voice. 3 suggested or intended meaning, implication.

ధ్వనించు **dhwanincu** *v.i. and t.* 1 to sound, produce a sound. 2 to echo, resound. 3 (of a meaning) to be suggested or implied.

ధ్వనిక **dhwanika** *adj. phys.* acoustic.

ధ్వనితరంగశాస్త్రం **dhwanitarangaśaastram** *n.* acoustics.

ధ్వనినిరోధక **dhwaniniroodhaka** *adj.* soundproof.

ధ్వనిలిపి **dhwanilipi** *n.* phonetic writing.

ధ్వనివిధేయ **dhwaniwidheeya** *adj.* phonetic; **~ leekhanam** phonetic writing.

ధ్వనిశాస్త్రం **dhwaniśaastram** *n.* phonetics.

ధ్వన్యనుకరణం **dhwanyanukaraNam** *n. ling.* onomatopoeia.

ధ్వానం **dhwaanam** *n.* sound, noise.

న - na

న **na** *p.p.* in, at, on; **aayana naayakatwaana** under his leadership; **balawantaana** by force.

నంగనాచి **nanganaaci** *n.* 1 hypocrite. 2 person who attempts to hide the commission of a daring act; **abbaayi dongatanam ceesi ~kaburlu ceptunnaaDu** the boy has committed a theft but is pretending to be innocent.

నంగి **nangi** *adj.* (of words) 1 unclear (in sound), vague, imprecise (in meaning). 2 spoken through the nose, nasal sounding.

నంగితనం **nangitanam** *n.* pretence of innocence.

నంగిరి **nangiri** *n.* 1 timidity. 2 stupidity.

నంగిరిపింగిరివాడు **nangiripingiriwaaDu** *n.* person who cannot decide what to say or do, weakminded person.

నంగిరోడు **nangirooDu** *v.i.* to be shy or hesitant.

నంజ **nanja** *n.* irrigated land.

నంజు **nanju** *v.t.* to nibble, eat by small morsels, eat as a relish to a principal dish.

నంజుకురుపు **nanjukurupu** *n.* gum boil.

నంజుడుముక్క **nanjuDumukka** *n.* piece of mutton.

నంద **nanda** *n.* large jar for storing grain.

నందన **nandana** *n.* twenty-sixth year of the Hindu cycle of sixty years.

నందనం **nandanam** *class.* garden.

నందనవనం **nandanawanam** *n.* 1 temple garden. 2 Indra's pleasure garden.

నందనోద్యానం **nandanoodyaanam** *n.* Indra's pleasure garden.

నంది **nandi** *n.* the bull on which Siva rides; **~ ni pandi ceeyu** to declare that black is white (i.e., to say s.g that is a complete travesty of the truth; *lit.* to make a bull into a pig).

నందివర్ధనం **nandiwardhanam** *n.* kind of white flower used as a remedy to give relief to the eyes.

నకనకలాడు **nakanakalaaDu** *v.i.* 1 to be very hungry. 2 to be angry.

నకలు **nakalu** I. *n.* copy, replica, facsimile, duplicate; **lekka cuuci ~ tayaaru ceesEEDu** he looked at the account and prepared a duplicate. II. *adj.* counterfeit, imitation.

నకారం **nakaaram** *n.* the letter *n* in Telugu script.

నకారప్రయోగం **nakaaraprayoogam** *n.* 1 use of the sing. pron. **niiwu/nuwwu** when addressing a person. 2 refusing, saying 'no'; **neenu Dabbu aDigitee aayana ~ ceesEEDu** when I asked him for money, he refused.

నకిలీ **nakilii** *adj.* 1 artificial. 2 imitation, bogus, spurious, false, fake, counterfeit; **~ nooTLu cuusi moosapookaNDi** do not be deceived by the sight of counterfeit notes.

నకులం **nakulam** *n. class.* mongoose.

నక్క **nakka** *n.* jackal; **~nu tokki waccu** *lit.* to tread on a jackal (and escape without harm), i.e., to have a stroke of luck.

నక్కజిత్తులు **nakkajittulu** *n. pl.* crafty tricks.

నక్కదోస **nakkadoosa** *n.* short round cucumber sour in taste, *cucumis sp.*

నక్కబొక్క **nakkabokka** *n. colloq.* mistake, defect, omission.

నక్కలోళ్లు **nakkalooLLu** *n.pl.* tribe of wandering beggars.

నక్కవినయం **nakkawinayam** *n.* feigned or insincere humility.

నక్కిళ్లు **nakkiLLu** *n.pl.* joints of the jaws.

నక్కు **nakku**[1] I. *n.* 1 ploughshare. 2 *dial.* miser. II. *v.i.* to lurk, prowl, walk furtively, creep, crouch, hide o.s.

నక్కు **nakku**[2] *n.* chisel for chipping and boring stone.

నక్కేరు **nakkeeru** *n. cardia dichotoma,* a tree.

నక్తం **naktam** *n.* 1 *class.* night. 2 *same as* **nattam.**

నక్షత్రం **nakSatram** *n.* 1 star. 2 *astrol.* constellation, asterism. 3 *astrol.* lunar mansion. 4 (in printing) asterisk. 5 *pl.* **nakSatraalu** kind of firework.

నక్షత్రకుడు **nakSatrakuDu** *n.* 1 name of a mythological character who demanded repayment of debt. 2 *colloq.* person who pesters for anything.

నక్షత్రమండలం **nakSatramaNDalam** *n.* constellation.

నక్షత్రాకార **nakSatraakaara** *adj. bot.* stellate.

నక్షత్రాభం **nakSatraabham** *n. astron.* asteroid.

నఖం **nakham** *n. class.* 1 nail (of finger or toe). 2 claw, talon.

నఖక్షతం **nakhakSatam** *n.* nip made by a nail.

నఖముఖాల **nakhamukhaala** *adv.* in all directions.

నఖశిఖపర్యంతం **nakhaśikha paryantam** *adv.* all over, from top to toe (*lit.* from the nails of the toes to the hair of the head).

నగ **naga** *n.* jewel, ornament; *pl.* **~lu** jewellery.

నగం **nagam** *n. class.* hill, mountain.

నగదు **nagadu** *n.* cash, ready money.

నగనట్రా, నగానట్రా **naganaTraa, nagaanaTraa** *n.* jewellery and such things.

నగర **nagara** *adj.* urban: **~ paalaka samstha** city muncipal corporation.

నగరం **nagaram** *n.* city.

నగరీకరణ[o] **nagariikaraNa[m]** *n.* urbanisation.

నగరు **nagaru** *n.* 1 palace. 2 king's court. 3 harem.

నగవు **nagawu** *n.* smile, laugh.

నగానట్రా **nagaanaTraa** *same as* **naganaTraa.**

నగారా **nagaaraa** *n.* kettledrum.

నగిషీ **nagiSii** *n.* carving, engraving.

నగు **nagu** I. *n.* laugh, smile. II. *v.i.* to laugh, smile.

నగుబాటు, నవ్వుబాటు **nagubaaTu, nawwubaaTu** *n.* 1 s.g ridiculous, s.g to laugh at. 2 (of a person) laughing stock.

నగుమొగం, నగుమోము **nagumogam, nagumoomu** *n.* happy and smiling face.

నగ్న **nagna** *adj.* naked, nude.

నచ్చచెప్పు **naccaceppu** *v.i.* to persuade, convince; **ii carya tagadani waariki naccaceppaDaaniki waari tooTisahacarulu prayatnistunnaaru** their colleagues are trying to persuade them that this action is unseemly.

నచ్చు **naccu** *v.i.* 1 to be liked, be found pleasing or agreeable, be appreciated; **waaLLaloo okaDikoo iddarikoo nuwwu ceppindi ~ tundi** what you say will please one or two of them (*or* one or two of them will like what you say). 2 to be agreed with. 3 to be approved of.

నజరానా, నజరు **najaraanaa, najaru**[1] *n.* present, esp. a present offered in homage.

నజరు **najaru**[2] *n.* sight, view.

నజరు, నదరు, నదురు **najaru**[3]**, nadaru, naduru** *adj.* charming, delightful, beautiful, appealing, attractive.

నజరుబందీ **najarubandii** *n.* range of view.

నజ్జు **najju**[1] *n.* atom, particle.

నజ్జు **najju**[2] *n.* feeling of dullness or heaviness in the head.

నజ్జునజ్జు అవు **najjunajju awu** *v.i.* 1 *lit.* to be converted into small particles. 2 *fig.* to be reduced to pulp; **roojallaa śariiram najjunajju ayyeeTaTTu pani ceesindi** she worked all day till her body was reduced to pulp (*or* till she was dead tired).

నటకుడు **naTakuDu** *n.* 1 actor. 2 dancer.

నటన **naTana** *n.* 1 acting. 2 pretence.

నటబృందం **naTabṛndam** *n.* company of actors.

నటి **naTi** *n.* actress.

నటించు **naTincu** *v.i. and t.* 1 to act (on stage); **paatra ~** to act a part. 2 to pretend; **eraganaTTu naTincEEDu** he pretended that he did not know (*or* he pretended not to know).

నటుడు **naTuDu** *n.* actor.

నట్ట **naTTa** *adjvl. prefix meaning* mid[dle].

నట్టనడుమ **naTTanaDuma** *n.* the exact centre, the very middle.

నట్టిల్లు **naTTillu** *n.* 1 middle part of a house. 2 *fig.* emptiness, bare space (since the middle of a house is normally empty); **nelaakharuloo cuTTaalu wacciweLLEEka illu ~ ayindi** at the end of the month when the relatives had come and gone the house was left bare (i.e. they used up everything in the house and left the owner penniless).

నట్టు[పడు] **naTTu[paDu]** *v.i.* to hesitate, stumble for want of words.

నట్టేట **naTTeeTa** *adv.* in the middle of the stream, in midstream; ~ **muncu** to abandon in midstream *or* to leave in the lurch; **wyaapaaram** ~ **kalupu** to ruin a business.

నట్ర **naTra** *echo word suffixed to* **naga** *meaning* and other such things.

నడ **naDa** *alt. form of* **naDaka.**

నడక **naDaka** *n.* 1 walk, way of walking, gait, pace; **kaali** ~ **na waccEEDu** he came by walking *or* he came on foot. 2 movement, motion. 3 rhythm, cadence (in poetry). 4 move (in chess).

నడచు[కొను], నడపు **naDacu[konu], naDapu** *same as* **naDucu[konu], naDupu.**

నడత **naData** *n.* conduct, behaviour.

నడమంతరం, నడమంత్రం, నడుమంత్రం **naDamantaram, naDamantram, naDumantram** *n.* s.g that comes quite unexpectedly; **naDamantrapu siri naraalamiida kurupu** wealth that comes by a stroke of luck is like a boil on the nerves (i.e., it is sure to bring pain — proverb).

నడమంతరంగా **naDamantarangaa** *adv.* 1 unexpectedly. 2 by a stroke of luck.

నడయాడు **naDayaaDu** *v.i. class.* to roam, wander about, go about, move about.

నడబావి **naDabaawi** *n.* step well, well with steps for descending to the water.

నడవ, నడవా **naDawa[a]** *n.* 1 passage forming the entrance to a house; *see* **angaNam.** 2 passage connecting different parts of a house. 3 outlet for rain water from a field.

నడవడి[క] **naNawaDi[ka]** *n.* conduct, behaviour, demeanour.

నడి **naDi** *adj.* middle, centre; ~ **eNDaloo** in the middle of the hot weather; ~ **netti** crown of the head; **ataniki kaLLu** ~ **nettiki waccEEyi** he has grown very arrogant (*lit.* his eyes have come to the crown of his head); **samsaaram** ~ **wiidhilooki ekkindi** the affairs of the family are common knowledge.

నడికట్టు **naDikaTTu** *n.* girdle worn by a woman in the period following pregnancy.

నడికారు, నడికాలపు **naDikaaru, naDikaalapu** *adj.* middle-aged.

నడిపాత **naDipaata** *adj.* very old.

నడిపించు **naDipincu** *v.t.* 1 to cause to walk. 2 to lead, conduct, escort (a person). 3 to conduct, carry on, run, manage (institution, business). 4 to drive, steer (vehicle).

నడిపొద్దు **naDipoddu** *n.* noon.

నడిమధ్య **naDimadhya** *adv. and p.p.* in the very middle, right in the middle; **waakiTi**~ right in the middle of the doorway.

నడిమి **naDimi** *adj.* middle, central (referring to the middle one of several things); **telangaaNaa** ~ **jillaalu** the central districts of Telangana; **maa** ~ **waaDu** the middle one of our children.

నడిరాత్రి, నడిరేయి **naDiraatri, naDireeyi** *n.* midnight.

నడుం **naDum** *n.* waist, loins.

నడుం కట్టు **naDum kaTTu** *v.i.* to prepare o.s. to strive for some object (*lit.* to gird up o.'s loins).

నడుం తిప్పు **naDum tippu** *v.i.* to move affectedly, attitudinise; *cf.* **kuluku** *sense II. 2.*

నడుం బిగించు **naDum bigincu** *v.i.* (*stronger than* **naDum kaTTu**) to prepare o.s. to strive hard for some object.

నడుం వాల్చు, నడ్డి వాల్చు **naDum waalcu, naDDi waalcu** *v.i.* 1 to lie down for a rest. 2 to relax.

నడుచు, నడచు **naDucu, naDacu** *v.i.* 1 to walk. 2 to move, proceed, step. 3 to happen, occur. 4 to behave. 5 to go on, continue.

నడుచుకొను, నడచుకొను **naDucukonu, naDacukonu** *v.i.* to behave, act, conduct o.s.; **neenu ceppinaTTu naDucukoo** behave in the way that I say.

నడుపు, నడపు **naDupu, naDapu** *v.t.* 1 to lead. 2 to conduct, carry on, run, manage (institution, business). 3 to drive, steer (vehicle).

నడుమ **naDuma** I. *n. and adj.* middle. II. *adv.* 1 in the middle. 2 in the mean time, meanwhile. III. *p.p.* between, in the midst of, in the middle of.

నడుమంత్రం **naDumantram** *same as* **naDamantaram.**

నడ్డి **naDDi** *n.* small of the back; ~ **wiragagoTTu** to thrash, beat (s.o.).

నడ్డిపూస **naDDipuusa** *n.* lowest of the vertebrae.

నడ్డిముక్కు **naDDimukku** *n.* snub nose.

నడ్డి వాల్చు **naDDi waalcu** *same as* **naDum waalcu.**

నత[ం] **nata[m]** *adj. class.* bent, inclined.

నతి **nati** *n.* 1 *class.* bending of the body in salutation. 2 *sci.* dip.

నతిక్రమం **natikramam** *n. sci.* gradient.

నత్త **natta** *n.* snail; ~ **gulla** snail's shell.

నత్తం, నక్తం **nattam, naktam** *n.* custom of eating food only at nightfall, observed traditionally throughout the month of Kartika.

నత్తి **natti** *n.* stammer, stutter.

నత్తివాడు **nattiwaaDu** *n.* stammerer, one who stammers.

నత్తు **nattu**[1] *v.i.* to stammer, stutter.

నత్తు **nattu**[2] *n.* nose ornament.

నత్రజని **natrajani** *n. chem.* nitrogen.

నదం **nadam** *n.* river that flows from east to west.

నదరు **nadaru** *same as* **najaru**[3].

నది **nadi** *n.* river, stream.

నదీనదాలు **nadiinadaalu** *n.pl.* rivers and streams (in general).

నదీముఖద్వారం **nadiimukhadwaaram** *n.* estuary.

నదురు **naduru** *same as* **najaru**[3].

నదురుబెదురు **nadurubeduru** *n.* hesitation and fear.

నన **nana** *n.* bud.

నన్నూరు **nannuuru** *n. dial.* four hundred.

నపుంసక **napunsaka** *adj. gram.* neuter (gender).

నపుంసకత్వం **napunsakatwam** *n.* impotence.

నపుంసకుడు **napunsakuDu** *n.* eunuch, impotent man.

నప్పు **nappu**[1] *v.i. colloq. dial.* to suit, fit; **nalla rangu cokkaa niiku nappadu** a black shirt will not suit you; **waLLiddaruu okarikokaru napparu** those two persons will not suit each other.

నప్పు **nappu**[2] *v.t.* to move a piece in a game of shells.

నభం **nabham** *n. class.* sky.

నభోమండలం, నభోవీధి **nabhoomaNDalam, nabhoowiidhi** *n. class.* sky, heavens.

నమలు, నములు **namalu, namulu** *v.t.* to chew, munch.

నమస్కరించు **namaskarincu** *v.i.* to make a respectful salutation with folded hands.

నమస్కారం **namaskaaram** I. *n.* salutation. II. *polite form of address used as a greeting or on taking leave equivalent to* hallo *or* goodbye.

నమస్తే **namastee** *polite greeting equivalent to* hallo.

నమాజు **namaaju** *n.* namaz, Muslim prayer.

నమామి ! **namaami!** *interj. class.* hail!

నమూనా, నమోనా **namuunaa, namoonaa** *n.* **1** form (document with spaces to be filled up). **2** sample, pattern, specimen, model, prototype.

నమోదు **namoodu** *n.* entry in an account or register or similar document, enrolment.

నమోదు చేయు **namoodu ceeyu** *v.t.* to enter, specify, record or mention in an account or register or similar document.

నమ్మకం, నమ్మిక **nammakam, nammika** *n.* **1** trust, reliance. **2** confidence, assurance, belief, faith, credence.

నమ్మకంగా **nammakangaa** *adv.* **1** confidently. **2** assuredly, positively.

నమ్మకద్రోహం **nammakadrooham** *n. legal* breach of trust.

నమ్మకస్థుడు **nammakasthuDu** *n.* trustworthy person.

నమ్మదగిన **nammadagina** *adj.* reliable, dependable, trustworthy.

నమ్మపలుకు **nammapaluku** *v.i.* to lead s.o. to believe; **aadiwaaram naaDu tappakuNDaa wastaanani nammapalikEEDu** he led me to believe that he would come on Sunday without fail.

నమ్మశక్య **nammaśakya** *adj.* believable, credible.

నమ్మించు **nammincu** *v.t.* **1** to make s.o. believe or trust **2** to convince, persuade.

నమ్మిక **nammika** *same as* **nammakam.**

నమ్మిక కాపు **nammika kaapu** *n.* trustworthy guardian.

నమ్ము **nammu** *v.t.* to believe, trust, rely on, depend on, have faith in.

నమ్య **namya** *adj.* flexible, pliable.

నమ్యత **namyata** *n.* flexibility, pliability.

నమ్ర **namra** *adj.* humble, meek, modest, unassuming.

నమ్రంగా **namrangaa** *adv.* humbly, meekly, modestly.

నమ్రత **namrata** *n.* modesty, humility, meekness, deference.

నయ **naya** *n.* beauty.

నయం **nayam** I. *n.* **1** good, benefit, profit, advantage; **aame weLLakapoowaDam ~ ayindi** it was a good thing that she did not go. **2** improvement in health, recovery from illness. **3** justice, morality. **4** civility, politeness. II. *adj.* better, improved. III. *interj.* (i) *expressing joy or sarcasm* fine! (ii) **inkaa ~** *or* **~ kaaduu** it's a good thing (*gen. said with sarcasm*) **nelaakharuloo wanda ruupaayalaa? inkaa ~** (*or* **~ kaaduu**) **weyyi annaawu kaadu, naa daagira kaanii kuuDaa leedu** a hundred rupees at the end of the month? it's a good thing you did not say a thousand! I haven't even a pie.

నయం అవు **nayam awu** *v.i.* **1** to be better. **2** to get better, recover, be cured; **ataniki nayam awtundi** he will get better; **nayamkaani jabbu** incurable disease.

నయం చేయు **nayam ceeyu** *v.t.* to cure.

నయగారం **nayagaaram** I. *n.* **1** beauty. **2** playfulness, frivolity. II. *adj.* **1** frivolous. **2** mischievous, deceitful.

నయగారితనం **nayagaaritanam** *n.* pretence of innocence.

నయనం **nayanam** *n. class.* eye.

నయనానందకర **nayanaanandakara** *adj.* delightful to the eye.

నయవంచకుడు **nayawancakuDu** *n.* cheat, deceiver.

నయవంచన **nayawancana** *n.* cheating, deception, guile.

నయాన **nayaana** *adv.* in a fair and just manner, reasonably, politely, civilly.

నయానా భయానా **nayaanaa bhayaanaa** *adv.* by smooth or rough methods.

నర **nara**[1] *adjvl. prefix meaning* human; **~ hatya** manslaughter, homicide.

నర **nara**[2] *n.* grey hair.

నరం **naram** *n.* **1** nerve; **~ laa** very thin (*lit.* as thin as a nerve); **~ leeni naaluka** *expression used of s.o. who does not keep his word* (*lit.* tongue without a nerve); **naraalu toodeesinaTTu** *lit.* like tugging at the nerves, i.e., causing great distress or anguish. **2** vein. **3** pulse. **4** string of a bow (**kamaanu**) used for teasing cotton.

నరకు, నరుకు **naraku, naruku** *v.t.* **1** to cut [off], chop[off]. **2** *colloq.* to kill; **waaNNi narikinaa nijam ceppaDu** nothing will make him tell the truth (*lit.* even if you kill him, he will not tell the truth). **3** *colloq.* to boast; **eedoo ~ tunnaaDu** he is boasting about s.g.

నరద, నెరద **narada, nerada** *n.* groove.

నరమాంసభక్షకులు **naramaamsabhakSakulu** *n.pl.* cannibals.

నరమాంసభక్షణ **naramaamsabhakSaNa** *n.* cannibalism.

నరమానవుడు **naramaanawuDu** *n.* human being.

నరమేధం **narameedham** *n.* human sacrifice.

నరహత్య **narahatya** *n.* manslaughter, homicide.

నరుడు **naruDu** *n.* man.

నర్తకి **nartaki** *n. class.* **1** dancer. **2** actress.

నర్తకుడు **nartakuDu** *n.* **1** dancer. **2** actor.

నర్తనం **nartanam** *n.* **1** dancing. **2** acting.

నర్తించు **nartincu** *v.i.* to dance.

నర్మ **narma** *n.* jesting, merriment.

నర్మసంభాషణ **narmasambhaaSaNa** *n.* joking remarks with a hidden meaning.

నర్మసచివుడు **narmasaciwuDu** *n. class.* king's jester or clown.

నఱ్ర **narra** *n.* bad tempered cow or bullock.

నల **nala** *n.* fiftieth year of the Hindu cycle of sixty years.

నలక **nalaka** *n.* particle, speck.

నలగగొట్టు **nalagagoTTu** *v.t.* to pound, crush to powder.

నలగు **nalagu** *same as* **nalugu** *v.i.*

నలత **nalata** *n.* 1 weakness, debility. 2 slight illness, indisposition; ~ **gaa uNDu** to be indisposed.

నలభై **nalabhay** *n.* forty.

నలికళ్లపాము **nalikaLLapaamu** *n.* kind of lizard (= **raktapucchika**).

నలిగిపోవు **naligipoowu** *v.i.* 1 to be crushed between opposing forces or objects. 2 to be[come] tired; **prayaaNamwalla waaDi oLLu naligipooyindi** he was tired on account of the journey.

నలిగులి **naliguli** *adj.* crushed, bruised, trampled.

నలు **nalu** *adjvl. prefix meaning* four *or* an indefinite number; *cf.* **naalugu.**

నలుగడల **nalugaDala** *adv.* in all directions.

నలుగు **nalugu** I. *n.* 1 rubbing the body with paste made of green gram, etc., to cleanse and purify the skin before washing and oiling the hair (**talaNTi**). 2 paste used for that purpose. II. *v.i.* (*also* **nalagu)** 1 to be broken, be crushed, be trampled, be bruised. 2 to be turned into powder. 3 (of cloth, paper) to be crumpled.

నలుగుడు **naluguDu** *n.* trouble, difficulty, suffering.

నలుగుడుపడు **naluguDupaDu** *v.i.* 1 to be beset with difficulties, be worried or anguished (= **mallaagullaalupaDu**). 2 **waaDiki paaTham naluguDu paDaleedu** he has not come to understand the lesson *or* he has not absorbed or assimilated the lesson.

నలుగుపెట్టు, నలుగుపూయు **nalugupeTTu, nalugupuuyu** *v.i.* to rub the body with paste before **talaNTi.**

నలుగురినోటపడు, నలుగురిచేత కాదనిపించుకొను **naluguri nooTapaDu, naluguri ceetakaadanipincukonu** *v.i.* to earn a bad reputation.

నలుగురు **naluguru** *n.pl.* 1 four persons. 2 several persons.

నలుచదరం **nalucadaram** *n.* square.

నలుచు **nalucu** *v.t.* 1 to rub off (powder, dust). 2 **mukku nalici diipam aNTincu** to trim the wick and light a lamp.

నలుదిక్కులు, నలుదిశలు, నలుదెసలు **naludikkulu, naludiśalu, naludesalu** *n.pl.* 1 four directions. 2 all directions.

నలుపు **nalupu**[1] *v.t.* 1 to crush, squeeze. 2 (of cloth, paper) to crumple. 3 **kaaLLatoo**~ to trample. 4 to rub; **kaLLu** ~ **konu** to rub o.'s eyes; **ceetulu** ~ **konu** to rub o.'s hands together in a nervous or apologetic gesture.

నలుపు **nalupu**[2] *n. and adj.* 1 black. 2 (of complexion) dark, swarthy; **eNDaloo tirigi** ~ **ekkEEDu** his complexion became dark by going about in the sun.

నలుమూలలకు **nalumuulalaku** *adv.* to every corner, in every direction.

నలుమూలలా **nalumuulalaa** *adv.* everywhere, throughout (*lit.* in all four corners).

నలువురు **naluwuru** *alt. form of* **naluguru.**

నలుసంత **nalusanta** *adj.* very little, very small, tiny.

నలుసు **nalusu** *n.* 1 small particle, atom. 2 *dial.* infant, baby.

నల్చదరంగా **nalcadarangaa** *adv.* square shaped.

నల్ల **nalla**[1] *adj.* 1 black. 2 (of complexion) dark, swarthy.

నల్ల **nalla**[2] *n. dial.* water tap.

నల్లకలువ **nallakaluwa** *n.* blue lotus.

నల్లకావురు **nallakaawuru** *n.* blackness (*gen.* of dark clouds); *see* **kaawuru.**

నల్లగుడ్డు **nallaguDDu** *n.* pupil of the eye.

నల్లజీడి **nallajiiDi** *n.* marking nut, fruit of *semicarpus anacardicum* whose stain is used for marking clothes; it produces a strong gum, hence **nannu** ~ **laa paTTukonnaaDu** he stuck to me like a leech; *cf.* **banka.**

నల్లజీలకర్ర **nallajiilakarra** *n.* black cummin seed.

నల్లనయ్య **nallanayya** *n.* epithet of Krishna.

నల్లనాగు **nallanaagu** *n.* black cobra (very poisonous).

నల్లనువ్వులు **nallanuwwulu** *n. pl.* black sesamum, a grain used in certain religious ceremonies.

నల్లపూస **nallapuusa** *n.* black bead; ~ **aypooyEEwu** you disappeared from view *or* you could not be found anywhere (*lit.* you became a black bead).

నల్లబడు **nallabaDu** *v.i.* to turn black.

నల్లబల్ల **nallaballa** *n.* blackboard.

నల్లమందు **nallamandu** *n.* opium; ~ **weesukonnaaDu** he consumed opium.

నల్లమందు భాయి **nallamandu bhaayi** *n. colloq.* opium addict.

నల్లమద్ది **nallamaddi** *n. terminalia tomentosa*, a timber tree.

నల్లరాయి **nallaraayi** *n.* black stone (proverbially said to be hard to break).

నల్లరేగడ **nallareegaDa** *n.* black cotton soil.

నల్లవడ్లు, నల్లార్లు **nallawaDLu, nallaarlu** *n.pl.* a coarse variety of paddy, blackish in colour.

నల్లసీసం **nallasiisam** *n.* graphite.

నల్లి **nalli** *n.* bug.

నల్లేరు **nalleeru** *n. vitis quadrangularis*, a creeper; ~ **pay baNDinaDaka** *is an expression used of s.g easy to accomplish*. **pay baNDi nadakawale puroogamanam saagutunnadi** the advance is proceeding without any difficulties.

నవ **nawa**[1] *adj.* new, fresh, modern.

నవ **nawa**[2] *n.* nine.

నవ **nawa**[3] *n.* itch[ing].

నవకం **nawakam** *adj.* 1 young, tender. 2 beautiful.

నవకల్పన **nawakalpana** *n.* inventiveness, ingenuity, innovation.

నవకాయ పిండివంటలు **nawakaayapiNDiwaNTalu** *same as* **naawakaayapiNDiwaNTalu.**

నవగ్రహాలు **nawagrahaalu** *n.pl.* the nine planets of Hindu astrology.

నవజాత **nawajaata** *adj.* nascent, newly born.

నవటాకు **nawaTaaku** *n.* one eighth of a seer.

నవత **nawata**[1] *n.* freshness.

నవత **nawata**[2] *n.* 1 languishing illness. 2 pain, sorrow.

నవదంపతులు **nawadampatulu** *n.pl.* newly married couple.

నవధాన్యాలు **nawadhaanyaalu** *n.pl.* mixture of nine different grains used in certain religious ceremonies.

నవనవలాడు **nawanawalaaDu** *v.i.* to be fresh, blooming or flourishing.

నవనాడులు, నవనాళ్లు **nawanaaDulu, nawanaaLLu** *n.pl.* the nine nerve centres of the body.

నవనిధులు **nawanidhulu** *n.pl.* nine kinds of wealth.

నవనీత **nawaniita** *adj.* kindly, gentle, generous; **~hrdayuDu** person with a kind and generous heart.

నవనీతం **nawaniitam** *n.* fresh butter.

నవమల్లిక **nawamallika** *n.* kind of jasmine.

నవమి **nawami** *n.* ninth day of a lunar fortnight.

నవయవ్వనం **nawayawwanam** *n.* prime of youth, fresh bloom of youth.

నవయువ **nawayuwa** *adj.* new, young.

నవయువకుడు **nawayuwakuDu** *n.* young man.

నవయువతి **nawayuwati** *n.* 1 young woman. 2 modern woman.

నవరంధ్రాలు **nawarandhraalu** *n.pl.* the nine apertures of the human body.

నవరత్నాలు **nawaratnaalu** *n.pl.* the nine principal gems (diamond, ruby, etc.)

నవరసాలు **nawarasaalu** *n.pl.* the nine *rasas*, i.e., the nine traditional sentiments or emotions in art and literature (**śrngaaram** sexual love, **karuNa** compassion, **haasyam** humour, etc.)

నవరసు, నవర్సు **nawarasu, nawarsu** *n. corrupt form of the word* sovereign (gold coin).

నవరాత్రి **nawaraatri** *n.* festival celebrated for nine nights, esp. the Dasara festival in September–October, *also known as* **śaran~**.

నవల **nawala**[1] *n. class.* woman.

నవల **nawala**[2] *n.* novel.

నవలాకర్త, నవలాకారుడు **nawalaakarta, nawalaakaaruDu** *n.* novelist.

నవాబు **nawaabu** *n.* nawab.

నవారు **nawaaru** *n.* broad cotton tape used for weaving the support for a mattress in a bed.

నవాసారం **nawaasaaram** *n.* sal ammoniac, chloride of ammonia.

నవీకరణం **nawiikaraNam** *n.* renewal, renovation.

నవీన **nawiina** *adj.* new, recent, modern, fresh.

నవీనత, నవీనత్వం **nawiinata, nawiinatwam** *n.* novelty, modernity.

నవుజు **nawuju** *adj. dial.* young, green, very tender.

నవోఢ **nawooDha** *n.* newly married girl.

నవ్య **nawya** *adj.* new, modern.

నవ్యత, నవ్యత్వం **nawyata, nawyatwam** *n.* newness, freshness, novelty.

నవ్యుడు **nawyuDu** *n.* 1 modern person. 2 (in literature) modernist.

నవ్వించు **nawwincu** *v.t.* to cause to laugh, amuse.

నవ్వు **nawwu** I. *n.* 1 laughter, laughing. 2 smile, smiling. II. *v.i.* 1 to laugh. 2 to smile.

నవ్వులాట, నవ్వుటాలు, నవ్వుతాలు **nawwulaaTa, nawwuTaalu, nawwutaalu** I. *n.* 1 laughter, amusement, fun. 2 s.g to laugh at, s.g amusing, s.g ridiculous. II. *adj.* funny, ludicrous, ridiculous.

నవ్వుబాటు **nawwubaaTu** *same as* **nagubaaTu.**

నవ్వులబండి **nawwulabaNDi** *n. colloq.* cheerful and humorous person.

నవ్వులబాజా **nawwulabaajaa** *n. colloq. dial. same as* **nawwulabaNDi.**

నశించు **naśincu** *v.i.* 1 to be ruined or destroyed. 2 to disappear, vanish, become extinct, be lost; **wyawahaaramloo arasunna palakaDam naśincindi** in colloquial speech the pronunciation of *arasunna* was lost; **naśincina jaati** extinct species.

నశింపజేయు **naśimpajeeyu** *v.t.* to destroy, annihilate.

నశింపు **naśimpu** *n.* destruction, annihilation, extinction.

నశ్యం, నస్యం **naśyam, nasyam** *n.* snuff.

నశ్వర **naśwara** *adj.* perishing, perishable.

నశ్వరం **naśwaram** *n.* s.g perishable or impermanent.

నశ్వరత, నశ్వరత్వం **naśwarata, naśwaratwam** *n.* perishableness, destructibility.

నష్టం **naSTam** *n.* 1 loss. 2 harm, damage, detriment.

నష్టజాతకుడు **naSTajaatakuDu** *n.* unlucky or illfated or illstarred person.

నష్టదాయక **naSTadaayaka** *adj.* 1 harmful, injurious, detrimental. 2 causing loss.

నష్టపడు, నష్టపోవు **naSTapaDu, naSTapoowu** *v.i.* to suffer loss or harm or damage.

నష్టపరిహారం **naSTaparihaaram** *n.* compensation.

నష్టపరిహార పత్రం **naSTaparihaara patram** *n.* indemnity bond.

నష్టపెట్టు **naSTapeTTu** *v.i.* to cause loss or harm or damage.

నస **nasa**[1] *n.* itching, irritation, esp. of the nose or throat.

నస **nasa**[2] *n.* boring talk.

నస **nasa**[3] *n.* 1 danger. 2 lust.

నసగొట్టు **nasagoTTu** *n.* lustful person.

నసపెట్టు **nasapeTTu** *v.i.* 1 to talk boringly. 2 to pester (s.o.).

నసాళం **nasaaLam** *n. class.* centre of the nervous system believed to be located in the head; *mod. only in* **nasaaLaaniki aNTu** *or* **nasaaLaaniki ekku** *lit.* to reach the centre of the nervous system, i.e., to constitute a severe blow or jolt or shock; **naa nasaaLaaniki aNTeeTaTTu maaTLaaDEEDu** *lit.* he talked so that his words reached the centre of my nervous system, i.e., his words were a severe blow to me.

నసీబు **nasiibu** *n.* destiny, fortune, fate.

నసుగు **nasugu** I. *n.* 1 murmuring, speaking indistinctly. 2 hesitation. II. *v.i.* 1 to murmur, mutter, say (s.g) indistinctly. 2 to hesitate, dither, shilly-shally, beat about the bush. 3 to grumble.

నసుగుగొసుగు **nasugugosugu** *n.* hesitation and so on.

నసుగుడు **nasuguDu** *n.* 1 hesitation. 2 murmuring.

నస్యం **nasyam** *same as* **naśyam.**

నా - naa

నా **naa** *pronom. possessive adj.* my.

నాంది **naandi** *n.* prelude.

నాందిగా **naandigaa** *adv.* as a preliminary.

నాందిపలుకు **naandipaluku** I. *n.* foreword, prologue. II. *v.i.* to speak a foreword or prologue.

నాందిప్రస్తావన **naandi prastaawana** *n. theat.* worship followed by prologue at a performance.

నాందీవాచకం **naandiiwaacakam** *n.* **1** first lesson book, primer. **2** *theat.* speaking a prologue.

నాకం, నాకలోకం **naakam, naakalookam** *n. class.* heaven, paradise; **nakka ekkaDa? naagalookam ekkaDa?** *lit.* where is the jackal and where is heaven? *rhetorical question meaning* there is no comparison between them; *this expression in which* **naakalookam** *is mispronounced as* **naagalookam** *is used of a person who aspires to s.g that he can never attain; see* **ekkaDa, naagalookam.**

నాకు **naaku**[1] *dative of pers. pron.* to me.

నాకు **naaku**[2] *v.t.* to lick.

నాగం **naagam**[1] *n.* **1** snake, serpent. **2** cobra.

నాగం **naagam**[2] *n.* tin, pewter.

నాగజెముడు, నాగతాళి **naagajemuDu, naagataaLi** *n.* kind of cactus, prickly pear, *opuntia dillenii.*

నాగదేవత **naagadeewata** *same as* **naaguDu.**

నాగపూర్‌సంత్రా **naagapuur santraa** *n.* Nagpur orange, kind of orange grown near Nagpur.

నాగమల్లె, నాగమల్లి **naagamalle, naagamalli** *n.* kind of jasmine.

నాగరం **naagaram** *n.* jewel worn by a woman on the head.

నాగరక, నాగరిక **naagaraka, naagarika** *adj.* **1** civilised. **2** refined, urbane. **3** smart, fashionable.

నాగరకత, నాగరికత **naagarakata, naagarikata** *n.* **1** civilisation. **2** civilised customs. **3** refinement, urbanity. **4** fashionableness.

నాగరికం **naagarikam** *n.* **1** refinement, urbanity. **2** fashionableness.

నాగరికుడు **naagarikuDu** *n.* civilised, cultured, urbane or refined person.

నాగలి **naagali** *n.* plough.

నాగలోకం **naagalookam** *n.* the underworld, hell; *see* **naakam.**

నాగవత్తు **naagawattu** *n.* article of a woman's jewellery worn on the upper arm.

నాగవల్లి **naagawalli** *n.* **1** betel vine. **2** final part of the wedding ceremony signifying the closeness of the union between the bride and bridegroom.

నాగవల్లిపిడతలు **naagawalli piDatalu** *n.pl.* small (miniature) cooking vessels used for the **naagawalli** ceremony.

నాగవాసం **naagawaasam** *n.* staple (for fastening).

నాగస్వరం **naagaswaram** *n.* kind of clarinet used by snake charmers.

నాగు [పాము] **naagu[paamu]** *n.* cobra.

నాగుడు, నాగదేవత **naaguDu, naagadeewata** *n.* serpent god.

నాగులచవితి **naagulacawiti** *n.* fourth day after Dipavali, when worship of snakes is performed.

నాగులుచీర, నాగులుకోక **naaguluciira, naagulukooka** *n.* checked sari (= **gaLLa ciira**).

నాచు **naacu** *n.* waterweed, moss, slime.

నాజరు **naajaru** *n.* nazir, official in a court of law.

నాజూకు **naajuuku** I. *n.* refinement. **2** stylishness, fashionableness. II. *adj.* **1** delicate, fine, soft, tender. **2** stylish, elegant, fashionable.

నాటకం **naaTakam** *n.* **1** drama, play. **2** play-acting, guile, trickery.

నాటకం ఆడు **naaTakam aaDu** *v.i.* **1** to act in a play. **2** to cause mischief.

నాటకం వేయు **naaTakam weeyu** *v.i.* **1** to perform a play. **2** to act in a play. **3** to practise guile.

నాటకకర్త **naaTakakarta** *n.* playwright, dramatist.

నాటకరంగం **naaTakarangam** *n.* stage.

నాటకశాల **naaTakaśaala** *n.* theatre.

నాటకీయం, నాటకీయత **naaTakiiyam, naaTakiiyata** *n.* dramatisation.

నాటకీయంగా **naaTakiiyangaa** *adv.* dramatically.

నాటి **naaTi** I. *genitive of* **naaDu** day; **~ nunci neeTiwaraku** from that day to this. II. *adj.* of that time, former.

నాటిక **naaTika** *n.* short play, one act play.

నాటికి **naaTiki** *adv.* by (the time of):**1901 loo 1.9 kooTLu unna aandhra pradeeś janaabhaa 1976~ 4.8 kooTLu ayindi** the population of Andhra Pradesh which was 1.9 crores in 1901 had become 4.8 crores by 1976.

నాటికీ నేటికీ **naaTikii neeTikii** *adv.* at that time and at this, then as now.

నాటు **naaTu**[1] *adj.* locally made or produced;~ **pogaaku** indigenous variety of tobacco; **ii palleTuuri ~paDucu** this country girl from a small hamlet.

నాటు **naaTu**[2] I. *n.* (*also* **~ pani** *and pl.* **naaTLu**) transplantation. II. *v.t.* **1** to plant. **2** to fix, insert. **3** to transplant (seedlings).

నాటు **naaTu**[3] *n. class.* wound, dent.

నాటుకాయ **naaTukaaya** *n.* fruit of a tree grown from seed, not grafted.

నాటుకొను **naaTukonu** *v.i.* (of a plant) to establish itself, strike root.

నాటుపడు **naaTupaDu** *v.i.* to receive a shock.

నాట్యం **naaTyam** *n.* dance, dancing.

నాట్యంచేయు **naaTyam ceeyu** *v.i.* to dance.

నాట్యకత్తె **naaTyakatte** *n.* woman dancer.

నాట్యగాడు **naaTyagaaDu** *n.* male dancer.

నాట్లు **naaTLu** *n.pl.* transplantation; **ninna maa polamloo naaTLaynaayi** yesterday my field was transplanted.

నాట్లు పెట్టు, నాట్లు వేయు **naaTLu peTTu, naaTLu weeyu** *v.i.* to transplant seedlings.

నాడం, నాడా, నాళం, లాడం, లాడా **naaDam, naaDaa**[1], **naaLam, laaDam, laaDaa** *n.* bullock-shoe, horseshoe.

నాడా **naaDaa**[2] *n.* ribbon, tape.

నాడి **naaDi**[1] *n.* 1 nerve. 2 pulse.

నాడి **naaDi**[2] *n.* sect; *cf.* **naaDu**[2].

నాడిచూచు, నాడిపరీక్షించు **naaDi cuucu, naaDi pariikSincu** *v.i.* to feel (s.o.'s) pulse.

నాడీమండలం **naaDiimaNDalam** *n.* nervous system.

నాడీసంధి **naaDiisandhi** *n. med.* ganglion.

నాడు **naaDu**[1] I. *n.* day, time; **ennaaLLu**? how many days? *or* how long? II. *adv.* 1 at a certain time, on a certain day or date; **aadiwaaram~** on Sunday; **wijayadaśami~ eem ceestaaru**? what will you do on Vijayadasami day? **~ii~unnantagaa saankeetika parijñaanam leedu** at that time there was not as much technical knowledge as there is today; **1926 loo ii wiśwawidyaalayam sthaapincina~** at the time of founding this university in 1926; **modaTLoo 1971-72 kaalam~raaSTramloo 192 juuniyar kaLaaśaalalu** uNDeewi at the beginning in 1971–72 there were 192 junior colleges in the State. 2 ago; **aayana naalugaydu roojula~ canipooyEEDu** he died four or five days ago. 3 *ironical usage* **wastaaDani miiru anukonnaaru, naaDee waccEEDu** *lit.* you expected him to come and he came on that very day (but the speaker means the opposite, i.e., he did not come then and he is not likely to come at all).

నాడు **naaDu**[2] *n.* 1 country, land, region. 2 **naaDibheedam** difference of sect among Vaidiki brahmans; the names of divisions, which are based on regions, are **telagaaNyulu, welanaaDulu, kasarnaaDulu, weeginaaDulu** and **mulakanaaDulu.**

నాడె **naaDe** *n.* weaver's shuttle.

నాణెం, నాణ్యం **naaNem, naaNyam** I. *n.* 1 quality, fineness, purity. 2 coin. II. *adj.* 1 fine, of good quality, superior. 2 honest.

నాణ్యత **naaNyata** *n.* quality, purity, fineness.

నాతం **naatam** *n.* batta, daily allowance of money; **jiitanaataalu** salary and allowances.

నాతి **naati** *n.* woman.

నాథుడు **naathuDu** *n.* 1 lord, king, master. 2 husband. 3 leader. 4 great person (said sarcastically); **neenu wacci gaNTaynaa nannu palakarincina~leedu** although I came an hour ago, not one great person has spoken to me (*the equivalent English expression would be* not a soul has spoken to me).

నాదం **naadam** *n.* 1 *same as* **naadu.** 2 *ling.* voiced sound.

నాదతంత్రి **naada tantri** *n.* vocal cord.

నాదరహిత **naadarahita** *adj. ling.* unvoiced.

నాదవంత **naadawanta** *adj. ling.* voiced.

నాదస్వరం **naadaswaram** *n.* shenai, musical instrument similar to an oboe.

నాదు, నాదం **naadu, naadam** *n.* 1 sound, musical note. 2 humming or ringing in the ears. 3 slight headache. 4 *dial.* gloom, depression.

నాన **naana** *n.* shame, feeling of guilt.

నానబెట్టు, నానవేయు **naanabeTTu, naanaweeyu** *v.t.* 1 to wet, moisten, soak. 2 *colloq.* to protract, prolong, drag out.

నానవేత **naanaweeta** *n.* 1 soaking. 2 *colloq.* dragging and protracting, prolonging; **inka nirNayam tiisukoowaDamloo~enduku**? why are you still dragging out the matter of taking a decision?

నానా **naanaa** *adj.* 1 many, various, several. 2 miscellaneous.

నానాజాతిసమితి **naanaa jaati samiti** *n.* League of Nations.

నానాటికి **naanaaTiki** *adv.* day by day, from day to day, gradually, by degrees.

నాను **naanu**[1] *n.* (*also* **~taaDu**) necklace of twisted gold thread.

నాను **naanu**[2] *v.i.* 1 to become wet. 2 to be drenched. 3 to be soaked, be steeped; **aame nooTLoo nuwwuginja kuuDaa naanadu** she cannot keep a secret (*lit.* even a gingelly seed will not get soaked in her mouth). 4 *fig.* (of proverbs, sayings, idioms) to evolve or take shape slowly; **likhitam kaakuNDaa prajala nooLLaloo naanutuu waccina caaTuwulni seekarincEEDu** he collected stray verses that were not written down but had slowly taken shape on the tongues of the people.

నానుడి **naanuDi** *n.* proverb.

నానుడు **naanuDu** *adj.* 1 wet, soaked. 2 protracted.

నానుడుబేరం **naanuDubeeram** *n. colloq.* indecisiveness.

నానుడువాన **naanuDuwaana** *n.* continuous light rain, steady drizzle.

నానుపుడు **naanupuDu** *n.* hesitating, protracting, prolonging.

నానుబ్రాయి **naanubraayi** *n.* (*also pl.* **naanubraalu, naanuwaalu**) rice not fully cooked.

నాన్చు **naancu** I. *v.i. colloq.* to hesitate or stumble for want of words, break off without finishing a sentence. II. *v.t.* 1 to wet, dampen. 2 to soak, steep, drench.

నాన్న **naanna** *n.* father.

నాన్నా! **naannaa!** *term of address used (i) by any person to a younger person or child (ii) by son or daughter to father.*

నాన్‌రొట్టె **naanrooTTe** *n.* bread.

నాప **naapa** I. *n.* 1 useless person, weaking (*used as a term of abuse to an inferior or a child*). 2 impotent person. II. *adj.* (of ears of grain) not fully developed.

నాపరాయి **naaparaayi** *n.* stone slab used for flooring.

నాపసాని **naapasaani** *n.* matron, dame, grand lady.

నాభి **naabhi**[1] *n.* 1 *class.* navel, umbilicus. 2 central hole in a wheel. 3 *phys.* focus.

నాభి **naabhi**[2] *n.* poison.

నాభిరజ్జువు **naabhirajjuwu** *n.* umbilical cord.

నామం **naamam** *n.* 1 name. 2 mark worn on the forehead by Vaishnavites. 3 *gram.* noun.

నామకరణం **naamakaraNam** *n.* naming, christening.

నామకరణ విధానం **naamakaraNa widhaanam** *n.* nomenclature.

నామకాగా, నామకార్థం **naamakaagaa, naamakaartham** *adv.* for name's sake, nominally.

నామగుంట **naamaguNTa** *n. med.* hollow at the base of the throat.

నామదుంప **naamadumpa** *n. rumex aponogeton*, a water plant.

నామధేయం **naamadheeyam** *n.* 1 name. 2 nomenclature.

నామనిర్దిష్ట **naamanirdiSTa** *adj. admin.* nominated.

నామనిర్దేశం **naamanirdeeśam** *n. admin.* nomination by a prescribed authority.

నామపద్ధతి **naamapaddhati** *n. ling.* nomenclature.

నామప్రతిపాదన **naamapratipaadana** *n. admin.* nomination for election.

నామమాత్రపు **naamamaatrapu** *adj.* titular, nominal, token.

నామమాత్రావశిష్ట **naamamaatraawaśiSTa** *adj.* vestigial.

నామమాల **naamamaala** *n.* list of names of a deity repeated during worship.

నామరూపం **naamaruupam** *n.* 1 name and form; **naamaruupa rahitam ceeyu** to blot out, wipe out, obliterate; **aa utsaaham naamaruupaalu leekuNDaa pootundi** that enthusiasm will vanish without a trace. 2 *ling.* nominal form.

నామర్దా, నామోషి **naamardaa, naamooSi** I. *n.* shame, disgrace, degradation, loss of dignity. II. *adj.* shameful, disgraceful, degrading.

నామవాచకం **naamawaacakam** *n. gram.* noun.

నామా **naamaa** *second part of a n. compound meaning* deed, document; **karaaru~** agreement; **wiilu~** will.

నామాంతరం **naamaantaram** *n.* another name.

నామాలకోడి **naamaalakooDi** *n.* coot (bird), *fulica atra.*

నామీకరణం **naamiikaraNam** *n. ling.* nominalisation.

నాము **naamu** *n.* 1 knee-high shoots of young cholam or sprouts growing from stumps of cholam, which are harmful for cattle to graze. 2 the cattle disease so caused (= **ungiDi**). 3 white powder used (i) to make **muggulu** (patterns on the ground), (ii) by Vaishnavites to make marks on the forehead.

నామోషి **naamooSi** *same as* **naamardaa.**

నాయకత్వం **naayakatwam** *n.* 1 leadership, hegemony. 2 captaincy (of a team).

నాయకమ్మన్యులు **naayakammanyulu** *n.pl., derogratory term* worthless leaders.

నాయకి, నాయిక **naayaki, naayika** *n.* heroine (of a story).

నాయకుడు **naayakuDu** *n.* 1 leader, chief. 2 hero (of a story).

నాయన **naayana** *n. dial.* father.

నాయనమ్మ **naayanamma** *n.* 1 grandmother, father's mother. 2 old woman.

నాయనా! **naayanaa!** *term of address* 1 *used familiarly to any male person* my friend! *or* my boy! 2 *dial.* father!

నాయాల **naayaala** *interj., term of abuse.*

నాయిబు **naayibu** *n.* naib, assistant.

నాయిబ్రాహ్మణుడు **naayibraahmaNuDu** *n.* barber.

నార **naara** *n.* fibre.

నారదుడు **naaraduDu** *n.* 1 Narada, musician and messenger of the gods. 2 *colloq.* person who tells tales about others and spreads quarrels.

నారపీచు, నారపీసు **naarapiicu, naarapiisu** *n.* 1 fibre. 2 *colloq.* hardhearted and miserly person.

నారి **naari**[1] *n.* woman.

నారి **naari**[2] *n. class.* bowstring.

నారింజ, నారంజి **naarinja, naaranji** *n.* bitter kind of orange.

నారికురుపు **naarikurupu** *same as* **tantikurupu.**

నారికేళం **naarikeeLam** *n.* coconut palm.

నారికేళపాకం **naarikeeLapaakam** *n.* style of literary composition which is hard to understand.

నారు **naaru** *n.* 1 young plant, sprout, seedling. 2 seedlings for transplanting.

నారు పోయు, నారు వేయు **naaru pooyu, naaru weeyu** *v.i.* to sow seedlings in a seedbed.

నారుమడి **naarumaDi** *n.* seedbed.

నాలి **naali** I. *n.* 1 mean work; *cf.* **kuuli~**. 2 slightness. 3 deceitfulness, hypocrisy. II. *adj.* 1 slight. 2 deceitful, hypocritical; ~ **maaTalu** deceitful words.

నాలిక, నాలుక **naalika, naaluka** *n.* tongue; **waaDiki~ tiragadu** he cannot pronounce words correctly; **iNTiki poodamani~piikkoNTunnaaDu** (*or* **perukkoNTunnaaDu**) he is yearning to go home; ~ **weLLabeTTu** to be speechless, be at a loss for an answer; **adi naalukaa, taaTi paTTEE?** *lit.* is that a tongue or a piece of palmyra wood in your mouth? (scornful reply to s.o. who tells a blatant lie).

నాలికబద్ద **naalikabadda** *n.* tongue cleaner.

నాలితనం **naalitanam** *n.* deceitfulness, hypocrisy.

నాలిముచ్చు **naalimuccu** *n.* deceitful person, hypocrite.

నాలుగందాలా **naalugandaalaa** *adv.* in all possible ways, by all possible means.

నాలుగు **naalugu** *n.* 1 four. 2 an indefinite number, a few, several, many; **naalukkaalaalapaaTu** for some time, for a fairly long time (*lit.* for four seasons); ~**raaLLu sampaadincu** to earn a little money; ~**kaayalu kaayu** to have many offspring; **waaNNi~peTTi pampEEnu** *or* **waaNNi~dulipi pampincEEnu** I scolded him and sent him away.

నాలుగుదిక్కులా **naalugudikkulaa** *adv.* on all four sides, all around.

నాలుగుమూలలాట **naalugumuulalaaTa** *n.* name of a children's game.

నాలుగో **naalugoo** *adj.* fourth.

నాళం **naaLam**[1] *same as* **naaDam.**

నాళం **naaLam**[2] *n.* 1 tube, pipe. 2 **rakta~** vein, blood vessel. 3 barrel (of a gun). 4 duct.

నాళిక **naaLika** *n.* tube; **pariikSa~** test tube.

నావ **naawa** *n.* ship, boat, vessel.

నావకాయపిండివంటలు **naawakaaya piNDiwaNTalu** *n.pl.* (of food) many kinds of delicacies.

నావిక **naawika** *adj.* nautical.

నావికదళం **naawikadaLam** *n.* navy.

నావికుడు **naawikuDu** *n.* sailor, seaman.

నాశక **naaśaka** *adj.* destroying, having power to destroy, destructive.

నాశనం **naaśanam** *n.* ruin, destruction, havoc.

నాశనం అవు **naaśanam awu** *v.i.* to be destroyed, be ruined.

నాశనం చేయు **naaśanam ceeyu** *v.t.* to destroy, ruin.

నాసామిరంగా! **naasaamirangaa!** *interj.* oh my lord! *or* oh my God! (*lit.* oh my God Ranga!).

నాసారంధ్రం **naasaarandhram** *n. class.* nostril.

నాసి[రకపు] **naasi[rakapu]** *adj.* of poor quality, worthless, useless, wretched.

నాసిక **naasika** *n. class.* nose.

నాసికాపుటం **naasikaapuTam** *n. class.* nostril.

నాస్తా **naastaa** *n.* 1 breakfast. 2 tiffin, snacks.

నాస్తి **naasti** *n.* non-existence.

నాస్తికత్వం **naastikatwam** *n.* atheism.

నాస్తికుడు **naastikuDu** *n.* atheist.

ని - ni

నింగి **ningi** *n.* sky, heavens.

నించి **ninci** *same as* **nunci.**

నించు, నింపు **nincu, nimpu** *v.t.* to fill.

నిండా **niNDaa** *adv.* 1 fully, completely, entirely; **waaDiki ~ paatikeeLLu leewu** he is not fully twenty-five years old *or* he is hardly twenty-five years old. 2 *post-positional use* so as to fill, so as to cover; **jeebu ~ Dabbulunnaayi** the pocket is full of money (*lit.* money is so as to fill the pocket); **baTTa ~ marakalunnaay** the cloth is covered with stains.

నిండు **niNDu** I. *n.* fullness, completeness, satisfaction; **pillalu wacceedaakaa iNTiki ~ raaleedu** until the children arrived the house felt empty. II. *adj.* (*also* **niNDayna**) 1 full, complete, perfect; **~ candruDu** full moon; **~ eNDaa kaalam** midsummer; **niNDayna erupu** bright red; **~ sunna** zero, nothing at all; **~ koluwu** open court, public audience in a royal palace; **niNDayna maaTa** *or* **niNDayna paluku** expressive word (*lit.* word that expresses a meaning with perfect adequacy); **~ manasutoo** with a heart full of emotion *or* with wholehearted dedication and devotion. 2 abundant, ample; **niNDayna wigraham** well-built *or* ample figure (of a person). 3 *other usages*: **~ cuulaalu** woman about to give birth; **~ maniSi** pregnant woman; **~ muttayduwu** grand old lady, dame (*lit.* woman of mature age whose husband is living); **~ samsaaram** happy and contented family; **pramaadamloo ~ praaNaalu koolpooyEEru** they lost their precious lives in an accident. III. *v.i.* 1 to be filled, be full, be covered; **niiLLatoo niNDina siisaa** a glass filled with water; **tellaTi nuugu niNDina paakuDu tiige** a spreading creeper covered with white down. 2 to be completed; **18 eeLLu niNDagaanee udyoogamloo praweeśincEEDu** as soon as he was 18 years old, he entered on employment; **waaDiki nuureeLLu niNDEEyi** (*lit.* 100 years were completed for him) *is a set phrase for* he died; **waaDiki mupphay eeLLakee nuureeLLu niNDEEyi** he passed away when he was just 30 years old.

నిండుకొను **niNDukonu** *v.i.* to be filled, be[come] full; **biyyam niNDukonnaayi** the rice is exhausted (*lit.* the rice is full — euphemism to avoid a taboo expression); *cf.* **golusu, diipam.**

నిండుగా **niNDugaa** *adv.* 1 fully, completely, entirely. 2 much, greatly, abundantly. 3 properly, satisfactorily, to (s.o.'s) satisfaction, gratifyingly, pleasingly; **sommu ekkuwa wyayaparacakuNDaa niraaDambarangaa ~ wiwaahaalu jaragaali** weddings should be celebrated in a proper and gratifying manner without ostentation or great expense.

నిండుతనం **niNDutanam** *n.* 1 fullness, completeness, satisfaction. 2 self-assurance, feeling of confidence.

నింద **ninda** *n.* blame, reproach, reproof, censure.

నిందారోపణ **nindaaroopaNa** *n.* allegation, accusation; **paraspara ~lu** mutual recriminations.

నిందాస్తుతి **nindaastuti** *n.* ironical praise, irony.

నిందించు **nindincu** *v.t.* 1 to blame, reproach, accuse. 2 to criticise, find fault with, abuse.

నిందితుడు **nindituDu** *n.* 1 one who is blamed or censured. 2 *legal* accused person.

నింద్య, నింద్యార్హ **nindya, nindyaarha** *adj.* blamable, blameworthy.

నింపాది **nimpaadi** I. *n.* 1 gentleness, mildness, calmness. 2 slowness; **~ ceesukoni maaTLaaDu** take your time and then speak. II. *adj.* 1 gentle, mild, calm. 2 slow, inactive, inert, sluggish.

నింపాదిగా **nimpaadigaa** *adv.* 1 in good health, fine, well; **antaa ~ unnaaraa?** are you all keeping well? 2 calmly, coolly. 3 carefully, taking o.'s time. 4 slowly, sluggishly. 5 gradually, by degrees.

నింపు **nimpu** *same as* **nincu.**

నింబోళి **nimbooLi** *n.* lemon yellow colour.

నికంటు[వు] **nikaNTu[wu]** *n.* 1 custom. 2 social convention.

నికట **nikaTa** *adj.* 1 unbroken, uninterrupted, continuous. 2 near, at hand.

నికర **nikara** *adj.* net; **~ laabham** net profit.

నికరం **nikaram** *n.* 1 balance left over, net balance. 2 pith, [quint]essence.

నికరంగా **nikarangaa** *adv.* clearly, definitely, explicitly.

నికషం, నికషోపలం **nikaSam, nikaSoopalam** *n. class.* 1 touchstone, criterion. 2 grinding stone.

నికషణం **nikaSaNam** *n. class.* rubbing, grinding.

నికాయం **nikaayam** *n. class.* 1 house, habitation. 2 multitude, collection, crowd.

నికార్సు, నిఖార్సు **nikaarsu, nikhaarsu** *adj.* pure, genuine, real; **nikaarsayna maniSi** straightforward person.
నికుంచకం, నికుంచనం **nikuncakam, nikuncanam** *n. class.* measure equal to one fourth of a manika.
నికుంజం **nikunjam** *n. class.* bower, arbour, thicket.
నికృష్టం **nikrSTam** *adj.* 1 wicked, vile, evil, base, mean. 2 wretched.
నికృష్టత **nikrSTata** *n.* 1 baseness. 2 wretchedness.
నికృష్టుడు **nikrSTuDu** *n.* useless person.
నిక్కం **nikkam** *n.* truth, certainty.
నిక్కంచేయు **nikkam ceeyu** *v.i.* to bring about, cause (s.g) to come true.
నిక్కచ్చి **nikkacci** I. *n.* pressure, forcing, compulsion: ~ **ceeyu** to apply pressure (for payment of dues, etc.); ~ **maniSi** strict person, person who has straight[forward] dealings.
నిక్కచ్చిగా **nikkaccigaa** *adv.* most definitely, without any doubt.
నిక్కనీలుగు **nikkaniilugu** *v.i.* to be proud or arrogant.
నిక్కపొడుచు **nikkapoDucu** *v.i.* to jut out, stick out, protrude, (of hair) to stand up.
నిక్కా **nikkaa** *n.* marriage according to Muslim rites.
నిక్కాక **nikkaaka** *n.* extreme heat.
నిక్కు **nikku** I. *n.* 1 conceit. 2 protrusion. 3 erectness. II. *v.i.* 1 to be conceited, be arrogant. 2 **Dabbu istaanani nikki niiligi ippuDu ceppEEDu** he has just now grudgingly (*or* reluctantly) said that he will give the money. 3 to strut about. 4 to jut out, protrude.
నిక్కుడు **nikkuDu** *n.* conceit, arrogance.
నిక్కువం **nikkuwam** *n.* truth, certainty.
నిక్కువంగా **nikkuwangaa** *adv.* truly, definitely.
నిక్షిప్త **nikSipta** *adj.* hidden, treasured up, stored.
నిక్షేపం **nikSeepam** *n.* 1 treasure; **eeraa** ~ ! hallo my treasure! (spoken to a child); ~ **laa unnaaDu** he is fine *or* he is quite all right; ~ **laaNTi** like a treasure, precious. 2 *geol.* deposit: *pl.* **nikSeepaalu** reserves.
నిక్షేపంగా **nikSeepangaa** *adv.* 1 nicely, finely. 2 comfortably, conveniently, without trouble.
నిక్షేపరాయుడు **nikSeeparaayuDu** *n.* 1 carefree person. 2 person who evades responsibility.
నిక్షేపించు **nikSeepincu** *v.t.* 1 to store, hide away. 2 to bury underground.
నిఖార్సు **nikhaarsu** *same as* **nikaarsu.**
నిఖిలం **nikhilam** *adj. class.* all, entire, complete, whole.
నిగడదన్ను **nigaDadannu** *v.t.* to stretch out; **kaaLLu** ~ to stretch out o.'s legs.
నిగనిగ **niganiga** *onom. adv. sug.* gleaming, glittering, shining brightly, shimmering.
నిగనిగలాడు, నిగనిగమను **niganigalaaDu, niganigamanu** *v.i.* to gleam, glitter, glisten.
నిగమనం **nigamanam** *n.* deduction, conclusion reached by reasoning.
నిగమనం చేయు **nigamanam ceeyu** *v.t.* to deduce, conclude by reasoning.
నిగర్వి **nigarwi** I. *n.* unassuming person. II. *adj.* unassuming, modest.
నిగళం **nigaLam** *n.* chain, fetter.
నిగా, నిఘా **nigaa, nighaa** *n.* 1 attention. 2 watching, observing, surveillance; ~ **weeyu** to keep watch; ~ **weesukkuurconu** *dial.* to sit idly.
నిగారించు **nigaarincu** *v.i.* to shine.
నిగారింపు **nigaarimpu** *n.* brightness, lustre.
నిగుడు **niguDu** I. *n.* pride. II. *v.i.* 1 to stretch, be extended. 2 to rise, stand up; **pilaka** (*or* **tooka**) ~ **tundeemiTi?** why are you so proud? (*lit.* why does your tuft of hair (*or* tail) stand up?).
నిగుడ్చు, నిగిడించు **niguDcu, nigiDincu** *v.t.* to stretch, extend; **drSTi** ~ to extend, direct or concentrate o.'s vision; **pilaka** (*or* **tooka**) ~ to display pride (*lit.* to make o.'s tuft of hair (*or* tail) stand up).
నిగురు **niguru** *same as* **niwuru.**
నిగూఢ **niguuDha** *adj.* 1 hidden, concealed. 2 (of meaning) obscure.
నిగ్గదీయు **niggadiiyu** *v.i.* to ask emphatically, demand an answer.
నిగ్గు **niggu** *n.* 1 brilliancy, brightness. 2 pith, essence. 3 extract.
నిగ్గుతేర్చు **nigguteercu** *v.i.* to extract essence.
నిగ్రహం **nigraham** *n.* [self]control, restraint.
నిగ్రహించు[కొను] **nigrahincu[konu]** *v.t.* to control, restrain, curb.
నిఘంటు[వు] **nighaNTu[wu]** *n.* dictionary, lexicon.
నిఘంటుకారుడు **nighaNTukaaruDu** *n.* lexicographer.
నిఘా **nighaa** *same as* **nigaa.**
నిచ్చ **nicca** *alt. colloq. form of* **nitya.**
నిచ్చెన **niccena** *n.* ladder.
నిజ[మైన] **nija[mayna]** *adj.* true, real, genuine, actual, factual; **nija jiiwitamloo** in real life; **nijamayna katha** true story.
నిజం **nijam** *n.* truth, reality, certainty.
నిజంగా **nijangaa** *adv.* truly, really, actually.
నిజాం, నిజాము **nijaam[u]** the Nizam of Hyderabad.
నిజాయితీ, నిజాయతీ **nijaayitii, nijaayatii** I. *n.* honesty, integrity, truthfulness, straightforwardness, uprightness. II. *adj.* honest, upright.
నిజానికి **nijaaniki** *adv.* in fact, actually, as a matter of fact.
నిజానిజాలు **nijaanijaalu** *n.pl.* truth and falsehood.
నిటారు **niTaaru** *adj.* straight.
నిటారుగా **niTaarugaa** *adv.* vertically, erect, upright; ~ **nilabaDi** standing straight up.
నిట్ట, నిట్టాడి[గుంజ], నిట్టరాట, నిట్రాట **niTTa[1], niTTaaDi[gunja], niTTaraaTa, niTraaTa** *n.* upright central pole supporting a house roof which has no beams.
నిట్ట **niTTa[2]** *adj.* erect.
నిట్టనిలువు **niTTaniluwu** *adj.* straight up, erect.

నిట్టుపవాసం **niTTupawaasam** *n.* complete fasting.

నిట్టూర్చు **niTTuurcu** *v.i.* to sigh.

నిట్టూర్పు **niTTuurpu** *n.* sigh.

నిట్రం **niTram** *adj. class.* steep, precipitous, vertical.

నిడివి **niDiwi** *n.* 1 length. 2 **~ miida** in the long run, eventually.

నిడుద **niDuda** *adj.* long, lengthy.

నిడుపు **niDupu** I. *n.* length. II. *adj.* (*also* **niDupaaTi**) long: **niDupaaTi weNTrukalu** long hair.

నితంబం **nitambam** *n. class.* buttocks.

నితంబిని **nitambini** *n. class.* beautiful woman.

నిత్య **nitya** *adj.* 1 eternal, permanent. 2 constant, regular, fixed, usual, daily; **~waaDakam** *gram.* regular usage.

నిత్యం **nityam** *adv.* always, continually, constantly.

నిత్యకర్మ **nityakarma** *n.* 1 daily ritual, daily routine. 2 ritual performed daily for ten days after a person's death.

నిత్యకృత్యాలు **nityakṛtyaalu** *n.pl.* daily duties, chores, daily routine.

నిత్యత, నిత్యత్వం **nityata, nityatwam** *n.* continuity, continuance.

నిత్యనిత్యపూజ **nityanityapuuja** *n.* 1 daily worship in a temple. 2 *colloq.* **aayana nannu ~ ceestunnaaDu** he scolds me repeatedly.

నిత్యప్రవాహిని **nityaprawaahini** *n.* perennial river.

నిత్యమల్లె **nityamalle** *n.* creeper with red and white flowers, *aibicus hirtus.*

నిత్యశంకితుడు **nityaśankituDu** *n.* timid, nervous or distrustful person.

నిత్యశ్యామల **nityaśyaamala** *adj.* evergreen.

నిత్యాగ్నిహోత్రుడు **nityaagnihootruDu** *n.* 1 person who maintains a sacred fire continually in his house. 2 *colloq.* chain smoker.

నిత్యామృతం **nityaamṛtam** *n.* food that is offered every day to the god in a temple.

నిదర్శకుడు **nidarśakuDu** *n.* director.

నిదర్శనం **nidarśanam** *n.* instance, example, illustration, evidence, proof; **pragatiki~** evidence of progress.

నిదానం **nidaanam**[1] I. *n.* slowness, calmness, steadiness, deliberation, patience, gentleness. II. *adj.* 1 slow, steady, deliberate. 2 *dial.* flat, level.

నిదానం **nidaanam**[2] *n.* 1 original cause. 2 source, origin. 3 study of causes and origins; **rooga~** diagnosis of a disease.

నిదానంగా **nidaanangaa** *adv.* slowly, steadily, deliberately.

నిదానాత్మక **nidaanaatmaka** *adj.* diagnostic.

నిదానించు **nidaanincu** *v.i.* to pause, ponder, consider carefully.

నిద్ర, నిద్దర, నిదుర **nid[da]ra, nidura** *n.* sleep; **oka nidra tiiyu** to take a nap.

నిద్ర కాచు **nidra kaacu** *v.i.* to stay awake, keep a vigil.

నిద్రగన్నేరు **nidraganneeru** *n. enterolobium saman,* a tree.

నిద్ర పుచ్చు **nidra puccu** *v.t.* 1 to put to sleep, lull to sleep. 2 to pacify.

నిద్రపోతు **nidrapootu** *n., mild term of abuse* sleepyhead, slothful person.

నిద్రపోవు **nidra poowu** *v.i.* to go to sleep, fall asleep.

నిద్రమత్తు, నిద్రమబ్బు **nidramattu, nidramabbu** *n.* drowsiness.

నిద్రమొఖం **nidramokham** *n.* dull fellow, good for nothing person.

నిద్ర లేచు **nidra leecu** *v.i.* to wake up, be awakened.

నిద్రవాటుగా **nidrawaaTugaa** *adv.* with a feeling of drowsiness; **neenu ~ kuurcuNTee dongalu naa sanci ettukupooyEEru** thieves stole my bag when I was sitting and feeling drowsy.

నిద్రాణం **nidraaNam** *adj.* 1 dormant. 2 sleepy, drowsy.

నిద్రాణమై ఉండు **nidraaNamay uNDu** *v.i.* to lie dormant.

నిద్రించు, నిదురించు **nidrincu, nidurincu** *v.i.* to sleep, fall asleep, go to sleep.

నిధనం **nidhanam** *n. class.* death, destruction.

నిధానం **nidhaanam** *class.* treasure.

నిధి **nidhi** *n.* 1 fund. 2 treasure house, repository. 3 *pl.* **nidhulu** reserves. 4 *fig.* fund or store of good qualities; **cadarangamloo~** expert at chess.

నినదించు **ninadincu** *v.t.* to chant, intone.

నినాదం, నినదం **ninaadam, ninadam** *n.* slogan.

నిన్న **ninna** *adv.* yesterday.

నిన్నమొన్న **ninnamonna** *adv.* recently; **~ TiwaaDu** young man.

నిపాతం **nipaatam** *n. gram.* 1 indeclinable word. 2 irregular word.

నిపుణ **nipuNa** *adj.* clever, skilful, expert.

నిపుణత, నిపుణత్వం **nipuNata, nipuNatwam** *n.* 1 skill, ability, expertness. 2 special skill, speciality.

నిపుణతగా **nipuNatagaa** *adv.* skilfully, cleverly, artfully.

నిపుణుడు **nipuNuDu** *n.* 1 expert. 2 specialist.

నిప్పచ్చ **nippacca** *n.* 1 *class.* ruin. 2 *colloq.* **~niraamayam** the state of living contentedly on a pittance after losing a fortune.

నిప్పట్టు **nippaTTu** *n.* kind of pancake.

నిప్పు **nippu** *n.* fire, live coal; **akka kaapuramloo ~lu poosindi** she ruined her elder sister's family life; **~laaNTiwaaDu** staunch or pious person (*lit.* person who is as pure as fire); **talaki nippeTTu** *or* **talaki koriwi peTTu** to light a funeral pyre; **~too celagaaTam** playing with fire.

నిప్పుకోడి **nippukooDi** *n.* ostrich.

నిప్పుపుల్ల, నిప్పుల్ల **nippupulla, nippulla** *n.* match[stick].

నిప్పుపెట్టె, నిప్పెట్టె **nippupeTTe, nippeTTe** *n.* matchbox.

నిప్పులు కక్కు **nippulu kakku** *v.i.* 1 to spit fire, burn fiercely; **eNDa~ tunnadi** the sun is scorching. 2 to rage with anger.

నిబంధన **nibandhana** *n.* 1 rule, regulation. 2 restriction, restraint. 3 testament, covenant.

నిబంధనావళి **nibandhanaawaLi** *n.* code of rules or regulations.

నిబంధించు **nibandhincu** *v.t.* 1 to bind. 2 to restrict.

నిబద్ది **nibaddi** *n.* truth, certainty, reality; ~**maniSi** plain-spoken person.

నిబద్దించు **nibaddincu** *v.t.* to make (s.g) true or real.

నిబద్ధ **nibaddha** *adj.* **1** bound. **2** restricted. **3** committed.

నిబిడ **nibiDa** *adj. class.* thick, dense; **nibiDaandhakaaram** pitch darkness.

నిబిడీకృత **nibiDiikrta** *adj. class.* thickened.

నిబ్బ **nibba** *n.* truth.

నిబ్బరం **nibbaram** I. *n.* **1** steadfastness. **2** composure. **3** confidence, assurance. **4** courage. II. *adj.* **1** steady, firm, steadfast. **2** assured, confident.

నిబ్బరంగా **nibbarangaa** *adv.* **1** firmly, staunchly. **2** confidently.

నిబ్బరించుకొను **nibbarincukonu** *v.i.* to keep o.'s composure.

నిభాయించు **nibhaayincu** *v.i. and t.* to endure, withstand, manage in face of difficulties.

నిమంత్రణం **nimantraNam** *n. class.* inviting, invitation.

నిమంత్రించు **nimantrincu** *v.t. class.* to invite.

నిమంత్రితుడు **nimantrituDu** *n. class.* invitee, guest.

నిమగ్నం **nimagnam** *adj.* **1** absorbed, engrossed, immersed, engaged, involved (**-loo**, in). **2** intent (**-loo**, on).

నిమజ్జనం **nimajjanam** *n.* submersion, immersion.

నిమిత్తం **nimittam** I. *n.* **1** cause, reason; **miikeem~ aDagaDaaniki?** what reason have you for asking? **~leekuNDaa naatoo pooTLaaTa peTTukonnaaDu** he entered into a quarrel with me without any cause. **2** need, requirement; **ika raayabaaraalatoo~leedu** there is no more need for negotiations; **patrikaa bhaaSaloo deeśyam, anyadeeśyam anee wicakSaNatoo ~leedu; wyawahaaramee pramaaNam** in newspaper language there is no need to distinguish between native and foreign; usage is the criterion. **3** connection, concern; **aastikii naakuu~leedu** there is no connection between me and the property; **aastitoo naaku~leedu** I have no concern with the property. **4** omen; **dur~** bad omen. **5** token, mark, sign. II. *advbl. particle* for [the sake of]; **niiTi paarudala sawkaryaalanu kalpincee~** for the sake of creating (*or* in order to create) irrigation facilities. III. *p.p.* on account of, because of; **andu~** on account of that, for that reason.

నిమిత్తమాత్రుడు **nimittamaatruDu** *n.* person whose actions are directed or manipulated by another.

నిమిషం, నిముషం **nimiSam, nimuSam** *n.* minute, moment; **gaNTaki araway nimiSaalu** there are sixty minutes in an hour; **nimiSaala miida** in a short time, within minutes.

నిమీలనం **nimiilanam** *n.* closing o.'s eyes.

నిమీలిత **nimiilita** *adj.* closed; **ardha~neetraalu** half-closed eyes.

నిమురు **nimuru** *v.t.* to pat, fondle, stroke.

నిమ్న **nimna** *adj.* **1** deep. **2** downward, low, depressed; **~jaati** low caste; **~pooTu** low tide.

నిమ్నోన్నత **nimnoonnata** *n.* unevenness, irregularity.

నిమ్మ[చెట్టు] **nimma[ceTTu]** *n.* lime tree.

నిమ్మకాయ, నిమ్మపండు **nimmakaaya, nimmapaNDu** *n.* lime fruit.

నిమ్మకినీరెత్తినట్లు **nimmaki niirettinaTLu** *lit.* like pouring water on a lime tree (whose stock must always be kept moist) *is a proverbial expression used to signify* doing s.g quietly, unobtrusively, without the knowledge of others.

నిమ్మళం **nimmaLam** I. *n.* **1** ease, comfort. **2** slowness. **3** carefulness, patience, gentleness. II. *adj.* **1** easy. **2** quiet. **3** happy, well, healthy.

నిమ్మళంగా, నిమ్మళం మీద **nimmaLangaa, nimmaLam miida** *adv.* **1** gently, softly. **2** slowly, carefully. **3** gradually, by degrees.

నిమ్మళించు **nimmaLincu** *v.i.* (of health) to get better, improve, recover.

నియంత **niyanta** *n.* dictator.

నియంతృత్వం **niyantrtwam** *n.* dictatorship.

నియంత్రకం **niyantrakam** *n.* regulator.

నియంత్రణ **niyantraNa** *n.* regulation, control, ordering; **kuTumba~** family planning.

నియంత్రించు **niyantrincu** *v.t.* to control, regulate.

నియత **niyata** *adj.* **1** regular, consistent. **2** fixed, regulated; **~kriiDalu** organised games. **3** finite; **~sankhya** finite number.

నియతంగా **niyatangaa** *adv.* in a regular manner, consistently.

నియతి **niyati** *n.* **1** control, restriction. **2** rule, regulation. **3** consistency.

నియతికాలికంగా **niyatikaalikangaa** *adv.* at regular intervals.

నియమం **niyamam** *n.* **1** principle, precept; **aayana caalaa ~unna maniSi** he is a man of strict principles. **2** rule, norm; **sthaana~** *gram.* placement rule; **niyamanibandhanalu** rules and regulations; **niyamabaddha** regulated. **3** social rule, convention. **4** religious precept, religious observance. **5** law of nature; **gurutwaakarSaNa~** law of gravity. **6** condition, stipulation (= **Saratu**).

నియమంగా **niyamangaa** *adv.* **1** regularly, punctually. **2** strictly according to social and religious principles; **maDikaTTukoni caalaa~bhoonceestaaDu** he puts on ceremonially pure clothes and takes his meals according to strict religious principles.

నియమనం **niyamanam** *n.* **1** controlling, restraining, regulating. **2** command, order, rule.

నియమానుసారంగా **niyamaanusaarangaa** *adv.* regularly.

నియమావళి **niyamaawaLi** *n.* set or code of rules, manual.

నియమించు **niyamincu** *v.t.* to appoint.

నియమిత **niyamita** *adj.* **1** appointed. **2** fixed, regulated.

నియమితుడు **niyamituDu** *n.* appointee.

నియామకం **niyaamakam** *n.* **1** appointment. **2** posting, stationing (of staff).

నియుక్త **niyukta** *adj.* allotted, assigned, designated.

నియోగి, నియ్యోగి **niyoogi, niyyoogi** *n.* name of a brahman sect.

నియోగించు **niyoogincu** *v.t.* 1 to employ, appoint, engage (s.o. to carry out a task): **ii panimiida nannu niyoogincEEDu** he has employed me on this work *or* he has given me this work to do. 2 to allot, allocate (funds).

నియోజకవర్గం **niyoojakawargam** *n. polit.* constituency.

నియోజకులు **niyoojakulu** *n. pl.* electors, electorate.

నియోజనం **niyoojanam** *n.* assignment, allotted task.

నిర్, నిశ్, నిష్, నిస్ **nir, niś, niS, nis** *prefix signifying* not *or* without, e.g., **nirupayooga** useless.

నిరంకుశ **nirankuśa** *adj.* 1 *polit.* authoritarian, totalitarian, dictatorial, autocratic, despotic. 2 unrestrained, uncontrolled.

నిరంకుశత్వం **nirankuśatwam** *n.* authoritarianism, totalitarianism, despotism.

నిరంజన **niranjana** *adj.* 1 unstained. 2 free from passion or emotion.

నిరంతర **nirantara** *adj.* 1 ceaseless, incessant, endless. 2 continuous.

నిరంతరం[గా] **nirantaram[gaa]** *adv.* continuously, ceaselessly, incessantly, perennially.

నిరంతరాయంగా **nirantaraayangaa** *adv.* without interruption, without intermission.

నిరక్షరకుక్షి **nirakSarakukSi** *n.* illiterate person (*term of contempt*; *lit.* stomach with no education).

నిరక్షరాస్యత **nirakSaraasyata** *n.* illiteracy.

నిరక్షరాస్యుడు **nirakSaraasyuDu** *n.* illiterate person.

నిరతి **nirati** *n. second part of a n. compound signifying* dedication, devotion; **seewaa**~ devotion to service.

నిరపరాధ **niraparaadha** *adj. legal* innocent, not guilty.

నిరపరాధం **niraparaadham** *n. legal* innocence.

నిరపరాధి **niraparaadhi** *n. legal* innocent person.

నిరపాయ **nirapaaya** *adj.* not dangerous, harmless.

నిరపేక్ష **nirapeekSa** I. *n.* detachment, indifference, freedom from wordly desire. II. *adj. sci.* absolute; ~**aardrata** absolute humidity.

నిరపేక్షత **nirapeekSata** *n.* absoluteness.

నిరభ్యంతరంగా **nirabhyantarangaa** *adv.* without any objection.

నిరయస్కాంతీకరణం **nirayaskaantiikaraNam** *n.* demagnetisation.

నిరర్గళ **nirargaLa** *adj.* 1 uninterrupted. 2 unrestrained.

నిరర్థక **nirarthaka** *adj.* 1 meaningless. 2 fruitless, useless; **tana jiiwitam** ~**paracukonnaaDu** he ruined his own life.

నిరవధిక **nirawadhika** *adj.* 1 boundless, limitless, unlimited. 2 (of time) indefinite.

నిరవధికంగా **nirawadhikangaa** *adv.* 1 boundlessly. 2 *legal* sine die.

నిరవశేష **nirawaśeeSa** *adj.* complete, with nothing left over.

నిరవాకం, నిర్వాకం **nirawaakam, nirwaakam** *n. colloq.* (< **nirwaahakam**) accomplishment, achievement (*used disparagingly*); **mottam Dabbu bajaaruku tiisukeLLi ii alugguDDalu paTTukoccEEwu! idee nii**~**! baTTalu eem baagunnaayi?** you took all the money to the bazaar and brought back these rags! what a great achievement! what good are these clothes?

నిరశనం **niraśanam** *n. class.* fasting.

నిరశన దీక్ష, నిరశన వ్రతం **niraśana diikSa, niraśana wratam** *n. class.* vow of abstinence from food, hunger strike.

నిరసన **nirasana** *n.* 1 protest. 2 contempt, scorn. 3 slighting, belittling, disregard.

నిరసన దీక్ష, నిరసన వ్రతం **nirasana diikSa, nirasana wratam** *colloq. alt. form of* **niraśana diikSa, niraśana wratam.**

నిరసించు **nirasincu** *v.i. and t.* 1 to protest. 2 to despise, disparage, belittle, disregard. 3 to censure, condemn. 4 to resist, oppose.

నిరసు **nirasu** *n.* obsolete gold coin.

నిరస్త **nirasta** *adj. class.* rejected, discarded, refused.

నిరహంకారం, నిరహంకృతి **nirahankaaram, nirahankrti** *n.* modesty, unpretentiousness.

నిరాకరణ[ం] **niraakaraNa[m]** *n.* 1 refusal: **sahaaya**~ non-cooperation. 2 rejection, disregard, repudiation.

నిరాకరించు **niraakarincu** *v.t.* 1 to refuse: **Dabbu iwwaDaaniki niraakarincEEDu** he refused to lend money. 2 to oppose (resolution). 3 to reject, repudiate, disregard.

నిరాకార **niraakaara** *adj.* without shape or form.

నిరాకారుడు **niraakaaruDu** *n.* God, the Supreme Spirit, who is without shape or form.

నిరాకృతి **niraakrti** *n.* 1 refusal. 2 rejection, disregard.

నిరాక్షేప **niraakSeepa** *adj.* incontestable, indisputable.

నిరాక్షేపణీయ **niraakSeepaNiiya** *adj.* unobjectionable.

నిరాఘాట **niraaghaaTa** *adj.* 1 unobstructed, unimpeded, unhindered, untrammelled. 2 boundless, unlimited.

నిరాఘాటంగా **niraaghaaTangaa** *adv.* 1 without obstruction, easily. 2 without limitation.

నిరాటంకంగా **niraaTankangaa** *adv.* without a hitch or hindrance, unrestrainedly.

నిరాడంబర **niraaDambara** *adj.* 1 unpretentious, modest, unostentatious. 2 (of dress) informal. 3 (of food) plain, simple.

నిరాడంబరంగా **niraaDambarangaa** *adv.* informally, simply, without pomp or ceremony, without ostentation.

నిరాడంబరత్వం **niraaDambaratwam** *n.* unpretentiousness, lack of ostentation.

నిరాడంబరుడు **niraaDambaruDu** *n.* modest and unpretentious person.

నిరాదరణ **niraadaraNa** *n.* want of interest or concern.

నిరాదరించు **niraadarincu** *v.t.* to disregard, neglect, pay no attention to.

నిరాదరువు **niraadaruwu** *adj.* without shelter or support.

నిరాధార **niraadhaara** *adj.* 1 baseless, unfounded, unsubstantiated. 2 without shelter or support.

నిరాపేక్ష **niraapeekSa** *n.* want of affection, indifference.

నిరామయం **niraamayam** *n.* enjoyment of a healthy and carefree life: *see* **nippacca.**

నిరాయాసంగా **niraayaasangaa** *adv.* easily, without exertion.

నిరాయుధ **niraayudha** *adj.* unarmed.

నిరాయుధీకరణ **niraayudhiikaraNa** *n.* disarmament.

నిరాలంబ **niraalamba** *adj.* without external means of support.

నిరాశ **niraaśa** *n.* despair, despondency, feeling of disappointment or frustration.

నిరాశ చేసుకొను **niraaśa ceesukonu** *v.i.* to lose hope, give up hope, be despondent, be disappointed.

నిరాశావాదం **niraaśaawaadam** *n.* pessimism.

నిరాశావాది **niraaśaawaadi** *n.* pessimist.

నిరాశ్రయ **niraaśraya** *adj.* without shelter or support, destitute.

నిరాశ్రయుడు **niraaśrayuDu** *n.* homeless person, destitute person.

నిరాహార **niraahaara** *adj.* fasting, abstaining from food.

నిరాహారదీక్ష **niraahaara diikSa** *n.* vow of abstinence from food, hunger strike.

నిరీక్షణ **niriikSaNa** *n.* expectation, waiting.

నిరీక్షించు **niriikSincu** *v.i.* to wait for, await: **phalitaala-koosam niriikSistunnaaDu** he is waiting for results.

నిరీశ్వర **niriiśwara** *adj.* atheistic.

నిరీశ్వరవాదం **niriiśwarawaadam** *n.* atheism.

నిరీశ్వరవాది **niriiśwarawaadi** *n.* atheist.

నిరుక్త **nirukta** *adj.* uttered, defined.

నిరుక్తం **niruktam** *n.* 1 that which is uttered, defined or explained. 2 name of Yaska's commentary on the Nighantus. 3 name of one of the Vedangas containing a glossary of obscure terms occurring in the Vedas.

నిరుక్తి **nirukti** *n.* name of a figure of speech.

నిరుడు **niruDu** *advbl. n.* last year: **niruTimiida ii eeDu cali ekkuwa** compared with last year this year is cooler.

నిరుత్తర **niruttara** *adj.* speechless, unable to answer.

నిరుత్సాహం **nirutsaaham** *n.* dejection, disappointment, discouragement, downheartedness, despondency.

నిరుత్సాహం చెందు **nirutsaaham cendu** *v.i.* to be disappointed.

నిరుత్సాహపరచు **nirutsaahaparacu** *v.t.* to discourage.

నిరుద్యోగం **nirudyoogam** *n.* unemployment.

నిరుద్యోగి **nirudyoogi** *n.* unemployed person.

నిరుపమాన **nirupamaana** *adj.* incomparable, matchless, unequalled.

నిరుపయోగ **nirupayooga** *adj.* useless.

నిరుపహతి **nirupahati** *adj. class.* undisturbed, untroubled.

నిరుపాధిక **nirupaadhika** *adj. class.* without attributes or qualities.

నిరూఢ **niruuDha** *adj. class.* 1 famous. 2 (of words, expressions) in current usage.

నిరూఢి **niruuDhi** *n. class.* fame.

నిరూపకం **niruupakam** *n. maths.* coordinate.

నిరూపణ[ం] **niruupaNa[m]** *n.* demonstration, exhibiting, display, proof.

నిరూపించు **niruupincu** *v.t.* to demonstrate, exhibit, determine, substantiate, prove.

నిరూప్య **niruupya** *adj. class.* proven, determined.

నిరోధం **niroodham** *n.* 1 obstruction, prevention. 2 restraint, check, constraint, resistance.

నిరోధక **niroodhaka** *adj.* preventive, inhibitory, resistant.

నిరోధకత **niroodhakata** *n.* inhibition.

నిరోధకుడు **niroodhakuDu** *n.* one who obstructs.

నిరోధించు **niroodhincu** *v.t.* to obstruct, prevent, resist, restrain, inhibit, impede, check, stop; **atanni loopaliki raakuNDaa niroodhincEEru** they prevented him from entering.

నిరోష్ఠ **nirooSTa** *adj. class.* without labial sounds (a device used in some poetical compositions).

నిర్గంధ **nirgandha** *adj.* odourless.

నిర్గంపెట్టు, నిర్గెంపెట్టు, నిర్ఘ్యంపెట్టు **nirgampeTTu, nirgempeTTu, nirghyampeTTu** *v.t.* to make a token start on a journey by going and depositing a package at some place on the way and then returning (this is done at an auspicious time to offset any bad effect if the actual start is due to be made later at an inauspicious time): **waaDu peTTe nirgempeTTi wenakki wacc-EEDu** he has deposited his box on the way and come back.

నిర్గమద్వారం **nirgamadwaaram** *n. sci.* outlet.

నిర్గమన[ం] **nirgamana[m]** *n.* exit, egress.

నిర్గమించు **nirgamincu** *v.t.* to depart.

నిర్గళనం **nirgaLanam** *n. class.* oozing, trickling.

నిర్గుణ **nirguNa** *adj.* devoid of attributes or qualities.

నిర్ఘాంతపడు, నిర్ఘాంతపోవు **nirghaantapaDu, nirgh-aantapoowu** *v.i.* to be amazed, be thunderstruck.

నిర్జన **nirjana** *adj.* deserted, unpopulated.

నిర్జల **nirjala** *adj.* waterless.

నిర్జలీకరణం **nirjaliikaraNam** *n. sci.* dehydration.

నిర్జీవ **nirjiiwa** *adj.* lifeless, inanimate.

నిర్ఝరం **nirjharam** *n.* torrent, cascade.

నిర్ఝరిణి **nirjhariNi** *n. class.* river.

నిర్ణయం **nirNayam** *n.* 1 decision, conclusion, determination, settlement. 2 *legal* **koorTu~** verdict: **neera~** conviction.

నిర్ణయంగా **nirNayangaa** *adv.* definitely, positively, for certain.

నిర్ణయమైన **nirNayamayna** *adj.* settled, determined, decided.

నిర్ణయించు **nirNayincu** *v.i. and t.* 1 to settle, decide. 2 to fix, determine, prescribe. 3 *legal* **dooSigaa~** to find guilty, convict.

నిర్ణయించుకొను **nirNayincukonu** *v.i.* to decide for o.s., make up o.'s mind, resolve, determine.

నిర్ణాయక **nirNaayaka** *adj.* deciding, decisive, definitive, conclusive: **~wooTu** deciding vote, (chairman's) casting vote.

నిర్ణిబద్ధ **nirNibaddha** *adj.* (of a rule) strict, invariable, hard and fast.

నిర్ణీత **nirNiita** *adj.* 1 definite, decided. 2 fixed, settled, prescribed. ~ **kaalamloo** within a fixed time.

నిర్ణేత nirNeeta *n.* person who decides, adjudicator.

నిర్దయ nirdaya *n.* unkindness, pitilessness, cruelty.

నిర్దయాత్మకుడు, నిర్దయుడు **nirdayaatmakuDu, nirdayuDu** *n.* pitiless person.

నిర్దాక్షిణ్య **nirdaakSiNya** *adj.* merciless, heartless.

నిర్దాక్షిణ్యం **nirdaakSiNyam** *n.* mercilessness, heartlessness.

నిర్దిష్ట **nirdiSTa** *adj.* 1 certain, particular, specific, such and such: **sankhyalu gurtincina uuLLaloo ~ padam waaDukaloo unnadani nirdhaaraNagaa ceppawaccu** we can say definitely that in villages marked with numbers a certain word (*or* such and such a word) is in use. 2 specified, indicated, prescribed, ~ **ruupamloo pramaaNam ceesEEDu** he took the oath in the prescribed manner. 3 clear, definite, exact.

నిర్దిష్టంగా **nirdiSTangaa** *adv.* specifically.

నిర్దిష్టం చేయు **nirdiSTam ceeyu** *v.t.* to specify.

నిర్దిష్టత **nirdiSTata** *n.* exactitude.

నిర్దుష్ట **nirduSTa** *adj.* 1 free from errors, free from defects, faultless, flawless. 2 unimpeachable. 3 pure, unpolluted.

నిర్దేశ **nirdeeśa** *adj. gram.* demonstrative: ~ **sarwanaamam** demonstrative pronoun.

నిర్దేశం **nirdeeśam** *n.* 1 order. 2 indication. 3 distinguishing mark.

నిర్దేశక **nirdeeśaka** *adj.* directive: ~ **suutraalu** directive principles: ~ **kaaryaalayam** directorate: ~ **maNDali** board of directors.

నిర్దేశకుడు **nirdeeśakuDu** *n.* director (of an institution or project).

నిర్దేశాంకం **nirdeesaankam** *n. maths.* coordinate.

నిర్దేశించు **nirdeeśincu** *v.t.* 1 to command, order, ordain direct, prescribe. 2 to designate, denote. 3 to indicate, point out, specify, set forth, lay down: **aayaa suutraalanu praadhaanya kramamloo nirdeesiddaam** we will set forth the various principles in order of importance.

నిర్దోషి **nirdooSi** *n. legal* innocent person, person found not guilty.

నిర్దోషిత్వం **nirdooSitwam** *n. legal* innocence.

నిర్ద్వంద్వంగా **nirdwandwangaa** *adv.* unequivocally, unambiguously.

నిర్ధనుడు **nirdhanuDu** *n.* penniless person, impoverished person.

నిర్ధరించు, నిర్ధారించు **nirdha[a]rincu** *v.t.* 1 to determine, establish. 2 to fix, settle. 3 to confirm, affirm.

నిర్ధరించుకొను, నిర్ధారించుకొను **nirdha[a]rincukonu** *v.i.* to decide, resolve, make up o.'s mind.

నిర్ధారకం **nirdhaarakam** *n. sci.* determinant.

నిర్ధారణ **nirdhaaraNa** *n.* 1 proof, certainty. 2 conclusion, decision. 3 confirmation, affirmation.

నిర్ధారణగా **nirdhaaraNagaa** *adv.* 1 definitely, undoubtedly, assuredly. 2 confidently, with conviction.

నిర్ధారణచేయు **nirdhaaraNaceeyu** *v.t.* 1 to prove, establish. 2 to confirm, affirm.

నిర్ధారణచేసుకొను **nirdhaaraNaceesukonu** *v.i.* to feel sure, feel convinced.

నిర్ధారిత **nirdhaarita** *adj.* determined, fixed.

నిర్ధూమ **nirdhuuma** *adj. class.* smokeless.

నిర్ధూమధామం **nirdhuumadhaamam** *n. lit.* abode from whose roof no smoke rises, i.e., abode which has been abandoned.

నిర్నిబంధ **nirnibandha** *adj.* 1 unconditional. 2 unrestricted.

నిర్నిమిత్తం **nirnimittam** *adj.* without cause, groundless.

నిర్పూచీ **nirpuucii** *dial. variant of* **niSpuucii.**

నిర్బంధ **nirbandha** *adj.* compulsory, obligatory: ~ **widya** compulsory education.

నిర్బంధం **nirbandham** *n.* 1 force, compulsion, duress. 2 restriction, restraint. 3 oppression. 4 detention in custody. 5 confinement, captivity. 6 *pl.* ~ **nirbandhaalu** sanctions (**aankSalu**).

నిర్బంధించు **nirbandhincu** *v.t.* 1 to force, compel. 2 to restrict, restrain. 3 to detain in custody.

నిర్బంధితుడు **nirbandhituDu** *n.* detenu, detainee.

నిర్బిందుకంగా **nirbindukangaa** *adv. class.* (of orthography) without using the symbol for **arasunna.**

నిర్భయ **nirbhaya** *adj.* fearless.

నిర్భయంగా **nirbhayangaa** *adv.* fearlessly.

నిర్భర **nirbhara** *adj.* 1 unbearable. 2 excessive, great.

నిర్భాగ్యుడు **nirbhaagyuDu** *n.* luckless or accursed person.

నిర్భీకంగా **nirbhiikangaa** *adv.* fearlessly.

నిర్భీకత, నిర్భీతి **nirbhiikata, nirbhiiti** *n.* fearlessness.

నిర్మల **nirmala** *adj.* 1 pure, clear. 2 clean, unsullied. 3 unclouded, serene.

నిర్మాణ **nirmaaNa** *adj.* 1 structural. 2 (*also* **nirmaaNaatmaka**) constructive: **nirmaana kaaryakramam** constructive programme: **nirmaaNaatmaka wimarśa** constructive criticism.

నిర్మాణం **nirmaaNam** *n.* 1 (abstract) construction, production, formation, creation, founding: **caTTa~** framing of laws. 2 (concrete) construction, structure, building.

నిర్మాణజీవక్రియ **nirmaaNajiiwakriya** *n. biol.* anabolism.

నిర్మాత nirmaata *n.* creator, originator, founder (of a movement), framer (of law), producer (of drama) maker, manufacturer.

నిర్మానుష్య **nirmaanuSya** *adj.* uninhabited.

నిర్మించు **nirmincu** *v.t.* to create, build, form, construct.

నిర్మిత **nirmita** *adj.* made, created.

నిర్మితి **nirmiti** *n. class. same as* **nirmaaNam.**

నిర్మూలం **nirmuulam** *n.* extinction, annihilation.

నిర్మూలం చేయు, నిర్మూలించు **nirmuulam ceeyu, nirmuulincu** *v.t.* to eradicate, extirpate, root out, annihilate, abolish.

నిర్మూలనం **nirmuulanam** *n.* rooting out, abolition, eradication, annihilation.

నిర్మొగమాటం, నిర్మొహమాటం **nirmogamaaTam, nirmohamaaTam** *n.* 1 boldness. 2 bluntness of manner.

నిర్మొహమాటంగా **nirmohamaaTangaa** *adv.* boldly, bluntly, uninhibitedly.

నిర్యాణం **niryaaNam** *n. class.* death, demise.

నిర్రనీలుగు **nirraniilugu** *v.i.* to be proud, be arrogant, be presumptuous.

నిర్లక్ష్య **nirlakSya** *adj.* 1 careless, reckless. 2 neglectful, inattentive, indifferent.

నిర్లక్ష్యం **nirlakSyam** *n.* 1 carelessness, not caring, recklessness. 2 inattention. disregard, neglect: **caduwumiida ~** neglect of studies.

నిర్లక్ష్యంగా **nirlakSyangaa** *adv.* 1 carelessly, recklessly. 2 casually, unconcernedly, indifferently.

నిర్లక్ష్యం చేయు **nirlakSyam ceeyu** *v.t.* to ignore neglect, disregard.

నిర్లజ్జ **nirlajja** *adj.* shameless, immodest.

నిర్లిప్త **nirlipta** *adj.* 1 indifferent, unconcerned. 2 detached, unattached.

నిర్లిప్తంగా **nirliptangaa** *adv.* indifferently, calmly, in a detached and unconcerned manner.

నిర్లిప్తత **nirliptata** *n.* 1 unconcernedness, indifference. 2 freedom from emotion, detachment.

నిర్వక్రత **nirwakrata** *n.* straightforwardness.

నిర్వచనం **nirwacanam** *n.* 1 definition, interpretation, description. 2 *class.* literary work that does not contain prose.

నిర్వచనీయ **nirwacaniiya** *adj.* describable, definable.

నిర్వచించు **nirwacincu** *v.t.* to define, explain, describe, interpret.

నిర్వర్తించు **nirwartincu** *v.t.* to perform, carry out, discharge (duty, responsibility).

నిర్వహణం **nirwahaNam** *n.* 1 performance, conduct, execution. 2 administration, management.

నిర్వహించు **nirwahincu** *v.t.* 1 to undertake, perform, carry out, carry on, execute, discharge (duty, function). 2 to manage, run, maintain, administer, conduct (organisation, business). 3 to hold (competition).

నిర్వాకం **nirwaakam** *see* **nirawaakam.**

నిర్వాణం **nirwaaNam** *n.* nirvana, extinction, merging with the infinite.

నిర్వాపణం **nirwaapaNam** *n. class.* slaughter, killing.

నిర్వాసితుడు **nirwaasituDu** *n.* expropriated or dispossessed or homeless person, displaced person, evacuee.

నిర్వాహక **nirwaahaka** *adj.* managerial: **~ wargam** managerial class.

నిర్వాహకం **nirwaahakam** *n. class.* 1 accomplishment, achievement. 2 management: *see* **nirawaakam.**

నిర్వాహకుడు **nirwaahakuDu** *n.* manager, organiser.

నిర్వికల్ప సమాధి **nirwikalpa samaadhi** *n.* state of complete mental absorption.

నిర్వికార **nirwikaara** *adj.* 1 changeless. 2 expressionless, emotionless. 3 unruffled.

నిర్వికారుడు **nirwikaaruDu** *n.* God, the Supreme Spirit.

నిర్విఘ్న **nirwighna** *adj.* unobstructed, uninterrupted, unimpeded.

నిర్విఘ్నంగా **nirwighnangaa** *adv.* without a hitch, without hindrance.

నిర్విచార **nirwicaara** *adj.* free from sorrow.

నిర్విణ్ణత **nirwiNNata** *n.* amazement, stupefaction.

నిర్విణ్ణుడు **nirwiNNuDu** *n.* person who is stupefied or nonplussed.

నిర్విరామ **nirwiraama** *adj.* ceaseless: **~ kṛSi** untiring effort.

నిర్వివాద **nirwiwaada** *adj.* indisputable, incontestable.

నిర్విశేష **nirwiśeeSa** *adj.* making no difference or distinction.

నిర్వీర్య **nirwiirya** *adj.* weak, feeble, unmanly.

నిర్వీర్యం **nirwiiryam** *n.* unmanliness.

నిర్వృత్తి **nirwṛtti** *n.* 1 death. 2 happiness.

నిర్వేదం, నిర్వేదన **nirweedam, nirweedana** *n.* grief, despair, despondency.

నిర్వ్యాజ్య **nirwyaajya** *adj.* true, unfeigned, sincere: **~ preema** true love.

నిర్హేతుక **nirheetuka** *adj.* 1 unreasonable. 2 unjustified, unmerited (accusation). 3 unfounded, groundless (allegation).

నిలకడ **nilakaDa** I. *n.* 1 steadiness, steadfastness, stability. 2 constancy, endurance. II. *adj.* 1 steady, stable: **aayana maaTa ~ leeDu** he does not keep to his word. 2 constant, enduring: **udyoogam ~ leedu** the job is not a permanent one.

నిలకడగా **nilakaDagaa** *adv.* ceaselessly, continuously: **waana ~ kurisindi** the rain poured continuously.

నిలకడమీద **nilakaDamiida** *adv.* eventually: **nijam ~ teelutundi** eventually the truth will come out.

నిలదీయు, నిలవేయు, నిలేయు **niladiiyu, nilaweeyu, nileeyu** *v.t.* to stop (s.o.); **niladiisi** (*or* **nilabeTTi** *or* **nileesi**) **aDugu** to stop s.o. and ask, ask point blank, ask insistently, question closely; **"saayam ceestee ceppu ceyyakapootee ceyyanani ceppeeyi" ani niladisindi aame** "if you will help, say so, if not, say you will not" she demanded point blank; **anumaanam tooci waaNNi niladiisi gaTTigaa aDigEEnu, raasEEnani oppukonnaaDu** being suspicious I questioned him closely and he admitted having written it.

నిలదొక్కుకొను **niladokkukonu** *v.t.* to recover o.s., rally o.s., stabilise o.s.: **kaalu ~** to establish o.s.

నిలబడు **nilabaDu** *v.t.* 1 to stand. 2 to stay, remain, wait: **jwaram aTLaa nilabadi undi** the fever remains (in the same condition) as it was: **aa mandu aa jabbu maniSiki istee praaNam nilabaDutundaTa** if you give that medicine to that sick man, they say his life will be saved. 3 to last, endure; **tumma karra nilabaDi kaalutundi, migataa kaTTelu surasura kaalutaayi** babulwood burns slowly, other firewood burns very fast.

నిలబెట్టి **nilabeTTi** *past participle of* **nilabeTTu** *used adverbially* continuously, nonstop; **waana ~ kurisindi** the rain poured continuously.

నిలబెట్టు, నిలువబెట్టు, నిల్వబెట్టు **nilabeTTu, niluwabeTTu, nilwabeTTu** *v.t.* 1 to set up, establish. 2 to stop; **nannu naDiwiidhiloo nilabeTTEEDu** he stopped me in the middle of the street. 3 to uphold, maintain, sustain. 4 to save; **praaNam ~** to save (s.o.'s) life; **maa illu nilabeTTEEDu** he come to the help of my family in trouble. 5 **samsaaram ~ konu** to set right o.'s family affairs. 6 to confront: *see* **niladiiyu.**

నిలయం **nilayam** *n.* abode, house, residence.

నిలవ **nilawa** *same as* **niluwa.**

నిలవనీడ **nilawaniiDa** *n.* shelter, protection.

నిలవరించు **nilawarincu** *v.i. and t.* 1 to support, sustain, manage. 2 to bear, endure.

నిలవరించుకొను **nilawarincukonu** *v.i.* 1 to summon up o.'s courage. 2 to suppress o.'s emotions.

నిలవేయు **nilaweeyu** *v.t.* 1 *same as* **niladiiyu.** 2 *colloq.* to collect, accumulate; **Dabbu nilaweesukonnaaDu** he accumulated money.

నిలిచి **nilici** *past participle of* **nilucu** *used adverbially* slowly; **cintakarra boggu ~ kaalutundi** charcoal made from tamarind wood burns slowly.

నిలుచు **nilucu** *v.i.* 1 to stand. 2 to rise, get up. 3 to stop, halt, cease. 4 to last, endure, remain, be retained.

నిలుచుండు, నిలుచును **nilucuNDu, nilucunu** *stylistic variants of* **nilucu.**

నిలుపు **nilupu** I. *n.* (*also* **~ dala**) 1 stopping. 2 *legal* stay. II. *v.t.* 1 to cause to stand, set up, erect, fix, put in place; *see* **diipampeTTu.** 2 to stop, detain, restrain. 3 to post, station (troops).

నిలుపుకొను **nilupukonu** *v.t.* to keep, preserve, maintain.

నిలువ, నిలవ, నిల్వ **niluwa, nil[a]wa** *n.* 1 remainder, balance left over. 2 storage: **~ śakti** storage capacity. 3 reservation, preservation. 4. *geol. pl.* **~ lu** reserves. 5 **~ niiTi maDugu** pool of still water.

నిలువ చేయు **niluwa ceeyu** *v.t.* 1 to accumulate. 2 to store, keep, preserve. 3 to hoard. 4 to keep back, reserve.

నిలువబెట్టు **niluwabeTTu** *same as* **nilabeTTu.**

నిలువు **niluwu** I. *n.* six feet, one fathom. II. *adj.* 1 upright, erect, standing, vertical: **~ gunja** upright post. 2 lengthwise, longitudinal.

నిలువుగా **niluwugaa** *adv.* 1 vertically, upright. 2 lengthwise: **~ aDDangaa dunnaDam** ploughing (a field) lengthwise and crosswise.

నిలువుటద్దం **niluwuTaddam** *n.* full length mirror, upright mirror.

నిలువుదోపిడీ **niluwudoopiDii** *n.* type of offering in which everything on o.'s person is taken off and offered to the deity.

నిలువున, నిలువునా **niluwuna[a]** *adv.* 1 upright, erect; **~ nilabaDi** standing straight up. 2 throughout, all through, all over, completely, from top to bottom.

నిలువెత్తు **niluwettu** *adj.* 1 life-size. 2 as high as a man. 3 of full stature.

నిలువెల్లా **niluwellaa** *adv.* throughout, all through.

నిలేయు **nileeyu** *same as* **niladiiyu.**

నిల్వబెట్టు **nilwabeTTu** *same as* **nilabeTTu.**

నివర్తి **niwarti** *n. class.* 1 doing away with, removal, abolition. 2 *alt. form of* **niwṛtti.**

నివర్తించు **niwartincu** *v.t.* to do away with.

నివసించు **niwasincu** *v.i.* to live, reside, dwell.

నివహం **niwaham** *n. class.* 1 crowd, multitude, group, collection: **wṛkSa ~** cluster of trees. 2 large quantity: **andhakaara ~** thick pall of darkness.

నివాత **niwaata** *adj. class.* airless, close, confined.

నివారక **niwaaraka** *adj.* preventive, protective.

నివారణ **niwaaraNa** I. *n.* prevention, protection, remedy. II. *adj.* preventive, protective, remedial.

నివారణి **niwaaraNi** *n.* cure, remedy: **sarwarooga** panacea.

నివారణీయ **niwaaraNiiya** *adj.* preventible, remediable.

నివారించు **niwaarincu** *v.t.* 1 to prevent, stop, avert, ward off: **waaNNi raakuNDaa niwaarincEEnu** I prevented him from coming. 2 to do away with, dissipate.

నివాళి, నివ్వాళి **niwaaLi, niwwaaLi** *n.* 1 waving lighted camphor before a deity as an offering. 2 tribute; **~ arpincu** to pay tribute (to a person): *cf.* **haarati.**

నివాసం **niwaasam** *n.* house, dwelling, residence, abode.

నివాసయోగ్య **niwaasayoogya** *adj.* [in]habitable.

నివాసస్థలం **niwaasasthalam** *n.* place of residence.

నివాసి **niwaasi** *n.* inhabitant, resident.

నివురు, నిగురు **niwuru, niguru** *n. class.* ashes; **~ kappina nippu** burning embers covered by ashes, hidden fire.

నివృత్తి **niwṛtti** *n.* 1 removal, abolition. 2 cessation. 3 salvation: **waaDu ceesina paapaalaki ~ leedu** there will be no salvation for him owing to the sins he has committed.

నివృత్తి చేయు **niwṛtti ceeyu** *v.t.* to remove, clear away, dispel (doubt).

నివేదన[ం] **niweedana[m]** *n.* 1 offering, oblation. 2 proclaiming.

నివేదించు **niweedincu** *v.t.* 1 to make known, report. 2 to submit, represent: **saakSyam ~** to adduce evidence. 3 to offer, present, deliver: **atithulaku swaagatam ~** to bid welcome to guests.

నివేదిక **niweedika** *n.* report, memorandum.

నివేశం **niweeśam** *n.* 1 house. 2 house site.

నివేశనస్థలం **niweeśanasthalam** *n.* 1 dwelling place. 2 house site.

నివ్వరి **niwwari** *same as* **niiwaaram.**

నివ్వాళి **niwwaaLi** *same as* **niwaaLi.**

నివ్వెర[పాటు] **niwwera[paaTu]** *n.* astonishment, amazement, shock, alarm.

నివ్వెరపడు, నివ్వెరపోవు **niwwerapaDu, niwwerapoowu** *v.i.* to be astonished, be alarmed, be thunderstruck.

నిశ, నిశి, నిసి **niśa, niśi, nisi** *n. class.* night.

నిశాంతం **niśaantam** *n. class.* dawn, daybreak.
నిశాకరుడు **niśaakaruDu** *n. class.* moon.
నిశాచరి **niśaacari** *n. class.* adulteress.
నిశాచరుడు **niśaacaruDu** *n.* fiend, ghost.
నిశాని **niśaani** *n.* mark, sign (= **gurtu**): ~ **peTTina cooTa santakam peTTaNDi** please sign in the place where a mark has been put.
నిశానిపద్దు, నిశానివాడు **niśaanipaddu, niśaaniwaaDu**[1] *n.* illiterate person.
నిశానివాడు **niśaaniwaaDu**[2] *n. class.* drummer employed in olden times to precede an important person on a journey.
నిశిత **niśita** *adj.* **1** sharp, keen, acute. **2** (of criticism) severe. **3** specific, precise.
నిశితంగా **niśitangaa** *adv.* sharply, keenly, intently, acutely.
నిశితత్వం **niśitatwam** *n.* sharpness, keenness, acuteness.
నిశిరాత్రి **niśiraatri** *n.* midnight, dead of night.
నిశీథం, నిశీధి **niśiidham, niśiidhi** *n. class.* night.
నిశ్చయ **niścaya** *adj.* certain, sure.
నిశ్చయం **niścayam** *n.* **1** certainty, definiteness. **2** determination, resolution, decision.
నిశ్చయంగా **niścayangaa** *adv.* definitely, for certain.
నిశ్చయం చేయు **niścayam ceeyu** *v.t.* to confirm, make definite.
నిశ్చయతాంబూలం, నిశ్చితార్థం **niścayataambuulam, niścitaartham** *n.* betrothal.
నిశ్చయార్థకం **niścayaarthakam** *n. gram.* indicative mood.
నిశ్చయించు **niścayincu** *v.t.* to settle, decide, determine, resolve: **teedii** ~ to fix a date.
నిశ్చల **niścala** *adj.* **1** fixed, firm, steady, steadfast. **2** immovable, immobile, motionless. **3** still, calm, undisturbed.
నిశ్చలం **niścalam** *n. class.* the earth.
నిశ్చలంగా **niścalangaa** *adv.* steadily, calmly.
నిశ్చలత **niścalata** *n.* **1** steadiness, steadfastness. **2** calmness. **3** motionlessness, immobility.
నిశ్చింత **niścinta** *n.* freedom from grief and anxiety.
నిశ్చింతగా **niścintagaa** *adv.* **1** showing no interest, unconcernedly. **2** without grief or anxiety.
నిశ్చిత **niścita** *adj.* **1** definite, certain. **2** settled, confirmed.
నిశ్చిత[త్వ]ం **niścita[twa]m** *n.* certainty.
నిశ్చితంగా **niścitangaa** *adv.* definitely.
నిశ్చితార్థం **niścitaartham** *same as* **niścayataambuulam.**
నిశ్చేతన **nisceetana** *adj. class.* motionless.
నిశ్చేష్ట **nisceeSTa** *adj.* aghast, dumbfounded.
నిశ్రేణి **niśreeNi** *n. class.* ladder.
నిశ్వసనం, నిశ్వాసం **niśwasanam, niśwaasam** *n.* exhalation, breathing out.
నిశ్వసించు **niświasincu** *v.i.* to breathe out, exhale.
నిశ్శంక **niśśanka** *n.* absence of doubt.
నిశ్శంకగా **niśśankagaa** *adv.* without doubt.
నిశ్శక్త **niśśakta** *adj.* powerless.
నిశ్శక్తి **niśśakti** *n.* powerlessness.
నిశ్శబ్ద **niśśabda** *adj.* silent.
నిశ్శబ్దం **niśśabdam** *n.* silence.
నిశ్శబ్దంగా **niśśabdangaa** *adv.* silently, in silence.
నిశ్శేష **niśśeeSa** *adj.* without any remainder, entire, complete.
నిశ్శేషంగా **niśśeeSangaa** *adv.* completely, with nothing left over, with nothing outstanding; ~ **baakii cellincees-EEnu** I have repaid the debt leaving no balance.
నిషా **niSaa** *n.* intoxication; **waaDiki** ~ **ekkindi** he became intoxicated.
నిషాదం **niSaadam** *n. ni,* the highest of the seven musical notes.
నిషాదుడు **niSaaduDu** *n. class.* member of a tribe of hunters.
నిషాపదార్థం **niSaapadaartham** *n.* intoxicant.
నిషిద్ధ **niSiddha** *adj.* forbidden, prohibited, banned; ~ **padam** taboo word.
నిషేకం **niSeekam** *n. class.* consummation of marriage.
నిషేధం **niSeedham** *n.* **1** prohibiting, banning; **madya-[paana]** ~ prohibition of alcoholic liquor. **2** veto. **3** *ling.* taboo.
నిషేధాజ్ఞ **niSeedhaajña** *n. legal* injunction.
నిషేధార్థం **niSeedhaartham** *n. gram.* future habitual negative tense.
నిషేధించు **niSeedhincu** *v.t.* to forbid, prohibit, ban, proscribe.
నిష్కం **niSkam** *n. class.* gold coin.
నిష్కంటక **niSkaNTaka** *adj.* free from obstacles (*lit.* free from thorns).
నిష్కపట **niSkapaTa** *adj.* simple, sincere, guileless.
నిష్కపటం **niSkapaTam** *n.* simplicity, guilelessness.
నిష్కపటి **niSkapaTi** *n.* simple and guileless person.
నిష్కరుణ **niSkaruNa** *adj. class.* pitiless.
నిష్కలంక, నిష్కళంక **niSkalanka, niSkaLanka** *adj.* clear, pure, spotless, undefiled.
నిష్కర్ష **niSkarSa** *n.* determination, decision.
నిష్కర్షగా **niSkarSagaa** *adv.* **1** definitely, indisputably, without room for doubt. **2** decisively, finally, once for all.
నిష్కర్షణం **niSkarSaNam** *n. sci.* extraction (of minerals).
నిష్కర్షించు **niSkarSincu** *v.t. sci.* to extract (minerals).
నిష్కల్మష **niSkalmaSa** *adj.* **1** untainted, unpolluted, without blemish. **2** pure, sincere; **wiiri wimarśalu enta niśitangaa unnaayoo anta** ~ **gaanuu uNTaayi** his criticisms are as sincere as they are keen.

నిష్కాపట్యం **niSkaapaTyam** *n.* sincerity, straightforwardness, candour.

నిష్కామ **niSkaama** *adj.* without sexual desire.

నిష్కామకరంగా **niSkaamakarangaa** *adv.* dispassionately.

నిష్కారణ **niSkaaraNa** *adj.* groundless, unreasonable.

నిష్కారణంగా **niSkaaraNangaa** *adv.* for no reason, groundlessly.

నిష్కృతి **niSkṛti** *n.* atonement, expiation.

నిష్క్రమణం **niSkramaNam** *n.* departure, exit, egress.

నిష్క్రమించు **niSkramincu** *v.i.* 1 to depart. 2 *theat.* to leave the stage, exit.

నిష్క్రియ **niSkriya** *adj.* inactive, passive, torpid: ~ **pratighaTana** passive resistance.

నిష్ట, నిష్ఠ **niSTa, niSTha** *n.* 1 religious devotion. 2 devotedness, dedication, commitment: ~ **too** with devotion, scrupulously. 3 austerity.

నిష్టగా **niSTagaa** *adv.* regularly, as a matter of routine: **roojuu saayantram eeDu gaNTalaki ~ weLLi bhoonceeseewaaDu** he would go and take his meal regularly at seven o'clock every evening.

నిష్ఠుర, నిష్ఠూర **niSThu[u]ra** *adj.* 1 harsh, rough. 2 stern, severe, grim.

నిష్ఠురం, నిష్ఠూరం **niSThu[u]ram** *n.* 1 harshness, severity, sternness. 2 taunt, gibe, reproach.

నిష్ఠురంగా **niSThurangaa** *adv.* 1 harshly, rudely. 2 severely, sternly, grimly.

నిష్ణాతుడు **niSNaatuDu** *n.* skilful or learned or scholarly person, expert.

నిష్ణాతృత్వం **niSNaatṛtwam** *n.* expertise, scholarship.

నిష్పక్షపాతంగా **niSpakSapaatangaa** *adv.* impartially, objectively, dispassionately.

నిష్పత్తి **niSpatti** *n.* 1 ratio. 2 derivation: **bahuwacana ruupa** ~ derivation of plural forms.

నిష్పత్రణం **niSpatraNam** *n. bot.* defoliation.

నిష్పన్న **niSpanna** *adj.* derived, produced.

నిష్పన్నం చేయు **niSpannam ceeyu** *v.t. gram.* to derive, form: **'ceeyu' modalayna anubandhaalu ceerci naamawaacakaalanunci kriyalu niSpannam ceeyawaccu** by adding 'ceeyu' and other auxiliaries verbs can be derived from nouns.

నిష్పూచీ **niSpuucii** *adj.* free from responsibility.

నిష్ప్రయోజకుడు **niSprayoojakuDu** *n.* useless person.

నిష్ప్రయోజన **niSprayoojana** *adj.* useless, vain, fruitless.

నిష్ప్రయోజనం **niSprayoojanam** *n.* uselessness.

నిష్ప్రయోజనకర **niSprayoojanakara** *adj.* ineffective.

నిష్పాక్షిక **niSpaakSika** *adj.* impartial, unbiassed.

నిష్ఫల **niSphala** *adj.* unsuccessful, fruitless, useless, abortive, futile.

నిష్ఫలం చేయు **niSphalam ceeyu** *v.t.* to thwart, frustrate.

నిసర్గ **nisarga** *n.* nature, natural state.

నిసి **nisi** *same as* **niśi.**

నిసువు, నిసుగు **nisuwu, nisugu** *n.* 1 the young of an animal or bird. 2 *dial.* child, infant.

నిస్తంత్రం **nistantram** *adj. class.* easy.

నిస్తంత్రి **nistantri** *n. and adj.* wireless.

నిస్తంద్ర **nistandra** *adj. class.* unwearied.

నిస్తబ్ధ **nistabdha** *adj.* motionless, still.

నిస్తబ్ధత **nistabdhata** *n.* 1 motionless state, stillness. 2 standstill, stalemate.

నిస్తరంగ **nistaranga** *adj.* waveless, calm (sea).

నిస్తుల **nistula** *adj.* unequalled, unmatched.

నిస్తేజ **nisteeja** *adj.* lustreless.

నిస్త్రాణ **nistraaNa** *n* feebleness, lack of vigour.

నిస్పృహ **nispṛha** *n.* despair, despondency, depression, dejection, hopelessness.

నిస్వనం, నిస్వానం **niswa[a]nam** *n.* musical note.

నిస్వార్థ **niswaartha** *adj.* unselfish, selfless.

నిస్వార్థం **niswaartham** *n.* unselfishness.

నిస్సంకోచంగా **nissankoocangaa** *adv.* without hesitation, uninhibitedly.

నిస్సంగం **nissangam** *n. class.* freedom from attachment.

నిస్సంతు **nissantu** *adj.* without an heir, without offspring.

నిస్సందేహ, నిస్సంశయ **nissandeeha, nissamśaya** *adj.* undoubted.

నిస్సత్తువ **nissattuwa** I. *n.* weakness, debility, want of nerve. II. *adj.* weak, feeble.

నిస్సరణం **nissaraNam** *n. chem.* effusion.

నిస్సహాయ **nissahaaya** *adj.* helpless, forlorn.

నిస్సహాయత, నిస్సహాయత్వం **nissahaayata, nissahaayatwam** *n.* helplessness.

నిస్సాకారం **nissaakaaram** *n. dial.* contempt, scorn.

నిస్సాకారంగా **nissaakaarangaa** *adv. dial,* contemptuously.

నిస్సార **nissaara** *adj.* 1 sapless, spiritless, weak, feeble, lacking vitality. 2 boring, uninteresting, insipid, vapid.

నిస్సైన్యీకరణం **nissaynyiikaraNam** *n.* demilitarisation.

నీ - nii

నీ **nii** *pronom. possessive adj. sing.* your.

నీచ **niica** *adj.* low, base, mean, despicable, squalid.

నీచ[త్వ]ం **niica[twa]m** *n.* baseness, meanness.

నీచు **niicu**[1] *n.* **1** (*also* ~ **kampu**) foul smell, stench, smell of fish. **2** *slang* meat.

నీచు, నీచుడు **niicu**[2], **niicuDu** *n.* base or mean or vile person.

నీటి **niiTi** *genitive of* **niiru** water; ~ **maTTam** water level; ~ **paarudala** irrigation; ~ **wanarulu** water resources.

నీటు **niiTu** I. *n.* stylishness, elegance, neatness. II. *adj.* elegant, stylish, fashionable, neat and trim; **maniSi ~ gaa unnaaDu gadaa ani loopaliki raaniccEEnu, naa gaDiyaaram ettuku pooyEEDu** I let him in because he was neat and trim in appearance, but he stole my watch.

నీడ **niiDa** *n.* **1** shade, shadow; **appuDee ~ tirugutunnadi neenu iNTLooki weLLEEnu** I entered the house just when shadows were lengthening (i.e., at dusk). **2** reflection, image. **3** shelter, protection. **4** concealment.

నీడపట్టు **niiDapaTTu** *n.* shade.

నీడపట్టున **niidapaTTuna** *adv.* **1** *lit.* in the shade. **2** in comfort, at ease.

నీతం **niitam** *n.* principle, rule.

నీతి **niiti** *n.* **1** morality, morals. **2** right, righteousness. **3 kathaloo ~** the moral of a story.

నీతిగా **niitigaa** *adv.* morally, honestly, in a principled manner.

నీతిదూరుడు, నీతిమాలినవాడు **niitiduuruDu, niitimaalinawaaDu** *n.* person with no morals or principles.

నీతిపరుడు, నీతిమంతుడు **niitiparuDu, niitimantuDu** *n.* virtuous or scrupulous or righteous person.

నీతివచనం **niitiwacanam** *n.* aphorism.

నీతిశాస్త్రం **niitiśaastram** *n.* ethics.

నీతీనిజాయితీ **niitiinijaayitii** *n. pl.* honesty and morality.

నీర, నీరా **niira[a]** *n.* sweet toddy, unfermented juice of the date or palmyra or coconut palm

నీరం **niiram** *n. class.* water.

నీరజం **niirajam** *n. class.* lotus.

నీరదం **niiradam** *n. class.* cloud.

నీరధి **niiradhi** *n. class.* sea.

నీరవం **niirawam** *n. class.* calmness, quiet, silence; **niirawa niśiidhiloo** in the silence of the night.

నీరవుడు **niirawuDu** *n. class.* speechless or silent or dumbfounded person.

నీరస **niirasa** *adj.* weak, feeble.

నీరసం **niirasam** *n.* weakness, debility.

నీరసించు, నీరసిల్లు **niirasincu, niirasillu** *v.i.* **1** to become weak or feeble or exhausted. **2** to be depressed, be downhearted.

నీరాజనం **niiraajanam** *n.* **1** offering of lighted camphor to a deity. **2** tribute; **niiraajanaalu paTTu** to pay tributes.

నీరు **niiru** *n.* **1** (*gen. pl.* **niiLLu**) water. **2** any fluid. **3** urine; **~ paTTeesindi** the flow of urine has stopped. **4** *idiomatic usages:* **aa dṛśyam cuuDagaanee waaDi guNDelu niirayipooyEEyi** as soon as he saw that sight his courage deserted him (*lit.* his heart turned into water); **neenu ceppindantaa wini niiLLu kaari pooyEEDu** when he heard all that I said, his strength and courage gave up; **pradarśanam niiLLu kaaripooyindi** the performance was a disaster; **annii ceestaanani ceppi ciwaraku niiLLu kaarceesEEDu** having promised to do everything, in the end he disappointed us; **wṛddhaapyamloo taNDriki niiru pooyaDam pillala dharmam** it is the duty of children to support their father in old age; **niiLLu poosukonu** (i) to take a bath; (ii) to become pregnant; **niiLLu tooDu** (i) to draw water from a well; (ii) to mix hot and cold water for a bath; **naaku niiLLu tooDutunnaaDu** he is creating some trouble for me; **niiLLu namulu** to hesitate; **niLLaku poowu** *dial.* to go to the latrine; **aa Dabbuku niiLLu wadulukonnaanu** I have said goodbye to that money (i.e., I do not expect to get that money back); *cf.* **tiloodakaalu iccu**; *see also* **niiTi**.

నీరుకాకి **niirukaaki** *n.* cormorant.

నీరుకావి, నీరుకాయ[రంగు] **niirukaawi, niirukaaya [rangu]** *n.* reddish or yellowish tinge found on a white cloth that has been washed many times.

నీరుగంటి **niirugaNTi** *n.* nirganti, village servant entrusted with the work of distribution of water to fields for irrigation in former times.

నీరుగన్నేరు **niiruganneeru** *n.* kind of oleander.

నీరుడు, నీరుడి **niiruDu, niiruDi** *n.* urine.

నీరుల్లి **niirulli** *n.* onion.

నీరెండ, నీరుటెండ **niireNDa, niiruTeNDa** *n.* soft light, weak sunlight.

నీలం **niilam** *n.* **1** blue colour. **2** indigo colour. **3** sapphire. **4** a variety of mango.

నీలకంఠం **niilakaNTham** *n. class.* peacock.

నీలకంఠుడు **niilakaNThuDu** *n.* epithet of Siva.

నీలమణి **niilamaNi** *n.* sapphire.

నీలలోహిత **niilaloohita** *adj. sci.* violet coloured.

నీలాంబరం **niilaambaram** *n. class.* **1** bell-shaped blue flower. **2** sky, heavens.

నీలాపనింద **niilaapaninda** *n.* undeserved blame.

నీలాలు **niilaalu** *n.pl.* **1** tears. **2** hair of the head cut and offered as a vow in a temple.

నీలి **niili** I. *n.* indigo plant. II. *adj.* **1** dark blue, indigo coloured; **~ mabbu** dark cloud. **2** false; **~ waartalu** faked or concocted news or information.

నీలితుత్తం **niilituttam** *n. chem.* copper sulphate.

నీలిమందు **niilimandu** *n.* **1** indigo dye. **2** blue colour used for whitening cloth at the time of washing.

నీలుగు **niilugu** I. *n.* audacity, impudence. II. *v.i.* 1 to be haughty or proud or impudent. 2 to mutter, grumble.

నీలుగుడు **niiluguDu** *n.* impudence, audacity.

నీళ్లాడు **niiLLaaDu** *v.i.* to give birth.

నీళ్లు **niiLLu** *see* **niiru.**

నీవారం, నివ్వరి **niiwaaram, niwwari** *n. class.* rice which grows wild.

నీవు, నువ్వు **niiwu, nuwwu** *pron. sing.* you.

నీహారం **niihaaram** *n.* snow.

ను - nu

నుంచి, నుండి, నించి **nunci, nuNDi, ninci** *p.p.* 1 from. 2 since, for: **padeeLLa~** for the last ten years. 3 due to, as a result of; **miiru raawaDam~ pani jarigindi** the work has been done as a result of your coming.

నుంచును **nuncunu** *colloq. form of* **nilucu; waaNNi nuncunaTTugaa tiisukuraa** bring him instantly (*lit.* bring him just as he is standing).

నుజ్యర్థం **nuǰyartham** *n. gram.* infinitive.

నుక్సాను **nuksaanu** *n.* loss.

నుగ్గు **nuggu** *n.* 1 bit, fragment. 2 powder.

నుగ్గుగా **nuggugaa** *adv.* as fine as powder.

నుగ్గుచేయు **nugguceeyu** *v.t.* 1 to break into pieces, reduce to powder. 2 to kill.

నుచ్చు **nuccu**[1] *n.* dung of sheep and goats.

నుచ్చు **nuccu**[2] *n.* foam.

నుజ్జు **nujju** *adj.* crushed, trampled.

నుడి **nuDi** *n.* 1 word. 2 saying, expression.

నుడికారం **nuDikaaram** *n.* 1 idiom. 2 saying, expression. 3 idiomaticness, style or manner of speech.

నుడుగు, నుడువు **nuDugu, nuDuwu** I. *n.* word, phrase, sentence, line of verse or poetry. II *v.t. class.* to say, tell.

నుడువరి **nuDuwari** *n.* 1 speaker. 2 talkative person, babbler, chatterer.

నుదురు **nuduru** *n.* forehead; **nuduTi raata** fate, destiny.

నును **nunu** *adj.* smooth, gentle, slight, soft; **~siggu** slight blush.

నునుపు, నున్న **nunupu, nunna** *adj.* smooth.

నునుపు చేయు **nunupu ceeyu** *v.t.* to smooth[en].

నునుపుతనం, నున్నతనం **nunuputanam, nunnatanam** *n.* smoothness.

నుయ్యి, నూయి **nuyyi, nuuyi** *n.* well; **nuutiloo kappa** *same as* **kuupastha maNDuukam.**

నురిపిడి, నూర్పిడి **nuripiDi, nuurpiDi** *n.* threshing.

నురుగు, నురగ, నురువు **nurugu, nuraga, nuruwu** *n.* foam, froth, lather.

నురుగులు కక్కు **nurugulu kakku** *v.i.* 1 to foam at the mouth (as a horse does). 2 to be hot and tired. 3 to be in a state of great excitement.

నురుచు, నురుపు **nurucu, nurupu** *same as* **nuurpu.**

నులక **nulaka** *n.* string or cord or tape used for lacing the underside of a bed or cot.

నులక మంచం **nulaka mancam** *n.* bed or cot whose underside is laced with **nulaka.**

నులి **nuli** I. *n.* 1 twist. 2 (*also* **~noppi**) stomach pain, griping pain. II. *adj.* gentle, slight, small.

నులితీగ **nulitiigaa** *n. bot.* tendril.

నులిపాము **nulipaamu** *n.* round worm, nematode.

నులిపురుగు **nulipurugu** *n.* hair worm, a parasite.

నులివెచ్చ **nuliwecca** *adj.* luke warm.

నులుచు, నులుపు **nulucu, nulupu** *v.t.* 1 to twist. 2 to squeeze.

నులుపుకొను **nulupukonu** *v.t.* 1 to twist. 2 to squeeze. 3 to rub: **kaLLu~** to rub o.'s eyes; **ceetulu~** to wring o.'s hands, rub o.'s hands together in an apologetic gesture.

నులుము **nulumu** *v.t.* 1 to twist, wring: **miisaalu ~konu** to twist o.'s moustache: **meDa** (*or* **gontu**)~ to wring a neck. 2 to rub: **kaLLu~konu** to rub o.'s eyes.

నువ్వు **nuwwu**[1] *same as* **niiwu.**

నువ్వు **nuwwu**[2] *n.* (*gen. pl.* **~lu**) gingelly, sesamum; **~ginjanta** *colloq.* a small amount of, a modicum of; *see* **naanu**[2].

నుసి **nusi** *n.* 1 powder made by boring insects. 2 ashes. 3 *same as* **usi**[2].

నూ - nuu

నూ **nuu** *alt. form of* **nuwwu**[2].

నూకలు **nuukalu** *n.pl.* **1** broken rice, rice grains broken while being milled. **2** the grains of rice allotted by fate to each human being at birth; when they are exhausted his life will end; **waaDiki bhuumi miida ~unnaayi** he is still alive; **R.ki ii lookamloo ~tiirEEyi ii naaTitoo** the life ordained for R. by fate has ended today.

నూకాలమ్మ **nuukaalamma** *n.* **1** name of a village goddess. **2** chicken pox.

నూకు **nuuku** *v.t.* **1** to push. **2** *slang* to steal.

నూగారు **nuugaaru** *n.* line of hair on the body above the abdomen.

నూగు **nuugu** I. *n.* **1** soft down, downiness. **2** *bot.* tomentum, hairy covering of leaves and stalks of some plants. II. *adj.* downy; **~miisaalu** downy moustache appearing on the lip of a young man; **~~ gaa paTTina** fluffy.

నూటికీ కోటికీ **nuuTikii kooTikii** *see* **nuuru.**[1]

నూతన, నూత్న **nuutana, nuutna** *adj.* new, fresh, modern.

నూతనత్వం **nuutanatwam** *n.* novelty.

నూనూగు **nuunuugu** *n.* soft down starting to appear on a young man's lips; **~praayam** adolescence, early manhood; **~miisaalawaaDu** adolescent.

నూనె **nuune** *n.* oil; **~suddhi karmaagaaram** oil refinery.

నూపిండి **nuupiNDi** *n.* gingelly seed flour.

నూపురం **nuupuram** *n.* anklet.

నూయి **nuuyi** *same as* **nuyyi.**

నూరు **nuuru**[1] *n.* a hundred; **nuuTiki tombhay** ninety out of a hundred, ninety percent; **nuuTiki~paaLLu** a hundred percent; **nuuTikii kooTikii** hardly ever; **nuuTikoo kooTikoo mahaanubhaawulu puDataaru** great men are born very rarely; *see* **niNDu** *v.i.*; **nuureeLLu miiku!** may you live to be a hundred! (*this is said to s.o. who arrives just when the speaker is talking about him*).

నూరు **nuuru**[2] *v.t.* **1** to grind into powder. **2** to sharpen, whet; **katti~** to sharpen a knife. **2** (*also* **nuuripooyu**) to din s.g into s.o. by constant repetition; **pillalaku paaThaalu baagaa~taaDu** he dins lessons into the children; **neenu daani taatanu aneedi daani manasuloo baagaa inkeeTaTTu nuuripooyi** repeat to her over and over again that I am her grandfather so that it sinks well into her mind; **tammuNNi ii sambandham ceesukoomani nuuripoosEEDu** by dint of constant urging he induced his younger brother to contract this marriage. **4 aaphiisuloo mammalni nuurukoni taagutunnaaDu** he is constantly harassing us in the office.

నూరురాయి **nuururaayi** *n. dial.* whetstone.

నూరువరహాలు **nuuruwarahaalu** *n. pl. plumeria*, a flowering plant.

నూరో **nuuroo** *adj.* hundredth.

నూర్పిడి **nuurpiDi** *same as* **nuripiDi.**

నూర్పు **nuurpu** I. *n.* threshing; **kuppa~lu ayyEEyi** threshing is over. II. *v.t.* (*also* **nurupu, nurucu, nuurcu**) to thresh with a roller or by trampling.

నూలు **nuulu**[1] *n.* cotton thread; **~waDaku** *or* **~tiiyu** to spin thread; **~waasiloo tappipoowu** to escape by a hair's breadth (*lit.* to escape by the width of a thread).

నూలు **nuulu**[2] *alt. form of* **nuwwulu.**

నూలుకొను **nuulukonu** *v.i. class.* to agree, consent.

నూలుకొలుపు **nuulukolupu** *v.t. class.* to cause to agree or consent.

నూలుపోగు **nuulupoogu** *n.* a single thread; **candrunikoo~** (an offering of) one thread to the moon; *this expression means* a small contribution, but as much as one is able to give; *cf.* **uDutabhakti.**

నృ - nṛ

నృత్తం, నృత్యం **nṛttam, nṛtyam** *n.* dance, dancing.

నృత్యకారిణి **nṛtyakaariNi** *n.* woman dancer.

నృత్యకారుడు **nṛtyakaaruDu** *n.* male dancer.

నృపాలకుడు **nṛpaalakuDu** *n. class.* king, ruler.

నె - ne

నెంజిలి **nenjili** *n. class.* sorrow, anguish.

నెంబర్లు **nembarlu** *n. pl.* variety of rice renowned for its fineness, so called from the well-known official numer of its strain GEB 24, otherwise known as **kiciDii.**

నెగడు, నెగడి **negaDu**[1], **negaDi** *n.* fire lit for warmth or to scare away animals, bonfire.

నెగడు **negaDu**[2] *v.i. class.* (of fame) to increase, spread.

నెగ్గించు **neggincu** *v.t.* to cause to win, cause to succeed.

నెగ్గు **neggu** *v.i.* to succeed, be successful, win.

నెగ్గుకొను **neggukonu** *v.i.* to carry on, get along, manage: **telugu munSiila dwaaraa uttara pratyuttaraalu jaripincukoNTuu neggukuwacceewaaDu** he would manage to conduct correspondence through the help of Telugu munshis.

నెచ్చు **neccu** *n.* rice flour.

నెచ్చెలి **necceli** *n. class.* close friend.

నెటికలు **neTikalu** *alt. form of* **meTikalu.**

నెట్టు **neTTu** *v.t.* to push, thrust, shove: **pakkaku ~** to put on one side, push aside, brush aside.

నెట్టుకొను **neTTukonu** *v.i. and t.* 1 *lit.* to push for o.s. 2 **loopaliki neTTukuwaccu** to push o.'s way inside. 3 *fig.* **eedoo roojulu neTTukuwastunnanu** somehow I am making the days go by *or* somehow I am carrying on my life.

నెత్తి **netti** *n.* 1 head: **nii ~**! your head! (*mild expletive*), **nii ~ki kaLLu waccEEyi** *lit.* your eyes have come to (the top of) your head, i.e., you are very arrogant; **naa ~na ekki kuurcunnaaDu** he is domineering over me; **~ni kaTTukoni pootaanaa**? (said of wealth, etc.) *lit.* can I tie it in a bundle and go with it on my head? i.e., can I take it with me when I die? **naa ~ni ceetulu peTTEEDu** he deceived me: **wyaapaaramloo ~na guDDa weesukoni pooyEEDu** he lost everything in his business (*lit.* in his business he went away after putting a cloth over his head —a reference to departing from a funeral with a cloth over o.'s head): **~na noorupeTTukoni marii ceppEEDu** he stressed emphatically *or* he stressed repeatedly; **aame ~ miida niiLLakuNDa pagilindi** she burst out crying: **reepu pariikSa ~miida peTTukoni sinimaaku weLL-EEwaa?** did you go to the cinema when you have to face an examination tomorrow? **nettii nooruu koTTukunnaaDu** he grieved *or* he lamented; **~waaceeTaTTu ciwaaTLu peTTu** to scold s.o. severely. 2 hair of the head: **~duuwukonu** to comb o.'s hair.

నెత్తురు **netturu** *n.* blood.

నెత్తురుకందు, నెత్తురుగుడ్డు **netturukandu, netturuguDDu** *n.* newborn infant.

నెత్తురుకూడు **netturukuuDu** *n.* blood money, money earned by a hired assassin.

నెత్తురుగడ్డ **netturugaDDa** *n.* boil, abscess.

నెత్తురుపోడ **netturupoDa** *n.* kind of red snake.

నెత్తురుబంక **netturubanka** *n.* dysentery.

నెనరు **nenaru** *n. class.* love, affection.

నెన్నడుము **nennaDumu** *n. class.* slender waist.

నెన్నుదురు **nennuduru** *n. class.* fine forehead.

నెపం **nepam** *n.* 1 blame. 2 pretext, excuse.

నెపమిడు **nepamiDu** *v.t.* to blame.

నెప్పి **neppi** *same as* **noppi.**

నెమకు **nemaku** *v.t. dial.* to search, investigate.

నెమరు **nemaru** *n.* 1 cud. 2 rumination. 3 memory.

నెమరువేయు, నెమరేయు **nemaruweeyu, nemareeyu** *v.t.* 1 to chew the cud. 2 to ruminate. 3 to recall to o.'s mind, ponder over.

నెమలి, నెమిలి **nemali, nemili** *n.* peacock.

నెమలికన్ను **nemalikannu** *n.* eye in a peacock's feather.

నెమలిపింఛం చీర **nemalipincham ciire** *n.* peacock blue sari, woven with blue threads lengthwise and green threads crosswise.

నెమురు **nemuru** *v.i. and t.* 1 to rub oil on the body. 2 to grope with o.'s hands.

నెమ్మది **nemmadi** I. *n.* 1 quiet, calm. 2 ease, comfort. 3 composure. II. *adj.* 1 quiet, calm, peaceful. 2 slow. 3 gentle.

నెమ్మదిగా **nemmadigaa** *adv.* 1 quietly, slowly, calmly. 2 at ease, at leisure. 3 in good health.

నెమ్మదిపడు **nemmadipaDu** *v.i.* to become quiet, become calm, subside

నెమ్మదిపరచు **nemmadiparacu** *v.t.* to quieten, soothe, pacify.

నెమ్మదిమీద **nemmadimiida** *adv.* 1 slowly. 2 gradually.

నెమ్మి **nemmi** *n.* 1 love, affection. 2 happiness.

నెమ్ము **nemmu**[1] *n.* 1 iron nail. 2 iron bar, iron strip.

నెమ్ము **nemmu**[2] *n.* dampness, moisture.

నెమ్ము, నెమ్మ **nemmu**[3], **nemma** *n.* cold in the head, catarrh.

నెయ్యం **neyyam** *n.* love, affection, friendliness.

నెయ్యం ఆడు **neyyam aaDu** *v.i.* to be affectionate or friendly.

నెయ్యపు కినుక, నెయ్యపుటలుక **neyyapu kinuka, neyyapuTaluka** *n.* lovers' quarrel.

నెయ్యి, నేయి **neyyi, neeyi** *n.* ghee; liquefied butter; **neeti ginneloo gariTe uNDaraadu** no spoon should be used in the bowl of ghee (i.e., expense should not be stinted—proverbial saying).

నెయ్యురాలు **neyyuraalu** *n.* woman friend or companion.

నెరజాణ **nerajaaNa** *n.* 1 intelligent or skilful woman. 2 deceitful woman.

నెరద **nerada** *same as* **narada.**

నెరపు, నెరుపు **nerapu**[1], **nerupu**[1] *n.* greyness, whiteness (of hair).

నెరపు, నెరుపు **nerapu²**, **nerupu²** *v.t.* 1 to spread: **kaLLamloo kankulu neripee koyya panimuTTu** a wooden implement for spreading out the heads of corn on the threshing floor. 2 to fulfil, perform (a function): **raayabaaram~** to fulfil the function of an intermediary: **wiyyaalawaaritanam~** to perform the duties of parents-in-law, take on the role of parents-in-law. 3 to extend, provide: **sahakaaram~** to extend cooperation.

నెరయు, నెరియు **nerayu, neriyu** *v.i.* (of hair) to become grey or white.

నెరవ **nerawa** *n.* width: **ii baTTa~enta**? what is the width of this cloth?

నెరవారు **nerawaaru** *v.i.* to crack, split.

నెరవేరు **neraweeru** *v.i.* to be accomplished, be fulfilled.

నెరవేర్చు **neraweercu** *v.t.* 1 to accomplish, effect, discharge. 2 to carry out, fulfil.

నెరసు **nerasu** *n.* 1 particle (= **nalusu**). 2 mistake, error.

నెరి **neri¹** *n.* beauty.

నెరి **neri²** *n.* crookedness.

నెరీడిగా **neriidigaa** *adv.* openly, publicly.

నెఱ్ఱ, నెఱ్ఱి, నెఱ్ఱె **nerra, nerri, nerre** *n.* crack, split.

నెల **nela** *n.* 1 month: **~paTTu** to observe a month of ritual leading upto an important festival such as Sankranti; **~muriki** pink colour of a newborn baby which disappears after a month (= **cawa**). 2 period of menstruation: **~baala** woman in menses: **~la maniSi** pregnant woman: **aameki~niNDaleedu** her time for delivery has not yet come: **~takkuwa biDDa** child born prematurely: **~tappu** to become pregnant. 3 moon: **~poDupu** moonrise: **~wanka** crescent moon: **~welugu** moonlight.

నెల[వు]కొను **nela[wu] konu** *v.i.* 1 to be established, be set up, come into being. 2 to become firmly settled. 3 to stay, remain.

నెల[వు]కొల్పు **nela[wu]kolpu** *v.t.* 1 to establish, set up. 2 to establish firmly, make secure.

నెలత, నెలతుక **nelata, nelatuka** *n. class.* 1 woman. 2 wife.

నెలవు, నెలకువ **nelawu, nelakuwa** *n. class.* place, abode, home.

నెలవొందు **nelawondu** *v.i.* to become established.

నెలసరి **nelasari** *adj.* 1 sufficient for a month. 2 relating to a month, monthly.

నెల్లి **nelli** *n. phyllunthus emblica*, a tree whose leaves are used as a green vegetable.

నెల్లూరికంద **nelluurikanda** *n.* kind of root vegetable commonly grown in Nellore District.

నెసుళ్లు **nesuLLu** *n. pl.* 1 kind of insect which appears during the rains. 2 weak persons, weaklings.

నే - nee

నే **nee¹** *abbreviated form of* **neenu**.

నే **nee²** *alt. form of* **neyyi.**

నేటి **neeTi** *genitive of* **neeDu** of today, present, existing.

నేటితో సరి **neeTitoo sari** *minor sentence* that is all, that is enough.

నేడు **neeDu** *advbl. n.* 1 today. 2 nowadays.

నేత **neeta¹** *n.* leader.

నేత **neeta²** *n.* 1 weaving: **~ciire** handloom sari. 2 texture (of cloth). 3 thatching with palm leaves.

నేతకాడు **neetakaaDu** *n.* weaver.

నేతయంత్రం **neetayantram** *n.* loom.

నేతి **neeti** *adj.* of ghee: **~miThaayi** sweet made with ghee.

నేతిగోకుడు **neetigookuDu** *n.* residue formed in the process of making ghee.

నేతిదాక **neetidaaka** *n.* earthen pot with a wide mouth made for holding ghee.

నేతిబీరకాయ **neetibiirakaaya** *n.* 1 butter cucumber, *luffa aegyptica. 2 this term can be used of any object which belies its name.*

నేతృత్వం **neetṛtwam** *n.* leadership.

నేత్రం **neetram** *n.* eye.

నేత్రపటలం **neetrapaTalam** *n. med.* retina.

నేత్రరోగశాస్త్రం **neetraroogaśaastram** *n.* (science of) ophthalmology.

నేత్రవైద్యశాల **neetrawaydyaśaala** *n.* eye hospital.

నేత్రశోష **neetraśooSa** *n. med.* xerophthalmia.

నేత్రేంద్రియం **neetreendriyam** *n.* sense of sight.

నేను **neenu** *pron.* I, myself.

నేపథ్యం **neepathyam** *n. theat.* background: **~loo, neepathyaana** (i) in the background; (ii) off stage.

నేపథ్యగానం **neepathyagaanam** *n.* playback music.

నేపాళం **neepaaLam¹** *n.* Nepal.

నేపాళం **neepaaLam²** *n. jatropha curcas*, a tree whose seeds are used medicinally.

నేబు **neebu** *n.* an obsolete coin.

నేమించు **neemincu** *alt. form of* **niyamincu.**

నేయి **neeyi** *same as* **neyyi.**

నేయు **neeyu** *v.t.* 1 to weave. 2 to thatch (roof).

నేరం **neeram** *n.* crime, offence.

నేరం మోపు **neeram moopu** *v.i.* to impute a crime, accuse: **waaDimiida neeram moopEEru** they accused him of a crime.

నేరక **neeraka** *neg. participle of* **neeranu** *used adverbially* (*also* **~pooyi**) unawares, involuntarily, unconsciously, unwittingly: **~pooyi atanni kadilincEEnu** unwittingly I stirred him up.

నేరను **neeranu** *defective vb. class.* I cannot: *mod. only in the form* **neeraka.**

నేరమి **neerami** *n.* 1 mistake, fault, failing. 2 ignorance. 3 inability.

నేరశాస్త్రం **neeraśaastram** *n.* (science of) criminology.

నేరస్థుడు, నేరగాడు **neerasthuDu, neeragaaDu** *n.* **1** guilty person. **2** criminal, offender, culprit.

నేరారోపణ **neeraaroopaNa** *n.* accusation.

నేరుగా **neerugaa** *adv.* **1** straight, directly. **2** straightforwardly, straight out, openly.

నేరేడు **neereeDu** *n.* wild black plum, *eugenia jambolana.*

నేర్చు[కొను] **neercu[konu]** *v.t.* to learn; **ingliiSu maaTLaaDaDam neerucukonnaaDu** he learn to speak English.

నేర్పరి **neerpari** *n.* skilful or accomplished person, expert.

నేర్పరితనం **neeparitanam** *n.* expertness.

నేర్పించు **neerpincu** *v.t.* to teach.

నేర్పు **neerpu** I. *n.* **1** art, skill, craft. **2** cunning. II. *v.t.* to teach.

నేర్పుగా **neerpugaa** *adv.* skilfully, deftly, expertly.

నేల **neela** *n.* land, earth, soil, ground; ~ **karacu** to fall to the ground, be defeated; ~ **kaliyu** to be ruined; ~ **cuucu** to cast o.'s eyes downwards; ~ **naalugu ceragulaa** in all corners of the land, all around; ~ **paalawu** (i) to become part of the earth; (ii) to be wasted; ~ **paalu ceeyu** to drop, cause of fall; ~ **maTTam ceeyu** to raze to the ground; ~ **muccu** *colloq.* person with his eyes fixed on the ground, hypocrite; ~ **raalu** (i) to fall to the ground (ii) to prostrate o.s.; ~ **wiDicina saamu** activity which lacks support (*lit.* gymnastics performed in midair); *see* **iinu.**

నేలకోత **neelakoota** *n.* soil erosion.

నేలగుమ్మడి **neelagummaDi** *n.* kind of pumpkin.

నేలబారు **neelabaaru** *adj.* ordinary, not outstanding, mediocre.

నేలబొగ్గు **neelaboggu** *n.* coal.

నేలమళిగ **neelamaLiga** *n.* underground granary, cellar.

నేవళం **neewaLam** *n.* **1** bloom, brightness. **2** *class.* necklace of precious stones.

నేస్తం **neestam** *n.* **1** friend. **2** friendship; **o.-i too ~ kaTTu** to make friends with s.o.

నేస్తగాడు **neestagaaDu** *n.* man friend.

నేస్తురాలు **neesturaalu** *n.* woman friend.

నై - nay

నైగనిగ్యం **nayganigyam** *n.* brilliancy, gleam, sparkle.

నైచ్యం **naycyam** *n.* baseness, meanness.

నైజం **nayjam** *n.* nature, characteristic, natural disposition.

నైజాం **nayjaam** *n.* alt. name of the Telangana region.

నైతిక **naytika** *adj.* moral, ethical.

నైతికంగా **naytikangaa** *adv.* morally.

నైపథ్యం **naypathyam** *n. class. alt. form of* **neepathyam.**

నైపుణి, నైపుణ్యం **naypuNi, naypuNyam** *n.* skill, talentedness, dexterity, cleverness, expertness, expertise.

నైరాశ్యం **nayraaśyam** *n.* hopelessness, despair.

నైరుతి, నైఋతి **nayruti, nayṛti** *n.* southwest.

నైరూప్య **nayruupya** *adj.* abstract; ~ **citrakaLa** abstract art.

నైర్మల్యం, నైర్మల్యత **nayrmalyam, nayrmalyata** *n.* purity, spotlessness, stainlessness.

నైవాసిక **naywaasika** *adj.* residential.

నైవేద్యం **nayweedyam** *n.* offering of food made to a deity.

నైశిత్యం **nayśityam** *n. class.* sharpness, keenness.

నైశ్చల్యం **nayścalyam** *n.* fixedness, fixity, steadiness.

నైషధం **naySadham** *n.* name of a celebrated Sanskrit poem.

నైష్ఠిక **naySTika** *adj.* firm, constant, adhering to rule or principle.

నైష్ఠికుడు **naySTikuDu** *n.* **1** person who strictly adheres to religious principles and observances. **2** disciple who stays with his guru after his education is over.

నైష్పత్తిక **naySpattika** *adj.* proportional; ~ **praatinidhyam** proportional representation.

నైసర్గిక **naysargika** *adj.* **1** natural, inborn. **2** *geog.* physical; **ii praantapu ~ swaruupam** the physical features of this region.

నొ - no

నొక్కి చెప్పు, నొక్కి వక్కాణించు **nokki ceppu, nokki wakkaaNincu** *v.t.* 1 to stress, emphasise; **nokki ceppadalacinappuDu maaTa ciwara 'ee' ceerutundi** 'ee' is added at the end of a word when the intention is to emphasise it. 2 to assert, say emphatically, affirm.

నొక్కి పలుకు **nokki paluku** *v.t.* 1 to utter (a sound) with emphasis. 2 to stress, emphasise; **aayana ii wiSayaanni nokki palikEEDu** he stressed this point.

నొక్కిపెట్టు **nokkipeTTu** *v.t.* to suppress.

నొక్కు **nokku** I. *n.* 1 pressure, squeeze. 2 dent, impression, notch, tooth (of a saw). 3 ~**la juTTu** curly or wavy hair. II. *v.t.* to press, squeeze, compress, pinch, make a dent; **o.-i nooru~** to silence s.o.; **gontuka nokkiweeyu** to strangle.

నొగ **noga** *n.* shaft[s] or pole[s] connecting the body of a cart or plough or harrow to the yoke.

నొచ్చు **noccu** *v.i.* 1 to ache, smart, pain. 2 to be grieved, feel sad.

నొచ్చుకొను **noccukonu** *v.i.* 1 to grieve, lament, feel sad. 2 to regret, take to heart. 3 to resent, feel aggrieved, feel offended or hurt. 4 to repent, feel sorry (for a mistake or fault).

నొచ్చుకోలు **noccukoolu** *n.* repentance.

నొచ్చుకోలుగా **noccukoolugaa** *adv.* penitently.

నొట్ట **noTTa** *n. dial.* forehead.

నొప్పి, నెప్పి **noppi, neppi** *n.* pain, ache; *pl.* **noppulu** labour pains.

నొప్పించు **noppincu** *v.t.* to hurt, cause grief or pain to.

నొప్పిపెట్టు, నొప్పివేయు, నొప్పిపుట్టు, నొప్పిఎత్తు, నొప్పిలేచు **noppi peTTu, noppi weeyu, noppi puTTu, noppi ettu, noppi leecu** *v.i.* to be painful.

నొల్ల **nolla** *n.* harrow used on irrigated land after ploughing.

నొల్లు **nollu**[1] *v.t.* (of children) to suck fingers.

నొల్లు, నొల్లుకొను **nollu**[2], **nollukonu** *v.i. and t.* 1 to scrape together into a heap. 2 to amass (wealth) greedily.

నొవ్వు **nowwu** *n.* pain.

నొసలు, నొష్ట **nosalu, noSTa** *n.* forehead.

నొసలు చిట్లించు, నొసలు ముడివేయు **nosalu ciTLincu, nosalu muDiweeyu** *v.i.* to frown, wrinkle o.'s brow.

నో, నౌ - noo, naw

నోకు **nooku** *n. dial.* point of a pencil.

నోచు[కొను] **noocu[konu]** *v.i.* 1 to perform a vow or other meritorious act; **reNDu puuTalaa bhoojanam ceeyaDaaniki Dabbu uNDagaanee sarikaadu, noocukoni uNDaali** in order to eat two meals a day (i.e., in order to live in comfort) it is not enough that you have money, you must have performed a meritorious act (in this life or a previous life). 2 to be blessed with, have the good fortune to achieve or attain (with the underlying meaning that good fortune only comes from a meritorious act performed earlier in this life or in a previous life); **akSaraasyataku noocukooleeni abhaagyulu caalaamandi unnaaru** there are many unfortunate persons who have not been able to attain literacy; **taageenduku manci niiLLaku noocukooni uuLLunnaayi** there are villages which are not blessed with good water for drinking; *cf.* **daLam.**[1]

నోటు **nooTu** *n. colloq.* promissory note; ~**raasi iccEEDu** he wrote a promissory note (for a debt).

నోము **noomu** *n.* religious vow; ~**noocu** to perform a vow or other meritorious act; **naa~paNDindi** my prayers have been answered; **naa~ phalam** *or* **naa~paNTa** the reward of my good deeds and vows (gen. referring to o.'s family members).

నోరారా **nooraaraa** *adv., always used with ref. to speech* 1 heartily, affectionately; **nannu bajaaruloo kalusukoni~palakarincEEDu** he met me in the bazaar and had a hearty talk with me; **nannu~'akkayya' ani pilicindi** she called me **'akkayya'** affectionately. 2 as much as one wishes; **waaNNi~paccibuutulu tiTTEEnu** I cursed him loud and long.

నోరు **nooru** *n.* mouth; ~**uuru** to water at the mouth, salivate; ~**ettu** to open o.'s mouth, venture to speak; ~**muuyu,** ~**kaTTukonu** to keep o.'s mouth shut, keep silent, keep quiet; ~**terici** (*or* ~**wiDici**) **appu aDigEEDu** he summoned up courage and asked for a loan; ~**cincukoni keekalu weeyu** to shout at the top of o.'s voice, yell; **niiku~paDipooyindaa?** have you lost the power of speech? i.e., cannot you reply? (said as a rebuke); ~**paareesukonu** to hurl abuse (**-pay** *or* **-miida**, at); **o.-i nooTa gaDDa/maTTi/dummu koTTu** to deprive s.o. of his livelihood; **nooTa gaDDi peTTu** to teach (s.o.) a lesson, punish (s.o.); **nooTa naaluka leeniwaaDu** simpleton; **o.-i nooTikaaDidi tiiyu** to deprive s.o. of his livelihood; **nooTiki kaLLam weeyu** to bridle or curb (s.o.); **nooTiki muuta leekuNDaa eeDcu** to weep uncontrolledly; **nooTi lekkalu** oral calculations made without using pen and paper; **naaku padyam nooTi-**

ki waccu I know the poem by heart; ~ **tuttara** talkativeness, loquaciousness; ~ **puuta** disease of the mouth involving boils on the tongue; **waaDi nooTLoo karakkaaya paDindi** he sustained a loss; *see* **naanu**[2], **waayi, weLLabeTTu.**

నౌక **nawka** *n.* ship, vessel.

నౌకరి **nawkarii** *n.* service, job, employment.

నౌకరు **nawkaru** *n.* servant.

నౌకాదళం **nawkaadaLam** *n.* navy, fleet.

నౌకాదళాధికారి **nawkaadaLaadhikaari** *n.* admiral.

నౌకానిర్మాణం **nawkaanirmaaNam** *n.* shipbuilding.

నౌకానిర్మాణకేంద్రం **nawkaanirmaaNakeendram** *n.* shipyard.

నౌకాభంగం **nawkaabhangam** *n.* shipwreck.

నౌకాయాత్ర **nawkaayaatra** *n.* voyage.

నౌకాయానం **nawkaayaanam** *n.* 1 navigation. 2 voyage.

నౌకారవాణా **nawkaarawaaNaa** *n.* water transport.

నౌకాశ్రయం **nawkaaśrayam** *n.* port, harbour.

నౌబత్తు **nawbattu** *n.* large kettledrum.

న్యా, న్యూ - nyaa, nyuu

న్యాయ **nyaaya** *adj.* 1 judicial, legal. 2 real, true, genuine, legitimate; ~**mayna carcaa weedika** a true forum for discussion.

న్యాయం **nyaayam** *n.* 1 justice, law, equity. 2 justification. 3 name of one of the six systems of Indian philosophy. 4 logic. 5 logical relationship; **guruśiSya**~ teacher-pupil relationship. 6 *advbl. use* ~ **[gaa]** *is used colloquially in the sense of* like *in certain phrases which recall a proverb or fable*, e.g., **muuSika maajaala**~ like the cat and the mouse; **uddhaalakuDu caNDika** ~**gaa kaapuram ceestunnaaru** their family life is like Uddhalaka's and Chandika's (a puranic story tells how Chandika was constantly contradicting Uddhalaka).

న్యాయంగా **nyaayangaa** *adv.* 1 really, by right, in fact, as a matter of fact. 2 *same as* **nyaayam** *sense 6.*

న్యాయత **nyaayata** *n.* legality.

న్యాయతః **nyaayatah** *adj. de jure*; ~ **gurtimpu** *de jure* recognition.

న్యాయనిర్ణయం, న్యాయనిర్ణాయం **nyaayanirNa[a]yam** *n.legal* adjudication.

న్యాయనిర్ణేత **nyaayanirNeeta** *n. legal* adjudicator.

న్యాయపాలన **nyaayapaalana** *n.* administration of justice.

న్యాయబద్ధ **nyaayabaddha** *adj.* ruled by law, legal.

న్యాయబద్ధంగా, న్యాయరీత్యా **nyaayabaddhangaa, nyaayariityaa** *adv.* legally, in accordance with law.

న్యాయబద్ధీకరణ **nyaayabaddhiikaraNa** *n.* legalisation.

న్యాయమూర్తి *n.* **nyaayamuurti** *n.* judge.

న్యాయవాదవృత్తి **nyaayawaadawrtti** *n.* legal profession.

న్యాయవాది **nyaayawaadi** *n.* advocate, lawyer.

న్యాయవిరుద్ధ **nyaayawiruddha** *adj.* illegal.

న్యాయవిరుద్ధత **nyaayawiruddhata** *n.* illegality.

న్యాయశాఖ **nyaayaśaakha** *n.* judiciary.

న్యాయశాస్త్రం **nyaayaśaastram** *n.* science of law, jurisprudence.

న్యాయశాస్త్రవేత్త **nyaayaśaastraweetta** *n.* jurist.

న్యాయసమ్మత **nyaayasammata** *adj.* just, in accordance with law.

న్యాయసూత్రావళి **nyaayasuutraawaLi** *n.* code of laws.

న్యాయస్థానం **nyaayasthaanam** *n.* court of law, law court.

న్యాయాధికారి, న్యాయాధిపతి, న్యాయాధీశుడు **nyaayaadhikaari, nyaayaadhipati, nyaayaadhiiśuDu** *n.* judge.

న్యాసం **nyaasam** *n. class. gen. occurring in the compounds* **anga**~ *and* **kara**~ ritual performed at the time of **sandhya** and **abhiSeekam** involving assignment of parts of the body to tutelary divinities.

న్యూన **nyuuna** *adj.* 1 inferior, of poor quality. 2 belitting; ~ **bhaawam** belittlement.

న్యూనం, న్యూనత **nyuunam, nyuunata** *n.* 1 inferiority. 2 belittlement; **aatma nyuunata** self-belittlement, inferiority complex.

ప - pa

పంకం **pankam** *n.* 1 mud, mire. 2 *fig.* sin.
పంకజం **pankajam** *n.* lotus.
పంకా, పంఖా **pankaa, pankhaa** *n.* fan.
పంకించు **pankincu** *v.t.* to move, shake, nod.
పంకిల **pankila** *adj.* muddy.
పంకిలం **pankilam** *n.* muddy place, mire, bog, morass.
పంక్తి **pankti** *n.* line, row, series: **parwata panktulu** mountain ranges.
పంక్తిభోజనం **pankti bhoojanam** *n.* 1 *lit.* meal eaten by persons sitting in a line. 2 meal eaten by a group of persons together: **waaLLaku maaku pankti bhoojanaalu leewu** we and they do not dine together, *i.e.*, we and they belong different communities: *see* **saha ~**.
పంక్తిలోబలపక్షం **panktiloo balapakSam** *colloq.* (< **panktiloo walapakSam**) partiality, favouritism, unfair treatment (*lit.* favouritism shown to an individual when distributing food among persons dining together).
పంగ **panga** *n.* 1 two pronged fork. 2 parting the legs wide.
పంగచాచు, పంగచాపు **panga caacu, panga caapu** *v.t.* **kaaLLu ~** to stretch o.'s legs wide apart, spread out o.'s legs.
పంగటించు **pangaTincu** *v.t.* to straddle.
పంగటించుకొను **pangaTincukonu** *v.i.* to stretch o.'s legs wide apart: **pangaTincukonNTuu wastunnaaDu** he is coming striding along; **kaaLLu pangaTincuku kuurcuNTee panulu elaa awutaayi?** if you sit with your legs spread out how will the work be done?
పంగటికాళ్లవాడు **pangaTikaaLLawaaDu** *n.* bowlegged person, bandy legged person.
పంగనామం **panganaamam** *n.* mark worn on the forehead by Vaishnavites: **o.-ki ~ peTTu** *colloq.* to deceive s.o., cheat s.o.
పంగల కఱ్ఱ, పంగల కొయ్య, పంగల కట్టె, పంగల గుంజ **pangala karra, pangala koyya, pangala kaTTe, pangala gunja** *n.* forked stick, forked post.
పంగు **pangu**[1] *n.* 1 work turned out in a day by a person engaged for digging a well or canal. 2 *colloq.* **eem pani ceesEEwu? ~ pani?** *lit.* what work have you done? is it a day's work? (*said with sarcasm, meaning* 'you have done very little').
పంగు **pangu**[2] *n.* vagina.
పంగు **pangu**[3] *n.* fear.
పంచ, పంచె **panca**[1], **pance** *n.* dhoti, man's skirt.
పంచ **panca**[2] *n.* 1 porch, verandah. 2 shelter, asylum: *see* **aa pancaa aa pancaa.**
పంచకజ్జాయం **pancakajjaayam** *n.* mixture of grated coconut and sugar.
పంచకల్యాణి, పంచకళ్యాణి **pancakalyaaNi, pancakaLyaaNi** *n.* horse (or other animal) with auspicious markings—white legs and a white spot on the forehead.
పంచకావ్యాలు **pancakaawyaalu** *n.pl.* five famous literary works prescribed for study by a student of Sanskrit.
పంచకోణ **pancakooNa** *adj. maths.* pentagular.
పంచకోళ్లకషాయం **pancakooLLa kaSaayam** *n.* mixture (deprecatory term), mixture of incompatible ingredients, illassorted collection.
పంచదార **pancadaara** *n.* sugar.
పంచదార పాకం **pancadaara paakam** *n.* syrup.
పంచనామ **pancanaama** *n.* report of an enquiry by mediators into an unexplained or sudden or violent death, inquest report.
పంచపాత్ర **pancapaatra** *n.* kind of cup used in worship.
పంచపాళీ **pancapaaLii** *n.* covered verandah in front of a house.
పంచప్రాణాలు **pancapraaNaalu** *n.pl.* 1 the five vital airs of the body. 2 life: **cellelaNTee ataDiki ~** his sister is very dear to him (*lit.* his sister is (as dear as) life to him).
పంచభుజం **pancabhujam** *n. maths.* pentagon.
పంచభూతాలు **pancabhuutaalu** *n.pl.* the five primordial elements: **aayana aatma pancabhuutaalaloo kalisipooyindi** *lit* his spirit has mingled with the elements, i.e., he has died.
పంచమ **pancama** *adj.* 1 fifth. 2 belonging to the harijan community.
పంచమం **pancamam** *n.* name of a certain musical note.
పంచమి **pancami** *n.* 1 fifth day of a lunar fortnight. 2 (*also* **pancamii wibhakti**) *gram.* ablative case.
పంచముడు **pancamuDu** *n.* harijan.
పంచాంగం **pancaangam** *n.* the Hindu almanac.
పంచాంగం చెప్పు **pancaangam ceppu** *v.i.* to make an astrological forecast.
పంచాంగం విప్పు **pancaangam wippu** *v.i. colloq.* to expatiate on s.g at length and in detail (because a **pancaangam** is wordy and diffuse); **neenu oka cinna praśna aDigEEnu. waaDu pancaangam wippEEDu** when I asked a brief question, he started a long narration; **tiTLa pancaangam wippEEDu** he abused me at great length.
పంచాంగ శ్రవణం **pancaanga śrawaNam** *n.* listening to the reading of the almanac, performed annually on Hindu New Year's day, the first day of the month of Chaitra.
పంచామృతం **pancaamṛtam** *n.* the five nectars which are mixed and used for anointing the idol in temple worship and distributed to the devotees.
పంచాయతి **pancaayati** *n.* 1 panchayat, court or committee of five arbitrators. 2 the lowest tier of local government, a committee of villagers invested with certain powers.
పంచాయతి చేయు **pancaayati ceeyu** *v.i.* to create a clamour; **neenu Dabbu waapasu iwwaleedani waaDu pancaayati ceesEEDu** he created a clamour because I had not repaid his money.

పంచాయతిదారు[డు] **pancaayatidaaru[Du]** *n.* panchayatdar, member of a panchayat.

పంచాయతి పెట్టించు **pancaayati peTTincu** *v.i.* to call upon a panchayat of arbitrators to settle a dispute.

పంచాయతి సమితి **pancaayati samiti** *n.* panchayat samiti, the middle tier of local government, in charge of many developmental activities.

పంచాళి మనిషి **pancaaLimaniSi** *n.* quarrelsome person.

పంచికట్టు **pancikaTTu** *n.* style or way of tying a dhoti; **maDi~** way of tying a dhoti when performing religious duties; **saykilu~** way of tying a dhoti in preparation for riding a bicycle.

పంచితం **pancitam** *n.* cow's urine.

పంచిపెట్టు, పంచు **pancipeTTu, pancu** *v.t.* **1** to divide, share[out], distribute. **2** to deal (playing cards).

పంచె **pance** *same as* **panca**[1].

పంచేంద్రియాలు **panceendriyaalu** *n.pl.* the five senses—sight, hearing, touch, taste, smell.

పంజా **panjaa** *n.* **1** animal's paw. **2** *dial.* rake (= **dante**).

పంట **paNTa** *n.* crop, produce.

పంటకాలువ **paNTakaaluwa** *n.* branch channel for irrigation leading from a main channel (**pedda kaaluwa**).

పంటగడ్డి **paNTagaDDi** *n.* unthreshed straw.

పంటగాలి **paNTagaali** *n.* gentle wind from the northeast which benefits crops.

పంటపొలం **paNTapolam** *n.* cultivated field.

పంటలువేయు **paNTalu weeyu** *v.i.* *child language* children's method of choosing one of their number to be **donga** or 'odd man out' in a game like hide and seek: hands are held out with the palms either upwards or downwards; of the two groups of children so formed the term for the minority group is **'paNDindi'** and they are eliminated: for the others it is **'paNDaleedu'** and they repeat the process until all are eliminated except for one child, who becomes the **donga.**

పంట్లాం **paNTLaam** *n.* trousers.

పండబారు **paNDabaaru** *v.i.* to ripen, mature.

పండబెట్టు **paNDabeTTu**[1] *v.t.* to ripen.

పండబెట్టు **paNDabeTTu**[2] *v.t.* to lay down.

పండా **paNDaa** *n.* **1** member of a subcommunity of temple priests. **2** guide who escorts devotees into a temple and arranges for performance of ceremonies desired by them.

పండించు **paNDincu** *v.t.* **1** to grow, cultivate, raise (a crop). **2** to ripen.

పండిత **paNDita** *adj.* scholarly; **~janam** scholarly people; **~bhaaSa** scholarly language.

పండితపుత్రుడు **paNDita putruDu** *n.* **1** *lit.* scholar's son. **2** *colloq.* foolish or brainless person, idiot.

పండితమ్మన్యుడు **paNDitammanyuDu** *n.* conceited person who poses as a scholar, bogus scholar, self-styled scholar.

పండితుడు **paNDituDu** *n.* **1** learned man, scholar, pandit. **2** Telugu language teacher in a school.

పండు **paNDu**[1] I. *n.* ripe fruit; **paNDaa? kaayaa?** *lit.* is it a ripe fruit or an unripe fruit? i.e., is it good news or bad news? *or* is it success or failure? **paNDaNTi/paNDuwaNTi kaapuram** *lit.* a household like a ripe fruit, i.e., a happy home. II. *adj.* **1** bright, fair; **~ wennela** bright moonlight; **paNDerupu** bright red. **2 ~ musali** (*or* **musali ~**) very old person. **3 ~ naayana** dear boy (used as a term of affection or endearment with reference to a male person younger than the speaker) **mii pillakeemaNDii, ratnam laaNTi pilla! daaniki ~ naayanaNTi moguDostaaDu!** your daughter? she's treasure! she will find a lovely husband! III. *v.i.* **1** to ripen, mature. **2** to yield a crop; **naa polam paNDaleedu** my field produced no crop; **innaaLLaki aame kaDupu paNDindi** after so many days she has been blessed with a child. **3** (of a vow) to be fulfilled; **naa noomu paNDindi** my prayers have been answered. **4** (of hair) to turn grey; **paNDina/paNDutunna juTTu** hair that has turned/is turning grey. **5** to be full of experience; **neenu ii wyawahaaramloo paNDipooyEEnu** I am an old hand at this business. **6** to be reddened by betel juice; **taambuulam weesukoowaDamwalla paNDina nooru** mouth reddened by chewing betel and nut. **7 paNDindi** *and* **paNDaleedu** *in child language: see* **paNTalu weeyu.**

పండు **paNDu**[2] (*also* **~ konu**) *v.i.* **1** to lie down. **2** to sleep.

పండుగ, పండగ, పండువు **paNDuga, paNDaga, paNDuwu** *n.* festival, feast.

పండ్రెండు **paNDreNDu** *n. class.* twelve (= **panneNDu**).

పంతం **pantam** *n.* **1** bet, wager. **2** resolve, determination. **3** perseverance, obstinacy. **4** vow. **5** rivalry.

పంతం పట్టు, పంతగించు **pantam paTTu, pantagincu** *v.t.* **1** to resolve, vow. **2** to be determined, insist.

పంతులు **pantulu** *n.* **1** (*also* **baDi~**) school teacher. **2** name suffix added to certain brahman names. **3** term of address to a respectable man.

పంతులమ్మ **pantulamma** *n.* schoolmistress.

పంథ, పంథా **pantha[a]** *n.* **1** *class.* way. **2** manner, method, system.

పంద **panda**[1] *n.* (*also* **piriki~**) coward.

పంప **panda**[2] *n. dial.* sheaf of corn.

పంది **pandi** *n.* pig; **~maamsam** pork.

పందికొక్కు **pandikokku** *n.* bandicoot, a large kind of rat.

పందిరి **pandiri** *n.* **1** canopy, pandal. **2** shed or awning made of leaves; **illu piiki ~ weesEEru** they turned the house into a shambles: *lit.* they pulled down the house and put an awning (in its place).

పందుం **pandum** *n.* **1** ten tooms, half a candy. **2** an indefinite large quantity; **~ tinnaa paragaDupee** in spite of eating ten tooms his stomach is still empty (*colloquial saying*).

పందెం **pandem** *n.* **1** bet, wager. **2** (*also* **parugu~**) race; **gurrapu~** horse race.

పందెంకట్టు, పందెంకాచు **pandem kaTTu, pandem kaacu** *v.t.* to bet, wager.

పందేరం **pandEEram** *n.* **1** distribution to devotees of **prasaadam** which has been offered to a deity. **2** *colloq.* free distribution.

పందొమ్మిది **pandommidi** *n.* nineteen.

పంపకం **pampakam** *n.* **1** despatch[ing]. **2** division, distribution, partition: **aasti pampakaala dastaaweeju** *legal* partition deed.

పంపకం చేయు **pampakam ceeyu** *v.t.* to distribute.

పంపర **pampara** *n.* (*also* **~panasa**) pomello, *citrus decumana.*

పంపర **pampara**[2] *n.* a cattle disease.

పంపించు **pampincu** *v.t.* to send [away].

పంపిణి **pampiNi** *n.* distribution, partition.

పంపు **pampu**[1] *n.* 1 pump. 2 *dial.* tap.

పంపు **pampu**[2] *v.t.* to send, despatch.

పంపుకొట్టు **pampukoTTu** *v.i.* 1 to pump (a tyre). 2 *colloq.* to flatter: **aayanaki pampu koDutunnaaDu** he is flattering him.

పంబ **pamba** *n.* 1 flock cotton cleaned and made soft by teasing. 2 small drum carried by fortune-telling beggars at the Sankranti festival.

పంబకొట్టు **pambakoTTu** *v.t.* to tease cotton by twanging a bow-like instrument (**kamaanu**).

పంబరేగకొట్టు **pambareegakoTTu** *v.t.* to beat (s.o.) so as to raise bruises.

పకడ్బందీగా **pakaDbandiigaa** *adv.* strongly, powerfully, forcefully, effectively.

పకపక **pakapaka** *onom. n. sug.* laughter: **~ nawwu** to laugh loudly, burst out laughing: **~ laadu** to laugh aimlessly, giggle, snigger.

పకాల్మనినవ్వు **pakaalmani nawwu** *v.i.* to burst out laughing.

పకోడీ **pakooDii** *n.* fried snack of bengalgram flour and onions.

పక్క, ప్రక్క **pakka**[1], **prakka** I. *n.* side, direction, way: **~ lu cekkalayeeTaTTu nawwu** to laugh so as to burst o.'s sides. II. *adj.* nearby, adjoining, next, neighbouring: **pakkillu** the next-door house; **pakkuuru** the next village *or* the adjoining village; **~ waadyam** instrumental music which accompanies a singer. III. *p.p.* (also **~ na**) by the side of: **rooDDu~** by the roadside.

పక్క **pakka**[2] *n.* bed[ding]: **~ cuTTa** bedding roll.

పక్కం **pakkam** *n.* side: **waaDiki saayam enduku ceestunnaawu? waaDu nii cuTTamaa, ~ aa?** why are you helping him? is he your relative or your close friend? **cuTTa pakkaalu** kith and kin.

పక్కగా, ప్రక్కగా **pakkagaa, prakkagaa** *adv.* at the side, by the side.

పక్కదారి **pakkadaari** *n.* side road, byway.

పక్కపక్కన, పక్కపక్కల్ని **pakkapakkana, pakkapakkalni** *adv.* side by side, next to each other.

పక్కవాటుగా **pakkawaaTugaa** *see* **waaTugaa.**

పక్కా **pakkaa** *adj.* 1 thorough, complete. 2 durable, substantial. 3 real, genuine.

పక్కాగా **pakkaagaa** *adv.* 1 thoroughly. 2 durably, substantially. 3 definitely, without fail: **~ wastaanu** I will come without fail.

పక్కాపేగూ **pakkaapeeguu** *n.* o.'s close relations, i.e., o.'s brothers and sisters and o.'s direct descendants.

పక్కి **pakki** *substandard form of* **pakSi.**

పక్కు **pakku** *n.* 1 dried up grains of cooked rice. 2 **mukkuloo~** snot. 3 scab (= **errapuNDu**).

పక్కెముక **pakkemuka** *n.* rib.

పక్వ **pakwa** *adj.* 1 ripe, matured. 2 cooked: **pakwaahaaram** cooked food.

పక్షం **pakSam** *n.* 1 side, part (in an argument); **o.-i ~ wahincu** to take s.o.'s part, side with s.o. 2 party (in a dispute). 3 fortnight. 4 *class.* wing.

పక్షంలో, పక్షాన **pakSamloo, pakSaana** *adv.* in the case of, in the event of: **aa~** in that case, in that event; **leeni~** if not, otherwise: **miiru raani ~ ceppaNDi** in case you are not coming, tell me.

పక్షపాతం **pakSapaatam** *n.* 1 bias, partisanship, prejudice. 2 partiality, preference (**-pay[na]**, for).

పక్షవాతం **pakSawaatam** *n.* paralysis.

పక్షాంతరం **pakSaantaram** *n.* alternative.

పక్షి **pakSi** *n.* 1 bird. 2 *colloq.* wretched person: **anaatha~ aypootaaDu** he will become a helpless wretch.

పక్ష్మం **pakSmam** *n. class.* 1 eyelash. 2 wing.

పగ **paga** *n.* enmity, hostility, hatred, dislike.

పగటిపూట, పగటిపొద్దు, పగటివేళ **pagaTipuuTa, pagaTipoddu, pagaTiweeLa** *n.* daytime, daylight hours.

పగటి వేషాలు **pagaTi weeSaalu** *n.pl.* eccentric style of dress (referring to wearing theatrical costume during daytime).

పగడం, పవడం, పొగడం **pagaDam, pawaDam, pogaDam** *n.* coral.

పగడాల దండ **pagaDaala daNDa** *n.* coral necklace.

పగడాల దీవి **pagaDaala diiwi** *n.* coral island.

పగ తీర్చుకొను **paga tiircukonu** *v.i.* to assuage o.'s anger, take revenge.

పగపట్టు **pagapaTTu** *v.i.* to bear a grudge, cherish enmity (**-miida**, against).

పగపట్టే **pagapaTTee** *adj.* vindictive.

పగలగొట్టు **pagalagoTTu** *v.t.* to break, smash, shatter.

పగలబడు **pagalabaDu** *v.i.* 1 to burst with laughter: **pagalabaDi nawwEEDu** he burst out laughing. 2 *colloq.* to be proud and boastful: **tanadaggira Dabbu unnadani~ tunnaaDu** he is boasting that he has money: **eem cuusukoni ~ tunnaaDu?** what has he got to be proud of?

పగలు **pagalu** I. *n.* day[time]. II *adv.* in the daytime, by day.

పగవాడు **pagawaaDu** *n.* enemy.

పగిడీ **pagiDii** *n.* 1 turban. 2 *dial.* deposit of money.

పగిది, పవిది **pagidi, pawidi** *n. class.* manner, way.

పగులు **pagulu** I. *n.* break, crack, crevice: **~ baarina** full of cracks or crevices. II. *adj.* (of glass, china) cracked; **~ jaaDi** cracked jar. III. *v.i.* to break, crack, burst: **pagili pagili eeDcu** to weep copiously.

పగ్గం **paggam** *n.* 1 rope, cord. 2 tether, halter. 3 rein, rope used to guide bullocks when pulling a cart or ploughing.

పచనం **pacanam** *n. class.* 1 cooking. 2 digestion.

పచారీ **pacaarii** *n.* petty shopkeeper.

పచారీ కొట్టు **pacaarii koTTu** *n.* petty shop selling condiments, etc.

పచారు **pacaaru** *n.* 1 walk, stroll. 2 pacing up and down.

పచారు చేయు, పచార్లు చేయు **pacaaru ceeyu, pacaarlu ceeyu** *v.i.* 1 to take a walk, go for a walk. 2 to pace up and down.

పచీ pacii *see* **rucii.**

పచ్చ **pacca** I. *n.* 1 greenish yellow colour; **aaku~** green (like a leaf): **pasupu~**yellow (like turmeric). 2 emerald. 3 tattoo mark. II. *adj.* 1 green; **~kaagitam** *colloq.* hundred rupee note (being green in colour). 2 yellow. 3 fair in complexion. 4 bright, shining; **aarubayaTa eNDa~gaa weccagaa undi** out in the open the sunshine is bright and hot. 5 prosperous, flourishing.

పచ్చ కర్పూరం **pacca karpuuram** *n.* fragrant kind of camphor used as a cooling eye lotion; **naa kaLLaloo~ peTTukonnaTLunnadi** (*lit.* it is as if my eyes were bathed in cooling camphor) *is a stock phrase meaning* I am happy at s.o. else's misfortune.

పచ్చ కామెర్లు **pacca kaamerlu** *n.* jaundice.

పచ్చ గడ్డి **pacca gaDDi** *n.* green grass; **waaLLa madhya~ weestee bhaggumaNTundi** they are on very bad terms with each other (*lit.* if you put green grass between them, it will catch fire—colloq. expression).

పచ్చ గన్నేరు **pacca ganneeru** *n.* yellow oleander.

పచ్చ జొన్న **pacca jonna** *n.* yellow cholam.

పచ్చడం **paccaDam** *n.* 1 bed sheet. 2 cloth covering. 3 *class.* dress.

పచ్చడి **paccaDi** *n.* chutney.

పచ్చడి అవు **paccaDi awu** *v.i.* to be pounded, be crushed (*lit.* to be pounded into chutney): **oLLantaa paccaDi ayyeTaTTu koTTEEru** they beat him soundly (*lit.* they pounded his whole body into chutney).

పచ్చబడు, పచ్చబారు **paccabaDu, paccabaaru** *v.i.* to turn green, turn yellow; **waaDi kaLLu paccabaDDaayi/ paccabaarEEyi** (i) he is suffering from jaundice (ii) his eyes are green with envy.

పచ్చి **pacci**[1] *adj.* 1 raw, uncooked, untreated, undried; **~pulusu** kind of soup that is not cooked; **~carmam** raw hide; **~puNDu** open wound. 2 (of wood) green, not dried or seasoned: **~kaTTelu** freshly cut sticks; **~baddalu** green bamboo slats (used for making a funeral bier). 3 unripe. 4 downright, blatant, rank, barefaced; **~abaddham** barefaced lie; **~buutulu** obscene language; *see* **baalintaraalu.**

పచ్చి **pacci**[2] *n. substandard form of* **pakSi.**

పచ్చి ఒళ్లు **pacci oLLu** *n.* state of convalescence (often with ref. to post-natal cases); **~. bayTa tiragaku** you are still convalescing. do not go outside.

పచ్చిక **paccika** *n.* (*also* **~biiDu**) green grass, lawn, pasture.

పచ్చిక బయలు **paccika bayalu** *n.* grassy meadow, grassland, pasture.

పచ్చీసు **pacciisu** *n.* a game played with twenty-five coins per player.

పజ్ఝెనిమిది, పద్ధెనిమిది, పదునెనిమిది **pajjhenimidi, paddhenimidi, padunenimidi** *n.* eighteen.

పటం **paTam** *n.* 1 picture, map, sketch, illustration, diagram. 2 *class.* cloth.

పటం కట్టించు **paTam kaTTincu** *v.t.* to frame (a picture).

పటకా **paTakaa** *n.* 1 belt. 2 collar.

పటకారు, పట్టకారు **pa[T]Takaaru** *n.* pair of tongs; **cinna~** pincers.

పటపట **paTapaTa** *onom.n.sug.* any rattling or crackling sound, e.g., grinding or chattering of teeth, creaking of wood, etc.; **~maNTuu mooTaarusaykil okaTi pooyindi** one motorcycle went past with a pop-popping sound: **uppuni penammiida weeyistee ~mani śabdam ceestundi** if you fry salt in a pan it makes a crackling sound.

పటపటాంగం **paTapaTaangam** *n. dial.* combat.

పటలం **paTalam** *n.* 1 coating, covering. 2 membrane. 3 group, collection.

పటవ **paTawa** *same as* **paTuwa.**

పటహం, పటాహం **paTaham, paTaaham** *n. class.* kettledrum.

పటాకీ **paTaakii** *n.* firework, cracker.

పటాటోపం **paTaaToopam** *n.* pomp, show.

పటాపంచలు **paTaapancalu** *n.* scattering, dispersing.

పటాపంచలు అవు **paTaapancalu awu** *v.i.* to be scattered, be dispersed, be dissipated.

పటాపంచలు చేయు **paTaapancalu ceeyu** *v.t.* to scatter, disperse, break up.

పటారం **paTaaram** *adj.* big, showy, ostentatious; **payna ~loopala loTaaram** *lit.* showy outside but empty within—*expression used of anything which is outwardly magnificent but contains nothing of worth internally.*

పటాలం **paTaalam** *n.* regiment, battalion; **~loo ceerEEDu** he enlisted in the army.

పటాహం **paTaaham** *same as* **paTaham.**

పటిక **paTika** *n.* alum.

పటిక బెల్లం **paTika bellam** *n.* sugar candy.

పటిమ **paTima** *n.* 1 cleverness, skilfulness. 2 strength, vigour, power.

పటిష్ఠ **paTiSTa** *adj.* strong, firm, sound.

పటిష్ఠం చేయు **paTiSTam ceeyu** *v.t.* to strengthen.

పటిష్ఠత **paTiSTata** *n.* strength, soundness.

పటు[వు] **paTu[wu]** *adj.* 1 clever, skilful, able. 2 strong, vigorous.

పటుత్వం **paTutwam** *n.* 1 skill, ability. 2 strength, vigour, forcefulness, effectiveness.

పటువ, పటవ **paTuwa, paTawa** *n. dial.* earthen pot, jar.

పటేల్ **paTeel** *n. dial.* patel, village headman.

పట్ట **paTTa** *same as* **paTTaa**[2].

పట్టం **paTTam** *n.* 1 (*also* **paTTaa**) academic degree; **gawrawa~** honorary degree. 2 crown, diadem; **waaLLiNT-Loo wiiDiki~ kaTTEEru** they treat him like a king (*lit.* they have crowned him as king) in their house.

పట్టంచు చీర **paTTancu ciira** *n.* sari woven with a border of gold or silver thread.

పట్టకం **paTTakam** *n.* prism.

పట్టకారు **paTTakaaru** *same as* **paTakaaru.**

పట్టణం, పట్నం **paTTaNam, paTNam** *n.* town, city.

పట్టపగలు **paTTapagalu** I. *n.* broad daylight. II. *adv.* in broad daylight.

పట్టపగ్గాలు **paTTapaggaalu** *n.pl.* restraints (*lit.* restraining ropes).

పట్టపుటేనుగు **paTTapuTeenugu** *n.* royal elephant, elephant on which the king rides.

పట్టభద్రుడు **pattabhadruDu** *n.* graduate.

పట్టమహిషి, పట్టపురాణి, పట్టపుదేవి **paTTamahiSi, paTTapuraaNi, paTTapudeewi** *n.* queen.

పట్టరాని **paTTaraani** *adj.* unrestrainable, uncontrollable.

పట్టా **paTTaa**[1] *n.* 1 patta, grant or lease specifying land held by a cultivator and revenue payable on it. 2 (*also* **paTTam**) academic degree. 3 (*also* **kaali~**) anklet. 4 iron tyre of a cart wheel. 5 (*also* **raylu~**) railway line. 6 *dial.* bullock's collar (= **paTTeDa**). 7 coarse cloth such as canvas or sacking. **kurcii~** canvas cloth used in a deck chair: **goone~** sacking.

పట్టా, పట్ట **paTTaa**[2], **paTTa** *n.* bark of a tree.

పట్టాకత్తి **paTTaakatti** *n.* broadsword.

పట్టాదారు **paTTaadaaru** *n.* pattadar, holder of a patta, holder of a right to cultivate land.

పట్టాభిషేకం **paTTaabhiSeekam** *n.* coronation.

పట్టాభూమి **paTTaabhuumi** *n.* land held by a cultivator subject to payment of land revenue.

పట్టి **paTTi**[1] *n. class.* child; **raaca~** royal child.

పట్టి **paTTi**[2] I. *past participle of* **paTTu.** II *following an infinitive, see* **baTTi.**

పట్టించు **paTTincu** I. *v.i.* to be unsuitable, have a bad effect, be contrary to s.o.'s tastes or likings; **waataawaraNamloo cinna maarpu waccinaa niiku paTTistundi jaagratta** be careful, even if there is a small change in the weather, it will upset you; **ii ceppulu naawi kaawu, paTTistunnaayi** these are not my shoes, they feel uncomfortable (*or* they do not fit properly); **naaku maamuulugaa bhoojanam ceeyaDaaniki endukoo paTTincinaTTayyindi** I somehow felt it awkward to eat a normal meal. II. *v.t. as causative of* **paTTu** ~ *has a wide range of usages. some examples are:* **nannu tappudoowa paTTincEEDu** he made me take a wrong road; **peTTe waaDiceeta paTTincuku waccEEnu** I got him to bring the box; **waaDiceeta amaram kaNThataa paTTincEEru** they made him learn the Amaram by heart; **waaDiki aa adrsTam paTTincEEru** they brought that good fortune upon him; **naaku aa picci paTTincEEDu** he initiated me into that craze; **waaDi waLLu paTTincEEru** they had his body massaged; **annam kaDupuniNDaa paTTincEEDu** he ate a hearty meal; *see* **egataaLi~, weeLaakooLam~, pani~.**

పట్టించుకొను **paTTincukonu** *v.t.* 1 to take heed of, pay attention to, treat seriously. 2 to take to heart, take amiss. 3 **manasuki~** to fix (s.g) in o.'s mind. 4 to make much of, think much of. 5 to rub (oil, soap) on o.'s body.

పట్టింపు **paTTimpu** *n.* 1 application, concern. 2 restriction, scruple: **kulam~la walla peLLi jaragaleedu** the marriage did not take place owing to community restrictions; **naaku~lu ekkuwa** I stand on formalities. 3 insistence; **miiree paaDaalani naaku~leedu, ewaru paaDinaa pharwaaleedu** I do not insist on your singing, anyone may sing. 4 preference. 5 superstition; **~unnawaaLLu pilli śakunam paaTistaaru** superstitious people consider a cat to be a bad omen. 6 taking offence, taking objection; **neenu aame tappu etti cuupitee aameku~waccindi** when I pointed out her mistake, she took offence.

పట్టింపుగా **paTTimpugaa** *adv.* 1 attentively, with concentration, with concern. 2 with reservations.

పట్టిక **paTTika** *see* **paTTii** *sense 6.*

పట్టి చూచు **paTTi cuucu** *v.t.* to try, test; **deewuDu nannu paTTi cuustunnaaDu** God is testing me.

పట్టిడి **paTTiDi** *n.* anvil.

పట్టీ **paTTii** n. 1 band, strap, belt. 2 (*also* **nawaaru~**) tape. 3 hem of a garment. 4 (*also* **malaam~, paalaastri~**) bandage, sticking plaster to cover a wound or boil. 5 rectangular strip of some material, *e.g.*, slab or bar of chocolate or other eatable, or a strip of masonry laid on a roof to secure the tiles. 6 (*also* **paTTika**) list, panel, inventory, statistical table. 7 label. 8 *dial.* field (= **maDi**).

పట్టు **paTTu** I. *n.* 1 hold, grip, grasp; **~tappi paDipooyEEnu** I lost my grip and fell; **paTTuu wiDupuu telisinawaaDu** s.o. who knows when to be firm and when to relax; **bhalluukapu~** bear's hug. 2 pertinacity, resolution, resolve; **gaTTi~ paTTEEDu** he made a firm resolve. 3 support, prop. 4 place, abode, dwelling place; **kuuDali~** meeting place, junction; *cf.* **aayuwu~, uniki~, palle~.** 5 plaster, poultice. 6 trick in a card game. 7 teat in wrestling. 8 polish of rice when milled. 9 *other idiomatic usages:* (i) **aaTa manci~loo unnappuDu paaripooyEEDu** he ran off just when the game was in full swing; **sinimaa manci~loo unnappuDu naakoosam ewaroo waccEEru** just when the movie was at an exciting point, someone came for me; (ii) **annam oka~paTTEEDu** he ate his fill *or* he had hearty meal; (iii) **~miida unnaaDu** he is drunk *or* he is intoxicated; (iv) **poDum~** pinch of snuff. II. *v.i.* 1 (of physical states, diseases, pests) to come to, affect; **ippuDee waaDiki nidra paTTindi** he has just fallen asleep; **naaku rompa paTTindi** I caught cold; **pustakaalaku cedalu paTTEEyi** white ants attacked the books; **tupaanu paTTina samudram** stormy sea; **poga paTTina illu** house filled with smoke; **mancu paTTina maamiDi puuta** mango flowers drenched with dew. 2 to be formed (by natural process); **mabbulu paTTeedendukuraa? waanalu kuriseeTandukuraa!** why are clouds formed? in order that rain may fall; **payrulaku adhika warSaalawalla ginja sarigaa paTTadu** due to excess of rain for the crops, the ear does not form properly. 3 to happen, befall; **waaDiki adrSTam paTTindi** fortune favoured him; **pekku pathakaalaku paTTina gatee diiniki paTTindi** the same fate which befell many plans befell this one also; **cokkaa korru paTTindi** there is a tear in the shirt; **candruDiki grahaNam paTTindi** the moon is eclipsed. 4 to be of interest, be of concern; **appu ewaru istaaroo sundaraaniki paTTaleedu** Sundaram was not concerned with who would give a loan; **naakeem paTTindi? neenenduku ceyyaali**? how am I concerned? why should I do it? 5 to fit, suit, apply to, be applicable to; **pustakam jeebuloo paTTadu** the book will not fit into the pocket; **aa maaTaku ee artham ~ tundoo eelaaguna telustundi**? how are we to know which meaning will fit that word? 6 to contain, hold, accommodate, take; **okee maniSi paTTee cooTundi** there is only enough space to take one man; **pulusuloo uppu paDutundEE? saripooyindEE?** will the soup take more salt or is that enough? 7 to take (time, money); **prayaaNam muuDu gaNTalu paDutundi** the journey will take three hours; **enta Dabbu**

paTTinaa peTTaDaniki neenu siddhangaa unnaanu however much it may cost I am willing to pay. **8** (of joints of the body) to be stiff; **mookaaLLu kaastaa paTTeesEEyi** the knees were a little stiff. **9** to adhere; **ii rangu gooDaku paTTadu** this colour will not adhere to the wall. **10** *examples of other idiomatic usages are* (i) **iNTimukham paTTEEDu** he turned his face towards home *or* he set out for home; (ii) **waaDi burraki paTTaDam leedu** it is not penetrating his mind *or* he is not able to understand it; (iii) **aDawulu paTTi tirugutunnaaru** they are keeping to the forests; (iv) **illu paTTina wedhawa aaDapaDucu** widowed daughter who has returned to her parents' home. III *v.t.* **1** to take, catch, capture, hold; **ceepalu~** to catch fish; **daari~** to take or follow a road; **mancam~** to take to o.'s bed due to illness; **daanam~** to receive charity; **idigoo Dabbu, paTTu!** here is the money, take it! **2** to bear, suffer, endure. **3** to stop, restrain; **santooSam paTTaleekuNDaa unnaanu** I cannot restrain my joy. **4** *~ is used with many nouns of Telugu origin to form intr. or tr. vbs.*, e.g., **cirugu~** to be torn; **gaanuga~** to crush (seeds, etc.) in an oil mill; **citrika~** to plane; **taggumokham~** to recede, decline; **tappu~** to find fault with, blame; **oopika~** to keep o.'s patience.

పట్టు **paTTu**[2] *n. and adj.* silk; **~ciire** silk sari.

పట్టు, పట్టండి **paTTu**[3], **paTTaNDi** *clitic following a hortative verb inviting participation between hearers and speaker* **manam tindaam~** come let us eat.

పట్టుకుపోవు, పట్టుకొనిపోవు **paTTukupoowu, paTTukoni poowu** I. *v.i.* (of joints of the body) to be stiff, be paralysed; **kaaLLu paTTukupooyEEyi** the legs are stiff. II. *v.t.* to take away.

పట్టుకువచ్చు, పట్టుకొనివచ్చు **paTTukuwaccu, paTTukoni waccu** *v.t.* to bring.

పట్టుకొను **paTTukonu** *v.i. and t.* to catch, grasp, take hold of; **naaku jabbu paTTukonnadi** I have been attacked by illness *or* I have been taken ill; *see* **weelaaDu, paakulaaDu.**

పట్టుగడ **paTTugaDa** *n.* **1** stick held for support by a man treading a picota (baling machine). **2** means of support, refuge.

పట్టుగొమ్మ **paTTugomma** *n.* **1** stick to lean on, refuge, means of support. **2** *class.* woman.

పట్టుదల **paTTudala** *n.* singlemindedness, persistence, determination, doggedness, insistence, perseverance.

పట్టుదలగా **paTTudalagaa** *adv.* determinedly.

పట్టున **paTTuna** *p.p.* in, at, near, by; **iNTi~** at home; **taNDri niiDa~** in the shadow of his father; **weeLa~** at the appropriate/appointed/fixed time; *cf.* **ii~, oka~**.

పట్టుపరిశ్రమ **paTTupariśrama** *n.* sericulture.

పట్టుపురుగు **paTTupurugu** *n.* silkworm.

పట్టుబట్ట **paTTubaTTa** *n.* **1** silk dhoti worn when the wearer puts on **maDi**; it is considered ceremonially pure. **2** any cloth made of silk.

పట్టుబట్టు **paTTubaTTu** *v.t.* to strive, press, insist, make a point of.

పట్టుబడి **paTTubaDi** *n.* s.g that is caught or grasped.

పట్టుబడు **paTTubaDu** *v.i. with dative* **1** to be seized, be caught, be held. **2** to be understood, be comprehended. **3** (of a habit, skill) to be acquired, be mastered; **sundaraaniki alawaaTu paTTubaDindi** Sundaram developed a habit; **appaTiki teluguloo okamoostarugaa maaTLaaDaDam paTTubaDindi** by then he had learnt to talk Telugu after a fashion.

పట్టుమని **paTTumani** *adv.* at the most, not even; **~padimandi waccEEru** at the most ten people came; **~padimandi raaleedu** not even ten people came.

పట్టె **paTTe** *n.* **1** strip of wood. **2** wood forming the frame of a cot. **3** tape, esp. strong nawar tape used for making a cot. **4** stripe or streak of paint.

పట్టెడ **paTTeDa** *n.* **1** woman's necklace or collar. **2** collar for attaching the yoke to a bull's neck when ploughing or pulling a cart.

పట్టెడు **paTTeDu** *adj.* single handful (*lit.* as much as can be held in the palm of one hand).

పట్టెమంచం **paTTemancam** *n.* cot made with woven nawar tape.

పట్టెవర్ధనాలు **paTTewardhanaalu** *n. pl.* broad white marks on the forehead worn by Vaishnavites.

పట్నం **paTNam** *same as* **paTTaNam.**

పట్నవాసం **paTNawaasam** *n.* urban area.

పట్నవాసి **paTNawaasi** *n.* town dweller.

పట్రా! **paTraa!** *colloq.* bring! (= **paTTukuraa!**).

పట్ల **paTLa** *p.p.* **1** with regard to, with reference to, about, concerning, towards; **aame~preema** love towards her; **wṛddhulu, yuwakulu ani neenu upayoogincina maaTalanu wayassu ~anwayincukooraadu** the words 'old persons' and 'young persons' which I have used should not be construed with reference to age. **2** in, at; **konniTi~** in some respects; **cuTTu~** in the neighbourhood, round about.

పట్వారీ **paTwaarii** *n.* patwari, village accountant (= **karaNam**).

పఠనం **paThanam** *n. class.* reading, studying.

పఠన మందిరం **paThana mandiram** *n. class.* reading room.

పఠించు **paThincu** *v.t. class.* **1** to learn. **2** to read. **3** to recite.

పడంగా, పళంగా, పడాన, పళాన, పాటున, పాట్న, పాడంగా, పాళంగా **p[a]aDangaa, p[a]aLangaa, paDaana, paaT[u]na** *advbl. particle* **1** *suffixed to a durative vbl. adj.* as it is/was, on the spot, then and there; **nannu nilucunna~Dabbu temmannaaDu** he demanded me to bring the money then and there; **kuurcunnawaaDu kuurcunna~nidra pooyEEDu** he fell asleep in the same position as he was sitting; **neenu cuustunna~pramaadam jarigindi** the accident happened just as I was watching; **adi ippuDuu unna ~nee undi** even now it is in that same condition *or* even now it is just as it was. **2** *suffixed to a n.* along with, together with, and all; **annam tina leedu, pleeTu~paareesEEDu** he did not eat his food, he threw it away, plate and all; **kobbari miThaayi kaagitam ~tinaali** coconut sweets should be eaten along with the paper; *see also* **paaTu[na]nee.**

పడక **paDaka** *n.* **1** bed[ding]. **2** sleep[ing]. **3** *dial.* sick bed.

పడక కుర్చీ, పడకుర్చీ **paDak[a]kurcii** *n.* easy chair.

పడకటిల్లు, పడగ్గది **paDakaTillu, paDaggadi** *n.* bedroom.

పడక వేయు, పడకేయు **paDaka weeyu, paDakeeyu** *v.i.* **1** to take to o.'s bed due to illness. **2** to sleep.

పడగ **paDaga** *n.* hood of a snake.

పడగొట్టు **paDagoTTu** *v.t.* to knock down, overthrow, demolish.

పడచు **paDacu** *same as* **paDucu.**

పడతి **paDati** *n. class.* woman.

పడదొబ్బు **paDadobbu** *v.t. slang.* to knock down, throw down.

పడపడ **paDapaDa** *onom. n. sug. sound of* (i) beating, thumping, tapping, clapping; (ii) chattering, jabbering.

పడపడలాడు **paDapaDalaaDu** *v.i. colloq.* to chatter, jabber.

పడమటి **paDamaTi** *adj.* western.

పడమర **paDamara** *n.* west.

పడయు **paDayu** *v.t. class.* 1 to obtain, acquire. 2 to beget.

పడవ **paDawa** *n.* boat.

పడవేయు, పడేయు **paDaweeyu, paDeeyu** *v.t.* 1 to cause to fall or drop, knock over. 2 to throw [down], cast [down]. 3 to put down, set down. 4 to give, present, hand over; **naa Dabbu naaku paDeeyi!** give me my money!; **darakhaastulu paDeestunnaaDu gaani udyoogam eemii raaleedu** he is making applications but no job has come his way.

పడాన **paDaana** *same as* **paDangaa.**

పడి **paDi**[1] *n.* 1 obsolete measure of volume varying from one area to another. 2 (with ref. to a person's age) period of ten years; **aayana enabhayyoo ~ loo** in his eighties (i.e., when aged between 80 and 89); **iTu yawwanaaniki aTu waardhakyaaniki incumincu samaana duuramloo nalabhayyoo ~ loo unna naawaNTi wyakti** an individual like me in his forties, about equally far from youth and old age (said by Sri Sri when aged 44).

పడి **paDi**[2] *past participle of* **paDu**; *see* **paDu** *I sense 15.*

పడి ఉండు, పడుండు **paDi uNDu, paDuNDu** *v.i.* 1 (of money, etc.) to be accumulated *or* to lie idle. 2 (of a room) to lie vacant. 3 to stay, be accomodated; **kaligindeedoo peDataanu, tini maa iNTLoo paDi uNDu** whatever I get I will share with you, take it for your meals and stay in my house.

పడికట్టు **paDikaTTu** *n.* 1 weight used in scales. 2 *dial.* step, stair.

పడికట్టు పదం **paDikaTTu padam** *n.* stock phrase, catch phrase.

పడికట్టు రాయి **paDikaTTu raayi** *n.* 1 weight used in scales. 2 standard for reference.

పడిగాపులు కాయు, పడిగాపులు పడు **paDigaapulu kaayu, paDigaapulu paDu** *v.i.* to wait patiently for a long time.

పడిదె **paDide** *n.* clothes hired from a washerman.

పడిపడి **paDipaDi** *adv.* 1 (of laughter, weeping) copiously; **~ nawwu** to laugh heartily; **~ eeDcu** to weep copiously. 2 **~ daNDaalu peTTu** to fall down and prostrate o.s. repeatedly before s.o. (either in reverence or from an insincere motive).

పడిసెం **paDisem** *n.* cold in the head, catarrh.

పడు **paDu** I. *v.i.* 1 to fall. 2 **-loo ~** *lit.* to fall into, *hence* to enter [upon], become immersed in; **waaDi burraloo eedannaa aaloocana paDitee** if any thought enters his head; **guDDeddu ceeloo paDDaTTu** like a blind bull rushing into a field (proverbial expression used of a person who acts precipitately and without discrimination); **kaburlaloo paDDaaru** they plunged into conversation; **ii saahityamloo paDipooyEEnu** I became immersed in literature; *colloq.* **bassuloo paDDaanu** I managed to get on a bus. 3 **-miida ~** to rush towards, fall upon; **kukkalu naamiida paDDaayi** the dogs rushed at me. 4 to occur, happen, come into being, appear; **ginne soTTa paDindi** a dent was formed in the vessel; **ceruwu kaTTaki gaNDi paDindi** a breach occurred in the tank bund; **punaadi paDindi** the foundation was laid; **maa uuriki bassu paDindi** a bus has been provided to our village *or* there is a bus to our village; **maa baawiloo niiLLu paDaleedu, raaLLu paDDaayi** water has not been struck in our well, only rock has been found; **kaalam gaDustunnakoddii, reyilu paDi, prayaaNa sawkaryaalu eerpaDDaayi** in the course of time the railway appeared and travel facilities were provided; **dongalu paDina aaru nelalaki kukkalu moriginaTTu** like dogs barking six months after the thieves came (proverb). 5 to be got, be obtained, be received; **kondaru kurraaLLu diipassemmEElu paTTukoni illilluu tirigi paaDeewaaLLu. prati iNTLoonuu diipaalaki nuune kaani Dabbulu paDeewi** some boys used to take lampstands and go from house to house singing. at every house they would receive oil for the lamps and some pie coins. 6 to be liked, be agreeable, suit, agree with; **aa jeyilu tiNDi aayanaku paDalEE** that jail food did not agree with him (*or* did not suit him). 7 *idiomatic usages*: **ceepa walaloo paDDadi** a fish was caught in the net; **inkaa naaTLu paDaleedu** transplantation has not been done yet; **daani nooru mancidi kaadu, daani nooTLoo paDaku** she has a sharp tongue, do not fall foul of her; **waaDi kuDi ceeyi paDipooyindi** his right hand has become paralysed; **rooDDuku aDDangaa paDipooyEEDu** *or* **rooDDuku aDDam paDDaaDu** he made his way along the road. 8 *impersonal, in neg. constr.* to be on friendly terms, get on well together; **twaraloonee aayanatoo paDaleeka aame weLLi pooyindi** very soon she went away being unable to get on with him; **wiiDikii waaDikii paDadu** these two do not get on well together. 9 *following a vbl. n. in neg. constr.* to be possible; **haydaraabaaduloo waaLLa iNTiki weLLaDaaniki naaku paDaleedu** it was not possible for me (*or* I could not manage) to visit his house when I was at Hyderabad. 10 (of literary work) to appear in print, be published. 11 **paDitee** *conditional form of* **paDu** *is used idiomatically as shown in these examples:* **eedi paDitee adi tiisukoo** take anything at all *or* take whatever you want; **ekkaDiki paDitee akkaDiki weLtaaDu** he will go anywhere; **eppuDu paDitee appuDu** at any time; **ewaru paDitee waaru** anyone, anybody. 12 *~ following an infinitive forms the passive voice of a transitive vb.*, e.g., **ceppa~** to be said. 13 *~ is used as a suffix to form vbs. from certain nouns and adjs.*, e.g., **accu~** to be printed, **pooTii~** to compete, **sadhya~** to be possible, **weeru~** to be separated. 14 **wacci~** *means* to arrive unexpectedly or unwanted; **poddunee tellawaarakuNDaa samsaaramtoo waccipaDDaaDu** he arrived before dawn with all his family; **eemi duSkaalam waccipaDindi!** what bad times have befallen us! 15 *idiomatic usages of* **paDi**, *past participle of ~* : **pillalu miThaayilu paDi tinnaaru** the children gobbled up the sweets; **Tii wii cuuDaDaaniki paDi castunnaaDu** he is crazy on watching T.V; **raatrallaa paDi cadiwEEDu** he read continuously all through the night; **neenu kaburu ceyyagaanee paDi waccEEDu** as soon as I sent word he came all the way; *see also* **paDi uNDu.** II. *v.t.* to suffer, bear, endure; **baadhanu paDaleeka pooyEEnu** I could not endure the pain.

పడుకొను **paDukonu** *v.i.* **1** to lie down, recline. **2** to go to bed. **3** to sleep.
పడుగాయ **paDugaaya** *n.* unripe fruit fallen from a tree.
పడుగు **paDugu** *n.* **1** woof. **2** heap of unthreshed corn. **3** corn and straw spread on the threshing floor for threshing. **4** straw bundles laid as foundation for a rick.
పడుచు, పడచు **paDucu**[1], **paDacu** *n.* young woman, girl. II *adj.* young, youthful.
పడుచు **paDucu**[2] *v.i.* to solicit (as a prostitute).
పడుచుకొను **paDucukonu** *v.i.* to commit adultery, live as a prostitute, earn money by prostitution.
పడుచుతనం, పడుచువయసు **paDucutanam, paDucuwayasu** *n.* [period of] youth.
పడుచువాడు **paDucuwaaDu** *n.* boy, youth.
పడుపు [వృత్తి] **paDupu[wṛtti]** *n.* prostitution.
పడుపుకత్తె **paDupukatte** *n.* prostitute.
పడె **paDe** *same as* **baaDe.**
పడ్డ **paDDa**[1] *n.* **1** three year old female buffalo. **2** (*also* ~**peyya**) heifer.
పడ్డ **paDDa**[2] *past vbl. adj. of* **paDu** (= **paDina).**
పణం **paNam**[1] *n.* **1** stake, bet, wager. **2** price. **3** commodity for sale.
పణం **paNam**[2] *n* fanam, an obsolete small silver coin.
పణంగా **paNangaa** *adv.* **1** as a wager, as a price. **2** at stake.
పణత **paNata** *n.* **1** upper part of the stock of a plough. **2** head (of an animal).
పణ్య **paNya** *adj.* saleable.
పణ్యస్త్రీ **paNyastrii** *n. class.* prostitute.
పతంగం **patangam** *n. class.* bird.
పతంగి **patangi** *n. dial.* kite (= **gaalipaTam**).
పతకం **patakam** *n.* **1** medal. **2** locket.
పతనం **patanam** *n.* **1** fall[ing]: **aadarśa**~ falling away from an ideal. **2** decline, decadence: **naytika**~ moral decline or degradation or deterioration.
పతనం అవు **patanam awu** *v.i.* **1** to fall. **2** to decline, become decadent.
పతనావస్థ **patanaawastha** *n.* decadence.
పతనోన్ముఖ **patanoonmukha** *adj.* about to fall, tottering, destined to fall.
పతాక **pataaka** *n.* flag, banner.
పతాకసన్నివేశం **pataakasanniweeśam** *n.* climax situation (in a drama).
పతాకహస్తం **pataakahastam** *n.* holding the fingers of the hand in a certain position (a gesture in dancing).
పతి **pati** *n. class.* **1** husband. **2** lord, master.
పతిత **patita** I. *n.* immoral woman. II. *adj.* fallen, destitute, sinful, immoral.
పతితుడు **patituDu** *n.* fallen person, destitute person, sinful person, immoral person.
పతివ్రత **patiwrata** *n.* chaste and virtuous wife.
పత్తా **pattaa** *n.* **1** trace, sign, clue. **2** address.
పత్తి, ప్రత్తి **p[r]atti** *n.* **1** cotton bush, *gossypium.* **2** raw cotton, uncleaned and unginned cotton: ~**too ceesina watti** lamp wick made of raw cotton (such wicks are used by orthodox persons): ~**pani** *lit.* work of cleaning cotton, *hence* tedious work.
పత్తికాయ **pattikaaya** *n.* cotton boll: **kaLLu** ~**llaagaa ceesukoni cuusindi** she gazed with eyes opened wide (in surprise or pleasure).
పత్తిరి, పత్రి **pattiri, patri** *n.* leaves and flowers used as an offering in worship, esp. of Ganesa.
పత్తెం, పథ్యం **pattem, pathyam** *n.* diet; ~**tinu** (i) to follow a prescribed diet; (ii) to take food for the first time after an illness; **ninnaTidaakaa jwaram undi, iwwEELa**~**tinnaDu** till yesterday he had fever, today he ate his first meal.
పత్తెదార్ **pattedaar** *n.* **1** holder of a patta or right cultivate land. **2** detective.
పత్ని **patni** *n.* wife.
పత్రం **patram** *n.* **1** leaf. **2** document, deed. **3** written bond. **4** *dial.* letter. **5** paper: **pariikSa**~ examination paper.
పత్రహరితం **patraharitam** *n. bot.* chlorophyll.
పత్రి **patri** *same as* **pattiri.**
పత్రించు **patrincu** *v.t.* **1** to trim, reduce in size. **2** to taper, narrow gradually.
పత్రింపు, బద్రింపు **patrimpu, badrimpu** *n.* **1** cutting, pruning. **2** trimming, tapering.
పత్రిక **patrika** *n.* **1** newspaper, journal. **2** **aahwaana**~ invitation card.
పత్రికా ప్రకటన **patrikaa prakaTana** *n.* press release, press communique.
పత్రికా రచన **patrikaa racana** *n.* journalism.
పత్రికావిక్రేత **patrikaa wikreeta** *n.* newsagent, newspaper seller.
పత్రికావిలేఖరి **patrikaa wileekhari** *n.* journalist.
పథం **patham** *n.* path, way.
పథకం **pathakam** *n.* scheme, plan.
పథికుడు **pathikuDu** *n.* traveller.
పథ్యం **pathyam** *same as* **pattem.**
పద, పదండి **pada, padaNDi** *defective vb. occurring only in the imperative* let us start!, let us go!
పదం **padam** *n.* **1** foot. **2** footstep, footmark. **3** word, term. **4** line in a stanza or verse. **5** kind of song: **palle padaalu** folk songs. **5** *class.* rank, station, degree: **parama**~ highest rank.
పదంపడి **padampaDi** *adv. class.* afterwards.
పదకొండు **padakoNDu** *n.* eleven.
పదకోశం **padakoośam** *n.* glossary, concordance.
పదచ్ఛేదం **padaccheedam** *n.* separation of the components of a compound word.
పదజాలం **padajaalam** *n.* **1** vocabulary. **2** terminology, nomenclature.
పదనిర్మాణశాస్త్రం **padanirmaaNaśaastram** *n.* (science of) morphology.
పదబంధం **padabandham** *n.* **1** phrase, expression. **2** compound word.
పదమూడు **padamuuDu** *n.* thirteen.
పదలం **padalam** *n.* obsolete weight equal to ten palams.

పదవి **padawi** *n.* position, designation, status, rank, office.

పదవీకాలం **padawiikaalam** *n.* term of office.

పదవీచ్యుతి **padawiicyuti** *n.* fall from power.

పదవీభ్రష్టుడు **padawiibhraSTuDu** *n.* deposed or dismissed person.

పదవీరీత్యా **padawiiriityaa** *adv. admin.* ex officio.

పదవీవిరమణ **padawiiwiramaNa** *n.* retirement from office.

పదవీవ్యామోహం **padawiiwyaamooham** *n.* lust for power and position.

పదసాహిత్యం **padasaahityam** *n.* verse, poetry.

పదసూచి **padasuuci** *n.* index.

పదహారణాలా **padahaaraNaalaa** *adv.* hundred per cent, out and out, outright.

పదహారు **padahaaru** *n.* sixteen.

పదాతిదళం, పదాతిబలం **padaatidaLam, padaatibalam** *n.* infantry, land forces.

పదాది **padaadi** *adj.* initial (letter or sound in a word).

పదార్థం **padaartham** *n.* **1** thing, article. **2** substance, constituent, ingredient. **3** *sci.* matter. **4** meaning of a word. **5** *colloq.* liquor.

పదావళి **padaawaLi** *n.* vocabulary, word list.

పది **padi** *n.* **1** ten. **2** many, a considerable number; **padi kaalaalapaaTu** for a long time (*lit.* for a length of ten seasons); **padi roojulu** ten days *or* a considerable length of time.

పదిమంది **padimandi** *n.pl.* **1** ten persons. **2** many persons, people in general; **padimandii eem anukoNTaaru?** what will people think?

పదిల[ం] **padila[m]** *adj.* **1** careful. **2** safe, secure.

పదిలం **padilam** *n.* care, caution, carefulness.

పదిలంగా **padilangaa** *adv.* carefully, cautiously, safely, securely.

పదిలం చేయు **padilam ceeyu** *v.t.* to keep, preserve.

పదిలపడు **padilapaDu** *v.i.* to be secured.

పదిలపరచు **padilaparacu** *v.t.* to secure, take care of, put or stow in a safe place.

పదిహేడు **padiheeDu** *n.* seventeen.

పదిహేను **padiheenu** *n.* fifteen.

పదుగురు **paduguru** *n. pl. class.* **1** ten persons. **2** many persons, people in general.

పదును **padunu** I. *n.* **1** sharpness. **2** cutting edge or blade of an axe, sickle or similar tool. **3** whetting. **4** wet[ness], moisture. **5** ripeness, maturity. II. *adj.* **1** sharp. **2** wet, damp, moist.

పదును చేయు, పదును పెట్టు **padunu ceeyu, padunu peTTu** *v.t.* **1** to wet, moisten. **2** to tan, cure (leather). **3** to sharpen.

పదునెనిమిది, పద్దెనిమిది **padunenimidi, paddhenimidi** *n.* eighteen.

పదేపదే **padee padee** *adv.* often, repeatedly, again and again.

పదో **padoo** *adj.* tenth.

పదోన్నతి **padoonnati** *n.* promotion.

పద్దు **paddu** *n.* **1** item (in an account). **2** account maintained in course of business. **3 caakali**~ list of clothes given to a washerman.

పద్ధతి **paddhati** *n.* **1** manner, method, custom, scheme, system; **waayidaala**~ system of instalments. **2** technique. **3** style in writing.

పద్ధతిగా **paddhatigaa** *adv.* systematically.

పద్ధెనిమిది **paddhenimidi** *same as* **padunenimidi.**

పద్నాలుగు **padnaalugu** *n.* fourteen.

పద్మ[ం] **padma[m]** *n.* lotus, waterlily.

పద్మరాగం **padmaraagam** *n. class.* ruby.

పద్మవ్యూహం **padmawyuuham** *n. class.* kind of military manoeuvre first described in the Mahabharata.

పద్మశాలి **padmaśaali** *n.* name of a community of weavers.

పద్మాకరం **padmaakaram** *n. class.* tank or pond full of lotuses, lotus pond.

పద్మాసనం **padmaasanam** *same as* **baasipiiTa.**

పద్యం **padyam** *n.* **1** verse or stanza in a poem. **2** poem. **3** verse, poetry.

పద్యకావ్యం **padyakaawyam** *n.* verse, poetry.

పద్యాత్మక **padyaatmaka** *adj.* composed in verse.

పన **pana** *n.* **1** sheaf of corn. **2** bundle of sticks. **3** tuber of ginger or turmeric. **4** horn of a cow or bull.

పనబారు **panabaaru** *v.i.* (of root crops) to grow in size, swell, come to maturity.

పనస **panasa** *n.* **1** jack fruit, *artocarpus heterophyllus.* **2** *class.* verse in a chapter of the Vedas.

పని **pani** *n.* **1** work, task, job, labour, business, employment, profession. **2** act, deed, affair, matter, thing; **manci** ~ **ceesEEwuraa!** you have done the right thing! **aTuwaNTi panulu ceeyaku** do not do such things. **3** care, concern; **naaku ewaritooTi**~ **leedu** I have no concern with anyone; **nii koopamtoo naaku** ~ **eemiTi?** what concern have I with your anger? *or* what do I care for your anger? **4** *following an infinitive in neg. constr.* need, necessity, purpose; **waaDu ii wiSayam ceppiweeya**~ **leedu** he need not disclose this matter. **5** *idiomatic usages:* (i) *a past vbl. adj. followed by* **anta**~ **ayindi** *signifies that an action almost took place*, e.g., **neenu rooDDu daaTutuuNDagaa kaaru wacci nannu koTTinanta**~ **ayindi** when I was crossing the road a car came and almost struck me; **raamuki muurcha waccinanta**~ **ayindi** Ramu almost fainted; (ii) **nii**~ **ayipootundi** you (*lit.* your affair) will be finished or ruined; **maa annayya**~ **sarisari anukonnaamu** we thought it was all over with my brother (*lit.* we thought that my brother's affair was finished).

పనికట్టుకొని **panikaTTukoni** *adv. lit.* having stopped o.'s (other) work (for a special purpose or reason), *hence* making a special point of, purposefully, deliberately; **nuwwu prati raatrii**~ **uurantaa cuTTawalasindee** every night you must make a special point of going round the whole town; ~ **waaLLiNTiki weLLi ceppEEnu** I went specially to his house and told him.

పనికివచ్చు **paniki waccu** *v.i.* to be of use, be useful, serve a purpose; **paniki waccee** useful; **paniki raani** (*or* **paniki maalina**) useless.

పనిగాపెట్టుకొను panigaapeTTukonu *v.i., following a vbl. n.* to make (s.g) o.'s object or business, make a point of, be intent on; **kaangres waadulanu samarthincaDaannee idiwaraloo daadaapu anni patrikalu panigaa peTTukonnaayi** hitherto almost all newspapers have made it their business to support the Congressites.

పనిచేయించుకొను paniceeyincukonu *v.i. colloq.* to get o.'s hair cut.

పనిచేయు paniceeyu *v.i.* to work, act, function, produce a result, be effective: **aayana kinda pani ceestunnaanu** I am working under him; **mandu pani ceestunnadi** the medicine is acting (*or* the medicine is proving effective).

పనితనం panitanam *n.* workmanship, craftsmanship.

పని దొంగ pani donga *n.* one who avoids work, shirker, truant.

పనిపట్టించు panipaTTincu *v.i.* to deal severely with s.o., punish s.o., teach s.o. a lesson; **allari ceesee pillala pani paTTistaanu** I will punish the children who are making a noise.

పనిపాట్లు panipaaTLu *n.pl.* jobs, work.

పనిపెట్టుకొను panipeTTukonu *v.i.* 1 to undertake a work. 2 to have business dealings: **sarkaar kacceeriitoo panipeTTukoNTee** if you have dealings with a government office. 3 **panipeTTukoni** (*advbl. phrase*) intentionally, deliberately, on purpose.

పని మనిషి, పని చేసేది pani maniSi, pani ceeseedi *n.* woman servant.

పనిముట్టు panimuTTu *n.* tool, implement.

పనిలోపని[గా] paniloo pani[gaa] *adv.* in the course of o.'s work, journey, etc. *or* while (some action) is/was happening: **maambaLam weLLaalani bayaldeerEEnu, ~ mandawalli poosTaaphiisulooki weLLEEnu** I set out for Mambalam, in the course of my journey (*or* on my way) I went into Mandavalli post office.

పనివాడితనం paniwaaDitanam *n.* workmanship, craftsmanship, artistry.

పనివాడు paniwaaDu *n.* workman, labourer.

పనుచు panucu *v.t. class.* to send.

పనుపు panupu *n. class.* order, command, commission, errand.

పనుపున panupuna *adv.* at the command of; **aayana ~ waccEEnu** I have come at his command.

పన్న panna[1] *n. class.* 1 servant. 2 person of nó consequence.

పన్న panna[2] *n.* 1 frame used in weaving. 2 (*also* **pannaa**) breadth of a cloth.

పన్నం pannam *n. class.* 1 verse in a chapter of the Vedas. 2 question.

పన్నగం pannagam *n. class.* snake, serpent.

పన్నాగం pannaagam[1] *n.* canopy over a palanquin.

పన్నాగం, పన్నుగడ pannaagam[2], **pannugaDa** *n.* 1 plot, trick. 2 device, contrivance.

పన్నారు pannaaru *n.* small pot shaped like a tortoise shell.

పన్నీరు panniiru *n.* rose water.

పన్ను, పల్లు pannu[1], **pallu** (*pl.* **paLLu**) *n.* tooth.

పన్ను pannu[2] (*pl.* **pannulu**) *n.* tax.

పన్ను pannu[3] *v.t.* 1 to make, form. 2 to invent, contrive: **kuTra ~, wala ~** to hatch a plot.

పన్నుగడ pannugaDa *same as* **pannaagam**[2].

పన్నె panne *n. dial.* comb.

పన్నెండు panneNDu *n.* twelve.

పప్ప pappa *n. child language* food, drink.

పప్పడం pappaDam *same as* **appaDam.**

పప్పన్నం pappannam *n. colloq.* feast, banquet; **~ eppuDu peDataawu?** (i) when are you going to give us a feast? (ii) *when said to a young man, the meaning is* when are you going to get married?

పప్పు pappu *n.* 1 kernel. 2 dhall (= kernel of a gram or pulse) either raw or cooked: **maa baawi niiLLaloo ~ uDukutundi** dhall will cook in our well water, i.e., our well water is soft and does not contain calcium; **aa ~ lu naa daggira uDakawu** those tricks do not deceive me; **~ loo kaalu weeyu** to make a mistake, commit a blunder.

పప్పుగుత్తి pappugutti *n.* dhall pounder (kitchen implement).

పప్పుగోంగుర చీరె pappugoonguura ciire *n.* sari woven with yellow threads for woof and black threads for warp.

పప్పుదినుసులు, పప్పుధాన్యాలు pappudinusulu, pappudhaanyaalu *n.pl.* grams, pulses.

పప్పుసుద్ద pappu sudda *n.* 1 *lit.* lump of dhall. 2 idle or slothful person.

పబ్బ pabba *n.* rattan creeper, *calamus rotang*.

పబ్బం pabbam *n.* festival, feast; **~ gaDupukoni weLLEEDu** he left after managing to complete his work.

పమిట, పమిటకొంగు, పమిటచెంగు pamiTa, pamiTa kongu, pamiTa cengu *n.* loose end of a sari worn over the shoulder (= **payTa**).

పయనం payanam *n.* journey.

పయనం అవు payanam awu *v.i.* to set forth, start on a journey.

పయనించు payanincu *v.i.* to travel.

పయోధి payoodhi *n. class.* ocean.

పయ్య payya[1] *n. dial.* wheel.

పయ్య payya[2] *n.* reddish or pinkish colour.

పయ్యె payye *n. dial.* pinkish white colour in cattle.

పర para[1] *adjvl. prefix* 1 alien, other, foreign: **~ deeśam** foreign country. 2 next, succeeding, following: **~ lookam** the next world; **~ hallu** *gram.* succeeding, following or suffixed consonant; **padaadyaccu hraswamay ~ hallu dwiruktamaynappuDu** when the initial vowel of a word is short and the succeeding consonant is doubled.

పర para[2] *n.* obsolete measure of volume.

పరం param[1] *n.* (*also* **paralookam**) the next world: *cf.* **iham.**

పరం param[2] *n.* frame of a cart.

పరం param[3] *p.p.* in the possession or custody of, under the control of, at the disposal of; **pooliisula ~** in the custody of police; **jaanaki taanu ceesee pani puurtigaa kaTTipeTTi tananu taanu śakuntala ~ ceesukonnadi** Janaki stopped all the work that she was doing and put herself at Sakuntala's disposal.

పరంగా parangaa *advbl. suffix* 1 on behalf of, in the name of: **aayanaki naa ~ ceppaNDi** please tell him on my behalf. 2 in terms of, in relation to, from the point of view of, with reference to, in connection with: **ippuDu S. manuSyula raabaDi gurinci jiitaala ~ aaloocinca saagEEDu** now S. began to think of people's incomes in terms of their salaries; **śaastriiya ~ pariikSincu** to investigate scientifically *or* to investigate from the point of view of science; **paariśraamika waaNijya ~ pekku deeśaalu sandarśincEEru** he toured many countries in connection with industry and commerce; **ucchaaraNa ~ akSaraaniki** '*syllable*' **ani artham, leekhana ~** '*letter*' **ani artham** in relation to pronunciation **'akSaram'** means a syllable, in relation to script it means a letter; **nighaNTuwu anee padam samskṛta mawlikamaynadi, toluta waydika ~ nee waaDabaḌindi** the word **'nighaNTuwu'** has a Sanskrit root, it was indeed first used in connection with the Vedas. 3 in the sense of, with the meaning of; **'ayyawaarlu' kramasyaa 'upaadhyaayula' ~ waaDabaDaDam eerpaDiṇdi 'ayyawaarlu'** gradually came to be used in the sense of 'teachers': *cf.* **gatangaa.**

పరంజా **paranjaa** *n.* 1 bamboo sunshade projecting from the eaves of a house. 2 *dial.* scaffolding.

పరంజ్యోతి **paranjyooti** *n.* divine light.

పరంపర **parampara** *n.* 1 series, sequence, succession: **~ gaa waccina** handed down in succession. 2 stream, train (of thought). 3 volley (of questions).

పరంపరాగత **paramparaagata** *adj.* hereditary, handed down from generation to generation.

పరంగి **parangi** *adj. obs.* foreign, European.

పరక **paraka** *n.* 1 (*also* **gaDDi ~**) blade of grass. 2 one eighth of a rupee. 3 trifle; *expressions like* **beeDoo parakoo, padoo parakoo** *and* **paatikoo parakoo** *mean* some small amount of money. 4 *same as* **poraka.**

పరకాయప్రవేశం **parakaaya praweeśam** *n.* transmigration from one body to another, transferring life from one body to another (dead) body by magic.

పరకాయించు **parakaayincu** *v.t.* to look carefully at, examine closely.

పరకీయ **parakiiya** *n. class.* another man's wife.

పర[లోక] క్రియలు **para[looka]kriyalu** *n.pl.* obsequies, funeral rites.

పరగణా **paragaNaa** *n. obs.* territory, territorial division, area, district.

పరగు **paragu** *v.i. class.* to be, exist.

పరచు, పరుచు **paracu, parucu** *v.t.* 1 to spread (cloth, grain in the sun). 2 to scatter. 3 to extend. 4 ~ *is used in composition to form tr. vbs. from nouns and adjs.*, e.g., **teliya ~** to make known, **siddha ~** to make ready.

పరచుకొను **paracukonu** *v.i.* to spread, extend.

పరజా **parajaa** *n. dial.* balcony.

పరతంత్ర **paratantra** *adj.* dependent.

పరతంత్రుడు **paratantruDu** *n.* dependant.

పరతత్త్వం **paratattwam** *n.* all-embracing philosophy.

పరతెంచు **paratencu** *v.i. class.* to come running.

పరదా **paradaa** *n.* 1 screen, curtain. 2 veil.

పరదేశం **paradeeśam** *n.* foreign country.

పరదేశి **paradeesi** *n.* stranger, foreigner, alien.

పరధ్యానం **paradhyaanam** *n.* absentmindedness, diversion of o.'s attention.

పరధ్యానంగా **paradhyaanangaa** *adv.* 1 inattentively, without paying attention, off-handedly, unawares. 2 absent-mindedly, casually, listlessly.

పరనారి **paranaari** *n.* 1 another man's wife. 2 woman stranger.

పరనింద **paraninda** *n.* blaming others.

పరపతి **parapati** *n.* 1 loan. 2 credit[worthiness].

పరపర **parapara** *onom. adv. sug. sound of* (i) tearing paper; (ii) scribbling on paper; (iii) speaking fast; (iv) cutting with a saw.

పరపీడన **parapiiDaana** *n.* oppression of other persons.

పరపు, పరుపు **parapu, parupu** I. *n.* laying out, spreading. II. *v.t.* 1 to spread. 2 to cast; **dṛSTi ~** to cast a glance.

పరపురుషుడు **parapuruSuDu** *n.* 1 another woman's husband. 2 man stranger.

పరప్రభుత్వం **paraprabhutwam** *n.* foreign government.

పరబ్రహ్మ **parabrahma** *n.* God, the Supreme Spirit.

పరభాష **parabhaaSa** *n.* foreign language.

పరమ **parama** I. *adjvl. prefix meaning* very; **~ palleTuuru** tiny hamlet; **~ rahasyangaa** very secretly; **~ samarthangaa** very competently. II. *adj.* greatest, most, best, highest, supreme, principal, chief.

పరమపదం **paramapadam** *n.* heaven.

పరమపదసోపానపటం **paramapadasoopaana paTham** *n.* game of snakes and ladders.

పరమపదించు, పరమపదం చేరుకొను **paramapadincu, paramapadam ceerukonu** *v.i.* to die, expire.

పరమహంస **paramahamsa** *n. class.* ascetic of the highest order.

పరమాణు **paramaaNu** *adj.* atomic.

పరమాణురచన **paramaaNuracana** *n. phys.* atomic structure.

పరమాణువు **paramaaNuwu** *n.* atom.

పరమాణ్వంకం **paramaaNwankam** *n. phys.* atomic number.

పరమాత్మ, పరమేశ్వరుడు **paramaatma, parameeśwaruDu** *n.* God, the Supreme Being.

పరమానందం **paramaanandam** *n.* supreme happiness, rapture.

పరమాన్నం, పరవాన్నం, పర్వాన్నం **paramaannam, par[a]waannam** *n.* sweetened rice pudding.

పరమార్థం **paramaartham** *n.* greatest good, highest truth: **jiiwita ~** highest meaning or object of life.

పరమావధి **paramaawadhi** *n.* highest goal, ultimate aim.

పరమేష్ఠి **parameeSTi** *n.* epithet of Brahma.

పరమైన **paramayna** *adjvl. suffix* 1 relating to, connected with, for; **saahitya ~ noobel bahumati** Nobel prize for literature; **raajyaanga ~ samasyalu** constitutional problems; **nyaaya ~ cikkulu** legal difficulties; **paalanaa ~ sardubaaTLu** administrative adjustments; *cf.* **gata.** 2 applicable to, associated with. 3 under the control of, in the possession of, vested in; **boorDu ~ adhikaaraalu** powers vested in the Board. 4 *gram.* following after, suffixed to.

పరలోకం **paralookam** *n.* the next world.

పరలోకక్రియలు **paralooka kriyalu** *same as* **parakriyalu.**

పరవళ్లు **parawaLLu** *n.pl.* frenzy, excitement, rushing, turbulence; **koopamtoo ~ tokkutunnaaDu** he is dancing with rage; **ninna kurisina waanalaki nadi ~ tokkutunnadi** the river is flowing turbulently owing to yesterday's rains.

పరవశం, పరవశత, పరవశత్వం **parawaśam, parawaśata, parawaśatwam** *n.* entrancement, rapture, delight.

పరవశం అవు, పరవశించు **parawaśam awu, parawasincu** *v.i.* to be entranced, be enraptured, be enthralled, be delighted.

పరవశింప చేయు **parawaśimpa ceeyu** *v.t.* to entrance, enrapture, enthral, delight.

పరవా, పర్వా, ఫరవా, ఫర్వా **parawaa, parwaa, pharawaa, pharwaa** *n.* concern, care, worry, regard *occurring only in the phrase* ~ **leedu** (i) never mind, it does not matter, it is all right; **"neenu ceppuleesukoni loopaliki raawaccaa?" "~ leedu raNDi"** "can I come in with my shoes on?" "it does not matter, come in!" (ii) all right, fairly good, not bad; **"sinimaa elaagundi?" "~ leedu, oka saari cuuDawaccu"** "what is the movie like?" "not bad, worth seeing once".

పరవాన్నం **parawaannam** *same as* **paramaannam.**

పరశు[వు] **paraśu[wu]** *n. class.* battle-axe.

పరశురామ **paraśuraama** *n.* Parasurama, an incarnation of Vishnu holding an axe.

పరశురామక్షేత్రం **paraśuraamakSeetram** *n.* classical name of Kerala.

పరశురామప్రీతి **paraśuraamapriiti** *n.* **1** *lit.* Parasurama's delight, i.e., destruction. **2** *colloq.* destruction by burning, conflagration, holocaust.

పరశ్రేయస్సు **paraśreeyassu** *n.* welfare of other persons.

పరస **parasa** *n. dial.* annual festival of a village goddess.

పరసతి **parasati** *n.* another man's wife.

పరస్నాలు **parasanaalu** *n.pl. dial.* purging, loose motions.

పరస్త్రీ **parastrii** *n.* woman stranger, woman who is not o.'s wife.

పరస్థలం **parasthalam** *n.* strange place, foreign place.

పరస్పర **paraspara** *adj.* reciprocal, mutual; ~ **sambandham** mutual relationship, interrelationship.

పరస్పరం **parasparam** *adv.* mutually.

పరస్పరవిరుద్ధ, పరస్పరవ్యతిరేక **paraspara wiruddha, paraspara wyatireeka** *adj.* mutually opposed, contradictory, conflicting, incompatible.

పరహిత **parahita** *adj.* devoted to the welfare of others.

పరాకాష్ఠ **paraakaaSTha** *n.* **1** maximum limit, climax. **2** crest, peak, highest point, zenith. **3** greatest achievement, summit of excellence.

పరాకు **paraaku** I. *n.* **1** inattention, carelessness, neglect. **2** absent-mindedness. II. *adj.* **1** inattentive, uninterested. **2** absent-minded. **3** distracted, mentally disturbed. III. ~ ! *or* **bahu paraak!** *interj. uttered at the end of a prayer addressed to a God or a king and meaning* pray be attentive !

పరాకుగా, పరాగ్గా **paraakugaa, paraaggaa** *adv.* inattentively, absentmindedly, casually.

పరాకు చెప్పు **paraaku ceppu** *v.i.* to call the attention of a God or a king to a prayer that is being uttered.

పరాకు పడు **paraaku paDu** *v.i. and t.* to be negligent, forget, overlook.

పరాక్రమం **paraakramam** *n.* valour, prowess, strength, heroism.

పరాక్రమశాలి **paraakramaśaali** *n.* warrior.

పరాగం **paraagam** *n.* pollen.

పరాగరేణువు **paraagareeNuwu** *n.* grain of pollen.

పరాచకం, పరాచికం, పరియాచకం **paraacakam, paraacikam, pariyaacakam** *n.* joking, making fun.

పరాచికాలాడు **paraacikaalaaDu** *v.t.* to poke fun (at s.o.).

పరాజయం **paraajayam** *n.* defeat, overthrow.

పరాజయం పొందు **paraajayam pondu** *v.i.* to be defeated, be overthrown.

పరాజితుడు **paraajituDu** *n.* defeated or vanquished person.

పరాఙ్ముఖత్వం **paraaŋmukhatwam** *n. class.* turning o.'s face away, aversion.

పరాత్పరుడు **paraatparuDu** *n.* God, the Supreme Being.

పరాధీన **paraadhiina** *adj.* dependent, subject, subservient.

పరాధీనం, పరాధీనత **paraadhiinam, paraadhiinata** *n.* dependence, subjection, subservience.

పరాన **paraana** *advbl. suffix* following; **'j' ku ~ waccina accu** the vowel that follows 'j'; *cf.* **paramayna** *sense 4.*

పరాన్న **paraanna** *adj.* parasitic.

పరాన్నజీవి, పరాన్నభుక్కు **paraannajiiwi, paraannabhukku** *n. sci.* parasite.

పరాపేక్ష **paraapeekSa** *n.* dependence on help from others.

పరాభవ **paraabhawa** *n.* fortieth year of the Hindu cycle of sixty years.

పరాభవం **paraabhawam** *n.* insult, humiliation, disgrace, discredit.

పరాభవించు **paraabhawincu** *v.t.* to insult, disgrace, humiliate, discredit.

పరాభూతుడు **paraabhuutuDu** *n.* person who is insulted, disgraced, humiliated or discredited

పరామర్శ[ం] **paraamarśa[m]** *n.* **1** attention, care. **2** scrutiny, enquiry, examination, criticism. **3** consolation, condolence.

పరామర్శించు **paraamarśincu** *v.t.* **1** to enquire about, examine, investigate. **2** to tend, take care of, pay polite attention to, converse with. **3** to console, condole with.

పరాయణత్వం **paraayaNatwam** *n.* dedication, devotion.

పరాయణుడు **paraayaNuDu** *n.* dedicated or devoted person..

పరాయత్త **paraayatta** *adj.* subject, dependent.

పరాయి **paraayi** *adj.* another, foreign, strange; ~ **waaDu** stranger.

పరారి అవు **paraari awu** *v.i.* to abscond.

పరారు, పరారి **paraaru, paraari** *n.* absconding.

పరారుచిత్తగించు **paraaru cittagincu** *v.i.* **1** to run away, flee, abscond; **waaNNi gaTTigaa aDigitee paraaru cittagincEEDu** when he was questioned sternly, he fled away. **2** to become scarce, vanish, disappear.

పరారుణ **paraaruNa** *adj.* infrared.

పరార్థం **paraartham**[1] *n.* other persons' interests; **paraartha cintana** unselfishness.

పరార్థం **paraartham**[2] *n.* the second half.

పరావర్త **paraawarta** *adj.* changed, transformed.

పరావర్తనం **paraawartanam** *n. sci.* reflection.

పరాశ్రయ **paraaśraya** *adj.* dependent.

పరాసు **paraasu** *adj. obs.* French.

పరాస్త **paraasta** *adj.* (of a theory, belief) rejected, refuted, discredited, outmoded.

పరి **pari**[1] *n.* time, occasion; **oka~** once.

పరి **pari**[2] *Sanskrit prefix* (i) *signifying* around, fully, completely; (ii) *lending intensive force, often with only slight alteration of meaning*, e.g., **śuddha** pure, **~śuddha** [very] pure.

పరికరం **parikaram** *n.* 1 implement, instrument, tool. 2 apparatus, equipment. 3 device, means.

పరికర్మ[ం] **parikarma[m]** *n. class.* cleansing, purifying.

పరికల్పన **parikalpana** *n.* 1 *sci.* hypothesis. 2 contriving, inventing.

పరికించు **parikincu** *v.t.* to examine, look carefully at, scrutinise.

పరికిణీ **parikiNii** *n.* skirt (inner garment).

పరిగణన[ం] **parigaNana[m]** *n.* 1 estimation, consideration, regard. 2 counting, reckoning. 3 recognition.

పరిగణనంగా **parigaNanangaa** *adv.* in consideration of.

పరిగణించు **parigaNincu** *v.t.* 1 to consider, regard, treat, look upon. 2 to calculate, reckon. 3 to take into consideration, have in mind.

పరిగృహీత **parigrhiita** *adj.* 1 accepted. 2 grasped.

పరిగె **parige**[1] *n.* kind of fish.

పరిగె **parige**[2] *n.* corn remaining on the ground in a field after reaping.

పరిగ్రహణం **parigrahaNam** *n.* 1 taking, accepting. 2 *class.* accepting in marriage.

పరిగ్రహించు **parigrahincu** *v.t.* 1 to take, seize, grasp. 2 to take over, embrace, adopt (custom). 3 to receive, accept. 4 to abstract.

పరిఘ **parigha** *n.* 1 club studded with iron. 2 iron bar used for securing a door.

పరిచయం **paricayam** *n.* 1 acquaintance, familiarity. 2 introduction; **paricaya paaTham** introductory lesson.

పరిచయం చేయు **paricayam ceeyu** *v.t.* to introduce; **nannu tana mitrulaki paricayam ceesEEDu** he introduced me to his friends.

పరిచయకర్త **paricayakarta** *n.* 1 person who introduces. 2 *journ.* interviewer.

పరిచయస్థుడు, పరిచయుడు, పరిచితుడు **paricayasthuDu, paricayuDu, paricituDu** *n.* acquaintance, known person.

పరిచరుడు **paricaruDu** *n.* servant, attendant.

పరిచర్య **paricarya** *n.* service, attendance.

పరిచారకుడు **paricaarakuDu** *n.* 1 servant, attendant. 2 cook (in a Vaisnavite household).

పరిచారిక **paricaarika** *n.* woman servant.

పరిచిత **paricita** *adj.* acquainted, familiar, known; **cira~ mohaalu** familiar faces.

పరిచ్ఛిన్న **paricchinna** *adj. class.* cut off, divided, detached.

పరిచ్ఛేదం **pariccheedam** *n. class.* section or chapter of a book; **sandhi~** chapter on sandhi.

పరిజనం **parijanam** *n.pl.* attendants, servants, retinue.

పరిజ్ఞాత **parijñaata** *n.* learned person, scholar; **bahuwiSaya~** person with a wide range of knowledge.

పరిజ్ఞానం **parijñaanam** *n.* 1 knowledge. 2 technical knowledge, know-how.

పరిఢవం **pariDhawam** *n.* greatness.

పరిఢవించు, పరిఢవిల్లు **pariDhawincu, pariDhawillu** *v.i. class.* 1 to shine. 2 to flourish.

పరిణత **pariNata** *adj. class.* 1 ripe, matured. 2 transformed, developed.

పరిణతి **pariNati** *n.* 1 state of development. 2 transformation, development, evolution. 3 stage of full development, maturity. 4 result, outcome.

పరిణమించు **pariNamincu** *v.i.* 1 to become ripe, become mature. 2 to be changed, be transformed, develop. 3 to turn out to be, be found to be; **paTamloo gurtincina konni uuLLu aayaa praantaalaku weLLeeTappaTiki durgamaalugaa pariNamincEEyi** certain villages that were marked on the map turned out to be difficult of access when those areas were visited.

పరిణయం **pariNayam** *n. class.* marriage.

పరిణయం ఆడు, పరిణయంచేసుకొను **pariNayam aaDu, pariNayam ceesukonu** *v.t.* to marry.

పరిణామం **pariNaamam** *n.* 1 change, transformation, development; **pariNaama daśa** development stage. 2 evolution. 3 result, consequence, eventuality, outcome. 4 *class.* digestion; **pariNaama śuula** griping pain (caused by indigestion).

పరిణాహం **pariNaaham** *n. class.* breadth, width, extent.

పరిణీత **pariNiita** *n. class.* wife.

పరితపించు **paritapincu** *v.i.* 1 to grieve, lament. 2 to regret, yearn for. 3 to reflect ruefully.

పరితాపం **paritaapam** *n.* affliction, sorrow, pain, anguish.

పరితుష్టి, పరితృప్తి **parituSTi, paritrpti** *n.* complete satisfaction, contentment.

పరిత్యజనం, పరిత్యాగం **parityajanam, parityaagam** *n.* abandonment, renunciation.

పరిత్యజించు **parityajincu** *v.t.* 1 to abandon, quit. 2 to give up, renounce. 3 to reject, discard, disclaim.

పరిత్యాగి **parityaagi** *n.* 1 *class.* one who abandons. 2 *mod. in the phrase* **sarwasanga~** one who abandons all worldly things.

పరిత్యాజ్య **parityaajya** *adj.* fit to be abandoned or renounced or rejected.

పరిత్రాణ **paritraaNa** *adj. class.* protective.

పరిత్రాత **paritraata** *n. class.* preserver, saviour, deliverer.

పరిధి **paridhi** *n.* 1 circumference, perimeter, periphery. 2 limit, parameter, scope, range. 3 field, jurisdiction. 4 domain, confines, purview.

పరిపక్వ **paripakwa** *adj.* mature, fully developed.
పరిపక్వత **paripakwata** *n.* maturity, fulfilment, full development.
పరిపరి **paripari** *adj.* diverse, various, sundry; **naa manasu ~ widhaala pooyindi** my thoughts strayed in many directions; **~ widhaala aaloocinca saagEEDu** he proceeded to think along various lines.
పరిపాకం **paripaakam** *n.* 1 ripeness, maturity. 2 state of being completely cooked.
పరిపాటి **paripaaTi** I. *n.* common occurrence, commonplace, common practice, regular habit, s.g normal, s.g usual. II. *adj.* common, normal, usual.
పరిపాలక **paripaalaka** *adj.* administrative.
పరిపాలకుడు **paripaalakuDu** *n.* 1 ruler. 2 administrator.
పరిపాలన **paripaalana** *n.* rule, administration.
పరిపాలనాదక్షుడు **paripaalanaadakSuDu** *n.* administrator.
పరిపాలించు **paripaalincu** *v.t.* to rule, govern, administer.
పరిపీడన **paripiiDana** *n.* oppression.
పరిపీడితుడు **paripiiDituDu** *n.* oppressed or downtrodden person.
పరిపుష్ట **paripuSTa** *adj.* 1 strengthened. 2 well developed.
పరిపుష్టి **paripuSTi** *n.* strength, vigour.
పరిపూర్ణ **paripuurNa** *adj.* 1 full, complete, total. 2 fulfilled. 3 absolute (majority).
పరిపూర్ణత, పరిపూర్ణత్వం **paripuurNata, paripuurNatwam** *n.* perfection, completeness.
పరిపూర్తి **paripuurti** *n.* fulfilment, fulfilling.
పరిపోషణ **paripooSaNa** *n.* nourishment, fostering.
పరిభాష **paribhaaSa** *n. sci.* terminology, technical language, parlance, jargon.
పరిభ్రమణం **paribhramaNam** *n.* revolving, revolution, rotation.
పరిభ్రమించు **paribhramincu** *v.i.* 1 to revolve, circle round. 2 to rotate, gyrate. 3 to wander about, go from place to place. 4 **waaDi mati paribhramincindi** his mind became unstable.
పరిమళ **parimaLa** *adj.* scented; **~ drawyaalu** perfumery.
పరిమళం **parimaLam** *n.* perfume, scent, fragrance.
పరిమళించు **parimaLincu** *v.i.* to be fragrant.
పరిమాణం **parimaaNam** *n.* 1 quantity, amount, size, magnitude, volume. 2 scale; **adhika ~ loo** on a larger scale. 3 dimension.
పరిమాణాత్మక **parimaaNaatmaka** *adj.* quantitative.
పరిమార్చు **parimaarcu** *v.t.* to kill, slay, murder; **pillalu nannu paTTi parimaarustunnaaru** the children are worrying the life out of me.
పరిమిత **parimita** *adj.* limited, restricted, finite.
పరిమితంగా **parimitangaa** *adv.* to a limited extent.
పరిమితం చేయు **parimitam ceeyu** *v.t.* to limit, restrict.
పరిమితి **parimiti** *n.* limit, restriction.
పరియ, పర్రె **pariya, parre** *n.* 1 piece, bit, fragment. 2 crack (in glass).
పరియవాయు **pariyawaayu** *v.i.* to crack, split, break.
పరియాచకం **pariyaacakam** *same as* **paraacakam.**
పరియోజన **pariyoojana** *n.* project.
పరిరంభ[ణ]ం **parirambha[Na]m** *n. class* embrace, embracing.
పరిరక్షణ **parirakSaNa** *n.* safeguarding, protection, preservation.
పరిరక్షించు **parirakSincu** *v.t.* to safeguard, protect, preserve.
పరిలబ్ధ **parilabdha** *adj.* attainable.
పరివర్తకం **pariwartakam** *n. phys.* transformer.
పరివర్తన[ం] **pariwartana[m]** *n.* 1 change, conversion, alteration, modification, transformation, transition. 2 **hrdaya ~** change of heart, repentance: 3 **bhaaSaa ~** translation; **naalugu pradhaana bhaaSalalooki ~** translation into four important languages.
పరివర్తన కాలం **pariwartana kaalam** *n.* transition[al] period.
పరివర్తించు **pariwartincu** *v.i.* to revolve, move in a cycle.
పరివారం **pariwaaram** *n.* 1 followers, supporters, dependants. 2 train, retinue. 3 staff. 4 crew.
పరివాహ ప్రదేశం, పరివాహ ప్రాంతం **pariwaaha pradeeśam, pariwaaha praantam** *n.* area irrigated by an irrigation source.
పరివీక్షించు **pariwiikSincu** *v.t.* to monitor.
పరివృత **pariwṛta** *adj.* 1 surrounded, enveloped. 2 pervaded.
పరివేదన **pariweedana** *n.* 1 pain, grief. 2 emotions, feelings.
పరివేషం **pariweeSam** *n.* halo round the sun or moon.
పరివేష్టించు **pariweeSTincu** *v.t.* to surround, encompass, envelop.
పరివ్యాప్త **pariwyaapta** *adj.* spread wide, disseminated.
పరివ్రాజకుడు **pariwraajakuDu** *n.* wandering ascetic.
పరిశిష్టం **pariśiSTam** *n.* miscellaneous items such as those remaining at the end of a list.
పరిశీలన **pariśiilana** *n.* enquiry, investigation, examination, scrutiny.
పరిశీలనగా **pariśiilanagaa** *adv.* carefully, studiously, intently, keenly, observantly.
పరిశీలించు **pariśiilincu** *v.t.* 1 to enquire into, investigate, examine, scrutinise, study. 2 to regard, look [up]on; **andaruu adi wijayootsawangaa pariśiilistunnaaru** they all look upon it as a victory celebration.
పరిశుద్ధ **pariśuddha** *adj.* 1 clean, pure, purified. 2 holy.
పరిశుద్ధత **pariśuddhata** *n.* 1 cleanliness, purity, purification. 2 holiness.
పరిశుద్ధాత్మ **pariśuddhaatma** *n.* Holy Spirit (in Christian theology).
పరిశుద్ధి **pariśuddhi** *n.* 1 purity. 2 cleansing, purification.
పరిశుభ్ర **pariśubhra** *adj.* [very] clean.

పరిశేషించు **pariśeeSincu** *v.i.* to remain over, be left over.

పరిశోధకుడు **pariśoodhakuDu** *n.* 1 research worker. 2 investigator.

పరిశోధన **pariśoodhana** *n.* 1 research. 2 enquiry, investigation: ~ **keendram** research station.

పరిశోధించు **pariśoodhincu** *v.i. and t.* 1 to examine, investigate. 2 to conduct research.

పరిశ్రమ **pariśrama** *n.* 1 industry. 2 industriousness, assiduousness. 3 labour, exertion: **deeha**~ bodily exertion.

పరిశ్రమించు **pariśramincu** *v.i.* to work hard, toil, labour.

పరిశ్రాంతం, పరిశ్రాంతి **pariśraantam, pariśraanti** *n. class.* fatigue.

పరిషత్తు **pariSattu** *n.* parishat, assembly, council, conference, meeting: **paNDita**~ assembly of scholars.

పరిషదులు **pariSadulu** *n.pl.* members of a parishat.

పరిషేచనం **pariSeecanam** *n.* ceremony of sanctifying food at a meal by sprinkling water round it.

పరిష్కరణ[ం] **pariSkaraNa[m]** *n.* critical examination, critical editing (of literary work).

పరిష్కరించు **pariSkarincu** *v.t.* 1 to settle, arrange, adjust. 2 to set right, remedy, rectify, correct. 3 to [re]solve (problem). 4 to examine carefully, scrutinise. 5 to dispose of, finish.

పరిష్కర్త **pariSkarta** *n.* 1 scrutiniser. 2 person who prepares a critical edition. 3 person who settles or decides a dispute.

పరిష్కారం **pariSkaaram** *n.* 1 decision, settlement: **madhyawartula**~ settlement reached by mediators. 2 (*also* **pariSkaara maargam**) solution, way out (of a problem). 3 scrutiny, critical editing (of literary work).

పరిష్వంగం **pariSwangam** *n. class.* embrace: **gaaDha**~ close embrace.

పరిసమాప్తి **parisamaapti** *n.* end, conclusion.

పరిసర **parisara** *adj.* 1 neighbouring. 2 surrounding, environmental.

పరిసరం **parisaram** (*also pl.* **parisaraalu**) *n.* 1 neighbourhood, vicinity. 2 surroundings, environment.

పరిస్థితి **paristhiti** *n.* state, situation, condition.

పరిస్పందనం **parispandanam** *n.* throbbing.

పరిస్ఫుట **parisphuTa** *adj.* clear, distinct, manifest.

పరిస్ఫురణం **parisphuraNam** *n.* quivering, throbbing.

పరిహరణం **pariharaNam** *n.* deletion.

పరిహరించు **pariharincu** *v.t.* 1 to reject, remove, discard, delete. 2 to avoid: **karmaNi prayoogam saadhyamaynantawaraku pariharincaali** you must avoid the use of the passive voice as far as possible. 3 to ward off, get rid of (ill health).

పరిహరించుకొను **pariharincukonu** *v.i.* to withdraw: **pooTiiloonunci pariharincukonnaaDu** he withdrew from the contest.

పరిహసించు **parihasincu** *v.t.* to laugh at, deride, mock, ridicule.

పరిహారం **parihaaram** *n.* 1 recompense, compensation, requital. 2 counteracting means, remedy.

పరిహారక **parihaaraka** *adj.* 1 remedial. 2 compensatory.

పరిహార్య **parihaarya** *adj.* fit to be given up.

పరిహాసం **parihaasam** *n.* joking, mocking, ridicule, derision, raillery.

పరిహా[సా]స్పద **parihaa[saa]spada** *adj.* ridiculous.

పరీక్ష **pariikSa** *n.* examination, test.

పరీక్షగా **pariikSagaa** *adv.* 1 questioningly, curiously, enquiringly. 2 intently, keenly. 3 inquisitively.

పరీక్షనాళిక **pariikSanaaLika** *n.* test tube.

పరీక్షాపత్రం **pariikSaapatram** *n.* examination paper, i.e., question paper.

పరీక్షించు **pariikSincu** *v.t.* to examine, enquire, scrutinise, test: **prayoogaśaalaloo pariikSincEEru** they tested it in a laboratory.

పరీధావి **pariidhaawi** *n.* forty-sixth year of the Hindu cycle of sixty years.

పరుండబెట్టు **paruNDabeTTu** *v.t.* to lay down.

పరుండు **paruNDu** *v.i.* 1 to lie down, recline, repose. 2 to sleep.

పరుగు **parugu** *n.* 1 run[ning]: **okka**~**na** *or* **okka**~**loo** (i) at one stretch, without stopping; (ii) in haste, very fast. 2 (*also* **paruwu**) obsolete measure of distance, about four kilometres.

పరుగున, పరుగులమీద **paruguna, parugula miida** *adv.* running, very quickly, in a hurry: **waaLLa ammani cuuDaDaaniki pillalu** ~ **waccEEru** the children came running to see their mother; **idi parugula miida ceesee pani kaadu** this is not a work that can be done in a hurry; **naaku wanda ruupaayalu kaawaalaNTee** ~ **tecci iccEEDu** when I wanted a hundred rupees he brought it in a matter of minutes.

పరుగుపందెం **parugu pandem** *n.* running race.

పరుగులెత్తు, పరుగు[లు]తీయు **parugulettu, parugu[lu]tiiyu** *v.i.* to run, make haste: **parugulettee nadi** fast flowing river.

పరుగెత్తు, పరుగెట్టు, పరుగిడు **parugettu, parugeTTu, parugiDu** *v.i.* (of humans, animals, vehicles) to run.

పరుచు **parucu** *same as* **paracu.**

పరుడు **paruDu** I. *n.* another person, stranger; **induku parulanu nindincanakkara leedu** there is no need to blame others for this. II. *second part of a n. compound meaning* person possessing a certain character or quality: **jaagratta**~ cautious person; **aaloocanaa**~ reflective person; **awiniiti**~ corrupt person; **bhajana**~ (i) worshipper (ii) *colloq.* sycophant, yes man.

పరుపు **parupu** I. *n.* 1 same as **parapu** *sense I.* 2 bedding, mattress. II. *adj.* flat, level, even.

పరువం **paruwam** *n.* 1 youth, bloom, prime of life. 2 ripeness.

పరువు **paruwu**[1] *n.* dignity, respectability, self-respect, prestige: ~ **pratiSTa** respectability and good name.

పరువు **paruwu**[2] *n.* ripeness: ~**ku waccina maamiDi paNDu** half ripe mango fruit.

పరువు **paruwu**[3] *class. alt. form of* **parugu.**

పరువు తీయు **paruwu tiiyu** *v.i.* to disgrace, put to shame.

పరువునష్టం **paruwunaSTam** *n.* defamation.

పరుషం **paruSam** I. *n.ling.* unvoiced stop. II. *adj.* 1 harsh, rough. 2 severe, stern.

పరుషత్వం **paruSatwam** *n.* harshness, roughness.

పరుసవేది **parusaweedi** *n.* philosopher's stone which turns things into gold.

పరేంగితజ్ఞుడు **pareengitajñuDu** *n.* thought-reader.

పరేత **pareeta** *alt. form of* **preeta.**

పరోక్ష **parookSa** *adj.* indirect.

పరోక్షంగా **parookSangaa** *adv.* indirectly.

పరోక్షంలో, పరోక్షాన **parookSamloo, parookSaana** *adv.* in the absence of; **naa~** (i) in my absence (ii) behind my back, secretly without my knowledge.

పరోపకారం **paroopakaaram** *n.* giving help to others; **paroopakaaraartham idam śariiram** this body (i.e., o.'s life), is for the purpose of helping others (proverbial saying).

పరోపకారి **paroopakaari** *n.* benefactor, one who helps others.

పర్జన్యం **parjanyam** *n.* thunder[cloud].

పర్ణం **parNam** *n. class.* 1 leaf. 2 feather.

పర్ణశాల **parNaśaala** *n.* bower of leaves, hut, hermitage.

పర్యంతం **paryantam** *advbl. particle and p.p.* until, as far as, up to, near: **aayana waccee~neenu tinanu** until he comes I will not eat; **kaLLaniiLLa~ayi** on the verge of tears.

పర్యటక **paryaTaka** *adj.* touring, roving, wandering.

పర్యటకుడు, పర్యాటకుడు **parya[a]TakuDu** *n.* person making a tour, tourist.

పర్యటన **paryaTana** *n.* tour[ing].

పర్యటించు **paryaTincu** *v.i.* to tour, travel.

పర్యయం **paryayam** *n.* 1 inversion, inverted order. 2 deviation.

పర్యవసానం **paryawasaanam** *n.* 1 result, outcome. 2 end, conclusion, termination.

పర్యవసించు **paryawasincu** *v.i.* to result.

పర్యవేక్షకుడు **paryaweekSakuDu** *n.* 1 supervisor. 2 superintendent.

పర్యవేక్షణ **paryaweekSaNa** *n.* 1 supervision. 2 superintendence.

పర్యవేక్షించు **paryaweekSincu** *v.t.* to supervise, superintend, monitor.

పర్యాటకుడు **paryaaTakuDu** *same as* **paryaTakuDu.**

పర్యాప్తం **paryaaptam** I. *n.* spreading, extending. II. *second part of an adjvl. compound meaning* spread; **wiśwa~** spread far and wide; **deeśa~**countrywide.

పర్యాయం **paryaayam** *n.* occasion, time; **reNDu paryaayaalu** twice.

పర్యాయంగా **paryaayangaa** *adv.* in turn, successively.

పర్యాయపదం **paryaayapadam** *n.* 1 synonym. 2 corresponding word; **aa anya bhaaSa padaaniki mana bhaaSaloo~** a word in our language corresponding to that foreign word.

పర్యాయ రూపం **paryaaya ruupam** *n.* alternant, alternative form.

పర్యాయోక్తి **paryaayookti** *n.* a certain figure of speech.

పర్యాలోచించు **paryaaloocincu** *v.t.* to consider carefully, consider from all aspects, ponder over, deliberate upon.

పఱ్ఱ **parra** *n.* infertile elevated land; **isaka~** sandy waste; **uppu~** salt marsh.

పఱ్ఱం, పఱ్ఱాం **parram, parraam** *n. dial.* driver's seat in a bullock cart.

పఱ్ఱు **parru** *onom. n. sug. sound of* tearing.

పఱ్ఱె **parre** *same as* **pariya.**

పర్వం **parwam**[1] *n.* 1 festival, feast. 2 (*also* **parwadinam**) minor festival day during a lunar fortnight.

పర్వం **parwam**[2] *n.* one of the eighteen divisions or sections of the Mahabharata; **udyooga~** name of the fifth **parwam** in which plans for war are made; **caduwu ayipooyindi, ippuDu udyooga~loo unnaaDu** *colloq.* his education is over, now he is at the stage of looking for a job.

పర్వం **parwam**[3] *n.* joint in a cane or corn stalk.

పర్వకాలం **parwakaalam** *n. astrol.* a certain period occurring every fortnight which is considered auspicious.

పర్వతం **parwatam** *n.* mountain.

పర్వతమయ **parwatamaya** *adj.* mountainous, hilly.

పర్వతరాజు **parwataraaju** *n.* epithet of the Himalayas.

పర్వా **parwaa** *same as* **parawaa.**

పర్వాన్నం **parwaannam** *same as* **paramaannam.**

పర్శుక **parśuka** *n. class.* rib.

పలం **palam** *n.* an obsolete weight of one fortieth of a viss.

పలక **palaka** *n.* 1 plank, board, slab, sheet, pane; **gaaju~** sheet or pane of glass. 2 facet or flat side of an object like a pyramid or crystal; **~la murugulu** bangles made with flat facets, not rounded; **~la glEEsu** tumbler with flat sides. 3 slate for writing on. 4 (*also* **~raayi**) slate, smooth rock that can be split into thin layers.

పలకబారు **palakabaaru** *v.i.* to begin to become ripe.

పలకమారు **palakamaaru** *same as* **polamaaru.**

పలకరించు **palakarincu** *v.t.* to greet, address, talk to, engage in conversation, enquire from s.o. about their welfare.

పలకరింపు **palakarimpu** *n.* greeting.

పలకసరులు **palakasarulu** *n.pl.* kind of necklace.

పలచని, పలుచని **palacani, palucani** *adj.* 1 (of liquid) thin, weak, diluted. 2 (of cloth, sheets of paper) thin. 3 (of persons) thin, spare, lean.

పలచబడు, పలచబారు **palacabaDu, palacabaaru** *v.i.* to become weak or diluted or sparse.

పలచబార్చు **palacabaarcu** *v.t.* to dilute.

పలవ **palawa** *n. class.* forked branch.

పలవరం, పలవరింపు, పలవరింత **palawaram, palawarimpu, palawarinta** *n.* talking in o.'s sleep.

పలవరించు **palawarincu** *v.t.* 1 to talk in o.'s sleep. 2 to talk confusedly. 3 to talk on and on about the same matter.

పలహారం[చేయు], పలారం[చేయు] **palahaaram [ceeyu], palaaram[ceeyu]** *same as* **phalahaaram [ceeyu].**

పలాయనం **palaayanam** *n.* flight, fleeing, rout.

పలాయనం అవు **palaayanam awu** *v.i.* to run away, flee.

పలాయనం చిత్తగించు, పలాయన మంత్రం పఠించు **palaayanam cittagincu, palaayana mantram paThincu** *v.i.* to run away, flee, abscond.

పలావు **palaawu** *same as* **pulaawu.**

పలికించు **palikincu** *v.t.* to cause to speak, cause to sound: **wiiNa** ~ to play the vina.

పలిత **palita** *adj.* grey: ~ **keesam** grey hair.

పలు **palu**[1] *adj.* many, several, various.

పలు **palu**[2] *n.* tooth: ~ **warasa** row of teeth, set of teeth.

పలుకు **paluku** I. *n.* 1 sound, note, voice. 2 speaking, speech. 3 saying, pronouncement, utterance. 4 word. 5 speech in a play. 6 piece, bit: **kalakaNDa ~ kanna telugu ~ tiyyana** words of Telugu are sweeter than a piece of sugar candy. 7 firmness, substance: **ii tegulu ginjalaku ~ eerpaDakuNDaa ceestundi** this pest prevents the seeds from developing firmness. 8 *fig.* solidness, toughness: **maniSiloo ~ uNTee racanaku iiDu waccinaTTuNTundi** if there is toughness in a man, his writings will appear mature. 9 hardness of rice, etc., not properly cooked: **annam ~ gaa undi** the rice is hard, i.e., it is only partially cooked. II. *v.i and t.* 1 to speak, say, utter, enunciate: **waaDu sarigaa palakaleeni maaTalu caala unnaayi** there are many words which he cannot enunciate correctly: **saakSyam ~** to give evidence. 2 to sound, be heard: **aame kaNTham niirasangaa palikindi** her voice sounded weak. 3 (of a price) to be quoted: **bajaaruloo dhaanyaaniki manci dhara ~ tunnadi** a good rate for grain is being quoted in the market.

పలుదోంపుడకలు **paludoompuDakalu** *n.pl.* a part of the marriage ceremony.

పలుదోంపుల్ల, పలుదోంపుడక **paludoompulla, paludoompuDaka** *n.* twig for cleaning o.'s teeth.

పలుకుబడి **palukubaDi** *n.* 1 influence. 2 reputation. 3 *dial.* idiomatic usage, idiomatic expression.

పలుగాకి **palugaaki** *n.* evil person, mean-minded person.

పలుగు **palugu**[1] *n.* 1 crowbar. 2 iron tooth of a harrow. 3 iron head of a sickle, spade, pickaxe, etc.

పలుగు **palugu**[2] *dial. variant of* **pagulu.**

పలుగురాయి **palugu raayi** *n.* 1 small broken piece of stone: ~ **paNTikinda paDDaTTu** like getting piece of stone in o.'s teeth while eating (= something irritating or disagreeable). 2 kind of crystalline rock.

పలుపు **palupu** *n.* 1 halter for cattle or horses. 2 rope collar for a bullock in a cart.

పలువురు, పలుగురు **paluwuru, paluguru** *n.pl.* many people, several people.

పల్టీ **palTii** *n.* 1 somersault. 2 a fall in wrestling.

పల్టీ కొట్టు **palTii koTTu** *v.i.* to turn somersaults.

పల్ల **palla** *adj.* reddish brown: ~ **geede** ash coloured buffalo.

పల్లం **pallam** *n.* 1 low ground. 2 depression in the ground: **ettu pallaalu** high and low level places; **pallapu praantam** low lying area; **pallapu neela** *dial.* irrigated land; **ceruwu kaTTaku ~ gaa unna cooTu** a place situated at a lower level than the tank bund.

పల్లకి, పల్లకీ, పాలకి **pallaki[i], paalaki** *n.* palanquin.

పల్లకొను **pallakonu** *v.i. dial.* to keep silent, be quiet.

పల్లద[న]ం, ప్రల్లద[న]ం **p[r]allada[na]m** *n.* pride, boasting, showing off.

పల్లపు **pallapu** *see* **pallam.**

పల్లవ **pallawa** *adj.* sprouting: ~ **patram** sprouting leaf.

పల్లవం **pallawam** *n.* sprout, shoot.

పల్లవి **pallawi** *n.* refrain of a song.

పల్లవించు **pallawincu** *v.i.* 1 to sprout new leaves. 2 to sing a refrain. 3 to become clear, become apparent.

పల్లా **pallaa** *n.* obsolete grain measure of about a hundred seers.

పల్లాండు **pallaaNDu** *n.* benediction recited at the end of a prayer.

పల్లి, పల్లికాయ **palli**[1], **pallikaaya** *n.* groundnut.

పల్లి **palli**[2] *n. class.* village *occurring mod. only in names of villages,* e.g., **anakaa ~, kotta ~.**

పల్లిక, పళ్లిక **pallika, paLLika** *n.* 1 basket woven in a flat shape for winnowing, carrying earth, etc. 2 large basket for storing grain.

పల్లినూనె **pallinuune** *n.* groundnut oil.

పల్లీ **pallii** *n. dial.* name of a community of fishermen.

పల్లీయులు **palliiyulu** *n. pl.* villagers.

పల్లు **pallu** *n.* 1 tooth. 2 cutting edge of a pickaxe. 3 *substandard form of* **paLLu.**

పల్లె **palle** *n.* village.

పల్లెటూరి గబ్బిలాయి **palleTuuri gabbilaayi** *n.* uncultured person, rustic.

పల్లెటూరిమేళం **palleTuuri meeLam** *n. colloq.* country people, village folk.

పల్లెటూరు **palleTuuru** *n.* hamlet.

పల్లెత్తు **pallettu** *adj. occurring in neg. constr. in phrases like* ~ **maaTa,** ~ **sahaayam** very little, hardly any, least; ~ **sahaayam ceeyaleedu** he gave not even the least help; **aame ~ maaTa anadu** she will not speak even a word.

పల్లెపట్టులు **pallepaTTulu** *n. pl.* villages, rural parts.

పల్లెమనుషులు **pallemanuSulu** *n. pl.* country people, village folk.

పల్లెమాటలు **pallemaaTalu** *n.pl.* villagers' dialect.

పల్లెవాడు **pallewaaDu** *n.* 1 villager. 2 *dial.* fisherman.

పల్లేరు **palleeru** *n.* caltrop, *tribulus sp.*, a creeping plant.

పల్లేరుకాయ **palleerukaaya** *n.* fruit of the plant **palleeru,** caltrop, which is covered with burrs and is used in worship.

పళాన, పళంగా **paLaana, paLangaa** *same as* **paDangaa.**

పళ్లబిగువున **paLLa biguwuna** *advbl. phrase* by gritting o.'s teeth.

పళ్లిక **paLLika** *same as* **pallika.**

పళ్లు **paLLu** *n.pl.of* **pannu, pallu** *and* **paNDu.**

పళ్లుతోంపుడకలు **paLLu toompuDakalu** *alt. form of* **paludoompuDakalu.**

పళ్లెం **paLLem** *n.* 1 plate, dish, saucer; **ginnemiida ~ boorlincindi** she placed a saucer upside down over the vessel (to serve as a lid). 2 **baawi~** platform round a well.

పళ్లెత్తు **paLLettu** (*also* **ettu paLLu**) *n.* prominent or protruding teeth.

పళ్లెరం **paLLeram** *class. alt. form of* **paLLem.**

పవడం **pawaDam** *same as* **pagaDam.**

పవనం **pawanam** *n. class.* air, breeze, wind.

పవనుడు **pawanuDu** *n.* epithet of Vayu, god of the wind.

పవళించు, పవ్వళించు **pawaLincu, pawwaLincu** *v.i. class.* 1 to lie down. 2 to sleep.

పవళింత, పవళింపు **pawaLinta, pawaLimpu** *n. class.* sleep[ing].

పవళింపు సేవ **pawaLimpu seewa** *n.* final act of worship performed each day in a temple.

పవిడి **pawiDi** *same as* **pagiDi.**

పవిత్ర **pawitra** *adj.* 1 holy, sacred, sanctified. 2 pure, clean, purified, undefiled.

పవిత్రం **pawitram** *n. class.* 1 sacred thread (= **jandhyam**). 2 ring of darbha grass tied round the fourth finger of the right hand when performing a sacrifice.

పవిత్రయుద్ధం **pawitrayuddham** *n.* holy war, crusade.

పవిత్రత **pawitrata** *n.* 1 purity. 2 holiness, sanctity.

పవులు **pawulu** *substandard form of* **pagulu.**

పశుగణం **paśugaNam** *n.* cattle, livestock.

పశుత్వం, పశుప్రవృత్తి **paśutwam, paśuprawṛtti** *n.* brutality, bestiality.

పశుపతి **paśupati** *n.* epithet of Siva.

పశుపాలన, పశుపోషణ **paśupaalana, paśupooSaNa** *n.* animal husbandry, cattle breeding.

పశుప్రవర్తన **paśuprawartana** *n.* brutish or bestial behaviour.

పశుప్రాయుడు **paśupraayuDu** *n.* beast-like person, brutish person.

పశుబలం **paśubalam** *n.* brute force.

పశువు **paśuwu** *n.* 1 animal, beast; **reNDu kaaLLa~** *or* **nara~** brute (applied to a human); **oori paśuwaa!** you brute! 2 *class.* cow. 3 *pl.* **~lu** cattle, farm animals.

పశువుల దొడ్డి **paśuwula doDDi** *n.* cattle pen.

పశువైద్యశాల **paśuwaydyaśaala** *n.* veterinary hospital.

పశువైద్యశాస్త్రం **paśuwaydyaśaastram** *n.* veterinary science.

పశుసంపద **paśusampada** *n.* cattle wealth.

పశ్చాత్ **paścaat** *adjvl. prefix. meaning later*, subsequent; **~ kaaryakramam** later programme.

పశ్చాత్తాపం **paścaattaapam** *n.* remorse, repentance, penitence, regret; **naaku ~ paTTukonnadi** I felt remorse.

పశ్చాత్తాపపడు **paścattaapapaDu** *v.i.* to feel regret or remorse.

పశ్చాద్గమనం **paścaadgamanam** *n.* retreat[ing], retrogression; **idi puroogamanamaa ~ aa anee wiSayam aaloocincaali** we must consider the question whether this is an advance or a retreat.

పశ్చిమ **paścima** *adj.* west[ern].

పశ్చిమం **pascimam** *n.* west.

పశ్చిమార్థం **paścimaartham** *n.* latter half; **jiiwitam ~ loo unnaaDu** he is in the latter half of his life.

పశ్యతోహరుడు **paśyatooharuDu** *n.* person who steals before o.'s very eyes, pilferer.

పస **pasa** *n.* 1 sap, essence. 2 bloom, vigour, vitality, strength, brilliance, worth, value; **~ leeni waadam** weak or worthless argument. 3 artistic merit, artistry; **maaTLaaDinaTTee sarigaa raayaDam kuuDaa ewariki saadhyam? adhawaa raasinappaTikii 'anduloo eemi~ uNTundi?** who is able to write exactly as people speak? or if he can, what artistic merit is there in it?

పసందు **pasandu** I. *n.* pleasure, delight. II. *adj.* 1 pleasing, appealing, agreeable, enjoyable, delightful. 2 approved, commended. 3 preferred.

పసందు చేయు **pasandu ceeyu** *v.t.* 1 to like, enjoy. 2 to prefer.

పసరం **pasaram** *n. class.* head of cattle.

పసరిక **pasarika** *same as* **pasirika.**

పసరు **pasaru** I. *n.* 1 sap; **aaku~** juice of a leaf. 2 bile. II. *adj.* tender, unripe, immature; **~ kaaya** *or* **~ pinde** unripe fruit; **~ mogga** immature bud.

పసి **pasi**[1] *adj.* little, young, tender; **~ pillalu** little children; **~ paapa, ~ guDDu, ~ kandu** baby, infant.

పసి **pasi**[2] *n.* scent, smell.

పసి **pasi**[3], **pase** *n. dial.* pinkish white colour in cattle (= **payye**).

పసి **pasi**[4] *n. class.* hunger.

పసికట్టు, పసిపట్టు **pasikaTTu, pasipaTTu** *v.t.* 1 to scent, smell, get the scent or smell of. 2 to smell out, track or trace by sense of smell; **pilli elukanu pasikaDutundi** (*or* **pasipaDutundi**) the cat will smell out the rat. 3 to perceive, sense, get wind of, discern, spot, identify; **S. attawaari yathaartha paristhiti pasikaTTaleeka pooyEEDu** S. could not discern his parents-in-law's true situation.

పసిడి **pasiDi** I. *n.* 1 gold. 2 wealth. II. *adj.* 1 golden. 2 rich; **~ paNTa** rich harvest.

పసితనం **pasitanam** *n.* childhood.

పసిమి **pasimi** *adj.* 1 fair (in complexion). 2 golden yellow.

పసిమిరోగం **pasimiroogam** *n.* jaundice.

పసిరిక, పసరిక **pasirika, pasarika** *adj.* green; **~ bayalu** green meadow; **~ paamu** green snake.

పసిరిక పిట్ట **pasirika piTTa** *n.* green bee-eater (bird).

పసిరికలు **pasirikalu** *n. pl.* jaundice.

పసుపు **pasupu** *n.* turmeric.

పసుపుకుంకుమ, పసుపుకుంకం **pasupukunkuma, pasupukunkam** *n.* 1 *lit.* turmeric and red powder; **~ peTTu-**

konnaaru *in Telangana signifies that a betrothal has taken place* (*cf.* **taambuulam**); **~ceesEEru** *in coastal dialect signifies that a conception cermony has been performed.* 2 *fig.* maintenance; **wiilunaamaaloo tana kuuturi ~la nimittam oka ekaram polam raasEEDu** in his will he left one acre of land to his daughter for her maintenance.

పసుపుపచ్చ **pasupupacca** *n. and adj.* yellow.

పసుపుబొట్టు **pasupuboTTu** *dial. same as* **peeraNTam.**

పసులకాపరి **pasulakaapari** *n.* cowherd.

పసులు **pasulu** *alt. form of* **paśuwulu.**

పసె **pase** *same as* **pasi.**[3]

పస్కిర్లు **paskirlu** *n.pl.* jaundice (‹ **pasirikalu**).

పస్తాయించు **pastaayincu** *v.i.* 1 to pause, hesitate. 2 to regret, feel sorry; **maaTa anna taruwaata endukannaanaa ani pastaayincEEnu** after saying it I wondered why I had said it and felt sorry.

పస్తు **pastu** *n.* 1 starving, starvation. 2 *dial* fasting.

పస్తుండు **pastuNDu** *v.i.* to starve, be starving.

పహరా, పారా **paharaa, paaraa** *n.* 1 guard. 2 patrol.

పహరా ఇచ్చు, పారా ఇచ్చు **paharaa iccu, paraa iccu** *v.i.* 1 to stand sentry, mount guard. 2 to patrol.

పహరా హుషార్! **paharaa huSaar!** *interj.* cry of a night watchman as he goes on his rounds.

పహలా పచీస్ **pahalaa paccíis** *same as* **paylaa pacciisu.**

పహాణీ **pahaaNii** *n. dial.* village register in Telangana in which the crops cultivated in each field are noted annually after inspection.

పా - paa

పాంకోడు **paankooDu** *n.* 1 wooden sandal (this kind of sandal is worn by sanyasis and also by the bridegroom at the time of **snaatakam** in the marriage ceremony). 2 *colloq.* **~laa mukham** a face like a wooden sandal, i.e., ugly and bony.

పాంగెం **paangem** *n. class.* relationship (= **cuTTarikam**).

పాంగొట్టు **paangoTTu** *v.t. dial.* to damage, spoil.

పాంచజన్యం **paancajanyam** *n.* Vishnu's conch.

పాంచభౌతిక **paancabhawtika** *adj.* made up of the five primordial elements; **~prapancam** the natural world.

పాంచాలి **paancaali** *n.* epithet of Draupadi.

పాంచాలిక **paancaalika** *n. class.* doll, puppet, image carved on a pillar.

పాంజేబు[పట్టీ] **paanjeebu[paTTii]** *n.* silver anklet.

పాండవులు **paaNDawulu** *n.pl.* Pandavas, the sons of king Pandu of the Mahabharata.

పాండిత్యం, పాండితి **paaNDityam, paaNDiti** *n.* scholarship, proficiency in learning.

పాండు[రోగం] **paaNDu[roogam]** *n.* anaemia.

పాంథుడు **paanthuDu** *n. class.* traveller.

పాంశువు **paamśuwu** *n. class.* dust.

పాక **paaka** *n.* hut, shed.

పాకం **paakam** *n.* 1 cooking; **śaaka paakaalu** vegetarian cooking. 2 (*also* **pancadaara~**) syrup; **~paTTu** to make syrup; **maysuur~** Mysorepak, a kind of sweet made from syrup and bengalgram flour; *see* **piiku.** 3 maturity; **paakaaniki waccu** to come to maturity, be[come] fully developed. 4 style of writing; *see* **draakSaa~, kadaLii~.**

పాకీ **paakii** *n.* sweeper, scavenger.

పాకీదొడ్డి **paakiidoDDi** *n.* latrine, toilet.

పాకు, ప్రాకు **paaku**[1], **praaku** *v.i.* 1 to creep, crawl. 2 (of plants) to climb. 3 *fig.* to spread, extend, find its way to, affect: **matawibheedaalu deeśamloo wiwidha praantaalaku paakEEyi** religious differences spread to various parts of country; **pleeg wyaadhi prapancam antaTaa paakindi** plague spread over the whole world; **unna peTTubaDulu paTTaNaalaku~tunnaayi** what capital there is finds its way to the towns; **nayraaśyam iiyanaku kuuDaa praakindi** despair affected him also.

పాకు **paaku**[2] *same as* **paakuDu** *sense I.*

పాకు **paaku**[3] *same as* **paakam** *sense 2.*

పాకుడు **paakuDu** I. *n.* 1 moss, slime, scum; **raayiki~paTTindi** the stone is covered with moss/slime. 2 prop or trellis for a creeper. II. *adj.* 1 mossy, slimy. 2 (of a plant) creeping, climbing; **~tiige** creeper, climber.

పాకులాట, ప్రాకులాట **p[r]aakulaaTa** *n.* anxious search, earnest striving, yearning.

పాకులాడు, ప్రాకులాడు **p[r]aakulaaDu** *v.i.* 1 to creep, crawl. 2 to scramble. 3 to search anxiously, strive earnestly, yearn, crave (**-koosam**, for). 4 (*also* **paTTukoni~**) to cling to, hang on to, adhere to; **eemiTraa nannu wadalakuNDaa~tunnaawu?** why are you clinging to me? **paata wiśwaasaalanu paTTukoni ~** to adhere to old beliefs; *cf.* **weelaaDu** *sense 3.*

పాక్షిక **paakSika** *adj.* 1 partial. 2 biassed.

పాక్షికంగా **paakSikangaa** *adv.* partially, partly.

పాగా **paagaa** *n.* turban; **~cuTTukonu** to tie o.'s turban.

పాచకం **paacakam** *n.* pepsin.

పాచకుడు **paacakuDu** *n.* 1 cook. 2 *class.* God of fire.

పాచి **paaci**[1] *n.* 1 moss, slime. 2 rot, foulness. 3 tartar (in teeth).

పాచి **paaci**[2] *adj.* 1 (of food) stale; **~roTTe** stale bread; **~annam** stale food remaining from the previous day. 2 uncleansed, unwashed; **~mukham** unwashed face; **~naalika** coated tongue.

పాచిక **paacika** *n.* 1 dice. 2 plan, device, stratagem; **naa~paarindi** my plan worked (i.e., proved successful).

పాచిక పన్ను, పాచిక వేయు **paacika pannu, paacika weeyu** *v.i.* to devise a stratagem, lay a trap.

పాచి చేయు, పాచి తీయు paaci ceeyu, paaci tiiyu *v.i.* to clean and tidy a house and its surroundings by dusting and sweeping.

పాచిపని paacipani *n.* work of cleaning and tidying a house.

పాచిరంగు paacirangu *n.* dull green colour.

పాట paaTa *n.* 1 song. 2 bid in auction.

పాటక్ paaTak *n. dial.* gate.

పాటకచేరి paaTakaceeri *n.* concert.

పాటగత్తె, పాటకి paaTagatte, paaTaki *n.* singer (female).

పాటగాడు paaTagaaDu *n.* singer (male).

పాటక[పు]జనం paaTaka[pu] janam *n. pl.* people who toil for a living, esp. people of the countryside who work in the fields.

పాటపాడు paaTapaaDu *v.i.* 1 to sing a song. 2 to make a bid at an auction. 3 to say something repeatedly.

పాటవం paaTawam *n.* 1 energy, strength, power, vigour. 2 skill, ability, dexterity. 3 proficiency, talent.

పాటి paaTi[1] I. *n., gen. preceded by an interrog. or det.adj. or a basic adj. or a pron.* extent, amount, quantity, degree; **ee~ Dabbu kaawaali? ii~caalu** how much money do you want? this much will be enough: **aa~teliyadaa miiku?** don't you know that much? **waaDi~caduwu naakuu undi** *or* **waaDi~ neenuu caduwukonnaanu** I have as much education as he has: **tagu~** (*or* **oka~**) **ettayna muLLa ceTTu** a fairly tall thorny tree: **pramaadam koddi ~loo tappi pooyindi** the accident was narrowly avoided; **neenu miiku buddhi ceppee~ waaNNi kaadu** I am not a fit person to give you advice: **miiku ceppee~loo neenee weLLi ceeseewaaNNi** in the (amount of) time taken for telling you, I might have gone and done it myself: **reNDeeLLa caduwuki saripaDee ~Dabbu** an amount of money sufficient for two years study: **aa ammaayi niiku ceesina~seewa neenu ceeyaleeka pooyEEnu** the amount of service that girl did for you (was something that) I could not do: **naa~ki neenu** I for my part *or* so far as I am concerned: **ewari~ waaru caduwukooNDi** each of you study for yourself *or* each of you study on your own; *see* **koddi~, ii~ki.** II. *as a particle~may be suffixed to certain adjvl. roots without contributing to the meaning,* e.g., **sanna~** thin: **laawu~** stout.

పాటి paaTi[2] *n.* slightly elevated land in a village site.

పాటించు paaTincu *v.t.* 1 to heed, pay attention to, be mindful of (an appeal). 2 to accept (a recommendation). 3 to care about, have regard for, take notice of (pain). 4 to observe, follow (rules). 5 to keep to, adhere to; **weeLa~** to keep to time, observe punctuality.

పాటింపు paaTimpu *n.* 1 heeding, paying attention. 2 observing, following. 3 adherence.

పాటికంద paaTikanda *n.* kind of yam, *arum campanulatum.*

పాటిమట్టి, పాటిమన్ను paaTimaTTi, paaTimannu *n.* soil found in an abandoned village site which is extra fertile and used as manure.

పాటు paaTu I. *n.* 1 labour, toil. 2 misfortune, hardship. 3 *pl.* troubles; **waaLLa paaTLu waaLLu paDataaru** they will manage for themselves. 4 fall; **piDugu~** thunderstroke; **gaali~** gust of wind; **kanureppa~** wink. 5 **samudrapu~** ebbing or falling of tide. II. *as a suffix~forms nouns from vbl. and adjvl. roots,* e.g., **diddubaaTu** correction; **eDabaaTu** separation (*here~*) **baaTu** *in sandhi*). III. *p.p.* for (a period of time); **naalugu roojula~** for a few days; **eeDaadi~** for a year's time.

పాటుగా paaTugaa *adv.* 1 sloping downwards; **~uNDee neela** downward sloping land. 2 in or from a certain direction; **wenaka~wacci** coming in the rear *or* coming from behind: *cf.* **waaTugaa.**

పాటున, పాట్న paaTuna, paaTNa *same as* **paDangaa.**

పాటునపడు paaTunapaDu *v.i.* to return to a normal condition, recover.

పాటు[న]నే paaTu[na]nee *advbl. particle suffixed to a past vbl. adj.* as soon as; **paDDa~leeci nilabaDDaaDu** as soon as he fell down, he got up again; *cf.* **aapaaTa.**

పాటుపడు paaTupaDu *v.i.* to work hard, labour, toil, strive, struggle; **jiiwanaaniki paaTupaDeewaaru** people who struggle for a livelihood.

పాటూ్నలు paaTNuulu *n.* finely spun thread: **~pancelu** dhotis of fine quality.

పాట్లమారి paTLamaari *n.* drudge.

పాఠం paaTham *n.* 1 lesson. 2 reading. 3 text; **prasangaa~** text of a speech.

పాఠకలోకం paaThakalookam *n.* the reading public.

పాఠకుడు paaThakuDu *n.* reader.

పాఠన paaThana *adj.* teaching; **~saamagri** teaching materials.

పాఠశాల paaThaśaala *n.* school.

పాఠాంతరం paaThaantaram *n.* variant reading.

పాఠ్యక్రమం paaThyakramam *n.* course of studies, curriculum, syllabus.

పాఠ్యగ్రంథం paaThyagrantham *n.* text book.

పాఠ్యప్రణాళిక, పాఠ్యవివరణ paaThyapraNaalika, paaThyawiwaraNa *n.* syllabus.

పాఠ్యవిషయం paaThyawiSayam *n.* subject matter (in a syllabus).

పాడంగా paaDangaa *same as* **paDangaa.**

పాడా paaDaa *echo word*; **teeDaa~eemii leedu** no difference of any kind *or* no difference whatever.

పాడి paaDi[1] *n.* dairy farming; **~paNTalu** dairy farming and cultivation, mixed farming; **maaku ~undi** we have cattle and all kinds of dairy products; **~aawu** milch cow; **~pariśrama** dairy industry.

పాడి paaDi[2] *n.* justice, decency, right; **idi niiku paaDEE?** is this a right thing for you? *or* is it right for you to act like this?

పాడించు paaDincu *v.t.* 1 to cause to sing, cause (s.g) to be sung. 2 **weelam~** to have (s.g) auctioned.

పాడి చేయు paaDi ceeyu *v.i.* to do dairy work, i.e., milking the cows or buffaloes, boiling the milk and making butter and ghee.

పాడు paaDu[1] *v.t.* 1 to sing. 2 to bid (at an auction).

పాడు paaDu[2] I. *n.* 1 waste, desolation, ruin. 2 *class.* village, *occurring mod. in names of villages,* e.g., **pedapaaDu.** 3 *idiomatic usages*: (i) (noun) **leedu ~leedu** *or* (noun) **paaDuuleedu** *means* no (noun) at all *or* no (noun) or anything of that kind; **waaDiki caduwu leedu ~leedu, uurikee tirugutunnaaDu** he has no education at all, he is spending his time aimlessly; **tiNDi leedu ~leedu, aTLaagee padiNTiki paDukonnaanu** I had no food or anything, I just went to bed at ten o'clock; "**kaaleejiiki weLLEEraa?**" "**kaaleejii leedu~ leedu, uurikee nadicipooyiwaccEEnu**" "did you go to the college"? "I did nothing like that, I just went for a walk"; **caduwuu paaDuu leedaa niiku?** have not you any studies to attend to? **waaDiki oNTimiida cokkaa paaDuu eemii leedu** there was no shirt or anything like that on his body; *cf.* **tiiruwa**; (ii) **eempaaDoo** perhaps *indicates both doubt and apprehension in the speaker's mind;* **waana wastundoo eempaaDoo, tondaragaa weLLu** go quickly, perhaps it is going to rain (I hope not); *cf.* **eemoo, karNapiśaacam.** II. *adj.* bad, shocking, wretched, miserable, rotten; **ii~alawaaTu ekkaDa neercukoonnaawu?** where did you learn this bad habit?

పాడు అవు, పాడవు **paaDu awu, paaDawu** *v.i.* to be spoilt or damaged (referring to a particular event, not to a lengthy process); **iwwEELa kaaphii paaDayindi** today the coffee got spoilt; **wastuuNTee bassu paaDayindi** when I was coming the bus broke down.

పాడు చేయు **paaDu ceeyu** *v.t.* **1** to spoil, damage, make unfit for use; **pillalu annam paaDu ceesEEru** the children wasted their food. **2** to destroy, ruin. **3** to rape.

పాడుపడు **paaDupaDu** *v.i.* to degenerate, deteriorate, become dilapidated, fall into disrepair, go to ruin, be spoilt or damaged due to neglect or natural causes; **tooTa paaDu paDindi** the garden went to ruin.

పాడుపెట్టు **paaDupeTTu** *v.t.* **1** to spoil, damage. **2** to destroy, ruin. **3 illu/gadi paaDupeTTu** to leave a house/room empty for a period prescribed by religion because a death has occurred there.

పాడె **paaDe** *n.* funeral bier. **2** ~ *is used in swear terms,* e.g., **nii~!** *or* **nii~pacci baddalu!** = blast you!

పాడ్యమి **paaDyami** *n.* first day of a lunar fortnight.

పాణి **paaNi** *n. class.* **1** hand. **2** (*in composition*) wielder of; **rathaanga~** holder or wielder of the reins of a chariot, epithet of Krishna.

పాణిగ్రహణం **paaNigrahaNam** *n. class.* marriage (*lit.* taking the hand of the bride, a part of the wedding ceremony).

పాత, ప్రాత **p[r]aata** *adj.* **1** (of things) old, ancient, decayed, worn out, outmoded; **~baTTa** (*or simply~*) an old cloth; *cf.* **gooci~, masi~.** **2** (of persons) former, previous; **~mEESTaru** former schoolmaster.

పాతం **paatam** *n. class.* fall; *mod. in compounds,* e.g., **jala~** waterfall.

పాతకం **paatakam** *n.* sin, crime.

పాతకాలపు **paatakaalapu** *adj.* of olden times, ancient, old-fashioned.

పాతకి **paataki** *n.* sinner, criminal (female).

పాతకుడు **paatakuDu** *n.* sinner, criminal (male).

పాతబడు, పాతగిలు **paatabaDu, paatagilu** *v.i.* to become old[fashioned] or outmoded, become out of date or archaic.

పాతర **paatara** *n.* grain pit, granary.

పాతరలాడు **paataralaaDu** *v.i.* to dance about, move about agitatedly.

పాతాళం **paataaLam** *n.* the underworld in Hindu mythology.

పాతాళగంగ **paataaLaganga** *n.* **1** river of the underworld in Hindu mythology. **2** name given to the River Krishna at Srisailam.

పాతిక **paatika** *n.* **1** quarter; **okaTim~** one and a quarter; *cf.* **paraka.** **2** quarter of a rupee. **3** twenty-five.

పాతిపెట్టు, పాతివేయు **paatipeTTu, paatiweeyu** *v.t.* **1** to plant, fix. **2** to bury. **3.** *fig.* to finish off, bring to an end.

పాతివ్రత్యం **paatiwratyam** *n.* matrimonial fidelity, chastity.

పాతు **paatu** I. *n.* **1** the part of a post or pillar or other standing object which is buried in the ground. **2** *dial.* **oka paateesEEDu sTeejii miida** he scored a success (*or* he made his mark) on the stage. II. *v.t.* **1** to plant, fix in the ground. **2** to bury.

పాతుకొను **paatukonu** *v.i.* to become firm, become deep-rooted, become fixed.

పాత్ర **paatra** *n.* **1** character (in a play). **2** part, role (in an undertaking). **3** cooking pot.

పాత్రం **paatram** *n. class.* metal vessel or utensil, cooking pot.

పాత్రధరించు, పాత్రవేయు **paatradharincu, paatraweeyu** *v.i.* to play a part.

పాత్రధారి **paatradhaari** *n.* actor, performer, player of a part.

పాత్రికేయవృత్తి **paatrikeeyawṛtti** *n.* journalism.

పాత్రికేయుడు **paatrikeeyuDu** *n.* journalist.

పాత్రుడు **paatruDu** *n.* **1** worthy or fit or deserving person. **2** *gen. as second part of a compound,* e.g., **wiśwaasa~** trustworthy person.

పాదం **paadam** *n.* **1** foot. **2** *astrol.* quarter. **3** line of verse in a poem.

పాదచారి **paadacaari** *n.* **1** pedestrian. **2** foot soldier.

పాదపూరణం **paadapuuraNam** *n.* completing a line of verse.

పాదరక్ష **paadarakSa** *n.* shoe.

పాదరసం **paadarasam** *n* mercury.

పాదసేవ **paadaseewa** *n.* doing personal service, e.g., to a guru.

పాదాక్రాంతం అవు **paadaakraantam awu** *v.i.* to be under the heel of, be subjected to.

పాదిష్టి **paadiSTi** *n.* moss, slime, scum.

పాదు **paadu** *n.* **1** bed for plants in a garden. **2** circular trough formed round garden plants or shrubs to retain water for them. **3** creeper.

పాదుకొను **paadukonu** *v.i.* **1** to be[come] established, take root. **2** to be implanted.

పాదుకొల్పు **paadukolpu** *v.t.* **1** to fix, establish. **2** to implant.

పాదుషా **paaduSaa** *n.* emperor.

పానం **paanam**[1] *n. class.* **1** drink[ing]. **2 snaanam~ayyEEka** *or* **snaanam~ceesEEka** after taking a bath and a drink, i.e., after having refreshed o.s.; **caalaa duuram prayaaNam ceesEEnu, snaanam ~ ceesi mii iNTiki wastaanu** I have had a long journey, I will refresh myself and then come to your house. **3 madya~** drinking liquor; **dhuuma~** smoking (cigarette, etc.)

పానం **paanam**[2] *substandard form of* **praaNam.**

పానకం **paanakam** *n.* sweet drink made of jaggery and other ingredients; **ceruku~** sugarcane juice; **~loo pu-Dakallee** like a fly in the ointment (*lit.* like a piece of stick in a sweet drink).

పానకం బిందెలు **paanakam bindelu** *n.pl.* two jars given to the bride and bridegroom by the bride's parents as part of the wedding ceremony.

పానవట్టం **paanawaTTam** *n.* pedestal supporting the lingam in a Saivite temple.

పానీయం **paaniiyam** *n. class.* 1 water. 2 drink, beverage.

పాన్పు, పానుపు **paanpu, paanupu** *n. class.* bed, couch.

పాప **paapa**[1] *n.* 1 child, baby; **pasi~** infant. 2 (*also* **kaNTi~**, **kanu~**) pupil of the eye.

పాప, పాపపు **paapa**[2], **paapapu** *adj.* sinful.

పాపం **paapam** I. *n.* 1 sin, crime (*often contrasted with* **puNyam**); **puNyam entoo~entoo teliyadu gaani jarigindi idi** I do not know the rights or wrongs of the matter, but this is what happened; **puNyaaniki pootee~edurayindi** I attempted to do good (to s.o.) but I only suffered for my pains; **ceppina paapaaniki neenee ceesEEnu** *lit.* for the sin of telling (how to do s.g) I did it myself, i.e., I explained how to do s.g, but after all I had to do it myself. 2 *past vbl. adj.* + **paapaana pooleedu** *gives the sense of a strong negative* **eppuDuu aayana maa iNTiki waccina papaana pooleedu** never has he come to my house (*the underlying meaning is*: thinking it a sin, he has not committed the sin of coming to my house); **pooyina eeDaadi neenoka pustakamayanaa raasina paapaana pooleedu** I have not written a single book in the past year. II. *interj.* (i) *expressing a mild degree of sorrow, disappointment, regret, sympathy* oh dear!, alas!, what a pity! **~naDici waccEED-aNDii**! poor fellow, he has come walking! (ii) *with little meaning except to draw attention to the remark that follows* **~waaLLiNTiloo roojuu kaaphii taagutaaraNDii**! they drink coffee at home daily! (iii) **istaanaa**? **~neeniwwanu do**, you think I will give it? I will not—*here* ~ *signals that the reply will be negative*.

పాపం తలచు **paapam talacu** *v.t.* to sympathise with, feel sorry for, take pity on; **waaNNi paapam talaci udyoo-gam iccEEnu** I took pity on him and gave him a job.

పాపకూపం **paapakuupam** *n. class.* the pit of hell.

పాపట, పాపిడి **paapaTa, paapiDi** *n.* parting of hair on the head; **pakka~tiiyu** to part o.'s hair on the side of o.'s head.

పాపటం **paapaTam** *n.* kind of harrow.

పాపటబొట్టు **paapaTaboTTu** *n.* ornament worn by a woman on the parting of her hair.

పాపడ్ **paapaD** *same as* **appaDam.**

పాపఫలం **paapaphalam** *n.* retribution.

పాపభయం, పాపభీతి **paapabhayam, paapabhiiti** *n.* fear of sinning.

పాపాత్ముడు **paapaatmuDu** *n.* sinner.

పాపాయి **paapaayi** *n.* 1 child. baby. 2 *term of endearment* dear child.

పాపాలభైరవుడు **paapaalabhayrawuDu** *n.* 1 great sinner 2 one who is considered as sinful.

పాపిడి **paapiDi** *same as* **paapaTa.**

పాపిడిబిందెలు, పాపిడిపిందిరీలు **paapiDibinde-lu, paapiDipindiriilu** *n.pl.* kind of jewellery.

పాపిడిబిళ్ల **paapiDibiLLa** *dial. same as* **paapaTaboTTu.**

పాపిష్టి **paapiSTi** *adj.* wicked, sinful, tainted with sin; **~ Dabbu** tainted money.

పాపు **paapu** *v.t.* 1 to separate, divide. 2 *dial.* to dig up root-crops such as groundnut.

పామర **paamara** *adj.* common, ordinary; **~bhaaSa** common speech, colloquial language.

పామరులు **paamarulu** *n.pl.* common people, ordinary folk.

పాము **paamu**[1] *n.* snake, serpent; **waaDiwi~cewulu** he has keen ears.

పాము **paamu**[2] *v.t.* to rub, smear, dab; **nuune oNTiki~konnaaDu** he rubbed oil on his body.

పాములవాడు **paamulawaaDu** *n.* snake catcher, snake charmer.

పాయ **paaya** *n.* 1 branch or section into which s.g is split or divided. 2 stream, strand or plait of hair; **waaDi juTTu~kaDutunnadi** his hair is plaited. 3 branch of a river in a delta. 4 **wellulli~** clove of garlic.

పాయకారి **paayakaari** *n.* person who cultivates land on lease.

పాయఖానా **paayakhaanaa** *n.* latrine.

పాయల, పాయలాకు **paayala, paayalaaku** *n. dial.* kind of spinach (= **baccali**).

పాయసం **paayasam**[1] *n.* rice pudding made with milk and sugar; *cf.* **waradapaasem.**

పాయసం, పాశం **paayasam,**[2] **paaśam** *second part of a n. compound* **toDa~** thigh pinching, a form of punishment.

పాయా **paayaa** *same as* **phaayaa.**

పాయు **paayu** *v.t. class.* to leave, quit; **asuwulu baasinaaDu** (*formal and literary style*) he lost his life.

పాయువు **paayuwu** *n.* anus.

పార **paara** *n.* 1 spade. 2 iron head of a tool such as a spade or pickaxe or sickle.

పారం **paaram** *n. class.* 1 opposite bank or shore of a river. 2 end, limit, furthest extent.

పారంగతుడు **paarangatuDu** *n. lit.* person who has reached the further shore, *hence* person who is well versed or adept or expert.

పారంపర్యం **paaramparyam** *n.* 1 succession. 2 order, series.

పారంపర్యంగా **paaramparyangaa** *adv.* in succession, hereditarily, successively.

పారకాడు **paarakaaDu** *n. dial.* labourer.

పారగొట్టు, పారదోలు, పారద్రోలు **paaragoTTu, paarad[r]oolu** *v.t.* to drive away, beat off.

పారచూచు **paaracuucu** *v.t.* to observe carefully.

పారజల్లు **paarajallu** *v.t.* to scatter.

పారణ **paaraNa** *n.* 1 breaking o.'s fast, taking food after a religious fast. 2 *same as* **paaraayaNam** *sense 1.*

పారతంత్ర్యం **paaratantryam** *n.* dependence.

పారదం **paaradam** *n.* mercury, quicksilver.

పారదర్శక **paaradarśaka** *adj.* transparent.

పారదోలు, పారద్రోలు **paarad[r]oolu** *same as* **paara-goTTu.**

పారపట్టు **paarapaTTu** *v.t.* to abuse, rebuke, scold.

పారపని **paarapani** *n. dial.* manual work.

పారపళ్ళు **paarapaLLu** *n. pl.* uncleaned discoloured teeth.

పారబోయు **paarabooyu** *v.t.* to pour away, empty out.

పారమార్థిక **paaramaarthika** *adj.* spiritual, otherworldly; ~ **jñaanam** divine knowledge.

పారమార్థికం **paaramaarthikam** *n.* piety, devotion, otherworldliness.

పారలౌకిక **paaralawkika** *adj.* otherworldly, spiritual.

పారవశ్యం **paarawaśyam** *n.* ecstasy, rapture, state of being overwhelmed with emotion; **aananda** ~ being entranced with joy; **duhkha** ~ being beside o.s. with sorrow.

పారవేయు, పారేయు **paaraweeyu, paareeyu** *v.t.* 1 to throw away. 2 *colloq.* to throw, give, hand over; **naa baakii naaku paareeyaNDi** pay me my dues. 3 *following a past participle ~ gives the sense of action done thoroughly and completely*, e.g., **annam mottam tini paareesEEru** they ate up all the food; **pani ceeṣi paareesEEDu** he finished all the work; **gooDalu asahyam ceesipaareeSEEru** they disfigured the walls completely.

పారవేసుకొను, పారేసుకొను **paaraweesukonu, paareesukonu** *v.t.* to misplace, lose; **naa kaLLajooDu paareesukonnaanu** I have lost my glasses; **hṛdayam paareesukonnaaDu** he lost his heart (in love).

పారవైచు **paarawaycu** *alt. form of* **paaraweeyu.**

పారశీక **paaraśiika** *adj.* Persian, Iranian.

పారశీకం **paaraśiikam** *n.* the Persian language.

పారా[ఇచ్చు] **paaraa[iccu]** *same as* **paharaa[iccu].**

పారాణి **paaraaNi** *n.* red dye made from turmeric and powdered lime, used for decorating the feet on certain auspicious occasions and also applied as a remedy for boils and cuts.

పారాయణ[ం] **paaraayaNa[m]** *n.* 1 reciting the Vedas or another sacred book in daily sessions as a religious exercise. 2 constant reading, regular study; **paaraśiika saahitya ~ loo paDDaaDu** he engaged on the regular study of Persian literature.

పారావారం **paaraawaaram** *n. class.* sea, ocean.

పారి **paari** *n. dial.* time, occasion; **oka ~** once.

పారించు **paarincu** *v.t.* 1 to cause to flow. 2 *see* **dṛSTi ~.**

పారిజాతం **paarijaatam** *n.* 1 name of a flowering tree. 2 name of one of the five mythical trees of heaven.

పారితోషికం **paaritooSikam** *n.* 1 award, prize. 2 honorarium. 3 reward.

పారిపోవు **paaripoowu** *v.i.* 1 to run away, flee. 2 to escape.

పారిభాషిక **paaribhaaSika** *adj.* terminological, technical; ~ **padam** technical term.

పారిశుద్ధ్య **paariśuddhya** *adj.* sanitary.

పారిశుద్ధ్యం **paariśuddhyam** *n.* 1 clean[li]ness. 2 sanitation.

పారిశ్రామిక **paariśraamika** *adj.* industrial.

పారిశ్రామికక్షేత్రం, పారిశ్రామికవాడ **paariśraamikakSeetram, paariśraamikawaaDa** *n.* industrial estate.

పారిశ్రామికవేత్త **paariśraamikaweetta** *n.* industrialist.

పారిశ్రామికీకరణ **paariśraamikiikaraNa** *n.* industrialisation.

పారు **paaru**[1] *n.* trash in the form of grit and similar impurities; **padi kiloola biyyam testee ~ pooyEEka tommidi kiloolu migulutundi** if you bring home ten kilos of rice only nine kilos will be left after the trash has been removed.

పారు **paaru**[2] *v.i.* 1 to flow. 2 to run [away]. 3 *dial.* (of bowels) to purge. 4 (of charm, stratagem, etc.) to work, take effect, have an effect; **naa ettu** (*or* **naa yukti**) **paarindi** my trick worked; **atanimiida aawiDa sambhaaSaNa aaTee paaraleedu** her conversation had no effect at all on him. 5 (of a glance) to fall; **waaDi dṛSTi naa miidaki paarindi** his glance fell on me. 6 *following a vb. in the infinitive or a n. or an adj. and becoming* **baaru** *or* **waaru** *in sandhi ~ means* to become, e.g., **nallabaaru** to turn black; **pagulubaaru** to split, break into pieces; **paNDabaaru** to ripen; **errawaaru** to turn red.

పారుకొను **paarukonu** *v.i.* (of bowels) to purge.

పారుడు **paaruDu** *n.* purging of the bowels.

పారుదల **paarudala** *n.* flow[ing]; **niiTi ~** irrigation; **muruguniiTi ~** drainage.

పారుపత్తెందారు **paarupattendaaru** *n.* person who supervises and manages a temple.

పారుబాకీ **paarubaakii** *n.* bad debt.

పారువేట **paaruweeTa** *n.* 1 hunting. 2 rite performed in Vaishnavite temples symbolic of hunting.

పారుష్యం **paaruSyam** *n.* harshness, roughness.

పార్థివ **paarthiwa**[1] *n.* nineteenth year of the Hindu cycle of sixty years.

పార్థివ **paarthiwa**[2] *adj. class.* belonging to the earth.

పార్థివుడు **paarthiwuDu** *n. class.* king.

పార్శ్వ[ం] **paarśwa[m]** *n.* side, flank; **parwata ~** mountain side.

పాల **paala**[1] *adj.* pale brown, milky white (in colour).

పాల **paala**[2] *locative of* **paalu** *n.* share; **waaDi ~ paDindi** it fell to his lot.

పాల **paala**[3] *genitive of* **paalu** *n.pl.* milk.

పాల ఉబ్బసం **paala ubbasam** *n.* kind of asthma which affects infants.

పాలక **paalaka** *adj.* 1 executive. 2 ruling, governing.

పాలకాయలు **paalakaayalu** *n.pl.* kind of sweet.

పాలకి **paalaki** *same as* **pallaki.**

పాలకుడు **paalakuDu** *n.* 1 ruler, administrator. 2 guardian, protector.

పాలకూర, పాలాకు **paalakuura, paalaaku** *n.* spinach, *oxystelma esculentum.*

పాలగచ్చు **paalagaccu** *same as* **paalasunnam.**

పాలదాయి **paaladaayi** *n.* wet nurse.

పాలన[ం] **paalana[m]** *n.* 1 preserving, guarding, cherishing, caring. 2 administration, rule; **paalanaa wyawastha** administrative system.

పాలపళ్ళు **paalapaLLu** *n.pl.* milk teeth.

పాలపాపడు **paalapaapaDu** *n.* suckling baby.

పాలపిట్ట **paalapiTTa** *n.* blue jay (bird); ~ **rangu** bluish grey colour.

పాలబాటు, పాలపుంత **paalabaaTa, paalapunta** *n. astron.* milky way.

పాలబుగ్గలవాడు **paalabuggalawaaDu** *n.* bonny baby.

పాలరాయి **paalaraayi** *n.* marble (rock).

పాలవు **paalawu** (<paalu + awu) *v.i.* **1** *lit.* to become the share of, *hence* to be subjected to, become a victim of, become a prey to; **warada~** to become a victim of floods; **ninda~** to incur blame; **appula~** to fall into debt; **nawwula~** to become a laughing stock. **2** to become a part of; **maTTi/ganga~** *lit.* to become a part of earth/water, *hence* to be totally ruined or destroyed. **3 kanjiniiLLu neela paalayyEEyi** the cunjee was spilt on the ground.

పాలవెల్లి **paalawelli** *n.* **1** *astron.* milky way. **2** canopy made of bamboo strips decorated and placed over an idol in a house at times of worship.

పాలసుగంధి **paalasugandhi** *n.* flavoured milk shake.

పాలసున్నం, పాలగచ్చు **paalasunnam, paalagaccu** *n.* fine lime plaster.

పాలాకు **paalaaku** *same as* **paalakuura.**

పాలాస్త్రి **paalaastri** *n.* plaster.

పాలాస్త్రి పట్టి **paalaastri paTTi** *n.* sticking plaster for covering a wound or boil.

పాలాస్త్రీ పెంకులు, బిళ్ల పెంకులు **paalaastrii penkulu, biLLa penkulu** *n.pl.* thin square tiles laid between the reepers and the outer layer of roof titles of a building for the purpose of insulation.

పాలి **paali**[1] *genitive of* **paalu** *n.* share (*also* **~Ti, ~Ta**) *lit.* being the share of, falling to the lot of, *hence* pertaining to, connected with; **naa~waram** the boon conferred on me; **naa~raakSasi** the demon that I am a prey to.

పాలి **paali**[2] *n. dial.* time, occasion; **okka~** once.

పాలించు **paalincu** *v.t.* **1** to rule, govern. **2** to observe, follow, adhere to. **3** *class.* to protect, cherish.

పాలిక **paalika** *n. dial.* rimless earthen pot containing soil in which **nawadhaanyaalu** (nine kinds of grain) are sown and left to sprout as part of the wedding ceremony and the sacred thread ceremony (**upanayanam**).

పాలికాడు **paalikaaDu** *n.* crop sharing tenant.

పాలికాపు **paalikaapu** *n.* field labourer, agricultural labourer.

పాలిత **paalita** *adj.* ruled, governed, administered; **keendra ~praantam** Centrally administered area.

పాలితులు **paalitulu** *n.pl.* persons who are ruled or governed.

పాలిపగ **paalipaga** *n.* blood feud.

పాలిపోవు **paalipoowu** *v.i.* to turn pale.

పాలివాడు **paaliwaaDu** *n.* (*pl.* **paaliwaaru, paaliwaaLLu, paalooLLu**) co-sharer, person who has a right to a share in ancestral property.

పాలిసేద్యం **paaliseedyam** *n.* cultivation by crop sharing between landowner and cultivator.

పాలు **paalu**[1] *n.* **1** share; **paaliki ceesee seedyam** cultivation by crop sharing. **2** part, portion; **nuuTiki aydu paaLLu** five parts in a hundred, five per cent. **3** (of ingredients in a mixture) quantity, proportion; **daani rasaayanika padaarthaalanuu bhawtika lakSaNaalanuu pasikaTTi tagu paaLLaloo miśramam ceesEEru** they identified its chemical ingredients and physical properties and combined them in the right proportions.

పాలు **paalu**[2] *n.pl.* **1** milk; **~wiDicina duuDa** weaned calf. **2** milky juice found in unripe grains of paddy, maize, etc.; **~paTTina ginjalu** tender unripe grains.

పాలుపంచుకొను **paalupancukonu** *v.i.* to share, take part in; **naaku ewaruu paalu pancukonee waaLLu leeru** there is none to share with me.

పాలుపడు, పాల్పడు **paalupaDu, paalpaDu** *v.i.* **1** to take part in, engage in, indulge in, resort to, go in for **2** to descend to, stoop to; **swaamidroohaaniki~** to stoop to treachery.

పాలుపోవు **paalupoowu** *v.i. with dat., in neg. constr.* to be decided or determined, to occur to the mind; **eem ceeyaaloo naaku eemii paalupoowaDam leedu** I cannot make up my mind what to do *or* I am at a loss what to do (*lit.* it does not occur to me what I should do).

పాలుమాలిక **paalumaalika** *n.* lethargy.

పాలుమాలు **paalumaalu** *v.i.* to be idle, relax; **ninna koncem paalumaali paTTincukooleedu, paniwaaLLu pani ceyyaleedu** yesterday I relaxed a little and did not pay attention, and the workers did not do their work.

పాలుమాల్చు **paalumaalcu** *v.t.* to wean.

పాలె **paale** *n. dial.* plough tail.

పాలెం, పాళెం **paalem, paaLem** *n.* hamlet, small village.

పాలెగాడు, పాళెగాడు **paalegaaDu, paaLegaaDu** *n.* poligar, petty feudal chief.

పాలేరు **paaleeru** *n.* farm labourer, farm servant.

పాలోళ్లు **paalooLLu** *see* **paaliwaaDu.**

పాల్గొను **paalgonu** *v.i.* to take part, participate, partake; **calam brahmasamaajamloo paalgonee kaalamloo** during the time when Chalam was participating in the Brahmasamaj.

పాల్పడు **paalpaDu** *same as* **paalupaDu.**

పాళం **paaLam** *n.* **1** manner, state, condition, degree; **oka paaLapu maniSi** a mediocre sort of person; **biDDa aakali ~erigi** knowing the degree of the child's hunger; **waana waccee~gaa undi** it looks as if rain will come. **2** proportion; **miThaayiloo paalu, cakkera, neyyi sama paaLaalaloo poostaaru** they mix milk, sugar and ghee in equal proportions in the sweet; **niiLLu paaLaalu ceesi poosukonnaanu** I mixed (hot and cold) water in the right proportions (i.e., to the right temperature) and took my bath.

పాళంగా **paaLangaa** *same as* **paDangaa.**

పాళా **paaLaa** I. *n.* ingot. II. *adj.* pure; **~bangaaram** pure gold.

పాళీ **paaLii** *n.* nib of a pen.

పాళెం **paaLem** *same as* **paalem.**

పావంచ **paawanca** *n.* steps forming the front entrance to a house flanked by a veranda on either side.

పావడ **paawaDa** *n.* woman's skirt (undergarment).

పావన **paawana** *adj.* pure, clean, holy, sanctified.

పావనం **paawanam** *n.* purification, sanctification; **maa illu~ ceesEEDu** he graced our house by his presence.

పావలా **paawalaa** *n.* quarter of a rupee.

పావు **paawu** *n.* **1** quarter. **2** pawn (in chess). **3** any piece or man' in a game like caroms or draughts.

పావురం, పావురాయి **paawuram, paawuraayi** *n.* pigeon, dove.

పావురాయి రంగు **paawuraayi rangu** *n.* grey colour.

పాశం **paaśam**[1] *n.* 1 cord, rope. 2 Yama's noose. 3 **keeśa-paaśaalu** strands of hair.

పాశం **paaśam**[2] *same as* **paayasam.**[2]

పాశవిక **paaśawika** *adj.* cruel, brutal, beastlike, bestial.

పాశుపత **paaśupata** *adj.* pertaining to Siva.

పాశుపతం, పాశుపతాస్త్రం **paaśupatam, paaśupataa-stram** *n.* magic arrow presented by Siva to Arjuna, which would unfailingly hit its mark.

పాశ్చాత్య **paaścaatya** *adj.* western; ~ **prapancam** the western world.

పాశ్చాత్యుడు **paaścaatyuDu** *n.* westerner.

పాషండుడు **paaSaNDuDu** *n.* 1 atheist, heretic. 2 adamant or headstrong person.

పాషాణం **paaSaaNam** *n.* 1 stone, rock. 2 poison.

పాషాణపాకం **paaSaaNapaakam** *n.* style of writing that is highly obscure.

పాషాణాలు **paaSaaNaalu** *n.pl. dial.* purging, loose motions.

పాసి **paasi** *n. substandard alt. form of* **paaci.**

పాసిన **paasina** *adj.* stale.

పాసిపోవు **paasipoowu** *v.i.* 1 to become stale. 2 *colloq.* (of work) to need to be done, wait to be done; **ikkaDa eem pani paasipoowaDam leedu, poo!** there is no work waiting to be done here, go away! **eem panulu paasipootunnaayani anta tondaragaa weLLEEwu?** what made you go away so quickly? (*lit.* thinking, "what work needs to be done?" did you go away so quickly?)

పాసిమొహం **paasimoham** *n.* unwashed face.

పాసు **paasu** *n.* miser.

పాసెం **paasem** *n.* very soft pulp of fruit.

పాస్పీస్ **paaspiis** *n.* (*imitation of the sound of English as heard by a Telugu speaker*) unintelligible language.

పాహి! **paahi!** *Sanskrit interj. used in prayer* save me!

పి - pi

పింగళ **pingaLa** *n.* fifty-first year of the Hindu cycle of sixty years.

పింగాణి **pingaaNi** *n.* 1 china, porcelain, ceramics. 2 *med.* enamel (white substance covering a tooth).

పింఛం **pincham** *n.* 1 crest, plume. 2 **nemili** ~ peacock's tail.

పింఛను **pinchanu** *n.* pension.

పింఛనుదారు **pinchanudaaru** *n.* pensioner.

పింజ, పింజె **pinja, pinje**[1] *n.* flock of cotton, cotton-wool: **poTTi/poDugu ~ patti** short / long staple cotton.

పింజారీ **pinjaarii** *n.* 1 name of a community of cotton cleaners. 2 **~ wedhawa** a term of abuse.

పింజె **pinje**[2] *dial. alt. form of* **pinde.**

పింజెలు **pinjelu** *n. pl. dial. same as* **kucciLLu.**

పిండం **piNDam** *n.* 1 embryo, foetus. 2 ball of food offered ceremonially to spirits of dead ancestors. 3 food (spoken of deprecatingly) **~ tinnaawaa?** have you had a bite of food? **neenu ~ tini leeceesariki aydu gaNTalayindi** by the time I had something eat it was five o'clock.

పిండాకూడు **piNDaakuuDu** *n.* 1 *same as* **piNDam** *senses 2 and 3.* 2 **waaDi ~!** may he drop dead! (term of abuse implying a wish to offer a **piNDam** to s.o.'s departed spirit).

పిండి **piNDi** *n.* 1 flour, powder; **wennela ~ aarapoosinaT-Tundi** the moonlight is very bright (*lit.* the moonlight is as if flour was spread out for drying). 2 (*also* **telaka ~**) oilcake. 3 starch. 4 *see* **koTTu** *sense II. 1.*

పిండికట్టు **piNDikaTTu** *n.* poultice.

పిండికూర **piNDikuura** *n.* curry made largely of flour.

పిండి చేయు **piNDi ceeyu** *v.t.* to grind to powder, pulverise.

పిండి జల్లెడ **piNDi jalleDa** *n.* fine sieve for sifting flour.

పిండితార్థం **piNDitaa.:ham** *n.* essential meaning, gist.

పిండిపదార్థం **piNDipadaartham** *n. biol.* starch, carbohydrate.

పిండిపిండయిపోవు **piNDipiNDaypoowu** *v.i.* to be crushed, be smashed to pieces; **kaaru piNDipiNDay pooyindi** the car was a total wreck.

పిండిబలపం **piNDibalapam** *n.* kind of soft slate pencil.

పిండిబొమ్మ **piNDibomma** *n.* objec. used by a sorcerer when casting a spell.

పిండిమిరియం **piNDimiriyam** *n.* spiced dish made with dhall and chillies.

పిండివంట **piNDiwaNTa** *n.* any cooked food made of flour.

పిండు **piNDu** *v.t.* 1 to squeeze; **naa daggira Dabbu ~ kun-naaDu** he squeezed money out of me. 2 **aawunu ~** to milk a cow. 3 to press out, pinch, wring (clothes to remove moisture); **cewulu ~** to pinch s.o.'s ears (as a punishment); **waaDidaggira mukku piNDi Dabbu wasuulu ceesEEnu** I collected the money.forcibly from him (*lit.* by pinching his nose).

పిండోత్పత్తి శాస్త్రం **piNDootpattiśaastram** *n.* (science of) embryology.

పిందె **pinde** *n.* tender unripe fruit (the stage before that c **kaaya**).

పికం **pikam** *n. class.* coel, Indian cuckoo.

పికాసి **pikaasi** *n.* pickaxe.

పికిలి[పిట్ట], పిగిలి[పిట్ట] **pikili[piTTa], pigili[piTTa]** *n.* bulbul.

పిక్క **pikka** *n.* **1** calf of the leg. **2** thigh. **3** stone, nut or kernel of a fruit. **4** *dial. alt. of* **paawu** *senses 2 and 3.* **5** *slang* money.

పిక్కబలం **pikkabalam** *n. lit.* strength of the legs; ~ **cuupincEEDu** *colloq.* he ran away.

పిక్కలాంటి **pikkalaaNTi** *adj.* healthy, flourishing, strong, well-built.

పిక్కు **pikku** *v.i.* **1** to draw back, withhold. **2** *dial.* to be miserly.

పిగులు **pigulu** *v.i.* (of clothes) to suffer from wear and tear, become threadbare, burst at the seams.

పిచపిచ **picapica** *onom. n.* pit-a-pat; **guNDe ~ laaDindi** his heart beat fast *or* his heart went pit-a-pat.

పిచిక, పిచ్చుక, పిచికి **picika, piccuka, piciki** *n.* **1** sparrow; ~ **miida brahmaastram** (using) a thunderbolt to kill a sparrow (*cf. the English expression* taking a sledge-hammer to crack a nut). **2** *slang* girl. **3** *slang* **bangaaru ~** very rich person.

పిచికారి, పిచ్చికారి **picikaari, piccikaari** *n.* syringe, sprayer.

పిచికారి చేయు **picikaari ceeyu** *v.t.* to spray.

పిచోడీలు **picooDiilu** *n.pl.* fine variety of rice grown in the second crop period.

పిచ్చ **picca**[1] *n.* testicle.

పిచ్చ **picca**[2] *same as* **picci.**

పిచ్చకాయ **piccakaaya** *n.* testicle.

పిచ్చకాయలు కొట్టు **piccakaayulu koTTu** *v.i.* to castrate.

పిచ్చటిల్లు **piccaTillu** *v.i.* **1** to tremble. **2** to misbehave.

పిచ్చాపాటీ **piccaapaaTii** *n.* gossip.

పిచ్చి **picci** I. *n.* **1** madness, insanity; **ataniki ~ paTTindi/ekkindi** he became mad. **2** eccentricity, craze, fad; **ataniki sangiitam ~** he is crazy about music. II. *adj.* **1** mad, insane, demented; **~ waaDu** insane person; **~ burra** crazed or deranged or wandering mind. **2** stupid, foolish, senseless; **~ panulu/maaTalu** senseless deeds/words. **3** silly, simple; **~ waaDaa!** silly boy! (spoken affectionately). **4 ~ cuupu** blank look, vacant stare, look of bewilderment or distress. **5** violent, overpowering, excessive; **~ preema/balam** overpowering love/strength; **~ talanoppi** terrible headache; **~ waana** excessive rain. **6** stray, casual; **~ paaTalu** snatches of song. **7** (of coinage, weights, measures) false, counterfeit. **8** (of plants) wild, uncultivated; **~ mokkalu** weeds. **9** (of plants) bitter; **~ doNDa/doosa** bitter [variety of] gourd/cucumber.

పిచ్చికారి **piccikaari** *same as* **picikaari.**

పిచ్చుక **piccuka** *same as* **picika.**

పిటకం **piTakam** *n.* hindrance, obstruction.

పిటపిటలాడు **piTapiTalaaDu** *v.i.* to be full of youth and vitality.

పిట్ట **piTTa** *n.* **1** bird; **oka guuTi ~ lu** *lit.* birds of the same nest, i.e., persons of the same category. **2** *slang* girl.

పిట్టకథ **piTTakatha** *n.* anecdote, generally humorous, told during the narration of a longer story.

పిట్టగోడ **piTTagooDa** *n.* low wall, parapet wall.

పిట్టమనిషి **piTTamaniSi** *n.* puny person.

పిట్టు **piTTu**[1] *n.* door stopper.

పిట్టు **piTTu**[2] *n.* **1** steamed flour made into balls. **2** oilcake remaining after oil is extracted.

పిట్టెం **piTTem** *n.* hard lump; **waaDi pani ~ kaTTindi** *lit.* his affairs became a hard lump, i.e., he was plunged into difficulties.

పిడక **piDaka** *n.* dried cowdung cake; **raamaayaNamloo ~ la weeTa** *is a stock phrase meaning* wasting time on trivialities when important events are taking place.

పిడచ, పిడుచ **piDaca, piDuca** *n.* **1** handful. **2** small lump of anything semi-solid; **annam ~ lu** lumps of cooked rice.

పిడచకట్టు [కొను] **piDacakaTTu[konu]** *v.i.* to become parched, become caked; **piDacakaTTuku pooyina naaluka** parched tongue.

పిడత, పిడుత **piData, piDuta** *n.* small earthen pot.

పిడతమొహం! **piDatamoham!** *interj.* ugly face! (*term of abuse*).

పిడి **piDi** *n.* **1** handle, hilt. **2** fist; **~ bigincu** to clench o.'s fist.

పిడికిలి **piDikili** *n.* **1** hold, grasp. **2** fist; *see* **praaNam** *sense 6 (i).*

పిడికుచ్చులాంటి **piDikucculaaNTi** *adj.* strong, sturdy.

పిడికెడు **piDikeDu** *adj.* **1** fistful of, handful of. **2** a small amount of.

పిడిగుద్దు **piDiguddu** *n.* punch.

పిడివాటు, పిడేటు **piDiwaaTu, piDeeTu** *n.* beating grain out of sheaves of corn (a form of threshing).

పిడివాదం **piDiwaadam** *n.* **1** obstinacy, obduracy. **2** dogmatic assertion.

పిడుగు **piDugu** *n.* thunderbolt, lightning stroke.

పిడుచు **piDucu** *v.t.* **1** to squeeze, press. **2** to wring out (wet clothes).

పిణ్యాకం **piNyaakam** *n. class.* **1** oilcake. **2** asafoetida.

పిత **pita** *n.* father; **jaati ~** father of the nation.

పితపితలాడు **pitapitalaaDu** *v.i.* to be soft.

పితరుడు **pitaruDu** *n. class.* father.

పితలాటకం **pitalaaTakam** *n.* **1** petty difficulty or inconvenience. **2** quarrelsomeness, trickery.

పితలాటకంపెట్టు **pitalaaTakampeTTu** *v.i.* **1** to create a petty difficulty, raise a trivial objection. **2** to cause a dispute or quarrel.

పితామహుడు **pitaamahuDu** *n.* father's father, grandfather.

పితుకు, పిదుకు **pituku, piduku** *v.t.* **1** to milk. **2** *colloq.* to squeeze.

పితూరీ, ఫితూరీ **p[h]ituurii** *n.* **1** rebellion, disturbance, outcry. **2** talebearing, slandering.

పితృ **pitṛ** *adj. class.* paternal; **~ preema** father's love.

పితృకర్మ, పితృకార్యం, పితృక్రియ **pitṛkarma, pitṛkaaryam, pitṛkriya** *n.* father's funeral obsequies.

పితృగణం **pitṛgaNam** *n.* spirits of departed ancestors.

పితృతిథి **pitrtithi** *n.* rite performed each year on the anniversary of a father's death.
పితృత్వం **pitrtwam** *n.* paternity.
పితృలు **pitrlu** *n.pl. class.* ancestors.
పితృస్వామిక **pitrswaamika** *adj.* patriarchal.
పితృస్వామికం n. **pitrswaamikam** *n.* patriarchy.
పిత్తం **pittam** *n.* bile, gall.
పిత్తలం, పిత్తళం, పిత్తడి, పిత్తళి **pittalam, pittaLam, pittaDi, pittaLi** *n.* brass.
పిత్తవాయువు **pittawaayuwu** *n. class.* flatulence.
పిత్తాశయం, పిత్తకోశం **pittaaśayam, pittakoośam** *n.* gall bladder.
పిత్తు **pittu** I. *n.* breaking wind, fart (vulgar). II. *v.i.* to break wind, fart (vulgar).
పిత్రార్జిత **pitraarjita** *adj.* (of property) ancestral.
పిత్రార్జితం **pitraarjiitam** *n.* ancestral property.
పిదప **pidapa** *adv.* afterwards, later.
పిదపకాలం **pidapakaalam** *n.* bad times: **araTipaNDu padiheenu paysalaa? eem ~ waccindi!** fifteen paise for a plantain? what bad times have come upon us!
పిదపబుద్ధులు **pidapabuddhulu** *n.pl.* mean thoughts.
పిదుకు **piduku** *same as* **pituku.**
పిన **pina** *alt. form of* **cinna.**
పినతండ్రి **pinataNDri** *n.* uncle, father's younger brother or mother's younger sister's husband.
పినతల్లి **pinatalli** *n.* 1 aunt, mother's younger sister or father's younger brother's wife. 2 stepmother.
పినమామ **pinamaama** *n.* 1 pinnatta's husband. 2 father-in-law's younger brother.
పినాకం **pinaakam** *n.* Siva's trident.
పినాకపాణి **pinaakapaaNi** *n.* epithet of Siva.
పినాకిని **pinaakini** *n.* name of the River Pennar.
పిన్న **pinna** *alt. form of* **cinna; ~ lu peddalu** younger and elder people, juniors and seniors.
పిన్నతనం **pinnatanam** *n.* childhood.
పిన్ననాడు **pinnanaaDu** *adv.* in (o.'s) childhood.
పిన్నత్త **pinnatta** *n.* mother-in-law's younger sister or father-in-law's younger brother's wife.
పిన్నమ్మ, పిన్నాం **pinnamma, pinnaam** *n.* mother's younger sister.
పిన్నయ్య **pinnayya** *n.* father's younger brother.
పిన్నరికం **pinnarikam** *n.* infancy, childhood; **~ peddarikam akkaralEE?** *lit.* ought there not to be (consideration of) youth and age? i.e., ought you not to have respect for your elders?
పిన్ని **pinni** *n.* 1 *same as* **pinnamma.** 2 (*also* **~ gaaruu**) *mode of address to a woman conveying both respect and familiarity.*
పిన్నీసు **pinniisu** *n.* safety pin.
పిపాస **pipaasa** *n. class.* thirst; **widyaa ~** thirst for learning.
పిపాసి **pipaasi** *n. class.* thirsty person.
పిపీలి, పిపీల, పిపీలికం **pipiili, pipiila, pipiilikam** *n. class* ant.
పిపీలికాదిబ్రహ్మపర్యంతం **pipiilikaadibrahmaparyantam** *adv.* from the lowest to the highest *or* from the smallest to the greatest (*lit.* from an ant to Brahma himself).
పిప్పలం **pippalam** *n. class.* banyan tree.
పిప్పలి **pippali** *n.* long pepper, *chavica roxburghii*; **pippaLLa basta** *colloq.* very fat person.
పిప్పళ్ల మోడికారం **pippaLLa mooDikaaram** *n.* medicine prepared from **pippali** taken by women after childbirth.
పిప్పి **pippi** I. *n.* trash, e.g., of sugarcane after removal of juice by crushing; *see* **piilci ~ ceeyu.** II. *adj.* rotten, decayed; **~ pannu** decayed tooth.
పిమ్మట **pimmaTa** I. *p.p.* after. II. *adv.* afterwards, later, subsequently.
పిమ్మటి **pimmaTi** *adj.* subsequent.
పియ్య, పియ్యి **piyya, piyyi** *n.* dung, excrement.
పిరం **piram** *adj. dial.* costly (‹ **priyam**).
పిరికి **piriki** *adj.* 1 cowardly, timid. 2 nervous, uneasy.
పిరికి[పంద] **piriki [panda]** *n.* 1 coward. 2 nervous or uneasy person; **sabhaapiriki** person who is nervous of speaking in public.
పిరికితనం **pirikitanam** *n.* 1 cowardice, cowardliness. 2 nervousness, uneasiness.
పిరియాది, ఫిర్యాది **piriyaadi, phiryaadi** *n.* complainant.
పిరియాదు, ఫిర్యాదు **piriyaadu, phiryaadu** *n.* complaint.
పిరుదులు **pirudulu** *n.pl. class.* buttocks.
పిర్ర **pirra** *n.* buttocks, rump.
పిలక, పిలుక **pilaka, piluka** *n.* 1 tuft of hair (*lit.* a tuft left to grow on the top of the head, the rest of the head being shaved); **o.-ni ~ paTTukonu** to hold s.o. by the hair; *cf.* **nigiDincu, niguDu.** 2 young shoot, side shoot (of plantain, etc.).
పిలవనంపు **pilawanampu** *v.i.* to send for; **naakoosam pilawanampEEDu** he sent for me.
పిలాయించు **pilaayincu** *v.t. dial.* 1 to cause (s.o.) to drink. 2 to pay out more thread so as to enable a kite to fly higher.
పిలిపించు **pilipincu** *v.t.* to send for, summon.
పిలుచు **pilucu** *v.t.* 1 to call. 2 to call by name or kinship term; **pillalu nannu maamayyaa ani pilustaaru** the children call me uncle. 3 to invite.
పిలుపు **pilupu** *n.* 1 call, cry. 2 invitation; **peNDLi ~** marriage invitation. 3 **~ iccu** to issue a call, issue an appeal.
పిల్ల **pilla** I. *n.* 1 girl. 2 *pl.* **~ lu** children (boys and girls), offspring; **~ lanu kanu** to produce offspring (human); **~ lanu peTTu** to produce offspring (nonhuman). 3 *colloq.* **ii pustakam mii daggira uNTee ~ lanu peDutundEE? maaku iwwaNDi** if this book remains with you will it be of any use to you? (*lit.* will it produce any offspring?) please give it to me. II. *adj.* 1 childlike, childish; **~ maaTalu** words like those of a child; **~ weeSaalu** childish or immature behaviour; *see* **sancu**[2]. 2 small; **~ kaaluwa** small channel or canal; **~ gaali** gentle breeze.

పిల్లంగ్రోవి, పిల్లనగ్రోవి **pillan[a]groowi** *n.* flute.

పిల్లకాయ **pillakaaya** *n.* 1 *dial.* child. 2 childish or immature person.

పిల్లపెత్తనం **pillapettanam** *n.* misrule by young and inexperienced persons.

పిల్లలకోడి **pillalakooDi** *n.* 1 mother hen with a brood of chickens. 2 *astrol.* a name of the third lunar mansion.

పిల్లాడు, పిల్లవాడు, పిల్లడు **pillaaDu, pillawaaDu, pillaDu** *n.* boy, lad.

పిల్లాపాపా **pillaapaapaa** *n.pl.* o.'s children both old and young (*lit.* children and infants); ~ **kulaasaagaa unnaaraa**? are all your children well?

పిల్లాపీచూ **pillaapiicuu** *n.pl.* o.'s children and other family members; ~ **ewaruu leeru. waaLLu iddaree** there are only two of them, they have no children or other family members.

పిల్లామేకా, పిల్లాజెల్లా **pillaamEEkaa, pillaajellaa** *n.pl.* o.'s children (gen. said with ref. to a large family); ~ **too kalakalalaaDutuu uNDeewaaru** they used to have a flourishing family of children.

పిల్లి **pilli** *n.* cat; ~ **ettukupootundEE?** *lit.* will a cat run away with it?, i.e., will (s.g) be lost or stolen very easily?

పిల్లి అడుగులు **pilli aDugulu** *n.pl.* 1 noiseless steps. 2 small footprints.

పిల్లి కళ్లు **pilli kaLLu** *n.pl. lit.* cat's eyes, i.e., light coloured eyes (considered as a sign of ugliness).

పిల్లి నడక **pilli naDaka** *n.* cat's walk, noiseless steps; ~ **naDustuu waccEEDu** he came on tiptoe.

పిల్లిపెసర, పిల్లిపిసర **pillipesara, pillipisara** *n. phaseolus trilobus*, a leguminous crop.

పిల్లిమొగ్గలు **pillimoggalu** *n.pl.* somersaults; ~ **weeyu** to turn somersaults.

పిళ్లారి **piLLaari** *n.* epithet of the God Vinayaka.

పిశాచం, పిశాచి **piśaacam, piśaaci** *n.* demon, devil.

పిశాచిభాష **piśaaci bhaaSa** *n.* unintelligible language.

పిషాణం **piSaaNam** *n.* name of a fine variety of rice.

పిష్టం **piSTam** *n. class.* flour.

పిష్టపేషణం **piSTa peeSaNam** *n.* 1 *class.* grinding flour. 2 wasted effort, useless repetition.

పిసరంత **pisaranta** *adj.* only very little, hardly any.

పిసరు **pisaru** *n.* trifle, small amount, small quantity; **oka**~ a little, somewhat; **cinna**~ just a little; **poDum**~ pinch of snuff.

పిసరూపిప్పీ **pisaruupippii** *n.* 1 scrap, very small quantity. 2 trash.

పిసికిళ్లు **pisikiLLu** *n.pl.* 1 grain not quite ripe. 2 *same as* **pisukuLLu.**

పిసినారి, పిసిని[గొట్టు], పీసినారి, పీనాసి **pisinaari, pisini[goTTu], piisinaari, piinaasi** *n.* miser.

పిసినారితనం **pisinaaritanam** *n.* miserliness.

పిసుకు **pisuku** *v.t.* 1 to squeeze; **o.-i piike**~ *or* **o.-i gontu**~ to strangle s.o. 2 to massage; **kaaLLu**~ to massage the legs. 3 **piNDi**~ to knead flour.

పిసుకుడు **pisukuDu** *n.* 1 squeezing. 2 massaging. 3 (*also pl.* **pisukuLLu**) mixing by hand, kneading.

పిసుక్కొను **pisukkonu** *v.i. and t.* 1 to feel distressed. 2 **ceetulu**~ to wring o.'s hands.

పీ - pii

పీక **piika** *same as* **piike.**

పీకు **piiku** I. *n.* (*also* **piikuDu**) ache, aching II. *v.i. and t.* 1 to pull out, pluck out, tear out, uproot. 2 to pull, drag, draw. 3 to torment, worry, cause anxiety; **pillalu naamiida paDi piikeesEEru** the children rushed to me and worried me; **piiki paakam peTTu** to cause extreme trouble (to s.o.); *see* **praaNam**, *sense 5.*

పీకుకొను, పీక్కొను **piikukonu, piikkonu** *v.i. and t.* 1 to pull out, pluck out; *see* **naaluka.** 2 to be drawn or haggard; **eNDaloo tirigaDamwalla waaDi moham piikku pooyindi** his face was drawn due to going about in the sun. 3 to grumble, murmur; **tanu tappu ceeyakapooyinaa tanani tiTTEErani piikkoNTunnaaDu** he is grumbling because they abused him although he had done nothing wrong.

పీకుడు[గాడు] **piikuDu[gaaDu]** *n.* quarrelsome or contentious person; *see also* **piiku** *sense I.*

పీకుదానా, పీకుదాను **piikudaanaa, piikudaanu** *n. dial.* spitoon.

పీకులాట **piikulaaTa** *n.* entanglement, wrangle; **naaku ii**~ **peTTaku** do not involve me in this wrangle.

పీకులాటపంచాంగం **piikulaaTa pancaangam** *n. slang* long and protracted wrangle.

పీకులాట బేరం చేయు **piikulaaTa beeram ceeyu** *v.i.* to haggle.

పీకె, పీక **piike, piika** *n.* 1 windpipe, throat, gullet, neck; **aa paapam naa**~**ki cuTTukondi / paTTukondi** that sin has fastened on me *or* I am being held responsible for that sin; **Dabbu istaawaa castaawaa ani naa**~**la miida kuurcunnaaDu** he is threatening me violently (*or* he is terrorising me) into paying money; **naa**~ **la moyya pani undi** (*lit.* there is work up to my throat) *corresponds to the English expression* I am up to my eyes in work; *see* **pisuku.** 2 **naa**~**la miida [katti] teccEEDu** *lit.* he brought a knife to my throat, i.e., he put me in extreme difficulty; **naa**~**la miidaki[katti] waccindi** *lit.* a knife came to my throat, i.e., I was in dire straits. 3 voice. 4 reed or tongue of a musical instrument. 5 nipple of a baby's milk bottle. 6 stub or stump of a cigar or cigarette.

పీచం **piicam** *n.* pride.

పీచు **piicu** *n.* fibre; **kobbari**~ coconut fibre; ~**juTTu** hair like fibre.

పీచుపీచుమను **piicupiicumanu** *v.i.* to tremble or quake with fear; **naa guNDelu piicupiicumaNTunnaayi** my heart is quaking.

పీట **piiTa** *n.* 1 wooden plank. 2 stool or plank to sit or stand on. 3 wooden bar. 4 **pedda~** high seat, seat of honour: *see* **piiTham** *sense 4*.

పీటముడి **piiTamuDi** *n.* knot that is hard to untie. Gordian knot.

పీఠం **piiTham** *n.* 1 *class.* seat of honour, guru's chair, throne; **adhikaara~** seat of power. 2 institute of studies; **wijñaana~** seat of learning. 3 a certain sitting posture. 4 *colloq.* **maa iNTLoo~ weesukoni kuurcunnaaDu** *or* **maa iNTLoo piiTa peTTi kuurcunnaaDu** he settled down in my house *or* he made himself at home in my house.

పీఠభూమి **piiThabhuumi** *n.* plateau, uplands.

పీఠిక **piiThika** *n.* preface, introduction.

పీడ **piiDa** *n.* 1 pain, annoyance, trouble, torment, harassment; **appulawaaLLa ~ paTTukondi waaDiki** he was afflicted by creditors. 2 *legal* nuisance.

పీడకల **piiDakala** *n.* nightmare.

పీడనం **piiDanam** *n.* 1 pressure. 2 oppression.

పీడనమాపకం **piiDanamaapakam** *n.* pressure gauge.

పీడాకర **piiDaakara** *adj.* oppressive, troublesome.

పీడానాడా **piiDaanaaDaa** *n.* pest, plague, curse (**naaDaa** is an echo word).

పీడించు **piiDincu** *v.t.* 1 to plague, persecute, harass, distress, oppress, pester, torment. 2 to exploit.

పీడిత **piiDita** I. *adj.* oppressed, afflicted. II. *second part of an adjvl. compound* affected; **anaawrṢTi~ praantaalu** drought affected areas.

పీత **piita**[1] *n.* crab.

పీత **piita**[2] *adj. class.* yellow; **~wastradhaari** person who wears ceremonial yellow robes.

పీతకర్మ **piitakarma** *n. class.* alchemy.

పీతాంబరం **piitaambaram** *n.* yellow robe, gen. made of silk, used for **maDi**.

పీతి **piiti** *adj.* yellow; **~guDDalu** soiled clothes of a baby.

పీత్వాపీత్వా **piitwaa piitwaa** *adv. class.* as drinking continues or proceeds; *cf.* **gatwaa gatwaa.**

పీనాసి **piinaasi** *same as* **pisinaari.**

పీనాసితనం **piinaasitanam** *n.* miserliness.

పీనుగ, పీనుగు **piinuga, piinugu** *n.* 1 dead body, corpse, carcass. 2 *colloq.* **moNDi~** obstinate rascal.

పీపా **piipaa** *n.* cask or drum for containing liquid.

పీపి, పీపె **piipi, piipe** *n.* head of corn at a very early stage.

పీయూష **piiyuuSa** *n. class.* 1 nectar, ambrosia. 2 beestings.

పీర్ **piir** *n.* Muslim saint.

పీల **piila** *adj.* 1 lean, thin. 2 weak.

పీలిక **piilika** *n.* 1 small piece, bit. 2 **guDDa~** scrap of cloth, rag.

పీలు **piilu** *alt. form of* **pigulu.**

పీల్చిపిప్పిచేయు **piilcipippiceeyu** *v.t.* 1 *lit.* to suck (s.g) dry and leave only trash. 2 to drain all the essence from. prey upon, exploit. 3 **ninnu piilcipippi ceesi paareestaanu** I will make trash of you (a threat).

పీల్చు **piilcu** *v.t.* 1 to breathe in, inhale; **gaali~** to draw breath; **mukku poDum~** to inhale snuff; **mukku~konu** to sniff; **mukku ega~** to snivel. 2 to suck the juice from s.g, suck s.g dry; **sTraatoo~konu** to drink through a straw.

పీల్పు **piilpu** *n.* inhalation, draught of air or cigarette smoke.

పీల్‌మట్టి **piilmaTTi** *n.* yellow ochre wash applied to walls of buildings.

పీసినారి **piisinaari** *same as* **pisinaari.**

పు - pu

పుం **pum** *adj. gram.* male, masculine.

పుంఖం **punkham** *n. class.* feathered end of an arrow.

పుంఖానుపుంఖంగా **punkhaanupunkhangaa** *adv.* in rapid succession, one after another.

పుంగవుడు **pungawuDu** *second part of a n. compound, class.* eminent or venerable person; **ṛSi~** venerable rishi.

పుంజ **punja** *adj.* dry, unirrigated (land, crop).

పుంజం **punjam** *n.* 1 *class.* heap, group, collection. 2 **kaanti~** beam of light. 3 **punjaalu tempukoni parugettu** to cut o.'s bonds (i.e., to free o.s.) and run away.

పుంజీ **punjii** *n. dial.* 1 four. 2 a few.

పుంజు **punju** *n.* cock.

పుంజుకొను **punjukonu** *v.i.* 1 to gather strength. 2 to pick up, revive, improve; **gata samwatsaram pragati maLLi punjukondi** last year progress picked up again.

పుంజెడు **punjeDu** *adj.* 1 four. 2 a few.

పుంటికూర **puNTikuura** *n. dial. hibiscus cannabinus*, a green vegetable (= **goonguura**).

పుండాకోరు **puNDaakooru** *n.* rowdy, villain, bad character.

పుండి, పుండేకు **puNDi, puNDEEku** *dial. alt. forms of* **puNTikuura.**

పుండు **puNDu** *n.* boil, abscess, ulcer, sore; **kotta ceppulu weesukoNTee kaali miida~paDindi** I got a sore on my foot from wearing new shoes.

పుండ్రం **puNDram** *n.* mark on the forehead denoting religious sect.

పుంత **punta** *n.* 1 path. 2 small channel carrying irrigation water from field to field.

పుంబీజకోశాలు **pumbiijakoośaalu** *n.pl.* testes.

పుంభావం **pumbhaawam** *n.* 1 *class.* scholarship, learning. 2 maleness, masculinity.

పుంభావ సరస్వతి **pumbhaawa saraswati** *n.* embodiment of the goddess Saraswati, very scholarly person.

పుంలింగం **pumlingam** *n. gram.* masculine gender.

పుకారు **pukaaru** *n.* rumour.

పుక్కిట పెట్టుకొను **pukkiTa peTTukonu** *v.i.* to preserve (*lit.* to keep stored up in o.'s cheek); **ii pallepaaTalu ententa kawitaa sampadanu pukkiTa peTTukonnaayoo**! what a wealth of poetry has been preserved in these folk songs!

పుక్కిటిపురాణం **pukkiTi puraaNam** *n.* myth, legend, fable.

పుక్కిలి **pukkili** *n.* inside of the cheek.

పుక్కిలించు **pukkilincu** *v.t.* to rinse o.'s mouth, gargle.

పుక్కిలింపు **pukkilimpu** *n.* gargling.

పుక్కెడు **pukkeDu** *n.* mouthful.

పుచ్చ[కాయ] **pucca[kaaya]** *n.* **1** bitter melon, *cucumus sp.*. **2** water melon, *citrullus vulgaris.*

పుచ్చపువ్వు **puccapuwwu** *n.* white flower of a **pucca**; ~**laaNTi wennela** bright moonlight.

పుచ్చాకు **puccaaku** *n.* name of a medicinal plant; *see* **gaccakaaya.**

పుచ్చు **puccu**[1] I. *n.* **1** rot[tenness], decay. **2** *pl.* ~**lu** rotten things. II *adj.* rotten, decayed, decaying, putrid. III. (*also* **puccipoowu**) *v.i.* to decay, rot, be rotten.

పుచ్చు **puccu**[2] *v.t.* **1** *class.* to take. **2** *mod. only in composition* (i) *with certain nouns and adjs. to form vbs.*, e.g., **moosa**~ to cheat; **cinna**~ to offend, humiliate; (ii) *as an auxiliary in place of* **peTTu**, e.g., **wiDici**~ to omit.

పుచ్చుకొను **puccukonu** *v.t.* **1** to take, receive, accept; *see* **sanyaasam**~. **2** *in the Godavari and northern coastal regions of Andhra Pradesh*~ *is regularly used for* **tiisukonu** *in the sense of* 'to take'; *in other areas only* (i) *in certain set phrases*, e.g., **iNTi doowa puccukonnaanu** I set out for home; **parugu puccukonnaanu** I took to my heels *or* I started to run; (ii) *where a degree of formality is involved*, e.g., **loopaliki eem puccukonnaaru iwwEELa?** what nourishment have you taken today? (said by a doctor to a patient); **selawu puccukoNTaanu** I will take leave of you (polite formula used on departure); **kaphii puccukoNTaaraa Tii puccukoNTaaraa?** will you take coffee or tea?

పుచ్చుకోలు **puccukoolu** *n.* taking, receiving; *cf.* **icci**~.

పుచ్చె **pucce** *n.* **1** skull. **2** small unripe coconut. **3** half coconut shell with the kernel.

పుచ్ఛం **puccham** *n. class.* tail.

పుట **puTa** *n.* page.

పుటం, పుఠం **puT[h]am** *n.* the operation of refining precious metal or calcining a drug in a crucible; **naa**~ **aarustunnaaDu** *colloq.* he is worrying me to death (*lit.* he is quenching the fire of my crucible).

పుటం పెట్టు, పుటం వేయు, పుఠం పెట్టు, పుఠం వేయు **puT[h]am peTTu, puT[h]am weeyu** *v.t.* **1** to refine a precious metal. **2** to calcine a drug.

పుటక **puTaka** *n.* birth; ~**too waccina alawaaTu puDakalatoo gaani poodu** a habit acquired at birth will only depart at death (*lit.* will only depart at cremation—proverbial saying).

పుటపుట **puTapuTa** *onom. adv. sug.* quickness in running, speaking, etc.

పుటికీలు **puTikiilu** *n. pl. dial.* children's game played by bouncing a ball on the ground.

పుటుక్కున **puTukkuna** *adv.* **1** with a snapping sound; **taaDu**~ **tegi pooyindi** the cord broke with a snap. **2** abruptly; **maaTalu** ~ **aneesEEDu** he blurted out the words.

పుట్ట **puTTa** *n.* anthill; ~**laku** ~**lu janam unnaaru** crowds upon crowds of people were present; ~ **pagilinaTLu janam waccEEru** swarms of people came (imagery derived from ants swarming).

పుట్టం **puTTam** *n. class.* cloth, garment.

పుట్టకాలు **puTTakaalu** *n.* elephantiasis, filariasis.

పుట్టకురుపు, పుట్టవ్యాధి; పుట్టరణం **puTTakurupu, puTTawyaadhi, puTTaraNam** *n.* cancer.

పుట్టకొక్కు, పుట్టగొడుగు **puTTakokku, puTTagoDugu** *n.* mushroom, toadstool.

పుట్టకోట **puTTakooTa** *n.* buttress, bulwark.

పుట్టగతులు **puTTagatulu** *n.pl.* hope for the future; **waaDi nooTidaggira kuuDu tiistee**~**uNDawu** if you deprive him of his livelihood you will have no hope for the future (*meaning* retribution will come to you in this life or the next).

పుట్టమట్టి, పుట్టమన్ను **puTTamaTTi, puTTamannu** *n.* earth dug from an anthill.

పుట్టలమ్మ **puTTalamma** *n.* goitre.

పుట్టి **puTTi**[1] *n.* **1** obsolete grain measure equal to twenty tooms. **2** obsolete measure of land varying in extent regionwise.

పుట్టి **puTTi**[2] *n.* round coracle or raft made of wickerwork and leather; **nuwwu ippuDu weLLakapootee**~**munigipootundEE?** if you do not go now will everything be lost? (*lit.* will your raft be sunk?); *see also* ~**muncu.**

పుట్టించు **puTTincu** *v.t.* **1** to create, generate, cause (laughter, surprise, fear, etc.). **2** to make, form. **3** to give rise to, fabricate (rumour). **4** to raise (loan).

పుట్టి[ని]ల్లు **puTTi[ni]llu** *n.* parents' home (of a woman).

పుట్టి ముంచు **puTTi muncu** *v.i.* **1** *lit.* to sink (s.o.'s) raft. **2** *fig.* to ruin (s.o.); **naa puTTi muncEEwuraa bhagawantuDaa!** oh God! you have ruined me!

పుట్టు **puTTu**[1] *v.i.* **1** to be born; **puTTina rooju** birthday. **2** to be produced, be caused, originate, come into existence, happen, occur, appear; **nippu puTTindi** a fire occurred; **appu puTTindi** a loan was raised; **naaku talanoppi puTTindi** I developed a headache; **utsaaham puTTindi** excitement was aroused; **cawDu puTTi gooDalu kuuli pootunnaayi** salt has appeared and the walls are collapsing. **3** (of a river, star) to rise; **goodaawari nadi naasikdaggara puDutundi** the River Godavari rises (*or* takes its source) near Nasik.

పుట్టు **puTTu**[2] *n. dial.* dish made of rice.

పుట్టుక **puTTuka** *n.* birth, origin.

పుట్టుకల్లరి **puTTukallari** *n.* born liar.

పుట్టుకుంక **puTTukunka** *n.* born idiot (*term of abuse*).

పుట్టుకువచ్చు, పుట్టుకవచ్చు, పుట్టుకొనివచ్చు, పుట్టుకొచ్చు **puTTuku waccu, puTTukawaccu, puTTukoniwaccu, puTTukoccu** *v.i.* to arise, originate, be born.

పుట్టుగుడ్డి **puTTuguDDi** *n.* person born blind.

పుట్టుపూర్వోత్తరాలు **puTTupuurwoottaraalu** *n.pl.* origin and antecedents.

పుట్టుమచ్చ **puTTumacca** *n.* birth mark.

పుట్టుమూగ **puTTumuuga** *n.* person born dumb.

పుట్టువెంట్రుకలు **puTTuweNTrukalu** *n.pl.* child's hair at the time of birth; ~ **tiiyu** to cut a child's hair for the first time (ceremony performed at the age of three or five years).

పుట్టెడు **puTTeDu** *adj.* 1 *lit.* a **puTTi** (twenty tooms) of. 2 *fig.* a large measure of, abundance of.

పుట్ర, పుట్రా **puTra[a]** *echo word, see* **puli**[1], **pulii puTraa, polam puTraa, puruguupuTraa.**

పుట్రేపులు పెట్టు **puTreepulu peTTu** *v.i.* to instigate, incite.

పుఠం **puTham** *same as* **puTam.**

పుడక **puDaka** *n.* small stick; *see* **paanakam; mukku**~ stick-shaped nose ornament.

పుడమి **puDami** *n. class.* the earth, the world.

పుడమి రేడు **puDami reeDu** *n. class.* king.

పుడిసెడు **puDiseDu** *adj.* palmful of (some liquid); **ikkaDa ~ niiLLu kuuDaa leewu** there is not even a palmful of water here.

పుడిసెలి **puDiseli** *n.* hollow of the hand.

పుడీ **puDii** *n. dial.* small package.

పుడీలు **puDiilu** *n.pl. dial.* bluffing, boasting.

పుణికి **puNiki** *n. dial.* 1 skull. 2 vessel, bowl.

పుణికిపుచ్చుకొను **puNiki puccukonu** *v.t.* to become imbued with, acquire (trends, features).

పుణుకు, పుడుకు **puNuku, puDuku** *v.t.* 1 to touch with the fingers; **paapa buggalu**~ to hold a child's cheek in o.'s fingers. 2 to squeeze; **naa daggara Dabbu puNukkonnaaDu/puDukkonnaaDu** he squeezed money out of me.

పుణుకులు, పునకలు **puNukulu, punakalu** *n.pl.* savoury snacks made of groundnut flour or any gram flour.

పుణ్య **puNya** *adj.* 1 good, excellent, charitable, meritorious. 2 holy, sacred, pious, blessed. 3 auspicious.

పుణ్యం **puNyam** *n.* 1 virtue, goodness, excellence. 2 credit, merit; **nii[ku]~ uNTundi** (*lit.* there will be merit for you) *is used to reinforce a request,* e.g., **astamaanam bhujam alaa egareeyaDam maaneedduu niiku~ uNTundi!** stop shrugging your shoulders like that all day long, I beg you! 3 good deed, meritorious deed; **naa~ paNDindi** *lit.* my good deed has come to fruition, i.e., I have reaped the reward of my good deed; **waaDi puNyaphalam waaDiki wastundi** he will earn the reward of his good deed; *see* **paapam** *sense I.1.*

పుణ్యం కట్టుకొను **puNyam kaTTukonu** *v.i.* to earn or acquire merit (*lit.* to credit merit to o.'s account); *this vb. is used of present or future action,* e.g., **naaku ii pani ceesipeTTi puNyam kaTTukoNDi** please do this for me and thereby earn some merit.

పుణ్యం చేసుకొను **puNyam ceesukonu** *v.i.* to earn or acquire merit; *this vb. is used of past actions,* e.g., **waaDu eppuDoo puNyam ceesukonnaaDu, ippuDu naalugu ruupaayalu sampaadistunnaaDu** he acquired merit some time in the past whereby he is able to earn a living now.

పుణ్యకాలం **puNyakaalam** *n.* 1 auspicious time. 2 *colloq.* fixed or appointed time; **waaDu wacceesariki ~ daaTi pooyindi** by the time he arrived the appointed time was over. 3 *astrol.* time fixed for carrying out certain ceremonies, esp. during eclipses and equinoxes and on certain other occasions.

పుణ్యక్షేత్రం **puNyakSeetram** *n.* place of pilgrimage, pilgrimage centre.

పుణ్యపురుషుడు, పుణ్యవంతుడు, పుణ్యాత్ముడు **puNyapuruSuDu, puNyawantuDu, puNyaatmuDu** *n.* virtuous person.

పుణ్యభూమి **puNyabhuumi** *n.* land of piety (gen. with reference to India).

పుణ్యమా అని, పుణ్యమా అంటూ, పుణ్యాన **puNyamaa ani, puNyamaa aNTuu, puNyaana** *advbl. phrase.* thanks to, by the grace of.

పుణ్యవంశం **puNyawamśam** *n.* pious family.

పుణ్యస్త్రీ **puNyastrii** *n.* wife, married woman.

పుణ్యానికి **puNyaaniki** *adv. dial.* 1 free of cost. 2 **utti**~ without any cause, for no reason at all.

పుణ్యాహవాచనం **puNyaahawaacanam** *n.* ceremony of purification and invoking welfare, gen. performed after a birth or death in a house.

పుత్తడి, పుత్తళి **puttaDi, puttaLi** *n.* gold.

పుత్తెంచు **puttencu** *v.t. class.* to send, despatch.

పుత్ర **putra** *adj.* relating to a son.

పుత్ర కామేష్టి **putra kaameeSTi** *n.* religious sacrifice made by a person desiring the birth of a son.

పుత్రభిక్ష **putrabhikSa** *n.* saving of a son's life; **DaakTaru maaku~ peTTEEDu** the doctor has saved my son's life.

పుత్రసంతానం **putrasantaanam** *n.* male offspring.

పుత్ర హీనుడు **putrahiinuDu** *n.* person who has no son.

పుత్రి[క] **putri[ka]** *n. class.* daughter.

పుత్రుడు **putruDu** *n. class.* son.

పుత్రోత్సవం **putrootsawam** *n. class.* function held to celebrate a son's birth.

పుదీన **pudiina** *n.* mint, *mentha arvensis.*

పునః **punaḥ** I. *adjvl. prefix; same as* **punar.** II. *adv.* (*also* **punaa**) *colloq.* again; **neenu ceppina tarawaata ~ maLLii aDigEEDu** after I had told him he asked me again.

పునఃప్రారంభించు **punaḥ praarambhincu** *v.i. and t.* to begin again, restart.

పునఃస్థాపించు **punaḥsthaapincu** *v.t.* to re-establish.

పునకలు **punakalu** *same as* **puNukulu.**

పునర్, పునః **punar, punaḥ** *Sanskrit adjvl. prefix meaning* again, re-, e.g., **punarnirmaaNam** reconstruction.

పునరంకితం **punarankitam** *n.* rededication.

పునరభ్యసన **punarabhyasana** *adj.* retraining, refreshing, orientation: ~ **taragati** refresher course.

పునరభ్యాసం **punarabhyaasam** *n.* revision exercise.

పునరారంభించు **punaraarambhincu** *v.i. and t.* to begin again, restart, resume.

పునరావలోకనం **punaraawalookanam** *n.* retrospection.

పునరావాసం **punaraawaasam** *n.* rehabilitation, resettlement.

పునరావృత్తం, పునరావృత్తి **punaraawṛttam, punaraawṛtti** *n.* repetition, recurrence.

పునరుక్తి, పునరుక్తం **punarukti, punaruktam** *n.* repetition.

పునరుక్తిదోషం **punaruktidooSam** *n. ling.* redundancy.

పునరుజ్జీవనం **punarujjiiwanam** *n.* reviving, revitalising.

పునరుత్థానం **punarutthaanam** *n.* resurrection.

పునరుత్థాన దినం **punarutthaana dinam** *n.* Easter day.

పునరుద్ఘాటించు **punarudghaaTincu** *v.t.* to reaffirm, reiterate.

పునరుద్ధరణ **punaruddharaNa** *n.* **1** refurbishment. **2** reclamation (of land). **3** renewal, renovation.

పునరుద్ధరించు **punaruddharincu** *v.t.* to revive, restore, regenerate (vegetation), reclaim (land).

పునరుద్ధారణ **punaruddhaaraNa** *n.* revival, restoration, regeneration, reclamation.

పునరేకీకరణ[ం] **punnareekiikaraNa[m]** *n.* reunification.

పునర్జన్మ **punarjanma** *n.* **1** rebirth. **2** new life; **waaDiki ~ iccEEru** they gave him new life *or* they revived him.

పునర్జీవం **punarjiiwam** *n.* revival, bringing back to life.

పునర్నవం **punarnawam** *n.* rebirth, rejuvenation, renewal.

పునర్నిర్మాణం **punarnirmaaNam** *n.* reconstruction.

పునర్నిర్మించు **punarnirmincu** *v.t.* to reconstruct.

పునర్భవం **punarbhawam** *n.* rebirth, regeneration.

పునర్భవించు **punarbhawincu** *v.i.* (of a rumour, suspicion) to revive, reappear.

పునర్ముద్రణ **punarmudraNa** *n.* reprint[ing], new edition, revised edition.

పునర్యవ్వనం **punaryawwanam** *n.* rejuvenation.

పునర్వసు **punarwasu** *n. astrol.* seventh lunar mansion.

పునర్వికాసం **punarwikaasam** *n.* redevelopment.

పునర్వ్యవస్థీకరణ **punarwyawasthiikaraNa** *n.* reorganisation.

పునర్వ్యవస్థీకరించు **punarwyawasthiikarincu** *v.t.* to reorganise.

పునశ్చరణ **punaścaraNa** *n.* revision; ~ **taragati** refresher course; ~ **paaTham** revision lesson; **ślooka / mantra ~** *class.* repetition of a verse/prayer.

పునస్కారాలు **punaskaaraalu** *echo word*: *see* **puujaa ~**.

పునస్సంధానం **punassandhaanam** *n.* ceremony of consummation of marriage.

పునా **punaa** *same as* **punaḥ** *sense II.*

పునాది **punaadi** *n.* foundation, base on which a structure stands.

పునాసపంట **punaasa paNTa** *n.* **1** crop sown at the start of the rainy season. **2** third crop of paddy sown in May. **3** out of season crop (e.g., very early mangoes).

పునిస్త్రీ **punistrii** *n.* married woman (whose husband is living).

పునీత **puniita** *adj.* holy, sacred, sanctified.

పునుగు **punugu** *n.* civet.

పున్నమ, పూర్ణిమ, పున్నమి, పౌర్ణమి **punnama, puurNima, punnami, pawrNami** *n.* full moon day.

పున్నాగం **punnaagam**[1] *n. class.* serpent.

పున్నాగం **punnaagam**[2] *same as* **ponna**[2].

పున్నామ[నరకం] **punnaama[narakam]** *n.* hell to which persons who have no sons are consigned.

పున్నురాలు **punnuraalu** *n.* ghost of a **puNyastrii.**

పున్నెం **punnem** *alt. form of* **puNyam.**

పుప్పి, పిప్పి **puppi, pippi** *adj.* rotten, decayed; ~ **pannu** decayed tooth.

పుప్పుస **puppusa** *adj. med.* pulmonary.

పుప్పుసం **puppusam** *n. med.* lung.

పుప్పొడి **puppoDi** *n. bot.* pollen.

పుబ్బ **pubba** *n. astrol.* eleventh lunar mansion.

పుయిలోడు **puyilooDu** *v.i. obs.* to hesitate, be diffident.

పురం **puram** *n. class.* city, town; *mod. only as n. suffix in* names of towns, e.g., **piiThaapuram** Pithapuram.

పురఃపతనం **puraḥpatanam** *n.* downfall.

పురజనులు **purajanulu** *n.pl.* townspeople, citizens, the public.

పురపాలక **purapaalaka** *adj. admin.* municipal; ~ **maNDali** municipal council; ~ **sangham** municipality.

పురపుర **purapura** *onom. adv. expressing greatness or intensity* (i) of swelling; **piNDi ~ pongindi** the dough swelled very much (due to action of yeast); (ii) of emotion; ~ **cuucu** to stare angrily.

పురపురలాడు **purapuralaaDu** *v.i.* to desire strongly, be eager; **weLLi cuuDaalani ~ tunnaaDu** he is eager to go and see.

పురమాయించు **puramaayincu** *v.t.* to entrust or assign (a task).

పురమాయింపు **puramaayimpu** *n.* instruction.

పురస్కరించుకొని **puraskarincukoni** *adv.* in view of, in the light of, in pursuance of, taking account of, out of; **sneeham ~** out of friendship.

పురస్కారం **puraskaaram** *n.* present, gift.

పురస్సరంగా **purassarangaa** *adv.* by way of, out of; **gawrawa ~** out of respect.

పురా **puraa** *adj.* ancient, earlier, former; ~ **waybhawam** former splendour.

పురాకృత **puraakṛta** *adj.* previously done; ~ **karma** past deeds.

పురాకృతం **puraakṛtam** *n. class.* deeds done in a former birth.

పురాణ **puraaNa** *adj.* old, ancient; ~ **kaalam** ancient times.

పురాణం **puraaNam** *n.* 1 old story, legend, myth, fable. 2 *colloq.* lengthy narration; **paata ~ wippEEDu** he started narrating all the past history.

పురాణదంపతులు **puraaNa dampatulu** *n.pl.* the primeval couples among the Gods, Vishnu and Lakshmi, Siva and Parvati.

పురాణపురుషుడు **puraaNa puruSuDu** *n.* 1 epithet of Vishnu. 2 very old man.

పురాతత్వ **puraatatwa** *adj.* archaeological.

పురాతత్వశాస్త్రం **puraatatwaśaastram** *n.* archaeology.

పురాతత్వ శాస్త్రజ్ఞుడు **puraatatwa śaastrajñuDu** *n.* archaeologist.

పురాతన **puraatana** *adj.* old, ancient.

పురాలేఖనశాస్త్రం **puraaleekhanaśaastram** *n.* palaeography.

పురావస్తు **puraawastu** *adj.* archaeological.

పురావస్తు శాస్త్రం **puraawastuśaastram** *n.* archaeology.

పురి **puri** *n.* 1 peacock's tail; ~ **wippina nemali** peacock which has spread its tail. 2 storage place made of straw ropes and mats for keeping grain. 3 string, twine.

పురికొలుపు **purikolupu** *v.t.* 1 to stir up, excite, incite, instigate. 2 to spur on, inspire.

పురికొస[దారం] **purikosa[daaram]** *n.* thread made of jute.

పురిటిల్లు **puriTillu** *n.* house where a birth has taken place within twelve days; **nela ~** house where a birth took place between twelve days and a month previously.

పురిపెట్టు **puripeTTu** *v.t.* **taaDu ~** to twist a rope.

పురివిప్పుకు తిరుగు **puri wippuku tirugu** *v.i. slang* to behave shamelessly.

పురీషం **puriiSam** *n. class.* faeces, excrement.

పురుగు **purugu** *n.* any reptile or non-flying insect, e.g., worm, weevil, snail, snake; **waaNNi ~ muTTindi** *dial.* a snake bit him.

పురుగూపుట్రా **puruguu puTraa** *collective n.* creeping things.

పురుటాలు, పురుటియాలు **puruTaalu, puruTiyaalu** *n.* woman in childbirth.

పురుడు **puruDu** *n.* 1 childbirth, delivery. 2 *colloq.* period of ceremonial pollution for a family lasting for twelve days after a child's birth; for the mother this period is known as **pedda ~** and the period from 12 days to a month after the birth is known as **nela ~**.

పురుడుపోయు **puruDupooyu** *v.i.* 1 (of a midwife) to deliver a child. 2 to meet the expenses of delivery; **naa celleliki puruDu poosEEnu** I met the expenses of my younger sister's delivery.

పురుడుపోసుకొను **puruDupoosukonu** *v.i.* to give birth to a child; **aame aasupatriloo puruDupoosukonnadi** she had her delivery in the hospital.

పురుడూపుణ్యం **puruDuupuNyam** *collective n.* delivery and related matters; **neenu aame ~ cuustaanu** I will see to her delivery and all the connected matters.

పురుళ్లగది **puruLLagadi** *n.* lying-in room.

పురుష **puruSa** I. *n. gram.* person (in vbs.) II. *adj.* male, men's, manly.

పురుషకారం **puruSakaaram** *n.* 1 manly effort. 2 human endeavour.

పురుషత్వం **puruSatwam** *n.* masculinity, virility, maleness.

పురుషబీజకణాలు **puruSa biijakaNaalu** *n.pl. biol.* spermatozoa.

పురుషసింహం **puruSasimham** *n.* valiant man, hero.

పురుషసూక్తం **puruSasuuktam** *n.* a hymn of the Rigveda in praise of the first manifestation of the Supreme Spirit.

పురుషాంతరం **puruSaantaram** *n.* generation (= **taram**).

పుషార్థం **puruSaartham** *n.* 1 object of desire. 2 highest aim or object of life; **idi ceestee puNyamaa ~ aa**? if you do this, will it bring you satisfaction in this life or merit in the next?

పురుషుడు **puruSudu** *n. n.* 1 man. 2 husband.

పురుషోత్తముడు **puruSoottamuDu** *n.* the Supreme Being.

పురెక్కించు, పుర్రెక్కించు **pur[r]ekkincu** *v.t.* to incite, spur on, instigate.

పురోగతి, పురోగమనం **puroogati, puroogamanam** *n.* progress, advancement, development.

పురోగమించు **puroogamincu** *v.i.* to go forward, advance, progress.

పురోగామి **puroogaami** *n.* 1 leader. 2 pioneer. 3 progressive-minded person.

పురోభాగం **puroobhaagam** *n.* front.

పురోభివృద్ధి **puroobhiwṛddhi** *n.* progress, development, advancement; ~ **daśa** advanced stage.

పురోహితుడు **puroohituDu** *n.* purohit, family priest.

పుర్ర **purra** *adj.* left.

పుర్ర చేయి **purra ceeyi** *n. slang* left hand.

పుర్రచేయివాటం **purraceeyiwaaTam** *n.* lefthandedness.

పుర్రాకులు **purraakulu** *n.pl. dial.* troubles, difficulties.

పుర్రు **purru**[1] *n.* 1 loose motion of the bowels. 2 semiliquid substance.

పుర్రు **purru**[2] *onom. n. sug.* sound of tearing cloth.

పుర్రుమన్ను **purrumannu** *n.* soft mud, slush.

పుర్రె **purre** *n.* skull.

పుర్రెక్కించు **purrekkincu** *same as* **purekkincu.**

పులక[ం], పులకరం, పులకరింత **pulaka[m], pulakaram, pulakarinta** *n.* thrill, tingling, glowing sensation due to excitement.

పులకాంకురం **pulakaankuram** *n.* tingling, thrill, bristling of hair on the body.

పులకించు, పులకరించు **pulakincu, pulakarincu** *v.i.* to tingle, feel a thrill of excitement.

పులగం **pulagam** *n.* dish made of rice boiled with green-gram.

పులగంపెట్టుగా **pulagampeTTugaa** *adv.* jumbled up, in a hash, in a hotch potch.

పులావు, పలావు **pulaawu, palaawu** *n.* pilau, a preparation made of[meat,] rice and spices.

పులి **puli**[1] *n.* (*also* **pedda ~**) tiger; **ciruta ~** panther, leopard, cheetah; **~ miida puTra laagaa** *is a stock phrase meaning* to add to the difficulty *or* to make matters worse; **nel-aakharu roojulaloo ceetuloo paysalu leewu, ~ miida puTra laagaa cuTTaalu waccipaDDaaru** I had no ready cash at the end of the month and to make matters worse my relatives arrived.

పులి **puli**[2] *adj.* sour, acid.

పులికాపు **pulikaapu** *n.* cleaning of temple idols and images performed in the early morning; *colloq.* **abbaayi ippuDee leecEEDu. waaDiki ~ peTTi mii iNTiki tiisuku wastaanu** the boy has just woken. I will tidy him up and bring him to your house.

పులిగోరు **puligooru** *n.* locket shaped like a tiger's claw, worn as an ornament.

పులిచల్ల **pulicalla** *n.* sour buttermilk.

పులిచింత **pulicinta** *n.* *oxalis corniculata*, a tree whose pods contain edible seeds.

పులిజూదం **pulijuudam** *n.* a game like draughts.

పులితేనువు, పులితేన్పు **puliteen[u]pu** *n.* belching caused by indigestion.

పులినీళ్ళు **puliniiLLu** *n.* rice gruel or cunji left overnight to turn sour.

పులిపిరి[కాయ] **pulipiri[kaaya]** *n.* wart.

పులిబొంగరం **pulibongaram** *n.* preparation made from dough left overnight, mixed with spices and then fried.

పులియబెట్టు **puliyabeTTu** *v.t.* to make sour, cause to ferment.

పులియు **puliyu** *v.i.* to turn sour, ferment.

పులిసిపోవు **pulisipoowu** *v.i.* 1 to be[come] sour. 2 *colloq.* to be[come] rich and proud.

పులి[వి]స్తరాకు **puli[wi]staraaku** *n.* leaf plate which has been used and is therefore defiled.

పులిహోర **pulihoora** *n.* rice mixed with tamarind or lime juice and spices.

పులీపుట్రా **puliipuTraa** *collective n.* tigers and other wild animals.

పులుకుపులుకు **pulukupuluku** *n.* blinking.

పులుకుపులుకు చూచు **pulukupuluku cuucu** *v.i.* 1 to blink. 2 to look angrily. 3 *slang* to look invitingly.

పులుగు **pulugu** *n.* bird.

పులుపు **pulupu** *n.* acidity, sourness.

పులుము **pulumu** *v.t.* 1 to smear, splash, daub, dab (paint, powder, etc.). 2 *fig.* to foist; **tana tappu naa nettina pulimi tanu tappukonnaaDu** he foisted his fault on to me and escaped himself.

పులుముకొను **pulumukonu** *v.t.* 1 to smear or dab on o.s. 2 *fig.* to put on an insincere expression; **wicaaram mukh-aana pulumukonnaaDu** he put a sad expression on his face (although he felt glad); **mukhaana balawantaana nawwu pulumukonnaaDu** he forced himself to smile.

పులుసు **pulusu** I. *n.* 1 acid juice or sap, e.g., of tamarind or soapnut. 2 tamarind soup; **naa pani ~ loo paDDaTTayin-di** *lit.* it is as if my affair had fallen in the soup; i.e., I am in a helpless state.

పుల్ల **pulla** I. *n.* small stick, twig; **~ lu** small sticks, firewood; **nippu ~** match stick. II *adj.* 1 sour, acid. 2 dun coloured, pale red, yellowish white.

పుల్లకూర **pullakuura** *n.* 1 (*also* **pulusu kuura**) curry cooked in tamarind juice or lime juice. 2 kind of spinach.

పుల్లన **pullana** *n.* acidity, sourness.

పుల్లరి **pullari** *n.* pasture tax (obsolete).

పుల్లవిరుపు **pullawirupu** *same as* **kaTTewirupu.**

పుల్ల[లు] వేయు **pulla[lu] weeyu** *v.i.* *colloq.* to raise difficulties, put difficulties in the way.

పుల్లాట **pullaaTa** *n.* a children's game.

పుల్లింగం **pullingam** *n.* 1 *corrupt form of* **sphulingam**; *mod. only in the expression* **pullingaalu ceppu** to carry tales or make malicious allegations (**-miida**, against). 2 *gram.* masculine gender.

పుల్లుడు **pulluDu** *adj.* pale reddish coloured.

పుళింద **puLinda** *n.* a legendary kingdom in India.

పువ్వు, పూవు **puwwu, puuwu** *n.* flower; **puulu paLLu peTTukonnaaru** *is a phrase meaning* they finalised the engagement (for a marriage).

పువ్వుబోడి, పూబోడి **puwwubooDi, puubooDi** *n. class.* beautiful woman.

పుష్కరం **puSkaram** *n* 1 auspicious occasion celebrated once every twelve years along the banks of a river, e.g., **goodaawari ~, krSNaa ~**, at which offerings are made to the spirits of departed ancestors. 2 period of twelve years. 3 name of a pilgrimage centre in Ajmer.

పుష్కరిణి **puSkariNi** *n.* 1 lotus pond. 2 temple tank.

పుష్కలం **puSkalam** I. *n.* abundance, plenty. II *adj.* abundant, many, plentiful.

పుష్కలంగా **puSkalangaa** *adv.* plentifully.

పుష్టి **puSTi** *n.* strength, vigour, plumpness, wellbeing; **aarthika ~** economic wellbeing, prosperity.

పుష్టిగల, పుష్టివంత **puSTigala, puSTiwanta** *adj.* vigorous, sturdy, well nourished, plump.

పుష్పం **puSpam** *n.* flower.

పుష్పకం, పుష్పకవిమానం **puSpakam, puSpaka-wimaanam** *n.* 1 *class.* Kubera's aerial chariot. 2 *colloq.* conveyance which can accommodate a large number of persons.

పుష్పదళం **puSpadaLam** *n.* petal.

పుష్పబాణుడు **puSpabaaNuDu** *n.* epithet of Manmatha or Cupid.

పుష్పలావిక **puSpalaawika** *n. class.* woman flower gatherer and garland maker.

పుష్పవతి **puSpawati** *n.* 1 girl who has attained puberty. 2 menstruous woman.

పుష్పవృష్టి **puSpawrSTi** *n. class.* shower of flowers.

పుష్పాంజలి **puSpaanjali n.** offering of flowers made as a token of worship or respect.

పుష్పించు **puSpincu** *v.i.* 1 to flower, bloom, blossom. 2 to be in menses.

పుష్యం **puSyam** *n.* the tenth lunar month (= January).

పుష్యమి **puSyami** *n. astrol.* the eighth lunar mansion.

పుష్యరాగం **puSyaraagam** *n.* topaz.

పుసలాయించు **pusalaayincu** *v.t.* to coax, cajole.

పుసి **pusi** *n.* rheum of the eyes; **kaLLu ~ kaTTEEyi** rheum formed in the eyes.

పుసికిపోవు **pusikipoowu** *v.i.* 1 to slip from o.'s grasp. 2 *fig.* to fail to materialise; **sambandham pusiki pooyindi** the marriage alliance did not come off; *cf.* **besuku.**

పుసుకున, పుసుక్కున **pusuk[k]una** *adv.* suddenly, hastily, unexpectedly, abruptly; **~ rahasyam ceppeesEEDu** he blurted out the secret.

పుస్తకం **pustakam** *n.* book.

పుస్తు **pustu** *n.* stench, foul smell.

పుస్తె **puste** *same as* **taaLiboTTu.**

పూ - puu

పూ **puu** *adjvl. prefix meaning* of a flower, floral; **puutooTa** flower garden.

పూచిక **puucika** *n. aristida setacea,* a shrub whose twigs are tied in a bundle to make a broom.

పూచిక[ల]కట్ట **puucika[la]kaTTa** *n.* broom.

పూచికపుల్ల **puucikapulla** *n.* 1 twig of a broom. 2 *colloq.* minute quantity, s.g trifling.

పూచీ **puucii** *n.* 1 responsibility. 2 security, recognizance.

పూచీకత్తు **puuciikattu** *n.* security bond.

పూచు, పూయు **puucu[1], puuyu[1]** *v.i.* to flower, bloom, blossom.

పూచు, పూయు **puucu[2], puuyu[2]** *v.i.* (of tongue, mouth) to blister, be sore.

పూజ **puuja** *n.* worship, adoration; **~ lu andukonu** to receive adoration, receive the highest degree of honour; *colloq.* **pustakaalu guuTLoo peTTi ~ ceestunnaaDu** he puts his books in a pigeonhole and thinks no more about them: *see* **baDite, nityanitya ~, yaamayaama**

పూజనీయ **puujaniiya** *adj.* fit to be worshipped, worthy of worship, venerable.

పూజనీయుడు, పూజ్యుడు **puujaniiyuDu, puujyuDu** *n.* respected person, venerable person.

పూజాపునస్కారాలు **puujaapunaskaaraalu** *n.pl.* worship and other rituals.

పూజారి **puujaari** *n.* temple priest.

పూజించు, పూజ చేయు **puujincu, puuja ceeyu** *v.t.* to worship, adore, venerate, do homage or reverence to.

పూజు **puuju** *n.* yoke.

పూజె కుండ **puuje kuNDa** *n.* painted pot used in worship of a village goddess.

పూజ్యం **puujyam** I. *n.* nothing, nil. II *adj.* 1 *class.* venerable. 2 non-existent.

పూట **puuTa** *n.* 1 a period of time, part of a day of twenty-four hours: **pagaTi ~** daytime: **raatri ~** night time: **podduna ~** morning time; **madhyaana ~** afternoon time; **saayantram ~** evening time. 2 time, occasion; **roojuu muuDu ~ la sandhya waarustunnaanu** I am performing sandhya at the three appointed times each day; **eppuDannaa selawulaloo oo ~ maa iNTiki raNDi** come to my house sometime during the holidays. 3 meal time; **pillalaki reNDu ~ laa ganjiniiLLannaa iwwaali** children must at least be given cunjee water at two meal times each day; **oka ~ upawaasam** fasting at one meal time, i.e., missing a meal. 4 (of a school) session; **oNTi ~ baDi** school having only one session per day.

పూటకూళ్లమ్మ **puuTakuuLLamma** *n.* woman who keeps a **puuTakuuLLillu.**

పూటకూళ్లిల్లు **puuTakuuLLillu** *n.* house where meals are supplied to customers on payment.

పూటీ **puuTii** *n.* felloe of a wheel.

పూటుగా **puuTugaa** *adv.* completely, fully; **~ tinu** to eat o.'s fill; **~ taagu** to be fully drunk.

పూటుపడు **puuTupaDu** *v.i.* to grow rich, prosper.

పూడిక **puuDika** *n.* silt; **baawi ~ tiisEEru** they desilted the well.

పూడు **puuDu** *v.i.* 1 (of a well, tank) to be filled up, be silted up, collapse, fall in. 2 **waaDi kaNTham puuDi pooyindi** his voice became choked.

పూడ్చు **puuDcu** *v.t.* 1 to fill up, cover up, close (pit, gap, breach). 2 to bury, inter.

పూడ్పించు **puuDpincu** *v.t.* to block up, fill up (pit, hole).

పూడ్పు **puuDpu** *n.* 1 silting. 2 filling up; **gaNDi ~** closing a breach.

పూత **puuta[1]** *n.* flowering, blooming, blossoming; **ceTTu ~ paTTindi** the tree started to flower; **ceTTu ~ puusindi** the tree flowered.

పూత **puuta[2]** *n.* thrush, a disease of the mouth.

పూత **puuta**[3] *n.* painting, smearing, rubbing on, applying; **rangu inkoo ~ puuyaali** you must apply another coat of paint; **bangaaru / weNDi ~ puusina ginne** gold / silver plated vessel; **ii mandu pay ~ kee** this medicine is for external application only.

పూతన **puutana** *n.* demoness.

పూతరేకులు **puutareekulu** *n.pl.* a sweet dish.

పూతిక **puutika** *dial. variant form of* **puucika.**

పూనకం **puunakam** *n.* possession by a spirit or goddess.

పూనిక **puunika** *n.* determination, resolve, undertaking.

పూను **puunu**[1] *v.i. and t.* 1 to undertake; **diikSa ~** to undertake a vow. 2 (of a spirit or goddess) to take possession of; **ammawaaru puunina maniSi** a person possessed by the goddess.

పూను, పూన **puunu**[2], **puuna** *n. dial.* diversion weir.

పూనుకొను **puunukonu** *v.i.* 1 to undertake, venture upon, attempt; **akaDami accuku puunukondi** the Academy undertook the printing. 2 to go in for, indulge in. 3 to take up for, stand up for, lend support to; **aa wedhawa pakSaana puunukoni waccEEDu** he took up for that wretch; **niigroolaku caTTaprakaaram waari hakkula rakSaNaku aayana puunukonnaaru** he stood up for the defence of the rights of blacks in accordance with law.

పూన్చు **puuncu** *v.t.* to harness horses / bullocks to a cart; **baNDi ~ koni weLLEEDu** he harnessed the cart and left.

పూప **puupa** *n.* 1 very young fruit (at the stage just after blossoming). 2 **oree ~ !** fool! (*term of abuse*).

పూపం **puupam** *n.* kind of sweet cake.

పూపు **puupu** *n. dial.* similarity, comparison.

పూబోడి **puubooDi** *same as* **puwwubooDi.**

పూయు **puuyu**[1],[2] *same as* **puucu**[1],[2].

పూయు **puuyu**[3] *v.t.* to smear, daub, apply (paint, etc.); **gooDaku sunnam ~** to whitewash a wall; **citraaniki rangu ~** to paint a picture; *see* **puuta**[3], **masi.**

పూరకం **puurakam** *n.* 1 filling, completing. 2 supplement.

పూరణం **puuraNam** *n.* 1 filling up, completing; *cf.* **paada ~ samasyaa ~** . 2 *same as* **puurNam.**

పూరా[గా] **puuraa[gaa]** *adv.* fully, completely.

పూరి **puuri**[1] *n.* kind of wheat puff.

పూరి **puuri**[2] *n.* grass, thatch; **~ karacu** to be defeated, accept defeat (*lit.* to bite grass).

పూరించు **puurincu** *v.t.* 1 to fill [up], complete; **khaaLii ~** to fill a vacancy; **looTu ~** to make good a deficiency. 2 to puff out, blow; **buggalu ~** to puff out o.'s cheeks; **śanku ~** to blow a conch.

పూరికొంప, పూరిపాక, పూరిల్లు **puurikompa, puuripaaka, puurillu** *n.* thatched house or hut.

పూరిత **puurita** *second part of an adjvl. compound meaning* full of; **santooSa ~** full of joy; **paapa ~** sinful.

పూరీడుపిట్ట **puuriiDupiTTa** *n.* 1 (*also* **puureeDu**) quail (bird). 2 *dial.* short person.

పూరేకు **puureeku** *n.* 1 *bot.* petal. 2 kind of jewellery. 3 *pl.* **~ lu** name of a variety of paddy.

పూర్ణ **puurNa** *adj.* 1 full, complete; **~ suuryagrahaNam** total eclipse of the sun. 2 *maths.* integral.

పూర్ణం, పూరణం **puurNam, puuraNam** *n.* stuffing inside a cooked dish such as a cake or pie.

పూర్ణకుంభం **puurNakumbham** *n.* 1 ornamental jar filled with water used in welcoming ceremonies. 2 emblem of of prosperity, the state emblem of Andhra Pradesh.

పూర్ణబిందువు, పూర్ణానుస్వారం **puurNabinduwu, puurNaanuswaaram** *n. gram.* full sunna or anusvara.

పూర్ణమాసం **puurNamaasam** *n.* monthly sacrifice or ceremony performed on full moon day.

పూర్ణాంకం **puurNaankam** *n. maths.* integer.

పూర్ణిమ **puurNima** *alt. form of* **punnama.**

పూర్ణుడు **puurNuDu** *second part of a n. compound meaning* person who is full of, e.g., **widyaa ~** person full of learning.

పూర్తి **puurti** *n.* 1 fullness, completion. 2 end, conclusion.

పూర్తి అవని, పూర్తికాని **puurti awani, puurti kaani** *adj.* unfinished, incomplete.

పూర్తి అవు **puurti awu** *v.i.* 1 to be finished, be completed; **appatikii mugguruu kaaphii taagaDam puurti ayindi** by then all three of them finished drinking coffee. 2 (of a vow) to be fulfilled.

పూర్తి చేయు **puurti ceeyu** *v.t.* to finish, complete (work), fill up (form).

పూర్వ **puurwa** *adj.* 1 preceding, previous, prior, former; **~ prakaraNam** previous chapter. 2 ancient; **~ kawulu** ancient poets. 3 east[ern].

పూర్వం **puurwam** I. *n.* 1 preceding time, previous time, former time. 2 ancient times. 3 east. II. *adv.* formerly, previously, of old. III. *advbl. particle suffixed to negative vbl. adj.* before; **miiru raaka ~** before you came.

పూర్వక **puurwaka** *adjvl. suffix meaning* full of, accompanied by, e.g., **gawrawa ~ mayna** respectful.

పూర్వకంగా **puurwakangaa** *advbl. suffix meaning* arising from, accompanied by, in accordance with, by way of, as a token of, e.g., **samanwaya ~** in a coordinated manner; **prayatna ~** with an effort; **waatsalya ~** affectionately; **buddhi ~** intentionally; **wraata ~** in writing; **mantra ~** accompanied by charms.

పూర్వగత **puurwagata** *adj.* preceding, bygone.

పూర్వచరిత్ర **puurwacaritra** *n.* past history.

పూర్వజన్మ **puurwajanma** *n.* a former birth.

పూర్వజన్మఫలం **puurwajanmaphalam** *n.* a person's destiny (*lit.* result of deeds in a former birth).

పూర్వపక్షం **puurwapakSam** *n.* 1 *class.* first fortnight in a lunar month. 2 first or opening argument in a discussion. 3 question or issue raised in a discussion. 4 antithesis.

పూర్వపదం **puurwapadam** *n. ling.* first part of a compound word.

పూర్వపరాలు, పూర్వాపరాలు **puurwa[a]paraalu** *n.pl.* attendant circumstances.

పూర్వపరిశీలన చేయు **puurwapariśiilana ceeyu** *v.t.* to censor.

పూర్వపరిశీలనాధికారి **puurwapariśiilanaadhikaari** *n.* censor.

పూర్వప్రమాణం **puurwapramaaNam** *n.* precedent.

పూర్వఫల్గుని **puurwaphalguni** *n. astrol.* eleventh lunar mansion.

పూర్వభాద్ర **puurwabhaadra** *n. astrol.* twenty-fifth lunar mansion.

పూర్వమీమాంస **puurwamiimaamsa** *n.* treatise on the ritual portion of the Vedas.

పూర్వరంగం **puurwarangam** *n.* 1 earlier phase, earlier stage. 2 prelude to a drama; ~ **siddham ceeyu** to complete the preliminaries.

పూర్వశ్రుతి **puurwaśruti** *n. ling.* on-glide.

పూర్వస్మృతులు **puurwasmṛtulu** *n.pl.* memoirs.

పూర్వాధికారి **puurwaadhikaari** *n.* predecessor.

పూర్వార్థం **puurwaartham** *n.* first half.

పూర్వాషాఢ **puurwaaSaaDha** *n. astrol.* twentieth lunar mansion..

పూర్వాహ్ణం **puurwaahNam** *n. class.* forenoon.

పూర్వీక **puurwiika** *adj.* ancestral.

పూర్వులు, పూర్వీకులు **puurwulu, puurwiikulu** *n.pl.* 1 ancestors, forefathers. 2 predecessors, forerunners.

పూర్వోత్తర **puurwoottara** *adj.* 1 north-east (point of the compass). 2 old-fashioned (person).

పూలచెల్లాట, బంతులాట **puulaceLLaaTa, bantulaaTa** *n.* game played by the bride and bridegroom with a ball of flowers during the wedding ceremony.

పూలజడ **puulajaDa** *n.* girl's pigtail woven with flowers for its entire length.

పూళ్లు **puuLLu** *pair word, see* **eeDu.**[2]

పూవు **puuwu** *same as* **puwwu.**

పూస **puusa** *n.* 1 bead, globule; ~ **guccinaTTu** *lit.* like stringing beads, i.e., in regular order, carefully and comcompletely, meticulously; *see* **nalla ~, wenna ~.** 2 joint of the body; *see* **wennu ~.** 3 *dial.* joint in a sugarcane or bamboo.

పూసుకు తిరుగు **puusuku tirugu** *v.i. colloq.* to be on intimate terms.

పృ - pṛ

పృచ్ఛించు, పృచ్ఛచేయు **pṛcchincu, pṛcchaceeyu** *v.t. class.* to question, enquire.

పృథక్కరణం **pṛthakkaraNam** *n. chem.* separation.

పృథక్త్వం **pṛthaktwam** *n. class.* isolation.

పృథ్వి **pṛthwi** *n. class.* the earth.

పృథ్వీపతి **pṛthwiipati** *n. class.* king.

పృష్ఠం **pṛSTham** *n.* back, rear, buttocks.

పె - pe

పెం, పెను **pem, penu** *adjvl. prefix meaning* great, intense; **penjiikaTi, penuciikaTi** pitch darkness.

పెంక **penka** *see* **penku,** *sense 4.*

పెంకి, పెంకె **penki, penke** *adj.* obstinate, stubborn, ill-natured, impertinent, badly behaved; **~ghaTam** stubborn person; **~pillalu** naughty children.

పెంకితనం **penkitanam** *n.* obstinacy, stubbornness, ill-nature, naughtiness.

పెంకు **penku** *n.* **1** tile; **maaDu~** *colloq.* top of the head. **2** piece of broken pottery or glass. **3** shell of a fruit; **welaga~** shell of a wood apple. **4** (*also* **penka**) flat pan for parching grain or for frying.

పెంకుటిల్లు **penkuTillu** *n.* tiled house.

పెంకెపురుగు **penkepurugu** *n.* **1** weevil in grain. **2** insect which attacks crops.

పెంచు **pencu** *v.t.* **1** to nourish, nurture. **2** to foster, adopt, rear, bring up. **3** to raise, increase, inflate (prices). **4** to expand, enhance, extend, enlarge. **5** to exaggerate.

పెంచుకొను **pencukonu** *v.t.* **1** to adopt, bring up (child). **2** to rear (animals), raise (crops). **3** to nourish, promote (good feelings). **4 gaDDam~** to grow a beard.

పెంట **peNTa** *n.* **1** manure, dung of cattle, etc. **2** (*also* **~kuppa, ~poogu**) manure heap, rubbish heap.

పెంట చేయు **peNTa ceeyu** *v.i. colloq.* to make a mess or muddle.

పెంటా **peNTaa** *echo word, see* **waNTaa~.**

పెంటి **peNTi** *adj.* female.

పెంటికలు **peNTikalu** *n.pl.* sheep and goats' droppings.

పెండ **peNDa** *n. dial.* dung of cattle.

పెండలం **peNDalam** *n.* yam, *dioscoria alata.*

పెండె **peNDe** *n.* lath, reeper, small strip of wood laid across the rafters to support the tiles of a sloping roof.

పెండెం **peNDem** *n.* wooden door or gate.

పెండెకట్టు **peNDekaTTu** *n.* row of trees or houses.

పెండెకట్లు **peNDekaTLu** *n.pl.* (*also* **wibhuuti~**) white lines of **wibhuuti** worn by Saivite men on the forehead and upper arms.

పెండ్లాం, పెండ్లాడు, పెండ్లి **peNDLaam, peNDLaaDu, peNDLi** *same as* **peLLaam, peLLaaDu, peLLi.**

పెందరాళే, పెందరాడే, పెందలాడే **pendaraaLee, pendaraaDee, pendalaaDee** adv. **1** early. **2** [very] soon.

పెందలకడ **pendalakaDa** *n.* **1** early in the morning. **2** early, in advance, in good time.

పెందిలి **pendili** *adv. dial.* at dawn.

పెంపకం **pempakam** *n.* **1** rearing, nurturing, upbringing (of humans). **2** breeding, rearing (of animals). **3** raising, maintenance (of trees, crops, gardens).

పెంపు **pempu** *n.* **1** rearing, nourishing. **2** adoption, fostering; **~ku kudirEEDu** he was adopted. **3** increase, growth.

పెంపు చేయు **pempu ceeyu** *v.t.* **1** to adopt, foster. **2** to increase, enlarge, expand.

పెంపుడు **pempuDu** *adj.* **1** reared, adopted, fostered; **~koDuku** adopted son. **2** adoptive; **~taNDri** adoptive father. **3** tame, domestic[ated]; **~jantuwu** domestic animal.

పెంపుదల **pempudala** *n.* growth, increase.

పెంపొందించు **pempondincu** *v.t.* **1** to increase. **2** to foster, promote, encourage, nourish.

పెంపొందు **pempondu** *v.i.* to increase, grow, be encouraged, be promoted.

పెకలించు, పెగలించు, పెకల్చు, పెగల్చు **pekalincu, pegalincu, pekalcu, pegalcu** *v.t.* **1** to pull up by the roots, root up, eradicate. **2** to pull out, draw out, extract.

పెకలు, పెగలు **pekalu, pegalu** *v.i.* **1** to be pulled up by the roots, be pulled out, be extracted; **paysaa pegaladu waaDidaggira** not a pie can be extracted from him *or* he will not part with even a pie. **2** to be got or obtained; **Dabbu pegalaka neenu weLLa leedu** being unable to raise money, I did not go; **raayaDaaniki samayam pekalaleedu** I could not find time to write. **3** (of voice, words) to come out, emerge, be uttered; **guNDe daDadaDalaaDindi, bhayam weesindi, gontu pekalaleedu** his heart beat fast, he felt afraid, he could not utter a word.

పెక్కు **pekku** *adj.* many, a good number of.

పెచ్చరిల్లు **peccarillu** *v.i.* to increase, grow.

పెచ్చు **peccu**[1] *n.* **1** skin, peel or rind of fruit or vegetable. **2** crust of bread. **3** flake; **gooDa~lu uuDutunnadi** plaster is flaking off the wall.

పెచ్చు **peccu**[2] I. *n.* **1** surplus, excess, s.g additional or extra; **konni maaTala ciwara 'Ti'~gaa wacci ceerutundi** at the end of some words 'Ti' occurs as an addition. **2** *dial.* **~lu** boasting. II. *adj.* much, more, great[er]; **~jiitam miida paniki kudirEEnu** I was employed in a job on a higher salary.

పెచ్చుపెరుగు **peccuperugu** *v.i.* to increase, grow.

పెచ్చుమీరు **peccumiiru** *v.i.* to exceed the limit, go out of control.

పెటకం **peTakam** *n.* trouble, problem, difficulty, hitch, snag.

పెటకొర్రు **peTakorru** *dial. form of* **peDakoyya.**

పెటపెట **peTapeTa** *onom. adv. sug. sound of* cracking, snapping or crackling; **~wirugu** to break with a snap[ping sound]; **~laaDu** (i) (of fire) to crackle; (ii) (of a person) to be in a rage.

పెటాకులు **peTaakulu** *echo word; see* **peLLii~.**

పెటుకు **peTuku** I. *n.* roughness, curtness, discourteousness. II. *adj.* rough, curt, discourteous.

పెటులు, పెట్లు **peTulu, peTLu** *v.i.* to crack, burst, split; **gaaju palaka peTLipooyindi** the pane of glass cracked.

పెటేల్నా **peTeelna** *adv.* suddenly, loudly; ~ **nawwEEDu** he burst out laughing.

పెటేల్మను **peTeelmanu** *v.i.* (of a gun being fired) to explode with a loud report or crack.

పెట్ట **peTTa** *n.* hen.

పెట్టిందిపేరు **peTTindi peeru** *n.* well-known person, byword; **paalalloo niiLLu kalapaDaaniki paalawaaLLu** ~ milk sellers are well known for mixing water with milk.

పెట్టిపుట్టినవాడు **peTTipuTTinawaaDu** *n.* person blest with good fortune (*underlying meaning*: a person who gave liberally in a former birth and is rewarded in this birth).

పెట్టిపోయు **peTTipooyu** *v.i.* to give food (to s.o.) for maintenance.

పెట్టు **peTTu** I. *n.* **1** blow, stroke, slap; **goDDali** ~ (i) stroke of an axe; (ii) *fig.* severe blow; **okka** ~**na** at one stroke, suddenly, all at once; **cempa** ~ slap on the cheek; **naaku gooDa** ~ **cempa** ~ **reNDuu waccEEyi** I was between the devil and the deep sea (*lit.* a blow from the wall (on one side) and a slap on the cheek (from the other) both struck me). **2** equivalent; **naa balam padimandi** ~ my strength is equal to the strength of ten persons; **mugguri** ~ **waaDee tinnaaDu** he alone ate as much as three persons. II. *v.i.* to occur, happen, arise, form, be caused; **gontuloo uNDa peTTinaTTundi** it is as if (*or* I feel as if) a lump had formed in my throat; **naaku koddigaa cali peTTindi** I felt rather cold. III. *v.t.* **1** to place, put; *this root meaning varies idiomatically according to the context*, e.g., **ceTTu** ~ to plant a tree; **gooDa** ~ to build a wall; **guDLu** ~ to lay eggs; **baDi** ~ to establish a school; **mEESTarni** ~ to appoint a teacher; **naa miida tappu peTTEEru** they put the blame on me; **pani naa miida peTTi uuriki weLLEEDu** he entrusted the work to me and went to his village; **baaNam naamiida guri peTTEEDu** he aimed the arrow at me; **iSTam leenaTTu mokham peTTEEDu** he wore an unwilling look on his face; **waaNNi naaluguu peTTEEnu** I scolded him. **2** to give, present; **annam** ~ to give food; **nagalu** ~ to present jewellery. **3** to pay, spend, invest; **aydu ruupaayalu peTTi pustakam konnaanu** I spent five rupees on a book *or* I paid five rupees for a book; ~ **baDi** ~ to invest capital. **4** ~ *is used with certain nominal roots to form vbs.*, e.g., **santooSa** ~ to please; **bhaya** ~ to frighten. **5** *as an auxiliary* ~ *is used with a past participle* (i) *to give intensive force*, e.g., **wiDici** ~ to leave off; **daaci** ~ to hide; (ii) *to convey a request* **okka sahaayam ceesi peTTaNDi** please help me in just one thing *or* please do me just one favour.

పెట్టుకొను **peTTukonu** I. *v.i.* to have a relationship (with s.o.); **waaDitoo peTTukoni kuurconnaaDu** he established a rapport with him *or* he entered into an argument with him *or* he got talking to him; **waaDitoo peTTukoNTee laabham leedu, miiree ceeyaali** it is no use depending on him, you must do it yourself. II. *v.t.* **1** to put or keep for o.s.; **pillalni peTTukoni aa uuLLoo unnaaDu** he is living in that town keeping his children with him. **2** to put on things other than clothes, e.g., jewellery, bangles, glasses, watch. **3** to feel, experience, suffer from; **paścaattaapam** ~ to feel remorse; **benga** ~ *or* **digulu** ~ to worry; **jwaram** ~ to suffer from illness, have fever. **4** to undertake, busy o.s. with, be engaged upon, be[come] involved in; **eeweewoo wyaapakaalu peTTukonnaaDu** he engaged himself in several activities; **waccee nelaloo prayaaNam peTTukonnaanu** I plan to make a journey next month; **naatoo tagaadaa peTTukonnaaDu** he entered into a quarrel with me. **5** *other usages*: **panimaniSini** ~ to engage a servant maid; **umpuDukatteni** ~ to keep a mistress; **kampenii** ~ to set up a company; **peLLi muhuurtaalu** ~ to fix a date for a marriage; **mokhaana nawwu tecci peTTukonnaaDu** he forced himself to smile; **ee mukham peTTukoni naatoo maaTLaaDataawu?** how have you the face to speak to me?; **kanniiLLu** ~ to shed tears; **jñaapakam** ~ to remember; **kaaru naDipeeTappuDu oLLu daggira peTTukoni naDapaali** when you drive a car you must drive it cautiously; **oLLu daggira peTTukoni maaTLaaDu** be careful what you say (this implies a warning); **neenu ceppeedi burra daggira peTTukoni winu** listen attentively to what I am telling you; *see also* **panigaa** ~.

పెట్టుకోలు **peTTukoolu** I. *n.* simulating, pretending. II. *adj.* simulated, pretended, insincere; ~ **praśamsa** insincere praise; ~ **gaambhiiryam** feigned or pretended seriousness.

పెట్టుబడి **peTTubaDi** *n.* **1** investment, outlay. **2** capital.

పెట్టుబడిదారీ **peTTubaDidaarii** *adj.* capitalist[ic]; **wyawastha** capitalist system.

పెట్టుబడిదారు **peTTubaDidaaru** *n.* capitalist.

పెట్టుమందు **peTTumandu** *n.* love potion.

పెట్టె **peTTe** *n.* **1** box, chest. **2** compartment in a train.

పెట్టెబండి **peTTebaNDi** *n.* covered carriage.

పెట్టేబేడా **peTTeebeeDaa** *n.* luggage.

పెట్లదిమ్మె **peTLadimme** *n.* crude gun used for scaring birds and beasts from crops.

పెట్లు **peTLu** *same as* **peTulu.**

పెట్లుప్పు **peTLuppu** *n.* saltpetre, potassium nitrate.

పెడ **peDa** I. *n.* **1** side, direction. **2** cluster (part of a bunch) of plantains. II *adj.* **1** wrong, bad; ~ **daari** wrong road; ~ **bobba** dreadful yell. **2** back, hind, rear (of hand, ear, etc.); *cf.* **eDaapeDaa, eDamukham peDamukham.**

పెడ[సరం]కట్టె **peDa[saram]kaTTe** *n.* stubborn or obstinate person.

పెడకట్లు **peDakaTLu** *n.* tying a person's hands behind his back; **waaNNi** ~ **wirici kaTTEEru** they tied his hands behind his back.

పెడకొయ్య **peDakoyya** *adj.* (of persons, words, actions) arrogant, conceited.

పెడగా **peDagaa** *adv.* apart, at a distance; ~ **kuurconnawaaDu** person who is sitting apart.

పెడచెవిని పెట్టు **peDacewini peTTu** *v.t.* to turn a deaf ear to (*lit.* to turn the back of the ear to); **manam aayana sandeeśaanni peDacewini peDitee** if we turn a deaf ear to his message.

పెడసరం **peDasaram** *n.* stubbornness, obstinacy, perverseness.

పెడసరపు, పెడసరి **peDasarapu, peDasari** *adj.* stubborn, obstinate, perverse.

పెడాకులు **peDaakuḷu** *echo word, see* **peLLii** ~.

పెడుసు, పెళుసు **peDusu, peLusu** *adj.* **1** brittle, fragile. **2** (of words) harsh.

పెడ్డ **peDDa** *same as* **beDDa.**

పెణక **peNaka** *n.* 1 pent roof, one side of a sloping roof. 2 sunshade over a window.

పెత్తండ్రి, పెద్దయ్య **pettaNDri, peddayya** *n.* father's elder brother *or* mother's elder sister's husband.

పెత్తందారు **pettandaaru** *n.* 1 village elder. 2 respectable gentleman of a village. 3 *colloq.* **peLLi~** person who conducts negotiations for a wedding and presides over the wedding ceremonies.

పెత్తనం **pettanam** *n.* 1 old age (= **peddatanam**). 2 authority, control.

పెత్తనం చేయు **pettanam ceeyu** *v.i.* 1 to be in overall charge, supervise. 2 (*also* **pettanaaniki weLLu**) to go for a walk.

పెత్తనాలు **pettanaalu** *n.pl.* wandering about, paying visits.

పెత్తల్లి **pettalli** *n.* mother's elder sister *or* father's elder brother's wife.

పెద **peda** *alt. form of* **pedda.**

పెదవి **pedawi** *n.* (*pl.* **pedawulu** *or* **pedaalu**) lip.

పెద్ద **pedda** I. *n.* 1 senior, elder; **uuLLoo~lu** village elders. 2 chief, leader, head, principal person; **kula~** leader of a community; **baDi~** head boy of a school. 3 *idiomatic usage*: great person; **~raaya waccEEDu [kaani raayaleeka pooyEEDu]** he gave the impression (*or* he made people believe) that he could write, but he was not able to; *the underlying meaning is* he came forward as if he was a great person to write, but he could not write; *so also* **~naDustaanannaawu akkaNNinci [kaani naDawa leeka pooyEEwu]** you said you would walk from there, but you could not; **niikeem telusu ani ceppawaccEEwu~?** *lit.* what did you come to tell us that you know, as if you were a great person? i.e., what do you think you can tell us? (said sarcastically). II. *adj.* great, big, large, long (of distance, time), loud (of sound); **~wiidhi** broad street where the temple car is taken in procession in a town or village; **~roogam** serious disease; **~maaTalu** (i) boasting, (ii) disrespectful words; **~nooru** sharp tongue; **aayana ii wiSayamloo~tala paNDina tala** he is a man of wisdom and experience in this matter; **aame atanikaNTe aaru nelalu~** she is six months older than he.

పెద్ద కాపు **pedda kaapu** *n.* title given to a village headman in some areas.

పెద్ద కాలువ **pedda kaaluwa** *n.* main irrigation channel or canal.

పెద్దగా **peddagaa** *adv.* 1 much, to a great extent; **waaDu~ eemii tinaleedu** he did not eat to any great extent; **naaku aayanatoo~paricayam leedu** I am not very familiar with him; **reepu wastaanoo raanoo~ceppaleenu** I cannot say with any certainty whether I will come tomorrow or not. 2 loudly; **~maaTLaaDu/nawwu** to talk/laugh loudly.

పెద్దచెయ్యి **peddaceyyi** *n.* 1 experienced person. 2 generous nature or disposition (= **bhaarii ceyyi**).

పెద్దచేయు **peddaceeyu** *v.t.* 1 to glorify, make much of (a person). 2 to magnify.

పెద్దనిద్ర **peddanidra** *n.* death.

పెద్దనిద్ర పోవు **peddanidra poowu** *v.i.* to die.

పెద్దన్న **peddanna** *n.* 1 eldest brother in a family. 2 *colloq.* idiot, fool. 3 name of a poet in the emperor Krishnadevaraya's court.

పెద్ద పండగ **pedda paNDaga** *n.* chief day of a festival which lasts for several days.

పెద్ద పీట **pedda piiTa** *n.* seat of honour.

పెద్దపులి **peddapuli** *n.* tiger.

పెద్దపులుగు **peddapulugu** *n. class.* owl.

పెద్దపేగు **peddapeegu** *n. med.* colon, large intestine.

పెద్దబుద్ధి **peddabuddhi** *n.* bigheartedness, good heartedness, generosity.

పెద్దమనిషి **peddamaniSi** *n.* 1 gentleman; *pl.* **peddamanuSulu** gentlemen, gentry. 2 girl who has attained puberty.

పెద్దమనిషితనం **peddamaniSitanam** *n.* gentlemanliness.

పెద్దమ్మ **peddamma** *n.* 1 mother's elder sister *or* father's elder brother's wife. 2 respectable term used in referring to an elderly woman. 3 (*also* **peddi**) senior woman in a community; **caakali~** head woman member of a community of washermen. 4 a name of Jyeshta, elder sister of Lakshmi and goddess of poverty, misery and misfortune.

పెద్దయు **peddayu** *adv. class.* much, exceedingly.

పెద్దయ్య **peddayya** *same as* **pettaNDri.**

పెద్దరికం **peddarikam** *n.* 1 adulthood. 2 headship, leadership, authority; *see* **pinnarikam.**

పెద్దరోగం **peddaroogam** *n. colloq.* serious disease, dreadful disease.

పెద్ది **peddi** *see* **peddamma** *sense 3.*

పెద్దింటమ్మ **peddiNTamma** *n.* 1 name of a village goddess. 2 woman belonging to a wealthy family.

పెద్దల అమావాస్య, మహాలయ అమావాస్య **peddala amaawaasya, mahaalaya amaawaasya** *n.* new moon day in the month of Bhadrapadam when spirits of ancestors are worshipped.

పెన **pena** *n.* twist.

పెనం **penam** *n.* 1 frying pan. 2 iron plate for roasting grain.

పెనగు **penagu** *v.i.* 1 to be twisted, be twined. 2 to struggle.

పెనగులాట **penagulaaTa** *n.* 1 struggling. 2 wrangling.

పెనగులాడు **penagulaaDu** *v.i.* 1 to struggle, tussle. 2 to wrangle.

పెనగొను **penagonu** *v.i.* 1 to be twisted. 2 to be mixed or mingled.

పెనయు **penayu** *class. alt. form of* **penagu.**

పెనవేయు **penawweeyu** *v.t.* to twist, twine.

పెనవేసుకొను **penaweesukonu** *v.i. and t.* (*also* **penaweesukoni uNDu**) to be intertwined, be mixed, be mingled; **okadaannokaTi penaweesukoNTuu** each embracing (*or* each intertwining with) the other.

పెనిమిటి **penimiTi** *n.* husband.

పెను **penu** *adj.* great, big, strong, mighty; **~keeka** loud cry; **~gaali** strong wind; **~tuphaanu** severe cyclone; **~ciikaTi** pitch darkness.

పెనులోయ **penulooya** *n.* canyon.

పెనుసుకుపోవు **penusukupoowu** *v.i.* (of persons) to be on friendly terms with each other.

పెన్న **penna** *n.* River Pennar.

పెన్నిధి **pennidhi** *n.* treasure.

పెయ్య **peyya** *n.* **1** young cow, heifer. **2 kooDe~** young bull.

పెరటి చెట్టు **peraTi ceTTu** *n. lit.* tree or plant growing in o.'s own backyard; **~manduku paniki raadu** the tree in o.'s own backyard is no use for medicine (proverbial saying which conveys the meaning 'familiarity breeds contempt').

పెరటిదారి **peraTi daari** *n. lit.* road leading to the backyard: **~loo unnnaawu** you are on the wrong track.

పెరడు **peraDu** *n.* backyard.

పెరుకు **peruku** *v.t.* to pull up by the roots, pull out.

పెరుగు **perugu**[1] *n.* curds, yogurt; **~paccaDi** curds mixed with spices and vegetables.

పెరుగు **perugu**[2] *v.i.* **1** to grow, increase, accumulate. **2** (of temperature, prices) to rise. **3 golusu perigi pooyindi** the chain broke—*euphemistic expression*; *see* **golusu.**

పెరుగుతోటకూర **perugutooTakuura** *n.* a kind of green vegetable, *amaranthus gangeticus.*

పెరుగుదల **perugudala** *n.* growth, increase, development.

పెల్ల, పెళ్ల **pella, peLLa** *n.* **1** lump, clod; **maTTi~** clod of earth; **iTika~** broken piece of brick; **annam~** lump of cooked rice. **2** flake of plaster. **3 ii ~wirigi waaDimiida paDDadi** this misfortune has befallen him (*lit.* this clod has broken and fallen on him).

పెల్లగించు, పెళ్లగించు **pellagincu, peLLagincu** *v.t.* to dig up, uproot.

పెల్లున **pelluna** *same as* **peLLuna.**

పెల్లుబుకు **pellubuku** *v.i.* to well up, burst forth.

పెళపెళ **peLapeLa** *onom. adv.sug. sound of* crackling or rustling.

పెళుసు **peLusu** *same as* **peDusu.**

పెళ్ళాం, పెండ్లాం **peLLaam, peNDLaam** *n.* wife.

పెళ్లాడు, పెళ్లి చేసుకొను **peLLaaDu, peLLi ceesukonu** *v.t.* to marry (a spouse).

పెళ్లి, పెండ్లి **peLLi, peNDLi** *n.* marriage, wedding.

పెళ్లికాని **peLLikaani** *adj.* unmarried.

పెళ్లికూతురు **peLLikuuturu** *n.* bride.

పెళ్లికొడుకు **peLLikoDuku** *n.* **1** bridegroom. **2 ~**is also used of a young man in other auspicious ceremonies; *see* **kaaryam~, baarasaala~, waDaka~.**

పెళ్లి చీర **peLLi ciire** *n.* wedding sari.

పెళ్లిచూపులు **peLLicuupulu** *n.pl.* visit to look over a prospective bride.

పెళ్లి చేయు **peLLi ceeyu** *v.t.* **1** to perform a marriage. **2** to marry off (a son or daughter). **3** *colloq.* to punish; **allari ceestee nii peLLi ceestaanu cuuDu!** if you make a noise I will punish you, be careful!

పెళ్లితంతు **peLLitantu** *n.* wedding ceremony and all the connected ceremonies.

పెళ్లి నడక **peLLi naDaka** *n. colloq.* very slow walk (as in a marriage procession).

పెళ్లి పెద్ద **peLLi pedda** *n.* person who conducts negotiations and makes arrangements for a wedding.

పెళ్లివారు **peLLiwaaru** *n.pl.* persons assembled for a wedding, wedding party; **aaDa/moga~** bride's/bridegroom's party at a wedding.

పెళ్లీ పెటాకులు, పెళ్లీ పెడాకులు **peLLii peTaakulu, peLLii peDaakulu** *n. pl. colloq.* marriage; **niiku~ eemii leewaa**? are you not married?

పెళ్లీ పేరంటం **peLLii peeraNTam** *n.* wedding ceremony and the accompanying social ceremonies.

పెళ్లున, పెల్లున **peLLuna, pelluna** *adv.* **1** loudly; **~nawwEEDu** he burst out laughing. **2** much, greatly, excessively; **eNDa ~ kaasindi** the sunshine was extremely hot.

పెసర **pesara** *n.* (*gen. pl.* **pesalu**) greengram, *phaseolus mungo.*

పెసరట్టు **pesaraTTu** *n.* kind of pancake made with greengram flour.

పెసరపప్పు **pesarapappu** *n.* greengram dhall.

పే - pee

పేంబెత్తం, పేకబెత్తం **peembettam, peekabettam** *n.* cane.

పేక **peeka** *n.* **1** warp. **2** playing card.

పేకమేడ **peekameeDa** *n.* house of cards.

పేకాట **peekaaTa** *n.* game of cards.

పేకాడు **peekaaDu** *v.i.* to play cards.

పేగు, ప్రేగు **p[r]eegu** *n.* guts, intestines, entrails; **naa ~lu tiistunnaaDu** *or* **naa ~lu tooDeestunnaaDu** he is torturing me (*lit.* he is pulling at my entrails).

పేగు జారు **peegu jaaru** *v.i. with dative subject* to suffer from hernia.

పేగూపక్కా **peeguupakkaa** *same as* **pakkaapeeguu.**

పేచీ **peecii** *n.* **1** quarrel, dispute. **2** worry, trouble. **3** objection.

పేచీకోరు **peeciikooru** *n.* quarrelsome person.

పేచీపెట్టు **peeciipeTTu** *v.i.* **1** to cause a quarrel; **waari madhya peecii peTTEEDu** he created a quarrel between them. **2** (of a child) to cry for, keep on demanding; **mottam biskaT pEEkeT kaawaalani peecii peDutunnaaDu** he is crying to be given the whole biscuit packet. **3** to give trouble, cause worry. **4** to object; *see* **ippuDappuDee.**

పేచీ పెట్టుకొను, పేచీ తెచ్చుకొను **peecii peTTukonu, peecii teccukonu** *v.i.* to start a dispute, enter into a quarrel.

పేట **peeTa**[1] *n.* string or strand in a necklace; **oNTi~ golusu** necklace consisting of one strand.

పేట **peeTa**[2] *n.* ward or division of a town.

పేటిక **peeTika** *n. class.* chest, box.

పేటు **peeTu** *n.* patterned border of a cloth; **jarii~ciire** sari with a silver or gold lace border.

పేట్రేగు **peeTreegu** *v.i.* to exceed the limit (in anger).

పేడ **peeDa** *n.* dung of cattle.

పేడనీళ్లు **peeDaniiLLu** *n.* **1** water mixed with cowdung (used for sprinkling the front yard of a house). **2** *colloq.* **waaDi mokhaana~koTTEEru** they insulted him.

పేడపురుగు **peeDapurugu** *n.* beetle.

పేడవేయు **peeDaweeyu** *v.t.* to excrete.

పేడసుద్ద **peeDasudda** *n. colloq.* stick-in-the-mud person, one who does not move with the times.

పేడి **peeDi** I. *n.* impotent man. II *adj.* effeminate.

పేడు **peeDu** *n.* **1** thin strip or slat or splinter of wood; **kaTTe peeLLu weeyu** *or* **kaTTe peeLLeeyu** to split firewood into strips. **2** strip of bamboo or date palm leaf. **3** peel or rind of a gourd.

పేద **peeda** *adj.* poor; **~waaDu** poor man; **~raalu** poor woman.

పేదకోపం **peedakoopam** *n.* helpless anger, frustration.

పేదపడు **peedapaDu** *v.i.* **1** to become poor. **2** to become dejected.

పేదరాసిపెద్దమ్మ కథలు **peedaraasi peddamma kathalu** *n.pl.* fairy tales.

పేదరికం **peedarikam** *n.* poverty.

పేదాసాదా, పేదసాదలు **peedaasaadaa, peedasaadalu** *collective n.* the poor.

పేనం **peenam** *substandard form of* **praaNam.**

పెనా **peenaa** *n.* pen.

పేను **peenu**[1] *n.* **1** louse; *see* **kukku. 2** mite. **3** aphis.

పేను **peenu**[2] *v.i. and t.* to twist, entwine.

పేనుగుడ్డు, పేనుపిల్ల **peenuguDDu, peenupilla** *n.* nit.

పేప **peepa** *adj.* made of rattan cane.

పేము **peemu**[1] *n.* rattan cane.

పేము **peemu**[2] *v.t.* to smear; **ayskriimu tiNTuu mukham antaa ~ konnaaDu** while eating ice cream he smeared it all over his face.

పేయం **peeyam** *n. class.* s.g acceptable, s.g enjoyable.

పేర[ట], పేరిట **peera[Ta], peeriTa** *adv.* **1** in the name of; **aasti tana kuuturi~raasEEDu** he put (*lit.* he wrote) his property in his daughter's name. **2** bearing the name of, by the name of. **3** by name; **aayana~konnaaLLa kritam oka leekha raasEEnu** I wrote a letter to him by name some time ago.

పేరంటం **peeraNTam** *n.* married woman's visit to another's house on an auspicious occasion.

పేరంటాలు **peeraNTaalu**[1] *n.* **1** woman who attends a **peeraNTam. 2** woman who dies during her husband's lifetime.

పేరంటాలు **peeraNTaalu**[2] *second part of a n. compound* woman peddler; **mandula~** woman who goes from village to village peddling quack medicines.

పేరంటాలాకు, పేరంటాలికూర **peeraNTaalaaku, peeraNTaalikuura** *n. corchorus clitorius*, a herb used in cooking and for medicine.

పేరక్క **peerakka** *n. colloq.* elderly woman.

పేరణం, పేరిణి **peeraNam, peeriNi** *n.* kind of dance performed on an earthen pot.

పేరలుక **peeraluka** *n.* extreme offence, extreme displeasure.

పేరా **peeraa** *n.* paragraph.

పేరాస **peeraasa** *n.* extreme greed.

పేరిట **peeriTa** *same as* **peera.**

పేరిమి **peerimi** *same as* **peermi.**

పేరు **peeru**[1] *n.* **1** name; **~ettu** to mention a name; **naa~ deewuDu tirupati koNDa miida unnaaDu** the god after whose name I am called dwells on the Tirupati hill; **~peTTi pilucu** to call (s.o.) by name; **~ ~warasana andarinii pilicEEDu** he invited each and every one of them; **waaDi~phalam** *or* **waaDi~balam** his luck, his good or bad fortune: *see* **peTTindi ~**, **uuru**[1]. 2 fame, renown, celebrity, repute: **ceDDa ~** notoriety; **~ pondina, peerondina, ~ paDDa, ~ moosina** famous, renowned, celebrated, reputed: **panca paaNDawulaloo balaaniki ~ moosinawaaDu bhiimuDu** among the Pandava brothers the one renowned for strength was Bhima.

పేరు **peeru**[2] *n.* necklace of things strung together; **puusala ~** necklace of beads.

పేరు **peeru**[3] *adj. class.* great; *mod. only in certain phrases*, e.g., **peeraluka, peeraasa.**

పేరుకు **peeruku** *adv.* 1 nominally, in name. 2 for name's sake.

పేరుకొను **peerukonu** *v.i.* 1 to coagulate, curdle. 2 to congeal, solidify. 3 (of silt, rubbish) to collect, gather. 4 (of work, debt) to accumulate, mount up, pile up.

పేరోలగం **peeroolagam** *n. class.* king's court.

పేర్కొనదగిన **peerkonadagina** *adj.* worthy of mention, notable, noteworthy.

పేర్కొను **peerkonu** *v.t.* 1 to mention, state, point out. 2 to refer to, call; **aagam ceesee waarini aakataayigaa peerkonaDam undi** persons who create disturbance (**aagam**) are referred to as (*or* are called) **aakataayi.** 3 to cite (example). 4 to commend. 5 to denote, name, designate, nominate.

పేర్చు **peercu** *v.t.* 1 to pile up, heap up, stack. 2 to arrange, place in position. 3 **iTikalu ~** to lay bricks. 4 to lay out (chessmen or caroms on a board in preparation for a game or dolls in preparation for **bommala koluwu**).

పేర్నెయ్యి **peerneyyi** *n.* solidified ghee.

పేర్పు **peerpu** *n.* 1 heaping, piling up. 2 arranging, arrangement.

పేర్మి, పేరిమి **peer[i]mi** *n. class.* 1 greatness. 2 eminence. 3 affection, love.

పేలగింజలు, పేలాలు **peelaginijalu, peelaalu** *n.pl.* fried or roasted grain, popcorn.

పేలపిండి **peelapiNDi** *n.* flour made from roasted grain; **~ muuTa gaTTukonu** (i) to get ready for a journey, taking **peelapiNDi** for food on the way; (ii) *colloq.* to be on the point of death; **~ muuTa gaTTukoni kuurcunnaaDu** he is on the point of death, he is ready to travel to the next world.

పేలవ **peelawa** *adj.* weak, faint, feeble, gentle; **~ haasam** slight smile.

పేలాపన, ప్రేలాపన **p[r]eelaapana** *n.* rambling talk, aimless talk.

పేలిక **peelika** *n.* scrap of cloth or paper; **guDDa ~** rag.

p[r]eelu[1] *v.i.* 1 to burst, explode. 2 to erupt; **oLLu peelindi** the body erupted (with prickly heat rash). 3 (of a gun) to be fired, go off. 4 *colloq.* **mii jooku peela leedu** your joke misfired (colloq.) 5 **cempa peela koTTu** to give a hard slap on the cheek.

పేలు, ప్రేలు **p[r]eelu**[2] *v.i. and t.* to babble, prate, talk nonsense.

పేలు **peelu**[3] *pl. of* **peenu.**

పేల్చు **peelcu** *v.t.* 1 to explode, detonate; **tupaaki ~** to fire a gun (**-miida,** at). 2 to blow up. 3 *colloq.* **naa miida jooku peelcEEru** they played a joke on me.

పేవు **peewu** *alt. form of* **peegu.**

పేషకం **peeSakam** *n.* crusher, pulveriser.

పేషణం **peeSaNam** *n. class.* grinding, crushing, pulverising.

పేసం **peesam** *n.* fruit pulp.

పై - pay

పై **pay** I. *adj.* **1** upper, higher; ~ **adhikaarulu** higher authorities; ~ **caduwulu** higher studies; ~ **ceeyi** upper hand, superiority. **2** outer, external; ~ **sambandham** marriage alliance with s.o. outside the family circle. **3** coming, next; ~ **paNTa** next harvest; ~ **eeDaadi** the coming year. **4** strange, unfamiliar; ~ **waaDu** stranger; ~ **uuru** strange or unfamiliar town. **5** additional, extra; **ayduguru** ~ **manuSulu bhoojanaaniki waccEEru** five extra people came to dinner; **muuDu kiloola** ~ **ciluku** three kilos and odd; **pratii ettukii** ~ **ettu uNTundi** for every trick there will be a counter trick; ~ **sampaadana** extra earnings (i.e., illegal gratification). **6** excessive; **aDigeewaaLLu ewaruu leeru,** ~ **tiruguLLu tirugutunnaaDu** there is no one to question him, he roams about excessively. II. *p.p.* above, on top of, over, on.

పైకం **paykam** *n.* money.

పైకప్పు **paykappu** *n.* **1** roof. **2** ceiling.

పైకి **payki** *adv.* **1** upwards. **2** outwardly, externally; ~ **baagaanee unnaaDu** outwardly he appears quite all right; ~ **kanipincaleedu** it was not visible from outside. **3** aloud, out loud; ~ **caduwu** to read aloud; ~ **ceppaNDi** (i) please speak out loud, (ii) please speak out openly.

పైకి ఎత్తు, పైకెత్తు **payki ettu, payketttu** *v.t.* to raise up, hoist.

పైకొను **paykonu** *v.i. class.* to attack, rush upon.

పైగంబరు **paygambaru** *n.* Muslim prophet.

పైగా **paygaa** *adv.* **1** besides, moreover. **2** nevertheless. **3** more than; **sagam**~ more than half; **nuuTiki**~ more than a hundred; **reNDu gaNTalaku**~ for more than two hours.

పైజామా **payjaamaa** *n.* **1** loose trousers made of plain material for daily wear. **2** pyjamas for night wear.

పైట **payTa** *n.* loose end of a sari worn over the left shoulder (= **pamiTa**).

పైఠాన్ **payThaan** *n.* kind of cloth.

పైడి **payDi** *n.* gold.

పైతృక **paytṛka** *adj.* **1** paternal. **2** ancestral (referring to paternal ancestors).

పైత్యం **paytyam** *n.* **1** *med.* biliousness. **2** eccentricity, craziness; **paytyaana paDinaTLu maaTLaaDutunnaaDu** he talks as if he was out his mind . **3 kaaLidaasu kawitwam konta naa** ~ **konta** Kalidas' verse (the truth) is such and such, my version (partly fiction) is such and such (proverb meaning 'I have not stuck strictly to the truth').

పైత్యకారి **paytyakaari** *n.* crazy person.

పైత్యప్రకోపం **paytyaprakoopam** *n.* bilious or irritable temperament.

పైత్యరసం **paytyarasam** *n.* bile.

పైత్యవికారం **paytyawikaaram** *n.* **1** biliousness. **2** morning sickness.

పైత్యాంతకం **paytyaantakam** *n.* Ayurvedic remedy against biliousness; *see* **antakam.**

పైన **payna** I. *p.p.* **1** on, above, over; **tiNDi** ~ **kharcupeTTu** to spend money on food; **bassu/reyilu**~ **waccEEDu** he came on (*or* by) the bus/train; **bhagawantuDi** ~ **bhaaram** it is in God's hands (*lit.* the burden is upon God). **2** on top of, over and above, in addition to; **aa** ~ in addition to that. **3** more than; **aayana daggira wanda ruupaayala** ~ **undi** he has more than a hundred rupees on him. II. *adv.* **1** on top, above, upstairs. **2** in addition, over and above; **idi kharcu peTTaNDi,** ~ **paDitee neenu cuustaanu** you spend this amount, over and above that I will see to it.

పైనవాడు **paynawaaDu** *n.* He who is above, i.e., God.

పైని **payni** *alt. form of* **payna**, *sense I.*

పైపంచె **paypance** *n.* man's upper cloth (**uttariiyam**).

పైపూత **paypuuta** *n.* ointment.

పైపెచ్చు **paypeccu** I. *n.* outer skin or peel of fruit. II *adv.* **1** in addition, furthermore, moreover. **2** on the other hand.

పైపై **paypay** *adj.* superficial, cursory.

పైపైన **paypayna** *adv.* on the surface, superficially, outwardly.

పైపై మెరుగులు **paypay merugulu** *n.pl.* glamour.

పైప్రాణాలు **paypraaNaalu** *n.pl. colloq.* o.'s senses; **waarini cuuDagaanee naa** ~ **paynee [egiri] pooyEEyi** as soon as I saw them, I fainted.

పైబడు **paybaDu** *v.i.* **1** to attack, fall upon; **naa miidaku paybaDDaaru** they attacked me. **2** to exceed, be in excess of; **nuuru ekaraalu paybaDDa aasti** property in excess of a hundred acres; **araway eeLLu paybaDinawaaru** persons over sixty years of age.

పైరగాలి, పైరుగాలి **payragaali, payrugaali** *n.* **1** fresh wind. **2** cool breeze from the southeast which is beneficial to crops.

పైరు **payru** *n.* crop.

పైలా పచ్చీసు, పహలా పచ్చీస్ **paylaa pacciisu, pahalaa pacciis** *n.* prime of life (*lit.* the first twenty-five years of a man's life); **ceppina maaTa winaleedu,** ~ **gaa tirugutunnaaDu** he does not listen to what people say, he acts as he pleases.

పైశాచి **payśaaci** *n.* name of one of the Prakrit languages.

పైశాచిక **payśaacika** *adj.* devilish.

పైసా **paysaa** *n.* **1** paisa, one hundredth of a rupee. **2** pie, an obsolete coin, one twelfth of an anna.

పొ - po

పొంకం **ponkam** *n.* 1 beauty, grace, elegance. 2 appropriateness. 3 pride, haughtiness.

పొంకంగా **ponkangaa** *adv.* 1 beautifully, gracefully, elegantly. 2 properly, effectively. 3 proudly.

పొంకణం **ponkaNam** *n.* 1 purse. 2 pouch.

పొంగరాలు **pongaraalu** *n.pl.* kind of cake.

పొంగలి **pongali** *n.* 1 rice cooked with milk and dhall presented to a deity by persons entering a new house or embarking on a new undertaking. 2 sacrifice of a goat or fowl to a village goddess. 3 Pongal, a name for the Sankranti festival.

పొంగలి పెట్టు **pongali peTTu** *v.i.* to make an animal sacrifice.

పొంగారు **pongaaru** *v.i.* 1 to be full. 2 to excel. 3 to rejoice. 4 to be proud.

పొంగించు **ponginicu** *v.t.* to boil, cook by boiling; **paalu ponginci iNTLooki weLLEEru** (i) they boiled milk and entered the house; (ii) they prepared **pongali** and entered the house for the first time.

పొంగు **pongu**[1] I. *n.* boiling, bubbling up; **paalu ~ raagaanee** as soon as the milk bubbles up *or* as soon as the milk boils. II. *v.i.* 1 to boil. 2 (*also* **pongipor[a]lu**) to bubble up, overflow, boil over. 3 to surge, swell. 4 (of a river) to be in full spate. 5 to be thrilled, be overjoyed, exult. 6 to be proud, be elated; **aa wiirulu neeDu batiki uNTee enta pongipooyi uNDeewaaroo**! if those heroes were alive today, how proud they would be!

పొంగు **pongu**[2] *n.* chicken pox.

పొంగు **pongu**[3] *n. dial.* cheap kind of cake.

పొంచి[ఉండి]చూచు **ponci[uNDi]cuucu** *v.i.* to peep.

పొంచి[ఉండి]దూకు **ponci[uNDi]duuku** *v.i.* to pounce.

పొంచి[ఉండి]విను **ponci[uNDi]winu** *v.i.* to eavesdrop.

పొంచు, పొంచి ఉండు **poncu, ponci uNDu** *v.i.* 1 to lie in wait, crouch, lurk. 2 to impend.

పొంత **ponta**[1] *n.* large pot for boiling water.

పొంత **ponta**[2] *n. class.* nearness; *cf.* **antupontu.**

పొంత **ponta**[3] *dial. variant of* **weNTa.**

పొంతన **pontana** *n.* 1 matching, suitability (e.g., of the horoscopes of a prospective bride and bridegroom). 2 convenience, feasibility; **miiku ~ aytee, naaku ii pani ceesi peTTaNDi** if it is convenient for you, please do this for me; **maa iNTLoo raatri puuTa caduwukooDaaniki ~ kaawaDam leedu** in our house it is not feasible to study in the night time. 3 agreeability of temperament; **waaDikii naakuu ~ leedu** he and I do not get on well together.

పొందించు **pondincu** *v.t.* to cause to obtain, cause to acquire, cause to experience.

పొందిక **pondika** *n.* 1 fitness, suitability, convenience, appropriateness. 2 agreement, harmony, compatibility, coherence.

పొందికగా **pondikagaa** *adv.* 1 fitly, conveniently, suitably, to suit; **nalugurikii ~ naalugu gadulu unnaayi iNTLoo** there are four rooms in the house for four persons (*or* to suit four persons); **~ naalugu jatala baTTalu uNTee caalu** if you have four sets of clothes, that will be enough (*or* that will suit). 2 neatly, tidily, properly; **~ peercina ginnelu** vessels piled up tidily; **~ kuurcoo**! sit up properly!

పొందు **pondu** I. *n.* 1 fitness, suitability, aptness. 2 harmony, friendship; **waaLLa madhya ~ kudirindi** friendship arose between them. 3 obtaining. 4 sexual intercourse. II. *v.t.* 1 to gain, acquire, get, attain, obtain, achieve. 2 to experience, feel, undergo, suffer, derive. 3 to receive, win, be granted, be accorded.

పొందుపడు **pondupaDu** *v.i.* to suit, be appropriate, be convenient, be practicable; **miiku pondupaDitee naaku aa pustakaalu koni iwwaNDi** if it is convenient to you please buy those books for me; **pondupaDitee reNDu peLLiLLu kalipi ceestaanu** if it turns out to be practicable I will perform both the marriages at the same time.

పొందుపరచు **ponduparacu** *v.t.* 1 to provide, furnish, supply. 2 to make available, present, set forth (information).

పొక్క **pokka** *n.* pit, hole.

పొక్కిలి **pokkili** *n.* navel.

పొక్కు **pokku**[1] *n.* boil, blister, pimple.

పొక్కు **pokku**[2] *v.i.* 1 to be blistered. 2 (of boils, blisters) to erupt, break out. 3 (of news) to emerge, come out, come to light; **prajala samasyalanu patrikalu pratibimbincaali gaani payki pokkakuNDaa aNacakuuDadu** newspapers must reflect the people's problems and not prevent their coming to light.

పొగ **poga** *n.* smoke; *see* **sega.**

పొగగూడు, పొగగొట్టం **pogaguuDu, pogagoTTam** *n.* chimney.

పొగచుట్ట **pogacuTTa** *n.* cigar.

పొగచూరు **pogacuuru** *v.i.* to be begrimed, be sooty, be black with smoke.

పొగడ **pogaDa** *n.* a tree, *mimusops elengi.*

పొగడం **pogaDam** *same as* **pagaDam.**

పొగడిక **pogaDika** *n.* praise, commendation.

పొగడికోలు **pogaDikoolu** *n.* self-praise.

పొగడు **pogaDu** *v.t.* to praise, applaud, commend, eulogise, compliment.

పొగడ్త **pogaDta** *n.* act of praising, praise.

పొగతాగు, పొగత్రాగు **pogat[r]aagu** *v.i.* to smoke (cigarettes, etc.); **~ t[r]aagaraadu** no smoking (public notice).

పొగపు **pogapu** *dial. form of* **poopu.**

పొగపెట్టు **pogapeTTu** *v.i.* 1 to make smoke; **poga peDitee doomalu pootaayi** if you make smoke the mosquitoes will go. 2 *colloq.* to give a hint; **pommanakkaraleedu pogapeDitee caalu** you need not tell him to go, if you give a hint it will be enough.

పొగమంచు **pogamancu** *n.* fog.

పొగరు **pogaru** I. *n.* pride, presumption, arrogance, insolence. II. *adj.* 1 proud, insolent. 2 headstrong, unruly.

పొగరుపోతు, పొగరుబోతు, పొగరుమోతు **pogarupootu, pogarubootu, pogarumootu** I. *n.* arrogant or insolent person. II *adj.* arrogant, insolent.

పొగరుబోత్తనం, పొగరుమోత్తనం **pogaruboottanam, pogarumoottanam** *n.* arrogance.

పొగ వదులు **poga wadulu** *v.i.* to puff smoke.

పొగాకు **pogaaku** *n.* tobacco.

పొటమరించు **poTamarincu** *v.i.* 1 (of a young shoot, boil) to swell. 2 *fig.* to well up, burst forth.

పొటమరింపు **poTamarimpu** *n.* protruberance, swelling.

పొటికిపోవు **poTikipoowu** *v.i.* to rot or decay internally.

పొటేలు **poTeelu** *same as* **poTTeelu.**

పొట్ట **poTTa**[1] *n.* 1 stomach, belly; ~ **kaalitee** (*or* ~ **maaDitee**) **waaDee wastaaDu** when he is hungry (*lit.* when his stomach burns) he will come of his own accord; **waaDidi jaaneDu** ~ *lit.* his stomach is only a span in size, *meaning* his is a very small stomach (expression used of a person with a small appetite); ~ **pagileelaa tinnaaDu** he ate like a glutton; ~ **pagileelaa nawwEEDu** he burst his sides with laughing; ~ **ciilistee** (*or* ~ **koostee**) **akSaram mukka leeniwaaDu** person with no trace of education in him, illiterate person; ~ **maaDcukoni Dabbu sampaadincEEDu** he earned money by depriving himself; **tala** ~ **loo peTTukonnaaDu** he hid his head due to shame; ~ **[loo annam] kadalakuNDaa kuurcunnaaDu** he is sitting at ease; ~ **pencu** to grow prosperous by illegal means; **nuwwu** ~ **ku tineedi annamaa?gaDDEE?** do you eat rice or grass? i.e., are you a man or a beast? 2 subsistence, living, livelihood; ~ **gaDupukonu** (*or* ~ **poosukonu**) to earn a livelihood; ~ **ceetitoo puccukoni** (*or* ~ **ceetitoo paTTukoni**) **ii uuru waccEEnu** I have come here to earn my living; ~ **miida koTTu** to deprive (s.o.) of his livelihood; **waaDi** ~ **karigincaali** you must make him work hard; ~ **peTTukonu**(i) to kill; (ii) to steal; **naa Dabbu** ~ **peTTukonnaaDu** he swallowed my money.

పొట్ట **poTTa**[2] *n.* unopened ear of corn.

పొట్ట పోసుకొను **poTTa poosukonu** *v.i. lit.* to nourish o.'s own stomach, i.e., (i) to earn o.'s livelihood; (ii) to appropriate (s.g) to o.'s own use.

పొట్టి **poTTi** I. *n.* shortness (of stature). II. *adj.* short; ~ **waaDu** short person.

పొట్టు **poTTu** *n.* 1 s.g that has been reduced to trash or dust or pulp, such as husk of grain or trash left after threshing pulses (used as cattle fodder). 2 **panasa** ~ **kuura** curry made of minced jackfruit. 3 **rampam** ~ sawdust.

పొట్టుకొట్టు **poTTukoTTu** *v.t.* to mince (meat, etc.).

పొట్టుపప్పు **poTTupappu** *n.* pulses with their husk.

పొట్టుపొయ్యి **poTTupoyyi** *n.* hearth in which husk is burnt as fuel.

పొట్టేలు, పొటేలు **poTTeelu, poTeelu** *n.* ram.

పొట్ల [కాయ] **poTLa[kaaya]** *n.* snake gourd.

పొట్లం **poTLam** *n.* 1 parcel, package. 2 packet.

పొట్లెం **poTLem** *n.* pampered child.

పొడ **poDa** *n.* 1 appearance, trace, form; **ippuDee eNDa** ~ **waccindi** a trace of sunshine has just appeared. 2 spot or mark of one colour on the background of another colour; **ii mokka nallaTi** ~ **la tellaTi puulu puustundi** this plant produces white flowers with black spots on them. 3 scab on skin due to ringworm or similar disease.

పొడకట్టు **poDakaTTu** *v.i.* 1 to appear, be visible, be in sight. 2 to be[come] evident.

పొడగు, పొడవు, పొడుగు, పొడువు **poDagu, poDawu, poDugu, poDuwu** I. *n.* 1 height, tallness. 2 length. II. *adj.* 1 high, tall. 2 long.

పొడచూపు **poDacuupu** *v.i.* to appear.

పొడము **poDamu** *v.i. class.* to occur, arise; **anumaanamu poDaminadi** suspicion arose.

పొడవునా **poDawunaa** *adv.* for the entire length of, all along, all through, throughout; **komma** ~ all along the branch; **katha** ~ all through the story; **samwatsaram** ~ throughout the year.

పొడి **poDi** I. *n.* 1 powder, dust. 2 *same as* **poDum.** 3 precious stone; **erra poLLa tammeTLu** earnings set with red stones. 4 *colloq.* telling remark; **wiiDu ceppina maaTaki waaDu koncem** ~ **tagilincEEDu** in response to what A said, B made a telling remark. II. *adj.* 1 dry; **waataawaraNam** ~ **gaa uNTundi** the weather will be dry; ~ **bellam** dry jaggery or powdered jaggery (unrefined sugar); ~ **daggu** dry cough. 2 *fig.* plain, bare; ~ **metukulu** plain cooked rice with nothing added; ~ **akSaraalu** initials; **sneehitulu okarinokaru** ~ **akSaraalatoo pilucukonee waaLLu. pii naageeśwara raawu 'PNR'** friends used to call each other by their initials. P. Nageswara Rao was PNR; ~ **mukkalu** (i) (*also* ~ **maaTalu**) plain words, simple words; (ii) playing cards which are neither aces nor court cards (i.e. cards bearing numbers from 2 to 10).

పొడిగించు **poDigincu** *v.t.* to lengthen, increase, extend, stretch out, prolong.

పొడిచి వేయు, 'పొడిచేయు **poDici weeyu, poDiceeyu** I. *v.i. colloq.* to excel, surpass, do better; **waaDu cadawaleedu saree, nuwwu eem poDiceesEEwu? niikuu mupphayi maarkulee waccEEyi** I grant that he did not study, but were you any better? you also only got thirty marks; **waaDu weLLi Dabbu teeleedu, ika nuwwu weLLi poDiceeyaali** he went but did not bring the money, now you must go and do better. II. *v.t.* to prick, pierce, stab, jab.

పొడి చేయు **poDi ceeyu**[1] *v.t.* to make (s.g) into powder, pulverise.

పొడిచేయు **poDiceeyu**[2] *see* **poDiciweeyu.**

పొడుం, పొడి **poDum, poDi** *n.* snuff.

పొడుంపట్టు **poDumpaTTu** *n.* pinch of snuff.

పొడుం పీల్చు **poDum piilcu** *v.i.* to inhale or take snuff.

పొడుగు **poDugu** *same as* **poDagu.**

పొడుచు **poDucu** I. *v.i.* (of sun, moon, star) to rise. II. *v.t.* 1 to prick, pierce, stab, jab. 2 to punch, prod (with fist, elbow). 3 (of a crow) to peck. 4 (of a bull, ram) to butt, gore.

పొడుచుకొను, పొడుచుకు వచ్చు **poDucukonu, poDucuku waccu** *v.i.* to stick up, stick out, protrude; **wittanaalu molici payki poDucuku waccEEyi** the seeds sprouted and sprang up; **waaNNi tiDitee koopam poDucuku waccindi** when he was abused his wrath flared up.

పొడుపు **poDupu** *n.* **1** piercing, stabbing. **2** rising (of sun, moon, star).

పొడుపు[డు] కథ **poDupu[Du]katha** *n.* riddle, conundrum, enigma.

పొడువు **poDuwu** *same as* **poDagu.**

పొణక **poNaka** *n.* **1** large grain storage basket. **2** basket for carrying articles on a cart.

పొణుకు **poNuku** *n.* (*also* **~ karra, ~ kalapa**) kind of light wood from which Kondapalle dolls are made.

పొతక **potaka** *n.* bundle of leaves; **~ laaNTi** fat, stout.

పొత్తం **pottam** *corrupt form of* **pustakam.**

పొత్తర **pottara** *n.* bundle of leaves.

పొత్తరం **pottaram** *same as* **potram.**

పొత్తి **potti** *n.* **1** old and soft piece of cloth. **2 araTi~** soft skin round the trunk of a plantain tree. **3 pooka~** sheath round the crown of an arecanut palm.

పొత్తికడుపు **pottikaDupu** *n.* abdomen, part of the stomach below the navel.

పొత్తిగుడ్డ **pottiguDDa** *n.* baby linen.

పొత్తిళ్లు **pottiLLu** *n.pl.* **1** baby linen. **2** dolls' clothes.

పొత్తు **pottu** *n.* **1** friendship. **2** partnership, association, cooperation; **oNTeddu~** joint cultivation in which each cultivator contributes one working bullock.

పొత్తు కుడుపు **pottu kuDupu** *n.* eating together from the same plate.

పొత్తు సేద్యం **pottu seedyam** *n.* joint cultivation.

పొత్రం, పొత్తరం **potram, pottaram** *n.* upper grinding stone of a mortar.

పొద **poda** *n.* bush, shrub.

పొదరిల్లు **podarillu** *n.* bower, arbour.

పొది **podi** *n.* **1** box, case; **mangali~** barber's box containing his equipment. **2 ammula~** quiver.

పొదివిపట్టుకొను **podiwi paTTukonu** *v.t.* **1** to hold under one arm; **pustakam podiwi paTTukoni weLLEEDu** he went away with the book under his arm. **2** to carry in both arms; **pillani podiwi paTTukoni meTLu ekkEEDu** he climbed the stairs with the child in his arms.

పొదుగు **podugu**[1] *n.* udder.

పొదుగు, పొదువు **podugu**[2]**, poduwu** *v.t.* **1** to cover, surround, envelop. **2** to embrace, clasp. **3** to set (precious stones). **4** to hatch, incubate (eggs). **5** *fig.* to ponder, brood over, ruminate on.

పొదుపరి **podupari** *n.* thrifty or frugal person.

పొదుపరితనం **poduparitanam** *n.* thrift, frugality.

పొదుపు **podupu** *n.* **1** savings; **jaatiiya ~ udyamam** national savings movement. **2** thrift, frugality, economy.

పొదుపుచేయు **podupuceeyu** *v.t.* **1** to save. **2** to economise.

పొదుపైన **podupayna** *adj.* thrifty, economical.

పొద్దస్తమానం, పొద్దుగూకులు **poddastamaanam, podduguukulu** *adv. colloq.* all day long.

పొద్దు, ప్రొద్దు **p[r]oddu** *n.* **1** sun; **~ poDupu** sunrise. **2** time; **ciikaTi~** night time; **okka ~ uNDu** to eat only one meal per day. **3** *pl.* **~ lu** time for a woman's delivery.

పొద్దుకాల, పొద్దుగాల, పొద్దున **poddukaala, poddugaala, podduna** *adv.* in the morning.

పొద్దుతిరుగుడు పువ్వు **poddutiruguDu puwwu** *n.* sunflower, *helianthus annuus* (= **suuryakaantam**).

పొద్దు పుచ్చు **poddu puccu** *v.i.* to pass the time, spend time.

పొద్దుపోవు **poddu poowu** *v.i.* **1** to be late; **tommidi gaNTalaku rammaNTee, poddu pooyEEka waccEEDu** when he had been told to come at nine o'clock, he came late; **miiru raawaDam poddu pooyindi** *lit.* the time of your coming is late; i.e., you have come late; **raatri baagaa poddu pooyEEka** very late at night. **2** *colloq.* (of time) to pass; **poddu poowaDamkoosam eeweewoo wyaapakaalu peTTukonnaanu** I undertook various activities in order to make the time pass.

పొద్దూకుమాట్ల **podduukumaaTLa** *adv. colloq.* at sunset.

పొద్దూకులూ **podduukuluu** *adv. colloq.* all day long.

పొద్దెదురు **poddeduru** *n. colloq.* adverse or inauspicious circumstances; **waaDu ee pani ceeyapoyinaa poddeduree** whatever work he proceeded to undertake, circumstances were against him.

పొన్న **ponna**[1] *adj. obs.* golden.

పొన్న, పొన్నాగం, పున్నాగం **ponna**[2]**, ponnaagam, punnaagam** *n.* alexandrian laurel, *carophyllum inophyllum*, a bush with scented yellow flowers.

పొన్నగంటికూర **ponnagaNTi kuura** *n. alternanthera sessilis*, a green vegetable.

పొన్నారి **ponnaari** *adj.* golden; *mod. only in* **cinnaari baalalu/pillalu** darling little children.

పొన్ను **ponnu** *n.* **1** gold. **2** ring or ferrule on a pestle or stick.

పొన్నుకర్ర **ponnukarra** *n.* walking stick.

పొప్పర **poppara** *n. dial.* outer skin of a fruit.

పొయ్యి, ప్రొయ్యి **p[r]oyyi** *n.* hearth, fireplace.

పొయ్యిల్లు **poyyillu** *n. dial.* kitchen.

పొర **pora** *n.* **1** layer; **~ lu ~ lugaa** in layers. **2** stratum. **3** film, membrane. **4** thin skin, e.g., of an onion; **ulli~ laalcii** shirt made of very fine cloth. **5** snake's skin.

పొరంబోకు **porambooku** *n. same as* **poorambooku** *sense I.*

పొరక, పరక **poraka, paraka** *n.* **1** broom. **2** *dial.* green leaf manure.

పొరపడు **porapaDu** *v.i.* to be mistaken, make a mistake, be wrong, blunder.

పొరపాటు **porapaaTu** I. *n.* mistake, error, oversight, fault. II *adj.* wrong, mistaken.

పొరపాటున **porapaaTuna** *adv.* **1** by mistake, mistakenly, wrongly. **2** accidentally, by chance.

పొరపొచ్చెం, పొరపు, పొరుపు **porapoccem, porapu, porupu** *n.* dispute, disagreement, difference of opinion, quarrel.

పొరపోవు **porapoowu** *same as* **polamaaru.**

పొరుగు **porugu** I. *n.* neighbourhood, vicinity. II. *adj.* neighbouring; *cf.* **irugu~**

పొర్లిపోవు, పొరలిపోవు **por[a]li poowu** *v.i.* to overflow, flow away, pour out.

పొర్లివచ్చు, పొరలివచ్చు **por[a]li waccu** *v.i.* to come pouring out.

పొర్లు, పొరలు **por[a]lu** I. *n.* **1** overflowing. **2** weir which allows excess water to escape from an irrigation tank. II. (*also* **por[a]laaDu**) *v.i.* **1** to roll. **2** to overflow; *cf.* **pongi-por[a]lu.** **3** (of a cow) to be crossed.

పొర్లుదండాలుపెట్టు, పొరలుదండాలు పెట్టు **por[a]lu daNDaalu peTTu** *v.i.* to perform a vow by going round the perimeter of a temple rolling over and over on the ground.

పొలం **polam** *n.* cultivated land, field.

పొలంపుట్ర **polampuTra** *n.* fields and so on; **maa tammu-Du iNTidaggiree uNDi ~ cuucukoNTunnaaDu** my younger brother stays at home and looks after our fields and so on.

పొలతి **polati** *n. class.* woman.

పొలపొల **polapola** *onom. adv. sug.* severe blistering; **eNDawEELa isakaloo naDistee arikaaLLu ~ pokkutaayi** if you walk on the sand in sunshine, the soles of your feet will be severely blistered.

పొలమారు, పొరపోవు, పలకమారు **polamaaru, porapoowu, palakamaaru** *v.i.* (of food, drink) to go down the wrong way when being swallowed; **annam tiNTunnap-puDu polamaarindi waaDiki** when he was eating some rice, it went down the wrong way (= **korapoowu**),

పొలి **poli** *n.* **1** sacrifice made to village deities at harvest time. **2** ceremony performed in honour of village deities at harvest time. **3** name of the demon who presides over the harvest; he was conquered by Vishnu and is also known as Bali or Mahabali.

పొలికట్టె **polikaTTe** *n.* broom made of redgram branches for sweeping a threshing floor.

పొలికేక **polikeeka** *n.* **1** loud shout or yell. **2** cry uttered during the poli ceremony at harvest time, e.g., the words **poliyoo poli!** or **raaraa poli!** by a man walking round the threshing floor carrying a tray of grain.

పొలితిరుగు **politirugu** *v.i.* **1** to walk round the threshing floor at harvest time uttering the words of the **polikeeka.** **2** *colloq.* to wander about freely; **pariikSalu ayipooyEEka uurantaa poli (or bali) tirigi waccEEDu** when the examinations were over he went about the town just as he pleased.

పొలిమేర **polimeera** *n.* territorial limit, boundary, village boundary.

పొలుసు **polusu** *n.* (of fish) scale.

పొల్లు **pollu** *n.* **1** empty ears of corn. **2** chaff, trash left over after threshing. **3** worthless stuff. **4** *gram.* (*also* ~ **hallu**) bare consonant with no vowel attached. **5 akSaram ~ pookuNDaa jarigindantaa naaku ceppEEDu** he told me everything that had happened without omitting the smallest detail.

పొల్లుకాడు **pollukaaDu** *n.* s.o. not worthy of consideration, useless person.

పొల్లుమాట **pollumaaTa** *n.* **1** trashy or worthless remark or saying. **2** improper or objectionable remark or saying.

పొసగించు **posagincu** *v.i.* to cause to agree, bring to terms.

పొసగు, పొసుగు **posagu, posugu** *v.i.* to agree, suit, be compatible, be consistent; **waaLLa iddarikii posagaDam leedu** those two are not getting on well together.

పొసుగుడు **posuguDu** *n. slang* procuring for prostitution.

పో - poo

పోక **pooka**[1] *n.* arecanut; ~**cekka** *dial.* piece of arecanut; ~**tooTa** arecanut plantation.

పోక **pooka**[2] *n.* going, departure; **weLLi aydu nimiSaalaloo rammaNTee adee~pooyEEDu** I told him to go and come back in five minutes but he went away for good (*or* but he has been away for a long time).

పోక ఉండ **pooka uNDa** *n. dial.* cake made with rice flour and jaggery.

పోకడ **pookaDa** *n.* 1 going, departure. 2 behaviour, conduct. 3 method, way of proceeding, way of going about o.'s work. 4 *often pl.* ~**lu** departures, directions, trends, tendencies. 5 *often pl.* signs, indications, traces.

పోకదల **pookadala** *n.* arrogance.

పోకిరి **pookiri** I. *n.* scoundrel, rogue. II *adj.* wicked, mischievous.

పోకిరితనం **pookiritanam** *n.* wickedness, mischievousness.

పోగా **poogaa** *advbl. particle* 1 besides, in addition to, apart from, excluding, after deducting; **aayana weLLaka ~nannu weLLaniwwaleedu** besides not going himself, he did not let me go either; **idigoo padi rupaayalu, caarjiiki ~Dabbu uNTundi** here is ten rupees, after deducting what is charged, some money will remain over. 2 in addition, moreover. 3 but, however. 4 omitting, excluding; **goodaawari DeLTaa wistiirNam reNDu weela cadarapu mayLLu. isuka bhuumulu, graamaalu, rahadaarulu wagayraa~ nikarangaa padi lakSala ekaraalu saaguku wiilugaa unnaayi** the Godavari delta is two thousand square miles in extent. excluding sandy areas, village sites, roads and so on, ten lakhs of acres net are cultivable.

పోగు, ప్రోగు **p[r]oogu** *n.* 1 heap, pile. 2 food (in a derogatory sense); ~**cellindi kaanii pani jaraga leedu** food was swallowed but no work done; ~**cellincaDaanikee gaanii dammiDi ettu pani ceeyaDu** he gets through his food but he does not get through any work. 3 thread, string, fibre, filament; *see* **candruDu. 4 cewi~** earring; **mukku~** nose ring.

పోగు అవు, పోగవు, పోగుపడు **poog[u]awu, poogupaDu** *v.i.* 1 to be collected. 2 (of a crowd) to assemble, gather together.

పోగు చేయు **poogu ceeyu** *v.t.* to collect, assemble, gather together, accumulate, amass; *see* **gaali.**

పోగు పెట్టు **poogu peTTu** *v.t.* to make a heap; **kaagitaalu cimpi poogu peTTEEDu** he tore up the papers and made a heap of them.

పోగొట్టు **poogoTTu** *v.t.* 1 to lose. 2 to dispel, get rid of, remove, drive away, banish, eliminate (illness, pain, grief).

పోచ **pooca** *n., gen. second part of a compound* 1 **gaDDi~** blade of dry grass, trifle. 2 *sci.* fibre; **daaru~lu** wood fibres. 3 thread; **jandhyam~** sacred thread; **niiku meDaloo ~undaa?** are you wearing a sacred thread? i.e., has your **upanyanam** been performed? *or* are you a brahman?

పోచీ **poocii** *n. obs.* kind of bracelet.

పోచుకోలు కబుర్లు **poocukoolu kaburlu** *n. pl.* gossip, idle talk.

పోజు **pooju** *n.* pose; ~**koTTu** to give o.s. airs.

పోటకత్తి **pooTakatti** *n.* billhook, knife for cutting wood.

పోటాపోటీలు **pooTaapooTiilu** *n.pl.* rivalry, competition

పోటి **pooTi** *class. alt. form of* **booTi.**

పోటీ **pooTii** *n.* 1 competition, rivalry, contest (~**ki**, for); ~**pariikSalu** competitive examinations. 2 **parugu~** race. 3 prop, support; **gaDDamkinda ceeyi ~ peTTukoni kuurcunnaaDu** he sat resting his chin on his hand.

పోటీ చేయు **pooTii ceeyu** *v.i.* to compete, contest (**-ki**, for).

పోటీ[లు]పడు **pooTii[lu]paDu** *v.i.* to compete, vie (**-too**, with).

పోటు **pooTu** *n.* 1 thrust, stab, blow. 2 shooting or throbbing pain; **cewi/pannu/kaDupu~** shooting or throbbing pain in the ear/tooth/stomach. 3 tide; **samudram ~ miida undi** the tide is rising. 4 **raktapu~** blood pressure.

పోటుగాడు **pooTugaaDu** *n. slang* ruffian, villain.

పోటుమగడు **pooTumagaDu** *n. slang* fighter.

పోట్లాట **pooTLaaTa** *n.* fight, struggle, quarrel.

పోట్లాట పెట్టుకొను, పోట్లాట వేసుకొను **pooTLaaTa peTTukonu, pooTLaaTa weesukonu** *v.i.* to pick up a quarrel.

పోట్లాడు **pooTLaaDu** *v.i.* to fight, struggle, quarrel, dispute.

పోడు **pooDu** *n.* land cleared of jungle for cultivation by slashing and burning.

పోత **poota** I. *n.* 1 pouring. 2 casting of metal. 3 eruption of a disease; **taDapara~** eruption of chicken pox. II. *adj.* (of a statue) cast in metal.

పోత ఇనుము **poota inumu** *n.* cast iron.

పోతపోయు **pootapooyu** *v.t.* to cast (statue).

పోతు **pootu** *n.* male of certain species, e.g., **meeka~** he-goat.

పోతుతాడు **pootutaaDu** male palmyra tree.

పోతురాజు **pooturaaju** *n.* name of a village god.

పోతే **pootee** I. *conditional form of* **poowu.** II. *advbl. particle, often as sentence opener* 1 however. 2 besides, moreover. 3 after that, next.

పోనిచ్చు **pooniccu** *v.t.* 1 to let go [by], let pass. 2 to ride, drive (vehicle).

పోనీ, పోనీండి, పోనీలే, పోనిస్తూ, పోనిద్దూ **poonii[NDi], pooniilee, poonistuu, poonidduu** *clitic* 1 well [then], never mind, let it be, don't worry; **iwwEELa raaleedu, ~reepaynaawastaaDaa?** he did not come today. well, will he at least come tomorrow? 2 further, what is more; **loopaliki weLLeewaaDu kaaDu,~saaluwaa annaa tecci kappukonee waaDu kaadu** he would not go indoors; what is more, he would not even fetch a shawl to cover himself; *note: of these alternative forms* **pooniiNDi** *is formal:* **poonistuu** *and* **poonidduu** *are semi-formal;* **poonii** *and* **pooniilee** *are informal.*

పోనీ[ండి]గదా **poonii[NDi]gadaa** *clitic* well, after all; **~ pillalu tiNTaarani miThaayi tiisuku waccEEnu** I brought some sweets thinking that after all the children would eat them.

పోను **poonu** *advbl. particle* apart from, over and above, after deducting; **aayanaki iwwawalasina Dabbu ~ naadaggira eemii migaladu** take away the money that is due to him and nothing will be left with me.

పోను పోను **poonu poonu** *adv.* gradually, by degrees, as one proceeds.

పోనున్న **poonunna** *adj.* about to go.

పోపు **poopu** *n.* seasoning, spicing.

పోబిడి **poobiDi** *n.* trace.

పోయి **pooyi** I. *past participle of* **poowu.** II. *advbl. particle* whereas; **aayana naaku uttaram raayawalasindi ~ neenu raasina uttaraaniki jawaabu iwwaleedu** whereas he ought to have written a letter to me (in the first place), he has not even answered the letter that I wrote to him.

పోయించు **pooyincu** *v.i.* 1 to have (s.g) poured. 2 *slang* to make (s.o.) drunk; **waaDiki baagaa pooyinci kaagitam raayincukonnaaDu** he made him very drunk and got him to write the deed.

పోయిన **pooyina** *adj.* last, gone by, previous; **~ samwatsaram** last year.

పోయిపోయి **pooyi pooyi** *adv.* eventually, finally, in the end.

పోయు **pooyu** I. *v.i.* (of a disease) to occur, break out, appear, attack; **waaDiki taDapara poosindi** he was attacked by chicken pox. II. *v.t.* 1 to pour; **biDDaki niiLLu poostunnadi** she is giving the child a bath; **bhoogi** (*or* **reegi**) **paLLu pooyu** to pour reegi fruits on the heads of children on Sankranti day; **naaru ~** to transplant seedlings. 2 to cast (metal). 3 to construct (s.g) by pouring; **dhaanyam kuppa ~** to pile up a heap of grain; **gaTTu ~** to construct a bank *or* to raise a dam. 4 to tie; **mukkuku taaDu ~** to tie a leading rope to the nose; *see* **kacca, kaase.** 5 *with certain past participles ~ gives intensive force,* e.g., **aame atanni baagaa tiTTipoosindi** she abused him roundly; **biiDiilu taagipoostunnaaDu** he smokes beedies continuously; *see also* **poosukonu.**

పోయేకాలపు **pooyeekaalapu** *adj. slang* damnable; *see* **kaalam** *sense 1.*

పోరంబోకు **poorambooku** I. *n.* (*also* **porambooku**) 1 government land reserved for communal use in a village. 2 uncultivable waste land. II. *adj.* idle, useless; **~ sthalam** waste or useless land; **~ maniSi** useless person; *colloq.* **~ wedhawa** waster.

పోరంబోకుగా **poorambookugaa** *adv.* wastefully, uselessly, to no purpose; **~ tirugutunnaaDu** he is wandering aimlessly.

పోర[గా]డు **poora[gaa]Du** *n. dial.* boy, young man.

పోరాటం **pooraaTam** *n.* fight, struggle, conflict.

పోరాడు **pooraaDu** *v.i.* to fight, contend, struggle, grapple.

పోరి **poori** *n. dial.* girl; *cf.* **pooli.**

పోరు **pooru** I. *n.* 1 fight, struggle, dispute, quarrel. 2 insistence, urging. 3 teasing, troubling, pestering, harassment, nagging; **uuLLoowaaLLa ~ paDaleeka tana kuuturiki peLLi ceesEEDu** being unable to endure the villagers' harassment he performed his daughter's marriage. II. *v.i. and t.* 1 to fight, quarrel, struggle, strive. 2 to urge, pester, nag; **"naaku manci paNTLaam kuTTincu naannaa" ani waaDu taNDrini roojuu pooreewaaDu** every day he used to pester his father saying "get nice pair of pants made for me".

పోరుకాడు **poorukaaDu** *v.i. dial. and class.* to fight, strive.

పోరుపెట్టు **poorupeTTu** *v.i.* to worry or pester continuously.

పోలడు **poolaDu** *n. class.* eagle.

పోలాల పండుగ **poolaala paNDaga** *n. dial.* festival held on the day after Sankranti (= **kaNum**).

పోలి **pooli** *n. dial.* girl; *cf.* **poori.**

పోలిక **poolika** *n.* likeness, resemblance, similarity, comparison; **maa ammaayi waaLLa amma ~** my daughter resembles her mother; **iddaru kawala pillalu okka ~ nee unnaaru** the two twins are exactly alike; **waaDikii naakuu ~ leedu** there is no comparison between him and me.

పోలిన **poolina** *past vbl. adj. of* **poolu** like, resembling.

పోలు, పోలి ఉండు **poolu, pooli uNDu** *v.t.* 1 to resemble, be like, be similar to. 2 to be comparable to; **waaDu mii kaali gooTiki [sari]poolaDu** he is not fit to be compared to your toenail, i.e., he is far inferior to you.

పోలె **poole** *class. alt. form of* **wale**[1].

పోలేరమ్మ **pooleeramma** *n.* goddess who presides over village boundaries.

పోల్చదగిన **poolcadagina** *adj.* comparable.

పోల్చిపట్టు **poolcipaTTu** *v.t.* to recognise.

పోల్చు **poolcu** *v.t.* 1 to compare. 2 to recognise, identify.

పోళీ **pooLii** *n.* kind of sweet (= **hooLiga**).

పోవు **poowu** *v.i.* 1 to go, proceed; *note: in some parts of Andhra Pradesh, particularly the central coastal districts,* **weLLu** *replaces* **poowu** *in the sense of 'to go' because of the association of* **poowu** *with the meaning 'to die'; similarly* **pooyi raNDi** please go (*lit.* please go and come) *and* **pooyi wastaanu** I will go *or* I will take leave of you (*lit.* I will go and come) *are more acceptable than* **poNDi** *and* **pootaanu.** 2 to depart, pass off, cease, vanish, disappear. 3 to be lost. 4 to die. 5 to become; **tella ~** to turn pale; **cillulu ~** to become cracked. 6 to be subtracted; **padiNTLoo naalugu pootee aaru** ten minus four equals six. 7 *as an auxiliary (vb.) ~ is used* (i) *with an infinitive to give the sense of* to be about to, be going to **ceppabootunnaaDu** he is about to say; (ii) *with a durative participle to indicate continuity of action* **uuhincukoNTuu pooyEEDu** he went on imagining *or* he continued to imagine; (iii) *with a past participle to give intensive force* **taDisEEDu** he got wet, **taDisi pooyEEDu** he got drenched; (iv) *with a negative participle to give the sense of* to omit or fail to do (s.g) **neenu ceppina maaTa winaka pooyEEDu** he failed to take my advice; (v) *~ in the negative with a negative participle gives a double negative meaning* **aayana aaloocincaka pooleedu** he did not fail to consider; **aanandam kanipincaka poodu** joy will not fail to appear. 8 *~ following a noun in the dative gives the sense of* to go in for, venture on, resort to, indulge in **ii goppalaku mari poogalamaa?** can we still indulge in these boastings?: **leenipooni laanchanaalaku poowaDam endukani neenee corawa tiisukoni okasaari aawiDa iNTiki weLLEEnu** thinking why bother about needless formalities I myself summoned up courage and went to her house; *see* **jooli, binkam, paapam** *sense I. 2,* **leeka.**

పోషక **pooSaka** *adj.* nutritious, nutritional, nutritive.

పోషకగ్రంథి **pooSakagranthi** *n. med.* pituitary gland.

పోషకాహారం **pooSakaahaaram** *n.* nourishing food, nutriment, nutrition; **pooSakaahaara pariśoodhana** nutrition research.

పోషకుడు **pooSakuDu** *n.* patron, protector, supporter; **mahaaraaja~** chief patron.

పోషకురాలు **pooSakuraalu** *n.* patroness, protectress.

పోషణ[ం] **pooSaNa[m]** *n.* **1** nourishing, nourishment, nutrition, nutriment. **2** cherishing, maintaining, rearing, bringing up, support, maintenance. **3** patronage. **4** delineation, portrayal (of a part or character in a drama).

పోషించు **pooSincu** *v.t.* **1** to nourish, cherish, support, maintain, rear, bring up; **pillalaki peTTi pooSistunnaaDu** he is bringing up the children. **2** to patronise, protect. **3** to delineate, portray (a part or character in a drama).

పోసుకొను **poosukonu** *v.t.* **1** *lit.* to pour on o.s.; **naa aayuS-Su poosukoni batuku!** may my lifetime be added to yours! (a blessing); *see* **usuru. 2** to bathe, take a bath. **3** *colloq.* **laabhaalu~** to amass profits. **4** *colloq.* **aawiDa niiLLu poosukondi** she has become pregnant.

పౌ - paw

పౌజు **pawju** *alt. form of* **phawju.**

పౌత్రి **pawtri** *n.* granddaughter, son's daughter.

పౌత్రుడు **pawtruDu** *n.* grandson, son's son.

పౌనఃపున్యం **pawnahpunyam** *n. phys.* frequency.

పౌనరుక్త్యం **pawnaruktyam** *n. class.* repetition.

పౌను **pawnu** *n.* **1** pound (weight). **2** pound (sterling).

పౌర **pawra** *adj.* people's, civic, civil, public.

పౌరకర్తవ్య భావన **pawrakartawya bhaawana** *n.* civic sense.

పౌరశాస్త్రం **pawraśaastram** *n.* (science of) civics.

పౌరసంబంధాలు **pawrasambandhaalu** *n. pl.* public relations.

పౌరసత్వం **pawrasatwam** *n.* citizenship.

పౌరసన్మానం **pawrasanmaanam** *n.* civic reception.

పౌరసరఫరాలు **pawrasarapharaalu** *n.pl.* civil supplies.

పౌర[సత్వ]హక్కులు **pawra[satwa]hakkulu** *n.pl.* civil rights.

పౌరాణిక **pawraaNika** *adj.* mythological, legendary.

పౌరాణికుడు **pawraaNikuDu** *n.* person well versed in the Puranas.

పౌరాతన్యం **pawraatanyam** *n.* antiquity.

పౌరుడు **pawruDu** *n.* citizen.

పౌరుషం **pawruSam** *n.* **1** manliness, courage. **2** resentment or indignation at being belittled or insulted. **3** self-esteem, self-assertion. **4** *class.* human activity, man's work.

పౌరుషంగా **pawruSangaa** *adv.* indignantly, feeling hurt or insulted.

పౌరుషానికి **pawruSaaniki** I. *dative of* **pawruSam.** II. *adv.* out of bravado; **"iitaku wastaawaa?" ani aDigEEDu. mundu bhayapaDDaa, "wastaanu" ani ceppEEnu** - "will you come swimming?" he asked. "I will come" I said out of bravado, although I was afraid at first; *cf.* **binkangaa** *sense 2.*

పౌరోహితం, పౌరోహిత్యం **pawroohit[y]am** *n.* priesthood, office of family priest.

పౌర్ణమి **pawrNami** *same as* **punnama.**

పౌష్టిక **pawSTika** *adj.* nutritious; **~aahaaram** nutriment, nutrious diet.

ప్ర - pra

ప్రకంపనం **prakampanam** *n.* quake, tremor.

ప్రకంపించు **prakampincu** *v.i.* to vibrate, pulsate.

ప్రకట **prakaTa** *adj. class.* public, made known.

ప్రకటన **prakaTana** *n.* 1 publication, notification, notice, announcement, proclamation. 2 declaration, disclosure, pronouncement, expression; **bhaawa~** expression of ideas. 3 advertisement.

ప్రకటించు **prakaTincu** *v.t.* 1 to publish, proclaim, notify, announce, promulgate. 2 to declare, disclose, express. 3 to advertise, publicise. 4 to show, display, exhibit.

ప్రకరణం **prakaraNam** *n.* chapter or section in a book.

ప్రకర్ష **prakarSa** *n.* 1 pre-eminence, distinction, excellence. 2 **paaNDitya~** pedantry.

ప్రకాండం **prakaaNDam** *n. bot.* trunk of a tree.

ప్రకాండుడు **prakaaNDuDu** *second part of a n. compound meaning* excellent person; **paNDita~** excellent scholar.

ప్రకారం **prakaaram** *p.p. and advbl. particle* according to, in accordance with, [in the same way] as, in terms of; **maamuulu paddhati~** according to the usual system; **miiru ceppina~** as you say; **1981 dharala~** in terms of 1981 prices.

ప్రకాశం **prakaaśam** *n.* light, splendour, brightness, gleam.

ప్రకాశంగా **prakaaśangaa** *adv.* 1 *theat.* aloud (of words spoken by an actor intended to be heard by other characters on the stage after an aside). 2 brightly.

ప్రకాశకుడు **prakaaśakuDu** *n.* publisher.

ప్రకాశవంత **prakaaśawanta** *adj.* bright, shining, brilliant, radiant, gleaming.

ప్రకాశించు **prakaaśincu** *v.i.* to shine, gleam, glow, radiate.

ప్రకీర్ణ **prakiirNa** *adj.* miscellaneous.

ప్రకీర్ణం **prakiirNam** *n. class.* fly whisk.

ప్రకృత **prakṛta** *adj.* present; **~paristhitulaloo** in present circumstances.

ప్రకృతం **prakṛtam** I. *n.* the present time. II. *adv.* at present, now.

ప్రకృతి **prakṛti** *n.* 1 nature, the natural world; **~ loo paDu** (*or* **mana lookamloo paDu**) to come back to o.'s senses (after fainting or suffering a shock). 2 nature, character, temperament, disposition. 3 *gram.* the original or natural form of a word.

ప్రకృతి శాస్త్రాలు **prakṛti śaastraalu** *n.pl.* natural sciences.

ప్రకోపం **prakoopam** *n.* excitement, vehemence, fury; **paytya~** excess of bile; **uSNa~** overheating.

ప్రకోపనం **prakoopanam** *n.* provocation.

ప్రకోపించు **prakoopincu** *v.i.* (of bile, etc.) to be in excess.

ప్రకోపింప చేయు **prakoopimpa ceeyu** *v.t.* to arouse, excite, provoke.

ప్రక్క[గా] **prakka[gaa]** *same as* **pakka[gaa]**.

ప్రక్రియ **prakriya** *n.* 1 process; **śiitooSNasthiti~.prawṛttulu** climatic processes and patterns; **tayaaruceeyu ~loo** in the process of manufacture. 2 procedure; **praNaaLika~loo deeśamlooni wiwidha raaSTraalu bhaagaswaamulu** the various States in the country are partners in the planning procedure. 3 method, technique; **adhunaatana~lu** modern techniques. 4 *sci.* reaction; **rasaayana ~lu** chemical reactions. 5 experiment. 6 class, type or form of literature; **kathakuluu, nawalaa racayitaluu, itara saahitya~laloo aariteerinawaaruu** story writers, novelists and persons skilled in other forms of literature. 7 *class.* chapter in a traditional grammar; **sandhi~** chapter on sandhi.

ప్రక్వణం **prakwaNam** *n. class.* sound of a lute.

ప్రక్షాళన[ం] **prakSaaLana[m]** *n.* washing, cleansing; **mukha/danta/paada~** washing or cleansing o.'s face/teeth/feet.

ప్రక్షాళన చేయు **prakSaaLana ceeyu** *v.t.* to clean, cleanse, wash, purify.

ప్రక్షిప్త **prakSipta** *adj. literary* spurious, interpolated.

ప్రక్షేప[ణ]ం **prakSeepa[Na]m** *n. sci.* 1 scattering, diffusion. 2 projection.

ప్రఖ్యాత **prakhyaata** *adj.* famous, renowned, illustrious.

ప్రఖ్యాతి **prakhyaati** *n.* fame, renown, celebrity.

ప్రగతి **pragati** *n.* progress.

ప్రగతిశీల **pragatiśiila** *adj.* progressive.

ప్రగతిసూచక **pragatisuucaka** *adj.* indicative of progress.

ప్రగల్భం **pragalbham** *n.* boasting.

ప్రగల్భాలు పలుకు, ప్రగల్భించు **pragalbhaalu paluku, pragalbhincu** *v.i.* to boast.

ప్రగాఢ **pragaaDha** *adj.* strong, powerful, intense (love, faith, loyalty).

ప్రచండ **pracaNDa** *adj.* fierce, violent, tremendous, terrible, vehement.

ప్రచలిత **pracalita** *adj.* 1 widespread, rife. 2 popular.

ప్రచారం **pracaaram** *n.* 1 publicity. 2 (of news, ideas, opinions) currency, spreading; **~ looki waccu** to become current, be disseminated, be accepted, become widely known. 3 popularity, acceptability. 4 propaganda. 5 circulation (of a newspaper). 6 **ennika~** election campaign.

ప్రచారం అవు **pracaaram awu** *v.i.* (of news, ideas, opinions) to be spread, be diffused, be disseminated.

ప్రచారం చేయు **pracaaram ceeyu** *v.t.* to propagate, disseminate, publicise, popularise.

ప్రచారకుడు **pracaarakuDu** *n.* 1 propagandist, publicity man. 2 proclaimer, proponent.

ప్రచారసాధనాలు **pracaara saadhanaalu** *n.pl.* publicity media.

ప్రచురం **pracuram** *adj.* (of a word) widely used, commonly used, frequent.

ప్రచురణ **pracuraNa** *n.* 1 publication, publishing. 2 edition.

ప్రచురణకర్త **pracuraNakarta** *n.* publisher.

ప్రచురించు **pracurincu** *v.t.* to publish.

ప్రచోదనం **pracoodanam** *n.* 1 motivation, stimulation. 2 *phys.* impulse.

ప్రచోదనం చేయు **pracoodanam ceeyu** *v.t.* to motivate, stimulate, inspire, instigate.

ప్రచ్ఛన్న **pracchanna** *adj.* secret, covert, disguised; ~ **bhaaSa** secret language, code language; ~ **yuddham** 'cold war'.

ప్రచ్ఛన్నంగా **pracchannangaa** *adv.* stealthily, covertly, in disguise.

ప్రచ్ఛాదనం **pracchaadanam** *n.* covering, concealing, hiding.

ప్రజ **praja** *n., gen. pl.* ~ **lu** people, folk.

ప్రజననం **prajananam** *n.* 1 breeding, propagation. 2 procreation.

ప్రజా **prajaa** *adj.* people's, public.

ప్రజా ఋణం **prajaa ṛNam** *n. econ.* public debt.

ప్రజాతి **prajaati** *n. sci.* genus.

ప్రజా నిర్మాణాల శాఖ **prajaa nirmaaNaala śaakha** *n.* Public Works Department.

ప్రజానీకం, ప్రజాబాహుళ్యం **prajaaniikam, prajaabaahuLyam** *n.* the people, the masses, the general public.

ప్రజాభిప్రాయం **prajaabhipraayam** *n.* public opinion.

ప్రజాభిప్రాయ సేకరణ **prajaabhipraaya seekaraNa**. *n.* plebiscite, referendum.

ప్రజారోగ్య శాఖ **prajaaroogya śaakha** *n.* Public Health Department.

ప్రజా[వ]ళి **prajaa[wa]Li** *n.* the people as a whole; **prapanca** ~ all the people in the world.

ప్రజాసామాన్యం **prajaasaamaanyam** *n.* the common people.

ప్రజాస్వామిక **prajaaswaamika** *adj.* democratic.

ప్రజాస్వామ్యం **prajaaswaamyam** *n.* democracy.

ప్రజాస్వామ్యవాది **prajaaswamyawaadi** *n.* democrat.

ప్రజాహిత **prajaahita** *adj.* beneficial to the public; ~ **kaaryakramaalu** public utility programmes.

ప్రజోత్పత్తి **prajootpatti** *n.* fifth year of the Hindu cycle of sixty years.

ప్రజ్ఞ **prajña** *n.* understanding, intelligence, talent, skill, artistry; **prajñaawiśeeSam** special talent.

ప్రజ్ఞాశాలి, ప్రజ్ఞావంతుడు, ప్రజ్ఞుడు **prajñaaśaali, prajñaawantuDu, prajñuDu** *n.* talented person, distinguished person, learned person.

ప్రజ్వరిల్లు **prajwarillu** *v.i.* to burn or shine brightly.

ప్రజ్వలన **prajwalana** *n.* 1 burning, blazing, shining. 2 ignition. 3 (of war, strife) outbreak, flaring up.

ప్రజ్వలించు **prajwalincu** *v.i.* 1 to burn, blaze, gleam, shine. 2 to ignite. 3 (of war, strife) to break out, flare up.

ప్రజ్వలింప చేయు **prajwalimpa ceeyu** *v.t.* to cause to burn or shine brightly.

ప్రణతి **praNati** *n. class.* 1 bow, salutation. 2 obeisance, reverence.

ప్రణమిల్లు **praNamillu** *v.i. class.* to bow down, prostrate o.s.

ప్రణయం **praNayam** *n.* love, passion.

ప్రణయ కలహం **praNaya kalaham** *n.* lovers' quarrel.

ప్రణయి **praNayi** *n. class.* lover.

ప్రణవం **praNawam** *n. class.* the sacred syllable OM, symbol of the Supreme Being.

ప్రణామం **praNaamam** *n. class.* bow, salutation.

ప్రణాళిక **praNaaLika** *n.* 1 plan. 2 project.

ప్రణాళికాబద్ధ **praNaaLikaabaddha** *adj. econ.* planned, systematic; ~ **mayna kṛSi** planned activity.

ప్రణాళికాసంఘం **praNaaLikaa sangham** *n.* Planning Commission.

ప్రణీత[ం] **praNiita[m]** *adj. class.* written, composed, compiled.

ప్రణుతి **praNuti** *n. class.* great praise.

ప్రణుతించు **praNutincu** *v.t. class.* to praise highly.

ప్రతాపం **prataapam** *n.* 1 power, force, energy. 2 prowess, valour.

ప్రతి **prati**[1] *n.* copy, facsimile.

ప్రతి **prati**[2] *Sanskrit prefix meaning* against, in return; ~ **waadam** counterargument; **pratyupakaaram** return favour.

ప్రతి **prati**[3] *adj.* each, every.

ప్రతికక్షి **pratikakSi** *n.* opponent, enemy.

ప్రతికూల **pratikuula** *adj.* 1 contrary, adverse, unfavourable, inconvenient, disagreeable, inauspicious. 2 *legal* repugnant.

ప్రతికూలంగా **pratikuulangaa** *adv.* in opposition (**-ki**, to).

ప్రతికూలించు **pratikuulincu** *v.i.* to oppose, be unfavourable.

ప్రతికూలుడు **pratikuuluDu** *n.* opponent.

ప్రతిక్రియ **pratikriya** *n.* reaction, counteraction, remedy.

ప్రతిగా **pratigaa** *adv.* 1 in return, in exchange (**-ki**, for). 2 instead, in place, in lieu (**-ki**, of). 3 in opposition (**-ki**, to).

ప్రతిగృహీత **pratigṛhiita** *n.* donee, person who receives a gift.

ప్రతిగ్రహించు **pratigrahincu** *v.t.* to accept or receive (donation, alms).

ప్రతిగ్రాహ్య **pratigraahya** *adj.* acceptable, receivable.

ప్రతిఘటన **pratighaTana** *n.* resistance.

ప్రతిఘటించు **pratighaTincu** *v.t.* to oppose, resist, withstand, fight back.

ప్రతిఘాతం **pratighaatam** *n.* blow struck in return.

ప్రతిచర్య **praticarya** *n.* countermeasure, reprisal, reaction: **anduku~gaa** as a countermeasure to that *or* in reaction to that.

ప్రతిచ్ఛాయ **praticchaaya** *n.* reflected image, reflection.

ప్రతిజ్ఞ **pratijña** *n.* **1** vow, resolution, promise. **2** asseveration, affirmation.

ప్రతిజ్ఞేయం **pratijñeeyam** *n.* s.g that is to be admitted or promised or decided on.

ప్రతి దినం **prati dinam** *adv.* every day, daily.

ప్రతిద్వంద్వి **pratidwandwi** *n.* opponent.

ప్రతిధ్వని **pratidhwani** *n.* echo, reverberation.

ప్రతిధ్వనించు **pratidhwanincu** *v.i.* **1** to resound, re-echo, reverberate. **2** *colloq.* to initate, mimic.

ప్రతిన **pratina** *colloq. alt. form of* **pratijña.**

ప్రతినాదం **pratinaadam** *n.* echo, reverberation.

ప్రతినామం **pratinaamam** *n.* alias, another name.

ప్రతినిత్యం **pratinityam** *adv.* **1** continuously, ceaselessly. **2** every day, daily.

ప్రతినిధి **pratinidhi** *n.* representative, proxy.

ప్రతినిధి వర్గం **pratinidhi wargam** *n.* group of representatives, deputation.

ప్రతిపక్షం **pratipakSam** *n.* opposite party, opposition.

ప్రతిపక్షి **pratipakSi** *n.* **1** opponent. **2** member of the opposite party in a dispute.

ప్రతిపత్తి **pratipatti** *n.* status; **swatantra~** independent status.

ప్రతిపత్తు **pratipattu** *n. class.* first day of a lunar fortnight.

ప్రతిపదార్థం **pratipadaartham** *n.* detailed explanation of the meaning of words in a poetical text.

ప్రతిపదార్థ వ్యాఖ్య **pratipadaartha wyaakhya** *n.* commentary explaining each word in detail in a poetical text.

ప్రతిపాదకుడు **pratipaadakuDu** *n.* proposer, proponent.

ప్రతిపాదన **pratipaadana** *n.* **1** proposal, suggestion. **2** exposition.

ప్రతిపాదించు **pratipaadincu** *v.t.* **1** to propose. **2** to propound, proffer, set forth, put forward (idea, theory).

ప్రతిపాదిత **pratipaadita** *adj.* **1** proposed, put forward. **2** *admin.* **keendra~pathakam** Centrally sponsored scheme.

ప్రతిపాలనం **pratipaalanam** *n.* protection.

ప్రతిఫలం **pratiphalam** *n.* return, reward, requital, remuneration, recompense, retribution.

ప్రతిఫలించు **pratiphalincu** I. *v.i.* to be reflected. II. *v.t.* to reflect.

ప్రతిబంధ[క]ం, ప్రతిబంధనం **pratibandha[ka]m, pratibandhanam** *n.* impediment, obstacle, hindrance.

ప్రతిబంధక **pratibandhaka** *adj.* impeding, obstructing.

ప్రతిబంధించు **pratibandhincu** *v.t.* to obstruct, hinder, impede.

ప్రతిబలం **pratibalam** *n.* **1** opposing force. **2** hostile army.

ప్రతిబింబం **pratibimbam** *n.* reflection, image.

ప్రతిబింబించు **pratibimbincu** I. *v.i.* to be reflected. II. (*also* **pratibimbimpa ceeyu**) *v.t.* to reflect.

ప్రతిభ **pratibha** *n.* **1** understanding, intelligence, intellect. **2** genius, talent. **3** grandeur, splendour, eminence. **4** skill, aptitude. merit: **~nu baTTi** on merit.

ప్రతిభావంత **pratibhaawanta** *adj.* intelligent, skilled, gifted.

ప్రతిమ **pratima** *n.* image, idol, statue, figure.

ప్రతిముఖ **pratimukha** *adj. zool.* aboral.

ప్రతిరక్షకం **pratirakSakam** *n. biol.* antibody.

ప్రతిరూపం **pratiruupam** *n.* **1** image, picture, representation, likeness. **2** facsimile, replica, counterpart. **3** pattern. **4** symbol.

ప్రతిరోధి **pratiroodhi** *n.* adversary, opponent.

ప్రతిరోధించు **pratiroodhincu** *v.t.* to oppose, resist.

ప్రతిలేఖనం **pratileekhanam** *n.* transliteration.

ప్రతిలోమ **pratilooma** *adj.* against the grain; *cf.* **anulooma.**

ప్రతివాక్యం **pratiwaakyam** *n.* answer, response.

ప్రతివాదం **pratiwaadam** *n.* counterargument.

ప్రతివాది **pratiwaadi** *n. legal* respondent, defendant.

ప్రతివిమర్శ **pratiwimarśa** *n.* countercriticism.

ప్రతిశతి **pratiśati** *n.* per cent.

ప్రతిషిద్ధ **pratiSiddha** *adj.* forbidden, prohibited.

ప్రతిషేధించు **pratiSeedhincu** *v.t.* to forbid, prohibit.

ప్రతిష్టంభం, ప్రతిష్టంభన **pratiSTambham, pratiSTambhana** *n.* deadlock, stalemate, standstill, stagnation; **~ eerpaDindi** a deadlock arose.

ప్రతిష్ఠ **pratiSTha** *n.* **1** reputation, standing, good name, prestige. **2** setting up, installing; **wigraha~** erecting a statue, installing an idol in a temple; *see* **praaNa~.**

ప్రతిష్ఠాకరమైన **pratiSThaakaramayna** *adj.* prestigious.

ప్రతిష్ఠానం **pratiSThaanam** *n.* **1** foundation, basis. **2** foundation, charitable endowment.

ప్రతిష్ఠాపన[ం] **pratiSThaapana[m]** *n.* setting up, erection, installation.

ప్రతిష్ఠాపించు, ప్రతిష్ఠించు **pratiSThaapincu, pratiSThincu** *v.t.* **1** to set up, erect. **2** to establish, instal.

ప్రతిష్ఠిత **pratiSThita** *adj.* well established, firmly established.

ప్రతిసృష్టి **pratisṛSTi** *n.* imitation of creation, artificial creation; **brahma srSTiki~ceesina mahaniiyuDu wiśwaamitra maharSi** Viswamitra the sage who made an imitation of Brahma's creation.

ప్రతిస్పర్ధి **pratisparthi** *n.* opponent, rival, competitor.

ప్రతిస్పర్ధించు **pratisparthincu** *v.i.* to compete.

ప్రతిహత[ం] **pratihata[m]** *adj.* repulsed, beaten back, averted.

ప్రతిహారి, ప్రతీహారి, ప్రతిహారుడు **prati[i]haari, pratihaaruDu** *n. class.* doorkeeper, porter.

ప్రతీక **pratiika** *n.* **1** symbol, symbolic representation. **2** reflection.

ప్రతీకాత్మకంగా **pratiikaatmakangaa** *adv.* symbolically.

ప్రతీకాత్మకత **pratiikaatmakata** *n.* symbolism.

ప్రతీకారం **pratiikaaram** *n.* retaliation, revenge, requital, reprisal, retribution.

ప్రతీకారేచ్ఛ **pratiikaareeccha** *n.* longing for revenge.

ప్రతీక్ష[ణం] **pratiikSa[Nam]** *n.* waiting, expectation.

ప్రతీక్షించు **pratiikSincu** *v.i.* to wait for, look out for, hope for, expect.

ప్రతీత **pratiita** *adj.* famous, celebrated, renowned.

ప్రతీతి **pratiiti** *n.* what is widely known or generally believed; **aayana taagutaaDani ~ undi** it is common knowledge (*or* it is commonly believed) that he drinks.

ప్రతీప **pratiipa** *adj.* 1 hostile, adverse. 2 reactionary; **~ saktulu** reactionary forces.

ప్రతీహారి **pratiihaari** *same as* **pratihaari.**

ప్రత్తి **pratti** *same as* **patti.**

ప్రత్యక్ష **pratyakSa** *adj.* 1 perceptible, perceivable, visible. 2 clear, evident, manifest, distinct. 3 direct; **~ sambandham** direct connection.

ప్రత్యక్షం **pratyakSam** *n.* 1 appearance, manifestation, presence; **~loo** in the presence of; **naa ~ loo okalaa naa parookSamloo okalaa ceppEEDu** he said one thing to my face and another thing behind my back. 2 **~** *is used colloq. with* **awu** *understood but not expressed*, e.g., **talacukoogaanee ~** as soon as I thought of him, he appeared; **waaDiki ippuDu pani leedu, ekkaDa paDitee akkaDa ~** he has no work to do now, he turns up anywhere and everywhere; **aa patrikaki giraakii caalaa undi ippuDu, ekkaDa paDitee akkaDa ~** that newspaper is in good demand now, you find it everywhere.

ప్రత్యక్షం అవు **pratyakSam awu** *v.i.* to appear, become visible, become manifest; **ataniki deewuDu pratyakSam ayyEEDu** the god appeared visibly to him.

ప్రత్యక్షంగా **pratyakSangaa** *adv.* 1 directly, in person; **~ neenu cuusEEnu** I saw it in person *or* I saw it with my own eyes. 2 clearly, distinctly.

ప్రత్యక్ష ప్రమాణం **pratyakSa pramaaNam** *n.* direct proof which can be verified by the senses.

ప్రత్యక్షవాది **pratyakSawaadi** *n.* one who rejects any belief that cannot be verified by the senses.

ప్రత్యక్షవ్యాఖ్యానం **pratyakSawyaakhyaanam** *n.* running commentary.

ప్రత్యక్ష సాక్షి **pratyakSa saakSi** *n.* eyewitness.

ప్రత్యభివందనం **pratyabhiwandanam** *n.* return of greetings; *see* **abhiwandanam.**

ప్రత్యయం **pratyayam** *n.* 1 *gram.* affix. 2 *class.* belief, confidence.

ప్రత్యర్థి **pratyarthi** *n.* 1 enemy, opponent. 2 opposite party. 3 rebel.

ప్రత్యహం **pratyaham** *adv. class.* every day, daily.

ప్రత్యామ్నాయ **pratyaamnaaya** *adj.* alternative.

ప్రత్యామ్నాయం **pratyaamnaayam** *n.* 1 substitute. 2 alternative.

ప్రత్యుత్తరం **pratyuttaram** *n.* answer, reply, response, rejoinder.

ప్రత్యుత్థానం చేయు **pratyutthaanam ceeyu** *v.i.* to rise and greet a visitor on arrival.

ప్రత్యుత్పత్తి **pratyutpatti** *n.* reproduction.

ప్రత్యుత్పన్నమతి **pratyutpannamati** *n.* quick-witted person.

ప్రత్యుపకారం **pratyupakaaram** *n.* return favour.

ప్రత్యూష **pratyuuSa** *n.* dawn, daybreak.

ప్రత్యేక **pratyeeka** *adj.* 1 special, particular. 2 separate, distinct, independent. 3 specific.

ప్రత్యేకంగా **pratyeekangaa** *adv.* 1 specially, particularly. 2 separately, distinctly.

ప్రత్యేకత **pratyeekata** *n.* 1 speciality, peculiarity, special feature, special significance, uniqueness. 2 separateness, distinctness.

ప్రత్యేక హక్కు **pratyeeka hakku** *n.* privilege.

ప్రత్యేకించి **pratyeekinci** I. *past. participle of* **pratyeekincu**; **~ ceppu** (i) to make special mention of; (ii) to emphasise. II. *adv.* separately, specifically, particularly; **eDwaarD Taamsan naalugaydu roojulanaaDu canipoowaDam iNDiyaaku ~ santaapa kaaraNam** the death of Edward Thompson four or five days ago is particularly a cause of mourning for India.

ప్రత్యేకించు **pratyeekincu** *v.t.* 1 to set apart, separate. 2 to set aside, reserve.

ప్రథ **pratha** *n. class.* fame, repute.

ప్రథమ **prathama** *adj.* first.

ప్రథమంగా **prathamangaa** *adv.* for the first time, initially.

ప్రథమగణ్య **prathamagaNya** *adj.* first of all, first and foremost.

ప్రథమచికిత్స **prathamacikitsa** *n.* first aid.

ప్రథమపురుష **prathamapuruSa** *n. gram.* third person.

ప్రథమావిభక్తి **prathamaawibhakti** *n. gram.* nominative case.

ప్రద **prada** *adjvl. termination signifying* giving, conferring, bestowing, e.g., **gawrawa ~** honourable; **jaya ~** successful.

ప్రదక్షిణం **pradakSiNam** *n.* 1 circumambulation of a temple keeping it on o.'s right hand. 2 *colloq.* **udyoogamkoosam naa cuTTuu pradakSiNaalu ceestunnaaDu** he is constantly running after me in search of a job.

ప్రదర్శకుడు **pradarśakuDu** *n.* demonstrator, exhibitor.

ప్రదర్శనం **pradarśanam** *n.* exhibition, performance, show, demonstration, presentation, display.

ప్రదర్శించు **pradarśincu** *v.t.* to exhibit, display, show, reveal, evince.

ప్రదాత **pradaata** *n.* giver, donor.

ప్రదానం **pradaanam** *n.* presentation, conferring.

ప్రదానం చేయు **pradaanam ceeyu** *v.i.* to present, confer.

ప్రదీప్తం అవు **pradiiptam awu** *v.i.* to shine brightly.

ప్రదీప్తి **pradiipti** *n.* shining, brightness.

ప్రదేశం **pradeesam** *n.* place, locality, region, country.

ప్రదోష **pradooSa** *n. class.* evening twilight.

ప్రధనం **pradhanam** *n. class.* fight, battle.

ప్రధనభూమి **pradhanabhuumi** *n. class.* battlefield.

ప్రధాన **pradhaana** *adj.* **1** principal, chief, main, prominent, salient, predominant, pre-eminent. **2** *as second part of an adjvl. compound* concentrating on, laying stress on; **sangiita ~ citram** musical (movie); **haasya ~ citram** comic (movie).

ప్రధానం **pradhaanam** *n.* **1** importance, s.g important. **2** *dial.* betrothal.

ప్రధానం అవు **pradhaanam awu** *v.i.* **1** to be important. **2** to predominate.

ప్రధానంగా **pradhaanangaa** *adv.* **1** mainly, chiefly, predominantly. **2** *as second part of an advbl. compound* concentrating on, laying stress on; **wyakti duuSaNa leekuNDaa wiSaya~ raastee weesukoNTaam** if the writing concentrates on material facts without vilifying individuals we will publish it.

ప్రధానం చేయు **pradhaanam ceeyu** *v.t. dial.* to betroth.

ప్రధాన న్యాయమూర్తి **pradhaana nyaayamuurti** *n.* Chief Justice.

ప్రధాన మంత్రి, ప్రధాని **pradhaana mantri, pradhaani** *n.* Prime Minister.

ప్రపంచం **prapancam** *n.* world.

ప్రపంచించు **prapancincu** *v.t.* to spread (s.g) around the world, make (s.g) universal.

ప్రపత్తి **prapatti** *n. class.* paying respect; **mana bhaaSaku raanunna gawrawa prapattulawalla** on account of the honour and respect that will be paid to our language.

ప్రపూర్ణ **prapuurNa** *adj.* full; **~ candruDu** full moon.

ప్రప్రథమ **praprathama** *adj.* the very first.

ప్రప్రథమంగా **praprathamangaa** *adv.* first of all, at the very start.

ప్రఫుల్ల **praphulla** *adj. class.* in full bloom, blooming, fully blown: **~ candruDu** full moon: **atani mukham ~ maynadi** his face was blooming with happiness.

ప్రబంధం **prabandham** *n.* tale or fable composed partly in verse and partly in ornate prose; this style of Telugu literature was developed in the fifteenth and sixteenth centuries, a period known as **prabandha yugam.**

ప్రబల **prabala** *adj.* **1** mighty, powerful, strong, potent. **2** prevailing, prevalent. **3** [pre]dominant. **4** important.

ప్రబలం అవు, ప్రబలు **prabalam awu, prabalu** *v.i.* **1** to become strong or powerful. **2** to prevail, [pre]dominate, preponderate. **3** to grow, increase, spread, intensify.

ప్రబలంగా **prabalangaa** *adv.* predominantly.

ప్రబుద్ధ **prabuddha** *adj.* (intellectually) awakened.

ప్రబుద్ధంచేయు **prabuddham ceeyu** *v.t.* to awaken, arouse, bring to light (mental faculties).

ప్రబుద్ధుడు **prabuddhuDu** *n.* wise, enlightened person (may be used sarcastically).

ప్రబోధం **praboodham** *n.* moral teaching, preaching, message.

ప్రబోధకుడు **praboodhakuDu** *n.* preacher; **mata~** religious preacher.

ప్రబోధించు **praboodhincu** *v.t.* **1** to preach, teach. **2** to advise, counsel.

ప్రభ **prabha**[1] *n.* brightness, splendour; **ippuDu aayana~ weligipootunnadi** at present he is in the limelight.

ప్రభ **prabha**[2] *n.* kind of canopy offered to Siva in the annual festival at Kotappakonda in Guntur district.

ప్రభంజనం **prabhanjanam** *n. class.* strong wind, gale.

ప్రభవ **prabhawa** *n.* first year of the Hindu cycle of sixty years.

ప్రభవం **prabhawam** *n. class.* birth.

ప్రభవించు **prabhawincu** *v.i. class.* to be born, be produced, come into being, come into existence.

ప్రభవిల్లు **prabhawillu** *v.i. class.* to flourish.

ప్రభాకరుడు **prabhaakaruDu** *n. class.* sun.

ప్రభాత[ం] **prabhaata[m]** *n.* dawn.

ప్రభావం **prabhaawam** *n.* **1** influence, effect. **2** power, might, strength.

ప్రభావిత **prabhaawita** *adj.* influenced, affected.

ప్రభు[వు] **prabhu[wu]** *n.* lord, master, ruler.

ప్రభుత **prabhuta** *n.* authority, power, mastery, dominion, rulership, governance.

ప్రభుత్వ **prabhutwa** *adj.* government, state; **prabhutwoodyoogi** government employee; **~rangam** state sector, public sector.

ప్రభుత్వం **prabhutwam** *n.* **1** government. **2** power, authority, supremacy.

ప్రభువర్గం **prabhuwargam** *n.* ruling class.

ప్రభృతులు **prabhṛtulu** *n. phrase* and other persons.

ప్రమత్త **pramatta** *adj. class.* heedless, negligent, neglectful of duty.

ప్రమత్తుడు **pramattuDu** *n. class.* person who is negligent or not conscientious, person who is unmindful of duty.

ప్రమథలు, ప్రమథగణాలు **pramathalu, pramathagaNaalu** *n.pl.* mythological servants of Siva.

ప్రమద **pramada** *n. class.* woman.

ప్రమదావనం **pramadaawanam** *n.* park set apart for the ladies of a palace.

ప్రమాణం **pramaaNam** *n.* **1** standard, criterion, norm; **pramaaNaruupam** standard form; **antaTaa wartincee saamaanya~** common standard that is applicable everywhere. **2** measure, scale, extent, size, quantity, bulk; **ciru caapa ~gala kaagitam** a paper the size of a small mat; **kuura boggu pramaaNaaniki maaDindi** the curry was burnt to [the extent of] a cinder; **bhuuwasatiki gariSTa~ nirNayincu** to set a maximum extent for the enjoyment of land. **3** proof, testimony, authority; **tikkana kaalamuloonee aa śabdaaniki aa arthamu kaliginaTTu aayana prayoogamee pramaaNamu** his own usage is proof that the word bore that meaning in Tikkana's time. **4** oath.

ప్రమాణం చేయు **pramaaNam ceeyu** *v.i.* to swear, take an oath.

ప్రమాణపత్రం **pramaaNapatram** *n. legal* affidavit.

ప్రమాణపూర్వకంగా , ప్రమాణపూర్తిగా **pramaaNapuurwakangaa, pramaaNapuurtigaa** *adv.* on oath.

ప్రమాణీకరణం **pramaaNiikaraNam** *n.* standardisation.

ప్రమాణీకరించు **pramaaNiikarincu** *v.t.* to standardise.

ప్రమాద **pramaada** *adj.* dangerous, hazardous, risky; ~ **paristhitulu** dangerous circumstances.

ప్రమాదం **pramaadam** *n.* 1 danger. 2 mishap, accident, mischance, hazard, risk. 3 chance; **aayana waccee ~ undi** there is a chance of his coming.

ప్రమాదకర **pramaadakara** *adj.* dangerous, fraught with danger, liable to cause danger; **widyucchaktitoo aaDukoowaDam ~ m** it is dangerous to play with electricity.

ప్రమాది **pramaadi** *n.* thirteenth year of the Hindu cycle of sixty years.

ప్రమాదీచ **pramaadiica** *n.* forty-seventh year of the Hindu cycle of sixty years.

ప్రమిద **pramida** *n.* earthenware saucer containing oil and a wick, used as a lamp.

ప్రముక్త **pramukta** *adj. class.* (of a weapon) released, fired.

ప్రముఖ **pramukha** *adj.* 1 chief, principal. 2 prominent, important, leading.

ప్రముఖుడు **pramukhuDu** *n., gen. pl.* **pramukhulu** important persons.

ప్రమేయం **prameeyam** *n.* 1 concern, connection, involvement; **induloo naa[ku] ~ leedu** this is no concern of mine; **idi naa wyawahaaram, ewaDi ~ eemii leedu** this is my affair, no-one else has any involvement in it; **waaDi ~ leekuNDaa** without involving him *or* without consulting him *or* without reference to him. 2 plan, move, steps, measures; **mii pilla peLLi ~ eemaynaa undaa**? are you taking any steps about your daughter's marriage? "**bhoojanam ~ undaa leedaa? muuDawutunnadi**" "**aa ~ miidanee unnaam**" "is there any move to have lunch? it is nearly three o'clock". "we were just thinking about it". 3 *maths. sci.* function.

ప్రమేయాత్మక **prameeyaatmaka** *adj. maths. sci.* functional.

ప్రమోదం **pramoodam** *n. class.* joy, delight.

ప్రమోదూత **pramooduuta** *n.* fourth year of the Hindu cycle of sixty years.

ప్రయత్నం **prayatnam** *n.* attempt, endeavour, effort; *see also* **prayatnaalu**.

ప్రయత్నపూర్వకంగా **prayatnapuurwakangaa** *adv.* with a great effort.

ప్రయత్నాలు **prayatnaalu** *n.pl.* 1 efforts. 2 preparations, arrangements; **peLLi ~** marriage arrangements; **yuddha ~** preparations for war; **waNTa ~** cooking operations.

ప్రయత్నించు **prayatnincu** *v.i.* to try, attempt, endeavour, make an effort.

ప్రయాణం **prayaaNam** *n.* journey, travel.

ప్రయాణం అవు, ప్రయాణం కట్టు **prayaaNam awu, prayaaNam kaTTu** *v.i.* to embark on a journey, start on a journey.

ప్రయాణంపెట్టుకొను **prayaaNam peTTukonu** *v.i.* to plan to make a journey.

ప్రయాణించు, ప్రయాణం చేయు **prayaaNincu, prayaaNam ceeyu** *v.i.* to make a journey, travel.

ప్రయాణికుడు **prayaaNikuDu** *n.* traveller, passenger.

ప్రయాస[ం] **prayaasa[m]** *n.* toil, effort, exertion, trouble, strain.

ప్రయాసపడు **prayaasapaDu** *v.i.* to strive hard, make an effort.

ప్రయాసపెట్టు **prayaasa peTTu** *v.t.* to harass, cause trouble (to s.o.).

ప్రయుక్త **prayukta** *adj. class.* associated, connected; *cf.* **bhaaSaa ~**.

ప్రయుక్తం **prayuktam** *n.* established usage; **kawi ~** poetic usage; **ii padaalu wiśeeSaNaalugaa kuuDaa ~ awtaayi** these words are also used as adjectives.

ప్రయుక్తి **prayukti** *n. class.* use, application.

ప్రయోక్త **prayookta** *n. theat.* 1 prompter. 2 promoter. 3 person who speaks the **prastaawana** or introduction to a drama.

ప్రయోగం **prayoogam** *n.* 1 application, use. 2 usage. 3 practice (as opposed to theory). 4 experiment. 5 launch[ing] (of a missile).

ప్రయోగపాత్ర **prayoogapaatra** *n. chem.* beaker, retort.

ప్రయోగశాల **prayoogaśaala** *n.* laboratory.

ప్రయోగశీలి **prayoogaśiili** *n.* innovator, experimenter.

ప్రయోగాత్మక **prayoogaatmaka** *adj.* experimental.

ప్రయోగించు **prayoogincu** *v.t.* 1 to use, make use of, employ. 2 to launch, discharge (missile).

ప్రయోజకత్వం **prayoojakatwam** *n.* capability, capacity, usefulness.

ప్రయోజకుడు **prayoojakuDu** *n.* able or capable or competent person; **waaDu ~ ayyEEDu** he has become capable of earning his living.

ప్రయోజనం **prayoojanam** *n.* 1 use[fulness], advantage, profit, benefit, interest; **eeDistee eem ~**? what is the use of crying? **daaniwalla maaku eemii ~ leedu** there is no advantage in that to us; **jaatiiya prayoojanaalu** national interests. 2 aim, purpose, motive; **sangha prayoojanaalu** social purposes.

ప్రయోజనకర **prayoojanakara** *adj.* useful, profitable, beneficial, expedient, advantageous, serviceable.

ప్రయోజనకారి **prayoojanakaari** *n.* s.g that is beneficial, advantageous, useful, helpful, expedient or serviceable.

ప్రయోజనాత్మక **prayoojanaatmaka** *adj.* 1 functional, practical. 2 verifiable by experiment.

ప్రలాపం **pralaapam** *n.* vain or idle talk.

ప్రలుబ్ధి **pralubdhi** *n. second part of a n. compound meaning* one who is avid for, one who craves for.

ప్రలోభం **praloobham** *n.* 1 greed, avidity, lust. 2 allurement, enticement.

ప్రలోభనం **praloobhanam** *n.* allurement, enticement.

ప్రలోభపడు, ప్రలోభించు **praloobhapaDu , praloobhincu** *v.i.* to be lured, be enticed.

ప్రలోభ పెట్టు **praloobhapeTTu** *v.t.* to lure, entice.

ప్రల్లదనం **pralladanam** *same as* **palladanam.**

ప్రళయం **praLayam** *n.* 1 destruction, calamity. 2 destruction of the world at the end of an epoch (**kalpa**).

ప్రళయంగా **praLayangaa** *adv.* 1 prodigiously. 2 grandly; **waaDi pani ~ undi** he lives in a grand style; **~ maaTLaaDataaDu** he talks pompously.

ప్రవక్త **prawakta** *n.* prophet.

ప్రవచనం **prawacanam** *n.* 1 proclaiming, expounding. 2 saying, proclamation, pronouncement. 3 sacred text, the Vedas.

ప్రవచించు **prawacincu** *v.t.* 1 to declaim, pronounce (discourse). 2 to proclaim, preach.

ప్రవర **prawara** *n.* family, lineage; **~ ceppu** to recite the name of o.'s ancestors for seven generations.

ప్రవరుడు **prawaruDu** *n. class.* 1 excellent person. 2 name of a character in Allasani Peddana's poetical work 'Manucaritra' renowned for his self-control.

ప్రవర్తకుడు **prawartakuDu** *n.* 1 originator, initiator, founder. 2 proponent, promoter.

ప్రవర్తన **prawartana** *n.* conduct, behaviour.

ప్రవర్తించు **prawartincu** *v.i.* to behave, conduct o.s.; **naatoo sneehangaa prawartincEEDu** he behaved towards me in a friendly manner.

ప్రవర్తిల్లు **prawartillu** *v.i. class.* to happen, occur, take place.

ప్రవర్ధమాన **prawardhamaana** *adj.* 1 increasing, growing, developing. 2 flourishing.

ప్రవర్ధిల్లు **prawardhillu** *v.i.* to increase, grow, flourish, prosper.

ప్రవహించు **prawahincu** *v.i.* to flow.

ప్రవాదం **prawaadam** *n.* 1 rumour, report. 2 popular saying.

ప్రవాళం **prawaaLam** *n. class.* coral.

ప్రవాసం **prawaasam** *n.* living away from home, living abroad.

ప్రవాసి **prawaasi** *n.* person living away from home, exile.

ప్రవాహం **prawaaham** *n.* stream, flow, current.

ప్రవీణత **prawiiNata** *n.* skill, proficiency.

ప్రవీణుడు **prawiiNuDu** *n.* skilful or clever or accomplished person, expert; *see* **ubhaya.**

ప్రవృత్తి **prawṛtti** *n.* 1 nature, character, disposition, tendency, propensity; **maanawa ~** human nature; **manaḥ ~** nature of the mind, mentality. 2 conduct, behaviour. 3 pattern; **śiitooSNasthiti prakriyalu prawṛttulu** climatic processes and patterns.

ప్రవేశం **praweeśam** *n.* 1 entrance, entry; **praweeśa pariikSa** entrance examination; *see* **gṛha ~**. 2 access, admission. 3 slight knowledge of or acquaintance with a language or skill; **ataniki malayaaLam bhaaSa baagaa waccu, kannaDamloo ataniki ~ undi** he knows the Malayalam language well and has a smattering of Kannada; **jaanapada geeyaalni seekarincee waariloo caalaamandiki sangiitamloo tagina ~ leedu** many of those persons who collect folk songs do not have a sufficient acquaintance with music.

ప్రవేశపెట్టు **praweeśapeTTu** *v.t.* 1 to introduce, bring forward (proposal). 2 to bring in, usher in, admit (person from outside).

ప్రవేశించు **praweeśincu** *v.i.* 1 to enter. 2 **madhyaloo ~** to intervene, interfere. 3 (*also* **praweeśam awu**) to arrive; **kaalam maarindi, paariśraamika yugam praweeśincindi** (*or* **praweeśam ayindi**) times changed, the industrial age arrived.

ప్రవేశిక **praweeśika** *n. class.* introduction (to a book).

ప్రవ్రజ్య **prawrajya** *n. class.* wandering as a religious mendicant.

ప్రవ్రాజకుడు **prawraajakuDu** *n. class.* wandering ascetic.

ప్రశంస **praśamsa** *n.* 1 praise, commendation. 2 mention; **anduloo mii ~ waccindi** in that connection mention was made of you.

ప్రశంసనీయ **praśamsaniiya** *adj.* praiseworthy, commendable, laudable.

ప్రశంసించు **praśamsincu** *v.t.* to praise, commend, extol.

ప్రశమనం **praśamanam** *n. class.* calming, soothing.

ప్రశస్త **praśasta** *adj.* 1 famous, renowned, celebrated. 2 best, excellent, optimum. 3 superior.

ప్రశస్తి **praśasti** *n.* 1 fame, celebrity, renown. 2 excellence. 3 glory, eminence.

ప్రశాంత **praśaanta** *adj.* quiet, serene, calm, tranquil, peaceful.

ప్రశాంతి, ప్రశాంతత **praśaanti, praśaantata** *n.* peace [of mind], tranquillity, quiet, calm[ness], serenity.

ప్రశాఖ **praśaakha** *n.* small branch, twig.

ప్రశిష్యుడు **praśiSyuDu** *n.* disciple of a disciple.

ప్రశ్న **praśna** *n.* 1 question, query, enquiry. 2 divination.

ప్రశ్న పత్రం **praśna patram** *n.* question paper.

ప్రశ్న వాచకం **praśna waacakam** *n. gram.* interrogative (form, sentence).

ప్రశ్నార్థక **praśnaarthaka** *adj. gram.* interrogative.

ప్రశ్నార్థకం **praśnaarthakam** *n.* 1 interrogative (form, sentence). 2 question mark.

ప్రశ్నార్థకంగా **praśnaarthakangaa** *adv.* questioningly, enquiringly.

ప్రశ్నావళి **praśnaawaLi** *n.* 1 questionnaire. 2 volley of questions.

ప్రశ్నించు **praśnincu** *v.i. and t.* to question, ask, enquire, interrogate, put a question.

ప్రష్ట **praSTa** *n. class.* person who asks questions.

ప్రసంగం **prasangam** *n.* 1 speech, lecture, address, discourse. 2 talk, conversation.

ప్రసంగవశాత్తు **prasangawaśaattu** *adv.* in the course of conversation.

ప్రసంగించు **prasangincu** *v.i.* to lecture, deliver a speech.

ప్రసక్తం **prasaktam** *n.* s.g that is mentioned.

ప్రసక్తి **prasakti** *n.* 1 subject, topic. 2 mention, consideration, thought, idea; **sambhaaSaNaloo aayana ~ waccindi** mention was made of him in the conversation; **kula ~ leekuN-**

Daa keewalam meriTpay aadhaarapaDi based solely on merit without consideration of community. 3 relationship, connection, concern, involvement, reference: **induloo waaDi ~ eemii leedu** he has no involvement in this affair; **tana talli śaktisaamarthyaalatoo sundaraaniki ~ leedu** Sundaram was not concerned with his mother's means or resources.

ప్రసన్న **prasanna** *adj.* 1 joyful, happy, cheerful, genial. 2 kind, gracious.

ప్రసన్నత **prasannata** *n.* joy, happiness, cheerfulness, geniality, good humour.

ప్రసన్నుడు **prasannuDu** *n.* one who is pleased or happy.

ప్రసరణం **prasaraNam** *n.* 1 spreading, extending. 2 circulation: **rakta ~** circulation of blood.

ప్రసరించు **prasarincu** I. *v.i.* to spread, extend, radiate. II. *v.t.* (*also* **prasarimpa ceeyu**) to spread, emit (ideas, influence).

ప్రసవం **prasawam** *n.* delivery, childbirth, confinement: **prasawa strii** woman in childbirth.

ప్రసవించు **prasawincu** *v.t.* to bear, give birth to.

ప్రసాదం **prasaadam** *n.* 1 food offered to a deity and subsequently distributed to devotees. 2 *class.* kindness, favour, grace. 3 *class.* gift, grant: **bhagawat ~ ayna** granted by God.

ప్రసాదించు **prasaadincu** *v.t.* to bestow, grant.

ప్రసాధనం **prasaadhanam** *n.* 1 decoration, adornment. 2 decor, get up: **ee grantha wikrayaśaalaloo aynaa kaLLanu aakarSincagala andamayna ~ prasphuTangaanee undi** in any bookshop the attractive and handsome get up (of a certain book) is conspicuous.

ప్రసారం **prasaaram** *n.* 1 spreading, extension. 2 broadcasting.

ప్రసారం చేయు **prasaaram ceeyu** *v.t.* to broadcast.

ప్రసార కేంద్రం **prasaara keendram** *n.* broadcasting station.

ప్రసిద్ధ **prasiddha** *adj.* famous, celebrated, illustrious, wellknown.

ప్రసిద్ధార్థం **prasiddhaartham** *n.* principal or current or commonly understood meaning.

ప్రసిద్ధి **prasiddhi** *n.* fame, celebrity, renown.

ప్రసిద్ధికి ఎక్కు **prasiddhiki ekku** *v.i.* to become famous.

ప్రసిద్ధుడు **prasiddhuDu** *n.* famous or wellknown person.

ప్రసూతి **prasuuti** *n.* childbirth.

ప్రసూతిక **prasuutika** *n. class.* woman who has borne a child within the previous twelve days.

ప్రసూతిగృహం **prasuutigṛham** *n.* maternity home.

ప్రసూనం **prasuunam** *n. class.* flower, bud, fruit: **puujaa prasuunaalu** flowers offered to a deity in worship.

ప్రస్తావన **prastaawana** *n.* 1 subject, topic. 2 mention, reference; **~ ettu** to make mention. 3 introduction, preface (to a book). 4 prologue to a drama which is spoken by the **prayookta** and follows the **naandi** (prelude).

ప్రస్తావించు **prastaawincu** *v.t.* 1 to mention, make mention of, refer to. 2 to speak of, talk about, discuss. 3 to deal with, dwell on (a subject for discussion).

ప్రస్తుత **prastuta** *adj.* present: **~ paristhitulu** present circumstances.

ప్రస్తుతం **prastutam** *adv.* at present.

ప్రస్తుతి **prastuti** *n.* praise, applause, eulogy.

ప్రస్తుతించు **prastutincu** *v.t.* to praise, applaud, extol.

ప్రస్థం **prastham** *n. class.* tableland on the summit of a mountain.

ప్రస్థానం **prasthaanam** *n. class.* 1 start of a journey. 2 journey, march, progress.

ప్రస్థానభేరి **prasthaana bheeri** *n. class.* great drum announcing an army's march.

ప్రస్థానించు **prasthaanincu** *v.i. class.* to set out on a march or journey.

ప్రస్ఫుట **prasphuTa** *adj.* clearly discernible, conspicuous, manifest, plain, obvious.

ప్రస్ఫోటనం **prasphooTanam** *n.* splitting or cracking noise.

ప్రస్వనం **praswanam** *n. class.* loud resounding noise.

ప్రహరి[గోడ] **prahari[gooDa]** *n.* compound wall, boundary wall.

ప్రహర్షం **praharSam** *n.* joy, exultation.

ప్రహసనం **prahasanam** *n.* farce, satire, burlesque.

ప్రహారం **prahaaram** *n.* heavy blow.

ప్రహేళి[క] **praheeLi[ka]** *n.* 1 *class.* poem with a hidden meaning. 2 riddle, conundrum.

ప్రహ్లాదం **prahlaadam** *n.* joy, happiness.

ప్రా - praa

ప్రాంగణం **praangaNam** *n. class.* **1** courtyard in front of a house. **2** precincts, campus.

ప్రాంతం **praantam** *n.* neighbourhood, vicinity, locality, territory, region, area; **maa ~ loo allarlu jarugutunnayi** affrays are taking place in our neighbourhood; **kaDapa jillaaloo mottam paNTala ~ 4,33,000 hekTaarlu** the total area of crops in Cuddapah district is 4,33,000 hectares; **maa iNTiki sTeeSanuki madhya ~ loo ekkaDoo uNTaaDu waaDu** he lives somewhere in between our house and the station; **oNTigaNTa naalugu gaNTala madhya ~ loo cuT-Taalu waccEEru** our relations came sometime between one and four o'clock; **wela nuuru ruupaayalu leedaa aa ~ loo aytee koni tiisukuraNDi** if the cost is in the region of (*or* if the cost is round about) a hundred rupees, please buy and bring it.

ప్రాంతీయ **praantiiya** *adj.* regional, territorial.

ప్రాంతీయతావాదం **praantiiyataawaadam** *n.* regionalism.

ప్రాంతీయుడు **praantiiyuDu** *n.* inhabitant of a region, local person.

ప్రాక్ **praak** *Sanskrit adjvl. prefix meaning* (i) east; **praagdiśa** easterly direction; (ii) in front, before; **praakcaritra** prehistory.

ప్రాకారం **praakaaram** *n.* **1** rampart. **2** encircling or surrounding wall.

ప్రాకు **praaku** *same as* **paaku.**

ప్రాకులాట, ప్రాకులాడు **praakulaaTa, praakulaaDu** *same as* **paakulaaTa, paakulaaDu.**

ప్రాకృతం **praakṛtam** *n.* Prakrit, name given to a number of colloquial languages derived from Sanskrit.

ప్రాకృతిక **praakṛtika** *adj.* natural.

ప్రాకృతుడు **praakṛtuDu** *n.* simple peasant, rustic.

ప్రాక్కల్పన **praakkalpana** *n.* hypothesis.

ప్రాగల్భ్యం **praagalbhayam** *n.* **1** skill, ability. **2** boldness, resolution. **3** energy, spiritedness.

ప్రాగ్రూపం **praagruupam** *n.* original form, primary form.

ప్రాఘాతం **praaghaatam** *n. phys.* percussion.

ప్రాచీన **praaciina** *adj.* **1** old, ancient, archaic, antiquated. **2** eastern.

ప్రాచీన[తమ] ఆంధ్రం **praaciina[tama] aandhram** *n.* Old Telugu.

ప్రాచుర్యం **praacuryam** *n.* **1** wide distribution, abundance. **2** fame, publicity, wide publication. **3** importance, prominence.

ప్రాచ్య **praacya** *adj.* eastern, oriental.

ప్రాచ్యం **praacyam** *n.* east, orient.

ప్రాజ్ఞ **praajna** *class. alt. form of* **prajña.**

ప్రాజ్ఞత **praajñata** *n. class.* prudence.

ప్రాజ్ఞుడు **praajñuDu** *n. class.* wise, learned and scholarly man, sage.

ప్రాడ్వివాకుడు **praaDwiwaakuDu** *n. class.* judge, adjudicator.

ప్రాణం **praaNam** *n.* **1** life; **naa bondiloo ~ uNDagaa** as long as there is life in my body *or* so long as I remain alive; **~ pooyinaa ceppanu** I will not say it even at the cost of my life; **pulini praaNaalatoo paTTukonnaaru** they caught the tiger alive. **2** s.g as dear as o.'s life; **nuwwaNTee naaku ~** you are as dear as life to me; **cakrawartiki tooTaNTee ~** Chakravarti is devoted to his garden. **3** breath; **praaNaalu** (*or* **uupiri**) **bigapaTTukonu** to hold o.'s breath. **4** the first of the five vital airs (**panca praaNaalu**) in traditional medicine. **5** heart, mind, conscience; **abaddham aaDEEnani naa ~** (*or* **naa manassu**) **piikutunnadi** my conscience is worrying me because I told a lie; **aNaa kharcu peTTaalaNTee ~ piikeedi aameki** her mind would be upset if she had to spend (even) one anna; **paapam, aayana ~ manawaraalni oka saari cuuDaalani mahaa piikutunnadi** poor man, his heart is tormenting him because he yearns to see his granddaughter just once. **6** *idiomatic usages*: (i) **~ araceeta/guppeTLoo/piDikiTa paTTukonu** (*or* **peT-Tukonu**) *lit.* to hold o.'s life in o.'s hands, i.e., to be in great fear for o.'s life, be in suspense; (ii) **aayanaku ~ caali waccindi** he was greatly vexed *or* he was greatly distressed; (iii) **aayanni cuuDagaanee naa ~ leeci waccindi** as soon as I saw him I cheered up *or* as soon as I saw him I brightened up; (iv) **~ pooyu** *lit.* to pour life into, *hence* to bring to life, resuscitate, revive, nourish; **kotta aaśalaku ~** (*or* **uupiri**) **poosEEDu** he nourished fresh hopes; (v) **naa ~ tooDeestunnaaDu/tiistunnaaDu** he is worrying me to death; (vi) **~ wisugu** (*or* **~ rooyu**) to feel disgusted; (vii) **~ wiDucu** to pass away, die; (viii) **naa ~ koTTukoNTunnadi** I feel very agitated; (ix) **roogiki ~ miidiki waccindi** the patient is/was on the point of death; *see* **alpa ~, mahaa ~, kaDabaTTu, paypraaNaalu;** *see also* **praaNaaniki.**

ప్రాణగొడ్డం **praaNagoDDam** *n.* danger to life.

ప్రాణత్యాగం **praaNatyaagam** *n.* sacrificing o.'s life.

ప్రాణదానం **praaNadaanam** *n.* **1** saving of life. **2** sparing of life.

ప్రాణప్రతిష్ఠ **praaNapratiSTa** *n.* **1** bringing to life, vitalising. **2** ceremony by which a god is invoked and installed in an image or idol.

ప్రాణప్రదంగా **praaNapradangaa** *adv.* very dearly, very carefully, preciously.

ప్రాణప్రదమైన **praaNapradamayna** *adj.* **1** precious. **2** vital[ly important].

ప్రాణవాయువు **praaNawaayuwu** *n.* oxygen.

ప్రాణసంకటం **praaNasankaTam** *n.* danger to life, mortal danger.

ప్రాణస్నేహితుడు **praaNasneehituDu** *n.* close friend, bosom friend.

ప్రాణహాని **praaNahaani** *n.* destruction of life, loss of life.

ప్రాణాంతక **praaNaantaka** *adj.* deadly, lethal.

ప్రాణాధికంగా **praaNaadhikangaa** *adv.* more than o.'s life: ~ **preemincina bharta** the husband whom she loves more than her own life.

ప్రాణానికి **praaNaaniki** *dative of* **praaNam 1** *idiomatic usages*: (i) **praaNaalaku tegincu** to be in fear for o.'s life, risk losing o.'s life, act in a desperate manner; **ubhaya pakSaaluu praaNaalaku teginci pooraaDutunnaayi** both sides are fighting desperately; (ii) **naa ~ ii kharcu kuuDaa ippuDee raawaalEE?** must this expense come just now, to add to my misfortune?; **naa ~ waccindi** I am completely disheartened *or* I cannot stand any more *or* this is the last straw (*the underlying meaning is* this problem has come to take away my life). **2** ~ *following a n. or pron. in the genitive forms an advbl. phrase meaning* in o.'s personal capacity, as regards o.s., personally, for o.'s own part; **nijaaniki idi eemanta pedda pani kaadu gaanii naa ~ idi pedda panee** this is really not such a big task but for me considering my capacity it is a big task; **waaDu itaratraa pedda teliwigalawaaDu kaadu gaanii sundaram ~ waaDi sangiitamloo cepparaani aakarSaNa uNDeedi** in other respects he was not a very intelligent boy but for Sundaram personally there was an inexpressible attraction in his music.

ప్రాణాయామం **praaNaayaamam** *n.* ritual mode of controlling o.'s breathing by yogic methods.

ప్రాణావసర **praaNaawasara** *adj.* vitally necessary.

ప్రాణి **praaNi** *n.* living creature.

ప్రాణోత్క్రమణం **praaNootkramaNam** *n.* departure from life, death.

ప్రాత **praata** *same as* **paata.**

ప్రాతఃకాలం **praatahkaalam** *n.* early morning.

ప్రాతస్సంధ్య **praatassandhya** *n.* **1** early morning twilight. **2** sandhya prayers said at dawn.

ప్రాతికూల్యం **praatikuulyam** *n.* objection, opposition, antipathy, hostility.

ప్రాతినిధ్యం **praatinidhyam** *n.* representation.

ప్రాతిపదిక **praatipadika** *n.* base, basis.

ప్రాథమిక **praathamika** *adj.* primary, elementary.

ప్రాథమిక విద్య **praathamika widya** *n.* elementary or primary education.

ప్రాథమిక సత్వాలు, ప్రాథమిక హక్కులు **praathamika satwaalu, praathamika hakkulu** *n.pl.* fundamental rights.

ప్రాథమికాచ్చు **praathamikaaccu** *n. ling.* cardinal vowel.

ప్రాదుర్భవించు **praadurbhawincu** *v.i.* to come into existence.

ప్రాదుర్భావం **praadurbhaawam** *n.* coming into existence, emergence, birth.

ప్రాదేశిక **praadeeśika** *adj.* local, regional, provincial, territorial.

ప్రాధాన్యం **praadhaanyam** *n.* **1** primary importance. **2** preference, priority. **3** predominance.

ప్రాధాన్యక్రమం, **praadhaanyakramam** *n.* **1** order of importance. **2** system of priorities.

ప్రాధాన్యత **praadhaanyata** *n.* priority.

ప్రాధేయపడు **praadheeyapaDu** *v.i and t.* to entreat, beg, beseech.

ప్రాధేయ పూర్వకంగా **praadheeya puurwakangaa** *adv.* full of entreaty, imploringly.

ప్రాపంచిక **praapancika** *adj. class.* worldly, mundane; ~ **sukhaalu** worldly pleasures.

ప్రాపకం **praapakam** *n.* **1** protection, patronage, support. **2** refuge.

ప్రాపు **praapu** *n.* **1** prop, support. **2** patronage.

ప్రాప్తం **praaptam** I. *n.* that which falls to o.'s lot, fate, luck, fortune; **adi naaku ~ leedu** I was not fated for that: **waaDiki iraway naaku padi ruupaayalu waccEEyi. ewaDiki enta praaptamoo antee anukonnnaanu** he got twenty rupees and I got ten. I reflected that (in life) each person receives only as much as is ordained for him (by his fate). II. *adj.* **1** obtained, acquired, received. **2** (of a disease) caught, contracted.

ప్రాప్తి **praapti** *n.* **1** luck, fortune; **deenikaynaa ~ uNDaali** in order to obtain anything you must be favoured by fortune; **ippaTiki intee ~ anukoni weLLipooyEEDu** thinking that this was as much as he could expect (*lit.* thinking 'this much is my good fortune') he went away. **2** [the good fortune of] getting, obtaining, attaining, acquiring, achieving, receiving, procuring (always with ref. to s.g abstract) **santaana ~** good fortune of getting offspring; **iSTawastu ~ kay tahatahapaDuwaaDu** one who strives hard for the good fortune of getting what he desires; **punardarśana ~ rastu** may you have the good fortune of coming for darshan again (words uttered by a priest to a devotee on leaving a temple); **swarga ~** attaining heaven; **wijaya ~** achieving success; **dhana ~** acquisition of wealth.

ప్రాప్తించు **praaptincu** *v.i.* **1** to happen, occur, befall, fall to o.'s lot. **2** to accrue, be procured. **3** to devolve, be inherited. **4** (of a disease) be caught, be contracted.

ప్రాప్యం **praapyam** *adj.* attainable, obtainable, procurable.

ప్రాబల్యం **praabalyam** *n.* **1** power, strength; **paristhitula ~** force of circumstances. **2** [pre]dominance, pre-eminence. **3** impact.

ప్రాభవం **praabhawam** *n.* **1** ability, competence. **2** grandeur; **adhikaara ~** display of authority.

ప్రామాణిక **praamaaNika** *adj.* standard, authoritative; **praamaaNikaandhram** standard Telugu.

ప్రామాణికం, ప్రామాణ్యం **praamaNikam, praamaaNyam** *n.* **1** standard, authority. **2** standard form, authoritative form.

ప్రామాణికుడు **praamaaNikuDu** *n.* person who may be accepted as an authority.

ప్రాముఖ్యం **praamukhyam** *n.* **1** importance, significance. **2** prominence, pre-eminence.

ప్రాయం **praayam** I. *n.* **1** age. **2** bloom, prime of life; ~ **loo unna barre** she buffalo of age for mating. II. *second part of an adjvl. or advbl. compound* like, as if; **teene kalupukoni awSadha ~ gaa daanni digamingaali** you must mix it with honey and swallow it like medicine; **andha ~ gaa sancarincu** to wander about blindly; **sthira ~ ayna** quasi-permanent; **aadarśa ~ ayna** ideal; **udaaharaNa ~ ayna** exemplary; **reekhaa ~ gaa** in outline; *see* **suucana ~ gaa, suutra ~ gaa.**

ప్రాయశః **praayaśaḥ** *adv. class.* generally, for the most part.

ప్రాయశ్చిత్తం **praayaścittam** *n.* expiation, propitiation, atonement.

ప్రాయికంగా **praayikangaa** *adv.* in general, commonly, generally.

ప్రాయుడు **praayuDu** *second part of a n. compound meaning* person who has the characteristics of; **paśu**~ person who behaves like a beast, bestial person.

ప్రాయోగికంగా **praayoogikangaa** *adv.* experimentally.

ప్రాయోపవేశం **praayoopaweeśam** *n.* vow to undertake a fast to death.

ప్రారంభ **praarambha** *adj.* beginning, starting, opening, inaugural; **praarambhootsawam** inaugural ceremony.

ప్రారంభం **praarambham** *n.* beginning, start, inception, onset.

ప్రారంభం అవు **praarambham awu** *v.i.* to begin.

ప్రారంభకుడు **praarambhakuDu** *n.* 1 person who starts or begins; **sabhaa**~ opening speaker at a meeting. 2 originator, founder.

ప్రారంభించు **praarambhincu** *v.i. and t.* to begin, start.

ప్రారబ్ధం **praarabdham** *n.* 1 fate, destiny, fortune. 2 predestination.

ప్రార్థన **praarthana** *n.* prayer, request.

ప్రార్థించు **praarthincu** *v.t.* to pray, request; **bhagawantuNNi**~ to pray to God.

ప్రాలు **praalu** *n.pl. class.* rice.

ప్రావాహిక **praawaahika** *adj.* flowing.

ప్రావిర్భవించు **praawirbhawincu** *v.i.* to arise, originate.

ప్రావీణ్యం, ప్రావీణ్యత **praawiiNyam, praawiiNyata** *n.* skill, expertness, competence, expertise, proficiency, accomplishment.

ప్రాశన[ం] **praaśana[m]** *n. class.* eating, tasting; *cf.* **anna**~

ప్రాశస్త్యం **praaśastyam** *n.* excellence.

ప్రాస **praasa** *n.* rule observed in composing classical and some modern Telugu poetry by which the consonant in the second syllable of each line (**paadam**) of a stanza (**padyam**) must be the same.

ప్రాసాదం **praasaadam** *n. class.* king's palace.

ప్రాస్తావిక శ్లోకాలు **praastaawika ślookaalu** *n.pl.* introductory verses recited by the **prayookta** in the introduction (**prastaawana**) to a drama.

ప్రి, ప్రీ, ప్రే - pri, prii, pree

ప్రియం **priyam** I. *n.* love, affection; **śuSka priyaalu** meaningless niceties. II. *adj.* 1 dear, [be]loved, liked, desired. 2 (of price) dear, expensive, costly.

ప్రియంగా **priyangaa** *adv.* 1 lovingly, affectionately, fondly. 2 with liking; **wankaayalu**~ **tiNTaaDu** he likes to eat brinjals.

ప్రియత్వం **priyatwam** *n.* love, affection, liking; **sangiita**~ love of music.

ప్రియుడు **priyuDu** *n.* lover (male).

ప్రియురాలు **priyuraalu** *n.* lover (female).

ప్రీతి **priiti** *n.* love, affection, fondness, liking.

ప్రీతికర **priitikara** *adj.* much liked.

ప్రీతిపాత్రుడు **priitipaatruDu** *n.* person who is loved or liked; **widyaarthulaku priitipaatruDayna upaadhyaayuDu** teacher who is popular with the students.

ప్రేక్షకజనం, ప్రేక్షకలోకం **preekSakajanam, preekSakalookam** *n. pl.* spectators, audience, onlookers.

ప్రేక్షకుడు **preekSakuDu** *n.* spectator, onlooker.

ప్రేగు **preegu** *same as* **peegu.**

ప్రేత[ం] **preeta[m]** *n.* ghost, phantom.

ప్రేమ **preema** *n.* love, affection.

ప్రేమగా **preemagaa** *adv.* kindly, lovingly, affectionately.

ప్రేమపాత్రుడు **preemapaatruDu** *n.* person who is loved or liked.

ప్రేమించు **preemincu** *v.t.* to love, fall in love with.

ప్రేమికుడు **preemikuDu** *n.* lover (male).

ప్రేముడి **preemuDi** *n. class.* love, affection.

ప్రేమైకజీవి **preemaykajiiwi** *n.* one who lives only for love, one who is the embodiment of love.

ప్రేయసి **preeyasi** *n.* lover (female).

ప్రేరకం **preerakam** *n.* inducement, inspiration, encouragement.

ప్రేరణ[ం] **preeraNa[m]** *same as* **preereepaNa.**

ప్రేరణార్థక **preeraNaarthaka** *adj. gram.* causative.

ప్రేరణార్థకం **preeraNaarthakam** *n. gram.* causative form (of a vb.).

ప్రేరిత **preerita** *adj.* incited, spurred on, inspired, encouraged, instigated.

ప్రేరేపణ **preereepaNa** *n.* instigation, incitement, inducement, prompting, encouragement, exhortation, urge.

ప్రేరేపించు **preereepincu** *v.t.* to instigate, incite, induce, urge, impel, prompt, encourage, exhort.

ప్రేలాపన **preelaapana** *same as* **peelaapana.**

ప్రేలు **preelu**[1,2] *same as* **peelu**[1,2].

ప్రేవు **preewu** *class. alt. form of* **peegu.**

ప్రేషకం **preeSakam** *n.* radio transmitter.

ప్రేషక ధనం **preeSaka dhanam** *n.* money remitted, remittance.

ప్రేషణం **preeSaNam** *n. class.* sending.

ప్రో to ప్లు - pro to plu

ప్రొద్దు **proddu** *same as* **poddu.**

ప్రొయ్యి **proyyi** *same as* **poyyi.**

ప్రోక్త **prookta** *n.* one who ordains or proclaims.

ప్రోక్తం **prooktam** *adj.* declared, ordained, proclaimed.

ప్రోక్షణం **prookSaNam** *n. class.* sprinkling.

ప్రోగు **proogu** *same as* **poogu.**

ప్రోచు **proocu** *v.t. class.* to protect, preserve, save.

ప్రోత్సహించు **prootsahincu** *v.t.* to encourage, promote, stimulate, incite, induce.

ప్రోత్సాహం **prootsaaham** *n.* encouragement, incitement, inducement, stimulation; **egumati~** export promotion.

ప్రోత్సాహకుడు **prootsaahakuDu** *n.* one who encourages, promotes, incites or stimulates.

ప్రోది చేయు **proodi ceeyu** *v.i. and t.* to nourish, support, lend support to.

ప్రోద్బలం **proodbalam** *n.* encouragement, support, instigation.

ప్రోవు **proowu** *class. alt. form of* **poogu.**

ప్రౌఢ **prawDha** I. *n. class.* adult woman. II. *adj. class.* 1 mature, bold; **prawDhookti** confident assertion. 2 skilful, masterly.

ప్రౌఢత్వం **prawDhatwam** *n.* 1 maturity. 2 masterliness, skilled craftsmanship.

ప్రౌఢ దశ **prawDha daśa** *n.* stage of maturity, adulthood.

ప్రౌఢి[మ] **prawDhi[ma]** *n.* 1 maturity. 2 skilfulness.

ప్లవ **plawa** *n.* thirty-fifth year of the Hindu cycle of sixty years.

ప్లవంగ **plawanga** *n.* forty-first year of the Hindu cycle of sixty years.

ప్లవకం **plawakam** *n. biol.* plankton.

ప్లీహం **pliiham** *n.* 1 spleen. 2 disease of the spleen.

ప్లుతం **plutam** *n. gram.* extra long vowel having a value one and a half times the length of a long vowel or **diirgham.**

ఫ, ఫా - pha, phaa

ఫకీరు **phakiiru** *n.* 1 Muslim religious mendicant. 2 *fig.* very poor person, destitute person.

ఫక్కీ **phakkii** *n.* manner, mode, style, fashion.

ఫక్కున **phakkuna** *onom. adv.* **~ nawwu** to burst out laughing.

ఫక్కుమను **phakkumanu** *v.i.* to burst out laughing.

ఫక్తు **phaktu** I. *adj.* real, genuine, pucca. II. *adv.* 1 only, merely, simply. 2 completely, absolutely, actually, in fact.

ఫడేల్మని **phaDeelmani** *onom. adv.* with a bang, with a crash (of a door shutting, wave breaking).

ఫణి **phaNi** *n.* [hooded] snake.

ఫణితి **phaNiti** *n.* way, style, manner, fashion.

ఫరకు **pharaku** *n.* 1 meaning, intention. 2 skill, trick, stratagem. 3 difference of opinion.

ఫర్మానా **pharmaanaa** *n.* royal mandate, order.

ఫర్మాయిషి **pharmaayiSi** *n.* order, commission.

ఫరవా, ఫర్వా **pharawaa, pharwaa** *same as* **parawaa, parwaa.**

ఫలం **phalam** *n.* 1 fruit. 2 benefit. 3 result, consequence, outcome. 4 *maths.* quotient.

ఫలంపాటు **phalampaaTu** *n.* fruitful labour.

ఫలకం **phalakam** *n. class.* 1 slab or sheet of stone or metal. 2 shield.

ఫలదీకరణం **phaladiikaraNam** *n. biol.* fertilisation.

ఫలప్రద **phalaprada** *adj.* fruitful, productive.

ఫలవంత **phalawanta** *adj.* fruitful.

ఫలశర్కర **phalaśarkara** *n. bot.* fructose.

ఫలసాయం **phalasaayam** *n.* 1 produce, yield. 2 usufruct. 3 proceeds.

ఫలసిద్ధి **phalasiddhi** *n.* successful result, fulfilment, fruition.

ఫలహారం, పలహారం, పలారం **phalahaaram, palahaaram, palaaram** *n.* light refreshment, snack.

ఫలహారం చేయు, పలహారం చేయు, పలారం చేయు **phalahaaram ceeyu, pala[ha]aram ceeyu** *v.t.* 1 to eat a snack. 2 *slang* to misappropriate.

ఫలానా, ఫలాని **phalaanaa, phalaani** *adj.* a particular (person or thing), such and such (a person or thing).

ఫలించు **phalincu** *v.i.* 1 to be fruitful, bear fruit, come to bearing, fructify. 2 (of a vow, desire) to be fulfilled. 3 (of a dream) to come true.

ఫలితం **phalitam** *n.* result, consequence, effect, outcome; **diini[ki] ~ gaa** as a result of this.

ఫలితార్థం **phalitaartham** *n.* purport or point of a passage as distinguished from its literal meaning.

ఫల్గునుడు, ఫాల్గునుడు **phalgunuDu, phaalgunuDu** *n.* epithet of Arjuna.

ఫసలి **phasali** *n.* the official revenue year running from 1st July to 30th June.

ఫాయా, పాయా **phaayaa, paayaa** *n.* 1 style, manner. 2 status, standing; **naa ~ ekkaDa waaDi ~ ekkaDa?** *lit.* where is his status and where is mine? i.e., how does his status compare with mine?

ఫాయిదా **phaayidaa** *n.* 1 interest on capital; **asalu ~ lu** principal and interest. 2 *dial.* benefit, advantage.

ఫాలం, ఫాలభాగం **phaalam, phaalabhaagam** *n. class.* forehead.

ఫాలాక్షుడు **phaalaakSuDu** *n.* epithet of Siva: **phaalaakSuDiki kuuDaa teliyakuNDaa weLLi pooyEEDu** *lit.* he went away without even Siva's knowledge, i.e., he went away without the knowledge of anyone.

ఫాల్గునం **phaalgunam** *n.* the twelfth lunar month.

ఫి to ఫౌ - phi to phaw

ఫికరు **phikaru** *n.* 1 worry, caring; **~ ceeyaku!** do not worry! 2 *dial.* trace, clue.

ఫితూరి **phituurii** *same as* **pituurii.**

ఫిరంగి **phirangi** *n.* cannon.

ఫిరాయించు **phiraayincu** *v.t.* 1 to change, exchange. 2 **pleeTu ~** (i) to turn over a gramophone record; (ii) to tell a different story, change o.'s version of events. 3 **paarTii ~** to change sides in politics. 4 to give back, return (s.g borrowed).

ఫిరాయింపు **phiraayimpu** *n.* 1 shifting, defecting, changing o.'s stand or position. 2 rotation (of capital). 3 giving back, returning (s.g borrowed).

ఫిర్కా **phirkaa** *n.* firka, group of villages, subdivision of a taluk (now obsolete).

ఫిర్యాది, ఫిర్యాదు **phiryaadi, phiryaadu** *same as* **piriyaadi, piriyaadu.**

ఫురుసత్తు **phurusattu** *n. dial.* stamina, energy.

ఫూత్కారం **phuutkaaram** *n.* 1 sound of hissing. 2 screaming, shrieking.

ఫెడీమని **pheDiimani** *adv.* resoundingly; **~ jawaabu ceppu** to answer sternly, retort.

ఫేణీ **pheeNii** *n.* sweet dish gen. eaten on Diwali day.

ఫేనం **pheenam** *n. class.* foam.

ఫైసలా **phaysalaa** *n.* 1 settlement, decision. 2 disposal.

ఫైసలా అవు, ఫైసలవు **phaysalaa awu, phaysalawu** *v.i.* 1 to be fixed, be settled, be decided, be determined. 2 to be finished off, be disposed of.

ఫైసలా చేయు **phaysalaa ceeyu** *v.t.* 1 to fix, settle, decide, determine. 2 to finish off, dispose of. 3 *colloq.* to do away with, kill.

ఫౌజు, పౌజు **phawju, pawju** *n.* army.

బ - ba

బంక **banka** I. *n.* 1 gum, glue. 2 mucus, slime. 3 anything sticky or clammy; **waaDu oo~laagaa wadalakuNDaa nannu paTTukonnaaDu** he clung to me like glue without letting go; *cf. the English expression* he stuck to me like a leech. II. *adj.* sticky, slimy.

బంకతుత్తర **bankatuttara** *n.* kind of okra plant covered with hairs which cling to clothes, etc.

బంకతెగులు **bankategulu** *n.* pest which affects millets, cotton and other crops.

బంకనక్కిడి, బంకనక్కెర **bankanakkiDi, bankanakkera** *n.* name of a plant covered with hairs which cling to clothes, etc.

బంకపురుగు **bankapurugu** *n.* snail.

బంకమట్టి, బంకమన్ను **bankamaTTi, bankamannu** *n.* clay.

బంకవిరోచనాలు **bankawiroocanaalu** *n.pl.* dysentery.

బంకసాగు **bankasaagu** *v.i.* 1 to be[come] sticky, slimy or mushy; **miThaayi~tunnadi, paareeyi!** the sweet has become soft and sticky, throw it away! 2 (of a naughty child) to be obstinate or persistent. 3 to make a show of affection; **attaa kooDaLLu~tunnaaru** the mother-in-law and daughter-in-law are making a show of being affectionate to each other.

బంగనపల్లి **banganapalli** *n.* 1 name of a town in Andhra Pradesh. 2 name of a kind of mango large in size, sweet and with little fibre.

బంగనబైలు **banganabaylu** *n.* wide open space.

బంగళా **bangaLaa** *n.* bungalow.

బంగళాపెంకు **bangaLaapenku** *n.* large factory-made roof tile, commonly called Mangalore tile.

బంగారం **bangaaram** *n.* 1 gold. 2 (*also* **bangaaru koNDa**) *term of endearment to a child* precious darling.

బంగారక్క **bangaarakka** *n.* name of stock character in a puppet show; *see* **keetigaaDu.**

బంగారు **bangaaru** I. *n.* gold. II. *adj.* 1 gold[en]. 2 *colloq.* excellent, grand, fine, noble, beautiful, admirable; **~paapa** good child, well-behaved child; *see* **bangaaram.**

బంగారుతీగె **bangaarutiige** *n.* name of a variety of sugar cane.

బంగారుతీగెలు **bangaarutiigelu** *n.pl.* name of a fine long-grained variety of rice grown in the second crop season.

బంగాళం **bangaaLam** *n.* Bengal.

బంగాళా ఖాతం **bangaaLaa khaatam** *n.* Bay of Bengal.

బంగాళా దుంప **bangaaLaa dumpa** *n. dial.* potato.

బంగీ **bangii** *n.* parcel, package, packet.

బంగీకాగితం **bangiikaagitam** *n.* packing paper.

బంచెరాయి **banceraayi** *n. dial.* government land reserved for communal use in a village.

బంజరు **banjaru** *n.* waste land.

బంజార, బంజారి, లంబాడ, లంబాడి **banjaara, banjaari, lambaaDa, lambaaDi** *n.* name of a scheduled tribe in Andhra Pradesh, originally gipsies.

బంటి **baNTi** *adjvl. suffix meaning* as high as, up to, as deep as; **mookaali~niiLLu** knee-deep water.

బంటు **baNTu** *n.* 1 soldier. 2 servant; **nammina~** trusted servant, trusted lieutenant. 3 pawn in chess.

బంట్రోతు **baNTrootu** *n.* peon, attendant.

బండ **baNDa** I. *n.* 1 (*also* **~raayi** *or* **raati~**) rock, boulder, stone, lump of rock or stone, stone block or slab. 2 *colloq.* (*also* **~raayi**) crude, obstinate, slovenly, stupid or dull-witted person. 3 (*also* **rookali~**) pestle. II. *adj.* 1 (of language) indecent, foul, obscene; **~buutulu** obscenities; **o.-ni ~ buutulu tiTTu** to abuse s.o. with foul language. 2 hard, tedious; **~pani** heavy manual work; **~caakiri** drudgery. 3 (of a cutting edge or point) worn away, worn down, blunted; **~mukku** bulbous nose.

బండబారు **baNDabaaru** *v.i.* 1 (of a cutting edge or point) to be worn away, become blunted. 2 to become obstinate, become intractable.

బండలు చేయు **baNDalu ceeyu** *v.t. colloq.* to ruin.

బండారం **baNDaaram** *n.* 1 treasury. 2 hidden wealth. 3 secret.

బండారు, బందారు **baNDaaru, bandaaru** *n.* karum, a timber tree.

బండి **baNDi** *n.* 1 any conveyance that moves on land—cart, carriage, car, train, bicycle, etc. 2 (*also* **daaram~**) bobbin, reel.

బండి ర **baNDi ra** *n.* a name for **śakaTa reepha**, the obsolete letter 'ఱ'.

బండిసున్న **baNDi sunna** *n. colloq.* a big zero, i.e., nothing at all.

బండెడు **baNDeDu** *adj.* a cartload of, a quantity of; **~pustakaalu** a quantity of books.

బంతి **banti**[1] *n.* 1 ball (to play with). 2 (*also* **~puwwu**) marigold.

బంతి **banti**[2] *n.* 1 line, row (= **pankti**). 2 ceremony held when a girl attains puberty, at which she and others of her age take a meal together.

బంతి భోజనం **banti bhoojanam** *see* **pankti bhoojanam.**

బంతులాట **bantulaaTa** *same as* **puulaceLLaaTa.**

బంద్ **band** *n.* closure of shops, offices, etc., in token of a strike.

బంద **banda** *n.* 1 small pond or tank. 2 mud.

బందం **bandam** *n.* 1 rope used to hobble animals or tie them together. 2 cord used by toddy tappers to tie their feet together when climbing. 3 *colloq.* **o.-i mundari kaaLLaku bandaalu weeyu** to obstruct or hinder s.o.'s progress.

బందాకు **bandaaku** *n.* mortgage.

బందారు **bandaaru** *same as* **baNDaaru.**

బంది **bandi** *n.* 1 imprisonment, confinement. 2 prisoner.

బందికాన, బందీఖానా **bandikaana, bandiikhaanaa** *n.* prison.

బందిపోటు **bandipooTu** *n.* dacoity, gang robbery.

బందిపోటు దొంగ **bandipooTu donga** *n.* dacoit.

బందు **bandu** *n.* 1 bond, restriction. 2 (*also* **raa**~) vulture. 3 (*also* **maData**~) hinge.

బందూకు **banduuku** *n. dial.* gun.

బందె **bande** *n.* 1 confinement of stray cattle. 2 fine imposed for trespassing by cattle.

బందెలదొడ్డి **bandeladoDDi** *n.* cattle pound.

బందోబస్తు **bandoobastu** I. *n.* arrangements, preparations. II. *adj.* strong, well built, sturdy; **maniSi ~ gaa unnaaDu** he has a sturdy figure.

బందోబస్తు చేయు **bandoobastu ceeyu** *v.i.* to make arrangements for safety and security.

బంద్ చేయు **band ceeyu** *v.i. and t.* to close, shut.

బంధం **bandham** *n.* 1 binding, tying, bond[age]. 2 rope for tying. 3 kind of poetic metre; *see* **anjali**~.

బంధనం **bandhanam** *n.* 1 binding, tying. 2 restriction. 3 *phys.* insulation.

బంధించు **bandhincu** *v.t.* 1 to tie, bind, hold together. 2 to hold fast or tight. 3 to lock up, imprison, incarcerate.

బంధుత్వం **bandhutwam** *n.* relationship, consanguinity.

బంధుపక్షపాతం **bandhupakSapaatam** *n.* nepotism.

బంధుప్రీతి **bandhupriiti** *n.* 1 fondness for o.'s relations. 2 showing favouritism towards o.'s relations, nepotism.

బంధుమిత్రులు **bandhumitrulu** *n.pl.* relations and friends.

బంధుర **bandhura** *adjvl. suffix meaning* filled with, full of; **rasa**~ full of elegance.

బంధువు **bandhuwu** *n.* relation, relative.

బకం **bakam** *n.* crane, heron.

బకధ్యానం **bakadhyaanam** *n. lit.* crane's meditation, a proverbial phrase for hypocrisy, because a crane, while it appears to be meditating and praying, is in fact aiming to catch fish; *cf.* **konga japam.**

బకాయి **bakaayi** I. *n.* arrears, dues, backlog. II. *adj.* outstanding, overdue, in arrears.

బకాయి పడు **bakaayi paDu** *v.i.* to fall into arrears.

బకాసురుడు **bakaasuruDu** *n.* 1 name of a demon in the Mahabharata. 2 *colloq.* person with a voracious appetite.

బక్క **bakka** *adj.* 1 thin, lean, slim. 2 poor, weakly, undernourished, emaciated; ~ **deeśaalu** poverty-stricken countries.

బక్కచిక్కు **bakkacikku** *v.i.* to be[come] thin, lean or emaciated.

బక్కురు **bakkuru** *v.i. dial.* 1 to scratch, scrape. 2 *slang* to write.

బక్రీద్ **bakriid** *n.* the Muslim festival of Bakrid.

బగ్గంపాడు **baggampaaDu** *adj.* utterly ruined.

బగ్గి **baggi** *n.* 1 carriage. 2 *dial.* stripe.

బగ్గున **bagguna** *same as* **bhagguna.**

బగ్గుమను **baggumanu** *same as* **bhaggumanu.**

బచ్చలపండురంగు **baccalapaNDu rangu** *n.* magenta colour.

బచ్చలి **baccali** *n.* spinach.

బచ్చాలాట **baccaalaaTa** *n.* boys' game played with a disc made from a stone or tile (**baccaa**).

బజ్జీ **bajjii** *n.* 1 snack made of bengalgram flour. 2 kind of chutney.

బజంత్రీలు, భజంత్రీలు **b[h]ajantriilu** *n.pl.* band of pipers and drummers traditionally belonging to the barbers' community.

బజంత్రీవాడు, భజంత్రీవాడు **b[h]ajantriiwaaDu** *n.* 1 member of a band composed of **b[h]ajantriilu.** 2 barber.

బజకడుగు **bajakaDugu** *v.i.* to expose s.o. in his true colours.

బజాయించు **bajaayincu** *v.i.* 1 to beat, thrash. 2 to beat a drum.

బజారు **bajaaru** *n.* 1 street; **pedda**~ high street, main street; ~**na paDu** to come out into the open, do s.g openly or publicly. 2 market, bazaar; ~ **ceeyu** to go shopping.

బజీతు, భజీతు **b[h]ajiitu** *n.* disgrace, shame.

బజ్జుండు **bajjuNDu** *v.i. child language* to lie down, sleep; **bajjoo**! go to sleep!

బటానీ, బఠానీ **baT[h]aanii** *n.* pea.

బటారం **baTaaram** *class. alt. form of* **paTaaram.**

బటుడు, భటుడు **b[h]aTuDu** *n.* 1 soldier. 2 servant, page.

బటువు **baTuwu** *n.* ring presented to a young man at his **upanayanam** ceremony and to a bridegroom at his wedding; *cf.* **unkuTungaram.**

బట్ట **baTTa**[1] *n.* cloth; ~ **[lu] kaTTu** to wear clothes; **batiki ~ kaTTu** to live, be alive, remain alive, survive (*lit.* to live and wear clothes); **batiki ~ kaDitee koNDaki wastaanu** if I live (*or* if I survive) I will come to the hill (i.e., to the temple at Tirupati) *are the words of a vow.*

బట్ట **baTTa**[2] *adj.* bald; ~ **tala waaDu** baldheaded person.

బట్ట **baTTa**[3] *adj.* dappled, mottled.

బట్ట **baTTa**[4] *n. med.* whites, leucorrhoea.

బట్టబయలుగా **baTTabayalugaa** *adv.* openly, publicly.

బట్టబయలు చేయు **baTTabayalu ceeyu** *v.t.* to reveal, expose, bring into the open.

బట్టబైలు, బట్టబయలు **baTTabay[a]lu** *n.* wide open space.

బట్టి **baTTi** I. *p.p. attached to a n. in the accusative* 1 for, because of, on account of, by reason of, based on; **awi pondee maarpulni ~ naalugu wibhaagaalugaa ceyyoccu** we can divide them into four classes by reason of the changes that they undergo. 2 in accordance with, according to, from; **dinni ~ miiru grahincawaccu** from this you can understand. II. *particle suffixed to an infinitive* because; **goDuguNDa ~ taDawakuNDaa waccEEnu** because I had an umbrella I came without getting wet.

బట్టీ **baTTii** *n.* 1 kiln; **iTika ~** brick kiln. 2 still; **saaraayi ~** still for distilling liquor.

బట్టీ పట్టు **baTTii paTTu** *v.t.* 1 to distil (liquor). 2 (*also* **baTTii peTTu**) to memorise, learn by heart, commit to memory.

బట్టె **baTTe** *n.* flow, stream.

బట్టె కట్టు **baTTe kaTTu** *v.i.* to flow.

బట్వాడా **baTwaaDaa** *n.* 1 disbursement. 2 acquittance. 3 distribution, delivery (of mail). 4 conveying, communication (of ideas).

బఠానీ **baThaanii** *same as* **baTaanii.**

బడబడమను **baDabaDamanu** *v.i.* to prattle.

బడబాగ్ని, బడబానలం **baDabaagni, baDabaanalam** *n.* inextinguishable fire.

బడలిక **baDalika** *n.* tiredness, fatigue, weariness.

బడలు **baDalu** *v.i.* to be tired, be weary.

బడవ, భడవ **b[h]aDawa** *n.* 1 pimp, procurer. 2 wicked person, villain. 3 useless person.

బడాయి **baDaayi** *n.* 1 boasting, bragging, pretentiousness. 2 egoism, pride, vanity.

బడాయించు **baDaayincu** *v.i.* to advance, increase.

బడి **baDi**[1] *n.* school.

బడి **baDi**[2] *adj.* little, smaller, minor, lesser.

బడితె, బడిత **baDite, baDita** *n.* thick stick, cudgel; **~ puuja ceesteegaani winaDu** unless you take a stick to him, he will not listen; **baTTalu leekuNDaa ~ laagaa nilcunnaaDu** he stood stark naked without any clothes.

బడిపంతులు **baDipantulu** *n.* schoolmaster.

బడుగు **baDugu** *adj.* weak, poor, poverty-stricken, underdeveloped.

బడుద్ధాయి **baDuddhaayi** *n.* useless person, good for nothing person.

బడ్డీ **baDDii** *n.* (*also* **~ koTTu, ~ dukaaNam, kiLLii ~**) pan shop, petty shop selling betel and nut (pan) and other sundries.

బడ్డు **baDDu** *n.* 1 thick rope. 2 *slang* male sex organ.

బడ్డుగాడు **baDDugaaDu** *n.* *slang* stupid or useless person.

బతకమ్మ, బ్రతకమ్మ **b[r]atakamma** *n.* village festival held at Dasara time in Telangana.

బతికించు, బ్రతికించు **b[r]atikincu** *v.t.* 1 to cause s.o. to survive, save s.o's life, bring s.o. back to life, revive s.o. who has lost consciousness. 2 *~ is sometimes used in a weak sense* **miiru raareemoo anukunnaanu. batikincEEru!** I thought you might not come; you have saved me (by coming)!

బతిమాలు, బతిమిలాడు **batimaalu, batimilaaDu** *v.t.* to beg, beseech, entreat.

బతిమిలాట **batimilaaTa** *n.* entreaty.

బతుకు, బ్రతుకు **b[r]atuku** I. *n.* 1 life: **tana tammuDiloo nippulu poosEEDu** he ruined his younger brother's life. 2 livelihood, subsistence. II. *v.i.* 1 to live. 2 to carry on o.'s livelihood, subsist. 3 to be alive. 4 to survive, be saved, escape; **waana raakamundu iNTLooki waccEEnu: batikEEnu!** I reached home before the rain came; I was saved!; *cf.* **baTTa**[1], **ceDu** *sense 6*, **ceDDa** *sense 2.*

బతుకుజీవుడా! **batukujiiwuDaa!** *interj. expressing relief* I've escaped! *or* I've been saved!

బతుకు తెరువు **batuku teruwu** *n.* means of livelihood, subsistence.

బత్తాయి **battaayi** *n.* sweet kind of orange (originally introduced from Batavia).

బత్తి **battii** *n.* wick (= **watti**).

బత్తుడు **battuDu** *n.* honorific community title of certain village artificers, e.g., **waDLa ~** carpenter; **kamsaali ~** goldsmith.

బత్తెం, భత్తెం **b[h]attem** *n.* batta, daily allowance for expenses; **jiitam ~** salary and allowances.

బదనాం, బదలాం **badanaam, badalaam** *n.* disgrace, infamy.

బదనాం చేయు **badanaam ceeyu** *v.t.* to disgrace, defame (s.o.).

బదరి **badari**[1] *n.* jujube tree, *zyzyphus jujuba* (= **reegu**).

బదరి **badari**[2] *n.* Badrinath, a place of pilgrimage in the Himalayas.

బదలా **badalaa** *n. dial.* revenge.

బదలాయించు **badalaayincu** *v.t. dial.* to transfer.

బదిలీ **badilii** *n.* transfer.

బదిలీ అవు **badilii awu** *v.i.* to be transferred.

బదిలీ చేయు **badilii ceeyu** *v.t.* to transfer.

బదులు **badulu** *n.* 1 exchange. 2 substitute. 3 reply. 4 (*also* **ceyyi ~**) hand loan, loan for which no bond is executed.

బదులుగా **badulugaa** *adv.* 1 in exchange. 2 as a substitute.

బదులు చెప్పు, బదులు ఇచ్చు **badulu ceppu, badulu iccu** *v.i.* to reply.

బద్ద, బ్రద్ద **b[r]adda** *n.* 1 piece, bit, section, fragment, slice, chip, chunk; **nimma ~** slice of lime pickle (= **nimma dabba**). 2 thin flat stick or strip of wood, etc.; **weduru ~** bamboo slat; **kaawiDi ~** carrying pole; **kolata ~** measuring rod; **taaTEEku ~** strip of palmyra leaf, tongue cleaner.

బద్దలు అవు **baddalu awu** *v.i.* 1 to break into pieces. 2 to crack open, erupt, burst, explode; **agni parwatam baddalayindi** the volcano erupted; **enta paapam baddalayindi!** what a misfortune has burst upon us! **paccikaaya baddalayindi** *lit.* an unripe fruit has burst open (expression used of a sudden death of a young person or other unexpected misfortune).

బద్దలు కొట్టు **baddalu koTTu** *v.t.* to smash, break into pieces.

బద్దింపులు **baddimpulu** *n.pl.* conditions, restrictions.

బద్దీ **baddii** *n.* flat bar, slat; **kiTikii ~** window bar; **reyilu ~** railway line; **weduru ~** bamboo slat.

బద్దు **baddu** *n. dial.* lie, untruth.

బద్దె **badde** *n.* 1 thin flat strip of wood, etc.; **weduru~** bamboo slat; **nawaaru~** cotton tape. 2 iron tip fixed to the wooden tooth of a harrow.

బద్ధ **baddha** *adj.* 1 tied, bound. 2 intense; **~ wayram** intense hostility; **~ wiroodhulu, ~ śatruwulu** deadly enemies; **~ wiśwaasam** intense conviction; **~ wyatireekhata** intransigeance.

బద్ధం **baddham** *adjvl. suffix meaning* 1 tied, bound. 2 confined. 3 linked; **praNaaLikaa~** linked to planning; **praNaaLikaa~ ayna kṛSi** planned activity; **śaastra~** scientific; **raajyaanga~** constitutional.

బద్ధం చేయు **baddham ceeyu** *v.t.* 1 to bind. 2 to confine, restrict.

బద్ధకం **baddhakam** *n.* 1 laziness, indolence. 2 lethargy, drowsiness.

బద్ధకంగా **baddhakangaa** *adv.* lethargically, drowsily.

బద్ధకంకణుడు **baddhakankaNuDu** *n.* person who has bound himself by an oath.

బద్ధకస్తుడు **baddhakastuDu** *n.* lazy or idle person.

బద్ధకించు **baddhakincu** *v.i.* to feel lazy; **weLLaDaaniki baddhakincEEnu** I felt too lazy to go.

బద్ధుడు **baddhuDu** *second part of a n. compound meaning* person who is bound or confined; **kaaraagaara~** person who is confined to prison.

బద్రింపు **badrimpu** *same as* **patrimpu.**

బధిర **badhira** *adj.* deaf.

బధిరత్వం **badhiratwam** *n.* deafness.

బధిరుడు **badhiruDu** *n.* deaf person.

బనాయించు **banaayincu** *v.t.* 1 to forge, fabricate. 2 *dial.* to heckle. 3 *dial.* to ridicule, caricature.

బనాయింపు **banaayimpu** *n.* 1 forgery, fabrication. 2 *dial.* heckling.

బనారసు **banaarasu** *n.* Benares; **~ ciire** silk sari made in Benares.

బనియన్ **baniyan** *n.* vest.

బబ్బుండు, బొబ్బుండు **babbuNDu, bobbuNDu** *v.i. child language* to lie down, sleep; **babboo!** *or* **bobboo!** go to sleep!

బభ్రాజమానం **babhraajamaanam** *n.* fool, idiot.

బమ్మెర **bammera** *n. class.* confusion, perplexity.

బమ్మెర పోవు **bammera poowu** *v.i. class.* to be confused, be perplexed.

బయట, బైట **bayaTa, bayTa** *p.p. and adv.* outside.

బయటపడు **bayaTapaDu** *v.i.* 1 to make o.'s way out, extricate o.s., escape, emerge. 2 (of s.g hidden or secret) to come out, be revealed, be discovered, become publicly known. 3 (of a book) to appear in print.

బయట పెట్టు **bayaTa peTTu** *v.t.* to reveal, let out, divulge, disclose.

బయర్లు, బైర్లు **bayarlu, bayrlu** *n.pl.* darkness; **waaDiki balahiinamwalla kaLLu~ kammEEyi** his eyes were blurred (*lit.* his eyes were covered with darkness) on account of weakness; **Dabbuwalla waaDi kaLLu~ kammEEyi** he was blinded (*lit.* his eyes were darkened) by so much wealth.

బయల్పడు **bayalpaDu** *same as* **bayaTapaDu.**

బయలు, బైలు **bayalu, baylu** *n.* open place, open space.

బయలుకుపోవు, బయలుకువెళ్లు **bayaluku poowu, bayaluku weLLu** *v.i.* to go out in order to ease o.s.

బయలుదేరతీయు **bayaludeeratiiyu** *v.t.* to (start out and) take with one; **andarinii naaTakaaniki bayaludeera tiisEEDu** he took them all to the play; **tooDugaa nannu kuuDaa bayaludeera tiisEEDu** he took me too as a companion.

బయలుదేరు **bayaludeeru** *v.i.* 1 to set out, start on a journey. 2 to come into existence, come forward, appear, emerge, come to light, occur; **oka aaloocana naa manasuloo bayaludeerindi** an idea took shape in my mind; **naaTakaalu weeseeTappuDu ennoo anukooni awaantaraalu bayaludeera waccunu** when plays are being staged ever so many unforeseen mishaps may occur.

బయానా **bayaanaa** *n.* advance of money paid when a bargain is struck, earnest money.

బయ్యంకలు **bayyankalu** *n.pl.* morning sickness.

బయ్యడు **bayyaDu** *n.* dull witted or stupid person.

బరంపురం **barampuram** *n.* 1 the town of Berhampore. 2 **manam manam~** *is a colloquial expression meaning* 'we are all alike'.

బరక **baraka** *adj.* rough, coarse (sand, soil, flour).

బరకగా **barakagaa** *adv.* roughly, coarsely, unevenly.

బరణి, భరిణె **baraNi, bhariNe** *n.* little box, casket.

బరబర **barabara** *onom. adv. sug. sound of* dragging.

బరమా, బర్మా **baramaa, barmaa** *n.* 1 gimlet, drill. 2 blasting with dynamite.

బరాతం **baraatam** *n.* sanction for payment.

బరాబరిచేయు **baraabari ceeyu** *v.i.* to respond in a like manner, reciprocate.

బరాయించు, భరాయించు **b[h]araayincu** *v.t.* 1 to bear, tolerate, sustain, endure. 2 *dial.* to fill; **buDDiloo saaraa~** to fill a bottle with arrack.

బరావత్తు **baraawattu** *n.* paybill, slary bill.

బరి **bari** *n.* line drawn to mark a limit or boundary; **~ miidi paamulaa tala ettukoni nilabaDDaaDu** he stood rearing up his head like a snake on a line (comparing s.o. to a snake which rears its head when it cannot cross a line drawn round it by a snake charmer).

బరికె, బరిక **barike, barika** *n.* 1 small stick or switch. 2 dried palmyra stalk. 3 coconut shell.

బరిణెపురుగు **bariNe purugu** *n.* cockroach.

బరి తెగించు **bari tegincu** *v.i.* to go beyond the limit, behave without decorum.

బరిసె **barise** *n.* spear, lance.

బరుకు **baruku** *v.t.* 1 to scratch. 2 *slang* to scribble.

బరువు **baruwu** I. *n.* 1 weight, load, burden. 2 responsibility, obligatory duty; **baruwu baadhyatalu** duty and responsibility. II. *adj.* heavy, weighty, burdensome, onerous; *cf.* **baLuwu.**

బర్తరఫు **bartaraphu** *n.* dismissal, discharge.

బర్బర **barbara** *adj.* harsh, barbarian.

బర్బరత్వం **barbaratwam** *n.* crudeness, barbarity.

బర్మా **barmaa** *same as* **baramaa.**

బర్రున, బర్రుమని **barruna, barrumani** *onom. adv. sug.* making a roaring sound, e.g., like a motor car.

బర్రె **barre** *n.* she buffalo.

బర్హి **barhi** *n. class.* peacock.

బలం **balam** *n.* 1 strength, power, might, force, stamina. 2 army; **saynika balaalu** military forces. 3 set of chessmen. ~ **peercu** to arrange a set of chessmen on a board.

బలగం **balagam** *n.* 1 retinue, supporters. 2 group, gang, party, troupe.

బలపం **balapam** *n.* slate pencil; *see* **kaalu** *sense I. 2.*

బలపడు **balapaDu** *v.i.* 1 to grow stronger, be strengthened. 2 to be reinforced.

బలపరచు **balaparacu** *v.t.* 1 to support, strengthen. 2 to reinforce. 3 to second (resolution).

బలపరాయి **balaparaayi** *n.* slate (rock).

బలప్రయోగం **balaprayoogam** *n.* use of force.

బలబల **balabala** *onom.adv.sug.* oozing, trickling; **gaayam nunci raktam ~ kaarindi** blood trickled from the wound.

బలవంత **balawanta** *adj.* 1 strong, forceful. 2 violent.

బలవంతం **balawantam** *n.* 1 strength, force. 2 violence. 3 compulsion, duress.

బలవంతంగా **balawantangaa** *adv.* 1 forcefully. 2 forcibly, by[means of] force. 3 violently.

బలవంతం చేయు, బలవంతపెట్టు **balawantam ceeyu, balawantapeTTu** *v.t.* to compel.

బలవంతుడు, బలశాలి **balawantuDu, balaśaali** *n.* strong person.

బలవత్తర **balawattara** *adj.* very strong.

బలవిన్యాసం **balawinyaasam** *n.* drawing up a battle line.

బలసమతౌల్యం **balasamatawlyam** *n.* balance of power.

బలహీన **balahiina** *adj.* (physically or mentally) weak or feeble.

బలహీనం **balahiinam** *n.* (physical or mental) weakness or feebleness or debility.

బలహీనత **balahiinata** *n.* weakness (gen. with ref. to mental weakness).

బలాత్కరించు **balaatkarincu** *v.t.* 1 to force, compel. 2 to rape.

బలాత్కారం **balaatkaaram** *n.* 1 violence, force. 2 rape.

బలాబలాలు **balaabalaalu** *n.pl.* strengths and weaknesses, comparative strengths.

బలి **bali** *n.* 1 sacrifice. 2 (*also* **mahaa ~**) name of a demon king associated with harvest ceremonies; *see* **poli**[1].

బలి అవు **bali awu** *v.i* 1 to be sacrificed. 2 to become a victim (of), fall a prey (to).

బలి ఇచ్చు **bali iccu** *v.t.* to sacrifice.

బలిగుడి **baliguDi** *n. dial.* boys' game also called **kabaDDi** or **ceDuguDu.**

బలిగొను **baligonu** *v.t.* to take as a sacrifice, claim as a victim; **mahammaari inni praaNaalu baligonnadi** the pestilence has claimed so many lives as its victims.

బలిజ, బలిజె **balija, balije** *n.* name of a community in Andhra Pradesh.

బలిపశువు **balipaśuwu** *n.* sacrificial animal, scapegoat.

బలిపించు **balipincu** *v.t.* to fatten up (an animal).

బలిపిడత **balipiData** *n.* small earthen pot marked with white spots, displayed in a field to ward off evil influences.

బలిపీఠం **balipiiTham** *n.* sacrificial altar.

బలిపెట్టు **balipeTTu** *v.t.* 1 to sacrifice. 2 to kill, slay.

బలిమి **balimi** *n.* 1 strength. 2 force, compulsion.

బలిమిని **balimini** *adv.* by force, forcibly.

బలియు, బలిసిపోవు **baliyu, balisipoowu** *v.i.* 1 to grow fat, be[come] stout, be[come] corpulent. 2 *colloq.* to be[come] arrogant. 3 to be[come] strong.

బలిష్ఠ **baliSTa** *adj.* staunch, very strong, very sturdy.

బలీయ[ం] **baliiya[m]** *adj.* very strong, powerful; **widhi baliiyam** destiny is very powerful.

బలీయత **baliiyata** *n.* strength, force, power, might.

బలుపు **balupu** *n.* 1 fat[ness], stoutness. 2 strength.

బలువు[గా] **baluwu[gaa]** *same as* **baLuwu[gaa].**

బలుస **balusa** *n. plectronia parviflora*, a plant whose edible leaves provide a proverbially poor diet; **batiki uNTee balusaaku tinawaccani paaripooyEEDu** *lit.* he ran away saying 'if I remain alive (after this), I will (be content to) eat balusa leaves' *meaning* anything will be better than what I am enduring now.

బలే, భలే **b[h]alee** I. *adj.* 1 very: ~ **ettayna kaTTaDaalu** very tall buildings 2 very good: ~ **maarkulu waccEEyi** he got very good marks. II. *adv.* 1 much, very, greatly: **waNTa ~ baagundi** the cooking is very good; ~ **poddunnee waccEEDu** he came very early in the morning. 2 very well: ~ **paaDEEDu** he sang very well. III. *interj.* good!, well done!

బల్ల **balla** *n.* 1 bench. 2 table. 3 plank, board; **nalla ~** blackboard. 4 *dial.* slate. 5 *med.* enlargement of spleen.

బల్లకట్టు **ballakaTTu** *n.* flat-bottomed boat, raft, pontoon.

బల్లపరపు **ballaparapu** *adj.* 1 flat. 2 level.

బల్లి **balli** *n.* lizard.

బల్లిదం **ballidam** *adj. class.* strong, powerful.

బల్లెం **ballem** *n.* spear, lance; **waariki pakkaloo ~ laa unnaaDu** *lit.* he is like a spear in their side, i.e., he is a source of imminent danger to them.

బళా!, బళిరా! **baLaa!, baLiraa!** *interj. class.* well done!, bravo!

బళువు, బలువు **baLuwu, baluwu** I. *n.* 1 weight, load, burden. 2 responsibility, obligatory duty. II. *adj.* 1 heavy, weighty, burdensome, onerous; **naa tala ~ gaa unnadi** I have a heavy feeling in my head (due to a cold). 2 (of illness) acute, severe; **ninna - gaa unnaaDu, iwwEELa ninnaTikanna suLuwu** yesterday he was seriously ill, today he is better than yesterday; *cf.* **baruwu.**

బళువుగా, బలువుగా **baLuwugaa, baluwugaa** *adv.* 1 heavily. 2 (of illness) seriously, acutely. 3 **aayana illu ikkaNNunci ~ reNDu mayLLa duuram unnadi** his house is fully two miles from here.

బళ్లు **baLLu**[1] *n.pl.* combinations of primary symbols of consonants with secondary symbols of vowels to form graphic syllables (**akSaraalu**): **padeeLLu daaTi padakoN-**

DeeLLu waccinaa waaDiki anni baLLuu raawu although he has passed ten and come to eleven years (of age) he still does not know all his **baLLu**; *cf.* **guDintam, guNintam.**

బళ్లు **baLLu**[2] *plural of* **baNDi** *and of* **baDi.**

బళ్లున **baLLuna,** *same as* **bhaLLuna.**

బవిరి[గడ్డం] **bawiri[gaDDam]** *n.* bushy beard.

బస **basa** *n.* lodging, place to stay temporarily.

బసంగి **basangi** *n.* variety of paddy grown in the Godavari delta, maturing early, inferior in quality but suitable for converting into parboiled rice.

బసచేయు **basaceeyu** *v.i.* to stay, stop, lodge.

బసవ, బసవడు **basawa,basawaDu**[1] *n.* name of the saint who established the Lingayat sect in Karnataka.

బసవడు, బసవన్న **basawaDu**[2], **basawanna** *n.* bull on which Siva rides.

బసివి **basiwi** *n.* temple prostitute.

బస్కీలు **baskiilu** *n.pl.* kind of physical exercise.

బస్తా **bastaa** *n.* gunny bag, sack.

బస్తాడు **bastaaDu** *adj.* sackful of.

బస్తీ **bastii** *n.* **1** city, town; **tana uuru wiDici pillala caduwukoosam ~ ceerEEDu** he left his village and came to town for his children's education. **2** locality (in a town). **3** slum area.

బహిః, బహిర్ **bahih, bahir** *adjvl. prefix meaning* outward, external, outside, outer; **bahih prapancam** the outside world; **bahiraakrti** external shape or form.

బహిరంగ **bahiranga** *adj.* open, public.

బహిరంగంగా **bahirangangaa** *adv.* publicly, openly.

బహిరంగంచేయు **bahirangam ceeyu** *v.t.* to divulge, reveal (secret).

బహిరంగపరచు **bahirangaparacu** *v.t.* to publicise, expose, reveal, bring to public notice.

బహిర్భూమి **bahirbhuumi** *n. class.* public area reserved for use as latrine.

బహిష్కరణం, బహిష్కారం **bahiSkaraNam, bahiSkaaram** *n.* **1** excommunication, expulsion, banishment. **2** boycott.

బహిష్కరించు **bahiSkarincu** *v.t.* **1** to excommunicate, expel, banish. **2** to boycott.

బహిష్కృతుడు **bahiSkrtuDu** *n.* person who is excommunicated, expelled, banished or boycotted.

బహిష్ఠు **bahiSThu** *n.* menstruation.

బహిష్ఠు అవు **bahiSThu awu** *v.i.* to be in menses.

బహు **bahu** *adj.* **1** many; **~ widhaalu** many types. **2** very; **~ takkuwa** very little. **3** great.

బహుధా **bahudhaa** *adv.* in many ways.

బహుధాకరణ **bahudhaakaraNa** *n.* proliferation.

బహుధాన్య **bahudhaanya** *n.* twelfth year of the Hindu cycle of sixty years.

బహునాయకత్వం **bahunaayakatwam** *n.* multiplicity of leaders.

బహుపక్షీయ **bahupakSiiya** *adj.* multi-party.

బహుపరాక్ **bahuparaak** *see* **paraaku**, *sense III.*

బహుపాక్షిక **bahupaakSika** *adj.* multilateral.

బహుప్రయోజక **bahuprayoojaka** *adj.* multipurpose.

బహుభార్యత్వం **bahubhaaryaatwam** *n.* polygamy.

బహుభాషాభాషి **bahubhaaSaabhaaSi** *n.* polyglot.

బహుమతం **bahumatam** *adj.* highly esteemed, highly respected.

బహుమతి, బహుమానం **bahumati, bahumaanam** *n.* **1** present, gift. **2** reward, prize.

బహుముఖ **bahumukha** *adj.* many faceted, many sided, having many aspects; **~ prajnaaśaali** scholar with great and varied learning.

బహుముఖం చేయు **bahumukham ceeyu** *v.t.* to diversify.

బహుముఖంగా **bahumukhangaa** *adv.* in many ways.

బహుమూత్రవ్యాధి **bahumuutrawyaadhi** *n.* diabetes.

బహుళ **bahuLa** *adj.* **1** plentiful, abundant, copious. **2** mass; **~ pracaaram** mass publicity. **3** multiple; **~ winimaya reeTLu** multiple exchange rates.

బహుళం, బహుళపక్షం **bahuLam, bahuLa pakSam** - *n.* dark fortnight, fortnight of the waning moon.

బహుళంగా **bahuLangaa** *adv.* abundantly, plentifully.

బహుళత్వం **bahuLatwam** *n.* multiplicity.

బహుళార్థ[సాధ]క **bahuLaartha[saadha]ka** *adj.* multipurpose.

బహువచనం **bahuwacanam** *n. gram.* plural.

బహువిధ **bahuwidha** *adj.* various, diverse, multiple, multifarious.

బహువ్యాప్త **bahuwyaapta** *adj.* widespread.

బహువ్రీహి **bahuwriihi** *n. gram.* two nouns put together to form a compound with a different meaning. e.g., **padmabaandhawuDu** *lit.* friend of the lotus, i.e., the sun.

బహుశా **bahuśaa** *adv.* probably, perhaps.

బహుసంఖ్య **bahusankhya** *n.* multitude.

బహూకరణ **bahuukaraNa** *n.* presentation.

బహూకరించు **bahuukarincu** *v.t.* to present, bestow, confer.

బా - baa

బాంచ **baanca** *dial. alt. form of* **baanisa.**

బాండీ **baaNDii** *n.* wide mouthed cooking pot used for frying.

బాంధవుడు **baandhawuDu** *n.* 1 relation, kinsman. 2 friend; **aapad~** friend in need.

బాంధవ్యం **baandhawyam** *n.* 1 kinship, relationship; **maa~looni waaDee** he is one of our relations. 2 connection, bond; **anuraaga baandhawyaalu** bonds of love.

బాకా **baakaa** *n.* long trumpet.

బాకీ **baakii** I. *n.* 1 remainder, rest, balance. 2 balance due, arrears; **waaDi~ tiiripooyindi** his arrears (i.e., either the balance due to him or the balance due from him) have been paid. II. *adj.* 1 remaining, left over; **~pani** the remaining work. 2 due; **~sommu** the amount due.

బాకీ ఉండు **baakii uNDu** *v.i.* to owe, be in arrears, be indebted; **miiru naaku padi ruupaayalu baakii unnaaru** you owe me ten rupees.

బాకీదారు[డు] **baakiidaaru[Du]** *n.* 1 creditor; **baakiidaarulu waakiTLooki wacci nilabaDDaaru** the creditors have come to the door. 2 *in some contexts* debtor, e.g., **baakiidaarlani enni kaSTaalu peTTaaloo annii peTTi dayaadaakSiNyaalu cuupakuNDaa tana Dabbu piNDukonee waaDu** by troubling his debtors in every way that he could and by showing them no favour or clemency he would extract his money from them.

బాగా **baagaa** *adv.* 1 well, properly, duly, satisfactorily. 2 in good health. 3 much, greatly, thoroughly. 4 round about, approximately; **~reNDu gaNTala seepu maaTLaaDEEDu** he talked for round about two hours.

బాగు **baagu** I. *n.* good, welfare, wellbeing; **nii~koosam ceppEEnu** I said it for your good. II. *adj.* 1 good. 2 beautiful. III. *interj.* quite right!, fine!

బాగుండు, బాగా ఉండు **baaguNDu, baagaa uNDu** *v.i.* 1 to be good, be well, be all right, be satisfactory. 2 to thrive, flourish, be prosperous. 3 to be beautiful, be goodlooking. 4 to be in good health; **naaku oNTLoo baagu leedu/baagaa leedu** I do not feel well. 5 to be to o.'s liking; **ii bhajana sundaraaniki baaguNDeedi** Sundaram used to enjoy this chanting of prayers; **miiru raakapootee naaku baaguNDadu** if you do not come I shall be unhappy about it.

బాగుచేయు, బాగుపడేయు, బాగుపరచు **baaguceeyu, baagupaDeeyu, baaguparaacu** *v.t.* 1 to do good to, benefit. 2 to mend, repair, put right, set right. 3 to restore (health). 4 to clean[up], tidy. 5 to purify. 6 to improve, reform; **ewaruu waaNNi baaguceeya leeru** no-one can reform him.

బాగుపడు **baagupaDu** *v.i.* 1 to thrive, prosper. 2 to be improved. 3 to be reformed. 4 to be put right. 5 to recover, get better (health). 6 to turn out well.

బాగులు **baagulu** *n.pl.* 1 repairs. 2 exorcising; **ceetabaDiki guri ayna pillaki mandulu ippinci eem prayoojanam? ~ceeyincaNDi** what use are medicines to a girl upon whom a spell has been cast? you should have it exorcised.

బాగోగులు **baagoogulu** *n.pl.* general welfare, general state or condition.

బాజా **baajaa** *n.* 1 kind of drum. 2 drum music, drum beating; **caawu~lu** mournful drum beating at a funeral. 3 *colloq.* beating.

బాజాబందు **baajaabandu** *n. dial.* kind of jewellery worn on the shoulder.

బాజాభజంత్రీలు **baajaabhajantriilu** *n.pl.* band of drummers.

బాజారు **baajaaru** *dial. alt. form of* **bajaaru.**

బాజావాయించు **baajaawaayincu** *v.i.* 1 to play a drum. 2 *colloq.* **nii wiipu baajaa waayistaanu** I will give you a beating.

బాట **baaTa** *n.* road, [high]way.

బాటసారి **baaTasaari** *n.* traveller by road, wayfarer, passer by.

బాటు **baaTu** *n. dial.* weighing scales.

బాడఖో **baaDakhoo** I. *n.* cheat, swindler. II. *adj.* useless, wretched; **~pani, ~caakiri** drudgery.

బాడవ **baaDawa** *n.* lowlying swampy or boggy land; **~neela** morass, bog.

బాడిగ, బాడుగ **baaDiga, baaDuga** *n.* rent.

బాడిద, బాడిస **baaDida, baaDisa** *n.* carpenter's adze.

బాడీ **baaDii** *n.* bodice, brassiere, bra.

బాడె, బాడి, పడె **baaDe, baaDi, paDe** *n.* ulcer, sore, scab (due to disease, burning, scalding, etc.); **tamalapaakulloo sunnam ekkuwa aytee naalika~paDutundi** if there is too much lime in the betel and nut, the tongue will develop sores.

బాణం **baaNam** *n.* arrow, dart; **naa miida praśnala baaNaalu kuripincEEDu** he fired volleys of questions at me; **namaskaara~** casual bow, token gesture of respect.

బాణాకత్తి **baaNaakatti** *n.* two handed sword.

బాణాకర్ర **baaNaakarra** *n.* heavy stick used in gymnastics and for self-defence.

బాణాసంచా **baaNaasancaa** *n.* fireworks.

బాణీ **baaNii** *n.* style, manner; **karNaaTaka~**Carnatic style (of music); **waaDi maaTala~ naaku naccaleedu** I did not like the manner of his speaking.

బాతాఖాని **baataakhaani** *n.* gossip, chitchat, conversation.

బాతాఖాని కొట్టు **baataakhaani koTTu** *v.i.* to have a chat.

బాతు **baatu** *n.* duck.

బాదం[కాయ], బాదాం **baadam[kaaya], baadaam** *n.* almond nut.

బాదం[చెట్టు] **baadam[ceTTu]** *n.* almond tree.

బాదం పప్పు **baadam pappu** *n.* almond kernel.

బాదరబందీ **baadarabandii** *n.* entanglements, troubles, worries.

బాదరాయణ సంబంధం **baadaraayaNa sambandham** *n.* imaginary or farfetched relationship (*lit.* relationship traced through Badarayana, from whom all men are reputed to be descended).

బాదరాయణుడు **baadaraayaNuDu** *n.* Badarayana, another name of the sage Vyasa.

బాదాం **baadaam** *same as* **baadam[kaaya].**

బాదామి **baadaami** *adj.* almond shaped.

బాదు **baadu** I.*n.* blow, stroke, beating. II. *v.i.* (of rain) to beat down, pour incessantly; **ninna raatrantaa waana baadutuunee undi** the rain was beating down all through last night. III. *v.t.* **1** to beat, thrash. **2** to bang, thump; **kaaLLu~** to stamp o.'s feet.

బాధ **baadha** *n.* **1** pain, trouble, affliction, suffering. **2** grief, distress, grievance. **3** annoyance, nuisance; **waaDitoo naaku pedda~wacci paDindi** he has become a great nuisance to me. **4** impatience; **eemiTi nii~? aaTalaki tondaragaa poowaalEE?** why are you impatient? are you in a hurry to go and play?

బాధకం **baadhakam** *n.* obstacle, hindrance.

బాధపడు **baadha paDu** *v.i.* **1** to be in pain or trouble, grieve, fret, feel sorrow, feel worried. **2** to regret, feel sorry. **3** to suffer (from), be afflicted (by); **kSayawyaadhitoo~** to be afflicted by tuberculosis.

బాధపెట్టు, బాధించు **baadhapeTTu, baadhincu** *v.t.* to trouble, worry, torment, afflict, oppress, harass.

బాధామయ **baadhaamaya** *adj.* distressful.

బాధితుడు **baadhituDu** *n.* sufferer, victim; **warada baadhitulu** flood victims.

బాధ్యత **baadhyata** *n.* responsibility, liability.

బాధ్యతలేని **baadhyataleeni** *adj.* irresponsible.

బాధ్యతాయుత **baadhyataayuta** *adj.* bearing responsibility; **~prabhutwam** responsible government.

బాధ్యతాయుతంగా **baadhyataayutangaa** *adv.* responsibly; **~prawartincu** to behave responsibly.

బాధ్యుడు **baadhyuDu** *n.* person who is responsible or liable.

బాన **baana** *n.* **1** cauldron. **2** large earthen pot. **3** leather baling bucket used for drawing well water for irrigation.

బానకడుపు, బానపొట్ట **baanakaDupu, baanapoTTa** *n.* pot belly.

బానిస **baanisa** *n.* **1** servant. **2** slave.

బానిసత్వం, బానిసతనం, బానిసబంధం **baanisatwam, baanisatanam, baanisabandham** *n.* slavery, servitude.

బాపడు **baapaDu** *n.* brahman.

బాపతు **baapatu** I. *n.* kind, sort, type (=**rakam**); **ceppina maaTa winani~** type (of person) who will not listen to what is said: **aa ~manuSulatoo sneeham ceeyaDam naaku iSTam leedu** I do not want to make friends with persons of that type. II. *p.p. and advbl. particle* pertaining to, relating to, concerning, belonging to; **waaDi~ saamaanu naa gadiloo unnadi** the luggage belonging to him is in my room; **paNTa ammina~ Dabbu naa jeebuloo unnadi** the money that pertains to the sale of the crop is in my pocket; **aa pustakam tarjumaa ceesina ~ Dabbu konta muTTindi** some of the money relating to the translation of that book has been received.

బాపన **baapana** *adj.* brahman.

బాపనోడు **baapanooDu** *n. slang* brahman.

బాపు **baapu**[1] *v.t. class.* to relieve; **kaSTaalu~** to relieve difficulties; **kSudhaartini~** to assuage hunger; **bhayaanni~** to alleviate fear.

బాపు **baapu**[2] *n.* **1** *dial.* father. **2** a name for Mahatma Gandhi.

బాపురే!, బాబోయి! **baapuree!, baabooyi!** *interj. expressive of various emotions*, e.g., horror, sorrow, surprise, fear, joy.

బాబయ్య **baabayya** I. *substandard form of* **baabaayi.** II. *substandard term of address* sir!

బాబా **baabaa** *n.* **1** saintly person. **2** religious mendicant.

బాబాయి **baabaayi** I. *n.* **1** father's younger brother. **2** mother's younger sister's husband. II. *informal mode of address to a man conveying both respect and familiarity.*

బాబు **baabu** *n.* **1** father. **2** son. **3** *dial.* father's younger brother. **4** man, boy; (*used respectfully for a male person of any age*).

బాబూ! **baabuu!** *respectful and friendly term of address to a male person of any age* sir!, young man!

బాము **baamu** *n.* **1** grief. **2** embarrassment, entanglement.

బాముకొను, బావుకొను **baamukonu, baawukonu** *v.i.* to be benefited.

బామ్మ, మామ్మ **baamma, maamma** I. *n.* **1** father's mother, grandmother. II. *respectful and affectionate term of address to an old woman.*

బాయి **baayi** *n.* **1** milk. **2** breast.

బార **baara** *n.* **1** two stretched arms, six feet, two yards, one fathom. **2** stroke (in swimming); **ceruwulooki duuki naalugu ~ lu weesEEnu** I jumped into the tank and swam a few strokes.

బారకాసు **baarakaasu** *n.* barracks.

బారచాచు **baaracaacu** *v.t.* to stretch out (o.'s legs or arms).

బారసాల **baarasaala** *n.* ceremony of naming a child.

బారసాల పెళ్లికొడుకు **baarasaalapeLLikoDuku** *n.* father who is present at his son's **baarasaala.**

బారాఖడీ **baaraakhaDii** *n.* chart of the Telugu alphabet containing all the combinations of consonants and vowels (**baLLu**).

బారి **baari** *n.* **1** assault, onslaught. **2** sloping path made for bullocks to walk up and down when baling water from a well by means of a mhote.

బారికి **baariki** *n.* village servant, attendant on the village headman or village accountant.

బారు **baaru**[1] *n.* line, row; **~tiirci naDucu** to march in line; **~tiirci nilabaDu** to stand in a row.

బారు **baaru**[2] *see* **paaru**[2] *sense 6.*

బారుగా **baarugaa** *adv.* **1** straight; **~weLLaNDi** go straight on; *see* **melika.** **2** loudly; **~ nawwu** to laugh aloud. **3** wide[ly]; **kiTikiilannii~terici unnaayi** all the windows are wide open.

బారుచేయు **baaru ceeyu** *v.t.* **tupaaki**~ to point or aim a gun (-**miida**, at).

బారున **baaruna** *adv.* all along, along the whole length of, for the full length of: **rooDDu** ~ **ceTLu unnaayi** all along the road there are trees: **reNDu peejiila** ~ **piiThika unnadi** there is a preface covering two pages *or* there is a preface two pages long; *cf.* **aa**~.

బారువ **baaruwa** *n.* obsolete measure of weight equal to one candy or twenty maunds.

బారువడ్డీ **baaruwaDDii** *n.* simple interest.

బారెడు **baareDu** *adj.* ~**duuram** a short distance (*lit.* two yards distance); **maa illu ikkaNNinci** ~ **duuramloo unnadi** our house is a short distance from here.

బార్లా[గా] **baarlaa[gaa]** *adv.* ~**terici** wide open.

బాల **baala** I. *n.* child under sixteen years of age. II. *adj.* **1** young, fresh. **2** juvenile.

బాలకుడు, బాలుడు **baalakuDu, baaluDu** *n.* boy.

బాలతొడుగు **baalatoDugu** *n.* jewellery which is assigned to a daughter at birth and will accompany her on her marriage.

బాలనాయకం **baalanaayakam** *n.* leadership by inexperienced persons.

బాలభటుడు **baalabhatuDu** *n.* boy scout.

బాలభానుడు, బాలసూర్యుడు **baalabhaanuDu, baalasuuryuDu** *n.* the rising sun.

బాలశిక్ష **baalasikSa** *n.* primer, first lesson book for children

బాలారిష్టం **baalaariSTam** *n.* **1** *astrol.* period which may be dangerous to the life a child. **2** *journ.* teething trouble.

బాలాజీ **baalaajii** *n.* a name of Sri Venkateswara, the God worshipped on Tirupati hill.

బాలింత[రాలు], బాలెంత[రాలు] **baalinta[raalu], baalenta[raalu]** *n.* woman with a newborn child: **pacci** (*or* **pedda**) ~ woman whose child is less than twelve days old: **nela**~ woman whose child is less than a month old.

బాలిక **baalika** *n.* girl, lass.

బాలీసు **baaliisu** *n.* large pillow or bolster to recline against.

బాలుడు **baaluDu** *same as* **baalakuDu.**

బాల్చీ **baalcii** *n.* bucket.

బాల్చీ తన్ను **baalcii tannu** *v.i. slang* to kick the bucket (slang), die.

బాల్య **baalya** *adj.* juvenile.

బాల్యం **baalyam** *n.* childhood.

బాళి **baaLi** *n.* desire, love, passion.

బావ **baawa** *n.* **1** man's sister's husband whether older or younger than himself, man's father's sister's son if older than himself, man's mother's brother's son if older than himself. **2** woman's husband's elder brother, woman's father's sister's son whether older or younger than herself, woman's mother's brother's son whether older or younger than herself, woman's elder sister's husband. **3** *for an unmarried woman any man whom she is eligible to marry may be called* ~ *or* **maama.**

బావమరిది **baawamaridi** *n.* man's wife's brother whether older or younger than himself, man's father's sister's son if younger than himself, man's mother's brother's son if younger than himself.

బావాజి **baawaaji** *n.* religious mendicant.

బావి **baawi** *n.* well.

బావిలీ **baawilii** *n.* kind of ear ornament.

బావుండు, బావుచేయు, బావుపడు, బావుపడేయు, బావుపరచు **baawuNDu, baawuceeyu, baawupaDu, baawupaDeeyu, baawuparacu** *colloq. alt. forms of* **baaguNDu, baaguceeyu, baagupaDu, baagupaDeeyu, baaguparacu.**

బావుకొను **baawukonu** *same as* **baamukonu.**

బావుటా **baawuTaa** *n. class.* flag.

బావురుపిల్లి **baawurupilli** *n.* wild cat.

బావురుమను **baawurumanu** *v.i.* **1** to sob, weep, be miserable, be dismal. **2** (of an empty house) to echo, resound, be dreary, be desolate.

బాషికాలు **baaSikaalu** *same as* **baasikaalu.**

బాష్పం **baaSpam** *n.* **1** tear: **aananda baaSpaalu** tears of joy. **2** *sci.* vapour.

బాష్పవాయువు **baaSpawaayuwu** *n.* tear gas.

బాష్పశీల, బాష్పశీలి **baaSpasiila, baaSpasiili** *adj. chem.* volatile.

బాష్పశీలత **baaSpasiilata** *n. chem.* volatility.

బాష్పీభవనం **baaSpiibhawanam** *n.sci.* evaporation.

బాష్యం, భాష్యం **b[h]aaSyam** *n.* commentary, interpretation, exposition.

బాష్యకారుడు, భాష్యకారుడు **b[h]aaSyakaaruDu** *n.* commentator.

బాస **baasa**[1] *n.* language (= **bhaaSa**).

బాస **baasa**[2] *n.* vow, promise.

బాసచేయు **baasaceeyu** *v.i.* to promise.

బాసట **baasaTa** *n.* aid, help, support.

బాసికాలు, బాషికాలు **baasikaalu, baaSikaalu** *n.pl.* lockets (one for each) tied to the bride's and bridegroom's foreheads during the wedding ceremony.

బాసిపీట, బాసిక[ప]ట్టు, సకలం ముకలం **baasipiiTa, baasika[pa]TTu, sakalam mukalam** *n.* sitting cross-legged, sitting in the lotus pose with the legs crossed: ~**peTTu**, ~ **weeyu** to sit with o.'s legs crossed (= **padmaasanam**).

బాస్మతి **baasmati** *n.* superior kind of scented rice.

బాహాటం **baahaaTam** I. *n.* publicity, openness. II. *adj.* **1** public, open. **2** loud. **3** undisguised.

బాహాటంగా **baahaaTangaa** *adv.* openly, publicly.

బాహాబాహీ **baahaabaahii** *adj.* (of fighting) hand to hand.

బాహిరం **baahiram** *adj.* public, known.

బాహుదండం **baahudaNDam** *n.* arm as strong as a rod, very strong arm.

బాహుమూలం **baahumuulam** *n.* armpit.

బాహుళ్యం **baahuLyam** *n.* plenty, abundance, wealth, multitude: **pada**~ wealth of words: **wyawahaara**~**unna ruupam** most commonly used form.

బాహుళ్యంగా **baahuLyangaa** *adv.* liberally.

బాహువు **baahuwu** *n.* **1** arm. **2** *maths.* side of a geometrical figure: **cadaramloo unna anni ~luu samaanamaynawee** all the sides of a square are equal.

బాహ్య **baahya** I. *adj.* outer, outward, outside, exterior, external, public. II. *second part of an adjvl. compound meaning* excluded from, devoid of: **niiti ~ mayna** amoral.

బాహ్యంగా **baahyangaa** *adv.* outwardly, externally.

బి - bi

బింకం **binkam** *n.* stiffness, pride, arrogance, conceitedness, vanity, boastfulness: **binkaalu paluku** to boast, talk arrogantly: **kappu weeDigaa uNTee peTTeeseyyi, binkaaniki pookuNDaa ceppu** if the cup is too hot put it down, don't be too proud to say so: *see also* **~gaa**.

బింకంగా **binkangaa** *adv.* **1** proudly, arrogantly, conceitedly. **2** (*also* **binkaaniki**) out of bravado, making a show of bravery; **paynunci paDi~** (*or* **binkaaniki**) **debbatagalaleedani ceppEEDu** after falling down he said out of of bravado that he had not been hurt: *cf.* **pawruSaaniki.**

బింకి **binki** *n. dial.* small pot used for toddy.

బిందువు **binduwu** *n.* **1** drop, dot. **2** *gram.* anusvara, represented in writing by a small circle o. **3** *maths.* point.

బిందె **binde** *n.* large brass pot for carrying or storing water.

బింబం **bimbam** *n.* **1** image, reflection. **2 suurya/candra~** face or disc of the sun/moon: *cf.* **mukha~**.

బికారి **bikaari** *n.* beggar.

బిక్కచచ్చిపోవు **bikkacacci poowu** *v.i.* to be terrified, be aghast, be greatly frightened.

బిక్కమొహం **bikkamoham** *n.* blank or expressionless face.

బిక్కమొహం పెట్టు, బిక్కమొహం వేయు **bikkamoham peTTu, bikkamoham weeyu** *v.i.* to look distressed, look miserable.

బిక్కు[వు] **bikku[wu]** *n.* wandering Buddhist monk (= **bhikSuwu**).

బిక్కు బిక్కు **bikkubikku** *adv.* nervously, anxiously.

బిక్కుబిక్కుమను **bikkubikkumanu** *v.i.* **1** to feel scared, feel nervous, feel anxious: **naaku bikkubikkumaNTunnadi** I am feeling scared. **2** (of an empty house) to be lonely and desolate.

బిగ **biga** *adv.* tightly, firmly, stiffly: *always prefixed to a vb.*, e.g., **~tiiyu, ~paTTu.**

బిగం, బీగం, బీగా, బీఘా **bigam, biigam[1], biigaa, biighaa** *n.* bigha, an obsolete measure of land, about three quarters of an acre.

బిగడాయించు **bigaDaayincu** *v.i.* to be on bad terms, have bad mutual relations; **waaLLa iddarikii bigaDaayincindi** they are on bad terms with each other.

బిగతొక్కు **bigatokku** *v.t.* to tread down tightly.

బిగదీయు **bigadiiyu** *v.i.* to become tense, become stiff: **mukku bigadiisindi jalubuwalla** the nose is blocked up due to a cold: **poddunee leewagaanee meDa bigadiisindi** my neck was stiff when I woke in the morning: **aayana naatoo bigadiisukonnaaDu** he has become stiff in manner towards me.

బిగపట్టు **bigapaTTu** I. *v.i.* to keep off, hold off: **waana bigapaTTindi** the rain held off. II. *v.t.* **1** to hold tightly. **2** to hold back, restrain, withhold: **uupiri~konu** to hold o.'s breath: **jiitam~** to withhold (s.o.'s) pay.

బిగి **bigi** *n.* **1** firmness of flesh. **2** vitality, physical well-being: **yawwanapu ~** bloom of youth.

బిగించు **bigincu** *v.t.* **1** to hold tightly, hold firmly. **2** to tighten. **3** to fasten (bolt). **4** to fit in place, fix, set: **ungaramloo raayi~** to have a stone set in a ring: **phooTooki phreem ~** to frame a photo. **5** to clench(fist). **6** to tuck in: **laaguu loopaliki cokkaa bigincEEDu** he tucked his shirt into his pants. **7** to stick (s.g) into o.'s mouth: **kiLLii bigincEEDu** he stuck a roll of pan into his mouth: **oka peggu wiskii bigincEEDu** he gulped down a peg of whisky. **8 muuti~** to purse o.'s lips.

బిగియు, బిగిసిపోవు **bigiyu, bigisipoowu** *v.i., of non-human things* **1** to be tight, be stiff, be rigid, be hard: **laDDu bigisindi** the laddu has become hard. **2** to stick, get stuck: **calla gaaliki talupu bigisipooyindi** the door got stuck due to the cold wet air.

బిగుతు **bigutu** I. *n.* **1** tightness (e.g., of clothes). **2** tension. II. *adj.* tight.

బిగుమానం **bigumaanam** *n.* firmness, strength (of materials).

బిగువు **biguwu** *n.* **1** tightness (of clothes or of a grip or grasp): **laaguu naDumdaggira ~gaa undi** the trousers are tight round the waist: **kaalu noppigaa unnaa paNTi ~na naDicEEnu** although my leg was painful, I gritted my teeth and walked. **2** tautness (of a rope). **3** tenseness (of style in writing). **4** liveliness (of a look or expression). **5** firmness (of flesh).

బిగుసుకొను **bigusukonu** *v.i., gen. of human beings* **1** to be stiff, be tense: **aa maaTalu wini naatoo bigusuku pooyEEDu** on hearing those words he became stiff in his manner towards me. **2** to be adamant, be obstinate, be determined. **3** to be[come] rigid with fear.

బిగ్గరగా **biggaragaa** *adv.* loudly.

బిచానా, బిచాణా **bicaanaa, bicaaNaa** *n.* bedding.

బిచానా వేయు **bicaanaa weeyu** *v.i.* to camp or stay at a place: **maa iNTLoo bicaanaa weesEEDu** he is staying in my house.

బిచ్చం **biccam** *n.* alms.

బిచ్చం ఇచ్చు, బిచ్చం పెట్టు, బిచ్చం వేయు **biccam iccu, biccam peTTu, biccam weeyu** *v.i.* to give alms.

బిచ్చగాడు **biccagaaDu** *n.* beggar.

బిడాయించు **biDaayincu** *v.t.* **1** to shut (door). **2** to cover completely: **duppaTi biDaayincEEDu** he covered himself from head to foot in a sheet.

బిడారం **biDaaram** *n.* caravan.
బిడాలం **biDaalam** *n.* cat.
బిడియం **biDiyam** *n.* **1** shyness, self-consciousness, diffidence, modesty. **2** shame.
బిడియపడు **biDiyapaDu** *v.i.* to feel shy, feel embarrassed, feel shamefaced.
బిడ్డ **biDDa** *n.* child, infant, son, daughter; **caNTi~** baby in arms; **~ talli** mother of a child.
బిడ్డి **biDDi** *n. dial.* small pot or cup.
బితుకూబితుకూ **bitukuu bitukuu** *adv.* timidly, nervously.
బిత్తరపు, బిత్తరి **bittarapu, bittari** *adj.* quickly changing, fleeting; **~ cuupulu** fleeting glances.
బిత్తరపోవు **bittarapoowu** *v.i.* to be astonished, be taken aback.
బిత్తలి, బిత్తళి **bittali, bittaLi** *n. dial.* naked person.
బిబ్బోకం **bibbookam** *n.* refusing or despising what one was previously contented with, presumptuousness, capriciousness.
బియ్యం **biyyam** *n.pl.* uncooked rice; **~ niNDukonnaayi** the rice is exhausted (*lit.* the rice is full—paraphrase to avoid a taboo expression); *cf.* **golusu, diipam.**
బియ్యాన **biyyana** *adv. dial.* quickly.
బిరడా **biraDaa** *n.* cork, stopper, plug.
బిరబిర, బిరాన, బిరాలున, బిరాల **birabira, biraana, biraaluna, biraala** *adv.* quickly.
బిరుదు, బిరుదం **birudu, birudam** *n.* title, award.
బిరుసు **birusu** *adj.* **1** hard, firm; **annam ~ gaa undi** the rice is hard (not fully cooked). **2** stiff. **3** rough. **4** tight.
బిర్రబిగియు **birrabigiyu** *v.i.* **1** to be very tight or stiff. **2** to be stubborn. **3** to be firmly established.
బిర్రు **birru** *adj.* **1** tight. **2** tense. **3** stiff, inflexible.
బిర్రున బిగదీయు **birruna bigadiiyu** *v.i.* to become tense.
బిలం **bilam** *n.* **1** hole, cavity, crater. **2** burrow. **3** cave.
బిలబిలా **bilabilaa** *onom. adv. sug.* crowding, swarming, teeming; **tallini cuustuunee ~ parigettukoccEEru pillalantaa** all the children ran swarming towards their mother as soon as they saw her.
బిలబిలాక్షులు **bilabilaakSulu** *n.pl.* kind of small sparrow-like bird.
బిలిబిలి పలుకులు **bilibili palukulu** *n.pl.* lisping words of a child learning to speak.
బిళ్ల **biLLa** *n.* **1** disc. **2** anything shaped like a disc, e.g., pill, tablet, toffee. **3** washer, pulley wheel. **4** playing piece (in caroms). **5** piece of soap. **6** locket. **7** lump or bump; **~ kaTTu** to form a lump; **gawaDa ~ lu** mumps. **8** (*also* **tapaala ~**) postage stamp.
బిళ్లంగోడు **biLLangooDu** *n.* a boys' game (= **karraabiLLaa** *or* **gilliidaNDu**).
బిళ్లపురుగు **biLLa purugu** *n.* red-winged stinging beetle.
బిళ్లపెంకులు **biLLapenkulu** *same as* **paalaastri penkulu.**
బిస **bisa** *n.* device, contrivance.
బిస ఎక్కించు **bisa ekkincu** *v.t. dial.* to incite, spur on.

బీ - bii

బీగం, బీగా, బీఘా **biigam**[1], **biigaa, biighaa** *same as* **bigam.**
బీగం **biigam**[2] *n.* **1** lock. **2** padlock.
బీజం **biijam** *n.* **1** seed. **2** testicle.
బీజకణం **biijakaNam** *n. bot.* spore.
బీజకోశం **biijakoośam** *n. biol.* ovary.
బీజగణితం **biijagaNitam** *n. maths.* algebra.
బీజదళం **biijadaLam** *same as* **daLabiijam.**
బీజమంత్రం, బీజాక్షరం **biijamantram, biijaakSaram** *n.* mystic syllable[s] forming a mantra.
బీజావాపం **biijaawaapam** *n.* scattering seed.
బీట **biiTa** *n.* crack, split, chink, crevice.
బీట[లు] వారు, బీట[లు]పోవు **biiTa[lu]waaru, biiTa[lu]poowu** *v.i.* (of glass) to be cracked.
బీడా **biiDaa** *n.* roll of betel and nut.
బీడీ **biiDii** *n.* beedi, tobacco wrapped in a leaf and smoked.
బీడు **biiDu** *n.* **1** uncultivated land, fallow or waste land. **2** pasture land.
బీతు **biitu** *n.* fear (= **bhiiti**).
బీతుకొను **biitukonu** *v.i.* to fear, be afraid.
బీతుకొలుపు **biitukolupu** *v.t.* to frighten.
బీద **biida** *adj.* poor, indigent; **~ waaDu** poor person; *pl.* **~ waaLLu** *or* **~ lu** poor persons, the poor.
బీదరికం, బీదతనం **biidarikam, biidatanam** *n.* poverty.
బీదసాదలు, బీదాబిక్కి **biidasaadalu, biidaabikkii** *n. pl.* the poor (used as a term of commiseration); **biidasaadalaku ucita waydya sahaayam kalpistaaru** they provide free medical aid to the poor.

బీబీ **biibii** *n.* Muslim lady.

బీభత్సం **biibhatsam** I. *n.* terror, horror. II. *adj.* terrible, terrifying, horrible, horrifying.

బీమా **biimaa** *n.* insurance.

బీర[కాయ] **biira[kaaya]** *n.* ridge cucumber, angled cucumber, *luffa acutangula.*

బీర[కాయ]పీచు **biira[kaaya]piicu** *n.* 1 *lit.* fibre of the ridge cucumber. 2 *colloq.* state of being interrelated; **welanaaTi braahmalantaa~** Velnad brahmans are all interrelated with one another.

బీరాలు **biiraalu** *n.pl.* boasting.

బీరు **biiru** *n.* beer.

బీరుపోవు **biirupoowu** *v.i.* 1 *class.* to become weak, become useless. 2 *mod. only in neg. and interrog. constr.* to flag, fail, be weakened; **biirupooni dhayryamtoo munduku naDicEEDu** with unflagging courage he walked forward; **eem jarigindoo biirupookuNDaa mottam ceppEEDu** without omitting anything (*lit.* without failing in anything) he told all that had happened; **aayana ceppinaTLu ceeyaDamwalla eem biirupooyinaawu? laabhamee waccindigaa!** what did you lose by doing as he said? you made a profit, didn't you?

బీరువా **biiruwaa** *n.* 1 almirah, wardrobe, cupboard. 2 bookcase, bookshelf.

బు - bu

బుంగ **bunga** *n.* pot with a narrow mouth.

బుంగమూతి **bungamuuti** *n.* sulky face; **~ peTTukonu** to put on a sulky look.

బుకాయించు **bukaayincu** *v.i. and t.* to bluff, hoodwink, elude.

బుకాయింపు **bukaayimpu** *n.* bluffing, hoodwinking.

బుక్క **bukka** *n.* 1 inside of the mouth. 2 (*also* **bukkeDu**) mouthful; **bukkeDu niiLLu** a mouthful of water; **reNDu bukkala annam tinnaaDu** he ate a little food (*lit.* he ate two mouthfuls of food).

బుక్కా[యి] **bukkaa[yi]** *n.* fragrant powder thrown by the bride and bridegroom (together with **wasantam**) on each other at a point in the wedding ceremony.

బుక్కాఫకీరు **bukkaaphakiiru** *n.* very poor person.

బుక్కు **bukku** *same as* **bokku.**

బుగత **bugata** *n.* 1 brahman landlord. 2 big landowner from any community.

బుగులు **bugulu** *dial. variant form of* **gubulu.**

బుగ్గ **bugga**[1] *n.* cheek; **~lu nokkukonu** to clutch o.'s cheeks (a gesture of surprise).

బుగ్గ **bugga**[2] *n.* spring or fountain of water; **weeDi niiTi~lu** hot[water] springs.

బుగ్గ **bugga**[3] *n.* 1 balloon. 2 *dial.* electric light bulb.

బుగ్గమీసాలు **buggamiisaalu** *n.pl.* bushy moustache.

బుగ్గి **buggi** *n.* ashes, dust; **~loo** (*or* **buuDidaloo**) **poosina panniiru** rose-water poured on ashes (a proverbial term for waste).

బుగ్గిచేయు **buggi ceeyu** *v.t.* to destroy, spoil (*lit.* to burn to ashes).

బుచ్చి, బుజ్జి **bucci, bujji** *adj.* little, small, young, miniature: **~paapa** little baby.

బుజ్జగించు **bujjagincu** *v.t.* 1 to coax, cajole, humour. 2 to caress.

బుటా, బుట్టా, బూటా **buTaa, buTTaa, buuTaa** *n.* flowered pattern in cloth; **~lu kuTTee pani** *dial.* embroidery.

బుట్ట **buTTa**[1] *n.* 1 basket with a narrow neck. 2 waste paper basket; **~daakhalaa ceeyu** *colloq.* to consign to the waste paper basket, discard, scrap.

బుట్ట **buTTa**[2] *n.* kind of ear ornament.

బుట్టలోవేయు **buTTaloo weeyu** *v.t.* 1 to dupe, hoodwink (s.o.). 2 to win over, gain the confidence of (s.o.).

బుడగ **buDaga** *n.* bubble.

బుడత, బుడుత **buData, buDuta** I. *n.* child; **~Du** little boy. II. *adj.* 1 short. 2 young.

బుడతకీచు **buDatakiicu** *adj.* Portuguese.

బుడబుక్క **buDabukka** *dial. variant form of* **DabuDakku.**

బుడమ **buDama**[1] *n. dial.* short round cucumber with a sour taste, *cucumis pubescense*; **waaDu poTTi~kaaya** he is as round and tubby as a **buDama.**

బుడమ **buDama**[2] *n.* variety of rainfed paddy maturing early in the agricultural year.

బుడిగి **buDigi** *n.* small pot.

బుడిప, బుడిపె, బొడిపె **buDipa, buDipe, boDipe** *n.* bump, swelling, knob, excrescence, nodule; **tala[miida] ~ kaTTindi** he got a bump on the head.

బుడిబుడి **buDibuDi** *adj.* trifling, petty; **~eeDupulu** whimpering.

బుడుంగున, బుడుక్కున **buDunguna, buDukkuna** *onom. adv. sug.* sound of plunging into water.

బుడుంగుమను, బుడుక్కుమను **buDungumanu, buDukkumanu** *v.i.* to plunge into water, sink with a gurgling sound.

బుడుగు **buDugu** *adj.* short.

బుడ్డ **buDDa**[1] *n. med.* hydrocele.

బుడ్డ **buDDa**[2] *adj. dial.* 1 short. 2 small, **~ginne** small vessel; **~bedirimpulu** empty threats.

బుడ్డకొట్టు **buDDakoTTu** *v.i.* to castrate.

బుడ్డలు **buDDalu** *n.pl. dial.* groundnut.

బుడ్డి **buDDi** *n.* 1 bottle. 2 vessel with a narrow neck; **gallaa~** money box.

బుడ్డికొట్టు **buDDikoTTu** *v.i. colloq.* to drink liquor.

బుడ్డిచెంబు **buDDicembu** *n.* metal jar shaped liked a bottle.

బుడ్డిదీపం **buDDidiipam** *n.* small kerosene lamp with an unprotected flame.

బుద్ధి **buddhi** *n.* **1** mind, intellect. **2** intelligence, wit, understanding, judgement, sense, wisdom, discernment; **neenu~ eriginappaTinunci** from the time that I reached the age of discernment. **3** thought, idea, conception; **weLLi cuuDaalani waaDiki~puTTindi** he conceived the idea of (*or* he thought of) going and seeing. **4** intention, wish, will, inclination; **~kaligina naaDu iNTiki wacci tiNTaaDu, leekapooTee hooTalloo eeDustaaDu** when the inclination comes to him (*or* when he feels like it) he comes home and eats, otherwise he eats in a hotel. **5** mental characteristics; **pedda~** bigheartedness; **cinna~** mean mentality, narrowmindedness; **manci buddhulu** good disposition, good behaviour; **alagaa~** low mental calibre; *see* **sari** *sense I. 3.*

బుద్ధిగల **buddhigala** *adj.* sensible, wise, intelligent.

బుద్ధి చెప్పు **buddhi ceppu** *v.i.* **1** to admonish, reprimand. **2** to give advice; *see* **kaalu** *sense I. 1.*

బుద్ధితక్కువ **buddhitakkuwa** I. *n.* stupidity, foolishness. II. *adj.* stupid, foolish, unintelligent.

బుద్ధి తెచ్చుకొను **buddhiteccukonu** *v.i.* **1** to learn a sound lesson. **2** to come to o.'s senses, recover o.'s wits.

బుద్ధిపూర్వకంగా **buddhipuurwakangaa** *adv.* **1** on purpose, deliberately, intentionally. **2** with full understanding.

బుద్ధిమంతనంగా **buddhimantanangaa** *adv.* in a well-behaved manner.

బుద్ధిమంతనంగా ఉండు **buddhimantanangaa uNDu** *v.i.* to be of good behaviour.

బుద్ధిమంతుడు **buddhimantuDu** *n.* well-behaved person.

బుద్ధిలేని **buddhileeni** *adj.* stupid, unintelligent, senseless.

బుద్ధిశాలి **buddhiśaali** *n.* clever person, intelligent person.

బుద్ధిస్థిరత **buddhisthirata** *n.* sanity, soundness of mind.

బుద్ధిహీనత **buddhihiinata** *n.* stupidity, foolishness, folly.

బుద్ధిహీనుడు **buddhihiinuDu** *n.* fool.

బుద్ధుడు **buddhuDu** *n.* Buddha.

బుద్బుదం **budbudam** *n. class.* bubble; **jiiwitam budbudapraayam** life is like a bubble.

బుద్బుదనం **budbudanam** *n.* effervescence.

బుధవారం **budhawaaram** *n.* Wednesday.

బుధుడు **budhuDu** *n.* **1** the planet Mercury. **2** *class.* sage.

బురకా, బురఖా **burak[h]aa** *n.* Muslim woman's veil.

బురద **burada** *n.* mud.

బురబుర **burabura** *adv.* quickly, in a hurry.

బురబురపొంగు **buraburapongu** *v.i.* to swell up, bubble up (as a **puuri** or wheat puff does when fried).

బురబురలాడు **buraburalaaDu** *v.i.* to come on suddenly; **waaDiki~tuu jwaram waccindi** the fever attacked him suddenly.

బురికి **buriki** *n. dial.* small bowl made from a coconut shell.

బురిడీ **buriDii** *n.* trickery, deception; **~koTTincu** to trick, dupe, make a fool of (s.o.).

బురుజు **buruju** *n.* tower in a fort, turret, bastion, rampart.

బుర్ర **burra** *n.* **1** shell of a nut or gourd. **2** skull. **3** head. **4** *colloq.* brains.

బుర్రకాయ **burrakaaya** *n. slang* head.

బుర్రతిరుగుడు **burratiruguDu** *n.* perverseness, wrongheadedness.

బుర్రముక్కు **burramukku** *n.* flared nostrils.

బులపాటం **bulapaaTam** *n.* **1** thrill, excitement. **2** keen enjoyment; *cf.* **ubalaaTam.**

బులాకి, బులాకీ **bulaaki[i]** *n.* nose ornament.

బులిపించు **bulipincu** *v.t.* to entice, cajole.

బులిబుచ్చికాలు **bulibuccikaalu** *n.pl.dial.* soft and winning words.

బులిసిపోవు **bulisipoowu** *v.i.* to be[come] loving and affectionate.

బులుగు **bulugu** *adj. dial.* blue.

బులుపు **bulupu** *n.* **1** delight, thrill, excitement. **2** resentment, offence; **waaDiki ceppa leedani~ waccindi** he took offence because he was not informed.

బుల్ల[కాయ], బుల్లపండు **bulla[kaaya], bullapaNDu** *n.* (used with ref. to a child) penis.

బుల్లాడు, బుల్లోడు **bullaaDu, bullooDu** *n.* small boy.

బువ్వ **buwwa** *n.* cooked rice.

బుస **busa** *n.* hiss of a snake.

బుస[లు] కొట్టు, బుస్సుమను **busa[lu]koTTu, bussumanu** *v.i.* **1** (of a snake) to hiss. **2** (of a person) *fig.* to hiss with anger.

బుసబుసపొంగు **busabusapongu** *v.i.* to effervesce.

బుసి **busi** *n. dial.* ashes.

బుస్సున **bussuna** *adv.* angrily (*lit.* with a hiss).

బూ - buu

బూందీ **buundii** *n.* sweet or savoury dish made with bengalgram.

బూకరం **buukaram** *n.* downright lie.

బూకరించు **buukarincu** *v.i.* **1** to browbeat. **2** to bluff, bluster.

బూకరింపు **buukarimpu** *n.* **1** browbeating. **2** bluffing, blustering.

బూగర **buugara** *n.* grain threshed but not yet winnowed.

బూచి **buuci** *n.* **1** ghost, evil spirit, monster. **2** (*also* ~ **waaDu. buucaaDu**) ogre, bugbear, bogey (a word used to frighten children).

బూజంబంతి **buujambanti** *n.* meal provided by the bride's party for the members of both parties at the end of the wedding ceremony.

బూజు **buuju** *n.* mould, mildew, cobwebs.

బూజుదులుపు **buujudulupu** *v.t.* **1** to dust; **pustakaalu buujudulipi caduwu modalu peTTEEnu** I dusted the books and started to study. **2** *colloq.* to give s.o. a beating, give s.o. a dressing down.

బూజుపట్టు **buujupaTTu** *v.i.* **1** to become mouldy or musty. **2** to become outmoded, become out of date.

బూటక **buuTaka** *adj.* false, delusive, bogus, sham; ~ **waydyuDu** quack doctor.

బూటకం **buuTakam** *n.* trick, fraud, deceit, sham.

బూటా **buuTaa** *same as* **buTaa.**

బూడిద, బూడిదె **buuDida, buuDide** *n.* **1** ashes; *see* **buggi. 2** *term of abuse* **waaDi ~ ! waaDiki eem telusu?** silly ass! what does he know?

బూడిద అవు **buuDida awu** *v.i.* to be ruined, be a failure (*lit.* to become ashes).

బూడిదగుమ్మడి **buuDidagummaDi** *n.* ash gourd, *cucurbita pepo.*

బూడిదరంగు **buuDidarangu** *n.* grey colour.

బూతు **buutu** I. *n.* **1** foul language, obscenity. **2** (in a milder sense) s.g unspeakable, s.g intolerable. II. *adj.* obscene, indecent; ~ **racanalu** pornography.

బూతు[లు] తిట్టు **buutu[lu] tiTTu** *v.t.* to abuse (s.o.) with foul language, swear at (s.o.).

బూబు **buubu** *n.* Muslim lady (= **biibii**).

బూర **buura** *n.* balloon.

బూరకాలు **buurakaalu** *n.* filariasis, elephantiasis.

బూరా **buuraa** *n.* **1** trumpet, bugle. **2** siren. **3 paamu ~** snake charmer's flute.

బూరుగ, బూరుగు[దూది] **buuruga, buurugu[duudi]** *n.* silk cotton, kapok.

బూరుగచెట్టు, బూరుగుచెట్టు **buurugaceTTu, buuruguceTTu** *n.* silk cotton tree, *bombax heptaphylla.*

బూరె **buure** I. *n.* kind of sweet cake made at the time of death ceremonies. II. *adj.* ~ **buggalu** (child's) cheeks that are bursting with health.

బూర్జువా **buurjuwaa** *n. and adj.* bourgeois.

బూర్నీసు **buurniisu** *n.* blanket, thick woollen cloth.

బూర్లెమూకుడు **buurle muukuDu** *n.* deep frying pan in which **buurelu** are made.

బూసట్లుపోవు **buusaTLupoowu** *v.i.* to pretend.

బూసరకాయ **buusarakaaya** *n.* Brazil cherry, *physalis peruviana.*

బూసి **buusi** *n.* dirt, cobwebs.

బృ - bṛ

బృంద **bṛnda** *n. class.* tulasi or sacred basil plant, *ocymum sanctum.*

బృందం **bṛndam** *n.* **1** team, troupe. **2 mitra ~** group or band of friends.

బృందగానం **bṛndagaanam** *n.* singing in chorus.

బృందభావం **bṛndabhaawam** *n.* team spirit

బృందావనం **bṛndaawanam** *n.* **1** *class.* place where Krishna spent his boyhood. **2** garden.

బృగువు **bṛguwu** *n. dial.* good relations, friendly terms.

బృహత్తర **bṛhattara** *adj.* huge, enormous.

బృహత్తు **bṛhattu** *adj.* large, huge, giant, monster; **bṛhatpathakam** overall plan, master plan.

బృహన్నల **bṛhannala** *n.* **1** epithet of Arjuna. **2** eunuch.

భృహస్పతి **bṛhaspati** *n.* **1** the planet Jupiter. **2** name of the priest and teacher of the gods in mythology.

బృహస్పతివారం **bṛhaspatiwaaram** *n.* Thursday (= **bestawaaram**).

బె - be

బెంగ **benga** *n.* worry, anxiety.

బెంగపెట్టుకొను, బెంగపడు **bengapeTTukonu, bengapaDu** *v.i.* **1** to worry, be anxious (**-koosam,** on account of). **2** to yearn, pine; **pillalamiida bengapeTTukonnaaDu** (*or* **bengapaDDaaDu**) he is pining for his children; **iNTimiida bengapeTTukonnaaDu** (*or* **bengapaDDaaDu**) he is feeling homesick.

బెండ[కాయ] **beNDa[kaaya]** *n.* vegetable known as okra or ladies' fingers, *hibiscus longifolius.*

బెండు **beNDu** *n.* **1** cork. **2** pith, pulp, trash.

బెందడు **bendaDu** *n.* stone chips inserted in a wall to fill the interstices.

బెంబేరుపడు, బెంబేలుపడు **bembeerupaDu, bembeelupaDu** *v.i.* to be worried, be alarmed, be in a panic.

బెకబెకలు **bekabekalu** *n.pl.* croaking of frogs.

బెక్కు **bekku** *v.i., alt. variant form of* **wekku.**

బెజ్జం **bejjam** *n.* hole, aperture.

బెట్టిదం **beTTidam** *n. class.* **1** hardness. **2** harshness, severity.

బెట్టు[సరి] **beTTu[sari]** I. *n.* stiffness, rigidity, haughtiness, reservedness. II. *adj.* stiff, haughty, reserved.

బెట్టు[సరి]గా **beTTu[sari]gaa** *adv.* stiffly, haughtily, with reserve.

బెట్టుచేయు **beTTuceeyu** *v.i.* to behave in a stiff or reserved manner.

బెడద **beDada** *n.* **1** trouble, complication, bother, problem. **2** misfortune, hardship. **3** threat, menace.

బెడియు, బెడిసిపోవు **beDiyu, beDisipoowu** *v.i.* **1** (of an affair, plan) to be spoilt, be unsuccessful, go wrong; **beDisina sambandhaalu** strained relations. **2** (of persons) to have a difference of opinion, have a misunderstanding.

బెడిసికొట్టు **beDisikoTTu** *v.i. same meanings as* **beDiyu** *but more emphatic,* e.g., **naa pathakam beDisi koTTindi** my plan misfired; **waaLLa iddarikii beDisi koTTindi** they are at loggerheads.

బెడ్డ, పెడ్డ **beDDa, peDDa** *n.* **1** clod, lump of earth. **2** *pl.* **~ lu** grit and other impurities (in rice).

బెణుకు **beNuku** I. *n.* sprain; **~ mantram** charm chanted to relieve a sprain. II. *v.i.* to be sprained; **kaalu beNikindi** the leg was sprained.

బెత్త **betta** *n.* width of four fingers, handbreadth; **betteDu duuram** distance of a handbreadth.

బెత్తం **bettam** *n.* cane, rattan.

బెత్తాయించు **bettaayincu** *v.t.* to assign, entrust (a job to s.o.).

బెత్తిక **bettika** *n.* flake (of paint, plaster); **gooDa ~ lu uuDindi** plaster flaked off the wall.

బెదరగొట్టు, బెదిరించు **bedaragoTTu, bedirincu** *v.t.* to frighten, intimidate, threaten, menace.

బెదిరింపు **bedirimpu** *n.* intimidation, threat; **~ caryalu** intimidatory actions.

బెదిరిన, బెదరిన **bedirina, bedarina** *adj.* frightened, alarmed, timid, nervous.

బెదురు, బెదరు **beduru, bedaru** I. *n.* fright, alarm, fear, timidity, nervousness. II. *v.i.* to be frightened or alarmed (**-ki,** by *or* of).

బెదురుకుండ, బెదురుబొమ్మ **bedurukuNDa, bedurubomma** *n.* scarecrow to protect crops from birds or animals or the effects of the evil eye.

బెదురుగొడ్డు **bedurugoDDu** *n.* frightened or timid animal; **waaDu oTTi ~** ; he is a timid wretch.

బెబ్బులి **bebbuli** *n.* tiger (= **peddapuli**).

బెరడు **beraDu** *n.* bark of a tree.

బెరుకు **beruku** *n.* inhibition, scruple, hesitation.

బెల్లం **bellam**[1] *n.* **1** gur, jaggery, boiled sugarcane juice; **~ uNDa** jaggery made into balls; **gaccu ~** jaggery made in slabs; **~ waNDu** to manufacture (*lit.* to cook) jaggery. **2** **~ koTTina raayilaaga** (*lit.* like a stone on which jaggery is powdered) *is an advbl. phrase meaning* noiselessly, without a sound.

బెల్లం, బెల్లకాయ **bellam**[2]**, bellakaaya** *n. slang* penis.

బెల్లపానకాయ కథలు **bellapaanakaayakathalu** *n.pl. slang* erotic stories.

బెల్లించు **bellincu** *v.t.* to coax, cajole, wheedle.

బెల్లింపు **bellimpu** *adj.* coaxing, enticing; **~ maaTalu/cuupulu** coaxing words/looks.

బెసుకు **besuku** *v.i.* to slip away; **niiLLakuNDa ceetiloonci besiki kinda paDipooyindi** the pot of water slipped out of my hand and fell; **dongani paTTukonnaanu, paTTu besiki waaDu paaripooyEEDu** I caught the thief but he slipped from my grasp and ran away; **bassu ekkabootuNTee paTTu besikindi, kinda paDDaanu** I lost my hold and fell down when getting onto the bus; *cf.* **pusikipoowu.**

బెస్త[వాడు] **besta[waaDu]** *n.* fisherman.

బెస్తవారం, బేస్తవారం **be[e]stawaaram** *n. dial.* Thursday.

బే - bee

బే **bee** *Urdu prefix conveying a negative meaning*, e.g., **bee-Saratu** without conditions.

బేకు **beeku**[1] (<Urdu **beewakuuf**) *term of abuse* fool, useless person.

బేకు **beeku**[2] *v.t.* to cane.

బేఖాతర్ **beekhaatar** *adj.* careless, carefree.

బేఖాతర్‌గా **beekhaatargaa** *adv.* carelessly, without caring, in a carefree manner, in an offhand or indifferent manner.

బేగా, బేగి **beegaa, beegi** *adv. dial.* quickly.

బేజారవు, బేజారుపడు, బేజారెత్తు **beejaarawu, beejaarupaDu, beejaarettu** *v.i.* to be worried, upset, confused or distracted.

బేజారుపెట్టు **beejaarupeTTu** *v.t.* to worry, upset, trouble, confuse, distract.

బేజోటు అవు **beejooTu awu** *v.i. dial.* (of a plan) to go wrong, misfire (colloq).

బేడ **beeDa** *n.* **1** *dial.* two anna coin (obsolete). **2** *dial.* (*also pl.* **beeLLu**) pulse, dhall (= **pappu**); **uddibeeLLu** blackgram dhall.

బేడిమూక **beeDimuuka** *n.* rabble.

బేడీలు **beeDiilu** *n.pl.* handcuffs.

బేతాళం **beetaaLam** *n.* demon, fiend, evil spirit believed to inhabit a corpse and make it move as if alive.

బేతాళుడు **beetaaLuDu** *n.* name of a servant of Yama, God of death.

బేదఖల్ **beedakhal** *n.* eviction, dispossession; **~ceeyu** to evict, dispossess.

బేది, భేది **b[h]eedi** *n.* purging of the bowels.

బేదిమందు, భేదిమందు **b[h]eedimandu** *n.* laxative, purgative.

బేపన **bEEpana** *adj. slang* brahman.

బేపర్వాగా **beeparwaagaa** *adv. dial.* carelessly, inattentively.

బేపి **beepi** *n. dial.* dog, hound.

బేబాకీ **beebaakii** *n.* absence of debt or arrears; **waaDikii naakuu~** he and I are quits *or* he and I do not owe each other anything.

బేరం **beeram** *n.* **1** business, trade. **2** bargain, business transaction, business deal; **~tegindi, ~kudirindi** a bargain was struck. **3** (in transport business) customer, paying passenger; **waana kurawaDam walla rikSaa waaL-Laki beeraalu leewu** on account of the rain the rickshaw men are not getting any passengers.

బేరం ఇచ్చు **beeram iccu** *v.i.* to settle the terms of a sale.

బేరం చేయు, బేరం ఆడు **beeram ceeyu, beeram aaDu** *v.i.* to bargain.

బేరం పెట్టు **beeram peTTu** *v.t.* to put up for sale; **illu beeram peTTEEDu** he put the house up for sale *or* he put the house on the market.

బేరసారాలు **beerasaaraalu** *n.pl.* business dealings and such things.

బేరీ **beerii** *n.* name of a subsect of the merchant community; *originally they were travelling salesmen who called out their wares, hence* **enduku aTLaa~koomaTilaa arustunnaawu?** why are you shouting like that, like a travelling salesman?

బేరీజు **beeriiju** *n.* total annual revenue assessment of a village.

బేరీజువేయు, బేరీజుకట్టు **beeriiju weeyu, beeriiju kaTTu** *v.t.* to weigh up, estimate, calculate, assess, work out (profit, loss, etc.).

బేరుమను **bEErumanu** *v.i.* **1** to gape with astonishment. **2** to exclaim with fear. **3** to weep, cry. **4** to speak out openly; *cf.* **Thaarumanu.**

బేల **beela** *adj.* **1** weak, mild. **2** simple, innocent. **3** dispirited, distressed.

బేలుదారి **beeludaari** **1** foreman. **2** mason.

బేళ్లు **beeLLu** *see* **beeDa** *sense 2.*

బేవారసు **beewaarasu** *adj.* **1** *lit.* without an heir. **2** *colloq.* without a job, with nothing to do; **~gaa tirugutunnaaDu** he is wandering about aimlessly.

బేషరతుగా **beeSaratugaa** *adv.* **1** unconditionally, unreservedly. **2** unequivocally.

బేసబబు **beesababu** *adj.* unreasonable, groundless, baseless.

బేసి **beesi** *adj. maths.* odd; **~sankhya** odd number.

బేసుమట్టం **beesumaTTam** *n.* lower portion of a building, from foundations up to groundfloor level.

బేస్తవారం **beestawaaram** *same as* **bestawaaram.**

బేస్తు **beestu** *n.* a card game, also called **kudeeLLu** *or* **beestulaaTa.**

బై - bay

బైజ **bayja** *n. obs.* ignorance.

బైట, బైలు **bayTa, baylu** *same as* **bayaTa, bayalu.**

బైఠాయించు **bayThaayincu** *v.i.* to sit, occupy a seat.

బైతు **baytu** *n. colloq.* uneducated uncivilised person: **palleTuuri~** country bumpkin, rustic, yokel.

బైరాగి **bayraagi** *n.* religious beggar (= **goosaayi**).

బైర్లు **bayrlu** *same as* **bayarlu.**

బైసి **baysi** *n. dial.* respect.

బైసితీయు **baysitiiyu** *v.i.* to disgrace, put to shame.

బైస్కోపు **bayskoopu** *n.* (‹ *bioscope*) cinema, movie.

బొ - bo

బొంకు **bonku** I. *n.* **1** lie, falsehood. **2** fraud, guile, deceit, falsity. II. *adj.* false, lying. III. *v.i.* to tell a lie.

బొంగరం **bongaram** *n.* **1** (spinning) top. **2** *pl.* **bongaraalu** kind of savoury dish.

బొంగు **bongu** *n.* **1** hollow bamboo pole. **2** *slang* penis.

బొంగురు **bonguru** *adj.* hoarse; **~gontu** hoarse voice.

బొండా, బోండా **boNDaa, booNDaa** *n.* savoury dish made of potato and spices.

బొండాం **boNDaam** *n.* **1** coconut with its husk. **2** baling bucket made of wood or iron. **3** *slang* stout individual.

బొండు **boNDu** *adj.* round, globular.

బొంత **bonta** *n.* quilted cloth, patched rug; **atukula~** rug made of patchwork.

బొంతకాకి **bonta kaaki** *n.* kind of cormorant (bird).

బొంతపురుగు **bontapurugu** *n.* shoot and capsule borer (insect).

బొంతరటి **bontaraTi** *n.* large kind of plantain or banana.

బొంతరాయి **bontaraayi** *n.* kind of pebbly rock.

బొంతు **bontu** *n.* husk surrounding seeds in an ear of millet.

బొంద **bonda**[1] *n.* **1** hole, pit, grave; **~lagaDDa** burial ground. **2** *used as a mild expletive or term of abuse* **anta annam peTTukonnaawu enduku? nii~ ! antaa tinaleewu** why have you taken so much rice, silly boy? you will not be able to eat it all.

బొంద **bonda**[2] *n.* channel for water.

బొంద **bonda**[3] *n.* small palmyra or date tree.

బొంది **bondi** *n.* human body; **naa ~loo praaNam uNDagaa** as long as there is life in my body.

బొందిలి **bondili** *n.* name of a community originating from Bundelkhand.

బొందు **bondu** *n.* cord tied round the waist to support a skirt.

బొందె **bonde** *n.* pith of a plantain tree.

బొక్క **bokka** *n.* **1** hole. **2** pit. **3** *colloq.* police lockup. **4** *slang* female sex organ. **5** *dial.* bone (= **bomike**).

బొక్కపడు **bokka paDu** *v.i.* **1** to be punctured; **Tayru bokka paDindi** the tyre was punctured. **2** *colloq.* (of expenditure) to be in deficit; **neenu idiwaraku ceesina appu tiircaDamwalla ii nela kharculoo bokka paDindi** because I repaid my previous debt, my expenditure was in deficit this month (*or* I was short of money this month).

బొక్కపెట్టు **bokka peTTu** *v.i.* to cause loss (to s.o.); **naa uppu tiNTuu naaku bokka peTTEEDu** while living at my expense he put me to loss.

బొక్కసం **bokkasam** *n.* treasury.

బొక్కి **bokki** *adj.* defective, broken; **~kurcii** rickety chair; **~paLLu** broken teeth.

బొక్కు, బుక్కు **bokku, bukku** *v.t. dial.* to eat greedily, gobble [up].

బొక్కెన **bokkena** *n.* bucket.

బొగ్గు **boggu** *n.* **1** charcoal. **2** (*also* **raakaasi~**, **raakSasi~**, **reyil~**) coal (from a mine).

బొగ్గుపులుసు గాలి **boggupulusu gaali** *n. sci.* carbon dioxide.

బొగ్గులు **boggulu** I. *n. colloq.* total failure, fiasco; **waaDu tiisina sinimaa iTLaa ~ayindi** the movie that he produced was a fiasco; **neenu ceppindi eemiTi? nuwwu ceesindi eemiTi? nii teliwi iTLaa ~ayindi** *lit.* what is it that I said? what is it that you have done? by acting like this your intelligence has totally failed, i.e., you have not done what I told you to do, you have been very stupid. II. *echo word* **bassu~ entaseepaTikii raaleedu** no bus or anything like that came after any length of time; **caduwuu ~leedaa niiku?** is not there any studying and so on for you to do?; *cf.* **maTTigaDDalu.**

బొచ్చు **boccu** I. *n.* **1** hair on the body. **2** wool. II. *adj.* woolly; **~kukka** woolly dog.

బొచ్చె **bocce**[1] *n.* **1** piece of broken pottery. **2** dish-shaped or bowl-shaped object, e.g., top part of a skull; **aDukkutinee~** begging bowl.

బొచ్చె **bocce**[2] *n.* kind of fish.

బొజ్జ **bojja** *n.* stomach, belly.

బొటనవేలు **boTanaweelu** *n.* **1** thumb. **2** big toe; **boTana weelitoo neela raastuu nilabaDDadi** she stood rubbing the ground with her big toe (a gesture of shyness or modesty).

బొటబొటా, చొటచొటా **boTaboTaa, coTacoTaa** *onom. adv. sug.* sound of drops falling; **kanniiru ~ kaarcEEDu** he shed tears plentifully.

బొటాబొటీగా **boTaaboTiigaa** *adv.* by a narrow margin, only just, barely; ~ **mupphay markulu waccEEyi** he only just got thirty marks; ~ **baNDi bayaludeeree samayaaniki waccEEDu** he only just arrived at the departure time of the train.

బొట్ట **boTTa** *n.* large basket with a narrow mouth for storing grain.

బొట్టిగాడు **boTTigaaDu** *n. dial.* little boy.

బొట్టు **boTTu** *n.* **1** drop; **niiTi~** water drop. **2** auspicious or cosmetic mark on a woman's forehead. **3** dot, spot; **sunnapu~** white dot made with whitewash; **waaDiki sunnapuboTLu peTTEEru** they insulted him.

బొట్టె **boTTe** *n. dial.* **1** child. **2** son. **3** daughter.

బొడిపె **boDipe** *same as* **buDipe.**

బొడ్డు **boDDu** *n.* **1** navel. **2** middle point, central point, pivotal point; **nagaram naDi~loo kancu wigraham undi** at the centre of the city there is a bronze statue.

బొడ్డు కోయు **boDDu kooyu** *v.i.* to cut the umbilical cord.

బొడ్డుతాడు **boDDutaaDu** *n.* umbilical cord.

బొడ్డుమల్లె **boDDumalle** *n.* double jasmine.

బొడ్డురాయి **boDDuraayi** *n.* stone planted in the middle of a village when it is founded.

బొత్తాం **bottaam** *n.* button.

బొత్తి **botti** *n.* bundle or sheaf or pack of things arranged in order.

బొత్తిగా **bottigaa** *adv.* **1** in a bundle; **kaayitaalu annii~ peTTu** keep all the papers in a bundle. **2** *always in neg. sense, either expressed or implied* completely, utterly, at all; **naa daggira~ Dabbu leedu** I have no money on me at all *or* I have absolutely no money on me; ~ **apuruupam aypooyEEwu** *lit.* you have become very scarce, i.e., you are hardly ever to be seen; **aayanaki ~ kanabaDaDam leedu** he cannot see at all.

బొద్దింక **boddinka** *n.* cockroach.

బొద్దు **boddu** *adj.* stout, fat, sturdy.

బొప్పాయి[పండు] **boppaayi[paNDu]** *n.* papaya fruit.

బొప్పాయి చెట్టు **boppaayi ceTTu** *n.* papaya tree, *carica papaya*

బొప్పి **boppi** *n.* **1** bump, swelling (gen. on the head); **talaki tagilina debbalaku boppulu kaTTEEyi** bumps formed due to the blows on the head that he received. **2** *fig.* **waaDiki paaTham ceppeesariki naa tala ~ kaTTindi** by the time I had taught him the lesson my head was aching (*lit.* my head had developed a bump). **3** small earthenware pot; **kallu~** toddy pot.

బొబ్బ **bobba**[1] *n.* shout, cry, yell; **~lu weeyu, ~lu peTTu** to shout.

బొబ్బ **bobba**[2] *n.* blister; **kaalina~laki mandu raayaali** you must rub ointment on blisters caused by burns.

బొబ్బ **bobba**[3] *n. child language* water (= **manci niiLLu**); **~taagu naayanaa!** drink some water!

బొబ్బట్టు **bobbaTTu** *n.* kind of sweet pancake.

బొబ్బరించు **bobbarincu** *v.i.* to shout, yell.

బొబ్బరింత **bobbarinta** *n.* yelling, shouting, clamour.

బొబ్బర్లు **bobbarlu** *n.pl.* minor kind of pulse, *dolichos catjang* (**alasandalu**).

బొబ్బుండు **bobbuNDu** *same as* **babbuNDu.**

బొమ **boma** *alt. form of* **bomma**[2].

బొమికె **bomike** *n.* bone.

బొమ్మ **bomma**[1] *n.* **1** doll. **2** picture, illustration; **~ weeyu** (*or* **~dincu**) to draw a picture. **3** statue, figure; **bangaaru~ laagaa** (of a human being) perfect in every way (*lit.* like a golden statue). **4** heads, the obverse side of a coin; *cf.* **borusu.**

బొమ్మ **bomma**[2] *n.* eyebrow; **~[lu] muDiweeyu** to frown; *cf.* **kanu~.**

బొమ్మంచుచీరె **bommancu ciire** *n.* white sari with a red border.

బొమ్మజెముడు **bommajemuDu** *same as* **brahmajemuDu.**

బొమ్మరిల్లు **bommarillu** *n.* miniature house for children to play in.

బొమ్మల పెళ్లిళ్లు **bommala peLLiLLu** *n.pl.* dolls' marriages, a children's game played with dolls.

బొమ్మలాట **bommalaaTa** *n.* puppet show

బొరిగ **boriga** *n.* small spade.

బొరియ **boriya** *n. class.* burrow, hole, pit.

బొరుగులు **borugulu** *n.pl.* puffed rice (= **maramaraalu**).

బొరుసు **borusu** *n.* tails, the reverse side of a coin; **prati naaNEENiki bommaa ~uNTaayi** *lit.* every coin has head and tail, i.e., there are two ways of looking at every problem (proverbial saying); *cf.* **bomma**[1] *sense 4.*

బొర్ర **borra** *n.* pot belly.

బొల్లి **bolli** I. *n.* leucoderma. II. *adj.* having white spots or patches.

బొల్లిబొల్లి **bolli bolli** *adj.* false, bogus, faked; **~eeDupulu** feigned weeping.

బొల్లు **bollu** I. *n.* lie, falsehood. II. *v.i.* to tell a lie.

బో - boo

బోండా **booNDaa** *same as* **boNDaa.**

బోకు **booku** *n.* 1 useless person. 2 woman of loose character.

బోగంమేళం **boogammeeLam** *n.* nautch dance.

బోగంవాళ్లు **boogamwaaLLu** *n.pl.* prostitutes.

బోటి **booTi** *p.p.* like; **naa ~ waaru** people like me.

బోడి **booDi** *adj.* 1 bare, plain, unadorned, unornamented, undecorated. 2 (of cattle) hornless. 3 blunt; **pensil mukku ~ gaa undi** the pencil point is blunt. 4 *colloq.* wretched, miserable; **ii ~ udyoogam ewaru ceestaaru?** who will do this wretched job? **pani antaa ceesEEka ~ padi ruupaayalu iccEEDu** when I had done all the work he gave me a miserable ten rupees.

బోడెమ్మ **booDemma** *n.* widow.

బోణీ **booNii** *n.* first money transaction in a day's business; **neenu weLLi ~ ceesEEnu** I went and made the first purchase for that day.

బోదకాలు, బోదవ్యాధి **boodakaalu, boodawyaadhi** *n.* filariasis, elephantiasis.

బోదురుకప్ప **boodurukappa** *n.* kind of large green frog.

బోదె **boode**[1] *n.* small channel bringing irrigation water to fields.

బోదె **boode**[2] *n.* trunk of a palm tree.

బోదెకాళ్లు **boodekaaLLu** *n.pl.* stumpy legs.

బోధ **boodha** *n.* 1 understanding, intellect, knowledge. 2 teaching, explaining, instruction, advice; **caritra ~ lu** teachings of history; **hita ~** good advice. 3 preaching. 4 *gram.* expression of sense or meaning; **telugu bhaaSaloo tara tama ~ suucincee pratyayaalu leewu** in the Telugu language there are no suffixes which express degrees of comparison. 5 consciousness, awareness, recognition; **kinda paDipooyEEDu, manam weLLi palakaristee mana ~ loo leeDu** he fell down, when we went and spoke to him, he was not aware of us (*or* he could not recognise us).

బోధక **boodhaka** *adjvl. suffix with the meaning of* connoting, expressing, signifying, e.g., **bandhutwa ~ padaalu** words expressing relationship; **puruSa ~ pratyayaalu** personal suffixes.

బోధకుడు **boodhakuDu** *n.* instructor.

బోధ చేయు, బోధ పరచు, బోధించు **boodha ceeyu, boodha paracu, boodhincu** *v.t.* 1 to teach, preach. 2 to explain, expound, inform.

బోధన **boodhana** *n.* teaching, preaching, instruction.

బోధపడు, బోధ అవు **boodhapaDu, boodha awu** *v.i.* to be understood, be learnt, be known; **miiru ceppinadi naaku boodhapaDindi** I understood what you said; **ii paaTiki miiku aame tatwam boodhapaDee uNTundi** by this time you will indeed have understood her nature.

బోధపరచుకొను **boodhaparacukonu** *v.t.* to learn, understand, comprehend.

బోధి **boodhi** *n.* sacred fig tree, *ficus religiosa*, under which Buddha attained enlightenment.

బోనం **boonam** *n. dial.* (<**bhoojanam**) food cooked in new earthenware pots and offered to a village deity.

బోనం తీయు **boonam tiiyu** *v.i.* to take pots containing **boonam** to a village temple in procession.

బోనం పెట్టు **boonam peTTu** *v.i.* to offer **boonam** to a village deity.

బోను **boonu** *n.* 1 trap, cage. 2 dock for prisoners in court. 3 witness box.

బోయ **booya** *n.* 1 member of the Boya community. 2 professional hunter or trapper of birds or animals.

బోయీ[డు] **booyii[Du]** *n.* palanquin bearer.

బోర **boora** *n. colloq.* chest, breast.

బోర విరుచుకొను **boora wirucukonu** *v.i.* to puff out o.'s chest (with pride or self-importance).

బోరు **booru** *adj. colloq.(Eng.)* boring; **sinimaa mahaa ~ gaa undi** the movie is very boring.

బోరుకాడు **boorukaaDu** *v.i. dial.* (of children) to bathe, take a bath.

బోరుకొట్టు **boorukoTTu** *v.i. colloq. (Eng.)* to be boring.

బోరెం **boorem** *n.* 1 large sack for grain. 2 kind of granary with a conical thatched roof.

బోర్లగిలు **boorlagilu** *v.i.* to capsize, overturn.

బోర్లా **boorlaa** *adv.* upside down, topsy-turvy, fac downwards.

బోర్లాతోయు **boorlaatooyu** *v.t.* to push over, tip over, overturn.

బోర్లాపడు **boorlaapaDu** *v.i.* 1 to overturn, tip over, capsize. 2 to fall face downwards, fall on o.'s face.

బోర్లించు **boorlincu** *v.t.* 1 to turn (s.g) upside down, overturn, invert. 2 to lay or place (s.g) upside down or on its face; **ginnemiida paLLem boorlincindi** she placed a saucer upside down over a vessel.

బోలి, బోలె **booli, boole** *n.* 1 *derogatory term* earthen pot, esp. one used for performing a funeral ceremony. 2 **nii ~ !** *is a mild expletive or term of abuse.*

బోలు **boolu** *adj.* hollow.

బోలెడు, బోలెడంత **booleDu, booleDanta** *adj.* 1 *lit.* as much as a **boole** or potful of. 2 plenty of, ever so much.

బోలెడన్ని **booleDanni** *adj.* ever so many.

బోల్తా **booltaa** *adv.* upside down, topsy-turvy.

బోల్తా కొట్టించు **booltaa koTTincu** *v.t.* 1 to knock over, overturn. 2 to dupe, cheat.

బోల్తా కొట్టు, బోల్తాపడు **booltaa koTTu, booltaa paDu** *v.i.* to fall over, overturn, capsize.

బోళా, భోళా **b[h]ooLaa** *adj.* frank, forthright, unreserved, openhearted, naïve.

బోళా బోళీ **booLaabooLii** *n.* frank or openhearted or naïve or straightforward person.

బోళాశంకరుడు **booLaaśankaruDu** *n.* 1 person who can be easily appeased or flattered. 2 epithet of Siva.

బోషాణం, భోషాణం **b[h]ooSaaNam** *n.* large chest.

బోసి **boosi** *adj.* bare; **~ meDa** neck without ornaments; **illu ~ gaa undi** the house is empty and deserted; **~ nooru** toothless mouth.

బౌ, బ్ర, బ్రా - baw, bra, braa

బౌద్ధ **bawddha** *adj.* Buddhist.

బౌద్ధం **bawddham** *n.* Buddhism.

బ్రతకమ్మ **bratakamma** *same as* **batakamma.**

బ్రతికించు **bratikincu** *same as* **batikincu.**

బ్రతుకు **bratuku** *same as* **batuku.**

బ్రద్ద **bradda** *same as* **badda.**

బ్రహ్మ **brahma** I. *n.* **1** God Brahma, Creator of the world, the primordial Supreme Being. **2** *n. suffix* **jaanapada saahitya~** originator of folk literature. II. *adj.* great, superior: **~teejassu** superior brilliancy.

బ్రహ్మచర్యం **brahmacaryam** *n.* bachelorhood, bachelordom, celibacy.

బ్రహ్మచారి **brahmacaari** *n.* bachelor.

బ్రహ్మచారిణి **brahmacaariNi** *n.* spinster.

బ్రహ్మజెముడు, బ్రమ్మజెముడు, బొమ్మజెముడు **brahmajemuDu, brammajemuDu, bommajemuDu** *n.* kind of cactus.

బ్రహ్మత్వం **brahmatwam** *n.* merging or identification with Brahma, the Supreme Being.

బ్రహ్మదండి **brahmadaNDi** *n.* prickly poppy, *argemone mexicana*, an annual weed.

బ్రహ్మపదార్థం **brahmapadaartham** *n.* **1** the universal divine spirit. **2** *colloq.* s.g that cannot be perceived by any of the senses.

బ్రహ్మబీజం **brahmabiijam** *n.* the mystic syllable **oom.**

బ్రహ్మభేద్యం **brahma bheedyam** *n.* s.g very difficult to accomplish.

బ్రహ్మముడి **brahmamuDi** *n.* Brahma's knot, i.e., wedlock, marriage; **~ni ewaruu wippaleeru** no one can untie the bond of marriage.

బ్రహ్మరంధ్రం **brahmarandhram** *n.* suture in the top of the head through which the soul is believed to quit the body at death.

బ్రహ్మరథం పట్టు **brahmaratham paTTu** *v.i.* to praise greatly.

బ్రహ్మరాకాసి **brahmaraakaasi** *n.* **1** aloe plant. **2** ghoul, devil.

బ్రహ్మరాక్షస **brahmaraakSasa** *adj.* ghoulish, devilish.

బ్రహ్మరాక్షసి **brahmaraakSasi** *n.* ghoul, devil.

బ్రహ్మరాత **brahmaraata** *n.* **1** mysterious lines on the sutures of a person's skull believed to be writings which contain the person's destiny. **2** (*also* **brahmalipi**) indecipherable writing, hieroglyphics.

బ్రహ్మర్షి **brahmarSi** *n.* **1** brahman who has reached the status of rishi. **2** great or illustrious rishi.

బ్రహ్మవర్చస్సు **brahmawarcassu** *n.* eminence in holiness and sacred knowledge.

బ్రహ్మవాది **brahmawaadi** *n.* pantheist, follower of the Vedanta system of philosophy.

బ్రహ్మవిద్య **brahmawidya** *n.* impossible task (of doing or learning).

బ్రహ్మవేళ, బ్రహ్మముహూర్తం, బ్రాహ్మీముహూర్తం **brahmaweeLa, brahmamuhuurtam, braahmiimuhuurtam** *n.* very early morning before dawn.

బ్రహ్మశక్యం, బ్రహ్మతరం **brahmaśakyam, brahmataram** *n., lit.* s.g that is possible (only) for Brahma; *used only in neg. constr.* **adi ~kaadu** that is not even possible for Brahma, i.e., that is impossible.

బ్రహ్మసూత్రం **brahmasuutram** *n.* **1** sacred thread (= **jandhyam**). **2** set of aphorisms on the true nature of spiritual knowledge.

బ్రహ్మసృష్టి **brahmasṛSTi** *n.* the world created by Brahma.

బ్రహ్మహత్య **brahmahatya** *n.* slaying of a brahman.

బ్రహ్మాండం **brahmaaNDam** I. *n.* **1** *class.* the universe (*lit* the primordial egg out of which the whole universe came). **2** *colloq.* s.g very difficult to accomplish; **aayanaki caalaa pani undi, uttaram raayaDaaniki ~aypooyindi** he has a great deal of work, it is very difficult for him to write a letter. II. *adj.* **1** huge, vast, enormous. **2** *colloq.* excellent, wonderfully good, first class; **~ayna sinimaa** a wonderfully good movie.

బ్రహ్మాస్త్రం **brahmaastram** *n.* **1** unerring and irresistible weapon. **2** thunderbolt; *cf.* **picika.**

బ్రహ్మి **brahmi** *n.* epithet of Saraswati, wife of Brahma.

బ్రహ్మిగాళ్లు **brahmigaaLLu** *n.pl. colloq., used in a derogatory sense* brahmans.

బ్రహ్మోత్సవం **brahmootsawam** *n.* religious celebration held in a temple lasting for seven days.

బ్రాహ్మణార్థం **braahmaNaartham** *n.* attendance at a feast held as part of a death ceremony.

బ్రాహ్మణీకం **braahmaNiikam** *n.* brahmans collectively, the brahman community; **ii uuLLoo unna~** the brahmans of this town.

బ్రాహ్మణుడు, బ్రాహ్మడు **braahmaNuDu, braahmaDu** *n.* brahman.

బ్రాహ్మణేతర **braahmaNeetara** *adj.* non-brahman.

బ్రాహ్మణ్యం **braahmaNyam** *n.* brahmanhood.

బ్రాహ్మీముహూర్తం **braahmiimuhuurtam** *same as* **brahmamuhuurtam.**

భ - bha

భంగం **bhangam** *n.* 1 breaking, disrupting, violating; **niśśabda~** breaking of silence; **maana~** violation of modesty; **aaśaa~** disappointment, frustration; **wyaktigata hakkulaki~ leekuNDaa/kalagakuNDaa** without prejudice to individual rights. 2 impediment, hindrance, obstruction, interference. 3 spoiling, damage, harm.

భంగకర **bhangakara** *adj.* violating, disruptive.

భంగపడు **bhangapaDu** *v.i.* 1 to be broken, be shattered, be disrupted, be interrupted. 2 to be disappointed, be frustrated. 3 to be spoilt, be damaged, be harmed.

భంగపరచు **bhangaparacu** *v.t.* 1 to break, shatter, disrupt, interrupt. 2 to disappoint, frustrate. 3 to spoil, damage, harm.

భంగపాటు **bhangapaaTu** *n.* 1 failure, defeat. 2 disappointment.

భంగి **bhangi** *n.* manner, mode, way.

భంగిమ **bhangima** *n.* 1 manner, way. 2 attitude, pose, posture, (facial) expression.

భంగు **bhangu** *n.* bhang, Indian hemp, *cannabis indica.*

భంగుర **bhangura** *adj.* fragile, transient.

భంజక **bhanjaka** *adj. class.* breaking, destroying.

భండనం **bhaNDanam** *n. class.* battle, fight.

భండారం **bhaNDaaram** *n.* 1 treasury. 2 hidden wealth. 3 store room.

భక్తి **bhakti** *n.* devotion, reverence, piety.

భక్తిగా **bhaktigaa** *adv.* 1 reverently, piously. 2 respectfully, deferentially.

భక్తిమార్గం **bhaktimaargam** *n.* way to salvation through devotion to God.

భక్తియోగం **bhaktiyoogam** *n.* practice of devotion to God as the means to salvation.

భక్తిరంజని **bhaktiranjani** *n.* recitation of prayer.

భక్తుడు **bhaktuDu** *n.* devotee, worshipper, votary.

భక్షక కణాలు **bhakSaka kaNaalu** *n.pl. biol.* phagocytes.

భక్షకుడు **bhakSakuDu** *n.* one who eats or devours or feeds upon.

భక్షణ[ం] **bhakSaNa[m]** *n.* eating, devouring, consuming; **waaDiki waayu~ jala~ tappa tiNDi leedu** *lit.* he has nothing to eat except air and water, i.e., he lives on a very abstemious diet.

భక్షించు **bhakSincu** *v.t.* to eat, feed on, devour.

భక్ష్యం **bhakSyam** *n.* 1 s.g eatable. 2 cake, sweet.

భగం **bhagam** *n. med.* vagina.

భగందరం **bhagandaram** *n. med.* fistula.

భగభగ **bhagabhaga** *onom. adv. sug.* blazing (of flame or anger).

భగభగమండు **bhagabhaga maNDu** *v.i.* 1 to blaze. 2 to rage with anger. 3 to smart, feel a stinging sensation: **kaaram tinnaaka waaDi nooru bhagabhaga maNDindi** his mouth smarted after eating spices.

భగవంతుడు **bhagawantuDu** *n.* God, the Supreme Being.

భగవతి **bhagawati** *n.* 1 goddess. 2 venerable lady.

భగిని **bhagini** *n. class.* sister.

భగీరథ ప్రయత్నం **bhagiiratha prayatnam** *n.* herculean task, task involving tremendous effort.

భగీరథుడు **bhagiirathuDu** *n.* Bhagiratha, a mythological king who brought the river Ganges from heaven to earth by prayers and penance.

భగోణి **bhagooNii** *n.* deep frying pan.

భగ్గున, బగ్గున **bhagguna, bagguna** *adv.* blazing, ablaze (with fire or anger).

భగ్గుమను, బగ్గుమను **bhaggumanu, baggumanu** *v.i.* (of fire, anger) to flare up, burst forth, blaze; *see* **paccagaDDi.**

భగ్న **bhagna** *adj.* broken, shattered, frustrated.

భగ్నహృదయుడు **bhagnahrdayuDu** *n.* brokenhearted person.

భజంత్రీలు, భజంత్రీవాడు **bhajantriilu, bhajantriiwaaDu** *same as* **bajantriilu, bajantriiwaaDu.**

భజన **bhajana** *n.* 1 worship accompanied by music, chanting or prayers. 2 *colloq.* **o.-ki~ceeyu** to pander or pay court to s.o.

భజనపరుడు **bhajanaparuDu** *n.* 1 person who performs **bhajana.** 2 *colloq.* person who worships indiscriminately.

భజించు, భజియించు **bhajincu, bhajiyincu** *v.t.* to worship, adore.

భజీతు **bhajiitu** *same as* **bajiitu.**

భటుడు **bhaTuDu** *same as* **baTuDu.**

భట్టాచారి **bhaTTaacaari** *n.* name of a class of Vaishnavite temple priests in South India.

భట్టారకుడు **bhaTTaarakuDu** *n. class.* 1 scholarly person, sage. 2 saint. 3 king.

భట్రాజు **bhaTraaju** *n. class.* chanter of titles, panegyrist in a king's court.

భడవ **bhaDawa** *same as* **baDawa.**

భత్తెం **bhattem** *same as* **battem.**

భద్ర **bhadra** *n.* name of a river which combines with the Tunga to form the Tungabhadra.

భద్రం **bhadram** I. *adj.* safe, secure, intact. II. *interj.* **be** careful!, take care!

భద్రంగా **bhadrangaa** *adv.* safely, securely, carefully.

భద్రంచేయు, భద్రపరచు **bhadramceeyu, bhadraparacu** *v.t.* to keep securely, preserve carefully, look after, put in a safe place.

భద్రకాళి **bhadrakaaLi** *n.* epithet of Parvati; **~laa wacc-EEDu** *lit.* he came like Bhadrakali, i.e., he came looking very terrible.

భద్రగజం **bhadragajam** *n. class.* elephant on which the king rides, royal elephant.

భద్రత **bhadrata** *n.* safety, security.
భద్రతా మండలి, భద్రతా సమితి **bhadrataa maNDali, bhadrataa samiti** *n. polit.* Security Council.
భద్రాసనం, భద్రపీఠం **bhadraasanam, bhadrapiiTham** *n.* chair of state, throne.
భయం **bhayam** *n.* fear, fright, alarm, dread, terror.
భయంకర **bhayankara** *adj.* terrible, fearful, dreadful, frightful, frightening.
భయంకరంగా **bhayankarangaa** *adv.* terrifyingly, frighteningly.
భయకంపితుడు **bhayakampituDu** *n.* person trembling with fear.
భయగ్రస్థుడు **bhayagrasthuDu** *n.* person overcome by fear.
భయపడు **bhayapaDu** *v.i.* to be afraid (**-ki,** of).
భయపెట్టు, భయపడేయు **bhayapeTTu, bhayapaDeeyu** *v.t.* to frighten, alarm, scare, terrify.
భయభక్తులు **bhayabhaktulu** *n.pl.* respect[fulness], deference.
భయభీత **bhayabhiita** *adj.* aghast with fear.
భయభ్రాంతుడు **bhayabhraantuDu** *n.* terrified person.
భయవిహ్వలిత **bhayawihwaalita** *adj.* terrorised.
భయస్థుడు **bhayasthuDu** *n.* timid person.
భయాందోళన **bhayaandooLana** *n.* panic.
భయానక **bhayaanaka** *adj.* dreadful, terrible, alarming, frightening.
భయానకం **bhayaanakam** *n.* terror, one of the nine emotions (**rasaalu**) aroused by poetical or dramatic compositions.
భరణం **bharaNam** *n.* **1** *class.* maintenance, support. **2** alimony. **3 raaja~** privy purse.
భరణి **bharaNi** *n. astrol.* second lunar asterism.
భరతంపట్టు **bharatampaTTu** *v.i. slang* to finish off, see the end of.
భరతఖండం, భరతవర్షం **bharatakhaNDam, bharatawarSam** *n.* India.
భరతనాట్యం **bharatanaaTyam** *n.* Bharata Natyam, a South Indian style of classical dancing.
భరతపక్షి, భరతపిట్ట **bharatapakSi, bharatapiTTa** *n.* lark.
భరతవాక్యం **bharatawaakyam** *n. theat.* epilogue.
భరతశాస్త్రం **bharataśaastram** *n.* treatise written by the sage Bharatamuni on music, dancing and drama.
భరతుడు **bharatuDu** *n.* **1** one of the brothers of Sri Rama. **2** king who gave his name to **bharatawarSam.**
భరాయించు **bharaayincu** *same as* **baraayincu.**
భరించు **bharincu** *v.t.* **1** to bear, tolerate, sustain, endure. **2** to defray (expense).
భరిణె **bhariNe** *same as* **baraNi.**
భరిత **bharita** *adjvl. suffix meaning* full of, filled with.
భరోసా, భరవసా **bharoosaa, bharawasaa** *n.* **1** faith, confidence (**-miida,** in), assurance, reliance, trust. **2** support; **naa ~ eppuDuu uNTundi** my support will always be there. **3** guarantee.
భర్జించు **bharjincu** *v.t. class.* to fry, roast.
భర్త **bharta** *n.* husband.
భర్తీ **bhartii** *n.* filling up, replenishing; **sibbandi~** recruitment of staff.
భర్తీ అవు **bhartii awu** *v.i.* to be filled up.
భర్తీ చేయు **bhartii ceeyu** *v.t.* **1** to fill up (vacancy), recruit (staff), fill in (blank space), make good (deficiency). **2** to replenish, reimburse: **naSTapooyina aadaayaanni~** to reimburse lost income.
భర్తృత్వ **bhartrtwa** *adj.* pertaining to a husband, husband's.
భర్తృదారిక **bhartṛdaarika** *n. class. theat.* princess.
భలే **bhalee** *same as* **balee.**
భల్లూకం **bhalluukam** *n.* bear.
భల్లూకపట్టు **bhalluukapaTTu** *n.* bear's hug, tight and stifling embrace.
భళ్లున, బళ్లున **bhaLLuna, baLLuna** *onom. adv.* **1** *sug. a sudden loud sound* with a crash, with a smash, with a splash. **2 ~ tellaarindi** day dawned brightly.
భళ్లుమను **bhaLLumanu** *v.i.* to make a crashing/smashing/splashing sound.
భవం **bhawam** I. *n.* being, existence, earthly or worldly existence; **bhawa bandhaalu** earthly ties. II. *second part of an adjvl. compound meaning* arising from, originating from, produced by.
భవంతి **bhawanti** *n.* palatial building.
భవదీయ **bhawadiiya** *adj. class.* your; **~ sahoodaruDu** your brother.
భవదీయుడు **bhawadiiyuDu** *n.* yours (used in ending a letter).
భవనం **bhawanam** *n.* **1** house, dwelling, mansion. **2** building.
భవితవ్యం **bhawitawyam** *n.* the future, the state or condition of things in the future; **maanawa jaati~** the future of the human race.
భవిష్యం **bhawiSyam** *n.* **1** status, rank. **2** future prosperity, future wellbeing.
భవిష్యత్తు, భవిష్యత్కాలం **bhawiSyattu, bhawiSyatkaalam** *n.* **1** future time. **2** *gram.* future tense.
భవిష్యనిధి **bhawiSyanidhi** *n.* provident fund.
భస్మం **bhasmam** *n.* **1** ashes. **2** ayurvedic medicine made by calcining.
భస్మం చేయు, భస్మీకరించు **bhasmam ceeyu, bhasmiikarincu** *v.t.* to reduce to ashes, incinerate.
భస్మాసుర హస్తం **bhasmaasura hastam** *n. colloq.* bungler.
భస్మాసురుడు **bhasmaasuruDu** *n.* mythological demon who was granted a boon enabling him to destroy his enemies by turning them to ashes.
భస్మీకరణం **bhasmiikaraNam** *n.* **1** incineration. **2** *sci.* calcination.
భస్మీపటలం **bhasmiipaTalam** *n.* layer of ashes.

భా - bhaa

భాంచోత్! **bhaancoot!** *interj. used as a term of abuse.*

భాండం **bhaaNDam** *n. class.* pot, vessel; *mod. only in* **amrta~** pot of nectar.

భాండాగారం **bhaaNDaagaaram** *n.* **1** treasury. **2** repository, storehouse.

భాండీ **bhaaNDii** *n.* deep frying pan.

భాగం **bhaagam** *n.* **1** part, portion; **pay~loo** (i) in the upper part; (ii) on the top. **2** section, division. **3** share; **naaku~ peTTEEDu** he gave me a share. **4** side; **eDama~** left side.

భాగంపంచుకొను **bhaagam pancukonu** *v.i.* to share, participate, take part (**-loo**, in); **bhaagam pancukoneewaaLLu** co-sharers; *see also* **bhaagaalu pancukonu.**

భాగలబ్ధం, భాగఫలం **bhaagalabdham, bhaagaphalam** *n. maths.* quotient.

భాగవతం **bhaagawatam** *n.* **1** the Bhagavatam, a religious and mythological poetical work recounting the ten incarnations of Vishnu. **2** *colloq. same as* **bhaagootam.**

భాగవతారు **bhaagawataaru** *n.* person who narrates stories from the Bhagawatam or other mythological work.

భాగస్థుడు, భాగస్వామి **bhaagasthuDu, bhaagaswaami** *n.* partner, sharer.

భాగస్వామ్యం **bhaagaswaamyam** *n.* partnership, sharing.

భాగహారం **bhaagahaaram** *n. maths.* division.

భాగాలు పంచుకొను **bhaagaalu paancukonu** *v.i.* to partition a family property into separate shares.

భాగాలుపడు **bhaagaalupaDu** *v.i.* **1** to be divided. **2** (of family property) to be partitioned into separate shares.

భాగించు **bhaagincu** *v.t.* to divide.

భాగీరథి **bhaagiirathi** *n. class.* River Ganges.

భాగోతం **bhaagootam** *n.* **1** kind of informal dramatic production in which a mythological story is freely interpreted by actors; **wiidhi~** street drama. **2** story, fable. **3** long rambling tale; *see* **tirageeyu** *sense 2.*

భాగోతులు **bhaagootulu** *n.pl.* persons who perform street dramas.

భాగ్యం **bhaagyam** *n.* **1** fortune, luck, destiny. **2** good fortune. **3** happiness, welfare, prosperity.

భాగ్యవంత **bhaagyawanta** *adj.* prosperous, wealthy.

భాగ్యవంతుడు **bhaagyawantuDu** *n.* **1** fortunate person. **2** prosperous or well-off person.

భాగ్యవతి **bhaagyawati** *n.* fortunate woman.

భాజకం **bhaajakam** *n. maths.* divisor.

భాజన **bhaajana** *adjvl. suffix meaning* worthy of, deserving of; **apratiSThaa~** deserving of disrepute.

భాజనం **bhaajanam** *n. class.* dish, vessel.

భాద్రపదం **bhaadrapadam** *n.* the sixth Telugu lunar month.

భానుడు **bhaanuDu** *n. class.* sun.

భానువారం **bhaanuwaaram** *n. class.* Sunday.

భానూదయం **bhaanuudayam** *n. class.* rising of the sun, dawn.

భామ **bhaama** *n.* passionate woman.

భామిని **bhaamini** *n. class.* woman.

భారం **bhaaram** *n.* **1** weight, heaviness. **2** burden. **3** responsibility.

భారంగా **bhaarangaa** *adv.* **1** heavily. **2** gloomily, feeling depressed.

భారతం **bhaaratam** *n.* **1** the great Sanskrit epic known as the Mahabharata. **2** *colloq.* long and tedious recital. **3** India.

భారతి **bhaarati** *n.* **1** a name of Saraswati, goddess of speech and literature. **2** speech, literary composition.

భారతీయ **bhaaratiiya** *adj.* Indian.

భారమితి **bhaaramiti** *n.* barometer.

భారలేఖిని **bhaaraleekhini** *n.* barograph.

భారీ **bhaarii** *adj.* **1** big, large; **cinna, madhya, ~tarahaa praajekTulu** minor, medium and major projects; **~pariśrama** large scale industry; **~utpatti** mass production; **~ettuna** on a big scale, on a mass scale. **2** hefty, weighty. **3** *fig.* heavy; **~warSaalu** heavy rains.

భారీచెయ్యి **bhaariiceyyi** *n.* generous nature or disposition (= **pedda ceyyi**).

భార్య **bhaarya** *n.* wife.

భార్యాభర్తలు **bhaaryaabhartalu** *n.pl.* wife and husband.

భావ **bhaawa**[1] *n.* eighth year of the Hindu cycle of sixty years.

భావ **bhaawa**[2] *adj. gram.* affirmative, positive.

భావం **bhaawam** *n.* **1** thought, idea, impression; **manasuloo bhaawaalanu payki tecceedi maatrbhaaSa** it is the mother tongue that gives expression to the thoughts in the mind; **bhaawa prakaTanaa swaatantryam** freedom to express ideas. **2** feeling, sense, sentiment; **sneeha~** feeling of friendliness; **bhadrataa~** sense of security. **3** intention, desire, purpose, inclination; **seewaa~** desire to be of service. **4** emotion; **bhaawasamaykyata~** emotional integration. **5** nature, disposition. **6** meaning, purport; **bhaawawiwaraNa** explanation of meaning (of a word); **diini~eemi tirumaleeśa**? what meaning does it convey, oh lord of Tirumala? (stock phrase used when inviting a person to guess the answer to a riddle). **7** conjecture, surmise, supposition.

భావకవి **bhaawakawi** *n.* romantic poet.

భావగర్భితంగా **bhaawagarbhitangaa** *adv.* conveying a hidden meaning, meaningfully.

భావగీతం **bhaawagiitam** *n.* **1** lyrical poem, lyric. **2** romantic poem.

భావన **bhaawana** *n.* **1** thought, thinking, idea, concept; **oka pratyeeka paaribhaaSika ~ku oka bhaaSaloo sarayna** maaTa leekapoowaccu a language may not have the right word for a particular technical concept; **pekkumandi madhyawargaalawaari ~ loo swaraajyam sukhajiiwanaaniki paryaayapadam aypooyindi** in the thinking of many middle class people self-government became synonymous with wellbeing. **2** feeling; **preema ~ lu** feelings of love. **3** process followed in Ayurvedic medicine of steeping an ingredient many times in the juice of another (e.g., ginger or cummin seed in limejuice).

భావనాత్మక **bhaawanaatmaka** *adj.* romantic.

భావార్థం **bhaawaartham** *n.* **1** gist, summary. **2** implication. **3** *gram.* affirmative or positive sense or form of a verb.

భావార్థకం **bhaawaarthakam** *n.gram.* verbal noun ending in **-aDam / -aTam.**

భావావేశం **bhaawaaweeśam** *n.* emotion[al feeling].

భావి **bhaawi** I. *n.* future. II. *adj.* future, later, subsequent.

భావించు **bhaawincu** *v.t.* to think, deem, fancy, feel, imagine, consider, suppose, surmise.

భావిసూచన **bhaawisuucana** *n.* forecast.

భావుకత **bhaawukata** *n.* meaningfulness.

భావుకుడు **bhaawukuDu** *n.* man of ideas, thinker.

భావురచన **bhaawuracana** *n.* sentimental writing, sobstuff.

భావ్యం **bhaawyam** *adj.* proper, fit[ting].

భాష **bhaaSa** *n.* language.

భాషణం **bhaaSaNam** *n.* **1** speech, speaking. **2** lecture.

భాషాంతరీకరణం **bhaaSaantariikaraNam** *n.* translation.

భాషాతత్వం **bhaaSaatatwam** *n.* (science of) philology.

భాషాప్రయుక్త **bhaaSaaprayukta** *adj. lit.* connected with language; **~ raaSTram** linguistic state.

భాషాప్రాంతం **bhaaSaapraantam** *n.* language area, linguistic region.

భాషాభాగం **bhaaSaabhaagam** *n. gram.* part of speech, grammatical class (noun, verb, adjective, etc.).

భాషాశాస్త్రం **bhaaSaaśaastram** *n.* (science of) linguistics.

భాషాశాస్త్రజ్ఞుడు, భాషాశాస్త్రవేత్త **bhaaSaaśaastrajñuDu, bhaaSaaśaastraweetta** *n.* linguist.

భాషి, భాషీయుడు **bhaaSi, bhaaSiiyuDu** *n.* speaker (of a language).

భాషించు **bhaaSincu** *v.i.* to speak, talk, converse.

భాషికం **bhaaSikam** *same as* **baasikam.**

భాష్యం, భాష్యకారుడు **bhaaSyam, bhaaSyakaaruDu** *same as* **baasyam, baasyakaaruDu.**

భాసం **bhaasam** *n. class.* **1** light. **2** brilliancy.

భాసించు, భాసిల్లు **bhaasincu, bhaasillu** *v.i.* **1** *class.* to shine brightly, shine forth. **2** to appear, become evident.

భాసుర **bhaasura** *adj. class.* brightly shining, splendid; **~ kiirti** brightly shining fame.

భాస్కరుడు **bhaaskaruDu** *n. class.* sun.

భాస్వర **bhaaswara** *adj. sci.* phosphoric.

భాస్వరం **bhaaswaram** *n. sci.* phosphorus.

భి. - bhi

భిక్ష[ం] **bhikSa[m]** *n.* **1** alms. **2** boon, great favour.

భిక్ష[ం] పెట్టు **bhikSa[m] peTTu** *v.i.* **1** to give alms to a beggar. **2** to give alms ceremonially to a young man at his **upanayanam** ceremony; the first offering is **maatrbhikSa,** given by his mother, which he in turn passes on to his teacher. **3** to confer or bestow a boon; **wiiru naaku widyaa bhikSa peTTina guruwulu** he is the teacher who conferred the boon of education on me.

భిక్షుకవృత్తి **bhikSukawrtti** *n.* the profession of begging.

భిక్షుకుడు **bhikSukuDu** *n.* beggar.

భిక్షువు **bhikSuwu** *n.* **1** sanyasi, wandering religious beggar. **2** wandering Buddhist monk (= **bikku[wu]**).

భిత్తి **bhitti** *n. class.* wall.

భిన్న **bhinna** *adj.* **1** separate, divided, distinct. **2** other, different. **3** differing, varying, contrary; **daaniki ~ ngaa** contrary to that.

భిన్నం **bhinnam** *n.* **1** change, alteration, variation. **2** (*also* **bhinnaankam**) *maths.* fraction.

భిన్నత్వం **bhinnatwam** *n.* **1** difference, variation. **2** variety, diversity.

భిన్నాభిప్రాయం **bhinnaabhipraayam** *n.* disagreement, dissent.

భిల్లు **bhillu** *n.* Bhil, name of a hill tribe.

భిషక్కు **bhiSakku** *n.class.* ayurvedic physician.

భీ - bhii

భీకర **bhiikara** *adj.* fearful, frightening, terrible.

భీత **bhiita** *adj. class.* frightened; ~ **hariNi**·frightened deer.

భీతాహం, భీతావహం **bhiitaaham, bhiitaawaham** *n. class.* panic.

భీతి **bhiiti** *n.* fear, alarm.

భీతిల్లు, భీతికొను, భీతిచెందు **bhiitillu, bhiitikonu, bhiiti cendu** *v.i.* to be afraid.

భీమ **bhiima** *adj.* frightful, terrible, tremendous.

భీముడు, భీమసేనుడు **bhiimuDu, bhiimaseenuDu** *n.* Bhima, second of the five Pandava brothers in the Mahabharata, famous for his strength.

భీరువు **bhiiruwu** *n.* coward.

భీషణ, భీష్మ **bhiiSaNa, bhiiSma** *adj.* terrible, dreadful, alarming.

భీషణం, భీష్మం **bhiiSaNam, bhiiSmam** *n.* horror, fright, alarm.

భీష్మప్రతిజ్ఞ **bhiiSmapratijña** *n.* very strong oath, such as was sworn by Bhishma.

భీష్మాచార్యుడు **bhiiSmaacaaryuDu** *n. colloq.* seniormost member, oldest living member (of a family, community, society).

భీష్మించు[కొను] **bhiiSmincu[konu]** *v.i.* **1** to insist obstinately, assert forcibly. **2** to refuse (a request) churlishly. **3** to refuse to communicate, refuse to respond.

భీష్ముడు **bhiiSmuDu** *n.* Bhishma, grandfather of the Pandavas and Kauravas in the Mahabharata.

భు - bhu

భుక్త **bhukta** *adj.* **1** eaten, consumed. **2** enjoyed, made use of.

భుక్తం **bhuktam** *n.* enjoyment; **aasti naaku hakku bhuktaalatoo raasi iccEEDu** he made over the property to me with the rights of ownership and enjoyment.

భుక్తంచేసుకొను, భుక్తపరచుకొను **bhuktamceesukonu, bhuktaparacukonu** *v.t.* **1** to enjoy, have the benefit of, have the use of. **2** to take or appropriate for o.'s use or enjoyment.

భుక్తాయాసం **bhuktaayaasam** *n.* sleepiness felt after a meal.

భుక్తి **bhukti** *n.* **1** food, livelihood; *see* **kaDacu** *sense 3.* **2** *astrol.* daily motion of a planet.

భుజం **bhujam** *n.* **1** shoulder, arm. **2** side of a geometrical figure: **tri**~ triangle.

భుజకీర్తి **bhujakiirti** *n.* shoulder ornament shaped like a wing worn by kings or great warriors.

భుజ[ం]గం **bhuja[n]gam** *n. class.* snake, serpent.

భుజశాలి **bhujaśaali** *adj.* physically strong, powerful.

భుజస్కంధం **bhujaskandham** *n. class.* shoulder.

భుజాలు తడుముకొను **bhujaalu taDumukonu** *v.i. colloq.* to react to a chance remark, display a guilty feeling.

భుజించు **bhujincu** *v.t.* to eat, consume.

భువనం **bhuwanam** *n. class.* world; **caturdaśa bhuwanaalu** the fourteen worlds of Hindu mythology.

భువి **bhuwi** *n. class.* the earth (as opposed to **diwi** heaven).

భూ - bhuu

భూకంపం **bhuukampam** *n.* earthquake.

భూకంపశాస్త్రం **bhuukampaśaastram** *n.* seismology.

భూకమతం **bhuukamatam** *n.* land-holding.

భూకామందు **bhuukaamandu** *n.* landowner, wealthy cultivator.

భూక్షయం **bhuukSayam** *n.* soil erosion.

భూఖండం **bhuukhaNDam** *n.* plot of land.

భూగర్భ **bhuugarbha** *adj.* subterranean, underground.

భూగర్భశాస్త్రం **bhuugarbhaśaastram** *n.* geology.

భూగృహం **bhuugṛham** *n.* cellar.

భూగోళం **bhuugooLam** *n.* the earth, the world, the globe.

భూగోళశాస్త్రం **bhuugooLaśaastram** *n.* geography.

భూచక్రం **bhuucakram** *n.* **1** the earth, the world, the globe. **2** kind of firework.

భూతం **bhuutam** *n.* **1** ghost, spectre, phantom. **2** living being. **3** one of the five primordial elements—earth, water, fire, air and ether — known as **panchabhuutaalu.**

భూతకల్పన **bhuutakalpana** *n.* phantasm.

భూతకాలం **bhuutakaalam** *n.* **1** past. **2** *gram.* past tense.

భూతగణాలు **bhuutagaNaalu** *n.pl.* mythological servants of Siva.

భూతదయ **bhuutadaya** *n.* humaneness, humanity, kindness, kindheartedness.

భూతద్దం **bhuutaddam** *n.* magnifying glass.

భూతలం **bhuutalam** *n.* the earth's surface.

భూతవైద్యుడు **bhuutawaydyuDu** *n.* exorcist.

భూతుడు **bhuutuDu** *n. suffix meaning* a person who is or who constitutes (s.g), e.g., **kaaraNa~** person who is a cause (of s.g).

భూనభోంతరాళాలు **bhuunabhoontaraaLaalu** *n.pl.* earth and heaven (‹ **bhuumi** earth, **nabham** heaven, **antaraaLam** intervening space).

భూనిక్షిప్తనిధి **bhuunikSiptanidhi** *n.* treasure trove.

భూప్రపంచం **bhuuprapancam** *n.* the world.

భూభాగం **bhuubhaagam** *n.* **1** territory. **2** area, extent.

భూభౌతిక శాస్త్రం **bhuubhawtikaśaastram** *n.* geophysics.

భూమండలం **bhuumaNDalam** *n.* the earth, the world.

భూమధ్య రేఖ **bhuumadhyareekha** *n.* equator.

భూమి **bhuumi** *n.* **1** earth, land, ground, soil. **2** site.

భూమిక **bhuumika** *n. class.* **1** part or role in a drama. **2** preface.

భూమిశిస్తు **bhuumiśistu** *n.* land revenue.

భూమీపుట్రా **bhuumiipuTraa** *n.* land and so on; *cf.* **polampuTra.**

భూమ్యాకర్షణశక్తి **bhuumyaakarSaNaśakti** *n. sci.* force of gravity.

భూయిష్ఠ **bhuuyiSTa** *second part of an adjvl. compound meaning* full of, abounding in.

భూరి **bhuuri** *adj.* generous, liberal; **~sambhaawanalu** generous gifts to brahmans.

భూలోకం **bhuulookam** *n.* the world.

భూవసతి **bhuuwasati** *n.* enjoyment of land.

భూవిజ్ఞానశాస్త్రం **bhuuwijñaanaśaastram** *n.* geology.

భూశయనం **bhuuśayanam** *n.* laying a person on the ground, esp. one who is on the point of death.

భూషణ **bhuuSaNa** *n.* praise.

భూషణం **bhuuSaNam** *n. class.* ornament.

భూషించు **bhuuSincu** *v.t.* to praise, applaud.

భూసంధి **bhuusandhi** *n.* isthmus.

భూసంబంధ **bhuusambandha** *adj.* agrarian.

భూసారం **bhuusaaram** *n.* fertility (of soil).

భూసార సంరక్షణ **bhuusaara samrakSaNa** *n.* soil conservation.

భూస్థాపనం **bhuusthaapanam** *n.* burial (of a corpse).

భూస్థాపితం **bhuusthaapitam** *n.* burial (of anything non-human).

భూస్వాధీనత **bhuuswaadhiinata** *n.* acquisition of land.

భూస్వామి **bhuuswaami** *n.* landlord, landowner, wealthy cultivator.

భూస్వామ్యం **bhuuswaamyam** *n.* landownership.

భృ, భే - bhṛ, bhee

భృంగం **bhṛngam** *n.* large black bee.

భృతి **bhṛti** *n.* allowance; **nirudyooga~** unemployment benefit, unemployment relief.

భృత్యుడు **bhṛtyuDu** *n. class.* servant.

భేకం **bheekam** *n. class.* frog.

భేటీ **bheeTii** *n.* **1** audience, interview. **2** formal call, meeting.

భేదం **bheedam** *n.* **1** difference, distinction; **cinnaa peddaa~ leekuNDaa** without distinction between young and old. **2** divergence, deviation. **3** variation, alteration. **4** dividing, separating. **5** dissension, disagreement, rift, schism. **6** *class.* creating dissension among o.'s enemies, enticing an enemy's ally to join o.'s own party. **7** variety; **uttara aaphirikaaloo aneeka arabik bhaaSaa bheedaalu waaDukaloo unnaayi** in North Africa many varieties of the Arabic language are current.

భేదక **bheedaka** *adj.* dividing, separating.

భేదకరేఖ **bheedakareekha** *n.* **1** dividing line. **2** *ling.* isogloss.

భేదనం **bheedanam** *n.* **1** dividing, separating. **2** breaking [open].

భేదభావం **bheedabhaawam** *n.* discrimination.

భేది **bheedi** *same as* **beedi.**

భేదించు **bheedincu** I. *v.i.* to vary, differ; **wadhuuwarula kulam okkaTee kaawaali, aacaara wyawahaaraalu rawwantagaanaynaa bheedincaraadu** the community of the bride and bridegroom must be one and the same, their customs and practices must not differ in the slightest degree. II. *v.t.* **1** to divide, separate. **2** to cleave apart, break open. **3** to break, penetrate (a secret).

భేదిమందు **bheedimandu** *same as* **beedimandu.**

భేద్య **bheedya** *adj.* **1** penetrable. **2** fragile.

భేరీ **bheerii** *n.* kettledrum.

భేష్! **bheeS!** *interj.* fine!, excellent!

భేషజం **bheeSajam** *n.* **1** deceit, pretence, humbug; **waaLLaki bastii bheeSajaalu leewu** they do not make a pretence of being townsfolk. **2** *class.* medicine.

భేషుగా, భేషుగ్గా **bheeSug[g]aa** *adv.* very well, excellently.

భై, భో - bhay, bhoo

భైరవ **bhayrawa** *adj.* frightful, terrible, terrifying.

భైరవమూర్తి **bhayrawamuurti** *n.* epithet of Siva.

భైరవి **bhayrawi** *n.* the Goddess Kali.

భైరవుడు **bhayrawuDu** *n.* **1** the God Siva. **2** terrible or terrifying person.

భోంచేయు **bhoonceeyu** *v.i. and t.* to eat, dine, take a meal.

భోక్త **bhookta** *n.* **1** person who eats. **2** *pl.* **~lu** brahmans who are fed at a death ceremony as representatives of the spirits of departed ancestors.

భోక్తవ్య **bhooktawya** *adj.* **1** eatable, edible. **2** enjoyable.

భోగం **bhoogam** *n.* **1** enjoyment, possession. **2** pleasure. **3** indulgence, luxury; **bhoogawastuwu** luxury item. **4** offering of food to an idol in a temple. **5** *class.* expanded hood of a snake.

భోగగృహం **bhoogagṛham** *n. class.* bedroom.

భోగట్టా **bhoogaTTaa** *n.* information, news, facts.

భోగట్టా చేయు **bhoogaTTaa ceeyu** *v.i.* to enquire, make enquiries, investigate.

భోగపరాయణుడు **bhoogaparaayaNuDu** *n.* person who lives in luxury.

భోగపురుషుడు **bhoogapuruSuDu** *n.* man of pleasure, playboy.

భోగబంధ **bhoogabanda** *n.* usufructuary mortgage.

భోగభాగ్యాలు **bhoogabhaagyaalu** *n.pl.* **1** luxuries. **2** state of luxury.

భోగలాలసత, భోగలాలసత్వం **bhoogalaalasata, bhoogalaalasatwam** *n.* luxury, indulgence.

భోగలాలసుడు **bhoogalaalasuDu** *n.* **1** person living in luxury. **2** immoral person, depraved person.

భోగస్త్రీ **bhoogastrii** *n.* prostitute, concubine.

భోగి **bhoogi**[1] *n.* the day before Makara Sankranti.

భోగి **bhoogi**[2] *n.* person with luxurious tastes.

భోగి **bhoogi**[3] *n. class.* snake, serpent.

భోగిని **bhoogini** *n. class.* concubine, kept woman.

భోగిమంట **bhoogimaNTa** *n.* bonfire which is lit before dawn every day in the month called **dhanurmaasam** ending with the Sankranti festival.

భోగ్య **bhoogya** *adj.* enjoyable.

భోగ్యం **bhoogyam** *n.* s.g that is enjoyed.

భోజనం **bhoojanam** *n.* **1** meal. **2** food.

భోజనం చేయు **bhoojanam ceeyu** *v.i. and t.* to eat, dine, take a meal.

భోజుడు **bhoojuDu** *n.* name of a legendary king who was a bountiful patron of art and literature.

భోరున **bhooruna** *onom. adv. sug.* loud continuous noise; ~ **eeDcEEDu** he wept loud and long; ~ **waana kurisindi** the rain poured in torrents.

భోళా **bhooLaa** *same as* **booLaa.**

భోషాణం **bhooSaaNam** *same as* **booSaaNam.**

భౌ, భ్ర - bhaw, bhra

భౌగోళిక **bhawgooLika** *adj.* geographical.

భౌతిక **bhawtika** *adj.* 1 physical, material. 2 materialistic.

భౌతికవాదం **bhawtikawaadam** *n.* materialism.

భౌతికవాది **bhawtikawaadi** *n.* materialist.

భౌతికశాస్త్రం **bhawtikaśaastram** *n.* physics.

భౌమ **bhawma** *adj.* 1 underground; ~ **jala sampada** underground water resources. 2 geological; ~ **sarweekSaNa** geological survey.

భ్రంశం **bhramśam** *n.* falling, slipping.

భ్రమ **bhrama** *n.* 1 illusion, delusion, misconception, misapprehension, mistaken belief, false idea. 2 desire, fondness, liking. 3 whirling, revolving.

భ్రమం **bhramam** *n. class. alt. form of* **bhrama.**

భ్రమక కీలకం **bhramaka kiilakam** *n. phys.* pivot.

భ్రమణం **bhramaNam**[1] *n.* whirling, revolving, rotating, rotation.

భ్రమణం, భ్రమరం **bhramaNam**[2], **bhramaram** *n.* large black bee.

భ్రమపడు **bhramapaDu** *v.i.* to be mistaken, be deluded.

భ్రమపరచు, భ్రమపెట్టు, భ్రమింపచేయు **bhramaparacu, bhrama peTTu, bhramimpa ceeyu** *v.t.* to deceive, delude, mislead.

భ్రమించు **bhramincu** *v.i.* 1 to believe wrongly, be mistaken. 2 to be deceived, be deluded. 3 to circle round, revolve.

భ్రమియు, భ్రమయు **bhramiyu, bhramayu** *v.i.* 1 to believe wrongly. 2 to be deluded, be misled, be captivated (-**ki**, by).

భ్రష్ట **bhraSTa** I. *n.* unchaste or immoral woman. II. *adj.* 1 degenerate, depraved. 2 sunken, fallen, ruined. 3 *ling.* ~ **ruupam** corrupt form.

భ్రష్టత, భ్రష్టత్వం **bhraSTata, bhraSTatwam** *n.* 1 degeneration, depravity. 2 ruin: **ubhaya bhraSTatwam, upari sanyaasam** two-fold ruin followed by beggary; *this is a strong proverbial expression to describe s.o. who falls between two stools; he suffers disaster on both counts and in addition becomes a wandering beggar (sanyasi).*

భ్రష్టాకారి **bhraSTaakaari** *n.* person of depraved habits.

భ్రష్టుచేయు, భ్రష్టుపట్టించు **bhraSTuceeyu, bhraSTupaTTincu** *v.t.* 1 to corrupt, deprave. 2 to ruin.

భ్రష్టుడు **bhraSTuDu** *n.* 1 wretched person. 2 fallen person; **kula**~ outcaste.

భ్రష్టుపట్టు **bhraSTupaTTu** *v.i.* 1 to be corrupted 2 to be ruined.

భ్రా, భ్రు, భ్రూ - bhraa, bhru, bhruu

భ్రాంతి **bhraanti** *n.* 1 illusion, delusion. 2 desire, fancy (**-miida** *or* **-payna**, for).

భ్రాంతికారక **bhraantikaaraka** *adj.* delusive, misleading.

భ్రాంతికొను **bhraantikonu** *v.i.* to be deluded, be beguiled.

భ్రాంతి చెందు **bhraanti cendu** *v.i.* to believe mistakenly, get a wrong impression.

భ్రాంతిపడు **bhraantipaDu** *v.i.* to be deluded, be misled, be captivated.

భ్రాత **bhraata** *n. class.* brother.

భ్రాతృ **bhraatṛ** *Sanskrit adjvl. prefix meaning* brotherly, fraternal.

భ్రాతృహత్య **bhraatṛhatya** *n.* fratricide.

భ్రుకుటి **bhrukuTi** *n.* frown; ~ **muDucukonnaaDu** he wrinkled his brows *or* he frowned.

భ్రూణం **bhruuNam** *n.* foetus, embryo.

భ్రూణహత్య **bhruuNahatya** *n. lit.* killing an embryo, abortion.

మ - ma

మంకుతనం **mankutanam** *n.* obstinacy, stubbornness.
మంకుపట్టు **mankupaTTu** *n.* obstinacy, obdurateness, stubbornness.
మంకుపట్టు పట్టు **mankupaTTu paTTu** *v.i.* to be obstinate, be stubborn.
మంకెన **mankena** *n.* name of a red coloured flower.
మంగలం **mangalam** *n.* earthen vessel for parching grain, often blackened by soot, *hence* **aawiDa mukham ~ laa ayindi** her face went black with rage.
మంగలి **mangali** *n.* barber.
మంగళ **mangaLa** *adj.* auspicious.
మంగళం **mangaLam** *n.* 1 auspiciousness, happiness, good fortune. 2 welfare, wellbeing, prosperity. 3 s.g auspicious. 4 prayer in praise of a deity at end of a recitation or performance.
మంగళం పాడు, మంగళహారతి పాడు **mangaLam paaDu, mangaLahaarati paaDu** *v.i.* 1 to sing a song and pray to God for a blessing at the end of an auspicious ceremony; *cf.* **haaratipaLLem.** 2 *colloq.* to bid farewell to; **aasti antaa mangaLam paaDEEDu** (*or* **mangaLahaarati paaDEEDu**) he bade farewell to his property *or* he lost all his property.
మంగళవాద్యం **mangaLawaadyam** *n.* music for an auspicious occasion.
మంగళవారం **mangaLawaaram** *n.* Tuesday.
మంగళసూత్రం **mangaLasuutram** *see* **taaLi.**
మంగళహారతి **mangaLahaarati** *same as* **haarati.**
మంచం **mancam** *n.* bed, cot, bedstead.
మంచం ఎక్కు, మంచం పట్టు **mancam ekku, mancam paTTu** *v.i.* to take to o.'s bed, become bedridden, fall sick.
మంచం [మీదనుంచి] దించు **mancam [miidanunci] dincu** *v.t.* to take a person from his bed and lay him on the ground (a custom followed when he is about to die).
మంచి **manci** I. *n.* 1 good[ness]; **maniSilooni ~ni pencu** to foster the good[ness] in man; **waaDi ~ ceDDalu waaDiki teliyadu** he does not know what is good and what is bad for him. II. *adj.* 1 good *in varying senses depending on the noun qualified*, e.g., **~ rooju** auspicious day; **waaLLadi ~ kuTumbam** theirs is a well-reputed family; **aayanaki ~ peeru unnadi** he has a good reputation *or* he is widely known; **~ ruupaayi** genuine (not counterfeit) rupee; **~ mutyaalu** real pearls; **~ waana** heavy shower of rain; **~ neela** fertile soil; **~ guDDalu** clean newly-washed clothes; **~ gummaDi** sweet pumpkin; **~ debba** severe blow; **~ tappu** big mistake, blunder. 2 **~ maaTa ceesukoniweLLu** take a meal and then go *is used by some persons instead of* **bhoojanam ceesi weLLu** *which could be inauspicious.*
మంచిగంధం **mancigandham** *n.* sandalwood [paste].
మంచిగా **mancigaa** *adv.* 1 well. 2 kindly, in a kindly way.
మంచిచేసుకొను **manciceesukonu** *v.t.* to get round s.o., win over s.o.; **waaNNi manciceesukoni pani ceeyincEEnu** I humoured him and got the work done.
మంచితనం **mancitanam** *n.* 1 goodness. 2 kindness.
మంచిది!, మంచిదండీ! **mancidi!, mancidaNDii!** *minor sentence* good!, all right!, O.K! *cf.* **aNDi** *sense II.*
మంచినీళ్లప్రాయంగా **manciniiLLapraayangaa** *adv.* 1 easily and promptly; **ee panaynaa ~ ceestaaDu** he will do any work easily and promptly. 2 fluently; **telugu ~ maaTLaaDataaDu** he talks Telugu fluently.
మంచినీళ్ళు **manciniiLLu** *n.pl.* 1 drinking water. 2 fresh water (as opposed to salt water).
మంచినూనె **mancinuune** *n.* cooking oil (gen. gingelly oil or groundnut oil).
మంచు **mancu** *n.* 1 dew. 2 mist. 3 ice. 4 snow.
మంచు గడ్డ **mancu gaDDa** *n.* block of ice, lump of ice, ice cube.
మంచు యుగం **mancu yugam** *n.* ice age.
మంచు రేకు **mancu reeku** *n.* snow flake.
మంచుసంచీ **mancu sancii** *n.* ice bag.
మంచె **mance** *n.* 1 elevated platform for watching crops. 2 dais, platform.
మంజరి **manjari** *n.* bunch of flowers, cluster of flowers and leaves; **gaana ~** collection of songs.
మంజరీఛందస్సు **manjarii chandassu** *n.* kind of poetic metre.
మంజీర **manjiira** *n.* 1 *class.* anklet. 2 name of a river in Andhra Pradesh.
మంజుల **manjula** *adj.* sweet, delicate, beautiful.
మంజూరు **manjuuru** *n.* approval, sanction.
మంజూరు అవు **manjuuru awu** *v.i.* to be sanctioned.
మంజూరు చేయు **manjuuru ceeyu** *v.t.* to sanction.
మంజూష **manjuuSa** *n. class.* large basket or box.
మంట **maNTa** *n.* 1 flame, blaze, burning. 2 burning or smarting sensation; **nidra leeka naaku kaLLu ~gaa unnaayi** my eyes are burning (*or* smarting) due to lack of sleep; **aakali ~lu** pangs of hunger; **waaDaNTee naaku oLLu ~** I am furiously angry with him; *see* **kaDupu ~.**
మంటకలియు, మంటకలిసిపోవు **maNTakaliyu, maNTakalisipoowu** *v.i. fig.* to be ruined, be destroyed.
మంటకలుపు **maNTakalupu** *v.t.* to ruin, destroy.
మంటపం **maNTapam** *same as* **maNDapam.**
మంటపెట్టు **maNTapeTTu** *v.t.* 1 to set on fire. 2 *fig.* to ruin, destroy.
మంటలబాంబు **maNTalabaambu** *n.* incendiary bomb.
మంటిగడ్డలు **maNTigaDDalu** *same as* **maTTigaDDalu.**
మండ **maNDa**[1] *n.* branch or twig or stalk with leaves attached.
మండ **maNDa**[2] *n.* 1 ankle. 2 back of the hand.

మండనం **maNDanam** *n. class.* **1** adorning, decorating. **2** ornament, jewel.

మండపం, మంటపం **maNDapam, maNTapam** *n.* **1** pillared hall or covered veranda in a temple. **2** pavilion. **3** temporary building erected and decorated for wedding and other festivities.

మండబూరెలు **maNDabuurelu** *n.pl.* sweet dish made by steaming.

మండబెట్టు **maNDabeTTu** *v.t.* **1** to set on fire, burn. **2** *same as* **tagalabeTTu** *sense 2 but more emphatic.*

మండల్ **maNDal** *n. admin.* territorial division within a district.

మండలం **maNDalam** *n.* **1** region, zone, province, country. **2** orb, globe, ring. **3** disc of the sun or moon. **4** (*also* **maNDalakaalam**) period of forty days prescribed for taking a course of Ayurvedic medicine; *see* **candra ~**, **sawra ~**, **nakSatra ~**, **bhuu ~**, **waayu ~**, **naaDii ~**.

మండలి **maNDali** *n.* **1** society, association, committee, council.

మండలేశ్వరుడు **maNDaleeśwaruDu** *n. class.* king, sovereign.

మండి **maNDi** *n.* **1** wholesale market. **2** storehouse, warehouse, godown.

మండించు **maNDincu** *v.t.* **1** to burn, consume by burning. **2** *colloq.* to sell for a high price; **bajaarloo kuuragaayalu maNDistunnaaru** they are charging exorbitant prices for vegetables in the bazaar.

మండికం, మండిగం **maNDikam**[1], **maNDigam** *n.* threshold.

మండికం **maNDikam**[2] *n.* small pottery bowl.

మండిపడు **maNDipaDu** *v.i. fig.* to be very angry: **bhagguna ~** to blaze with anger, flare up in anger.

మండిపోవు **maNDipoowu** *v.i.* **1** *intensive form of* **maNDu**, *see* **poowu** *sense 7 (iii)*. **2** *idiomatic usages:* (i) **kaalam maNDipootunnadi** these are very bad times; (ii) **dharalu maNDipootunnaayi** prices are soaring; (iii) *impersonal, with dative* **andarikii maNDipooyindi** everyone was very angry.

మండీవేయు **maNDiiweeyu** *v.i.* to trip up (a person); **neenu parigettutuuNTee kaaLLaki maNDiiweesi paDagoTTEEDu** when I was running he tripped me up and made me fall.

మండు **maNDu** *v.i.* **1** to burn, blaze, scorch; **eNDalu ~ tunnaayi** the sun's heat is scorching. **2** to smart, feel a burning sensation; **kaaram tinnaaka naaku nooru ~ tunnadi** my mouth is burning after eating hot spices; **naaku oLLu ~ tunnadi** I feel angry. **3** *colloquially ~ may substitute for other verbs*, e.g., **waaDu Dabbu aDigEEDu, naaku eem maNDindi ganaka** (*for* **naaku eem unnadi ganaka**) **waaDiki iwwaDaaniki?** he asked for money, but what did I have to give him? *cf.* **tagalabaDu** *sense 3.*

మండుకువచ్చు **maNDukuwaccu** *v.i. lit.* to come to burning; **mii maaTa wiNTee naaku maNDukoccindi** when I heard what you said I was very angry (*lit.* when I heard what you said, it came to burning for me).

మండుటెండ **maNDuTeNDa** *n.* scorching heat of the sun.

మండువా **maNDuwaa** *n.* covered veranda surrounding the central courtyard of a house.

మండువా ఇల్లు **maNDuwaa illu** *n.* house with a central courtyard.

మండువేసవి **maNDuweesawi** *n.* very hot summer.

మండూకం **maNDuukam** *n. class.* frog.; *cf.* **kuupastha ~**

మండె **maNDe** *n.* heap of unthreshed grain, tobacco leaves or other harvested produce.

మండ్రగబ్బ **maNDragabba** *n.* large black scorpion.

మంతనాలాడు **mantanaalaaDu** *v.i.* to hold consulations or negotiations.

మంతనాలు **mantanaalu** *n.pl.* consultations, negotiations.

మంత్రం **mantram** *n.* **1** spell, charm, incantation; **mantraaniki kaTTabaDi** spellbound. **2** mantra, sacred text, hymn, chant.

మంత్రగాడు **mantragaaDu** *n.* sorcerer.

మంత్రపఠనం **mantrapaThanam** *n.* recitation of mantras.

మంత్రపూర్వకంగా **mantrapuurwakangaa** *adv.* ceremonially, ceremoniously, accompanied by chants or incantations.

మంత్రమహిమ **mantramahima** *n.* effect of a charm.

మంత్రముగ్ధ **mantramugdha** *adj.* spellbound, enchanted, entranced, bewitched.

మంత్రసాని **mantrasaani** *n.* midwife.

మంత్రాంగం **mantraangam** *n.* advice and assistance.

మంత్రి **mantri** *n.* **1** minister. **2** queen (in chess). **3** *dial.* barber.

మంత్రించు **mantrincu** *v.t.* **1** to charm, bewitch, entrance, cast a magic spell over. **2** to conjure up.

మంత్రిత్వ శాఖ **mantritwa śaakha** *n. admin.* ministry.

మంత్రి మండలి **mantrimaNDali** *n. admin.* cabinet, council of ministers.

మంత్రి వర్గం **mantriwargam** *n. admin.* cabinet.

మంత్రోపదేశం **mantroopadeeśam** *n.* guru's precept in the form of a sacred mantra given to a pupil who has completed his studies satisfactorily.

మంథనం **manthanam** *same as* **mathanam.**

మంథర, మందర **manthara, mandara** *n.* the legendary Mount Mandara, used by the Gods as a staff for churning the ocean of milk.

మంద **manda**[1] *n.* **1** flock, herd. **2** troupe; **baDinunci pillalu ~ gaa bayTaku waccEEru** the children came out of school in a troupe.

మంద **manda**[2] *adj.* **1** slow, tardy, sluggish, torpid, listless, inactive. **2** (of business) slack; (of appetite) poor[ly]; **kaDupuloo ~ ngaa undi** I have no appetite *or* I have indigestion. **3** dull, stupid. **4** (of light, sound) weak, soft, faint, subdued; **~ swaram** faint sound. **5** mild, gentle; **~ maarutam** gentle breeze. **6** thick.

మందం **mandam** *n.* **1** slowness, tardiness, sluggishness. **2** dullness. **3** thickness; **nuulu ~** the thickness (*or* width) of a thread. **4** indigestion, want of appetite; **naaku ~ ceesindi** I have indigestion *or* I have no appetite.

మందకొడి **mandakoDi** *adj.* slow, sluggish, inactive, listless; **pillawaaDu ~ gaa unnaaDu** the boy is listless.

మందగతి mandagati *n.* slow motion.
మందగమన mandagamana *n. class.* woman.
మందగామి mandagaami *n.* person who walks slowly, thing which moves slowly.
మందగించు mandagincu *v.i.* **1** to become dull, become sluggish. **2** (of progress) to be retarded. **3** (of interest, activity) to slow down, decline.
మందట mandaTa *n.* nearness.
మందడి mandaDi *n.* gap between bricks or stones in a wall.
మందడిగట్టు mandaDigaTTu *n.* ridge or bund between two fields.
మందడిగా mandaDigaa *adv.* in the middle, between; **reNDu stambhaalaki ~** between two pillars.
మందడ్డిగోడ mandaDigooDa *n.* partition wall.
మందడిరాయి mandaDi raayi *n.* boundary stone.
మందబుద్ధి, మందమతి mandabuddhi, mandamati *n.* dull wit[ted person].
మందభాగి, మందభాగ్యుడు mandabhaagi, mandabhaagyuDu *n.* unlucky person.
మందమతితనం mandamatitanam *n.* dull-wittedness.
మందమరపు mandamarapu *n.* absent-mindedness, forgetfulness.
మంధర mandara *same as* **manthara.**
మందల mandala *n.* limit, boundary.
మందలవాడు mandalawaaDu *alt. form of* **mandulawaaDu.**
మందలించు mandalincu *v.t.* to blame, scold, admonish, rebuke, upbraid.
మందలింపు mandalimpu *n.* scolding, rebuking, rebuke.
మందవారం mandawaaram *n. class.* Saturday.
మందస[ం] mandasa[m] *n.* chest, box, safe.
మందస్మితం, మందహాసం mandasmitam, mandahaasam *n.* gentle smile.
మందహాసం చేయు mandahaasam ceeyu *v.i.* to smile.
మందాకిని mandaakini *n.* **1** the heavenly river Ganges in mythology. **2** woman over sixty years old.
మందాగ్ని mandaagni *n. class.* indigestion, dyspepsia, want of appetite; *cf.* **agnimaandyam.**
మందారం mandaaram *n. hibiscus rosa sinensis*, red hibiscus; **reeka ~, reeku ~** single hibiscus (i.e., having a single whorl of petals); **mudda ~** double hibiscus.
మంది mandi I. *suffix added to numerals and det. nouns* persons, people; **padi ~** ten persons; **padi ~ sneehitulu** ten friends; **anta ~** so many persons. II. *n.pl.* others, persons other than o.s.; **tana Dabbu tanaku gaTTi, ~ Dabbu baagaa kharcu peDataaDu** he keeps a tight hold on his own money but spends other people's money freely.
మందిరం mandiram *n.* **1** mansion; **raaja ~** king's palace. **2** temple, shrine.
మందీమార్బలం mandiimaarbalam *n.* retinue.
మందు mandu *n.* **1** medicine, drug. **2** alcoholic drink, liquor. **3** chemical fertiliser. **4** insecticide. **5** love potion, love powder. **6** gunpowder; *pl.* **~ lu** fireworks; **diipaawaLi ~ lu teccEEnu** I have brought fireworks for Dipavali. **7** *in certain types of medicine only a tiny quantity is needed, hence ~ comes to mean* s.g very scarce, s.g that cannot be seen; **pancadaara bajaaruloo ~ aypooyindi** sugar has almost vanished from the bazaar; **waaDu bottigaa kanabadaDam leedu, ~ aypooyEEDu** he does not appear at all, he can seldom be seen; *cf.* **kalikam** *sense 3.*
మందుకొట్టు mandukoTTu *v.i. slang* to drink liquor.
మందుగుండు సామగ్రి, మందుగుండు సామాను manduguNDu saamagri, manduguNDu saamaanu *n.* ammunition, explosives.
మందుడు manduDu *n.* **1** fool, blockhead. **2** the planet Saturn.
మందుపట్టుమీద mandupaTTumiida *adv. slang* in a drunken state.
మందుపెట్టు mandupeTTu *v.i.* to give s.o. a love potion, infatuate s.o., cast a spell over s.o.
మందుభాయీ mandubhaayii *n. slang* drug addict.
మందుమాకు mandumaaku *n.* medicines and such things.
మందులవాడు, మందలవాడు mandulawaaDu, mandalawaaDu *n.* **1** chemist, person who sells drugs and medicines. **2** member of a community which lives by selling herbal and other medicines.
మకమకలాడు makamakalaaDu *v.i.* to lack lustre (*opposite of* **taLataLalaaDu**).
మకర[ం] makara[m] *n.* **1** *astrol.* the sign Capricorn. **2** crocodile, alligator.
మకరందం, మరందం makarandam, marandam *n. class.* nectar of flowers.
మకర కుండలాలు makarakuNDalaalu *n.pl. class.* earrings set with red stones and bearing the figure of a crocodile's head, worn by eminent persons.
మకరరేఖ makarareekha *n.* tropic of Capricorn.
మకరసంక్రమణం, మకరసంక్రాంతి makarasankramaNam, makarasankraanti *see* **sankraanti.**
మకాం makaam *n.* camp, halting place.
మకాం ఎత్తివేయు makaam ettiweeyu *v.i.* to move camp.
మకాంచేయు makaam ceeyu *v.i.* to camp or stay at a place; **maa iNTLoo makaam ceesEEDu** he stayed in our house.
మకాంపెట్టు, మకాంవేయు makaam peTTu, makaam weeyu *v.i.* to camp, set up a camp (military).
మకిల makila I. *n.* dirt[iness]. II. *adj.* (*also* **makili**) **1** dirty, tarnished. **2** dim, obscure.
మకుటం makuTam *n.* **1** crown. **2** refrain (in a poem or song).
మకురుతనం makurutanam *n.* stubbornness, obstinacy.
మక్క makka[1] *n.* small of the back.
మక్క makka[2] *dial. variant form of* **mokkajonna.**
మక్కలు, మక్కెలు makkalu, makkelu *n.pl.* body bones below the waist; **o.-i ~ wiragatannu** to break s.o.'s bones, beat s.o. up.
మక్కీకిమక్కీ makkiikimakkii *adj.* slavish (imitation); **~ anuwaadam** word for word translation.
మక్కు makku[1] *n.* mastic, resinous substance used to fill cracks in wood.

మక్కు, మాగు **makku²**, **maagu** *v.i. dial* (of fruit, crops) to become fully ripe.

మక్కువ **makkuwa** *n.* **1** fondness, affection. **2** desire, lust.

మక్తా **maktaa** *n.* **1** lease. **2** rent.

మక్తేదారు **makteedaaru** *n.* lessee.

మక్షికం **makSikam** *n. class.* fly.

మక్షికడింభం **makSikaDimbham** *n.* maggot.

మఖ, మఘ **makha, magha** *n. astrol.* tenth lunar mansion.

మఖం, మఘం **makham, magham** *n. class.* sacrifice.

మఖమల్, ముఖమల్ **makhamal, mukhamal** *n.* velvet.

మగ, మొగ **maga, moga** *adj.* male, man's.

మగజాతి **magajaati** I. *n.* menfolk, men in general, males. II. *adj.* male; **~ puSpaalu** male flowers; **~ aśwam** stallion.

మగజీర **magajiira** *n.* masculine sound (of a voice).

మగటిమి **magaTimi** *n.* manliness.

మగడు **magaDu** *n.* husband.

మగత[నిద్ర] **magata¹[nidra]** *n.* drowsiness, dozing.

మగత **magata²** *n.* lease.

మగతనం **magatanam** *n.* manliness.

మగది **magadi** *n.* male of any kind of animal or bird.

మగనాలి **maganaali** *n.* wife, married woman.

మగరాయుడు **magaraayuDu** *n.* man, male; **~ allee maaTLaaDutunnadi** she is talking like a man; **magaraayuLLanu kannawaaDu rommuna ceeyiDi nidra pootaaDu** the man who begets sons sleeps undisturbed (*lit.* sleeps with his hands on his chest).

మగవాడు **magawaaDu** *n.* man, male.

మగిడి, మగుడ **magiDi, maguDa** *adv. class.* again.

మగిడించు **magiDincu** *same as* **maralincu.**

మగులు **magulu** *n.* coping of a wall.

మగువ **maguwa** *n.* woman.

మగ్గం **maggam** *n.* loom.

మగ్గరి **maggari** *n.* weaver.

మగ్గు, మ్రగ్గు **m[r]aggu v.i. 1** to feel stifled or suffocated for want of fresh air. **2** (of fruit) to go mouldy. **3** to be distressed, be dejected. **4** *class.* to die, perish.

మగ్న **magna** *adj.* immersed.

మగ్నుడు **magnuDu** *n.* person who is immersed.

మఘ[ం] **magha[m]** *same as* **makha[m].**

మచ్చ **macca** *n.* **1** (*also* **puTTu~**) mole, birth mark. **2** mark or scar on the skin; **kaalina~** scar caused by a burn. **3** stain, spot, blot, blemish.

మచ్చపడు **maccapaDu** *v.i.* **1** to be stained, be scarred. **2** to lose o.'s good name, incur reproach.

మచ్చమాపు **macca maapu** *v.i.* to cause trouble (to s.o.); **waaNNi tiisukuweLtee tappakuNDaa nii~taaDu** if you take him with you he is certain to cause you trouble.

మచ్చలేని **maccaleeni** *adj.* **1** spotless, without a mark or scar. **2** (of character) unblemished.

మచ్చిక **maccika** *n.* **1** attachment, fondness, affection (**-miida,** for). **2** tameness, domestication.

మచ్చికచేయు **maccikaceeyu** *v.t.* **1** to tame, domesticate.

మచ్చికచేసుకొను **maccikaceesukonu** *v.t.* to get acquainted with, come to know, come to understand, make friends with, learn how to manage or control; **pillalanu maccika ceesukoni waaLLatoo kaburlu ceptuu kuurconnaanu** I made friends with the children and sat talking to them.

మచ్చికపడు **maccikapaDu** *v.i.* to become tame or domesticated.

మచ్చు **maccu** *n.* **1** sample, model, specimen, example. **2** love powder.

మచ్చుకత్తి **maccukatti** *n.* billhook.

మచ్చుకు **maccuku** *adv.* as an example or specimen; **maccukaynaa leedu** not even as an example, i.e., not at all.

మచ్చు చూచు **maccu cuucu** *v.t.* to sample, test, taste; **maa aawakaaya maccu cuuci ceppaNDi** taste some of our **aawakaaya** and tell me your opinion.

మచ్చుతునక **maccutunaka** *n.* **1** specimen, sample piece, example; **atani teliwiki idi~** this is an example of his intelligence; **~ llaaNTi widyaarthulu** exemplary students, model students.

మచ్చెం **maccem** *substandard form of* **matsyam.**

మచ్చెకంటి **maccekaNTi** *n.* woman with beautiful eyes.

మచ్చెరం **macceram** *n.* jealousy, rivalry.

మజరా **majaraa** *n.* hamlet.

మజా **majaa** *n.* **1** pleasant taste, good flavour; **saambaar~ gaa undi** the sambar is very tasty. **2** pleasure, delight, fun, charm; **cuTTa muTTistee eem~!** what a pleasure it is to light a cigar! **niiku teliyakuNDaa niiloo anni~luu unnaayi** without your knowing it, you possess all the charms. **3** s.g thrilling, wonderful, remarkable, amazing; **aakaaśamloo ewaruu egarananta ettuki egaraDam~gaa uNDaduu?** won't it be thrilling to fly higher than anyone else in the sky? **DayrekTaru: treetaayugamloo teeyaakeemiTayyaa? kawi: adee~! sinimaakawitwam alaagee uNTundi** director: how could there have been tea in the silver age? author: that's the amazing thing! cinema poetry is like that. **5** meaning, point, significance; **modaTi saari naa muulugu artham kaaleedanna maaTa! kaanii maLLii adee muulugutoo jawaabu iccEEnu. wiNTunnaananee artham waccindi. reNDoo maaTLoo uNTundi kaaboolu~** so he had not understood my groan the first time! but I answered again with the same groan and then he understood that I was listening. on the second occasion he seems to have got my meaning; **naa gadiloo pustakaalu maTuku muTTukooku, adee~** do not touch any of the books in my room, that is the point to remember.

మజాకా **majaakaa** *n.* **1** strength, power (= **taDaakhaa**). **2** joke (< *Hindi* majaak).

మజా చేయు **majaa ceeyu** *v.i.* to act in a wasteful manner; **majaaceesi Dabbu paaDuceesEEDu** he squandered the money; **majaa ceesi samayam wrdhaa ceestunnaaDu** he is frittering away the time.

మజిలీ **majilii** *n.* **1** stage in a journey. **2** camping, halting, stop for a night; **kaaśii~kathalu** *lit.* stories told at stages on a pilgrimage to Benares (title of a wellknown story book).

మజూరి **majuuri** *n.* cost of labour for making jewellery charged by a goldsmith.

మంజ్కూరు **majkuuru** *adj.* aforesaid, above mentioned.

మజ్జ **majja** *n.* **1** pith or sap of plants. **2** bone marrow.

మజ్జనం **majjanam** *n. class.* bath[ing].

మజ్జిగ **majjiga** *n.* buttermilk.

మజ్జిగతెగులు **majjigategulu** *n.* mildew.

మజ్జిగపులుసు **majjigapulusu** *n.* soup made with buttermilk.

మజ్జుగుజ్జులు పడు **majjugujjulupaDu** *same as* **gunjaaTanapaDu.**

మజ్దూర్ **majduur** *n.* labourer.

మజ్దూరీ **majduurii** *n.* cost of labour, labour charge.

మటం వేసుకొను, మఠం వేసుకొను **maT[h]am weesukonu** *v.i.* **1** to sit crosslegged in the lotus pose: *cf.* **padmaasanam. 2** *colloq.* to sit idly; **iNTLoo caduwukookuNDaa maT[h]am weesukoni kuurconnaaDu** he sat idly at home without studying.

మటమటలాడు **maTamaTalaaDu** *v.i.* **1** to burn fiercely, blaze. **2** to rage or blaze with anger.

మటిక[కాయ] **maTika[kaaya]** *n. dial.* kind of bean (= **goorucikkuDu**).

మటుకు, మట్టుకు **maT[T]uku** *particle* **1** [just] so much, [just] so far: **anta ~ naaku telusu** I know just so much; **lisTuloonunci konni maatram eeri 500 ruupaayalaku saripaDee pustakaalu ~ konamani siphaarsu ceesEEDu** choosing only a few from the list he recommended buying books amounting to just Rs. 500 in value; **inta ~ waccEEka daacaDam eem prayoojanam?** when things have gone so far, what is the use of hiding? **waaDi oLLu caalaa ~ nayam ayindi** his health has improved to a large extent; **dorikinanta ~ sampaadincukonu** to acquire as much as is available; **ippaTi ~ ikkaDee unnaaDu** he was here till just now; **appaTi ~ naaku eemii teliyadu** up to that time I did not know anything; **appaTi ~ adhikaaramloo unna waaru** people in power for the time being. **2** *~ may serve to emphasise or particularise a preceding n., pron., adv. or conditional clause,* e.g., **Dabbu~ naaku waddu** as for money, I do not want it; **andarinii pilicEEnu, waaDu~ waccEEDu** I invited them all, but only he came; **Tii~ taagutaanu** I will just drink some tea (nothing else); **enni piTiiSanlu peDitee ~ eem laabham? dammiDii ettu laabham uNDadu** however many petitions he sends, what profit will there be? not even a pie of profit. **3** *for strong emphasis the n., pron. or adv. may be repeated after ~,* e.g., **iiwEELa~iiwEELa** on this very day; **naa~ naaku** as for me *or* so far as I am concerned. **4** *idiomatic usages:* (i) **ewaDi~waaDu caduwukonnaaDu** each of them studied separately; **bhoojanaalu ceeyaDaaniki ewari~waaru weL-LipooyEEru** they went away separately to have dinner; (ii) **gontu ~ tinnaaDu** he stuffed himself with food (*lit.* he ate up to the limit of his throat); **waaDiki naamiida gontu~ unnadi** he is full of animosity towards me.

మటుమాయం **maTumaayam** *n.* unaccountable disappearance.

మటుమాయం అవు **maTumaayam awu** *v.i.* **1** to disappear unaccountably. **2** to vanish totally, disappear without a trace.

మట్ట **maTTa** *n.* **1** bough or frond of a palm tree. **2** branch of a cactus. **3** leaf of an aloe.

మట్టం **maTTam** I. *n.* **1** level: **samudra~** sea level; **~ cuuDu, tarawaata sanci kudinci inkaa pooyi!** look at the level (of the contents), then shake the bag and pour in some more. **2** levelling instrument, spirit level. **3** *dial.* bottom of a round pot or basket. **4** width, diameter. **5** *dial.* one rupee. II *adj.* **1** level, flat. **2** *dial. slang* having broad hips.

మట్టం చేయు **maTTam ceeyu** *v.t.* to raze to the ground.

మట్టగించు **maTTagincu** *v.t.* to trample [on]; **waaNNi maTTagistee nijam ceppEEDu** when they gave him a pounding (*lit.* when they trampled on him) he told the truth.

మట్టగిడస **maTTagiDasa** *n.* kind of fish.

మట్టసం **maTTasam** *adj.* **1** *same as* **maTTam** *sense II.* **2** dwarfish.

మట్టి **maTTi** I.*n.* earth, soil, clay. II. *adj.* made of clay or earthenware: **~kuNDa** earthenware pot.

మట్టి కలియు **maTTikaliyu** *v.i.* **1** to be ruined, be destroyed. **2** to lose o.'s life, die.

మట్టి కలుపు **maTTi kalupu** *v.t.* to ruin, destroy, spoil.

మట్టికొట్టుకొను **maTTikoTTukonu** *v.i.* **1** to be covered with dust or mud; **naa kaaLLu maTTi koTTuku pooyEEyi** my feet are caked with mud. **2** to be ruined, be destitute; **caduwukookapootee maTTikoTTukuNTaawu** if you do not study your future will be ruined.

మట్టి పాలవు **maTTipaalawu** *v.i. see* **paalawu** *sense 2.*

మట్టిమశానం **maTTimaśaanam** *n.* rubbish.

మట్టిగడ్డలు, మంటిగడ్డలు **maTTigaDDalu, maNTigaDDalu** *n.pl.* **1** particles of earth, grains of sand. **2** *~ may be suffixed to an other n. to give a derisory sense:* e.g., **waaDiki caduwuu~ eemii leedu** he has no education of any kind; **maryaadaa~ leeni kuTumbam** a family with no status whatever.

మట్టు **maTTu**[1] *n.* **1** limit, measure, extent, degree; **unna ~ tinaNDi, neenu maLLii waNDanu** eat what there is, I will not cook again; **eedoo unna ~ talaa kaastaa pancukondaam** let us share what there is equally among us. **2** time: **ii~ miiru paaDaali** this time you must sing (= **maaTu**): *cf.* **unna ~ na, aa ~ nee.**

మట్టు **maTTu**[2] *n.* **1** ring-shaped carrying pad worn on the head. **2** ring of straw placed on the ground for a round bottomed pot to rest on (= **cuTTakuduru**).

మట్టు **maTTu**[3] *v.t.* to tread on, stamp on, trample.

మట్టుకు **maTTuku** *same as* **maTuku.**

మట్టు పెట్టు **maTTu peTTu** *v.t.* **1** to suppress, conceal (information). **2** to kill.

మట్టూ మర్యాదా **maTTuu maryaadaa** *n.* respect and politeness.

మట్టె **maTTe** *n.* woman's toe ring.

మట్టేయు **maTTeeyu** I. *v.i.* **1** to throng together, come in crowds. **2** (of illness) to intensify, grow worse. II. *v.t.* to trample [on], crush.

మఠం **maTham** *n.* 1 monastery, mutt, home of a religious order. 2 **bayraagi**~ home for religious beggars; **ataniki satram bhoojanam** ~ **nidra** he has his meals in a choultry and sleeps in a beggars' home *is a conventional expression for* he leads a lonely life with no-one to care for him.

మఠం వేసుకొను **maTham weesukonu** *same as* **maTam weesukonu.**

మడ **maDa**[1] (*also* ~**ceTTu**) *n.* mangrove; ~**aDawi** tidal forest.

మడ **maDa**[2] *n.* small channel for taking irrigation water from main channel to field.

మడక **maDaka** *n.* plough complete with bullocks.

మడచు **maDacu** *v.t.* 1 to fold. 2 to roll up; **cokkaa ceetulu**~ to roll up o.'s shirtsleeves.

మడత **maData** *n.* 1 fold, crease; ~**kaagitam** piece of folded paper; **istri**~ crease made by an iron; ~**ceesina baTTalu** ironed clothes. 2 tuck or pleat in a garment. 3 **waaDidi**~**naaluka** (i) he cannot pronounce words; (ii) he is a habitual liar.

మడతకుర్చీ **maDatakurcii** *n.* folding chair.

మడత తీయు, మడత విప్పు **maData tiiyu, maDaTa wippu** *v.t.* to unfold.

మడతపడు **maDatapaDu** *v.i.* 1 to be folded. 2 **kaalu maDatapaDindi** the leg was sprained.

మడతపెట్టు, మడతవేయు **maDatapeTTu, maDataweeyu** *v.t.* to fold; **naalugu maDatalu peTTina** folded four times; **o.-ni maData peTTi koTTu** to strike s.o. with the side of o.'s hand (not with the flat of the hand).

మడతపేచీ **maDatapeecii** *n.* petty or trivial objection.

మడతబందు **maDatabandu** *n.* hinge; ~**kiilu** hinge joint.

మడతమాను **maDatamaanu** *n.* porcelain pot for serving pickles.

మడతవడ్డీ **maDatawaDDii** *n. dial.* compound interest.

మడమ **maDama** *n.* heel.

మడవ **maDawa** *n.* gap made in a boundary ridge to allow water to flow from one irrigated plot of land to the next.

మడి **maDi**[1] *n.* 1 plot of wet (i.e., irrigated) land surrounded by a ridge to retain the water. 2 seedbed.

మడి **maDi**[2] *n.* ceremonial purity.

మడికట్టుకొను **maDikaTTukonu** *v.i.* 1 to wear ceremonially pure clothes. 2 **maDikaTTukoni kuurcuNDu** to keep aloof from others in order to preserve o.'s purity. 3 ~ *may be used derisively,* e.g., **anyadeeśyaalanu egumati ceesukoowaDam walla telugu bhaaSalooni śuciiśubhrataa mayla paDipootaayanee maDikaTTukonna waaLLani cuusi manam jaali paDaali** we ought to feel sorry for those pure-minded persons who say that the purity of the Telugu language will be defiled by importing foreign words.

మడికాళ్లు వేసుకొని కూర్చుండు **maDikaaLLu weesukoni kuurcuNDu** *v.i.* to sit with one knee crossed over the other.

మడిగట్టు **maDigaTTu** *n.* ridge formed round a plot of irrigated land (**maDi**) in order to retain the water.

మడిగా **maDigaa** *adv.* in a state of ceremonial purity.

మడిగుడ్డలు, మడిబట్టలు **maDiguDDalu, maDibaTTalu** *n.pl.* ceremonially pure clothes worn by orthodox persons when taking meals or worshipping.

మడినీళ్లు **maDiniiLLu** *n.* water that is drawn in a ceremonially pure manner and kept for the use of persons wearing **maDi.**

మడిమాన్యాలు, మళ్లూమాన్యాలూ **maDimaanyaalu, maLLuumaanyaaluu** *n.pl.* lands, landed property; **taatalu sampaadincina**~ lands that his ancestors acquired.

మడియు **maDiyu** *v.i. class.* to die, perish.

మడివేలు, మడేలు **maDiweelu, maDeelu** *n. dial.* washerman; **caduwukonna waaDikanna maDeeluwaaDu minna** better a washerman than an educated person (if you want a job done properly).

మడిసి **maDisi** *substandard form of* **maniSi.**

మడీ ఆచారం **maDii aacaaram** *n.* ceremonial purity and traditional observance.

మడీదడీ **maDiidaDii** (*also* **maDulu daDulu**) *n.* hampering, obstructiveness.

మడుగు **maDugu** *n.* pond, lake, pool, puddle; **waana kurustunnadi, illantaa**~**ayindi** it is raining and the whole house has become a lake; **aayana[ki] aDugulaki** ~**lu ottEEru** they paid him the greatest respect.

మడుగులు **maDugulu** *n.pl.* 1 ponds, lakes, puddles. 2 times (= **reTLu**); **weyyi**~ a thousand times.

మడుపు **maDupu** *n.* 1 fold. 2 **kaali**~ front part of the ankle.

మడేలు **maDeelu** *same as* **maDiweelu.**

మడ్డి **maDDi** I. *n.* 1 sediment, dregs, lees. 2 scum. 3 dullness, stupidity. 4 slovenliness. II. *adj.* 1 dull, stupid. 2 heedless, inattentive. 3 dirty, slovenly, dishevelled.

మడ్డితనం **maDDitanam** *n.* 1 dullness, stupidity. 2 slovenliness.

మణి **maNi** *n.* 1 jewel, gem. 2 *used as a complimentary affix to certain feminine nouns,* e.g., **naTii**~ actress; **widuSii**~ scholarly woman; **sahoodariimaNulaaraa**! ladies! (*formal term of address, lit.* sisters!)

మణికట్టు **maNikaTTu** *n.* wrist.

మణిపూస **maNipuusa** *n.* gem, jewel.

మణిప్రవాళం **maNiprawaaLam** *n.* hybrid literary language composed, e.g., of Sanskrit and Malayalam.

మణీలా, మణేలా **maNiilaa, maNeelaa** *n.* card (in a pack of cards) bearing the number nine.

మణుగు **maNugu** *n.* maund, a measure of weight now obsolete, in some areas $82\frac{2}{7}$ pounds, in others about 28 pounds.

మణుగుబూరెలు **maNugubuurelu** *n.pl.* kind of savoury dish.

మతం **matam** *n.* 1 religion, creed. 2 opinion, belief. 3 idea, thought, intention, wish, purpose; **koDukki iSTamleeni peLLi ceeyaDam aawiDa**~**kaadu** it was not her intention to perform her son's marriage against his will.

మతమౌఢ్యం **matamawDhyam** *n.* religious obscurantism.

మతయుద్ధం **matayuddham** *n.* religious war, crusade.

మతలబు **matalabu** *n.* 1 purport, meaning. 2 hidden meaning.

మతస్థుడు, మతీయుడు **matasthuDu, matiiyuDu** *n.* follower of a religion.

మతాంతరీకరణ **mataantariikaraNa** *n.* religious conversion.

మతాబా **mataabaa** *n.* kind of firework emitting a brilliant white light.

మతి **mati** *n.* **1** mind, intellect. **2** understanding, consciousness, judgement, sense; **aa maaTalu winnaaka naa~ pooyindi** (*or* **naa~ ~loo leedu**) when I heard those words my mind was in a daze; **~suti leekuNDaa** without any sense at all.

మతింపు, మదింపు **matimpu, madimpu** *n.* estimate, valuation.

మతింపు చేయు/వేయు, మదింపు చేయు/వేయు **matimpu ceeyu/weeyu, madimpu ceeyu/weeyu** *v.t.* to estimate.

మతిభ్రమ **matibhrama** *n.* **1** confusion of mind. **2** unsoundness of mind, madness.

మతిభ్రమించు **matibhramincu** *v.i. with dative* to become mad; **waaDiki matibhramincindi** he became mad.

మతిమరపు **matimarapu** *n.* absent-mindedness, forgetfulness.

మతీయుడు **matiiyuDu** *same as* **matasthuDu.**

మతుబర్థకం **matubarthakam** *n. gram.* suffix for forming agent nouns, e.g., **-kaaDu, -katte.**

మత్కుణం **matkuNam** *n. class.* bug, flea.

మత్తకాసిని **mattakaasini** *n. class.* very fascinating woman.

మత్తకోకిల **mattakookila** *n.* name of a poetic metre.

మత్తగజం **mattagajam** *n.* elephant in must.

మత్తడి **mattaDi** *n. dial.* surplus weir of an irrigation reservoir.

మత్తిల్లు, మత్తుచెందు **mattillu, mattucendu** *v.i.* **1** to be entranced. **2** to be intoxicated.

మత్తు **mattu** *n.* **1** intoxication, inebriation, drunkenness. **2** sleepiness, dreaminess; **gadiloo praśaantata eerpaDaDamtoo goopaalam tirigi tana talapula~loo paDDaDu** as soon as his room became calm Gopalam fell into a reverie again. **3** anaesthetic; **~iccu** to give an anaesthetic; **~loo uNDu** to be under an anaesthetic *or* to be in a state of intoxication. **4** passion, lust; **mattekkina kaLLu** lustful eyes. **5** spell, entrancement; **atanu aame ~loo unnaaDu** he is under her spell *or* he is entranced by her.

మత్తుగా **mattugaa** *adv.* **1** drunkenly. **2** dazedly, dreamily, sleepily. **3** lustfully, passionately.

మత్తుగొను **mattugonu** *v.i.* to be intoxicated.

మత్తుడు **mattuDu** *second part of a n. compound* person who is drunk or intoxicated; **dhana/adhikaara~** person who is drunk with riches/power.

మత్తుపదార్థం **mattupadaartham** *n.* intoxicating substance, drug.

మత్తుమందు **mattumandu** *n.* **1** anaesthetic, narcotic, sedative, drug. **2** love potion, love powder.

మత్తేభం **matteebham** *n. class.* **1** elephant in must. **2** kind of poetic metre.

మత్సరం **matsaram** *n. class.* jealousy, rivalry.

మత్స్యం **matsyam** *n. class.* fish.

మత్స్యకారుడు **matsyakaaruDu** *n.* fisherman.

మత్స్యపాలనం **matsyapaalanam** *n.* pisciculture.

మత్స్యయంత్రం **matsyayantram** *n.* **1** magical diagram inscribed on a copper plate and laid beneath the foundation stone of a building. **2** test of ability in archery described in the Mahabharata.

మత్స్యావతారం **matsyaawataaram** *n.* the first of the ten incarnations of Vishnu, in the form of a fish.

మథన **mathana** *adj.* agitated, distressed, grieved.

మథనం, మంథనం **mathanam, manthanam** *n.* **1** *class.* churning. **2** deep or thorough study; **weedaanta~** deep study of the Vedanta.

మథనపడు **mathanapaDu** *v.i.* **1** to be distressed, be agitated, be disturbed. **2** to be restless, be restive. **3** to consider carefully, ponder deeply.

మథించు **mathincu** *v.t.* **1** to churn, stir. **2** (of literature, science) to study thoroughly and completely, be immersed in, absorb, devour; **brawn appaTikee basawa puraaNaanni puuraagaa mathinci unnaaDu** by then Brown had absorbed the whole of the Basava Purana; **reepu udayam ingliiSu parikSa anagaa aa raatri DitekTiw Sarlaak hoomsnu mathincEEnu, aynaa pariikSaloo uttiirNuDanayyEEnu** the night before the English examination I devoured a Sherlock Holmes detective story, yet I passed the examination.

మదం **madam** *n.* **1** pride, arrogance. **2** lust. **3** fat.

మదగజం, మదపుటేనుగు **madagajam, madapuTeenugu** *n.* elephant in must.

మదవతి **madawati** *n.* **1** amorous woman. **2** wanton woman.

మదద్గారు **madadgaaru** *n. dial* assistant.

మదనం **madanam** *n. dial.* grain threshed but not yet winnowed.

మదనకామరాజు కథలు **madana kaamaraaju kathalu** *n.pl.* tales about the folk hero Madana Kamaraju.

మదనుడు **madanuDu** *n.* Cupid.

మదాం **madaam** *n.* queen (in playing cards).

మది **madi** *n.* mind, heart, emotional feelings; **nii ~loo eemundoo naaku telusu** I know how you feel in your heart.

మదించు **madincu** *v.i.* **1** to be swollen with pride or arrogance. **2** to be intractable, be unmanageable. **3** to be passionate.

మదింపు **madimpu** *same as* **matimpu.**

మదిర **madira** *n. class.* alcoholic liquor.

మదుం **madum** *n.* sluice of an irrigation reservoir.

మదుపు **madupu** *n.* capital investment, outlay.

మదుపు పెట్టు, మదుపు చేయు **madupu peTTu, madupu ceeyu** *v.i. and t.* **1** to provide funds for investment. **2** to invest; **padi weelu madupu peTTi dukaaNam peTTEEDu** he invested ten thousand rupees and started a shop.

మదురు **maduru** *n.* coping on a wall; **~miidi pilli eTu duukutundoo teliyadu** no one knows which way the cat on the wall will jump (common saying).

మద్దతు **maddatu** *n.* support, help, assistance; **kaLaakaarula sanghaaniki~gaa** in support of the artists' association.

మద్దతుదారు **maddatudaaru** *n.* supporter, seconder.

మద్దిచెట్టు **maddiceTTu** *n.* a timber tree, *terminalia alata* (= **saalam**)

మద్దినేల **maddineela** *substandard form of* **madhyaanam wEELa** (= **madhyaanam**).

మద్దెల **maddela** *n.* kind of small drum.

మద్యం **madyam** *n.* intoxicating drink, alcoholic liquor.

మద్య[పాన] నిషేధం **madya[paana] niSeedham** *n.* prohibition (of liquor).

మధుకరం **madhukaram** *n.* 1 *class.* bee. 2 food obtained by begging.

మధుపం **madhupam** *n. class.* bee.

మధుపర్కం **madhuparkam** *n.* (*also pl.* **madhuparkaalu**) 1 wedding clothes dipped in turmeric and given to the bride and bridegroom to wear during the wedding ceremony up to the time of **appagintalu.** 2 flock of raw cotton (**patti**) smeared with turmeric and offered to a deity at the beginning of worship when the deity is invoked. 3 *colloq.* clothes worn for a long time; *cf.* **diikSaa-wastraalu.**

మధుపాత్ర **madhupaatra** *n. class.* wine cup.

మధుమాసం **madhumaasam** *n. class.* spring time.

మధుమేహం **madhumeeham** *n. med.* diabetes.

మధుర **madhura** *adj.* 1 sweet, delicious, delightful. 2 (of sound) melodious.

మధురం **madhuram** *n.* sweetness.

మధురత **madhurata** *n.* sweetness, agreeableness.

మధురసం **madhurasam** *n.* wine.

మధురిమ **madhurima** *n. poet.* sweetness.

మధువు **madhuwu** *n.* 1 nectar of flowers. 2 intoxicating drink, liquor. 3 honey.

మధుస్వనం **madhuswanam** *n. class.* cuckoo.

మధ్య **madhya** I. *n, class.* young woman aged between about eighteen and thirty years. II. *adj.* 1 mid[dle], central: ~ **bhaagam** middle or central part. 2 medium; ~ **tarahaa pariśrama** medium scale industry. III. *p.p.* in the middle of, at the centre of, admist, between, among. IV. *adv.* (*also* ~ **na,** ~ **loo**) 1 in the middle, at the centre, in between. 2 *idiomatically in a situation where two persons are concerned and a third person is affected in spite of not being directly concerned* ~ *is used to convey the sense of the third person being* 'in the middle', e.g., **waaLLakeem? śubh-rangaa unnaaru,** ~ **naa pani ayindi** they are quite all right, but it was I who suffered; **waaDu wastaanannaaDu, raalee-du;** ~ **naSTam naaku, niikenduku koopam**? he said he would come but he did not come; it was I who suffered loss, then why are you angry? *cf.* **aa** ~, **ii** ~, **naDi** ~.

మధ్యం **madhyam** *n.* middle, centre.

మధ్యంతర **madhyantara** *adj.* intermediate; ~ **ennikalu** mid-term elections.

మధ్యంతరంగా **madhyantarangaa** *adv.* 1 in the intervening period. 2 unexpectedly; ~ **waccipaDDa wiSayam** an item that turned up unexpectedly.

మధ్యకాలం **madhyakaalam** *n.* intervening time.

మధ్యకాలీన **madhyakaaliina** *adj.* interim.

మధ్యగోడ **madhyagooDa** *n.* partition wall.

మధ్యచ్ఛేదనం **madhyaccheedanam** *n.* cross-section.

మధ్యదళారీ **madhyadaLaari** *n.* middleman.

మధ్యధరా సముద్రం **madhyadharaa samudram** *n.* Mediterranean Sea.

మధ్యన **madhyana** *see* **madhya** *sense IV.*

మధ్యనుంచి **madhyanunci** *p.p.* 1 through; **janam** ~ **doowa ceesukoni weLLEEnu** I made my way though a crowd of people. 2 along the middle of; **rooDDu** ~ **naDistee kaaru-kinda paDataawu** if you walk in the middle of the road you will be run over by a car.

మధ్యమ **madhyama** *n. class.* middle finger.

మధ్యమం **madhyamam** *n.* fourth musical note in the seven note scale.

మధ్యమపురుష **madhyama puruSa** *n. gram.* second person.

మధ్యమధ్య **madhyamadhya** *adv.* now and then, now and again, from time to time.

మధ్యయుగం **madhya yugam** *n.* the Middle Ages.

మధ్యరకం **madhyarakam** *adj.* medium (in size, duration, quality).

మధ్యవర్తి **madhyawarti** *n.* 1 arbitrator. 2 mediator. 3 middleman.

మధ్యవర్తిత్వం **madhyawartitwam** *n.* 1 arbitration. 2 mediation.

మధ్యస్థ **madhyastha** *adj.* intermediate.

మధ్యస్థంగా **madhyasthangaa** *adv.* halfway, midway, in between, in the middle; **haalu** ~ **kuurcunnaaDu** he sat in the middle of the hall.

మధ్యాకార **madhyaakaara** *n.* kind of classical poetic metre (employed by Viswanatha Satyanarayana in modern times).

మధ్యాహ్నం, మధ్యాన్నం **madhyaahnam, madhyaan-nam** *n.* midday, noon, afternoon; ~ **paNDreNDu** (*or* ~ **panneNDu**) **gaNTalaki** at twelve noon; ~ **muuDu ga-NTalaki** at three p.m.; ~ **bhoojanam** midday meal, lunch; ~ **baDi** afternoon session of school.

మన **mana** *pronom. adj.* our (*inclusive of the person*[*s*] *addressed*).

మనం **manam**[1] *personal pron.* we (*inclusive of the person*[*s*] *addressed*).

మనం **manam**[2] *n.* mind.

మనః **manaḥ** *Sanskrit adjvl. prefix meaning* of the mind, mental.

మనఃక్లేశం **manaḥkleeśam** *n.* mental distress.

మనఃపూర్వకంగా, మనోపూర్వకంగా **manaḥpuur-wakangaa, manoopuurwakangaa** *adv.* wholeheartedly.

మనఃప్రవృత్తి **manaḥprawṛtti** *n.* mental attitude.

మనఃఫలకం **manaḥphalakam** *same as* **manoophalakam.**

మననం **mananam** *n.* 1 consideration, reflection. 2 recalling.

మననంచేసుకొను **mananam ceesukonu** *v.i.* 1 to reflect on, consider, think over, ponder over. 2 to keep in mind, bear in mind. 3 to recall.

మనమడు, మనమరాలు **manamaDu, manamaraalu** *same as* **manumaDu, manumaaraalu.**

మనవి **manawi** *n.* request, submission, petition, representation.

మనవి చేయు **manawi ceeyu** *v.t.* to represent, submit.

మనశ్శాంతి **manaśśaanti** *n.* peace of mind.

మనసా **manasaa** *adv.* 1 in the mind, mentally. 2 with o.'s whole mind; **~nammu** to believe steadfastly.

మనసారా **manasaaraa** *adv.* with all o.'s heart, wholeheartedly; **~koorukonu** to desire earnestly.

మనసావాచాకర్మణా **manasaawaacaakarmaNaa** *adv.* by thought, word and deed (i.e., wholeheartedly).

మనసు, మనస్సు **manasu, manassu** *n.* 1 mind, heart, emotions, feelings; **~ki paTTincukonu** to fix (s.g) in o.'s mind *or* to take (s.g) to heart; **atani~ ~loo leedu** he is not in his right mind *or* his mind is in a daze; **~nilupukonu** *or* **~aapukonu** to keep a steady mind *or* to control o.'s emotions; **~wippu** to lay bare o.'s heart *or* to make o.'s feelings known; **o.-i~noppincu** to hurt s.o.'s feelings. 2 inclination, liking; **idantaa talliki wiwarinci ceppaDaaniki waaDiki~ pooleedu** he had no inclination (*or* he did not feel inclined) to explain all this to his mother; **maamiDi paNDumiida ~paDDaanu** *or* **naaku maamiDi paNDu miida~ayindi** I felt like eating a mango. 3 fondness, affection; **~icci maaTLaaDu** to talk affectionately; **waaDimiida~too unnaTTundi paapam!** she seems to have a fondness for him; **o.-ki~icci sneeham ceeyu** to get on affectionate terms with s.o.; **o.-i~doocukonu** to capture s.o.'s affections. 4 human feelings, compassion; **~uNTee ewaDuu ii pani ceeyaDu** no-one will do a thing like this if he has any human feelings.

మనస్కరించు **manaskarincu** *v.i.* 1 *with dative* to feel inclined, have an inclination; **aa taragatiloo uNDaDaaniki S.-ki manaskarinca leedu** S. had no inclination to remain in that class. 2 to appeal to the mind, seem fitting; **niiku ii maaTa anaDaaniki elaa manaskaristoondi?** how does it seem fitting to you to say this?

మనస్కుడు **manaskuDu** *second part of a n. compound connoting* with a .... mind/heart, e.g., **wyadhita manaskuDay weLLipooyEEDu** he went away with a distressed heart.

మనస్తత్వం **manastatwam** *n.* 1 psychological state, mentality, temperament. 2 state of mind, frame of mind, mood.

మనస్తత్వశాస్త్రం **manastatwaśaastram** *n.* (science of) psychology.

మనస్తత్వ[శాస్త్ర]వేత్త **manastatwa[śaastra]weetta** *n.* psychologist.

మనస్తాపం **manastaapam** *n.* mental distress, sorrow.

మనస్పర్థ **manaspartha** *n.* 1 disagreement. 2 ill feelings.

మనస్ఫూర్తిగా **manasphuurtigaa** *adv.* willingly, wholeheartedly, sincerely, earnestly.

మనస్సాక్షి **manassaakSi** *n.* conscience.

మనస్సు **manassu** *same as* **manasu.**

మనా, మన్నా **manaa, mannaa** *n.* prohibition, prevention, stoppage; **raajugaaru waaDiki deewiDii~ceppeesEEru** the king banished him from court.

మనికి **maniki** *n.* 1 living, existence. 2 abode.

మనిషి **maniSi** *n.* 1 man, woman, person; **~wEE? paśuwwEE?** are you a man or beast? i.e., do you call yourself a man? **~ki oka maaTa cebutaaDu** he tells a different story to every person; **jalubu~ki kaaka maanuku wastundEE?** *lit.* will a cold be caught by a tree and not by a man? i.e., (colds are so common that) anyone may catch a cold. 2 (human) body, frame, figure; **phooTooloo~baagaa kanapaDaDam leedu** the figure has not come out well in the photo; **nuwwu~wi maaraleedu** your appearance has not altered; *see* **tiiyu** *sense I. 2,* **niiTu, bandoobastu.** 3 *pl.* **manuSulu** people, persons, human beings.

మనిషెత్తు **maniSettu** *adj.* life-size[d] (picture, statue).

మనీషి **maniiSi** *n.* learned person, scholar.

మను, మనుం **manu[1], manum** *same as* **manuwu[1].**

మను **manu[2]** *v.i.* to live, exist.

మనుగడ **manugaDa** *n.* 1 life, living, existence; **ii prapancamloo maanawula~unnanta kaalam** as long as human life remains on this earth. 2 way of life, livelihood; **aayana aa Dabbutoo ~konasaagistunnaaDu** he is maintaining himself on that (amount of) money.

మనుగుడుపులు **manuguDupulu** *n.pl.* final entertainment given by the bride's family to the bridegroom's family for three days after the marriage is over.

మనుధర్మశాస్త్రం **manudharmaśaastram** *n.* code of Manu; *see* **manuwu[2].**

మనుమడు, మనమడు **manumaDu, manamaDu** *n.* grandson.

మనుమరాలు, మనమరాలు **manumaraalu, manamaraalu** *n.* granddaughter.

మనువర్తి, మనోవర్తి, మనోవృత్తి **manuwarti, manoowarti, manoowṛtti** *n.* 1 allowance paid to a widow for her maintenance. 2 *colloq.* allowance paid to an unemployed person, unemployment relief.

మనువాడు **manuwaaDu** *v.t.* to marry.

మనువు, మను[ం] **manuwu[1], manu[1], manum** *n.* 1 married life, matrimony; **aayanatoo~weLLindi** she went to live with him as his wife. 2 marriage alliance; **manci~cikkitee kuuturuni istaaDu** he will give his daughter in marriage if a good alliance can be found; **maaru~** second marriage, remarriage of a widow.

మనువు **manuwu[2]** *n.* Manu, name of a legendary sage, reputed to have been the progenitor of mankind and author of the **manudharmaśaastram** or code of Manu, the basis of Hindu jurisprudence; fourteen Manus are believed to have held sway successively over the earth in past ages.

మనుష్యుడు **manuSyuDu** *n.* 1 man. 2 *pl.* **manuSyulu** people, persons, human beings.

మనో **manoo** *first part of a n. or adjvl. compound meaning* of the mind *or* of the emotions, e.g., **~nigraham.**

మనోగత **manoogata** *adj.* deeply felt (emotion, desire).

మనోగతం **manoogatam** *n.* wish, intention.

మనోజ్ఞ **manoojña** *adj.* 1 pleasing, appealing. 2 lovely, delightful.

మనోజ్ఞత **manoojñata** *n.* loveliness.

మనోధర్మం **manoodharmam** *n.* psychological characteris-stics, mentality.

మనోనిగ్రహం **manoonigraham** *n.* control over the mind, control over the emotions.

మనోపూర్వకంగా **manoopuurwakangaa** *same as* **manaḥ-puurwakangaa.**

మనోఫలకం, మనఃఫలకం **manoophalakam, man-ahphalakam** *n.* mind, the mind's eye (*lit.* the 'slate' of the mind, on which experiences are recorded); **ii bhaawananu reepaTinunci manam mana ~ paynunci puurtigaa ceripi-weesukoowaali** from tomorrow we must totally obliterate this idea from our minds.

మనోభావం **manoobhaawam** *n.* emotional feelings.

మనోరంజక **manooranjaka** *adj.* charming, appealing, attractive.

మనోరంజని **manooranjani** *adj.* stirring, piquant.

మనోవర్తి **manoowarti** *same as* **manuwarti.**

మనోవాక్కాయకర్మలా **manoowaakkaayakarmalaa** *adv.* wholeheartedly, with all o.'s might.

మనోవిజ్ఞానశాస్త్రం **manoowijñaanaśaastram** *n.* (science of) psychology.

మనోవిజ్ఞాన శాస్త్రజ్ఞుడు **manoowijñaanaśaastrajñuDu** *n.* psychologist.

మనోవిశ్లేషణ **manoowiśleeSaNa** *n.* psychoanalysis.

మనోవృత్తి **manoowṛtti** *same as* **manuwarti.**

మనోవైజ్ఞానిక **manoowayjñaanika** *adj.* psychological.

మనోవ్యాధి **manoowyaadhi** *n.* sadness of heart.

మనోస్థైర్యం, మనోధైర్యం **manoosthayryam, manoo-dhayram** *n.* self-confidence.

మనోహర **manoohara** *adj.* charming, fascinating, enchant-ing; (*lit.* heart-stealing).

మన్నన **mannana** *n.* 1 respect, regard. 2 approbation, commendation.

మన్ననచేయు **mannanaceeyu** *v.t.* to treat with respect.

మన్నా **mannaa** *same as* **manaa.**

మన్నించు **manninicu** *v.t.* 1 to forgive, pardon, excuse. 2 to respect, honour. 3 **uttaruwunu ~** to obey an order. 4 **koorikanu ~** to accede to a request.

మన్నిక **mannika** *n.* 1 durability. 2 respect, regard.

మన్నికగల, మన్నికైన **mannikagala, mannikayna** *adj.* long-lasting, durable.

మన్ను **mannu**[1] *n.* earth, soil, mud, dirt.

మన్ను **mannu**[2] *v.i.* to last, endure, remain; **ii baTTa caalaa kaalam mannindi** this cloth has lasted for a long time.

మన్మథబాణం **manmathabaaNam** *n.* 1 Cupid's arrow. 2 name of a flowering plant.

మన్మథ భాష **manmathabhaaSa** *n.* 1 *lit.* Cupid's lan-guage. 2 foul language.

మన్మథావస్థ **manmathaawastha** *n. slang* state of being head over heels in love.

మన్మథుడు **manmathuDu** *n.* Manmatha, Cupid.

మన్యం, మన్నెం **manyam, mannem** *n.* 1 mountainous country. 2 Agency tracts of Andhra Pradesh.

మన్వంతరం **manwantaram** *n.* period of one Manu's rule, amounting according to legend to 4,320,000 years.

మప్పితం **mappitam** *adj.* well trained, well behaved.

మప్పు **mappu** *v.t.* 1 to teach, train, habituate. 2 to break in an animal, e.g., to train a bullock or horse to draw a cart, obey a rider, etc.; *cf.* **marapu**[2].

మఫసిల్ **maphasil** *n.* mafassil, up-country area.

మబ్బు **mabbu** *n.* 1 cloud; **~ tunakalu** flecks of cloud; **~ ekkindi / paTTindi / weesindi** clouds have gathered; **~ kammukoni waana wastunnadi** the sky is becoming over-cast and rain is approaching. 2 darkness, dimness, dull-ness; **~ rangu** dark tint (in colour); **kanu ~** dimness of sight; **nidra ~** drowsiness. 3 (*also* **~ weeLa**) *dial.* early dawn, morning twilight; **~ la leeciNDu** he got up very early in the morning.

మభ్యపరచు **mabhyaparacu** *v.t.* to cover up, conceal with a view to deceive.

మమకారం **mamakaaram** *n.* fondness, affection, attach-ment; **waaDaNTee naaku ~** I am very attached to him.

మమత **mamata** *n.* love, attachment, affection.

మమేకంగా **mameekangaa** *adv.* at one with; **udyoogulu janamtoo ~ uNDaali** officials must be at one with the people.

మయ **maya** *second part of an adjvl. compound meaning* full of, consisting of, composed of, immersed in, e.g., **dayaa ~** full of graciousness; **aananda ~** joyful; **aśaanti ~** unpeaceful, disturbed; **jala ~** full of water, watery, sub-merged in water; **andhakaara ~** enveloped in darkness.

మయం **mayam** *n. colloq.* middle, centre (= **madhyam**).

మయం అవు **mayam awu** *v.i.* to be full of; **uppenawalla manci niiLLa baawulannii uppuniiLLa mayam ayyEEyi** all the drinking water wells were filled with salt water as a result of the tidal wave.

మయసభ **mayasabha** *n.* palace of wonders (*lit.* palace constructed by Maya described in the Mahabharata).

మయాన **mayaana** *adv. colloq.* in the middle (= **madhya-loo**).

మయూరం, మయూరి **mayuuram, mayuuri** *n.* pea-cock.

మర **mara** *n.* 1 screw. 2 mill; **piNDi ~** flour mill, **biyyam ~** rice mill.

మరందం **marandam** *same as* **makarandam.**

మరక **maraka** *n.* stain, spot, mark, smudge, blotch.

మరకం **marakam** *n. dial.* a grain measure now obsolete equivalent to four or five seers.

మరకతం **marakatam** *n.* emerald.

మరగబెట్టు **maragabeTTu** *v.t.* to boil.

మరగు **maragu** *v.i. and t.* 1 to have a liking or fondness for. 2 to have a taste for, be addicted to, be keen on, go in for; **sukham ~** to be fond of living at ease, take life easy; **pillalloo caduwukonee waaLLu aaTalu maragaranii, aa-**

Talu marigina waaLLu cadawaranii aawiDaki gaTTi nammakam it was her firm belief that children who studied were not keen on games, while those who were keen on games did not study; *see* **ruci~**.

మరగొట్టం **maragoTTam** *n.* Archimedes' screw, water lifting device using a rotating spiral inside an inclined cylinder.

మరచు **maracu** *v.t.* to forget; *see* **oLLu** *sense 3.*

మరచెంబు **maracembu** *n.* small round metal waterpot with a screw top.

మరచేప **maraceepa** *n.* kind of shark.

మరణం **maraNam** *n.* death.

మరణశాసనం **maraNaśaasanam** *n legal* will.

మరణానంతర **maraNaanantara** *adj.* posthumous.

మరణించు **maraNincu** *v.i.* to die.

మరతకం **maratakam** *variant form of* **marakatam.**

మరతుపాకి **maratupaaki** *n.* **1** rifle. **2** machine gun.

మరదలు **maradalu** *n.* **1** woman's younger brother's wife, woman's father's sister's daughter or mother's brother's daughter if younger than herself. **2** man's younger brother's wife, man's wife's younger sister, man's father's sister's daughter or mother's brother's daughter if younger than himself. **3** *colloq.* for an unmarried man, any woman whom he is eligible to marry may be called~.

మరది **maradi** *same as* **maridi.**

మరపట్టించు, మరపోయించు **marapaTTincu, marapooyincu** *v.t.* to mill (grain).

మరపించు **marapincu** *same as* **maripincu.**

మరపు, మరుపు **marapu[1], marupu[1]** *n.* forgetfulness.

మరపు, మరుపు **marapu[2], marupu[2]** *v.t.* **1** to habituate, accustom; **biccagaaDiki roojuu maa iNTLoo biccam maripi iwEELa leedu pommaNTee waaDu tiTTi pooyEEDu** having accustomed a beggar to receiving alms at our house every day, when we told him there was nothing for him today, he went away abusing us. **2** to train or break in animal; **edduku kaaDi~** to train a bullock to become accustomed to a yoke; *cf.* **mappu.**

మరపురాని **marapuraani** *adj.* unforgettable.

మరఫిరంగి **maraphirangi** *n.* machine gun.

మరమగ్గం **maramaggam** *n.* power loom.

మరమనిషి **maramaniSi** *n.* puppet, robot.

మరమరాలు **maramaraalu** *n.pl.* puffed rice (= **borugulu**).

మరమేకు **marameeku** *n.* screw used in carpentry, etc.

మరమ్మతు **marammatu** *n.* repairs.

మరమ్మతు చేయు **marammatu ceeyu** *v.t.* to repair.

మరల **marala** *alt. variant form of* **maLLii.**

మరలించు, మరల్చు, మళ్లించు, మగిడించు **maralincu, maralcu, maLLincu, magiDincu** *v.t.* **1** to turn back, cause to return. **2** to turn to one side, divert, turn away.

మరలు, మళ్ళు **maralu, maLLu[1]** *v.i.* to turn; **wenu~** to turn back, return, go back; **pakkaku~** to turn aside, change direction, be diverted.

మరల్పు **maralpu** *v.t.* to divert, turn away.

మరవ **marawa** *n.* small pot used for water.

మరాటీ, మరాఠీ **maraaT[h]ii** *n.* the Marathi language.

మరాళం **maraaLam** *n. class.* swan.

మరి **mari** I. *adj. and adv. often prefixed to a numeral or det. adj.* other, more, again; **maroka maaTu** another time *or* one more time; **~reNDu pustakaalu** two more books; **marinta** some more (quantity); **marinni** some more (number); **mareemi?** what else? **marewaru?** who else? **marewaroo** s.o. else; **mareppuDu?** at what other time? **naadaggira~Dabbu leedannaanu** I said I had no more money with me; **~ikkaDiki raaDu** he will not come here again. II. *clitic* **1** but, then, now, well, really; **~naaku selawu ippincaNDi** now let me take leave of you; **adi saahasamee~!** well, that is courage indeed! **miiku eTLaa ceppaaloo teliyaDam leedu~** I really do not know how to tell you. **2 paapam~** *signals a negative reply to a question,* e.g., **"bassuloo waccEEraa?" "paapam~ bassuleedu, naDici waccEEnu"** "did you come by bus?" "no indeed, there was no bus, I came walking".

మరింక **marinka** *adv.* **1** and so, therefore. **2** moreover, besides. **3** again. **4** *in neg. constr.* any more, any longer, any further.

మరింత **marinta** *adj.* more, some more, even more (quantity).

మరిడి **mariDi** *n.* village goddess reputed to bring various infectious diseases.

మరిడిజాడ్యం **mariDijaaDyam** *n. colloq.* infectious disease.

మరిది, మరది **maridi, maradi** *n.* woman's husband's younger brother, woman's younger sister's husband, woman's father's sister's son or mother's brother's son if younger than herself.

మరిపించు, మరపించు **maripincu, marapincu** *v.t.* to make (s.o.) forget.

మరియాద **mariyaada** *same as* **maryaada.**

మరియు **mariyu** *conjunction class.* and.

మరీ **marii** *adj. and adv.* too [much], very [much], even [more], still [more], yet again; **aa naDawaDika ~ hiinam anipincindi** that conduct seemed too mean; **puurwam pallepaTTulannii sarayna doowalu leeka caalaa awastha paDeewaaru, warSaakaalam~nu** formerly every small village used to suffer much from want of proper roads, even more so in the wet weather; **waaDiki~tondara** he is in a great hurry; **sabhaku rammani~ ~ceppEEDu** he was insistent that I should come to the meeting.

మరీచి **mariici** *n.* ray of light.

మరీచిక **mariicika** *n.* mirage.

మరు **maru** *adjvl. prefix meaning* next, immediately following; **~naaDu** next day; **~nimiSamloo** in the next moment.

మరుకేళి **marukeeLi** *n.* amorous game.

మరుగు **marugu[1]** I. *n.* concealment, cover; *cf.* **kanu~.** II. *adj.* hidden, concealed. III. *v.i. class.* to be hidden, be concealed.

మరుగు **marugu[2]** *v.i.* **1** to boil. **2** *class.* to grieve.

మరుగుజ్జు **marugujju** *n.* dwarf, pygmy.

మరుగుదొడ్డి **marugudoDDi** *n.* latrine.

మరుగున **maruguna** *adv.* in hiding, hidden by, concealed by; **ciikaTi~** under cover of darkness.

మరుగు[న]పడు **marugu[na]paDu** *v.i.* 1 to be hidden. 2 to vanish, disappear, be obscured, be obliterated.

మరుగుపరచు, మరుగునపెట్టు **maruguparacu, marugunapeTTu** *v.t.* to hide, conceal, obscure, obliterate.

మరుచటి **marucaTi** *same as* **marusaTi.**

మరుడు **maruDu** *n.* epithet of Manmatha or Cupid.

మరునాడు, మర్నాడు **marunaaDu, marnaaDu** *adv.* next day.

మరపు **marupu**[1],[2] *same as* **marapu**[1],[2].

మరుభూమి **marubhuumi** *n.* 1 barren land. 2 burial ground.

మరులు **marulu** *n.* 1 love, passion, lust. 2 seduction.

మరులుకొను **marulukonu** *v.i.* to fall in love.

మరులుకొల్పు **marulukolpu** *v.t* 1 to enamour, charm, captivate. 2 to seduce.

మరులుమందు **marulumandu** *n.* love potion.

మరవం **maruwam** *n.* sweet marjoram.

మరుసంధ్య **marusandhya** *n.* evening twilight.

మరుసటి, మరుచటి **marusaTi, marucaTi** *adj.* next (in time); ~ **rooju** next day.

మరే **maree** *clitic* 1 *serving to draw attention to a remark that will follow* ~ **ippuDu TEEksii wastundi** here is a taxi coming; ~ **neenu sTeeSanuku weLtaanu, nuwwu bajaaruku weLLu** look, I will go to the station, you go to the bazaar. 2 yes; "**wastaaraa**?" "~, **wastaanu**" "will you come?" "yes, I will come".

మరొక, మరో **maroka, maroo** *adj.* one more, another.

మరొకప్పుడు **marokappuDu** *adv.* at another time.

మరొకలాగా, మరోలా **marokalaagaa, maroolaa** *adv.* in another way, differently; ~ **anukonu** to take amiss; **neenu ilaa ceppinanduku** ~ **anukookaNDi** please do not take it amiss that I have spoken like this.

మరొచ్చిగంటే, మరేవచ్చి, మళ్లావచ్చి **marocciga-NTee, mareewacci, maLLaawacci** *a throwaway phrase used by s.o. who forgets what he was meaning to say next,* e.g., **araTipaLLu, aakulu, wakkalu,** ~ **nuwwu ceppinawannii teccEEnu** plantains, betel, arecanuts, let me see what else?—I have brought everything you said (*the three forms are current in different dialects*).

మర్కటం **markaTam** *n.* monkey.

మర్జీ **marjii** *n. dial.* 1 pleasure, inclination. 2 temper, disposition.

మర్త్య **martya** *adj. class.* mortal.

మర్త్యుడు **martyuDu** *n. class.* man, mortal.

మర్దన[ం] **mardana[m]** *n.* rubbing, pounding, beating, grinding; **nuune**~ oil massage.

మర్దనచేయు **mardanaceeyu** *v.t.* to massage.

మర్దించు **mardincu** *v.t.* 1 to rub, pound, grind. 2 to massage.

మర్నాడు **marnaaDu** *same as* **marunaaDu.**

మర్మం **marmam** *n.* 1 secrecy, mystery. 2 secret; ~ **wiDici ceppu** to let out a secret. 3 hidden meaning.

మర్మస్థానం, మర్మస్థలం **marmasthaanam, marmasthalam** *n.* vital point in the body.

మర్మాఘాతం **marmaaghaatam** *n.* hidden blow.

మర్యాద, మరియాద **maryaada, mariyaada** *n.* 1 respect [fulness]. 2 respectability, dignity. 3 politeness, courtesy, good behaviour. 4 *pl.* ~**lu** manners, conventions. 5 hospitable nature.

మర్యాదకు **maryaadaku** *adv.* out of politeness, for politeness' sake.

మర్యాదగల **maryaadagala** *adj.* polite, courteous, respectful.

మర్యాదగా **maryaadagaa** *adv.* 1 respectfully. 2 politely, courteously. 3 respectably, in a dignified manner. 4 hospitably.

మర్యాదచేయు **maryaadaceeyu** *v.t.* to treat (s.o.) respectfully.

మర్యాదరామన్న **maryaadaraamanna** *n.* 1 honourable and upright person. 2 very hospitable person.

మర్యాదస్థుడు **maryaadasthuDu** *n.* respectable person.

మర్రి **marri** *n.* banyan tree, *ficus indica.*

మల **mala** *n. class.* mountain, hill; *mod. only as second part of a n. compound,* e.g., **tiru**~ Tirumala (name of the hill at Tirupati).

మలం **malam** *n.* faeces, excrement, dung, filth.

మలకపుట్టి **malakapuTTi** *n.* obsolete measure of grain equal to 960 seers.

మలచు **malacu** *v.t.* 1 to turn. 2 to mould, fashion; **maT-Tiloonunci maaNikyaanni**~ to fashion a pearl out of clay; **paristhitulanu**~ to mould circumstances; **aadarśaalanu**~ to give shape to ideals. 3 to formulate, adapt; **widhaanaalanu**~ to formulate policies. 4 to carve, chip, inscribe (wood, stone). 5 **biyyam**~ to separate rice from sand, pebbles, etc., by winnowing, washing or shaking in a tray.

మలబద్ధకం **malabaddhakam** *n.* constipation.

మలమలమాడు **malamalamaaDu** *v.i.* 1 to burn fiercely. 2 to be consumed by fire, hunger or jealousy; **iirSyatoo**~ to be consumed by jealousy.

మలమూత్రాలు **malamuutraalu** *n.pl.* dung and urine, filth.

మలయపర్వతం **malaya parwatam** *n.* traditional name of the part of the western Ghats lying in Kerala state.

మలయమారుతం, మలయపవనం, మలయానిలం **malaya maarutam, malayapawanam, malayaanilam** *n.* cool breeze from the mountains.

మలయాళం **malayaaLam** *n.* the Malayalam language.

మలాం, మలామా **malaam[aa]** *n.* 1 plating; **weNDi**~ silver plating; **bangaaru**~ gold plating, gilding. 2 ointment, balm.

మలాం చేయు **malaam ceeyu** *v.t.* to plate (with gold, silver, etc.)

మలాం పట్టి **malaam paTTi** *n.* plaster for dressing a boil or wound.

మలారం **malaaram** *n.* bunch of glass bangles tied together by a string.

మలి, మలు **mali, malu** *adj.* 1 next; ~ **majilii** next camp. 2 second; ~ **cuulu** second pregnancy.

మలిన **malina** *adj.* 1 dirty, foul. 2 black.

మలినం **malinam** *n.* dirt, filth. 2 foulness.

మలిసంధ్య **malisandhya** *n.* evening twilight.

మలుగు **malugu n.** small of the back.

మలుపు **malupu** I. *n.* turn, turning [point]: **rooDDu** ~ corner, bend or curve in a road. II. *v.t.* 1 to turn, divert. 2 to put out, extinguish.

మలోమలికితం **maloomalikitam** *n.* dirt, dust.

మల్లయుద్ధం **mallayuddham** *n.* wrestling.

మల్లవీరుడు **mallawiiruDu** *n.* wrestling champion.

మల్లాగుల్లాలుపడు **mallaagullaalu paDu** *same as* **gunjaaTanapaDu.**

మల్లి **malli** *n.* woman who carries tales.

మల్లిగాడు **malligaaDu** *n.* mean fellow.

మల్లు **mallu** *n.* 1 wrestler. 2 wrestling.

మల్లుడు **malluDu** *n.* wrestler.

మల్లె, మల్లిక **malle**[1], **mallika** *n.* jasmine; ~ **puwwu** jasmine flower; ~ **tiige** jasmine creeper.

మల్లె, మల్లే **malle**[2], **mallee** *adv. and p.p.* like; **waaLLu kuuDaa manaku ~ mEESTarlee** they too are teachers like us.

మల్ర **malra** *dial. alt. form of* **marala.**

మళిగ **maLiga** *n.* 1 godown, warehouse, wholesale shop. 2 *dial.* shop.

మళ్ళావచ్చి **maLLaawacci** *same as* **mareewacci.**

మళ్ళించు **maLLincu** *same as* **maralincu.**

మళ్ళింపు **maLLimpu** *n.* diversion; **kṛSNaa nadiijalaala** ~ diversion of Krishna river waters.

మళ్ళీ, మళ్ళా **maLLii, maLLaa** *advbl. particle* 1 again. 2 but still, and yet, however; **tanaku raamaayaNam aNTee nijam katha ani nammakam leedanii; ~ bhaarataanni wiśwasistaananii ceppEEru** he said he did not believe that the Ramayana was a true story, but still he believed in the Mahabharata; **nannu tiTTEEDu, ~ neenaNTee aayanaki preema leedani kaadu** he scolded me but that is not to say that he had no love towards me.

మళ్ళు **maLLu**[1] *v.i. same as* **maralu.**

మళ్ళు **maLLu**[2] *pl.* of **maDi**[1,2].

మళ్ళూమాన్యాలూ **maLLuu maanyaaluu** *same as* **maDimaanyaalu.**

మళ్ళేసుకొను **maLLeesukonu** *v.t.* to turn back, drive back; **goDLanu maLLeesuku wastaanu** I will go and drive the cattle back.

మశకం **maśakam** *n. class.* mosquito, gnat.

మశానం **maśaanam** *alt. form of* **smaśaanam.**

మశూచి[కం] **maśuuci[kam]** *n.* smallpox.

మషాలు **maSaalu** *n. class.* torch.

మషాల్జీ, మషాల్తీ **maSaaljii, maSaaltii** *n.* lamp-lighter, torch bearer.

మషి **maSi** *n. dial.* ink.

మస[కం] **masa[kam]** *n.* lust; **waaDi kaLLu ~ weesEEyi** his eyes were filled with lust.

మసక **masaka**[1] I. *n.* dimness, obscurity, sombreness, slight darkness. II. *adj.* dim, obscure, sombre.

మసక **masaka**[2] (*also* ~ **neela**) *n.* mixed type of soil containing red earth and loam; *cf.* **masara.**

మసక చీకటి **masaka ciikaTi** *n.* semi-darkness.

మసకబారు, మసక[లు] కమ్ము **masakabaaru, masaka[lu]kammu** *v.i.* to grow dim, be obscured.

మసటు, మసడు, మస్టు, మష్టు **masaTu, masaDu, masTu, maSTu** *n.* dirt, sediment, dross.

మసర **masara** I. *n.* (*also* ~ **neela**) *same as* **masaka**[2]. II. *adj.* (of colours) mixed, variegated.

మసలు **masalu**[1] *v.i.* 1 to move about, go about; **iNTLoo caalaamandi ~ tunnaaru** many people are moving about inside the house. 2 to mix, consort (**-too**, with). 3 to be alive, exist, live. 4 to linger, be slow, be sluggish.

మసలు, మసులు **masalu**[2], **masulu** *v.i.* to boil violently.

మసలుకొను **masalukonu** *v.i.* to behave; **jaagrattagaa masalukoowaali nuwwu** you must behave cautiously.

మసాలా **masaalaa** *n.* a mixture of spices including cinnamon.

మసాల్చి **masaalci** *n.* servant in an office.

మసి **masi** I. *n.* 1 soot. 2 blackness, black stain; ~ **puusi maareeDukaaya ceeyu** to hoodwink people by making s.g useless appear to be good and desirable (*lit.* to apply soot so as to make s.g look like **maareeDukaaya**, a black fruit). II. *adj.* 1 sooty. 2 black.

మసిపాత, మసిగుడ్డ, మసిబట్ట **masipaata, masiguDDa, masibaTTa** *n.* 1 piece of old cloth tied above a heap of harvested produce to avert the evil eye. 2 kitchen towel. 3 *pl.* ~ **lu** dirty clothes.

మసిబారు **masibaaru** *v.i.* to be covered with soot, be blackened; **masibaarina addam** smoked glass.

మసీదు **masiidu** *n.* mosque.

మసూచి[కం] **masuuci[kam]** *alt. variant form of* **maśuuci-[kam].**

మసూరి **masuuri** *n.* name of a superior variety of paddy.

మసృణ **masṛNa** *adj. class.* glossy, smooth, soft, mild.

మస్కా **maskaa** *n.* (< Hindi **maśkaa**) butter.

మస్కాకొట్టు **maskaakoTTu** *v.i. colloq.* 1 to flatter. 2 to cheat, hoax.

మస్త[క]ం **masta[ka]m** *n. class.* head, skull.

మస్తిష్కం **mastiSkam** *n. class.* brain.

మస్తు **mastu** *n.* 1 plenty, abundance. 2 pride. 3 fat. 4 intoxication; ~ **miida unnaaDu** he is intoxicated.

మస్తుగా **mastugaa** *adv.* plentifully, abundantly, in abundance.

మహ **maha** *see* **mahaa.**

మహం **maham** *n. class.* 1 religious rite. 2 religious festival.

మహంతు **mahantu** *n.* 1 head of a body of religious mendicants. 2 title of the head priest in certain temples.

మహజరు **mahajaru** *n.* petition or memorial signed by many people.

మహత్ **mahat** *Sanskrit adjvl. prefix meaning* great, e.g., **~ kaaryam** great deed.

మహతి **mahati** *n. class.* Narada's legendary hundred-stringed vina.

మహతీవాచకం **mahatiiwaacakam** *n. gram.* feminine noun.

మహత్తమం **mahattamam** *n. maths.* maximum.

మహత్తర **mahattara** *adj.* **1** greater, major. **2** great. **3** excellent, fine.

మహత్తు **mahattu** *n.* **1** greatness. **2** *gram.* masculine noun.

మహనాడు **mahanaaDu** *n.* meeting held by members of different communities to decide matters of common interest.

మహనీయ **mahaniiya** *adj.* **1** sacred, holy. **2** excellent, superb.

మహనీయుడు **mahaniiyuDu** *n.* great person, venerable person.

మహన్మహతీ వాచకం **mahanmahatii waacakam** *n. gram.* a n. that is both masculine and feminine, e.g., a pl. n. like **pawrulu** citizens (male and female) *or* **waaru** they (women and men).

మహమ్మారి, మహామారి **mahammaari, mahaamaari** *n.* smallpox.

మహర్నవమి **maharnawami** *same as* **mahaanawami.**

మహర్నాటకం **maharnaaTakam** *n.* grand drama.

మహర్షి **maharSi** *n.* great rishi or saint.

మహల్, మహాల్ **maha[a]l** *n.* house, mansion.

మహలావు, మాలావు **mahalaawu, maalaawu** *adv. colloq., used in a sarcastic or derogatory sense* very much, very greatly.

మహసూలు, మాసూలు **mahasuulu, maasuulu** *n.* **1** produce, crop. **2** tax, revenue.

మహస్సు **mahassu** *n. class.* light, lustre.

మహా, మహ, మా **mahaa, maha, maa** I. *adj.* (*note: the form* **maa** *is not used before a n. of Sanskrit origin*) very, great, much; **~ baagundi** it is very good; **aa maha[a] samstha caritraloo** in the history of that great organisation. II. *particle* **1** at the most; **aameki ~ uNTee oo paatikeeLLu uNTaayeemoo** at the most she may be about twenty-five years old; **akkaDinunci sTeeSanu duuram uNTundi annaaDu, ~ enta duuram uNTundilee ani naDaka modalu peTTEEnu** he said the station was far from there. thinking, "how far will it be at the most?" I started to walk; **mookaallootu marinka ~ entekkuwa uNTundilee ani mari koncem dhayryam ceesEEDu** thinking, "how much deeper than knee-deep will it be at the most?" he plucked up a little more courage. **2** *idiomatic usage* (*the form* **maa** *is not used in this sense*): **iraway mayLLu naDawagalanannaaDu, maha[a] naDiceewaaDi laagaa** "I can walk twenty miles" he said, as if he was a great walker; **monna ii maaTa cebitee naalugu ruupaayalu peTTikaawalasinanni bommalu tecci paDeesee waaNNi annaanu, maha[a] teccipaDeeseewaaDilaagaa** "if you had told me this the other day, I would have spent a few rupees and brought as many toys as were needed" I said, as if I was s.o. who could easily afford to bring them.

మహాకాయుడు **mahaakaayuDu** *n* person of gigantic stature.

మహాకాళి **mahaakaaLi** *n.* Goddess Kali, the fiercest incarnation of Parvati.

మహాకావ్యం **mahaakaawyam** *n.* great poetic work.

మహాజనులు **mahaajanulu** *n.pl.* respectable people.

మహాత్యం, మహాత్మ్యం **mahaatyam, mahaatmyam** *same as* **maahaatmyam.**

మహాద్భుతం **mahaadbhutam** *n.* miracle.

మహాద్వారం **mahaadwaaram** *n.* portal.

మహాధమని **mahaadhamani** *n. med.* aorta.

మహానవమి, మహార్నవమి **mahaanawami, maharnawami** *n.* second day of the Dasara festival.

మహానసం **mahaanasam** *n. class.* kitchen.

మహానీయుడు **mahaaniiyuDu** *n.* person worthy of honour and respect.

మహానుభావుడు **mahaanubhaawuDu** *n.* great person, great soul.

మహాపాతకం **mahaapaatakam** *n.* heinous sin.

మహాపురుషుడు **mahaapuruSuDu** *n.* **1** great hero. **2** the Supreme Spirit.

మహాప్రభూ! **mahaaprabhuu!** *interj.* my lord!

మహాప్రళయం **mahaapraLayam** *n.* **1** total destruction of the universe at the end of a kalpa or mythological age. **2** any severe and destructive natural calamity.

మహాప్రసాదం **mahaaprasaadam** *n.* great favour.

మహాప్రస్థానం **mahaaprasthaanam** *n.* journey leading to enlightenment.

మహాప్రాణం **mahaapraaNam** *n. ling.* aspirate sound.

మహాబలి **mahaabali** *see* **poli.**

మహాబలుడు **mahaabaluDu** *n.* powerful or mighty man.

మహాబోధి **mahaaboodhi** *n.* the bodhi or pipal tree under which Buddha attained enlightenment.

మహాభారతం **mahaabhaaratam** *n.* the great Sanskrit epic known as the Mahabharata.

మహామహానాడు **mahaamahaanaaDu** *adv.* never at any time in the past, present or future.

మహామహుడు **mahaamahuDu** *n.* very great person.

మహామారి **mahaamaari** *same as* **mahammaari.**

మహాయుగం **mahaayugam** *n.* **1** age, era, period of history. **2** *in mythology* a Great Yuga comprising the **krita, treeta, dwaapara** and **kali** yugas and amounting to 4,320,000 years.

మహారాజశ్రీ **mahaarajaśrii** *obs. title equivalent to* Mr.: *the modern form is* **śrii.**

మహారాజు **mahaaraaju** *n.* **1** maharaja, king, sovereign. **2** *colloq.* nobleman, great person (often used sarcastically).

మహారాజుగా **mahaaraajugaa** *adv. colloq.* easily, comfortably; **padi ruupaayalatoo ~ reNDu puuTalu bhoojanam ceeyawaccu** for ten rupees you can easily get two meals per day. **2** certainly, by all means; **"mii iNTiki padi gaNTalaku raawaccaa?" "~ raawaccu"** "may I come to your house at ten o'clock?" "certainly you may come" *or* "you are welcome to come".

మహారాజ్ఞి **mahaaraajñi** *n.* empress.

మహారాష్ట్రం **mahaaraaSTram** *n.* State of Maharashtra.

మహార్ణవం **mahaarNawam** *n. class.* ocean.

మహాల్ **mahaal** *same as* **mahal.**

మహాలయ అమావాస్య **mahaalaya amaawaasya** *n.* name of the fortnight of the waning moon in the month of Bhadrapada.

మహావీరుడు **mahaawiiruDu** *n.* 1 great hero. 2 Mahavir, name of the founder of the Jain religion.

మహాశయులారా! **mahaaśayulaaraa!** *formal term used in addressing an audience* ladies and gentlemen!

మహాశయులు **mahaaśayulu** *n.pl. formal* great persons.

మహాసభ **mahaasabha** *n.* conference, esp. a conference organized on a large scale.

మహాసముద్రం **mahaasamudram** *n.* 1 ocean. 2 *fig.* sea of troubles; **~loo unnaanu** *or* **naDisamudramloo unnaanu** I am in the midst of a sea of troubles.

మహి **mahi** *n.* the earth, the world.

మహిత **mahita** *adj.* 1 great. 2 revered.

మహితాత్ముడు **mahitaatmuDu** *n.* great soul.

మహిమ **mahima** *n.* 1 power of working wonders or miracles: **mantra ~ walla paamu kaaTu nayam ayindi** due to the magical effect of a charm the snakebite was cured; **aa yoogiki ~lu unnaayi** that yogi possesses supernatural powers; **caawu tappi maLLii ii lookamloo paDDaawaNTee nii peLLaam ~ walla** it is by the grace of your wife that you have escaped death and come back to this world (from a coma). 2 greatness, glory.

మహిమాన్విత **mahimaanwita** *adj.* imbued with glory.

మహిమాన్వితుడు **mahimaanwituDu** *n.* person who possesses supernatural or mystical or magical powers.

మహిళ **mahiLa** *n.* lady, woman.

మహిళామండలి **mahiLaamaNDali** *n.* women's association.

మహిషం **mahiSam** *n. class.* he-buffalo.

మహిషి **mahiSi** *n. class.* 1 queen; **paTTa~** crowned queen. 2 she-buffalo.

మహీతలం **mahiitalam** *n. class.* the earth, the world.

మహీధరం **mahiidharam** *n. class.* mountain.

మహీరుహం **mahiiruham** *n. class.* tree.

మహేశ్వరుడు **maheeśwaruDu** *n.* God Siva.

మహోచ్చ **mahoocca** *adj.* highest.

మహోజ్జ్వల **mahoojjwala** *adj.* bright, shining, gleaming.

మహోత్కృష్ట **mahootkṛSTa** *adj.* excellent, outstanding.

మహోత్తమ **mahoottama** *adj.* excellent, splendid.

మహోత్తుంగ **mahoottunga** *adj.* very great.

మహోత్సవం **mahootsawam** *n.* feast, festival.

మహోదయం **mahoodayam** *n.* eminence.

మహోద్యమం **mahoodyamam** *n.* great effort.

మహోన్నత **mahoonnata** *adj.* very high, highest.

మహోన్నతి **mahoonnati** *n.* high position.

మహోపాధ్యాయుడు **mahoopaadhyaayuDu** *n.* 1 great teacher. 2 an academic title.

మహౌషధం **mahawSadham** *n.* sovereign medicine, panacea, an epithet applied to **śoNThi** (dried ginger).

మా - maa

మా **maa**[1] *pronom. adj.* **1** our (*excluding the person[s] addressed*) **2 maa** *is used for* **naa** (i) *in speaking of s.g which is or can be shared with others*, e.g., **maa tammuDu** my younger brother; **maa illu** my house; (ii) *in the expressions* **maa waaru** my husband *and* **maa aawiDa** my wife.

మా **maa**[2] *colloq. alt. form of* **maha[a]** (*adj.*) occurring before Telugu words; **maa baagaa ceppEEwu**! well said!

మాంగల్యం **maangalyam** *n.* **1** auspiciousness. **2** tali, woman's marriage token; *see* **taaLi.**

మాంజా **maanjaa** *n. dial.* kite thread coated with powdered glass.

మాండలిక **maaNDalika** *adj.* dialectal.

మాండలికం **maaNDalikam** *n.* dialect.

మాంత్రికుడు **maantrikuDu** *n.* wizard, sorcerer, magician.

మాంద్యం **maandyam** *n.* dullness, sluggishness, torpor, apathy; **aarthiká~** economic depression, economic stagnation.

మాంసం **maamsam** *n.* meat, flesh.

మాంసకృత్తులు **maamsakrttulu** *n. pl.* proteins.

మాంసల **maamsala** *adj.* **1** stout, fat, fleshy; **~phalam** fleshy fruit. **2** strong, lusty.

మాంసాహార **maamsaahaara** *adj.* non-vegetarian, meat eating.

మాకు, మ్రాకు **m[r]aaku** *n. class.* tree.

మాక్షికం **maakSikam** *n. class.* honey.

మాగధుడు **maagadhuDu** *n.* bard employed to sing in praise of a king, panegyrist (= **wandi~**).

మాగపెట్టు **maagapeTTu** *v.t.* to ripen.

మాగన్ను, మ్రాగన్ను **m[r]aagannu** *n.* half open eyes, half shut eyes; **naaku ~gaa nidra paTTindi** I was half asleep.

మాగాణం **maagaaNam** *n. literary form of* **maagaaNi; telugu saahitya~loo** in the fertile field of Telugu literature.

మాగాణి **maagaaNi** *n.* irrigated land, wet land.

మాగాయ **maagaaya** *n.* **1** unripe mango fruit. **2** mango pickle made from mango slices dried in the sun and mixed with fenugreek (**mentulu**).

మాగు **maagu** *same as* **makku**[2].

మాగుడు **maaguDu** *n.* **1** blackness. **2** dirtiness.

మాగుడుకాలం **maaguDukaalam** *n.* murky weather.

మాఘం **maagham** *n.* Magha, the eleventh Telugu lunar month (January-February).

మాఘభోజనం **maagha bhoojanam** *n.* meal eaten in a garden as part of a religious ceremony in the month of Magha.

మాచకమ్మ **maacakamma** *n.* woman of mannish appearance.

మాచికాయ **maacikaaya** *n.* gallnut.

మాచిపత్రి **maacipatri** *n. artemisia indica*, a bush used in the wo ship of Ganesha.

మాజీ **maajii** *adj.* former, late, ex-.

మాట **maaTa** *n.* **1** word; **naa~winu** *lit.* listen to my word, i.e., listen to what I say *or* follow my advice; **naa~tiiseeyaku** do not disregard what I say; **enta~**! what a thing to say! *or* good heavens! (exclamation expressing surprise); **aayana~pay~** *or* **aayana~ku eduruleedu** his is the deciding word; **~lu kooTalu daaTutaayi, manuSulu gummam daaTaru** their words overcome forts (*lit.* their words cross over forts) but they themselves do not cross their own thresholds — proverb applied to those who are braver in word than in deed; **~la poogu** talkative person. **2** mention; **uttaramloo peLLi ~ekkaDaa leedu** there is no mention of marriage anywhere in the letter. **3** promise; **~nilabeTTukonu** to stand by o.'s word; **~iccu** to give o.'s word, give o.'s promise; **~tappu** to break o.'s word, break o.'s promise; **nooTi~** oral promise; **~dakkincu** to preserve o.'s word of honour. **4** subject, topic, matter, affair; **selawu~ettindi** she mentioned the topic of leave; **aa~ku wastee** if it comes to that, for that matter, as a matter of fact; **idi weeree~** this is a different matter; **Dabbu~eem ceesEEwu**? what did you do about the money? (*lit.* what did you do in the matter of the money?) **5** fact; **neenu aayanni cuusina~nijamee** the fact that I saw him is true *or* it is fact that I saw him; **neenu weLLina~waaDiki eTLaa telisindi**? how did he know (the fact) that I had gone?; **naaku kaligee naSTam~ aTLaa unci** setting aside the fact of my incurring loss; A: "**kaalu baagaa noppigaa undEE?**" B: "**noppi~saree! kaalu wiragabaDindi, neenu naDawaleenu**" A: "is the leg very painful?" B: "the (fact of the) pain does not matter, but the leg is sprained and I cannot walk" (*note: in this sense* **maaTa** *lit. means* 'word' *or* 'saying', *but* 'fact' *is the appropriate English translation*). **6** idea, thought, intention; **nuwwu cadiwee~leekapootee, diipam aapeeseeyi** if there is no intention of your reading (*or* if you are not intending to read), put out the light; **nuwwu weLLee~uNDee~ ceppu, waNTa cestaanu** tell me whether you are intending to go or stay, then I will start to cook (*note: in these examples ~ lit. means* 'word' *but is translated* 'intention' *to bring out the meaning in English*). **7** blame, rebuke; **~[lu]paDu** to be blamed, be rebuked; **nii muulaana maaku kuuDaa ~wastundi** owing to you we will also incur blame. **8 pay~** *is used with a numeral in the dative to mean* more than, e.g., **kooTiki pay~** more than a crore (ten millions); **wiiTi sankhya nuuTiki pay~kaadaa**? do they not number more than a hundred? **9** *other idiomatic usages*: **manaloo mana~** s.g strictly between ourselves, s.g off the record; **~la sandarbhamloo** in the course of conversation; **maaTalloonee wacceesEEDu** he came just when we were speaking about him; **~ki ~jawaabu ceppu** to answer back, have an altercation; **maaTaamaaTaa anukonnaaru** they had an exchange of words; **maa naannakuu wakiilukii ippuDu~lu leewu** my father and the lawyer are not on speaking terms now; **~lu migulu, ~tuulu** to talk wildly, talk unrestrainedly; **ii gaDDu roojulloo peLLi ceeyaDam aNTee ~laa**? in these hard days it is no easy matter to perform a marriage — *here* **~laa** (*meaning* is it only a matter of words?, i.e., is it an easy matter?) *turns the sentence into a rhetorical question which implies a negative answer*; **~teelcu** *or*

~ **teelciweeyu** (i) to settle or decide a matter; (ii) *see* **teelcu** *sense 5*: ~**lu namileesEEDu** he mumbled his words; **musalaayanaki ~ paDipooyindi** the old man is unable to speak (due to paralytic shock): **ee ~ ku aa maaTee ceppukoowaali** (*advbl.phrase*) to tell the truth, really and truly; **naa ~ keem leNDi, mii sangati cuusukooNDi** do not worry about me, look after yourself; **manci ~ ceppEEwu** you have spoken rightly *or* you have given me good news; **manci ~ ceesukoni weLLu** *see* **manci** *sense II. 2.*

మాటకాడు, మాటకారి **maaTakaaDu, maaTakaari** *n.* good talker, good speaker, eloquent person.

మాటకారితనం **maaTakaaritanam** *n.* eloquence.

మాటవరసకి, మాటసామెతకి **maaTawaarasaki,maaTasaametaki** *adv.* 1 for example, for instance. 2 hypothetically, for the sake of argument.

మాటవరసగా **maaTawarasagaa** *adv.* in the course of conversation, casually.

మాటామంతీ **maaTaamantii** *n.* talk, conversation.

మాటికి **maaTiki** *adv.* every now and then, from time to time.

మాటిమాటికీ **maaTimaaTikii** *adv.* again and again.

మాటు **maaTu**[1] *n.* 1 concealment, hiding. 2 screen, covering. 3 ambush.

మాటు **maaTu**[2] *n.* time, occasion; **ii ~** this time; **oka ~** once.

మాటు **maaTu**[3] *n.* 1 welding, soldering. 2 patch for repairing a metal vessel.

మాటుగా, మాటున **maaTugaa, maaTuna** *adv.* hidden by, screened by, behind.

మాటుమణుగు **maaTumaNugu** *v.i.* to become quiet, quieten down, stay silent, stay mute.

మాటువేయు **maaTuweeyu**[1] *v.i.* to ambush.

మాటువేయు **maaTuweeyu**[2] *v.i.* to weld, solder.

మాట్లాడు **maaTLaaDu** I. *v.i.* to speak, talk; **talallaa ~ taaDu** (of a child) he talks without understanding his own words. II. *v.t.* 1 to engage (vehicle). 2 to arrange, negotiate (marriage alliance).

మాడ **maaDa** *n.* small obsolete coin; **maaDanta mabbu kanipincindi saayantraaniki uuranta waana kurisindi** a tiny cloud appeared and by evening there was a deluge of rain; **srii raama ~** coin considered to be lucky which is kept and worshipped by a family.

మాడి **maaDi** *n. dial.* upper storey of a house.

మాడు **maaDu**[1] *n.* middle of the crown of the head; **nii ~ pagulutundi jaagratta!** take care, otherwise I will break your head!

మాడు **maaDu**[2] I. *n.* food burnt while cooking. II. *v.i.* 1 to be burnt, be scorched; *see* **pramaaNam** *sense 2.* 2 to become black due to scorching; *also fig.*, e.g., **waaDi mokham maaDindi** his face grew black (with anger, jealousy or shame). 3 to starve; **waaLLu annam leeka maaDi castunnaaru** they are starving to death. 4 to be ruined; *see* **aDugumaaDipoowu.**

మాడుమచ్చ **maaDumacca** *n.* scar caused by burning or branding.

మాడ్చు **maaDcu** *v.t.* to burn, scorch; **moham ~ konu** *lit.* to make o.'s face black, *hence* to wear an expression of grief, anger, shame or envy; **poTTa ~ konu** *lit.* to starve o.'s stomach, *hence* to tighten o.'s belt, live very frugally.

మాణిక్యం **maaNikyam** *n.* 1 ruby. 2 jewel.

మాత **maata** *n. class.* mother.

మాతంగ[ం] **maatanga[m]** *n. class.* elephant.

మాతంగి **maatangi** *n.* 1 epithet of Parvati. 2 *colloq.* woman who lets her hair hang loose. 3 woman wine seller.

మాతామహి **maataamahi** *n.class.* maternal grandmother.

మాతామహుడు **maataamahuDu** *n. class.* maternal grandfather.

మాతృ **maatṛ** *Sanskrit adjvl. prefix* maternal, mother-; ~ **bhuumi** motherland.

మాతృక **maatṛka** *n.* source, origin, original (of a written copy). 2 (*also* **maatrika**) *maths.* matrix.

మాతృత్వం **maatṛtwam** *n.* motherhood.

మాతృభాష **maatṛbhaaSa** *n.* mother tongue.

మాతృస్వామిక **maatṛswaamika** *adj.* matriarchal.

మాతృస్వామ్యం **maatṛswaamyam** *n.* matriarchy.

మాత్ర **maatra** *n.* pill, tablet.

మాత్రం **maatram** I. *n.* 1 measure, amount, quantity; **waaDi ~ neenuu caduwukonnaanu** I have studied as much as he has; **aNu ~ anumaanam leedu** there is not the least suspicion (*lit.* there is not an atom quantity of suspicion). 2 *when ~ follows a demonstrative or det. adj. it has a limiting force equivalent to* only, even, at least, e.g., **aa ~ niiku teliyaduu**? don't you know that much at least? *see* **enta ~, ee ~**. II. *advbl. particle, never as first word in a sentence* 1 only, alone, merely, simply; **aayanaku ~ cuupincu** show it only to him; **maaTa ~ cepitee Dabbu pampinceewaaNNi** if you had only told me I would have sent money. 2 however, nevertheless, still, yet; **simeNTu phyaakTariila sankhya antagaa peraganapaTikii, waaTi utpatti śakti ~ pencaDam jarigindi** although the number of cement factories did not increase much, nevertheless their productive capacity increased. 3 *~ may emphasise the word that precedes it*, e.g., **"miiru ~ deeśaalannii tirigi raawaali, neenu ~ ikkaDee uNDaali" ani gabagabaa eekaruwu peTTeesindi** "you go to all the countries while I have to remain here" she went on repeating.

మాత్రంగా **maatrangaa** *adv.* at least, even; **maaTa ~ naatoo ceppakuuDaduu**? could you not have said a word to me at least?

మాత్రాన, మాత్రానికి **maatraana, maatraaniki** *see* **antamaatraana, antamaatraaniki.**

మాత్రిక **maatrika** *same as* **maatṛka** *sense 2.*

మాత్రుడు **maatruDu** *second part of a n. compound meaning* mere, plain, ordinary; **maanawa ~** a mere man; *cf.* **anguSTa ~.**

మాత్సర్యం **maatsaryam** *n. class.* envy, malice, jealousy.

మాద **maada** *n.* kind of cattle disease.

మాదక **maadaka** *adj.* intoxicating.

మాదకద్రవ్యం **maadakadrawyam** *n.* intoxicating substance.

మాదాకబళం! **maadaakabaLam!** ((maataa kabaLam) *interj.* alms! (a beggar's cry).

మాదాకబళం అడుగు **maadaakabaLam aDugu** *v.i.* to beg.

మాదాకబళంవాడు *n.* **maadaakabaLam waaDu** *n.* beggar (*lit.* one who cries out **maadaakabaLam!**).

మాదిగ **maadiga** *n.* name of a community of harijans, also called Arundhatiyas, whose hereditary occupations include cobbling and playing music at village ceremonies.

మాదిరి **maadiri** *n.* 1 model, sample, example, specimen. 2 type, pattern, kind, sort; **ii ~ pustakam** this kind of book *or* a book like this; **mii ~ cokkaa naakundi** I have a shirt like yours. 3 **oka ~** *lit.* a kind of; **oka ~ aaTakaaDu** a fairly good player *or* a mediocre player; **oka ~ nalupu rangu** a fairly dark colour; **oka ~ gaa (***or* **adoo ~ gaa) nannu cuusEEDu** he looked at me in an odd way.

మాదీఫలం **maadiiphalam** *n. med. citrus medica,* a kind of lime fruit used in Ayurvedic medicine.

మాదీఫలరసాయనం **maadiiphala rasaayanam** *n.* medicine made from **maadiiphalam** considered to be a panacea.

మాదు **maadu** *n.* boil, ulcer, sore.

మాధవి **maadhawi** *n.* a white flowered climbing plant.

మాధవుడు **maadhawuDu** *n.* 1 God. 2 a name of Vishnu.

మాధుర్యం **maadhuryam** *n.* sweetness.

మాధ్యం, మాధ్యమం **maadhyam[am]** *n.* medium; **boodhanaa ~** medium of instruction.

మాధ్యమిక **maadhyamika** *adj.* middle, central.

మానం **maanam** *n.* 1 measure; *cf.* **kaala ~**, **kola ~**. 2 sense of respect, self-respect, honour, modesty, dignity.

మానచిత్రం **maanacitram** *n.* map.

మానచిత్రలేఖనశాస్త్రం **maanacitra leekhanaśaastram** *n.* cartography.

మానన **maanana** *class. alt. form of* **mannana.**

మాననీయ **maananiiya** *adj.* deserving honour, venerable.

మానభంగం **maanabhangam** *n.* 1 disgrace, dishonour. 2 violation of a woman's modesty, rape.

మానవ **maanawa** *adj.* human; **~ prayatnam** human endeavour.

మానవత **maanawata** *n.* 1 mankind, humanity, the human race. 2 humaneness, kindliness.

మానవతావాదం **maanawataawaadam** *n.* humanism.

మానవతావాది **maanawataawaadi** *n.* humanist.

మానవతి **maanawati** *n.* modest woman.

మానవత్వ **maanawatwa** *adj.* human: **~ pu wiluwalu** human values.

మానవత్వం **maanawatwam** *n.* humanity, kindliness.

మానవమాత్రుడు **maanawamaatruDu** *see* **maatruDu.**

మానవశాస్త్రం **maanawaśaastram** *n.* (science of) anthropology.

మానవశాస్త్రజ్ఞుడు **maanawaśaastrajñuDu** *n.* anthropologist.

మానవాతీత **maanawaatiita** *adj.* superhuman.

మానవాళి **maanawaaLi** *n.* humanity, mankind, the human race.

మానవీయశాస్త్రాలు **maanawiiyaśaastraalu** *n.pl.* humanities.

మానవుడు **maanawuDu** *n.* man.

మానస **maanasa** *adj.* mental, of the mind: **~ putruDu** devoted follower.

మానసం **maanasam** *n.* 1 mind. 2 heart (= **manasu).**

మానసి **maanasi** *substandard form of* **maniSi.**

మానసిక **maanasika** *adj.* mental, psychological.

మానసిక చికిత్స **maanasika cikitsa** *n.* psychotherapy.

మానసిక శాస్త్రవేత్త **maanasika śaastraweetta** *n.* psychologist.

మానహాని **maanahaani** *n.* disgrace.

మానాన, మానాన్న **maanaan[n]a** *locative case of* **maanam** *used idiomatically with a personal or reflexive pron. in the sense of* by o.s., on o.'s own; **naa ~ nannu batakanii!** allow me to live by myself! **aame tana gadi talupulu biDaayincukoni tana ~ tanu kuurcundi** she shut the doors of her room and sat by herself; **kukkanu daani ~ daanni wadileestee adi karustundi** if you let the dog go free on its own it will bite.

మానానికి **maanaaniki** *dative of* **maanam** *used idiomatically with a time adv. repeated; the phrase emphasises that a previous action or occurrence has taken place again:* **niruDu ~ niruDu waanalu leewu** last year also there were no rains (just like this year): **niruDu ~ niruDu ilaagee analEE?** did you not say the same thing last year also? **appaTi ~ appuDu ilaa ceppEEDu** he said the same thing then also.

మానిక, మానికె **maanika, maanike** *n.* measure of volume approximately equal to two and a half kilograms of grain.

మానికవాయి **maanikawaayi** *n.* low level sluice of an irrigation reservoir.

మానిని **maanini** *n.* woman.

మాను, మ్రాను **maanu**[1], **mraanu** *n.* 1 tree. 2 trunk of a tree. 3 wood.

మాను **maanu**[2] I. *v.i. and t.* to be healed, be cured; **maanipooyina gaayam maLLii reepEEDu** he reopened a wound that had been healed. II. *v.t.* 1 (*in this sense the intensive form* **maaneeyu** *is gen. used*) to stop, put a stop to, cease from, desist from, leave off; **sigareTLu taagaDam maaneesEEnu** I stopped smoking cigarettes; **pani maaneeyu** to cease from work; **baDi maaneeyu** to stop going to school. 2 *the neg. participle of a vb. followed by a neg. form of* ~ *produces a strong affirmative,* e.g., **waaDu raaka maanaDu** he will not fail to come *or* he will certainly come: **neenu angiikaarincaka maanaleenu** I cannot but accept. 3 ~ *is used in the constr.* whether (to do s.g) or not, e.g., **weLLaDamaa maanaDamaa anee praśna** the question whether to go or not; **aa puwwulu talloo peTTukoonaa maananaa?** should I put those flowers in my hair or not?

మానుగాయరంగు **maanugaaya rangu** *n.* olive green colour.

మానుముంత **maanumunta** *n.* small wooden pot used for serving pickles.

మానుష **maanuSa** *adj.* human.

మానె **maane**[1] *n.* large basket.

మానె **maane**[2] *irregular impersonal form of* **maanu**[2] it does not matter, never mind: **waaru tiTTinaa ~, ilaa ceyyaNDi** never mind if they abuse you, do it in this way; **biccam peTTakapootee ~, kukkanu kaTTeeyaNDi** it does not matter if you give no alms, but please tie up your dog.

మాన్పించు **maanpincu** *v.t.* to stop; **waaNNi pani maanpincEEnu** I stopped him from coming to work.

మాన్పడు , మ్రాన్పడు **m[r]aanpaDu** *v.i.* to be dumbfounded, be astounded.

మాన్పు **maanpu** *v.t.* **1** to stop. **2** to heal, cure.

మాన్య **maanya** *adj.* honoured, venerable.

మాన్యం **maanyam** *n.* **1** land granted on favourable terms for services rendered. **2** land in general; *cf.* **maDimaanyaalu.**

మాన్యత **maanyata** *n.* venerability.

మాన్యుడు **maanyuDu** *n.* honoured or venerable person.

మాపకం, మాపిని **maapakam, maapini** *n.* measuring instrument, gauge.

మాపు **maapu**[1] *n.* **1** evening; **maapaTa** *or* **maapaTiki** in the evening; **reepaTikoo maapaTikoo wastaaDu** he will come tomorrow or the day after; *see* **reepoomaapoo.**

మాపు **maapu**[2] I. *n.* dirt, grime, soiling (on clothes, etc.) **cokkaa ceetula miida ~ kanipistunnadi** the shirt is soiled at the sleeves. II. *v.t.* **1** to soil, dirty; **baTTalu ~ konnaaDu** he dirtied his clothes. **2** to destroy, ruin, put an end to. **3** to efface, erase.

మాఫీ **maaphii** *n.* **1** exemption, cancellation. **2** forgiveness, pardon, condonation. **3** remission (of fees, tax, sentence).

మాఫీ చేయు **maaphii ceeyu** *v.i. and t.* **1** to excuse, forgive, pardon, condone. **2** to remit (fees, tax, sentence).

మాబాగు! **maabaagu!** *interj.* very good!

మామ, మావ **maama, maawa** *n.* **1** maternal uncle, father-in-law, father-in-law's brother. **2** for an unmarried woman, any man whom she is eligible to marry may be called ~ or **baawa.**

మామిడల్లం **maamiDallam** *n.* mango-ginger, a tuberous plant, wild or cultivated, eaten for its flavour and medicinal qualities, *cucurma amada.*

మామిడి ఆకు **maamiDi aaku** *n.* **1** mango leaf. **2** festoon of mango leaves strung across an entrance (= **tooraNam**).

మామిడి కాయ **maamiDi kaaya** *n.* unripe mango.

మామిడి చెట్టు **maamiDi ceTTu** *n.* mango tree.

మామిడి పండు **maamiDi paNDu** *n.* ripe mango.

మామిడి పిందెలు **maamiDi pindelu** *n.pl.* **1** unripe mango fruit at a very early stage. **2** ornamental string of gold worn around the waist by a young child.

మామీ **maamii** *n.* *Tamil* term of affection to an elderly woman.

మామూలు **maamuulu** I. *n.* **1** custom, normal usage; **~ eemiTi?** what is the usual practice? **2** *colloq.* bribe. II. *adj.* ordinary, common, usual.

మామూలుగా **maamuulugaa** *adv.* usually, as usual, normally, generally, as a rule.

మామ్మ **maamma** *same as* **baamma.**

మాయ **maaya** I. *n.* **1** fraud, trickery, deceit, deception. **2** unreality, illusion. **3** hypnotic or psychic power. **4 deewuDi ~** God's mystical power. **5** *med.* placenta (= **maawi**). II. *adj.* false, deceitful; **~ maaTalu** deceitful words.

మాయం **maayam** *n.* disappearance, vanishing.

మాయం అవు **maayam awu** *v.i.* to disappear, vanish.

మాయం చేయు **maayam ceeyu** *v.t.* to make (s.g) disappear or vanish.

మాయచేయు **maaya ceeyu** *v.t.* **1** to deceive, hoodwink. **2** to put (s.o.) in a hypnotic trance.

మాయజాలం **maayajaalam** *n.* juggling, conjuring.

మాయదారి **maayadaari** *adj.* **1** deceitful. **2** *colloq.* bothersome, wretched; **~ bassu entakii raaleedu** the wretched bus did not come for ever so long.

మాయదారితనం **maayadaaritanam** *n.* deceitfulness.

మాయరోగం **maayaroogam** *n.* **1** mysterious disease; **waaDu iwwEELa peeparu iwwaleedu, eem ~ oo!** he has not brought the paper today, what can have come over him? **2** pretended illness.

మాయలాడి **maayalaaDi** *n.* deceitful woman.

మాయామర్మం **maayaamarmam** *n.* deception and concealment.

మాయావాదం **maayaawaadam** *n.* the doctrine that the world of the senses is an illusion.

మాయావి, మాయలమారి **maayaawi, maayalamaari** *n.* **1** cheat, deceiver. **2** juggler, conjurer.

మాయు **maayu** *v.i.* **1** to become dirty, soiled, stained, discoloured or tarnished; **waaDi tella paNTLaamu Treyin prayaaNaaniki baagaa maasindi** his white pants got very dirty on the railway journey; **maasipooyina gaDDam** unkempt beard; **tala maasina** (of a woman) widowed; **talaku maasina waaDu** brainless person, idiot. **2** to fade [away], be wiped off, be effaced, disappear; **macca maasipooyindi** the scar on the skin faded away. **3 nii macca maaya!** *lit.* may your blemish be wiped away! *hence* may you be blessed!

మాయోపాయం **maayoopaayam** *n.* guile, trickery; **balaprayoogamwalla gaanii maayoopaayaalawalla gaanii** by force or by guile.

మారకం **maarakam** *n.* **1** exchange; *see* **wideeśii. 2** deadly disease, plague. **3 jaatakamloo ~** source of danger forecast by a horoscope.

మారణ **maaraNa** *adj.* deadly, lethal; **maaraNaayudham** deadly weapon.

మారణం **maaraNam** *n.* killing, slaughter.

మారణకాండ **maaraNakaaNDa** *n.* cruel treatment, atrocities.

మారణహోమం **maaraNahoomam** *n.* holocaust.

మారాం **maaraam** *n.* (gen. of children) worrying, pestering, crying out (for), craving (for), hankering (after).

మారాంచేయు **maaraamceeyu** *v.i.* (gen. of children) to worry, pester, cry out (for), crave (for), hanker (after).

మారాకు **maaraaku** *n.* fresh young leaf, sprouting leaf.

మారాముళ్లు **maaraamuLLu** *n.pl.* **1** knots which cannot be untied. **2** problems, difficulties, complications.

మారామేకు **maaraameeku** *n.* punishment.

మారి, మారెమ్మ **maari, maaremma** *n.* **1** village goddess reputed to bring infectious diseases. **2** goddess of death.

మారీచం **maariicam** *n.* deception, guile, dissembling.

మారీచుడు **maariicuDu** *n.* Maricha, a giant and friend of Ravana in the Ramayana.

మారు **maaru** I. *n.* time, occasion; **oka~** once; **mum~** three times. II. *adj., as first part of a n. compound* **1** other: **~peeru** another name. **2** returning, answering; **~beeram** exchange. **3** turned, averted; **~mogam** face turned away. III. *v.i.* **1** to change, turn, alter, shift; **okka samwatsaram-loonee uuru paTTaNangaa maarindi** in a single year the village changed into a town; **lookam antaa narakam kinda maarindi** the whole world turned into hell; **kotta iNTiki~** to move (*or* to shift) to a new house. **2** (of money) to pass, be current.

మారుకొను **maarukonu** *same as* **maarkonu.**

మారుగా **maarugaa** *adv.* instead of, in lieu of, in place of, as a substitute for.

మారుడు **maaruDu** *n. class.* a name of Manmatha or Cupid.

మారుతం **maarutam** *n. class.* wind.

మారు[టి]తల్లి **maaru[Ti]talli** *n.* stepmother.

మారుపడు **maarupaDu** *v.i.* to go astray, get lost; **cinna pillawaaDu sTeeSanuloo maarupaDDaaDu** the little boy got lost in the station.

మారుపేరు **maarupeeru** *n.* another name, nickname, false name, pseudonym; **ii pani ceeyakapootee nannu~too pilawaNDi** if I do not do this call me by a different name (*colloq. expression meaning* I will definitely do this).

మారుబేరం **maarubeeram** *n.* exchange, barter; **maarubee-raaniki teccEEnu** (i) I got this in exchange; (ii) I brought this for retail sale.

మారుబేరకాడు **maarubeerakaaDu** *n.* retail dealer.

మారుమనువు **maarumanuwu** *n.* woman's second marriage.

మారుమాట **maarumaaTa** *n.* reply, rejoinder.

మారుమాట్లాడు **maarumaaTLaaDu** *v.i.* to answer, reply.

మారుమూల **maarumuula** *adj.* out of the way, off the beaten track, in a remote corner.

మారుమోగు, మారుమ్రోగు **maarum[r]oogu** *v.i.* to echo, resound.

మారురూపు **maaruruupu** *n.* new appearance, change of form.

మారువడ్డన **maaruwaDDana** *n.* second helping of food at a meal.

మారువేషం **maaruweeSam** *n.* disguise.

మారెమ్మ **maaremma** *same as* **maari.**

మారేడు **maareeDu** *n.* bael fruit tree, *aegle marmelos, cf.* **masi.**

మార్కొను, మారుకొను **maar[u]konu** *v.t. class.* to oppose, confront, attack.

మార్గం **maargam** *n.* **1** way, road, path; **reyilu~** railway line, railway track. **2** means, manner, method.

మార్గదర్శక **maargadarśaka** *adj.* **1** pioneering, pointing the way. **2** exemplary, giving guidance; **~suutraalu** guiding principles.

మార్గదర్శకుడు **margadarśakuDu** *n.* **1** guide, pilot. **2** pioneer.

మార్గదర్శని **maargadarśani** *n.* guidebook.

మార్గదర్శి **maargadarśi** *n.* pattern, model, exemplar.

మార్గశిరం, మార్గశీర్షం **maargaśiram, maargaśiirSam** *n.* the ninth Telugu lunar month.

మార్చు **maarcu** *v.t.* **1** to change, alter, turn, convert, transform. **2** *class.* to kill.

మార్చుకొను **maarcukonu** *v.t.* **1** to change; **baTTalu~** to change o.'s clothes. **2** to exchange.

మార్జాలం **maarjaalam** *n. class.* cat.

మార్తాండుడు **maartaaNDuDu** *n. class.* sun.

మార్దాంగికుడు **maardaangikuDu** *n.* mrudangam player.

మార్దవ **maardawa** *adj.* soft, mild, gentle, kind, good-natured.

మార్దవం, మార్దవత **maardawam, maardawata** *n.* softness, mildness, gentleness, kindness, good nature.

మార్పాటు **maarpaaTu** *n.* change.

మార్పిడి **maarpiDi** *n.* **1** change, exchange, alteration; **talala~** change of personnel; **pada~** alteration of words. **2** permutation.

మార్పిడిచేయు **maaripiDiceeyu** *v.t.* to change, exchange, alter.

మార్పు **maarpu** *n.* change, alteration, variation, modification.

మార్వాడీ **maarwaaDii** *n.* name of a merchant community.

మాల **maala**[1] *n.* harijan, member of a scheduled caste also called Adi Andhra.

మాల **maala**[2] *n.* garland.

మాల కట్టు **maala kaTTu** *v.t.* to make a garland.

మాల గుచ్చు **maala guccu** *v.t.* to thread a garland.

మాలతి, మాలతీలత **maalati, maalatiilata** *n. class.* jasmine creeper.

మాలపల్లె **maalapalle** *n.* harijan hamlet of a village.

మాలావు **maalaawu** *same as* **mahalaawu.**

మాలి **maali** *n.* gardener.

మాలిక **maalika** *n.* **1** garland. **2 raaga~** collection of ragas.

మాలిన **maalina** **1** *past vbl. adj. of* **maalu; tanaku~** (*or* **tananu~**) **dharmam modalu ceDDa beeram** a code of conduct that is against o.'s interest is a bad bargain (proverb). **2** *second part of an adjvl. compound signifying* lacking, devoid of, without, -less; **siggu~** shameless, **paniki~** useless; **dikku~** helpless, wretched.

మాలిన్యం **maalinyam** *n.* **1** dirt[iness], foulness, impurity. **2** defilement.

మాలిమి **maalimi** *n.* affection, attachment.

మాలీసు **maaliisu** *n.* **1** massage. **2** grooming of a horse.

మాలు **maalu** *v.i. class.* **1** to be destroyed. **2** to be devoid of, be without; *see* **maalina, paalumaalu, aDugumaali poowu.**

మాలోకం **maalookam** *n.* simple person, innocent-minded person.

మాల్గాడీ **maalgaaDii** *n.* goods train.

మాల్చు **maalcu** *see* **paalumaalcu.**

మాల్యం **maalyam** *n. class.* garland.

మాళవం **maaLawam** *n.* Malwar, a district in Rajasthan.

మావ **maawa** *same as* **maama.**

మావి **maawi**[1] *n.* placenta, afterbirth.

మావి **maawi²** *n.* mango tree; **gunna**~ young mango tree.

మావిడి **maawiDi** *colloq. alt. form of* **maamiDi.**

మాషం **maaSam¹** *n. class.* blackgram.

మాషం **maaSam²** *n. obs.* small weight equal to 5 guriginja seeds.

మాషచక్రం **maaSacakram** *n.* spiced blackgram cake (= **waDa²**, **gaare**).

మాస **maasa** *adj.* monthly; ~**patrika** monthly journal.

మాసం **maasam** *n.* 1 month. 2 *same as* **maaSam²**.

మాసరా **maasaraa** *n.* sample, specimen.

మాసిక **maasika** *n.* patch (on a garment); **cirigina ciireki~ weesindi** she sewed a patch on her torn sari.

మాసికం **maasikam** *n.* death ceremony performed every month for twelve months after a death.

మాసూలు **maasuulu** *same as* **mahasuulu.**

మాహాత్మ్యం, మహాత్యం, మహాత్మ్యం **maahaat-myam, mahaat[m]yam** *n.* 1 might, greatness, mystical power, glory. 2 the special greatness or efficacy of a deity, shrine or other sacred place. 3 graciousness, magnanimity.

మి - mi

మింగు, మ్రింగు **m[r]ingu** *v.t.* 1 to swallow. 2 *slang* to eat; **waaDu ippuDee mingi weLLEEDu** he has just had his food and gone away. 3 **mingaleeka kakkaleeka** *lit.* unable to swallow or to vomit up, *hence* unable to decide what to do.

మింగుడు పడు **minguDupaDu** *v.i.* 1 to be swallowed. 2 *in neg. constr.* to be distasteful, be impossible to swallow; **ii mandu naaku minguDu paDakuNDaa undi** I cannot stomach this medicine; **aayana maaTalu naaku minguDu paDaleedu** his words were distasteful to me.

మించు **mincu¹** *v.i. and t.* 1 to surpass, excel. 2 (of time) to pass the limit, expire; **wEELa mincipooleeDu** the time has not expired *or* it is not too late. 3 to go beyond the limit, exceed; **ruupaayiki minci neenu iwwanu** I will not pay more than a rupee; **talaku mincina pani nettiki ettukonnaa-Du** he took on work that exceeded his capacity; **okka saari iNTiki weLLi kaasta bhoonceesi raa! ii loopuna minci-pooyeedeemii leedu** please go home and have a meal, in the mean time nothing will go wrong (*lit.* in the mean time nothing will go beyond its limit); A: **abboo! caalaa Taym ayindi! ika neenu iNTiki weLLaali.** B: **eemippuDu eemanta mincipooyindi? kaaphii taagi poowaccu** A: oh dear, it's very late. I must go home. B: what is the hurry? (*lit.* what has exceeded its limit now?) drink some coffee and go.

మించు **mincu²** *n. class.* 1 brightness. 2 flash of lightning.

మించుగా **mincugaa** *adv.* chiefly, mainly, predominantly.

మింజుమల **minjumala** *n.* part, share.

మింట **miNTa** *class., locative of* **minnu.**

మిండకత్తె **miNDakatte** *n.* lover, paramour (female).

మిండడు, మిండగాడు **miNDaDu, miNDagaaDu** *n.* lover, paramour (male).

మిండతనం **miNDatanam** *n.* adultery.

మిండప్రాయం **miNDapraayam** *n.* youth, manhood.

మిక్కిలి **mikkili** *adj. and adv.* much, very, greatly.

మిక్కుటం **mikkuTam** I. *n.* abundance, excess. II. *adj.* great, extreme, excessive.

మిగత, మిగతా **migata[a]** *adj.* remaining, other.

మిగతాప్పుడు **migataappuDu** *adv.* at other times.

మిగిలించు **migilincu** *v.t.* to save, set aside, set apart.

మిగిలిన **migilina** *past vbl. adj. of* **migulu** remaining, left over.

మిగుల, మిగల **migula, migala** *adv.* much, greatly.

మిగులపెట్టు **migulapeTTu** *v.t.* 1 to save. 2 *colloq.* **pani~koni kuurcunnaaweemiTi?** why are you bottling up the work? *or* why are you letting the work accumulate?

మిగులు **migulu** I. *n.* remainder, balance, surplus. II. *adj.* remaining, surplus. III. *v.i.* 1 to remain over, be left over, remain behind. 2 (of money) to be saved.

మిగుల్చు **migulcu** *v.t.* 1 to save, preserve, keep, retain. 2 to set apart, set aside. 3 to leave behind, leave as a legacy.

మిటకరించు **miTakarincu** *v.t.* **guDLu~** to stare with wide open eyes; **guDLu miTakarincEEDu** his eyes protruded (with amazement, anger, fear).

మిటమిట **miTamiTa** *onom. adv. sug.* fierceness, brightness (e.g., of sunlight).

మిటమిటలాడు **miTamiTalaaDu** *v.i.* 1 to shine brightly. 2 to be arrogant, be insolent.

మిటారం **miTaaram** *n.* beauty, charm, attractiveness.

మిటారపు **miTaarapu** *adj.* beautiful, charming, attractive.

మిటుకు **miTuku** *v.i. alt. variant form of* **miNuku.**

మిట్ట **miTTa** I. *n.* 1 high ground. 2 mound, hillock. II. *adj.* (of land) high, elevated.

మిట్టకాయ **miTTakaaya** *n. dial.* second, moment of time.

మిట్టమధ్యాహ్నం, మిడిమధ్యాహ్నం **miTTama-dhyaahnam, miDimadhyaahnam** *n.* high noon, the hottest part of the day.

మిట్టారు **miTTaaru** *v.i.* to roam, wander about.

మిట్టిపడు, మిట్టిపాటు **miTTipaDu, miTTipaaTu** *same as* **miDisipaDu, miDisipaaTu.**

మిఠాయి **miThaayi** *n.* sweet, confection; ~**rangu** colouring used for a sweet.

మిడత **miData** *n.* 1 locust. 2 grasshopper, cricket.

మిడసరిలగ్నం **miDasarilagnam** *n. colloq.* high noon; **enduku inta~loo waccEEwu?** why have you come at such a hot time of day?

మిడి **miDi** *adj.* 1 proud, arrogant. 2 raised up, projecting.

మిడిగుడ్లు **miDiguDLu** *n.pl.* staring eyes, protruding eyes.

మిడిమిడి **miDimiDi** *adj.* slight, meagre; ~**jñaanam** superficial knowledge, smattering of knowledge.

మిడిమేళం **miDimeeLam** *n.* haughtiness, arrogance.

మిడిసిపడు, మిట్టిపడు **miDisipaDu, miTTipaDu** *v.i.* to be haughty, be arrogant, be insolent, be presumptuous.

మిడిసిపాటు, మిట్టిపాటు **miDisipaaTu, miTTipaaTu** *n.* haughtiness, arrogance, insolence, presumption.

మిణకరించు **miNakarincu** *v.i.* to stare with wide open eyes due to fear or hesitation.

మిణుకు, మినుకు **miNuku, minuku** I. *n.* gleam[ing], flicker[ing]. II. *v.i.* to gleam, flicker.

మిణుకుమిణుకుమను, మినుకుమినుకుమను **miNukumiNukumanu, minukuminukumanu** *v.i.* to twinkle, flicker, glimmer.

మిణుగురు, మిడుగురు, మినుగురు **miNuguru, miDuguru, minuguru** *n.* 1 spark of fire. 2 flicker, twinkle, glimmer.

మిణుగురు పురుగు **miNuguru purugu** *n.* glow worm, firefly.

మిణ్ణాగు, మిన్నాగు **miNNaagu, minnaagu** *n.* deadly snake which springs on its prey.

మిత **mita** *adj.* 1 moderate, temperate. 2 limited.

మితం **mitam** *n.* 1 moderation, temperance. 2 limit, bound.

మితవాది **mitawaadi** *n. polit.* moderate.

మితవ్యయం **mitawyayam** *n.* economy, moderation in expenditure.

మితభాషి **mita bhaaSi** *n.* person who is reticent in speech.

మితభాషిత్వం **mita bhaaSitwam** *n.* reticence in speech.

మితి **miti** *n.* end, limit.

మితి మీరు **miti miiru** *v.i.* to exceed the limit: **miti miirina** boundless.

మిత్త **mitta** *n. dial.* friend.

మిత్తి **mitti** *n.* 1 death. 2 goddess of death. 3 *dial.* interest (= **waDDii**).

మిత్ర **mitra** *adj.* friendly, allied: ~ **deeśaalu** friendly (or allied) countries: ~ **saynyaalu** allied armies.

మిత్రం, మిత్రుడు **mitram, mitruDu** *n.* friend.

మిత్రద్రోహి **mitradroohi** *n.* one who betrays a friend.

మిత్రభావం **mitrabhaawam** *n.* friendliness.

మిత్రభేదం **mitrabheedam** *n.* 1 break-up of friendship. 2 causing dissension between friends.

మిత్రమండలి **mitramaNDali** *n.* group of friends.

మిథునం **mithunam** *n.* 1 pair, couple. 2 *astrol.* constellation of Gemini.

మిథ్య **mithya** *n.* 1 illusion, unreality. 2 nothingness. II *adj.* false, unreal, sham.

మిద్దె **midde** *n.* 1 house with a flat or terraced roof. 2 flat or terraced roof of a house.

మినప **minapa** *genitive of* **minumu.**

మినపసున్ని **minapasunni** *n.* preparation of blackgram flour, mixed with ghee and jaggery, traditionally sent by the bride's family to the bridegroom's family at the time of a wedding.

మినహా **minahaa** I. *n.* deduction, exception. II *adv.* except, with the exception of.

మినహాయించు **minahaayincu** *v.t.* 1 to deduct, subtract. 2 to except, make an exception of. 3 to exclude. 4 to exempt.

మినహాయింపు **minahaayimpu** *n.* 1 exception. 2 deduction, discount, rebate.

మిను **minu** *alt. form of* **minnu.**

మినుకు **minuku** *same as* **miNuku.**

మినుకుమినుకుమను **minukuminukumanu** *same as* **miNukumiNukumanu.**

మినుగురు **minuguru** *same as* **miNuguru.**

మినుము **minumu** *n., gen. pl.* ~ **lu** blackgram, *phaseolus mungo.*

మిన్న **minna** *adj.* better, superior.

మిన్నక **minnaka** *adv.* quietly, silently.

మిన్నకుండు **minnakuNDu** *v.i.* to stay quiet, stay silent.

మిన్నగా **minnagaa** *adv.* better, more.

మిన్నాగు **minnaagu** *same as* **miNNaagu.**

మిన్ను **minnu** *n. class.* sky, heavens; *mod. in certain expressions,* e.g., **aanandam** ~ **muTTindi** his joy was sky high (*lit.* his joy touched the heavens): **kharcu munduNDagaa Dabbu poowaDam** ~ **wirigi miida paDDaTTayindi** when expenses were facing him the loss of his money was calamitous (*lit.* was like the sky breaking and falling on him); **miNTa peTTina diipamlaa unnaaDu** *lit.* he is (shining) like a lamp placed in the sky, i.e., he shines like the moon (a phrase used sarcastically of a boastful or pretentious person).

మిరపకాయ **mirapakaaya** *n.* chilli: **eNDu**~ dried chilli.

మిరప[కాయ]పొడి **mirapa[kaaya]poDi** *n.* chilli powder.

మిరపపండు, మిరప్పండు **mirap[a]paNDu** *n.* ripe chilli.

మిరప్పళ్లకారం **mirappaLLakaaram** *n.* pickle made from ripe chillies.

మిరప్పళ్లరంగు **mirappaLLarangu** *n.* bright red colour.

మిరాసీ **miraasii** *n.* hereditary right, hereditary property.

మిరాసీదారు **miraasiidaaru** *n.* landowner.

మిరియాలపొడి **miriyaalapoDi** *n.* ground black pepper.

మిరియాలు **miriyaalu** *n.pl.* black pepper.

మిరుమిట్లు కొలుపు **mirumiTLukolupu** *v.t.* to dazzle.

మిర్చి **mirci** *n. dial.* red chillies.

మిర్రిచూచు **mirricuucu** *v.i.* to stare with wide open eyes (due to amazement, fear, etc.).

మిర్రు **mirru** *n.* high ground: ~ **gaa unna maDikii pallangaa unna maDikii madhya** between a high level plot and a low level plot.

మిలమిలమెరయు **milamila merayu** *v.i.* to gleam, shine, sparkle, shimmer.

మిలాయించు, మిళాయించు **milaayincu, miLaayincu** *v.t.* to mix, combine.

మిల్లి[గరిటె] **milli[gariTe]** *n.* very small spoon used for serving ghee.

మిళిత **miLita** *adj.* mixed, combined.

మిశ్ర, మిశ్రిత **miśra, miśrita** *adj.* mixed, mingled, blended.
మిశ్రణం **miśraNam** *n. chem.* blending.
మిశ్రపదం **miśrapadam** *n.* hybrid word.
మిశ్రమం **miśramam** *n.* mixture.
మిశ్రమజాతి **miśramajaati** *n. and adj.* mixed race.
మిశ్ర[మ] మంత్రివర్గం **misra[ma]mantriwargam** *n.polit.* coalition ministry.
మిశ్ర[మ] లోహం **misra[ma]looham** *n.* alloy.
మిశ్రి **miśri** *n. dial.* sugar candy (paTika bellam).
మిష **miSa** *n.* excuse, pretext.
మిషను **miSanu** *n.* 1 machine. 2 mission.
మిసిమి **misimi** *n.* brilliance, lustre, brightness.

మీ - mii

మీ **mii** *pronom. adj.* your (polite sing. or pl.)
మీంచి **miinci** *same as* **miidanunci.**
మీగడ **miigaDa** *n.* 1 **paalamiida~** cream on the surface of milk. 2 **perugumiida~** curds which set on the top of the whey (**perugu**) when milk coagulates.
మీట **miiTa** *n.* 1 switch, bell push, lever, key of a typewriter, door latch, handle. 2 balancing arm of a picotah which swings up and down when baling water.
మీట నొక్కు **miiTa nokku** *v.i.* to press a switch.
మీటు **miiTu** *v.t.* 1 to pluck the string of a musical instrument with the fingernail; **wiiNa~** to play the vina. 2 to tap a child's cheek with the finger. 3 *dial.* (of a scorpion) to sting.
మీద **miida** *p.p. and adv.* 1 above, on, upon, on top [of], up, over; **rooDDu~** on the road; **~unnaaDaa, kinda unnaaDaa?** is he upstairs or downstairs? **Treyn~ waccEEDu** he came by train; **weeLLa~lekkapeTTa waccu** you can count them on your fingers; **aa pani~ waccEEDu** he came on that business; **uttaram~ uttaram raasEEnu** I wrote letter after letter; **Teligraamula~peLLi jarigindi** the wedding came about on the strength of telegrams. 2 because of, out of, due to; **kakSa~** due to spite; **alasaTa~ aameki nidra waccindi** she fell asleep out of tiredness. 3 against; **naa~maa naannagaaritoo ceppEEDu** he spoke against me to my father; **wankaayakuura~asahyam** dislike of brinjal curry. 4 compared with; **ninnaTi~ iwwEELa caalaamandi waccEEru** compared with yesterday many more have come today. 5 *usages relating to mental or physical states*: **aame oNTi~ spṛha leedu** she is in a state of unconsciousness; **nidramattu~unnaaDu** he is in a state of drowsiness; **miiru prayaaNam baDalika~ unnaTTunnaaru** you seem to be tired after your journey; *slang* **waaDu gurram~unnaaDu** he is drunk. 6 *other usages*: **naa ceetula~perigEEDu** he grew up under my care; **ceetula~weesi ikkaDiki tiisuku waccEEru** they carried him here in their arms; **lakSala~wyaapaaram ceestunnaaru** they transact business in lakhs (of rupees); **waayidaala~kaTTu** to pay by instalments; **takkuwa waDDii~ parapati** a loan at a lower rate of interest; **aaphiisuloo pani nimiSaala~jarigindi** at the office the business was over in a matter of minutes; **parugula~waccEEDu** he came running; **kaSTam~** with difficulty; **nemmadi~** slowly, gradually; **asprśyata~paaTa** a song about untouchability; *colloq.* **waaDu uuri~paDDaaDu** he went into town (implying that it was a casual visit); **iddari~waDDanaki naalugu kuuralu kaawaalEE?** do you need four vegetables to serve two persons? *see* **mottam~, nilakaDa~**
మీదగా **miidagaa** *same as* **miidugaa.**
మీదట **miidaTa** *advbl. particle suffixed to past vbl. adj.* after; **maaTa iccina~neenu wenakki poonu** after giving my word I will not go back on it.
మీదటికి **miidaTiki** *adv.* next year.
మీదను **miidanu** *stylistic variant form of* **miida.**
మీదనుంచి, మీంచి **miidanunci, miinci** *p.p.* 1 from over, from above. 2 through, across, by way of, via.
మీది **miidi**[1] *pronominalised adj., neuter sing.* yours.
మీది **miidi**[2] *adj.* 1 upper, higher, top; **~komma** the top[most] branch. 2 **~panulu** sundry or miscellaneous affairs.
మీదికి **miidiki** *p.p. and adv.* 1 up to, on to. 2 upwards. 3 **waaDiki praaNam~waccindi** (i) he is in great difficulty; (ii) he is at the point of death.
మీదిమిక్కిలి, మీదుమిక్కిలి **miidimikkili, miidumikkili** *adv.* in addition, furthermore.
మీదుకట్టు **miidukaTTu** *v.t.* to devote or set aside (s.g) in the name of a deity; **miLTan mahaa kaawya racana koosam tana jiiwitam~konnaaDu** Milton devoted his life to writing a great poem.
మీదుగా, మీదగా **miidugaa, miidagaa** *p.p. and adv.* 1 along, past, through, over, across (a bridge), by way of, via. 2 by means of, through the efficacy of; **okka ceeti~** single-handed.
మీనం **miinam** *n.* 1 *class.* fish. 2 the first incarnation of Vishnu, in the form of a fish. 3 *astrol.* Pisces; **miinameeSaalu lekkapeTTu** to make calculations of auspicious and inauspicious times by astrology (*colloq. expression for* a way of delaying matters).
మీనరాశి **miinaraaśi** *n. astrol.* constellation of Pisces.
మీనాక్షి **miinaakSi** *n.* 1 woman with beautiful eyes. 2 the goddess of the temple at Madurai.
మీను **miinu** *n.* fish.
మీమాంస **miimaamsa** *n.* 1 controversy, disputation, argument. 2 problem. 3 one of the six systems of Hindu philosophy.
మీమాంసకుడు **miimaamsakuDu** *n.* 1 enquirer, ponderer. 2 philosopher. 3 one who is versed in Mimamsa philosophy.
మీరు **miiru**[1] *personal pron., polite sing. or pl.* you.
మీరు **miiru**[2] *v.t.* to exceed, excel, transgress, pass, go beyond; **ceeyi miiri poowu** to go out of control; **wayasu miirina** elderly, overaged, age-barred.
మీసం **miisam** *gen.pl.* **miisaalu** *n.* moustache; *cf.* **sampangi nuune.**
మీసం దువ్వు, మీసం మెలివేయు, మీసం మెలిపెట్టు **miisam duwwu, miisam meliweeyu, miisam melipeTTu** *v.i.* to stroke o.'s moustache, twist o.'s moustache (as a challenge to a fight).
మీసకట్టు **miisakaTTu** *n.* style or fashion of trimming a moustache.

ము - mu

ము **mu** *adjvl. prefix meaning* three, e.g., **mukkaalu** three quarters: **mullookaalu** three worlds.

ముంగర **mungara** *n.* woman's nose ring.

ముంగల **mungala** I. *p.p.* **1** in front of. **2** before (place or time). II. *adv.* **1** in front. **2** previously.

ముంగలి **mungali** *adj.* **1** front, foremost. **2** previous.

ముంగారి **mungaari** *adj.* (of crops) sown in the south-west moonsoon season.

ముంగాలు **mungaalu** *n.* **1** toe. **2** shin.

ముంగి[స] **mungi[sa]** *n.* mongoose.

ముంగిట **mungiTa** *adv.* in front.

ముంగిముశాణం **mungimuśaaNam** *n.* unfriendly and unsociable person.

ముంగిలి **mungili** *n.* front yard, courtyard in front of a house.

ముంగురులు **mungurulu** *n.pl.* curls that fall over the forehead.

ముంగోపం, ముంగోపి **mungoopam, mungoopi** *same as* **mukkoopam, mukkoopi.**

ముంగోరు **mungooru** *n. dial.* cropsharing system under which two thirds goes to the landlord and one third to the tenant.

ముంచు **muncu** *v.t.* **1** to dip, plunge, immerse, submerge **kalam siraa buDDiloo muncEEDu** he dipped his pen in the inkbottle. **2** to draw (water): **glEESuloo niiLLu muncEEnu** I drew water in a glass. **3** *fig.* to ruin; **ii wyaapaaramloo nannu muncEEDu** he ruined me in this business.

ముంచుకుపోవు, ముంచుకువచ్చు **muncukupoowu, muncukuwaccu** *v.i.* **1** to submerge, engulf; **naaku nidra muncuku wastunnadi** sleep is engulfing me. **2** to plunge in ruin, overwhelm; **sankSoobhaalu muncukuwaccinappuDu tappa mundu aaloocana ceeyaleeru** they cannot think ahead except when disasters plunge them in ruin; **kottagaa tericina kaaleejii, muncukupooyee paaThaaleemii leewu** it was a newly opened college and the workload was not overwhelming. **3 puTTi muncukupootundi** *is equivalent to* **puTTi munigipootundi** (*see* **puTTi**[2]).

ముంచెత్తు **muncettu** *v.t.* to submerge, engulf, overwhelm, swamp

ముంజం **munjam** *n.* munja, a kind of grass, *saccharum munja.*

ముంజి, మౌంజి **munji, mawnji** *n.* girdle made of three strands of munja grass worn by a brahman boy from the time of his **upanayanam** until his **upaakarma.**

ముంజూరు **munjuuru** *n.* eaves above the front wall of a house.

ముంజె, ముంజ **munje, munja** *n.* kernel of an unripe palmyra fruit.

ముంజెయ్యి **munjeyyi** *n.* forearm.

ముంజేతి కంకణం **munjeeti kankaNam** *n.* **1** *lit.* bracelet worn on the forearm. **2** *fig.* s.g plain to see, s.g obvious.

ముండ **muNDa** *n.* **1** widow. **2** prostitute, slut. **3** ~ *is used as a term of abuse; also as a term of endearment with ref. to a child,* e.g., **picci** ~ ! silly boy! *or* silly girl!

ముండ[న]ం **muNDa[na]m** *adj.* **1** shaven. **2** bald.

ముండజబ్బు **muNDajabbu** *n. slang* syphilis.

ముండమోపి **muNDamoopi** *n.* widow (*term of abuse*).

ముండమోయు **muNDamooyu** *v.i.* **1** *lit.* to become a widow, be widowed. **2** ~ *is used disparagingly or abusively,* e.g., **sinimaa muNDamoosinaTLu undi** the cinema was wretched: **nii muNDa mooya!** *is a mild term of abuse.*

ముండలముఠాకోరు **muNDala muThaakooru** *n.* philanderer, womaniser.

ముండి, ముండుడు **muNDi, muNDuDu** *n.* **1** shaven headed person. **2** bald person.

ముండ్లకంచె **muNDLakance** *same as* **muLLakance.**

ముండ్లకంప, ముండ్లపంది **muNDLakampa, muNDLapandi** *same as* **muLLakampa, muLLapandi.**

ముంత **munta** *n.* small pot; **callaku wacci** ~ **daacaDam enduku**? if you come to ask for buttermilk, why hide the pot? *proverbial expression equivalent to* why beat about the bush? ~ **kindi pappu** roasted nuts kept warm under a pot containing hot charcoal.

ముంతమామిడి **muntamaamiDi** *n.* cashewnut.

ముందంజ **mundanja** *n.* forward step.

ముందంజవేయు, ముందడుగువేయు **mundanjaweeyu, mundaDuguweeyu** *v.i.* to advance, progress, prosper.

ముందటికి **mundaTiki** *adv.* next time, on the next occasion.

ముందర, ముందట **mundara, mundaTa** I. *p.p.* **1** (of place) before, in front of. **2** (of time) (i) before; (ii) after. **3** compared with; **mii** ~ **atanu paniki raaDu** compared with you he is of no use. II. *adv.* **1** (of place) before, in front. **2** (of time) (i) before; (ii) in future, hereafter.

ముందరి, ముందటి **mundari, mundaTi** *adj.* **1** (of place) front; ~ **bhaagam** front part, forward part; ~ **kaaLLu** front legs. **2** (of time) (i) past, previous, earlier; (ii) future, coming, later; ~ **roojulu** previous days *or* coming days.

ముందు **mundu** I. *adj.* **1** (of place) front; ~ **waakili** front entrance; ~ **cakram** front wheel. **2** (of time) (i) previous, earlier; (ii) future, coming, later; ~ **eeDaadi** the previous year *or* the coming year; ~ **heccarika** advance warning. II. *p.p.* before, in front of; **naa kaLLa** ~ before my eyes. III *adv.* **1** (of place) in front, at the front; **uureegimpuku** ~ **naDicEEDu** he walked at the head of the procession. **2** (of time) (i) before, previously, in the first instance; ~ **annam tinu tarawaata maaTLaaDadaam** first eat your food, then let us talk; (ii) in future, later; ~ **elaa raasipeTTindoo naaku teliyadu** I do not know what my future fate will be. IV. *advbl. particle following fut. hab. or neg. vbl. adj.* before; **neenu ceppaka** ~ **raakaNDi** do not come before I say; **miiru waccee** ~ **naaku phoon ceyyaNDi** telephone to me before you come.

ముందుకు **munduku** *adv.* forwards, to the front.

ముందుకు పోవు, ముందుకు పడు **munduku poowu, munduku paDu** *v.i.* to go forward, advance, fare well, prosper.

ముందుకు వచ్చు **munduku waccu** *v.i.* **1** to come forward, advance. **2** *fig.* to emerge.

ముందు జాగ్రత్తలు **mundujaagrattalu** *n.pl.* precautions.

ముందునుడి **mundunuDi** *same as* **munnuDi.**

ముందుమాట **mundumaaTa** *n.* foreword.

ముందు ముందు **mundumundu** *adv.* hereafter, in future, in course of time.

ముందువెనక చూచుకొను **munduwenaka cuucukonu** *same as* **wenakamundu cuucukonu.**

ముందువెనుకలుగా **munduwenukalugaa** *same as* **wenakamundugaa.**

ముంపు[డు] **mumpu[Du]** *n.* flooding, submersion.

ముకుటం **mukuTam** *n.* crown, diadem.

ముకుతాడు, ముక్కుతాడు, ముగుదాడు **muk[k]utaaDu, mugudaaDu** *n.* controlling rope or rein attached to the nose or mouth of a bullock or horse to guide or control it.

ముకురం **mukuram**[1] *n. class.* mirror.

ముకురం, ముకుళం **mukuram**[2], **mukuLam** *n.* half-closed bud.

ముకుళించు **mukuLincu** *v.i.* to shut, close.

ముకుళిత **mukuLita** *adj.* 1 closed (like a bud). 2 ~ **hastaalu** folded hands (i.e., with the palms held together as in prayer).

ముక్క **mukka**[1] *n.* 1 bit, piece: ~ **cekkalugaa egiripoowu** to be blown to pieces; **uttaram** ~ short note or brief letter consisting of just a few lines; **peeka** ~ playing card; **sigareTTu** ~ stub of a cigarette; **akSaram** ~ syllable; *see* **poTTa**[2]. 2 word, a few words; **aa** ~ **waaDiki ceppaNDi** tell him that bit of news; **oka** ~ **winapaDaDam leedu aa reeDiyooloo** you cannot hear a word from that radio. 3 meat: ~ **lu tineewaaDu** meat eater.

ముక్క **mukka**[2] *adj.* foul, musty; ~ **waasana** state smell; ~ **ciiwaaTLu** foul abuse.

ముక్కంటి **mukkaNTi** I. *n.* epithet of Siva. II. *adj.* having three eyes.

ముక్కద్దమా **mukkaddamaa** *n.* 1 affair, matter, business. 2 *dial.* court case.

ముక్కద్దాలు **mukkaddaalu** *n.pl. dial.* spectacles.

ముక్కపురుగు **mukkapurugu** *n.* weevil.

ముక్కాక **mukkaaka** *n.* trouble, distress (*lit.* threefold heat); ~ **lu tiirina** well proven, experienced (*lit.* thrice tested in fire).

ముక్కాలిపీట **mukkaalipiiTa** *n.* three-legged stool.

ముక్కాలు **mukkaalu** *n.* three quarters.

ముక్కిడి **mukkiDi** *adj.* snubnosed.

ముక్కు **mukku**[1] *n.* 1 nose; ~ **miida weelu weesukonu** to hold o.'s finger to o.'s nose (*a gesture which betokens* (i) surprise *or* (ii) forbidding); **mukkuu mokham teliyaniwaaDu** a completely unknown person; ~ **na peTTukonu** to treat with scant attention; **pustakam cadiwi** ~ **na peTTukoni pariikSaku weLLEEDu** he glanced through the book and sat for the exam; **waaDiki eppuDuu [koopam]** ~ **miida uNTundi** he is a quick-tempered person (*lit.* for him there is always anger on his nose); **peLLaam waaNNi** ~ **paTTi aaDistunnadi** his wife leads him by the nose; **ii wiSayam telistee naa** ~ **koostaaDu** if he knows about this he will insult me. 2 **nii** ~ you fool! *is a dial. variant of* **nii mukham**! 3 beak. 4 end, tip; **pensilu** ~ point of a pencil.

ముక్కు **mukku**[2] *v.i.* 1 to moan, groan, grumble. 2 to strain at stool or in child-labour.

ముక్కు **mukku**[3] *v.i.* to become musty, become mouldy.

ముక్కుకమ్మి, ముక్కుకాడ, ముక్కుపుల్ల, ముక్కుపుడక, ముక్కుపోగు **mukkukammi, mukkukaaDa, mukkupulla, mukkupuDaka, mukkupoogu** *n.* woman's nose ornament.

ముక్కుకు సూటిగా **mukkuku suuTigaa** *adv.* in a straightforward manner.

ముక్కుతాడు **mukkutaaDu** *same as* **mukutaaDu.**

ముక్కు నలుచు **mukku nalucu** *v.t.* to trim the wick of a lamp.

ముక్కునానోటనా **mukkunaanooTanaa** *see* **kukku** *sense 2.*

ముక్కుపచ్చలారని **mukkupaccalaarani** *adj.* young and tender.

ముక్కుపొడి **mukkupoDi** *n.* snuff.

ముక్కుబంతి **mukkubanti** *n.* kind of cattle disease.

ముక్కుమూసుకొను **mukku muusukonu** *v.i.* 1 to cover the nose with the fingers. 2 to adopt this pose during meditation. 3 to remain quiet (as if in meditation).

ముక్కురంధ్రం **mukkurandhram** *n.* nostril.

ముక్కెర **mukkera** *n.* nose ring.

ముక్కోటి **mukkooTi** *n.* three crores, thirty millions; ~ **deewatalu** the three crores of gods comprising the Hindu pantheon.

ముక్కోణం **mukkooNam** *n.* triangle.

ముక్కోపం, ముంగోపం **mukkoopam, mungoopam** *n.* irritability.

ముక్కోపి, ముంగోపి **mukkoopi, mungoopi** *n.* quick-tempered person, irritable person.

ముక్త **mukta**[1] *n. class.* pearl.

ముక్త **mukta**[2] *adj.* released, freed, liberated.

ముక్తకంఠంతో **muktakaNThamtoo** *adv.* in a chorus, with one voice.

ముక్తసరి **muktasari** *adj.* brief, curt, succinct.

ముక్తసరిగా **muktasarigaa** *adv.* 1 briefly, curtly, succinctly. 2 disinterestedly.

ముక్తాఫలం **muktaaphalam** *n.* 1 result, outcome. 2 pearl. 3 custard apple.

ముక్తాయింపు **muktaayimpu** *n.* 1 finale of a musical performance generally given by drummers playing together. 2 final remark, conclusion.

ముక్తావళి **muktaawaLi** *n. class.* pearl necklace.

ముక్తి **mukti** *n.* release, liberation, salvation.

ముక్తుడు **muktuDu** *n.* released or liberated person.

ముక్త్యారు **muktyaaru** *n. obs.* authorised agent.

ముఖం, మొఖం, ముగం, మొగం, ముహం, మొహం **mukham, mokham, mugam, mogam, muham, moham** *n.* 1 face, **nawwu** ~ **too waccEEDu** he came with a smiling face; **pedda** ~ (*or* **weDalpu** ~) **ceesukonnaaDu** his face looked cheerful; **cinna ~ ceesukonnaaDu** he looked unhappy (*or* he looked depressed): **tella ~ wesEEDu** he looked blank; **koopangaa ~ peTTEEDu** he put on an angry expression; **iNTi ~ paTTEEDu** he set his face for home *or* he headed for home; **jwaram taggu ~ paTTindi** the fever subsided; **waaDiki weLLaDaaniki ~ cella leedu** he had not the face to go; **~ tiisukuweLLi poTTaloo peTTukonnaaDu** he hid his face for shame; **iddaruu mukhamukhaalu cuucukonnaaru** they looked each other in the face *or* they looked one another in the eye; **nii ~** ! *or* **waaDi ~** ! silly ass! (a mild expletive). 2 mouth: **poddunee leeci ~ kaDukkonnaanu** I got up in the morning and washed my mouth. 3 front; *gen. as first part of a n. compound*, e.g., **mukhamaNDapam.** 4 direction; **naanaa mukhaala wiiru parugettutunnaaru** these people are running off in many directions.

ముఖంగా **mukhangaa** *p.p.* 1 through [the medium of], by means of: **patrikaa ~** through the newspapers; **leekhaa ~** by means of a letter. 2 **sabhaa ~** in an open meeting.

ముఖం మొత్తు **mukham mottu** *v.i.* to have had enough of, be tired of, lose o.'s taste for; **naaku aa pani aNTee mukham mottipooyindi** I have had enough of that work; **gaarelu tinagaa tinagaa mukham mottutaayi** if you go on eating blackgram cakes you will lose the taste for them (proverbial saying).

ముఖంవాచు **mukhamwaacu** *v.i.* 1 to yearn for, long for, crave for: **kuuTikii guDDakii mukham waacina prajalu** the people who crave for food and clothing; **o.-ni mukham waaceeTaTLu** (*or* **tala waaceeTaTLu**) **ciiwaaTLu peTTu** to scold s.o. severely.

ముఖకవళికలు **mukhakawaLikalu** *n.pl.* facial expressions.

ముఖచిత్రం **mukhacitram** *n.* 1 frontispiece of a book. 2 picture on the front cover of a book.

ముఖతా **mukhataa** *adv.* from the mouth of: **guru ~ neercukonnaanu** I learnt it from the mouth of my guru.

ముఖద్వారం **mukhadwaaram** *n.* 1 mouth of a river. 2 front gate of a fort.

ముఖపత్రం **mukhapatram** *n.* 1 front cover of a book. 2 title page.

ముఖపరిచయం **mukhaparicayam** *n.* knowing a person by sight, nodding acquaintance.

ముఖప్రీతి మాటలు **mukhapriiti maaTalu** *n.pl.* soft and winning words, ingratiating words, cajolery.

ముఖబింబం **mukhabimbam** *n. literary* face.

ముఖమండపం **mukhamaNDapam** *n.* pillared portico at the front entrance of a temple.

ముఖమల్ **mukhamal** *same as* **makhamal.**

ముఖమై **mukhamay** *adv.* facing [towards]; **miiTingu ~ kuurcuNDu** to sit facing the meeting.

ముఖరిత **mukharita** *adj. class.* resonant, resounding.

ముఖస్థం **mukhastam** *adj.* learnt by heart.

ముఖస్తుతి **mukhastuti** *n.* flattery, adulation, sycophancy.

ముఖాముఖి[ని] **mukhaamukhi[ni]** *adv.* face to face, in person; **meem okarinokaram ~ kalusukooleedu** we did not meet one another in person.

ముఖుడు **mukhuDu** *second part of a n. compound* person who is headed for or inclined for; **tiroomukhuDayyEEDu** he turned back; *cf.* **unmukham.**

ముఖ్య **mukhya** *adj.* 1 chief, principal, main. 2 important, prominent, salient.

ముఖ్యంగా **mukhyangaa** *adv.* 1 chiefly, principally, mainly. 2 particularly, especially, primarily.

ముఖ్యకేంద్రం **mukhyakeendram** *n.* headquarters.

ముఖ్యపట్టణం **mukhyapaTTaNam** *n.* principal town, headquarters town, capital.

ముఖ్యావసర **mukhyaawasara** *adj.* of prime importance.

ముఖ్యుడు **mukhyuDu** *n.* 1 chief, leader. 2 important person: **naaku mukhyulu** those who are most important to me, i.e., my closest family members.

ముగం **mugam** *same as* **mukham.**

ముగించు **mugincu** *v.t.* to finish [off], end, close, complete, conclude, terminate.

ముగింపు **mugimpu** *n.* end, conclusion, finish.

ముగియు **mugiyu** *v.i.* to end, be finished, come to an end; **samayam mugisindi** the time expired.

ముగుదాడు **mugudaaDu** *same as* **mukutaaDu.**

ముగ్గు **muggu**[1] *n.* 1 (*also* **rangawalli**) ornamental pattern drawn on the ground with white flour, esp. at a house entrance. 2 white powder (of flour, lime, etc.); **~ pooyu** to mark out a plan on the ground (e.g., of a building) with lines of white powder; **~ buTTa waNTi tala** snow white hair (*lit.* head like a basket of white lime powder).

ముగ్గు **muggu**[2] *v.i.* 1 to become ripe; **paLLu muggaweeyu** to ripen fruit artificially. 2 to become overripe, become musty, become mouldy.

ముగ్గురాయి **mugguraayi** *n.* limestone.

ముగ్గురు, ముగ్వురు **mugguru, muwwuru** *n.pl.* three persons.

ముగ్ధ **mugdha** I. *n.* adolescent girl. II. *adj.* lovely, beautiful.

ముగ్ధత, ముగ్ధత్వం **mugdhata, mugdhatwam** *n.* 1 simplicity. 2 loveliness.

ముగ్ధుడు **mugdhuDu** *n.* dumbfounded person, speechless person.

ముచిక **mucika** *same as* **muccika** *sense 2.*

ముచ్చు **mucca** *n.* lower part of the spine; **nii ~ pagulutundi jaagratta!** be careful or I will give a thrashing!

ముచ్చంగి **muccangi** *n.* kind of fish.

ముచ్చట **muccaTa** I. *n.* (*pl.* **muccaTLu**) 1 wish, desire, pleasure, taste, liking; **idi maa ~, kaadanakaNDi** this is our pleasure, do not deny it to us; **naa ~ tiirindi** my desire is fulfilled *or* I am content; **muunnaaLLa ~** a short lived pleasure. 2 attractiveness, charm, pleasantness, beauty; **idi caduwutuuNTee ~ weestundi** when you are reading this you will be charmed. 3 story, anecdote. 4 conversation, talk, chat; **peLLiceeyaDam aNTee ~ anukoNTunnaawaa?** do you think that performing a marriage is just a matter of talk? i.e., do you think marriage is a small matter? 5 *dial.* news; **eem ~ ?** what is the news? II. *adj.* (*also* **muccaTayna, ~ gaa uNDee**) 1 pleasant, pleasurable, to o.'s liking. 2 delightful, charming, attractive, handsome, fine, beautiful; **waaLLu muccaTayna iNTLoo uNTunnaaru** they are living in a fine house; **parisaraalu annii cuuDa ~ gaa andangaa unnaayi** all the surroundings are charming and beautiful to see. 3 entertaining, fascinating; *cf.* **accaTamuccaTa, accaTLumuccaTLu.**

ముచ్చటపడు **muccaTapaDu** *v.i.* to be pleased with, have a liking or fancy or desire for, be fond of: **aame koDuku ceppina samaadhaanaaniki muccaTapaDindi** she was pleased with the answer that her son gave; **bajaarloo kalam cuusi muccaTapaDi konnaanu** I saw the pen in the bazaar and took a fancy to it and bought it.

ముచ్చటముడి **muccaTamuDi** *n.* hair braided and tied in a knot.

ముచ్చట వచ్చు, ముద్దు వచ్చు **muccaTa waccu, mudduwaccu** *v.i.* (of persons) to be pleasant, nice, sweet, charming, goodlooking; **aa paapaayi muddu wastunnadi** that baby is very sweet; **entoo muccaTa wastuu** (*or* **entoo muddu wastuu**) **uNDeewaaDu** he used to be ever so pleasant; **oka muccaTa wastunna** (*or* **oka muddu wastunna**) **pillawaaDu naa edurugaa kuurcunnaaDu** a nice boy sat opposite me.

ముచ్చటవేయు **muccaTaweeyu** *v.i.* to be pleasant, delightful, enjoyable, charming; **aa ammaayi maaTalu caalaa muccaTa weesEEyi** the girl's words were very charming.

ముచ్చటించు **muccaTincu** *v.i. and t.* to converse [about], talk[about], refer to.

ముచ్చట్లాడు **muccaTLaaDu** *v.i.* to talk, chat, converse.

ముచ్చి, ముచ్చెబంగారం **mucci**[1], **muccebangaaram** *n.* **1** tinsel. **2** silver paper.

ముచ్చి **mucci**[2] *n. class.* thief.

ముచ్చిక **muccika** *n.* **1** small basket. **2** *bot.* (*also* **mucika** calyx of a fruit.

ముచ్చిలించు, మ్రుచ్చిలించు **m[r]uccilincu** *v.t.* to steal.

ముచ్చిలిక **muccilika** *n.* **1** agreement made by a cultivator (counterpart of a patta). **2** agreement to pay a fixed rent.

ముచ్చిలిగుంట **mucciliguNTa** *n.* nape of the neck, hollow at the back of the neck.

ముచ్చివక, ముచ్చివుక **mucciwaka, mucciwuka** *n. dial.* three quarters, esp. three quarters of a rupee.

ముచ్చు **muccu** *n.* **1** thief, rogue; ~ **sanyaasi** bogus sanyasi. **2** monkey.

ముచ్చె **mucce** *n. dial.* shoe, slipper.

ముచ్చెమట **muccemaTa** *n., often pl.* ~**lu** sweat.

ముచ్చెమటలు పోయు **muccemaTalu pooyu** *v.i.* to sweat profusely, pour with sweat.

ముజ్జిడ్డు **mujjiDDu** *n.* state of being beset with problems.

ముట్టగించు **muTTagincu** *v.i.* **1** to set on fire, set fire to. **2** *colloq.* to create quarrels, stir up enmity.

ముట్టచెప్పు **muTTaceppu** *v.i. and t.* **1** to give, assign, hand over, entrust. **2** to pay money. **3** *colloq.* to pay a bribe.

ముట్టడి **muTTaDi** *n.* **1** siege, blockade. **2** attack, assault, storming.

ముట్టడించు, ముట్టడిచేయు **muTTaDincu, muTTaDiceeyu** *v.t.* **1** to besiege, blockade. **2** to surround. **3** to attack, assault, storm.

ముట్టవు **muTTawu** *v.i.* to be menstruous.

ముట్టించు **muTTincu** *v.i. and t.* **1** to light, ignite, (fire, lamp, cigarette). **2** to create enmity or anger; **waLLiddarikii muTTincEEDu** he created enmity between them; **waaDiki muTTincEEDu** he put him in a rage, made him very angry.

ముట్టించుకొను **muTTincukonu** *v.t.* to touch; **muTTincukonee aaTa** tag, a children's game in which one player chases the rest and tries to touch one of them.

ముట్టికాళ్లవాడు **muTTikaaLLawaaDu** *n.* knock-kneed person.

ముట్టికాళ్లు **muTTikaaLLu** *n.pl.* knock-knees, knees that touch each other.

ముట్టికాళ్లు వేసుకొని కూర్చుండు **muTTikaaLLu weesukoni kuurcuNDu** *v.i. colloq.* to sit idly doing no work.

ముట్టికాళ్లు వేసుకొను **muTTikaaLLu weesukonu** *v.i.* to kneel.

ముట్టు **muTTu** I. *n.* **1** touch[ing], contact. **2** defilement by touching. **3** menses; ~ **kooka** sari defiled by menses; ~ **jabbu** *colloq.* syphilis. II. *v.i.* (of s.g despatched) to arrive, be received; **uttaram muTTindi, Dabbu muTTaleedu** the letter was received but not the money. III. *v.t.* (*also* ~ **konu**) **1** to touch. **2** *dial* (of a snake, scorpion) to bite, sting.

ముట్టుది **muTTudi** (*also dial.* **muTTuta**) *n.* woman in menses.

ముట్టునీళ్లు **muTTuniiLLu** (*also colloq.* **niiLLu**) purificatory bath taken by a woman after menses; *colloq.* **niiLLarooju** day on which a purificatory bath is taken.

ముట్టె **muTTe** *n.* **1** animal's snout or muzzle. **2** stone or kernel of a fruit.

ముట్లకొట్టు, ముట్లగది **muTLakoTTu, muTLagadi** *n.* room for a woman to stay in during a period of menses.

ముఠా **muThaa** *n.* **1** gang, clique, group. **2** mutta, obsolete territorial division in the Agency area (hill area) of Andhra Pradesh.

ముఠాకోరు **muThaakooru** *n.* gang leader; **muNDala** ~ frequenter of brothels, womaniser.

ముఠానాయకుడు **muThaanaayakuDu** *n.* ringleader.

ముడత **muData** *n.* wrinkle.

ముడతలుపడు **muDatalupaDu** *v.i.* to be wrinkled, be crumpled.

ముడి **muDi**[1] *n.* **1** knot. **2** bun of hair. **3** marriage, wedlock; *cf.* ~ **peTTu, brahma** ~. **4 oka** ~ **ki teccu** to bring together, unite.

ముడి **muDi**[2] *adj.* **1** raw, untreated, unrefined; ~ **saraku,** ~ **padaartham** raw material; ~ **nuwwulu** gingelly seeds uncleaned and with the husk; ~ **bellam** unrefined jaggery; ~ **biyyam** unpolished rice, handpounded rice; ~ **khanijam** mineral ore; ~ **inum** iron ore. **2** whole, unbroken; ~ **wakkalu** whole arecanuts. **3** unopened; ~ **puwwu** unopened bud.

ముడి **muDi**[3] *same as* **muDDi.**

ముడిపడు **muDipaDu** *v.i.* to be tied in a knot, be united (with), be linked (with), be combined (with), be bound up (with), be tied (to).

ముడిపెట్టు **muDipeTTu** *v.t.* **1** to link together, tie together; **kongu** ~ (*or* **kongu muDiweeyu**) to tie the loose end of the bride's sari and bridegroom's dhoti together during the wedding ceremony; **waaLLakii wiiLLakii [juTTu] muDipeTTi** (*or* **[juTTu] muDiweesi) cuustuu kuurcunnaaDu** he created a quarrel between them and sat looking on. 2 to perform a marriage; **manci sambandham cuusi muDipeTTEEnu** I found a good match and performed the marriage (of a son or daughter or a dependant).

ముడివేయు **muDiweeyu** *v.t.* to join or link together; **kanubommalu~** to knit o.'s brows, wrinkle o.'s forehead, frown: *see also* **muDipeTTu** *sense 1*.

ముడుకు, మునుకు, ముడుసు **muDuku, muNuku, muDusu** *n.* 1 elbow. 2 knee.

ముడుచు **muDucu** *v.t.* 1 to fold. 2 to tie in a knot, tie in a bundle. 3 to adorn hair with flowers, set flowers in hair.

ముడుచుకొను **muDucukonu** I. *v.i.* to fold up, contract; **ceyyi tagilitee diini aakulu muDucukupootaayi** the leaves of this (plant) contract if the hand touches them. II. *v.t.* 1 to fold; **juTTu koppugaa muDucukonnadi** she did up her hair in a bun. 2 to cause to wrinkle; **kanubommalu~** to wrinkle o.'s forehead, frown. 3 *fig.* to cause to contract; **mokham** (*or* **muuti**)~ to look downcast, look glum, look sullen. 4 to fold or bend o.'s limbs, contract o.'s limbs, crouch; **mookaaLLu muDucukoni kuurcuNDu** to sit with knees bent, sit doubled up; **ceetulu muDucukoni kuurcuNDu** to sit with folded arms (i.e., to sit without taking part or without interfering). 5 *slang* **mookaaLLu muDucukoni waccu** to go and pass urine.

ముడుపు **muDupu** *n.* 1 *lit.* folding. 2 ~ *is used in other senses corresponding to those of* **muDucu[konu]**, e.g., **puwwula~** setting flowers in the hair; **enduku aa mokham~**? why that downcast look? 3 purse (gen. a yellow cloth) containing money or other articles dedicated as a vow to a deity; **aa sommu~kaTTi miidukaTTipeTTEEnu** I dedicated the money and set it aside to be offered to the deity: *cf.* **miidukaTTu.** 4 *colloq.* **~kaTTu** (*or* **~cellincu**) to pay a bribe; **entoo konta~cellincanidee pani jaragadu** unless some amount is paid as a bribe the work will not be done.

ముడ్డి, ముడి **muDDi, muDi**[3] *n.* rump.

ముడ్డిపూస **muDDipuusa** *n.* coccyx, last bone of the spinal column.

మునుగు **muNugu** *dial. alt. form of* **munugu.**

ముతక, ముతుక **mutaka, mutuka** *adj.* coarse.

ముత్త **mutta** *n.* old person.

ముత్తరాలు **muttaraalu** *n.pl.* three generations.

ముత్తరాసి **muttaraasi** *n.* name of a community in Andhra Pradesh.

ముత్తవ్వ **muttawwa** *n.* 1 mother's mother; **~kaTNam** present given by the bridegroom to the bride's mother's mother at the time of a wedding. 2 old woman.

ముత్తాత **muttaata** *n.* great grandfather.

ముత్తుం **muttum** *n.* weight of three tooms.

ముత్యాలమ్మ **mutyaalamma** *n.* 1 kind of chickenpox. 2 name of a village goddess.

ముత్తైద, ముత్తైదు[వ] **muttayda, muttaydu[wa]** *n.* married woman.

ముత్యం, ముత్తెం **mutyam, muttem** *n.* pearl.

ముత్యపుచిప్ప, ముత్తెపుచిప్ప **mutyapucippa; muttepucippa** *n.* 1 pearl oyster. 2 mother of pearl.

ముదం **mudam** *n. class.* delight, pleasure, joy; **~andu** to be pleased, be happy.

ముదనష్టం **mudanaSTam** *n.* 1 illgotten gain. 2 unexpected gain.

ముదనష్టపు **mudanaSTapu** *adj.* 1 wretched, miserable, illfated. 2 wrongful.

ముదర, ముదురు **mudara, muduru** *adj.* no longer young or fresh or tender, fully grown, of mature age.

ముదరా **mudaraa** *n.* remission, discount, rebate.

ముదలకించు **mudalakincu** *v.i.* 1 to speak tauntingly. 2 to remonstrate.

ముదావహం **mudaawaham** *n.* matter for rejoicing, s.g gratifying.

ముది **mudi** I. *n.* old age. II. *adj.* old.

ముదిత **mudita** *n.* woman.

ముదిమి **mudimi** *n.* old age, decrepitude.

ముదియు **mudiyu** *v.i.* to become old, grow old.

ముదుగు **mudugu** *adj.* 1 coarse. 2 (of hair) stiff.

ముదురు **muduru** I. *adj.* 1 (of colour) dark; **~aaku pacca** dark green. 2 **~paakam** thick syrup. 3 *same as* **mudara.** II. *v.i.* 1 to coarsen, become coarse, become overgrown; **beNDakaaya mudiri pooyindi** the okra has become coarse. 2 (of disease) to take a firm hold, become established. 3 (of a feeling, attitude, situation) to become more acute, harden; **ciraaku mudiri koopangaa maarindi** irritation hardened and turned into anger.

ముదుసలి **mudusali** I. *n.* old man, old woman. II. *adj.* old.

ముద్గరం **mudgaram** *n. class.* 1 hammer. 2 club, mace.

ముద్ద **mudda** I. *n.* 1 lump, mass, clot; **naa baTTalannii taDisi~ayyEEyi** all my clothes were soaking wet (*lit.* all my clothes got wet and became a mass). 2 morsel; **annam~** morsel of rice. II. *adj.* like a lump or ball; **~pappu** dhall stirred into a paste; **~banti puwwu** double flowered marigold (shaped like a ball).

ముద్దకట్టు **muddakaTTu** *v.i.* to solidify, congeal, form into a lump.

ముద్దకవ్వం **muddakawwam** *m.* wooden implement for stirring dhall.

ముద్దగా **muddagaa** *adv.* in a solid mass or lump, tightly packed together; **waaDi maaTalu ~waccEEyi** his words were mumbled (said of s.o. who is drunk).

ముద్దరాలు **muddaraalu** *n. class.* beautiful woman.

ముద్దాడు, ముద్దు పెట్టుకొను **muddaaDu, muddupeTTukonu** *v.t.* to kiss.

ముద్దాయి **muddaayi** *n.* accused person.

ముద్దిచ్చు **muddiccu** (< **muddu** + **iccu**) *v.i.* to give a kiss (to s.o.).

ముద్దిడు **muddiDu** *v.t. class.* to kiss.

ముద్దు **muddu** I. *n.* 1 kiss, caress. 2 love, fondness, affection; **aayanaku pillalu aNTee~** he loves children; **aameki nannu cuustee koncem~** she is rather fond of me. 3 sweetness, delightfulness, beauty, charm; **~lu olikee cinnapaapalu** little children who overflow with sweetness. 4 wish, desire; **daani~tiircaali** (*or* **daani~cellincaali**) we must satisfy her wish (*or* we must indulge her). II. *adj.* sweet, lovely, dear, darling, beloved: ~ **cellelu** darling sister.

ముద్దుగా **muddugaa** *adv.* 1 affectionately, fondly. 2 sweetly, delightfully.

ముద్దుచేయు **mudduceeyu** *v.t.* to be very fond of, dote on, pamper; **pillalanu mudduceesi paaDuceestunnaaru** they are spoiling the children by pampering them.

ముద్దుటుంగరం **mudduTungaram** *n.* seal ring, signet ring.

ముద్దుపెట్టు[కొను] **muddupeTTu[konu]** *same as* **muddaaDu.**

ముద్దుపేరు **muddupeeru** *n.* pet name.

ముద్దులాడు **muddulaaDu** *v.t.* to kiss, caress, fondle.

ముద్దువచ్చు **mudduwaccu** *same as* **muccaTawaccu.**

ముద్ర **mudra** *n.* 1 print, stamp, impression; **weelu~** thumb impression; **kaali~** footprint. 2 seal; ~ ~**gaa undi kaanii kawaruloo Dabbu pooyindi** the seal is intact but the money in the cover has gone. 3 gesture, pose, posture. 4 emblem.

ముద్రవేయు **mudraweeyu** *v.t.* 1 to stamp, make an impression. 2 to seal.

ముద్రణ[ం] **mudraNa[m]** *n.* 1 print[ing], impression. 2 publication. 3 edition: *see* **punar~**.

ముద్రణ యంత్రం **mudraNayantram** *n.* printing press.

ముద్రాక్షర శాల **mudraakSaraśaala** *n.* print shop.

ముద్రాపకుడు **mudraapakuDu** *n.* 1 printer. 2 publisher.

ముద్రారాక్షసం **mudraaraakSasam** *n.* printer's devil.

ముద్రించు **mudrincu** *v.t.* 1 to print. 2 to publish. 3 to seal, stamp, impress. 4 to form, model (sculpture).

ముద్రిక **mudrika** *n.* signet ring.

మునక, మునుక **munaka, munuka** *n.* 1 plunge, dip; **eeTiloo reNDu ~lu weesi waccEEDu** he went and had a quick bath in the stream. 2 submersion, sinking.

మునగ, ములగ **munaga, mulaga** *n. hyperanthera moringa*, drumstick tree (whose wood is proverbially brittle); ~ **kaaya,** ~ **kaaDa** drumstick (a vegetable).

మునసబు **munasabu** *n.* 1 village munsiff, village headman. 2 munsiff, civil court judge.

ముని **muni**[1] *n.* hermit, sage, ascetic, saint, holy man.

ముని **muni**[2] *n. class.* point, tip; *mod. in a few expressions,* e.g., ~ **weeLLu** tips of the fingers.

మునిదోసకాయ **munidoosakaaya** *n.* kind of cucumber.

మునిమనమడు **munimanamaDu** *n.* great grandson.

మునిమనమరాలు **munimanamaraalu** *n.* great granddaughter.

మునిమాపు **munimaapu** *n.* early evening.

మునిముచ్చు **munimuccu** *n.* sanctimonious person, deceiver, hypocrite.

మును **munu** *adv.* formerly, previously, first.

మునుం **munum** *n.* 1 tip of the leaf or shoot of a plant. 2 furrows assigned to a man to reap, one man's share of harvest work.

మునుక **munuka** *same as* **munaka.**

మునుగు, ములుగు **munugu, mulugu** *v.i.* 1 to plunge, dive. 2 to sink, be submerged, be drowned; **niiLLaloo munigi pooyEEDu** (i) he plunged into the water; (ii) he was drowned. 3 *fig.* to be immersed, be engrossed, be busily engaged; **tana caduwulloo munigipooyEEDu** he was immersed in his studies. 4 to be ruined, be lost; **aa suutraalu leekapootee eemii muligipooyeedi leedu** if those guiding principles were abolished nothing would be lost; *cf.* **kompa** *sense 4.*

మునుపటి **munupaTi** *adj.* former, previous.

మునుపటికి **munupaTiki** *adv.* formerly, previously.

మునుపు **munupu** I. *p.p.* before (in time). II. *adv.* formerly, previously.

మున్నగు **munnagu** *adj. class.* and other (= **modalayna**).

మున్నీరు **munniiru** *n. class.* sea; *mod. in* **kanniiru ~gaa eeDcu** to weep a torrent of tears.

మున్నుడి, ముందునుడి **munnuDi, mundunuDi** *n.* preface, foreword.

మున్నూరు **munnuuru** *n.* three hundred.

మున్నూరుకాపు **munnuuru kaapu** *n.* name of a community of agriculturists in Andhra Pradesh.

మున్ముందు **munmundu** *adv.* 1 first of all, at the very beginning. 2 in future, in course of time.

ముప్పందుం **muppandum** *n.* 1 obsolete grain measure of thirty tooms. 2 **taDisi ~ awu** *is a colloq. expression meaning lit.* to get wet (with rain) and weigh thirty tooms; *hence* to be very heavy due to soaking with rain *or* to be a very heavy burden: **pustakaala sanci taDisi ~ ayindi** the satchel of books was soaking wet and very heavy; **tiisukonna appu taDisi ~ ayindi** the debt which he incurred was a heavy burden. 3 (in Rayalaseema) obsolete measure of area varying from seven and a half to thirty acres.

ముప్పతిప్పలు **muppatippalu** *n.pl.* hardship, suffering, distress, troubles; **waarini ~ peTTi muuDu ceruwula niiLLu taagincEEru** they caused them great distress *or* they plunged them into misfortune; *cf.* **ceruwu.**

ముప్పది **muppadi** *class alt. form of* **mupphay.**

ముప్పాతిక **muppaatika** *n.* three quarters; ~ **muuDu wantulu neenu wastaanu** I am almost certain to come.

ముప్పావు **muppaawu** *n.* three quarters.

ముప్పావులా **muppaawulaa** *n.* three quarters of a rupee.

ముప్పిడి **muppiDi** *n. class.* dagger.

ముప్పిరిగొను **muppirigonu** *v.i.* 1 to be twisted together. 2 to be combined, be intermingled.

ముప్పు **muppu** *n.* 1 danger, peril. 2 distress, misfortune, disaster, calamity. 3 *obs.* old age.

ముప్పొద్దులా **muppoddulaa** *adv. lit.* in all the three periods of the day, i.e., morning, noon and evening; *hence* all day long.

ముప్పై **mupphay** *n.* thirty.

ముబ్బడి **mubbaDi** *adv.* three times.

ముభావం **mubhaawam** *adj.* aloof, standoffish, reserved, withdrawn, indifferent.

ముముక్షువు **mumukSuwu** *n.* one who strives for final emancipation or salvation.

ముమ్మడి **mummaDi** *adj.* threefold.

ముమ్మడించు **mummaDincu** *v.i.* to increase threefold, triple.

ముమ్మరం **mummaram** *n.* intenseness, intensity, vehemence; **wyawasaaya panula ~ loo raytulaku tiirika dorakadu** in the rush of agricultural work the cultivators can find no leisure time.

ముమ్మరంగా **mummarangaa** *adv.* intensely, intensively, briskly, at a brisk rate, energetically, vehemently, vigorously; **kṛSi ~ saagutunnadi** work is proceeding briskly: **waanalu ~ kurisEEyi** rain fell in torrents.

ముమ్మరం చేయు **mummaram ceeyu** *v.i.* to intensify.

ముమ్మరించు **mummarincu** *v.i.* to increase, become intense.

ముమ్మాటికి **mummaaTiki** *adv.* assuredly, definitely, certainly: **~ wastaaDu** he will certainly come.

ముమ్మారు **mummaaru** *n.* three times.

ముమ్మూర్తులా **mummuurtulaa** *adv.* exactly like: **aame taNDri ~ poolikee** she is exactly like her father.

ముయ్యేరు **muyyeeru** *n.* another name for **triweeNi.**

మురగపెట్టు **muragapeTTu** *v.t.* 1 to allow (s.g) to rot, decay or stagnate. 2 to let (s.g) go to ruin.

మురబ్బా **murabbaa** *n.* (*also* **allam ~**) kind of sweet conserve made with ginger.

మురళి **muraLi** *n.* flute.

మురికి **muriki** I. *n.* dirt, filth. II. *adj.* dirty, filthy.

మురికికాలువ, మురిక్కాల్వ **murikikaalawa, murikkaalwa** *n.* drain[age channel], sewer.

మురికివాడ **murikiwaaDa** *n.* slum.

మురిగిపోవు **murigipoowu** *v.i.* 1 to putrefy, rot, decay. 2 (of water) to become stagnant. 3 to go for waste, be wasted, count for nothing: **appaTi maaTalu appuDee murigipooyEEyi** the words that I said then are no longer relevant (*meaning* I am not bound by what I said then).

మురిడీగొలుసు **muriDiigolusu** *n.* chain worn round the wrist as an ornament.

మురిపించు **muripincu** *v.t.* to arouse interest or expectation, provoke excitement, arouse curiosity, tantalise, whet the appetite.

మురిపించుకొను **muripincukonu** *v.i.* to let o.s. be coaxed or persuaded.

మురిపెం **muripem** *n.* 1 coaxing, tantalising. 2 gracefulness.

మురియు **muriyu** *v.i.* to be pleased, be happy, be delighted, rejoice (**-ki**, at).

మురుగు **murugu**[1] I. *n.* rotting, putrefying, stagnation. II. *adj.* rotten, putrid, decaying, rancid, stagnant; **~ niiLLu** stagnant water; **~ niiTi paarudala** drainage. III. *v.i.* to rot, putrefy, decay, become rancid, stagnate.

మురుగు **murugu**[2] *n.* kind of bangle or bracelet worn by a young child.

మురుగు **murugu**[3] (*pl.* **murukulu**) *n.* kind of savoury dish made of bengalgram and rice flour, shaped like a ring.

మురుగుకాలువ **murugukaaluwa** *n.* drain[age channel], sewer.

ముర్రుపాలు **murrupaalu** *n.* beestings, milk of a cow or buffalo that has recently calved (= **junnupaalu**).

ములగ **mulaga** *same as* **munaga.**

ములికి **muliki** *n.* sharp point, thorn.

ములుకోల **mulukoola** *n.* goad.

ములుగు **mulugu** *same as* **munugu.**

ముల్లంగి **mullangi** *n.* radish.

ముల్లా **mullaa** *n.* Muslim scholar.

ముల్లు **mullu** *n.* 1 thorn. 2 spike. 3 fishbone. 4 hour or minute hand of a clock or watch. 5 pointer, indicator, needle.

ముల్లె, ముల్లే **mulle[e]** *n.* 1 bag or bundle or purse of money or jewels. 2 property, wealth: **waaDiki reNDu ruupaayalu istee, nii ~ eem pootundi?** if he is paid two rupees what does it matter to you? (*lit.* if he is paid two rupees, how will your property be lost?): *cf.* **muuTaa ~**. 3 (obsolete term referring to a quantity of fruit) ten thousand: **reNDu ~ araTikaayalu pampincEEnu** I sent (a consignment of) twenty thousand plantains.

ముల్లోకాలు **mullookaalu** *n.pl.* the three worlds, i.e., heaven, earth and hell.

ముళ్లకంచె, ముండ్లకంచె **muLLakance, muNDLakance** *n.* 1 thorn fence. 2 barbed wire fence.

ముళ్లకంప, ముండ్లకంప **muLLakampa, muNDLakampa** *n.* thorn bush.

ముళ్లతీగ, ముండ్లతీగ **muLLatiiga, muNDLatiiga** *n.* barbed wire.

ముళ్ళపంది, ముండ్లపంది **muLLapandi, muNDLapandi** *n.* porcupine.

ముళ్లాట్లుపెట్టు **muLLaaTLupeTTu** *v.i. dial.* to start quarrels.

మువ్వ **muwwa** *n.* 1 small tinkling bell: **kaali ~ lu** anklet of small tinkling bells worn by dancers. 2 town in Krishna district which is the home of the Kuchipudi style of dancing.

మువ్వన్నెమెకం **muwwannemekam** *n. class.* tiger.

మువ్వపట్టెడ **muwwapaTTeDa** *n.* collar with small tinkling bells worn by a bullock.

మువ్వీసం **muwwiisam** *n.* three sixteenths.

మువ్వురు **muwwuru** *same as* **mugguru.**

ముషలకం **muSalakam** *n.* piston.

ముషిణి **muSiNi** *n.* ayurvedic skin lotion.

ముష్కర **muSkara** *adj.* 1 obstinate, stubborn. 2 wicked, rude.

ముష్కరత్వం **muSkaratwam** *n.* 1 obstinacy, perverseness. 2 wickedness.

ముష్కరుడు **muSkaruDu** *n.* 1 obstinate person. 2 wicked person.

[ముష్టా]ముష్టియుద్ధం **[muSTaa]muSTiyuddham** *n.* fist fight.

ముష్టి **muSTi** I. *n.* 1 fist. 2 alms (*lit.* fistful of grain given as alms). II. *adj.* wretched, miserable: **~ muuDu weelaki waaDicuTTuu mupphay saarlu tiragaalsiwaccindi** for a miserable three thousand (rupees) I had to go and ask him thirty times.

ముష్టి ఎత్తు [కొను] **muSTi ettu[konu]** *v.i.* to live by begging.

ముష్టిపెట్టు, ముష్టివేయు **muSTi peTTu, muSTi weeyu** *v.i.* to give alms.

ముష్టివాడు **muSTiwaaDu** *n.* beggar.

ముసద్దీ **musaddii** *n. class.* clerk, writer; ~ **peecii** *colloq.* mistakes committed deliberately by an employee dissatisfied with his remuneration.

ముసముసలాడు, మొసమొసలాడు **musamusalaaDu, mosamosalaaDu** *v.i.* 1 to be angry. 2 sniff or snuffle due to a cold.

ముసర **musara** *n.* kind of cattle disease involving loose motions.

ముసరు, ముసురు **musaru, musuru** *v.i.* 1 to collect, gather; **ciikaTi ~ tunnadi** darkness is gathering; **mabbulu ~ tunnaayi** clouds are gathering. 2 to crowd round, swarm; **iiagalu ~ tunnaayi** flies are swarming; *see also* **musuru** *n.*

ముసలం **musalam** *n.* 1 *class.* pestle, mace, club. 2 *colloq.* threat of disaster.

ముసలమ్మ **musalamma** *n.* old woman.

ముసలయ్య **musalayya** *n.* old man.

ముసలవాయి **musalawaayi** *n.* high level sluice of a tank (irrigation reservoir).

ముసలి **musali** *adj.* (of animate things) old, aged.

ముసలితనం **musalitanam** *n.* old age, senility.

ముసలిపండు **musalipaNDu** *see* **paNDu**[1] *sense II.*

ముసలిముతక, ముసలిముదుక **musalimutaka, musalimuduka** *n.pl.* old people.

ముసలివగ్గు **musaliwaggu** *n.* doddering old person.

ముసల్మాన్ **musalmaan** *n.* Musalman, Muslim.

ముసళ్లపండగ, మొసళ్లపండగ **musaLLapaNDaga, mosaLLapaNDaga** *n.* 1 *obs.* dog days, the hottest part of the year. 2 *colloq.* **mundu unnadi ~** days of trouble lie ahead.

ముసాంబరం **musaambaram** *n.* bitter aloes, a purgative.

ముసాఫిర్ **musaaphir** *n.* traveller.

ముసాయిదా **musaayidaa** *n. and adj.* draft.

ముసిముసి నవ్వు **musimusi nawwu** *n.* slight smile, gentle laugh, giggle, titter, simper.

ముసుగు **musugu** *n.* 1 cover[ing]; ~ **tanni** (*or* ~ **peTTukoni**) **paDukonu** to cover o.s. from head to foot and go to sleep. 2 veil for the head.

ముసురు **musuru** I. *n.* 1 (of the sky) cloudiness, being overcast. 2 drizzle, continuous light rain. II. *v.i. same as* **musaru.**

ముసురుపట్టు **musurupaTTu** *v.i.* (of the sky) to be cloudy, be overcast.

ముస్తాబు **mustaabu** *n.* 1 dress, style of dressing. 2 fine clothes, finery.

ముస్తాబు అవు **mustaabu awu** *v.i.* to be dressed for an occasion.

ముస్లిం **musliim** *n. and adj.* Muslim.

ముహం **muham** *same as* **mukham.**

ముహూర్తం **muhuurtam** *n.* 1 an auspicious time fixed for a ceremony. 2 lucky moment. 3 (*also* **muhuurtakaalam**) *class.* period of 48 minutes, a thirtieth part of a day and night.

మూ - muu

మూక **muuka**[1] *n.* **1** crowd, mob. **2** swarm.

మూక **muuka**[2] *adj.* silent, dumb.

మూక ఉమ్మడిని, మూకుమ్మడిని **muuka ummaDini, muukummaDini** *adv.* all together, en masse.

మూకాభినయం **muukaabhinayam** *n.* mime.

మూకీ **muukii** *n.* silent film; *cf.* **Taakii.**

మూకీభావం **muukiibhaawam** *n.* silence, dumbness.

మూకుడు **muukuDu** *n.* **1** earthen pan used as a lid. **2** **buurla~** frying pan.

మూగ **muuga** *adj.* **1** dumb. **2** inexpressible; **~koorika** inexpressible wish.

మూగపోవు **muugapoowu** *v.i. colloq.* to be dumbfounded, be struck dumb.

మూగనోముపట్టు **muuganoomupaTTu** *v.i.* **1** to take a religious vow of silence. **2** *colloq.* **naatoo muuganoomu paTTEEDu** he refuses to talk to me.

మూగు **muugu** *v.i.* **1** to crowd around. **2** to swarm.

మూచూచు **muucuucu** *v.t.* to sniff, smell.

మూజువాణీ **muujuwaaNii** *adj.* oral; **~kharaaru** oral agreement.

మూట **muuTa** *n.* bundle, pack, load; **waaDi maaTalannii niiTiloo ~lu** his words cannot be relied on (*lit.* all his words are like bundles in water, i.e., they sink and get lost).

మూటకట్టు[కొను] **muuTakaTTu[konu]** *v.i. and t.* **1** to tie together in a bundle. **2** to collect, amass, accumulate; **Dabbu muuTakaTTu** to accumulate wealth; **paapam muuTakaTTukonu** to bear a load of sin (*lit.* to tie together a bundle of sin).

మూటాముల్లే, మూటలుముల్లెలు **muuTaamullee, muuTalumullelu** *n.pl.* bag and baggage, all o.'s belongings.

మూడంకె వేసుకొను **muuDanke weesukonu** *v.i.* to curl o.s. up, double up; **kaTika neelamiida caliki muuDanke weesukoni aame sukhangaa nidrapooyindi** curling herself up against the cold on the hard floor she slept comfortably.

మూడు **muuDu**[1] *n.* three.

మూడు **muuDu**[2] *v.i.* **1** to end, terminate; **aayuwu muuDina waaDiki mandulatoo pani leedu** medicines are of no use to s.o. whose life span has come to its end. **2** to approach, come near; **nii antu muuDindi** your end is approaching; **debbalu muuDinaayi** blows are coming (*these two colloq. expressions mean* I will give you a beating); **kiiDu** (*or* **aapada**) **~tunnadi** some harm is approaching. **3** to come over (colloq.) **niikeem muuDindiraa naaku anyaayam ceesEEwu?** what has come over you that you have done me an injustice?

మూడుపూలు ఆరుకాయలుగా **muuDupuulu aarukaayalugaa** *adv.* flourishingly, abundantly, very successfully (as if three flowers had produced six fruits).

మూడుముళ్లు **muuDumuLLu** *n.* **1** *lit.* three knots. **2** *colloq.* marriage; **aameki~weesEEDu** he married her.

మూడొంతులు **muuDontulu** (< **muuDu wantulu**) *adv.* in all probability.

మూడో **muuDoo** *adj.* third.

మూడోకంటి వాడు **muuDookaNTi waaDu** *n.* he who possesses a third eye, i.e., Siva; **muuDookaNTi waaDiki teliyakuNDaa weLLipooyEEDu** he went away without anyone's knowledge (*lit.* he went away without the knowledge of even Siva himself).

మూడో కన్ను **muuDoo kannu** *n.* the third eye of Siva which possesses the power of destruction.

మూఢ **muuDha** *adj.* dull, stupid, foolish, ignorant; **~nammakam, ~wiśwaasam** blind faith, blind belief, superstition.

మూఢం, మూఢమి, మౌఢ్యం **muuDham[i], mawDhyam**[1] *n. astrol.* obscuration of a planet by the sun's rays.

మూఢత, మూఢత్వం, మౌఢ్యం **muuDhata, muuDhatwam, mawDhyam**[2] *n.* **1** stupidity, foolishness. **2** ignorance.

మూఢుడు, మూఢమతి **muuDhuDu, muuDhamati** *n.* **1** fool, stupid person. **2** ignorant person.

మూణ్ణాళ్లపట్టపగలు **muuNNaaLLapaTTapagalu** *n. colloq.* a short time.

మూణ్ణిద్దరలు **muuNNiddaralu** (= **muuDu** + **nidralu**) *n. pl.* social custom whereby the bride spends three nights at the bridegroom's home and the bridegroom in turn spends three nights at the bride's home at the end of the wedding ceremonies.

మూత **muuta**[1] *n.* cover[ing], lid.

మూత **muuta**[2] *n. dial.* large-sized ear ornament.

మూతపడు **muutapaDu** *v.i.* **1** to be shut, be closed. **2** to be stopped, be ended; **wyaapaaram muuta paDindi** the business was wound up.

మూతపెట్టు **muutapeTTu** *v.t.* to cover; **migilina annam muutapeTTi saayantram tiNTaanu** I will cover the rest of the food and eat it in the evening.

మూతముప్పిడి **muutamuppiDi** *n.* hiding, concealment.

మూతి **muuti** *n.* **1** (outer part of the) mouth; **~kaDukkonu** to wash the outside of o.'s mouth; **~muDucukonu** to look sour, look sullen; **~muuDu wampulu tippu** *or* **~muuDu wankaralu ceeyu** to purse o.'s lips (in dislike or anger). **2** *in some areas* **~** *is used for* **mukham** *as in* **nii~!** *for* **nii mukham!** you silly ass! **3 kukka~** dog's mouth or muzzle.

మూత్ర[ం] **muutra[m]** *n.* urine.

మూత్రనాళం **muutranaaLam** *n. med.* urinary tract.

మూత్రపిండం **muutrapiNDam** *n. med.* kidney.

మూత్రాశయం **muutraaśayam** *n. med.* urinary bladder.

మూపు **muupu** *n.* **1** shoulder. **2** bull's hump.

మూపురం **muupuram** *n.* bull's hump.

మూయు **muuyu** *v.t.* **1** to shut, close. **2** to cover, hide; **suuryuNNi muusina mabbulu** the clouds which covered (*or* hid) the sun.

మూర **muura** *n.* **1** lower arm. **2** cubit, a measure of eighteen inches.

మూర్కొను **muurkonu** *v.t.* to sniff, smell, esp. to sniff a child's head, equivalent to kissing.

మూర్ఖ **muurkha** *adj.* **1** foolish, stupid. **2** stubborn, obstinate. **3** rude.

మూర్ఖంగా **muurkhangaa** *adv.* **1** obstinately, stubbornly. **2** rudely.

మూర్ఖత, మూర్ఖత్వం **muurkhata, muurkhatwam** *n.* **1** foolishness, stupidity, ignorance. **2** obstinacy. **3** rudeness.

మూర్ఖుడు **muurkhuDu** *n.* **1** fool, blockhead. **2** obstinate person. **3** rude person.

మూర్ఛ **muurcha** *n.* swoon, fainting, epileptic fit.

మూర్ఛపోవు, మూర్ఛిలు **muurchapoowu, muurchilu** *v.i.* to swoon, faint.

మూర్ఛితుడు **muurchituDu** *n.* person who swoons; **mooha~** one who swoons from passion or lust.

మూర్త **muurta** *adj.* concrete (*as opposed to* **a ~** abstract).

మూర్తం **muurtam** *substandard variant form of* **muhuurtam.**

మూర్తి **muurti** I. *n.* figure, form, shape, image. II. *second part of a n. compound* **1** embodiment of; **sawjanya~** embodiment of good nature; **paramaśaanta~** very peaceable person. **2** *~ is added to certain nouns as a literary variant without alteration of meaning,* e.g., **strii~** woman.

మూర్తిమంత **muurtimanta** *adj.* having a bodily form.

మూర్తిమత్వం **muurtimatwam** *n.* personification.

మూర్తీపటం **muurtiipaTam** *n. med.* retina.

మూర్తీభవించు **muurtiibhawincu** I. *v.i.* to be embodied, be personified. II. *v.t.* to embody, personify.

మూర్ధం **muurdham** *n. class.* crown of the head.

మూర్ధన్యం **muurdhanyam** *n. ling.* retroflex consonant.

మూర్ధాఘ్రాణం చేయు **muurdhaaghraaNam ceeyu** *v.t.* to sniff a child's head, equivalent to kissing.

మూర్ధాభిషిక్తుడు **muurdhaabhiSiktuDu** *n.* **1** one who is anointed. **2** king.

మూల **muula**[1] *n.* **1** corner; **rooDDu~** corner of a road; **gadiloo oka~** in a corner of a room; **~nunna musalamma** old woman who cannot move about *or* old woman who sits in one place; **mii saamaanu oka ~[gaa] peTTaNDi** please keep your things aside *or* please put your things out of the way; *see* **~peTTu. 2 ee~ki?** *lit.* to what corner (will it reach)? i.e., how far it will go? *or* what use will it be? **wanda ruupaayalu aDigitee ruupaayi iccEEDu, ee~ki?** when I asked for a hundred rupees he gave one rupee, what use will it be? *see* **gampa.**

మూల **muula**[2] *adj., gen. as first part of a n. compound* **1** basic, fundamental; **~suutram** basic principle. **2** original, earliest; **~ruupam** prototype. **3** main, principal; **~wiraaTTu** principal idol in a temple.

మూల, మూలానక్షత్రం **muula**[3], **muulaanakSatram** *n. astrol.* nineteenth lunar mansion.

మూలం **muulam** *n.* **1** root; **warga~** square root. **2** beginning, origin. **3** source, basis. **4** bare text (without a commentary). **5** cause.

మూల[కం]గా, మూలాన **muula[ka]ngaa, muulaana** *p.p.* through, by means of, due to, as a result of.

మూలక **muulaka** *adj. chem.* inorganic.

మూలకం **muulakam** *n.* **1** *chem.* basic element. **2** *class.* radish.

మూలకందం **muulakandam** *n.* root cause, basis.

మూలగ, మూలుగ **muulaga, muuluga** *n.* bone marrow.

మూలద్రవ్యం **muuladrawyam** *n. chem.* basic element.

మూలద్రావిడ భాష **muuladraawiDa bhaaSa** *n.* proto-Dravidian (language).

మూలధనం **muuladhanam** *n. econ.* capital, principal.

మూలనాశనం **muulanaaśanam** *n.* total destruction.

మూలపడు **muulapaDu** *v.i.* **1** to be put aside. **2** to fall sick. **3** (of a machine, apparatus) to break down, go out of order, go out of action. **4** (of business enterprise) to collapse, be on the rocks.

మూలపురుషుడు **muulapuruSuDu** *n.* originator, founder; **wamśaaniki~** founder of a dynasty.

మూలపెట్టు **muulapeTTu** *v.t.* to put away, put aside, give up, abandon; **skuuTaru muulapeTTEEDu** he has stopped using his scooter; **caduwu muulapeTTi wyaapaaram ceestunnaaDu** he has given up his studies and is doing business.

మూలప్రకృతి **muulaprakṛti** *n.* matter in its primordial state.

మూలభాష **muulabhaaSa** *n.* original language, source language (from which a translation is made).

మూలభూత **muulabhuuta** *adj.* forming the origin or cause.

మూలభూతుడు **muulabhuutuDu** *n.* one who is the root cause of (s.g).

మూలమంత్రం **muulamantram** *n.* principal or most powerful mantra.

మూలమట్టం **muulamaTTam** *n.maths.* set square.

మూలమట్టంగా **muulamaTTangaa** *adv.* entirely, completely; **~pekalincu** to pull up by the roots.

మూలమట్టు [గా] **muulamaTTu[gaa]** *adv.* entirely, completely.

మూలరూపం **muularuupam** *n.* prototype.

మూలవిరాట్టు **muulawiraaTTu** *n.* principal idol in a temple.

మూలవ్యాధి, మూలశంక **muulawyaadhi, muulaśanka** *n.med.* piles, haemarrhoids.

మూలసిద్ధాంతం **muulasiddhaantam** *n.* basic doctrine, basic principle.

మూలసూత్రం **muulasuutram** *n.* basic principle.

మూలస్థానం **muulasthaanam** *n.* **1** sanctum sanctorum, innermost shrine of a temple (= **garbhaguDi**). **2** original location.

మూలాధర **muulaadhaara** *adj.* fundamental.

మూలాధారం **muulaadhaaram** *n.* source, basis.

మూలాన **muulaana** *same as* **muula[ka]ngaa.**

మూలానక్షత్రం **muulaanakSatram** *same as* **muula**[3]**.**

మూలిక **muulika** *n.* medicinal root, medicinal herb.

మూలుగ **muuluga** *same as* **muulaga.**

మూలుగు, మూల్గు **muul[u]gu** I. *n.* 1 groan, moan. 2 grumbling, complaint. II. *v.i.* 1 to groan, moan. 2 to grumble, complain. 3 **waaDidaggira Dabbu ~ tunnadi** he is rolling in money (colloq.) *or* he is very well off (*lit.* money is groaning with him).

మూల్యం **muulyam** *n.* price, value, cost.

మూల్యనిర్ధారణ చేయు **muulyanirdhaaraNa ceeyu** *v.t.* to evaluate, appraise.

మూల్యనిర్ణేత **muulyanirNeeta** *n.* appraiser.

మూల్యన్యూనీకరణం **muulyanyuuniikaraNam** *n.* devaluation (of currency).

మూల్యాంకనం **muulyaankanam** *n.* appraisal, evaluation.

మూవురు **muuwuru** *n.pl.* three persons.

మూషికం **muuSikam** *n.class.* rat, mouse.

మూస, మూష **muusa, muuSa** *n.* 1 crucible. 2 mould; **iddaru annadammuluu okka ~loo poosinaTTunnaaru** the two brothers look exactly alike (*lit.* the two brothers are as if they had been cast in the same mould.)

మూసపోయు **muusapooyu** *v.t.* to mould, cast.

మూసివేత **muusiweeta** *n.* shutting, shutdown, closure.

మృ - mr̥

మృగం **mr̥gam** *n.* 1 wild animal, beast. 2 *class.* (i) deer; (ii) any wild animal.

మృగతృష్ణ **mr̥gatr̥SNa** *n.* mirage.

మృగనాభి, మృగమదం **mr̥ganaabhi, mr̥gamadam** *n.* musk.

మృగపతి, మృగరాజు **mr̥gapati, mr̥garaaju** *n.* king of the beasts, lion.

మృగయవినోదం **mr̥gayawinoodam** *n. class.* hunting.

మృగశిర **mr̥gaśira** *n. astrol.* fifth lunar mansion.

మృగశిరకార్తె **mr̥gaśirakaarte** *n.* fortnight in the second half of June when the rains are due to begin.

మృగాక్షి **mr̥gaakSi** *n.* beautiful woman.

మృగ్యం **mr̥gyam** *adj.* non-existent, not to be found; **waaDiloo samskr̥ti~** no culture is to be found in him *or* there is no trace of culture in him.

మృచ్ఛిలించు, మృచ్చు **mr̥ccilincu, mr̥ccu** *class. alt. forms of* **muccilincu, muccu.**

మృణాళిని **mr̥NaaLini** *n.* lotus pond.

మృణ్మయ **mr̥Nmaya** *adj.* earthen, made of earth; **~ paatra** clay pot.

మృత **mr̥ta** *adj.* dead.

మృతదేహం **mr̥tadeeham** *n.* dead body, corpse.

మృతప్రాయం **mr̥tapraayam** *adj.* looking as if dead, moribund.

మృతభాష **mr̥tabhaaSa** *n.* dead language.

మృతసంజీవి, మృతసంజీవని **mr̥tasanjiiwi, mr̥tasanjiiwani** *n.* medicinal plant believed to have the power of restoring the dead to life.

మృతి **mr̥ti** *n.* death.

మృతి చెందు **mr̥ti cendu** *v.i.* to die.

మృతుడు **mr̥tuDu** *n.* dead person.

మృత్తిక **mr̥ttika** *n.* earth, clay, soil.

మృత్తికశాస్త్రం **mr̥ttikaśaastram** *n.* soil science.

మృత్పరికరవిజ్ఞానం **mr̥tparikarawijñaanam** *n.*(science of) ceramics.

మృత్యుంజయుడు **mr̥tyunjayuDu** *n.* 1 one who has overcome death. 2 epithet of Siva.

మృత్యువు **mr̥tyuwu** *n. class.* 1 death; **akaala~** untimely death. 2 the God of death.

మృదంగం **mr̥dangam** *n.* small drum played as a musical instrument.

మృదుత్వం **mr̥dutwam** *n.* softness, gentleness.

మృదుల **mr̥dula** *adj.* soft, tender.

మృదులత **mr̥dulata** *n.* softness, tenderness.

మృదులాస్థి **mr̥dulaasthi** *n. med.* cartilage.

మృదువు **mr̥duwu** *adj.* 1 soft, tender. 2 mild, gentle. 3 smooth.

మృష్టాన్నం **mr̥STaannaam** *n.* 1 *lit.* sweet rice pudding. 2 *fig.* wholesome food.

మె - me

మెండు **meNDu**[1] *adj.* much, abundant, plentiful.
మెండు **meNDu**[2] I. *n.* turn, twist. II. *v.t. dial.* to lever up.
మెండుగా **meNDugaa** *adv.* plentifully, copiously, abundantly.
మెంతి **menti** *n., gen.pl.* **mentulu** fenugreek seeds; **araTikaaya ~ peTTi waNDu** to cook bananas with fenugreek.
మెంతికాయ **mentikaaya** *n.* mango pickle flavoured with fenugreek powder.
మెంతికూర **mentikuura** *n.* fenugreek plant, *trigonella foenumgraecum.*
మెంతిపెరుగు **mentiperugu** *n.* chutney made with fenugreek and curds.
మెకం **mekam** *n.* beast.
మెక్కు **mekku** *v.t. colloq.* to eat, swallow, gobble up.
మెచ్చు[కొను] **meccu[konu]** *v.t.* 1 to praise, commend. 2 to appreciate, admire.
మెచ్చుకోలు **meccukoolu** *n.* 1 praise, commendation. 2 appreciation, admiration.
మెచ్చులాడి **mecculaaDi** *n.* woman deserving of praise.
మెటిక **meTika** *n.* 1 knuckle. 2 cracking of the knuckles, making a cracking sound with the knuckles.
మెటికలు విరుచుకొను **meTikalu wirucukonu** *v.i.* to crack o.'s knuckles over the head of a child as an expression of joy and affection.
మెట్ట **meTTa** *n.* 1 high ground, uplands. 2 dry (unirrigated) land. 3 hillock, small hill.
మెట్టతామర **meTTataamara** *n. cassia alata,* a flowering plant.
మెట్టపంచాంగం **meTTapancaangam** *n.* vain and foolish talk.
మెట్టపైరు **meTTapayru** *n.* dry (unirrigated) crop.
మెట్టవడ్లు **meTTawaDLu** *n.pl.* rainfed (unirrigated) paddy.
మెట్టవేదాంతం **meTTaweedaantam** *n.* false logic.
మెట్టిక **meTTika** *dial. variant form of* **meTTu** *n.*
మెట్టినిల్లు **meTTinillu** *n., lit.* the house into which a bride steps after her marriage, i.e., her husband's house or her mother-in-law's house.
మెట్టు **meTTu** I. *n.* 1 step in a staircase, rung of a ladder. 2 stage, point, juncture; **pani oka ~ na paDindi** the work has reached a certain stage. 3 stop or fret in a stringed instrument like a vina. 4 *dial.* slipper, sandal. II. *v.i.* to step, walk, tread.
మెట్టుపన్ను **meTTupannu** *n.* toll levied on road vehicles.
మెట్న **meTNa** *n. dial.* set square (= **muulamaTTam**).
మెట్లబావి **meTLabaawi** *n.* step well, large well with steps leading down to the water.
మెట్లు, మెట్లవరస **meTLu, meTLawarasa** *n.* flight of steps, staircase.
మెడ **meDa** *n.* neck.
మెడకాయ **meDakaaya** *alt. variant form of* **meDa.**
మెడకొంకులు **meDakonkulu** *n.pl.* collar bones.
మెడ పిసుకు **meDa pisuku** *v.t.* to throttle, strangle.
మెడ్డాయించు **meDDaayincu** *v.t. dial.* 1 to dig up, unearth. 2 to disregard.
మెతక, మెతుక **metaka, metuka** *adj.* 1 soft. 2 soft-hearted, weak, pliable. 3 (of soil) fine, loose. 4 ~ **waasana** dank smell.
మెతకబారు **metakabaaru** *v.i.* to become soft, be softened.
మెతుకు, మెదుకు **metuku, meduku** *n.* 1 a grain of cooked rice. 2 *fig.* morsel; **reNDu ~ lu tinnaaDu** he ate a small amount of food.
మెత్త **metta** I. *n.* 1 cushion, pad. 2 quilted cloth. II. *adj.* 1 soft, tender. 2 mild, gentle. 3 (of soil) fine, loose.
మెత్తగిలు **mettagilu** *v.i.* to become soft.
మెత్తదనం **mettadanam** *n.* 1 softness, tenderness. 2 mildness, gentleness.
మెత్తపడు **mettapaDu** *v.i.* 1 to become soft, be softened. 2 to be soothed, be calmed, be mollified, be pacified.
మెత్తు **mettu** I. *n.* plastering, daubing, smearing. II. *v.t.* to plaster, daub, smear.
మెదగించు **medagincu** *v.t.* to crush, reduce to powder.
మెదడు **medaDu** *n.* brain.
మెదడువాపు **medaDuwaapu** *n.* meningitis.
మెదపు, మెదుపు **medapu, medupu** *v.t.* to move, stir; **pedawi ~** to move o.'s lips *or* to utter a sound.
మెదలాడు **medalaaDu** *v.i.* 1 to move a little, stir, sway. 2 (of an image) to linger; *cf.* **medalu.**
మెదలు **medalu** *v.i.* 1 to stir, move a little. 2 to behave. 3 to take shape, appear, present itself; **tirigi aa praśna aayana manassuloo medilindi** again that question presented itself to his mind. 4 *fig.* to remain, continue to exist, linger; **baabu naa kaLLamundu medulutuu uNTaaDu** the child's image lingers before my eyes; **aayana tiTLu Dokkaloo ~ tunnaayi** his abuse is still rankling.
మెదల్చు **medalcu** *v.t.* to move, stir.
మెదుకు **meduku** *same as* **metuku.**
మెదుగు **medugu** *v.i.* 1 to be pounded, be crushed, be reduced to powder; **kaaLLakinda ~** to be trampled underfoot. 2 (of straw) to be threshed. 3 to be trained; **aayanadaggira medigina widyaarthi** a student trained under him. 4 to be accustomed, be habituated.
మెప్పించు **meppincu** *v.t.* to gratify, please, gladden, satisfy, win the approval or admiration of.
మెప్పు **meppu** *n.* 1 praise, commendation. 2 appreciation, approval.
మెప్పుకోలు, మెప్పుదల **meppukoolu, meppudala** *n.* appreciation, admiration.
మెరక **meraka** *n.* 1 high ground, raised ground. 2 dry (unirrigated) land.

మెరప **merapa** *alt. form of* **mirapa.**

మెరపు **merapu** *same as* **merupu.**

మెరమెచ్చు మాటలు **meramecu maaTalu** *n.pl.* flattery.

మెరమెరలాడు **merameralaaDu** *v.i.* to cause irritation (mental or physical).

మెరయు **merayu** *v.i.* to flash, gleam, glitter, shine; **merupulu merustunnaayi** lightning is flashing.

మెరసిపోవు, మెరిసిపోవు **merasipoowu, merisipoowu** *v.i.* to gleam, look radiant.

మెరికలు **merikalu** *n.pl.* grains of paddy (**waDLu**) which in pounding resist the pestle and remain unbroken: **merikallaaNTiwaaDu** choice favourite; **merikallaaNTi saynyaalu** picked troops.

మెరుగు **merugu** *n.* **1** polish. **2** brightness, lustre. **3** improvement: **tudi~lu** finishing touches.

మెరుగు కాయితం **merugu kaayitam** *n.* sandpaper.

మెరుగుదల **merugudala** *n.* improvement, betterment.

మెరుగు[లు]దిద్దు **merugu[lu] diddu** *v.i.* to improve[on], make improvements to, refine, revise; **gurajaaDa tana racanalaku ennoo saarlu~konnaTLu manaku telusu** we know that Gurajada revised his writings many times; **diinipay inkaa merugulu diddaDaaniki awakaaśam uNTundi** there will be an opportunity to improve on it still further.

మెరుగుపడు, మెరుగు అవు **merugupaDu, merugu awu** *v.i.* to improve, get better.

మెరుగుపరచు **meruguparacu** *v.t.* to improve.

మెరుగుపెట్టు **merugupeTTu** *v.i. and t.* **1** to polish: **nagalani** (or **nagalaki**) ~ to polish jewels. **2** (*also* **merugulupeTTu**) to improve [on], make improvements to, refine, revise, put finishing touches to.

మెరుపు, మెరపు **merupu, merapu** I. *n.* **1** brightness, brilliance. **2** gleam, glitter. **3** lightning. II. *adj.* **1** shiny, polished. **2** gleaming, glittering.

మెరుపుతీగ **meruputiiga** *n.* flash or streak of lightning.

మెలకువ, మెళుకువ **melakuwa, meLukuwa** *n.* **1** waking from sleep, being awake, wakefulness. **2** watchfulness, wariness, cautiousness, caution. **3** *pl.* ~**lu** (of an art or skill) technique, fine points, intricacies.

మెలకువగా, మెళుకువగా **melakuwagaa, meLukuwagaa** *adv.* **1** wakefully. **2** cautiously. **3** skilfully.

మెలగబడు **melagabaDu** *v.i.* (of a limb) to be twisted, be sprained.

మెలగు, మెలుగు **melagu, melugu** *v.i.* **1** to behave, conduct o.s. **2** to move about, go about (among), consort (with).

మెలత **melata** *n. class.* woman.

మెలమెల్లగా, మెల్లమెల్లగా **mel[l]amellagaa** *adv.* **1** slowly. **2** quietly. **3** gently.

మెలి **meli** *n.* twist: *only occurring prefixed to certain vbs.*, e.g., ~**tippu,** ~**tirugu,**~**peTTu,** ~**weeyu.**

మెలిక **melika** *n.* **1** turn, twist, curve. **2** s.g twisted, winding or tortuous: **rooDDu baarugaa leedu, ~lu tirigi undi** the road is not straight, it is winding. **3** difference of opinion, misunderstanding. **4** hitch, snag.

మెలి[కలు]తిప్పు **meli[kalu]tippu** *v.t.* to twist, turn, contort.

మెలి[కలు]తిరుగు **meli[kalu]tirugu** *v.i.* **1** to be twisted, be contorted. **2** to writhe, squirm.

మెలి[కలు]పడు **meli[kalu]paDu** *v.i.* **1** to be twisted. **2** to be entwined, be entangled.

మెలి[కలు]పెట్టు **meli[kalu]peTTu** *v.i. and t.* to twist, be twisted; **o.-i ceyyi/cewi melipeTTu** to twist s.o's arm/ear; **waaDiki kaDupuloo boDDucuTTuu melipeTTindi** he felt griping pains in his stomach around the navel.

మెలుగు **melugu** *same as* **melagu.**

మెలుపు **melupu** *v.t. dial.* to bend.

మెల్ల **mella**[1] *n.* (*also*~**cuupu,** ~**kannu**) squint, squinting eye, eye that squints.

మెల్ల **mella**[2] *adj.* **1** gentle, soft. **2** slow.

మెల్లగా, మెల్లిగా **mellagaa, melligaa** *adv.* **1** gently, softly. **2** slowly, gradually. **3** ~**aDugutunnaawaa**? are you asking that question seriously? *or* do you really mean to ask that question? (*implying* don't you know the answer already?).

మెల్లమెల్లగా **mellamellagaa** *same as* **melamellagaa.**

మెల్లా **mellaa** *n.* front courtyard of a house.

మెళుకువ[గా] **meLukuwa[gaa]** *same as* **melakuwa[gaa].**

మెసవు **mesawu** *v.t.* to eat, feed on.

మెసులు **mesulu** *v.i.* **1** to move about, go about, shift, stir. **2** to behave, comport o.s.

మెస్తా **mestaa** *n.* jute fibre.

మే - mee

మేం, మేము **meem[u]** *personal pron.* we (exclusive of the person[s] addressed).

మేక **meeka** *n.* goat; ~ **wanne puli** *is a phrase equivalent to* wolf in sheep's clothing.

మేకపిల్ల **meekapilla** *n.* kid.

మేకపోతు **meekapootu** *n.* he goat, billy goat; ~ **gaambhiir-yam** sham courage, blustering.

మేకు **meeku** *n.* 1 nail. 2 peg, stake.

మేఖల **meekhala** *n. class.* belt, zone, girdle.

మేఘం **meegham** *n.* cloud.

మేఘాచ్ఛాదిత **meeghaacchaadita** *adj.* clouded, covered in cloud, overcast.

మేజా **meejaa** *n.* table.

మేజువాడీ **meejuwaaDii** *adj.* oral; ~ **kawlu** oral lease; *cf.* **muujuwaaNii.**

మేజువాణి **meejuwaaNi** *n.* 1 nautch, music and dancing performance by professional dancing girls. 2 social gathering of women held towards the end of a wedding cere ony.

మేజోడు **meejooDu** *n.* (*gen.pl.* **meejooLLu**) socks, stockings.

మేట **meeTa** *n.* heap of soil; ~ **weesina** silted up; **isaka** ~ sandhill.

మేటి **meeTi** I. *n.* person in the forefront, leader, chief. II. *adj.* chief, principal, leading, foremost; ~ **wimarśakulu** leading critics; ~ **jaTTu** foremost team.

మేటికొయ్య **meeTikoyya** *n.* post planted in the middle of a threshing floor, round which the threshing revolves.

మేటు **meeTu** *n.* rick of threshed straw.

మేడ **meeDa** *n.* 1 house with more than one floor or storey. 2 upper floor or storey of a house; ~ **miidi gadi** upstairs room; ~ **miida** on the upper floor; ~ **meeTLu** stairs leading to the upper floor[s].

మేడి **meeDi** *n.* species of fig tree, *ficus glomerata*, whose fruit is proverbially attractive in appearance but inwardly worthless.

మేడికర్ర **meeDikarra** *n.* ploughshaft.

మేడితోక **meeDitooka** *n.* ploughtail.

మేడెం **meeDem** *n.* heap of cut corn before threshing.

మేత **meeta** *n.* 1 grazing, pasture. 2 fodder, feed (for cattle, poultry, etc.)

మేతర **meetara** *n. dial.* scavenger.

మేదకుడు **meedakuDu** *n.* mild person, simple and artless person.

మేదర **meedara** *n.* member of the basketmakers' community.

మేదిని **meedini** *n. class.* the earth.

మేధ[స్సు] **meedha[ssu]** *n.* 1 memory, retentiveness. 2 understanding, intellect, intelligence.

మేధం **meedham** *n.* sacrifice, esp. of an animal.

మేధావంతుడు **meedhaawantuDu** *n.* intelligent person.

మేధావి **meedhaawi** *n.* 1 intellectual. 2 learned person.

మేనక **meenaka** *n.* Menaka, a celestial courtesan.

మేనకోడలు **meenakooDalu** *n.* niece, man's sister's daughter or woman's brother's daughter.

మేనత్త **meenatta** *n.* paternal aunt, father's sister.

మేనబావ **meenabaawa** *n.* man's/woman's father's sister's son if older than himself/herself.

మేనమరదలు **meenamaradalu** *n.* man's /woman's father's sister's daughter.

మేనమరిది **meenamaridi** *n.* man's/woman's father's sister's son if younger than himself/herself.

మేనమామ **meenamaama** *n.* maternal uncle, mother's brother.

మేనరికం **meenarikam** *n.* 1 (of a man) marriage with his maternal uncle's daughter. 2 (of a woman) marriage with her paternal aunt's son.

మేనల్లుడు **meenalluDu** *n.* nephew, man's sister's son or woman's brother's son.

మేనా **meenaa** *n.* palanquin.

మేను **meenu** *n. class.* body.

మేపు **meepu** *v.t.* to graze cattle, tend cattle.

మేము **meemu** *same as* **meem.**

మేయు **meeyu** *v.t.* (of cattle) to graze, feed on.

మేర **meera** *n.* 1 limit; **kanucuupu** ~ **loo** within (the limit of) sight, as far as the eye can see. 2 space, area; **waaLLa iNTiki maa iNTiki madhya unna kaastaa** ~ **loo guDise wesukonnaaDu** he built a hut in the little space between their house and ours. 3 extent; **koddi** ~ **ku** to a small extent. 4 period, span of time; **muuDu śataabdaala** ~ **ku mugguru kawulu mahaabhaarataanni anuwadincEEru** over a span of three centuries three poets translated the Mahabharata. 5 *dial.* boundary ridge between two fields.

మేరకు **meeraku** *adv., used as p.p. and as an advbl. particle* 1 up to (the limit of), to the extent of, as much as; **muuDu eeLLa** ~ **selawupeTTEEDu** he took leave for up to three years; **ii samstha 25.51 lakSala ruupaayala wiluwa** ~ **dustulanu wideeśaalaku egumati ceesindi** this organisation exported garments worth as much as Rs. 25.51 lakhs to foreign countries; **naaku saadhyamaynanta** ~ to the extent that is possible for me *or* as far as I am able; **waaDu kuurcunnanta** ~ **kaphii poosEEDu** he spilt coffee all round the place where he was sitting; **nibandhanala** ~ **pani** *journ.* work to rule. 2 in accordance with, in compliance with, in line with, to suit; **miiru ceppina** ~ **aayanni kalusukonnaanu** I met him in accordance with your instructions; **aayana koorika** ~ **weLLEEnu** I went in compliance with his wish; **anni tarahaala caduwarula abhirucula** ~ to suit the tastes of all classes of readers.

మేరుపు **meerupu** *n.* spinal cord.

మేరువు **meeruwu** *n.* Meru, a legendary mountain; **naaku adee mahaa** ~ that is a great mountain of help to me (an expression of gratitude).

మేలం **meelam** *n.* 1 joking, fun, sport (as between members of families which are connected by marriage or are eligible to be so connected). 2 festivity, festive occasion, mela.

మేలమాడు **meelamaaDu** *v.i.* to joke, make fun, have sport (as between members of families which are connected by marriage or are eligible to be so connected).

మేలి[మి] **meeli[mi]** *adj.* fine, pure; ~ **bangaaram** pure gold.

మేలిచీరె **meeliciire** *n.* kind of sari eight yards in length worn by elderly women.

మేలిముసుగు **meelimusugu** *n.* end of a sari draped over the head like a veil.

మేలు **meelu** I. *n.* 1 good, benefit, profit, advantage, superiority; **mii ~ koori ceppEEnu** I said it for your good: *see* **encu.** 2 goodness, kindness; **padi ruupaayalu ippincEEraa, mii ~ marawanu** if you lend me ten rupees I will be obliged to you (*lit.* I will not forget your kindness). II. *adj.* 1 good, fine, excellent. 2 superior, preferable, better, best: **waana paDeeTaTTundi, miiru weLLaDam ~** it looks like rain, you had better go.

మేలుకొను, మేల్కొను **meelukonu, meelkonu** *v.i.* 1 to wake up, rise. 2 (*also* **meel[u]koni uNDu**) to be awake, stay awake.

మేలుకొలుపు, మేల్కొలుపు **meelukolupu, meelkolpu** I. *n.* 1 (*gen. pl.* ~ **lu**) music played at dawn. 2 awakening. II. *v.t.* to wake, awaken.

మేలు చేయు **meelu ceeyu** *v.i.* to give help to, do good to, benefit; **naluguriki meelu ceeyaDam aayana alawaaTu** he is in the habit of helping people; **daywam meelu ceestee waanalu paDataayi** if God favours us, there will be rain.

మేలుబంతి **meelubanti** *n.* 1 top line written by a teacher in a copy book as an example to be copied by a pupil (= **ojjabanti**). 2 pattern, example.

మేలుమేలు! **meelumeelu!** *interj.* fine!, excellent!, well done!

మేలురకం **meelurakam** *n. and adj.* fine variety.

మేలురాసి **meeluraasi** *n.* heap of clean grain formed on the ground after winnowing.

మేళం **meeLam** *n.* 1 band or troupe of music players, singers and dancers. 2 *as second part of a n. compound* group of persons or an individual of a certain kind, e.g., **palleTuuri ~** group of village people; **tikka ~** (i) group of crazy people, (ii) simpleton; **jaagu ~** procrastinator. 3 *dial.* festivity involving extravagant expenditure.

మేళనం **meeLanam** *n.* 1 meeting, union. 2 mixing, mingling.

మేళవించు **meeLawincu** *v.t.* to unite (in harmony), combine, mingle.

మేళవింపు **meeLawimpu** *n.* combination, uniting, mixing, mingling.

మేషం **meeSam** *n.* 1 ram. 2 *astrol.* Aries.

మేషాండుడు **meeSaaNDuDu** *n. class.* epithet of Indra.

మేస్త్రి **meestri** *n.* head of a band of workmen, overseer.

మేహం **meeham** *n.* 1 disease of the urinal tract. 2 gonorrhoea. 3 (in Ayurvedic medicine) excessive heat in the body.

మేహనం **meehanam** *n. class.* penis.

మై - may

మై **may** *n. class.* body.

మైకం **maykam** *n.* 1 intoxication. 2 insensitivity. 3 forgetting o.s. 4 infatuation. 5 drowsiness. 6 unconsciousness: **taaguDu ~** drunken stupor.

మైత్రి **maytri** *n.* friendship.

మైథునం **maythunam** *n.* coition, sexual intercourse.

మైదా[పిండి] **maydaa[piNDi]** *n.* wheat flour.

మైదానం **maydaanam** *n.* open level ground, plain, flat stretch of land.

మైదు **maydu** *n.* love powder, love potion.

మైనం **maynam** *n.* wax.

మైనపువత్తి **maynapuwatti** *n.* candle.

మైమరచు **maymaracu** *v.i.* 1 to be transported or overcome by joy, sorrow or other emotion. 2 to be enchanted, be entranced. 3 to lose consciousness. 4 to be engrossed, be absorbed (**-loo**, in).

మైమరపించు **maymarapincu** *v.t.* to entrance.

మైమరపు **maymarapu** *n.* entrancement, ecstasy.

మైరావణుడు **mayraawaNuDu** *n.* 1 villain. 2 name of a demon in the Ramayana.

మైల **mayla** I. *n.* 1 ceremonial pollution or defilement. 2 *dial.* dirt, uncleanness. II. *adj.* 1 ceremonially impure, polluted or defiled. 2 *dial.* dirty, unclean. 3 black (with ref. to a black spot on some other colour).

మైలపడు **maylapaDu** *v.i.* 1 to be[come] ceremonially impure, polluted or defiled. 2 *dial.* to be[come] dirty or unclean.

మైలు **maylu** *n.* mile: **mayLLaku mayLLu naDicEEDu** he walked for miles and miles.

మైలుతుత్తం **maylututtam** *n.* copper sulphate.

మైలురాయి **mayluraayi** *n.* mile stone.

మొ - mo

మొండి **moNDi** *adj.* 1 maimed, lame; ~ **kaalu** lame leg. 2 bare; ~ **meDa/ceetulu** bare neck/arms (without ornaments); **Dabbu istaanannaaDu, ciwariki ~ ceyyi cuupincEEDu** he said he would give me money but in the end he showed me an empty hand (i.e., he gave me nothing); ~ **gooDalu** bare walls (of an unfinished or ruined building). 3 stubborn, obstinate, wilful, obdurate, intractable, unmanageable; ~ **eddu** stubborn or unmanageable bullock; **pillawaaDu ~ eeDupu eeDustunnaaDu** the boy is crying obdurately; ~ **praaNam** life which clings to one obstinately and does not depart; *see* **ghaTam.** 4 blunt; ~ **katti** blunt knife.

మొండికట్టె **moNDikaTTe** *n.* stubborn person, obstinate person.

మొండికిపడు **moNDikipaDu** *v.i.* to persist or insist resolutely, refuse to be dissuaded.

మొండికివేయు, మొండికేయు, మొండికెత్తు **moNDikiweeyu, moNDikeeyu, moNDikettu** *v.i.* to insist or persist obstinately; **DaakTaru annam tinawaddannaa tiNTaanani moNDikeesEEDu** (*or* **moNDikettEEDu**) he persisted in eating rice although the doctor had forbidden it.

మొండిగా **moNDigaa** *adv.* stubbornly, obstinately, persistently, determinedly, refusing to be deterred.

మొండిచేయు **moNDiceeyu** I. *v.i.* to behave stubbornly or obstinately. II. *v.t.* 1 to make (s.g) blunt. 2 to make (s.g) bare or empty.

మొండితనం **moNDitanam** *n.* stubbornness, wilfulness, obstinacy.

మొండితేరు, మొండిపారు **moNDiteeru, moNDipaaru** *v.i.* to become blunt.

మొండిపట్టు **moNDipaTTu** *n.* obstinacy, obduracy, wilfulness, stubbornness, persistence.

మొండిపీనుగు **moNDipiinugu** *n.* person who will not listen to others, very stubborn person.

మొండిమొల **moNDimola** *adj.* naked, nude.

మొండిరకం **moNDirakam** *adj.* persistent, obdurate.

మొండెం **moNDem** *n.* 1 stump, stub. 2 trunk, headless body.

మొక్క **mokka**[1] *n.* 1 plant. 2 young plant, shoot, sprout. 3 *same as* ~ **jonna.**

మొక్క **mokka**[2] *adj.* blunt.

మొక్కజొన్న **mokkajonna** *n* maize, *zea mays.*

మొక్కట్టు **mokkaTTu** *n.* features, lineaments.

మొక్కపారు **mokkapaaru** *v.i.* to become blunt.

మొక్కపోవు, మొక్కవోవు **mokkapoowu, mokkawoowu** *v.i.* 1 to be blunted, become blunt. 2 *fig.* to fail, flag, wane; **mokkawooni aatmawiśwaasamtoo munduku naDicipooyEEDu** he stepped forward with unflagging courage. 3 *colloq.* to suffer loss, be harmed; **ii pani ceestee mokkapootaawaa?** if you do this will you lose anything? *or* is there any harm in your doing this? (*lit.* if you do this will you be blunted?).

మొక్కరం **mokkaram** *n.* upright pillar or column.

మొక్కలం **mokkalam** *n.* 1 stubbornness, obstinacy. 2 ruffian, villain.

మొక్కు, మ్రొక్కు **m[r]okku** I. *n.* 1 religious vow. 2 offering to a god. II. *v.i.* to bow down, do reverence, make obeisance.

మొక్కుకొను **mokkukonu** *v.i.* to [make a] vow.

మొక్కుబడి **mokkubaDi** *n.* 1 vow. 2 offering to a god.

మొక్కుబడితీర్చినట్లు, మొక్కుబడిగా **mokkubaDi tiircinaTLu, mokkubaDigaa** *adv. colloq.* perfunctorily, mechanically, in a perfunctory or mechanical manner; ~ **paaTham cebataaDu** he teaches in a mechanical manner.

మొక్కుబడి తీర్చు **mokkubaDi tiircu** *v.i.* to fulfil a vow.

మొఖం **mokham** *same as* **mukham.**

మొఖాసా **mokhaasaa** *n.* mokhasa, village granted under a system now obsolete to a person on favourable tenure for services rendered or to be rendered.

మొఖాసాదారు **mokhaasaadaaru** *n.* 1 holder of a mokhasa. 2 landowner.

మొఖిరీ **mokhirii** *n.* kind of plantain or banana..

మొగ **moga**[1] *n.* 1 tip, point, end. 2 beginning, entrance **wiidhi ~ loo** at the entrance to a street *or* at the end of a street.

మొగ **moga**[2] *adj.* male, man's.

మొగం **mogam** *same as* **mukham.**

మొగదల **mogadala** I. *n.* front part. II. *adv. used postpositionally* in front of; **gummam ~** in front of the doorway.

మొగమాటం, మొగమోటమి **mogamaaTam, mogamootami** *same as* **mohamaaTam.**

మొగలాయీ **mogalaayii** *n. and adj.* Moghul.

మొగలి **mogali** *n.* screw pine, *pandanus odoratissimus.*

మొగసాల **mogasaala** *n.* porch or covered veranda in front of a house.

మొగుడు **moguDu** *n.* 1 husband. 2 *colloq.* **naa ~** my boss.

మొగులు, మొయిలు **mogulu, moyilu** *n. poet. and dial.* cloud.

మొగ్గ **mogga** *n.* 1 bud. 2 acrobatic feat, somersault.

మొగ్గ తొడుగు **mogga toDugu** *v.i.* to issue, sprout, arise, emanate; **anumaanam mogga toDigindi** a suspicion arose.

మొగ్గవేయు **mogga weeyu** *v.i.* 1 to somersault. 2 *same as* **mogga toDugu.**

మొగ్గు **moggu** I. *n.* 1 tilting of a balance. 2 inclination, leaning. 3 favour[itism]. II. *v.i.* to lean, be inclined.

మొగ్గుచూపు **moggucuupu** *v.i.* 1 to show an inclination, show partiality, show favour. 2 to show favouritism.

మొగ్గుదల **moggudala** *n.* inclination, preference, partiality.

మొటమొటలాడు **moTamoTalaaDu** *v.i.* to frown, be in an angry mood.

మొటిమ **moTima** *n.* pimple.

మొట్టమొదట **moTTamodaTa** *adv.* at the very beginning.

మొట్టమొదటి **moTTamodaTi** *adj.* the very first.

మొట్టికాయ **moTTikaaya** *n.* rap with the knuckles.

మొట్టు **moTTu** *v.t.* to rap with the knuckles, esp. on the head.

మొత **motta**[1] *n.* **1** distance from a doorway to the end of the wall in which the doorway is set. **2** side, edge.

మొత్త **motta**[2] *n. slang* hips; **~ cuusi piiTa weesinaTTu** like giving s.o. only as much respect as is due to his status (*lit.* like seeing the hips and then offering a suitable seat—proverbial saying); **waaDi ~ balisindi** he has become proud (*lit.* his hips have become fat); **eem nii ~ laawaa? neenu enduku ceeyaali?** are you such a great person? (*lit.* are your hips so broad?) why should I do this for you?

మొత్తం **mottam** I. *n.* whole, total, total amount, total quantity. II. *adj.* whole, entire, all; **~ raaSTramloo** *or* **raaSTram ~ miida** in the entire state; **raaSTram looni ~ widyaasamsthalaloo muuDoo wantu** one third of all the educational institutions in the state.

మొత్తంమీద **mottammiida** I. *adv.* **1** in all, in total, taken as a whole: **krSNaanadi raaSTramloo ~ 720 kilomiiTarlu prawahistundi** the river Krishna flows through the state for 720 kilometres in all; **graamiiNa praantaalaloo raaSTram ~ janasaandrata cadarapu kiloomiiTaruki 128 mandi** the density of population in rural areas taking the state as a whole is 128 per square kilometre. **2** on [an] average; **rooju ~ irawaymandi janam wastaaru** twenty persons come per day on an average. **3** on the whole, by and large, in general, in short, to sum up; **aa abbaayi talee uupEEDoo, ceyyee uupEEDoo, eemi ceesEEDoo teliyadu kaanii ~ andaruu baawamaruduleenani niścayincukonnaaru** the young man may have nodded his head or waved his hand or I do not know what he may have done, but in short they all concluded that these two persons were cousins; **ii saari kuuDaa DaakTaru gaariNTa peeSaNTLu leeru; ~ roogulanu aakarSincee śakti aayanaloo leedu** again there were no patients at the doctor's house; by and large he lacked the power to attract patients.

మొత్తన, మొత్తను, మొత్తనే **mottaha, mottanu, mottanee** *p.p. and adv.* by the side of, next to; **kaaluwa ~ unnapolam naadee** the field by the side of the canal is mine: **aa mottanee** next to that.

మొత్తా **mottaa** *n.* driver's seat (made of rope) on a bullock cart.

మొత్తానికి **mottaaniki** *adv.* **1** on the whole, in all, in total, in general, whatever it may be. **2** at least, at any rate, anyhow.

మొత్తు **mottu** *v.t.* to beat, smite.

మొత్తుకొను **mottukonu** *v.i.* **1** to beat o.'s head in despair. **2** to grieve, lament, be distressed.

మొత్తుకోలు **mottukoolu** *n.pl.* telling o.'s troubles, expressing o.'s grief; **eeDupuluu mottukooLLuu** weeping and lamentation.

మొదట **modaTa** *adv.* **1** at first, at the very beginning. **2** at the foot of; **ceTTu ~** at the foot of the tree.

మొదటి **modaTi** *adj.* first.

మొదలగు **modalagu** *class. alt. form of* **modalayna.**

మొదలవు **modalawu** *v.i.* to begin, start.

మొదలిడు **modaliDu** *class. alt. form of* **modalupeTTu.**

మొదలు **modalu** I. *n.* **1** beginning, origin, source, root, base, basis; **aaku ~** base of a leaf; **kaaluwa ~** starting point of a canal; **koNDa ~** foot of a hill. **2 mokka ~** stem of a plant; **ceTTu ~** trunk (or foot) of a tree. **3** *econ.* principal, capital. II. *adv.* beginning with, starting from.

మొదలుకొని **modalukoni** I. *adv.* beginning with, starting from; **nannaya ~ ippaTiwaraku** starting from Nannaya up to the present time. II. *advbl. particle* from the time of, since; **aayana waccina ~** since his arrival.

మొదలుపెట్టు, మొదలెట్టు **modalupeTTu, modaleTTu** *v.i. and t.* to begin, start; **maarci raagaanee cali taggi eNDalu kaayaDam modalu peDataayi** as soon as March comes the coolness diminishes and the sun's heat begins to scorch.

మొదలే **modalee** *adv.* **1** to begin with, for a start; **~ naaku caalaa appu undi, inkaa neenu ekkaDa testaanu?** for a start I am heavily in debt, so how will I be able to borrow more? **2** *in neg. constr.* at all; **waaDu ~ raaDu** he will not come at all.

మొదలైన **modalayana** *adj.* and other: **tooDeeLLu ~ jantuwulu** wolves and other animals.

మొదవ **modawa** *n.* cow that has borne its first calf.

మొద్దు **moddu** I. n. **1** block, stump; **koyya ~** block of wood; **tolacina taaTi ~** hollowed out stump of a palmyra tree. **2** blockhead, dunce, stupid person. II. *adj.* **1** blunt. **2** (of cloth, skin, hide) thick. **3** dull-witted, stupid. **4 ~ nidra** heavy sleep. **5 ~ miisaalu** bushy moustache.

మొద్దుబారు **moddubaaru** *v.i.* to become blunt or insensible or dull in mind.

మొన **mona** *n.* point, end, tip.

మొనగాడు **monagaaDu** *n.* hero, champion, leader, chief; **dongalloo ~** ringleader among thieves.

మొనతేరు **monateeru** *v.i.* **1** to be sharp or pointed. **2** (of a boil, ulcer) to come to a head.

మొన్న **monna** *n. and adv.* **1** the day before yesterday. **2** the other day, very recently.

మొన్నటి **monnaTi** *adj.* **1** of the day before yesterday. **2** very recent. **3** (of a day, week or month) last; **~ aadiwaaram** *or* **monna aadiwaaram** last Sunday; **~ waaram** last week; **~ nela** last month.

మొప్ప **moppa** *n.* gill (of a fish).

మొయిలు **moyilu** *same as* **mogulu.**

మొర, మొర్ర **mora, morra** *n.* cry, wail, lament, complaint.

మొరం, మొరుం **moram, morum** *n.* gravel, grit, rubble.

మొరటు **moraTu** *adj.* **1** rude, unmannerly, uncultured. **2** rough, harsh, crude.

మొరపెట్టుకొను **morapeTTukonu** *v.i.* to wail, lament, complain; **tana baadhalannii naatoo morapeTTukonnaaDu** he poured out all his woes to me.

మొరమొరాలు **moramoraalu** *same as* **maramaraalu.**

మొరలిడు **moraliDu** *v.i. class.* to cry out in complaint.

మొరవ **morawa** *adj.* blunt.

మొరాయించు **moraayincu** *v.i. and t.* **1** to resist, oppose. **2** to refuse.

మొరి, మొ్రి **mor[r]i** I. *n.* defect, imperfection, deformity. II. *adj.* defective, imperfect, deformed.
మొ్ర **morra** *same as* **mora.**
మొ్రో! **morroo!** *interj.* alas!
మొల **mola** *n.* **1** waist, loins. **2** nail, spike, clamp.
మొలక **molaka** *n.* germ, sprout, seedling, young plant; ~ **miisam** sprouting moustache.
మొలకెత్తు **molakettu** *v.i.* **1** to sprout, spring up. **2** to germinate.
మొలగజ్జెలు **molagajjelu** *n.pl.* small bells tied round a young child's waist.
మొలగొలుకులు **molagolukulu** *n.pl.* kind of paddy grown in Rayalaseema and Nellore having a short grain.
మొలతాడు **molataaDu** *n.* cord worn round the waist.
మొలతాయెత్తు **molataayettu** *n.* charm in the form of a locket tied round the waist.
మొలనూలు **molanuulu** *n.* girdle round the waist worn by women.
మొలలు **molalu** *n.pl. med.* piles.
మొలిపించు **molipincu** *v.t.* to cause to sprout; **cirunawwu molipincEEDu** he summoned up a smile.
మొలుచు **molucu** *v.i.* to sprout, germinate.
మొల్ల **molla[1]** *n.* kind of double jasmine.
మొల్ల **molla[2]** *n.* name of a Telugu poetess of the 15th century.
మొవ్వు, మొవు, మోవు **mow[w]u, moowu** *n.* unopened sprout or shoot of a palm tree or banana (plantain) or reed.
మొసమొసలాడు **mosamosalaaDu** *same as* **musamusalaaDu.**
మొసలి **mosali** *n.* crocodile.
మొసలికన్నీరు కార్చు **mosalikanniiru kaarcu** *v.i.* to shed crocodile's tears, make an insincere display of grief.
మొసళ్లపండగ **mosaLLapaNDaga** *same as* **musaLLapaNDaga.**
మొహం **moham** *same as* **mukham.**
మొహమాటం, మొగమాటం, మొగమోటమి **mohamaaTam, mogamaaTam, mogamooTami** *n.* **1** hesitation, reserve, diffidence, shyness. **2** *pl.* **mohamaaTaalu** obligations.
మొహమాటంలో పెట్టు **mohamaaTamloo peTTu** *v.t.* to cause embarrassment (to s.o.).
మొహమాటపడు **mohamaaTapaDu** *v.i.* to hesitate, feel diffident, feel shy, feel embarrassed.
మొహరీ **moharii** *n.* mohur, an obsolete gold coin.
మొహరు **moharu** *n.* seal, stamp.

మో - moo

మోంబత్తి **moombatti** *n. dial.* wax candle.
మోకరించు, మోకరిల్లు **mookarincu, mookarillu** *v.i.* to kneel.
మోకాలు **mookaalu** *n.* knee.
మోకాలుచిప్ప, మోకాటిచిప్ప **mookaalucippa, mookaaTicippa** *n.* knee cap.
మోకు **mooku** *n.* thick rope.
మోక్షం **mookSam** *n.* **1** final liberation of the soul from bodily ties. **2** salvation.
మోక్షకాలం **mookSakaalam** *n.* time of passing off of an eclipse.
మోగించు, మ్రోగించు, మ్రోయించు **m[r]oogincu, mrooyincu** *v.t.* **1** to ring (bell), sound (motor horn, siren, etc.). **2** to play (musical instrument). **3** to cause (s.g) to resound.
మోగు, మ్రోగు, మ్రోయు **m[r]oogu, mrooyu** *v.i.* **1** to sound, ring, tinkle. **2** to resound, reverberate.
మోచెయ్యి **mooceyyi** *n.* elbow.
మోజు **mooju** *n.* great liking, keenness, fondness, passion, predilection, fancy, taste (**-miida/-payna/-paTLa/-aNTee** for); **antadaakaa naaku paaścaatya saahityam miidanee~uNDeedi** hitherto I had had a predilection for western literature; **naakanta~leedu aa puwwulaNTee; koyyawaddu** I have not got such a great liking for those flowers; please do not cut them.
మోజుపడు **moojupaDu** *v.i.* to be keen (on), be devoted (to), be attracted (by).
మోట **mooTa[1]** *n.* mhote, apparatus for baling water from a well for irrigation.
మోట **mooTa[2]** *dial. variant form of* **mooTu.**
మోటబావి **mooTabaawi** *n.* baling well.
మోటాయించు **mooTaayincu** *v.i.* to be stubborn, insist.
మోటించు **mooTincu** *v.i.* to lean; **naaku mooTinci kuurcunnaaDu** he sat leaning against me.
మోటు **mooTu** I. *n.* stupid person, obstinate person, blockhead. II. *adj.* **1** rough, coarse, crude, uncultured. **2** dull, stupid. **3** (of a knife) blunt.
మోటుగాడు **mooTugaaDu** *n. slang* ruffian, villain.
మోటుతనం **mooTutanam** *n.* roughness, coarseness, crudeness.
మోటుతిండి **mooTutiNDi** *n.* eating to excess, guzzling; **waaDu~tiNTaaDu** he is in the habit of guzzling *or* he is a guzzler.
మోటుపని **mooTupani** *n.* rough manual work, e.g., carrying stones.
మోటుసరసం **mooTusarasam** *n.* horse play.
మోటుహాస్యం **mooTuhaasyam** *n.* practical joking.
మోడం **mooDam** *n.* cloud[iness].
మోడా **mooDaa** *n.* round-shaped cane stool.
మోడి **mooDi** *n.* **1** trickery, jugglery. **2** way, manner, style. **3** ill humour, crossness. **4** handwriting.
మోడికారం **mooDikaaram** *see* **pippaLLa~.**

మోడిచేయు **mooDiceeyu** *v.i.* to practise magic or jugglery.

మోడు **mooDu** I. *n.* dead or dry wood, stump of a tree or plant. II *adj.* dried, withered.

మోడుచరచు **mooDucaracu** *v.i.* 1 to become stiff or motionless. 2 (of a limb) to lose sensation, become numb.

మోడుబారు **mooDubaaru** *v.i.* 1 to become like dead wood, wither. 2 to become stiff or rigid.

మోడ్చు **mooDcu** *v.t.* 1 *class.* to join or fold together. 2 **kay ~ koni** with the hands joined together in greeting or salutation.

మోడ్పు **mooDpu** *n.* joining or folding together, esp. of the palms of the hands in greeting or salutation; *cf.* **kay-mooDpu.**

మోత **moota**[1] *n.* load.

మోత **moota**[2] *n.* loud sound, noise; **iigala ~** buzzing of flies.

మోత **moota**[3] I. *adj. colloq.* fine, excellent; **sinimaa ~ gaa undi** the movie is fine. II. *interj. colloq.* fine!, splendid!, excellent! **~ ! niiku manci maarkulu waccEEyi** excellent! you have got good marks.

మోతాదు **mootaadu**[1] *n.* 1 dose (of medicine). 2 moderate amount, moderate quantity.

మోతాదు **mootaadu**[2] *n.* village servant working under a village headman or accountant (now obsolete).

మోతాదుగా **mootaadugaa** *adv.* moderately.

మోతుబరి **mootubari** I. *n.* wealthy person, man of means. II. *adj.* rich, wealthy.

మోద[న]ం **mooda[na]m** *n. class.* pleasure, joy.

మోదకం **moodakam** *n. class.* coconut.

మోదకాలు **moodakaalu** *n.pl.* kind of sweet cake (= **uNDraaLLu**).

మోదు **moodu** *v.t.* to beat, strike, hit or thump with a heavy instrument or stone.

మోదుగ, మోదుగు **mooduga, moodugu** *n.* tree called flame of the forest, *butea frondosa.*

మోపి **moopi** *n.* widow.

మోపు **moopu** I. *n.* bundle, load, burden; **kaTTela ~** bundle of firewood. II. *adj.* heavy, severe; **moopayna gaayam** severe wound. III. *v.t.* 1 to load. 2 to place, put, set, lay; **candramaNDalam payna maanawuDu tolisaarigaa kaalu moopina naaDu** the day when man first set foot on the moon; **neeram ~** to lay a charge *or* to impute a crime (**-miida**, against).

మోపుకొను **moopukonu** *v.t.* to take (a burden) upon o.s.

మోపుగా **moopugaa** *adv.* heavily, severely; **debbalu waaDiki ~ tagilEEyi** the blows struck him heavily.

మోపెడు **moopeDu** *adj.* load of, bundle of; **~ gaDDi** bundle of straw.

మోమాటం **moomaaTam** *alt. variant form of* **mohamaa-Tam.**

మోము **moomu** *n. class.* face, countenance, visage (= **mukham**).

మోయిన **mooyina** *locative of* **mooyinu** *used colloq. as an advbl. particle meaning* amounting to, to the extent of: **aa ~ tiNTee jabbu raakeem ceestundi?** if you eat as much as that you are sure to get ill (*lit.* if you eat to that extent, what else will illness do except come?); **waaLLiddariki kaawalasina ~ saamanulu kaTTi iccEEnu** I gave them equipment sufficient for (*lit.* amounting to what is necessary for) two people; **yuuniwarsiTiila paribhaaSaloo ceppaalaNTee, ii krSi okaTi reNDu Ph.D.la ~ wyawahaaram awtundi** expressed in university parlance this work is a matter amounting to one or two Ph.D.'s.

మోయిను **mooyinu** *n.* 1 *same as* **sadaawrtti.** 2 sample. 3 manner.

మోయు **mooyu** *v.t.* to bear, sustain, carry, convey.

మోర **moora** *n.* 1 face of an animal having a projecting snout or muzzle, such as a horse. 2 **~** *is used disparagingly of a human face in certain expressions,* e.g., **peddawaaLLu maaTLaaDukoNTuuNTee pillalu ~lu etti wiNTunnaaru** when the grownups were talking together, the children were listening in to what was being said.

మోరీ **moorii** *n.* drainage pipe, waste pipe, gutter.

మోళీ **mooLii** *n.* jugglery, conjuring.

మోవి **moowi** *n. class.* lip.

మోవు **moowu** *same as* **mow[w]u.**

మోసం **moosam** *n.* 1 deceit, fraud, trick[ery], imposture, cheating. 2 danger, peril, harm; **tarugu jillaala pooSaNa baadhyatanu migulu jillaalaku appagincaDam, modaTikee ~ gaa unna praantaala pooSaNaku digumati dhaanyaalanu keeTaayincaDam jarigindi** the responsibility for supporting the deficit districts was assigned to the surplus districts (of the State) and imported food grains (from abroad) were allotted for the support of areas that were in dire straits.

మోసం చేయు, మోసగించు, మోసపుచ్చు **moosam ceeyu, moosagincu, moosapuccu** *v.t.* to cheat, defraud, deceive, mislead, betray.

మోసంబి **moosambi** *n.* sweet orange, batavian orange (= **battaayi**).

మోసకాడు **moosakaaDu** *n.* deceiver, swindler, cheat, impostor, rogue.

మోసపడు **moosapaDu** *v.i.* to be cheated, be deceived; **aa wyawahaaramloo neenu moosapaDDaanu** I was cheated in that deal.

మోసపు **moosapu** *adj.* deceitful, fraudulent.

మోసపోవు **moosapoowu** *v.i.* to be cheated, be deceived, be misled, be betrayed; **aayanaki** (*or* **aayana walla**) **neenu moosapoyEEnu** I was deceived by him; **aayana maaTalaki neenu moosapooyEEnu** I was deceived by his words.

మోసు **moosu** *n.* shoot, sprout.

మోసులెత్తు **moosulettu** *v.i.* to sprout, grow.

మోస్తరు **moostaru** *n.* sample, specimen, model; **oka ~ paaTakaaDu** a fairly good singer; **oka ~ saarangala neela** moderately fertile soil; **oka ~ gaa tiNDi baaguNTundi** the food is fairly good.

మోహం **mooham** *n.* 1 enchantment, fascination, infatuation. 2 love, lust, passion.

మోహన **moohana** *adj.* fascinating, enchanting.

మోహరించు **mooharincu** *v.i.* to prepare for battle, mobilise.

మోహరింపచేయు **mooharimpaceeyu** *v.t.* to mobilise.

మోహాన్వితుడు moohaanwituDu *n.* one who is possessed by lust.

మోహించు moohincu *v.t.* to fall in love with, be passionately fond of.

మోహిని moohini *n.* fascinating woman, enchantress, siren.

మోహినిపిశాచం moohinipiśaacam *n.* she devil.

మౌ to మ్లే - maw to mlee

మౌంజి mawnji *same as* **munji.**

మౌఖిక mawkhika *adj.* oral; ~ **pariikSa** viva voce examination.

మౌగ్ధ్యం mawgdhyam *n.* youthful simplicity.

మౌఢ్యం mawDhyam[1] *n. same as* **muuDhata, muuDhatwam.**

మౌఢ్యం mawDhyam[2] *same as* **muuDham[i].**

మౌన mawna *adj.* silent.

మౌనం mawnam *n.* silence.

మౌనం వహించు, మౌనం దాల్చు mawnam wahincu, mawnam daalcu *v.i.* to keep silence, be silent.

మౌనవ్రతం mawnawratam *n.* vow of silence.

మౌని mawni *n.* hermit, ascetic, recluse.

మౌలిక mawlika *adj.* basic, fundamental.

మౌళి mawLi *n.class.* 1 lock of hair on the crown of the head. 2 diadem.

మ్రగ్గు mraggu *same as* **maggu.**

మ్రాకు, మ్రాగన్ను, మ్రాను, మ్రాన్పడు mraaku, mraagannu, mraanu, mraanpaDu *same as* **maaku, maagannu, maanu, maanpaDu.**

మ్రింగు, మ్రుచ్చిలించు mringu, mruccilincu *same as* **mingu, muccilincu.**

మ్రొక్కు mrokku *same as* **mokku.**

మ్రోగించు, మ్రోయించు, మ్రోగు, మ్రోయు mroogincu, mrooyincu, mroogu, mrooyu *same as* **moogincu, moogu.**

మ్రోల mroola *p.p.* in front of, in the presence of, before; **deewuni** ~ in the presence of God.

మ్లాన mlaana *adj.* 1 faded, withered. 2 faint, feeble, weak, languishing. 3 dejected, downcast.

మ్లాని mlaani *n.* 1 fading, withering. 2 faintness, feebleness, weakness, languor. 3 dejection.

మ్లేచ్ఛ mleeccha *adj.* 1 foreign. 2 barbarous.

మ్లేచ్ఛుడు mleecchuDu *n.* barbarian.

య - ya

యంత్ర yantra *adj.* pertaining to machinery, mechanical.

యంత్రం yantram *n.* 1 engine, machine[ry]. 2 apparatus, contrivance. 3 astrological diagram inscribed on a copper plate.

యంత్రపరికరాలు, యంత్రసాధనాలు yantraparikaraalu, yantrasaadhanaalu *n.pl.* machine tools.

యంత్రసజ్జితం చేయు yantrasajjitam ceeyu *v.t* to mechanise.

యంత్ర సజ్జిత సేన yantrasajjita seena *n.* mechanised army.

యంత్రసామగ్రి yantrasaamagri *n.* mechanical equipment.

యంత్రాంగం yantraangam *n.* 1 machinery (abstract, not concrete); **prabhutwa** ~ machinery of government. 2 mechanism.

యంత్రీకరణ yantriikaraNa *n.* mechanisation.

యంత్రీకరించు yantriikarincu *v.t.* to mechanise.

యక్షగానం yakSagaanam *n.* 1 kind of dance drama performed in parts of Karnataka and Andhra Pradesh. 2 *class.* music of a band of celestial singers (**yakSulu**).

యక్షులు yakSulu *n.pl.* band of celestial singers, attendants on Kubera.

యక్ష్మం, రాజయక్ష్మం yakSmam, raajayakSmam *n. class.* tuberculosis, consumption.

యజనం yajanam *n.* 1 sacrifice. 2 sacrificing, worshipping.

యజమాని, యజమానుడు yajamaani, yajamaanuDu *n.* 1 master, lord. 2 owner, proprietor.

యజమానురాలు yajamaanuraalu *n.* mistress.

యజుర్వేదం yajurweedam *n.* Yajurveda, the second of the four Vedas, containing hymns and texts arranged for use at sacrifices.

యజ్ఞం, యాగం yajñam, yaagam *n.* 1 religious sacrifice. 2 act of devotion, act of worship. 3 *in literary usage* work, task, undertaking. 4 *colloq.* affair; **praNaya** ~ love affair.

యజ్ఞకాండ yajñakaaNDa *n.* 1 great sacrifice. 2 great undertaking.

యజ్ఞపశువు yajñapaśuwu *n.* sacrificial animal, scapegoat.

యజ్ఞపురుషుడు yajñapuruSuDu *n.* 1 divine being who grants a boon when propitiated by a sacrifice. 2 epithet of Vishnu.

యజ్ఞయాగాదులు yajñayaagaadulu *n.pl.* sacrifices and offerings.

యజ్ఞోపవీతం **yajñoopawiitam** *n.* sacred thread worn by Brahmans, Kshatriyas and Vysyas.

యజ్వ, యజ్వి, యాజి **yajwa, yajwi, yaaji** *n.* one who has performed Vedic sacrifices.

యతాత్ముడు **yataatmuDu** *n.* one who has curbed his emotions.

యతి **yati**[1] *n.* one who has curbed his emotions, ascetic.

యతి **yati**[2] *n.* rule observed in composing classical and some modern Telugu poetry by which there is a pause after the ninth, tenth or eleventh syllable of each line (depending on the metre) and the vowel in the immediately following syllable is in euphonic agreement with a syllable in a specific place in the same line.

యత్కించిత్తు **yatkincittu** *Sanskrit adj.* just a little, such small amount as there is; **naaku ~ koopam kuuDaa waccindi** I was also just a little annoyed; **ii kaaryabhaaranni naakunna yatkincit śakti saamarthyaalatoo nirwahistaanu** I will perform this responsibility with whatever little ability I possess.

యత్తదర్థక ప్రయోగం **yattadarthaka prayoogam** *n. gram.* correlative construction.

యత్నం **yatnam** *n.* 1 effort, endeavour, attempt. 2 *pl.* **yatnaalu** *colloq.* preparations, getting ready; **naa pilla peLLi yatnaalloo unnaanu** I am making preparations for my daughter's wedding.

యత్నించు **yatnincu** *v.i.* to try, attempt, endeavour, make an effort.

యథాతథంగా, ఉన్నదున్నట్లుగా **yathaatathangaa, unnadunnaTLugaa** *adv.* 1 just as he/she/it is *and connected forms* (just as he/she/it/was, just as they are/were, etc.). 2 word for word, verbatim.

యథాతథ్యస్థితి **yathaatathyasthiti** *n.* status quo.

యథాపూర్వ **yathaapuurwa** *adj.* previously existing; ~ **sthiti** previously existing situation, status quo; ~ **ruupam** previous shape.

యథాప్రకారంగా **yathaaprakaarangaa** *adv.* as usual.

యథార్థ **yathaartha** *adj.* 1 true, real, genuine, factual, actual. 2 accurate.

యథార్థం **yathaartham** *n.* 1 truth, fact. 2 real facts, true situation.

యథార్థంగా **yathaarthangaa** *adv.* really, truly, actually.

యథార్థత **yathaarthata** *n.* 1 truth, reality. 2 accuracy.

యథాలాపంగా **yathaalaapangaa** *adv.* casually, spontaneously, involuntarily, by chance; **mii maaTa ~ winnaanu, maLLii ceppaNDi** I half heard what you said, please repeat it.

యథావిధిగా **yathaawidhigaa** *adv.* 1 according to rule, duly. 2 normally, in the normal manner, in the usual course.

యథాశక్తిగా, యథాశక్తిని, యథాశక్తీ **yathaaśaktigaa, yathaaśaktini, yathaaśaktii** *adv* according to o.'s means, to the extent of o.'s ability; **iTuwaNTi samasyalanniTinii drSTiloo peTTukoni ~ arthanirNayam ceeyaDam jarigindi** bearing in mind all the problems of this nature we have determined the meanings to the best of our ability.

యథాస్థానం **yathaasthaanam** *n.* former place, place where (s.g) was previously.

యథాస్థితి **yathaasthiti** *n.* existing situation, actual situation, true state of affairs.

యథేచ్ఛ[ం]గా **yatheeccha[n]gaa** *adv.* freely, at will, at random: ~ **tirugutunnaaDu** he roams about as he pleases.

యథోచిత **yathoocita** *adj.* fitting, appropriate, suitable.

యథోచితంగా **yathoocitangaa** *adv.* fittingly, appropriately, suitably.

యద **yada** *alt, variant form of* **eda.**

యమ **yama**[1] *adj.* of or relating to Yama, the God of death.

యమ **yama**[2] *adj. colloq.* very great, extreme; **pillalu ~ goola ceestunnaaru** the children are making a terrible noise; **waaDiki ~ gaNDam undi** he is in mortal danger; **~ aakali weesindaNDii** I was extremely hungry, sir; **sinimaa ~ gaa unnadi** the movie is excellent.

యమకం **yamakam** *n.* a figure of speech in prosody.

యమకింకరుడు **yamakinkaruDu** *n.* angel of death, servant of Yama, the God of death.

యమకూపం **yamakuupam** *n.* hell.

యమచాకిరీ **yamacaakirii** *n.* drudgery, menial work.

యమడలు **yamaDalu** *n.pl. colloq.* twins.

యమబాధ **yamabaadha** *n.* great distress, severe pain.

యమయాతన **yamayaatana** *n.* extreme torment.

యముడు, జముడు, యమధర్మరాజు **yamuDu, jamuDu, yamadharmaraaju** *n.* Yama, the God of death.

యమున **yamuna** *n.* River Jamna.

యవక్షారం **yawakSaaram** *n.* saltpetre, potassium nitrate.

యవన **yawana** *adj.* Greek.

యవనిక **yawanika** *n. class.* curtain, screen.

యవనుడు **yawanuDu** *n.* Greek.

యవలు **yawalu** *n.pl.* barley.

యవ్వన **yawwana** *adj.* young, youthful.

యవ్వనం **yawwanam** *n.* youth, manhood.

యవ్వని **yawwani** *n.* young woman, maiden.

యవ్వనుడు **yawwanuDu** *n.* young man.

యవ్వారం **yawwaaram** *colloq. alt. form of* **wyawahaaram.**

యశదం **yaśadam** *n.* zinc.

యశస్కాముడు **yaśaskaamuDu** *n.* person desirous of fame or renown.

యశస్కాయుడు **yaśaskaayuDu** *same as* **kiirtikaayuDu.**

యశస్సు **yaśassu** *n.* fame, renown, celebrity.

యశస్వి **yaśaswi** *adj.* 1 famous, renowned. 2 excellent.

యా - yaa

యాంత్రిక **yaantrika** *adj.* mechanical, automatic.

యాంత్రికంగా **yaantrikangaa** *adv.* mechanically, automatically.

యాంత్రికశాస్త్రం **yaantrikaśaastram** *n.* (science of) mechanics.

యాంత్రికీకరణ, యాంత్రీకరణ **yaantrikiikaraNa, yaantriikaraNa** *n.* mechanisation.

యాంత్రికీకరించు **yaantrikiikarincu** *v.t.* to mechanise.

యాగం **yaagam** *same as* **yajñam.**

యాగీ **yaagii** *n.* loud and angry complaining, expostulation.

యాగీచేయు **yaagiiceeyu** *v.t. colloq.* to defame, make false allegations against.

యాచకం, యాచన **yaacakam, yaacana** *n.* begging.

యాచించు **yaacincu** *v.t.* to beg, request.

యాచితం **yaacitam** *adj.* begged, requested.

యాజకుడు **yaajakuDu** *n.* officiating priest.

యాజమాన్యం **yaajamaanyam** *n.* 1 management. 2 ownership.

యాజి **yaaji** *same as* **yajwa.**

యాజ్ఞికుడు **yaajñikuDu** *n.* one who performs a sacrifice.

యాతన **yaatana** *n.* **1** agony, torment, torture. **2** pain, anguish, affliction. **3** *colloq., in a weaker sense* troubles, difficulties, problems; **niiku saayam ceeyanu, nii ~ eedoo nuwwu paDu** I will not help you, you must put up with your own difficulties.

యాతావాతా **yaataawaataa** *adv.* by and large, in general, when all is said and done; **~ neenu ceppawaccindi eemaNTee**. . . finally what I have to say is . . .

యాత్ర **yaatra** *n.* **1** pilgrimage. **2** journey, march, expedition.

యాత్రికుడు **yaatrikuDu** *n.* **1** pilgrim. **2** traveller. **3** tourist: **yaatrikula raakapookalu** tourist traffic.

యాథార్థ్యం **yaathaarthyam** *n.* truth, reality, genuineness.

యాద **yaada** *n. dial.* memory.

యాదస్తు **yaadastu** *n.* **1** *dial.* memory. **2** *obs.* memorandum.

యాదికివచ్చు **yaadikiwaccu** *v.i. dial.* to come to mind, be remembered.

యాదృచ్ఛిక **yaadṛcchika** *adj.* casual, accidental, unexpected, impromptu.

యాద్‌చేయు **yaadceeyu** *v.t. dial.* to recall, remember.

యానం **yaanam** *n.* **1** travelling. **2** journey, voyage.

యానకం **yaanakam** *n. sci.* medium.

యాపన[ం] **yaapana[m]** *second part of a n. compound meaning* extension, prolonging; **kaala ~** extension of time.

యాభై *n.* fifty.

యామం **yaamam** *n. class.* watch, a period of three hours.

యామయామ పూజ **yaamayaama puuja** *n.* **1** worship at regular intervals in a temple. **2** *colloq.* **aayana nannu ~ ceestunnaaDu** he scolds me repeatedly.

యామిని **yaamini** *n. class.* night.

యాయవారం, ఆయవారం **yaayawaaram, aayawaaram** *n.* alms; **~ ettukonu** to ask for alms.

యావ **yaawa** *n.* inordinate desire, longing, passion, obsession.

యావగా **yaawagaa** *adv.* longingly, passionately.

యావచ్ఛక్తి **yaawacchakti** *n.* all o.'s might.

యావజ్జీవ **yaawajjiiwa** *adj.* lifelong; **~ kaaraagaara śikSa** life imprisonment.

యావత్ **yaawat** *first part of a n. compound signifying* all, whole; **~ prapancam** the whole world.

యావత్తు **yaawattu** I. *n. and adj.* whole, all, entire. II. *adv.* entirely, altogether.

యావన్మంది **yaawanmandi** *n.pl.* everyone, all the people, all persons.

యావర్తి **yaawarti** *colloq alt. form of* **wyaawṛtti.**

యాష్ట **yaaSTa** *dial. variant form of* **weesaTa.**

యాస **yEEsa** *same as* **eesa.**

యు - yu

యుక్త **yukta** I. *second part of an adjvl. compound meaning* joined with, combined with; **artha ~ waakyam** meaningful sentence; **yukti ~ waadam** logical argument. II. *adj.* **1** fit, proper. **2** allotted, assigned.

యుక్తవయస్కత **yuktawayaskata** *n.* adulthood.

యుక్తవయస్సు **yuktawayassu** *n.* **1** proper age for performing a ceremony such as marriage. **2** age of majority.

యుక్తి **yukti** *n.* **1** reason, logic, sound argument. **2** skill, cleverness, cunning. **3** trick, artifice, stratagem, ruse. **4** tactics. **5** bright idea (colloq.); *see* **śakti** *sense 1.*

యుక్తిగా **yuktigaa** *adv.* cleverly, artificially, cunningly.

యుక్తిచేయు **yukticeeyu** *v.t.* to manoeuvre.

యుక్తివిన్యాసం **yuktiwinyaasam** *n.* manoeuvre.

యుగం **yugam** *n.* **1** age, period. **2** *class.* pair, couple.

యుగంధరుడు **yugandharuDu** *n.* Yugandhara, name of a famous minister in the court of king Prataparudra.

యుగకర్త **yugakarta** *n.* leading creative artist, literary or artistic innovator.

యుగధర్మం **yugadharmam** *n.* spirit or character of an age.
యుగపురుషుడు **yugapuruSuDu** *n.* great man or leading figure of an age.
యుగళం **yugaLam** *n. class.* pair, couple.
యుగళగీతం **yugaLagiitam** *n.* duet.
యుగళపదం **yugaLapadam** *n.*word with two meanings.
యుగసంధి **yugasandhi** *n.* transitional period.
యుగ్మం **yugmam** *n. class.* pair, couple.
యుత **yuta** *second part of an advbl. or adjvl. compound meaning* endowed with, possessed of; **adhikaara~ngaa** officially: **alankaara~mayna śayli** ornamental style; *cf.* **baadhyataa~**.
యుద్ధం **yuddham** *n.* 1 war. 2 battle, fight.
యుద్ధతంత్రం, యుద్ధనీతి, యుద్ధకళ **yuddhatantram, yuddhaniiti, yuddhakaLa** *n.* strategy, generalship.
యుద్ధనౌక **yuddha nawka** *n.* warship.
యుద్ధపన్నాగం **yuddhapannaagam** *n.* stratagem.
యుద్ధరంగం, యుద్ధభూమి **yuddharangam, yuddhabhuumi** *n.* battlefield.
యుద్ధసామగ్రి **yuddhasaamagri** *n.* war materials, armaments.
యుద్ధోన్మాది **yuddhoonmaadi** *n.* warmonger.
యునాని **yunaani** *n.* the Yunani system of medicine.
యువ **yuwa**[1] *first part of a n. or adjvl. compound meaning* young; **~janulu** young persons.
యువ **yuwa**[2] *n.* ninth year of the Hindu cycle of sixty years.
యువక **yuwaka** *adj.* of young persons; **yuwakoodyamam** young persons' movement, youth movement.
యువకుడు **yuwakuDu** *n.* youth, young man.
యువగండం **yuwagaNDam** *n.* pimple.
యువజన **yuwajana** *adj.* of young persons; **~saahitii samiti** young persons' literary association.
యువత **yuwata** *n.* youth, young people, the younger generation.
యువతి **yuwati** *n.* young woman.
యువరాజు **yuwaraaju** *n.* prince, Yuvaraja, ruler's eldest son, heir apparent to a ruler.

యూ to యౌ - yuu to yaw

యూదు **yuudu** *adj.* Jewish.
యూదుడు, యూదీయుడు **yuuduDu, yuudiiyuDu** *n.* Jew.
యొక్క **yokka** *p.p.* of; *bookish form, as in* **deeśam~ kSeemam** welfare of the country.
యోక్త **yookta** *n.* one who joins.
యోగం **yoogam** *n.* 1 joining, junction, combining, combination, union. 2 systematic practice of abstraction, contemplation, concentration of the mind, meditation, devotion. 3 the Yoga system of philosophy established by Patanjali. 4 fate, fortune; **dhana~** fortune of acquiring wealth; **wiwaaha~** fortune of getting married; **nii~ baaguNTee caduwu wastundi** if your fate is favourable you will acquire education; **adṛSTa~ paTTindi** a time of good fortune arrived; **waaDi~baagundi** this is a propitious time for him. 5 expedient, device, plan. 6 *med.* prescription, remedy, cure. 7 *gram.* root meaning or literal sense of a word based on its etymology; *cf.* **yawgikam, ruuDhyaartham.**
యోగక్షేమం **yoogakSeemam** (*gen.pl.* **yoogakSeemaalu**) *n.* welfare, wellbeing.
యోగదండం **yoogadaNDam** *n.* stick or staff carried by a yogi.
యోగనిద్ర **yooganidra** *n.* state of supernatural sleep attained by a yogi.
యోగమాయ **yoogamaaya** *n.* power of the Almighty in creation.
యోగశాలి **yoogaśaali** *n.* fortunate person.
యోగాసనం **yoogaasanam** *n.* posture in performing yoga.
యోగి **yoogi** *n.* yogi, devotee, hermit, ascetic.
యోగిని **yoogini** *n.* 1 woman yogi. 2 minor female deity attendant on Durga, normally malevolent but conferring special powers when propitiated.
యోగ్య **yoogya** I. *second part of an adjvl. compound meaning* suitable for; **seedya~** suitable for cultivation, cultivable; **aacaraNa~** practicable; **utpatti~** productive. II *adj.* worthy, fit, suitable.
యోగ్యత **yoogyata** *n.* 1 fitness, worthiness, merit. 2 competence, ability, cleverness. 3 eligibility, qualification. 4 **anubhawa~** right of enjoyment.
యోగ్యతాపత్రం **yoogyataapatram** *n.* certificate (of eligibility, competence, etc.), testimonial.
యోగ్యుడు **yoogyuDu** *n.* 1 deserving person, worthy person. 2 estimable person.
యోచన **yoocana** *n.* 1 consideration, deliberation, reflection. 2 *pl.* **~lu** views, ideas.
యోచించు **yoocincu** *v.t.* to consider, reflect, ponder.
యోజన **yoojana** *n.* plan[ning].
యోజనం **yoojanam** *n.* obsolete measure of distance, about eight or ten miles.
యోజనగంధం **yoojanagandham** *n. class.* musk.
యోజిత **yoojita** *adj.* planned; **~aarthika wyawastha** planned economy.
యోధానుయోధులు **yoodhaanuyoodhulu** *n.pl.* host of heroes.
యోధుడు **yoodhuDu** *n.* 1 warrior, hero. 2 feudal chieftain.

యోని **yooni** *n. class.* 1 vagina. 2 womb, uterus.
యోష **yooSa** *n. class.* woman.
యౌకం **yawkam** *n. class.* stitch in the side (= **uupirikuTTu**).
యౌగికం **yawgikam** *n.* 1 *chem.* compound. 2 *gram.* etymological or literal meaning of a word; *see* **ruuDhyaartham.**
యౌవరాజ్యం **yawwaraajyam** *n.* state of being Yuvaraja or heir apparent to a ruler.
యౌవరాజ్య పట్టాభిషేకం **yawwaraajya paTTaabhiSeekam** *n.* installation as Yuvaraja or heir apparent to a ruler.

ర - ra

రంకు **ranku** *n.* adultery, fornication, lechery.
రంకుటాలు, రంకులాడి **rankuTaalu, rankulaaDi** *n.* adulteress.
రంకుపోతు **rankupootu** *n.* adulterer.
రంకు ముండ **ranku muNDa** *n. slang* adulteress, prostitute (*term of abuse*).
రంకుమొగుడు **ranku moguDu** *n.* lover, paramour.
రంకె **ranke** *n.* 1 bellow (of a bull). 2 roar, shout, yell.
రంకెవేయు **ranke weeyu** *v.i.* 1 to bellow. 2 to roar, shout, yell.
రంగం **rangam**[1] *n.* 1 *theat.* stage, setting. 2 *theat.* scene in a play. 3 area, sector, field, sphere, arena; **yuddha ~** battlefield; **raajakiiya ~** political field or arena; **prabhutwa ~** public sector.
రంగం **rangam**[2] *n. colloq.* Rangoon, capital of Burma.
రంగమంటపం **rangamaNTapam** *n.* 1 decorated hall in a temple. 2 theatre.
రంగరించు **rangarincu** *v.t.* to mix solid and liquid ingredients (esp. in Ayurvedic medicine) by stirring them together.
రంగవల్లి **rangawalli** *same as* **muggu**[1] *sense 1.*
రంగస్థలం **rangasthalam** *n.* stage in a theatre.
రంగు **rangu** *n.* 1 colour, paint, tint, dye; **ii gooDaku leeta niilam ~ weeyaali** you must paint this wall pale blue; **~ weesukonu** to make o.s. up (for a drama); **~ kaDigeesukonu** to remove o.'s make-up (after a drama). 2 suit (in a game of cards). 3 **~ ~la janam** many and varied types of people.
రంగులరాట్నం **rangularaaTNam** *n.* merry-go-round.
రంజక **ranjaka** *second part of an adjvl. compound meaning* pleasing; **jana ~, prajaa ~** popular.
రంజకం **ranjakam** *n.* 1 inflammable or incendiary substance. 2 *class.* priming of a gun.
రంజకుడు **ranjakuDu** *n.* 1 one who pleases. 2 *class.* painter, decorator, dyer.
రంజని **ranjani** *n. class.* indigo plant.
రంజించు, రంజింపచేయు **ranjincu, ranjimpa ceeyu** *v.t.* to please, gladden, give pleasure to.
రంజిత **ranjita** *adj* reddened.
రంజిల్లు **ranjillu** *v.i.* to be pleased, be glad.
రంజు **ranju** *v.i. dial.* (of a quarrel) to spread, intensify.
రంజుగా **ranjugaa** *adv.* pleasantly, enjoyably.
రండ, రండి **raNDa, raNDi**[1] *n. slang* 1 widow. 2 shrewish woman (*term of abuse*).
రండి **raNDi**[2] *imperative pl. and polite sing. of* **waccu** please come!
రండికీ మొండికీ ఓర్చు **raNDikii moNDikii oorcu** *v.i. colloq.* to be hardened, be toughened, put up with difficulties.
రండు **raNDu** *class. alt. form of* **raNDi**[2].
రంధి **randhi** *n.* 1 craze, passion, urge, intemperate yearning, lust. 2 fight, quarrel.
రంధ్రం **randhram** *n.* hole, aperture.
రంధ్రకం **randhrakam** *n.* boring implement, borer.
రంధ్రాన్వేషణ[ం] **randhraanweeSaNa[m]** *n.* censoriousness, fault-finding.
రంపం **rampam** *n.* saw.
రంపపుకోత **rampapukoota** *n. lit.* 1 cutting with a saw. 2 *fig.* causing long-drawn-out pain.
రంపపు పొట్టు **rampapu poTTu** *n.* sawdust.
రంపపు ముళ్లు **rampapu muLLu** *n.pl.* teeth of a saw.
రంభ **rambha** *n.* 1 Rambha, a celestial courtesan. 2 *colloq.* very beautiful woman.
రంభాఫలం **rambhaaphalam** *n. class.* plantain, banana.
రంభారావిడి **rambhaaraawiDi** *n. dial.* quarrelling, uproar.
రంయిన, రయ్యిన **ramyina, rayyina** *adv.* with a rush, with a whizzing sound.
రకం **rakam** *n.* 1 kind, sort, variety, type, quality; **rakaaniki oka cokkaa konnaanu** I bought one shirt of each type; **aayana manassu** (*or* **aayana aaloocana**) **aneeka rakaala pooyindi** his mind pursued various thoughts *or* his thoughts strayed in various directions. 2 kind of person, type of person; **waaDu ceppina maaTa winee ~ kaadu** he is not the kind of person to listen to advice. 3 **oka ~ gaa** (i) in a manner, in a way, in a fashion; (ii) fairly, moderately; (iii) **oka ~ gaa ceppaalaNTee** to put it in a nutshell.
రకరకాల **rakarakaala** *adj.* many kinds of.
రకరకాలుగా **rakarakaalugaa** *adv.* 1 in many ways. 2 (of thoughts straying) in various directions.
రక్కసి, రాకాసి, రాక్షసి **rakkasi, raakaasi, raakSasi** I. *n.* demon, devil. II. *adj.* devilish.
రక్కిస **rakkisa** *n.* medicinal plant with yellow flowers.
రక్కు **rakku** I. *n.* scratch; *pl.* **~ lu** marks on the skin made by scratching or biting. II. *v.t.* to scratch, tear with nails or claws.
రక్తం **raktam** I. *second part of a n. compound meaning* love of, devotion to, passion for; **heetuwaada ~** devotion to rationalism. II. *n.* blood; **nii ~ kaLLa cuustaanu** (*lit.* I will see your blood with my eyes) *is a threat.*

రక్తకణం **raktakaNam** *n.* blood corpuscle.

రక్తచందనం **raktacandanam** *n.* red sandalwood.

రక్తదానం **raktadaanam** *n.* donation of blood.

రక్తనాళం **raktanaaLam** *n.* 1 vein. 2 blood vessel.

రక్తనిధి **raktanidhi** *n.* blood bank.

రక్తపాతం **raktapaatam** *n.* bloodshed.

రక్తపిపాసి **raktapipaasi** *adj.* bloodthirsty, sanguinary.

రక్తపీడనం, రక్తపోటు **raktapiiDanam, raktapooTu** *n.* blood pressure.

రక్తపుచ్ఛిక **raktapucchika** *n.* kind of lizard (= **nalikaL-Lapaamu**).

రక్తసంబంధీకుడు **raktasambandhiikuDu** *n.* blood relation.

రక్తస్రావం **raktasraawam** *n.* bleeding, loss of blood, haemorrhage.

రక్తహీనత **raktahiinata** *n. med.* anaemia.

రక్తాక్షి **raktaakSi** *n.* fifty-eighth year of the Hindu cycle of sixty years.

రక్తి **rakti** *n.* 1 aesthetic pleasure, charmingness, loveliness. 2 affection, love, devotion. 3 liking, taste.

రక్తికట్టు **raktikaTTu** *v.i.* to give aesthetic pleasure, be charming, be appealing, be attractive.

రక్తికట్టించు **raktikaTTincu** *v.t.* to make (a drama, etc.) attractive or appealing.

రక్ష **rakSa** *n.* 1 protection. 2 amulet, charm.

రక్షక **rakSaka** *adj.* relating to defence, defensive, protective, preserving.

రక్షకపత్రం **rakSakapatram** *n. bot.* calyx.

రక్షకభటుడు „ **rakSakabhaTuDu** *n.* policeman, police constable.

రక్షక[భట]శాఖ **rakSaka[bhaTa] śaakha** *n.* police department, police force.

రక్షకుడు **rakSakuDu** *n.* protector, preserver, saviour.

రక్షణ[ం] **rakSaNa[m]** *n.* 1 protection; ~ **kalpincu** to provide protection. 2 safeguard. 3 rescue. 4 immunity, immunisation.

రక్షరేకు **rakSareeku** *n.* 1 amulet, talisman. 2 protective charm.

రక్షాకవచం **rakSaakawacam** *n.* protective armour.

రక్షించు **rakSincu** *v.t.* 1 to protect, safeguard. 2 to save, rescue.

రక్షిత **rakSita** *adj.* protected.

రక్షితప్రాంతం **rakSitapraantam** *n.* 1 protected area. 2 *polit.* protectorate.

రగడ **ragaDa**[1] *n.* quarrel, altercation, row.

రగడ **ragaDa**[2] *n. dial.* savoury dish made with bengal-gram.

రగడ **ragaDa**[3] *n. class.* a kind of verse.

రగడాయించు **ragaDaayincu** *v.t. dial.* to rub.

రగలబెట్టు, రగిలించు, రగుల్చు **ragalabeTTu, ragilincu, ragulcu** *v.t.* 1 to kindle, light, ignite (fire). 2 to set fire to (s.g that will burn). 3 *fig.* to inflame (passions).

రగులుకొను **ragulukonu** *v.i.* to be kindled, be inflamed, be set on fire.

రగులుకొల్పు **ragulukolpu** *v.t.* to kindle, inflame (passions).

రచన **racana** *n.* 1 writing. 2 composing, composition, formation, creation; **wyuuha**~ strategy. 3 *sci.* structure; **paramaaNu**~ atomic structure.

రచయిత **racayita** *n.* author, writer.

రచయిత్రి **racayitri** *n.* authoress.

రచించు **racincu** *v.t.* 1 to write. 2 to compose, form, create.

రచిత **racita** *adj. class.* written [down], composed.

రచ్చ **racca** *n.* 1 open place, public place; **iNTa gelici ~gelawaali** command at home before you command abroad (proverb). 2 place where disputes are heard and settled in public by a council of elders or other adjudicators.

రచ్చకి ఎక్కించు, రచ్చకి ఈడ్చు **raccaki ekkincu, raccaki iiDcu** *v.t.* 1 to drag (s.g) into the open, expose (s.g) to public view. 2 to bring a disputed matter (or the opposite party in a dispute) before a council of elders or other adjudicators in order to have the dispute settled.

రచ్చకి ఎక్కు **raccaki ekku** *v.i.* 1 to engage in a dispute. 2 to go before a council of elders or other adjudicators to have a dispute settled.

రచ్చచేయు **raccaceeyu** *v.i.* to create a hubbub, make a fuss.

రచ్చబండ **raccabaNDa** *n.* stone bench where village elders meet in council.

రచ్చమాను **raccamaanu** *n.* tree under which meetings of village elders are held.

రజం, రజస్సు **rajam, rajassu** *n.* 1 dust, pollen. 2 *rajas*, activity or passion, one of the three *gunas*; *see* **guNam**.

రజకుడు **rajakuDu** *n. class.* washerman.

రజతం **rajatam** *n. class.* silver.

రజతోత్సవం **rajatootsawam** *n.* silver jubilee.

రజని **rajani** *n. class.* night.

రజనీగంధ **rajaniigandha** *n.* queen of the night, a flower with a strong scent at night time.

రజను **rajanu** *n.* filings; **inapa**~ iron filings.

రజస్వల **rajaswala** *n.* girl's attainment of puberty.

రజస్వల అవు **rajaswala awu** *v.i.* (of a girl) to attain puberty.

రజస్సు **rajassu** *same as* **rajam.**

రజాయి **rajaayi** *n.* quilt, blanket.

రజ్జు **rajju** *n.* vain talk.

రజ్జువు **rajjuwu** *n.* string, cord, rope; **naabhi**~ umbilical cord.

రజ్జుసర్పభ్రాంతి **rajjusarpabhraanti** *n.* deceiving the eye by making a rope appear to be a snake.

రట్టు **raTTu** *n.* divulging a secret; *see* **guTTu.**

రట్టుచేయు **raTTuceeyu** *v.t.* 1 to divulge a secret. 2 to spread scandal.

రణం **raNam** *n.* war, battle.

రణగొణధ్వని **raNagoNadhwani** *n.* sustained and continous noise, clamour.

రణనం **raNanam** *n.* resonant sound.

రణపెంకె **raNapenke** *n.* mischievous person, obstinate person.

రణభేరి **raNabheeri** *n.* war drum, battle drum.

రణరంగం **raNarangam** *n.* battle-field.

రతం **ratam** *n.* coition, copulation, intercourse.

రతి **rati** *n.* **1** name of the wife of Manmatha, goddess of beauty. **2** lust, desire, passion. **3** *slang* coition, copulation, intercourse.

రత్నం **ratnam** *n.* jewel, precious stone, gem; **~ laaNTi pilla** a jewel of a girl.

రత్నకంబళం, రత్నకంబళి **ratnakambaLam, ratnakambaLi** *n.* carpet.

రత్నపురిగడ్డ **ratnapurigaDDa** *n.dial.* sweet potato, *ipomoea batatas* (= **cilagaDadumpa**).

రత్నాకరం **ratnaakaram** *n. class.* sea, ocean.

రత్నావళి **ratnaawaLi** *n.* **1** *lit.* necklace of gems. **2** title given to a collection of songs or poems, e.g., **padya~**.

రథం **ratham** *n.* **1** chariot. **2** temple car: *colloq.* any driven vehicle.

రథచోదకుడు **rathacoodakuDu** *n.* **1** charioteer. **2** *colloq.* any driver of a vehicle.

రథసప్తమి **rathasaptami** *n.* seventh day of the bright (**śuddha**) fortnight in the month of **maagha**.

రథుడు **rathuDu** *n.class.* warrior who fights from a chariot.

రథోత్సవం **rathootsawam** *n.* temple car festival.

రద్ది, రద్దీ **raddi[i]** *n.* commotion, rush, [over]crowding, congestion of traffic.

రద్దిగా **raddigaa** *adv.* [over]crowded, noisy, packed with people, busy with traffic, congested; **bhaaratiiya raylu maargaalaloo ati~uNDee ii maargamloo kotta wantenawaLLa raddii taggutundi** on this line which is the most overcrowded of Indian railway lines the congestion will be relieved by the new bridge.

రద్దు **raddu**[1] *n.* **1** cancellation. **2** abolition; **jamiindaariila~** abolition of zamindaris.

రద్దు **raddu**[2] *n. dial.* waste material, scrap; **~raayi** stone chippings; **loohaala~** scrap metal.

రద్దుచేయు, రద్దుపరచు **radduceeyu, radduparacu** *v.t.* **1** to cancel. **2** to abolish, obliterate, eliminate. **3** *admin.* to dissolve (legislature). **4** to quash, annul, revoke (order). **5** to repeal, rescind (law).

రప్ప **rappa** *n.* small stone; (*note: ~ occurs only as an echo word in* **raayiirappaa, raaLLu~lu**).

రప్పించు **rappincu** *v.t.* **1** to summon, call, send for. **2** to bring back, summon back, recall.

రప్పు **rappu** *n.* mending clothes, darning.

రప్పుతీయు **rappu tiiyu** *v.t.* to mend or darn (clothes).

రబీ **rabii** *n.* rabi, the north-east moonsoon agricultural season starting in September-October.

రభస **rabhasa** *n.* altercation, row, commotion, turmoil.

రమ **rama** *n. class.* a name of the goddess Lakshmi.

రమణీయ **ramaNiiya** *adj.* charming, pleasant, pleasing, attractive.

రమారమి **ramaarami** *adv.* approximately, about, nearly.

రమించు, రమియించు **ramincu, ramiyincu** *v.i.* **1** to be pleased, rejoice. **2** to play. **3** to have sexual intercourse.

రమ్య **ramya**[1] *adj.* charming, pleasing.

రమ్య **ramya**[2] *n. class.* night.

రయం **rayam** *n. class.* quickness, speed.

రయమున **rayamuna** *adv. class.* quickly.

రయితాంగం, రయితు[వారీ] **rayitaangam, rayitu [waarii]** *same as* **raytaangam, raytu[waarii].**

రయ్యిన **rayyina** *same as* **ramyina.**

రవ **rawa**[1,2,3] *same as* **rawwa**[1,2,3].

రవం **rawam** *n.* sound, noise.

రవంత, రవన్ని **rawanta, rawanni** *same as* **rawwanta, rawwanni.**

రవరవలాడు **rawarawalaaDu** *v.i.* to be furiously angry.

రవళి **rawaLi** *n.* sound, noise; **gajjela~** jingling of little bells.

రవసెల్లా **rawasellaa** *n.* fine kind of muslin.

రవాణా **rawaaNaa** *n.* transport.

రవాణాచేయు **rawaaNaa ceeyu** *v.t.* to transport.

రవి **rawi** *n. class.* sun.

రవిక **rawika** *n.* bodice, blouse.

రవికారట్రా **rawikaaraTraa** *n.* blouses and such things.

రవ్వ, రవ **rawwa**[1], **rawa**[1] *n.* diamond.

రవ్వ, రవ **rawwa**[2], **rawa**[2] *n.* small piece, particle, speck; **nippu~** spark of fire; **okka~** just a little, a very little.

రవ్వ, రవ **rawwa**[3], **rawa**[3] *n.* coarse wheat flour.

రవ్వ **rawwa**[4] *n. dial.* fever.

రవ్వంత, రవంత **rawwanta, rawanta** *det. adj.* just a little, slightly; **~spaSTam** fairly clear.

రవ్వన్ని, రవన్ని **rawwanni, rawanni** *det. n.pl.* a very few.

రశీదు, రసీదు **raśiidu, rasiidu** *n.* receipt, acknowledgement.

రశ్మి **raśmi** *n.* ray (of light).

రసం **rasam** *n.* **1** juice; **nimma~** lime juice. **2** pepper water. **3** any liquid or fluid. **4** liquid extract or essence. **5** mercury, quicksilver (= **paada~**). **6** taste, flavour, savour; *cf.* **SaDrasaalu. 7** emotion, sentiment; *cf.* **nawarasaalu. 8** aesthetic taste or pleasure. **9** literary or artistic beauty.

రసకందాయం **rasakandaayam** *n.* (*also* **rasakandaaya[pu]paTTu**) most interesting or exciting stage (in a story, game, undertaking, etc.), climax.

రసజ్ఞ **rasajña** *n. class.* tongue (*lit.* that which tastes).

రసజ్ఞుడు **rasajñuDu** *n.* person of taste.

రసతాళీ, రస్తాళీ **rasataaLii, rastaaLii** *n.* kind of plantain or banana, small in size with a sweet taste.

రసన **rasana** *n.class.* tongue.

రసనేంద్రియం **rasaneendriyam** *n.* organ of taste.

రసపతి, రసరాట్టు **rasapati, rasaraaTTu** *n. class.* mercury, quicksilver.

రసపుత్ర, రాజపుత్ర **rasaputra, raajaputra** *adj.* Rajput.

రసపోషణ **rasapooSaNa** *n.* expression or portrayal of emotion.

రసభంగం **rasabhangam** *n.* disturbance of privacy.

రసమయ **rasamaya** *adj.* charged with emotion (*lit.* replete with all the emotions; *cf.* **nawarasaalu**).

రసవంత **rasawanta** *adj.* tasteful, artistic.

రసవాదం **rasawaadam** *n.* alchemy.

రసవాది **rasawaadi** *n.* alchemist.

రసాతలం **rasaatalam** *n.* one of the seven mythical regions under the earth.

రసాత్మక **rasaatmaka** *adj.* tasteful, graceful, artistic.

రసాధిదేవత **rasaadhideewata** *n.* the presiding deity of a particular rasa or emotion, *cf.* **nawarasaalu.**

రసాభాసం **rasaabhaasam** *n.* **1** fiasco, s.g that has been fouled up, s.g gone wrong. **2** s.g which looks like elegance but is not so.

రసాభాసం అవు **rasaabhaasam awu** *v.i.* to be spoilt, be upset, go wrong; **sabha rasaabhaasam ayindi** the meeting ended in failure.

రసాయన, రసాయనిక **rasaayan[ik]a** *adj.* chemical.

రసాయనం **rasaayanam** *n.* **1** chemical (substance). **2** *obs.* elixir, panacea.

రసాయనికం **rasaayanikam** *n.* chemical (substance).

రసాయనశాస్త్రం **rasaayanaśaastram** *n.* chemistry.

రసాలం **rasaalam** *n. class.* mango tree.

రసాలు **rasaalu** *n.* kind of mango, juicy and sweet but with much fibre.

రసాస్వాదన **rasaaswaadana** *n.* aesthetic enjoyment.

రసి[క] **rasi[ka]**[1] *n.* pus.

రసిక **rasika**[2] I. *n.* **1** cultured woman, woman of taste. **2** sugarcane juice. II. *adj.* full of flavour, tasty.

రసికత, రసికత్వం **rasikata, rasikatwam** *n.* culture, elegance, good taste, aesthetic sense.

రసికుడు **rasikuDu** *n.* **1** cultured person; **sangiita~** music lover. **2** *colloq.* womaniser, philanderer.

రసీదు **rasiidu** *same as* **raśiidu.**

రస్తా **rastaa** *n.* road, highway.

రస్తాళి **rastaaLi** *same as* **rasataaLi.**

రహదారి, రాదారి **rahadaari, raadaari** *n.* public way, road, highway, thoroughfare.

రహదారిపడవ **rahadaari paDawa** *n.* ferry.

రహస్య **rahasya** *adj.* private, confidential, secret; **~ samaalooc̄ana** private consultation; **~ niweedika** confidential report; **~ wooTu widhaanam** secret ballot.

రహస్యం **rahasyam** *n.* **1** secret. **2** secrecy, privacy, confidentiality.

రహస్యంగా **rahasyangaa** *adv.* **1** secretly, confidentially, privately. **2** stealthily.

రహిత **rahita** *second part of an adjvl. compound meaning* without, devoid of, deprived of, lacking; **warga~** classless; **loopa~** without defects; **widyaa~** devoid of education.

రా - raa

రా **raa**[1] *adj. alt. form of* **raati** made of stone.

రా **raa**[2] *adj. used in compounds* of a king, royal; **~ kumaaruDu** king's son, prince.

రా **raa**[3] **1** *imperative sing. of* **waccu. 2** *infinitive of* **waccu.**

రా **raa**[4] *clitic, informal mode of address to a younger person or an inferior* **eem~!** hey!

రాక **raaka** I. *n.* coming. II. *negative participle of* **waccu.**

రాకడ, రాకట **raakaDa, raakaTa** *n.* **1** coming, arrival, approach. **2** manner, demeanour; **waaDi~cuustee baakii eggoTTeelaa unnaaDu** judging from his demeanour he will evade paying his debt.

రాకపోకలు **raakapookalu** *n.pl.* coming and going, travelling to and fro; **waahanaala~** vehicular traffic.

రాకా **raakaa** *n.* day of the full moon.

రాకాచంద్రుడు **raakaacandruDu** *n.* full moon.

రాకాసి **raakaasi** *same as* **raakSasi.**

రాకాసిగడ్డి **raakaasigaDDi** *n.* kind of grass grown for fodder, introduced from Africa, *penisetum clandestinum.*

రాకుమారుడు **raakumaaruDu** *n.* king's son, prince.

రాకుమార్తె, రాకుమారిత **raakumaarte, raakumaarita** princess.

రాకులం **raakulam** *n.* Kshatriya community.

రాక్షస **raakSasa** I. *n.* forty-ninth year of the Hindu cycle of sixty years. II. *adj.* devilish.

రాక్షసం, రాక్షసవివాహం **raakSasam, raakSasawiwaaham** *n.* marriage by seizure, one of the eight traditional types of marriage.

రాక్షసత్వం **raakSasatwam** *n.* devilry.

రాక్షసి, రాకాసి **raakSasi, raakaasi** *n.* female demon, she devil.

రాక్షసిబొగ్గు **raakSasiboggu** *n.* coal (produced from a mine).

రాక్షసుడు **raakSasuDu** *n.* demon, fiend, devil.

రాగం **raagam** *n.* **1** raga, a conventional pattern of melody and rhythm forming the basis for freely interpreted compositions in Indian music. **2** love, affection: **raagadweeSaalu** love and hatred, likes and dislikes. **3** colour, tint, hue; **aruNa~** red colour; *see also* **raagaalu tiiyu, raagaalu peTTu.**

రాగమాల **raagamaala** *n. poet.* garland of ragas.

రాగరంజిత **raagaranjita** *adj.* gleaming with love.

రాగల **raagala** *adj.* about to come, future; **~ kaalam** time that lies ahead; *see* **kala**[2] *sense 3.*

రాగవరసని **raagawarasani** *adv.* **1** *lit.* correctly according to the notes of the raga, i.e., in a musical manner;**~ paaTa paaDEEDu** he sang the song melodiously. **2** in a sing-song voice; **muSTidi peTTemadhya catikilabaDi~ modaleTTindi** the beggar woman slumped down in the middle of the compartment and began (to say) in a sing-song voice. . . .

రాగాపోగా **raagaapoogaa** *adv.* as a net result.

రాగాలు తీయు, రాగాలు పెట్టు **raagaalu tiiyu, raagaalu peTTu** *v.i.* to scream, sob, cry, weep, wail.

రాగి **raagi**[1] *n.* copper.

రాగి **raagi**[2] *n.* (*gen. pl.* **raagulu**) ragi, a millet, *eleusine coracana* (= **cooDi, tamida**).

రాగిడిబిళ్ల **raagiDibiLLa** *n.* round ornament worn by a woman on the crown of the head.

రాగోల **raagoola** *n.* forked stick.

రాచ **raaca** *adj.* **1** royal, princely. **2** pertaining to the Kshatriya community.

రాచకార్యాలు **raacakaaryaalu** *n.pl.* **1** important business. **2** affairs of state.

రాచకురుపు, రాచపుండు **raacakurupu, raacapuNDu** *n.* cancerous tumour.

రాచనగరు **raacanagaru** *n.* quarter of a city containing the royal palace.

రాచపట్టి **raacapaTTi** *n.* royal child.

రాచపుట్టుక **raacapuTTuka** *n.* birth in a noble family.

రాచబాట **raacabaaTa** *n.* highway, thoroughfare.

రాచరికం, రాజరికం **raacarikam, raajarikam** *n.* monarchy, kingly rule.

రాచవారు **raacawaaru** *n.pl.* **1** royal family. **2** community of Kshatriyas.

రాచిప్ప **raacippa** *n.* stone bowl, stone crucible.

రాచిరాచి **raaciraaci** *adv.* persistently; **~aDugu** to ask again and again; **~pani ceeyincu** to get work done by applying persistent pressure (on s.o.).

రాచు **raacu** *v.t.* **1** to crush. **2** to rub. **3** to scrub; **waNTillu raaci kaDagaali** you must scrub and wash the kitchen.

రాచుకుపోవు **raacukupoowu** *v.i.* **1** (of throat) to become hoarse. **2** to be bruised.

రాచుకొను **raacukonu** *same as* **raasukonu**[1].

రాజ **raaja** *adj.* royal.

రాజం **raajam** *second part of a n. compound signifying* s.g that is best out of a class or group; **grantha~** great book: **naaTaka~** masterpiece of a play; **wrSabha~** prize-winning bull.

రాజకం **raajakam** *n.* **1** assembly of princes. **2** assembly of Kshatriyas.

రాజకీయ **raajakiiya** *adj.* political.

రాజకీయవాది, రాజకీయవేత్త **raajakiiyawaadi, raajakiiyaweetta** *n.* politician.

రాజకీయాలు **raajakiiyaalu** *n.pl.* politics.

రాజగృహం **raajagrham** *n.* palace.

రాజతంత్రాలు **raajatantraalu** *n.pl.* machinations.

రాజదంతం **raajadantam** *n.* front tooth, incisor.

రాజధాని **raajadhaani** *n.* capital, metropolis.

రాజనాలు **raajanaalu** *n.pl.* name of a superior variety of rice.

రాజనీతి[జ్ఞత] **raajaniiti[jñata]** *n.* statesmanship, statecraft.

రాజనీతిజ్ఞుడు **raajaniitijñuDu** *n.* **1** statesman. **2** political scientist.

రాజనీతిశాస్త్రం **raajaniitiśaastram** *n.* political science.

రాజనీతి సిద్ధాంతం **raajaniiti siddhaantam** *n.* political theory.

రాజపుత్ర **raajaputra** *adj.* Rajput.

రాజభక్తి **raajabhakti** *n.* loyalty.

రాజభాష **raajabhaaSa** *n.* official language.

రాజభృతి, రాజభరణం **raajabhrti, raajabharaNam** *n. polit.* privy purse.

రాజమర్యాదలు **raajamaryaadalu** *n.pl.* highest respect, highest honour.

రాజమార్గం **raajamaargam** *n.* highway, high road.

రాజయక్ష్మం **raajayakSmam** *same as* **yakSmam.**

రాజయోగం **raajayoogam** *n.* **1** form of yoga or religious meditation less austere than **haThayoogam.** **2** *astrol.* destiny of becoming a king.

రాజయోగి **raajayoogi** *n.* one who practises **raajayoogam.**

రాజరాజు **raajaraaju** *n.* king of kings, emperor.

రాజరికం **raajarikam** *same as* **raacarikam.**

రాజర్షి **raajarSi** *n.* Kshtriya who has attained the status of a rishi.

రాజలాంఛనాలు **raajalaanchanaalu** *n.pl.* royal regalia.

రాజవీధి **raajawiidhi** *n.* main street.

రాజశ్రీ **raajaśrii** *obs. title equivalent to* Mr.; *the modern form is* **śrii.**

రాజసం **raajasam** *n.* domineering spirit, haughtiness, arrogance.

రాజసంగా **raajasangaa** *adv.* **1** proudly, haughtily. **2** lavishly, extravagantly; **DabbuNTee~ kharcupeDataaDu** if he has any money he spends it lavishly.

రాజసభ **raajasabha** *n.* king's court.

రాజసూయ యాగం, రాజసూయం **raajasuuya yaagam, raajasuuyam** *n.* Vedic ceremony in which a king declares himself to be emperor superior to other kings.

రాజహంస, రాయంచ **raajahamsa, raayanca** *n.* swan.

రాజిత **raajita** *adj.* **1** shining. **2** adorned.

రాజిల్లు **raajillu** *v.i.* to shine, be bright.

రాజీ **raajii**[1] *n.* reconciliation, compromise.

రాజీ, రాజీనామా **raajii**[2], **raajiinaamaa** *n.* resignation.

రాజీ చేయు **raajii ceeyu** *v.i.* to arrange or bring about a compromise.

రాజీనామా చేయు, రాజీనామా ఇచ్చు **rajiinaamaa ceeyu, raájiinaamaa iccu** *v.i.* to resign; **padawiki raajiinaamaa ceesEEDu/iccEEDu** he resigned from office.

రాజీపడు **raajiipaDu** *v.i.* to compromise, be reconciled, come to an agreement; **raajiipaDee gontutoo maTLaaDu** to speak in a conciliatory tone.

రాజీవం **raajiiwam** *n. class.* blue lotus.

రాజు **raaju** *n.* king, raja; **weesi~** *or* **teraci~** check (in chess); **koTTi~** checkmate (in chess).

రాజుకొను **raajukonu** *v.i.* **1** to catch fire, begin to burn. **2** *fig.* to flare up; **yuddham raajukondi** war flared up.

రాజేయు **raajeeyu** *v.t.* to set on fire; **poyyi~** to light or kindle fire in a hearth.

రాజ్ఞి **raajñi** *n.* queen, princess.

రాజ్యం **raajyam** *n.* 1 rule, government, rulership. 2 power; **raajyaaniki waccu** to come to power; **raajya kuuTami** power bloc; **raajya kaankSa** lust for power. 3 kingdom, state, nation, country; **aykya raajya samiti** United Nations Organisation.

రాజ్యచక్రం తిప్పు **raajyacakram tippu** *v.i.* to wield power.

రాజ్యతంత్రం **raajyatantram** *n.* political theory, science of government.

రాజ్యపాలన **raajyapaalana** *n.* rule, government, rulership.

రాజ్యపాలుడు **raajyapaaluDu** *n.* Governor (of an Indian State).

రాజ్యాంగం **raajyaangam** *n. polit.* constitution.

రాజ్యాంగ చట్టం, రాజ్యాంగ విధానం **raajyaanga caTTam, raajyaanga widhaanam** *n. polit.* legally enacted constitution.

రాజ్యాంగ పరిషత్తు, రాజ్యాంగ నిర్ణయసభ **raajyaanga pariSattu, raajyaanga nirNayasabha** *n. polit.* constituent assembly.

రాజ్యాంగవిరుద్ధ **raajyaangawiruddha** *adj.* unconstitutional.

రాజ్యాంగ వేత్త **raajyaanga weetta** *n.* constitutional expert.

రాజ్యాధికారం **raajyaadhikaaram** *n.* political power.

రాట **raaTa** *n.* peg for tying cattle.

రాటం, రాట్నం **raaTam, raaTNam** *n.* spinning wheel.

రాటుతేరు, రాటుతేలు **raaTuteeru, raaTuteelu** *v.i.* 1 to be rubbed, be worn down, become blunted. 2 to become experienced.

రాటుపడు **raaTupaDu** *v.i.* 1 *lit.* to be worn down. 2 to be troubled, be afflicted; **raaTupaDi gaaTupaDi paNTa paNDincee raytulu** cultivators who raise crops in spite of troubles and afflictions (**gaaTupaDi** is an echo word lending intensive force).

రాటుపోటులు **raaTupooTulu** *n.pl.* friction and strife, hurlyburly, rough and tumble.

రాణి **raaNi** *n.* queen.

రాణించు **raaNincu** *v.i.* 1 to shine. 2 to thrive, do well, be a success.

రాణింపు **raaNimpu** *n.* (of a mental quality or characteristic) displaying itself, showing itself to advantage.

రాణివాసం **raaNiwaasam** *n.* queen's apartment in a palace.

రాత, వ్రాత **raata, wraata** *n.* 1 writing, document. 2 (*also* **tala** ~) destiny (popularly believed to be written on the forehead).

రాతం **raatam** *advbl. n., Telangana dial.* (of services provided or goods supplied and paid for at fixed intervals) on a regular basis, at regular intervals, on a running account; **aa dukaaNamloo maaku ~ unnadi** we have a running account at that shop; **~ gaa paalu poosee narasamma ii madhya maaneesindi** Narasamma who supplies us regularly with milk has just recently stopped coming; **~ rikSaawaaDu Dabbutoo paaripooyEEDu** the rickshaw man whom we employ regularly (*or* our regular rickshaw man) has run away with the money; *cf.* **watanugaa.**

రాతకోతలు **raatakootalu** *n. pl.* writing work; *see* **tiNDi.**

రాతగాడు **raatagaaDu** *n.* writer, clerk.

రాతప్రతి **raataprati** *n.* manuscript.

రాతబల్ల **raataballa** *n.* writing table.

రాతమూలకంగా, రాతపూర్వకంగా **raatamuulakangaa, raatapuurwakangaa** *adv.* in writing.

రాతి **raati** *adj.* made of stone.

రాతి ఉప్పు **raati uppu** *n.* rock salt.

రాతికడీలు **raatikaDiilu** *n.pl.* stone slabs forming the edge of a roadside footpath for pedstrians.

రాతినార **raatinaara** *n.* asbestos.

రాత్రి **raatri** *n.* night.

రాత్రించరుడు **raatrincaruDu** *n.* 1 demon. 2 thief. 3 homeless wanderer.

రాత్రింబగళ్లు **raatrimbagaLLu** *adv.* day and night.

రాత్రికి రాత్రి **raatriki raatri** *adv.* 1 on the same night, that very night. 2 only last night; **~ eem jarigindoo telusaa**? do you know what happened only last night?

రాత్రిపూట **raatripuuTa** I. *n.* night time. II. *adv.* at night, in the night.

రాదారి **raadaari** *same as* **rahadaari.**

రాద్ధాంతం చేయు **raaddhaantam ceeyu** *v.i.* to make a big issue (of s.g), make a fuss, get worked up (colloq.); **oo ruupaayi iwwaDaaniki inta raaddhaantam ceeyaalaa**? should you make so much fuss over paying a rupee?

రాద్ధాంతసిద్ధాంతాలు, సిద్ధాంతరాద్ధాంతాలు **raaddhaanta siddhaantaalu, siddhaanta raaddhaantaalu** *n. pl.* theories and counter-theories.

రాధామనోహరం **raadhaamanooharam** *n.* name of a flowering creeper.

రాని **raani** *neg. vbl. adj. of* **waccu** 1 *lit.* not coming. 2 *idiomatic usages*; (i) ~ **ingliiSu** broken English; (ii) ~ **nawwu** a forced smile. 3 *following the infinitive of another verb* incapable of being, e.g., **ceppa** ~ unsayable, inexpressible, unutterable.

రానున్న **raanunna** *adj.* likely to come; ~ *is more indefinite than* **wastunna**; *forms like* ~ **di** *and* ~ **waaDu** *also occur*; **gaaliwaana ~ di** a storm is likely to come; **tana graamaanni payki tiisuku ~ waaDu** one who is likely to uplift his village.

రానుపోను **raanupoonu** *adv.* going and coming back, to and fro; ~ **caalaa paysalu awutaayi** the to and fro journey will be very expensive; **raanu nuwwu peTTukoo, poonu neenu istaanu** you pay for coming, I will pay for going back.

రానురాను **raanuraanu** *adv.* gradually.

రాపడు **raapaDu** *v.i.* to be petrified (with fear, shock, etc.).

రాపాడు **raapaaDu** *v.t.* 1 to make (s.g) smooth by rubbing. 2 *fig.* to put pressure on (s.o.); **waaNNi raapaaDitee Dabbu istaaDu** if you press him he will pay.

రాపాషాణాలు **raapaaSaaNaalu** *n.pl. colloq.* very hard stones.

రాపిడి **raapiDi** *n.* rubbing, friction.

రాబందు **raabandu** *n.* vulture.

రాబట్టుకొను **raabaTTukonu** *v.t.* 1 to get back, recover, regain. 2 to extract, exact, obtain, secure; **samaacaaram** ~ to gather information.

రాబడి **raabaDi** *n.* income, yield; **heccu ~ wangaDaalu** high yielding varieties (of crops).

రాబోయే **raabooyee** *adj.* about to come, approaching; **~ samwatsaram** ensuing year.

రామ **raama** *n.* 1 *class.* beautiful woman. 2 *same as* **raamuDu.**

రామకోటి రాయు **raamakooTi raayu** *v.i.* to write the name of Sri Rama one crore of times as a devotional exercise.

రామచిలుక **raamaciluka** *n.* kind of parrot.

రామణీయకం, రామణీయకత **raamaNiiyakam, raamaNiiyakata** *n.* loveliness, charm.

రామతులసి **raamatulasi** *n.* plant known as *ocymum gratissimum.*

రామదండు **raamadaNDu** *n.* 1 village ceremony performed in order to bring rain. 2 (*lit.* Rama's army) name given to a group of śatyagrahis during the independence movement. 3 *colloq.* group of naughty children (so called from the troop of monkeys that accompanied Rama on his invasion of Lanka).

రామదాడీ[గా], రావంధాళీ[గా] **raamadaaDii [gaa], raawandhaaLii[gaa]** *adv.* freely without question, freely in large numbers or crowds; **karphyuu peTTinaa wiidhulloo janam ~ tirugutunnaaru** although a curfew is in force, people are freely going about in the streets.

రామదాసు **raamadaasu** *n.* 1 Ramadas, name of a devotee who founded the temple at Bhadrachalam. 2 *colloq.* person who misappropriates government money.

రామనామం **raamanaamam** *n.* 1 the name Rama, which is recited over and over again as a devotional exercise; **udyoogam leedu, iNTLoo kuurconi ~ ceesukoNTunnaaDu** he has no job, he stays at home doing nothing (*lit.* he has no job, he sits at home reciting the name of Rama). 2 a name that is on everyone's lips; **aayana peeru paTTaNam antaTaa ~ aypooyindi** all over the town his name was on everyone's lips.

రామబాణం **raamabaaNam** *n.* 1 *lit.* Rama's arrow, an unfailing weapon. 2 unfailing means or device; **ii mandu ~ laa paniceestundi** this medicine will work like Rama's arrow, i.e., this medicine will work unfailingly.

రామములగ **raamamulaga** *n.* tomato, *lycopersicum esculentum.*

రామరామ! **raamaraama!** *interj.* alas!, how sad!

రామానుజకూటం **raamaanujakuuTam** *n.* choultry or lodging place for Vaishnavite wanderers.

రామానుజుడు **raamaanujuDu** *n.* Ramanuja, founder of the Visishtadwaita school of philosophy.

రామాఫలం **raamaaphalam** *n.* bull's heart (a fruit), *anona reticulata.*

రామాయణం **raamaayaNam** *n.* 1 the great Sanskrit epic known as the Ramayana. 2 *colloq.* long and tedious story.

రామి **raami** *n. class.* non-arrival, not coming.

రామీగా **raamiigaa** *adv.* cheaply.

రాముడు, రామ **raamuDu, raama** *n.* Rama, the hero of Ramayana.

రాయంగీసలు **raayangiisalu** *n.pl. dial.* two annas, one eighth of a rupee.

రాయంచ **raayanca** *same as* **raajahamsa.**

రాయంమట్టం **raayammaTTam** *n. dial.* two rupees.

రాయబడు **raayabaDu** *passive of* **raayu** to be written.

రాయబారం **raayabaaram** *n.* 1 embassy, legation. 2 ambassadorship. 3 negotiation, mediation; **raayabaaraalanu saagincu** to conduct negotiations; **~ nerapu** to act as an intermediary. 4 message.

రాయబార కార్యాలయం **raayabaara kaaryaalayam** *n.* embassy office building.

రాయబారవర్గం **raayabaarawargam** *n.* delegation.

రాయబారి **raayabaari** *n.* ambassador, envoy.

రాయలసీమ **raayalasiima** *n.* the Rayalasima region of Andhra Pradesh comprising Anantapur, Cuddapah, Kurnool and Chi   or districts.

రాయసం **raayasam** *n.* clerkship, secretaryship.

రాయసకాడు **raayasakaaDu** *n.* writer, clerk.

రాయి **raayi** *n.* 1 stone, rock. 2 *slang* rupee (*gen.pl.* **raaLLu**); **naalugu raaLLu sampaadistunnaaDu** he earns a few rupees *or* he earns a little money.

రాయించు, వ్రాయించు **raayincu**[1], **wraayincu** *v.t.* to cause to write, have s.g written.

రాయించు **raayincu**[2] *v.t.* to cause to rub or smear, have s.g rubbed or smeared.

రాయితీ **raayitii** I. *n.* concession, favour. II. *adj.* concessional.

రాయితీగా **raayitiigaa** *adv.* cheaply, at a low price.

రాయీరప్పా **raayiirappaa** *n.* little stones, small particles, grit; **biyyamloo ~ uNTee tiiseestaanu** if there is any grit in the rice I will remove it; *cf.* **raaLLu rappalu.**

రాయు, వ్రాయు **raayu**[1], **wraayu** *v.t.* to write; *see* **peera.**

రాయు **raayu**[2] *v.t.* 1 to rub. 2 to smear. 3 to scrape.

రాయుడు **raayuDu** *n.* king, master, lord; *sometimes used sarcastically*, e.g., **kootala ~** master of boasting.

రారాజు **raraaju** *n.* 1 king of kings. 2 title of Duryoodhana in the Mahabharata.

రాలిపడిపోవు **raalipaDipoowu** *v.i.* 1 to fall. 2 *colloq.* to behave in an arrogant way.

రాలు **raalu**[1] *n. suffix denoting the female sex* **sneehitu ~** girl friend; **yajamaanu ~** mistress.

రాలు **raalu**[2] *v.t.* to fall, drop.

రాలు **raalu**[3] *dial. pl. of* **raayi** stones.

రాలుగాయ **raalugaaya** *n.* 1 fruit that falls before it is ripe. 2 mischievous boy.

రాలుబడి **raalubaDi** *n.* yield.

రాల్చు **raalcu** *v.t.* to cause to fall, knock down, drop, shed.

రాళ్లగని **raaLLagani** *n.* stone quarry.

రాళ్లురప్పలు **raaLLurappalu** *n.pl.* stones and such things; **wiidhiloo ~ unnaayi jaagratta!** be careful, there are stones and things like that in the street; *cf.* **raayiirappaa.**

రావం **raawam** *alt. form of* **rawam.**

రావంధాళీ[గా] **raawandhaaLii[gaa]** *same as* **raamadaaDii [gaa].**

రావణుడు **raawaNuDu** *n.* Rawana, demon king of Lanka in the Ramayana, who carried off Sita and was defeated and killed by Rama.

రావి **raawi** *n.* peepal tree, *ficus religiosa*

రావించు **raawincu** *v.t.* **1** to summon, call (more formal and polite than **rappincu**). **2** (of a number of persons) to assemble.

రావు **raawu** *name suffix* Rao *or* Rau; *see* **iNTipeeru.**

రాశి, రాసి **raaśi, raasi** *n.* **1** heap, pile. **2** *astrol.* constellation, astrological house, sign of the zodiac. **3** mass, quantity. **4** collection, multitude; *cf.* **jiiwa~**. **5** *fig.* embodiment; **sadguNaaLa~** embodiment (*lit.* collection) of good qualities; **wijñaana~** embodiment (*lit.* mass) of knowledge.

రాశిచక్రం **raaśicakram** *n. astrol.* zodiac circle showing the positions of the planets.

రాశిపోయు **raaśipooyu** *v.t.* to heap up, pile up.

రాష్ట్రం **raaSTram**[1] *n.* State; **keeraLa~** Kerala State; **amerikaa samyukta raaSTraalu** United States of America.

రాష్ట్రం **raaSTram**[2] *n. class.* disaster, calamity.

రాష్ట్రపతి **raaSTrapati** *n.* President of India.

రాష్ట్రీయ **raaSTriiya** *adj.* belonging or pertaining to a State.

రాష్ట్రీయుడు **raaSTriiyuDu** *n. theat.* king's brother-in-law.

రాసకేళి, రాసక్రీడ **raasakeeLi, raasakriiDa** *n.* **1** amorous sport. **2** dance of Krishna with the Gopikas.

రాసి, రాస్తా **raasi, raastaa** *alt. forms of* **raaśi, rastaa.**

రాసిరంపాన పెట్టు **raasirampaana peTTu** *v.t.* to inflict mental and physical torture.

రాసుకొను, రాచుకొను **raasukonu**[1], **raacukonu** *v.t.* **1** to rub against, brush against: **meTLu digutunnappuDu nannu raasukoNTuu** (*or* **raacukoNTuu**) **pooyEEDu** he brushed against me as he went downstairs. **2** to rub, smear: **talaki nuune~** to rub or smear oil on o.'s head; **mukhaaniki pawDaru~** to dab powder on o.'s face.

రాసుకొను **raasukonu**[2] *v.t.* **1** to write for o.s. **2** (of two or more persons) to write to each other.

రాహిత్యం **raahityam** *class. second part of a n. compound signifying* absence (of), want (of), lack (of): **wiśwaasa~** absence of trust or confidence: **janma~** freedom from rebirth.

రాహువు **raahuwu** *n. astrol.* Rahu, name of the eighth planet, considered to be unlucky; *see* **keetuwu.**

రి, రీ - ri, rii

రింగుమను **ringumanu** *v.i.* (of the ears) to ring, resound.

రికాబు **rikaabu** *n.* stirrup.

రికామీగా **rikaamiigaa** *adv.* free from responsibilities.

రిక్క **rikka** *n. class.* star.

రిక్కించు **rikkincu** *v.t.* **cewulu~** to prick up the ears, listen attentively.

రిక్త **rikta** *adj.* empty: **~hastaalatoo tirigi waccEEDu** he returned empty-handed.

రిక్థం **riktham** *n.* bequest, property left at death.

రిక్షా **rikSaa** *n.* rickshaw.

రిపుడు **ripuDu** *n. class.* enemy, foe.

రిమ్మ **rimma** *n.* peturbation.

రిమ్మతెగులు **rimmategulu** *n. colloq.* **1** passion, lust. **2** pride, arrogance.

రిమ్ము **rimmu** *v.t. dial.* to scatter, spurt.

రిమ్మెత్తు **rimmettu** *v.i. with dative* to be shocked or amazed: **aa waarta wini waaDiki rimmettipooyindi** he was shocked on hearing that news.

రివట **riwaTa** *n.* small branch or twig growing from a larger branch.

రివాజు **riwaaju** *n.* **1** custom, convention, usage, practice: **idi maa iNTLoo~** this is the custom in our house. **2** s.g usual or customary.

రివ్వున, రివ్వుమని **riwwuna, riwwumani** *adv.* **1** (of a bird) swooping, diving. **2** (in general) very swiftly, with a rush.

రీతి **riiti** *n.* **1** manner, mode, method, way, fashion. **2** system: **miiru ceesee paniloo koncemaynaa~uNDodduu?** should there not be a system in your way of working? **3** practice, custom, usage. **4** type, style: **chandooriitulu** types of poetic metre: **hindustaanii, karNaaTaka sangiita riitulu** Hindustani and Carnatic musical styles.

రీత్యా **riityaa** *p.p. and adv.* **1** in accordance with, based on, in terms of: **caTTa~ idi tappu** as per the rules (*or* by law) this is wrong: **anubhawa~** based on experience: **saagu wistiirNam~ bhaaratadeeśamloo mana raaSTraaniki aaroo sthaanam, utpatti~reNDoo sthaanam labhistundi** in India our State holds sixth place in terms of area cultivated (with paddy) and second place in terms of production. **2** in the course of, in pursuance of: **kaarya~ aa uuru weLLEEnu** I went to that town on business. **3 wṛtti~** (i) on account of o.'s profession; **wṛtti~aa uuLLoo uNDipooyEEDu** he remained in that town on account of his profession (ii) by profession: **wṛtti~aaayana mEESTaru** he is a teacher by profession.

రీపరు కట్టె **riiparu kaTTe** *n.* reeper, thin slat laid lengthwise across the rafters and under the tiles of a roof to provide insulation.

రు - ru

రుంజ **runja** *n.* brass drum.

రుంజాయించు **runjaayincu** *v.t.* 1 to shake; **ceTTu komma~** to shake the branch of a tree. 2 to reproach, upbraid.

రుంజుకొను **runjukonu** *v.i.* to grumble, show disliking or disgust.

రుగ్మత **rugmata** *n.* illness, sickness, disease.

రుచి **ruci** *n.* 1 taste, flavour. 2 wish, desire, inclination, liking; **naaku kawitwamloo~unnadi** I have a liking (*or* I have a taste) for poetry. 3 lustre, splendour.

రుచించు **rucincu** *v.i.* to be agreeable, be to (o.'s) liking; **waaDiki naa maaTalu rucincaleedu** he did not like what I said.

రుచిగల, రుచియైన **rucigala, ruciyayna** *adj.* tasty, delicious.

రుచిచూచు **rucicuucu** *v.t.* to taste.

రుచిమరగు **rucimaragu** *v.i.* 1 to develop a taste (for). 2 to fall in love (with).

రుచిలేని **rucileeni** *adj.* tasteless, insipid.

రుచీపచీ **ruciipacii** *n., only in neg. constr.* **tiNDiki~leedu** the food is tasteless.

రుచ్యం, రుచ్యమైన **rucyam[ayna]** *adj. obs.* tasty.

రుజ **ruja** *n. class.* disease, sickness.

రుజాగ్రస్త **rujaagrasta** *adj. class.* diseased, sick.

రుతం **rutam** *n. class.* sound, noise, esp. humming of bees.

రుద్దు **ruddu** *v.t.* 1 to rub, scrub, scour. 2 to force, impose, inflict; **panikiraani graanthikaanni mana widyaarthula nettipay neeTikii~tunnaaru** they are still inflicting the useless classical language on our students. 3 to din (s.g) into (s.o.); **waaNNi kuurcoobeTTi paaThaalu ruddEEnu** I made him sit down and dinned the lessons into him. 4 to foist; **tappu naamiida ruddEEDu** he foisted the offence on me.

రుద్ధ **ruddha** *adj.* (of a voice) choked.

రుద్రభూమి **rudrabhuumi** *n.* cemetery, graveyard, burial ground.

రుద్రవీణ **rudrawiiNa** *n.* vina played as accompaniment to Siva's dance.

రుద్రాక్షచెట్టు **rudraakSaceTTu** *n.* tree known as rudraksha or bastard cedar.

రుద్రాక్షపిల్లి **rudraakSapilli** *n.* thief, cheat, hypocrite.

రుద్రాక్షమాల **rudraakSamaala** *n.* necklace of rudraksha seeds.

రుద్రాక్షలు **rudraakSalu** *n.pl.* seeds of the rudraksha tree, used as rosary beads.

రుద్రాణి **rudraaNi** *n.* a name of Parvati, wife of Siva.

రుద్రుడు **rudruDu** *n.* a name of Siva; **brahma rudrulu wacci ceppinaa ii pani ceeyanu** *lit.* I will not do this even if Brahma and Siva both come and tell me to do it, i.e., under no circumstances (*or* on no account) will I do this.

రుధిరం **rudhiram** *n. class.* blood.

రుధిరోద్గారి **rudhiroodgaari** *n.* fifty-seventh year of the Hindu cycle of sixty years.

రుబ్బు **rubbu** *v.t.* 1 to grind into paste in a mortar. 2 *colloq.* to learn (s.g) by heart.

రుబ్బురాయి **rubburaayi** *n.* upper (revolving) grinding stone of a mortar.

రుబ్బురోలు **rubburoolu** *n.* lower (fixed) grinding stone of a mortar.

రుమాలు **rumaalu** *n.* handkerchief.

రువ్వ **ruwwa** *n.* 1 cane. 2 *colloq.* rupee.

రువ్వు **ruuwwu** *v.t.* to throw.

రుసరుసలాడు **rusarusalaaDu** *v.i.* to be in a bad temper, be sulky, murmur, grumble.

రుసుం **rusum** *n.* fee, charge; **praweeśa~** entrance fee.

రూ - ruu

రూక **ruuka** *n.* 1 (*gen. pl.* ~**lu**) money. 2 *obs.* old silver coin.

రూఢ **ruuDha** *adj.* (popularly) accepted, established; **prayooga~** established by usage.

రూఢి **ruuDhi** I. *n.* 1 certainty, definiteness. 2 *gram.* common usage, day to day usage; **DikSanaarii nirmaaNamloo kaawyaprayoogaalni maatramee kaLLakaddukoni looka wyawahaaraannii ruuDhinii tṛNiikarincaleedu** in compiling the dictionary he did not fix his attention only on literary practice, despising colloquialisms and day to day usage. II. *adj.* certain, definite, established.

రూఢిగా **ruuDhigaa** *adv.* definitely, certainly, positively.

రూఢిచేసుకొను **ruuDhiceesukonu** *v.t.* to assure o.s., convince o.s.

రూఢిపడు **ruuDhipaDu** *v.i.* to be established, be confirmed, be substantiated.

రూఢిపరచు **ruuDhiparacu** *v.t.* 1 to confirm, establish, substantiate. 2 to ratify.

రూఢ్యార్థం **ruuDhyaartham** *n.* usual or commonly understood meaning; e.g., *the usual meaning* (~) *of* **pankajam** *is* lotus *but its literal meaning based on its etymology* (**yoogam** *or* **yawgikam**) *is* mud-born.

రూపం **ruupam** *n.* figure, shape, form.

రూపంగా, రూపంలో **ruupangaa, ruupamloo** *adv.* in the shape of, in the form of; **dhana~** in the form of money, **wastu~** in kind.

రూపం దాల్చు, రూపు దాల్చు **ruupam daalcu, ruupu daalcu** *v.i.* **1** to assume a shape or form; **tiiwra ruupam daalcu** to assume a serious form, become acute. **2** to take shape, materialise.

రూపకం **ruupakam**[1] *n.* form of drama often used on radio in which discourse on a subject alternates with dialogue between characters illustrating and dwelling on points in the discourse.

రూపకం **ruupakam**[2] (*also* **ruupaka alankaaram**) *n.* metaphor.

రూపకంగా **ruupakangaa** *adv.* **1** in the shape of, in the form of. **2** in connection with; **ii~maa iNTiki waccEEDu** he has come to our house in connection with this affair.

రూపకల్పన **ruupakalpana** *n.* **1** formulation, giving form, giving shape, expression. **2** portrayal, portraying; **~loo sajiiwatanu ceekuurcaDam wiiri pratyeekata** in portraying (a figure) his speciality was to achieve vitality.

రూపకల్పన చేయు **ruupakalpana ceeyu** *v.i.* to formulate, give shape, give expression; **bhaawaaniki~** to give expression to an idea; **pathakaaniki~** to give shape to a project.

రూపచిత్రణ **ruupacitraNa** *n.* sketch.

రూపనిర్మాణశాస్త్రం **ruupanirmaaNaśaastram** *n. biol.* (science of) morphology.

రూపవంతుడు, రూపశాలి **ruupawantuDu, ruupaśaali** *n.* handsome man.

రూపవతి, రూపశాలిని **ruupawati, ruupaśaalini** *n.* beautiful woman.

రూపసి **ruupasi** *n.* handsome man, beautiful woman.

రూపాంతరం **ruupaantaram** *n.* **1** modification. **2** alternative form, variant.

రూపాంతరణ, రూపాంతరీకరణ **ruupaantaraNa, ruupaantariikaraNa** *n.* transformation.

రూపాంతరత **ruupaantarata** *n. chem.* allotropy, allotropism.

రూపాయి **ruupaayi** *n.* rupee.

రూపు **ruupu** *n.* **1** form, figure, shape. **2** complexion: **eNDaloo tirigi nalla~paDipooyEEDu** his complexion has turned dark from going about in sunshine.

రూపుకట్టు **ruupukaTTu** *v.i.* (of an image, idea) to take shape, be formed.

రూపు దాల్చు **ruupu daalcu** *same as* **ruupam daalcu.**

రూపుమాపు **ruupumaapu** *v.t.* to blot out, wipe out, destroy, kill, eradicate, do away with.

రూపుమాయు **ruupumaayu** *v.i.* to perish, be destroyed.

రూపుమారు **ruupumaaru** *v.i.* to be changed in appearance, be transformed.

రూపురేఖ **ruupureekha** *n.* **1** outline, configuration. **2** *pl.* **~lu** outlines, features, appearance.

రూపేణా **ruupeeNaa** *adv.* in the form of, in the shape of.

రూపొందించు **ruupondincu** *v.t.* **1** to formulate (plan). **2** to compile, draw up (programme). **3** to design, set up (project). **4 caTTaalanu~** to frame laws. **5 aarDinensu caTTangaa~** to convert an ordinance into an enactment. **6** to mould (public opinion). **7 kotta wangaDaalanu~** to evolve new strains (of crops).

రూపొందు **ruupondu** *v.i.* to be formed, take shape, be constituted, be converted, develop (**-gaa**, into); **billu caTTangaa ruupondindi** the bill was passed into law.

రూప్యం **ruupyam** *n. class.* silver rupee.

రూళ్లకర్ర **ruuLLakarra** *n.* ruler (for ruling lines).

రె - re

రెండు **reNDu** *n.* two.

రెక్క **rekka** *n.* **1** wing: **~lu muDucukonu** (of a bird) to fold its wings; **~la purugu** flying or jumping insect; **neenu uttaram raayagaanee ~lu kaTTukoni waccEEDu** when I wrote a letter he came with the utmost speed (*lit.* he tied on wings and came). **2** anything resembling a wing; **reNDu ~la talupu** door with two leaves; **muuDu~la phEEnu** fan with three blades. **3** arm, shoulder blade; **o.-ni~paTTukonu** to catch s.o. by the arm; **o.-ni peDa~lu wiricikaTTu** to tie s.o.'s arms behind his back; **~lu mukkalu ceesukoni kaTTelu koDataaDu** he works very hard at cutting firewood.

రెచ్చగొట్టు **reccagoTTu** *v.t.* to arouse, stir up, instigate, incite.

రెచ్చు, రెచ్చిపోవు **reccu, reccipoowu** *v.i.* **1** to be stirred up, be aroused, grow excited. **2** (of cattle) to become agitated, get out of control. **3** to increase, swell.

రెట్ట **reTTa** *n.* **1** birds' dung. **2** filth.

రెట్టమతం **reTTamatam** *n.* tendency to object and contradict, argumentativeness.

రెట్టించు **reTTincu** *v.t.* **1** to double. **2** to repeat; **adee pallawi padeepadee~** to repeat the same refrain again and again. **3** to oppose; **reTTinci aDugu** to ask a counterquestion.

రెట్టింపు **reTTimpu** *n. and adj.* twice as much, double; **japaanu janasankhya incumincugaa telugu deeśam kaNTe~ undi** the population of Japan is about double that of the Telugu country.

రెట్లు **reTLu** *n.pl.* times; **intaku naalugu~istaaDu** he will give four times as much as this.

రెడ్డి **reDDi** *n.* **1** Reddi, name of a community in Andhra Pradesh. **2** (in Rayalaseema and Nellore districts) village head man: **reDDocce modalaaDu** the Reddi has arrived (late): start the performance all over again! (*commonly quoted example of paying undue deference to s.o. in authority*).

రెడ్డిగం **reDDigam** *n.* sitting on the ground with one knee up and a knotted cloth tied round the knee and the body; ~ **weesukonu** to sit in that posture.

రెణ్ణీళ్లు పోయు **reNNiiLLu pooyu** *v.i.* to spoil a work that has been undertaken.

రెపరెప **reparepa** *onom. adv. suggesting* flickering *or* fluttering.

రెపరెపలాడు **reparepalaaDu** *v.i.* to flicker, flutter.

రెప్ప **reppa** *n.* eyelid; ~ **waalcaka cuucu,** ~ **lu aarpaka cuucu,** ~ **weeyakuNDaa cuucu** to stare without blinking, stare fixedly.

రెప్పపాటు **reppapaaTu** *n.* 1 wink, blink. 2 instant, moment of time; ~ **loo raylu tappipooyindi** I missed the train by a fraction of a second.

రెబ్బ **rebba** *n.* compound leaf consisting of a main stalk with leaflets attached (e.g., a neem or margosa leaf).

రెమ్మ **remma** *n.* 1 twig, sub-branch of a main branch. 2 *same as* **rebba.**

రెల్లు **rellu** *n.* kind of reed, *saccharum spontaneum*, used for thatching and as fodder.

రెళ్ల **reLLa** *n.* stalk or sheath holding the grain in an ear of corn.

రే - ree

రే **ree** ! *interj.* 1 *expressing surprise* **ree paapam**! how sad!, what a pity! 2 *form of address to inferiors or young persons* hey!

రే **ree**[2] *first part of a n. compound meaning* night.

రేక **reeka** *n. dial.* bucket for drawing water.

రేకు **reeku** *n.* 1 thin sheet, strip or plate of metal; ~ **Dabbaa,** ~ **paatra** pot or vessel of tin or other metal; **mucci**~ sheet of tinsel; **paara**~ blade of a spade. 2 petal. 3 *dial.* sheet of cloth.

రేకెత్తించు **reekettincu** *v.t.* to arouse, stir up, excite, stimulate.

రేకెత్తు **reekettu** *v.i.* 1 to be aroused, be excited, be stimulated. 2 to increase.

రేఖ **reekha** *n.* 1 line, streak, stripe. 2 ray (of light). 3 (in palmistry) line on the palm of the hand.

రేఖాంశం **reekhaamśam** *n.* longitude.

రేఖాగణితం **reekhaagaNitam** *n.* geometry.

రేఖాచిత్రం, రేఖాపటం **reekhaacitram, reekhaapaTam** *n.* drawing, sketch, outline, diagram.

రేఖాప్రాయంగా **reekhaapraayangaa** *adv.* in outline.

రేగడ, రేగడి, రేవడి **regaDa, reegaDi, reewaDi** *n.* clay soil; **nalla**~ black cotton soil.

రేగి, రేగు **reegi, reegu**[1] *n.* jujube tree, *ziziphus jujuba.*

రేగు **reegu**[2] *v.i.* 1 to [a]rise, be [a]roused, be stirred up. 2 (of hair) to be dishevelled.

రేచీకటి **reeciikaTi** *n.* night blindness.

రేచుకుక్క **reecukukka** *n.* 1 hound, hunting dog. 2 wild dog.

రేడియోధార్మిక శక్తి **reeDiyoodhaarmika śakti** *n.* radio activity.

రేడు **reeDu** *n. class.* 1 king, lord, master. 2 husband.

రేణువు **reeNuwu** *n.* grain, speck, particle.

రేతస్సు **reetassu** *n.* semen, sperm.

రేపకడ **reepakaDa** *adv.* in the morning.

రేపటి **reepaTi** *adj.* 1 of tomorrow. 2 future, next; ~ **taram** next generation.

రేపు **reepu**[1] *n. and adv.* 1 tomorrow; **reepiipaaTiki** by this time tomorrow. 2 morning; **maa geede reepuu maapuu seeru paalistundi** our buffalo gives a seer of milk morning and evening.

రేపు, రేపెట్టు **reepu**[2], **reepeTTu** *v.t.* 1 to arouse, stir up. 2 to incite, excite, provoke.

రేపోమాపో **reepoomaapoo** *adv.* 1 in the morning or in the evening. 2 tomorrow or the next day, very soon.

రేఫ **reepha** *n.* the letter *r*. Old Telugu had two distinct sounds, (i) **saadhu**~ and (ii) an archaic sound **sakaTa**~ which has merged with **saadhu**~ in Modern Telugu.

రేయి **reeyi** *n.* night.

రేయి[ం]బవళ్లు **reeyi[m]bawaLLu** *adv.* night and day, continually.

రేల[చెట్టు] **reela[ceTTu]** *n.* laburnum, *cassia fistula.*

రేవ **reewa** *n.* silt, alluvial soil.

రేవడి **reewaDi**[1] *n. class.* washerman; **reNTiki ceDDa**~ *is a proverbial expression for s.o. who gets the worst of both worlds.*

రేవడి **reewaDi**[2] *same as* **reegaDa.**

రేవతి **reewati** *n. astrol.* twenty-seventh asterism or lunar mansion.

రేవు **reewu** *n.* 1 port, harbour. 2 landing place on a river bank or canal bank or sea shore; *see* **caaki**~

రేషం **reeSam** *n.* silk.

రై, రొ - ray, ro

రైతాంగం, రయితాంగం **raytaangam, rayitaangam** *n.* cultivators (in general), peasantry.

రైతు, రయితు **raytu, rayitu** *n.* cultivator, farmer, ryot, agriculturist.

రైతువారీ, రయితువారీ **raytuwaarii, rayituwaarii** *n.* ryotwari system of land tenure under which a cultivator holds land directly under the government.

రైలు **raylu** *n.* **1** railway. **2** train.

రైలుపట్టాలు **raylupaTTaalu** *n.pl.* rails (of a railway line).

రైలుబండి **raylubaNDi** *n.* train.

రైలుమార్గం **raylumaargam** *n.* railway line, railway track.

రొండి **roNDi** *n.* side of the waist, haunch.

రొండు **roNDu** *informal variant form of* **reNDu.**

రొంప **rompa** *n. dial.* cold in the head.

రొంపి **rompi** *n.* **1** mud. **2** morass, quagmire.

రొక్కం **rokkam** *n.* cash, ready money.

రొక్కపు పైరు **rokkapu payru** *n.* cash crop.

రొక్కించు **rokkincu** *v.i. and t.* to demand, press for (money, answer to a question, etc.).

రొచ్చు **roccu** *n.* **1** foul mud smelling of drains or cattle urine. **2** muddy or marshy place.

రొజ్జ **rojja** *n.* drizzle; ~ **gaali** cold damp wind.

రొట్టె **roTTe** *n.* bread; ~ **wirigi neetiloo paDDadaTa** *lit.* the bread broke and fell into the ghee, so they say (proverb used of s.o. who benefits from a lucky chance or stroke of fortune).

రొడ్డ **roDDa** *n.* greenery, green manure, green leaves trampled and used as manure for irrigated lands.

రొడ్డు, లొడ్డు **roDDu, loDDu** *adj.* much, very; ~ **pulupu** very sour.

రొద **roda** *n.* **1** noise, sound. **2** clamour.

రొప్పు **roppu** I. *n.* panting, gasping. II. *v.i.* to pant, gasp.

రొమ్ము **rommu** *n.* **1** chest, breast, bosom; ~ **lamiida kumpaTi** (*lit.* a stove on o.'s chest) *is a proverbial expression signifying a heavy or burdensome responsibility.* **2** teat of an animal.

రొయ్య **royya** *n.* prawn.

రొయ్యి **royyi** *n.* ashes covering smouldering embers (= **niwuru**).

రొళ్లు **roLLu** *v.t. dial.* to gather, pick up, amass (scattered materials).

రొష్టు **roSTu** *n.* **1** annoyance, outrage. **2** trouble, worry. **3** disturbance, quarrelling.

రొష్టుచేసుకొను **roSTuceesukonu** *v.t.* to divulge, make public.

రొష్టుపెట్టు **roSTupeTTu** *v.t.* to trouble, worry, pester.

రో, రౌ - roo, raw

రోకంటిపాట **rookaNTipaaTa** *n.* **1** repetitive song sung by women pounding paddy. **2** *colloq.* s.g repeated monotonously and mechanically.

రోకటిబండ **rookaTibaNDa** *n.* **1** centipede (= **śatapadi**). **2** *same as* **rookali.**

రోకలి **rookali** *n.* pestle, rice pounder.

రోకు **rooku** *n.* love, passion, infatuation.

రోగం **roogam** *n.* disease, sickness, illness; **ii nelaloo jiitaalu inkaa iwwaleedu. waaLLakeem ~ waccindoo!** they have not yet paid the wages for this month. what has come over them?

రోగనిదానశాస్త్రం **rooganidaanaśaastram** *n. med.* pathology.

రోగి **roogi** *n.* sick person, patient.

రోగిష్టి **roogiSTi** I. *n.* sick person, invalid. II. *adj.* sick, ill.

రోజల్లా **roojallaa** *adv.* all day long.

రోజా **roojaa** *n.* fast observed by Muslims during Ramzan.

రోజాచెట్టు **roojaa ceTTu** *n.* rose tree.

రోజు **rooju**[1] *n.* day.

రోజు **rooju**[2] I. *n.* panting, gasping. II. *v.i.* to pant, breathe hard, gasp.

రోజువారీ **roojuwaarii** *adv.* daily, day to day.

రోజూ **roojuu** *adv.* every day, daily, day by day.

రోత **roota** I. *n.* **1** foulness, filth, nastiness, loathsomeness. **2** loathing, disgust; **kotta oka winta, paata oka ~** anything new is counted as a marvel, anything old is detested (common saying). II. *adj.* **1** nasty, loathsome. **2** hateful, detestable.

రోతపడు **rootapaDu** *v.i. and t.* to abhor, loathe.

రోతపుట్టించే **rootapuTTincee** *adj.* squalid, disgusting.

రోదన[ం] **roodana[m]** *n.* crying, wailing.

రోదసి **roodasi** *n.* **1** space. **2** sky, heavens.

రోదించు **roodincu** *v.i.* to weep, wail, cry aloud.

రోధం **roodham** *n.* obstruction, hindrance.

రోమం **roomam** *n.* hair on the body.

రోమాంచం **roomaancam** *n.* **1** tingling. **2** (of hair) standing on end from shock, etc.

రోయు **rooyu** *v.i. and t.* to dislike, abhor, be disgusted with; **praaNam ~** to feel disgusted.

రోలు **roolu** *n.* **1** mortar; *cf.* **rubbu ~**. **2** socket in which the lower pivot of an oldfashioned door turns. **3** *dial.* sluice of an irrigation tank.

రోషం **rooSam** *n.* anger, indignation, resentment, pique.
రోహం **rooham** *n. class.* bud, blossom, flower.
రోహిణి **roohiNi** *n. astrol.* fourth lunar mansion or asterism: *see* **kaarte.**
రౌతు **rawtu** *n.* **1** rider, horseman, cavalier. **2** *dial.* stone.
రౌద్ర **rawdra** *adj.* terrifying.
రౌద్రం **rawdram** *n.* fury, wrath, ferocious anger.
రౌద్రి **rawdri** *n.* fifty-fourth year of the Hindu cycle of sixty years.
రౌరవ **rawrawa** *adj.* fearsome, terrible, frightful, dreadful.
రౌరవనరకం **rawrawa narakam** *n.* the deepest of all the hells of mythology.

ల - la

లంక **lanka** *n.* **1** island; **lankanta illu** huge house (*lit.* house as big as an island). **2** classical name for the island of Sri Lanka. **3** ~ is the name given to islands of alluvial soil formed in the beds of the Krishna and Godavari rivers in their delta areas during the flood season.
లంకణం, లంఖణం, లంఘనం **lankaNam, lankhaNam, langhanam** *n.* fasting in order to relieve illness (an Ayurvedic remedy).
లంకణం చేయు, లంకణాలు చేయు **lankaNam ceeyu, lankaNaalu ceeyu** *v.i.* to fast in order to relieve illness.
లంకణం పెట్టు **lankaNam peTTu** *v.t.* to prescribe fasting in order to relieve illness.
లంక పొగాకు **lanka pogaaku** *n.* cheroot tobacco grown on delta lankas.
లంకించు **lankincu** I. *v.i.* (*also* ~**konu**) to begin, start, proceed, embark on, launch into: **adi eeDupuki lankincukoNTee kaaśiiloo gaaDida kuusinaa wadaladu** once she starts to cry nothing will stop her. II. *v.t.* to join, link or couple together.
లంకిణి **lankiNi** *n.* **1** fierce-tempered woman. **2** *class.* fierce she devil who guarded Lanka in the Ramayana.
లంకె **lanke** *n.* link, connection, bond.
లంకెపడు **lankepaDu** *v.i.* to be linked, be joined.
లంకెపీట **lankepiiTa** *n.* wooden hobble to prevent cattle from straying.
లంకెబిందెలు **lankebindelu** *n.pl.* **1** pair of pots containing buried treasure (*in former times when treasure was buried for safety it was customary to bury two pots together*). **2** *colloq.* a closely attached pair of persons; **akkacelleLLu iddaruu lankebindellaa unnaaru** the two sisters are an inseparable pair.
లంఖణం **lankhaNam** *same as* **lankaNam.**
లంగరు **langaru** *n.* anchor.
లంగరు అందు **langaru andu** *v.i.* to agree, be in harmony, be in consonance; **rikSaabatukkii lookam naDakkii langarandaka atanu andari miidaa caalaa kasigaa unnaaDu** because there was no harmony between a rickshaw man's life and the demeanour of the public he was very spiteful towards everyone; **adhyayanaaniki anubhawaaniki langarandaali. ii lakSyaanni saadhincinanaaDu kramaśikSaNa ewaruu ceppakuNDaanee abbutundi** studying and practical experience must be in consonance with each other. when that goal is achieved, discipline will be secured without anyone's instructions.
లంగరుఖానా **langarukhaanaa** *n.* poor house, beggars' home.
లంగరువేయు **langaruweeyu** *v.i.* to cast anchor.
లంగా **langaa**[1] *n.* woman's skirt.
లంగా **langaa**[2] *n. dial.* libertine.
లంగోటి **langooTi** *n.* loincloth tied in a truss.
లంఘనం **langhanam** *n.* **1** jump, leap. **2** *same as* **lankaNam.**
లంఘించు **langhincu** *v.i. and t.* **1** to jump [over], leap [over]. **2** to pass over, traverse.
లంచం **lancam** *n.* bribe[ry].
లంచం తిను, లంచం మేయు, లంచం కొట్టు, లంచం పట్టు **lancam tinu, lancam meeyu, lancam koTTu, lancam paTTu** *v.i.* to take bribes.
లంచగొండి **lancagoNDi** *n.* corrupt person, one who takes bribes.
లంచగొండితనం **lancagoNDitanam** *n.* corruption, bribery.
లంజ, లంజె **lanja, lanje** *n.* prostitute, harlot, whore.
లంజకొడుకా! **lanjakoDukaa!** *interj., term of abuse* son of a whore!
లంజరికం **lanjarikam** *n.* prostitution.
లండాచోరీ **laNDaacoorii** *n.* dispute, altercation.
లండీ **laNDii** *n.* mean, obstinate or wicked person.
లంపటం **lampaTam** *n.* **1** difficulty, trouble, entanglement. **2** hindrance, obstruction, clog, impediment.
లంపటుడు **lampaTuDu** *n.* **1** one who is fond of or attached to (s.g). **2** libertine.
లంబ **lamba** *adj.* perpendicular: ~**reekha** perpendicular line: ~**kooNam** right angle.
లంబకర్ణం **lambakarNam** *n. class.* ass, donkey.
లంబాచౌడా **lambaacawDaa** *adj. colloq.* big, hefty (*lit.* tall and broad).
లంబాడ, లంబాడి **lambaaDa, lambaaDi** *same as* **banjaara, banjaari.**
లంబు **lambu** *n.* **1** tallness. **2** largeness.
లంబోదరుడు **lamboodaruDu** *n.* **1** epithet of Vinayaka. **2** potbellied person.
లకారం **lakaaram** *n.* **1** the Telugu letter ల. **2** *colloq.* lakh of rupees; **oka ~ sampaadincEEDu** he earned a lakh of rupees; **waaDidaggira lakaaraalu muulugutunnaayi** he is worth lakhs. **3** *colloq.* ~ **ceppu** to say 'no', reply in the negative.
లకుముకి **lakumuki** *n.* kingfisher (bird).
లకోటా **lakooTaa** *n.* **1** envelope, cover. **2** seal.

లక్క **lakka** *n.* 1 lac, a resinous substance secreted by some insects. 2 sealing wax. 3 lacquer, a hard glossy finish applied to wooden furniture, toys, etc. 4 red colour, red dye.

లక్కంచు **lakkancu** *n.* border of a sari or dhoti woven with coloured yarn.

లక్కపిడత **lakkapiData** *n.* toy-sized lacquered pot for a child to play with.

లక్కపిడతనోరు **lakkapiData nooru** *n.* small finely sculptured mouth (*lit.* lacquered toy-like mouth, a sign of beauty, opposite of **daakanooru**).

లక్కబొమ్మ **lakkabomma** *n.* lacquered toy.

లక్కాకు **lakkaaku** *n.* bush of a cartwheel.

లక్కి **lakki** *substandard form of* **lakSmi.**

లక్ష **lakSa** *n.* 1 lakh, a hundred thousand. 2 a very large but indefinite number or quantity (*cf. English expressions like* millions of, any number of, any amount of) **nuwwu~ [saarlu] ceppinaa saree, iTLaagee ceestaanu** even if you tell me a lakh of times (i.e., even if you tell me any number of times) I will still do it this way; **waaNNi~tiTTEEnu** I scolded him thoroughly; **~loo okaru** one in a million (i.e., s.o. outstanding); **diinikii daanikii~ teeDaa undi** there is a huge difference between this and that.

లక్షణం **lakSaNam** *n.* 1 sign, mark, symptom, indication. 2 feature, characteristic, property, attribute, trait. 3 **mukha lakSaNaalu** facial features. 4 trace, vestige. 5 definition. 6 classification, categorisation. 7 rule of art or science; **kaawyabhaaSa lakSaNaalu** rules of prosody in poetical works. 8 grammar, grammatical science; **lakSaNawiruddha** ungrammatical.

లక్షణంగా **lakSaNangaa** *adv.* 1 properly, in the right way, fittingly. 2 handsomely, beautifully, finely.

లక్షణగ్రంథం **lakSaNagrantham** *n.* 1 standard work of literature. 2 book of reference.

లక్షణమైన **lakSaNamayna** *adj.* fine, excellent, beautiful, handsome.

లక్షవత్తులనోము, లక్షవర్తినోము **lakSawattulanoomu, lakSawartinoomu** *n.* vow performed by women involving lighting a lakh of wicks.

లక్షాధికారి **lakSaadhikaari** *n.* owner of property worth a lakh of rupees.

లక్షించు **lakSincu** *v.t.* to aim at.

లక్షోపలక్షలు **lakSoopalakSalu** *n.pl.* lakhs upon lakhs.

లక్ష్మణుడు **lakSmaNuDu** *n.* Lakshman, younger brother of Rama in the Ramayana.

లక్ష్మి **lakSmi** *n.* Lakshmi, Goddess of wealth, wife of Vishnu.

లక్ష్మీవారం **lakSmiiwaaram** *n.* Thursday.

లక్ష్యం **lakSyam** *n.* 1 aim, object[ive], target, purpose. 2 care, concern, regard, esteem. 3 instance, example.

లక్ష్యం చేయు, లక్ష్యపెట్టు **lakSyam ceeyu, lakSyapeTTu** *v.t.* to esteem, pay regard to, pay attention to, care for, respect; **naa salahaani lakSyapeTTaleedu** (*or* **lakSyam ceeyaleedu**) he did not heed my advice.

లక్ష్యప్రాయుడు **lakSyapraayuDu** *n.* one who serves as a perfect model.

లక్ష్యశుద్ధి **lakSyaśuddhi** *n.* pureness of motive.

లక్ష్యసాధన **lakSyasaadhana** *n.* attaining a goal, achieving an object.

లక్ష్యసిద్ధి **lakSyasiddhi** *n.* successful achievement.

లగాం **lagaam** *n.* bridle, reins.

లగాయించు **lagaayincu** *v.t.* 1 to pile up. 2 *slang* to take for o.s., make away with. 3 *slang* to eat or drink freely; **kuura baagundi, lagaayincEEDu** (*or* **lagaayinci tinnaaDu**) the curry was good and he ate heartily.

లగాయితు, లగాయతు **lagaayitu, lagaayatu** *adv.* [ever] since, beginning from.

లగువుబిగువు **laguwubiguwu** *n.* give and take, readiness to compromise; **~leekuNTee beeram ceDipootundi** if there is no give and take the bargain will not come off.

లగెత్తు **lagettu** *v.i. dial.* to run.

లగ్గం **laggam** *n. colloq.* marriage.

లగ్గసరి **laggasari** *n. colloq.* marriage season.

లగ్నం **lagnam** *n.* 1 auspicious time for a religious ceremony, esp. a marriage. 2 concentration (of attention).

లగ్నం అవు **lagnam awu** *v.i.* (of attention) to be fixed, be concentrated.

లగ్నం చేయు **lagnam ceeyu** *v.t.* to concentrate; **manassu/drsTi~** to concentrate o.'s mind/sight (**-pay** *or* **-miida**, on).

లగ్నపత్రం **lagnapatram** *n.* letter proposing a marriage.

లఘిమ **laghima** *n.* weightlessness, supernatural power of floating in the air, levitation.

లఘు **laghu** I. *n.* (*also* **~wu**) 1 *gram.* short syllable. 2 *dial.* leap, jump. II. *adj.* light; **~pariśrama** light industry, small-scale industry. 2 slight, trifling, small; **~kooNam** *geom.* acute angle. 3 **~śanka** (*lit.* small suspicion) *is a euphemism for wanting to pass urine*; **~śankaku weLLi kaaLLu kaDukku waccEEDu** he eased himself, washed his feet and returned.

లఘువేయు **laghuweeyu** *v.i. dial.* to jump, leap.

లఘ్వాంత్రం **laghwantram** *n. med.* duodenum.

లచ్చి **lacci** *substandard form of* **lakSmi.**

లజుగుజులుపడు **lajugujulupaDu** *v.i.* to argue this way and that.

లజ్జ **lajja** *n.* 1 modesty, shyness, bashfulness. 2 shame, disgrace.

లజ్జాకర **lajjaakara** *adj.* disgraceful, shameful, scandalous.

లజ్జాళువు **lajjaaLuwu** *n.* modest or bashful person.

లజ్జించు **lajjincu** *v.i.* to feel ashamed.

లజ్జితం అవు **lajjitam awu** *v.i.* 1 to feel ashamed, feel shy. 2 to feel belittled, feel slighted.

లజ్జు **lajju** *n.dial.* softness.

లటపటలు **laTapaTalu** *n.pl.* bickering.

లటుక్కున **laTukkuna** *adv.* suddenly, all at once.

లడాయి **laDaayi** *n.* fight, quarrel.

లడీ **laDii** *n. dial.* kind of fire cracker.

లడ్డు **laDDu** *n.* kind of sweet.

లత **lata** *n.* creeper, climbing plant.

లతాంగి lataangi *n.* slender woman.

లతాంతం lataantam *n. class.* flower.

లత్తుక lattuka *n.* red colour, red dye.

లద్ధి, లద్దె laddi, ladde *n.* horse's dung, elephant's dung.

లద్ధి పురుగు laddi purugu *n.* dung beetle.

లపక, లప్ప lapaka, lappa *n. dial.* money.

లబలబ labalaba *onom. adv. sug. the sound of beating o.'s mouth in grief;* **~ mottukonu** to lament passionately.

లబోదిబోమను laboodiboomanu *v.i.* to wail loudly.

లబ్జుగా labjugaa *adv.* 1 jokingly. 2 slyly.

లబ్ధ labdha *first part of a n. compound meaning* gained, acquired; **~ pratiSThuDu** person with an established reputation; **labdhaawakaaśuDu** one who has gained an opportunity or advantage.

లబ్ధం labdham *n. maths.* (*also* **guNakaara ~**) quotient.

లబ్ధి labdhi *n.* gain, acquisition.

లబ్బీ, లబ్బె labbii, labbe *n.* name of a Muslim sect in South India.

లబ్బున labbuna *adv. dial., used with certain vbs. to give intensive force,* e.g., **~ parigettu** to run fast; **~ eeDcu** to weep copiously; **~ nawwu** to burst out laughing.

లభించు labhincu *v.i.* 1 to be acquired, be gained, be obtained, be won; **deeśa swaatantryam labhincina tarwaata** after the achievement of the country's independence; **padi weela ruupaayala bahumati labhincindi** an award of ten thousand rupees was won. 2 to be accorded; **aayanaku swaagatam labhincindi** a welcome was accorded to him *or* he was accorded a welcome. 3 to occur, be found; **krii. puu. 5000 naaTi panimuTLu giddaluuru wadda labhincEEyi** tools dating from 5000 B.C. have been found near Giddalur. 4 to be available; **manaku labhincina caaritrakaadhaaraalanu baTTi** according to historical sources that are available to us.

లభింప చేయు labhimpa ceeyu *v.t.* to make available.

లభ్య labhya *adj.* 1 available, obtainable. 2 found, obtained.

లమిడీ lamiDii *n.* prostitute (term of abuse).

లయ laya *n.* rhythm (in music, dancing, poetry); **gaaliki bhujampay egiree uttariyam aa gaanaaniki ~ weestunnaTTundi** the cloth over his shoulder playing in the wind seems to be keeping in rhythm with the music.

లయం layam *n.* 1 merging, fusion. 2 vanishing; **aame andhakaaramloo ~ ayindi** she disappeared into the darkness. 3 destruction.

లయగా layagaa *adv.* keeping in rhythm, keeping in time, rhythmically.

లలన lalana *n.* beautiful girl.

లలాటం lalaaTam *n.* forehead.

లలాట రేఖలు lalaaTa reekhalu *n.pl., lit.* lines on the forehead, *hence* destiny (since a person's fate is commonly believed to be written on his forehead).

లలాట లిఖితం lalaaTa likhitam *n., lit.* what is written on the forehead, *hence* what is fated or destined.

లలామ lalaama *second part of a n. compound meaning* beautiful, lovely; **yuwatii ~** beautiful girl.

లలిత lalita *adj.* 1 beautiful, charming, lovely, graceful, soft, gentle. 2 epithet of Parvati.

లలిత కళ lalita kaLa *n.* fine art.

లలిత సంగీతం lalita sangiitam *n.* light music.

లవం lawam *n.* 1 small quantity. 2 *maths.* numerator.

లవంగం lawangam *n.* clove.

లవంగ పట్ట lawanga paTTa *n.* cinnamon.

లవంగ తైలం lawanga taylam *n.* clove oil.

లవకుశులు lawakuśulu *n.pl.* Lava and Kusa, twin sons of Rama in the Ramayana.

లవణం lawaNam *n.* salt.

లవణజనకం lawaNajanakam *n. chem.* halogen.

లవణజలం lawaNajalam *n.* brine.

లవణిమ lawaNima *n. class.* 1 loveliness. 2 saltiness.

లవలేశం lawaleeśam *n.* very little, very small quantity.

లవింత lawinta *n. dial.* some more (quantity).

లశునం, లశూనం laśu[u]nam *n.* garlic.

లసిక lasika *n. class.* saliva.

లహరి lahari *n.* large wave.

లా - laa

లా[గ], లాగా, లాగు laa[ga], laagaa, laagu[1] *advbl. suffix and p.p.* like, as; **mii annayya ~ kanabaDataaDu** he looks like your elder brother.

లాంగలం laangalam *n. class.* plough.

లాంగూలం laanguulam *n. class.* tail.

లాంగూలి laanguuli *n. class.* monkey.

లాంఛనం laanchanam *n.* mark, sign, token, emblem; *see also* **laanchanaalu.**

లాంఛనంగా laanchanangaa *adv.* 1 formally, in a formal manner. 2 for the sake of formality, for form's sake, for name's sake.

లాంఛనప్రాయ, లాంఛనబద్ధ laanchanapraaya, laanchanabaddha *adj.* formal.

లాంఛనప్రాయంగా laanchanapraayangaa *adv.* 1 *same as* **laanchanangaa.** 2 as a token.

లాంఛనాలు laanchanaalu *n.pl.* 1 formalities; **attagaaru/aaDabiDDa ~** formalities due to be observed towards (*i.e.* marks of respect due to be shown to) o.'s mother-in-law/sister-in-law. 2 obligatory gifts to members of the bridegroom's family agreed to as part of a wedding settlement; **kaTNamuu laanchanaaluu leekuNDaa peLLiki oppukunnaaDu** he (bridegroom) agreed to a wedding without a dowry or gifts to members of his family; *see* **raaja ~.**

లాంఛనుడు **laanchanuDu** *n.* one who is awarded: **kiirtipataka ~** one who is awarded (*or* recipient of) **kiirti** medal.

లాంటి **laaNTi** *same as* **laaTi.**

లాంతరు **laantaru** *n.* lantern.

లాక్ష **laakSa** *class. alt. form of* **lakka.**

లాక్షణికుడు **laakSaNikuDu** *n.* grammarian, classical scholar.

లాక్షాగృహం **laakSaagrham** *n.* palace of wax in the Mahabharata made by Duryodhana in order to destroy the Pandavas.

లాగించు **laagincu** *v.t.* **1** to cause (s.g) to be pulled. **2** *slang* to take away, remove. **3** *slang* to eat, drink. **4** *slang* to carry on (business).

లాగు **laagu**[1] *same as* **laa.**

లాగు **laagu**[2] *n.* short trousers, shorts.

లాగు[కోను], లాక్కొను **laagu**[3] **[konu], laakkonu** I. *v.i.* to ache; **naDicinanduku naa kaaLLu laagutunnaayi** (*or* **laakku pootunnaayi**) because I walked my legs are aching. II. *v.t.* **1** to pull, draw, drag; **duppaTi kaaLLamiidiki laakkonnaaDu** he pulled the sheet over his legs. **2** to seize, snatch, obtain by force, carry off, make off with; **Dabbu laagEEDu** (*or* **laakkonnaaDu**) he made off with the money. **3** to carry on with difficulty, manage to look after; **eedoo ii samsaaram neenee laagutunnaanu** (*or* **laakku wastunnaanu**) somehow I am managing to look after this family.

లాఘవం **laaghawam** *n.* lightness, levity.

లాఘవంగా **laaghawangaa** *adv.* skilfully, cleverly.

లాచేరీపడు **laaceeriipaDu** *v.i. dial.* to grovel, demean o.s.; **laaceerii paDi aDugu** to beg on o.'s bended knees.

లాజలు **laajalu** *n.pl.* fried grain.

లాటం **laaTam** *n.* kind of alliteration in classical Telugu.

లా[ం]టి **laa[N]Ti** *adjvl. suffix* like; **mii ~ pedda maniSi** a gentleman like you.

లాఠీ **laaThii** *n.* stick, club, baton.

లాడం, లాడా **laaDam, laaDaa** *same as* **naaDam.**

లాభం **laabham** *n.* gain, profit, advantage; **waaDitoo ceppi ~ leedu** there is no point/use/advantage/good in telling it to him; **wagaci eem ~** ? what is the use of lamenting?

లాభకర, లాభదాయక, లాభసాటి, లాభప్రద **laabhakara, laabhadaayaka, laabhasaaTi, laabhaprada** *adj.* profitable, advantageous, gainful.

లాభకారి **laabhakaari** *n.* s.g advantageous, s.g profitable.

లాభదాయకంగా **laabhadaayakangaa** *adv.* profitably.

లాభపడు, లాభం పొందు **laabhapaDu, laabham pondu** *v.i.* to earn a profit; **ii wyaapaaramloo laabhapaDDaaDu** (*or* **laabham pondEEDu**) he earned a profit in this business *or* he made a profit on this transaction.

లాభించు **laabhincu** *v.i.* **1** to be profited, be benefited, derive benefit. **2** to be beneficial.

లాయం **laayam** *n. class.* horse's stable.

లాయకు, లాయఖు **laayak[h]u** *adj.* fit, suitable.

లాల **laala** *n.* **1** saliva. **2** *child language* water; **~ poosukunnaawaa?** have you taken a bath?

లాలన **laalana** *n.* **1** wheedling, coaxing. **2** caressing.

లాలనగా **laalanagaa** *adv.* beseechingly.

లాలస **laalasa** *n.* **1** eager longing. **2** greed, cupidity.

లాలసుడు **laalasuDu** *n.* **1** one who eagerly desires. **2** lustful person, greedy person.

లాలాజలం **laalaajalam** *n. class.* saliva, spittle.

లాలి **laali** *n.* **1** cradle. **2** (*also* **~ paaTa**) cradle song, lullaby.

లాలించు **laalincu** *v.t.* **1** to wheedle, coax. **2** to fondle, caress, fuss over, show great affection for.

లాలింపుగా **laalimpugaa** *adv.* **1** coaxingly. **2** caressingly.

లాలిత్యం **laalityam** *n.* **1** beauty, grace, loveliness. **2** gentleness.

లాలూచీ, లాలోచీ **laaluucii, laaloocii** *n.* clandestine dealings, underhand dealings.

లాలూచీపడు **laaluuciipaDu** *v.i.* to have clandestine or underhand dealings.

లాల్చీ **laalcii** *n.* loose-fitting shirt.

లావణ్యం **laawaNyam** *n.* **1** beauty, loveliness. **2** *class.* saltiness.

లావాదేవీ **laawaadeewii** *n.* transactions, dealings.

లావు **laawu** I. *n.* **1** fatness, stoutness; **~ ekku** to grow fat. **2** bigness, largeness. **3** thickness. II. *adj.* **1** fat, stout. **2** large, big. **3** thick. **4** blunt. **5** much, many, plentiful; **waaDiki asuuya ~** he is very jealous.

లాస్యం **laasyam** *n. class.* dance, dancing.

లాహిరి **laahiri** *n. class.* intoxication.

లి, లీ - li, lii

లింగం **lingam** *n.* 1 phallus, male organ of generation, emblem of Siva. 2 *slang* penis. 3 *gram.* gender. 4 sex: **lingabheedam leekuNDaa** without discrimination of sex.

లింగకాయ **lingakaaya** *n.* small case containing a lingam, emblem of Siva, worn on a cord round the neck by Saivites.

లింగధారి **lingadhaari** *n.* Saivite who wears a symbol in the shape of a lingam.

లింగాయత్ **lingaayat** *n.* name of a Saivite sect in Karnataka founded by Basawa in the 12 century A.D.

లింగిలింగడు **lingilingaDu** *n. colloq.* man and wife.

లింగులింగుమని **lingulingumani** *adv.* quietly, unostentatiously.

లింగూలిటుకూ **linguuliTukuu** *alliterative phrase used of two persons regarded as petty and unimportant* **iNTLoo iddaree unnaaru kadaa~, waNTa paawugaNTaloo aypootundi** there are just two of them in the house, their cooking takes only a quarter of an hour.

లిక్కి[కొడవలి] **likki[koDawali]** *n.* kind of small sickle used for removing weeds; **likkanta maniSi** little man (i.e., small in stature).

లిఖించు **likhincu** *v.t.* 1 to write. 2 *class.* to portray.

లిఖిత **likhita** *adj.* 1 written. 2 *class* portrayed.

లిఖితం **likhitam** *n.* writing; **naa swahasta~** written by my own hand (*formula signifying that a document is in the handwriting of the signatory*).

లిపి **lipi** *n.* script.

లిపిశాస్త్రం **lipiśaastram** *n.* grammatology.

లిప్త **lipta**[1] *n.* moment; **maru~ loo** next moment; **~ paaTu-kaalam** a moment of time.

లిప్త **lipta**[2] *second part of a class. adjvl. compound meaning* anointed with, smeared with: **cuuDagaanee mukham darahaasa ~ mayindi** at the sight his face was wreathed in (*lit.* anointed with) smiles.

లిఫాఫా **liphaaphaa** *n. dial.* envelope, cover.

లీన **liina** *adj.* 1 absorbed, merged, rapt. 2 disappeared, vanished.

లీనం **liinam** *n.* absorption.

లీనీకరణ **liiniikaraNa** *n.* amalgamation, merging.

లీల **liila** *n.* 1 play, sport, diversion. 2 deed, action. 3 amorous sport.

లీలగా **liilagaa** *adv.* 1 easily. 2 playfully. 3 faintly, vaguely, dimly, indistinctly.

లీలామాత్రంగా **liilaamaatrangaa** *adv.* indistinctly, only faintly.

లీలామానుషరూపుడు **liilaamaanuSa ruupuDu** *n.* 1 god who assumes human guise in order to intervene in human activities. 2 *colloq.* person who changes his views and attitudes to fit in with changing circumstances.

లు, లూ - lu, luu

లుంగచుట్టు **lungacuTTu** *v.t.* to bundle up, roll up carelessly: **cokkaa lungacuTTi paareesEEDu** he rolled the shirt up carelessly in a bundle and threw it away.

లుంగ[లు] చుట్టుకొను **lunga[lu]cuTTukonu** *v.i.* 1 to roll up; coil up. 2 to curl o.s. up; **lungalucuTTukoni nidra pooyEEDu** he curled himself up and went to sleep.

లుంగీ **lungii** *n.* cloth worn by a man draped round the waist.

లుకలుక **lukaluka** *n.* sound made by insects boring in wood.

లుగసాను **lugasaanu** *n.* loss (= **nuksaanu**).

లుచ్చా **lucchaa** I. *n.* mean fellow. II. *adj.* mean, base.

లుప్త **lupta** *adj.* lost.

లుబ్ధ **lubdha** *adj.* 1 covetous, greedy, avaricious. 2 miserly.

లుబ్ధుడు **lubdhuDu** *n.* 1 greedy person. 2 miser.

లుమ్మ[లు] చుట్టు[కొను] **lumma[lu] cuTTu[konu]** *dial. variant form of* **lunga[lu]cuTTu[konu]**.

లులాయం **lulaayam** *n. class.* wild buffalo.

లూటీ **luuTii** *n.* loot[ing].

లూత **luuta** *n. class.* 1 spider. 2 ant.

లెంక **lenka** *n. class.* servant; **telugu**~ *lit.* servant of Telugu, a title awarded for scholarship in Telugu.

లెండి **leNDi** *see* **lee**[2],[4].

లెంప **lempa** *dial. variant of* **cempa** *occurring only in the sense of* cheek.

లెంపకాయ, లెంపలేసుకొను **lempakaaya, lempaleesukonu** *dial. variants of* **cempakaaya, cempaleesukonu.**

లెక్క **lekka** *n.* **1** account; **laabhanaSTaala**~ profit and loss account. **2** counting, calculation, sum (in arithmetic); **miiru tiTTinaa naaku aaśiissukindee**~ even if you scold me I shall count it as a blessing. **3** reckoning, consideration; **okkoo raatri eeDu enimidi daaTinatarwaata iNTiki wacceewaaDu. aawiDa**~ **prakaaram iwi ceDipooyee lakSaNaalu** on some nights he would come home after seven or eight o'clock. by her way of reckoning these were signs of degeneration. **4** amount; **ninna niiku** ~ **icceesEEnu** yesterday I paid you the amount; **paalaloo konta**~ **wenna kalipi tayaaru ceesEEnu** I prepared it by mixing some amount of butter with milk. **5** number; ~ **leen[ann]i** countless, innumerable; ~ **ku mikkiligaa janam waccEEru** people came in countless numbers. **6** rate; **jiitamnunci padiheenu ruupaayala** ~**na nelanelaa guDDi kuNTi modalayna wikalaangulaku istuu wacceewaaDu** he used to give from his salary at the rate of fifteen rupees per month to blind, lame and other incapacitated persons. **7** regard, esteem, heeding, paying attention; **waaDiki naa maaTa**~ **leedu** he has no regard for what I say; **naaku nii**~ **eemiTi**? why should I heed you? **Y-ki X aNTee**~ **leedu** Y does not take X into account *or* Y cares nothing for X. **8** ~ *is used idiomatically in the following senses* (i) s.g to be considered, assumed or taken; **idi ceesinappuDee telugu deeśam aayana ruNaanni kontaynaa tiirucukonnaTTu**~ only when this is done can the Telugu country's debt to him be taken as having been partly repaid; **mis preema eeDawa leedu, hEEnkiitoo kaLLottukundi, anduceeta eeDcinaTTee** ~ Miss Prema did not cry, but she wiped her eyes with a hanky, so it was assumed that she had cried; (ii) s.g deserving concern or consideration, s.g important, a great matter; **saree, konta kaSTapaDawalasi wasteeneem? adoo**~ **loonidi kaadu** all right, what if I did have to suffer a little? it is not a matter for concern; **nijaaniki aa nagalu manakanta** ~ **looniwi kaawu** to tell the truth those jewels are not of such great importance to us; **aayana eppuDu waccEEDannadi**~ **kaadu, waccii eem ceesEEDoo ceppaNDi** when he came is not the important thing. tell me what he did after he came; **aTu pimmaTa mottam deeśaanni waśaparacukonaDam waariki oka** ~**gaa toocaleedu** after that it seemed to them to be no great matter to take possession of the whole country; *see* **jama.**

లెక్కకట్టు **lekkakaTTu** *v.t.* to work out, calculate; **waDDii aaru śaatam coppuna lekkakaTTi Dabbu icceesEEnu** I worked out the interest at six percent and paid the money.

లెక్కచేయు **lekkaceeyu** *v.t.* **1** to count, calculate, compute. **2** to take into account, take account of, care for, heed, pay attention to. **3** to esteem, respect.

లెక్కపక్కలు **lekkapakkalu** *n.pl.* accounts and such things.

లెక్కపెట్టు **lekkapeTTu** *v.t.* to count, calculate, reckon, compute.

లెక్కలేనన్ని **lekkaleenanni** *adj.* countless, innumerable.

లెక్కాడొక్కా **lekkaaDokkaa** *n* accounts and such things.

లెక్కాపత్రమా? **lekkaapatramaa?** *rhetorical question, lit.* is there an account or a document? **caalaa uuLLu cuusEEnu,**~? I have visited many towns — too many to count; **waaDiki oka weyyi ruupaayalu paDeestee niiku oka**~? if you give him a thousand rupees that is a mere nothing to you (*implication*: for you it is too trivial a sum to require an account or document).

లెక్కించు **lekkincu** *v.t.* to count, calculate, reckon, compute.

లెగ, లెగు, లెగిసి **lega, legu, legisi** *dial. forms of the infinitive, imperative sing. and past participle of* **leecu.**

లెద్దురు **ledduru** *see* **lee**[2].

లెస్స **lessa** *adj.* **1** good, excellent. **2** best. **3** more.

లెస్సగా **lessagaa** *adv.* well, throughly.

లే - lee

లే **lee**[1] *adj.* young, tender: **lee** *occurs only with certain nouns*, e.g., **leeduuDa** young calf; **leewayasu** tender age; *cf.* **leeta.**

లే, లెండి, లెద్దురు **lee**[2], **leNDi, ledduru** *clitic conveying indefiniteness combined with light-heartedness or irony*; you know, for sure; **nuwwu ii pani ceeyaleewulee!** you won't be able to do this work, you know!

లే **lee**[3] *basic stem of defective vb. meaning* not to be, not to exist.

లే **lee**[4], **leNDi** *imperative sing. pl. of* **leecu** rise! get up!

లేక **leeka** I. *neg. participle of* **lee**[1] **1** *lit.* there not being; **illu leeka kaSTapaDutunnaanu** *lit.* there not being a house (for me), I am suffering; i.e., I am suffering without a house *or* I am suffering for want of a house. **2** 'could not' *is expressed by an infinitive* + ~ + **poo** (*auxiliary vb.*); **waaDu maaTLaaDa~ pooyEEDu** he could not speak. II. *advbl. particle* or, otherwise.

లేకపోవు **leekapoowu** *v.i.* to be wanting, be absent; *see also* **leeka** *sense I. 2.*

లే[త]కాల్పు **lee[ta]kaalpu** *see* **leeta** *sense 3.*

లేకి **leeki** *n.* **1** grain left on the ground after harvesting. **2** person who scrounges for food.

లేకుండా **leekuNDaa** *neg. participle of* **lee** there not being, without there being, without . . . being there; **miiru~ pani awutundEE?** without you being there will the work be finished? *see* **kuNDaa.**

లేకేం? **leekeem?** *rhetorical question conveying a strong affirmative meaning* "**maaku cooTu undEE?**" "~ ?" "will there be room for us?" "of course there will!"; *see* **eem.**

లేఖ **leekha** *n. class.* letter, epistle.

లేఖన[ం] **leekhana[m]** *n.* writing, script; **śilaaleekhanam** inscription on stone.

లేఖన సామగ్రి **leekhana saamagri** *n.* stationery.

లేఖాంకితుడు, లేఖితుడు, లేఖ్యుడు **leekhaankituDu, leekhituDu, leekhyuDu** *n.* addressee of a letter.

లేఖావతారిక **leekhaawataarika** *n.* formal set of words at the beginning of a letter setting out the relationship between the writer and addressee.

లేఖిని **leekhini** *n. class.* pen.

లేగ[దూడ] **leega[duuDa]** *n.* sucking calf.

లేగటి ఆవు **leegaTi aawu** *n.* cow with a sucking calf.

లేచిపోవు **leecipoowu** *v.i.* **1** to elope, run away (**-too**, with). **2** to desert, quit, abandon; **aa paragaNaalanunci leecipoowalasiwaccindi** they had to quit those areas.

లేచు **leecu** *v.i.* to rise, get up, stand up.

లేడి **leeDi** *n.* deer.

లేత **leeta** *adj.* **1** young, fresh, soft, tender. **2** (of colour) pale. **3** light, slight; **lee[ta]kaalpu waccina doosa** (i) dosa that is lightly baked (ii) dosa that is underbaked (i.e., insufficiently baked). **4 lee[ta]paakam** thin syrup.

లేతతనం **leetatanam** *n.* **1** freshness, tenderness. **2** lightness, slightness. **3** paleness.

లేదా **leedaa** *advbl. particle* or, otherwise.

లేని **leeni** *neg. vbl. adj. of* **lee 1** not being, not existing; **appuDu~ śookam ippuDenduku?** why do you show grief now which you did not show then? **2** non-existent, imaginary; **~ bhuutaanni śrsTincEEru** they created an imaginary bogey. **3** forced, unnatural, uncharacteristic; **~ nawwu teccukonnaaDu** he put on a forced smile; **~ kaaThinyam** uncharacteristic sternness.

లేనిపోని **leenipooni** *adj.* useless, pointless, needless, unnecessary, unwanted; **~ kalatalu** pointless disputes.

లేపం **leepam** *n. class.* ointment.

లేపనం **leepanam** *n.* **1** smearing, plastering. **2** anointing. **3** painting.

లే[త]పాకం **lee[ta]paakam** *see* **leeta** *sense 4.*

లేపు **leepu** *v.t.* **1** to rouse, make s.o. get up. **2** to wake up. **3** to raise, stir up.

లేబగలు **leebagalu** *n.* early morning.

లేమ **leema** *n.* woman.

లేమి **leemi** *n.* **1** not being. **2** want, poverty; **nidra~** want of sleep; *cf.* **kalimi.**

లేమిడి **leemiDi** *n.* want, poverty; **~ batuku** life of want.

లేవగొట్టు **leewagoTTu** *v.t.* **1** to raise, arouse, stir up. **2** to make s.o. give up or leave (a place); **waaNNi iNTinunci leewagoTTEEDu** he made him leave the house.

లేవదీయు **leewadiiyu** *v.t.* **1** to lift up, raise. **2** to erect, set up (shed). **3** to carry off, run away with. **4** to stir up (agitation).

లేవదీసుకుపోవు **leewadiisukupoowu** *v.t.* to elope with.

లేవనెత్తు **leewanettu** *v.t.* **1** to raise, bring up (point for discussion, problem). **2** to stir up (agitation).

లేవిడీ **leewiDii** *n.* jeering.

లేవిడీకొట్టు **leewiDiikoTTu** *v.i.* to jeer.

లేశం **leeśam** *n.* tiny portion, particle, very little; **aa dhanaaniki naa miida leeśamaatramuu adhikaaram leedu** that wealth has not the slightest power over me.

లేహ్యం **leehyam** *n.* ayurvedic medicine.

లై, లొ - lay, lo

లైంగిక **layngika** *adj.* **1** sexual. **2** about or concerning sex.

లైంగికవ్యాధి **layngika wyaadhi** *n.* veneral disease, syphilis.

లొంగదీయు **longadiiyu** *v.t.* **1** to tame, humble, cause to submit. **2** to win over, bring round to o.'s point of view.

లొంగదీసుకొను **longadiisukonu** *v.t.* to captivate, seduce.

లొంగు **longu** *v.i.* to yield, submit, surrender, succumb, capitulate.

లొంగుబాటు **longubaaTu** *n.* yielding, surrender, capitulation.

లొండ **loNDa** *n. dial.* cave, hole.

లొంప **lompa** *n.* hut, hovel (in a deprecatory sense): *cf.* **kompa.**

లొచ్చు **loccu** *adj.* inferior, deficient, defective.

లొటలొట **loTaloTa** *onom. adv. sug.* sound made by a pot when struck abruptly.

లొటారం **loTaaram** I. *n.* hole, emptiness. II. *adj.* empty, pithless: *see* **paTaaram.**

లొటిపిట, లొటిపిట్ట **loTipiTa, loTipiTTa** *n. obs.* camel.

లొట్ట **loTTa** I. *n.* **1** click of the tongue. **2** pit, hollow, dent; **ginne ~ paDindi** there is a dent in the bowl. **3** hollow tube or pipe. II. *adj.* **1** sunken, hollow; **~ kaLLu** sunken eyes. **2 ~ kaalu** withered leg.

లొట్టకాయ **loTTakaaya** *n. slang* penis.

లొట్ట[లు]వేయు **loTTa[lu]weeyu** *v.i.* to click o.'s tongue (at the prospect of food; *cf. the English expression* to smack o.'s lips).

లొట్టి **loTTi** *n.* small earthen pot used for toddy; **~ laaTi maniSi** short and stout person.

లొడబిడ **loDabiDa** I. *n.* confusion, disturbance, noise. II. *adv.* confusedly, in confusion.

లొడలొడ **loDaloDa** *adv.* **1** loosely, confusedly. **2** (of water or words pouring out) in a stream, continuously.

లొడిత **loDita** *n.* span from tip of thumb to tip of forefinger, about twenty centimetres; **loDiteDu maniSi** diminutive person.

లొడుపు **loDupu** *v.t. dial.* to stir with a ladle.

లొడ్డు **loDDu** *same as* **roDDu.**

లొత్త **lotta** I. *n.* hole, dent, hollow. II. *adj.* **1** (of eyes, cheeks) hollow, sunken. **2 ~ cewi** malformed ear.

లొల్ల **lolla** *n.* kind of harrow.

లొల్లి **lolli** *n. dial.* **1** sound made by dogs barking. **2** shouting, clamour.

లొల్లిచేయు, లొల్లిపెట్టు **lolliceeyu, lollipeTTu** *v.i. dial.* to shout, clamour.

లొసుగు **losugu** I. *n.* fault, defect, deficiency. II. *adj.* inferior.

లో, లౌ - loo, law

లో **loo** I. *adj.* inner, inmost; **loogadi** inner room; **looguTTu** deep secret; **loopaawaDa** underskirt. II. *p.p.* **1** in, inside, within, among; **Dilliiloo** in Delhi; **naa anubhawamloo** within my experience; **lakSamandiloo** among a lakh of people. **2** *English usage sometimes requires a different preposition in translation*, e.g., **aandhra pradeeSloo muuDoo wantu** one third of Andhra Pradesh; **tanaloo taanu goNukkonnaaDu** he muttered to himself; **maalanu deewuDi meDaloo weestundi** she places the garland round the god's neck; **maaloo andaruu udyoogastulee** all of us are employees; **paniloo unnaanu** I am at work *or* I am busy. **3** *other idiomatic usages*: **dhaanyam pasimiranguloo uNTundi** the grain will be golden yellow in colour; **waaDiki naaloo sagam wayasu undi** he is half my age.

లోంచి **loonci** *same as* **loonunci.**

లోక **looka** *adj., gen. as first part of a n. compound* **1** of the world. **2** of mankind, of society, common, general.

లోకం **lookam** *n.* **1** the world. **2** mankind, the human race, society.

లోకకల్యాణం **lookakalyaaNam** *adj.* beneficial to the world.

లోకజ్ఞానం, లోకజ్ఞత **lookajñaanam, lookajñata** *n.* common sense, worldly knowledge.

లోకత్రయం **lookatrayam** *n.* the three worlds, i.e., heaven, earth and hell (= **mullookaalu**).

లోకనం **lookanam** *n.* seeing, sight.

లోకప్పు **lookappu** *n.* ceiling.

లోకప్రవాదం **lookaprawaadam** *n.* common talk.

లోకప్రసిద్ధ **lookaprasiddha** *adj.* world-famous.

లోకప్రియ **lookapriya** *adj.* attractive to the public, popular.

లోకప్రియం చేయు **lookapriyam ceeyu** *v.t.* to popularise.

లోకబాంధవుడు **lookabaandhawuDu** *n.class.* sun.

లోకమర్యాద **lookamaryaada** *n.* convention, established custom.

లోకయాత్ర **lookayaatra** *n.* life's journey.

లోకవ్యవహారం **lookawyawahaaram** *n.* common or general usage.

లోకసాక్షి **lookasaakSi** *n.class.* sun.

లోకాపవాదం **lookaapawaadam** *n.* public scandal.

లోకాభిరామాయణం **lookaabhiraamaayaNam** *n.* leisurely conversation, gossip, chit chat, talking about this and that.

లోకులు **lookulu** *n.pl.* people, the public; ~ **palugaakulu** *is a stock phrase meaning* the public are very mean-minded.

లోకువ **lookuwa** *adj.* inferior, subordinate, subject; **waaLLani ~ gaa cuustaaDu** he looks on them as inferior *or* he looks down on them; **waaLLaku** (or **waaLLamundu**) ~ **ayyEEnu** I was humiliated before them.

లోకేశ్వరుడు **lookeeśwaruDu** *n.* God, the Supreme Being.

లోకోక్తి **lookookti** *n.* proverbial saying.

లోకోత్తర **lookoottara** *adj.* excellent, best of all.

లోకోపకారి **lookoopakaari** I *n.* philanthropist. II. *adj.* philanthropic.

లోగడ **loogaDa** *adv.* previously, formerly, some time ago.

లోగడప **loogaDapa** *n.* inner part of a threshold.

లోగా **loogaa** *advbl. particle* **1** by (a certain date), within (a certain period). **2** *affixed to a fut. vbl. adj.* before; **waanawaccee ~ iNTikipoowaali** you must go home before it rains.

లోగిలి **loogili** *n.* house with living rooms opening on to a central courtyard.

లోగుండా **looguNDaa** *p.p.* through, by way of.

లోచనం **loocanam** *n. class.* eye.

లోచెయ్యి **looceyyi** *n.* palm of the hand.

లోటా **looTaa** *n.* drinking vessel, lota.

లోటు **looTu** *n.* **1** shortage, want, lack, deficiency; **Dabbuku ~ leedu** there is no shortage of money. **2** shortfall, deficit. **3** loss, detriment, harm.

లోటుపాట్లు **looTupaaTLu** *n.pl.* defects, shortcomings.

లోతక్కువ **lootakkuwa** *n.* balance remaining to be made up.

లోతట్టు **lootaTTu** *n.* inner surface, inside.

లోతు **lootu** I. *n.* depth, profundity. II. *adj.* deep, profound.

లోతులేని **lootuleeni** *adj.* shallow.

లోన **loona** *adv.* within, inside, internally.

లోనవు **loonawu** *v.i.* to be subjected to, be exposed to; **kaalaanugatangaa maarpulaku ~ tuu waccina ii widyaaśaakha** this education department which has been subjected to changes in course of time.

లోని **looni** *adj.* inner, inside, internal.

లోనుంచి, లోంచి **loonunci, loonci** *p.p.* **1** from [out of]: **ummaDi kuTumbam ~ weerupaDDaaDu** he separated from his joint family. **2** through.

లోనుచేయు **loonuceeyu** *v.t.* to subject.

లోపం **loopam** *n.* dearth, want, absence, omission, lack, deficiency, shortcoming; **tiNDikii baTTakii ~ leedu** there is no dearth of food or clothing; **niikeem ~ ceesEEnu ippuDu**? now what have I deprived you of? **waaLLa [śaktiki] ~ leekuNDaa ceesEEru** they have done it to the best of their ability.

లోపల **loopala** I. *p.p. and adv.* **1** inside, within, inwardly; ~ **anukonnaaDu** he thought to himself; ~ **caduwukonnaaDu** he read to himself. **2** before (of time): **nelaakharu ~** before the end of the month. II. *advbl. particle suffixed to fut. vbl. adj.* by the time that, before; **aayana waccee ~ weLLi pooyEEnu** by the time he came, I had gone away.

లోపలి **loopali** *adj.* inner, interior.

లోపాయకారీ **loopaayakaarii** *adj.* **1** secret, private. **2** furtive, clandestine, underhand.

లోపాయకారీగా **loopaayakaariigaa** *adv.* **1** secretly, privately **2** clandestinely, furtively.

లోపించు **loopincu** *v.i.* **1** to lack, be lacking, be missing, be wanting, be absent. **2** to vanish, disappear. **3** *gram.* to be dropped, be elided.

లోపు[గా], లోపున, లోపులో **loopu**[1]**[gaa], loopuna, loopuloo** *advbl. particle affixed to fut. vbl. adj.* by the time that, before; **aayana waccee ~ neenu bhoonceestaanu** I will take my meal before he comes.

లోపు **loopu**[2] *p.p. and adv.* within, less than; **dhara wanda ruupaayala ~ aytee, koNTaanu** if the cost is less than a hundred rupees, I will buy it; **panneNDu samwatsaraala ~ [wayasugala] pillalu** children under the age of twelve years.

లోబడు **loobaDu** *v.i.* **1** to yield, submit, succumb, surrender. **2** to come within, fall within; **aadaaya parimitiki loobaDinawaaru** those who fall within an income limit.

లోబరచుకొను **loobaracukonu** *v.t.* to master, conquer, subject, subjugate, bring under control.

లోభం, లోభత్వం **loobham, loobhatwam** *n.* **1** miserliness, stinginess. **2** greed, avarice.

లోభి **loobhi** *n.* miser.

లోభించు **loobhincu** *v.i.* to be miserly, be stingy; **Dabbuku ~** to grudge or stint money, be stingy with money.

లోయ **looya** *n.* valley.

లోల **loola** *adj.* **1** trembling, agitated. **2** wishing, desiring.

లోలకం **loolakam** *n. sci.* pendulum.

లోలకులు, లోలాకులు **loolakulu, loolaakulu** *n.pl.* earrings.

లోలత, లోలత్వం **loolata, loolatwam** *n.* intense desire.

లోలలోచన, లోలాక్షి **loolaloocana, loolaakSi** *n.class.* woman with roving eyes.

లోలుడు **looluDu** *second part of a n. compound meaning* one who is devoted to or enamoured of; **strii ~** philanderer.

లోలోన **looloona** *adv.* inwardly, to o.s.

లోలోపల **looloopala** *adv.* **1** deep inside, inwardly. **2** secretly, clandestinely. **3** ~ **caduwu** to read to o.s.

లోవ **loowa** *n.* **1** valley. **2** burrow, hole in the ground.

లోవంక **loowanka** *adj.* bent inwards.

లోష్టం **looSTam** *n.class.* clod, lump of earth.

లోహ **looha** *adj.* of metal, metallic.

లోహం **looham** *n.* metal.

లోహచూర్ణం **loohacuurNam** *n.* iron filings.

లోహితము **loohitam** *n.* red colour.

లోహోత్పత్తిశాస్త్రం **loohootpatti śaastram** *n.* metallurgy

లౌకిక **lawkika** *adj.* 1 secular, temporal. 2 mundane, worldly. 3 common, in general use; ~ **bhaaSa** everyday speech, colloquial language.
లౌకికం **lawkikam** *n.* worldly wisdom, worldliness.
లౌకికవాదం **lawkikawaadam** *n.* secularism.
లౌకికుడు, లౌక్యుడు **lawkikuDu, lawkyuDu** *n.* worldly-wise person.
లౌక్యం **lawkyam** *n.* 1 worldliness, worldly wisdom. 2 prudence, tact.
లౌక్యంగా **lawkyangaa** *adv.* prudently, tactfully.
లౌల్యం **lawlyam** *n.* lustfulness, passion.

వ - wa

వంక **wanka** I. *n.* 1 side, direction. 2 curve, bend; **candra**~ *or* **nela**~ crescent moon. 3 stream, watercourse. 4 pretext, excuse. 5 fault; ~ **lu peTTu** to complain, grumble. II. *p.p.* in the direction of, towards; **ii**~ in this direction.
వంకదారి **wankadaari** *n.* winding path leading to a fort gate.
వంకర **wankara** I. *n.* 1 crookedness, bend, curve; ~ **lutirugu** to be bent, be twisted, be contorted. 2 *dial.* nose ornament. II. *adj.* crooked, bent, curved, twisted, warped, distorted.
వంకరటింకరగా **wankaraTinkaragaa** *adv.* crookedly, twistedly, (of walking) erratically, (of writing) shakily; **paapiDi**~ **undi** the parting (of the hair) is crooked.
వంకసన్నాలు **wankasannaalu** *n.pl.* superior kind of rice.
వంకాయ **wankaaya** *n.* brinjal, aubergine, egg plant.
వంకీ **wankii** *n.* 1 hook, latch. 2 armlet of crooked shape.
వంకెలు **wankelu** *n.pl.* name of a coarse variety of rice having a grain with a slightly curved tip.
వంగ **wanga**[1] *adj.* Bengali; ~ **bhaaSa** the Bengali language.
వంగ **wanga**[2] *n.* brinjal plant; ~ **tooTa** brinjal garden.
వంగం, వంగదేశం **wangam**[1], **wangadeešam** *n.* Bengal.
వంగం **wangam**[2] *n. class.* tin.
వంగడం **wangaDam** *n.* 1 *biol.* strain, variety. 2 pedigree, lineage, ancestry.
వంగదీయు **wangadiiyu** *v.t.* to bend, cause to bow.
వంగపండు గువ్వ **wangapaNDu guwwa** *n.* black-headed oriole (bird).
వంగపండు రంగు **wangapaNDu rangu** *n.* purple colour.
వంగలేపనం **wangaleepanam** *n.* tinning.
వంగసం **wangasam** *n. biol.* strain, variety.
వంగీయుడు **wangiiyuDu** *n.* Bengali.
వంగు, ఒంగు **wangu, ongu** *v.i.* 1 to bend, bow, stoop; **panilooki ongaNDi, telustundi enta kaSTamoo** get down to the work, then you will understand how hard it is. 2 to be bent. 3 to be[come] low or humble.
వంగుడుగుడిసె **wanguDu guDise** *n.* small hut (too low for standing upright).
వంగుని **wanguni** *irregular past participle of* **wangu.**
వంచకత్వం **wancakatwam** *n.* deceit, cheating, fraud.
వంచకుడు **wancakuDu** *n.* deceiver, cheat, rogue, impostor.
వంచతగిన **wancatagina** *adj.* flexible, pliable.
వంచన[ం] **wancana[m]** *n.* fraud, deceit, deception, cheating.
వంచనబారిపడు **wancanabaaripaDu** *v.i.* to be tricked or cheated.
వంచించు **wancincu** *v.t.* to cheat, deceive, defraud, trick, dupe.
వంచితుడు **wancituDu** *n.* one who is deceived or cheated.
వంచు, వంపు **wancu, wampu** *v.t.* 1 to bend, make s.o. bend or stoop; **ammaa naannaa waaDi meDalu wanci peLLi ceesEEru** his mother and father made him submit and get married. 2 to humble, demean. 3 **tala**~ (i) to bow o.'s head; (ii) to hang o.'s head in shame. 4 **willu**~ to draw a bow. 5 to pour off, drain off (water, etc.); **ganjini caTTilooki wancutoondi** she drains off cunjee (from the cooked rice) into a pot.
వంట **waNTa** *n.* cooking, cookery; **waNTalu ayyEEyi** cooking is over (i.e., the meal is ready).
వంటకం **waNTakam** (*also pl.* **waNTakaalu**) cookery; **kottimiira ginjalu waNTakaalloo masaalaa dinusugaa upayoogistaaru** they use coriander seeds a condiment in cooking.
వంటకాడు **waNTakaaDu** *n.* professional cook.
వంటగది, వంటిల్లు, వంటసాల **waNTagadi, waNTillu, waNTasaala** *n.* kitchen.
వంటచమురు **waNTacamuru** *n.* oil in which food has been fried.
వంటచెరకు **waNTaceraku** *n.* firewood.
వంటపట్టు **waNTapaTTu** *same as* **oNTapaTTu.**
వంటప్రయత్నం **waNTaprayatnam** *n.* cooking operations.
వంటబ్రాహ్మడు **waNTabraahmaDu** *n.* 1 brahman cook. 2 cook.
వంటసరుకు **waNTasaruku** *n.* fuel for domestic use.
వంటసారాయి **waNTasaaraayi** *n. slang* illicitly distilled arrack.
వంటా పెంటా, వంటాపెట్టూ **waNTaa peNTaa, waNTaa peTTuu** *n.* cooking and serving, catering; *cf.* **tiNDi.**
వంటావార్పూ **waNTaa waarpuu** *n.* preparation of food.
వంటి **waNTi**[1] *p.p. and adjvl. suffix* like; **mii**~ **waaru** people like you.
వంటి **waNTi**[2] *same as* **oNTi**[2].
వంటిల్లు **waNTillu** *same as* **waNTagadi.**

వండలి **waNDali** *n.* alluvium; ~**neelalu** alluvial soils.

వండు, ఒండు **waNDu**[1], **oNDu**[1] *v.t.* to cook.

వండు, వండ్రు **waNDu**[2], **waNDru** *same as* **oNDu**[2], **oNDru.**

వంత **wanta** *n. class.* sorrow, grief.

వంతపాట **wantapaaTa** *n.* chorus, refrain; ~**kaaDu** yes man.

వంతపాడు **wantapaaDu** *v.i.* 1 to sing along with s.o. else, sing in a chorus. 2 to echo what s.o. else has said.

వంతు **wantu** *n.* 1 share, part, portion; **muuDoo**~ one third (*lit.* a third part); **iccina appulu wasuulu ceesukoowaDamloo saayapaDi ciwaraki**~**kuuDEEDu** after helping me to collect my dues in the end he demanded a share for himself; **naa**~**kartawyangaa aydu ruupaayalu iccEEnu** I gave five rupees as my due share. 2 turn; **nii**~**waccindi** your turn has come. 3 competition, rivalry; **aayanaki naatoo**~ he is in competition with me; **naaku Taym dorakka uttaram raayaleedu, naatoo**~ **peTTukoni aayana uttaram raayaDam maaneesEEDu** for want of time I did not write him a letter, and he in his turn stopped writing to me.

వంతుడు **wantuDu** *n. suffix meaning* s.o. who is possessed of or is gifted with; **pratibhaa**~ person of intelligence; **aaroogya**~ healthy person; *cf.* **wati.**

వంతున **wantuna** *adv.* at the rate of.

వంతెన **wantena** *n.* bridge.

వంద **wanda** *n.* 1 a hundred. 2 an indefinite number; ~**manditoo ceppEEDu** he told scores of people.

వందనం **wandanam** *n.* 1 *class.* salutation, obeisance, praise. 2 *pl.* **wandanaalu** thanks.

వందనీయ **wandaniiya** *adj.* worthy of praise.

వందితుడు **wandituDu** *n. class.* one who is praised or saluted.

వందిమాగధుడు **wandi maagadhuDu** *n.* 1 *class.* panegyrist employed in a king's court in olden days. 2 *colloq.* flatterer.

వందించు **wandincu** *v.t. class.* to praise, salute.

వందేమాతరం **wandeemaataram** *n.* patriotic song composed by Bankim Chandra Chatterjee, adopted as national anthem by the Calcutta Congress in 1906.

వంద్య **wandya** *adj.* laudable, praiseworthy.

వంధ్య **wandhya** *n.* barren woman, sterile woman.

వంధ్యాత్వం **wandhyaatwam** *n.* sterility.

వంపు **wampu** I. *n.* 1 bend, curve. 2 *dial.* hill stream. II. *v.t. same as* **wancu.**

వంపుతిరిగి ఉన్న **wampu tirigi unna** *adj.* curved, bent, twisted, curled.

వంపులు తిరుగు **wampulu tirugu** *v.i.* to twist, turn, writhe.

వంశం **wamśam** *n.* 1 family. 2 dynasty. 3 pedigree. 4 parentage, line of descent, lineage.

వంశక్రమానుగత **wamśakramaanugata** *adj.* following the hereditary principle.

వంశజ **wamśaja** *adj.* born of a family; **uttama**~ born of a noble family; **wamśajulu** descendants.

వంశపరంపర **wamśaparampara** *n.* family succession.

వంశపారంపర్య **wamśapaaramparya** *adj.* hereditary, ancestral.

వంశపారంపర్యం **wamśapaaramparyam** *n.* ancestry.

వంశపూర్వికుడు **wamśapuurwikuDu** *n.* ancestor.

వంశస్థుడు **wamśasthuDu** *n.* member of a family or dynasty, descendant.

వంశాంకురం **wamśaankuram** *n.* descendant or offspring of a dynasty or family.

వంశానుగతంగా **wamśaanugatangaa** *adv.* hereditarily; ~**wastunna aacaaram** a custom handed down from generation to generation.

వంశావళి **wamśaawaLi** *n.* genealogy.

వంశి **wamśi** *n.* flute.

వంశీకుడు, వంశీయుడు **wamśiikuDu, wamśiiyuDu** *n.* member of a family.

వంశీధరుడు **wamśiidharuDu** *n.* 1 epithet of Krishna. 2 flute player.

వకాలతు **wakaalatu** *n.* attorneyship.

వకాలతునామా **wakaalatunaamaa** *n.* deed of attorneyship.

వకాల్తీ **wakaaltii** *n.* lawyership.

వకీలు **wakiilu** *n.* vakil, lawyer, advocate.

వకుళం **wakuLam** *n. mimosops elengi*, a flower.

వక్క **wakka** *n.* 1 bit of arecanut; **o.-ki wakkaa mukkaa iccu** to make friends with s.o. 2 (*also* **wrakka**) bit, piece, fragment.

వక్కపలుకు, వక్కముక్క **wakkapaluku, wakkamukka** *n.* bit of arecanut.

వక్కపొడి **wakkapoDi** *n.* arecanut powder.

వక్కాణించు **wakkaaNincu** *v.t.* to assert, say emphatically.

వక్కి **wakki** *adj.* lean, thin, emaciated.

వక్కికట్టె **wakkikaTTe** *n.* lean or starved-looking person.

వక్కు **wakku** I. *n.* (*also* ~**pakSi**) 1 crane (bird). 2 lean and emaciated person (*used colloquially as a mild term of abuse*); *cf.* **akkupakSi.** II. *v.i.* to become lean or thin or emaciated.

వక్త **wakta** *n.* orator, speaker.

వక్తవ్య **waktawya** *adj.* fit to be spoken, worth saying.

వక్తృత్వ **waktṛtwa** *adj.* oratorical; ~**pooTii** elocution competition.

వక్తృత్వం **waktṛtwam** *n.* oratory.

వక్త్రం **waktram** *n. class.* mouth, face.

వక్ర **wakra** *adj.* 1 curved. 2 crooked, bent, warped, twisted, awry. 3 winding, meandering, tortuous. 4 perverse, perverted. 5 evasive, equivocating.

వక్రం **wakram** *n.* curve.

వక్రగతి **wakragati** *n.* 1 twist, contortion. 2 shifting and changing of direction, irregular motion.

వక్రత, వక్రత్వం **wakrata, wakratwam** *n.* 1 crookedness. 2 perversity.

వక్రతమములు **wakratamamulu** *n.pl.* name given to the diphthongs *ay* and *aw* in Sanskrit grammar.

వక్రదృష్టి **wakradrsTi** *n.* **1** squinting. **2** malicious look.

వక్రములు **wakramulu** *n.pl.* name given to the vowels *ee* and *oo* in Sanskrit grammar.

వక్రరేఖ **wakrareekha** *n.* curved line.

వక్రాకృతి **wakraakrti** *n.* curvature.

వక్రించు **wakrincu** *v.i.* **1** to go astray, deviate. **2** *astrol.* (of planets) to follow an irregular course, be malignant. **3** (of time, fortune) to be unfavourable.

వక్రిత **wakrita** *adj.* twisted, distorted.

వక్రీకరణ **wakriikaraNa** *n.* distortion, misinterpretation, misrepresentation.

వక్రీకరించు **wakriikarincu** *v.t.* to misrepresent, misinterpret, distort (facts).

వక్రీభవన **wakriibhawana** *n. sci.* refraction (of light).

వక్రీభవించు **wakriibhawincu** *v.i. sci.* (of light) to be deflected, be refracted.

వక్రోక్తి **wakrookti** *n.* **1** hint, insinuation. **2** pun. **3** sarcasm.

వక్షం **wakSam** *n.* breast, chest, bosom.

వక్షస్థలం **wakSasthalam** *n.* chest.

వక్షోజం, వక్షోరుహం **wakSoojam, wakSooruham** *n. class.* woman's breast.

వగ **waga** *n.* **1** grief, sorrow. **2** dissimulation, pretence.

వగచు, వగయు **wagacu, wagayu** *v.i.* to be sad, grieve, lament.

వగరు **wagaru**[1] *n.* hard breathing, panting.

వగరు **wagaru**[2] *same as* **ogaru.**

వగర్చు **wagarcu** *v.i.* to breathe hard, pant, gasp.

వగైరా **wagayraa** I. *n.* (*also* ~**lu**) and other things, and the like, etcetera. II. *adj.* and other [such]; **jawaraalu, muddaraalu ~ telugu maaTalu taatala kaalam naaTiwi, waaDa waddu** *jawaraalu, muddaraalu* and other such Telugu words belong to our grandfathers' time, they should not be used.

వచనం **wacanam** *n.* **1** saying, remark, utterance. **2** word, sentence. **3** text, quotation. **4** prose. **5** *gram.* number.

వచించు **wacincu** *v.t.* to say, speak, tell, utter; **wacinca raani** unspeakable, unutterable.

వచ్చిపడు **waccipaDu** *see* **paDu** *sense I. 12.*

వచ్చీరాని **wacciiraani** *vbl. adj.* scarcely coming, scarcely appearing; ~**nawwu** a hesitating smile.

వచ్చు, ఒచ్చు **waccu, occu** *v.i.* **1** to come; **waccee waaram** the coming week, next week; **mii[ku] iSTam waccinaTTugaa raayaNDi** write in the way that you like (*lit.* write in the way that liking comes to you); **maa iSTam waccina baTTalu** clothes that we like; **kaLLaki koTToccee** (*or* **kaLLaki koTTawaccee**) **ciire** a sari that strikes the eye *or* an attractive sari; **balee nawwoccee** (*or* **nawwuwaccee**) **kathalu** very laughable stories; **ewariki waccina laabham idi**? to whom is this of any use? **endukoccina batuku**! what a purposeless life this is! **weLLiwastaanu** I will take leave of you (said on departing; here **wastaanu** substitutes for **pootaanu**). **2** to appear, happen, occur, take place; **iwwEELa eNDa waccindi** today it is sunny (*lit.* today sunshine has appeared); **naaku nawwoccindi** I laughed; **saynyamloo tirugubaaTu waccindi** a revolt took place in the army; **'La' waccee maaTala sankhya takkuwa** the number of of words in which (the syllable) 'La' occurs is small. **3** to be got, be obtained, be procured; **naaku manci maarkulu waccEEyi** I got good marks; **manci dharoccee sarukulu** commodities that fetch good prices; **reNDaNaalaku buTTeDu waccee beNDakaayalu wiise reNDaNaalayyEEyi** okra which you could (formerly) get for two annas a basket has become two annas a viss. **4** to last; **ceppulu caalaa roojulu waccEEyi** the shoes lasted for a long time. **5** (of a skill or facility) to be learnt or acquired; **ataniki iita** (*or* **ataniki iidaDam**) ~**nu** he knows how to swim *or* he can swim; **miiku telugu** ~**naa**? do you know Telugu? (*in these two examples* ~**nu** *is the 3rd per. sing. of an obsolete indef. tense*); **cuustuNDagaanee S.-ki aa paaTantaa waccindi** in a very short time S. learnt the whole song. **6** (of an activity) to be carried on continuously or habitually; **padakoNDu gaNTalaku kaaphii taagaDam alawaaTugaa wastunnadi** it is habitual to drink coffee at 11 o'clock. **7** to appear in print, be published. **8** *as an auxiliary verb* ~ *occurs* (i) *in the obsolete indef. tense with an infinitive to express* 'may'; **miiru raa**~ you may come (probability or permission); **miiru raakapoo**~ you may not come (probability only); (ii) *with an infinitive to express* 'to be about to'; **suurya astamaanam kaawastunnadi** sunset is about to happen; (iii) *in constr. with* **aalsi** *to express* 'had to / will have to'; **neenu ceppaalsi waccindi** I had to say; **neenu ceppaalsi wastundi** I will have to say; (iv) *with a present participle to express continuance of a state or action*; **caalaa wiswaasangaa uNTuuwastunnaaDu** he continues to be very faithful; **pleegrawND oka muula uNTuu waccina weepa ceTTu** the neem tree that always used to stand in a corner of the playground.

వచ్చుబడి, రాబడి **waccubaDi, raabaDi** *n.* income.

వజను **wajanu** *n. dial.* weight.

వజవజ, వడవడ **wajawaja, waDawaDa** *onom. adv. sug.* trembling.

వజ్రం **wajram** *n.* diamond.

వజ్రగుణకారం **wajraguNakaaram** *n. maths.* cross multiplication.

వజ్రవైడూర్యాలు **wajrawayDuuryaalu** *n. pl.* precious stones (in general).

వజ్రాయుధం **wajraayudham** *n.* Indra's weapon, thunderbolt.

వటం, వటవృక్షం **waTam, waTawrkSam** *n.* banyan tree.

వటుకం **waTukam** *n. class.* pill.

వటుడు **waTuDu** *n.* unmarried youth whose thread ceremony (**upanayanam**) has been performed.

వట్ట, వట్టకాయ **waTTa[kaaya]** *n. slang.* testicle.

వట్టం **waTTam** *n.* discount, amount deducted from the regular price of an article.

వట్టలు కొట్టు **waTTalu koTTu** *v.t.* **1** to castrate. **2** *slang* to deceive, cheat.

వట్టి **waTTi** *same as* **utta**.

వట్టినే **waTTinee** *same as* **uttanee.**

వట్టిపోవు **waTTipoowu** *v.i.* to go dry, dry up.

వట్టివేరు **waTTiweeru** *n.* cuscus, a fragrant grass root from which screens are made.

వట్రతలం **waTratalam** *n. maths.* curved surface.

వట్రసుడి **waTrasuDi** *n. gram.* secondary symbol of the semi vowel ṛ written as ృ.

వడ **waDa**[1] *n.* heat (of sun or wind).

వడ **waDa**[2] *n.* kind of spiced cake made with blackgram.

వడంబం **waDambam** *n.* builder's plumb line.

వడకపెళ్లికొడుకు **waDakapeLLikoDuku** *n.* boy for whom the ceremony of **waDugu** is being performed.

వడకు, వణకు **waDaku, waNaku** I. *n.* trembling, shaking, quivering, shuddering. II. *v.i.* 1 to tremble, shake, quiver, shudder, shiver; **caliki~** to shiver with cold. 2 (of voice) to waver.

వడగండ్లు, వడగళ్లు **waDagaNDLu, waDagaLLu** *n. pl.* hailstones.

వడగళ్లవాన **waDagaLLawaana** *n.* hailstorm.

వడగాడ్పు, వడగాల్పు **waDagaaDpu, waDagaalpu** *n.* strong hot wind.

వడదెబ్బ **waDadebba** *n.* heat stroke.

వడపప్పు **waDapappu** *n.* greengram soaked overnight and offered next day to a deity as **nayweedyam.**

వడపిందెలు **waDapindelu** *n.pl.* unripe mangoes which fall from a tree due to heat and are collected and pickled in salt water.

వడపోత **waDapoota** *n.* 1 straining, filtering. 2 filtration.

వడబోయు **waDabooyu** *v.t.* to strain [off], filter; *see* **kaaci~.**

వడలు **waDalu** *v.i.* to fade [away], wither, dry up; **eNDaku~** to wither due to the sun's heat.

వడలుతెగులు **waDalutegulu** *n.* wilt, a plant disease.

వడవడ **waDawaDa** *same as* **waja waja.**

వడసారం **waDasaaram** *adv.* totally, completely, in entirety.

వడి **waDi** *n.* 1 speed, velocity, quickness, briskness. 2 sharpness, severity (of words).

వడిగా **waDigaa** *adv.* quickly, speedily, fast.

వడిబియ్యం **waDibiyyam** *same as* **oDibiyyam.**

వడియం **waDiyam** *same as* **oDiyam.**

వడిసిపట్టు **waDisipaTTu** *same as* **oDisipaTTu.**

వడిసె[ల] **waDise[la]** *n.* 1 sling. 2 catapult.

వడుకు **waDuku** *v.t.* to spin (thread).

వడుక్కొను **waDukkonu** *v.t. slang* to grasp, grab, take forcibly.

వడుగు **waDugu** *n.* ceremony of investiture with the sacred thread.

వడేయు **waDeeyu** *v.t.* to strain, filter.

వడ్డన **waDDana** *n.* serving food.

వడ్డాణం **waDDaaNam** *n.* gold waistbelt worn by a woman.

వడ్డించు **waDDincu** *v.t.* 1 to serve food. 2 *colloq.* to scold, beat; **waaNNi naaluguu waDDinci pampincEEnu** I gave him a scolding (*or* I gave him a beating) and sent him away.

వడ్డీ **waDDii** *n.* interest on capital; **~wyaapaaram** money-lending business; **~wyaapaari** moneylender.

వడ్డెర **waDDera** *same as* **oDDe.**

వడ్రంగం **waDrangam** *n.* carpenter's trade.

వడ్రంగి **waDrangi** *n.* carpenter.

వడ్రంగిపని **waDrangipani** *n.* carpentry.

వడ్రంగిపిట్ట **waDrangipiTTa** *n.* woodpecker.

వడ్లచిలుక **waDLaciluka** *n.* insect pest which attacks grain in storage.

వడ్లవాళ్లు **waDLawaaLLu** *n.pl.* carpenters.

వడ్లు **waDLu** *see* **wari.**

వణకు **waNaku** *same as* **waDaku.**

వణిక్ప్రముఖులు **waNikpramukhulu** *n.pl.* leading merchants.

వణిజ **waNija** *adj.* commercial.

వణ్ణం **waNNam** *n. slang* food (= **annam**).

వతంసం **watamsam** *same as* **awatamsam.**

వతంసుడు **watamsuDu** *same as* **awatamsuDu.**

వతనుగా **watanugaa** *adv.* on regular basis, at regular intervals (of services, delivery of supplies, etc., performed and paid for regularly); **maaku~ paalu pooseewaaDu iwwEELa raaleedu** our regular milkman has not come today; *cf.* **raatam.**

వతి **wati** *n. suffix denoting* a woman possessed of a certain quality, e.g., **widyaa~** woman of learning; *cf.* **wantuDu.**

వతు, వతుగా **watu[gaa]**[1] *adv.* like; **pilli eluka~** like cat and mouse; *cf.* **nyaayam.**

వతుగా, వత్తుగా **watugaa**[2], **wattugaa** *adv.* in accordance with; **aayana ceppina~undi** it is in accordance with what he has said *or* it is as he says.

వత్తరి **wattari** *same as* **ottari.**

వత్తాసు, ఒత్తాసు **wattaasu, ottaasu** *n.* support, backing; **aayana naaku~ waccEEDu** he came to my aid; **ii wiSayamloo aayana waaDiki~ palikEEDu** he backed him up in this affair.

వత్తి **watti** *n.* wick; **agaru~** incense stick; **kaLLaku wattulu peTTi wetuku** to search diligently and with great care; **kaLLaku wattulu peTTukonu** to keep awake all night.

వత్తు **wattu** *same as* **ottu.**

వత్తుగా **wattugaa** *same as* **watugaa.**

వత్తులు **wattulu** *n.pl.* 1 children's gold or silver bracelets or bangles, traditionally given to them by their grandparents. 2 *pl. of* **watti.**

వత్సరం **watsaram** *n. class.* year.

వదంతి **wadanti** *n.* rumour.

వదనం **wadanam** *n.* 1 face, countenance. 2 mouth.

వదరు, వదురు **wadaru, waduru** *v.i.* 1 to talk indiscriminately, prattle. 2 to brag, boast.

వదలు, వదులు **wadalu, wadulu** I. *adj.* loose; **~Saraayi** loose trousers. II. *v.i.* 1 to be loosened, be slackened, be untied, be freed, be separated. 2 (of grief, illness) to pass off, cease, disappear. III. *v.t.* 1 to leave, relinquish, abandon; **daari~** to leave the way free, get out of the way.

2 to give up, renounce, quit, abstain from. 3 to let go, let loose, release; **buDagalu**~ to blow bubbles; **poga**~ to puff smoke. 4 **praaNaalu**~ to leave o.'s life, die.

వదాన్యుడు **wadaanyuDu** *n. class.* 1 generous or liberal minded person. 2 person who talks affably.

వది **wadi** *n. class.* elephant pit.

వదినె **wadine** *n.* 1 elder brother's wife. 2 spouse's elder sister. 3 mother's brother's daughter or father's sister's daughter if older than o.s.

వదిలించు, వదల్చు, వదుల్చు **wadilincu, wadalcu, wadulcu** *v.t.* 1 to loosen, slacken, release, untie, free, separate. 2 to get rid of, shed. 3 *slang* **naaku Dabbu wadilincEEDu** he made me lose money.

వదిలించుకొను **wadilincukonu** *v.t.* to get rid of, shed, shake off, break free from, disengage o.s. from.

వదిలిపెట్టు **wadilipeTTu** *v.t.* 1 to give up; **taaguDu wadilipeTTEEDu** he gave up drinking. 2 to discard. 3 *colloq.* to divorce. 4 to close (school, office).

వదిలివేయు **wadiliweeyu** *v.t.* 1 to leave behind. 2 to depart from. 3 to untie. 4 to leave out of account, overlook, ignore. 5 to discard, desert.

వదురు **waduru** *same as* **wadaru.**

వదులు **wadulu** *same as* **wadalu.**

వద్ద **wadda** *p.p. obs.* near, with, by, at.

వద్దు **waddu** I. *auxiliary vb. with infinitive equivalent to neg. imperative* **[miiru] ceppa**~! do not say! II. *minor sentence* no! *or* you must not (refusing permission).

వధ **wadha** *n.* killing, slaughter.

వధించు **wadhincu** *v.t.* to kill, slay.

వధువు **wadhuwu** *n.* 1 bride. 2 wife; **wadhuuwarulu** bride and bridegroom.

వధూజనం **wadhuujanam** *n.pl.* womenfolk, ladies.

వధూటి **wadhuuTi** *n.* daughter-in-law.

వధూప్రవేశం **wadhuupraweeśam** *n.* ceremony performed when a bride enters the bridegroom's house for the first time.

వధ్య **wadhya** *adj.* 1 deserving of death. 2 condemned to death.

వన[ం] **wana[m]** *n.* 1 wood, forest, grove. 2 garden.

వనచరం **wanacaram** *n. class.* wild animal.

వనచరుడు **wanacaruDu** *n.* forest dweller.

వనజ **wanaja** *n.* lotus.

వనజాక్షి **wanajaakSi** *n. class.* woman.

వనట **wanaTa** *n. class.* grief.

వనభోజనం **wanabhoojanam** *n.* 1 picnic. 2 meal eaten in a garden or forest as part of a religious ceremony in the month of Kartika.

వనమహోత్సవం **wanamahootswam** *n.* national festival of tree planting celebrated annually during the rainy season.

వనమాల **wanamaala** *n. class.* garland of wild flowers, esp. one worn by Krishna.

వనమాలి **wanamaali** *n.* epithet of Krishna.

వనరు **wanaru**[1] *v.i.* to grieve, lament.

వనరు **wanaru**[2] *n.* 1 provision, convenience; **miiru weLLee doowaloo niiDa**~**dorakadu** on the road that you will travel there is no convenience of shade. 2 *pl.* ~**lu** resources.

వనరుహం **wanaruham** *n. class.* lotus.

వనలక్ష్మి **wanalakSmi** *n.* natural beauty of the forest.

వనవాసం **wanawaasam** *n.* dwelling in a forest.

వనవిహారం **wanawihaaram** *n.* picnic.

వనాటం **wanaaTam** *n. class.* wild animal.

వని **wani** *n. class.* park, grove, garden.

వనిత **wanita** *n.* woman.

వన్నారు **wannaaru** *n. dial.* vacant space between houses.

వన్నె **wanne** *n.* 1 colour, tint, hue. 2 nuance, variation in shade of colour or tone of sound. 3 beauty, brightness. 4 fame. 5 carat; **pajjhenimidi**~**la bangaaram** eighteen carat gold. 6 manner, way; **ii**~**na ceestee pani awutundaa**? if you do it in this way, will the work get finished?

వన్నెకెక్కు **wannekekku** *v.i.* to achieve fame, become famous.

వన్నెలవిసనకర్ర **wannelawisanakarra** *n.colloq.* fashionable and stylish woman.

వన్నెలాడి **wannelaaDi** *n.* woman who gives herself airs.

వన్నెలు చిన్నెలు **wannelucinnelu** *n.pl.* marks of beauty, adornments, embellishments; ~**ceerci katha ceppEEDu** he told the story with some embellishments of his own.

వన్య **wanya** *adj.* of the forest, wild.

వన్యమృగం **wanyamrgam** *n.* wild animal.

వప **wapa** *n. class.* caul of fat.

వపాహోమం **wapaahoomam** *n. class.* kind of sacrifice; ~**ceeyu** *colloq.* to punish severely.

వప్పగించు, వప్పచెప్పు **wappagincu, wappaceppu** *same as* **appagincu, appaceppu.**

వమనం **wamanam** *n. class.* vomiting.

వమనేచ్ఛ **wamaneeccha** *n.* nausea.

వమ్ము **wammu** I *n.* ruin, destruction, overthrow (of a belief, intention or similar abstraction). II. *adj.* vain, fruitless.

వమ్ము చేయు **wammu ceeyu** *v.t.* to destroy, nullify (a belief, intention, etc.).

వయఃపరిమితి **wayaḥparimiti** *same as* **wayooparimiti.**

వయనం **wayanam** *n.* weaving.

వయసు, వయస్సు **waya[s]su** *n.* 1 age; **atani**~**enta**? how old is he? 2 any time or period of life; ~**maLLina** elderly; **pedda**~**waaDu** old person; **madhya**~ middle age. 3 prime of life; ~**loo unna kurrawaaDu** young man; ~**loo unna pilla** young woman; ~**kaalamloo** in the prime of life.

వయస్య **wayasya** *n. class.* woman's female companion, confidante.

వయస్యుడు **wayasyuDu** *n. class.* man's male companion, confidant.

వయోజన **wayoojana** *adj.* adult; ~**widya** adult education.

వయోజనుడు **wayoojanuDu** *n.* adult.

వయోపరిమితి, వయఃపరిమితి **wayooparimiti, wayahparimiti** *n.* age limit.

వయోవృద్ధులు **wayoowrddhulu** *n.pl.* elderly persons, elders.

వయోసమూహం **wayoosamuuham** *n.* age group.

వయ్యారం[గా] **wayyaaram[gaa]** *same as* **oyyaaram[gaa].**

వర[ం] **waram**[1], **wara** *n.* dial. ridge or bund between two plots of irrigated land.

వరం **waram**[2] *n.* boon, divine gift.

వరండం **waraNDam** *n. class.* pimple on the face.

వరకం **warakam** *n.* rigorous imprisonment.

వరకట్టు **warakaTTu** *v.t.* 1 to reclaim waste land and claim occupancy right. 2 *colloq.* **~konu** to corner for o.'s own use; **mottam kurciilu ~koni kuurcunnaaDu, inkewarinii kuurcooniwwaDaTa** he has cornered all the chairs for himself and says he will not let anyone else sit on them.

వరకట్నం **warakaTNam** *n.* dowry.

వరకు **waraku** *p.p. and advbl. particle* until, till, as far as, upto.

వరగలు, వరిగలు **waragalu, warigalu** *n.pl.* variga, a small-grained millet.

వరణం **waraNam** *n.* 1 surrounding wall, boundary wall. 2 selection, choosing. 3 choosing a bride. 4 **kanyaa-waraNaalu** part of the wedding ceremony in which the names of the bride's ancestors for seven generations are recited by a priest.

వరణాత్మక **waraNaatmaka** *adj.* selective.

వరద **warada**[1] *n.* flood, inundation.

వరద **warada**[2] *n. class.* unmarried girl, virgin.

వరదక్షిణ **waradakSiNa** *n.* present made to the bridegroom by the bride's father on giving her away.

వరదగుడి, వరదగూడు **waradaguDi, waradaguuDu** *n.* halo round the sun or moon in moist or misty weather.

వరదపాసెం **waradapaasem** *n.* distribution of **paasem** or **paayasam** (rice cooked with milk and sugar) in a ceremony to bring rain.

వరదుడు **waraduDu** *n.* one who gives a boon, benefactor.

వరపు **warapu** *n.* drought, lack of rain.

వరపోయు **warapooyu** *v.i.* (of a boil, ulcer) to come to a head; **kurupu warapoosuku waccindi** the boil came to a head.

వరప్రసాదం **waraprasaadam** *n.* boon, blessing; **idi deewuDi~** this is God's blessing.

వరలక్ష్మి **waralakSmi** *n.* Lakshmi, giver of boons.

వరలక్ష్మీవ్రతం **waralakSmii wratam** *n.* vow performed by a woman annually in the first fortnight of Sravana on a Friday.

వరవ **warawa** *n.* channel bringing water to an irrigation reservoir.

వరవడి **warawaDi** *n.* 1 top line in a copy book set as an example to be copied. 2 example to be followed. 3 convention, custom; **maa iNTi~** the custom followed in our house.

వరవేయు **waraweeyu** *v.i.* to collect in a heap, accumulate.

వరస **warasa** *n.* 1 line, row, queue, series; **~loo nilabaDu** to stand in line, stand in a queue; **eeka~ni** in succession, continuously; **kaawyaalannii~beTTi caduwutuu waccEEDu** he went on reading all the poetical works one after another. 2 order, sequence; **~nambaru** serial number; **~kramamloo** in serial order; **telugu ingliiSu~loo padajaalam weluwaristunnaaru** they are publishing a Telugu-into-English glossary. 3 manner, way; **idii~!** this is the way! *or* that is how it is! (gen. said with disapproval); **muuDu waaraala nuncii roojuu idee~** for three weeks it has been just like this. 4 relationship, kinship; **DaakTaru naaku anna~** the doctor is related to me as a brother (*or* cousin); **o.-i too~kalupu** to call s.o. by a kinship term (e.g. **anna** *or* **tammuDu** *or* **maama** *or* **baawa**, *a sign of familiarity or affection*); **nannu wadine~ peTTi pilicindi** she addressed me as **'wadine'**; **warasayna waaLLu** relatives between whom intermarriage in permissible.

వరసగా **warasagaa** *adv.* in a line, one after another, in succession.

వరహా, వరా **warahaa, waraa** *n.* obsolete gold coin.

వరహాలమూట **warahaalamuuTa** *n.* treasure.

వరహీనం **warahiinam** *n.* situation where a bridegroom is inferior to his bride in looks, stature, etc.

వరాంగం **waraangam** *n. class.* 1 head. 2 name of an ayurvedic preparation.

వరాహం **waraaham** *n. class.* boar.

వరాహమిహిరుడు **waraahamihiruDu** *n.* name of a celebrated astrologer and poet.

వరి **wari** *n. gen. pl.* **waDLu** paddy, rice in the husk; *the singular form occurs in compounds,* e.g., **~gaDDi** paddy straw; **~ceenu** paddy field.

వరించు **warincu** *v.t.* 1 to choose, select. 2 to choose as o.'s spouse, bestow o.s.

వరిగలు **warigalu** *same as* **waragalu.**

వరిణె **wariNe** *n. dial.* sieve used for winnowing at harvest time.

వరిబీజం **waribiijam** *n. med.* hernia.

వరుగు **warugu**[1,2] *same as* **orugu**[1,2].

వరుడు **waruDu** *n.* bridegroom.

వరుణుడు **waruNuDu** *n.* Varuna, god of the ocean and of the sky and the rain.

వరుమానం **warumaanam** *n.* 1 income. 2 *dial.* gift of money.

వరువాత **waruwaata** *adj. class.* in the early morning.

వరేణ్యుడు **wareeNyuDu** I. *n.* great person, eminent person. II. *n. suffix meaning* great, e.g., **guru~** great guru.

వర్గం **wargam** *n.* 1 group, class, category, party in a dispute; **adhikaara~** officialdom; **mantri~** cabinet. 2 *maths.* square.

వర్గమూలం **wargamuulam** *n. maths.* square root.

వర్గయుక్కులు **wargayukkulu** *n.pl.* name given to the aspirated consonants in Sanskrit grammar.

వర్గీకరణం **wargiikaraNam** *n.* classification, categorisation.

వర్గీకరించు **wargiikarincu** *v.t.* to classify.

వర్గీకృత **wargiikṛta** *adj.* classificatory.

వర్చస్వి **warcaswi** *n.* bright, animated and goodlooking person.

వర్చస్సు **warcassu** *n.* brightness, lustre, radiance.

వర్జనం **warjanam** *n.* exclusion.

వర్జించు **warjincu** *v.t.* **1** to give up, abandon. **2** to avoid, shun.

వర్జ్యం **warjyam** *n. astrol.* inauspicious time of the day.

వర్జ్యనీయ **warjyaniiya** *adj.* (s.g) which should be shunned or avoided.

వర్ణం **warNam** *n.* **1** colour, hue. **2** paint, dye. **3** caste, community. **4** letter of the alphabet. **5** syllable. **6** *ling.* phoneme. **7** kind of composition in Carnatic music.

వర్ణకం, వర్ణదం, వర్ణద్రవ్యం **warNakam, warNadam, warNadrawyam** *n.* pigment.

వర్ణకల్పన **warNakalpana** *n.* colour scheme.

వర్ణక్రమం **warNakramam** *n.* **1** alphabetical order. **2** spelling.

వర్ణగ్రాహకం **warNagraahakam** *n. sci.* chromosome.

వర్ణన **warNana** *n.* **1** description. **2** panegyric.

వర్ణనాతీత **warNanaatiita** *adj.* beyond description.

వర్ణనాత్మక **warNanaatmaka** *adj.* descriptive.

వర్ణనిర్మాణశాస్త్రం **warNanirmaaNaśaastram** *n. ling.* (science of) phonology.

వర్ణపటం **warNapaTam** *n. sci.* spectrum.

వర్ణపటదర్శిని **warNapaTadarśini** *n.* spectroscope.

వర్ణపటమాపకం **warNapaTamaapakam** *n.* spectrometer.

వర్ణమాల **warNamaala** *n.* **1** alphabet. **2** *sci.* colours of the spectrum.

వర్ణరహితత **warNarahitata** *n. sci.* albinism.

వర్ణవ్యత్యయం **warNawyatyayam** *n. ling.* metathesis.

వర్ణసమామ్నాయం **warNasamaamnaayam** *n.* alphabetical chart.

వర్ణస్తుడు **warNastuDu** *n.* member of a caste or community; **waaLLantaa okee warNastulu** they all belong to the same community.

వర్ణాంతర **warNaantara** *adj.* intercaste, between castes or communities (= **antarwarNa**).

వర్ణాంధత **warNaandhata** *n.* colour blindness.

వర్ణాదేశం **warNaadeeśam** *n.* transformation of one consonant into another according to a sandhi rule, e.g., c > s before t (*wac-tuu > wastuu).

వర్ణాశ్రమధర్మాలు **warNaaśramadharmaalu** *n.pl.* characteristic features of an individual's caste **(warNam)** and the period of life **(aaśramam)** through which he is passing.

వర్ణించు **warNincu** *v.t.* to describe, depict, portray.

వర్తకం **wartakam** *n.* trade, business.

వర్తక మార్గాలు **wartaka maargaalu** *n.pl.* trade routes.

వర్తకసంస్థ **wartakasamstha** *n.* business organisation, trading firm.

వర్తకుడు **wartakuDu** *n.* merchant, dealer, trader.

వర్తన[ం] **wartana[m]** *n.* conduct, behaviour.

వర్తనీయత **wartaniiyata** *n.* applicability.

వర్తమాన **wartamaana** *adj.* present, current, existing.

వర్తమానం **wartamaanam** *n.* **1** news, information. **2** the present time. **3** *gram.* present tense.

వర్తమానం చేయు **wartamaanam ceeyu** *v.i.* to send word, send information.

వర్తమానించు **wartamaanincu** *v.i.* to send word requesting s.o. to attend and be present.

వర్తి **warti**[1] *n. class.* wick.

వర్తి **warti**[2] *second part of a n. compound meaning* person who behaves or acts in a certain way, e.g., **duSTa~** badly behaved person.

వర్తించు **wartincu** *v.i.* **1** to be in force, apply, be applicable. **2** to act, behave.

వర్తింపచేయు **wartimpaceeyu** *v.t.* to apply, cause to apply.

వర్తుల **wartula** *adj.* round, circular.

వర్దీ **wardii** *n.* care, protection, guardianship.

వర్ధంతి **wardhanti** *n.* death anniversary.

వర్ధక **wardhaka** *adjvl. suffix meaning* causing an increase, e.g., **bala~** giving more strength; **aayuS~** conferring longevity.

వర్ధనం **wardhanam** *n.* increase, growth, improvement.

వర్ధమాన **wardhamaana** *adj.* **1** increasing, growing. **2** developing; **~deeśaalu** developing countries.

వర్ధిత **wardhita** *adj.* increased, improved.

వర్ధిల్లచేయు, వర్ధింపచేయు **wardhilla ceeyu, wardhimpa ceeyu** *v.t.* to cause to prosper, cause to flourish.

వర్ధిల్లు **wardhillu** *v.i.* to grow, increase, improve, thrive, prosper, flourish.

వర్ధిష్ణుడు **wardhiSNuDu** *n. class.* person who improves or thrives; **wardhiSNulayna racayitalu** budding writers.

వర్యుడు **waryuDu** I. *n.* chief, leader. II. *second part of a n. compound meaning* leading, chief, principal; **aacaarya-waryulu** leading professors.

వర్ర **warra** *n.* pungent taste, spicy taste; **~guNDa** chilly powder.

వర్రె **warre**[1] *n. dial.* stream, watercourse.

వర్రె **warre**[2] *n. dial.* unmanageable and stubborn bullock.

వర్రె **warre**[3] *n.* rick of straw.

వర్షం **warSam** *n.* **1** rain. **2** shower. **3** *class.* year. **4** *class.* part of the world, country; **bharata~** India.

వర్షపాతం **warSapaatam** *n.* rainfall.

వర్షమాపకం **warSamaapakam** *n.* rain gauge.

వర్షాధారం **warSaadhaaram** *n.* dependence on rainfall.

వర్షాభావం **warSaabhaawam** *n.* failure of rains.

వర్షించు **warSincu** *v.i. and t.* **1** to rain. **2** to shower.

వల **wala** *n.* net; **~pannu** to hatch a plot; **~weesi cuuDu** *dial.* to ponder or consider carefully; **~loo paDu** *colloq.* to be entrapped or entangled; **~loo weeyu** *colloq.* to entrap, entangle.

వలం **walam** I. *n.* stoutness, fatness. II *adj.* stout, fat.

వలకపోయు **walakapooyu** *same as* **ulakapooyu.**

వలకాక **walakaaka** *n. colloq.* lovesickness.

వలచు **walacu** *v.t.* to love, fall in love with.

వలజ **walaja** *n. class.* **1** the earth. **2** beautiful woman.

వలతి **walati** *n.* clever or skilful woman.

వలతిరుగు **walatirugu** *v.i.* **1** to walk round and round (a place). **2** *colloq.* to frequent.

వలన **walana** *literary form of* **walla.**

వలను **walanu** *n.* **1** method, manner. **2** convenience, practicability; **miiku ~ aytee oka saari maa iNTiki raNDi** please come to our house if it is convenient to you.

వలపక్షం **walapakSam** *n. colloq.* partiality.

వలపట **walapaTa** *adv.* on the right hand.

వలపల **walapala** *n.* right hand side.

వలపించు **walapincu** *v.t.* to captivate, fascinate, enamour.

వలపు **walapu** *n.* **1** love, affection, fondness. **2** desire, wish. **3** fragrance.

వలయం **walayam** *n.* **1** circle, ring, circumference. **2** rim of a wheel. **3** circuit. **4** cycle. **5** circular spreading ripple. **6** *class.* bracelet, armlet.

వలయాకార **walayaakaara** *adj.* round, circular.

వలయు **walayu** *v.i. class.* to be wanted, be needed; *parts of this verb, e.g.,* **[w]aali**, *which occur mod. are cited separately.*

వలవల, వలవలా **walawala[a]** *onom. adv. sug.* tears falling from the eyes; **aame ~ eeDcindi** she wept copiously.

వలస **walasa** *n.* **1** migration. **2** colony.

వలసపోవు **walasapoowu** *v.i.* to emigrate, migrate.

వలసరాజ్యం **walasaraajyam** *n.* colony.

వలసిందిగా **walasindigaa** *advbl. phrase, formal and literary* in order to; **briTiiSwaaLLu waaNijya sawkaryaalanu kalpinca ~ waccEEru** the Britishers came in order to create facilities for commerce.

వలసిన **walasina** *vbl. adj. of* **walayu** wanted, needed, required; **anta jaagrattagaa kolawa ~ awasaram** the need to measure so carefully; **taanu kuuDaa eeDawa ~ paristhiti wastundani ataDu eppuDuu uuhincukoo leedu** he never guessed that the situation would arise in which he too would have to weep; *cf.* **kaa ~**.

వలసినది, వలె, వలెను **walasinadi, wale, walenu** *alt. forms of* **[w]aali** *used in the written language.*

వలి **wali** *n.* **1** cold, chill (= **cali**). **2** fold of skin on a woman's stomach, considered as a mark of beauty.

వలిగం **waligam** *n.* iron ring or hoop round the lip of a leather baling bucket.

వలితిరుగు **walitirugu** *v.i.* to walk round; **uurantaa ~ tunnaaDu** he is going all round the village.

వలిపిరి **walipiri** *n.* cold, shivering.

వలిపిరిగొట్టు **walipirigoTTu** *n.* shiverer (term used to express contempt).

వలువ **waluwa** *n.* garment, cloth.

వలె **wale**[1] I. *p.p.* like. II. *adv.* as, just as.

వలె, వలెను **wale**[2], **walenu** *alt. forms of* **[w]aali.**

వల్కలం **walkalam** *n.* **1** *biol.* cortex. **2** hermit's garb made of tree bark.

వల్మీకం **walmiikam** *n. class.* anthill.

వల్ల **walla** *p.p.* **1** by [means of], due to, owing to, from; **mii daya ~** by your grace; **anubhawam ~** from (*or* by) experience. **2** by the ability of; **aa pani naa ~ jarigindi** I was able to do that work (*lit.* that work happened or was done through my ability); **adi naa ~ awutundaa?** shall I be able to do that? **3 adi ~ kaadu** that is impossible; **waaDu uNTeegaani ~ kaadu** I cannot do without him (emphatic); **miiru tiNTeegaani ~ kaadu** you must eat (emphatic) *or* I insist on your eating.

వల్లం **wallam** *n.* cloth purse.

వల్లకాటి **wallakaaTi** *genitive of* **wallakaaDu** *and adj., used to express* disgust, scorn or mere indefiniteness; **ii ~ daggu taggadu** this wretched cough will not go away; **eewoo ~ pustakaalu caduwutunnaaDu** he is reading some books or other.

వల్లకాడు **wallakaaDu** *n.* cemetery, burial ground.

వల్లడి **wallaDi** *n. class.* **1** trouble, violence. **2** plunder.

వల్లదు **walladu** *dial. form of* **waddu.**

వల్లభ **wallabha** *n. class.* **1** wife. **2** mistress.

వల్లభుడు **wallabhuDu** *n. class.* **1** husband. **2** lover. **3** chief, lord, master.

వల్లమాలిన **wallamaalina** *adj.* **1** immense, tremendous, unimaginable. **2** dreadful, unbearable. **3** impracticable.

వల్లరి **wallari** *n. class.* **1** creeper. **2** bunch of flowers.

వల్లి **walli** *n. class.* creeper, twining plant.

వల్లించు **wallincu** *same as* **walle weeyu.**

వల్లిక **wallika** *n. class.* creeper, twining plant.

వల్లె **walle**[1] *n.* repetition.

వల్లె **walle**[2] *interj.* yes.

వల్లెయను **walleyanu** *v.i. class.* to say yes, agree, assent.

వల్లెవాటు **wallewaaTu** *n. dial.* half-sari (= **ooNii**).

వల్లెవేయు, వల్లించు **walleweeyu, wallincu** *v.t.* **1** to learn by heart. **2** to repeat from memory. **3** to recite.

వళాసం **waLaasam** *n.* sack.

వశం **waśam** *n.* **1** possession, custody. **2** charge, control, power.

వశంచేయు **waśam ceeyu** *v.t.* to put (s.o.) in possession of or in control of.

వశం చేసుకొను, వశపరచుకొను **waśam ceesukonu, waśaparacukonu** *v.t.* to take charge of, get possession of, confiscate.

వశాత్తు, వశాన **waśaattu, waśaana** *advbl. suffix* **1** by, through, in consequence of; **duradṛSTa ~** unfortunately; **pramaada ~** by accident. **2** in the course of; **prasaṅga ~** in the course of conversation.

వశీకరణ **waśiikaraNa** *n.* overpowering by means of spells or charms.

వశీకరించు **waśiikarincu** *v.t.* **1** to overcome by spells or charms. **2** to subjugate, subdue.

వశీకృతుడు **waśiikṛtuDu** *n.* one who is inspired or possessed or overcome.

వశ్య[ం] waśya[m] *adj.* 1 overpowered by spells or charms. 2 subdued, subject, dependent.

వషట్కారం waSaTkaaram *n. class.* burnt sacrifice.

వస wasa *n.* sweet flag, *acorus calamus*, a medicinal root; ~ **poosinaTLu maaTLaaDutunnaaDu** he is very talkative (*lit.* he is talking as if he had been overdosed with **wasa**, which is given to infants to assist their powers of speech).

వసంతం wasantam *n.* 1 spring time. 2 pink powder sprinkled by the bride and bridegroom on each other at a point during the marriage ceremony. 3 pink powder or spray thrown during the Holi festival.

వసంతుడు wasantuDu *n.* 1 God of spring. 2 *colloq.* handsome man.

వసంతోత్సవం wasantootsawam *n.* Holi, the festival of spring.

వసతి wasati *n.* 1 convenience, comfort, facility, amenity. 2 accomodation, lodging.

వసతిగృహం wasatigrham *n.* 1 hotel, boarding house, lodging house. 2 hostel.

వసనం wasanam *same as* **wasnam.**

వసారా wasaaraa *n.* veranda, balcony, front porch.

వసి wasi *n.* pointed wooden peg, spike.

వసికొను wasikonu *v.i.* 1 to attempt. 2 to undertake.

వసిలిపోవు, వసులు wasilipoowu, wasulu *v.i.* 1 to be loosened, be dislocated, become slack. 2 to slip out; **naa ceetilooNci kuNDa wasilipooyindi** the jar slipped out of my hand. 3 to be[come] tired; **eNDaloo tirigi wasilipooyEEDu** he became tired after walking about in the sun.

వసివాడు wasiwaaDu *v.i.* to fade.

వసుధ, వసుంధర, వసుమతి wasudha, wasundhara, wasumati *n. class.* the earth.

వసుధైవ, వసుధైక wasudhaywa, wasudhayka *adj.* embracing the entire world, worldwide, universal; ~ **bhraatrtwam** universal brotherhood.

వసువు wasuwu *n. class.* 1 gold. 2 wealth. 3 name of a class of demigods in mythology.

వసూలు wasuulu *n.* collection (of money due to be paid, etc.).

వసూలు చేయు wasuulu ceeyu *v.t.* to collect (money due to be paid, etc.).

వస్తాదు wastaadu *n.* 1 gymnast, stalwart. 2 *colloq.* rowdy character.

వస్తుగత, వస్తుపర wastugata, wastupara *adj.* objective.

వస్తుతః wastutah I. *adj.* de facto; ~ **prabhutwam** de facto government. II *adv.* basically, fundamentally; ~ **aayana manciwaaDu** basically he is a good man.

వస్తుప్రదర్శనం wastupradarśanam *n.* exhibition.

వస్తురూపంలో wasturuupamloo *adv.* in kind.

వస్తువినిమయ పద్ధతి wastuwinimaya paddhati *n. econ.* barter system.

వస్తువు wastuwu *n.* 1 thing, article, object. 2 substance, material. 3 subject matter, content, plot (of a story). 4 *pl.* ~ **lu** goods, commodities.

వస్త్రం wastram *n.* cloth; *see* **wastraalu.**

వస్త్రకాయితం పట్టు wastrakaayitam paTTu *v.t.* to strain a liquid through cloth.

వస్త్రగాలితం wastragaalitam *n.* straining a liquid through cloth.

వస్త్రధారణ wastradhaaraNa *n.* dressing, putting on clothes.

వస్త్రధారి wastradhaari *n.* person who wears (a garment).

వస్త్ర పరిశ్రమ wastra pariśrama *n.* textile industry.

వస్త్రాలయం wastraalayam *n.* cloth shop.

వస్త్రాలు wastraalu *pl. of* **wastram** 1 garments, clothes, dress. 2 textiles. 3 *either* a flock of raw cotton **(patti)** smeared with turmeric *or* some cotton thread coloured with turmeric and kumkum; this is offered to deities at the time of worship as a token representing an offering of clothes.

వస్నం, వసనం wasnam, wasanam *n. class.* cloth.

వహనం wahanam *n.* bearing, carrying.

వహించు wahincu *v.t.* 1 to bear, sustain, support. 2 to take on, assume, undertake; **paatra**~ to play a part; **mawnam**~ to observe silence; **ghanata**~ to achieve fame; **jaagratta** ~ to take due care and precautions; **śraddha wahinci ceeyu** to do (s.g) diligently; *see* **śirasaa**~

వహ్ని wahni *n. class.* fire.

వహ్వా! wahwaa! *interj. expressive of appreciation.*

వా - waa

వాంఛ **waancha** *n.* **1** desire, longing, craving. **2** *slang* sexual desire.
వాంఛనీయ **waanchaniiya** *adj.* desirable.
వాంఛించు **waanchincu** *v.t.* to desire, wish for, long for.
వాంఛిత **waanchita** *adj.* longed for, desired.
వాంతి **waanti** *n.* vomiting.
వాంతిచేసుకొను **waanti ceesukonu** *v.i.* to vomit.
వాక **waaka** *n.* stream, watercourse.
వాకట్టు **waakaTTu** *n.* gag; *see* **taakaTTu.**
వాకబు **waakabu** *n.* enquiry; **ippuDu ~ loo unnadi** it is under enquiry now.
వాకబు చేయు **waakabu ceeyu** *v.i.* **1** to make enquiries, ascertain by enquiry or investigation. **2** to verify, check.
వాకిలి **waakili** *n.* **1** gateway. **2** door[way]. **3** front entrance to a house, front courtyard. **4 waakiTa uNDu** to be in menses.
వాకొను **waakonu** *v.t.* **1** to say, speak. **2** to tell of, state, mention.
వాక్కాయ **waakkaaya** *n. carissa carandas*, a tree with a sour edible fruit.
వాక్కు **waakku** *n.* **1** speech, speaking. **2** word. **3** saying, utterance.
వాక్చాతుర్యం **waakcaaturyam** *n.* oratorical skill, eloquence.
వాక్పటిమ **waakpaTima** *n.* power of speech, eloquence.
వాక్యం **waakyam** *n.* **1** sentence. **2** clause. **3** phrase.
వాక్యనిర్మాణం **waakyanirmaaNam** *n.* syntax.
వాక్రుచ్చు **waakruccu** *v.t. class.* to speak, say, utter.
వాక్సరణి **waaksaraNi** *n.* manner of speech, way of talking; **aayana ~ cuustee aayana wastaaDani neenu anukooleedu** judging from his way of talking, I did not think he would come.
వాక్సహాయం **waaksahaayam** *n.* help in the form of words, verbal intervention.
వాక్స్వాతంత్ర్యం **waakswaatantryam** *n.* freedom of speech.
వాగడుపు **waagaDupu** *n.* swollen stomach.
వాగనుశాసనుడు **waaganuśaasanuDu** *n.* title given to Nannaya (*lit.* he who regulated the Telugu language).
వాగు **waagu**[1] *n.* stream, watercourse, torrent.
వాగు **waagu**[2] *v.i.* to babble, prattle.
వాగుడు **waaguDu** *n.* talkativeness, babbling, prattling, garrulousness.
వాగుర **waagura** *n.* noose, trap, snare.
వాగ్గేయకారుడు **waaggeeyakaaruDu** *n.* song writer.
వాగ్ఝరి **waagjhari** *n.* flow of words.
వాగ్దానం **waagdaanam** *n.* promise, word of honour.
వాగ్ధాటి **waagdhaaTi** *n.* readiness of speech, eloquence.
వాగ్బంధ[న]ం **waagbandha[na]m** *n.* silencing, reducing (s.o.) to silence.
వాగ్యుద్ధం **waagyuddham** *n.* altercation.
వాగ్రూపంలో **waagruupamloo** *adv.* orally, in words.
వాగ్వాదం **waagwaadam** *n.* dispute, altercation, argument.
వాగ్వివాదం **waagwiwaadam** *n.* debate.
వాగ్వివాద పోటీ **waagwiwaada pooTii** *n.* debating competition.
వాఙ్మయ **waaŋmaya** *adj.* literary.
వాఙ్మయం **waaŋmayam** *n.* literature.
వాఙ్మూలం **waaŋmuulam** *n.* statement, deposition.
వాచకం **waacakam** *n.* **1** learning book, reader. **2** *gram.* term, form; **naama ~** noun; **sankhyaa ~** numeral; **gawrawa ~** honorific term; **strii/puruSa waacaka sarwanaamaalu** feminine/masculine forms of pronouns. **3** *theat.* speech, recitation; **naandi ~** speaking a prologue. **4** *theat.* elocution, delivery; **aa paatradhaari ~ baagaa leedu** that actor's delivery is not good. **5** name; **wṛkSa waacakaalu** names of trees; *cf.* **swasti ~**.
వాచచ్చిన **waacaccina** *adj.* having lost taste for food.
వాచవి **waacawi** *n.* taste, flavour, relish.
వాచా **waacaa** *adv. class.* orally, verbally, in words; *see* **karmaNaa.**
వాచాలత, వాచాలత్వం **waacaalata, waacaalatwam** *n.* talkativeness, wordiness.
వాచాలుడు **waacaaluDu** *n.* talkative person, garrulous person.
వాచు **waacu**[1] *v.i.* to swell.
వాచు **waacu**[2] *v.i.* to pine, crave, yearn (**-koosam**, for); *see* **tala** *sense 2* (*v*), **mukham ~**.
వాచ్యం **waacyam** *adj.* **1** fit to be uttered, spoken or said. **2** called, named; **kawi śabda waacyuDayna pratiwaaDu** everyone who is named as a poet.
వాజ[మ్మ] **waaja[mma]** *n. colloq.* incapable person.
వాజపేయం **waajapeeyam** *n.* a Vedic sacrifice.
వాజసనేయం **waajasaneeyam** *n.* a name of the Yajurveda.
వాజి **waaji** *n. class.* **1** horse. **2** bird. **3** arrow.
వాజిమేధం **waajimeedham** *n. class.* traditional horse sacrifice (= **aśwameedham**).
వాజీకర **waajiikara** *adj.* stimulating sexual desire, aphrodisiac.
వాటం **waaTam** *n.* **1** way, course, path, direction (of wind, running water); **niiLLu waccee waaTaana nilabaDaku** do not stand in the way of the running water; **siisaa gaali waaTaana paTTukunnaaDu** he held the bottle up in the

direction of the wind *or* he held the bottle up to the wind. 2 manner; **nii ~ cuustee** judging from your manner. 3 custom, habit: **purra ceyyi ~** habit of using o.'s left hand, lefthandedness. 4 suitability, adjustment: **iddarikii ~ kudirindi** they are made for each other. 5 convenient position or condition: **~ cuucukoni paTTuku laagaali** hold it at the right place and pull; **wiipu miida baruwuuNTee ~ [kudaraDam]koosam koncem wangutaaru** if there is a heavy burden on the back, they lean forward a little for comfort and convenience.

వాటా **waaTaa** *n.* 1 share: **~ lu weesukonu** to contribute shares. 2 portion. 3 **~ dhanam** share capital (in a company). 4 part of a house; **maa iNTLoo ~ addeki iccEEru** they gave part of our house on rent.

వాటాదారు **waaTaadaaru** *n.* 1 owner of a share (in property). 2 shareholder (in a company). 3 tenant.

వాటారు **waaTaaru** *v.i.* to decline, sink, set; **poddu ~ tunnadi** the sun is setting.

వాటి[క] **waaTi[ka]** *n.* 1 area, locality, quarter. 2 place, site; **smaśaana ~** burial ground, cemetery; **yajña ~** place of sacrifice. 3 garden; **puSpa ~** flower garden.

వాటిల్లు **waaTillu** *v.i.* to happen unexpectedly, befall.

వాటు **waaTu** *n.* 1 blow, stroke, force; **kaagitaalu gaali ~ na koTTukupooyEEyi** the papers were blown away by the force of the wind; **saykil tokkakuNDaaNee gaali ~ na munduku pooyindi** the cycle moved forward without pedalling due to the force of the wind; *see* **katti ~**. 2 manner; **ceeti ~ maniSi** thievish or light-fingered person. 3 direction, side; **naa kaaLLaku ~ na** (*or* **naa kaaLLa-kaaTuna**) **kuurcunnaaDu** he sat beside my feet.

వాటుగా **waaTugaa** *adv.* in the direction of, by the side of; **naDawaDamloo pakka ~ pooyee kaalu** a lame or limping leg (*lit.* a leg that has a sideways motion when walking); **kaaluwapakka ~ baNDi doowa undi** adjacent to the canal there is a cart track; **diwaanuki pakkagaanuu koncem wenaka ~ nuu nuncunnaaDu** he stood by the side of and a little behind the dewan.

వాటుపడు **waaTupaDu** *v.i.* to be troubled, be perturbed, be perplexed.

వాటేసుకొను **waaTeesukonu** *v.t.* 1 to throw o.'s arms around, clasp in o.'s arms, embrace. 2 to cling [on] to.

వాడ **waaDa** *n.* 1 locality or quarter in a town. 2 area; **paariśraamika ~** industrial area. 3 *second part of a proper name indicating a township,* e.g., **wijaya ~** Vijayawada.

వాడకం **waaDakam** *n.* 1 use, usage. 2 consumption.

వాడకట్టు **waaDakaTTu** *n.* 1 row or line of houses. 2 street. 3 local custom, custom observed in a particular locality.

వాడి **waaDi** I. *n.* sharpness. II. *adj.* sharp.

వాడిగా **waaDigaa** *adv.* sharply, keenly.

వాడు **waaDu**[1] *v.i.* to wither, fade.

వాడు **waaDu**[2] *v.t.* to use.

వాడు **waaDu**[3] I. *pron.* he, that man. II. *~ is used as second part of a n. compound with certain names of professions, trades, etc.*: **golla ~** shepherd; **caakali ~** washerman; **koTTu ~** shopkeeper; **paala ~** milkman, milk vendor.

వాడుక, వాడిక **waaDuka, waaDika** I. *n.* 1 custom, habit, practice. 2 use, utilisation. 3 usage (in speech); **gaajupuruganTee jonna mokkala daNTulooni saaraanni tinee dolupuDu purugu; sunkunu naaki poyyee puruguku kuuDaa ii ~ undi** '**gaajupurugu**' means a boring insect which consumes the sap in cholam stems; this term is also used for an insect which attacks the blossom. 4 regular patronage (of a shop or business): **aayana ~ maa daggiree** his regular custom is with us *or* his regular dealings are with us. II *adj.* customary, habitual, usual, commonly used: **~ bhaaSa** colloquial language.

వాడుకగా **waaDukagaa** *adv.* 1 commonly, usually. 2 regularly.

వాడుకొను **waaDukonu** *v.t.* to use, make use of.

వాణి **waaNi** *n.* 1 epithet of Saraswati, goddess of speech. 2 voice, speech, sound: *cf.* **aakaaśa ~**

వాణిజ్య **waaNijya** *adj.* commercial: **~ nawka** merchant ship.

వాణిజ్యం **waaNijyam** *n.* commerce.

వాణిజ్య పన్ను **waaNijya pannu** *n.* commercial tax, sales tax.

వాణిజ్యమండలి **waaNijyamaNDali** *n.* Chamber of Commerce.

వాణిజ్యవేత్త **waaNijya weetta** *n.* businessman, merchant.

వాణీ **waaNii** *colloq. and dial. variant of* **ooNii.**

వాత **waata**[1] *n.* 1 branding, burning. 2 mark caused by branding.

వాత **waata**[2] *obsolete locative case of* **waayi** *occurring mod. in* **~ paDu** *lit.* to fall into the mouth of, *hence* to fall a prey to: **kalaraa** (*or* **waradala**) **~ paDi caccipooyEEDu** he fell a prey to cholera (*or* floods) and died; **puli ~ paDDaaDu** *lit.* he fell into a tiger's mouth, *hence* he was destroyed.

వాతం **waatam** *n.* 1 *class.* air, wind. 2 *med.* (*also* **waataroogam**) rheumatism.

వాత పెట్టు, వాత వేయు **waata peTTu, waata weeyu** *v.t.* 1 to brand. 2 to cauterise.

వాతాపి **waataapi** *n.* name of a demon who was swallowed and digested by the sage Agastya; **jiirNam jiirNam ~ jiirNam** *are words of a lullaby originating from this legend.*

వాతాయనం **waataayanam** *n.* ventilator.

వాతావరణం **waataawaraNam** *n.* 1 weather. 2 atmosphere.

వాతావరణశాస్త్రం **waataawaraNaśaastram** *n.* meteorology.

వాతావరణ సూచన **waataawaraNa suucana** *n.* weather forecast.

వాత్సల్యం **waatsalyam** *n.* 1 parental love. 2 affection.

వాదం **waadam** *n.* 1 doctrine, principle. 2 *equivalent to* -ism: **waastawika ~** realism. 3 theory. 4 discussion, debate. 5 argument, contention.

వాదోపవాదాలు **waadoopawaadaalu** *n. pl.* arguments and counter-arguments.

వాదన **waadana** *n.* 1 argument, contention. 2 advocacy.

వాదర **waadara** *n. class.* knife-edge.

వాది **waadi** *n.* 1 *legal* plaintiff, complainant. 2 proponent or supporter of a creed or cause or doctrine; **kaangres ~** Congressite; **aadarśa ~** idealist.

వాదించు **waadincu** *v.t.* 1 to argue, debate, dispute, discuss. 2 to advocate, contend.

వాదు **waadu** *n.* 1 unconfirmed rumour, unsubstantiated allegation: **aayana taagutaaDani ~ undi** people say that he drinks. 2 argument, contention.

వాదులాడుకొను **waadulaaDukonu** *v.i.* (of two or more persons) to argue or dispute among themselves.

వాదోడుగా **waadooDugaa** *adv.* giving verbal support: *cf.* **ceedooDu ~**.

వా[యి]ద్యం **waa[yi]dyam** *n.* 1 musical instrument. 2 playing an instrument; **waa[yi]dyasangiitam** instrumental (i.e., non-vocal) music.

వాన **waana** *n.* rain; *see* **eNDa.**

వానకాలం **waanakaalam** *n.* rainy season; **waanakaalapu caduwulu** studying off and on, desultory study.

వానచినుకు **waanacinuku** *n.* rain drop.

వానజల్లు **waanajallu** *n.* shower of rain.

వానపాము **waanapaamu** *n.* earthworm.

వానప్రస్థం **waanaprastham** *n.* stage or **aaśrama** in a man's life when he goes to live a life of meditation in the woods.

వానప్రస్థుడు **waanaprasthuDu** *n.* man who has entered the stage of **waanaprastham**, hermit.

వానరం, వానరుడు **waanaram, waanaruDu** *n.* monkey.

వానరాయి **waanaraayi** *n.* hailstone.

వాను **waanu** *v.t.* to make pots, bricks, etc., in a kiln.

వాపసు **waapasu** *n.* giving back, returning.

వాపసు చేయు **waapasu ceeyu** *v.t.* to return, refund, give back.

వాపి **waapi**[1] *n.* 1 greed[iness]; **~ koddii miThaayilannii tinnaaDu** he ate all the sweets out of greediness. 2 longing, yearning, pining.

వాపి **waapi**[2] *n. class.* well with steps leading down to the water, step well.

వాపిరిగొట్టు **waapirigoTTu** *n.* greedy person, glutton.

వాపు **waapu** *n.* swelling.

వాపోక **waapooka** *n.* crying out, lamenting, bewailing, deploring.

వాపోవు **waapoowu** *v.i. and t.* to lament, bewail, deplore.

వామ **waama** I. *n. class.* beautiful woman. II. *adj.* 1 left (opposite of right); **~ pakSa** *polit.* the left. 2 *class.* beautiful.

వామన **waamana** *adj.* short, dwarfish.

వామనకాయ **waamana kaaya** *n.* tender fruit, esp. of tamarind or **waakkaaya.**

వామనగుంటలు **waamanaguNTalu** *n.pl.* girls' game played on a board.

వామనుడు **waamanuDu** *n.* 1 dwarf. 2 epithet of Vishnu.

వామాంగి, వామాక్షి **waamaangi, waamaakSi** *n. class.* woman.

వామి, వాము **waami, waamu**[1] *n.* stack of straw, rick of hay.

వాము, ఓమం **waamu**[2], **oomam** *n.* bishop's weed, *carum copticum*, a home remedy for indigestion.

వాయ **waaya**[1] *n.* 1 trayful of idlies in the pot in which they are cooked (a pot may contain two or three trays). 2 a helping of food. 3 *colloq.* a generous helping of food; **oo ~ annam aawakaayatoo tinnaaDu** he ate a generous helping of rice with mango pickle. 4 as much grain as can be poured into a mortar at one time for pounding.

వాయ **waaya**[2] *n.* fainting: **waaDiki ~ waccindi** he fainted.

వాయనం **waayanam** *n.* betel and nut with fruit and soaked bengalgram and other food items first offered to a deity and then distributed to persons present on a festival day or to mark the end of a religious vow or penance (a custom observed by women).

వాయవ్యం **waayawyam** *n. and adj.* north-west.

వాయసం **waayasam** *n. class.* crow.

వాయి **waayi** *n.* 1 mouth. 2 face; **nooruu waayii leeni waaDu** meek person, person who cannot argue on his own behalf. 3 (*also* **~ daara**) cutting edge of a knife.

వాయించు **waayincu** *v.t.* 1 to play (musical instrument). 2 to beat (drum). 3 *colloq.* to beat, scold.

వాయింపు **waayimpu** *n.* 1 playing (musical instrument). 2 beating (drum). 3 *colloq.* beating, scolding.

వాయిదా **waayidaa** *n.* 1 time allowed for making payment or for some other purpose. 2 adjournment, postponement. 3 instalment: **~ la paddhatini cellincu** to pay in instalments; **muuDoo ~ kaTTEEnu** I have paid the third instalment.

వాయిదా పడు **waayidaa paDu** *v.i.* to be postponed, be put off, be adjourned.

వాయిదా వేయు **waayidaa weeyu** *v.t.* to postpone, put off, adjourn, defer: **guNTuuru prayaaNam reNDu nelalu waayidaa weeyaali** you must put off the journey to Guntur for two months.

వాయిద్యం **waayidyam** *same as* **waadyam.**

వాయుగతిశాస్త్రం **waayugatiśaastram** *n.* aerodynamics.

వాయుగుండం **waayuguNDam** *n.* 1 whirlwind. 2 cyclone.

వాయుపదార్థం **waayupadaartham** *n. chem.* gas.

వాయుపూరకం **waayupuurakam** *n.* inflator.

వాయుమండలం **waayumaNDalam** *n.* atmosphere.

వాయుయంత్రం **waayuyantram** *n.* windmill.

వాయువు **waayuwu** *n.* 1 air, wind. 2 gas.

వాయుస్తంభనం **waayustambhanam** *n.* 1 power to float in the air by supernatural means, levitation. 2 power to maintain life while withholding breath.

వాయుస్థితి **waayusthiti** *n.* 1 *met.* weather. 2 *chem.* gaseous state.

వార **waara** I. *n.* 1 side; **cinna balla tiisukeLLi waraNDaaloo oo ~ ki uncEEDu** he took a small table and placed it to one side on the veranda; **geeTu teraci cuusee sariki oo rikSaa gooDa ~ ni kanipincindi** as soon as she opened the gate and looked out, she saw a rickshaw by the side of the wall. 2 difference, variation; **pillaki pillaki madhya ~ leedu** there is not much difference in age between the two children. II. *post-positional use* **ekkaDoo ceTTu ~ kuurcundi** she sat beside a tree somewhere. III. *advbl. use* 1 **gadiki oo ~ kiTikii undi** on one side of the room there is a window. 2 **aa ~** so as to compensate *or* [so as] to make up the difference; **neenu kharcupeTTinaa aa ~ konta laabham waccindi** although I spent money I got some profit as a compensation: **pooyina waaram raaleedu, aa ~ ii waaram reNDu roojulu wastaaDu** last week he did not come but to make up for it he will come on two days this week.

వారం **waaram** *n.* 1 week. 2 day of the week: **aadi~** Sunday; **~roojulu** a week's time; **waaraalu ceesukonu** to take meals with a different family on each day of the week (a practice followed by poor students); **~warjyam cuucu** to make enquiries about auspicious and inauspicious times of the day.

వారకాంత **waarakaanta** *n.* prostitute.

వారధి **waaradhi** *n.* bridge.

వార పత్రిక **waara patrika** *n.* weekly newspaper.

వారవనిత **waarawanita** *n.* prostitute.

వారసత్వం **waarasatwam** *n.* 1 inheritance. 2 succession.

వారసత్వపు **waarasatwapu** *adj.* hereditary.

వారసుడు **waarasuDu** *n.* heir, successor.

వారాశి **waaraaśi** *n. class.* ocean.

వారి, వారీ **waari**[1], **waarii**[1] *suffix* according to, by: **jillaala~gaa** by districts, districtwise; **ancela~** by stages.

వారి! వారీ! **waari!**[2] **waarii!**[2] *interj. of surprise* oh!

వారి **waari**[3] *genitive of* **waaru**[1].

వారించు **waarincu** *v.i. and t.* 1 to drive away, warn off, ward off. 2 to avert, prevent, hinder. 3 to forbid, stop, restrain, dissuade. 4 to elude.

వారిజం **waarijam** *n. class.* lotus.

వారు **waaru**[1] *pron.pl.* 1 they, those persons. 2 **maa~** my husband.

వారు **waaru**[2] *n.* leather strap or thong.

వారు **waaru**[3] *v.i.* (of water used for cooking rice) to be poured off or strained off.

వారు **waaru**[4] *see* **paaru**[2] *sense 6.*

వారుపోయు **waarupooyu** *v.i.* to pour cooked rice in a heap (referring to a custom at temple car festivals of pouring a heap of cooked rice before the temple car which starts its journey in procession by passing over the heap); **kancamcuTTuu waarupoosEEweemiTi**? why have you made a heap of rice all round your plate? (said to a child who eats untidily).

వారుణి **waaruNi** *n. class.* 1 west, region of Varuna. 2 alcoholic liquor.

వారెన **waarena** *n.* rope or leather thong used to tie the baling rope of a mhote to the bullocks' yoke.

వార్చు **waarcu** *v.t.* 1 to strain off water from cooked rice. 2 **sandhya~** to perform the ritual of **sandhya,** which includes allowing water to drain through the fingers.

వార్త **waarta** *n., often pl.* **~lu** news, intelligence, tidings.

వార్తాదర్శిని **waartaadarśini** *n.* newsreel.

వార్తాప్రసారం **waartaa prasaaram** *n.* news broadcast.

వార్తాసంస్థ **waartaasamstha** *n.* news agency.

వార్తాహరుడు **waartaa haruDu** *n.* messenger.

వార్ధక్యం, వార్ధకం **waardhakyam, waardhakam** *n.* old age, senility.

వార్పు **waarpu** *n.* 1 straining off water from boiling rice. 2 water so strained off. 3 **waNTaa~u** cooking, cookery.

వార్షిక **waarSika** *adj.* annual.

వార్షికం **waarSikam** *n.* yearly payment, annuity.

వార్షికోత్సవం **waarSikootsawam** *n.* anniversary.

వాలం **waalam** *n. class.* 1 tail. 2 sword.

వాలకం **waalakam** *n.* (often used in a derogatory sense) 1 attitude, behaviour, demeanour, manner. 2 appearance, facial expression.

వాలాడిపోవు **waalaaDipoowu** *v.i. colloq.* to be available in plenty; **bajaaruloo maamiDipaLLu waalaaDipootunnaayi** there are lots of mangoes in the market; **naa daggira Dabbulu waalaaDipootunnaayanukoNTunnaawaa?** do you think I have plenty of money?

వాలాయం **waalaayam** *n.* force, compulsion.

వాలాయంగా **waalaayangaa** *adv.* 1 certainly, undoubtedly. 2 necessarily.

వాలి **waali**[1] *form of* **aali** *used after an infinitive ending* in a vowel.

వాలి **waali**[2] Vali, brother of Sugriva, who was slain by Rama.

వాలికలు **waalikalu** *n.pl.* tattered clothes; **ciilikalu~** rags and tatters.

వాలు **waalu** I. *n.* 1 slope, slant, incline, inclination, gradient. 2 direction of flow of air or water; **akkaDa paDDa niiLLaki~iTee undi. taDustaawu, jaagrata**! the water that fell there will run off in this direction. you will get wet, be careful! **waaDiki iita raaka niiTi~loo koTTukupooyEEDu** not knowing how to swim he was swept away by the current; **gaali~loo aa śabdam egasi wacci naa cewina paDDadi** the sound came floating downwind and struck my ear. 3 sword. II. *adj.* sloping, slanting, drooping, descending; **~cuupu** downcast glance. III *v.i.* 1 to lean, slope, slant, incline; **munduku waali kuurcunnaaDu** he sat leaning forwards; **paDawa koncem aa pakkaki waalindi** the boat heeled over a little to that side. 2 to droop. 3 to fall down; **o.-i paadaala miida~** to fall at s.o.'s feet. 4 to alight, perch. 5 *colloq.* to arrive unexpectedly; **kaburu ceeyakuNDaanee wacci waalEEDu** he descended on us without notice.

వాలుక **waaluka** *n. class.* sand.

వాలుకంటి **waalukaNTi** *n.* beautiful woman.

వాలుకుర్చీ **waalukurcii** *n.* easy chair.

వాలుగ **waaluga** *n.* catfish.

వాలుగపాము **waalugapaamu** *n.* kind of eel.

వాలుపొద్దు **waalupoddu** *n.* afternoon, evening (*lit.* setting sun).

వాలుబల్ల, వాలుతలం **waaluballa, waalutalam** *n. phys.* inclined plane.

వాలుమెకం **waalumekam** *n.* wild boar.

వాల్చు **waalcu** *v.t.* 1 to bend, incline, lean; **tala baagaa wenakku waalceesi** bending the head well back; **meenu~** (*literary phrase*) to lie down and rest; **naDum~** to rest, take a nap; **reppa~** to blink. 2 to set down, place on the ground; **mancam** (or **piiTa**) **~** to place a cot (or wooden seat) on the ground.

వాల్మీకి **waalmiiki** *n.* 1 name of the reputed author of the Ramayana. 2 name of a hill tribe in Andhra Pradesh.

వాల్లభ్యం **waallabhyam** *n.* 1 authority, rule. 2 love, affection. 3 *class.* influence.

వావి **waawi** *n.* blood relationship, consanguinity; **warasaleeni waaDu** person who disregards the rules of consanguinity.

వావిక **waawika** *n.* hollow at the bottom of the throat.

వాసం **waasam** *n.* 1 house, habitation, abode, dwelling; **raaNi~** queen's quarters in a palace; *see* **graasawaasaalu, janaa~, paTNa~**. 2 rafter.

వాసంతం **waasantam** *adj.* pertaining to spring.

వాసంతి **waasanti** *n.* a flower, *jasminum auriculatum.*

వాసగృహం **waasagrham** *n.* living quarters.

వాసన **waasana** *n.* 1 smell, scent, odour, fragrance. 2 influence; **padeeLLugaa aa deeśamloo kaapuram unnaa aa~lu aNTaleedu** although he has lived in that country for ten years, its influence has not affected him; **paata~lu** old habits, old characteristics; **puurwa janma~lu** characteristics hailing from o.'s past life or from a previous birth.

వాసన కొట్టు, వాసన వేయు **waasana koTTu, waasana weeyu** *v.i.* to emit a smell.

వాసన చూచు **waasana cuucu** *v.t.* to smell, scent.

వాసన పట్టు **waasana paTTu** I. *v.i.* to acquire a smell. II *v.t.* 1 to smell, scent. 2 to track or trace out s.g by means of its scent. 3 *colloq.* to smell out, detect; **neenu uuLLooki waccina wiSayam aayana waasana paTTEEDu** he smelt out the reason for my coming to town.

వాసయోగ్య **waasayoogya** *adj.* [in]habitable.

వాసరం **waasaram** *n. class.* day (= **waaram**).

వాసి **waasi**[1] I. *n.* 1 difference. 2 extent; **weNTruka~ loo** (*or* **nuulu~loo) tappipoowu** to escape by a hair's breadth; **wiiDikaNTe waaDu oka cuupu ~ poDuggaa kanipistaaDu** this boy appears a shade taller than that boy. 3 amelioration, improvement. 4 greatness, superior quality. 5 splendour, glory. 6 fame, renown; **~ki ekku** to become great, become famous; *see* **hasta~**. II. *adj.* better, improved (in health or quality); **ninnaTikaNTe roogi paristhiti koncem~** the patient's condition is a little better than yesterday.

వాసి **waasi**[2] *second part of a n. compound meaning* inhabitant, dweller; **paTNa~** town dweller.

వాసెన **waasena** *n.* 1 cloth tied over the mouth of a jar in which pickles are stored. 2 cloth tied over the mouth of a jar in which cakes are steamed. 3 cloth tied round the head for protection from heat, rain, etc.

వాసెన కుడుములు **waasena kuDumulu** *n.pl.* steamed cakes made of rice and blackgram.

వాస్తవ **waastawa** *adj.* 1 real, actual, true, genuine. 2 substantial, material.

వాస్తవం **waastawam** *n.* truth, reality.

వాస్తవంగా, వాస్తవానికి **waastawangaa, waastawaaniki** *adv.* really, truly, actually, in fact, as a matter of fact.

వాస్తవవాదం **waastawawaadam** *n.* realism.

వాస్తవవాది **waastawawaadi** *n.* realist.

వాస్తవిక **waastawika** *adj.* 1 true, real, genuine, actual, factual. 2 realistic, objective.

వాస్తవికత **waastawikata** *n.* 1 reality. 2 objectivity. 3 realism.

వాస్తవికవాదం **waastawikawaadam** *n.* realism.

వాస్తవికవాది **waastawikawaadi** *n.* realist.

వాస్తవిక విజ్ఞానం **waastawika wijñaanam** *n.* objective knowledge.

వాస్తవికతావాదం **waastawikataawaadam** *n.* realism.

వాస్తవ్యుడు **waastawyuDu** *n.* inhabitant, resident; **X graama~** resident of X village.

వాస్తు **waastu** I *n.* science or art of building, architecture; II *adj.* architectural.

వాస్తుపురుషుడు **waastupuruSuDu** *n.* deity who presides over the site where a dwelling exists.

వాస్తుపూజ **waastupuuja** *n.* ceremony performed at laying of foundation of a building.

వాస్తుశాంతి **waastuśaanti** *n.* ceremony performed at the time of entering and occupying a new home.

వాస్తుశాస్త్రం **waastuśaastram** *n.* (science of) architecture.

వాస్తుశిల్పం **waastuśilpam** *n.* architectural work.

వాస్తుశిల్పి **waastuśilpi** *n.* architect.

వాహకం **waahakam** *n. sci.* carrier, conductor; **widyud~** conductor of electricity.

వాహకత్వం **waahakatwam** *n.sci.* conductivity.

వాహకుడు **waahakuDu** *n.* bearer, carrier; **śawa~** corpse bearer.

వాహనం **waahanam** *n.* vehicle, conveyance, carriage.

వాహనారూఢుడు **waahanaaruuDhuDu** *n.* person seated on a vehicle or carriage.

వాహిక **waahika** *n.* vehicle, medium (of expression).

వాహిని **waahini** *n. class.* 1 river. 2 army.

వాహ్యాళి **waahyaaLi** *n.* 1 trip, outing. 2 walk, stroll.

వాహ్వా! వహ్వా! **waahwaa! wahwaa!** *interj. of appreciation and approval* well done!, excellent!

వి - wi

వి **wi** *prefix expressing* (i) *intensification*, e.g., **khyaati** fame, **wikhyaati great** fame; (ii) *negation*, e.g., **śramam** toil, trouble, **wiśramam** rest.

వింగడించు **wingaDincu** *v.t.* to separate, distinguish, differentiate, analyse; **ii roojulloo eedi wacanam eedi kawanam ani manam wingaDincanakkaraleedu** in these days there is no need for us to distinguish between what is poetry and what is prose.

వింజామర **winjaamara** *n.* white flywhisk used in court or temple ceremonies.

వింత **winta** I. *n.* 1 s.g strange or rare or extraordinary, a marvel. 2 strangeness, curiousness, oddness. II. *adj.* strange, odd, curious, quaint, wonderful.

వింతగా **wintagaa** *adv.* 1 strangely, oddly, in a strange or peculiar way or manner. 2 curiously, wonderingly, enquiringly.

విందు **windu** *n.* dinner, feast, banquet: **teeniiTi~** tea party; **kaLLaku/cewulaku~** feast for the eyes/ears.

వింధ్య **windhya** *n.* the Vindhya mountains.

వింశతి **wimśati** *n. class.* twenty; **eeka ~ patraalu** leaves of 21 species of plants used in the worship of Ganesha.

వికట **wikaTa** *adj.* 1 ugly, uncouth. 2 crooked, awkward. 3 repulsive, unpleasant. 4 contrary, obstinate; *cf.* **akaTaa-wikaTam.**

వికటంగా **wikaTangaa** *adv.* spitefully; **~nawwu** to laugh spitefully.

వికటించు **wikaTincu** *v.i.* (of circumstances, health) to become unfavourable, grow worse.

వికరణం **wikaraNam** *n. sci.* radiation.

వికర్ణం **wikarNam** *n. maths.* diagonal.

వికర్షించు **wikarSincu** *v.t.* to repel.

వికల **wikala** *adj.* 1 defective, imperfect. 2 mutilated, disabled. 3 (of a limb) withered, deformed. 4 agitated, perturbed, confused.

వికలత, వికలత్వం, వైకల్యం **wikalata, wikalatwam, waykalyam** *n.* 1 defect, imperfection. 2 mutilation, disability. 3 deformity. 4 agitation, perturbation.

వికలాంగుడు **wikalaanguDu** *n.* disabled person.

వికల్పం **wikalpam** I. *n.* 1 change, alteration. 2 doubt, uncertainty. II *adj. gram.* optional.

వికల్పార్థక **wikalpaarthaka** *adj. gram.* disjunctive.

వికల్మష **wikalmaSa** *adj.* sinless, guiltless, stainless.

వికవిక **wikawika** *onom. adv. sug.* sound of laughter.

వికసించు **wikasincu** *v.i.* 1 (of a flower) to open, bloom. 2 to develop, grow, expand. 3 *fig.* to light up, beam (with joy); **aame mukham wikasincindi** her face lit up *or* she beamed with joy.

వికసిత **wikasita** *adj.* 1 expanded, developed. 2 (of a face) beaming, smiling.

వికార **wikaara** *adj.* 1 ugly, awkward, unshapely. 2 odd, strange, uncouth. 3 nasty, unpleasant.

వికారం **wikaaram** *n.* 1 change, transformation, alteration. 2 distortion, ugliness. 3 perturbation, emotion, passion; **kaama ~** lust; **manoo ~** mental perturbation, mental instability. 4 aversion, repulsion. 5 nausea; **kaDupuloo ~** queasiness in the stomach.

వికారంగా **wikaarangaa** *adv.* 1 oddly. 2 awkwardly. **3~ mukham peTTu** to put on a look of distaste.

వికారి **wikaari** *n.* thirty-third year of the Hindu cycle of sixty years.

వికాసం **wikaasam** *n.* 1 expanding, expansion. 2 blooming, blossoming. 3 cheerfulness, brightness. 4 developing, development.

వికీర్ణ **wikiirNa** *adj.* diffused, scattered.

వికీర్ణ తాపం **wikiirNa taapam** *n. sci.* radiant heat.

వికృత **wikṛta** *adj.* 1 changed, altered, transformed, modified. 2 deformed, distorted. 3 imperfect, uncouth, strange, odd, ugly.

వికృతంగా **wikṛtangaa** *adv.* 1 hideously, in an ugly manner. 2 hoarsely, harshly; **kaakulu ~ kuusEEyi** the crows cawed harshly. 3 crookedly, misshapenly.

వికృతి **wikṛti** *n.* 1 change, alteration, distortion. 2 *gram.* modification, corruption (of a word). 3 name of the twenty-fourth year of the Hindu cycle of sixty years.

వికేంద్రీకరణ **wikeendriikaraNa** *n.* decentralisation.

వికేంద్రీకరించు **wikeendriikarincu** *v.t.* to decentralise.

విక్కు **wikku** *v.i. class.* 1 to swell with pride. 2 to stretch out the limbs.

విక్రమ **wikrama** *n.* name of the fourteenth year of the Hindu cycle of sixty years.

విక్రమం **wikramam** *n.* heroism, valour.

విక్రమార్కుడు **wikramaarkuDu** *n.* name of a king famous for his persistence; **paTTu wadalani ~** Vikramarka who would not give up (proverbial saying).

విక్రమించు **wikramincu** *v.i.* to display strength, be energetic.

విక్రయం **wikrayam** *n.* sale, selling.

విక్రయదారుడు **wikrayadaaruDu** *n.* seller, vendor.

విక్రయధనం **wikrayadhanam** *n.* sale proceeds.

విక్రయపత్రం **wikrayapatram** *n.* sale deed.

విక్రయించు **wikrayincu** *v.t.* to sell.

విక్రాంతి **wikraanti** *n.* valour.

విక్రియ **wikriya** *n.* change, alteration, transformation.

విక్రేత **wikreeta** *n.* seller.

విక్షిప్త **wikSipta** *adj* 1 *class.* thrown, cast, flung, tossed up. 2 *sci.* dispersed.

విక్షేపణ[ం] **wikSeepaNa[m]** *n. sci.* 1 dispersion. 2 deflection.

విక్షేపించు **wikSeepincu** *v.t.* to throw, fling, toss up.

విఖ్యాత **wikhyaata** *adj.* famous, celebrated.

విఖ్యాతి **wikhyaati** *n.* fame, celebrity.

విఖ్యాతి కను **wikhyaati kanu** *v.i.* to win fame.

విఖ్యాతుడు **wikhyaatuDu** *n.* wellknown person.

విగడియ, విఘడియ **wigaDiya, wighaDiya** *n.* 1 moment, instant. 2 one sixtieth of a **gaDiya**, i.e., 24 seconds.

విగళనం **wigaLanam** *n.* 1 flowing, trickling. 2 melting away. 3 dispersion.

విగుణ **wiguNa** *adj.* without merit, worthless.

విగ్రహం **wigraham** *n.* 1 statue, image. 2 body, figure: **poDuguu poTTii kaaka niNDayna ~** ample figure, neither tall nor short. 3 *gram.* separation of a compound word into its constituent parts.

విఘటనం **wighaTanam** *n. sci.* disintegration, dissolution, decomposition.

విఘడియ **wighaDiya** *same as* **wigaDiya.**

విఘాతం **wighaatam** *n.* 1 hindrance, obstacle. 2 heavy blow.

విఘ్నం **wighnam** *n.* impediment, obstacle, hindrance, obstruction.

విచక్షణం **wicakSaNam** *n.* discretion, discernment, discrimination.

విచక్షణగల **wicakSaNagala** *adj.* discriminating, judicious.

విచలనం **wicalanam** *n.* 1 stirring, moving about. 2 unsteadiness. 3 deviation, variation.

విచారం **wicaaram** *n.* 1 grief, regret, sorrow. 2 distress, worry, care. 3 pondering, reflection, consideration: **kuTumbaadaayam taggindanna ~ toopaaTu takkuwa kharcutoo kaalayaapana eTLaagaa anna ~ kuuDaa aawiNNi paTTukonnadi** along with her grief that the family income had become less, consideration of how to spin out the time on a reduced budget also assailed her.

విచారణ **wicaaraNa** *n.* 1 enquiry, investigation. 2 *legal* trial. 3 *legal* examination of a witness.

విచారమయ, విచారమైన **wicaaramaya, wicaaramayna** *adj.* sad, sorrowful.

విచారించు **wicaarincu** *v.i. and t.* 1 to feel sad, feel sorry, regret. 2 to investigate, examine, enquire into. 3 to think about, consider.

విచికిత్స **wicikitsa** *n.* doubt, uncertainty.

విచిత్ర **wicitra** *adj.* 1 strange, wonderful, prodigious, marvellous, remarkable, fantastic, surprising. 2 special, particular, peculiar. 3 **~ warNaalu** variegated colours.

విచిత్రం **wicitram** *n.* wonder, marvel, s.g strange, s.g surprising.

విచిత్రంగా **wicitrangaa** *adv.* 1 strangely, unusually, exceedingly: **aayanaki ~ koopam waccindi** he was exceedingly angry. 2 curiously, with curiosity, with surprise: **nannu ~ cuusEEru** they looked at me curiously *or* they looked at me with surprise.

విచ్చలవిడిగా **wiccalawiDigaa** *adv.* freely, unrestrainedly, independently, at will.

విచ్చు **wiccu** I. *adj.* 1 expanding, opening: **~ mogga** opening bud. 2 unsheathed: **~ kattulu** unsheathed swords, drawn swords. II. (*also* **~ konu**) *v.i.* 1 to open: **pedawulu ~ konnaayi** the lips parted. 2 (of flowers) to expand, blossom. 3 (of ripe fruit) to burst open. 4 **aameni cuuDagaanee waaDi mukham ~ kondi** as soon as he saw her, his face beamed with joy. 5 (of new earthenware pots) to burst as soon as used due to faulty firing: *cf.* **iDugu.** 6 to be scattered, be dispersed.

విచ్చురూపాయి, విచ్చరూపాయి **wiccuruupaayi, wiccaruupaayi** *same as* **iccaruupaayi.**

విచ్చేయు **wicceeyu** *v.i. class.* 1 to pay a visit (-**ki**, to). 2 to come, go, proceed.

విచ్ఛిత్తి **wicchitti** *n.* 1 partition, separation: **kuTumba ~** family partition. 2 cutting off, interruption. 3 splitting. 4 *sci.* fission. 5 **garbha ~** abortion, miscarriage.

విచ్ఛిన్న **wicchinna** *adj.* 1 separated, split [up], discontinuous, broken, interrupted. 2 destroyed, shattered.

విచ్ఛిన్నం చేయు **wicchinnam ceeyu** *v.t.* to shatter, destroy

విచ్ఛిన్నత **wicchinnata** *n.* splitting, breaking [up].

విచ్ఛేద[న]ం **wiccheeda[na]m** *n.* 1 cutting, separation, severance. 2 disintegration, splitting. 3 interruption.

విచ్యుతి **wicyuti** *n. class.* decline, downfall.

విజయ **wijaya** *n.* twenty-seventh year of the Hindu cycle of sixty years.

విజయం **wijayam** *n.* 1 victory, triumph. 2 success.

విజయం చేయు, వేంచేయు **wijayam ceeyu, weemceeyu** *v.i. class.* 1 to condescend to come. 2 to visit.

విజయదశమి **wijayadaśami** *n.* tenth day of the first lunar fortnight of Aswiyuja: *see* **dasaraa.**

విజయవంత **wijayawanta** *adj.* victorious, successful.

విజాతీయ **wijaatiiya** *adj.* 1 foreign. 2 of a different type or origin.

విజిగీష **wijigiiSa** *n.* desire to conquer, desire to win.

విజితుడు **wijituDu** *n.* loser, defeated person.

విజృంభణ **wijṛmbhaNa** *n.* 1 expansion, intensification: **aarthika ~** economic boom. 2 pride, ostentation. 3 outburst of anger.

విజృంభించు **wijṛmbhincu** *v.i.* 1 to flourish, bloom, boom, prosper. 2 to swell, expand, intensify. 3 to be presumptuous, be audacious. 4 to explode or burst out with anger.

విజేత **wijeeta** *n.* victor, conqueror, winner.

విజ్ఞత **wijñata** *n.* good sense, commonsense, prudence, wisdom, understanding.

విజ్ఞప్తి, విజ్ఞాపన[ం] **wijñapti, wijñaapana[m]** *n.* 1 petition, representation, appeal. 2 prayer, request.

విజ్ఞానం **wijñaanam** *n.* 1 knowledge, learning. 2 wisdom. 3 science.

విజ్ఞానసర్వస్వం **wijñaanasarwaswam** *n.* encyclopedia.

విజ్ఞానశాస్త్రం **wijñaanasaastram** *n.* science.

విజ్ఞాపన పత్రం **wijñaapana patram** *n.* memorial, statement of facts accompanying a representation.

విజ్ఞుడు **wijñuDu** *n.* **1** scholar. **2** learned person. **3** experienced person.

విటుడు, విటకాడు **wiTuDu, wiTakaaDu** *n.* paramour.

విడంబం **wiDambam** *n.* **1** imitation. **2** delay.

విడగొట్టు **wiDagoTTu** *v.t.* to separate, detach.

విడదీయు **wiDadiiyu** *v.t.* **1** to separate. **2** to sort out, disentangle, undo, unravel: **cikkupaDDa daaram~** to unravel a tangled thread.

విడనాడు **wiDanaaDu** *v.t.* **1** to desert. **2** to give up, abandon, relinquish.

విడమరచు **wiDamaracu** *v.t.* (*also* **wiDamaraci ceppu**) to explain clearly, explain in detail, explain point by point.

విడాకులు **wiDaakulu** *n. pl.* divorce: **bhaaryaku~iccu** to divorce o.'s wife.

విడి **wiDi** *adj.* **1** separate, distinct, isolated: **~maniSi** person living on his own without encumbrances: **waaLLaku kharceemundi? ~manuSulu, moguDuupeLLaamee** what expenses do they have? they live by themselves, just husband and wife. **2** loose, spare: **~Dabbulu** loose cash, small change: **~bhaagaalu** spare parts. **3** single: **nelasari candaa padi ruupaayalu, ~patrika artharuupaayi** monthly subscription ten rupees, single copy fifty paise.

విడిగా **wiDigaa** *adv.* **1** separately, severally, singly. **2** loosely.

విడిచి **wiDici** *past participle of* **wiDucu** *used adverbially* **1** *lit.* having left. **2 uuru~uuru tirigEEDu** he moved from village to village. **3 dinam~dinam ikkaDiki wastaaDu** he comes here on alternate days *or* he comes here every other day.

విడిచిపెట్టు **wiDicipeTTu** *v.t.* **1** to relinquish, quit, abandon, desert, give up, omit. **2** to let go, leave off, leave behind. **3** to close (school, office).

విడిది **wiDidi** *n.* **1** lodging, lodging house. **2** temporary accommodation: **adi mogapeLLiwaari~** that is the bridegroom's party's temporary accommodation.

విడిపించు **wiDipincu** *v.t.* **1** to set free, set loose, let go, extricate, release (from custody, mortgage). **2** to separate (quarrelling persons). **3** to pick (cotton, groundnuts).

విడిపించుకొను **wiDipincukonu** *v.i.* to free o.s., get free, break loose.

విడిపోవు **wiDipoowu** *v.i.* **1** to separate, part: **aayanatoo konnaaLLu paniceesi taruwaata wiDipooyEEru** having worked with him for some time, later on they parted from him. **2** to cease, be resolved: **pratiSTambhana wiDipooyindi** the deadlock was resolved. **3** to secede.

విడియ[ం] **wiDiya[m]** *same as* **wiDem.**

విడివడు, విడువడు **wiDiwaDu, wiDuwaDu** *v.i.* **1** to part, come apart, separate: **annadammulu wiDiwaDDaaru** the brothers separated from each other. **2** to get separated, stray (from a flock, herd or group). **3** to get free, break loose, escape.

విడు **wiDu** I. *v.i.* **1** to separate, part, be separated, be parted. **2** to be loosened, be untied. **3** (of a door, lock) to be opened. **4** (of a flower) to open, bloom. **5** to be scattered, be dispersed: **mabbu wiDindi** the cloud dispersed. II. *v.t.* **1** to separate, part. **2** to leave, abandon, give up: **doowa~** to give way, make way. **3** to loosen, undo, untie. **4** to let go, release.

విడుచు **wiDucu** I. *v.i.* to stop, end, pass off, cease: **waana/cali wiDicindi** the rain/the cold has passed off: **grahaNam wiDicindi** the eclipse is over. II. *v.t.* **1** to leave [behind], relinquish, quit, abandon. **2** to loosen, slacken, untie, undo. **3** to omit, leave out. **4** to release, let go, leave: **uupiri~** to breathe out: **niTTuurpu~** to heave a sigh: **aayana paTTu wiDawaDu** *lit.* he will not let go his hold, i.e., he is very stubborn: **praaNaaLu~** to leave o.'s life, die. **5 niiLLu~** to make an offering of water to deceased ancestors. **6 baTTalu/ceppulu~** to take off o.'s clothes/shoes. **7 kaTTiwiDicina baTTalu** cast off (or discarded) clothes. **8** (of trees, plants) to produce, put forth (branches, sprouts, shoots).

విడుత **wiDuta** *n.* time, occasion: **reNDu~lu annam peTTukonnaaDu** he helped himself to rice twice.

విడుదల **wiDudala** *n.* release, freeing, liberation.

విడుదల చేయు **wiDudala ceeyu** *v.t.* to release, free.

విడుదలవు **wiDudalawu** *v.i.* to be freed, be released.

విడుపు **wiDupu** *n.* **1** leaving, quitting. **2** loosening. **3** release: **paTTuu wiDupuu uNDakkaraleedaa?** ought there not to be give and take? (*lit.* ought there not to be holding and releasing?): **grahaNam~** passing off of an eclipse: *see* **aaTa~**. **4 poDupukatha~** solution of a riddle. **5** almsgiving, charity.

విడువడు **wiDuwaDu** *same as* **wiDiwaDu.**

విడువమి **wiDuwami** *n.* persistence.

విడెం **wiDem** *n.* (*also* **wiDiya[m], wiiDiyam, wiiDem**) betel and nut.

విడ్డూరం **wiDDuuram** I. *n.* **1** wonder, marvel, strange event. **2** supernatural occurrence, miracle. II. *adj.* peculiar, strange, remarkable, curious, astonishing, fantastic.

విడ్డూరంగా **wiDDuurangaa** *adv.* in astonishment, in amazement: **uurantaa ~ceppukonnaaru** the whole town talked about it in astonishment.

వితండం, వితండవాదం **witaNDam, witaNDawaadam** *n.* frivolous or fallacious argument, sophistry.

వితంతువు **witantuwu** *n.* widow.

వితరణ **witaraNa** *n.* liberality, munificence.

వితర్కం **witarkam** *n.* **1** reasoning. **2** argument, discussion. **3** doubt.

వితర్కించు **witarkincu** *v.i.* **1** to reflect, ponder. **2** to hesitate.

వితానం **witaanam** *n. class.* **1** canopy, awning. **2** collection, group.

విత్త **witta** *adj.* financial.

విత్తం **wittam** *n.* **1** money, wealth. **2** finance.

విత్తనం **wittanam** *n.* seed.

విత్తనపు కోడె **wittanapu kooDe** *n.* breeding bull.

విత్తు **wittu** I. *n.* seed. II. *v.t.* to sow.

విదగ్ధ **widagdha** *adj.* burnt up.

విదరం **widaram** *n.* fissure.

విదల్చు **widalcu** *same as* **widilincu.**

విదళనం **widaLanam** *n.* breaking, rending, splitting, cleaving.

విదారక **widaaraka** *adj.* splitting, tearing, rending, cleaving: **hṛdaya~dṛśyam** heart-rending sight.

విదారణం **widaaraNam** *n. bot.* dehiscence, bursting (of a seed pod).

విదాహం **widaaham** *n.* excessive thirst.

విదిక్కు, విదిశ **widikku, widiśa** *n.* intermediate point of the compass between cardinal points.

విదిత **widita** *adj.* **1** known, understood. **2** plain, clear, evident.

విదియ **widiya** *n.* second day of a lunar fortnight.

విదిలించు, విదల్చు, విదుల్చు **widilincu, widalcu, widulcu** *v.t.* **1** to shake off, brush off, get rid of. **2** to shake loose. **3** to repulse, reject angrily. **4** to brandish, flourish (whip). **5** to flap (wings).

విదిలించుకొను **widilincukonu** *v.t.* **1** to free, loosen, disengage (e.g., o.'s hands). **2** to shake off, get rid of, free o.s. from. **3** to shake o.s. (in order to remove dust, water).

విదిలింపు **widilimpu** *n.* spurning, rejection.

విదుపు **widupu** *v.t.* to shake, sprinkle, spatter; **kalam~** to shake a pen (in order to make it write); **siraa~** to spatter ink.

విదుపుకొను **widupukonu** *v.i.* to shake off (dust, water) from o.'s body.

విదురుడు, విధురుడు **widuruDu[1], widhuruDu** *n.* widower.

విదురుడు **widuruDu[2]** *n.* name of the brother of king Pandu in the Mahabharata renowned for his discourse on moral principles.

విదులు **widulu** *v.i. and t. dial. variant of* **wadalu.**

విదుల్చు **widulcu** *same as* **widilincu.**

విదుషి, విదుషీమణి **widuSi, widuSiimaNi** *n.* learned woman.

విదూషకుడు **widuuSakuDu** *n.* jester, clown.

విదేశం **wideeśam** *n.* foreign country.

విదేశాంగ **wideeśaanga** *adj. polit.* relating to foreign affairs; **~mantri** Foreign Affairs Minister; **~widhaanam** foreign policy.

విదేశీ **wideeśii** *adj.* foreign; **~maaraka drawyam** *econ.* foreign exchange.

విదేశీయుడు **wideeśiiyuDu** *n.* foreigner.

విద్య **widya** *n.* **1** knowledge, learning. **2** education. **3** art, skill; **naaTyam neercukonnaawu kadaa ippuDu nii~cuupincu** you have studied dancing, now demonstrate your skill. **4** conjuring, juggling.

విద్యాధరులు **widyaadharulu** *n.pl.class.* name of a class of demigods.

విద్యాధికుడు **widyaadhikuDu** *n.* **1** educated person; **aangla~** English-educated person. **2** *pl.* **widyaadhikulu** intellectuals, intelligentsia.

విద్యాపీఠం **widyaapiiTham** *n.* seat of traditional Indian learning.

విద్యాప్రణాళిక **widyaapraNaaLika** *n.* plan for education.

విద్యాభ్యాసం **widyaabhyaasam** *n.* education; **~ceeyu** to get or acquire education.

విద్యార్థి **widyaarthi** *n.* student (man or woman).

విద్యార్థిని **widyaarthini** *n.* woman student.

విద్యాలయం **widyaalayam** *n.* school, place of education.

విద్యావంతుడు **widyaawantuDu** *n.* educated person.

విద్యావతి **widyaawati** *n.* educated woman.

విద్యావిధానం **widyaawidhaanam** *n.* **1** educational system. **2** educational policy.

విద్యావేత్త **widyaaweetta** *n.* educationist.

విద్యావ్యాప్తి **widyaawyaapti** *n.* spread of education.

విద్యాసంబంధ **widyaasambandha** *adj.* relating to education, academic.

విద్యా సంవత్సరం **widyaasamwatsaram** *n.* academic year.

విద్యుక్త, విధ్యుక్త **widyukta, widhyukta** *adj.* ordained.

విద్యుక్తం, విధ్యుక్తం **widyuktam, widhyuktam** *n.* obligation.

విద్యుక్త ధర్మం **widyukta dharmam** *n.* **1** bounden duty. **2** duty prescribed by social conventions, courtesy.

విద్యుచ్ఛక్తి **widyucchakti** *n.* electricity.

విద్యుత్తు **widyuttu** *n.* **1** electricity. **2** flash of lightning.

విద్యుదయస్కాంతం **widyudayaskaantam** *n.* electromagnet.

విద్యుదీకరణ **widyudiikaraNa** *n.* electrification.

విద్యుదోత్పాదన కేంద్రం **widyudootpaadana keendram** *n.* electric generating station.

విద్యుద్ఘాతం, విద్యుదాఘాతం **widyudghaatam, widyudaaghaatam** *n.* electric shock.

విద్యుద్దీపం **widyuddiipam** *n.* electric light.

విద్యుల్లత **widyullata** *n.* streak of lightning.

విద్యోతన **widyootana** *adj.* illuminating, throwing light on, elucidating.

విద్రోహం **widrooham** *n.* treachery, subversion.

విద్రోహకర **widroohakara** *adj.* treacherous, traitorous, subversive.

విద్రోహి **widroohi** *n.* traitor.

విద్వజ్జనం **widwajjanam** *n.pl.* wise persons, sages.

విద్వత్తు **widwatta** *n.* learning, knowledge, scholarship.

విద్వాంసుడు **widwaamsuDu** *n.* learned person, scholar.

విద్వేషం **widweeSam** *n.* hatred, abhorrence, enmity.

విద్వేషి **widweeSi** *n.* enemy, foe.

విద్వేషించు **widweeSincu** *v.t.* to hate, abhor.

విధ **widha** *adjvl. suffix meaning* kind, e.g., **dwi~** of two kinds; **naanaa~patrapuSpaalatoo puujincu** to perform worship with many kinds of (*or* with an assortment of) leaves and flowers.

విధం **widham** *n.* **1** kind, sort, type, form, category. **2** way, manner, method, means; **anni widhaalaa** by every means, in all respects; **appu ee widhaana tiirustaawu?** how will you discharge the debt?

విధంగా **widhangaa** *adv.* **1** in the manner of, like: **ii~** in this way, thus. **2** in order to, as a means to, with a view to: **bhuumula utpaadakatanu pencaDaaniki tooDpaDee~ baawulanu amarcukoNTaaru** they will provide wells in order to assist in increasing the productivity of land.

విధవ **widhawa** *n.* widow: *cf.* **wedhawa.**

విధవతనం **widhawatanam** *n.* widowhood.

విధాత, విధాతృడు **widhaata, widhaatrDu** *n. class.* God the Creator.

విధానం **widhaanam** *n.* **1** manner, mode, method, means. **2** policy. **3** process. **4** system: **widyaa~** educational system: **jiiwana~** way of life.

విధాన పరిషత్, విధాన మండలి **widhaana pariSat, widhaana maNDali** *n.* **1** Legislative Council. **2** Legislature.

విధాన సభ **widhaana sabha** *n.* Legislative Assembly.

విధాయకం **widhaayakam** I. *n.* s.g obligatory: **maa iNTLoo idi~** in our family this is obligatory *or* this is the rule in our family. II. *adj.* obligatory, ordained, enjoined.

విధి **widhi** *n.* **1** rule. **2** order, command: **~niSeedhaalu** commands and prohibitions, do's and don'ts. **3** duty: **widhulu baadhyatalu** duties and responsibilities. **4** fate, destiny, providence.

విధించు **widhincu** *v.t.* **1** to order, command, ordain. **2** to impose, inflict. **3** to assign, allot. **4** to levy (tax). **5** to lay down, prescribe (conditions).

విధింపు **widhimpu** *n.* **1** ordering, commanding. **2** imposition, infliction, prescription.

విధిగా **widhigaa** *adv.* of necessity, necessarily, perforce, compulsorily, without fail: *see* **yathaa~.**

విధిలిఖిత **widhilikhita** *adj.* ordained by fate, preordained, fated.

విధిలేక **widhileeka** *adv.* there being no alternative, having no alternative.

విధివిధానం **widhi widhaanam** *n.* **1** providence. **2** regular practice.

విధి విపాకం **widhi wipaakam** *n.* merit earned or retribution suffered by an individual in consequence of an act committed earlier in his present life or in a previous birth.

విధివిరామం లేకుండా **widhiwiraamam leekuNDaa** *advbl. phrase* continuously, without resting, without a break.

విధురుడు **widhuruDu** *same as* **widuruDu**[1].

విధేయం **widheeyam** I. *n. gram.* predicate. II. *adj.* obedient.

విధేయంగా **widheeyangaa** *adv.* in accordance with, in consonance with: **telugu lipi meeraku saadhyamaynanta waraku padaalanu ucchaaraNa~ nee sangraahakulu raasEEru** as far as is possible within the bounds of Telugu script the compilers have written down the words in accordance with their pronunciation.

విధేయత **widheeyata** *n.* obedience.

విధ్యర్థం **widhyartham** *n. gram.* imperative mood.

విధ్యుక్త[ం] **widhyukta[m]** *same as* **widyukta[m].**

విధ్వంసం, విధ్వంసన **widhwamsam, widhwamsana** *n.* ruin, destruction.

విధ్వంసం అవు **widhwamsam awu** *v.i.* to be destroyed.

విధ్వంసక[ర] **widhwamsaka[ra]** *adj.* destructive.

విధ్వంసకాండ **widhwamsakaaNDa** *n.* carnage.

వినతి **winati** *n.* **1** appeal, entreaty, humble request. **2** bowing, salutation.

వినతిపత్రం **winatipatram** *n.* written appeal or representation.

వినతుడు **winatuDu** *n.* modest, unassuming person.

వినబడు **winabaDu** *v.i.* to be heard, be audible.

వినమ్ర **winamra** *adj.* modest, humble.

వినమ్రత **winamrata** *n.* modesty, humility.

వినమ్రుడు **winamruDu** *n.* humble or modest person.

వినయం **winayam** *n.* **1** humility, modesty, deference. **2** good behaviour, decorum: **winayawidheeyatalugala** well-behaved, decorous.

వినవచ్చు **winawaccu** *v.i.* to be heard, come to the ears (of s.o.): **maaTimaaTikii reyilubaLLu parigettina cappuDu winawastunnadi** again and again the sound of passing trains reaches his ears.

వినా **winaa** *adv.* apart from, except for, but for: **okaTi reNDu sampuTaalu~ migataawannii naSTamay pooyinaTTee ani iimadhya winnaanu** I heard recently that except for one or two issues, all the rest appear to have been destroyed.

వినాయకుడు **winaayakuDu** *n.* a name of the God Ganesha.

వినాయించు **winaayincu** *v.t.* to except, exempt.

వినాయింపు **winaayimpu** *n.* exception, exclusion, exemption.

వినాశ[న]ం **winaaśa[na]m** *n.* ruin, destruction.

వినాశక **winaaśaka** *adj.* destructive.

వినికిడి **winikiDi** *n.* **1** hearing: **~duuramloo** within hearing, within earshot: **iNTLoo alikiDi leedu~ leedu** not a sound could be heard in the house. **2** hearsay, rumour.

వినిపించు **winipincu** I. *v.i.* **1** to be heard: **cinna śabdam winipincindi** a slight sound was heard. **2** to sound (like s.g) **aa gontu maa tammuDilaagaa winipistuunnadi** that voice sounds like my younger brother's. II. *v.t.* **1** to cause to hear, cause to be heard: **oo paaTa winipincaNDi** please sing us a song: **haydaraabaadu aakaaśawaaNi rikaarDulu winipincindi** Hyderabad radio played records. **2 cadiwi~** to read out, read aloud.

వినిపించుకొను **winipincukonu** *v.i. and t.* **1** *in affirmative and neg. senses* to listen [to], hear. **2** *in neg. sense only* to pay heed [to], pay attention [to]: **waaDu naa salahaa winipincukooleedu** he paid no heed to my advice.

వినిమయం **winimayam** *n.* **1** consumption, use. **2** exchange, interchange: **bhaawa~** exchange of ideas: **paraspara winimaya warNaalu** mutually interchangeable sounds.

వినిమయదారు **winimayadaaru** *n.* consumer.

వినియమాలు **winiyamaalu** *n.pl.* regulations.

వినియుక్త **winiyukta** *adj.* used, utilised, employed.

వినియోగం **winiyoogam** *n.* **1** use, utilisation, consumption. **2** allocation, distribution: **prasaadaala~** distribution of **prasaadam** to worshippers at a temple.

వినియోగం అవు **winiyoogam awu** *v.i.* **1** to be used. **2** to be allotted, be devoted, be allocated, be distributed.

వినియోగదారుడు, వినియోక్త **winiyoogadaaruDu, winiyookta** *n.* consumer.

వినియోగ పరచు, వినియోగం చేయు **winiyoogaparacu, winiyoogam ceeyu** *v.t.* to make use of, utilise.

వినియోగించు **winiyoogincu** *v.t.* to use, make use of, utilise.

వినిర్మల **winirmala** *adj.* very bright, very clear.

వినీల **winiila** *adj.* **1** jet black. **2** deep blue, dark blue.

విను **winu**[1] *n. class.* sky.

విను **winu**[2] *v.i. and t.* **1** to hear, listen[to]. **2** to pay attention [to], heed, obey; **naa maaTa winaru** they will not heed what I say *or* they will not obey me.

వినుతి **winuti** *n.* great praise, commendation.

వినుతించు **winutincu** *v.t.* to praise, commend.

వినూత్న **winuutna** *adj.* new, novel, modern, up-to-date.

వినోదం **winoodam** *n.* amusement, recreation, entertainment, pleasure, enjoyment.

వినోదక్రీడ **winoodakriiDa** *n.* pastime.

వినోదపరచు, వినోదపెట్టు **winoodaparacu, winoodapeTTu** *v.t.* to please, amuse, divert.

వినోదపు పన్ను **winoodapu pannu** *n.* entertainment tax.

వినోది **winoodi** *n.* **1** amusing or entertaining person. **2** easy going person. **3** person who lives for pleasure.

వినోదించు **winoodincu** *v.i.* to enjoy o.s., amuse o.s.

విన్నతనం **winnatanam** *n.* dejection, sorrow.

విన్నపం **winnapam** *n.* petition, request, submission, representation.

విన్నపోవు **winnapoowu** *v.i.* to be dejected, be sorrowful.

విన్నవించు **winnawincu** *v.t.* to represent, submit, tell or say s.g respectfully or politely.

విన్ను **winnu** *n. class.* sky.

విన్యాసం **winyaasam** *n.* **1** arrangement, configuration. **2** pose, posture, gesture (in dancing), feat (in acrobatics). **3** demonstration, display, performance; **kaLaa**~ artistic performance. **4** **seenaa**~ military manoeuvre; **saynika winyaasootsawam** ceremonial military parade. **5** (*in literature*) picture, display; **atani apasmaara manassulooni swapna**~**cuuddaam raNDi** let us watch the picture that arises in his subconscious mind while he sleeps. **6** **racanaa**~ style in writing, literary craftsmanship.

విపంచి[క] **wipanci[ka]** *n.* lute.

విపక్షం **wipakSam** *n.* **1** exception to a rule. **2** instance cited on the opposite side in an argument.

విపణి, విఫణి **wip[h]aNi** *n.* shop, market place.

విపత్కర **wipatkara** *adj.* dangerous, perilous.

విపత్తు **wipattu** *n.* **1** calamity, disaster. **2** misfortune.

విపథం **wipatham** *n.* deviation.

విపన్నుడు **wipannuDu** *n.* distressed or afflicted or unfortunate person.

విపరిణామం **wipariNaamam** *n.* deterioration, change for the worse, turn for the worse.

విపరీత **wipariita** *adj.* **1** unusual, unnatural, abnormal, exceptional, peculiar, incongruous. **2** contrary, opposite. **3** extreme, excessive. **4** abundant.

విపరీతంగా **wipariitangaa** *adv.* **1** greatly, exceedingly, extremely, abundantly: **aayanaku**~**koopam waccindi** he was extremely angry; ~**waana kurisindi** rain fell very heavily. **2** excessively. **3** abnormally, incongruously; ~**maaTLaaDutunnaaDu** he is talking excessively *or* he is talking in a strange (*or* unexpected) manner.

విపరీతవాది **wipariitawaadi** *n.* extremist.

విపర్యయం **wiparyayam** *n.* **1** difference, change, reversal. **2** misfortune. **3** contrariness; **widhi**~ perverseness of (s.o.'s) fate. **4** *maths.* converse.

విపర్యయంగా, విపర్యయంలో **wiparyayangaa, wiparyayamloo** *adv.* conversely, vice versa.

విపర్యస్త **wiparyasta** *adj.* **1** opposite, contrary, converse. **2** unfavourable, adverse. **3** wrongly considered to be real.

విపర్యాసం **wiparyaasam** *n.* inversion.

విపాకం **wipaakam** *n. class.* **1** spoilt cooking. **2** thorough cooking. **3** maturing: ~ *occurs mod. only as a bound form in* **widhi**~.

విపినం **wipinam** *n. class.* forest.

విపుల **wipula** *adj.* extensive, copious, big, large, lengthy, broad, capacious.

విపులంగా **wipulangaa** *adv.* **1** widely, extensively. **2** in detail, thoroughly; ~**carcincEEDu** he discussed it in detail.

విపులీకరించు **wipuliikarincu** *v.t.* **1** to explain, expound, elucidate, clarify. **2** to elaborate, enlarge on, expatiate on, dilate on.

విప్పసారా **wippasaaraa** *n. colloq.* arrack made from mohwa flowers (= **ippa saaraa[yi]**).

విప్పారు **wippaaru** *v.i.* **1** to open, expand; **wippaarina kaLLatoo** with wide open eyes; **wippaarani puwwu** flower not yet opened. **2** **waaDi mukham wippaarindi** he smiled broadly *or* he beamed with joy.

విప్పించు **wippincu** *v.t.* to dismantle, take to pieces; **illu**~ to remove the roof of a tiled or thatched house in order to rebuild.

విప్పు **wippu** *v.t.* **1** to open, untie, loosen, undo, unroll, unwind; **muDi**~ to untie a knot; **juTTu**~**konu** to let down o.'s hair; **rekkalu** ~ **konu** to spread o.'s wings. **2** to take off (clothes). **3** **wippi ceppu** to explain, expound; **adantaa wippi ceppaDaaniki ippuDu wyawadhi leedu** there is no time to explain all that now.

విప్రతిపత్తి **wipratipatti** *n.* **1** enmity. **2** disbelief. **3** discrepancy, conflict of interest.

విప్రయోగం **wiprayoogam** *n.* separation, esp. of lovers.

విప్రలంభం **wipralambham** *n.* **1** deceiving by a false affirmation or by not keeping a promise. **2** separation of lovers.

విప్రలబ్ధ **wipralabdha** *n.* woman disappointed by a lover who fails to keep his appointment.

విప్రవినోదులు **wiprawinoodulu** *n.pl.* class of jugglers or conjurers.

విప్రుడు **wipruDu** *n.* brahman.

విప్లవం **wiplawam** *n.* revolution.

విప్లవకారుడు, విప్లవవాది **wiplawakaaruDu, wiplawawaadi** *n.* revolutionary.

విప్లవాత్మక **wiplawaatmaka** *adj.* revolutionary.

విప్లవించు **wiplawincu** *v.i.* to rebel, mutiny, revolt.

విఫణి **wiphaNi** *same as* **wipaNi.**

విఫల **wiphala** *adj.* fruitless, vain, ineffective.

విఫలం అవు **wiphalam awu** *v.i.* to fail, be unsuccessful.

విఫలత, విఫలత్వం **wiphalata, wiphalatwam** *n.* 1 failure. 2 uselessness.

విబూది, వీబూది, విభూతి **wi[i]buudi, wibhuuti** *n.* sacred ashes made from cowdung used by Saivites to make white markings on the forehead.

విభక్త **wibhakta** *adj.* divided, partitioned.

విభక్తి **wibhakti** *n. gram.* 1 case. 2 **kriyaa~** inflection of a verb.

విభజన **wibhajana** *n.* 1 separation, partition, severance. 2 splitting, division into sections. 3 classification.

విభజనగా **wibhajanagaa** *adv.* in detail; **antaa ~ raasEEDu** he wrote down everything item after item.

విభజించు **wibhajincu** *v.t.* 1 to separate, divide, split. 2 to distinguish. 3 to classify.

విభవ **wibhawa** *n.* second year of the Hindu cycle of sixty years.

విభవం **wibhawam** *n. class.* wealth, riches.

విభాకరుడు **wibhaakaruDu** *n. class.* sun.

విభాగం **wibhaagam** *n.* 1 part, portion, division, section. 2 class, category. 3 department. 4 partition, dividing, division: **kuTumba~** family partition; **pada~** division of a word into constituent parts.

విభాగించు **wibhaagincu** *v.t.* 1 to share out. 2 to divide.

విభాజక **wibhaajaka** *adj.* separating, dividing, divisive.

విభాజకం **wibhaajakam** *n. maths.* divisor.

విభాజిత **wibhaajita** *adj.* divided.

విభాజ్య **wibhaajya** *adj.* divisible.

విభాత **wibhaata** *adj. class.* bright, shining.

విభాతం **wibhaatam** *n. class.* dawn.

విభావనం **wibhaawanam** *n.* 1 clear perception. 2 name of a figure of speech.

విభావరి **wibhaawari** *n.* night; **sangiita~** a night of musical entertainment.

విభావసుడు **wibhaawasuDu** *n. class.* 1 sun. 2 fire.

విభాసించు **wibhaasincu** *v.i.* to shine.

విభిన్న **wibhinna** *adj.* 1 different, differing. 2 various, diverse.

విభీషణం **wibhiiSaNam** *n.* changing sides in a dispute or a war, treachery.

విభీషణుడు **wibhiiSaNuDu** *n.* name of the brother of Ravana, who committed treachery by going over to Rama's side in the war between Rama and Ravana in the Ramayana.

విభుడు **wibhuDu** *n. class.* 1 lord, master. 2 husband.

విభూతి **wibhuuti**[1] *same as* **wibuudi.**

విభూతి **wibhuuti**[2] *n. class.* wealth, riches.

విభూషణం **wibhuuSaNam** *n.* ornament, decoration.

విభేదం **wibheedam** *n.* 1 distinction, difference. 2 separation. 3 disagreement, difference of opinion, cleavage, rift, schism. 4 *biol.* new strain, variation.

విభేదనం **wibheedanam** *n.* differentiation.

విభేదపడు **wibheedapaDu** *v.i.* to fall out with, have differences with: **naatoo wibheedapaDDaaru** they had differences with me.

విభేదించు **wibheedincu** *v.i.* to differ.

విభ్రంశం **wibhramśam** *n.* decay, decline.

విభ్రమం **wibhramam** *n.* 1 roaming, wandering. 2 whirling, turning. 3 confusion, bewilderment, agitation: **~ gaa cuusEEDu** he looked in a bewildered manner. 4 beauty, grace. 5 amorous feelings; **wibhrama wilaasaalu** sensual delights.

విభ్రాంతి **wibhraanti** *n.* 1 shock, confusion, puzzlement, perplexity, bewilderment. 2 error.

విభ్రాంతికర **wibhraantikara** *adj.* shocking, confusing, bewildering, perplexing.

విభ్రాంతుడు **wibhraantuDu** *n.* shocked or dazed or confused or nonplussed person.

విమందనం **wimandanam** *n. phys. chem.* retarding, retardation.

విమతుడు **wimatuDu** *n.* dissenter.

విమనస్కుడు **wimanaskuDu** *n.* disconsolate or distressed person

విమర్శ[ం], విమర్శన[ం] **wimarśa[m], wimarśana[m]** *n.* 1 criticism: **saahitya~** literary criticism. 2 review; **grantha~** book review.

విమర్శక **wimarśaka** *adj.* critical.

విమర్శకుడు **wimarśakuDu** *n.* 1 critic. 2 reviewer.

విమర్శించు **wimarśincu** *v.t.* to criticise.

విమల **wimala** *adj.* pure, clear, stainless, spotless.

విమానం **wimaanam** *n.* 1 aeroplane, aircraft. 2 small **goopuram** over the innermost part of a temple. 3 *class.* palace with seven or more stories.

విమానవాహకం **wimaanawaahakam** *n.* aircraft carrier.

విమానశాస్త్రం **wimaanaśaastram** *n.* (science of) aeronautics.

విమానాశ్రయం **wimaanaaśrayam** *n.* airport, aerodrome, airfield.

విముక్త **wimukta** *adj.* liberated, freed, released.

విముక్త జాతి **wimukta jaati** *n.* name given to a community formerly designated as a criminal tribe.

విముక్తి **wimukti** *n.* 1 release, liberation, deliverance, redemption. 2 relief; **rNa~** debt relief. 3 *legal* acquittal.

విముక్తుడు **wimuktuDu** *n.* 1 liberated or released person. 2 *legal* acquitted person.

విముఖ **wimukha** *adj.* 1 indifferent, neglectful. 2 averse.

విముఖత, విముఖత్వం **wimukhata, wimukhatwam** *n.* 1 indifference, lack of interest, lack of concern. 2 dislike, disfavour, antagonism, aversion.

విముఖుడు **wimukhuDu** *n.* one who is opposed or hostile or antipathetic.

విమూఢుడు **wimuuDhuDu** *see* **kimkartawyam.**

విమోచనం **wimoocanam** *n.* 1 release, liberation, deliverance, redemption, emancipation. 2 relief (from pain). 3 **paapa~** absolution from sin.

విమోహం **wimooham** *n.* strong passion, ardent love.

విమోహించు **wimoohincu** *v.i.* to love ardently.

విమోహితుడు **wimoohituDu** *n.* person who is ardently in love.

వియచ్చరుడు **wiyaccaruDu** *n. class.* god, deity, demigod.

వియత్తలం **wiyattalam** *n. class.* sky, heavens.

వియుక్త **wiyukta** *adj.* separated, disunited.

వియోగం **wiyoogam** *n.* **1** detachment, parting, separation. **2** *sci.* decomposition. **3** *literary* separation of lovers. **4** loss caused by death; **pitr**~ loss of o.'s father.

వియోజనం **wiyoojanam** *n. sci.* separation, resolution.

వియ్యం **wiyyam** *n.* relationship existing between the parents of a married couple (i.e., between the husband's parents and the wife's parents); ~ **andu** to contract such a relationship (i.e., to intermarry); **sagootriikulu ~ andakuuDadu** people who belong to the same clan should not intermarry; **ewaritoo ~ andaaloo teliyaDam leedu** I do not know whom I should decide to have as my son's/daughter's parents-in-law (i.e., I do not know to whom I should marry my son/daughter); **kayyaanikaynaa wiyyaanikaynaa sama ujjii kaawaali** in fighting and matchmaking there must be equality between parties (proverb).

వియ్యంకుడు **wiyyankuDu** *n.* father-in-law of o.'s son or daughter.

వియ్యంకురాలు, వియ్యపురాలు **wiyyankuraalu, wiyyapuraalu** *n.* mother-in-law of o.'s son or daughter.

విరంజనం **wiranjanam** *n.* bleaching.

విరక్తి **wirakti** *n.* **1** aversion, dislike. **2** lack of affection. **3** detachment, indifference to worldly life.

విరక్తుడు **wiraktuDu** *n.* one who is free from passion and indifferent to worldly life.

విరగకాయు **wiragakaayu** *v.i.* (of plants, trees) to bear fruit profusely, yield a heavy crop.

విరగడ **wiragaDa** *n.* **1** release, liberation. **2** relief; ~ **awu** (of pain, affliction) to pass off, be at an end, be removed; **waaDiki śani ~ ayindi** the unlucky period of his life is over; **maaku waaDi piiDa ~ ayindi** we are rid of the nuisance caused by him.

విరగపూయు **wiragapuuyu** *v.i.* (of plants, trees) to flower profusely.

విరగబడు **wiragabaDu** *v.i.* **1** to collect in a crowd; **janam wiragabaDDaaru, cooTu caalaleedu** people came in crowds, there was not enough room. **2** to be crowded, be thronged; **darbaaru antaa wiragabaDi pooyindi** the entire court hall was thronged with people. **3** *colloq.* to be proud, be presumptuous. **4 wiragabaDi nawwu** to burst out laughing, laugh heartily.

విరగబాటు **wiragabaaTu** *n.* pride, arrogance, presumption.

విరచించు **wiracincu** *v.t.* to compose, write.

విరజిమ్ము **wirajimmu** *v.i. and t.* **1** to spread, scatter, sprinkle, spurt. **2** to spend extravagantly, squander (wealth).

విరజిల్లు, విరాజిల్లు **wira[a]jillu** *v.i.* **1** to shine. **2** to flourish.

విరతి **wirati** *n.* **1** break, pause, interval. **2** pause in a line

విరథుడు **wirathuDu** *n. class.* warrior who has been thrown from his chariot.

విరపూచు **wirapuucu** *v.i.* to bloom, blossom.

విరపోయు **wirapooyu** *v.t.* to scatter, sprinkle.

విరపోసుకొను, విరియపోసుకొను **wirapoosukonu, wiriyapoosukonu** *v.t.* to allow (o.'s hair) to hang loose or be dishevelled; **juTTu** (*or* **tala**) **wirapoosukoni tirugu** to wander about with o.'s hair dishevelled.

విరమణ **wiramaNa** *n.* **1** relinquishing. **2 udyoga ~ [m]** retirement from employment.

విరమించు[కొను] **wiramincu[konu]** I. *v.i.* **1** to cease, stop, desist. **2** to withdraw, retire. II. *v.t.* **1** to give up, discontinue, abandon. **2** to put an end to. **3** to withdraw (proposal, resolution).

విరమింప చేయు **wiramimpa ceeyu** *v.t.* to dissuade, deter.

విరళ[ం] **wiraLa[m]** *adj.* **1** rare. **2** separated by an interval; *cf.* **awiraLa.**

విరసం **wirasam** *n.* **1** illwill, disagreement, unpleasantness. **2** lack of aesthetic taste.

విరహం **wiraham** *n.* **1** separation of lovers. **2** lovers' grief at being separated.

విరహతాపం **wirahataapam** *n.* lovesickness.

విరహాగ్ని, విరహానలం **wirahaagni, wirahaanalam** *n.* lovers' feeling of anguish at being separated.

విరహిణి **wirahiNi** *n.* woman separated from her lover, lovesick woman.

విరాగం, వైరాగ్యం **wiraagam, wayraagyam** *n.* detachment, renunciation of worldly desires, asceticism, stoicism.

విరాగి, వైరాగి **wiraagi, wayraagi** *n.* one who is free from passion, one who has suppressed worldly desires, stoic, ascetic.

విరాజమానం **wiraajamaanam** *adj.* very bright, very brilliant, very splendid.

విరాజిత **wiraajita** *adj.* splendid, shining.

విరాజిల్లు **wiraajillu** *same as* **wirajillu.**

విరాట్టు **wiraaTTu** *n.* God, the Supreme Being in his primary manifestation as an entity with a form.

విరాడ్రూపం **wiraaDruupam** *n.* primary form.

విరామం **wiraamam** *n.* **1** rest, respite. **2** interval, intermission.

విరామచిహ్నం **wiraamacihnam** *n.* **1** full stop. **2** punctuation mark.

విరామతీర్మానం **wiraamatiirmaanam** *n. polit.* adjournment motion.

విరాళం **wiraaLam** *n.* contribution, donation.

విరాళి **wiraaLi** *n. class.* state of being fascinated or captivated.

విరి **wiri** *n. class.* flower.

విరించి **wirinci** *n.* epithet of Brahma.

విరిచికట్టు **wiricikaTTu** *v.t.* to pinion; **ceetulu ~** to fasten a person's hands behind his back.

విరిబోడి **wiribooDi** *n. class.* beautiful woman.

విరియపూయు **wiriyapuuyu** *v.i.* to be in full bloom.

విరియపోసుకొను **wiriyapoosukonu** *same as* **wirapoosukonu.**

విరియు **wiriyu** *v.i.* 1 (of a flower) to open, bloom, blossom. 2 to burst or crack open. 3 **waaDi mukhamloo cirunawwulu wirisEEyi** his face was wreathed in smiles (*lit.* smiles bloomed in his face).

విరివి **wiriwi** I. *n.* abundance, extensiveness, extension. II. *adj.* extensive, wide, broad, large.

విరివిగా **wiriwigaa** *adv.* freely, extensively, widely, plentifully, in abundance.

విరుగు **wirugu** *v.i.* 1 to break, snap, be broken: **kaalu wirigindi** the leg was broken: **naDum wirigeelaa pani ceesEEDu** he toiled strenuously (*lit.* he worked in a such a way as to break his back). 2 to curdle: **paalu wirigEEyi** the milk has curdled. 3 (of poison) to be counteracted. 4 **waaDiki manasu wirigindi** he lost heart *or* he became downcast.

విరుగుడు **wiruguDu** *n.* remedy, cure, antidote: ~ **kinda paniceesindi** it acted as a remedy.

విరుచు **wirucu** *v.t.* 1 to break [off], snap [off]: **naa maaTalu madhyaloonee wiriceesEEDu** he interrupted what I was saying. 2 to break to pieces. 3 to twist: **o.-i ceyyi**~ to twist s.o.'s arm. 4 **pedawi**~ to curl o.'s lip in scorn or disapproval. 5 to curdle (milk). 6 to counteract (poison). 7 to separate words from each other: **akkaDakkaDa maaTalu tappugaa wirustuu sundaram uttaram antaa cadiwEEDu** making mistakes in some places over the separation of words, Sundaram read the whole letter.

విరుచుకుపడు **wirucukupaDu** *v.i.* 1 to burst upon, burst out against, make a sudden attack on. 2 to explode in anger (**-pay** *or* **-miida**, against). 3 to fall down in a fit. 4 to collect in crowds, throng, jostle together.

విరుచుకొను **wirucukonu** *v.t.* to stretch, expand: **oLLu**~ to stretch o.'s limbs: **chaatii/rommu**~ to puff out o.'s chest, expand o.'s chest (from pride or self-importance).

విరుద్ధ **wiruddha** *adj.* opposed, opposing, antagonistic, contrary, hostile: **caTTaaniki**~ unlawful: **raajyaanga**~ unconstitutional.

విరుద్ధం **wiruddham** *n.* contrariness, opposition.

విరుద్ధార్థకం **wiruddhaarthakam** *n. ling.* antonym.

విరుపు **wirupu** *n.* 1 break[ing], gap, pause. 2 separation of words from each other. 3 **pedawi/muuti**~ curling of the lip in scorn or disapproval; *see* **kaTTe**~, **pulla**~.

విరూప **wiruupa** *adj.* deformed, truncated.

విరేచనం **wireecanam** *n.* purging, loose motion.

విరేచనకారి **wireecanakaari** *n. and adj.* purgative.

విరోధం **wiroodham** *n.* 1 enmity, hostility. 2 hatred, animosity. 3 obstruction, hindrance. 4 antithesis, contrariness.

విరోధం కట్టు **wiroodham kaTTu** *v.i.* to be on bad terms (**-too**, with).

విరోధాభాస **wiroodhaabhaasa** *n.* paradox.

విరోధి **wiroodhi** *n.* 1 enemy. 2 twenty-third year of the Hindu cycle of sixty years.

విరోధించు **wiroodhincu** *v.i.* to oppose, withstand, be hostile to.

విరోధికృత్తు **wiroodhikrttu** *n.* forty-fifth year of the Hindu cycle of sixty years.

విర్రవీగు **wirrawiigu** *v.i.* to give o.s. airs, be excessively proud and boastful.

విలంబ[ం], విలంబన[ం] **wilamba[m], wilambana[m]** *n.* delay, tardiness.

విలంబశుల్కం **wilambasulkam** *n.* late fee.

విలక్షణ **wilakSaNa** *adj.* 1 different, separate, distinct. 2 distinctive, typical. 3 special, particular, peculiar: **intawaraku ceppina dhwanula maarpulu telugu bhaaSaku**~**maynawi** the sound changes hitherto mentioned are peculiar to the Telugu language. 4 remarkable, outstanding, phenomenal.

విలక్షణం **wilakSaNam** *n.* difference, distinguishing feature, distinction.

విలక్షణంగా **wilakSaNangaa** *adv.* 1 handsomely, properly, excellently. 2 differently, separately.

విలక్షణత **wilakSaNata** *n.* peculiarity, speciality, distinctiveness.

విలపించు **wilapincu** *v.i.* to lament.

విలయం **wilayam** *n.* dissolution, destruction, ruin, annihilation.

విలవిల **wilawila** *onom. adv. sug.* convulsive movement.

విలవిల్లాడు **wilawillaaDu** *v.i.* 1 to be convulsed. 2 to struggle violently or convulsively. 3 to yearn (for s.g) anxiously and impetuously, hanker after.

విలసత్ **wilasat** *adj. first part of a compound meaning* bright, shining.

విలసనం **wilasanam** *n.* brightness, illumination.

విలసిత **wilasita** *adj.* shining, gleaming, full of light.

విలసిల్లు **wilasillu** *v.i.* 1 to shine, gleam. 2 to flourish.

విలాతి, విలాయతి **wilaati, wilaayati** *n.* 1 foreign country. 2 *colloq.* Britain.

విలాపం **wilaapam** *n.* grief, sorrow, lamentation.

విలాసం **wilaasam** *n.* 1 (on letters) address. 2 grace, elegance. 3 game, sport: **widhi**~ game played by fate.

విలాసంగా **wilaasangaa** *adv.* merrily, cheerfully, jovially, gaily.

విలాసపురుషుడు **wilaasapuruSuDu** *n.* playboy.

విలాసవస్తువు **wilaasawastuwu** *n.* plaything.

విలీన **wiliina** *adj.* merged, absorbed, amalgamated.

విలీనం **wiliinam** *n.* merger, merging, amalgamation, absorption.

విలీనం అవు **wilinam awu** *v.i.* to merge, be absorbed, be amalgamated.

విలీనం చేయు **wiliinam ceeyu** *v.t.* to absorb, amalgamate.

విలీన ద్రావణం **wiliina draawaNam** *n. chem.* dilute solution.

విలు, విల్లు **wilu, willu** *n.* bow.

విలుకాడు **wilukaaDu** *n.* bowman, archer.

విలుప్త **wilupta** *adj.* obsolete, vanished, wanting, extinct: **~jaati** extinct species.

విలుప్తం అవు **wiluptam awu** *v.i.* to become obsolete, vanish, disappear.

విలువ **wiluwa** *n.* price, cost, value, worth; *see* **kaTTu** *sense IV. 5.*

విలువ చేయు **wiluwa ceeyu** *v.t.* to cost, be worth.

విలువిద్య **wiluwidya** *n.* archery.

విలువైన **wiluwayna** *adj.* valuable.

విలేకరి **wileekari** *n.* reporter, representative, correspondent (of a newpaper).

విలేపనం **wileepanam** *n.* **1** smearing. **2** ointment.

విలోకనం **wilookanam** *n.* seeing, viewing, observing.

విలోకించు **wilookincu** *v.t.* to see, behold, view.

విలోచనం **wiloocanam** *n. class.* eye.

విలోమ **wilooma** *adj.* **1** against the lie of the hair, against the grain. **2** inverse, reverse; **~niSpatti** inverse ratio; **wiloomaanupaatam** inverse proportion.

విలోమం **wiloomam** *n.* inversion.

విలోమంగా **wiloomangaa** *adv.* inversely, in the opposite way, in reverse, contrariwise.

విలోల **wiloola** *adj.* shaking, moving, agitated.

విల్లంబులు, విల్లమ్ములు **willambulu, willammulu** *n. pl.* bow and arrows.

విల్లు **willu** *same as* **wilu.**

విల్లు వంచు **willu wancu** *v.i.* to draw a bow.

విళంబి **wiLambi** *n.* thirty-second year of the Hindu cycle of sixty years.

వివక్ష **wiwakSa** *n.* **1** intention or meaning of a speaker. **2** distinction, difference.

వివక్షత **wiwakSata** *n.* distinction, discrimination; **strii-puruSa ~leekuNDaa** without making a distinction between men and women.

వివక్షించు **wiwakSincu** *v.i.* to express or convey a distinct meaning: **taratama lakSaNaalu wiwakSincaDamloo kaNTe/kanna waaDukaloo unnaayi 'kaNTe/kanna'** are used to express the comparative and superlative degrees.

వివక్షిత **wiwakSita** *adj.* intended to be spoken; **wiwakSitaartham** intended meaning.

వివరం **wiwaram** *n.* **1** explanation, description. **2** detail. **3** *pl.* **wiwaraalu** details, particulars.

వివరంగా **wiwarangaa** *adv.* with full particulars, in detail.

వివరణ **wiwaraNa** *n.* **1** explanation, description, elucidation, detailed account, specification. **2** caption or legend accompanying an illustration.

వివరణగా **wiwaraNagaa** *adv.* in detail.

వివరణాత్మకంగా **wiwaraNaatmakangaa** *adv.* in detail, descriptively, elaborately, at full length, *in extenso*: **arthanirNayam suutrapraayangaa ceeyaDamaa~ ceeyaDamaa?** should the meaning (of a word in a glossary) be defined in broad terms or in detail?

వివరణపటం **wiwaraNapaTam** *n.* chart.

వివరించు **wiwarincu** *v.t.* to describe, explain, elucidate; **wiwarinci ceppu** to describe or explain or narrate in detail.

వివర్ణం **wiwarNam I.** *n.* (*also* **wiwarNanam**) bleaching. **II.** *adj.* pale, pallid, discoloured, colourless.

వివర్ణుడు **wiwarNuDu** *n.* **1** person who has turned pale. **2** person who has no caste.

వివర్తనం **wiwartanam** *n. sci.* diffraction.

వివశత, వివశత్వం **wiwaśata, wiwaśatwam** *n.* **1** ecstasy, rapture. **2** trance.

వివశుడు **wiwaśuDu** *n.* person in ecstasy, person who is overwhelmed or beside himself with joy or sorrow.

వివస్త్ర **wiwastra** *adj.* nude.

వివాదం **wiwaadam** *n.* **1** controversy, dispute, altercation, quarrel, dissension. **2** discussion, debate.

వివాదగ్రస్త **wiwaadagrasta** *adj.* subject to dispute, disputed.

వివాదాస్పద **wiwaadaaspada** *adj.* liable to be disputed, controversial, debatable, contentious.

వివాహం **wiwaaham** *n.* marriage, matrimony, wedding.

వివాహం ఆడు **wiwaaham aaDu** *v.t.* to marry, get married to.

వివాహం చేయు **wiwaaham ceeyu** *v.i.* to perform a marriage.

వివాహిత **wiwaahita** *n.* married woman.

వివిక్త **wiwikta** *adj.* **1** lonely, solitary. **2** separate, discrete.

వివిధ **wiwidha** *adj.* varied, various, diverse, different, assorted.

వివిధంగా **wiwidhangaa** *adv.* in different ways.

వివిధీకరణ **wiwidhiikaraNa** *n.* diversification.

వివృత **wiwṛta** *adj.* **1** revealed, explained, unfolded. **2** *ling.* (of a vowel) open.

వివేకం **wiweekam** *n.* wisdom, discretion, prudence, sagacity.

వివేకంగల **wiweekangala** *adj.* **1** wise. **2** rational.

వివేకజ్ఞానం **wiweekajñaanam** *n.* power of distinguishing reality from the semblance of it.

వివేకి **wiweeki** *n.* cautious or prudent or wise person.

వివేచన **wiweecana** *n.* **1** discretion. **2** investigation, enquiry, examination, consideration.

వివేచనీయ **wiweecaniiya** *adj.* requiring consideration, worthy of consideration.

వివేచించు **wiweecincu** *v.t.* **1** to differentiate, distinguish. **2** to probe, analyse.

వివ్వచ్చుడు **wiwwaccuDu** *n.* **1** *class.* epithet of Arjuna in the Mahabharata. **2** one who slays.

విశద **wiśada** *adj.* clear, evident, apparent, plain, manifest.

విశదం **wiśadam** *n.* clearness, clarity.

విశదం చేయు, విశదపరచు, విశదీకరించు **wiśadam ceeyu, wiśadaparacu, wiśadiikarincu** *v.t.* to clarify, elucidate, explain.

విశదీకరణ **wiśadiikaraNa** *n.* clarifying, clarification, elucidation.

విశల్యకరణి **wiśalyakaraNi** *n.* name of a herbal medicine for healing fractures.

విశాఖ **wiśaakha** *n.* 1 *astrol.* name of the sixteenth asterism or lunar mansion. 2 *colloq. name of* the town Visakhapatnam.

విశారదుడు **wiśaaraduDu** *n.* eminent scholar, renowned exponent or master of an art; **ubhayabhaaSaa~** scholar in both languages, i.e., Telugu and Sanskrit.

విశాల **wiśaala** *adj.* 1 large, wide, broad. 2 extensive, spacious. 3 noble, generous; **~hṛdayam** generous heart.

విశాలత, విశాలత్వం **wiśaalata, wiśaalatwam** *n.* breadth, width, spaciousness.

విశిష్ట **wiśiSTa** *adj.* 1 superior, excellent. 2 outstanding, eminent, distinguished, important. 3 specific. 4 special, particular, peculiar. 5 *second part of an adjvl. compound meaning* endowed with.

విశిష్టగురుత్వం **wiśiSTagurutwam** *n. sci.* specific gravity.

విశిష్టత **wiśiSTata** *n.* 1 excellence, eminence, greatness. 2 noteworthiness. 3 special quality or feature or characteristic. 4 peculiarity, particularity.

విశిష్టాద్వైతం **wiśiSTaadwaytam** *n.* Vedanta system of philosophy.

విశిష్టీకరణం **wiśiSTiikaraNam** *n.* specialisation.

విశిష్టుడు **wiśiSTuDu** *n.* 1 excellent person. 2 *in composition* one who is endowed with.

విశుద్ధ **wiśuddha** *adj.* very pure.

విశుష్క **wiśuSka** *adj.* 1 very empty. 2 very dry.

విశృంఖల **wiśṛnkhala** *adj.* 1 unhindered, unchecked, unrestrained. 2 unfettered by laws of morality.

విశేష **wiśeeSa** *adj.* 1 much, plentiful, abundant. 2 unusual, extraordinary, remarkable.

విశేషం **wiśeeSam** *n.* 1 special or particular feature, matter of interest; **ii pustakamloo ~ eemii leedu** there is nothing special in this book. 2 *pl.* **wiśeeSaalu** particulars, details, news, information; **eemiTi wiśeeSaalu**? what is the [latest] news? 3 point, matter, thing, object. 4 (*in apposition*) something special or excellent; **pratibhaa~** special skill; **mana bhaagya~** our great good fortune. 5 kind, sort, variety; **idi oka wṛkSa~** this is a kind of tree; *see* **weeLa.**

విశేషంగా **wiśeeSangaa** *adv.* 1 especially, particularly, in particular. 2 plentifully, very much, abundantly.

విశేషచిహ్నం **wiśeeSacihnam** *n. ling.* diacritical mark.

విశేషణం **wiśeeSaNam** *n. gram.* 1 adjective. 2 attribute. 3 epithet.

విశేషించి **wiśeeSinci** *adv.* especially, particularly, in particular.

విశేష్యం **wiśeeSyam** *n. gram.* noun.

విశ్రమం **wiśramam** *n.* rest, repose.

విశ్రమించు **wiśramincu** *v.i.* to rest, repose, take rest.

విశ్రాంతి **wiśraanti** *n.* 1 rest, repose. 2 *theat.* interval, intermission.

విశ్రుతి **wiśruti** *n.* celebrity, fame.

విశ్లేషక **wiśleeSaka** *adj.* analytical.

విశ్లేషణ **wiśleeSaNa** *n.* analysis.

విశ్లేషణ చేయు, విశ్లేషించు **wiśleeSaNa ceeyu, wiśleeSincu** *v.t.* to analyse.

విశ్లేషణాత్మక **wiśleeSaNaatmaka** *adj.* analytical.

విశ్వ **wiśwa** *adj.* universal, entire.

విశ్వం **wiśwam** *n.* the universe, the cosmos.

విశ్వకళాపరిషత్తు **wiśwakaLaapariSattu** *n.* university.

విశ్వకవి **wiśwakawi** *n.* world-renowned poet, a title given to Rabindranath Tagore.

విశ్వకిరణం **wiśwakiraNam** *n. sci.* cosmic ray.

విశ్వజనీన **wiśwajaniina** *adj.* agreeable to all, universally approved.

విశ్వజనీనత **wiśwajaniinata** *n.* universality; **sangiita~** universality of music.

విశ్వదాత **wiśwadaata** *n.* philanthropist.

విశ్వపర్యాప్త **wiśwaparyaapta** *adj.* pervading the universe.

విశ్వప్రయత్నం **wiśwaprayatnam** *n.* immense or unprecedented effort; **~ceesi saadhincEEDu** he succeeded after making an unprecedented effort.

విశ్వరూపం **wiśwaruupam** *n.* existence in many forms, many-sidedness.

విశ్వవిద్యాలయం **wiśwawidyaalayam** *n.* university.

విశ్వశాస్త్రం **wiśwaśaastram** *n.* cosmology.

విశ్వసనీయ **wiśwasaniiya** *adj.* reliable, trustworthy, credible.

విశ్వసించు **wiśwasincu** *v.t.* to trust, believe, give credence to, confide in, have faith in, rely on.

విశ్వామిత్రం **wiśwaamitram** *n. colloq.* deceit, fraud, trickery (*lit.* a deed typical of the sage Viswamitra, who created an artificial heaven).

విశ్వామిత్రసృష్టి **wiśwaamitrasṛSTi** *n.* s.g imitated or counterfeit, s.g artificially created.

విశ్వావసు **wiśwaawasu** *n.* thirty-ninth year of the Hindu cycle of sixty years.

విశ్వాసం **wiśwaasam** *n.* 1 trust, faith, credence, reliance, confidence, belief. 2 faithfulness, loyalty, trustworthiness. 3 recognition, gratitude; **Dabbu tiisukonna ~ leedaa niiku**? do not you feel any gratitude in return for the money you have received? **naaku sahaayam ceesEEDanna ~ too tirigi neenukuuDaa awasaramloo aadukonnaanu** out of gratitude for the help he had given me, I too helped him when he was in need.

విశ్వాసంగల **wiśwaasangala** *adj.* faithful, trusting, loyal.

విశ్వాసకర **wiśwaasakara** *adj.* inspiring faith, inspiring trust.

విశ్వాసతీర్మానం **wiśwaasatiirmaaNam** *n.* confidence resolution, vote of confidence.

విశ్వాసపాత్రుడు **wiśwaasapaatruDu** *n.* trustworthy or dependable person.

విశ్వాససూత్రం **wiśwaasasuutram** *n.* creed.

విశ్వేశ్వరుడు **wiśweeśwaruDu** *n.* lord of the universe, an epithet of Siva.

విష **wiSa** *adj.* 1 poisonous, venomous, toxic; ~ **krimi** poisonous insect. 2 malignant, virulent; ~ **jwaram** malignant disease.

విషం **wiSam** *n.* 1 poison, venom. 2 anything hurtful or destructive.

విషణ్ణ **wiSaNNa** *adj.* dejected, sad, pensive; ~ **wadanam** dejected face.

విషతుల్యం **wiSatulyam** *n.* s.g equivalent to poison.

విషపు **wiSapu** *adj.* 1 poisonous, venomous. 2 malignant, unfavourable; ~ **ghaDiyaloo bayaludeeritee kaalu wirigindi** because he started at an inauspicious time he broke his leg.

విషపూరిత, విషభరిత, విషతుల్య, విషయుక్త **wiSapuurita, wiSabharita, wiSatulya, wiSayukta** *adj.* poisonous, toxic.

విషమ **wiSama** *adj.* 1 irregular, uneven. 2 crucial, critical: ~ **paristhiti** critical situation, crisis. 3 troublesome, vexatious.

విషమ బాహుచతురస్రం **wiSama baahucaturasram** *n. maths.* unequal-sided quadrilateral.

విషమించు **wiSamincu** *v.i.* 1 to be critical, be crucial. 2 (of a situation) to deteriorate, worsen.

విషయం **wiSayam** *n.* 1 object, matter, subject, affair, thing; **konni wiSayaalaloo** in some matters, in some particulars. 2 material, subject matter, content. 3 respect, relation, case, instance; **adee naa ~loonuu jarigindi** the same thing happened in my case also. 4 sensuality, sensual pleasure, sexual pleasure.

విషయక **wiSayaka** *adjvl. suffix meaning* relating to, having to do with, in the matter of: **widyaa~ sawkaryaalu** educational facilities; **bhaaSaa ~ngaa** in the matter of language, so far as language is concerned, linguistically.

విషయపరిజ్ఞానం **wiSayaparijñaanam** *n.* material knowledge.

విషయమై **wiSayamay** *see* **ay.**

విషయలంపటుడు, విషయలోలుడు **wiSayalampaTuDu, wiSayaloolu Du** *n.* womaniser, libertine, rake.

విషయసుఖం **wiSayasukham** *n.* sexual pleasure.

విషయసూచిక **wiSayasuucika** *n.* table of contents.

విషయాసక్తి, విషయవాంఛ **wiSayaasakti, wiSayawaancha** *n.* desire for sexual pleasure.

విషాణం **wiSaaNam** *n. class.* horn, tusk.

విషాద **wiSaada** *adj.* 1 sad, gloomy, sorrowful; ~ **kaalam** period of grief. 2 tragic; **wiSaadaantam** tragic ending.

విషాదం **wiSaadam** *n.* 1 sorrow, sadness, grief, gloom, dejection. 2 tragic event.

విషాదగాథ **wiSaadagaatha** *n.* tragedy.

విషాదించు **wiSaadincu** *v.i.* to be sad, grieve, mourn.

విషు **wiSu** *n.* fifteenth year of the Hindu cycle of sixty years.

విషువం, విషువత్తు *n.* **wiSuwam, wiSuwattu** equinox.

విషూచి[క] **wiSuuci[ka]** *n.* cholera.

విష్కంభం **wiSkambham** *n.* 1 *theat.* introduction to a scene in a play. 2 hindrance, obstacle.

విష్ణుకాంత, విష్ణుక్రాంత **wiSNuk[r]aanta** *n.* creeping plant with a blue flower used in the worship of Ganesha, *evolvulus alsinoides.*

విష్ణువు **wiSNuwu** *n.* God Vishnu.

విసం **wisam** *alt. form of* **wiSam.**

విసంకేతనం **wisankeetanam** *n.* decoding.

విసంకేతించు **wisankeetincu** *v.t.* to decode.

విసంధి **wisandhi** *n. gram.* absence of sandhi.

విసనకర్ర **wisanakarra** *n.* hand fan.

విసరణం **wisaraNam** *n. sci.* diffusion.

విసరికొట్టు, విసరివేయు **wisarikoTTu, wisariweeyu** *same as* **wisirikoTTu, wisiriweeyu.**

విసరు **wisaru** *same as* **wisuru.**

విసర్గ **wisarga** *n.* the character *ḥ* representing voiced *h,* which occurs in certain words of Sanskrit origin, e.g., **praataḥkaalam.**

విసర్జన[ం] **wisarjana[m]** *n.* 1 relinquishing, renouncing, giving up, abandoning; *see* **kankaNam.** 2 bidding farewell to a deity when worship comes to an end. 3 **mala~** voiding of excreta.

విసర్జనీయ **wisarjaniiya** *adj.* fit or deserving to be given up, relinquished, renounced or abandoned.

విసర్జించు **wisarjincu** *v.t.* 1 to give up, drop, abandon. 2 to leave off, discard, desert. 3 to lay down (weapons).

విసవిస **wisawisa** *adv.* fast, quickly, hurriedly.

విసిగించు **wisigincu** *v.t.* 1 to weary, tire. 2 to sicken, disgust. 3 to trouble, bother, annoy. 4 to bore.

విసిరికొట్టు, విసరికొట్టు **wisirikoTTu, wisarikoTTu** *v.t.* 1 to throw away. 2 to wave off, thrust away, push away.

విసిరివేయు, విసరివేయు **wisiriweeyu, wisariweeyu** *v.t.* 1 to throw away, discard; **ekkaDoo wisireesinaTTundi aayana illu** his house is in some remote corner (*lit.* it is as if his house was thrown away somewhere). 2 to toss, shake; **tala wisireesEEDu** he tossed his head.

విసుక్కొను **wisukkonu** *v.i.* to be annoyed, be irritated, grumble; **taracuu waaLLamiida wisukkoNTaaDu** he often gets irritated with them *or* he often grumbles at them.

విసుగు I. *n.* (*also* **wisuwu**) 1 disgust, dislike, vexation. 2 boredom, tedium, tediousness. 3 weariness, tiredness; ~ **puTTincee** irksome. II. *v.i.* (*also* **wisigipoowu**) 1 to grow tired (of), grow disgusted (with); **jiiwitammiida wisigipooyEEDu** he grew tired of life. 2 to be sick of (colloq.), be fed up with (colloq.).

విసుగుదల **wisigudala** *n.* 1 disgust. 2 irritation, annoyance. 3 boredom.

విసుగ్గా **wisuggaa** *adv.* 1 irritatedly, with vexation. 2 boringly, tediously.

విసుపు **wisupu** *n. dial. variant of* **wisugu** *sense I.*

విసురు, విసరు **wisuru, wisaru** I. *n.* 1 blow, stroke, swipe (colloq.), sweep; **ceeti~too** with a sweep of the arm. 2 throwing, casting. 3 waving. 4 disparaging remark, retort, reproach, rebuke. II. *v.i.* (of wind) to blow. III. *v.t.* 1 to throw, fling, hurl, cast. 2 to wave (fan, flag). 3 to flourish, brandish (knife). 4 to grind in a mill. 5 to utter (retort, harsh word). 6 **chatookti~** to make a joke.

విసురుగా **wisurugaa** *adv.* 1 quickly, hastily. 2 bad temperedly, in a huff. 3 freely, casually, carelessly; **eDama**

bhujam miida oo daLasari unni sweTTaru ~ weesukoni unnaaDu he had casually thrown a thick woollen sweater over his left shoulder.

విసుర్రాయి **wisurraayi** *n.* handmill.

విసువు **wisuwu** *same as* **wisugu.**

విస్తంత్రి **wistantri** *n. and adj.* wireless, radio.

విస్తరం **wistaram** *n.* 1 spreading, expanding. 2 prolixity, longwindedness, diffuseness.

విస్తరణ **wistaraNa** *n.* 1 spreading, extent. 2 extension, expansion.

విస్తరాకు **wistaraaku** *n.* 1 eating plate made of leaves stitched together. 2 plantain (banana) leaf used as an eating plate.

విస్తరి **wistari** *n.* 1 eating plate made of leaves stitched together. 2 plantain (banana) leaf used as an eating plate. 3 eating plate of any kind: **ee puuTaa maa iNTLoo wanda ~ leestundi** *lit.* at each mealtime a hundred plates are picked up in our house, i.e., a hundred people are served with food in our house at every mealtime.

విస్తరించు **wistarincu** *v.i. and t.* 1 to extend, spread out, expand, increase, amplify. 2 to be widened, be broadened. 3 to particularise, detail.

విస్తరింప చేయు **wistarimpa ceeyu** *v.t.* to expand, extend.

విస్తరిల్లు **wistarillu** *v.i.* to be enlarged, expand, spread.

విస్తారం **wistaaram** I. *n.* plenty, abundance. II. *adj.* plentiful, abundant.

విస్తారంగా **wistaarangaa** *adv.* 1 plentifully, abundantly, extensively. 2 in detail.

విస్తీర్ణం **wistiirNam** *n.* extent, area.

విస్తీర్ణత **wistiirNata** *n.* extent, area.

విస్తీర్ణమైన **wistiirNamayna** *adj.* great, large, extensive.

విస్తు **wistu** *n.* surprise, wonder[ment], astonishment.

విస్తుపోవు, విస్తుపడు **wistupoowu, wistupaDu** *v.i.* to be astonished, be bewildered, be taken aback.

విస్తృత **wistrta** *adj.* extended, extensive, widespread.

విస్తృతంగా **wistrtangaa** *adv.* widely, extensively.

విస్తృతపరచు **wistrtaparacu** *v.t.* to extend, amplify.

విస్తృతి **wistrti** *n.* spreading, extension, extent, distribution.

విస్పష్ట, సుస్పష్ట **wispaSTa, suspaSTa** *adj.* plain, clear-cut, definite.

విస్పష్టత, సుస్పష్టత **wispaSTata, suspaSTata** *n.* clearness, definiteness.

విస్ఫారం **wisphaaram** *n. sci.* dilation.

విస్ఫారిత **wisphaarita** *adj.* wide open; **~ nayanaalu** staring eyes, wide open eyes.

విస్ఫుట **wisphuTa** *adj.* very clear, very definite.

విస్ఫులింగం **wisphulingam** *n. class.* spark of fire.

విస్ఫోటం **wisphooTam** *n.* boil, pustule, abscess.

విస్ఫోటనం **wisphooTanam** *n.* explosion, detonation.

విస్మయం **wismayam** I. *n.* surprise, astonishment, wonder, amazement. II. *adj.* surprised.

విస్మయకర **wismayakara** *adj.* surprising, astonishing, amazing, marvellous.

విస్మయాకుల **wismayaakula** *adj.* dismayed.

విస్మయావహ **wismayaawaha** *adj.* overcome by surprise.

విస్మరం **wismaram** *n.* discordant sound.

విస్మరణ **wismaraNa** *n.* neglect[fulness]; **baadhyataa ~** neglect of responsibilities.

విస్మరించు **wismarincu** *v.t.* to disregard, ignore, overlook (defects), neglect (duties), forget (sorrows).

విస్మిత **wismita** *adj.* amazed, astonished, dismayed.

విస్మృత **wismrta** *adj.* forgotten, neglected.

విస్మృతి **wismrti** *n.* forgetfulness, oblivion.

విస్రంభం **wisrambham** *n.* affection, kind regard.

విస్సాటంగా **wissaaTangaa** *adv. dial.* carelessly, inattentively.

విహంగం **wihangam** *n. class.* bird; **wihangawiikSaNam** *colloq.* bird's eye view.

విహరణం **wiharaNam** *n.* wandering, roaming.

విహరించు **wiharincu** *v.i.* to wander, roam, move about.

విహాయసం **wihaayasam** *n. class.* 1 sky. 2 bird.

విహాయితం **wihaayitam** *n. class.* gift, donation.

విహారం **wihaaram** *n.* 1 *class.* buddhist monastery. 2 relaxation, recreation. 3 wandering, roaming.

విహారయాత్ర **wihaarayaatra** *n.* excursion.

విహారి **wihaari** *n.* one who rambles or roves or roams.

విహిత **wihita** *adj.* prescribed, enjoined.

విహితరూపం **wihitaruupam** *n. ling.* canonical form.

విహితుడు **wihituDu** *n.* friend, companion, ally.

విహీన **wihiina** *second part of an adjvl. compound meaning* devoid of, destitute of: **kaLaa ~** devoid of brightness, dull, gloomy.

విహ్వల **wihwala** *adj.* perturbed, discomposed, agitated, overwhelmed.

విహ్వలత, విహ్వలత్వం **wihwalata, wihwalatwam** *n.* disquiet, perturbation.

విహ్వలించు **wihwalincu** *v.i.* to be agitated, be perturbed, be overcome by fear or other emotion.

విహ్వాలుడు **wihwaluDu** *n.* one who is agitated or perturbed or overcome by fear or other emotion.

వీ - wii

వీక్షణం **wiikSaNam** *n.* seeing, sight, view.

వీక్షించు **wiikSincu** *v.t.* 1 to view, observe. 2 to watch, look out (for); **aayanakoosam wiikSistunnaanu** I am looking out for him.

వీగు **wiigu**[1] *v.i.* 1 to be proud, be vain, be swoollen with pride. 2 to protrude.

వీగు **wiigu**[2] *v.i.* (*also* **wiigipoowu**) 1 to be beaten, be defeated. 2 (of a bill, resolution) to be set aside.

వీచి[క] **wiici[ka]** *n.* 1 breeze. 2 *fig.* wave, ripple; **madhura bhaawa wiicikalu** sweet waves of thought; **gaana wiicikalu** strains of music.

వీచు **wiicu** I. *v.i.* (of wind) to blow. II. *v.t.* to wave (fan).

వీడియం, వీడెం **wiiDiyam, wiiDem** *same as* **wiDem.**

వీడు **wiiDu**[1] *pron.* he, this man.

వీడు **wiiDu**[2] *n. class.* 1 town, city. 2 troupe of rope dancers and jugglers.

వీడు **wiiDu**[3] I. *v.i.* 1 to be separated. 2 to be loosened. II *v.t.* (*also* **wiiDipoowu**) to give up, abandon, leave.

వీడుకొలుపు **wiiDukolupu** I. *n.* send off, farewell (= **wiiDkoolu**). II. *v.t.* to send away, bid farewell to.

వీడ్కోలు **wiiDkoolu** n. [bidding] farewell.

వీడ్కోలు ఇచ్చు, వీడ్కోలు చెప్పు **wiiDkoolu iccu, wiiDkoolu ceppu** *v.i.* to say goodbye, bid farewell; **waariki wiiDkoolu iwwaDaaniki neenu wicaarapaDDaanu** I was sorry to say goodbye to them.

వీణ **wiiNa** *n.* vina, stringed musical instrument with a long neck and rounded body.

వీతరాగి **wiitaraagi** *n.* ascetic.

వీధి **wiidhi** *n.* street, road; **~na paDu** to come out into the open, do s.g openly or publicly.

వీధినాటకం **wiidhi naaTakam** *n.* play performed on a street corner, gen. without stage or costumes.

వీధిబడి **wiidhibaDi** *n.* informally run school, gen. with a single teacher and intended for children living nearby.

వీధిబేరగాడు **wiidhibeeragaaDu** *n.* street vendor.

వీధివాకిలి **wiidhiwaakili** *n.* front entrance of a house.

వీను **wiinu** *n. class.* ear; **~ la windu** a feast for the ears.

వీపు **wiipu** *n.* back; **~ miida taTTu** to pat (s.o.) on the back.

వీబూది **wiibuudi** *same as* **wibuudi.**

వీరంగం **wiirangam** *n.* wild dance performed by worshippers of Siva.

వీరగంధం **wiiragandham** *n. class.* scented paste smeared on the body of a hero before he goes to war.

వీరగాథ **wiiragaatha** *n.* heroic tale, epic.

వీరచరితం **wiiracaritam** *n.* tale of heroes, epic; **palanaaTi~** the epic of Palnad.

వీరణం **wiiraNam** *n.* double drum.

వీరత్వం **wiiratwam** *n.* heroism, valour, prowess.

వీరపత్ని **wiirapatni** *n.* wife of a hero.

వీరమాత **wiiramaata** *n.* mother of heroes.

వీరముష్టి **wiiramuSTi** *n.* member of a community of Saivite religious beggars.

వీరరసం **wiirarasam** *n.* heroic sentiment in literature.

వీరవిహారం **wiirawihaaram** *n.* campaigning, a warrior's roving life.

వీరవైష్ణవుడు **wiirawaySNawuDu** *n.* member of a strictly orthodox sect of Vaishnavites.

వీరశైవం **wiiraśaywam** *n.* Virasaivate or Lingayat creed.

వీరశైవుడు **wiiraśaywuDu** *n.* Lingayat.

వీరాంగం **wiiraangam** *n.* wild passionate dance.

వీరాంగన **wiiraangana** *n.* heroic woman, heroine.

వీరాధివీరుడు **wiiraadhiwiiruDu** *n.* greatest of heroes.

వీరావేశం **wiiraaweeśam** *n.* 1 bravery, heroism. 2 fury.

వీరు, వీళ్లు **wiiru, wiiLLu** *pron. pl.* they, these persons.

వీరుడు **wiiruDu** *n.* hero, warrior.

వీరోచిత **wiiroocita** *adj.* befitting a hero; **~swaagatam** hero's welcome.

వీరోచితంగా **wiiroocitangaa** *adv.* heroically.

వీర్యం **wiiryam** *n.* 1 heroism, valour. 2 sperm, semen. 3 virility, potency.

వీర్యపటుత్వం **wiiryapaTutwam** *n.* virility.

వీర్యవృద్ధి **wiiryawṛddhi** *n.* increase in virility.

వీలు **wiilu** I. *n.* convenience, practicability, possibility, opportunity; **~nubaTTi** (*or* **~cuucukoni** *or* **~ceesukoni**) **raNDi** come at your convenience *or* come when you get an opportunity; **nuwwu ceesee paniki wiiluu waaluu undaa?** is there any system in what you are doing? II. *adj.* convenient, practicable, possible; **maa haasTalloo uNDaDam anniTikii~** staying in our hostel is convenient for all purposes; **eeDu gaNTalaki raNDi, andarikii ~** come at seven o'clock, it will be convenient for everyone.

వీలుగా **wiilugaa** *adv.* conveniently, so as to be convenient; **naluguruu paTTukooDaaniki~naalugu muuTalu kaTTEEm** we tied up four parcels so as to be convenient for all four of us to carry them.

వీలుపడు, వీలు అవు **wiilupaDu, wiilu awu** *v.i.* to be possible, be practicable.

వీలునామా **wiilunaamaa** *n.* will, testament.

వీలైనంత **wiilaynanta** *adj.* as much as possible.

వీలైనన్ని **wiilaynanni** *adj.* as many as possible.

వీళ్లు **wiiLLu**[1] *pron.pl.* of **wiiDu**[1].

వీళ్లు **wiiLLu**[2] *n.pl* of **wiiDu**[2].

వీళ్లు **wiiLLu**[3] *n.pl.* of **wiilu.**

వీవన **wiiwana** *n. class.* fan.

వీశ, వీసె **wiiśa, wiise** *n.* viss, a weight equal to 120 tolas.

వీశగుద్దులు **wiiśaguddulu** *n.pl. colloq.* severe blows.

వీసం **wiisam** *n.* **1** one sixteenth part. **2** a small quantity. **3** a measure of land varying in extent in different regions.

వీసమెత్తు **wiisamettu** *see* **ettu.**

వృ - wṛ

వృంతం **wṛntam** *n.* stalk of a leaf or flower, pedicel.

వృకం **wṛkam** *n. class.* wolf.

వృకోదరుడు **wṛkoodaruDu** *n.* **1** *colloq.* person with a wolf's appetite. **2** epithet of Bhima.

వృక్క **wṛkka** *adj.* renal.

వృక్కలు **wṛkkalu** *n.pl.* kidneys.

వృక్షం **wṛkSam** *n.* tree.

వృక్షకోటి, వృక్షసంతతి **wṛkSakooTi, wṛkSasantati** *n.* **1** vegetable kingdom. **2** vegetation.

వృక్షజాలం **wṛkSajaalam** *n.* flora.

వృక్షశాస్త్రం **wṛkSaśaastram** *n.* botany.

వృక్షశాస్త్రజ్ఞుడు **wṛkSaśaastrajñuDu** *n.* botanist.

వృత **wṛta** *adj.* covered, screened, surrounded.

వృత్త **wṛtta** *adj.* round, circular.

వృత్తం **wṛttam** *n.* **1** circle. **2** news. **3** account. **4** subject matter or plot of a story. **5** kind of poetic metre.

వృత్తఖండం **wṛttakhaNDam** *n. maths.* segment of a circle.

వృత్తలేఖిని **wṛttaleekhini** *n.* compass for drawing circles.

వృత్తాంతం **wṛttaantam** *n.* **1** news, particulars. **2** story, narrative. **3** occurrence, incident.

వృత్తాకార **wṛttaakaara** *adj.* circular.

వృత్తి **wṛtti** *n* **1** livelihood, means of subsistence. **2** profession, occupation, vocation. **3** craft; **ceeti~** handicraft. **4** share of a village granted as a free gift to a brahman in former times.

వృత్తికళ **wṛttikaLa** *n.* professional skill.

వృత్తిగా **wṛttigaa** *adv.* as a profession, as a livelihood.

వృత్తివిద్య **wṛttiwidya** *n.* vocational education.

వృథా **wṛthaa** I. *adj.* vain, empty, fruitless, of no avail, useless, wasted. II. *adv.* in vain.

వృథా అవు **wṛthaa awu** *v.i.* to be wasted, be in vain, be of no use, be of no avail.

వృథా చేయు **wṛthaa ceeyu** *v.t.* to waste.

వృద్ధ **wṛddha** *adj.* old, aged.

వృద్ధత్వం, వృద్ధాప్యం **wṛddhatwam, wṛddhaapyam** *n.* old age, senility.

వృద్ధి **wṛddhi** *n.* **1** increase, accumulation, growth. **2** improvement, development. **3** prosperity. **4** interest (on money). **5** waxing (of moon).

వృద్ధి అవు, వృద్ధి పొందు, వృద్ధి చెందు **wṛddhi awu, wṛddhi pondu, wṛddhi cendu** *v.i.* to progress, develop, accumulate, grow, attain growth.

వృద్ధి చేయు **wṛddhi ceeyu** *v.t.* **1** to increase, enhance, develop. **2** to accumulate.

వృద్ధుడు **wṛddhuDu** *n.* old man; **wayoo~** man of great age; **jñaana~** man of mature wisdom.

వృశ్చికం **wṛścikam** *n.* **1** scorpion. **2** *astrol.* constellation of Scorpio.

వృషణం **wṛSaNam** *n.* scrotum, testicle.

వృషణాయాసం **wṛSaNaayaasam** *n. colloq.* wasted effort.

వృషభం **wṛSabham** *n.* **1** bull. **2** *astrol.* constellation of Taurus.

వృష్టి **wṛSTi** *n. class.* rain.

వె - we

వెంకటేశుడు **wenkaTeesuDu** *same as* **weenkaTeesuDu.**

వెంగలి, వెర్రివెంగళప్ప **wengali, werriwengaLappa** *n.* fool, stupid person, innocent-minded person.

వెంట **weNTa** *p.p.* 1 along with, in company with. 2 behind, following after; **caalu ~ caalubaTTi dunnaDam** ploughing one furrow after another. 3 along, through; **tellaarluu wiidhuleNTa tirigi tirigi** wandering on and on through the streets all night long; **krSNaa goodaawarii tiiraala ~ gala aDawulu** forests along the banks of the Krishna and Godavari. 4 from (the eyes, nose or mouth); **kaLLa ~ niiLLu kaarEEyi** tears poured from the eyes; **mukku ~ raktam cimmindi** blood ran from the nose; **naa nooTi ~ maaTa raawaDam aalasyam aa pani ayikuur-cuNTundi** as soon as I give the word, the work will be done.

వెంట తగులు **weNTa tagulu** *v.t.* to persist in following, chase after.

వెంట తరుము **weNTa tarumu** *v.t.* to chase, pursue.

వెంట తెచ్చు, వెంట పెట్టుకొను **weNTa teccu, weNTa peTTukonu** *v.t.* to bring along with one.

వెంటనే **weNTanee** I. *adv.* immediately, forthwith. II. *advbl. particle following a past vbl. adj.* immediately, as soon as; **aayana anna ~ bayaludeerEEm kaanii baNDi andaleedu** we started as soon as he said but we did not catch the train.

వెంటపడు **weNTapaDu** *v.i.* to follow persistently, chase after; **nuwweemiTraa naaweNTa paDDaawu?** why do you dog my footsteps?

వెంటవేసుకొను, వెంటేసుకొను **weNTaweesukonu, weNTeesukonu** *v.t.* to take (s.o.) with one for company: *see* **weesukonu** *sense 9.*

వెంటాడు **weNTaaDu** *v.t.* to chase, hunt, follow, pursue.

వెంటి **weNTi** same as **eNTi.**

వెంట్రుక **weNTruka** *n.* 1 a single hair. 2 *pl.* **~ lu** hair of the head.

వెండి **weNDi**[1] *n. and adj.* silver.

వెండి, వెండియు **weNDi**[2], **weNDiyu** *adv. class.* again, once more.

వెండికొండ **weNDikoNDa** *n.* a name for Mount Kailash in the Himalayas.

వెంపరలాట **wemparalaaTa** *n* 1 quarrelling. 2 harassing.

వెంపరలాడు **wemparalaaDu** *v.i.* to make an attempt by all possible means; **aa padawikoosam ~ tunnaaDu** he is trying by hook or by crook to get that post; **waaDi wenaka wemparalaaDi pani ceeyincEEnu** I tried by all the means in my power and got him to do the work.

వెంపలి **wempali** *n.* purple galega, a wild leguminous plant.

వెంబడి **wembaDi** *p.p. and adv.* 1 along with, accompanying. 2 behind, after, following. 3 along; **samudra tiiram ~** along the seashore. 4 from out of; **nooTi ~** from out of the mouth; *cf.* **ambaDi.**

వెంబడించు **wembaDincu** *v.t.* 1 to follow, pursue, hunt, chase. 2 to accompany.

వెంబడే **wembaDee** I. *p.p. and adv.* along with; **wari payru ~ perigee kalupu mokka** a weed that grows along with the paddy crop. II. *advbl. particle following a past vbl. adj.* immediately after; **baNDiwaccina ~ aayana kanabaDDaaDu** immediately after the train came he appeared.

వెకసక్కెం, ఎకసక్కెం **wekasakkem, ekasakkem** *n.* mockery, ridicule.

వెకసక్కేలాడు, ఎకసక్కేలాడు **wekasakkEElaaDu, ekasakkEElaadu** *v.t.* to mock, ridicule.

వెకిలి **wekili** *adj.* 1 illbred, unmannered, common, vulgar. 2 clownish. 3 absurd.

వెకిలిగా **wekiligaa** *adv.* rudely, coarsely, abusively, sarcastically.

వెక్కసం, ఎక్కసం **wekkasam, ekkasam** I. *n.* 1 excess, superfluity. 2 repugnance, disgust, abhorrence. II. *adj.* 1 too much, too many, excessive, superfluous. 2 repugnant, disgusting, abhorrent, sickening, tedious, unbearable, intolerable; **pani ~ ayindi** the work was tedious.

వెక్కసపడు, ఎక్కసపడు **wekkasapaDu, ekkasapaDu** *v.i.* to be disgusted (by), be sickened (by), be unable to tolerate; **waaDi goppalu winaleeka wekkasapaDDaanu** I was disgusted by his boastings and could not listen to them.

వెక్కిరించు **wekkirincu** *v.i. and t.* 1 to mock [at], jeer at, tease, laugh at, ridicule. 2 to grimace, make an ugly face.

వెక్కిరింత **wekkirinta** *n.* 1 jeering, ridiculing, mocking. 2 mockery, ridicule.

వెక్కిరింతగా **wekkirintagaa** *adv.* mockingly.

వెక్కిళ్లు **wekkiLLu** *same as* **ekkiLLu.**

వెక్కు **wekku** *v.i.* to sob; **wekki wekki eeDcu** to sob convulsively.

వెగటు **wegaTu** I. *n.* dislike, aversion, repugnance. II. *adj.* repulsive, nasty, having a bad taste.

వెగడు **wegaDu** *n.* 1 astonishment. 2 mental confusion.

వెచ్చ **wecca** I. *n.* (*also* **~ na, ~ tanam**) heat, warmth. II. *adj.* (*also* **~ ni**) hot, warm.

వెచ్చం **weccam** *n.* 1 sundry expenditure; **dina ~** daily expenditure; **kharcu weccaalu raasipeTTEEnu** I have listed all the expenses. 2 *pl.* **weccaalu** purchases, provisions.

వెచ్చంచేయు, వెచ్చించు **weccam ceeyu, weccincu** *v.t.* 1 to spend. 2 to squander.

వెచ్చపెట్టు **weccapeTTu** *v.t.* to heat, warm; **kaaphii weccapeTTEEnu** I have warmed the coffee.

వెటకారం **weTakaaram** *n.* sarcasm, scorn.

వెట్టి[వాడు] **weTTi[waaDu]** *n.* village servant who attended on the village headman in former times.

వెట్టిచాకిరీ **weTTicaakirii** *n.* drudgery, menial work.

వెడలు **weDalu** *v.i. classical form of* **weLLu** *sometimes occurring mod. with the meaning* to come out, go out, issue:

certain parts of this verb, namely, **weDataanu, weDutunnaanu, weDutuu, weDali** *and* **weDitee** *occur freely as alternatives of* **weLtaanu, weLtunnaanu, weLtuu, weLLi** *and* **weLtee; reepoo maapoo mundugaa baalaśikSa accupaDutundi, baDulaloo paaThya pustakam awutundi ani aaśalu puTTeeTaTTu prakaTanalu ceesinaaru; ippaTiki irawayaaru eeNDLayindi pariSattu garbhamloonuNDi adi payki weDali raanee leedu, wastundani aaśaaleedu** in order to arouse expectations they published notices that a primer (of classical Telugu) would be printed shortly and would become a text book in schools; that was twenty-six years ago but the primer has not issued from the womb of the Parishat and there is no hope that it will.

వెడల్పు **weDalpu** I. *n.* breadth, width. II. *adj.* broad, wide.

వెత **weta** *n.* pain, grief.

వెతుకు, వెదకు, వెదుకు **wetuku, wedaku, weduku** *v.i. and t.* to seek, search [for], look for.

వెతుకులాట **wetukulaaTa** *n.* 1 search. 2 groping with the hands.

వెతుకులాడు **wetukulaaDu** *v.i.* to search for.

వెద **weda** *n. class.* 1 sowing of seed. 2 rutting season.

వెదగొర్రు **wedagorru** *n.* drill plough, instrument for sowing seed in drills.

వెదచల్లు, వెదజల్లు **wedacallu, wedajallu** *v.t.* 1 to sow. 2 to scatter, sprinkle.

వెదురు **weduru** *n.* bamboo.

వెదురుకాడ, వెదురుబొంగు **wedurukaaDa, wedurubongu** *n.* strong bamboo stick.

వెదురుబియ్యం **wedurubiyyam** *n.* kind of forest produce.

వెధవ **wedhawa** I. *n.* 1 (*also* **widhawa**) widow. 2 *colloq., used as a mild term of abuse* wretch. II. *adj. colloq., used as a mild term of abuse* wretched.

వెధవతనం **wedhawatanam** *n.* widowhood.

వెనక, వెనుక **wenaka, wenuka** I. *adv. and p.p.* 1 behind, after[wards]; **mundu nuyyi ~ goyyi** a well in front, a pit behind (proverb meaning it is dangerous both ways); **mundu nuwwu tinu, aa ~ neenu tiNTaanu** you eat first, I will eat afterwards. 2 before, previously; **sundaram ii graamaaniki ~ okka saaree waccEEDu** Sundaram had only come to this village once before. II. *advbl. particle following past vbl. adj.* after; **modaTi bharta pooyina ~ witantu wiwaaham ceesukoni reNDoo bhartatoo caala sukhapaDindi** after her first husband died she married again as a widow and lived very happily with her second husband.

వెనకంజవేయు, వెనకడుగువేయు **wenakanjaweeyu, wenakaDuguweeyu** *v.i.* 1 to step back, draw back, withdraw, retreat. 2 to hesitate, be reluctant.

వెనకచిక్కు **wenaka cikku** *v.i.* to fall behind, lag behind, be left behind.

వెనకటి **wenakaTi** *adj.* 1 back, hind, rear; **~ kaaLLu** hind legs; **~ bhaagam** rear portion. 2 past, last, former, previous; **~ saari** the last time (i.e., the previous time). 3 following, subsequent, latter, later; **~ waaru** those who precede *or* those who come after.

వెనకటికి **wenakaTiki** *adv.* in the past, some time ago; **~ ewaroo ceppinaTTu** as s.o. said in the past.

వెనకదీయు, వెనుదీయు **wenakadiiyu, wenudiiyu** *v.i.* 1 to retreat, retire, retract, withdraw. 2 to draw back, shrink, hesitate, be reluctant; **wenudiiyakuNDaa** without hesitating, without shrinking.

వెనకనుంచి **wenakanunci** *adv. colloq.* afterwards, later on.

వెనకనుంచు, వెనకుంచు **wenakanuncu, wenakuncu** *v.t. colloq.* to keep aside, set aside, keep separately.

వెనకపెట్టు **wenakapeTTu** I. *n.* blow struck from behind. II. *v.t.* 1 *same as* **wenakaweeyu.** 2 to lay aside, leave behind.

వెనకబడు **wenakabaDu** I. *v.i.* to fall or lag behind, be left behind; **wenakabaDina** backward (*opposite of* advanced). II. *v.t.* to follow persistently, chase after.

వెనకబాటు **wenakabaaTu** *n.* backwardness.

వెనకముందవు **wenakamundawu** *v.i.* to be confused, be in confusion.

వెనకముందు చూచుకొను, ముందువెనక చూచుకొను **wenakamundu cuucukonu, munduwenaka cuucukonu** *v.i.* to be cautious, be prudent, be circumspect (*lit.* to look before and behind).

వెనకముందులుగా, ముందువెనకలుగా **wenakamundulugaa, munduwenakalugaa** *adv.* a little before or after, about the same time; **miiru waccee ~ aayana weLLipooyEEDu** he left at about the same time as you arrived.

వెనకముఖం పట్టు **wenakamukham paTTu** *v.i.* 1 to regress, decline (= **taggumukham paTTu**). 2 to turn o.'s face away, turn back.

వెనకల, వెనకాల **wenakala, wenakaala** *adv. and p.p.* behind, after[wards], later [on]; **naa wenakaalee** just behind me; **neenu mundu laNDanu waccEEnu, ~ maa pillalu waccEEru** I came to London first, my children came later on.

వెనకవేయు, వెనకేయు **wenakaweeyu, wenakeeyu** *v.t.* 1 to save, put by (money). 2 to acquire or accumulate (wealth) by underhand means.

వెనకవేసుకొను, వెనకేసుకొను **wenakaweesukonu, wenakeesukonu** *v.t.* 1 to shield, protect, give support or protection to. 2 to save (money) for o.s.

వెనకాడు **wenakaaDu** *v.i.* 1 to be hesitant, be reluctant, hesitate. 2 to hang back, draw back, shrink, lag behind; **śramakugaani Dabbukugaani wenakaaDakuNDaa** without grudging either trouble or expense. 3 to retreat.

వెనుతిరుగు **wenutirugu** *v.i.* to turn round, turn back.

వెనుదీయు **wenudiiyu** *same as* **wenakadiiyu.**

వెనువెంట[నే] **wenuweNTa[nee]** *adv.* immediately afterwards.

వెన్న **wenna** *n.* 1 butter. 2 **~ laaNTi manasu** kindly or amiable nature or disposition. 3 **~ too peTTina widya** *lit.* knowledge imparted along with butter, *hence* knowledge imparted at a very early age (because butter was traditionally given to infants).

వెన్నపూస **wennapuusa** *n.* small globule or ball of butter.

వెన్నముద్ద **wennamudda** *n.* 1 lump of butter. 2 name of a superior variety of paddy.

వెన్నాడు **wennaaDu** *v.t.* to pursue, chase, follow closely.

వెన్నిచ్చు **wenniccu** *v.i.* to run away, flee; **śatruwulaku wenniccEEDu** he fled from the enemy.

వెన్ను **wennu**[1] *n.* back.

వెన్ను, ఎన్ను **wennu**[2], **ennu** *n.* ear of corn.

వెన్నుగాడి **wennugaaDi** *n.* beam supporting the ridge of a hipped roof of a house.

వెన్నుపాము **wennupaamu** *n.* spinal cord.

వెన్నుపూస **wennupuusa** *n.* **1** backbone, spine. **2** one joint of the spine, vertebra.

వెన్నుపోటు **wennupooTu** *n.* stab in the back.

వెన్నెముక, వెన్నుపట్టె **wennemuka, wennupaTTe** *n.* backbone, spine.

వెన్నెల **wennela** *n.* moonlight.

వెన్నెలపులుగు **wennelapulugu** *n.* greek partridge (= **cakooram**).

వెయ్యి, వేయి **weyyi, weeyi** *n.* **1** thousand; **weyyiNTa enimidi** eight per mille, eight out of a thousand. **2** *fig.* a great number, a great amount; ~ **eenugula balam** great strength (*lit.* strength of a thousand elephants); ~ **eenugula maaTa** very firm promise; ~ **kaLLatoo kaapalaa kaayu** to guard very strictly (*lit.* to guard with a thousand eyes); ~ **ceppinaa winanu** however much you say, I will not listen to you; ~ **uuLLa puujaari** *colloq.* s.o. who is always wandering about, s.o. who can never be found at home; *see* **eela.**

వెయ్యి ఏళ్లు ఆయుష్షు!, వెయ్యేళ్లాయుష్షు! **weyyi eeLLu aayuSSu!, weyyeeLLaayuSSu!** *interj. lit.* may your life be for a thousand years! (i) this is said to a person who arrives just when the speaker is talking about him; (ii) **śrii raamarakSa!~ !** is a blessing spoken by a mother daily after bathing her child.

వెర[పు] **wera[pu]** *n.* fear.

వెరగు **weragu** *n.* surprise.

వెరచు **weracu** *v.i.* to fear, be afraid; **lookaaniki weraci ii pani ceesEEnu** I did this fearing what people might say.

వెరవు **werawu** *n.* **1** cleverness, skill, skilfulness. **2** contrivance.

వెరసి **werasi** *n.* total.

వెర్రి **werri** I. *n.* **1** craziness, eccentricity, folly. **2** simple-mindedness, foolishness. **3** wrongheadedness, obstinacy, perverseness. II. *adj.* **1** nonsensical, meaningless, silly, inane, foolish; ~ **mokham** (i) foolish or blank expression; (ii) simple or innocent-minded or foolish person; ~ **nawwu** involuntary laugh or smile. **2** crazy, wild, uncontrolled, violent; ~ **keeka** wild cry; ~ **koopam** violent anger; ~ **talanoppi** terrible headache; ~ **uuha** wild speculation, fantasy; ~ **aaweeśam** frenzy; ~ **piiru** *colloq.* eccentric person, s.o. who behaves unpredictably. **3** wild (undomesticated, uncultivated); ~ **pucca** wild bitter melon; ~ **ceruku** wild sugarcane. **4** senseless, wrong, misconceived; ~ **samaasam** wrongly formed compound; ~ **ancanaa** wrong estimation; ~ **tala** shoot of a plant that is not true to type; **waaDi buddhi ~ talalu weesindi** his mind has produced wrongheaded notions; *see* **tala** *sense I. 5.* **5** poor (term used to indicate sympathy); **daanikiipuuTa oLLu kaasta weccagaa undaNDii! nidraloo ~ talli ulikkipaDutunnadi** just now her body is rather feverish, she shakes violently in her sleep, poor little girl!

వెర్రిబాగుల **werribaagula** (*also* ~ **maari**) *adj.* crazy, foolish ~ **ceeSTalu** foolish deeds.

వెర్రిబాగులమారి **werribaagulamaari** *n.* crazy or foolish woman.

వెర్రిబాగులవాడు **werribaagula waaDu** *n.* fool, simpleton, crazy person.

వెర్రిమొర్రి **werrimorri** *adj.* crazy.

వెర్రివాడు **werriwaaDu** *n.* **1** crazy or eccentric person. **2** foolish or simple or innocent-minded person. **3** perverse or senseless or obstinate person.

వెర్రివెంగళప్ప **werriwengaLappa** *same as* **wengali.**

వెల **wela** *n.* price, cost; ~ **kaTTu** to estimate the price (of s.g); ~ **leeni** priceless, invaluable.

వెలంది **welandi** *n.* woman.

వెలక్కాయ **welakkaaya** *n.* wood apple.

వెలగ **welaga** *n.* wood apple tree, *feronia elephantum.*

వెలగపెట్టు **welagapeTTu** *v.t. colloq., used disparagingly* to do some work, have an occupation: **Dilliiloo eem wyaapaaram welagapeDutunnaawu**? what are you doing in Delhi? *or* what is your business in Delhi? *cf.* **weligincu.**

వెలనాటివారు **welanaaTiwaaru** *n.pl.* name of a subsect of Vaidiki brahmans.

వెలనాడు **welanaaDu** *n.* coastal region of Andhra Pradesh stretching between Guntur and East Godavari districts.

వెలపరం **welaparam** *n.* aversion.

వెలపల **welapala** *same as* **welupala.**

వెలమ **welama** *n.* name of a community in Andhra Pradesh.

వెలయాలు **welayaalu** *n.* prostitute.

వెలయించు **welayincu** *v.t.* to brighten, cause to shine.

వెలయు **welayu** *v.i.* **1** to come into existence, come into being, spring up. **2** (of a deity) to appear, become manifest.

వెలవరించు **welawarincu** *v.t.* to feel aversion or nausea towards (s.g).

వెలవెల **welawela** I. *n.* paleness. II. *adj.* pale.

వెలవెలపోవు, వెలవెలలాడు, వెలవెలపారు **welawelapoowu, welawelalaaDu, welawelapaaru** *v.i.* to become pale, turn pale.

వెలార్చు **welaarcu** I. *v.i.* to shine. II. *v.t.* **1** to brighten. **2** to express (a meaning).

వెలి **weli** I. *n.* excommunication. II. *adj.* white; ~ **sunnam** whitewash. III. *adv.* outside.

వెలి అవు **weli awu** *v.i.* to be excommunicated.

వెలికిల, వెల్లకిల **welikila, wellakila** *adv.* lying on o.'s back.

వెలికిలబడు **welikilabaDu** *v.i.* **1** to fall down backwards, fall on o.'s back. **2 baNDi welikilabaDindi** the cart overturned.

వెలిగారం **weligaaram** *n.* borax.

వెలిగించు **weligincu** *v.t.* **1** to light (lamp, cigarette). **2** *colloq., used disparagingly* to do some work, have an occupation: **Dilliiloo eem weligistunnaawu**? what are you doing in Delhi? **maa waaDu biiyee weligistunnaaDu** my son is doing his B.A.; **gumaastaagiri weligistunnaanu** I am working as a clerk; *cf.* **welagapeTTu.**

వెలిగ్రక్కు, వెళ్లగ్రక్కు **weligrakku, weLLagrakku** *v.t.* **1** *lit.* to vomit. **2** *fig.* to pour out, give out, utter; **baadha weligrakkEEDu** he poured out his sorrow; **abhipraayam weligrakkEEDu** he gave out his opinion.

వెలిజిమ్ము **welijimmu** *v.t.* to emit, spurt out.

వెలితి, వెల్తి **weliti, welti** I. *n.* 1 deficiency, want. 2 degradation, loss of esteem: **naluguriloo ~ paDDaaDu** he suffered loss of esteem among the public. II. *adj.* 1 deficient, wanting; **katha raayaDam mugincEEnu; maLLii caduwukoNTee naakee ~ gaa unnaTTu toocindi** I finished writing the story; when I read it again I myself felt there was something lacking in it. 2 short in measurement: **kappuloo kaaphii ~ gaa undi** the coffee in the cup is less than the full quantity. 3 degrading, undignified; **~ maaTalu** undignified words.

వెలితిగా, వెల్తిగా **welitigaa, weltigaa** *adv.* deficiently, faintly, weakly, dimly; **~ nawwEEDu** he smiled faintly; **candruDu ~ welugutunnaaDu** the moon is shining dimly.

వెలి[కి]తీయు **weli[ki]tiiyu** *v.t.* 1 to bring to light, reveal. 2 to take out (s.g covered or hidden). 3 to extract (minerals).

వెలిపడు **welipaDu** *v.i.* to abstain from associating (with others), cut o.s. off (from others).

వెలిపుచ్చు, వెలిపరచు **welipuccu, weliparacu** *v.t.* to reveal, make known, display, express.

వెలిబూడిద **welibuuDida** *n.* white powder made from burnt cowdung cakes, used by weavers and others to absorb sweat on the hands.

వెలియు **weliyu** *v.i.* 1 (of rain) to stop, cease, clear up, pass off. 2 to fade; **welisipooyina cokkaa** faded shirt.

వెలివాడ **weliwaaDa** *n.* harijans' quarter in a village.

వెలివేయు, వెలిపెట్టు **weliweeyu, welipeTTu** *v.t.* 1 to excommunicate. 2 to outlaw, ostracise.

వెలుగు **welugu**[1] I. *n.* light, brightness. II. *v.i.* 1 to shine, gleam, give light. 2 to be alight, be lighted. 3 (of a cigar, cigarette) to burn.

వెలుగు, ఎలుగు **welugu**[2], **elugu** *n.* fence.

వెలుగొందు **welugondu** *v.i.* 1 to shine. 2 to flourish. 3 to exist, be in existence.

వెలుతురు, వెల్తురు **weluturu, welturu** *n.* light.

వెలుపల, వెలపల **welupala, welapala** *adv.* outside; **aame ~ undi** she is in menses.

వెలుపలి **welupali** *adj.* outer, external.

వెలువడు **weluwaDu** *same as* **welwaDu.**

వెలువరించు, వెలువర్చు **weluwar[in]cu** *v.t.* 1 to make known, make public, divulge, disclose. 2 to issue, publish (book). 3 to display, express (pleasure).

వెల్తి **welti** *same as* **weliti.**

వెల్ల **wella** I. *n.* 1 whiteness. 2 whitewash; **gooDaku ~ weeyu** to whitewash a wall. II. *adj.* 1 white. 2 **~ mokham** blank face (= **tella mokham**).

వెల్లకిల **wellakila** *same as* **welikila.**

వెల్లడి అవు, వెల్లడవు **wellaDi awu, wellaDawu** *v.i.* to be visible, be apparent, be revealed, become known.

వెల్లడి చేయు, వెల్లడించు **wellaDi ceeyu, wellaDincu** *v.t.* 1 to announce, proclaim. 2 to divulge, reveal, let out (secret). 3 to display, express (o.'s feelings).

వెల్లిగడ్డ, వెల్లిపాయ **welligaDDa, wellipaaya** *n.* garlic.

వెల్లివిరియు **welliwiriyu** *v.i.* 1 to break forth, burst forth, shine forth, overflow. 2 to burst into flower, blossom. 3 to be scattered.

వెల్లుల్లి **wellulli** *n.* garlic.

వెల్లువ **welluwa** *n.* flood, inundation.

వెల్వడు, వెలువడు **wel[u]waDu** *v.i.* 1 to come out, emerge. 2 to become known. 3 (of sound) to be uttered. 4 (of a book) to appear, be published. 5 (of rays) to be emitted. 6 to be freed, be released.

వెళ్లగొట్టు **weLLagoTTu** *v.t.* to drive away, drive out, banish, evict.

వెళ్లగ్రక్కు **weLLagrakku** *same as* **weligrakku.**

వెళ్లదీయు **weLLadiiyu** *v.t.* 1 to take out, extract. 2 **kaalam ~** to pass the time, spend o.'s days.

వెళ్లపోయు, వెళ్లపోసుకొను **weLLapooyu, weLLapoosukonu** *v.t.* to pour out, pour forth (o.'s grief, troubles).

వెళ్లబుచ్చు **weLLabuccu** *v.t.* to pass (o.'s lifetime), spend (o.'s days); **jiiwitam antaa deeśa seewaloo weLLabuccEEDu** he passed his whole life in the service of his country.

వెళ్లబెట్టు **weLLabeTTu** *v.t.* **nooru ~** to stare blankly, be unable to speak or act.

వెళ్లమారు **weLLamaaru** *v.i.* (of life) to pass, be spent; **waaLLaki jiiwitam eppuDuu okeelaagaa ~ tundaa**? will their life always be spent in the same way?

వెళ్లమార్చు **weLLamaarcu** *v.t.* to spend (o.'s life), pass (o.'s days); **pustakaalu raasukoni naa migilina jiiwitaanni ~ koogalanu** I can pass the rest of my life in writing books.

వెళ్లిపోవు **weLLipoowu** *v.i.* 1 to go away, depart. 2 to pass off, pass away; **ceDu roojulu weLLipooyEEyi** the days of misfortune have passed away.

వెళ్లు **weLLu** *v.i.* 1 to go, proceed. 2 to depart. 3 (of time) to pass, elapse. 4 (of crops, plants, trees) to sprout; **kommalu weLLEEyi** branches have sprouted; **kanki weLLani warigaDDi goDLa meetagaa upayoogistundi** paddy straw in which the ears have not sprouted is used for cattle fodder.

వెసనం **wesanam** *alt. form of* **wyasanam.**

వెసులుబాటు **wesulubaaTu** *n.* 1 ease, convenience; **mii ~ cuucukoni raNDi** please come at your convenience. 2 adaptability, flexibility, accommodative nature.

వే - wee

వే **wee** *adjvl. prefix* (= **weeyi**) *meaning* thousand; *see* **weeceetulaa.**

వేంకటేశుడు, వెంకటేశుడు **weenkaTeeśuDu, wenkaTeeśuDu** *n.* name of the God worshipped on the Tirumala hills above Tirupati.

వేంచేయు **weemceeyu** *same as* **wijayam ceeyu.**

వేండ్రం **weeNDram** *n. class.* heat.

వేండ్రపడు **weeNDrapaDu** *v.i.* **1** to feel hot. **2** to be angry, be enraged.

వేకువ[జాము] **weekuwa[jaamu]** *n.* dawn, early morning.

వేగం **weegam** *n. sci.* speed, swiftness, velocity, pace.

వేగవంత **weegawanta** *adj.* fast, speedy.

వేగవృద్ధి **weegawṛddhi** *n.* acceleration.

వేగిరం **weegiram** I. *n.* speed, haste. II. *adv.* quickly, soon.

వేగిరపడు **weegirapaDu** *v.i.* to hurry, hasten.

వేగిరపాటు **weegirapaaTu** *n.* **1** speed, swiftness. **2** hastening, hurrying.

వేగు, వేగువాడు, వేగులవాడు **weegu**[1], **weegu[la]waaDu** *n.* spy.

వేగు **weegu**[2] *v.i.* **1** to be fried. **2** to endure, tolerate, put up with; **pillala allaritoo weegaleeka** being unable to endure the children's mischief.

వేగుచుక్క **weegucukka** *n.* morning star, Venus.

వేగురు **weeguru** *n.pl. class.* many persons.

వేచి ఉండు **weeci uNDu** *v.i.* to wait (expectantly); **nii koosam enta kaalam weeci unnaanoo!** how long I have waited for you!

వేచి చూచు **weeci cuucu** *v.i.* to wait and watch, wait and see; **enta kSuNNangaa ii uttaruwu amalu jaraganunnadoo weeci cuuDaali** we must wait and see how completely this order will be enforced.

వేచు **weecu**[1] *v.t. class.* to wait for, expect, watch for.

వేచు **weecu**[2] *v.t.* to fry, grill.

వేచేతులా **weeceetulaa** *adv. lit.* with a thousand hands: ~ **sahaayam ceesEEru** they gave a very great amount of help.

వేట **weeTa** *n.* **1** hunt, hunting. **2** animal sacrifice. **3** *colloq.* sheep or goat intended for slaughter. **4** *colloq.* mutton; ~ **tini waccEEnu** I have eaten mutton; **aayana** ~ **muTTaDu** he will not eat (*lit.* touch) mutton.

వేటకాడు **weeTakaaDu** *n.* hunter, huntsman.

వేటాడు **weeTaaDu** *v.t.* to hunt, pursue, chase.

వేటు **weeTu** *n.* blow, stroke (= **eeTa**).

వేడబం **weeDabam** *n.* trickery, deceit.

వేడి **weeDi** I. *n.* **1** heat, warmth. **2** mild fever. II. *adj.* hot, warm.

వేడిమి **weeDimi** *n.* heat, warmth.

వేడు[కొను] **weeDu[konu]** *v.t.* to pray, beg, beseech, implore, entreat, plead.

వేడుక **weeDuka** *n.* **1** spectacle, display, show: **alluDi alaka oo** ~ **anteegaani adee paTTuku kuurcooku** a son-in-law's grumblings are just for show (*or* just a formality) and should not be taken amiss; ~ **pilupu** invitation issued only for name's sake (not seriously meant). **2** fun, joy, mirth, merriment, pleasure; ~ **ki** for fun, in jest. **3** festivity, festive occasion, celebration; **baarasaala** ~ the naming of a child is a festive occasion (not a religious ceremony).

వేడుకకత్తె **weeDukakatte** *n.* prostitute, adulteress.

వేడుకకాడు **weeDukakaaDu** *n.* adulterer.

వేడుకగా **weeDukagaa** *adv.* **1** finely, grandly, in style: **peLLi** ~ **jarigindi** the wedding was celebrated ceremoniously. **2** for pleasure, for enjoyment, for fun's sake: **pratyeekam eemii leedu, oo saari** ~ (*or* **muccaTagaa) maa iNTiki bhoojanaaniki raNDi** it is not a special occasion, but please come and have dinner at our house and give us the pleasure of your company.

వేడుకపడు **weeDukapaDu** *v.i.* to itch, yearn, long (to do s.g); **manawi manam wekkirincukooDaaniki weeDuka paDaDam kanabaDutundi** we appear to be longing to ridicule those things that are our own.

వేడుకోలు **weeDukoolu** *n.* entreaty, prayer, plea.

వేడెక్కించు **weeDekkincu** *v.t.* to heat, warm.

వేడెక్కు **weeDekku** *v.i.* to be heated, grow hot; **niiLLu weeDekkEEyi** the water has been heated *or* the water is hot; **waaDu uttaram cuusi weeDekkEEDu** after seeing the letter he grew angry.

వేణి **weeNi** *n. class.* **1** plait or braid of hair. **2** stream.

వేణీసంహారం **weeNiisamhaaram** *n. class.* **1** gathering up loose hair and tying it in a braided knot. **2** the title of a Sanskrit play.

వేణునాదం, వేణుగానం **weeNunaadam, weeNugaanam** *n.* music of the flute.

వేణువు **weeNuwu** *n.* flute.

వేణ్ణీళ్ళు **weeNNiiLLu** *n.pl.* hot water (= **weeDi niiLLu**).

వేత **weeta**[1] *n.* **1** throwing, casting. **2** knock, blow.

వేత **weeta**[2] *suffix used for forming nouns from vbs.*, e.g., **tiisi~** subtraction; **aNaci~** suppression.

వేతనం **weetanam** *n.* wages, salary; **widyaarthi~** student's scholarship or stipend; *see* **upakaara weeta[na]m.**

వేత్త **weetta** *n. suffix meaning* one is who is well versed in or acquainted with; **aarthikaśaastra~** economist.

వేత్రం **weetram** *n. class.* rattan cane.

వేత్రహస్తుడు, వేత్రధరుడు **weetrahastuDu, weetradharuDu** *n. class.* cane bearer, person who clears the way for a dignitary.

వేదం **weedam** *n.* 1 knowledge. 2 divine knowledge. 3 sacred scripture, the Vedas.

వేదండం **weedaNDam** *n. class.* elephant.

వేదచోదిత **weedacoodita** *adj.* prompted or inspired by the Vedas.

వేదజ్ఞుడు **weedajñuDu** *n.* person well versed in the Vedas.

వేదత్రయం **weedatrayam** *n.* name given to the first three Vedas, the Rigveda, Yajurveda and Samaveda.

వేదన **weedana** *n.* 1 pain. 2 distress, suffering.

వేదభూమి **weedabhuumi** *n.* land where the Vedas were revealed, India.

వేదవాక్యం **weedawaakyam** *n.* 1 quotation from the Vedas. 2 indisputable statement. 3 *colloq.* gospel truth.

వేదాంగం **weedaangam** *n.* name given to certain treatises considered as auxiliary to the Vedas.

వేదాంత **weedaanta** *adj.* philosophic[al].

వేదాంతం **weedaantam** *n.* 1 philosophy. 2 doctrine. 3 Vedanta, the Advaita system of philosophy based on the Upanishads.

వేదాంతి **weedaanti** *n.* 1 philosopher. 2 follower of the Advaita system.

వేదాంతీకరించు **weedaantiikarincu** *v.t.* to philosophise.

వేది[క] **weedi[ka]** *n.* 1. dais, platform. 2. forum for discussion. 3 altar.

వేదోక్త **weedookta** *adj.* declared or ordained in the Vedas.

వేద్య **weedya** *adj.* knowable; **anubhawayka~** capable of being known through experience.

వేద్యుడు **weedyuDu** *n.* he who may be known.

వేధ, వేధం **weedha[m]** *n.* 1 pain, grief. 2 evil influence of a star.

వేధశాల **weedhaśaala** *n. astron.* 1 observatory. 2 planetarium.

వేధి **weedhi** *n. class.* missile.

వేధించు **weedhincu** *v.t.* to tease, torment, trouble, nag, worry; **~ku tinu** to pester, harass.

వేనవేలు **weenaweelu** *n.pl.* thousands upon thousands.

వేనోళ్ల **weenooLLa** *adv.* (= **weyyi nooLLatoo**) 1 *lit.* with a thousand mouths. 2 (praising, proclaiming) loudly, forcefully; **ee kSaamapiiDitula sahaayaanikanoo candaalakoosam waccinawaariki prati wartakuDuu tana pakkawaaDinee cuupinci ataDee goppawaaDani~poguDutaaDu** every merchant who is approached by persons collecting subscriptions on behalf of the famine stricken points to his neighbour and loudly commends him as being a rich man; **taamu tama gooDalaku tagilincee cawkabaaru keelaNDaru bommalu tama samskaara daaridryaanni lookaaniki~ caaTutaayani wiiriki toocanaynaa toocadu** these people are quite unaware that the cheap calendar pictures that they hang on their walls proclaim forcefully to the world their lack of culture.

వేప[చెట్టు] **weepa[ceTTu]** *n.* neem tree, margosa tree.

వేపపుల్ల **weepapulla** *n.* margosa twig, used for cleaning the teeth.

వేపు **weepu** *v.t.* to fry.

వేపుడు **weepuDu** I. *n.* 1 fried curry. 2 act of frying. II. *adj.* fried, baked.

వేయి **weeyi** *same as* **weyyi.**

వేయించు **weeyincu**[1] *v.t.* to fry.

వేయించు **weeyincu**[2] *causative of* **weeyu** to cause to throw, put, etc.

వేయు **weeyu** I. *v.i.* 1 (of a physical or mental state) to be felt or experienced; **naaku aakali/cali weestunnadi** I feel hungry/cold; **naaku bhayam weestunnadi** I am afraid; **naaku anumaanam weesindi** I felt suspicious. 2 to appear, come on; **ceTTu kaaDaku aakuku madhya ciguru weesindi** a shoot appeared between the stalk and the leaf of the plant. 3 to collect, gather; **mabbu weestunnadi, waana paDutundi** clouds are gathering, it is going to rain; **isuka meeTa weesindi** sand collected into a heap; *cf.* **waraweeyu.** II. *v.t.* 1 to throw. 2 to strike, hit, knock. 3 to place, put. 4 to let fall, drop. 5 to shut; **talupu~** to shut a door; **reppa weeyakuNDaa cuucu** to stare without closing an eyelid *or* to stare fixedly. 6 to plant, sow (crop, seed). 7 to appoint; **aayanni maa baLLoo kotta pantulugaa weesEEru** they appointed him as a new teacher in our school. 8 *as an auxiliary ~ is used with a past participle to give intensive force*, e.g., **aapu** (imperative) stop! **aapiweeyi!** *or* **aapeeyi!** stop! (emphatic); **tinu** to eat; **tini~** to eat up, devour. 9 *~ is used idiomatically with a wide range of meanings which vary according to the context*, e.g., **illu~** (i) to thatch a house; (ii) to build a house; **citram~** to paint a picture; **naaTakam~** to enact a play; **pathakaalu~** to draw up or make plans; **baNDi~** to ply a cart for hire; **praśnalu~** to put questions; **layT~** to turn on a light; **gantulu~** to leap; **Tiikaalu~** to inoculate; **baaNam~** to shoot an arrow; **aawu duuDa weesindi** the cow calved; **reNDu aDugulu wenakaki weesEEDu** he took two steps backwards; **lekkalu weesEEDu** he added up (*or* he worked out) the account; **oTTu weesEEDu** he promised on oath; **naatoo pandem weesEEDu** he made a bet with me *or* he challenged me; **injin kuuta weesindi** the engine sounded its siren; *see also* **weesukonu.**

వేరవు **weerawu** *v.i.* to part, separate, be[come] separated.

వేరు **weeru**[1] *n.* root.

వేరు **weeru**[2] I. *n.* separation, division, difference. II. *adj.* other, separate, distinct, different; **deeśa prayoojanaalu ~, wyakti prayoojanaalu ~** the country's interests and an individual's interests are different from each other.

వేరుగా **weerugaa** *adv.* separately, apart.

వేరు చేయు, వేరుపరచు **weeru ceeyu, weeruparacu** *v.t.* to separate, detach, isolate, segregate, keep apart.

వేరు తన్ను, వేరూను, వేళ్లూను **weeru tannu, weeruunu, weeLLuunu** *v.i.* to strike root, take root; *cf.* **uunu.**

వేరు పట్టు **weeru paTTu** *v.i.* to take root.

వేరుపురుగు **weerupurugu** *n.* worm which attacks the roots of plants.

వేరు పోవు, వేరుపడు **weeru poowu, weerupaDu** *v.i.* 1 to separate, part, secede. 2 to be separated, be disassociated.

వేరువేరు **weeruweeru** *adj.* different, separate, differing.

వేరుశనగ, వేరుసెనగ **weeruśanaga, weerusenaga** *n.* groundnut.

వేరే **weeree** I. *adj.* other, separate, distinct. II. *adv.* separately, specially, particularly; **aa maaTa ~ ceppanakkaraleedu** that need not be mentioned specially *or* that need not be emphasised.

వేరొక **weeroka** *adj.* another.

వేర్పాటు **weerpaaTu** *n.* separation, secession, segregation.

వేర్పాటువాదం **weerpaaTuwaadam** *n.* separatism.

వేలం, ఏలం **weelam, eelam** *n.* auction.

వేలంపాట **weelampaaTa** *n.* bidding in auction.

వేలంవెర్రి **weelamwerri** *n.* 1 recklessness when bidding in auction. 2 *colloq.* passion, craze; **waaDiki sinimaalaNTee ~** he is mad on movies.

వేలతరబడి **weelatarabaDi** *adj.* thousands upon thousands of.

వేలబడు **weelabaDu** *v.i.* to hang [down], be suspended.

వేలవేయు, వేలదీయు, వేలాడవేయు, వేలాడదీయు **weelaweeyu, weeladiiyu, weelaaDaweeyu, weelaaDadiiyu** *v.t.* to hang, suspend; **tala** (*or* **mukham**) **weelaweesukonu** to hang o.'s head (in tiredness or shame or distress); **weNTrukalu weelaweesukoni tirugu** to go about with o.'s hair hanging loose.

వేలా **weelaa** *n.* tide; **~ nadi** tidal river.

వేలాడు, వేళాడు, వేళ్లాడు **weelaaDu, weeLaaDu, weeLLaaDu** *v.i.* 1 to hang, dangle, be suspended. 2 to hang down, droop. 3 **paTTukoni ~** to hang onto, cling to, adhere to; **ii aadarśaanni paTTukoni ~ tunna waariloonee eekiibhaawam leedu** even among those who cling to this ideal there is no agreement.

వేలాది **weelaadi** *adj.* at the rate of thousands, in thousands, thousands of.

వేలార్చు **weelaarcu** *v.t.* to hang, suspend.

వేలిముద్ర **weelimudra** *n.* 1 fingerprint. 2 thumb impression; **~ gaaDu** *colloq.* person who cannot sign his name, uneducated person.

వేలు **weelu**[1] *pl. of* **weyyi** thousands.

వేలు **weelu**[2] *n.* finger, toe; **~ etticuupu** to point a finger at, point out; **~ wiDicina** distant by one degree of relationship; **~ wiDicina meenamaama** mother's cousin; **waaLLa aydu weeLLuu nooTLooki elaa pootaayi?** how will they get food to eat? (*lit.* how will their five fingers go into their mouths?) **naa kaaLLaa weeLLaa paDi aDigEEDu** he fell at my feet and begged.

వేలు **weelu**[3] *v.i.* to hang, be suspended, dangle.

వేలుపు, వేల్పు **weelupu, weelpu** *n.* 1 god, goddess. 2 **ila ~, ilu ~** household god or goddess, tutelary deity.

వేలెడెత్తు **weeleDettu** *see* **ettu.**

వేళ **weeLa** *n.* time; **pagaTi ~** daytime; **raatri ~** night time; **~ ku** at the right time, in time, puncutually; **~ minci pooyindi, ika bhoonceeyanu** the time (for a meal) is past, I will not take food now; **leecina weeLaa wiśeeSam** the singular effect of the hour of o.'s getting up (this refers to a belief that the hour of rising influences a person's fortune for good or ill during the day); **leecina weeLaa wiśeeSam walla ciiwaaTLu tinnaaDu** due to his having got up at an unlucky hour he had to endure being scolded.

వేళాకోళం **weeLaakooLam** *n.* 1 joking. 2 ridicule, mockery, foolery, derision. 3 something laughable.

వేళాకోళం ఆడు, వేళాకోళం చేయు, వేళాకోళం పట్టించు **weeLaakooLam aaDu, weeLaakooLam ceeyu, weeLaakooLam paTTincu** *v.t.* to make fun of, play a joke on.

వేళాడు, వేళ్లాడు **weeLaaDu, weeLLaaDu** *same as* **weelaaDu.**

వేళాపాళా **weeLaapaaLaa** *n.* (**paaLaa** *is an echo word*) *in neg. constr.* proper or regular time; **~ leekuNDaa tinakuuDadu** do not take meals at irregular hours.

వేళ్లు తన్ను, వేళ్లూను **weeLLu tannu, weeLLuunu** *same as* **weeru tannu, weeruunu.**

వేవిళ్లు **weewiLLu** *n.pl.* morning sickness.

వేశం **weeśam** *n. class.* house.

వేశ్య **weeśya** *n.* prostitute.

వేశ్యావృత్తి **weeśyawrtti** *n.* prostitution.

వేషం **weeSam** *n.* 1 dress, garb. 2 trick, pretence; **naa daggira ii weeSaalu panikiraawu telusaa?** don't you know you cannot play these tricks on me? 3 *theat.* costume, make up. 4 part or role in a play; **sinimaalaloo cillara weeSaalu weesi Dabbu sampaadistaaDu** he earns money by playing small parts in movies.

వేషభాషలు **weeSabhaaSalu** *n.pl.* manner of dressing and talking.

వేషాలమారి **weeSaalamaari** *n.* pretender.

వేష్టనం **weeSTanam** *n. class.* girdle; **siroo ~** turban.

వేసంకాలం, వేసవికాలం **weesamkaalam, weesawikaalam** *n.* summertime.

వేసంగి, వేసవి **weesangi, weesawi** *n.* summer, hot season, the hot weather; **~selawalu** summer holidays.

వేసట **weesaTa** *n.* tiredness, fatigue.

వేసరు, వేసారు **weesaru, weesaaru** *v.i.* (*also* **wisigi weesaari poowu**) to be tired or bored or disgusted.

వేసుకొను **weesukonu** *v.t.* 1 to place or put (s.g) for o.s. 2 to put on, wear (clothes made to measure, shoes, jewellery). 3 **paaka~** to build a hut for o.s. 4 to arrange a vehicle for travelling; **kaaru weesukoni waccEEDu** he came by car (*lit.* he arranged for a car and came). 5 to collect, accumulate; **saruku~** to collect a supply of goods for carrying on business; **laabham~** to accumulate a profit. 6 to eat, consume; **annamloo eem weesukoni tiNTaawu?** what will you take to eat along with the rice? 7 **taambuulam~** to chew betel and nut. 8 *colloq.* to drink liquor; **weesukoni** (*or* **mandu weesukoni**) **waccEEDu** he came after drinking liquor. 9 (*equivalent to* **weNTa~**) **pillaajellaa weesukoni paDi waccEEDu** he came all the way accompanied by his children.

వై, వో - way, woo

వైకల్పం **waykalpam** *n. gram.* s.g optional.

వైకల్పిక **waykalpika** *adj.* 1 optional. 2 alternative.

వైకల్యం **waykalyam** *same as* **wikalata.**

వైకుంఠం **waykuNTham** *n.* Vishnu's paradise.

వైకుంఠపాళీ **waykuNThapaaLii** *n.* game of snakes and ladders.

వైకృత **waykṛta** *adj.* 1 altered, modified. 2 corrupted.

వైకృతం **waykṛtam** *n.* modification, alteration; **deeśya waykṛtaalu** regional variations.

వైక్రాంతం **waykraantam** *n.* kind of precious stone.

వైక్లబ్యం **wayklabyam** *n.* confusion, perplexity.

వైఖరి **waykhari** *n.* 1 attitude, demeanour. 2 manner, style. 3 look, appearance.

వైచిత్రం **waycitram** *n.* wonder, peculiarity, oddity.

వైచిత్రి, వైచిత్ర్యం **waycitri, waycitryam** *n.* 1 diversity. 2 strangeness, peculiarity.

వైచు **waycu** *class. form of* **weeyu.**

వైజయంతం **wayjayantam** *n.* 1 Indra's palace. 2 Indra's banner or emblem.

వైజ్ఞానిక **wayjñaanika** *adj.* scientific.

వైజ్ఞానికశాస్త్రం **wayjñaanikaśaastram** *n.* science.

వైజ్ఞానికశాస్త్రవేత్త, వైజ్ఞానికుడు **wayjñaanikaśaastraweetta, wayjñaanikuDu** *n.* scientist.

వైడూర్యం **wayDuuryam** *n.* lapis lazuli.

వైణికుడు **wayNikuDu** *n.* vina player.

వైతరణి **waytaraNi** *n.* name of the mythical river which the soul must cross after death in order to reach heaven.

వైతాళికుడు **waytaaLikuDu** *n.* 1 *class.* bard who awakens a king with music in the morning. 2 one who inspires or stirs up other persons.

వైతొలగు **waytolagu** *v.i.* to withdraw (from), break away (from).

వైదగ్ధ్యం **waydagdhyam** *n.* skill, dexterity.

వైదిక **waydika** *adj.* Vedic, pertaining to the Vedas; **~bhaaSa** Vedic Sanskrit, the language of the Vedas.

వైదికుడు, వైదీకుడు **waydi[i]kuDu** *n. colloq.* **śuddha~** simple-minded person.

వైదికులు, వైదీకులు **waydi[i]kulu** *n.pl.* name of a subsect of brahmans.

వైదుష్యం **wayduSyam** *n.* learning, wisdom, knowledge, scholarship.

వైదేశిక **waydeeśika** *adj.* pertaining to foreign affairs; **~widhaanam** foreign policy.

వైద్యం **waydyam** *n.* 1 medical science. 2 medical treatment; **~ceeyincukonnaaDu** he got himself medically treated.

వైద్యశాల **waydyaśaala** *n.* hospital, dispensary, clinic.

వైద్యుడు **waydyuDu** *n.* doctor, physician.

వైధవ్యం **waydhawyam** *n.* widowhood.

వైనం **waynam** *n.* 1 information, detail. 2 matter, affair. 3 item, instance.

వైనంగా **waynangaa** *adv.* 1 in detail, minutely; **cuusinadantaa~ceppEEDu** he described in detail all that he had seen. 2 with careful attention, with concentration, intently, singlemindedly, methodically; **~wiNTunnaaDu** he is listening intently.

వైపరీత్యం **wayparíityam** *n.* 1 abnormality, absurdity, preposterousness. 2 disaster, calamity, catastrophe; **prakṛti~** natural calamity.

వైపు **waypu** I. *n.* side, direction; **iru~laa** *or* **reNDu~laa** on two sides, on both sides. II. *p.p.* towards, in the direction of.

వైఫల్యం **wayphalyam** *n.* failure.

వైభవం **waybhawam** *n.* 1 wealth, riches. 2 grandeur, splendour.

వైభవంగా **waybhawangaa** *adv.* grandly, splendidly, in [fine] style.

వైభవోపేత **waybhawoopeeta** *adj.* grand, splendid.

వైమనస్యం **waymanasyam** *n.* 1 strife, discord. 2 aversion, dislike, illwill.

వైమానిక **waymaanika** *adj.* aeronautical.

వైమానికుడు **waymaanikuDu** *n.* airman, aviator.

వైముఖ్యం **waymukhyam** *n.* unwillingness.

వైయక్తిక **wayyaktika** *adj.* individual.

వైయాకరణుడు **wayyaakaraNuDu** *n.* grammarian.

వైరం, వైరభావం **wayram, wayrabhaawam** *n.* 1 enmity, hostility. 2 spite.

వైరస్యం **wayrasyam** *n.* illwill, enmity.

వైరాగి **wayraagi** *same as* **wiraagi.**

వైరాగ్యం **wayraagyam** *same as* **wiraagam.**

వైరాగ్యంగా **wayraagyangaa** *adv.* stoically.

వైరి **wayri** *n.* enemy, adversary, opponent, rival.

వైరుధ్యం **wayrudhyam** *n.* 1 difference. 2 contrariness, inconsistency. 3 enmity, hostility.

వైరూప్యం **wayruupyam** *n.* ugliness, deformity.

వైలక్షణ్యం **waylakSaNyam** *n.* 1 difference, disparity. 2 special quality or ability, distinctiveness.

వైళం **wayLam** *adv. class.* quickly, fast.

వైవస్వతం **waywaswatam** *n. class.* name of the current **manwantaram.**

వైవాహిక **waywaahika** *adj.* marital, matrimonial, conjugal; **~jiiwitam** married life.

వైవిధ్య **waywidhya** *adj.* diverse.

వైవిధ్యం **waywidhyam** *n.* difference, variety, diversity, variation.

వైశాఖం **wayśaakham** *n.* second Telugu lunar month corresponding to April-May.

వైశాల్యం **wayśaalyam** *n.* 1 breadth, width. 2 extent, area.

వైశిష్ట్యం **wayśiSTyam** *n.* speciality, special nature, peculiarity.

వైశ్యుడు **wayśyuDu** *n.* 1 member of the Vaisya community. 2 merchant, trader.

వైషమ్యం, వైషమ్యత **waySamyam, waySamyata** *n.* 1 unevenness, inequality. 2 dissimilarity. 3 enmity, hostility.

వైష్ణవ **waySNawa** *adj.* Vaishnavite.

వైష్ణవం **waySNawam** *n.* the Vaishnavite religion, Vaishnavism.

వోటరు **wooTaru** *n.* voter.

వోటు **wooTu** *n.* vote.

వోటుహక్కు **wooTu hakku** *n.* voting right, franchise, suffrage; **saarwajaniina~** universal suffrage.

వ్య - wya

వ్యంగ్య **wyangya** *adj.* 1 sarcastic, mocking, scornful. 2 insinuating.

వ్యంగ్యం **wyangyam** *n.* 1 sarcasm. 2 insinuation. 3 (*also* **wyangyakaawyam**) satire.

వ్యంగ్యంగా **wyangyangaa** *adv.* 1 sarcastically, sardonically, ironically, cynically. 2 suggestively, insinuatingly.

వ్యంగ్య చిత్రం **wyangya citram** *n.* satirical cartoon.

వ్యంగ్య చిత్రకారుడు **wyangya citrakaaruDu** *n.* cartoonist.

వ్యంగ్యరచన **wyangya racana** *n.* satire, satirical writing.

వ్యంజక **wyanjaka** *adjvl. suffix meaning* expressive of; **artha~padam** word expressing a meaning.

వ్యంజనం **wyanjanam**[1] *n. gram.* consonant.

వ్యంజనం **wyanjanam**[2] *n.* item of food which accompanies rice at a meal.

వ్యక్తం **wyaktam** *adj.* 1 apparent, clear, evident, manifest. 2 disclosed, revealed. 3 expressed, specified.

వ్యక్తం అవు **wyaktam awu** *v.i.* to be expressed.

వ్యక్తంగా **wyaktangaa** *adv.* clearly, plainly.

వ్యక్తం చేయు, వ్యక్తపరచు **wyaktam ceeyu, wyaktaparacu** *v.t.* to express (feeling, thought).

వ్యక్తత **wyaktata** *n.* 1 distinctness. 2 manifestation.

వ్యక్తరాసి **wyaktaraasi** *n. maths.* known quantity.

వ్యక్తి **wyakti** *n.* 1 individual. 2 adult, grown-up person.

వ్యక్తిగత **wyaktigata** *adj.* personal, individual.

వ్యక్తిత్వం **wyaktitwam** *n.* individuality, personality, nature, character.

వ్యక్తివాదం, వ్యష్టివాదం **wyaktiwaadam, wyaSTiwaadam** *n.* individualism.

వ్యక్తీకరణ **wyaktiikaraNa** *n.* expression; **bhaawa~** expression of an idea.

వ్యక్తీకరించు **wyaktiikarincu** *v.t.* to express.

వ్యక్తురాలు అవు **wyakturaalu awu** *v.i. colloq.* (of a girl) to attain puberty.

వ్యగ్రత **wyagrata** *n.* 1 concentration; **eekaamśa~** concentration on a single topic. 2 bewilderment, puzzlement.

వ్యగ్రుడు **wyagruDu** *second part of a n. compound meaning* one who is intent upon.

వ్యతికరం **wyatikaram** *n. class.* 1 grief. 2 misfortune, calamity.

వ్యతికరణ **wyatikaraNa** *n.* dissimilation.

వ్యతిక్రమం **wyatikramam** *n.* disorder, deviation, transgression.

వ్యతిచ్ఛేదనం **wyaticcheedanam** *n. maths. sci.* intersection.

వ్యతిరిక్త **wyatirikta** *adj.* different, opposite, contrary.

వ్యతిరేక **wyatireeka** I. *adjvl. suffix equivalent to* anti-; **warakaTNa ~ udyamam** anti-dowry movement. II. *adj.* 1 opposite, opposed, contrary, converse. 2 *gram.* negative; **~ waakyam** negative sentence. 3 reverse; **~ kramam** reverse order.

వ్యతిరేకం **wyatireekam** *n.* 1 opposition, contrariness, difference. 2 disagreement, antagonism.

వ్యతిరేకంగా **wyatireekangaa** *adv.* against, on the opposite side, in opposition to, contrary to; **miiru anukoneedaaniki ~** contrary to what you suppose.

వ్యతిరేకత **wyatireekata** *n.* opposition, antipathy, antagonism.

వ్యతిరేకార్థకం **wyatireekaarthakam** *n. gram.* negative.

వ్యతిరేకి **wyatireeki** *n.* antagonist, opponent.

వ్యతిరేకించు **wyatireekincu** *v.i. and t.* 1 to oppose. 2 to disagree.

వ్యత్యయం **wyatyayam** *class. alt. form of* **wyatyaasam.**

వ్యత్యస్త **wyatyasta** *adj.* reversed, contrary, opposite.

వ్యత్యస్తంగా **wyatyastangaa** *adv.* conversely, *vice versa.*

వ్యత్యాసం **wyatyaasam** *n.* difference, disparity, discrepancy.

వ్యథ **wyadha** *n.* pain, anguish, distress.

వ్యథిత **wyadhita** *adj.* 1 pained. 2 agitated, alarmed.

వ్యభిచరించు **wyabhicarincu** *v.i.* to commit adultery.

వ్యభిచారం **wyabhicaaram** *n.* adultery, prostitution.

వ్యభిచారి **wyabhicaari** *n.* adulterer.

వ్యభిచారిణి **wyabhicaariNi** *n.* adulteress.

వ్యయ **wyaya** *n.* twentieth year of the Hindu cycle of sixty years.

వ్యయం **wyayam** *n.* 1 expense, expenditure. 2 *pl.* **wyayaalu** expenses, charges.

వ్యయపరచు, వ్యయం చేయు **wyayaparacu, wyayam ceeyu** *v.t.* 1 to spend. 2 to squander.

వ్యయపూరిత **wyayapuurita** *adj.* expensive.

వ్యయించు **wyayincu** *v.t.* to spend, expend.

వ్యర్థ **wyartha** *adj.* 1 useless, vain, fruitless, futile, ineffectual, wasted. 2 meaningless: **~ padam** meaningless word.

వ్యర్థం చేయు, వ్యర్థపుచ్చు **wyartham ceeyu, wyarthapuccu** *v.t.* to waste; **mii samayam wyarthapuccaDam leedu gadaa**? I am not wasting your time, am I?

వ్యర్థత **wyarthata** *n.* wastage.

వ్యర్థుడు **wyarthuDu** *n.* waster, good-for-nothing person.

వ్యవకలనం **wyawakalanam** *n. maths.* subtraction.

వ్యవధానం **wyawadhaanam** *n.* 1 *same as* **wyawadhi.** 2 *gram.* insertion of a letter or syllable for euphony, e.g., **aakaaśapu-T-anculu** the borders of the sky, **teene-T-iiga** bee.

వ్యవధి **wyawadhi** *n.* available time, intervening time; **koncem ~ kaawaali** some time is needed.

వ్యవసాయం **wyawasaayam** *n.* 1 agriculture, cultivation. 2 activity, effort, exertion.

వ్యవసాయదారుడు **wyawasaayadaaruDu** *n.* agriculturist, farmer, cultivator.

వ్యవసాయిక **wyawasaayika** *adj.* agricultural, agrarian.

వ్యవస్థ **wyawastha** *n.* 1 system, order, method: **pani ~ leekuNDaa jarigindi** the work was done without any system *or* the work was done unsystematically; **saamaajika ~** social system. 2 organisation, institution. 3 regime; **saynika ~** military regime.

వ్యవస్థాపకుడు **wyawasthaapakuDu** *n.* founder, establisher.

వ్యవస్థాపన **wyawasthaapana** *n.* 1 organisation; **aarthika/paaThaśaala ~** economic/school organisation. 2 **~ sawkaryaalu** *econ.* infrastructure. 3 founding, establishing.

వ్యవస్థాపనాత్మక, వ్యవస్థాపరమైన **wyawasthaapanaatmaka, wyawasthaaparamayna** *adj.* organisational.

వ్యవస్థాపించు **wyawasthaapincu** *v.t.* to establish, organise.

వ్యవస్థీకరణ **wyawasthiikaraNa** *n.* organising, setting up.

వ్యవస్థీకరించు **wyawasthiikarincu** *v.t.* to organise.

వ్యవహరించు **wyawaharincu** I. *v.i.* 1 to behave, act, function. 2 to be current. 3 to have dealings, do business (**-too**, with). II. *v.t.* 1 to conduct, practise, carry out (policy). 2 to use, employ, make use of: **neeDu manam wyawaharistunna koostaa jillaalu, telangaaNaa, raayalasiima anee wibhaagam raajakiiyamaynadee gaaka sthuulangaa bhaaSaawiSayakangaa kuuDaa saripootundi** the division which we employ nowadays into coastal districts, Telangana and Rayalaseema is not only political, broadly speaking it also applies linguistically. 3 to call, term, name, describe, refer to; **aa padi jillaalanu telangaaNaa** praantangaa wyawaharistaaru they call those ten districts the Telangana region.

వ్యవహర్త, వ్యవహార్త **wyawaha[a]rta** *n.* 1 practical or capable person. 2 manager. 3 *colloq.* organiser. 4 *ling.* informant.

వ్యవహారం **wyawahaaram** *n.* 1 custom, practice. 2 use, usage; **kaasta gaTTi wiSayaalu raayawalasiwastee nitya~loo leeni maaTalu upayoogincaka tappadu** if you have to write about somewhat difficult subjects you are bound to employ words that are not in constant use. 3 affair, matter, transaction, business; **adhikaarawyawahaaraalu** official business. 4 trade, occupation. 5 behaviour; **nii~ eem baagaa leedu** your behaviour is not at all good.

వ్యవహారచ్యుతి **wyawahaaracyuti** *n.* falling out of use, obsolescence.

వ్యవహారజ్ఞానం **wyawahaarajñaanam** *n.* 1 understanding of worldly matters, common sense. 2 (*also* **wyawahaarawaadam**) pragmatism.

వ్యవహారభ్రష్ట **wyawahaarabhraSTa** *adj.* out of use, obsolete.

వ్యవహిత **wyawahita** *adj.* 1 discontinuous. 2 separated, parted.

వ్యష్టి **wyaSTi** *adj.* individual, personal, private (often contrasted with **samiSTi**); **~prayoojanam** private advantage; **~dṛSTi** individual or selfish outlook.

వ్యష్టివాదం **wyaSTiwaadam** *same as* **wyaktiwaadam.**

వ్యసనం **wyasanam** *n.* 1 *class.* grief, sorrow. 2 passion, addiction; **strii~** weakness for women, womanising; **madyapaana~** addiction to drink. 3 vice, bad habit.

వ్యసనపడు **wyasanapaDu** *v.i.* to regret, feel sorry.

వ్యసనపరుడు **wyasanaparuDu** *n.* addict.

వ్యసని **wyasani** *n.* 1 addict. 2 **strii~** womaniser, adulterer.

వ్యస్త **wyasta** *adj.* separate, single, simple.

వ్యస్తపదం **wyastapadam** *n.* non-compound word, simple word.

వ్యా - wyaa

వ్యాకరణం **wyaakaraNam** *n.* grammar.

వ్యాకరణయుక్త **wyaakaraNayukta** *adj.* grammatically acceptable.

వ్యాకరణరూపం **wyaakaraNaruupam** *n.* 1 part of speech (noun, adjective, verb, etc.). 2 grammatical form.

వ్యాకరించు **wyaakarincu** *v.t.* to explain or analyse grammatically.

వ్యాకుల, వ్యాకులిత **wyaakul[it]a** *adj.* afflicted, sorrowful, disturbed, troubled, uneasy, agitated.

వ్యాకులత **wyaakulata** *n.* sorrow, anxiety, affliction, agitation, uneasiness.

వ్యాకులపడు **wyaakulapaDu** *v.i.* to be perturbed.

వ్యాకులపాటు **wyaakulapaaTu** *n.* perturbation, agitation.

వ్యాకోచం **wyaakoocam** *n. sci.* expansion.

వ్యాకోచత్వం **wyaakoocatwam** *n. econ.* elasticity (of demand).

వ్యాఖ్య **wyaakhya** *n.* 1 comment. 2 caption accompanying an illustration.

వ్యాఖ్యాత **wyaakhyaata** *n.* commentator.

వ్యాఖ్యానం **wyaakhyaanam** *n.* 1 comment; **wyaakhyaana sweeccha** freedom of comment. 2 commentary, gloss, note, exposition, explanation, interpretation, criticism. 3 **pratyakSa~** running commentary.

వ్యాఖ్యానించు **wyaakhyaanincu** *v.t.* to comment.

వ్యాఘాతం **wyaaghaatam** *n.* 1 striking, beating. 2 blow, stroke.

వ్యాఘ్రం **wyaaghram** *n. class.* tiger.

వ్యాఘ్రి **wyaaghri** *n. class.* tigress.

వ్యాజం **wyaajam** *n.* cunning, deceit, pretence.

వ్యాజ్యం **wyaajyam** *n.* 1 law suit. 2 litigation.

వ్యాధి **wyaadhi** *n.* disease, sickness, illness, ailment; **~nirNayam** diagnosis of a disease.

వ్యాధితుడు **wyaadhituDu** *n.* sick person, patient.

వ్యానం **wyaanam** *n.* one of the five vital airs pervading the body according to traditional medicine.

వ్యాపక **wyaapaka** *adj.* widespread.

వ్యాపకం **wyaapakam** *n.* 1 distribution, spreading; **wiriwigaa~loo unnappaTikii** although they are widely distributed. 2 activity, avocation, interest; **aayanaku ennoo wyaapakaalu unnaayi** he has ever so many activities; **iiyana manastatwam, abhiruci, ~annii saahityaaniki anukuulamayinaTTiwee** his bent of mind, tastes and interests all appeared to favour literature.

వ్యాపనం **wyaapanam** *n.* 1 spreading. 2 **iinela~** *bot.* venation. 3 circulation (of news, books).

వ్యాపారం **wyaapaaram** *n.* 1 business, trade, commerce. 2 *colloq.* business (in the widest sense), matter, affair, concern; **inta aalasyam ayindi! eem ~ ceestunnaawu?** it is so late! what business have you been up to? **roojuu aydu ruupaayalu sampaayinci jiiwita ~** (*or* **jiiwita wyaasangam**) **naDipistunnaaDu** he is eking out his existence by earning five rupees per day; **ii ~ loo naSTapaDDaanu** I have lost money in this affair. 3 action, activity, function: **kriya dwaaraa suucincadalacina ~ puurti aytee, samaapakam** if the action indicated by the verb is complete, (the verb) is finite; *see* **welagapeTTu.**

వ్యాపార చిహ్నం **wyaapaara cihnam** *n.* brand, trade mark.

వ్యాపార పవనాలు **wyaapaara pawanaalu** *n.pl.* trade winds.

వ్యాపార వేత్త **wyaapaaraweetta** *n.* businessman.

వ్యాపారి, వ్యాపారస్థుడు **wyaapari, wyaapaarasthuDu** *n.* merchant, trader.

వ్యాపి **wyaapi** I. *n. class.* that which pervades. II. *adj. class.* pervading, all-pervading.

వ్యాపించు **wyaapincu** *v.i. and t.* to expand, spread.

వ్యాపింపచేయు, వ్యాప్తంచేయు **wyaapimpaceeyu, wyaaptamceeyu** *v.t.* to spread, extend, disseminate.

వ్యాప్తం **wyaaptam** *adjvl. suffix meaning* pervading, spreading through, extending over; **deeśa ~ gaa** extending over the whole country, covering the whole country, countrywide.

వ్యాప్తి **wyaapti** *n.* 1 spreading, pervading, extension, expansion. 2 dissemination, diffusion, distribution; **abhipraayam baagaa ~ loo undi** the opinion prevails widely *or* the opinion is widely disseminated.

వ్యాప్తిచెందు, వ్యాప్తిపొందు **wyaapticendu, wyaaptipondu** *v.i.* to be spread, be extended, be disseminated, be diffused.

వ్యాప్తిలోకి తెచ్చు **wyaaptilooki teccu** *v.t.* to disseminate, popularise.

వ్యామోహం **wyaamooham** *n.* 1 inordinate desire, lust. 2 passion, infatuation, craze.

వ్యాయామం **wyaayaamam** *n.* 1 physical exercise. 2 gymnastics.

వ్యాయామవిద్య, వ్యాయామశిక్షణ **wyaayaamawidya, wyaayaamaśikSaNa** *n.* physical education.

వ్యాయోగం **wyaayoogam** *n.* type of one act play dealing with a hero's exploits excluding any love interest.

వ్యావర్తక **wyaawartaka** *adj.* 1 surrounding. 2 revolving.

వ్యావర్తనం **wyaawartanam** *n.* 1 turning back. 2 surrounding. 3 revolving.

వ్యావసాయిక **wyaawasaayika** *adj.* agricultural.

వ్యావహారిక **wyaawahaarika** *adj.* in common use; **~ bhaaSa** colloquial language.

వ్యావహారికం **wyaawahaarikam** *n.* colloquial language.

వ్యావృత, వ్యావృత్త **wyaawṛt[t]a** *adj.* covered, screened, surrounded, encompassed.

వ్యావృత్తి **wyaawṛtti** *n.* business, occupation, avocation.

వ్యాసం **wyaasam**[1] *n. maths.* diameter.

వ్యాసం **wyaasam**[2] *n.* 1 essay, dissertation; **pariśoodhana ~** thesis. 2 newspaper article.

వ్యాసంగం **wyaasangam** *n.* 1 pursuit of or involvement in literature, art, science or scholarship; **racanaa ~ oka saamaajika baadhyata anaDam suluwee** it is easy to say that literary activity is a social obligation; **pariśoodhana wyaasangaaniki phelooSip paddhatini praweeśapeTTaDam mancidee** it is a good thing to introduce the fellowship system for research activity; **aa roojulloo neenu, puripaNDaa modalayna waaLLam kawitaa ~ ceeseewaaLLam** in those days Puripanda, myself and others used to conduct poetic pursuits. 2 **jiiwita ~** day to day activities, routine daily life; **roojuu aydu ruupaayalu sampaayinci jiiwita ~** (*or* **jiiwitawyaapaaram**) **naDipistunnaaDu** he is eking out his existence by earning five rupees per day; **jiiwita ~ loo alasipooyEEDu** he is tired of the routine of daily life.

వ్యాసంగి **wyaasangi** *n.* person who is active or involved in a subject; **saahitya ~** person involved in literary activities.

వ్యాసకర్త **wyaasakarta** *n.* essayist.

వ్యాసపీఠం **wyaasapiiTham** *n.* book rest.

వ్యాసరేఖ **wyaasareekha** *n.* diameter.

వ్యాసార్థం **wyaasaartham** *n. maths.* radius.

వ్యాసుడు **wyaasuDu** *n.* Vyasa, the sage who is reputed to have composed the Mahabharata.

వ్యాహత **wyaahata** *adj. class.* beaten down, subdued.

వ్యు to వ్రే - wyu to wree

వ్యుత్క్రమ **wyutkrama** *adj. maths.* reciprocal.

వ్యుత్క్రమం **wyutkramam** *n.* **1** reverse order. **2** irregular arrangement.

వ్యుత్పత్తి **wyutpatti** *n.* **1** *gram.* derivation, etymology. **2** critical knowledge, learning, scholarship.

వ్యుత్పత్తిశాస్త్రం **wyutpattiśaastram** *n.* (science of) etymology.

వ్యుత్పన్న **wyutpanna** *adj.* derived, derivative.

వ్యుత్పన్నుడు **wyutpannuDu** *n.* person who is well versed in the study of a subject, esp. language and literature.

వ్యూహం, వ్యూహరచన **wyuuham, wyuuharacana** *n.* strategy.

వ్యోమం **wyoomam** *n.* sky, heavens, space.

వ్యోమగామి **wyoomagaami** *n.* astronaut.

వ్రక్క, వక్క **wrakka, wakka** *n.* bit, piece, fragment.

వ్రజం **wrajam** *n. class.* flock, herd, multitude, collection.

వ్రణం **wraNam** *n.* **1** tumour. **2** boil, ulcer, sore.

వ్రతం **wratam** *n.* vow to undertake certain religious obligations or perform certain religious ceremonies.

వ్రతకల్పం **wratakalpam** *n.* treatise on religious vows.

వ్రతగ్రంథం **wratagrantham** *n.* book of religious observances and ceremonies.

వ్రతుడు **wratuDu** *last part of a n. compound meaning* one who has taken a vow; **satyawacana~** one who has vowed to speak only the truth.

వ్రాత **wraata** *alt. class. form of* **raata.**

వ్రాయసకాడు **wraayasakaaDu** *n.* writer, clerk.

వ్రాయు **wraayu** *alt. class. form of* **raayu.**

వ్రాలు **wraalu** *n.* signature.

వ్రేలు **wreelu** *alt. form of* **weelu**[2]**.**

వ్రేల్మిడి **wreelmiDi** *n.* **1** snap of the fingers. **2** instant of time.

శ - śa

శంక **śanka** *n.* **1** doubt, hesitation, suspicion. **2** ~ *is a euphemism for wanting to pass urine* **~tiircukoni wastaanu** I will go to the toilet; *cf.* **laghu** *sense 3.*

శంకపడు **śankapaDu** *v.i.* to doubt, hesitate, have scruples.

శంకరగిరి మాన్యాలు **śankaragiri maanyaalu** *n.pl.* **1** graveyard, burial ground. **2** *colloq.* **~ paTTu** *is used scornfully to mean* to be in a wretched state, be reduced to a miserable condition.

శంకరాభరణం **śankaraabharaNam** *n.* name of a raga in music.

శంకాకార **śankaakaara** *adj.* conical (in shape).

శంకించు **śankincu** *v.i. and t.* to doubt, hesitate, suspect.

శంకితుడు **śankituDu** *n.* **1** timid or hesitant or apprehensive person. **2** person who is under suspicion.

శంకు[వు] **sanku[wu]** *n.* **1** stake, peg, esp. a stake planted ceremonially at the north-east corner of a building site before starting construction of the building. **2** *maths. sci.* cone. **3** *colloq. alt. form of* **śankhu[wu].**

శంకుచ్ఛేదం **śankuccheedam** *n. maths.* conic section.

శంకుస్థాపన[ం] **śankusthaapana[m],** *n.* ceremony performed before starting construction of a building, consisting of either planting a stake (**śanku**) or laying a foundation stone.

శంఖం, శంఖు[వు] **śankham, śankhu[wu]** *n.* conch shell.

శంఖనాదం **śankhanaadam** *n.* sound made by blowing a conch shell.

శంఖారావం **śankhaaraawam** *n.* clarion call sounded on a conch shell before battle.

శంప **śampa** *n. class.* lightning.

శంబలం **śambalam** *n. class.* provision made for a journey.

శంసనం **śamsanam** *n. class.* praising.

శకం **śakam** *n.* epoch, era.

శకటం **śakaTam** *n.* **1** cart, carriage. **2** (*also* **śakaTu**) bishop in chess.

శకటరేఫ **śakaTareepha** *n.* the obsolete Telugu letter ఱ, also called **baNDi ra.**

శకటికం **śakaTikam** *n. class.* small cart.

శకపురుషుడు **śakapuruSuDu** *n.* person after whom an era is called (as the Vikramarka era is called after king Vikramarka).

శకలం **śakalam** *n.* fragment, broken piece, part.

శకాబ్దం **śakaabdam** *n.* a year of an era.

శకారుడు **śakaaruDu** *n.* **1** name of a boastful character in Sanskrit drama. **2** *colloq.* person who boasts habitually.

శకుంతం, శకుంతి **śakuntam, śakunti** *n. class.* kind of bird.

శకుంతలం **śakuntalam** *n.* **~ cadiwEEDu** he has embarked on the study of Sanskrit (*lit.* he has studied the play Sakuntala. **abhijñaana ~**, a play by Kalidasa, is the first of **panca mahaa kaawyaalu** or five Sanskrit masterpieces whose study is essential for all Sanskrit scholars).

శకునం **śakunam** *n.* **1** omen, augury, esp. one derived from the cry or flight of a bird. **2** evil omen, s.g inauspicious. **3** *class.* kind of bird.

శకునం చెప్పు **śakunam ceppu** *v.i.* to prophesy, [make a] forecast.

శకునపక్షి **śakunapakSi** *n.* **1** bird that brings misfortune. **2** *term used as a mild form of abuse.*

శకుని **śakuni** *n.* **1** name of the uncle of Duryodhana, who was the chief cause of the Pandavas being defeated in dice at the beginning of the Mahabharata. **2** *colloq.* person who indulges in trickery and mischief-making. **3** *class.* kind of bird.

శక్త[ం] **śakta[m]** *adj.* strong, powerful, capable.

శక్తత **śaktata** *n.* power, ability, capability.

శక్తి **śakti** *n.* **1** power, strength, force, energy: **~ yuktulu** talents, powers, capabilities; **~ saamarthyaalu** strength and skill, ability; **~ wancana leekuNDaa** without stinting o.'s efforts. **2** ability, capability, capacity, potential; **niluwa ~** storage capacity. **3** means, competence; **naa śaktyaanusaaram candaa iccEEnu** I subscribed according to my means. **4** the energy or active power of a god personified as his wife. **5** a name of Parvati, wife of Siva. **6** female deity, goddess; **~ puuja ceeyu** to worship a goddess, gen. Parvati or Kali.

శక్తిపరిమాణం **śaktiparimaaNam** *n.* capacity, ability.

శక్తిమంత **śaktimanta** *adj.* strong, powerful, mighty, energetic, effectual, efficacious.

శక్తియుత **śaktiyuta** *adj.* powerful, forceful, energetic.

శక్తిసంపన్న **śaktisampanna** *adj.* endowed with power, powerful.

శక్తిసమతులనం **śaktisamatulanam** *n.* balance of power.

శక్మ **śakma** *n. sci.* potential.

శక్యం **śakyam** *adj.* possible, practicable.

శఠం **śaTham** *adj.* wicked, perverse.

శఠగోపం **śaThagoopam** *n.* cover made of precious metal and shaped like a bowl, inscribed with the marks of Vishnu's feet and placed on the head of a devotee by the priest when uttering a blessing at the end of worship in a temple.

శఠించు **śaThincu** *v.i.* to be stubborn, be obstinate.

శఠుడు **śaThuDu** *n.* **1** obstinate person. **2** rascal.

శతం **śatam** *n.* hundred.

శతకం **śatakam** *n.* **1** hundred. **2** collection of a hundred stanzas.

శతకోటి **śatakooTi** *n.* **1** a hundred crores (a thousand million). **2** *colloq.* a very large number.

శతగుణం **śataguNam** *adj.* hundredfold.

శతఘ్ని **śataghni** *n.* **1** tank or other armoured vehicle. **2** *class.* heavy weapon or missile.

శతఘ్నిదళం **śataghnidaLam** *n.* artillery.

శతజయంతి **śatajayanti** *n.* centenary.

శతతార, శతభిష **śatataara, śatabhiSa** *n. astrol.* name of the twenty-fourth lunar mansion.

శతథా **śatathaa** *adv.* **1** a hundred times. **2** *colloq.* over and over again.

శతపత్ర **śatapatra** *n. class.* **1** lotus. **2** peacock. **3** parrot.

శతపత్రసుందరి **śatapatrasundari** *n.* beautiful woman.

శతపది, శతపాదజీవి **śatapadi, śatapaadajiiwi** *n.* centipede.

శతపోరు **śatapooru** *v.i and t.* to try again and again, strive by repeated efforts; **śatapoori pampincEEnu** after making repeated efforts I induced him to go; **cewiloo illu kaTTukoni śatapoori salahaa ceppEEnu** I urged advice on him by constant repetition.

శతమానం **śatamaanam** *n.* **1** tali, woman's marriage token. **2** weight of one palam. **3** hundred. **4** a hundred rupees.

శతవర్ధంతి **śatawardhanti** *n.* hundredth anniversary of a person's death.

శతవార్షికం, శతవార్షికోత్సవం **śatawaarSik[ootsaw]am** *n.* centenary.

శతవిధాల **śatawidhaala** *adv.* **1** *lit.* in a hundred ways. **2** *gen. in neg. constr.* by all possible means, by any means, on all accounts, on any account; **Dabbukoosam ~ prayatnincinaa dorakaleedu** although I tried by all possible means to get money, it was not forthcoming; **~ aayana raaDu** he will not come on any account.

శతాంశం **śataamśam** *n.* hundredth part.

శతాధిక **śataadhika** *adj.* more than a hundred; **~ granthakarta** author of more than a hundred books.

శతాబ్దం, శతాబ్ది **śataabdam, śataabdi** *n.* century.

శతాయుష్మంతుడు **śataayuSmantuDu** *n.* centenarian.

శతాయుష్యం **śataayuSyam** *n.* life span of a hundred years.

శతావధాని **śataawadhaani** *n.* **1** *lit.* person who can attend to a hundred things at the same time. **2** person with a prodigious memory and a very alert mind.

శత్రర్థక **śatrarthaka** *adj. gram.* durative; **~ pratyayam** durative suffix.

శత్రుత్వం **śatrutwam** *n.* enmity, hostility.

శత్రుభీకర **śatrubhiikara** *adj.* frightening, terrifying.

శత్రువు **śatruwu** *n.* enemy, foe.

శనగలు **śanagalu** *same as* **senagalu**.

శని, సని **śani, sani** *n.* 1 the planet Saturn, whose baneful influence is said to last for seven years; **eelnaaTi ~** seven years of misfortune caused by the planet Saturn. 2 god of misfortune. 3 misfortune, ill luck, period of ill luck; **naa kompaki ~ paTTindi** ill luck has come upon my household; **~ roojulu** evil days, days of misfortune; *see* **wiragaDa awu.**

శనిగొట్టు **śanigoTTu** *n.* ill-starred wretch, unlucky person.

శనిగ్రహం **śanigraham** *n.* 1 the planet Saturn. 2 *colloq.* unlucky person.

శనిదానం **śanidaanam** *n.* bestowing certain objects and a gift of money on another person in the belief that o.'s ill luck will thereby pass off.

శపథం **śapatham** *n.* oath, promise.

శపథం పట్టు **śapatham paTTu** *v.i.* to swear an oath.

శపించు **śapincu** *v.t.* 1 to curse. 2 *colloq.* to abuse.

శబర **śabara** *n.* name of a hill tribe in Andhra Pradesh.

శబ్దం **śabdam** *n.* 1 sound, noise. 2 word, term.

శబ్దచిత్రం **śabdacitram** *n.* sound track (of a movie).

శబ్దజాలం **śabdajaalam** *n.* vocabulary.

శబ్దరత్నాకరం **śabdaratnaakaram** *n.* 1 *lit.* ocean of words. 2 name of a famous dictionary of classical Telugu.

శబ్దలేఖనం **śabdaleekhanam** *n. ling.* logogram.

శబ్దవేధి **śabdaweedhi** *n. class.* person who can shoot an arrow in the dark and hit a mark, locating it by sound alone.

శబ్దసంగ్రహం **śabdasangraham** *n.* list of selected words, vocabulary, glossary.

శబ్దసాగరం **śabdasaagaram** *n.* 1 *lit.* ocean of words. 2 lexicon, dictionary.

శబ్దానుశాసనుడు **śabdaanuśaasanuDu** *n.* title given to Nannaya (*lit.* he who regulated the Telugu language).

శబ్దావళి **śabdaawaLi** *n.* vocabulary, glossary.

శమం **śamam** *n.* 1 tranquillity, calm; **raamuDu raajyam śama damaadulatoo paalincenu** Rama ruled the kingdom with calmness and sternness. 2 absence of passion, quietism, stoicism.

శమనం **śamanam** *n.* 1 calming, soothing. 2 calmness, tranquillity.

శమి **śami** *n. class.* 1 calm and quiet person. 2 *alt. form of* **jammi.**

శమించు **śamincu** *v.i.* 1 to become quiet or tranquil. 2 to pass away, pass off, be alleviated. 3 (of illness) to subside.

శమీధాన్యం **śamiidhaanyam** *n.* pulse, bean or other leguminous crop.

శయనం **śayanam** *n.* 1 bed, couch. 2 lying down; *cf.* **bhuu ~**

శయనాగారం **śayanaagaaram** *n. class.* bedroom.

శయనించు **śayanincu** *v.i.* to lie down, repose.

శయ్య **śayya** *n.* bed, couch.

శరం **śaram**[1] *n.* 1 arrow. 2 kind of grass or reed.

శరం **śaram**[2] *n. gen. occurring in the compound* **sigguu ~** shame.

శరణం, శరణు **śaraNam, śaraNu** *n.* 1 refuge, shelter, asylum. 2 protection, deliverance.

శరణాగతుడు **śaraNaagatuDu** *n.* one who appeals for shelter or protection.

శరణార్థి **śaraNaarthi** *n.* refugee.

శరణాలయం **śaraNaalayam** *n.* place of refuge, asylum, sanctuary.

శరణుకోరు **śaraNu kooru** I. *v.i.* to surrender, capitulate. II. *v.t.* to beg s.o. for asylum, beg s.o. for protection.

శరణు చొచ్చు **śaraNu coccu** *alt. class form of* **śaraNu kooru.**

శరణ్యం **śaraNyam** *n.* 1 protection, shelter. 2 refuge, asylum, sanctuary. 3 *colloq., following* **-ee** (*emphatic marker*) the only recourse, the only solution, the only way; **peTrooliyam dinusula dharalu aakaaśaanni aNTutunna ii roojulaloo ilaaNTi jala rawaaNaa paddhatee ~** in these days of skyhigh prices for petroleum products a water transport system of this kind is the only solution; **maamiDi paNDu ruci eTLaa unnadoo ceppaDaaniki tinaDamee ~** the only way to tell how a mango will taste is to eat it.

శరణ్యుడు **śaraNyuDu** *n.* 1 protector. 2 one who needs protection.

శరత్కాలం, శరదృతువు, శరత్తు **śaratkaalam, śaradṛtuwu, śarattu** *n.* autumn, the season which follows the rainy season.

శరపరంపరగా **śaraparamparagaa** *adv.* in volleys, in quick succession (*lit.* like a stream of arrows).

శరభం **śarabham** *n. class.* a mythological animal.

శరాభ్యాసం **śaraabhyaasam** *n.* practice of archery.

శరీరం **śariiram** *n.* body.

శరీరధర్మశాస్త్రం **śariiradharmaśaastram** *n.* physiology.

శరీరనిర్మాణ శాస్త్రం **śariiranirmaaNaśaastram** *n.* anatomy.

శరీరయాత్ర **śariirayaatra** *n.* a person's journey through life.

శరీరాభివృద్ధి **śariiraabhiwṛddhi** *n.* physical growth.

శరీరి **śariiri** *n. class.* embodied soul, embodied spirit.

శర్కర **śarkara** *n. class.* sugar (= **cakkera**).

శర్మ **śarma** *n.* honorific title among brahmans, also used as a personal name.

శర్వాణి **śarwaaNi**[1] *n.* epithet of the Goddess Parvati.

శర్వాణీ, షేర్వాణీ **śarwaaNi², SeerwaaNi** *n.* man's long coat fastening upto the collar.

శలగ **śalaga** *same as* **selaga.**

శలభం **śalabham** *n.* **1** cricket, grasshopper, locust. **2** moth.

శలవు **śalawu** *same as* **selawu.**

శలాక **śalaaka** *n.* **1** thin bar or rod. **2** sharp piece of bone. **3** toothpick. **4** pointed surgical instrument. **5** rib of an umbrella. **6** *class.* javelin.

శల్యం **śalyam** *n.* **1** *class.* bone. **2** *colloq.* **cikki ~ awu** to become as thin as a rake; *see* **awaśiSTa.**

శల్యపరీక్ష **śalyapariikSa** *n.* close scrutiny, close observation.

శల్యసారథ్యం **śalyasaarathyam** *n.* discouragement; **~ ceesi nannu weLLaniwwakuNDaa ceesEEDu** he discouraged me and stopped me from going.

శవం **śawam** *n.* corpse.

శవఖననం **śawakhananam** *n.* burial.

శవజాగరణం **śawajaagaraNam** *n.* nightlong vigil beside a corpse.

శవదహనం **śawadahanam** *n.* cremation.

శవపరీక్ష **śawapariikSa** *n.* postmortem examination, autopsy.

శవపేటిక **śawapeeTika** *n.* coffin.

శశ[క]ం **śaśa[ka]m** *n. class.* hare.

శశవిషాణం **śaśawiSaaNam** *n. lit.* a hare's horn, *hence* an absurdity, s.g that does not exist (= **kundeeTi kommu).**

శశి, శశాంకుడు **śaśi, śaśaankuDu** *n. class.* moon.

శషభిషలు **śaSabhiSalu** *n.pl. colloq.* **1** pretence, disguise; **ii ~ naa daggira saagawu** this pretence will not fool me. **2** futile discussion, vain disputes.

శస్త్ర **śastra** *adj.* surgical.

శస్త్రం **śastram** *n.* **1** weapon. **2** surgical instrument. **3** *class.* iron.

శస్త్రచికిత్స **śastracikitsa** *n.* surgical treatment.

శస్త్రవైద్యం **śastrawaydyam** *n.* (art of) surgery.

శస్త్రవైద్యుడు **śastrawaydyuDu** *n.* surgeon.

శష్పం **śaSpam** *n.* **1** young grass. **2** *colloq.* pubic hair.

శహనాయి **śahanaayi** *n.* shenai (musical instrument).

శా - śaa

శాంతం **śaantam** *n.* **1** gentleness. **2** tranquillity. **3** peace, quiet.

శాంతపరచు **śaantaparacu** *v.t.* **1** to pacify, placate. **2** to tranquillise.

శాంతి **śaanti** *n.* **1** peace, tranquillity, calmness, quiet[ness], rest. **2** warding off the evil influence of a star or spell or curse.

శాంతించు **śaantincu** *v.i.* to become calm, calm down, be pacified.

శాంతింపచేయు **śaantimpa ceeyu** *v.t.* **1** to calm, soothe, pacify. **2** to propitiate, placate. **3** to appease, mollify.

శాంతిభంగం **śaantibhangam** *n.* breach of peace.

శాంతిభద్రతలు **śaantibhadratalu** *n.pl.* law and order.

శాంతియుత **śaantiyuta** *adj.* peaceful.

శాంతి వహించు **śaanti wahincu** *v.i.* to keep calm, preserve an even temper.

శాంతివాది **śaantiwaadi** *n.* pacifist.

శాకం **śaakam** *n. class.* vegetable.

శాకతైలం **śaakataylam** *n.* vegetable oil.

శాకపాకాలు **śaakapaakaalu** *n.pl.* vegetable dishes and sweet preparations.

శాకాహారి **śaakaahaari** *n.* vegetarian.

శాకిని **śaakini** *n.* female evil spirit (= **Dhaakini).**

శాకునం **śaakunam** *n. class.* science of interpreting omens.

శాక్తేయుడు **śaakteeyuDu** *n.* member of a sect which worships Kali.

శాఖ **śaakha** *n.* **1** branch. **2** department. **3** sect, subsect (in religion or caste).

శాఖాచంక్రమణం **śaakhaacankramaNam** *n.* **1** *lit.* moving from one branch to another. **2** shifting from one place or state to another; **~ ceestunnaaDu, inkaa ekkaDaa udyoogamloo kudiripoowaDam leedu** he skips from one thing to another, he has not yet settled down to a job anywhere. **3** diversion, digression.

శాఖాధిపతి **śaakhaadhipati** *n.* head of a department.

శాఖామృగం **śaakhaamrgam** *n.* monkey.

శాఖాహారి **śaakhaahaari** *incorrect alt. form of* **śaakaahaari.**

శాఖోపశాఖలు **śaakhoopaśaakhalu** *n.pl.* branches and sub branches, ramifications.

శాఖోపశాఖలుగా **śaakhoopaśaakhalugaa** *adv.* spreading far and wide, diverging in all directions.

శాణం **śaaNam** *same as* **seeNam.**

శాతం **śaatam** *n.* percent[age].

శాన **śaana** *colloq. alt. form of* **caalaa** *(adj.) or* **caalu** *(impersonal vb.).*

శాపం **śaapam** *n.* curse, malediction, imprecation.

శాపగ్రస్తుడు **śaapagrastuDu** *n.* one who is accursed.

శాపనార్థం **śaapanaartham** *n.* cursing, swearing, abusive language.

శాపనార్థాలు పెట్టు **śaapanaarthaalu peTTu** *v.t* to curse, swear at, hurl abuse at.

శాయశక్తులా, సాయశక్తులా **śaayaśaktulaa, saayaśaktulaa** *adv.* with all (o.'s) might; ~ **prayatnistaanu** I will try my hardest.

శారద **śaarada** *n.* epithet of Saraswati, goddess of literature.

శారి[క] **śaari[ka]** *n. class.* myna (bird).

శారీరక **śaariiraka** *adj.* physical, relating to the body, bodily, corporeal.

శారీరకం **śaariirakam** *n.* physical features, physique.

శారీరకంగా **śaariirakangaa** *adv.* physically.

శాత్రవం **śaatrawam** *n.* enmity, hostility.

శాత్రవుడు **śaatrawuDu** *n.* enemy.

శార్దూలం **śaarduulam** *n.* 1 tiger. 2 (*also* **śaarduula wikriiDitam**) a kind of poetic metre.

శార్ధం **śaardham** *colloq. alt. form of* **śraaddham.**

శార్వరి **śaarwari** *n.* 1 *class.* night. 2 thirty-fourth year of the Hindu cycle of sixty years.

శాల, సాల **śaala, saala** *second part of a n. compound meaning* house, edifice, building, shed; *the form* **śaala** *is used in conjunction with Sanskrit nouns*, e.g., **paaThaśaala** school, *and the form* **saala** *in conjunction with Telugu nouns or nouns derived from other languages*, e.g., **cerasaala** prison, **Tankasaala** mint.

శాలి **śaali** *n.suffix meaning* one who is possessed of: **adrsTa** ~ fortunate person.

శాలిబియ్యం **śaalibiyyam** *n.pl.* paddy, rice in husk.

శాలివాహన **śaaliwaahana** *n.* Salivahana, founder of the Satawahana dynasty after whom the Salivahana era is named.

శాలివాహన శకం **śaaliwaahana śakam** *n.* Salivahana era.

శాలువ **śaaluwa** *n.* shawl.

శాల్తి **śaalti** *n. colloq.* 1 item, object. 2 person, individual; **ippaTidaakaa kurciiloo kuurcunna** ~ **gallantu ayyindi** the person who was sitting in the chair till a moment ago is not to be seen.

శాశ్వత **śaaśwata** *adj.* permanent, perpetual, eternal, everlasting; ~ **kiirti** undying fame.

శాశ్వతంగా **śaaśwatangaa** *adv.* permanently, eternally, perpetually.

శాశ్వతత్వం **śaaśwatatwam** *n.* permanence, perpetuity.

శాసనం **śaasanam** *n.* 1 law, act, statute. 2 order, command, edict; **daana** ~ order confirming a grant. 3 inscription (on stone, copper plate).

శాసననిర్మాణం **śaasananirmaaNam** *n.* legislation, enactment of laws.

శాసనమండలి **śaasana maNDali** *n.* Legislative Council.

శాసనవిరుద్ధ **śaasanawiruddha** *adj.* illegal, unlawful.

శాసనసభ **śaasana sabha** *n.* Legislative Assembly.

శాసనస్థ **śaasanastha** *adj.* used in inscriptions, occurring in inscriptions; ~ **bhaaSa** inscriptional language.

శాసనాత్మక, శాసనబద్ధ, శాసనప్రోక్త, శాసనవిహిత **śaasanaatmaka, śaasanabaddha, śaasanaprookta, śaasanawihita** *adj.* statutory.

శాసనోల్లంఘన **śaasanoollanghana** *n.* civil disobedience.

శాసించు **śaasincu** *v.t.* to order, command, decree, ordain. 2 to regulate. 3 to rule, govern.

శాస్తి **śaasti** *n.* punishment, retribution; **waaDiki manci** ~ **ceesEEDu** he taught him a good lesson.

శాస్త్ర **śaastra** *adj.* scientific; ~ **saadhanaalu** scientific instruments.

శాస్త్రం **śaastram** *n.* 1 science; **waydya** ~ science of medicine. 2 sacred precept, spiritual injunction. 3 sacred writings, scripture, the Hindu Sastras.

శాస్త్రజ్ఞుడు, శాస్త్రవేత్త **śaastrajñuDu, śaastraweetta** *n.* scientist.

శాస్త్రవిజ్ఞానం **śaastrawijñaanam** *n.* science, scientific knowledge.

శాస్త్రి **śaastri** *n.* 1 person who is learned in the Sastras. 2 honorific title among brahmans, also used as a personal name. 3 title awarded to a scholar in a classical language of India.

శాస్త్రీయ **śaastriiya** *adj.* 1 scientific. 2 belonging to the Sastras. 3 according to the Sastras, classical; ~ **sangiitam** classical music.

శాస్త్రీయంగా **śaastriiyangaa** *adv.* scientifically.

శాస్త్రోక్త **śaastrookta** *adj.* 1 declared, ordained or decreed by the Sastras. 2 ordained by law, lawful.

శాస్త్రోక్తంగా **śaastrooktangaa** *adv.* 1 in accordance with the Sastras, as laid down in the Sastras. 2 lawfully.

శి - śi

శిక్ష **śikSa** *n.* **1** punishment, penalty, retribution, sentence. **2** training, education. **3** title of the Vedanga which teaches correct pronunciation of the language of the Vedas.

శిక్షణ **śikSaNa** *n.* **1** training, coaching; ~ **pondu** to undergo training. **2** punishment; *see* **śiSTa**.

శిక్షా[సంబంధి] **śikSaa[sambandhi]** *adj.* penal; **bhaarata śikSaa smṛti** Indian Penal Code.

శిక్షాత్మక **śikSaatmaka** *adj.* punitive.

శిక్షార్హ **śikSaarha** *adj.* punishable.

శిక్షించు **śikSincu** *v.t.* to punish.

శిక్షిత **śikSita** *adj.* trained, disciplined.

శిక్షితుడు **śikSituDu** *n.* **1** person who is trained. **2** person who is punished.

శిఖ **śikha** *n.* **1** crest, peacock's crest. **2** tuft of hair on the top of the head. **3** (*also* **agni**~) flame.

శిఖండి **śikhaNDi** *n.* **1** name of the son of king Drupada in the Mahabharata who changed from a female into a male. **2** *colloq.* obstinate person.

శిఖరం **śikharam** *n.* **1** top, peak, summit. **2** pinnacle, apex. **3** tower.

శిఖరాగ్రం **śikharaagram** *n.* summit; **śikharaagra samaaweeśam** summit conference.

శిఖామణి **śikhaamaNi** *n.* **1** jewel worn on the head, chief gem in a diadem. **2** *second part of a n. compound* best, finest,. noblest, grandest.

శిఖి **śikhi** *n.* fire.

శితాగ్రం **śitaagram** *n. class.* thorn, prickle.

శిథిల **śithila** *adj.* ruined, dilapidated.

శిథిలాలు **śithilaalu** *n.pl.* ruins.

శిబిరం **śibiram** *n.* **1** camp. **2** tent. **3** **saynika**~ barracks.

శిర **śira** *n.* rib or vein of a leaf.

శిరం, శిరసు, శిరస్సు **śiram, śirasu, śirassu** *n. class.* head.

శిరఃకంప[న]ం **śirahkampa[na]m** *n.* nodding the head (in approval or appreciation).

శిరచ్ఛేదం **śiraccheedam** *n.* beheading, decapitation.

శిరసావహించు **śirasaawahincu** I. *v.i.* to bow the head (in obedience or acknowledgement). II. *v.t.* to receive or accept with respect (a blessing), defer to (advice).

శిరస్త్రాణం, శిరస్త్రం **śirastraaNam, śirastram** *n.* helmet.

శిరోగృహం **śiroogrham** *n. class.* upper room in a house.

శిరోజాలు **śiroojaalu** *n.pl.* hair of the head, locks.

శిరోధార్య **śiroodhaarya** *adj.* acceptable with respect.

శిరోభారం **śiroobhaaram** *n.* **1** headache. **2** cold in the head. **3** anger, displeasure.

శిరోభూషణం **śiroobhuuSaNam** *n.* ornament for the head.

శిరోమణి **śiroomaNi** *n.* **1** jewel worn on the head. **2** title awarded to a scholar who passes a prescribed test in Sanskrit learning.

శిరోవేదన **śirooweedana** *n.* headache.

శిరోవేష్టనం **śirooweeSTanam** *n.* any headwear, e.g., turban, helmet.

శిల **śila** *n.* stone, rock.

శిలాఖండం **śilaakhaNDam** *n.* piece of stone, block of stone.

శిలాక్షరం **śilaakSaram** *n.* **1** writing on stone. **2** *colloq.* s.g not to be disputed.

శిలాజ **śilaaja** *adj.* petro-, petrified, fossil; ~ **indhanaalu** fossil fuels.

శిలాజం **śilaajam** *n.* fossil.

శిలాతైలం **śilaataylam** *n.* petroleum.

శిలాద్రవం **śilaadrawam** *n.* lava.

శిలాయుగం **śilaayugam** *n.* stone age.

శిలావరణం **śilaawaraNam** *n.* lithosphere.

శిలావిగ్రహం **śilaawigraham** *n.* stone statue.

శిలాశాసనం **śilaaśaasanam** *n.* inscription on stone.

శిలీంధ్రం **śiliindram** *n.* mushroom, fungus.

శిలీంధ్రనాశకం **śiliindranaaśakam** *n.* fungicide.

శిలీంధ్రశాస్త్రం **śiliindraśaastram** *n.* mycology.

శిల్పం **śilpam** *n.* **1** sculpture (the art of carving *or* a carved object). **2** any manual art or fine art. **3** artistry. **4** technique; **kaawyamloo śilpaanni wastuwunu wiDamaracaleemu** in literary composition we cannot separate technique from form and content; **wancanaa**~ the technique of cheating.

శిల్పకళ **śilpakaLa** *n.* art of sculpture.

శిల్పి **śilpi** *n.* **1** sculptor. **2** artist.

శివం **śiwam** *n.* **1** prosperity, happiness, wellbeing, blessedness. **2** auspiciousness. **3** emancipation. **4** inspiration, elation of spirit. 5 energy. 6 possession by a demon. 7 *pl.* **śiwaalu** (or **siwaalu**) wild dancing; *see* **ankamma.**

శివమెత్తించు **śiwamettincu** *v.t.* to arouse a feeling of strong or violent emotion such as elation, frenzy, fury.

శివమెత్తు **śiwamettu** *v.i.* (of strong or violent emotion) to be aroused; **śiwametti gantulu weestunnaaDu, waaNNi ippuDu palakarincaku** he is dancing with rage, do not speak to him now.

శివరాత్రి **śiwaraatri** *n.* 1 (*also* **mahaa~**) festival in honour of Siva held annually on the fourteenth day and night of the second fortnight of Magha; **naaku aa raatri~ aypooyindi** *colloq.* I stayed awake all that night (*lit.* for me that night became Sivaratri—because people stay awake all night for that festival). 2 **maasa~** fourteenth day of the second fortnight of every month, which is sacred to Siva.

శివలింగం **śiwalingam** *n.* the phallus worshipped as the emblem of Siva.

శివలోకం **śiwalookam** *n.* Siva's heaven.

శివాయనమః **śiwaayanamaḥ** *n.* invocation of the name of Siva.

శివాయిజమా **śiwaayijamaa** *n.* term used in revenue accounts for unauthorised cultivation of government land.

శివారు **śiwaaru** *n.* 1 hamlet, offshoot of a main village. 2 *pl.* **śiwaarlu** outskirts; **paTTaNa śiwaarlaloo dongatanaalu** thefts in the outskirts of the town.

శివాలయం **śiwaalayam** *n.* temple of Siva.

శివుడు **śiwuDu** *n.* God Siva.

శిశినం **śiśinam** *n.* penis.

శిశిరం **śiśiram** *n.* cold season, winter.

శిశుచికిత్స **śiśucikitsa** *n. med.* pediatrics.

శిశుపక్షవాతం **śiśupakSawaatam** *n.* infantile paralysis, poliomyelitis.

శిశువు **śiśuwu** *n.* infant, baby.

శిశుసంరక్షణ **śiśusamrakSaNa** *n.* child care.

శిశుహత్య **śiśuhatya** *n.* infanticide.

శిశూత్పాదక **śiśuutpaadaka** *adj.* viviparous.

శిష్ట **śiSTa** *adj.* 1 trained, disciplined. 2 educated, polite, refined, cultured; **~bhaaSa** educated speech. 3 good, sound, highminded, virtuous; **duSTaśikSaNa ~rakSaNa kSatriya dharmam** a warrior's duty is to punish the wicked and protect the virtuous; **wiirandarikii eewoo konni spaSTamayna sthiramayna ~mayna jiiwitapu wiluwalu uNDeewi** all of these persons had some clear, steady and highminded values to guide their lives; **prabhutwa wyawasthaloo ii~ siddhaantaanni praweeśapeTTaDam wiSayamloo agranaayakulu konta awdaasiinyaanni pradarśincEEru** the leaders have shown some indifference in the matter of applying this sound doctrine to the administrative system.

శిష్టం **śiSTam** *second part of a n.compound* remainder, residue; *cf.* **awa~.**

శిష్టజనులు **śiSTajanulu** *n.pl.* elite.

శిష్టత్వం **śiSTatwam** *n.* good behaviour, good qualities.

శిష్టాచారం **śiSTaacaaram** *n.* 1 established rule of conduct. 2 good manners, good conduct.

శిష్టాచారపరుడు, శిష్టాచారపరాయణుడు **śiSTaacaarapar[aayaN]uDu** *n.* traditionalist, one who follows traditional beliefs.

శిష్టుడు **śiSTuDu** *n.* 1 educated, cultured person. 2 good, upright, honest person.

శిష్టేతరుడు **śiSTeetaruDu** *n.* uneducated, uncultured person.

శిష్టోక్తి **śiSTookti** *n.* euphemism.

శిష్యరికం **śiSyarikam** *n.* period of studentship, period of discipleship, tutelage.

శిష్యుడు **śiSyuDu** *n.* disciple, pupil.

శిస్తు **śistu** *n.* 1 kist, tax assessed on land, land revenue. 2 rent paid by a tenant to a landowner.

శీ -śii

శీఘ్ర **śiighra** *adj.* quick, rapid, swift, fast.

శీఘ్రంగా, శీఘ్రగతిని **śiighrangaa, śiighragatini** *adv.* swiftly, quickly, rapidly, speedily.

శీత **śiita** *adj.* cold, frigid, cool, chilly; **naamiida~kannu weesEEDu** he behaved coldly towards me.

శీతం **śiitam** *n.* cold[ness].

శీతకాలం, శీతాకాలం **śiita[a]kaalam** *n.* cold weather, cold season, winter.

శీతనగం **śiitanagam** *n. class.* Himalayas.

శీతల[ం] **śiitala[m]** *n. class.* cold[ness].

శీతల **śiitala** *adj.* cold; **~waayuwu** cold wind; **~giDDangi** cold store.

శీతలీకరణ **śiitaliikaraNa** *n.* refrigeration.

శీతశ్వాసం **śiitaśwaaswam** *n. zool.* hibernation.

శీతాంశువు **śiitaamśuwu** *n. class.* moon.

శీతోష్ణ. **śiitooSNa** *adj.* climatic.

శీతోష్ణస్థితి **śiitooSNasthiti** *n.* climate.

శీర్షం **śiirSam** *n.* 1 *class.* head. 2 *maths.* vertex. 3 apex.

శీర్షిక **śiirSika** *n.* 1 title, heading. 2 headline (of a newspaper).

శీల[క] **śiila[ka]** *second part of an adjvl. compound meaning* inclined to, prone to; **pragati~** progressive.

శీలం **śiilam** *n.* 1 nature, character, conduct. 2 good conduct, morality. 3 chastity; **~ ceracu** to rape.

శీలత **śiilata** *second part of a n. compound meaning* proneness, disposition, inclination.

శీలనం **śiilanam** *n.* examination, research, study.

శీలవంతుడు **śiilawantuDu** *n.* person of good conduct and character.

శీలవతి **śiilawati** *n.* chaste woman.

శీలి, శీలుడు **śiili, śiiluDu** *second part of a n. compound meaning* one who is inclined towards; **witaraNa~** bountiful or liberal person; **daana~** philanthropic person.

శు - śu

శుంఠ **śuNTha** I. *n.* blockhead, stupid person, fool. II. *adj.* stupid, senseless; **~ praśnalu** rubbishy questions.

శుంఠుడు **śuNThuDu** *n.* blockhead, stupid person, fool.

శుక[మహర్షి] **śuka[maharSi]** *n.* sage who is reputed to have composed the Bhagawatam.

శుకం **śukam** *n.* parrot.

శుకనాడి **śukanaaDi** *n.* book of astrological predictions.

శుక్తి **śukti** *n.* pearl oyster.

శుక్రం **śukram** *n.* sperm, semen.

శుక్రధారణ **śukradhaaraNa** *n.* insemination.

శుక్రవారం **śukrawaaram** *n.* Friday.

శుక్రాశయం **śukraaśayam** *n.* testicle.

శుక్రుడు **śukruDu** *n.* 1 (*also* **śukragraham**) the planet Venus. 2 name of the teacher of the Asuras (demons) in mythology.

శుక్ల **śukla** *n.* third year of the Hindu cycle of sixty years.

శుక్లపక్షం **śuklapakSam** *n.* fortnight of the moon's waxing, bright lunar fortnight.

శుక్లపటలం **śuklapaTalam** *n.* cataract (eye disease).

శుక్లాలు **śuklaalu** *n.pl.* cataract (eye disease).

శుచి **śuci** I. *n.* purity, cleanliness. II. *adj.* pure, clean.

శుచీశుభ్రం, శుచీశుభ్రత **śuciiśubhram, śuciśubhrata** *n.* cleanliness, hygiene.

శుద్ధ **śuddha** *adj.* 1 pure, clean, undefiled; **~ prati** fair copy. 2 unmixed, unadulterated. 3 downright, utter, sheer; **~ abaddham** downright lie. 4 *class.* pertaining to the bright lunar fortnight (when the moon is waxing); **~ cawiti** fourth day of the bright lunar fortnight.

శుద్ధం **śuddham** *n.* 1 purity. 2 bright lunar fortnight (when the moon is waxing).

శుద్ధంగా **śuddhangaa** *adv.* 1 cleanly, purely. 2 *colloq.* wholly, entirely, completely.

శుద్ధాంతం **śuddhaantam** *n. class.* harem.

శుద్ధి **śuddhi** *n.* 1 cleanliness, purity. 2 cleansing, purification; **waaLLaki puriTi ~ ayndi** the period of defilement is over for them (referring to the ceremonial defilement incurred by family members for eleven days after a birth in the family).

శుద్ధి చేయు **śuddhi ceeyu** *v.t.* to cleanse, purify, refine.

శుద్ధి పెట్టు **śuddhi peTTu** *v.t. colloq.* to clean a place where s.o. has been taking food by sprinkling water.

శుద్ధీకరించు **śuddhiikarincu** *v.t.* to purify.

శునకం **śunakam** *n. class.* dog.

శుభ **śubha** *adj.* good, happy, lucky, blessed, fortunate, auspicious.

శుభం **śubham** I. *n.* 1 auspicious ceremony. 2 s.g auspicious. 3 auspiciousness; **~ astu**! may it be fortunate! *is a form of words used to invoke the blessing of Providence on an auspicious occasion.* 4 right, good; *see* **abham.** II. *interj.* that's good!, that's fine!

శుభకార్యం **śubhakaaryam** *n.* auspicious occasion, happy occasion.

శుభకృతు **śubhakrtu** *n.* thirty-sixth year of the Hindu cycle of sixty years.

శుభచింతనం **śubhacintanam** *n.* kind thoughts, good wishes.

శుభప్రద **śubhaprada** *adj.* bringing good fortune.

శుభలేఖ **śubhaleekha** *n.* 1 note or letter giving news of a happy event. 2 invitation card.

శుభవార్త **śubhawaarta** *n.* 1 good news. 2 (Christian) gospel.

శుభసూచకం, శుభసూచన **śubhasuucakam, śubhasuucana** *n.* happy augury.

శుభస్యశీఘ్రం **śubhasyaśiighram** *Sanskrit phrase meaning* the sooner the better.

శుభాంతం **śubhaantam** *n.* happy ending (to a story).

శుభాకాంక్షలు **śubhaakaankSalu** *n.pl.* good wishes, greetings.

శుభావహం **śubhaawaham** *n.* s.g auspicious.

శుభాశుభాలు **śubhaaśubhaalu** *n.pl.* **1** good and evil. **2** auspicious and inauspicious events.

శుభుడు **śubhuDu** *n. astrol.* one who is auspicious; **ii jaatakuDiki rawi ~** the sun is auspicious for the person whose horoscope this is.

శుభ్రం **śubhram** I. *n.* cleanliness, hygiene; **waaDiki ~ leedu** he does not observe cleanliness. II. *adj.* **1** pure, clean. **2** neat, tidy. **3** fresh; **~ ayna gaali** fresh cool breeze.

శుభ్రంగా **śubhrangaa** *adv.* **1** purely, cleanly. **2** neatly, tidily; **sTeeSan ~ uncaNDi** please keep the station tidy. **3** *colloq.* completely; **nippu ~ nusi aypooyindi** the fire has completely turned to ashes. **4** *colloq.* readily, without hesitation; **tanu tappu ceesEEnani ~ ceppEEDu** he readily admitted that he had made a mistake. **5** fine, quite all right; **waaDikeem? ~ unnaaDu; madhyaloo naa pani ayindi** what of him? he is quite all right; meanwhile I am in trouble.

శుభ్రంచేయు **śubhram ceeyu** *v.t.* to clean, purify.

శుభ్రత **śubhrata** *n.* **1** cleanliness. **2** neatness, tidiness.

శుభ్రపరచు **śubhraparacu** *v.t.* to clean, cleanse, purify.

శుల్కం **śulkam** *n.* toll, duty, tax, fee.

శుశ్రూష **śuśruuSa** *n.* **1** service. **2** obedience. **3** willingness to listen.

శుష్క **śuSka** *adj.* **1** dry, arid, dried up. **2** mere, empty, useless, vain, pointless.

శుష్కించు **śuSkincu** *v.i.* **1** to dry up. **2** to become lean. **3** to wither away.

శూ - śuu

శూకం **śuukam** *n. class.* **1** beard or awn of barley, etc. **2** scorpion's sting.

శూద్ర **śuudra** *adj.* belonging to the Sudra or fourth caste.

శూద్రుడు **śuudruDu** *n.* member of the Sudra caste.

శూన్య **śuunya** I. *adj.* empty, void, hollow, blank. II. *second part of an adjvl. compound meaning* destitute of, devoid of; **anubhawa ~** devoid of experience.

శూన్యం **śuunyam** *n.* **1** nothing, nil, zero, cypher. **2** emptiness, void, vacuum.

శూన్యత్వం **śuunyatwam** *n.* emptiness, hollowness.

శూన్యప్రదేశం, శూన్యస్థానం **śuunyapradeeśam, śuunyasthaanam** *n.* vacuum.

శూన్యవాదం **śuunyawaadam** *n.* nihilism.

శూన్యుడు **śuunyuDu** *second part of a n. compound meaning* person devoid of; **samskaara ~** s.o. devoid of culture.

శూరత, శూరత్వం **śuurata, śuuratwam** *n.* heroism, bravery, valour.

శూరుడు **śuuruDu** *n.* hero, champion, warrior.

శూర్పణఖ **śuurpaNakha** *n.* a female demon, sister of Ravana in the Ramayana.

శూల **śuula** *n.* (*also* **~ noppi**) shooting or stabbing pain.

శూలం **śuulam** *n.* **1** trident. **2** dart. **3** spike, pointed weapon.

శృ - śṛ

శృంఖలం **śrnkhalam** *n.* chain, fetter.

శృంఖలాప్రక్రియ **śrnkhalaaprakriya** *n. sci.* chain reaction.

శృంగం **śrngam** *n.* **1** horn, trumpet. **2** peak, summit.

శృంగాటకం **śrngaaTakam** *n.* crossroads, road junction.

శృంగార **śrngaara** *adj.* **1** ornamented, decorated. **2** ornamental, graceful, elegant, beautiful. **3** romantic. **4** erotic; **~ kawitwam** love poetry; **~ rasam** sentiment or emotion of love or sex.

శృంగారం **śrngaaram** *n.* **1** ornament, decoration. **2** grace, elegance, beauty. **3** romanticism. **4** sexual attractiveness, sexual love, eroticism.

శృగారంగా **śrngaarangaa** *adv.* **1** ornamentally. **2** charmingly, attractively; **~ nawwEEDu** he smiled beguilingly.

శృంగార పురుషుడు **śrngaarapuruSuDu** *n.* philanderer, womaniser.

శే, శై - śee, śay

శేఖరం **śeekharam** *n.* 1 chaplet or garland worn on top of the head. 2 (*also* **śeekharuDu**) one who wears such a chaplet or garland; **candra~** he who wears the crescent moon on his head (epithet of Siva). 3 *second part of a n. compound* (*also* **śeekharuDu**) one who is pre-eminent; **raaja~** chief among kings.

శేముషి **śeemuSi** *n.* intellect, intellectual power, intellectual eminence.

శేరీ, సేరీ **śeerii, seerii** *n.* 1 cultivation. 2 home farm land of the proprietor of an estate.

శేరీదారు **śeeriidaaru** *n.* middleman who gets a landholder's land cultivated through tenants.

శేరు, సేరు **śeeru, seeru** *n.* 1 seer, a weight equal to 80 tolas or four fifths of a kilogram. 2 measure of grain by volume, varying from one region to another.

శేష **śeeSa** *adj.* remaining, residual; **~bhaagam** remaining part.

శేషం **śeeSam** *n.* rest, remainder, residue, remnant, vestige; **pada~** vestige of a word.

శేషతోలనపట్టిక **seeSatoolana paTTika** *n. econ.* trial balance.

శేషాంత్రం **śeeSaantram** *n. med.* ileum.

శేషించు **śeeSincu** *v.i.* to be left, remain over.

శేషుడు **śeeSuDu** *n.* the serpent Sesha, Vishnu's couch.

శైత్యం, సైచ్చం **śaytyam, sayccam** *n.* 1 cold, chilliness. 2 cold in the head, catarrh.

శైత్యోపచారం **śaytyoopacaaram** *n.* ceremony of offering rosewater, etc., to alleviate heat.

శైథిల్యం **śaythilyam** *n.* ruin, decay, disintegration.

శైలం **śaylam** *n. class.* mountain.

శైలి **śayli** *n.* style.

శైవ **śaywa** *adj.* pertaining to Siva, Saivite.

శైవం **śaywam** *n.* the Saivite religion, Saivism.

శైవలం **śaywalam** *n. bot.* alga.

శైవుడు **śaywuDu** *n.* Saivite.

శైశవం **śayśawam** *n.* 1 infancy. 2 childhood.

శొ, శో, శౌ - śo, śoo, śaw

శొంఠి, సొంఠి **śoNThi, soNThi** *n.* dried ginger.

శోకం **śookam** *n.* grief, sorrow.

శోకగ్రస్త, శోకపూర్ణ, శోకమయ **śookagrasta, śookapuurNa, śookamaya** *adj.* sad, mournful, plaintive.

శోకాలు తీయు, శోకాలు పెట్టు **śookaalu tiiyu, śookaalu peTTu** *v.i.* to sob (often said of insincere sobbing); **neenu koTTaka mundee śookaalu peTTEEDu** he began sobbing before I hit him.

శోకావేశం **śookaaweeśam** *n.* utter misery.

శోకించు, శోకిల్లు **śookincu, śookillu** *v.i.* to grieve, lament.

శోచనీయ **śoocaniiya** *adj.* regrettable, lamentable, deplorable.

శోణితం **śooNitam** *n. class.* blood.

శోధన[ం] **śoodhana[m]** *n.* 1 cleaning, purifying. 2 *chem.* purification. 3 search, enquiry, investigation. 4 test.

శోధననాళం, శోధననాళిక **śoodhananaaLam, śoodhananaaLika** *n.* test tube.

శోధించు **śoodhincu** *v.t.* 1 to search. 2 to test.

శోఫ **śoopha** *n.med.* swelling, oedema.

శోభ **śoobha** *n.* lustre, brightness, splendour, radiance, light.

శోభకృత్తు **śoobhakrttu** *n.* thirty-seventh year of the Hindu cycle of sixty years.

శోభన **śoobhana** *adj.* 1 auspicious. 2 bright, shining.

శోభనం **śoobhanam** *n.* 1 happiness, good fortune. 2 ceremony of consummation of marriage, nuptial ceremony.

శోభనం పెళ్ళి కొడుకు **śoobhanam peLLikoDuku** *n.* the groom at the nuptial ceremony.

శోభాయమాన **śoobhaayamaana** *adj.* glorious, splendid.

శోభించు, శోభిల్లు **śoobhincu, śoobhillu** *v.i.* to shine, be splendid.

శోభిత **śoobhita** *second part of an adjvl. compound meaning* adorned with, beautified by.

శోష **śooSa** *n.* 1 drying up. 2 weakness or weariness due to hunger or exhaustion. 3 **waaDiki aa pani ceeyawaddani ceppaDam naa kaNTha~ayindi** my telling him not to do that was a waste of breath (*lit.* was just causing dryness in my throat).

శోషక **śooSaka** *adj. sci.* absorbent; **~taylam** drying oil.

శోషణం **śooSaNam** *n. sci.* 1 absorption. 2 dryness, drying, dessication.

శోషణపాత్ర **śooSaNapaatra** *n. chem.* dessicator.

శోషరసం śooSarasam *n. biol.* lymph.

శోషరసమండలం śooSarasa maNDalam *n. biol.* lymphatic system.

శోషించు, శోషణ చేయు śooSincu, śooSaNa ceeyu *v.t.* to absorb.

శౌచం śawcam *n.* cleanliness, purity.

శౌరసేని śawraseeni *n.* a dialect of Prakrit.

శౌర్యం śawryam *n.* heroism, bravery, valour, gallantry, prowess.

శ్మ to శ్ర - śma to śra

శ్మశానం, శ్మశానవాటిక śmaśaanam, śmaśaanawaaTika *n.* burial ground.

శ్మశానవైరాగ్యం śmaśaanawayraagyam *n.* shortlived sense of the vanity of human wishes and resolve to renounce worldly life, induced by attendance at a funeral.

శ్యామ śyaama *n.* girl, young woman.

శ్యామల[ం] śyaamala[m] *adj.* 1 black. 2 dark blue. 3 green.

శ్యేనం śyeenam *n. class.* hawk, falcon.

శ్రద్ధ śraddha *n.* 1 care, diligence; **bhakti ~ lu** *or* **śraddhaabhaktulu** care and devotion. 2 interest, attention. 3 zeal.

శ్రద్ధగా śraddhagaa *adv.* carefully, painstakingly.

శ్రద్ధవహించు śraddhawahincu *v.i.* 1 to be attentive. 2 to bestow care. 3 to be zealous.

శ్రద్ధాంజలి śraddhaanjali *n.* offering of reverence, tribute.

శ్రద్ధాళువు śraddhaaLuwu *n.* attentive, diligent or zealous person.

శ్రమ śrama *n.* 1 labour, toil. 2 trouble. 3 tiredness, weariness, fatigue.

శ్రమ ఇచ్చు śrama iccu *v.i.* to cause trouble (to s.o.).

శ్రమజీవి śramajiiwi *n.* person who toils, person who works hard for a living.

శ్రమణి śramaNi *n.* Buddhist nun.

శ్రమణుడు śramaNuDu *n.* 1 Buddhist monk. 2 ascetic.

శ్రమదానం śramadaanam *n.* giving o.'s labour free for a good cause.

శ్రమ పడు śrama paDu *v.i.* 1 to be troubled. 2 to take trouble, take pains, strive, work hard.

శ్రమ పెట్టు śrama peTTu *v.t.* to trouble, worry, distress, annoy, torment.

శ్రమశీల śramaśiila *adj.* industrious, hardworking.

శ్రమసాంద్ర śramasaandra *adj.* labour intensive.

శ్రవణ śrawaNa *adj. sci.* acoustic, auditory.

శ్రవణం śrawaNam *n.* 1 ear. 2 hearing, listening. 3 *astrol.* twenty-second asterism or lunar mansion.

శ్రవణపేయ śrawaNapeeya *adj.* sweet, charming, appealing.

శ్రవణేంద్రియం śrawaNeendriyam *n.* sense of hearing.

శ్రవ్య śrawya *adj.* audible.

శ్రా - śraa

శ్రాంతి śraanti *n.* fatigue, tiredness.

శ్రాద్ధం śraaddham *n.* obsequies, funeral ceremonies; **M.-too sneehaaniki ~ peTTeesi** having put an end to his friendship with M.

శ్రామిక śraamika *adj.* labour[ing], working; **~ janaabhaa** working population.

శ్రామిక సంఘవాదం śraamika sanghawaadam *n. polit.* syndicalism.

శ్రామికుడు śraamikuDu *n.* labourer, worker.

శ్రావణం śraawaNam[1] *n. astrol.* fifth lunar month of the Hindu calendar corresponding to August-September.

శ్రావణం śraawaNam[2] *n. sci.* forceps.

శ్రావణి śraawaNi *n.* night of the full moon in the month of Sravana.

శ్రావ్య śraawya *adj.* harmonious, melodious, tuneful.

శ్రావ్యత śraawyata *n.* melodiousness.

శ్రీ - śrii

శ్రీ śrii I. *n.* **1** epithet of Lakshmi, goddess of wealth. **2** wealth, riches, prosperity, good fortune. **3** name of a raga. **4** poison. II. *adj.* holy, blessed, sacred. III. *honorific prefix equivalent to* Mr.; **śrii** *is also prefixed to names of deities and sacred places as an honorific title.*

శ్రీకంఠుడు śriikaNThuDu *n.* epithet of Siva (*lit.* poison-throated).

శ్రీకారం śriikaaram *n.* the letter **śrii** in Telugu script.

శ్రీకారం చుట్టు śriikaaram cuTTu *v.i.* to begin, start, undertake, embark on, enter upon: **nissandeehangaa ii naaDu maanawuDu tana caritraloo oka apuurwaadhyaa-yaaniki śriikaaram cuTTEEDu** today without doubt man has entered upon an unprecedented chapter in his history.

శ్రీగంధం śriigandham *n.* scented sandalwood.

శ్రీఘనం śriighanam *n.* kind of sweet made with curds.

శ్రీపుత్రుడు śriiputruDu *n.* one born with a silver spoon in his mouth, one who is fortunate and well off all through his life.

శ్రీమంత śriimanta *adj.* fortunate, prosperous, well off.

శ్రీమంతం, సీమంతం śriimantam, siimantam *n.* ceremony performed during pregnancy to ensure the welfare of the mother and the safe delivery and future wellbeing of the expected child.

శ్రీమంతుడు śriimantuDu *n.* prosperous or wealthy person.

శ్రీమతి śriimati I. *n.* wife; **naa~** my wife. II. *honorific prefix equivalent to* Mrs.

శ్రీముఖ śriimukha *n.* seventh year of the Hindu cycle of sixty years.

శ్రీముఖం śriimukham *n.* **1** letter from a guru (spiritual preceptor). **2** *colloq.* memorandum or note calling for an explanation. **3** *colloq.* memorandum or note conveying a reminder.

శ్రీయుతులు śriiyutulu *honorific prefix equivalent to* Messrs.

శ్రీరంగనీతులు śriiranganiitulu *n.pl. lit.* moral teachings of (the temple of) Srirangam, *a proverbal expression for precepts which the preacher himself does not observe.*

శ్రీరస్తు! śriirastu! *interj.* may it be blessed! *form of words used to invoke the blessing of Providence on an auspicious occasion.*

శ్రీరామరక్ష! śriiraamarakSa! *interj. lit.* may Sri Rama protect you! *said as a blessing; see* **weyyi eeLLaayuSSu!**

శ్రీవారు śriiwaaru *n.* **1** term of respect when referring to a high personage. **2** husband; **maa~** my husband.

శ్రు, శ్రే - śru, śree

శ్రుత śruta *adj.* heard.

శ్రుతం śrutam *n.* that which is heard by revelation, the Vedas.

శ్రుతపాండిత్యం śrutapaaNDityam *n.* **1** scholarship acquired orally. **2** *colloq.* superficial knowledge, hearsay.

శ్రుతి śruti *n.* **1** *class.* ear. **2** that which is heard by revelation, the Vedas. **3** interval of a quarter tone in the musical scale. **4** (of a musical instrument) state of being in tune, state of having the strings correctly tuned; **wiiNaa~ceeyu** to tune a vina. **5** **~miiru, ~mincu** *lit.* (of a musical instrument) to go out of tune, *hence in general* to transgress or exceed the proper limit, get out of hand; **~mincina sneeham** friendship that exceeds the proper limit; **pillawaaDi penkitanam ~minci raagaana paDindi** the boy's naughtiness went beyond all bounds. **6** musical accompaniment in the form of a drone.

శ్రుతిదండం śrutidaNDam *n.* tuning fork.

శ్రేఢి śreeDhi *n. maths.* progression.

శ్రేణి śreeNi *n.* **1** row, line; **~tiircu** to form a row or line. **2** range of mountains. **3** series. **4** rank, grade. **5** tier. **6** class, category. **7** group whose members are considered collectively; **ooriyaNTalisTula~loo brawnuku oka agras-thaanam undi** Brown has a very high place in the ranks of Orientalists; **hinduu deewataa~looni deewuLLanda-rikii aalayaalu leewu** not all the gods in the Hindu pantheon have temples. **8** *maths.* progression.

శ్రేణీకరణ śreeniikaraNa *n.* grading, ranking.

శ్రేణీకరణ చేయు śreeNiikaraNa ceeyu *v.t.* to grade.

శ్రేయస్కర śreeyaskara *adj.* beneficial, advantageous.

శ్రేయస్సు, శ్రేయం śreeyassu, śreeyam *n.* good fortune, prosperity, happiness, wellbeing, welfare.

శ్రేయోదాయక śreeyoodaayaka *adj.* beneficent.

శ్రేయోభిలాషి śreeyoobhilaaSi *n.* wellwisher.

శ్రేయోరాజ్యం śreeyooraajyam *n. polit.* welfare state.

శ్రేష్ఠ[ం] śreeSTa[m] *adj.* excellent, best.

శ్రేష్ఠుడు śreeSTuDu *second part of a n. compound meaning* best; **upaadhyaaya~** best of teachers.

శ్రేష్ఠి śreeSThi *n.* name denoting a member of the Vaisya community (= **seTTi** *or* **ceTTi**).

శ్రో to శ్లో - śroo to śloo

శ్రోణి **śrooNi** *n. med.* pelvis.

శ్రోత **śroota** *n.* listener, hearer.

శ్రోతవ్య **śrootawya** *adj.* **1** audible. **2** fit to be heard.

శ్రోత్రం **śrootram** *n. class.* ear.

శ్రోత్రియం **śrootriyam** *n.* village donated by a landowner to a learned man for his maintenance on favourable terms in former times.

శ్రోత్రియుడు **śrootriyuDu** *n.* **1** follower of the classical tradition, orthodox person. **2** simple-minded person. **3** brahman learned in the Vedas.

శ్రోత్రేంద్రియం **śrootreendriyam** *n. class.* sense of hearing.

శ్లాఘించు **ślaaghincu** *v.t.* to praise, applaud.

శ్లాఘ్య, శ్లాఘనీయ **ślaaghya, ślaaghaniiya** *adj.* praiseworthy, laudable, commendable.

శ్లిష్ట **śliSTa** *adj.* connected, joint, combined.

శ్లేష[ం] **śleeSa[m]** *n.* **1** double meaning, pun. **2** irony, sarcasm.

శ్లేష[ం]గా **śleeSa[n]gaa** *adv.* **1** enigmatically. **2** sarcastically.

శ్లేషించు **śleeSincu** *v.i.* to speak or write so as to convey a double meaning.

శ్లేష్మం **śleeSmam** *n.* mucus, phlegm.

శ్లోకం **ślookam** *n.* verse, stanza or couplet in Sanskrit poetry.

శ్వ to శ్వే - śwa to śwee

శ్వశుర **śwaśura** *adj.* belonging or pertaining to o.'s parents-in-law; ~**gṛham** o.'s parents-in-law's house.

శ్వసనం **śwasanam** *n. class.* **1** breath. **2** air, wind.

శ్వానం **śwaanam** *n. class.* dog.

శ్వాస[ం] **śwaasa[m]** *n.* **1** breath, breathing. **2** respiration.

శ్వాసకాశం **śwaasakaaśam** *n.* asthma.

శ్వాసకోశం **śwaasakoośam** *n.* lung.

శ్వాసక్రియ **śwaasakriya** *n. sci.* respiration.

శ్వాసనాళం **śwaasanaaLam** *n. med.* trachea, windpipe.

శ్వాసమండలం **śwaasamaNDalam** *n. med.* respiratory system.

శ్వాసవంత **śwaasawanta** *adj. ling.* unvoiced.

శ్వాసావరోధన **śwaasaawaroodhana** *n.* suffocation.

శ్వేత **śweeta** *adj.* white.

శ్వేతకం **śweetakam** *n. zool.* albumen.

శ్వేతకణాలు **śweetakaNaalu** *n.pl. med.* white blood corpuscles, leucocytes.

శ్వేతతప్త **śweetatapta** *adj. chem.* white hot.

శ్వేతపత్రం **śweetapatram** *n. polit.* White Paper containing proposals for legislation.

శ్వేతాంబరుడు **śweetaambaruDu** *n.* member of an order of Jain monks who wear white clothing.

ష, షా - Sa, Saa

షండుడు **SaNDuDu** *n.* eunuch, impotent man.

షట్ **SaT** *Sanskrit adj.* six.

షట్కర్మాలు **SaTkarmaalu** *n.pl. class.* the six kinds of activity by which a brahman may earn his living.

షట్పది **SaTpadi** *n.* stanza consisting of six lines.

షడంగములు **SaDangamulu** *n.pl. class.* the six treatises considered as auxiliary to the Vedas.

షడ్జం **SaDjam** *n.* name of a note in the musical scale.

షడ్డకుడు, సడ్డకుడు **SaDDakuDu, saDDakuDu** *n.* fellow son-in-law (= **tooDalluDu**).

షడ్భుజి, షట్కోణం **SaDhhuji, SaTkooNam** *n.* hexagon.

షడ్రసాలు **SaDrasaalu** *n.pl.* the six flavours which can be tasted; **ogaru** (astringent), **tiipi** (sweet), **uppu** (salt), **kaaram** (pungent), **ceedu** (bitter), **pulusu** (sour).

షడ్రసోపేతం **SaDrasoopeetam** *adj.* superb, sumptuous (gen. of food, *lit.* containing all the six flavours).

షడ్రసోపేతంగా **SaDrasoopeetangaa** *adv.* sumptuously.

షరతు **Saratu** *n.* **1** condition (s.g required as part of an agreement). **2** proviso, stipulation.

షరబత్ **Sarabat** *n.* fruit-flavoured drink.

షరా **Saraa** *n.* note, comment.

షరాబు **Saraabu** *same as* **saraabu.**

షరాయి **Saraayi** *n.* trousers.

షష్టి **SaSTi** *n.* sixty.

షష్టిపూర్తి **SaSTipuurti** *n.* celebration on completing sixty years of age.

షష్ఠి **SaSThi** *n.* **1** sixth day of a lunar fortnight. **2** *gram.* sixth or genitive case.

షాణ్మాసిక **SaaNmaasika** *adj.* half-yearly, six monthly.

షాణ్మాసికం **SaaNmaasikam** *n.* half-yearly ceremony performed for a dead person.

షామియానా **Saamiyaanaa** *n.* shamiana, large tent erected for marriages and other functions.

షావుకారు, షాకారు **Saawukaaru, Sawkaaru** *n.* **1** moneylender. **2** businessman. **3** rich person.

షి to షౌ - Si to Saw

షికం **Sikam** *n.* **1** government land reserved for communal use in a village. **2** tankbed land.

షికారి **Sikaari** *n.* hunting.

షికారు **Sikaaru** *n.* walk, trip, outing; ~ **[ku]weLLu** to go for a walk or trip or outing; **paDawa~** boat trip; **Sikaarlu koTTu** to stroll about.

షుమారు **Sumaaru** *same as* **sumaaru.**

షేర్వాణి **SeerwaaNi** *same as* **śarwaaNi**[2].

షైరువెళ్లు **Sayru weLLu** *v.i.* to go for a walk or trip or outing.

షోకు, సోకు **Sooku, sooku** I. *n.* **1** fashionable appearance, fashionable dress, stylishness. **2** display, show; **sommokaridi ~ weerokaridi** one person owns the wealth, another person (enjoys and) displays it — proverbial saying. II. *adj.* fashionable, stylish.

షోకుగా, షోగ్గా **Sookugaa, Sooggaa** *adv.* fashionably, stylishly.

షోకులాడి **SookulaaDi** *n. colloq.* fashionable woman.

షోడశ **SooDaśa** *adj.* sixteenth.

షోడశం **SooDaśam** *n.* sixteen.

షోడశ బ్రాహ్మణుడు **SooDaśa braahmaNuDu** *n.* **1** one of a group of sixteen brahmans who are invited to a meal by the family of a deceased person on the eleventh day after a funeral. **2** *colloq.* glutton.

షోలంగిరాజు **Soolangiraaju** *n. colloq.* person who wanders about with nothing to do.

షౌకారు **Sawkaaru** *n. same as* **Saawukaaru.**

స - sa

స **sa** *Sanskrit prefix meaning* (i) with, accompanied by, e.g., **sakuTumbangaa** with (o.'s) family; **sawyaakhyaanangaa** accompanied by a commentary; (ii) having, possessing, e.g., **sabala** strong (*lit.* possessing strength); **saputruDu** person who has a son.

సం **sam** Sanskrit prefix giving intensive force, often used for stylistic reasons with very little alteration of meaning, e.g., **puurtigaa** and **sampuurtigaa** both mean 'fully, completely'; **rakSincu** and **samrakSincu** both mean 'to rescue', but the forms with **sam** prefixed have a slightly stronger connotation.

సంకట **sankaTa** *adj.* difficult, troublesome.

సంకటం **sankaTam** *n.* **1** difficulty, trouble. **2** danger, peril, risk, hazard, jeopardy; **praaNa~** mortal peril. **3** disease, illness.

సంకటపడు **sankaTapaDu** *v.i.* to be troubled.

సంకటపెట్టు **sankaTapeTTu** *v.t.* to cause trouble (to s.o.).

సంకటి **sankaTi** *n.* porridge made from millet or rice.

సంకర **sankara** *adj.* mixed, crossbred, hybrid; **~bhaaSa** hybrid language.

సంకరం **sankaram** *n.* mixing; **warNa~** mixing of castes.

సంకరణం **sankaraNam** *n. sci.* hydridisation, crossbreeding.

సంకలనం **sankalanam** *n.* **1** *maths.* addition. **2** compilation, collection. **3** selection, anthology; **padya~** anthology of verse.

సంకలనరాశి **sankalanaraaśi** *n.* sum total.

సంకలిత **sankalita** *adj.* added together, aggregated.

సంకల్పం **sankalpam** *n.* **1** resolution, resolve, determination, will, intention. **2** (*also* **daywa~**) the will of God, destiny. **3** vow to undertake a religious ceremony or observance.

సంకల్పబలం **sankalpabalam** *n.* determination, strength of purpose.

సంకల్పశుద్ధి **sankalpaśuddhi** *n.* unblemished intentions.

సంకల్పించు **sankalpincu** I. *v.i.* to determine, decide, resolve, intend; **reepu uuriki weLLaalani sankalpincEEnu** I have decided to go to my village tomorrow. II. *v.t.* to plan, design, think of, invent, formulate (scheme, policy).

సంకీర్ణ **sankiirNa** *adj.* **1** mixed; **~prabhutwam** coalition government. **2** complex. **3** dense, crowded. **4** adulterated.

సంకీర్తన **sankiirtana** *n.* hymn of praise.

సంకు **sanku** *n.* conch shell; *cf.* **śankham.**

సంకుచిత **sankucita** *adj.* narrow, contracted, constricted, restricted; **~swabhaawam** narrowmindedness, narrowness of outlook, parochialism.

సంకుచితత్వం **sankucitatwam** *n.* **1** meanness. **2** pettiness, narrowmindedness.

సంకుచితపరచు **sankucitaparacu** *v.t.* to restrict.

సంకురాత్రి **sankuraatri** *corrupt form of* **sankraanti.**

సంకురుమియ్య **sankurumiyya** *n., colloq. alt. form of* **sankraanti puruSuDu.**

సంకులసమరం **sankulasamaram** *n.* fierce battle, bitter struggle.

సంకెళ్లు **sankeLLu** *n. pl.* fetters, shackles, handcuffs.

సంకేత **sankeeta** *adj.* **1** appointed, fixed, ordained; **~sthalam** fixed or appointed place. **2** code; **~sandeeśam** code message; **~padam** code word, pass word; **~lipi** code writing.

సంకేతం **sankeetam** *n.* **1** sign, signal, token, symbol. **2** code.

సంకేతనం **sankeetanam** *n.* encoding.

సంకేతించు **sankeetincu** *v.t.* to encode.

సంకోచం **sankoocam** I. *n.* **1** hesitation, reluctance, **2** worry, concern, trepidation. **3** shrinking, contraction. **4** diffidence, bashfulness.

సంకోచించు **sankoocincu** *v.i.* **1** to hesitate, falter, be hesitant, show reluctance. **2** to be bashful. **3** to shrink, contract.

సంక్రమం, సంక్రామం **sankramam, sankraamam** *n.* **1** transit of a planetary body through the zodiac. **2** difficult progress.

సంక్రమణం **sankramaNam** *n.* **1** coming together. **2** passing through, transit[ion]. **3** *astrol.* day on which the sun passes from one zodiacal constellation to another. **4** devolution (= **sankramimpu**). **5** infection; **sankramaNa wyaadhi** infectious disease. **6** *same as* **sankraanti.**

సంక్రమించు **sankramincu** *v.i.* **1** (of a tradition) to be handed down, be passed on, be inherited. **2** *legal* to devolve, be devolved, be conferred, be made over. **3** to infect; **aayana baddhakam andarikii aNTuwyaadhilaa sankramincindi** his laziness infected everyone like an epidemic.

సంక్రమింపు **sankramimpu** *n.* **1** transition. **2** *legal* devolution.

సంక్రాంతి **sankraanti** *n.* **1** *astrol.* (*also* **makara~** *or* **[makara] sankramaNam**) day in mid-January when the sun passes into the sign of Capricorn. **2** a rural festival in mid-January, known as Sankranti or Pongal.

సంక్రాంతి పురుషుడు, సంకురుమియ్య **sankraantipuruSuDu, sankurumiyya** *n.* name of a deity who is believed to appear annually at the time of Sankranti; details concerning him, such as the direction in which he travels, mode of his conveyance, colour which he wears, etc., are interpreted in the almanac as indicating good or bad fortune to be expected in the year ahead; **aa sankurumiyya waaDimiidagaa pooyindi** (*lit.* **sankurumiyya** has passed over him) *is equivalent to* he has suffered a great misfortune.

సంక్రామిక, సాంక్రామిక **sankraamika, saankraamika** *adj.* contagious, infectious.

సంక్లిష్ట **sankliSTa** *adj.* complicated

సంక్షారణం **sankSaaraNam** *n. sci.* corrosion.

సంక్షిప్త **sankSipta** *adj.* 1 brief, concise, terse, summary. 2 abridged, abbreviated: ~**ruupam** abbreviated form.

సంక్షిప్తం **sankSiptam** *n.* abbreviation.

సంక్షిప్తత **sankSiptata** *n.* conciseness.

సంక్షిప్తీకరణ[ం] **sankSiptiikaraNa[m]** *n.* abridgement, précis.

సంక్షుభిత, సంక్షోభిత **sankSubhita, sankSoobhita** *adj.* 1 agitated, disturbed. 2 grieved, alarmed.

సంక్షేపం, సంక్షేపణ[ం] **sankSeepam, sankSeepaNa[m]** *n.* 1 abridging, condensing, summarising. 2 abridgement, abstract, summary, synopsis, digest. 3 abbreviation: **wiilaytee śiirSikaloo sankSeepaNalu waaDawaddu** if possible do not use abbreviations in a headline.

సంక్షేపరూపం **sankSeepa ruupam** *n.* abbreviated form.

సంక్షేపించి చెప్పు **sankSeepinci ceppu** *v.t.* to sum up.

సంక్షేపించు **sankSeepincu** *v.t.* to abridge, summarise, condense, abstract.

సంక్షేమం **sankSeemam** *n.* welfare.

సంక్షేమ రాజ్యం **sankSeema raajyam** *n.* welfare state.

సంక్షోభం **sankSoobham** *n.* agitation, disturbance, upheaval, turmoil, crisis; **indhana**~ fuel crisis.

సంక్షోభపెట్టు **sankSoobhapeTTu** *v.t.* to disturb, agitate, alarm.

సంక్షోభించు **sankSoobhincu** *v.i.* to be disturbed, be agitated.

సంక్షోభిత **sankSoobhita** *same as* **sankSubhita.**

సంఖ్య **sankhya** *n.* number, numeral, digit, figure; **jana**~ population; **itara bhaaSalanunci wandala**~**loo** (*or* **wandalakoddii**) **padaalanu dincukonnaamu** we have imported hundreds of words from other languages.

సంఖ్యాత్మక **sankhyaatmaka** *adj.* numerical.

సంఖ్యాధికత **sankhyaadhikata** *n.* numerical superiority.

సంఖ్యాబలం **sankhyaabalam** *n.* numerical strength.

సంఖ్యావాచకం **sankhyaawaacakam** *n. gram.* numeral: **ankelatoo konta, akSaraalatoo konta sankhyaawaacakaalu raayawaddu** do not write numerals partly in figures and partly in words.

సంఖ్యాశాస్త్రం **sankhyaaśaastram** *n.* (science of) statistics.

సంగం **sangam** *n.* 1 junction, meeting, union. 2 **nadii**~ confluence of rivers.

సంగడి **sangaDi** *n.* couple, pair.

సంగడికత్తె **sangaDikatte** *n.* woman friend.

సంగడికాడు **sangaDikaaDu** *n.* man friend.

సంగడిమోట **sangaDimooTa** *n.* pair of mhotes baling from a single well.

సంగత **sangata** *adj.* consistent, proper, appropriate, relevant, pertinent.

సంగతంగా **sangatangaa** *adv.* consistently, appropriately.

సంగతత్వం **sangatatwam** *n.* consistency.

సంగతి **sangati** I. *n.* 1 subject, affair, thing, matter. 2 circumstance, event, occurrence. 3 contents of a letter. 4 sexual intercourse. 5 *pl.* **sangatulu** news. II. *p.p.* about, concerning.

సంగమం **sangamam** *n.* 1 junction, union, meeting. 2 touch, contact. 3 association, society. 4 sexual intercourse. 5 confluence of rivers.

సంగమదోషం **sangama dooSam** *n. class.* veneral disease.

సంగమల **sangamala** *n. chem.* marble.

సంగమ స్థానం **sangama sthaanam** *n.* meeting place, point of juncture.

సంగమించు **sangamincu** *v.i.* to join, unite, link up.

సంగరం **sangaram** *n., colloq. form of* **sangraamam** *used in certain set phrases*, e.g., **peLLi aNTee nuureeLLa paNTa weyyeeLLa**~ marriage is like a crop that yields after a hundred years or a battle that lasts for a thousand years.

సంగాతం **sangaatam** *n. obs.* 1 friendship. 2 bond of friendship created and cemented by a religious rite.

సంగాతి **sangaati** *n. obs.* 1 friend. 2 person who becomes a friend through a religious rite.

సంగీతం **sangiitam** *n.* music.

సంగీతరూపకం **sangiitaruupakam** *n.* kind of musical drama based on a Puranic story.

సంగోరు **sangooru** *n.* 1 half share, half portion. 2 system of cultivation in which cultivator and landowner get equal shares in the crop.

సంగ్రహ **sangraha** *adj.* 1 short, brief, concise. 2 *class.* stolen: ~**drawyam** stolen wealth.

సంగ్రహం **sangraham** *n.* 1 summary, abridgement, abstract, synopsis, digest. 2 grasping, seizing. 3 *class.* stealing.

సంగ్రహంగా **sangrahangaa** *adv.* in brief, concisely.

సంగ్రహణం **sangrahaNam** *n.* 1 collection, gathering. 2 acquisition, procurement.

సంగ్రహాలయం **sangrahaalayam** *n.* museum.

సంగ్రహించు **sangrahincu** *v.t.* 1 to obtain, acquire, procure, get, earn. 2 to seize, grasp, snatch, steal. 3 to abridge, summarise, condense, compress. 4 to collect, compile, assemble.

సంగ్రామం **sangraamam** *n.* 1 strife, conflict, fight[ing]. 2 war, battle.

సంగ్రాహకుడు **sangraahakuDu** *n.* compiler, collector.

సంఘ **sangha** *adj.* social: **maanawuDu**~**jiiwi** man is a social animal: ~**sankSeemam** social welfare, the welfare of society.

సంఘం **sangham** *n.* 1 society, *meaning the people at large, as in* 'the welfare of society'. 2 society, union, association; **sahakaara~** cooperative society; **widyaarthi~** students' union. 3 group; **~peTTukonnaaru** they formed a group. 4 committee.

సంఘటన[ం] **sanghaTana[m]** *n.* 1 event, occurrence, incident, happening. 2 encounter[ing]. 3 *polit.* front; **aykya~** united front. 4 consolidation; **kamataala~** consolidation of holdings.

సంఘటనాంశం, సంఘటకం **sanghatanaamśam, sanghaTakam** *n. sci.* component.

సంఘటించు, సంఘటిల్లు **sanghaTincu, sanghaTillu** *v.i.* to happen, occur, take place.

సంఘటిత **sanghaTita** *adj.* 1 united. 2 integrated. 3 consolidated. 4 compact. 5 organised; **~śrama** organised labour.

సంఘననం **sanghananam** *n. chem.* condensation (of moisture).

సంఘనియమావళి **sanghaniyamaawaLi** *n.* articles of association.

సంఘర్షణ[ం] **sangharSaNa[m]** *n.* 1 friction. 2 conflict, strife, struggle. 3 dispute. 4 *phys.* collision.

సంఘర్షించు **sangharSincu** *v.i.* to fight, struggle, dispute.

సంఘవిద్రోహక **sanghawidroohaka** *adj.* anti-social.

సంఘీభవించు **sanghiibhawincu** *v.i.* to unite, join together, become united into one society or association.

సంఘీభావం **sanghiibhaawam** *n.* fellow feeling, solidarity, comradeship.

సంచకారం **sancakaaram** *n. class.* advance money, earnest money.

సంచయం **sancayam** *n.* collecting, gathering.

సంచయనం **sancayanam** *n.* 1 collecting, gathering, accumulation. 2 collection of ashes after cremation for immersion in water.

సంచరించు **sancarincu** *v.i.* 1 to wander, roam, rove; **intagaa haddu miiri sancarincaDam sigguceeTu pani kaadaa**? is it not a disgraceful act to exceed the limits to such an extent? 2 to go about, move about. 3 to behave; **atighooramayna pramaadamloo cikkukonnaa, mugguru roodasii yaatrikulu entoo dhayryangaa niścalangaa sancaristunnaaru** although they are in terrible danger, the three astronauts are behaving with great courage and calmness.

సంచలనం **sancalanam** *n.* 1 shaking, moving. 2 stir[ring], movement, shake up (colloq.).

సంచలించు **sancalincu** *v.i.* to shake, move, tremble.

సంచార **sancaara** *adj.* 1 travelling, touring, mobile. 2 nomadic, wandering.

సంచారం **sancaaram** *n.* 1 travel[ling]. 2 *colloq.* wandering about, straying; **iNTLoo leeDu, eToo sancaaraaniki weLLEEDu** he is not at home, he has wandered off somewhere. 3 *astrol.* movement of the sun or moon from one zodiacal sign to another.

సంచారి **sancaari** *n.* wanderer.

సంచాలక **sancaalaka** *adj.* managing, organising.

సంచాలకుడు **sancaalakuDu** *n.* organiser, convener.

సంచి **sanci** *n.* 1 bag, sack. 2 purse.

సంచిక **sancika** *n.* volume or number or issue of a magazine or newspaper; **aandhra prabha ugaadi~** Telugu New Year's Day number of the Andhra Prabha weekly.

సంచికట్టు **sancikaTTu** *n.* unqualified physician who goes about carrying his remedies in a bag.

సంచిత **sancita** *adj.* 1 cumulative. 2 accumulated.

సంచితనిధి **sancita nidhi** *n. admin.* consolidated fund.

సంచిమొదలు **sanci modalu** *n. colloq.* financial capital.

సంచు **sancu**[1] *n.* 1 trace. 2 manner, way. 3 stratagem.

సంచు **sancu**[2] *n.* group or collection or party of persons; **allari~** group of rowdy persons; **pilla~paatikamandi maatoo bhoojanaaniki waccEEru** a group of 25 children came along with us for a meal.

సంజయ రాయబారం **sanjaya raayabaaram** *n.* 1 *lit.* the embassy of Sanjaya in the Mahabharata. 2 lukewarm negotiations.

సంజ, సందె **sanja, sande** *n.* (*also* **~weeLa**) twilight; **mali~** (*or*~) evening twilight, dusk; **toli~** morning twilight, dawn.

సంజనిత, సంజాత **sanjanita, sanjaata** *adj.* born, created, produced.

సంజాయిషి **sanjaayiSi** *n.* explanation in response to an accusation.

సంజీవి, సంజీవకరణి **sanjiiwi, sanjiiwakaraNi** *n.* mythical herbal medicine believed to have the power to bring the dead back to life; **naa maaTalu waaDimiida~laa paniceesEEyi** my words acted as a revivifier for him.

సంజ్ఞ, సన్న **sanjña, sanna** *n.* 1 gesture, sign, token, symbol. 2 **kanusanna** wink.

సంఝాయించు **sanjhaayincu** *v.i. dial.* to make s.o. understand, bring home (a point) to s.o.

సంత **santa** *n.* 1 market, fair. 2 (*also* **~goola**) commotion, hubbub, uproar, confusion. 3 recitation of the Vedas. 4 concern, business, affairs; **waaDi ~niikenduku**? what have you to do with his affairs? *cf.* **goDawa.**

సంతకం **santakam** *n.* signature.

సంతచెప్పు **santaceppu** *v.t.* to recite many times what has been taught by a teacher in order to commit it to memory.

సంతత **santata** *adj.* continual, perpetual.

సంతతం **santatam** *adv.* always, unceasingly.

సంతతి **santati** *n.* 1 offspring, progeny. 2 descent, lineage; **aayana~waaLLu** his descendants; **ikSawaakula~waaLLu** those of the lineage of the Ikshavakus.

సంతన **santana** *n.* 1 joining, uniting. 2 adjustment. 3 agreement, concord. 4 cooperating, helping; **mottam pani waaDokkaDee ceyyaali, maniSi~leedu** he has to do all the work himself, no one cooperates with him; **uNDaDaaniki caalaamandi unnaaru gaani awasaraaniki maniSi~**

leedu as a matter of fact there are many people, but at a time of need there is no one to give any help.

సంతనకట్టు **santanakaTTu** *v.i.* to join, unite.

సంతనచేయు **santanaceeyu** *v.i. and t.* 1 to fit together closely. 2 to persuade persons to agree or adjust; **waaLLakuu maakuu santanaceesi peLLi ceesEEDu** he performed the marriage after persuading their family and ours to agree to it; **bassuloo cooTu leedu, pakkawaaLLatoo santanaceesi wiiDini kuurcoobeTTEEnu** there was no room in the bus, but I persuaded the nearby people to adjust and give him a seat.

సంతనపడు **santanapaDu** *v.i.* to agree, be satisfactorily adjusted; **ii eeDaadi santanapaDitee maa abbaayi peLLi ceestaanu** if things work out well, I will perform my son's marriage this year.

సంతప్త **santapta** *adj.* 1 heated. 2 pained, grieved, afflicted.

సంతప్తుడు **santaptuDu** *n.* one who is pained or grieved.

సంతరణం **santaraNam** *n. class.* passing across, passing through.

సంతరించు **santarincu** *v.t.* 1 to earn, get, acquire, procure, obtain. 2 to compose, write. 3 to collect, compile. 4 *class.* to wear.

సంతరించుకొను **santarincukonu** *v.t.* 1 to put on, clothe o.s. with. 2 to acquire, develop; **krimulu DDT-ki taTTukonee śaktini santarincukonnawi** the germs developed a resistance to DDT.

సంతర్పణ **santarpaNa** *n.* 1 satisfying, satiating. 2 feast given to brahmans.

సంతసం **santasam** *n.* pleasure, joy, gladness.

సంతసించు, సంతసపడు **santasincu, santasapaDu** *v.i.* to be happy, rejoice.

సంతానం **santaanam** *n.* offspring, progeny; **niiku entamandi ~**? how many children have you?

సంతాపం **santaapam** *n.* 1 distress, grief, sorrow. 2 condolence; **santaapa tiirmaanam** condolence resolution. 3 mourning; **santaapa dinaalu** days of mourning.

సంతాపార్థకం **santaapaarthakam** *n. gram.* exclamation expressing grief.

సంతు **santu** *n.* offspring, progeny.

సంతులిత **santulita** *adj.* well balanced, evenly balanced.

సంతుష్ట **santuSTa** *adj.* satisfied, pleased, content.

సంతుష్టి **santuSTi** *n.* pleasure, satisfaction, contentment.

సంతృప్త **santr̥pta** *adj.* 1 satisfied, content. 2 *chem.* saturated; **~draawaNam** saturated solution.

సంతృప్తి **santr̥pti** *n.* satisfaction, contentment.

సంతృప్తిగా **santr̥ptigaa** *adv.* satisfactorily.

సంతృప్తిపడు **santr̥tipaDu** *v.i.* to be satisfied.

సంతృప్తిపరచు **santr̥ptiparacu** *v.t.* to satisfy.

సంతోషం **santooSam** I. *n.* 1 joy, happiness, pleasure, delight, jubilation. 2 satisfaction. II. *minor sentence* I'm glad! *or* that's good!

సంతోషంగల **santooSangala** *adj.* happy, joyful, jubilant, glad.

సంతోషంగా **santooSangaa** *adv.* joyfully, happily, gladly.

సంతోషకర **santooSakara** *adj.* causing joy or happiness or pleasure, delightful.

సంతోషపడు **santooSapaDu** *v.i.* to be happy, rejoice, be jubilant.

సంతోషపెట్టు, సంతోషపరచు **santooSapeTTu, santooSaparacu** *v.t.* to please, delight.

సంతోషమయ **santooSamaya** *adj.* full of joy, festive.

సంతోషించు **santooSincu** *v.i.* to be glad, be pleased.

సంత్ర, సంత్రా **santra[a]** *n.* sweet orange.

సందంశం **sandamśam** *n.* tool which grips, vice, clamp.

సందడి **sandaDi** *n.* 1 confused sound or noise; **manuSulu unna ~ iNTLoo leedu** there is no sound of people in the house. 2 crowding, thronging, stir[ring], bustle, confusion, disturbance. 3 excitement, state of being intent on or immersed in (s.g); **naanna wastunnaaDu anna ~ loo pillalu caduwulu maaneesEEru** in their excitement that their father was arriving the children stopped studying; **maLLii naaluka karacukonnaaDu kaanii maaTala ~ loo adi ewaruu gamaninacaleedu** again he bit his tongue (in self-reproach) but in the midst of conversation (*or* being immersed in conversation) nobody noticed it.

సందడికాడు **sandaDikaaDu** *n.* person who gets confused himself and confuses others.

సందడిపడు **sandaDipaDu** *v.i.* 1 to get excited. 2 to crowd together.

సందరం, సంద్రం **sandaram, sandram** *n.* sea.

సందర్భం **sandarbham** *n.* 1 circumstance, event, happening, occurrence, occasion; **sandarbhoocita** suitable to the occasion. 2 context. 3 **maaTala sandarbhaana** in the course of conversation.

సందర్భంగా **sandarbhangaa** *adv.* on the occasion of, in the context of, in the matter of, in connection with, with regard to.

సందర్భపడు **sandarbhapaDu** *v.i. with dative* to get an opportunity, meet by chance; **miiku sandarbhapaDitee phoonu ceeyaNDi** if you get a convenient opportunity please telephone; **aayana miiku sandarbhapaDitee maa iNTiki rammani ceppaNDi** if you come across him, ask him to come to my house.

సందర్భవశాత్తూ **sandarbhawaśaattuu** *adv.* in some connection, somehow or other; **meemu eeewoo kaburlu ceppukoNTuu uNTee ~ aayana maaTa waccindi** when we were chatting together, in some connection he was mentioned.

సందర్భశుద్ధి **sandarbhaśuddhi** *n.* appropriateness of context.

సందర్శకుడు **sandarśakuDu** *n.* visitor.

సందర్శనం **sandarśanam** *n.* 1 sight, view, appearance. 2 visit.

సందర్శించు **sandarśincu** *v.t.* 1 to visit, call on. 2 to look at, view, behold, survey.

సందలు **sandalu** *n.pl. obs.* children's anklets.

సందిగ్ధ **sandigdha** *adj.* 1 doubtful, uncertain, dubious. 2 ambiguous, equivocal. 3 critical, crucial; **ii ~ samayamloo śatruwulu manamiida wirucukupaDDaaru** at this critical time the enemy has made a sudden attack on us.

సందిగ్ధ[ం] **sandigdha[m]** *n.* 1 doubt, uncertainty. 2 ambiguity, equivocation.

సందియం **sandiyam** *n.* doubt.

సందిలి **sandili** *n.* upper arm (from shoulder to elbow): **sandiTLooki pillani tiisukonnaaDu** he took the child in his arms.

సందు **sandu** *n.* 1 small narrow opening, chink, crevice, crack, fissure. 2 interval, gap; **weeLLa ~** space or gap between the fingers; **~ leekuNDaa** without intermission. 3 lane, alley way. 4 opportunity.

సందుకా **sandukaa** *n.* strong box, safe.

సందువాకిలి **sanduwaakili** *n.* side or back door of a house opening on to a lane.

సందె **sande** *same as* **sanja.**

సందేశం **sandeeśam** *n.* message.

సందేశాత్మక **sandeeśaatmaka** *adj.* conveying or containing a message.

సందేహం **sandeeham** *n.* doubt, suspicion.

సందేహంగా **sandeehangaa** *adv.* 1 doubtfully. 2 hesitantly.

సందేహపూరిత **sandeehapuurita** *adj.* doubtful, sceptical.

సందేహాస్పద **sandeehaaspada** *adj.* doubtful, giving rise to doubt or suspicion, dubious.

సందేహించు **sandeehincu** *v.i.* 1 to doubt, suspect. 2 to hesitate.

సందోహం **sandooham** *n.* assemblage, multitude.

సంద్రం **sandram** *same as* **sandaram.**

సంధాత **sandhaata** *n.* one who unites.

సంధానం **sandhaanam** *n.* joining, uniting, linking together, welding.

సంధానకరణి **sandhaanakaraNi** *n.* 1 that which [re-] unites or heals. 2 name of a herbal medicine for healing fractures.

సంధానభాష **sandhaanabhaaSa** *n.* link language.

సంధాయక **sandhaayaka** *adj.* connective.

సంధి **sandhi** *n.* 1 joining, linking, uniting. 2 junction, connection, union, combination. 3 *gram.* modification of a phonetic unit (sound) by a following phonetic unit. 4 treaty. 5 agreement, compact, peace; **~ ceesukonnaaru** they came to an agreement *or* they made peace with each other. 6 joint of the body. 7 critical juncture. 8 critical stage of an illness, delirium; **~ maaTalu maaTLaaDutunnaawaa?** are you talking deliriously? (said as a rebuke).

సంధించు **sandhincu** I. *v.i.* 1 to be joined, be united. 2 to be attached, be appended. 3 (of an arrow) to be fitted to a bowstring. 4 *colloq., with dative* (*also* **sandhipuTTu, sandhikoTTu**) to become critically ill, become delirious; **pillaaDiki sandhincindeemoo anukoni gaabharaa- paDindi** thinking that the child might have become delirious she was greatly disturbed. II. *v.t.* 1 to unite. 2 to fit together, attach, (e.g., to fit an arrow to a bowstring). 3 (*also* **sandhiceeyu**) to cause persons to agree or come to terms with each other.

సంధికార్యం **sandhikaaryam** *n. gram.* instance of sandhi, occurrence of sandhi.

సంధికాలం **sandhikaalam** *n.* 1 interval, interim period. 2 critical point in time, turning point, juncture.

సంధికొట్టు, సంధిపుట్టు, సంధిచేయు **sandhikoTTu, sandhipuTTu, sandhiceeyu** see **sandhincu.**

సంధిబద్ధమైన రాజ్యం **sandhibaddhamayna raajyam** *n. polit.* confederation.

సంధియుగం **sandhiyugam** *n.* period of transition.

సంధివాతం **sandhiwaatam** *n. med.* rheumatism.

సంధిసమయం **sandhisamayam** *n.* critical point in time, juncture.

సంధ్య **sandhya** *n.* 1 morning or evening twilight. 2 (*also* **sandhyaawandanam**) a brahman's prayers said three times a day; *cf.* **waarcu, nyaasam.**

సంధ్యారాగం **sandhyaaraagam** *n.* redness in the sky at dusk or dawn.

సంపంగి, సంపెంగ **sampangi, sampenga** *n.* champak tree, *michelia champaca.*

సంపంగి నూనె **sampangi nuune** *n.* fragrant champak oil: **minga metuku leedu miisaalaku ~** not a grain of rice to eat, but champak oil (an expensive commodity) for his moustache, i.e., extravagance in spite of dire poverty (proverb).

సంపత్తి, సంపత్తు, సంపద **sampatti, sampattu, sampada** *n.* wealth, prosperity, riches.

సంపదలు **sampadalu** *n.pl.* resources; **prakṛti ~** natural resources.

సంపన్న **sampanna** *adj.* 1 wealthy, prosperous, opulent, affluent. 2 possessed of, endowed with.

సంపన్నుడు **sampannuDu** *n.* one who is endowed with; **sadguNa ~** person who has a wealth of good qualities.

సంపర్కం **samparkam** *n.* 1 contact. 2 connection. 3 mingling, mixing. 4 sexual intercourse.

సంపర్కుడు **samparkuDu** *n. class.* relative, kinsman.

సంపాదకత్వం **sampaadakatwam** *n.* editorship.

సంపాదకీయం **sampaadakiiyam** *n.* editorial.

సంపాదకుడు **sampaadakuDu** *n.* 1 editor. 2 person who earns or acquires.

సంపాదన **sampaadana** *n.* earning[s], income; **pay ~** illicit receipts on top of regular earnings.

సంపాదనపరుడు, సంపాద్యపరుడు **sampaadanaparuDu, sampaadyaparuDu** *n.* earner, one who earns.

సంపాదించు **sampaadincu** *v.t.* 1 to obtain, procure,

acquire, get. 2 to earn. 3 to secure, bring about. 4 to edit.

సంపాదిత **sampaadita** *adj.* obtained, acquired, procured.

సంపాయించు **sampaayincu** *colloq. alt. form of* **śampaadincu.**

సంపీడన **sampiiDana** *n.* compression.

సంపీడ్య **sampiiDya** *adj.* compressible.

సంపుటం, సంపుటి **sampuTam, sampuTi** *n.* 1 volume of a book or magazine. 2 mixture or combination of ingredients.

సంపుటిత **sampuTita** *adj.* collected (literary works).

సంపుటీకరించు **sampuTiikarincu** *v.t.* to collect, assemble, gather together (literary material).

సంపూరకం **sampuurakam** *n. sci.* complement.

సంపూర్ణ **sampuurNa** *adj.* full, complete, overall, comprehensive, plenary: ~ **grahaNam** total eclipse: ~ **hakku** absolute right.

సంపూర్ణత **sampuurNata** *n.* completeness, plenitude.

సంపూర్ణాధికారంగల **sampuurNaadhikaarangala** *adj.* plentipotentiary.

సంపూర్తి **sampuurti** *n.* 1 fulfilment. 2 completion.

సంపూర్తిగా **sampuurtigaa** *adv.* fully, completely.

సంపెంగ **sampenga** *same as* **sampangi.**

సంప్రతించు **sampratincu** *v.t.* 1 to consult. 2 to discuss, negotiate.

సంప్రతింపు **sampratimpu** *n.* 1 consultation: ~ **grantham** reference book. 2 *pl.* ~ **lu** discussions, negotiations.

సంప్రదానం **sampradaanam** *n.* 1 giving, presenting. 2 *gram.* dative case.

సంప్రదాయం, సాంప్రదాయం **sampradaayam, saampradaayam** *n.* 1 established doctrine transmitted from teacher to pupil. 2 custom, convention, practice, tradition.

సంప్రదాయక **sampradaayaka** *adj.* 1 traditional. 2 conventional: ~ **kuTumbam** family with good reputation and fine traditions, respectable family.

సంప్రదాయకుడు **sampradaayakuDu** *n.* follower of of tradition.

సంప్రదాయవాదం **sampradaayawaadam** *n.* 1 traditionalism. 2 conservatism.

సంప్రదాయవాది **sampradaayawaadi** *n.* 1 traditionalist. 2 conservative.

సంప్రదాయసిద్ధ **sampradaayasiddha** *adj.* 1 traditional. 2 conventional.

సంప్రధారణ **sampradhaaraNa** *n.* 1 substantiating a statement. 2 determining the propriety of anything.

సంప్రహారం **samprahaaram** *n. class.* 1 war. 2 battle.

సంప్రాప్తి **sampraapti** *n.* obtaining, acquiring, achieving, attaining.

సంప్రాప్తించు **sampraaptincu** *same as* **praaptincu.**

సంప్రీతి **sampriiti** *same as* **priiti.**

సంప్రేరణ[ం] **sampreeraNa[m]** *same as* **preeraNa[m].**

సంప్రోక్షణం **samprookSaNam** *n.* ceremony of consecration by sprinkling with water.

సంప్రోక్షించు **samprookSincu** *v.t.* to consecrate by a ceremonial sprinkling of water.

సంబంధం **sambandham** *n.* 1 connection, relation[ship]: **kaarmika sambandhaala śaakha** labour relations department. 2 kinship, family relationship. 3 relevancy, affinity. 4 union. 5 marriage alliance. 6 *slang* wife. 7 concern: **naaku waaDitoo ~ leedu** I have no concern with him.

సంబంధంగా **sambandhangaa** *adv.* in connection with: **aa wyawahaaram ~ wiśaakhapaTNam weLLEEnu** I went to Visakhapatnam in connection with that business.

సంబంధం లేని **sambandham leeni** *adj.* unconnected, extraneous.

సంబంధబాంధవ్యాలు **sambandhabaandhawyaalu** *n.pl.* connections and relationships.

సంబంధి **sambandhi** *n.* 1 person who is related by marriage. 2 *dial.* relationship existing between the parents of a married couple (= **wiyyam**).

సంబంధించి **sambandhinci** *past participle of* **sambandhincu** *used adverbially* connected with, concerned with, concerning, pertaining to, relevant to, relating to, for: **wyaktigata kamataalaku ~ utpatti praNaaLikalu** production plans for (*or* pertaining to) individual holdings: **iNDoor kriiDalaku ~ jaatiiya pooTiilu** national competitions for (*or* concerning) indoor games: **aayana raakaku ~ naaku eemii teliyadu** I know nothing concerning his coming.

సంబంధించిన **sambandhincina** *past vbl. adj. of* **sambandhincu** connected with, concerned with, relating to, relevant to, pertaining to, having to do with: **aa wrttiki ~ kulamloo janmincina prati wyakti widhigaa aa wrttinee awalambincawalasi uNDeedi** each individual who was born into the caste relating to that profession used to be bound to adopt that profession: **maanasika jiiwitaaniki sambandhincinantawaraku mana deeśam irawayyoo sataabdiloo leedu** so far as intellectual life is concerned, our country is not living in the twentieth century.

సంబంధించు **sambandhincu** *v.i.* to be connected with, be related to, be concerned with, have to do with, pertain to: **ii pani ewariki sambandhistundi?** to whom does this work relate/pertain? (*or simply*) whose task is this?

సంబంధీకుడు **sambandhiikuDu** *n.* 1 person who is connected with or has a relationship with. 2 person who is related by marriage.

సంబడం **sambaDam** *n.* 1 *dial.* pay, salary, wages. 2 *alt. form of* **sambaram.**

సంబరం **sambaram** *n.* 1 festive occasion, festivity. 2 festive mood, excitement, thrill, delight, rejoicing, merriment. 3 eagerness, impatience. 4 surprise, astonishment, bewilderment.

సంబరపడు **sambarapaDu** *v.i.* 1 to be thrilled, be excited. 2 to rejoice, be delighted. 3 to be eager.

సంబరాల రాంబాబు **sambaraala raambaabu** *n. colloq.* happy-go-lucky person.

సంబారం **sambaaram** *n., gen.pl.* **sambaaraalu** 1 spices, condiments. 2 ingredients (in cookery).

సంబాళించు[కొను] **sambaaLincu[konu]** *v.i. and t.* 1 to take care of, manage, control; **nooru sambaaLincukoo!** control your tongue! i.e., speak politely! 2 to recover o.'s composure, calm o.s., steady o.'s nerve, control o.s.

సంబోధన **samboodhana** *n.* 1 addressing. 2 form of address.

సంబోధన ప్రథమావిభక్తి **samboodhana prathamaa wibhakti** *n. gram.* vocative case.

సంబోధించు **samboodhincu** *v.t.* 1 to address; **aame tanani 'nuwwu' ani samboodhincinanduku aaścaryapooyEEDu** he was astonished that she addressed him as 'nuwwu'. 2 to call, term, refer to.

సంభవ **sambhawa** *adj.* possible, potential.

సంభవం **sambhawam** *n.* 1 happening, occurrence. 2 possibility.

సంభవం అవు, సంభవించు **sambhawam awu, sambhawincu** *v.i.* 1 to happen, occur, arise. 2 to be possible.

సంభారం **sambhaaram** *n.* equipment, materials, necessaries, supplies.

సంభావన **sambhaawana** *n.* money presented to brahmans in return for invoking blessings at a wedding or other religious or social ceremony.

సంభావించు **sambhaawincu** *v.t.* 1 to consider, reckon. 2 *class.* to honour, revere.

సంభావ్య **sambhaawya** *adj.* 1 conceivable, possible. 2 probable.

సంభావ్యత **sambhaawyata** *n.* 1. possibility, potential. 2 probability. 3 *maths. sci.* statistical probability.

సంభాషణ **sambhaaSaNa** *n.* conversation, dialogue.

సంభాషించు **sambhaaSincu** *v.i.* to converse, talk.

సంభూతుడు **sambhuutuDu** *n. class.* one who is born or created.

సంభోగం **sambhoogam** *n.* 1 enjoyment. 2 sensual pleasure. 3 sexual intercourse.

సంభ్రమం **sambhramam** *n.* 1 thrill, excitement. 2 surprise, astonishment, bewilderment.

సంయమ[న]ం **samyama[na]m** *n.* 1 control over o.'s emotions, self-discipline, sobriety, restraint, forbearance. 2 humanity, compassion.

సంయమి **samyami** *n.* one who controls his emotions, dispassionate person.

సంయుక్త **samyukta** *adj.* combined, joined, united, connected; **~raaSTraalu** United States; **~rangam** *econ.* joint sector (of the economy); **samyuktaakSaram** *ling.* cluster of consonants.

సంయోగం **samyoogam** *n.* 1 union, association. 2 conjunction, combination (of letters). 3 *chem.* compound. 4 synthesis. 5 **sthalakaalaala~** space-time continuum.

సంయోజనం **samyoojanam** *n.* 1 uniting, joining, connecting. 2 combining, combination. 3 *ling.* agglutination.

సంయోజిత **samyoojita** *adj.* conjoined, attached, annexed.

సంయోజితం **samyoojitam** *n. chem.* valency.

సంరంభం **samrambham** *n.* 1 excitement, festive feeling, festive mood. 2 haste, flurry. 3 agitation, perturbation.

సంరక్షకవాదం **samrakSakawaadam** *n.* conservatism.

సంరక్షకుడు **samrakSakuDu** *n.* 1 protector, guardian. 2 saviour, rescuer.

సంరక్షణ **samrakSaNa** *n.* 1 protection, support, care, patronage. 2 preservation, conservation.

సంరక్షించు **samrakSincu** *v.t.* 1 to support, protect, maintain. 2 to save, preserve, conserve.

సంరక్షితరాజ్యం **samrakSitaraajyam** *n.* protectorate.

సంలీనం **samliinam** *n.* amalgamation, merger.

సంవత్సరం **samwatsaram** *n.* year.

సంవత్సరాది **samwatsaraadi** *n.* beginning of the year, Telugu New Year's Day.

సంవత్సరీకం **samwatsariikam** *same as* **saamwatsarikam.**

సంవరణం **samwaraNam** *n.* choice, selection.

సంవర్గమానం **samwargamaanam** *n.* logarithm.

సంవర్గీకరణం **samwargiikaraNam** *n.* categorisation.

సంవర్ధనం **samwardhanam** *n.* improvement, development; **śiśu~** child development.

సంవాదం **samwaadam** *n.* 1 argument, dispute. 2 dialogue.

సంవిత్తు **samwittu** *n.* wisdom, understanding, intellect.

సంవిధానం **samwidhaanam** *n.* 1 constitution (of a state). 2 literary craftsmanship. 3 (of a literary work) form, structure; **kathaa~** narrative structure.

సంవిధాన విరుద్ధ **samwidhaana wiruddha** *adj.* unconstitutional.

సంవృత **samwṛta** *adj.* 1 *ling.* closed: **samwṛtaaccu** closed vowel. 2 enclosed, surrounded, covered, concealed.

సంవేగం **samweegam** *n.* haste.

సంవేదక **samweedaka** *adj. sci.* sensory; **~naaDulu** sensory nerves.

సంవేదనం **samweedanam** *n. sci.* sensation.

సంశప్తకులు **samśaptakulu** *n.pl.class.* picked soldiers who have sworn never to flee from the enemy.

సంశయం **samśayam** *n.* doubt, uncertainty, hesitation, suspicion.

సంశయాత్ముడు **samśayaatmuDu** *n.* waverer.

సంశయాళువు **samśayaaLuwu** *n.* irresolute person.

సంశయాస్పద **samśayaaspada** *adj.* open to question, questionable, doubtful.

సంశయించు **samśayincu** *v.i. and t.* to doubt, suspect, hesitate.

సంశోధన **samśoodhana** *n.* 1 search, enquiry; **aatma~** self-examination. 2 correction.

సంశోధించు samśoodhincu *v.t.* 1 to search for. 2 to scrutinise, correct.

సంశోధిత samśoodhita *adj.* scrutinised, corrected; **~ prati** scrutinised copy; **~ mudraNa** critical edition.

సంశ్లిష్ట samśliSTa *adj.* 1 complex. 2 synthetic.

సంశ్లేషణ samśleeSaNa *n.* synthesis.

సంసక్త samsakta *adj.* adjoining, connected.

సంసక్తక samsaktaka *adj.* cohesive.

సంసక్తి samsakti *n.* 1 close connection, proximity. 2 cohesion.

సంసత్తు samsattu *n. class.* assembly, meeting, audience.

సంసర్గం samsargam *n. class.* contact.

సంసారం samsaaram *n.* 1 domestic life, married life, family life; **~ ceeyu** to live a family life. 2 family, household. 3 family affairs; **~ diddu** *or* **~ nilabeTTu** to set right o.'s family affairs. 4 the world, secular life; **palu duḥkhaalaku nilayam ii~** this world is the abode of many miseries. 5 *colloq.* wife: *see* **iidu.**

సంసారి samsaari *n.* householder, family man.

సంసారిక samsaarika *adj.* domestic, family.

సంసిద్ధ samsiddha *adj.* fully prepared or ready.

సంసిద్ధత samsiddhata *n.* readiness, preparedness.

సంసిద్ధి samsiddhi *n.* accomplishment, achievement, attainment.

సంసిద్ధించు samsiddhincu *v.i.* to be accomplished, be achieved, be attained.

సంస్కరణ samskaraNa *n.* reform.

సంస్కరించు samskarincu *v.t.* 1 to reform. 2 to revise (a book).

సంస్కర్త samskarta *n.* 1 reformer. 2 reviser (of a book).

సంస్కారం samskaaram *n.* 1 reform[ation]. 2 culture, refinement. 3 education, training. 4 memory. 5 any faculty or capacity. 6 **puurwajanma~** traits of character lingering from a previous birth. 7 sacrament. 8 purificatory ceremony. 9 **dahana~** cremation.

సంస్కృత samskṛta *adj.* refined, polished, purified.

సంస్కృతం samskṛtam *n.* the Sanskrit language.

సంస్కృతి samskṛti *n.* 1 culture; **aandhrula caritra~** the history and culture of the Andhras. 2 nature and upbringing, character; **waaDi~loo durmaargam annadaaniki taawu leedu** there was no place for such a thing as wickedness in his character.

సంస్కృతీకరించు samskṛtiikarincu *v.t.* to Sanskritise.

సంస్తవం samstawam *n. class.* praise.

సంస్తవనీయ samstawaniiya *adj. class.* praiseworthy.

సంస్తవించు samstawincu *v.t. class.* to praise.

సంస్తుతించు samstutincu *v.t.* to praise.

సంస్థ samstha *n.* 1 institute, institution. 2 organisation, corporation, authority; **rooDDu rawaaNaa~** Road Transport Corporation; **nagaraabhiwṛddhi~** Urban Development Authority.

సంస్థానం samsthaanam *n.* 1 land-holder's estate held under the former zamindari settlement, now obsolete. 2 princely state under the British raj. 3 *colloq.* family: **waaDu maatram ii~loowaaDu kaaDuu? waaDu kuudaa adee ceesEEDu** isn't he a member of this family? he did just the same (as the others did).

సంస్థానాధీశుడు samsthaanaadhiiśuDu *n.* 1 owner of a landed estate. 2 ruler of a princely state.

సంస్థాపకుడు samsthaapakuDu *n.* founder.

సంస్థాపన samsthaapana *n.* placing, fixing, establishing, installing, instituting, founding.

సంస్థాపించు samsthaapincu *v.t.* to found, establish, instal.

సంస్థిత samsthita *adj.* fixed, established.

సంస్పర్శ samsparśa *n.* close touch, close contact.

సంస్పృశించు samspṛśincu *v.t. class.* to touch.

సంస్ఫుట samsphuTa *adj.* clear, plain, distinct.

సంస్మరణ samsmaraNa *adj.* memorial; **~ sancika** memorial volume.

సంస్మరణ[ం] samsmaraNa[m] *n.* remembrance, recollection, memory; **aame samsmaraNaartham** in memory of her.

సంస్మరించు samsmarincu *v.t.* 1 to recall, remember. 2 to bring to mind.

సంస్మృతి samsmṛti *n.* mental faculties.

సంహతి samhati *n. class.* assemblage, agglomeration, collection.

సంహరణ[ం] samharaNa[m] *n.* killing, slaying.

సంహరించు samharincu *v.t.* to kill, slay, destroy.

సంహారం samhaaram *n.* killing, destruction.

సంహిత samhita *n.* 1 digest, condensed version of a piece of writing. 2 *ling.* juncture. 3 collection, compilation, code; **hinduu dharma~** code of Hindu Law.

సంహితాబద్ధంచేయు samhitaabaddham ceeyu *v.t.* to codify.

సకర్మక sakarmaka *adj. gram.* transitive; **~ kriya** transitive verb.

సకల sakala *adj.* all, entire, whole.

సకలం sakalam *n.* all, everything, the whole.

సకలం ముకలం sakalammukalam *adv. dial.* sitting with o.'s legs crossed, sitting cross-legged; *cf.* **padmaasanam, baasipiiTa.**

సకలార్థ sakalaartha *adj.* all-purpose.

సకశేరుకం sakaśeerukam *n. sci.* vertebrate.

సకామప్రేమ sakaama preema *n.* sexual love.

సకాలంలో, సకాలానికి sakaalamloo, sakaalaaniki *adv.*

1 at the right time, at the appropriate time. 2 on time, punctually.

సకిలించు, సగిలించు **sakilincu, sagilincu** *v.i.* 1 to neigh. 2 *colloq.* to laugh scornfully.

సకిలింపు, సగిలింపు **sakilimpu, sagilimpu** *n.* neighing.

సకృత్తుగా **sakrttugaa** *adv.* rarely, seldom.

సక్రమ **sakrama** *adj.* proper, correct, regular, orderly.

సక్రమంగా **sakramangaa** *adv.* 1 correctly, properly, duly. 2 regularly. 3 punctually.

సఖా! **sakhaa!** *interj.* my dear!

సఖియ **sakhiya** *n. class.* woman friend.

సఖుడు **sakhuDu** *n.* male friend or companion.

సఖ్యం **sakhyam** *n.* friendship, intimacy.

సఖ్యత **sakhyata** *n.* friendliness, amicableness.

సఖ్యపడు **sakhyapaDu** *v.t.* to come to terms, be reconciled.

సఖ్యపరచు **sakhyaparacu** *v.t.* to reconcile.

సగం, సహం **sagam, saham** *n.* half; ~ **loo** in the middle, halfway through.

సగటు **sagaTu**[1] *n.* average; ~ **naa** on average.

సగటు **sagaTu**[2] *n.* bishop in chess.

సగపాలు **sagapaalu** *n.* half share.

సగర్వంగా **sagarwangaa** *adv.* proudly, with pride.

సగిలించు, సగిలింపు **sagilincu, sagilimpu** *same as* **sakilincu, sakilimpu.**

సగుణం **saguNam** *adj.* possessing attributes or qualities or properties.

సగోత్రీకులు **sagootriikulu** *n.pl.* members of the same clan.

సగ్గుబియ్యం **saggubiyyam** *n.* sago.

సచిత్ర **sacitra** *adj.* illustrated; ~ **waarapatrika** illustrated weekly paper.

సచివాలయం **saciwaalayam** *n.* secretariat.

సచివుడు **saciwuDu** *n. class.* minister.

సచేతన **saceetana** *adj.* lively, active, astir, alert.

సచ్ఛిద్ర **sacchidra** *adj.* 1 perforated. 2 porous.

సచ్ఛీలం **sacchiilam** *n.* good conduct.

సజల **sajala** *adj. sci.* diluted.

సజాతి, సజాతీయ **sajaati, sajaatiiya** *adj.* 1 like, belonging to the same class or category; **sajaatii dhruwaalu wikarSistaayi** like poles repel one another. 2 homogeneous.

సజాతీయత **sajaatiiyata** *n.* feeling of homogeneity.

సజావు **sajaawu** *adj.* honest, plain, straightforward.

సజావుగా **sajaawugaa** *adv.* 1 plainly, straightforwardly. 2 in an orderly manner. 3 even-temperedly, civilly.

సజీవ **sajiiwa** *adj.* 1 alive, living. 2 animate.

సజీవత **sajiiwata** *n.* vitality.

సజీవుడు **sajiiwuDu** *n.* living person.

సజ్జ **sajja**[1] *n.* spiked millet, *holcus spicatus, also called* **kambu** *or* **gaNTi.**

సజ్జ **sajja**[2] *n.* basket; **puula** ~ flower basket.

సజ్జ **sajja**[3] *adj. dial.* fresh; **kuuragaayalu ~ gaa unnaayi** the vegetables are fresh.

సజ్జ, సజ్జా **sajja**[4], **sajjaa** *n. dial.* lintel.

సజ్జ **sajja**[5] *n.* 1 dress, decoration. 2 equipment. 3 armour. 4 harness.

సజ్జనుడు **sajjanuDu** *n.* virtuous and upright person.

సజ్జిత **sajjita** *adj. class.* armed, equipped, made ready.

సజ్జీకరించు **sajjiikarincu** *v.t.* 1 to equip, arm. 2 to decorate. 3 to harness.

సజ్జు **sajju** *n.* kind, type.

సటీక **saTiika** *adj. class.* with a commentary or notes, annotated.

సట్టా [వ్యాపారం] **saTTaa[wyaapaaram]** *n.* speculation, betting.

సట్టావ్యాపారి **saTTaawyaapaari** *n.* speculator.

సడలించు **saDalincu** *v.t.* to loosen, relax, untie.

సడలింపు **saDalimpu** *n.* relaxation.

సడలు, సడలిపోవు **saDalu, saDalipoowu** *v.i.* 1 to become slack or loose. 2 to be relaxed. 3 *fig.* to fade away, melt away, vanish, dissolve, be exhausted; **andhawiśwaasaalu saDalipootunnaayi** superstitious beliefs are fading away; **oorpu saDalipooyindi** patience was exhausted.

సడి **saDi** *n.* 1 sound, noise; *cf.* **caDi.** 2 disrepute, blame. 3 trace.

సడ్డకుడు **saDDakuDu** *same as* **SaDDakuDu.**

సణుగు **saNugu** *v.i.* 1 to murmur, mutter. 2 to grumble.

సణుగుడు **saNuguDu** *n.* 1 murmuring, muttering. 2 grumbling.

సత్, సద్ **sat, sad** *adjvl. prefix meaning* good, true; **sadud-deeśam** good intention.

సతతం **satatam** I. *adj.* continuous, permanent, eternal. II. *adv.* always, for ever, permanently.

సతతహరిత **satataharita** *adj.* evergreen.

సతమతం అవు **satamatam awu** *v.i.* 1 to be harassed, be distraught; **pillalatoo iNTicaakiriitoo ~ tunnadi** she is distraught on account of the children and the housework. 2 to be worried, be disturbed, be afflicted; **wastaa-Daa raaDaa anna aaloocanatoo satamatam awtuu kuur-cunnaanu** I waited in suspense to know whether he would come or not.

సతర్కంగా **satarkangaa** *adv.* logically.

సతాయించు **sataayincu** *v.t.* to tease, torment, pester.

సతి **sati** *n.* 1 *class.* virtuous woman. 2 wife; **satipatulu** wife and husband. 3 *same as* **sahagamanam.** 4 a name of Parvati.

సతీతిలకం **satiitilakam** *n. class.* 1 virtuous woman. 2 wife.

సతీమణి **satiimaNi** *n.* wife.

సత్కరించు **satkarincu** *v.t.* to honour, felicitate.

సత్కారం **satkaaram** *n.* 1 honouring, felicitation. 2 **atithi ~** hospitality.

సత్కార్యం **satkaaryam** *n.* good deed.

సత్తా, సత్తువ **sattaa, sattuwa** *n.* 1 strength, vigour, force, power, energy; **sattuwapuuraa koTTu** to strike with all o.'s force. 2 capacity, capability.

సత్తు **sattu** *n.* pewter; **~ ruupaayi** counterfeit rupee.

సత్పథం **satpatham** *n.* path of righteousness.

సత్య **satya** *adj.* true, real.

సత్యం **satyam** *n.* 1 truth, reality. 2 fact.

సత్యకాలం, సత్తెకాలం **satyakaalam, sattekaalam** *n.* age of truth, age of innocence (an imaginary golden age in the past; *cf.* the English expression 'the good old days').

సత్యకాలపు మనిషి, సత్తెకాలపు మనిషి **satyakaalapu maniSi, sattekaalapu maniSi** *n.* simple-minded, innocent and old fashioned person.

సత్యనిష్ఠతో **satyaniSThatoo** *adv., lit.* with devotion to the truth; **~ pramaaNam ceeyu** to swear solemnly.

సత్యప్రమాణం **satyapramaaNam** *n.* oath.

సత్యవరం **satyawaram** *n.* Satyavaram, a town in East Godavari District famous for growing betel leaves, also known as Annavaram; **satyawarapu kawaTaakulu** betel leaves grown in Satyavaram.

సత్యవర్తనం **satyawartanam** *n.* honesty, probity, integrity.

సత్యసంకల్పం **satyasankalpam** *n.* dedication to truthfulness.

సత్యాగ్రహం **satyaagraham** *n.polit.* satyagraha, the policy of non-violent resistance to British rule formulated by Mahatma Gandhi.

సత్రం **satram** *n.* choultry, rest house for travellers, inn.

సత్రకాయ **satrakaaya** *n.* 1 extra player in a game, gen. a child who does not belong to either side but is allowed to join in for his own satisfaction. 2 person who can be dispensed with, unncessary person.

సత్రయాగం **satrayaagam** *n. class.* kind of **yajña** or sacrifice performed by kings in olden times.

సత్రసాముచేయు **satrasaamuceeyu** *v.i. colloq.* to make a strenuous effort; **satrasaamuceesi sinimaaki Dabbulu sampaadincEEDu** he made a great effort and got money for going to the cinema.

సత్వం **satwam** *n.* 1 *class.* being, existence. 2 *class.* essence, nature. 3 strength, courage; *mod. mainly in compounds,* e.g. **jawasatwaalu** youthful vigour. 4 *sattwa*, goodness or purity, one of the three *gunas*; *see* **guNam.**

సత్వర **satwara** *adj.* swift, speedy.

సత్వరంగా **satwarangaa** *adv.* quickly, swiftly.

సత్సంగం **satsangam** *n.* group of devotees joining together.

సత్సంబంధాలు **satsambandhaalu** *n.pl.* good relations.

సదనం **sadanam** *n.* 1 house, dwelling, residence. 2 refuge, home; **wayassu maLLina striila ~** home for elderly women.

సదయుడు **sadayuDu** *n.* one who is kind or merciful.

సదరు **sadaru**[1] *adj.* [afore]said, above mentioned.

సదరు, సదరుకొను **sadaru**[2], **sadarukonu** *dial. variant of* **sardu[konu].**

సదవకాశం **sadawakaaśam** *n.* favourable opportunity.

సదవగాహన **sadawagaahana** *n.* good or clear understanding.

సదసద్వివేచన **sadasadwiweecana** *n.* discrimination between good and evil.

సదస్యం **sadasyam** *n.* part of the wedding ceremony in which learned pandits are invited to bless the bride and bridegroom in return for which they receive presents.

సదస్యుడు **sadasyuDu** *n.* 1 member of a meeting or conference. 2 *pl.* **sadasyulu** persons attending a meeting, audience.

సదస్సు **sadassu** *n.* conference, seminar, symposium.

సదా **sadaa** *adv.* 1 always. 2 continuously.

సదాచారం **sadaacaaram** *n.* good behaviour, good conduct, morality.

సదావృత్తి **sadaawṛtti** *n.* uncooked food given to a person who for reasons of religious orthodoxy will not eat food cooked by others (= **mooyinu, swayampaakam**); *cf.* **swahastam.**

సదిశ **sadiśa** *n. maths. sci.* vector.

సదుపాయం **sadupaayam** *n.* 1 arrangement, expedient, means. 2 facility, convenience.

సదుపాయంగా **sadupaayangaa** *adv.* with ease, with facility, conveniently.

సదృశం **sadṛśam** *adj.* similar, like, comparable.

సద్గతి **sadgati** *n.* salvation.

సద్దణుగు **saddaNugu** *v.i.* to die down, become quiet.

సద్దన్నం **saddannam** *n.* 1 cold rice, stale food (= **caldi annam**). 2 food served for breakfast.

సద్దు **saddu**[1] *n.* sound, noise.

సద్దు **saddu**[2] *same as* **sardu.**

సద్భావం, సద్భావన **sadbhaawam, sadbhaawana** *n.* good heartedness, good feelings, cordial feelings, good will; **sadbhaawa yaatra** good will mission.

సద్యః **sadyaḥ** *adv. class.* immediately.

సద్యోగం **sadyoogam** *echo word* **niiku udyoogam ~ eemaynaa undEE**? have you any job at all?

సద్యోజాతం **sadyoojaatam** *adj. chem.* nascent.

సద్వర్తన **sadwartana** *n.* good conduct, uprightness.

సద్వినియోగం **sadwiniyoogam** *n.* proper distribution, proper utilisation.

సద్వినియోగం చేయు **sadwiniyoogam ceeyu** *v.t.* to put to good use, make good use of.

సనాతన **sanaatana** *adj.* 1 ancient. 2 traditional. 3 *class.* fixed, permanent, eternal.

సనాతనుడు **sanaatanuDu** *n.* traditionally-minded person.

సనాతనులు **sanaatanulu** *n.pl. class.* the gods Brahma, Vishnu and Maheshwara (Siva).

సనాథ **sanaatha** *n. class.* married woman.

సని **sani** *same as* **śani.**

సన్న **sanna**[1] *same as* **sanjña.**

సన్న **sanna**[2] *adj.* 1 thin, slim. 2 narrow. 3 fine, sharp. 4 gentle. 5 (of sound) faint, soft. 6 *dial.* little, small; ~ **pillagaaDu** little boy; *see* **kaaru**[1] *sense I. 6.*

సన్నన, సన్నతనం **sannana, sannatanam** *n.* 1 thinness, slimness. 2 narrowness. 3 fineness. 4 gentleness. 5 softness.

సన్నగిలు, సన్నగిల్లు **sannagil[l]u** *v.i.* 1 to become lean or thin, pine away. 2 to become narrow. 3 to decrease, diminish.

సన్నజాజి **sannajaaji** *n.* jasmine, *jasminum ariculatum.*

సన్నదు **sannadu** *n.* written grant or patent, title deed.

సన్నద్ధం **sannaddham** *adj.* ready, prepared.

సన్నద్ధపడు **sannaddhapaDu** *v.i.* to get ready, get prepared.

సన్నని, సన్నపాటి **sannani, sannapaaTi** *alt. forms of* **sanna**[2].

సన్నాయి **sannaayi** *n.* kind of clarinet.

సన్నాసి **sannaasi** *see* **sanyaasi.**

సన్నాహం **sannaaham** *n.* 1 plans, preparations; **haydaraabaadu weLLee ~ loo unnaaDu** he has plans for going to Hyderabad; *see* **eduru ~ , saynya ~ .**

సన్నికల్లు **sannikallu** *n.* stone for grinding condiments; (in some communities it is the custom for the bridegroom to place his foot on a **sannikallu** when tying the bride's tali at the wedding ceremony).

సన్నికృష్ట **sannikṛSTa** *adj.* very close; ~ **kaaraNam** proximate cause.

సన్నిధానం, సన్నిధి **sannidhaanam, sannidhi** *n.* 1 nearness, proximity. 2 presence. 3 *dial.* temple, e.g., **goowindaraajula ~** temple of the God Govindarajulu.

సన్నిపాతం **sannipaatam** *n.* 1 dangerous fever involving delirium. 2 typhoid fever.

సన్నిపాతించు **sannipaatincu** *v.i.* to be delirious.

సన్నిబద్ధ **sannibaddha** *adj.* bound firmly, tied fast.

సన్నిభ **sannibha** *adj. class.* like, similar to, resembling.

సన్నిభుడు **sannibhuDu** *n. class.* one who resembles.

సన్నిహిత **sannihita** *adj.* 1 near, close. 2 intimate.

సన్నిహిత[త్వ]ం **sannihita[twa]m** *n.* 1 nearness, closeness. 2 intimacy.

సన్నిహితుడు **sannihituDu** *n.* one who is close, close relative, close friend, ally.

సన్నుత **sannuta** *adj.* praised, commended.

సన్నుతి **sannuti** *n.* praise, commendation.

సన్నుతించు **sannutincu** *v.t.* to praise, commend.

సన్మానం, సమ్మానం **sanmaanam, sammaanam** *n.* honouring, conferring honour (on s.o.).

సన్మానపత్రం **sanmaanapatram** *n.* address conferring honour (on s.o.).

సన్మానించు **sanmaanincu** *v.t.* to honour (s.o.).

సన్మార్గం **sanmaargam** *n.* good conduct, right doing.

సన్మార్గి **sanmaargi** *n.* one who pursues a virtuous way of life.

సన్యసించు **sanyasincu** *v.i. and t.* 1 to enter the fourth and final **aaśramam** or a period of a man's life, in which he becomes an ascetic. 2 to relinquish or resign or abandon any position or occupation.

సన్యాసం **sanyaasam** *n.* 1 asceticism, life of renunciation, the fourth and final **aaśramam** or period in a man's life, in which he becomes an ascetic. 2 relinquishment, abandonment.

సన్యాసం ఇచ్చు **sanyaasam iccu** *v.i.* (of a guru) to confer the status of **sanyaasam** on a person desiring to become a **sanyaasi.**

సన్యాసం పుచ్చుకొను **sanyaasam puccukonu** *v.i.* to renounce the world and become an ascetic (*lit.* to receive the status of **sanyaasam**, which is conferred by a guru).

సన్యాసి **sanyaasi** *n.* 1 ascetic, religious mendicant. 2 useless person (term of abuse). 3 **picci ~** *or* **picci sannaasi** dear fellow, dear child (term of affection).

సపత్ని **sapatni** *n. class.* co-wife.

సపదాంశం **sapadaamśam** *n. ling.* allomorph.

సపర్య **saparya** *n.* service.

సపిండీకరణం **sapiNDiikaraNam** *n.* funeral rite performed on the twelfth day after death, investing the spirit of the deceased with the rights of a sapinda.

సపిండుడు **sapiNDuDu** *n.* sapinda, agnatic kinsman to the seventh generation in descent from a common male ancestor, who has the right to offer a **piNDam** at the **sapiNDiikaraNam** of a deceased person.

సపోటా **sapooTaa** *n.* sapota fruit.

సప్త **sapta** *adj.* seven; ~ **swaraalu** the seven notes of the musical scale *sa, ri, ga, ma, pa, da, ni.*

సప్తపది **saptapadi** *n.* seven steps performed as part of the wedding ceremony; *cf.* **eeDaDugulu.**

సప్తమ **saptama** *adj.* seventh.

సప్తమి **saptami** *n.* 1 seventh day of a lunar fortnight;

cf. **ratha**~ 2 (*also* **saptamii wibhakti**) *gram.* locative case.

సప్తర్షిమండలం **saptarSimaNDalam** *n.* a name of the constellation called the Plough or the Great Bear in English.

సప్తాహం **saptaaham** *n.* 1 week. 2 period of seven days and nights devoted to fulfilment of a vow or other religious purpose.

సప్రయత్నంగా **saprayatnangaa** *adv.* with an effort.

సఫల **saphala** *adj.* fruitful, successful, effective, effectual.

సఫలత, సఫలత్వం **saphalata, saphalatwam** *n.* 1 success, fruition, fulfilment. 2 efficacy.

సఫలీకరణం **saphaliikaraNam** *n.* fulfilment, realisation.

సఫలీకృత **saphaliikṛta** *adj.* 1 fulfilled, realised. 2 successful, fruitful.

సఫాచేయు **saphaaceeyu** *v.t. colloq.* to kill.

సబబు **sababu** I. *n.* reason, ground, cause: ~**kaani** unreasonable. II. *adj.* fitting, proper, reasonable, appropriate.

సబల **sabala** *adj.* strong.

సబిందుకంగా **sabindukangaa** *adj. class.* spelt with an arasunna.

సబ్బందులు **sabbandulu** *echo word* **ibbandulu**~ inconveniences and the like.

సబ్బర **sabbara** *n.* bad, evil.

సబ్బు **sabbu** *n.* soap; ~**biLLa** cake of soap.

సభ **sabha** *n.* 1 meeting, conference, assembly; **eguwa/diguwa**~ upper/lower house of the legislature. 2 audience present at a meeting.

సభర్తృక **sabhartṛka** *n.* married woman.

సభాపతి **sabhaapati** *n.* 1 Speaker of the Legislative Assembly. 2 chairman of a meeting.

సభాసదులు, సభాస్తారులు, సభికులు **sabhaasadulu, sabhaastaarulu, sabhikulu** *n.pl.* members present at a meeting or assembly.

సభ్య **sabhya** *adj.* 1 polite, polished. 2 cultured, civilised: ~**maanawuDu** civilised person.

సభ్యత **sabhyata** *n.* 1 politeness, good manners. 2 culture, civilisation.

సభ్యత్వం **sabhyatwam** *n.* membership of a committee or assembly or similar body.

సభ్యుడు **sabhyuDu** *n.* 1 polite, civilised person. 2 (*also* **sabhikuDu**) member of a committee or assembly or similar body.

సభ్యోక్తి **sabhyookti** *n.* euphemism.

సమ **sama** *adj.* 1 like, similar. 2 same, equal, even.

సమ ఉజ్జీ, సముజ్జీ **sama ujjii, samujjii** *n.* equal; **sampanna praantaalanu mincaleeka pooyinaa,~laynaa kaagalugutaayi** although they cannot surpass the wealthy regions, they can at least be their equals.

సమం **samam** *n.* equality, evenness; **aaTa~aypootundi** the game will be a tie.

సమంగా **samangaa** *adv.* 1 properly; **ataniki telugu~teliyadu** (*or* **raadu**) he does not know Telugu properly. 2 evenly, equally; ~**wibhajincu** to divide equally; **praaNa~preemincina wyakti** a person whom one loves as much as o.'s own life.

సమం చేయు **samam ceeyu** *v.t.* to equalise.

సమంజసం **samanjasam** I. *n.* 1 propriety, justice, fitness. 2 reasonableness. II. *adj.* 1 just, right, proper, fit. 2 fair, reasonable. 3 correct, accurate.

సమంత్ర[పూర్వ]కంగా **samantra[puurwa]kangaa** *adv.* accompanied by incantations.

సమకట్టు **samakaTTu** *v.i. and t.* 1 to attempt. 2 to prepare, make ready. 3 to arrange.

సమకాలిక, సమకాలీన **samakaalika, samakaaliina** *adj.* contemporary.

సమకాలికుడు, సమకాలీనుడు **samakaalikuDu, samakaaliinuDu** *n.* contemporary.

సమకూడు, సమకూరు **samakuuDu, samakuuru** *v.i.* to accrue, accumulate, be gained, be obtained, be generated.

సమకూర్చు **samakuurcu** *v.t.* 1 to cause, bring about. 2 to provide, furnish, supply (facilities). 3 to yield (income). 4 to accord (approval). 5 to gather, collect, amass (profits). 6 to collect, assemble.

సమకోణం **samakooNam** *n. maths.* right angle.

సమక్షం **samakSam** *n.* presence.

సమగ్ర **samagra** *adj.* 1 entire, whole, complete, overall. 2 comprehensive, integrated.

సమగ్రత **samagrata** *n.* entirety.

సమగ్రాకృతి **samagraakṛti** *n.* configuration.

సమచతురస్ర **samacaturasra** *adj.* four square.

సమచతుర్భుజం **samacaturbhujam** *n. maths.* rhombus.

సమత, సమత్వం **samata, samatwam** *n.* equality, sameness.

సమతల **samatala** *adj.* plain, level; ~**praantam**, ~**pradeeśaalu** plains.

సమతలం **samatalam** *n.* level ground.

సమతావాదం **samataawaadam** *n.* egalitarianism.

సమతావాది **samataawaadi** *n.* egalitarian.

సమతాస్థితి **samataasthiti** *same as* **samasthiti.**

సమతులిత **samatulita** *adj.* balanced; ~**aahaaram** balanced diet.

సమతూకం **samatuukam** *n.* balance, equilibrium.

సమతౌల్యం **samatawlyam** *n.* even balance, equilibrium.

సమ[బాహు] త్రిభుజం **sama[baahu] tribhujam** *n. maths.* equilateral triangle.

సమదర్శి **samadarśi** *n.* person who regards all things with impartiality and equanimity.

సమదృష్టి, సమబుద్ధి, సమభావం **samadṛSTi, samabuddhi, samabhaawam** *n.* balanced outlook, impartial attitude, giving equal consideration to both sides.

సమధిక **samadhika** *adj.* very great, very much.

సమను **samanu** *n. legal* court summons.

సమన్వయం **samanwayam** *n.* 1 coordination. 2 reconciliation or synthesis of opposing propositions in logic.

సమన్వయం చేయు **samanwayam ceeyu** *v.t.* to reconcile opposing propositions.

సమన్వయపరచు, సమన్వయించు **samanwayaparacu, samanwayincu** *v.t.* to coordinate.

సమన్వయకర్త **samanwayakarta** *n.* coordinator.

సమన్విత **samanwita** *adj.* joined, united.

సమపదం **samapadam** *n.* unassimilated loan word (= **tatsamam**).

సమపాళంగా, సమపాళంలో **samapaaLangaa, samapaaLamloo** *adv.* in equal quantities.

సమపీడనరేఖ **samapiiDanareekha** *n. met.* isobar.

సమబాహుత్రిభుజం **samabaahutribhujam** *same as* **samatribhujam.**

సమబుద్ధి, సమభావం **samabuddhi, samabhaawam** *same as* **samadṛSTi.**

సమయం **samayam** *n.* 1 time, occasion. 2 right or proper time; **samayaaniki waccu** (i) to arrive in time, arrive punctually; (ii) to arrive at the right moment. 3 **kawi samayaalu** poetic conventions.

సమయసారణి **samayasaaraNi** *n.* timetable.

సమయస్ఫూర్తి **samayasphuurti** *n.* 1 proper sense of timing. 2 quick wittedness, presence of mind. 3 spontaneity.

సమయాసమయాలు లేకుండా **samayaasamayaalu leekuNDaa** *advbl. phrase* in season and out of season.

సమయించు **samayincu** *v.t. class.* to destroy, kill.

సమయు **samayu** *v.i. class.* to be destroyed, be killed; *cf.* **samasipoowu.**

సమయోచిత **samayoocita** *adj.* suited to the occasion, proper to the occasion, timely, topical.

సమయోచితంగా **samayoocitangaa** *adv.* at the appropriate time, when needed, suitably to the occasion, seasonably.

సమరం **samaram** *n.* battle, war, struggle.

సమరసం **samarasam** *n.* amicableness, amicability.

సమరూపం **samaruupam** *n. ling.* homonym.

సమరూపత **samaruupata** *n.* 1 uniformity. 2 *sci.* isomorphism.

సమర్త **samarta** *n.* girl's attainment of puberty.

సమర్త ఆడు **samarta aaDu** *v.i.* (of a girl) to attain puberty.

సమర్థ[వంత] **samartha[wanta]** *adj.* 1 able, capable. 2 efficacious, effective, efficient. 3 skilled, well versed.

సమర్థ[వంత]ంగా **samartha[wanta]ngaa** *adv.* 1 capably. 2 effectively, efficiently. 3 skilfully, competently.

సమర్థకుడు **samarthakuDu** *n.* supporter, backer.

సమర్థత **samarthata** *n.* ability, capability, competence, skilfulness.

సమర్థన **samarthana** *n.* 1 support. 2 seconding (of a proposal). 3 justification. 4 perseverance, persistence.

సమర్థనీయ **samarthaniiya** *adj* worthy of support, sustainable, justifiable, justified.

సమర్థించు **samarthincu** *v.i. and t.* 1 to support, stand up for. 2 to second (a proposal). 3 to justify (conduct). 4 to establish, substantiate; **M. amaayakuDaynappaTikii atani aaśaki kaaraNam leeka pooleedani samarthincaDaaniki R. ilaa annaaDu** to establish that although M. was a simple minded person his desire was not without a reason, R. spoke as follows.

సమర్థించుకువచ్చు **samarthincukuwaccu** *v.i. and t.* to manage, cope; **enta kaSTamayna pani aynaa waaDu samarthincukuraagalaDu** no matter how difficult the work is he will be able to manage it.

సమర్థుడు **samarthuDu** *n.* able, talented, competent or capable person.

సమర్పణ **samarpaNa** *n.* act of making an offering, presentation; **krti~** dedication of a literary work.

సమర్పించు **samarpincu** *v.t.* to offer, present, submit, dedicate.

సమవయస్కుడు **samawayaskuDu** *n.* contemporary.

సమవర్తి **samawarti** *adj. legal* concurrent.

సమశీతోష్ణ **samaśiitooSNa** *adj. geog.* temperate; **~ maNDalam** temperate zone.

సమష్టి **samaSTi** *same as* **samiSTi.**

సమసంబంధం **samasambandham** *n.* correlation.

సమసిపోవు **samasipoowu** *v.i.* to be abolished, be destroyed, be dispelled, disappear, vanish, die out, be lost; **twaraloonee ii duraacaaram tanantataanee samasipootundi** very soon this bad custom will die out of its own accord.

సమస్త **samasta** *adj.* 1 all, whole, entire, complete; **~ mayna sampadalu** all kinds of resources. 2 *gram.* compound; **~ padam** compound word; **~ waakyam** compound sentence.

సమస్తం **samastam** *n.* all, the whole, everything.

సమ[తా]స్థితి **sama[taa]sthiti** *n.* equilibrium.

సమస్య **samasya** *n.* problem, enigma.

సమస్యాత్మక **samasyaatmaka** *adj.* problematical.

సమస్యాపూరణం **samasyaapuuraNam** *n.* poetical problem, in which part of a stanza is proposed by one person to be completed by another as a trial of skill.

సమాంతర **samaantara** *adj. maths. phys.* parallel; **~ balaalu** parallel forces.

సమాంతర చతుర్భుజం **samaantara caturbhujam** *n. maths.* parallelogram.

సమాకలనం **samaakalanam** *n.* **1** integration. **2** *ling.* collation.

సమాకలన గణితం **samaakalana gaNitam** *n. maths.* integral calculus.

సమాఖ్య **samaakhya** *n.* federation.

సమాగత **samaagata** *adj.* approached, arrived.

సమాగమం **samaagamam** *n.* **1** opportune arrival. **2** meeting. **3** union, junction.

సమాచారం **samaacaaram** *n.* **1** news, information, intelligence. **2** report, message.

సమాజ **samaaja** *adj.* **1** relating to the community; **~ wikaasam** *or* **~ abhiwrddhi** community development. **2** social; **~ seewa** social service.

సమాజం **samaajam** *n.* **1** society, association, club. **2** religious congregation. **3** society in general, the community.

సమాజశాస్త్రం **samaaja śaastram** *n.* (science of) sociology.

సమాజికుడు **samaajikuDu** *n.* member of a society or religious congregation.

సమాదరం **samaadaram** *n.* **1** respect, regard. **2** kindness, love, attachment (< **sam** + **aadaram**).

సమాదరణ **samaadaraNa** *n.* equal regard, equal favour (< **sama** + **aadaraNa**).

సమాదరించు **samaadarincu** *v.t.* **1** to treat kindly. **2** to show respect for.

సమాధానం **samaadhaanam** *n.* **1** answer. **2** explanation (to a charge or accusation). **3** explanation, solution (to a problem). **4** consent, agreement.

సమాధానం అవు, సమాధానపడు **samaadhaanam awu, samaadhaanapaDu** *v.i.* **1** to be reconciled. **2** to come to terms.

సమాధానపరచు **samaadhaanaparacu** *v.t.* **1** to reconcile. **2** to soothe, calm.

సమాధానపరచుకొను **samaadhaanaparacukonu** *v.i.* to reconcile o.s., satisfy o.'s mind.

సమాధి **samaadhi** *n.* **1** grave, tomb. **2** state of deep meditation. **3** reverie.

సమాధిరాయి **samaadhi raayi** *n.* tombstone.

సమానం **samaanam** *adj.* **1** like, similar. **2** same, equal, equivalent; **X -too~** equal to **X**.

సమానం చేయు **samaanam ceeyu** *v.t.* to equalise, make equal.

సమానత, సమానత్వం **samaanata, samaanatwam** *n.* equality, parity.

సమానాంతర **samaanaantara** *adj.* parallel; **~ reekhalu** parallel lines.

సమానార్థక **samaanaarthaka** *adj.* synonymous, having the same meaning.

సమానుడు **samaanuDu** *n.* one who is equal.

సమాపక **samaapaka** *adj. gram.* finite; **~ kriya** finite verb.

సమాపనం **samaapanam** *n.* finishing, completing.

సమాప్తం, సమాప్తి **samaaptam, samaapti** *n.* end, conclusion, finish.

సమామ్నాయం **samaamnaayam** *n.* group; **rSi~** group of rishis; **warNa~** alphabet.

సమాయత్త **samaayatta** *adj.* ready, prepared.

సమాయత్తం **samaayattam** *n.* readiness, preparation.

సమాయోజనం **samaayoojanam** *n. phys.* adjustment.

సమారాధకుడు **samaaraadhakuDu** *n.* **1** one who takes part in a **samaaraadhana**. **2** one who adores, one who worships.

సమారాధన **samaaraadhana** *n.* ceremonial feasting of brahmans on certain religious occasions, e.g., **waykuNTha ~** performed on the thirteenth day after a death.

సమార్హత **samaarhata** *n.* parity.

సమాలోచనలు **samaaloocanalu** *n.pl.* **1** consultations. **2** negotiations.

సమావేశం **samaaweeśam** *n.* **1** meeting, consorting together; **samaaweeśa sweeccha** freedom of association. **2** conference. **3** sitting, session (of assembly or parliament).

సమావేశం అవు **samaaweeśam awu** *v.i.* **1** to meet. **2** to hold a meeting.

సమావేశకాలం **samaaweeśakaalam** *n.* session (of assembly or parliament).

సమాశ్రిత **samaaśrita** *adj.* dependent, depending.

సమాశ్వాసం **samaaśwaasam** *n.* consoling, comforting.

సమాసం **samaasam** *n. gram.* compound word.

సమాసోక్తి **samaasookti** *n.* model metaphor.

సమాహారం **samaahaaram** *n.* **1** collecting, gathering. **2** collection, assemblage.

సమితి **samiti** *n.* association, league, union, assembly; **naanaa jaati~** League of Nations.

సమిధ **samidha** *n.* sacrificial fuel, firewood for a sacrifice.

సమిష్టి, సమష్టి **samiSTi, samaSTi** I. *n.* **1** the whole. **2** the people in general, the public. II. *adj.* joint, united, common, collective; **~ kuTumba paddhati** joint family system; **~ bhaaSa** common language; *cf.* **wyaSTi.**

సమిష్టిగా, సమిష్టిమీద **samiSTigaa, samiSTimiida** *adv.* jointly, collectively.

సమీకరణ[ం] **samiikaraNa[m]** *n.* **1** *maths.* equation. **2** *ling.* assimilation.

సమీకరించు **samiikarincu** *v.t.* to collect, gather, assemble, bring together, pool.

సమీకృత **samiikrta** *adj.* **1** unified, integrated. **2** *ling.* assimilated.

సమీక్ష **samiikSa** *n.* review.

సమీక్షకుడు **samiikSakuDu** *n.* reviewer.

సమీక్షించు **samiikSincu** *v.t.* to review.

సమీప **samiipa** *adj.* near, close, adjoining, adjacent.

సమీపం **samiipam** *n.* nearness, closeness, proximity.

సమీపస్థ **samiipastha** *adj.* adjoining, adjacent, nearby.

సమీపించు **samiipincu** *v.i. and t.* to approach, come near, be imminent.

సముఖం **samukham** *n.* presence.

సముచిత **samucita** *adj.* right, fit, proper, appropriate, suitable, felicitous.

సముచ్చయం **samuccayam** *n.* 1 *gram.* conjunction. 2 collection, assemblage, group. 3 aggregate.

సముచ్చయార్థక **samuccayaarthaka** *adj. gram.* conjunctive.

సముజ్జీ **samujjii** *same as* **sama ujjii.**

సముజ్వల **samujwala** *adj.* radiant, splendid.

సముత్సాహం **samutsaaham** *n.* enthusiasm.

సముదాయం **samudaayam** *n.* 1 collection, accumulation, assemblage. 2 group. 3 cluster. 4 community.

సముదాయక **samudaayaka** *adj.* collective, relating to the community; ~**wasatigṛham** community rest house.

సముదాయించు **samudaayincu** *v.t.* 1 to calm, quieten, lull. 2 to comfort, soothe, console, appease.

సముద్ధరణ **samuddharaNa** *n.* 1 raising, uplift. 2 restoration, rehabilitation.

సముద్ధరించు **samuddharincu** *v.t.* 1 to uplift. 2 to revive, restore.

సముద్రం **samudram** *n.* sea; **mahaa**~ ocean.

సముద్రపు దొంగ **samudrapu donga** *n.* pirate.

సముద్రవాహక **samudrawaahaka** *adj.* seaborne.

సమున్నత **samunnata** *adj.* highest, noblest, very high.

సమున్నతంగా **samunnatangaa** *adv.* high up, on high.

సమున్నతి **samunnati** *n.* elevation, raising.

సముపార్జన **samupaarjana** *n.* acquiring, earning, gaining, achieving.

సముపార్జించు **samupaarjincu** *v.t.* to earn, acquire, gain.

సమూలంగా **samuulangaa** *adv.* totally, completely, right from the roots.

సమూహ **samuuha** *adj.* collective.

సమూహం **samuuham** *n.* 1 crowd, multitude, number, flock, group. 2 cluster (of stars).

సమూహీకృత **samuuhiikṛta** *adj. sci.* agglutinative.

సమృద్ధి **samṛddhi** *n.* abundance, plenty, copiousness, affluence; **swayam**~ self-sufficiency.

సమృద్ధిగా **samṛddhigaa** *adv.* plentifully, in abundance.

సమేతంగా **sameetangaa** *adv., used postpositionally* accompanied by, together with, along with; **bandhumitra**~ accompanied by relatives and friends.

సమైక్య **samaykya** *adj.* joint, united, integrated; ~**kṛSi** concerted effort.

సమైక్యం **samaykyam** *n.* unity, unification.

సమైక్యంగా **samaykyangaa** *adv.* unitedly.

సమైక్యత **samaykyata** *n.* unity, integration; **jaatiiya**~ national integration.

సమైక్యపరచు **samaykyaparacu** *v.t.* to unite, bring together.

సమైక్యభావం **samaykyabhaawam** *n.* thinking alike.

సమ్మత[ం] **sammata[m]** *adj.* agreed to, assented to, concurred in, liked, approved of, countenanced, acquiesced in; **uttaraalu raayaDam waaDiki sammatam kaaleedu** writing letters was not agreeable to him.

సమ్మతంగా **sammatangaa** *advbl. suffix* in consonance with, in accordance with; **caTTa/nyaaya**~ in accordance with law.

సమ్మతి, సమ్మతం **sammati, sammatam** *n.* consent, agreement, assent, approval.

సమ్మతించు **sammatincu** *v.i. and t.* to consent, agree, concur, approve, acquiesce.

సమ్మదం **sammadam** *n. class.* joy.

సమ్మర్దం **sammardam** *n.* crowd, throng, rush, overcrowding.

సమ్మానం **sammaanam** *same as* **sanmaanam.**

సమ్మిత **sammita** *adj.* of equal dimensions.

సమ్మిళిత **sammiLita** *adj.* 1 well mixed, well mingled. 2 complex.

సమ్ముఖం **sammukham** *n.* presence; ~**loo** in the presence of, before, in front of.

సమ్మె **samme** *n.* strike.

సమ్మె కట్టు, సమ్మె చేయు **samme kaTTu, samme ceeyu** *v.i.* to go on strike.

సమ్మెట **sammeTa** *n.* sledgehammer, large hammer.

సమ్మేళనం **sammeeLanam** *n.* 1 mixing, mingling, fusing, blending. 2 *chem.* compound. 3 **kawi**~ gathering of poets for recital of poetry; **sangiita**~ gathering of musicians for performance of music.

సమ్మోహన[ం] **sammoohana[m]** *n.* 1 love, passion. 2 charm, enchantment, entrancement, fascination.

సమ్మోహ[న]పరచు, సమ్మోహింప చేయు **sammooha[na] paracu, sammoohimpa ceeyu** *v.t.* to charm, enchant, fascinate, enthral.

సమ్మోహిత **sammoohita** *adj.* 1 charmed, enchanted, fascinated, enthralled. 2 *fig.* hypnotised, mesmerised.

సమ్యక్ **samyak** *adj. class.* comprehensive, all embracing.

సమ్రాట్టు, సామ్రాట్టు **samraaTTu, saamraaTTu** *n.* emperor, lord: **kawi**~ great poet; **naTa**~ great actor.

సయానా, స్వయానా, సయాం **sayaanaa, swayaanaa, sayaam** *adj.* o.'s own: ~**naa tammuDu** my own younger brother; *cf.* **saakSaattu.**

సయించు **sayincu** *v.i.* to be agreeble, be palatable, be pleasing, be to o.'s taste; **miiku pulupu sayistee** if you like sour things; **naaku annam sayincadu** I have lost my appetite.

సయితం **sayitam** *same as* **sahitam.**

సయీశ్వరవాదం **sayiiśwarawaadam** *n.* theism.

సయుక్తిక **sayuktika** *adj.* reasonable, logical.

సయుక్తికంగా **sayuktikangaa** *adv.* reasonably, logically.

సయోధ్య **sayoodhya** *n. journ.* friendly relations, amity.

సయ్యాట[ం] **sayyaaTa[m]** *n.* sport, amorous play.

సరం **saram** *n.* garland, necklace; **mutyaala saraalu** 'Strings of Pearls', title of a book of lyrics by Gurajada Appa Rao.

సరంగు **sarangu** *n.* boatman.

సరంజాం **saranjaam** *n. dial.* preparation, getting ready.

సరంజామా **saranjaamaa** *n.* 1 equipment, outfit. 2 articles, paraphernalia. 3 goods, merchandise.

సరంబి **sarambi** *n.* loft, ceiling; **balla**~ loft or ceiling made of planks.

సరకు, సరుకు **saraku, saruku** *n.* 1 commodity, merchandise, goods, cargo. 2 article, thing, object. 3 *slang* prostitute.

సరకుచేయు **sarakuceeyu** *v.t.* to care for, regard, esteem.

సరణి **saraNi** *n. class.* 1 course, way, path, channel. 2 series.

సరదా **saradaa** *n.* 1 fondness, affection. 2 joy, pleasure, delight; **waaDi snehitulu naluguruu caalaa**~**aynawaaLLu** his friends are delightful people. 3 liking; **sinimaaki weLLaDamkoosam pillawaaDu**~**paDutunnaaDu** the boy is keen on going to the cinema.

సరదాగా **saradaagaa** *adv.* 1 cheerfully, happily, jokingly. 2 for fun, for the sake of amusement.

సరఫరా **sarapharaa** *n.* supply.

సరఫరాచేయు **sarapharaa ceeyu** *v.t.* to supply.

సరఫరాదారు[డు] **sarapharaadaaru[Du]** *n.* supplier.

సరళ **saraLa** *adj.* 1 straight, direct; ~**reekha** straight line. 2 simple, straightforward. 3 simplified, moderated; ~**graanthika bhaaSa** simplified or moderated form of the classical style of Telugu. 4 *maths.* linear. 5 ~ **waDDii** simple interest.

సరళత **saraLata** *n.* straightforwardness, clarity, simplicity.

సరళి **saraLi** *n.* 1 trend, course. 2 method, style, manner; **niipaTLa waari**~**elaa undi**? how was his manner towards you? 3 ~**swaraalu** simple tunes learnt by beginners in Carnatic music.

సరవ **sarawa** *same as* **sariwi.**

సరస, సరసన, సరసని **sarasa[1], sarasana, sarasani** I. *adv.* nearby, close. II. *p.p.* alongside, side by side with.

సరస **sarasa[2]** *adj.* 1 funny, facetious, amusing (with sexual connotations). 2 pleasant, agreeable. 3 fair, reasonable; ~**dharala dukaaNam** fair price shop. 4 *class.* elegant, tasteful.

సరసం **sarasam** *n.* 1 joking, fun, amusement (with sexual overtones); **sarasaalu aaDu** to make sexual advances, practise lewd behaviour. 2 *class.* joking, jesting, pleasantry, merriment.

సరసత్వం, సారస్యం, స్వారస్యం **sarasatwam, saarasyam, swaarasyam** *n.* 1 good taste, good manners, gentlemanliness. 2 elegance, beauty of composition.

సరసర **sarasara** *adv.* quickly, rapidly.

సరసీరుహం **sarasiiruham** *n. class.* lotus.

సరసుడు **sarasuDu** *n.* 1 man of good taste, connoisseur. 2 playboy, womaniser (colloq.), libertine.

సరసురాలు **sarasuraalu** *n.* 1 woman of good taste and refinement. 2 libertine.

సరసోదంతం **sarasoodantam** *n.* love affair.

సరస్వతి **saraswati** *n.* 1 name of the Goddess of speech and learning, wife of Brahma. 2 *see* **triweeNi.**

సరస్సు **sarassu** *n.* lake, pond, pool.

సరా? **sarEE?** (<**sari** + **aa** *interrog. suffix*) *part of a rhetorical question, lit.* is it enough if. . . .? **neenu, naa sneehitulu tanatoo maaTaaDatagani waaLLamani aame bhaawam. caduwukoogaanee (***or* **caduwukoNTee)** ~? **maryaadalu teliyawadduu**? she thinks that my friends and I are not good enough to talk to her. even though she is educated (*lit.* is it enough if she is educated?) ought she not to be polite?

సరాగం **saraagam** *n. gen. pl.* **saraagaalu** friendly exchange of words, friendly talk.

సరాబు, షరాబు **saraabu, Saraabu** *n.* 1 shroff, money changer, cash keeper. 2 *dial.* goldsmith.

సరాసరి **saraasari** I. *n.* average. II *adv.* directly, straight; ~**baadhyuDu** person directly responsible.

సరాసరిని **saraasarini** *adv.* on average.

సరి **sari** I. *n.* 1 end[ing], finish, completion; **selawalu reepaTitoo**~ the holidays will come to an end tomorrow; **atani wamśam antaTitoo**~ his line of descent ended there; **niikuu naakuu**~ (*or* **niikuu naakuu cellu**) the association (*or* the friendship) between you and me is over. 2 equality, matching, evenness, similarity, likeness; **waaDikii wiiDikii**~ that man and this man are a match for each other; **aayana sampaadanaki aawiDa kharcuki**~ **ki**~ what she spends is equal to what he earns; ~**leeni** *or* ~**kaani** matchless, unequalled; **éeTi iitaku lanka meetaku**~ the reward is worth the effort (*proverb meaning lit.* the grazing to be had on the island and the effort of swimming the river to reach it are equal). 3 correctness, propriety; **daanni gurinci miiru winnadi**~**kaadu** what you have heard about it is not correct; **siggu leekapootee** ~ *lit.* if there is no shame, it is all right (said with sarcasm, *meaning* you/he/she/they ought to feel ashamed); *so also* **buddhi**

leekapootee~ you/he/she/they ought to have more sense). 4 s.g appropriate, fitting, typical or characteristic: **aa pani ceyyaDam aayanakee**~ (*or* **aayanakee cellu**) only he is a fit person to do that work: **adi niikee**~ *or* **adi niikee cellu** that is typical of you. II. *adj.* equal, even: ~**sankhya** even number: ~**ujjii** an equal (= **sama ujjii**): *see also* **sariyayna.** III *minor sentence, in reply to a demand or request* yes!, all right!, o.k! (colloq).

సరికదా **sari kadaa** *minor sentence* not only that: **aapay waaTiki ekkaleem**~, **kaniisam kannetti kuuDaa cuuDaleem** not only can we not rise to higher things than that but we cannot even raise our eyes to look at them (*lit.* we cannot rise to higher things than that — not only that but we cannot even. . .).

సరికి **sariki** *adv.* 1 by [the time that]: **nuwwu nidra leecee**~ by the time that you wake up: **tommidiNTiki raNDi, aa**~ **neenu siddhangaa uNTaanu** come at 9 o'clock, I will be ready by that time: **saayantram**~by evening: **podduna**~ by morning. 2 when: **inta peddammaayi ilaa aDigee**~ **neenu aaścarya paDDaanu** I was astonished when such a grown up girl asked this question.

సరికొత్త **sarikotta** *adj.* 1 fresh, brand new. 2 strange, unfamiliar.

సరిగ **sariga** *n.* gold or silver lace (= **jarii, jaltaaru**): **sarigancu ciire** sari woven with a gold border.

స-రి-గ-మ-ప-ద-ని **sa-ri-ga-ma-pa-da-ni** *n.* the seven notes of the musical scale (*cf.* do/re/mi etc.).

సరిగా, సరిగ్గా **sarigaa, sariggaa** *adv.* 1 properly, rightly, correctly. 2 completely, fully. 3 exactly. 4 corresponding to: **konni maaTalu konni praantaalakee parimitangaa uNTaayi, waaTiki**~ **migilina praantaalloo weeruweeru padaalu waaDukaloo uNTaayi** some words are restricted to certain regions: corresponding to them, different words are in use in the remaining regions.

సరిచూచు[కొను] **saricuucu[konu]** *v.t.* 1 to observe carefully. 2 to check, verify. 3 to compare.

సరిచేయు **sariceeyu** *v.t.* 1 to correct, set right. 2 to adjust. 3 to arrange, put in order, make fit: **wittanaalu naaTaDaaniki neela sariceesEEDu** he made the land fit for sowing seeds. 4 to tidy (hair, clothes). 5 **manassu sariceesukonu** to calm or compose o.'s mind.

సరితూగు **sarituugu** *v.* 1 to be of equal weight or value. 2 to balance. 3 to be comparable.

సరిదిద్దు **sarididdu** *v.t.* to correct, set right, rectify, put in order: ~**koowalasina** (*or* **sardukoowalasina**) **panulu** affairs that need to be tided up.

సరిపడా **saripaDaa** *adj.* 1 enough, sufficient; **waaLLa awasaraalaku**~**Dabbu icci pampincEEnu** I gave them enough money for their needs and sent them away. 2 equal, equivalent.

సరిపడు **saripaDu** *v.t.* 1 to fit in with, conform with, be in accordance with: **aawiDa tatwaaniki goppalu ceppukoowaDam saripaDadu** boasting is not in accordance with her nature. 2 to be enough, be sufficient; **mupphay mandi atithulaku saripaDee aahaaram** enough food for thirty guests: **intamandiki saripaDee guNDiga undaa mii iNTLoo**? is there a pot big enough (to cook) for so many people in your house? 3 to equal, be equal to; **aynuuru ruupaayalaku saripaDee pustakaalu tiisukuraNDi** please bring books to the value of five hundred rupees. 4 to suit, agree with, be agreeable, pass muster: **naaku kottabiyyam saripaDawu** new rice does not agree with my constitution; **miiku ikkaDi niiLLu saripaDDaayaa**? does the water here suit you? 5 to fit: **cokkaa miiku saripaDitee uncukooNDi** if the shirt fits you, keep it (*but* **saripootee** *is commoner in this sense*). 6 *impersonal, with dative* to be on friendly terms, get on well together: **atanikii raamuukii modaTinunci saripaDaleedu** from the start he and Ramu did not get on well together.

సరిపుచ్చుకొను **saripuccukonu** *v.i.* 1 to content o.s. with, make do with, manage with: **ippaTiki diinitoo saripuccukooNDi** please manage with this for the present. 2 to put up with.

సరిపెట్టు **saripeTTu** *v.t.* 1 to equalise. 2 to adjust, set off (one thing against another). 3 to make s.g suffice: **idigoo baTTa: oka kooTu ayeeTaTTugaa**~ here is the cloth: make it do for one coat. 4 to finish: **caduwu saripeTTi udyoogamloo praweeśincu** finish your studies and enter employment.

సరిపెట్టుకొను **saripeTTukonu** *v.i* 1 to manage with, make do with: **wiiru reeSanu metukulatoonee saripeTTukoowaDam leedani andarikii telusu** everyone knows that these people do not manage with only the few grains of ration rice. 2 to be content with, satisfy o.s. with. 3 to persuade o.s., console o.s., calm o.s., reassure o.s., tell o.s., reflect: **raanu raanu aame uttaraalu karuway pooyEEyi. "samsaaramloo paDindi lemm" ani saripeTTukonnaaru naannagaaru, kaanii naakeedoo śanka toocindi** gradually her letters became scarce. my father reassured himself by saying, "she is busy with her family life", but a doubt still lurked for me.

సరిపోను **saripoonu** *adj.* just enough: **waaDiki**~**Dabbu iccEEnu** I gave him just enough money.

సరిపోలు **saripoolu** *v.i.* to be comparable, resemble.

సరిపోల్చు **saripoolcu** *v.t.* to compare.

సరిపోవు **saripoowu** *v.i.* 1 to be equal, be equivalent, match. 2 to fit, suit, be suitable: **ii cokkaa miiku saripootee uncukooNDi** if this shirt fits you, keep it: **naaku saripooyee ceppulu leewu** there are no shoes that will fit me. 3 to accord (**-ki,** with), fit in (**-ki,** with), correspond (**-ki,** with *or* to), be applicable (**-ki,** to); **ii wibhaagam raajakiiyamaynadee gaaka sthuulangaa bhaaSaawiSayikangaa kuuDaa saripootundi** this division is not only political but broadly speaking it also corresponds (*or* applies) linguistically. 4 to be right or proper or fitting. 5 **saripooyindi** *is used idiomatically to mean* it was all right, it was overlooked, it did not matter: **waaLLantaa atithulu kaabaTTee saripooyindi, kaanii siitammaku waaLLanu naaluguu peTTa buddhayindi** they were all guests, so she overlooked it (what they said), but Sitamma felt like boxing their ears; **iwwEELa pillalaku selawu kaabaTTi saripooyindi kaani leekapootee iNTipanulatoo nijangaa caccipooyuNDunu** the children have a holiday today so it does not matter (*or* it is a good thing that the children have a holiday today), otherwise I would have been really overwhelmed by housework. 6 to be appropriate (for), be typical or characteristic (of): **adi miikee saripooyindi** (*or* **adi miikee cellindi**) that is typical of you. 7 to be enough: **intamandiki annam saripootundEE**? will the food be enough for so many people? **8** to be just enough (for), be taken up (with): **roojantaa kaburlatooTee saripooyindi, panuleemii kaaleedu** the whole day was taken up with talk and no work was done. **9** to be finished, be exhausted, run out (colloq.): **miiru iccina Dabbu ninnaTitoo saripooyindi** the money that you gave was finished yesterday.

సరియైన, సరైన **sariyayna, sarayna** *adj.* right, correct, fitting, appropriate.

సరివచ్చు **sariwaccu** *v.i.* to be a match, be equal; **neenu waaDitoo sariraagalanaa?** can I be a match for him?

సరివి,సరవ,సర్వి **sariwi, sarawa, sarwi** *n.* small round bottomed vessel for boiling water or cooking.

సరిసమాన[ం] **sarisamaana[m]** *adj.* equal, equivalent.

సరిసమానంగా **sarisamaanangaa** *adv.* **1** equally. **2** on a par (**-ki** or **-too**, with).

సరిసరి **sarisari** I. *adj.* finished, all over; **maa annayya pani ~ anukonnaamu** we thought it was all over for my brother. II. *interj.* very well!, all right! **~ nuwwu ceppinadi caalu** all right, what you have said is enough.

సరిహద్దు **sarihaddu** *n.* **1** frontier. **2** boundary, limit.

సరీబేసీ **sarii beesii** *n.* a boys' game.

సరీసృపం **sariisrpam** *n.* reptile, snake, serpent.

సరుకు **saruku** *same as* **saraku.**

సరుగుడు **saruguDu** *n.* casuarina tree.

సరువు **saruwu** *n.* lustfulness (*a literary word used of tigers*): **~ ku waccina pulilaagaa** like a tiger lusting for a mate.

సరే **saree** (‹ *sari* + *ee emphatic suffix*) I. *minor sentence, in reply to a demand or request* yes!, all right! II. *particle* **1 ~** *is used in construction with an* **e-** *question word + vb. in the concessive form to give an indefinite meaning*: **aayana iNTiki ewaru waccinaa ~ oka paaTa winipistaaDu** whoever comes to his house, he will sing him a song; **eppuDaynaa ~** whenever it may be, at any time; **eemaynaa ~** whatever may happen, come what may, in any case. **2 ~** *following a verb in the concessive form in contrasting clauses gives the meaning* whether or not; **aayana waccinaa ~ raaka pooyinaa ~ naaku okaTee** whether he comes or not it is all the same to me.

సరేసరి **sareesari** *particle* **1** and also, in addition, besides, likewise. **2** without mentioning, not to mention, let alone, apart from.

సరైన **sarayna** *same as* **sariyayna.**

సరోజం **saroojam** *n. class.* lotus.

సరోవరం **saroowaram** *n.* pond, pool.

సర్కాయించు **sarkaayincu** *v.i. dial.* to adjust o.s., make room (e.g., for other passengers).

సర్కారు **sarkaaru** *n.* government.

సర్కారు జిల్లాలు **sarkaaru jillaalu** *n.pl.* the Northern Circars districts (i.e the northern and central coastal districts) of Andhra Pradesh.

సర్జం **sarjam** *n. bot.* resin.

సర్దార్ **sardaar** *n.* **1** leader. **2** title used before the name of a Sikh.

సర్దిచెప్పు **sardiceppu** *v.i.* to speak soothing words, speak in a calming manner.

సర్దిపుచ్చుకొను **sardipuccukonu** *v.i.* to be content with, satisfy o.s. with.

సర్దు, సద్దు **sardu, saddu** *v.t.* **1** to arrange, adjust, set right, tidy. **2** to pack (luggage), tuck in (blanket). **3** to arrange for, provide: **naaku Dabbu sardEEDu** he provided (*or* he obliged) me with money. **4** to distribute evenly or proportionately.

సర్దుకొను **sardukonu** I. *v.i.* **1** to adjust o.s., make room, fit o.s. in. **2** to manage, cope; **pani entunnaa sardukoogalaDu** no matter how heavy the work is, he can cope with it. **3** to manage with, make do with. **4** to put up with; **waaNNi enni tiTTinaa sardukupootaaDu, eemii maaTLaaDaDu** however much he is abused, he puts up with it without saying a word. **5** to settle down, be calmed, be soothed, be pacified. **6** (of laughter) to subside, die down. **7** (of illness) to be cured. II. *v.t.* **1** to arrange, adjust; **wyawahaaraalu ~** to tidy up o.'s affairs. **2** to settle (disputes). **3** to compose (o.'s mind), overcome (confusion). **4** *slang* to steal, make away with.

సర్దుబాటు **sardubaaTu** *n.* **1** arranging, adjustment. **2** soothing, calming, pacifying. **3 Dabbu ~** accommodating (s.o.) with money.

సర్దుమణుగు **sardumaNugu** *v.i.* to calm down, be quiet, subside.

సర్పం **sarpam** *n.* snake, serpent.

సర్పంచ్ **sarpanc** *n.* chairman or president of a panchayat.

సర్పదష్టుడు **sarpadaSTuDu** *n.* person bitten by a snake; **baadhaa ~** one who is bitten by the snake of affliction.

సర్రున **sarruna** *adv.* quickly, suddenly.

సర్వ **sarwa** *Sanskrit adjvl. prefix meaning* all, total[ly], very; **~ śwaamyaalu** all rights; **~ naaśanam** total destruction; **~ samartha** entirely capable; **~ saadhaaraNa** very common.

సర్వం **sarwam** *r* all, everything, the whole.

సర్వంకషమైన **sarwankaSamayna** *adj.* all-embracing, all-pervading.

సర్వంసహ **sarwamsaha** *n. class.* the earth.

సర్వకాలీన **sarwakaaliina** *adj.* pertaining to every age, timeless.

సర్వజనీన, సార్వజనీన, సార్వజనిక **sarwajaniina, saarwajaniina, saarwajanika** *adj.* pertaining to all humanity, universal.

సర్వజనులు **sarwajanulu** *n. pl.* all the people, the whole population.

సర్వజిత్తు **sarwajittu** *n.* twenty-first year of the Hindu cycle of sixty years.

సర్వజ్ఞత **sarwajñata** *n.* omniscience.

సర్వజ్ఞుడు **sarwajñuDu** *n.* omniscient person.

సర్వతంత్ర స్వతంత్ర **sarwatantraswatantra** *n.* complete freedom.

సర్వతోముఖ **sarwatoomukha** *adj.* **1** all-round, multifarious, many faceted. **2** universal, all-embracing.

సర్వతోముఖంగా **sarwatoomukhangaa** *adv.* comprehensively, on all fronts.

సర్వత్రా, సర్వేసర్వత్రా **sarwatraa, sarweesarwatraa** *adv.* everywhere.

సర్వథా **sarwathaa** *adv.* in every way, by every means.

సర్వదా **sarwadaa** *adv.* always.

సర్వధారి **sarwadhaari** *n.* twenty-second year of the Hindu cycle of sixty years.

సర్వనామం **sarwanaamam** *n. gram.* pronoun.

సర్వపక్షసమావేశం **sarwapakSa samaaweeśam** *n.* all party conference.

సర్వభక్షక **sarwabhakSaka** *adj.* omnivorous.

సర్వభక్షకుడు **sarwabhakSakuDu** *n.* **1** *colloq.* person whose diet is unrestricted. **2** *class.* epithet of fire.

సర్వవ్యాపక **sarwawyaapaka** *adj.* all-pervading.

సర్వశక్తిగల, సర్వశక్తిమంత **sarwaśaktigala, sarwaśaktimanta** *adj.* all-powerful, almighty, omnipotent.

సర్వశక్తులూ **sarwaśaktuluu** *n.pl.* all (o.'s) powers.

సర్వసంగపరిత్యాగం **sarwasangaparityaagam** *n.* total renunciation.

సర్వసంపన్న **sarwasampanna** *adj.* fully equipped, equipped in every aspect.

సర్వసత్తాక **sarwasattaaka** *adj.* sovereign, independent.

సర్వసభ్య సమావేశం **sarwasabhya samaaweeśam** *n.* general body meeting.

సర్వసమన్వయం **sarwasamanwayam** *n.* generalisation.

సర్వసాధారణ **sarwasaadhaaraNa** *adj.* very common.

సర్వసాధారణంగా **sarwasaadhaaraNangaa** *adv.* normally, usually, generally.

సర్వసామాన్య **sarwasaamanya** *adj.* common to all, universal.

సర్వసామాన్యంగా **sarwasaamaanyangaa** *adv.* generally, universally.

సర్వసిద్ధ **sarwasiddha** *adj.* ready in all respects.

సర్వసేనాని, సర్వసేనాధిపతి **sarwaseenaani, sarwaseenaadhipati** *n.* commander in chief.

సర్వస్వం **sarwaswam** *n.* a person's entire property, the whole of a person's possessions; **wijñaana~** encyclopedia.

సర్వాంగ సుందర **sarwaangasundara** *adj.* perfect in all respects (*lit.* every limb being beautiful).

సర్వాంగీకారంగా **sarwaangiikaarangaa** *adv.* in a manner acceptable to all.

సర్వాంగీన **sarwaangiina** *adj. class.* thorough, complete, entire (*lit.* pertaining to all limbs).

సర్వాంతర్యామి **sarwaantaryaami** *n.* the Supreme Spirit, God.

సర్వాత్మకత్వం **sarwaatmakatwam** *n.* omnipresence.

సర్వాత్మనా **sarwaatmanaa** *adv.* with all o.'s power, by all possible means.

సర్వాధికార **sarwaadhikaara** *adj.* supreme.

సర్వాధికారం **sarwaadhikaaram** *n.* supreme power, supremacy.

సర్వాధికారి **sarwaadhikaari** *n.* supreme ruler.

సర్వి **sarwi** *same as* **sariwi.**

సర్వీ **sarwii** *n.* casuarina tree.

సర్వులూ **sarwuluu** *n.pl.* everyone, all people.

సర్వే[క్షణ] **sarwee[kSaNa]** *n.* survey.

సర్వే రాయి **sarwee raayi** *n.* survey stone, governmental boundary stone.

సర్వేసర్వత్రా **sarweesarwatraa** *same as* **sarwatraa.**

సర్వోత్తమ **sarwoottama** *adj.* best of all, optimum.

సర్వోన్నత **sarwoonnata** *adj.* highest of all, supreme.

సర్వోన్నతం **sarwoonnatam** *n.* supremacy.

సలక **salaka** *n.* small sack of two and a half tooms capacity.

సలక్షణ **salakSaNa** *adj.* of good quality, up to the mark.

సలక్షణం **salakSaNam** *n.* good or desirable quality or characteristic.

సలక్షణంగా **salakSaNangaa** *adv.* in a proper manner, correctly, in the right way.

సలపరం **salaparam** *n.* feeling of slight feverishness.

సలపరించు **salaparincu** *impersonal vb. with dative* **biDDaki salaparincindi** the child was slightly feverish.

సలపరింత **salaparinta** *n.* moaning due to pain from fever or other cause.

సలపు **salapu** *same as* **salupu**[1].

సలలిత **salalita** *adj. class.* beautiful, lovely.

సలసలా **salasalaa** *onom. adv. suggesting* (i) boiling violently; **niiLLu~kaagutunnaayi** the water is boiling; (ii) feverish bodily heat; **oLLu~ kaalutunnadi** his body is very hot with fever *or* he has a high temperature.

సలహా **salahaa** *n.* advice, counsel; **~sangham** advisory body.

సలహా చెప్పు, సలహా ఇచ్చు **salahaa ceppu, salahaa iccu** *v.i.* to give advice.

సలాం **salaam** *n.* salutation meaning peace, used chiefly by Muslims.

సలాం కొట్టు **salaam koTTu** *v.i.* to salute.

సలాక **salaaka** *n. dial.* iron bar or rod.

సలిలం **salilam** *n. class.* water.

సలీసు **saliisu** *adj. dial.* easy, light.

సలుగుడు **saluguDu** *n.* sledge, vehicle without wheels.

సలుపు, సలపు **salupu**[1], **salapu** I. *n.* shooting pain, pang, throb, ache. II. *v.i.* to throb, ache.

సలుపు **salupu**[2] *v.t.* 1 *class., also mod. in high-flown literary style* to do, make, perform, practise, carry on (an activity). 2 *mod. in* **uupiri** ~ ; *see* **uupiri.**

సలువు **saluwu** *n.* light ploughing.

సల్లాపం **sallaapam** *n.* conversation, friendly talk; **sarasa** ~ (i) agreeable conversation; (ii) flirting.

సళ్లు **saLLu**[1] *substandard form of* **caLLu** breasts.

సళ్లు **saLLu**[2] I. *n.* looseness, slackness. II. *adj.* loose; ~ **neela** loose soil. III. *v.i., colloq. form of* **saDalu.**

సవటు **sawaTa** *substandard form of* **cawaTa.**

సవతి, సవితి **sawati, sawiti** *n.* co-wife.

సవతి తల్లి, సవితి తల్లి **sawatitalli, sawititalli** *n.* stepmother.

సవర **sawara** *n.* name of a hill tribe in Andhra Pradesh.

సవరం **sawaram** *n.* false hair or wig worn by a woman.

సవరణ **sawaraNa** *n.* correction, amendment.

సవరణ చేయు **sawaraNa ceeyu** *v.t.* to amend, correct.

సవరించు **sawarincu** *v.t.* 1 to arrange, adjust. 2 to correct, rectify. 3 to revise, update. 4 to tidy; **baTTalu ~ konu** to tidy o.'s clothes. 5 **gontuka ~ konu** to clear o.'s throat. 6 to tune, modulate (musical instrument). 7 *slang* **jeebulu** ~ to pick pockets.

సవరింత **sawarinta** *n.* 1 arranging, adjusting. 2 correcting, rectifying. 3 revising.

సవరుడు[చెట్టు] **sawaruDu[ceTTu]** *n.* casuarina tree.

సవర్ణం **sawarNam** *n. ling.* allophone.

సవాలక్ష **sawaa lakSa** *n. and adj. lit.* one and a quarter lakhs, *hence colloq.* innumerable; **ceeyaDaaniki ~ panluNTaayi** there are a thousand and one jobs to be done.

సవాయి[రోగం], సవామేహం **sawaayi[roogam], sawaameeham** *n.* syphilis, venereal disease.

సవారీ, స్వారీ **sawaarii, swaarii** *n.* riding (in a cart or carriage or on an animal); **eDLabaNDi** ~ travelling in a bullock cart; **gurrapu** ~ riding on horseback.

సవారీచేయు, స్వారీచేయు **sawaariiceeyu, swaariiceeyu** *v.i.* to ride (in a cart or carriage or on an animal).

సవాలు **sawaalu** *n.* 1 challenge. 2 question, query. 3 *pl. legal* **sawaaLLu** cross-questions.

సవితి[తల్లి] **sawiti[talli]** *same as* **sawati[talli].**

సవిత్రి **sawitri** *n. class.* 1 mother. 2 cow.

సవినయంగా **sawinayangaa** *adv.* humbly, modestly.

సవిమర్శ[క]ంగా **sawimarśa[ka]ngaa** *adv.* critically.

సవిస్తరంగా, సవిస్తారంగా **sawistarangaa, sawistaarangaa** *adv.* in detail, in full, at length.

సవ్య **sawya** *adj.* 1 proper, correct. 2 left *or* right *according to the context*, e.g., **jandem sawyangaa weesukonnaaDu** he wore the sacred thread over the correct (i.e., left) shoulder; ~ **hastamtoo tiNTaaDu** he eats with his right hand.

సవ్యంగా **sawyangaa** *adv.* 1 correctly, in the proper manner. 2 clockwise.

సవ్యసాచి **sawyasaaci** *n.* 1 *class.* epithet of Arjuna. 2 ambidextrous person. 3 versatile person.

సవ్వడి **sawwaDi** *n.* noise, sound.

సశాస్త్రీయంగా **saśaastriiyangaa** *adv.* scientifically, by scientific means.

ససవ **sasawa** *dial. variant of* **cawaTa.**

ససి **sasi**[1] *adj.* 1 palatable; **waNTa ~ gaa leedu** the cooking is not palatable; **aayana maaTalu naaku ~ gaa leewu** his words are not palatable to me. 2 healthy; **aame oLLu ~ gaa leedu** (*or* **aame oLLu sarigaa leedu**) she is not keeping well.

ససి **sasi**[2] *n.* 1 young plants or seedlings of paddy, chillies, etc. 2 fully grown crop.

ససేమిరా, ససేమీ **saseemiraa, saseemii** *adv.* by no means, on no account; **anduku aawiDa saseemiraa oppukoodu** on no account will she agree to that.

సస్యం **sasyam** *n.* crop, produce, grain.

సస్యభ్రమణం **sasyabhramaNam** *n.* rotation of crops.

సస్యశ్యామల **sasyaśyaamala** *adj.* evergreen.

సస్య శ్యామలం **sasyaśyaamalam** *n. fig.* carpet of greenery.

సహ **saha** *Sanskrit prefix meaning* joint, fellow, co-; ~ **sabhyuDu** co-member; ~ **widyaarthi** fellow student.

సహం **saham** *same as* **sagam.**

సహకరించు **sahakarincu** *v.i.* to cooperate.

సహకార **sahakaara** *adj.* cooperative; ~ **sangham** cooperative society.

సహకారం **sahakaaram** *n.* cooperation.

సహకారి **sahakaari** *n.* helper, assistant.

సహగమనం **sahagamanam** *n.* suttee.

సహగామి **sahagaami** *n. and adj.* concomitant.

సహచరుడు **sahacaruDu** *n.* 1 comrade, companion. 2 colleague, associate.

సహచర్యం, సాహచర్యం **sahacaryam, saahacaryam** *n.* companionship, living together, association.

సహచారి **sahacaari** *n.* associate.

సహ[ధర్మ]చారిణి **saha[dharma]caariNi** *n.* wife.

సహజ **sahaja** *adj.* 1 innate, natural; ~ **kawi** poet by nature, born poet; ~ **deeśabhakti** patriot by nature, true patriot; ~ **wanarulu** natural resources. 2 ordinary, customary, normal, usual.

సహజంగా **sahajangaa** *adv.* naturally, normally, in the ordinary course.

సహజజ్ఞానం, సహజబుద్ధి, సహజాతం **sahajajñaanam, sahajabuddhi, sahajaatam** *n.* instinct.

సహజత్వం **sahajatwam** *n.* naturalness, true nature.

సహజశక్తి **sahajaśakti** *n.* intrinsic energy.

సహజసామర్థ్యం **sahajasaamarthyam** *n.* aptitude.

సహజాత **sahajaata** *adj. ling.* cognate.

సహజార్థం **sahajaartham** *n.* connotation.

సహజీవనం **sahajiiwanam** *n.* 1 living side by side, coexistence. 2 *biol.* symbiosis.

సహధర్మచారిణి **sahadharmacaariNi** *same as* **sahacaariNi.**

సహనం **sahanam** *n.* patience, endurance, forbearance, tolerance, toleration.

సహపంక్తి భోజనం **sahapankti bhoojanam** *n.* 1 *lit.* meal eaten by persons sitting in one line. 2 meal eaten by persons sitting together without consideration of community, creed or status.

సహపాఠి **sahapaaThi** *n.* fellow student.

సహవాసం, సావాసం **sahawaasam, saawaasam** *n.* 1 living together. 2 fellowship, association, friendship; **neenu nii saawaasam uNDanu** I will not be friends with you.

సహసంబంధం **sahasambandham** *n.* 1 collocation. 2 correlation.

సహస్రం **sahasram** *n.* thousand.

సహస్రపాది **sahasrapaadi** *n.* millipede.

సహస్రాబ్దం **sahasraabdam** *n.* period of a thousand years, millenium.

సహా **sahaa** *adv.* 1 even, also. 2 including; **naatoo ~ mugguru waccEEru** three persons came including myself.

సహాక్ష **sahaakSa** *adj. phys.* coaxial.

సహాధ్యాయి, సహాధ్యాయుడు **sahaadhyaayi, sahaadhyaayuDu** *n.* 1 associate, comrade, companion. 2 classmate.

సహాయ **sahaaya** *adj.* assistant; **~ kaaryadarśi** assistant secretary.

సహాయం, సాయం **sahaayam, saayam** *n.* help, aid, assistance; **diiniki saayam** over and above this, in addition to this.

సహాయంగా, సాయంగా **sahaayangaa, saayangaa** *adv.* as an aid.

సహాయక **sahaayaka** *adj.* 1 assistant. 2 auxiliary. 3 subsidiary.

సహాయకారి **sahaayakaari** *adj.* helpful, conducive.

సహాయకుడు, సహాయుడు **sahaayakuDu, sahaayuDu** *n.* helper, assistant.

సహాయత, సహాయత్వం **sahaayata, sahaayatwam** *n.* help, assistance, helpfulness.

సహాయనిరాకరణ **sahaayaniraakaraNa** *n. polit.* non-cooperation.

సహాయపడు, సాయపడు **sahaayapaDu, saayapaDu** *v.i.* to be helpful, be of help.

సహాయభూత **sahaayabhuuta** *adj.* helpful.

సహాయార్థం **sahaayaartham** *adv.* in aid of; **waradabaadhitula ~ Dabbu iccEEm** we gave money in aid of the flood victims.

సహించు **sahincu** *v.t.* 1 to bear, suffer, tolerate, endure. 2 *same as* **sayincu.**

సహిత **sahita** *adjvl. suffix meaning* with, containing; **kriyaa ~ waakyam** sentence containing a verb.

సహితం, సయితం, సైతం **sahitam, sayitam, saytam** *adv.* along with, even, also, too.

సహిష్ణుత **sahiSNuta** *n.* patience, endurance, tolerance.

సహిష్ణువు **sahiSNuwu** *n.* patient, enduring, resigned person.

సహృదయం **sahṛdayam** *n.* good nature, good temper, amiability.

సహృదయంగా **sahṛdayangaa** *adv.* good-naturedly.

సహృదయత **sahṛdayata** *n.* 1 good nature, good will. 2 generosity, big heartedness.

సహృదయుడు **sahṛdayuDu** *n.* 1 good-natured or understanding or sympathetic person. 2 person of good taste.

సహేతుక **saheetuka** *adj.* reasonable, sensible.

సహేతుకత **saheetukata** *n.* reasonableness.

సహోదరి **sahoodari** *n.* uterine sister.

సహోదరుడు **sahoodaruDu** *n.* uterine brother.

సహ్య **sahya** *adj.* bearable, tolerable.

సా - saa

సాంకర్యం **saankaryam** *n.* hybridisation, intermixing.

సాంకేతిక **saankeetika** *adj.* technical.

సాంకేతికం **saankeetikam** *n. sci.* formula.

సాంకేతికత **sankeetikata** *n.* technicality.

సాంకేతికజ్ఞుడు **saankeetikajñuDu** *n.* technician.

సాంకేతికశాస్త్రం **saankeetikaśaastram** *n.* (science of) technology.

సాంక్రామిక **saankraamika** *adj.* contagious, infectious.

సాంఖ్య **saankhya** *adj.* statistical; **~ seekaraNa** collection of statistics.

సాంఖ్యక **saankhyaka** *adj.* numerical, statistical.

సాంఖ్యకశాస్త్రం **saankhyaka śaastram** *n.* (science of) statistics.

సాంఖ్యకశాస్త్రజ్ఞుడు **saankhyaka śaastrajñuDu** *n.* statistician.

సాంఖ్యకాలు **saankhyakaalu** *n.pl.* statistics.

సాంగంగా **saangangaa** *adv. class.* completely.

సాంగత్యం **saangatyam** *n.* **1** association, company. **2** intercourse.

సాంగోపాంగం **saangoopaangam** *adj.* entire, complete from beginning to end.

సాంగోపాంగంగా **saangoopaangangaa** *adv.* completely, through and through, from beginning to end; **weedam ~ abhyasincEEDu** he has studied the whole of the Vedas, including the subsidiary portions.

సాంఘిక **saanghika** *adj.* social; **~ wyawastha** social order.

సాంతం[గా] **saantam[gaa]** *adv.* to the very end, right through, completely, in full; **uttaram ~ cadiwEEDu** he read the letter right through.

సాంతం అవు **saantam awu** *v.i.* to be finished.

సాంతం చేయు **saantam ceeyu** *v.t.* **1** to finish [off]. **2** *colloq.* to kill.

సాంత్వన[ం] **saantwana[m]** *n.* **1** appeasing, comforting, soothing. **2** solace, consolation.

సాంద్ర **saandra** *adj.* **1** thick, dense. **2** compact. **3** intensive.

సాంద్రత **saandrata** *n.* **1** density. **2** compactness. **3** intensiveness, intensity.

సాంద్రీకరణం **saandriikaraNam** *n. chem.* concentration.

సాంద్రీకృత **saandriikrta** *adj. chem.* concentrated.

సాంప్రదాయం, సాంప్రదాయక, సాంప్రదాయకుడు **saampradaayam, saampradaayaka, saampradaayakuDu** *same as* **sampradaayam, sampradaayaka, sampradaayakuDu.**

సాంబ[లు] **saamba[lu]** *n.* suffix added to names of certain kinds of fine rice.

సాంబారు **saambaaru** *n.* lentil soup.

సాంబ్రాణి **saambraaNi** *n.* benzoin; **~ watti, ~ kaDDi, ~ pulla** incense stick.

సాంవత్సరిక **saamwatsarika** *adj.* annual.

సాంవత్సరికం, సంవత్సరీకం **saamwatsarikam, samwatsariikam** *n.* annual death ceremony.

సాంసారిక **saamsaarika** *adj.* conjugal, domestic, pertaining to a family; **~ jiiwitam** family life.

సాంసారికంగా **saamsaarikangaa** *adv.* domestically.

సాంస్కృతిక **saamskrtika** *adj.* cultural.

సాకల్యం **saakalyam** *n.* **1** the whole, entirety. **2** completeness.

సాకల్యంగా **saakalyangaa** *adv.* completely, comprehensively, fully, in detail.

సాకీను **saakiinu** *n.* inhabitant, resident.

సాకు **saaku**[1] *n.* excuse, pretext, plea.

సాకు **saaku**[2] *v.t.* **1** to bring up, rear, foster, nourish, nurture, support. **2** to tend, look after. **3** (*also* **~ konu**) to adopt (a child).

సాకుడు **saakuDu** *n.* rearing, bringing up.

సాకూతంగా **saakuutangaa** *adv. class.* (of a gesture or glance) meaningfully.

సాక్షాత్కరించు **saakSaatkarincu** *v.i.* to become manifest, appear in visible form.

సాక్షాత్కారం, సాక్షాత్కృతి **saakSaatkaaram, saakSaatkrti** *n.* manifestation.

సాక్షాత్తు, సాక్షాత్తూ **saakSaattu[u]** I. *adj.* **1** real, actual, very; **~ waaDee** that very person; **~ subbaaraawu waccEEDu** Subba Rao came himself *or* Subba Rao came in person; **~ lakSmii deewilaa kaLakaLalaaDee sudhanu cuuci murisi pooyEEnu** when I saw Sudha shining like the goddess Lakshmi herself I was filled with joy. **2** the very same; **meem ~ oka taNDri biDDalam** we are children of the very same father. II. *adv.* **1** really, actually; **waaDu ~ naa meenalluDu** he is actually my nephew *or* he is my very own nephew. **2** just, exactly; **~ kawulu warNincinaTLu kaluwa reekulawaNTi neetraalu** eyes like lotus petals, just as poets describe them.

సాక్షి **saakSi** *n.* witness.

సాక్షేపంగా **saakSeepangaa** *adv.* reproachfully, scornfully.

సాక్ష్యం **saakSyam** *n.* evidence, testimony.

సాక్ష్యాధారాలు **saakSyaadhaaraalu** *n.pl.* sources of evidence.

సాగదీయు **saagadiiyu** *v.t.* 1 to extend, stretch [out], draw out, lengthen, prolong, elongate. 2 *colloq.* to soothe, calm, mollify.

సాగనంపు **saaganampu** *v.t.* to send (s.o.) away, see (s.o.) off, start (s.o.) on a journey; **atanni gummamwaraku saaganampindi** she escorted him as far as the doorway.

సాగనార **saaganaara** *n., colloq.* form of **caaganaara**, a kind of aloe, *sansviera roxburghiana*, whose leaf is proverbially tough and hard to break off; ~ **maTTalaagaa saagutunnaaDu** he is as tough and unyielding as an aloe leaf.

సాగరం **saagaram** *n.* 1 sea, ocean. 2 large lake or reservoir.

సాగరగర్భం **saagaragarbham** *n.* seabed.

సాగరశాస్త్రం **saagaraśaastram** *n.* (science of) oceanography.

సాగించు **saagincu** *v.t.* to conduct, pursue, carry on, proceed with, cause to continue; **wyaapaaram saagistunnaaDu** he is carrying on business; **samsaaram saagistunnaaDu** he is managing to support his family.

సాగిపోవు **saagipoowu** *v.i.* to start off, depart; **kaalam saagipootunnadi** time is passing.

సాగిలబడు, జాగిలపడు **saagilabaDu, jaagilapaDu** *v.i.* 1 to prostrate o.s. 2 to bow down.

సాగివచ్చు **saagiwaccu** *v.i.* (of a crowd, army) to advance.

సాగు, సాగుబడి, సాగుదల **saagu**[1], **saagubaDi, saagudala** *n.* cultivation, tillage.

సాగు **saagu**[2] *v.i.* 1 to continue, last, go on, be carried on. 2 to be prolonged, be extended. 3 (of a crowd, army) to advance. 4 to proceed; **ilaa ceppa saagEEDu** he proceeded to say as follows. 5 to have effect, prevail, be successful; **nii nakka jittulu naa daggira saagawu** your jackal's tricks will not succeed with me; **waaDi maaTa iNTLoo saagadu** his word does not prevail at home *or* he does not get his way at home; **maaTa ~tunnawaLLu** (*or simply* ~ **tunnawaaLLu**) **ennaynaa aNTaaru** people whose word prevails (*or* people with influence) will say anything they like. 6 *colloq.* to be obstinate.

సాగు అవు **saagu awu** *v.i.* to be cultivated.

సాగు చేయు **saagu ceeyu** *v.t.* to cultivate.

సాజాత్యం **saajaatyam** *n.* 1 likeness, similarity. 2 homogeneity.

సాటి **saaTi** I. *n.* equal; **daanikadee**~ unequalled, matchless, II. *adj.* equal, similar; ~**waaLLu** o.'s equals, o.'s fellows, o.'s companions; ~**pillawaaLLatoo aaDaDu** he does not play with children of his own age.

సాటిగా **saaTigaa** *adv.* equal to, on a par with.

సాటిలేని **saaTileeni** *adj.* unequalled, incomparable, matchless.

సాతాని **saataani** *n.* a class of Vaishnavites.

సాతాళించు **saataaLincu** *same as* **taaLincu** *sense 2.*

సాత్విక **saatwika** *adj.* mild, gentle, kindly, amiable.

సాత్వికం **saatwikam** *n.* amiability, goodness, gentleness.

సాత్త్వికుడు **saatwikuDu** *n.* good-natured or amiable person.

సాదం **saadam** *n.* cooked rice, food in general (term used by Vaishnavites).

సాదర **saadara** *adj.* 1 respectful. 2 kind.

సాదరంగా **saadarangaa** *adv.* 1 respectfully. 2 kindly, cordially.

సాదరు ఖర్చులు **saadarukharculu** *n.pl.* petty expenses, incidental expenses.

సాదా **saadaa** *adj.* plain, ordinary; ~ **doośa** plain dosa (not spiced).

సాదు, సాధు **saadu, saadhu** *adj.* tame, mild, gentle, good.

సాదృశ్య **saadṛśya** *adj.* analogous.

సాదృశ్యం **saadṛśyam** *n.* 1 similarity, resemblance. 2 example, instance. 3 analogy.

సాధక **saadhaka** *second part of an adjvl. compound meaning* effecting, effective; **bahuLaartha**~ multipurpose.

సాధకం **saadhakam** *n.* 1 practice. 2 instrument, means.

సాధకం చేయు **saadhakam ceeyu** *v.i. and t.* to practise (e.g., on a musical instrument).

సాధకబాధకాలు **saadhakabaadhakaalu** *n.pl.* problems.

సాధకుడు **saadhakuDu** 1 one who practises. 2 one who achieves.

సాధన **saadhana** *n.* 1 practice. 2 achievement (of an aim).

సాధనం **saadhanam** *n.* 1 way, means, medium. 2 instrument, tool, implement. 3 contrivance, expedient; **eemiTi** ~? what is the way out? *or* what is the solution?

సాధనంగా **saadhanangaa** *adv.* as a means, as an instrument.

సాధనచేయు **saadhanaceeyu** *v.i. and t.* to practise.

సాధనసంపత్తి **saadhanasampatti** *n.* facilities and resources.

సాధనసామగ్రి **saadhanasaamagri** *n.* equipment.

సాధారణ **saadhaaraNa**[1] *n.* forty-fourth year of the Hindu cycle of sixty years.

సాధారణ **saadhaaraNa**[2] *adj.* usual, ordinary, customary, common, normal, general; ~ **ennikalu** general elections; ~ **sankSeemam** general welfare.

సాధారణంగా **saadharaNangaa** *adv.* ordinarily, normally, commonly, generally, in general.

సాధించు **saadhincu** *v.t.* 1 to achieve or attain by perseverance; **cacci**~ to achieve s.g after o.'s death. 2 to accomplish, effect. 3 **artham**~ to convey a sense or meaning. 4 to master, overcome, conquer, defeat. 5 *colloq.* to nag, reproach.

సాధింపు **saadhimpu** *n.* 1 achievement. 2 *colloq.* nagging.

సాధికార, సాధికారిక **saadhikaara, saadhikaarika** *adj.* 1 official. 2 authoritative.

సాధు **saadhu** *same as* **saadu.**

సాధు జంతువు **saadhu jantuwu** *n.* tame animal, domestic animal.

సాధుత్వం **saadhutwam** *n. gram.* correctness.

సాధురేఫ **saadhureepha** *n.* the Telugu letter ర as distinguished from ఱ (**śakaTareepha**).

సాధువు **saadhuwu** I. *n.* holy person, saint, religious mendicant. II. *adj.* **1** gentle, mild. **2** tame, docile. **3** right, correct, proper.

సాధ్యం **saadhyam** I. *n.* s.g that is possible. II. *adj.* possible, attainable, practicable, achievable, feasible.

సాధ్యపడు **saadhyapaDu** *v.i.* to be possible, be feasible.

సాధ్యాసాధ్యాలు **saadhyaasaadhyaalu** *n.pl.* those things that are possible and those that are not.

సాధ్వి **saadhwi** *n. class.* virtuous woman.

సాన **saana** *n.* **1** whetstone. **2** stone on which sandal paste is prepared.

సానందంగా **saanandangaa** *adv.* happily, with pleasure.

సానకత్తి **saanakatti** *n.* kind of sword.

సానతీరు **saanatiiru** *v.t. fig.* to sharpen, polish up (wits).

సానపట్టు, సానపెట్టు **saanapaTTu, saanapeTTu** *v.t.* **1** to cut or polish (precious stone). **2** to sharpen (knife).

సాని **saani** I. *n.* (*also* ~ **di**) prostitute. II. *n. suffix signifying the female sex,* e.g., **mantra**~ midwife.

సానిక, సానికె **saanika, saanike** *n.* earthen dish or plate.

సానుకూల **saanukuula** *adj.* **1** favourable; ~ **waataawaraNam** favourable atmosphere. **2** successful; **pani saanukuulamayndi** the job has been done successfully.

సానుకూలంగా **saanukuulangaa** *adv.* **1** favourably. **2** successfully, to o.'s liking.

సానుకూలత **saanukuulata** *n.* **1** favourability. **2** suitability.

సానుక్రోశం **saanukroośam** *n.* compassion, pity.

సానునయ **saanunaya** *adj.* soothing.

సానుపు, సాన్పు **saan[u]pu** *n.* sweeping the courtyard of a house and sprinkling it with **kaLLaapu.**

సానుపు చేయు, సాన్పు చేయు **saan[u]puceeyu** *v.i.* to sweep the courtyard of a house and sprinkle **kaLLaapu.**

సానుభూతి **saanubhuuti** *n.* sympathy.

సానుభూతిపరుడు **saanubhuutiparuDu** *n.* sympathiser.

సానుమోదం **saanumoodam** *n. legal* accord.

సానువు **saanuwu** *n.* level ground at the top of a mountain, tableland.

సాన్నిధ్యం **saannidhyam** *n.* nearness, vicinity, proximity.

సాన్నిహిత్యం **saannihityam** *n.* **1** closeness, affinity. **2** intimacy.

సాన్పు **saanpu** *same as* **saanupu.**

సాపత్యం **saapatyam** *n.* likeness, similarity.

సాపాడు, సాపాటు **saapaaDu, saapaaTu** *n.* a meal (term used by Vaishnavites).

సాపు **saapu** *colloq. variant of* **saaphu.**

సాపేక్ష **saapeekSa** *adj.* relative; ~ **siddhaantam** theory of relativity.

సాపేక్షత **saapeekSata** *n.* relativity.

సాప్తపదీనం **saaptapadiinam** *n. class.* friendship.

సాఫల్యం **saaphalyam** *n.* **1** success, fruitfulness, efficacy. **2** fulfilment, accomplishment, achievement.

సాఫీగా **saaphiigaa** *adv.* **1** smoothly, evenly, calmly, without obstruction; ~ **naDicipooyee jiiwitam** life which goes on smoothly. **2** plainly, in a straightforward manner; ~ **maaTLaaDu, DonkatiruguDugaa maaTLaaDaku** talk plainly, not in a roundabout fashion.

సాఫు, సాపు **saaphu, saapu** I. *n.* (*also* ~ **prati**) fair copy of s.g written. II. *adj.* **1** smooth, not wrinkled. **2** straight; ~ **gaa niDupugaa unnakarra** a long straight stick. **3** level.

సాఫుచేయు **saaphuceeyu** *v.t.* **1** to smooth (cloth). **2** to clean (room). **3** to level (ground). **4** *colloq.* **nii wiipu saaphuceestaanu** I will thrash you.

సాఫుపట్టు **saaphupaTTu** *v.t.* to make s.g smooth, e.g., to plane wood with a carpenter's plane.

సాభిప్రాయంగా **saabhipraayangaa** *adv.* in token of o.'s agreement, indicating agreement.

సామంతరాజు, సామంతుడు **saamantaraaju, saamantuDu** *n.* feudatory prince.

సామంతరాజ్యం **saamantaraajyam** *n.* subordinate kingdom.

సామగానం **saamagaanam** *n.* recital of the Sama Veda.

సామగ్రి **saamagri** *n.* articles required for carrying out an operation; **aaTa**~ sports equipment, sports materials; **waNTa**~ cooking ingredients and/or utensils.

సామరస్య **saamarasya** *adj.* amicable, friendly.

సామరస్యం **saamarasyam** *n.* **1** amicableness, friendliness. **2** harmony, compatibility. **3 mata**~ religious toleration.

సామరస్యంగా **saamarasyangaa** *adv.* **1** amicably. **2** harmoniously.

సామజం **saamajam** *n. class.* elephant.

సామర్థ్యం **saamarthyam** *n.* skill, ability, capability, competence, efficiency, effectiveness.

సామాజిక **saamaajika** *adj.* social.

సామాజిక భాష **saamaajika bhaaSa** *n. ling.* colloquial language.

సామాజికుడు **saamaajikuDu** *n.* **1** member of a society. **2** member of society (in general); **idi tappu kaawaccu kaanii saamaajikulaloo ii waaDuka undi** it may be wrong, but this usage does exist among members of society.

సామాను **saamaanu** *n.* things, baggage, luggage, goods,

wares, tools, implements: **waNTa ~ lu** any of the things needed for cooking, i.e., ingredients, utensils, fuel.

సామాన్య **saamaanya** *adj.* common, general, normal, ordinary: **~ śaastram** general science; **~ waakyam** *gram.* simple sentence: **lawkika bhaaSa andarikii ~ maynadi** everyday speech is common to all (*or* is shared by all).

సామాన్యంగా **saamaanyangaa** *adv.* 1 usually, ordinarily, generally, normally. 2 plainly, simply.

సామాన్యుడు **saamaanyuDu** *n.* 1 ordinary citizen. 2 layman. 3 *pl.* **saamaanyulu** common people, the masses.

సామి **saami** *colloq. variant form of* **swaami.**

సామీప్యం **saamiipyam** *n.* nearness, proximity.

సాము **saamu** *n.* 1 gymnastics, bodily exercise. 2 fencing, sword play: *see* **neela.**

సాముదాయక **saamudaayaka** *adj.* communal, relating to the whole community.

సాముదాయకంగా **saamudaayakangaa** *adv.* collectively.

సాముద్రికం **saamudrikam** *n.* palmistry.

సాముద్రికం చెప్పు **saamudrikam ceppu** *v.i.* to tell fortunes by palmistry, forecast by palmistry.

సాముద్రికుడు **saamudrikuDu** *n.* palmist.

సామూహిక **saamuuhika** *adj.* common, collective, mass: **~ praarthana** group prayer; **~ hatya** mass murder, massacre.

సామూహికంగా **saamuuhikangaa** *adv.* collectively, *en bloc, en masse.*

సామెత **saameta** *n.* proverb; **eedoo ~ ceppinaTTu** as the proverb says (this phrase may be used casually without reference to any particular proverb).

సామ్యం **saamyam** *n.* 1 equality, parity. 2 likeness, similarity, comparison, affinity. 3 analogy.

సామ్యత **saamyata** *n.* similarity.

సామ్యవాద **saamyawaada** *adj.* socialist.

సామ్యవాదం **saamyawaadam** *n.* socialism.

సామ్యవాది **saamyawaadi** *n.* socialist.

సామ్రాజ్ఞి **saamraajñi** *n.* empress.

సామ్రాజ్య **saamraajya** *adj.* imperial.

సామ్రాజ్యం **saamraajyam** *n.* 1 empire. 2 rule, sway.

సామ్రాజ్యవాదం **saamraajyawaadam** *n.* imperialism

సామ్రాజ్యవాది **saamraajyawaadi** *n.* imperialist.

సామ్రాట్టు **saamraaTTu** *same as* **samraaTTu.**

సాయం **saayam**[1] *n.* evening; *mod. always in adjvl. position,* e.g., **~ kaalam** evening[time]; **~ kaLaaśaala** evening college.

సాయం **saayam**[2] *same as* **sahaayam.**

సాయంగా **saayangaa** *same as* **sahaayangaa.**

సాయంత్రం **saayantram** *n.* evening.

సాయంవేళ, సాయంసమయం **saayamweeLa, saayamsamayam** *n.* evening[time].

సాయంసంధ్య **saayamsandhya** *n.* 1 evening twilight. 2 evening prayer.

సాయపడు **saayapaDu** *same as* **sahaayapaDu.**

సాయశక్తులా **saayaśaktulaa** *same as* **śaayaśaktulaa.**

సాయిమేకు **saayimeeku** *n.* linch pin.

సాయిలాఫాయిలాగా **saayilaaphaayilaagaa** *adv.* amicably, on friendly terms.

సాయుజ్యం **saayujyam** *n.* ultimate union with the deity; **śiwa ~** ultimate union with Siva.

సాయుధ **saayudha** *adj.* armed.

సారం **saaram** *n.* 1 essence, extract. 2 sap (of a plant). 3 fertility (of soil). 4 pith, substance; **daanni sampratincaDam praarambhincEEDu kaanii anduloo tanaku aaTTee ~ kanabaLLeedu** he started to consult it (a dictionary) but found no substance in it at all.

సారంగి **saarangi** *n.* fiddle with five strings.

సారథి **saarathi** *n.* charioteer.

సారథ్యం **saarathyam** *n.* leadership, headship (*lit.* the status of a charioteer or one who holds the reins): **saarathyasangham** steering committee.

సారపప్పు **saarapappu** *n.* the fruit of a certain forest tree.

సారళ్యం **saaraLyam** *n.* 1 softness, gentleness. 2 simplicity (of style).

సారవంత **saarawanta** *adj.* fertile.

సారస్యం **saarasyam** *same as* **sarasatwam.**

సారస్యంలేని **saarasyam leeni** *adj.* ill-mannered.

సారస్వత్ **saaraswat** *n.* a sect of brahmans.

సారస్వత **saaraswata** *adj.* literary.

సారస్వతం **saaraswatam** *n.* literature.

సారా[యి], సారాయం **saaraa[yi], saaraayam** *n.* arrack, locally made intoxicating spirit.

సారా[యి]బట్టీ **saaraa[yi]baTTii** *n.* still for distillation.

సారాంశం **saaraamśam** *n.* 1 essence, gist, purport. 2 sum and substance, summary; **~ ceppu** to sum up.

సారి **saari** *n.* time, occasion; **nelakoka ~** once [in] a month; **ii ~** (i) this time, (ii) next time: **ippuDu naa daggira leedu, ii ~** (*or* **waccee ~**) **miiru waccinappuDu istaanu** I have not got it now, the next time that you come, I will give it.

సారించు **saarincu** *v.t.* 1 to extend, stretch, spread. 2 **dṛSTi ~** to cast a glance. 3 *class.* **naari ~** to string a bow.

సారువా **saaruwaa** *n.* the main paddy crop, grown in the southwest monsoon season; cf. **daaLawaa.**

సారూప్యం **saaruupyam** *n.* similarity of form.

సారె **saare**[1] *n.* presents from the bride's parents to the bridegroom's family and neighbours, brought by the bride when she goes to the bridegroom's house for the first time.

సారె **saare**[2] *n.* potter's wheel (= **aare**[1]).

సార్థం **saartham** *n.* *class.* caravan.

సార్థక **saarthaka** *adj.* 1 meaningful, significant, purposeful. 2 (of a word, name, title) fitting, appropriate.

సార్థకంగా **saarthakangaa** *adv.* (referring to use of words) effectively.

సార్థకత, సార్థక్యత **saarthak[y]ata** *n.* 1 meaningfulness, significance. 2 aim, purpose.

సార్థకనామం **saarthaka naamam** *n.* appropriate name.

సార్థకనామధేయుడు **saarthaka naamadheeyuDu** *n.* one who is appropriately named, one who is true to his name.

సార్థక్యం **saarthakyam** *n.* meaningfulness, significance.

సార్ద్ర **saardra** *adj.* wet, damp, moist, humid.

సార్లా **saarlaa** *adv. dial.* thoroughly, properly, completely.

సార్వకాలిక, సార్వకాలీన **saarwakaalika, saarwakaaliina** *adj.* perennial, enduring for all time, pertaining to all time.

సార్వజనిక, సార్వజనీన **saarwajanika, saarwajaniina** *same as* **sarwajaniina.**

సార్వత్రిక **saarwatrika** *adj.* general, universal; **~ ennikalu** general elections, **~ wiśwawidyaalayam** open university.

సార్వభౌమ అధికారం **saarwabhawma adhikaaram** *n.* sovereignty, sovereign power.

సార్వభౌముడు **saarwabhawmuDu** *n.* emperor, universal monarch.

సార్వభౌమ్యం **saarwabhawmyam** *n.* emperorship.

సాల **saala** *see* **śaala.**

సాలం **saalam** *n.* 1 sal tree. 2 wall or fence round a building. 3 *same as* **maddi ceTTu.**

సాలగ్రామం **saalagraamam** *n.* kind of black ammonite stone with circular or spiral markings, an object of worship in Hinduism.

సాలభంజిక **saalabhanjika** *n.* doll, puppet, **aame ~ laa undi** she is as pretty as a doll; **~ lu ceppina kathalu** stories told by Salabhanjikas.

సాలీడు **saaliiDu** *n.* 1 spider. 2 *dial.* weaver.

సాలీనా **saaliinaa** *adv.* annually.

సాలు **saalu** *n.* year.

సాలుకు **saaluku** *adv.* annually, per year.

సాలుసరి **saalusari** *adj.* annual.

సాలె **saale** *n.* weaving.

సాలెగూడు, సాలెపట్టు **saaleguuDu, saalepaTTu** *n.* spider's web, cobweb.

సాలెపురుగు **saalepurugu** *n.* spider.

సాలెబత్తులు **saalebattulu** *n.pl.* name of a sub-community of weavers.

సాలెవాడు **saalewaaDu** *n.* weaver.

సాలోచనగా **saaloocanagaa** *adv.* thoughtfully, pensively; **~ tala pankincEEDu** he nodded his head thoughtfully.

సావకాశం **saawakaaśam** *n.* 1 leisure. 2 ease, comfort.

సావకాశంగా **saawakaaśangaa** *adv.* 1 in a leisurely manner. 2 at ease, comfortably.

సావధానం, సావధానత **saawadhaanam, saawadhaanata** *n.* attention.

సావధానం అవు, సావధానంగా ఉండు **saawadhaanam awu, saawadhaanangaa uNDu** *v.i.* 1 to be attentive. 2 to be careful, be cautious. 3 to be calm, be patient.

సావధానంగా **saawadhaanangaa** *adv.* 1 attentively. 2 carefully. 3 calmly, patiently.

సావధానతీర్మానం **saawadhaana tiirmaanam** *n. polit.* call attention motion.

సావాసం **saawaasam** *colloq. alt. form of* **sahawaasam.**

సావాసి **saawaasi** *n.* friend, companion, associate.

సావిడి **saawiDi** *same as* **caawiDi.**

సావు **saawu** *colloq. alt. form of* **caawu.**

సాష్టాంగం **saaSTaangam** *n.* prostration.

సాష్టాంగపడు **saaSTaangapaDu** *v.i.* to prostrate o.s.

సాసవలు **saasawalu** *n.pl. dial.* mustard seeds.

సాస్న **saasna** *n.* bull's dewlap.

సాహచర్యం **saahacaryam** *same as* **sahacaryam.**

సాహస, సాహసిక **saahasa, saahasika** *adj.* bold, daring, adventurous.

సాహసం **saahasam** *n.* 1 daring, boldness, courage. 2 temerity, rashness, impetuosity. 3 daring act, bold deed.

సాహసకృత్యం **saahasakr̥tyam** *n.* adventure.

సాహసించు **saahasincu** *v.i.* to dare, venture, be bold, pluck up courage.

సాహసుడు, సాహసికుడు **saahasuDu, saahasikuDu** *n.* bold, daring, intrepid or adventurous person, daredevil.

సాహసోపేత **saahasoopeeta** *adj.* bold, daring.

సాహసోపేతంగా **saahasoopeetangaa** *adv.* boldly, daringly.

సాహిణం **saahiNam** *n. class.* horse's stable.

సాహిణి **saahiNi** *n.class.* groom.

సాహితి **saahiti** I. *n.* literature. II. *adj.* literary.

సాహితీపరుడు, సాహిత్యపరుడు **saahitiiparuDu, saahityaparuDu** *n.* 1 writer, author. 2 person interested in literature.

సాహిత్య **saahitya** *adj.* literary.

సాహిత్యం **saahityam** *n.* literature.

సి - si

సింగం **singam** *colloq. alt. form of* **simham.**

సింగడు **singaDu** *n.* gipsy.

సింగారం **singaaram** *colloq. alt. form of* **śrngaaram.**

సింగారించుకొను, సింగారం చేసుకొను **singaarincukonu, singaaram ceesukonu** *v.i. and t.* to adorn o.s. with jewellery and fine clothes, dress up, put on finery.

సింగి **singi** *n.* gipsy woman.

సింగినాదం **singinaadam** *n.* 1 *class.* horn, trumpet made from a stag's horn. 2 *colloq.* nonsense. 3 *colloq.* **eemiTi** ~ ? what does it matter? *or* why make a fuss (over s.g trivial)?

సిందురం, సిందూరం **sinduram, sinduuram** *n.* vermilion.

సింధువు **sindhuwu** *n.* 1 River Indus. 2 *class.* river. 3 *class.* ocean.

సింధుశాఖ **sindhuśaakha** *n.* gulf.

సింహం **simham** *n.* 1 lion. 2 *astrol.* constellation of Leo.

సింహద్వారం **simhadwaaram** *n.* main entrance, front door.

సింహనాదం **simhanaadam** *n.* 1 lion's roar. 2 loud cry or roar.

సింహళం **simhaLam** *n. class.* Sri Lanka.

సింహస్వప్నం **simhaswapnam** *n.* object of terror, s.g terrifying (*lit.* a dream about a lion).

సింహాణం **simhaaNam** *n. class.* 1 rust. 2 mucus of the nose.

సింహావలోకనం **simhaawalookanam** *n.* survey, review.

సింహాసనం **simhaasanam** *n.* throne.

సిక్కు **sikku** *n. and adj.* Sikh; ~ **matam** the Sikh religion.

సిక్త[ం] **sikta[m]** *adj.* wetted, moistened; **rakta** ~ drenched with blood.

సిగ **siga** *n.* 1 lock of hair uncut on top of a man's head. 2 woman's bun of hair.

సిగ్గరి **siggari** *n.* 1 s.o. who is ashamed. 2 shy person.

సిగ్గరితనం **siggaritanam** *n.* 1 shame. 2 shyness.

సిగ్గిలు **siggilu** *v.i. class.* 1 to feel ashamed. 2 to feel shy.

సిగ్గు **siggu** *n.* 1 shame; **naaku ~ weesindi** I felt ashamed. 2 shyness, modesty.

సిగ్గుచేటు **sigguceeTu** I. *n.* shame. II. *adj.* shameful.

సిగ్గుపడు **siggupaDu** *v.i.* 1 to feel ashamed; **ippuDu tama maaTalaku taamee ~tunnaaru** now they are feeling ashamed of their own words. 2 to feel shy.

సిగ్గుమాలిన, సిగ్గులేని **siggumaalina, sigguleeni** *adj.* shameless.

సిగ్గుసిగ్గు! **siggusiggu!** *interj.* what a disgrace! **ceppukoNTee** ~ ! what a disgrace to say it! *or* I feel ashamed to say it.

సిగ్గొయ్య! **siggoyya!** (< **siga kooya!**) *term of abuse, lit.* may (your) hair be cut off! i.e., may (you) be put to shame: **nii** ~ ! *is equivalent to* damn you!

సిటం **siTam** *n. dial.* moment, instant.

సిడె **siDe** *n.* balancing arm of a picota, which swings up and down when water is raised for irrigation.

సిద్ది, సిద్దీ **siddi[i]** *n.* 1 Abyssinian, person of black complexion. 2 ruffian.

సిద్ధం **siddham** I. *adj.* 1 ready, prepared. 2 (of fruit) ripe. II. *as second part of an adjvl. compound* ~ *has the force of* in accordance with; **sahaja** ~ *or* **swabhaawa** ~ in accordance with nature, natural; **sampraadaaya** ~ in accordance with tradition, traditional.

సిద్ధం అవు **siddham awu** *v.i.* to get ready, be ready.

సిద్ధంగా **siddhangaa** *adv.* ready.

సిద్ధం చేయు **siddham ceeyu** *v.t.* to make ready.

సిద్ధపడు **siddhapaDu** *v.i.* 1 to be ready, be prepared. 2 to come forward; **waaDu deenikaynaa ~ taaDu, Dabbu paDeestee caalu** he will come forward to do anything if you offer him money.

సిద్ధపరచు **siddhaparacu** *v.t.* to prepare, make ready.

సిద్ధబీజం **siddhabiijam** *n. bot.* spore.

సిద్ధసంకల్పుడు **siddhasankalpuDu** *n.* one who can work miracles; **miiru siddhasankalpulu, annii mii iSTaprakaaramee jarugutaayi** you are a regular magician, everything happens in the way that you want.

సిద్ధహస్తుడు **siddhahastuDu** *n.* skilled and dexterous and expert person who is also favoured by good fortune.

సిద్ధాంతం **siddhaantam** *n.* 1 doctrine, principle, axiom. 2 theory. 3 theorem.

సిద్ధాంతకర్త **siddhaantakarta** *n.* theoretician.

సిద్ధాంతపరమైన **siddhaantaparamayna** *adj.* theoretical.

సిద్ధాంతరాద్ధాంతాలు **siddhaanta raaddhaantaalu** *same as* **raaddhaanta siddhaantaalu.**

సిద్ధాంతరీత్యా **siddhaantariityaa** *adv.* in theory, theoretically.

సిద్ధాంతి **siddhaanti** *n.* 1 theoretician. 2 astrologer.

సిద్ధాంతీకరించు **siddhaantiikarincu** *v.i. and t.* 1 to propound a theory. 2 to theorise.

సిద్ధాన్నం **siddhaannam** *n.* 1 ready-cooked food. 2 *fig.* s.g ready for use.

సిద్ధార్థి **siddhaarthi** *n.* fifty-third year of the Hindu cycle of sixty years.

సిద్ధి **siddhi** *n.* accomplishment, attainment, achievement, realisation.

సిద్ధించు **siddhincu** I. *v.i.* **1** to be achieved, be accomplished, be effected. **2** to be attained, be fulfilled, be realised. II. *v.t.* to produce, bring about, achieve.

సిద్ధుడు **siddhuDu** *n.* **1** holy person, saintly person. **2** *class.* demigod.

సినిమా **sinimaa** *n.* cinema film, movie.

సిపాయి **sipaayi** *n.* soldier.

సిఫార్సు **siphaarsu** *n.* recommendation.

సిబ్బంది **sibbandi** *n.* **1** staff, personnel. **2** retinue.

సిబ్బి **sibbi** *n.* **1** strainer, cullender. **2** brass lid of a pot.

సిర **sira** *n.* vein.

సిరం **siram** *n.* **1** udder. **2** teat.

సిరస్తదారు **sirastadaaru** *n.* sheristadar, head clerk in a court or Collector's office.

సిరా **siraa** *n.* ink.

సిరి **siri** *n.* **1** wealth, prosperity, good fortune. **2** a name of Lakshmi, goddess of wealth.

సిరిపాదం **siripaadam** *n. class.* the right foot; *occurring mod. in* **sirassununci ~ daakaa** from head to foot.

సిరిబొజ్జ **sribojja** *n.* round belly (regarded as a sign of wealth).

సిరిసంపదలు **sirisampadalu** *n.pl.* wealth, riches.

సిలువ **siluwa** *n.* cross.

సిలువాకార **siluwaakaara** *adj.* cruciform.

సిల్వరు **silwaru** *n.* German silver, nickel silver (an alloy once used for making cups, etc.).

సివంగి **siwangi** *n.* hunting cheetah.

సివారు **siwaaru** *n.* **1** *dial. form of* **śiwaaru. 2** *dial.* village boundary.

సివా[యి] **siwaa[yi]** *adv.* except; **aayanadaggira wanda ruupaayalu ~ inkeemii leedu** he has nothing on him except a hundred rupees.

సివాలు **siwaalu** *n.pl.* lurching and swaying due to drunkenness or anger or being possessed by a goddess; **koopamtoo ~ weestunnaaDu** *or* **koopamtoo ~ tokkutunnaaDu** he is dancing with rage; **taagi ~ weestunnaaDu** *or* **taagi ~ tokkutunnaaDu** he is reeling with drunkenness; *see* **ankamma.**

సిసలు **sisalu** *adj.* **1** pure, unadulterated. **2** real: **sisalayna jiiwitam** real life (not fiction). **3** true, genuine: **atani sisalayna waarasulu** his true heirs.

సిసింద్రీ **sisindrii** *n.* **1** kind of jumping firework. **2** person with a vivacious and effervescent nature.

సీ - sii

సీకాయ **siikaaya** *n. acacia concinna,* a tree whose fruit is used for soap.

సీకు **siiku** *n.* iron bar.

సీటి **siiTi** *n.* whistling; **~ weeyu, ~ koTTu** to whistle.

సీత **siita** *n.* **1** name of Rama's wife. **2** furrow.

సీతభేది **siitabheedi** *n.* dysentery.

సీతాకోకచిలుక **siitaakookaciluka** *n.* butterfly.

సీతాఫలం **siitaaphalam** *n.* custard apple, *annona squamosa.*

సీతు **siitu** *n.* **1** cold, cold season, winter. **2** *dial.* quarrel, misunderstanding.

సీత్కారం **siitkaaram** *n.* hissing sound made when drawing in o.'s breath.

సీదా[గా] **siidaa[gaa]** *adv.* **1** straight, directly. **2** honestly.

సీదాసాదా **siidaasaadaa** *adj.* plain and honest, straightforward.

సీపిచేప **siipiceepa** *n.* shellfish.

సీమ **siima** I. *n.* **1** country, area; **telugu ~** the Telugu country; **graama ~** rural area. **2** foreign country, Europe, Britain. **3** region; **puurwam kaasula daNDalu gaLa ~ loo alankarincukoneewaaLLu** in former times they used to adorn themselves with necklaces of gold coins about the region of the neck; *see* **kaTi. 4** limit, boundary. II. *adj.* **1** foreign, European, British. **2** hybrid, crossbred.

సీమంతం **siimantam** *same as* **śriimantam.**

సీమంతిని **siimantini** *n.* young married woman.

సీమచింత **siimacinta** *n.* Manila tamarind, *pithecolobium dulce,* a tree with fruit containing edible seeds.

సీమజమ్మి **siimajammi** *n.* a thorny hedge plant, *prosopis juliflora.*

సీమటపాకాయ **siimaTapaakaaya** *n.* explosive firework.

సీమమిరప **siimamirapa** *n.* kind of capsicum, very hot to taste; **~ kaaya laaNTi maniSi** hot tempered person.

సీమసున్నం **siimasunnam** *n.* chalk.

సీల **siila** *n.* **1** plug, stopper. **2** screw; **~ jaari kaalipaTTaa paDipooyindi** the screw came loose and the anklet fell off.

సీలమండ **siilamaNDa** *n.* ankle.

సీసం **siisam**[1] *n.* lead (metal).

సీసం, సీసపద్యం **siisam**[2], **siisapadyam** *n.* a metre used in poetry.

సీసా **siisaa** *n.* bottle.

సు - su

సు **su** *Sanskrit prefix* (i) *signifying* good, well; **suguNam** good quality; **sudinam** lucky day; (ii) *lending intensive force* (*often amounting to only slight emphasis*) *to an adj.*, e.g., **sudiirgha** long.

సుంకం **sunkam** *n.* toll, tax, fee, customs duty, excise duty; **daari** ~ toll levied on road vehicles.

సుంకరి **sunkari** *n.* toll collector.

సుంకు **sunku** *n.* **1** blossom of corn and pulses. **2** flowery part of an ear of millet.

సుంత **sunta** *det. adj.* little, small, slight, trifling.

సుంతి **sunti** *same as* **sunnati.**

సుంతైనా **suntaynaa** *adv.*, *always in neg. constr.* in the least, at all; ~ **naaku iSTam leedu** I do not like it in the least.

సుందర **sundara** *adj.* beautiful, handsome.

సుందరం **sundaram** *n.* beauty, handsomeness.

సుందరాంగి, సుందరి **sundaraangi, sundari** *n.* beautiful woman.

సుందరుడు **sundaruDu** *n.* handsome man.

సుకరం **sukaram** *adj.* **1** easy, practicable. **2** convenient, manageable.

సుకుమార **sukumaara** *adj.* tender, delicate, gentle.

సుకుమారం **sukumaaram** *n.* delicacy, tenderness.

సుకుమారి **sukumaari** *n.* person who has been delicately reared.

సుకృతం **sukṛtam** *n.* good deeds, meritorious actions; **puurwajanma** ~ **walla caduwu abbindi waaDiki** he has been blessed with education as a result of his good deeds in a former life.

సుకృతాత్ముడు **sukṛtaatmuDu** *n.* virtuous person.

సుకృతి **sukṛti** *n.* good deed or act.

సుక్తా అవు **suktaa awu** *v.i.* to be finished; **iiwEELaTiki pani suktaa ayindi** work is over for today.

సుక్షేత్రం **sukSeetram** *n.* fertile land.

సుఖ **sukha** *adj.* **1** happy, joyful. **2** pleasant, sweet, agreeable. **3** easy. **4** comfortable.

సుఖం **sukham** *n.* **1** joy, happiness. **2** wellbeing, contentment, comfort, ease, peacefulness.

సుఖపడు **sukhapaDu** *v.i.* to feel happy and contented.

సుఖపెట్టు **sukhapeTTu** *v.t.* to make (s.o.) happy and contented.

సుఖమయ **sukhamaya** *adj.* joyful, happy, harmonious; ~ **samsaaram** happy and harmonious family life.

సుఖరోగం, సుఖవ్యాధి **sukharoogam, sukhawyaadhi** *n.* venereal disease.

సుఖించు **sukhincu** *v.i.* **1** to be happy. **2** *slang* to have intercourse.

సుఖోపవిష్టులు **sukhoopawiSTulu** *n.pl. class.* persons seated at ease.

సుగంధ **sugandha** *adj.* aromatic, perfumed.

సుగంధం **sugandham** *n.* good or pleasant scent or smell.

సుగంధిపాల **sugandhi paala** *n.* **1** Indian sarsaparilla, *hemidesmus indicus.* **2** *colloq.* flavoured milk shake.

సుగమ **sugama** *adj.* accessible, attainable; ~ **maargam** easy way or method.

సుగమం **sugamam** *n.* access.

సుగుణం **suguNam** *n.* good point, good quality.

సుగ్రాహ్య **sugraahya** *adj.* easily intelligible.

సుచరిత్రుడు **sucaritruDu** *n.* person of good character.

సుజనుడు **sujanuDu** *n.* good or virtuous person.

సుజినీ, సుజనా **sujinii, sujanaa** *n.* cotton rug used either as a hanging or a cover or a carpet, woven in a pattern called peacock's eye.

సుజ్ఞానం **sujñaanam** *n.* sound knowledge.

సుడి **suDi** *n.* **1** eddy, vortex, whirlpool, whirlwind. **2** twist or whirl of hair or other mark, e.g., spot of colour, particularly on bodies of cattle or horses, regarded as an auspicious or inauspicious sign. **3** *colloq.* luck, fortune; **waaDi** ~ **tirigindi** his luck has turned (from good to bad or *vice versa*); **aa ammaayiki** ~ **unnadi** that girl is a lucky person *or* that girl is an unlucky person (depending on circumstances). **4** leading shoot of a sprouting plant.

సుడిగాలి **suDigaali** *n.* whirlwind.

సుడిగుండం **suDiguNDam** *n.* whirlpool.

సుడిపడు **suDipaDu** *v.i. colloq.* to be worn out, be exhausted, be overcome (with an implication of being overcome by a spell cast by others).

సుడిపెట్టు **suDipeTTu** *v.i. colloq.* to cause a hindrance, interfere; **induloo aDDangaa wacci suDipeTTaku** do not get in the way and interfere in this.

సుత **suta**[1] *n. class.* daughter.

సుత **suta**[2] *adv. Telangana dial.* too, also; **neenu** ~ **wasta** I will come too.

సుతరాము, సుతరామూ **sutaraamu[u]** *adv.* **1** utterly, completely, totally. **2** *in neg. constr.* at all; **N. raaka K.-ki** ~ **kiTTaleedu** K. did not at all like N.'s coming.

సుతార **sutaara** *adj.* soft, gentle, meek, mild, delicate.

సుతారి **sutaari** *n.* building worker who attends to plastering.

సుతిమెత్తని **sutimettani** *adj.* mild, meek, gentle.

సుతీక్ష్ణంగా **sutiikSNangaa** *adv.* fiercely (burning, shining).

సుతుడు **sutuDu** *n. class.* son.

సుత్తి, సుత్తె **sutti, sutte** *n.* hammer.

సుత్తికొట్టు, సుత్తివేయు **suttikoTTu, suttiweeyu** *v.i. colloq.* 1 to say (s.g) persistently and tediously: **eedoo DabbukaawaalaTa, reNDu roojulanunci suttiweestunnaaDu** (*or* **suttikoDutunnaaDu**) he says he needs some money, he has been hammering at it for the last two days. 2 to coax, wheedle: **waaDiki suttikoTTi** (*or* **waaDiki suttiweesi**) **pani ceeyincEEDu** he coaxed/wheedled him and got the work done *or* he coaxed/wheedled him into doing the work.

సుదతి **sudati** *n.* beautiful woman.

సుదర్శనం **sudarśanam** *n.* Vishnu's discus.

సుదామ **sudaama** *see* **kuceeluDu.**

సుదీర్ఘ **sudiirgha** *adj.* long.

సుదూర **suduura** *adj.* distant, far off, remote.

సుదృఢ **sudṛDha** *adj.* strong.

సుద్ద **sudda**[1] *n.* chalk; ~ **mukka** piece of chalk.

సుద్ద **sudda**[2] *n.* lump: **pappu**~ *or* ~ **pappu** lump of dhall.

సుద్ది **suddi**[1] *n. dial.* 1 news, talk, gossip: **eemiTi suddulu**? what is the news? (= **eemiTi sangatulu**?) 2 story.

సుద్ది, సుద్దిచేయు సుద్దిపెట్టు **suddi**[2], **suddiceeyu, suddipeTTu** *dial. variant forms of* **śuddhi, śuddhiceeyu, śuddhipeTTu.**

సుద్దులోళ్లు **suddulooLLu** *n.* a community of beggars who tell stories to weavers and beg from them.

సుధ **sudha** *n.* nectar.

సుధాకరుడు, సుధాంశువు **sudhaakaruDu, sudhaamśuwu** *n. class.* moon.

సుధి **sudhi** *n. class.* 1 good sense, intelligence. 2 learned person, scholar.

సునాదం **sunaadam** *n. class.* sweet sound, good sound.

సునాముఖి **sunaamukhi** *n.* senna.

సునాయాసంగా **sunaayaasangaa** *adv.* easily, without any effort.

సునారి **sunaari** *n.* goldsmith; ~ **nyaayam** like a goldsmith (phrase used of s.o. who cheats, because some goldsmiths are said to habitually cheat their customers).

సున్న **sunna** *n.* 1 nil, nought, zero, nothing. 2 *gram.* homorganic nasal letter also called **anuswaaram**,written as a small circle o; *see* **haLLi.**

సున్నం **sunnam** *n.* lime, lime mortar.

సున్నం కొట్టు, సున్నం వేయు **sunnam koTTu, sunnam weeyu** *v.i.* to whitewash.

సున్నం పెట్టు **sunnam peTTu** *v.i. colloq.* to harm s.o., insult s.o.

సున్న చుట్టించు **sunna cuTTincu** *v.t.* to put an end to.

సున్న చుట్టు **sunna cuTTu** *v.i. and t.* to make a small circle like a zero; **muuti**~ to purse o.'s lips; **waaDi pariikSa sunna cuTTindi** he failed his examination.

సున్నతి, సుంతి **sunnati, sunti** *n.* circumcision.

సున్నపుబట్టీ **sunnapubaTTii** *n.* lime kiln.

సున్నపురాయి **sunnapuraayi** *n.* limestone.

సున్ని, సున్నిపొడి **sunni[poDi]** *n.* dish made of (i)redgram flour or greengram flour with spices *or* (ii) blackgram flour with jaggery and ghee.

సున్నిత **sunnita** *adj.* 1 delicate, gentle, sensitive. 2 fine, exact, precise. 3 touchy, peevish.

సున్నితంగా **sunnitangaa** *adv.* 1 delicately. 2 gently, lightly; **wiipumiida**~ **taTTEEDu** he patted (him) gently on the back.

సున్నితత్వం **sunnitatwam** *n.* 1 gentleness. 2 sensitivity.

సున్నిపిండి **sunnipiNDi** *n.* greengram flour; this is used for rubbing on the body when bathing.

సున్నుండలు **sunnuNDalu** *n.pl.* balls of blackgram flour, jaggery and ghee; these are sent by the bride's family to the bridegroom's family at the time of a wedding.

సుపరిచిత **suparicita** *adj.* wellknown, well acquainted, familiar.

సుపరిచితుడు **suparicituDu** *n.* wellknown or familiar person.

సుపుత్రి[క] **suputri[ka]** *n.* daughter.

సుప్త[మైన] **supta[mayna]** *adj.* sleeping, dormant.

సుప్త చైతన్యం **suptacaytanyam** *n.* subconscious mind.

సుప్తావస్థ **suptaawastha** *n.* dormancy.

సుప్తి **supti** *n. class.* sleep.

సుప్రసిద్ధ **suprasiddha** *adj.* famous, wellknown.

సుబంతం **subantam** *n. gram. class.* name given to a noun in Sanskrit grammar.

సుబద్ధం **subaddham** *n.* truth; *occurring only in* **abaddhaalu subaddhaalu** half truths (*lit.* mixture of truths and falsehoods).

సుబా **subaa** *n.* 1 portion of a kingdom. 2 Suba or province of the Mogul Empire.

సుబేదారు **subeedaaru** *n.* 1 non-commissioned officer in the army. 2 ruler of a Suba. 3 Viceroy under the Moghul Emperor.

సుబోధంగా **suboodhangaa** *adv.* intelligibly.

సుబోధకమైన **suboodhakamayna** *adj.* easily understood, intelligible, comprehensible.

సుబోధన **suboodhana** *n.* ease of understanding, ease of comprehension, intelligibility.

సుభాషితం **subhaaSitam** *n.* adage, precept.

సుభిక్షం **subhikSam** I.*n.* plenty, abundance (*opposite of* **durbhikSam**): **śaanti~** peace and plenty. II. *adj.* prosperous, well off.

సుమం **sumam** *n. class.* flower, blossom: **sumabaala** child as fair as a flower.

సుమంగళి **sumangaLi** *n.* married woman.

సుమతి **sumati** *n. class.* good sense.

సుమతీశతకం **sumatii śatakam** *n.* name of a book of moral teachings.

సుమా!, సుమీ! **sumaa!, sumii!** *interj.* indeed!, to be sure!

సుమారు, షుమారు **sumaaru, Sumaaru** *adv.* about, approximately.

సుమారుగా **sumaarugaa** *adv.* **1** roughly, approximately. **2** moderately.

సుముఖ **sumukha** *adj.* favourable; **~mayna dhooraNi** favourable disposition.

సుముఖంగా **sumukhangaa** *adv.* in a friendly manner, favourably.

సుముఖత **sumukhata** *n.* favour[ableness].

సుముహూర్తం **sumuhuurtam** *n.* auspicious time.

సుర **sura** *n. class.* **1** intoxicating liquor. **2** nectar.

సురంగం **surangam** *same as* **sorangam.**

సురక **suraka** *same as* **curaka.**

సురకత్తి **surakatti** *same as* **curakatti.**

సురక్షత **surakSata** *n.* safety, security.

సురక్షిత **surakSita** *adj.* safe, secure, protected.

సురతం **suratam** *n. class.* copulation, coition.

సురపొన్న **suraponna** *n. calophyllum longifolium,* a yellow flower.

సురభి **surabhi**[1] *n. class.* cow.

సురభి, సురభిళం **surabhi**[2], **surabhiLam** *n.* perfume, fragrance.

సురలు **suralu** *n.pl.* demigods, celestials.

సురలోకం **suralookam** *n. class.* heaven.

సురసుర **surasura** *same as* **curacura.**

సురసురలాడు **surasuralaaDu** *v.i.* (of fireworks, soda water) to hiss, sizzle, fizz.

సురాధిపతి, సురేశ్వరుడు **suraadhipati, sureeśwaruDu** *n. class.* epithet of Indra.

సురాయి **suraayi** *n. dial.* goglet (= **kuujaa**).

సురాళించు **suraaLincu** *v.i.* **1** to make scornful comments, administer a rebuke. **2** *dial., same as* **digatuDucu.**

సురుగు **surugu** *v.i. class.* to disappear, fade away, run away.

సురుచి **suruci** *n.* good taste, good flavour.

సురుచిర **surucira** *adj. class.* beautiful, lovely.

సురుమా, సుర్మా **surumaa, surmaa** *n.* collyrium.

సురేకారం **sureekaaram** *n.* nitrate of potash, saltpetre.

సురేశ్వరుడు **sureeśwaruDu** *same as* **suraadhipati.**

సులభ[ం] **sulabha[m]** *adj.* easy, convenient, simple; **sulabha waayidaalu** easy instalments; **ceppaDam sulabham ceeyaDam kaSTam** it is simple (or easy) to say but hard to do.

సులభుడు **sulabhuDu** *n.* accessible person, affable person.

సులోచనం **suloocanam** *n., gen.pl.* **suloocanaalu** spectacles.

సుళువు, సులువు **suLuwu, suluwu** I. *n.* ease, facility. II. *adj.* easy, light, simple, convenient; **ninnaTidaakaa jwaram undi, iwwEELa koncem~gaa undi** there was fever till yesterday but today it is a little better.

సుళుసూత్రంగా **suLusuutrangaa** *adv.* very easily; **~ceesEEDu** he did it very easily (*lit.* like an easy grammatical principle).

సువర్ణ **suwarNa** *adj.* golden.

సువర్ణం **suwarNam** *n.* gold.

సువార్త **suwaarta** *n.* gospel.

సువార్తికుడు **suwaartikuDu** *n.* evangelist.

సువాసన **suwaasana** *n.* scent, perfume.

సువాసిని **suwaasini** *n. class.* married woman whose husband is living; *mod. only in* **puurwa~** widow.

సువిదిత **suwidita** *adj.* plain, clear.

సువిశాల **suwiśaala** *adj.* wide, extensive.

సువిస్పష్ట **suwispaSTa** *adj.* very clear.

సువ్యవస్థ **suwyawastha** *n.* good condition, orderly state.

సువ్యవస్థిత **suwyawasthita** *adj.* well organised.

సుశిక్షిత **suśikSita** *adj.* trained.

సుశోభిత **suśoobhita** *adj.* well decorated, ornamented.

సుశ్రావ్య **suśraawya** *adj.* melodious.

సుషమ **suSama** *n. class.* beauty, splendour.

సుషుప్తి **suSupti** *n.* deep or sound sleep.

సుషుమ్న **suSumna** *n. class.* **1** spinal cord. **2** artery supposed to be one of the passages of the breath or spirit within the body.

సుష్టు **suSTu** *adj.* good, satisfying (gen. with reference to food).

సుష్టుగా **suSTugaa** *adv.* (gen. with ref. to food) satisfying; **~tinu** to eat heartily, eat o.'s fill, eat till one is satisfied; **~tiNDi peTTu** to give (s.o.) a good meal.

సుసంగత **susangata** *adj.* relevant.

సుసంఘటిత **susanghaTita** *adj.* integrated, consolidated.

సుసంఘటిత పరచు, సుసంఘటితం చేయు **susanghaTita paracu, susanghaTitam ceeyu** *v.t.* to consolidate.

సుసంపన్న **susampanna** *adj.* well provided, well equipped.

సుసంపన్నం చేయు **susampannam ceeyu** *v.t.* to enrich: **anyabhaaSaa padaalu aayaa awasaraalaku anuguNangaa wacci ceeri bhaaSanu susampannam ceesEEyi** foreign words were incorporated to meet various needs and they enriched the language.

సుసాధ్య **susaadhya** *adj.* attainable, achievable, possible.

సుస్తి, సుస్తీ **susti[i]** *n.* 1 minor illness, indisposition; **ataniki ~ ceesindi** *or* **atanu ~ paDDaDu** he was unwell *or* he was indisposed. 2 *dial.* laziness, indolence, idleness; **eppuDuu ~ gaa kuurcuNTaawenduku?** why do you sit idle all the time?

సుస్థాపిత **susthaapita** *adj.* well established, firmly founded.

సుస్థిర **susthira** *adj.* stable.

సుస్థిరత, సుస్థిరత్వం **susthirata, susthiratwam** *n.* stability.

సుస్పష్ట[త] **suspaSTa[ta]** *same as* **wispaSTa[ta].**

సుస్వాగతం **suswaagatam** *n.* welcome; **o.-ki ~ paluku** *or* **o.-ki ~ ceppu** to welcome s.o.

సుహాసిని **suhaasini** *n.* married woman.

సుహృద్ **suhrd** *adjvl. prefix meaning* friendly; **suhrlleekhalu** friendly letters.

సుహృదుడు **suhrduDu** *n. class.* friend, wellwisher.

సుహృద్భావం **suhrdbhaawam** *n.* friendly feeling, favour, goodwill; **suhrdbhaawa paryaTana** goodwill tour.

సూ - suu

సూక్తం **suuktam** *n.* Vedic hymn.

సూక్తి **suukti** *n.* moral saying.

సూక్తిముక్తావళి **suuktimuktaawaLi** *n.* collection of moral sayings.

సూక్ష్మ **suukSma** *adj.* 1 little, small, minute, micro-, microscopic. 2 fine, sharp, keen, subtle.

సూక్ష్మం **suukSmam** *n.* 1 tiny particle. 2 fine point. 3 fineness, nicety, delicacy, subtlety.

సూక్ష్మంగా **suukSmangaa** *adv.* concisely, in a few words.

సూక్ష్మక్రిమి, సూక్ష్మజీవి **suukSmakrimi, suukSmajiiwi** *n.* bacterium, microbe, micro-organism.

సూక్ష్మజగత్తు **suukSmajagattu** *n.* microcosm.

సూక్ష్మజీవశాస్త్రం **suukSmajiiwaśaastram** *n.* microbiology.

సూక్ష్మజీవినాశక **suukSmajiiwinaaśaka** *adj.* antibiotic.

సూక్ష్మదర్శిని **suukSmadarśini** *n.* microscope.

సూక్ష్మనియమ **suukSmaniyama** *adj.* minute, tiny.

సూక్ష్మబుద్ధి **suukSmabuddhi** *n.* keen intellect.

సూచక **suucaka** *second part of an adjvl. compound meaning* indicating, denoting, suggesting.

సూచకం **suucakam** *n.* hint, indication, intimation; **śubha ~** happy augury.

సూచకంగా **suucakangaa** *advbl. suffix meaning* as a sign of, as an indication of, in token of.

సూచన **suucana** I. *n.* 1 indication, suggestion, hint, sign, representation; **reekhaacitra ~** map reference, indication of position on a map. 2 *pl.* **~ lu** guideliness. 3 citation (of words in a dictionary). II. *clitic* take note (= *nota bene*, N.B.).

సూచనగా, సూచనాత్మకంగా, సూచనప్రాయంగా **suucanagaa, suucanaatmakangaa, suucanapraayangaa** *adv.* implicitly, by implication.

సూచించు **suucincu** *v.i. and t.* 1 to indicate, show, cite, mention, make mention of, make a note of; **kinda suucincina jaagratalu tiisukoNTee caalu** if you take the precautions indicated/shown/cited/mentioned below, it will be enough. 2 to hint, suggest, imply, represent.

సూచీ **suucii** *n.* 1 (*also* **suucika**) index, indicator. 2 *class.* needle.

సూటి **suuTi** *adj.* 1 straight[forward], direct. 2 plain, clear: **~ udaaharaNa** clear instance; **~ maaTalu** plain words.

సూటిగా **suuTigaa** *adv.* straight, directly, in a straight line; **mukkuku ~ pootaaDu** he is a straightforward person.

సూటితనం **suuTitanam** *n.* directness.

సూటీపోటీ **suuTiipooTii** *adj.* mocking, scornful.

సూటూబూటూ **suuTuubuuTuu** *n.* suit and boots, western style clothes.

సూడిద **suuDida** *n.* gift, offering.

సూతకం **suutakam** *n.* ceremonial impurity arising from a death in the family; **eeTi ~** ceremonial impurity lasting for a year during which no auspicious ceremony such as a marriage should be performed.

సూతిక **suutika** *n. class.* woman who has recently delivered a child.

సూతికాగృహం **suutikaagrham** *n. class.* lying-in chamber.

సూతికావాయువు **suutikaawaayuwu** *n.. class.* vitiated wind humour which is believed to cause uterine troubles after childbirth.

సూతుడు **suutuDu** *n. class.* **1** charioteer. **2** bard.

సూత్రం **suutram** *n.* **1** *sci. gram.* principle, law, rule. **2** *sci. maths.* formula. **3** precept, maxim, aphorism. **4** point: **iraway suutraala aarthika kaaryakramam** twenty point economic programme. **5** thread. **6** *same as* **taaLi.**

సూత్రధారణ **suutradhaaraNa** *n.* putting on the bride's tali at a wedding ceremony.

సూత్రధారి, సూత్రధారుడు **suutradhaari, suutradhaaruDu** *n.* **1** actor who speaks the introduction to a drama. **2** stage manager, person who supervises from behind the scenes. **3 jagannaaTaka~** God, the unseen conductor of the universe.

సూత్రప్రాయంగా **suutrapraayangaa** *adv.* **1** in principle; **~ angiikarincu** to accept in principle. **2** in broad terms.

సూత్రీకరణ **suutriikaraNa** *n.* rule, principle.

సూత్రీకరించు **suutriikarincu** *v.t.* to reduce to principles, define in terms of principles.

సూదంటురాయి **suudaNTuraayi** *n.* **1** *colloq.* magnet. **2** *phys.* lodestone.

సూదనం **suudanam** *n. class.* killing, destroying.

సూది **suudi** *n.* needle; **~ mukku** pointed nose.

సూదిమందు **suudimandu** *n. colloq.* injection.

సూదిమందు వేయు **suudimandu weeyu** *v.i. colloq.* to give an injection.

సూనృతం **suunṛtam** *n. class.* truth[fulness], veracity, sincerity.

సూరకత్తి **suurakatti** *same as* **curakatti.**

సూరి **suuri** *n. class.* learned person, scholar, esp. a Sanskrit scholar.

సూర్యకాంతం **suuryakaantam** *n.* **1** sunflower. **2** girl's name.

సూర్యనమస్కారాలు **suuryanamaskaaraalu** *n.pl.* worship of the sun at dawn involving yogic exercises and postures.

సూర్యాస్తమానం **suuryaastamaanam** *n.* sunset.

సూర్యుడు, సూరీడు **suuryuDu, suuriiDu** *n.* sun.

సూర్యోదయం **suuryoodayam** *n.* sunrise.

సృ - sṛ

సృజన **sṛjana** *n.* creation; **~śakti** creative power.

సృజనాత్మక **sṛjanaatmaka** *adj.* creative.

సృజనాత్మకత **sṛjanaatmakata** *n.* creativity, originality.

సృజించు **sṛjincu** *v.t.* to create, make, form.

సృష్టి **sṛSTi** *n.* creation, formation.

సృష్టికర్త **sṛSTikarta** *n.* creator.

సృష్టిచేయు, సృష్టించు **sṛSTiceeyu, sṛSTincu** *v.t.* **1** to create, make, form, invent, contrive, produce: **artharaatri cuTTaalu waccEEka appaTikappuDu eedoo tinaDaaniki sṛSTincindi** when relatives arrived at midnight she contrived something for them to eat then and there. **2** to concoct, fabricate (falsehoods).

సృష్టిస్థితిలయకారకుడు **sṛSTisthitilayakaarakuDu** ~ the creator, preserver and destroyer. i.e., God, the Almighty.

సె - se

సెంటు **seNTu**[1] *n.* scent, perfume.

సెంటు **seNTu**[2] *n.* cent, one hundredth of an acre; **naaku ~ bhuumi leedu** I haven't even a cent of land.

సెగ **sega** *n.* **1** heat, warmth; **eNDa ~ lupogalugaa undi** the sun is scorching hot. **2** *dial.* flame; **pogaloonunci ~ looki** *lit.* out of the smoke into the flame (= *the English expression* 'out of the frying pan into the fire').

సెగగడ్డ **segagaDDa** *n.* boil.

సెగరోగం, సెగసంకటం **segaroogam, segasankaTam** *n. slang* gonorrhoea.

సెటకారీ, సెట్కారీ **seT[a]kaarii** I. *n. used as term of abuse, equivalent to* bastard *in English.* II. *adj.* vile, worthless, execrable.

సెట్టి **seTTi** *n.* **1** merchant. **2** name suffix gen. denoting a member of the Vysya community.

సెనక్కాయలు **senakkaayalu** *n.pl.* **1** *same as* **senagalu. 2** *dial.* groundnut, *arachis hypogea.*

సెనగలు, శనగలు **senagalu, śanagalu** *n.pl.* chickpea, bengalgram, *cicer arietinum.*

సెబాస్ ! **sebaas!** *interj.* excellent!, well done!

సెమ్మె **semme** *n.* 1 brass lampstand. 2 *dial.* brass spitoon.

సెల **sela** *n.* boil or abscess from which pus is discharging.

సెలగ, శలగ **selaga, śalaga** *n.* 1 double palmful of grain set aside to denote that a certain number of measures has been counted at the time of measuring grain. 2 word used in place of the last number when counting in a series, e.g., **tombhaytommidi** ~ instead of **tombhaytommidi nuuru** when counting upto a hundred.

సెలగటనిచ్చు **selagaTaniccu** *v.t., gen. in neg. or conditional constr.* to allow (s.o.) to speak or carry on work; **naa maaTa selagaTanistee cebtaanu** if you allow me to speak, I will tell you; **podduTinuncii pillawaaDu selagaTaniwwaDam leedu, okaTee eeDustunnaaDu** the boy has not allowed me to do any work since the early morning, he has been crying all the time.

సెలగపార **selagapaara** *n.* spade.

సెలయేరు **selayeeru** *n.* hill stream, mountain torrent.

సెలవు, శలవు **selawu, śalawu** *n.* 1 leave, permission. 2 holiday (from work or school): **krismas** ~ **lu** Christmas holidays. 3 order, command. 4 saying.

సెలవు ఇచ్చు, సెలవు ఇప్పించు **selawu iccu, selawu ippincu** *v.i. and t.* 1 to give leave, grant permission, allow, permit. 2 to give (s.o.) permission to depart. 3 to order, command. 4 to speak, say, tell (gen. used deferentially, sometimes mockingly): **ii raamacandra raawu intawarakuu ceesina ghanakaaryaaleemiToo selawistaaraa**? will you tell us what great deeds this Ramachandra Rao has performed upto now?

సెలవు తీసుకొను, సెలవు పుచ్చుకొను **selawu tiisukonu, selawu puccukonu** *v.i.* to take leave, bid farewell; **andaridaggaraa** (*or* **andariwadda**) **selawu puccukonnaaDu** he took leave of (*or* he bade farewell to) them all.

సెలవు పెట్టు **selawu peTTu** *v.i.* 1 to apply for leave. 2 to go on leave; **udyoogaaniki selawu peTTEEDu** he he applied for leave (*or* he went on leave) from his job.

సెలవేయు **selaweeyu** *v.i.* (of an ulcer) to break out; **puNDu maanutuu selaweestuu unnadi** the ulcer keeps on subsiding and breaking out again; **paata pagalu selaweestunnaayi** old enmities are reappearing.

సెల్లా **sellaa** *n.* plain unbleached cloth; **tera** ~ **lu** two pieces of plain cloth which are held up between the bride and bridegroom before the tying of the tali at a wedding.

సే - see

సేంద్రియ **seendriya** *adj. sci.* organic.

సేకరణ **seekaraNa** *n.* collection, gathering (of materials).

సేకరించు **seekarincu** *v.t.* to collect, procure, gather.

సేణం, శాణం, సేనం **seeNam, śaaNam, seenam** *n.* chisel for cutting stone.

సేత **seeta** *n.* adaptation, rendering, translation; **'karapucca' karbuujaaki telugu** ~ **kaawaccu** '*karapucca*' may be the Telugu rendering of *karbuujaa*; **malayaaLam muulam keeśawadeew, telugu** ~ **wenkateeśwara śaastri** Malayalam original by Keshav Dev, Telugu translation by Venkateswara Sastry.

సేతుబంధనం **seetubandhanam** *n.* stopping a flow by means of a dam or causeway; **gatajala** ~ building a dam after the water has flowed away (= locking the stable door after the horse is stolen).

సేతువు **seetuwu** *n. class.* bridge, causeway.

సేత్సింద్ **seetsind** *n. dial.* village watchman.

సేద **seeda** *n.* weariness, fatigue.

సేదతీరు **seedatiiru** *v.i.* to overcome fatigue, take rest; **reNDu roojulu seedatiiri maLLii panilooki digEEDu** he returned to work after taking two days' rest.

సేద్యం **seedyam** *n.* cultivation, farming, agriculture.

సేద్యగాడు **seedyagaaDu** *n.* cultivator, farmer, agriculturist.

సేద్యయోగ్య **seedyayoogya** *adj.* cultivable.

సేన **seena** *n.* 1 army. 2 band, troop: **baDipillalu waanara** ~ **laa tooTalooki wacci paDDaaru** the school-children invaded the garden like a troop of monkeys.

సేనాంగం **seenaangam** *n. mil.* corps.

సేనాధిపతి **seenaadhipati** *n. mil.* commandant.

సేనా నాయకుడు **seenaanaayakuDu** *n. mil.* general.

సేనాని **seenaani** *n. mil.* commanding officer.

సేనావిన్యాసం **seenaawinyaasam** *n.* military exercises, manoeuvres.

సేపు **seepu**[1] *n., always suffixed to an adj.* period of time; **kaa[s]** ~ a short time; **gaNTa** ~ an hour's time; **caalaseepaTiki** after a long time.

సేపు **seepu**[2] *n.* kind of fruit.

సేరీ **seerii** *same as* **śeerii**.

సేరు **seeru** *same as* **śeeru**.

సేవ **seewa** *n.* 1 service. 2 worship; *pl.* ~ **lu** different kinds of worship performed in a temple.

సేవక వృత్తి **seewaka wrtti** *n.* 1 living by performing social service. 2 life of servitude.

సేవకుడు **seewakuDu** *n.* 1 sevak, social worker. 2 servant.

సేవనం **seewanam** *n. class.* 1 service, serving. 2 partaking of food or drink, esp. medicine: *see* **awSadhaseewa[nam]**.

సేవి **seewi** *n. class.* servant.

సేవించు **seewincu** *v.t.* 1 to serve. 2 to worship. 3 to drink. 4 to take medicine: **ii mandu muuDu puuTalaa naalugu roojulu seewincaNDi** take this medicine three times a day for four days.

సేవిత **seewita** *adj.* 1 served. 2 worshipped.

సేసలు **seesalu** *n.pl. same as* **tala[m]braalu.**

సై - say

సై! **say!** *minor sentence, pronounced with nasalisation* 1 ready! 2 all right!, o.k! (=**sari** *sense III*); "**manam saayantram kaluskondaam, sayaa?**" **aNTee, "say" ani bayaldeerEEDu** when I said, "we will meet in the evening, is that all right?" he said, "all right" and started out.

సైంధవ **sayndhawa** *adj.* of or belonging to Sind.

సైంధవ లవణం **sayndhawa lawanam** *n.* rock salt.

సైంధవుడు **sayndhawuDu** *n.* 1 name of a king in the Mahabharata who obstructed the Pandavas from protecting Abhimanya, son of Arjuna. 2 *colloq.* person who creates an obstacle or obstruction.

సైకతం **saykatam** *n.* sandhill, sand dune.

సైకిలు **saykilu** *n.* [bi]cycle; ~**tokku,** ~**naDupu** to ride a cycle.

సైగ **sayga** *n.* sign, gesture.

సైచ్చం **sayccam** *same as* **satyam.**

సైతాను **saytaanu** *n.* devil, Satan.

సైదోడు **saydooDu** *n.* backer, supporter.

సైద్ధాంతిక **sayddhaantika** *adj.* theoretical.

సైనిక **saynika** *adj.* military: ~**daLaalu** troops, forces; ~**saasanam** martial law.

సైనికుడు **saynikuDu** *n.* soldier.

సైనుగుడ్డ **saynuguDDa** *n.* kind of plain coarse cloth.

సైన్యం **saynyam** *n.* army; *pl.* **saynyaalu** troops.

సైన్య సన్నాహం **saynya sannaaham** *n.* mobilisation.

సైరంధ్రి **sayrandri** *n. class.* maid servant, woman attendant.

సొ - so

సొంటు **soNTu** *n.* 1 *class.* fault, defect: *in the singular it occurs mod. only in* **aNTuu soNTuu** (*or* **aNTuu śoNTuu**) impurity. 2 *pl.* **soNTLu** defects: **soNTLu** (*or* **soNTannaalu**) **wetukutunnaaDu** he is searching for defects *or* he is finding fault.

సొంఠి **soNThi** *same as* **śoNThi.**

సొంత **sonta** *adj.* own, private, personal: *with a few nouns the form is either* ~ *or* **sontam**, e.g., **sontillu** *or* **sontam illu** o.'s own house.

సొంతంగా, సొంతాన **sontangaa, sontaana** *adv.* by o.s., on o.'s own, alone, unaided; **aa naaTakam neenu sontaana cadawaleeka daaTeesina naaTakaalaloo okaTi** that play was one of those which I passed over being unable to read it by myself.

సొంపారు, సొంపిల్లు **sompaaru, sompillu** *v.i.* to be beautiful, be pleasant.

సొంపు **sompu** I. *n.* elegance, grace, beauty, fineness, grandeur. II. *adj.* elegant, graceful, beautiful, pleasing, fine, grand.

సొక్కు **sokku** *v.i.* 1 to stagger with tiredness or drunkenness: **alisi sokki** staggering on account of tiredness. 2 *dial. alt. form of* **cokku.**

సొగసరి **sogasari** *n.* handsome man, beautiful woman.

సొగసు **sogasu** I. *n.* beauty, handsomeness, elegance, attractiveness. II. *adj.* beautiful, handsome, elegant, attractive.

సొజ్జ **sojja** *n.* kind of porridge made with rice flour or wheat flour.

సొజ్జభక్ష్యాలు, సొజ్జప్పాలు **sojjabhakSyaalu, sojjappaalu** *n.pl.* kind of sweet made with wheat flour.

సొటసొట **soTasoTa** *n.* leanness, thinness.

సొటసొటలాడు **soTasoTalaadu** *v.i.* 1 to languish, be weak. 2 to be hungry.

సొట్ట, చొట్ట **soTTa**[1], **coTTa** *adj.* lame, crippled.

సొట్ట **soTTa**[2] *n.* 1 dent: **ginne** ~ **paDindi / pooyindi** the bowl was dented: ~ **tiiyu** to remove a dent. 2 dimple: **nawwitee aame buggalu** ~ **lu paDDaayi** when she laughed her cheeks were dimpled.

సొడ్డు **soDDu** *n.* defect, fault.

సొడ్డు పెట్టు **soDDu peTTu** *v.i.* **1** to find fault with s.o.; **waaDu naamiida soDDu** (*or* **soDLu**) **peDutunnaaDu** he is finding fault with me. **2** to crow over s.o. (colloq.), boast o.'s superiority over s.o.; **waaDu mundu ceestee niimiida soDDu peDataaDu** if he does it first, he will crow over you.

సొత్తు **sottu** *n.* property.

సొద **soda** *n.* **1** long woeful story, tale of woe. **2** long boring story.

సొన **sona** *n.* **1** yolk; **kooDiguDDu~** yolk of egg. **2** juice of plants.

సొబగు **sobagu** *n.* beauty, prettiness.

సొమ్మ[రోగం] **somma[roogam]** *n.* fainting fit.

సొమ్మసిల్లు **sommasillu** *v.i.* to faint, lose consciousness; **sommasilli nidrapoowu** to sleep soundly, be sound asleep, be fast asleep.

సొమ్ము **sommu** *n.* **1** money. **2** wealth, property. **3** *pl. dial.* **~lu** cattle.

సొర[కాయ] **sora**[1], **sorakaaya** *n.* bottle gourd, *lagenarius vulgaris.*

సొర[చేప] **sora**[2], **soraceepa** *n.* shark.

సొరకాయలు నరుకు, సొరకాయలు కోయు **sorakaayalu naruku, sorakaayalu kooyu** *v.i.* to boast extravagantly (*lit.* to cut bottle gourds).

సొరంగం, సురంగం **sorangam, surangam** *n.* tunnel.

సొరపియ్యి **sorapiyyi** *n.* cuttlebone, shell of a cuttlefish.

సొరుగు, చొరుగు **sorugu, corugu** *n.* drawer in a table or box.

సొలయు, సొలిసిపోవు **solayu, solisipoowu** *v.i.* to languish, feel faint, feel exhausted; **alisi solisi** tired and exhausted.

సో - SOO

సోంచాయించు **sooncaayincu** *v.i. dial.* to reflect, ponder, think over.

సోంపు **soompu** *n.* aniseed, *pimpinella anisum.*

సోకు **sooku**[1] *v.i. and t.* **1** to touch or strike lightly, come into contact with; **eNDaweeDi sookagaanee mancu karugutundi** ice melts as soon as the sun's heat strikes it; **aayana badilii ayyEEDani naa cewini sookindi** I heard vaguely (*or* it came to my ears) that he had been transferred. **2** to infect, contaminate; **waaDiki kuSTuroogam sookindi** he caught (*or* he was infected by) leprosy; **X moNDitanam Y-ki sookindi** X's stubborness infected Y.

సోకు **sooku**[2] *same as* **Sooku.**

సోకుడు **sookuDu** *n.* infection.

సోగ **sooga**[1] *adj.* long, elongated; **~kaLLu** elongated eyes (a mark of beauty).

సోగ **sooga**[2] *n.* short wooden grip or handle attached to the ploughtail and used for guiding a plough.

సోదర **soodara** *adj.* brotherly, fraternal; **~preema** brotherly love.

సోదరత్వం, సోదర భావం **soodaratwam, soodara bhaawam** *n.* brotherhood, fraternity.

సోదరి **soodari** *n.* sister.

సోదరుడు **soodaruDu** *n.* brother.

సోదా **soodaa** *n.* search.

సోదా చేయు **soodaa ceeyu** *v.t.* to search.

సోదాహరణగా **soodaaharaNagaa** *adv.* accompanied by an illustration or example.

సోది, సోదె **soodi, soode** *n.* **1** spiritualism, attempting to receive messages from the dead through a spiritualist medium. **2** boring or senseless talk, drivel.

సోదెకత్తె **soodekatte** *n.* woman spiritualist medium.

సోదెలోకైనారాకుండాపోవు **soodelookaynaa raakuNDaa poowu** *v.i.* to vanish completely (*this idiomatic phrase refers lit. to the failure of a spirit to appear at a seance when summoned by a medium*). **brawnu taaTiyaakula granthaalanu mudrincaDam kanuka praarambhincaka pooyinaTTaytee telugu saahityamloo caalaa granthaalu manaku iinaaDu labhinceewi kaaweemoo. weemana śatakamlaaTi śatakaalu soodilooki kuuDaa wacceewi kaaweemoo** if Brown had not begun to print the palmleaf manuscripts, many works of Telugu literature might not be available to us today and collections of verses like Vemana's might have disappeared completely.

సోద్దెం **sooddem** *n. colloq. form of* **coodyam** wonder, marvel, s.g. wonderful; **~cuustunnaaraa?** is what you are looking at s.g wonderful? (said to idle onlookers); **niidantaa~raa!** what wonderful things you think of! (spoken sarcastically).

సోన **soona** *n.* rain, drizzle.

సోపా soopaa *n.* covered veranda running along the front of a house, flanking the main entrance (= **panca**).

సోపానం soopaanam *n.* **1** step. **2** flight of steps, stairway.

సోమ[రసం] sooma[rasam] *n.* **1** nectar, the drink of the gods. **2** juice of the moon plant.

సోమమ్మ, సోమదేవమ్మ soomamma, soomadeewamma *n.* **1** *lit.* wife of a **soomayaaji. 2** *colloq.* talkative or boastful woman.

సోమయాగం, సోమయజ్ఞం soomayaagam, soomayajñam *n.* a certain Vedic ritual.

సోమయాజి soomayaaji *n.* **1** *lit.* person who has performed a certain Vedic sacrifice. **2** *~ and pl.* **soomayaajulu** are name suffixes of different brahman subsects.

సోమరి soomari I. *n.* (*also* **~ pootu**) idle or lazy person. II. *adj.* idle, lazy.

సోమరితనం soomaritanam *n.* laziness, idleness.

సోమలత, సోమవల్లి soomalata, soomawalli *n.* moon plant, *asclepias acida.*

సోమవారం soomawaaram *n.* Monday.

సోమసూత్రం soomasuutram *n.* **1** vessel with a spout or similar outlet. **2** receptacle to receive water in which an idol has been bathed. **3** channel for conveying water from a Sivalinga.

సోయగం sooyagam *n.* beauty, elegance, charm.

సోయగపు sooyagapu *adj.* beautiful, handsome.

సోల soola *n.* measure of volume varying in different areas

సోలు soolu *v.i.* to reel, stagger, faint, swoon.

సోహం sooham *Sanskrit phrase meaning* 'I am He' *or* 'the Deity and I are one'.

సౌ - saw

సౌందర్యం sawndaryam *n.* beauty, good looks, handsomeness.

సౌకర్యం sawkaryam *n.* comfort, convenience; **illu~ gaa undi** the house is comfortable *or* the house is convenient.

సౌకర్యం కలిగించు sawkaryam kaligincu *v.i.* to make provision.

సౌకుమార్యం sawkumaaryam *n.* delicacy, tenderness, grace.

సౌఖ్యం sawkhyam *n.* bliss, happiness.

సౌఖ్యవంత sawkhyawanta *adj.* blissful, happy.

సౌగంధిక sawgandhika *adj.* fragrant, sweet scented.

సౌగంధికం sawgandhikam *n. class.* white lotus.

సౌజన్యం sawjanyam *n.* good nature, kindness; **aaliNDiyaa reeDiyoo ~ too** by courtesy of All India Radio.

సౌదాగరు sawdaagaru *n.* **1** shopkeeper. **2** horse dealer.

సౌదామిని sawdaamini *n. class.* lightning.

సౌధం sawdham *n.* mansion, palace.

సౌభాగ్యం sawbhaagyam *n.* good fortune.

సౌభాగ్యవతి sawbhaagyawati *n.* fortunate woman; **ciranjiiwi lakSmi~** long life, prosperity and good fortune (connoting long life for her husband)—a conventional blessing invoked on a woman.

సౌభ్రాత్రం, సౌభ్రాతృత్వం sawbhraatram, sawbhraatṛtwam *n.* brotherhood, fraternity.

సౌమనస్య sawmanasya *adj.* friendly, cordial; **~ waataawaraNamloo carcalu jarigEEyi** discussions were conducted in a cordial atmosphere.

సౌమనస్యం sawmanasyam *n.* good feeling, good will, cordiality, friendliness.

సౌమ్య sawmya I. *n.* forty-third year of the Hindu cycle of sixty years. II. *adj.* mild, gentle.

సౌమ్యత sawmyata *n.* mildness, gentleness.

సౌమ్యుడు sawmyuDu *n.* good-natured or mild natured person.

సౌర sawra *adj.* solar.

సౌరకుటుంబం, సౌరమండలం sawrakuTumbam, sawramaNDalam *n.* solar system.

సౌరమానం sawramaanam *n.* solar calendar.

సౌరమాసం sawramaasam *n.* solar month.

సౌరభం, సౌరభ్యం sawrabh[y]am *n.* fragrance.

సౌరు sawru *n. class.* **1** bloom, beauty. **2** manner.

సౌలభ్యం sawlabhyam *n.* convenience, ease, facility.

సౌవర్ణకరణి sawwarNakaraNi *n. class.* name of a legendary herb believed to bring health and vigour to the body.

సౌవిదుడు sawwiduDu *n. class.* attendant or guard at women's quarters.

సౌశీల్యం sawśiilyam *n.* good nature.

సౌష్ఠవ sawSThawa *adj.* symmetrical.

సౌష్ఠవం sawSThawam *n.* **1** beauty, good proportions. **2** symmentry. **3** goodness, excellence; **aarthika ~** economic wellbeing.

సౌహార్దం, సౌహార్ద్రం sawhaard[r]am *n.* friendship, friendliness, goodheartedness.

స్క to స్త - ska to sta

స్కందం **skandam** *n. sci.* clot.

స్కందావారం **skandaawaaram** *n. class.* **1** military camp, bivouac. **2** army.

స్కంధం **skandham** *n. class.* **1** shoulder. **2** trunk of a tree. **3** chapter or canto in a classical literary work.

స్ఖలనం **skhalanam** *n.* **1** stumbling, tripping. **2** dripping, effusion, emission.

స్ఖాలిత్యం **skhaalityam** *n.* error, mistake, omission; **mudra-Na~** printer's error, printing mistake.

స్తంభం **stambham** *n.* pillar, post.

స్తంభనం **stambhanam** *n.* **1** stopping, obstructing. **2** stupefying, putting a person in a trance by occult means; *see* **jala~**, **waayu~**.

స్తంభించు **stambhincu** I. *v.i.* **1** to be stopped, be brought to a halt, be made immobile. **2** to be paralysed. II. *v.t.* **1** to halt, stop. **2** to stupefy.

స్తంభింపచేయు **stambhimpaceeyu** *v.t.* **1** to halt, stop. **2** *fig.* to freeze (profits, etc.).

స్తనం **stanam** *n.* breast, nipple.

స్తన్యం **stanyam** *n.* breast milk.

స్తన్యదం **stanyadam** *n. zool.* mammal.

స్తబ్ధ, స్తబ్ధు **stabdha, stabdhu** *adj.* **1** fixed, firm. **2** stiff, rigid. **3** steady, immovable, immobile, motionless, inactive. **4** unable to move, stupefied, paralysed. **5** dull, boring. **6** stupid, slow-witted, dim-witted.

స్తబ్ధత **stabdhata** *n.* **1** inactivity, immobility, inertia. **2** stiffness, frigidity (of manner). **3** dullness, stagnation, sluggishness.

స్తరం **staram** *n.* layer, stratum.

స్తబ్ధుడు **stabdhuDu** *n.* **1** person who is struck dumb or senseless. **2** stupid person, blockhead.

స్తరిత **starita** *adj.* stratified.

స్తవం **stawam** *n. class.* praise (gen. of the gods); **durgaa~** collection of stanzas in praise of Durga.

స్తవనీయ **stawaniiya** *adj. class.* praiseworthy.

స్తి to స్త్రీ - sti to strii

స్తిమిత **stimita** *adj.* **1** steady, unmoving. **2** calm, stable.

స్తిమితం **stimitam** *n.* steadiness, calm[ness].

స్తిమితపడు, స్తిమితంకుదురు **stimitapaDu, stimitam kuduru** *v.i.* **1** to get settled. **2** to feel calm. **3** (of health) to get better, improve.

స్తుతి **stuti** *n. class.* praise.

స్తుతించు **stutincu** *v.t.* to praise.

స్తూపం **stuupam** *n.* **1** cylinder. **2** Buddhist monument in the form of a hemispherical mound.

స్తూపాకార **stuupaakaara** *adj.* cylindrical.

స్తోత్రం **stootram** *n.* **1** praise. **2** hymn of praise.

స్తోత్రం చేయు **stootram ceeyu** *v.t.* to praise.

స్తోమత **stoomata** *n.* capacity, capability; **aarthika~** economic capacity; **nii~telisi kharcu peTTukoo** know your capacity before you spend money.

స్త్రీ **strii** *n.* woman, lady.

స్త్రీజనం **striijanam** *n.pl.* women; **akkaDa caalaamandi~ poogayyEEru** many women collected there.

స్త్రీజాతి **striijaati** *n.* womenfolk, women in general.

స్త్రీత్వం **striitwam** *n.* femininity, womanliness.

స్త్రీధనం **striidhanam** *n.* woman's personal property over which she has independent control.

స్త్రీబీజకోశం **striibiijakoośam** *n. biol.* ovary.

స్త్రీరోగశాస్త్రం **striiroogaśaastram** *n.* gynaecology.

స్త్రీలింగం **striilingam** *n. gram.* feminine gender.

స్త్రీవాచకం **striiwaacakam** *n. gram.* feminine noun.

స్థ, స్థా - stha, sthaa

స్థండిలం **sthaNDilam** *n. class.* **1** site that has been levelled and purified for performance of a sacrifice. **2** levelled ground spread with darbha grass to be lain on by a person performing a religious vow.

స్థపతి **sthapati** *n.* architect, builder.

స్థలం **sthalam** *n.* **1** place, spot. **2** space, room.

స్థలపురాణం **sthalapuraaNam** *n.* legend associated with a particular place.

స్థలమహాత్మ్యం **sthalamahatmyam** *n.* greatness, sanctity, renown, etc., associated with a place.

స్థలాకృతి **sthalaakṛti** *n.* topography.

స్థలాభావం **sthalaabhaawam** *n.* lack of space.

స్థలి **sthali** *n. class.* place.

స్థాణువు **sthaaNuwu** *adj. and n.* **1** firmly fixed. **2** epithet of Siva.

స్థానం **sthaanam** *n.* **1** place, spot; **naaku kuurcooDaaniki ~ cuupincaNDi** please show me a place to sit down. **2** site, situation, position. **3** office, post, rank. **4** seat (in college, etc.).

స్థానభ్రంశం **sthaanabhramśam** *n. phys. chem.* displacement.

స్థానిక **sthaanika** *adj.* local.

స్థానికంగా **sthaanikangaa** *adv.* locally.

స్థానికుడు **sthaanikuDu** *n.* local person.

స్థానే **sthaanee** *advbl. particle* in [the] place of; **X badilii aytee Y aayana ~ waccEEDu** when X was transferred, Y came in his place.

స్థాపకుడు **sthaapakuDu** *n.* founder.

స్థాపన **sthaapana** *n.* establishment, founding, setting up.

స్థాపించు **sthaapincu** *v.t.* **1** to set up, erect, instal. **2** to found, establish.

స్థాయి **sthaayi** *n.* **1** level, status, rank, standing; **cuuDaNDi, manawaaLLa naTanaa ~ elaa undoo!** see what the level of acting is like among our people!; **raaSTra ~** state level. **2** scale; **ii pariśoodhana kṛSi nyaayangaa mana wiśwawidyaalayaalu bṛhattara ~ loo ceepaTTawalasindi** really our universities ought to undertake this research effort on a huge scale. **3** pitch (in music).

స్థాయీసంఘం **sthaayiisangham** *n. polit.* standing committee.

స్థాయీసేన **sthaayiiseena** *n.* standing army.

స్థాలి **sthaali** *n. class.* cooking pot.

స్థాలీపాకం **sthaaliipaakam** *n.* part of the wedding ceremony in which the bride and bridegroom are introduced to domestic life.

స్థాలీపులాక న్యాయం[గా] **sthaaliipulaakanyaayam[gaa]** *advbl. phrase meaning lit.* like judging the contents of a whole pot (of rice) by examining one grain, i.e., using a random sample to come to a conclusion.

స్థావర **sthaawara** *adj.* **1** fixed, stationary, immovable. **2** settled, not wandering.

స్థావరం **sthaawaram** *n.* **1** military base. **2** settlement.

స్థావరం చేయు **sthaawaram ceeyu** *v.t.* to base, station (troops).

స్థి to స్థై - sthi to sthay

స్థితప్రజ్ఞ **sthitaprajña** *n.* indifference to worldly joys and sorrows.

స్థితప్రజ్ఞుడు **sthitaprajñuDu** *n.* **1** one who treats good and bad fortune alike with equanimity and indifference. **2** person with a mature and balanced outlook.

స్థితి **sthiti** *n.* **1** state, condition. **2** status, standing; **uccha ~** high status. **3** position, location. **4** existence.

స్థితిగతులు **sthitigatulu** *n. pl.* circumstances, general well-being, economic or social status or condition.

స్థితిపరుడు, స్థితిమంతుడు **sthitiparuDu, sthitimantuDu** *n.* wealthy person; **pedda ~** man of means; **aydu lakSala ~** s.o. worth five lakhs of rupees.

స్థితిశక్తి **sthitiśakti** *n. phys.* potential energy.

స్థితిశాస్త్రం **sthitiśaastram** *n.* (science of) statics.

స్థితిస్థాపక **sthitisthaapaka** *adj.* elastic.

స్థితిస్థాపకత **sthitisthaapakata** *n.* elasticity.

స్థిర[ం] **sthira[m]** *adj.* 1 fixed, firm. 2 steady, stable. 3 enduring, lasting, permanent. 4 settled, established. 5 constant, unchanging. 6 static.

స్థిరం చేసుకొను **sthiram ceesukonu** *v.i. and t.* to resolve, decide, make up o.'s mind.

స్థిరచిత్తంగలవాడు **sthiracittangalawaaDu** *n.* person of sound mind, sane person.

స్థిరత, స్థిరత్వం **sthirata, sthiratwam** *n.* 1 steadiness. 2 durability, constancy, permanence.

స్థిరపడు **sthirapaDu** *v.i.* 1 to come to live, settle down (in a village). 2 to be confirmed, be ratified. 3 (*also* **sthiram awu**) to be[come] fixed or settled or established.

స్థిరపరచు **sthiraparacu** *v.t.* to confirm, ratify.

స్థిరరాశి **sthiraraaśi** *n. maths.* constant.

స్థిరవారం **sthirawaaram** *n. class.* Saturday.

స్థిరాస్తి **sthiraasti** *n.* immoveable property.

స్థిరీకరణ **sthiriikaraNa** *n.* 1 stabilisation, fixing. 2 **dharala** ~ freezing of prices.

స్థిరీకరించు **sthiriikarincu** *v.t.* to stabilise, fix.

స్థిరుడు **sthiruDu** *n. class.* 1 person who is firmly settled. 2 person of strong determination.

స్థూల **sthuula** *adj.* 1 thick, stout, large, bulky. 2 macro-; ~ **aarthika wiśleeSaNam** (study of) macro-economics. 3 broad, rough, not detailed; ~ **nirwacanam** broad definition.

స్థూలంగా **sthuulangaa** *adv.* 1 stoutly. 2 broadly, roughly, in general terms, generally speaking. 3 in all, overall.

స్థూలకాయుడు **sthuulakaayuDu** *n.* stout or heavily built person.

స్థూలజగత్తు **sthuulajagattu** *n.* the macrocosm, the universe.

స్థూలదృష్టి **sthuuladrSTi** *n.* superficial or cursory glance.

స్థైర్యం **sthayryam** *n.* firmness, steadiness, stability.

స్నా to స్నే - snaa to snee

స్నాతకం, స్నాతకవ్రతం **snaatakam, snaatakawratam** *n. class.* first part of the marriage ceremony, which involves a man's taking a ceremonial bath to mark the completion of his studies and of the first **aaśramam** of his life (**brahmacaryam**).

స్నాతకుడు **snaatakuDu** *n. class.* man who has taken a ceremonial bath to mark the completion of his studies and of the first **aaśramam** of his life.

స్నాతకోత్తర **snaatakoottara** *adj.* postgraduate.

స్నాతకోత్సవం **snaatakootsawam** *n.* 1 *class.* ceremony involving the taking of a ceremonial bath by a man who has completed the first **aaśramam** of his life or who has performed a Vedic sacrifice. 2 convocation ceremony held by a university for conferring degrees.

స్నానం **snaanam** *n.* bath[ing].

స్నానం చేయు **snaanam ceeyu** *v.i.* to take a bath, bathe.

స్నాయు బంధనం **snaayubandhanam** *n. med.* tendon, sinew.

స్నాయువు **snaayuwu** *n. med.* ligament.

స్నిగ్ధ **snigdha** *adj.* 1 bright, shining. 2 soft, tender. 3 kind, amiable. 4 sticky, viscous.

స్నిగ్ధత **snigdhata** *n.* 1 brightness. 2 tenderness, softness. 3 kindness. 4 viscosity.

స్నేహం **sneeham** *n.* 1 friendship, friendliness; **aawiDa naatoo ~ kaTTindi** she made friends with me. 2 *class.* oil[iness].

స్నేహకం **sneehakam** *n.* lubricant.

స్నేహనం **sneehanam** *n.* lubrication.

స్నేహపాత్రుడు **sneehapaatruDu**, *n.* likeable person.

స్నేహపూర్వకంగా, స్నేహపురస్సరంగా **sneehapuurwakangaa, sneehapurassarangaa** *adv.* in a friendly manner, cordially.

స్నేహశీలి **sneehaśiili** *n.* good-natured or warm hearted person.

స్నేహితుడు **sneehituDu** *n.* friend (male).

స్నేహితురాలు **sneehituraalu** *n.* friend (female).

స్ప, స్పృ - spa, spṛ

స్పంద[న]ం **spanda[na]m** *n.* 1 throbbing, vibrating. 2 vibration, pulsation. 3 quivering, fluttering.

స్పందించు **spandincu** *v.i.* 1 to throb, vibrate, pulsate. 2 to palpitate, quiver, be agitated.

స్పర్ధ **spardha** *n.* rivalry, emulation, competition.

స్పర్ధి **spardhi** *n.* competitor, rival.

స్పర్శ[నం] **sparśa[nam]** *n.* touch[ing], contact; **sparśamuulaana grahincu** to feel (*lit.* to perceive by touching).

స్పర్శకం **sparśakam** *n.* tentacle.

స్పర్శకాలం **sparśakaalam** *n.* time of onset of an eclipse.

స్పర్శజ్ఞానం **sparśajñaanam** *n.* sense of touch, sense of feeling.

స్పర్శజ్ఞేయ **sparśajñeeya** *adj. class.* palpable.

స్పర్శధ్వని **sparśadhwani** *n. ling.* occlusive sound.

స్పర్శమణి, స్పర్శవేధి **sparśamaNi, sparśaweedhi** *n. class.* philosopher's stone.

స్పర్శరేఖ **sparśareekha** *n. maths.* tangent.

స్పర్శశృంగం **sparśaśṛngam** *n. zool.* antenna.

స్పర్శించు **sparśincu** *v.t.* to touch.

స్పర్శేంద్రియం **sparśeendriyam** *n.* sensory organ.

స్పష్ట **spaSTa** *adj.* 1 clear, plain, distinct, explicit. 2 evident, apparent, manifest.

స్పష్టత **spaSTata** *n.* clearness, clarity, distinctness, explicitness.

స్పష్టపరచు **spaSTaparacu** *v.t.* to make clear, clarify.

స్పష్టీకరణ **spaSTiikaraNa** *n.* clarification.

స్పష్టీకరించు **spaSTiikarincu** *v.t.* to clarify.

స్పృశించు **spṛśincu** *v.t.* to touch.

స్పృహ **spṛha** *n.* consciousness, awareness; **ataniki ~ tappindi/waccindi** he lost/regained consciousness; **aame oNTimiida ~ leedu** she is unconscious; **saamaajika ~** social consciousness, social awareness.

స్ఫ to స్ఫో -spha to sphoo

స్ఫటికం **sphaTikam** *n.* crystal, quartz.

స్ఫటికీకరణం **sphaTikiikaraNam** *n.* crystallisation.

స్ఫాటిక **sphaaTika** *adj.* crystalline.

స్ఫీతం **sphiitam** *adj. class.* 1 swollen, turgid. 2 much, many.

స్ఫుట[ం] **sphuTa[m]** *adj.* 1 clear, plain, distinct. 2 prominent, striking, manifest, conspicuous.

స్ఫురణ **sphuraNa** *n.* (of a concept or thought) occurring to the mind.

స్ఫురణకు వచ్చు **sphuraNaku waccu** *v.i.* to occur to the mind.

స్ఫురద్రూపి **sphuradruupi** *n.* handsome person.

స్ఫురించు **sphurincu** I. *v.i.* to occur to the mind, appear, strike the mind; **aa maaTaloo koncem weTakaaram sphurincindi R.-ki** it occurred to R. that there was some scorn in that word; **ayśwaryam cuuDani waaDiki daaridryam baadha kaligincadu, leemigaa sphurincadu** for one who has not seen wealth, poverty does not cause distress or strike him as want. II. *v.t.* to show, exhibit, suggest, express.

స్ఫురింపచేయు **sphurimpaceeyu** *v.t.* to call to mind, suggest, convey (meaning, idea).

స్ఫులింగం **sphulingam** *n. class.* spark of fire.

స్ఫూర్తి **sphuurti** *n.* 1 manifestation, becoming evident. 2 spirit; **prajaaswaamya ~** spirit of democracy. 3 shining, brilliance; *cf.* **samaya ~**.

స్ఫూర్తిమంతంగా **sphuurtimantangaa** *adv.* brilliantly, vividly, meaningfully.

స్ఫోటకం **sphooTakam** *n.* smallpox.

స్ఫోటనం **sphooTanam** *n.* explosion, detonation.

స్ఫోరకం **sphoorakam** *n.* that which indicates; **bahuwacana sphoorakaalu** signs which indicate the plural.

స్ఫోరకంగా **sphoorakangaa** *adv.* as an indication of, as a sign of.

స్మ to స్రో - sma to sroo

స్మరణ[ం] **smaraNa[m]** *n.* **1** memory, recollection, remembrance. **2** repeating a sacred name many times (a form of prayer).

స్మరణీయ, స్మరించతగ్గ **smaraNiiya, smarincatagga** *adj.* worth remembering, memorable.

స్మరించు **smarincu** *v.t.* **1** to recollect, recall, remember. **2** to think of, reflect on.

స్మరింప చేయు **smarimpa ceeyu** *v.t.* to remind.

స్మారక **smaaraka** *adj.* memorial, commemorative; **~ nidhi** memorial fund; **~ cihnam** memorial statue or tablet, monument.

స్మారకం **smaarakam** *n.* consciousness, awareness of o.'s surroundings; **cuTTuu unnawaaLLa ~ loo leeDu** he is not conscious of the people around him.

స్మార్త **smaarta** *adj.* agreeable to or based on the smritis.

స్మార్తులు **smaartulu** *n.pl.* followers of the doctrine of Sankaracharya which inculcates worship of both Vishnu and Siva.

స్మిత **smita** *adj. class.* smiling; **~ wadanam** smiling face.

స్మితం **smitam** *n. class.* smile, smiling.

స్మృతి **smrti** *n.* **1** consciousness. **2** memory, recollection, remembrance. **3** tradition, law. **4** law book, code of law; **manu ~** Manu's code of Hindu law.

స్మృతిచిహ్నం **smrticihnam** *n.* memorial, monument.

స్మృతికావ్యం **smrti kaawyam** *n.* elegy.

స్యందనం **syandanam** *n. class.* chariot.

స్రవంతి **srawanti** *n. class.* river; *mod. in* **jiiwana ~** the river of life.

స్రవించు **srawincu** *v.i.* to flow, trickle, ooze.

స్రష్ట **sraSTa** *n.* **1** creator; **sangiita ~** composer of music. **2** epithet of Brahma.

స్రావం, స్రవం **sraawam, srawam** *n.* secretion, flow[ing]; **rakta ~** flow of blood; **garbha ~** abortion.

స్రోతస్సు **srootassu** *n. class.* **1** stream **2** flow, current.

స్వ - swa

స్వ **swa** *adjvl. prefix* own, personal, individual; **swagraamam** o.'s own village.

స్వకపోలకల్పిత **swakapoolakalpita** *adj.* (of an idea, story) made up or created or thought of by o.s., original, not borrowed (*lit.* created in o.'s own cheek).

స్వకార్యం **swakaaryam** *n.* o.'s own affairs, o.'s business; **swaamikaaryam ~ ceesukoni waccEEDu** he came after attending to both his master's business and his own.

స్వకీయ **swakiiya** I. *n. class.* o.'s own wife. II. *adj.* own, personal, private.

స్వగతం **swagatam** *n.* **1** *theat.* aside. **2** *theat.* monologue. **3** talking to o.s., s.g said to o.s.; **swagataalu gaTTigaa anukooru** people do not talk to themselves aloud.

స్వగతంగా **swagatangaa** *adv.* (saying) to o.s., in o.'s own mind.

స్వగ్రామం **swagraamam** *n.* o.'s own village.

స్వచ్ఛ **swaccha** *adj.* **1** clean, pure, unadulterated. **2** clear, transparent.

స్వచ్ఛంద **swacchanda** *adj.* **1** free, independent. **2** spontaneous. **3** voluntary; **~ samstha** voluntary organisation.

స్వచ్ఛందంగా **swacchandangaa** *adv.* **1** voluntarily, of o.'s own accord, spontaneously. **2** independently.

స్వచ్ఛత, స్వచ్ఛత్వం **swacchata, swacchatwam** *n.* purity, cleanliness.

స్వజనం **swajanam** *n.* o.'s own family/people/friends.

స్వజనోద్ధారకుడు **swajanooddhaarakuDu** *n.* **1** one who shows favouritism towards his relatives, nepotist. **2** one who strives to uplift his fellow countrymen.

స్వజాతి **swajaati** *n.* o.'s own nation or race or kind.

స్వతంత్ర **swatantra** *adj.* free, independent; **~ racana** original writing.

స్వతంత్రం, స్వతంత్రత, స్వాతంత్ర్యం **swatantram, swatantrata, swaatantryam** *n.* independence, liberty, freedom.

స్వతంత్రంగా **swatantrangaa** *adv.* independently, freely.

స్వతంత్రించు **swatantrincu** *v. i.* **1** to please o.s., do as one likes, experiment. **2** to act on o.'s own initiative, act independently.

స్వతంత్రుడు **swatantruDu** *n.* free or independent person.

స్వతః, స్వతహాగా **swatah, swatahaagaa** *adv.* of itself, by nature, naturally, inherently, spontaneously, *ipso facto.*

స్వతస్సిద్ధ **swatassiddha** *adj.* 1 natural, inherent. 2 self-evident.

స్వతస్సిద్ధంగా **swatassiddhangaa** *adv.* naturally, by nature, inherently.

స్వత్వం **swatwam** *n.* right; **praathamika swatwaalu** fundamental rights; **samaana swatwaalu** equal rights.

స్వదేశీ[యు] **swadeeśii[ya]** *adj.* indigenous, native, belonging to the country.

స్వదేశీయుడు **swadeeśiiyuDu** *n.* compatriot, fellow countryman.

స్వధర్మం **swadharmam** *n.* o.'s own duty or characteristic or religion.

స్వనం **swanam** *n. class.* sound, noise; **pakSula kalakala swanaalu** sound of birds chirruping.

స్వనించు **swanincu** *v.i.* to echo, resound.

స్వపరభేదం **swaparabheedam** *n.* discrimination between o.s. and others.

స్వపరాగసంపర్కం **swaparaagasamparkam** *n. bot.* self-pollination.

స్వపరిపాలన **swaparipaalana** n. self-government, self-rule.

స్వప్నం **swapnam** *n.* dream.

స్వప్రయోజనం **swaprayoojanam** *n.* o.'s own interest, o.'s own advantage.

స్వబుద్ధిగల **swabuddhigala** *adj.* self-willed.

స్వభాను **swabhaanu** *n.* seventeenth year of the Hindu cycle of sixty years.

స్వభావం **swabhaawam** *n.* nature, quality, character, disposition, temperament; **swabhaawa citraNaśakti** power of characterisation (in a writer).

స్వభావతః, స్వభావసిద్ధంగా **swabhaawatah, swabhaawasiddhangaa** *adv.* by nature, naturally.

స్వభావరీత్యా **swabhaawariityaa** *adv.* by its very nature.

స్వభావి **swabhaawi** *n. suffix meaning* person having a certain nature or temperament; **koopa~** person with an irritable temperament.

స్వభావికత **swabhaawikata** *same as* **swaabhaawikata.**

స్వయం **swayam** *adjvl. prefix meaning* o.'s own, self-, auto-.

స్వయంకృతం **swayankṛtam** *n.* s.g done or caused by o.s. personally; **swayankṛtaaparaadham** o.'s own fault, fault committed by an individual personally.

స్వయంకృషి **swayankṛSi** *n.* o.'s own effort.

స్వయంగమన, స్వయంచలన **swayangamana, swayamcalana** *adj.* 1 automatic. 2 self-propelled.

స్వయంగా **swayangaa** *adv.* personally, in person; **taanee waccEEDu** *or* **~ waccEEDu** he himself came.

స్వయం నిర్ణయం **swayam nirNayam** *n.* self-determination.

స్వయంపాకం **swayampaakam** *n.* 1 cooking o.'s own meals; **idi waaDi ~ ee** he cooked this himself *or* (in general) he did this with his own hands. 2 *same as* **sadaawṛtti.**

స్వయంపాలక **swayampaalaka** *adj.* autonomous, self-governing.

స్వయంపూర్ణ **swayampuurNa** *adj.* self-contained.

స్వయంపోషక **swayampooSaka** *adj.* self-supporting, self-sustaining.

స్వయం ప్రతిపత్తి **swayam pratipatti** *n.* autonomy, self-governing status.

స్వయంభువు **swayambhuwu** *n. class.* self-existent being (epithet of Brahma or Siva or Vishnu or Manmatha).

స్వయంవరం **swayamwaram** *n.* 1 choice of partner for o.s. in marriage. 2 *class.* choice of a husband for herself by a princess or a Kshatriya bride.

స్వయంవివరణాత్మక **swayamwiwaraNaatmaka** *adj.* self-explanatory.

స్వయంశక్తి **swayamśakti** *same as* **swaśakti.**

స్వయంసమృద్ధ **swayamsamṛddha** *adj.* self-sufficient.

స్వయంసమృద్ధి **swayamsamṛddhi** *n.* self-sufficiency.

స్వయంసిద్ధ **swayamsiddha** *adj.* 1 natural, inherent. 2 self-evident.

స్వయానా **swayaanaa** *same as* **sayaanaa.**

స్వరం **swaram** *n.* 1 voice, sound. 2 musical note; *see* **sapta.** 3 tone. 4 pitch in Vedic recitation.

స్వరక్షణ **swarakSaNa** *n.* self-defence.

స్వరపరచు **swaraparacu** *v.t.* to set (words of a poem) to music.

స్వరపేటిక **swarapeeTika** *n. med.* larynx.

స్వరభక్తి **swarabhakti** *n. ling.* anaptyxis, insertion of a short vowel between consonants for ease of pronunciation.

స్వర సమ్మేళనం **swarasammeeLanam** *n.* harmony of notes, harmony of tones.

స్వరాజ్యం **swaraajyam** *n.* swaraj, self-government, independence.

స్వరితస్వరం **swaritaswaram** *n. ling.* voiced tone in Vedic recitation.

స్వరూపం **swaruupam** *n.* 1 form, shape, nature. 2 **bhawgooLika~** geographical features (of a region).

స్వరూపనాశం **swaruupanaaśam** *n.* annihilation.

స్వరూపశాస్త్రం **swaruupaśaastram** *n. ling.* (science of) morphology.

స్వరూపి **swaruupi** *n.suffix meaning* embodiment; **aayana dharma~** he is the embodiment of justice.

స్వర్గం, స్వర్లోకం **swargam, swarlookam** *n.* Indra's heaven.

స్వర్గతుల్య **swargatulya** *adj.* like heaven, heavenly.

స్వర్గధామం **swargadhaamam** *n.* heavenly abode.

స్వర్గస్థుడవు **swargasthuDawu** *v.i.* to go to heaven, i.e., to die.

స్వర్గీయ **swargiiya** *adj.* late, deceased.

స్వర్ణ **swarNa** *adj.* golden.

స్వర్ణం **swarNam** *n.* gold.

స్వర్ణకారుడు **swarNakaaruDu** *n. class.* goldsmith.

స్వర్ణోత్సవం **swarNootsawam** *n.* golden jubilee.

స్వర్లోకం **swarlookam** *same as* **swargam.**

స్వల్ప **swalpa** *adj.* **1** little, small. **2** few. **3** trifling, insignificant.

స్వల్పకాలిక **swalpakaalika** *adj.* short-term; **~ ṛNam** short-term loan.

స్వల్పత **swalpata** *n.* paucity.

స్వశక్తి, స్వయంశక్తి **swaśakti, swayamśakti** *n.* o.'s own means, o.'s own ability.

స్వస్తి **swasti** I. *Sanskrit phrase meaning* may it be well with you! *or* (at the end of a prayer) may it be so! II. *n.class.* welfare, wellbeing.

స్వస్తిచెప్పు, స్వస్తిపలుకు **swasticeppu, swastipaluku** *v.i.* to bid farewell to, give up, abandon; **caduwuki swasti ceppEEDu** he abandoned his studies.

స్వస్తివాచకం, స్వస్తివాచనం **swastiwaacakam, swastiwaacanam** *n. class.* benedictory hymn or prayer; **swastiwaacanaalu ceeyu** to invoke the blessings of God at the end of a religious sacrifice.

స్వస్థం, స్వస్థత, స్వాస్థ్యం **swastham, swasthata, swaasthyam** *n.* **1** good health. **2** sound condition.

స్వస్థపరచు **swasthaparacu** *v.t.* to cure, heal, restore to health, relieve; **kalatabaDina antaraatmanu ~** to relieve an anxious mind.

స్వస్థలం, స్వస్థానం **swasthalam, swasthaanam** *n.* home town, own village; **mii ~ eemiTi**? *or* **mii ~ eedi**? what is your home town?

స్వహస్తం **swahastam** *n.* **1** *lit.* o.'s own hand. **2** the custom of eating only food cooked by o.s.; *cf.* **sadaawṛtti, mooyinu.**

స్వహస్తాలవారు **swahastaalawaaru** *n.pl.* persons who for reasons of religious orthodoxy will eat only food cooked by themselves.

స్వా - swaa

స్వాంతం **swaantam** *n.* mind.

స్వాంతన[ం] **swaantana[m]** *n.* peace, quiet; **manasuku ~ cikka leedu** the mind found no peace.

స్వాగతం **swaagatam** *n.* welcome; **o.-ki ~ iccu/ceppu** to welcome s.o.

స్వాతంత్ర, స్వాతంత్ర్య **swaatantra, swaantrya** *adj.* of or relating to independence; **~ samaram** independence struggle.

స్వాతంత్ర్యం **swaatantryam** *n.* independence, freedom, liberty (= **swatantra.n**).

స్వాతి **swaati** *n. astrol.* the fifteenth lunar asterism, through which the sun passes in the month of Kartika (end of October); **~ waanalaku nooru terucukoni mutyapu cippalu edurucuucinaTTu** as pearl oysters gape open waiting for rain when the sun is in the **swaati** constellation (proverbial saying).

స్వాదు[వు] **swaadu[wu]** *adj. class.* sweet, pleasant, agreeable.

స్వాధీనం **swaadhiinam** *n.* **1** possession. **2** power, control, custody.

స్వాధీనత **swaadhiinata** *n. legal* acquisition (of property).

స్వాధీనపడు **swaadhiinapaDu** *v.i.* to come into (s.o.'s) possession or control; **naa aasti waaDiki swaadhiina paDindi** my property came into his possession.

స్వాధీనపతిక **swaadhiinapatika** *n. class.* woman who rules her husband.

స్వాధీనపరచు, స్వాధీనం చేయు **swaadhiinaparacu, swaadhiinam ceeyu** *v.t.* to give possession of, hand over.

స్వాధీనపరచుకొను, స్వాధీనం చేసుకొను **swaadhiinaparacukonu, swaadhiinam ceesukonu** *v.t.* to take possession of, take charge of, take over.

స్వాధీనపు **swaadhiinapu** *adj.* with or involving possession; **~ tanakhaa** mortgage with possession, usufructory mortgage.

స్వాధీనుడు **swaadhiinuDu** *n.* subservient or docile person.

స్వాధ్యాయం **swaadhyaayam** *n.* **1** *class.* repetition of the Vedas, study of the Vedas. **2** acquiring knowledge by studying on o.'s own. **3** repeating to o.s.

స్వానుభవం **swaanubhawam** *n.* direct experience, personal experience.

స్వాప్నిక **swaapnika** *adj.* dreamlike; **~ jagattu** world of dreams.

స్వాభావిక **swaabhaawika** *adj.* natural, innate, inherent, inborn, intrinsic.

స్వాభావికత, స్వభావికత **swaabhaawikata, swabhaawikata** *n.* naturalness.

స్వాభిమానం **swaabhimaanam** *n.* **1** self-respect. **2** self-pride.

స్వామి **swaami** *n.* **1** *class.* lord, presiding deity. **2** master, owner, proprietor. **3** *dial.* (*also* **saami**) sir! (*form of address*). **4** religious leader.

స్వామిద్రోహం **swaamidrooham** *n.* treachery to a master.

స్వామిని **swaamini** *n.* proprietrix.

స్వామి భోగం **swaami bhoogam** *n.* landlord's share of harvest produce.

స్వాములవారు **swaamulawaaru** *n. hon. pl.* title given to a religious leader equivalent to His Grace or His Holiness.

స్వాములు **swaamulu** *n. hon. pl.* **1** *class.* Vaishnavite priest. **2** wandering sanyasi.

స్వామ్యం **swaamyam** *n.* ownership, right, title.

స్వాయత్తం చేసుకొను **swaayattam ceesukonu** *v.t.* to make o.'s own, incorporate, acquire; **alaagee ingliiSu modalayna prapanca bhaaSala wijñaana sampadanu swaayattam ceesukoogaligina śakti telugu bhaaSaki unnadi** in the same way Telugu has the power to acquire the wealth of technical terminology possessed by English and the other world languages.

స్వారస్యం **swaarasyam** *same as* **sarasatwam.**

స్వారీ[చేయు] **swaarii[ceeyu]** *same as* **sawaarii[ceeyu].**

స్వార్జిత **swaarjiita** *adj.* self-earned, self-acquired.

స్వార్జితం **swaarjitam** *n.* self-earned property.

స్వార్థం **swaartham** *n.* self-interest, self[ish] motive; **waakyamloo okee karta unnappuDu 'konu' ceerika ~ suucistundi** when the subject of a sentence is singular, the addition of 'konu' gives the meaning '(doing s.g) for o.s.'

స్వార్థకం **swaarthakam** *n. gram. class.* indicative mood.

స్వార్థచింత **swaarthacinta** *n.* self-interest, selfishness.

స్వార్థత్యాగం **swaarthatyaagam** *n.* self-sacrifice.

స్వార్థపర **swaarthapara** *adj.* selfish, self-centred.

స్వార్థపరత, స్వార్థపరత్వం **swaarthaparata, swaarthaparatwam** *n.* **1** self-interest. **2** self-seeking. **3** selfishness.

స్వార్థపరుడు **swaarthaparuDu** *n.* selfish or self-centred person.

స్వార్థాశయం **swaarthaaśayam** *n.* selfish intention, selfish motive.

స్వావలంబన **swaawalambana** *n.* self-reliance.

స్వాస్థ్యం **swaasthyam** *same as* **swastham.**

స్వాహా **swaahaa** I. *n. class.* name of the wife of the God of fire. II. *interj. used when making an offering to a God.*

స్వాహాచేయు **swaahaaceeyu** *v.t. colloq.* to misappropriate, make away with.

స్వి to స్వో - swi to swoo

స్విన్న జలం **swinna jalam** *n. sci.* distilled water.

స్వీకరణ **swiikaraNa** *n.* adoption, selection, choice; **wastu~** choice of subject matter (for a literary work).

స్వీకరించు **swiikarincu** *v.t.* **1** to adopt, appropriate. **2** to receive, accept; **baadhyata~** to accept or undertake responsibility. **3** to choose (subject matter for a literary work). **4 pramaaNam~** to take the oath on assumption of office.

స్వీకారం, స్వీకృతి **swiikaaram, swiikrti** *n.* **1** adoption, adopting, appropriating, accepting. **2 pramaaNa~** swearing in, taking the oath of office.

స్వీయ **swiiya** *adjvl. prefix meaning* own, personal, self-.

స్వీయచరిత్ర **swiiyacaritra** *n.* autobiography.

స్వీయప్రయోజనం **swiiyaprayoojanam** *n.* self-interest, personal advantage.

స్వీయోపాధికల్పన **swiiyoopaadhi kalpana** *n.* self-employment.

స్వేచ్ఛ **sweeccha** *n.* **1** freedom, liberty; **sweecchaa wyaapaaram** free trade. **2** free will.

స్వేచ్ఛగా **sweecchagaa** *adv.* **1** freely, independently. **2** voluntarily.

స్వేచ్ఛాయుత **sweecchaayuta** *adj.* free, independent.

స్వేదం **sweedam** *n.* sweat, perspiration.

స్వేదనం **sweedanam** *n. sci.* distillation; **sweedana jalam** distilled water.

స్వైరవిహారం **swayrawihaaram** *n.* **1** roaming about at o.'s will and pleasure. **2** unchastity, adultery.

స్వైరిణి **swayriNi** *n.* adulteress.

స్వోత్కర్ష **swootkarSa** *n.* self-conceit, boasting, bragging.

హ - ha

హంకరించు, హంకారం **hankarincu, hankaaram** *same as* **ahankarincu, ahankaaram.**

హంగామా **hangaamaa** *n.* **1** pomp and show. **2** fuss, stir, bustle, pother, furore.

హంగు **hangu** *n.* **1** pomp and show. **2** support or backing organised for a person from behind the scenes.

హంగుదారు **hangudaaru** *n.* prompter or backer who organises support for a person from behind the scenes.

హంగులు **hangulu** *n.pl.* **1** facilities, conveniences. **2** outward trappings and paraphernalia associated with a profession or occupation (such as suitable accommodation, equipment, reference materials, etc.).

హండీ **haNDii** *n. dial.* large wide-mouthed vessel.

హంత **hanta** *n. class.* slayer, murderer.

హంతకుడు **hantakuDu** *n.* murderer.

హంశ **hamśa** *variant form of* **amśa.**

హంస[ం] **hamsa[m]** *n.* **1** swan. **2** spirit, soul; **DaakTaru wacceeloogaa ~leeci pooyindi** by the time the doctor arrived he had expired (*lit.* his soul had departed). **3** ascetic.

హంసగమన **hamsagamana** *n. class.* woman who walks elegantly.

హంసతూలికాతల్పం **hamsatuulikaatalpam** *n. class.* swan's down couch.

హంసపాదు **hamsapaadu** *n.* omission; **aDuguloonee~** *proverbial expression meaning* a mistake or omission occurring right at the start.

హకీము, హకీం **hakiimu, hakiim** *n.* Unani physician.

హక్కు **hakku** *n.* **1** lawful right, claim, title. **2 pratyeeka~** privilege.

హక్కుదారుడు **hakkudaaruDu** *n.* **1** title holder, rightful owner. **2** claimant.

హజం **hajam** *n.* arrogance.

హజారం **hajaaram** *n. class.* hall of audience.

హఠ **haTha** *adj.* stubborn, obstinate, adamant, insistent.

హఠం **haTham** *n.* obstinacy, insistence.

హఠయోగం **haThayoogam** *n.* method of attaining abstract contemplation by means of austere practices.

హఠయోగి **haThayoogi** *n.* ascetic who practices **haThayoogam.**

హఠాత్ **haThaat** *adjvl. prefix signifying* sudden; **~prayaaNam** sudden journey.

హఠాత్తు **haThaattu** *adj.* sudden, abrupt.

హఠాత్తుగా **haThaattugaa** *adv.* suddenly.

హడలకొట్టు, అడలకొట్టు **haDalakoTTu, aDalakoTTu** *v.t.* to frighten.

హడలిపోవు, అడలిపోవు **haDalipoowu, aDalipoowu** *v.i.* to be frightened, be scared, be in a panic.

హడలు, అడలు **haDalu, aDalu** I. *n.* fright, terror. II. *v.i.* to be frightened, be alarmed, be terror-struck.

హడావిడి **haDaawiDi** *n.* **1** commotion, stir, bustle, excitement. **2** haste, hurry; **iNTiki weLLee ~ loo Dabbu maricipooyEEDu** in his hurry to go home he forgot his money.

హడావిడిగా **haDaawiDigaa** *adv.* in a hurry, in haste.

హడావిడిచేయు **haDaawiDiceeyu** *v.t.* **1** to hustle, bestir. **2** (of a critically ill person) to cause anxiety.

హతం **hatam** *adj.* killed, slain.

హతం అవు **hatam awu** *v.i.* to be killed, be slaughtered.

హతమారు **hatamaaru** *v.i.* to die.

హతమార్చు **hatamaarcu** *v.t.* to kill, slay, destroy.

హతమార్చుకుపోవు **hatamaarcukupoowu** *v.i.* to get o.s. killed by doing s.g dangerous or foolish; **taagi taagi hatamaarcukupootunnaaDu** he is drinking himself to death.

హతవిధి **hatawidhi** I. *n.* irony of fate. II. *interj.* alas!

హతాశుడు **hataaśuDu** *n.* person whose hopes have been dashed, despairing person.

హతోడ **hatooDa** *same as* **atooDa.**

హతోస్మి! **hatoosmi!** *interj. expressing hopelessness and helplessness* (*lit.* I am slain!).

హత్తించు **hattincu** *v.t.* to stamp, imprint.

హత్తుకొను **hattukonu** *v.t.* **1** to press, clasp. **2** to imprint, impress.

హత్య **hatya** *n.* **1** killing, slaying; **aatma~** suicide. **2** murder, assassination.

హత్య చేయు **hatya ceeyu** *v.t.* **1** to kill, slay. **2** to murder.

హత్యాకాండ **hatyaakaaNDa** *n.* slaughter, massacre, carnage.

హద్దు, అద్దు **haddu, addu** *n.* boundary, limit; **~paddu leekuNDaa** unrestrainedly (*lit.* without limit or account).

హద్దురాయి **hadduraayi** *n.* boundary stone.

హనుమ, హనుమంతుడు **hanuma, hanumantuDu** *n.* Hanuman, the monkey god.

హనువు **hanuwu** *n.* jaw.

హమాలీ **hamaalii** *n.* porter in a market.

హమేషా **hameeSaa** *adv.* always.

హమ్మయ్య! **hammayya!** *interj. expressive of relief.*

హయం **hayam** *n. class.* horse, steed.

హయాం **hayaam** *n.* **1** period of authority, period of office. **2** tenure of office.

హరణం **haraNam** *n.* **1** removal by force, carrying off. **2** theft.

హరశోఠం **harasooTham** *n.* gypsum.

హరహరా! **haraharaa!** *interj.* (i) *chanted by pall bearers when carrying a corpse to the burial ground;* (ii) *uttered on hearing bad news.*

హరహరా అవు **haraharaa awu** *v.i. colloq.* **1** to die. **2** to be destroyed.

హరాయించుకొను **haraayincukonu** *same as* **araayincucukonu.**

హరి **hari** *n.* epithet of Vishnu; ~**miida giri paDDaa** (*lit.* even if a mountain falls on Hari) *is a proverbial phrase meaning* come what may.

హరిఓంఅను **hari oom anu** *v.i.* to make a beginning (*lit.* to say 'Hari oom!'—*a formula used in starting prayer or worship*).

హరించు **harincu** I. *v.i.* **1** to perish, waste away, disappear, vanish. **2** to be digested. II. *v.t.* to steal, make away with, carry off, misappropriate.

హరింపు **harimpu** *n.* **1** waste, loss. **2** misappropriation.

హరికథ **harikatha** *n.* ballad recounting a story taken from mythology.

హరిచందనం **haricandanam** *n. class.* kind of yellow fragrant sandalwood.

హరిజనుడు **harijanuDu** *n.* harijan, member of a scheduled caste.

హరిణం **hariNam** *n. class.* deer, antelope.

హరిణి **hariNi** *n. class.* doe, female antelope.

హరిత **harita** *adj.* green.

హరితకణం, హరితరేణువు **haritakaNam, haritareeNuwu** *n. bot.* chloroplast.

హరిదాసు **haridaasu** *n.* reciter of **harikatha.**

హరిద్ర **haridra** *adj. class.* yellow.

హరివాణం **hariwaaNam** *same as* **ariwaaNam.**

హరివిల్లు **hariwillu** *n.* rainbow.

హరిహరి! **harihari!** *interj. expressing horror at some sinful act.*

హరీ అను **harii anu** *v.i.* to die (*lit.* to say, Hari!).

హర్తాల్, హర్తాళ్ **hartaal, hartaaL** *n.* act of closing shops and suspending work, esp. in political protest.

హర్మ్యం **harmyam** *n.* palace, mansion.

హర్రాజు **harraaju** *same as* **arraaju.**

హర్షం **harSam** *n.* joy, gladness, delight, happiness.

హర్షధ్వనులు, హర్షధ్వానాలు **harSadhwanulu, harSadhwaanaalu** *n.pl.* applause.

హర్షించు **harSincu** I. *v.i.* to be glad, be delighted, be pleased. II. *v.t.* to appreciate, admire, approve.

హలం **halam** *n. class.* plough.

హలంత **halanta** *adj. gram.* ending in a consonant.

హలఫ్‌నామా **halaphnaamaa** *n.* affidavit.

హలాది **halaadi** *adj. gram.* beginning with a consonant.

హలాహలం, హాలాహలం **halaahalam, haalaahalam** *n. class.* poison, venom.

హల్లు **hallu** *n. ling.* consonant.

హళాహళి **haLaahaLi** *n.* confused noise, tumult.

హళ్లి **haLLi** *n.* cipher, zero; *occurring mod. only in the expression* **sunnaku sunna ~ ki~** *meaning* nothing at all.

హవాయి చెప్పులు **hawaayi ceppulu** *n.pl.* sandals made of thin light material such as plastic.

హవాలా **hawaalaa** *n.* charge, custody, care.

హవి, హవిష్యం, హవిస్సు **hawi, hawiSyam, hawissu** *n. class.* ghee or any other object intended as an oblation.

హవేలీ **haweelii** *n.* mansion, palace.

హవ్య **hawya** *adj.* fit to be offered as an oblation.

హసం, హసనం, హాసం **hasam, hasanam, haasam** *n.* laugh[ter].

హసాదు! **hasaadu!** *minor sentence, class.* as you wish! *or* as you please!

హసించు **hasincu** *v.i.* to laugh, smile.

హస్కుకొట్టు **haskukoTTu** *v.i. colloq.* to talk of trivial things (*lit.* to pound husk).

హస్త **hasta** *n. astrol.* thirteenth lunar mansion or asterism.

హస్తం **hastam** *n.* **1** *class.* hand. **2** palm of the hand. **3** *colloq.* five rupees. **4** kind of ladle in the shape of a hand used for serving rice.

హస్తప్రయోగం **hastaprayoogam** *n.* masturbation.

హస్తముద్ర **hastamudra** *n.* gesture (of a dancer).

హస్తవాసి **hastawaasi** *n.* skill, competence (esp. of a doctor).

హస్తసాముద్రికం **hastasaamudrikam** *n.* palmistry.

హస్తాక్షరం **hastaakSaram** *n.* **1** handwriting. **2** signature.

హస్తి **hasti** *n. class.* elephant.

హస్తినాపురం **hastinaapuram** *n.* capital city of the Kauravas in the Mahabharata situated near Delhi.

హస్తిమశకాంతరం **hastimasakaantaram** *n.* huge difference (*lit.* difference between an elephant and a gnat).

హా - haa

హాజరీ **haajarii** *n.* presence.

హాజరు **haajaru** *adj.* present, at hand; **sabhaki ~ ayyEEDu** he was present at the meeting.

హాజరు పట్టీ **haajaru paTTii** *n.* muster roll.

హాటక **haaTaka** *adj. class.* made of gold.

హాని **haani** I. *n.* **1** damage, harm, injury, detriment. **2** danger. II. *second part of a n. compound meaning* loss; **praaNa ~** loss of life.

హానికర **haanikara** *adj.* **1** damaging, harmful, detrimental, injurious, maleficent, prejudicial; **~ prabhaawam** prejudicial effect. **2** dangerous.

హామీ **haamii** *n.* **1** assurance, promise. **2** security, surety.

హామీ[గా] నిలుచు **haamii[gaa] nilucu** *v.i.* to stand surety, stand security.

హామీపడు **haamiipaDu** *v.i.* to [serve as a] guarantee; **sampaadakula sweecchaku ~ tuu** guaranteeing the independence of editors.

హాము **haamu** *n. colloq., corruption of* **aham** pride, self-conceit, egoism; **waaDi waNTLoo ~ waaDiceeta aTLaa maaTLaaDistunnadi** his egoism is making him speak like that.

హాయి **haayi** *n.* happiness, peace, quiet, comfort, pleasantness.

హాయిగా **haayigaa** *adv.* happily, cheerfully, comfortably at ease, without any trouble.

హారం **haaram** *n.* **1** garland, necklace. **2** *maths.* denominator.

హారతి **haarati** *n.* (*also* **mangaLa ~**) offering of lighted camphor to a deity or of a lighted lamp to an individual, e.g., a householder, on an auspicious occasion.

హారతికర్పూరం **haaratikarpuuram** *n.* camphor (a substance which evaporates and disappears quickly); **aasti ~ laa aypooyindi** the property vanished in no time.

హారతిపట్టు **haaratipaTTu** *v.i.* to pay tribute (to a person as a sign of admiration): **sabhaloo waktalu andaruu aayanaki haaratulu paTTEEru** all the speakers at the meeting paid tributes to him.

హారతిపళ్లెం **haaratipaLLem** *n.* tray containing a lighted lamp held by the **iNTi aaDapaDucu** of a householder when she invokes blessings on the household on an auspicious occasion, after which the householder places a gift for her in the tray.

హార్దం **haardam** *n.* sincerity, cordiality.

హార్దిక **haardika** *adj.* sincere, heartfelt, cordial.

హాలాహలం **haalaahalam** *same as* **halaahalam.**

హాలికుడు **haalikuDu** *n.* cultivator, agriculturist.

హావభావాలు **haawabhaawaalu** *n.pl.* expressions and gestures.

హాలీసిక్కా **haaliisikkaa** *n.* coinage issued by the Nizam of Hyderabad.

హాసం **haasam** *same as* **hasam.**

హాస్య **haasya** *adj.* funny, comic.

హాస్యం **haasyam** *n.* **1** laughter, fun, joking, humour; **haasyaaniki** for fun, as a joke, in jest. **2** joke, jest. **3** ridicule.

హాస్యం ఆడు **haasyam aaDu** *v.i.* to make a joke.

హాస్యంగా **haasyangaa** *adv.* laughingly, jokingly, jestingly.

హాస్యం చేయు, హాస్యం పట్టించు **haasyam ceeyu, haasyam paTTincu** *v.t.* to laugh at, make fun of, ridicule.

హాస్యగాడు **haasyagaaDu** *n.* clown, jester.

హాస్యపూరిత **haasyapuurita** *adj.* facetious.

హాస్యరసం **haasyarasam** *n.* (sentiment of) humour.

హాస్యాస్పదం **haasyaaspadam** *n.* s.g laughable or ridiculous.

హాహాకారం **haahaakaaram** *n.* **1** cry for help. **2** cry of alarm. **3** booing.

హి, హీ - hi, hii

హింగారి **hingaari** *adj.* (crops) sown in the north-east monsoon season.

హింగుళం **hinguLam** *n.* cinnabar.

హింతాళం **hintaaLam** *n.* kind of date tree.

హిందీ **hindii** *n.* the Hindi language.

హిందూస్థానం **hindusthaanam** *n.* Hindusthan, an old name for India; **uttara~** North India.

హిందువు **hinduwu** *n.* Hindu.

హిందూమహాసముద్రం **hinduu mahaasamudram** *n.* the Indian ocean.

హిందోళం **hindooLam** *n.* 1 swing. 2 name of a raga.

హింస **himsa** *n.* 1 harm, violence. 2 cruelty; **jantu~** cruelty to animals. 3 persecution, oppression.

హింసకుడు **himsakuDu** *n.* persecutor.

హింసాకర **himsaakara** *adj.* violent, cruel, hurtful.

హింసాకాండ **himsaakaaNDa** *n.* (deeds of) violence, violent activity.

హింసాత్మక **himsaatmaka** *adj.* violent, imbued with violence.

హింసాయుత **himsaayuta** *adj.* violent.

హింసించు **himsincu** *v.t.* to injure, harm, do violence to, plague, torment, treat cruelly, persecute, oppress.

హిజరా, హిజ్ర **hijaraa, hijra** *n.* the departure of Mahommed from Mecca for Medina in 622 A.D., the start of the Muslim era.

హిజ్రి **hijri** *n.* year of the Muslim era counted from the hijra.

హిత **hita** *adj.* 1 good, beneficial, helpful, useful, wholesome, salutary. 2 kind, friendly.

హితం **hitam** *n.* good, benefit, welfare, wellbeing; **nii~ koori ceppEEnu** I said it for your good; **prajaahita kaaryakramaalu** programmes for the good of the people.

హితబోధ **hitaboodha** *n.* good advice, sound advice.

హితవరి **hitawari** *same as* **itawari.**

హితవు **hitawu** *n.* 1 *same as* **hitam.** 2 s.g agreeable, s.g that is to o.'s liking, s.g that one can bear or tolerate; **śaantamma majjiga annam tindi, adi aameki~ kaaleedu** Santamma ate some buttermilk and rice, it was not to her liking; **nidraloo leewagaanee widyuddiipapu welugu aame kaL-Laku~ kaaleedu, kaaseepu eemii kanipincaleedu** on waking her eyes could not bear the electric light, so she could not see anything for a little time.

హితుడు, హితైషి **hituDu, hitaySi** *n.* friend, wellwisher; **mii hitaySi** *is sometimes used as a formula for ending a letter, equivalent to* 'yours truly'.

హితోపదేశం **hitoopadeeśam** *n.* good advice, title of a book of fables with morals.

హిమ, హిమానీ **hima, himaanii** *adj.* 1 of ice, icy. 2 glacial.

హిమం **himam** *n.* 1 dew. 2 frost, snow, ice.

హిమకరుడు, హిమాంశువు **himakaruDu, himaamśuwu** *n. class.* moon.

హిమనదం, హిమానీనదం **himanadam, himaaniinadam** *n.* glacier.

హిమప్రవాహం **himaprawaaham** *n.* avalanche.

హిమయుగం, హిమానీయుగం **himayugam, himaaniiyugam** *n.* ice age.

హిమాలయ **himaalaya** *n.* the Himalayas.

హిమ్రూ **himruu** *n.* kind of embroidered cloth woven in the Hyderabad area.

హిరణ్యం **hiraNyam** *n. class.* gold.

హిరణ్యాక్షవరాలు **hiraNyaakSawaraalu** *n.pl.* 1 boons which Hiranyaksha asked of the gods in order to make himself immortal. 2 *colloq.* impossible demands, demands which are too difficult to concede.

హిరణ్యాక్షుడు **hiraNyaakSuDu** *n.* Hiranyaksha, a demon king who was killed by Vishnu.

హీన **hiina** *adj.* 1 low, poor, abject, wretched; **~sthiti** low state, poor condition. 2 mean, vile, base. 3 *second part of an adjvl. compound meaning* lacking in, bereft of; **bala~** weak; **kula~** casteless, **guNa~** without virtue.

హీనంగా **hiinangaa** *adv.* 1 poorly, meanly; **~cuucu** to look down on, despise; **wiiTi wiluwa enta~ ancanaa weesinaa mupphay weela ruupaayala payciluku uNTundi** however low a valuation you put on these (books) their value will be thirty thousand rupees or more. 2 weakly, faintly; **~nawwu** to smile faintly; **ewaroo gontuka nokkeestee~ maaTLaaDinaTTu maaTLaaDindi** she spoke as faintly as if s.o. was gripping her throat.

హీనత, హీనత్వం **hiinata, hiinatwam** *n.* lowness, meanness, baseness, wretchedness.

హీనధాతువు **hiina dhaatuwu** *n.* base metal.

హీనపక్షం **hiinapakSam** *adv. colloq.* at least, at the minimum; **wiiTini accuweestee~padiheenu weela peejiilaku wistaristaayi** if these are printed they will extend to 15,000 pages at the minimum.

హీనుడు **hiinuDu** *n.* 1 wretch, vile person. 2 *second part of a n. compound meaning* person who lacks (s.g); **buddhi~** senseless person.

హీరం **hiiram** *n. obs.* diamond.

హు, హూ, హృ - hu, huu, hr̥

హుంకరించు **hunkarincu** *v.i.* **1** to speak in an authoritative tone. **2** to speak arrogantly.

హుంకారం **hunkaaram** *n.* shout, yell.

హుండీ, ఉండీ **huNDii, uNDii** *n.* **1** money box. **2** cash box in a temple. **3** bill or cheque or draft on a bank.

హుందా, హుందాతనం **hundaa[tanam]** *n.* dignity, solemnity, gravity, seriousness.

హుందాగా **hundaagaa** *adv.* **1** solemnly, gravely, with dignity. **2** stylishly, grandly.

హుకుం **hukum** *n.* order, command.

హుక్కా **hukkaa** *n.* huqqa, hubble bubble; **~piilcu** to smoke a huqqa.

హుజూర్ **hujuur** I. *n. obs.* headquarters. II. *form of address, obs.* **~jii!** yes sir!

హుటాహుటీగా **huTaahuTiigaa** *adv.* rapidly, quickly, in a great hurry.

హుళక్కి, ఉళక్కి **huLakki, uLakki** *n.* **1** falsehood, lie. **2** nil, nothingness.

హుషార్! **huSaar!** *interj. expressing appreciation* how clever! *or* well done!

హుషారు **huSaaru** I. *n.* **1** cheerful or joyful mood, cheerfulness. **2** liveliness. **3** alertness, watchfulness, caution. II. *adj.* **1** cheerful, in a good mood. **2** bright, active, lively, full of life. **3** alert, watchful, cautious.

హుషారు ఇచ్చు **huSaaru iccu** *v.i.* **1** to give encouragement, **2** to give a warning, put (s.o.) on the alert.

హుషారు చేయు **huSaaru ceeyu** *v.t.* to encourage, stimulate, urge on.

హూణుడు **huuNuDu** *n.* hun, barbarian.

హూనం అవు **huunam awu** *v.i.* to be beaten or broken or crushed out of shape, be reduced to pulp, be broken into fragments; **kaaru huunam aypooyindi** the car was totally wrecked; **oLLu huunam ayyeelaa koDataaDu** he will beat you to pulp.

హృదయం **hr̥dayam** *n.* **1** heart. **2** mind.

హృదయంగమ **hr̥dayangama** *adj.* heart-stirring, touching, affecting.

హృదయంగమంగా **hr̥dayangamangaa** *adv.* **1** *lit.* so as to stir the heart. **2** attractively, appealingly.

హృదయపూర్వక **hr̥dayapuurwaka** *adj.* sincere, heartfelt, wholehearted, cordial.

హృదయపూర్వకంగా **hr̥dayapuurwakangaa** *adv.* sincerely, wholeheartedly, cordially.

హృదయవిదారక **hr̥dayawidaaraka** *adj.* heartbreaking, heart-rending.

హృదయవేదన **hr̥dayaweedana** *n.* mental agony.

హృదయస్పందనం **hr̥dayaspandanam** *n.* heart beat.

హృదయాంతర్గత **hr̥dayaantargata** *adj.* heartfelt, innermost (emotions).

హృదయాకార **hr̥dayaakaara** *adj. bot.* cordate, heart shaped.

హృదయుడు **hr̥dayuDu** *second part of a n. compound*; **kaThina~** hard-hearted person.

హృది **hr̥di** *n. class.* **1** heart. **2** mind.

హృద్గతం చేసుకొను **hr̥dgatam ceesukonu** *v.t.* to take to heart, give due consideration to.

హృద్యం **hr̥dyam** *adj.* loving, amicable.

హృద్రోగం **hr̥droogam** *n.* heart attack, heart disease.

హె, హే, హై - he, hee, hay

హెక్టారు **hekTaaru** *n.* hectare.

హెగ్గడికత్తె **heggaDikatte** *n. class.* maid of honour, principal lady in waiting.

హెచ్చరించు **heccarincu** *v.t.* 1 to warn, caution. 2 to urge. 3 to bring to mind, draw attention. 4 to remind.

హెచ్చరిక **heccarika** *n.* 1 warning, caution. 2 remark, mention, intimation.

హెచ్చవేత **heccaweeta** *n.* multiplication.

హెచ్చవేయు **heccaweeyu** *v.t.* to multiply.

హెచ్చించి చెప్పు **heccinci ceppu** *v.t.* to exaggerate.

హెచ్చించు **heccincu** *v.t.* to increase, augment, raise, enhance.

హెచ్చు **heccu** I. *n.* 1 increase. 2 greatness. 3 excess. II. *adj.* 1 much, great. 2 more, greater; **ataniki caalaa mandi pillalunnaaru, anduloo aaDapillalu** ~ he has many children, more of them are girls than boys. 3 excessive. III. *v.i.* to increase, grow.

హెచ్చు అవు **heccu awu** *v.i.* to increase; **naa paTTudala heccaypooyindi** my determination increased.

హెచ్చుగా **heccugaa** *adv.* 1 greatly, much. 2 more.

హెచ్చు చేయు **heccu ceeyu** *v.t.* to increase; **tondara heccu ceesEEDu** he increased his speed.

హెచ్చుతక్కువ **heccutakkuwa** *adv.* round about, approximately; ~ **160 eeLLa kritam** round about 160 years ago.

హెచ్చుతగ్గులు **heccutaggulu** *n.pl.* 1 unevenness, inequalities. 2 differences in status.

హెచ్చులు **hecculu** *same as* **ecculu.**

హేతుక **heetuka** *second part of an adjvl. compound meaning* causing.

హేతుదృష్టి, హేతువాదదృష్టి **heetudrSTi, heetuwaadadrSTi** *n.* rational or logical attitude.

హేతుబద్ధ **heetubaddha** *adj.* rational, reasonable, logical.

హేతుభూత **heetubhuuta** *adj.* being the cause of, causing.

హేతువాదం **heetuwaadam** *n.* 1 rationalism. 2 reasoning.

హేతువాది **heetuwaadi** *n.* rationalist.

హేతువు **heetuwu** *n.* cause, reason, ground.

హేత్వర్థం **heetwartham** *n. gram.* causative sense, causative meaning.

హేమం **heemam** *n. class.* gold.

హేమంతం **heemantam** *n. class.* winter.

హేమవిద్య **heemawidya** *n.* alchemy.

హేమాహేమీలు **heemaa heemiilu** *n.pl.* 1 eminent persons. 2 stalwarts. 3 experts.

హేయ **heeya** *adj.* mean, vile, abominable, hateful, loathsome.

హేయం **heeyam** *n.* dislike, disgust, revulsion (**-pay,** towards).

హేయత **heeyata** *n.* hatefulness, vileness.

హేయపడు **heeyapaDu** *v.i.* to be disgusted.

హేల **heela** *n.* 1 sport, play. 2 frowning.

హేళన[ం] **heeLana[m]** *n.* mockery, ridicule, derision, sneering.

హేళనగా **heeLanagaa** *adv.* mockingly, sarcastically, derisively, sneeringly.

హేళనచేయు **heeLana ceeyu** *v.t.* to ridicule, mock, laugh at, deride, sneer at.

హేవిళంబి **heewiLambi** *n.* thirty-first year of the Hindu cycle of sixty years.

హేష **heeSa** *n.* neigh[ing].

హైందవ **hayndawa** *adj.* Hindu.

హైన్యం **haynyam** *n.* 1 meanness, baseness. 2 ignominy, degradation.

హైరాన్, హైరాన **hayraan[a]** *n.* 1 fatigue, strain. 2 worry, trouble: **prayaaNam caalaa** ~ ayndi the journey was very troublesome.

హైరానపడు **hayraana paDu** *v.i.* to undergo physical or mental strain: **caalaa hayraana paDi sampaadincEEDu** he got it after much tribulation.

హైరానపెట్టు **hayraana peTTu** *v.t.* to worry, trouble, torment.

హొ to హ్లా - ho to hlaa

హొయలు, హోయలు **hoyalu, hooyalu** *n.* grace, charm.

హోత **hoota** *n.* priest who recites prayers from the Rigveda at a sacrifice.

హోత్రి **hootri** *n.* sacrificer.

హోదా **hoodaa** *n.* **1** office, authority. **2** rank, status.

హోమం **hoomam** *n.* sacrifice performed by casting ghee and other objects on a fire accompanied by recital of prayers from the Rigveda.

హోమగుండం **hoomanguNDam** *n.* pit for a sacrificial fire.

హోర **hoora** *n. class.* hour.

హోరాహోరీ **hooraahoorii** *adv.* (of fighting, quarrelling) fiercely and continuously: **~ mrtyudeewatatoo raatrimbawaLLu poori praaNaalu nilabeTTEEnu** fighting fiercely by day and by night with the God of Death, I have saved lives.

హోరు **hooru** *n.* roar[ing], raucous sound: **samudrapu ~** roar of the sea.

హోరుమను **hoorumanu** *v.i.* to make a roaring noise.

హోరుగాలి, ఓరుగాలి **hoorugaali, oorugaali** *n.* storm, tempest.

హోరెత్తు **hoorettu** *v.i.* to ring, resound, reverberate: **aydu roojuluu peLLi wiDidi narusu paaTalatoo hooretti pooyindi** on all the five days the wedding party's lodging place resounded with Narasu's songs.

హోళి **hooLi** *n.* spring festival celebrated on the full moon day of Phalguna in March/April.

హోళిగ **hooLiga** *n.* kind of sweet (= **pooLi**).

హోసు **hooSu** *n.* false prestige, posing.

హౌజు **hawju** *n.* water tank made of masonry or cement.

హౌదా **hawdaa** *n.* howdah, seat on an elephant's back.

హ్రస్వ **hraswa** *adj.* **1** short. **2** little, small.

హ్రస్వం, హ్రస్వాచ్చు **hraswam, hraswaaccu** *n. gram.* short vowel.

హ్లాదం **hlaadam** *n.* joy, pleasure.

INT BH 5003 17/9/12
HB
E1